WHO A[M I]

A FULL TIME BASEBALL CARD DEALER F[OR ...]

MW00823581

MY ACCOMPLISHMENTS

- I am the largest cash buyer of vintage baseball cards in the world. In the past 30 years I have spent over 150 million dollars in vintage cards and related memorabilia.
- I am the dealer who purchased the greatest discovery of baseball cards ever found, a 1952 Topps High Number vending case.
- I am the dealer who purchased in Paris, Tennessee over 250 1954-1955 baseball and football wax boxes.
- I have been featured on hundreds of live TV and radio talk shows over the past 30 years including Good Morning America, The Today Show and ESPN.
- I have appeared in over 300 magazines and newspaper articles across the U.S. including front page stories on the Wall Street Journal, The New York Times and the New York Daily News. I have been featured in major national magazines such as Sports Illustrated and Sport and Archie Comics.
- I have participated in 24 National Sports Collectors Conventions in addition to almost 1,000 regional baseball card shows.
- I was inducted into the National Baseball Card Hall of Fame 2002.
- I have been voted by Krause Publications as one of the Sports Collectible Industry's 20 most influential people.

MY SERVICES

- I can purchase your cards for cold cash, check, money order, bank wire or whatever your needs might be.
- Appraised collections or individual cards on a percentage basis.
- Counsel collectors at any time in the privacy of your home or by phone on any questions you might have about the hobby.
- I can assist in any tax situation you might encounter when liquidating your collection.

**BUYING SPORTS CARDS
1869-1969 ONLY!!!!**

**NOBODY DOES IT BETTER
THAN THE BUYING MACHINE!!**

**P.O. Box 500, Montvale, NJ 07645
Phone: (201) 307-0700
Fax: (201) 962-2155**

Email: **mrmint@optonline.net**

Website: **www.mrmint.com**

TOP COLLECTOR GUIDES
FOR ANY HOBBYIST

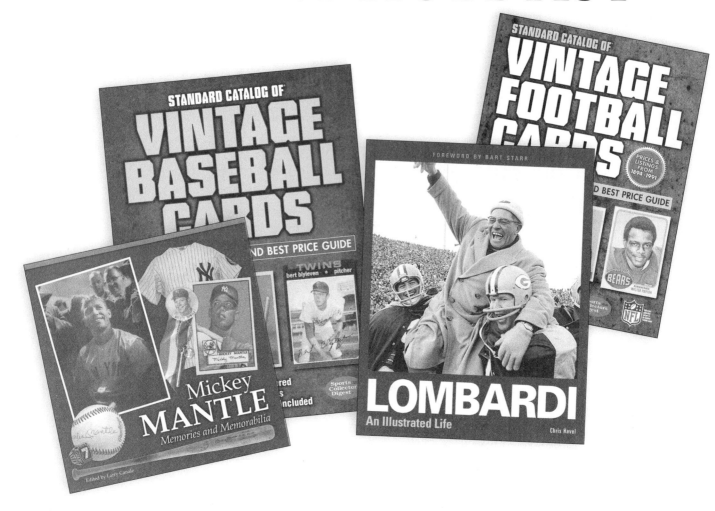

KrauseBooks.com is your one-stop shop for all of your hobby and collecting needs. Whether you are just getting started or have been collecting for years, our products will help you build, identify, appraise and maintain your collections.

You'll find great products at great prices throughout the site and we even offer **FREE SHIPPING** on purchases over $49.

Be sure to sign up to receive exclusive offers and discounts!

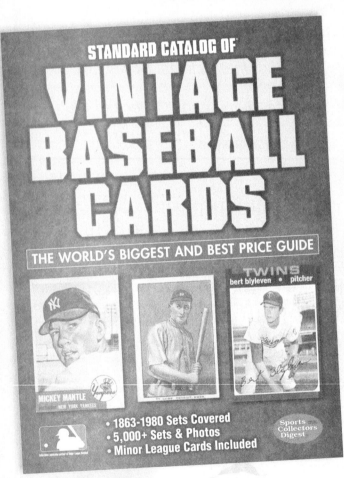

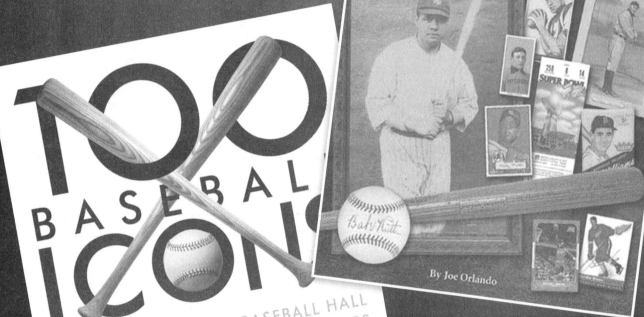

The Authority in Antiques & Collectibles

For nearly 30 years, Antique Trader Antiques & Collectibles has served as the leading source for information on antiques and collectibles. Eric Bradley brings you 816 pages full of pictures, pricing information, and more on this amazingly diverse and glorious market.

In This Antiques Price Guide You'll Find:

- Expert advice along with market and collecting trends
- 4,500 high quality color images
- Vetted values and pricing guide information

Antique Trader Antiques & Collectibles is the undisputed best-selling annual guide in the hobby.

Item # V8192 • Retail: $22.99

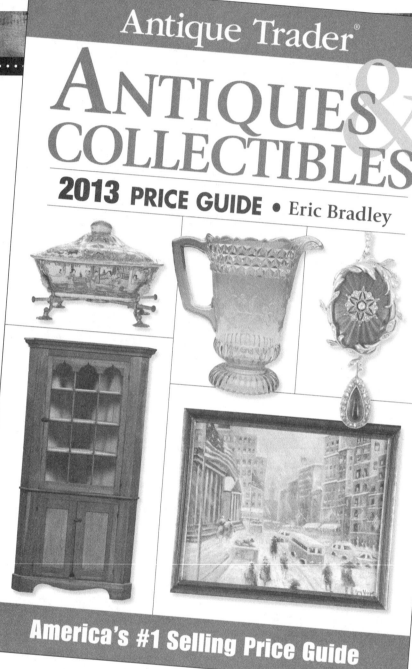

Antique Trader®
ANTIQUES & COLLECTIBLES
2013 PRICE GUIDE • Eric Bradley

America's #1 Selling Price Guide

STANDARD CATALOG OF
VINTAGE FOOTBALL CARDS

Edited by the Staff of *Sports Collectors Digest*

Published by

Krause Publications, a division of F+W Media, Inc.
700 East State Street • Iola, WI 54990-0001
715-445-2214 • 888-457-2873
www.krausebooks.com

To order books or other products call toll-free 1-800-258-0929
or visit us online at www.krausebooks.com

ISBN-13: 978-1-4402-3289-3
ISBN-10: 1-4402-3289-X

Cover Design by Kevin Ulrich
Designed by Sandi Carpenter
Edited by Staff of Sports Collectors Digest

Printed in the United States of America

Welcome! Guide to Using This Catalog

GREETINGS!

Thank you for purchasing the *Standard Catalog of Vintage Football Cards*. This catalog is one of the most comprehensive football card price guides available, complete with listings for more than 100,000 cards and checklists for more than 1,000 sets cover the years 1894-1991.

This catalog has been designed to serve the needs of collectors and dealers at all levels from beginning to advanced. It provides a comprehensive guide for 100 years of football card issues, arranged so that even the most novice hobbyist can consult the book without difficulty.

The following explanations summarize the general practices used in preparing the Standard Catalog of Vintage Football Cards' listings. However, because of specialized requirements which might vary from card set to card set, these must not be considered ironclad. Where these standards have been set aside, appropriate notations are usually incorporated.

ARRANGEMENT

Because the most important feature in identifying and pricing a sports card is its set of origin, this catalog has been alphabetically arranged according to the name by which the set is most popularly known.

Those sets that were issued for more than one year are then listed chronologically, from earliest to most recent.

Within each set, the cards are listed by their designated card number, or in the absence of card numbers, alphabetically according to the last name of the player pictured.

IDENTIFICATION

While the date and issue of most modern sports cards are well identified on front, back or both, such has not always been the case. In general, the back of the card is more useful in identifying the set of origin than the front. The issuer or sponsor's name will usually appear on the back since, after all, sports cards were first produced as a promotional item to stimulate sales of other products. As often as not, that issuer's name is the name by which the set is known to collectors and under which it will be found listed in this catalog.

In some difficult cases identifying a sports card's general age, if not specific year of issue, can be fixed by studying the biological or statistical information on the back of the card. The last year mentioned in either the biography or stats is usually the year that preceded the year of issue.

PHOTOGRAPHS

A photograph of the front of at least one representative card from many of the sets listed in this catalog has been incorporated into the listings to aid in identification.

Photographs have been printed in reduced size. The actual size of cards in each set is given in the introductory text preceding its listing, unless the card is the standard size 1-1/2" by 3-1/2".

DATING

The dating of sports cards by year of issue on the front or back of the card itself is a relatively new phenomenon. In most cases, to accurately determine a date of issue for an unidentified card, it must be studied for clues.

As mentioned, the biography, career summary or statistics on the back of the card are the best way to pinpoint a year of issue. In most cases, the year of issue will be the year after the last season mentioned on the card.

Luckily for today's collector, earlier generations have done much of the research in determining your year of issue for those cards which bear no clues. The painstaking task of matching players' listed and/or pictured teams against their career records often allowed an issue date to be determined.

In some cases, particular card sets were issued over a period of more than one calendar year, but since they are collected together as a single set, their specific year of issue is not important. Such sets will be listed with their complete known range of issue years.

NUMBERING

While many sports card issues as far back as the early 1900s have contained card numbers assigned by the issuer to facilitate the collecting of a complete set, the practice has by no means been universal. Even today, not every set bears card numbers.

Logically, those sports cards which were numbered by their manufacturer are presented in that numerical order within the listings of this catalog.

The many unnumbered issues, however, have been assigned *Standard Catalog* numbers to facilitate their universal identification within the hobby, especially when buying and selling by mail.

In all cases, numbers which have been assigned or which otherwise do not appear on the card through error or by design, are shown in this catalog within parentheses. In virtually all cases, unless a more natural system suggested itself by the unique matter of a particular set, the assignment of *Standard Catalog* numbers by the cataloging staff has been done by alphabetical arrangement of the players' last names or the card's principal title.

Significant collectible variations for any particular card are noted within the listings by the application of a suffix letter within parentheses. In instances of variations, the suffix "a" is assigned to the variation which was created first.

NAMES

The identification of a player by full name on the front of his sports card has been a common practice only since the 1940s. Prior to that, the player's name and team were the usual information found on the card front.

As a general practice, the listings in the *Standard Catalog of Vintage Football Cards* present the player's name as it is more commonly known. If the player's name only appears on the back, rather than on the front of the card, the listing corresponds to that designation.

In cases where only the player's last name is given on the card, the cataloging staff has included the first name by which he was most often known for ease of identification.

Cards which contain misspelled first or last names, or even wrong initials, will have included in their listings the incorrect information, with a correction accompanying in parentheses. This extends, also, to cases where the name on the card does not correspond to the player actually pictured.

GRADING

The vast majority of cards in this book were issued between 1970 and 1991 and feature NFL players only. The term "card" is used rather loosely as in this context it is construed to include virtually any series of cardboard or paper product, of whatever size and/or shape, depicting football players.

Further, "cards" printed on wood, metal, plastic and other materials are either by their association with other issues or by their compatibility in size with the current 2-1/2" x 3-1/2" card standard also listed here.

In general, post-1980 cards which grade Near Mint (NM) will retail at about 75% of the Mint price, while Excellent (EX) condition cards bring 40%.

Here is a more detailed look at grading procedures:

Mint (MT): A perfect card. Well-centered, with parallel borders which appear equal to the naked eye. Four sharp, square corners. No creases, edge dents, surface scratches, paper flaws, loss of luster, yellowing or fading, regardless of age. No imperfectly printed card - out of register, badly cut or ink flawed - or card stained by contact with gum, wax or other substances can be considered truly Mint, even if new out of the pack.

Near Mint (NR MT): A nearly perfect card. At first glance, a Near Mint card appears perfect; upon a closer examination, however, a minor flaw will be discovered. On well-centered cards, three of the four corners must be perfectly sharp; only one corner shows a minor imperfection upon close inspection. A slightly off-center card with one or more borders being noticeably unequal - but still present - would also fit this grade.

Excellent (EX): Corners are still fairly sharp with only moderate wear. Card borders may be off center. No creases. May have very minor gum, wax or product stains, front or back. Surfaces may show slight loss of luster from rubbing across other cards.

Very Good (VG): Show obvious handling. Corners rounded and/or perhaps showing minor creases. Other minor creases may be visible. Surfaces may exhibit loss of luster, but all printing is intact. May show major gum, wax or other packaging stains. No major creases, tape marks or extraneous markings or writing. Exhibit honest wear.

Good (G - generally 50% of the VG price): A well-worn card, but exhibits no intentional damage or abuse. May have major or multiple creases. Corners rounded well beyond the border.

Fair (F - generally 50% of the Good price): Shows excessive wear, along with damage or abuse. Will show all the wear characteristics of a Good card, along with such damage as thumb tack holes in or near margins, evidence of having been taped or pasted, perhaps small tears around the edges, or creases so heavy as to break the cardboard. Backs may show minor added pen or pencil writing, or be missing small bits of paper. Still, basically a complete card.

Poor (P): A card that has been tortured to death. Corners or other areas may be torn off. Card may have been trimmed, show holes from a paper punch or have been used for BB gun practice. Front may have extraneous pen or pencil writing, or other defacement. Major portions of front or back design may be missing. In other words, cards that are Poor are not a pretty sight.

In addition to these terms, collectors may encounter intermediate grades, such as VG-EX or EX-MT. These cards usually have characteristics of both the lower and higher grades, and are generally priced midway between those two values.

VALUATIONS

Values quoted in this book represent the current retail market and are compiled from recommendations provided and verified through the authors' involvement in the publication of the hobby's leading advertising periodicals, as well as the input of specialized consultants.

It should be stressed, however, that this book is intended to serve only as an aid in evaluating cards; actual market conditions are constantly changing. This is especially true of the cards of current players, whose on-field performance during the course of a season can greatly affect the value of their cards - upward or downward.

Publication of this book is not intended as a solicitation to buy or sell the listed cards by the editors, publishers or contributors. Again, the values here are retail prices - what a collector can expect to pay when buying a card from a dealer. The wholesale price, that which a collector can expect to receive from a dealer when selling cards, will be significantly lower.

Most dealers operate on a 100 percent mark-up, generally paying about 50 percent of a card's retail value. On some high demand cards, dealers will pay up to 75 percent or even 100 percent or more of retail value, anticipating continued price increases. Conversely, for many low-demand cards, such as common players' cards of recent years, dealers may pay 25 percent or even less of retail.

SETS

Collectors may note that the complete set prices for newer issues quoted in these listings are usually significantly lower than the total of the value of the individual cards which comprise the set. This reflects two factors in the sports card market. First, a seller is often willing to take a lower composite price for a complete set as a "volume discount" and to avoid inventorying a large number of common player or other lower-demand cards.

Second, to a degree, the value of common cards can be said to be inflated as a result of having a built-in overhead charge to justify the dealer's time in sorting cards, carrying them in stock and filling orders. This accounts for the fact that even brand new sports cards, which cost the dealer around 1 cent each when bought in bulk, carry individual price tags of 3 cents or higher.

ERRORS/VARIATIONS

It is often hard for the beginning collector to understand that an error on a sports card, in and of itself, does not usually add premium value to that card. It is usually only when the correcting of an error in the subsequent printing creates a variation that premium value attaches to an error.

Minor errors, such as wrong stats or personal data, create a variation that attaches to an error. Misspellings, inconsistencies, etc. - usually affecting the back of the card - are very common, especially in recent years. Unless a corrected variation was also printed, these errors are not noted in the listings of this book because they are not generally perceived by collectors to have premium value.

On the other hand, major effort had been expended to include the most complete listings ever for collectible variation cards. Many scarce and valuable variations are included in these listings because they are widely collected and often have significant premium value.

COUNTERFEITS/REPRINTS

As the value of sports cards has risen in the past 10-20 years, certain cards and sets have become too expensive for the average collector to obtain. This, along with changes in the technology of color printing, has given rise to increasing numbers of counterfeit and reprint cards.

While both terms describe essentially the same thing - a modern day copy which attempts to duplicate as closely as possible an original sports card - there are differences which are important to the collector.

Generally, a counterfeit is made with the intention of deceiving somebody into believing it is genuine, and thus paying large amounts of money for it. The counterfeiter takes every pain to try to make his fakes look as authentic as possible.

A reprint, on the other hand, while it may have been made to look as close as possible to an original card, is made with the intention of allowing collectors to buy them as substitutes for cards they may never be otherwise able to afford. The big difference is that a reprint is generally marked as such, usually on the back of the card.

In other cases, like the Topps 1952 baseball reprint set, the replicas are printed in a size markedly different from the originals. Collectors should be aware, however, that unscrupulous persons will sometimes cut off or otherwise obliterate the distinguishing word - "Reprint," "Copy" - or modern copyright date on the back of a reprint card in an attempt to pass it as genuine. A collector's best defense against reprints and counterfeits is to acquire knowledge of the look and feel of genuine sports cards of various eras and issues.

UNLISTED CARDS

Readers who have cards or sets which are not covered in this edition are invited to correspond with the editor for purposes of adding to the compilation of work now in progress. Address: Standard Catalog of Vintage Football Cards, 700 E. State St., Iola, WI 54990.

COLLECTOR ISSUES

Many cards do not fall under the scope of this catalog because they were issued solely for the collector market. Known as, "collector issues," these cards and sets are distinguished from "legitimate" issues by not having been created as a sales promotional item for another product - bubble gum, soda, snack cakes, dog food, cigarettes, gasoline, etc.

Because of their nature - the person issuing them is always free to print and distribute more if they should ever attain any real value - collector issues are generally regarded as having little or no premium value.

NEW ISSUES

Because new sports cards are being issued all the time, the cataloging of them is an ongoing challenge. Readers are invited to submit news of new issues, especially limited-edition or regionally issued cards, to the editors. Address: Standard Catalog of Vintage Football Cards, 700 E. State St., Iola, WI 54990.

ACKNOWLEDGMENTS

The editors wish to thank the many collectors, dealers and hobbyists (too many to list) who helped us compile, list and price the data in this edition.

A

1987 Ace Fact Pack Chicago Bears

Ace Fact Pack in West Germany printed card sets for 12 National Football League teams. The cards, which have rounded corners, were distributed throughout Great Britain and England. They were designed to look like a deck of playing cards and are unnumbered. There were 33 cards created for each of the 12 teams, which are listed below alphabetically. Twenty-two cards are players; 11 are informational. All but the cards for the Chicago Bears (2-1/2" x 3-1/2") measure 2-1/4" x 3-5/8".

		NM/M	NM	E
	Complete Set (33):	175.00	131.00	70.00
	Common Player:	4.00	3.00	1.50
(1)	Todd Bell	5.00	3.75	2.00
(2)	Mark Bortz	4.00	3.00	1.50
(3)	Kevin Butler	5.00	3.75	2.00
(4)	Jim Covert	6.00	4.50	2.50
(5)	Richard Dent	10.00	7.50	4.00
(6)	Dave Duerson	4.00	3.00	1.50
(7)	Gary Fencik	5.00	3.75	2.00
(8)	Willie Gault	8.00	6.00	3.25
(9)	Dan Hampton	10.00	7.50	4.00
(10)	Jay Hilgenberg	4.00	3.00	1.50
(11)	Wilber Marshall	6.00	4.50	2.50
(12)	Jim McMahon	10.00	7.50	4.00
(13)	Steve McMichael	6.00	4.50	2.50
(14)	Emery Moorehead	4.00	3.00	1.50
(15)	Keith Ortega	4.00	3.00	1.50
(16)	Walter Payton	70.00	52.00	28.00
(17)	William Perry	8.00	6.00	3.25
(18)	Mike Richardson	4.00	3.00	1.50
(19)	Mike Singletary	10.00	7.50	4.00
(20)	Matt Suhey	5.00	3.75	2.00
(21)	Keith Van Horne	4.00	3.00	1.50
(22)	Otis Wilson	5.00	3.75	2.00
(23)	Bears Helmet	4.00	3.00	1.50
(24)	Bears Information	4.00	3.00	1.50
(25)	Bears Uniform	4.00	3.00	1.50
(26)	Game Record Holders	4.00	3.00	1.50
(27)	Season Record Holders	4.00	3.00	1.50
(28)	Career Record Holders	4.00	3.00	1.50
(29)	Bears 1967-86	4.00	3.00	1.50
(30)	1986 Team Statistics	4.00	3.00	1.50
(31)	All-Time Greats	4.00	3.00	1.50
(32)	Roll of Honour	4.00	3.00	1.50
(33)	Soldier Field	4.00	3.00	1.50

1987 Ace Fact Pack Dallas Cowboys

Measuring 2-1/4" x 3-5/8", the 33-card set follows the same design as the Bears and Broncos. The set was released in Great Britain. It has 22 player cards in the set and 11 organizational cards. The cards are unnumbered.

		NM/M	NM	E
	Complete Set (33):	200.00	150.00	80.00
	Common Player:	4.00	3.00	1.50
(1)	Bill Bates	5.00	3.75	2.00
(2)	Doug Cosbie	5.00	3.75	2.00
(3)	Tony Dorsett	25.00	18.50	10.00
(4)	Michael Downs	4.00	3.00	1.50
(5)	John Dutton	5.00	3.75	2.00
(6)	Ron Fellows	4.00	3.00	1.50
(7)	Mike Hegman	4.00	3.00	1.50
(8)	Tony Hill	6.00	4.50	2.50
(9)	Jim Jeffcoat	5.00	3.75	2.00
(10)	Ed "Too Tall" Jones	12.00	9.00	4.75
(11)	Crawford Ker	4.00	3.00	1.50
(12)	Eugene Lockhart	5.00	3.75	2.00
(13)	Phil Pozderac	4.00	3.00	1.50
(14)	Tom Rafferty	5.00	3.75	2.00
(15)	Jeff Rohrer	4.00	3.00	1.50
(16)	Mike Sherrard	6.00	4.50	2.50
(17)	Glen Titensor	4.00	3.00	1.50
(18)	Mark Tuinei	5.00	3.75	2.00
(19)	Herschel Walker	15.00	11.00	6.00
(20)	Everson Walls	5.00	3.75	2.00
(21)	Danny White	8.00	6.00	3.25
(22)	Randy White	16.00	12.00	6.50
(23)	Cowboys Helmet	4.00	3.00	1.50
(24)	Cowboys Information	4.00	3.00	1.50
(25)	Cowboys Uniform	4.00	3.00	1.50
(26)	Game Record Holders	4.00	3.00	1.50
(27)	Season Record Holders	4.00	3.00	1.50
(28)	Career Record Holders	4.00	3.00	1.50
(29)	1967-86 Team Record	4.00	3.00	1.50
(30)	1986 Team Statistics	4.00	3.00	1.50
(31)	All-Time Greats	4.00	3.00	1.50
(32)	Roll of Honour	4.00	3.00	1.50
(33)	Texas Stadium	4.00	3.00	1.50

1987 Ace Fact Pack Denver Broncos

Measuring 2-1/4" x 3-5/8", the 33-card set features 22 player cards and 11 organizational cards. The front showcases the team's logo and player's name at the top, with a photo and the player's bio filling the remainder of the card front. The opposite side of the card has a playing card design. The cards are unnumbered. The set was released in Great Britain.

		NM/M	NM	E
	Complete Set (33):	175.00	131.00	70.00
	Common Player:	4.00	3.00	1.50
(1)	Keith Bishop	4.00	3.00	1.50
(2)	Bill Bryan	4.00	3.00	1.50
(3)	Mark Cooper	4.00	3.00	1.50
(4)	John Elway	90.00	67.00	36.00
(5)	Steve Foley	5.00	3.75	2.00
(6)	Mike Harden	4.00	3.00	1.50
(7)	Rick Hunley	4.00	3.00	1.50
(8)	Vance Johnson	5.00	3.75	2.00
(9)	Rulon Jones	5.00	3.75	2.00
(10)	Rich Karlis	4.00	3.00	1.50
(11)	Clarence Kay	5.00	3.75	2.00
(12)	Ken Lanier	5.00	3.75	2.00
(13)	Karl Mecklenburg	8.00	6.00	3.25
(14)	Chris Norman	4.00	3.00	1.50
(15)	Jim Ryan	4.00	3.00	1.50
(16)	Dennis Smith	5.00	3.75	2.00
(17)	Dave Studdard	4.00	3.00	1.50
(18)	Andre Townsend	4.00	3.00	1.50
(19)	Steve Watson	5.00	3.75	2.00
(20)	Gerald Wilhite	4.00	3.00	1.50
(21)	Sammy Winder	5.00	3.75	2.00
(22)	Louis Wright	5.00	3.75	2.00
(23)	Team Helmet	4.00	3.00	1.50
(24)	Team Information	4.00	3.00	1.50
(25)	Broncos Uniform	4.00	3.00	1.50
(26)	Game Record Holders	4.00	3.00	1.50
(27)	Season Record Holders	4.00	3.00	1.50
(28)	Career Record Holders	4.00	3.00	1.50
(29)	Record 1967-86	4.00	3.00	1.50
(30)	Roll of Honour	4.00	3.00	1.50
(31)	All-Time Greats	4.00	3.00	1.50
(32)	1986 Team Statistics	4.00	3.00	1.50
(33)	Denver Mile High Stadium	4.00	3.00	1.50

1987 Ace Fact Pack Detroit Lions

Measuring 2-1/4" x 3-5/8", the 33-card set follows the same design as the other teams in the series. Issued in Great Britain, the set includes 22 player cards and 11 highlight cards. The cards are unnumbered.

		NM/M	NM	E
	Complete Set (33):	120.00	90.00	48.00
	Common Player:	4.00	3.00	1.50
(1)	Carl Bland	4.00	3.00	1.50
(2)	Lomas Brown	6.00	4.50	2.50
(3)	Jeff Chadwick	5.00	3.75	2.00
(4)	Mike Cofer	6.00	4.50	2.50
(5)	Keith Dorney	4.00	3.00	1.50
(6)	Keith Ferguson	4.00	3.00	1.50
(7)	William Gay	6.00	4.50	2.50
(8)	James Harrell	4.00	3.00	1.50
(9)	Eric Harrell	5.00	3.75	2.00
(10)	Garry James	5.00	3.75	2.00
(11)	Demetrious Johnson	4.00	3.00	1.50
(12)	James Jones	6.00	4.50	2.50
(13)	Chuck Long	5.00	3.75	2.00
(14)	Vernon Maxwell	5.00	3.75	2.00
(15)	Bruce McNorton	4.00	3.00	1.50
(16)	Devon Mitchell	4.00	3.00	1.50
(17)	Steve Lott	4.00	3.00	1.50
(18)	Eddie Murray	6.00	4.50	2.50
(19)	Harvey Smith	4.00	3.00	1.50
(20)	Rich Stenger	4.00	3.00	1.50
(21)	Eric Williams	4.00	3.00	1.50
(22)	Jimmy Williams	4.00	3.00	1.50
(23)	Detroit Lions Helmet	4.00	3.00	1.50
(24)	Team Information	4.00	3.00	1.50
(25)	Uniform Design	4.00	3.00	1.50
(26)	Game Record Holders	4.00	3.00	1.50
(27)	Season Record Holders	4.00	3.00	1.50
(28)	Career Record Holders	4.00	3.00	1.50
(29)	1986 Team Statistics	4.00	3.00	1.50
(30)	Team Record 1967-86	4.00	3.00	1.50
(31)	Championship Seasons	4.00	3.00	1.50
(32)	Pontiac Silverdome	4.00	3.00	1.50
(33)	All-Time Greats	4.00	3.00	1.50

1987 Ace Fact Pack Green Bay Packers

Measuring 2-1/4" x 3-5/8", the 33-card set follows the same design as the other teams in the series. Issued in Great Britain, there are 22 player cards and 11 highlight cards. The cards are unnumbered.

		NM/M	NM	E
	Complete Set (33):	120.00	90.00	48.00
	Common Player:	4.00	3.00	1.50
(1)	John Anderson	6.00	4.50	2.50
(2)	Robbie Bosco	5.00	3.75	2.00
(3)	Don Bracken	4.00	3.00	1.50
(4)	John Cannon	5.00	3.75	2.00
(5)	Alphonso Carreker	4.00	3.00	1.50
(6)	Kenneth Davis	8.00	6.00	3.25
(7)	Al Del Greco	4.00	3.00	1.50
(8)	Gary Ellerson	4.00	3.00	1.50
(9)	Gerry Ellis	5.00	3.75	2.00
(10)	Phillip Epps	6.00	4.50	2.50
(11)	Ron Hallstrom	4.00	3.00	1.50
(12)	Mark Lee	5.00	3.75	2.00
(13)	Bobby Leopold	4.00	3.00	1.50
(14)	Charles Martin	4.00	3.00	1.50
(15)	Brian Noble	5.00	3.75	2.00
(16)	Ken Ruettgers	5.00	3.75	2.00
(17)	Randy Scott	4.00	3.00	1.50
(18)	Walter Stanley	5.00	3.75	2.00
(19)	Ken Stills	4.00	3.00	1.50
(20)	Keith Uecker	4.00	3.00	1.50
(21)	Ed West	5.00	3.75	2.00
(22)	Randy Wright	5.00	3.75	2.00
(23)	Packer Helmet	4.00	3.00	1.50
(24)	Packer Information	4.00	3.00	1.50
(25)	Packer Uniform	4.00	3.00	1.50
(26)	Game Record Holders	4.00	3.00	1.50
(27)	Season Record Holders	4.00	3.00	1.50
(28)	Career Record Holders	4.00	3.00	1.50
(29)	1967-86 Team Record	4.00	3.00	1.50
(30)	1986 Team Statistics	4.00	3.00	1.50
(31)	All-Time Greats	4.00	3.00	1.50
(32)	Roll of Honour	4.00	3.00	1.50
(33)	Lambeau Field/Milwaukee County Stadium	4.00	3.00	1.50

1987 Ace Fact Pack Los Angeles Rams

Measuring 2-1/4" x 3-5/8", the 33-card set follows the same design as the other teams in the series. Issued in Great Britain, it contains 22 player cards and 11 highlight cards, which are unnumbered.

		NM/M	NM	E
	Complete Set (33):	120.00	90.00	48.00
	Common Player:	4.00	3.00	1.50
(1)	Nolan Cromwell	6.00	4.50	2.50
(2)	Eric Dickerson	18.00	13.50	7.25
(3)	Reggie Doss	4.00	3.00	1.50
(4)	Carl Ekern	4.00	3.00	1.50
(5)	Henry Ellard	10.00	7.50	4.00
(6)	Jim Everett	10.00	7.50	4.00
(7)	Jerry Gray	5.00	3.75	2.00
(8)	Dennis Harrah	5.00	3.75	2.00
(9)	David Hull	4.00	3.00	1.50
(10)	Kevin House	5.00	3.75	2.00
(11)	LeRoy Irvin	5.00	3.75	2.00
(12)	Mark Jerue	4.50	3.50	1.75
(13)	Shawn Miller	4.00	3.00	1.50
(14)	Tom Newberry	5.00	3.75	2.00
(15)	Vince Newsome	4.50	3.50	1.75
(16)	Mel Owens	5.00	3.75	2.00
(17)	Irv Pankey	4.00	3.00	1.50
(18)	Doug Reed	5.00	3.75	2.00
(19)	Doug Smith	5.00	3.75	2.00
(20)	Jackie Slater	6.00	4.50	2.50
(21)	Charles White	6.00	4.50	2.50
(22)	Mike Wilcher	4.00	3.00	1.50
(23)	Rams Helmet	4.00	3.00	1.50
(24)	Rams Information	4.50	3.50	1.75
(25)	Rams Uniform	4.00	3.00	1.50
(26)	Game Record Holders	4.00	3.00	1.50
(27)	Season Record Holders	4.00	3.00	1.50
(28)	Career Record Holders	5.00	3.75	2.00
(29)	Team Record 1967-86	4.00	3.00	1.50
(30)	1986 Team Statistics	4.00	3.00	1.50
(31)	All-Time Greats	4.00	3.00	1.50
(32)	Rams Roll of Honour	4.50	3.50	1.75
(33)	Anaheim Stadium	4.00	3.00	1.50

1987 Ace Fact Pack Miami Dolphins

Measuring 2-1/4" x 3-5/8", the 33-card set follows the same design as the others. It was released in Great Britain. There are 22 player cards and 11 highlight cards. The cards are unnumbered.

		NM/M	NM	E
	Complete Set (33):	300.00	220.00	120.00
	Common Player:	4.00	3.00	1.50

(1)	Bob Baumhower	5.00	3.75	2.00
(2)	Woody Bennett	4.00	3.00	1.50
(3)	Doug Betters	5.00	3.75	2.00
(4)	Glenn Blackwood	5.00	3.75	2.00
(5)	Bud Brown	4.00	3.00	1.50
(6)	Bob Brudzinski	4.00	3.00	1.50
(7)	Mark Clayton	7.00	5.25	2.75
(8)	Mark Duper	7.00	5.25	2.75
(9)	Roy Foster	4.00	3.00	1.50
(10)	Jon Giesler	4.00	3.00	1.50
(11)	Hugh Green	6.00	4.50	2.50
(12)	Lorenzo Hampton	5.00	3.75	2.00
(13)	Bruce Hardy	4.00	3.00	1.50
(14)	William Judson	4.00	3.00	1.50
(15)	Greg Koch	4.00	3.00	1.50
(16)	Paul Lankford	4.00	3.00	1.50
(17)	George Little	4.00	3.00	1.50
(18)	Dan Marino	175.00	131.00	70.00
(19)	John Offerdahl	5.00	3.75	2.00
(20)	Dwight Stephenson	6.00	4.50	2.50
(21)	Don Strock	5.00	3.75	2.00
(22)	T.J. Turner	4.00	3.00	1.50
(23)	Dolphins Helmet	4.00	3.00	1.50
(24)	Team Information	4.00	3.00	1.50
(25)	Dolphins Uniform	4.00	3.00	1.50
(26)	Game Record Holders	4.00	3.00	1.50
(27)	Season Record Holders	4.00	3.00	1.50
(28)	Career Record Holders	4.00	3.00	1.50
(29)	Dolphins 1967-86	4.00	3.00	1.50
(30)	1986 Team Statistics	4.00	3.00	1.50
(31)	Dolphin Greats	4.00	3.00	1.50
(32)	Roll of Honour	4.00	3.00	1.50
(33)	Joe Robbie Stadium	4.00	3.00	1.50

1987 Ace Fact Pack New York Giants

Measuring 2-1/4" x 3-5/8", the 33-card set follows the same design as the other teams in the series. Released in Great Britain, the set includes 22 player cards and 11 highlight cards. The cards are unnumbered.

		NM/M	NM	E
Complete Set (33):		150.00	112.00	60.00
Common Player:		4.00	3.00	1.50
(1)	Billy Ard	4.00	3.00	1.50
(2)	Carl Banks	8.00	6.00	3.25
(3)	Mark Bavaro	5.00	3.75	2.00
(4)	Brad Benson	4.00	3.00	1.50
(5)	Harry Carson	8.00	6.00	3.25
(6)	Maurice Carthon (misspelled Morris)	5.00	3.75	2.00
(7)	Mark Collins	5.00	3.75	2.00
(8)	Chris Godfrey	4.00	3.00	1.50
(9)	Kenny Hill	4.00	3.00	1.50
(10)	Erik Howard	5.00	3.75	2.00
(11)	Bobby Johnson	4.00	3.00	1.50
(12)	Leonard Marshall	6.00	4.50	2.50
(13)	George Martin	5.00	3.75	2.00
(14)	Joe Morris	5.00	3.75	2.00
(15)	Karl Nelson	4.00	3.00	1.50
(16)	Bart Oates (misspelled Oakes)	5.00	3.75	2.00
(17)	Gary Reasons	5.00	3.75	2.00
(18)	Stacy Robinson	4.00	3.00	1.50
(19)	Phil Simms	20.00	15.00	8.00
(20)	Lawrence Taylor	30.00	22.00	12.00
(21)	Herb Welch	4.00	3.00	1.50
(22)	Perry Williams	4.00	3.00	1.50
(23)	Giants Helmet	4.00	3.00	1.50
(24)	Giants Information	4.00	3.00	1.50
(25)	Giant Uniforms	4.00	3.00	1.50
(26)	Game Record Holders	4.00	3.00	1.50
(27)	Season Record Holders	4.00	3.00	1.50
(28)	Career Record Holders	4.00	3.00	1.50
(29)	Giants 1967-86	4.00	3.00	1.50
(30)	1986 Team Statistics	4.00	3.00	1.50
(31)	All-Time Greats	4.00	3.00	1.50
(32)	Roll of Honour	4.00	3.00	1.50
(33)	Giants Stadium	4.00	3.00	1.50

1987 Ace Fact Pack New York Jets

Measuring 2-1/4" x 3-5/8", the 33-card set follows the same design as the other teams in the series. Released in Great Britain, there are 22 player cards and 11 highlight cards. The cards are unnumbered.

		NM/M	NM	E
Complete Set (33):		120.00	90.00	48.00
Common Player:		4.00	3.00	1.50
(1)	Dan Alexander	4.00	3.00	1.50
(2)	Tom Baldwin	4.00	3.00	1.50
(3)	Barry Bennett	4.00	3.00	1.50
(4)	Russell Carter	5.00	3.75	2.00
(5)	Kyle Clifton	6.00	4.50	2.50
(6)	Bob Crable	4.00	3.00	1.50
(7)	Joe Fields	5.00	3.75	2.00
(8)	Rusty Guilbeau	4.00	3.00	1.50
(9)	Harry Hamilton	5.00	3.75	2.00
(10)	Johnny Hector	7.00	5.25	2.75
(11)	Jerry Holmes	4.00	3.00	1.50
(12)	Gordon King	4.00	3.00	1.50
(13)	Lester Lyles	4.00	3.00	1.50
(14)	Marty Lyons	5.00	3.75	2.00
(15)	Kevin McArthur	4.00	3.00	1.50
(16)	Freeman McNeil	8.00	6.00	3.25
(17)	Ken O'Brien	7.00	5.25	2.75
(18)	Tony Paige	6.00	4.50	2.50
(19)	Mickey Shuler	5.00	3.75	2.00
(20)	Jim Sweeney	4.00	3.00	1.50
(21)	Al Toon	8.50	6.50	3.50
(22)	Wesley Walker	9.50	7.25	3.75
(23)	Jets Helmet	4.00	3.00	1.50
(24)	Jets Team Information	4.00	3.00	1.50
(25)	Jets Uniform	4.00	3.00	1.50
(26)	Game Record Holders	4.00	3.00	1.50
(27)	Season Record Holders	4.00	3.00	1.50
(28)	Career Record Holders	4.00	3.00	1.50
(29)	1986 Team Statistics	4.00	3.00	1.50
(30)	Jets 1967-86	4.00	3.00	1.50
(31)	All-Time Greats	4.00	3.00	1.50
(32)	Roll of Honour	4.00	3.00	1.50
(33)	Giants Stadium	4.00	3.00	1.50

1987 Ace Fact Pack San Francisco 49ers

Measuring 2-1/4" x 3-5/8", this 33-card set was released in Great Britain. The design follows the same format of the other teams in the set. There are 22 player cards and 11 highlights cards. The cards are unnumbered.

		NM/M	NM	E
Complete Set (33):		400.00	300.00	160.00
Common Player:		4.00	3.00	1.50
(1)	John Ayers	4.00	3.00	1.50
(2)	Dwaine Board	4.00	3.00	1.50
(3)	Michael Carter	6.00	4.50	2.50
(4)	Dwight Clark	12.00	9.00	4.75
(5)	Roger Craig	12.00	9.00	4.75
(6)	Joe Cribbs	5.00	3.75	2.00
(7)	Randy Cross	5.00	3.75	2.00
(8)	Riki Ellison	4.00	3.00	1.50
(9)	Jim Fahnhorst	4.00	3.00	1.50
(10)	Keith Fahnhorst	4.00	3.00	1.50
(11)	Russ Francis	5.00	3.75	2.00
(12)	Don Griffin	5.00	3.75	2.00
(13)	Ronnie Lott	14.00	10.50	5.50
(14)	Milt McColl	4.00	3.00	1.50
(15)	Tim McKyer	5.00	3.75	2.00
(16)	Joe Montana	175.00	130.00	70.00
(17)	Bubba Paris	4.00	3.00	1.50
(18)	Fred Quinlan	4.00	3.00	1.50
(19)	Jerry Rice	150.00	112.00	60.00
(20)	Manu Tuiasosopo	4.00	3.00	1.50
(21)	Keena Turner	6.00	4.50	2.50
(22)	Carlton Williamson	4.00	3.00	1.50
(23)	49er Helmet	4.00	3.00	1.50
(24)	49er Information	4.00	3.00	1.50
(25)	49er Uniform	4.00	3.00	1.50
(26)	Game Record Holders	4.00	3.00	1.50
(27)	Season Record Holders	4.00	3.00	1.50
(28)	Career Record Holders	4.00	3.00	1.50
(29)	49ers History 1967-86	4.00	3.00	1.50
(30)	1986 Team Statistics	4.00	3.00	1.50
(31)	All-Time Greats	4.00	3.00	1.50
(32)	Roll of Honour	4.00	3.00	1.50
(33)	Candlestick Park	4.00	3.00	1.50

1987 Ace Fact Pack Seattle Seahawks

Measuring 2-1/4" x 3-5/8", the 33-card set follows the same design as the other teams in the series. Issued in Great Britain, the set is broken up into 22 player and 11 highlight cards, which are unnumbered.

		NM/M	NM	E
Complete Set (33):		150.00	112.00	60.00
Common Player:		4.00	3.00	1.50
(1)	Edwin Bailey	4.00	3.00	1.50
(2)	Dave Brown	6.00	4.50	2.50
(3)	Jeff Bryant	4.00	3.00	1.50
(4)	Blair Bush	5.00	3.75	2.00
(5)	Keith Butler	4.00	3.00	1.50
(6)	Kenny Easley	5.00	3.75	2.00
(7)	Greg Gaines	4.00	3.00	1.50
(8)	Jacob Green	6.00	4.50	2.50
(9)	Norm Johnson	5.00	3.75	2.00
(10)	Dave Krieg	8.00	6.00	3.25
(11)	Steve Largent	30.00	22.00	12.00
(12)	Reggie Kinlaw	4.00	3.00	1.50
(13)	Ron Mattes	4.00	3.00	1.50
(14)	Bryan Millard	4.00	3.00	1.50
(15)	Eugene Robinson	5.00	3.75	2.00
(16)	Bruce Scholtz	4.00	3.00	1.50
(17)	Terry Taylor	4.00	3.00	1.50
(18)	Mike Tice	5.00	3.75	2.00
(19)	Daryl Turner	5.00	3.75	2.00
(20)	Curt Warner	7.50	5.75	3.00
(21)	John L. Williams	12.00	9.00	4.75
(22)	Fredd Young	5.00	3.75	2.00
(23)	Seattle Helmet	4.00	3.00	1.50
(24)	Seahawk Information	4.00	3.00	1.50
(25)	Seahawk Uniform	4.00	3.00	1.50
(26)	Game Record Holder	4.00	3.00	1.50
(27)	Season Record Holders	4.00	3.00	1.50
(28)	Career Record Holders	4.00	3.00	1.50
(29)	1977-86 Team Record	4.00	3.00	1.50
(30)	1986 Team Statistics	4.00	3.00	1.50
(31)	All-Time Greats	4.00	3.00	1.50
(32)	Roll of Honour	4.00	3.00	1.50
(33)	Kingdome	4.00	3.00	1.50

1987 Ace Fact Pack Washington Redskins

Measuring 2-1/4" x 3-5/8", the 33-card set follows the same design as the other teams in the series. Issued in Great Britain, the set is broken up into 22 player cards and 11 highlight cards, which are unnumbered.

		NM/M	NM	E
Complete Set (33):		175.00	130.00	70.00
Common Player:		4.00	3.00	1.50
(1)	Jeff Bostic	5.00	3.75	2.00
(2)	Dave Butz	6.00	4.50	2.50
(3)	Gary Clark	20.00	15.00	8.00
(4)	Monte Coleman	5.00	3.75	2.00
(5)	Vernon Dean	4.00	3.00	1.50
(6)	Clint Didier	5.00	3.75	2.00
(7)	Darryl Grant	4.00	3.00	1.50
(8)	Darrell Green	7.50	5.75	3.00
(9)	Russ Grimm	6.00	4.50	2.50
(10)	Joe Jacoby	6.00	4.50	2.50
(11)	Curtis Jordan	4.00	3.00	1.50
(12)	Dexter Manley	5.00	3.75	2.00
(13)	Charles Mann	6.00	4.50	2.50
(14)	Mark May	5.00	3.75	2.00
(15)	Rich Milot	4.00	3.00	1.50
(16)	Art Monk	30.00	22.00	12.00
(17)	Neal Olkewicz	4.00	3.00	1.50
(18)	George Rogers	8.00	6.00	3.25
(19)	Jay Schroeder	8.00	6.00	3.25
(20)	R.C. Thielemann	4.00	3.00	1.50
(21)	Alvin Walton	4.00	3.00	1.50
(22)	Don Warren	4.00	3.00	1.50
(23)	Redskin Helmet	4.00	3.00	1.50
(24)	Redskin Information	4.00	3.00	1.50
(25)	Redskin Uniforms	4.00	3.00	1.50
(26)	Game Record Holders	4.00	3.00	1.50
(27)	Season Record Holders	4.00	3.00	1.50
(28)	Career Record Holders	4.00	3.00	1.50
(29)	Redskins 1867-86	4.00	3.00	1.50
(30)	1986 Team Statistics	4.00	3.00	1.50
(31)	All-Time Redskins	4.00	3.00	1.50
(32)	Roll of Honour	4.00	3.00	1.50
(33)	Robert F. Kennedy Stadium	4.00	3.00	1.50

1989 Action Packed Prototypes

These cards were produced as prototypes before Action Packed released its 1989 30-card test set. The gold-bordered front has a raised color action photo on it; the back has stats, a head shot, notes, a card number and a space for an autograph. These cards, numbered 72 and 101, can be distinguished from the test set by where the card number appears. On these cards, they are on the same side as the mug shot; on the test cards they are on the opposite side.

Complete Set (2):		40.00	56.00	30.00
Common Player:		20.00	34.00	15.00
72	Freeman McNeil	20.00	15.00	8.00
101	Phil Simms	20.00	15.00	8.00

1989 Action Packed Test

These 30 cards are standard size and were packaged in packs of six. Ten players from the Chicago Bears, New York Giants and Washington Redskins are represented in the set, which was copyrighted by Hi-Pro Marketing of Northbrook, Ill. Each front has a gold-border and a raised color action photo; the back has a head shot, statistics, informational notes, a card number and a space for an autograph.

Complete Set (30):		20.00	18.50	10.00
Common Player:		.50	.40	.20
1	Neal Anderson	1.00	.70	.40
2	Trace Armstrong	.60	.45	.25
3	Kevin Butler	.50	.40	.20
4	Richard Dent	.75	.60	.30
5	Dennis Gentry	.50	.40	.20
6	Dan Hampton	.75	.60	.30
7	Jay Hilgenberg	.60	.45	.25
8	Thomas Sanders	.60	.45	.25
9	Mike Singletary	.75	.60	.30
10	Mike Tomczak	.75	.60	.30

11	Raul Allegre	.50	.40	.20
12	Ottis Anderson	.75	.60	.30
13	Mark Bavaro	.60	.45	.25
14	Terry Kinard	.50	.40	.20
15	Lionel Manuel	.50	.40	.20
16	Leonard Marshall	.60	.45	.25
17	Dave Meggett	1.00	.70	.40
18	Joe Morris	.75	.60	.30
19	Phil Simms	1.00	.70	.40
20	Lawrence Taylor	1.75	1.25	.70
21	Kelvin Bryant	.75	.60	.30
22	Darrell Green	1.00	.70	.40
23	Dexter Manley	.60	.45	.25
24	Charles Mann	.60	.45	.25
25	Wilber Marshall	.60	.45	.25
26	Art Monk	1.50	1.25	.60
27	Jamie Morris	.60	.45	.25
28	Tracy Rocker	.60	.45	.25
29	Mark Rypien	2.00	1.50	.80
30	Ricky Sanders	1.00	.70	.40

1990 Action Packed

BARRY SANDERS

LIONS™

Action Packed was released in two series over the summer, with the first available in June and the second available in August. The total of 280 cards was randomly split up between the two series. In the first series, 126 players were issued; 154 came out in Series II. A factory set was also issued. The cards are embossed, with a gold foil and rounded corners. Special cards included those honoring the retired Reggie Williams and Steve Largent; a card back for Christian Okoye with a phrase written in Nigerian; and a Braille card featuring the retired Jim Plunkett.

	NM/M	NM	E
Complete Set (280):	20.00	15.00	8.00
Complete Factory (281):	20.00	15.00	8.00
Common Player:	.10	.08	.04
Minor Stars:	.20	.15	.08
Series 1 Foil Pack (6):	.50		
Series 1 Foil Wax Box (36):	10.00		
Series 2 Foil Pack (6):	.50		
Series 2 Foil Wax Box (36):	10.00		

1	Aundray Bruce	.10	.08	.04
2	Scott Case	.10	.08	.04
3	Tony Casillas	.10	.08	.04
4	Shawn Collins	.10	.08	.04
5	Marcus Cotton	.10	.08	.04
6	Bill Fralic	.10	.08	.04
7	Tim Green	.10	.08	.04
8	Chris Miller	.20	.15	.08
9	Deion Sanders	1.25	.90	.50
10	John Settle	.10	.08	.04
11	Cornelius Bennett	.20	.15	.08
12	Shane Conlan	.10	.08	.04
13	Kent Hill	.10	.08	.04
14	Jim Kelly	.50	.40	.20
15	Mark Kelso	.10	.08	.04
16	Scott Norwood	.10	.08	.04
17	Andre Reed	.20	.15	.08
18	Fred Smerlas	.10	.08	.04
19	Bruce Smith	.20	.15	.08
20	Thurman Thomas	.50	.40	.20
21	Neal Anderson	.20	.15	.08
22	Kevin Butler	.10	.08	.04
23	Richard Dent	.20	.15	.08
24	Dennis Gentry	.10	.08	.04
25	Dan Hampton	.10	.08	.04
26	Jay Hilgenberg	.10	.08	.04
27	Steve McMichael	.10	.08	.04
28	Brad Muster	.10	.08	.04
29	Mike Singletary	.20	.15	.08
30	Mike Tomczak	.10	.08	.04
31	James Brooks	.10	.08	.04
32	Rickey Dixon	.10	.08	.04
33	Boomer Esiason	.20	.15	.08
34	David Fulcher	.10	.08	.04
35	Rodney Holman	.10	.08	.04
36	Tim Krumrie	.10	.08	.04
37	Tim McGee	.10	.08	.04
38	Anthony Munoz	.20	.15	.08
39	Reggie Williams	.10	.08	.04
40	Ickey Woods	.10	.08	.04
41	Thane Gash	.10	.08	.04
42	Mike Johnson	.10	.08	.04
43	Bernie Kosar	.20	.15	.08
44	Reggie Langhorne	.10	.08	.04
45	Clay Matthews	.10	.08	.04
46	Eric Metcalf	.20	.15	.08
47	Frank Minnifield	.10	.08	.04
48	Ozzie Newsome	.20	.15	.08
49	Webster Slaughter	.10	.08	.04
50	Felix Wright	.10	.08	.04
51	Troy Aikman	2.00	1.50	.80
52	James Dixon	.10	.08	.04
53	Michael Irvin	.50	.40	.20
54	Jim Jeffcoat	.10	.08	.04
55	Ed Jones	.10	.08	.04
56	Eugene Lockhart	.10	.08	.04
57	Danny Noonan	.10	.08	.04
58	Paul Palmer	.10	.08	.04
59	Everson Walls	.10	.08	.04
60	Steve Walsh	.20	.15	.08
61	Steve Atwater	.10	.08	.04
62	Tyrone Braxton	.10	.08	.04
63	John Elway	2.00	1.50	.80
64	Bobby Humphrey	.10	.08	.04
65	Mark Jackson	.10	.08	.04
66	Vance Johnson	.10	.08	.04
67	Greg Kragen	.10	.08	.04
68	Karl Mecklenburg	.10	.08	.04
69	Dennis Smith	.10	.08	.04
70	David Treadwell	.10	.08	.04
71	Jim Arnold	.10	.08	.04
72	Jerry Ball	.10	.08	.04
73	Bennie Blades	.10	.08	.04
74	Mel Gray	.10	.08	.04
75	Richard Johnson	.10	.08	.04
76	Eddie Murray	.10	.08	.04
77	Rodney Peete	.10	.08	.04
78	Barry Sanders	5.00	3.75	2.00
79	Chris Spielman	.10	.08	.04
80	Walter Stanley	.10	.08	.04
81	Dave Brown	.10	.08	.04
82	Brent Fullwood	.10	.08	.04
83	Tim Harris	.10	.08	.04
84	Johnny Holland	.10	.08	.04
85	Don Majkowski	.10	.08	.04
86	Tony Mandarich	.10	.08	.04
87	Mark Murphy	.10	.08	.04
88	Brian Noble	.10	.08	.04
89	Ken Ruettgers	.10	.08	.04
90	Sterling Sharpe	.20	.15	.08
91	Ray Childress	.10	.08	.04
92	Ernest Givins	.10	.08	.04
93	Alonzo Highsmith	.10	.08	.04
94	Drew Hill	.10	.08	.04
95	Bruce Matthews	.10	.08	.04
96	Bubba McDowell	.10	.08	.04
97	Warren Moon	.50	.40	.20
98	Mike Munchak	.10	.08	.04
99	Allen Pinkett	.10	.08	.04
100	Mike Rozier	.10	.08	.04
101	Albert Bentley	.10	.08	.04
102	Duane Bickett	.10	.08	.04
103	Bill Brooks	.10	.08	.04
104	Chris Chandler	.20	.15	.08
105	Ray Donaldson	.10	.08	.04
106	Chris Hinton	.10	.08	.04
107	Andre Rison	.20	.15	.08
108	Keith Taylor	.10	.08	.04
109	Clarence Verdin	.10	.08	.04
110	Fredd Young	.10	.08	.04
111	Deron Cherry	.10	.08	.04
112	Steve DeBerg	.10	.08	.04
113	Dino Hackett	.10	.08	.04
114	Albert Lewis	.10	.08	.04
115	Nick Lowery	.10	.08	.04
116	Christian Okoye	.10	.08	.04
117	Stephone Paige	.10	.08	.04
118	Kevin Ross	.10	.08	.04
119	Derrick Thomas	.20	.15	.08
120	Mike Webster	.10	.08	.04
121	Marcus Allen	.20	.15	.08
122	Eddie Anderson	.10	.08	.04
123	Steve Beuerlein	.20	.15	.08
124	Tim Brown	.50	.40	.20
125	Mervyn Fernandez	.10	.08	.04
126	Bob Golic	.10	.08	.04
127	Bo Jackson	.50	.40	.20
128	Howie Long	.20	.15	.08
129	Greg Townsend	.10	.08	.04
130	Willie Anderson	.10	.08	.04
131	Greg Bell	.10	.08	.04
132	Robert Delpino	.10	.08	.04
133	Henry Ellard	.10	.08	.04
134	Jim Everett	.20	.15	.08
135	Jerry Gray	.10	.08	.04
136	Kevin Greene	.20	.15	.08
138	Tom Newberry	.10	.08	.04
139	Jackie Slater	.10	.08	.04
140	Doug Smith	.10	.08	.04
141	Mark Clayton	.10	.08	.04
142	Jeff Cross	.10	.08	.04
143	Mark Duper	.10	.08	.04
144	Ferrell Edmunds	.10	.08	.04
145	Jim Jensen	.10	.08	.04
146	Dan Marino	3.50	2.75	1.50
147	John Offerdahl	.10	.08	.04
148	Louis Oliver	.10	.08	.04
149	Reggie Roby	.10	.08	.04
150	Sammie Smith	.10	.08	.04
151	Joey Browner	.10	.08	.04
152	Anthony Carter	.10	.08	.04
153	Chris Doleman	.10	.08	.04
154	Steve Jordan	.10	.08	.04
155	Carl Lee	.10	.08	.04
156	Randall McDaniel	.10	.08	.04
157	Keith Millard	.10	.08	.04
158	Herschel Walker	.20	.15	.08
159	Wade Wilson	.10	.08	.04
160	Gary Zimmerman	.10	.08	.04
161	Hart Lee Dykes	.10	.08	.04
162	Irving Fryar	.20	.15	.08
163	Steve Grogan	.10	.08	.04
164	Maurice Hurst	.10	.08	.04
165	Fred Marion	.10	.08	.04
166	Stanley Morgan	.10	.08	.04
167	Robert Perryman	.10	.08	.04
168	John Stephens	.10	.08	.04
169	Andre Tippett	.10	.08	.04
170	Brent Williams	.10	.08	.04
171	John Fourcade	.10	.08	.04
172	Bobby Hebert	.20	.15	.08
173	Dalton Hilliard	.10	.08	.04
174	Rickey Jackson	.10	.08	.04
175	Vaughan Johnson	.10	.08	.04
176	Eric Martin	.10	.08	.04
177	Robert Massey	.10	.08	.04
178	Rueben Mayes	.10	.08	.04
179	Sam Mills	.10	.08	.04
180	Pat Swilling	.10	.08	.04
181	Ottis Anderson	.20	.15	.08
182	Carl Banks	.10	.08	.04
183	Mark Bavaro	.10	.08	.04
184	Mark Collins	.10	.08	.04
185	Leonard Marshall	.10	.08	.04
186	Dave Meggett	.10	.08	.04
187	Gary Reasons	.10	.08	.04
188	Phil Simms	.20	.15	.08
189	Lawrence Taylor	.50	.40	.20
190	Odessa Turner	.10	.08	.04
191	Kyle Clifton	.10	.08	.04
192	James Hasty	.10	.08	.04
193	Johnny Hector	.10	.08	.04
194	Jeff Lageman	.10	.08	.04
195	Pat Leahy	.10	.08	.04
196	Erik McMillan	.10	.08	.04
197	Ken O'Brien	.10	.08	.04
198	Mickey Shuler	.10	.08	.04
199	Al Toon	.10	.08	.04
200	JoJo Townsell	.10	.08	.04
201	Eric Allen	.10	.08	.04
202	Jerome Brown	.10	.08	.04
203	Keith Byars	.10	.08	.04
204	Cris Carter	1.00	.70	.40
205	Wes Hopkins	.10	.08	.04
206	Keith Jackson	.20	.15	.08
207	Seth Joyner	.10	.08	.04
208	Mike Quick	.10	.08	.04
209	Andre Waters	.10	.08	.04
210	Reggie White	.50	.40	.20
211	Rich Carmarillo	.10	.08	.04
212	Roy Green	.10	.08	.04
213	Ken Harvey	.10	.08	.04
214	Gary Hogeboom	.10	.08	.04
215	Tim McDonald	.10	.08	.04
216	Stump Mitchell	.10	.08	.04
217	Luis Sharpe	.10	.08	.04
218	Vai Sikahema	.10	.08	.04
219	J.T. Smith	.10	.08	.04
220	Ron Wolfley	.10	.08	.04
221	Gary Anderson	.10	.08	.04
222	Bubby Brister	.10	.08	.04
223	Merril Hoge	.10	.08	.04
224	Tunch Ilken	.10	.08	.04
225	Louis Lipps	.10	.08	.04
226	David Little	.10	.08	.04
227	Greg Lloyd	.10	.08	.04
228	Dwayne Woodruff	.10	.08	.04
229	Rod Woodson	.20	.15	.08
230	Tim Worley	.10	.08	.04
231	Marion Butts	.10	.08	.04
232	Gill Byrd	.10	.08	.04
233	Burt Grossman	.10	.08	.04
234	Jim McMahon	.20	.15	.08
235	Anthony Miller	.20	.15	.08

236	Leslie O'Neal	.10	.08	.04
237	Gary Plummer	.10	.08	.04
238	Billy Ray Smith	.10	.08	.04
239	Tim Spencer	.10	.08	.04
240	Lee Williams	.10	.08	.04
241	Mike Cofer	.10	.08	.04
242	Roger Craig	.20	.15	.08
243	Charles Haley	.10	.08	.04
244	Ronnie Lott	.20	.15	.08
245	Guy McIntyre	.10	.08	.04
246	Joe Montana	2.50	2.00	1.00
247	Tom Rathman	.10	.08	.04
248	Jerry Rice	2.00	1.50	.80
249	John Taylor	.20	.15	.08
250	Michael Walter	.10	.08	.04
251	Brian Blades	.10	.08	.04
252	Jacob Green	.10	.08	.04
253	Dave Krieg	.10	.08	.04
254	Steve Largent	.20	.15	.08
255	Joe Nash	.10	.08	.04
256	Rufus Porter	.10	.08	.04
257	Eugene Robinson	.20	.15	.08
258	Paul Skansi	.10	.08	.04
259	Curt Warner	.10	.08	.04
260	John L. Williams	.10	.08	.04
261	Mark Carrier	.10	.08	.04
262	Reuben Davis	.10	.08	.04
263	Harry Hamilton	.10	.08	.04
264	Bruce Hill	.10	.08	.04
265	Donald Igwebuike	.10	.08	.04
266	Eugene Marve	.10	.08	.04
267	Kevin Murphy	.10	.08	.04
268	Mark Robinson	.10	.08	.04
269	Lars Tate	.10	.08	.04
270	Vinny Testaverde	.50	.40	.20
271	Gary Clark	.10	.08	.04
272	Monte Coleman	.10	.08	.04
273	Darrell Green	.20	.15	.08
274	Charles Mann	.10	.08	.04
275	Wilbur Marshall	.10	.08	.04
276	Art Monk	.20	.15	.08
277	Gerald Riggs	.10	.08	.04
278	Mark Rypien	.20	.15	.08
279	Rickey Sanders	.10	.08	.04
280	Alvin Walton	.10	.08	.04
NNO	Jim Plunkett BR (Braille)	4.00	3.00	1.50
NNO	Checklist	.10	.08	.04

1990 Action Packed All-Madden

This 58-card set pictures players selected by CBS analyst and former coach John Madden. Cards were released in late February of 1991. Cards were issued in six-card wax packs and in complete sets. The set features Action Packed's first borderless set, previewing the 1991 set. Cards are standard-sized, embossed, and feature Madden's comments about each player on the back.

		NM/M	NM	E
	Complete Set (58):	20.00	15.00	8.00
	Common Player:	.25	.20	.10
	Wax Box:	20.00		
1	Joe Montana	3.00	2.25	1.25
2	Jerry Rice	3.00	2.25	1.25
3	Charles Haley	.40	.30	.15
4	Steve Wisniewski	.25	.20	.10
5	Dave Meggett	.40	.30	.15
6	Ottis Anderson	.40	.30	.15
7	Nate Newton	.25	.20	.10
8	Warren Moon	1.00	.75	.40
9	Emmitt Smith	6.00	4.50	2.50
10	Jackie Slater	.25	.20	.10
11	Pepper Johnson	.25	.20	.10
12	Lawrence Taylor	.75	.60	.30
13	Sterling Sharpe	1.00	.70	.40
14	Sean Landeta	.25	.20	.10
15	Richard Dent	.40	.30	.15
16	Neal Anderson	.50	.40	.20
17	Bruce Matthews	.25	.20	.10
18	Matt Millen	.25	.20	.10
19	Reggie White	.50	.40	.20
20	Greg Townsend	.25	.20	.10
21	Troy Aikman	3.00	2.25	1.25
22	Don Mosebar	.25	.20	.10
23	Jeff Zimmerman	.25	.20	.10
24	Rod Woodson	.50	.40	.20
25	Keith Byars	.40	.30	.15
26	Randall Cunningham	.75	.60	.30
27	Reyna Thompson	.40	.30	.15
28	Marcus Allen	.60	.45	.25
29	Gary Clark	.50	.40	.20
30	Anthony Carter	.40	.30	.15
31	Bubba Paris	.25	.20	.10
32	Ronnie Lott	.50	.40	.20
33	Erik Howard	.25	.20	.10
34	Ernest Givins	.25	.20	.10
35	Mike Munchak	.25	.20	.10
36	Jim Lachey	.25	.20	.10

37	Merril Hoge	.25	.20	.10
38	Darrell Green	.25	.20	.10
39	Pierce Holt	.25	.20	.10
40	Jerome Brown	.25	.20	.10
41	William Perry	.25	.20	.10
42	Michael Carter	.25	.20	.10
43	Keith Jackson	.40	.30	.15
44	Kevin Fagan	.25	.20	.10
45	Mark Carrier	.40	.30	.15
46	Fred Barnett	.75	.60	.30
47	Barry Sanders	3.00	2.25	1.25
48	Pat Swilling, Rickey Jackson	.50	.40	.20
49	Sam Mills, Vaughan Johnson	.25	.20	.10
50	Jacob Green	.25	.20	.10
51	Stan Brock	.25	.20	.10
52	Dan Hampton	.25	.20	.10
53	Brian Noble	.25	.20	.10
54	John Elliott	.25	.20	.10
55	Matt Bahr	.25	.20	.10
56	Bill Parcells	.25	.20	.10
57	Art Shell	.25	.20	.10
58	All-Madden Team Trophy	.25	.20	.10

1990 Action Packed Rookie Update

Issued in November 1990, the Update set includes each of the 1990 first-round draft choices, rookie prospects, and traded players. Randall Cunningham, who did not appear in the regular 1990 Action Packed set, signed a late contract with the NFL Players Association and does not appear in the Update set. Cards were issued in both wax packs and factory sets.

		NM/M	NM	E
	Complete Set (84):	15.00	11.00	6.00
	Complete Factory (84):	15.00	11.00	6.00
	Common Player:	.10	.08	.04
	Minor Stars:	.20	.15	.08
	Foil Pack (6):	2.00		
	Foil Box (36):	55.00		
1	Jeff George RC	1.00	.70	.40
2	Richmond Webb RC	.20	.15	.08
3	James Williams RC	.10	.08	.04
4	Tony Bennett RC	.20	.15	.08
5	Darrell Thompson RC	.10	.08	.04
6	Steve Broussard RC	.10	.08	.04
7	Rodney Hampton RC	.75	.60	.30
8	Rob Moore RC	3.00	2.25	1.25
9	Alton Montgomery RC	.10	.08	.04
10	Leroy Butler RC	.50	.40	.20
11	Anthony Johnson RC	.50	.40	.20
12	Scott Mitchell RC	1.00	.70	.40
13	Mike Fox RC	.10	.08	.04
14	Robert Blackmon RC	.10	.08	.04
15	Blair Thomas RC	.10	.08	.04
16	Tony Stargell RC	.10	.08	.04
17	Peter Tom Willis RC	.10	.08	.04
18	Harold Green RC	.20	.15	.08
19	Bernard Clark RC	.10	.08	.04
20	Aaron Wallace RC	.10	.08	.04
21	Dennis Brown RC	.10	.08	.04
22	Johnny Johnson RC	.20	.15	.08
23	Chris Calloway RC	.50	.40	.20
24	Walter Wilson RC	.10	.08	.04
25	Dexter Carter RC	.10	.08	.04
26	Percy Snow RC	.10	.08	.04
27	Johnny Bailey RC	.10	.08	.04
28	Mike Bellamy RC	.10	.08	.04
29	Ben Smith RC	.10	.08	.04
30	Mark Carrier RC	.50	.40	.20
31	James Francis RC	.10	.08	.04
32	Lamar Lathon RC	.10	.08	.04
33	Bern Brostek RC	.10	.08	.04
34	Emmitt Smith RC	3.00	1.50	.90
35	Andre Collins RC	.10	.08	.04
36	Alexander Wright RC	.10	.08	.04
37	Fred Barnett RC	.20	.15	.08
38	Junior Seau RC	3.00	2.25	1.25
39	Cortez Kennedy RC	.50	.40	.20
40	Terry Wooden RC	.10	.08	.04
41	Eric Davis RC	.10	.08	.04

42	Fred Washington RC	.10	.08	.04
43	Reggie Cobb RC	.10	.08	.04
44	Andre Ware RC	.20	.15	.08
45	Anthony Smith RC	.10	.08	.04
46	Shannon Sharpe RC	8.00	6.00	3.25
47	Harlon Barnett RC	.10	.08	.04
48	Greg McMurty RC	.10	.08	.04
49	Stacey Simmons RC	.10	.08	.04
50	Calvin Williams RC	.20	.15	.08
51	Anthony Thompson RC	.10	.08	.04
52	Ricky Proehl RC	.50	.40	.20
53	Tony James RC	.10	.08	.04
54	Ray Agnew RC	.10	.08	.04
55	Tom Hodson RC	.10	.08	.04
56	Ron Cox RC	.10	.08	.04
57	Leroy Hoard RC	.10	.08	.04
58	Eric Green RC	.50	.40	.20
59	Barry Foster RC	.10	.08	.04
60	Keith McCants RC	.10	.08	.04
61	Oliver Barnett RC	.10	.08	.04
62	Chris Warren RC	.10	.08	.04
63	Pat Terrell RC	.10	.08	.04
64	Renaldo Turnbull RC	.10	.08	.04
65	Chris Chandler	.20	.15	.08
66	Everson Walls	.10	.08	.04
67	Alonzo Highsmith	.10	.08	.04
68	Gary Anderson	.20	.15	.08
69	Fred Smerlas	.10	.08	.04
70	Jim McMahon	.50	.40	.20
71	Curt Warner	.20	.15	.08
72	Stanley Morgan	.10	.08	.04
73	Dave Waymer	.10	.08	.04
74	Billy Joe Tolliver	.20	.15	.08
75	Tony Eason	.10	.08	.04
76	Max Montoya	.10	.08	.04
77	Greg Bell	.10	.08	.04
78	Dennis McKinnon	.10	.08	.04
79	Raymond Clayborn	.10	.08	.04
80	Broderick Thomas	.10	.08	.04
81	Timm Rosenbach	.10	.08	.04
82	Tim McKyer	.10	.08	.04
83	Andre Rison	.50	.40	.20
84	Randall Cunningham	.75	.60	.30

1991 Action Packed

Action Packed issued a borderless card with a gold stripe protecting the back seam, both improving on the previous year's design. Cards are arranged in alphabetical order by city and player. Two unnumbered prototype cards were also created, for Randall Cunningham and Emmitt Smith. The cards are labeled on the back as being 1991 prototypes. Cunningham's is valued at $10; Smith's is $15. Eight Braille cards, numbers 281-288, were also produced. The cards, similar in design to the regular issue, feature statistical leaders but have different photos than the players' regular cards. The backs are written in Braille. The Braille cards were only available in factory sets.

		NM/M	NM	E
	Complete Set (280):	15.00	11.00	6.00
	Complete Factory (291):	15.00	11.00	6.00
	Common Player:	.10	.08	.04
	Minor Stars:	.20	.15	.08
	Pack (6):	1.00		
	Wax Box (24):	20.00		
1	Steve Broussard	.10	.08	.04
2	Scott Case	.10	.08	.04
3	Brian Jordan	.20	.15	.08
4	Darion Conner	.10	.08	.04
5	Tim Green	.10	.08	.04
6	Chris Miller	.20	.15	.08
7	Andre Rison	.50	.40	.20
8	Mike Rozier	.10	.08	.04
9	Deion Sanders	1.00	.70	.40
10	Jessie Tuggle	.10	.08	.04
11	Leonard Smith	.10	.08	.04
12	Shane Conlan	.10	.08	.04
13	Kent Hull	.10	.08	.04
14	Keith McKeller	.10	.08	.04
15	James Lofton	.20	.15	.08

16	Andre Reed	.20	.15	.08
17	Bruce Smith	.20	.15	.08
18	Darryl Talley	.10	.08	.04
19	Steve Tasker	.10	.08	.04
20	Thurman Thomas	.50	.40	.20
21	Neal Anderson	.10	.08	.04
22	Trace Armstrong	.10	.08	.04
23	Mark Bortz	.10	.08	.04
24	Mark Carrier (Chi.)	.10	.08	.04
25	Wendell Davis	.10	.08	.04
26	Richard Dent	.10	.08	.04
27	Jim Harbaugh	.20	.15	.08
28	Jay Hilgenberg	.10	.08	.04
29	Brad Muster	.10	.08	.04
30	Mike Singletary	.20	.15	.08
31	Harold Green	.10	.08	.04
32	James Brooks	.10	.08	.04
33	Eddie Brown	.10	.08	.04
34	Boomer Esiason	.20	.15	.08
35	James Francis	.10	.08	.04
36	David Fulcher	.10	.08	.04
37	Rodney Holman	.10	.08	.04
38	Tim McGee	.10	.08	.04
39	Anthony Munoz	.10	.08	.04
40	Ickey Woods	.10	.08	.04
41	Rob Burnett RC	.10	.08	.04
42	Thane Gash	.10	.08	.04
43	Mike Johnson	.10	.08	.04
44	Brian Brennan	.10	.08	.04
45	Reggie Langhorne	.10	.08	.04
46	Kevin Mack	.10	.08	.04
47	Clay Matthews	.10	.08	.04
48	Eric Metcalf	.20	.15	.08
49	Anthony Pleasant	.10	.08	.04
50	Ozzie Newsome	.10	.08	.04
51	Troy Aikman	2.00	1.50	.80
52	Issiac Holt	.10	.08	.04
53	Michael Irvin	.50	.40	.20
54	Jimmie Jones	.10	.08	.04
55	Eugene Lockhart	.10	.08	.04
56	Kelvin Martin	.10	.08	.04
57	Ken Norton Jr.	.10	.08	.04
58	Jay Novacek	.10	.08	.04
59	Emmitt Smith	4.00	3.00	1.50
60	Daniel Stubbs	.10	.08	.04
61	Steve Atwater	.10	.08	.04
62	Michael Brooks	.10	.08	.04
63	John Elway	2.00	1.50	.80
64	Simon Fletcher	.10	.08	.04
65	Bobby Humphrey	.10	.08	.04
66	Mark Jackson	.10	.08	.04
67	Vance Johnson	.10	.08	.04
68	Karl Mecklenburg	.10	.08	.04
69	Dennis Smith	.10	.08	.04
70	Greg Kragen	.10	.08	.04
71	Jerry Ball	.10	.08	.04
72	Lomas Brown	.10	.08	.04
73	Robert Clark	.10	.08	.04
74	Michael Coper	.10	.08	.04
75	Mel Gray	.10	.08	.04
76	Richard Johnson	.10	.08	.04
77	Rodney Peete	.20	.15	.08
78	Barry Sanders	4.00	3.00	1.50
79	Chris Spielman	.10	.08	.04
80	Andre Ware	.10	.08	.04
81	Matt Brock	.10	.08	.04
82	Leroy Butler	.10	.08	.04
83	Tim Harris	.10	.08	.04
84	Perry Kemp	.10	.08	.04
85	Don Majkowski	.10	.08	.04
86	Mark Murphy	.10	.08	.04
87	Brian Noble	.10	.08	.04
88	Sterling Sharpe	.20	.15	.08
89	Darrell Thompson	.10	.08	.04
90	Ed West	.10	.08	.04
91	Ray Childress	.10	.08	.04
92	Ernest Givins	.10	.08	.04
93	Drew Hill	.10	.08	.04
94	Haywood Jeffires	.10	.08	.04
95	Richard Johnson	.10	.08	.04
96	Sean Jones	.10	.08	.04
97	Bruce Matthews	.10	.08	.04
98	Warren Moon	.20	.15	.08
99	Mike Munchak	.10	.08	.04
100	Lorenzo White	.10	.08	.04
101	Albert Bentley	.10	.08	.04
102	Duane Bickett	.10	.08	.04
103	Bill Brooks	.10	.08	.04
104	Jeff George	.50	.40	.20
105	Jon Hand	.10	.08	.04
106	Jeff Herrod	.10	.08	.04
107	Jessie Hester	.10	.08	.04
108	Mike Prior	.10	.08	.04
109	Rohn Stark	.10	.08	.04
110	Clarence Verdin	.10	.08	.04
111	Steve Deberg	.10	.08	.04
112	Dan Saleaumua	.10	.08	.04
113	Albert Lewis	.10	.08	.04
114	Nick Lowery	.10	.08	.04
115	Christian Okoye	.10	.08	.04
116	Stephone Paige	.10	.08	.04
117	Kevin Ross	.10	.08	.04
118	Dino Hackett	.10	.08	.04
119	Derrick Thomas	.20	.15	.08
120	Barry Word	.10	.08	.04
121	Marcus Allen	.25	.20	.10
122	Mervyn Fernandez	.10	.08	.04
123	Willie Gault	.10	.08	.04
124	Bo Jackson	.25	.20	.10
125	Terry McDaniel	.10	.08	.04
126	Don Mosebar	.10	.08	.04
127	Jay Schroeder	.10	.08	.04
128	Greg Townsend	.10	.08	.04
129	Aaron Wallace	.10	.08	.04
130	Steve Wisniewski	.10	.08	.04
131	Willie Anderson	.10	.08	.04
132	Henry Ellard	.10	.08	.04
133	Jim Everett	.20	.15	.08
134	Cleveland Gary	.10	.08	.04
135	Jerry Gray	.10	.08	.04
136	Kevin Greene	.10	.08	.04
137	Buford McGee	.10	.08	.04
138	Vince Newsome	.10	.08	.04
139	Jackie Slater	.10	.08	.04
140	Frank Stams	.10	.08	.04
141	Jeff Cross	.10	.08	.04
142	Mark Duper	.10	.08	.04
143	Ferrell Edmunds	.10	.08	.04
144	Dan Marino	3.00	2.25	1.25
145	Louis Oliver	.10	.08	.04
146	John Offerdahl	.10	.08	.04
147	Tony Paige	.10	.08	.04
148	Sammie Smith	.10	.08	.04
149	Richmond Webb	.10	.08	.04
150	Jarvis Williams	.10	.08	.04
151	Joey Browner	.10	.08	.04
152	Anthony Carter	.10	.08	.04
153	Chris Doleman	.10	.08	.04
154	Hassan Jones	.10	.08	.04
155	Steve Jordan	.10	.08	.04
156	Carl Lee	.10	.08	.04
157	Randall McDaniel	.10	.08	.04
158	Mike Merriweather	.10	.08	.04
159	Herschel Walker	.20	.15	.08
160	Wade Wilson	.10	.08	.04
161	Ray Agnew	.10	.08	.04
162	Bruce Armstrong	.10	.08	.04
163	Mary Cook	.10	.08	.04
164	Hart Lee Dykes	.10	.08	.04
165	Irving Fryar	.10	.08	.04
166	Tom Hodson	.10	.08	.04
167	Ronnie Lippett	.10	.08	.04
168	Fred Marion	.10	.08	.04
169	John Stephens	.10	.08	.04
170	Brent Williams	.10	.08	.04
171	Morten Andersen	.10	.08	.04
172	Gene Atkins	.10	.08	.04
173	Craig Heyward	.10	.08	.04
174	Rickey Jackson	.10	.08	.04
175	Vaughan Johnson	.10	.08	.04
176	Eric Martin	.10	.08	.04
177	Rueben Mayes	.10	.08	.04
178	Pat Swilling	.10	.08	.04
179	Renaldo Turnbull	.10	.08	.04
180	Steve Walsh	.10	.08	.04
181	Ottis Anderson	.10	.08	.04
182	Rodney Hampton	.20	.15	.08
183	Jeff Hostetler	.20	.15	.08
184	Pepper Johnson	.10	.08	.04
185	Sean Landeta	.10	.08	.04
186	Dave Meggett	.10	.08	.04
187	Bart Oates	.10	.08	.04
188	Phil Simms	.10	.08	.04
189	Lawrence Taylor	.20	.15	.08
190	Reyna Thompson	.10	.08	.04
191	Brad Baxter	.10	.08	.04
192	Dennis Byrd	.10	.08	.04
193	Kylce Clifton	.10	.08	.04
194	James Hasty	.10	.08	.04
195	Pat Leahy	.10	.08	.04
196	Erik McMillan	.10	.08	.04
197	Rob Moore	.50	.40	.20
198	Ken O'Brien	.10	.08	.04
199	Mark Boyer	.10	.08	.04
200	Al Toon	.10	.08	.04
201	Fred Barnett	.10	.08	.04
202	Jerome Brown	.10	.08	.04
203	Keith Byars	.10	.08	.04
204	Randall Cunningham	.50	.40	.20
205	Wes Hopkins	.10	.08	.04
206	Keith Jackson	.10	.08	.04
207	Seth Joyner	.10	.08	.04
208	Heath Sherman	.10	.08	.04
209	Reggie White	.50	.40	.20
210	Calvin Williams	.10	.08	.04
211	Roy Green	.10	.08	.04
212	Ken Harvey	.10	.08	.04
213	Luis Sharpe	.10	.08	.04
214	Ernie Jones	.10	.08	.04
215	Tim McDonald	.10	.08	.04
216	Freddie Joe Nunn	.10	.08	.04
217	Ricky Proehl	.10	.08	.04
218	Timm Rosenbach	.10	.08	.04
219	Anthony Thompson	.10	.08	.04
220	Lonnie Young	.10	.08	.04
221	Gary Anderson	.10	.08	.04
222	Bubby Brister	.10	.08	.04
223	Eric Green	.10	.08	.04
224	Merril Hoge	.10	.08	.04
225	Carnell Lake	.10	.08	.04
226	Louis Lipps	.10	.08	.04
227	David Little	.10	.08	.04
228	Greg Lloyd	.10	.08	.04
229	Gerald Williams	.10	.08	.04
230	Rod Woodson	.10	.08	.04
231	Marion Butts	.10	.08	.04
232	Gill Byrd	.10	.08	.04
233	Burt Grossman	.10	.08	.04
234	Courtney Hall	.10	.08	.04
235	Ronnie Harmon	.10	.08	.04
236	Anthony Miller	.10	.08	.04
237	Leslie O'Neal	.10	.08	.04
238	Junior Seau	.50	.40	.20
239	Billy Joe Tolliver	.10	.08	.04
240	Lee Williams	.10	.08	.04
241	Dexter Carter	.10	.08	.04
242	Kevin Fagan	.10	.08	.04
243	Charles Haley	.10	.08	.04
244	Brent Jones	.10	.08	.04
245	Ronnie Lott	.20	.15	.08
246	Guy McIntyre	.10	.08	.04
247	Joe Montana	2.50	2.00	1.00
248	Jerry Rice	2.00	1.50	.80
249	John Taylor	.10	.08	.04
250	Roger Craig	.20	.15	.08
251	Brian Blades	.10	.08	.04
252	Derrick Penner	.10	.08	.04
253	Nesby Glasgow	.10	.08	.04
254	Jacob Green	.10	.08	.04
255	Tommy Kane	.10	.08	.04
256	Dave Krieg	.10	.08	.04
257	Rufus Porter	.10	.08	.04
258	Eugene Robinson	.10	.08	.04
259	Cortez Kennedy	.10	.08	.04
260	John L. Williams	.10	.08	.04
261	Gary Anderson	.10	.08	.04
262	Mark Carrier	.10	.08	.04
263	Steve Christie	.10	.08	.04
264	Reggie Cobb	.10	.08	.04
265	Paul Gruber	.10	.08	.04
266	Wayne Haddix	.10	.08	.04
267	Bruce Hill	.10	.08	.04
268	Keith McCants	.10	.08	.04
269	Vinny Testaverde	.50	.40	.20
270	Broderick Thomas	.10	.08	.04
271	Earnest Byner	.10	.08	.04
272	Gary Clark	.10	.08	.04
273	Darrell Green	.10	.08	.04
274	Jim Lachey	.10	.08	.04
275	Chip Lohmiller	.10	.08	.04
276	Charles Mann	.10	.08	.04
277	Wilber Marshall	.10	.08	.04
278	Art Monk	.20	.15	.08
279	Mark Rypien	.10	.08	.04
280	Alvin Walton	.10	.08	.04
281	Randall Cunningham (Braille)	.50	.40	.20
282	Warren Moon (Braille)	.20	.15	.08
283	Barry Sanders (Braille)	5.00	3.75	2.00
284	Thurman Thomas (Braille)	.50	.40	.20
285	Jerry Rice (Braille)	2.00	1.50	.80
286	Haywood Jeffires (Braille)	.20	.15	.08
287	Charles Haley (Braille)	.20	.15	.08
288	Derrick Thomas (Braille)	.20	.15	.08
289	NFC Logo Card	.20	.15	.08
290	AFC Logo Card	.20	.15	.08
291	Checklist	.10	.08	.04

1991 Action Packed 24K Gold

These cards were randomly issued in foil packs of 1991 Action Packed cards. Cards feature the regular-issue fronts, but the stripe has been done in 24k gold. Cards have also been stamped 24k on the front and are numbered 1G-42G on the back. It's estimated that less than 8,000 were made of each card. Generally, the cards are valued at about 15 times the amount of the corresponding regular Action Packed card.

		NM/M	NM	E
Complete Set (42):		200.00	370.00	200.00
Common Player:		3.00	3.75	2.00
Minor Stars:		10.00	7.50	4.00
1	Andre Rison	4.00	3.00	1.50
2	Deion Sanders	12.00	9.00	4.75
3	Andre Reed	3.00	3.75	2.00
4	Bruce Smith	3.00	3.75	2.00
5	Thurman Thomas	6.00	4.50	2.50
6	Neal Anderson	3.00	3.75	2.00
7	Mark Carrier	3.00	3.75	2.00
8	Mike Singletary	3.00	3.75	2.00
9	Boomer Esiason	3.00	3.75	2.00
10	James Francis	3.00	3.75	2.00
11	Anthony Munoz	3.00	3.75	2.00
12	Troy Aikman	20.00	15.00	8.00
13	Emmitt Smith	35.00	26.00	14.00
14	John Elway	25.00	18.50	10.00
15	Bobby Humphrey	3.00	3.75	2.00
16	Barry Sanders	35.00	26.00	14.00
17	Don Majikowski	3.00	3.75	2.00
18	Sterling Sharpe	4.00	3.00	1.50
19	Warren Moon	6.00	4.50	2.50
20	Jeff George	4.00	3.00	1.50
21	Christian Okoye	3.00	3.75	2.00
22	Derrick Thomas	4.00	3.00	1.50
23	Barry Word	3.00	3.75	2.00
24	Marcus Allen	10.00	7.50	4.00
25	Bo Jackson	10.00	7.50	4.00
26	Jim Everett	3.00	3.75	2.00
27	Cleveland Gary	3.00	3.75	2.00
28	Dan Marino	35.00	26.00	14.00
29	Herschel Walker	3.00	3.75	2.00
30	Ottis Anderson	3.00	3.75	2.00
31	Rodney Hampton	3.00	3.75	2.00
32	Dave Meggett	3.00	3.75	2.00
33	Marion Butts	3.00	3.75	2.00
34	Randall Cunningham	4.00	3.00	1.50
35	Reggie White	4.00	3.00	1.50
36	Jerry Rice	25.00	18.50	10.00
37	Eric Green	3.00	3.75	2.00
38	Charles Haley	3.00	3.75	2.00
39	Ronnie Lott	3.00	3.75	2.00
40	Joe Montana	35.00	26.00	14.00
41	Vinny Testaverde	4.00	3.00	1.50
42	Gary Clark	3.00	3.75	2.00

1991 Action Packed All-Madden

This 52-card set is John Madden's second issue featuring the All-Madden team. The borderless fronts feature embossed color photos with gold and aqua border stripes. Cards, which are standard size, have the Madden logo and team helmet on the front. The back, which is numbered, has stats and a mug shot.

		NM/M	NM	E
Complete Set (52):		25.00	18.50	10.00
Common Player:		.20	.15	.08
Wax Box:		15.00		
1	Mark Rypien	.40	.30	.15
2	Erik Kramer	1.00	.70	.40
3	Jim McMahon	.40	.30	.15
4	Jesse Sapolu	.20	.15	.08
5	Jay Hilgenberg	.20	.15	.08
6	Howard Ballard	.20	.15	.08
7	Lomas Brown	.20	.15	.08
8	John Elliott	.20	.15	.08
9	Joe Jacoby	.20	.15	.08
10	Jim Lachey	.20	.15	.08
11	Anthony Munoz	.30	.25	.12
12	Nate Newton	.20	.15	.08
13	Will Wolford	.20	.15	.08
14	Jerry Ball	.20	.15	.08
15	Jerome Brown	.20	.15	.08
16	William Perry	.25	.20	.10
17	Charles Mann	.20	.15	.08
18	Clyde Simmons	.20	.15	.08
19	Reggie White	1.50	1.25	.60
20	Eric Allen	.20	.15	.08
21	Darrell Green	.25	.20	.10
22	Bennie Blades	.20	.15	.08
23	Chuck Cecil	.20	.15	.08
24	Rickey Dixon	.30	.25	.12
25	David Fulcher	.20	.15	.08
26	Ronnie Lott	.75	.60	.30
27	Emmitt Smith	6.00	4.50	2.50
28	Neal Anderson	.30	.25	.12
29	Robert Delpino	.30	.25	.12
30	Barry Sanders	4.00	3.00	1.50
31	Thurman Thomas	1.00	.70	.40
32	Cornelius Bennett	.35	.25	.14
33	Rickey Jackson	.20	.15	.08
34	Seth Joyner	.20	.15	.08
35	Wilber Marshall	.20	.15	.08
36	Clay Matthews	.20	.15	.08
37	Chris Spielman	.20	.15	.08
38	Pat Swilling	.25	.20	.10
39	Fred Barnett	.50	.40	.20
40	Gary Clark	.40	.30	.15
41	Michael Irvin	1.50	1.25	.60
42	Art Monk	.50	.40	.20
43	Jerry Rice	2.50	2.00	1.00
44	John Taylor	.50	.40	.20
45	Tom Waddle	.20	.15	.08
46	Kevin Butler	.20	.15	.08
47	Bill Bates	.20	.15	.08
48	Greg Manusky	.20	.15	.08
49	Elvis Patterson	.20	.15	.08
50	Steve Tasker	.20	.15	.08
51	John Daly	1.00	.75	.40
52	All-Madden Trophy	1.50	1.25	.60

1991 Action Packed NFLPA Awards

1990 NFL award winners are recognized in this 16-card set produced by Action Packed. The cards, similar in design to the regular 1991 issue, were available as a boxed set; 5,000 individually-numbered sets were produced. Each box has the set number on it, plus "NFLPA/MDA Awards Dinner March 12, 1991" inscribed on it. Each card back has the award he won listed under his name.

		NM	E	VG
Complete Set (16):		40.00	56.00	30.00
Common Player:		2.00	3.00	1.50
1	Jim Lachey	2.00	3.00	1.50
2	Anthony Munoz	5.00	3.75	2.00
3	Bruce Smith	6.00	4.50	2.50
4	Reggie White	6.00	4.50	2.50
5	Charles Haley	2.00	3.00	1.50
6	Derrick Thomas	3.00	2.25	1.25
7	Albert Lewis	2.00	3.00	1.50
8	Mark Carrier	2.00	1.50	.80
9	Reyna Thompson	2.00	1.50	.80
10	Steve Tasker	2.00	3.00	1.50
11	James Francis	2.00	1.50	.80
12	Mark Carrier	3.00	2.25	1.25
13	Johnny Johnson	3.00	2.25	1.25
14	Eric Green	4.00	3.00	1.50
15	Warren Moon	6.00	4.50	2.50
16	Randall Cunningham	6.00	4.50	2.50

1991 Action Packed Rookie Update

This set features the first 26 top draft picks among its 74 rookie cards, plus 10 traded and update cards. Each card has an embossed helmet with a white "R" inside to indicate the player is a rookie. The backs are written in red and have the player's collegiate statistics. An Emmitt Smith prototype card was included in each case of 1991 Action Packed Rookie/Update foil or factory set ordered. Special 24K gold cards were also made for the 26 first-round draft draft picks. They were inserted into update packs.

		NM/M	NM	E
Complete Set (84):		15.00	11.00	6.00
Complete Factory (84):		20.00	15.00	8.00
Common Player:		.05	.04	.02
Minor Stars:		.10	.08	.04
Pack (6):		1.25		
Wax Box (24):		25.00		
1	Herman Moore RC	3.00	2.25	1.25
2	Eric Turner RC	.10	.08	.04
3	Mike Croel RC	.10	.08	.04
4	Alfred Williams RC	.05	.04	.02
5	Stanley Richard RC	.10	.08	.04
6	Russell Maryland RC	.25	.20	.10
7	Pat Harlow RC	.05	.04	.02
8	Alvin Harper RC	.10	.08	.04
9	Mike Pritchard RC	.25	.20	.10
10	Leonard Russell RC	.25	.20	.10
11	Jarrod Bunch RC	.10	.08	.04
12	Dan McGwire RC	.10	.08	.04
13	Bobby Wilson RC	.05	.04	.02
14	Vinnie Clark RC	.05	.04	.02
15	Kelvin Pritchett RC	.05	.04	.02
16	Harvey Williams RC	.25	.20	.10
17	Stan Thomas RC	.05	.04	.02
18	Todd Marinovich RC	.10	.08	.04
19	Antone Davis RC	.05	.04	.02
20	Greg Lewis RC	.05	.04	.02
21	Brett Favre RC	10.00	7.50	4.00
22	Wesley Carroll RC	.05	.04	.02
23	Ed McCaffrey RC	3.00	2.25	1.25
24	Reggie Barrett RC	.05	.04	.02
25	Chris Zorich RC	.05	.04	.02
26	Kenny Walker RC	.05	.04	.02
27	Aaron Craver RC	.05	.04	.02
28	Browning Nagle RC	.05	.04	.02
29	Nick Bell RC	.05	.04	.02
30	Anthony Morgan RC	.05	.04	.02
31	Jesse Campbell RC	.05	.04	.02
32	Eric Bieniemy RC	.10	.08	.04
33	Ricky Ervins RC	.10	.08	.04
34	Kanavis McGhee RC	.05	.04	.02
35	Shawn Moore RC	.05	.04	.02
36	Todd Lyght RC	.10	.08	.04
37	Eric Swann RC	.25	.20	.10
38	Henry Jones RC	.05	.04	.02
39	Ted Washington RC	.05	.04	.02
40	Charles McRae RC	.05	.04	.02
41	Randal Hill RC	.10	.08	.04
42	Huey Richardson RC	.05	.04	.02
43	Roman Phifer RC	.05	.04	.02
44	Ricky Watters RC	2.00	1.50	.80
45	Esera Tuaolo RC	.05	.04	.02
46	Michael Jackson RC	.25	.20	.10
47	Shawn Jefferson RC	.05	.04	.02
48	Tim Barnett RC	.05	.04	.02
49	Chuck Webb RC	.05	.04	.02
50	Moe Gardner RC	.05	.04	.02
51	Mo Lewis RC	.05	.04	.02
52	Mike Dumas RC	.05	.04	.02
53	Jon Vaughn RC	.05	.04	.02
54	Jerome Henderson RC	.05	.04	.02
55	Harry Colon RC	.05	.04	.02
56	David Daniels RC	.05	.04	.02
57	Phil Hansen RC	.05	.04	.02
58	Ernie Mills RC	.05	.04	.02
59	John Kasay RC	.05	.04	.02
60	Darren Lewis RC	.05	.04	.02
61	James Joseph RC	.05	.04	.02
62	Robert Wilson RC	.05	.04	.02
63	Lawrence Dawsey RC	.05	.04	.02

64	Mike Jones RC	.05	.04	.02
65	Dave McCloughan RC	.05	.04	.02
66	Erric Pegram RC	.10	.08	.04
67	Aeneas Williams RC	.25	.20	.10
68	Reggie Johnson RC	.05	.04	.02
69	Todd Scott RC	.05	.04	.02
70	James Jones RC	.05	.04	.02
71	Lamar Rogers RC	.05	.04	.02
72	Darryll Lewis RC	.05	.04	.02
73	Bryan Cox RC	.25	.20	.10
74	Leroy Thompson RC	.05	.04	.02
75	Mark Higgs RC	.05	.04	.02
76	John Friesz	.25	.20	.10
77	Tim McKyer	.05	.04	.02
78	Roger Craig	.10	.08	.04
79	Ronnie Lott	.25	.20	.10
80	Steve Young	1.00	.70	.40
81	Percy Snow	.05	.04	.02
82	Cornelius Bennett	.10	.08	.04
83	Johnny Johnson	.10	.08	.04
84	Blair Thomas	.05	.04	.02

1991 Action Packed Rookie Update 24K Gold

These insert cards were randomly included in 1991 Action Packed Rookie Update foil packs and are devoted to first-round draft picks. Each card front has an embossed color photo, plus gold foil stamping. A "24K" is also stamped on the card to distinguish it as an insert card. The card back is in a horizontal format and includes the player's collegiate statistics, a color mug shot, a panel for an autograph, and a card number. The card is numbered according to the order the player was drafted and uses a "G" suffix.

		NM/M	NM	E
Complete Set (26):		100.00	220.00	120.00
Common Player:		4.00	7.50	4.00
Minor Stars:		6.00	15.00	8.00
1	Russell Maryland	4.00	7.50	4.00
2	Eric Turner	4.00	7.50	4.00
3	Mike Croel	4.00	7.50	4.00
4	Todd Lyght	4.00	7.50	4.00
5	Eric Swann	6.00	4.50	2.50
6	Charles McRae	4.00	7.50	4.00
7	Antone Davis	4.00	7.50	4.00
8	Stanley Richard	4.00	7.50	4.00
9	Herman Moore	20.00	15.00	8.00
10	Pat Harlow	4.00	7.50	4.00
11	Alvin Harper	4.00	7.50	4.00
12	Mike Pritchard	4.00	7.50	4.00
13	Leonard Russell	4.00	7.50	4.00
14	Huey Richardson	4.00	7.50	4.00
15	Dan McGwire	4.00	7.50	4.00
16	Bobby Wilson	4.00	7.50	4.00
17	Alfred Williams	4.00	7.50	4.00
18	Vinnie Clark	4.00	7.50	4.00
19	Kelvin Pritchett	4.00	7.50	4.00
20	Harvey Williams	5.00	3.75	2.00
21	Stan Thomas	4.00	7.50	4.00
22	Randal Hill	4.00	7.50	4.00
23	Todd Marinovich	4.00	7.50	4.00
24	Ted Washington	4.00	7.50	4.00
25	Henry Jones	4.00	7.50	4.00
26	Jarrod Bunch	4.00	7.50	4.00

1991 Action Packed Whizzer White Greats

The 25 winners of the Justice Byron "Whizzer" White Humanitarian Award from 1967 to 1991 were pictured in this special Action Packed set issued in conjunction with the 1991 awards banquet in Chicago. The White award is given annually to a single NFL player who serves his team, community and country in the spirit of former NFL player and U.S. Supreme Court Justice Byron White. The card set features Action Packed's 1991 gold standard design with full color, embossed action photos. For the first time, however, the indicia is silver with the award year inscribed in a silver helmet. The card backs feature a color head shot, player biographical information, career and community contributions. A total of 3,500 sets were distributed at the dinner; another 5,000 were made available to collectors through Rotman Productions.

		NM/M	NM	E
Complete Set (25):		25.00	56.00	30.00
Common Player:		.50	1.50	.80
1	Bart Starr (1967)	4.00	3.00	1.50
2	Willie Davis (1968)	2.00	1.50	.80
3	Ed Meador (1969)	.50	1.50	.80
4	Gale Sayers (1970)	4.00	3.00	1.50
5	Kermit Alexander (1971)	.50	1.50	.80
6	Ray May (1972)	.50	1.50	.80
7	Andy Russell (1973)	1.00	.70	.40
8	Floyd Little (1974)	1.00	.70	.40
9	Rocky Bleier (1975)	1.00	.70	.40
10	Jim Hart (1976)	1.00	.70	.40
11	Lyle Alzado (1977)	1.00	.70	.40
12	Archie Manning (1978)	1.00	.70	.40
13	Roger Staubach (1979)	5.00	3.75	2.00
14	Gene Upshaw (1980)	1.00	.70	.40

15	Ken Houston (1981)	1.00	.70	.40
16	Franco Harris (1982)	2.00	1.50	.80
17	Doug Dieken (1983)	.60	1.50	.80
18	Rolf Benirschke (1984)	.50	1.50	.80
19	Reggie Williams (1985)	.50	1.50	.80
20	Nat Moore (1986)	.50	1.50	.80
21	George Martin (1987)	.50	1.50	.80
22	Deron Cherry (1988)	.50	1.50	.80
23	Mike Singletary (1989)	1.00	.70	.40
24	Ozzie Newsome (1990)	1.00	.70	.40
25	Mike Kenn (1991)	.50	1.50	.80

1971 Alabama Team Sheets

	NM	E	VG
Complete Set (6):	45.00	22.00	13.50
Common Player:	6.00	3.00	1.75

		NM	E	VG
1	Mike Raines, Pat Raines, Terry Rowell, Gary Rutledge, Bubba Sawyer, Bill Sexton, Wayne Wheeler, Jack White, Steve Williams, Dexter Wood	8.00	4.00	2.50
2	Johnny Musso, Lanny Norris, Robin Parkhouse, Jim Patterson, Steve Root, Jimmy Rosser, Jeff Rouzie, Robby Rowan, Chuck Strickland, Tom Surlas, Steve Wade, David Watkins	10.00	5.00	3.00
3	Fred Marshall, Noah Miller, John Mitchell, Randy Moore, Gary Reynolds, Benny Rippetoe, Ronny Robertson, John Rogers, Jim Simmons, Paul Spivey, Steve Sprayberry, Rod Steakley	6.00	3.00	1.75
4	Richard Bryan, Chip Burke, Jerry Cash, Don Cokely, Greg Gantt, Jim Grammer, Wayne Hall, John Hannah, Rand Lambert, Tom Lusk, Bobby McKinney, David McMakin	8.00	4.00	2.50
5	Ellis Beck, Steve Bisceglia, Jeff Blitz, Buddy Brown, Steve Dean, Mike Denson, Joe Doughty, Mike Eckenrod, Pat Keever, David Knapp, Jim Krapf, Joe LaBue	6.00	3.00	1.75
6	Wayne Adkinson, David Bailey, Marvin Barron, Jeff Beard, Andy Cross, John Croyle, Bill Davis, Terry Davis, Steve Higginbotham, Ed Hines, Jimmy Horton, Wilbur Jackson	7.00	3.50	2.00

1972 Alabama

	NM	E	VG
Complete Set (54):	95.00	47.00	28.00
Common Player:	1.50	.70	.45

		NM	E	VG
1C	Skip Kubelius	1.50	.70	.45
1D	Terry Davis	2.50	1.25	.70
1H	Robert Fraley	1.50	.70	.45
1S	Paul "Bear" Bryant (CO)	25.00	12.50	7.50
2C	David Watkins	1.50	.70	.45
2D	Bobby McKinney	1.50	.70	.45
2H	Dexter Wood	1.50	.70	.45
2S	Chuck Strickland	1.50	.70	.45
3C	John Hannah	15.00	7.50	4.50
3D	Tom Lusk	1.50	.70	.45
3H	Jim Krapf	1.50	.70	.45
3S	Warren Dyar	1.50	.70	.45
4C	Greg Gantt	2.50	1.25	.70
4D	Johnny Sharpless	1.50	.70	.45
4H	Steve Wade	1.50	.70	.45
4S	John Rogers	1.50	.70	.45
5C	Doug Faust	1.50	.70	.45
5D	Jeff Rouzie	1.50	.70	.45
5H	Buddy Brown	1.50	.70	.45
5S	Randy Moore	1.50	.70	.45
6C	David Knapp	2.50	1.25	.70
6D	Lanny Norris	1.50	.70	.45
6H	Paul Spivey	1.50	.70	.45
6S	Pat Raines	1.50	.70	.45
7C	Pete Pappas	1.50	.70	.45
7D	Ed Hines	1.50	.70	.45
7H	Mike Washington	1.50	.70	.45
7S	David McMakin	2.50	1.25	.70
8C	Steve Dean	1.50	.70	.45

8D	Joe LaBue	1.50	.70	.45
8H	John Croyle	1.50	.70	.45
8S	Noah Miller	1.50	.70	.45
9C	Bobby Stanford	1.50	.70	.45
9D	Sylvester Croom	2.50	1.25	.70
9H	Wilbur Jackson	6.00	3.00	1.75
9S	Ellis Beck	1.50	.70	.45
10C	Steve Bisceglia	1.50	.70	.45
10D	Andy Cross	1.50	.70	.45
10H	John Mitchell	2.50	1.25	.70
10S	Bill Davis	1.50	.70	.45
11C	Gary Rutledge	2.50	1.25	.70
11D	Randy Billingsley	1.50	.70	.45
11H	Randy Hall	1.50	.70	.45
11S	Ralph Stokes	1.50	.70	.45
12C	Jeff Blitz	1.50	.70	.45
12D	Robby Rowan	1.50	.70	.45
12H	Mike Raines	1.50	.70	.45
12S	Terry Wheeler	1.50	.70	.45
13C	Steve Sprayberry	1.50	.70	.45
13D	Wayne Hall	2.50	1.25	.70
13H	Morris Hunt	1.50	.70	.45
13S	Butch Norman	1.50	.70	.45
JK	Denny Stadium	1.50	.70	.45
JK	Memorial Coliseum	1.50	.70	.45

1973 Alabama

	NM	E	VG
Complete Set (54):	80.00	40.00	24.00
Common Player:	1.50	.70	.45

		NM	E	VG
1C	Skip Kubelius	1.50	.70	.45
1D	Mark Prudhomme	1.50	.70	.45
1H	Robert Fraley	1.50	.70	.45
1S	Paul "Bear" Bryant (CO)	20.00	10.00	6.00
2C	David Watkins	1.50	.70	.45
2D	Richard Todd	12.00	6.00	3.50
2H	Buddy Pope	1.50	.70	.45
2S	Chuck Strickland	1.50	.70	.45
3C	Bob Bryan	1.50	.70	.45
3D	Gary Hanrahan	1.50	.70	.45
3H	Greg Montgomery	1.50	.70	.45
3S	Warren Dyar	1.50	.70	.45
4C	Greg Gantt	2.50	1.25	.70
4D	Johnny Sharpless	1.50	.70	.45
4H	Rick Watson	1.50	.70	.45
4S	John Rogers	1.50	.70	.45
5C	George Pugh	2.50	1.25	.70
5D	Jeff Rouzie	1.50	.70	.45
5H	Buddy Brown	1.50	.70	.45
5S	Randy Moore	1.50	.70	.45
6C	Ray Maxwell	1.50	.70	.45
6D	Alan Pizzitola	1.50	.70	.45
6H	Paul Spivey	1.50	.70	.45
6S	Ron Robertson	1.50	.70	.45
7C	Pete Pappas	1.50	.70	.45
7D	Steve Kulback	1.50	.70	.45
7H	Mike Washington	1.50	.70	.45
7S	David McMakin	2.50	1.25	.70
8C	Steve Dean	1.50	.70	.45
8D	Jerry Brown	1.50	.70	.45
8H	John Croyle	1.50	.70	.45
8S	Noah Miller	1.50	.70	.45
9C	Leroy Cook	1.50	.70	.45
9D	Sylvester Croom	2.50	1.25	.70
9H	Wilbur Jackson	6.00	3.00	1.75
9S	Ellis Beck	1.50	.70	.45
10C	Tyrone King	1.50	.70	.45
10D	Mike Stock	1.50	.70	.45
10H	Mike Dubose	1.50	.70	.45
10S	Bill Davis	1.50	.70	.45
11C	Gary Rutledge	2.50	1.25	.70
11D	Randy Billingsley	1.50	.70	.45
11H	Randy Hall	1.50	.70	.45
11S	Ralph Stokes	1.50	.70	.45
12C	Woodrow Lowe	6.00	3.00	1.75
12D	Marvin Barron	1.50	.70	.45
12H	Mike Raines	1.50	.70	.45
12S	Wayne Wheeler	1.50	.70	.45
13C	Steve Sprayberry	1.50	.70	.45
13D	Wayne Hall	2.50	1.25	.70
13H	Morris Hunt	1.50	.70	.45
13S	Butch Norman	1.50	.70	.45
JKO	Denny Stadium	1.50	.70	.45
JKO	Memorial Coliseum	1.50	.70	.45

1988 Alabama Winners

		NM/M	NM	E
Complete Set (73):		10.00	7.50	4.00
Common Player:		.15	.11	.06
1	Title Card (Schedule on back)	.25	.20	.10
2	Charlie Abrams	.15	.11	.06
3	Sam Atkins	.15	.11	.06
4	Marco Battle	.15	.11	.06
5	George Bethune	.15	.11	.06
6	Scott Bolt	.15	.11	.06

		NM/M	NM	E
7	Tommy Bowden	.25	.20	.10
8	Danny Cash	.15	.11	.06
9	John Cassimus	.15	.11	.06
10	David Casteal	.15	.11	.06
11	Terrill Chatman	.15	.11	.06
12	Andy Christoff	.15	.11	.06
13	Tommy Cole	.15	.11	.06
14	Tony Cox	.15	.11	.06
15	Howard Cross	.75	.60	.30
16	Bill Curry (CO)	.25	.20	.10
17	Johnny Davis	.25	.20	.10
18	Vantreise Davis	.15	.11	.06
19	Joe Demos	.15	.11	.06
20	Philip Doyle	.15	.11	.06
21	Jeff Dunn	.15	.11	.06
22	John Fruhmorgen	.15	.11	.06
23	Jim Fuller	.15	.11	.06
24	Greg Gilbert	.15	.11	.06
25	Pierre Goode	.25	.20	.10
26	John Guy	.15	.11	.06
27	Spencer Hammond	.15	.11	.06
28	Stacy Harrison	.15	.11	.06
29	Murry Hill	.15	.11	.06
30	Byron Holdbrooks	.15	.11	.06
31	Ben Holt	.15	.11	.06
32	Bobby Humphrey	.75	.60	.30
33	Gene Jelks	.50	.40	.20
34	Kermit Kendrick	.15	.11	.06
35	William Kent	.15	.11	.06
36	David Lenoir	.15	.11	.06
37	Butch Lewis	.15	.11	.06
38	Don Lindsey	.15	.11	.06
39	John Mangum	.50	.40	.20
40	Tim Matheny	.15	.11	.06
41	Mac McWhorter	.25	.20	.10
42	Chris Mohr	.25	.20	.10
43	Larry New	.15	.11	.06
44	Gene Newberry	.15	.11	.06
45	Lee Ozmint	.15	.11	.06
46	Trent Patterson	.15	.11	.06
47	Greg Payne	.15	.11	.06
48	Thomas Rayam	.15	.11	.06
49	Chris Robinette	.15	.11	.06
50	Larry Rose	.15	.11	.06
51	Derrick Rushton	.15	.11	.06
52	Lamonde Russell	.15	.11	.06
53	Craig Sanderson	.15	.11	.06
54	Wayne Shaw	.15	.11	.06
55	Willie Shepherd	.15	.11	.06
56	Roger Shultz	.15	.11	.06
57	David Smith	.15	.11	.06
58	Homer Smith	.15	.11	.06
59	Mike Smith	.15	.11	.06
60	Byron Sneed	.15	.11	.06
61	Robert Stewart	.15	.11	.06
62	Vince Strickland	.15	.11	.06
63	Brian Stutson	.15	.11	.06
64	Vince Sutton	.15	.11	.06
65	Derrick Thomas	5.00	3.75	2.00
66	Steve Turner	.15	.11	.06
67	Alan Ward	.15	.11	.06
68	Lorenzo Ward	.15	.11	.06
69	Steve Webb	.15	.11	.06
70	Woody Wilson	.15	.11	.06
71	Chip Wisdom	.15	.11	.06
72	Willie Wyatt	.15	.11	.06
73	Mike Zuga	.15	.11	.06

1989 Alabama Coke 20

		NM/M	NM	E
	Complete Set (20):	10.00	7.50	4.00
	Common Player:	.35	.25	.14
C1	Paul "Bear" Bryant (CO)	1.50	1.25	.60
C2	John Hannah	.75	.60	.30
C3	Fred Sington	.35	.25	.14
C4	Derrick Thomas	1.50	1.25	.60
C5	Dwight Stephenson	.75	.60	.30
C6	Cornelius Bennett	1.00	.70	.40
C7	Ozzie Newsome	1.00	.70	.40
C8	Joe Namath (Art)	2.00	1.50	.80
C9	Steve Sloan	.60	.45	.25
C10	Bill Curry (CO)	.35	.25	.14
C11	Paul "Bear" Bryant (CO)	1.50	1.25	.60
C12	**Big Al** (Mascot)	.35	.25	.14
C13	Scott Hunter	.50	.40	.20
C14	Lee Roy Jordan	.75	.60	.30
C15	Walter Lewis	.35	.25	.14
C16	Bobby Humphrey	.35	.25	.14
C17	John Mitchell	.35	.25	.14
C18	Johnny Musso	.75	.60	.30
C19	Pat Trammell	.35	.25	.14
C20	Ray Perkins (CO)	.60	.45	.25

1989 Alabama Coke 580

		NM/M	NM	E
	Complete Set (580):	35.00	26.00	14.00
	Common Player:	.08	.06	.03
1	Paul "Bear" Bryant (CO)	.75	.60	.30
2	W.T. Van De Graff	.08	.06	.03
3	A.T.S. Hubert	.08	.06	.03
4	Bill Buckler	.08	.06	.03
5	Hoyt (Wu) Winslett	.08	.06	.03
6	Tony Holm	.08	.06	.03
7	Fred Sington Sr.	.15	.11	.06
8	John Suther	.08	.06	.03
9	Johnny Cain	.08	.06	.03
10	Tom Hupke	.15	.11	.06
11	Millard Howell	.25	.20	.10
12	Steve Wright	.08	.06	.03
13	Bill Searcey	.08	.06	.03
14	Riley Smith	.08	.06	.03
15	Arthur "Tarzan" White	.08	.06	.03
16	Joe Kilgrow	.08	.06	.03
17	Leroy Monsky	.08	.06	.03
18	James Ryba	.08	.06	.03
19	Carey Cox	.08	.06	.03
20	Holt Rast	.08	.06	.03
21	Joe Domnanovich	.08	.06	.03
22	Don Whitmire	.15	.11	.06
23	Harry Gilmer	.25	.20	.10
24	Vaughn Mancha	.08	.06	.03
25	Ed Salem	.08	.06	.03
26	Bobby Marlow	.30	.25	.12
27	George Mason	.08	.06	.03
28	Billy Neighbors	.25	.20	.10
29	Lee Roy Jordan	.50	.40	.20
30	Wayne Freeman	.08	.06	.03
31	Dan Kearley	.08	.06	.03
32	Joe Namath	1.00	.70	.40
33	David Ray	.15	.11	.06
34	Paul Crane	.08	.06	.03
35	Steve Sloan	.25	.20	.10
36	Richard Cole	.08	.06	.03
37	Cecil Dowdy	.15	.11	.06
38	Bobby Johns	.08	.06	.03
39	Ray Perkins	.30	.25	.12
40	Dennis Homan	.25	.20	.10
41	Ken Stabler	.60	.45	.25
42	Robert W. Boylston	.08	.06	.03
43	Mike Hall	.08	.06	.03
44	Alvin Samples	.08	.06	.03
45	Johnny Musso	.25	.20	.10
46	**Bryant-Denny Stadium**	.08	.06	.03
47	Tom Surlas	.08	.06	.03
48	John Hannah	.30	.25	.12
49	Jim Krapf	.08	.06	.03
50	John Mitchell	.15	.11	.06
51	Buddy Brown	.08	.06	.03
52	Woodrow Lowe	.15	.11	.06
53	Wayne Wheeler	.08	.06	.03
54	Leroy Cook	.08	.06	.03
55	Sylvester Croom	.15	.11	.06
56	Mike Washington	.08	.06	.03
57	Ozzie Newsome	.50	.40	.20
58	Barry Krauss	.15	.11	.06
59	Marty Lyons	.25	.20	.10
60	Jim Bunch	.08	.06	.03
61	Don McNeal	.15	.11	.06
62	Dwight Stephenson	.30	.25	.12
63	Bill Davis	.08	.06	.03
64	E.J. Junior	.15	.11	.06
65	Tommy Wilcox	.15	.11	.06
66	Jeremiah Castille	.15	.11	.06
67	Bobby Swafford	.08	.06	.03
68	Cornelius Bennett	.50	.40	.20
69	David Knapp	.15	.11	.06
70	Bobby Humphrey	.30	.25	.12
71	Van Tiffin	.08	.06	.03
72	Sid Smith	.08	.06	.03
73	Pat Trammell	.25	.20	.10
74	Mickey Andrews	.08	.06	.03
75	Steve Bowman	.08	.06	.03
76	Bob Baumhower	.25	.20	.10
77	Bob Cryder	.08	.06	.03
78	Bryon Braggs	.15	.11	.06
79	Warren Lyles	.08	.06	.03
80	Steve Mott	.08	.06	.03
81	Walter Lewis	.15	.11	.06
82	Ricky Moore	.08	.06	.03
83	Wes Neighbors	.08	.06	.03
84	Derrick Thomas	.75	.60	.30
85	Kermit Kendrick	.08	.06	.03
86	Larry Rose	.08	.06	.03
87	Charlie Marr	.08	.06	.03
88	James Whatley	.08	.06	.03
89	Erin Warren	.08	.06	.03
90	Charlie Holm	.08	.06	.03
91	Fred Davis	.08	.06	.03
92	John Wyhonic	.08	.06	.03
93	Jimmy Nelson	.08	.06	.03
94	Roy Steiner	.15	.11	.06
95	Tom Whitley	.08	.06	.03
96	John Wozniak	.08	.06	.03
97	Ed Holdnak	.08	.06	.03
98	Al Lary	.08	.06	.03
99	Mike Mizerany	.08	.06	.03
100	Pat O'Sullivan	.08	.06	.03
101	Jerry Watford	.08	.06	.03
102	Cecil Ingram	.15	.11	.06
103	Mike Fracchia	.08	.06	.03
104	Benny Nelson	.08	.06	.03
105	Tommy Tolleson	.08	.06	.03
106	Creed Gilmer	.08	.06	.03
107	John Calvert	.08	.06	.03
108	Derrick Slaughter	.08	.06	.03
109	Mike Ford	.08	.06	.03
110	Bruce Stephens	.08	.06	.03
111	Danny Ford	.25	.20	.10
112	Jimmy Grammer	.08	.06	.03
113	Steve Higginbotham	.08	.06	.03
114	David Bailey	.08	.06	.03
115	Greg Gantt	.25	.20	.10
116	Terry Davis	.15	.11	.06
117	Chuck Strickland	.08	.06	.03
118	Bobby McKinney	.08	.06	.03
119	Wilbur Jackson	.25	.20	.10
120	Mike Raines	.08	.06	.03
121	Steve Sprayberry	.08	.06	.03
122	David McMakin	.15	.11	.06
123	Ben Smith	.08	.06	.03
124	Steadman Shealy	.25	.20	.10
125	John Rogers	.08	.06	.03
126	Ricky Davis	.15	.11	.06
127	Conley Duncan	.08	.06	.03
128	Wayne Rhodes	.08	.06	.03
129	Buddy Seay	.08	.06	.03
130	Alan Pizzitola	.08	.06	.03
131	Richard Todd	.25	.20	.10
132	Charlie Ferguson	.08	.06	.03
133	Charley Hannah	.15	.11	.06
134	Wiley Barnes	.08	.06	.03
135	Mike Brock	.08	.06	.03
136	Murray Legg	.08	.06	.03
137	Wayne Hamilton	.08	.06	.03
138	David Hannah	.08	.06	.03
139	Jim Bob Harris	.08	.06	.03
140	Bart Krout	.08	.06	.03
141	Bob Cayavec	.08	.06	.03
142	Joe Beazley	.08	.06	.03
143	Mike Adcock	.08	.06	.03
144	Albert Bell	.08	.06	.03
145	Mike Shula	.40	.30	.15
146	Curt Jarvis	.08	.06	.03
147	Freddie Robinson	.08	.06	.03
148	Bill Condon	.08	.06	.03
149	Howard Cross	.30	.25	.12
150	Joe Demyanovich	.08	.06	.03
151	Major Ogilvie	.25	.20	.10
152	Perron Shoemaker	.08	.06	.03
153	Ralph Jones	.08	.06	.03
154	Vic Bradford	.08	.06	.03
155	Ed Hickerson	.08	.06	.03
156	Mitchell Olenski	.08	.06	.03
157	George Hecht	.08	.06	.03
158	Russ Craft	.08	.06	.03
159	Joey Jones	.25	.20	.10
160	Jack Green	.08	.06	.03
161	Lowell Tew	.15	.11	.06
162	Lamar Moye	.08	.06	.03
163	Jesse Richardson	.15	.11	.06
164	Harold Lutz	.08	.06	.03
165	Travis Hunt	.08	.06	.03
166	Ed Culpepper	.08	.06	.03
167	Nick Germanos	.08	.06	.03
168	Billy Rains	.08	.06	.03
169	Don Cochran	.08	.06	.03
170	Cotton Clark	.08	.06	.03
171	Gaylon McCollogh	.08	.06	.03
172	Tim Bates	.08	.06	.03
173	Wayne Cook	.08	.06	.03
174	Jerry Duncan	.08	.06	.03
175	Steve Davis	.08	.06	.03

176	Donnie Sutton	.08	.06	.03
177	Randy Barron	.08	.06	.03
178	Frank Mann	.08	.06	.03
179	Jeff Rouzie	.08	.06	.03
180	John Croyle	.08	.06	.03
181	Skip Kubelius	.08	.06	.03
182	Steve Bisceglia	.08	.06	.03
183	Gary Rutledge	.15	.11	.06
184	Mike Dubose	.08	.06	.03
185	Johnny Davis	.25	.20	.10
186	K.J. Lazenby	.08	.06	.03
187	Jeff Rutledge	.25	.20	.10
188	Mike Tucker	.08	.06	.03
189	Tony Nathan	.25	.20	.10
190	Buddy Aydelette	.08	.06	.03
191	Steve Whitman	.08	.06	.03
192	Ricky Tucker	.08	.06	.03
193	Randy Scott	.08	.06	.03
194	Warren Averitte	.08	.06	.03
195	Doug Vickers	.08	.06	.03
196	Jackie Cline	.08	.06	.03
197	Wayne Davis	.08	.06	.03
198	Hardy Walker	.08	.06	.03
199	Paul Ott Carruth	.15	.11	.06
200	Paul "Bear" Bryant (CO)	.75	.60	.30
201	Randy Rockwell	.08	.06	.03
202	Chris Mohr	.15	.11	.06
203	Walter Merrill	.08	.06	.03
204	Johnny Sullivan	.08	.06	.03
205	Harold Newman	.08	.06	.03
206	Erskine Walker	.08	.06	.03
207	Ted Cook	.08	.06	.03
208	Charles Compton	.08	.06	.03
209	Bill Cadenhead	.08	.06	.03
210	Butch Avinger	.08	.06	.03
211	Bobby Wilson	.08	.06	.03
212	Sid Youngelman	.25	.20	.10
213	Leon Fuller	.08	.06	.03
214	Tommy Brooker	.15	.11	.06
215	Richard Williamson	.25	.20	.10
216	Riggs Stephenson	.25	.20	.10
217	Al Clemens	.08	.06	.03
218	Grant Gillis	.08	.06	.03
219	Johnny Mack Brown	.40	.30	.15
220	Major Ogilvie	.25	.20	.10
221	Fred Pickhard	.08	.06	.03
222	Herschel Caldwell	.08	.06	.03
223	Emile Barnes	.08	.06	.03
224	Mike McQueen	.08	.06	.03
225	Ray Abruzzese	.15	.11	.06
226	Jesse Bendross	.25	.20	.10
227	Lew Bostick	.08	.06	.03
228	Jimmy Bowdoin	.08	.06	.03
229	Dave Brown	.08	.06	.03
230	Tom Calvin	.08	.06	.03
231	Ken Emerson	.08	.06	.03
232	Calvin Frey	.08	.06	.03
233	Thornton Chandler	.15	.11	.06
234	George Weeks	.08	.06	.03
235	Randy Edwards	.08	.06	.03
236	Phillip Brown	.08	.06	.03
237	Clay Whitehurst	.08	.06	.03
238	Chris Goode	.08	.06	.03
239	Preston Gothard	.08	.06	.03
240	Herb Hannah	.08	.06	.03
241	John M. Snoderly	.08	.06	.03
242	Scott Hunter	.25	.20	.10
243	Bobby Jackson	.08	.06	.03
244	Bruce Jones	.08	.06	.03
245	Robbie Jones	.08	.06	.03
246	Terry Jones	.08	.06	.03
247	Leslie Kelley	.08	.06	.03
248	Larry Lauer	.08	.06	.03
249	'61 National Champs (Tommy Brooker, Pat Trammell, Lee Roy Jordan, Paul "Bear" Bryant, Mike Fracchia, Billy Neighbors)	.25	.20	.10
250	Bobby Luna	.08	.06	.03
251	Keith Pugh	.08	.06	.03
252	Alan McElroy	.08	.06	.03
253	'25 National Champs (Team Photo)	.15	.11	.06
254	Curtis McGriff	.25	.20	.10
255	Norman Mosley	.08	.06	.03
256	Herky Mosley	.08	.06	.03
257	Ray Ogden	.15	.11	.06
258	Pete Jilleba	.08	.06	.03
259	Benny Perrin	.08	.06	.03
260	Claude Perry	.08	.06	.03
261	Tommy Cole	.08	.06	.03
262	Ed Versprille	.08	.06	.03
263	'30 National Champs (Team Photo)	.15	.11	.06
264	Don Jacobs	.08	.06	.03
265	Robert Skelton	.08	.06	.03
266	Joe Curtis	.08	.06	.03
267	Bart Starr	.75	.60	.30
268	Young Boozer	.08	.06	.03
269	Tommy Lewis	.15	.11	.06
270	Woody Umphrey	.08	.06	.03
271	Carney Laslie	.08	.06	.03
272	Russ Wood	.08	.06	.03
273	David Smith	.08	.06	.03
274	Paul Spivey	.08	.06	.03
275	Linnie Patrick	.08	.06	.03
276	Ron Durby	.08	.06	.03
277	'26 National Champs (Team Photo)	.15	.11	.06
278	Robert Higginbotham	.08	.06	.03
279	William Oliver	.08	.06	.03
280	Stan Moss	.08	.06	.03
281	Eddie Propst	.08	.06	.03
282	Laurien Stapp	.08	.06	.03
283	Clem Gryska	.08	.06	.03
284	Clark Pearce	.08	.06	.03
285	Pete Cavan	.08	.06	.03
286	Tom Newton	.08	.06	.03
287	Rich Wingo	.15	.11	.06
288	Rickey Gilliland	.08	.06	.03
289	Conrad Fowler	.08	.06	.03
290	Rick Neal	.08	.06	.03
291	James Blevins	.08	.06	.03
292	Dick Flowers	.08	.06	.03
293	Marshall Brown	.08	.06	.03
294	Jeff Beard	.08	.06	.03
295	Pete Moore	.08	.06	.03
296	Vince Boothe	.08	.06	.03
297	Charley Boswell	.08	.06	.03
298	Van Marcus	.08	.06	.03
299	Randy Billingsley	.15	.11	.06
300	Paul "Bear" Bryant (CO)	.75	.60	.30
301	Gene Blackwell	.08	.06	.03
302	Johnny Mosley	.08	.06	.03
303	Ray Perkins (CO)	.25	.20	.10
304	Harold Drew (CO)	.08	.06	.03
305	Frank Thomas (CO) (Not the Frank Thomas that went to Auburn)	.25	.20	.10
306	Wallace Wade	.15	.11	.06
307	Newton Godfree	.08	.06	.03
308	Steve Williams	.08	.06	.03
309	Al Lewis	.08	.06	.03
310	Fred Grant	.08	.06	.03
311	Jerry Brown	.08	.06	.03
312	Mal Moore	.15	.11	.06
313	Tilden Campbell	.08	.06	.03
314	Jack Smalley	.08	.06	.03
315	Paul "Bear" Bryant (CO)	.75	.60	.30
316	C.B. Clements	.08	.06	.03
317	Billy Piper	.08	.06	.03
318	Robert Lee Hamner	.08	.06	.03
319	Donnie Faust	.08	.06	.03
320	Gary Bramblett	.08	.06	.03
321	Peter Kim	.08	.06	.03
322	Fred Berrey	.08	.06	.03
323	Paul "Bear" Bryant (CO)	.75	.60	.30
324	John Fruhmorgen	.08	.06	.03
325	Jim Fuller	.08	.06	.03
326	Doug Allen	.08	.06	.03
327	Russ Mosley	.08	.06	.03
328	Ricky Thomas	.08	.06	.03
329	Vince Sutton	.08	.06	.03
330	Larry Roberts	.15	.11	.06
331	Rick McLain	.08	.06	.03
332	Charles Eckerly	.08	.06	.03
333	'34 National Champs (Team Photo)	.15	.11	.06
334	Eddie McCombs	.08	.06	.03
335	Scott Allison	.08	.06	.03
336	Vince Cowell	.08	.06	.03
337	David Watkins	.08	.06	.03
338	Jim Duke	.08	.06	.03
339	Don Harris	.08	.06	.03
340	Lanny Norris	.08	.06	.03
341	Thad Flanagan	.08	.06	.03
342	Albert Elmore	.08	.06	.03
343	Alan Gray	.08	.06	.03
344	David Gilmer	.08	.06	.03
345	Hal Self	.08	.06	.03
346	Ben McLeod	.08	.06	.03
347	Clell (Butch) Hobson	.50	.40	.20
348	Jimmy Carroll	.08	.06	.03
349	Frank Canterbury	.08	.06	.03
350	John Byrd Williams	.08	.06	.03
351	Marvin Barron	.08	.06	.03
352	William Stone	.08	.06	.03
353	Barry Smith	.15	.11	.06
354	Jerrill Sprinkle	.08	.06	.03
355	Hank Crisp (CO)	.08	.06	.03
356	Bobby Smith	.08	.06	.03
357	Charles Gray	.08	.06	.03
358	Marlin Dyess	.08	.06	.03
359	'41 National Champs (Team Photo)	.15	.11	.06
360	Robert Moore	.08	.06	.03
361	1961 National Champs (Billy Neighbors, Pat Trammell, Darwin Holt) (Team Photo)	.15	.11	.06
362	Tommy White	.08	.06	.03
363	Earl Wesley	.08	.06	.03
364	John O'Linger	.08	.06	.03
365	Bill Battle	.08	.06	.03
366	Butch Wilson	.08	.06	.03
367	Tim Davis	.08	.06	.03
368	Larry Wall	.08	.06	.03
369	Hudson Harris	.08	.06	.03
370	Mike Hopper	.08	.06	.03
371	Jackie Sherrill	.40	.30	.15
372	Tom Somerville	.08	.06	.03
373	David Chatwood	.08	.06	.03
374	George Ranager	.08	.06	.03
375	Tommy Wade	.25	.20	.10
376	'64 National Champs (Joe Namath)	.60	.45	.25
377	Reid Drinkard	.08	.06	.03
378	Mike Hand	.08	.06	.03
379	Ed White	.25	.20	.10
380	Angelo Stafford	.08	.06	.03
381	Ellis Beck	.08	.06	.03
382	Wayne Hall	.15	.11	.06
383	Randy Lee Hall	.08	.06	.03
384	Jack O'Rear	.08	.06	.03
385	Colenzo Hubbard	.08	.06	.03
386	Gus White	.08	.06	.03
387	Rich Watson	.08	.06	.03
388	Steve Allen	.08	.06	.03
389	John David Crow Jr.	.15	.11	.06
390	Britton Cooper	.08	.06	.03
391	Mike Rodriguez	.08	.06	.03
392	Steve Wade	.08	.06	.03
393	William J. Rice	.08	.06	.03
394	Greg Richardson	.08	.06	.03
395	Joe Jones	.15	.11	.06
396	Todd Richardson	.08	.06	.03
397	Anthony Smiley	.08	.06	.03
398	Duff Morrison	.08	.06	.03
399	Jay Grogan	.08	.06	.03
400	Steve Booker	.08	.06	.03
401	Larry Abney	.08	.06	.03
402	Bill Abston	.08	.06	.03
403	Wayne Adkinson	.08	.06	.03
404	Charles Allen	.08	.06	.03
405	Phil Allman	.08	.06	.03
406	1965 National Champs (1965 Seniors)	.25	.20	.10
407	James Angelich	.08	.06	.03
408	Troy Barker	.08	.06	.03
409	George Bethune	.08	.06	.03
410	Bill Blair	.08	.06	.03
411	Clark Boler	.08	.06	.03
412	Duffy Boles	.08	.06	.03
413	Ray Bolden	.08	.06	.03
414	Bruce Bolton	.08	.06	.03
415	Alvin Davis	.08	.06	.03
416	Baxter Booth	.08	.06	.03
417	Paul Boschung	.08	.06	.03
418	1979 National Champs (Team Photo)	.25	.20	.10
419	Richard Brewer	.08	.06	.03
420	Jack Brown	.08	.06	.03
421	Larry Brown	.08	.06	.03
422	David Brungard	.08	.06	.03
423	Jim Burkett	.08	.06	.03
424	Auxford Burks	.08	.06	.03
425	Jim Cain	.08	.06	.03
426	Dick Turpin	.08	.06	.03
427	Neil Callaway	.08	.06	.03
428	David Casteal	.08	.06	.03
429	Phil Chaffin	.08	.06	.03
430	Howard Chappell	.08	.06	.03
431	Bob Childs	.08	.06	.03
432	Knute Rockne Christian	.08	.06	.03
433	Richard Ciemny	.08	.06	.03
434	J.B. Whitworth	.08	.06	.03
435	Mike Clements	.08	.06	.03
436	1973 National Champs (Coaching Staff)	.08	.06	.03
437	Rocky Colburn	.08	.06	.03
438	Danny Collins	.08	.06	.03
439	James Taylor	.08	.06	.03
440	Joe Compton	.08	.06	.03
441	Bob Conway	.08	.06	.03
442	Charlie Stephens	.08	.06	.03
443	Kerry Goode	.15	.11	.06
444	Joe LaBue	.08	.06	.03
445	Allen Crumbley	.08	.06	.03
446	Bill Curry (CO)	.15	.11	.06
447	David Bedwell	.08	.06	.03
448	Jim Davis	.08	.06	.03
449	Mike Dean	.08	.06	.03
450	Steve Dean	.08	.06	.03

451	Vince DeLaurentis	.08	.06	.03
452	Gary Deniro	.08	.06	.03
453	Jim Dildy	.08	.06	.03
454	Joe Dildy	.08	.06	.03
455	Jimmy Dill	.08	.06	.03
456	Jamie Dismuke	.08	.06	.03
457	Junior Davis	.08	.06	.03
458	Warren Dyar	.08	.06	.03
459	Hugh Morrow	.08	.06	.03
460	Grady Elmore	.08	.06	.03
461	1978 National Champs (Jeff Rutledge, Tony Nathan, Barry Krauss, Marty Lyons, Rich Wingo)	.25	.20	.10
462	Ed Hines	.08	.06	.03
463	D. Joe Gambrell	.08	.06	.03
464	Kavanaugh (Kay) Francis	.08	.06	.03
465	Robert Fraley	.08	.06	.03
466	Milton Frank	.08	.06	.03
467	Jim Franko	.08	.06	.03
468	Buddy French	.08	.06	.03
469	Wayne Rhoads	.08	.06	.03
470	Ralph Gandy	.08	.06	.03
471	Danny Gilbert	.08	.06	.03
472	Greg Gilbert	.08	.06	.03
473	Joe Godwin	.08	.06	.03
474	Richard Grammer	.08	.06	.03
475	Louis Green	.08	.06	.03
476	Gary Martin	.08	.06	.03
477	Bill Hannah	.08	.06	.03
478	Allen Harpole	.08	.06	.03
479	Neb Hayden	.08	.06	.03
480	Butch Henry	.08	.06	.03
481	Norwood Hodges	.08	.06	.03
482	Earl Smith	.08	.06	.03
483	Darwin Holt	.08	.06	.03
484	Scott Homan	.08	.06	.03
485	Nathan Rustin	.08	.06	.03
486	Gene Raburn	.08	.06	.03
487	Ellis Houston	.08	.06	.03
488	Frank Howard	.08	.06	.03
489	Larry Hughes	.08	.06	.03
490	Joe Kelley	.08	.06	.03
491	Charlie Harris	.08	.06	.03
492	Legion Field	.08	.06	.03
493	Tim Hurst	.08	.06	.03
494	Hunter Husband	.08	.06	.03
495	Lou Ikner	.08	.06	.03
496	Craig Epps	.08	.06	.03
497	Jug Jenkins	.08	.06	.03
498	Billy Johnson	.08	.06	.03
499	David Johnson	.08	.06	.03
500	Jon Hand	.25	.20	.10
501	Max Kelley	.08	.06	.03
502	Terry Killgore	.08	.06	.03
503	Eddie Lowe	.08	.06	.03
504	Noah Langdale	.08	.06	.03
505	Ed Lary	.08	.06	.03
506	Foy Leach	.08	.06	.03
507	Harry Lee	.08	.06	.03
508	Jim Loftin	.08	.06	.03
509	Curtis Lynch	.08	.06	.03
510	John Mauro	.08	.06	.03
511	Ray Maxwell	.08	.06	.03
512	Frank McClendon	.08	.06	.03
513	Tom McCrary	.08	.06	.03
514	Sonny McGahey	.08	.06	.03
515	John McIntosh	.08	.06	.03
516	David McIntyre	.08	.06	.03
517	Wes Thompson	.08	.06	.03
518	James Melton	.08	.06	.03
519	John Miller	.08	.06	.03
520	Fred Mims	.08	.06	.03
521	Dewey Mitchell	.08	.06	.03
522	Lydell Mitchell (Linebacker)	.08	.06	.03
523	Greg Montgomery	.15	.11	.06
524	Jimmie Moore	.08	.06	.03
525	Randy Moore	.08	.06	.03
526	Ed Morgan	.08	.06	.03
527	Norris Hamer	.08	.06	.03
528	Frank Mosely	.08	.06	.03
529	Sidney Neighbors	.08	.06	.03
530	Rod Nelson	.08	.06	.03
531	James Nisbet	.08	.06	.03
532	Mark Nix	.08	.06	.03
533	L.W. Noonan	.08	.06	.03
534	Louis Thompson	.08	.06	.03
535	William Oliver	.08	.06	.03
536	Gary Otten	.08	.06	.03
537	Wayne Owen	.08	.06	.03
538	Steve Patterson	.08	.06	.03
539	Charley Pell	.25	.20	.10
540	Bob Pettee	.08	.06	.03
541	Gordon Pettus	.08	.06	.03
542	Gary Phillips	.08	.06	.03
543	Clay Walls	.08	.06	.03
544	Douglas Potts	.08	.06	.03
545	Mike Stock	.08	.06	.03

546	John Mark Prudhomme	.08	.06	.03
547	George Pugh	.15	.11	.06
548	Pat Raines	.08	.06	.03
549	Joe Riley	.08	.06	.03
550	Wayne Trimble	.08	.06	.03
551	Darryl White	.08	.06	.03
552	Bill Richardson	.08	.06	.03
553	Ray Richeson	.08	.06	.03
554	Danny Ridgeway	.08	.06	.03
555	Terry Sanders	.08	.06	.03
556	Kenneth Roberts	.08	.06	.03
557	Jimmy Watts	.08	.06	.03
558	Ronald Robertson	.08	.06	.03
559	Norbie Ronsonet	.08	.06	.03
560	Jimmy Lynn Rosser	.08	.06	.03
561	Terry Rowell	.08	.06	.03
562	Larry Joe Ruffin	.08	.06	.03
563	Jack Rutledge	.08	.06	.03
564	Al Sabo	.08	.06	.03
565	David Sadler	.08	.06	.03
566	Donald Sanford	.08	.06	.03
567	Hayward Sanford	.08	.06	.03
568	Paul Tripoli	.08	.06	.03
569	Lou Scales	.08	.06	.03
570	Kurt Schmissrauter	.08	.06	.03
571	Willard Scissum	.08	.06	.03
572	Joe Sewell	.15	.11	.06
573	Jimmy Sharpe	.08	.06	.03
574	Willie Shepherd	.08	.06	.03
575	Jack Smalley Jr.	.08	.06	.03
576	Jim Simmons (Tight End)	.08	.06	.03
577	Jim Simmons (Tackle)	.08	.06	.03
578	Malcolm Simmons	.08	.06	.03
579	Dave Sington	.08	.06	.03
580	Fred Sington Jr.	.15	.11	.06

1991 All-World CFL

		NM/M	NM	E
Complete Set (110):		3.00	2.25	1.25
Common Player:		.04	.03	.02
1	Raghib (Rocket) Ismail	.25	.20	.10
2	Bruce McNall (owner)	.04	.03	.02
3	Ray Alexander	.08	.06	.03
4	Matt Clark	.08	.06	.03
5	Bobby Jurasin	.08	.06	.03
6	Dieter Brock (LEG)	.08	.06	.03
7	Doug Flutie	.75	.60	.30
8	Stewart Hill	.04	.03	.02
9	James Mills	.08	.06	.03
10	Raghib (Rocket) Ismail, With Bruce McNall	.25	.20	.10
11	Tom Clements (LEG)	.15	.11	.06
12	Lui Passaglia	.20	.15	.08
13	Ian Sinclair	.08	.06	.03
14	Chris Skinner	.08	.06	.03
15	Joe Theismann (LEG)	.15	.11	.06
16	Jon Volpe	.30	.25	.12
17	Deatrich Wise	.04	.03	.02
18	Danny Barrett	.08	.06	.03
19	Warren Moon (LEG)	.25	.20	.10
20	Leo Blanchard	.04	.03	.02
21	Derrick Crawford	.08	.06	.03
22	Lloyd Fairbanks	.08	.06	.03
23	David Beckman (CO)	.04	.03	.02
24	Matt Finlay	.04	.03	.02
25	Darryl Hall	.04	.03	.02
26	Ron Hopkins	.08	.06	.03
27	Wally Buono (CO)	.04	.03	.02
28	Kenton Leonard	.08	.06	.03
29	Brent Matich	.04	.03	.02
30	Greg Peterson	.04	.03	.02
31	Steve Goldman (CO)	.04	.03	.02
32	Allen Pitts	.25	.20	.10
33	Raghib (Rocket) Ismail	.25	.20	.10
34	Danny Bass	.08	.06	.03
35	John Gregory (CO)	.04	.03	.02
36	Rod Connop	.04	.03	.02
37	Craig Ellis	.08	.06	.03
38	Raghib (Rocket) Ismail (Rookie)	.25	.20	.10

39	Ron Lancaster (CO)	.08	.06	.03
40	Tracy Ham	.25	.20	.10
41	Ray Macoritti	.08	.06	.03
42	Willie Pless	.08	.06	.03
43	Bob O'Billovich (CO)	.04	.03	.02
44	Michael Soles	.08	.06	.03
45	Reggie Taylor	.15	.11	.06
46	Henry Williams	.20	.15	.08
47	Adam Rita (CO)	.04	.03	.02
48	Larry Wruck	.08	.06	.03
49	Grover Covington	.08	.06	.03
50	Rocky DePietro	.08	.06	.03
51	Darryl Rogers (CO)	.04	.03	.02
52	Pete Giftopoulus	.08	.06	.03
53	Herman Heard	.08	.06	.03
54	Mike Kerrigan	.08	.06	.03
55	Reggie Barnes (AS)	.08	.06	.03
56	Derrick McAdoo	.08	.06	.03
57	Paul Osbaldiston	.08	.06	.03
58	Earl Winfield	.08	.06	.03
59	Greg Battle (AS)	.08	.06	.03
60	Damon Allen	.08	.06	.03
61	Reggie Barnes	.15	.11	.06
62	Bob Molle	.04	.03	.02
63	Raghib (Rocket) Ismail	.25	.20	.10
64	Irv Daymond	.04	.03	.02
65	Andre Francis	.04	.03	.02
66	Bart Hull	.15	.11	.06
67	Stephen Jones	.08	.06	.03
68	Raghib (Rocket) Ismail	.25	.20	.10
69	Glenn Kulka	.08	.06	.03
70	Loyd Lewis	.04	.03	.02
71	Rob Smith	.04	.03	.02
72	Roger Aldag	.08	.06	.03
73	Kent Austin	.25	.20	.10
74	Ray Elgaard	.08	.06	.03
75	Mike Clemons (AS)	.25	.20	.10
76	Jeff Fairholm	.08	.06	.03
77	Richie Hall	.04	.03	.02
78	Willis Jacox	.08	.06	.03
79	Eddie Lowe	.04	.03	.02
80	Ray Elgaard (AS)	.08	.06	.03
81	Donald Narcisse	.15	.11	.06
82	James Mills (AS)	.08	.06	.03
83	Dave Ridgway	.08	.06	.03
84	Ted Wahl	.08	.06	.03
85	Carl Brazley	.08	.06	.03
86	Mike Clemons	.35	.25	.14
87	Matt Dunigan	.35	.25	.14
88	Grey Cup (Checklist 1)	.04	.03	.02
89	Harold Hallman	.08	.06	.03
90	Rodney Harding	.08	.06	.03
91	Don Moen	.08	.06	.03
92	Raghib (Rocket) Ismail	.25	.20	.10
93	Reggie Pleasant	.08	.06	.03
94	Darrell Smith (UER) (One L on front, two on back)	.15	.11	.06
95	Group Shot (Checklist 2)	.04	.03	.02
96	Chris Schultz	.08	.06	.03
97	Don Wilson	.04	.03	.02
98	Greg Battle	.08	.06	.03
99	Lyle Bauer	.04	.03	.02
100	Less Browne	.08	.06	.03
101	Raghib (Rocket) Ismail	.25	.20	.10
102	Tom Burgess	.15	.11	.06
103	Mike Gray	.04	.03	.02
104	Rod Hill	.08	.06	.03
105	Warren Hudson	.08	.06	.03
106	Tyrone Jones	.15	.11	.06
107	Stan Mikawos	.04	.03	.02
108	Robert Mimbs	.15	.11	.06
109	James West	.08	.06	.03
110	Raghib (Rocket) Ismail	.25	.20	.10
P1	Rocket Ismail Promo# (numbered P)	1.00	.70	.40
NNO	Raghib (Rocket) Ismail (Autographed card/1600)	50.00	37.00	20.00

1991 All-World Troy Aikman Promos

The six-card, regular size set used the same Troy Aikman photo, but with different crops and biography versions (English, French and Spanish). Each card is numbered with a "1" and A-F is used to distinguish the cards.

		NM/M	NM	E
Complete Set (6):		15.00	11.00	6.00
Common Player:		2.50	2.00	1.00
1A	Troy Aikman (Green border, English bio)	2.50	2.00	1.00
1B	Troy Aikman (Green border, French bio)	2.50	2.00	1.00
1C	Troy Aikman (Green border, Spanish bio)	2.50	2.00	1.00
1D	Troy Aikman (Speckled border, English bio)	2.50	2.00	1.00

| 1E | Troy Aikman (Speckled border, French bio) | 2.50 | 2.00 | 1.00 |
| 1F | Troy Aikman (Speckled border, Spanish bio) | 2.50 | 2.00 | 1.00 |

1966 American Oil All-Pro

Released in 1966, the 15/16" x 1-1/8" 20-stamp set could be affixed to an 8-1/2" x 11" collection sheet. American Oil dealers distributed the stamps and collectors could win cash prizes and a 1967 Ford Mustang as a top prize. The stamps feature headshots of top players such as Bob Lilly, Deacon Jones, Alex Karras, Johnny Unitas and Gale Sayers.

		NM	E	VG
Complete Set (15):		300.00	220.00	120.00
Common Player:		10.00	7.50	4.00
1	Herb Adderley (Winner 5.00)			
2	Gary Ballman	10.00	5.00	3.00
3	Dick Butkus (Winner 250.00)			
4	Gary Collins (Winner Car)			
5	Willie Davis	20.00	10.00	6.00
6	Tucker Frederickson	10.00	5.00	3.00
7	Sam Huff	28.00	14.00	8.50
8	Charlie Johnson	10.00	5.00	3.00
9	Deacon Jones	30.00	15.00	9.00
10	Alex Karras	30.00	15.00	9.00
11	Bob Lilly	35.00	17.50	10.50
12	Lenny Moore	35.00	17.50	10.50
13	Tommy Nobis	20.00	10.00	6.00
14	Dave Parks	10.00	5.00	3.00
15	Pete Retzlaff	10.00	5.00	3.00
16	Frank Ryan	10.00	5.00	3.00
17	Gale Sayers	45.00	22.00	13.50
18	Mick Tinglehoff	10.00	5.00	3.00
19	Johnny Unitas (Winner 25.00)			
20	Wayne Walker (Winner 1.00)			
NNO	**Saver Sheet**	25.00	12.50	7.50
---	**Envelope**	20.00	15.00	8.00

1968 American Oil Mr. and Mrs.

The 32-card, 2-1/8" x 3-7/16" set featured 16 players and their wives. The cards were distributed by American Oil stations and collectors could win cash or a 1969 Ford. The player card fronts feature a horizontal action shot with the wife cards in domestic-type poses.

		NM	E	VG
Complete Set (16):		100.00	75.00	40.00
Common Player:		5.00	3.75	2.00
Common Wife:		2.50	2.00	1.00
1	Kermit Alexander (Winner 100.00)			
2	**Mrs. Kermit Alexander** (Jogging with Family)	2.50	1.25	.70
3	Jim Bakken	5.00	2.50	1.50
4	**Mrs. Jim Bakken** (Winner 1.00)			
5	Gary Collins (Winner 500.00)			
6	**Mrs. Gary Collins** (Enjoying the Outdoors)	2.50	1.25	.70
7	Jim Grabowski (Winner 1969 Ford)			
8	**Mrs. Jim Grabowski** (At the Fireside)	2.50	1.25	.70
9	Earl Gros (Winner 1.00)			
10	**Mrs. Earl Gros** (At the Park)	2.50	1.25	.70
11	Deacon Jones	20.00	10.00	6.00
12	**Mrs. Deacon Jones** (Winner 500.00)			
13	Billy Lothridge (Winner 10.00)			
14	**Mrs. Billy Lothridge and Baby Daughter**	2.50	1.25	.70
15	Tom Matte	10.00	5.00	3.00
16	**Mrs. Tom Matte** (Winner 50 cents)			
17	Bobby Mitchell (Winner 5.00)			
18	**Mrs. Bobby Mitchell** (At a Backyard Barbecue)	2.50	1.25	.70
19	Joe Morrison	10.00	5.00	3.00
20	**Mrs. Joe Morrison** (Winner 1969 Ford)			
21	Dave Osborn	5.00	2.50	1.50
22	**Mrs. Dave Osborn** (Winner 5.00)			
23	Dan Reeves (Winner 50 cents)			
24	**Mrs. Dan Reeves** (Enjoying the Children)	2.50	1.25	.70
25	Gale Sayers	30.00	15.00	9.00
26	**Mrs. Gale Sayers** (Winner 100.00)			
27	Norm Snead (Winner 1.00)			
28	**Mrs. Norm Snead** (On the Family Boat)	2.50	1.25	.70
29	Steve Stonebreaker	5.00	2.50	1.50
30	**Mrs. Steve Stonebreaker** (Winner 10.00)			
31	Wayne Walker (Winner 50 cents)			
32	**Mrs. Wayne Walker** (At a Family Picnic)	2.50	1.25	.70

1980 Arizona Police

		NM	E	VG
Complete Set (24):		90.00	45.00	27.00
Common Player:		3.00	1.50	.90
1	Brian Clifford	3.00	1.50	.90
2	Mark Fulcher	3.00	1.50	.90
3	Bob Gareeb	3.00	1.50	.90
4	Marcellus Green	4.00	2.00	1.25
5	Drew Hardville	3.00	1.50	.90
6	Neal Harris	3.00	1.50	.90
7	Richard Hersey	3.00	1.50	.90
8	Alfondia Hill	3.00	1.50	.90
9	Tim Holmes	3.00	1.50	.90
10	Jack Housley	3.00	1.50	.90
11	Glenn Hutchinson	3.00	1.50	.90
12	Bill Jensen	3.00	1.50	.90
13	Frank Kalil	3.00	1.50	.90
14	Dave Liggins	3.00	1.50	.90
15	Tom Manno	3.00	1.50	.90
16	Bill Nettling	3.00	1.50	.90
17	Hubert Oliver	6.00	3.00	1.75
18	Glenn Perkins	3.00	1.50	.90
19	John Ramseyer	3.00	1.50	.90
20	Mike Robinson	3.00	1.50	.90
21	Chris Schultz	4.00	2.00	1.25
22	Larry Smith (CO)	4.00	2.00	1.25
23	Reggie Ware (SP)	30.00	15.00	9.00
24	Bill Zivic	3.00	1.50	.90

1981 Arizona Police

		NM/M	NM	E
Complete Set (27):		40.00	30.00	16.00
Common Player:		2.00	1.50	.80
1	Moe Ankney (ACO)	3.00	2.25	1.25
2	Van Brandon	2.00	1.50	.80
3	Bob Carter	2.00	1.50	.80
4	Brian Christiansen	2.00	1.50	.80
5	Mark Fulcher	2.00	1.50	.80
6	Bob Gareeb	2.00	1.50	.80
7	Gary Gibson	2.00	1.50	.80
8	Mark Gobel	2.00	1.50	.80
9	Alfred Gross	2.00	1.50	.80
10	Kevin Hardcastle	2.00	1.50	.80
11	Neal Harris	2.00	1.50	.80
12	Brian Holland	2.00	1.50	.80
13	Ricky Hunley	4.00	3.00	1.50
14	Frank Kalil	2.00	1.50	.80
15	Jeff Kiewel	2.00	1.50	.80
16	Chris Knudsen	2.00	1.50	.80
17	Ivan Lesnik	2.00	1.50	.80
18	Tony Neely	2.00	1.50	.80
19	Glenn Perkins	2.00	1.50	.80
20	Randy Robbins	2.00	1.50	.80
21	Gerald Roper	2.00	1.50	.80
22	Chris Schultz	3.00	2.25	1.25
23	Gary Shaw	2.00	1.50	.80
24	Larry Smith (CO)	3.00	2.25	1.25
25	Tom Tunnicliffe	3.00	2.25	1.25
26	Sergio Vega	2.00	1.50	.80
27	Brett Weber	3.00	2.25	1.25

1982 Arizona Police

		NM/M	NM	E
Complete Set (26):		35.00	26.00	14.00
Common Player:		1.50	1.25	.60
1	Brad Anderson	1.50	1.25	.60
2	Steve Boadway	1.50	1.25	.60
3	Bruce Bush	1.50	1.25	.60
4	Mike Freeman	1.50	1.25	.60
5	Marsharne Graves	1.50	1.25	.60
6	Courtney Griffin	1.50	1.25	.60
7	Al Gross	2.00	1.50	.80
8	Julius Holt	1.50	1.25	.60
9	Lamonte Hunley	2.00	1.50	.80
10	Ricky Hunley	2.50	2.00	1.00
11	Vance Johnson	5.00	3.75	2.00
12	Chris Kaesman	1.50	1.25	.60
13	John Kaiser	1.50	1.25	.60
14	Mark Keel	1.50	1.25	.60
15	Jeff Kiewell	1.50	1.25	.60
16	Ivan Lesnik	1.50	1.25	.60
17	Glenn McCormick	1.50	1.25	.60
18	Ray Moret	1.50	1.25	.60
19	Tony Neely	1.50	1.25	.60
20	Byron Nelson	2.00	1.50	.80
21	Glenn Perkins	1.50	1.25	.60
22	Randy Robbins	1.50	1.25	.60
23	Larry Smith (CO)	2.00	1.50	.80
24	Tom Tunnicliffe	2.00	1.50	.80
25	Kevin Ward	1.50	1.25	.60
26	David Wood	1.50	1.25	.60

1983 Arizona Police

		NM/M	NM	E
Complete Set (24):		35.00	26.00	14.00
Common Player:		1.50	1.25	.60
1	John Barthalt	1.50	1.25	.60
2	Steve Boadway	1.50	1.25	.60
3	Chris Brewer	1.50	1.25	.60
4	Lynnden Brown	1.50	1.25	.60
5	Charlie Dickey	1.50	1.25	.60
6	Jay Dobins	1.50	1.25	.60
7	Joe Drake	1.50	1.25	.60
8	Allan Durden	2.00	1.50	.80
9	Byron Evans	5.00	3.75	2.00
10	Nils Fox	1.50	1.25	.60
11	Mike Freeman	1.50	1.25	.60
12	Marsharne Graves	1.50	1.25	.60
13	Lamonte Hunley	2.00	1.50	.80
14	Vance Johnson	4.00	3.00	1.50
15	John Kaiser	1.50	1.25	.60
16	Ivan Lesnik	1.50	1.25	.60
17	Byron Nelson	2.00	1.50	.80
18	Randy Robbins	1.50	1.25	.60
19	Craig Schiller	1.50	1.25	.60
20	Larry Smith (CO)	2.00	1.50	.80
21	Tom Tunnicliffe	2.00	1.50	.80
22	Mark Walczak	1.50	1.25	.60
23	David Wood	1.50	1.25	.60
24	Max Zendejas	2.00	1.50	.80

1984 Arizona Police

		NM/M	NM	E
Complete Set (25):		15.00	11.00	6.00
Common Player:		.75	.60	.30
1	Alfred Jenkins	2.00	1.50	.80
8	John Connor	1.00	.70	.40
13	Max Zendejas	1.00	.70	.40
15	Gordon Bunch	.75	.60	.30
19	Allen Durden	1.00	.70	.40
23	Lynnden Brown	.75	.60	.30
25	Vance Johnson	2.00	1.50	.80
28	Tom Bayse	.75	.60	.30
35	Brent Wood	.75	.60	.30
40	Greg Turner	.75	.60	.30
47	Steve Boadway	.75	.60	.30
52	Nils Fox	.75	.60	.30
54	Craig Vesling	.75	.60	.30
62	David Connor	.75	.60	.30
67	Charlie Dickey	.75	.60	.30
71	Brian Denton	.75	.60	.30
78	John DuBose	.75	.60	.30
79	Joe Drake	.75	.60	.30
82	Joy Dobyns	.75	.60	.30
85	Mark Walczak	.75	.60	.30
86	Jon Horton	.75	.60	.30
92	David Wood	.75	.60	.30
98	Lamonte Hunley	1.00	.70	.40
99	John Barthalt	.75	.60	.30
NNO	Larry Smith (CO)	1.00	.70	.40

1985 Arizona Police

		NM/M	NM	E
Complete Set (23):		15.00	11.00	6.00
Common Player:		.75	.60	.30
1	Alfred Jenkins	1.50	1.25	.60
2	David Adams	.75	.60	.30
6	Chuck Cecil	2.00	1.50	.80
13	Max Zendejas	1.00	.70	.40
15	Gordon Bunch	.75	.60	.30
18	Jeff Fairholm	1.00	.70	.40
19	Allen Durden	1.00	.70	.40
29	Don Be'ans	.75	.60	.30
32	Joe Prior	.75	.60	.30
42	Blake Custer	.75	.60	.30
44	Boomer Gibson	.75	.60	.30
48	Byron Evans	3.00	2.25	1.25
50	Val Bichekas	.75	.60	.30
52	Joe Tofflemire	1.00	.70	.40
54	Craig Vesling	.75	.60	.30
59	Jim Birmingham	.75	.60	.30
72	Curt DiGiacomo	.75	.60	.30
73	Lee Brunelli	.75	.60	.30
78	John DuBose	.75	.60	.30
83	Gary Parrish	.75	.60	.30
95	Cliff Thorpe	.75	.60	.30
96	Glenn Howell	.75	.60	.30
NNO	Larry Smith (CO)	1.00	.70	.40

1986 Arizona Police

		NM/M	NM	E
Complete Set (24):		15.00	11.00	6.00
Common Player:		.75	.60	.30
1	David Adams	.75	.60	.30
2	Frank Arriola	.75	.60	.30
3	Val Biehekas	.75	.60	.30
4	Jim Birmingham	.75	.60	.30
5	Chuck Cecil	1.50	1.25	.60
6	James Debow	.75	.60	.30
7	Brian Denton	.75	.60	.30
8	Byron Evans	2.00	1.50	.80
9	Jeff Fairholm	1.00	.70	.40
10	Boomer Gibson	.75	.60	.30
11	Eugene Hardy	.75	.60	.30
12	Derek Hill	1.50	1.25	.60
13	Jon Horton	.75	.60	.30
14	Alfred Jenkins	1.25	.90	.50
15	Danny Lockett	1.00	.70	.40
16	Stan Mataele	.75	.60	.30
17	Chris McLemore	.75	.60	.30
18	Jeff Rinehart	.75	.60	.30
19	Ruben Rodriguez	1.00	.70	.40
20	Martin Rudolph	.75	.60	.30
21	Larry Smith (CO)	1.00	.70	.40
22	Joe Tofflemire	1.00	.70	.40
23	Dana Wells	.75	.60	.30
24	Brent Wood	.75	.60	.30

1987 Arizona Police

		NM/M	NM	E
Complete Set (23):		15.00	11.00	6.00
Common Player:		.75	.60	.30
2	Bobby Watters	1.00	.70	.40
3	Doug Pfaff	.75	.60	.30
6	Chuck Cecil	1.50	1.25	.60
11	Gary Coston	.75	.60	.30
18	Jeff Fairholm	1.00	.70	.40
22	Eugene Hardy	.75	.60	.30
26	Troy Cephers	.75	.60	.30
34	Charles Webb	.75	.60	.30
38	James Debow	.75	.60	.30
40	Art Greathouse	.75	.60	.30
43	Jerry Beasley	.75	.60	.30
44	Boomer Gibson	.75	.60	.30
47	Gallen Allen	.75	.60	.30
52	Joe Tofflemire	1.00	.70	.40
60	Jeff Rinehart	.75	.60	.30
64	Kevin McKinney	.75	.60	.30
68	Tom Lynch	.75	.60	.30
82	Derek Hill	1.25	.90	.50
84	Kevin Singleton	1.00	.70	.40
87	Chris Singleton	3.00	2.25	1.25
97	George Hinkle	.75	.60	.30
99	Dana Wells	.75	.60	.30
NNO	Dick Tomey (CO)	1.25	.90	.50

1988 Arizona Police

		NM/M	NM	E
Complete Set (25):		15.00	11.00	6.00
Common Player:		.75	.60	.30
2	Bobby Watters	1.00	.70	.40
4	Darryl Lewis	2.00	1.50	.80
5	Durrell Jones	.75	.60	.30
8	Reggie McGill	.75	.60	.30
10	Ronald Veal	1.00	.70	.40
15	Jeff Hammerschmidt	.75	.60	.30
22	Scott Geyer	.75	.60	.30
24	R. Groppenbacher	.75	.60	.30
25	David Eldridge	.75	.60	.30
35	Mario Hampton	.75	.60	.30
38	James Debow	.75	.60	.30
40	Art Greathouse	.75	.60	.30
50	Darren Case	.75	.60	.30
51	Doug Penner	.75	.60	.30
52	Joe Tofflemire	1.00	.70	.40
63	John Brandom	.75	.60	.30
65	Ken Hakes	.75	.60	.30
74	Glenn Parker	1.25	.90	.50
78	Rob Woods	.75	.60	.30
82	Derek Hill	1.25	.90	.50
84	Kevin Singleton	1.00	.70	.40
87	Chris Singleton	2.00	1.50	.80
96	Brad Henke	.75	.60	.30
99	Dana Wells	.75	.60	.30
NNO	Dick Tomey (CO)	1.00	.70	.40

1989 Arizona Police

		NM/M	NM	E
Complete Set (26):		12.00	9.00	4.75
Common Player:		.60	.45	.25
1	Zeno Alexander	.60	.45	.25
2	John Brandom	.60	.45	.25
3	Todd Burden	.60	.45	.25
4	Darren Case	.60	.45	.25
5	David Eldridge	.60	.45	.25
6	Nick Fineanganofo	.60	.45	.25
7	Scott Geyer	.60	.45	.25
8	Art Greathouse	.60	.45	.25
9	Richard Griffith	.60	.45	.25
10	Ken Hakes	.60	.45	.25
11	Jeff Hammerschmidt	.60	.45	.25
12	Mario Hampton	.60	.45	.25
13	Darryl Lewis	1.50	1.25	.60
14	Kip Lewis	.60	.45	.25
15	George Malauulu	.75	.60	.30
16	Reggie McGill	.60	.45	.25
17	John Nies	.60	.45	.25
18	Glenn Parker	1.00	.70	.40
19	Mike Parker	.60	.45	.25
20	Doug Pfaff	.60	.45	.25
21	David Roney	.60	.45	.25
22	Pete Russell	.60	.45	.25
23	Chris Singleton	1.50	1.25	.60
24	Paul Tofflemire	.60	.45	.25
25	Dick Tomey (CO)	.75	.60	.30
26	Ronald Veal	.75	.60	.30

1988 Athletes in Action

The 12-card, regular-sized set features six Dallas Cowboys and six Texas Rangers from 1988. The card fronts have a color action shot while the backs contain a player quote, a religious message and the player's favorite Bible verse. The top card in the set is Dallas head coach Tom Landry, featured one year before leaving the Cowboys after 29 years.

		NM/M	NM	E
Complete Set (12):		10.00	7.50	4.00
Common Player:		.50	.40	.20
1	Pete O'Brien	.50	.40	.20
2	Scott Fletcher	.50	.40	.20
3	Oddibe McDowell	.75	.60	.30
4	Steve Buechele	.50	.40	.20
5	Jerry Browne	.50	.40	.20
6	Larry Parrish	.50	.40	.20
7	Tom Landry (CO)	3.00	2.25	1.25
8	Steve Pelluer	.50	.40	.20
9	Gordon Banks	.50	.40	.20
10	Bill Bates	.75	.60	.30
11	Doug Cosbie	.50	.40	.20
12	Herschel Walker	1.50	1.25	.60

1972 Auburn Tigers

		NM	E	VG
Complete Set (54):		70.00	35.00	21.00
Common Player:		1.50	.70	.45
1C	Ken Calleja	1.50	.70	.45
1D	James Owens	1.50	.70	.45
1H	Mac Lorendo	1.50	.70	.45
1S	Ralph (Shug) Jordan (CO)	6.00	3.00	1.75
2C	Rick Neel	1.50	.70	.45
2D	Ted Smith	1.50	.70	.45
2H	Eddie Welch	1.50	.70	.45
2S	Mike Neel	1.50	.70	.45
3C	Larry Taylor	1.50	.70	.45
3D	Rett Davis	1.50	.70	.45
3H	Rusty Fuller	1.50	.70	.45
3S	Lee Gross	1.50	.70	.45
4C	Bruce Evans	1.50	.70	.45
4D	Rusty Deen	1.50	.70	.45
4H	Johnny Simmons	1.50	.70	.45
4S	Bill Newton	1.50	.70	.45
5C	David Beverly	2.00	1.00	.60
5D	Dave Lyon	1.50	.70	.45
5H	Mike Fuller	3.00	1.50	.90
5S	Bill Luka	1.50	.70	.45
6C	Ken Bernich	1.50	.70	.45
6D	Andy Steele	1.50	.70	.45
6H	Wade Whatley	1.50	.70	.45
6S	Bob Newton	2.00	1.00	.60
7C	Benny Sivley	2.00	1.00	.60
7D	Gardner Jett	2.00	1.00	.60
7H	Rob Spivey	2.00	1.00	.60
7S	Jay Casey	1.50	.70	.45
8C	David Langner	1.50	.70	.45
8D	Terry Henley	1.50	.70	.45
8H	Thomas Gossom	1.50	.70	.45
8S	Joe Tanory	1.50	.70	.45
9C	Chris Linderman	1.50	.70	.45
9D	Harry Unger	1.50	.70	.45
9H	Kenny Burks	1.50	.70	.45
9S	Sandy Cannon	1.50	.70	.45
10C	Roger Mitchell	1.50	.70	.45
10D	Jim McKinney	1.50	.70	.45
10H	Gaines Lanier	1.50	.70	.45
10S	Dave Beck	1.50	.70	.45
11C	Bob Farrior	1.50	.70	.45
11D	Miles Jones	1.50	.70	.45
11H	Tres Rogers	1.50	.70	.45
11S	David Hughes	1.50	.70	.45
12C	Sherman Moon	1.50	.70	.45
12D	Danny Sanspree	1.50	.70	.45
12H	Steve Taylor	1.50	.70	.45
12S	Randy Walls	1.50	.70	.45
13C	Steve Wilson	1.50	.70	.45
13D	Bobby Davis	1.50	.70	.45
13H	Hamlin Caldwell	1.50	.70	.45
13S	Dan Nugent	1.50	.70	.45
JK	**Joker - Auburn Memorial Coliseum**	1.50	.70	.45
JK	**Joker - Cliff Hare Stadium**	1.50	.70	.45

1973 Auburn Tigers

		NM	E	VG
Complete Set (54):		60.00	30.00	18.00
Common Player:		1.50	.70	.45
1C	Ken Calleja	1.50	.70	.45
1D	Chris Wilson	1.50	.70	.45
1H	Lee Hayley	1.50	.70	.45
1S	Ralph (Shug) Jordan (CO)	5.00	2.50	1.50
2C	Rick Neel	1.50	.70	.45
2D	Johnny Sumner	1.50	.70	.45
2H	Mitzi Jackson	1.50	.70	.45
2S	Jim Pitts	1.50	.70	.45
3C	Steve Stanaland	1.50	.70	.45
3D	Rett Davis	1.50	.70	.45
3H	Rusty Fuller	1.50	.70	.45
3S	Lee Gross	1.50	.70	.45
4C	Bruce Evans	1.50	.70	.45
4D	Rusty Deen	1.50	.70	.45
4H	Liston Eddins	1.50	.70	.45
4S	Bill Newton	1.50	.70	.45
5C	Jimmy Sirmans	1.50	.70	.45
5D	Harry Ward	1.50	.70	.45
5H	Mike Fuller	2.50	1.25	.70
5S	Bill Luka	1.50	.70	.45
6C	Ken Bernich	1.50	.70	.45
6D	Andy Steele	1.50	.70	.45
6H	Wade Whatley	1.50	.70	.45
6S	Bob Newton	2.00	1.00	.60
7C	Benny Sivley	2.00	1.00	.60
7D	Rick Telhiard	2.00	1.00	.60
7H	Rob Spivey	2.00	1.00	.60
7S	David Williams	1.50	.70	.45
8C	David Langner	1.50	.70	.45
8D	Chuck Fletcher	1.50	.70	.45
8H	Thomas Gossom	1.50	.70	.45
8S	Holley Caldwell	1.50	.70	.45
9C	Chris Linderman	1.50	.70	.45
9D	Ed Butler	1.50	.70	.45
9H	Kenny Burks	1.50	.70	.45
9S	Mike Flynn	1.50	.70	.45
10C	Roger Mitchell	1.50	.70	.45
10D	Jim McKinney	1.50	.70	.45
10H	Gaines Lanier	1.50	.70	.45
10S	Carl Hubbard	1.50	.70	.45
11C	Bob Farrior	1.50	.70	.45
11D	Ronnie Jones	1.50	.70	.45
11H	Billy Woods	1.50	.70	.45
11S	David Hughes	1.50	.70	.45
12C	Sherman Moon	1.50	.70	.45
12D	Mike Gates	1.50	.70	.45
12H	Steve Taylor	1.50	.70	.45
12S	Randy Walls	1.50	.70	.45
13C	Roger Pruett	1.50	.70	.45
13D	Bobby Davis	1.50	.70	.45
13H	Hamlin Caldwell	1.50	.70	.45
13S	Dan Nugent	1.50	.70	.45
JK	**Joker - Auburn Memorial Coliseum**	1.50	.70	.45
JK	**Joker - Cliff Hare Stadium**	1.50	.70	.45

1989 Auburn Coke 20

		NM/M	NM	E
Complete Set (20):		8.00	6.00	3.25
Common Player:		.35	.25	.14
C1	Pat Dye (CO)	.50	.40	.20
C2	Zane Smith	.35	.25	.14
C3	**War Eagle** (Mascot)	.50	.40	.20
C4	Tucker Frederickson	.50	.40	.20
C5	John Heisman	.50	.40	.20
C6	Ralph (Shug) Jordan (CO)	.50	.40	.20
C7	Pat Sullivan	.50	.40	.20
C8	Terry Beasley	.35	.25	.14
C9	Punt Bama Punt (Ralph (Shug) Jordan, Paul "Bear" Bryant)	.50	.40	.20
C10	Retired Jerseys (Pat Sullivan, Terry Beasley)	.50	.40	.20
C11	Bo Jackson	2.00	1.50	.80
C12	Lawyer Tillman	.75	.60	.30
C13	Gregg Carr	.35	.25	.14
C14	Lionel James	.50	.40	.20
C15	Joe Cribbs	.60	.45	.25

C16	Heisman Winners			
	(Pat Sullivan, Bo			
	Jackson, Pat Dye CO)	1.00	.70	.40
C17	Aundray Bruce	.50	.40	.20
C18	Aubie (Mascot)	.35	.25	.14
C19	Tracy Rocker	.35	.25	.14
C20	James Brooks	1.00	.70	.40

1989 Auburn Coke 580

AUBURN TIGERS
BOOZER PITTS

		NM/M	NM	E
	Complete Set (580):	30.00	22.00	12.00
	Common Player:	.07	.05	.03
1	Pat Dye (CO)			
	(His First Game)	.25	.20	.10
2	Auburn's First Team			
	(1892 Team Photo)	.15	.11	.06
3	Pat Sullivan	.25	.20	.10
4	Over The Top(Bo Jackson)	.75	.60	.30
5	Jimmy Hitchcock	.07	.05	.03
6	Walter Gilbert	.07	.05	.03
7	Monk Gafford	.07	.05	.03
8	Frank D'Agostino	.07	.05	.03
9	Joe Childress	.15	.11	.06
10	Jim Pyburn	.15	.11	.06
11	Tex Warrington	.07	.05	.03
12	Travis Tidwell	.15	.11	.06
13	Fob James	.07	.05	.03
14	Jim Phillips	.15	.11	.06
15	Zeke Smith	.07	.05	.03
16	Mike Fuller	.15	.11	.06
17	Ed Dyas	.07	.05	.03
18	Jack Thornton	.07	.05	.03
19	Ken Rice	.07	.05	.03
20	Freddie Hyatt	.07	.05	.03
21	Jackie Burkett	.15	.11	.06
22	Jimmy Sidle	.15	.11	.06
23	Buddy McClinton	.07	.05	.03
24	Larry Willingham	.15	.11	.06
25	Bob Harris	.07	.05	.03
26	Bill Cody	.07	.05	.03
27	Lewis Colbert	.07	.05	.03
28	Brent Fullwood	.25	.20	.10
29	Tracy Rocker	.15	.11	.06
30	Kurt Grain	.07	.05	.03
31	Walter Reeves	.15	.11	.06
32	Jordan-Hare Stadium	.07	.05	.03
33	Ben Tamburello	.07	.05	.03
34	Benji Roland	.07	.05	.03
35	Chris Knapp	.07	.05	.03
36	Dowe Aughtman	.07	.05	.03
37	Auburn Tigers Logo	.07	.05	.03
38	Tommie Agee	.15	.11	.06
39	Bo Jackson	.75	.60	.30
40	Freddy Weygand	.15	.11	.06
41	Rodney Garner	.07	.05	.03
42	Brian Shulman	.07	.05	.03
43	Jim Thompson	.07	.05	.03
44	Shan Morris	.07	.05	.03
45	Ralph (Shug) Jordan (CO)	.15	.11	.06
46	Stacy Searels	.07	.05	.03
47	1957 Champs (Team Photo)	.15	.11	.06
48	Mike Kolen	.15	.11	.06
49	A Challenge Met(Pat Dye)	.15	.11	.06
50	Mark Dorminey	.07	.05	.03
51	Greg Staples	.07	.05	.03
52	Randy Campbell	.07	.05	.03
53	Duke Donaldson	.07	.05	.03
54	Yann Cowart	.07	.05	.03
55	Second Blocked Punt			
	(vs. Alabama 1972)	.15	.11	.06
56	Keith Uecker	.15	.11	.06
57	David Jordan	.07	.05	.03
58	Tim Drinkard	.07	.05	.03
59	Connie Frederick	.07	.05	.03
60	Pat Arrington	.07	.05	.03
61	Willie Howell	.07	.05	.03
62	Terry Page	.07	.05	.03
63	Ben Thomas	.07	.05	.03
64	Ron Stallworth	.15	.11	.06
65	Charlie Trotman	.07	.05	.03
66	Ed West	.15	.11	.06
67	James Brooks	.50	.40	.20
68	Changing of the Guard			
	(Doug Barfield, Ralph			
	(Shug) Jordan)	.15	.11	.06
69	Ken Bernich	.07	.05	.03
70	Chris Woods	.07	.05	.03
71	Ralph (Shug) Jordan (CO)	.15	.11	.06
72	Steve Dennis (CO)	.07	.05	.03
73	Reggie Herring (CO)	.07	.05	.03
74	Al Del Greco	.15	.11	.06
75	Wayne Hall (CO)	.07	.05	.03
76	Langdon Hall	.07	.05	.03
77	Donnie Humphrey	.07	.05	.03
78	Jeff Burger	.15	.11	.06
79	Vernon Blackard	.07	.05	.03
80	Larry Blakeney (CO)	.07	.05	.03
81	Doug Smith	.07	.05	.03
82	Two Eras Meet			
	(Ralph (Shug) Jordan,			
	Vince Dooley)	.15	.11	.06
83	Kyle Collins	.07	.05	.03
84	Bobby Freeman	.07	.05	.03
85	Pat Sullivan (CO)	.25	.20	.10
86	Neil Callaway (CO)	.07	.05	.03
87	William Andrews	.25	.20	.10
88	Curtis Kuykendall	.07	.05	.03
89	David Campbell	.07	.05	.03
90	Seniors of '83	.25	.20	.10
91	Bud Casey (CO)	.07	.05	.03
92	Jay Jacobs (CO)	.07	.05	.03
93	Al Del Greco	.15	.11	.06
94	Pate Mote	.07	.05	.03
95	Rob Shuler	.07	.05	.03
96	Jerry Beasley	.07	.05	.03
97	Pat Washington	.07	.05	.03
98	Ed Graham	.07	.05	.03
99	Leon Myers	.07	.05	.03
100	Paul Davis (CO)	.07	.05	.03
101	Tom Banks Jr.	.15	.11	.06
102	Mike Simmons	.07	.05	.03
103	Alex Bowden	.07	.05	.03
104	Jim Bone	.07	.05	.03
105	Wincent Harris	.07	.05	.03
106	James Daniel	.07	.05	.03
107	Jimmy Carter	.07	.05	.03
108	Leading Passers			
	(Pat Sullivan)	.25	.20	.10
109	Alvin Mitchell	.07	.05	.03
110	Mark Clement	.07	.05	.03
111	Bob Brown	.07	.05	.03
112	Shot Senn	.07	.05	.03
113	Loran Carter	.07	.05	.03
114	Pat Dye's First Team			
	(Team Photo)	.15	.11	.06
115	Bob Hix	.07	.05	.03
116	Bo Russell	.07	.05	.03
117	Mike Mann	.07	.05	.03
118	Mike Shirey	.07	.05	.03
119	Pat Dye (CO)	.15	.11	.06
120	Kevin Greene	.25	.20	.10
121	Auburn Creed	.07	.05	.03
122	Jordan's All-Americans			
	(Ralph (Shug) Jordan,			
	Tucker Frederickson,			
	Jimmy Sidle)	.15	.11	.06
123	Dave Blanks	.07	.05	.03
124	Scott Bolton	.07	.05	.03
125	Vince Dooley	.15	.11	.06
126	Tim Jessie	.07	.05	.03
127	Joe Davis	.07	.05	.03
128	Clayton Beauford	.07	.05	.03
129	Wilbur Hutsell (AD)	.07	.05	.03
130	Joe Whit (CO)	.07	.05	.03
131	Gary Kelley	.07	.05	.03
132	Bo Jackson	.75	.60	.30
133	Aundray Bruce	.25	.20	.10
134	Ronny Bellew	.07	.05	.03
135	Hindman Wall	.07	.05	.03
136	Frank Warren	.07	.05	.03
137	Abb Chrietzberg	.07	.05	.03
138	Collis Campbell	.07	.05	.03
139	Randy Stokes	.07	.05	.03
140	Teedy Faulk	.07	.05	.03
141	Reese McCall	.15	.11	.06
142	Jeff Jackson	.07	.05	.03
143	Bill Burgess	.07	.05	.03
144	Willie Huntley	.07	.05	.03
145	Doug Huntley	.07	.05	.03
146	Bacardi Bowl(Walter			
	Gilbert)	.07	.05	.03
147	Russ Carreker	.07	.05	.03
148	Joe Moon	.07	.05	.03
149	A Look Ahead			
	(Pat Dye) (CO)	.15	.11	.06
150	Joe Sullivan	.07	.05	.03
151	Scott Riley	.07	.05	.03
152	Larry Ellis	.07	.05	.03
153	Jeff Parks	.07	.05	.03
154	Gerald Williams	.07	.05	.03
155	Mike Griffith	.07	.05	.03
156	First Blocked Punt (vs.			
	Alabama 1972)	.15	.11	.06
157	Bill Beckwith (ADMIN)	.07	.05	.03
158	Celebration			
	(1957 Action Photo)	.15	.11	.06
159	Tommy Carroll	.15	.11	.06
160	John Dailey	.07	.05	.03
161	George Stephenson	.07	.05	.03
162	Danny Arnold	.07	.05	.03
163	Mike Edwards	.07	.05	.03
164	1894 Auburn-Alabama			
	Trophy	.15	.11	.06
165	Don Anderson	.07	.05	.03
166	Alvin Briggs	.07	.05	.03
167	Herb Waldrop (CO)	.07	.05	.03
168	Jim Skuthan	.07	.05	.03
169	Alan Hardin	.07	.05	.03
170	Coaching Generations(Pat			
	Sullivan, Bobby Freeman)	.25	.20	.10
171	Georgia Celebration (1971			
	Locker Room)	.07	.05	.03
172	Auburn 17, Alabama 16 (1972)	.15	.11	.06
173	Nat Ceasar	.07	.05	.03
174	Billy Hitchcock	.15	.11	.06
175	SEC Championship			
	Trophy	.15	.11	.06
176	Dr. James E. Martin (PRES)	.07	.05	.03
177	Ricky Westbrook	.15	.11	.06
178	Fob James	.15	.11	.06
179	Stacy Dunn	.07	.05	.03
180	Tracy Turner	.07	.05	.03
181	Pat Dye (CO)	.15	.11	.06
182	In the Record Book			
	(Terry Beasley)	.07	.05	.03
183	Ed "Foots" Bauer	.07	.05	.03
184	1984 Sugar Bowl			
	Scoreboard	.07	.05	.03
185	Mark Robbins	.07	.05	.03
186	Paul White (CO)	.07	.05	.03
187	Hindman Wall (AD)	.07	.05	.03
188	David Beverly	.15	.11	.06
189	Sugar Bowl Trophy	.07	.05	.03
190	Edmund Nelson	.07	.05	.03
191	Edmund Nelson	.07	.05	.03
192	Cliff Hare	.07	.05	.03
193	Byron Franklin	.15	.11	.06
194	Richard Manry	.07	.05	.03
195	Malcolm McCary	.07	.05	.03
196	Patrick Waters (ADMIN)	.07	.05	.03
197	Chester Willis	.07	.05	.03
198	Alex Dudchock	.07	.05	.03
199	In the Record Book			
	(Pat Sullivan)	.25	.20	.10
200	Victory Ride(Pat Dye) (CO)	.15	.11	.06
201	Dr. George Petrie (CO)	.07	.05	.03
202	D.M. Balliet (CO)	.07	.05	.03
203	G.H. Harvey (CO)	.07	.05	.03
204	F.M. Hall (CO)	.07	.05	.03
205	John Heisman (CO)	.25	.20	.10
206	Billy Watkins (CO)	.07	.05	.03
207	J.R. Kent (CO)	.07	.05	.03
208	Mike Harvey (CO)	.07	.05	.03
209	Billy Bates (CO)	.07	.05	.03
210	Mike Donahue (CO)	.07	.05	.03
211	W.S. Kienholz (CO)	.07	.05	.03
212	Mike Donahue (CO)	.07	.05	.03
213	Boozer Pitts (CO)	.07	.05	.03
214	David Morey (CO)	.07	.05	.03
215	George Bohler (CO)	.07	.05	.03
216	John Floyd (CO)	.07	.05	.03
217	Chet Wynne (CO)	.07	.05	.03
218	Jack Meagher (CO)	.07	.05	.03
219	Carl Voyles (CO)	.07	.05	.03
220	Earl Brown (CO)	.07	.05	.03
221	Ralph (Shug) Jordan (CO)	.15	.11	.06
222	Doug Barfield (CO)	.15	.11	.06
223	Most Career Points			
	(Bo Jackson)	.35	.25	.14
224	Sonny Ferguson	.07	.05	.03
225	Ronnie Ross	.07	.05	.03
226	Gardner Jett	.15	.11	.06
227	Jerry Wilson	.07	.05	.03
228	Dick Schmatz	.07	.05	.03
229	Morris Savage	.07	.05	.03
230	James Owens	.07	.05	.03
231	Eddie Welch	.07	.05	.03
232	Lee Hayley	.07	.05	.03

233	Dick Hayley	.07	.05	.03
234	Jeff McCollum	.07	.05	.03
235	Rick Freeman	.07	.05	.03
236	Bobby Freeman (CO)	.07	.05	.03
237	**Auburn 32, Alabama 22** (Trophy)	.15	.11	.06
238	Chip Powell	.07	.05	.03
239	Nick Ardillo	.07	.05	.03
240	Don Bristow	.07	.05	.03
241	Bucky Waid	.07	.05	.03
242	Greg Robert	.07	.05	.03
243	Ray Rollins	.07	.05	.03
244	Tommy Hicks	.07	.05	.03
245	Steve Wallace	.15	.11	.06
246	David Hughes	.07	.05	.03
247	Chuck Hurston	.07	.05	.03
248	Jimmy Long	.07	.05	.03
249	John Cochran (AD)	.07	.05	.03
250	Bobby Davis	.07	.05	.03
251	G.W. Clapp	.07	.05	.03
252	Jere Colley	.07	.05	.03
253	Tim James	.07	.05	.03
254	Joe Dolan	.07	.05	.03
255	Jerry Gordon	.07	.05	.03
256	Billy Edge	.07	.05	.03
257	Lawyer Tillman	.25	.20	.10
258	John McAfee	.07	.05	.03
259	Scotty Long	.07	.05	.03
260	Billy Austin	.07	.05	.03
261	Tracy Rocker	.15	.11	.06
262	Mickey Sutton	.07	.05	.03
263	Tommy Traylor	.07	.05	.03
264	Billy Van Dyke	.07	.05	.03
265	Sam McClurkin	.07	.05	.03
266	Mike Flynn	.07	.05	.03
267	Jim Sirmans	.07	.05	.03
268	Reggie Ware	.15	.11	.06
269	Bill Luke	.07	.05	.03
270	Don Machen	.07	.05	.03
271	Bill Grisham	.07	.05	.03
272	Bruce Evans	.07	.05	.03
273	Hank Hall	.07	.05	.03
274	Tommy Lunceford	.07	.05	.03
275	Pat Thomas	.07	.05	.03
276	Marvin Trott	.07	.05	.03
277	Brad Everett	.07	.05	.03
278	Frank Reeves	.07	.05	.03
279	Bishop Reeves	.07	.05	.03
280	Carver Reeves	.07	.05	.03
281	Billy Haas	.07	.05	.03
282	Dye's First AU Bowl (Pat Dye) (CO)	.15	.11	.06
283	Nate Hill	.07	.05	.03
284	Bucky Howard	.07	.05	.03
285	Tim Christian	.07	.05	.03
286	Tim Christian (CO)	.07	.05	.03
287	Tom Nettleman	.07	.05	.03
288	Carl Hubbard	.07	.05	.03
289	**Auburn's Biggest Wins** (Chart)	.07	.05	.03
290	Jay Jacobs	.07	.05	.03
291	Jimmy Pettus	.07	.05	.03
292	**Cliff Hare Stadium**	.07	.05	.03
293	Richard Wood	.15	.11	.06
294	Sandy Cannon	.07	.05	.03
295	Bill Braswell	.07	.05	.03
296	Foy Thompson	.07	.05	.03
297	Robert Margeson	.07	.05	.03
298	**Pipeline to the Pros** (Seven Pro Players)	.25	.20	.10
299	Bill Evans	.07	.05	.03
300	Marvin Tucker	.07	.05	.03
301	Jack Locklear	.07	.05	.03
302	Mike Locklear	.07	.05	.03
303	Harry Unger	.07	.05	.03
304	Lee Marke Sellers	.07	.05	.03
305	Ted Foret	.07	.05	.03
306	Bobby Foret	.07	.05	.03
307	Mike Neel	.07	.05	.03
308	Rick Neel	.07	.05	.03
309	Mike Alford	.07	.05	.03
310	Mac Crawford	.07	.05	.03
311	Bill Cunningham	.07	.05	.03
312	**Legends** (Pat Sullivan, Jeff Burger)	.25	.20	.10
313	Frank LaRussa	.07	.05	.03
314	Chris Vacarella	.07	.05	.03
315	Gerald Robinson	.15	.11	.06
316	Ronnie Baynes	.07	.05	.03
317	Dave Edwards	.07	.05	.03
318	Steve Taylor	.07	.05	.03
319	Phillip Gilchrist	.07	.05	.03
320	Ben McCurdy	.07	.05	.03
321	Dave Hill	.07	.05	.03
322	Jimmy Reynolds	.07	.05	.03
323	Chuck Fletcher	.07	.05	.03
324	Bogue Miller	.07	.05	.03
325	Dave Beck	.07	.05	.03
326	Johnny Simmons	.07	.05	.03
327	Howard Simpson	.07	.05	.03
328	Benny Sivley	.15	.11	.06
329	**1987 SEC Champions** (Team Photo)	.15	.11	.06
330	Frank Cox	.07	.05	.03
331	Phil Gargis	.07	.05	.03
332	Don Webb	.07	.05	.03
333	Dan Presley	.07	.05	.03
334	Al Giffin	.07	.05	.03
335	Don Lewis	.07	.05	.03
336	Eric Floyd	.15	.11	.06
337	Stadium (Ralph (Shug) Jordan)	.15	.11	.06
338	Terry Hendly	.07	.05	.03
339	Billy Atkins	.07	.05	.03
340	Tony Long	.07	.05	.03
341	Jimmy Clemmer	.07	.05	.03
342	John Valentine	.07	.05	.03
343	Bruce Bylsma	.07	.05	.03
344	Merrill Shirley	.07	.05	.03
345	Kenny Howard (CO)	.07	.05	.03
346	Hal Hamrick	.07	.05	.03
347	Greg Zipp	.07	.05	.03
348	Mac Champion	.07	.05	.03
349	Most Tackles in One Game (Kurt Crain)	.07	.05	.03
350	Leading Career Rushers (Bo Jackson)	.35	.25	.14
351	Homer Williams	.07	.05	.03
352	Mike Gates	.07	.05	.03
353	Rusty Fuller	.07	.05	.03
354	Rusty Deen	.07	.05	.03
355	Stalwart Defenders (Bob Harris, Mark Dorminey)	.07	.05	.03
356	Heroes of '56 (Ralph (Shug) Jordan, Jerry Elliott, Frank Reeves)	.15	.11	.06
357	**Road to the Top** (Cartoon)	.15	.11	.06
358	Cleve Wester	.07	.05	.03
359	Line Stars (Jackie Burkett, Zeke Smith)	.15	.11	.06
360	Bob Scarbrough	.07	.05	.03
361	Jimmy Speigner	.07	.05	.03
362	Danny Speigner	.07	.05	.03
363	Alvin Bresler	.07	.05	.03
364	Wade Whatley	.07	.05	.03
365	Lance Hill	.07	.05	.03
366	Andy Steele	.07	.05	.03
367	John Whatley	.07	.05	.03
368	Alton Shell	.07	.05	.03
369	Larry Blakeney	.07	.05	.03
370	Mickey Zofko	.07	.05	.03
371	Gene Lorendo (CO)	.07	.05	.03
372	Mac Lorendo	.07	.05	.03
373	Buddy Davidson (CO)	.07	.05	.03
374	Dave Woodward	.07	.05	.03
375	Richard Guthrie	.07	.05	.03
376	George Rose	.07	.05	.03
377	Alan Bollinger	.07	.05	.03
378	Danny Sanspree	.07	.05	.03
379	Winky Giddens	.07	.05	.03
380	Franklin Fuller	.07	.05	.03
381	Charles Collins	.07	.05	.03
382	**Auburn, 23-22** (Scoreboard)	.07	.05	.03
383	Jeff Weekley	.07	.05	.03
384	Larry Haynie	.07	.05	.03
385	Miles Jones	.07	.05	.03
386	Bobby Wilson	.15	.11	.06
387	Bobby Lauder	.07	.05	.03
388	Charlie Glenn	.07	.05	.03
389	Claude Saia	.07	.05	.03
390	Tom Bryan	.07	.05	.03
391	Lee Gross	.07	.05	.03
392	Jerry Popwell	.07	.05	.03
393	Tommy Groat	.07	.05	.03
394	Neal Dettmering	.07	.05	.03
395	Dr. W.S. Bailey (ADMIN)	.07	.05	.03
396	Jim Pitts	.07	.05	.03
397	**College Football History** (Cliff Hare Stadium)	.07	.05	.03
398	Doc Griffith	.07	.05	.03
399	Liston Eddins	.07	.05	.03
400	Woody Woodall	.07	.05	.03
401	**Auburn Helmet**	.07	.05	.03
402	Skip Johnston	.07	.05	.03
403	Trey Gainous	.07	.05	.03
404	Randy Walls	.07	.05	.03
405	Jimmy Partin	.07	.05	.03
406	Dick Ingwerson	.07	.05	.03
407	David Shelby	.07	.05	.03
408	Harry Ward	.07	.05	.03
409	Thomas Gossom	.07	.05	.03
410	Sanford T. Gower	.07	.05	.03
411	Architects of the Future (Jeff Beard, Ralph (Shug) Jordan)	.15	.11	.06
412	Ed Butler	.07	.05	.03
413	Bob Butler	.07	.05	.03
414	Ben Strickland	.07	.05	.03
415	Jeff Lott	.07	.05	.03
416	Harris Rabren	.07	.05	.03
417	Mike McQuaig	.07	.05	.03
418	Steve Wilson	.07	.05	.03
419	Jorge Portela	.07	.05	.03
420	Dave Middleton	.15	.11	.06
421	Tommy Yearout	.07	.05	.03
422	Gusty Yearout	.07	.05	.03
423	**The Auburn Stadium**	.07	.05	.03
424	**Cliff Hare Stadium**	.07	.05	.03
425	Oscar Burford	.07	.05	.03
426	**Cliff Hare Stadium**	.07	.05	.03
427	**Cliff Hare Stadium**	.07	.05	.03
428	**Jordan-Hare Stadium**	.07	.05	.03
429	Jack Meagher (CO)	.07	.05	.03
430	Jeff Beard (AD)	.07	.05	.03
431	Frank Young (ADMIN)	.07	.05	.03
432	Frank Riley	.07	.05	.03
433	Ernie Warren	.07	.05	.03
434	Brian Atkins	.07	.05	.03
435	George Atkins	.07	.05	.03
436	Ricky Sanders	.35	.25	.14
437	George Kenmore	.07	.05	.03
438	Don Heller	.07	.05	.03
439	Pat Meagher	.07	.05	.03
440	Tim Davis	.07	.05	.03
441	**Tiger Meat** (Cooks)	.07	.05	.03
442	Joe Connally (CO)	.07	.05	.03
443	Bob Newton	.15	.11	.06
444	Bill Newton	.07	.05	.03
445	David Langner	.07	.05	.03
446	Charlie Langner	.07	.05	.03
447	Brownie Flournoy (ADMIN)	.07	.05	.03
448	Mike Hicks	.07	.05	.03
449	Larry Hill	.07	.05	.03
450	Tim Baker	.07	.05	.03
451	Danny Bentley	.07	.05	.03
452	Tommy Lowry	.07	.05	.03
453	Jim Price	.07	.05	.03
454	Lloyd Nix	.07	.05	.03
455	Kenny Burks	.07	.05	.03
456	Rusty Deen, Sallie Deen (ADMIN)	.07	.05	.03
457	Johnny Sumner	.07	.05	.03
458	Scott Blackmon	.07	.05	.03
459	Chuck Maxime	.07	.05	.03
460	**Big SEC Wins** (Chart)	.07	.05	.03
461	Bo Davis	.07	.05	.03
462	George Rose	.07	.05	.03
463	Bob Bradley	.07	.05	.03
464	Steve Osburne	.07	.05	.03
465	George Gross	.07	.05	.03
466	Andy Gross	.07	.05	.03
467	M.L. Brackett	.07	.05	.03
468	Herman Wilkes	.07	.05	.03
469	Roger Mitchell	.07	.05	.03
470	Bobby Beaird	.07	.05	.03
471	Sammy Oates	.07	.05	.03
472	Jimmy Ricketts	.07	.05	.03
473	Bucky Ayters	.07	.05	.03
474	Bill James	.07	.05	.03
475	Johnny Wallis	.07	.05	.03
476	Chris Jornson	.07	.05	.03
477	Joe Overton	.07	.05	.03
478	Tommy Lorino	.07	.05	.03
479	James Warren	.07	.05	.03
480	Lynn Johnson	.07	.05	.03
481	Sam Mitchell	.07	.05	.03
482	Sedrick McIntyre	.07	.05	.03
483	Mike Holtzclaw	.07	.05	.03
484	Dave Ostrowski	.07	.05	.03
485	Jim Walsh	.07	.05	.03
486	Mike Henley	.07	.05	.03
487	Roy Tatum	.07	.05	.03
488	Al Parks	.07	.05	.03
489	Billy Wilson	.15	.11	.06
490	Ken Luke	.07	.05	.03
491	Phillip Hall	.07	.05	.03
492	Bruce Yates	.07	.05	.03
493	Dan Hataway	.07	.05	.03
494	Joe Leichtnam	.07	.05	.03
495	Danny Fulford	.07	.05	.03
496	Ken Hardy	.07	.05	.03
497	Rob Spivey	.07	.05	.03
498	Rick Telhiard	.07	.05	.03
499	Ron Yarbrough	.07	.05	.03
500	Leo Sexton	.07	.05	.03

501	Dick McGowen (CO)	.07	.05	.03
502	Lee Kidd	.07	.05	.03
503	Rex McKissick	.07	.05	.03
504	Fagen Canzoneri, Zach Jenkins	.07	.05	.03
505	Jim Bouchillon	.07	.05	.03
506	Forrest Blue	.25	.20	.10
507	Mike Helms	.07	.05	.03
508	Bobby Hunt	.15	.11	.06
509	John Liptak	.07	.05	.03
510	James McKinney	.07	.05	.03
511	Ed Baker	.07	.05	.03
512	**Heisman Trophies**	.25	.20	.10
513	Eddy Jackson	.07	.05	.03
514	Jimmy Powell	.07	.05	.03
515	Jerry Elliott	.07	.05	.03
516	Jimmy Jones	.07	.05	.03
517	Jimmy Laster	.07	.05	.03
518	Larry Laster	.07	.05	.03
519	Jerry Sansom	.07	.05	.03
520	Don Downs	.07	.05	.03
521	Danny Skutack	.07	.05	.03
522	Keith Green	.07	.05	.03
523	Spence McCracken	.07	.05	.03
524	Lloyd Cheattom	.07	.05	.03
525	Mike Shows	.07	.05	.03
526	Spec Kelley	.07	.05	.03
527	Dick McGowen	.07	.05	.03
528	Jon Kilgore	.07	.05	.03
529	Frank Gatski	.25	.20	.10
530	Joel Eaves	.07	.05	.03
531	John Adcock	.07	.05	.03
532	Jimmy Fenton	.07	.05	.03
533	Mike McCartney	.07	.05	.03
534	Harrison McCraw	.07	.05	.03
535	Mailon Kent	.07	.05	.03
536	Dickie Flournoy	.07	.05	.03
537	Coker Barton	.07	.05	.03
538	Scotty Elam	.07	.05	.03
539	Tim Wood	.07	.05	.03
540	Terry Fuller	.07	.05	.03
541	Johnny Kern	.07	.05	.03
542	Mike Currier	.07	.05	.03
543	Richard Cheek	.07	.05	.03
544	Dan Dickerson	.07	.05	.03
545	Arnold Fagen	.07	.05	.03
546	John "Rat" Riley	.07	.05	.03
547	Jimmy Burson	.15	.11	.06
548	Bob Fleming	.07	.05	.03
549	Mike Fitzhugh	.07	.05	.03
550	Jim Patton	.25	.20	.10
551	Bryant Harvard	.07	.05	.03
552	Leon Cochran	.07	.05	.03
553	Wayne Frazier	.07	.05	.03
554	Phillip Dembowski	.07	.05	.03
555	Alex Spurlin, Ed Spurlin	.07	.05	.03
556	Bill Kilpatrick	.07	.05	.03
557	Gaines Lanier	.07	.05	.03
558	Johnny McDonald	.07	.05	.03
559	Ray Powell	.07	.05	.03
560	Jimmy Putman	.07	.05	.03
561	Bobby Wasden	.07	.05	.03
562	Roger Pruett	.07	.05	.03
563	Don Braswell	.07	.05	.03
564	Jim Jeffery	.07	.05	.03
565	Auburn - A TV Favorite (Pat Dye) (CO)	.15	.11	.06
566	Lamar Rawson	.07	.05	.03
567	Larry Rawson	.07	.05	.03
568	David Rawson	.07	.05	.03
569	Hal Herring (CO)	.07	.05	.03
570	Pat Sullivan	.25	.20	.10
571	John Cochran	.07	.05	.03
572	Jerry Gulledge	.07	.05	.03
573	Steve Stanaland	.15	.11	.06
574	Greg Zipp	.07	.05	.03
575	John Trotman	.07	.05	.03
576	Clyde Baumgartner	.07	.05	.03
577	Jay Casey	.07	.05	.03
578	Ralph O'Gwynne	.07	.05	.03
579	Sid Scarborough	.07	.05	.03
580	Tom Banks Sr.	.15	.11	.06

1991 Auburn Hoby

		NM/M	NM	E
Complete Set (42):		9.00	6.75	3.50
Common Player:		.25	.20	.10
523	Thomas Bailey	.25	.20	.10
524	Corey Barlow	.35	.25	.14
525	Reggie Barlow	.35	.25	.14
526	Fred Baxter	.35	.25	.14
527	Eddie Blake	.35	.25	.14
528	Herbert Casey	.25	.20	.10
529	Pedro Cherry	.25	.20	.10
530	Darrel Crawford	.35	.25	.14

531	Tim Cromartie	.35	.25	.14
532	Juan Crum	.25	.20	.10
533	Karekin Cunningham	.25	.20	.10
534	Alonzo Etheridge	.25	.20	.10
535	Joe Frazier	.25	.20	.10
536	Pat Dye (AD/CO)	.35	.25	.14
537	Thery George	.25	.20	.10
538	Chris Gray	.35	.25	.14
539	Victor Hall	.25	.20	.10
540	Randy Hart	.25	.20	.10
541	Chris Holland	.25	.20	.10
542	Chuckie Johnson	.25	.20	.10
543	Anthony Judge	.25	.20	.10
544	Corey Lewis	.25	.20	.10
545	Reid McMillion	.25	.20	.10
546	Bob Meeks	.25	.20	.10
547	Dale Overton	.25	.20	.10
548	Mike Pelton	.35	.25	.14
549	Bennie Pierce	.25	.20	.10
550	Mike Pina	.25	.20	.10
551	Anthony Redmon	.25	.20	.10
552	Tony Richardson	.25	.20	.10
553	Richard Shea	.25	.20	.10
554	Fred Smith	.35	.25	.14
555	Otis Mounds	.25	.20	.10
556	Ricky Sutton	.25	.20	.10
557	Alex Thomas	.25	.20	.10
558	Greg Thompson	.25	.20	.10
559	Tim Tillman	.25	.20	.10
560	Jim Von Wyl	.25	.20	.10
561	Stan White	.50	.40	.20
562	Darrell Williams	.25	.20	.10
563	James Willis	.25	.20	.10
564	Jon Wilson	.25	.20	.10

B

1990 Bandits Smokey

The Fresno Bandits, a semi-pro team, are featured in this 25-card set. The fronts feature a black-and-white player photo with the Smokey the Bear logo in the upper left and the team logo in the bottom right. The card backs have a black-and-white photo of the player with Smokey and a safety message.

		NM/M	NM	E
Complete Set (25):		12.00	22.00	12.00
Common Player:		.50	.90	.50
1	Allan Blades	.50	.90	.50
2	Corey Clark	.50	.90	.50
3	Darryl Duke	.50	.90	.50
4	Heikoti Fakava	.50	.90	.50
5	Charles Frazier	.50	.90	.50
6	Chris Geile	.50	.90	.50
7	Mike Henson	.50	.90	.50
8	James Hickey	.50	.90	.50
9	Anthony Howard	.50	.90	.50
10	Derrick Jinks	.50	.90	.50
11	Anthony Jones	.50	.90	.50
12	Marvin Jones	.50	.90	.50
13	Mike Jones	.50	.90	.50
14	Steve Loop	.50	.90	.50
15	Thomas Ireland	.50	.90	.50
16	Jay Lynch	.50	.90	.50
17	Sheldon Martin	.50	.90	.50
18	Chuckie McCutchen	.50	.90	.50
19	Lance Oberparleiter	.50	.90	.50
20	Darrell Rosette	.50	.90	.50
21	Fred Sims	.50	.90	.50
22	Bryan Turner	.50	.90	.50
23	Jim Woods CO	.50	.90	.50
24	Rick Zumwalt	.50	.90	.50
25	**Coaching Staff**	.50	.90	.50

1982 Bantam/FBI CFL Discs

		NM/M	NM	E
Complete Set (31):		300.00	225.00	120.00
Common Player:		5.00	3.75	2.00
1	Junior Ah You	10.00	7.50	4.00
2	Zenon Andrusyshyn	10.00	7.50	4.00
3	Leon Bright	10.00	7.50	4.00
4	Bob Cameron	5.00	3.75	2.00
5	Tom Clements	35.00	26.00	14.00
6	Jim Corrigall	10.00	7.50	4.00
7	Tom Cousineau	15.00	11.00	6.00
8	Carl Crennell	10.00	7.50	4.00
9	Dave Cutler	10.00	7.50	4.00
10	Peter Dalla Riva	15.00	11.00	6.00
11	Dave Fennell	5.00	3.75	2.00
12	Vince Ferragamo	25.00	18.50	10.00
13	Tom Forzani	10.00	7.50	4.00
14	Tony Gabriel	25.00	18.50	10.00
15	Gabriel Gregoire	5.00	3.75	2.00
16	Billy Hardee	5.00	3.75	2.00
17	Larry Highbaugh	10.00	7.50	4.00
18	Condredge Holloway	25.00	18.50	10.00
19	Mark Jackson	5.00	3.75	2.00
20	Billy Johnson (White Shoes)	25.00	18.50	10.00
21	Larry Key	5.00	3.75	2.00
22	Marc Lacelle	5.00	3.75	2.00
23	Ian Mofford	5.00	3.75	2.00
24	Gerry Organ	10.00	7.50	4.00
25	Tony Petruccio	5.00	3.75	2.00
26	Tony Proudfoot	10.00	7.50	4.00
27	Randy Rhino	15.00	11.00	6.00
28	Ian Santer	5.00	3.75	2.00
29	Jerry Tagge	15.00	11.00	6.00
30	Jim Washington	10.00	7.50	4.00
31	Tom Wilkinson	15.00	11.00	6.00

1959 Bazooka

These cards were found on the backs of Bazooka Bubble Gum boxes in 1959. The unnumbered cards are blank-backed and are checklisted alphabetically. Each card measures 2-13/16" x 4-15/16" and is part of the display box. Intact boxes are worth more than if the cards have been cut out.

		NM	E	VG
Complete Set (18):		5,000	2,500	1,500
Common Player:		150.00	75.00	45.00
(1)	Alan Ameche	190.00	95.00	57.00
(2)	Jon Arnett	150.00	75.00	45.00
(3)	Jim Brown	675.00	335.00	200.00
(4)	Rick Casares	150.00	75.00	45.00
(5A)	Charley Connerly (error, Baltimore Colts)	450.00	225.00	135.00
(5B)	Charley Conerly (correct, New York Giants)	325.00	162.00	97.00
(6)	Howard Ferguson	150.00	75.00	45.00
(7)	Frank Gifford	450.00	225.00	135.00
(8)	Lou Groza	475.00	235.00	140.00
(9)	Bobby Layne	325.00	162.00	97.00
(10)	Eddie LeBaron	200.00	100.00	60.00
(11)	Woodley Lewis	150.00	75.00	45.00
(12)	Ollie Matson	250.00	125.00	75.00
(13)	Joe Perry	250.00	125.00	75.00
(14)	Pete Retzlaff	150.00	75.00	45.00
(15)	Kyle Rote	225.00	112.00	67.00
(16)	Y.A. Tittle	325.00	162.00	97.00
(17)	Tom Tracy	300.00	150.00	90.00
(18)	Johnny Unitas	500.00	250.00	150.00

1971 Bazooka

These cards were issued on the backs of Bazooka Bubble Gum as panels of three. The panels are 2-5/8" x 5-7/8"; each individual card is 1-15/16" x 2-5/8". The card front has a number, plus a color head shot of the player. The back is blank. Panels generally command a premium price which would be greater than the total of the three players combined. Individual card prices are listed.

		NM	E	VG
Complete Set (36):		200.00	100.00	60.00
Common Player:		3.00	1.50	.90
1	Joe Namath	35.00	17.50	10.50
2	Larry Brown	5.00	2.50	1.50
3	Bobby Bell	5.00	2.50	1.50
4	Dick Butkus	15.00	7.50	4.50
5	Charlie Sanders	3.00	1.50	.90
6	Chuck Howley	4.00	2.00	1.25
7	Gale Gillingham	3.00	1.50	.90
8	Leroy Kelly	6.00	3.00	1.75
9	Floyd Little	6.00	3.00	1.75
10	Dan Abramowicz	3.50	1.75	1.00
11	Sonny Jurgensen	15.00	7.50	4.50
12	Andy Russell	3.00	1.50	.90
13	Tommy Nobis	3.00	1.50	.90
14	O.J. Simpson	30.00	15.00	9.00
15	Tom Woodeshick	3.00	1.50	.90
16	Roman Gabriel	4.50	2.25	1.25
17	Claude Humphrey	3.00	1.50	.90
18	Merlin Olsen	8.00	4.00	2.50
19	Daryle Lamonica	4.00	2.00	1.25
20	Fred Cox	3.00	1.50	.90
21	Bart Starr	16.00	8.00	4.75
22	John Brodie	8.00	4.00	2.50
23	Jim Nance	3.00	1.50	.90
24	Gary Garrison	3.00	1.50	.90
25	Fran Tarkenton	17.00	8.50	5.00
26	Johnny Robinson	3.00	1.50	.90

27	Gale Sayers	18.00	9.00	5.50
28	John Unitas	20.00	10.00	6.00
29	Jerry LeVias	3.00	1.50	.90
30	Virgil Carter	3.00	1.50	.90
31	Bill Nelsen	3.00	1.50	.90
32	Dave Osborn	3.00	1.50	.90
33	Matt Snell	3.00	1.50	.90
34	Larry Wilson	6.00	3.00	1.75
35	Bob Griese	15.00	7.50	4.50
36	Lance Alworth	8.00	4.00	2.50

1972 Bazooka Official Signals

The 12-card, 6-1/4" x 2-7/8" set was issued by Bazooka on the bottoms of its bubble gum boxes in 1972. The first eight cards define football lingo for juveniles while cards 9-12 describe the responsibilities of the referees.

		NM	E	VG
Complete Set (12):		85.00	64.00	34.00
Common Player:		8.00	6.00	3.25
1	Football Lingo (Automatic through Bread and Butter Play)	8.00	4.00	2.50
2	Football Lingo (Broken-Field Runner through Dive)	8.00	4.00	2.50
3	Football Lingo (Double-Coverage through Interference)	8.00	4.00	2.50
4	Football Lingo (Game Plan through Lateral Pass)	8.00	4.00	2.50
5	Football Lingo (Interception through Man-to-Man Coverage)	8.00	4.00	2.50
6	Football Lingo (Killing the Clock through Punt)	8.00	4.00	2.50
7	Football Lingo (Belly Series through Quick Whistle)	8.00	4.00	2.50
8	Football Lingo (Prevent Defense through Primary Receiver)	8.00	4.00	2.50
9	Officials' Duties (Reveree through Line Judge)	8.00	4.00	2.50
10	Officials' Duties	8.00	4.00	2.50
11	Officials' Signals	8.00	4.00	2.50
12	Officials' Signals	8.00	4.00	2.50

1976 Bears Coke Discs

The 24 circular-card set was issued in 1976 as part of a local Coca-Cola promotion in Chicago. Each one of the 3-3/8" (diameter) discs feature Chicago Bears players, including a noteworthy disc of Walter Payton, whose rookie Topps card was also issued in 1976. The card front features a headshot with the Coca-Cola logo and a Bears helmet while the back has another Coca-Cola logo with the "Coke adds life to ... halftime fun."

		NM	E	VG
Complete Set (24):		60.00	45.00	24.00
Common Player:		1.50	.70	.45
1	Lionel Antoine	1.50	.70	.45
2	Bob Avellini	3.00	1.50	.90
3	Waymond Bryant	1.50	.70	.45
4	Doug Buffone	2.00	1.00	.60
5	Wally Chambers	2.00	1.00	.60
6A	Craig Clemons (Yellow border)	1.50	.70	.45
6B	Craig Clemons (Orange border)	1.50	.70	.45
7	Allan Ellis	1.50	.70	.45
8	Roland Harper	2.50	1.25	.70
9	Mike Hartenstine	1.50	.70	.45
10	Noah Jackson	2.50	1.25	.70
11	Virgil Livers	1.50	.70	.45
12	Jim Osborne	1.50	.70	.45
13	Bob Parsons	1.50	.70	.45
14	Walter Payton	45.00	22.00	13.50
15	Dan Peiffer	1.50	.70	.45
16A	Doug Plank (Yellow border)	3.00	1.50	.90
16B	Doug Plank (Green border)	3.00	1.50	.90
17	Bo Rather	1.50	.70	.45
18	Don Rives	1.50	.70	.45
19	Jeff Sevy	1.50	.70	.45
20	Ron Shanklin	1.50	.70	.45
21	Revie Sorey	1.50	.70	.45
22	Roger Stillwell	1.50	.70	.45

1981 Bears Police

64 • Ted Albrecht

The 24-card, 2-5/8" x 4-1/8" set was released in 1981 and sponsored by the Kiwanis Club, the local law enforcement agency and the Chicago Bears. The card fronts feature an action shot while the backs have a Bears helmet and tips geared toward younger fans.

		NM/M	NM	E
Complete Set (24):		25.00	18.50	10.00
Common Player:		.50	.25	.15
1	Ted Albrecht	.50	.25	.15
2	Neil Armstrong CO	.50	.40	.20
3	Brian Baschnagel	.50	.40	.20
4	Gary Campbell	.50	.25	.15
5	Robin Earl	.50	.25	.15
6	Allan Ellis	.50	.25	.15
7	Vince Evans	2.00	1.50	.80
8	Gary Fencik	1.50	1.25	.60
9	Dan Hampton	5.00	3.75	2.00
10	Roland Harper	.75	.60	.30
11	Mike Hartenstine	.50	.25	.15
12	Tom Hicks	.50	.25	.15
13	Noah Jackson	.75	.60	.30
14	Dennis Lick	.50	.25	.15
15	Jerry Muckensturm	.50	.25	.15
16	Dan Neal	.50	.25	.15
17	Jim Osborne	.50	.25	.15
18	Alan Page	3.50	2.75	1.50
19	Walter Payton	18.00	13.50	7.25
20	Doug Plank	.50	.40	.20
21	Terry Schmidt	.50	.25	.15
22	James Scott	.50	.25	.15
23	Revie Sorey	.50	.40	.20
24	Rickey Watts	.50	.25	.15

1968 Bengals Team Issue

The Cincinnati Bengals team-issued set consisted of 8-1/2" x 11" cards with a black and white player photo. The player's name and position are below the photo.

		NM	E	VG
Complete Set (7):		35.00	17.50	10.50
Complete Player:		5.00	2.50	1.50
1	Frank Buncom	5.00	2.50	1.50
2	Sherrill Headrick	5.00	2.50	1.50
3	Warren McVea	5.00	2.50	1.50
4	Fletcher Smith	5.00	2.50	1.50
5	John Stofa	7.00	3.50	2.00
6	Dewey Warren	5.00	2.50	1.50
7	Ernie Wright	7.00	3.50	2.00

1969 Bengals Tresler Comet

The 20-card, standard-size cards were distributed by Tresler Comet gas stations. The card fronts feature a simulated autograph while the backs contain bio and career highlights. The card backs are not numbered and Bob Johnson's card is unusually higher in value than the other 19 because of its scarcity. Also, future Bengals' coach Sam Wyche is included along with football announcer Bob Trumpy.

	NM	E	VG
Complete Set (20):	300.00	220.00	120.00
Common Player:	5.00	3.75	2.00

1	Al Beauchamp	5.00	3.75	2.00
2	Bill Bergey	10.00	5.00	3.00
3	Royce Berry	5.00	3.75	2.00
4	Paul Brown CO	35.00	17.50	10.50
5	Frank Buncom	5.00	3.75	2.00
6	Greg Cook	10.00	5.00	3.00
7	Howard Fest SP	25.00	12.50	7.50
8	Harry Gunner SP	20.00	10.00	6.00
9	Bobby Hunt	5.00	3.75	2.00
10	Bob Johnson SP	125.00	62.00	37.00
11	Charley King	5.00	3.75	2.00
12	Dale Livingston	5.00	3.75	2.00
13	Warren McVea SP	25.00	12.50	7.50
14	Bill Peterson	5.00	3.75	2.00
15	Jess Phillips	5.00	3.75	2.00
16	Andy Rice	5.00	3.75	2.00
17	Bill Staley	5.00	3.75	2.00
18	Bob Trumpy	20.00	10.00	6.00
19	Ernie Wright	5.00	3.75	2.00
20	Sam Wyche	25.00	12.50	7.50

1960 Bills Team Issue

Issued by the team, this set of 40 black and white 5" x 7" cards were delivered to the 1960 Buffalo Bills season ticketholders. The photos are not numbered and were frequently found autographed.

		NM	E	VG
Complete Set (40):		180.00	135.00	72.50
Common Player:		5.00	2.50	1.50
1	Bill Atkins	5.00	2.50	1.50
2	Bob Barrett	5.00	2.50	1.50
3	Phil Blazer	5.00	2.50	1.50
4	Bob Brodhead	5.00	2.50	1.50
5	Dick Brubacher	5.00	2.50	1.50
6	Bernie Burzinski	5.00	2.50	1.50
7	Wray Carlton	8.00	4.00	2.50
8	Don Chelf	5.00	2.50	1.50
9	Monte Crockett	5.00	2.50	1.50
10	Bob Dove	5.00	2.50	1.50
11	Elbert Dubenion	10.00	5.00	3.00
12	Fred Ford	5.00	2.50	1.50
13	Dick Gallagher	5.00	2.50	1.50
14	Darrell Harper	5.00	2.50	1.50
15	Harvey Johnson	5.00	2.50	1.50
16	John Johnson	5.00	2.50	1.50
17	Billy Kinard	5.00	2.50	1.50
18	Joe Kulbacki	5.00	2.50	1.50
19	John Laraway	5.00	2.50	1.50
20	Richie Lucas	10.00	5.00	3.00
21	Archie Matsos	8.00	4.00	2.50
22	Richie McCabe	8.00	4.00	2.50
23	Dan McGrew	5.00	2.50	1.50
24	Chuck McMurtry	5.00	2.50	1.50
25	Ed Meyer	5.00	2.50	1.50
26	Ed Muelhaupt	5.00	2.50	1.50
27	Tom O'Connell	5.00	2.50	1.50
28	Harold Olson	5.00	2.50	1.50
29	Buster Ramsey CO	5.00	2.50	1.50
30	Floyd Reid	5.00	2.50	1.50
31	Tom Rychlec	5.00	2.50	1.50
32	Joe Schaeffer	5.00	2.50	1.50
33	John Scott	5.00	2.50	1.50
34	Bob Sedlock	5.00	2.50	1.50
35	Carl Smith	5.00	2.50	1.50
36	Jim Sorey	5.00	2.50	1.50
27	Lavern Torczon	5.00	2.50	1.50
38	Jim Wagstaff	5.00	2.50	1.50
39	Ralph Wilson OWN	8.00	4.00	2.50
40	Mack Yoho	5.00	2.50	1.50

1963 Bills Jones Dairy

The 40-card, circular cards were available as cardboard cut-outs on milk cartons. The 1" (diameter) discs are frequently found miscut and off-centered and are not numbered.

		NM	E	VG
Complete Set (40):		1,000	500.00	300.00
Common Player:		20.00	15.00	8.00
1	Ray Abruzzese	20.00	15.00	8.00
2	Art Baker	20.00	15.00	8.00
3	Stew Barber	20.00	10.00	6.00
4	Glenn Bass	20.00	15.00	8.00
5	Dave Behrman	20.00	10.00	6.00
6	Al Bemiller	20.00	15.00	8.00
7	Wray Carlton	20.00	10.00	6.00
8	Carl Charon	20.00	15.00	8.00
9	Monte Crockett	20.00	10.00	6.00
10	Wayne Crow	20.00	15.00	8.00
11	Tom Day	20.00	10.00	6.00
12	Elbert Dubenion	25.00	12.50	7.50
13	Jim Dunaway	20.00	10.00	6.00
14	Booker Edgerson	20.00	10.00	6.00
15	Cookie Gilchrist	30.00	15.00	9.00
16	Dick Hudson	20.00	10.00	6.00
17	Frank Jackunas	20.00	15.00	8.00
18	Harry Jacobs	20.00	10.00	6.00

19	Jack Kemp	375.00	185.00	110.00
20	Roger Kochman	20.00	15.00	8.00
21	Daryle Lamonica	85.00	42.00	25.00
22	Charley Leo	20.00	15.00	8.00
23	Marv Matuszak	20.00	10.00	6.00
24	Bill Miller	20.00	15.00	8.00
25	Leroy Moore	20.00	15.00	8.00
26	Harold Olson	20.00	15.00	8.00
27	Herb Paterra	20.00	15.00	8.00
28	Ken Rice	20.00	15.00	8.00
29	Henry Rivera	20.00	15.00	8.00
30	Ed Rutkowski	20.00	15.00	8.00
31	George Saimes	25.00	12.50	7.50
32	Tom Sestak	25.00	12.50	7.50
33	Billy Shaw	25.00	12.50	7.50
34	Mike Stratton	20.00	10.00	6.00
35	Gene Sykes	20.00	15.00	8.00
36	John Tracey	20.00	15.00	8.00
37	Ernie Warlick	20.00	10.00	6.00
38	Willie West	20.00	10.00	6.00
39	Mack Yoho	20.00	10.00	6.00
40	Sid Youngelman	20.00	10.00	6.00

1965 Bills Super Duper Markets

The 10-card, 8-1/2" x 11" set was offered as a giveaway from Super Duper food stores in 1965. The fronts contain black and white action (posed) photos and the set is not numbered.

		NM	E	VG
Complete Set (10):		180.00	135.00	72.50
Common Player:		5.00	3.75	2.00
1	Glenn Bass	5.00	3.75	2.00
2	Elbert Dubenion	10.00	5.00	3.00
3	Billy Joe	10.00	5.00	3.00
4	Jack Kemp	100.00	50.00	30.00
5	Daryle Lamonica	30.00	15.00	9.00
6	Tom Sestak	5.00	3.75	2.00
7	Billy Shaw	10.00	5.00	3.00
8	Mike Stratton	5.00	3.75	2.00
9	Ernie Warlick	5.00	3.75	2.00
10	**Team Photo**	25.00	12.50	7.50

1967 Bills Jones-Rich Milk

Through a special mail-in offer, Jones-Rich Milk offered the set of six Buffalo Bills 8-1/2" x 11" cards in 1967.

		NM	E	VG
Complete Set (6):		100.00	50.00	30.00
Common Player:		15.00	7.50	4.50
1	George (Butch) Byrd	20.00	10.00	6.00
2	Wray Carlton	20.00	10.00	6.00
3	Hagood Clarke	15.00	7.50	4.50
4	Paul Costa	20.00	10.00	6.00
5	Jim Dunaway	20.00	10.00	6.00
6	Jack Spikes	20.00	10.00	6.00

1974 Bills Team Issue

The 12-card, 8-1/2" x 11" photo cards were issued through concession sales at Rich Stadium in Buffalo during the 1974 season.

		NM	E	VG
Complete Set (12):		80.00	60.00	32.00
Common Player:		5.00	3.75	2.00
1	Jim Braxton	5.00	2.50	1.50
2	Bob Chandler	8.00	4.00	2.50
3	Jim Cheyunski	5.00	2.50	1.50
4	Earl Edwards	5.00	3.75	2.00
5	Joe Ferguson	12.00	6.00	3.50
6	Dave Foley	5.00	3.75	2.00
7	Robert James	5.00	3.75	2.00
8	Reggie McKenzie	5.00	2.50	1.50
9	Jerry Patton	5.00	3.75	2.00
10	Walt Patulski	5.00	2.50	1.50
11	John Skorupan	5.00	2.50	1.50
12	O.J. Simpson	30.00	15.00	9.00

1976 Bills McDonald's

The three-card set was issued by McDonald's in conjunction with WBEN-TV and was given away free with a purchase of a Quarter Pounder hamburger at particpating restaurants. The 8" x 10" color photos included statistical information on the backs.

		NM	E	VG
Complete Set (3):		30.00	22.00	12.00
Common Player:		8.00	6.00	3.25
1	Bob Chandler	10.00	5.00	3.00
2	Joe Ferguson	15.00	7.50	4.50
3	Reggie McKenzie	8.00	4.00	2.50

1979 Bills Bell's Market

The 11-card, 7-5/8" x 10" photo cards were issued weekly by Bell's Markets during the 1979 season. The cards were printed on thin stock and were not numbered.

		NM	E	VG
Complete Set (11):		50.00	37.00	20.00
Common Player:		4.00	3.00	1.50
(1)	Curtis Brown	4.00	3.00	1.50
(2)	Bob Chandler	5.00	2.50	1.50
(3)	Joe DeLamielleure	4.00	2.00	1.25
(4)	Joe Ferguson	10.00	5.00	3.00
(5)	Reuben Gant	4.00	2.00	1.25
(6)	Dee Hardison	4.00	3.00	1.50
(7)	Frank Lewis	4.00	2.00	1.25
(8)	Reggie McKenzie	5.00	2.50	1.50
(9)	Terry Miller	4.00	2.00	1.25
(10)	Shane Nelson	4.00	3.00	1.50
(11)	Lucius Sanford	4.00	3.00	1.50

1980 Bills Bell's Market

The 20-card, regular-sized set was issued by Bell's Markets in 1980 and arrived in 20-card packs or two-pack perforation sets. The card fronts contain color shots while the backs have career statistics.

		NM/M	NM	E
Complete Set (20):		12.00	9.00	4.75
Common Player:		.50	.40	.20
1	Curtis Brown	.50	.40	.20
2	Shane Nelson	.50	.40	.20
3	Jerry Butler	1.00	.40	.20
4	Joe Ferguson	1.25	.40	.20
5	Joe Cribbs	1.00	.40	.20
6	Reggie McKenzie	.75	.40	.20
7	Joe Devlin	.75	.40	.20
8	Ken Jones	.50	.40	.20
9	Steve Freeman	.50	.40	.20
10	Mike Kadish	.50	.40	.20
11	Jim Haslett	.50	.40	.20
12	Isiah Robertson	.50	.40	.20
13	Frank Lewis	.50	.40	.20
14	Jeff Nixon	.50	.40	.20
15	Nick Mike-Mayer	.50	.40	.20
16	Jim Ritcher	.50	.40	.20
17	Charles Romes	.50	.40	.20
18	Fred Smerlas	.75	.40	.20
19	Ben Williams	.50	.40	.20
20	Roland Hooks	.50	.40	.20

1986 Bills Sealtest

The six-card, 3-5/8" x 7-5/8" set was issued on sides of half-gallon Sealtest milk containers. The Freeman and Marve cards were found on vitamin D cartons while the Kelly and Romes cards appeared on lowfat (2%) cartons. The cards featured a black and white player headshot with bio information and stats.

		NM/M	NM	E
Complete Set (6):		30.00	22.00	12.00
Common Player:		1.50	1.25	.60
1	Greg Bell SP	5.00	3.75	2.00
2	Jerry Butler SP	5.00	3.75	2.00
3	Steve Freeman	1.50	1.25	.60
4	Jim Kelly	20.00	15.00	8.00
5	Eugene Marve	1.50	1.25	.60
6	Charles Romes	1.50	1.25	.60

1987 Bills Police

The eight-card, 2-5/8" x 4-1/8" set was sponsored by the Bills, Erie and Niagara County Sheriff's Departments, Louis Rich Turkey products, Claussen Pickles and WBEN radio. The black and white photos on the card fronts were taken by Robert L. Smith, the Bills' official team photographer.

		NM/M	NM	E
Complete Set (8):		8.00	9.00	4.75
Common Player:		.50	.70	.40
1	Marv Levy CO	1.00	.70	.40
2	Bruce Smith	2.00	1.50	.80
3	Joe Devlin	.50	.70	.40
4	Jim Kelly	3.00	2.25	1.25
5	Eugene Marve	.50	.70	.40
6	Andre Reed	1.00	.70	.40
7	Pete Metzelaars	.50	.70	.40
8	John Kidd	.50	.70	.40

1988 Bills Police

The eight-card, 2-5/8" x 4-1/8" set was sponsored by the Bills, Erie and Niagara County Sheriff's Departments, Louis Rich Turkey Products and WBEN radio. The fronts feature an action photo while the backs have bio and stat information.

		NM/M	NM	E
Complete Set (8):		5.00	6.00	3.25
Common Player:		.75	.60	.30

1	Steve Tasker	1.50	1.25	.60
2	Cornelius Bennett	2.00	1.50	.80
3	Shane Conlan	.75	.60	.30
4	Mark Kelso	.75	.60	.30
5	Will Wolford	.75	.60	.30
6	Chris Burkett	.75	.60	.30
7	Kent Hull	.75	.60	.30
8	Art Still	.75	.60	.30

1989 Bills Police

The eight-card, regular-sized set was issued in conjunction with the Bills, Erie County Sheriff's Department and Louis Rich Turkey Products. The card fronts feature an action shot while the backs contain bio and stat information.

		NM/M	NM	E
Complete Set (8):		8.00	7.50	4.00
Common Player:		.75	.60	.30
1	Leon Seals	.75	.60	.30
2	Thurman Thomas	4.00	3.00	1.50
3	Jim Ritcher	.75	.60	.30
4	Scott Norwood	.75	.60	.30
5	Darryl Talley	1.00	.70	.40
6	Nate Odomes	.75	.60	.30
7	Leonard Smith	.75	.60	.30
8	Ray Bentley	.75	.60	.30

1990 Bills Police

The eight-card, 4" x 6" set was sponsored by Blue Shield of New York. The card fronts feature a color action photo and the card backs contain highlights and career statistics.

		NM/M	NM	E
Complete Set (8):		8.00	7.50	4.00
Common Player:		.50	.40	.20
1	Carlton Bailey	.50	.40	.20
2	Kirby Jackson	.50	.40	.20
3	Jim Kelly	4.00	3.00	1.50
4	James Lofton	1.00	.70	.40
5	Keith McKeller	.50	.40	.20
6	Mark Pike	.50	.40	.20
7	Andre Reed	1.00	.70	.40
8	Jeff Wright	.50	.40	.20

1991 Bills Police

The eight-card, regular-sized set was sponsored by Blue Shield of New York. The card fronts feature an action shot and bio information while the backs contain highlights and career statistics.

		NM/M	NM	E
Complete Set (8):		5.00	3.75	2.00
Common Player:		.75	.60	.30
1	Howard Ballard	.75	.60	.30
2	Don Beebe	1.50	1.25	.60
3	John Davis	.75	.60	.30
4	Kenneth Davis	1.00	.70	.40
5	Mark Kelso	.75	.60	.30
6	Frank Reich	1.50	1.25	.60
7	Butch Rolle	.75	.60	.30
8	J.D. Williams	.75	.60	.30

1983 Blitz Chicago

The eight-sheet, 10" x 8" set featured the United States Football League team. One set contains the coaching staff, including head coach George Allen, while the other seven feature the players. The sheets are unnumbered and the individual photos on the sheets are approximately 2-1/4" x 2-1/2".

		NM/M	NM	E
Complete Set (8):		35.00	26.00	14.00
Common Player:		4.50	3.50	1.75
1	Coaching Staff(George Allen, Joe Haering, Paul Lanham, John Payne, John Teerlink, Dick Walker, Charlie Waller, Ray Wietecha)	4.50	3.50	1.75
2	Luther Bradley, Eddie Brown, Virgil Livers, Frank Minnifield, Lance Sheilds, Don Schwartz, Maurice Tyler, Ted Walton	4.50	3.50	1.75
3	Mack Boatner, Frank Collins, Frank Corral, Doug Cozen, Doug Dennison, John Roveto, Jim Stone, Tim Wrightman	4.50	3.50	1.75
4	Robert Barnes, Bruce Branch, Nick Eyre, Tim Norman, Wally Pesuit, Mark Stevenson, Rob Taylor, Steve Tobin	4.50	3.50	1.75

5	Junior Ah You, Mark Buben, Bob Cobb, Joe Ehrmann, Kit Lathrop, Karl Lorch, Troy Thomas	4.50	3.50	1.75
6	Jim Fahnhorst, Joe Federspiel, Doak Field, Bruce Gheesling, Andy Melontree, Ed Smith, Stan White, Kari Yli-Renko	4.50	3.50	1.75
7	Marcus Anderson, Larry Douglas, Mark May, Pat Schmidt, Lenny Willis, Warren Anderson, Chris Pagnucco, Bruce Allen GM	4.50	3.50	1.75

1954 Blue Ribbon Tea CFL

		NM	E	VG
Complete Set (80):		9,000	4,500	2,700
Common Player:		100.00	50.00	30.00
1	Jack Jacobs	250.00	125.00	75.00
2	Neil Armstrong	150.00	75.00	45.00
3	Lorne Benson	100.00	50.00	30.00
4	Tom Casey	125.00	62.00	37.00
5	Vincent Drake	100.00	50.00	30.00
6	Tommy Ford	100.00	50.00	30.00
7	Bud Grant	500.00	250.00	150.00
8	Dick Huffman	125.00	62.00	37.00
9	Gerry James	150.00	75.00	45.00
10	Bud Korchak	100.00	50.00	30.00
11	Thomas Lumsden	100.00	50.00	30.00
12	Steve Patrick	100.00	50.00	30.00
13	Keith Pearce	100.00	50.00	30.00
14	Jesse Thomas	100.00	50.00	30.00
15	Buddy Tinsley	125.00	62.00	37.00
16	Alan Scott Wiley	100.00	50.00	30.00
17	Winty Young	100.00	50.00	30.00
18	Joseph Zaleski	100.00	50.00	30.00
19	Ron Vaccher	100.00	50.00	30.00
20	John Gramling	100.00	50.00	30.00
21	Bob Simpson	150.00	75.00	45.00
22	Bruno Bitkowski	125.00	62.00	37.00
23	Kaye Vaughan	125.00	62.00	37.00
24	Don Carter	100.00	50.00	30.00
25	Gene Roberts	100.00	50.00	30.00
26	Howie Turner	100.00	50.00	30.00
27	Avatus Stone	100.00	50.00	30.00
28	Tom McHugh	100.00	50.00	30.00
29	Clyde Bennett	100.00	50.00	30.00
30	Bill Berezowski	100.00	50.00	30.00
31	Eddie Bevan	100.00	50.00	30.00
32	Dick Brown	100.00	50.00	30.00
33	Bernie Custis	125.00	62.00	37.00
34	Merle Hapes	125.00	62.00	37.00
35	Tip Logan	100.00	50.00	30.00
36	Vince Mazza	125.00	62.00	37.00
37	Pete Neumann	125.00	62.00	37.00
38	Vince Scott	125.00	62.00	37.00
39	Ralph Toohy	100.00	50.00	30.00
40	Frank Anderson	100.00	50.00	30.00
41	Bob Dean	100.00	50.00	30.00
42	Leon Manley	100.00	50.00	30.00
43	Bill Zock	125.00	62.00	37.00
44	Frank Morris	150.00	75.00	45.00
45	Jim Quondamatteo	100.00	50.00	30.00
46	Eagle Keys	150.00	75.00	45.00
47	Bernie Faloney	400.00	200.00	120.00
48	Jackie Parker	500.00	250.00	150.00
49	Ray Willsey	100.00	50.00	30.00
50	Mike King	100.00	50.00	30.00
51	Johnny Bright	300.00	150.00	90.00
52	Gene Brito	125.00	62.00	37.00
53	Stan Heath	125.00	62.00	37.00
54	Roy Jenson	100.00	50.00	30.00
55	Don Loney	100.00	50.00	30.00
56	Eddie Macon	100.00	50.00	30.00
57	Peter Maxwell-Muir	100.00	50.00	30.00
58	Tom Miner	100.00	50.00	30.00
59	Jim Prewett	100.00	50.00	30.00
60	Lowell Wagner	100.00	50.00	30.00
61	Red O'Quinn	125.00	62.00	37.00
62	Ray Poole	125.00	62.00	37.00
63	Jim Staton	100.00	50.00	30.00
64	Alex Webster	200.00	100.00	60.00
65	Al Dekdebruin	100.00	50.00	30.00
66	Ed Bradley	100.00	50.00	30.00
67	Tex Coulter	150.00	75.00	45.00
68	Sam Etcheverry	500.00	250.00	150.00
69	Larry Grigg	100.00	50.00	30.00
70	Tom Hugo	100.00	50.00	30.00
71	Chuck Hunsinger	100.00	50.00	30.00
72	Herb Trawick	125.00	62.00	37.00
73	Virgil Wagner	125.00	62.00	37.00
74	Phil Adrian	100.00	50.00	30.00
75	Bruce Coulter	100.00	50.00	30.00
76	Jim Miller	100.00	50.00	30.00
77	Jim Mitchener	100.00	50.00	30.00
78	Tom Moran	100.00	50.00	30.00
79	Doug McNichol	100.00	50.00	30.00
80	Joey Pal	100.00	50.00	30.00
---	**Album**	500.00	250.00	150.00

1988 Bootlegger B.C. Lions

		NM/M	NM	E
Complete Set (13):		15.00	11.00	6.00
Common Player:		1.00	.70	.40
1	Jamie Buis	1.00	.70	.40
2	Jan Carinci	1.00	.70	.40
3	Dwayne Derban	1.00	.70	.40
4	Roy Dewalt	3.00	2.25	1.25
5	Andre Francis	1.25	.90	.50
6	Rick Klassen	2.00	1.50	.80
7	Kevin Konar	1.25	.90	.50
8	Scott Lecky	1.00	.70	.40
9	James Parker	3.00	2.25	1.25
10	John Ulmer	1.00	.70	.40
11	Peter VandenBos	1.00	.70	.40
12	Todd Wiseman	1.00	.70	.40
13	**NNO Title Card** (Corporate Sponsors)	1.25	.90	.50

1948 Bowman

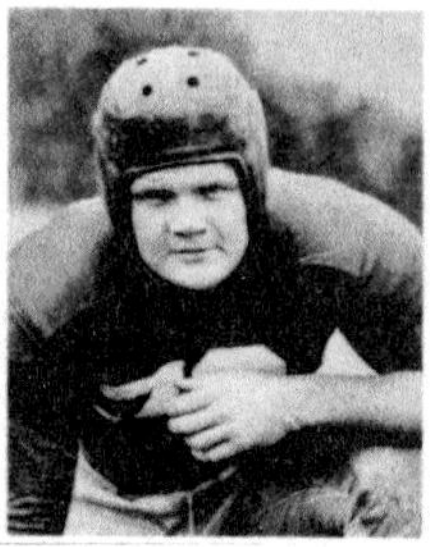

Considered to be the first true football set of the modern era, the 1948 Bowman set included only players from the National Football League (the first set to do so). Each of the 108 cards measures 2-1/16" x 2-1/2" and shows a player photo on the front with no name or team name. Backs have biographical information. This set was printed on three separate sheets, with the first sheet being plentiful, the second a little scarcer, and the third very difficult to find. So cards numbered 1, 4, 7, 10, etc., are easiest to find; cards numbered 2, 5, 8, 11, etc., are somewhat harder, and those divisble by three (3, 6, 9, 12, etc.) are extremely tough to find. Rookie cards in this set include Hall of Famers Steve Van Buren, Charley Trippi, Sammy Baugh, Bob Waterfield, Bulldog Turner, Alex Wojciechowicz, Pete Pihos, Bill Dudley, George McAfee and Sid Luckman. Other star rookie cards include Johnny Lujack and Charlie Conerly.

		NM	E	VG
Complete Set (108):		8,000	4,000	2,000
Common Player (1, 4, 7...):		40.00	20.00	12.00
Common Player (2, 5, 8...):		25.00		
Common Player (3, 6, 9...):		100.00		
SP Cards:		110.00	50.00	30.00
1	Joe Tereshinski **RC**	165.00	85.00	51.00
2	Larry Olsonoski	40.00	20.00	12.00
3	John Lujack SP **RC**	400.00	200.00	120.00
4	Ray Poole	40.00	20.00	12.00
5	Bill DeCorrevont	40.00	20.00	12.00
6	Paul Briggs	100.00	50.00	30.00
7	Steve Van Buren **RC**	200.00	100.00	60.00
8	Kenny Washington **RC**	60.00	30.00	18.00
9	Nolan Luhn	100.00	50.00	30.00
10	Chris Iversen	40.00	20.00	12.00
11	Jack Wiley	40.00	20.00	12.00
12	Charlie Conerly SP **RC**	300.00	150.00	90.00
13	Hugh Taylor **RC**	40.00	20.00	12.00
14	Frank Seno	40.00	20.00	12.00
15	Gil Bouley	100.00	50.00	30.00
16	Tommy Thompson **RC**	40.00	20.00	12.00
17	Charlie Trippi **RC**	120.00	60.00	30.00
18	Vince Banonis	100.00	50.00	30.00
19	Art Faircloth	40.00	20.00	12.00
20	Clyde Goodnight	40.00	20.00	12.00
21	Bill Chipley	100.00	50.00	30.00
22	Sammy Baugh **RC**	450.00	225.00	135.00
23	Don Kindt	40.00	20.00	12.00
24	John Koniszewski	100.00	50.00	30.00
25	Pat McHugh	40.00	20.00	12.00
26	Bob Waterfield **RC**	275.00	150.00	75.00
27	Tony Compagno	100.00	50.00	30.00
28	Paul Governali	40.00	20.00	12.00
29	Pat Harder **RC**	60.00	30.00	18.00
30	Vic Lindskog	100.00	50.00	30.00
31	Salvatore Rosato	40.00	20.00	12.00
32	John Mastrangelo	40.00	20.00	12.00
33	Fred Gehrke	100.00	50.00	30.00
34	Bosh Pritchard	40.00	20.00	12.00
35	Mike Micka	40.00	20.00	12.00
36	Bulldog Turner SP **RC**	275.00	140.00	90.00
37	Len Younce	40.00	20.00	12.00
38	Pat West	40.00	20.00	12.00
39	Russ Thomas	100.00	50.00	30.00
40	James Peebles	40.00	20.00	12.00
41	Bob Skoglund	40.00	20.00	12.00
42	Wat Stickle	100.00	50.00	30.00
43	Whitey Wistert **RC**	40.00	20.00	12.00
44	Paul Christman **RC**	40.00	20.00	12.00
45	Jay Rhodemyre	100.00	50.00	30.00
46	Skip Minisi	40.00	20.00	12.00
47	Bob Mann	40.00	20.00	12.00
48	Mal Kutner SP **RC**	110.00	55.00	33.00
49	Dick Poillon	40.00	20.00	12.00
50	Charles Cherundolo	40.00	20.00	12.00
51	Gerald Cowhig	100.00	50.00	30.00
52	Neil Armstrong **RC**	40.00	20.00	12.00
53	Frak Maznicki	40.00	20.00	12.00
54	John Sanchez	100.00	50.00	30.00
55	Frank Reagan	40.00	20.00	12.00
56	Jim Hardy	40.00	20.00	12.00
57	John Badaczewski	100.00	50.00	30.00
58	Robert Nussbaumer	40.00	20.00	12.00
59	Marvin Pregulman	40.00	20.00	12.00
60	Elbert Nickel SP **RC**	150.00	75.00	45.00
61	Alex Wojciechowicz **RC**	175.00	90.00	54.00
62	Walt Shclinkman	40.00	20.00	12.00
63	Pete Pihos SP **RC**	275.00	140.00	85.00
64	Joseph Sulaitis	40.00	20.00	12.00
65	Mike Holovak **RC**	50.00	25.00	15.00
66	Cecil Souders	100.00	50.00	30.00
67	Paul McKee	40.00	20.00	12.00
68	Bill Moore	40.00	20.00	12.00
69	Frank Minini	100.00	50.00	30.00
70	Jack Ferrante	40.00	20.00	12.00
71	Leslie Horvath **RC**	50.00	25.00	15.00
72	Ted Fritsch, Sr. SP **RC**	100.00	50.00	25.00
73	Tex Coulter	40.00	20.00	12.00
74	Boley Dancewicz	40.00	20.00	12.00
75	Dante Mangani	100.00	50.00	30.00
76	James Hefti	40.00	20.00	12.00
77	Paul Sarringhaus	40.00	20.00	12.00
78	Joe Scott	100.00	50.00	30.00
79	Bucko Kilroy **RC**	40.00	20.00	12.00
80	Bill Dudley **RC**	150.00	75.00	40.00
81	Marshall Goldberg SP **RC**	100.00	50.00	25.00
82	John Cannady	40.00	20.00	12.00
83	Perry Moss	40.00	20.00	12.00
84	Harold Crisler SP **RC**	100.00	50.00	25.00
85	Bill Gray	40.00	20.00	12.00
86	John Clement	40.00	20.00	12.00
87	Dan Sandifer	100.00	50.00	30.00
88	Ben Kish	40.00	20.00	12.00
89	Herbert Banta	40.00	20.00	12.00
90	Bill Garnaas	100.00	50.00	30.00
91	Jim White	40.00	20.00	12.00
92	Frank Barzilauskas	40.00	20.00	12.00
93	Vic Sears	100.00	50.00	30.00
94	John Adams	40.00	20.00	12.00
95	George McAfee **RC**	100.00	50.00	25.00
96	Ralph Heywood	100.00	50.00	30.00
97	Joe Muha	40.00	20.00	12.00
98	Fred Enke	40.00	20.00	12.00
99	Harry Gilmer SP **RC**	200.00	100.00	60.00
100	Bill Miklich	40.00	20.00	12.00
101	Joe Gottlieb	40.00	20.00	12.00
102	Bud Angsman SP **RC**	100.00	50.00	25.00
103	Tom Farmer	40.00	20.00	12.00
104	Bruce F. Smith **RC**	50.00	25.00	15.00
105	Bob Cifers	100.00	50.00	30.00
106	Ernie Steele	40.00	20.00	12.00
107	Sid Luckman **RC**	275.00	150.00	90.00
108	Buford Ray SP **RC**	400.00	200.00	120.00
---	**Album**	500.00	250.00	150.00

1950 Bowman

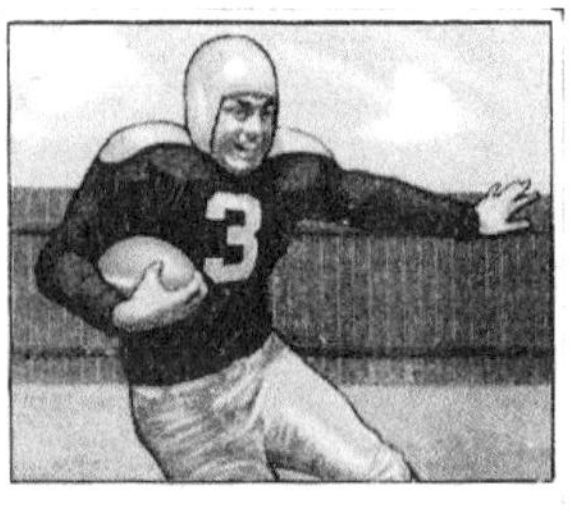

After a one-year absence, Bowman returned to football cards with the first of four straight 144-card sets. As with the '48 Bowman set, cards showed only the player on the front without any identification. Cards again measured 2-1/16" x 2-1/2". Rookie cards in this set include Y.A. Tittle, Lou Groza, Tony Canadeo, Joe Perry, Marion Motley, Otto Graham, Tom Fears, Elroy Hirsch, Dante Lavelli, Tobin Rote and Dub Jones.

	NM	E	VG
Complete Set (144):	5,000	2,500	1,225
Common Player:	35.00	17.00	8.00
Minor Stars:	50.00		

		NM	E	VG
1	Doak Walker	300.00	150.00	75.00
2	John Greene	35.00	17.00	8.00
3	Bob Nowasky	35.00	17.00	8.00
4	Jonathan Jenkins	35.00	17.00	8.00
5	Y.A. Tittle **RC**	400.00	200.00	100.00
6	Lou Groza **RC**	175.00	87.00	52.00
7	Alex Agase **RC**	35.00	17.00	8.00
8	Mac Speedie **RC**	50.00	25.00	15.00
9	Tony Canadeo **RC**	170.00	85.00	43.00
10	Larry Craig	35.00	15.00	8.00
11	Ted Fritsch, Sr.	35.00	17.00	8.00
12	Joe Goldring	35.00	17.00	8.00
13	Martin Ruby	35.00	17.00	8.00
14	George Taliaferro	35.00	17.00	8.00
15	Tank Younger **RC**	50.00	25.00	15.00
16	Glenn Davis **RC**	150.00	75.00	38.00
17	Bob Waterfield	150.00	75.00	37.00
18	Val Jansante	35.00	17.00	8.00
19	Joe Geri	35.00	17.00	8.00
20	Jerry Nuzum	30.00	10.00	6.00
21	Elmer Angsman	35.00	17.00	8.00
22	Billy Dewell	35.00	17.00	8.00
23	Steve Van Buren	90.00	45.00	27.00
24	Cliff Patton	35.00	17.00	8.00
25	Bosh Pritchard	35.00	17.00	8.00
26	John Lujack	80.00	40.00	24.00
27	Sid Luckman	125.00	62.00	37.00
28	Bulldog Turner	60.00	30.00	18.00
29	Bill Dudley	40.00	20.00	10.00
30	Hugh Taylor	35.00	17.00	8.00
31	George Thomas	35.00	17.00	8.00
32	Ray Poole	35.00	17.00	8.00
33	Travis Tidwell	35.00	17.00	8.00
34	Gail Bruce	35.00	17.00	8.00
35	Joe Perry **RC**	200.00	100.00	60.00
36	Frankie Albert **RC**	35.00	17.00	8.00
37	Bobby Layne	200.00	100.00	60.00
38	Leon Hart	35.00	17.00	8.00
39	Bob Hoernschemeyer	35.00	17.00	8.00
40	Dick Barwegan **RC**	35.00	17.00	8.00
41	Adrian Burk **RC**	35.00	17.00	8.00
42	Barry French	35.00	17.00	8.00
43	Marion Motley **RC**	250.00	125.00	75.00
44	Jim Martin	35.00	17.00	8.00
45	Otto Graham **RC**	400.00	200.00	110.00
46	Al Baldwin	35.00	17.00	8.00
47	Larry Coutre	35.00	17.00	8.00
48	John Rauch	35.00	17.00	8.00
49	Sam Tamburo	35.00	17.00	8.00
50	Mike Swistowicz	35.00	17.00	8.00
51	Tom Fears **RC**	100.00	50.00	28.00
52	Elroy Hirsch **RC**	230.00	115.00	60.00
53	Dick Huffman	35.00	17.00	8.00
54	Bob Cage	35.00	17.00	8.00
55	Bob Tinsley	35.00	17.00	8.00
56	Bill Blackburn	35.00	17.00	8.00
57	John Cochran	35.00	17.00	8.00
58	Bill Fischer	35.00	17.00	8.00
59	Whitey Wistert	35.00	8.00	17.00
60	Clyde Scott	35.00	17.00	8.00
61	Walter Barnes	35.00	17.00	8.00
62	Bob Perina	35.00	17.00	8.00
63	Bill Wightkin	35.00	17.00	8.00
64	Bob Goode	35.00	17.00	8.00
65	Al Demao	35.00	17.00	8.00
66	Harry Gilmer	35.00	17.00	8.00
67	Bill Austin	35.00	17.00	8.00
68	Joe Scott	30.00	10.00	6.00
69	Tex Coulter	35.00	17.00	8.00
70	Paul Salata	35.00	17.00	8.00
71	Emil Sitko	35.00	17.00	8.00
72	Bill Johnson	35.00	17.00	8.00
73	Don Doll **RC**	35.00	17.00	8.00
74	Dan Sandifer	35.00	17.00	8.00
75	John Panelli	35.00	17.00	8.00
76	Bill Leonard	35.00	17.00	8.00
77	Bob Kelly	35.00	17.00	8.00
78	Dante Lavelli **RC**	140.00	70.00	35.00
79	Tony Adamle	35.00	17.00	8.00
80	Dick Wildung	35.00	17.00	8.00
81	Tobin Rote **RC**	40.00	20.00	10.00
82	Paul Burris	35.00	17.00	8.00
83	Lowell Tew	35.00	17.00	8.00
84	Barney Poole	35.00	17.00	8.00
85	Fred Naumetz	35.00	17.00	8.00
86	Dick Hoerner	35.00	17.00	8.00
87	Bob Reinhard	35.00	17.00	8.00
88	Howard Hartley	35.00	17.00	8.00
89	Darrell Hogan	35.00	17.00	8.00
90	Jerry Shipkey	35.00	17.00	8.00
91	Frank Tripucka	35.00	17.00	8.00
92	Garrard Ramsey	35.00	17.00	8.00
93	Pat Harder	35.00	17.00	8.00
94	Vic Sears	35.00	17.00	8.00
95	Tommy Thompson	35.00	17.00	8.00
96	Bucko Kilroy	35.00	17.00	8.00
97	George Connor	35.00	17.00	8.00
98	Fred Morrison	35.00	17.00	8.00
99	Jim Keane	35.00	17.00	8.00
100	Sammy Baugh	250.00	125.00	75.00
101	Harry Ulinski	35.00	17.00	8.00
102	Frank Spaniel	35.00	17.00	8.00
103	Charlie Conerly	75.00	37.00	18.00
104	Dick Hensley	35.00	17.00	8.00
105	Eddie Price	35.00	17.00	8.00
106	Ed Carr	35.00	17.00	8.00
107	Leo Nomellini	75.00	37.00	22.00
108	Verl Lillywhite	35.00	17.00	8.00
109	Wallace Triplett	35.00	17.00	8.00
110	Joe Watson	35.00	17.00	8.00
111	Cloyce Box **RC**	35.00	15.00	8.00
112	Billy Stone	35.00	17.00	8.00
113	Earl Murray	35.00	17.00	8.00
114	Chet Mutryn **RC**	35.00	15.00	8.00
115	Ken Carpenter	35.00	17.00	8.00
116	Lou Rymkus **RC**	35.00	17.00	8.00
117	Dub Jones **RC**	35.00	17.00	8.00
118	Clayton Tonnemaker	35.00	17.00	8.00
119	Walt Schlinkman	35.00	17.00	8.00
120	Billy Grimes	35.00	17.00	8.00
121	George Ratterman **RC**	35.00	15.00	8.00
122	Bob Mann	35.00	17.00	8.00
123	Buddy Young **RC**	50.00	25.00	15.00
124	Jack Zilly	35.00	17.00	8.00
125	Tom Kalmanir	35.00	17.00	8.00
126	Frank Sinkovitz	35.00	17.00	8.00
127	Elbert Nickel	35.00	17.00	8.00
128	Jim Finks **RC**	70.00	35.00	18.00
129	Charlie Trippi	70.00	35.00	18.00
130	Tom Wham	35.00	17.00	8.00
131	Ventan Yablonski	35.00	17.00	8.00
132	Chuck Bednarik	125.00	62.00	37.00
133	Joe Muha	35.00	17.00	8.00
134	Pete Pihos	80.00	40.00	24.00
135	Washington Serini	35.00	17.00	8.00
136	George Gulyanics	35.00	17.00	8.00
137	Ken Kavanaugh	35.00	17.00	8.00
138	Howie Livingston	35.00	17.00	8.00
139	Joe Tereshinski	35.00	17.00	8.00
140	Jim White	35.00	17.00	8.00
141	Gene Roberts	35.00	17.00	8.00
142	William Swiacki	35.00	17.00	8.00
143	Norm Standlee	35.00	17.00	8.00
144	Knox Ramsey **RC**	125.00	65.00	35.00

1951 Bowman

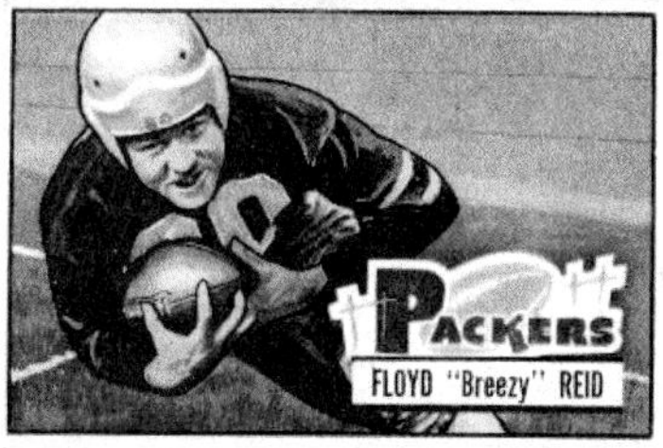

Bowman's third set was again 144 cards, but cards were increased in size to 2-1/16" x 3-1/8". Cards bear a close similarity to this year's Bowman baseball set on both fronts and backs. Rookies in this set include Norm Van Brocklin, Tom Landry, Arnie Weinmeister, Bill Walsh, Emlen Tunnell, and Ernie Stautner.

	NM	E	VG
Complete Set (144):	4,000	2,000	1,200
Common Player:	35.00	18.00	10.00
Minor Stars:	50.00		

		NM	E	VG
1	Weldon Humble **RC**	115.00	60.00	36.00
2	Otto Graham	200.00	100.00	60.00
3	Mac Speedie	35.00	18.00	10.00
4	Norm Van Brocklin **RC**	325.00	165.00	95.00
5	Woodley Lewis	35.00	18.00	10.00
6	Tom Fears	35.00	18.00	10.00
7	George Musacco	35.00	18.00	10.00
8	George Taliaferro	35.00	18.00	10.00
9	Barney Poole	35.00	18.00	10.00
10	Steve Van Buren	60.00	30.00	18.00
11	Whitey Wistert	35.00	18.00	10.00
12	Chuck Bednarik	90.00	45.00	27.00
13	Bulldog Turner	70.00	35.00	21.00
14	Bob Williams	35.00	18.00	10.00
15	John Lujack	70.00	35.00	21.00
16	Roy "Rebel" Steiner	35.00	18.00	10.00
17	Earl "Jug" Girard	35.00	18.00	10.00
18	Bill Neal	35.00	18.00	10.00
19	Travis Tidwell	35.00	18.00	10.00
20	Tom Landry **RC**	365.00	180.00	105.00
21	Arnie Weinmeister **RC**	125.00	65.00	39.00
22	Joe Geri	35.00	18.00	10.00
23	Bill Walsh **RC**	35.00	18.00	10.00
24	Fran Rogel	35.00	18.00	10.00
25	Doak Walker	70.00	35.00	21.00
26	Leon Hart	35.00	18.00	10.00
27	Thurman McGraw	35.00	18.00	10.00
28	Buster Ramsey	35.00	18.00	10.00
29	Frank Tripucka	35.00	18.00	10.00
30	Don Paul	35.00	18.00	10.00
31	Alex Loyd	35.00	18.00	10.00
32	Y.A. Tittle	150.00	75.00	45.00
33	Verl Lillywhite	35.00	18.00	10.00
34	Sammy Baugh	160.00	80.00	48.00
35	Chuck Drazenovich	35.00	18.00	10.00
36	Bob Goode	35.00	18.00	10.00
37	Horace Gillom	35.00	18.00	10.00
38	Lou Rymkus	35.00	18.00	10.00
39	Ken Carpenter	35.00	18.00	10.00
40	Bob Waterfield	90.00	45.00	27.00
41	Vitamin Smith	35.00	18.00	10.00
42	Glenn Davis	60.00	30.00	18.00
43	Dan Edwards	35.00	18.00	10.00
44	John Rauch	35.00	18.00	10.00
45	Zollie Toth	35.00	18.00	10.00
46	Pete Pihos	50.00	25.00	15.00
47	Russ Craft	35.00	18.00	10.00
48	Walter Barnes	35.00	18.00	10.00
49	Fred Morrison	35.00	18.00	10.00
50	Ray Bray	35.00	18.00	10.00
51	Ed Sprinkle **RC**	35.00	18.00	10.00
52	Floyd Reid	35.00	18.00	10.00
53	Billy Grimes	35.00	18.00	10.00
54	Ted Fritsch, Sr.	35.00	18.00	10.00
55	Al DeRogatis	35.00	18.00	10.00
56	Charlie Conerly	90.00	45.00	27.00
57	Jon Baker	35.00	18.00	10.00
58	Tom McWilliams	35.00	18.00	10.00
59	Jerry Shipkey	35.00	18.00	10.00
60	Lynn Chandnois	35.00	18.00	10.00
61	Don Doll	35.00	18.00	10.00
62	Lou Creekmur	35.00	18.00	10.00
63	Bob Hoernschemeyer	35.00	18.00	10.00
64	Tom Wham	35.00	18.00	10.00
65	Bill Fischer	35.00	18.00	10.00
66	Robert Nussbaumer	35.00	18.00	10.00
67	Gordon Soltau	35.00	18.00	10.00
68	Visco Grgich	35.00	18.00	10.00
69	John Strzykalski	35.00	18.00	10.00
70	Pete Stout	35.00	18.00	10.00
71	Paul Lipscomb	35.00	18.00	10.00
72	Harry Gilmer	35.00	18.00	10.00
73	Dante Lavelli	75.00	45.00	27.00
74	Dub Jones	35.00	18.00	10.00
75	Lou Groza	100.00	50.00	30.00
76	Elroy Hirsch	90.00	45.00	27.00
77	Tom Kalmanir	35.00	18.00	10.00
78	Jack Zilly	35.00	18.00	10.00
79	Bruce Alford	35.00	18.00	10.00
80	Art Weiner	35.00	18.00	10.00
81	Brad Ecklund	35.00	18.00	10.00
82	Bosh Pritchard	35.00	18.00	10.00
83	John Green	35.00	18.00	10.00
84	H. Ebert Van Buren	35.00	18.00	10.00
85	Julie Rykovich	35.00	18.00	10.00
86	Fred Davis	35.00	18.00	10.00
87	John Hoffman	35.00	18.00	10.00
88	Tobin Rote	35.00	18.00	10.00
89	Paul Burris	35.00	18.00	10.00
90	Tony Canadeo	50.00	25.00	15.00
91	Emlen Tunnell **RC**	140.00	70.00	42.00
92	Otto Schnellbacher	35.00	18.00	10.00
93	Ray Poole	35.00	18.00	10.00
94	Darrell Hogan	35.00	18.00	10.00
95	Frank Sinkovitz	35.00	18.00	10.00
96	Ernie Stautner	140.00	70.00	42.00
97	Elmer Angsman	35.00	18.00	10.00
98	Jack Jennings	35.00	18.00	10.00
99	Jerry Groom	35.00	18.00	10.00
100	John Prchlik	35.00	18.00	10.00
101	J. Robert Smith	35.00	18.00	10.00
102	Bobby Layne	140.00	70.00	42.00
103	Frankie Albert	35.00	18.00	10.00
104	Gail Bruce	35.00	18.00	10.00
105	Joe Perry	95.00	48.00	29.00
106	Leon Heath	35.00	18.00	10.00
107	Ed Quirk	35.00	18.00	10.00
108	Hugh Taylor	35.00	18.00	10.00
109	Marion Motley	100.00	50.00	30.00
110	Tony Adamle	35.00	18.00	10.00
111	Alex Agase	35.00	18.00	10.00
112	Tank Younger	35.00	18.00	10.00
113	Bob Boyd	35.00	18.00	10.00

114	Jerry Williams	35.00	18.00	10.00
115	Joe Goldring	35.00	18.00	10.00
116	Sherman Howard	35.00	18.00	10.00
117	John Wozniak	35.00	18.00	10.00
118	Frank Reagan	35.00	18.00	10.00
119	Vic Sears	35.00	18.00	10.00
120	Clyde Scott	35.00	18.00	10.00
121	George Gulyanics	35.00	18.00	10.00
122	Bill Wightkin	35.00	18.00	10.00
123	Chuck Hunsinger	35.00	18.00	10.00
124	Jack Cloud	35.00	18.00	10.00
125	Abner Wimberly	35.00	18.00	10.00
126	Dick Wildung	35.00	18.00	10.00
127	Eddie Price	35.00	18.00	10.00
128	Joe Scott	35.00	18.00	10.00
129	Jerry Nuzum	35.00	18.00	10.00
130	Jim Finks	50.00	25.00	15.00
131	Bob Gage	35.00	18.00	10.00
132	William Swiacki	35.00	18.00	10.00
133	Joe Watson	35.00	18.00	10.00
134	Ollie Cline	35.00	18.00	10.00
135	Jack Lininger	35.00	18.00	10.00
136	Fran Polsfoot	35.00	18.00	10.00
137	Charlie Trippi	50.00	25.00	15.00
138	Ventan Yablonski	35.00	18.00	10.00
139	Emil Sitko	40.00	12.00	20.00
140	Leo Nomellini	60.00	40.00	18.00
141	Norm Standlee	35.00	18.00	10.00
142	Eddie Saenz	35.00	18.00	10.00
143	Al Demao	35.00	18.00	10.00
144	Bill Dudley	195.00	100.00	60.00

1952 Bowman Large

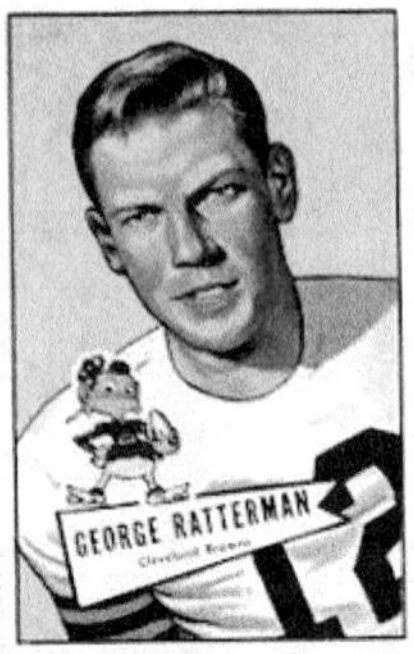

The player selection in the "Large" set exactly matches Bowman's 1952 "Small" issue. The card size, however, was increased from 2-1/16" x 3-1/8" to 2-1/2" x 3-3/4". A problem surfaced for Bowman while trying to produce the larger set: the company could not fit all the larger cards on one sheet the way it could with the smaller set. So certain cards were pulled. The short-printed cards are those with a factor of nine plus the card immediately following that number. In addition, the second series was issued in lesser quantities than the first. The 1952 Bowman Large set is easily the most valuable football card set ever produced. Card #144, Jim "Buck" Lansford, is practically impossible to find in mint condition, first because it was an odd number on the last sheet, second because it was the last card in the set.

	NM	E	VG
Complete Set (144):	19,500	9,750	5,850
Common Player (1-72):	60.00	30.00	18.00
Minor Stars (1-72):	45.00		
Unlisted Stars (1-72):	50.00		
Common Player (73-144):	70.00	35.00	21.00
Minor Stars (73-144):	50.00		
Unlisted Stars (73-144):	70.00		

1	Norm Van Brocklin	600.00	300.00	180.00
2	Otto Graham	325.00	165.00	100.00
3	Doak Walker	150.00	75.00	45.00
4	Steve Owen **RC**	150.00	75.00	45.00
5	Frankie Albert	60.00	30.00	18.00
6	Laurie Niemi	60.00	30.00	15.00
7	Chuck Hunsinger	60.00	30.00	18.00
8	Ed Modzelewski	60.00	30.00	18.00
9	Joe Spencer (SP)	600.00	300.00	180.00
10	Chuck Bednarik (SP)	300.00	150.00	90.00
11	Barney Poole	60.00	30.00	18.00
12	Charlie Trippi	125.00	65.00	39.00
13	Tom Fears	125.00	65.00	39.00
14	Paul Brown **RC**	250.00	125.00	75.00
15	Leon Hart	60.00	30.00	15.00
16	Frank Gifford **RC**	500.00	250.00	150.00
17	Y.A. Tittle	300.00	150.00	90.00
18	Charlie Justice (SP)	230.00	115.00	69.00
19	George Connor (SP)	225.00	115.00	69.00
20	Lynn Chandnois	60.00	30.00	18.00
21	Bill Howton **RC**	60.00	30.00	18.00
22	Kenneth Snyder	60.00	30.00	15.00
23	Gino Marchetti **RC**	250.00	125.00	75.00
24	John Karras	60.00	30.00	18.00
25	Tank Younger	60.00	30.00	18.00
26	Tommy Thompson	60.00	30.00	18.00
27	Bob Miller **RC** (SP)	400.00	200.00	120.00
28	Kyle Rote **RC** (SP)	200.00	100.00	60.00
29	Hugh McElhenny **RC**	250.00	125.00	75.00
30	Sammy Baugh	400.00	200.00	120.00
31	Jim Dooley	60.00	30.00	18.00
32	Ray Matthews	60.00	30.00	18.00
33	Fred Cone	60.00	30.00	15.00
34	Al Pollard	60.00	30.00	18.00
35	Brad Ecklund	60.00	30.00	18.00
36	John Lee Hancock **RC**	400.00	200.00	120.00
37	Elroy Hirsch (SP)	250.00	125.00	75.00
38	Keever Jankovich	60.00	30.00	18.00
39	Emlen Tunnell	125.00	62.00	37.00
40	Steve Dowden	60.00	30.00	18.00
41	Claude Hipps	60.00	30.00	18.00
42	Norm Standlee	60.00	30.00	18.00
43	Dick Todd	60.00	30.00	18.00
44	Babe Parilli	60.00	30.00	18.00
45	Steve Van Buren (SP)	350.00	175.00	105.00
46	Art Donovan **RC** (SP)	365.00	185.00	111.00
47	Bill Fischer	60.00	30.00	18.00
48	George Halas **RC**	300.00	150.00	90.00
49	Jerrell Price	60.00	30.00	18.00
50	John Sandusky **RC**	60.00	30.00	18.00
51	Ray Beck	60.00	30.00	18.00
52	Jim Martin	60.00	30.00	18.00
53	Joe Back	60.00	30.00	18.00
54	Glen Christian (SP)	175.00	90.00	54.00
55	Andy Davis (SP)	125.00	65.00	39.00
56	Tobin Rote	60.00	30.00	18.00
57	Wayne Millner **RC**	150.00	75.00	45.00
58	Zollie Toth	60.00	30.00	18.00
59	Jack Jennings	40.00	12.50	7.50
60	Bill McColl	60.00	30.00	18.00
61	Les Richter **RC**	60.00	30.00	18.00
62	Walt Michaels **RC**	60.00	30.00	18.00
63	Charlie Conerly (SP)	550.00	225.00	135.00
64	Howard Hartley (SP)	125.00	65.00	39.00
65	Jerome Smith	60.00	30.00	18.00
66	James Clark	60.00	30.00	18.00
67	Dick Logan	60.00	30.00	18.00
68	Wayne Robinson	60.00	30.00	18.00
69	James Hammond	60.00	30.00	18.00
70	Gene Schroeder	60.00	30.00	18.00
71	Tex Coulter	60.00	30.00	18.00
72	John Schweder **RC** (SP)	650.00	325.00	195.00
73	Vitamin Smith (SP)	200.00	100.00	60.00
74	Joe Campanella	70.00	35.00	21.00
75	Joe Kuharich **RC**	70.00	35.00	21.00
76	Herman Clark	70.00	35.00	21.00
77	Dan Edwards	70.00	35.00	21.00
78	Bobby Layne	250.00	125.00	75.00
79	Bob Hoernschemeyer	70.00	35.00	21.00
80	John Carr Blount	70.00	35.00	21.00
81	John Kastan (SP)	200.00	100.00	60.00
82	Harry Minarik **RC** (SP)	200.00	100.00	60.00
83	Joe Perry	150.00	75.00	45.00
84	Ray Parker	70.00	35.00	21.00
85	Andy Robustelli **RC**	225.00	115.00	69.00
86	Dub Jones	70.00	35.00	21.00
87	Mal Cook	70.00	35.00	21.00
88	Billy Stone	70.00	35.00	21.00
89	George Taliaferro	70.00	35.00	21.00
90	Thomas Johnson (SP)	225.00	115.00	69.00
91	Leon Heath (SP)	150.00	75.00	45.00
92	Pete Pihos	150.00	75.00	45.00
93	Fred Benners	70.00	35.00	21.00
94	George Tarasovic	70.00	35.00	21.00
95	Lawrence Shaw	70.00	35.00	21.00
96	Bill Wightkin	70.00	35.00	21.00
97	John Wozniak	70.00	35.00	21.00
98	Bobby Dillon	70.00	35.00	21.00
99	Joe Stydahar **RC** (SP)	950.00	475.00	285.00
100	Dick Alban (SP)	175.00	90.00	54.00
101	Arnie Weinmeister	70.00	35.00	21.00
102	Robert Joe Cross	70.00	35.00	21.00
103	Don Paul	70.00	35.00	21.00
104	Buddy Young	70.00	35.00	21.00
105	Lou Groza	175.00	90.00	54.00
106	Ray Pelfrey	70.00	35.00	21.00
107	Maurice Nipp	70.00	35.00	21.00
108	Hubert Johnston **RC**	750.00	375.00	225.00
109	Volney Quinlan (SP)	150.00	75.00	45.00
110	Jack Simmons	70.00	35.00	21.00
111	George Ratterman	70.00	35.00	21.00
112	John Badaczewski	70.00	35.00	21.00
113	Bill Reichardt	70.00	35.00	21.00
114	Art Weiner	70.00	35.00	21.00
115	Keith Flowers	70.00	35.00	21.00
116	Russ Craft	70.00	35.00	21.00
117	Jim O'Donahue (SP)	225.00	115.00	69.00
118	Darrell Hogan (SP)	225.00	115.00	69.00
119	Frank Ziegler	70.00	35.00	21.00
120	Deacon Dan Towler	70.00	35.00	21.00
121	Fred Williams	70.00	35.00	21.00
122	Jimmy Phelan	70.00	35.00	21.00
123	Eddie Price	70.00	35.00	21.00
124	Chet Ostrowski	70.00	35.00	21.00
125	Leo Nomellini	150.00	75.00	45.00
126	Steve Romanik **RC** (SP)	350.00	175.00	105.00
127	Ollie Matson **RC** (SP)	400.00	200.00	120.00
128	Dante Lavelli	130.00	65.00	39.00
129	Jack Christiansen **RC**	300.00	150.00	90.00
130	Dom Moselle	70.00	35.00	21.00
131	John Rapacz	70.00	35.00	21.00
132	Chuck Ortman	70.00	35.00	21.00
133	Bob Williams	70.00	35.00	21.00
134	Chuck Ulrich	70.00	35.00	21.00
135	Gene Ronzani **RC** (SP)	900.00	450.00	270.00
136	Bert Rechichar (SP)	200.00	100.00	60.00
137	Bob Waterfield	175.00	90.00	54.00
138	Bobby Walston **RC**	70.00	35.00	21.00
139	Jerry Shipkey	70.00	35.00	21.00
140	Yale Lary **RC**	250.00	125.00	75.00
141	Gordon Soltau	70.00	35.00	21.00
142	Tom Landry	525.00	265.00	159.00
143	John Papit	70.00	35.00	21.00
144	Jim Lansford **RC** (SP)	3,000	1,500	900.00

1952 Bowman Small

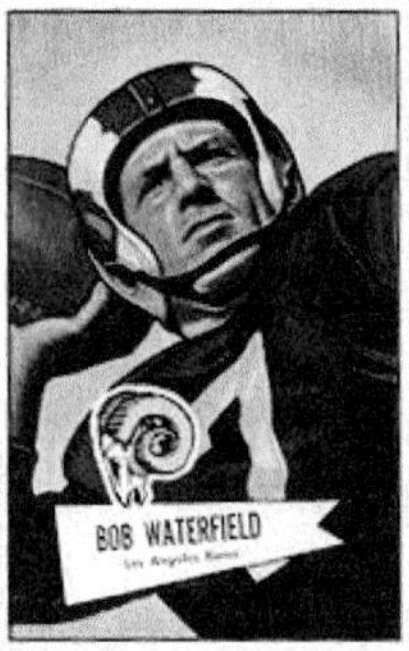

This set was issued in two sizes, large and small, with the large size being much more scarce and expensive. The Bowman Small set measures 2-1/16" x 3-1/8", and cards feature a flag motif, with flags pointing to the right (two years later, Bowman would use about the same theme, with flags pointing left). This 144-card set features an abdundance of rookie cards. They include Steve Owen, Paul Brown, Frank Gifford, Gino Marchetti, Kyle Rote, Hugh McElhenny, George Halas, Wayne Millner, Walt Michaels, Andy Robustelli, Joe Stydahar, Ollie Matson and Yale Lary.

	NM	E	VG
Complete Set (144):	8,500	4,250	2,550
Common Player (1-72):	45.00	23.00	14.00
Minor Stars (1-72):	35.00		
Common Player (73-144):	50.00	25.00	15.00
Minor Stars (73-144):	45.00		

1	Norm Van Brocklin	375.00	200.00	120.00
2	Otto Graham	200.00	100.00	60.00
3	Doak Walker	80.00	40.00	24.00
4	Steve Owen **RC**	100.00	50.00	30.00
5	Frankie Albert	45.00	23.00	14.00
6	Laurie Niemi	45.00	23.00	14.00
7	Chuck Hunsinger	45.00	23.00	14.00
8	Ed Modzelewski	45.00	23.00	14.00
9	Joe Spencer	45.00	23.00	14.00
10	Chuck Bednarik	75.00	37.00	22.00
11	Barney Poole	45.00	23.00	14.00
12	Charlie Trippi	70.00	35.00	21.00
13	Tom Fears	70.00	35.00	21.00
14	Paul Brown **RC**	170.00	85.00	50.00
15	Leon Hart	45.00	23.00	14.00
16	Frank Gifford **RC**	325.00	165.00	100.00
17	Y.A. Tittle	170.00	85.00	51.00
18	Charlie Justice	45.00	23.00	14.00
19	George Connor	45.00	23.00	14.00
20	Lynn Chandnois	45.00	23.00	14.00
21	Bill Howton **RC**	45.00	23.00	14.00
22	Kenneth Snyder	45.00	23.00	14.00
23	Gino Marchetti **RC**	150.00	75.00	45.00
24	John Karras	45.00	23.00	14.00
25	Tank Younger	45.00	23.00	14.00
26	Tommy Thompson	45.00	23.00	14.00
27	Bob Miller	45.00	23.00	14.00
28	Kyle Rote **RC**	75.00	38.00	23.00
29	Hugh McElhenny **RC**	175.00	87.00	52.00
30	Sammy Baugh	200.00	100.00	60.00
31	Jim Dooley	45.00	23.00	14.00
32	Ray Matthews	45.00	23.00	14.00
33	Fred Cone	45.00	23.00	14.00
34	Al Pollard	45.00	23.00	14.00
35	Brad Ecklund	45.00	23.00	14.00
36	John Lee Hancock	45.00	23.00	14.00
37	Elroy Hirsch	75.00	38.00	23.00

38	Keever Jankovich	45.00	23.00	14.00
39	Emlen Tunnell	45.00	23.00	14.00
40	Steve Dowden	45.00	23.00	14.00
41	Claude Hipps	45.00	23.00	14.00
42	Norm Standlee	45.00	23.00	14.00
43	Dick Todd	45.00	23.00	14.00
44	Babe Parilli	45.00	23.00	14.00
45	Steve Van Buren	80.00	40.00	25.00
46	Art Donovan **RC**	225.00	115.00	70.00
47	Bill Fischer	45.00	23.00	14.00
48	George Halas **RC**	200.00	100.00	60.00
49	Jerrell Price	45.00	23.00	14.00
50	John Sandusky	45.00	23.00	14.00
51	Ray Beck	45.00	23.00	14.00
52	Jim Martin	45.00	23.00	14.00
53	Joe Back	45.00	23.00	14.00
54	Glen Christian	45.00	23.00	14.00
55	Andy Davis	45.00	23.00	14.00
56	Tobin Rote	45.00	23.00	14.00
57	Wayne Millner **RC**	100.00	50.00	30.00
58	Zollie Toth	45.00	23.00	14.00
59	Jack Jennings	45.00	23.00	14.00
60	Bill McColl	45.00	23.00	14.00
61	Les Richter **RC**	50.00	25.00	15.00
62	Walt Michaels **RC**	50.00	25.00	15.00
63	Charlie Conerly	75.00	37.00	22.00
64	Howard Hartley	45.00	23.00	14.00
65	Jerome Smith	45.00	23.00	14.00
66	James Clark	45.00	23.00	14.00
67	Dick Logan	45.00	23.00	14.00
68	Wayne Robinson	45.00	23.00	14.00
69	James Hammond	45.00	23.00	14.00
70	Gene Schroeder	45.00	23.00	14.00
71	Tex Coulter	45.00	23.00	14.00
72	John Schweder	45.00	23.00	14.00
73	Vitamin Smith	50.00	25.00	15.00
74	Joe Campanella	50.00	25.00	15.00
75	Joe Kuharich	50.00	25.00	15.00
76	Herman Clark	50.00	25.00	15.00
77	Dan Edwards	50.00	25.00	15.00
78	Bobby Layne	200.00	100.00	60.00
79	Bob Hoernschemeyer	50.00	25.00	15.00
80	John Carr Blount	50.00	25.00	15.00
81	John Kastan	50.00	25.00	15.00
82	Harry Minarik	50.00	25.00	15.00
83	Joe Perry	75.00	37.00	22.00
84	Ray Parker	50.00	25.00	15.00
85	Andy Robustelli **RC**	125.00	62.00	37.00
86	Dub Jones	50.00	25.00	15.00
87	Mal Cook	50.00	25.00	15.00
88	Billy Stone	50.00	25.00	15.00
89	George Taliaferro	50.00	25.00	15.00
90	Thomas Johnson	50.00	25.00	15.00
91	Leon Heath	50.00	25.00	15.00
92	Pete Pihos	75.00	38.00	23.00
93	Fred Benners	50.00	25.00	15.00
94	George Tarasovic	50.00	25.00	15.00
95	Lawrence Shaw	50.00	25.00	15.00
96	Bill Wightkin	50.00	25.00	15.00
97	John Wozniak	50.00	25.00	15.00
98	Bobby Dillon **RC**	50.00	25.00	15.00
99	Joe Stydahar **RC**	175.00	90.00	54.00
100	Dick Alban	50.00	25.00	15.00
101	Arnie Weinmeister	50.00	25.00	15.00
102	Robert Joe Cross	50.00	25.00	15.00
103	Don Paul	50.00	25.00	15.00
104	Buddy Young	50.00	25.00	15.00
105	Lou Groza	75.00	37.00	22.00
106	Ray Pelfrey	50.00	25.00	15.00
107	Maurice Nipp	50.00	25.00	15.00
108	Hubert Johnston	50.00	25.00	15.00
109	Volney Quinlan	50.00	25.00	15.00
110	Jack Simmons	50.00	25.00	15.00
111	George Ratterman	50.00	25.00	15.00
112	John Badaczewski	50.00	25.00	15.00
113	Bill Reichardt	50.00	25.00	15.00
114	Art Weiner	50.00	25.00	15.00
115	Keith Flowers	50.00	25.00	15.00
116	Russ Craft	50.00	25.00	15.00
117	Jim O'Donahue	50.00	25.00	15.00
118	Darrell Hogan	50.00	25.00	15.00
119	Frank Ziegler	50.00	25.00	15.00
120	Deacon Dan Towler	50.00	25.00	15.00
121	Fred Williams	50.00	25.00	15.00
122	Jimmy Phelan	50.00	25.00	15.00
123	Eddie Price	50.00	25.00	15.00
124	Chet Ostrowski	50.00	25.00	15.00
125	Leo Nomellini	75.00	37.00	22.00
126	Steve Romanik	50.00	25.00	15.00
127	Ollie Matson **RC**	200.00	100.00	60.00
128	Dante Lavelli	75.00	38.00	23.00
129	Jack Christiansen **RC**	80.00	40.00	24.00
130	Dom Moselle	50.00	25.00	15.00
131	John Rapacz	50.00	25.00	15.00
132	Chuck Ortman	50.00	25.00	15.00
133	Bob Williams	50.00	25.00	15.00
134	Chuck Ulrich	50.00	25.00	15.00
135	Gene Ronzani **RC**	50.00	25.00	15.00
136	Bert Rechichar	50.00	25.00	15.00
137	Bob Waterfield	100.00	50.00	30.00
138	Bobby Walston **RC**	50.00	25.00	15.00
139	Jerry Shipkey	50.00	25.00	15.00
140	Yale Lary **RC**	100.00	50.00	30.00
141	Gordon Soltau	50.00	25.00	15.00
142	Tom Landry	325.00	165.00	100.00
143	John Papit	50.00	25.00	15.00
144	Jim Lansford **RC**	250.00	125.00	75.00

1953 Bowman

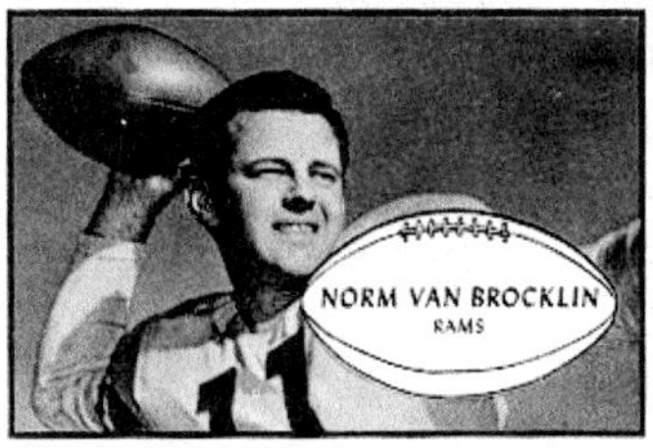

The "name in a football" theme was one that would next be used by Topps in its 1960 set and again in the 1976 set. Bowman was the only company to issue football cards, but only a 96-card issue was produced (and 24 of those were short-printed).

	NM	E	VG
Complete Set (96):	6,400	3,200	1,920
Common Player:	50.00	25.00	15.00
Minor Stars:	45.00		
Unlisted Stars:	40.00		
SP Cards:	75.00	38.00	23.00

1	Eddie LeBaron **RC**	325.00	165.00	100.00
2	John Dottley	50.00	25.00	15.00
3	Babe Parilli	50.00	25.00	15.00
4	Bucko Kilroy	50.00	25.00	15.00
5	Joe Tereshinski	50.00	25.00	15.00
6	Doak Walker	95.00	50.00	30.00
7	Fran Polsfoot	50.00	25.00	15.00
8	Sisto Averno	50.00	25.00	15.00
9	Marion Motley	90.00	45.00	27.00
10	Pat Brady	50.00	25.00	15.00
11	Norm Van Brocklin	175.00	90.00	54.00
12	Bill McColl	50.00	25.00	15.00
13	Jerry Groom	50.00	25.00	15.00
14	Al Pollard	50.00	25.00	15.00
15	Dante Lavelli	90.00	45.00	27.00
16	Eddie Price	50.00	25.00	15.00
17	Charlie Trippi	90.00	45.00	27.00
18	Elbert Nickel	50.00	25.00	15.00
19	George Taliaferro	50.00	25.00	15.00
20	Charlie Conerly	100.00	50.00	30.00
21	Bobby Layne	175.00	90.00	54.00
22	Elroy Hirsch	100.00	50.00	30.00
23	Jim Finks	75.00	38.00	23.00
24	Chuck Bednarik	100.00	50.00	30.00
25	Kyle Rote	80.00	40.00	24.00
26	Otto Graham	250.00	125.00	75.00
27	Harry Gilmer	50.00	25.00	15.00
28	Tobin Rote	50.00	25.00	15.00
29	Billy Stone	50.00	25.00	15.00
30	Buddy Young	75.00	38.00	23.00
31	Leon Hart	75.00	38.00	23.00
32	Hugh McElhenny	100.00	50.00	30.00
33	Dale Samuels	50.00	25.00	15.00
34	Lou Creekmur	80.00	40.00	24.00
35	Tom Catlin	50.00	25.00	15.00
36	Tom Fears	80.00	40.00	24.00
37	George Connor	80.00	40.00	24.00
38	Bill Walsh	50.00	25.00	15.00
39	Leo Sanford (SP)	75.00	38.00	23.00
40	Horace Gillom	50.00	25.00	15.00
41	John Schweder (SP)	75.00	38.00	23.00
42	Tom O'Connell	50.00	25.00	15.00
43	Frank Gifford (SP)	250.00	125.00	75.00
44	Frank Continetti (SP)	75.00	38.00	23.00
45	John Olszewski (SP)	75.00	38.00	23.00
46	Dub Jones	50.00	25.00	15.00
47	Don Paul (SP)	75.00	38.00	23.00
48	Gerald Weatherly	50.00	25.00	15.00
49	Fred Bruney (SP)	75.00	38.00	23.00
50	Jack Scarbath	50.00	25.00	15.00
51	John Karras	50.00	25.00	15.00
52	Al Conway	50.00	25.00	15.00
53	Emlen Tunnell (SP)	175.00	90.00	54.00
54	Gern Nagler (SP)	75.00	38.00	23.00
55	Kenneth Snyder (SP)	75.00	38.00	23.00
56	Y.A. Tittle	175.00	90.00	54.00
57	John Rapacz (SP)	75.00	38.00	23.00
58	Harley Sewell	50.00	25.00	15.00
59	Don Bingham	50.00	25.00	15.00
60	Darrell Hogan	50.00	25.00	15.00
61	Tony Curcillo	50.00	25.00	15.00
62	Ray Renfro **RC** (SP)	90.00	45.00	27.00
63	Leon Heath	50.00	25.00	15.00
64	Tex Coulter (SP)	75.00	38.00	23.00
65	Dewayne Douglas	50.00	25.00	15.00
66	J. Robert Smith (SP)	75.00	38.00	23.00
67	Bob McChesney (SP)	75.00	38.00	23.00
68	Dick Alban (SP)	75.00	38.00	23.00
69	Andy Kozar	50.00	25.00	15.00
70	Merwin Hodel (SP)	75.00	38.00	23.00
71	Thurman McGraw	50.00	25.00	15.00
72	Cliff Anderson	50.00	25.00	15.00
73	Pete Pihos	90.00	45.00	27.00
74	Julie Rykovich	50.00	25.00	15.00
75	John Kreamcheck (SP)	75.00	38.00	23.00
76	Lynn Chandnois (SP)	75.00	38.00	15.00
77	Cloyce Box (SP)	75.00	38.00	23.00
78	Ray Matthews	50.00	25.00	15.00
79	Bobby Walston	50.00	25.00	15.00
80	Jim Dooley	50.00	25.00	15.00
81	Pat Harder (SP)	75.00	38.00	23.00
82	Jerry Shipkey	50.00	25.00	15.00
83	Bobby Thomason	50.00	25.00	15.00
84	Hugh Taylor	50.00	25.00	15.00
85	George Ratterman	50.00	25.00	15.00
86	Don Stonesifer	50.00	25.00	15.00
87	John Williams (SP)	75.00	38.00	23.00
88	Leo Nomellini	90.00	45.00	27.00
89	Frank Ziegler	50.00	25.00	15.00
90	Don Paul	50.00	25.00	15.00
91	Tom Dublinski	50.00	25.00	15.00
92	Ken Carpenter	50.00	25.00	15.00
93	Ted Marchibroda **RC**	60.00	30.00	18.00
94	Chuck Drazenovich	50.00	25.00	15.00
95	Lou Groza (SP)	175.00	90.00	54.00
96	William Cross (SP)	200.00	100.00	60.00

1954 Bowman

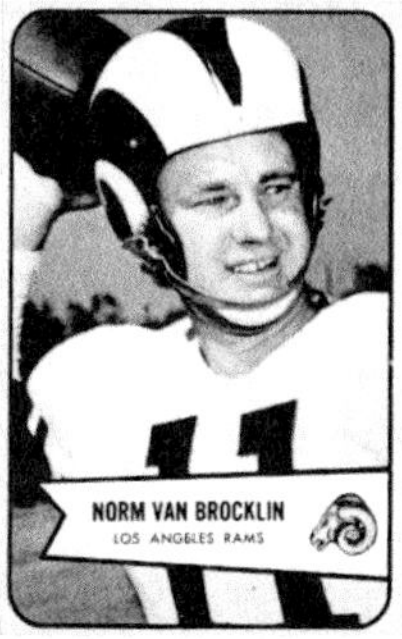

This 128-card set has a flag motif that points left, almost a reversal of the 1952 theme. Issued in four series of 32 cards, numbers 65-96 are much tougher to find than the other three. Rookies in this set include Doug Atkins, George Blanda, Hawg Hanner and Whizzer White (actually not Whizzer White; see below). There's an error and a variation in this set. The error is on card #125 "Whizzer" White, his rookie card. It shows not the future Supreme Court Justice, but Wilford White. The variation involves #97, Tom Finnan. On the scarcer error version, his name was incorrectly spelled "Finnin." This was corrected.

	NM	E	VG
Complete Set (128):	2,500	1,250	750.00
Common Player (1-64):	15.00	7.50	4.50
Minor Stars (1-64):	20.00		
Unlisted Stars (1-64):	10.00		
Common Player (65-96):	25.00	12.50	7.50
Minor Stars (65-96):			
Common Player (97-128):	5.00	3.00	1.75
Minor Stars (97-128):	20.00		
Unlisted Stars (97-128):	20.00		

1	Ray Matthews	40.00	20.00	12.00
2	John Huzvar	15.00	7.50	4.50
3	Jack Scarbath	15.00	7.50	4.50
4	Doug Atkins **RC**	55.00	28.00	17.00
5	Bill Stits	15.00	7.50	3.50
6	Joe Perry	35.00	18.00	10.00
7	Kyle Rote	20.00	10.00	6.00
8	Norm Van Brocklin	45.00	23.00	14.00
9	Pete Pihos	30.00	15.00	9.00
10	Babe Parilli	15.00	7.50	4.50
11	Zeke Bratkowski **RC**	25.00	12.50	7.50
12	Ollie Matson	25.00	12.50	7.50
13	Pat Brady	15.00	7.50	4.50
14	Fred Enke	15.00	7.50	4.50
15	Harry Ulinski	15.00	7.50	4.50
16	Bobby Garrett	15.00	7.50	4.50
17	Bill Bowman	15.00	7.50	4.50
18	Leo Rucka	15.00	7.50	4.50
19	John Cannady	15.00	7.50	4.50
20	Tom Fears	35.00	18.00	10.00
21	Norm Willey	15.00	7.50	4.50

22	Floyd Reid	15.00	7.50	4.50
23	George Blanda **RC**	180.00	90.00	54.00
24	Don Doheney	15.00	7.50	4.50
25	John Schweder	15.00	7.50	4.50
26	Bert Rechichar	15.00	7.50	4.50
27	Harry Dowda	15.00	7.50	4.50
28	John Sandusky	15.00	7.50	4.50
29	Les Bingaman **RC**	18.00	9.00	5.50
30	Joe Arenas	15.00	7.50	4.50
31	Ray Wietecha	16.00	8.00	5.00
32	Elroy Hirsch	30.00	15.00	9.00
33	Harold Giancanelli	15.00	7.50	4.50
34	Bill Howton	18.00	9.00	5.50
35	Fred Morrison	15.00	7.50	4.50
36	Bobby Cavazos	15.00	7.50	4.50
37	Darrell Hogan	15.00	7.50	4.50
38	Buddy Young	15.00	7.50	4.50
39	Charlie Justice	25.00	13.00	8.00
40	Otto Graham	80.00	40.00	24.00
41	Doak Walker	35.00	17.50	10.50
42	Y.A. Tittle	75.00	38.00	23.00
43	Buford Long	15.00	7.50	4.50
44	Volney Quinlan	15.00	7.50	4.50
45	Bobby Thomason	15.00	7.50	4.50
46	Fred Cone	15.00	7.50	4.50
47	Gerald Weatherly	15.00	7.50	4.50
48	Don Stonesifer	15.00	7.50	4.50
49a	Lynn Chandnois ("Chadnois" on back)	15.00	7.50	4.50
49b	Lynn Chandnois (correct)	15.00	7.50	4.50
50	George Taliaferro	15.00	7.50	4.50
51	Dick Alban	15.00	7.50	4.50
52	Lou Groza	35.00	17.50	10.50
53	Bobby Layne	55.00	28.00	17.00
54	Hugh McElhenny	30.00	15.00	9.00
55	Frank Gifford	75.00	38.00	23.00
56	Leon McLaughlin	15.00	7.50	4.50
57	Chuck Bednarik	35.00	18.00	10.00
58	Art Hunter	15.00	7.50	4.50
59	Bill McColl	15.00	7.50	4.50
60	Charlie Trippi	30.00	15.00	9.00
61	Jim Finks **RC**	25.00	13.00	8.00
62	Bill Lange	15.00	7.50	4.50
63	Laurie Niemi	15.00	7.50	4.50
64	Ray Renfro	15.00	7.50	4.50
65	Dick Chapman	25.00	12.50	7.50
66	Bob Hantla	25.00	12.50	7.50
67	Ralph Starkey	25.00	12.50	7.50
68	Don Paul	25.00	12.50	7.50
69	Kenneth Snyder	25.00	12.50	7.50
70	Tobin Rote	25.00	12.50	7.50
71	Arthur DeCarlo	25.00	12.50	7.50
72	Tom Keane	25.00	12.50	7.50
73	Hugh Taylor	25.00	12.50	7.50
74	Warren Lahr **RC**	25.00	12.50	7.50
75	Jim Neal	25.00	12.50	7.50
76	Leo Nomellini	75.00	38.00	23.00
77	Dick Yelvington	25.00	12.50	7.50
78	Les Richter	30.00	15.00	9.00
79	Bucko Kilroy	30.00	15.00	9.00
80	John Martinkovic	25.00	12.50	7.50
81	Dale Dodrill **RC**	25.00	12.50	7.50
82	Ken Jackson	25.00	12.50	7.50
83	Paul Lipscomb	25.00	12.50	7.50
84	John Bauer	25.00	12.50	7.50
85	Lou Creekmur	40.00	20.00	12.00
86	Eddie Price	25.00	12.50	7.50
87	Kenneth Farragut	25.00	12.50	7.50
88	Dave Hanner **RC**	25.00	12.50	7.50
89	Don Boll	25.00	12.50	7.50
90	Chet Hanulak	25.00	12.50	7.50
91	Thurman McGraw	25.00	12.50	7.50
92	Don Heinrich **RC**	25.00	12.50	7.50
93	Dan McKown	25.00	12.50	7.50
94	Bob Fleck	25.00	12.50	7.50
95	Jerry Hilgenberg	25.00	12.50	7.50
96	Bill Walsh	25.00	12.50	7.50
97	Tom Finnin Error	75.00	38.00	23.00
97	Tom Finnan	15.00	7.50	4.50
98	Paul Barry	15.00	7.50	4.50
99	Harry Jagade	15.00	7.50	4.50
100	Jack Christiansen	25.00	13.00	8.00
101	Gordon Soltau	15.00	7.50	4.50
102a	Emlen Tunnel (Tunnell)	25.00	12.50	7.50
102b	Emlen Tunnell (correct)	20.00	10.00	6.00
103	Stan West	15.00	7.50	4.50
104	Jerry Williams	15.00	7.50	4.50
105	Veryl Switzer	15.00	7.50	4.50
106	Billy Stone	15.00	7.50	4.50
107	Jerry Watford	15.00	7.50	4.50
108	Elbert Nickel	15.00	7.50	4.50
109	Ed Sharkey	15.00	7.50	4.50
110	Steve Meilinger	15.00	7.50	4.50
111	Dante Lavelli	25.00	13.00	8.00
112	Leon Hart	20.00	10.00	6.00
113	Charlie Conerly	35.00	18.00	10.00
114	Richard Lemmon	15.00	7.50	4.50
115	Al Carmichael	15.00	7.50	4.50
116	George Conner	30.00	15.00	9.00
117	John Olszewski	15.00	7.50	4.50
118	Ernie Stautner	25.00	12.50	7.50
119	Ray Smith	15.00	7.50	4.50
120	Neil Worden	15.00	7.50	4.50
121	Jim Dooley	15.00	7.50	4.50
122	Arnold Galiffa	15.00	7.50	4.50
123	Kline Gilbert	15.00	7.50	4.50
124	Bob Hoernschemeyer	15.00	7.50	4.50
125	Whizzer White **RC**	20.00	10.00	6.00
126	Art Spinney	15.00	7.50	4.50
127	Joe Koch	15.00	7.50	4.50
128	John Lattner **RC**	90.00	45.00	27.00

1955 Bowman

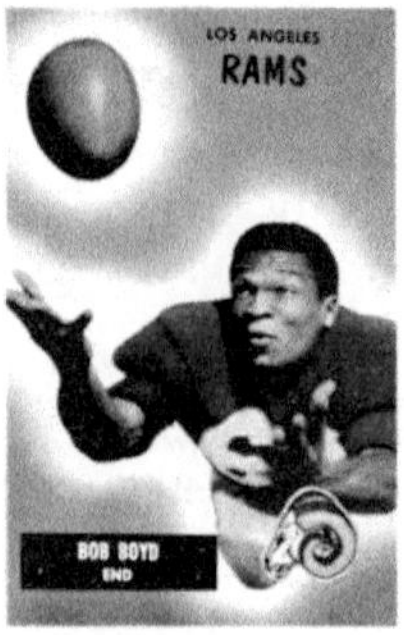

An excellent run of football cards ended after this year when the Bowman Co. released its last set of 160 cards. (Its competitor, Topps Chewing Gum Co., bought it early in 1956). The first 64 cards are relatively easy to find, compared to numbers 65-160. Rookies in this set include Hall of Famers Mike McCormick, Len Ford, John Henry Johnson, Bob St. Clair, Jim Ringo, and Frank Gatski. Other rookies include Pat Summerall and Alan Ameche.

	NM	E	VG
Complete Set (160):	2,200	1,100	660.00
Common Player (1-64):	15.00	7.50	4.50
Minor Stars (1-64):	15.00		
Unlisted Stars (1-64):	25.00		
Common Player (65-160):	25.00	12.50	7.50
Minor Stars (65-160):	20.00		
Unlisted Stars (65-160):	35.00		

1	Doak Walker	90.00	45.00	27.00
2	Mike McCormack **RC**	50.00	25.00	15.00
3	John Olszewski	15.00	7.50	4.50
4	Dorne Dibble	15.00	7.50	4.50
5	Lindon Crow	15.00	7.50	4.50
6	Hugh Taylor	15.00	7.50	4.50
7	Frank Gifford	80.00	40.00	24.00
8	Alan Ameche **RC**	50.00	25.00	15.00
9	Don Stonesifer	15.00	7.50	4.50
10	Pete Pihos	25.00	13.00	8.00
11	Bill Austin	15.00	7.50	4.50
12	Dick Alban	15.00	7.50	4.50
13	Bobby Walston	15.00	7.50	4.50
14	Len Ford **RC**	45.00	23.00	14.00
15	Jug Girard	15.00	7.50	4.50
16	Charlie Conerly	35.00	18.00	10.00
17	Volney Peters	15.00	7.50	4.50
18	Max Boydston	15.00	7.50	4.50
19	Leon Hart	25.00	13.00	8.00
20	Bert Rechichar	15.00	7.50	4.50
21	Lee Riley	15.00	7.50	4.50
22	Johnny Carson	15.00	7.50	4.50
23	Harry Thompson	15.00	7.50	4.50
24	Ray Wietecha	15.00	7.50	4.50
25	Ollie Matson	35.00	10.00	18.00
26	Eddie LeBaron	30.00	15.00	9.00
27	Jack Simmons	15.00	7.50	4.50
28	Jack Christiansen	30.00	15.00	9.00
29	Bucko Kilroy	15.00	7.50	4.50
30	Tom Keane	15.00	7.50	4.50
31	Dave Leggett	15.00	7.50	4.50
32	Norm Van Brocklin	50.00	25.00	15.00
33	Harlon Hill	20.00	10.00	6.00
34	Robert Haner	15.00	7.50	4.50
35	Veryl Switzer	15.00	7.50	4.50
36	Dick Stanfel	25.00	13.00	8.00
37	Lou Groza	35.00	18.00	10.00
38	Tank Younger	25.00	12.50	7.50
39	Dick Flanagan	15.00	7.50	4.50
40	Jim Dooley	15.00	7.50	4.50
41	Ray Collins	15.00	7.50	4.50
42	John Henry Johnson **RC**	50.00	25.00	15.00
43	Tom Fears	25.00	12.50	7.50
44	Joe Perry	40.00	20.00	12.00
45	Gene Brito	15.00	7.50	4.50
46	Bill Johnson	15.00	7.50	4.50
47	Deacon Dan Towler	15.00	7.50	4.50
48	Dick Moegle	15.00	7.50	4.50
49	Kline Gilbert	15.00	7.50	4.50
50	Les Gobel	15.00	7.50	4.50
51	Ray Krouse	15.00	7.50	4.50
52	Pat Summerall **RC**	50.00	25.00	15.00
53	Ed Brown **RC**	25.00	12.50	7.50
54	Lynn Chandnois	15.00	7.50	4.50
55	Joe Heap	15.00	7.50	4.50
56	John Hoffman	15.00	7.50	4.50
57	Howard Ferguson	15.00	7.50	4.50
58	Bobby Watkins	15.00	7.50	4.50
59	Charlie Ane	15.00	7.50	4.50
60	Ken MacAfee **RC**	25.00	12.50	7.50
61	Ralph Guglielmi **RC**	25.00	12.50	7.50
62	George Blanda	70.00	35.00	21.00
63	Kenneth Snyder	15.00	7.50	4.50
64	Chet Ostrowski	15.00	7.50	4.50
65	Buddy Young	30.00	15.00	9.00
66	Gordon Soltau	25.00	12.50	7.50
67	Eddie Bell	25.00	12.50	7.50
68	Ben Agajanian **RC**	25.00	12.50	7.50
69	Tom Dahms	25.00	12.50	7.50
70	Jim Ringo **RC**	90.00	45.00	27.00
71	Bobby Layne	80.00	40.00	24.00
72	Y.A. Tittle	80.00	40.00	24.00
73	Bob Gaona	25.00	12.50	7.50
74	Tobin Rote	25.00	12.50	7.50
75	Hugh McElhenny	40.00	20.00	12.00
76	John Kreamcheck	25.00	12.50	7.50
77	Al Dorow	25.00	12.50	7.50
78	Bill Wade	25.00	12.50	7.50
79	Dale Dodrill	25.00	12.50	7.50
80	Chuck Drazenovich	25.00	12.50	7.50
81	Billy Wilson **RC**	25.00	12.50	7.50
82	Les Richter	25.00	12.50	7.50
83	Pat Brady	25.00	12.50	7.50
84	Bob Hoernschemeyer	25.00	12.50	7.50
85	Joe Arenas	25.00	12.50	7.50
86	Len Szafaryn	25.00	12.50	7.50
87	Rick Casares **RC**	25.00	12.50	7.50
88	Leon McLaughlin	25.00	12.50	7.50
89	Charley Toogood	25.00	12.50	7.50
90	Tom Bettis	25.00	12.50	7.50
91	John Sandusky	25.00	12.50	7.50
92	Bill Wightkin	25.00	12.50	7.50
93	Darrell Brewster	25.00	12.50	7.50
94	Marion Campbell	25.00	12.50	7.50
95	Floyd Reid	25.00	12.50	7.50
96	Harry Jagade	25.00	12.50	7.50
97	George Taliaferro	25.00	12.50	7.50
98	Carleton Massey	25.00	12.50	7.50
99	Fran Rogel	25.00	12.50	7.50
100	Alex Sandusky	25.00	12.50	7.50
101	Bob St. Clair **RC**	90.00	45.00	27.00
102	Al Carmichael	25.00	12.50	7.50
103	Carl Taseff	25.00	12.50	7.50
104	Leo Nomellini	40.00	20.00	12.00
105	Tom Scott	25.00	12.50	7.50
106	Ted Marchibroda	25.00	12.50	7.50
107	Art Spinney	25.00	12.50	7.50
108	Wayne Robinson	25.00	12.50	7.50
109	Jim Ricca	25.00	12.50	7.50
110	Lou Ferry	25.00	12.50	7.50
111	Roger Zatkoff	25.00	12.50	7.50
112	Lou Creekmur	30.00	15.00	9.00
113	Kenny Konz	25.00	12.50	7.50
114	Doug Eggers	25.00	12.50	7.50
115	Bobby Thomason	25.00	12.50	7.50
116	Bill McPeak	25.00	12.50	7.50
117	William Brown	25.00	12.50	7.50
118	Royce Womble	25.00	12.50	7.50
119	Frank Gatski **RC**	80.00	40.00	24.00
120	Jim Finks	25.00	12.50	7.50
121	Andy Robustelli	25.00	12.50	7.50
122	Bobby Dillon	25.00	12.50	7.50
123	Leo Sanford	25.00	12.50	7.50
124	Elbert Nickel	25.00	12.50	7.50
125	Wayne Hansen	25.00	12.50	7.50
126	Buck Lansford	25.00	12.50	7.50
127	Gern Nagler	25.00	12.50	7.50
128	Jim Salsbury	25.00	12.50	7.50
129	Dale Atkeson	25.00	12.50	7.50
130	John Schweder	25.00	12.50	7.50
131	Dave Hanner	25.00	12.50	7.50
132	Eddie Price	25.00	12.50	7.50
133	Vic Janowicz	25.00	12.50	7.50
134	Ernie Stautner	35.00	18.00	10.00
135	James Parmer	25.00	12.50	7.50
136	Emlen Tunnell	35.00	18.00	10.00
137	Kyle Rote	25.00	12.50	7.50
138	Norm Willey	25.00	12.50	7.50
139	Charlie Trippi	25.00	12.50	7.50
140	Bill Howton	25.00	12.50	7.50
141	Bobby Clatterbuck	25.00	12.50	7.50
142	Bob Boyd	25.00	12.50	7.50
143	Bob Toneff **RC**	25.00	12.50	7.50
144	Jerry Helluin	25.00	12.50	7.50
145	Adrian Burk	25.00	12.50	7.50
146	Walt Michaels	25.00	12.50	7.50

147	Zillie Toth	25.00	12.50	7.50
148	Frank Varrichione RC	25.00	12.50	7.50
149	Dick Bielski	25.00	12.50	7.50
150	George Ratterman	25.00	12.50	7.50
151	Mike Jarmoluk	25.00	12.50	7.50
152	Tom Landry	200.00	100.00	60.00
153	Ray Renfro	25.00	12.50	7.50
154	Zeke Bratkowski	25.00	12.50	7.50
155	Jerry Norton	25.00	12.50	7.50
156	Maurice Bassett	25.00	12.50	7.50
157	Volney Quinlan	25.00	12.50	7.50
158	Chuck Bednarik	30.00	15.00	9.00
159	Don Colo	25.00	12.50	7.50
160	L.G. Dupre RC	50.00	25.00	15.00

1991 Bowman

CHRIS DOLEMAN

Topps produced this 561-card set in 1991 under the Bowman name. The standard-size cards have color photos on the front, with blue and orange borders. The player's name is in white in a purple stripe at the bottom. The grey backs, in green and black type, have a player profile, biography and statistics. The cards are numbered alphabetically by team, beginning with Atlanta and ending with Washington. Subsets include League Leaders (#s 273-283), Rookie Superstars (#s 1-11), and Road to the Super Bowl (#s 547-557). These 33 subset cards are gold-foil embossed, with one appearing in every pack.

	NM/M	NM	E
Complete Set (561):	10.00	7.50	4.00
Common Player:	.03	.02	.01
Pack:	.50		
Wax Box (36):	10.00		

1	Jeff George (RS)	.10	.08	.04
2	Richmond Webb (RS)	.03	.02	.01
3	Emmitt Smith (RS)	1.00	.70	.40
4	Mark Carrier (RS)	.05	.04	.02
5	Steve Christie (RS)	.03	.02	.01
6	Keith Sims (RS)	.03	.02	.01
7	Rob Moore (RS)	.15	.11	.06
8	Johnny Johnson (RS)	.10	.08	.04
9	Eric Green (RS)	.03	.02	.01
10	Ben Smith (RS)	.03	.02	.01
11	Tory Epps (RS)	.03	.02	.01
12	Andre Rison	.25	.20	.10
13	Shawn Collins	.03	.02	.01
14	Chris Hinton	.03	.02	.01
15	Deion Sanders	.50	.40	.20
16	Darion Conner	.03	.02	.01
17	Michael Haynes	.30	.25	.12
18	Chris Miller	.03	.02	.01
19	Jessie Tuggle	.03	.02	.01
20	Scott Fulhage	.03	.02	.01
21	Bill Fralic	.03	.02	.01
22	Floyd Dixon	.03	.02	.01
23	Oliver Barnett	.03	.02	.01
24	Mike Rozier	.03	.02	.01
25	Tory Epps	.03	.02	.01
26	Tim Green	.03	.02	.01
27	Steve Broussard	.03	.02	.01
28	Bruce Pickens	.03	.02	.01
29	Mike Pritchard RC	.50	.40	.20
30	Andre Reed	.10	.08	.04
31	Darryl Talley	.03	.02	.01
32	Nate Odomes	.03	.02	.01
33	Jamie Mueller	.03	.02	.01
34	Leon Seals	.03	.02	.01
35	Keith McKeller	.03	.02	.01
36	Al Edwards	.03	.02	.01
37	Butch Rolle	.03	.02	.01
38	Jeff Wright	.10	.08	.04
39	Will Wolford	.03	.02	.01
40	James Williams	.03	.02	.01
41	Kent Hull	.03	.02	.01
42	James Lofton	.03	.02	.01
43	Frank Reich	.03	.02	.01
44	Bruce Smith	.03	.02	.01
45	Thurman Thomas	.50	.40	.20
46	Leonard Smith	.03	.02	.01
47	Shane Conlan	.03	.02	.01
48	Steve Tasker	.03	.02	.01
49	Ray Bentley	.03	.02	.01
50	Cornelius Bennett	.03	.02	.01

51	Stan Thomas	.03	.02	.01
52	Shaun Gayle	.03	.02	.01
53	Wendell Davis	.10	.08	.04
54	James Thornton	.03	.02	.01
55	Mark Carrier	.03	.02	.01
56	Richard Dent	.03	.02	.01
57	Ron Morris	.03	.02	.01
58	Mike Singletary	.03	.02	.01
59	Jay Hilgenberg	.03	.02	.01
60	Donnell Woolford	.03	.02	.01
61	Jim Covert	.03	.02	.01
62	Jim Harbaugh	.10	.08	.04
63	Neal Anderson	.10	.08	.04
64	Brad Muster	.03	.02	.01
65	Kevin Butler	.03	.02	.01
66	Trace Armstrong	.03	.02	.01
67	Ron Cox	.03	.02	.01
68	Peter Tom Willis	.03	.02	.01
69	Johnny Bailey	.03	.02	.01
70	Mark Bortz	.03	.02	.01
71	Chris Zorich RC	.25	.20	.10
72	Lamar Rogers	.03	.02	.01
73	David Grant	.03	.02	.01
74	Lewis Billups	.03	.02	.01
75	Harold Green	.15	.11	.06
76	Ickey Woods	.03	.02	.01
77	Eddie Brown	.03	.02	.01
78	David Fulcher	.03	.02	.01
79	Anthony Munoz	.03	.02	.01
80	Carl Zander	.03	.02	.01
81	Rodney Holman	.03	.02	.01
82	James Brooks	.03	.02	.01
83	Tim McGee	.03	.02	.01
84	Boomer Esiason	.15	.11	.06
85	Leon White	.03	.02	.01
86	James Francis	.10	.08	.04
87	Mitchell Price	.03	.02	.01
88	Ed King RC	.10	.08	.04
89	Eric Turner RC	.25	.20	.10
90	Rob Burnett RC	.10	.08	.04
91	Leroy Hoard	.10	.08	.04
92	Kevin Mack	.03	.02	.01
93	Thane Gash	.03	.02	.01
94	Gregg Rakoczy	.03	.02	.01
95	Clay Matthews	.03	.02	.01
96	Eric Metcalf	.03	.02	.01
97	Stephen Braggs	.03	.02	.01
98	Frank Minnifield	.03	.02	.01
99	Reggie Langhorne	.03	.02	.01
100	Mike Johnson	.03	.02	.01
101	Brian Brennan	.03	.02	.01
102	Anthony Pleasant	.03	.02	.01
103	Godfrey Myles	.03	.02	.01
104	Russell Maryland RC	.50	.40	.20
105	James Washington RC	.10	.08	.04
106	Nate Newton	.03	.02	.01
107	Jimmie Jones	.03	.02	.01
108	Jay Novacek	.15	.11	.06
109	Alexander Wright	.10	.08	.04
110	Jack Del Rio	.03	.02	.01
111	Jim Jeffcoat	.03	.02	.01
112	Mike Saxon	.03	.02	.01
113	Troy Aikman	1.00	.70	.40
114	Issiac Holt	.03	.02	.01
115	Ken Norton	.03	.02	.01
116	Kelvin Martin	.03	.02	.01
117	Emmitt Smith	2.00	1.50	.80
118	Ken Willis	.03	.02	.01
119	Daniel Stubbs	.03	.02	.01
120	Michael Irvin	.15	.11	.06
121	Danny Noonan	.03	.02	.01
122	Alvin Harper RC	.50	.40	.20
123	Reggie Johnson RC	.10	.08	.04
124	Vance Johnson	.03	.02	.01
125	Steve Atwater	.03	.02	.01
126	Greg Kragen	.03	.02	.01
127	John Elway	.40	.30	.15
128	Simon Fletcher	.03	.02	.01
129	Wymon Henderson	.03	.02	.01
130	Ricky Nattiel	.03	.02	.01
131	Shannon Sharpe	.10	.08	.04
132	Ron Holmes	.03	.02	.01
133	Karl Mecklenburg	.03	.02	.01
134	Bobby Humphrey	.03	.02	.01
135	Clarence Kay	.03	.02	.01
136	Dennis Smith	.03	.02	.01
137	Jim Juriga	.03	.02	.01
138	Melvin Bratton	.03	.02	.01
139	Mark Jackson	.03	.02	.01
140	Michael Brooks	.03	.02	.01
141	Alton Montgomery	.03	.02	.01
142	Mike Croel RC	.15	.11	.06
143	Mel Gray	.03	.02	.01
144	Michael Cofer	.03	.02	.01
145	Jeff Campbell	.03	.02	.01
146	Dan Owens	.03	.02	.01
147	Robert Clark	.03	.02	.01
148	Jim Arnold	.03	.02	.01

149	William White	.03	.02	.01
150	Rodney Peete	.03	.02	.01
151	Jerry Ball	.03	.02	.01
152	Bennie Blades	.03	.02	.01
153	Barry Sanders	1.50	1.25	.60
154	Andre Ware	.10	.08	.04
155	Lomas Brown	.03	.02	.01
156	Chris Spielman	.03	.02	.01
157	Kelvin Pritchett	.03	.02	.01
158	Herman Moore RC	3.50	2.75	1.50
159	Chris Jacke	.03	.02	.01
160	Tony Mandarich	.03	.02	.01
161	Perry Kemp	.03	.02	.01
162	Johnny Holland	.03	.02	.01
163	Mark Lee	.03	.02	.01
164	Anthony Dilweg	.03	.02	.01
165	Scott Stephen	.03	.02	.01
166	Ed West	.03	.02	.01
167	Mark Murphy	.03	.02	.01
168	Darrell Thompson	.15	.11	.06
169	James Campen	.03	.02	.01
170	Jeff Query	.03	.02	.01
171	Brian Noble	.03	.02	.01
172	Sterling Sharpe	.15	.11	.06
173	Robert Brown	.03	.02	.01
174	Tim Harris	.03	.02	.01
175	LeRoy Butler	.03	.02	.01
176	Don Majkowski	.03	.02	.01
177	Vinnie Clark	.03	.02	.01
178	Esera Tuaolo	.03	.02	.01
179	Lorenzo White	.10	.08	.04
180	Warren Moon	.25	.20	.10
181	Sean Jones	.03	.02	.01
182	Curtis Duncan	.03	.02	.01
183	Al Smith	.04	.02	.01
184	Richard Johnson	.03	.02	.01
185	Tony Jones	.03	.02	.01
186	Bubba McDowell	.03	.02	.01
187	Bruce Matthews	.03	.02	.01
188	Ray Childress	.03	.02	.01
189	Haywood Jeffires	.25	.20	.10
190	Ernest Givins	.03	.02	.01
191	Mike Munchak	.03	.02	.01
192	Greg Montgomery	.03	.02	.01
193	Cody Carlson RC	.30	.25	.12
194	Johnny Meads	.03	.02	.01
195	Drew Hill	.03	.02	.01
196	Mike Dumas	.03	.02	.01
197	Darryll Lewis RC	.10	.08	.04
198	Rohn Stark	.03	.02	.01
199	Clarence Verdin	.03	.02	.01
200	Mike Prior	.03	.02	.01
201	Eugene Daniel	.03	.02	.01
202	Dean Biasucci	.03	.02	.01
203	Jeff Herrod	.03	.02	.01
204	Keith Taylor	.03	.02	.01
205	Jon Hand	.03	.02	.01
206	Pat Beach	.03	.02	.01
207	Duane Bickett	.03	.02	.01
208	Jessie Hester	.03	.02	.01
209	Chip Banks	.03	.02	.01
210	Ray Donaldson	.03	.02	.01
211	Bill Brooks	.03	.02	.01
212	Jeff George	.30	.25	.12
213	Tony Siragusa	.03	.02	.01
214	Albert Bentley	.03	.02	.01
215	Joe Valerio	.03	.02	.01
216	Chris Martin	.03	.02	.01
217	Christian Okoye	.03	.02	.01
218	Stephone Paige	.03	.02	.01
219	Percy Snow	.03	.02	.01
220	David Scott	.03	.02	.01
221	Derrick Thomas	.25	.20	.10
222	Todd McNair	.03	.02	.01
223	Albert Lewis	.03	.02	.01
224	Neil Smith	.03	.02	.01
225	Barry Word	.10	.08	.04
226	Robb Thomas	.03	.02	.01
227	John Alt	.03	.02	.01
228	Jonathan Hayes	.03	.02	.01
229	Kevin Ross	.03	.02	.01
230	Nick Lowery	.03	.02	.01
231	Tim Grunhard	.03	.02	.01
232	Dan Saleaumua	.03	.02	.01
233	Steve DeBerg	.03	.02	.01
234	Harvey Williams RC	.50	.40	.20
235	Nick Bell RC	.15	.11	.06
236	Mervyn Fernandez	.03	.02	.01
237	Howie Long	.03	.02	.01
238	Marcus Allen	.03	.02	.01
239	Eddie Anderson	.03	.02	.01
240	Ethan Horton	.03	.02	.01
241	Lionel Washington	.03	.02	.01
242	Steve Wisniewski	.03	.02	.01
243	Bo Jackson	.25	.20	.10
244	Greg Townsend	.03	.02	.01
245	Jeff Jaeger	.03	.02	.01
246	Aaron Wallace	.03	.02	.01

247	Garry Lewis	.03	.02	.01
248	Steve Smith	.03	.02	.01
249	Willie Gault	.03	.02	.01
250	Scott Davis	.03	.02	.01
251	Jay Schroeder	.03	.02	.01
252	Don Mosebar	.03	.02	.01
253	Todd Marinovich **RC**	.10	.08	.04
254	Irv Pankey	.03	.02	.01
255	Flipper Anderson	.03	.02	.01
256	Tom Newberry	.03	.02	.01
257	Kevin Greene	.03	.02	.01
258	Mike Wilcher	.03	.02	.01
259	Bern Brostek	.03	.02	.01
260	Buford McGee	.03	.02	.01
261	Cleveland Gary	.03	.02	.01
262	Jackie Slater	.03	.02	.01
263	Henry Ellard	.03	.02	.01
264	Alvin Wright	.03	.02	.01
265	Darryl Henley **RC**	.10	.08	.04
266	Damone Johnson	.03	.02	.01
267	Frank Stams	.03	.02	.01
268	Jerry Gray	.03	.02	.01
269	Jim Everett	.03	.02	.01
270	Pat Terrell	.03	.02	.01
271	Todd Lyght **RC**	.15	.11	.06
272	Aaron Cox	.03	.02	.01
273	Barry Sanders (LL)	.50	.40	.20
274	Jerry Rice (LL)	.40	.30	.15
275	Derrick Thomas (LL)	.10	.08	.04
276	Mark Carrier (LL)	.05	.04	.02
277	Warren Moon (LL)	.15	.11	.06
278	Randall Cunningham (LL)	.10	.08	.04
279	Nick Lowery (LL)	.03	.02	.01
280	Clarence Verdin (LL)	.03	.02	.01
281	Thurman Thomas (LL)	.25	.20	.10
282	Mike Horan (LL)	.03	.02	.01
283	Flipper Anderson (LL)	.03	.02	.01
284	John Offerdahl	.03	.02	.01
285	Dan Marino	2.00	1.50	.80
286	Mark Clayton	.03	.02	.01
287	Tony Paige	.03	.02	.01
288	Keith Sims	.03	.02	.01
289	Jeff Cross	.03	.02	.01
290	Pete Stoyanovich	.03	.02	.01
291	Ferrell Edmunds	.03	.02	.01
292	Reggie Roby	.03	.02	.01
293	Louis Oliver	.03	.02	.01
294	Jarvis Williams	.03	.02	.01
295	Sammie Smith	.03	.02	.01
296	Richmond Webb	.03	.02	.01
297	J.B. Brown	.03	.02	.01
298	Jim Jensen	.03	.02	.01
299	Mark Duper	.03	.02	.01
300	David Griggs	.03	.02	.01
301	Randal Hill **RC**	.35	.25	.14
302	Aaron Craver **RC**	.10	.08	.04
303	Keith Millard	.03	.02	.01
304	Steve Jordan	.03	.02	.01
305	Anthony Carter	.03	.02	.01
306	Mike Merriweather	.03	.02	.01
307	Audray McMillian **RC**	.35	.25	.14
308	Randall McDaniel	.03	.02	.01
309	Gary Zimmerman	.03	.02	.01
310	Carl Lee	.03	.02	.01
311	Reggie Rutland	.03	.02	.01
312	Hassan Jones	.03	.02	.01
313	Kirk Lowdermilk	.03	.02	.01
314	Herschel Walker	.08	.06	.03
315	Chris Doleman	.03	.02	.01
316	Joey Browner	.03	.02	.01
317	Wade Wilson	.03	.02	.01
318	Henry Thomas	.03	.02	.01
319	Rich Gannon	.08	.06	.03
320	Al Noga	.03	.02	.01
321	Pat Harlow **RC**	.08	.06	.03
322	Bruce Armstrong	.03	.02	.01
323	Maurice Hurst	.03	.02	.01
324	Brent Williams	.03	.02	.01
325	Chris Singleton	.03	.02	.01
326	Jason Staurovsky	.03	.02	.01
327	Marvin Allen	.03	.02	.01
328	Hart Lee Dykes	.03	.02	.01
329	Johnny Rembert	.03	.02	.01
330	Andre Tippett	.03	.02	.01
331	Greg McMurtry	.03	.02	.01
332	John Stephens	.03	.02	.01
333	Ray Agnew	.03	.02	.01
334	Tommy Hodson	.03	.02	.01
335	Ronnie Lippett	.03	.02	.01
336	Marv Cook	.03	.02	.01
337	Tommy Barnhardt **RC**	.08	.06	.03
338	Dalton Hilliard	.03	.02	.01
339	Sam Mills	.03	.02	.01
340	Morten Andersen	.03	.02	.01
341	Stan Brock	.03	.02	.01
342	Brett Maxie	.03	.02	.01
343	Steve Walsh	.03	.02	.01
344	Vaughan Johnson	.03	.02	.01
345	Rickey Jackson	.03	.02	.01
346	Renaldo Turnbull	.03	.02	.01
347	Joel Hilgenberg	.03	.02	.01
348	Toi Cook **RC**	.10	.08	.04
349	Robert Massey	.03	.02	.01
350	Pat Swilling	.03	.02	.01
351	Eric Martin	.03	.02	.01
352	Rueben Mayes	.03	.02	.01
353	Vince Buck	.03	.02	.01
354	Brett Perriman	.03	.02	.01
355	Wesley Carroll **RC**	.25	.20	.10
356	Jarrod Bunch **RC**	.10	.08	.04
357	Pepper Johnson	.03	.02	.01
358	Dave Meggett	.03	.02	.01
359	Mark Collins	.03	.02	.01
360	Sean Landeta	.03	.02	.01
361	Maurice Carthon	.03	.02	.01
362	Mike Fox	.03	.02	.01
363	Jeff Hostetler	.15	.11	.06
364	Phil Simms	.08	.06	.03
365	Leonard Marshall	.03	.02	.01
366	Gary Reasons	.03	.02	.01
367	Rodney Hampton	.50	.40	.20
368	Greg Jackson **RC**	.08	.06	.03
369	Jumbo Elliott	.03	.02	.01
370	Bob Kratch **RC**	.08	.06	.03
371	Lawrence Taylor	.10	.08	.04
372	Erik Howard	.03	.02	.01
373	Carl Banks	.03	.02	.01
374	Stephen Baker	.03	.02	.01
375	Mark Ingram	.03	.02	.01
376	Browning Nagle **RC**	.25	.20	.10
377	Jeff Lageman	.03	.02	.01
378	Ken O'Brien	.03	.02	.01
379	Al Toon	.03	.02	.01
380	Joe Prokop	.03	.02	.01
381	Tony Stargell	.03	.02	.01
382	Blair Thomas	.10	.08	.04
383	Erik McMillan	.03	.02	.01
384	Dennis Byrd	.03	.02	.01
385	Freeman McNeil	.03	.02	.01
386	Brad Baxter	.08	.06	.03
387	Mark Boyer	.03	.02	.01
388	Terance Mathis	.10	.08	.04
389	Jim Sweeney	.03	.02	.01
390	Kyle Clifton	.03	.02	.01
391	Pat Leahy	.03	.02	.01
392	Rob Moore	.15	.11	.06
393	James Hasty	.03	.02	.01
394	Blaise Bryant	.03	.02	.01
395	Jesse Campbell (Error-Photo actually Dan McGwire, see 509 Corrected)	.03	.02	.01
396	Keith Jackson	.15	.11	.06
397	Jerome Brown	.03	.02	.01
398	Keith Byars	.03	.02	.01
399	Seth Joyner	.03	.02	.01
400	Mike Bellamy	.03	.02	.01
401	Fred Barnett	.20	.15	.08
402	Reggie Singletary	.03	.02	.01
403	Reggie White	.15	.11	.06
404	Randall Cunningham	.15	.11	.06
405	Byron Evans	.03	.02	.01
406	Wes Hopkins	.03	.02	.01
407	Ben Smith	.03	.02	.01
408	Roger Ruzek	.03	.02	.01
409	Eric Allen	.03	.02	.01
410	Anthony Toney	.03	.02	.01
411	Clyde Simmons	.03	.02	.01
412	Andre Waters	.03	.02	.01
413	Calvin Williams	.15	.11	.06
414	Eric Swann **RC**	.15	.11	.06
415	Eric Hill	.03	.02	.01
416	Tim McDonald	.03	.02	.01
417	Luis Sharpe	.03	.02	.01
418	Ernie Jones	.03	.02	.01
419	Ken Harvey	.03	.02	.01
420	Ricky Proehl	.15	.11	.06
421	Johnny Johnson	.25	.20	.10
422	Anthony Bell	.03	.02	.01
423	Timm Rosenbach	.03	.02	.01
424	Rich Camarillo	.03	.02	.01
425	Walter Reeves	.03	.02	.01
426	Freddie Joe Nunn	.03	.02	.01
427	Anthony Thompson	.03	.02	.01
428	Bill Lewis	.03	.02	.01
429	Jim Wahler **RC**	.08	.06	.03
430	Cedric Mack	.03	.02	.01
431	Michael Jones **RC**	.08	.06	.03
432	Ernie Mills	.03	.02	.01
433	Tim Worley	.03	.02	.01
434	Greg Lloyd	.03	.02	.01
435	Dermontti Dawson	.03	.02	.01
436	Louis Lipps	.03	.02	.01
437	Eric Green	.08	.06	.03
438	Donald Evans	.03	.02	.01
439	David Johnson	.03	.02	.01
440	Tunch Ilkin	.03	.02	.01
441	Bubby Brister	.08	.06	.03
442	Chris Calloway	.03	.02	.01
443	David Little	.03	.02	.01
444	Thomas Everett	.03	.02	.01
445	Carnell Lake	.03	.02	.01
446	Rod Woodson	.05	.04	.02
447	Gary Anderson	.03	.02	.01
448	Merril Hoge	.03	.02	.01
449	Gerald Williams	.03	.02	.01
450	Eric Moten **RC**	.08	.06	.03
451	Marion Butts	.05	.04	.02
452	Leslie O'Neal	.03	.02	.01
453	Ronnie Harmon	.03	.02	.01
454	Gill Byrd	.03	.02	.01
455	Junior Seau	.25	.20	.10
456	Nate Lewis **RC**	.25	.20	.10
457	Leo Goeas	.03	.02	.01
458	Burt Grossman	.03	.02	.01
459	Courtney Hall	.03	.02	.01
460	Anthony Miller	.06	.05	.02
461	Gary Plummer	.03	.02	.01
462	Billy Joe Tolliver	.03	.02	.01
463	Lee Williams	.03	.02	.01
464	Arthur Cox	.03	.02	.01
465	John Kidd	.03	.02	.01
466	Frank Cornish	.03	.02	.01
467	John Carney	.03	.02	.01
468	Eric Bieniemy **RC**	.10	.08	.04
469	Don Griffin	.03	.02	.01
470	Jerry Rice	1.00	.70	.40
471	Keith DeLong	.03	.02	.01
472	John Taylor	.10	.08	.04
473	Brent Jones	.03	.02	.01
474	Pierce Holt	.03	.02	.01
475	Kevin Fagan	.03	.02	.01
476	Bill Romanowski	.03	.02	.01
477	Dexter Carter	.03	.02	.01
478	Guy McIntyre	.03	.02	.01
479	Joe Montana	1.00	.70	.40
480	Charles Haley	.03	.02	.01
481	Mike Cofer	.03	.02	.01
482	Jesse Sapolu	.03	.02	.01
483	Eric Davis	.03	.02	.01
484	Mike Sherrard	.03	.02	.01
485	Steve Young	.75	.60	.30
486	Darryl Pollard	.03	.02	.01
487	Tom Rathman	.03	.02	.01
488	Michael Carter	.03	.02	.01
489	Ricky Watters **RC**	1.50	1.25	.60
490	John Johnson **RC**	.08	.06	.03
491	Eugene Robinson	.03	.02	.01
492	Andy Heck	.03	.02	.01
493	John L. Williams	.03	.02	.01
494	Norm Johnson	.03	.02	.01
495	David Wyman	.03	.02	.01
496	Derrick Fenner	.10	.08	.04
497	Rick Donnelly	.03	.02	.01
498	Tony Woods	.03	.02	.01
499	Derek Loville **RC**	.75	.60	.30
500	Dave Krieg	.03	.02	.01
501	Joe Nash	.03	.02	.01
502	Brian Blades	.03	.02	.01
503	Cortez Kennedy	.25	.20	.10
504	Jeff Bryant	.03	.02	.01
505	Tommy Kane	.03	.02	.01
506	Travis McNeal	.03	.02	.01
507	Terry Wooden	.03	.02	.01
508	Chris Warren	.50	.40	.20
509	Dan McGwire **RC** (Error-Photo actually Jesse Campbell; see 395 Corrected)	.50	.40	.20
510	Mark Robinson	.03	.02	.01
511	Ron Hall	.03	.02	.01
512	Paul Gruber	.03	.02	.01
513	Hary Hamilton	.03	.02	.01
514	Keith McCants	.03	.02	.01
515	Reggie Cobb	.25	.20	.10
516	Steve Christie	.03	.02	.01
517	Broderick Thomas	.03	.02	.01
518	Mark Carrier	.03	.02	.01
519	Vinny Testaverde	.10	.08	.04
520	Ricky Reynolds	.03	.02	.01
521	Jesse Anderson	.03	.02	.01
522	Reuben Davis	.03	.02	.01
523	Wayne Haddix	.03	.02	.01
524	Gary Anderson	.03	.02	.01
525	Bruce Hill	.03	.02	.01
526	Kevin Murphy	.03	.02	.01
527	Lawrence Dawsey **RC**	.25	.20	.10
528	Ricky Ervins **RC**	.35	.25	.14
529	Charles Mann	.03	.02	.01
530	Jim Lachey	.03	.02	.01
531	Mark Rypien	.10	.08	.04
532	Darrell Green	.03	.02	.01
533	Stan Humphries	.40	.30	.15
534	Jeff Bostic	.03	.02	.01

		NM	E	VG
535	Earnest Byner	.03	.02	.01
536	Art Monk	.08	.06	.03
537	Don Warren	.03	.02	.01
538	Darryl Grant	.03	.02	.01
539	Wilber Marshall	.03	.02	.01
540	Kurt Gouveia **RC**	.10	.08	.04
541	Markus Koch	.03	.02	.01
542	Andre Collins	.03	.02	.01
543	Chip Lohmiller	.03	.02	.01
544	Alvin Walton	.03	.02	.01
545	Gary Clark	.10	.08	.04
546	Ricky Sanders	.03	.02	.01
547	**Redskins vs. Eagles** (Gary Clark)	.03		.01
548	**Bengals vs. Oilers** (Cody Carlson)	.03	.02	.01
549	**Dolphins vs. Chiefs** (Mark Clayton)	.03	.02	.01
550	**Bears vs. Saints** (Neal Anderson)	.03	.02	.01
551	**Bills vs. Dolphins** (Thurman Thomas)	.10	.08	.04
552	**49ers vs. Redskins** (Line Play)	.03	.02	.01
553	**Giants vs. Bears** (Ottis Anderson)	.03	.02	.01
554	**Raiders vs. Bengals** (Bo Jackson)	.10	.08	.04
555	**AFC Championship** (Andre Reed)	.03	.02	.01
556	**NFC Championship** (Jeff Hostetler)	.03	.02	.01
557	**Super Bowl XXV** (Ottis Anderson)	.03	.02	.01
558	**Checklist 1-140**	.03	.02	.01
559	**Checklist 141-280**	.03	.02	.01
560	**Checklist 281-420**	.03	.02	.01
561	**Checklist 421-561**	.03	.02	.01

1952 Bread For Health

These early 1950s bread end labels feature 32 NFL players. The cards, which measure 2-3/4" x 2-3/4", were found in loaves of Fisher's Bread (New Jersey, New York and Pennsylvania) and NBC Bread in Michigan. The cards are unnumbered and are blank-backed. A B.E.B. copyright is on the card front, along with an informational note.

		NM	E	VG
Complete Set (32):		4,300	2,150	1,290
Common Player:		90.00	45.00	27.00
(1)	Frankie Albert	250.00	125.00	75.00
(2)	Elmer Angsman	200.00	100.00	60.00
(3)	Dick Barwegan	200.00	100.00	60.00
(4)	Sammy Baugh	800.00	400.00	240.00
(5)	Charley Conerly	500.00	250.00	150.00
(6)	Glenn Davis	250.00	125.00	75.00
(7)	Don Doll	200.00	100.00	60.00
(8)	Tom Fears	250.00	125.00	75.00
(9)	Harry Gilmer	200.00	100.00	60.00
(10)	Otto Graham	800.00	400.00	240.00
(11)	Pat Harder	200.00	100.00	60.00
(12)	Bobby Lane	600.00	300.00	180.00
(13)	Sid Luckman	600.00	300.00	180.00
(14)	Johnny Lujack	400.00	200.00	120.00
(15)	John Panelli	200.00	100.00	60.00
(16)	Barney Poole	200.00	100.00	60.00
(17)	George Ratterman	200.00	100.00	60.00
(18)	Tobin Rote	250.00	125.00	75.00
(19)	Jack Russell	200.00	100.00	60.00
(20)	Lou Rymkus	200.00	100.00	60.00
(21)	Joe Signiago	200.00	100.00	60.00
(22)	Mac Speedie	250.00	125.00	75.00
(23)	Bill Swiacki	200.00	100.00	60.00
(24)	Tommy Thompson	250.00	125.00	75.00
(25)	Y.A. Tittle	600.00	300.00	180.00
(26)	Clayton Tonnemaker	200.00	100.00	60.00
(27)	Charlie Trippi	300.00	150.00	90.00
(28)	Clyde Turner	250.00	125.00	75.00
(29)	Steve Van Buren	250.00	125.00	75.00
(30)	Bill Walsh	200.00	100.00	60.00
(31)	Bob Waterfield	500.00	250.00	150.00
(32)	Jim White	200.00	100.00	60.00

1990 British Petroleum

This 36-card set featured color fronts and black backs (with either contest rules or advertising). The cards were handed out two at a time in California, with the goal of the game to collect two adjacent numbers (1-2, 3-4). One of the two was difficult to find, with the contest expiring in October of 1991. There were also five instant win cards: Andre Tippett, Freeman McNeil, Clay Matthews, Tim Harris and Deion Sanders. Numbers 1, 3, 6, 8 and 10 had six different possible players.

		NM/M	NM	E
Complete Set (36):		45.00	34.00	18.00
Common Player:		.50	.40	.20

		NM/M	NM	E
1A	John Elway	3.00	2.25	1.25
1B	Boomer Esiason	.50	.40	.20
1C	Jim Everett	.50	.40	.20
1D	Bernie Kosar	.50	.40	.20
1E	Karl Mecklenburg	.50	.40	.20
1F	Bruce Smith	.50	.40	.20
2	Deion Sanders			
3A	Roger Craig	.50	.40	.20
3B	Randall Cunningham	.50	.40	.20
3C	Keith Jackson	.50	.40	.20
3D	Dan Marino	10.00	7.50	4.00
3E	Freddie Joe Nunn	.50	.40	.20
3F	Jerry Rice	5.00	3.75	2.00
3G	Vinny Testaverde	.50	.40	.20
3H	John L. Williams	.50	.40	.20
4	Tim Harris			
5	Clay Matthews			
6A	Neal Anderson	.50	.40	.20
6B	Duane Bickett	.50	.40	.20
6C	Ronnie Lott	.50	.40	.20
6D	Anthony Munoz	.50	.40	.20
6E	Christian Okoye	.50	.40	.20
6F	Barry Sanders	5.00	3.75	2.00
7	Freeman McNeil			
8A	Cornelius Bennett	.50	.40	.20
8B	Anthony Carter	.50	.40	.20
8C	Jim Kelly	1.00	.70	.40
8D	Louis Lipps	.50	.40	.20
8E	Phil Simms	.50	.40	.20
8F	Billy Ray Smith	.50	.40	.20
8G	Lawrence Taylor	1.00	.70	.40
9	Andre Tippett			
10A	Bo Jackson	1.50	1.25	.60
10B	Howie Long	.50	.40	.20
10C	Don Majkowski	.50	.40	.20
10D	Art Monk	1.00	.70	.40
10E	Warren Moon	1.00	.70	.40
10F	Mike Singletary	1.00	.70	.40
10G	Al Toon	.50	.40	.20
10H	Herschel Walker	1.00	.70	.40
10I	Reggie White	1.50	1.25	.60

1968-70 Broncos

This 53-card set contains black and white photos and black, unnumbered card backs. The cards measure 5" x 7" and include mostly posed shots.

		NM	E	VG
Complete Set (53):		130.00	97.50	52.50
Common Player:		2.00	1.50	.80
1	Bob Anderson	4.00	2.00	1.25
2	Tom Beer	4.00	2.00	1.25
3	Phil Brady	2.00	1.50	.80
4	Sam Brunelli	3.00	1.50	.90
5	George Burrell	2.00	1.50	.80
6	Carter Campbell	2.00	1.50	.80
7	Grady Cavness	3.00	1.50	.90
8	Barney Chavous	6.00	3.00	1.75
9	Dave Costa	3.00	1.50	.90
10	Ken Criter (Head shot)	2.00	1.50	.80
11	Ken Criter (Head-and-shoulders)	2.00	1.50	.80
12	Carl Cunningham	2.00	1.50	.80
13	Mike Current (Left-side shot)	4.00	2.00	1.25
14	Mike Current (Right-side shot)	4.00	2.00	1.25
15	Joe Dawkins	4.00	2.00	1.25
16	Al Denson (Offensive end)	4.00	2.00	1.25
17	Al Denson (Wide receiver)	4.00	2.00	1.25
18	Wallace Dickey	2.00	1.50	.80
19	John Embree	2.00	1.50	.80
20	Fred Forsberg	2.00	1.50	.80
21	Jack Gehrke	2.00	1.50	.80
22	Cornell Gordon	3.00	1.50	.90
23	John Grant	2.00	1.50	.80
24	Charlie Greer (Head shot)	2.00	1.50	.80
25	Charlie Greer (Head-and-shoulders)	2.00	1.50	.80
26	Dwight Harrison	2.00	1.50	.80
27	Walter Highsmith	2.00	1.50	.80
28	Gus Hollomon	2.00	1.50	.80
29	Larron Jackson (Left-side shot)	2.00	1.50	.80
30	Larron Jackson (Right-side shot)	2.00	1.50	.80
31	Calvin Jones	4.00	2.00	1.25
32	Larry Kaminski (Left-side shot)	2.00	1.50	.80
33	Larry Kaminski (Right-side shot)	2.00	1.50	.80
34	Bill Laskey	2.00	1.50	.80
35	Pete Liske	4.00	2.00	1.25
36	Fran Lynch	2.00	1.50	.80
37	Tom Lyons (Guard on front)	2.00	1.50	.80
38	Tommy Lyons (Center on front)	2.00	1.50	.80
39	Rex Mirich	2.00	1.50	.80

40	Randy Montgomery (Left-side shot)	2.00	1.50	.80
41	Randy Montgomery (Right-side shot)	2.00	1.50	.80
42	Tom Oberg	2.00	1.50	.80
43	Steve Ramsey	6.00	3.00	1.75
44	Frank Richter	2.00	1.50	.80
45	Mike Schnitker	2.00	1.50	.80
46	Roger Shoals	2.00	1.50	.80
47	Jerry Simmons (Looking toward upper left corner of picture)	4.00	2.00	1.25
48	Jerry Simmons (Head turned slightly toward right)	4.00	2.00	1.25
49	Paul Smith (Head shot)	4.00	2.00	1.25
50	Paul Smith (Head-and-shoulders)	4.00	2.00	1.25
51	Olen Underwood	2.00	1.50	.80
52	Dave Washington	2.00	1.50	.80
53	Bob Young	2.00	1.50	.80

1980 Broncos Stamps Police

This unnumbered set contains nine different stamps, with each stamp containing two players with a Broncos logo in between. The stamps were given away (one per week) at Albertson's food stores in the Denver area. The set measures 3" x 3" and is tri-sponsored by Albertson's, the Kiwanis Club and local police. There is a poster that the stamps fit on that sold at the time for 99 cents.

		NM	E	VG
Complete Set (9):		12.00	9.00	4.75
Common Player:		1.00	.70	.40
1	Barney Chavous, Rubin Carter	1.00	.70	.40
2	Bernard Jackson, Haven Moses	1.00	.50	.30
3	Tom Jackson, Riley Odoms	3.00	1.50	.90
4	Brison Manor, Steve Foley	1.00	.70	.40
5	Claudie Minor, Randy Gradishar	1.00	.50	.30
6	Craig Morton, Tom Glassic	2.00	1.00	.60
7	Jim Turner, Bob Swenson	1.00	.50	.30
8	Rick Upchurch, Billy Thompson	1.00	.50	.30
9	Louis Wright, Joe Rizzo	1.00	.70	.40

1982 Broncos Police

Measuring 2-5/8" x 4-1/8", the 15-card set boasts the player's jersey number, name, position, team and Broncos' helmet under a photo. The unnumbered card backs feature Broncos Tips inside a box, which is topped by a Broncos' helmet. The set's sponsor is listed at the bottom center.

		NM/M	NM	E
Complete Set (15):		120.00	110.00	60.00
Common Player:		2.00	1.50	.80
7	Craig Morton	8.00	6.00	3.25
11	Luke Prestridge	2.00	1.50	.80
20	Louis Wright	4.00	3.00	1.50
24	Rick Parros	2.00	1.50	.80
36	Bill Thompson	4.00	3.00	1.50
41	Rob Lytle	2.00	1.50	.80
46	Dave Preston (SP)	5.00	3.75	2.00
51	Bob Swenson	2.00	1.50	.80
53	Randy Gradishar (SP)	30.00	22.00	12.00
57	Tom Jackson	12.00	9.00	4.75
60	Paul Howard	2.00	1.50	.80
68	Rubin Carter	2.00	1.50	.80
79	Barney Chavous (SP)	30.00	22.00	12.00
80	Rick Upchurch	8.00	6.00	3.25
88	Riley Odoms (SP)	12.00	9.00	4.75

1984 Broncos KOA

Handed out at Safeway or Dairy Queen stores, this 24-card set was part of the KOA Match 'N Win and KOA/Denver Broncos Silver Anniversary Sweepstakes. Measuring 2" x 4", with a bottom tab measuring 1-1/8", the card fronts showcase a black-and-white photo, with the player's name, number and position inside a banner under the photo. The American Football League and various sponsor logos appear under the photo. The card's tab featured three silver footballs that could be scratched off with a coin. The card backs feature the sweepstakes' rules. Besides the player's jersey number, the cards are unnumbered.

		NM/M	NM	E
Complete Set (24):		90.00	67.00	36.00
Common Player:		1.00	.70	.40
7	Craig Morton	5.00	3.75	2.00
11	Bob Anderson (SP)	10.00	7.50	4.00
12	Charlie Johnson	4.00	3.00	1.50
15	Jim Turner	2.00	1.50	.80

21	Gene Mingo	1.00	.70	.40
22	Fran Lynch	1.00	.70	.40
23	Goose Gonsoulin	2.00	1.50	.80
24	Otis Armstrong	4.00	3.00	1.50
24	Willie Brown	6.00	4.50	2.50
25	Haven Moses	2.00	1.50	.80
36	Billy Thompson	2.00	1.50	.80
42	Bill Van Heusen	1.00	.70	.40
44	Floyd Little (SP)	16.00	12.00	6.50
53	Randy Gradishar (SP)	14.00	10.50	5.50
71	Claudie Minor (SP)	5.00	3.75	2.00
72	Sam Brunelli	1.00	.70	.40
74	Mike Current	1.00	.70	.40
75	Eldon Danenhauer	1.00	.70	.40
78	Marv Montgomery	1.00	.70	.40
81	Billy Masters	1.00	.70	.40
82	Bob Scarpitto	1.00	.70	.40
87	Lionel Taylor	2.00	1.50	.80
87	Rich Jackson	1.00	.70	.70
88	Riley Odoms	2.00	1.50	.80

1987 Broncos Orange Crush

This standard sized nine-card set honors former Denver Broncos players who are featured in the stadium's Ring of Fame. The card fronts feature a black-and-white photo bordered with blue and orange. The Orange Crush logo is on an angle at the top of the card front. The player's number, name, position and years played with the Broncos are printed underneath the photo. The Broncos' Ring of Fame logo is located at the bottom right. The backs feature "1st Annual Collector's Edition Ring of Famer" at the top, with his name, number, position, years played and highlights printed below. The info is packaged inside a box, with the Crush logo appearing at the bottom. The KOA Radio logo is printed at the very bottom of the card back. The cards were handed out for three weeks at 7-11 and Albertsons stores in the Denver area.

		NM/M	NM	E
Complete Set (9):		4.50	3.50	1.75
Common Player:		.50	.40	.20
1	Billy Thompson	.50	.40	.20
2	Lionel Taylor	.50	.40	.20
3	Goose Gonsoulin	.50	.40	.20
4	Paul Smith	.50	.40	.20
5	Rich Jackson	.50	.40	.20
6	Charlie Johnson	.50	.40	.20
7	Floyd Little	.75	.60	.30
8	Frank Tripucka	.50	.40	.20
9	Gerald Phipps (Owner 1960-1981)	.50	.40	.20

1986 Brownell Heisman

Measuring 7-15/16" x 10", the black-and-white cards feature Art Brownell artwork of Heisman Trophy winners. The blank-backed cards are unnumbered. The cards are listed in chronological order. Even though Archie Griffin won the Heisman in both 1974 and 1975, he is featured on only one card. The fronts feature the year the player won the Heisman, plus a short write-up.

		NM/M	NM	E
Complete Set (50):		250.00	187.00	100.00
Common Player:		5.00	3.75	2.00
1	Jay Berwanger	4.00	3.00	1.50
2	Larry Kelley	4.00	3.00	1.50
3	Clint Frank	4.00	3.00	1.50
4	Davey O'Brien	4.00	3.00	1.50
5	Niles Kinnick	10.00	7.50	4.00
6	Tom Harmon	5.00	3.75	2.00
7	Bruce Smith	4.00	3.00	1.50
8	Frank Sinkwich	4.00	3.00	1.50
9	Angelo Bertelli	4.00	3.00	1.50
10	Les Horvath	4.00	3.00	1.50
11	Doc Blanchard	8.00	6.00	3.25
12	Glenn Davis	8.00	3.00	3.25
13	Johnny Lujack	12.00	9.00	4.75
14	Doak Walker	10.00	7.50	4.00
15	Leon Hart	4.00	3.00	1.50
16	Vic Janowicz	10.00	7.50	4.00
17	Dick Kazmaier	4.00	3.00	1.50
18	Billy Vessels	4.00	3.00	1.50
19	John Lattner	8.00	6.00	3.25
20	Alan Ameche	6.00	4.50	2.50
21	Howard Cassady	5.00	3.75	2.00
22	Paul Hornung	18.00	13.50	7.25
23	John David Crow	4.00	3.00	1.50
24	Pete Dawkins	4.00	3.00	1.50
25	Billy Cannon	4.00	3.00	1.50
26	Joe Bellino	4.00	3.00	1.50
27	Ernie Davis	30.00	22.00	12.00
28	Terry Baker	4.00	3.00	1.50
29	Roger Staubach	35.00	26.00	14.00
30	John Huarte	4.00	3.00	1.50
31	Mike Garrett	4.00	3.00	1.50

32	Steve Spurrier	15.00	11.00	6.00
33	Gary Beban	4.00	3.00	1.50
34	O.J. Simpson	20.00	15.00	8.00
35	Steve Owens	5.00	3.75	2.00
36	Jim Plunkett	10.00	7.50	4.00
37	Pat Sullivan	4.00	3.00	1.50
38	Johnny Rodgers	4.00	3.00	1.50
39	John Cappelletti	4.00	3.00	1.50
40	Archie Griffin	6.00	4.50	2.50
41	Tony Dorsett	18.00	13.50	7.25
42	Earl Campbell	18.00	13.50	7.25
43	Billy Sims	8.00	6.00	3.25
44	Charles White	4.00	3.00	1.50
45	George Rogers	4.00	3.00	1.50
46	Marcus Allen	10.00	7.50	4.00
47	Herschel Walker	8.00	6.00	3.25
48	Mike Rozier	4.00	3.00	1.50
49	Doug Flutie	8.00	6.00	3.25
50	Bo Jackson	10.00	7.50	4.00

1946 Browns Sears

Measuring 2-1/2" x 4", the eight-card set was released by Sears and Roebuck. The set showcases players from the Cleveland Browns' initial season. Card fronts boast a black-and-white photo of the player and a slogan to follow the Browns and shop at Sears. The cards are unnumbered.

		NM	E	VG
Complete Set (8):		375.00	280.00	150.00
Common Player:		35.00	26.00	14.00
(1)	Ernie Blandin	35.00	26.00	14.00
(2)	Jim Daniell	35.00	26.00	14.00
(3)	Fred Evans	35.00	26.00	14.00
(4)	Frank Gatski	50.00	25.00	15.00
(5)	Otto Graham	150.00	75.00	45.00
(6)	Dante Lavelli	75.00	37.00	22.00
(7)	Mel Maceau	35.00	26.00	14.00
(8)	George Young	35.00	26.00	14.00

1950 Browns Team Issue

Measuring 6-1/2" x 9", the five-card set showcases a black-and-white posed player photo, which is bordered in white. The player's name, printed in cursive, also is on the front of the blank-backed and unnumbered cards.

		NM	E	VG
Complete Set (5):		75.00	56.00	30.00
Common Player:		10.00	5.00	3.00
1	Frank Gatski	15.00	7.50	4.50
2	Tommy James	10.00	5.00	3.00
3	Don Moselle	10.00	5.00	3.00
4	Marion Motley	30.00	15.00	9.00
5	Derrell F. Palmer	10.00	5.00	3.00

1951 Browns White Border

Measuring 6-1/2" x 9", the 25-card team-issued set was anchored by a posed black-and-white photo on the front, bordered in white. The player's name is printed in cursive on the front of the unnumbered and blank-backed cards. The set was housed in an off-white envelope with brown and orange trim. "Cleveland Browns Photographs" is also printed on the envelopes.

		NM	E	VG
Complete Set (25):		250.00	125.00	75.00
Common Player:		5.00	2.50	1.50
1	Tony Adamle	8.00	4.00	2.50
2	Alex Agase	8.00	4.00	2.50
3	Rex Bumgardner	5.00	2.50	1.50
4	Emerson Cole	5.00	2.50	1.50
5	Len Ford	12.00	6.00	3.50
6	Frank Gatski	12.00	6.00	3.50
7	Horace Gillom	5.00	2.50	1.50
8	Ken Gorgal	5.00	2.50	1.50
9	Otto Graham	45.00	22.00	13.50
10	Forrest Gregg	5.00	2.50	1.50
11	Lou Groza	20.00	10.00	6.00
12	Hal Herring	5.00	2.50	1.50
13	Lin Houston	5.00	2.50	1.50
14	Weldon Humble	5.00	2.50	1.50
15	Tommy James	5.00	2.50	1.50
16	Dub Jones	8.00	4.00	2.50
17	Warren Lahr	5.00	2.50	1.50
18	Dante Lavelli	20.00	10.00	6.00
19	Cliff Lewis	5.00	2.50	1.50
20	Marion Motley	20.00	10.00	6.00
21	Lou Rymkus	8.00	4.00	2.50
22	Mac Speedie	10.00	5.00	3.00
23	Tommy Thompson	10.00	5.00	3.00
24	Bill Willis	15.00	7.50	4.50
25	George Young	15.00	7.50	4.50

1954-55 Browns White Border

Measuring 8-1/2" x 10", the 20-card set showcases posed player shots on the front, which are bordered in white. The unnumbered and blank-backed cards feature the player's name and position at the bottom inside a white border.

		NM	E	VG
Complete Set (20):		125.00	95.00	50.00
Common Player:		5.00	2.50	1.50
1	Maurice Bassett	5.00	2.50	1.50
2	Harold Bradley	5.00	2.50	1.50
3	Darrell Brewster	5.00	2.50	1.50
4	Don Colo	5.00	2.50	1.50
5	Len Ford	10.00	5.00	3.00
6	Bob Gain	5.00	2.50	1.50
7	Frank Gatski	10.00	5.00	3.00
8	Abe Gibron	5.00	2.50	1.50
9	Tommy James	5.00	2.50	1.50
10	Dub Jones	7.00	3.50	2.00
11	Ken Konz	5.00	2.50	1.50
12	Warren Lahr	5.00	2.50	1.50
13	Dante Lavelli	15.00	7.50	4.50
14	Carlton Massey	5.00	2.50	1.50
15	Mike McCormack	10.00	5.00	3.00
16	Walt Michaels	5.00	2.50	1.50
17	Chuck Noll	25.00	12.50	7.50
18	Don Paul	5.00	2.50	1.50
19	Ray Renfro	10.00	5.00	3.00
20	George Ratterman	5.00	2.50	1.50

1955 Browns Carling Beer

Measuring 8-1/2" x 11-1/2", the 10-card set featured a large black-and-white photo on the front of the white-bordered cards. Carling's Black Label Beer and team name are printed below the photo in black. "DBL 54" is printed in the bottom right corner.

		NM	E	VG
Complete Set (10):		250.00	150.00	80.00
Common Player:		10.00	7.50	4.00
1	Darrell Brewster	10.00	7.50	4.00
2	Tom Catlin	10.00	7.50	4.00
3	Len Ford	20.00	10.00	6.00
4	Otto Graham	75.00	37.00	22.00
5	Lou Groza	40.00	20.00	12.00
6	Kenny Konz	10.00	7.50	4.00
7	Dante Lavelli	25.00	12.50	7.50
8	Mike McCormack	20.00	10.00	6.00
9	Fred Morrison	10.00	7.50	4.00
10	Chuck Noll	60.00	30.00	18.00

1955 Browns Color Postcards

These six postcards, which measure 6" x 9", boast a full-bleed color photo on the front. The unnumbered backs have the player's name and team at the top left, with the "place stamp here" box in the upper left and "Giant Post Card" centered on the right. The cards feature rounded corners.

		NM	E	VG
Complete Set (6):		140.00	90.00	47.50
Common Player:		10.00	7.50	4.00
1	Mo Bassett	10.00	7.50	4.00
2	Don Colo	10.00	7.50	4.00
3	Frank Gatski	20.00	10.00	6.00
4	Lou Groza	70.00	35.00	21.00
5	Dante Lavelli	40.00	20.00	12.00
6	George Ratterman	15.00	7.50	4.50

1959 Browns Carling Beer

Measuring 8-1/2" x 11-1/2", the nine-card set featured a black-and-white posed photo, which was bordered in white. The player's name and position are printed in black inside a white rectangle inside the photo. Printed under the photo are "Carling Black Label Beer" and "The Cleveland Browns." The backs are usually blank, but can be stamped with "Henry M. Barr Studios, Berea, Ohio BE4-1330." The card fronts are numbered in the lower right corner, except for Jim Brown's photo card. The set was also reprinted in the late 1980s on thinner paper and most likely show the Henry M. Barr stamp on the back. Some sources say the Brown photo is only available in the reprint set.

		NM	E	VG
Complete Set (9):		130.00	97.50	52.50
Common Player:		10.00	7.50	4.00
A	Leroy Bolden	10.00	7.50	4.00
B	Vince Costello	10.00	7.50	4.00
C	Galen Fiss	10.00	7.50	4.00
E	Lou Groza	30.00	15.00	9.00
F	Walt Michaels	15.00	7.50	4.50
G	Bobby Mitchell	30.00	15.00	9.00
J	Bob Gain	10.00	7.50	4.00
K	Billy Howton	15.00	7.50	4.50
NNO	Jim Brown (DP)	8.00	4.00	2.50

1961 Browns Carling Beer

Measuring 8-1/2" x 11-1/2", the 10 black-and-white cards feature posed photos on the front, with the player's name and position printed inside a white rectangle inside the photo. "Carling Back Label Beer" and "The Cleveland Browns" are printed underneath the photo on the card front. The card numbers appear in the lower right corner on the front, while the backs are blank.

		NM	E	VG
Complete Set (10):		200.00	100.00	60.00
Common Player:		10.00	7.50	4.00
A	Milt Plum	20.00	10.00	6.00
B	Mike McCormack	20.00	10.00	6.00
C	Bob Gain	10.00	7.50	4.00
D	John Morrow	10.00	7.50	4.00
E	Jim Brown	80.00	40.00	24.00
F	Bobby Mitchell	35.00	17.50	10.50
G	Bobby Franklin	10.00	7.50	4.00
H	Jim Ray Smith	10.00	7.50	4.00
K	Jim Houston	18.00	9.00	5.50
L	Ray Renfro	15.00	7.50	4.50

1961 Browns National City Bank

Measuring 2-1/2" x 3-9/16", the 36-card set was released in sheets of six cards. Each sheet was numbered, while each individual card was numbered. The card fronts feature "Quarterback Club Brownie Card 1961 Cleveland Browns" at the top. The posed photos anchor the front, with "issued in 1961 by Cleveland's Oldest Bank National City Bank" printed underneath. The card backs are numbered at the top with a set number and a player (card) number. The player's name, position, bio and write-up are also on the back. The bottom of the card back includes the National City Bank logo.

		NM	E	VG
Complete Set (36):		2,000	1,000	600.00
Common Player:		40.00	30.00	16.00
1	Mike McCormack	80.00	40.00	24.00
2	Jim Brown	575.00	287.00	172.00
3	Leon Clarke	40.00	30.00	16.00
4	Walt Michaels	40.00	20.00	12.00
5	Jim Ray Smith	40.00	30.00	16.00
6	**Quarterback Club Membership Card**	220.00	110.00	66.00
7	Len Dawson	225.00	112.00	67.00
8	John Morrow	40.00	30.00	16.00
9	Bernie Parrish	40.00	20.00	12.00
10	Floyd Peters	40.00	20.00	12.00
11	Paul Wiggin	40.00	20.00	12.00
12	John Wooten	40.00	20.00	12.00
13	Ray Renfro	40.00	20.00	12.00
14	Galen Fiss	40.00	30.00	16.00
15	Dave Lloyd	40.00	30.00	16.00
16	Dick Schafrath	40.00	20.00	12.00
17	Ross Fichtner	40.00	30.00	16.00
18	Gern Nagler	40.00	30.00	16.00
19	Rich Kreitling	40.00	30.00	16.00
20	Duane Putnam	40.00	30.00	16.00
21	Vince Costello	40.00	30.00	16.00
22	Jim Shofner	40.00	20.00	12.00
23	Sam Baker	40.00	20.00	12.00
24	Bob Gain	40.00	20.00	12.00
25	Lou Groza	100.00	50.00	30.00
26	Don Fleming	40.00	20.00	12.00
27	Tom Watkins	40.00	30.00	16.00
28	Jim Houston	40.00	20.00	12.00
29	Larry Stephens	40.00	30.00	16.00
30	Bobby Mitchell	100.00	50.00	30.00
31	Bobby Franklin	40.00	30.00	16.00
32	Charlie Ferguson	40.00	30.00	16.00
33	Johnny Brewer	40.00	30.00	16.00
34	Bob Crespino	40.00	30.00	16.00
35	Milt Plum	40.00	20.00	12.00
36	Preston Powell	40.00	30.00	16.00

1961 Browns White Border

Measuring 8-1/2" x 10-1/2", the 20-card set showcased black-and-white photos on the front, with the player's name and position listed inside a white box inside the photo. The fronts are bordered in white. The cards are unnumbered and blank-backed.

		NM	E	VG
Complete Set (20):		160.00	120.00	65.00
Common Player:		5.00	3.75	2.00
1	Jim Brown	75.00	37.00	22.00
2	Galen Fiss	5.00	3.75	2.00
3	Don Fleming	5.00	2.50	1.50
4	Bobby Franklin	5.00	3.75	2.00
5	Bob Gain	5.00	2.50	1.50
6	Jim Houston	5.00	2.50	1.50
7	Rich Kreitling	5.00	3.75	2.00
8	Dave Lloyd	5.00	3.75	2.00
9	Mike McCormack	12.00	6.00	3.50
10	Bobby Mitchell	16.00	8.00	4.75
11	John Morrow	5.00	3.75	2.00
12	Bernie Parrish	5.00	2.50	1.50
13	Milt Plum	5.00	2.50	1.50
14	Ray Renfro	5.00	2.50	1.50
15	Dick Schafrath	5.00	2.50	1.50
16	Jim Shofner	5.00	2.50	1.50
17	Jim Ray Smith	5.00	3.75	2.00
18	Tom Watkins	5.00	3.75	2.00
19	Paul Wiggin	5.00	2.50	1.50
20	John Wooten	5.00	2.50	1.50

1963 Browns White Border

Measuring 7-1/2" x 9-1/2", the 26-card set showcases black-and-white photos on the front. The card backs are blank. Each card is unnumbered.

		NM	E	VG
Complete Set (26):		120.00	90.00	47.50
Common Player:		5.00	3.75	2.00
1	Johnny Brewer	5.00	3.75	2.00
2	Monte Clark	5.00	2.50	1.50
3	Gary Collins	10.00	5.00	3.00
4	Vince Costello	5.00	2.50	1.50
5	Bob Crespino	5.00	3.75	2.00
6	Ross Fichtner	5.00	3.75	2.00
7	Galen Fiss	5.00	3.75	2.00
8	Bob Gain	5.00	3.75	2.00
9	Bill Glass	5.00	2.50	1.50
10	Ernie Green	10.00	5.00	3.00
11	Lou Groza	16.00	8.00	4.75
12	Gene Hickerson	7.00	3.50	2.00
13	Jim Houston	5.00	2.50	1.50
14	Tom Hutchinson	5.00	3.75	2.00
15	Rich Kreitling	5.00	3.75	2.00
16	Mike Lucci	5.00	2.50	1.50
17	John Morrow	5.00	3.75	2.00
18	Jim Ninowski	5.00	2.50	1.50
19	Frank Parker	5.00	3.75	2.00
20	Bernie Parrish	5.00	2.50	1.50
21	Ray Renfro	5.00	2.50	1.50
22	Dick Schafrath	5.00	2.50	1.50
23	Jim Shofner	5.00	2.50	1.50
24	Ken Webb	5.00	3.75	2.00
25	Paul Wiggin	5.00	2.50	1.50
26	John Wooten	5.00	2.50	1.50

1985 Browns Coke/Mr. Hero

Measuring 2-3/4" x 3-1/4", the 48-card set was released on six sheets of eight cards. The card fronts are anchored by a photo, with the player's name and position listed at the bottom center. The player's jersey number is printed in large numerals in the lower left. The unnumbered card backs spotlight the player's name, position, bio and career highlights. Coupons were included on each complete sheet.

		NM/M	NM	E
Complete Set (48):		25.00	18.50	10.00
Common Player:		.50	.40	.20
7	Jeff Gossett (4)	.75	.60	.30
9	Matt Bahr (1)	.75	.60	.30
16	Paul McDonald (4)	.50	.40	.20
18	Gary Danielson (5)	.50	.40	.20
19	Bernie Kosar (6)	2.50	2.00	1.00
20	Don Rogers (4)	.50	.40	.20
22	Felix Wright (2)	.50	.40	.20
26	Greg Allen (3)	.50	.40	.20
27	Al Gross (2)	.50	.40	.20
29	Hanford Dixon (5)	.50	.40	.20
30	Boyce Green (1)	.50	.40	.20
31	Frank Minnifield (1)	.50	.40	.20
34	Kevin Mack (3)	1.00	.70	.40
37	Chris Rockins (1)	.50	.40	.20
38	Johnny Davis (5)	.50	.40	.20
44	Earnest Byner (2)	1.25	.90	.50
47	Larry Braziel (4)	.50	.40	.20
50	Tom Cousineau (6)	.50	.40	.20
51	Eddie Johnson (2)	.50	.40	.20
55	Curtis Weathers (1)	.50	.40	.20
56	Chip Banks (6)	.75	.60	.30
57	Clay Matthews (5)	1.75	1.25	.70
58	Scott Nicolas (1)	.50	.40	.20
61	Mike Baab (4)	.50	.40	.20
62	George Lilja (5)	.50	.40	.20
63	Cody Risien (6)	.50	.40	.20
65	Mark Krerowicz (3)	.50	.40	.20
68	Robert Jackson (4)	.50	.40	.20
69	Dan Fike (2)	.50	.40	.20
72	Dave Puzzuoli (1)	.50	.40	.20
74	Paul Farren (2)	.50	.40	.20
77	Rickey Bolden (3)	.50	.40	.20
78	Carl Hairston (2)	.50	.40	.20
79	Bob Golic (6)	.50	.40	.20
80	Willis Adams (2)	.50	.40	.20
81	Harry Holt (3)	.50	.40	.20
82	Ozzie Newsome (3)	1.75	1.25	.70
83	Fred Banks (3)	.50	.40	.20
84	Glen Young (1)	.50	.40	.20
85	Clarence Weathers (6)	.50	.40	.20
86	Brian Brennan (5)	.50	.40	.20
87	Travis Tucker (6)	.50	.40	.20
88	Reggie Langhorne (5)	.50	.40	.20
89	John Jefferson (4)	1.00	.70	.40
91	Sam Clancy (4)	.50	.40	.20
96	Reggie Camp (5)	.50	.40	.20
99	Keith Baldwin (6)	.50	.40	.20
NNO	**Action Photo** (Clay Matthews tackling Eric Dickerson)(3)	1.75	1.25	.70

1987 Browns Louis Rich

Louis Rich produced this set to be a promotion in its products. After the cards were printed the promotion was pulled. After the set's cancellation, Oscar Mayer gave collectors who stopped into the Cleveland corporate office a set. The cards measure 5" x 7-1/8".

		NM/M	NM	E
Complete Set (5):		45.00	34.00	18.00
Common Player:		5.00	3.75	2.00
1	Jim Brown, Bobby Mitchell	22.00	16.50	8.75
2	Otto Graham	15.00	11.00	6.00
3	Lou Groza	10.00	7.50	4.00
4	Dante Lavelli (Question Mark)	5.00	3.75	2.00
5	Marion Motley	5.00	3.75	2.00

1980 Buccaneers Police

Measuring 2-5/8" x 4-1/8", the 56-card set boasts a photo on the front, with the player's name, position and bio underneath on the left. The Bucs' helmet is printed in the lower right. The unnumbered card backs have "Kids and Kops tips from the Buccaneers" at the top. A definition of a football term and a safety tip are included, while the Coca-Cola logo is printed above the various sponsor names at the bottom. Cards including the Paradyne Corp. name on the back are scarce variations, which are valued at two to three times more.

		NM	E	VG
Complete Set (56):		150.00	110.00	60.00
Common Player:		3.00	2.25	1.25
1	Ricky Bell	8.00	4.00	2.50
2	Rick Berns	3.00	1.50	.90
3	Tom Blanchard	3.00	2.25	1.25
4	Scot Brantley	3.00	2.25	1.25
5	Aaron Brown	3.00	2.25	1.25
6	Cedric Brown	3.00	2.25	1.25
7	Mark Cotney	3.00	2.25	1.25
8	Randy Crowder	3.00	2.25	1.25
9	Gary Davis	3.00	2.25	1.25
10	Johnny Davis	3.00	1.50	.90
11	Tony Davis	3.00	2.25	1.25
12	Jerry Eckwood	5.00	2.50	1.50
13	Chuck Fusina	3.00	1.50	.90
14	Jimmie Giles	5.00	2.50	1.50
15	Isaac Hagins	3.00	2.25	1.25
16	Charley Hannah	3.00	2.25	1.25
17	Andy Hawkins	3.00	2.25	1.25
18	Kevin House	3.00	1.50	.90
19	Cecil Johnson	3.00	2.25	1.25
20	Gordon Jones	3.00	1.50	.90
21	Curtis Jordan	3.00	2.25	1.25
22	Bill Kollar	3.00	2.25	1.25
23	Jim Leonard	3.00	2.25	1.25
24	David Lewis	3.00	1.50	.90
25	Reggie Lewis	3.00	2.25	1.25
26	David Logan	3.00	1.50	.90
27	Larry Mucker	3.00	2.25	1.25
28	Jim O'Bradovich	3.00	1.50	.90
29	Mike Rae	3.00	2.25	1.25
30	Dave Reavis	3.00	2.25	1.25
31	Danny Reece	3.00	2.25	1.25
32	Greg Roberts	3.00	2.25	1.25
33	Gene Sanders	3.00	2.25	1.25
34	Dewey Selmon	5.00	2.50	1.50
35	Lee Roy Selmon	15.00	7.50	4.50
36	Ray Snell	3.00	2.25	1.25
37	Dave Stalls	3.00	2.25	1.25
38	Norris Thomas	3.00	2.25	1.25
39	Mike Washington	3.00	2.25	1.25
40	Doug Williams	10.00	5.00	3.00
41	Steve Wilson	3.00	2.25	1.25
42	Richard Wood	3.00	1.50	.90
43	George Yarno	3.00	2.25	1.25
44	Garo Yepremian	6.00	3.00	1.75
45	**Logo Card**	3.00	2.25	1.25
46	**Team Photo**	5.00	2.50	1.50
47	Hugh Culverhouse (OWN)	3.00	1.50	.90
48	John McKay (CO)	3.00	1.50	.90
49	**Mascot Capt. Crush**	3.00	2.25	1.25
50	**Cheerleaders: Swash-Buc-Lers**	3.00	1.50	.90
51	**Swash-Buc-Lers** (Buzz)	3.00	1.50	.90

		NM/M	NM	E
52	**Swash-Buc-Lers** (Check with me)	3.00	1.50	.90
53	**Swash-Buc-Lers** (Gap Two)	3.00	1.50	.90
54	**Swash-Buc-Lers** (Gas)	3.00	1.50	.90
55	**Swash-Buc-Lers** (Pass Protection)	3.00	1.50	.90
56	**Swash-Buc-Lers** (Post Pattern)	3.00	1.50	.90

1982 Buccaneers Shell

Measuring 1-1/2" x 2-1/2", the 32-card set boasts a full-bleed color photo on the front, with a white stripe at the bottom which includes the Buccaneers' helmet on the left, the player's name in the center and Shell logo on the right. The card backs are blank and unnumbered.

		NM/M	NM	E
	Complete Set (32):	30.00	22.00	12.00
	Common Player:	.50	.40	.20
1	Theo Bell	.75	.60	.30
2	Scot Brantley	.75	.60	.30
3	Cedric Brown	.50	.40	.20
4	Bill Capece	.50	.40	.20
5	Neal Colzie	.75	.60	.30
6	Mark Cotney	.50	.40	.20
7	Hugh Culverhouse	.75	.60	.30
8	Jeff Davis	.75	.60	.30
9	Jerry Eckwood	.75	.60	.30
10	Sean Farrell	.75	.60	.30
11	Jimmie Giles	1.00	.70	.40
12	Hugh Green	1.50	1.25	.60
13	Charley Hannah	.50	.40	.20
14	Andy Hawkins	.50	.40	.20
15	John Holt	.50	.40	.20
16	Kevin House	1.00	.70	.40
17	Cecil Johnson	.50	.40	.20
18	Gordon Jones	.50	.40	.20
19	David Logan	.75	.60	.30
20	John McKay	1.50	1.25	.60
21	James Owens	1.00	.70	.40
22	Greg Roberts	.50	.40	.20
23	Gene Sanders	.50	.40	.20
24	Lee Roy Selmon	4.00	3.00	1.50
25	Ray Snell	.50	.40	.20
26	Larry Swider	.50	.40	.20
27	Norris Thomas	.50	.40	.20
28	Mike Washington	.50	.40	.20
29	James Wilder	1.50	1.25	.60
30	Doug Williams	2.00	1.50	.80
31	Steve Wilson	.50	.40	.20
32	Richard Wood	1.00	.70	.40

1984 Buccaneers Police

Measuring 2-5/8" x 4-1/8", the 56-card set boasts a photo on the card front, with the player's name, position and bio on the bottom left. The Bucs' helmet is located in the lower right. The unnumbered card backs have "Kids and Kops tips from the Buccaneers" at the top, with a football term definition and safety tip below it. The various sponsors are listed at the bottom.

		NM/M	NM	E
	Complete Set (56):	65.00	49.00	26.00
	Common Player:	1.00	.70	.40
1	**Swash-Buc-Lers**	2.00	1.50	.80
2	Hugh Culverhouse (OWN)	1.75	1.25	.70
3	John McKay (25 Years as Head Coach)	1.50	1.25	.60
4	John McKay (CO)	1.50	1.25	.60
5	**Defensive Action**	1.25	.90	.50
6	Fred Acorn	1.00	.70	.40
7	Obed Ariri	1.00	.70	.40
8	Adger Armstrong	1.00	.70	.40
9	Jerry Bell	1.00	.70	.40
10	Theo Bell	2.50	2.00	1.00
11	Byron Braggs	1.00	.70	.40
12	Scot Brantley	1.00	.70	.40
13	Cedric Brown	1.00	.70	.40
14	Keith Browner	1.50	1.25	.60
15	John Cannon	1.00	.70	.40
16	Jay Carroll	1.00	.70	.40
17	Gerald Carter	1.00	.70	.40
18	Melvin Carter	1.00	.70	.40
19	Jeremiah Castille	1.50	1.25	.60
20	Mark Cotney	1.00	.70	.40
21	Steve Courson	1.50	1.25	.60
22	Jeff Davis	1.00	.70	.40
23	Steve DeBerg	5.00	3.75	2.00
24	Sean Farrell	1.75	1.25	.70
25	Frank Garcia	1.00	.70	.40
26	Jimmie Giles	2.50	2.00	1.00
27	Hugh Green	3.00	2.25	1.25
28	Hugh Green (1A)	1.50	1.25	.60
29	Randy Grimes	1.00	.70	.40
30	Ron Heller	1.50	1.25	.60
31	John Holt	1.00	.70	.40

		NM/M	NM	E
32	Kevin House	2.00	1.50	.80
33	Noah Jackson	2.00	1.50	.80
34	Cecil Johnson	1.00	.70	.40
35	Ken Kaplan	1.00	.70	.40
36	Blair Kiel	1.50	1.25	.60
37	David Logan	1.50	1.25	.60
38	Brison Manor	1.00	.70	.40
39	Michael Morton	1.00	.70	.40
40	James Owens	1.00	.70	.40
41	Beasley Reece	1.50	1.25	.60
42	Gene Sanders	1.00	.70	.40
43	Lee Roy Selmon	5.00	3.75	2.00
44	Lee Roy Selmon (1A)	3.00	2.25	1.25
45	Danny Spradlin	1.00	.70	.40
46	Kelly Thomas	1.00	.70	.40
47	Norris Thomas	1.00	.70	.40
48	Jack Thompson	1.50	1.25	.60
49	Perry Tuttle	1.00	.70	.40
50	Chris Washington	1.00	.70	.40
51	Mike Washington	1.00	.70	.40
52	James Wilder	2.50	2.00	1.00
53	James Wilder (1A)	1.25	.90	.50
54	Steve Wilson	1.00	.70	.40
44	Mark White	1.00	.70	.40
56	Richard Wood	1.50	1.25	.60

1989 Buccaneers Police

Measuring 2-5/8" x 4-1/8", the 10-card set showcases a color action photo at the top, with the player's name, position and team, along with the Bucs' helmet printed inside a box under the photo. The card backs have the Polk County Sheriff's name at the top, with the card number underneath. Located in the center of the card back are the player's name, number, bio, highlights and stats. A safety tip and IMC Fertilizer are listed at the bottom of the card back.

		NM/M	NM	E
	Complete Set (10):	20.00	15.00	8.00
	Common Player:	1.50	1.25	.60
1	Vinny Testaverde	6.00	4.50	2.50
2	Mark Carrier (WR)	4.00	3.00	1.50
3	Randy Grimes	1.50	1.25	.60
4	Paul Gruber	3.00	2.25	1.25
5	Ron Hall	2.00	1.50	.80
6	William Howard	1.50	1.25	.60
7	Curt Jarvis	1.50	1.25	.60
8	Ervin Randle	1.50	1.25	.60
9	Ricky Reynolds	1.50	1.25	.60
10	Rob Taylor	1.50	1.25	.60

1976 Buckmans Discs

Measuring 3-3/8 inches in diameter, the 20-disc set features a black-and-white headshot of the player on the front, with four stars printed at the top. The player's name is printed on the right side of the photo, with his team name on the left. His position is printed under the photo. A colored border surrounds the disc, except where the stars are at the top. Printed inside the border are the player's bio and "National Football League Players 1976." The unnumbered disc backs have "A collectors and traders item" at the top, with Buckmans and its address and phone number underneath.

		NM	E	VG
	Complete Set (20):	45.00	34.00	18.00
	Common Player:	.50	.40	.20
1	Otis Armstrong	1.00	.50	.30
2	Steve Bartkowski	1.00	.50	.30
3	Terry Bradshaw	10.00	5.00	3.00
4	Doug Buffone	.50	.40	.20
5	Wally Chambers	.50	.40	.20
6	Chuck Foreman	1.00	.50	.30
7	Roman Gabriel	1.00	.50	.30
8	Mel Gray	1.00	.50	.30
9	Franco Harris	7.00	3.50	2.00
10	James Harris	.50	.25	.15
11	Jim Hart	1.00	.50	.30
12	Gary Huff	.50	.40	.20
13	Billy Kilmer	1.00	.50	.30
14	Terry Metcalf	1.00	.50	.30
15	Jim Otis	.50	.40	.20
16	Jim Plunkett	1.50	.70	.45
17	Greg Pruitt	.50	.25	.15
18	Roger Staubach	10.00	5.00	3.00
19	Jan Stenerud	1.00	.50	.30
20	Roger Wehrli	.50	.40	.20

1984 BYU All-Time Greats

		NM/M	NM	E
	Complete Set (15):	18.00	13.50	7.25
	Common Player:	.50	.40	.20
1	Steve Young	10.00	7.50	4.00
2	Eldon Fortie	.50	.40	.20
3	Bart Oates	1.50	1.25	.60
4	Pete Van Valkenburg	.60	.45	.25
5	Mike Mees	.50	.40	.20
6	Wayne Baker	.50	.40	.20

		NM/M	NM	E
7	Gordon Gravelle	.60	.45	.25
8	Gordon Hudson	.60	.45	.25
9	Kurt Gunther	.50	.40	.20
10	Todd Shell	.60	.45	.25
11	Chris Farasopoulos	1.00	.70	.40
12	Paul Howard	.50	.40	.20
13	Dave Atkinson	.50	.40	.20
14	Paul Linford	.50	.40	.20
15	Phil Odle	.60	.45	.25

1984-85 BYU National Champions

		NM/M	NM	E
	Complete Set (15):	25.00	18.50	10.00
	Common Player:	1.50	1.25	.60
1	Mark Allen	1.50	1.25	.60
2	Adam Hysbert	1.50	1.25	.60
3	Larry Hamilton	1.50	1.25	.60
4	Jim Hermann	1.50	1.25	.60
5	Kyle Morrell	2.00	1.50	.80
6	Lee Johnson	1.50	1.25	.60
7	David Mills	1.50	1.25	.60
8	Garrick Wright, Matich Wright, Anae Wright, Louis Wong	3.00	2.25	1.25
9	Jim Hermann, Larry Hamilton	2.00	1.50	.80
10	Louis Wong	1.50	1.25	.60
11	Bosco in Holiday Bowl (Robbie Bosco)	5.00	3.75	2.00
12	**BYU Cougar Stadium**	1.50	1.25	.60
13	**UPI Final Top 20**	1.50	1.25	.60
14	**BYU National Championship Roster**	1.50	1.25	.60
15	**Schedule and Scores For 1984**	1.50	1.25	.60

1990 BYU Safety

		NM/M	NM	E
	Complete Set (12):	15.00	11.00	6.00
	Common Player:	1.00	.70	.40
1	Rocky Beigel	1.00	.70	.40
2	Matt Bellini	1.50	1.25	.60
3	Tony Crutchfield	1.00	.70	.40
4	Ty Detmer	6.00	4.50	2.50
5	Norm Dixon	1.00	.70	.40
6	Earl Kauffman	1.00	.70	.40
7	Rich Kaufusi	1.50	1.25	.60
8	Bryan May	1.00	.70	.40
9	Brent Nyberg	1.00	.70	.40
10	Chris Smith	1.50	1.25	.60
11	Mark Smith	1.00	.70	.40
12	Robert Stephens	1.00	.70	.40

1991 BYU Safety

		NM/M	NM	E
	Complete Set (16):	10.00	7.50	4.00
	Common Player:	.75	.60	.30
1	Josh Arnold	.75	.60	.30
2	Rocky Beigel	.75	.60	.30
3	Scott Charlton	.75	.60	.30
4	Tony Crutchfield	.75	.60	.30
5	Ty Detmer	3.00	2.25	1.25
6	LaVell Edwards (CO)	1.50	1.25	.60
7	Scott Giles	.75	.60	.30
8	Derwin Gray	1.00	.70	.40
9	Shad Hansen	.75	.60	.30
10	Brad Hunter	.75	.60	.30
11	Earl Kauffman	.75	.60	.30
12	Jared Leavitt	.75	.60	.30
13	Micah Matsuzaki	.75	.60	.30
14	Bryan May	.75	.60	.30
15	Peter Tuipulotu	.75	.60	.30
16	Matt Zundel	.75	.60	.30

C

1988 California Smokey

		NM/M	NM	E
	Complete Set (12):	12.00	9.00	4.75
	Common Player:	1.25	.90	.50
1	Rob Bimson	1.25	.90	.50
2	Joel Dickson	1.25	.90	.50
3	Robert DosRemedios	1.25	.90	.50
4	Mike Ford	1.25	.90	.50
5	Darryl Ingram	1.25	.90	.50
6	David Ortega	1.25	.90	.50

		NM/M	NM	E
7	Chris Richards	1.25	.90	.50
8	Bruce Snyder (CO)	1.50	1.25	.60
9	Troy Taylor	2.00	1.50	.80
10	Natu Tuatagaloa	2.00	1.50	.80
11	Majett Whiteside	1.25	.90	.50
12	Dave Zawatson	1.25	.90	.50

1989 California Smokey

		NM/M	NM	E
Complete Set (16):		12.00	9.00	4.75
Common Player:		1.00	.70	.40
1	John Hardy	1.00	.70	.40
2	Mike Ford	1.00	.70	.40
10	Robbie Keen	1.00	.70	.40
11	Troy Taylor	1.25	.90	.50
20	Dwayne Jones	1.00	.70	.40
21	Travis Oliver	1.00	.70	.40
34	Darrin Greer	1.00	.70	.40
40	David Ortega	1.00	.70	.40
41	Dan Slevin	1.00	.70	.40
52	Troy Auzenne	3.00	2.25	1.25
69	Tony Smith	1.00	.70	.40
80	Junior Tagaloa	1.00	.70	.40
83	Michael Smith	1.00	.70	.40
95	DeWayne Odom	1.00	.70	.40
99	Joel Dickson	1.00	.70	.40
NNO	Bruce Snyder (CO)	1.25	.90	.50

1990 California Smokey

		NM/M	NM	E
Complete Set (16):		10.00	7.50	4.00
Common Player:		.75	.60	.30
1	Troy Auzenne (52)	2.00	1.50	.80
2	John Belli (61)	.75	.60	.30
3	Joel Dickson (99)	.75	.60	.30
4	Ron English (42)	.75	.60	.30
5	Rhett Hall (57)	2.00	1.50	.80
6	John Hardy (1)	.75	.60	.30
7	Robbie Keen (10)	.75	.60	.30
8	DeWayne Odom (95)	.75	.60	.30
9	Mike Pawlawski (9)	1.50	1.25	.60
10	Castle Redmond (37)	.75	.60	.30
11	James Richards (64)	.75	.60	.30
12	Ernie Rogers (68)	.75	.60	.30
13	Bruce Snyder (CO)	1.00	.70	.40
14	Brian Treggs (3)	1.00	.70	.40
15	Anthony Wallace (6)	.75	.60	.30
16	Greg Zomalt (28)	.75	.60	.30

1991 California Smokey

		NM/M	NM	E
Complete Set (16):		14.00	10.50	5.50
Common Player:		.75	.60	.30
1	Troy Auzenne	1.50	1.25	.60
2	Chris Cannon	.75	.60	.30
3	Cornell Collier	.75	.60	.30
4	Sean Dawkins	3.00	2.25	1.25
5	Steve Gordon	.75	.60	.30
6	Mike Pawlawski	1.25	.90	.50
7	Bruce Snyder (CO)	1.00	.70	.40
8	Todd Steussie	2.00	1.50	.80
9	Mack Travis	.75	.60	.30
10	Brian Treggs	1.00	.70	.40
11	Russell White	2.00	1.50	.80
12	Jason Wilborn	.75	.60	.30
13	David Wilson	.75	.60	.30
14	Brent Woodall	.75	.60	.30
15	Eric Zomalt	1.25	.90	.50
16	Greg Zomalt	.75	.60	.30

1960 Cardinals Mayrose Franks

Measuring 2-1/2" x 3-1/2", the 11-card set showcases a black-and-white photo printed over a red background. A box in the upper left includes the Cardinals' logo and card number. The player's name, position and bio are printed under the photo. The card backs describe the Mayrose Franks football contest. The cards are coated in plastic because they were inserted in hot dog and bacon packages. The cards feature rounded corners.

		NM	E	VG
Complete Set (11):		100.00	75.00	40.00
Common Player:		8.00	6.00	3.25
1	Don Gillis	8.00	6.00	3.25
2	Frank Fuller	8.00	6.00	3.25
3	George Izo	10.00	5.00	3.00
4	Woodley Lewis	8.00	6.00	3.25
5	King Hill	12.00	6.00	3.50
6	John David Crow	16.00	8.00	4.75
7	Bill Stacy	8.00	6.00	3.25
8	Ted Bates	8.00	6.00	3.25
9	Mike McGee	8.00	6.00	3.25
10	Bobby Joe Conrad	12.00	6.00	3.50
11	Ken Panfil	8.00	6.00	3.25

1961 Cardinals Jay Publishing

Measuring 5" x 7", the 12-card set spotlights posed black-and-white photos on the front, while the backs were blank and unnumbered. The set was sold in 12-card packs for 25 cents in 1961.

		NM	E	VG
Complete Set (12):		50.00	25.00	15.00
Common Player:		5.00	2.50	1.50
1	Joe Childress	5.00	2.50	1.50
2	Sam Etcheverry	5.00	2.50	1.50
3	Ed Henke	5.00	2.50	1.50
4	Jimmy Hill	5.00	2.50	1.50
5	Bill Koman	5.00	2.50	1.50
6	Roland McDole	5.00	2.50	1.50
7	Mike McGee	5.00	2.50	1.50
8	Dale Meinert	5.00	2.50	1.50
9	Jerry Norton	5.00	2.50	1.50
10	Sonny Randle	5.00	2.50	1.50
11	Joe Robb	5.00	2.50	1.50
12	Billy Stacy	5.00	2.50	1.50

1965 Cardinals Big Red Biographies

Half-gallon milk cartons from St. Louis' Adams Dairy featured these biographies on side panels. When cut from the carton, the panels measure 3-1/16" x 5-9/16". The panels spotlight "Big Red Biographies" in the upper left, with the Cardinals' logo in the upper right. The player's photo is printed on the left center, with his name, number, position and bio listed on the right. His highlights are printed under the photo. "Enjoy Cardinal Football get your tickets now!" and the team's address are printed at the bottom. The card backs are blank.

		NM	E	VG
Complete Set (17):		1,000	500.00	300.00
Common Player:		50.00	37.00	20.00
1	Monk Bailey	50.00	37.00	20.00
2	Jim Bakken	100.00	50.00	30.00
3	Jim Burson	50.00	37.00	20.00
4	Willis Crenshaw	50.00	37.00	20.00
5	Bob DeMarco	50.00	37.00	20.00
6	Pat Fischer	100.00	50.00	30.00
7	Billy Gambrell	50.00	37.00	20.00
8	Ken Gray	75.00	37.00	22.00
9	Irv Goode	50.00	37.00	20.00
10	Mike Melinkovich	50.00	37.00	20.00
11	Bob Reynolds	50.00	37.00	20.00
12	Marion Rushing	50.00	37.00	20.00
13	Carl Silvestri	50.00	37.00	20.00
14	Dave Simmons	50.00	37.00	20.00
15	Jackie Smith	150.00	75.00	45.00
16	Bill (Thunder) Thornton	50.00	37.00	20.00
17	Herschel Turner	50.00	37.00	20.00

1965 Cardinals Team Issue

Measuring 7-3/8" x 9-3/8", the 10-card set is anchored by a black-and-white photo inside a white border on the front. The player's name, position and team are listed in the white border at the bottom. The unnumbered backs are also blank.

		NM	E	VG
Complete Set (10):		40.00	30.00	16.00
Common Player:		4.00	3.00	1.50
1	Don Brumm	4.00	2.00	1.25
2	Bobby Joe Conrad	5.00	2.50	1.50
3	Bob DeMarco	4.00	2.00	1.25
4	Charley Johnson	7.00	3.50	2.00
5	Ernie McMillan	5.00	2.50	1.50
6	Dale Meinert	4.00	2.00	1.25
7	Luke Owens	4.00	2.00	1.25
8	Sonny Randle	4.00	2.00	1.25
9	Joe Robb	4.00	2.00	1.25
10	Jerry Stovall	4.00	2.00	1.25

1980 Cardinals Police

Measuring 2-5/8" x 4-1/8", the 15-card set showcases the player's name, jersey number, position, bio and team name under the photo. The Cardinals' helmet is printed in the lower left. The card backs feature Cardinal Tips inside a box, with the Cards' helmet at the top of it. The various sponsors are listed, along with their logos, at the bottom of the unnumbered card backs.

		NM	E	VG
Complete Set (15):		16.00	12.00	6.50
Common Player:		.75	.40	.25
17	Jim Hart	2.00	1.00	.60
22	Roger Wehrli	1.00	.50	.30
24	Wayne Morris	.75	.40	.25
32	Ottis Anderson	2.00	1.00	.60
33	Theotis Brown	.75	.40	.25
37	Kevin Green	.75	.40	.25
55	Eric Williams	.75	.40	.25
56	Tim Kearney	.75	.40	.25

		NM	E	VG
59	Calvin Favron	.75	.40	.25
68	Terry Stieve	.75	.40	.25
72	Dan Dierdorf	2.50	1.25	.70
73	Mike Dawson	.75	.40	.25
82	Bob Pollard	.75	.40	.25
83	Pat Tilley	1.50	.70	.45
85	Mel Gray	2.00	1.00	.60

1988 Cardinals Holsum

The standard sized 12-card set showcases the Holsum logo in the upper left, with "1988 Annual Collectors' Edition" in the upper right. The color headshot anchors the front, with the player's name and team listed in a box at the bottom. The backs have the player's facsimile autograph at the top, along with his jersey number, bio and card number. His stats are listed in the center. The NFLPA, MSA and Holsum logos are printed at the bottom of the card backs.

		NM/M	NM	E
Complete Set (12):		50.00	37.00	20.00
Common Player:		4.00	3.00	1.50
1	Roy Green	7.00	5.25	2.75
2	Stump Mitchell	6.00	4.50	2.50
3	J.T. Smith	5.00	3.75	2.00
4	E.J. Junior	5.00	3.75	2.00
5	Cedric Mack	4.00	3.00	1.50
6	Curtis Greer	4.00	3.00	1.50
7	Lonnie Young	4.00	3.00	1.50
8	David Galloway	4.00	3.00	1.50
9	Luis Sharpe	4.00	3.00	1.50
10	Leonard Smith	4.00	3.00	1.50
11	Ron Wolfley	4.00	3.00	1.50
12	Earl Ferrell	4.00	3.00	1.50

1989 Cardinals Holsum

The standard-sized 16-card set showcases the Holsum logo in the upper left, with "1989 Annual Collectors' Edition" in the upper right. The player's name and team are printed inside a stripe underneath the photo. The card backs have the player's name, jersey number, card number, position and bio at the top. His stats are listed in the center, while the NFLPA logo is in the lower left.

		NM/M	NM	E
Complete Set (16):		6.00	4.50	2.50
Common Player:		.25	.20	.10
1	Roy Green	1.00	.70	.40
2	J.T. Smith	.50	.40	.20
3	Neil Lomax	1.00	.70	.40
4	Stump Mitchell	.50	.40	.20
5	Vai Sikahema	.25	.20	.10
6	Lonnie Young	.25	.20	.10
7	Robert Awalt	.25	.20	.10
8	Cedric Mack	.25	.20	.10
9	Earl Ferrell	.25	.20	.10
10	Ron Wolfley	.25	.20	.10
11	Bob Clasby	.25	.20	.10
12	Luis Sharpe	.25	.20	.10
13	Steve Alvord	.25	.20	.10
14	David Galloway	.25	.20	.10
15	Freddie Joe Nunn	.25	.20	.10
16	Niko Noga	.25	.20	.10

1989 Cardinals Police

Measuring 2-5/8" x 4-3/16", the 15-card set has a photo bordered in white. The player's name and position are printed under the photo on the left, with his jersey number on the right. The bottom of the card front features the Phoenix Cardinals' logo. The unnumbered card backs feature the Cardinals' logo at the top, with his jersey number, name, position, bio and career highlights listed. The Cardinals rule is printed inside a box. The KTSP-TV and Louis Rich logos also appear at the bottom. The cards are listed here by uniform number. Two cards were distributed each week. Overall, 100,000 of each card was produced.

		NM/M	NM	E
Complete Set (15):		25.00	18.50	10.00
Common Player:		1.00	.70	.40
5	Gary Hogeboom	1.25	.90	.50
24	Ron Wolfley	1.00	.70	.40
30	Stump Mitchell	1.25	.90	.50
31	Earl Ferrell	1.00	.70	.40
36	Vai Sikahema	1.00	.70	.40
43	Lonnie Young	1.00	.70	.40
46	Tim McDonald	1.50	1.25	.60
65	David Galloway	1.00	.70	.40
67	Luis Sharpe	1.00	.70	.40
70	Derek Kennard (SP)	10.00	7.50	4.00
79	Bob Clasby	1.00	.70	.40
80	Robert Awalt	1.00	.70	.40
81	Roy Green	1.50	1.25	.60
84	J.T. Smith	1.25	.90	.50
85	Jay Novacek	5.00	3.75	2.00

1990 Cardinals Police

Measuring 2-5/8" x 4-1/4", the 16-card set is bordered in maroon, with the Cardinals' logo in the upper left and NFL shield in upper right. Underneath the photo are the player's name, position and jersey number. The unnumbered card backs feature the Phoenix Cardinals' logo at the top, with the player's number, name, position, bio highlights underneath. The center of the card back has the Cardinal Rule in a box. KTSP, McGruff the Crime Dog and Louis Rich logos are printed at the bottom.

		NM/M	NM	E
Complete Set (16):		10.00	7.50	4.00
Common Player:		.25	.20	.10
1	Anthony Bell	.25	.20	.10
2	Joe Bugel (CO)	.50	.40	.20
3	Rich Camarillo	.25	.20	.10
4	Roy Green	1.25	.90	.50
5	Ken Harvey	1.00	.70	.40
6	Eric Hill	1.25	.90	.50
7	Tim McDonald	.50	.40	.20
8	Tootie Robbins	.25	.20	.10
9	Timm Rosenbach	.75	.60	.30
10	Luis Sharpe	.50	.40	.20
11	Vai Sikahema	.50	.40	.20
12	J.T. Smith	.75	.60	.30
13	Lance Smith	.25	.20	.10
14	Jim Wahler	.25	.20	.10
15	Ron Wolfley	.25	.20	.10
16	Lonnie Young	.25	.20	.10

1989 CBS Television Announcers

Measuring 2-3/4" x 3-7/8", this 10-card set showcases the 1989 CBS NFL announcers. The card fronts spotlight a color action shot from the announcer's pro career. The photo is bordered in orange and placed over a green and white football field. "Going the extra yard" is printed in red at the top. "NFL on CBS" is located in the bottom right. The horizontal card backs feature a black-and-white head shot of the announcer, with his bio and highlights bordered in red. Approximately 500 sets, which were divided into two five-card series, were given to CBS affiliates.

		NM/M	NM	E
Complete Set (10):		250.00	185.00	100.00
Common Player:		10.00	7.50	4.00
1	Terry Bradshaw	50.00	37.00	20.00
2	Dick Butkus	45.00	34.00	18.00
3	Irv Cross	10.00	7.50	4.00
4	Dan Fouts	25.00	18.50	10.00
5	Pat Summerall	15.00	11.00	6.00
6	Gary Fencik	10.00	7.50	4.00
7	Dan Jiggetts	10.00	7.50	4.00
8	John Madden	45.00	34.00	18.00
9	Ken Stabler	35.00	26.00	14.00
10	Hank Stram	15.00	11.00	6.00
---	Wrappers	.45	.35	.20

1961 Chargers Golden Tulip

The 22-card, 2" x 3" set was found in bags of Golden Tulip potato chips. The cards featured top players from the San Diego Chargers in black and white with brief bio information also on the card fronts. The back explains how to upgrade to an 8" x 10" photo and win tickets to a Chargers home game. The set was also sponsored by XETV, an independent television station in San Diego.

		NM	E	VG
Complete Set (22):		1,500	1,100	600.00
Common Player:		40.00	30.00	16.00
1	Ron Botchan	40.00	30.00	16.00
2	Howard Clark	40.00	30.00	16.00
3	Fred Cole	40.00	30.00	16.00
4	Sam DeLuca	40.00	30.00	16.00
5	Orlando Ferrante	40.00	30.00	16.00
6	Charlie Flowers	40.00	30.00	16.00
7	Dick Harris	40.00	20.00	12.00
8	Emil Karas	40.00	30.00	16.00
9	Jack Kemp	550.00	275.00	165.00
10	Dave Kocourek	40.00	20.00	12.00
11	Bob Laraba	40.00	30.00	16.00
12	Paul Lowe	60.00	30.00	18.00
13	Paul Maguire	70.00	35.00	21.00
14	Charlie McNeil	40.00	20.00	12.00
15	Ron Mix	100.00	50.00	30.00
16	Ron Nery	40.00	30.00	16.00
17	Don Norton	40.00	30.00	16.00
18	Volney Peters	40.00	30.00	16.00
19	Don Rogers	40.00	30.00	16.00
20	Maury Schleicher	40.00	30.00	16.00
21	Ernie Wright	40.00	20.00	12.00
22	Bob Zeman	40.00	30.00	16.00

1962 Chargers Union Oil

The 14-card, 6" x 8" set, sponsored by Union 76, features black and white player sketches by the artist, "Patrick." The card backs include a player bio and the Union 76 logo.

		NM	E	VG
Complete Set (14):		450.00	340.00	180.00
Common Player:		8.00	6.00	3.25
1	Chuck Allen	10.00	5.00	3.00
2	Lance Alworth	100.00	50.00	30.00
3	John Hadl	30.00	15.00	9.00
4	Dick Harris	10.00	5.00	3.00
5	Bill Hudson	8.00	6.00	3.25
6	Jack Kemp	225.00	112.00	67.00
7	Dave Kocourek	10.00	5.00	3.00
8	Ernie Ladd	25.00	12.50	7.50
9	Keith Lincoln	18.00	9.00	5.50
10	Paul Lowe	18.00	9.00	5.50
11	Charlie McNeil	10.00	5.00	3.00
12	Ron Mix	25.00	12.50	7.50
13	Ron Nery	8.00	6.00	3.25
14	Team Photo	25.00	12.50	7.50

1966 Chargers White Border

The 50-card, 5-1/2" x 8-1/2" set was issued by the team and features black and white headshots of top players, such as Lance Alworth, with facsimile autographs. With the exception of card No. 16 (George Gross), the card backs are blank.

		NM	E	VG
Complete Set (50):		225.00	167.00	90.00
Common Player:		3.00	1.50	.90
1	Chuck Allen	5.00	2.50	1.50
2	James Allison	3.00	1.50	.90
3	Lance Alworth	30.00	15.00	9.00
4	Tom Bass	3.00	1.50	.90
5	Joe Beauchamp	3.00	1.50	.90
6	Frank Buncom	5.00	2.50	1.50
7	Richard Degen	3.00	1.50	.90
8	Steve DeLong	5.00	2.50	1.50
9	Les Duncan	3.00	1.50	.90
10	John Farris	3.00	1.50	.90
11	Gene Foster	3.00	1.50	.90
12	Willie Frazier	5.00	2.50	1.50
13	Gary Garrison	5.00	2.50	1.50
14	Sid Gillman (CO)	10.00	5.00	3.00
15	Kenny Graham	3.00	1.50	.90
16	George Gross	3.00	1.50	.90
17	Sam Gruineisen	3.00	1.50	.90
18	Walt Hackett (CO)	3.00	1.50	.90
19	John Hadl	15.00	7.50	4.50
20	Dick Harris	5.00	2.50	1.50
21	Dan Henning	10.00	5.00	3.00
22	Bob Horton	3.00	1.50	.90
23	Harry Johnston (CO)	3.00	1.50	.90
24	Howard Kindig	3.00	1.50	.90
25	Keith Lincoln	5.00	2.50	1.50
26	Paul Lowe	3.00	1.50	.90
27	Jacque MacKinnon	3.00	1.50	.90
28	Joseph Madro (CO)	3.00	1.50	.90
29	Ed Mitchell	3.00	1.50	.90
30	Bob Mitinger	3.00	1.50	.90
31	Ron Mix	10.00	5.00	3.00
32	Fred Moore	3.00	1.50	.90
33	Don Norton	3.00	1.50	.90
34	Terry Owen	5.00	2.50	1.50
35	Bob Petrich	3.00	1.50	.90
36	Dave Plump	3.00	1.50	.90
37	Rick Redman	3.00	1.50	.90
38	Houston Ridge	3.00	1.50	.90
39	Pat Shea	3.00	1.50	.90
40	Walt Sweeney	5.00	2.50	1.50
41	Sammy Taylor	3.00	1.50	.90
42	Steve Tensi	3.00	1.50	.90
43	Herb Travenio	3.00	1.50	.90
44	John Travis	3.00	1.50	.90
45	Dick Van Raaphorst	3.00	1.50	.90
46	Charlie Waller (CO)	3.00	1.50	.90
47	Bud Whitehead	3.00	1.50	.90
48	Nat Whitmyer	3.00	1.50	.90
49	Ernie Wright	3.00	1.50	.90
50	Bob Zeman	3.00	1.50	.90

1976 Chargers Dean's Photo

The 10-card, 5" x 8" set was sponsored by Dean's Photo Service and featured top Chargers players such as Dan Fouts and Joe Washington. The card fronts are black and white while the Chargers helmet in the lower left corner is in color. The backs are blank.

		NM	E	VG
Complete Set (10):		28.00	21.50	11.50
Common Player:		2.00	1.00	.60
1	Pat Currin	2.00	1.00	.60
2	Chris Fletcher	2.00	1.00	.60
3	Dan Fouts	12.00	6.00	3.50

4	Gary Garrison	2.00	1.00	.60
5	Louie Kelcher	3.00	1.50	.90
6	Joe Washington	3.00	1.50	.90
7	Russ Washington	2.00	1.00	.60
8	Doug Wilkerson	2.00	1.00	.60
9	Don Woods	2.00	1.00	.60
10	Schedule Card	2.00	1.00	.60

1981 Chargers Police

The 24-card, 2-5/8" x 4-1/8" set was sponsored by San Diego law enforcement, Pepsi and Kiwanis. The card fronts feature an action shot with the player's name and position, along with the Chargers team logo. The backs contain a law enforcement tip. The Fouts and Winslow cards have two versions with different safety tips. The cards are numbered by the player's jersey number.

		NM/M	NM	E
Complete Set (24):		50.00	37.00	20.00
Common Player:		1.00	.70	.40
6	Rolf Benirschke	2.00	1.50	.80
14A	Dan Fouts (After a team...)	14.00	10.50	5.50
14B	Dan Fouts (Once you've...)	7.00	5.25	2.75
18	Charlie Joiner	4.00	3.00	1.50
25	John Cappelletti	2.00	1.50	.80
28	Willie Buchanon	1.00	.70	.40
29	Mike Williams	1.00	.70	.40
43	Bob Gregor	1.00	.70	.40
44	Pete Shaw	1.00	.70	.40
46	Chuck Muncie	2.00	1.50	.80
51	Woodrow Lowe	1.00	.70	.40
57	Linden King	1.00	.70	.40
59	Cliff Thrift	1.00	.70	.40
62	Don Macek	1.00	.70	.40
63	Doug Wilkerson	1.00	.70	.40
66	Billy Shields	1.00	.70	.40
67	Ed White	1.00	.70	.40
68	Leroy Jones	1.00	.70	.40
70	Russ Washington	1.00	.70	.40
74	Louie Kelcher	1.00	.70	.40
79	Gary Johnson	1.00	.70	.40
80A	Kellen Winslow (Go all out...)	14.00	10.50	5.50
80B	Kellen Winslow (The length of ...)	7.00	5.25	2.75
NNO	Don Coryell (CO)	2.00	1.50	.80

1982 Chargers Police

The 16-card, 2-5/8" x 4-1/8" set is nearly identical in design with the 1981 Chargers Police set. The card fronts feature a Chargers player with his postion and San Diego helmet. The backs contain a law enforcement tip and are sponsored by San Diego law enforcement, Pepsi and Kiwanis.

		NM/M	NM	E
Complete Set (16):		45.00	34.00	18.00
Common Player:		2.00	1.50	.80
1	Rolf Benirschke	2.00	1.50	.80
2	James Brooks	4.00	3.00	1.50
3	Wes Chandler	5.00	3.75	2.00
4	Dan Fouts	10.00	7.50	4.00
5	Tim Fox	2.00	1.50	.80
6	Gary Johnson	2.00	1.50	.80
7	Charlie Joiner	8.00	6.00	3.25
8	Louie Kelcher	2.00	1.50	.80
9	Linden King	2.00	1.50	.80
10	Bruce Laird	2.00	1.50	.80
11	David Lewis	2.00	1.50	.80
12	Don Macek	2.00	1.50	.80
13	Billy Shields	2.00	1.50	.80
14	Eric Sievers	2.00	1.50	.80
15	Russ Washington	2.00	1.50	.80
16	Kellen Winslow	10.00	7.50	4.00

1985 Chargers Kodak

The 15-card, 5-1/2" x 8-1/2" set, sponsored by Kodak, features color action shots and San Diego helmet in the lower left corner. The backs contain bio information.

		NM/M	NM	E
Complete Set (15):		40.00	30.00	16.00
Common Player:		2.00	1.50	.80
1	Carlos Bradley	2.00	1.50	.80
2	Wes Chandler	6.00	4.50	2.50
3	Chuck Ehin	2.00	1.50	.80
4	Mike Green	2.00	1.50	.80
5	Pete Holohan	2.00	1.50	.80
6	Lionel James	2.00	1.50	.80
7	Charlie Joiner	12.00	9.00	4.75
8	Woodrow Lowe	2.00	1.50	.80
9	Dennis McKnight	2.00	1.50	.80
10	Miles McPherson	2.00	1.50	.80
11	Derrie Nelson	2.00	1.50	.80
12	Vince Osby	2.00	1.50	.80
13	Billy Ray Smith	2.00	1.50	.80
14	Danny Walters	2.00	1.50	.80
15	Ed White	2.00	1.50	.80

1986 Chargers Kodak

The 36-card, 5-1/2" x 8-1/2" set are similar to the 1985 Kodak Chargers cards, but have blank backs. The bio information is featured on the card fronts below the player's name and between the Chargers helmet and the Kodak logo.

		NM/M	NM	E
	Complete Set (36):	45.00	34.00	18.00
	Common Player:	1.00	.70	.40
1	Curtis Adams	1.00	.70	.40
2	Gary Anderson (RB)	3.00	2.25	1.25
3	Jesse Bendross	1.00	.70	.40
4	Gill Byrd	1.00	.70	.40
5	Sam Claphan	1.00	.70	.40
6	Don Coryell (CO)	2.00	1.50	.80
7	Jeffery Dale	1.00	.70	.40
8	Wayne Davis	1.00	.70	.40
9	Jerry Doerger	1.00	.70	.40
10	Chris Faulkner	1.00	.70	.40
11	Mark Fellows	1.00	.70	.40
12	Dan Fouts	8.00	6.00	3.25
13	Mike Guendling	1.00	.70	.40
14	John Hendy	1.00	.70	.40
15	Mark Hermann	1.00	.70	.40
16	Lionel James	1.00	.70	.40
17	Trumaine Johnson	1.00	.70	.40
18	David King	1.00	.70	.40
19	Linden King	1.00	.70	.40
20	Jim Lachey	2.00	1.50	.80
21	Don Macek	1.00	.70	.40
22	Buford McGee	1.00	.70	.40
23	Dennis McKnight	1.00	.70	.40
24	Ralf Mojsiejenko	1.00	.70	.40
25	Ron O'Bard	1.00	.70	.40
26	Fred Robinson	1.00	.70	.40
27	Eric Sievers	1.00	.70	.40
28	Tony Simmons	1.00	.70	.40
29	Billy Ray Smith	1.00	.70	.40
30	Lucious Smith	1.00	.70	.40
31	Alex G. Spanos (PRES)	1.00	.70	.40
32	Tim Spencer	1.00	.70	.40
33	Rich Umphrey	1.00	.70	.40
34	Ed White	1.00	.70	.40
35	Lee Williams	1.00	.70	.40
36	Earl Wilson	1.00	.70	.40

1987 Chargers Junior Coke Tickets

The 12-card, 1-7/8" x 4-1/4" set was issued to members of the Coca-Cola Junior Chargers. The cards are in the form of a ticket, which was exchanged by members for actual game tickets. The card fronts included a color action photo, and had imitation ticket information, such as section, row and seat number. The card backs contain a Chargers logo and a description of how to exchange the coupon for a real ticket.

		NM/M	NM	E
	Complete Set (12):	12.00	9.00	4.75
	Common Player:	1.00	.70	.40
1	Gary Anderson (RB)	1.50	1.25	.60
2	Rolf Benirschke	1.00	.70	.40
3	Wes Chandler	1.75	1.25	.70
4	Jeffery Dale	1.00	.70	.40
5	Dan Fouts	3.00	2.25	1.25
6	Pete Holohan	1.00	.70	.40
7	Lionel James	1.00	.70	.40
8	Don Macek	1.00	.70	.40
9	Dennis McKnight	1.00	.70	.40
10	Al Saunders (CO)	1.00	.70	.40
11	Billy Ray Smith	1.00	.70	.40
12	Kellen Winslow	3.00	2.25	1.25

1987 Chargers Police

The 21-card, 2-5/8" x 4-1/8" set, sponsored by the Chargers, Oscar Meyer and San Diego law enforcement, features top players from the 1987 Chargers squad. Even though the cards are numbered, there was no card No. 13 issued and card Nos. 3 and 17 were pulled during distribution. The card fronts feature an action shot and bio information while the backs have a brief player description with a safety tip.

		NM/M	NM	E
	Complete Set (22):	20.00	15.00	8.00
	Common Player:	.75	.60	.30
1	Alex G. Spanos (OWN)	.75	.60	.30
2	Gary Anderson (RB)	1.00	.70	.40
3	Rolf Benirschke (SP)	5.00	3.75	2.00
4	Gill Byrd	.75	.60	.30
5	Wes Chandler	1.50	1.25	.60
6	Sam Claphan	.75	.60	.30
7	Jeffery Dale	.75	.60	.30
8	Pete Holohan	.75	.60	.30
9	Lionel James	.75	.60	.30
10	Jim Lachey	.75	.60	.30
11	Woodrow Lowe	.75	.60	.30
12	Don Macek	.75	.60	.30

14	Dan Fouts	3.50	2.75	1.50
15	Eric Sievers	.75	.60	.30
16	Billy Ray Smith	.75	.60	.30
17	Danny Walters (SP)	4.00	3.00	1.50
18	Lee Williams	.75	.60	.30
19	Kellen Winslow	2.50	2.00	1.00
20	Al Saunders (CO)	.75	.60	.30
21	Dennis McKnight	.75	.60	.30
22	Chip Banks	.75	.60	.30

1987 Chargers Smokey

The 48-card, 5-1/2" x 8-1/2" sets were issued by the California Forestry Department and fronted color action shots. The card backs contain a safety tip cartoon with Smokey The Bear. Coach Don Coryell's card was pulled after the initial distribution after he was replaced. Also, the cards of Donald Brown, Mike Douglas and Fred Robinson were pulled after they were cut.

		NM/M	NM	E
	Complete Set (48):	100.00	75.00	40.00
	Common Player:	1.00	.70	.40
	Common SP:	8.00	6.00	3.25
1	Curtis Adams	1.00	.70	.40
2	Ty Allert	1.00	.70	.40
3	Gary Anderson (RB)	2.50	2.00	1.00
4	Rolf Benirschke	2.00	1.50	.80
5	Thomas Benson	1.00	.70	.40
6	Donald Brown (SP)	8.00	6.00	3.25
7	Gill Byrd	1.50	1.25	.60
8	Wes Chandler	4.00	3.00	1.50
9	Sam Claphan	1.00	.70	.40
10	Don Coryell (CO)(SP)	10.00	7.50	4.00
11	Jeffery Dale	1.00	.70	.40
12	Wayne Davis	1.00	.70	.40
13	Mike Douglass (SP)	8.00	6.00	3.25
14	Chuck Ehin	1.00	.70	.40
15	James Fitzpatrick	1.00	.70	.40
16	Tom Flick	1.00	.70	.40
17	Dan Fouts	12.00	9.00	4.75
18	Dee Hardison	1.00	.70	.40
19	Andy Hawkins	1.00	.70	.40
20	John Hendy	1.00	.70	.40
21	Mark Hermann	1.00	.70	.40
22	Pete Holohan	1.00	.70	.40
23	Lionel James	1.50	1.25	.60
24	Trumaine Johnson	1.00	.70	.40
25	Charlie Joiner	8.00	6.00	3.25
26	Gary Kowalski	1.00	.70	.40
27	Jim Lachey	1.50	1.25	.60
28	Jim Leonard	1.00	.70	.40
29	Woodrow Lowe	1.00	.70	.40
30	Don Macek	1.00	.70	.40
31	Buford McGee	1.00	.70	.40
32	Dennis McKnight	1.00	.70	.40
33	Ralf Mojsiejenko	1.00	.70	.40
34	Derrie Nelson	1.00	.70	.40
35	Leslie O'Neal	5.00	3.75	2.00
36	Gary Plummer	1.50	1.25	.60
37	Fred Robinson (SP)	8.00	6.00	3.25
38	Eric Sievers	1.00	.70	.40
39	Billy Ray Smith	1.50	1.25	.60
40	Tim Spencer	1.50	1.25	.60
41	Kenny Taylor	1.00	.70	.40
42	Terry Unrein	1.00	.70	.40
43	Jeff Walker	1.00	.70	.40
44	Danny Walters	1.00	.70	.40
45	Lee Williams	1.50	1.25	.60
46	Earl Wilson	1.00	.70	.40
47	Kellen Winslow	8.00	6.00	3.25
48	Kevin Wyatt	1.00	.70	.40

1988 Chargers Police

The 12-card, 2-5/8" x 4" set features white and blue borders with color action shots. The card backs have career highlights and safety tips.

		NM/M	NM	E
	Complete Set (12):	12.00	9.00	4.75
	Common Player:	.50	.40	.20
1	Gary Anderson (RB)	.75	.60	.30
2	Rod Bernstine	1.00	.70	.40
3	Gill Byrd	.75	.60	.30
4	Vencie Glenn	.75	.60	.30
5	Lionel James	.75	.60	.30
6	Babe Laufenberg	.75	.60	.30
7	Don Macek	.50	.40	.20
8	Mark Malone	1.00	.70	.40
9	Dennis McKnight	.50	.40	.20
10	Anthony Miller	5.00	3.75	2.00
11	Billy Ray Smith	.75	.60	.30
12	Lee Williams	.75	.60	.30

1988 Chargers Smokey

The 52-card, 5" x 8" set features color action shots on the card fronts and a forestry safety tip, along with a Smokey The Bear cartoon on the back. Two Alex Spanos cards exist, one stating incorrectly that he purchased the Chargers in 1987, and one stating the correct 1984. Also, 18 of the cards were short printed (Nos. 9, 23, 27, 36, 55, 56, 57, 74, 77, 78, 79, 81, 88, 89, 92, 96 and 98) as some of the players were cut, traded or put on injured reserve.

		NM/M	NM	E
	Complete Set (52):	45.00	34.00	18.00
	Common Player:	.50	.40	.20
2	Ralf Mojsiejenko	.50	.40	.20
9	Mark Hermann (SP)	1.50	1.25	.60
10	Vince Abbott	.50	.40	.20
13	Mark Vlasic	.50	.40	.20
14	Dan Fouts	4.00	3.00	1.50
20	Barry Redden	.50	.40	.20
22	Gill Byrd	.75	.60	.30
23	Danny Walters (SP)	1.50	1.25	.60
25	Vencie Glenn	.50	.40	.20
26	Lionel James	.75	.60	.30
27	Daniel Hunter (SP)	1.50	1.25	.60
34	Elvis Patterson	.50	.40	.20
36	Mike Davis (SP)	1.50	1.25	.60
40	Gary Anderson (RB)	.75	.60	.30
42	Curtis Adams	.50	.40	.20
43	Tim Spencer	.50	.40	.20
44	Martin Bayless	.50	.40	.20
50	Gary Plummer	.50	.40	.20
52	Jeff Jackson	.50	.40	.20
54	Billy Ray Smith	.50	.40	.20
55	Steve Busick (SP)	1.50	1.25	.60
56	Chip Banks (SP)	2.00	1.50	.80
57	Thomas Benson (SP)	1.50	1.25	.60
58	David Brandon	.50	.40	.20
60	Dennis McKnight	.50	.40	.20
61	Ken Dallafior	.50	.40	.20
62	Don Macek	.50	.40	.20
68	Gary Kowalski	.50	.40	.20
69	Les Miller	.50	.40	.20
70	James Fitzpatrick	.50	.40	.20
71	Mike Charles	.50	.40	.20
72	Karl Wilson	.50	.40	.20
74	Jim Lachey (SP)	2.00	1.50	.80
75	Joe Phillips	.50	.40	.20
76	Broderick Thompson	.50	.40	.20
77	Sam Claphan (SP)	1.50	1.25	.60
78	Chuck Ehin (SP)	1.50	1.25	.60
79	Curtis Rouse (SP)	1.50	1.25	.60
80	Kellen Winslow	4.00	3.00	1.50
81	Timmie Ware (SP)	1.50	1.25	.60
82	Rod Bernstine	.75	.60	.30
85	Eric Sievers	.50	.40	.20
86	Jamie Holland	.50	.40	.20
88	Pete Holohan (SP)	1.50	1.25	.60
89	Wes Chandler (SP)	4.00	3.00	1.50
92	Dee Hardison (SP)	1.50	1.25	.60
94	Randy Kirk	.50	.40	.20
96	Keith Baldwin (SP)	1.50	1.25	.60
98	Terry Unrein (SP)	1.50	1.25	.60
99	Lee Williams	.50	.40	.20
NNO	Al Saunders (CO)	.50	.40	.20
NNO	Alex G. Spanos (ERR SP Chairman of the Board) (Purchased team 1987)	4.00	3.00	1.50
NNO	Alex G. Spanos (COR Chairman of the Board) (Purchased team 1984)	.50	.40	.20

1989 Chargers Junior Ralph's Tickets

The 12-card, 1-7/8" x 3-5/8" set was delivered in a perforated sheet which has all 12 cards. The set was sponsored by Ralph's and XTRA and the backs of the cards had coupons to local attractions. The fronts have a color action shot with the coupon description.

		NM/M	NM	E
	Complete Set (12):	10.00	7.50	4.00
	Common Player:	.50	.40	.20
1	Gary Anderson (RB)	.75	.60	.30
2	Gill Byrd	.75	.60	.30
3	Quinn Early	1.50	1.25	.60
4	Vencie Glenn	.75	.60	.30
5	Jamie Holland	.50	.40	.20
6	Don Macek	.50	.40	.20
7	Dennis McKnight	.50	.40	.20
8	Anthony Miller	5.00	3.75	2.00
9	Ralf Mojsiejenko	.50	.40	.20
10	Leslie O'Neal	1.75	1.25	.70
11	Billy Ray Smith	.50	.40	.20
12	Lee Williams	.50	.40	.20

1989 Chargers Police

The 12-card, 2-5/8" x 4-3/16" set has white borders with color action shots while the backs have bio information, career highlights and safety messages and are sponsored by Louis Rich. The cards were distributed in two, six-card sheets on Oct. 22 and Nov. 5 at Chargers home games.

		NM/M	NM	E
Complete Set (12):		10.00	7.50	4.00
Common Player:		.50	.40	.20
1	Tim Spencer	.50	.40	.20
2	Vencie Glenn	.75	.60	.30
3	Gill Byrd	.75	.60	.30
4	Jim McMahon	1.50	1.25	.60
5	David Richards	.50	.40	.20
6	Don Macek	.50	.40	.20
7	Billy Ray Smith	.75	.60	.30
8	Gary Plummer	.75	.60	.30
9	Lee Williams	.50	.40	.20
10	Leslie O'Neal	1.00	.70	.40
11	Anthony Miller	3.00	2.25	1.25
12	Broderick Thompson	.50	.40	.20

1989 Chargers Smokey

The 48-card, 5" x 8" set has white borders with color action shots while the backs have bio information, career highlights and safety tips.

		NM/M	NM	E
Complete Set (48):		45.00	34.00	18.00
Common Player:		1.00	.70	.40
2	Ralf Mojsiejenko	1.00	.70	.40
6	Steve DeLine	1.00	.70	.40
10	Vince Abbott	1.00	.70	.40
13	Mark Vlasic	1.00	.70	.40
16	Mark Malone	1.00	.70	.40
20	Barry Redden	1.00	.70	.40
22	Gill Byrd	1.00	.70	.40
23	Roy Bennett	1.00	.70	.40
25	Vencie Glenn	1.00	.70	.40
26	Lionel James	1.00	.70	.40
30	Sam Seale	1.00	.70	.40
31	Leonard Coleman	1.00	.70	.40
34	Elvis Patterson	1.00	.70	.40
40	Gary Anderson (RB)	1.50	1.25	.60
42	Curtis Adams	1.00	.70	.40
43	Tim Spencer	1.00	.70	.40
44	Martin Bayless	1.00	.70	.40
48	Pat Miller	1.00	.70	.40
50	Gary Plummer	1.00	.70	.40
51	Cedric Figaro	1.00	.70	.40
52	Jeff Jackson	1.00	.70	.40
53	Chuck Faucette	1.00	.70	.40
54	Billy Ray Smith	1.00	.70	.40
57	Keith Browner	1.00	.70	.40
58	David Brandon	1.00	.70	.40
59	Ken Woodard	1.00	.70	.40
60	Dennis McKnight	1.00	.70	.40
61	Ken Dallafior	1.00	.70	.40
65	David Richards	1.00	.70	.40
66	Dan Rosado	1.00	.70	.40
69	Les Miller	1.00	.70	.40
70	James Fitzpatrick	1.00	.70	.40
71	Mike Charles	1.00	.70	.40
72	Karl Wilson	1.00	.70	.40
73	Darrick Brilz	1.00	.70	.40
75	Joe Phillips	1.00	.70	.40
76	Broderick Thompson	1.00	.70	.40
82	Rod Bernstine	1.50	1.25	.60
83	Anthony Miller	6.00	4.50	2.50
86	Jamie Holland	1.00	.70	.40
87	Quinn Early	1.50	1.25	.60
88	Arthur Cox	1.00	.70	.40
89	Darren Flutie	2.50	2.00	1.00
91	Leslie O'Neal	2.50	2.00	1.00
93	Tyrone Keys	1.00	.70	.40
95	Joe Campbell	1.00	.70	.40
97	George Hinkle	1.00	.70	.40
99	Lee Williams	1.00	.70	.40

1990 Chargers Police

The 12-card, 2-5/8" x 4-1/8" set was sponsored by Louis Rich Meats. The card fronts have blue borders with color action shots while the backs have player descriptions and bio information, along with a safety tip.

		NM/M	NM	E
Complete Set (12):		10.00	7.50	4.00
Common Player:		.75	.60	.30
1	Martin Bayless	.75	.60	.30
2	Marion Butts	1.25	.90	.50
3	Gill Byrd	.75	.60	.30
4	Burt Grossman	.75	.60	.30
5	Ronnie Harmon	1.00	.70	.40

6	Anthony Miller	3.00	2.25	1.25
7	Leslie O'Neal	1.50	1.25	.60
8	Joe Phillips	.75	.60	.30
9	Gary Plummer	.75	.60	.30
10	Billy Ray Smith	.75	.60	.30
11	Billy Joe Tolliver	1.00	.70	.40
12	Lee Williams	.75	.60	.30

1990 Chargers Smokey

The 36-card, 5" x 8" set was similar to the 1989 set with a fire safety cartoon and brief bio information on the back.

		NM/M	NM	E
Complete Set (36):		30.00	22.00	12.00
Common Player:		.75	.60	.30
11	Billy Joe Tolliver	1.25	.90	.50
13	Mark Vlasic	.75	.60	.30
15	David Archer	1.50	1.25	.60
20	Darrin Nelson	.75	.60	.30
22	Gill Byrd	1.00	.70	.40
24	Lester Lyles	.75	.60	.30
25	Vencie Glenn	1.25	.90	.50
30	Sam Seale	.75	.60	.30
31	Craig McEwen	.75	.60	.30
35	Marion Butts	1.25	.90	.50
43	Tim Spencer	.75	.60	.30
44	Martin Bayless	.75	.60	.30
46	Joe Caravello	.75	.60	.30
50	Gary Plummer	.75	.60	.30
51	Cedric Figaro	.75	.60	.30
53	Courtney Hall	.75	.60	.30
54	Billy Ray Smith	1.00	.70	.40
58	David Brandon	.75	.60	.30
59	Ken Woodard	.75	.60	.30
60	Dennis McKnight	.75	.60	.30
65	David Richards	.75	.60	.30
69	Les Miller	.75	.60	.30
75	Joe Phillips	.75	.60	.30
76	Broderick Thompson	.75	.60	.30
78	Joel Patten	.75	.60	.30
79	Joey Howard	.75	.60	.30
80	Wayne Walker	.75	.60	.30
82	Rod Bernstine	1.00	.70	.40
83	Anthony Miller	5.00	3.75	2.00
85	Andy Parker	.75	.60	.30
87	Quinn Early	1.75	1.25	.70
88	Arthur Cox	.75	.60	.30
91	Leslie O'Neal	1.75	1.25	.70
92	Burt Grossman	.75	.60	.30
97	George Hinkle	.75	.60	.30
99	Lee Williams	.75	.60	.30

1991 Chargers Vons

RONNIE HARMON   33

The twelve standard-sized cards were distributed by Vons in three-card sheets (6-5/8" x 3-1/2") with each sheet containing one card, one Junior Chargers Official Membership Card and a Sea World of California discount coupon. The card fronts have a color shot with a white border while the backs have bio and stat information.

		NM/M	NM	E
Complete Set (12):		10.00	7.50	4.00
Common Player:		.75	.60	.30
1	Rod Berstine	.75	.60	.30
2	Gill Byrd	1.00	.70	.40
3	Burt Grossman	.75	.60	.30
4	Ronnie Harmon	1.00	.70	.40
5	Anthony Miller	2.00	1.50	.80
6	Leslie O'Neal	1.50	1.25	.60
7	Gary Plummer	.75	.60	.30
8	Junior Seau	2.50	2.00	1.00
9	Billy Ray Smith	.75	.60	.30
10	Broderick Thompson	.75	.60	.30
11	Billy Joe Tolliver	1.00	.70	.40
12	Lee Williams	.75	.60	.30

1971 Chevron B.C. Lions

		NM	E	VG
Complete Set (50):		225.00	112.00	67.00
Common Player:		3.00	1.50	.90
Common SP:		12.00	6.00	3.50
1	George Anderson	3.00	1.50	.90
2	Josh Ashton	4.00	2.00	1.25
3	Ross Boice (SP)	12.00	6.00	3.50
4	Paul Brothers	3.00	1.50	.90
5	Tom Cassese	3.00	1.50	.90
6	Roy Cavallin	3.00	1.50	.90
7	Rusty Clark (SP)	12.00	6.00	3.50
8	Owen Dejanovich (CO)	3.00	1.50	.90
9	Dave Denny	3.00	1.50	.90
10	Brian Donnelly	3.00	1.50	.90
11	Steve Duich (SP)	12.00	6.00	3.50
12	Jim Duke	3.00	1.50	.90
13	Dave Easley	3.00	1.50	.90
14	Trevor Ekdahl	4.00	2.00	1.25
15	Jim Evenson	4.00	2.00	1.25
16	Greg Findlay	3.00	1.50	.90
17	Ted Gerela	3.00	1.50	.90
18	Dave Golinsky	3.00	1.50	.90
19	Lefty Hendrickson	3.00	1.50	.90
20	Lach Heron	3.00	1.50	.90
21	Gerry Herron	3.00	1.50	.90
22	Larry Highbaugh (SP)	12.00	6.00	3.50
23	Wayne Holm	3.00	1.50	.90
24	Bob Howes	3.00	1.50	.90
25	Max Huber	3.00	1.50	.90
26	Garrett Hunsperger	3.00	1.50	.90
27	Lawrence James (SP)	12.00	6.00	3.50
28	Brian Kelsey (SP)	12.00	6.00	3.50
29	Eagle Keys (CO)	4.00	2.00	1.25
30	Mike Leveille	3.00	1.50	.90
31	John Love	3.00	1.50	.90
32	Ray Lychak	3.00	1.50	.90
33	Dick Lyons (SP)	12.00	6.00	3.50
34	Wayne Matherne	3.00	1.50	.90
35	Ken McCullough (CO)	3.00	1.50	.90
36	Don Moorhead	3.00	1.50	.90
37	Peter Palmer	3.00	1.50	.90
38	Jackie Parker (GM)	12.00	6.00	3.50
39	Ken Phillips	3.00	1.50	.90
40	Cliff Powell	3.00	1.50	.90
41	Gary Robinson	3.00	1.50	.90
42	Ken Sugarman	4.00	2.00	1.25
43	Bruce Taupier	3.00	1.50	.90
44	Jim Tomlin (SP)	12.00	6.00	3.50
45	Bud Tynes (CO)	3.00	1.50	.90
46	Carl Weathers (SP)	12.00	6.00	3.50
47	Jim White	3.00	1.50	.90
48	Mike Wilson	3.00	1.50	.90
49	Jim Young	8.00	4.00	2.50
50	Contest Card (For Chevron)	3.00	1.50	.90

1964-69 Chiefs Fairmont Dairy

The 19-card, 3-3/8" x 2-3/8" set was available on milk cartons by Fairmont Dairy between the years 1964-69. Most cards are printed in red ink, with some cards printed in black (3-7/16" x 1-9/16"). Although there are 19 cards listed below, there could have been more than that produced in the 1960s. The card fronts feature a player closeup with brief bio information, as well as a Chiefs schedule.

		NM	E	VG
Complete Set (19):		1,800	1,350	725.00
Common Player:		75.00	37.00	22.00
1	Fred Arbanas (Red printing)	75.00	37.00	22.00
2	Bobby Bell (Red printing)	175.00	87.00	52.00
3	Buck Buchanan (Black print)	160.00	80.00	48.00
4	Chris Burford (Red printing)	75.00	37.00	22.00
5	Len Dawson (Red printing)	260.00	130.00	78.00
6	Dave Grayson (Red printing)	75.00	37.00	22.00
7	Abner Haynes (Red printing)	100.00	50.00	30.00
8	Sherrill Headrick (Red printing)	100.00	50.00	30.00
9	Bobby Hunt (Red printing)	75.00	37.00	22.00
10	Frank Jackson (Red printing)	75.00	37.00	22.00
11	Curtis McClinton (Red printing)	75.00	37.00	22.00
12	Bobby Ply (Red printing)	75.00	37.00	22.00
13	Al Reynolds (Red printing)	75.00	37.00	22.00

		NM	E	VG
14	Johnny Robinson			
	(Red printing)	125.00	62.00	37.00
15	Noland Smith	75.00	37.00	22.00
16	Smokey Stover			
	(Red printing)	75.00	37.00	22.00
17	Otis Taylor	150.00	75.00	45.00
18	Jim Tyrer (Red printing)	100.00	50.00	30.00
19	Jerrel Wilson			
	(Red printing)	75.00	37.00	22.00

1969 Chiefs Kroger

The eight-card, 8" x 9-3/4" set was sponsored by Kroger and features card fronts with color paintings by artist John Wheeldon. The backs have biographical and statistical information and a brief note about the artist.

		NM	E	VG
Complete Set (8):		75.00	56.00	30.00
Common Player:		5.00	3.75	2.00
1	Buck Buchanan	10.00	5.00	3.00
2	Len Dawson	25.00	12.50	7.50
3	Mike Garrett	10.00	5.00	3.00
4	Willie Lanier	15.00	7.50	4.50
5	Jerry Mays	5.00	3.75	2.00
6	Johnny Robinson	10.00	5.00	3.00
7	Jan Stenerud	15.00	7.50	4.50
8	Jim Tyrer	5.00	3.75	2.00

1971 Chiefs Team Issue

The 10-card, 7" x 10" set features Chiefs players in black and white headshots with white borders. The backs contain bio information and career highlights and limited statistics.

		NM	E	VG
Complete Set (10):		45.00	34.00	18.00
Common Player:		5.00	2.50	1.50
1	Bobby Bell	10.00	5.00	3.00
2	Wendell Hayes	5.00	2.50	1.50
3	Ed Lothamer	5.00	2.50	1.50
4	Jim Lynch	5.00	2.50	1.50
5	Jack Rudnay	5.00	2.50	1.50
6	Sid Smith	5.00	2.50	1.50
7	Bob Stein	5.00	2.50	1.50
8	Jan Stenerud	12.00	6.00	3.50
9	Otis Taylor	10.00	5.00	3.00
10	Jim Tyrer	5.00	2.50	1.50

1973-74 Chiefs Team Issue

The 18-card, 5" x 7" set features black and white photos on the card fronts with white borders. The card backs are blank.

		NM	E	VG
Complete Set (18):		50.00	37.00	20.00
Common Player:		3.00	1.50	.90
1	Robert Briggs	3.00	1.50	.90
2	Larry Brunson	3.00	1.50	.90
3	Gary Butler	3.00	1.50	.90
4	Dean Carlson	3.00	1.50	.90
5	Tom Condon	3.00	1.50	.90
6	George Daney	3.00	1.50	.90
7	Andy Hamilton	3.00	1.50	.90
8	Dave Hill	3.00	1.50	.90
9	Jim Kearney	3.00	1.50	.90
10	Mike Livingston	3.00	1.50	.90
11	Jim Marsalis	3.00	1.50	.90
12	Barry Pearson	3.00	1.50	.90
13	Francis Peay	3.00	1.50	.90
14	Kerry Reardon	3.00	1.50	.90
15	Mike Sensibaugh	3.00	1.50	.90
16	Bill Thomas	3.00	1.50	.90
17	Marvin Upshaw	3.00	1.50	.90
18	Clyde Werner	3.00	1.50	.90

1979 Chiefs Police

The 10-card, 2-5/8" x 4-1/8" set was issued by Hardee's Restaurants, the Chiefs and the Kansas City Police Department. The card fronts feature an action shot with the backs offering a safety tip.

		NM	E	VG
Complete Set (10):		10.00	7.50	4.00
Common Player:		1.00	.70	.40
1	Bob Grupp	1.00	.70	.40
4	Steve Fuller	1.00	.50	.30
22	Ted McKnight	1.00	.70	.40
24	Gary Green	1.00	.50	.30
26	Gary Barbaro	1.50	.70	.45
32	Tony Reed	1.00	.50	.30
58	Jack Rudnay	1.00	.70	.40
67	Art Still	1.50	.70	.45
73	Bob Simmons	1.00	.70	.40
NNO	Marv Levy (CO)	3.00	1.50	.90

1980 Chiefs Police

The 10-card, 2 5/8" x 4-1/8" set, sponsored by Frito-Lay, Kiwanis and area law enforcement, features action fronts with "Chiefs Tips" on the backs. The Stenerud card was limited in distribution.

		NM	E	VG
Complete Set (10):		12.00	9.00	4.75
Common Player:		1.00	.50	.30
1	Bob Grupp	1.00	.50	.30
3	Jan Stenerud (SP)	3.00	1.50	.90
32	Tony Reed	1.00	.50	.30
53	Whitney Paul	1.00	.50	.30
59	Gary Spani	1.00	.50	.30
67	Art Still	1.75	.90	.50
86	J.T. Smith	1.00	.50	.30
99	Mike Bell	1.00	.50	.30
NNO	Defensive Team	1.50	.70	.45
NNO	Offensive Team	1.50	.70	.45

1981 Chiefs Police

The 10-card, 2-5/8" x 4-1/8" set, sponsored by Frito-Lay, Kiwanis and local law enforcement, features action shots on the card fronts and "Chiefs Tips" on the backs.

		NM/M	NM	E
Complete Set (10):		6.00	4.50	2.50
Common Player:		.50	.40	.20
1	Warpaint and Carla			
	(Mascots)	.50	.40	.20
2	Art Still	.75	.60	.30
3	Steve Fuller, Jack Rudnay	.75	.60	.30
4	Gary Green	.50	.40	.20
5	Tom Condon, Marv Levy			
	(CO)	1.00	.70	.40
6	J.T. Smith	.75	.60	.30
7	Gary Spani, Whitney Paul	.50	.40	.20
8	Nick Lowery, Steve Fuller	.75	.60	.30
9	Gary Barbaro	.50	.40	.20
10	Henry Marshall	.50	.40	.20

1982 Chiefs Police

37 • JOE DELANEY
Running Back
HI 170 WT 184
kansas city chiefs

The 10-card, 2-5/8" x 4-1/8" set, sponsored by Frito-Lay, Kiwanis and local law enforcement, features action fronts while the backs contain cartoons in addition to "Chiefs Tips." Some of the card fronts feature two players (card Nos. 1 and 2).

		NM/M	NM	E
Complete Set (10):		6.00	4.50	2.50
Common Player:		.50	.40	.20
1	Bill Kenney, Jack Rudnay	.75	.60	.30
2	Steve Fuller, Nick Lowery	.75	.60	.30
3	Matt Herkenhoff	.50	.40	.20
4	Art Still	.75	.60	.30
5	Gary Spani	.50	.40	.20
6	James Hadnot	.50	.40	.20
7	Mike Bell	.50	.40	.20
8	Carol Canfield (Chiefette)	.50	.40	.20
9	Gary Green	.50	.40	.20
10	Joe Delaney	.75	.60	.30

1983 Chiefs Police

The 10-card, 2-5/8" x 4-1/8" set, sponsored by Frito-Lay, KCTV-5, Kiwanis and local law enforcement, features action fronts with "Crime Tip" cartoons on the backs.

		NM/M	NM	E
Complete Set (10):		6.00	4.50	2.50
Common Player:		.50	.40	.20
1	John Mackovic (CO)	.75	.60	.30
2	Tom Condon	.50	.40	.20
3	Gary Spani	.50	.40	.20
4	Carlos Carson	.75	.60	.30
5	Brad Budde	.50	.40	.20
6	Lloyd Burruss	.50	.40	.20
7	Gary Green	.50	.40	.20
8	Mike Bell	.50	.40	.20
9	Nick Lowery	.75	.60	.30
10	Sandi Byrd (Chiefette)	.50	.40	.20

1984 Chiefs Police

The 10-card, 2-5/8" x 4-1/8" set, sponsored by Frito-Lay and KCTV, features a "Chiefs Tip" and "Crime Tip" on the card backs.

		NM/M	NM	E
Complete Set (10):		6.00	4.50	2.50
Common Player:		.50	.40	.20
1	John Mackovic (CO)	.75	.60	.30
2	Deron Cherry	.75	.60	.30
3	Bill Kenney	.50	.40	.20
4	Henry Marshall	.50	.40	.20
5	Nick Lowery	.75	.60	.30
6	Theotis Brown	.50	.40	.20
7	Stephone Paige	1.00	.70	.40
8	Gary Spani, Art Still	.75	.60	.30
9	Albert Lewis	.75	.60	.30
10	Carlos Carson	.75	.60	.30

1984 Chiefs QuikTrip

The 16-card, 5" x 7" set was sponsored by QuickTrip and features black and white fronts with blank backs.

		NM/M	NM	E
Complete Set (16):		48.00	36.00	19.20
Common Player:		2.00	1.50	.80
1	Mike Bell	2.00	1.50	.80
2	Todd Blackledge	3.00	2.25	1.25
3	Brad Budde	2.00	1.50	.80
4	Lloyd Burruss	2.00	1.50	.80
5	Carlos Carson	3.00	2.25	1.25
6	Gary Green	2.00	1.50	.80
7	Anthony Hancock	2.00	1.50	.80
8	Eric Harris	2.00	1.50	.80
9	Lamar Hunt (OWN)	5.00	3.75	2.00
10	Bill Kenney	3.00	2.25	1.25
11	Ken Kremer	2.00	1.50	.80
12	Nick Lowery	4.50	3.50	1.75
13	John Mackovic (CO)	3.00	2.25	1.25
14	J.T. Smith	3.00	2.25	1.25
15	Gary Spani	2.00	1.50	.80
16	Art Still	3.00	2.25	1.25

1985 Chiefs Police

The 10-card, 2-5/8" x 4-1/8" set, sponsored by Frito-Lay, KCTV and local law enforcement, features a "Chiefs Tip" and "Crime Tip" on the card backs.

		NM/M	NM	E
Complete Set (10):		6.00	4.50	2.50
Common Player:		.50	.40	.20
1	John Mackovic (CO)	.75	.60	.30
2	Herman Heard	.50	.40	.20
3	Bill Kenney	.75	.60	.30
4	Deron Cherry, Lloyd			
	Burruss	.75	.60	.30
5	Jim Arnold	.50	.40	.20
6	Kevin Ross	.50	.40	.20
7	David Lutz	.50	.40	.20
8	Chiefettes Cheerleaders	.75	.60	.30
9	Bill Maas	.75	.60	.30
10	Art Still	1.00	.70	.40

1986 Chiefs Police

The 10-card, 2-5/8" x 4-1/8" set was sponsored by Frito-Lay, KCTV and local law enforcement and features "Chiefs Tip" and "Crime Tip" on the backs.

		NM/M	NM	E
Complete Set (10):		6.00	4.50	2.50
Common Player:		.50	.40	.20
1	John Mackovic	.50	.40	.20
2	Willie Lanier (Hall of			
	Fame)	1.50	1.25	.60
3	Stephone Paige	1.00	.70	.40
4	Brad Budde	.50	.40	.20
5	Nick Lowery	.75	.60	.30
6	Scott Radecic	.50	.40	.20
7	Mike Pruitt	.50	.40	.20
8	Albert Lewis	.75	.60	.30
9	Todd Blackledge	.75	.60	.30
10	Deron Cherry	1.25	.90	.50

1987 Chiefs Louis Rich

		NM/M	NM	E
Complete Set (16):		20.00	15.00	8.00
Common Player:		1.00	.70	.40
1	John Alt	1.50	1.25	.60
2	Carlos Carson	1.50	1.25	.60
3	Deron Cherry	2.00	1.50	.80
4	Sherman Cocroft	1.00	.70	.40
5	Irv Eatman	1.00	.70	.40
6	Frank Gansz	1.00	.70	.40
7	Dino Hackett	1.50	1.25	.60
8	Jonathan Hayes	1.00	.70	.40

		NM/M	NM	E
9	Bill Kenney	1.50	1.25	.60
10	Albert Lewis	2.00	1.50	.80
11	Nick Lowery	1.50	1.25	.60
12	Bill Maas	1.00	.70	.40
13	Christian Okoye	1.75	1.25	.70
14	Stephone Paige	1.75	1.25	.70
15	Paul Palmer	1.00	.70	.40
16	Kevin Ross	1.50	1.25	.60

1987 Chiefs Police

The 10-card, 2-5/8" x 4-1/8" set, sponsored by Frito-Lay, US Sprint, KCTV and local law enforcement, features a "Chiefs Tip" and "Crime Tip" on the backs.

		NM/M	NM	E
Complete Set (10):		5.00	3.75	2.00
Common Player:		.50	.40	.20
1	Frank Gansz (CO)	.50	.40	.20
2	Tim Cofield	.50	.40	.20
3	Deron Cherry, Albert Lewis	.75	.60	.30
4	Chiefs Cheerleaders	.50	.40	.20
5	Jeff Smith	.50	.40	.20
6	Rick Donnalley	.50	.40	.20
7	Lloyd Burruss, Kevin Ross	.50	.40	.20
8	Dino Hackett	.50	.40	.20
9	Bill Maas	.50	.40	.20
10	Carlos Carson	.75	.60	.30

1988 Chiefs Police

The 10-card, 2-5/8" x 4-1/8" set was sponsored by Frito-Lay, KCTV, US Sprint and local law enforcement and has "Chiefs Tip" and "Crime Tip" on the backs.

		NM/M	NM	E
Complete Set (10):		6.00	4.50	2.50
Common Player:		.50	.40	.20
1	Frank Gansz (CO)	.50	.40	.20
2	Bill Kenney	.75	.60	.30
3	Carlos Carson	.75	.60	.30
4	Paul Palmer	.50	.40	.20
5	Christian Okoye	1.00	.70	.40
6	Mark Adickes	.50	.40	.20
7	Bill Maas	.50	.40	.20
8	Albert Lewis	.75	.60	.30
9	Deron Cherry	.75	.60	.30
10	Stephone Paige	.75	.60	.30

1989 Chiefs Police

The 10-card, 2-5/8" x 4-1/8" set, sponsored by Western Auto, KCTV and local law enforcement, features a "Chiefs Tip" and "Crime Tip" on the card backs.

		NM/M	NM	E
Complete Set (10):		5.00	3.75	2.00
Common Player:		.50	.40	.20
1	Marty Schottenheimer (CO)	1.00	.70	.40
2	Irv Eatman	.50	.40	.20
3	Kevin Ross	.50	.40	.20
4	Bill Maas	.50	.40	.20
5	Chiefs Cheerleaders	.50	.40	.20
6	Carlos Carson	.75	.60	.30
7	Steve DeBerg	1.00	.70	.40
8	Jonathan Hayes	.50	.40	.20
9	Deron Cherry	.75	.60	.30
10	Dino Hackett	.50	.40	.20

1971 Chiquita CFL All-Stars

		NM	E	VG
Complete Set (13):		200.00	112.00	67.00
Common Pair:		15.00	7.50	4.50
1	Bill Baker, 2 Ken Sugarman	20.00	10.00	6.00
3	Wayne Giardino, 4 Peter Dalla Riva	20.00	10.00	6.00
5	Leon McQuay, 6 Jim Thorpe	25.00	12.50	7.50
7	George Reed, 8 Jerry Campbell	20.00	10.00	6.00
9	Tommy Joe Coffey, 10 Terry Evanshen	25.00	12.50	7.50
11	Jim Young, 12 Mark Kosmos	20.00	10.00	6.00
13	Ron Forwick, 14 Jack Abendschan	15.00	7.50	4.50
15	Don Jonas, 16 Al Marcellin	20.00	10.00	6.00
17	Joe Theismann, 18 Jim Corrigall (Toronto Argonauts)	50.00	25.00	15.00
19	Ed George, 20 Dick Dupuis	15.00	7.50	4.50
21	Ted Dushinski, 22 Bob Swift	15.00	7.50	4.50
23	John Lagrone, 24 Bill Danychuk	15.00	7.50	4.50
25	Garney Henley, 26 John Williams	20.00	10.00	6.00
NNO	Yellow Viewer	40.00	20.00	12.00

1972 Chiquita NFL Slides

The 13-slide, 3-9/16" x 1-3/4" set features two players on each slide. The slides have a slide image in each of the four corners with a player summary in the middle. The top two images are of the same player, while the bottom two are of the second player. A yellow viewer was also issued.

		NM	E	VG
Complete Set (13):		325.00	240.00	130.00
Common Player:		20.00	10.00	6.00
1	Joe Greene, Bob Lilly (2)	50.00	25.00	15.00
3	Bill Bergey, Gary Collins (4)	30.00	15.00	9.00
5	Walt Sweeney, Bubba Smith (6)	30.00	15.00	9.00
7	Larry Wilson, Fred Carr (8)	20.00	10.00	6.00
9	Mac Percival, John Brodie (10)	30.00	15.00	9.00
11	Lem Barney, Ron Yary (12)	30.00	15.00	9.00
13	Curt Knight, Alvin Haymond (14)	20.00	10.00	6.00
15	Floyd Little, Gerry Philbin (16)	30.00	15.00	9.00
17	Jim Mitchell, Paul Costa (18)	20.00	10.00	6.00
19	Jake Kupp, Ben Hawkins (20)	20.00	10.00	6.00
21	Johnny Robinson, George Webster (22)	20.00	10.00	6.00
23	Mercury Morris, Willie Brown (24)	40.00	20.00	12.00
25	Ron Johnson, Jon Morris (26)	20.00	10.00	6.00
NNO	Yellow Viewer	30.00	15.00	9.00

1961 CKNW B.C. Lions

		NM	E	VG
Complete Set (30):		200.00	100.00	60.00
Common Player:		6.00	3.00	1.75
1	By Bailey	15.00	7.50	4.50
2	Nub Beamer	6.00	3.00	1.75
3	Bob Belak (Kings Drive-In)	6.00	3.00	1.75
4	Neil Beaumont	6.00	3.00	1.75
5	Bill Britton (Nestle's Quik)	6.00	3.00	1.75
6	Tom Brown (Kings Drive-In)	8.00	4.00	2.50
7	Mike Cacic	6.00	3.00	1.75
8	Jim Carphin	6.00	3.00	1.75
9	Bruce Claridge	6.00	3.00	1.75
10	Pat Claridge	6.00	3.00	1.75
11	Steve Cotter	6.00	3.00	1.75
12	Lonnie Dennis (Nestle's Quik)	6.00	3.00	1.75
13	Norm Fieldgate	8.00	4.00	2.50
14	Willie Fleming	18.00	9.00	5.50
15	George Grant	6.00	3.00	1.75
16	Sonny Homer (Nestle's Quik)	8.00	4.00	2.50
17	Bob Jeter	10.00	5.00	3.00
18	Dick Johnson	6.00	3.00	1.75
19	Earl Keeley	6.00	3.00	1.75
20	Vic Kristopatis	6.00	3.00	1.75
21	Gordie Mitchell	6.00	3.00	1.75
22	Rae Ross (Nestle's Quik)	6.00	3.00	1.75
23	Bob Schloredt	8.00	4.00	2.50
24	Gary Schwertfeger	6.00	3.00	1.75
25	Mel Semenko (Kings Drive-In)	6.00	3.00	1.75
26	Ed Sullivan	8.00	4.00	2.50
27	Barney Therrien (Nestle's Quik)	6.00	3.00	1.75
28	Ed Vereb	6.00	3.00	1.75
29	Don Vicic	6.00	3.00	1.75
30	Ron Watton	6.00	3.00	1.75

1962 CKNW B.C. Lions

		NM	E	VG
Complete Set (32):		200.00	100.00	60.00
Common Player:		5.00	2.50	1.50
1	By Bailey	15.00	7.50	4.50
2	Nub Beamer	5.00	2.50	1.50
3	Neil Beaumont	5.00	2.50	1.50
4	Bob Belak	5.00	2.50	1.50
5	Walt Bilicki	5.00	2.50	1.50
6	Tom Brown (Shop-Easy)	8.00	4.00	2.50
7	Mark Burton (Shop-Easy)	8.00	4.00	2.50
8	Mike Cacic	5.00	2.50	1.50
9	Jim Carphin	5.00	2.50	1.50
10	Pat Claridge	5.00	2.50	1.50
11	Steve Cotter	5.00	2.50	1.50
12	Lonnie Dennis	5.00	2.50	1.50
13	Norm Fieldgate	8.00	4.00	2.50
14	Willie Fleming (Shop-Easy)	18.00	9.00	5.50
15	Dick Fouts	8.00	4.00	2.50
16	George Grant	5.00	2.50	1.50
17	Ian Hagemoen	5.00	2.50	1.50

		NM	E	VG
18	Tommy Hinton	8.00	4.00	2.50
19	Sonny Homer	8.00	4.00	2.50
20	Joe Kapp	25.00	12.50	7.50
21	Earl Keeley	5.00	2.50	1.50
22	Vic Kristopatis (Shop-Easy)	5.00	2.50	1.50
23	Tom Larscheid	5.00	2.50	1.50
24	Mike Martin	5.00	2.50	1.50
25	Gordie Mitchell	5.00	2.50	1.50
26	Baz Nagle	5.00	2.50	1.50
27	Bob Schloredt	8.00	4.00	2.50
28	Gary Schwertfeger	5.00	2.50	1.50
29	Willie Taylor	8.00	4.00	2.50
30	Barney Therrien	5.00	2.50	1.50
31	Don Vicic	5.00	2.50	1.50
32	Tom Walker	5.00	2.50	1.50

1970 Clark Volpe

The 66-card, 7-1/2" x 9-15/16" set includes cards for eight of the teams in the league in 1970. The Chicago Bears (1-8), Cincinnati Bengals (9-14), Cleveland Browns (15-21), Detroit Lions (22-30), Green Bay Packers (31-39), Kansas City Chiefs (40-48), Minnesota Vikings (49-57) and St. Louis Cardinals (58-66). Cards with the mail tabs measure 7-1/2" x 14" and the backs have mail-in offers for other merchandise while the fronts feature player drawings by artist Nicholas Volpe.

		NM	E	VG
Complete Set (66):		325.00	240.00	130.00
Common Player:		3.00	2.25	1.25
1	Ron Bull	3.00	2.25	1.25
2	Dick Butkus	18.00	9.00	5.50
3	Lee Roy Caffey	3.00	2.25	1.25
4	Bobby Douglass	6.00	3.00	1.75
5	Dick Gordon	3.00	2.25	1.25
6	Bennie McRae	3.00	2.25	1.25
7	Ed O'Bradovich	3.00	2.25	1.25
8	George Seals	3.00	2.25	1.25
9	Bill Bergey	6.00	3.00	1.75
10	Jess Phillips	3.00	2.25	1.25
11	Mike Reid	6.00	3.00	1.75
12	Paul Robinson	6.00	3.00	1.75
13	Bob Trumpy	8.00	4.00	2.50
14	Sam Wyche	12.00	6.00	3.50
15	Erich Barnes	3.00	2.25	1.25
16	Gary Collins	6.00	3.00	1.75
17	Gene Hickerson	3.00	2.25	1.25
18	Jim Houston	3.00	2.25	1.25
19	Leroy Kelly	12.00	6.00	3.50
20	Ernie Kellerman	3.00	2.25	1.25
21	Bill Nelsen	6.00	3.00	1.75
22	Lem Barney	10.00	5.00	3.00
23	Mel Farr	6.00	3.00	1.75
24	Larry Hand	3.00	2.25	1.25
25	Alex Karras	12.00	6.00	3.50
26	Mike Lucci	6.00	3.00	1.75
27	Bill Munson	6.00	3.00	1.75
28	Charlie Sanders	6.00	3.00	1.75
29	Tommy Vaughn	3.00	2.25	1.25
30	Wayne Walker	6.00	3.00	1.75
31	Lionel Aldridge	3.00	2.25	1.25
32	Donny Anderson	6.00	3.00	1.75
33	Ken Bowman	3.00	2.25	1.25
34	Carroll Dale	6.00	3.00	1.75
35	Jim Grabowski	6.00	3.00	1.75
36	Ray Nitschke	15.00	7.50	4.50
37	Dave Robinson	6.00	3.00	1.75
38	Travis Williams	6.00	3.00	1.75
39	Willie Wood	10.00	5.00	3.00
40	Fred Arbanas	3.00	2.25	1.25
41	Bobby Bell	10.00	5.00	3.00
42	Aaron Brown	3.00	2.25	1.25
43	Buck Buchanan	10.00	5.00	3.00
44	Len Dawson	16.00	8.00	4.75
45	Jim Marsalis	3.00	2.25	1.25
46	Jerry Mays	3.00	2.25	1.25
47	Johnny Robinson	6.00	3.00	1.75
48	Jim Tyrer	6.00	3.00	1.75
49	Bill Brown	6.00	3.00	1.75
50	Fred Cox	3.00	2.25	1.25
51	Gary Cuozzo	6.00	3.00	1.75
52	Carl Eller	10.00	5.00	3.00
53	Jim Marshall	10.00	5.00	3.00
54	Dave Osborn	6.00	3.00	1.75
55	Alan Page	12.00	6.00	3.50
56	Mick Tingelhoff	6.00	3.00	1.75
57	Gene Washington	6.00	3.00	1.75
58	Pete Beathard	6.00	3.00	1.75
59	John Gilliam	6.00	3.00	1.75
60	Jim Hart	8.00	4.00	2.50
61	Johnny Roland	6.00	3.00	1.75
62	Jackie Smith	10.00	5.00	3.00
63	Larry Stallings	3.00	2.25	1.25
64	Roger Wehrli	6.00	3.00	1.75
65	Dave Williams	3.00	2.25	1.25
66	Larry Wilson	10.00	5.00	3.00

1991 Classic

Mike Pritchard

Classic's first venture into the football field resulted in this 50-card boxed set released in June. Classic reportedly paid several players for exclusive rights to appear in the set, including Raghib Ismail. No team names or college names are listed on the cards, which have a grey marble-like border on the front, plus the Classic logos. Each back has biographical information, plus a player profile.

		NM/M	NM	E
Complete Set (50):		6.00	4.50	2.50
Common Player:		.05	.04	.02
1	Rocket Ismail	.50	.40	.20
2	Russell Maryland	.30	.25	.12
3	Eric Turner	.30	.25	.15
4	Bruce Pickens	.10	.08	.04
5	Mike Croal	.10	.08	.04
6	Todd Lyght	.10	.08	.04
7	Eric Swann	.30	.25	.12
8	Antone Davis	.10	.08	.04
9	Stanley Richard	.10	.08	.04
10	Pat Harlow	.10	.08	.04
11	Alvin Harper	.50	.40	.20
12	Mike Pritchard	.30	.25	.12
13	Leonard Russell	.10	.08	.04
14	Dan McGwire	.10	.08	.04
15	Bobby Wilson	.10	.08	.04
16	Alfred Williams	.10	.08	.04
17	Vinnie Clark	.10	.08	.04
18	Kelvin Pritchett	.10	.08	.04
19	Harvey Williams	.50	.40	.20
20	Stan Thomas	.10	.08	.04
21	Randal Hill	.25	.20	.10
22	Todd Marinovich	.10	.08	.04
23	Henry Jones	.05	.04	.02
24	Jarrod Bunch	.05	.04	.02
25	Mike Dumas	.10	.08	.04
26	Ed King	.05	.04	.02
27	Reggie Jackson	.05	.04	.02
28	Roman Phifer	.10	.08	.04
29	Mike Jones	.10	.08	.04
30	Brett Favre	5.00	3.75	2.00
31	Browning Nagle	.10	.08	.04
32	Esera Tualolo	.10	.08	.04
33	George Thornton	.10	.08	.04
34	Dixon Edwards	.10	.08	.04
35	Darryl Lewis	.10	.08	.04
36	Eric Bieniemy	.20	.15	.08
37	Shane Curry	.10	.08	.04
38	Jerome Henderson	.10	.08	.04
39	Wesley Carroll	.10	.08	.04
40	Nick Bell	.10	.08	.04
41	John Flannery	.05	.04	.02
42	Ricky Watters	1.00	.70	.40
43	Jeff Graham	.50	.40	.20
44	Eric Moten	.05	.04	.02
45	Jesse Campbell	.05	.04	.02
46	Chris Zorich	.20	.15	.08
47	Doug Thomas	.05	.04	.02
48	Phil Hansen	.05	.04	.02
49	Kanavis McGhee	.10	.08	.04
50	Reggie Barrett	.10	.08	.04

1991 Classic Promos

Raghib "Rocket" Ismail WR

These promotional cards preview Classic's design for its debut set in 1991. The card back only has trademark information. The card back only has trademark information with the words "For Promotional Purposes Only! Not For Resale." The five cards were also featured together on a 7-1/2" x 7-1/8" promo sheet which was made available to collectors who attended the 12th National Sports Collectors Convention in Anaheim, Calif., in July 1991. Each sheet is serially-numbered (1 of 10,000, etc.) and is labeled on the back as being a promotional sheet.

		NM	E	VG
Complete Set (7):		15.00	11.00	6.006.00
Common Player (1-5):		1.50	1.25	6.00.60
1	Antone Davis	1.50	1.25	1.25 .60
2A	Raghib Rocket Ismail	5.00	3.75	2.002.00
2B	Raghib Rocket Ismail	5.00	3.75	2.002.00
3A	Todd Lyght	2.00	1.50	.80 .80
3B	Todd Lyght	2.00	1.50	.80 .80
4	Russell Maryland	2.00	1.50	.80 .80
5	Eric Turner	2.00	1.50	.80 .80

1989 Clemson

		NM/M	NM	E
Complete Set (32):		20.00	15.00	8.00
Common Player:		.75	.60	.30
1	Wally Ake (CO)	.75	.60	.30
2	Larry Beckman (CO)	.75	.60	.30
3	Mitch Belton (32)	.75	.60	.30
4	Scott Beville (61)	.75	.60	.30
5	Doug Brewster (92)	.75	.60	.30
6	Larry Brinson (CO)	1.00	.70	.40
7	Reggie Demps (30)	.75	.60	.30
8	Robin Eaves (44)	.75	.60	.30
9	Barney Farrar (CO)	.75	.60	.30
10	Stacy Fields (46)	.75	.60	.30
11	Vance Hammond (90)	.75	.60	.30
12	Eric Harmon (76)	.75	.60	.30
13	Ken Hatfield (CO)	1.50	1.25	.60
14	Jerome Henderson (36)	1.50	1.25	.60
15	Les Herrin (CO)	.75	.60	.30
16	Roger Hinshaw (CO)	.75	.60	.30
17	John Johnson (12)	1.50	1.25	.60
18	Reggie Lawrence (34)	.75	.60	.30
19	Stacy Long (67)	.75	.60	.30
20	Eric Mader (82)	.75	.60	.30
21	Arlington Nunn (39)	.75	.60	.30
22	David Puckett (68)	.75	.60	.30
23	Danny Sizer (54)	.75	.60	.30
24	Robbie Spector (2)	.75	.60	.30
25	Rick Stockstill (CO)	1.00	.70	.40
26	Bruce Taylor (6)	.75	.60	.30
27	Doug Thomas (41)	.75	.60	.30
28	**The Tiger** (Mascot)	.75	.60	.30
29	**Tiger Paw Title Card**	.75	.60	.30
30	Bob Trott (CO)	.75	.60	.30
31	Larry Van Der Heyden (CO)	.75	.60	.30
32	Richard Wilson (CO)	.75	.60	.30

1964 Coke Caps All-Stars AFL

The 44-cap, 1-1/8" in diameter set, found on bottles of Coca-Cola, was distributed in AFL cities. The cap outsides have a Coke logo with a football icon, while the inside of the cap features the player's face in black with surrounding text. A cap saver sheet was issued and could be redeemed for various prizes. Other Coke products, such as Fresca and Tab, also had the football caps.

		NM	E	VG
Complete Set (44):		175.00	87.00	52.00
Common Player:		2.50	2.00	1.00
1	Tommy Addison	2.50	2.00	1.00
2	Dalva Allen	2.50	2.00	1.00
3	Lance Alworth	10.00	5.00	3.00
4	Houston Antwine	2.50	2.00	1.00
5	Fred Arbanas	2.50	2.00	1.00
6	Tony Banfield	2.50	2.00	1.00
7	Stew Barber	2.50	2.00	1.00
8	George Blair	2.50	2.00	1.00
9	Mel Branch	2.50	2.00	1.00
10	Nick Buoniconti	8.00	4.00	2.50
11	Doug Cline	2.50	2.00	1.00
12	Eldon Danehauer	2.50	2.00	1.00
13	Clem Daniels	5.00	2.50	1.50
14	Larry Eisenhauer	2.50	2.00	1.00
15	Earl Faison	2.50	2.00	1.00
16	Cookie Gilchrist	5.00	2.50	1.50
17	Freddy Glick	2.50	2.00	1.00
18	Larry Grantham	5.00	2.50	1.50
19	Ron Hall	2.50	2.00	1.00
20	Charlie Hennigan	5.00	2.50	1.50
21	E.J. Holub	2.50	2.00	1.00
22	Ed Husmann	2.50	2.00	1.00
23	Jack Kemp	25.00	12.50	7.50
24	Dave Kocourek	2.50	2.00	1.00
25	Keith Lincoln	5.00	2.50	1.50
26	Charlie Long	2.50	2.00	1.00
27	Paul Lowe	5.00	2.50	1.50
28	Archie Matsos	2.50	2.00	1.00

29	Jerry Mays	5.00	2.50	1.50
30	Ron Mix	5.00	2.50	1.50
31	Tom Morrow	2.50	2.00	1.00
32	Billy Neighbors	2.50	2.00	1.00
33	Jim Otto	5.00	2.50	1.50
34	Art Powell	5.00	2.50	1.50
35	Johnny Robinson	5.00	2.50	1.50
36	Tobin Rote	2.50	2.00	1.00
37	Bob Schmidt	2.50	2.00	1.00
38	Tom Sestak	2.50	2.00	1.00
39	Billy Shaw	2.50	2.00	1.00
40	Bob Talamini	2.50	2.00	1.00
41	Lionel Taylor	5.00	2.50	1.50
42	Jim Tyrer	5.00	2.50	1.50
43	Dick Westmoreland	2.50	2.00	1.00
44	Fred Williamson	5.00	2.50	1.50

1964 Coke Caps All-Stars NFL

The 44-cap, 1-1/8" in diameter set is virtually identical to the 44-cap AFL set of the same year. The outside of each cap has the Coke logo with a football, with the inside having the player's facial image. As with the AFL set, a Cap Saver sheet was issued with potential prizes for collectors. Other Coke products, such as Fresca and Tab, also had the football caps.

		NM	E	VG
Complete Set (44):		160.00	120.00	65.00
Common Player:		2.50	1.25	.70
1	Doug Atkins	5.00	2.50	1.50
2	Terry Barr	2.50	1.25	.70
3	Jim Brown	25.00	12.50	7.50
4	Roger Brown	5.00	2.50	1.50
5	Roosevelt Brown	6.00	3.00	1.75
6	Timmy Brown	5.00	2.50	1.50
7	Bobby Joe Conrad	5.00	2.50	1.50
8	Willie Davis	6.00	3.00	1.75
9	Bob DeMarco	2.50	1.25	.70
10	Darrell Dess	2.50	1.25	.70
11	Mike Ditka	15.00	7.50	4.50
12	Bill Forester	2.50	1.25	.70
13	Joe Fortunato	2.50	1.25	.70
14	Bill George	5.00	2.50	1.50
15	Ken Gray	2.50	1.25	.70
16	Forrest Gregg	8.00	4.00	2.50
17	Roosevelt Grier	6.00	3.00	1.75
18	Hank Jordan	5.00	2.50	1.50
19	Jim Katcavage	5.00	2.50	1.50
20	Jerry Kramer	7.00	3.50	2.00
21	Ron Kramer	2.50	1.25	.70
22	Dick "Night Train" Lane	5.00	2.50	1.50
23	Dick Lynch	2.50	1.25	.70
24	Gino Marchetti	6.00	3.00	1.75
25	Tommy Mason	2.50	1.25	.70
26	Ed Meador	2.50	1.25	.70
27	Bobby Mitchell	7.00	3.50	2.00
28	Larry Morris	2.50	1.25	.70
29	Merlin Olsen	8.00	4.00	2.50
30	Jim Parker	5.00	2.50	1.50
31	Jim Patton	5.00	2.50	1.50
32	Myron Pottios	2.50	1.25	.70
33	Jim Ringo	5.00	2.50	1.50
34	Dick Schafrath	2.50	1.25	.70
35	Joe Schmidt	5.00	2.50	1.50
36	Del Shofner	5.00	2.50	1.50
37	Bob St. Clair	5.00	2.50	1.50
38	Jim Taylor	8.00	4.00	2.50
39	Roosevelt Taylor	5.00	2.50	1.50
40	Y.A. Tittle	10.00	5.00	3.00
41	Johnny Unitas	16.00	8.00	4.75
42	Larry Wilson	5.00	2.50	1.50
43	Willie Wood	5.00	2.50	1.50
44	Abe Woodson	5.00	2.50	1.50

1964 Coke Caps Browns

The 35-cap, 1-1/8" in diameter set was issued in Ohio and featured top Browns players, including a a first-year cap of receiver Paul Warfield. The cap tops feature a football stamp while the inside depicts a Browns player. A Cap Saver sheet, featuring Frank Ryan, was also issued.

		NM	E	VG
Complete Set (35):		125.00	95.00	50.00
Common Player:		2.50	2.00	1.00
1	Walter Beach	2.50	2.00	1.00
2	Larry Benz	2.50	2.00	1.00
3	Johnny Brewer	2.50	2.00	1.00
4	Jim Brown	30.00	15.00	9.00
5	John Brown	2.50	2.00	1.00
6	Monte Clark	5.00	2.50	1.50
7	Gary Collins	5.00	2.50	1.50
8	Vince Costello	5.00	2.50	1.50
9	Ross Fichtner	2.50	2.00	1.00
10	Galen Fiss	2.50	2.00	1.00
11	Bobby Franklin	2.50	2.00	1.00
12	Bob Gain	2.50	2.00	1.00
13	Bill Glass	5.00	2.50	1.50
14	Ernie Green	2.50	2.00	1.00

15	Lou Groza	8.00	4.00	2.50
16	Gene Hickerson	2.50	2.00	1.00
17	Jim Houston	2.50	2.00	1.00
18	Tom Hutchinson	2.50	2.00	1.00
19	Jim Kanicki	2.50	2.00	1.00
20	Mike Lucci	5.00	2.50	1.50
21	Dick Modzelewski	5.00	2.50	1.50
22	John Morrow	2.50	2.00	1.00
23	Jim Ninowski	2.50	1.25	.70
24	Frank Parker	2.50	2.00	1.00
25	Bernie Parrish	5.00	2.50	1.50
26	Frank Ryan	5.00	2.50	1.50
27	Charlie Scales	2.50	2.00	1.00
28	Dick Schafrath	5.00	2.50	1.50
29	Roger Shoals	2.50	2.00	1.00
30	Jim Shorter	2.50	2.00	1.00
31	Billy Truax	5.00	2.50	1.50
32	Paul Warfield	16.00	8.00	4.75
33	Ken Webb	2.50	2.00	1.00
34	Paul Wiggin	2.50	2.00	1.00
35	John Wooten	5.00	2.50	1.50
NNO	**Browns Saver Sheet Frank Ryan pictured**	20.00	10.00	6.00

1964 Coke Caps Chargers

The 35-cap, 1-1/8" set was issued in Southern California and featured top players from the AFL Chargers. As with other cap sets, a Cap Saver sheet was also available and when completed, collectors could redeem it for various prizes.

		NM	E	VG
Complete Set (35):		100.00	50.00	30.00
Common Player:		2.50	2.00	1.00
1	Chuck Allen	5.00	2.50	1.50
2	Lance Alworth	16.00	8.00	4.75
3	George Blair	2.50	2.00	1.00
4	Frank Buncom	2.50	2.00	1.00
5	Earl Faison	5.00	2.50	1.50
6	Kenny Graham	2.50	2.00	1.00
7	George Gross	2.50	2.00	1.00
8	Sam Gruneison	2.50	2.00	1.00
9	John Hadl	10.00	5.00	3.00
10	Dick Harris	2.50	1.25	.70
11	Bob Jackson	2.50	2.00	1.00
12	Emil Karas	2.50	2.00	1.00
13	Dave Kocourek	2.50	2.00	1.00
14	Ernie Ladd	6.00	3.00	1.75
15	Bobby Lane	2.50	2.00	1.00
16	Keith Lincoln	5.00	2.50	1.50
17	Paul Lowe	5.00	2.50	1.50
18	Jacque MacKinnon	2.50	2.00	1.00
19	Gerry McDougall	2.50	2.00	1.00
20	Charlie McNeil	5.00	2.50	1.50
21	Bob Mitinger	2.50	2.00	1.00
22	Ron Mix	6.00	3.00	1.75
23	Don Norton	2.50	2.00	1.00
24	Ernie Park	2.50	2.00	1.00
25	Bob Petrich	2.50	2.00	1.00
26	Jerry Robinson	2.50	2.00	1.00
27	Don Rogers	2.50	2.00	1.00
28	Tobin Rote	5.00	2.50	1.50
29	Henry Schmidt	2.50	2.00	1.00
30	Pat Shea	2.50	2.00	1.00
31	Walt Sweeney	5.00	2.50	1.50
32	Jimmy Warren	2.50	2.00	1.00
33	Dick Westmoreland	2.50	2.00	1.00
34	Bud Whitehead	2.50	2.00	1.00
35	Ernie Wright	5.00	2.50	1.50
NNO	**Chargers Saver Sheet**	20.00	10.00	6.00

1964 Coke Caps Lions

The 35-cap, 1-1/8" set was distributed in Michigan and contains Detroit Lions players' images on the inside of each cap. A Cap Saver sheet was also issued and the caps could also be found on Coke products such as Fresca and Tab.

		NM	E	VG
Complete Set (35):		100.00	50.00	30.00
Common Player:		2.50	2.00	1.00
1	Terry Barr	2.50	2.00	1.00
2	Carl Brettschneider	2.50	2.00	1.00
3	Roger Brown	5.00	2.50	1.50
4	Mike Bundra	2.50	2.00	1.00
5	Ernie Clark	2.50	2.00	1.00
6	Gail Cogdill	5.00	2.50	1.50
7	Larry Ferguson	2.50	2.00	1.00
8	Dennis Gaubatz	2.50	2.00	1.00
9	Jim Gibbons	5.00	2.50	1.50
10	John Gonzaga	2.50	2.00	1.00
11	John Gordy	2.50	2.00	1.00
12	Tom Hall	2.50	2.00	1.00
13	Alex Karras	10.00	5.00	3.00
14	Dick "Night Train" Lane	8.00	4.00	2.50
15	Dan LaRose	2.50	2.00	1.00
16	Yale Lary	8.00	4.00	2.50
17	Dick LeBeau	5.00	2.50	1.50
18	Dan Lewis	2.50	2.00	1.00
19	Gary Lowe	2.50	2.00	1.00
20	Bruce Maher	2.50	2.00	1.00
21	Darris McCord	2.50	2.00	1.00
22	Max Messner	2.50	2.00	1.00
23	Earl Morrall	7.00	3.50	2.00
24	Nick Pietrosante	2.50	1.25	.70
25	Milt Plum	2.50	1.25	.70
26	Daryl Sanders	2.50	2.00	1.00
27	Joe Schmidt	6.00	3.00	1.75
28	Bob Scholtz	2.50	2.00	1.00
29	J.D. Smith	5.00	2.50	1.50
30	Pat Studstill	5.00	2.50	1.50
31	Larry Vargo	2.50	2.00	1.00
32	Wayne Walker	5.00	2.50	1.50
33	Tom Watkins	2.50	2.00	1.00
34	Bob Whitlow	2.50	2.00	1.00
35	Sam Williams	2.50	2.00	1.00
NNO	**Lions Saver Sheet**	20.00	10.00	6.00

1964 Coke Caps National NFL

		NM	E	VG
Complete Set (68):		250.00	125.00	75.00
Common Player:		3.00	1.50	.90
1	Herb Adderley	5.00	2.50	1.50
2	Grady Alderman	3.00	1.50	.90
3	Doug Atkins	6.00	3.00	1.75
4	Sam Baker	3.00	1.50	.90
5	Erich Barnes	3.00	1.50	.90
6	Terry Barr	3.00	1.50	.90
7	Dick Bass	3.00	1.50	.90
8	Maxie Baughan	3.00	1.50	.90
9	Ray Berry	6.00	3.00	1.75
10	Charley Bradshaw	3.00	1.50	.90
11	Jim Brown	25.00	12.50	7.50
12	Roger Brown	3.00	1.50	.90
13	Tim Brown	3.00	1.50	.90
14	Gail Cogdill	3.00	1.50	.90
15	Tommy Davis	3.00	1.50	.90
16	Willie Davis	3.00	1.50	.90
17	Bob DeMarco	3.00	1.50	.90
18	Darrell Dess	3.00	1.50	.90
19	Buddy Dial	4.00	2.00	1.25
20	Mike Ditka	15.00	7.50	4.50
21	Galen Fiss	3.00	1.50	.90
22	Lee Folkins	3.00	1.50	.90
23	Joe Fortunato	3.00	1.50	.90
24	Bill Glass	3.00	1.50	.90
25	John Gordy	3.00	1.50	.90
26	Ken Gray	3.00	1.50	.90
27	Forrest Gregg	6.00	3.00	1.75
28	Rip Hawkins	3.00	1.50	.90
29	Charlie Johnson	4.00	2.00	1.25
30	John Henry Johnson	5.00	2.50	1.50
31	Hank Jordan	5.00	2.50	1.50
32	Jim Katcavage	3.00	1.50	.90
33	Jerry Kramer	5.00	2.50	1.50
34	Joe Krupa	3.00	1.50	.90
35	John Lovetere	3.00	1.50	.90
36	Dick Lynch	3.00	1.50	.90
37	John Mackey	6.00	3.00	1.75
38	Gino Marchetti	5.00	2.50	1.50
39	Joe Marconi	3.00	1.50	.90
40	Tommy Mason	3.00	1.50	.90
41	Dale Meinert	3.00	1.50	.90
42	Lou Michaels	4.00	2.00	1.25
43	Bobby Mitchell	6.00	3.00	1.75
44	John Morrow	3.00	1.50	.90
45	Merlin Olsen	8.00	4.00	2.50
46	Jack Pardee	4.00	2.00	1.25
47	Jim Parker	3.00	1.50	.90
48	Bernie Parrish	3.00	1.50	.90
49	Don Perkins	4.00	2.00	1.25
50	Richie Petibon	3.00	1.50	.90
51	Myron Pottios	3.00	1.50	.90
52	Vince Promuto	3.00	1.50	.90
53	Mike Pyle	3.00	1.50	.90
54	Pete Retzlaff	4.00	2.00	1.25
55	Jim Ringo	5.00	2.50	1.50
56	Joe Rutgens	3.00	1.50	.90
57	Dick Schafrath	3.00	1.50	.90
58	Del Shofner	3.00	1.50	.90
59	Jim Taylor	7.50	3.75	2.25
60	Roosevelt Taylor	3.00	1.50	.90
61	Clendon Thomas	3.00	1.50	.90
62	Y.A. Tittle	10.00	5.00	3.00
63	Johnny Unitas	15.00	7.50	4.50
64	Bill Wade	3.00	1.50	.90
65	Wayne Walker	3.00	1.50	.90
66	Jesse Whittenton	4.00	2.00	1.25
67	Larry Wilson	5.00	2.50	1.50
68	Abe Woodson	4.00	2.00	1.25
---	**NFL All-Star Saver Sheet**	30.00	15.00	9.00

1964 Coke Caps Oilers

		NM	E	VG
Complete Set (35):		125.00	62.00	37.00
Common Player:		3.00	1.50	.90
1	Scott Appleton	3.00	1.50	.90
2	Johnny Baker	3.00	1.50	.90
3	Tony Banfield	3.00	1.50	.90
4	George Blanda	15.00	7.50	4.50
5	Danny Brabham	3.00	1.50	.90
6	Ode Burrell	3.00	1.50	.90
7	Billy Cannon	6.00	3.00	1.75
8	Doug Cline	3.00	1.50	.90
9	Bobby Crenshaw	3.00	1.50	.90
10	Gary Cutsinger	3.00	1.50	.90
11	Willard Dewveall	3.00	1.50	.90
12	Mike Dukes	3.00	1.50	.90
13	Staley Faulkner	3.00	1.50	.90
14	Don Floyd	3.00	1.50	.90
15	Freddy Glick	3.00	1.50	.90
16	Tom Goode	3.00	1.50	.90
17	Charlie Hennigan	6.00	3.00	1.75
18	Ed Husmann	3.00	1.50	.90
19	Bobby Jancik	3.00	1.50	.90
20	Mark Johnston	3.00	1.50	.90
21	Jacky Lee	4.00	2.00	1.25
22	Bob McLeod	3.00	1.50	.90
23	Dudley Meredith	3.00	1.50	.90
24	Rich Michael	3.00	1.50	.90
25	Benny Nelson	3.00	1.50	.90
26	Jim Norton	4.00	2.00	1.25
27	Larry Onesti	3.00	1.50	.90
28	Bob Schmidt	3.00	1.50	.90
29	Dave Smith	3.00	1.50	.90
30	Walt Suggs	3.00	1.50	.90
31	Bob Talamini	3.00	1.50	.90
32	Charley Tolar	3.00	1.50	.90
33	Don Trull	4.00	2.00	1.25
34	John Varnell	3.00	1.50	.90
35	Hogan Wharton	3.00	1.50	.90

1964 Coke Caps Rams

The 35-cap, 1-1/8" set, issued in the Los Angeles area, had top Rams players and their image on the Coke bottle cap insides. The Cap Saver sheet could be redeemed for prizes and other Coke products also had the Rams bottle caps.

		NM	E	VG
Complete Set (35):		85.00	64.00	34.00
Common Player:		2.50	2.00	1.00
1	Jon Arnett	5.00	2.50	1.50
2	Pervis Atkins	2.50	2.00	1.00
3	Terry Baker	5.00	2.50	1.50
4	Dick Bass	5.00	2.50	1.50
5	Charley Britt	2.50	2.00	1.00
6	Willie Brown	5.00	2.50	1.50
7	Joe Carollo	2.50	2.00	1.00
8	Don Chuy	2.50	2.00	1.00
9	Charlie Cowan	2.50	2.00	1.00
10	Lindon Crow	2.50	2.00	1.00
11	Carroll Dale	5.00	2.50	1.50
12	Roman Gabriel	6.00	3.00	1.75
13	Roosevelt Grier	6.00	3.00	1.75
14	Mike Henry	2.50	2.00	1.00
15	Art Hunter	2.50	2.00	1.00
16	Ken Iman	2.50	2.00	1.00
17	Deacon Jones	10.00	5.00	3.00
18	Cliff Livingston	2.50	2.00	1.00
19	Lamar Lundy	5.00	2.50	1.50
20	Marlin McKeever	2.50	2.00	1.00
21	Ed Meador	5.00	2.50	1.50
22	Bill Munson	5.00	2.50	1.50
23	Merlin Olsen	8.00	4.00	2.50
24	Jack Pardee	5.00	2.50	1.50
25	Art Perkins	2.50	2.00	1.00
26	Jim Phillips	2.50	1.25	.70
27	Roger Pillath	2.50	2.00	1.00
28	Mel Profit	2.50	2.00	1.00
29	Joe Scibelli	2.50	2.00	1.00
30	Carver Shannon	2.50	2.00	1.00
31	Bobby Smith	2.50	2.00	1.00
32	Bill Swain	2.50	2.00	1.00
33	Frank Varrichione	2.50	2.00	1.00
34	Danny Villanueva	2.50	2.00	1.00
35	Nat Whitmyer	2.50	2.00	1.00
NNO	**Rams Saver Sheet**	20.00	10.00	6.00

1964 Coke Caps Redskins

The 32-cap, 1-1/8" in diameter set featured top players from the Redskins. Collectors who assembled the entire set before a specific expiration date could redeem it for prizes. The outside of the cap features the Coke logos with a stamp of a football, while the inside has the player's likeness. There may have been more of the 32 unnumbered caps issued than are listed below.

	NM	E	VG
Complete Set (32):	85.00	64.00	34.00
Common Player:	2.50	2.00	1.00

		NM	E	VG
1	Bill Barnes	2.50	2.00	1.00
2	Don Bosseler	2.50	2.00	1.00
3	Rod Breedlove	2.50	2.00	1.00
4	Frank Budd	2.50	2.00	1.00
5	Henry Butsko	2.50	2.00	1.00
6	Jimmy Carr	2.50	2.00	1.00
7	Angelo Coia	2.50	2.00	1.00
8	Fred Dugan	2.50	2.00	1.00
9	Fred Hageman	2.50	2.00	1.00
10	Sam Huff	8.00	4.00	2.50
11	Sonny Jurgensen	10.00	5.00	3.00
12	Carl Kammerer	2.50	2.00	1.00
13	Gordon Kelley	2.50	2.00	1.00
14	Bob Khayat	2.50	2.00	1.00
15	Paul Krause	5.00	2.50	1.50
16	J.W. Lockett	2.50	2.00	1.00
17	Riley Mattson	2.50	2.00	1.00
18	Bobby Mitchell	8.00	4.00	2.50
19	John Nisby	2.50	2.00	1.00
20	Fran O'Brien	2.50	2.00	1.00
21	John Paluck	2.50	2.00	1.00
22	Jack Pardee	5.00	2.50	1.50
23	Vince Promuto	2.50	2.00	1.00
24	Pat Richter	5.00	2.50	1.50
25	Johnny Sample	5.00	2.50	1.50
26	Lonnie Sanders	2.50	2.00	1.00
27	Dick Shiner	5.00	2.50	1.50
28	Ron Snidow	2.50	2.00	1.00
29	Jim Steffen	2.50	2.00	1.00
30	Charley Taylor	10.00	5.00	3.00
31	Tom Tracy	5.00	2.50	1.50
32	Fred Williams	2.50	2.00	1.00

1964 Coke Caps Steelers

		NM	E	VG
Complete Set (35):		110.00	55.00	32.50
Common Player:		3.00	1.50	.90
1	Art Anderson	3.00	1.50	.90
2	Frank Atkinson	3.00	1.50	.90
3	Gary Ballman	4.00	2.00	1.25
4	John Baker	4.00	2.00	1.25
5	Charley Bradshaw	4.00	2.00	1.25
6	Jim Bradshaw	3.00	1.50	.90
7	Ed Brown	4.00	2.00	1.25
8	John Burrell	3.00	1.50	.90
9	Preston Carpenter	5.00	2.50	1.50
10	Lou Cordileone	3.00	1.50	.90
11	Willie Daniel	3.00	1.50	.90
12	Dick Haley	3.00	1.50	.90
13	Bob Harrison	3.00	1.50	.90
14	Dick Hoak	5.00	2.50	1.50
15	Dan James	3.00	1.50	.90
16	Tom Jenkins	3.00	1.50	.90
17	John Henry Johnson	8.00	4.00	2.50
18	Jim Kelly	3.00	1.50	.90
19	Brady Keys	3.00	1.50	.90
20	Joe Krupa	3.00	1.50	.90
21	Ray Lemek	3.00	1.50	.90
22	Paul Martha	4.00	2.00	1.25
23	Lou Michaels	4.00	2.00	1.25
24	Bill Nelsen	5.00	2.50	1.50
25	Terry Nofsinger	3.00	1.50	.90
26	Buzz Nutter	3.00	1.50	.90
27	Clarence Peaks	4.00	2.00	1.25
28	Myron Pottios	4.00	2.00	1.25
29	John Reger	4.00	2.00	1.25
30	Mike Sandusky	3.00	1.50	.90
31	Theron Sapp	3.00	1.50	.90
32	Bob Schmitz	3.00	1.50	.90
33	Ron Stehouwer	3.00	1.50	.90
34	Clendon Thomas	4.00	2.00	1.25
35	Joe Womack	3.00	1.50	.90

1964 Coke Caps Team Emblems NFL

The 14-cap, 1-1/8" in diameter set features a cap for each of the NFL teams. The Cap Saver sheet had a section for collecting the team emblem caps which were also available with other Coke products such as Fresca and Tab.

		NM	E	VG
Complete Set (14):		50.00	37.00	20.00
Common Player:		5.00	2.50	1.50
1	**Baltimore Colts**	5.00	2.50	1.50
2	**Chicago Bears**	5.00	2.50	1.50
3	**Cleveland Browns**	5.00	2.50	1.50
4	**Dallas Cowboys**	7.00	3.50	2.00
5	**Detroit Lions**	5.00	2.50	1.50
6	**Green Bay Packers**	7.00	3.50	2.00
7	**Los Angeles Rams**	5.00	2.50	1.50
8	**Minnesota Vikings**	5.00	2.50	1.50
9	**New York Giants**	5.00	2.50	1.50
10	**Philadelphia Eagles**	5.00	2.50	1.50
11	**Pittsburgh Steelers**	5.00	2.50	1.50
12	**San Francisco 49ers**	6.00	3.00	1.75
13	**St. Louis Cardinals**	5.00	2.50	1.50
14	**Washington Redskins**	6.00	3.00	1.75

1965 Coke Caps All-Stars AFL

The 34-cap, 1-1/8" set features All-Stars from the AFL and was distributed in AFL cities along with local team caps. As with other caps, the outside features a Coke logo with a football icon and the inside depicts a facial image of an AFL All-Star. The caps are numbered with the "C" prefix.

		NM	E	VG
Complete Set (34):		130.00	65.00	40.00
Common Player:		2.50	1.25	.70
37	Jerry Mays	2.50	1.25	.70
38	Cookie Gilchrist	4.00	2.00	1.25
39	Lionel Taylor	2.50	1.25	.70
40	Goose Gonsoulin	4.00	2.00	1.25
41	Gino Cappelletti	4.00	2.00	1.25
42	Nick Buoniconti	6.00	3.00	1.75
43	Larry Eisenhauer	2.50	1.25	.70
44	Babe Parilli	2.50	1.25	.70
45	Jack Kemp	20.00	10.00	6.00
46	Billy Shaw	2.50	1.25	.70
47	Scott Appleton	2.50	1.25	.70
48	Matt Snell	2.50	1.25	.70
49	Charlie Hennigan	2.50	1.25	.70
50	Tom Flores	5.00	2.50	1.50
51	Clem Daniels	2.50	1.25	.70
52	George Blanda	8.00	4.00	2.50
53	Art Powell	2.50	1.25	.70
54	Jim Otto	5.00	2.50	1.50
55	Larry Grantham	2.50	1.25	.70
56	Don Maynard	8.00	4.00	2.50
57	Gerry Philbin	2.50	1.25	.70
58	E.J. Holub	2.50	1.25	.70
59	Chris Burford	2.50	1.25	.70
60	Ron Mix	5.00	2.50	1.50
61	Ernie Ladd	8.00	4.00	2.50
62	Fred Arbanas	2.50	1.25	.70
63	Tom Sestak	2.50	1.25	.70
64	Elbert Dubenion	2.50	1.25	.70
65	Mike Stratton	2.50	1.25	.70
66	Willie Brown	5.00	2.50	1.50
67	Sid Blanks	2.50	1.25	.70
68	Len Dawson	8.00	4.00	2.50
69	Lance Alworth	8.00	4.00	2.50
70	Keith Lincoln	2.50	1.25	.70

1965 Coke Caps All-Stars NFL

The 34-cap, 1-1/8" set featured NFL All-Stars and was distributed in NFL cities along with a Cap Saver sheet and local player caps. The completed sheet could be redeemed for various prizes. The caps are numbered with the "C" prefix.

		NM	E	VG
Complete Set (34):		125.00	95.00	50.00
Common Player:		2.50	1.25	.70
37	Sonny Jurgensen	8.00	4.00	2.50
38	Fran Tarkenton	12.00	6.00	3.50
39	Frank Ryan	2.50	1.25	.70
40	Johnny Unitas	12.00	6.00	3.50
41	Tommy Mason	2.50	1.25	.70
42	Mel Renfro	5.00	2.50	1.50
43	Ed Meador	2.50	1.25	.70
44	Paul Krause	4.00	2.00	1.25
45	Irv Cross	4.00	2.00	1.25
46	Bill Brown	2.50	1.25	.70
47	Joe Fortunato	2.50	1.25	.70
48	Jim Taylor	6.00	3.00	1.75
49	John Henry Johnson	5.00	2.50	1.50
50	Pat Fischer	2.50	1.25	.70
51	Bob Boyd	2.50	1.25	.70
52	Terry Barr	2.50	1.25	.70
53	Charley Taylor	5.00	2.50	1.50
54	Paul Warfield	8.00	4.00	2.50
55	Pete Retzlaff	2.50	1.25	.70
56	Maxie Baughan	2.50	1.25	.70
57	Matt Hazeltine	2.50	1.25	.70
58	Ken Gray	2.50	1.25	.70
59	Ray Nitschke	6.00	3.00	1.75
60	Myron Pottios	2.50	1.25	.70
61	Charlie Krueger	2.50	1.25	.70
62	Deacon Jones	7.00	3.50	2.00
63	Bob Lilly	7.00	3.50	2.00
64	Merlin Olsen	7.00	3.50	2.00
65	Jim Parker	5.00	2.50	1.50
66	Roosevelt Brown	5.00	2.50	1.50
67	Jim Gibbons	2.50	1.25	.70
68	Mike Ditka	12.00	6.00	3.50
69	Willie Davis	5.00	2.50	1.50
70	Aaron Thomas	2.50	1.25	.70

1965 Coke Caps Bills

The 35-cap, 1-1/8" set featuring the Bills was issued in western New York with a Cap Saver sheet, which could be redeemed for prizes such as an AFL leather football, a mini Bills megaphone, or a set of mini plastic AFL helmets. The cap tops have the Coke logo and a football stamp while the insides have the player's likeness. Hall of Fame quarterback Jack Kemp was the key player featured in the cap set. The caps are numbered with the "B" prefix.

		NM	E	VG
Complete Set (35):		120.00	90.00	47.50
Common Player:		2.50	2.00	1.00
1	Ray Abbruzzese	2.50	2.00	1.00
2	Joe Auer	2.50	2.00	1.00
3	Stew Barber	2.50	2.00	1.00
4	Glenn Bass	2.50	2.00	1.00
5	Dave Behrman	2.50	2.00	1.00
6	Al Bemiller	2.50	2.00	1.00
7	George (Butch) Byrd	2.50	1.25	.70
8	Wray Carlton	2.50	1.25	.70
9	Hagood Clarke	2.50	2.00	1.00
10	Jack Kemp	25.00	12.50	7.50
11	Oliver Dobbins	2.50	2.00	1.00
12	Elbert Dubenion	2.50	1.25	.70
13	Jim Dunaway	2.50	2.00	1.00
14	Booker Edgerson	2.50	2.00	1.00
15	George Flint	2.50	2.00	1.00
16	Pete Gogolak	5.00	2.50	1.50
17	Dick Hudson	5.00	2.50	1.50
18	Harry Jacobs	2.50	2.00	1.00
19	Tom Keating	2.50	2.00	1.00
20	Tom Day	2.50	2.00	1.00
21	Daryle Lamonica	10.00	5.00	3.00
22	Paul Maguire	8.00	4.00	2.50
23	Roland McDole	2.50	2.00	1.00
24	Dudley Meredith	2.50	2.00	1.00
25	Joe O'Donnell	2.50	2.00	1.00
26	Willie Ross	2.50	2.00	1.00
27	Ed Rutkowski	2.50	2.00	1.00
28	George Saimes	5.00	2.50	1.50
29	Tom Sestak	5.00	2.50	1.50
30	Billy Shaw	5.00	2.50	1.50
31	Bobby Smith	2.50	2.00	1.00
32	Mike Stratton	2.50	1.25	.70
33	Gene Sykes	2.50	2.00	1.00
34	John Tracey	2.50	2.00	1.00
35	Ernie Warlick	2.50	2.00	1.00
NNO	**Bills Saver Sheet**	20.00	10.00	6.00

1965 Coke Caps CFL

		NM	E	VG
Complete Set (230):		600.00	300.00	180.00
Common Player:		3.00	1.50	.90
1	Neal Beaumont	3.00	1.50	.90
2	Tom Brown	6.00	3.00	1.75
3	Mack Burton	3.00	1.50	.90
4	Mike Cacic	3.00	1.50	.90
5	Pat Claridge	3.00	1.50	.90
6	Steve Cotter	3.00	1.50	.90
7	Norm Fieldgate	6.00	3.00	1.75
8	Greg Findlay	3.00	1.50	.90
9	Willie Fleming	7.50	3.75	2.25
10	Dick Fouts	3.00	1.50	.90
11	Tom Hinton	6.00	3.00	1.75
12	Sonny Homer	3.00	1.50	.90
13	Joe Kapp	15.00	7.50	4.50
14	G. Kasapis	3.00	1.50	.90
15	Peter Kempf	3.00	1.50	.90
16	Bill Lasseter	3.00	1.50	.90
17	Mike Martin	3.00	1.50	.90
18	Ron Morris	3.00	1.50	.90
19	Bill Munsey	3.00	1.50	.90
20	Paul Seale	3.00	1.50	.90
21	Steve Shafer	3.00	1.50	.90
22	Ken Sugarman	3.00	1.50	.90
23	Bob Swift	3.00	1.50	.90
24	J. Williams	3.00	1.50	.90
25	Ron Albright (UER) (misspelled Albright)	3.00	1.50	.90
26	Lu Bain	3.00	1.50	.90
27	Frank Budd	3.00	1.50	.90
28	Lovell Coleman	4.00	2.00	1.25
29	Eagle Day	6.00	3.00	1.75
30	P. Dudley	3.00	1.50	.90
31	Jim Furlong	3.00	1.50	.90
32	George Hansen	3.00	1.50	.90
33	Wayne Harris	9.00	4.50	2.75
34	Herman Harrison	6.00	3.00	1.75
35	Pat Holmes	3.00	1.50	.90
36	Art Johnson	3.00	1.50	.90
37	Jerry Keeling	6.00	3.00	1.75
38	Roger Kramer	4.00	2.00	1.25
39	Hal Krebs	3.00	1.50	.90
40	Don Luzzi	6.00	3.00	1.75
41	Pete Manning	3.00	1.50	.90
42	Dale Parsons	3.00	1.50	.90

43	R. Payne	3.00	1.50	.90
44	Larry Robinson	3.00	1.50	.90
45	Gerry Shaw	3.00	1.50	.90
46	Don Stephenson	3.00	1.50	.90
47	Bob Taylor	3.00	1.50	.90
48	Ted Woods	3.00	1.50	.90
49	Jon Anabo	3.00	1.50	.90
50	R. Ash	3.00	1.50	.90
51	Jim Battle	3.00	1.50	.90
52	Charlie Brown	3.00	1.50	.90
53	Tommy Joe Coffey	9.00	4.50	2.75
54	Marcel Deleeuw	3.00	1.50	.90
55	Al Ecuyer	3.00	1.50	.90
56	Ron Forwick	3.00	1.50	.90
57	Jim Higgins	3.00	1.50	.90
58	H. Huth	3.00	1.50	.90
59	R. Kerbow	3.00	1.50	.90
60	Oscar Kruger	3.00	1.50	.90
61	T. Machan	3.00	1.50	.90
62	G. McKee	3.00	1.50	.90
63	Bill Mitchell	3.00	1.50	.90
64	Barry Mitchelson	3.00	1.50	.90
65	Roger Nelson	6.00	3.00	1.75
66	Bill Redell	3.00	1.50	.90
67	M. Rohliser	3.00	1.50	.90
68	Howie Schumm	3.00	1.50	.90
69	E.A. Sims	3.00	1.50	.90
70	John Sklopan	3.00	1.50	.90
71	Jim Stinnette	3.00	1.50	.90
72	Barney Therrien	3.00	1.50	.90
73	Jim Thomas	3.00	1.50	.90
74	Neil Thomas	3.00	1.50	.90
75	B. Tobin	3.00	1.50	.90
76	Terry Wilson	3.00	1.50	.90
77	Art Baker	3.00	1.50	.90
78	John Barrow	6.00	3.00	1.75
79	Gene Ceppetelli	3.00	1.50	.90
80	J. Cimba	3.00	1.50	.90
81	Dick Cohee	3.00	1.50	.90
82	Frank Cosentino	4.00	2.00	1.25
83	Johnny Counts	3.00	1.50	.90
84	Stan Crisson	3.00	1.50	.90
85	Tommy Grant	7.50	3.75	2.25
86	Garney Henley	7.50	3.75	2.25
87	H. Hoerster	3.00	1.50	.90
88	Zeno Karcz	3.00	1.50	.90
89	Ellison Kelly	7.50	3.75	2.25
90	Bob Krouse	3.00	1.50	.90
91	Billy Ray Locklin	3.00	1.50	.90
92	Chet Miksza	3.00	1.50	.90
93	Angelo Mosca	15.00	7.50	4.50
94	Bronko Nagurski	7.50	3.75	2.25
95	Ted Page	3.00	1.50	.90
96	Don Sutherin	6.00	3.00	1.75
97	Dave Viti	3.00	1.50	.90
98	Dick Walton	3.00	1.50	.90
99	Billy Wayte	3.00	1.50	.90
100	Joe Zuger	3.00	1.50	.90
101	Jim Andreotti	3.00	1.50	.90
102	John Baker	4.00	2.00	1.25
103	G. Beretta	3.00	1.50	.90
104	Bill Bewley	3.00	1.50	.90
105	Garland Boyette	4.00	2.00	1.25
106	Doug Daigneault	3.00	1.50	.90
107	George Dixon	7.50	3.75	2.25
108	D. Dolatri	3.00	1.50	.90
109	Ted Elsby	3.00	1.50	.90
110	Don Estes	3.00	1.50	.90
111	Terry Evenshen	9.00	4.50	2.75
112	Clare Exelby	3.00	1.50	.90
113	Larry Fairholm	4.00	2.00	1.25
114	Bernie Faloney	15.00	7.50	4.50
115	Don Fuell	3.00	1.50	.90
116	M. Gibbons	3.00	1.50	.90
117	Ralph Goldston	3.00	1.50	.90
118	Al Irwin	3.00	1.50	.90
119	John Kenerson	3.00	1.50	.90
120	Ed Learn	3.00	1.50	.90
121	Moe Levesque	3.00	1.50	.90
122	Bob Minihane	3.00	1.50	.90
123	Jim Reynolds	3.00	1.50	.90
124	Billy Roy	3.00	1.50	.90
125	L. Tominson	3.00	1.50	.90
126	Ernie White	3.00	1.50	.90
127	Rick Black	3.00	1.50	.90
128	Mike Blum	3.00	1.50	.90
129	Billy Joe Booth	3.00	1.50	.90
130	Jim Cain	3.00	1.50	.90
131	Bill Cline	3.00	1.50	.90
132	Merv Collins	3.00	1.50	.90
133	Jim Conroy	3.00	1.50	.90
134	Larry DeGraw	3.00	1.50	.90
135	Jim Dillard	3.00	1.50	.90
136	Gene Gaines	6.00	3.00	1.75
137	Don Gilbert	3.00	1.50	.90
138	Russ Jackson	15.00	7.50	4.50
139	Ken Lehmann	3.00	1.50	.90
140	Bob O'Billovich	3.00	1.50	.90
141	John Pentecost	3.00	1.50	.90
142	Joe Poirier	3.00	1.50	.90
143	Moe Racine	3.00	1.50	.90
144	Sam Scoccia	3.00	1.50	.90
145	Bo Scott	7.50	3.75	2.25
146	Jerry Selinger	3.00	1.50	.90
147	Marshall Shirk	3.00	1.50	.90
148	Bill Siekierski	3.00	1.50	.90
149	Ron Stewart	7.50	3.75	2.25
150	Whit Tucker	6.00	3.00	1.75
151	Ron Atchison	6.00	3.00	1.75
152	Al Benecick	3.00	1.50	.90
153	Clyde Brock	3.00	1.50	.90
154	Ed Buchanan	3.00	1.50	.90
155	R. Cameron	3.00	1.50	.90
156	Hugh Campbell	7.50	3.75	2.25
157	Henry Dorsch	3.00	1.50	.90
158	Larry Dumelie	3.00	1.50	.90
159	Garner Ekstran	3.00	1.50	.90
160	Martin Fabi	3.00	1.50	.90
161	Bob Good	3.00	1.50	.90
162	Bob Kosid	3.00	1.50	.90
163	Ron Lancaster	9.00	4.50	2.75
164	Hal Ledvard	3.00	1.50	.90
165	Len Legault	3.00	1.50	.90
166	Ron Meadmore	3.00	1.50	.90
167	Bob Ptacek	3.00	1.50	.90
168	George Reed	9.00	4.50	2.75
169	Dick Schnell	3.00	1.50	.90
170	Wayne Shaw	3.00	1.50	.90
171	Ted Urness	6.00	3.00	1.75
172	Dale West	3.00	1.50	.90
173	Reg Whitehouse	3.00	1.50	.90
174	Gene Wlasiuk	3.00	1.50	.90
175	Jim Worden	3.00	1.50	.90
176	Dick Aldridge	3.00	1.50	.90
177	Walt Balasiuk	3.00	1.50	.90
178	Ron Brewer	3.00	1.50	.90
179	W. Dickey	3.00	1.50	.90
180	B. Dugan	3.00	1.50	.90
181	L. Ferguson	3.00	1.50	.90
182	Don Fuell	3.00	1.50	.90
183	Ed Harrington	3.00	1.50	.90
184	Ron Howell	3.00	1.50	.90
185	F. Laroue	3.00	1.50	.90
186	Sherman Lewis	7.50	3.75	2.25
187	Marv Luster	6.00	3.00	1.75
188	Dave Mann	4.00	2.00	1.25
189	Pete Martin	3.00	1.50	.90
190	Marty Martinello	3.00	1.50	.90
191	Lamar McHan	6.00	3.00	1.75
192	Danny Nykoluk	3.00	1.50	.90
193	Jackie Parker	20.00	10.00	6.00
194	Dave Pivec	3.00	1.50	.90
195	Jim Rountree	3.00	1.50	.90
196	Dick Shatto	7.50	3.75	2.25
197	Billy Shipp	3.00	1.50	.90
198	Len Sparks	3.00	1.50	.90
199	D. Still	3.00	1.50	.90
200	Norm Stoneburgh	3.00	1.50	.90
201	Dave Thelan	6.00	3.00	1.75
202	J. Vilanus	3.00	1.50	.90
203	J. Walter	3.00	1.50	.90
204	P. Watson	3.00	1.50	.90
205	John Wydareny	3.00	1.50	.90
206	Billy Cooper	3.00	1.50	.90
207	Wayne Dennis	3.00	1.50	.90
208	Paul Desjardins	3.00	1.50	.90
209	N. Dunford	3.00	1.50	.90
210	Farrell Funston	3.00	1.50	.90
211	Herb Gray	7.50	3.75	2.25
212	Roger Hamelin	3.00	1.50	.90
213	Barrie Hansen	3.00	1.50	.90
214	Henry Janzen	3.00	1.50	.90
215	Hal Ledyard	3.00	1.50	.90
216	Leo Lewis	7.50	3.75	2.25
217	Brian Palmer	3.00	1.50	.90
218	Art Perkins	3.00	1.50	.90
219	Cornel Piper	3.00	1.50	.90
220	Ernie Pitts	3.00	1.50	.90
221	Kenny Ploen	7.50	3.75	2.25
222	Dave Raimey	4.00	2.00	1.25
223	Norm Rauhaus	3.00	1.50	.90
224	Frank Rigney	6.00	3.00	1.75
225	Roger Savoie	3.00	1.50	.90
226	Jackie Simpson	6.00	3.00	1.75
227	Dick Thornton	4.00	2.00	1.25
228	Sherwyn Thorson	3.00	1.50	.90
229	Ed Elmer	3.00	1.50	.90
230	Bill Whisler	3.00	1.50	.90

1965 Coke Caps Eagles

		NM	E	VG
Complete Set (36):		110.00	55.00	32.50
Common Player:		3.00	1.50	.90
1	Norm Snead	5.00	2.50	1.50
2	Al Nelson	3.00	1.50	.90
3	Jim Skaggs	3.00	1.50	.90
4	Glenn Glass	3.00	1.50	.90
5	Pete Retzlaff	4.00	2.00	1.25
6	Bill Mack	3.00	1.50	.90
7	Ray Rissmiller	3.00	1.50	.90
8	Lynn Hoyem	3.00	1.50	.90
9	King Hill	4.00	2.00	1.25
10	Timmy Brown	5.00	2.50	1.50
11	Ollie Matson	10.00	5.00	3.00
12	Dave Lloyd	4.00	2.00	1.25
13	Jim Ringo	7.00	3.50	2.00
15	Riley Gunnels	3.00	1.50	.90
16	Claude Crabb	3.00	1.50	.90
17	Earl Gros	4.00	2.00	1.25
18	Fred Hill	3.00	1.50	.90
19	Don Hultz	3.00	1.50	.90
20	Ray Poage	3.00	1.50	.90
21	Irv Cross	5.00	2.50	1.50
22	Mike Morgan	3.00	1.50	.90
23	Maxie Baughan	4.00	2.00	1.25
24	Ed Blaine	3.00	1.50	.90
25	Jack Concannon	4.00	2.00	1.25
26	Sam Baker	3.00	1.50	.90
27	Tom Woodeshick	4.00	2.00	1.25
29	John Meyers	3.00	1.50	.90
30	Nate Ramsey	3.00	1.50	.90
31	George Tarasovic	3.00	1.50	.90
32	Bob Brown	5.00	2.50	1.50
33	Willie Brown	3.00	1.50	.90
34	Ron Goodwin	3.00	1.50	.90
35	Dave Graham	3.00	1.50	.90
36	**Team Logo**	3.00	1.50	.90
---	**Eagles Saver Sheet**	30.00	15.00	9.00

1965 Coke Caps Giants

The 35-cap, 1-1/8" set was distributed in the metropolitan New York area and featured key players from the Giants. The outside of the cap features a Coke logo and a football while the inside depicts one of the Giants players. A Cap Saver sheet was also available and completed sheets could be redeemed for prizes (NFL leather football, mini plastic NFL helmet set, mini Giants megaphone). The caps are numbered with the "G" prefix.

		NM	E	VG
Complete Set (35):		100.00	50.00	30.00
Common Player:		2.50	2.00	1.00
1	Joe Morrison	2.50	2.00	1.00
2	Dick Lynch	2.50	1.25	.70
3	Andy Stynchula	2.50	2.00	1.00
4	Clarence Childs	2.50	2.00	1.00
5	Aaron Thomas	2.50	2.00	1.00
6	Mickey Walker	2.50	2.00	1.00
7	Bill Winter	2.50	2.00	1.00
8	Bookie Bolin	2.50	2.00	1.00
9	Tom Scott	2.50	2.00	1.00
10	John Lovetere	2.50	2.00	1.00
11	Jim Patton	5.00	2.50	1.50
12	Darrell Dess	2.50	2.00	1.00
13	Dick James	2.50	2.00	1.00
14	Jerry Hillebrand	2.50	2.00	1.00
15	Dick Personen	2.50	2.00	1.00
16	Del Shofner	2.50	1.25	.70
17	Erich Barnes	2.50	1.25	.70
18	Roosevelt Brown	6.00	3.00	1.75
19	Greg Larson	2.50	2.00	1.00
20	Jim Katcavage	2.50	1.25	.70
21	Frank Lasky	2.50	2.00	1.00
22	Lou Slaby	2.50	2.00	1.00
23	Jim Moran	2.50	2.00	1.00
24	Roger Anderson	2.50	2.00	1.00
25	Steve Thurlow	2.50	2.00	1.00
26	Ernie Wheelwright	2.50	2.00	1.00
27	Gary Wood	5.00	2.50	1.50
28	Tony Dimidio	2.50	2.00	1.00
29	John Contoulis	2.50	2.00	1.00
30	Tucker Fredrickson	5.00	2.50	1.50
31	Bob Timberlake	2.50	2.00	1.00
32	Chuck Mercein	2.50	1.25	.70
33	Ernie Koy	2.50	1.25	.70
34	Tom Costello	2.50	2.00	1.00
35	Homer Jones	5.00	2.50	1.50
NNO	**Giants Saver Sheet**	20.00	10.00	6.00

1965 Coke Caps Jets

The 35-cap, 1-1/8" in diameter set was issued in the New York City area and was highlighted by top players from the Jets. Collectors who redeemed the complete set were awarded either a leather AFL football, a mini plastic AFL helmet set, or a Jets mini megaphone. The caps were numbered with the "J" prefix. Joe Namath's cap is the key to the set.

		NM	E	VG
Complete Set (35):		150.00	75.00	45.00
Common Player:		2.50	2.00	1.00
1	Don Maynard	10.00	5.00	3.00
2	George Sauer Jr.	5.00	2.50	1.50

3	Cosmo Iacavazzi	2.50	2.00	1.00
4	Jim O'Mahoney	2.50	2.00	1.00
5	Matt Snell	5.00	2.50	1.50
6	Clyde Washington	2.50	2.00	1.00
7	Jim Turner	2.50	1.25	.70
8	Mike Taliaferro	2.50	2.00	1.00
9	Marshall Starks	2.50	2.00	1.00
10	Mark Smolinski	2.50	2.00	1.00
11	Bob Schweickert	2.50	2.00	1.00
12	Paul Rochester	2.50	2.00	1.00
13	Sherman Plunkett	2.50	1.25	.70
14	Gerry Philbin	2.50	1.25	.70
15	Pete Perreault	2.50	2.00	1.00
16	Dainard Paulson	2.50	2.00	1.00
17	Joe Namath	50.00	25.00	15.00
18	Winston Hill	2.50	1.25	.70
19	Dee Mackey	2.50	2.00	1.00
20	Curley Johnson	2.50	2.00	1.00
21	Mike Hudock	2.50	2.00	1.00
22	John Huarte	5.00	2.50	1.50
23	Gordy Holz	2.50	2.00	1.00
24	Gene Heeter	5.00	2.50	1.50
25	Larry Grantham	5.00	2.50	1.50
26	Dan Ficca	2.50	2.00	1.00
27	Sam DeLuca	2.50	2.00	1.00
28	Bill Baird	2.50	2.00	1.00
29	Ralph Baker	2.50	2.00	1.00
30	Wahoo McDaniel	10.00	5.00	3.00
31	Jim Evans	2.50	2.00	1.00
32	Dave Herman	2.50	2.00	1.00
33	John Schmitt	2.50	2.00	1.00
34	Jim Harris	2.50	2.00	1.00
35	Bake Turner	5.00	2.50	1.50
NNO	**Jets Saver Sheet**	20.00	10.00	6.00

1965 Coke Caps Lions

		NM	E	VG
	Complete Set (36):	100.00	50.00	30.00
	Common Player:	2.50	2.00	1.00
1	Pat Studstill	5.00	2.50	1.50
2	Bob Whitlow	2.50	2.00	1.00
3	Wayne Walker	5.00	2.50	1.50
4	Tom Watkins	2.50	2.00	1.00
5	Jim Simon	2.50	2.00	1.00
6	Sam Williams	2.50	2.00	1.00
7	Terry Barr	2.50	2.00	1.00
8	Jerry Rush	2.50	2.00	1.00
9	Roger Brown	2.50	1.25	.70
10	Tom Nowatzke	5.00	2.50	1.50
11	Dick "Night Train" Lane	7.00	3.50	2.00
12	Dick Compton	2.50	2.00	1.00
13	Yale Lary	5.00	2.50	1.50
14	Dick LeBeau	5.00	2.50	1.50
15	Dan Lewis	5.00	2.50	1.50
16	Wally Hilgenberg	5.00	2.50	1.50
17	Bruce Maher	2.50	2.00	1.00
18	Darris McCord	2.50	2.00	1.00
19	Hugh McInnis	2.50	2.00	1.00
20	Ernie Clark	2.50	2.00	1.00
21	Gail Cogdill	5.00	2.50	1.50
22	Wayne Rasmussen	2.50	2.00	1.00
23	Joe Don Looney	8.00	4.00	2.50
24	Jim Gibbons	5.00	2.50	1.50
25	John Gonzaga	2.50	2.00	1.00
26	John Gordy	2.50	2.00	1.00
27	Bobby Thompson	2.50	2.00	1.00
28	J.D. Smith	5.00	2.50	1.50
29	Earl Morrall	6.00	3.00	1.75
30	Alex Karras	8.00	4.00	2.50
31	Nick Pietrosante	2.50	1.25	.70
32	Milt Plum	2.50	1.25	.70
33	Daryl Sanders	2.50	2.00	1.00
34	Joe Schmidt	8.00	4.00	2.50
35	Bob Scholtz	2.50	2.00	1.00
36	**Team Logo**	2.50	2.00	1.00
NNO	**Lions Saver Sheet**	20.00	10.00	6.00

1965 Coke Caps National NFL

The 70-cap, 1-1/8" set was issued in metropolitan areas that did not have (in 1965) an NFL team. The caps have red liners and depict a player's facial image on the inside. The top of the cap had a Coke logo and a football icon. The caps are numbered with the "C" prefix.

		NM	E	VG
	Complete Set (70):	200.00	150.00	80.00
	Common Player:	2.50	1.25	.70
1	Herb Adderley	5.00	2.00	1.50
2	Yale Lary	5.00	2.50	1.50
3	Dick LeBeau	2.50	2.00	1.00
4	Bill Brown	5.00	2.50	1.50
5	Jim Taylor	8.00	4.00	2.50
6	Joe Fortunato	2.50	2.00	1.00
7	Bill Boyd	2.50	2.00	1.00
8	Terry Barr	2.50	2.00	1.00
9	Dick Szymanski	2.50	2.00	1.00

10	Mick Tinglehoff	2.50	1.25	.70
11	Wayne Walker	2.50	2.00	1.00
12	Matt Hazeltine	2.50	2.00	1.00
13	Ray Nitschke	7.00	3.50	2.00
14	Grady Alderman	2.50	2.00	1.00
15	Charlie Krueger	2.50	2.00	1.00
16	Tommy Mason	2.50	2.00	1.00
17	Willie Wood	5.00	2.50	1.50
18	Johnny Unitas	14.00	7.00	4.25
19	Lenny Moore	5.00	2.50	1.50
20	Fran Tarkenton	12.00	6.00	3.50
21	Deacon Jones	7.00	3.50	2.00
22	Bob Vogel	2.50	2.00	1.00
23	John Gordy	2.50	2.00	1.00
24	Jim Parker	2.50	1.25	.70
25	Jim Gibbons	2.50	2.00	1.00
26	Merlin Olsen	7.00	3.50	2.00
27	Forrest Gregg	6.00	3.00	1.75
28	Roger Brown	2.50	2.00	1.00
29	Dave Parks	2.50	2.00	1.00
30	Raymond Berry	5.00	2.50	1.50
31	Mike Ditka	12.00	6.00	3.50
32	Gino Marchetti	5.00	2.50	1.50
33	Willie Davis	5.00	2.50	1.50
34	Ed Meador	2.50	2.00	1.00
35	**Browns Logo**	2.50	2.00	1.00
36	**Colts Logo**	2.50	2.00	1.00
37	Sam Baker	2.50	2.00	1.00
38	Irv Cross	5.00	2.50	1.50
39	Maxie Baughan	2.50	2.00	1.00
40	Vince Promuto	2.50	2.00	1.00
41	Paul Krause	2.50	2.00	1.00
42	Charley Taylor	5.00	2.50	1.50
43	John Paluck	2.50	2.00	1.00
44	Paul Warfield	8.00	4.00	2.50
45	Dick Modzelewski	2.50	2.00	1.00
46	Myron Pottios	2.50	2.00	1.00
47	Erich Barnes	2.50	2.00	1.00
48	Bill Koman	2.50	2.00	1.00
49	Art Thomas	2.50	2.00	1.00
50	Gary Ballman	2.50	2.00	1.00
51	Sam Huff	5.00	2.50	1.50
52	Ken Gray	2.50	2.00	1.00
53	Roosevelt Brown	6.00	3.00	1.75
54	Bobby Joe Conrad	2.50	2.00	1.00
55	Pat Fischer	2.50	2.00	1.00
56	Irv Goode	2.50	2.00	1.00
57	Floyd Peters	2.50	2.00	1.00
58	Charlie Johnson	5.00	2.50	1.50
59	John Henry Johnson	5.00	2.50	1.50
60	Charley Bradshaw	2.50	2.00	1.00
61	Jim Ringo	5.00	2.50	1.50
62	Pete Retzlaff	5.00	2.50	1.50
63	Sonny Jurgensen	8.00	4.00	2.50
64	Don Meredith	12.00	6.00	3.50
65	Bob Lilly	8.00	4.00	2.50
66	Bill Glass	2.50	2.00	1.00
67	Dick Schafrath	2.50	2.00	1.00
68	Mel Renfro	5.00	2.50	1.50
69	Jim Houston	2.50	2.00	1.00
70	Frank Ryan	2.50	1.25	.70

1965 Coke Caps Packers

The 36-cap, 1-1/8" in diameter set featured Packers players and was issued in the greater metropolitan areas of Wisconsin, such as Milwaukee, Green Bay and Madison areas. Completed sets on a Cap Saver sheet could be redeemed for a variety of prizes before an expiration date. The caps are numbered with a "C" prefix.

		NM	E	VG
	Complete Set (36):	160.00	120.00	65.00
	Common Player:	2.50	2.00	1.00
1	Herb Adderley	5.00	2.50	1.50
2	Lionel Aldridge	2.50	2.00	1.00
3	Hank Gremminger	2.50	2.00	1.00
4	Willie Davis	6.00	3.00	1.75
5	Boyd Dowler	5.00	2.50	1.50
6	Marv Fleming	2.50	2.00	1.00
7	Ken Bowman	2.50	2.00	1.00
8	Tom Brown	2.50	2.00	1.00
9	Doug Hart	2.50	2.00	1.00
10	Steve Wright	2.50	2.00	1.00
11	Dennis Claridge	2.50	2.00	1.00
12	Dave Hanner	2.50	2.00	1.00
13	Tommy Crutcher	2.50	2.00	1.00
14	Fred Thurston	5.00	2.50	1.50
15	Elijah Pitts	5.00	2.50	1.50
16	Lloyd Voss	2.50	2.00	1.00
17	Lee Roy Caffey	5.00	2.50	1.50
18	Dave Robinson	5.00	2.50	1.50
19	Bart Starr	14.00	7.00	4.25
20	Ray Nitschke	10.00	5.00	3.00
21	Max McGee	6.00	3.00	1.75
22	Don Chandler	2.50	2.00	1.00
23	Norm Masters	2.50	2.00	1.00
24	Ron Kostelnik	2.50	2.00	1.00

25	Carroll Dale	5.00	2.50	1.50
26	Hank Jordan	5.00	2.50	1.50
27	Bob Jeter	2.50	2.00	1.00
28	Bob Skoronski	2.50	2.00	1.00
29	Jerry Kramer	6.00	3.00	1.75
30	Willie Wood	6.00	3.00	1.75
31	Paul Hornung	14.00	7.00	4.25
32	Forrest Gregg	8.00	4.00	2.50
33	Zeke Bratkowski	5.00	2.50	1.50
34	Tom Moore	2.50	2.00	1.00
35	Jim Taylor	10.00	5.00	3.00
36	**Team Logo**	2.50	2.00	1.00
NNO	**Packers Saver Sheet**	20.00	10.00	6.00

1965 Coke Caps Patriots

The 36-cap, 1-1/8" set was issued in the New England area and a completed set on a Cap Saver sheet could be redeemed for a prize. The cap tops feature a Coke logo and an image of a football, while the inside has the facial image of a Patriots player. Other Coke products, such as Fresca and Tab, also had the player caps. The caps are numbered with a "C" prefix.

		NM	E	VG
	Complete Set (36):	100.00	50.00	30.00
	Common Player:	2.50	2.00	1.00
1	Jon Morris	5.00	2.50	1.50
2	Don Webb	2.50	2.00	1.00
3	Charles Long	5.00	2.50	1.50
4	Tony Romeo	2.50	2.00	1.00
5	Bob Dee	2.50	2.00	1.00
6	Tommy Addison	5.00	2.50	1.50
7	Bob Yates	2.50	2.00	1.00
8	Ron Hall	2.50	2.00	1.00
9	Billy Neighbors	2.50	2.00	1.00
10	Jack Rudolph	2.50	2.00	1.00
11	Don Oakes	2.50	2.00	1.00
12	Tom Yewcic	2.50	2.00	1.00
13	Ron Burton	5.00	2.50	1.50
14	Jim Colclough	2.50	2.00	1.00
15	Larry Garron	5.00	2.50	1.50
16	Dave Watson	2.50	2.00	1.00
17	Art Graham	5.00	2.50	1.50
18	Babe Parilli	5.00	2.50	1.50
19	Jim Hunt	2.50	2.00	1.00
20	Don McKinnon	2.50	2.00	1.00
21	Houston Antwine	2.50	2.00	1.00
22	Nick Buoniconti	8.00	4.00	2.50
23	Ross O'Hanley	2.50	2.00	1.00
24	Gino Cappelletti	5.00	2.50	1.50
25	Chuck Shonta	2.50	2.00	1.00
26	Dick Felt	2.50	2.00	1.00
27	Mike Dukes	2.50	2.00	1.00
28	Larry Eisenhauer	2.50	2.00	1.00
29	Bob Schmidt	2.50	2.00	1.00
30	Len St. Jean	2.50	2.00	1.00
31	J.D. Garrett	2.50	2.00	1.00
32	Jim Whalen	2.50	2.00	1.00
33	Jim Nance	5.00	2.50	1.50
34	Eddie Wilson	2.50	2.00	1.00
35	Lonnie Farmer	2.50	2.00	1.00
36	**Boston Patriots Logo**	2.50	2.00	1.00
NNO	**Patriots Saver Sheet**	20.00	10.00	6.00

1965 Coke Caps Redskins

The 36-cap, 1-1/8" set was distributed in the Washington, D.C. area and featured top players from the Redskins. As with other Coke cap sets, the Redskins set could be collected on a Cap Saver sheet and redeemed for prizes. Other Coke products, such as Fresca and Tab, also had the player caps. The caps are numbered with a "C" prefix.

		NM	E	VG
	Complete Set (36):	100.00	50.00	30.00
	Common Player:	2.50	2.00	1.00
1	Jimmy Carr	2.50	2.00	1.00
2	Fred Mazurek	2.50	2.00	1.00
3	Lonnie Sanders	2.50	2.00	1.00
4	Jim Steffen	2.50	2.00	1.00
5	John Nisby	2.50	2.00	1.00
6	George Izo	5.00	2.50	1.50
7	Vince Promuto	2.50	2.00	1.00
8	Johnny Sample	5.00	2.50	1.50
9	Pat Richter	5.00	2.50	1.50
10	Preston Carpenter	2.50	2.00	1.00
11	Sam Huff	8.00	4.00	2.50
12	Pervis Atkins	2.50	2.00	1.00
13	Fred Barnett	2.50	2.00	1.00
14	Len Hauss	5.00	2.50	1.50
15	Bill Anderson	2.50	2.00	1.00
16	John Reger	2.50	2.00	1.00
17	George Seals	2.50	2.00	1.00
18	J.W. Lockett	2.50	2.00	1.00
19	Tom Walters	2.50	2.00	1.00
20	Joe Rutgens	2.50	2.00	1.00
21	John Paluck	2.50	2.00	1.00
22	Fran O'Brien	2.50	2.00	1.00

23	Joe Rutgens	2.50	2.00	1.00
24	Rod Breedlove	2.50	2.00	1.00
25	Bob Pellegrini	2.50	2.00	1.00
26	Bob Jencks	2.50	2.00	1.00
27	Joe Hernandez	2.50	2.00	1.00
28	Sonny Jurgensen	10.00	5.00	3.00
29	Bob Toneff	2.50	2.00	1.00
30	Charley Taylor	8.00	4.00	2.50
31	Bob Shiner	2.50	2.00	1.00
32	Bobby Williams	2.50	2.00	1.00
33	Angelo Coia	2.50	2.00	1.00
34	Ron Snidow	2.50	2.00	1.00
35	Paul Krause	5.00	2.50	1.50
36	**Team Logo**	2.50	2.00	1.00
NNO	**Redskins Saver Sheet**	20.00	10.00	6.00

1965 Coke Caps Vikings

		NM	E	VG
	Complete Set (36):	125.00	62.50	37.50
	Common Player:	3.00	1.50	.90
1	Jerry Reichow	4.00	2.00	1.25
2	Jim Prestel	3.00	1.50	.90
3	Jim Marshall	6.00	3.00	1.75
4	Errol Linden	3.00	1.50	.90
5	Bob Lacey	3.00	1.50	.90
6	Rip Hawkins	3.00	1.50	.90
7	John Kirby	3.00	1.50	.90
8	Roy Winston	4.00	2.00	1.25
9	Ron Vanderkelen	4.00	2.00	1.25
10	Gordon Smith	3.00	1.50	.90
11	Larry Bowie	3.00	1.50	.90
12	Paul Flatley	4.00	2.00	1.25
13	Grady Alderman	4.00	2.00	1.25
14	Mick Tingelhoff	5.00	2.50	1.50
15	Lee Calland	3.00	1.50	.90
16	Fred Cox	4.00	2.00	1.25
17	Bill Brown	4.00	2.00	1.25
18	Ed Sharockman	3.00	1.50	.90
19	George Rose	3.00	1.50	.90
20	Paul Dickson	3.00	1.50	.90
21	Tommy Mason	4.00	2.00	1.25
22	Carl Eller	5.00	2.50	1.50
23	Bill Jobko	3.00	1.50	.90
24	Hal Bedsole	3.00	1.50	.90
25	Karl Kassulke	3.00	1.50	.90
26	Fran Tarkenton	12.00	6.00	3.50
27	Tom Hall	3.00	1.50	.90
28	Archie Sutton	3.00	1.50	.90
29	Jim Phillips	3.00	1.50	.90
30	Bill Swain	3.00	1.50	.90
31	Larry Vargo	3.00	1.50	.90
32	Bobby Walden	3.00	1.50	.90
33	Bob Berry	4.00	2.00	1.25
34	Jeff Jordan	3.00	1.50	.90
35	Lance Rentzel	4.00	2.00	1.25
36	**Vikings Logo**	3.00	1.50	.90
---	**Vikings Saver Sheet**	30.00	15.00	9.00

1966 Coke Caps 49ers

The 36-cap, 1-1/8" set was issued to highlight members of the 49ers. A Cap Saver sheet was also available and could be redeemed for prizes upon completion. Tab and Fresca also had player caps. The cap tops featured the Coke logo with a football icon while the bottom had the player's image. The caps are numbered with a "C" prefix.

		NM	E	VG
	Complete Set (36):	80.00	60.00	32.00
	Common Player:	2.00	1.50	.80
1	Bernie Casey	3.00	1.50	.90
2	Bruce Bosley	2.00	1.50	.80
3	Kermit Alexander	3.00	1.50	.90
4	John Brodie	8.00	4.00	2.50
5	Dave Parks	3.00	1.50	.90
6	Len Rohde	2.00	1.50	.80
7	Walter Rock	2.00	1.50	.80
8	George Mira	4.00	2.00	1.25
9	Karl Rubke	2.00	1.50	.80
10	Ken Willard	3.00	1.50	.90
11	John David Crow (UER) (Name misspelled Crowe)	3.00	1.50	.90
12	George Donnelly	2.00	1.50	.80
13	Dave Wilcox	3.00	1.50	.90
14	Vern Burke	2.00	1.50	.80
15	Wayne Swinford	2.00	1.50	.80
16	Elbert Kimbrough	2.00	1.50	.80
17	Clark Miller	2.00	1.50	.80
18	Dave Kopay	3.00	1.50	.90
19	Joe Cerne	2.00	1.50	.80
20	Roland Lakes	2.00	1.50	.80
21	Charlie Krueger	2.00	1.50	.80
22	Billy Kilmer	4.00	2.00	1.25
23	Jim Johnson	5.00	2.50	1.50
24	Matt Hazeltine	2.00	1.50	.80
25	Mike Dowdle	2.00	1.50	.80
26	Jim Wilson	2.00	1.50	.80
27	Tommy Davis	3.00	1.50	.90
28	Jim Norton	2.00	1.50	.80
29	Jack Chapple	2.00	1.50	.80
30	Ed Beard	2.00	1.50	.80
31	John Thomas	2.00	1.50	.80
32	Monty Stickles	2.00	1.50	.80
33	Kay McFarland	2.00	1.50	.80
34	Gary Lewis	2.00	1.50	.80
35	Howard Mudd	2.00	1.50	.80
36	**49ers Logo**	2.00	1.50	.80
NNO	**49ers Saver Sheet**	20.00	10.00	6.00

1966 Coke Caps All-Stars AFL

The 34-cap, 1-1/8" in diameter set was issued in AFL cities and could be collected on Cap Saver sheets, some of which had separate sections to place both the local and All-Star caps. The caps are virtually identical to previous Coke caps sets and were also found on Fresca and Tab products. The caps are numbered with a "C" prefix.

		NM	E	VG
	Complete Set (34):	120.00	90.00	47.50
	Common Player:	2.00	1.00	.60
37	Babe Parilli	4.00	2.00	1.25
38	Mike Stratton	2.00	1.00	.60
39	Jack Kemp	18.00	9.00	5.50
40	Len Dawson	8.00	4.00	2.50
41	Fred Arbanas	2.00	1.00	.60
42	Bobby Bell	4.00	2.00	1.25
43	Willie Brown	4.00	2.00	1.25
44	Buck Buchanan	4.00	2.00	1.25
45	Frank Buncom	2.00	1.00	.60
46	Nick Buoniconti	4.00	2.00	1.25
47	Gino Cappelletti	4.00	2.00	1.25
48	Eldon Danenhauer	2.00	1.00	.60
49	Clem Daniels	4.00	2.00	1.25
50	Les Duncan	4.00	2.00	1.25
51	Willie Frazier	2.00	1.00	.60
52	Cookie Gilchrist	4.00	2.00	1.25
53	Dave Grayson	2.00	1.00	.60
54	John Hadl	5.00	2.50	1.50
55	Wayne Hawkins	2.00	1.00	.60
56	Sherrill Headrick	2.00	1.00	.60
57	Charlie Hennigan	4.00	2.00	1.25
58	E.J. Holub	2.00	1.00	.60
59	Curley Johnson	2.00	1.00	.60
60	Keith Lincoln	2.00	1.00	.60
61	Paul Lowe	4.00	2.00	1.25
62	Don Maynard	6.00	3.00	1.75
63	Jon Morris	2.00	1.00	.60
64	Joe Namath	20.00	10.00	6.00
65	Jim Otto	4.00	2.00	1.25
66	Dainard Paulson	2.00	1.00	.60
67	Art Powell	4.00	2.00	1.25
68	Walt Sweeney	4.00	2.00	1.25
69	Bob Talamini	2.00	1.00	.60
70	Lance Alworth (UER) (Name misspelled Alsworth)	8.00	4.00	2.50

1966 Coke Caps All-Stars NFL

The 34-cap, 1-1/8" set was issued in mostly NFL cities and some Cap Saver sheets had separate sections for both the local and All-Star caps. As with previous Cap Saver sheets, collectors could turn in a completed set for prizes. The caps are identical in design with other caps issues and could be found with Tab and Fresca products as well. The caps are numbered with a "C" prefix.

		NM	E	VG
	Complete Set (34):	120.00	90.00	47.50
	Common Player:	2.00	1.00	.60
37	Frank Ryan	4.00	2.00	1.25
38	Timmy Brown	4.00	2.00	1.25
39	Tucker Frederickson	2.00	1.00	.60
40	Cornell Green	4.00	2.00	1.25
41	Bob Hayes	4.00	2.00	1.25
42	Charley Taylor	4.00	2.00	1.25
43	Pete Retzlaff	4.00	2.00	1.25
44	Jim Ringo	6.00	3.00	1.75
45	John Wooten	2.00	1.00	.60
46	Dale Meinert	2.00	1.00	.60
47	Bob Lilly	8.00	4.00	2.50
48	Sam Silas	2.00	1.00	.60
49	Roosevelt Brown	6.00	3.00	1.75
50	Gary Ballman	2.00	1.00	.60
51	Gary Collins	2.00	1.00	.60
52	Sonny Randle	2.00	1.00	.60
53	Charlie Johnson	2.00	1.00	.60
54	Herb Adderley	4.00	2.00	1.25
55	Doug Atkins	4.00	2.00	1.25
56	Roger Brown	2.00	1.00	.60
57	Dick Butkus	14.00	7.00	4.25
58	Willie Davis	4.00	2.00	1.25
59	Tommy McDonald	2.00	1.00	.60
60	Alex Karras	6.00	3.00	1.75
61	John Mackey	4.00	2.00	1.25
62	Ed Meador	2.00	1.00	.60
63	Merlin Olsen	6.00	3.00	1.75
64	Dave Parks	2.00	1.00	.60
65	Gale Sayers	14.00	7.00	4.25
66	Fran Tarkenton	10.00	5.00	3.00
67	Mick Tingelhoff	2.00	1.00	.60
68	Ken Willard	2.00	1.00	.60
69	Willie Wood	4.00	2.00	1.25
70	Bill Brown	4.00	2.00	1.25

1966 Coke Caps Bills

The 36-cap, 1-1/8" in diameter set was distributed in western New York and was highlighted by Bills players. The caps are nearly identical in design as previous sets, except that the insides are numbered with a "B" prefix.

		NM	E	VG
	Complete Set (36):	120.00	90.00	47.50
	Common Player:	2.00	1.50	.80
1	Bill Laskey	2.00	1.50	.80
2	Marty Schottenheimer	8.00	4.00	2.50
3	Stew Barber	2.00	1.50	.80
4	Glenn Bass	2.00	1.50	.80
5	Remi Prudhomme	2.00	1.50	.80
6	Al Bemiller	2.00	1.50	.80
7	George (Butch) Byrd	3.00	1.50	.90
8	Wray Carlton	2.00	1.50	.80
9	Hagood Clarke	2.00	1.50	.80
10	Jack Kemp	25.00	12.50	7.50
11	Charlie Warner	2.00	1.50	.80
12	Elbert Dubenion	3.00	1.50	.90
13	Jim Dunaway	2.00	1.50	.80
14	Booker Edgerson	2.00	1.50	.80
15	Paul Costa	2.00	1.50	.80
16	Henry Schmidt	2.00	1.50	.80
17	Dick Hudson	2.00	1.50	.80
18	Harry Jacobs	2.00	1.50	.80
19	Tom Janik	2.00	1.50	.80
20	Tom Day	2.00	1.50	.80
21	Daryle Lamonica	5.00	2.50	1.50
22	Paul Maguire	6.00	3.00	1.75
23	Roland McDole	2.00	1.50	.80
24	Dudley Meredith	2.00	1.50	.80
25	Joe O'Donnell	2.00	1.50	.80
26	Charlie Ferguson	2.00	1.50	.80
27	Ed Rutkowski	2.00	1.50	.80
28	George Saimes	2.00	1.50	.80
29	Tom Sestak	3.00	1.50	.90
30	Billy Shaw	2.00	1.50	.80
31	Bobby Smith	2.00	1.50	.80
32	Mike Stratton	3.00	1.50	.90
33	Gene Sykes	2.00	1.50	.80
34	John Tracey	2.00	1.50	.80
35	Ernie Warlick	2.00	1.50	.80
36	**Bills Logo**	2.00	1.50	.80
NNO	**Bills Saver Sheet**	20.00	10.00	6.00

1966 Coke Caps Broncos

		NM	E	VG
	Complete Set (36):	125.00	62.50	37.50
	Common Player:	3.00	1.50	.90
1	Fred Forsberg	3.00	1.50	.90
2	Willie Brown	10.00	5.00	3.00
3	Bob Scarpitto	4.00	2.00	1.25
4	Butch Davis	3.00	1.50	.90
5	Al Denson	4.00	2.00	1.25
6	Ron Sbranti	3.00	1.50	.90
7	John Bramlett	3.00	1.50	.90
8	Mickey Slaughter	4.00	2.00	1.25
9	Lionel Taylor	5.00	2.50	1.50
10	Jerry Sturm	3.00	1.50	.90
11	Jerry Hopkins	3.00	1.50	.90
12	Charlie Mitchell	3.00	1.50	.90
13	Ray Jacobs	3.00	1.50	.90
14	Lonnie Wright	3.00	1.50	.90
15	Goldie Sellers	3.00	1.50	.90
16	Ray Kubala	3.00	1.50	.90
17	John Griffin	3.00	1.50	.90
18	Bob Breitenstein	3.00	1.50	.90
19	Eldon Danenhauer	3.00	1.50	.90
20	Wendell Hayes	4.00	2.00	1.25
21	Max Leetzow	3.00	1.50	.90
22	Nemiah Wilson	4.00	2.00	1.25
23	Jim Thibert	3.00	1.50	.90
24	Gerry Bussell	3.00	1.50	.90
25	Bob McCullough	3.00	1.50	.90
26	Jim McMillin	3.00	1.50	.90
27	Abner Haynes	6.00	3.00	1.75
28	Darrell Lester	3.00	1.50	.90
29	Cookie Gilchrist	6.00	3.00	1.75
30	John McCormick	4.00	2.00	1.25
31	Lee Bernet	3.00	1.50	.90
32	Goose Gonsoulin	5.00	2.50	1.50
33	Scotty Glacken	3.00	1.50	.90
34	Bob Hadrick	3.00	1.50	.90
35	Archie Matsos	4.00	2.00	1.25
36	**Broncos Logo**	3.00	1.50	.90

1966 Coke Caps Browns

The 36-cap, 1-1/8" set was part of Coke's 14-cap NFL set. The caps have a Coke logo and football icon on the outside with a the player's image on the inside. A Cap Saver sheet was also issued and, as with previous releases, a completed sheet could be redeemed for prizes. The caps are numbered with a "C" prefix.

		NM	E	VG
	Complete Set (36):	100.00	50.00	30.00
	Common Player:	2.00	1.50	.80
1	Jim Ninowski	3.00	1.50	.90
2	Leroy Kelly	6.00	3.00	1.75
3	Lou Groza	6.00	3.00	1.75
4	Gary Collins	3.00	1.50	.90
5	Bill Glass	3.00	1.50	.90
6	Dale Lindsey	2.00	1.50	.80
7	Galen Fiss	2.00	1.50	.80
8	Ross Fichtner	2.00	1.50	.80
9	John Wooten	2.00	1.50	.80
10	Clifton McNeil	2.00	1.50	.80
11	Paul Wiggin	2.00	1.50	.80
12	Gene Hickerson	3.00	1.50	.90
13	Ernie Green	2.00	1.50	.80
14	Mike Howell	2.00	1.50	.80
15	Dick Schafrath	2.00	1.50	.80
16	Sidney Williams	2.00	1.50	.80
17	Frank Ryan	3.00	1.50	.90
18	Bernie Parrish	3.00	1.50	.90
19	Vince Costello	2.00	1.50	.80
20	John Brown (CO)	2.00	1.50	.80
21	Monte Clark	2.00	1.50	.80
22	Walter Roberts	2.00	1.50	.80
23	Johnny Brewer	2.00	1.50	.80
24	Walter Beach	2.00	1.50	.80
25	Dick Modzelewski	2.00	1.50	.80
26	Gary Lane	2.00	1.50	.80
27	Jim Houston	2.00	1.50	.80
28	Milt Morin	2.00	1.50	.80
29	Erich Barnes	2.00	1.50	.80
30	Tom Hutchinson	2.00	1.50	.80
31	John Morrow	2.00	1.50	.80
32	Jim Kanicki	2.00	1.50	.80
33	Paul Warfield	8.00	4.00	2.50
34	Jim Garcia	2.00	1.50	.80
35	Walter Johnson	2.00	1.50	.80
36	**Browns Logo**	2.00	1.50	.80
NNO	**Browns Saver Sheet**	20.00	10.00	6.00

1966 Coke Caps Cardinals

The 36-cap, 1-1/8" set was issued in conjunction with other NFL, AFL and All-Star sets. Cap Saver sheets were also issued and completed sheets could be redeemed for prizes. The caps are virtually identical in design to previous sets. The caps are numbered with a "C" prefix.

		NM	E	VG
	Complete Set (36):	80.00	60.00	32.00
	Common Player:	2.00	1.50	.80
1	Pat Fischer	3.00	1.50	.90
2	Sonny Randle	2.00	1.50	.80
3	Joe Childress	2.00	1.50	.80
4	Dave Meggyesy (UER) (Name misspelled Meggyesy)	4.00	2.00	1.25
5	Joe Robb	2.00	1.50	.80
6	Jerry Stovall	3.00	1.50	.90
7	Ernie McMillan	3.00	1.50	.90
8	Dale Meinert	2.00	1.50	.80
9	Irv Goode	2.00	1.50	.80
10	Bob DeMarco	2.00	1.50	.80
11	Mal Hammack	2.00	1.50	.80
12	Jim Bakken	3.00	1.50	.90
13	Bill Thornton	2.00	1.50	.80
14	Buddy Humphrey	2.00	1.50	.80
15	Bill Koman	2.00	1.50	.80
16	Larry Wilson	5.00	2.50	1.50
17	Charles Walker	2.00	1.50	.80
18	Prentice Gautt	3.00	1.50	.90
19	Charlie Johnson (UER) (Name misspelled Charley)	3.00	1.50	.90
20	Ken Gray	2.00	1.50	.80
21	Dave Simmons	2.00	1.50	.80
22	Sam Silas	2.00	1.50	.80
23	Larry Stallings	2.00	1.50	.80
24	Don Brumm	2.00	1.50	.80
25	Bobby Joe Conrad	3.00	1.50	.90
26	Bill Triplett	2.00	1.50	.80
27	Luke Owens	2.00	1.50	.80
28	Jackie Smith	5.00	2.50	1.50
29	Bob Reynolds	2.00	1.50	.80
30	Abe Woodson	3.00	1.50	.90
31	Jim Burson	2.00	1.50	.80
32	Willis Crenshaw	2.00	1.50	.80
33	Billy Gambrell	2.00	1.50	.80
34	Ray Ogden	2.00	1.50	.80
35	Herschel Turner	2.00	1.50	.80
36	**Cardinals Logo**	2.00	1.50	.80
NNO	**Cardinals Saver Sheet**	20.00	10.00	6.00

1966 Coke Caps Chiefs

The 36-cap, 1-1/8" set featured key players from the Chiefs and had the Coke logo with a football stamp on the top and a player's image on the inside. Player caps could also be found on Fresca and Tab bottles. The caps are numbered with a "C" prefix.

		NM	E	VG
	Complete Set (36):	100.00	50.00	30.00
	Common Player:	2.00	1.50	.80
1	E.J. Holub	3.00	1.50	.90
2	Al Reynolds	2.00	1.50	.80
3	Buck Buchanan	5.00	2.50	1.50
4	Curt Merz (SP)	8.00	4.00	2.50
5	Dave Hill	2.00	1.50	.80
6	Bobby Hunt	2.00	1.50	.80
7	Jerry Mays	3.00	1.50	.90
8	Jon Gilliam	2.00	1.50	.80
9	Walt Corey	2.00	1.50	.80
10	Soloman Brannan	2.00	1.50	.80
11	Aaron Brown	2.00	1.50	.80
12	Bert Coan	2.00	1.50	.80
13	Ed Budde	2.00	1.50	.80
14	Tommy Brooker	2.00	1.50	.80
15	Bobby Bell	5.00	2.50	1.50
16	Smokey Stover	2.00	1.50	.80
17	Curtis McClinton	3.00	1.50	.90
18	Jerrel Wilson	2.00	1.50	.80
19	Ron Burton	3.00	1.50	.90
20	Mike Garrett	5.00	2.50	1.50
21	Jim Tyrer	3.00	1.50	.90
22	Johnny Robinson	3.00	1.50	.90
23	Bobby Ply	2.00	1.50	.80
24	Frank Pitts	2.00	1.50	.80
25	Ed Lothamer	2.00	1.50	.80
26	Sherrill Headrick	3.00	1.50	.90
27	Fred Williamson	5.00	2.50	1.50
28	Chris Burford	3.00	1.50	.90
29	Willie Mitchell	2.00	1.50	.80
30	Otis Taylor	5.00	2.50	1.50
31	Fred Arbanas	2.00	1.50	.80
32	Hatch Rosdahl	2.00	1.50	.80
33	Reg Carolan	2.00	1.50	.80
34	Len Dawson	8.00	4.00	2.50
35	Pete Beathard	3.00	1.50	.90
36	**Chiefs Logo**	2.00	1.50	.80
NNO	**Chiefs Saver Sheet**	20.00	10.00	6.00

1966 Coke Caps Colts

The 36-cap, 1-1/8" in diameter set was issued along with a Cap Saver sheet that, when completed, could be redeemed for various prizes. The caps are numbered with the "C" prefix.

		NM	E	VG
	Complete Set (36):	100.00	50.00	30.00
	Common Player:	2.00	1.50	.80
1	Ted Davis	2.00	1.50	.80
2	Bob Boyd	2.00	1.50	.80
3	Lenny Moore	8.00	4.00	2.50
4	Jackie Burkett	2.00	1.50	.80
5	Jimmy Orr	3.00	1.50	.90
6	Andy Stynchula	2.00	1.50	.80
7	Mike Curtis	4.00	2.00	1.25
8	Jerry Logan	2.00	1.50	.80
9	Steve Stonebreaker	2.00	1.50	.80
10	John Mackey	6.00	3.00	1.75
11	Dennis Gaubatz	2.00	1.50	.80
12	Don Shinnick	2.00	1.50	.80
13	Dick Szymanski	2.00	1.50	.80
14	Ordell Braase	2.00	1.50	.80
15	Lenny Lyles	2.00	1.50	.80
16	Rick Kestner	2.00	1.50	.80
17	Dan Sullivan	2.00	1.50	.80
18	Lou Michaels	3.00	1.50	.90
19	Gary Cuozzo	3.00	1.50	.90
20	Butch Wilson	2.00	1.50	.80
21	Willie Richardson	3.00	1.50	.90
22	Jim Welch	2.00	1.50	.80
23	Tony Lorick	2.00	1.50	.80
24	Billy Ray Smith	3.00	1.50	.90
25	Fred Miller	2.00	1.50	.80
26	Tom Matte	4.00	2.00	1.25
27	Johnny Unitas	12.00	6.00	3.50
28	Glenn Ressler	2.00	1.50	.80
29	Alvin Haymond	3.00	1.50	.90
30	Jim Parker	5.00	2.50	1.50
31	Butch Allison	2.00	1.50	.80
32	Bob Vogel	2.00	1.50	.80
33	Jerry Hill	2.00	1.50	.80
34	Raymond Berry	8.00	4.00	2.50
35	Sam Ball	2.00	1.50	.80
36	**Colts Team Logo**	2.00	1.50	.80
NNO	**Colts Saver Sheet**	20.00	10.00	6.00

1966 Coke Caps Cowboys

The 36-cap, 1-1/8" set was issued to highlight the Cowboys. A Cap Saver sheet was also available, and when completed, could be redeemed for prizes. Fresca and Tab bottles also had the player caps. Key players in the set are Don Meredith, Dan Reeves and Bob Hayes. The caps are numbered with a "C" prefix.

		NM	E	VG
	Complete Set (36):	140.00	70.00	42.50
	Common Player:	2.50	1.25	.70
1	Mike Connelly	2.50	1.25	.70
2	Tony Liscio	2.50	1.25	.70
3	Jethro Pugh	2.50	1.25	.70
4	Larry Stephens	2.50	1.25	.70
5	Jim Colvin	2.50	1.25	.70
6	Malcolm Walker	2.50	1.25	.70
7	Danny Villanueva	2.50	1.25	.70
8	Frank Clarke	4.00	2.00	1.25
9	Don Meredith	12.00	6.00	3.50
10	George Andrie	4.00	2.00	1.25
11	Mel Renfro	6.00	3.00	1.75
12	Pettis Norman	4.00	2.00	1.25
13	Buddy Dial	4.00	2.00	1.25
14	Pete Gent	4.00	2.00	1.25
15	Jerry Rhome	5.00	2.50	1.50
16	Bob Hayes	10.00	5.00	3.00
17	Mike Gaechter	2.50	1.25	.70
18	Joe Bob Isbell	2.50	1.25	.70
19	Harold Hays	2.50	1.25	.70
20	Craig Morton	5.00	2.50	1.50
21	Jake Kupp	2.50	1.25	.70
22	Cornell Green	4.00	2.00	1.25
23	Dan Reeves	12.00	6.00	3.50
24	Leon Donohue	2.50	1.25	.70
25	Dave Manders	2.50	1.25	.70
26	Warren Livingston	2.50	1.25	.70
27	Bob Lilly	8.00	4.00	2.50
28	Chuck Howley	5.00	2.50	1.50
29	Don Bishop	2.50	1.25	.70
30	Don Perkins	4.00	2.00	1.25
31	Jim Boeke	2.50	1.25	.70
32	Dave Edwards	2.50	1.25	.70
33	Lee Roy Jordan	5.00	2.50	1.50
34	Obert Logan	2.50	1.25	.70
35	Ralph Neely	4.00	2.00	1.25
36	**Cowboys Logo**	2.50	1.25	.70
NNO	**Cowboys Saver Sheet**	20.00	10.00	6.00

1966 Coke Caps Eagles

The 36-card, 1-1/8" set was issued with a Cap Saver sheet that could be redeemed for various prizes. The top of the caps had the Coke logo and a football icon while the inside had the player's image. The caps are numbered with the "C" prefix.

		NM	E	VG
	Complete Set (36):	75.00	37.00	22.00
	Common Player:	2.00	1.50	.80
1	Norm Snead	4.00	2.00	1.25
2	Al Nelson	2.00	1.50	.80
3	Jim Skaggs	2.00	1.50	.80
4	Glenn Glass	2.00	1.50	.80
5	Pete Retzlaff	4.00	2.00	1.25
6	John Osmond	2.00	1.50	.80
7	Ray Rissmiller	2.00	1.50	.80
8	Lynn Hoyem	2.00	1.50	.80
9	King Hill	4.00	2.00	1.25
10	Timmy Brown	4.00	2.00	1.25
11	Ollie Matson	6.00	3.00	1.75
12	Dave Lloyd	2.00	1.50	.80
13	Jim Ringo	6.00	3.00	1.75
14	Floyd Peters	2.00	1.50	.80
15	Gary Pettigrew	2.00	1.50	.80
16	Frank Molden	2.00	1.50	.80
17	Earl Gros	2.00	1.50	.80
18	Fred Hill	2.00	1.50	.80
19	Don Hultz	2.00	1.50	.80
20	Ray Poage	2.00	1.50	.80
21	Aaron Martin	2.00	1.50	.80
22	Mike Morgan	2.00	1.50	.80
23	Lane Howell	2.00	1.50	.80
24	Ed Blaine	2.00	1.50	.80
25	Jack Concannon	4.00	2.00	1.25
26	Sam Baker	2.00	1.50	.80
27	Tom Woodeshick	4.00	2.00	1.25
28	Joe Scarpati	2.00	1.50	.80
29	John Meyers	2.00	1.50	.80
30	Nate Ramsey	2.00	1.50	.80
31	Ben Hawkins	2.00	1.50	.80
32	Bob Brown	4.00	2.00	1.25
33	Willie Brown	2.00	1.50	.80
34	Ron Goodwin	2.00	1.50	.80
35	Randy Beisler	2.00	1.50	.80
36	**Team Logo**	2.00	1.50	.80
NNO	**Eagles Saver Sheet**	20.00	10.00	6.00

1966 Coke Caps Falcons

The 36-cap, 1-1/8" in diameter set highlights top members of the Falcons. A Cap Saver sheet was also available which could be redeemed for prizes. Coke products, such as Fresca and Tab, also came with player caps. The final cap in the set, which is numbered with the "C" prefix, is the Falcons team cap.

		NM	E	VG
	Complete Set (36):	80.00	60.00	32.00
	Common Player:	2.00	1.50	.80
1	Tommy Nobis	7.00	3.50	2.00
2	Ernie Wheelwright	3.00	1.50	.90
3	Lee Calland	2.00	1.50	.80
4	Chuck Sieminski	2.00	1.50	.80
5	Dennis Claridge	2.00	1.50	.80
6	Ralph Heck	2.00	1.50	.80
7	Alex Hawkins	3.00	1.50	.90
8	Dan Grimm	2.00	1.50	.80
9	Marion Rushing	2.00	1.50	.80
10	Bobbie Johnson	2.00	1.50	.80
11	Bobby Franklin	2.00	1.50	.80
12	Bill McWatters	2.00	1.50	.80
13	Billy Lothridge	3.00	1.50	.90
14	Billy Martin	2.00	1.50	.80
15	Tom Wilson	2.00	1.50	.80
16	Dennis Murphy	2.00	1.50	.80
17	Randy Johnson	3.00	1.50	.90
18	Guy Reese	2.00	1.50	.80
19	Frank Marchlewski	2.00	1.50	.80
20	Don Talbert	2.00	1.50	.80
21	Errol Linden	2.00	1.50	.80
22	Dan Lewis	2.00	1.50	.80
23	Ed Cook	2.00	1.50	.80
24	Hugh McInnis	2.00	1.50	.80
25	Frank Lasky	2.00	1.50	.80
26	Bob Jencks	2.00	1.50	.80
27	Bill Jobko	2.00	1.50	.80
28	Nick Rassas	2.00	1.50	.80
29	Bob Riggle	2.00	1.50	.80
30	Ken Reaves	2.00	1.50	.80
31	Bob Sanders	2.00	1.50	.80
32	Steve Sloan	3.00	1.50	.90
33	Ron Smith	2.00	1.50	.80
34	Bob Whitlow	2.00	1.50	.80
35	Roger Anderson	2.00	1.50	.80
36	**Falcons Logo**	2.00	1.50	.80
NNO	**Falcons Saver Sheet**	20.00	10.00	6.00

1966 Coke Caps Giants

The 35-cap, 1-1/8" set highlights top Giants players and was issued with a Cap Saver sheet, which when completed, could be redeemed for various prizes. The cap is similar in design to previous cap issues, complete with the Coke logo. The caps are numbered with a "G" prefix.

		NM	E	VG
	Complete Set (35):	80.00	60.00	32.00
	Common Player:	2.00	1.50	.80
1	Joe Morrison	3.00	1.50	.90
2	Dick Lynch	3.00	1.50	.90
3	Pete Case	2.00	1.50	.80
4	Clarence Childs	2.00	1.50	.80
5	Aaron Thomas	2.00	1.50	.80
6	Jim Carroll	2.00	1.50	.80
7	Henry Carr	3.00	1.50	.90
8	Bookie Bolin	2.00	1.50	.80
9	Roosevelt Davis	2.00	1.50	.80
10	John Lovetere	2.00	1.50	.80
11	Jim Patton	3.00	1.50	.90
12	Wendell Harris	2.00	1.50	.80
13	Roger LaLonde	2.00	1.50	.80
14	Jerry Hillebrand	2.00	1.50	.80
15	Spider Lockhart	3.00	1.50	.90
16	Del Shofner	3.00	1.50	.90
17	Earl Morrall	5.00	2.50	1.50
18	Roosevelt Brown	5.00	2.50	1.50
19	Greg Larson	2.00	1.50	.80
20	Jim Katcavage	3.00	1.50	.90
21	Smith Reed	2.00	1.50	.80
22	Lou Slaby	2.00	1.50	.80
23	Jim Moran	2.00	1.50	.80
24	Bill Swain	2.00	1.50	.80
25	Steve Thurlow	2.00	1.50	.80
26	Olen Underwood	2.00	1.50	.80
27	Gary Wood	3.00	1.50	.90
28	Larry Vargo	2.00	1.50	.80
29	Jim Prestel (Cap saver sheet reads Ed Prestel)	2.00	1.50	.80
30	Tucker Frederickson	3.00	1.50	.90
31	Bob Timberlake	2.00	1.50	.80
32	Chuck Mercein	3.00	1.50	.90
33	Ernie Koy	3.00	1.50	.90
34	Tom Costello	2.00	1.50	.80
35	Homer Jones	3.00	1.50	.90
NNO	**Giants Saver Sheet**	20.00	10.00	6.00

1966 Coke Caps Jets

The 35-cap, 1-1/8" in diameter set, distributed in western New York, featured key Jets players, including Joe Namath. A Cap Saver sheet was issued to help collectors complete the set and when completed, could be redeemed for prizes. The caps are numbered with a "J" prefix.

		NM	E	VG
	Complete Set (35):	120.00	90.00	47.50
	Common Player:	2.00	1.50	.80
1	Don Maynard	10.00	5.00	3.00
2	George Sauer Jr.	4.00	2.00	1.25
3	Paul Crane	2.00	1.50	.80
4	Jim Colclough	2.00	1.50	.80
5	Matt Snell	4.00	2.00	1.25
6	Sherman Lewis	2.00	1.50	.80
7	Jim Turner	4.00	2.00	1.25
8	Mike Taliaferro	2.00	1.50	.80
9	Cornell Gordon	2.00	1.50	.80
10	Mark Smolinski	2.00	1.50	.80
11	Al Atkinson	4.00	2.00	1.25
12	Paul Rochester	2.00	1.50	.80
13	Sherman Plunkett	2.00	1.50	.80
14	Gerry Philbin	4.00	2.00	1.25
15	Pete Lammons	4.00	2.00	1.25
16	Dainard Paulson	2.00	1.50	.80
17	Joe Namath	45.00	22.00	13.50
18	Winston Hill	4.00	2.00	1.25
19	Dee Mackey	2.00	1.50	.80
20	Curley Johnson	2.00	1.50	.80
21	Verlon Biggs	2.00	1.50	.80
22	Bill Mathis	4.00	2.00	1.25
23	Carl McAdams	2.00	1.50	.80
24	Bert Wilder	2.00	1.50	.80
25	Larry Grantham	4.00	2.00	1.25
26	Bill Yearby	2.00	1.50	.80
27	Sam DeLuca	2.00	1.50	.80
28	Bill Baird	2.00	1.50	.80
29	Ralph Baker	2.00	1.50	.80
30	Ray Abruzzese	2.00	1.50	.80
31	Jim Hudson	2.00	1.50	.80
32	Dave Herman	2.00	1.50	.80
33	John Schmitt	2.00	1.50	.80
34	Jim Harris	2.00	1.50	.80
35	Bake Turner	4.00	2.00	1.25
NNO	**Jets Saver Sheet**	20.00	10.00	6.00

1966 Coke Caps Lions

		NM	E	VG
	Complete Set (36):	100.00	50.00	30.00
	Common Player:	2.50	1.25	.70
1	Pat Studstill	3.50	1.75	1.00
2	Ed Flanagan	3.50	1.75	1.00
3	Wayne Walker	3.50	1.75	1.00
4	Tom Watkins	2.50	1.25	.70
5	Tommy Vaughn	2.50	1.25	.70
6	Jim Kearney	2.50	1.25	.70
7	Larry Hand	3.50	1.75	1.00
8	Jerry Rush	2.50	1.25	.70
9	Roger Brown	3.50	1.75	1.00
10	Tom Nowatzke	3.50	1.75	1.00
11	John Henderson	2.50	1.25	.70
12	Tom Myers	2.50	1.25	.70
13	Ron Kramer	3.50	1.75	1.00
14	Dick LeBeau	3.50	1.75	1.00
15	Amos Marsh	3.50	1.75	1.00
16	Wally Hilgenberg	3.50	1.75	1.00
17	Bruce Maher	2.50	1.25	.70
18	Darris McCord	3.50	1.75	1.00
19	Ted Karras	2.50	1.25	.70
20	Ernie Clark	2.50	1.25	.70
21	Gail Cogdill	3.50	1.75	1.00
22	Wayne Rasmussen	2.50	1.25	.70
23	Joe Don Looney	8.00	4.00	2.50
24	Jim Gibbons	3.50	1.75	1.00
25	John Gonzaga	2.50	1.25	.70
26	John Gordy	2.50	1.25	.70
27	Bobby Thompson	2.50	1.25	.70
28	J.D. Smith	2.50	1.25	.70
29	Roger Shoals	2.50	1.25	.70
30	Alex Karras	7.00	3.50	2.00
31	Nick Pietrosante	3.50	1.75	1.00
32	Milt Plum	4.00	2.00	1.25
33	Daryl Sanders	2.50	1.25	.70
34	Mike Lucci	3.50	1.75	1.00
35	George Izo	3.50	1.75	1.00
36	**Lions Logo**	2.50	1.25	.70

1966 Coke Caps National NFL

The 70-cap, 1-1/8" set was available in mostly non-NFL cities in addition to a Cap Saver sheet, which when redeemed, could earn collectors prizes. The cap tops have the Coke logo and a football icon, while the bottoms have the player's image in black. The caps are numbered with a "C" prefix.

		NM	E	VG
	Complete Set (70):	200.00	150.00	80.00
	Common Player:	2.00	1.50	.80
1	Larry Wilson	5.00	2.50	1.50
2	Frank Ryan	4.00	2.00	1.25
3	Norm Snead	4.00	2.00	1.25
4	Mel Renfro	4.00	2.00	1.25
5	Timmy Brown	4.00	2.00	1.25
6	Tucker Frederickson	2.00	1.50	.80
7	Jim Bakken	2.00	1.50	.80
8	Paul Krause	4.00	2.00	1.25
9	Irv Cross	2.00	1.50	.80
10	Cornell Green	4.00	2.00	1.25
11	Pat Fischer	2.00	1.50	.80
12	Bob Hayes	4.00	2.00	1.25
13	Charley Taylor	5.00	2.50	1.50
14	Pete Retzlaff	4.00	2.00	1.25
15	Jim Ringo	5.00	2.50	1.50
16	Maxie Baughan	2.00	1.50	.80
17	Chuck Howley	4.00	2.00	1.25
18	John Wooten	2.00	1.50	.80
19	Bob DeMarco	2.00	1.50	.80
20	Dale Meinert	2.00	1.50	.80
21	Gene Hickerson	2.00	1.50	.80
22	George Andrie	2.00	1.50	.80
23	Joe Rutgens	2.00	1.50	.80
24	Bob Lilly	6.00	3.00	1.75
25	Sam Silas	2.00	1.50	.80
26	Bob Brown (OT)	2.00	1.50	.80
27	Dick Schafrath	2.00	1.50	.80
28	Roosevelt Brown	6.00	3.00	1.75
29	Jim Houston	2.00	1.50	.80
30	Paul Wiggin	2.00	1.50	.80
31	Gary Ballman	2.00	1.50	.80
32	Gary Collins	4.00	2.00	1.25
33	Sonny Randle	2.00	1.50	.80
34	Charlie Johnson	4.00	2.00	1.25
35	**Browns Logo**	2.00	1.50	.80
36	**Packers Logo**	2.00	1.50	.80
37	Herb Adderley	6.00	3.00	1.75
38	Grady Alderman	2.00	1.50	.80
39	Doug Atkins	4.00	2.00	1.25
40	Bruce Bosley	2.00	1.50	.80
41	John Brodie	6.00	3.00	1.75
42	Roger Brown	2.00	1.50	.80
43	Bill Brown	2.00	1.50	.80
44	Dick Butkus	15.00	7.50	4.50
45	Lee Roy Caffey	2.00	1.50	.80
46	John David Crow	4.00	2.00	1.25
47	Willie Davis	6.00	3.00	1.75
48	Mike Ditka	12.00	6.00	3.50
49	Joe Fortunato	2.00	1.50	.80
50	John Gordy	2.00	1.50	.80
51	Deacon Jones	6.00	3.00	1.75
52	Alex Karras	6.00	3.00	1.75
53	Dick LeBeau	2.00	1.50	.80
54	Jerry Logan	2.00	1.50	.80
55	John Mackey	4.00	2.00	1.25
56	Ed Meador	2.00	1.50	.80
57	Tommy McDonald	4.00	2.00	1.25
58	Merlin Olsen	6.00	3.00	1.75
59	Jimmy Orr	4.00	2.00	1.25
60	Jim Parker	4.00	2.00	1.25
61	Dave Parks	2.00	1.50	.80
62	Walter Rock	2.00	1.50	.80
63	Gale Sayers	14.00	7.00	4.25
64	Pat Studstill	2.00	1.50	.80
65	Fran Tarkenton	12.00	6.00	3.50
66	Mick Tinglehoff	2.00	1.50	.80
67	Bob Vogel	2.00	1.50	.80
68	Wayne Walker	2.00	1.50	.80
69	Ken Willard	2.00	1.50	.80
70	Willie Wood	5.00	2.50	1.50
NNO	**National Saver Sheet**	20.00	10.00	6.00

1966 Coke Caps Oilers

The 36-cap, 1-1/8" set featured the top players from the Oilers and was distributed in the Houston area. A Cap Saver sheet was also issued, and when redeemed, the collector could earn prizes. Fresca and Tab products also had the player caps. The caps are numbered with a "C" prefix.

		NM	E	VG
	Complete Set (36):	100.00	50.00	30.00
	Common Player:	2.00	1.50	.80
1	Scott Appleton	2.00	1.50	.80
2	George Allen	4.00	2.00	1.25
3	Don Floyd	2.00	1.50	.80
4	Ronnie Caveness	2.00	1.50	.80

5	Jim Norton	2.00	1.50	.80
6	Jacky Lee	4.00	2.00	1.25
7	George Blanda	10.00	5.00	3.00
8	Tony Banfield	4.00	2.00	1.25
9	George Rice	2.00	1.50	.80
10	Charley Tolar	2.00	1.50	.80
11	Bobby Jancik	2.00	1.50	.80
12	Freddy Glick	2.00	1.50	.80
13	Ode Burrell	2.00	1.50	.80
14	Walt Suggs	2.00	1.50	.80
15	Bob McLeod	2.00	1.50	.80
16	Johnny Baker	2.00	1.50	.80
17	Danny Bradshaw	2.00	1.50	.80
18	Gary Cutsinger	2.00	1.50	.80
19	Doug Cline	2.00	1.50	.80
20	Hoyle Granger	2.00	1.50	.80
21	Bob Talamini	2.00	1.50	.80
22	Don Trull	4.00	2.00	1.25
23	Charlie Hennigan	4.00	2.00	1.25
24	Sid Blanks	2.00	1.50	.80
25	Pat Holmes	2.00	1.50	.80
26	John Frongillo	2.00	1.50	.80
27	John Whitehorn	2.00	1.50	.80
28	George Kinney	2.00	1.50	.80
29	Charles Frazier	2.00	1.50	.80
30	Ernie Ladd	6.00	3.00	1.75
31	W.K. Hicks	2.00	1.50	.80
32	Sonny Bishop	2.00	1.50	.80
33	Larry Elkins	2.00	1.50	.80
34	Glen Ray Hines	2.00	1.50	.80
35	Bobby Maples	4.00	2.00	1.25
36	**Oilers Logo**	2.00	1.50	.80
NNO	**Oilers Saver Sheet**	20.00	10.00	6.00

1966 Coke Caps Packers

The 36-cap, 1-1/8" set, issued in metropolitan areas in Wisconsin, was virtually identical in design to previous Coke player cap sets. A Cap Saver sheet was also available and a collector could redeem the completed sheet for various prizes. The caps are numbered with a "C" prefix.

		NM	E	VG
Complete Set (36):		150.00	110.00	60.00
Common Player:		2.50	1.25	.70
1	Herb Adderley	6.00	3.00	1.75
2	Lionel Aldridge	4.00	2.00	1.25
3	Bob Long	2.50	1.25	.70
4	Willie Davis	6.00	3.00	1.75
5	Boyd Dowler	4.00	2.00	1.25
6	Marv Fleming	2.50	1.25	.70
7	Ken Bowman	2.50	1.25	.70
8	Tom Brown	2.50	1.25	.70
9	Doug Hart	2.50	1.25	.70
10	Steve Wright	2.50	1.25	.70
11	Bill Anderson	2.50	1.25	.70
12	Bill Curry	4.00	2.00	1.25
13	Tommy Crutcher	2.50	1.25	.70
14	Fred Thurston	5.00	2.50	1.50
15	Elijah Pitts	5.00	2.50	1.50
16	Lloyd Voss	2.50	1.25	.70
17	Lee Roy Caffey	4.00	2.00	1.25
18	Dave Robinson	2.50	1.25	.70
19	Bart Starr	14.00	7.00	4.25
20	Ray Nitschke	8.00	4.00	2.50
21	Max McGee	5.00	2.50	1.50
22	Don Chandler	2.50	1.25	.70
23	Richard Marshall	2.50	1.25	.70
24	Ron Kostelnik	2.50	1.25	.70
25	Carroll Dale	4.00	2.00	1.25
26	Hank Jordan	5.00	2.50	1.50
27	Bob Jeter	4.00	2.00	1.25
28	Bob Skoronski	2.50	1.25	.70
29	Jerry Kramer	6.00	3.00	1.75
30	Willie Wood	6.00	3.00	1.75
31	Paul Hornung	14.00	7.00	4.25
32	Forrest Gregg	8.00	4.00	2.50
33	Zeke Bratkowski	4.00	2.00	1.25
34	Tom Moore	2.50	1.25	.70
35	Jim Taylor	12.00	6.00	3.50
36	**Packers Team Emblem**	2.50	1.25	.70
NNO	**Packers Saver Sheet**	20.00	10.00	6.00

1966 Coke Caps Patriots

The 36-cap, 1-1/8" in diameter set, distributed in the New England area, featured key players from the Patriots roster. A Cap Saver sheet was also issued to aid collectors in completing the set, which could then be redeemed for various prizes. The caps are numbered with a "C" prefix.

		NM	E	VG
Complete Set (36):		75.00	56.00	30.00
Common Player:		2.00	1.50	.80
1	Jon Morris	2.00	1.50	.80
2	Don Webb	2.00	1.50	.80
3	Charles Long	2.00	1.50	.80
4	Tony Romeo	2.00	1.50	.80
5	Bob Dee	2.00	1.50	.80
6	Tommy Addison	4.00	2.00	1.25
7	Tom Neville	2.00	1.50	.80
8	Ron Hall	2.00	1.50	.80
9	White Graves	2.00	1.50	.80
10	Ellis Johnson	2.00	1.50	.80
11	Don Oakes	2.00	1.50	.80
12	Tom Yewcic	2.00	1.50	.80
13	Tom Hennessey	2.00	1.50	.80
14	Jay Cunningham	2.00	1.50	.80
15	Larry Garron	4.00	2.00	1.25
16	Justin Canale	2.00	1.50	.80
17	Art Graham	4.00	2.00	1.25
18	Babe Parilli	4.00	2.00	1.25
19	Jim Hunt	2.00	1.50	.80
20	Karl Singer	2.00	1.50	.80
21	Houston Antwine	2.00	1.50	.80
22	Nick Buoniconti	6.00	3.00	1.75
23	John Huarte	4.00	2.00	1.25
24	Gino Cappelletti	4.00	2.00	1.25
25	Chuck Shonta	2.00	1.50	.80
26	Dick Felt	2.00	1.50	.80
27	Mike Dukes	2.00	1.50	.80
28	Larry Eisenhauer	2.00	1.50	.80
29	Jim Fraser	2.00	1.50	.80
30	Len St. Jean	2.00	1.50	.80
31	J.D. Garrett	2.00	1.50	.80
32	Jim Whalen	2.00	1.50	.80
33	Jim Nance	4.00	2.00	1.25
34	Rick Arrington	2.00	1.50	.80
35	Lonnie Farmer	2.00	1.50	.80
36	**Patriots Logo**	2.00	1.50	.80
NNO	**Patriots Saver Sheet**	20.00	10.00	6.00

1966 Coke Caps Rams

The 36-cap, 1-1/8" set features a Coke logo and a football icon on the cap top, as do the previous player cap sets. The cap insides depict a facial image of the player in black. Other Coke products, such as Fresca and Tab, also had the player caps. The caps are numbered with a "C" prefix.

		NM	E	VG
Complete Set (36):		100.00	50.00	30.00
Common Player:		2.00	1.50	.80
1	Tom Mack	5.00	2.50	1.50
2	Tom Moore	2.00	1.50	.80
3	Bill Munson	3.00	1.50	.90
4	Bill George	5.00	2.50	1.50
5	Joe Carollo	2.00	1.50	.80
6	Dick Bass	3.00	1.50	.90
7	Ken Iman	2.00	1.50	.80
8	Charlie Cowan	2.00	1.50	.80
9	Terry Baker	4.00	2.00	1.25
10	Don Chuy	2.00	1.50	.80
11	Jack Pardee	5.00	2.50	1.50
12	Lamar Lundy	3.00	1.50	.90
13	Bill Anderson	2.00	1.50	.80
14	Roman Gabriel	6.00	3.00	1.75
15	Roosevelt Grier	6.00	3.00	1.75
16	Billy Truax	3.00	1.50	.90
17	Merlin Olsen	8.00	4.00	2.50
18	Deacon Jones	7.00	3.50	2.00
19	Joe Scibelli	2.00	1.50	.80
20	Marlin McKeever	2.00	1.50	.80
21	Doug Woodlief	2.00	1.50	.80
22	Chuck Lamson	2.00	1.50	.80
23	Dan Currie	2.00	1.50	.80
24	Maxie Baughan	3.00	1.50	.90
25	Bruce Gossett	3.00	1.50	.90
26	Les Josephson	3.00	1.50	.90
27	Ed Meador	2.00	1.50	.80
28	Anthony Guillory	2.00	1.50	.80
29	Irv Cross	4.00	2.00	1.25
30	Tommy McDonald	3.00	1.50	.90
31	Bucky Pope	2.00	1.50	.80
32	Jack Snow	4.00	2.00	1.25
33	Joe Wendryhoski	2.00	1.50	.80
34	Clancy Williams	2.00	1.50	.80
35	Ben Wilson	2.00	1.50	.80
36	**Rams Logo**	2.00	1.50	.80
NNO	**Rams Saver Sheet**	20.00	10.00	6.00

1966 Coke Caps Steelers

The 36-cap, 1-1/8" set featured key players from the Steelers squad with the Coke logo and a football stamp on the cap top. The player's image was printed in black on the cap inside. A Cap Saver sheet was also issued and a completed sheet could be redeemed for various prizes. The caps are numbered with a "C" prefix.

		NM	E	VG
Complete Set (36):		80.00	60.00	32.00
Common Player:		2.00	1.50	.80
1	John Baker	2.00	1.50	.80
2	Mike Lind	3.00	1.50	.90
3	Ken Kortas	2.00	1.50	.80
4	Willie Daniel	2.00	1.50	.80
5	Roy Jefferson	3.00	1.50	.90
6	Bob Hohn	2.00	1.50	.80
7	Dan James	2.00	1.50	.80
8	Gary Ballman	3.00	1.50	.90
9	Brady Keys	2.00	1.50	.80
10	Charley Bradshaw	2.00	1.50	.80
11	Jim Bradshaw	2.00	1.50	.80
12	Jim Butler	2.00	1.50	.80
13	Paul Martha	4.00	2.00	1.25
14	Mike Clark	2.00	1.50	.80
15	Ray Lemek	2.00	1.50	.80
16	Clarence Peaks	3.00	1.50	.90
17	Theron Sapp	2.00	1.50	.80
18	Ray Mansfield	2.00	1.50	.80
19	Chuck Hinton	2.00	1.50	.80
20	Bill Nelsen	3.00	1.50	.90
21	Rod Breedlove	2.00	1.50	.80
22	Frank Lambert	2.00	1.50	.80
23	Ben McGee	2.00	1.50	.80
24	Myron Pottios	2.00	1.50	.80
25	John Campbell	2.00	1.50	.80
26	Andy Russell	4.00	2.00	1.25
27	Mike Sandusky	2.00	1.50	.80
28	Bob Schmitz	2.00	1.50	.80
29	Riley Gunnels	2.00	1.50	.80
30	Clendon Thomas	3.00	1.50	.90
31	Tommy Wade	2.00	1.50	.80
32	Dick Hoak	3.00	1.50	.90
33	Marv Woodson	2.00	1.50	.80
34	Bob Nichols	2.00	1.50	.80
35	John Henry Johnson	5.00	2.50	1.50
36	**Steelers Logo**	2.00	1.50	.80
NNO	**Steelers Saver Sheet**	20.00	10.00	6.00

1966 Coke Caps Vikings

		NM	E	VG
Complete Set (34):		100.00	50.00	30.00
Common Player:		2.50	1.25	.70
1	Milt Sunde	3.50	1.75	1.00
2	Don Hansen	2.50	1.25	.70
3	Jim Marshall	6.00	3.00	1.75
4	Jerry Shay	2.50	1.25	.70
5	Ken Byers	2.50	1.25	.70
6	Rip Hawkins	2.50	1.25	.70
7	John Kirby	2.50	1.25	.70
8	Roy Winston	3.50	1.75	1.00
9	Ron Vanderkelen	3.50	1.75	1.00
10	Jim Lindsey	2.50	1.25	.70
11	Paul Flatley	3.50	1.75	1.00
12	Larry Bowie	2.50	1.25	.70
13	Grady Alderman	3.50	1.75	1.00
14	Mick Tingelhoff	5.00	2.50	1.50
15	Lonnie Warwick	3.50	1.75	1.00
16	Fred Cox	3.50	1.75	1.00
17	Bill Brown	3.50	1.75	1.00
18	Ed Sharockman	3.50	1.75	1.00
19	George Rose	2.50	1.25	.70
20	Paul Dickson	2.50	1.25	.70
21	Tommy Mason	3.50	1.75	1.00
22	Carl Eller	6.00	3.00	1.75
23	Jim Young	2.50	1.25	.70
24	Hal Bedsole	2.50	1.25	.70
25	Karl Kassulke	5.00	2.50	1.50
26	Fran Tarkenton	10.00	5.00	3.00
27	Tom Hall	2.50	1.25	.70
28	Archie Sutton	2.50	1.25	.70
29	Jim Phillips	2.50	1.25	.70
30	Gary Larsen	3.50	1.75	1.00
31	Phil King	2.50	1.25	.70
32	Bobby Walden	2.50	1.25	.70
33	Bob Berry	3.50	1.75	1.00
34	**Team Logo**	2.50	1.25	.70
35	**Vikings Saver Sheet**	30.00	15.00	9.00

1971 Coke Caps Packers

The 22-cap, 1-1/8" set, issued in 1971, featured twist-off caps as well as the basic bottle opener cap. The twist-off cap is valued at twice the listings below. As with past Coke player sets, a Cap Saver sheet was issued to help collectors in completing the set.

		NM	E	VG
Complete Set (22):		50.00	37.00	20.00
Common Player:		1.50	.70	.45
1	Ken Bowman	1.50	.70	.45
2	John Brockington	3.00	1.50	.90
3	Bob Brown (DT)	1.50	.70	.45
4	Fred Carr	1.50	.70	.45
5	Jim Carter	1.50	.70	.45
6	Carroll Dale	1.50	.70	.45
7	Ken Ellis	1.50	.70	.45
8	Gale Gillingham	1.50	.70	.45
9	Dave Hampton	1.50	.70	.45
10	Doug Hart	1.50	.70	.45
11	Jim Hill	1.50	.70	.45
12	Dick Himes	1.50	.70	.45
13	Scott Hunter	1.50	.70	.45

14	MacArthur Lane	3.00	1.50	.90
15	Bill Lueck	1.50	.70	.45
16	Al Matthews	1.50	.70	.45
17	Rich McGeorge	1.50	.70	.45
18	Ray Nitschke	5.00	2.50	1.50
19	Francis Peay	1.50	.70	.45
20	Dave Robinson	3.00	1.50	.90
21	Alden Roche	1.50	.70	.45
22	Bart Starr	14.00	7.00	4.25

1971 Coke Fun Kit Photos

		NM	E	VG
Complete Set (9):		100.00	50.00	30.00
Common Player:		6.00	3.00	1.75

1	Donny Anderson	8.00	4.00	2.50
2	John Brodie	12.00	6.00	3.50
3	Fred Carr	6.00	3.00	1.75
4	Carroll Dale	6.00	3.00	1.75
5	Len Dawson	20.00	10.00	6.00
6	Carl Eller	8.00	4.00	2.50
8	Jim Marshall	12.00	6.00	3.50
9	Dave Osborn	6.00	3.00	1.75

1973 Coke Prints

		NM	E	VG
Complete Set (5):		30.00	15.00	9.00
Common Player:		5.00	2.50	1.50

1	Danny Abramowicz	5.00	2.50	1.50
2	Walter Johnson	5.00	2.50	1.50
3	Leroy Kelly	10.00	5.00	3.00
4	Archie Manning	10.00	5.00	3.00
5	Royce Smith	5.00	2.50	1.50

1981 Coke

Players from seven NFL teams are represented in this 84-card set produced by Topps for Coca-Cola. Each card is numbered from 1-11 within its own team, but has been checklisted below using #s 1-77, plus seven unnumbered header cards (one for each team). The Coca-Cola logo appears on both sides of the card, making it identifiable from the regular 1981 Topps card, which the set is patterned after.

		NM/M	NM	E
Complete Set (77):		50.00	37.00	20.00
Common Player:		.20	.15	.08

(1)	Raymond Butler	.40	.30	.15
(2)	Roger Carr	.30	.25	.12
(3)	Curtis Dickey	.40	.30	.15
(4)	Nesby Glasgow	.20	.15	.08
(5)	Bert Jones	1.00	.70	.40
(6)	Bruce Laird	.20	.15	.08
(7)	Greg Landry	.40	.30	.15
(8)	Reese McCall	.20	.15	.08
(9)	Don McCauley	.20	.15	.08
(10)	Herb Orvis	.20	.15	.08
(11)	Ed Simonini	.20	.15	.08
(12)	Pat Donovan	.20	.15	.08
(13)	Tony Dorsett	2.50	2.00	1.00
(14)	Billy Joe DuPree	.40	.30	.15
(15)	Tony Hill	.40	.30	.15
(16)	Ed "Too Tall" Jones	.75	.60	.30
(17)	Harvey Martin	.35	.25	.14
(18)	Robert Newhouse	.30	.25	.12
(19)	Drew Pearson	.40	.30	.15
(20)	Charlie Waters	.30	.25	.12
(21)	Danny White	.70	.50	.30
(22)	Randy White	1.75	1.25	.70
(23)	Mike Barber	.30	.25	.12
(24)	Elvin Bethea	.30	.25	.12
(25)	Gregg Bingham	.20	.15	.08
(26)	Robert Brazile	.30	.25	.12
(27)	Ken Burrough	.30	.25	.12
(28)	Rob Carpenter	.30	.25	.12
(29)	Leon Gray	.30	.25	.12
(30)	Vernon Perry	.20	.15	.08
(31)	Mike Renfro	.30	.25	.12
(32)	Carl Roaches	.30	.25	.12
(33)	Morris Towns	.20	.15	.08
(34)	Harry Carson	.75	.60	.30
(35)	Mike Dennis	.20	.15	.08
(36)	Mike Friede	.20	.15	.08
(37)	Earnest Gray	.20	.15	.08
(38)	Dave Jennings	.30	.25	.12
(39)	Gary Jeter	.30	.25	.12
(40)	George Martin	.30	.25	.12
(41)	Roy Simmons	.20	.15	.08
(42)	Phil Simms	2.50	2.00	1.00
(43)	Billy Taylor	.20	.15	.08
(44)	Brad Van Pelt	.30	.25	.12
(45)	Ottis Anderson	1.50	1.25	.60
(46)	Rush Brown	.20	.15	.08
(47)	Theotis Brown	.30	.25	.12
(48)	Dan Dierdorf	.75	.60	.30
(49)	Mel Gray	.30	.25	.12
(50)	Ken Greene	.20	.15	.08

(51)	Jim Hart	.50	.40	.20
(52)	Doug Marsh	.20	.15	.08
(53)	Wayne Morris	.20	.15	.08
(54)	Pat Tilley	.20	.15	.08
(55)	Roger Wehrli	.30	.25	.12
(56)	Rolf Bernirschke	.30	.25	.12
(57)	Fred Dean	.30	.25	.12
(58)	Dan Fouts	1.25	.90	.50
(59)	John Jefferson	.40	.30	.15
(60)	Gary Johnson	.30	.25	.12
(61)	Charlie Joiner	.75	.60	.30
(62)	Louie Kelcher	.30	.25	.12
(63)	Chuck Muncie	.30	.25	.12
(64)	Doug Wilkerson	.20	.15	.08
(65)	Clarence Williams	.20	.15	.08
(66)	Kellen Winslow	1.75	1.25	.70
(67)	Coy Bacon	.20	.15	.08
(68)	Wilbur Jackson	.20	.15	.08
(69)	Karl Lorch	.20	.15	.08
(70)	Rich Milot	.20	.15	.08
(71)	Art Monk	5.00	3.75	2.00
(72)	Mark Moseley	.30	.25	.12
(73)	Mike Nelms	.30	.25	.12
(74)	Lemar Parrish	.30	.25	.12
(75)	Joe Theismann	1.25	.90	.50
(76)	Ricky Thompson	.20	.15	.08
(77)	Joe Washington	.30	.25	.12

1981 Coke Caps

The 15-cap set was issued by Coke in conjuction with a collector contest, which distributed prizes to consumers who completed a column on the Cap Saver sheet. The prize for finding all seven caps from the middle row was $1,000, while the five caps in the third row earned the collector a "Mean" Joe Greene jersey. The first column required four caps and awarded a T-shirt. The most difficult caps to obtain were Ed "Too Tall" Jones, Steve Fuller and Gene Upshaw. The caps were skip numbered.

		NM/M	NM	E
Complete Set (15):		30.00	22.00	12.00
Common Player:		1.00	.70	.40

1	Joe Greene	3.00	2.25	1.25
3	Steve Grogan	1.50	1.25	.60
6	Mike Siani	1.00	.70	.40
11	Dan Fouts	3.00	2.25	1.25
12	Wesley Walker	1.50	1.25	.60
23	Harold Carmichael	1.50	1.25	.60
30	Greg Pruitt	1.00		
38	Gene Upshaw (SP)			
47	Steve Fuller (SP)			
49	Walter Payton	7.00	5.25	2.75
53	Ed "Too Tall" Jones (SP)			
107	Benny Barnes	1.00	.70	.40
108	Billy Sims	2.00	1.50	.80
127	Robert Newhouse	1.00	.70	.40
146	Charlie Waters	1.00	.70	.40

1973 Colorado State

1973 CSU FOOTBALL

JIM KENNEDY
Tight End

		NM	E	VG
Complete Set (8):		75.00	37.00	22.00
Common Player:		6.00	3.00	1.75

1	Wes Cerveny	6.00	3.00	1.75
2	Mark Driscoll	6.00	3.00	1.75
3	Jim Kennedy	6.00	3.00	1.75
4	Greg Kuhn	6.00	3.00	1.75
5	Willie Miller	20.00	10.00	6.00
6	Al Simpson (SP)	12.00	6.00	3.50
7	Jan Stuebbe (SP)	12.00	6.00	3.50
8	Tom Wallace	6.00	3.00	1.75

1990 Colorado Smokey

		NM/M	NM	E
Complete Set (16):		16.00	12.00	6.50
Common Player:		.75	.60	.30

1	Eric Bieniemy	2.50	2.00	1.00
2	Joe Garten	1.00	.70	.40
3	Darian Hagan	2.00	1.50	.80

4	George Hemingway	.75	.60	.30
5	Garry Howe	.75	.60	.30
6	Tim James	.75	.60	.30
7	Charles Johnson	2.50	2.00	1.00
8	Bill McCartney (CO)	2.00	1.50	.80
9	Dave McCloughan	1.00	.70	.40
10	Kanavis McGhee	1.00	.70	.40
11	Mike Pritchard	5.00	3.75	2.00
12	Tom Rouen	1.00	.70	.40
13	Michael Simmons	.75	.60	.30
14	Mark Vander Poel	1.00	.70	.40
15	Alfred Williams	2.50	2.00	1.00
16	**Ralphie** (Mascot)	.75	.60	.30

1961 Colts Jay Publishing

Measuring 5" x 7", the 12-card set showcases black-and-white posed photos on the front. The 12 cards were included in a package and sold for 25 cents. The backs are blank and unnumbered.

		NM	E	VG
Complete Set (12):		80.00	60.00	32.00
Common Player:		5.00	2.50	1.50

1	Raymond Berry	14.00	7.00	4.25
2	Art Donovan	12.00	6.00	3.50
3	Weeb Ewbank (CO)	5.00	2.50	1.50
4	Alex Hawkins	5.00	2.50	1.50
5	Gino Marchetti	10.00	5.00	3.00
6	Lenny Moore	12.00	6.00	3.50
7	Jim Mutscheller	5.00	2.50	1.50
8	Steve Myhra	5.00	2.50	1.50
9	Jimmy Orr	5.00	2.50	1.50
10	Jim Parker	7.00	3.50	2.00
11	Joe Perry	10.00	5.00	3.00
12	Johnny Unitas	25.00	12.50	7.50

1967 Colts Johnny Pro

Measuring 4-1/8" x 2-7/8", each player punchout featured a color photo, with the player's name, number and position inside a white box near the bottom. By inserting the punchout into a stand, which was included with each punchout, the player punchout stood upright. The punchouts are unnumbered.

		NM	E	VG
Complete Set (41):		750.00	560.00	300.00
Common Player:		15.00	7.50	4.50

1	Sam Ball	15.00	7.50	4.50
2	Raymond Berry	40.00	20.00	12.00
3	Bob Boyd	15.00	7.50	4.50
4	Ordell Braase	15.00	7.50	4.50
5	Barry Brown	15.00	7.50	4.50
6	Bill Curry	20.00	10.00	6.00
7	Mike Curtis	20.00	10.00	6.00
8	Norman Davis	15.00	7.50	4.50
9	Jim Detwiler	15.00	7.50	4.50
10	Dennis Gaubatz	15.00	7.50	4.50
11	Alvin Haymond	15.00	7.50	4.50
12	Jerry Hill	15.00	7.50	4.50
13	Roy Hilton	15.00	7.50	4.50
14	David Lee	15.00	7.50	4.50
15	Jerry Logan	15.00	7.50	4.50
16	Tony Lorick	15.00	7.50	4.50
17	Lenny Lyles	15.00	7.50	4.50
18	John Mackey	30.00	15.00	9.00
19	Tom Matte	20.00	10.00	6.00
20	Lou Michaels	15.00	7.50	4.50
21	Fred Miller	15.00	7.50	4.50
22	Lenny Moore	40.00	20.00	12.00
23	Jimmy Orr	20.00	10.00	6.00
24	Jim Parker	30.00	15.00	9.00
25	Ray Perkins	20.00	10.00	6.00
26	Glenn Ressler	15.00	7.50	4.50
27	Willie Richardson	20.00	10.00	6.00
28	Don Shinnick	15.00	7.50	4.50
29	Billy Ray Smith	20.00	10.00	6.00
30	Bubba Smith	40.00	20.00	12.00
31	Charlie Stukes	15.00	7.50	4.50
32	Andy Stynchula	15.00	7.50	4.50
33	Dan Sullivan	15.00	7.50	4.50
34	Dick Szymanski	15.00	7.50	4.50
35	Johnny Unitas	75.00	37.00	22.00
36	Bob Vogel	15.00	7.50	4.50
37	Rick Volk	20.00	10.00	6.00
38	Bob Wade	15.00	7.50	4.50
39	Jim Ward	15.00	7.50	4.50
40	Jim Welch	15.00	7.50	4.50
41	Butch Wilson	15.00	7.50	4.50

1978 Colts Team Issue

Measuring 5" x 7", the 28-photo set featured a player photo on the front, with the player's name, team and position listed under the photo. The blank backs are also unnumbered.

		NM	E	VG
Complete Set (28):		45.00	34.00	18.00
Common Player:		1.50	1.25	.60

1	Mack Alston	2.00	1.00	.60
2	Ron Baker	1.50	1.25	.60
3	Mike Barnes	1.50	1.25	.60
4	Tim Baylor	1.50	1.25	.60
5	Randy Burke	1.50	1.25	.60
6	Glenn Doughty	2.00	1.00	.60
7	Joe Ehrmann	2.00	1.00	.60
8	Wade Griffin	1.50	1.25	.60
9	Don Hardeman	1.50	1.25	.60
10	Dwight Harrison	1.50	1.25	.60
11	Ken Huff	1.50	1.25	.60
12	Marshall Johnson	1.50	1.25	.60
13	Bert Jones	8.00	4.00	2.50
14	Bruce Laird	1.50	1.25	.60
15	Roosevelt Leaks	2.50	1.25	.70
16	David Lee	1.50	1.25	.60
17	Ron Lee	1.50	1.25	.60
18	Toni Linhart	1.50	1.25	.60
19	Derrel Luce	1.50	1.25	.60
20	Reese McCall	1.50	1.25	.60
21	Ken Mendenhall	1.50	1.25	.60
22	Don Morrison	1.50	1.25	.60
23	Lloyd Mumphord	1.50	1.25	.60
24	Calvin O'Neal	1.50	1.25	.60
25	Robert Pratt	1.50	1.25	.60
26	Mike Siani	1.50	.70	.45
27	Bill Troup	1.50	1.25	.60
28	Stan White	1.50	.70	.45

1985 Colts Kroger

Measuring 5-1/2" x 8-1/2", the 17-photo set spotlighted a large photo on the front, with the Colts' helmet, player name, position, number and Kroger logo underneath from left to right. The card backs have the Indianapolis Colts at the top, with the player's name, position, number and bio underneath. The NFL logo and Kroger logos are also printed on the backs. The cards are unnumbered.

		NM/M	NM	E
Complete Set (17):		30.00	22.00	12.00
Common Player:		1.00	.70	.40
1	Karl Baldischwiler	1.00	.70	.40
2	Pat Beach	1.00	.70	.40
3	Albert Bentley	2.00	1.50	.80
4	Duane Bickett	3.00	2.25	1.25
5	Matt Bouza	1.00	.70	.40
6	Nesby Glasgow	1.00	.70	.40
7	Chris Hinton	2.00	1.50	.80
8	Lamonte Hunley	1.00	.70	.40
9	Barry Krauss	1.00	.70	.40
10	Orlando Lowry	1.00	.70	.40
11	Tate Randle	1.00	.70	.40
12	Tim Sherwin	1.00	.70	.40
13	Ron Solt	1.00	.70	.40
14	Rohn Stark	1.50	1.25	.60
15	Ben Utt	1.00	.70	.40
16	Brad White	1.00	.70	.40
17	Anthony Young	1.50	1.25	.60

1988 Colts Police

Measuring 2-5/8" x 4-1/8", the eight-card set boasts a large photo, with the photo credit, player's name, number, position and bio beneath it. The Colts' helmet and name are at the bottom of the card front. The card backs feature two cartoon drawings -- one is a Colts Tip, while the other is a Crime Stoppers Tip. The card backs are numbered "of 8." Oscar Mayer and WTHR-TV logos are printed at the bottom of the card backs.

		NM/M	NM	E
Complete Set (8):		8.00	6.00	3.25
Common Player:		1.00	.70	.40
1	Eric Dickerson	3.00	2.25	1.25
2	Barry Krauss	1.00	.70	.40
3	Bill Brooks	1.50	1.25	.60
4	Duane Bickett	1.00	.70	.40
5	Chris Hinton	1.00	.70	.40
6	Eugene Daniel	1.00	.70	.40
7	Jack Trudeau	1.00	.70	.40
8	Ron Meyer (CO)	1.00	.70	.40

1989 Colts Police

Measuring 2-5/8" x 4-1/8", the nine-card set showcases a photo on the front, with a photo credit, player's name, number, position, bio, Colts' helmet and "Indianapolis Colts" printed beneath the photo. The card backs feature two cartoon drawings -- one being a Colts Tip and the other a Crime Stoppers Tip. The cards are numbered. The Indiana Law Enforcement, Louis Rich and WTHR logos are at the bottom of the card backs.

		NM/M	NM	E
Complete Set (9):		8.00	6.00	3.25
Common Player:		.50	.40	.20
1	**Colts Team Card**	.50	.40	.20
2	Dean Biasucci	.50	.40	.20
3	Andre Rison	1.75	1.25	.70
4	Chris Chandler	1.25	.90	.50

5	O'Brien Alston	.50	.40	.20
6	Ray Donaldson	.75	.60	.30
7	Donnell Thompson	.50	.40	.20
8	Fredd Young	.50	.40	.20
9	Eric Dickerson	1.50	1.25	.60

1990 Colts Police

Measuring 2-5/8" x 4-1/8", the eight-card set features a large photo on the front, with a photo credit, player's name, position, bio, Colts' helmet and "Indianapolis Colts" printed underneath. The card backs have a Colts Tip and a Crime Stoppers Tip. The Indiana Law Enforcement, Louis Rich and WTHR logos are printed at the bottom of the card backs.

		NM/M	NM	E
Complete Set (8):		6.00	4.50	2.50
Common Player:		.50	.40	.20
1	Harvey Armstrong	.50	.40	.20
2	Pat Beach	.50	.40	.20
3	Albert Bentley	.75	.60	.30
4	Kevin Call	.50	.40	.20
5	Jeff George	3.00	2.25	1.25
6	Mike Prior	.50	.40	.20
7	Rohn Stark	.50	.40	.20
8	Clarence Verdin	.50	.40	.20

1991 Colts Police

Measuring 2-5/8" x 4-1/4", the eight-card set showcases a photo on the front, with a photo credit, player's name, Colts' helmet, "Indianapolis Colts" and Indiana Law Enforcement logo beneath it. The card backs feature the player's name, number, position and bio at the top and Colts quiz in the center. An anti-drug message, WTHR and Coke logos are printed at the bottom. The cards are numbered in the lower right corner.

		NM/M	NM	E
Complete Set (8):		5.00	3.75	2.00
Common Player:		.75	.60	.30
1	Jeff George	1.75	1.25	.70
2	Jack Trudeau	1.00	.70	.40
3	Jeff Herrod	.75	.60	.30
4	Eric Dickerson	1.50	1.25	.60
5	Bill Brooks	1.25	.90	.50
6	Jon Hand	.75	.60	.30
7	Keith Taylor	.75	.60	.30
8	Randy Dixon	.75	.60	.30

1950 C.O.P. Betsy Ross

		NM	E	VG
Complete Set (6):		75.00	37.00	22.00
Common Player:		8.00	4.00	2.50
1	Don Campora	8.00	4.00	2.50
2	Don Hardey	8.00	4.00	2.50
3	Robert Klein	8.00	4.00	2.50
4	Eddie LeBaron	35.00	17.50	10.50
5	Eddie Macon	15.00	7.50	4.50
6	John Rohde	8.00	4.00	2.50

1969 Cowboys Team Issue

Measuring 7" x 10", the card fronts showcase color action shots of players. The photos have black rounded-corner borders. The player's name and team are printed below the photo. The unnumbered backs are blank.

		NM	E	VG
Complete Set (5):		35.00	17.50	10.50
Common Player:		5.00	2.50	1.50
1	Walt Garrison	5.00	2.50	1.50
2	Lee Roy Jordan	7.00	3.50	2.00
3	Bob Lilly	10.00	5.00	3.00
4	Dave Manders	5.00	2.50	1.50
5	Mel Renfro	8.00	4.00	2.50

1971 Cowboys Team Issue

Measuring 5" x 6-1/2", the 40-card set showcases black-and-white posed shots on the front, bordered in white. The player's name and team are printed below the photo. The cards are unnumbered and have blank backs.

		NM	E	VG
Complete Set (40):		150.00	75.00	45.00
Common Player:		2.00	1.00	.60
1	Herb Adderley	5.00	2.50	1.50
2	Lance Alworth	12.00	6.00	3.50
3	George Andrie	2.00	1.00	.60
4	Mike Clark	2.00	1.00	.60
5	Larry Cole	2.00	1.00	.60
6	Mike Ditka	16.00	8.00	4.75
7	Dave Edwards	2.00	1.00	.60
8	John Fitzgerald	2.00	1.00	.60
9	Toni Fritsch	2.00	1.00	.60
10	Walt Garrison	2.00	1.00	.60
11	Cornell Green	2.00	1.00	.60
12	Bill Gregory	2.00	1.00	.60
13	Cliff Harris	3.00	1.50	.90

14	Bob Hayes	6.00	3.00	1.75
15	Calvin Hill	5.00	2.50	1.50
16	Chuck Howley	3.00	1.50	.90
17	Lee Roy Jordan	4.00	2.00	1.25
18	D.D. Lewis	2.00	1.00	.60
19	Bob Lilly	10.00	5.00	3.00
20	Tony Liscio	2.00	1.00	.60
21	Dave Manders	2.00	1.00	.60
22	Craig Morton	5.00	2.50	1.50
23	Ralph Neely	2.00	1.00	.60
24	John Niland	2.00	1.00	.60
25	Jethro Pugh	2.00	1.00	.60
26	Dan Reeves	12.00	6.00	3.50
27	Mel Renfro	8.00	4.00	2.50
28	Gloster Richardson	2.00	1.00	.60
29	Tody Smith	2.00	1.00	.60
30	Roger Staubach	30.00	15.00	9.00
31	Don Talbert	2.00	1.00	.60
32	Duane Thomas	2.00	1.00	.60
33	Isaac Thomas	2.00	1.00	.60
34	Pat Toomay	2.00	1.00	.60
35	Billy Truax	2.00	1.00	.60
36	Rodney Wallace	2.00	1.00	.60
37	Mark Washington	2.00	1.00	.60
38	Charlie Waters	3.00	1.50	.90
39	Claxton Welch	2.00	1.00	.60
40	Ron Widby	2.00	1.00	.60

1972 Cowboys Team Issue

Measuring 4-1/4" x 5-1/2", the 13-card set showcases black-and-white photos on the front, bordered in white. The player's name is printed underneath the photo. The cards are unnumbered and have blank backs.

		NM	E	VG
Complete Set (13):		50.00	25.00	15.00
Common Player:		2.00	1.00	.60
1	Herb Adderley	4.00	2.00	1.25
2	Mike Ditka	15.00	7.50	4.50
3	Toni Fritsch	2.00	1.00	.60
4	Walt Garrison	2.00	1.00	.60
5	Cornell Green	2.00	1.00	.60
6	Cliff Harris	3.00	1.50	.90
7	Bob Hayes	6.00	3.00	1.75
8	Calvin Hill	5.00	2.50	1.50
9	Robert Newhouse	2.00	1.00	.60
10	Billy Parks	2.00	1.00	.60
11	Mel Renfro	6.00	3.00	1.75
12	Dan Reeves	10.00	5.00	3.00
13	Charlie Waters	3.00	1.50	.90

1979 Cowboys Police

89 • Billy Joe DuPree
DALLAS COWBOYS

Measuring 2-5/8" x 4-1/8", the 15-card set showcases a player photo on the front, with a photo credit, player's name, number, position and team listed below. The Cowboys logo is in the lower left. The card backs have Cowboys Tips in a box, with the Cowboys' helmet at the top. The sponsors are listed at the bottom of the card back. D.D. Lewis replaced Thomas "Hollywood" Henderson during the season, which means lesser amounts were printed of both cards.

		NM	E	VG
Complete Set (15):		25.00	18.50	10.00
Common Player:		.50	.40	.20
12	Roger Staubach	6.00	3.00	1.75
33	Tony Dorsett	4.00	2.00	1.25
41	Charlie Waters	.75	.40	.25
43	Cliff Harris	.50	.40	.20
44	Robert Newhouse	.50	.40	.20
50	D.D. Lewis (SP)	2.00	1.00	.60
53	Bob Breunig	.50	.40	.20
54	Randy White	2.00	1.00	.60
56	Thomas Henderson (SP)	2.00	1.00	.60
67	Pat Donovan	.50	.40	.20
79	Harvey Martin	.50	.40	.20
80	Tony Hill	.50	.40	.20
88	Drew Pearson	1.00	.50	.30
89	Billy Joe DuPree	.50	.40	.20
NNO	Tom Landry (CO)	2.50	1.25	.70

1980 Cowboys Police

Measuring 2-5/8" x 4-1/8", the 14-card set is anchored by a large photo on the front, with the player's name, number, position and team printed under the photo. A photo credit is also listed beneath the photo. The Cowboys' helmet is printed in the lower left, while a Kiwanis logo is located in the lower right. The card backs feature Cowboys Tips inside a box, which features the Cowboys' helmet at the top. The sponsor names are printed at the bottom of the card backs. The cards are numbered by the player's jersey numbers.

		NM	E	VG
Complete Set (14):		10.00	7.50	4.00
Common Player:		.50	.40	.20
1	Rafael Septien	1.00	.50	.30
11	Danny White	2.00	1.00	.60
25	Aaron Kyle	.50	.40	.20
26	Preston Pearson	1.00	.50	.30
31	Benny Barnes	.75	.40	.25
35	Scott Laidlaw	.50	.40	.20
42	Randy Hughes	.50	.40	.20
62	John Fitzgerald	.75	.40	.25
63	Larry Cole	.75	.40	.25
64	Tom Rafferty	.75	.40	.25
68	Herbert Scott	.50	.40	.20
70	Rayfield Wright	.75	.40	.25
78	John Dutton	.75	.40	.25
87	Jay Saldi	.75	.40	.25

1981 Cowboys Police

Measuring 2-5/8" x 4-1/8", the 14-card set showcases a photo on the front, with a photo credit, player's name, jersey number, position and team printed beneath the photo. The Cowboys' helmet is in the lower left corner, while the Kiwanis' logo is in the lower right. The card backs feature Cowboys Tips inside, a box with the Cowboys helmet at the top. The cards are numbered with the player's jersey number.

		NM/M	NM	E
Complete Set (14):		10.00	7.50	4.00
Common Player:		.50	.40	.20
18	Glenn Carano	.75	.60	.30
20	Ron Springs	1.00	.70	.40
23	James Jones	.50	.40	.20
26	Michael Downs	.75	.60	.30
32	Dennis Thurman	.75	.60	.30
45	Steve Wilson	.50	.40	.20
51	Anthony Dickerson	.50	.40	.20
52	Robert Shaw	.50	.40	.20
58	Mike Hegman	.50	.40	.20
59	Guy Brown	.50	.40	.20
61	Jim Cooper	.50	.40	.20
72	Ed "Too Tall" Jones	2.00	1.50	.80
84	Doug Cosbie	1.00	.70	.40
86	Butch Johnson	1.00	.70	.40

1981 Cowboys Thousand Oaks Police

Measuring 2-5/8" x 4-1/8", the 14-card set is anchored by a photo on the front. A photo credit, player's name, jersey number, position and team are printed below the photo. The Cowboys' helmet is in the lower left, while a sponsor's logo is in the lower right. The card backs feature Cowboys Tips inside a box, with the Cowboys' helmet at the top. The sponsors, including the Thousand Oaks Police Dept., are listed at the bottom of the card backs.

		NM/M	NM	E
Complete Set (14):		42.00	31.50	16.80
Common Player:		1.50	1.25	.60
11	Danny White	4.00	3.00	1.50
31	Benny Barnes	1.50	1.25	.60
33	Tony Dorsett	8.00	6.00	3.25
41	Charlie Waters	3.00	1.25	1.25
42	Randy Hughes	1.50	1.25	.60
44	Robert Newhouse	2.00	1.50	.80
54	Randy White	6.00	4.50	2.50
55	D.D. Lewis	1.50	1.25	.60
78	John Dutton	1.50	1.25	.60
79	Harvey Martin	3.00	2.25	1.25
80	Tony Hill	3.00	2.25	1.25
88	Drew Pearson	4.00	3.00	1.50
89	Billy Joe DuPree	2.00	1.50	.80
NNO	Tom Landry (CO)	7.00	5.25	2.75

1982 Cowboys Carrollton Park

Measuring 3" x 4", the six-card set showcases a large photo on the front, with "Carrollton Park Mall" printed below it inside a white border. The card backs spotlight the card's number at the top inside a circle. The player's name, position and stats are printed below the number. The Cowboys' 1982-83 scheduled takes up the bottom 2/3 of the card back. The set is also available in uncut sheets.

		NM/M	NM	E
Complete Set (6):		5.00	3.75	2.00
Common Player:		.50	.40	.20
1	Roger Staubach	2.00	1.50	.80
2	Danny White	.75	.60	.30
3	Tony Dorsett	1.00	.70	.40
4	Randy White	.75	.60	.30
5	Charlie Waters	.50	.40	.20
6	Billy Joe DuPree	.50	.40	.20

1983 Cowboys Police

Measuring 2-5/8" x 4-1/8", the 28-card set is anchored by a large photo on the front, with a photo credit, player's name, number, position and team printed underneath the photo. The Cowboys' helmet is printed in the lower right, while the Kiwanis' logo is in the lower right. The card backs have Cowboys Tips inside a box, with the Cowboys' helmet at the top. The sponsors are listed at the bottom of the card back.

		NM/M	NM	E
Complete Set (28):		25.00	18.50	10.00
Common Player:		.50	.40	.20
1	Rafael Septien	.50	.40	.20
11	Danny White	1.50	1.25	.60
20	Ron Springs	.50	.40	.20
24	Everson Walls	.50	.40	.20
26	Michael Downs	.50	.40	.20
30	Timmy Newsome	.50	.40	.20
32	Dennis Thurman	.50	.40	.20
33	Tony Dorsett	3.00	2.25	1.25
47	Dexter Clinkscale	.50	.40	.20
53	Bob Breunig	.50	.40	.20
54	Randy White	3.00	2.25	1.25
65	Kurt Petersen	.50	.40	.20
67	Pat Donovan	.50	.40	.20
70	Howard Richards	.50	.40	.20
72	Ed "Too Tall" Jones	2.00	1.50	.80
78	John Dutton	.50	.40	.20
79	Harvey Martin	1.00	.70	.40
80	Tony Hill	.75	.60	.30
83	Doug Donley	.50	.40	.20
84	Doug Cosbie	.50	.40	.20
86	Butch Johnson	.50	.40	.20
88	Drew Pearson	1.75	1.25	.70
89	Billy Joe DuPree	.50	.40	.20
NNO	Tom Landry (CO)	2.00	1.50	.80
NNO	Melinda May (CHEER)	.50	.40	.20
NNO	Dana Presley (CHEER)	.50	.40	.20
NNO	Judy Trammell (CHEER)	.50	.40	.20
NNO	Toni Washington (CHEER)	.50	.40	.20

1985 Cowboys Frito Lay

Measuring 4" x 5-1/2", this 41 card set is anchored on the front by a large black-and-white photo. The player's name, jersey number, position and bio are listed beneath the photo on the front. The Cowboys' helmet is printed in the lower left, with the Frito Lay logo in the lower right. The backs are unnumbered and blank.

		NM/M	NM	E
Complete Set (41):		50.00	37.00	20.00
Common Player:		1.00	.70	.40
1	Vince Albritton	1.00	.70	.40
2	Brian Baldinger	1.00	.70	.40
3	Dexter Clinkscale	1.00	.70	.40
4	Jim Cooper	1.00	.70	.40
5	Fred Cornwell	1.00	.70	.40
6	Doug Crosbie	1.50	1.25	.60
7	Steve DeOssie	1.00	.70	.40
8	John Dutton	1.00	.70	.40
9	Ricky Easmon	1.00	.70	.40
10	Ron Fellows	1.00	.70	.40
11	Leon Gonzalez	1.00	.70	.40
12	Gary Hogeboom	1.50	1.25	.60
13	Jim Jeffcoat	2.50	2.00	1.00
14	Ed "Too Tall" Jones	3.00	2.25	1.25
15	James Jones	1.00	.70	.40
16	Crawford Ker	1.00	.70	.40
17	Robert Lavette	1.00	.70	.40
18	Eugene Lockhart	1.00	.70	.40
19	Timmy Newsome	1.00	.70	.40
20	Drew Pearson (ACO)	2.00	1.50	.80
21	Steve Pelluer	1.50	1.25	.60
22	Jesse Penn	1.00	.70	.40
23	Kurt Petersen	1.00	.70	.40
24	Karl Powe	1.00	.70	.40
25	Phil Pozderac	1.00	.70	.40
26	Tom Rafferty	1.00	.70	.40
27	Mike Renfro	1.00	.70	.40
28	Howard Richards	1.00	.70	.40
29	Jeff Rohrer	1.00	.70	.40
30	Mike Saxon	1.00	.70	.40
31	Victor Scott	1.00	.70	.40
32	Rafael Septien	1.00	.70	.40
33	Don Smerek	1.00	.70	.40
34	Roger Staubach	10.00	7.50	4.00
35	Broderick Thompson	1.00	.70	.40
36	Dennis Thurman	1.00	.70	.40
37	Glen Titensor	1.00	.70	.40
38	Mark Tuinei	1.50	1.25	.60
39	Everson Walls	1.50	1.25	.60
40	John Williams	1.00	.70	.40
41	**Team Photo**	3.00	2.25	1.25

1976 Crane Discs

These circular cards measure 3-3/8" in diameter and were produced by Michael Schechter Associates, as noted by the MSA letters on the card back. Each card front has a black- and-white mug shot of a player, along with his team, name and position. The card has a colored border with the word "Crane" at the top, representing Crane Potato Chips, which offered the cards as a mail-in offer. The Crane logo appears on the card back, but there are a few other sponsors which may also appear on the back; these are slightly more valuable than their Crane counterparts. The cards are unnumbered.

		NM	E	VG
Complete Set (30):		15.00	7.50	4.50
Common Player:		.10	.05	.03
(1)	Ken Anderson	.50	.25	.15
(2)	Otis Armstrong	.15	.08	.05
(3)	Steve Bartkowski	.35	.20	.11
(4)	Terry Bradshaw	2.00	1.00	.60
(5)	John Brockington	.25	.13	.08
(6)	Doug Buffone	.10	.05	.03
(7)	Wally Chambers	.10	.05	.03
(8)	Isaac Curtis	.25	.13	.08
(9)	Chuck Foreman	.20	.10	.06
(10)	Roman Gabriel	.75	.40	.25
(11)	Mel Gray	.15	.08	.05
(12)	Joe Greene	.65	.35	.20
(13)	James Harris	.25	.13	.08
(14)	Jim Hart	.25	.13	.08
(15)	Billy Kilmer	.25	.13	.08
(16)	Greg Landry	.25	.13	.08
(17)	Ed Marinaro	.50	.25	.15
(18)	Lawrence McCutcheon	.25	.13	.08
(19)	Terry Metcalf	.15	.08	.05
(20)	Lydell Mitchell	.25	.13	.08
(21)	Jim Otis	.15	.08	.05
(22)	Alan Page	.35	.20	.11
(23)	Walter Payton	10.00	5.00	3.00
(24)	Greg Pruitt	.40	.20	.12
(25)	Charlie Sanders	.25	.13	.08
(26)	Ron Shanklin	.25	.13	.08
(27)	Roger Staubach	2.00	1.00	.60
(28)	Jan Stenerud	.40	.20	.12
(29)	Charley Taylor	.40	.20	.12
(30)	Roger Wehrli	.25	.13	.08

1952 Crown Brand

		NM	E	VG
Complete Set (48):		2,000	1,000	600.00
Common Player:		50.00	25.00	15.00
1	John Brown	50.00	25.00	15.00
2	Tom Casey	75.00	37.00	22.00
3	Tommy Ford	50.00	25.00	15.00
4	Ian Gibb	50.00	25.00	15.00
5	Dick Huffman	75.00	37.00	22.00
6	Jack Jacobs	100.00	50.00	30.00
7	Thomas Lumsden	50.00	25.00	15.00
8	George McPhail	50.00	25.00	15.00
9	Jim McPherson	50.00	25.00	15.00
10	Buddy Tinsley	75.00	37.00	22.00
11	Ron Vaccher	50.00	25.00	15.00
12	Al Wiley	50.00	25.00	15.00
13	Ken Charlton	75.00	37.00	22.00
14	Glenn Dobbs	75.00	37.00	22.00
15	Sully Glasser	50.00	25.00	15.00
16	Nelson Greene	50.00	25.00	15.00
17	Bert Iannone	50.00	25.00	15.00
18	Art McEwan	50.00	25.00	15.00
19	Jimmy McFaul	50.00	25.00	15.00
20	Bob Pelling	50.00	25.00	15.00
21	Chuck Radley	50.00	25.00	15.00
22	Martin Ruby	100.00	50.00	30.00
23	Jack Russell	50.00	25.00	15.00
24	Roy Wright	50.00	25.00	15.00
25	Paul Alford	50.00	25.00	15.00
26	Sugarfoot Anderson	50.00	25.00	15.00
27	Dick Bradley	50.00	25.00	15.00
28	Bob Bryant	50.00	25.00	15.00
29	Cliff Cyr	50.00	25.00	15.00
30	Cal Green	50.00	25.00	15.00
31	Stan Heath	50.00	25.00	15.00
32	Stan Kaluznick	50.00	25.00	15.00
33	Guss Knickerhm	50.00	25.00	15.00
34	Paul Salata	50.00	25.00	15.00
35	Murry Sullivan	50.00	25.00	15.00
36	Dave West	50.00	25.00	15.00
37	Joe Aquirre	50.00	25.00	15.00
38	Claude Arnold	50.00	25.00	15.00
39	Bill Briggs	50.00	25.00	15.00
40	Mario DeMarco	50.00	25.00	15.00

41	Mike King	50.00	25.00	15.00
42	Donald Lord	50.00	25.00	15.00
43	Frank Morris	75.00	37.00	22.00
44	Gayle Pace	50.00	25.00	15.00
45	Rod Pantages	50.00	25.00	15.00
46	Rollin Prather	50.00	25.00	15.00
47	Chuck Quilter	50.00	25.00	15.00
48	Jim Quondamatteo	50.00	25.00	15.00

D

1986 DairyPak Cartons

These cards were sponsored by various brands of milk across the country in 1986; different colors (purple, green, lavender, aqua, orange, red, light blue, dark blue, black and brown) were used for different sponsors. Each card is perforated and features a black-and-white head shot of the player, plus a facsimilie autograph and card number. Cards which have been cut from the milk carton measure 3-1/4" x 4-7/16", but generally are more valuable if they are left intact as a complete carton. The set was not licensed by the NFL, so no team logos are shown; the NFLPA, however, licensed the set. Below each card was an offer to receive a 24" x 32" poster featuring the 24 cards.

		NM/M	NM	E
Complete Set (24):		65.00	49.00	26.00
Common Player:		1.25	.90	.50
1	Joe Montana	10.00	7.50	4.00
2	Marcus Allen	3.00	2.25	1.25
3	Art Monk	2.00	1.50	.80
4	Mike Quick	1.25	.90	.50
5	John Elway	5.00	3.75	2.00
6	Eric Hipple	1.25	.90	.50
7	Louis Lipps	1.25	.90	.50
8	Dan Fouts	2.00	1.50	.80
9	Phil Simms	2.00	1.50	.80
10	Mike Rozier	1.25	.90	.50
11	Greg Bell	1.25	.90	.50
12	Ottis Anderson	1.50	1.25	.60
13	Dave Krieg	1.75	1.25	.70
14	Anthony Carter	1.25	.90	.50
15	Freeman McNeil	1.25	.90	.50
16	Doug Cosbie	1.25	.90	.50
17	James Lofton	6.00	4.50	2.50
18	Dan Marino	8.00	6.00	3.25
19	James Wilder	1.25	.90	.50
20	Cris Collinsworth	1.50	1.25	.60
21	Eric Dickerson	4.00	3.00	1.50
22	Walter Payton	6.00	4.50	2.50
23	Ozzie Newsome	2.00	1.50	.80
24	Chris Hinton	1.25	.90	.50

1971-72 Dell

This 48-player set, which measures 8-1/4" x 10-3/4", from the 1971-72 Dell Pro Football Guide includes a center insert that unfolds to show 48 color photos. The photos, bordered in black and yellow, each measure 1-3/4" x 3". The player's name and team name are located inside a rectangle under the photo. The backs boast action photos, which are bordered in black and white. The football guide includes bios on each of the players offered in the set. The photos are not numbered. A complete set which is still intact in the guides are valued at 25 percent over what is listed here.

		NM	E	VG
Complete Set (48):		100.00	50.00	30.00
Common Player:		1.00	.50	.30
1	Dan Abramowicz	1.00	.50	.30
2	Herb Adderley	2.00	1.00	.60
3	Lem Barney	1.00	.50	.30
4	Bobby Bell	1.00	.50	.30
5	George Blanda	3.00	1.50	.90
6	Terry Bradshaw	15.00	7.50	4.50
7	John Brodie	2.00	1.00	.60
8	Larry Brown	1.00	.50	.30
9	Dick Butkus	10.00	5.00	3.00
10	Fred Carr	1.00	.50	.30
11	Virgil Carter	1.00	.50	.30
12	Mike Curtis	1.00	.50	.30
13	Len Dawson	2.50	1.25	.70
14	Carl Eller	1.00	.50	.30
15	Mel Farr	1.00	.50	.30
16	Roman Gabriel	1.50	.70	.45
17	Gary Garrison	1.00	.50	.30
18	Dick Gordon	1.00	.50	.30
19	Bob Griese	5.00	2.50	1.50
20	Bob Hayes	1.50	.70	.45
21	Rich Jackson	1.00	.50	.30
22	Charlie Johnson	1.00	.50	.30
23	Ron Johnson	1.00	.50	.30
24	Deacon Jones	2.50	1.25	.70
25	Sonny Jurgensen	2.50	1.25	.70
26	Leroy Kelly	1.50	.70	.45
27	Daryle Lamonica	1.50	.70	.45
28	MacArthur Lane	1.00	.50	.30
29	Willie Lanier	1.50	.70	.45
30	Bob Lilly	3.00	1.50	.90
31	Floyd Little	1.00	.50	.30
32	Mike Lucci	1.00	.50	.30
33	Don Maynard	2.50	1.25	.70
34	Joe Namath	16.00	8.00	4.75
35	Tommy Nobis	1.50	.70	.45
36	Merlin Olsen	3.00	1.50	.90
37	Alan Page	2.00	1.00	.60
38	Gerry Philbin	1.00	.50	.30
39	Jim Plunkett	2.00	1.00	.60
40	Tim Rossovich	1.00	.50	.30
41	Gale Sayers	10.00	5.00	3.00
42	Dennis Shaw	1.00	.50	.30
43	O.J. Simpson	14.00	7.00	4.25
44	Fran Tarkenton	7.00	3.50	2.00
45	Johnny Unitas	12.00	6.00	3.50
46	Paul Warfield	3.00	1.50	.90
47	Gene Washington	1.00	.50	.30
48	Larry Wilson	1.50	.70	.45

1933 Diamond Matchbooks Silver

With covers measuring 1-1/2" x 4-1/2" when folded out, the 95-matchbook set has a photo of the player over a pink or green background, bordered in silver. Prices listed here are with the matches removed. The player's name and team are listed at the bottom of the cover fronts. The cover backs showcase the player's name and highlights inside a box. The matchbooks are not numbered. Matchbooks with the matches intact are worth 1-1/2 to 2 times more than what is listed.

		NM	E	VG
Complete Set (95):		6,500	3,000	1,000
Common Player:		65.00	30.00	15.00
1	**All-American Board of Football Seal**	65.00	35.00	15.00
2	Gene Alford	65.00	25.00	15.00
3	Marger Apsit	65.00	25.00	15.00
4	Morris "Red" Badgro	65.00	25.00	15.00
5	Cliff Battles	100.00	60.00	35.00
6	Morris (Maury) Bodenger	65.00	25.00	10.00
7	Jimmy Bowdoin	65.00	25.00	15.00
8	John Boylan	65.00	25.00	15.00
9	Hank Bruder	65.00	25.00	15.00
10	Carl Brumbaugh	65.00	35.00	15.00
11	Bill Buckler	65.00	25.00	15.00
12	Jerome Buckley	65.00	35.00	15.00
13	Dale Burnett	65.00	35.00	15.00
14	Ernie Caddel	65.00	35.00	20.00
15	Red Cagle	65.00	35.00	20.00
16	Glen Campbell	65.00	25.00	15.00
17	John Cannella	65.00	25.00	15.00
18	Zuck Carlson	65.00	25.00	15.00
19	George Christensen	65.00	35.00	20.00
20	Stu Clancy	65.00	25.00	15.00
21	Paul (Rip) Collins	65.00	25.00	15.00
22	John F. Connell	65.00	25.00	15.00
23	George Corbett	65.00	25.00	15.00
24	Orien Crow	65.00	25.00	15.00
25	Ed Danowski	65.00	25.00	15.00
26	Sylvester (Red) Davis	65.00	25.00	15.00
27	John Isola	65.00	35.00	20.00
28	John Doehring	65.00	25.00	15.00
29	Glen Edwards	65.00	35.00	20.00
30	Earl Elser	65.00	35.00	25.00
31	Ox Emerson	65.00	35.00	25.00
32	Tiny Feather	65.00	25.00	15.00
33	Ray Flaherty	65.00	25.00	15.00
34	Ike Frankian	65.00	25.00	15.00
35	Harold "Red" Grange	425.00	250.00	150.00
36	Len Grant	65.00	25.00	15.00
37	Ace Gutowsky	65.00	35.00	20.00
38	Mel Hein	65.00	35.00	25.00
39	Arnie Herber	65.00	35.00	25.00
40	Bill Hewitt	65.00	35.00	25.00
41	Herman Hickman	65.00	35.00	25.00
42	Clarke Hinkle	375.00	200.00	75.00
43	Cal Hubbard	425.00	215.00	105.00
44	George Hurley	65.00	25.00	15.00
45	Herman Hussey	65.00	25.00	15.00
46	Cecil (Tex) Irvin	65.00	25.00	15.00
47	Luke Johnson	65.00	25.00	25.00
48	Bruce Jones	65.00	25.00	15.00
49	Tom Jones	65.00	25.00	15.00
50	Thacker Kay	65.00	25.00	15.00
51	John Kelly	65.00	35.00	25.00
52	Joe (Doc) Kopcha	65.00	35.00	25.00
53	Joe Kurth	65.00	25.00	15.00
54	Milo Lubratevich	65.00	25.00	15.00
55	Father Lumpkin	65.00	35.00	25.00
56	Jim MacMurdo	65.00	25.00	15.00
57	Joe Maniaci	65.00	25.00	15.00
58	Jack McBride	65.00	25.00	15.00
59	Ookie Miller	65.00	25.00	15.00
60	Granville Mitchell	65.00	25.00	15.00
61	Keith Molesworth	65.00	35.00	25.00
62	Bob Monnett	65.00	25.00	15.00
63	Hap Moran	65.00	25.00	15.00
64	Bill Morgan	65.00	25.00	15.00
65	Maynard (Doc) Morrison	65.00	25.00	15.00
66	Mathew Murray	65.00	25.00	15.00
67	Jim Musick	65.00	25.00	15.00
68	Bronko Nagurski	800.00	425.00	225.00
69	Dick Nesbitt	65.00	25.00	15.00
70	Harry Newman	65.00	35.00	25.00
71	Steve Owen	65.00	35.00	25.00
72	Bill (Red) Owen	65.00	25.00	15.00
73	Andy Pavlicovic	65.00	25.00	15.00
74	Bert Pearson	65.00	25.00	15.00
75	William Pendergast	65.00	25.00	15.00
76	Jerry Pepper	65.00	25.00	15.00
77	Stan Piawlock	65.00	25.00	15.00
78	Ernie Pinckert	65.00	35.00	25.00
79	Glenn Presnell	65.00	25.00	15.00
80	Jess Quatse	65.00	25.00	15.00
81	Hank Reese	65.00	25.00	15.00
82	Dick Richards	65.00	25.00	15.00
83	Tony Sarausky	65.00	25.00	15.00
84	Elmer (Dutch) Schaake	65.00	25.00	15.00
85	John Schneller	65.00	25.00	15.00
86	Johnny Sisk	65.00	25.00	15.00
87	Mike Steponovich	65.00	25.00	15.00
88	Ken Strong	275.00	150.00	75.00
89	Charles Tackwell	65.00	25.00	15.00
90	Harry Thayer	65.00	35.00	25.00
91	Walt Uzdavinis	65.00	25.00	15.00
92	John Welch	65.00	25.00	15.00
93	William Whelan	65.00	25.00	15.00
94	Fay (Mule) Wilson	65.00	35.00	25.00
95	Frank (Babe) Wright	65.00	25.00	15.00

1934 Diamond Matchbooks

Measuring 1-1/2" x 4-1/2", each matchbook showcases four different colored borders, including blue, red, tan and green. Many players have each of the four color combinations. Other players have one or two variations of borders. The player's name and team are printed above the photo on the front. The backs spotlight the player's name and highlights. This set features "The Diamond Match Co., N.Y.C" above the striking strip on the matchbook backs. As a note, the 1935 matchbooks resemble this set, but do not have the "Diamond Match" tag line at the bottom. The books are unnumbered. If matches are intact in the book, they are worth 1-1/2 times more.

		NM	E	VG
Complete Set (121):		4,000	1,100	600.00
Common Player:		25.00	5.00	3.00
1	Arvo Antilla	25.00	5.00	3.00
2	Morris "Red" Badgro	40.00	20.00	12.00
3	Norbert Bartell	25.00	5.00	3.00
4	Cliff Battles	25.00	12.50	7.50
5	Chuck Bennis	25.00	5.00	3.00
6	Jack Beynon	25.00	5.00	3.00
7	Morris (Maury) Bodenger	25.00	5.00	3.00
8	John Bond	25.00	5.00	3.00
9	John Brown	25.00	5.00	3.00
10	Carl Brumbaugh	25.00	5.00	3.00
11	Dale Burnett	25.00	5.00	3.00
12	Ernie Caddel	25.00	5.00	3.00
13	Red Cagle	25.00	5.00	3.00
14	Glen Campbell	25.00	5.00	3.00
15	John Cannella	25.00	5.00	3.00
16	Joe Carter	25.00	5.00	3.00
17	Les Caywood	25.00	5.00	3.00
18	George (Buck) Chapman	25.00	5.00	3.00
19	Frank Christensen	25.00	5.00	3.00
20	Stu Clancy	25.00	5.00	3.00
21	Algy Clark	25.00	5.00	3.00
22	Paul (Rip) Collins	25.00	5.00	3.00
23	Jack Connell	25.00	5.00	3.00
24	Orien Crow	25.00	5.00	3.00
25	Lone Star Dietz (CO)	25.00	5.00	3.00
26	John Doehring	25.00	5.00	3.00
27	Glen Edwards	50.00	25.00	15.00
28	Ox Emerson	25.00	5.00	3.00
29	Tiny Feather	25.00	5.00	3.00
30	Ray Flaherty	50.00	25.00	15.00
31	Frank Froschauer	25.00	5.00	3.00
32	Chuck Galbreath	25.00	5.00	3.00
33	Elbert (Red) Gragg	25.00	5.00	3.00
34	Harold "Red" Grange	500.00	250.00	150.00
35	Cy Grant	25.00	5.00	3.00
36	Len Grant	25.00	5.00	3.00
37	Ross Grant	25.00	5.00	3.00

38	Jack Griffith	25.00	5.00	3.00
39	Ed Gryboski	25.00	5.00	3.00
40	Ace Gutowsky	25.00	5.00	3.00
41	Thomas (Swede) Hanson	25.00	5.00	3.00
42	Mel Hein	25.00	12.50	7.50
43	Warren Heller	25.00	5.00	3.00
44	Bill Hewitt	50.00	25.00	15.00
45	Cecil (Tex) Irvin	25.00	5.00	3.00
46	Frank Johnson	25.00	5.00	3.00
47	Jack Johnson	25.00	5.00	3.00
48	Bob Jones	25.00	5.00	3.00
49	Tom Jones	25.00	5.00	3.00
50	Carl Jorgensen	25.00	5.00	3.00
51	John Karcis	25.00	5.00	3.00
52	Eddie Kawal	25.00	5.00	3.00
53	John Kelly	25.00	5.00	3.00
54	George Kenneally	25.00	5.00	3.00
55	Walt Kiesling	50.00	25.00	15.00
56	Jack Knapper	25.00	5.00	3.00
57	Frank Knox	25.00	5.00	3.00
58	Joe (Doc) Kopcha	25.00	5.00	3.00
59	Joe Kresky	25.00	5.00	3.00
60	Joe Laws	25.00	5.00	3.00
61	Russ Lay	25.00	5.00	3.00
62	Biff Lee	25.00	5.00	3.00
63	Gil LeFebvre	25.00	5.00	3.00
64	Jim Leonard	25.00	5.00	3.00
65	Les Lindberg	25.00	5.00	3.00
66	John Lipski	25.00	5.00	3.00
67	Milo Lubratevich	25.00	5.00	3.00
68	Father Lumpkin	25.00	5.00	3.00
69	Jim MacMurdo	25.00	5.00	3.00
70	Ed Matesic	25.00	5.00	3.00
71	Dave McCollough	25.00	5.00	3.00
72	John McKnight	25.00	5.00	3.00
73	Johnny "Blood" McNally	100.00	50.00	30.00
74	Al Minot	25.00	5.00	3.00
75	Keith Molesworth	25.00	5.00	3.00
76	Jim Mooney	25.00	5.00	3.00
77	Leroy Moorehead	25.00	5.00	3.00
78	Bill Morgan	25.00	5.00	3.00
79	Bob Moser	25.00	5.00	3.00
80	Lee Mulleneaux	25.00	5.00	3.00
81	George Munday	25.00	5.00	3.00
82	George Musso	50.00	25.00	15.00
83	Harry Newman	25.00	5.00	3.00
84	Al Norgard	25.00	5.00	3.00
85	John (Cap) Oehler	25.00	5.00	3.00
86	Charlie Opper	25.00	5.00	3.00
87	Bill (Red) Owen	25.00	5.00	3.00
88	Steve Owen	20.00	10.00	6.00
89	Bert Pearson	25.00	5.00	3.00
90	Tom Perkinson	25.00	5.00	3.00
91	Mace Pike	25.00	5.00	3.00
92	Joe Pilconis	25.00	5.00	3.00
93	Lew Pope	25.00	5.00	3.00
94	Crain Portman	25.00	5.00	3.00
95	Glenn Presnell	25.00	5.00	3.00
96	Jess Quatse	25.00	5.00	3.00
97	Clare Randolph	25.00	5.00	3.00
98	Hank Reese	25.00	5.00	3.00
99	Paul Riblett	25.00	5.00	3.00
100	Dick Richards	25.00	5.00	3.00
101	Jack Roberts	25.00	5.00	3.00
102	John Rogers	25.00	5.00	3.00
103	Gene Ronzani	25.00	5.00	3.00
104	John Schueller	25.00	5.00	3.00
105	Bob Rowe	25.00	5.00	3.00
106	Alolph Schwammel	25.00	5.00	3.00
107	Earl (Red) Seick	25.00	5.00	3.00
108	Allen Shi	25.00	5.00	3.00
109	Ben Smith	25.00	5.00	3.00
110	Ken Strong	75.00	37.00	22.00
111	Elmer Taber	25.00	5.00	3.00
112	Charles Tackwell	25.00	5.00	3.00
113	Ray Tesser	25.00	5.00	3.00
114	John (Stumpy) Thomason	25.00	5.00	3.00
115	Charlie Turbyville	25.00	5.00	3.00
116	Claude Urevig	25.00	5.00	3.00
117	John (Harp) Vaughan	25.00	5.00	3.00
118	Henry Wagnon	25.00	5.00	3.00
119	John West	25.00	5.00	3.00
120	Lee Woodruff	25.00	5.00	3.00
121	Jim Zyntell	25.00	5.00	3.00

1934 Diamond Matchbooks College Rivals

The 12-matchbook set honors a college rivalry with text about the recent history of the games. Bordered in black or tan, matchbooks could be found in either variation. Matchbooks which still have the matches intact are worth 1-1/2 times more than what is listed here.

		NM	E	VG
Complete Set (12):		150.00	75.00	40.00
Common Player:		20.00	7.50	4.00
1	**Alabama vs. Fordham 1933**	20.00	7.50	4.00
2	**Army vs. Navy start to finish**	20.00	5.00	3.00
3	**lose by a 13-6 score**	20.00	7.50	4.00
4	**Bulldog Alumni and followers**	20.00	7.50	4.00
5	**in atoning for this one defeat**	20.00	7.50	4.00
6	**victory for Lafayette**	20.00	7.50	4.00
7	**Michigan vs. Ohio State Champions**	20.00	7.50	4.00
8	**leader of men, Knute Rockne**	35.00	17.50	10.50
9	**Penn vs. Cornell pass**	20.00	7.50	4.00
10	**USC vs. Notre Dame year**	35.00	17.50	10.50
11	**Yale vs. Harvard Harvard**	20.00	7.50	4.00
12	**Yale vs. Princeton scoring 27**	20.00	7.50	4.00

1935 Diamond Matchbooks

In 1935, three different colored borders were used for this set, including tan, green and red. However, this time players were only printed with one color border. Resembling the 1934 set, this set can be identified by the "Made in U.S.A./The Diamond Match Co., N.Y.C." tag line. The unnumbered matchbooks measure 1-1/2" x 4-1/2". The player photo is not bordered and a player position is not listed. Matchbooks with the matches intact are valued at 1-1/2 times the values listed here.

		NM	E	VG
Complete Set (96):		2,000	500.00	300.00
Common Player:		20.00	5.00	3.00
1	Alf Anderson	20.00	5.00	3.00
2	Alec Ashford	20.00	5.00	3.00
3	Gene Augusterfer	20.00	5.00	3.00
4	Morris "Red" Badgro	20.00	10.00	6.00
5	Cliff Battles	50.00	25.00	15.00
6	Harry Benson	20.00	5.00	3.00
7	Tony Blazine	20.00	5.00	3.00
8	John Bond	20.00	5.00	3.00
9	Maurice (Mule) Bray	20.00	5.00	3.00
10	Dale Burnett	20.00	5.00	3.00
11	Charles (Cocky) Bush	20.00	5.00	3.00
12	Ernie Caddel	20.00	5.00	3.00
13	Zuck Carlson	20.00	5.00	3.00
14	Joe Carter	20.00	5.00	3.00
15	Cy Casper	20.00	5.00	3.00
16	Paul Causey	20.00	5.00	3.00
17	Frank Christensen	20.00	5.00	3.00
18	Stu Clancy	20.00	5.00	3.00
19	Earl "Dutch" Clark	75.00	37.00	22.00
20	Paul (Rip) Collins	20.00	5.00	3.00
21	Dave Cook (Chicago Cardinals)	20.00	5.00	3.00
22	Fred Crawford	20.00	5.00	3.00
23	Paul Cuba	20.00	5.00	3.00
24	Harry Ebding	20.00	5.00	3.00
25	Glen Edwards	20.00	10.00	6.00
26	Marvin (Swede) Ellstrom	20.00	5.00	3.00
27	Beattie Feathers	20.00	10.00	6.00
28	Ray Flaherty	20.00	10.00	6.00
29	John Gildea	20.00	5.00	3.00
30	Tom Graham	20.00	5.00	3.00
31	Len Grant	20.00	5.00	3.00
32	Maurice Green	20.00	5.00	3.00
33	Norman Greeney	20.00	5.00	3.00
34	Ace Gutowsky	20.00	5.00	3.00
35	Julius Hall	20.00	5.00	3.00
36	Thomas (Swede) Hanson	20.00	5.00	3.00
37	Charles Harold	20.00	5.00	3.00
38	Tom Haywood	20.00	5.00	3.00
39	Mel Hein	20.00	10.00	6.00
40	Bill Hewitt	20.00	10.00	6.00
41	Cecil (Tex) Irvin	20.00	5.00	3.00
42	Frank Johnson	20.00	5.00	3.00
43	Jack Johnson	20.00	5.00	3.00
44	Luke Johnson	20.00	5.00	3.00
45	Tom Jones	20.00	5.00	3.00
46	Carl Jorgensen	20.00	5.00	3.00
47	George Kenneally	20.00	5.00	3.00
48	Roger Kirkman	20.00	5.00	3.00
49	Frank Knox	20.00	5.00	3.00
50	Joe (Doc) Kopcha	20.00	5.00	3.00
51	Rick Lackman	20.00	5.00	3.00
52	Jim Leonard	20.00	5.00	3.00
53	Joe (Hunk) Malkovich	20.00	5.00	3.00
54	Ed Manske	20.00	5.00	3.00
55	Bernie Masterson	20.00	5.00	3.00
56	James McMillen	20.00	5.00	3.00
57	Mike Mikulak	20.00	5.00	3.00
58	Ookie Miller	20.00	5.00	3.00
59	Milford (Dub) Miller	20.00	5.00	3.00
60	Al Minot	20.00	5.00	3.00
61	Buster Mitchell	20.00	5.00	3.00
62	Bill Morgan	20.00	5.00	3.00
63	George Musso	20.00	10.00	6.00
64	Harry Newman	20.00	5.00	3.00
65	Al Nichelini	20.00	5.00	3.00
66	Bill (Red) Owen	20.00	5.00	3.00
67	Steve Owen	30.00	15.00	9.00
68	Max Padlow	20.00	5.00	3.00
69	Hal Pangle	20.00	5.00	3.00
70	Melvin Pittman	20.00	5.00	3.00
71	William Pollock	20.00	5.00	3.00
72	Glenn Presnell	20.00	5.00	3.00
73	George Rado	20.00	5.00	3.00
74	Clare Randolph	20.00	5.00	3.00
75	Hank Reese	20.00	5.00	3.00
76	Ray Richards	20.00	5.00	3.00
77	Doug Russell	20.00	5.00	3.00
78	Sandy Sandberg	20.00	5.00	3.00
79	John Schneller	20.00	5.00	3.00
80	Michael Sebastian	20.00	5.00	3.00
81	Allen Shi	20.00	5.00	3.00
82	Johnny Sisk	20.00	5.00	3.00
83	Phil Sarboe	20.00	5.00	3.00
84	James Stacy	20.00	5.00	3.00
85	Ed Storm	20.00	5.00	3.00
86	Ken Strong	50.00	25.00	15.00
87	Art Strutt	20.00	5.00	3.00
88	Frank Sullivan	20.00	5.00	3.00
89	Charles Treadaway	20.00	5.00	3.00
90	John Turley	20.00	5.00	3.00
91	Claude Urevig	20.00	5.00	3.00
92	Charles Vaughan	20.00	5.00	3.00
93	Izzy Weinstock	20.00	5.00	3.00
94	Henry Wiesenbaugh	20.00	5.00	3.00
95	Joe Zeller	20.00	5.00	3.00
96	Vince Zizak	20.00	5.00	3.00

1935 Diamond Matchbooks College Rivals

With all the variations available, this set goes from 12 matchbooks to 36. Covers include highlights on recent games in the rivalry. The Diamond name is printed in tan with a double-lined company name or the Diamond name is printed on a single line with a tan or black border. Matchbooks with the matches intact are valued at 1-1/2 times more than what is listed here.

		NM	E	VG
Complete Set (12):		100.00	75.00	40.00
Common Player:		10.00	7.50	4.00
1	**Alabama vs. Fordham once championship**	10.00	7.50	4.00
2	**Army vs. Navy over the Cadets since 1921**	10.00	5.00	3.00
3	**the gamely fighting "Rams"**	10.00	7.50	4.00
4	**Georgia vs. Georgia Tech 7-0 defeat**	10.00	7.50	4.00
5	**Holy Cross vs. Boston College defeat**	10.00	7.50	4.00
6	**in a 13-7 victory for Lehigh**	10.00	7.50	4.00
7	**Michigan vs. Ohio State tory for State**	10.00	7.50	4.00
8	**Notre Dame vs. Army Cadets 12-6**	12.00	6.00	3.50
9	**Penn vs. Cornell from start to finish**	10.00	7.50	4.00
10	**carries of Elmer Layden**	12.00	6.00	3.50
11	**Yale vs. Harvard set back**	10.00	7.50	4.00
12	**Yale vs. Princeton ed still led 7-0**	10.00	7.50	4.00

1936 Diamond Matchbooks

Chicago Bears and Philadelphia Eagles players were featured in this matchbook set. The matchbooks, when folded out, measure 1-1/2" x 4-1/2". The words were printed in black or brown, while borders were in three different colors, tan, red and green. Ray Nolting is the lone exception to the rule, as matchbooks featuring him were printed with black and brown ink. The front of the books include a player picture, his name and team. The backs showcase his name and his highlights. With the different variations available, a complete set totals 96 matchbooks, which are unnumbered. Books with matches intact are worth 1-1/2 times more than what is listed here.

		NM	E	VG
Complete Set (47):		1,000	250.00	150.00
Common Player:		15.00	7.50	4.00
1	Carl Brumbaugh	15.00	5.00	3.00
2	Zuck Carlson	15.00	5.00	3.00
3	George Corbett (last line - Sigma Alpha Epsilon.)	15.00	5.00	3.00
4	John Doehring (last line - is a bachelor.)	15.00	5.00	3.00
5	Beattie Feathers (first line - ...will be 28 years)	25.00	12.50	7.50
6	Dan Fortmann (first line - ...April 11, 1916, at)	25.00	12.50	7.50

7	George Grosvenor	15.00	5.00	3.00
8	Bill Hewitt	15.00	4.00	4.50
9	Luke Johnson	15.00	5.00	3.00
10	William Karr (first line - ...in Ripley,)	15.00	5.00	3.00
11	Eddie Kawal	15.00	5.00	3.00
12	Jack Manders (last line - 200, Height 6 ft. 1 in.)	15.00	5.00	3.00
13	Bernie Masterson (last line - Alpha Epsilon, Single.)	15.00	5.00	3.00
14	Eddie Michaels	15.00	5.00	3.00
15	Ookie Miller	15.00	5.00	3.00
16	Keith Molesworth (last line - 5 ft. 9 1/2 in. Weight 168.)	15.00	5.00	3.00
17	George Musso (last line - Science degree, Is single.)	50.00	25.00	15.00
18	Bronko Nagurski	400.00	200.00	120.00
19	Ray Nolting (first line - ...three years of Cin-)	15.00	5.00	3.00
20	Vernon Oech	15.00	5.00	3.00
21	William Pollock	15.00	5.00	3.00
22	Gene Ronzani (last line - is married.)	15.00	5.00	3.00
23	Ted Rosequist	15.00	5.00	3.00
24	Johnny Sisk	15.00	5.00	3.00
25	Joe Stydahar (last line - is single.)	25.00	12.50	7.50
26	Frank Sullivan (first line - ...Loyola U.) (New)	15.00	5.00	3.00
27	Russell Thompson (last line - Sigma Nu fraternity.)	15.00	5.00	3.00
28	Milt Trost (last line - is single.)	15.00	5.00	3.00
29	Joe Zeller (last line - and is single, Sigma Nu.)	15.00	5.00	3.00
30	Bill Brian	15.00	5.00	3.00
31	Art Buss	15.00	5.00	3.00
32	Joe Carter	15.00	5.00	3.00
33	Thomas (Swede) Hanson	15.00	5.00	3.00
34	Don Jackson	15.00	5.00	3.00
35	John Kusko	15.00	5.00	3.00
36	Jim Leonard	15.00	5.00	3.00
37	Jim MacMurdo	15.00	5.00	3.00
38	Ed Manske	15.00	5.00	3.00
39	George McPherson	15.00	5.00	3.00
40	George Mulligan	15.00	5.00	3.00
41	Joe Pilconis	15.00	5.00	3.00
42	Hank Reese	15.00	5.00	3.00
43	Jim Russell	15.00	5.00	3.00
44	Dave Smukler	15.00	5.00	3.00
45	Pete Stevens	15.00	5.00	3.00
46	John Thomason	15.00	5.00	3.00
47	Vince Zizak	15.00	5.00	3.00

1937 Diamond Matchbooks

This time only Chicago Bears players were featured. Measuring 1-1/2" x 4-1/2" when folded out, the matchbooks resemble the 1936 set, however, this 1937 set has a smaller type size. With text printed in gray or black, the 24-matchbook set showcases three different colored borders - red, green and tan. The cover fronts feature a player photo, with his name and team printed above the photo. The backs of the matchbooks have the player's name and highlights inside a box. Matchbooks with the matches intact are valued at 1-1/2 times the prices listed here.

		NM	E	VG
Complete Set (24):		450.00	167.50	90.00
Common Player:		12.00	5.25	2.75
1	Frank Bausch	12.00	5.25	2.75
2	Delbert Bjork	12.00	5.25	2.75
3	William Conkright	12.00	5.25	2.75
4	George Corbett (last line - ion.)	12.00	5.25	2.75
5	John Doehring (last line - baseball.)	12.00	5.25	2.75
6	Beattie Feathers (first line - ...turned 29 years)	25.00	12.50	7.50
7	Dan Fortmann (first line - April 11, 1916, in)	30.00	15.00	9.00
8	Harrison Francis	12.00	5.25	2.75
9	Henry Hammond	12.00	5.25	2.75
10	William Karr (first line - in Ripley, W.)	12.00	5.25	2.75
11	Jack Manders (last line - height 6 ft. 1 in.)	12.00	6.00	3.50
12	Ed Manske	12.00	5.25	2.75
13	Bernie Masterson (last line - single.)	25.00	12.50	7.50
14	Keith Molesworth (last line - 9 1/2 in. Weight 168.)	25.00	12.50	7.50
15	George Musso (last line - married.)	40.00	20.00	12.00
16	Ray Nolting (first line - ... three years for)	12.00	5.25	2.75
17	Richard Plasman	12.00	5.25	2.75
18	Gene Ronzani (last line - married.)	20.00	10.00	6.00
19	Joe Stydahar (last line - ing. Is single.)	35.00	17.50	10.50
20	Frank Sullivan (first line - Loyola U. New)	12.00	5.25	2.75
21	Russell Thompson (last line - year.)	12.00	5.25	2.75
22	Milt Trost (last line - pounds. Is single.)	12.00	5.25	2.75
23	George Wilson	12.00	6.00	3.50
24	Joe Zeller (last line - Nu.)	12.00	5.25	2.75

1938 Diamond Matchbooks

Showcasing players from the Chicago Bears and Detroit Lions, the 24-matchbook set measures 1-1/2" x 4-1/2" when folded out. They are bordered in silver. The player's highlights feature different colored backgrounds for the two teams - Bears have red backgrounds, while the Lions have blue. No variations are known for this set. The unnumbered matchbooks are listed alphabetically. As always, matchbooks with the matches intact are valued at 1-1/2 times the values listed here.

		NM	E	VG
Complete Set (24):		450.00	112.50	67.50
Common Player:		15.00	5.25	2.75
1	Delbert Bjork	15.00	5.25	2.75
2	Raymond Buivid	15.00	5.25	2.75
3	Gary Famiglietti	15.00	2.50	5.25
4	Dan Fortmann	15.00	7.50	4.50
5	Bert Johnson	15.00	5.25	2.75
6	Jack Manders	20.00	10.00	6.00
7	Joe Maniaci	25.00	12.50	7.50
8	Lester McDonald	15.00	5.25	2.75
9	Frank Sullivan	15.00	5.25	2.75
10	Robert Swisher	15.00	5.25	2.75
11	Russell Thompson	15.00	5.25	2.75
12	Gus Zarnas	15.00	5.25	2.75
13	Ernie Caddel	25.00	12.50	7.50
14	Lloyd Cardwell	15.00	5.25	2.75
15	Earl "Dutch" Clark	50.00	25.00	15.00
16	Jack Johnson	15.00	5.25	2.75
17	Ed Klewicki	15.00	5.25	2.75
18	James McDonald	15.00	5.25	2.75
19	James (Monk) Moscrip	15.00	5.25	2.75
20	Maurice (Babe) Patt	15.00	5.25	2.75
21	Bob Reynolds	15.00	5.25	2.75
22	Kent Ryan	15.00	5.25	2.75
23	Fred Vanzo	15.00	5.25	2.75
24	Alex Wojciechowicz	50.00	25.00	15.00

1967 Dolphins Royal Castle

Measuring 3" x 4-3/8", the 27-card set was released by Royal Castle restaurants in South Florida. The fronts showcase a large black-and-white photo, with his facsimile signature under the photo in a white area. The card fronts are bordered in orange. Each card back includes the player's name, position and bio, along with the Royal Castle and Miami Dolphins' logos. A 28th card in the set, featuring George Wilson Jr., may have also been produced.

		NM	E	VG
Complete Set (27):		2,700	2,000	1,050
Common Player:		25.00	12.50	7.50
Common Player (SP):		100.00	50.00	30.00
1	Joe Auer (SP)	100.00	50.00	30.00
2	Tom Beier	25.00	12.50	7.50
3	Mel Branch	25.00	12.50	7.50
4	Jon Brittenum	35.00	17.50	10.50
5	George Chesser	25.00	12.50	7.50
6	Edward Cooke	25.00	12.50	7.50
7	Frank Emanuel (SP)	125.00	62.00	37.00
8	Tom Erlandson (SP)	100.00	50.00	30.00
9	Norm Evans (SP)	150.00	75.00	45.00
10	Bob Griese (SP)	800.00	400.00	240.00
11	Abner Haynes (SP)	175.00	87.00	52.00
12	Jerry Hopkins (SP)	100.00	50.00	30.00
13	Frank Jackson	25.00	12.50	7.50
14	Billy Joe	25.00	12.50	7.50
15	Wahoo McDaniel	150.00	75.00	45.00
16	Robert Neff	25.00	12.50	7.50
17	Billy Neighbors	25.00	12.50	7.50
18	Rick Norton	25.00	12.50	7.50
19	Bob Petrich	25.00	12.50	7.50
20	Jim Riley	25.00	12.50	7.50
21	John Stofa (SP)	150.00	75.00	45.00
22	Lavern Torczon	25.00	12.50	7.50
23	Howard Twilley	80.00	40.00	24.00
24	Jimmy Warren (SP)	100.00	50.00	30.00
25	Richard Westmoreland	25.00	12.50	7.50
26	Maxie Williams (SP)	150.00	75.00	45.00
27	George Wilson, Sr. (SP) (Head Coach)	150.00	75.00	45.00

1974 Dolphins All-Pro Graphics

Measuring 8-1/4" x 10-3/4", the 10-photo set showcases color action shots on the front, surrounded by a white border. The player's name, position and team are printed in the top left corner. The unnumbered photos have blank backs.

		NM	E	VG
Complete Set (10):		100.00	75.00	40.00
Common Player:		5.00	2.50	1.50
1	Dick Anderson	8.00	4.00	2.50
2	Nick Buoniconti	14.00	7.00	4.25
3	Larry Csonka	18.00	9.00	5.50
4	Manny Fernandez	6.00	3.00	1.75
5	Bob Griese	25.00	12.50	7.50
6	Jim Kiick	8.00	4.00	2.50
7	Earl Morrall	12.00	6.00	3.50
8	Mercury Morris	8.00	4.00	2.50
9	Jake Scott	6.00	3.00	1.75
10	Garo Yepremian	5.00	2.50	1.50

1980 Dolphins Police

Measuring 2-5/8" x 4-1/8", the 16-card set features a photo on the front, with the player's name and position under the photo. The Kiwanis logo appears in the lower right. The unnumbered card backs feature Miami Dolphins Tips inside a box, which has the Dolphins' logo at the top. Sponsors are listed at the bottom of the card backs.

		NM	E	VG
Complete Set (16):		75.00	56.00	30.00
Common Player:		2.50	2.00	1.00
5	Uwe Von Schamann	2.50	2.00	1.00
10	Don Strock	5.00	2.50	1.50
12	Bob Griese	12.00	6.00	3.50
22	Tony Nathan	5.00	2.50	1.50
24	Delvin Williams	5.00	2.50	1.50
25	Tim Foley	4.00	2.00	1.25
50	Larry Gordon	2.50	2.00	1.00
58	Kim Bokamper	2.50	2.00	1.00
64	Ed Newman	2.50	2.00	1.00
66	Larry Little (SP)	20.00	10.00	6.00
67	Bob Kuechenberg	5.00	2.50	1.50
73	Bob Baumhower	4.00	2.00	1.25
77	A.J. Duhe	5.00	2.50	1.50
82	Duriel Harris	4.00	2.00	1.25
89	Nat Moore	5.00	2.50	1.50
NNO	Don Shula (CO)	15.00	7.50	4.50

1981 Dolphins Police

Measuring 2-5/8" x 4-1/8", the 16-card set features a photo, with the player's name, number, position and bio under the photo. The Dolphins and Kiwanis logos appear on the lower left and right, respectively. The card backs, numbered in the upper left corner, have Dolphins Tips in a box, with the Dolphins logo at the top. The sponsors are listed at the bottom of the card backs.

		NM/M	NM	E
Complete Set (16):		25.00	18.50	10.00
Common Player:		1.00	.70	.40
1	Duriel Harris	1.00	.70	.40
2	Bob Kuechenberg	1.00	.70	.40
3	Don Bessillieu	1.00	.70	.40
4	Gerald Small	1.00	.70	.40
5	David Woodley	1.50	1.25	.60
6	Don McNeal	1.00	.70	.40
7	Nat Moore	2.00	1.50	.80
8	A.J. Duhe	1.75	1.25	.70
9	Glenn Blackwood	1.00	.70	.40
10	Don Strock	2.00	1.50	.80
11	Doug Betters	1.00	.70	.40
12	George Roberts	1.00	.70	.40
13	Bob Baumhower	1.75	1.25	.70
14	Kim Bokamper	1.00	.70	.40
15	Tony Nathan	2.00	1.50	.80
16	Don Shula (CO)	6.00	4.50	2.50

1982 Dolphins Police

Measuring 2-5/8" x 4-1/8", the 16-card set is anchored by a color photo on the front, with the player's name and number in the upper left corner. His position and college are located in a stripe above the photo. The Kiwanis logo is in the lower right. The card fronts are bordered in orange and aqua. The card backs, numbered in the lower right, showcase Dolphins Tips inside a box, with the Dolphins logo in the upper right. The sponsors names are listed in the lower left.

		NM/M	NM	E
Complete Set (16):		25.00	18.50	10.00
Common Player:		1.00	.70	.40
1	Don Shula (CO) (SP)	10.00	7.50	4.00
2	Uwe Von Schamann (SP)	5.00	3.75	2.00
3	Jimmy Cefalo	1.50	1.25	.60
4	Andra Franklin	1.50	1.25	.60
5	Larry Gordon	1.00	.70	.40
6	Nat Moore	1.75	1.25	.70

		NM/M	NM	E
7	Bob Baumhower	1.25	.90	.50
8	A.J. Duhe	1.25	.90	.50
9	Tony Nathan	1.75	1.25	.70
10	Glenn Blackwood	1.00	.70	.40
11	Don Strock	2.00	1.50	.80
12	David Woodley	1.25	.90	.50
13	Kim Bokamper	1.00	.70	.40
14	Bob Kuechenberg	1.25	.90	.50
15	Duriel Harris	1.25	.90	.50
16	Ed Newman	1.00	.70	.40

1983 Dolphins Police

Measuring 2-5/8" x 4-1/8", the 16-card set is anchored by a photo on the front, with the player's name in the upper left and his position near the bottom of the photo. The cards are bordered in aqua and orange. The card backs, numbered in the lower right, feature Dolphins Tips, with the Dolphins logo in the upper right. The sponsors are listed at the bottom of the card back. The Kiwanis and Burger King logos both are printed inside the photo on the front of the cards.

		NM/M	NM	E
Complete Set (16):		15.00	11.00	6.00
Common Player:		.50	.40	.20
1	Earnie Rhone	.50	.40	.20
2	Andra Franklin	.75	.60	.30
3	Eric Laakso	.50	.40	.20
4	Joe Rose	.50	.40	.20
5	David Woodley	1.00	.70	.40
6	Uwe Von Schamann	.50	.40	.20
7	Eddie Hill	.50	.40	.20
8	Bruce Hardy	.50	.40	.20
9	Woody Bennett	.50	.40	.20
10	Fulton Walker	.50	.40	.20
11	Lyle Blackwood	.50	.40	.20
12	A.J. Duhe	.75	.60	.30
13	Bob Baumhower	.75	.60	.30
14	Duriel Harris	.50	.40	.20
15	Bob Brudzinski	.50	.40	.20
16	Don Shula (CO)	3.00	2.25	1.25

1984 Dolphins Police

Measuring 2-5/8" x 4-1/8", the 17-card set is anchored by a photo on the front, with the player's number and name in the upper left and his position at the bottom center. Sponsor logos are printed in the two lower corners. The card backs, which are unnumbered, have a "Dolphins Say" safety tip, with the Dolphins logo in the upper right. The sponsors are listed at the bottom of the card backs. The Mark Clayton card was added to the set after it was released.

		NM/M	NM	E
Complete Set (17):		30.00	22.00	12.00
Common Player:		.50	.40	.20
1	Bob Baumhower	.75	.60	.30
2	Doug Betters	.50	.40	.20
3	Glenn Blackwood	.50	.40	.20
4	Kim Bokamper	.50	.40	.20
5	**Dolfan Denny** (Mascot)	.50	.40	.20
7	A.J. Duhe	.75	.60	.30
7	Mark Duper	1.75	1.25	.70
8	Jim Jensen	.50	.40	.20
9	Dan Marino	5.00	2.50	1.50
10	Don McNeal	.50	.40	.20
11	Nat Moore	1.00	.70	.40
12	Tony Nathan	1.00	.70	.40
13	Ed Newman	.50	.40	.20
14	Don Shula (CO)	2.00	1.50	.80
15	Dwight Stephenson	.75	.60	.30
16	Fulton Walker	.50	.40	.20
17	Mark Clayton (SP)	.50	.25	.15

1985 Dolphins Police

Measuring 2-5/8" x 4-1/8", the 16-card set is anchored by a large photo on the front, with the player's name, number and position listed at the bottom center. The Dolphins and Kiwanis logos are in the lower left and right, respectively. The card backs, which are numbered in the lower right, have a "Dolphins Say" safety tip, with the Dolphins logo in the upper right. The sponsors are printed at the bottom of the card backs.

		NM/M	NM	E
Complete Set (16):		20.00	15.00	8.00
Common Player:		.50	.40	.20
1	William Judson	.50	.40	.20
2	Fulton Walker	.50	.40	.20
3	Mark Clayton	1.25	.90	.50
4	Lyle & Glenn Blackwood, Glenn Blackwood (Bruise Brothers)	.50	.40	.20
5	Dan Marino	2.00	1.00	.60
6	Reggie Roby	.75	.60	.30
7	Doug Betters	.50	.40	.20
8	Jay Brophy	.50	.40	.20
9	**Dolfan Denny** (Mascot)	.50	.40	.20

		NM/M	NM	E
10	Kim Bokamper	.50	.40	.20
11	Mark Duper	1.00	.70	.40
12	Nat Moore	.75	.60	.30
13	Mike Kozlowski	.50	.40	.20
14	Don Shula (CO)	1.50	1.25	.60
15	Don McNeal	.50	.40	.20
16	Tony Nathan	.75	.60	.30

1986 Dolphins Police

Measuring 2-5/8" x 4-1/8", the 16-card set is anchored by a large photo on the front, with the player's name printed inside a stripe on the right, his number printed inside a helmet in the lower left and his position located inside a stripe in the lower right. Anon Anew and the Kiwanis logos are printed in the lower right, too. The card backs, which are numbered in the lower right, have a "Dolphins Say" safety tip, along with the sponsors names.

		NM/M	NM	E
Complete Set (16):		15.00	11.00	6.00
Common Player:		.50	.40	.20
1	Dwight Stephenson	.75	.60	.30
2	Bob Baumhower	.50	.40	.20
3	**Dolfan Denny** (Mascot)	.50	.40	.20
4	Don Shula (CO)	1.50	1.25	.60
5	Dan Marino	8.00	6.00	3.25
6	Tony Nathan	.75	.60	.30
7	Mark Duper	1.00	.70	.40
8	John Offerdahl	1.00	.70	.40
9	Fuad Reveiz	.50	.40	.20
10	Hugh Green	.50	.40	.20
11	Lorenzo Hampton	.50	.40	.20
12	Mark Clayton	1.50	1.25	.60
13	Nat Moore	.75	.60	.30
14	Bob Brudzinski	.50	.40	.20
15	Reggie Roby	.50	.40	.20
16	T.J. Turner	.50	.40	.20

1987 Dolphins Holsum

The cards in this Miami Dolphins' set were available in Holsum Bread packages. The fronts have a color photo inside a green border and the backs feature basic player information.

		NM/M	NM	E
Complete Set (22):		60.00	45.00	24.00
Common Player:		2.00	1.50	.80
1	Bob Baumhower	3.00	2.25	1.25
2	Mark Brown	2.00	1.50	.80
3	Mark Clayton	6.00	4.50	2.50
4	Mark Duper	4.00	3.00	1.50
5	Roy Foster	2.00	1.50	.80
6	Hugh Green	3.00	2.25	1.25
7	Lorenzo Hampton	2.00	1.50	.80
8	William Judson	2.00	1.50	.80
9	George Little	2.00	1.50	.80
10	Dan Marino	40.00	30.00	16.00
11	Nat Moore	3.00	2.25	1.25
12	Tony Nathan	3.00	2.25	1.25
13	John Offerdahl	4.00	3.00	1.50
14	James Pruitt	2.00	1.50	.80
15	Fuad Reveiz	2.00	1.50	.80
16	Dwight Stephenson	3.00	2.25	1.25
17	Glenn Blackwood	2.00	1.50	.80
18	Bruce Hardy	2.00	1.50	.80
19	Reggie Roby	2.00	1.50	.80
20	Bob Brudzinski	2.00	1.50	.80
21	Ron Jaworski	3.00	2.25	1.25
22	T.J. Turner	2.00	1.50	.80

1987 Dolphins Police

Measuring 2-5/8" x 4-1/8", the 16-card set resembles the 1986 set in design. This time, however, the player's name is printed in a stripe on the left, with his position printed inside a stripe under the photo. The player's number is located inside a helmet on the lower right. The Kiwanis and Fair Oaks Hospital logos appear in the lower left. The card backs, which are numbered in the lower right, have a "Dolphins Say" safety message and the sponsors listed.

		NM/M	NM	E
Complete Set (16):		20.00	15.00	8.00
Common Player:		.50	.40	.20
1	Joe Robbie (OWN)	.50	.40	.20
2	Glenn Blackwood	.50	.40	.20
3	Mark Duper	1.00	.70	.40
4	Fuad Reveiz	.50	.40	.20
5	**Dolfan Denny** (Mascot)	.50	.40	.20
6	Dwight Stephenson (SP)	5.00	3.75	2.00
7	Hugh Green	.50	.40	.20
8	Larry Csonka (All-Time Great)	3.00	2.25	1.25
9	Bud Brown	.50	.40	.20
10	Don Shula (CO)	1.50	1.25	.60
11	T.J. Turner	.50	.40	.20
12	Reggie Roby	.50	.40	.20

		NM/M	NM	E
13	Dan Marino	10.00	7.50	4.00
14	John Offerdahl	.75	.60	.30
15	Bruce Hardy	.50	.40	.20
16	Lorenzo Hampton	.50	.40	.20

1988 Dolphins Holsum

The standard sized cards in this 12-card set showcase the Holsum logo in the upper left corner, with "1988 Annual Collectors' Edition" printed in the upper right. The player's name and team are printed inside a rectangle at the bottom of the card, beneath the player's photo. The card backs, numbered "of 12," have the player's facsimile autograph at the top and his number, bio and stats printed underneath inside a box. Cards were available in specially marked packages of Holsum Bread.

		NM/M	NM	E
Complete Set (12):		30.00	22.00	12.00
Common Player:		1.50	1.25	.60
1	Mark Clayton	3.00	2.25	1.25
2	Dwight Stephenson	2.00	1.50	.80
3	Mark Duper	2.00	1.50	.80
4	John Offerdahl	2.00	1.50	.80
5	Dan Marino	20.00	15.00	8.00
6	T.J. Turner	1.50	1.25	.60
7	Lorenzo Hampton	1.50	1.25	.60
8	Bruce Hardy	1.50	1.25	.60
9	Fuad Reveiz	1.50	1.25	.60
10	Reggie Roby	1.50	1.25	.60
11	William Judson	1.50	1.25	.60
12	Bob Brudzinski	1.50	1.25	.60

1991 Domino's Quarterbacks

Upper Deck produced 50-card sets of NFL Quarterback cards in conjunction with a national promotion kicked off during the Aug. 3 NBC telecast of "NFL Quarterback Challenge". The set was sponsored by Dominos, sold in foil packs and feature 32 active quarterbacks, 14 retired quarterbacks and three multi-player cards. Cards were produced especially for this promotion and were distributed through the 5,000 Domino's stores across the country. Each franchise initially received 2,500 packs or two cases of 1,250. Stores could order additional packs in cases of 1,250 or 500. Stores could also order sets.

		NM/M	NM	E
Complete Set (50):		6.00	4.50	2.50
Common Player:		.05	.04	.02
1	Chris Miller	.05	.04	.02
2	Jim Kelly	.20	.15	.08
3	Jim Harbaugh	.10	.08	.04
4	Boomer Esiason	.10	.08	.04
5	Bernie Kosar	.10	.08	.04
6	Troy Aikman	1.00	.70	.40
7	John Elway	.50	.40	.20
8	Rodney Peete	.05	.04	.02
9	Andre Ware	.05	.04	.02
10	Anthony Dilweg	.05	.04	.02
11	Warren Moon	.10	.08	.04
12	Jeff George	.10	.08	.04
13	Jim Everett	.05	.04	.02
14	Jay Schroeder	.05	.04	.02
15	Wade Wilson	.05	.04	.02
16	Dan Marino	1.50	1.25	.60
17	Phil Simms	.05	.04	.02
18	Jeff Hostetler	.05	.04	.02
19	Ken O'Brien	.05	.04	.02
20	Timm Rosenbach	.05	.04	.02
21	Bubby Brister	.05	.04	.02
22	Steve DeBerg	.05	.04	.02
23	Randall Cunningham	.10	.08	.04
24	Steve Walsh	.10	.08	.04
25	Billy Joe Tolliver	.05	.04	.02
26	Steve Young	.50	.40	.20
27	Dave Krieg	.05	.04	.02
28	Dan McGwire	.05	.04	.02
29	Vinny Testaverde	.10	.08	.04
30	Stan Humphries	.10	.08	.04
31	Mark Rypien	.05	.04	.02
32	Terry Bradshaw	.75	.60	.30

		NM/M	NM	E
33	John Brodie	.10	.08	.04
34	Len Dawson	.10	.08	.04
35	Dan Fouts	.25	.20	.10
36	Otto Graham	.50	.40	.20
37	Bob Griese	.25	.20	.10
38	Sonny Jurgensen	.20	.15	.08
39	Daryle Lamonica	.20	.15	.08
40	Archie Manning	.20	.15	.08
41	Jim Plunkett	.10	.08	.04
42	Bart Starr	.40	.30	.15
43	Roger Staubach	.75	.60	.30
44	Joe Theismann	.25	.20	.10
45	Y.A. Tittle	.20	.15	.08
46	Johnny Unitas	.50	.40	.20
47	Cowboy Gunslingers (Troy Aikman, Roger Staubach)	.75	.60	.30
48	Cajun Connection (Bubby Brister, Terry Bradshaw)	.30	.25	.12
49	Dolphin Duo (Dan Marino, Bob Griese)	.75	.60	.30
50	**Checklist Card**	.05	.04	.02

1987 Duke Police

		NM/M	NM	E
	Complete Set (16):	25.00	18.50	10.00
	Common Player:	1.50	1.25	.60
1	Andy Andreasik (60)	1.50	1.25	.60
2	Brian Bernard (93)	1.50	1.25	.60
3	Bob Calamari (31)	1.50	1.25	.60
4	Jason Cooper (22)	1.50	1.25	.60
5	Dave Demore (92)	1.50	1.25	.60
6	Mike Dimitrio (21)	1.50	1.25	.60
7	Jim Godfrey (56)	1.50	1.25	.60
8	Doug Green (5)	1.50	1.25	.60
9	Stanley Monk (24)	1.50	1.25	.60
10	Chris Port (73)	2.00	1.50	.80
11	Steve Ryan (63)	1.50	1.25	.60
12	Steve Slayden (7)	2.00	1.50	.80
13	Steve Spurrier (CO)	9.00	6.75	3.50
14	Dewayne Terry (27)	1.50	1.25	.60
15	Fonda Williams (19)	1.50	1.25	.60
16	**Blue Devil** (Mascot)	2.00	1.50	.80

E

1959 Eagles Jay Publishing

Measuring 5" x 7", the 12-card set is anchored by a black-and-white photo on the front, with the player's name and team printed in the white border underneath. The cards are blank-backed and unnumbered. The set was originally sold in 12-card packs for 25 cents.

		NM	E	VG
	Complete Set (12):	75.00	56.00	30.00
	Common Player:	5.00	2.50	1.50
1	Bill Barnes	5.00	2.50	1.50
2	Chuck Bednarik	10.00	5.00	3.00
3	Tom Brookshier	5.00	2.50	1.50
4	Marion Campbell	5.00	2.50	1.50
5	Ted Dean	5.00	2.50	1.50
6	Tommy McDonald	8.00	4.00	2.50
7	Clarence Peaks	5.00	2.50	1.50
8	Pete Retzlaff	5.00	2.50	1.50
9	Jesse Richardson	5.00	2.50	1.50
10	Norm Van Brocklin	15.00	7.50	4.50
11	Bobby Walston	5.00	2.50	1.50
12	Chuck Weber	5.00	2.50	1.50

1960 Eagles White Border

Measuring 5" x 7", the 11-card set is anchored by a black-and-white photo on the front, wth the player's name and team printed in the white border underneath. The cards are blank-backed and unnumbered.

		NM	E	VG
	Complete Set (11):	50.00	37.00	20.00
	Common Player:	5.00	2.50	1.50
1	Maxie Baughan	7.00	3.50	2.00
2	Chuck Bednarik	10.00	5.00	3.00
3	Don Burroughs	5.00	2.50	1.50
4	Jimmy Carr	5.00	2.50	1.50
5	Howard Keys	5.00	2.50	1.50
6	Ed Khayat	5.00	2.50	1.50
7	Jim McCusker	5.00	2.50	1.50
8	John Nocera	5.00	2.50	1.50

		NM	E	VG
9	Nick Skorich	5.00	2.50	1.50
10	J.D. Smith	5.00	2.50	1.50
11	John Wittenborn	5.00	2.50	1.50

1961 Eagles Jay Publishing

Measuring 5" x 7", the 12-card set is anchored by a black-and-white photo on the front, with his name and team printed underneath in a white border. The backs are blank and un-numbered. Originally, the set was sold in packs for 25 cents.

		NM	E	VG
	Complete Set (12):	50.00	25.00	15.00
	Common Player:	5.00	2.50	1.50
1	Maxie Baughan	7.00	3.50	2.00
2	Jim McCusker	5.00	2.50	1.50
3	Tommy McDonald	7.00	3.50	2.00
4	Bob Pellegrini	5.00	2.50	1.50
5	Pete Retzlaff	5.00	2.50	1.50
6	Jesse Richardson	5.00	2.50	1.50
7	Joe Robb	5.00	2.50	1.50
8	Theron Sapp	5.00	2.50	1.50
9	J.D. Smith	5.00	2.50	1.50
10	Bobby Walston	5.00	2.50	1.50
11	Jerry Williams (ACO)	5.00	2.50	1.50
12	John Wittenborn	5.00	2.50	1.50

1971 Eagles Team Issue

Measuring 4-1/4" x 5-1/2", the 16-card set showcases a posed black-and-white photo on the front, with the player's name and team printed inside the white border at the bottom of the card. The cards are unnumbered and the backs are blank.

		NM	E	VG
	Complete Set (16):	45.00	34.00	18.00
	Common Player:	3.00	2.25	1.25
1	Gary Ballman	3.00	1.50	.90
2	Lee Bouggess	3.00	2.25	1.25
3	Kent Kramer	3.00	1.50	.90
4	Tom McNeill	3.00	2.25	1.25
5	Mark Nordquist	3.00	2.25	1.25
6	Ron Porter	3.00	2.25	1.25
7	Steve Preece	3.00	2.25	1.25
8	Tim Rossovich (Facing right edge of card)	3.00	1.50	.90
9	Tim Rossovich (Facing left edge of card)	3.00	1.50	.90
10	Jim Skaggs	3.00	2.25	1.25
11	Norm Snead	5.00	2.50	1.50
12	Jim Thrower	3.00	2.25	1.25
13	Mel Tom	3.00	1.50	.90
14	Jim Ward	3.00	2.25	1.25
15	Adrian Young	3.00	2.25	1.25
16	Don Zimmerman	3.00	2.25	1.25

1983 Eagles Frito Lay

Measuring 4-1/4" x 5-1/2", the 37-card set is anchored by an action photo on the front, with the player's facsimile autograph on the photo. The player's name, position and Frito Lay logo are printed inside the white border under the photo. The top white margin features the "Philadelphia Eagles" and their logo on the card front. The set is unnumbered. The backs of Harold Carmichael, Max Runager and Jerry Sisemore's cards are done in a postcard format, while the others are blank.

		NM/M	NM	E
	Complete Set (37):	45.00	34.00	18.00
	Common Player:	1.00	.70	.40
1	Harvey Armstrong	1.00	.70	.40
2	Ron Baker	1.00	.70	.40
3	Greg Brown	1.00	.70	.40
4	Marion Campbell (CO)	1.00	.70	.40
5	Harold Carmichael	3.00	2.25	1.25
6	Ken Clarke	1.00	.70	.40
7	Dennis DeVaughn	1.00	.70	.40
8	Herman Edwards	1.00	.70	.40
9	Ray Ellis	1.00	.70	.40
10	Major Everett	1.50	1.25	.60
11	Anthony Griggs	1.00	.70	.40
12	Michael Haddix	1.50	1.25	.60
13	Perry Harrington	1.00	.70	.40
14	Dennis Harrison	1.00	.70	.40
15	Wes Hopkins	1.50	1.25	.60
16	Ron Jaworski	4.00	3.00	1.50
17	Ron Johnson	1.00	.70	.40
18	Vyto Kab	1.00	.70	.40
19	Steve Kenney	1.00	.70	.40
20	Dean Miraldi	1.00	.70	.40
21	Leonard Mitchell	1.00	.70	.40
22	Wilbert Montgomery	4.00	3.00	1.50
23	Hubie Oliver	1.00	.70	.40
24	Joe Pisarcik	1.50	1.25	.60
25	Mike Quick	2.00	1.50	.80
26	Jerry Robinson	1.50	1.25	.60
27	Max Runager	1.00	.70	.40
28	Buddy Ryan (CO)	4.00	3.00	1.50
29	Lawrence Sampleton	1.00	.70	.40
30	Jody Schulz	1.00	.70	.40
31	Jerry Sisemore	1.00	.70	.40
32	John Spagnola	1.50	1.25	.60
33	Reggie Wilkes	1.00	.70	.40
34	Mike Williams	1.00	.70	.40
35	Tony Woodruff	1.00	.70	.40
36	Glen Young	1.00	.70	.40
37	Roynell Young	1.00	.70	.40

1984 Eagles Police

Measuring 2-5/8" x 4-1/8", this eight-card set is anchored on the front with a photo, with the player's name, number, position, team and Eagles' logo inside a box at the bottom. The backs have the card number, player's name, number, position, bio, safety tip and sponsors.

		NM/M	NM	E
	Complete Set (8):	6.00	4.50	2.50
	Common Player:	.50	.40	.20
1	Mike Quick	1.00	.70	.40
2	Dennis Harrison	.50	.40	.20
3	Jerry Robinson	.75	.60	.30
4	Wilbert Montgomery	1.50	1.25	.60
5	Herman Edwards	.50	.40	.20
6	Kenny Jackson	1.00	.70	.40
7	Anthony Griggs	.50	.40	.20
8	Ron Jaworski	1.75	1.25	.70

1985 Eagles Police

Measuring 2-5/8" x 4-1/8", the 16-card set is identical on the front to the 1984 set, with the large photo and the player's name, number, position, team and Eagles' logo in a box at the bottom. The backs have the card number, player's name, number, bio, highlights and a safety tip. The sponsors are listed at the bottom of the card back.

		NM/M	NM	E
	Complete Set (16):	6.00	4.50	2.50
	Common Player:	.50	.40	.20
1	Ken Clarke	.50	.40	.20
2	Roynell Young	.50	.40	.20
3	Ray Ellis	.50	.40	.20
4	Ron Baker	.50	.40	.20
5	John Spagnola	.50	.40	.20
6	Reggie Wilkes	.50	.40	.20
7	Ron Jaworski	1.00	.70	.40
8	Steve Kenney	.50	.40	.20
9	Paul McFadden	.50	.40	.20
10	Mike Quick	1.00	.70	.40
11	Hubie Oliver	.50	.40	.20
12	Greg Brown	.50	.40	.20
13	Anthony Griggs	.50	.40	.20
14	Michael Haddix	.50	.40	.20
15	Kenny Jackson	.75	.60	.30
16	Vyto Kab	.50	.40	.20

1985 Eagles Team Issue

Measuring 2-15/16" x 3-7/8", the 53-card set is anchored by a glossy color photo on the front, with the player's name, position and number in the white margin under the photo. The backs have the player's name, position and number at the top, with his career highlights located inside a box. The cards are unnumbered.

		NM/M	NM	E
	Complete Set (53):	50.00	37.00	20.00
	Common Player:	1.00	.70	.40
1	Harvey Armstrong	1.00	.70	.40
2	Ron Baker	1.00	.70	.40
3	Norman Braman (PRES)	1.00	.70	.40
4	Greg Brown	1.00	.70	.40
5	Marion Campbell (CO)	1.00	.70	.40
6	Jeff Christensen	1.00	.70	.40
7	Ken Clarke	1.00	.70	.40
8	Evan Cooper	1.00	.70	.40
9	Byron Darby	1.00	.70	.40
10	Mark Dennard	1.00	.70	.40
11	Herman Edwards	1.00	.70	.40
12	Ray Ellis	1.00	.70	.40
13	Major Everett	1.00	.70	.40
14	Gerry Feehery	1.00	.70	.40
15	Elbert Foules	1.00	.70	.40
16	Gregg Garrity	1.00	.70	.40
17	Anthony Griggs	1.00	.70	.40
18	Michael Haddix	1.00	.70	.40
19	Andre Hardy	1.00	.70	.40
20	Dennis Harrison	1.00	.70	.40
21	Joe Hayes	1.00	.70	.40
22	Melvin Hoover	1.00	.70	.40
23	Wes Hopkins	1.50	1.25	.60
24	Mike Horan	1.00	.70	.40
25	Kenny Jackson	1.50	1.25	.60

26	Ron Jaworski	4.00	3.00	1.50
27	Vyto Kab	1.00	.70	.40
28	Steve Kenney	1.00	.70	.40
29	Rich Kraynak	1.00	.70	.40
30	Dean May	1.00	.70	.40
31	Paul McFadden	1.00	.70	.40
32	Dean Miraldi	1.00	.70	.40
33	Leonard Mitchell	1.00	.70	.40
34	Wilbert Montgomery	3.00	2.25	1.25
35	Hubie Oliver	1.00	.70	.40
36	Mike Quick	2.00	1.50	.80
37	Mike Reichenbach	1.00	.70	.40
38	Jerry Robinson	1.00	.70	.40
39	Rusty Russell	1.00	.70	.40
40	Lawrence Sampleton	1.00	.70	.40
41	Jody Schulz	1.00	.70	.40
42	John Spagnola	1.50	1.25	.60
43	Tom Strauthers	1.00	.70	.40
44	Andre Waters	2.00	1.50	.80
45	Reggie Wilkes	1.00	.70	.40
46	Joel Williams	1.00	.70	.40
47	Michael Williams	1.00	.70	.40
48	Brenard Wilson	1.00	.70	.40
49	Tony Woodruff	1.00	.70	.40
50	Roynell Young	1.00	.70	.40
51	Logo Card (Eagle holding football on both sides)	1.50	1.25	.60
52	1985 Schedule Card (Both sides)	1.50	1.25	.60
53	Title Card 1985-86 (Eagles' Helmet)	1.50	1.25	.60

1986 Eagles Frito Lay

The cards in this set are 4-1/4" x 5-1/2". They can be distinguished from other Eagles Frito Lay sets by the Frito Lay logo in the lower right and the 3/8" borders on the sides. The cards are blank-backed and unnumbered.

		NM/M	NM	E
Complete Set (7):		12.00	9.00	4.75
Common Player:		1.00	.70	.40
1	Wes Hopkins	1.50	1.25	.60
2	Ron Jaworski	4.00	3.00	1.50
3	Ron Johnson WR	1.00	.70	.40
4	Mike Quick	2.00	1.50	.80
5	Buddy Ryan CO	4.00	3.00	1.50
6	Tom Strauthers	1.00	.70	.40
7	Andre Waters	1.50	1.25	.60

1986 Eagles Police

#12 RANDALL CUNNINGHAM
Quarterback
PHILADELPHIA EAGLES

Measuring 2-5/8" x 4-1/8", the 16-card set is anchored by a large photo on the front, with the player's name, number, position, team and Eagles' logo in a box at the bottom. The backs have the card number, player's name, number, bio, position, highlights, safety tip and sponsors. The Eagles' and Frito Lay logos are also shown on the backs.

		NM/M	NM	E
Complete Set (16):		10.00	7.50	4.00
Common Player:		.50	.40	.20
1	Greg Brown	.50	.40	.20
2	Reggie White	3.50	2.75	1.50
3	John Spagnola	.50	.40	.20
4	Mike Quick	.75	.60	.30
5	Ken Clarke	.50	.40	.20
6	Ken Reeves	.50	.40	.20
7	Mike Reichenbach	.50	.40	.20
8	Wes Hopkins	.75	.60	.30
9	Roynell Young	.50	.40	.20
10	Randall Cunningham	3.00	2.25	1.25
11	Paul McFadden	.50	.40	.20
12	Matt Cavanaugh	.50	.40	.20
13	Ron Jaworski	1.00	.70	.40
14	Byron Darby	.50	.40	.20
15	Andre Waters	.75	.60	.30
16	Buddy Ryan (CO)	1.00	.70	.40

1987 Eagles Police

Measuring 2-3/4" x 4-1/8", the 12-card set includes a photo on the front, along with the player's name, bio and position. The Eagles' helmet is printed in the bottom center. The backs have "Tips from the Eagles" printed at the top, with the New Jersey police force logos printed directly underneath. A safety tip is also included on the unnumbered backs, which feature the sponsor names at the bottom. Overall, 10,000 sets were handed out by New Jersey police officers.

		NM/M	NM	E
Complete Set (12):		60.00	45.00	24.00
Common Player:		3.00	2.25	1.25
1	Ron Baker	3.00	2.25	1.25
2	Keith Byars	7.00	5.25	2.75
3	Ken Clarke	3.00	2.25	1.25
4	Randall Cunningham	12.00	9.00	4.75
5	Paul McFadden	3.00	2.25	1.25
6	Mike Quick	5.00	3.75	2.00
7	Mike Reichenbach	3.00	2.25	1.25
8	Buddy Ryan (CO)	7.00	5.25	2.75
9	John Spagnola	3.00	2.25	1.25
10	Anthony Toney	5.00	3.75	2.00
11	Andre Waters	5.00	3.75	2.00
12	Reggie White	16.00	12.00	6.50

1988 Eagles Police

Measuring 2-3/4" x 4-1/8", the 12-card set is anchored on the front by a large photo. "Philadelphia Eagles" and two Eagles' helmets printed in each corner are at the top of the card fronts. Under the photo are the player's name, number, height, position and weight. The unnumbered backs feature "Tips from the Eagles" at the top, with the New Jersey police logos located directly underneath. The McGruff the Crime Dog logo is printed at the bottom, along with the sponsors.

		NM/M	NM	E
Complete Set (12):		60.00	45.00	24.00
Common Player:		3.00	2.25	1.25
1	Jerome Brown	5.00	3.75	2.00
2	Keith Byars	5.00	3.75	2.00
3	Randall Cunningham	8.00	6.00	3.25
4	Matt Darwin	3.00	2.25	1.25
5	Keith Jackson	8.00	6.00	3.25
6	Seth Joyner	5.00	3.75	2.00
7	Mike Quick	4.00	3.00	1.50
8	Buddy Ryan (CO)	6.00	4.50	2.50
9	Clyde Simmons	5.00	3.75	2.00
10	John Teltschik	3.00	2.25	1.25
11	Anthony Toney	4.00	3.00	1.50
12	Reggie White	10.00	7.50	4.00

1989 Eagles Daily News

Measuring 5-9/16" x 4-1/4", the 24-card set features the Eagles logo in the upper left corner, with "Philadelphia Eagles" on the right side above the photo on the card front. Beneath the photo are the player's name and position, along with McDonald's, KYW radio and the Philadelphia News logos. The unnumbered cards have blank backs.

		NM/M	NM	E
Complete Set (24):		25.00	18.50	10.00
Common Player:		1.00	.70	.40
1	Eric Allen	2.00	1.50	.80
2	Jerome Brown	2.00	1.50	.80
3	Keith Byars	2.00	1.50	.80
4	Cris Carter (UER) (Name misspelled Chris on front)	5.00	3.75	2.00
5	Randall Cunningham	3.00	2.25	1.25
6	Matt Darwin	1.00	.70	.40
7	Gerry Feehery	1.00	.70	.40
8	Ron Heller	1.00	.70	.40
9A	Terry Hoage (Solid color jersey)	1.00	.70	.40
9B	Terry Hoage (With white collar or undershirt)	1.00	.70	.40
10	Wes Hopkins	1.50	1.25	.60
11	Keith Jackson	3.00	2.25	1.25
12	Seth Joyner	2.00	1.50	.80
13	Mike Pitts	1.00	.70	.40
14	Mike Quick	1.50	1.25	.60
15	Mike Reichenbach	1.00	.70	.40
16	Clyde Simmons	2.00	1.50	.80
17	John Spagnola	1.00	.70	.40
18	Junior Tautalatasi	1.00	.70	.40
19	John Teltschik	1.00	.70	.40
20	Anthony Toney	1.00	.70	.40
21	Andre Waters	1.50	1.25	.60
22	Reggie White	6.00	4.50	2.50
23	Luis Zendejas	1.00	.70	.40

1989 Eagles Police

Measuring 8-1/2" x 11", the nine-card set is anchored by a photo on the front, with the player's name and bio underneath the photo between the New Jersey State Police Crime Prevention Resource Center and Security Savings Bank logos. The unnumbered backs have "Alcohol and Other Drugs: Facts and Myths" and five questions and answers. The team logo and sponsors' logos are on the back. This set was released after the season.

		NM/M	NM	E
Complete Set (9):		50.00	37.00	20.00
Common Player:		3.00	2.25	1.25
1	Cris Carter	15.00	11.00	6.00
2	Gregg Garrity	3.00	2.25	1.25
3	Mike Golic	4.00	3.00	1.50
4	Keith Jackson	7.00	5.25	2.75
5	Clyde Simmons	6.00	4.50	2.50
6	John Teltschik	3.00	2.25	1.25
7	Anthony Toney	3.00	2.25	1.25
8	Andre Waters	4.00	3.00	1.50
9	Luis Zendejas	3.00	2.25	1.25

1989 Eagles Smokey

Measuring 3" x 5", the 49-card set features a full-bleed photo on the front, with the player's name, number and position in the lower right. The unnumbered card backs have the player's name, number, position and bio at the top, with a Smokey the Bear cartoon underneath. The Eagles' and sponsor logos appear at the bottom of the card backs. Some cards were produced with two versions, which can be differentiated by the home and away jerseys.

		NM/M	NM	E
Complete Set (49):		125.00	95.00	50.00
Common Player:		1.50	1.25	.60
6	Matt Cavanaugh	2.00	1.50	.80
8	Luis Zendejas	1.50	1.25	.60
9	Don McPherson	2.00	1.50	.80
10	John Teltschik	1.50	1.25	.60
12A	Randall Cunningham (White jersey)	8.00	6.00	3.25
12B	Randall Cunningham (Green jersey)	8.00	6.00	3.25
20	Andre Waters	3.00	2.25	1.25
21	Eric Allen	3.00	2.25	1.25
25	Anthony Toney	2.00	1.50	.80
33	William Frizzell	1.50	1.25	.60
34	Terry Hoage	1.50	1.25	.60
35	Mark Konecny	1.50	1.25	.60
41	Keith Byars	3.00	2.25	1.25
42	Eric Everett	1.50	1.25	.60
43	Roynell Young	1.50	1.25	.60
46	Izel Jenkins	1.50	1.25	.60
48	Wes Hopkins	2.00	1.50	.80
50	Dave Rimington	1.50	1.25	.60
52	Todd Bell	1.50	1.25	.60
53	Dwayne Jiles	1.50	1.25	.60
55	Mike Reichenbach	1.50	1.25	.60
56	Byron Evans	1.50	1.25	.60
58	Ty Allert	1.50	1.25	.60
59	Seth Joyner	3.00	2.25	1.25
61	Ben Tamburello	1.50	1.25	.60
63	Ron Baker	1.50	1.25	.60
66	Ken Reeves	1.50	1.25	.60
68	Reggie Singletary	1.50	1.25	.60
72	David Alexander	1.50	1.25	.60
73	Ron Heller	1.50	1.25	.60
74	Mike Pitts	1.50	1.25	.60
78	Matt Darwin	1.50	1.25	.60
80	Cris Carter	8.00	6.00	3.25
81	Kenny Jackson	2.00	1.50	.80
82A	Mike Quick (White jersey)	2.50	2.00	1.00
82B	Mike Quick (Green jersey)	2.50	2.00	1.00
83	Jimmie Giles	1.50	1.25	.60
85	Ron Johnson	1.50	1.25	.60
86	Gregg Garrity	1.50	1.25	.60
88	Keith Jackson	5.00	3.75	2.00
89	David Little	2.00	1.50	.80
90	Mike Golic	2.00	1.50	.80
91	Scott Curtis	1.50	1.25	.60
92	Reggie White	14.00	10.50	5.50
96	Clyde Simmons	3.00	2.25	1.25
97	John Klingel	1.50	1.25	.60
99	Jerome Brown	4.00	3.00	1.50
NNO	Buddy Ryan (CO) (Wearing white cap)	7.00	5.25	2.75
NNO	Buddy Ryan (CO) (Wearing green cap)	7.00	5.25	2.75

1990 Eagles Police

Measuring 2-5/8" x 4-1/8", the 12-card set has "Philadelphia Eagles" and two Eagles' helmets at the top of the card fronts above the photo. Beneath the photo are the player's name, position and bio. The unnumbered card backs have "Tips from the Eagles" and sponsor logos at the top, with a tip and McGruff the Crime Dog logo at the bottom.

		NM/M	NM	E
	Complete Set (12):	30.00	22.00	12.00
	Common Player:	2.00	1.50	.80
1	David Alexander	2.00	1.50	.80
2	Eric Allen	3.00	2.25	1.25
3	Randall Cunningham	5.00	3.75	2.00
4	Keith Byars	3.00	2.25	1.25
5	James Feagles	2.00	1.50	.80
6	Mike Golic	3.00	2.25	1.25
7	Keith Jackson	4.00	3.00	1.50
8	Rich Kotite (CO)	3.00	2.25	1.25
9	Roger Ruzek	2.00	1.50	.80
10	Mickey Shuler	3.00	2.25	1.25
11	Clyde Simmons	4.00	3.00	1.50
12	Reggie White	8.00	6.00	3.25

1990 Eagles Sealtest

Measuring 2" x 8", the set of six bookmarks showcases the Sealtest logo at the top, with "The Reading Team" inside a scoreboard above the player photo. The Eagles' logo, player name, number, bio and highlights are printed inside a box at the bottom of the card. The backs are unnumbered and contain the sponsor logos and give information on two books that are available at the public library. This set is identical to the the 1990 Knudsen 49ers and Chargers sets.

		NM/M	NM	E
	Complete Set (6):	15.00	11.00	6.00
	Common Player:	2.50	2.00	1.00
1	David Alexander	2.50	2.00	1.00
2	Eric Allen	3.50	2.75	1.50
3	Keith Byars	3.50	2.75	1.50
4	Randall Cunningham	4.00	3.00	1.50
5	Mike Pitts	2.50	2.00	1.00
6	Mike Quick	3.50	2.75	1.50

1981 Edmonton Journal Eskimos

		NM/M	NM	E
	Complete Set (16):	175.00	131.00	70.00
	Common Player:	5.00	3.75	2.00
1	Dave Fennell	7.50	5.75	3.00
2	Brian Fryer	5.00	3.75	2.00
3	Jim Germany	6.00	4.50	2.50
4	Gary Hayes	5.00	3.75	2.00
5	Larry Highbaugh	10.00	7.50	4.00
6	Joe Hollimon	5.00	3.75	2.00
7	Ed Jones	5.00	3.75	2.00
8	Dan Kearns	5.00	3.75	2.00
9	Brian Kelly	15.00	11.00	6.00
10	Dan Kepley	10.00	7.50	4.00
11	Neil Lumsden	6.00	4.50	2.50
12	Warren Moon	75.00	56.00	30.00
13	James Parker	15.00	11.00	6.00
14	Tom Scott	10.00	7.50	4.00
15	Waddell Smith	5.00	3.75	2.00
16	Bill Stevenson	6.00	4.50	2.50

1984 Edmonton Journal Eskimos

		NM/M	NM	E
	Complete Set (13):	40.00	30.00	16.00
	Common Player:	3.50	2.75	1.50
1	Leo Blanchard	3.50	2.75	1.50
2	Marco Cyncar	5.00	3.75	2.00
3	Blake Dermott	3.50	2.75	1.50
4	Brian Fryer	3.50	2.75	1.50
5	Joe Hollimon	3.50	2.75	1.50
6	James Hunter	3.50	2.75	1.50
7	Greg Marshall	5.00	3.75	2.00
8	Mike Nelson (CO)	3.50	2.75	1.50
9	Hector Pothier	3.50	2.75	1.50
10	Paul Rudzinski (ACO)	3.50	2.75	1.50
11	Bill Stevenson	5.00	3.75	2.00
12	Tom Towns	3.50	2.75	1.50
13	Eric Upton	3.50	2.75	1.50

1991 Enor Pro Football Hall of Fame

Photos from the NFL's files were used for the card fronts for this 160-card set, which features a blend of color and black-and-white photos bordered by black and gold frames. The Pro Football Hall of Fame logo also appears on the card front, in a purple square. The player's name and position are in the lower left corner in a black panel. The card back has a photo of the Hall of Fame on the bottom half, along with a card number. Biographical information, a career summary and the year of induction comprise the rest of the back. Special cards randomly inserted in packs allowed the holder to redeem them for a special Hall of Fame card album and free admission to the museum. Six different promo cards were also produced for the set. The cards, which are numbered on the back, do not match the numbers assigned to their counterparts in the regular set. Also, the cards have a different shade of color and the NFL logo on the back is black-and-white, not in color like those on the regular cards.

		NM/M	NM	E
	Complete Set (160):	12.00	9.00	4.75
	Common Player:	.10	.08	.04
1	**Pro Football Hall of Fame**	.15	.11	.06
1A	**Pro Football Hall of Fame**			
	(Canton, OH)	.15	.11	.06
2	Herb Adderley	.15	.11	.06
3	Lance Alworth	.20	.15	.08
4	Doug Atkins	.15	.11	.06
5	Morris "Red" Badgro	.10	.08	.04
6	Cliff Battles	.15	.11	.06
7	Sammy Baugh	.60	.45	.25
8	Chuck Bednarik	.25	.20	.10
9A	Bert Bell (FOUND/OWN)			
	(Factory set version in			
	coat and tie)	.20	.15	.08
9B	Bert Bell (FOUND/OWN)			
	(Wax pack version in			
	Steelers tee shirt)	.20	.15	.08
10	Bobby Bell	.10	.08	.04
11	Raymond Berry	.30	.25	.12
12	Charles W. Bidwill (OWN)	.10	.08	.04
13	Fred Biletnikoff	.25	.20	.10
14	George Blanda	.30	.25	.12
15	Mel Blount	.20	.15	.08
16	Terry Bradshaw	.75	.60	.30
17	Jim Brown	.75	.60	.30
18	Paul Brown			
	(CO/OWN/FOUND)	.20	.15	.08
19	Roosevelt Brown	.10	.08	.04
20	Willie Brown	.15	.11	.06
21	Buck Buchanan	.15	.11	.06
22	Dick Butkus	.50	.40	.20
23	Earl Campbell	.75	.60	.30
24	Tony Canadeo	.10	.08	.04
25	Joe Carr (PRES)	.10	.08	.04
26	Guy Chamberlin	.10	.08	.04
27	Jack Christiansen	.10	.08	.04
28	Earl "Dutch" Clark	.15	.11	.06
29	George Connor	.15	.11	.06
30	Jimmy Conzelman	.10	.08	.04
31	Larry Csonka	.30	.25	.12
32	Willie Davis	.10	.08	.04
33	Len Dawson	.25	.20	.10
34	Mike Ditka	.50	.40	.20
35	Art Donovan	.25	.20	.10
36	John (Paddy) Driscoll	.10	.08	.04
37	Billy Dudley	.15	.11	.06
38	Turk Edwards	.10	.08	.04
39	Weeb Ewbank (CO)	.10	.08	.04
40	Tom Fears	.10	.08	.04
41	Ray Flaherty (CO)	.10	.08	.04
42	Len Ford	.10	.08	.04
43	Dan Fortmann	.10	.08	.04
44	Frank Gatski	.10	.08	.04
45	Bill George	.10	.08	.04
46	Frank Gifford	.50	.40	.20
47	Sid Gillman (CO)	.10	.08	.04
48	Otto Graham	.50	.40	.20
49	Harold "Red" Grange	.50	.40	.20
50	Joe Greene	.20	.15	.08
51	Forrest Gregg	.15	.11	.06
52	Bob Griese	.30	.25	.12
53	Lou Groza	.20	.15	.08
54	Joe Guyon	.10	.08	.04
55	George Halas			
	(CO/OWN/FOUND)	.30	.25	.12
56	Jack Ham	.25	.20	.10
57	John Hannah	.10	.08	.04
58	Franco Harris	.30	.25	.12
59	Ed Healey	.10	.08	.04
60	Mel Hein	.10	.08	.04
61	Ted Hendricks	.15	.11	.06
62	Pete (Fats) Henry	.10	.08	.04
63	Arnie Herber	.10	.08	.04
64	Bill Hewitt	.10	.08	.04
65	Clarke Hinkle	.10	.08	.04
66	Elroy Hirsch	.20	.15	.08
67	Ken Houston	.15	.11	.06
68	Cal Hubbard	.10	.08	.04
69	Sam Huff	.20	.15	.08
70	Lamar Hunt (OWN/FOUND)	.10	.08	.04
71	Don Hutson	.20	.15	.08
72	John Henry Johnson	.15	.11	.06
73	Deacon Jones	.25	.20	.10
74	Stan Jones	.15	.11	.06
75	Sonny Jurgensen	.25	.20	.10
76	Walt Kiesling	.10	.08	.04
77	Frank "Bruiser" Kinard	.10	.08	.04
78	Earl (Curly) Lambeau			
	(CO/FOUND/OWN)	.25	.20	.10
79	Jack Lambert	.30	.25	.12
80	Tom Landry (CO)	.30	.25	.12
81	Dick "Night Train" Lane	.15	.11	.06
82	Jim Langer	.10	.08	.04
83	Willie Lanier	.15	.11	.06
84	Yale Lary	.10	.08	.04
85	Dante Lavelli	.15	.11	.06
86	Bobby Layne	.50	.40	.20
87	Tuffy Leemans	.10	.08	.04
88	Bob Lilly	.25	.20	.10
89	Sid Luckman	.25	.20	.10
90	William Roy Lyman	.10	.08	.04
91	Tim Mara (FOUND/OWN)	.10	.08	.04
92	Gino Marchetti	.20	.15	.08
93	Geo. Preston Marshall			
	(FOUND/OWN)	.10	.08	.04
94	Don Maynard	.20	.15	.08
95	George McAfee	.10	.08	.04
96	Mike McCormack	.10	.08	.04
97	Johnny "Blood" McNally	.10	.08	.04
98	Mike Michalske	.10	.08	.04
99	Wayne Millner	.10	.08	.04
100	Bobby Mitchell	.20	.15	.08
101	Ron Mix	.15	.11	.06
102	Lenny Moore	.20	.15	.08
103	Marion Motley (See also 130)	.20	.15	.08
104	George Musso	.10	.08	.04
105	Bronko Nagurski	.30	.25	.12
106	Earle "Greasy" Neale (CO)	.10	.08	.04
107	Ernie Nevers	.10	.08	.04
108	Ray Nitschke	.25	.20	.10
109	Leo Nomellini	.15	.11	.06
110	Merlin Olsen	.25	.20	.10
111	Jim Otto	.20	.15	.08
112	Steve Owen (CO)	.10	.08	.04
113	Alan Page	.15	.11	.06
114	Clarence "Ace" Parker	.10	.08	.04
115	Jim Parker	.10	.08	.04
116	**1958 NFL Championship**	.10	.08	.04
117	Pete Pihos	.10	.08	.04
118	Hugh (Shorty) Ray (OFF)	.10	.08	.04
119	Dan Reeves (OWN)	.10	.08	.04
120	Jim Ringo	.10	.08	.04
121	Andy Robustelli	.15	.11	.06
122	Art Rooney (FOUND/ADM)	.15	.11	.06
123	Pete Rozelle (COMM)	.20	.15	.08
124	Bob St. Clair	.15	.11	.06
125	Gale Sayers	.50	.40	.20
126	Joe Schmidt	.15	.11	.06
127	Tex Schramm (ADM)	.15	.11	.06
128	Art Shell	.20	.15	.08
129	Roger Staubach	.75	.60	.30
130	Ernie Stautner (UER)			
	(Numbered as 103)	.20	.15	.08
131	Jan Stenerud	.15	.11	.06
132	Ken Strong	.15	.11	.06
133	Joe Stydahar	.10	.08	.04
134	Fran Tarkenton	.30	.25	.12
135	Charley Taylor	.15	.11	.06
136	Jim Taylor	.15	.11	.06
137	Jim Thorpe	.50	.40	.20
138	Y.A. Tittle	.40	.30	.15
139	George Trafton	.10	.08	.04
140	Charlie Trippi	.10	.08	.04
141	Emlen Tunnell	.10	.08	.04
142	Clyde "Bulldog" Turner	.20	.15	.08
143	Johnny Unitas	.50	.40	.20
144	Gene Upshaw	.15	.11	.06
145	Norm Van Brocklin	.20	.15	.08
146	Steve Van Buren	.20	.15	.08
147	Doak Walker	.20	.15	.08
148	Paul Warfield	.20	.15	.08
149	Bob Waterfield	.20	.15	.08
150	Arnie Weinmeister	.10	.08	.04
151	Bill Willis	.10	.08	.04
152	Larry Wilson	.10	.08	.04
153	Alex Wojciechowicz	.10	.08	.04
154	Willie Wood	.15	.11	.06
155	**Enshrinement Day HOF**			
	Induction Ceremony	.10	.08	.04
156	**Mementoes Exhibit**	.10	.08	.04
157	**Checklist 1 -**			
	The Beginning	.10	.08	.04
158	**Checklist 2 -**			
	The Early Years	.10	.08	.04
159	**Checklist 3 -**			
	The Modern Era	.10	.08	.04
160A	**Checklist 4 - Evolution of**			
	Uniform (includes #133-			
	160)	.10	.08	.04

1991 Enor Pro Football HOF Promos

The six standard-sized cards were produced to show what the 1991 Enor set would look like. The cards are identical to the regular cards, except for the differences in numbering and color tones. To tell these cards apart from the regular cards, look at the Team NFL logo on the back. If the NFL logo is black and white it is a promo card. If it is red, white and blue, it is a card from the regular series.

	NM/M	NM	E
Complete Set (6):	8.00	6.00	3.25
Common Player:	1.00	.70	.40

		NM/M	NM	E
1	Pro Football Hall of Fame (Building) (Regular issue card number is also 1)	1.00	.70	.40
2	Earl Campbell (Regular issue card number is 23)	3.50	2.75	1.50
3	John Hannah (Regular issue card number is 57)	1.00	.70	.40
4	Stan Jones (Regular issue card number is 74)	1.00	.70	.40
5	Jan Stenerud (Regular issue card number is 131)	1.00	.70	.40
6	Tex Schramm ADM (Regular issue card number is 127)	1.00	.70	.40

1969 Eskimo Pie

These 2-1/2" x 3" panels each feature two mug shot stickers of American Football League players. The panels are in color but are unnumbered. Card 14 (Len Dawson/Jim Otto) has the players' names reversed under their pictures. The bottom half of each panel explains that these cards were also on other Eskimo "take home cartons."

	NM	E	VG
Complete Set (15):	850.00	425.00	255.00
Common Player:	50.00	25.00	15.00

		NM	E	VG
(1)	Lance Alworth, John Charles	95.00	47.00	28.00
(2)	Al Atkinson, George Goeddeke	50.00	25.00	15.00
(3)	Marlin Briscoe, Billy Shaw	50.00	25.00	15.00
(4)	Gino Cappelletti, Dale Livingston	50.00	25.00	15.00
(5)	Eric Crabtree, Jim Dunaway	50.00	25.00	15.00
(6)	Ben Davidson, Bob Griese	130.00	65.00	39.00
(7)	Hewritt Dixon, Pete Beathard	60.00	30.00	18.00
(8)	Mike Garrett, Bob Hunt	50.00	25.00	15.00
(9)	Daryle Lamonica, Willie Frazier	60.00	30.00	18.00
(10)	Jim Lynch, John Hadl	60.00	30.00	18.00
(11)	Kent McCloughan, Tom Regner	50.00	25.00	15.00
(12)	Jim Nance, Billy Neighbors	50.00	25.00	15.00
(13)	Rick Norton, Paul Costa	50.00	25.00	15.00
(14)	Jim Otto, Len Dawson (Names reversed)	125.00	62.00	37.00
(15)	Matt Snell, Dick Post	50.00	25.00	15.00

1948-52 Exhibit W468 Football

The 59-card set, which measures 3-1/4" x 5-3/8", was released by the Exhibit Supply Co. of Chicago in 1948-52. The thick cards were sold in vending machines. The cards, which have blank backs, were originally in black-and-white. In the following years they were released in sepia, blue, yellow and red. The cards that are colored carry a 3-4 times higher value than the black-and-white and sepia cards. Released in three groups of 32 in 1948, 1950 and 1951, the 1951 set is the easiest to find of the three. The 1951 cards were also reissued in sepia tone in 1952 and possibly 1953. A checklist card was produced in 1950. It was printed in black-and-white and green. It resembles the Bednarik card, however, it lists the 32 players from the 1950 set on the front. In addition, nine-card ad displays were produced, and feature the Bednarik checklist. In 1948, the words "Made in USA" measure 5/8 inch on the card. Also, 11 of the 1948 cards were single prints (Comp,

Jacobs, Cifers, Horvath, Mastrangelo, LeForce, Johnson, Pritko, Wedemeyer, Coulter and Schlinkman). In 1950, the single-print cards were Bednarik, Hoerner, Davis, Perry, Ruby and Justice. When the 1950 cards went into a second printing, 11 new cards were issued to replace the original 11 single prints. On the new cards, "Made in USA" measures 7/16 of an inch. The 1951 printing featured only 16 cards, with the six single-print cards from 1950 and 10 cards from 1948 shelved. The 1951 cards feature "Made in USA" in 1/2-inch high letters.

	NM	E	VG
Complete Set (59):	4,500	3,000	1,600
Common Player DP:	10.00	7.50	4.00
Minor Stars DP:	15.00	30.00	16.00
Common Player SP48:	300.00	87.00	52.00
Common Player SP50:	100.00	37.00	20.00

		NM	E	VG
1	Frankie Albert (DP) (48/50/51/52)	10.00	5.00	3.00
2	Dick Barwegan (DP) (51/52)	10.00	5.00	3.00
3	Sammy Baugh (DP) (48/50/51/52)	25.00	12.50	7.50
4	Chuck Bednarik (SP50)	150.00	75.00	45.00
5	Tony Canadeo (DP) (51/52)	15.00	7.50	4.50
6	Paul Christman (48/50)	40.00	20.00	12.00
7	Bob Cifers (SP48)	300.00	150.00	90.00
8	Irv Comp (SP48)	300.00	150.00	90.00
9	Charley Conerly (DP) (48/50/51/52)	15.00	7.50	4.50
10	George Connor (DP) (51/52)	15.00	7.50	4.50
11	Dewitt Coulter (SP50)	100.00	50.00	30.00
12	Glenn Davis (SP50)	100.00	50.00	30.00
13	Glenn Dobbs (48/50)	40.00	20.00	12.00
14	John Dottley (DP) (51/52)	10.00	5.00	3.00
15	Bill Dudley (48/50)	60.00	30.00	18.00
16	Tom Fears (DP) (51/52)	15.00	7.50	4.50
17	Joe Geri (DP) (51/52)	10.00	5.00	3.00
18	Otto Graham (DP) (48/50/51/52)	30.00	15.00	9.00
19	Pat Harder (48/50)	40.00	20.00	12.00
20	Elroy Hirsch (DP) (51/52)	20.00	10.00	6.00
21	Dick Hoerner (SP50)	100.00	50.00	30.00
22	Bob Hoernschemeyer (DP) (51/52)	10.00	5.00	3.00
23	Les Horvath (SP48)	300.00	150.00	90.00
24	Jack Jacobs (SP48)	300.00	150.00	90.00
25	Nate Johnson (SP48)	300.00	150.00	90.00
26	Charlie Justice (SP50)	150.00	75.00	45.00
27	Bobby Layne (DP) (48/50/51/52)	25.00	12.50	7.50
28	Clyde LeForce (SP48)	300.00	150.00	90.00
29	Sid Luckman (48/50)	80.00	40.00	24.00
30	John Lujack (48/50)	60.00	30.00	18.00
31	Bill McColl (DP) (51/52)	10.00	5.00	3.00
32	Ollie Matson (DP) (51/52)	15.00	7.50	4.50
33	Bill McColl (DP) (51/52)	10.00	5.00	3.00
34	Fred Morrison (DP) (50/51/52)	10.00	5.00	3.00
35	Marion Motley (DP) (48/50/51/52)	20.00	10.00	6.00
36	Chuck Ortmann (DP) (51/52)	10.00	5.00	3.00
37	Joe Perry (SP50)	135.00	67.00	40.00
38	Pete Pihos (48/50)	50.00	25.00	15.00
39	Steve Pritko (SP48)	300.00	150.00	90.00
40	George Ratterman (DP) (48/50/51/52)	10.00	5.00	3.00
41	Jay Rhodemyre (DP) (51/52)	10.00	5.00	3.00
42	Martin Ruby (SP50)	125.00	62.00	37.00
43	Julie Rykovich (DP) (51/52)	10.00	5.00	3.00
44	Walt Schlinkman (SP48)	300.00	150.00	90.00
45	Emil (Red) Sitko (DP) (51/52)	10.00	5.00	3.00
46	Vitamin Smith (DP) (50/51/52)	10.00	5.00	3.00
47	Norm Standlee (48/50)	40.00	20.00	12.00
48	George Taliaferro (DP) (51/52)	10.00	5.00	3.00
49	Y.A. Tittle (HOR) (48/50)	100.00	50.00	30.00
50	Charley Trippi (DP) (48/50/51/52)	15.00	7.50	4.50
51	Frank Tripucka (DP) (48/50/51/52)	12.00	6.00	3.50
52	Emlen Tunnell (DP) (51/52)	15.00	7.50	4.50
53	Bulldog Turner (DP) (48/50/51/52)	15.00	7.50	4.50
54	Steve Van Buren (48/50)	60.00	30.00	18.00
55	Bob Waterfield (DP) (48/50/51/52)	20.00	10.00	6.00
56	Herm Wedemeyer (SP48)	800.00	400.00	240.00
57	Bob Williams (DP) (51/52)	10.00	5.00	3.00
58	Claude Buddy Young (DP) (passing) (48/50/51/52)	10.00	5.00	3.00
59	Tank Younger (DP) (50/51/52)	10.00	5.00	3.00
NNO	Checklist Card SP50 (Chuck Bednarik)	800.00	400.00	240.00

F

1990 FACT Pro Set Cincinnati

Produced for 29 schools in the Cincinnati school district, the set was used as an educational tool for grade school students. The promotion ran for 15 straight weeks, with 25-card cello packs handed out to the students. The card fronts are identical to 1990 Pro Set Series I cards, while the backs have math, grammar and science questions. The card backs carry the card numbers in the lower right. The missing numbers from the first series are 338, 376 and 377.

	NM/M	NM	E
Complete Set (375):	550.00	410.00	220.00
Common Player:	1.00	.70	.40

		NM/M	NM	E
1	Barry Sanders (W1)	25.00	18.50	10.00
2	Joe Montana (W1)	20.00	15.00	8.00
3	Coach of the Year (Lindy Infante) (W1) (UER) (missing Coach next to Packers)	1.00	.70	.40
4	Man of the Year (Warren Moon) (W1) (UER) (missing R symbol)	2.00	1.50	.80
5	Defensive Player of the Year (Keith Millard) (W1)	1.00	.70	.40
6	Defensive Rookie of the Year (Derrick Thomas) (W1) (UER) (no 1989 on front banner of card)	2.00	1.50	.80
7	Comeback Player of the Year (Ottis Anderson) (W1)	1.50	1.25	.60
8	Passing Leader (Joe Montana) (W2)	20.00	15.00	8.00
9	Rushing Leader (Christian Okoye) (W2)	1.00	.70	.40
10	Total Yardage Leader (Thurman Thomas) (W2)	3.00	2.25	1.25
11	Kick Scoring Leader (Mike Cofer) (W2)	1.00	.70	.40
12	TD Scoring Leader (Dalton Hilliard) (W2) (UER) (O.J. Simpson not listed in stats, but is mentioned in text)	1.00	.70	.40
13	Receiving Leader (Sterling Sharpe) (W2)	3.00	2.25	1.25
14	Punting Leader (Rich Camarillo) (W3)	1.00	.70	.40
15	Punt Return Leader (Walter Stanley) (W3)	1.00	.70	.40
16	Kickoff Return Leader (Rod Woodson) (W3)	2.00	1.50	.80
17	Interception Leader (Felix Wright) (W3)	1.00	.70	.40
18	Sack Leader (Chris Doleman) (W3)	1.00	.70	.40
19	Heisman Trophy (Andre Ware) (W3)	1.00	.70	.40
20	Outland Trophy (Mohammed Elewonibi) (W4)	1.00	.70	.40
21	Lombardi Award (Percy Snow) (W4)	1.00	.70	.40
22	Maxwell Award (Anthony Thompson) (W4)	1.00	.70	.40
23	1990 HOF Selection (Buck Buchanan) (W4) (Sacking Bart Starr)	1.00	.70	.40
24	1990 HOF Selection (Bob Griese) (W4)	1.50	1.25	.60
25	1990 HOF Selection (Franco Harris) (W5)	1.50	1.25	.60
26	1990 HOF Selection (Ted Hendricks) (W4)	1.00	.70	.40
27	1990 HOF Selection (Jack Lambert) (W5)	1.00	.70	.40

28	1990 HOF Selection(Tom Landry) (W5)	1.50	1.25	.60
29	1990 HOF Selection(Bob St. Clair) (W5)	1.00	.70	.40
30	Aundray Bruce (W5) (UER) (Stats say Falcons)	1.00	.70	.40
31	Tony Casillas (W5) (UER) (Stats say Falcons)	1.00	.70	.40
32	Shawn Collins (W5)	1.00	.70	.40
33	Marcus Cotton (W6)	1.00	.70	.40
34	Bill Fralic (W6)	1.00	.70	.40
35	Chris Miller (W6)	1.50	1.25	.60
36	Deion Sanders (W6) (UER) (Stats say Falcons)	14.00	10.50	5.50
37	John Settle (W6)	1.00	.70	.40
38	Jerry Glanville (CO) (W6)	1.00	.70	.40
39	Cornelius Bennett (W7)	1.50	1.25	.60
40	Jim Kelly (W7)	3.00	2.25	1.25
41	Mark Kelso (W7) (UER) (No fumble rec. in '88; mentioned in '89)	1.00	.70	.40
42	Scott Norwood (W7)	1.00	.70	.40
43	Nate Odomes (W7)	1.50	1.25	.60
44	Scott Radecic (W7)	1.00	.70	.40
45	Jim Ritcher (W8)	1.00	.70	.40
46	Leonard Smith (W8)	1.00	.70	.40
47	Darryl Talley (W8)	1.00	.70	.40
48	Marv Levy (CO) (W8)	1.00	.70	.40
49	Neal Anderson (W8)	1.00	.70	.40
50	Kevin Butler (W8)	1.00	.70	.40
51	Jim Covert (W9)	1.00	.70	.40
52	Richard Dent (W9)	1.00	.70	.40
53	Jay Hilgenberg (W9)	1.00	.70	.40
54	Steve McMichael (W9)	1.00	.70	.40
55	Ron Morris (W9)	1.00	.70	.40
56	John Roper (W9)	1.00	.70	.40
57	Mike Singletary (W9)	1.50	1.25	.60
58	Keith Van Horne (W10)	1.00	.70	.40
59	Mike Ditka (CO) (W10)	3.00	2.25	1.25
60	Lewis Billups (W10)	1.00	.70	.40
61	Eddie Brown (W10)	1.00	.70	.40
62	Jason Buck (W10)	1.00	.70	.40
63	Rickey Dixon (W10)	1.00	.70	.40
64	Tim McGee (W11)	1.00	.70	.40
65	Eric Thomas (W11)	1.00	.70	.40
66	Ickey Woods (W11)	1.00	.70	.40
67	Carl Zander (W11)	1.00	.70	.40
68	Sam Wyche (CO) (W11)	1.00	.70	.40
69	Paul Farren (W11)	1.00	.70	.40
70	Thane Gash (W12)	1.00	.70	.40
71	David Grayson (W12)	1.00	.70	.40
72	Bernie Kosar (W12)	1.50	1.25	.60
73	Reggie Langhorne (W12)	1.00	.70	.40
74	Eric Metcalf (W12)	2.00	1.50	.80
75	Ozzie Newsome (W12)	1.50	1.25	.60
76	Felix Wright (W13)	1.00	.70	.40
77	Bud Carson (CO) (W13)	1.00	.70	.40
78	Troy Aikman (W13)	25.00	18.50	10.00
79	Michael Irvin (W13)	4.00	3.00	1.50
80	Jim Jeffcoat (W13)	1.00	.70	.40
81	Crawford Ker (W13)	1.00	.70	.40
82	Eugene Lockhart (W13)	1.00	.70	.40
83	Kelvin Martin (W14)	1.50	1.25	.60
84	Ken Norton Jr.	1.50	1.25	.60
85	Jimmy Johnson (CO) (W14)	2.00	1.50	.80
86	Steve Atwater (W14)	1.00	.70	.40
87	Tyrone Braxton (W14)	1.00	.70	.40
88	John Elway (W14)	14.00	10.50	5.50
89	Simon Fletcher (W15)	1.00	.70	.40
90	Ron Holmes (W15)	1.00	.70	.40
91	Bobby Humphrey (W15)	1.00	.70	.40
92	Vance Johnson (W15)	1.00	.70	.40
93	Ricky Nattiel (W15)	1.00	.70	.40
94	Dan Reeves (CO) (W15)	1.50	1.25	.60
95	Jim Arnold (W1)	1.00	.70	.40
96	Jerry Ball (W1)	1.00	.70	.40
97	Bennie Blades (W1)	1.00	.70	.40
98	Lomas Brown (W1)	1.00	.70	.40
99	Michael Cofer (W1)	1.00	.70	.40
100	Richard Johnson (W4)	1.00	.70	.40
101	Eddie Murray (W4)	1.00	.70	.40
102	Barry Sanders (W2)	25.00	18.50	10.00
103	Chris Spielman (W2)	1.00	.70	.40
104	William White (W2)	1.50	1.25	.60
105	Eric Williams (W2)	1.00	.70	.40
106	Wayne Fontes (CO) (W3) (UER) (Says born in MO, actually born in MA)	1.00	.70	.40
107	Brent Fullwood (W3)	1.00	.70	.40
108	Ron Hallstrom (W3)	1.00	.70	.40
109	Tim Harris (W8)	1.00	.70	.40
110	Johnny Holland (W8)	1.00	.70	.40
111	Perry Kemp (W8)	1.00	.70	.40
112	Don Majkowski (W9)	1.00	.70	.40
113	Mark Murphy (W9)	1.00	.70	.40
114	Sterling Sharpe (W9)	4.00	3.00	1.50
115	Ed West (W9)	1.50	1.25	.60
116	Lindy Infante (CO) (W9)	1.00	.70	.40

117	Steve Brown (W9)	1.00	.70	.40
118	Ray Childress (W10)	1.00	.70	.40
119	Ernest Givins (W10)	1.50	1.25	.60
120	John Grimsley (W10)	1.00	.70	.40
121	Alonzo Highsmith (W10)	1.00	.70	.40
122	Drew Hill (W10)	1.50	1.25	.60
123	Bubba McDowell (W10)	1.50	1.25	.60
124	Dean Steinkuhler (W10)	1.00	.70	.40
125	Lorenzo White (W11)	1.00	.70	.40
126	Tony Zendejas (W11)	1.00	.70	.40
127	Jack Pardee (CO) (W11)	1.00	.70	.40
128	Albert Bentley (W11)	1.00	.70	.40
129	Dean Biasucci (W11)	1.00	.70	.40
130	Duane Bickett (W11)	1.00	.70	.40
131	Bill Brooks (W12)	1.50	1.25	.60
132	Jon Hand (W12)	1.00	.70	.40
133	Mike Prior (W12)	1.00	.70	.40
134	Andre Rison (W12)	2.00	1.50	.80
135	Rohn Stark (W12)	1.00	.70	.40
136	Donnell Thompson (W12)	1.00	.70	.40
137	Clarence Verdin (W13)	1.00	.70	.40
138	Fredd Young (W13)	1.00	.70	.40
139	Ron Meyer (CO) (W14)	1.00	.70	.40
140	John Alt (W14)	1.00	.70	.40
141	Steve DeBerg (W14)	1.50	1.25	.60
142	Irv Eatman (W1)	1.00	.70	.40
143	Dino Hackett (W2)	1.00	.70	.40
144	Nick Lowery (W2)	1.00	.70	.40
145	Bill Maas (W2)	1.00	.70	.40
146	Stephone Paige (W5)	1.00	.70	.40
147	Neil Smith (W3)	2.00	1.50	.80
148	Marty Schottenheimer (CO) (W3)	1.00	.70	.40
149	Steve Beuerlein (W3)	1.00	.70	.40
150	Tim Brown (W4)	3.00	2.25	1.25
151	Mike Dyal (W4)	1.00	.70	.40
152	Mervyn Fernandez (W4)	1.00	.70	.40
153	Willie Gault (W4)	1.00	.70	.40
154	Bob Golic (W5)	1.00	.70	.40
155	Bo Jackson (W5)	3.00	2.25	1.25
156	Don Mosebar (W5)	1.00	.70	.40
157	Steve Smith (W5)	1.00	.70	.40
158	Greg Townsend (W5)	1.00	.70	.40
159	Bruce Wilkerson (W6)	1.00	.70	.40
160	Steve Wisniewski (W6) (Blocking for Bo Jackson)	1.00	.70	.40
161	Art Shell (CO) (W6)	2.00	1.50	.80
162	Flipper Anderson (W6)	1.00	.70	.40
163	Greg Bell (W6) (UER) (Stats have 5 catches, should be 9)	1.00	.70	.40
164	Henry Ellard (W6)	1.50	1.25	.60
165	Jim Everett (W6)	1.50	1.25	.60
166	Jerry Gray (W7)	1.00	.70	.40
167	Kevin Greene (W7)	2.00	1.50	.80
168	Pete Holohan (W13)	1.00	.70	.40
169	Larry Kelm (W13)	1.00	.70	.40
170	Tom Newberry (W13)	1.00	.70	.40
171	Vince Newsome (W13)	1.00	.70	.40
172	Irv Pankey (W14)	1.00	.70	.40
173	Jackie Slater (W14)	1.00	.70	.40
174	Fred Strickland (W14)	1.00	.70	.40
175	Mike Wilcher (W14) (UER) (Fumble rec. number different from 1989 Pro Set card)	1.00	.70	.40
176	John Robinson (CO) (W7) (UER) (Stats say Rams, should says L.A. Rams)	1.00	.70	.40
177	Mark Clayton (W7)	1.50	1.25	.60
178	Roy Foster (W7)	1.00	.70	.40
179	Harry Galbreath (W7)	1.00	.70	.40
180	Jim C. Jensen (W8)	1.00	.70	.40
181	Dan Marino (W15)	35.00	26.00	14.00
182	Louis Oliver (W15)	1.00	.70	.40
183	Sammie Smith (W15)	1.00	.70	.40
184	Brian Sochia (W15)	1.00	.70	.40
185	Don Shula (CO) (W15)	1.50	1.25	.60
186	Joey Browner (W8)	1.00	.70	.40
187	Anthony Carter (W15)	1.50	1.25	.60
188	Chris Doleman (W8)	1.00	.70	.40
189	Steve Jordan (W4)	1.00	.70	.40
190	Carl Lee (W4)	1.00	.70	.40
191	Randall McDaniel (W5)	1.00	.70	.40
192	Mike Merriweather (W5)	1.00	.70	.40
193	Keith Millard (W14)	1.00	.70	.40
194	Al Noga (W12)	1.00	.70	.40
195	Scott Studwell (W5)	1.00	.70	.40
196	Henry Thomas (W12)	1.50	1.25	.60
197	Herschel Walker (W5)	1.50	1.25	.60
198	Wade Wilson (W5)	1.50	1.25	.60
199	Gary Zimmerman (W5)	1.00	.70	.40
200	Jerry Burns (CO) (W6)	1.00	.70	.40
201	Vincent Brown (W6)	1.50	1.25	.60
202	Hart Lee Dykes (W14)	1.00	.70	.40
203	Sean Farrell (W6)	1.00	.70	.40
204	Fred Marion (W6)	1.00	.70	.40

205	Stanley Morgan (W15) (UER) (Text says he reached 10,000 yards fastest; 3 players did it in 10 seasons)	1.50	1.25	.60
206	Eric Sievers (W6)	1.00	.70	.40
207	John Stephens (W15)	1.00	.70	.40
208	Andre Tippett (W15)	1.00	.70	.40
209	Rod Rust (CO) (W15)	1.00	.70	.40
210	Morten Andersen (W6)	1.00	.70	.40
211	Brad Edelman (W12)	1.00	.70	.40
212	John Fourcade (W12)	1.00	.70	.40
213	Dalton Hilliard (W13)	1.00	.70	.40
214	Rickey Jackson (W13) (Forcing Jim Kelly fumble)	1.00	.70	.40
215	Vaughan Johnson (W13)	1.00	.70	.40
216	Eric Martin (W13)	1.50	1.25	.60
217	Sam Mills (W7)	1.00	.70	.40
218	Pat Swilling (W7) (UER) (Total fumble recoveries listed as 4, should be 5)	1.50	1.25	.60
219	Frank Warren (W7)	1.00	.70	.40
220	Jim Wilks (W7)	1.00	.70	.40
221	Jim Mora (CO) (W7)	1.00	.70	.40
222	Raul Allegre (W2)	1.00	.70	.40
223	Carl Banks (W1)	1.00	.70	.40
224	John Elliott (W1)	1.00	.70	.40
225	Erik Howard (W7)	1.00	.70	.40
226	Pepper Johnson (W2)	1.00	.70	.40
227	Leonard Marshall (W7) (UER) (In Super Bowl XXI, George Martin had the safety)	1.00	.70	.40
228	Dave Meggett (W2)	1.50	1.25	.60
229	Bart Oates (W3)	1.00	.70	.40
230	Phil Simms (W8)	1.50	1.25	.60
231	Lawrence Taylor (W8)	2.00	1.50	.80
232	Bill Parcells (CO) (W8)	1.50	1.25	.60
233	Troy Benson (W8)	1.00	.70	.40
234	Kyle Clifton (W8) (UER) (Born: Onley, should be Olney)	1.00	.70	.40
235	Johnny Hector (W8)	1.00	.70	.40
236	Jeff Lageman (W9)	1.50	1.25	.60
237	Pat Leahy (W9)	1.00	.70	.40
238	Freeman McNeil (W9)	1.00	.70	.40
239	Ken O'Brien (W9)	1.00	.70	.40
240	Al Toon (W9)	1.50	1.25	.60
241	Jo Jo Townsell	1.00	.70	.40
242	Bruce Coslet (CO) (W10)	1.00	.70	.40
243	Eric Allen (W10)	1.00	.70	.40
244	Jerome Brown (W10)	1.50	1.25	.60
245	Keith Byars (W10)	1.50	1.25	.60
246	Cris Carter (W13)	4.00	3.00	1.50
247	Randall Cunningham (W13)	2.00	1.50	.80
248	Keith Jackson (W14)	1.50	1.25	.60
249	Mike Quick (W14)	1.50	1.25	.60
250	Clyde Simmons (W14)	1.50	1.25	.60
251	Andre Waters (W14)	1.00	.70	.40
252	Reggie White (W15)	2.00	1.50	.80
253	Buddy Ryan (CO) (W15)	1.00	.70	.40
254	Rich Camarillo (W15)	1.00	.70	.40
255	Earl Ferrell (W10) (No mention of retirement on card front)	1.00	.70	.40
256	Roy Green (W10)	1.00	.70	.40
257	Ken Harvey (W3)	1.00	.70	.40
258	Ernie Jones	1.00	.70	.40
259	Tim McDonald (W11)	1.00	.70	.40
260	Timm Rosenbach (W11) (UER) (Born '67, should be '66)	1.50	1.25	.60
261	Luis Sharpe (W3)	1.00	.70	.40
262	Vai Sikahema (W3)	1.00	.70	.40
263	J.T. Smith (W1)	1.00	.70	.40
264	Ron Wolfley (W1) (UER) (Born Blaisdel, should be Blasdel)	1.00	.70	.40
265	Joe Bugel (CO) (W11)	1.00	.70	.40
266	Gary Anderson (W11)	1.00	.70	.40
267	Bubby Brister (W1)	1.00	.70	.40
268	Merril Hoge (W11)	1.00	.70	.40
269	Carnell Lake (W2)	1.00	.70	.40
270	Louis Lipps (W11)	1.00	.70	.40
271	David Little (W3)	1.00	.70	.40
272	Greg Lloyd (W3)	2.00	1.50	.80
273	Keith Willis (W11)	1.00	.70	.40
274	Tim Worley (W3)	1.00	.70	.40
275	Chuck Noll (CO) (W4)	1.50	1.25	.60
276	Marion Butts (W4)	1.00	.70	.40
277	Gill Byrd (W2)	1.00	.70	.40
278	Vencie Glenn (W2) (UER) (Sack total should be 2, not 2.5)	1.00	.70	.40
279	Burt Grossman (W4)	1.00	.70	.40
280	Gary Plummer (W4)	1.00	.70	.40
281	Bill Ray Smith (W12)	1.00	.70	.40

282	Billy Joe Tolliver (W12)	1.00	.70	.40
283	Dan Henning (CO) (W1)	1.00	.70	.40
284	Harris Barton (W1)	1.00	.70	.40
285	Michael Carter (W1)	1.00	.70	.40
286	Mike Cofer (W1)	1.00	.70	.40
287	Roger Craig (W1)	1.50	1.25	.60
288	Don Griffin (W1)	1.00	.70	.40
289	Charles Haley (W2)	1.50	1.25	.60
290	Pierce Holt (W2)	1.00	.70	.40
291	Ronnie Lott (W2)	1.50	1.25	.60
292	Guy McIntyre (W2)	1.00	.70	.40
293	Joe Montana (W2)	20.00	15.00	8.00
294	Tom Rathman (W2)	1.50	1.25	.60
295	Jerry Rice (W3)	20.00	15.00	8.00
296	Jesse Sapolu (W3)	1.00	.70	.40
297	John Taylor (W3)	1.50	1.25	.60
298	Michael Walter (W3)	1.00	.70	.40
299	George Seifert (CO) (W3)	2.00	1.50	.80
300	Jeff Bryant (W3)	1.00	.70	.40
301	Jacob Green (W4)	1.00	.70	.40
302	Norm Johnson (UER) (W4) (Card shop not in Garden Grove, should say Fullerton)	1.00	.70	.40
303	Bryan Millard (W4)	1.00	.70	.40
304	Joe Nash (W4)	1.00	.70	.40
305	Eugene Robinson (W4)	1.00	.70	.40
306	John L. Williams (W14)	1.00	.70	.40
307	Dave Wyman (W14) (NFL EXP is in caps, inconsisten with rest of the set)	1.00	.70	.40
308	Chuck Knox (CO) (W14)	1.00	.70	.40
309	Mark Carrier (C14)	1.50	1.25	.60
310	Paul Gruber (W14)	1.00	.70	.40
311	Harry Hamilton (W15)	1.00	.70	.40
312	Bruce Hill (W15)	1.00	.70	.40
313	Donald Igwebuike (W15)	1.00	.70	.40
314	Kevin Murphy (W15)	1.00	.70	.40
315	Ervin Randle (W12)	1.00	.70	.40
316	Mark Robinson (W12)	1.00	.70	.40
317	Lars Tate (W12)	1.00	.70	.40
318	Vinny Testaverde (W12)	2.00	1.50	.80
319	Ray Perkins (CO) (W12)	1.00	.70	.40
320	Earnest Byner (W12)	1.00	.70	.40
321	Gary Clark (W12) (Randall Cunningham looking on from sidelines)	2.00	1.50	.80
322	Darryl Grant (W13)	1.00	.70	.40
323	Darrell Green (W13)	1.00	.70	.40
324	Jim Lachey (W13)	1.00	.70	.40
325	Charles Mann (W13)	1.00	.70	.40
326	Wilber Marshall (W13)	1.00	.70	.40
327	Ralf Mojsiejenko (W13)	1.00	.70	.40
328	Art Monk (W15)	2.00	1.50	.80
329	Gerald Riggs (W15)	1.00	.70	.40
330	Mark Rypien (W14)	1.00	.70	.40
331	Ricky Sanders (W14)	1.00	.70	.40
332	Alvin Walton (W4)	1.00	.70	.40
333	Joe Gibbs (CO) (W5)	2.00	1.50	.80
334	**Aloha Stadium** (W5) (Site of Pro Bowl)	1.00	.70	.40
335	Brian Blades (PB) (W5)	1.50	1.25	.60
336	James Brooks (PB) (W5)	1.00	.70	.40
337	Shane Conlan (PB) (W5)	1.00	.70	.40
339	Ray Donaldson (PB) (W5)	1.00	.70	.40
340	Ferrell Edmunds (PB) (W6)	1.00	.70	.40
341	Boomer Esiason (PB) (W6)	1.50	1.25	.60
342	David Fulcher (PB) (W6)	1.00	.70	.40
343	Chris Hinton (PB) (W6)	1.00	.70	.40
344	Rodney Holman (PB) (W6)	1.00	.70	.40
345	Kent Hull (PB) (W6)	1.00	.70	.40
346	Tunch Ilkin (PB) (W7)	1.00	.70	.40
347	Mike Johnson (PB) (W7)	1.00	.70	.40
348	Greg Kragen (PB) (W7)	1.00	.70	.40
349	Dave Krieg (PB) (W7)	1.00	.70	.40
350	Albert Lewis (PB) (W7)	1.00	.70	.40
351	Howie Long (PB) (W7)	1.50	1.25	.60
352	Bruce Matthews (PB) (W8)	1.00	.70	.40
353	Clay Matthews (PB) (W8)	1.00	.70	.40
354	Erik McMillan (PB) (W8)	1.00	.70	.40
355	Karl Mecklenburg (PB) (W8)	1.00	.70	.40
356	Anthony Miller (PB) (W8)	2.00	1.50	.80
357	Frank Minnifield (PB) (W8)	1.00	.70	.40
358	Max Montoya (PB) (W8)	1.00	.70	.40
359	Warren Moon (PB) (W10)	2.00	1.50	.80
360	Mike Munchak (PB) (W9)	1.00	.70	.40
361	Anthony Munoz (PB) (W9)	1.00	.70	.40
362	John Offerdahl (PB) (W9)	1.00	.70	.40
363	Christian Okoye (PB) (W9)	1.00	.70	.40
364	Leslie O'Neal (PB) (W9)	1.00	.70	.40
365	Rufus Porter (PB) (W9) (UER) (TM logo missing)	1.00	.70	.40
366	Andre Reed (PB) (W10)	1.50	1.25	.60
367	Johnny Rembert (PB) (W10)	1.00	.70	.40
368	Reggie Roby (PB) (W10)	1.00	.70	.40
369	Kevin Ross (PB) (W10)	1.00	.70	.40
370	Webster Slaughter (PB) (W10)	1.00	.70	.40
371	Bruce Smith (PB) (W11)	1.50	1.25	.60
372	Dennis Smith (PB) (W11)	1.00	.70	.40
373	Derrick Thomas (PB) (W11)	2.00	1.50	.80
374	Thurman Thomas (PB) (W11)	2.00	1.50	.80
375	David Treadwell (PB) (W11)	1.00	.70	.40
376	Lee Williams (PB) (W11)	1.00	.70	.40

1991 FACT Pro Set Mobil

Each of the NFL cities received these cards, sponsored by Mobil Oil and Pro Set, to use as an educational tool for fourth grade students. The cards are identical to the 1990 Pro Set Series I cards, while the backs have questions for the students. Six different sets were issued throughout the program, each with a header card.

		NM/M	NM	E
	Complete Set (108):	130.00	97.50	52.50
	Common Player:	.75	.60	.30
3	Joe Montana (S1)	10.00	7.50	4.00
5	Mike Singletary (S2)	1.00	.70	.40
12	Jay Novacek (S3)	1.50	1.25	.60
20	Ottis Anderson (S2)	1.00	.70	.40
40	Tim Brown (S1)	1.50	1.25	.60
44	Herschel Walker (S1)	1.00	.70	.40
59	Eric Dorsey (S3)	.75	.60	.30
60	John Elliott (S1)	.75	.60	.30
63	Jeff Hostetler (S2)	1.00	.70	.40
69	Eric Moore (S4)	.75	.60	.30
70	Bart Oates (S3)	.75	.60	.30
71	Gary Reasons (S4)	.75	.60	.30
75	Shane Conlan (S3)	.75	.60	.30
78	Jim Kelly (S4)	2.50	2.00	1.00
84	Darryl Talley (S4)	.75	.60	.30
90	Marv Levy (CO) (S1)	.75	.60	.30
94	Tim Green (S2)	.75	.60	.30
99	Jerry Glanville (CO) (S3)	.75	.60	.30
101	Mark Carrier (S3)	.75	.60	.30
104	Jim Harbaugh (S6)	1.50	1.25	.60
105	Brad Muster (S4)	.75	.60	.30
107	Keith Van Horne (S6)	.75	.60	.30
111	Boomer Esiason (S1)	1.00	.70	.40
116	Anthony Munoz (S2)	1.00	.70	.40
117	Sam Wyche (CO) (S4)	.75	.60	.30
118	Paul Farren (S6)	.75	.60	.30
119	Thane Gash (S3)	.75	.60	.30
122	Clay Matthews (S2)	.75	.60	.30
123	Eric Metcalf (S6)	1.25	.90	.50
127	Tommie Agee (S6)	.75	.60	.30
128	Troy Aikman (S6)	12.00	9.00	4.75
132	Michael Irvin (S6)	3.00	2.25	1.25
134	Daniel Stubbs (S6)	.75	.60	.30
136	Steve Atwater (S1)	.75	.60	.30
138	John Elway (S2)	8.00	6.00	3.25
141	Mark Jackson (S6)	.75	.60	.30
142	Karl Mecklenburg (S3)	.75	.60	.30
143	Doug Widell (S2)	.75	.60	.30
153	Wayne Fontes (CO) (S2)	.75	.60	.30
156	Don Majkowski (S1)	.75	.60	.30
157	Tony Mandarich (S6)	.75	.60	.30
158	Mark Murphy (S6)	.75	.60	.30
161	Sterling Sharpe (S4)	2.00	1.50	.80
162	Lindy Infante (CO) (S3)	.75	.60	.30
163	Ray Childress (S6)	.75	.60	.30
166	Bruce Matthews (S3)	.75	.60	.30
167	Warren Moon (S6)	2.50	2.00	1.00
168	Mike Munchak (S4)	.75	.60	.30
169	Al Smith (S6)	.75	.60	.30
174	Bill Brooks (S1)	1.00	.70	.40
179	Clarence Verdin (S3)	.75	.60	.30
182	Steve DeBerg (S1)	1.00	.70	.40
185	Christian Okoye (S3)	.75	.60	.30
189	Marty Schottenheimer (CO) (S1)	.75	.60	.30
191	Howie Long (S2)	1.00	.70	.40
194	Steve Smith (S4)	.75	.60	.30
196	Lionel Washington (S6)	.75	.60	.30
198	Art Shell (CO) (S3)	1.00	.70	.40
203	Buford McGee (S2)	.75	.60	.30
204	Tom Newberry (S6)	.75	.60	.30
205	Frank Stams (S1)	.75	.60	.30
210	Dan Marino (S4)	18.00	13.50	7.25
212	John Offerdahl (S1)	.75	.60	.30
216	Don Shula (S4)	1.00	.70	.40
217	Darrell Fullington (S6)	.75	.60	.30
218	Tim Irwin (S2)	.75	.60	.30
219	Mike Merriweather (S3)	.75	.60	.30
231	Ed Reynolds (S3)	.75	.60	.30
238	Robert Massey (S4)	.75	.60	.30
246	James Hasty (S1)	.75	.60	.30
247	Erik McMillan (S2)	.75	.60	.30
249	Ken O'Brien (S4)	.75	.60	.30
260	Andre Waters (S2)	.75	.60	.30
270	Joe Bugel (CO) (S2)	.75	.60	.30
271	Gary Anderson (S1)	.75	.60	.30
272	Dermontti Dawson (S4)	.75	.60	.30
275	Tunch Ilkin (S2)	.75	.60	.30
282	Gill Byrd (S4)	.75	.60	.30
290	Michael Carter (S2)	.75	.60	.30
292	Pierce Holt (S3)	.75	.60	.30
297	George Seifert (CO) (S1)	1.25	.90	.50
306	Chuck Knox (CO) (S3)	.75	.60	.30
310	Harry Hamilton (S4)	.75	.60	.30
321	Martin Mayhew (S4)	.75	.60	.30
322	Mark Rypien (S1)	.75	.60	.30
NNO	**Title Card - Stay Fit** (S1)	.75	.60	.30
NNO	**Title Card - Eat Smart** (S2)	.75	.60	.30
NNO	**Title Card - Stay Off Drugs** (S3)	.75	.60	.30
NNO	**Title Card - Stay In Tune** (S4)	.75	.60	.30
NNO	**Title Card - Stay True to Yourself** (S5)	.75	.60	.30
NNO	**Title Card - Stay In School** (S6)	.75	.60	.30
NNO	**Title Card - Stay In School** (S6)	.75	.60	.30

1968 Falcons Team Issue

Measuring 7-1/2" x 9-1/2", the fronts feature a black-and-white photo, with the player's name and team printed in the white border at the bottom. The only card not using a posed action photo is Bob Berry's, which features a portrait. The cards are unnumbered and the backs are blank.

		NM	E	VG
	Complete Set (14):	65.00	32.00	19.50
	Common Player:	4.00	2.00	1.25
1	Bob Berry	4.00	2.00	1.25
2	Carlton Dabney	4.00	2.00	1.25
3	Bob Etter	4.00	2.00	1.25
4	Bill Harris	4.00	2.00	1.25
5	Ralph Heck	4.00	2.00	1.25
6	Claude Humphrey	4.00	2.00	1.25
7	Randy Johnson	4.00	2.00	1.25
8	George Kunz (White jersey 78)	6.00	3.00	1.75
9	George Kunz (Dark jersey 75)	6.00	3.00	1.75
10	Errol Linden	4.00	2.00	1.25
11	Billy Lothridge	4.00	2.00	1.25
12	Ken Reaves	4.00	2.00	1.25
13	Jerry Shay	4.00	2.00	1.25
14	Tommy Nobis	15.00	7.50	4.50

1978 Falcons Kinnett Dairies

Measuring 4-1/4" x 6", this six-card set showcases four black-and-white player head shots on the front. The Kinnett logo appears in the middle left, while "Atlanta Player Cards" and the NFLPA logo are printed to the right. The unnumbered cards have blank backs.

		NM	E	VG
	Complete Set (6):	35.00	17.50	10.50
	Common Player:	5.00	2.50	1.50
1	William Andrews, Jeff Yeates, Wilson Faumuina, Phil McKinnely	5.00	2.50	1.50
2	Warren Bryant, R.C. Thielemann, Steve Bartkowski, Frank Reed	10.00	5.00	3.00
3	Wallace Francis, Jim Mitchell, Jeff Van Note, Ray Easterling	5.00	2.50	1.50
4	Dewey McClain, Billy Ryckman, Paul Ryczek, Bubba Bean	5.00	2.50	1.50
5	Robert Pennywell, Dave Scott, Jim Bailey, John James	5.00	2.50	1.50
6	Haskel Stanback, Rick Byas, Mike Esposito, Tom Moriarty	5.00	2.50	1.50

1980 Falcons Police

Measuring 2-5/8" x 4-1/8", the 30-card set boasts a player photo on the front, with the Falcons' logo in the upper left and the player's name, number, position and bio under the photo on the left. Below the photo on the right is the Falcons' logo. The unnumbered card backs include "Tips from the Falcons" at the top, with the Atlanta Police Athletic League and Atlanta Jaycees logos underneath. A safety tip is printed in the center of the card, with the Coca-Cola logo at the bottom center of the card back.

		NM/M	NM	E
	Complete Set (30):	40.00	30.00	16.00
	Common Player:	1.25	.90	.50
1	William Andrews	4.00	3.75	2.00
2	Steve Bartkowski	8.00	7.50	4.00
3	Bubba Bean	2.50	2.00	1.00

4	Warren Bryant	1.25	.90	.50
5	Rick Byas	1.25	.90	.50
6	Lynn Cain	2.50	2.25	1.25
7	Buddy Curry	1.25	.90	.50
8	Edgar Fields	1.25	.90	.50
9	Wallace Francis	3.00	2.75	1.50
10	Alfred Jackson	2.50	2.25	1.25
11	John James	1.25	.90	.50
12	Alfred Jenkins	3.50	3.00	1.50
13	Kenny Johnson	1.25	.90	.50
14	Mike Kenn	2.50	2.25	1.25
15	Fulton Kuykendall	1.25	1.50	.80
16	Rolland Lawrence	1.25	1.50	.80
17	Tim Mazzetti	1.25	.90	.50
18	Dewey McLean	1.25	.90	.50
19	Jeff Merrow	1.25	1.50	.80
20	Junior Miller	2.50	2.25	1.25
21	Tom Pridemore	1.25	.90	.50
22	Frank Reed	1.25	.90	.50
23	Al Richardson	1.25	.90	.50
24	Dave Scott	1.25	.90	.50
25	Don Smith	1.25	.90	.50
26	Reggie Smith	1.25	.90	.50
27	R.C. Thielemann	2.00	1.50	.80
28	Jeff Van Note	2.50	2.25	1.25
29	Joel Williams	1.25	.90	.50
30	Jeff Yeates	1.25	.90	.50

1981 Falcons Police

Measuring 2-5/8" x 4-1/8", the 30-card set is anchored with a large photo on the front. The Atlanta Police Athletic League logo is printed in the upper left of the card front, while "NFC Western Division Champions 1980" is located in the upper right. Beneath the photo are the player's name, number, position, bio and Falcons' logo. The unnumbered card backs boast a Coca-Cola logo in the upper left and a Chevron logo in the upper right. The player's name and a highlight are printed in the center of the back, with a safety tip located beneath it. Photo and printing credits appear on the bottom of the card backs.

	NM/M	NM	E
Complete Set (30):	12.00	9.00	4.75
Common Player:	.50	.40	.20

6	John James	.50	.40	.20
10	Steve Bartkowski	3.00	2.25	1.25
16	Reggie Smith	.50	.40	.20
18	Mick Luckhurst	.50	.40	.20
21	Lynn Cain	1.00	.70	.40
23	Bobby Butler	.50	.40	.20
27	Tom Pridemore	.50	.40	.20
30	Scott Woerner	.50	.40	.20
31	William Andrews	1.25	.90	.50
36	Bob Glazebrook	.50	.40	.20
37	Kenny Johnson	.50	.40	.20
50	Buddy Curry	.50	.40	.20
51	Jim Laughlin	.50	.40	.20
54	Fulton Kuykendall	.50	.40	.20
56	Al Richardson	.50	.40	.20
57	Jeff Van Note	.50	.40	.20
58	Joel Williams	.50	.40	.20
65	Don Smith	.50	.40	.20
66	Warren Bryant	.50	.40	.20
68	R.C. Thielemann	.50	.40	.20
70	Dave Scott	.50	.40	.20
74	Wilson Faumuina	.50	.40	.20
75	Jeff Merrow	.50	.40	.20
78	Mike Kenn	.50	.40	.20
79	Jeff Yeates	.50	.40	.20
80	Junior Miller	.50	.40	.20
84	Alfred Jenkins	1.00	.70	.40
85	Alfred Jackson	.50	.40	.20
89	Wallace Francis	1.00	.70	.40
NNO	Leeman Bennett (CO)	.50	.40	.20

1960 Fleer

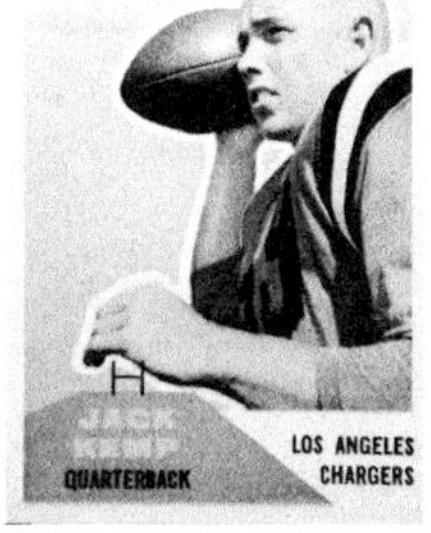

Fleer's first venture into football depicted cards of players from the newly-formed American Football League. Outside of George Blanda, Sammy Baugh and several rookie cards detailed below, the set basically features a lot of no-names, many of whom appeared on their only card with this issue. It's not surprising that this set includes the most rookie cards of any other set issued since football cards were issued. (Not coincidentally, Topps' 1984 USFL set ranks second because of the amount of rookies who played in that league.) Rookie cards in this set include Sid Gillman (as a coach - this was his only card), Lou Saban (only card), Hank Stram (only card until Pro Set announcer cards), Abner Haynes, and Ron Mix. The card that carries the set is Jack Kemp's rookie card.

	NM	E	VG
Complete Set (132):	900.00	450.00	270.00
Common Player:	8.00	4.00	2.40
Minor Stars:	4.00		
Unlisted Stars:	5.50		
Wax Pack (6):	225.00		

1	Harvey White **RC**	20.00	10.00	6.00
2	Tom "Corky" Tharp	4.00	2.40	8.00
3	Dan McGrew	8.00	4.00	2.40
4	Bob White	3.25	1.75	1.00
5	Dick Jamieson	8.00	4.00	2.40
6	Sam Salerno	8.00	4.00	2.40
7	Sid Gillman **RC**	25.00	13.00	8.00
8	Ben Preston	8.00	4.00	2.40
9	George Blanch	8.00	4.00	2.40
10	Bob Stransky	8.00	4.00	2.40
11	Fran Curci	8.00	4.00	2.40
12	George Shirkey	8.00	4.00	2.40
13	Paul Larson	8.00	4.00	2.40
14	John Stolte	8.00	4.00	2.40
15	Serafino Frazio **RC**	10.00	5.00	3.00
16	Tom Dimitroff	8.00	4.00	2.40
17	Elbert Dubenion **RC**	15.00	7.50	4.50
18	Hogan Wharton	8.00	4.00	2.40
19	Tom O'Connell	8.00	4.00	2.40
20	Sammy Baugh	50.00	25.00	15.00
21	Tony Sardisco	8.00	4.00	2.40
22	Alan Cann	8.00	4.00	2.40
23	Mike Hudock	8.00	4.00	2.40
24	Bill Atkins	8.00	4.00	2.40
25	Charlie Jackson	8.00	4.00	2.40
26	Frank Tripucka	10.00	5.00	3.00
27	Tony Teresa	8.00	4.00	2.40
28	Joe Amstutz	8.00	4.00	2.40
29	Bob Fee	8.00	4.00	2.40
30	Jim Baldwin	8.00	4.00	2.40
31	Jim Yates	8.00	4.00	2.40
32	Don Flynn	8.00	4.00	2.40
33	Ken Adamson	8.00	4.00	2.40
34	Ron Drzewiexki	8.00	4.00	2.40
35	J.W. Slack	8.00	4.00	2.40
36	Bob Yates	8.00	4.00	2.40
37	Gary Cobb	8.00	4.00	2.40
38	Jacky Lee **RC**	10.00	5.00	3.00
39	Jack Spikes **RC**	10.00	5.00	3.00
40	Jim Padgett	8.00	4.00	2.40
41	Jack Larsheid	8.00	4.00	2.40
42	Bob Reifsnyder	8.00	4.00	2.40
43	Fran Rogel	8.00	4.00	2.40
44	Ray Moss	8.00	4.00	2.40
45	Tony Banfield	10.00	5.00	3.00
46	George Herring	8.00	4.00	2.40
47	Willie Smith	8.00	4.00	2.40
48	Buddy Allen	8.00	4.00	2.40
49	Bill Brown	8.00	4.00	2.40
50	Ken Ford	8.00	4.00	2.40
51	Billy Kinard	8.00	4.00	2.40
52	Buddy Mayfield	8.00	4.00	2.40
53	Bill Krisher	8.00	4.00	2.40
54	Frank Bernardi	8.00	4.00	2.40
55	Lou Saban **RC**	10.00	5.00	3.00
56	Gene Cockrell	8.00	4.00	2.40
57	Sam Sanders	8.00	4.00	2.40
58	George Blanda	45.00	23.00	14.00
59	Sherrill Headrick **RC**	10.00	5.00	3.00
60	Carl Larpenter	8.00	4.00	2.40
61	Gene Prebola	8.00	4.00	2.40
62	Dick Chorovich	8.00	4.00	2.40
63	Bob McNamara	8.00	4.00	2.40
64	Tom Saidock	8.00	4.00	2.40
65	Willie Evans	8.00	4.00	2.40
66	Billy Cannon **RC**	20.00	10.00	6.00
67	Sam McCord	8.00	4.00	2.40
68	Mike Simmons	8.00	4.00	2.40
69	Jim Swink **RC**	10.00	5.00	3.00
70	Don Hitt	8.00	4.00	2.40
71	Gerhard Schwedes	8.00	4.00	2.40
72	Thurlow Cooper	8.00	4.00	2.40
73	Abner Haynes **RC**	25.00	13.00	8.00
74	Billy Shoemaker	8.00	4.00	2.40
75	Marv Lasater	8.00	4.00	2.40
76	Paul Lowe **RC**	15.00	7.50	4.50
77	Bruce Hartman	8.00	4.00	2.40
78	Blanche Martin	8.00	4.00	2.40
79	Gene Grabosky	8.00	4.00	2.40
80	Lou Rymkus	10.00	5.00	3.00
81	Chris Burford **RC**	10.00	5.00	3.00
82	Don Allen	8.00	4.00	2.40
83	Bob Nelson	8.00	4.00	2.40
84	Jim Woodard	8.00	4.00	2.40
85	Tom Rychlec	8.00	4.00	2.40
86	Bob Cox	8.00	4.00	2.40
87	Jerry Cornelison	8.00	4.00	2.40
88	Jack Work	8.00	4.00	2.40
89	Sam DeLuca	8.00	4.00	2.40
90	Rommie Loudd	8.00	4.00	2.40
91	Teddy Edmondson	8.00	4.00	2.40
92	Buster Ramsey	8.00	4.00	2.40
93	Doug Asad	8.00	4.00	2.40
94	Jimmy Harris	8.00	4.00	2.40
95	Lary Cundiff	8.00	4.00	2.40
96	Richie Lucas **RC**	10.00	5.00	3.00
97	Don Norwood	8.00	4.00	2.40
98	Larry Grantham **RC**	10.00	5.00	3.00
99	Bill Mathis **RC**	10.00	5.00	3.00
100	Mel Branch **RC**	10.00	5.00	3.00
101	Marvin Terrell	8.00	4.00	2.40
102	Charlie Flowers	8.00	4.00	2.40
103	John McMullan	8.00	4.00	2.40
104	Charlie Kaaihue	8.00	4.00	2.40
105	Joe Schaffer	8.00	4.00	2.40
106	Al Day	8.00	4.00	2.40
107	Johnny Carson	8.00	4.00	2.40
108	Alan Goldstein	8.00	4.00	2.40
109	Doug Cline	8.00	4.00	2.40
110	Al Carmichael	8.00	4.00	2.40
111	Bob Dee	8.00	4.00	2.40
112	John Bredice	8.00	4.00	2.40
113	Don Floyd	8.00	4.00	2.40
114	Ronnie Cain	8.00	4.00	2.40
115	Stan Flowers	8.00	4.00	2.40
116	Hank Stram **RC**	50.00	25.00	15.00
117	Bob Dougherty	8.00	4.00	2.40
118	Ron Mix **RC**	50.00	25.00	15.00
120	Elvin Caldwell	8.00	4.00	2.40
121	Bill Kimber	8.00	4.00	2.40
122	Jim Matheny	3.00	1.50	.90
123	Curley Johnson **RC**	8.00	4.00	2.40
124	Jack Kemp **RC**	100.00	50.00	30.00
125	Ed Denk	8.00	4.00	2.40
126	Jerry McFarland	8.00	4.00	2.40
127	Dan Lamphear	8.00	4.00	2.40
128	Paul Maguire **RC**	25.00	13.00	8.00
129	Ray Collins	8.00	4.00	2.40
130	Ron Burton **RC**	10.00	5.00	3.00
131	Eddie Erdelatz	8.00	4.00	2.40
132	Ron Beagle **RC**	20.00	10.00	6.00

1960 Fleer College Pennant Decals

This 19-decal set was also inserted into packs of 1960 Fleer Football along with the AFL Team Decals. These decals measured approximately 2-1/4" x 3" and included two colleges per card.

	NM	E	VG
Complete Set (19):	180.00	135.00	72.50
Common Player:	8.00	6.00	3.25

1	**Alabama/Yale**	10.00	5.00	3.00
2	**Army/Mississippi**	8.00	6.00	3.25
3	**California/Indiana**	8.00	6.00	3.25
4	**Duke/Notre Dame**	18.00	9.00	5.50
5	**Florida St./Kentucky**	10.00	5.00	3.00
6	**Georgia/Oklahoma**	10.00	5.00	3.00
7	**Houston/Iowa**	8.00	6.00	3.25
8	**Idaho St./Penn.**	8.00	6.00	3.25
9	**Iowa St./Penn State**	14.00	7.00	4.25
10	**Kansas/UCLA**	12.00	6.00	3.50
11	**Marquette/New Mexico**	8.00	6.00	3.25
12	**Maryland/Missouri**	8.00	6.00	3.25
13	**Miss.South./N.Carolina**	8.00	6.00	3.25
14	**Navy/Stanford**	10.00	5.00	3.00
15	**Nebraska/Purdue**	12.00	6.00	3.50
16	**Pittsburgh/Utah**	8.00	6.00	3.25
17	**SMU/West Virginia**	8.00	6.00	3.25
18	**So.Carolina/USC**	10.00	5.00	3.00
19	**Wake Forest/Wisconsin**	10.00	5.00	3.00

1960 Fleer Decals

This group of eight American Football League inserts was inserted in wax packs of Fleer football. The decals, which measure about 1-1/2" x 3-1/2", depict the logo of each AFL team. The decals were unnumbered.

	NM	E	VG
Complete Set (8):	50.00	25.00	15.00
Common Team:	4.00	2.00	1.25

1	**Boston Patriots**	4.00	2.00	1.25
2	**Buffalo Bills**	5.00	2.50	1.50
3	**Dallas Texans**	5.00	2.50	1.50
4	**Denver Broncos**	5.00	2.50	1.50
5	**Houston Oilers**	5.00	2.50	1.50
6	**Los Angeles Chargers**	4.00	2.00	1.25
7	**New York Titans**	5.00	2.50	1.50
8	**Oakland Raiders**	5.00	2.50	1.50

1961 Fleer Magic Message Blue Inserts

These 40 cards, which pose a trivia question on the front, instruct collectors to turn and wet the card to determine the answer. A line drawing also appears on the front, as does a card number, which is located in the lower right corner. Along the bottom of the card is a tag line which indicates the cards were printed by Business Service of Long Island, N.Y. The blank-backed cards, measuring 3" x 2-1/8", were inserts in 1961 Fleer football packs.

		NM	E	VG
Complete Set (40):		125.00	62.00	37.00
Common Player:		4.00	2.00	1.25
1	**First Sugar Bowl game**	4.00	2.00	1.25
2	**Point-A-Minute team**	4.00	2.00	1.25
3	**Gloomy Gil**	4.00	2.00	1.25
4	**College record for years coached**	4.00	2.00	1.25
5	**Two Platoon System**	4.00	2.00	1.25
6	**The only Sudden Death playoff**	4.00	2.00	1.25
7	**Sudden Death playoff**	4.00	2.00	1.25
8	**Longest field goal**	4.00	2.00	1.25
9	**Colorado All-American**	5.00	2.50	1.50
10	**Michigan All-American sportscaster**	5.00	2.50	1.50
11	**First North-South game**	4.00	2.00	1.25
12	**First Army-Navy game**	4.00	2.00	1.25
13	**Outfielder/All-American back**	5.00	2.50	1.50
14	**All-American Mr. Inside & Mr. Outside**	5.00	2.50	1.50
15	**The Thundering Herd**	4.00	2.00	1.25
16	**First NFL Championship playoff**	4.00	2.00	1.25
17	**Record for field goals dropkicked**	4.00	2.00	1.25
18	**Longest college winning streak**	4.00	2.00	1.25
19	**First collegian drafted**	4.00	2.00	1.25
20	**First team to use the huddle**	4.00	2.00	1.25
21	**The first Intercollegiate Champion**	4.00	2.00	1.25
22	**The first broadcast**	4.00	2.00	1.25
23	**The longest field goal**	4.00	2.00	1.25
24	**The tackling dummy**	4.00	2.00	1.25
25	**Greatest player in teh half-century**	5.00	2.50	1.50
26	**The most touchdowns in a game**	4.00	2.00	1.25
27	**Who ran the wrong way?**	4.00	2.00	1.25
28	**The first college field goal**	4.00	2.00	1.25
29	**The first All-American team**	4.00	2.00	1.25
30	**The forward pass**	4.00	2.00	1.25
31	**The first college to use numbers**	4.00	2.00	1.25
32	**The first professional football game**	4.00	2.00	1.25
33	**Where is the Football Hall of Fame?**	4.00	2.00	1.25
34	**The Four Horsemen**	5.00	2.50	1.50
35	**The first Rose Bowl**	4.00	2.00	1.25
36	**Record for forward passes in a prof gam**	4.00	2.00	1.25
37	**Galloping Ghost**	5.00	2.50	1.50
38	**Rose Bowl in California**	4.00	2.00	1.25
39	**Seven Blocks of Granite**	4.00	2.00	1.25
40	**First game in the U.S.**	4.00	2.00	1.25

1961 Fleer

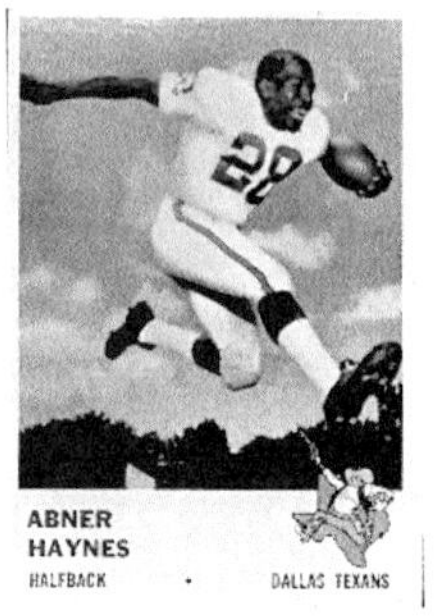
ABNER
HAYNES
HALFBACK • DALLAS TEXANS

This 220-card set by Fleer - its biggest of the four it produced was the last to include NFL players (future sets would include only AFL players). Cards 1-132 showcase NFL players; 133-up depict AFLers. Cards are again grouped alphabetically by city name. A number of cards in this set are short-printed, and are indicated by (SP) in the following checklist. Rookies in the '61 Fleer issue include Don Meredith, Tom Flores, Don Maynard, and Jim Otto. Second-year cards include Night Train Lane (his rookie card was in '57), Forrest Gregg, Jerry Kramer, Jack Kemp and Ron Mix. (Key: SP meads short-printed).

		NM	E	VG
Complete Set (220):		2,800	1,400	840.00
Common Player (1-132):		8.00	4.00	2.40
Minor Stars (1-132):		5.00		
Unlisted Stars (1-132):		7.00		
Common Player (133-220):		10.00	5.00	3.00
Minor Stars (133-220):		6.00		
Unlisted Stars (133-220):		8.00		
Series 1 Wax Pack (5):		215.00		
Series 2 Wax Pack (5):		250.00		
1	Ed Brown	20.00	10.00	6.00
2	Rick Casares	15.00	7.50	4.50
3	Willie Galimore	10.00	5.00	3.00
4	Jim Dooley	8.00	4.00	2.40
5	Harlon Hill	8.00	4.00	2.40
6	Stan Jones	10.00	5.00	3.00
7	J.C. Caroline	8.00	4.00	2.40
8	Joe Fortunato	8.00	4.00	2.40
9	Doug Atkins	15.00	7.50	4.50
10	Milt Plum	10.00	5.00	3.00
11	Jim Brown	110.00	55.00	33.00
12	Bobby Mitchell	15.00	7.50	4.50
13	Ray Renfro	10.00	5.00	3.00
14	Gern Nagler	8.00	4.00	2.40
15	Jim Shofner	8.00	4.00	2.40
16	Vince Costello	8.00	4.00	2.40
17	Galen Fiss	8.00	4.00	2.40
18	Walt Michaels	10.00	5.00	3.00
19	Bob Gain	8.00	4.00	2.40
20	Mal Hammack	8.00	4.00	2.40
21	Frank Mestnick	8.00	4.00	2.40
22	Bobby Joe Conrad	8.00	4.00	2.40
23	John David Crow	10.00	5.00	3.00
24	Sonny Randle **RC**	10.00	5.00	3.00
25	Don Gillis	10.00	5.00	3.00
26	Jerry Norton	8.00	4.00	2.40
27	Bill Stacy	8.00	4.00	2.40
28	Leo Sugar	8.00	4.00	2.40
29	Frank Fuller	8.00	4.00	2.40
30	John Unitas	70.00	35.00	21.00
31	Alan Ameche	10.00	5.00	3.00
32	Lenny Moore	20.00	10.00	6.00
33	Raymond Berry	20.00	10.00	6.00
34	Jim Mutscheller	8.00	4.00	2.40
35	Jim Parker	10.00	5.00	3.00
36	Bill Pellington	8.00	4.00	2.40
37	Gino Marchetti	15.00	7.50	4.50
38	Gene Lipscomb	10.00	5.00	3.00
39	Art Donovan	20.00	10.00	6.00
40	Eddie LeBaron	10.00	5.00	3.00
41	Don Meredith **RC**	120.00	60.00	36.00
42	Don McIlhenny	8.00	4.00	2.40
43	L.G. Dupre	8.00	4.00	2.40
44	Fred Dugan	8.00	4.00	2.40
45	Bill Howton	10.00	5.00	3.00
46	Duane Putnam	8.00	4.00	2.40
47	Gene Cronin	8.00	4.00	2.40
48	Jerry Tubbs	8.00	4.00	2.40
49	Clarence Peaks	8.00	4.00	2.40
50	Ted Dean **RC**	8.00	4.00	2.40
51	Tommy McDonald	10.00	5.00	3.00
52	Bill Barnes	8.00	4.00	2.40
53	Pete Retzlaff	10.00	5.00	3.00
54	Bobby Walston	8.00	4.00	2.40
55	Chuck Bednarik	20.00	10.00	6.00
56	Maxie Baughan	8.00	4.00	2.40
57	Bob Pellegrini	8.00	4.00	2.40
58	Jesse Richardson	8.00	4.00	2.40
59	John Brodie **RC**	50.00	25.00	15.00
60	J.D. Smith	10.00	5.00	3.00
61	Ray Norton **RC**	8.00	4.00	2.40
62	Monty Stickles	8.00	4.00	2.40
63	Bob St. Clair	10.00	5.00	3.00
64	Dave Baker	8.00	4.00	2.40
65	Abe Woodson	8.00	4.00	2.40
66	Matt Hazeltine	8.00	4.00	2.40
67	Leo Nomellini	15.00	7.50	4.50
68	Charley Conerly	15.00	7.50	4.50
69	Kyle Rote	10.00	5.00	3.00
70	Jack Stroud	8.00	4.00	2.40
71	Roosevelt Brown	10.00	5.00	3.00
72	Jim Patton	8.00	4.00	2.40
73	Erich Barnes	8.00	4.00	2.40
74	Sam Huff	20.00	10.00	6.00
75	Andy Robustelli	15.00	7.50	4.50
76	Dick Modzelewski	8.00	4.00	2.40
77	Roosevelt Grier	10.00	5.00	3.00
78	Earl Morrall	10.00	5.00	3.00
79	Jim Ninowski	8.00	4.00	2.40
80	Nick Pietrosante **RC**	10.00	5.00	3.00
81	Howard Cassady	10.00	5.00	3.00
82	Jim Gibbons	8.00	4.00	2.40
83	Gail Cogdill **RC**	10.00	5.00	3.00
84	Dick "Night Train" Lane	10.00	5.00	3.00
85	Yale Lary	10.00	5.00	3.00
86	Joe Schmidt	15.00	7.50	4.50
87	Darris McCord	8.00	4.00	2.40
88	Bart Starr	65.00	33.00	20.00
89	Jim Taylor	55.00	28.00	17.00
90	Paul Hornung	70.00	35.00	21.00
91	Tom Moore **RC**	15.00	7.50	4.50
92	Boyd Dowler **RC**	20.00	10.00	6.00
93	Max McGee	10.00	5.00	3.00
94	Forrest Gregg **RC**	15.00	7.50	4.50
95	Jerry Kramer	15.00	7.50	4.50
96	Jim Ringo	15.00	7.50	4.50
97	Bill Forester	10.00	5.00	3.00
98	Frank Ryan	10.00	5.00	3.00
99	Ollie Matson	15.00	7.50	4.50
100	Jon Arnett	10.00	5.00	3.00
101	Dick Bass **RC**	10.00	5.00	3.00
102	Jim Phillips	8.00	4.00	2.40
103	Del Shofner	10.00	5.00	3.00
104	Art Hunter	8.00	4.00	2.40
105	Lindon Crow	8.00	4.00	2.40
106	Les Richter	10.00	5.00	3.00
107	Lou Michaels	8.00	4.00	2.40
108	Ralph Guglielmi	8.00	4.00	2.40
109	Don Bosseler	8.00	4.00	2.40
110	John Olszewski	8.00	4.00	2.40
111	Bill Anderson	8.00	4.00	2.40
112	Joe Walton	8.00	4.00	2.40
113	Jim Schrader	8.00	4.00	2.40
114	Gary Glick	8.00	4.00	2.40
115	Ralph Felton	8.00	4.00	2.40
116	Bob Toneff	8.00	4.00	2.40
117	Bobby Layne	35.00	18.00	11.00
118	John Henry Johnson	10.00	5.00	3.00
119	Tom Tracy	10.00	5.00	3.00
120	Jimmy Orr **RC**	10.00	5.00	3.00
121	John Nisby	8.00	4.00	2.50
122	Dean Derby	8.00	4.00	2.40
123	John Reger	8.00	4.00	2.40
124	George Tarsovic	8.00	4.00	2.40
125	Ernie Stautner	15.00	7.50	4.50
126	George Shaw	8.00	4.00	2.40
127	Hugh McElhenny	15.00	7.50	4.50
128	Dick Haley	8.00	4.00	2.40
129	Dave Middleton	8.00	4.00	2.40
130	Perry Richards	8.00	4.00	2.40
131	Gene Johnson	8.00	4.00	2.40
132	Don Joyce	8.00	4.00	2.40
133	John "Chuck" Green	15.00	7.50	4.50
134	Wray Carlton **RC**	15.00	7.50	4.50
135	Richie Lucas	15.00	7.50	4.50
136	Elbert Dubenion	15.00	7.50	4.50
137	Tom Rychlec (SP)	10.00	5.00	3.00
138	Mark Yoho (SP)	10.00	5.00	3.00
139	Phil Blazer (SP)	10.00	5.00	3.00
140	Dan McGrew (SP)	10.00	7.50	4.50
141	Bill Atkins	10.00	5.00	3.00
142	Archie Matsos **RC**	10.00	5.00	3.00
143	Gene Grabosky	10.00	5.00	3.00
144	Frank Tripucka	15.00	7.50	4.50
145	Al Carmichael (SP)	10.00	5.00	3.00
146	Bob McNamara (SP)	10.00	5.00	3.00
147	Lionel Taylor **RC** (SP)	20.00	10.00	6.00
148	Eldon Danenhauer (SP)	10.00	5.00	3.00
149	Willie Smith	10.00	5.00	3.00
150	Carl Larpenter	10.00	5.00	3.00
151	Ken Adamson	10.00	5.00	3.00
152	Goose Gonsoulin **RC**	15.00	7.50	4.50
153	Joe Young (SP)	10.00	5.00	3.00
154	Gordy Molz (SP)	10.00	5.00	3.00
155	Jack Kemp (SP)	50.00	25.00	15.00
156	Charlie Flowers (SP)	10.00	5.00	3.00
157	Paul Lowe	10.00	5.00	3.00
158	Don Norton	10.00	5.00	3.00
159	Howard Clark	10.00	5.00	3.00
160	Paul Maguire	20.00	10.00	6.00
161	Ernie Wright **RC** (SP)	15.00	7.50	4.50
162	Ron Mix (SP)	20.00	10.00	6.00
163	Fred Cole (SP)	10.00	5.00	3.00
164	Jim Sears (SP)	10.00	5.00	3.00
165	Volney Peters	10.00	5.00	3.00
166	George Blanda	40.00	20.00	12.00
167	Jacky Lee	15.00	7.50	4.50
168	Bob White	10.00	5.00	3.00
169	Doug Cline (SP)	10.00	5.00	3.00
170	Dave Smith (SP)	10.00	5.00	3.00
171	Billy Cannon (SP)	15.00	7.50	4.50
172	Bill Groman (SP)	10.00	5.00	3.00
173	Al Jamison	10.00	5.00	3.00
174	Jim Norton	10.00	5.00	3.00
175	Dennit Morris	10.00	5.00	3.00
176	Don Floyd	10.00	5.00	3.00
177	Butch Songin (SP)	10.00	5.00	3.00
178	Billy Lott (SP)	10.00	5.00	3.00
179	Ron Burton (SP)	15.00	7.50	4.50
180	Jim Colchough (SP)	10.00	5.00	3.00
181	Charley Leo	10.00	5.00	3.00
182	Walt Cudzik	10.00	5.00	3.00

		NM	E	VG
183	Fred Bruney	10.00	5.00	3.00
184	Ross O'Hanley	10.00	5.00	3.00
185	Tony Sardisco (SP)	10.00	5.00	3.00
186	Harry Jacobs (SP)	10.00	5.00	3.00
187	Bob Dee (SP)	10.00	5.00	3.00
188	Tom Flores RC (SP)	35.00	17.50	10.50
189	Jack Larsheid	10.00	5.00	3.00
190	Dick Christy	10.00	5.00	3.00
191	Alan Miller	10.00	5.00	3.00
192	Jim Smith	10.00	5.00	3.00
193	Gerald Burch (SP)	10.00	5.00	3.00
194	Gene Prebola (SP)	10.00	5.00	3.00
195	Alan Goldstein (SP)	10.00	5.00	3.00
196	Don Manoukian (SP)	10.00	5.00	3.00
197	Jim Otto RC	45.00	23.00	14.00
198	Wayne Crow	10.00	5.00	3.00
199	Cotton Davidson RC	15.00	7.50	4.50
200	Randy Duncan RC	15.00	7.50	4.50
201	Jack Spikes (SP)	15.00	7.50	4.50
202	Johnny Robinson RC (SP)	20.00	10.00	6.00
203	Abner Haynes (SP)	20.00	10.00	6.00
204	Chris Burford (SP)	15.00	7.50	4.50
205	Bill Krisher	10.00	5.00	3.00
206	Marvin Terrell	10.00	5.00	3.00
207	Jimmy Harris	10.00	5.00	3.00
208	Mel Branch (SP)	15.00	7.50	4.50
209	Paul Miller (SP)	10.00	5.00	3.00
210	Al Dorow (SP)	10.00	5.00	3.00
211	Dick Jamieson (SP)	10.00	5.00	3.00
212	Pete Hart	10.00	5.00	3.00
213	Bill Shockley	10.00	5.00	3.00
214	Dewey Bohling	10.00	5.00	3.00
215	Don Maynard RC	45.00	23.00	14.00
216	Bob Mischak	10.00	5.00	3.00
217	Mike Hudock (SP)	10.00	5.00	3.00
218	Bob Reifsnyder (SP)	10.00	5.00	3.00
219	Tom Saidock (SP)	10.00	5.00	3.00
220	Sid Youngelman (SP)	25.00	13.00	8.00

1962 Fleer

WAYNE CROW
HALFBACK
OAKLAND RAIDERS

Fleer's third of four early '60s sets included only AFL players this time around. Cards are again grouped by team, alphabetically by city. The only rookie card of note in this set is Gino Cappelletti; second-year cards in this issue are Don Maynard, Tom Flores and Jim Otto.

	NM	E	VG
Complete Set (88):	900.00	450.00	270.00
Common Player:	10.00	5.00	3.00
Minor Stars:	8.00		
Unlisted Stars:	10.00		
Wax Pack (6):	400.00		

1	Billy Lott	25.00	13.00	8.00
2	Ron Burton	15.00	7.50	4.50
3	Gino Cappelletti RC	25.00	13.00	8.00
4	Babe Parilli	35.00	18.00	11.00
5	Jim Colclough	10.00	5.00	3.00
6	Tony Sardisco	10.00	5.00	3.00
7	Walt Cudzik	10.00	5.00	3.00
8	Bob Dee	10.00	5.00	3.00
9	Tommy Addison	10.00	5.00	3.00
10	Harry Jacobs	10.00	5.00	3.00
11	Ross O'Hanley	10.00	5.00	3.00
12	Art Baker	10.00	5.00	3.00
13	John "Chuck" Green	10.00	5.00	3.00
14	Elbert Dubenion	15.00	7.50	4.50
15	Tom Rychlec	10.00	5.00	3.00
16	Billy Shaw RC	65.00	33.00	20.00
17	Ken Rice	10.00	5.00	3.00
18	Bill Atkins	10.00	5.00	3.00
19	Richie Lucas	10.00	5.00	3.00
20	Archie Matsos	10.00	5.00	3.00
21	Lavern Torczon	10.00	5.00	3.00
22	Warren Rabb	10.00	5.00	3.00
23	Jack Spikes	10.00	5.00	3.00
24	Cotton Davidson	10.00	5.00	3.00
25	Abner Haynes RC	20.00	10.00	6.00
26	Jimmy Saxton	10.00	5.00	3.00
27	Chris Burford	10.00	5.00	3.00
28	Bill Miller	10.00	5.00	3.00
29	Sherrill Headrick	10.00	5.00	3.00

30	E.J. Holub RC	10.00	5.00	3.00
31	Jerry Mays RC	15.00	7.50	4.50
32	Mel Branch	10.00	5.00	3.00
33	Paul Rochester	10.00	5.00	3.00
34	Frank Tripucka	15.00	7.50	4.50
35	Gene Mingo	10.00	5.00	3.00
36	Lionel Taylor	15.00	7.50	4.50
37	Ken Adamson	10.00	5.00	3.00
38	Eldon Danenhauer	10.00	5.00	3.00
39	Goose Gonsoulin	15.00	7.50	4.50
40	Gordy Holz	10.00	5.00	3.00
41	Bud McFadin	10.00	5.00	3.00
42	Jim Stinnette	10.00	5.00	3.00
43	Bob Hudson	10.00	5.00	3.00
44	George Herring	10.00	5.00	3.00
45	Charley Tolar RC	10.00	5.00	3.00
46	George Blanda	50.00	25.00	15.00
47	Billy Cannon	20.00	10.00	6.00
48	Charlie Hennigan RC	20.00	10.00	6.00
49	Bill Groman	10.00	5.00	3.00
50	Al Jamison	10.00	5.00	3.00
51	Tony Banfield	10.00	5.00	3.00
52	Jim Norton	10.00	5.00	3.00
53	Dennit Morris	10.00	5.00	3.00
54	Don Floyd	10.00	5.00	3.00
55	Ed Husmann	10.00	5.00	3.00
56	Robert Brooks	10.00	5.00	3.00
57	Al Dorow	10.00	5.00	3.00
58	Dick Christy	10.00	5.00	3.00
59	Don Maynard	45.00	23.00	14.00
60	Art Powell	15.00	7.50	4.50
61	Mike Hudock	10.00	5.00	3.00
62	Bill Mathis	10.00	5.00	3.00
63	Butch Songin	10.00	5.00	3.00
64	Larry Grantham	10.00	5.00	3.00
65	Nick Mumley	10.00	5.00	3.00
66	Tom Saidock	10.00	5.00	3.00
67	Alan Miller	10.00	5.00	3.00
68	Tom Flores	20.00	10.00	6.00
69	Bob Coolbaugh	10.00	5.00	3.00
70	George Fleming	10.00	5.00	3.00
71	Wayne Hawkins RC	10.00	5.00	3.00
72	Jim Otto	30.00	15.00	9.00
73	Wayne Crow	10.00	5.00	3.00
74	Fred Willamson RC	35.00	18.00	12.00
75	Tom Lauderback	10.00	5.00	3.00
76	Volney Peters	10.00	5.00	3.00
77	Charley Powell	10.00	5.00	3.00
78	Don Norton	10.00	5.00	3.00
79	Jack Kemp	75.00	38.00	23.00
80	Paul Lowe	15.00	7.50	4.50
81	Dave Kocourek	10.00	5.00	3.00
82	Ron Mix	25.00	13.00	8.00
83	Ernie Wright	15.00	7.50	4.50
84	Dick Harris	10.00	5.00	3.00
85	Bill Hudson	10.00	5.00	3.00
86	Ernie Ladd RC	25.00	13.00	8.00
87	Earl Faison	10.00	5.00	3.00
88	Ron Nery RC	20.00	10.00	6.00

1963 Fleer

LARRY GARRON
FULLBACK
BOSTON PATRIOTS

After a four-year run, this 89-card set (88 player cards plus an unnumbered checklist) was the company's football farewell. (Fleer printed football "Teams in Action" sets in the '70s and '80s that featured NFL offenses and defenses, but apparently was unable to obtain a contract allowing the production of individual player cards. The 1963 Fleer football set showcases three of the most sought-after and rarest cards of the '60s - the checklist card (almost impossible to find in Mint condition), and cards #6 (Charles Long) and #64 (Bob Dougherty). The latter two cards were short-printed; it's believed both were pulled to make room for the checklist. The set includes AFL players only. Rookies featured in the set are Nick Buoniconti, Cookie Gilchrist, Keith Lincoln, Len Dawson and Lance Alworth. Gino Cappelletti's second-year card is in the set as well. (Key: SP means short-printed).

	NM	E	VG
Complete Set (88):	1,500	750.00	450.00
Common Player:	10.00	5.00	3.00
Minor Stars:	9.00		
Unlisted Stars:	10.00		

	Checklist:	275.00	138.00	83.00
	Wax Pack (5):	450.00		
1	Larry Garron RC	20.00	10.00	6.00
2	Babe Parilli	10.00	5.00	3.00
3	Ron Burton	15.00	7.50	4.50
4	Jim Colclough	10.00	5.00	3.00
5	Gino Cappelletti	15.00	7.50	4.50
6	Charles Long RC (SP)	85.00	43.00	26.00
7	Bill Neighbors RC	10.00	5.00	3.00
8	Dick Felt	10.00	5.00	3.00
9	Tommy Addison	10.00	5.00	3.00
10	Nick Buoniconti RC	115.00	58.00	35.00
11	Larry Eisenhauer	10.00	5.00	3.00
12	Bill Mathis	10.00	5.00	3.00
13	Lee Grosscup RC	10.00	5.00	3.00
14	Dick Christy	10.00	5.00	3.00
15	Don Maynard	40.00	20.00	12.00
16	Alex Kroll RC	10.00	5.00	3.00
17	Bob Mischak	10.00	5.00	3.00
18	Dainard Paulson	10.00	5.00	3.00
19	Lee Riley	10.00	5.00	3.00
20	Larry Grantham	10.00	5.00	3.00
21	Hubert Bobo	10.00	5.00	3.00
22	Nick Mumley	10.00	5.00	3.00
23	Cookie Gilchrist RC	40.00	20.00	12.00
24	Jack Kemp	80.00	40.00	24.00
25	Wray Carlton	10.00	5.00	3.00
26	Elbert Dubenion	10.00	5.00	3.00
27	Ernie Warlick	10.00	5.00	3.00
28	Billy Shaw	15.00	7.50	4.50
29	Ken Rice	10.00	5.00	3.00
30	Booker Edgerson	10.00	5.00	3.00
31	Ray Abbruzzese	10.00	5.00	3.00
32	Mike Stratton	15.00	7.50	4.50
33	Tom Sestak	10.00	5.00	3.00
34	Charlie Tolar	10.00	5.00	3.00
35	Dave Smith	10.00	5.00	3.00
36	George Blanda	50.00	25.00	15.00
37	Billy Cannon	15.00	7.50	4.50
38	Charlie Hennegan	10.00	5.00	3.00
39	Bob Talamini RC	10.00	5.00	3.00
40	Jim Norton	10.00	5.00	3.00
41	Tony Banfield	10.00	5.00	3.00
42	Doug Cline	10.00	5.00	3.00
43	Don Floyd	10.00	5.00	3.00
44	Ed Husmann	10.00	5.00	3.00
45	Curtis McClinton RC	15.00	7.50	4.50
46	Jack Spikes	10.00	5.00	3.00
47	Len Dawson RC	170.00	85.00	51.00
48	Abner Haynes	15.00	7.50	4.50
49	Chris Burford	10.00	5.00	3.00
50	Fred Arbanas RC	15.00	7.50	4.50
51	Johnny Robinson	10.00	5.00	3.00
52	E.J. Holub	10.00	5.00	3.00
53	Sherrill Headrick	10.00	5.00	3.00
54	Mel Branch	10.00	5.00	3.00
55	Jerry Mays	10.00	5.00	3.00
56	Cotton Davidson	10.00	5.00	3.00
57	Clem Daniels RC	15.00	7.50	4.50
58	Bo Roberson	10.00	5.00	3.00
59	Art Powell	15.00	7.50	4.50
60	Bob Coolbaugh	10.00	5.00	3.00
61	Wayne Hawkins	10.00	5.00	3.00
62	Jim Otto	35.00	18.00	11.00
63	Fred Williamson	15.00	7.50	4.50
64	Bob Dougherty (SP)	75.00	36.00	22.00
65	Dalva Allen	10.00	5.00	3.00
66	Chuck McMutry	10.00	5.00	3.00
67	Gerry McDougall	10.00	5.00	3.00
68	Tobin Rote	10.00	5.00	3.50
69	Paul Lowe	15.00	7.50	4.50
70	Keith Lincoln RC	45.00	23.00	14.00
71	Dave Kocourek	10.00	5.00	3.00
72	Lance Alworth RC	200.00	100.00	60.00
73	Ron Mix	25.00	13.00	8.00
74	Charles McNeil RC	10.00	5.00	3.00
75	Emil Karas	10.00	5.00	3.00
76	Ernie Ladd	20.00	10.00	6.00
77	Earl Faison	10.00	5.00	3.00
78	Jim Stinnette	10.00	5.00	3.00
79	Frank Tripucka	15.00	7.50	4.50
80	Don Stone	10.00	5.00	3.00
81	Bob Scarpitto	10.00	5.00	3.00
82	Lionel Taylor	15.00	7.50	4.50
83	Jerry Tarr	10.00	5.00	3.00
84	Eldon Danehauer	10.00	5.00	3.00
85	Goose Gonsoulin	10.00	5.00	3.00
86	Jim Fraser	10.00	5.00	3.00
87	Chuck Gavin	10.00	5.00	3.00
88	Bud McFadin	22.00	11.00	7.00

1970 Fleer Big Signs

Although this 26-card set carries the 1968 year in roman numerals on the back, it was actually issued in 1970. These blank-backed cards are unnumbered and measure 7 3/4" x 11 1/2" with rounded corners. The set was issued in a green box. Card fronts feature generic, faceless color drawings on a white bordered card. There is another version of Big Signs that also includes 1968 on the back in roman numerals, but was issued in a brown box in 1974. The 1974 versions are the same size, but feature different drawings, with the team name in large letters across the bottom, while the 1970 version has the team listed in small letters across the top.

		NM	E	VG
Complete Set (26):		60.00	30.00	18.00
Common Player:		3.00	1.50	.90
1	Atlanta Falcons	3.00	1.50	.90
2	Baltimore Colts	3.00	1.50	.90
3	Buffalo Bills	3.00	1.50	.90
4	Chicago Bears	5.00	2.50	1.50
5	Cincinnati Bengals	3.00	1.50	.90
6	Cleveland Browns	3.00	1.50	.90
7	Dallas Cowboys	5.00	2.50	1.50
8	Denver Broncos	3.00	1.50	.90
9	Detroit Lions	3.00	1.50	.90
10	Green Bay Packers	5.00	2.50	1.50
11	Houston Oilers	3.00	1.50	.90
12	Kansas City Chiefs	3.00	1.50	.90
13	Los Angeles Rams	3.00	1.50	.90
14	Miami Dolphins	5.00	2.50	1.50
15	Minnesota Vikings	3.00	1.50	.90
16	New England Patriots	3.00	1.50	.90
17	New Orleans Saints	3.00	1.50	.90
18	New York Giants	3.00	1.50	.90
19	New York Jets	3.00	1.50	.90
20	Oakland Raiders	5.00	2.50	1.50
21	Philadelphia Eagles	3.00	1.50	.90
22	Pittsburgh Steelers	5.00	2.50	1.50
23	St. Louis Cardinals	3.00	1.50	.90
24	San Diego Chargers	3.00	1.50	.90
25	San Francisco 49ers	5.00	2.50	1.50
26	Washington Redskins	5.00	2.50	1.50

1972 Fleer Quiz

This 28-card set was issued at a rate of one per pack with Fleer cloth team patches. Cards measure 2-1/2" x 4" and feature three questions about players and events, with answers upside down. Each card has the words "Official Football Quiz" across the top, a card number in the lower right hand corner and a blank back.

		NM	E	VG
Complete Set (28):		45.00	34.00	18.00
Common Player:		2.50	2.00	1.00
1	Questions 1-3	2.50	2.00	1.00
2	Questions 4-6	2.50	2.00	1.00
3	Questions 7-9	2.50	2.00	1.00
4	Questions 10-12	2.50	2.00	1.00
5	Questions 13-15	2.50	2.00	1.00
6	Questions 16-18	2.50	2.00	1.00
7	Questions 19-21	2.50	2.00	1.00
8	Questions 22-24	2.50	2.00	1.00
9	Questions 25-27	2.50	2.00	1.00
10	Questions 28-30	2.50	2.00	1.00
11	Questions 31-33	2.50	2.00	1.00
12	Questions 34-36	2.50	2.00	1.00
13	Questions 37-39	2.50	2.00	1.00
14	Questions 40-42	2.50	2.00	1.00
15	Questions 43-45	2.50	2.00	1.00
16	Questions 46-48	2.50	2.00	1.00
17	Questions 49-51	2.50	2.00	1.00
18	Questions 52-54	2.50	2.00	1.00
19	Questions 55-57	2.50	2.00	1.00
20	Questions 58-60	2.50	2.00	1.00
21	Questions 61-63	2.50	2.00	1.00
22	Questions 64-66	2.50	2.00	1.00
23	Questions 67-69	2.50	2.00	1.00
24	Questions 70-72	2.50	2.00	1.00
25	Questions 73-75	2.50	2.00	1.00
26	Questions 76-78	2.50	2.00	1.00
27	Questions 79-81	2.50	2.00	1.00
28	Questions 82-84	2.50	2.00	1.00

1973 Fleer Pro Bowl Scouting Report

The 14-card, blank backed set explains the ideal responsibilities and assignments of each player on an NFL team. These unnumbered cards were found at a rate of one per pack with two cloth football logos from 1972.

		NM	E	VG
Complete Set (14):		35.00	26.00	14.00
Common Player:		3.00	1.50	.90
1	Center	3.00	1.50	.90
2	Cornerback	3.00	1.50	.90
3	Defensive End	3.00	1.50	.90
4	Defensive Tackle	3.00	1.50	.90
5	Guard	3.00	1.50	.90
6	Kicker	3.00	1.50	.90
7	Linebacker	3.00	1.50	.90
8	Offensive Tackle	3.00	1.50	.90
9	Punter	3.00	1.50	.90
10	Quarterback	3.00	1.50	.90
11	Running Back	3.00	1.50	.90
12	Safety	3.00	1.50	.90
13	Tight End	3.00	1.50	.90
14	Wide Receiver	3.00	1.50	.90

1974 Fleer Hall of Fame

These cards were issued one per pack, along with two cloth stickers featuring team logos. Each card front has a black- and-white player action photo, with a set logo and "The Immortal Role" at the bottom of the card. The cards, which are unnumbered, are listed below alphabetically and feature 50 players who have been enshrined in the Pro Football Hall of Fame in Canton, Ohio. The Hall of Fame logo appears on the back of the card, along with biographical information about the player. Each card measures 2-1/2" x 4".

		NM	E	VG
Complete Set (50):		50.00	25.00	15.00
Common Player:		1.00	.50	.30
(1)	Cliff Battles	1.00	.50	.30
(2)	Sammy Baugh	1.50	.70	.45
(3)	Chuck Bednarik	1.00	.50	.30
(4)	Bert Bell	1.00	.50	.30
(5)	Paul Brown	1.00	.50	.30
(6)	Joe Carr	1.00	.50	.30
(7)	Guy Chamberlin	1.00	.50	.30
(8)	Earl "Dutch" Clark	1.00	.50	.30
(9)	Jimmy Conzelman	1.00	.50	.30
(10)	Art Donovan	1.00	.50	.30
(11)	John (Paddy) Driscoll	1.00	.50	.30
(12)	Billy Dudley	1.00	.50	.30
(13)	Dan Fortmann	1.00	.50	.30
(14)	Otto Graham	1.00	.50	.30
(15)	Harold "Red" Grange	2.00	1.00	.60
(16)	George Halas	1.00	.50	.30
(17)	Mel Hein	1.00	.50	.30
(18)	Fats Henry	1.25	.60	.40
(19)	Bill Hewitt	1.00	.50	.30
(20)	Clarke Hinkle	1.25	.60	.40
(21)	Elroy (Crazylegs) Hirsch	1.00	.50	.30
(22)	Robert "Cal" Hubbard	1.00	.50	.30
(23)	Lamar Hunt	1.00	.50	.30
(24)	Don Hutson	1.00	.50	.30
(25)	Earl (Curly) Lambeau	1.25	.60	.40
(26)	Bobby Layne	1.00	.50	.30
(27)	Vince Lombardi	2.00	1.00	.60
(28)	Sid Luckman	1.00	.50	.30
(29)	Gino Marchetti	1.25	.60	.40
(30)	Ollie Matson	1.00	.50	.30
(31)	George McAfee	1.00	.50	.30
(32)	Hugh McElhenny	1.00	.50	.30
(33)	Johnny "Blood" McNally	1.00	.50	.30
(34)	Marion Motley	1.00	.50	.30
(35)	Bronko Nagurski	1.50	.70	.45
(36)	Ernie Nevers	1.00	.50	.30
(37)	Leo Nomellini	1.25	.60	.40
(38)	Steve Owen	1.00	.50	.30
(39)	Joe Perry	1.00	.50	.30
(40)	Pete Pihos	1.25	.60	.40
(41)	Andy Robustelli	1.00	.50	.30
(42)	Ken Strong	1.00	.50	.30
(43)	Jim Thorpe	2.00	1.00	.60
(44)	Y.A. Tittle	1.00	.50	.30
(45)	Charlie Trippi	1.00	.50	.30
(46)	Emlen Tunnell	1.25	.60	.40
(47)	Clyde "Bulldog" Turner	1.00	.50	.30
(48)	Norm Van Brocklin	1.00	.50	.30
(49)	Steve Van Buren	1.00	.50	.30
(50)	Bob Waterfield	1.25	.60	.40

1974 Fleer Big Signs

The 1974 version of Big Signs is generally considered a Series II issue, but is credited to 1968 in roman numerals on the back. The cards measure 7-3/4" x 11-1/2" and have blank backs that are unnumbered. The 1974 set was issued in a brown box, while the fronts contain generic, faceless color drawings. Two 26-card Big Signs sets were produced by Fleer that carry a 1968 copyright on them, but one released in 1970 with this series releasing in 1974. The former version was issued in a green box and contains the team name in small letters across the top, while the 1974 version has the team name in bold letters across the card bottom.

		NM	E	VG
Complete Set (26):		45.00	34.00	18.00
Common Player:		2.50	1.25	.70
1	Atlanta Falcons	2.50	1.25	.70
2	Baltimore Colts	2.50	1.25	.70
3	Buffalo Bills	2.50	1.25	.70
4	Chicago Bears	4.00	2.00	1.25
5	Cincinnati Bengals	2.50	1.25	.70
6	Cleveland Browns	2.50	1.25	.70
7	Dallas Cowboys	4.00	2.00	1.25
8	Denver Broncos	2.50	1.25	.70
9	Detroit Lions	2.50	1.25	.70
10	Green Bay Packers	4.00	2.00	1.25
11	Houston Oilers	2.50	1.25	.70
12	Kansas City Chiefs	2.50	1.25	.70
13	Los Angeles Rams	2.50	1.25	.70
14	Miami Dolphins	4.00	2.00	1.25
15	Minnesota Vikings	2.50	1.25	.70
16	New England Patriots	2.50	1.25	.70
17	New Orleans Saints	2.50	1.25	.70
18	New York Giants	2.50	1.25	.70
19	New York Jets	2.50	1.25	.70
20	Oakland Raiders	4.00	2.00	1.25
21	Philadelphia Eagles	2.50	1.25	.70
22	Pittsburgh Steelers	4.00	2.00	1.25
23	St. Louis Cardinals	2.50	1.25	.70
24	San Diego Chargers	2.50	1.25	.70
25	San Francisco 49ers	4.00	2.00	1.25
26	Washington Redskins	4.00	2.00	1.25

1975 Fleer Hall of Fame

These 84 cards, which feature players who have been inducted into the Football Hall of Fame, can be distinguished from the 1974 cards by the card numbers which appear on the card backs. Fifty of the cards in the set are similar to the 1974 cards, except the fronts have brown borders, not white ones like the 1974 cards have. Each card measures 2-1/2" x 4". They were issued in wax packs along with cloth team logo stickers.

		NM	E	VG
Complete Set (84):		30.00	15.00	9.00
Common Player:		.35	.20	.11
1	Jim Thorpe	1.00	.50	.30
2	Cliff Battles	.35	.20	.11
3	Bronko Nagurski	.75	.40	.25
4	Harold "Red" Grange	1.00	.50	.30
5	Guy Chamberlin	.35	.20	.11
6	Joe Carr	.35	.20	.11
7	George Halas	.50	.25	.15
8	Jimmy Conzelman	.35	.20	.11
9	George McAfee	.35	.20	.11
10	Clarke Hinkle	.35	.20	.11
11	John Driscoll	.35	.20	.11
12	Mel Hein	.35	.20	.11
13	Johnny McNally	.35	.20	.11
14	Earl Clark	.35	.20	.11
15	Steve Owen	.35	.20	.11
16	Bill Hewitt	.35	.20	.11
17	Robert Hubbard	.35	.20	.11
18	Don Hutson	.50	.25	.15
19	Ernie Nevers	.50	.25	.15
20	Dan Fortmann	.35	.20	.11
21	Ken Strong	.35	.20	.11
22	Chuck Bednarik	.50	.25	.15
23	Bert Bell	.35	.20	.11
24	Paul Brown	.50	.25	.15
25	Art Donovan	.50	.25	.15
26	Bill Dudley	.35	.20	.11
27	Otto Graham	1.00	.50	.30
28	Fats Henry	.35	.20	.11
29	Elroy Hirsch	.50	.25	.15
30	Lamar Hunt	.50	.25	.15
31	Earl Lambeau	.75	.40	.25
32	Vince Lombardi	.75	.40	.25
33	Sid Luckman	.75	.40	.25
34	Gino Marchetti	.50	.25	.15
35	Ollie Matson	.50	.25	.15
36	Hugh McElhenny	.50	.25	.15
37	Marion Motley	.50	.25	.15
38	Leo Nomellini	.35	.20	.11
39	Joe Perry	.50	.25	.15
40	Andy Robustelli	.35	.20	.11
41	Pete Pihos	.35	.20	.11

42	Y.A. Tittle	.50	.25	.15
43	Charlie Trippi	.35	.20	.11
44	Emlen Tunnell	.35	.20	.11
45	Clyde Turner	.35	.20	.11
46	Norm Van Brocklin	.50	.25	.15
47	Steve Van Buren	.50	.25	.15
48	Bob Waterfield	.75	.40	.25
49	Bobby Layne	.50	.25	.15
50	Sammy Baugh	1.00	.50	.30
51	Joe Guyon	.35	.20	.11
52	William Roy Lyman	.35	.20	.11
53	George Trafton	.35	.20	.11
54	Albert G. Edwards	.35	.20	.11
55	Ed Healey	.35	.20	.11
56	Mike Michalske	.35	.20	.11
57	Alex Wojciechowicz	.35	.20	.11
58	Dante Lavelli	.35	.20	.11
59	George Connor	.35	.20	.11
60	Wayne Millner	.35	.20	.11
61	Jack Christiansen	.35	.20	.11
62	Roosevelt Brown	.35	.20	.11
63	Joe Stydahar	.35	.20	.11
64	Ernie Stautner	.50	.25	.15
65	Jim Parker	.50	.25	.15
66	Raymond Berry	.50	.25	.15
67	George Preston Marshall	.35	.20	.11
68	Clarence Parker	.50	.25	.15
69	Earle Neale	.35	.20	.11
70	Tim Mara	.35	.20	.11
71	Hugh Ray	.35	.20	.11
72	Tom Fears	.50	.25	.15
73	Arnie Herber	.35	.20	.11
74	Walt Kiesling	.35	.20	.11
75	Frank Kinard	.35	.20	.11
76	Tony Canadeo	.35	.20	.11
77	Bill George	.35	.20	.11
78	Art Rooney	.50	.25	.15
79	Joe Schmidt	.50	.25	.15
80	Dan Reeves	.35	.20	.11
81	Lou Groza	.50	.25	.15
82	Charles W. Bidwill	.35	.20	.11
83	Lenny Moore	.50	.25	.15
84	Dick "Night Train" Lane	.50	.25	.15

1976 Fleer Team Action

Beginning in 1976, and continuing through 1988, Fleer produced a series of "Team Action" cards showing football action shots but not identifying the individual players. All cards measure the standard 2-1/2" x 3-1/2". Because the sets did not contain individual player cards they have held little interest for collectors, and very few cards have any premium value. Generally, only the cards priced above common price are those with recognizable superstars prominently displayed in the action scene. The various years of issue can be determined by the border color on the front and the copyright date on the back. Sets from 1976 through 1984 and 1987 and 1988 feature an odd-numbered offensive card and an even-numbered defensive card for each NFL team. The backs list statistics from the previous year. In 1985 and 1986 each team had a third "In Action" card added - the backs of which show team schedules for the upcoming season. All sets (except 1988) are essentially numbered to correspond to team-city alphabetical order. The 1976 set is actually comprised of 66 stickercards and is quite scarce. For each subsequent year (up through 1980) the number of cards in the set was increased by one, adding a card for the most recent Super Bowl. Beginning in 1981, all sets were enlarged to 88 cards. Fleer's initial set in 1976 has two cards per team, plus 10 Super Bowl cards. The cards were issued in four-card wax packs, without inserts. It includes a Jack Lambert "rookie", a Joe Namath (not found in Topps) and the only team action card of O.J. Simpson.

		NM	E	VG
Complete Set (66):		375.00	185.00	110.00
Common Card:		5.00	2.50	1.50
Common SB Card:		7.50	3.75	2.25
1	**Baltimore Colts** (High Scorers)	5.25	2.75	1.50
2	**Baltimore Colts** (Effective Tackle)	5.00	2.50	1.50
3	**Buffalo Bills** (Perfect Blocking)	5.00	2.50	1.50
4	**Buffalo Bills** (The Sack)	5.00	2.50	1.50
5	**Cincinnati Bengals** (Being Hit Behind The Runner)	5.00	2.50	1.50
6	**Cincinnati Bengals** (Franco Harris) (A Little Help)	9.00	4.50	2.75
7	**Cleveland Browns** (Blocking Tight End)	5.00	2.50	1.50
8	**Cleveland Browns** (Stopping the Double Threat)	5.00	2.50	1.50
9	**Denver Broncos** (The Swing Pass)	5.00	2.50	1.50

10	**Denver Broncos** (The Gang Tackle)	5.00	2.50	1.50
11	**Houston Oilers** (Dan Pastorini) (Short Zone Flooded)	6.00	3.00	1.75
12	**Houston Oilers** (Franco Harris) (Run Stoppers)	9.00	4.50	2.75
13	**Kansas City Chiefs** (Off On the Ball)	5.00	2.50	1.50
14	**Kansas City Chiefs** (Forcing the Scramble)	5.00	2.50	1.50
15	**Miami Dolphins** (Bob Griese) (Pass Protection)	10.00	5.00	3.00
16	**Miami Dolphins** (Natural Turf)	6.00	3.00	1.75
17	**New England Patriots** (Quicker Than the Eye)	5.00	2.50	1.50
18	**New England Patriots** (The Rugby Touch)	5.00	2.50	1.50
19	New York Jets (John Riggins, Joe Namath) (They Run, Too)	16.50	8.25	5.00
20	New York Jets (O.J. Simpson) (The Buck Stops Here)	15.00	7.50	4.50
21	**Oakland Raiders** (A Strong Offense)	6.00	3.00	1.75
22	**Oakland Raiders** (High and Low)	6.00	3.00	1.75
23	Pittsburgh Steelers (Terry Bradshaw, Franco Harris, Rocky Bleier) (The Pitch-Out)	14.00	7.00	4.25
24	Pittsburgh Steelers (Jack Lambert) (The Takeaway)	15.00	7.50	4.50
25	**San Diego Chargers** (Run to Daylight)	5.00	2.50	1.50
26	**San Diego Chargers** (The Swarm)	5.00	2.50	1.50
27	**Tampa Bay Buccaneers** (Stadium)	5.00	2.50	1.50
28	**Tampa Bay Bucaneers** (Buccaneers Uniform)	5.00	2.50	1.50
29	**Atlanta Falcons** (A Key Block)	5.00	2.50	1.50
30	Atlanta Falcons (Robert Newhouse) (Breakthrough)	5.00	2.50	1.50
31	**Chicago Bears** (An Inside Look)	5.00	2.50	1.50
32	**Chicago Bears** (Defensive Emphasis)	5.00	2.50	1.50
33	Dallas Cowboys (Robert Newhouse) (Eight-Yard Burst)	6.00	3.00	1.75
34	**Dallas Cowboys** (The Big Return)	6.00	3.00	1.75
35	**Detroit Lions** (Power Sweep)	5.00	2.50	1.50
36	**Detroit Lions** (A Tough Defense)	5.00	2.50	1.50
37	**Green Bay Packers** (Tearaway Gain)	5.00	2.50	1.50
38	**Green Bay Packers** (Good Support)	5.00	2.50	1.50
39	**Los Angeles Rams**	5.00	2.50	1.50
40	**Los Angeles Rams** (Low-Point Defense)	5.00	2.50	1.50
41	Minnesota Vikings (Fran Tarkenton, Chuck Foreman) (The Running Guards)	10.00	5.00	3.00
42	Minnesota Vikings (A Stingy Defense)	5.00	2.50	1.50
43	**New York Giants** (The Quick Opener)	5.00	2.50	1.50
44	**New York Giants** (Defending a Tradition)	5.00	2.50	1.50
45	New Orleans Saints (Archie Manning) (Head for the Hole)	6.00	3.00	1.75
46	**New Orleans Saints** (The Contain Man)	5.00	2.50	1.50
47	**Philadelphia Eagles** (Line Signals)	5.00	2.50	1.50
48	**Philadelphia Eagles** (Don't Take Sides)	5.00	2.50	1.50
49	**San Francisco 49ers** (The Clues)	5.00	2.50	1.50
50	**San Francisco 49ers** (Goal-Line Stand)	5.00	2.50	1.50
51	St. Louis Cardinals (Jim Hart) (Nonskid Handoff)	6.00	3.00	1.75
52	**St. Louis Cardinals** (Strong Pursuit)	5.00	2.50	1.50

53	**Seattle Seahawks** (Stadium)	5.25	2.75	1.50
54	**Seattle Seahawks** (Uniform)	5.25	2.75	1.50
55	**Washington Redskins** (Billy Kilmer) (A Fancy Passing)	6.00	3.00	1.75
56	**Washington Redskins** (Chris Hanburger) (Let's Go Defense)	5.00	2.50	1.50
57	Super Bowl I (Jim Taylor) (Green Bay vs. Kansas City)	7.50	3.75	2.25
58	Super Bowl II (Ben Davidson) (Green Bay vs. Oakland)	7.50	3.75	2.25
59	Super Bowl III (New York vs. Baltimore)	7.50	3.75	2.25
60	Super Bowl IV (Kansas City vs. Minnesota)	7.50	3.75	2.25
61	Super Bowl V (Baltimore vs. Dallas)	7.50	3.75	2.25
62	Super Bowl VI (Roger Staubach, Walt Garrison) (Dallas vs. Miami)	16.00	8.00	4.75
63	Super Bowl VII (Larry Csonka) (Miami vs. Washington)	9.50	4.75	2.87
64	Super Bowl VIII (Larry Csonka) (Miami vs. Minnesota)	9.50	4.75	2.75
65	Super Bowl IX (Pittsburgh vs. Minnesota)	7.50	3.75	2.25
66	Super Bowl X (Terry Bradshaw, Franco Harris) (Pittsburgh vs. Dallas)	19.00	9.50	5.75

1977 Fleer Team Action

The 1977 set Fleer set has white borders and is complete at 67 cards, two for each NFL team and one for each Super Bowl. Odd-numbered cards picture offensive teams; defensive squads are on even-numbered cards. The set features Joe Namath (not found in 1977 Topps) and two different first-year Fleer Walter Payton cards. The packs had four cards and four team logo stickers.

		NM	E	VG
Complete Set (67):		80.00	40.00	24.00
Common Card:		1.00	.50	.30
Common SB Card:		1.50	.70	.45
1	Baltimore Colts (Bert Jones) (The Easy Chair)	1.75	.90	.50
2	**Baltimore Colts** (A Handy Solution)	1.00	.50	.30
3	**Buffalo Bills** (Blocking Tight End)	1.00	.50	.30
4	**Buffalo Bills** (Search and Destroy)	1.00	.50	.30
5	Cincinnati Bengals (Ken Anderson) (Cutting on a Rug)	1.50	.70	.45
6	**Cincinnati Bengals** (Strength in the Middle)	1.00	.50	.30
7	Cleveland Browns (Brian Sipe) (Snap, Drop, Set)	1.25	.60	.40
8	**Cleveland Browns** (High and Low)	1.00	.50	.30
9	**Denver Broncos** (Green Light)	1.25	.60	.40
10	**Denver Broncos** (Help From Behind)	1.25	.60	.40
11	**Houston Oilers** (Room to Move)	1.00	.50	.30
12	**Houston Oilers** (For The Defense)	1.00	.50	.30
13	**Kansas City Chiefs** (Chance to Motor)	1.00	.50	.30
14	**Kansas City Chiefs** (From the Ground Up)	1.00	.50	.30
15	**Miami Dolphins** (Eye of the Storm)	1.25	.60	.40

16	**Miami Dolphins** (When Man Takes Flight)	1.25	.60	.40
17	**New England Patriots** (Turning the Corner)	1.00	.50	.30
18	**New England Patriots** (A Matter of Inches)	1.00	.50	.30
19	New York Jets (Joe Namath) (Keeping Him Clean)	7.25	3.75	2.25
20	New York Jets (Plugging the Leaks)	1.00	.50	.30
21	**Oakland Raiders** (On Solid Ground)	1.25	.60	.40
22	**Oakland Raiders** (3-4 and Shut the Door)	1.25	.60	.40
23	Pittsburgh Steelers (Rocky Bleier) (Daylight Saving Time)	1.25	.60	.40
24	Pittsburgh Steelers (A Controlled Swarm)	1.25	.60	.40
25	San Diego Chargers (Dan Fouts) (Youth on the Move)	3.75	2.00	1.25
26	**San Diego Chargers** (A Rude Housewarming)	1.00	.50	.30
27	Seattle Seahawks (Jim Zorn) (Play Action Pass)	2.00	1.00	.60
28	**Seattle Seahawks** (Birds of Prey)	1.25	.60	.40
29	**Atlanta Falcons** (Ad-Libbing on Defense)	1.00	.50	.30
30	**Atlanta Falcons** (A Futile Chase)	1.00	.50	.30
31	Chicago Bears (Walter Payton) (Follow Me)	6.75	3.50	2.00
32	**Chicago Bears** (A Nose for the Ball)	1.00	.50	.30
33	**Dallas Cowboys** (The Plunge)	1.25	.60	.40
34	Dallas Cowboys (Ed "Too Tall" Jones) (Unassisted Sack)	3.00	1.50	.90
35	Detroit Lions (Motor City Might)	1.00	.50	.30
36	**Detroit Lions** (Block Party)	1.00	.50	.30
37	**Green Bay Packers** (Another Era)	1.00	.50	.30
38	Green Bay Packers (Walter Payton) (Face-to-Face)	6.50	3.25	2.00
39	Los Angeles Rams (Personal Escort)	1.00	.50	.30
40	Los Angeles Rams (A Closed Case)	1.00	.50	.30
41	**Minnesota Vikings** (Nothing Fancy)	1.00	.50	.30
42	**Minnesota Vikings** (Lending a Hand)	1.00	.50	.30
43	**New Orleans Saints** (Ample Protection)	1.00	.50	.30
44	**New Orleans Saints** (Well-Timed Contact)	1.00	.50	.30
45	**New York Giants** (Quick Pitch)	1.00	.50	.30
46	**New York Giants** (In a Pinch)	1.00	.50	.30
47	**Philadelphia Eagles** (When to Fly)	1.00	.50	.30
48	**Philadelphia Eagles** (Swooping Defense)	1.00	.50	.30
49	St. Louis Cardinals (Jim Hart) (Speed Outside)	1.25	.60	.40
50	**St. Louis Cardinals** (The Circle Tightens)	1.00	.50	.30
51	San Francisco 49ers (Gene Washington) (Sideline Route)	1.25	.60	.40
52	San Francisco 49ers (The Gold Rush)	1.00	.50	.30
53	**Tampa Bay Buccaneers** (A Rare Occasion)	1.00	.50	.30
54	**Tampa Bay Buccaneers** (Expansion Blues)	1.00	.50	.30
55	Washington Redskins (Joe Theismann) (Splitting the Seam)	2.75	1.50	.80
56	**Washington Redskins** (The Hands of Time)	1.00	.50	.30
57	**Super Bowl I** (Green Bay vs. Kansas City)	1.50	.70	.45
58	**Super Bowl II** (Green Bay vs. Oakland)	1.50	.70	.45
59	Super Bowl III (Tom Matte) (New York vs. Baltimore)	1.50	.70	.45
60	**Super Bowl IV** (Kansas City vs. Minnesota)	1.50	.70	.45

61	**Super Bowl V** (Baltimore vs. Dallas)	1.50	.70	.45
62	Super Bowl VI (Walt Garrison, Roger Staubach) (Dallas vs. Miami)	4.25	2.25	1.25
63	Super Bowl VII (Larry Csonka) (Miami vs. Washington)	2.25	1.25	.70
64	Super Bowl VIII (Larry Csonka) (Miami vs. Minnesota)	2.25	1.25	.70
65	**Super Bowl IX** (Pittsburgh vs. Minnesota)	1.50	.70	.45
66	Super Bowl X (Terry Bradshaw, Franco Harris) (Pittsburgh vs. Dallas)	3.75	2.00	1.25
67	Super Bowl XI (Ken Stabler) (Oakland vs. Minnesota)	3.75	2.00	1.25

1978 Fleer Team Action

The 1978 Fleer set contains 68 cards, two for each team and for each Super Bowl. The borders are yellow. Fleer continued with its odd-for-offense and even-for-defense numbering scheme. The set is highlighted by a Tony Dorsett "rookie" card. Seven cards and four team logo stickers were in each pack.

		NM	E	VG
	Complete Set (68):	50.00	25.00	15.00
	Common Card:	.55	.30	.15
	Common SB Card:	.70	.35	.20
1	**Atlanta Falcons** (Sticking to Basics)	.60	.30	.20
2	**Atlanta Falcons** (In Pursuit)	.55	.30	.15
3	**New England Colts** (Foward Plunge)	.55	.30	.15
4	**New England Colts** (Stacking It Up)	.55	.30	.15
5	**Buffalo Bills** (Daylight Breakers)	.55	.30	.15
6	**Buffalo Bills** (Swarming Defense)	.55	.30	.15
7	Chicago Bears (Walter Payton) (Up the Middle)	6.75	3.50	2.00
8	**Chicago Bears** (Rejuvenated Defense)	.55	.30	.15
9	Cincinnati Bengals (Ken Anderson) (Poise and Execution)	1.25	.60	.40
10	**Cincinnati Bengals** (Down-to-Earth)	.55	.30	.15
11	Cleveland Browns (Greg Pruitt) (Breakaway)	.80	.40	.25
12	Cleveland Browns (Ken Anderson) (Red Dogs)	1.00	.50	.30
13	Dallas Cowboys (Dorsett) (Up and Over)	7.50	3.75	2.25
14	**Dallas Cowboys** (Doomsday II)	.75	.40	.25
15	**Denver Broncos** (Mile-Hile Offense)	.75	.40	.25
16	Denver Broncos (Walter Payton) (Orange Crush)	5.25	2.75	1.50
17	**Detroit Lions** (End-Around)	.55	.30	.15
18	**Detroit Lions** (Special Teams)	.55	.30	.15
19	**Green Bay Packers** (Running Strong)	.55	.30	.15
20	**Green Bay Packers** (Tearin' em Down)	.55	.30	.15
21	**Houston Oilers** (Goal-Line Drive)	.55	.30	.15
22	**Houston Oilers** (Interception)	.55	.30	.15
23	Kansas City Chiefs (Ed Podolak) (Running Wide)	.60	.30	.20

24	**Kansas City Chiefs** (Armed Defense)	.55	.30	.15
25	**Los Angeles Rams** (Rushing Power)	.55	.30	.15
26	**Los Angeles Rams** (Backing the Line)	.55	.30	.15
27	Miami Dolphins (Bob Griese) (Protective Pocket)	2.50	1.25	.70
28	Miami Dolphins (Life in the Pit)	.75	.40	.25
29	Minnesota Vikings (Chuck Foreman) (Storm Breakers)	.80	.40	.25
30	Minnesota Vikings (Blocking the Kick)	.55	.30	.15
31	**New England Patriots** (Clearing the Way)	.55	.30	.15
32	**New England Patriots** (One-on-One)	.55	.30	.15
33	**New Orleans Saints** (Extra Yardage)	.55	.30	.15
34	**New Orleans Saints** (Drag-Down Defense)	.55	.30	.15
35	**New York Giants** (Ready, Aim, Fire)	.55	.30	.15
36	**New York Giants** (Meeting of Minds)	.55	.30	.15
37	**New York Jets** (Take-Off)	.55	.30	.15
38	**New York Jets** (Ambush)	.55	.30	.15
39	**Oakland Raiders** (Power 31 Left)	.75	.40	.25
40	**Oakland Raiders** (Welcoming Committee)	.75	.40	.25
41	**Philadelphia Eagles** (Taking Flight)	.55	.30	.15
42	**Philadelphia Eagles** (Soaring High)	.55	.30	.15
43	**Pittsburgh Steelers** (Ironclad Offense)	.75	.40	.25
44	Pittsburgh Steelers (Jack Lambert) (Curtain Closes)	2.00	1.00	.60
45	**St. Louis Cardinals** (A Good Bet)	.55	.30	.15
46	**St. Louis Cardinals** (Gang Tackle)	.55	.30	.15
47	**San Diego Chargers** (Circus Catch)	.55	.30	.15
48	**San Diego Chargers** (Charge)	.55	.30	.15
49	**San Francisco 49ers** (Follow the Block)	.55	.30	.15
50	**San Francisco 49ers** (Goal-Line Stand)	.55	.30	.15
51	**Seattle Seahawks** (Finding Daylight)	.60	.30	.20
52	**Seattle Seahawks** (Rushing the Pass)	.60	.30	.20
53	**Tampa Bay Buccaneers** (Play Action)	.55	.30	.15
54	**Tampa Bay Buccaneers** (Youth on the Move)	.55	.30	.15
55	**Washington Redskins** (Renegade Runners)	.55	.30	.15
56	**Washington Redskins** (Dual Action)	.55	.30	.15
57	Super Bowl I (Bart Starr) (Green Bay vs. Kansas City)	2.25	1.25	.70
58	**Super Bowl II** (Green Bay vs. Oakland)	.70	.35	.20
59	**Super Bowl III** (New York vs. Baltimore)	.70	.35	.20
60	**Super Bowl IV** (Kansas City vs. Minnesota)	.70	.35	.20
61	**Super Bowl V** (Baltimore vs. Dallas)	.70	.35	.20
62	**Super Bowl VI** (Dallas vs. Miami)	.70	.35	.20
63	**Super Bowl VII** (Miami vs. Washington)	.70	.35	.20
64	Super Bowl VIII (Larry Csonka) (Miami vs. Minnesota)	1.75	.90	.50
65	Super Bowl IX (Terry Bradshaw, Franco Harris) (Pittsburgh vs. Minnesota)	3.00	1.50	.90
66	**Super Bowl X** (Pittsburgh vs. Dallas)	.70	.35	.20
67	Super Bowl XI (Ken Stabler) (Oakland vs. Minnesota)	2.00	1.00	.60
68	**Super Bowl XII** (Roger Staubach, Tony Dorsett) (Dallas vs. Denver)	5.75	3.00	1.75

1979 Fleer Team Action

SUPER BOWL IX
PITTSBURGH (AFC) 16, MINNESOTA (NFC) 6

The 1979 white-bordered set contains 69 cards, two for each team plus one for each Super Bowl. The cards are numbered to correspond to team-city alphabetical order, followed by a chronological series of all 13 Super Bowls. An odd-offensive and even-defensive numbering format is used again. Earl Campbell's rookie card is the set's most significant. Packs were distributed with seven cards and three logo stickers.

		NM	E	VG
	Complete Set (69):	40.00	20.00	12.00
	Common Card:	.50	.25	.15
	Common SB Card:	.60	.30	.20
1	**Atlanta Falcons** (What's Up Front Counts)	.80	.40	.25
2	**Atlanta Falcons** (Following the Bouncing Ball)	.50	.25	.15
3	**Baltimore Colts** (Big Enough to Drive a Truck Through)	.50	.25	.15
4	**Baltimore Colts** (When the Defense Becomes the Offense)	.50	.25	.15
5	**Buffalo Bills** (Full Steam Ahead)	.50	.25	.15
6	**Buffalo Bills** (Three's a Crowd)	.50	.25	.15
7	**Chicago Bears** (Moving Out as One)	.50	.25	.15
8	**Chicago Bears** (Stack' Em Up)	.50	.25	.15
9	**Cincinnati Bengals** (Out in the Open Field)	.50	.25	.15
10	**Cincinnati Bengals** (Sandwiched)	.50	.25	.15
11	**Cleveland Browns** (Protective Pocket)	.50	.25	.15
12	**Cleveland Browns** (Shake Rattle and Roll)	.50	.25	.15
13	Dallas Cowboys (Tony Dorsett) (Paving the Way)	3.75	2.00	1.25
14	**Dallas Cowboys** (The Right Place at the Right Time)	.65	.35	.20
15	**Denver Broncos** (A Stable of Runners)	.65	.35	.20
16	**Denver Broncos** (Orange Crush)	.65	.35	.20
17	**Detroit Lions** (Through the Line)	.50	.25	.15
18	**Detroit Lions** (Tracked Down)	.50	.25	.15
19	**Green Bay Packers** (Power Play)	.50	.25	.15
20	**Green Bay Packers** (Four-To-One Odds)	.50	.25	.15
21	Houston Oilers (Earl Campbell) (Offensive Gusher)	7.00	3.50	2.00
22	**Houston Oilers** (Gotcha)	.50	.25	.15
23	**Kansas Chiefs** (Get Wings)	.50	.25	.15
24	**Kansas City Chiefs** (Ambushed)	.50	.25	.15
25	**Los Angeles Rams** (Men in the Middle)	.50	.25	.15
26	**Los Angeles Rams** (Nowhere To Go But Down)	.50	.25	.15
27	**Miami Dolphins** (Escort Service)	.65	.35	.20
28	**Miami Dolphins** (All For One)	.65	.35	.20
29	**Minnesota Vikings** (Up and Over)	.50	.25	.15
30	**Minnesota Vikings** (The Purple Gang)	.50	.25	.15
31	**New England Patriots** (Prepare For Takeoff)	.50	.25	.15
32	**New England Patriots** (Dept. of Defense)	.50	.25	.15
33	New Orleans Saints (Archie Manning) (Bombs Away)	.85	.45	.25
34	**New Orleans Saints** (Duel in the Dome)	.50	.25	.15
35	**New York Giants** (Battle of the Line of Scrimmage)	.50	.25	.15
36	**New York Giants** (Piled Up)	.50	.25	.15
37	**New York Jets** (Hitting the Hole)	.50	.25	.15
38	**New York Jets** (Making Sure)	.50	.25	.15
39	Oakland Raiders (Ken Stabler) (Left-Handed Strength)	2.00	1.00	.60
40	**Oakland Raiders** (Black Sunday)	.85	.45	.25
41	**Philadelphia Eagles** (Ready Aim Fire)	.50	.25	.15
42	**Philadelphia Eagles** (Closing In)	.50	.25	.15
43	**Pittsburgh Steelers** (Anchor Man)	.65	.35	.20
44	**Pittsburgh Steelers** (The Steel Curtain)	.85	.45	.25
45	St. Louis Cardinals (Jim Hart) (High Altitude Bomber)	.85	.45	.25
46	**St. Louis Cardinals** (Three On One)	.50	.25	.15
47	**San Diego Chargers** (Charge)	.50	.25	.15
48	**San Diego Chargers** (Special Teams Shot)	.50	.25	.15
49	**San Francisco 49ers** (In For the Score)	.50	.25	.15
50	**San Francisco 49ers** (Nothing But Red Shirts)	.50	.25	.15
51	**Seattle Seahawks** (North-South Runner)	.65	.35	.20
52	**Seattle Seahawks** (The Sting)	.65	.35	.20
53	**Tampa Bay Buccaneers** (Hitting Paydirt)	.50	.25	.15
54	**Tmpa Bay Buccaneers** (Making' Em Pay the Price)	.50	.25	.15
55	**Washington Redskins** (On the Warpath)	.50	.25	.15
56	**Washington Redskins** (Drawing a Crowd)	.50	.25	.15
57	Super Bowl I (Jim Taylor) (Green Bay vs. Kansas City)	.85	.45	.25
58	Super Bowl II (Bart Starr) (Green Bay vs. Oakland)	2.00	1.00	.60
59	**Super Bowl III** (New York vs. Baltimore)	.65	.35	.20
60	**Super Bowl IV** (Kansas City vs. Minnesota)	.65	.35	.20
61	**Super Bowl V** (Baltimore vs. Dallas)	.65	.35	.20
62	Super Bowl VI (Bob Griese, Bob Lilly) (Dallas vs. Miami)	2.00	1.00	.60
63	**Super Bowl VII** (Miami vs. Washington)	.65	.35	.20
64	Super Bowl VIII (Bob Griese, Larry Csonka) (Miami vs. Minnesota)	2.00	1.00	.60
65	Super Bowl IX (Terry Bradshaw, Franco Harris) (Pittsburgh vs. Minnesota)	3.00	1.50	.90
66	**Super Bowl X** (Pittsburgh vs. Dallas)	.65	.35	.20
67	**Super Bowl XI** (Oakland vs. Minnesota)	.65	.35	.20
68	**Super Bowl XII** (Dallas vs. Denver)	.65	.35	.20
69	**Super Bowl XIII** (Pittsburgh vs Dallas)	1.25	.60	.40

1980 Fleer Team Action

SAN FRANCISCO 49ers
FINDING A NUGGET

The 1980 Fleer set has white borders and is complete at 70 cards, two for each NFL team and one for each Super Bowl. The cards are numbered to correspond to team-city alphabetical order. Odds are offensive cards, evens are defensive plays. The last 14 picture Super Bowl action. A key card in the set is the Phil Simms "rookie" card. Seven cards and three logo stickers were in each pack.

	Complete Set (70):	38.00	19.25	11.50
	Common Card:	.40	.20	.12
	Common SB Card:	.25	.15	
1	**Atlanta Falcons** (Getting the Extra Yards)	.70	.35	.20
2	**Atlanta Falcons** (Falcons Get Their Prey)	.40	.20	.12
3	**Baltimore Colts** (Looking for Daylight)	.25	.14	
4	**Baltimore Colts** (Ready If Needed)	.40	.20	.12
5	**Buffalo Bills** (You Block For Me, I'll Block For You)	.40	.20	.12
6	**Buffalo Bills** (Stand 'Em Up and Push 'Em Back)	.40	.20	.12
7	**Chicago Bears** (Walter Payton) (Coming Through)	4.00	3.00	1.50
8	**Chicago Bears** (Four On One)	.40	.20	.12
9	**Cincinnati Bengals** (Power Running)	.20	.12	
10	**Cincinnati Bengals** (Out Of Running Room)	.40	.20	.12
11	**Cleveland Browns** (Ozzie Newsome) (End Around)	2.00	1.50	.80
12	**Cleveland Browns** (Rubber Band Defense)	.40	.20	.12
13	**Dallas Cowboys** (Tony Dorsett) (Point of Attack)	3.00	2.25	1.25
14	**Dallas Cowboys** (Bob Breunig) (Man in the Middle)	.60	.30	.20
15	**Denver Broncos** (Strong and Steady)	.45	.25	.14
16	**Denver Broncos** (Orange Power)	.45	.25	.14
17	**Detroit Lions** (On the March)	.40	.20	.12
18	**Detroit Lions** (The Silver Rush)	.40	.20	.12
19	**Green Bay Packers** (Getting Underway)	.40	.20	.12
20	**Green Bay Packers** (The Best Offense is a Good Defense)	.40	.20	.12
21	**Houston Oilers** (Airborne)	.40	.20	.12
22	**Houston Oilers** (Search and Destroy)	.40	.20	.12
23	**Kansas City Chiefs** (Blazing the Trail)	.40	.20	.12
24	**Kansas City Chiefs** (Making Sure)	.40	.20	.12
25	**Los Angeles Rams** (One Good Turn Deserves Another)	.40	.20	.12
26	**Los Angeles Rams** (Shedding the Block)	.40	.20	.12
27	**Miami Dolphins** (Sweeping the Flanks)	.50	.25	.15
28	**Miami Dolphins** (Keep 'Em Busy)	.50	.25	.15
29	**Minnesota Vikings** (One Man To Beat)	.40	.20	.12
30	**Minnesota Vikings** (Purple People Eaters II)	.40	.20	.12
31	**New England Patriots** (Hitting the Hole)	.40	.20	.12
32	**New England Patriots** (Getting to the Ball)	.40	.20	.12
33	**New Orleans Saints** (Splitting the Defenders)	.40	.20	.12
34	**New Orleans Saints** (Joe Theismann) (Don't Let Him Get Outside)	1.00	.70	.40
35	**New York Giants** (Phil Simms) (Audible)	4.00	2.00	1.25
36	**New York Giants** (Wrong Side Up)	.40	.20	.12
37	**New York Jets** (Make Him Miss)	.40	.20	.12

		NM/M	NM	E
38	**New York Jets** (Mark Gastineau) (The Only Way To Play)	.45	.25	.14
39	**Oakland Raiders** (Pulling Out All the Stops)	.60	.30	.20
40	**Oakland Raiders** (Right On)	.60	.30	.20
41	**Philadelphia Eagles** (Not Pretty, But Still Points)	.40	.20	.12
42	**Philadelphia Eagles** (Applying the Clamps)	.40	.20	.12
43	**Pittsburgh Steelers** (Franco Harris) (All Systems Go)	1.75	1.25	.70
44	**Pittsburgh Steelers** (Still the Steal Curtain)	.70	.35	.20
45	**St. Louis Cardinals** (Ottis Anderson) (On the Move)	2.00	1.50	.80
46	**St. Louis Cardinals** (Long Gone)	.40	.20	.12
47	**San Diego Chargers** (Short-Range Success)	.40	.20	.12
48	**San Diego Chargers** (Pursuit)	.40	.20	.12
49	**San Francisco 49ers** (Getting Field Position)	.40	.20	.12
50	**San Francisco 49ers** (Finding a Nugget)	.40	.20	.12
51	**Seattle Seahawks** (They'll Try Anything Once)	.45	.25	.14
52	**Seattle Seahawks** (Paying the Price)	.45	.25	.14
53	**Tampa Bay Buccaneers** (Coming of Age)	.40	.20	.12
54	**Tampa Bay Buccaneers** (Walter Payton) (3-4 Shut the Door)	3.00	2.25	1.25
55	**Washington Redskins** (Wide Open)	.40	.20	.12
56	**Washington Redskins** (Rude Reception)	.40	.20	.12
57	**Super Bowl I** (Green Bay vs. Kansas City)	.50	.25	.15
58	**Super Bowl II** (Bart Starr) (Green Bay vs. Oakland)	1.75	1.25	.70
59	**Super Bowl III** (Joe Namath) (New York vs. Baltimore)	3.75	2.00	1.25
60	**Super Bowl IV** (Kansas City vs. Minnesota)	.50	.25	.15
61	**Super Bowl V** (Baltimore vs. Dallas)	.50	.25	.15
62	**Super Bowl VI** (Roger Staubach) (Dallas vs. Miami)	3.00	2.25	1.25
63	**Super Bowl VII** (Miami vs. Washington)	.50	.25	.15
64	**Super Bowl VIII** (Miami vs. Minnesota)	.50	.25	.15
65	**Super Bowl IX** (Terry Bradshaw, Rocky Bleier) (Pittsburgh vs. Minnesota)	1.75	1.25	.70
66	**Super Bowl X** (Jack Lambert) (Pittsburgh vs. Dallas)	.70	.35	.20
67	**Super Bowl XI** (Chuck Foreman) (Oakland vs. Minnesota)	.60	.30	.20
68	**Super Bowl XII** (Dallas vs. Denver)	.50	.25	.15
69	**Super Bowl XIII** (Terry Bradshaw) (Pittsburgh vs. Dallas)	2.00	1.50	.80
70	**Super Bowl XIV** (Franco Harris) (Pittsburgh vs. Los Angeles)	2.00	1.50	.80

1981 Fleer Team Action

DALLAS COWBOYS   BIG "O" IN BIG "D"

The 1981 Fleer football set is complete at 88 cards, including two cards for each team, one for each Super Bowl, plus a series of extra cards at the end to round out the set. The front borders are white, while the backs are designed around a red, white and blue color scheme. Once again, Fleer used its alphabetical, offense/defense numbering scheme. Packs were marketed with eight cards and three logo stickers.

		NM/M	NM	E
	Complete Set (88):	26.50	20.00	10.50
	Common Card:	.30	.25	.12
	Common SB Card:	.35	.25	.14
1	**Atlanta Falcons** (Out In the Open)	.60	.45	.25

		NM/M	NM	E
2	**Atlanta Falcons** (Grits Blitz)	.30	.25	.12
3	**Baltimore Colts** (Sprung Through the Line)	.30	.25	.12
4	**Baltimore Colts** (Human Pyramid)	.30	.25	.12
5	**Buffalo Bills** (Buffalo Bills' Wild West Show)	.30	.25	.12
6	**Buffalo Bills** (Buffaloed)	.30	.25	.12
7	**Chicago Bears** (Walter Payton) (About to Hit Paydirt)	3.00	2.25	1.25
8	**Chicago Bears** (Bear Trap)	.30	.25	.12
9	**Cincinnati Bengals** (Pete Johnson) (Behind the Wall)	.35	.25	.14
10	**Cincinnati Bengals** (Black Cloud)	.30	.25	.12
11	**Cleveland Browns** (Mike Pruitt) (Point of Attack)	.45	.35	.20
12	**Cleveland Browns** (Rocky Bleier) (The Only Way to Go is Down)	.50	.40	.20
13	**Dallas Cowboys** (Ron Springs) (Big O in Big D)	.45	.35	.20
14	**Dallas Cowboys** (Headed Off at the Pass)	.45	.35	.20
15	**Dallas Cowboys** (Craig Morton) (Man Versus Elements)	.35	.25	.14
16	**Denver Broncos** (The Old High-Low Treatment)	.35	.25	.14
17	**Detroit Lions** (Billy Sims) (Play Action)	1.00	.70	.40
18	**Detroit Lions** (Into the Lions' Den)	.30	.25	.12
19	**Green Bay Packers** (A Packer Packs the Pigskin)	.30	.25	.12
20	**Green Bay Packers** (Sandwiched)	.30	.25	.12
21	**Houston Oilers** (Wait A Minute)	.30	.25	.12
22	**Houston Oilers** (3-4 Shut the Door)	.30	.25	.12
23	**Kansas City Chiefs** (On the Ball)	.30	.25	.12
24	**Kansas City Chiefs** (Seeing Red)	.30	.25	.12
25	**Los Angeles Rams** (The Point of Attack)	.30	.25	.12
26	**Los Angeles Rams** (Get Your Hands Up)	.30	.25	.12
27	**Miami Dolphins** (David Woodley) (Plenty of Time)	.45	.35	.20
28	**Miami Dolphins** (Pursuit)	.35	.25	.14
29	**Minnesota Vikings** (Tough Yardage)	.30	.25	.12
30	**Minnesota Vikings** (Pete Johnson) (Purple Avalanche)	.35	.25	.14
31	**New England Patriots** (In High Gear)	.30	.25	.12
32	**New England Patriots** (Ken Stabler) (Keep 'Em Covered)	1.50	1.25	.60
33	**New Orleans Saints** (Archie Manning) (Setting Up)	.45	.35	.20
34	**New Orleans Saints** (Air Ball)	.30	.25	.12
35	**New York Giants** (Off Tackle)	.30	.25	.12
36	**New York Giants** (In the Land of the Giants)	.30	.25	.12
37	**New York Jets** (Richard Todd) (Cleared for Launching)	.35	.25	.14
38	**New York Jets** (Airborne)	.30	.25	.12
39	**Oakland Raiders** (Off and Running)	.45	.35	.20
40	**Oakland Raiders** (Block that Kick)	.45	.35	.20
41	**Philadelphia Eagles** (About to Take Flight)	.30	.25	.12
42	**Philadelphia Eagles** (Robert Newhouse) (Birds of Prey)	.45	.35	.20
43	**Pittsburgh Steelers** (Franco Harris) (Here Comes the Infantry)	1.25	.90	.50
44	**Pittsburgh Steelers** (Like a Steel Trap)	.35	.25	.14

		NM/M	NM	E
45	St. Louis Cardinals (Run to Daylight)	.30	.25	.12
46	St. Louis Cardinals (Stacked Up and Up)	.30	.25	.12
47	San Diego Chargers (Straight-Ahead Power)	.30	.25	.12
48	San Diego Chargers (Stonewalled)	.30	.25	.12
49	San Francisco 49ers (Follow the Leader)	.30	.25	.12
50	San Francisco 49ers (Search and Destroy)	.30	.25	.12
51	Seattle Seahawks (Short-Range Success)	.30	.25	.12
52	Seattle Seahawks (Take Down)	.30	.25	.12
53	Tampa Bay Buccaneers (Jerry Eckwood) (Orange Blossom Special)	.35	.25	.14
54	Tampa Bay Buccaneers (Tropical Storm Buc)	.30	.25	.12
55	Washington Redskins (Alone for a Moment)	.30	.25	.12
56	Washington Redskins (Ambushed)	.30	.25	.12
57	Super Bowl I (Jim Taylor) (Green Bay vs. Kansas City)	.50	.40	.20
58	Super Bowl II (Green Bay vs. Oakland)	.30	.25	.12
59	Super Bowl III (New York vs. Baltimore)	.30	.25	.12
60	Super Bowl IV (Kansas City vs. Minnesota)	.30	.25	.12
61	Super Bowl V (Baltimore vs. Dallas)	.30	.25	.12
62	Super Bowl VI (Dallas vs. Miami)	.30	.25	.12
63	Super Bowl VII (Miami vs. Washington)	.30	.25	.12
64	Super Bowl VIII (Larry Csonka) (Miami vs. Minnesota)	1.00	.70	.40
65	Super Bowl IX (Franco Harris) (Pittsburgh vs. Minnesota)	1.00	.70	.40
66	Super Bowl X (Franco Harris) (Pittsburgh vs. Dallas)	.35	.25	.14
67	Super Bowl XI (Kenny Stabler) (Oakland vs. Minnesota)	1.50	1.25	.60
68	Super Bowl XII (Roger Staubach, Tony Dorsett) (Dallas vs. Denver)	2.25	1.75	.90
69	Super Bowl XIII (Roger Staubach, Tony Dorsett) (Pittsburgh vs. Dallas)	2.25	1.75	.90
70	Super Bowl XIV (Franco Harris) (Pittsburgh vs. Los Angeles)	1.00	.70	.40
71	Super Bowl XV (Jim Plunkett) (Oakland vs. Philadelphia)	.50	.40	.20
72	**Steeler Training Camp** (Chuck Noll)	.50	.40	.20
73	**Practice Makes Perfect**	.30	.25	.12
74	**Airborn Carrier**	.30	.25	.12
75	**The National Anthem Chargers**	.30	.25	.12
76	**Filling Up**	.30	.25	.12
77	**Terry Bradshaw** (Away in Time)	2.00	1.50	.80
78	**Flat Out**	.30	.25	.12
79	**Halftime** (Band playing)	.30	.25	.12
80	**Warm Ups Patriots**	.30	.25	.12
81	**Getting to the Bottom of It**	.30	.25	.12
82	**Souvenir** (Crowd)	.30	.25	.12
83	**A Game of Inches** (Officials measuring)	.30	.25	.12
84	**The Overview**	.30	.25	.12
85	**The Dropback**	.30	.25	.12
86	**Pregame Huddle** (Washington Redskins)	.30	.25	.12
87	**Every Way But Loose**	.30	.25	.12
88	**Mudders**	.50	.40	.20

1982 Fleer Team Action

ENCIRCLED

The 1982 Fleer set is again complete at 88 cards, but is slightly more valuable than other Fleer sets from this period, because it contains a couple of cards featuring Joe Montana. The same numbering scheme is used, but 16 NFL Team Highlight cards are included and added at the end. Seven cards and three logo stickers were in each pack.

	NM/M	NM	E
Complete Set (88):	45.00	34.00	18.00
Common Card:	.25	.20	.10
Common SB Card:	.30	.25	.12

1	**Atlanta Falcons** (Running to Daylight)	.50	.40	.20
2	**Atlanta Falcons** (Airborne Falcons)	.25	.20	.10
3	Baltimore Colts (Mark Gastineau, Bert Jones) (Plenty of Time to Throw)	.45	.35	.20
4	Baltimore Colts (Lassoing the Opponent)	.25	.20	.10
5	Buffalo Bills (Joe Ferguson) (Point of Attack)	.45	.35	.20
6	**Buffalo Bills** (Capturing the Enemy)	.25	.20	.10
7	Chicago Bears (Walter Payton) (Three on One)	2.50	2.00	1.00
8	Chicago Bears (Stretched Out)	.25	.20	.10
9	Cincinnati Bengals (Pete Johnson) (About to Hit Paydirt)	.30	.25	.12
10	**Cincinnati Bengals** (Tiger-Striped Attack)	.25	.20	.10
11	Cleveland Browns (Brian Sipe) (Reading the Field)	.45	.35	.20
12	Cleveland Browns (Covered From All Angles)	.25	.20	.10
13	Dallas Cowboys (Tony Dorsett) (Blocking Convoy)	1.50	1.25	.60
14	Dallas Cowboys (Encircled)	.45	.35	.20
15	Denver Broncos (Craig Morton) (Springing into Action)	.45	.35	.20
16	**Denver Broncos** (High and Low)	.30	.25	.12
17	**Detroit Lions** (Setting Up the Screen Pass)	.25	.20	.10
18	Detroit Lions (Doug Williams) (Poised and Ready to Attack)	.30	.25	.12
19	**Green Bay Packers** (Flying Through the Air)	.25	.20	.10
20	**Green Bay Packers** (Hitting the Pack)	.25	.20	.10
21	Houston Oilers (Earl Campbell) (Waiting for the Hole to Open)	3.25	2.50	1.37
22	**Houston Oilers** (Biting the Dust)	.25	.20	.10
23	**Kansas City Chiefs** (Going in Untouched)	.25	.20	.10
24	**Kansas City Chiefs** (No Place to Go)	.25	.20	.10
25	Los Angeles Rams (Wendell Tyler) (Getting to the Outside)	.30	.25	.12
26	Los Angeles Rams (John Riggins) (Double Team, Double Trouble)	.70	.50	.30
27	Miami Dolphins (Tony Nathan) (Cutting Back Against the Grain)	.45	.35	.20
28	Miami Dolphins (Taking Two Down)	.30	.25	.12
29	Minnesota Vikings (Running Inside for Tough Yardage)	.25	.20	.10
30	Minnesota Vikings (Bowling Over the Oppenent)	.25	.20	.10
31	New England Patriots (Leaping for the First Down)	.25	.20	.10
32	New England Patriots (Gang Tackling)	.25	.20	.10
33	New Orleans Saints (Breaking Into the Clear)	.45	.35	.20
34	New Orleans Saints (Double Jeopardy)	.25	.20	.10
35	New York Giants (Getting Ready to Hit the Opening)	.25	.20	.10
36	New York Giants (Tony Dorsett) (Negative Yardage)	1.25	.90	.50
37	New York Jets (Freeman McNeil) (Off to the Races)	1.00	.70	.40
38	New York Jets (Sandwiched)	.25	.20	.10
39	Oakland Raiders (Marc Wilson) (Throwing the Down and Out)	.45	.35	.20
40	**Oakland Raiders** (The Second Wave is on the Way)	.45	.35	.20
41	Philadelphia Eagles (Ron Jaworski) (Blasting Up the Middle)	.45	.35	.20
42	Philadelphia Eagles (Carl Hairston, John Riggins) (Triple Teaming)	.70	.50	.30
43	Pittsburgh Steelers (Stretching for the Score)	.30	.25	.12
44	Pittsburgh Steelers (Rising Above the Crowd)	.30	.25	.12
45	St. Louis Cardinals (Jim Hart) (Sweeping to the Right)	.45	.35	.20
46	**St. Louis Cardinals** (No Playe to go but Down)	.25	.20	.10
47	**San Diego Chargers** (Looking for Someone to Block)	.25	.20	.10
48	San Diego Chargers (Being in the Right Place)	.25	.20	.10
49	San Francisco 49ers (Joe Montana) (Giving Second Effort)	17.50	13.00	7.00
50	San Francisco 49ers (Steve Bartkowski) (In Your Face)	.50	.40	.20
51	Seattle Seahawks (Jack Lambert) (Nothing But Open Space)	.70	.50	.30
52	Seattle Seahawks (Brian Sipe) (Attacking From the Blind Side)	.45	.35	.20
53	Tampa Bay Buccaneers (Doug Williams) (Everyone in Motion)	.30	.25	.12
54	**Tampa Bay Buccaneers** (Ring Around the Running Back)	.25	.20	.10
55	Washington Redskins (Joe Theismann) (Knocking Them Down One-By-One)	.70	.50	.30
56	Washington Redskins (Coming From All Directions)	.25	.20	.10
57	Super Bowl I (Jim Taylor) (Green Bay vs. Kansas City)	.50	.40	.20
58	**Super Bowl II** (Green Bay vs. Oakland)	.25	.20	.10
59	**Super Bowl III** (New York vs. Baltimore)	.25	.20	.10
60	**Super Bowl IV** (Kansas City vs. Minnesota)	.25	.20	.10
61	**Super Bowl V** (Baltimore vs. Dallas)	.25	.20	.10
62	Super Bowl VI (Bob Griese, Bob Lilly) (Dallas vs. Miami)	.80	.60	.30
63	Super Bowl VII (Larry Csonka) (Miami vs. Washington)	.70	.50	.30
64	Super Bowl VIII (Larry Csonka, Paul Warfield) (Miami vs. Minnesota)	1.00	.70	.40
65	**Super Bowl IX** (Pittsburgh vs. Minnesota)	.25	.20	.10
66	Super Bowl X (Roger Staubach) (Pittsburgh vs. Dallas)	2.00	1.50	.80
67	Super Bowl XI (Mark Van Eeghen) (Oakland vs. Minnesota)	.30	.25	.12
68	Super Bowl XII (Roger Staubach) (Dallas vs. Denver)	2.00	1.50	.80
69	Super Bowl XIII (Lynn Swann) (Pittsburgh vs. Dallas)	1.00	.70	.40
70	**Super Bowl XIV** (Pittsburgh vs. Los Angeles)	.25	.20	.10
71	Super Bowl XV (Jim Plunkett) (Oakland vs. Philadelphia)	.45	.35	.20
72	Super Bowl XVI (Dwight Clark) (San Francisco vs. Cincinnati)	.85	.60	.35
73	NFL Team Highlights (Joe Montana) (Pro Bowl)	12.00	9.00	4.75
74	NFL Team Highlights (Ken Anderson, Anthony Munoz) (Pro Bowl)	2.50	2.00	1.00
75	**NFL Team Highlights** (Aloha Stadium)	.75	.60	.30
76	**NFL Team Highlights** (On the Field Meeting)	.25	.20	.10
77	NFL Team Highlights (Joe Theismann) (First Down)	.70	.50	.30
78	NFL Team Highlights (Jerry Markbright) (The Man in Charge)	.25	.20	.10
79	**NFL Team Highlights** (Coming Onto the Field)	.25	.20	.10
80	**NFL Team Highlights** (In the Huddle)	.30	.25	.12
81	**NFL Team Highlights** (Lying In Wait)	.25	.20	.10
82	**NFL Team Highlights** (Celebration)	.25	.20	.10
83	**NFL Team Highlights** (Men in Motion)	.25	.20	.10
84	**NFL Team Highlights** (Shotgun Formation)	.25	.20	.10
85	**NFL Team Highlights** (Training Camp)	.25	.20	.10
86	NFL Team Highlights (Bill Walsh) (Halftime Instructions)	.75	.60	.30
87	NFL Team Highlights (Rolf Bernirschke) (Field Goal Attempt)	.30	.25	.12
88	**NFL Team Highlights** (Free Kick)	.50	.40	.20

1983 Fleer Team Action

The 1983 Fleer football set is again complete at 88 cards, including two cards for each team, one for each Super Bowl, plus a series of "Highlights" cards at the end of the set. There is a numbering error in the set that was not corrected. The card depicting Super Bowl X, which should have been card number "66," was erroneously numbered "67," meaning there are two cards numbered "67" in the set and no card numbered "66." Collectors should be aware that the premium value attached to the Super Bowl X card is beacuse it pictures Terry Bradshaw, and not because of the numbering error. The set follows all of Fleer's usual numbering formats. A Jim McMahon "rookie" card highlights the set. Packs had seven cards and three logo stickers.

	NM/M	NM	E
Complete Set (88):	26.00	19.50	10.40
Common Card:	.25	.20	.10
Common SB Card:	.30	.25	.12

1	Atlanta Falcons (Ronnie Lott) (Breaking Away to Daylight)	2.50	2.00	1.00
2	**Atlanta Falcons** (Piles Up)	.25	.20	.10
3	**Baltimore Colts** (Cutting Back to Daylight)	.25	.20	.10
4	Baltimore Colts (Joe Ferguson) (Pressuring the QB)	.30	.25	.12
5	**Buffalo Bills** (Moving to the Outside)	.30	.25	.12
6	**Buffalo Bills** (Buffalo Stampede)	.25	.20	.10

7	Chicago Bears (Jim McMahon, Walter Payton) (Ready to Let it Fly)	2.25	1.75	.90
8	Chicago Bears (Jump Ball)	.25	.20	.10
9	Cincinnati Bengals (Hurdling Into Open)	.25	.20	.10
10	Cincinnati Bengals (Hands Up)	.25	.20	.10
11	Cleveland Browns (Mike Pruitt) (An Open Field Ahead)	.30	.25	.12
12	Cleveland Browns (Reacting to the Ball Carrier)	.25	.20	.10
13	Dallas Cowboys (Tony Dorsett) (Mid-Air Ballet)	1.50	1.25	.60
14	Dallas Cowboys (3, 2, 1 Takeoff)	.30	.25	.12
15	Denver Broncos (Clear Sailing)	.30	.25	.12
16	Denver Broncos (Stacking Up Offense)	.30	.25	.12
17	Detroit Lions (Hitting the Wall)	.25	.20	.10
18	Detroit Lions (Snapping into Action)	.25	.20	.10
19	Green Bay Packers (Ed "Too Tall" Jones) (Fingertip Control)	.60	.45	.25
20	Green Bay Packers (QB Sack)	.25	.20	.10
21	Houston Oilers (Sweeping to Outside)	.25	.20	.10
22	Houston Oilers (Freeman McNeil) (Halting Forward Progress)	.45	.35	.20
23	Kansas City Chiefs (Waiting for the Key Block)	.25	.20	.10
24	Kansas City Chiefs (John Hannah) (Going Head to Head)	.50	.40	.20
25	Los Angeles Raiders (Jim Plunkett) (Bowms Away)	.45	.35	.20
26	Los Angeles Raiders (Caged Bengal)	.45	.35	.20
27	Los Angeles Rams (Clearing Out Middle)	.25	.20	.10
28	Los Angeles Rams (One on One Tackle)	.25	.20	.10
29	Miami Dolphins (Skating Through Hole)	.30	.25	.12
30	Miami Dolphins (Follow the Bouncing Ball)	.30	.25	.12
31	Minnesota Vikings (Tommy Kramer) (Dropping into Pocket)	.30	.25	.12
32	Minnesota Vikings (Attacking from All Angles)	.25	.20	.10
33	New England Patriots (Touchdown)	.25	.20	.10
34	New England Patriots (Walter Payton) (Pouncing Patriots)	2.00	1.50	.80
35	New Orleans Saints (Only One Man to Beat)	.25	.20	.10
36	New Orleans Saints (Tony Dorsett) (Closing In)	1.25	.90	.50
37	New York Giants (Setting Up to Pass)	.25	.20	.10
38	New York Giants (In Pursuit)	.25	.20	.10
39	New York Jets (Just Enough Room)	.25	.20	.10
40	New York Jets (Warpping Up Runner)	.25	.20	.10
41	Philadelphia Eagles (Ron Jarowski, Harry Carson) (Play Action Fakers)	.30	.25	.12
42	Philadelphia Eagles (Archie Manning) (Step Away From Sack)	.45	.35	.20
43	Pittsburgh Steelers (Franco Harris, Terry Bradshaw) (Exploding Through a Hole)	1.50	1.25	.60
44	Pittsburgh Steelers (Jack Lambert) (Outnumbered)	.60	.45	.25
45	St. Louis Cardinals (Keeping His Balance)	.25	.20	.10

46	St. Louis Cardinals (Waiting for the Reinforcements)	.25	.20	.10
47	San Diego Chargers (Supercharged Charger)	.25	.20	.10
48	San Diego Chargers (Triple Team Tackle)	.25	.20	.10
49	San Francisco 49ers (There's No Stopping Him Now)	.25	.20	.10
50	San Francisco 49ers (Heading 'Em Off at the Pass)	.30	.25	.12
51	Seattle Seahawks (Jim Zorn) (Calling the Signals)	.45	.35	.20
52	Seattle Seahawks (The Hands Have it)	.30	.25	.12
53	Tampa Bay Buccaneers (Off to the Races)	.25	.20	.10
54	Tampa Bay Buccaneers (Buccaneer Sandwich)	.25	.20	.10
55	Washington Redskins (Looking for Daylight)	.25	.20	.10
56	Washington Redskins (Smothering the Ball Carrier)	.25	.20	.10
57	Super Bowl I (Jim Taylor) (Green Bay vs. Kansas City)	.60	.45	.25
58	Super Bowl II (Green Bay vs. Oakland)	.30	.25	.12
59	Super Bowl III (New York vs. Baltimore)	.30	.25	.12
60	Super Bowl IV (Kansas City vs. Minnesota)	.30	.25	.12
61	Super Bowl V (Johnny Unitas) (Baltimore vs. Dallas)	1.50	1.25	.60
62	Super Bowl VI (Bob Griese, Bob Lilly) (Dallas vs. Miami)	.75	.60	.30
63	Super Bowl VII (Manny Fernandez) (Miami vs. Washington)	.30	.25	.12
64	Super Bowl VIII (Larry Csonka) (Miami vs. Minnesota)	.60	.45	.25
65	Super Bowl IX (Franco Harris) (Pittsburgh vs. Minnesota)	1.00	.70	.40
66	Super Bowl X (Terry Bradshaw) (Pittsburgh vs. Dallas)	1.75	1.25	.70
67	Super Bowl XI (Oakland vs. Minnesota)	.45	.35	.20
68	Super Bowl XII (Dallas vs. Denver)	.30	.25	.12
69	Super Bowl XIII (Terry Bradshaw) (Pittsburgh vs. Dallas)	1.50	1.25	.60
70	Super Bowl XIV (Vince Ferragamo) (Pittsburgh vs. Los Angeles)	.30	.25	.12
71	Super Bowl XV (Oakland vs. Philadelphia)	.30	.25	.12
72	Super Bowl XVI (San Francisco vs. Cincinnati)	.30	.25	.12
73	Super Bowl XVII (John Riggins) (Washington vs. Miami)	.60	.45	.25
74	NFL Team Highlights (Dan Fouts) (Pro Bowl)	1.00	.70	.40
75	NFL Team Highlights (Super Bowl XVII Spectacular)	.30	.25	.12
76	NFL Team Highlights (Tampa Stadium: Super Bowl XVIII)	.30	.25	.12
77	NFL Team Highlights (Up, Up, and Away)	.30	.25	.12
78	NFL Team Highlights (Steve Bartkowski) (Sideline Conference)	.30	.25	.12
79	NFL Team Highlights (Mike Lansford) (Barefoot Follow-Through)	.30	.25	.12
80	NFL Team Highlights (Fourth and Long)	.30	.25	.12
81	NFL Team Highlights (Blocked Punt)	.30	.25	.12
82	NFL Team Highlights (Fumble)	.30	.25	.12
83	NFL Team Highlights (National Anthem)	.30	.25	.12

84	NFL Team Highlights (Tony Franklin) (Concentrating on the Ball)	.30	.25	.12
85	NFL Team Highlights (Splashing Around)	.30	.25	.12
86	NFL Team Highlights (Loading in Shotgun)	.30	.25	.12
87	NFL Team Highlights (Taking the Snap)	.30	.25	.12
88	NFL Team Highlights (Line of Scrimmage)	.45	.35	.20

1984 Fleer Team Action

The 1984 Fleer football set is again complete at 88 cards, using Fleer's typical numbering arrangement. However, the newly-relocated Indianapolis Colts are placed in Baltimore's usual position. A series of 18 Super Bowl and 14 NFL Team Highlight cards are included. The most signigicant cards are two of Earl Campbell, which are not found in the 1984 Topps set, a first-year Marcus Allen, and a Howie Long "rookie." Seven cards and three logo stickers were in each pack. Cards green borders.

		NM/M	NM	E
Complete Set (88):		23.50	17.50	9.40
Common Card:		.25	.20	.10
1	Atlanta Falcons	.50	.40	.20
2	Atlanta Falcons (Gang Tackle)	.25	.20	.10
3	Indianapolis Colts (About to Break Free)	.25	.20	.10
4	Indianapolis Colts (Cutting Off All the Angles)	.25	.20	.10
5	Buffalo Bills (Cracking the First Line of Defense)	.25	.20	.10
6	Buffalo Bills (Getting Help from a Friend)	.25	.20	.10
7	Chicago Bears (Jim McMahon, Walter Payton) (Over the Top)	1.75	1.25	.70
8	Chicago Bears (You Grab Him High I'll Grab Him Low)	.25	.20	.10
9	Cincinnati Bengals (Skipping Through an Opening)	.25	.20	.10
10	Cincinnati Bengals (Joe Ferguson) (Saying Hello to a QB)	.40	.30	.15
11	Cleveland Browns (Greg Pruitt) (Free Sailing into the End Zone)	.40	.30	.15
12	Cleveland Browns (Making Sure of the Tackle)	.25	.20	.10
13	Dallas Cowboys (Danny White)	.50	.40	.20
14	Dallas Cowboys (Ed "Too Tall" Jones) (Cowboy's Corral)	.60	.45	.25
15	Denver Broncos (Sprinting into the Open)	.40	.30	.15
16	Denver Broncos (Curt Warner) (Ready to Pounce)	.50	.40	.20
17	Detroit Lions (Billy Sims) (Lion on the Prowl)	.50	.40	.20
18	Detroit Lions (John Riggins) (Stacking Up the Ball Carrier)	.60	.45	.25
19	Green Bay Packers (Waiting for the Hole to Open)	.25	.20	.10
20	Green Bay Packers (Packing Up Your Opponent)	.25	.20	.10
21	Houston Oilers (Earl Campbell) (Nothing but Open Spaces Ahead)	2.50	2.00	1.00
22	Houston Oilers (Meeting Him Head On)	.25	.20	.10
23	Kansas City Chiefs (Going Outside for Extra Yardage)	.25	.20	.10
24	Kansas City Chiefs (A Running Back in Trouble)	.25	.20	.10
25	Los Angeles Raiders (Marcus Allen) (No Defenders in Sight)	2.75	2.00	1.00
26	Los Angeles Raiders (Howie Long, John Riggins) (Rampaging Raiders)	2.25	1.75	.90
27	Los Angeles Rams (Making the Cut)	.25	.20	.10

28	Los Angeles Rams (Caught From Behind)	.25	.20	.10
29	Miami Dolphins (Sliding Down the Line)	.40	.30	.15
30	Miami Dolphins (Making Sure)	.40	.30	.15
31	Minnesota Vikings (Stretching For Touchdown)	.25	.20	.10
32	Minnesota Vikings (Hitting the Wall)	.25	.20	.10
33	New England Patriots (Steve Grogan) (Straight Up the Middle)	.50	.40	.20
34	New England Patriots (Earl Campbell) (Come Here an Give Me a Hug)	2.00	1.50	.80
35	New Orleans Saints (One Defender to Beat)	.25	.20	.10
36	New Orleans Saints (Saints Sandwich)	.25	.20	.10
37	New York Giants (A Six Point Landing)	.25	.20	.10
38	New York Giants (Leaping to the Aid of a Teammate)	.25	.20	.10
39	New York Jets (Galloping Through Untouched)	.25	.20	.10
40	New York Jets (Capturing the Enemy)	.25	.20	.10
41	Philadelphia Eagles (One More Block and He's Gone)	.25	.20	.10
42	Philadelphoa Eagles (Meeting an Oppenent With Open Arms)	.25	.20	.10
43	Pittsburgh Steelers (The Play Begins to Develop)	.40	.30	.15
44	Pittsburgh Steelers (Rally Around the Ball Carrier)	.40	.30	.15
45	St. Louis Cardinals (Sprinting Around the Corner)	.25	.20	.10
46	St. Louis Cardinals (Overmatched)	.25	.20	.10
47	San Diego Chargers (Up, Up and Away)	.25	.20	.10
48	San Diego Chargers (Engulfing the Oppenent)	.25	.20	.10
49	San Francisco 49ers (Wendell Tyler) (Tunneling Up the Middle)	.40	.30	.15
50	San Francisco 49ers (John Riggins) (Nowhere to Go but Down)	.60	.45	.25
51	Seattle Seahawks (Jim Zorn) (Letting the Ball Fly)	.50	.40	.20
52	Seattle Seahawks (Handing Out Some Punishment)	.40	.30	.15
53	Tampa Bay Buccaneers (When He Hits the Ground He's Gone)	.25	.20	.10
54	Tampa Bay Buccaneers (One Leg Takedown)	.25	.20	.10
55	Washington Redskins (John Riggins) (Plenty of Room to Run)	.60	.45	.25
56	Washington Redskins (Squashing the Oppenent)	.25	.20	.10
57	Super Bowl I (Jim Taylor) (Green Bay vs. Kansas City)	.60	.45	.25
58	Super Bowl II (Bart Starr) (Green Bay vs. Oakland)	.80	.60	.30
59	Super Bowl III (New York vs. Baltimore)	.25	.20	.10
60	Super Bowl IV (Kansas City vs. Minnesota)	.25	.20	.10
61	Super Bowl V (Earl Morrall) (Baltimore vs. Dallas)	.75	.60	.30
62	Super Bowl VI (Roger Staubach) (Dallas vs. Miami)	1.50	1.25	.60
63	Super Bowl VII (Jim Kiick, Bob Griese) (Miami vs. Washington)	.50	.40	.20
64	Super Bowl VIII (Larry Csonka) (Miami vs. Minncsota)	.75	.60	.30
65	Super Bowl IX (Terry Bradshaw) (Pittsburgh vs. Minnesota)	1.25	.90	.50
66	Super Bowl X (Franco Harris) (Pittsburgh vs. Dallas)	.75	.60	.30
67	Super Bowl XI (Oakland vs. Minnesota)	.25	.20	.10
68	Super Bowl XII (Tony Dorsett) (Dallas vs. Denver)	1.00	.70	.40
69	Super Bowl XIII (Franco Harris) (Pittsburgh vs. Dallas)	.75	.60	.30
70	Super Bowl XIV (Franco Harris) (Pittsburgh vs. Los Angeles)	.75	.60	.30
71	Super Bowl XV (Jim Plunkett) (Oakland vs. Philadelphia)	.40	.30	.15
72	Super Bowl XVI (San Francisco vs. Cincinnati)	.25	.20	.10
73	Super Bowl XVII (Washington vs. Miami)	.25	.20	.10
74	Super Bowl XVIII (Howie Long) (Los Angeles vs. Washington)	1.75	1.25	.70
75	NFL Team Highlights (Official's Conference)	.25	.20	.10
76	NFL Team Highlights (Leaping for the Ball Carrier)	.25	.20	.10
77	NFL Team Highlights (Jim Plunkett) (Setting Up in the Passing Pocket)	.40	.30	.15
78	NFL Team Highlights (Field Goal Block)	.25	.20	.10
79	NFL Team Highlights (Steve Grogan) (Stopped for No Gain)	.40	.30	.15
80	NFL Team Highlights (Double Team Block)	.25	.20	.10
81	NFL Team Highlights (Kickoff)	.25	.20	.10
82	NFL Team Highlights (Punt Block)	.25	.20	.10
83	NFL Team Highlights (Coaches Signals)	.25	.20	.10
84	NFL Team Highlights (Training Camp)	.25	.20	.10
85	NFL Team Highlights (Dwight Stephenson) (Fumble)	.50	.40	.20
86	NFL Team Highlights (1984 AFC-NFC Pro Bowl)	.25	.20	.10
87	NFL Team Highlights (Cheerleaders)	.50	.40	.20
88	NFL Team Highlights (Joe Theismann) (In the Huddle)	.80	.60	.30

1960 49ers White Border

This 44-card set was available through a package offered to fans and is similar to other issues in that time span, and can be distinguished by the text on the back. Players are featured in black and white posed photos, with a facsimile signature across the photo.

#	Card	NM	E	VG
	Complete Set (44):	185.00	92.50	55.50
	Common Player:	3.00	1.50	.90
1	Dave Baker (David Lee Baker)	3.00	1.50	.90
2	Bruce Bosley (Born in Fresno)	3.00	1.50	.90
3	John Brodie (This could be)	14.00	7.00	4.25
4	Jack Christiansen (ACO)	8.00	4.00	2.50
5	Monte Clark (A special chapter)	5.00	2.50	1.50
6	Dan Colchico (Big Dan)	3.00	1.50	.90
7	Clyde Conner (Clyde Raymond)	3.00	1.50	.90
8	Ted Connolly (When Theodore)	3.00	1.50	.90
9	Tommy Davis (San Francisco)	4.00	2.00	1.25
10	Eddie Dove (Edward Everett)	3.00	1.50	.90
11	Mark Duncan (ACO A versatile)	3.00	1.50	.90
12	Bob Fouts (ANN)	3.00	1.50	.90
13	Bob Harrison (There is no more)	3.00	1.50	.90
14	Matt Hazeltine (Matthew Hazeltine)	3.00	1.50	.90
15	Ed Henke (Desire and)	3.00	1.50	.90
16	Red Hickey (CO Baseball)	3.00	1.50	.90
17	Russ Hodges (ANN)	3.00	1.50	.90
18	Bill Johnson (CO Bill Johnson)	3.00	1.50	.90
19	Gordon Kelley (This Southern)	3.00	1.50	.90
20	Charlie Krueger (The 49ers)	4.00	2.00	1.25
21	Lenny Lyles (Leonard Lyles)	3.00	1.50	.90
22	Hugh McElhenny (San Francisco's)	14.00	7.00	4.25
23	Mike Magac (Mike was)	3.00	1.50	.90
24	Jerry Mertens (Jerome William)	3.00	1.50	.90
25	Frank Morze (Anyone with)	3.00	1.50	.90
26	Leo Nomellini (Leo Joseph)	10.00	5.00	3.00
27	Clancy Osborne (Desire)	4.00	2.00	1.25
28	R.C. Owens (Few players)	5.00	2.50	1.50
29	Jim Ridlon (James Ridlon)	3.00	1.50	.90
30	C.R. Roberts (After trials)	3.00	1.50	.90
31	Len Rohde (Len, a three)	3.00	1.50	.90
32	Karl Rubke (Only 20 years)	3.00	1.50	.90
33	Bob St. Clair (Robert Bruce)	8.00	4.00	2.50
34	Henry Schmidt (After two years)	3.00	1.50	.90
35	Lon Simmons (ANN)	3.00	1.50	.90
36	J.D. Smith (In J.D. Smith)	4.00	2.00	1.25
37	Gordy Soltau (ANN)	3.00	1.50	.90
38	Monty Stickles (The football)	3.00	1.50	.90
39	John Thomas (Noted more)	3.00	1.50	.90
40	Y.A. Tittle (When Yelberton)	18.00	9.00	5.50
41	Lynn Waldorf (Director of Personnel)	3.00	1.50	.90
42	Bobby Waters (A smart)	5.00	2.50	1.50
43	Billy Wilson (Only Don Hutson)	4.00	2.00	1.25
44	Abe Woodson (A Big 10)	4.00	2.00	1.25

1968 49ers White Border

This 35-card oversized set measures 8-1/2" x 11" and displays different 49ers players in posed, black and white photos. Card backs are blank, with no card numbers listed either. In addition, Steve Spurrier's card in this set predates his rookie by four years.

#	Player	NM	E	VG
	Complete Set (35):	125.00	62.00	37.00
	Common Player:	2.50	1.25	.70
1	Kermit Alexander	2.50	1.25	.70
2	Cas Banaszek	2.50	1.25	.70
3	Ed Beard	2.50	1.25	.70
4	Forrest Blue	4.00	2.00	1.25
5	Bruce Bosley	4.00	2.00	1.25
6	John Brodie	10.00	5.00	3.00
7	Elmer Collett	2.50	1.25	.70
8	Doug Cunningham	2.50	1.25	.70
9	Tommy Davis	4.00	2.00	1.25
10	Kevin Hardy	2.50	1.25	.70
11	Matt Hazeltine	4.00	2.00	1.25
12	Stan Hindman	2.50	1.25	.70
13	Tom Holzer	2.50	1.25	.70
14	Jim Johnson	8.00	4.00	2.50
15	Charlie Krueger	4.00	2.00	1.25
16	Roland Lakes	2.50	1.25	.70
17	Gary Lewis	2.50	1.25	.70
18	Kay McFarland	2.50	1.25	.70
19	Clifton McNeil	4.00	2.00	1.25
20	George Mira	5.00	2.50	1.50
21	Howard Mudd	2.50	1.25	.70
22	Dick Nolan (CO)	4.00	2.00	1.25
23	Frank Nunley	2.50	1.25	.70
24	Don Parker	2.50	1.25	.70
25	Mel Phillips	4.00	2.00	1.25
26	Al Randolph	2.50	1.25	.70
27	Len Rohde	2.50	1.25	.70
28	Steve Spurrier	28.00	14.00	8.50
29	John Thomas	2.50	1.25	.70
30	Bill Tucker	2.50	1.25	.70
31	Dave Wilcox	4.00	2.00	1.25
32	Ken Willard	4.00	2.00	1.25
33	Bob Windsor	4.00	2.00	1.25

		NM/M	NM	E
34	Dick Witcher	4.00	2.00	1.25
35	**Team Photo**	10.00	5.00	3.00

1972 49ers Redwood City Tribune

This six-card set measures 3" x 5-1/2" and contains a head shot of the featured player in black and white with white borders. There is a large white space below the photo that contains a facsimile autograph. Cards are unnumbered and listed below in alphabetical order.

		NM	E	VG
Complete Set (6):		50.00	37.00	20.00
Common Player:		8.00	6.00	3.25
1	Frank Edwards	8.00	6.00	3.25
2	Frank Nunley	8.00	6.00	3.25
3	Len Rohde	8.00	6.00	3.25
4	Larry Schrieber	8.00	6.00	3.25
5	Steve Spurrier	30.00	15.00	9.00
6	Gene Washington	12.00	6.00	3.50

1982 49ers Team Issue

This 5" x 8" set has 44 cards in black and white with white borders. The backs of the cards are blank and unnumbered.

		NM/M	NM	E
Complete Set (44):		55.00	41.00	22.00
Common Player:		1.00	.70	.40
1	Dan Audick	1.00	.70	.40
2	John Ayers	1.00	.70	.40
3	Guy Benjamin	1.00	.70	.40
4	Dwaine Board	1.00	.70	.40
5	Ken Bungarda	1.00	.70	.40
6	Dan Bunz	1.00	.70	.40
7	Dwight Clark	4.00	3.00	1.50
8	Ricky Churchman	1.00	.70	.40
9	Earl Cooper	1.00	.70	.40
10	Randy Cross	1.50	1.25	.60
11	Johnny Davis	1.00	.70	.40
12	Fred Dean	1.00	.70	.40
13	Walt Downing	1.00	.70	.40
14	Walt Easley	1.00	.70	.40
15	Lenvil Elliott	1.00	.70	.40
16	Keith Fahnhorst	1.00	.70	.40
17	Rick Gervais	1.00	.70	.40
18	Willie Harper	1.00	.70	.40
19	John Harty	1.00	.70	.40
20	Pete Kugler	1.00	.70	.40
21	Amos Lawrence	1.00	.70	.40
22	Bobby Leopold	1.00	.70	.40
23	Saladin Martin	1.00	.70	.40
24	Milt McColl	1.00	.70	.40
25	Jim Miller	1.00	.70	.40
26	Joe Montana	22.00	16.50	8.75
27	Ricky Patton	1.00	.70	.40
28	Lawrence Pillers	1.00	.70	.40
29	Craig Puki	1.00	.70	.40
30	Fred Quillan	1.00	.70	.40
31	Eason Ramson	1.00	.70	.40
32	Archie Reese	1.00	.70	.40
33	Jack Reynolds	1.00	.70	.40
34	Mike Shumann	1.00	.70	.40
35	Freddie Solomon	1.50	1.25	.60
36	Scott Stauch	1.00	.70	.40
37	Jim Stuckey	1.00	.70	.40
38	Lynn Thomas	1.00	.70	.40
39	Keena Turner	1.25	.90	.50
40	Ray Wersching	1.00	.70	.40
41	Carlton Williamson	1.00	.70	.40
42	Mike Wilson	1.00	.70	.40
43	Eric Wright	1.00	.70	.40
44	Charlie Young	1.00	.70	.40

1984 49ers Police

This 12-card set was issued in three panels of four cards each and measures 2-1/2" x 4". The set is unnumbered and sponsored by 7-Eleven, Dr. Pepper and KCB's.

		NM/M	NM	E
Complete Set (12):		25.00	18.50	10.00
Common Player:		1.00	.70	.40
1	Dwaine Board	1.00	.70	.40
2	Roger Craig	3.50	2.75	1.50
3	Riki Ellison	1.00	.70	.40
4	Keith Fahnhorst	1.00	.70	.40
5	Joe Montana, Dwight Clark	10.00	7.50	4.00
6	Jack Reynolds	1.00	.70	.40
7	Freddie Solomon	1.00	.70	.40
8	Keena Turner	1.00	.70	.40
9	Wendall Tyler	1.00	.70	.40
10	Bill Walsh (CO)	3.00	2.25	1.25
11	Ray Wersching	1.00	.70	.40
12	Eric Wright	1.00	.70	.40

1985 49ers Police

This 16-card set was issued in four panels of four cards each, and is very similar to the 1984 set except its sponsored only by Dr. Pepper and 7-Eleven. The cards are unnumbered and measure 2-1/2" x 4".

		NM/M	NM	E
Complete Set (16):		18.00	13.50	7.25
Common Player:		.50	.40	.20
1	John Ayers	.50	.40	.20
2	Roger Craig	2.00	1.50	.80
3	Fred Dean	.75	.60	.30
4	Riki Ellison	.50	.40	.20
5	Keith Fahnhorst	.50	.40	.20
6	Russ Francis	.75	.60	.30
7	Dwight Hicks	.50	.40	.20
8	Ronnie Lott	1.75	1.25	.70
9	Dana McLemore	.50	.40	.20
10	Joe Montana	10.00	7.50	4.00
11	Todd Shell	.50	.40	.20
12	Freddie Solomon	.75	.60	.30
13	Keena Turner	.50	.40	.20
14	Bill Walsh (CO)	1.50	1.25	.60
15	Ray Wersching	.50	.40	.20
16	Eric Wright	.50	.40	.20

1985 49ers Smokey

This seven-card oversized set measures approximately 3" x 4-3/8". It was issued by the 49ers and Smokey Bear, and features a cartoon fire safety tip and a facsimile signature of the player on the back.

		NM/M	NM	E
Complete Set (7):		30.00	22.00	12.00
Common Player:		2.00	1.50	.80
1	**Group Picture with** (Smokey Player list on back of card)	6.00	4.50	2.50
2	Joe Montana	18.00	13.50	7.25
3	Jack Reynolds	3.00	2.25	1.25
4	Eric Wright	2.00	1.50	.80
5	Dwight Hicks	2.00	1.50	.80
6	Dwight Clark	4.00	3.00	1.50
7	Keena Turner	2.00	1.50	.80

1988 49ers Police

This 20-card set included 19 players and one coach card and was sponsored by 7-Eleven and Oscar Mayer. The fronts are almost full-bleed photos with a thin white border. Backs have a football tip and a McGruff crime tip.

		NM/M	NM	E
Complete Set (20):		20.00	15.00	8.00
Common Player:		.50	.40	.20
1	Harris Barton	.75	.60	.30
2	Dwaine Board	.50	.40	.20
3	Michael Carter	.75	.60	.30
4	Roger Craig	1.50	1.25	.60
5	Randy Cross	.75	.60	.30
6	Riki Ellison	.50	.40	.20
7	John Frank	.50	.40	.20
8	Jeff Fuller	.50	.40	.20
9	Pete Kugler	.50	.40	.20
10	Ronnie Lott	2.00	1.50	.80
11	Joe Montana	8.00	6.00	3.25
12	Tom Rathman	1.75	1.25	.70
13	Jerry Rice	8.00	6.00	3.25
14	Jeff Stover	.50	.40	.20
15	Keena Turner	.75	.60	.30
16	Bill Walsh (CO)	1.50	1.25	.60
17	Michael Walter	.50	.40	.20
18	Mike Wilson	.50	.40	.20
19	Eric Wright	.75	.60	.30
20	Steve Young	8.00	6.00	3.25

1988 49ers Smokey

This 35-card set was printed on a 5" x 8" format and is unnumbered, except for the uniform number. Fronts feature a full-bleed shot with a thin white border around the inside of the card. Backs have a fire safety cartoon usually featuring Smokey the Bear.

		NM/M	NM	E
Complete Set (35):		100.00	75.00	40.00
Common Player:		1.00	.70	.40
1	Harris Barton	1.50	1.25	.60
2	Dwaine Board (SP)	8.00	6.00	3.25
3	Michael Carter	1.50	1.25	.60
4	Bruce Collie	1.00	.70	.40
5	Roger Craig	3.50	2.75	1.50
6	Randy Cross	1.75	1.25	.70
7	Eddie DeBartolo (Jr Owner, President)	2.50	2.00	1.00
8	Riki Ellison	1.00	.70	.40
9	Kevin Fagan	1.00	.70	.40
10	Jim Fahnhorst	1.00	.70	.40

		NM/M	NM	E
11	John Frank	1.00	.70	.40
12	Jeff Fuller	1.00	.70	.40
13	Don Griffin	1.50	1.25	.60
14	Charles Haley	3.00	2.25	1.25
15	Ron Heller	1.00	.70	.40
16	Tom Holmoe	1.00	.70	.40
17	Pete Kugler	1.00	.70	.40
18	Ronnie Lott	4.00	3.00	1.50
19	Tim McKyer	1.50	1.25	.60
20	Joe Montana	20.00	15.00	8.00
21	Tory Nixon	1.00	.70	.40
22	Bubba Paris	1.00	.70	.40
23	John Paye	1.00	.70	.40
24	Tom Rathman	3.00	2.25	1.25
25	Jerry Rice	20.00	15.00	8.00
26	Jeff Stover	1.00	.70	.40
27	Harry Sydney	1.00	.70	.40
28	John Taylor	4.00	3.00	1.50
29	Keena Turner	1.50	1.25	.60
30	Steve Wallace	1.50	1.25	.60
31	Bill Walsh (CO)	3.00	2.25	1.25
32	Michael Walter	1.00	.70	.40
33	Mike Wilson	1.00	.70	.40
34	Eric Wright	1.50	1.25	.60
35	Steve Young	20.00	15.00	8.00

1990-91 49ers SF Examiner

This 16-card set was issued on two unperforated sheets measuring 14" x 11", and was issued by the San Francisco Examiner. Eight-card panels included a newspaper headline across the top reading "San Francisco Examiner Salutes the 49ers' Finest." Card fronts are in color with a thin orange border on the red-face card. Backs are horizontal and black and white with a head shot and stats.

		NM/M	NM	E
Complete Set (16):		10.00	7.50	4.00
Common Player:		.50	.40	.20
1	Harris Barton	.75	.60	.30
2	Michael Carter	.50	.40	.20
3	Mike Cofer	.50	.40	.20
4	Roger Craig	1.00	.70	.40
5	Kevin Fagan	.50	.40	.20
6	Don Griffin	.50	.40	.20
7	Charles Haley	1.25	.90	.50
8	Pierce Holt	.50	.40	.20
9	Brent Jones	1.25	.90	.50
10	Ronnie Lott	1.25	.90	.50
11	Guy McIntyre	.50	.40	.20
12	Matt Millen	.75	.60	.30
13	Joe Montana	4.00	3.00	1.50
14	Tom Rathman	1.00	.70	.40
15	Jerry Rice	4.00	3.00	1.50
16	John Taylor	1.50	1.25	.60

G

1989 Georgia 200

		NM/M	NM	E
Complete Set (200):		18.00	13.50	7.25
Common Player:		.10	.08	.04
1	Vince Dooley (AD)	.20	.15	.08
2	Ivy M. Shiver	.10	.08	.04
3	Vince Dooley (CO)	.20	.15	.08
4	Vince Dooley (CO)	.20	.15	.08
5	Ray Goff (CO)	.20	.15	.08
6	Ray Goff (CO)	.20	.15	.08
7	Wally Butts (CO)	.20	.15	.08
8	Wally Butts (CO)	.20	.15	.08
9	Herschel Walker	.75	.60	.30
10	Frank Sinkwich	.20	.15	.08
11	Bob McWhorter	.10	.08	.04
12	Joe Bennett	.10	.08	.04

13	Dan Edwards	.10	.08	.04
14	Tom A. Nash	.10	.08	.04
15	Herb Maffett	.10	.08	.04
16	Ralph Maddox	.10	.08	.04
17	Vernon Smith	.10	.08	.04
18	Bill Hartman Jr.	.10	.08	.04
19	Frank Sinkwich	.20	.15	.08
20	Joe O'Malley	.10	.08	.04
21	Mike Castronis	.10	.08	.04
22	Aschel M. Day	.10	.08	.04
23	Herb St. John	.10	.08	.04
24	Craig Hertwig	.10	.08	.04
25	Johnny Rauch	.20	.15	.08
26	Harry Babcock	.10	.08	.04
27	Bruce Kemp	.10	.08	.04
28	Pat Dye	.20	.15	.08
29	Fran Tarkenton	1.00	.70	.40
30	Larry Kohn	.10	.08	.04
31	Ray Rissmiller	.10	.08	.04
32	George Patton	.20	.15	.08
33	Mixon Robinson	.10	.08	.04
34	Lynn Hughes	.10	.08	.04
35	Bill Stanfill	.20	.15	.08
36	Robert Dicks	.10	.08	.04
37	Lynn Hunnicutt	.10	.08	.04
38	Tommy Lyons	.10	.08	.04
39	Royce Smith	.10	.08	.04
40	Steve Greer	.10	.08	.04
41	Randy Johnson	.20	.15	.08
42	Mike Wilson	.10	.08	.04
43	Joel Parrish	.10	.08	.04
44	Ben Zambiasi	.20	.15	.08
45	Allan Leavitt	.10	.08	.04
46	George Collins	.10	.08	.04
47	Rex Robinson	.10	.08	.04
48	Scott Woerner	.10	.08	.04
49	Herschel Walker	.75	.60	.30
50	Bob Burns	.10	.08	.04
51	Jimmy Payne	.10	.08	.04
52	Fred Brown	.10	.08	.04
53	Kevin Butler	.20	.15	.08
54	Don Porterfield	.10	.08	.04
55	Mac McWhorter	.10	.08	.04
56	John Little	.10	.08	.04
57	Marion Campbell	.20	.15	.08
58	Zeke Bratkowski	.30	.25	.12
59	Buck Belue	.20	.15	.08
60	Duward Pennington	.10	.08	.04
61	Lamar Davis	.10	.08	.04
62	Steve Wilson	.10	.08	.04
63	Leman L. Rosenberg	.10	.08	.04
64	Dennis Hughes	.10	.08	.04
65	Wayne Radloff	.10	.08	.04
66	Lindsay Scott	.20	.15	.08
67	Wayne Swinford	.10	.08	.04
68	Kim Stephens	.10	.08	.04
69	Willie McClendon	.20	.15	.08
70	Ron Jenkins	.10	.08	.04
71	Jeff Lewis	.10	.08	.04
72	Larry Rakestraw	.10	.08	.04
73	Spike Jones	.20	.15	.08
74	Tom Nash Jr.	.10	.08	.04
75	Vassa Cate	.10	.08	.04
76	Theron Sapp	.20	.15	.08
77	Claude Hipps	.20	.15	.08
78	Charley Trippi	.30	.25	.12
79	Mike Weaver	.10	.08	.04
80	Anderson Johnson	.10	.08	.04
81	Matt Robinson	.20	.15	.08
82	Bill Krug	.10	.08	.04
83	Todd Wheeler	.10	.08	.04
84	Mack Guest	.10	.08	.04
85	Frank Ros	.10	.08	.04
86	Jeff Hipp	.10	.08	.04
87	Milton Leathers	.10	.08	.04
88	George Morton	.10	.08	.04
89	Jim Broadway	.10	.08	.04
90	Tim Morrison	.10	.08	.04
91	Homer Key	.10	.08	.04
92	Richard Tardits	.20	.15	.08
93	Tommy Thurson	.10	.08	.04
94	Bob Kelley	.10	.08	.04
95	Bob McWhorter	.10	.08	.04
96	Vernon Smith	.10	.08	.04
97	Eddie Weaver	.10	.08	.04
98	Bill Stanfill	.20	.15	.08
99	Scott Williams	.10	.08	.04
100	**Checklist Card**	.10	.08	.04
101	Len Hauss	.20	.15	.08
102	Jim Griffith	.10	.08	.04
103	Nat Dye	.10	.08	.04
104	Quinton Lumpkin	.10	.08	.04
105	Mike Garrett	.10	.08	.04

106	Glynn Harrison	.10	.08	.04
107	Aaron Chubb	.10	.08	.04
108	John Brantley	.10	.08	.04
109	Pat Hodgson	.10	.08	.04
110	Guy McIntyre	.30	.25	.12
111	Keith Harris	.10	.08	.04
112	Mike Cavan	.10	.08	.04
113	Kevin Jackson	.10	.08	.04
114	Jim Cagle	.10	.08	.04
115	Charles Whittemore	.10	.08	.04
116	Graham Batchelor	.10	.08	.04
117	Art DeCarlo	.20	.15	.08
118	Kendall Keith	.10	.08	.04
119	Jeff Pyburn	.20	.15	.08
120	James Ray	.10	.08	.04
121	Mack Burroughs	.10	.08	.04
122	Jimmy Vickers	.10	.08	.04
123	Charley Britt	.10	.08	.04
124	Matt Braswell	.10	.08	.04
125	Jake Richardson	.10	.08	.04
126	Ronnie Stewart	.10	.08	.04
127	Tim Crowe	.10	.08	.04
128	Troy Sadowski	.10	.08	.04
129	Robert Honeycutt	.10	.08	.04
130	Warren Gray	.10	.08	.04
131	David Guthrie	.10	.08	.04
132	John Lastinger	.20	.15	.08
133	Chip Wisdom	.10	.08	.04
134	Butch Box	.10	.08	.04
135	Tony Cushenberry	.10	.08	.04
136	Vince Guthrie	.10	.08	.04
137	Floyd Reid	.20	.15	.08
138	Mark Hodge	.10	.08	.04
139	Joe Happe	.10	.08	.04
140	Al Bodine	.10	.08	.04
141	Gene Chandler	.10	.08	.04
142	Tommy Lawhorne	.10	.08	.04
143	Bobby Walden	.20	.15	.08
144	Douglas McFalls	.10	.08	.04
145	Jim Milo	.10	.08	.04
146	Billy Payne	.75	.60	.30
147	Paul Holmes	.10	.08	.04
148	Bob Clemens	.10	.08	.04
149	Kenneth Sims	.10	.08	.04
150	Reid Moseley Jr.	.10	.08	.04
151	Tim Callaway	.10	.08	.04
152	Rusty Russell	.10	.08	.04
153	Jim McCollough	.10	.08	.04
154	Wally Williamson	.10	.08	.04
155	John Bond	.10	.08	.04
156	Charley Trippi	.30	.25	.12
157	The Play (Lindsay Scott)	.20	.15	.08
158	Joe Boland	.10	.08	.04
159	Michael Babb	.10	.08	.04
160	Jimmy Poulos	.10	.08	.04
161	Chris McCarthy	.10	.08	.04
162	Billy Mixon	.10	.08	.04
163	Dicky Clark	.10	.08	.04
164	David Rholetter	.10	.08	.04
165	Chuck Heard	.10	.08	.04
166	Pat Field	.10	.08	.04
167	Preston Ridlehuber	.10	.08	.04
168	Heyward Allen	.10	.08	.04
169	Kirby Moore	.10	.08	.04
170	Chris Welton	.10	.08	.04
171	Bill McKenny	.10	.08	.04
172	Steve Boswell	.10	.08	.04
173	Bob Towns	.10	.08	.04
174	Anthony Towns	.10	.08	.04
175	Porter Payne	.10	.08	.04
176	Bobby Garrard	.10	.08	.04
177	Jack Griffith	.10	.08	.04
178	Herschel Walker	.75	.60	.30
179	Andy Perhach	.10	.08	.04
180	Dr. Charles Herty (CO)	.10	.08	.04
181	Kent Lawrence	.20	.15	.08
182	David McKnight	.10	.08	.04
183	Joe Tereshinski	.10	.08	.04
184	Cicero Lucas	.10	.08	.04
185	Glenn "Pop" Warner (CO)	.20	.15	.08
186	Tony Flack	.10	.08	.04
187	Kevin Butler	.20	.15	.08
188	Bill Mitchell	.10	.08	.04
189	Poulos vs. Tech (Jimmy Poulos)	.10	.08	.04
190	Pete Case	.20	.15	.08
191	Pete Tinsley	.10	.08	.04
192	Joe Tereshinski	.20	.15	.08
193	Jimmy Harper	.10	.08	.04
194	Don Leebern	.10	.08	.04
195	Harry Mehre (CO)	.10	.08	.04

196	Retired Jerseys (Herschel Walker, Theron Sapp, Charley Trippi, Frank Sinkwich)	.30	.25	.12
197	Terrie Webster	.10	.08	.04
198	George Woodruff (CO)	.10	.08	.04
199	**First Georgia Team** (1892 Team Photo)	.10	.08	.04
200	**Checklist Card**	.10	.08	.04

1988 Georgia McDag

GEORGIA BULLDOGS 1988

TIM WORLEY
Tailback

		NM/M	NM	E
	Complete Set (16):	65.00	49.00	26.00
	Common Player:	1.00	.70	.40
1	UGA IV (Mascot)	1.00	.70	.40
2	Vince Dooley (AD/CO)	3.00	2.25	1.25
3	Steve Crumley	1.00	.70	.40
4	Aaron Chubb	1.00	.70	.40
5	Keith Henderson	2.00	1.50	.80
6	Steve Harmon	1.00	.70	.40
7	Terrie Webster	1.00	.70	.40
8	John Kasay	4.00	3.00	1.50
9	Wayne Johnson	1.00	.70	.40
10	Tim Worley	2.00	1.50	.80
11	Wycliffe Lovelace	1.00	.70	.40
12	Brent Collins	1.00	.70	.40
13	Vince Guthrie	1.00	.70	.40
14	Todd Wheeler	1.00	.70	.40
15	Bill Goldberg	50.00	37.00	20.00
16	Rodney Hampton	7.00	5.25	2.75

1989 Georgia Police

		NM/M	NM	E
	Complete Set (16):	60.00	45.00	24.00
	Common Player:	.75	.60	.30
1	Hiawatha Berry (58)	.75	.60	.30
2	Brian Cleveland (37)	.75	.60	.30
3	Demetrius Douglas (53)	.75	.60	.30
4	Alphonso Ellis (33)	.75	.60	.30
5	Ray Goff (CO)	1.00	.70	.40
6	Bill Goldberg (95)	50.00	37.00	20.00
7	Rodney Hampton (7)	6.00	4.50	2.50
8	David Hargett (25)	.75	.60	.30
9	Joey Hester (1)	.75	.60	.30
10	John Kasay (3)	3.00	2.25	1.25
11	Mo Lewis	3.00	2.25	1.25
12	Arthur Marshall (12)	1.50	1.25	.60
13	Curt Mull (50)	.75	.60	.30
14	Ben Smith (26)	1.50	1.25	.60
15	Greg Talley (11)	.75	.60	.30
16	Kirk Warner (83)	.75	.60	.30

1990 Georgia Police

		NM/M	NM	E
	Complete Set (14):	10.00	7.50	4.00
	Common Player:	.75	.60	.30
1	John Allen (44)	.75	.60	.30
2	Brian Cleveland (37)	.75	.60	.30
3	Norman Cowins (59)	.75	.60	.30
4	Alphonso Ellis (33)	.75	.60	.30
5	Ray Goff (CO)	1.00	.70	.40
6	David Hargett (25)	.75	.60	.30
7	Sean Hunnings (6)	.75	.60	.30
8	Preston Jones (14)	1.00	.70	.40
9	John Kasay (3)	1.50	1.25	.60
10	Arthur Marshall (12)	1.50	1.25	.60
11	Jack Swan (76)	.75	.60	.30
12	Greg Talley (11)	.75	.60	.30
13	Lemonte Tellis (77)	.75	.60	.30
14	Chris Wilson (16)	.75	.60	.30

1991 Georgia Police

	NM/M	NM	E
Complete Set (16):	15.00	11.00	6.00
Common Player:	.75	.60	.30
1 John Allen	.75	.60	.30
2 Chuck Carswell	.75	.60	.30
3 Russell DeFoor	.75	.60	.30
4 Ray Goff (CO)	1.00	.70	.40
5 David Hargett	.75	.60	.30
6 Andre Hastings	2.50	2.00	1.00
7 Garrison Hearst	6.00	4.50	2.50
8 Arthur Marshall	1.25	.90	.50
9 Kevin Maxwell	.75	.60	.30
10 DeWayne Simmons	.75	.60	.30
11 Jack Swan	.75	.60	.30
12 Greg Talley	.75	.60	.30
13 Lemonte Tellis	.75	.60	.30
14 Chris Wilson	.75	.60	.30
15 George Wynn	.75	.60	.30
16 UGA V (Mascot)	.75	.60	.30

1991 Georgia Southern

	NM/M	NM	E
Complete Set (45):	30.00	22.00	12.00
Common Player:	.60	.45	.25
1 Tracy Ham	4.00	3.00	1.50
2 Tim Foley	1.50	1.25	.60
3 Vance Pike	.60	.45	.25
4 Dennis Franklin	.60	.45	.25
5 Ernest Thompson	.60	.45	.25
6 Giff Smith	.60	.45	.25
7 Flint Matthews	.60	.45	.25
8 Joe Ross	.60	.45	.25
9 Gerald Harris	.60	.45	.25
10 Monty Sharpe	.60	.45	.25
11 The Beginning (Erskine "Erk" Russell) (CO)	1.00	.70	.40
12 Mike West	.60	.45	.25
13 Jessie Jenkins	.60	.45	.25
14 '85 Championship (Ring)	.60	.45	.25
15 Erskine "Erk" Russell (CO)	1.00	.70	.40
16 Tim Brown	.75	.60	.30
17 Taz Dixon	.60	.45	.25
18 '86 Championship	.60	.45	.25
19 Sean Gainey	.60	.45	.25
20 James "Peanut" Carter	.75	.60	.30
21 Ricky Harris	.75	.60	.30
22 Fred Stokes	2.00	1.50	.80
23 Randell Boone	.60	.45	.25
24 Ronald Warnock	.60	.45	.25
25 Raymond Gross	.60	.45	.25
26 Robert Underwood	.60	.45	.25
27 Frank Johnson	.60	.45	.25
28 Darren Alford	.60	.45	.25
29 Darrell Hendrix	.60	.45	.25
30 Raymond Gross	.60	.45	.25
31 Hugo Rossignol	.60	.45	.25
32 Charles Carper	.60	.45	.25
33 Melvin Bell	.60	.45	.25
34 The Catch (Tracy Ham to Frank Johnson)	1.50	1.25	.60
35 Karl Miller	.60	.45	.25
36 Our House - Allen E. Paulson Stadium	.60	.45	.25
37 Danny Durham	.60	.45	.25
38 '89 Championship	.60	.45	.25
39 Tony Belser	.60	.45	.25
40 Nay Young	.60	.45	.25
41 Steve Bussoletti	.60	.45	.25
42 Tim Stowers (CO)	.60	.45	.25
43 Rodney Oglesby	.60	.45	.25
44 '90 Championship	.60	.45	.25
45 Tracy Ham	4.00	3.00	1.50

1973 Giants Color Litho

Measuring 8-1/2" x 11", the eight-card set showcased color lithographs on the front. A facsimile player signature is printed at the bottom right inside a white triangle. The unnumbered cards are not bordered and have blank backs.

	NM	E	VG
Complete Set (8):	50.00	25.00	15.00
Common Player:	5.00	2.50	1.50
1 Jim Files	5.00	2.50	1.50
2 Jack Gregory	5.00	2.50	1.50
3 Ron Johnson	7.50	3.75	2.25
4 Greg Larson	5.00	2.50	1.50
5 Spider Lockhart	7.50	3.75	2.25
6 Norm Snead	12.00	6.00	3.50
7 Bob Tucker	7.50	3.75	2.25
8 Brad Van Pelt	7.50	3.75	2.25

1960 Giants Jay Publishing

This 12-card set shows players in black and white on 5" x 7" cards. Cards were sold in 12-card packs and have blank, unnumbered backs.

	NM	E	VG
Complete Set (12):	85.00	42.00	25.00
Common Player:	4.00	2.00	1.25
1 Roosevelt Brown	8.00	4.00	2.50
2 Don Chandler	4.00	2.00	1.25
3 Charley Conerly	8.00	4.00	2.50
4 Frank Gifford	20.00	10.00	6.00
5 Roosevelt Grier	8.00	4.00	2.50
6 Sam Huff	10.00	5.00	3.00
7 Phil King	4.00	2.00	1.25
8 Andy Robustelli	6.00	3.00	1.75
9 Kyle Rote	6.00	3.00	1.75
10 Bob Schnelker	4.00	2.00	1.25
11 Pat Summerall	6.00	3.00	1.75
12 Alex Webster	5.00	2.50	1.50

1961 Giants Jay Publishing

Similar to the 1960 issue, this 12-card set is composed of black and white, 5" x 7" photos. It features traditional players and was available in 12-card packs.

	NM	E	VG
Complete Set (12):	65.00	32.00	19.50
Common Player:	4.00	2.00	1.25
1 Roosevelt Brown	10.00	5.00	3.00
2 Don Chandler	4.00	2.00	1.25
3 Charley Conerly	10.00	5.00	3.00
4 Roosevelt Grier	8.00	4.00	2.50
5 Sam Huff	10.00	5.00	3.00
6 Dick Modzelewski	4.00	2.00	1.25
7 Jimmy Patton	5.00	2.50	1.50
8 Jim Podoley	4.00	2.00	1.25
9 Andy Robustelli	8.00	4.00	2.50
10 Allie Sherman (CO)	4.00	2.00	1.25
11 Del Shofner	5.00	2.50	1.50
12 Y.A. Tittle	15.00	7.50	4.50

1987 Giants Police

Measuring 2-3/4" x 4-1/8", the 12-card set is anchored by a large photo on the front, with "New York Giants" printed at the top. Beneath the photo are the player's name and position printed between Giants' helmets. The card backs, which are unnumbered, have "Tips from the Giants" at the top, with two New Jersey law enforcement logos printed below. A safety tip and a McGruff the Crime Dog logo round out the backs. Overall, 10,000 sets were printed.

	NM/M	NM	E
Complete Set (12):	75.00	56.00	30.00
Common Player:	3.00	2.25	1.25
1 Carl Banks	5.00	3.75	2.00
2 Mark Bavaro	5.00	3.75	2.00
3 Brad Benson	3.00	2.25	1.25
4 Jim Burt	3.00	2.25	1.25
5 Harry Carson	5.00	3.75	2.00
6 Maurice Carthon	3.00	2.25	1.25
7 Sean Landeta	3.00	2.25	1.25
8 Leonard Marshall	5.00	3.75	2.00
9 George Martin	3.00	2.25	1.25
10 Joe Morris	6.00	4.50	2.50
11 Bill Parcells (CO)	8.00	6.00	3.25
12 Phil Simms	25.00	18.50	10.00

1988 Giants Police

Measuring 2-3/4" x 4-1/8", the card fronts are anchored by a large photo. A Giants' helmet is printed in both corners at the top, with "New York Giants" located at the top center. Beneath the photo are the player's name, number, position and bio. The unnumbered backs have "Tips from the Giants" at the top, with two New Jersey law enforcement logos located underneath. A safety tip and a McGruff the Crime Dog logo round out the card backs.

	NM/M	NM	E
Complete Set (12):	55.00	41.00	22.00
Common Player:	3.00	2.25	1.25
1 Billy Ard	3.00	2.25	1.25
2 Jim Burt	3.00	2.25	1.25
3 Harry Carson	5.00	3.75	2.00
4 Maurice Carthon	3.00	2.25	1.25
5 Leonard Marshall	5.00	3.75	2.00
6 George Martin	3.00	2.25	1.25
7 Phil McConkey	3.00	2.25	1.25
8 Joe Morris	6.00	4.50	2.50
9 Karl Nelson	3.00	2.25	1.25
10 Bart Oates	5.00	3.75	2.00
11 Bill Parcells (CO)	8.00	6.00	3.25
12 Phil Simms	16.00	12.00	6.50

1990 Giants Police

Measuring 2-3/4" x 4-1/8", the 12-card set is anchored by a large photo on the front, with a Giants' helmet in each of the top corners, with "New York Giants" printed at the top center. The player's name, position and bio are printed under the photo. The card backs, which are unnumbered, have "Tips from the Giants" at the top, with two New Jersey law enforcement logos beneath it. A safety tip and a McGruff the Crime Dog logo round out the card backs.

	NM/M	NM	E
Complete Set (12):	45.00	34.00	18.00
Common Player:	2.50	2.00	1.00
1 Ottis Anderson	5.00	3.75	2.00
2 Matt Bahr	2.50	2.00	1.00
3 Eric Dorsey	2.50	2.00	1.00
4 John Elliott	2.50	2.00	1.00
5 Ray Handley (CO)	2.50	2.00	1.00
6 Jeff Hostetler	7.00	5.25	2.75
7 Erik Howard	2.50	2.00	1.00
8 Pepper Johnson	4.00	3.00	1.50
9 Leonard Marshall	4.00	3.00	1.50
10 Bart Oates	4.00	3.00	1.50
11 Gary Reasons	2.50	2.00	1.00
12 Phil Simms	8.00	6.00	3.25

1960 Giants Shell/Riger Posters

This set features 10 black and white posters by Robert Siger and distributed by Shell Oil in 1960. Each poster measures approximately 11-3/4" x 13-3/4".

	NM	E	VG
Complete Set (10):	150.00	75.00	45.00
Common Player:	10.00	5.00	3.00
1 Charley Connerly	25.00	12.50	7.50
2 Frank Gifford	45.00	22.00	13.50
3 Sam Huff	20.00	10.00	6.00
4 Dick Modzelewski	10.00	5.00	3.00
5 Jim Patton	10.00	5.00	3.00
6 Andy Robustelli	16.00	8.00	4.75
7 Kyle Rote	16.00	8.00	4.75
8 Bob Schnelker	10.00	5.00	3.00
9 Pat Summerall	20.00	10.00	6.00
10 Alex Webster, Roosevelt Brown	16.00	8.00	4.75

1956 Giants Team Issue

This 36-card, black and white set contains posed player shots on the front surrounded by a white border and a facsimile signature. Backs are unnumbered, while each card measures approximately 5" x 7".

	NM	E	VG
Complete Set (36):	200.00	100.00	60.00
Common Player:	4.00	2.00	1.25
1 Bill Austin	4.00	2.00	1.25
2 Ray Beck	4.00	2.00	1.25
3 Roosevelt Brown	10.00	5.00	3.00
4 Hank Burnine	4.00	2.00	1.25
5 Don Chandler	4.00	2.00	1.25
6 Bobby Clatterbuck	4.00	2.00	1.25
7 Charley Conerly	20.00	10.00	6.00
8 Frank Gifford	30.00	15.00	9.00
9 Roosevelt Grier	10.00	5.00	3.00
10 Don Heinrich	5.00	2.50	1.50
11 John Hermann	4.00	2.00	1.25
12 Jim Lee Howell (CO)	5.00	2.50	1.50
13 Sam Huff	16.00	8.00	4.75
14 Ed Hughes	4.00	2.00	1.25
15 Gerald Huth	4.00	2.00	1.25
16 Jim Katcavage	6.00	3.00	1.75
17 Gene Kirby (ANN)	4.00	2.00	1.25
18 Ken MacAfee	5.00	2.50	1.50
19 Dick Modzelewski (Misspelled Modelewski on the reverse)	5.00	2.50	1.50
20 Henry Moore	4.00	2.00	1.25
21 Dick Nolan	5.00	2.50	1.50
22 Jimmy Patton	5.00	2.50	1.50
23 Andy Robustelli	10.00	5.00	3.00
24 Kyle Rote	10.00	5.00	3.00
25 Chris Schenkel (ANN)	5.00	2.50	1.50
26 Bob Schnelker	4.00	2.00	1.25
27 Jack Stroud	4.00	2.00	1.25
28 Harland Svare	5.00	2.50	1.50
29 Bill Svoboda	4.00	2.00	1.25
30 Bob Topp	4.00	2.00	1.25
31 Mel Triplett	5.00	2.50	1.50
32 Emlen Tunnell	10.00	5.00	3.00
33 Alex Webster	5.00	2.50	1.50
34 Ray Wietecha	4.00	2.00	1.25
35 Dick Yelvington	4.00	2.00	1.25
36 Walt Yowarsky	4.00	2.00	1.25

1957 Giants Team Issue

This 1957 Giants team set measures approximately 5" x 7", with black and white photos and a glossy finish. The set contains 40 unnumbered cards that are listed below in alphabetical order.

		NM	E	VG
Complete Set (40):		250.00	125.00	75.00
Common Player:		4.00	2.00	1.25
1	Ben Agajanian	4.00	2.00	1.25
2	Bill Austin	4.00	2.00	1.25
3	Ray Beck	4.00	2.00	1.25
4	John Bookman	4.00	2.00	1.25
5	Roosevelt Brown	8.00	4.00	2.50
6	Don Chandler	5.00	2.50	1.50
7	Bobby Clatterbuck	4.00	2.00	1.25
8	Charley Conerly	15.00	7.50	4.50
9	John Dell Isola (CO)	4.00	2.00	1.25
10	Gene Filipski	5.00	2.50	1.50
11	Frank Gifford	25.00	12.50	7.50
12	Don Heinrich	5.00	2.50	1.50
13	Jim Lee Howell (CO)	5.00	2.50	1.50
14	Sam Huff	10.00	5.00	3.00
15	Ed Hughes	4.00	2.00	1.25
16	Gerald Huth	4.00	2.00	1.25
17	Jim Katcavage	5.00	2.50	1.50
18	Ken Kavanaugh (CO)	5.00	2.50	1.50
19	Les Keiter (ANN)	4.00	2.00	1.25
20	Tom Landry (CO)	45.00	22.00	13.50
21	Cliff Livingston	4.00	2.00	1.25
22	Vince Lombardi (CO)	50.00	25.00	15.00
23	Ken MacAfee	5.00	2.50	1.50
24	Dennis Mendyk	4.00	2.00	1.25
25	Dick Modzelewski	5.00	2.50	1.50
26	Dick Nolan	5.00	2.50	1.50
27	Jim Patton	5.00	2.50	1.50
28	Andy Robustelli	10.00	5.00	3.00
29	Kyle Rote	10.00	5.00	3.00
30	Chris Schenkel (ANN)	5.00	2.50	1.50
31	Jack Spinks	4.00	2.00	1.25
32	Jack Stroud	4.00	2.00	1.25
33	Harland Svare	4.00	2.00	1.25
34	Bill Svoboda	4.00	2.00	1.25
35	Mel Triplett	5.00	2.50	1.50
36	Emlen Tunnell	8.00	4.00	2.50
37	Alex Webster	5.00	2.50	1.50
38	Ray Wietecha	5.00	2.50	1.50
39	Dick Yelvington	4.00	2.00	1.25
40	Walt Yowarsky	4.00	2.00	1.25

1969 Glendale Stamps

These unnumbered stamps, which measure 1-13/16" x 3-15/16", feature a color player photo on the front; the back has his name, team and instructions on how to apply the stamp to the corresponding album which was produced. "Dampen strip and affix in ablum" is on the back. The album measures 9" x 12" and is arranged alphabetically by team city.

		NM	E	VG
Complete Set (312):		200.00	100.00	60.00
Common Player:		.25	.13	.08
(1)	Bob Berry	.40	.20	.12
(2)	Clark Miller	.25	.13	.08
(3)	Jim Butler	.25	.13	.08
(4)	Junior Coffey	.25	.13	.08
(5)	Paul Flatley	.40	.20	.12
(6)	Randy Johnson	.45	.25	.14
(7)	Charlie Bryant	.25	.13	.08
(8)	Billy Lothridge	.25	.13	.08
(9)	Tommy Nobis	2.00	1.00	.60
(10)	Claude Humphrey	.40	.20	.12
(11)	Ken Reaves	.25	.13	.08
(12)	Jerry Simmons	.40	.20	.12
(13)	Mike Curtis	.75	.40	.25
(14)	Dennis Gaubatz	.25	.13	.08
(15)	Jerry Logan	.25	.13	.08
(16)	Lenny Lyles	.25	.13	.08
(17)	John Mackey	2.00	1.00	.60
(18)	Tom Matte	.50	.25	.15
(19)	Lou Michaels	.35	.20	.11
(20)	Jimmy Orr	.50	.25	.15
(21)	Willie Richardson	.35	.20	.11
(22)	Don Shinnick	.25	.13	.08
(23)	Dan Sullivan	.25	.13	.08
(24)	Johnny Unitas	15.00	7.50	4.50
(25)	Houston Antwine	.25	.13	.08
(26)	John Bramlett	.25	.13	.08
(27)	Aaron Marsh	.25	.13	.08
(28)	R.C. Gamble	.25	.13	.08
(29)	Gino Cappelletti	.75	.40	.25
(30)	John Charles	.25	.13	.08
(31)	Larry Eisenhauer	.35	.20	.11
(32)	Jon Morris	.25	.13	.08
(33)	Jim Nance	.50	.25	.15
(34)	Len St. Jean	.25	.13	.08
(35)	Mike Taliaferro	.25	.13	.08
(36)	Jim Whalen	.25	.13	.08
(37)	Stew Barber	.35	.20	.11
(38)	Al Bemiller	.25	.13	.08
(39)	George (Butch) Byrd	.35	.20	.11
(40)	Booker Edgerson	.25	.13	.08
(41)	Harry Jacobs	.35	.20	.11
(42)	Jack Kemp	18.00	9.00	5.50
(43)	Ron McDole	.35	.20	.11
(44)	Joe O'Donnell	.25	.13	.08
(45)	John Pitts	.25	.13	.08
(46)	George Saimes	.35	.20	.11
(47)	Mike Stratton	.35	.20	.11
(48)	O.J. Simpson	35.00	17.50	10.50
(49)	Ronnie Bull	.35	.20	.11
(50)	Dick Butkus	8.00	4.00	2.50
(51)	Jim Cadile	.25	.13	.08
(52)	Jack Concannon	.35	.20	.11
(53)	Dick Evey	.25	.13	.08
(54)	Bennie McRae	.25	.13	.08
(55)	Ed O'Bradovich	.25	.13	.08
(56)	Brian Piccolo	10.00	5.00	3.00
(57)	Mike Pyle	.25	.13	.08
(58)	Gale Sayers	10.00	5.00	3.00
(59)	Dick Gordon	.35	.20	.11
(60)	Roosevelt Taylor	.35	.20	.11
(61)	Al Beauchamp	.25	.13	.08
(62)	Dave Middendorf	.25	.13	.08
(63)	Harry Gunner	.25	.13	.08
(64)	Bobby Hunt	.25	.13	.08
(65)	Bob Johnson	.40	.20	.12
(66)	Charley King	.25	.13	.08
(67)	Andy Rice	.25	.13	.08
(68)	Paul Robinson	.35	.20	.11
(69)	Bill Staley	.25	.13	.08
(70)	Pat Matson	.25	.13	.08
(71)	Bob Trumpy	2.00	1.00	.60
(72)	Sam Wyche	5.00	2.50	1.50
(73)	Erich Barnes	.35	.20	.11
(74)	Gary Collins	.35	.20	.11
(75)	Ben Davis	.25	.13	.08
(76)	John Demarie	.25	.13	.08
(77)	Gene Hickerson	.35	.20	.11
(78)	Jim Houston	.35	.20	.11
(79)	Ernie Kellerman	.25	.13	.08
(80)	Leroy Kelly	3.00	1.50	.90
(81)	Dale Lindsey	.25	.13	.08
(82)	Bill Nelsen	.75	.40	.25
(83)	Jim Kanicki	.25	.13	.08
(84)	Dick Schafrath	.35	.20	.11
(85)	George Andrie	.75	.40	.25
(86)	Mike Clark	.25	.13	.08
(87)	Cornell Green	.50	.25	.15
(88)	Bob Hayes	1.50	.70	.45
(89)	Chuck Howley	.75	.40	.25
(90)	Lee Roy Jordan	1.25	.60	.40
(91)	Bob Lilly	3.00	1.50	.90
(92)	Craig Morton	1.00	.50	.30
(93)	John Niland	.25	.13	.08
(94)	Dan Reeves	5.00	2.50	1.50
(95)	Mel Renfro	1.00	.50	.30
(96)	Lance Rentzel	.50	.25	.15
(97)	Tom Beer	.25	.13	.08
(98)	Billy Van Heusen	.25	.13	.08
(99)	Mike Current	.25	.13	.08
(100)	Al Denson	.25	.13	.08
(101)	Pete Duranko	.25	.13	.08
(102)	George Goeddeke	.25	.13	.08
(103)	John Huard	.25	.13	.08
(104)	Richard Jackson	.25	.13	.08
(105)	Pete Jaquess	.35	.20	.11
(106)	Fran Lynch	.25	.13	.08
(107)	Floyd Little	2.00	1.00	.60
(108)	Steve Tensi	.50	.25	.15
(109)	Lem Barney	3.00	1.50	.90
(110)	Nick Eddy	.50	.25	.15
(111)	Mel Farr	.75	.40	.25
(112)	Ed Flanagan	.25	.13	.08
(113)	Larry Hand	.25	.13	.08
(114)	Alex Karras	2.50	1.25	.70
(115)	Dick LeBeau	.35	.20	.11
(116)	Mike Lucci	.35	.20	.11
(117)	Earl McCullouch	.35	.20	.11
(118)	Bill Munson	.40	.20	.12
(119)	Jerry Rush	.25	.13	.08
(120)	Wayne Walker	.35	.20	.11
(121)	Herb Adderley	2.00	1.00	.60
(122)	Donny Anderson	.50	.25	.15
(123)	Lee Roy Caffey	.25	.13	.08
(124)	Carroll Dale	.35	.20	.11
(125)	Willie Davis	1.50	.70	.45
(126)	Boyd Dowler	.35	.20	.11
(127)	Marv Fleming	.50	.25	.15
(128)	Bob Jeter	.35	.20	.11
(129)	Henry Jordan	.35	.20	.11
(130)	Dave Robinson	.35	.20	.11
(131)	Bart Starr	10.00	5.00	3.00
(132)	Willie Wood	1.50	.70	.45
(133)	Pete Beathard	.75	.40	.25
(134)	Jim Beirne	.25	.13	.08
(135)	Garland Boyette	.25	.13	.08
(136)	Woody Campbell	.25	.13	.08
(137)	Miller Farr	.25	.13	.08
(138)	Hoyle Granger	.25	.13	.08
(139)	Mac Haik	.25	.13	.08
(140)	Ken Houston	3.00	1.50	.90
(141)	Bobby Maples	.35	.20	.11
(142)	Alvin Reed	.25	.13	.08
(143)	Don Trull	.35	.20	.11
(144)	George Webster	.50	.25	.15
(145)	Bobby Bell	2.00	1.00	.60
(146)	Aaron Brown	.25	.13	.08
(147)	Buck Buchanan	2.00	1.00	.60
(148)	Len Dawson	5.00	2.50	1.50
(149)	Mike Garrett	.50	.25	.15
(150)	Robert Holmes	.35	.20	.11
(151)	Willie Lanier	3.00	1.50	.90
(152)	Frank Pitts	.25	.13	.08
(153)	Johnny Robinson	.75	.40	.25
(154)	Jan Stenerud	3.00	1.50	.90
(155)	Otis Taylor	.75	.40	.25
(156)	Jim Tyrer	.50	.25	.15
(157)	Dick Bass	.35	.20	.11
(158)	Maxie Baughan	.50	.25	.15
(159)	Rich Petitbon	.50	.25	.15
(160)	Roger Brown	.35	.20	.11
(161)	Roman Gabriel	1.50	.70	.45
(162)	Bruce Gossett	.25	.13	.08
(163)	David (Deacon) Jones	1.50	.70	.45
(164)	Tom Mack	1.25	.60	.40
(165)	Tommy Mason	.50	.25	.15
(166)	Ed Meador	.35	.20	.11
(167)	Merlin Olsen	3.00	1.50	.90
(168)	Pat Studstill	.35	.20	.11
(169)	Jack Clancy	.25	.13	.08
(170)	Maxie Williams	.25	.13	.08
(171)	Larry Csonka	10.00	5.00	3.00
(172)	Jimmy Warren	.25	.13	.08
(173)	Norm Evans	.35	.20	.11
(174)	Rick Norton	.25	.13	.08
(175)	Bob Griese	7.50	3.75	2.25
(176)	Howard Twilley	.50	.25	.15
(177)	Billy Neighbors	.35	.20	.11
(178)	Nick Buoniconti	1.25	.60	.40
(179)	Tom Goode	.25	.13	.08
(180)	Dick Westmoreland	.25	.13	.08
(181)	Grady Alderman	.25	.13	.08
(182)	Bill Brown	.75	.40	.25
(183)	Fred Cox	.35	.20	.11
(184)	Clint Jones	.35	.20	.11
(185)	Joe Kapp	1.00	.50	.30
(186)	Paul Krause	1.00	.50	.30
(187)	Gary Larsen	.25	.13	.08
(188)	Jim Marshall	1.50	.70	.45
(189)	Dave Osborn	.25	.13	.08
(190)	Alan Page	4.00	2.00	1.25
191	Mike Tingelhoff	.75	.40	.25
(192)	Roy Winston	.35	.20	.11
(193)	Dan Abramowicz	.50	.25	.15
(194)	Doug Atkins	1.50	.70	.45
(195)	Bo Burris	.25	.13	.08
(196)	John Douglas	.25	.13	.08
(197)	Don Shy	.25	.13	.08
(198)	Bill Kilmer	.75	.40	.25
(199)	Tony Lorick	.25	.13	.08
(200)	David Parks	.50	.25	.15
(201)	Dave Rowe	.25	.13	.08
(202)	Monty Stickles	.25	.13	.08
(203)	Steve Stonebreaker	.35	.20	.11
(204)	Del Williams	.25	.13	.08
(205)	Pete Case	.25	.13	.08
(206)	Tommy Crutcher	.35	.20	.11
(207)	Scott Eaton	.25	.13	.08
(208)	Tucker Frederickson	.75	.40	.25
(209)	Peter Gogolak	.35	.20	.11
(210)	Homer Jones	.35	.20	.11
(211)	Ernie Koy	.35	.20	.11
(212)	Carl (Spider) Lockhart	.35	.20	.11
(213)	Bruce Maher	.25	.13	.08
(214)	Aaron Thomas	.35	.20	.11
(215)	Fran Tarkenton	12.00	6.00	3.50
(216)	Jim Katcavage	.35	.20	.11
(217)	Al Atkinson	.25	.13	.08
(218)	Emerson Boozer	.35	.20	.11
(219)	John Elliott	.25	.13	.08
(220)	Dave Herman	.25	.13	.08

(221) Winston Hill	.35	.20	.11	
(222) Jim Hudson	.25	.13	.08	
(223) Pete Lammons	.35	.20	.11	
(224) Gerry Philbin	.35	.20	.11	
(225) George Sauer	.50	.25	.15	
(226) Joe Namath	20.00	10.00	6.00	
(227) Matt Snell	.50	.25	.15	
(228) Jim Turner	.35	.20	.11	
(229) Fred Biletnikoff	3.00	1.50	.90	
(230) Willie Brown	1.50	.70	.45	
(231) Billy Cannon	.50	.25	.15	
(232) Dan Conners	.25	.13	.08	
(233) Ben Davidson	.75	.40	.25	
(234) Hewritt Dixon	.35	.20	.11	
(235) Daryle Lamonica	1.00	.50	.30	
(236) Ike Lassiter	.25	.13	.08	
(237) Ken McCloughan	.25	.13	.08	
(238) Jim Otto	1.50	.70	.45	
(239) Harry Schuh	.25	.13	.08	
(240) Gene Upshaw	3.00	1.50	.90	
(241) Gary Ballman	.35	.20	.11	
(242) Joe Carollo	.25	.13	.08	
(243) Dave Lloyd	.25	.13	.08	
(244) Fred Hill	.25	.13	.08	
(245) Al Nelson	.25	.13	.08	
(246) Joe Scarpati	.25	.13	.08	
(247) Sam Baker	.35	.20	.11	
(248) Fred Brown	.25	.13	.08	
(249) Floyd Peters	.50	.25	.15	
(250) Nate Ramsey	.25	.13	.08	
(251) Norman Snead	.50	.25	.15	
(252) Tom Woodeshick	.25	.13	.08	
(253) John Hilton	.25	.13	.08	
(254) Kent Nix	.25	.13	.08	
(255) Paul Martha	.50	.25	.15	
(256) Ben McGee	.25	.13	.08	
(257) Andy Russell	.50	.25	.15	
(258) Dick Shiner	.25	.13	.08	
(259) J.R. Wilburn	.25	.13	.08	
(260) Marv Woodson	.25	.13	.08	
(261) Earl Gros	.25	.13	.08	
(262) Dick Hoak	.50	.25	.15	
(263) Roy Jefferson	.50	.25	.15	
(264) Larry Gagner	.25	.13	.08	
(265) Johnny Roland	.75	.40	.25	
(266) Jackie Smith	3.00	1.50	.90	
(267) Jim Bakken	.50	.25	.15	
(268) Don Brumm	.25	.13	.08	
(269) Bob DeMarco	.35	.20	.11	
(270) Irv Goode	.25	.13	.08	
(271) Ken Gray	.35	.20	.11	
(272) Charlie Johnson	1.00	.50	.30	
(273) Ernie McMillan	.35	.20	.11	
(274) Larry Stallings	.35	.20	.11	
(275) Jerry Stovall	.50	.25	.15	
(276) Larry Wilson	1.50	.70	.45	
(277) Chuck Allen	.25	.13	.08	
(278) Lance Alworth	3.00	1.50	.90	
(279) Kenny Graham	.25	.13	.08	
(280) Steve DeLong	.35	.20	.11	
(281) Willie Frazier	.35	.20	.11	
(282) Gary Garrison	.35	.20	.11	
(283) Sam Gruniesen	.25	.13	.08	
(284) John Hadl	.75	.40	.25	
(285) Brad Hubbert	.25	.13	.08	
(286) Ron Mix	2.00	1.00	.60	
(287) Dick Post	.35	.20	.11	
(288) Walt Sweeney	.35	.20	.11	
(289) Kermit Alexander	.50	.25	.15	
(290) Ed Beard	.25	.13	.08	
(291) Bruce Bosley	.35	.20	.11	
(292) John Brodie	3.00	1.50	.90	
(293) Stan Hindman	.25	.13	.08	
(294) Jim Johnson	1.50	.70	.45	
(295) Charlie Krueger	.35	.20	.11	
(296) Clifton McNeil	.35	.20	.11	
(297) Gary Lewis	.25	.13	.08	
(298) Howard Mudd	.25	.13	.08	
(299) Dave Wilcox	.50	.25	.15	
(300) Ken Willard	.50	.25	.15	
(301) Charlie Gogolak	.35	.20	.11	
(302) Len Hauss	.50	.25	.15	
(303) Sonny Jurgensen	3.50	1.75	1.00	
(304) Carl Kammerer	.25	.13	.08	
(305) Walt Rock	.25	.13	.08	
(306) Ray Schoenke	.25	.13	.08	
(307) Chris Hanburger	.75	.40	.25	
(308) Tom Brown	.50	.25	.15	
(309) Sam Huff	2.00	1.00	.60	
(310) Bob Long	.25	.13	.08	
(311) Vince Promuto	.25	.13	.08	
(312) Pat Richter	.50	.25	.15	

1989 Goal Line Hall of Fame

These postcard-size cards (4" x 6") feature full-color action paintings of inductees into the Pro Football Hall of Fame. The cards were part of an art series done by artist Gary Thomas and were offered by subscription. Each set was packaged in a custom box and was given a serial number (Set No. x of 5,000), which appears on each card, too. The back of the card is white and uses black ink. The player's name, college, position, biographical information, years he played, teams he played with and the year he was inducted are all listed, as well as a set and card number. A Football Hall of Fame logo is also given. Each of the first five series contains 30 cards; series 6 has 25. However, a card for Johnny Unitas (#174) was never issued. Series I was issued in 1989; a new series has followed each year since then. The cards are numbered alphabetically within each series.

	NM/M	NM	E
Complete Set (175):	400.00	300.00	160.00
Common Player:	2.00	1.50	.80
1 Lance Alworth	6.00	4.50	2.50
2 Morris "Red" Badgro	2.50	2.00	1.00
3 Cliff Battles	2.50	2.00	1.00
4 Mel Blount	2.50	2.00	1.00
5 Terry Bradshaw	10.00	7.50	4.00
6 Jim Brown	12.00	9.00	4.75
7 George Connor	2.50	2.00	1.00
8 Turk Edwards	2.50	2.00	1.00
9 Tom Fears	2.50	2.00	1.00
10 Frank Gifford	10.00	7.50	4.00
11 Otto Graham	6.00	4.50	2.50
12 Harold "Red" Grange	5.00	3.75	2.00
13 George Halas	4.00	3.00	1.50
14 Clarke Hinkle	2.50	2.00	1.00
15 Robert "Cal" Hubbard	2.50	2.00	1.00
16 Sam Huff	2.50	2.00	1.00
17 Frank "Bruiser" Kinard	2.50	2.00	1.00
18 Dick "Night Train" Lane	2.50	2.00	1.00
19 Sid Luckman	6.00	4.50	2.50
20 Bobby Mitchell	2.50	2.00	1.00
21 Merlin Olsen	4.00	3.00	1.50
22 Jim Parker	2.50	2.00	1.00
23 Joe Perry	3.00	2.25	1.25
24 Pete Rozelle	3.00	2.25	1.25
25 Art Shell	3.00	2.25	1.25
26 Fran Tarkenton	9.00	6.75	3.50
27 Jim Thorpe	6.00	4.50	2.50
28 Paul Warfield	3.00	2.25	1.25
29 Larry Wilson	2.50	2.00	1.00
30 Willie Wood	2.50	2.00	1.00
31 Doug Atkins	2.00	1.50	.80
32 Bobby Bell	2.00	1.50	.80
33 Raymond Berry	3.00	2.25	1.25
34 Paul Brown	2.00	1.50	.80
35 Guy Chamberlin	2.00	1.50	.80
36 Earl "Dutch" Clark	2.00	1.50	.80
37 Jimmy Conzelman	2.00	1.50	.80
38 Len Dawson	3.00	2.25	1.25
39 Mike Ditka	8.00	6.00	3.25
40 Dan Fortmann	2.00	1.50	.80
41 Frank Gatski	2.00	1.50	.80
42 Bill George	2.00	1.50	.80
43 Elroy Hirsch	3.00	2.25	1.25
44 Paul Hornung	4.00	3.00	1.50
45 John Henry Johnson	2.00	1.50	.80
46 Walt Kiesling	2.00	1.50	.80
47 Yale Lary	2.00	1.50	.80
48 Bobby Layne	3.00	2.25	1.25
49 Tuffy Leemans	2.00	1.50	.80
50 Geo. Preston Marshall	2.00	1.50	.80
51 George McAfee	2.00	1.50	.80
52 Wayne Millner	2.00	1.50	.80
53 Bronko Nagurski	4.00	3.00	1.50
54 Joe Namath	12.00	9.00	4.75
55 Ray Nitschke	3.00	2.25	1.25
56 Jim Ringo	2.00	1.50	.80
57 Art Rooney	2.00	1.50	.80

58 Joe Stydahar	2.00	1.50	.80
59 Charley Taylor	2.00	1.50	.80
60 Charlie Trippi	2.00	1.50	.80
61 Fred Biletnikoff	3.00	2.25	1.25
62 Buck Buchanan	2.00	1.50	.80
63 Dick Butkus	6.00	4.50	2.50
64 Earl Campbell	8.00	6.00	3.25
65 Tony Canadeo	2.00	1.50	.80
66 Art Donovan	3.00	2.25	1.25
67 Ray Flaherty	2.00	1.50	.80
68 Forrest Gregg	2.50	2.00	1.00
69 Lou Groza	3.00	2.25	1.25
70 John Hannah	2.00	1.50	.80
71 Don Hutson	2.50	2.00	1.00
72 David (Deacon) Jones	2.00	1.50	.80
73 Stan Jones	2.00	1.50	.80
74 Sonny Jurgensen	3.00	2.25	1.25
75 Vince Lombardi	3.00	2.25	1.25
76 Tim Mara	2.00	1.50	.80
77 Ollie Matson	2.00	1.50	.80
78 Mike McCormack	2.00	1.50	.80
79 John "Blood" McNally	2.00	1.50	.80
80 Marion Motley	2.00	1.50	.80
81 George Musso	2.00	1.50	.80
82 Earle "Greasy" Neale	2.00	1.50	.80
83 Clarence "Ace" Parker	2.00	1.50	.80
84 Pete Pihos	2.00	1.50	.80
85 Tex Schramm	2.00	1.50	.80
86 Roger Staubach	12.00	9.00	4.75
87 Jan Stenerud	2.00	1.50	.80
88 Y.A. Tittle	3.00	2.25	1.25
89 Clyde "Bulldog" Turner	2.00	1.50	.80
90 Steve Van Buren	2.00	1.50	.80
91 Herb Adderley	2.00	1.50	.80
92 Lem Barney	2.00	1.50	.80
93 Sammy Baugh	5.00	3.75	2.00
94 Chuck Bednarik	3.00	2.25	1.25
95 Charles W. Bidwill	2.00	1.50	.80
96 Willie Brown	2.00	1.50	.80
97 Al Davis	4.00	3.00	1.50
98 Bill Dudley	2.00	1.50	.80
99 Weeb Ewbank	2.00	1.50	.80
100 Len Ford	2.00	1.50	.80
101 Sid Gillman	2.00	1.50	.80
102 Jack Ham	2.00	1.50	.80
103 Mel Hein	2.00	1.50	.80
104 Bill Hewitt	2.00	1.50	.80
105 Dante Lavelli	2.00	1.50	.80
106 Bob Lilly	3.00	2.25	1.25
107 John Mackey	2.00	1.50	.80
108 Hugh McElhenny	3.00	2.25	1.25
109 Mike Michalske	2.00	1.50	.80
110 Ron Mix	2.00	1.50	.80
111 Leo Nomenllini	2.00	1.50	.80
112 Steve Owen	2.00	1.50	.80
113 Alan Page	2.50	2.00	1.00
114 Dan Reeves	2.00	1.50	.80
115 John Riggins	3.00	2.25	1.25
116 Gale Sayers	6.00	4.50	2.50
117 Ken Strong	2.00	1.50	.80
118 Gene Upshaw	3.00	2.25	1.25
119 Norm Van Brocklin	4.00	3.00	1.50
120 Alex Wojciechowicz	2.00	1.50	.80
121 Bert Bell	2.00	1.50	.80
122 George Blanda	4.00	3.00	1.50
123 Joe Carr	2.00	1.50	.80
124 Larry Csonka	4.00	3.00	1.50
125 John (Paddy) Driscoll	2.00	1.50	.80
126 Dan Fouts	3.00	2.25	1.25
127 Bob Griese	4.00	3.00	1.50
128 Ed Healy	2.00	1.50	.80
129 Wilbur "Fats" Henry	2.00	1.50	.80
130 Ken Houston	2.00	1.50	.80
131 Lamar Hunt	2.00	1.50	.80
132 Jack Lambert	2.50	2.00	1.00
133 Tom Landry	4.00	3.00	1.50
134 Willie Lanier	2.00	1.50	.80
135 Larry Little	2.00	1.50	.80
136 Don Maynard	3.00	2.25	1.25
137 Lenny Moore	3.00	2.25	1.25
138 Chuck Noll	3.00	2.25	1.25
139 Jim Otto	2.00	1.50	.80
140 Walter Payton	10.00	7.50	4.00
141 Hugh (Shorty) Ray	2.00	1.50	.80
142 Andy Robustelli	2.00	1.50	.80
143 Bob St. Clair	2.00	1.50	.80
144 Joe Schmidt	3.00	2.25	1.25
145 Jim Taylor	3.00	2.25	1.25
146 Doak Walker	3.00	2.25	1.25
147 Bill Walsh	3.00	2.25	1.25
148 Bob Waterfield	3.00	2.25	1.25
149 Arnie Weinmeister	2.00	1.50	.80
150 Bill Willis	2.00	1.50	.80

151	Roosevelt Brown	2.00	1.50	.80
152	Jack Christiansen	2.00	1.50	.80
153	Willie Davis	3.00	2.25	1.25
154	Tony Dorsett	6.00	4.50	2.50
155	Bud Grant	2.00	1.50	.80
156	Joe Greene	5.00	3.75	2.00
157	Joe Guyon	2.00	1.50	.80
158	Franco Harris	4.00	3.00	1.50
159	Ted Hendricks	2.00	1.50	.80
160	Arnie Herber	2.00	1.50	.80
161	Jimmy Johnson	2.00	1.50	.80
162	Leroy Kelly	2.00	1.50	.80
163	Curly Lambeau	2.00	1.50	.80
164	Jim Langer	2.00	1.50	.80
165	Link Lyman	2.00	1.50	.80
166	Gino Marchetti	3.00	2.25	1.25
167	Ernie Nevers	3.00	2.25	1.25
168	O.J. Simpson	12.00	9.00	4.75
169	Jackie Smith	2.00	1.50	.80
170	Bart Starr	6.00	4.50	2.50
171	Ernie Stautner	2.50	2.00	1.00
172	George Trafton	2.00	1.50	.80
173	Emien Tunnell	2.00	1.50	.80
174	Johnny Unitas (not issued)			
175	Randy White	2.00	1.50	.80
176	Jim Finks	2.00	1.50	.80
177	Henry Jordan	2.00	1.50	.80
178	Steve Largent	4.00	3.00	1.50
179	Lee Roy Selmon	2.00	1.50	.80
180	Kellen Winslow	2.00	1.50	.80

1939 Gridiron Greats Blotters

The 12-card, 3-7/8" x 9" blotter set was sponsored by Louis F. Dow Company. The blotter card fronts feature a headshot on the left side, superimposed over a football, with the collegiate player's school letter appearing in a pennant below. The right side of the card blotters feature a player profile and a monthly calendar, as each of the 12 blotter cards have a different month. The backs are blank. The cards are numbered with the "B" prefix.

		NM	E	VG
Complete Set (12):		3,500	1,750	1,050
Common Player:		150.00	75.00	45.00
3941	Jim Thorpe	700.00	350.00	210.00
3942	Walter Eckersall	150.00	75.00	45.00
3943	Edward Mahan	150.00	75.00	45.00
3944	Sammy Baugh	550.00	275.00	165.00
3945	Thomas Shevlin	150.00	75.00	45.00
3946	Harold "Red" Grange	600.00	300.00	180.00
3947	Ernie Nevers	325.00	162.00	97.00
3948	George Gipp	525.00	262.00	157.00
3949	Pudge Heffelfinger	150.00	75.00	45.00
3950	Bronko Nagurski	600.00	300.00	180.00
3951	Willie Heston	150.00	75.00	45.00
3952	Jay Berwanger	150.00	75.00	45.00

1991 GTE Super Bowl Theme Art

The 25-card, 4-5/8" x 6" set was distributed by GTE in correlation with the 25th anniversary of the Super Bowl. The card fronts feature the Super Bowl program art while the backs contain game summaries and a GTE Telefact.

		NM/M	NM	E
Complete Set (25):		5.00	3.75	2.00
Common Player:		.30	.25	.12
1	Super Bowl I	.50	.40	.20
2	Super Bowl II	.30	.25	.12
3	Super Bowl III	.30	.25	.12
4	Super Bowl IV	.30	.25	.12
5	Super Bowl V	.30	.25	.12
6	Super Bowl VI	.30	.25	.12
7	Super Bowl VII	.30	.25	.12
8	Super Bowl VIII	.30	.25	.12
9	Super Bowl IX	.30	.25	.12
10	Super Bowl X	.30	.25	.12
11	Super Bowl XI	.30	.25	.12
12	Super Bowl XII	.30	.25	.12
13	Super Bowl XIII	.30	.25	.12
14	Super Bowl XIV	.30	.25	.12
15	Suepr Bowl XV	.30	.25	.12
16	Super Bowl XVI	.30	.25	.12
17	Super Bowl XVII	.30	.25	.12
18	Super Bowl XVIII	.30	.25	.12
19	Super Bowl XIX	.30	.25	.12
20	Super Bowl XX	.30	.25	.12
21	Super Bowl XXI	.30	.25	.12
22	Super Bowl XXII	.30	.25	.12
23	Super Bowl XXIII	.30	.25	.12
24	Super Bowl XXIV	.30	.25	.12
25	Super Bowl XXV	.30	.25	.12

H

1990 Hall of Fame Stickers

These 80 stickers feature members of the Pro Football Hall of Fame. Each sticker measures 1-7/8" x 2-1/8" and was created for inclusion in a book titled "The Official Pro Football Hall of Fame Fun and Fact Sticker Book." Artist Mark Rucker did the original artwork which appears on each sticker. The player's name, position and sticker number are given on the front.

		NM/M	NM	E
Complete Set (80):		12.00	9.00	4.75
Common Player:		.15	.11	.06
1	Wilbur Henry	.20	.15	.08
2	George Trafton	.15	.11	.06
3	Mike Michalske	.15	.11	.06
4	Turk Edwards	.15	.11	.06
5	Bill Hewitt	.20	.15	.08
6	Mel Hein	.15	.11	.06
7	Joe Stydahar	.15	.11	.06
8	Dan Fortmann	.15	.11	.06
9	Alex Wojciechowicz	.15	.11	.06
10	George Connor	.20	.15	.08
11	Jim Thorpe	.75	.60	.30
12	Ernie Nevers	.35	.25	.14
13	John McNally	.25	.20	.10
14	Ken Strong	.15	.11	.06
15	Bronko Nagurski	.50	.40	.20
16	Clarke Hinkle	.15	.11	.06
17	Ace Parker	.15	.11	.06
18	Billy Dudley	.20	.15	.08
19	Don Hutson	.30	.25	.12
20	Dante Lavelli	.15	.11	.06
21	Elroy Hirsch	.25	.20	.10
22	Raymond Berry	.25	.20	.10
23	Bobby Mitchell	.15	.11	.06
24	Don Maynard	.25	.20	.10
25	Mike Ditka	.50	.40	.20
26	Lance Alworth	.25	.20	.10
27	Charley Taylor	.15	.11	.06
28	Paul Warfield	.30	.25	.12
29	Lou Groza	.35	.25	.14
30	Art Donovan	.25	.20	.10
31	Leo Nomellini	.15	.11	.06
32	Andy Robustelli	.20	.15	.08
33	Gino Marchetti	.15	.11	.06
34	Forrest Gregg	.15	.11	.06
35	Jim Otto	.20	.15	.08
36	Ron Mix	.15	.11	.06
37	Deacon Jones	.15	.11	.06
38	Bob Lilly	.25	.20	.10
39	Merlin Olsen	.25	.20	.10
40	Alan Page	.20	.15	.08
41	Joe Greene	.25	.20	.10
42	Art Shell	.25	.20	.10
43	Sammy Baugh	.35	.25	.14
44	Sid Luckman	.45	.35	.20
45	Bob Waterfield	.40	.30	.15
46	Bobby Layne	.25	.20	.10
47	Norm Van Brocklin	.25	.20	.10
48	Y.A. Tittle	.25	.20	.10
49	Johnny Unitas	.50	.40	.20
50	Bart Starr	.35	.25	.14
51	Sonny Jurgensen	.25	.20	.10
52	Joe Namath	.75	.60	.30
53	Roger Staubach	.75	.60	.30
54	Terry Bradshaw	.50	.40	.20
55	Steve Van Buren	.25	.20	.10
56	Marion Motley	.25	.20	.10
57	Joe Perry	.25	.20	.10
58	Hugh McElhenny	.25	.20	.10
59	Frank Gifford	.50	.40	.20
60	Jim Brown	1.00	.70	.40
61	Jim Taylor	.25	.20	.10
62	Gale Sayers	.35	.25	.14
63	Larry Csonka	.25	.20	.10
64	Emlen Tunnell	.15	.11	.06
65	Jack Christiansen	.15	.11	.06
66	Dick "Night Train" Lane	.15	.11	.06
67	Sam Huff	.25	.20	.10
68	Ray Nitschke	.15	.11	.06
69	Larry Wilson	.15	.11	.06
70	Willie Wood	.20	.15	.08
71	Bobby Bell	.15	.11	.06
72	Willie Brown	.20	.15	.08
73	Dick Butkus	.35	.25	.14
74	Jack Ham	.15	.11	.06
75	George Halas	.25	.20	.10
76	Steve Owen	.15	.11	.06
77	Art Rooney	.20	.15	.08
78	Bert Bell	.15	.11	.06
79	Paul Brown	.15	.11	.06
80	Pete Rozelle	.20	.15	.08

1989 Hawaii

		NM/M	NM	E
Complete Set (25):		10.00	7.50	4.00
Common Player:		.50	.40	.20
3	Michael Coulson	.50	.40	.20
4	Walter Briggs	.50	.40	.20
5	Gavin Robertson	.50	.40	.20
7	Jason Elam	3.00	2.25	1.25
16	Clayton Mahuka	.50	.40	.20
18	Garrett Gabriel	.60	.45	.25
19	Kim McCloud	.50	.40	.20
27	Kyle Ah Loo	.50	.40	.20
28	Dane McArthur	.50	.40	.20
30	Travis Sims	.50	.40	.20
31	David Maeva	.50	.40	.20
37	Mike Tresler	.50	.40	.20
43	Jamal Farmer	.60	.45	.25
56	Mark Odom	.50	.40	.20
61	Allen Smith	.50	.40	.20
66	Manly Williams	.50	.40	.20
67	Larry Jones	.50	.40	.20
71	Sean Robinson	.50	.40	.20
72	Shawn Alivado	.50	.40	.20
79	Leo Goeas	1.00	.70	.40
86	Larry Khan-Smith	.50	.40	.20
89	Chris Roscoe	.50	.40	.20
91	Augie Apelu	.50	.40	.20
97	Dana Directo	.50	.40	.20
NNO	Bob Wagner (CO)	.60	.45	.25

1990 Hawaii 7-Eleven

		NM/M	NM	E
Complete Set (50):		15.00	11.00	6.00
Common Player:		.35	.25	.14
1	Sean Abreu (40)	.35	.25	.14
2	Joaquin Barnett (53)	.35	.25	.14
3	Darrick Branch (87)	.35	.25	.14
4	David Brantley (9)	.35	.25	.14
5	Akili Calhoun (98)	.35	.25	.14
6	Michael Carter (3)	.35	.25	.14
7	Shawn Ching (72)	.35	.25	.14
8	Jason Elam (7)	2.00	1.50	.80
9	Jamal Farmer (43)	.50	.40	.20
10	Garrett Gabriel (18)	.50	.40	.20
11	Brian Gordon (15)	.35	.25	.14
12	Kenny Harper (6)	.35	.25	.14
13	Mitchell Kaaialii (57)	.35	.25	.14
14	Larry Khan-Smith (86)	.35	.25	.14
15	Haku Kahoano (94)	.35	.25	.14
16	Nuuanu Kaulia (94)	.35	.25	.14
17	Eddie Kealoha (38)	.35	.25	.14
18	Zerin Khan (14)	.35	.25	.14
19	David Maeva (31)	.35	.25	.14
20	Dane McArthur (28)	.35	.25	.14
21	Kim McCloud (19)	.35	.25	.14
22	Jeff Newman (1)	.35	.25	.14
23	Mark Odom (56)	.35	.25	.14
24	Louis Randall (51)	.35	.25	.14
25	Gavin Robertson (5)	.35	.25	.14
26	Sean Robinson (71)	.35	.25	.14
27	Tavita Sagapolu (77)	.35	.25	.14
28	Lyno Samana (45)	.35	.25	.14
29	Walter Santiago (12)	.35	.25	.14
30	Joe Sardo (21)	.35	.25	.14
31	Travis Sims (30)	.35	.25	.14
32	Allen Smith (61)	.35	.25	.14
33	Jeff Snyder (26)	1.50	1.25	.60
34	Richard Stevenson (33)	.35	.25	.14
35	David Tanuvasa (44)	.35	.25	.14
36	Mike Tresler (37)	.35	.25	.14
37	Lemoe Tua (60)	.35	.25	.14
38	Peter Viliamu (69)	.35	.25	.14
39	Bob Wagner (CO)	.50	.40	.20
40	Terry Whitaker (2)	.35	.25	.14
41	Manly Williams (66)	.35	.25	.14
42	Jerry Winfrey (90)	.35	.25	.14
43	**Aloha Stadium**	.35	.25	.14
44	**Assistant Coaches**	.35	.25	.14
45	Defense (Nuuanu Kaulia)	.35	.25	.14
46	Offense (Jamal Farmer)	.50	.40	.20
47	Special Teams (Jason Elam)	.75	.60	.30
48	BYU Victory (Jamal Farmer)	.50	.40	.20
49	**UH Logo**	.35	.25	.14
50	**WAC Logo**	.35	.25	.14

1991 Heisman Collection I

CHARLES WHITE

The 20-card, regular-sized set, produced by College Classics in association with The Downtown Athletic Club of New York, features 20 Heisman winners in skip-numbered order (based on chronological order). The card fronts feature a color or posed shot of the player with a Heisman trophy in the lower right corner. The card back informs collectors of the year the player won the award, player summary and a larger Heisman Trophy image. The production total was 100,000 sets and each case (1,000 sets) contained two player autograph cards. The set also had a serially numbered header card and a sample Bo Jackson card was also distributed.

	NM/M	NM	E
Complete Set (21):	5.00	3.75	2.00
Common Player:	.15	.11	.06

1	Jay Berwanger	.15	.11	.06
6	Tom Harmon	.25	.20	.10
9	Angelo Bertelli	.15	.11	.06
11	Doc Blanchard	.25	.20	.10
13	John Lujack	.25	.20	.10
15	Leon Hart	.25	.20	.10
16	Vic Janowicz	.25	.20	.10
19	John Lattner	.25	.20	.10
23	John David Crow	.15	.11	.06
26	Joe Bellino	.15	.11	.06
30	John Huarte	.15	.11	.06
32	Steve Spurrier	1.00	.70	.40
36	Jim Plunkett	.40	.30	.15
40	Archie Griffin	.25	.20	.10
42	Tony Dorsett	1.00	.70	.40
43	Earl Campbell	1.00	.70	.40
45	Charles White	.15	.11	.06
48	Herschel Walker	.50	.40	.20
51	Bo Jackson	1.00	.70	.40
53	Tim Brown	.40	.30	.15
NNO	**Title Card**	.15	.11	.06
SAM	Bo Jackson (Sample Promo)	3.00	2.25	1.25

1970 Hi-C Posters

These posters were featured on the insides of Hi-C drink can labels. The featured players were statistical leaders at their positions during the 1969 season. Each poster measures 6-5/8" x 13-3/4" and is numbered below the player photo.

	NM	E	VG
Complete Set (10):	700.00	350.00	210.00
Common Player:	75.00	37.00	22.00

(1)	Greg Cook	80.00	40.00	24.00
(2)	Fred Cox	75.00	37.00	22.00
(3)	Sonny Jurgensen	125.00	62.00	37.00
(4)	David Lee	75.00	37.00	22.00
(5)	Dennis Partee	75.00	37.00	22.00
(6)	Dick Post	75.00	37.00	22.00
(7)	Mel Renfro	90.00	45.00	27.00
(8)	Gale Sayers	175.00	87.00	52.00
(9)	Emmitt Thomas	80.00	40.00	24.00
(10)	Jim Turner	75.00	37.00	22.00

1991 Hoby SEC Stars

HERSCHEL WALKER

	NM/M	NM	E
Complete Set (396):	50.00	37.00	20.00
Common Player:	.15	.11	.06

1	Paul "Bear" Bryant (CO)	2.00	1.50	.80
2	Johnny Musso	.50	.40	.20
3	Keith McCants	.25	.20	.10
4	Cecil Dowdy	.15	.11	.06
5	Thomas Rayam	.15	.11	.06
6	Van Tiffin	.15	.11	.06
7	Efrum Thomas	.15	.11	.06
8	Jon Hand	.25	.20	.10
9	David Smith	.15	.11	.06
10	Larry Rose	.15	.11	.06
11	Lamonde Russell	.15	.11	.06
12	Mike Washington	.15	.11	.06
13	Tommy Cole	.15	.11	.06
14	Roger Shultz	.15	.11	.06
15	Spencer Hammond	.15	.11	.06
16	John Fruhmorgen	.15	.11	.06
17	Gene Jelks	.25	.20	.10
18	John Mangum	.25	.20	.10
19	George Thornton	.15	.11	.06
20	Billy Neighbors	.25	.20	.10
21	Howard Cross	.40	.30	.15
22	Jeremiah Castille	.25	.20	.10
23	Derrick Thomas	1.00	.70	.40
24	Terrill Chatman	.15	.11	.06
25	Ken Stabler	1.25	.90	.50
26	Lee Ozmint	.15	.11	.06
27	Philip Doyle	.15	.11	.06
28	Kermit Kendrick	.15	.11	.06
29	Chris Mohr	.15	.11	.06
30	Tommy Wilcox	.15	.11	.06
31	Gary Hollingsworth	.15	.11	.06
32	Sylvester Croom	.25	.20	.10
33	Willie Wyatt	.15	.11	.06
34	Pooley Hubert	.15	.11	.06
35	Bobby Humphrey	.25	.20	.10
36	Vaughn Mancha	.15	.11	.06
37	Reggie Slack	.40	.30	.15
38	Vince Dooley (CO)	.40	.30	.15
39	Ed King	.25	.20	.10
40	Connie Frederick	.15	.11	.06
41	Jeff Burger	.25	.20	.10
42	Monk Gafford	.15	.11	.06
43	David Rocker	.25	.20	.10
44	Jim Pyburn	.15	.11	.06
45	Bob Harris	.15	.11	.06
46	Travis Tidwell	.15	.11	.06
47	Ralph (Shug) Jordan (CO)	.40	.30	.15
48	Zeke Smith	.25	.20	.10
49	Terry Beasley	.25	.20	.10
50	Pat Sullivan	.40	.30	.15
51	Stacy Danley	.25	.20	.10
52	Jimmy Hitchcock	.15	.11	.06
53	John Wiley	.15	.11	.06
54	Greg Taylor	.15	.11	.06
55	Lamar Rogers	.25	.20	.10
56	Rob Selby	.15	.11	.06
57	James Joseph	.25	.20	.10
58	Mike Kolen	.15	.11	.06
59	Kevin Greene	.50	.40	.20
60	Ben Thomas	.15	.11	.06
61	Shayne Wasden	.15	.11	.06
62	Tex Warrington	.15	.11	.06
63	Tommie Agee	.25	.20	.10
64	Jim Phillips	.25	.20	.10
65	Lawyer Tillman	.40	.30	.15
66	Mark Dorminey	.15	.11	.06
67	Steve Wallace	.25	.20	.10
68	Ed Dyas	.15	.11	.06
69	Alexander Wright	.25	.20	.10
70	Lionel James	.25	.20	.10
71	Aundray Bruce	.25	.20	.10
72	Edmund Nelson	.15	.11	.06
73	Jack Youngblood	.50	.40	.20
74	Carlos Alvarez	.25	.20	.10
75	Ricky Nattiel	.25	.20	.10
76	Bill Carr	.15	.11	.06
77	Guy Dennis	.15	.11	.06
78	Charles Casey	.15	.11	.06
79	Louis Oliver	.40	.30	.15
80	John Reaves	.25	.20	.10
81	Wayne Peace	.25	.20	.10
82	Charlie LaPradd	.15	.11	.06
83	Wes Chandler	.40	.30	.15
84	Richard Trapp	.15	.11	.06
85	Ralph Ortega	.15	.11	.06
86	Tommy Durrance	.15	.11	.06
87	Burton Lawless	.25	.20	.10
88	Bruce Bennett	.15	.11	.06
89	Huey Richardson	.25	.20	.10
90	Larry Smith	.15	.11	.06
91	Trace Armstrong	.40	.30	.15
92	Nat Moore	.40	.30	.15
93	James Jones	.40	.30	.15
94	Kay Stephenson	.25	.20	.10
95	Scot Brantley	.15	.11	.06
96	Ray Criswell	.15	.11	.06
97	Steve Tannen	.25	.20	.10
98	Ernie Mills	.40	.30	.15
99	Bruce Vaughn	.15	.11	.06
100	Steve Spurrier	2.50	2.00	1.00
101	Crawford Ker	.25	.20	.10
102	David Galloway	.25	.20	.10
103	David Williams	.25	.20	.10
104	Lomas Brown	.40	.30	.15
105	Fernando Jackson	.15	.11	.06
106	Jeff Roth	.15	.11	.06
107	Mark Murray	.15	.11	.06
108	Kirk Kirkpatrick	.15	.11	.06
109	Ray Goff (CO)	.25	.20	.10
110	Quinton Lumpkin	.15	.11	.06
111	Royce Smith	.15	.11	.06
112	Larry Rakestraw	.25	.20	.10
113	Kevin Butler	.25	.20	.10
114	Aschel M. Day	.15	.11	.06
115	Scott Woerner	.25	.20	.10
116	Herb St. John	.15	.11	.06
117	Ray Rissmiller	.15	.11	.06
118	Buck Belue	.25	.20	.10
119	George Collins	.15	.11	.06
120	Joel Parrish	.15	.11	.06
121	Terry Hoage	.25	.20	.10
122	Frank Sinkwich	.40	.30	.15
123	Billy Payne	.50	.40	.20
124	Zeke Bratkowski	.25	.20	.10
125	Herschel Walker	1.00	.70	.40
126	Pat Dye (CO)	.40	.30	.15
127	Vernon Smith	.15	.11	.06
128	Rex Robinson	.15	.11	.06
129	Mike Castronis	.15	.11	.06
130	Pop Warner (CO)	.40	.30	.15
131	George Patton	.25	.20	.10
132	Harry Babcock	.15	.11	.06
133	Lindsay Scott	.25	.20	.10
134	Bill Stanfill	.25	.20	.10
135	Bill Hartman Jr.	.15	.11	.06
136	Eddie Weaver	.15	.11	.06
137	Tim Worley	.40	.30	.15
138	Ben Zambiasi	.40	.30	.15
139	Bob McWhorter	.15	.11	.06
140	Rodney Hampton	1.00	.70	.40
141	Len Hauss	.25	.20	.10
142	Wallace Butts	.25	.20	.10
143	Andy Johnson	.25	.20	.10
144	I.M. Shiver Jr.	.15	.11	.06
145	Clyde Johnson	.15	.11	.06
146	Steve Meilinger	.15	.11	.06
147	Howard Schnellenberger (CO)	.50	.40	.20
148	Irv Goode	.25	.20	.10
149	Sam Ball	.15	.11	.06
150	Babe Parilli	.40	.30	.15
151	Rick Norton	.25	.20	.10
152	Warren Bryant	.25	.20	.10
153	Mike Pfeifer	.15	.11	.06
154	Sonny Collins	.15	.11	.06
155	Mark Higgs	.40	.30	.15
156	Randy Holleran	.15	.11	.06
157	Bill Ransdell	.15	.11	.06
158	Joey Worley	.15	.11	.06
159	Jim Kovach	.25	.20	.10
160	Joe Federspiel	.25	.20	.10
161	Larry Seiple	.25	.20	.10
162	Darryl Bishop	.15	.11	.06
163	George Blanda	1.00	.70	.40
164	Oliver Barnett	.25	.20	.10
165	Paul Calhoun	.15	.11	.06
166	Dicky Lyons	.25	.20	.10
167	Tom Hutchinson	.25	.20	.10
168	George Adams	.25	.20	.10
169	Derrick Ramsey	.25	.20	.10
170	Rick Kestner	.15	.11	.06
171	Art Still	.40	.30	.15
172	Rick Nuzum	.15	.11	.06
173	Richard Jaffe	.15	.11	.06
174	Rodger Bird	.15	.11	.06
175	Jeff Van Note	.40	.30	.15
176	Herschel Turner	.15	.11	.06
177	Lou Michaels	.25	.20	.10
178	Ray Correll	.15	.11	.06
179	Doug Moseley	.15	.11	.06
180	Bob Gain	.25	.20	.10
181	Tommy Casanova	.40	.30	.15
182	Mike Anderson	.15	.11	.06
183	Craig Burns	.15	.11	.06
184	A.J. Duhe	.25	.20	.10
185	Lyman White	.15	.11	.06
186	Paul Dietzel (CO)	.40	.30	.15
187	Paul Lyons	.15	.11	.06
188	Eddie Ray	.15	.11	.06
189	Roy Winston	.25	.20	.10
190	Brad Davis	.15	.11	.06
191	Mike Williams	.15	.11	.06
192	Karl Wilson	.25	.20	.10
193	Ronnie Estay	.15	.11	.06
194	Malcolm Scott	.15	.11	.06
195	Greg Jackson	.15	.11	.06

196	Willie Teal	.25	.20	.10
197	Eddie Fuller	.15	.11	.06
198	Halph Norwood	.15	.11	.06
199	Bert Jones	.40	.30	.15
200	Y.A. Tittle	.50	.40	.20
201	Jerry Stovall	.40	.30	.15
202	Henry Thomas	.40	.30	.15
203	Lance Smith	.15	.11	.06
204	Doug Moreau	.25	.20	.10
205	Tyler LaFauci	.15	.11	.06
206	George Bevan	.15	.11	.06
207	Robert Dugas	.15	.11	.06
208	Carlos Carson	.25	.20	.10
209	Andy Hamilton	.25	.20	.10
210	James Britt	.15	.11	.06
211	Wendell Davis	.40	.30	.15
212	Ron Sancho	.15	.11	.06
213	Johnny Robinson	.40	.30	.15
214	Eric Martin	.40	.30	.15
215	Michael Brooks	.25	.20	.10
216	Toby Caston	.25	.20	.10
217	Jesse Anderson	.15	.11	.06
218	Jimmy Webb	.15	.11	.06
219	Mardye McDole	.15	.11	.06
220	David Smith	.15	.11	.06
221	Dana Moore	.15	.11	.06
222	Cedric Corse	.15	.11	.06
223	Louis Clark	.15	.11	.06
224	Walter Packer	.15	.11	.06
225	George Wonsley	.25	.20	.10
226	Billy Jackson	.25	.20	.10
227	Bruce Plummer	.15	.11	.06
228	Aaron Pearson	.15	.11	.06
229	Glen Collins	.15	.11	.06
230	Paul Davis (CO)	.15	.11	.06
231	Wayne Jones	.15	.11	.06
232	John Bond	.15	.11	.06
233	Johnnie Cooks	.25	.20	.10
234	Robert Young	.15	.11	.06
235	Don Smith	.15	.11	.06
236	Kent Hull	.40	.30	.15
237	Tony Shell	.15	.11	.06
238	Steve Freeman	.25	.20	.10
239	James Williams	.15	.11	.06
240	Tom Goode	.25	.20	.10
241	Stan Black	.15	.11	.06
242	Bo Russell	.15	.11	.06
243	Ricky Byrd	.15	.11	.06
244	Frank Dowsing	.15	.11	.06
245	Wayne Harris	.40	.30	.15
246	Richard Keys	.15	.11	.06
247	Artie Cosby	.15	.11	.06
248	Dave Marler	.15	.11	.06
249	Michael Haddix	.25	.20	.10
250	Jerry Clower	.25	.20	.10
251	Bill Bell	.15	.11	.06
252	Jerry Bouldin	.15	.11	.06
253	Parker Hall	.15	.11	.06
254	Allen Brown	.15	.11	.06
255	Bill Smith	.15	.11	.06
256	Freddie Joe Nunn	.25	.20	.10
257	John Vaught (CO)	.25	.20	.10
258	Buford McGee	.25	.20	.10
259	Kenny Dill	.15	.11	.06
260	Jim Miller	.15	.11	.06
261	Doug Jacobs	.15	.11	.06
262	John Dottley	.25	.20	.10
263	Willie Green	.40	.30	.15
264	Tony Bennett	.40	.30	.15
265	Stan Hindman	.15	.11	.06
266	Charles Childers	.15	.11	.06
267	Harry Harrison	.15	.11	.06
268	Todd Sandroni	.15	.11	.06
269	Glynn Griffing	.15	.11	.06
270	Chris Mitchell	.15	.11	.06
271	Shawn Cobb	.15	.11	.06
272	Doug Elmore	.15	.11	.06
273	Dawson Pruett	.15	.11	.06
274	Warner Alford	.15	.11	.06
275	Archie Manning	1.00	.70	.40
276	Kelvin Pritchett	.25	.20	.10
277	Pat Coleman	.15	.11	.06
278	Stevon Moore	.25	.20	.10
279	John Darnell	.15	.11	.06
280	Wesley Walls	.25	.20	.10
281	Billy Brewer	.25	.20	.10
282	Mark Young	.15	.11	.06
283	Andre Townsend	.25	.20	.10
284	Billy Ray Adams	.15	.11	.06
285	Jim Dunaway	.25	.20	.10
286	Paige Cothren	.25	.20	.10
287	Jake Gibbs	.40	.30	.15
288	Jim Urbanek	.15	.11	.06
289	Tony Thompson	.15	.11	.06
300	Johnny Majors (CO)	.40	.30	.15
301	Roland Poles	.15	.11	.06
302	Alvin Harper	.50	.40	.20
303	Doug Baird	.15	.11	.06
304	Greg Burke	.15	.11	.06
305	Sterling Henton	.15	.11	.06
306	Preston Warren	.15	.11	.06
307	Stanley Morgan	.50	.40	.20
308	Bobby Scott	.25	.20	.10
309	Doug Atkins	.40	.30	.15
310	Bill Young	.15	.11	.06
311	Bob Garmon	.15	.11	.06
312	Herman Weaver	.15	.11	.06
313	Dewey Warren	.15	.11	.06
314	John Boynton	.25	.20	.10
315	Bob Davis	.15	.11	.06
316	Pat Ryan	.15	.11	.06
317	Keith DeLong	.25	.20	.10
318	Bobby Dodd (CO)	.25	.20	.10
319	Ricky Townsend	.15	.11	.06
320	Eddie Brown	.25	.20	.10
321	Herman Hickman (CO)	.25	.20	.10
322	Nathan Dougherty	.15	.11	.06
323	Mickey Marvin	.15	.11	.06
324	Reggie Cobb	.40	.30	.15
325A	Condredge Holloway	.50	.40	.20
325B	Josh Cody	.15	.11	.06
326A	Anthony Hancock	.40	.30	.15
326B	Jack Jenkins	.15	.11	.06
327A	Steve Kiner	.15	.11	.06
327B	Bob Goodridge	.15	.11	.06
328A	Mike Mauck	.15	.11	.06
328B	Chris Gaines	.15	.11	.06
329A	Bill Bates	.40	.30	.15
329B	Willie Geny	.15	.11	.06
330A	Austin Denney	.25	.20	.10
330B	Bob Laws	.15	.11	.06
331A	Robert Nevland (CO)	.40	.30	.15
331B	Rob Monaco	.15	.11	.06
332A	Bob Suffridge	.15	.11	.06
332B	Chuck Scott	.15	.11	.06
333A	Abe Shires	.15	.11	.06
333B	Hek Wakefield	.15	.11	.06
334A	Robert Shaw	.40	.30	.15
334B	Ken Stone	.15	.11	.06
335	Mark Adams	.15	.11	.06
336	Ed Smith	.15	.11	.06
337	Dan McGugin (CO)	.15	.11	.06
338	Doug Mathews	.15	.11	.06
339	Whit Taylor	.40	.30	.15
340	Gene Moshier	.15	.11	.06
341	Christine Hauck	.15	.11	.06
342	Lee Nalley	.15	.11	.06
343	Wamon Buggs	.15	.11	.06
344	Jim Arnold	.25	.20	.10
345	Buford Ray	.25	.20	.10
346	Will Wolford	.25	.20	.10
347	Steve Bearden	.15	.11	.06
348	Frank Mordica	.15	.11	.06
349	Barry Burton	.15	.11	.06
350	Bill Wade	.40	.30	.15
351	Tommy Woodroof	.15	.11	.06
352	Steve Wade	.15	.11	.06
353	Preston Brown	.15	.11	.06
354	Ben Roderick	.15	.11	.06
355	Charles Horton	.15	.11	.06
356	DeMond Winston	.15	.11	.06
357	John North	.15	.11	.06
358	Don Orr	.15	.11	.06
359	Art Demmas	.15	.11	.06
360	Mark Johnson	.15	.11	.06
361	Hootie Ingram (AD)	.25	.20	.10
362	Gene Stallings (CO)	.50	.40	.20
363	**Alabama Checklist**	.15	.11	.06
364	Pat Dye (CO)	.25	.20	.10
365	**Auburn Checklist**	.15	.11	.06
366	Vince Dooley (AD)	.25	.20	.10
367	Ray Goff (CO)	.25	.20	.10
368	**Georgia Checklist**	.15	.11	.06
369	C.M. Newton (AD)	.25	.20	.10
370	Bill Curry (CO)	.25	.20	.10
371	**Kentucky Checklist**	.15	.11	.06
372	Joe Dean (AD)	.15	.11	.06
373	Curley Hallman (CO)	.25	.20	.10
374	**LSU Checklist**	.15	.11	.06
375	Warner Alford (AD)	.15	.11	.06
376	Billy Brewer (CO)	.25	.20	.10
377	**Ole Miss Checklist**	.15	.11	.06
378	Larry Templeton (AD)	.15	.11	.06
379	Jackie Sherrill (CO)	.40	.30	.15
380	**Mississippi State Checklist**	.15	.11	.06
381	Bill Arnsparger (AD)	.25	.20	.10
382	Steve Spurrier (CO)	1.25	.90	.50
383	**Florida Checklist**	.15	.11	.06
384	Doug Dickey (AD)	.15	.11	.06
385	Johnny Majors (CO)	.25	.20	.10
386	**Tennessee Checklist**	.15	.11	.06
387	Paul Hoolahan (AD)	.15	.11	.06
388	Gerry DiNardo (CO)	.25	.20	.10
389	**Vanderbilt Checklist**	.15	.11	.06

390	**The Iron Bowl - Alabama vs. Auburn**	.40	.30	.15
391	**Florida vs. Georgia**	.15	.11	.06
392	**Mississippi State vs. Ole Miss**	.15	.11	.06
393	**The Beer Barrel - Kentucky vs. Tennessee**	.15	.11	.06
394	**Drama on Halloween - LSU vs. Ole Miss**	.15	.11	.06
395	**Tennessee vs. Vanderbilt**	.15	.11	.06
396	Roy Kramer (COMM)	.15	.11	.06

1991 Hoby SEC Stars Signature

		NM/M	NM	E
	Complete Set (10):	375.00	281.00	150.00
	Common Player:	15.00	11.00	6.00
1	Carlos Alvarez	15.00	11.00	6.00
2	Zeke Bratkowski	25.00	18.50	10.00
3	Jerry Clower	15.00	11.00	6.00
4	Condredge Holloway	25.00	18.50	10.00
5	Bert Jones	50.00	37.00	20.00
6	Archie Manning	75.00	56.00	30.00
7	Ken Stabler	100.00	75.00	40.00
8	Pat Sullivan	50.00	37.00	20.00
9	Jeff Van Note	20.00	15.00	8.00
10	Bill Wade	25.00	18.50	10.00

1991 Homers

In 1991, boxes of QB's Cookies contained one of six different cards featuring Hall of Fame football players. Each standard-size card has a sepia-toned photograph on the front, with a bronze frame. The player's name is in a bronze panel in the lower left. The numbered back has a checklist for the set, plus information about the player's accomplishments, biographical information and the year he was inducted into the Hall of Fame. The set was sponsored by Legend Food Products.

		NM/M	NM	E
	Complete Set (6):	10.00	7.50	4.00
	Common Player:	1.00	.70	.40
1	Vince Lombardi	2.00	1.50	.80
2	Hugh McElhenny	2.00	1.50	.80
3	Elroy Hirsch	2.00	1.50	.80
4	Jim Thorpe	4.00	3.00	1.50
5	Dick "Night Train" Lane	1.00	.70	.40
6	Bart Starr	3.00	2.25	1.25

1988 Humboldt State Smokey

		NM/M	NM	E
	Complete Set (11):	12.00	9.00	4.75
	Common Player:	1.25	.90	.50
1	Richard Ashe (1)	1.25	.90	.50
2	Darin Bradbury (64)	1.25	.90	.50
3	Rodney Dorsett (7)	1.25	.90	.50
4	Dave Harper (55)	1.25	.90	.50
5	Earl Jackson (6)	1.25	.90	.50
6	Derek Mallard (82)	1.25	.90	.50
7	Scott Reagan (60)	1.25	.90	.50
8	Wesley White (1)	1.25	.90	.50
9	Paul Wienecke (40)	1.25	.90	.50
10	William Williams (14)	1.25	.90	.50
11	Kelvin Windham (30)	1.25	.90	.50

I

1989 Idaho

		NM/M	NM	E
	Complete Set (12):	12.00	9.00	4.75
	Common Player:	.75	.60	.30
3	Brian Smith	.75	.60	.30
11	Tim S. Johnson	.75	.60	.30
16	Lee Allen	.75	.60	.30
17	John Friesz	5.00	3.75	2.00
20	Todd Hoiness	.75	.60	.30
25	David Jackson	.75	.60	.30
53	Steve Unger	.75	.60	.30
58	John Rust	.75	.60	.30
63	Troy Wright	.75	.60	.30
67	Todd Neu	.75	.60	.30
83	Michael Davis	.75	.60	.30
93	Mike Zeller	.75	.60	.30

1990 Illinois Centennial

		NM/M	NM	E
	Complete Set (45):	25.00	18.50	10.00
	Common Player:	.35	.25	.14
1	Harold "Red" Grange	3.00	2.25	1.25
2	Dick Butkus	2.50	2.00	1.00
3	Ray Nitschke	1.50	1.25	.60
4	Jim Grabowski	.50	.40	.20
5	Alex Agase	.50	.40	.20
6	Claude Young	.50	.40	.20
7	Scott Studwell	.50	.40	.20
8	Tony Eason	.50	.40	.20
9	John Mackovic	.75	.60	.30
10	Jack Trudeau	.75	.60	.30
11	Jeff George	2.00	1.50	.80
12	Rose Bowl Coaches (Ray Eliot, Pete Elliott, Mike White)	.35	.25	.14
13	George Huff	.35	.25	.14
14	David Williams	.35	.25	.14
15	Bob Zuppke	.50	.40	.20
16	George Halas	2.00	1.50	.80
17	Dike Eddleman	.35	.25	.14
18	Dave Wilson	.35	.25	.14
19	Tab Bennett	.35	.25	.14
20	Jim Juriga	.35	.25	.14
21	John Karras	.35	.25	.14
22	Bobby Mitchell	1.00	.70	.40
23	Dan Beaver	.35	.25	.14
24	Joe Rutgens	.50	.40	.20
25	Bill Burrell	.35	.25	.14
26	J.C. Caroline	.50	.40	.20
27	Al Brosky	.35	.25	.14
28	Don Thorp	.35	.25	.14
29	First Football Team	.35	.25	.14
30	Harold "Red" Grange (Retired)	1.00	.70	.40
31	Memorial Stadium	.35	.25	.14
32	Chris White	.35	.25	.14
33	Early Stars (Ralph Chapman, Perry Graves, Bart Macomber)	.35	.25	.14
34	Early Stars (John Depler, Jim McMillen)	.35	.25	.14
35	Early Stars (Burt Ingwerson, Butch Nowack, Bernie Shively)	.35	.25	.14
36	Great Quarterbacks (Fred Custardo, Mike Wells, Tom O'Connell)	.35	.25	.14
37	Great Running Backs (Thomas Rooks, Abe Woodson, Keith Jones)	.50	.40	.20
38	Great Receivers (Mike Bellamy, Doug Dieken, John Wright)	.50	.40	.20
39	Great Offensive (Forrest Van Hook, Larry McCarren, Chris Babyar)	.35	.25	.14
40	Great Defensive Backs (Craig Swope, George Donnelly, Mike Gower)	.35	.25	.14
41	Great Linebackers (Charles Boerlo, Don Hansen, John Sullivan)	.35	.25	.14
42	Defensive Linemen (Archie Sutton, Chuck Studley, Scott Davis)	.35	.25	.14
43	Great Kickers (Mike Bass K, Bill Brown, Frosty Peters)	.35	.25	.14
44	Retired Numbers (Dick Butkus)	1.50	1.25	.60
45	Football Centennial Logo	.35	.25	.14

1982 Indiana State Police

		NM/M	NM	E
	Complete Set (64):	175.00	131.00	70.00
	Common Player:	3.00	2.25	1.25
1	David Allen	3.00	2.25	1.25
2	Doug Arnold	3.00	2.25	1.25
3	James Banks	3.00	2.25	1.25
4	Scott Bartel	3.00	2.25	1.25
5	Kurt Bell	3.00	2.25	1.25
6	Terry Bell	3.00	2.25	1.25
7	Steve Bidwell	3.00	2.25	1.25
8	Keith Bonney	3.00	2.25	1.25
9	Mark Boster	3.00	2.25	1.25
10	Bobby Boyce	3.00	2.25	1.25
11	Steve Brickey (CO)	3.00	2.25	1.25
12	Mark Bryson	3.00	2.25	1.25
13	Steve Buxton	3.00	2.25	1.25
14	Ed Campbell	3.00	2.25	1.25
15	Jeff Campbell	5.00	3.75	2.00
16	Tom Chapman	3.00	2.25	1.25

		NM/M	NM	E
17	Cheerleaders (Ruth Ann Medworth DIR)	4.00	3.00	1.50
18	Darrold Clardy	3.00	2.25	1.25
19	Wayne Davis	3.00	2.25	1.25
20	Herbert Dawson	3.00	2.25	1.25
21	Richard Dawson	4.00	3.00	1.50
22	Chris Delaplaine	3.00	2.25	1.25
23	Max Dillon	3.00	2.25	1.25
24	Rick Dwenger	3.00	2.25	1.25
25	Ed Foggs	3.00	2.25	1.25
26	Allen Hartwig	3.00	2.25	1.25
27	Pat Henderson (CO)	3.00	2.25	1.25
28	Don Hitz	3.00	2.25	1.25
29	Pete Hoener (CO)	3.00	2.25	1.25
30	Bob Hopkins	3.00	2.25	1.25
31	Kris Huber (Baton Twirler)	4.00	3.00	1.50
32	Leroy Irvin	20.00	15.00	8.00
33	Mike Johannes	3.00	2.25	1.25
34	Anthony Kimball	3.00	2.25	1.25
35	Gregg Kimbrough	3.00	2.25	1.25
36	Bob Koehne	3.00	2.25	1.25
37	Jerry Lasko (CO)	3.00	2.25	1.25
38	Kevin Lynch	3.00	2.25	1.25
39	Dan Maher	3.00	2.25	1.25
40	Ed Martin	3.00	2.25	1.25
41	Regis Mason	3.00	2.25	1.25
42	Rob McIntyre	3.00	2.25	1.25
43	Quintin Mikell	3.00	2.25	1.25
44	Jeff Miller	3.00	2.25	1.25
45	Mark Miller	3.00	2.25	1.25
46	Mike Osborne	3.00	2.25	1.25
47	Max Payne (CO)	3.00	2.25	1.25
48	Scott Piercy	3.00	2.25	1.25
49	Dennis Raetz (CO)	3.00	2.25	1.25
50	Kevin Ramsey	3.00	2.25	1.25
51	Dean Reader	3.00	2.25	1.25
52	Eric Robinson	3.00	2.25	1.25
53	Walter Seaphus	3.00	2.25	1.25
54	Sparkettes (Marthann Markler DIR)	4.00	3.00	1.50
55	John Spradley	3.00	2.25	1.25
56	Manual Studway	3.00	2.25	1.25
57	Sam Suggs	3.00	2.25	1.25
58	Larry Swart	3.00	2.25	1.25
59	Bob Tyree	3.00	2.25	1.25
60	Bob Turner (CO)	3.00	2.25	1.25
61	Brad Verdun	3.00	2.25	1.25
62	Keith Ward	3.00	2.25	1.25
63	Sean Whiten	3.00	2.25	1.25
64	Perry Willett	3.00	2.25	1.25

1984 Invaders Smokey

The five-card, 5" x 7" set featured four players and Smokey The Bear in a forestry promotion set. The card fronts feature a posed player shot with Smokey, as well as the player's signature. The card backs contain bio information. Notable in the set is future NFL linebacker Gary Plummer, who went on to play with San Diego and San Francisco.

		NM/M	NM	E
	Complete Set (5):	65.00	49.00	26.00
	Common Player:	10.00	7.50	4.00
1	Dupre Marshall	10.00	7.50	4.00
2	Gary Plummer	20.00	15.00	8.00
3	David Shaw	10.00	7.50	4.00
4	Kevin Shea	10.00	7.50	4.00
5	Smokey Bear (With players above)	10.00	7.50	4.00

1984 Iowa

		NM/M	NM	E
	Complete Set (60):	50.00	37.00	20.00
	Common Player:	.75	.60	.30
1	Kevin Angel	.75	.60	.30
2	Kerry Burt	.75	.60	.30
3	Fred Bush	.75	.60	.30
4	Craig Clark	.75	.60	.30
5	Zane Corbin	.75	.60	.30
6	Nate Creer	.75	.60	.30
7	Dave Croston	.75	.60	.30
8	George Davis	.75	.60	.30
9	Jeff Drost	.75	.60	.30
10	Quinn Early	4.00	3.00	1.50
11	Mike Flagg	.75	.60	.30
12	Hayden Fry (CO)	2.50	2.00	1.00
13	Bruce Gear	.75	.60	.30
14	Owen Gill	2.00	1.50	.80
15	Bill Glass	1.00	.70	.40
16	Mike Haight	1.50	1.25	.60
17	Bill Happel	.75	.60	.30
18	Kevin Harmon	1.00	.70	.40
19	Ronnie Harmon	4.00	3.00	1.50
20	Craig Hartman	.75	.60	.30
21	Jon Hayes	2.00	1.50	.80
22	Erric Hedgeman	.75	.60	.30
23	Scott Helverson	.75	.60	.30

		NM/M	NM	E
24	Mike Hooks	.75	.60	.30
25	Paul Hufford	.75	.60	.30
26	Keith Hunter	.75	.60	.30
27	George Little	.75	.60	.30
28	Chuck Long	2.00	1.50	.80
29	J.C. Love-Jordan	.75	.60	.30
30	George Millett	.75	.60	.30
31	Devon Mitchell	1.00	.70	.40
32	Tom Nichol	.75	.60	.30
33	Kelly O'Brien	.75	.60	.30
34	Hap Peterson	.75	.60	.30
35	Joe Schuster	1.00	.70	.40
36	Tim Sennott	.75	.60	.30
37	Ken Sims	.75	.60	.30
38	Mark Sindlinger	.75	.60	.30
39	Robert Smith	.75	.60	.30
40	Kevin Spitzig	.75	.60	.30
41	Larry Station	.75	.60	.30
42	Mike Stoops	.75	.60	.30
43	Dave Strobel	.75	.60	.30
44	Mark Vlasic	2.00	1.50	.80
45	Jon Vrieze	.75	.60	.30
46	Tony Wancket	.75	.60	.30
47	Herb Webster	.75	.60	.30
48	Coaching Staff	1.00	.70	.40
49	Captains	1.50	1.25	.60
50	Bowl Players	1.00	.70	.40
51	Harmon Brothers (Kevin Harmon, Ronnie Harmon)	1.50	1.25	.60
52	Cheerleaders	1.00	.70	.40
53	Pompons	1.00	.70	.40
54	Kinnick Stadium	.75	.60	.30
55	Herky the Hawk (Mascot)	.75	.60	.30
56	Rose Bowl Ring	.75	.60	.30
57	Peach Bowl Trophy	.75	.60	.30
58	Gator Bowl Stadium	.75	.60	.30
59	Floyd of Rosedale (Trophy)	.75	.60	.30
60	Checklist Card	.75	.60	.30

1987 Iowa

		NM/M	NM	E
	Complete Set (63):	40.00	30.00	16.00
	Common Player:	.60	.45	.25
1	Mark Adams	.60	.45	.25
2	Dave Alexander	1.00	.70	.40
3	Bill Anderson	.60	.45	.25
4	Tim Anderson	.60	.45	.25
5	Rick Bayless	.60	.45	.25
6	Jeff Beard	.60	.45	.25
7	Mike Burke	.60	.45	.25
8	Kerry Burt	.60	.45	.25
9	Malcolm Christie	.60	.45	.25
10	Craig Clark	.60	.45	.25
11	Marv Cook	2.00	1.50	.80
12	Jeff Croston	.60	.45	.25
13	Greg Divis	.60	.45	.25
14	Quinn Early	2.50	2.00	1.00
15	Greg Fedders	.60	.45	.25
16	Mike Flagg	.60	.45	.25
17	Melvin Foster	.60	.45	.25
18	Hayden Fry (CO)	2.00	1.50	.80
19	Grant Goodman	.60	.45	.25
20	Dave Haight	1.00	.70	.40
21	Merton Hanks	3.00	2.25	1.25
22	Deven Harberts	.60	.45	.25
23	Kevin Harmon	.75	.60	.30
24	Chuck Hartlieb	1.25	.90	.50
25	Tork Hook	.60	.45	.25
26	Rob Houghtlin	.60	.45	.25
27	David Hudson	.60	.45	.25
28	Myron Keppy	.60	.45	.25
29	Jeff Koeppel	.60	.45	.25
30	Bob Kratch	1.50	1.25	.60
31	Peter Marciano	.60	.45	.25
32	Jim Mauro	.60	.45	.25
33	Marc Mazzeri	.60	.45	.25
34	Dan McGwire	2.00	1.50	.80
35	Mike Miller	.60	.45	.25
36	Joe Mott	1.00	.70	.40
37	James Pipkins	.60	.45	.25
38	Tom Poholsky	.75	.60	.30
39	Jim Poynton	.60	.45	.25
40	J.J. Puk	.75	.60	.30
41	Brad Quast	.60	.45	.25
42	Jim Reilly	.60	.45	.25
43	Matt Ruhland	.60	.45	.25
44	Bob Schmitt	.60	.45	.25
45	Joe Schuster	.75	.60	.30
46	Dwight Sistrunk	.75	.60	.30
47	Mark Stoops	.60	.45	.25
48	Steve Thomas	.60	.45	.25
49	Kent Thompson	.60	.45	.25
50	Travis Watkins	.60	.45	.25

51	Herb Wester	.60	.45	.25
52	Anthony Wright	.60	.45	.25
53	**Ring and Rose Bowl Ring**	.60	.45	.25
54	**Cheerleaders**	.75	.60	.30
55	**Floyd of Rosedale** (Trophy)	.60	.45	.25
56	**Freedom Bowl**			
	(Game Action Photo)	.75	.60	.30
57	**Herky the Hawk** (Mascot)	.60	.45	.25
58	**Holiday Bowl**			
	(Game Action Photo)	.75	.60	.30
59	**Indoor Practice Facility**	.60	.45	.25
60	**Iowa Team Captains** (Quinn			
	Early and five others)	1.50	1.25	.60
61	**Kinnick Stadium**	.60	.45	.25
62	**Peach Bowl**			
	(Game Action Photo)	.60	.45	.25
63	**Pom Pons** (Cheerleaders)	1.00	.70	.40

1988 Iowa

#	Player	NM/M	NM	E
	Complete Set (64):	30.00	22.00	12.00
	Common Player:	.50	.40	.20
2	Travis Watkins	.60	.45	.25
4	James Pipkins	.50	.40	.20
5	Mike Burke	.50	.40	.20
8	Chuck Hartlieb	1.00	.70	.40
10	Anthony Wright	.50	.40	.20
14	Tom Poholsky	.60	.45	.25
16	Deven Harberts	.50	.40	.20
18	Leroy Smith	.50	.40	.20
20	David Hudson	.50	.40	.20
21	Tony Stewart	.50	.40	.20
22	Sean Smith	.50	.40	.20
23	Richard Bass	.50	.40	.20
26	Peter Marciano	.50	.40	.20
29	Greg Brown	.50	.40	.20
30	Grant Goodman	.50	.40	.20
31	John Derby	.50	.40	.20
32	Mike Saunders	1.00	.70	.40
35	Brad Quast	.50	.40	.20
38	Chet Davis	.50	.40	.20
40	Marc Mazzeri	.50	.40	.20
41	Mark Stoops	.50	.40	.20
42	Tork Hook	.50	.40	.20
44	Keaton Smiley	.50	.40	.20
45	Merton Hanks	2.00	1.50	.80
48	Tyrone Berrie	.50	.40	.20
50	Bill Anderson	.50	.40	.20
51	Jeff Koeppel	.50	.40	.20
53	Greg Fedders	.50	.40	.20
57	Matt Ruhland	.50	.40	.20
58	Greg Davis	.50	.40	.20
60	Bob Schmitt	.50	.40	.20
61	Dave Turner	.50	.40	.20
64	Dave Haight	.75	.60	.30
66	Melvin Foster	.50	.40	.20
67	Jim Poynton	.50	.40	.20
68	Tim Anderson	.50	.40	.20
70	Bob Kratch	1.00	.70	.40
71	Jim Johnson	.50	.40	.20
74	George Hawthorne	.50	.40	.20
75	Greg Aegerter	.50	.40	.20
77	Paul Glonek	.50	.40	.20
80	Steve Green	.50	.40	.20
81	Brian Wise	.50	.40	.20
82	Jon Filloon	.50	.40	.20
84	Marv Cook	1.50	1.25	.60
85	John Palmer	.60	.45	.25
87	Jeff Skillett	.50	.40	.20
88	Tom Ward	.50	.40	.20
95	Jim Reilly	.50	.40	.20
96	Ron Geater	.50	.40	.20
97	Joe Mott	.75	.60	.30
99	Moses Santos	.50	.40	.20
NNO	**Team Captains** (Marv			
	Crook and four others)	1.00	.70	.40
NNO	Hayden Fry (CO)	1.00	.70	.40
NNO	Holiday Bowl 1987			
	(Hayden Fry) (CO)	.75	.60	.30
NNO	**Peach Bowl**			
	(Game Action Photo)	.60	.45	.25
NNO	**Holiday Bowl 1986**			
	(Game Action Photo)	.60	.45	.25
NNO	**Herky the Hawk** (Mascot)	.50	.40	.20
NNO	**Cheerleaders**	.60	.45	.25
NNO	**Kinnick Stadium**	.50	.40	.20
NNO	**Pom Pons** (Cheerleaders)	.60	.45	.25
NNO	**Championship Rings**	.50	.40	.20
NNO	**Indoor Practice Facility**	.50	.40	.20
NNO	**Symbolic Tiger Hawk**			
	(Helmet)	.50	.40	.20

1989 Iowa

#	Player	NM/M	NM	E
	Complete Set (90):	30.00	22.00	12.00
	Common Player:	.40	.30	.15
1	Greg Aegerter	.40	.30	.15
2	Kevin Allendorf	.40	.30	.15
3	Bill Anderson	.40	.30	.15
4	Richard Bass	.40	.30	.15
5	Rob Baxley	.40	.30	.15
6	Nick Bell	1.50	1.25	.60
7	Phil Bradley	.40	.30	.15
8	Greg Brown	.40	.30	.15
9	Doug Buch	.40	.30	.15
10	Gary Clark	.40	.30	.15
11	Roderick Davis	.40	.30	.15
12	Scott Davis	1.00	.70	.40
13	John Derby	.50	.40	.20
14	Mike Devlin	.40	.30	.15
15	Jason Dumont	.40	.30	.15
16	Mike Ertz	.40	.30	.15
17	Ted Faley	.40	.30	.15
18	Greg Fedders	.40	.30	.15
19	Mike Ferroni	.50	.40	.20
20	Jon Filloon	.40	.30	.15
21	Melvin Foster	.50	.40	.20
22	Hayden Fry (CO)	1.00	.70	.40
23	Ron Geater	.40	.30	.15
24	Ed Gochenour	.40	.30	.15
25	Merton Hanks	2.00	1.50	.80
26	Jim Hartlieb	.50	.40	.20
27	George Hawthorne	.40	.30	.15
28	Tork Hook	.40	.30	.15
29	Danan Hughes	1.00	.70	.40
30	Jim Johnson	.40	.30	.15
31	Jeff Koeppel	.40	.30	.15
32	Marvin Lampkin	.40	.30	.15
33	Peter Marciano	.40	.30	.15
34	Ed Marshall	.40	.30	.15
35	Kirk McGowan	.40	.30	.15
36	Mike Miller	.40	.30	.15
37	Lew Montgomery	.40	.30	.15
38	George Murphy	.40	.30	.15
39	John Palmer	.50	.40	.20
40	James Pipkins	.40	.30	.15
41	Tom Poholsky	.50	.40	.20
42	Eddie Polly	.40	.30	.15
43	Jim Poyton	.40	.30	.15
44	Brad Quast	.40	.30	.15
45	Matt Rodgers	.75	.60	.30
46	Matt Ruhland	.40	.30	.15
47	Ron Ryan	.40	.30	.15
48	Moses Santos	.40	.30	.15
49	Mike Saunders	.75	.60	.30
50	Doug Scott	.40	.30	.15
51	Jeff Skillett	.40	.30	.15
52	Leroy Smith	.40	.30	.15
53	Sean Smith	.40	.30	.15
54	Sean Snyder	.40	.30	.15
55	Tony Stewart	.40	.30	.15
56	Mark Stoops	.40	.30	.15
57	Dave Turner	.40	.30	.15
58	Darin Vande Zande	.40	.30	.15
59	Ted Velicer	.40	.30	.15
60	Travis Watkins	.40	.30	.15
61	Dusty Weiland	.40	.30	.15
62	Ladd Wessles	.40	.30	.15
63	Matt Whitaker	.40	.30	.15
64	Brian Wise	.40	.30	.15
65	Anthony Wright	.40	.30	.15
66	**100 Years of Iowa Football**			
	(Logo)	.40	.30	.15
67	**The Tigerhawk** (School			
	Logo)	.40	.30	.15
68	**Herky the Hawk** (Mascot)	.40	.30	.15
69	**Kinnick Stadium**	.40	.30	.15
70	**Hawkeye Fans**	.40	.30	.15
71	**NFL Tradition** (Logo)	.40	.30	.15
72	**1982 Beach Bowl** (Logo)	.40	.30	.15
73	**1983 Gator Bowl** (Logo)	.40	.30	.15
74	**1984 Freedom Bowl** (Logo)	.40	.30	.15
75	**1986 Holiday Bowl** (Logo)	.40	.30	.15
76	**1986 Rose Bowl** (Logo)	.40	.30	.15
77	**1987 Holiday Bowl** (Logo)	.40	.30	.15
78	**1988 Beach Bowl** (Logo)	.40	.30	.15
79	**Big Ten Conference** (Logo)	.40	.30	.15
80	**Iowa Marching Band**	.40	.30	.15
81	**Indoor Practice Facility**	.40	.30	.15
82	**Iowa Locker Rooms**	.40	.30	.15
83	**Iowa Weight Room**	.40	.30	.15
84	**Iowa Class Rooms**	.40	.30	.15
85	**Players' Lounge**	.40	.30	.15
86	**Floyd of Rosedale** (Trophy)	.40	.30	.15
87	**Medical Facilities**	.40	.30	.15
88	**Media Coverage**	.40	.30	.15
89	**Television Coverage**			
	(Camera)	.40	.30	.15

1971 Iowa Team Photos

#		NM	E	VG
	Complete Set (4):	25.00	12.50	7.50
	Common Sheet:	6.00	3.00	1.75
1	Geoff Mickelson, Craig Clemons, Frank Holmes, Levi Mitchell, Charles Podolak, Lorin Lynch, Steve Penney, Larry Horton	8.00	4.00	2.50
2	Alan Schaefer, Dave Triplett, John Muller, Jim Kaiser, Wendell Bell, Clark Malmer, Rich Solomon, Kelly Disser	6.00	3.00	1.75
3	Bill Schoonover, Frank Sunderman, Craig Darling, Tom Cabalka, Dave Simms, Bill Rose, Buster Hoinkes, Charles Cross	6.00	3.00	1.75
4	Kyle Skogman, Jerry Reardon, Dave Harris, Rob Fick, Mike Dillner, Ike White, Mark Nelson, Harry Kokolus	6.00	3.00	1.75

J

1986 Jeno's Pizza

Two players from each of the 28 NFL teams were selected for this 58-card set offered by Jeno's Pizza. Specially-marked Jeno's Pizza boxes each contained one card inside, sealed in plastic. Current and former stars are represented in the set. Each card back has a number which corresponds to the location in a Terry Bradshaw Action Play Book which was created to display the cards. The Play Book was available through a mail-in coupon. Each card back also has a summary of the player's career accomplishments.

#	Player	NM/M	NM	E
	Complete Set (56):	25.00	18.50	10.00
	Common Player:	.40	.30	.15
1	Duane Thomas	.75	.60	.30
2	Butch Johnson	.40	.30	.15
3	Andy Headen	.40	.30	.15
4	Joe Morris	.60	.45	.25
5	Wilbert Montgomery	.50	.40	.20
6	Harold Carmichael	.75	.60	.30
7	Ottis Anderson	.60	.45	.25
8	Roy Green	.50	.40	.20
9	Mark Murphy	.40	.30	.15
10	Joe Theismann	1.50	1.25	.60
11	Jim McMahon	1.00	.70	.40
12	Walter Payton	3.00	2.25	1.25
13	Billy Sims	.75	.60	.30
14	James Jones	.40	.30	.15
15	Willie Davis	.75	.60	.30
16	Eddie Lee Ivery	.40	.30	.15
17	Fran Tarkenton	2.00	1.50	.80
18	Alan Page	.75	.60	.30
19	Ricky Bell	.60	.45	.25
20	Cecil Johnson	.40	.30	.15
21	Bubba Bean	.40	.30	.15
22	Gerald Riggs	.50	.40	.20
23	Eric Dickerson, Barry Redden	1.00	.70	.40
24	Jack Reynolds	.50	.40	.20
25	Archie Manning	1.00	.70	.40
26	Wayne Wilson	.60	.45	.25
27	Dan Bunz, Pete Johnson	.40	.30	.15
28	Roger Craig	1.00	.70	.40
29	O.J. Simpson	6.00	4.50	2.50
30	Joe Cribbs	.50	.40	.20
31	Rick Volk, Leroy Kelly	.60	.45	.25
32	Earl Morrall	.75	.60	.30
33	Jim Klick	.50	.40	.20
34	Dan Marino	5.00	3.75	2.00
35	Craig James	1.00	.70	.40
36	Julius Adams	.40	.30	.15
37	Joe Namath	4.00	3.00	1.50
38	Freeman McNeil	.60	.45	.25
39	Pete Johnson	.40	.30	.15
40	Larry Kinnebrew	.40	.30	.15
41	Brian Sipe	.50	.40	.20
42	Kevin Mack, Earnest Byner	.60	.45	.25
43	Dan Pastorini	.60	.45	.25

44	Elvin Bethea, Carter Hartwig	.40	.30	.15
45	Fran Tarkenton, Jack Lambert	1.00	.70	.40
46	Terry Bradshaw	3.00	2.25	1.25
47	Randy Gradishar, Steve Foley	.50	.40	.20
48	Sammy Winder	.40	.30	.15
49	Robert Holmes	.40	.30	.15
50	Buck Buchanan	.75	.60	.30
51	Willie Jones, Cedrick Hardman	.40	.30	.15
52	Marcus Allen	1.50	1.25	.60
53	Dan Fouts, Don Macek	.75	.60	.30
54	Dan Fouts	1.50	1.25	.60
55	Blair Bush	.40	.30	.15
56	Steve Largent	2.50	2.00	1.00
----	Play Book(Terry Bradshaw)	3.00		

1981 Jets Police

The 10-card, 2-5/8" x 4-1/8" set have green-bordered fronts and were sponsored by Frito-Lay, Kiwanis, local law enforcement and the Jets. The card backs contain a safety tip in red print. Apparently, four of the cards were short-printed and thus are more scarce.

		NM/M	NM	E
Complete Set (10):		20.00	15.00	8.00
Common Player:		1.00	.70	.40
14	Richard Todd (SP)	4.00	3.00	1.50
42	Bruce Harper	1.00	.70	.40
51	Greg Buttle	1.00	.70	.40
73	Joe Klecko	2.50	2.00	1.00
79	Marvin Powell	2.00	1.50	.80
80	Johnny Lam Jones (SP)	3.50	2.75	1.50
85	Wesley Walker (SP)	5.00	3.75	2.00
93	Marty Lyons	2.50	2.00	1.00
99	Mark Gastineau	2.50	2.00	1.00
xx0	**Team Effort** (SP)	2.50	2.00	1.00

1969 Jets Tasco Prints

The six-card, 11" x 16" set, produced by Tasco Associates, features an artist's depiction of the players with blank backs.

		NM	E	VG
Complete Set (6):		100.00	50.00	30.00
Common Player:		10.00	5.00	3.00
1	Winston Hill	10.00	5.00	3.00
2	Joe Namath	50.00	25.00	15.00
3	Gerry Philbin	15.00	7.50	4.50
4	Johnny Sample	10.00	5.00	3.00
5	Matt Snell	18.00	9.00	5.50
6	Jim Turner	10.00	5.00	3.00

1966 Jets Team Issue

The nine-card, 5" x 7" set features black and white player photos on the fronts with blank backs.

		NM	E	VG
Complete Set (9):		80.00	60.00	32.00
Common Player:		4.00	2.00	1.25
1	Ralph Baker	4.00	2.00	1.25
2	Larry Grantham	5.00	2.50	1.50
3	Bill Mathis	4.00	2.00	1.25
4	Don Maynard	15.00	7.50	4.50
5	Joe Namath	40.00	20.00	12.00
6	Gerry Philbin	5.00	2.50	1.50
7	Mark Smolinski	4.00	2.00	1.25
8	Matt Snell	8.00	4.00	2.50
9	Bake Turner	4.00	2.00	1.25

1984 JOGO CFL

		NM/M	NM	E
Complete Set (160):		275.00	206.00	110.00
Complete Series 1 (110):		150.00	112.00	60.00
Complete Series 2 (50):		125.00	94.00	50.00
Common Player (1-110):		1.00	.70	.40
Common Player (111-160):		2.50	2.00	1.00
1	Mike Hameluck	1.50	1.25	.60
2	Bob Bronk	1.00	.70	.40
3	Paul Pearson	1.00	.70	.40
4	Dan Ferrone	1.50	1.25	.60
5	Paul Bennett	1.00	.70	.40
6	Joe Barnes	4.00	3.00	1.50
7	Condredge Holloway	6.00	4.50	2.50
8	Terry Greer	5.00	3.75	2.00
9	Vince Goldsmith	3.00	2.25	1.25
10	Darrell Wilson	1.00	.70	.40
11	Tom Trifaux	1.00	.70	.40
12	Kelvin Pruenster	1.00	.70	.40
13	Earl Wilson	1.00	.70	.40
14	Hank Llesic	2.50	2.00	1.00
15	Stephen Del Col	1.00	.70	.40
16	Lamont Meacham	1.00	.70	.40
17	Lester Brown	1.00	.70	.40
18	Rob Forbes	1.00	.70	.40
19	Darrell Nicholson	1.00	.70	.40
20	James Curry	2.50	2.00	1.00
21	Skip Walker	2.50	2.00	1.00
22	J.C. Watts	25.00	18.50	10.00
23	Kevin Powell	1.00	.70	.40
24	Dean Dorsey	2.00	1.50	.80
25	Tyron Gray	2.00	1.50	.80
26	Mike Hudson	1.50	1.25	.60
27	Dan Rashovich	1.00	.70	.40
28	Rudy Phillips	1.50	1.25	.60
29	Larry Tittley	1.00	.70	.40
30	Ricky Barden (UER) (Number missing)	1.00	.70	.40
31	Mark Seale	1.00	.70	.40
32	Prince McJunkins	1.50	1.25	.60
33	Kevin Dalliday	1.00	.70	.40
34	Rick Sowieta	1.00	.70	.40
35	Roger Cattelan	1.00	.70	.40
36	Damir Dupin	1.00	.70	.40
37	Jack Williams	1.00	.70	.40
38	Dave Newman	1.00	.70	.40
39	Maurice Doyle	1.00	.70	.40
40	Tim Hook	1.00	.70	.40
41	Dieter Brock	12.00	9.00	4.75
42	Rufus Crawford	5.00	3.75	2.00
43	Steve Kearns	1.00	.70	.40
44	Ross Francis	1.00	.70	.40
45	Henry Waszczuk	1.00	.70	.40
46	Mark Streeter	1.00	.70	.40
47	Mike McIntyre	1.00	.70	.40
48	John Priestner	1.00	.70	.40
49	Paul Palma	1.00	.70	.40
50	Mike Walker	1.50	1.25	.60
51	Mike Barker	1.00	.70	.40
52	Todd Brown	1.00	.70	.40
53	Andre Francis	2.00	1.50	.80
54	Glenn Keeble	1.00	.70	.40
55	Turner Gill	10.00	7.50	4.00
56	Eugene Belliveau	1.00	.70	.40
57	Willie Hampton	1.00	.70	.40
58	Ken Ciancone	1.00	.70	.40
59	Preston Young	1.00	.70	.40
60	Stanley Washington	1.00	.70	.40
61	Denny Ferdinand	1.00	.70	.40
62	Steve Smith	1.00	.70	.40
63	Rick Klassen	1.50	1.25	.60
64	Larry Crawford	1.50	1.25	.60
65	John Henry White	1.00	.70	.40
66	Bernie Glier	1.00	.70	.40
67	Don Taylor	1.00	.70	.40
68	Roy DeWalt	3.00	2.25	1.25
69	Mervyn Fernandez	25.00	18.50	10.00
70	John Blain	1.00	.70	.40
71	James Parker	4.00	3.00	1.50
72	Henry Vereen	1.00	.70	.40
73	Gerald Roper	1.00	.70	.40
74	Jim Sandusky	12.00	9.00	4.75
75	John Pankratz	1.00	.70	.40
76	Tom Clements	10.00	7.50	4.00
77	Vernon Pahl	1.00	.70	.40
78	Trevor Kennerd	2.50	2.00	1.00
79	Stan Mikawos	1.00	.70	.40
80	Ken Hailey	1.00	.70	.40
81	James Murphy	4.00	3.00	1.50
82	Jeff Boyd	2.00	1.50	.80
83	Bob Cameron	1.00	.70	.40
84	Jerome Erdman	1.00	.70	.40
85	Tyrone Jones	2.50	2.00	1.00
86	John Bonk	1.00	.70	.40
87	John Sturdivant	1.00	.70	.40
88	Dan Huclack	1.00	.70	.40
89	Tony Norman	1.00	.70	.40
90	Kevin Neiles	1.00	.70	.40
91	Dave Kirzinger	1.00	.70	.40
92	Kevin Molle	1.00	.70	.40
93	Jerry DeBrouolny	1.00	.70	.40
94	Larry Hogue	1.00	.70	.40
95	Ken Moore	1.00	.70	.40
96	Jerry Friesen	1.00	.70	.40
97	Mike McTague	1.50	1.25	.60
98	Jason Riley	1.00	.70	.40
99	Roger Aldag	2.00	1.50	.80
100	Dave Ridgway	4.00	3.00	1.50
101	Eric Upton	1.00	.70	.40
102	Laurent DesLauriers	1.00	.70	.40
103	Brian Fryer	1.00	.70	.40
104	Brian DeRoo	1.00	.70	.40
105	Neil Lumsden	1.00	.70	.40
106	Hector Pothier	1.00	.70	.40
107	Brian Kelly	12.00	9.00	4.75
108	Dan Kepley	3.00	2.25	1.25
109	Danny Bass	5.00	3.75	2.00
110	Nick Arakgi	1.50	1.25	.60
111	Lyle Bauer	2.50	2.00	1.00
112	Al Washington	2.50	2.00	1.00
113	Michel Bourgeau	3.00	2.25	1.25
114	Keith Gooch	2.50	2.00	1.00
115	Sean Kehoe	2.50	2.00	1.00
116	Ken Clark	3.00	2.25	1.25
117	Orlando Flanagan	2.50	2.00	1.00
118	Greg Vavra	2.50	2.00	1.00
119	Mark Bragagnolo	2.50	2.00	1.00
120	Dave Cutler	7.50	5.75	3.00
121	Nick Hebeler	2.50	2.00	1.00
122	Harry Skipper	5.00	3.75	2.00
123	Frank Robinson	3.00	2.25	1.25
124	DeWayne Jett	3.00	2.25	1.25
125	Mark Young	2.50	2.00	1.00
126	Felix Wright	25.00	18.50	10.00
127	Bob Poley	2.50	2.00	1.00
128	Leo Ezerins	2.50	2.00	1.00
129	Johnny Shepherd	3.00	2.25	1.25
130	Jeff Inglis	2.50	2.00	1.00
131	Dwaine Wilson	2.50	2.00	1.00
132	Aaron Hill	2.50	2.00	1.00
133	Brian Dudley	2.50	2.00	1.00
134	Ned Armour	2.50	2.00	1.00
135	Darryl Hall	2.50	2.00	1.00
136	Vince Phason	2.50	2.00	1.00
137	Terry Lymon	2.50	2.00	1.00
138	Jerry Dobrovolny	2.50	2.00	1.00
139	Richard Nemeth	2.50	2.00	1.00
140	Matt Dunigan	60.00	45.00	24.00
141	Rick Mohr	2.50	2.00	1.00
142	Lawrie Skolrood	2.50	2.00	1.00
143	Craig Ellis	6.00	4.50	2.50
144	Steve Johnson	2.50	2.00	1.00
145	Glen Suitor	3.00	2.25	1.25
146	Jeff Roberts	2.50	2.00	1.00
147	Greg Fieger	2.50	2.00	1.00
148	Sterling Hinds	2.50	2.00	1.00
149	Willard Reaves	9.00	6.75	3.50
150	John Pitts	2.50	2.00	1.00
151	Delbert Fowler	3.00	2.25	1.25
152	Mark Hopkins	2.50	2.00	1.00
153	Pat Cantner	2.50	2.00	1.00
154	Scott Flagel	3.00	2.25	1.25
155	Don Rose	2.50	2.00	1.00
156	David Shaw	2.50	2.00	1.00
157	Mark Moors	2.50	2.00	1.00
158	Chris Walby	5.00	3.75	2.00
159	Eugene Belliveau	2.50	2.00	1.00
160	Trevor Kennerd	10.00	7.50	4.00

1985 JOGO CFL

		NM/M	NM	E
Complete Set (110):		150.00	112.00	60.00
Common Player:		1.00	.70	.40
1	Mike Hameluck	1.50	1.25	.60
2	Michel Bourgeau	1.50	1.25	.60
3	Waymon Alridge	1.00	.70	.40
4	Daric Zeno	1.50	1.25	.60
5	J.C. Watts	20.00	15.00	8.00
6	Kevin Gray	1.00	.70	.40
7	Steve Harrison	1.00	.70	.40
8	Ralph Dixon	1.00	.70	.40
9	Jo Jo Heath	1.00	.70	.40
10	Rick Sowieta	1.00	.70	.40
11	Brad Fawcett	1.00	.70	.40
12	Lamont Meacham	1.00	.70	.40
13	Dean Dorsey	1.50	1.25	.60
14	Bernard Quarles	1.00	.70	.40
15	Mike Caterbone	1.00	.70	.40
16	Bob Stephen	1.00	.70	.40
17	Nick Benjamin	1.50	1.25	.60
18	Tim McCray	1.50	1.25	.60
19	Chris Sigler	1.00	.70	.40
20	Tony Johns	1.00	.70	.40
21	Jason Riley	1.00	.70	.40
22	Ralph Scholz	1.00	.70	.40
23	Ken Hobart	2.50	2.00	1.00
24	Paul Bennett	1.00	.70	.40
25	Dan Ferrone	1.50	1.25	.60
26	Jim Kalafat	1.00	.70	.40
27	William Mitchell	1.00	.70	.40
28	Denny Ferdinand	1.00	.70	.40
29	James Curry	2.50	2.00	1.00
30	Jeff Inglis	1.00	.70	.40
31	Bob Bronk	1.00	.70	.40
32	Dan Petschenig	1.00	.70	.40
33	Terry Greer	4.00	3.00	1.50
34	Condredge Holloway	5.00	3.75	2.00
35	Ian Beckstead	1.00	.70	.40
36	James Parker	3.00	2.25	1.25
37	Tim Cowan	1.50	1.25	.60
38	Roy DeWalt	2.50	2.00	1.00
39	Mervyn Fernandez	15.00	11.00	6.00
40	Bernie Glier	1.00	.70	.40
41	Keyvan Jenkins	3.00	2.25	1.25
42	Melvin Byrd	2.00	1.50	.80
43	Ron Robinson	2.00	1.50	.80
44	Andre Jones	1.00	.70	.40
45	Jim Sandusky	6.00	4.50	2.50
46	Darnell Clash	2.50	2.00	1.00

47	Rick Klassen	1.50	1.25	.60
48	Brian Kelly	6.00	4.50	2.50
49	Rick House	1.50	1.25	.60
50	Stewart Hill	3.00	2.25	1.25
51	Chris Woods	3.00	2.25	1.25
52	Darryl Hall	1.50	1.25	.60
53	Laurent DesLauriers	1.00	.70	.40
54	Larry Cowan	1.00	.70	.40
55	Matt Dunigan	15.00	11.00	6.00
56	Andre Francis	1.50	1.25	.60
57	Roy Kurtz	1.00	.70	.40
58	Steve Raquet	1.00	.70	.40
59	Turner Gill	5.00	3.75	2.00
60	Sandy Armstrong	1.00	.70	.40
61	Nick Arakgi	1.50	1.25	.60
62	Mike McTague	1.50	1.25	.60
63	Aaron Hill	1.00	.70	.40
64	Brett Williams	2.00	1.50	.80
65	Trevor Bowles	1.50	1.25	.60
66	Mark Hopkins	1.00	.70	.40
67	Frank Kosec	1.00	.70	.40
68	Ken Ciancone	1.00	.70	.40
69	Dwaine Wilson	1.00	.70	.40
70	Mark Stevens	1.00	.70	.40
71	George Voelk	1.00	.70	.40
72	Doug Scott	1.00	.70	.40
73	Rob Smith	1.00	.70	.40
74	Alan Reid	1.00	.70	.40
75	Rick Mohr	1.00	.70	.40
76	Dave Ridgway	3.50	2.75	1.50
77	Homer Jordan	1.00	.70	.40
78	Terry Leschuk	1.00	.70	.40
79	Rick Goltz	1.00	.70	.40
80	Neil Quilter	1.00	.70	.40
81	Joe Paopao	2.50	2.00	1.00
82	Stephen Jones	2.50	2.00	1.00
83	Scott Redl	1.00	.70	.40
84	Tony Dennis	1.00	.70	.40
85	Glen Suitor	1.50	1.25	.60
86	Mike Anderson	1.00	.70	.40
87	Stewart Fraser	1.00	.70	.40
88	Fran McDermott	1.00	.70	.40
89	Craig Ellis	3.00	2.25	1.25
90	Eddie Ray Walker	2.00	1.50	.80
91	Trevor Kennerd	3.00	2.25	1.25
92	Pat Cantner	1.00	.70	.40
93	Tom Clements	10.00	7.50	4.00
94	Glen Steele	1.00	.70	.40
95	Willard Reaves	4.00	3.00	1.50
96	Tony Norman	1.00	.70	.40
97	Tyrone Jones	2.50	2.00	1.00
98	Jerome Erdman	1.00	.70	.40
99	Sean Kehoe	1.00	.70	.40
100	Kevin Neiles	1.00	.70	.40
101	Ken Hailey	1.00	.70	.40
102	Scott Flagel	1.50	1.25	.60
103	Mark Moors	1.00	.70	.40
104	Gerry McGrath	1.00	.70	.40
105	James Hood	1.00	.70	.40
106	Randy Ambrosie	1.00	.70	.40
107	Terry Irvin	1.00	.70	.40
108	Joe Barnes	3.00	2.25	1.25
109	Richard Nemeth	1.00	.70	.40
110	Darrell Patterson	1.00	.70	.40

1986 JOGO CFL

	NM/M	NM	E
Complete Set (169):	135.00	101.00	54.00
Common Series 1 (110):	75.00	56.00	30.00
Common Series 2 (59):	60.00	45.00	24.00
Common Player (1-110):	.75	.60	.30
Common Player (111-169):	.75	.60	.30

1	Ken Hobart	2.00	1.50	.80
2	Tom Porras	1.25	.90	.50
3	Jason Riley	.75	.60	.30
4	Ron Ingram	.75	.60	.30
5	Steve Stapler	1.25	.90	.50
6	Mike Derks	.75	.60	.30
7	Grover Covington	5.00	3.75	2.00
8	Lance Shields	1.25	.90	.50
9	Mike Robinson	.75	.60	.30
10	Mark Napiorkowski	.75	.60	.30
11	Romel Andrews	.75	.60	.30
12	Ed Gataveckas	.75	.60	.30
13	Tony Champion	5.00	3.75	2.00
14	Dale Sanderson	.75	.60	.30
15	Mark Barousse	.75	.60	.30
16	Nick Benjamin	1.25	.90	.50
17	Reginal Butts	.75	.60	.30
18	Tom Burgess	6.00	4.50	2.50
19	Todd Dillon	3.00	2.25	1.25
20	Jim Reid	1.25	.90	.50
21	Robert Reid	.75	.60	.30
22	Roger Cattelan	.75	.60	.30
23	Kevin Powell	.75	.60	.30
24	Randy Fabi	.75	.60	.30
25	Gerry Hornett	.75	.60	.30
26	Rick Sowieta	.75	.60	.30
27	Warren Hudson	1.25	.90	.50
28	Steven Cox	.75	.60	.30
29	Dean Dorsey	1.25	.90	.50
30	Michel Bourgeau	1.25	.90	.50
31	Ken Joiner	.75	.60	.30
32	Mark Seale	.75	.60	.30
33	Condredge Holloway	4.00	3.00	1.50
34	Bob Bronk	.75	.60	.30
35	Jeff Inglis	.75	.60	.30
36	Lance Chomyc	1.50	1.25	.60
37	Craig Ellis	2.00	1.50	.80
38	Marcellus Greene	.75	.60	.30
39	David Marshall	.75	.60	.30
40	Kerry Parker	.75	.60	.30
41	Darrell Wilson	.75	.60	.30
42	Walter Lewis	3.50	2.75	1.50
43	Sandy Armstrong	.75	.60	.30
44	Ken Ciancone	.75	.60	.30
45	Steve Raquet	.75	.60	.30
46	Lemont Jeffers	.75	.60	.30
47	Paul Gray	.75	.60	.30
48	Jacques Chapdelaine	.75	.60	.30
49	Rick Ryan	.75	.60	.30
50	Mark Hopkins	.75	.60	.30
51	Glenn Keeble	.75	.60	.30
52	Roy Kurtz	.75	.60	.30
53	Brian Dudley	.75	.60	.30
54	Mike Gray	.75	.60	.30
55	Tyrone Crews	.75	.60	.30
56	Roy DeWalt	2.50	2.00	1.00
57	Mervyn Fernandez	6.00	4.50	2.50
58	Bernie Glier	.75	.60	.30
59	James Parker	3.00	2.25	1.25
60	Bruce Barnett	.75	.60	.30
61	Keyvan Jenkins	1.50	1.25	.60
62	Alan Wilson	.75	.60	.30
63	Delbert Fowler	1.25	.90	.50
64	James Jefferson	5.00	3.75	2.00
65	James West	7.50	5.75	3.00
66	Laurent DesLauriers	.75	.60	.30
67	Damon Allen	10.00	7.50	4.00
68	Roy Bennett	3.00	2.25	1.25
69	Hasson Arbubakrr	.75	.60	.30
70	Tom Clements	7.50	5.75	3.00
71	Trevor Kennerd	1.50	1.25	.60
72	Perry Tuttle	3.50	2.75	1.50
73	Pat Cantner	.75	.60	.30
74	Mike Hameluck	.75	.60	.30
75	Rob Prodanovic	.75	.60	.30
76	James Bell	1.25	.90	.50
77	Hector Pothier	.75	.60	.30
78	Milson Jones	2.00	1.50	.80
79	Craig Shaffer	.75	.60	.30
80	Chris Skinner	1.25	.90	.50
81	Matt Dunigan	7.50	5.75	3.00
82	Tom Dixon	.75	.60	.30
83	Brian Pillman	1.25	.90	.50
84	Randy Ambrosie	.75	.60	.30
85	Rick Johnson	3.50	2.75	1.50
86	Larry Hogue	.75	.60	.30
87	Garrett Doll	.75	.60	.30
88	Stu Laird	1.25	.90	.50
89	Greg Fieger	.75	.60	.30
90	Sean McKeown	.75	.60	.30
91	Rob Bresciani	.75	.60	.30
92	Harold Hallman	2.50	2.00	1.00
93	Jamie Harris	.75	.60	.30
94	Dan Rashovich	.75	.60	.30
95	David Conrad	.75	.60	.30
96	Glen Suitor	1.25	.90	.50
97	Mike Siroishka	.75	.60	.30
98	Michael McGruder	3.00	2.25	1.25
99	Brad Calip	.75	.60	.30
100	Mike Anderson	.75	.60	.30
101	Trent Bryant	.75	.60	.30
102	Gary Lewis	.75	.60	.30
103	Tony Dennis	.75	.60	.30
104	Paul Tripoli	.75	.60	.30
105	Daric Zeno	.75	.60	.30
106	Michael Elarms	.75	.60	.30
107	Donohue Grant	.75	.60	.30
108	Ray Elgaard	15.00	11.00	6.00
109	Joe Paopao	2.00	1.50	.80
110	Dave Ridgway	2.50	2.00	1.00
111	Rudy Phillips	1.25	.90	.50
112	Carl Brazley	1.25	.90	.50
113	Andre Francis	.75	.60	.30
114	Mitchell Price	1.50	1.25	.60
115	Wayne Lee	.75	.60	.30
116	Tim McCray	1.50	1.25	.60
117	Scott Virkus	.75	.60	.30
118	Nick Hebeler	.75	.60	.30
119	Eddie Ray Walker	1.25	.90	.50
120	Bobby Johnson	.75	.60	.30
121	Mike McTague	.75	.60	.30
122	Jeff Inglis	.75	.60	.30
123	Joe Fuller	.75	.60	.30
124	Steve Crane	.75	.60	.30
125	Bill Henry	.75	.60	.30
126	Ron Brown	.75	.60	.30
127	Henry Taylor	.75	.60	.30
128	Greg Holmes	.75	.60	.30
129	Steve Harrison	.75	.60	.30
130	Paul Osbaldiston	3.00	2.25	1.25
131	Craig Walls	.75	.60	.30
132	Clorindo Grilli	.75	.60	.30
133	Marty Palazeti	.75	.60	.30
134	Darryl Hall	.75	.60	.30
135	David Black	.75	.60	.30
136	Bennie Thompson	2.50	2.00	1.00
137	Darryl Sampson	.75	.60	.30
138	James Murphy	2.50	2.00	1.00
139	Scott Flagel	.75	.60	.30
140	Trevor Kennerd	2.00	1.50	.80
141	Bob Molle	.75	.60	.30
142	Darrell Patterson	.75	.60	.30
143	Stan Mikawos	.75	.60	.30
144	John Sturdivant	.75	.60	.30
145	Tyrone Jones	2.00	1.50	.80
146	Jim Zorn	15.00	11.00	6.00
147	Steve Howlett	.75	.60	.30
148	Jeff Volpe	.75	.60	.30
149	Jerome Erdman	.75	.60	.30
150	Ned Armour	.75	.60	.30
151	Rick Klassen	1.25	.90	.50
152	Brett Williams	2.00	1.50	.80
153	Richie Hall	.75	.60	.30
154	Ray Alexander	2.50	2.00	1.00
155	Willie Pless	5.00	3.75	2.00
156	Marion Jones	.75	.60	.30
157	Danny Bass	3.50	2.75	1.50
158	Frank Balkovec	.75	.60	.30
159	Less Browne	4.00	3.00	1.50
160	Paul Osbaldiston	1.50	1.25	.60
161	Trevor Bowles	.75	.60	.30
162	David Daniels	.75	.60	.30
163	Kevin Konar	1.50	1.25	.60
164	Gary Allen	2.00	1.50	.80
165	Karlton Watson	.75	.60	.30
166	Ron Hopkins	1.25	.90	.50
167	Rob Smith	.75	.60	.30
168	Garrett Doll	.75	.60	.30
169	Rod Skillman	2.00	1.50	.80

1987 JOGO CFL

	NM/M	NM	E
Complete Set (110):	90.00	67.00	36.00
Common Player:	.60	.45	.25

1	Jim Reid	2.00	1.50	.80
2	Nick Benjamin	1.00	.70	.40
3	Dean Dorsey	1.00	.70	.40
4	Hasson Arbubakrr	.60	.45	.25
5	Gerald Alphin	6.00	4.50	2.50
6	Larry Willis	3.00	2.25	1.25
7	Rick Wolkensperg	.60	.45	.25
8	Roy DeWalt	2.00	1.50	.80
9	Michel Bourgeau	1.00	.70	.40
10	Anthony Woodson	.60	.45	.25
11	Marv Allemang	.60	.45	.25
12	Jerry Dobrovolny	.60	.45	.25
13	Larry Mohr	.60	.45	.25
14	Kyle Hall	.60	.45	.25
15	Irv Daymond	.60	.45	.25
16	Ken Ford	.60	.45	.25
17	Leo Groenewegen	.60	.45	.25
18	Michael Cline	.60	.45	.25
19	Gilbert Renfroe	3.00	2.25	1.25
20	Danny Barrett	6.00	4.50	2.50
21	Dan Petschenig	.60	.45	.25
22	Gill Fenerty (UER) (Misspelled Gil on card front)	10.00	7.50	4.00
23	Lance Chomyc	1.00	.70	.40
24	Jake Vaughan	.60	.45	.25
25	John Congemi	2.00	1.50	.80
26	Kelvin Pruenster	.60	.45	.25
27	Mike Siroishka	.60	.45	.25
28	Dwight Edwards	1.00	.70	.40
29	Darnell Clash	1.50	1.25	.60
30	Glenn Kulka	1.50	1.25	.60
31	Jim Kardash	.60	.45	.25
32	Selwyn Drain	.60	.45	.25
33	Ian Sinclair	1.00	.70	.40
34	Pat Cantner	.60	.45	.25
35	Trevor Kennerd	2.50	2.00	1.00
36	Bob Cameron	.60	.45	.25
37	Willard Reaves	3.00	2.25	1.25
38	Jeff Treftlin	.60	.45	.25
39	David Black	.60	.45	.25
40	Chris Walby	2.00	1.50	.80
41	Tom Clements	4.00	3.00	1.50
42	Mike Gray	.60	.45	.25
43	Bennie Thompson	1.50	1.25	.60
44	Tyrone Jones	2.00	1.50	.80

45	Ken Winey	.60	.45	.25
46	Nick Arakgi	1.00	.70	.40
47	James West	2.50	2.00	1.00
48	Ken Pettway	.60	.45	.25
49	James Murphy	2.50	2.00	1.00
50	Carl Fodor	.60	.45	.25
51	Tom Muecke	2.00	1.50	.80
52	Alvis Satele	.60	.45	.25
53	Grover Covington	2.00	1.50	.80
54	Tom Porras	1.00	.70	.40
55	Jason Riley	.60	.45	.25
56	Jed Tommy	.60	.45	.25
57	Bernie Ruoff	1.00	.70	.40
58	Ed Gataveckas	.60	.45	.25
59	Wayne Lee	.60	.45	.25
60	Ken Hobart	1.50	1.25	.60
61	Frank Robinson	1.00	.70	.40
62	Mike Robinson	.60	.45	.25
63	Ben Zambiasi (UER)			
	(No team listed on front			
	of card)	2.00	1.50	.80
64	Byron Williams	.60	.45	.25
65	Lance Shields	1.00	.70	.40
66	Ralph Scholz	.60	.45	.25
67	Earl Winfield	5.00	3.75	2.00
68	Terry Lehne	.60	.45	.25
69	Alvin Bailey	.60	.45	.25
70	David Sauve	.60	.45	.25
71	Bernie Glier	.60	.45	.25
72	Nelson Martin	.60	.45	.25
73	Kevin Konar	1.00	.70	.40
74	Greg Peterson	.60	.45	.25
75	Harold Hallman	1.50	1.25	.60
76	Sandy Armstrong	.60	.45	.25
77	Glenn Harper	.60	.45	.25
78	Rick Worman	1.50	1.25	.60
79	Darrell Toussaint	.60	.45	.25
80	Larry Hogue	.60	.45	.25
81	Rick Johnson	2.50	2.00	1.00
82	Richie Hall	.60	.45	.25
83	Stu Laird	1.00	.70	.40
84	Mike Emery	.60	.45	.25
85	Cliff Toney	.60	.45	.25
86	Matt Dunigan	6.00	4.50	2.50
87	Hector Pothier	.60	.45	.25
88	Stewart Hill	1.50	1.25	.60
89	Stephen Jones	1.50	1.25	.60
90	Dan Huclack	.60	.45	.25
91	Mark Napiorkowski	.60	.45	.25
92	Mike Derks	.60	.45	.25
93	Mike Walker	1.50	1.25	.60
94	Michael McGruder	2.00	1.50	.80
95	Terry Baker	3.00	2.25	1.25
96	Bobby Jurasin	4.00	3.00	1.50
97	James Curry	2.50	2.00	1.00
98	Tracey Mack	.60	.45	.25
99	Tom Burgess	3.50	2.75	1.50
100	Steve Crane	.60	.45	.25
101	Glen Suitor	1.00	.70	.40
102	Walter Bender	.60	.45	.25
103	Jeff Bentrim	2.00	1.50	.80
104	Eric Florence	.60	.45	.25
105	Terry Cochrane	.60	.45	.25
106	Tony Dennis	.60	.45	.25
107	Dave Albright	.60	.45	.25
108	David Sidoo	.60	.45	.25
109	Harry Skipper	1.00	.70	.40
110	Dave Ridgway	2.00	1.50	.80

1988 JOGO CFL

		NM/M	NM	E
Complete Set (110):		110.00	82.00	44.00
Common Player:		.60	.45	.25
1	Roy DeWalt	2.00	1.50	.80
2	Jim Reid	1.25	.90	.50
3	Patrick Wayne	.60	.45	.25
4	Jerome Erdman	.60	.45	.25
5	Tom Dixon	.60	.45	.25
6	Brad Fawcett	.60	.45	.25
7	Tom Muecke	1.25	.90	.50

8	Mike Hudson	.60	.45	.25
9	Orville Lee	1.50	1.25	.60
10	Michel Bourgeau	1.00	.70	.40
11	Dan Sellers	.60	.45	.25
12	Rob Pavan	.60	.45	.25
13	Rae Robirtis	.60	.45	.25
14	Rod Brown	.60	.45	.25
15	Ken Evraire	1.00	.70	.40
16	Irv Daymond	.60	.45	.25
17	Tim Jessie	1.00	.70	.40
18	Jim Sandusky	4.00	3.00	1.50
19	Blake Dermott	1.00	.70	.40
20	Brian Warren	.60	.45	.25
21	Mike Walker	3.00	2.25	1.25
22	Tom Porras	1.00	.70	.40
23	Less Browne	1.25	.90	.50
24	Paul Osbaldiston	1.00	.70	.40
25	Vernell Quinn	.60	.45	.25
26	Mike Derks	.60	.45	.25
27	Arnold Grevious	.60	.45	.25
28	Jim Lorenz	.60	.45	.25
29	Mike Robinson	.60	.45	.25
30	Doug Davies	.60	.45	.25
31	Earl Winfield	3.00	2.25	1.25
32	Wally Zatylny	2.00	1.50	.80
33	Martin Sartin	.60	.45	.25
34	Lee Knight	.60	.45	.25
35	Jason Riley	.60	.45	.25
36	Darrell Gorbin	.60	.45	.25
37	Tony Champion	2.50	2.00	1.00
38	Steve Stapler	1.00	.70	.40
39	Scott Flagel	1.00	.70	.40
40	Grover Covington	1.50	1.25	.60
41	Mark Napiorkowski	.60	.45	.25
42	Jacques Chapdelaine	.60	.45	.25
43	Lance Shields	1.00	.70	.40
44	Donohue Grant	.60	.45	.25
45	Henry Williams	25.00	18.50	10.00
46	Trevor Bowles	1.00	.70	.40
47	Don Wilson	.60	.45	.25
48	Tracy Ham	15.00	11.00	6.00
49	Richie Hall	1.00	.70	.40
50	Rob Bresciani	.60	.45	.25
51	James Curry	1.25	.90	.50
52	Kent Austin	15.00	11.00	6.00
53	Jeff Bentrim	1.00	.70	.40
54	Dave Ridgway	1.25	.90	.50
55	Terry Baker	1.00	.70	.40
56	Lance Chomyc	1.00	.70	.40
57	Paul Sandor	.60	.45	.25
58	Kevin Cummings	.60	.45	.25
59	John Congemi	1.25	.90	.50
60	Gilbert Renfroe	1.50	1.25	.60
61	Jake Vaughan	.60	.45	.25
62	Doran Major	.60	.45	.25
63	Dwight Edwards	1.00	.70	.40
64	Bruce Elliott	.60	.45	.25
65	Lorenzo Graham	.60	.45	.25
66	Jim Kardash	.60	.45	.25
67	Reggie Pleasant	1.50	1.25	.60
68	Carl Brazley	1.00	.70	.40
69	Gill Fenerty	5.00	3.75	2.00
70	Selwyn Drain	.60	.45	.25
71	Warren Hudson	1.00	.70	.40
72	Willie Fears	.60	.45	.25
73	Randy Ambrosie	.60	.45	.25
74	George Ganas	.60	.45	.25
75	Glenn Kulka	1.00	.70	.40
76	Kelvin Pruenster	.60	.45	.25
77	Darrell Smith	1.50	.45	.60
78	Jearld Baylis	1.50	1.25	.60
79	Blaine Schmidt	.60	.45	.25
80	Tony Visco	1.00	.70	.40
81	Carl Fodor	.60	.45	.25
82	Rudy Phillips	1.00	.70	.40
83	Craig Watson	1.00	.70	.40
84	Kent Warnock	1.00	.70	.40
85	Ken Ford	.60	.45	.25
86	Blake Marshall	2.00	1.50	.80
87	Terry Cochrane	.60	.45	.25
88	Shawn Faulkner	.60	.45	.25
89	Marshall Toner	.60	.45	.25
90	Darren Yewshyn	.60	.45	.25
91	Eugene Belliveau	.60	.45	.25
92	Jay Christensen	.60	.45	.25
93	Anthony Parker	1.25	.90	.50
94	Walter Ballard	.60	.45	.25
95	Matt Dunigan	6.00	4.50	2.50
96	Andre Francis	1.00	.70	.40
97	Rickey Foggie	6.00	4.50	2.50
98	Delbert Fowler	.60	.45	.25
99	Michael Allen	.60	.45	.25
100	Greg Battle	6.00	4.50	2.50
101	Mike Gray	.60	.45	.25
102	Dan Wicklum	.60	.45	.25
103	Paul Shorten	.60	.45	.25
104	Paul Clatney	.60	.45	.25
105	Rod Hill	2.00	1.50	.80

106	Steve Rodehutskors	.60	.45	.25
107	Sean Salisbury	4.00	3.00	1.50
108	Vernon Pahl	.60	.45	.25
109	Trevor Kennerd	1.00	.70	.40
110	David Williams	2.50	2.00	1.00

1989 JOGO CFL

		NM/M	NM	E
Complete Set (160):		95.00	71.00	38.00
Complete Series 1 (110):		60.00	45.00	24.00
Complete Series 2 (50):		35.00	26.00	14.00
Common Player (1-160):		.50	.40	.20
1	Mike Kerrigan	2.50	2.00	1.00
2	Ian Beckstead	.50	.40	.20
3	Lance Chomyc	.75	.60	.30
4	Gill Fenerty	3.50	2.75	1.50
5	Lee Morris	.50	.40	.20
6	Todd Wiseman	.50	.40	.20
7	John Congemi	.75	.60	.30
8	Harold Hallman	.75	.60	.30
9	Jim Kardash	.50	.40	.20
10	Kelvin Pruenster	.50	.40	.20
11	Blaine Schmidt	.50	.40	.20
12	Bruce Holmes	.50	.40	.20
13	Ed Berry	.50	.40	.20
14	Bobby McAllister	2.50	2.00	1.00
15	Frank Robinson	.75	.60	.30
16	Darrell Corbin	.50	.40	.20
17	Jason Riley	.50	.40	.20
18	Darrell Patterson	.50	.40	.20
19	Darrell Harle	.50	.40	.20
20	Mark Napiorkowski	.50	.40	.20
21	Derrick McAdoo	2.00	1.50	.80
22	Sam Loucks	.50	.40	.20
23	Ronnie Glanton	.50	.40	.20
24	Lance Shields	.75	.60	.30
25	Tony Champion	2.00	1.50	.80
26	Floyd Salazar	.50	.40	.20
27	Tony Visco	.75	.60	.30
28	Glenn Kulka	.75	.60	.30
29	Reggie Pleasant	.75	.60	.30
30	Rod Skillman	.50	.40	.20
31	Grover Covington	1.50	1.25	.60
32	Gerald Alphin	2.00	1.50	.80
33	Gerald Wilcox	.75	.60	.30
34	Daniel Hunter	.50	.40	.20
35	Tony Kimbrough	.75	.60	.30
36	Willie Fears	.75	.60	.30
37	Tyrone Thurman	4.00	3.00	1.50
38	Dean Dorsey	.75	.60	.30
39	Tom Schimmer	.50	.40	.20
40	Ken Evraire	.75	.60	.30
41	Steve Wiggins	.50	.40	.20
42	Donovan Wright	.50	.40	.20
43	Tuineau Alipate	.50	.40	.20
44	Richie Hall	.50	.40	.20
45	Rob Bresciani	.50	.40	.20
46	Tom Burgess	1.50	1.25	.60
47	Jeff Fairholm	4.00	3.00	1.50
48	John Hoffman	.50	.40	.20
49	Dave Ridgway	1.25	.90	.50
50	Terry Baker	.75	.60	.30
51	Mike Hildebrand	.50	.40	.20
52	Danny Bass	2.50	2.00	1.00
53	Jeff Braswell	.50	.40	.20
54	Michel Bourgeau	.75	.60	.30
55	Ken Ford	.50	.40	.20
56	Enis Jackson	.50	.40	.20
57	Tony Hunter	1.25	.90	.50
58	Andre Francis	.75	.60	.30
59	Larry Wruck	.75	.60	.30
60	Pierre Vercheval	1.00	.70	.40
61	Keith Wright	.50	.40	.20
62	Andrew McConnell	.50	.40	.20
63	Gregg Stumon	.75	.60	.30
64	Steve Taylor	3.00	2.25	1.25
65	Brett Williams	.75	.60	.30
66	Tracy Ham	5.00	3.75	2.00
67	Stewart Hill	.75	.60	.30
68	Eugene Belliveau	.50	.40	.20
69	Tom Porras	.75	.60	.30
70	Jay Christensen	.50	.40	.20
71	Michael Soles	1.00	.70	.40
72	John Mandarich	1.25	.90	.50
73	Dan Wicklum	.50	.40	.20
74	Shawn Daniels	.50	.40	.20
75	Marshall Toner	.50	.40	.20
76	Kent Warnock	.75	.60	.30
77	Terrence Jones	4.00	3.00	1.50
78	Damon Allen	2.00	1.50	.80
79	Kevin Konar	.75	.60	.30
80	Phillip Smith	.50	.40	.20
81	Marcus Thomas	.50	.40	.20
82	Jamie Taras	.50	.40	.20
83	Rob Moretto	.50	.40	.20
84	Eugene Mingo	.50	.40	.20
85	Matt Dunigan	5.00	3.75	2.00

		NM/M	NM	E
86	Jan Carinci	.50	.40	.20
87	Anthony Parker	2.00	1.50	.80
88	Keith Gooch	.50	.40	.20
89	Ron Howard	.50	.40	.20
90	David Williams	1.50	1.25	.60
91	Less Browne	.75	.60	.30
92	Quency Williams	.50	.40	.20
93	Tim McCray	.75	.60	.30
94	Jeff Croonen	.50	.40	.20
95	Greg Battle	2.00	1.50	.80
96	Moustafa Ali	.50	.40	.20
97	Michael Allen	.50	.40	.20
98	David Black	.50	.40	.20
99	Paul Randolph	.50	.40	.20
100	Trevor Kennerd	.75	.60	.30
101	Ken Pettway	.50	.40	.20
102	Sean Salisbury	2.50	2.00	1.00
103	Bob Cameron	.50	.40	.20
104	Tim Jessie	.75	.60	.30
105	Leon Hatzilioannou	.50	.40	.20
106	Matt Pearce	.50	.40	.20
107	Paul Clatney	.50	.40	.20
108	Randy Fabi	.50	.40	.20
109	Mike Gray	.50	.40	.20
110	James Murphy	2.00	1.50	.80
111	Danny Barrett	1.50	1.25	.60
112	Wally Zatylny	.75	.60	.30
113	Tony Truelove	.50	.40	.20
114	Leroy Blugh	.50	.40	.20
115	Reggie Taylor	1.50	1.25	.60
116	Mark Zeno	2.50	2.00	1.00
117	Paul Wetmore	.50	.40	.20
118	Mark McLoughlin	.50	.40	.20
119	Randy Ambrosie	.50	.40	.20
120	Will Johnson	.75	.60	.30
121	Brock Smith	.50	.40	.20
122	Willie Gillus	.50	.40	.20
123	Andy McVey	.50	.40	.20
124	Wes Cooper	.50	.40	.20
125	Tyrone Pope	.50	.40	.20
126	Craig Ellis	1.50	1.25	.60
127	Darrel Hopper	.50	.40	.20
128	Brad Fawcett	.50	.40	.20
129	Pat Miller	.50	.40	.20
130	Irv Daymond	.50	.40	.20
131	Bob Molle	.50	.40	.20
132	James Mills	3.00	2.25	1.25
133	Darrell Wallace	.75	.60	.30
134	Jerry Beasley	.50	.40	.20
135	Loyd Lewis	.50	.40	.20
136	Bernie Glier	.50	.40	.20
137	Eric Streater	2.00	1.50	.80
138	Gerald Roper	.50	.40	.20
139	Brad Tierney	.50	.40	.20
140	Patrick Wayne	.50	.40	.20
141	Craig Watson	.50	.40	.20
142	Doug Landry	3.50	2.75	1.50
143	Orville Lee	1.50	1.25	.60
144	Rocco Romano	.50	.40	.20
145	Todd Dillon	1.00	.70	.40
146	Michel Lamy	.50	.40	.20
147	Tony Cherry	3.50	2.75	1.50
148	Flint Fleming	.50	.40	.20
149	Kennard Martin	.50	.40	.20
150	Lorenzo Graham	.50	.40	.20
151	Junior Thurman	1.50	1.25	.60
152	Darnell Graham	.50	.40	.20
153	Dan Ferrone	.75	.60	.30
154	Matt Finlay	.50	.40	.20
155	Brent Matich	.50	.40	.20
156	Kent Austin	5.00	3.75	2.00
157	Will Lewis	.50	.40	.20
158	Mike Walker	1.50	1.25	.60
159	Tim Petros	.75	.60	.30
160	Stu Laird	1.50	1.25	.60

1990 JOGO CFL

RICKEY FOOGIE

	NM/M	NM	E
Complete Set (220):	60.00	45.00	24.00
Complete Series 1 (110):	30.00	22.00	12.00
Complete Series 2 (110):	30.00	22.00	12.00

	Common Player:	.25	.20	.10
1	**1989 Grey Cup Champs** (Saskatchewan)	1.00	.70	.40
2	Kent Austin	2.50	2.00	1.00
3	James Ellingson	.40	.30	.15
4	Vince Goldsmith	.40	.30	.15
5	Gary Lewis	.25	.20	.10
6	Bobby Jurasin	1.00	.70	.40
7	Tim McCray	.40	.30	.15
8	Chuck Klingbeil	1.50	1.25	.60
9	Albert Brown	.25	.20	.10
10	Dave Ridgway	.75	.60	.30
11	Tony Rice	3.00	2.25	1.25
12	Richie Hall	.25	.20	.10
13	Jeff Fairholm	1.00	.70	.40
14	Ray Elgaard	1.25	.90	.50
15	Sonny Gordon	.25	.20	.10
16	Peter Giftopoulos	.75	.60	.30
17	Mike Kerrigan	1.00	.70	.40
18	Jason Riley	.25	.20	.10
19	Wally Zatylny	.40	.30	.15
20	Derrick McAdoo	.40	.30	.15
21	Dale Sanderson	.25	.20	.10
22	Paul Osbaldiston	.40	.30	.15
23	Todd Dillon	.40	.30	.15
24	Miles Gorrell	.25	.20	.10
25	Earl Winfield	.75	.60	.30
26	Bill Henry	.25	.20	.10
27	Darrell Harle	.25	.20	.10
28	Ernie Schramayr	.25	.20	.10
29	Greg Peterson	.25	.20	.10
30	Marshall Toner	.25	.20	.10
31	Danny Barrett	1.50	1.25	.60
32	Mike Palumbo	.25	.20	.10
33	Ken Ford	.25	.20	.10
34	Brock Smith	.25	.20	.10
35	Tom Spoletini	.25	.20	.10
36	Will Johnson	.40	.30	.15
37	Terrence Jones	1.50	1.25	.60
38	Darcy Kopp	.25	.20	.10
39	Tim Petros	.40	.30	.15
40	Mitchell Price	.40	.30	.15
41	Junior Thurman	1.00	.70	.40
42	Kent Warnock	.40	.30	.15
43	Darrell Smith	1.00	.70	.40
44	Chris Schultz (UER) (No team on back)	.40	.30	.15
45	Kelvin Pruenster	.25	.20	.10
46	Matt Dunigan	3.00	2.25	1.25
47	Lance Chomyc	.40	.30	.15
48	John Congemi	.75	.60	.30
49	Mike Clemons	10.00	7.50	4.00
50	Glenn Harper	.25	.20	.10
51	Branko Vincic	.25	.20	.10
52	Tom Porras	.40	.30	.15
53	Reggie Pleasant	.40	.30	.15
54	Randy Marriott	.25	.20	.10
55	James Parker	.75	.60	.30
56	Don Moen	.40	.30	.15
57	James West	1.00	.70	.40
58	Trevor Kennerd	.75	.60	.30
59	Warren Hudson	.40	.30	.15
60	Tom Burgess	1.50	1.25	.60
61	David Black	.25	.20	.10
62	Matt Pearce	.25	.20	.10
63	Steve Rodehutskors	.40	.30	.15
64	Rod Hill	.40	.30	.15
65	Nick Benjamin	.40	.30	.15
66	Bob Cameron	.25	.20	.10
67	Leon Hatziioannou	.25	.20	.10
68	Robert Mimbs	2.50	2.00	1.00
69	Mike Gray	.25	.20	.10
70	Ken Winey	.25	.20	.10
71	Mike Hildebrand	.25	.20	.10
72	Brett Williams	.40	.30	.15
73	Tracy Ham	2.50	2.00	1.00
74	Danny Bass	.75	.60	.30
75	Mark Norman	.25	.20	.10
76	Andre Francis	.40	.30	.15
77	Todd Storme	.25	.20	.10
78	Henry Williams	5.00	3.75	2.00
79	Kevin Clark	.75	.60	.30
80	Enis Jackson	.25	.20	.10
81	Leroy Blugh	.25	.20	.10
82	Jeff Braswell	.40	.30	.15
83	Larry Wruck	.40	.30	.15
84A	Mike McLean (ERR) (Photo actually 24 Mike Hildebrand)	3.00	2.25	1.25
84B	Mike McLean (COR) (Two players shown)	5.00	3.75	2.00
85	Leo Groenewegen (UER) (Misspelled Groenewegan on card back)	.25	.20	.10
86	Mark Gastineau	1.50	1.25	.60
87	Larry Clarkson	.25	.20	.10

88	Major Harris	2.50	2.00	1.00
89	Ray Alexander	.40	.30	.15
90	Joe Paopao	.40	.30	.15
91	Ian Sinclair	.40	.30	.15
92	Tony Visco (UER) (British Columbia on front, correctly has team as Toronto on front)	.25	.20	.10
93	Lui Passaglia	.75	.60	.30
94	Doug Flutie	20.00	15.00	8.00
95	Glenn Kulka	.40	.30	.15
96	Bruce Holmes	.25	.20	.10
97	Stacey Dawsey	.25	.20	.10
98	Damon Allen	.75	.60	.30
99	Ken Evraire	.40	.30	.15
100	David Williams	.60	.45	.25
101	Gregg Stumon	.40	.30	.15
102	Scott Flagel	.40	.30	.15
103	Gerald Roper	.25	.20	.10
104	Tony Cherry	1.00	.70	.40
105	Jim Mills	.25	.20	.10
106	Dean Dorsey	.40	.30	.15
107	Patrick Wayne	.25	.20	.10
108	Reggie Barnes	2.00	1.50	.80
109	Kari Yli-Renko	.25	.20	.10
110	Ken Hobart	.75	.60	.30
111	Doug Flutie	15.00	11.00	6.00
112	Grover Covington	.75	.60	.30
113	Michael Allen	.25	.20	.10
114	Mike Walker	.75	.60	.30
115	Danny McManus	4.00	3.00	1.50
116	Greg Battle	1.25	.90	.50
117	Quency Williams	.25	.20	.10
118	Jeff Croonen	.25	.20	.10
119	Paul Randolph	.25	.20	.10
120	Rick House	.40	.30	.15
121	Rob Smith	.40	.30	.15
122	Mark Napiorkowski	.25	.20	.10
123	Ed Berry	.25	.20	.10
124	Rob Crifo	.25	.20	.10
125	Gord Weber	.25	.20	.10
126	Jeff Boyd	.40	.30	.15
127	Paul McGowan	.40	.30	.15
128	Reggie Taylor	.75	.60	.30
129	Warren Jones	.25	.20	.10
130	Blake Marshall	.40	.30	.15
131	Darrell Corbin	.25	.20	.10
132	Jim Rockford	.40	.30	.15
133	Richard Nurse	.25	.20	.10
134	Bryan Illerbrun	.25	.20	.10
135	Mark Waterman	.25	.20	.10
136	Doug Landry	1.25	.90	.50
137	Ronnie Glanton	.25	.20	.10
138	Mark Guy	.40	.30	.15
139	Mike Anderson	.25	.20	.10
140	Remi Trudel	.25	.20	.10
141	Stephen Jones	1.00	.70	.40
142	Mike Derks	.25	.20	.10
143	Michel Bourgeau (Edmonton Oilers)	.40	.30	.15
144	Jeff Bentrim	.40	.30	.15
145	Roger Aldag	.40	.30	.15
146	Donald Narcisse	2.50	2.00	1.00
147	Troy Wilson	.25	.20	.10
148	Glen Suitor	.40	.30	.15
149	Stewart Hill	1.00	.70	.40
150	Chris Johnstone	.25	.20	.10
151	Mark Mathis	.25	.20	.10
152	Blaine Schmidt	.25	.20	.10
153	Craig Ellis	.75	.60	.30
154	John Mandarich	.40	.30	.15
155	Steve Zatylny	.25	.20	.10
156	Michel Lamy	.25	.20	.10
157	Irv Daymond	.25	.20	.10
158	Tom Porras	.40	.30	.15
159	Rick Worman	.40	.30	.15
160	Major Harris	1.50	1.25	.60
161	Darryl Hall	.40	.30	.15
162	Terry Andrysiak	.40	.30	.15
163	Harold Hallman	.40	.30	.15
164	Carl Brazley	.25	.20	.10
165	Kevin Smellie	.25	.20	.10
166	Mark Campbell	.40	.30	.15
167	Andy McVey	.25	.20	.10
168	Derrick Crawford	.40	.30	.15
169	Howard Dell	.25	.20	.10
170	Dave Van Belleghem	.25	.20	.10
171	Don Wilson	.25	.20	.10
172	Robert Smith	.40	.30	.15
173	Keith Browner	.40	.30	.15
174	Chris Munford	.25	.20	.10
175	Gary Wilkerson	.25	.20	.10
176	Rickey Foggie (UER) (Misspelled Foogie on card front)	1.25	.90	.50
177	Robin Belanger	.25	.20	.10
178	Andrew Murray	.25	.20	.10
179	Paul Masotti	.40	.30	.15

180	Chris Gaines	.25	.20	.10
181	Joe Clausi	.25	.20	.10
182	Greg Harris	.25	.20	.10
183	David Bovell	.25	.20	.10
184	Eric Streater	.40	.30	.15
185	Larry Hogue	.25	.20	.10
186	Jan Carinci	.25	.20	.10
187	Floyd Salazar	.25	.20	.10
188	Alondra Johnson	.40	.30	.15
189	Jay Christensen (UER)			
	(Misspelled Christenson			
	on card front)	.40	.30	.15
190	Rick Ryan	.25	.20	.10
191	Willie Pless	1.50	1.25	.60
192	Walter Ballard	.25	.20	.10
193	Lee Knight	.25	.20	.10
194	Ray Macoritti	.40	.30	.15
195	Dan Payne	.25	.20	.10
196	Dan Sellers	.25	.20	.10
197	Rae Robirtis	.25	.20	.10
198	Dave Mossman	.25	.20	.10
199	Sam Loucks	.25	.20	.10
200	Derek MacCready	.25	.20	.10
201	Tony Cherry	.75	.60	.30
202	Ali Moustafa	.40	.30	.15
203	Terry Baker	.40	.30	.15
204	Matt Finlay	.25	.20	.10
205	Daniel Hunter	.25	.20	.10
206	Chris Major	2.00	1.50	.80
207	Henry Smith	.25	.20	.10
208	David Sapunjis	4.00	3.00	1.50
209	Darrell Wallace	.40	.30	.15
210	Mark Singer	.25	.20	.10
211	Tuineau Alipate	.25	.20	.10
212	Tony Champion	1.25	.90	.50
213	Mike Lazecki	.25	.20	.10
214	Larry Clarkson	.25	.20	.10
215	Lorenzo Graham	.25	.20	.10
216	Tony Martino	.25	.20	.10
217	Ken Watson	.25	.20	.10
218	Paul Clatney	.25	.20	.10
219	Ken Pettway	.25	.20	.10
220	Tyrone Jones	1.00	.70	.40

1991 JOGO CFL

		NM/M	NM	E
Complete Set (220):		6.00	4.50	2.50
Complete Series 1 (110):		3.00	2.25	1.25
Complete Series 2 (110):		3.00	2.25	1.25
Common Player:		.04	.03	.02
1	Tracy Ham	.35	.25	.14
2	Larry Wruck	.08	.06	.03
3	Pierre Vercheval	.04	.03	.02
4	Rod Connop	.04	.03	.02
5	Michel Bourgeau	.04	.03	.02
6	Leroy Blugh	.04	.03	.02
7	Mike Walker	.04	.03	.02
8	Ray Macoritti	.04	.03	.02
9	Michael Soles	.04	.03	.02
10	Brett Williams	.15	.11	.06
11	Blake Marshall	.15	.11	.06
12	David Williams	.08	.06	.03
13	Enis Jackson	.04	.03	.02
14	Craig Ellis	.15	.11	.06
15	Reggie Taylor	.15	.11	.06
16	Mike McLean	.04	.03	.02
17	Blake Dermott	.04	.03	.02
18	Henry Williams	.50	.40	.20
19	Jordan Gaertner	.04	.03	.02
20	Willie Pless	.15	.11	.06
21	Danny Bass	.15	.11	.06
22	Trevor Bowles	.04	.03	.02
23	Rob Davidson	.04	.03	.02
24	Mark Norman	.04	.03	.02
25	Ron Lancaster (CO)	.10	.08	.04
26	Chris Johnstone	.04	.03	.02
27	Randy Ambrosie	.04	.03	.02
28	Glenn Kulka	.04	.03	.02
29	Gerald Wilcox	.15	.11	.06
30	Kari Yli-Renko	.04	.03	.02
31	Daniel Hunter	.04	.03	.02
32	Bryan Illerbrun	.04	.03	.02
33	Terry Baker	.04	.03	.02
34	Jeff Braswell	.04	.03	.02
35	Andre Francis	.04	.03	.02
36	Irv Daymond	.04	.03	.02
37	Sean Foudy	.04	.03	.02
38	Brad Tierney	.04	.03	.02
39	Gregg Stumon	.04	.03	.02
40	Scott Flagel	.04	.03	.02
41	Gerald Roper	.04	.03	.02
42	Charles Wright	.04	.03	.02
43	Rob Smith	.04	.03	.02
44	James Ellingson	.04	.03	.02
45	Damon Allen	.08	.06	.03
46	John Congemi	.04	.03	.02
47	Reggie Barnes	.20	.15	.08
48	Stephen Jones	.15	.11	.06
49	Rob Prodanovic	.04	.03	.02
50	Steve Goldman	.04	.03	.02
51	Patrick Wayne	.04	.03	.02
52	David Conrad	.04	.03	.02
53	John Krupke	.04	.03	.02
54	Loyd Lewis	.04	.03	.02
55	Tony Cherry	.20	.15	.08
56	Terrence Jones	.25	.20	.10
57	Dan Wicklum	.04	.03	.02
58	Allen Pitts	.50	.40	.20
59	Junior Thurman	.04	.03	.02
60	Ron Hopkins	.04	.03	.02
61	Andy McVey	.04	.03	.02
62	Leo Blanchard	.04	.03	.02
63	Mark Singer	.04	.03	.02
64	Darryl Hall	.04	.03	.02
65	David McCrary	.04	.03	.02
66	Mark Guy	.04	.03	.02
67	Marshall Toner	.04	.03	.02
68	Derrick Crawford	.04	.03	.02
69	Danny Barrett	.20	.15	.08
70	Kent Warnock	.08	.06	.03
71	Brent Matich	.04	.03	.02
72	Mark McLoughlin	.04	.03	.02
73	Joe Clausi	.04	.03	.02
74	Wally Buono (CO)	.04	.03	.02
75	Will Johnson	.04	.03	.02
76	Walter Ballard	.04	.03	.02
77	Matt Finlay	.04	.03	.02
78	David Sapunjis	.35	.25	.14
79	Greg Peterson	.04	.03	.02
80	Paul Clatney	.04	.03	.02
81	Lloyd Fairbanks	.04	.03	.02
82	Herman Heard	.15	.11	.06
83	Richard Nurse	.04	.03	.02
84	Dave Richardson	.04	.03	.02
85	Ernie Schramayr	.04	.03	.02
86	Todd Dillon	.04	.03	.02
87	Tuineau Alipate	.04	.03	.02
88	Peter Giftopoulos	.04	.03	.02
89	Miles Gorrell	.04	.03	.02
90	Earl Winfield	.20	.15	.08
91	Paul Osbaldiston	.04	.03	.02
92	Dale Sanderson	.04	.03	.02
93	Jason Riley	.04	.03	.02
94	Ken Evraire	.04	.03	.02
95	Lee Knight	.04	.03	.02
96	Tim Lorenz	.04	.03	.02
97	Derrick McAdoo	.15	.11	.06
98	Bobby Dawson	.04	.03	.02
99	Rickey Royal	.04	.03	.02
100	Ronald Veal	.20	.15	.08
101	Grover Covington	.20	.15	.08
102	Mike Kerrigan	.20	.15	.08
103	Rocky DiPietro	.20	.15	.08
104	Mark Dennis	.04	.03	.02
105	Tony Champion	.20	.15	.08
106	Tony Visco	.04	.03	.02
107	Darrell Harle	.04	.03	.02
108	Wally Zatylny	.04	.03	.02
109	David Beckman (CO)	.04	.03	.02
110	**Checklist 1-110**	.04	.03	.02
111	Jeff Fairholm	.04	.03	.02
112	Roger Aldag	.04	.03	.02
113	Dave Albright	.04	.03	.02
114	Gary Lewis	.04	.03	.02
115	Dan Rashovich	.04	.03	.02
116	Lucius Floyd	.04	.03	.02
117	Bob Poley	.04	.03	.02
118	Donald Narcisse	.20	.15	.08
119	Bobby Jurasin	.15	.11	.06
120	Orville Lee	.15	.11	.06
121	Stacey Hairston	.04	.03	.02
122	Richie Hall	.04	.03	.02
123	John Gregory (CO)	.04	.03	.02
124	Rick Worman	.04	.03	.02
125	Dave Ridgway	.15	.11	.06
126	Wayne Drinkwater	.04	.03	.02
127	Eddie Lowe	.04	.03	.02
128	Mike Hogue	.04	.03	.02
129	Larry Hogue	.04	.03	.02
130	Milson Jones	.15	.11	.06
131	Ray Elgaard	.20	.15	.08
132	Dave Pitcher	.04	.03	.02
133	Vic Stevenson	.04	.03	.02
134	Albert Brown	.04	.03	.02
135	Mike Anderson	.04	.03	.02
136	Glen Suitor	.04	.03	.02
137	Kent Austin	.30	.25	.12
138	Mike Gray	.04	.03	.02
139	Steve Rodehutskors	.04	.03	.02
140	Eric Streater	.04	.03	.02
141	David Black	.04	.03	.02
142	James West	.15	.11	.06
143	Danny McManus	.30	.25	.12
144	Darryl Sampson	.04	.03	.02
145	Bob Cameron	.04	.03	.02
146	Tom Burgess	.35	.25	.14
147	Rick House	.04	.03	.02
148	Chris Walby	.15	.11	.06
149	Michael Allen	.04	.03	.02
150	Warren Hudson	.04	.03	.02
151	David Bovell	.04	.03	.02
152	Rob Crifo	.04	.03	.02
153	Lyle Bauer	.04	.03	.02
154	Trevor Kennerd	.20	.15	.08
155	Troy Johnson	.04	.03	.02
156	Less Browne	.04	.03	.02
157	Nick Benjamin	.04	.03	.02
158	Matt Pearce	.04	.03	.02
159	Tyrone Jones	.04	.03	.02
160	Rod Hill	.04	.03	.02
161	Bob Molle	.04	.03	.02
162	Lee Hull	.04	.03	.02
163	Greg Battle	.20	.15	.08
164	Robert Mimbs	.30	.25	.12
165	Giulio Caravatta	.04	.03	.02
166	James Mills	.15	.11	.06
167	Ian Sinclair	.04	.03	.02
168	Robin Belanger	.04	.03	.02
169	Deatrich Wise	.04	.03	.02
170	Chris Skinner	.04	.03	.02
171	Norman Jefferson	.04	.03	.02
172	Larry Clarkson	.04	.03	.02
173	Chris Major	.35	.25	.14
174	Stewart Hill	.04	.03	.02
175	Tony Hunter	.04	.03	.02
176	Stacey Dawsey	.04	.03	.02
177	Doug Flutie	1.00	.70	.40
178	Mike Trevathan	.04	.03	.02
179	Jearld Baylis	.04	.03	.02
180	Matt Clark	.25	.20	.10
181	Ken Pettway	.04	.03	.02
182	Lloyd Joseph	.04	.03	.02
183	Jon Volpe	1.00	.70	.40
184	Leo Groenewegen	.04	.03	.02
185	Carl Coulter	.04	.03	.02
186	O.J. Brigance	.35	.25	.14
187	Ryan Hanson	.04	.03	.02
188	Rocco Romano	.04	.03	.02
189	Ray Alexander	.04	.03	.02
190	Bob O'Billovich (CO)	.04	.03	.02
191	Paul Wetmore	.04	.03	.02
192	Harold Hallman	.04	.03	.02
193	Ed Berry	.04	.03	.02
194	Brian Warren	.04	.03	.02
195	Matt Dunigan	.40	.30	.15
196	Kelvin Pruenster	.04	.03	.02
197	Ian Beckstead	.04	.03	.02
198	Carl Brazley	.04	.03	.02
199	Trevor Kennerd	.15	.11	.06
200	Reggie Pleasant	.04	.03	.02
201	Kevin Smellie	.04	.03	.02
202	Don Moen	.04	.03	.02
203	Blaine Schmidt	.04	.03	.02
204	Chris Schultz	.04	.03	.02
205	Lance Chomyc	.04	.03	.02
206	Darrell Smith	.20	.15	.08
207	Dan Ferrone	.04	.03	.02
208	Chris Gaines	.04	.03	.02
209	Keith Castello	.04	.03	.02
210	Chris Munford	.04	.03	.02
211	Rodney Harding	.20	.15	.08
212	Darryl Ford	.04	.03	.02
213	Rickey Foggie	.20	.15	.08
214	Don Wilson	.04	.03	.02
215	Andrew Murray	.04	.03	.02
216	Jim Kardash	.04	.03	.02
217	Mike Clemons	1.25	.90	.50
218	Bruce Elliott	.04	.03	.02
219	Mike McCarthy	.04	.03	.02
220	**Checklist**	.04	.03	.02

1981 JOGO CFL B/W

		NM/M	NM	E
Complete Set (51):		200.00	150.00	80.00
Common Player:		1.00	.70	.40
1	Richard Crump	2.00	1.50	.80
2	Tony Gabriel	7.50	5.75	3.00
3	Gerry Organ	1.00	.70	.40
4A	Greg Marshall	2.50	2.00	1.00
4B	J.C. Watts (SP)	40.00	30.00	16.00
5	Mike Raines	1.00	.70	.40
6	Larry Brune	1.00	.70	.40
7	Randy Rhino	2.50	2.00	1.00
8	Bruce Clark	4.00	3.00	1.50
9	Condredge Holloway	7.50	5.75	3.00
10	Dave Newman	1.00	.70	.40
11	Cedric Minter	1.00	.70	.40
12	Peter Muller	1.00	.70	.40
13	Vince Ferragamo	8.00	6.00	3.25
14	James Scott	2.00	1.50	.80
15	Billy Johnson			
	(White Shoes)	6.00	4.50	2.50

		NM/M	NM	E
16	David Overstreet	6.00	4.50	2.50
17	Keith Gary	1.50	1.25	.60
18	Tom Clements	15.00	11.00	6.00
19	Keith Baker	1.00	.70	.40
20	David Shaw	1.00	.70	.40
21	Ben Zambiasi	3.00	2.25	1.25
22	John Priestner	1.00	.70	.40
23	Warren Moon	100.00	75.00	40.00
24	Tom Wilkinson	3.00	2.25	1.25
25	Brian Kelly	6.00	4.50	2.50
26	Dan Kepley	2.00	1.50	.80
27	Larry Highbaugh	2.50	2.00	1.00
28	David Boone	1.00	.70	.40
29	John Henry White	1.00	.70	.40
30	Joe Paopao	3.00	2.25	1.25
31	Larry Key	1.00	.70	.40
32	Glen Jackson	1.00	.70	.40
33	Joe Hollimon	1.00	.70	.40
34	Dieter Brock	6.00	4.50	2.50
35	Mike Holmes	1.00	.70	.40
36	William Miller	1.00	.70	.40
37	John Helton	3.00	2.25	1.25
38	Joe Poplawski	1.50	1.25	.60
39	Joe Barnes	5.00	3.75	2.00
40	John Hufnagel	6.00	4.50	2.50
41	Bobby Thompson	1.00	.70	.40
42	Steve Stapler	1.00	.70	.40
43	Tom Cousineau	6.00	4.50	2.50
44	Bruce Threadgill	1.00	.70	.40
45	Ed McAleney	1.00	.70	.40
46	Leif Petterson	1.50	1.25	.60
47	Paul Bennett	1.00	.70	.40
48	James Reed	1.00	.70	.40
49	Gerry Dattilio	1.50	1.25	.60
50	**Checklist Card**	1.50	1.25	.60

1988 JOGO CFL League

James Jefferson #20

		NM/M	NM	E
Complete Set (106):		250.00	187.00	100.00
Common Player:		1.25	.90	.50
1	Walter Ballard	1.25	.90	.50
2	Jan Carinci	1.25	.90	.50
3	Larry Crawford	1.25	.90	.50
4	Tyrone Crews	1.25	.90	.50
5	Andre Francis	2.00	1.50	.80
6	Bernie Glier	1.25	.90	.50
7	Keith Gooch	1.25	.90	.50
8	Kevin Konar	1.25	.90	.50
9	Scott Lecky	1.25	.90	.50
10	James Parker	3.00	2.25	1.25
11	Jim Sandusky (Traded)	10.00	7.50	4.00
12	Greg Stumon	1.25	.90	.50
13	Todd Wiseman (Not listed on checklist card)	1.25	.90	.50
14	Gary Allen	2.00	1.50	.80
15	Scott Flagel (Traded)	3.00	2.25	1.25
16	Harold Hallman	1.25	.90	.50
17	Larry Hogue (UER) (Misspelled Hogue)	1.25	.90	.50
18	Ron Hopkins	1.25	.90	.50
19	Stu Laird	2.00	1.50	.80
20	Andy McVey	1.25	.90	.50
21	Bernie Morrison	1.25	.90	.50
22	Tim Petros	1.25	.90	.50
23	Bob Poley	1.25	.90	.50
24	Tom Spoletini	1.25	.90	.50
25	Emmanuel Tolbert	4.00	3.00	1.50
26	Larry Willis	2.00	1.50	.80
27	Damon Allen	4.00	3.00	1.50
28	Danny Bass	4.00	3.00	1.50
29	Stanley Blair	1.25	.90	.50
30	Marco Cyncar	1.25	.90	.50
31	Tracy Ham	25.00	18.50	10.00
32	Milson Jones (Traded)	4.00	3.00	1.50
33	Stephen Jones	3.00	2.25	1.25
34	Jerry Kauric	3.00	2.25	1.25
35	Hector Pothier	1.25	.90	.50
36	Tom Richards	3.00	2.25	1.25
37	Chris Skinner	2.00	1.50	.80
38	Henry Williams	40.00	30.00	16.00
39	Larry Wruck	1.25	.90	.50
40	Pat Brady	1.25	.90	.50
41	Grover Covington	3.00	2.25	1.25
42	Rocky DiPietro	4.00	3.00	1.50
43	Howard Fields	1.25	.90	.50
44	Miles Gorrell	1.25	.90	.50
45	Johnnie Jones	1.25	.90	.50
46	Tom Porras	2.00	1.50	.80
47	Jason Riley	1.25	.90	.50
48	Dale Sanderson	1.25	.90	.50
49	Ralph Scholz	1.25	.90	.50
50	Lance Shields	2.00	1.50	.80
51	Steve Stapler	1.25	.90	.50
52	Mike Walker	3.00	2.25	1.25
53	Gerald Alphin	4.00	3.00	1.50
54	Nick Arakgi (SP) (Retired before season)	20.00	15.00	8.00
55	Nick Benjamin	2.00	1.50	.80
56	Tom Dixon	1.25	.90	.50
57	Leo Groenewegen	1.25	.90	.50
58	Will Lewis	2.00	1.50	.80
59	Greg Marshall (Injured and retired)	5.00	3.75	2.00
60	Larry Mohr	1.25	.90	.50
61	Kevin Powell (Traded)	3.00	2.25	1.25
62	Jim Reid	2.00	1.50	.80
63	Art Schlichter	8.00	6.00	3.25
64	Rick Wolkensperg	1.25	.90	.50
65	Anthony Woodson	1.25	.90	.50
66	Dave Albright	1.25	.90	.50
67	Roger Aldag	1.25	.90	.50
68	Mike Anderson	1.25	.90	.50
69	Kent Austin	25.00	18.50	10.00
70	Tom Burgess	6.00	4.50	2.50
71	James Curry	3.00	2.25	1.25
72	Ray Elgaard	4.00	3.00	1.50
73	Denny Ferdinand	1.25	.90	.50
74	Bobby Jurasin	6.00	4.50	2.50
75	Gary Lewis	1.25	.90	.50
76	Dave Ridgway	3.00	2.25	1.25
77	Harry Skipper	2.00	1.50	.80
78	Glen Suitor	2.00	1.50	.80
79	Ian Beckstead	1.25	.90	.50
80	Lance Chomyc	2.00	1.50	.80
81	John Congemi	3.00	2.25	1.25
82	Gill Fenerty	8.00	6.00	3.25
83	Dan Ferrone	2.00	1.50	.80
84	Warren Hudson	2.00	1.50	.80
85	Hank Llesic	3.50	2.75	1.50
86	Jim Kardash	1.25	.90	.50
87	Glenn Kulka	2.00	1.50	.80
88	Don Moen	1.25	.90	.50
89	Gilbert Renfroe	3.00	2.25	1.25
90	Chris Schultz	1.25	.90	.50
91	Darrell Smith	3.00	2.25	1.25
92	Lyle Bauer	1.25	.90	.50
93	Nick Bastaja	1.25	.90	.50
94	David Black	1.25	.90	.50
95	Bob Cameron	1.25	.90	.50
96	Randy Fabi	1.25	.90	.50
97	James Jefferson	6.00	4.50	2.50
98	Stan Mikawos	1.25	.90	.50
99	James Murphy	3.00	2.25	1.25
100	Ken Pettway	1.25	.90	.50
101	Willard Reaves (Signed with Redskins)	12.00	9.00	4.75
102	Darryl Sampson	1.25	.90	.50
103	Chris Walby	4.00	3.00	1.50
104	James West	5.00	3.75	2.00
105	Tom Clements (SP) (Retired before season)	20.00	15.00	8.00
106	**Checklist Card SP**	6.00	4.50	2.50

1983 JOGO CFL Limited

		NM/M	NM	E
Complete Set (110):		900.00	675.00	360.00
Common Player:		4.00	3.00	1.50
1	Steve Ackroyd	4.00	3.00	1.50
2	Joe Barnes	12.00	9.00	4.75
3	Bob Bronk	4.00	3.00	1.50
4	Jan Carinci	4.00	3.00	1.50
5	Gordon Elser	4.00	3.00	1.50
6	Dan Ferrone	5.00	3.75	2.00
7	Terry Greer	12.00	9.00	4.75
8	Mike Hameluck	4.00	3.00	1.50
9	Condredge Holloway	15.00	11.00	6.00
10	Greg Holmes	4.00	3.00	1.50
11	Hank Llesic	10.00	7.50	4.00
12	John Malinosky	4.00	3.00	1.50
13	Cedric Minter	4.00	3.00	1.50
14	Don Moen	4.00	3.00	1.50
15	Rick Mohr	4.00	3.00	1.50
16	Darrell Nicholson	4.00	3.00	1.50
17	Paul Pearson	5.00	3.75	2.00
18	Matthew Teague	4.00	3.00	1.50
19	Geoff Townsend	4.00	3.00	1.50
20	Tom Trifaux	4.00	3.00	1.50
21	Darrell Wilson	4.00	3.00	1.50
22	Earl Wilson	4.00	3.00	1.50
23	Ricky Barden	4.00	3.00	1.50
24	Roger Cattelan	4.00	3.00	1.50
25	Michael Collymore	4.00	3.00	1.50
26	Charles Cornelius	4.00	3.00	1.50
27	Mariet Ford	4.00	3.00	1.50
28	Tyron Gray	5.00	3.75	2.00
29	Steve Harrison	4.00	3.00	1.50
30	Tim Hook	4.00	3.00	1.50
31	Greg Marshall	5.00	3.75	2.00
32	Ken Miller	4.00	3.00	1.50
33	Dave Newman	4.00	3.00	1.50
34	Rudy Phillips	4.00	3.00	1.50
35	Jim Reid	4.00	3.00	1.50
36	Junior Robinson	4.00	3.00	1.50
37	Mark Seale	4.00	3.00	1.50
38	Rick Sowieta	4.00	3.00	1.50
39	Pat Stoqua	4.00	3.00	1.50
40	Skip Walker	10.00	7.50	4.00
41	Al Washington	4.00	3.00	1.50
42	J.C. Watts	50.00	37.00	20.00
43	Keith Baker	4.00	3.00	1.50
44	Dieter Brock	35.00	26.00	14.00
45	Rocky DiPietro	20.00	15.00	8.00
46	Howard Fields	4.00	3.00	1.50
47	Ron Johnson	6.00	4.50	2.50
48	John Priestner	4.00	3.00	1.50
49	Johnny Shepherd	4.00	3.00	1.50
50	Mike Walker	6.00	4.50	2.50
51	Ben Zambiasi	12.00	9.00	4.75
52	Nick Arakgi	5.00	3.75	2.00
53	Brian DeRoo	4.00	3.00	1.50
54	Denny Ferdinand	4.00	3.00	1.50
55	Willie Hampton	4.00	3.00	1.50
56	Kevin Starkey	4.00	3.00	1.50
57	Glen Weir	4.00	3.00	1.50
58	Larry Crawford	6.00	4.50	2.50
59	Tyrone Crews	4.00	3.00	1.50
60	James Curry	10.00	7.50	4.00
61	Roy DeWalt	12.00	9.00	4.75
62	Mervyn Fernandez	50.00	37.00	20.00
63	Sammy Green	4.00	3.00	1.50
64	Glen Jackson	4.00	3.00	1.50
65	Glenn Leonhard	4.00	3.00	1.50
66	Nelson Martin	4.00	3.00	1.50
67	Joe Paopao	8.00	6.00	3.25
68	Lui Passaglia	10.00	7.50	4.00
69	Al Wilson	4.00	3.00	1.50
70	Nick Bastaja	4.00	3.00	1.50
71	Paul Bennett	4.00	3.00	1.50
72	John Bonk	4.00	3.00	1.50
73	Aaron Brown	4.00	3.00	1.50
74	Bob Cameron	4.00	3.00	1.50
75	Tom Clements	60.00	45.00	24.00
76	Rick House	5.00	3.75	2.00
77	John Hufnagel	15.00	11.00	6.00
78	Sean Kehoe	4.00	3.00	1.50
79	James Murphy	12.00	9.00	4.75
80	Tony Norman	4.00	3.00	1.50
81	Joe Poplawski	4.00	3.00	1.50
82	Willard Reaves	15.00	11.00	6.00
83	Bobby Thompson	4.00	3.00	1.50
84	Wylie Turner	4.00	3.00	1.50
85	Dave Fennell	6.00	4.50	2.50
86	Jim Germany	5.00	3.75	2.00
87	Larry Highbaugh	6.00	4.50	2.50
88	Joe Hollimon	4.00	3.00	1.50
89	Dan Kepley	10.00	7.50	4.00
90	Neil Lumsden	4.00	3.00	1.50
91	Warren Moon	500.00	375.00	200.00
92	James Parker	12.00	9.00	4.75
93	Dale Potter	4.00	3.00	1.50
94	Angelo Santucci	4.00	3.00	1.50
95	Tom Towns	4.00	3.00	1.50
96	Tom Tuinei	5.00	3.75	2.00
97	Danny Bass	12.00	9.00	4.75
98	Ray Crouse	4.00	3.00	1.50
99	Gerry Dattilio	7.50	5.75	3.00
100	Tom Forzani	4.00	3.00	1.50
101	Mike Levenseller	4.00	3.00	1.50
102	Mike McTague	5.00	3.75	2.00
103	Bernie Morrison	4.00	3.00	1.50
104	Darrell Toussaint	4.00	3.00	1.50
105	Chris DeFrance	4.00	3.00	1.50
106	Dwight Edwards	5.00	3.75	2.00
107	Vince Goldsmith	10.00	7.50	4.00
108	Homer Jordan	4.00	3.00	1.50
109	Mike Washington	4.00	3.00	1.50
110A	Darrell Moir (Set number on back)	12.00	9.00	4.75
110B	Darrell Moir (Without set number)	50.00	37.00	20.00

1991 JOGO CFL Stamp Card Inserts

		NM/M	NM	E
Complete Set (3):		30.00	22.00	12.00
Common Player:		10.00	7.50	4.00
1	Albert H.G. Grey	10.00	7.50	4.00
2	Trevor Kennerd	10.00	7.50	4.00
NNO	**Grey Cup Trophy** (Grey Cup Winners listed on card back)	10.00	7.50	4.00

1983 JOGO Hall of Fame B

		NM/M	NM	E
Complete Set (25):		30.00	22.00	12.00
Common Player:		.75	.60	.30
B1	Bernie Faloney	3.50	2.75	1.50
B2	George Dixon	2.00	1.50	.80
B3	John Barrow	2.00	1.50	.80
B4	Jackie Parker	5.00	3.75	2.00
B5	Jack Jacobs	.75	.60	.30
B6	Sam Etcheverry (The Rifle)	4.00	3.00	1.50
B7	Norm Fieldgate	1.25	.90	.50
B8	John Ferrard	.75	.60	.30
B9	Tommy Joe Coffey	2.00	1.50	.80
B10	Martin Ruby	.75	.60	.30
B11	Ted Reeve	.75	.60	.30
B12	Kaye Vaughan	.75	.60	.30
B13	Ron Lancaster	2.50	2.00	1.00
B14	Smirle Lawson	.75	.60	.30
B15	Fritz Hanson	.75	.60	.30
B16	Vince Scott	.75	.60	.30
B17	Frank Morris	.75	.60	.30
B18	Normie Kwong	2.00	1.50	.80
B19	Dr. Tom Casey	1.25	.90	.50
B20	Herb Gray	2.00	1.50	.80
B21	Gerry James	1.25	.90	.50
B22	Pete Neumann	.75	.60	.30
B23	Joe Krol	.75	.60	.30
B24	Ron Stewart	1.25	.90	.50
B25	Buddy Tinsley	.75	.60	.30
NNO	**Title Card SP** (Map to HOF on back)	6.00	4.50	2.50

1982 JOGO Ottawa

		NM/M	NM	E
Complete Set (24):		8.00	6.00	3.25
Common Player:		.40	.30	.15
1	Jordan Case	.50	.40	.20
2	Larry Brune	.50	.40	.20
3	Val Belcher	.50	.40	.20
4	Greg Marshall	.75	.60	.30
5	Mike Raines	.40	.30	.15
6	Rick Sowieta	.40	.30	.15
7	John Glassford	.40	.30	.15
8	Bruce Walker	.40	.30	.15
9	Jim Reid	.50	.40	.20
10	Kevin Powell	.40	.30	.15
11	Jim Piaskoski	.50	.40	.20
12	Kelvin Kirk	.40	.30	.15
13	Gerry Organ	.50	.40	.20
14	Carl Brazley	.75	.60	.30
15	William Mitchell	.40	.30	.15
16	Billy Hardee	.40	.30	.15
17	Jonathan Sutton	.40	.30	.15
18	Doug Seymour	.40	.30	.15
19	Pat Staub	.40	.30	.15
20	Larry Tittley	.40	.30	.15
21	Pat Stoqua	.40	.30	.15
22	Sam Platt	.40	.30	.15
23	Gary Dulin	.40	.30	.15
24	John Holland	.50	.40	.20

1982 JOGO Ottawa Past

		NM/M	NM	E
Complete Set (16):		25.00	18.50	10.00
Common Player (1-12):		1.25	.90	.50
Common Player (13-16):		2.00	1.50	.80
Common DP:		.75	.60	.30
1	Tony Gabriel	3.00	2.25	1.25
2	Whit Tucker (DP)	1.50	1.25	.60
3	Dave Thelen	2.00	1.50	.80
4	Ron Stewart (DP)	1.50	1.25	.60
5	Russ Jackson (DP)	3.50	2.75	1.50
6	Kaye Vaughan	2.00	1.50	.80
7	Bob Simpson	2.00	1.50	.80
8	Ken Lehmann	1.50	1.25	.60
9	Lou Bruce	1.25	.90	.50
10	Wayne Giardino (DP)	.75	.60	.30
11	Moe Racine	1.25	.90	.50
12	Gary Schreider	1.25	.90	.50
13	Don Sutherin	4.00	3.00	1.50
14	Mark Kosmos (DP)	1.25	.90	.50
15	Jim Foley (DP)	2.00	1.50	.80
16	Jim Conroy	.75	.60	.30

1985 JOGO Ottawa Program Inserts

		NM/M	NM	E
Complete Set (9):		50.00	37.00	20.00
Common Player:		5.00	3.75	2.00
1	**1960 Grey Cup Team**	5.00	3.75	2.00
2	Russ Jackson	12.00	9.00	4.75
3	Angelo Mosca	10.00	7.50	4.00
4	Joe Poirier	5.00	3.75	2.00
5	Sam Scoccia	5.00	3.75	2.00
6	Gilles Archambeault	5.00	3.75	2.00
7	Ron Lancaster	5.00	3.75	2.00
8	Tom Jones	5.00	3.75	2.00
9	Gerry Nesbitt	5.00	3.75	2.00

1984 JOGO Ottawa Yesterday's Heroes

		NM/M	NM	E
Complete Set (22):		75.00	56.00	30.00
Common Player:		3.50	2.75	1.50
1	Tony Gabriel	5.00	3.75	2.00
2	Whit Tucker	3.50	2.75	1.50
3	Dave Thelen	3.50	2.75	1.50
4	Ron Stewart	3.50	2.75	1.50
5	Russ Jackson	10.00	7.50	4.00
6	Kaye Vaughan	3.50	2.75	1.50
7	Bob Simpson	3.50	2.75	1.50
8	Ken Lehmann	3.50	2.75	1.50
9	Lou Bruce	3.50	2.75	1.50
10	Wayne Giardino	3.50	2.75	1.50
11	Moe Racine	3.50	2.75	1.50
12	Gary Schreider	3.50	2.75	1.50
13	Don Sutherin	5.00	3.75	2.00
14	Mark Kosmos	3.50	2.75	1.50
15	Jim Foley	3.50	2.75	1.50
16	Jim Conroy	3.50	2.75	1.50
17	George Brancato	5.00	3.75	2.00
18	Art Green	5.00	3.75	2.00
19	Rudy Sims	5.00	3.75	2.00
20	Jim Coode	5.00	3.75	2.00
21	Jerry Campbell	5.00	3.75	2.00
22	Jim Piaskoski	5.00	3.75	2.00

1983 JOGO Quarterbacks

		NM/M	NM	E
Complete Set (9):		75.00	56.00	30.00
Common Player:		1.50	1.25	.60
1	Dieter Brock	5.00	3.75	2.00
2	Tom Clements	7.50	5.75	3.00
3	Gerry Dattilio	1.50	1.25	.60
4	Roy DeWalt	3.00	2.25	1.25
5	Johnny Evans	1.50	1.25	.60
6	Condredge Holloway	4.00	3.00	1.50
7	John Hufnagel	4.00	3.00	1.50
8	Warren Moon	40.00	30.00	16.00
9	J.C. Watts	25.00	18.50	10.00

K

1959 Kahn's

Kahn's Wieners produced this set, which features members of the Cleveland Indians and Pittsburgh Steelers. The card front contains the Kahn's slogan (The Wiener the World Awaited), plus a black-and-white photograph and a facsimile autograph. Each back has biographical and statistical information. Each unnumbered card measures 3-1/4" x 3-15/16".

		NM	E	VG
Complete Set (31):		1,250	625.00	375.00
Common Player:		30.00	15.00	9.00
(1)	Dick Alban	30.00	15.00	9.00
(2)	Jim Brown	375.00	185.00	110.00
(3)	Jack Butler	30.00	15.00	9.00
(4)	Lew Carpenter	35.00	17.50	10.50
(5)	Preston Carpenter	30.00	15.00	9.00
(6)	Vince Costello	30.00	15.00	9.00
(7)	Dale Dodrill	30.00	15.00	9.00
(8)	Bob Gain	30.00	15.00	9.00
(9)	Gary Glick	30.00	15.00	9.00
(10)	Lou Groza	75.00	37.00	22.00
(11)	Gene Hickerson	30.00	15.00	9.00
(12)	Billy Howton	35.00	17.50	10.50
(13)	Art Hunter	30.00	15.00	9.00
(14)	Joe Kruppa	30.00	15.00	9.00
(15)	Bobby Layne	65.00	32.00	19.50
(16)	Joe Lewis	30.00	15.00	9.00
(17)	Jack McClairen	30.00	15.00	9.00

		NM	E	VG
(18)	Mike McCormack	45.00	22.00	13.50
(19)	Walt Michaels	40.00	20.00	12.00
(20)	Bobby Mitchell	75.00	37.00	22.00
(21)	Jim Ninowski	35.00	17.50	10.50
(22)	Chuck Noll	110.00	55.00	33.00
(23)	Jimmy Orr	35.00	17.50	10.50
(24)	Milt Plum	35.00	17.50	10.50
(25)	Ray Renfro	35.00	17.50	10.50
(26)	Mike Sandusky	30.00	15.00	9.00
(27)	Billy Ray Smith	30.00	15.00	9.00
(28)	Jim Ray Smith	30.00	15.00	9.00
(29)	Ernie Stautner	50.00	25.00	15.00
(30)	Tom Tracy	30.00	15.00	9.00
(31)	Frank Varrichione	30.00	15.00	9.00

1960 Kahn's

Kahn's once again featured members of the Pittsburgh Steelers and Cleveland Browns in this 38-card set. The 3-1/4" x 3-15/16" cards had black-and-white photos on the front, along with the Kahn's slogan. The back has statistical and biographical information, plus an offer for collectors to send in for a free album and instructional booklet. The cards are not numbered and are listed alphabetically.

		NM	E	VG
Complete Set (38):		1,200	600.00	360.00
Common Player:		25.00	12.50	7.50
(1)	Sam Baker	25.00	12.50	7.50
(2)	Jim Brown	230.00	115.00	69.00
(3)	Ray Campbell	25.00	12.50	7.50
(4)	Preston Carpenter	25.00	12.50	7.50
(5)	Vince Costello	25.00	12.50	7.50
(6)	Willie Davis	65.00	32.00	19.50
(7)	Galen Fiss	25.00	12.50	7.50
(8)	Bob Gain	30.00	15.00	9.00
(9)	Lou Groza	50.00	25.00	15.00
(10)	Gene Hickerson	25.00	12.50	7.50
(11)	John Henry Johnson	55.00	27.00	16.50
(12)	Rich Kreitling	25.00	12.50	7.50
(13)	Joe Krupa	25.00	12.50	7.50
(14)	Bobby Layne	50.00	25.00	15.00
(15)	Jack McClairen	25.00	12.50	7.50
(16)	Mike McCormack	35.00	17.50	10.50
(17)	Walt Michaels	25.00	12.50	7.50
(18)	Bobby Mitchell	40.00	20.00	12.00
(19)	Dicky Moegle	25.00	12.50	7.50
(20)	John Morrow	25.00	12.50	7.50
(21)	Gern Nagler	25.00	12.50	7.50
(22)	John Nisby	25.00	12.50	7.50
(23)	Jimmy Orr	30.00	15.00	9.00
(24)	Bernie Parrish	25.00	12.50	7.50
(25)	Milt Plum	30.00	15.00	9.00
(26)	John Reger	25.00	12.50	7.50
(27)	Ray Renfro	30.00	15.00	9.00
(28)	Will Renfro	25.00	12.50	7.50
(29)	Mike Sandusky	30.00	15.00	9.00
(30)	Dick Schafrath	25.00	12.50	7.50
(31)	Jim Ray Smith	25.00	12.50	7.50
(32)	Billy Ray Smith	25.00	12.50	7.50
(33)	Ernie Stautner	40.00	20.00	12.00
(34)	George Tarasovic	25.00	12.50	7.50
(35)	Tom Tracy	30.00	15.00	9.00
(36)	Frank Varrichione	25.00	12.50	7.50
(37)	John Wooten	25.00	12.50	7.50
(38)	Lowe W. Wren	25.00	12.50	7.50

1961 Kahn's

In addition to featuring Cleveland Browns and Pittsburgh Steelers, as Kahn's sets from the two years before did, the 1961 set included players from the Baltimore Colts, Los Angeles Rams and Philadelphia Eagles. The cards are slightly larger than previous years' issues, measuring 3-1/4" x 4-1/16". The backs are similar to the 1961 backs, except the offer for the album and instructional booklet is slightly different. (The 1960 cards required two labels to be sent in for the album; the 1961 cards only required one.) The fronts are black-and-white and have a facsimile autograph and the Kahn's slogan. Once again, the cards are unnumbered.

		NM	E	VG
Complete Set (36):		1,000	500.00	300.00
Common Player:		20.00	10.00	6.00
(1)	Sam Baker	20.00	10.00	6.00
(2)	Jim Brown	225.00	112.00	67.00
(3)	Preston Carpenter	20.00	10.00	6.00
(4)	Vince Costello	20.00	10.00	6.00
(5)	Buddy Dial	25.00	12.50	7.50
(6)	Dean Derby	25.00	12.50	7.50
(7)	Don Fleming	25.00	12.50	7.50
(8)	Bob Gain	20.00	10.00	6.00
(9)	Bobby Joe Green	20.00	10.00	6.00
(10)	Gene Hickerson	25.00	12.50	7.50
(11)	Jim Houston	25.00	12.50	7.50
(12)	Dan James	20.00	10.00	6.00

(13)	John Henry Johnson	40.00	20.00	12.00
(14)	Rich Kreitling	20.00	10.00	6.00
(15)	Joe Krupa	20.00	10.00	6.00
(16)	Larry Krutko (photo actually Tom Tracy)	20.00	10.00	6.00
(17)	Bobby Layne	60.00	30.00	18.00
(18)	Joe Lewis	20.00	10.00	6.00
(19)	Gene Lipscomb	40.00	20.00	12.00
(20)	Mike McCormack	30.00	15.00	9.00
(21)	Bobby Mitchell	45.00	22.00	13.50
(22)	John Morrow	20.00	10.00	6.00
(23)	John Nisby	20.00	10.00	6.00
(24)	Jimmy Orr	25.00	12.50	7.50
(25)	Milt Plum	25.00	12.50	7.50
(26)	John Reger	20.00	10.00	6.00
(27)	Ray Renfro	30.00	15.00	9.00
(28)	Will Renfro	20.00	10.00	6.00
(29)	Mike Sandusky	20.00	10.00	6.00
(30)	Dick Schafrath	20.00	10.00	6.00
(31)	Jim Ray Smith	20.00	10.00	6.00
(32)	Ernie Stautner	45.00	22.00	13.50
(33)	George Tarasovic	20.00	10.00	6.00
(34)	Tom Tracy (photo actually Larry Krutko)	20.00	10.00	6.00
(35)	Frank Varrichione	20.00	10.00	6.00
(36)	John Wooten	20.00	10.00	6.00

1962 Kahn's

This Kahn's set adds three new teams to the mix - the Chicago Bears, Detroit Lions and Minnesota Vikings. The unnumbered cards are 3-1/4" x 4-3/16" and can be identified from previous issues by the player's name on the back, which is in bold. The stats on the back are also double-spaced. Basically, the card design is similar to previous issues.

		NM	E	VG
Complete Set (38):		1,000	500.00	300.00
Common Player:		20.00	10.00	6.00
(1)	Maxie Baughan	22.00	11.00	6.50
(2)	Charley Britt	20.00	10.00	6.00
(3)	Jim Brown	185.00	92.00	55.00
(4)	Preston Carpenter	20.00	10.00	6.00
(5)	Pete Case	22.00	11.00	6.50
(6)	Howard Cassady	25.00	12.50	7.50
(7)	Vince Costello	20.00	10.00	6.00
(8)	Buddy Dial	22.00	11.00	6.50
(9)	Gene Hickerson	20.00	10.00	6.00
(10)	Jim Houston	22.00	11.00	6.50
(11)	Dan James	20.00	10.00	6.00
(12)	Rich Kreitling	20.00	10.00	6.00
(13)	Joe Krupa	20.00	10.00	6.00
(14)	Bobby Layne	50.00	25.00	15.00
(15)	Ray Lemek	20.00	10.00	6.00
(16)	Gene Lipscomb	30.00	15.00	9.00
(17)	David Lloyd	20.00	10.00	6.00
(18)	Lou Michaels	22.00	11.00	6.50
(19)	Larry Morris	20.00	10.00	6.00
(20)	John Morrow	20.00	10.00	6.00
(21)	Jim Ninowski	20.00	10.00	6.00
(22)	Buzz Nutter	20.00	10.00	6.00
(23)	Jimmy Orr	25.00	12.50	7.50
(24)	Bernie Parrish	22.00	11.00	6.50
(25)	Milt Plum	22.00	11.00	6.50
(26)	Myron Pottios	22.00	11.00	6.50
(27)	John Reger	20.00	10.00	6.00
(28)	Ray Renfro	22.00	11.00	6.50
(29)	Frank Ryan	25.00	12.50	7.50
(30)	John Sample	22.00	11.00	6.50
(31)	Mike Sandusky	25.00	12.50	7.50
(32)	Dick Schafrath	20.00	10.00	6.00
(33)	Jim Shofner	22.00	11.00	6.50
(34)	Jim Ray Smith	20.00	10.00	6.00
(35)	Ernie Stautner	35.00	17.50	10.50
(36)	Fran Tarkenton	250.00	125.00	75.00
(37)	Paul Wiggin	22.00	11.00	6.50
(38)	John Wooten	20.00	10.00	6.00

1963 Kahn's

Kahn's included players from all 14 NFL teams this year, by adding players from the Dallas Cowboys, Green Bay Packers, New York Giants, St. Louis Cardinals, San Francisco 49ers and Washington Redskins to its 1963 lineup of eight teams. Although the backs are generally similar to those from previous sets, these cards can be distinguished from prior sets by the card front, which, for the first time, uses a white border around the black-and-white photo. Once again, the cards are unnumbered and measure 3-1/4" x 4-3/16".

		NM	E	VG
Complete Set (92):		2,300	1,150	690.00
Common Player:		18.00	9.00	5.50
(1)	Bill Barnes	18.00	9.00	5.50
(2)	Erich Barnes	20.00	10.00	6.00

(3)	Dick Bass	20.00	10.00	6.00
(4)	Don Bosseler	18.00	9.00	5.50
(5)	Jim Brown	200.00	100.00	60.00
(6)	Roger Brown	20.00	10.00	6.00
(7)	Roosevelt Brown	25.00	12.50	7.50
(8)	Ron Bull	20.00	10.00	6.00
(9)	Preston Carpenter	18.00	9.00	5.50
(10)	Frank Clarke	18.00	9.00	5.50
(11)	Gail Cogdill	18.00	9.00	5.50
(12)	Bobby Joe Conrad	18.00	9.00	5.50
(13)	John David Crow	30.00	15.00	9.00
(14)	Dan Currie	18.00	9.00	5.50
(15)	Buddy Dial	20.00	10.00	6.00
(16)	Mike Ditka	70.00	35.00	21.00
(17)	Fred Dugan	18.00	9.00	5.50
(18)	Galen Fiss	18.00	9.00	5.50
(19)	Bill Forester	20.00	10.00	6.00
(20)	Bob Gain	18.00	9.00	5.50
(21)	Willie Gailmore	20.00	10.00	6.00
(22)	Bill George	25.00	12.50	7.50
(23)	Frank Gifford	125.00	62.00	37.00
(24)	Bill Glass	22.00	11.00	6.50
(25)	Forrest Gregg	25.00	12.50	7.50
(26)	Fred Hageman	18.00	9.00	5.50
(27)	Jimmy Hill	18.00	9.00	5.50
(28)	Sam Huff	30.00	15.00	9.00
(29)	Dan James	18.00	9.00	5.50
(30)	John Henry Johnson	25.00	12.50	7.50
(31)	Sonny Jurgensen	35.00	17.50	10.50
(32)	Jim Katcavage	20.00	10.00	6.00
(33)	Ron Kostelnik	18.00	9.00	5.50
(34)	Jerry Kramer	25.00	12.50	7.50
(35)	Ron Kramer	22.00	11.00	6.50
(36)	Dick "Night Train" Lane	25.00	12.50	7.50
(37)	Yale Lary	25.00	12.50	7.50
(38)	Eddie LeBaron	25.00	12.50	7.50
(39)	Dick Lynch	18.00	9.00	5.50
(40)	Tommy Mason	20.00	10.00	6.00
(41)	Tommy McDonald	20.00	10.00	6.00
(42)	Lou Michaels	18.00	9.00	5.50
(43)	Bobby Mitchell	30.00	15.00	9.00
(44)	Dick Modzelewski	18.00	9.00	5.50
(45)	Lenny Moore	30.00	15.00	9.00
(46)	John Morrow	18.00	9.00	5.50
(47)	John Nisby	18.00	9.00	5.50
(48)	Ray Nitschke	40.00	20.00	12.00
(49)	Leo Nomellini	25.00	12.50	7.50
(50)	Jimmy Orr	20.00	10.00	6.00
(51)	John Paluck	18.00	9.00	5.50
(52)	Jim Parker	25.00	12.50	7.50
(53)	Bernie Parrish	18.00	9.00	5.50
(54)	Jim Patton	18.00	9.00	5.50
(55)	Don Perkins	20.00	10.00	6.00
(56)	Richie Petitbon	18.00	9.00	5.50
(57)	Jim Phillips	18.00	9.00	5.50
(58)	Nick Pietrosante	18.00	9.00	5.50
(59)	Milt Plum	20.00	10.00	6.00
(60)	Myron Pottios	18.00	9.00	5.50
(61)	Sonny Randle	18.00	9.00	5.50
(62)	John Reger	18.00	9.00	5.50
(63)	Ray Renfro	22.00	11.00	6.50
(64)	Pete Retzlaff	20.00	10.00	6.00
(65)	Pat Richter	22.00	11.00	6.50
(66)	Jim Ringo	25.00	12.50	7.50
(67)	Andy Robustelli	25.00	12.50	7.50
(68)	Joe Rutgens	18.00	9.00	5.50
(69)	Bob St. Clair	25.00	12.50	7.50
(70)	John Sample	18.00	9.00	5.50
(71)	Lonnie Sanders	18.00	9.00	5.50
(72)	Dick Schafrath	18.00	9.00	5.50
(73)	Joe Schmidt	30.00	15.00	9.00
(74)	Del Shofner	20.00	10.00	6.00
(75)	J.D. Smith	18.00	9.00	5.50
(76)	Norm Snead	20.00	10.00	6.00
(77)	Billy Stacy	18.00	9.00	5.50
(78)	Bart Starr	60.00	30.00	18.00
(79)	Ernie Stautner	30.00	15.00	9.00
(80)	Jim Steffen	18.00	9.00	5.50
(81)	Andy Stynchula	18.00	9.00	5.50
(82)	Fran Tarkenton	110.00	55.00	33.00
(83)	Jim Taylor	40.00	20.00	12.00
(84)	Clendon Thomas	18.00	9.00	5.50
(85)	Fred (Fuzzy) Thurston	25.00	12.50	7.50
(86)	Y.A. Tittle	50.00	25.00	15.00
(87)	Bob Toneff	18.00	9.00	5.50
(88)	Jerry Tubbs	18.00	9.00	5.50
(89)	John Unitas	130.00	65.00	39.00
(90)	Billy Wade	18.00	9.00	5.50
(91)	Willie Wood	25.00	12.50	7.50
(92)	Abe Woodson	18.00	9.00	5.50

1964 Kahn's

Kahn's introduced color to its 1964 set, making it distinctively different from its prior black-and-white efforts. The Kahn's slogan has also been removed from the card fronts; it has been placed on the card back instead. The card backs are generally the same as those in previous issues. The unnumbered cards measure 3" x 3-5/8".

		NM	E	VG
Complete Set (53):		1,400	700.00	420.00
Common Player:		15.00	7.50	4.50
(1)	Doug Atkins	25.00	12.50	7.50
(2)	Terry Barr	15.00	7.50	4.50
(3)	Dick Bass	20.00	10.00	6.00
(4)	Ordell Braase	15.00	7.50	4.50
(5)	Ed Brown	20.00	10.00	6.00
(6)	Jimmy Brown	160.00	80.00	48.00
(7)	Gary Collins	20.00	10.00	6.00
(8)	Bobby Joe Conrad	20.00	10.00	6.00
(9)	Mike Ditka	45.00	22.00	13.50
(10)	Galen Fiss	15.00	7.50	4.50
(11)	Paul Flatley	22.00	11.00	6.50
(12)	Joe Fortunato	18.00	9.00	5.50
(13)	Bill George	25.00	12.50	7.50
(14)	Bill Glass	18.00	9.00	5.50
(15)	Ernie Green	18.00	9.00	5.50
(16)	Dick Hoak	18.00	9.00	5.50
(17)	Paul Hornung	45.00	22.00	13.50
(18)	Sam Huff	35.00	17.50	10.50
(19)	Charlie Johnson	20.00	10.00	6.00
(20)	John Henry Johnson	30.00	15.00	9.00
(21)	Alex Karras	35.00	17.50	10.50
(22)	Jim Katcavage	18.00	9.00	5.50
(23)	Joe Krupa	15.00	7.50	4.50
(24)	Dick "Night Train" Lane	25.00	12.50	7.50
(25)	Tommy Mason	18.00	9.00	5.50
(26)	Don Meredith	60.00	30.00	18.00
(27)	Bobby Mitchell	30.00	15.00	9.00
(28)	Larry Morris	15.00	7.50	4.50
(29)	Jimmy Orr	18.00	9.00	5.50
(30)	Jim Parker	25.00	12.50	7.50
(31)	Bernie Parrish	20.00	10.00	6.00
(32)	Don Perkins	18.00	9.00	5.50
(33)	Jim Phillips	15.00	7.50	4.50
(34)	Sonny Randle			
(35)	Pete Retzlaff	18.00	9.00	5.50
(36)	Jim Ringo	25.00	12.50	7.50
(37)	Frank Ryan	20.00	10.00	6.00
(38)	Dick Schafrath	20.00	10.00	6.00
(39)	Joe Schmidt	25.00	12.50	7.50
(40)	Del Shofner	18.00	9.00	5.50
(41)	J.D. Smith	15.00	7.50	4.50
(42)	Norm Snead	18.00	9.00	5.50
(43)	Bart Starr	60.00	30.00	18.00
(44)	Fran Tarkenton	75.00	37.00	22.00
(45)	Jim Taylor	30.00	15.00	9.00
(46)	Clendon Thomas	15.00	7.50	4.50
(47)	Y.A. Tittle	50.00	25.00	15.00
(48)	Jerry Tubbs	18.00	9.00	5.50
(49)	John Unitas	80.00	40.00	24.00
(50)	Billy Wade	18.00	9.00	5.50
(51)	Paul Warfield	65.00	32.00	19.50
(52)	Alex Webster	18.00	9.00	5.50
(53)	Abe Woodson	15.00	7.50	4.50

1989 Kansas

MAURICE DOUGLAS

		NM/M	NM	E
	Complete Set (40):	12.00	9.00	4.75
	Common Player:	.35	.25	.14
1	Kelly Donohoe	.75	.60	.30
2	Roger Robben	.35	.25	.14
3	Tony Sands	.35	.25	.14
4	Paul Zaffaroni	.35	.25	.14
5	Lance Flachsbarth	.35	.25	.14
6	Brad Fleeman	.35	.25	.14
7	Chip Budde	.50	.40	.20
8	Bill Hundelt	.35	.25	.14
9	Dan Newbrough	.35	.25	.14
10	Gary Oatis	.35	.25	.14
11	B.J. Lohsen	.50	.40	.20
12	John Fritch	.35	.25	.14
13	Russ Bowen	.35	.25	.14
14	Smith Holland	.35	.25	.14
15	Jason Priest	.50	.40	.20
16	Scott McCabe	.35	.25	.14
17	Jason Tyrer	.35	.25	.14
18	Mongo Allen	.35	.25	.14
19	Glen Mason (CO)	1.00	.70	.40
20	Deral Boykin	.35	.25	.14
21	Quintin Smith	.35	.25	.14
22	Mark Koncz	.50	.40	.20
23	John Baker	.50	.40	.20
24	**Football Staff** (schedule on back)	.50	.40	.20
25	Maurice Hooks	.35	.25	.14
26	Frank Hatchett	.35	.25	.14
27	Paul Friday	.35	.25	.14
28	Doug Terry	.35	.25	.14
29	Kenny Drayton	.35	.25	.14
30	Jim New	.35	.25	.14
31	Chris Perez	.35	.25	.14
32	Maurice Douglas	1.25	.90	.50
33	Curtis Moore	.35	.25	.14
34	David Gordon	.35	.25	.14
35	Matt Nolen	.35	.25	.14
36	Dave Walton	.35	.25	.14
37	King Dixon	.50	.40	.20
38	**Memorial Stadium**	.35	.25	.14
39	Jayhawks in Action (Kelly Donohoe)	.50	.40	.20
40	Jayhawks in Action (John Baker) (OL)	.50	.40	.20
NNO	**Title Card**	.75	.60	.30

1970 Kellogg's

Kellogg's cereal entered the football card market in 1970 with a set of 60 cards featuring the 3D effect utilized for many of its baseball card issues from the same period. The cards, which measure approximately 2-1/4" x 3-1/2", could be obtained inside cereal boxes or through a mail-in offer. Because of the process used to make the 3D effect, the cards are susceptible to cracking and curling, making perfect condition somewhat difficult.

		NM	E	VG
	Complete Set (60):	50.00	25.00	15.00
	Common Player:	.40	.20	.12
1	Carl Eller	1.25	.60	.40
2	Jim Otto	1.25	.60	.40
3	Tom Matte	.60	.30	.20
4	Bill Nelson	.50	.25	.15
5	Travis Williams	.40	.20	.12
6	Len Dawson	2.00	1.00	.60
7	Gene Washington	.60	.30	.20
8	Jim Nance	.50	.25	.15
9	Norm Snead	.60	.30	.20
10	Dick Butkus	4.00	2.00	1.25
11	George Sauer	.50	.25	.15
12	Billy Kilmer	.75	.40	.25
13	Alex Karras	3.00	1.50	.90
14	Larry Wilson	1.25	.60	.40
15	Dave Robinson	.50	.25	.15
16	Bill Brown	.50	.25	.15
17	Bob Griese	4.00	2.00	1.25

18	Al Denson	.40	.20	.12
19	Dick Post	.40	.20	.12
20	Jan Stenerud	1.25	.60	.40
21	Paul Warfield	1.50	.70	.45
22	Mel Farr	.50	.25	.15
23	Mel Renfro	.60	.30	.20
24	Roy Jefferson	.40	.20	.12
25	Mike Garrett	.50	.25	.15
26	Harry Jacobs	.40	.20	.12
27	Carl Garrett	.40	.20	.12
28	Dave Wilcox	.50	.25	.15
29	Matt Snell	.60	.30	.20
30	Tom Woodeshick	.40	.20	.12
31	Leroy Kelly	.75	.40	.25
32	Floyd Little	.75	.40	.25
33	Ken Willard	.60	.30	.20
34	John Mackey	1.25	.60	.40
35	Merlin Olsen	3.50	1.75	1.00
36	David Grayson	.40	.20	.12
37	Lem Barney	2.00	1.00	.60
38	Deacon Jones	1.25	.60	.40
39	Bob Hayes	.75	.40	.25
40	Lance Alworth	2.00	1.00	.60
41	Larry Csonka	3.00	1.50	.90
42	Bobby Bell	1.25	.60	.40
43	George Webster	.50	.25	.15
44	John Roland	.50	.25	.15
45	Dick Shiner	.40	.20	.12
46	Charles (Bubba) Smith	2.00	1.00	.60
47	Daryle Lamonica	.75	.40	.25
48	O.J. Simpson	20.00	10.00	6.00
49	Calvin Hill	1.00	.50	.30
50	Fred Biletnikoff	1.50	.70	.45
51	Gale Sayers	5.00	2.50	1.50
52	Homer Jones	.50	.25	.15
53	Sonny Jurgensen	2.50	1.25	.70
54	Bob Lilly	2.00	1.00	.60
55	Johnny Unitas	6.00	3.00	1.75
56	Tommy Nobis	.75	.40	.25
57	Ed Meador	.50	.25	.15
58	Carl Lockhart	.40	.20	.12
59	Don Maynard	1.25	.60	.40
60	Greg Cook	.50	.25	.15

1971 Kellogg's

The 1971 Kellogg's football set was again complete at 60 cards and featured the 3D effect. The cards measure approximately 2-1/4" x 3-1/2", and again, because of the process used to achieve the 3D effect, are susceptible to cracking and curling. Cards from the 1971 set were available only in boxes of cereal. Because sets were not available through a mail-in offer, the '71 Kellogg's set is considerably scarcer and more valuable than the '70 set.

		NM	E	VG
	Complete Set (60):	360.00	180.00	108.00
	Common Player:	4.50	2.25	1.25
1	Tom Barrington	4.50	2.25	1.25
2	Chris Hanburger	5.00	2.50	1.50
3	Frank Nunley	4.50	2.25	1.25
4	Houston Antwine	4.50	2.25	1.25
5	Ron Johnson	5.00	2.50	1.50
6	Craig Morton	6.50	3.25	1.75
7	Jack Snow	5.00	2.50	1.50
8	Mel Renfro	5.00	2.50	1.50
9	Les Josephson	4.50	2.25	1.25
10	Gary Garrison	4.50	2.25	1.25
11	Dave Herman	4.50	2.25	1.25
12	Fred Dryer	6.50	3.25	1.75
13	Larry Brown	5.00	2.50	1.50
14	Gene Washington	4.50	2.25	1.25
15	Joe Greene	25.00	12.50	7.50
16	Marlin Briscoe	4.50	2.25	1.25
17	Bob Grant	4.50	2.25	1.25
18	Dan Conners	4.50	2.25	1.25
19	Mike Curtis	5.00	2.50	1.50
20	Harry Schuh	4.50	2.25	1.25
21	Rich Jackson	4.50	2.25	1.25
22	Clint Jones	4.50	2.25	1.25

23	Hewritt Dixon	4.50	2.25	1.25
24	Jess Phillips	4.50	2.25	1.25
25	Gary Cuozzo	4.50	2.25	1.25
26	Bo Scott	4.50	2.25	1.25
27	Glen Ray Hines	4.50	2.25	1.25
28	Johnny Unitas	27.00	13.50	8.25
29	John Gilliam	4.50	2.25	1.25
30	Harmon Wages	4.50	2.25	1.25
31	Walt Sweeney	4.50	2.25	1.25
32	Bruce Taylor	5.00	2.50	1.50
33	George Blanda	17.00	8.50	5.00
34	Ken Bowman	4.50	2.25	1.25
35	Johnny Robinson	5.00	2.50	1.50
36	Ed Podolak	4.50	2.25	1.25
37	Curley Culp	4.50	2.25	1.25
38	Jim Hart	6.50	3.25	1.75
39	Dick Butkus	20.00	10.00	6.00
40	Floyd Little	6.50	3.25	1.75
41	Nick Buoniconti	6.50	3.25	1.75
42	Larry Smith	4.50	2.25	1.25
43	Wayne Walker	4.50	2.25	1.25
44	MacArthur Lane	5.00	2.50	1.25
45	John Brodie	15.00	7.50	4.50
46	Dick LeBeau	4.50	2.25	1.25
47	Claude Humphrey	4.50	2.25	1.25
48	Jerry LeVias	4.50	2.25	1.25
49	Erich Barnes	4.50	2.25	1.25
50	Andy Russell	5.00	2.50	1.50
51	Donny Anderson	5.00	2.50	1.50
52	Mike Reid	7.50	3.75	2.25
53	Al Atkinson	4.50	2.25	1.25
54	Tom Dempsey	5.00	2.50	1.50
55	Bob Griese	18.00	9.00	5.50
56	Dick Gordon	4.50	2.25	1.25
57	Charlie Sanders	5.00	2.50	1.50
58	Doug Cunningham	4.50	2.25	1.25
59	Cyril Pinder	4.50	2.25	1.25
60	Dave Osborn	5.00	2.50	1.50

1982 Kellogg's

After a hiatus of more than a decade, Kellogg's returned in 1982 with a small (24-card) set that appeared in three-card panels on the backs of Raisin Bran boxes. The individual cards measure the standard 2-1/2" x 3-1/2", but the set is usually collected in panel-form, so it has little value if cut into individual cards. The prices below, therefore, are for complete panels. The cards are unnumbered and are checklisted here in alphabetical order based on the last name of the first player on each panel. Each panel measures approximately 4-1/8" x 7-1/2". Card fronts have the player's name, position and team on the bottom left, with the Kellogg's logo inside a football on the bottom right. Card backs feature the player's name and bio at the top, with his stats in the middle. His honors received are printed at the bottom, along with the team helmet and NFLPA and NFL logos. Billy Joe DuPree's photo is mistakenly labeled Harvey Martin, while Martin's is labeled DuPree.

		NM/M	NM	E
	Complete Set (8):	5.00	3.75	2.00
	Common Panel:	.60	.45	.25
1	Ken Anderson, Frank Lewis, Gifford Nielsen	.75	.60	.30
2	Ottis Anderson, Chris Collinsworth, Franco Harris	1.75	1.25	.70
3	William Andrews, Brian Sipe, Fred Smerlas	.60	.45	.25
4	Steve Bartkowski, Robert Brazile, Jack Rudnay	.60	.45	.25
5	Tony Dorsett, Eric Hipple, Pat McInally	1.25	.90	.50
6	Billy Joe DuPree, David Hill, John Stallworth	.75	.60	.30
7	Harvey Martin, Mike Pruitt, Joe Senser	.60	.45	.25
8	Art Still, Mel Gray, Tommy Kramer	.60	.45	.25

1978 Kellogg's Stickers

Measuring 2-1/2" x 2-5/8", the sticker fronts showcase the team's name beneath the team helmets. Spotlighted on the back are a brief history on each team and a referee's signals quiz. Each sticker is numbered on the back.

		NM	E	VG
	Complete Set (28):	30.00	15.00	9.00
	Common Player:	1.00	.70	.40
1	**Atlanta Falcons**	1.00	.70	.40
2	**Baltimore Colts**	1.00	.70	.40
3	**Buffalo Bills**	1.00	.70	.40
4	**Chicago Bears**	1.00	.70	.40
5	**Cincinnati Bengals**	1.00	.70	.40
6	**Cleveland Browns**	1.00	.70	.40
7	**Dallas Cowboys**	2.00	1.00	.60
8	**Denver Broncos**	1.00	.70	.40
9	**Detroit Lions**	1.00	.70	.40

10	Green Bay Packers	1.50	.70	.45
11	Houston Oilers	1.00	.70	.40
12	Kansas City Chiefs	1.00	.70	.40
13	Los Angeles Rams	1.00	.70	.40
14	Miami Dolphins	2.00	1.00	.60
15	Minnesota Vikings	1.00	.70	.40
16	New England Patriots	1.00	.70	.40
17	New Orleans Saints	1.00	.70	.40
18	New York Giants	1.00	.70	.40
19	New York Jets	1.00	.70	.40
20	Oakland Raiders	2.00	1.00	.60
21	Philadelphia Eagles	1.00	.70	.40
22	Pittsburgh Steelers	2.00	1.00	.60
23	St. Louis Cardinals	1.00	.70	.40
24	San Diego Chargers	1.00	.70	.40
25	San Francisco 49ers	2.00	1.00	.60
26	Seattle Seahawks	1.00	.70	.40
27	Tampa Bay Buccaneers	1.00	.70	.40
28	Washington Redskins	2.00	1.00	.60

1982 Kellogg's Teams

Inserted into specially marked boxes of Kellogg's Raisin Bran cereal, this 28-poster set measures 8" x 10-1/2". Inside a black border, color artwork of generic players is featured, with a smaller color painting inset on one side. The team name, helmet and NFL shield are located inside an oval at the bottom. The backs include the official rules and an entry form for the "Raisin Bran Super Bowl Sweepstakes." If the team showcased on the front won the 1983 Super Bowl, the collector had to fill out the form and mail the poster to Kellogg's to win various prizes.

		NM/M	NM	E
Complete Set (28):		100.00	75.00	40.00
Common Player:		5.00	3.75	2.00
1	Atlanta Falcons	5.00	3.75	2.00
2	Buffalo Bills	5.00	3.75	2.00
3	Chicago Bears	5.00	3.75	2.00
4	Cincinnati Bengals	5.00	3.75	2.00
5	Cleveland Browns	5.00	3.75	2.00
6	Dallas Cowboys	8.00	6.00	3.25
7	Denver Broncos	5.00	3.75	2.00
8	Detroit Lions	5.00	3.75	2.00
9	Green Bay Packers	8.00	6.00	3.25
10	Houston Oilers	5.00	3.75	2.00
11	Indianapolis Colts	5.00	3.75	2.00
12	Kansas City Chiefs	5.00	3.75	2.00
13	Los Angeles Raiders	8.00	6.00	3.25
14	Los Angeles Rams	5.00	3.75	2.00
15	Miami Dolphins	8.00	6.00	3.25
16	Minnesota Vikings	5.00	3.75	2.00
17	New England Patriots	5.00	3.75	2.00
18	New Orleans Saints	5.00	3.75	2.00
19	New York Giants	5.00	3.75	2.00
20	New York Jets	5.00	3.75	2.00
21	Philadelphia Eagles	5.00	3.75	2.00
22	Pittsburgh Steelers	5.00	3.75	2.00
23	St. Louis Cardinals	5.00	3.75	2.00
24	San Diego Chargers	5.00	3.75	2.00
25	San francisco 49ers	8.00	6.00	3.25
26	Seattle Seahawks	5.00	3.75	2.00
27	Tampa Bay Buccaneers	5.00	3.75	2.00
28	Washington Redskins	8.00	6.00	3.25

1982 Kentucky Schedules

		NM/M	NM	E
Complete Set (19):		45.00	34.00	18.00
Common Player:		3.00	2.25	1.25
1	Richard Abraham	3.00	2.25	1.25
2	Glenn Amerson	3.00	2.25	1.25
3	Effley Brooks	3.00	2.25	1.25
4	Shawn Donigan	3.00	2.25	1.25
5	Rod Francis	3.00	2.25	1.25
6	Terry Henry	3.00	2.25	1.25
7	Ben Johnson	3.00	2.25	1.25
8	Dave Lyons	3.00	2.25	1.25
9	John Maddox	3.00	2.25	1.25
10	Rob Mangas	4.00	3.00	1.50
11	David "Buzz" Meers	3.00	2.25	1.25
12	Andy Molls	3.00	2.25	1.25
13	Tom Petty	3.00	2.25	1.25
14	Don Roe	3.00	2.25	1.25
15	Todd Shadowen	3.00	2.25	1.25
16	Gerald Smyth	3.00	2.25	1.25
17	Pete Venable	3.00	2.25	1.25
18	Allan Watson	3.00	2.25	1.25
19	Steve Williams	3.00	2.25	1.25

1986 Kentucky Schedules

		NM/M	NM	E
Complete Set (4):		15.00	11.00	6.00
Common Player:		4.00	3.00	1.50
1	Jerry Claiborne (CO)	4.00	3.00	1.50
2	Mark Higgs	7.50	5.75	3.00
3	Marc Logan	6.00	4.50	2.50
4	Bill Ransdell	4.00	3.00	1.50

1989 KFC Calgary

		NM/M	NM	E
Complete Set (24):		10.00	7.50	4.00
Common Player:		.40	.30	.15
3	David McCrary	.40	.30	.15
4	Brent Matich	.40	.30	.15
8	Danny Barrett	1.50	1.25	.60
9	Terrence Jones	1.25	.90	.50
12	Tim Petros	.60	.45	.25
13	Mark McLoughlin	.40	.30	.15
15	Ron Hopkins	.60	.45	.25
20	Chris Major	1.25	.90	.50
24	Greg Peterson	.40	.30	.15
25	Shawn Faulkner	.40	.30	.15
32	Darcy Kopp	.40	.30	.15
34	Andy McVey	.40	.30	.15
39	Doug (Tank) Landry	1.00	.70	.40
59	Leo Blanchard	.40	.30	.15
61	Tom Spoletini	.40	.30	.15
65	Mike Palumbo	.40	.30	.15
66	Dan Ferrone	.60	.45	.25
74	Mitchell Price	.60	.45	.25
76	Marshall Toner	.40	.30	.15
84	Eugene Belliveau	.60	.45	.25
85	Brock Smith	.40	.30	.15
89	Larry Willis	.75	.60	.30
93	Kent Warnock	.75	.60	.30
97	Ken Ford	.40	.30	.15

1990 KFC Calgary

		NM/M	NM	E
Complete Set (24):		10.00	7.50	4.00
Common Player:		.50	.40	.20
1	Walter Ballard	.50	.40	.20
2	Danny Barrett	1.50	1.25	.60
3	Eddie Brown	.75	.60	.30
4	Joe Clausi	.50	.40	.20
5	Lloyd Fairbanks	.75	.60	.30
6	Matt Finlay	.75	.60	.30
7	Ken Ford	.50	.40	.20
8	Ron Hopkins	.75	.60	.30
9	Keyvan Jenkins	1.25	.90	.50
10	Will Johnson	.75	.60	.30
11	Terrence Jones	1.25	.90	.50
12	David McCrary	.50	.40	.20
13	Mark McLoughlin	.50	.40	.20
14	Andy McVey	.50	.40	.20
15	Brent Matich	.50	.40	.20
16	Mike Palumbo	.50	.40	.20
17	Greg Peterson	.50	.40	.20
18	Tim Petros	.75	.60	.30
19	Mitchell Price	.75	.60	.30
20	Brock Smith	.50	.40	.20
21	Tom Spoletini	.50	.40	.20
22	Junior Thurman	1.25	.90	.50
23	Marshall Toner	.50	.40	.20
24	Kent Warnock	.75	.60	.30

1989 King B Discs

These red-bordered discs, which feature 24 NFL stars, were included in specially-marked cans of King B beef jerky, one per can. The front has a color head shot of the player, along with the King B logo. "1st Annual Collectors Edition" is also written on the front. The back includes the King B and NFLPA logos, plus biographical information and 1988 and career statistics. A ring of stars runs along the border. The cards, produced by Michael Schechter Associates, are numbered on the back.

		NM/M	NM	E
Complete Set (24):		50.00	37.00	20.00
Common Player:		1.00	.70	.40
1	Chris Miller	2.50	2.00	1.00
2	Shane Conlan	1.25	.90	.50
3	Richard Dent	1.75	1.25	.70
4	Boomer Esiason	1.75	1.25	.70
5	Frank Minnifield	1.00	.70	.40
6	Herschel Walker	2.00	1.50	.80
7	Karl Mecklenburg	1.50	1.25	.60
8	Mike Cofer	1.00	.70	.40
9	Warren Moon	3.00	2.25	1.25
10	Chris Chandler	1.50	1.25	.60

11	Deron Cherry	1.00	.70	.40
12	Bo Jackson	2.00	1.50	.80
13	Jim Everett	1.50	1.25	.60
14	Dan Marino	12.00	9.00	4.75
15	Anthony Carter	1.25	.90	.50
16	Andre Tippett	1.50	1.25	.60
17	Bobby Hebert	1.50	1.25	.60
18	Phil Simms	1.75	1.25	.70
19	Al Toon	1.50	1.25	.60
20	Gary Anderson	1.50	1.25	.60
21	Joe Montana	14.00	10.50	5.50
22	Dave Krieg	1.50	1.25	.60
23	Randall Cunningham	2.50	2.00	1.00
24	Bubby Brister	1.00	.70	.40

1990 King B Discs

Once again, these discs were available in specially-marked cans of King B beef jerky, one per can. The front has a color mug shot of the player, surrounded by a red border with a yellow background. The year 1990 appears at the bottom of the card in green; the King B logo is underneath the year. Each card back is numbered and has a border of stars around it. Biographical information and a comment about the player's accomplishments are also given on the back, along with the King B and NFLPA logos.

		NM/M	NM	E
Complete Set (24):		45.00	34.00	18.00
Common Player:		1.00	.70	.40
1	Jim Everett	2.00	1.50	.80
2	Marcus Allen	2.00	1.50	.80
3	Brian Blades	1.50	1.25	.60
4	Bubby Brister	1.00	.70	.40
5	Mark Carrier	1.50	1.25	.60
6	Steve Jordan	1.00	.70	.40
7	Barry Sanders	7.00	5.25	2.75
8	Ronnie Lott	2.00	1.50	.80
9	Howie Long	2.00	1.50	.80
10	Steve Atwater	1.50	1.25	.60
11	Dan Marino	8.00	6.00	3.25
12	Boomer Esiason	2.00	1.50	.80
13	Dalton Hilliard	1.00	.70	.40
14	Phil Simms	2.50	2.00	1.00
15	Jim Kelly	3.00	2.25	1.25
16	Mike Singletary	1.50	1.25	.60
17	John Stephens	1.50	1.25	.60
18	Christian Okoye	1.50	1.25	.60
19	Art Monk	2.00	1.50	.80
20	Chris Miller	2.50	2.00	1.00
21	Roger Craig	2.00	1.50	.80
22	Duane Bickett	1.00	.70	.40
23	Don Majkowski	1.00	.70	.40
24	Eric Metcalf	2.50	2.00	1.00

1991 King B Discs

Specially-marked cans of King B beef jerky each contained a disc featuring one of 24 NFL stars. The front has a color mug shot of the player surrounded by a purple border. His name, team and position are printed in gold. The King B logo and 1991 are printed at the bottom of the disc. The back is numbered and includes 1990 and career statistics, plus brief biographical information, all in red ink. A ring of stars comprises the border. An NFLPA and King B logo are also included on the back. The discs were produced by Michael Schechter Associates.

		NM/M	NM	E
Complete Set (24):		35.00	26.00	14.00
Common Player:		1.00	.70	.40
1	Mark Rypien	1.25	.90	.50
2	Art Monk	2.00	1.50	.80
3	Sean Jones	1.00	.70	.40
4	Bubby Brister	1.00	.70	.40
5	Warren Moon	3.00	2.25	1.25
6	Andre Rison	2.00	1.50	.80
7	Emmitt Smith	9.00	6.75	3.50
8	Mervyn Fernandez	1.00	.70	.40
9	Rickey Jackson	1.00	.70	.40
10	Bruce Armstrong	1.00	.70	.40
11	Neal Anderson	1.25	.90	.50
12	Christian Okoye	1.00	.70	.40
13	Thurman Thomas	3.00	2.25	1.25
14	Bruce Smith	1.25	.90	.50
15	Jeff Hostetler	1.50	1.25	.60
16	Barry Sanders	6.00	4.50	2.50
17	Andre Reed	1.25	.90	.50
18	Derrick Thomas	2.50	2.00	1.00
19	Jim Everett	1.25	.90	.50
20	Boomer Esiason	1.50	1.25	.60
21	Merril Hoge	1.00	.70	.40
22	Steve Atwater	1.25	.90	.50
23	Dan Marino	8.00	6.00	3.25
24	Mark Collins	1.00	.70	.40

1991 Knudsen

Measuring 2" x 8", the 18-bookmark set was available to children who checked out books at San Diego, Los Angeles and San Francisco public libraries. The fronts have the Knudsen logo at the top, with "The Reading Team" printed below it. A photo of a player is included on a page of a book. The player's team name is superimposed over the photo. His name, position and bio are printed under the photo. The backs have the Knudsen and public library logos, along with information on two books. Each team's bookmarks were available only in its area. Nos. 1-6 are Chargers, Nos. 7-12 are Rams and Nos. 13-18 are 49ers.

		NM/M	NM	E
Complete Set (18):		30.00	22.00	12.00
Common Player:		1.50	1.25	.60
1	Gill Byrd	1.50	1.25	.60
2	Courtney Hall	1.50	1.25	.60
3	Ronnie Harmon	2.00	1.50	.80
4	Anthony Miller	3.00	2.25	1.25
5	Joe Phillips	1.50	1.25	.60
6	Junior Seau	5.00	3.75	2.00
7	Jim Everett	2.50	2.00	1.00
8	Kevin Greene	2.50	2.00	1.00
9	Damone Johnson	1.50	1.25	.60
10	Tom Newberry	1.50	1.25	.60
11	John Robinson (CO)	2.00	1.50	.80
12	Michael Stewart	1.50	1.25	.60
13	Michael Carter	1.50	1.25	.60
14	Charles Haley	2.50	2.00	1.00
15	Joe Montana	10.00	7.50	4.00
16	Tom Rathman	2.00	1.50	.80
17	Jerry Rice	10.00	7.50	4.00
18	George Seifert (CO)	3.00	2.25	1.25

1990 Knudsen 49ers

Measuring 2" x 8", this six-card bookmark set was given to children under 15 years of age at libraries in the San Francisco metro area. The design is basically the same as the Chargers set, with the Knudsen logo at the top and "The Reading Team" below it. The player's photo is in the center, above a box which contains the 49ers' logo and the player's name, uniform number and bio. The unnumbered backs have the Knudsen logo at the top and the San Francisco Public Library logo at the bottom. Two books are listed on the back of each bookmark.

		NM/M	NM	E
Complete Set (6):		25.00	18.50	10.00
Common Player:		1.50	1.25	.60

1	Roger Craig	2.50	2.00	1.00
2	Ronnie Lott	4.00	3.00	1.50
3	Joe Montana	12.00	9.00	4.75
4	Jerry Rice	12.00	9.00	4.75
5	George Siefert (CO)	3.00	2.25	1.25
6	Michael Walter	1.50	1.25	.60

1990 Knudsen Chargers

Measuring 2" x 8", the Chargers bookmarks were available at San Diego libraries. The fronts showcase the Knudsen logo at the top, with "The Reading Team" below it. The player photo is shown in the middle, with the Chargers' logo, player's name, uniform number and bio in a box under the photo. The unnumbered backs contain the Knudsen, American Library Association and San Diego libraries' logos.

		NM/M	NM	E
Complete Set (6):		10.00	7.50	4.00
Common Player:		1.50	1.25	.60
1	Marion Butts	2.50	2.00	1.00
2	Anthony Miller	3.50	2.75	1.50
3	Leslie O'Neal	2.50	2.00	1.00
4	Gary Plummer	1.50	1.25	.60
5	Billy Ray Smith	1.50	1.25	.60
6	Billy Joe Tolliver	2.00	1.50	.80

1989 Knudsen Raiders

Measuring 2" x 8", this bookmark set of 12 was introduced by Knudsen's Dairy of California. The bookmarks were available to children who checked out books from the Los Angeles Public Library during the 1989 season. The fronts featured a photo of a Raiders player, with "Knudsen presents Raiders Readers" at the top. The Raiders' logo, the player's name, position and bio, along with his highlights are listed below the photo. The unnumbered backs have reading tips, the player's name, L.A. Public Library, MCLS, Knudsen and Raiders' logos. The Mike Shanahan card is a tough one to locate, as it was not distributed or pulled after he left the Raiders for a position with another NFL team.

		NM/M	NM	E
Complete Set (14):		30.00	22.00	12.00
Common Player:		1.50	1.25	.60
6	Jeff Gossett	1.50	1.25	.60
13	Jay Schroeder	2.00	1.50	.80
26	Vann McElroy	1.50	1.25	.60
35	Steve Smith	2.00	1.50	.80
36	Terry McDaniel	2.00	1.50	.80
70	Scott Davis	1.50	1.25	.60
72	Don Mosebar	1.50	1.25	.60

75	Howie Long	2.50	2.00	1.00
76	Steve Wisniewski	2.00	1.50	.80
81	Tim Brown	6.00	4.50	2.50
83	Willie Gault	2.00	1.50	.80
NNO	Mike Shanahan (SP)			
	(CO)	16.00	12.00	6.50
NNO	**Raiders/Super Bowl**	1.50	1.25	.60
NNO	**Raiderettes** (SP)	2.00	1.50	.80

1990 Knudsen Rams

Measuring 2" x 8", the six-bookmark set promoted reading to children under 15 years of age in the Los Angeles area. The front design is the same as the Chargers, 49ers and Patriots sets of 1990.

		NM/M	NM	E
Complete Set (6):		25.00	18.50	10.00
Common Player:		4.00	3.00	1.50
1	Henry Ellard	8.00	6.00	3.25
2	Jim Everett	6.00	4.50	2.50
3	Jerry Gray	4.00	3.00	1.50
4	Pete Holohan	4.00	3.00	1.50
5	Mike Lansford	4.00	3.00	1.50
6	Irv Pankey	4.00	3.00	1.50

1990 Knudsen/Sealtest Patriots

Measuring 2" x 8", this six-card bookmark set was sponsored by Knudsen's and Sealtest. Those children under 15 years of age in the New England area received the bookmarks at their local libraries. The Knudsen or Sealtest logos were located at the top of the front, with "The Reading Team" below it. The player's photo is showcased above a box which contains the Patriots' logo, player's name, uniform number and bio. The backs have the sponsor logos and information on two books.

		NM/M	NM	E
Complete Set (6):		25.00	18.50	10.00
Common Player:		4.00	3.00	1.50
1	Steve Grogan	6.00	4.50	2.50
2	Ronnie Lippett	4.00	3.00	1.50
3	Eric Sievers	4.00	3.00	1.50
4	Mosi Tatupu	4.00	3.00	1.50
5	Andre Tippett	6.00	4.50	2.50
6	Garin Veris	4.00	3.00	1.50

L

1983 Latrobe Police

The black-and-white or sepia-toned standard sized cards were issued in Latrobe, Pa. Titled "Birthplace of Pro Football," the 30-card set featured a photo of the player in an oval, with his name and position in a box at the bottom of the card. The card backs, which came in two versions, have the 1895 "Birthplace of Pro Football" logo in the upper left, with the player's name and position at the right. A write-up of his career highlights also is included on the horizontal card backs. The cards were produced by Chess Promotions Inc. of Latrobe, Pa. The variation backs include safety tips.

		NM/M	NM	E
Complete Set (30):		8.00	6.00	3.25
Common Player:		.30	.25	.12
1	John Brallier	1.00	.70	.40
2	John K. Brallier	.50	.40	.20
3	**Latrobe YMCA Team 1895**	.50	.40	.20
4	**Brallier and Team at W and J 1895**	.50	.40	.20
5	**Latrobe A.A. Team 1896**	.50	.40	.20
6	**Latrobe A.A. 1897**	.50	.40	.20
7	**1st All Pro Team 1897**	.50	.40	.20
8	David Berry (Mgr.)	.30	.25	.12
9	Harry Ryan (RT)	.30	.25	.12
10	Walter Okeson (LE)	.30	.25	.12
11	Edward Wood (RE)	.30	.25	.12
12	E. Hammer (C)	.30	.25	.12
13	Marcus Saxman (LH)	.30	.25	.12
14	Charles Shumaker (SUB)	.30	.25	.12
15	Charles McDyre (LE)	.30	.25	.12
16	Edward Abbatticchio (FB)	.30	.25	.12
17	George Flickinger (C/LT)	.30	.25	.12
18	Walter Howard (RH)	.30	.25	.12
19	Thomas Trenchard	.50	.40	.20
20	John Kinport Brallier (QB)	.75	.60	.30
21	Jack Gass (LH)	.30	.25	.12
22	Dave Campbell (LT)	.30	.25	.12
23	Edward Blair (RH)	.30	.25	.12
24	John Johnston (RG)	.30	.25	.12
25	Sam Johnston (LG)	.30	.25	.12
26	Alex Laird (SUB)	.30	.25	.12
27	**Latrobe A.A. 1897 Team**	.50	.40	.20
28	**Pro Football Memorial Plaque**	.30	.25	.12
29	**Commemorative Medallion**	.30	.25	.12
30	**Birth of Pro Football Checklist Card**	.50	.40	.20

1975 Laughlin Flaky Football

Artist R.G. Laughlin created this 26-card set in 1975 as a parody to the NFL. Measuring 2-1/2" x 3-3/8", the card fronts have the city name and a parody NFL nickname, such as the Green Bay Porkers, with artwork relating to the nickname. "Flaky Football" is printed at the top of the cards, with the card number in a white circle in one of the corners of the horizontal fronts. The backs of the cards are blank.

		NM	E	VG
Complete Set (27):		125.00	62.00	37.00
Common Player:		4.50	3.50	1.75
1	Pittsburgh Stealers	8.00	4.00	2.50
2	Minnesota Spikings	6.00	3.00	1.75
3	Cincinnati Bungles	6.00	3.00	1.75
4	Chicago Bares	6.00	3.00	1.75
5	Miami Dullfins	8.00	4.00	2.50
6	Philadelphia Eggles	6.00	3.00	1.75
7	Cleveland Brawns	4.50	3.00	1.75
8	New York Gianuts	4.50	2.50	1.75
9	Buffalo Bulls	4.50	2.50	1.75
10	Dallas Plowboys	8.00	4.00	2.50
11	New England Pastry Nuts	4.50	2.50	1.75
12	Green Bay Porkers	8.00	4.00	2.50
13	Denver Bongos	4.50	2.50	1.75
14	St. Louis Cigardinals	4.50	2.50	1.75
15	New York Jests	4.50	2.50	1.75
16	Washington Redshins	8.00	4.00	2.50
17	Oakland Waders	8.00	4.00	2.50
18	Los Angeles Yams	4.50	2.50	1.75
19	Baltimore Kilts	4.50	2.50	1.75
20	New Orleans Scents	4.50	2.50	1.75
21	San Diego Charges	4.50	2.50	1.75
22	Detroit Loins	4.50	2.50	1.75
23	Kansas City Chefs	4.50	2.50	1.75
24	Atlanta Fakin's	4.50	2.50	1.75
25	Houston Owlers	4.50	2.50	1.75
26	San Francisco 40 Miners	8.00	4.00	2.50
NNO	Title Card Flaky Football	8.00	4.00	2.50

1948 Leaf

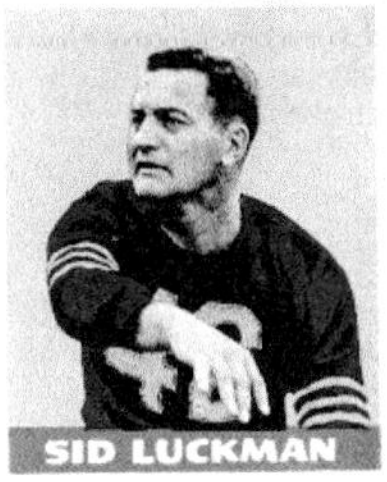

This 98-card set, the first of two Leaf sets to be issued in the late 1940s, features players posed in front of solid backgrounds (player hands and faces are in black and white). Cards measure 2-3/8" x 2-7/8", and the final 49 cards are more difficult to find than the first 49. Rookies in this set include Sid Luckman, Bulldog Turner, Doak Walker, Bobby Lane, Pete Pihos, George McAfee, Steve Van Buren, Bob Waterfield, Charlie Trippi, Sammy Baugh, Bill Dudley, George Connor, Frank Tripucka, Leo Nomellini, Charley Conerly, Leo Nomellini, Chuck Bednarik, and Jackie Jensen.

		NM	E	VG
Complete Set (98):		18,000	9,000	4,500
Common Player (1-49):		100.00	50.00	25.00
Minor Stars (1-49):		50.00		
Unlisted Stars (1-49):		60.00		
Common Player (50-98):		200.00	100.00	50.00
Unlisted Stars (50-98):		200.00		
1A	Sid Luckman **RC**	7,000	3,500	1,750
1B	Sid Luckman WB **RC**	500.00		
2	Steve Suhey	100.00	50.00	25.00
3A	Bulldog Turner **RC**	300.00	150.00	75.00
3B	Bulldog Turner WB **RC**	175.00		
4	Doak Walker **RC**	750.00	375.00	200.00
5	Levi Jackson	100.00	50.00	25.00
6A	Bobby Layne **RC**	2,500	1,125	575.00
6B	Bobby Layne RP **RC**	500.00		
7	Bill Fischer	100.00	50.00	25.00
8	Vice Banonis	100.00	50.00	25.00
9	Tommy Thompson **RC**	125.00	60.00	30.00
10	Perry Moss	100.00	50.00	25.00
11	Terry Brennan **RC**	100.00	50.00	25.00
12	William Swiacki **RC**	110.00	55.00	28.00
13A	Johnny Lujack **RC**	200.00	100.00	60.00
13B	Johnny Lujack ERR **RC**	700.00		
14	Mal Kutner	100.00	50.00	25.00
15	Charlie Justice **RC**	150.00	75.00	38.00
16A	Pete Pihos **RC**	175.00	80.00	40.00
16B	Pete Pihos BJN **RC**	175.00		
17A	Kenny Washington **RC**	60.00	30.00	15.00
17B	Kenny Washington WL **RC**	80.00		
18	Harry Gilmer **RC**	100.00	50.00	25.00
19A	George McAfee **RC**	250.00	125.00	65.00
19B	George McAfee ERR **RC**	500.00		
20	George Taliaferro **RC**	100.00	50.00	25.00
21	Paul Christman **RC**	50.00	25.00	15.00
22A	Steve Van Buren **RC**	400.00	200.00	100.00
22B	Steve Van Buren YJ **RC**	300.00		
23	Ken Kavanaugh **RC**	100.00	50.00	25.00
24	Jim Martin **RC**	100.00	50.00	25.00
25A	Bud Angsman **RC**	100.00	50.00	25.00
25B	Bud Angsman WL **RC**	60.00		
25C	Bud Angsman WB **RC**	60.00		
26A	Bob Waterfield **RC**	475.00	250.00	125.00
26B	Bob Waterfield WL **RC**	450.00		
27	Fred Davis	100.00	50.00	25.00
28	Whitey Wistert **RC**	100.00	50.00	25.00
29	Charlie Trippi **RC**	375.00	180.00	90.00
30	Paul Governali	100.00	50.00	25.00
31	Tom McWilliams	100.00	50.00	25.00
32	Larry Zimmerman	100.00	50.00	25.00
33	Pat Harder **RC**	140.00	70.00	35.00
34	Sammy Baugh **RC**	1,500	750.00	375.00
35	Ted Fritsch Sr.	100.00	50.00	25.00
36	Bill Dudley **RC**	200.00	100.00	50.00
37	George Connor **RC**	150.00	75.00	38.00
38	Frank Dancewicz	100.00	50.00	25.00
39	Billy Dewell	100.00	50.00	25.00
40	John Nolan	100.00	50.00	25.00
41	Harry Szulborski	100.00	50.00	25.00
42	Tex Coulter	100.00	50.00	25.00
43	Robert Nussbaumer	100.00	50.00	25.00
44	Bob Mann	100.00	50.00	25.00
45	Jim White	100.00	50.00	25.00
46	Jack Jacobs	100.00	50.00	25.00
47	John Clement	100.00	50.00	25.00
48	Frank Reagan	100.00	50.00	25.00
49	Frank Tripucka **RC**	100.00	50.00	25.00
50	John Rauch **RC**	200.00	100.00	50.00
51	Mike Dimitrio	200.00	100.00	50.00
52A	Leo Nomellini **RC**	700.00	350.00	175.00
52B	Leo Nomellini BBRJ **RC**	500.00		
52C	Leo Nomellini WB **RC**	500.00		
53	Charlie Conerly **RC**	1,200	600.00	300.00
54A	Chuck Bednarik **RC**	1,200	600.00	300.00
54B	Chuck Bednarik WB **RC**	500.00		
55	Chick Jagade	200.00	150.00	50.00
56	Bob Folsom **RC**	250.00	125.00	65.00
57	Eugene Rossides **RC**	250.00	125.00	65.00
58	Art Weiner	200.00	100.00	50.00
59	Alex Sarkistian	200.00	100.00	50.00
60	Dick Harris	200.00	100.00	50.00
61	Len Younce	200.00	100.00	50.00
62	Gene Derricotte	200.00	100.00	50.00
63	Roy Steiner	200.00	100.00	50.00
64	Frank Seno	200.00	100.00	50.00
65	Bob Hendreen	200.00	100.00	50.00
66	Jack Cloud	200.00	100.00	50.00
67	Harrell Collins	200.00	100.00	50.00
68	Clyde LeForce	200.00	100.00	50.00
69	Larry Joe	200.00	100.00	50.00
70	Phil O'Reilly	200.00	100.00	50.00
71	Paul Campbell	200.00	100.00	50.00
72	Ray Evans	200.00	100.00	50.00
73A	Jackie Jensen **RC**	500.00	250.00	125.00
73B	Jackie Jensen WB **RC**	450.00		
74	Russ Steger	200.00	100.00	50.00
75	Tony Minisi	200.00	100.00	50.00
76	Clayton Tonnemaker	200.00	100.00	50.00
77	George Savitsky	200.00	100.00	50.00
78	Clarence Self	200.00	100.00	50.00
79	Rod Franz	200.00	100.00	50.00
80	Jim Youle	200.00	100.00	50.00
81	Billy Bye	200.00	100.00	50.00
82	Fred Enke	200.00	100.00	50.00
83	Fred Folger	200.00	100.00	50.00
84	Jug Girard	200.00	100.00	50.00
85	Joe Scott	200.00	100.00	50.00
86	Bob Demoss	200.00	100.00	50.00
87	Dave Templeton	200.00	100.00	50.00
88	Herb Siegert	200.00	100.00	50.00
89	Bucky O'Conner	200.00	100.00	50.00
90	Joe Whisler	200.00	100.00	50.00
91	Leon Hart **RC**	350.00	175.00	90.00
92	Earl Banks	200.00	100.00	50.00
93	Frank Aschenbrenner	200.00	100.00	50.00
94	John Golddsberry	200.00	100.00	50.00
95	Porter Payne	200.00	100.00	50.00
96	Pete Perini	200.00	100.00	50.00
97	Jay Rhodemyre	200.00	100.00	50.00
98	Al DiMarco **RC**	450.00	225.00	115.00

1949 Leaf

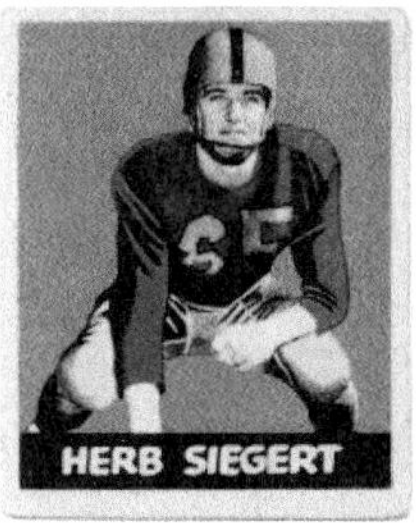

The 1949 Leaf issue is quite possibly the stupidest of what is considered the "major" football issues. There are but 49 cards in the set, but numerically the set jumps around until it reaches a 150 count. There are several gaps in the numbering sequence. Even less appealing is the fact that there is exactly one rookie card in the set - that of #1, Bob Hendren. Cards, which measure 2-3/8" x 2-7/8", bear close resemblance to the 1948 Leaf football set, as well as to the Leaf baseball sets of the era. The second-year cards in the set include those of Hall of Famers Sid Luckman, Charley Trippi, Bill Dudley, Sammy Baugh, Pete Pihos, George Connor, Ken McAfee (last card), Bobby Lane, Steve Van Buren, Bob Waterfield, Chuck Bednarik, and Bulldog Turner. Other sophomore cards include Charley Conerly, Johnny Lujack, and Frank Tripucka.

		NM	E	VG
Complete Set (49):		3,400	1,700	850.00
Common Player:		65.00	37.00	18.00
Minor Stars:		35.00		
1	Bob Hendren	100.00	50.00	25.00
2	Joe Scott	65.00	37.00	18.00
3	Frank Reagan	65.00	37.00	18.00
4	John Rauch	65.00	37.00	18.00
7	Bill Fischer	65.00	37.00	18.00
9	Bud Angsman	65.00	37.00	18.00
10	Billy Dewell	65.00	37.00	18.00
13	Tommy Thompson	65.00	37.00	18.00
15	Sid Luckman	150.00	75.00	38.00
16	Charlie Trippi	90.00	45.00	23.00
17	Bob Mann	65.00	37.00	18.00
19	Paul Christman	65.00	37.00	18.00

22	Bill Dudley	90.00	45.00	23.00
23	Clyde LeForce	65.00	37.00	18.00
26	Sammy Baugh	350.00	175.00	90.00
28	Pete Pihos	90.00	45.00	23.00
31	Tex Coulter	65.00	37.00	18.00
32	Mal Kutner	65.00	37.00	18.00
35	Whitey Wistert	65.00	37.00	18.00
37	Ted Fritsch Sr.	65.00	37.00	18.00
38	Vince Banonis	65.00	37.00	18.00
39	Jim White	65.00	37.00	18.00
40	George Connor	90.00	45.00	23.00
41	George McAfee	90.00	45.00	23.00
43	Frank Tripucka	65.00	37.00	18.00
47	Fred Enke	65.00	37.00	18.00
49	Charlie Conerly	150.00	75.00	38.00
51	Ken Kavanaugh	65.00	37.00	18.00
56	John Lujack	100.00	50.00	30.00
57	Jim Youle	65.00	37.00	18.00
62	Harry Gilmer	65.00	37.00	18.00
65	Robert Nussbaumer	65.00	37.00	18.00
67	Bobby Layne	250.00	125.00	65.00
70	Herb Siegert	65.00	37.00	18.00
74	Tony Minisi	65.00	37.00	18.00
79	Steve Van Buren	150.00	75.00	45.00
81	Perry Moss	65.00	37.00	18.00
89	Bob Waterfield	200.00	100.00	50.00
90	Jack Jacobs	65.00	37.00	18.00
95	Kenny Washington	65.00	37.00	18.00
101	Pat Harder	65.00	37.00	18.00
110	William Swiacki	65.00	37.00	18.00
118	Fred Davis	65.00	37.00	18.00
126	Jay Rhodemyre	65.00	37.00	18.00
134	Chuck Bednarik	250.00	125.00	65.00
144	George Savitsky	65.00	37.00	18.00
150	Bulldog Turner	250.00	125.00	65.00

1983 Leaf Football Facts Booklets

Leaf produced one Football Facts booklet for each NFL team. The unnumbered booklets were packaged in boxes of Leaf bubble gum and included team history and statistics.

		NM/M	NM	E
Complete Set (28):		70.00	52.00	28.00
Common Player:		3.00	2.25	1.25
1	Atlanta Falcons	3.00	2.25	1.25
2	Baltimore Colts	3.00	2.25	1.25
3	Buffalo Bills	3.00	2.25	1.25
4	Chicago Bears	6.00	4.50	2.50
5	Cincinnati Bengals	3.00	2.25	1.25
6	Cleveland Browns	3.00	2.25	1.25
7	Dallas Cowboys	6.00	4.50	2.50
8	Denver Broncos	3.00	2.25	1.25
9	Detroit Lions	3.00	2.25	1.25
10	Green Bay Packers	6.00	4.50	2.50
11	Houston Oilers	3.00	2.25	1.25
12	Kansas City Chiefs	3.00	2.25	1.25
13	Los Angeles Rams	3.00	2.25	1.25
14	Miami Dolphins	6.00	4.50	2.50
15	Minnesota Vikings	3.00	2.25	1.25
16	New England Patriots	3.00	2.25	1.25
17	New Orleans Saints	3.00	2.25	1.25
18	New York Giants	3.00	2.25	1.25
19	New York Jets	3.00	2.25	1.25
20	Oakland Raiders	6.00	4.50	2.50
21	Philadelphia Eagles	3.00	2.25	1.25
22	Pittsburgh Steelers	6.00	4.50	2.50
23	St. Louis Cardinals	3.00	2.25	1.25
24	San Diego Chargers	3.00	2.25	1.25
25	San Francisco 49ers	6.00	4.50	2.50
26	Seattle Seahawks	3.00	2.25	1.25
27	Tampa Bay Buccaneers	3.00	2.25	1.25
28	Washington Redskins	6.00	4.50	2.50

1961 Lions Jay Publishing

Measuring approximately 5" x 7", the 12-card set showcases black-and-white photos of players in the vintage football card poses. The blank-backed cards were sold in 12-card packs for 25 cents. The cards were unnumbered.

		NM	E	VG
Complete Set (12):		65.00	32.00	19.50
Common Player:		5.00	2.50	1.50
1	Carl Brettschneider	5.00	2.50	1.50
2	Howard Cassady	6.00	3.00	1.75
3	Gail Cogdill	5.00	2.50	1.50
4	Jim Gibbons	6.00	3.00	1.75
5	Alex Karras	12.00	6.00	3.50
6	Yale Lary	10.00	5.00	3.00
7	Jim Martin	5.00	2.50	1.50
8	Earl Morrall	8.00	4.00	2.50
9	Jim Ninowski	6.00	3.00	1.75
10	Nick Pietrosante	6.00	3.00	1.75
11	Joe Schmidt	10.00	5.00	3.00
12	George Wilson	5.00	2.50	1.50

1966 Lions Marathon Oil

The 5" x 7" photos showcase black-and-white photos on the front, surrounded by white borders. The player's name, position and Detroit Lions are printed under the photo. The backs are unnumbered and blank.

		NM	E	VG
Complete Set (7):		42.00	21.00	12.60
Common Player:		5.00	2.50	1.50
1	Gail Cogdill	5.00	2.50	1.50
2	John Gordy	5.00	2.50	1.50
3	Alex Karras	15.00	7.50	4.50
4	Ron Kramer	6.00	3.00	1.75
5	Milt Plum	8.00	4.00	2.50
6	Wayne Rasmussen	5.00	2.50	1.50
7	Daryl Sanders	5.00	2.50	1.50

1986 Lions Police

Measuring 2-5/8" x 4-1/8", this 14-card police set is sponsored by Oscar Mayer, WJR/WHYT, Detroit Lions, Claussen, Pontiac Police Athletic League and the Detroit Crime Prevention Section. Card fronts have the player's name, uniform number and position in a box at the bottom center, while the Lions' logo is at the top center. A white border surrounds the photo. The card backs have the player's name, bio and highlights in a box on the left of the horizontal backed cards. A safety tip is located on the right.

		NM/M	NM	E
Complete Set (14):		5.00	3.75	2.00
Common Player:		.50	.40	.20
1	William Gay	.50	.40	.20
2	**Pontiac Silverdome**	.60	.45	.25
3	Leonard Thompson	.60	.45	.25
4	Eddie Murray	1.00	.70	.40
5	Eric Hipple	1.00	.70	.40
6	James Jones	.75	.60	.30
7	Darryl Rogers (CO)	.50	.40	.20
8	Chuck Long	.75	.60	.30
9	Garry James	.60	.45	.25
10	Michael Cofer	.60	.45	.25
11	Jeff Chadwick	.60	.45	.25
12	Jimmy Williams	.50	.40	.20
13	Keith Dorney	.50	.40	.20
14	Bobby Watkins	.50	.40	.20

1987 Lions Police

Measuring 2-5/8" x 4-1/8", the 14-card set is sponsored by Oscar Mayer, WJR/WHYT, Claussen, Detroit Lions, Pontiac Police Athletic League and the Detroit Crime Prevention Section. The card fronts have the Lions and NFL logos at the top, with the photo in the center. The player's name, uniform number and position are printed inside a box at the bottom center. The Oscar Mayer and Claussen logos are in the lower corners of the card front. The card backs include a cartoon in the upper left, with the player's highlights. The upper left has a safety tip.

		NM/M	NM	E
Complete Set (14):		5.00	3.75	2.00
Common Player:		.40	.30	.15
1	Michael Cofer, Vernon			
	Maxwell, William Gay	.50	.40	.20
2	Rich Strenger	.40	.30	.15
3	Keith Ferguson	.40	.30	.15
4	James Jones	.50	.40	.20
5	Jeff Chadwick	.50	.40	.20
6	Devon Mitchell	.40	.30	.15
7	Eddie Murray	.75	.60	.30
8	Reggie Rogers	.50	.40	.20
9	Chuck Long	.60	.45	.25
10	Jimmie Giles	.60	.45	.25
11	Eric Williams	.40	.30	.15
12	Lomas Brown	.50	.40	.20
13	Jimmy Williams	.40	.30	.15
14	Garry James	.50	.40	.20

1988 Lions Police

Measuring 2-5/8" x 4-1/8", the 14-card set boasts 13 single-player cards which feature veterans. The remaining card has three of the Lions' top three 1988 draft picks. The card fronts have the Lions logo under the photo, which is opposite the 1987 Lions Police set. The card backs have the standard career highlights and safety tips.

		NM/M	NM	E
Complete Set (14):		5.00	3.75	2.00
Common Player:		.50	.40	.20
1	Rob Rubick	.50	.40	.20
2	Paul Butcher	.50	.40	.20
3	Pete Mandley	.60	.45	.25
4	Jimmy Williams	.50	.40	.20
5	Harvey Salem	.50	.40	.20
6	Chuck Long	.60	.45	.25
7	Pat Carter, Bennie			
	Blades, Chris Spielman	1.00	.70	.40

8	Jerry Ball	.75	.60	.30
9	Lomas Brown	.60	.45	.25
10	Dennis Gibson	.50	.40	.20
11	Jim Arnold	.50	.40	.20
12	Michael Cofer	.50	.40	.20
13	James Jones	.60	.45	.25
14	Steve Mott	.50	.40	.20

1989 Lions Police

Measuring 2-5/8" x 4-1/8", the 12-card set has the Lions logo and NFL shields at the top. The player's name, uniform number and position are printed in a box at the bottom, sandwiched between Oscar Mayer and Claussen logos. The backs feature a cartoon in the upper left, with a highlight directly under it. The horizontal backs also include a safety tip in the upper right. A WWJ logo is printed at the bottom left, with the card number located at bottom center. The cards are printed on thin paper stock. These cards were distributed in Michigan and Ontario.

		NM/M	NM	E
Complete Set (12):		14.00	10.50	5.50
Common Player:		.35	.25	.14
1	George Jamison	.35	.25	.14
2	Wayne Fontes (CO)	.75	.60	.30
3	Kevin Glover	.35	.25	.14
4	Chris Spielman	1.00	.70	.40
5	Eddie Murray	.75	.60	.30
6	Bennie Blades	.75	.60	.30
7	Joe Milinichik	.35	.25	.14
8	Michael Cofer	.35	.25	.14
9	Jerry Ball	.50	.40	.20
10	Dennis Gibson	.35	.25	.14
11	Barry Sanders	10.00	7.50	4.00
12	Jim Arnold	.35	.25	.14

1990 Lions Police

Measuring 2-5/8" x 4-1/8", the 12-card set includes the player's name and position at the bottom center, with his uniform number printed in much larger type. The Oscar Mayer and Claussen logos are in the lower left and right corners, respectively. The card backs have the player's name at the top, with a drawing of him and highlight directly under. A "Little Oscar" safety tip is included in the lower left. The card number is in the lower right, along with the WWJ Radio logo.

		NM/M	NM	E
Complete Set (12):		5.00	3.75	2.00
Common Player:		.35	.25	.14
1	William White	.35	.25	.14
2	Chris Spielman	.75	.60	.30
3	Rodney Peete	.75	.60	.30
4	Jimmy Williams	.35	.25	.14
5	Bennie Blades	.50	.40	.20
6	Barry Sanders	3.00	2.25	1.25
7	Jerry Ball	.50	.40	.20
8	Richard Johnson	.50	.40	.20
9	Michael Cofer	.35	.25	.14
10	Lomas Brown	.50	.40	.20
11	Joe Schmidt, Andre			
	Ware, Wayne Fontes	.50	.40	.20
12	Eddie Murray	.50	.40	.20

1991 Lions Police

Measuring 2-5/8" x 4-1/8", the 12-card set was available through Michigan police officers. The yellow-bordered cards feature a color action photo, with the Oscar Mayer logo in the lower left, the player's name in the lower center and Lions helmet in the lower right. Above and below the player's name are blue horizontal lines. Card backs include a player photo at the top, with his position and name below it. A Little Oscar safety tip is in the lower left. The cards are numbered and are located in the lower right. The WWJ Radio logo is in the lower right.

		NM/M	NM	E
Complete Set (12):		5.00	3.75	2.00
Common Player:		.35	.25	.14

1	Mel Gray	.50	.40	.20
2	Ken Dallafior	.35	.25	.14
3	Chris Spielman	.50	.40	.20
4	Bennie Blades	.50	.40	.20
5	Robert Clark	.50	.40	.20
6	Eric Andolsek	.50	.40	.20
7	Rodney Peete	.75	.60	.30
8	William White	.35	.25	.14
9	Lomas Brown	.50	.40	.20
10	Jerry Ball	.50	.40	.20
11	Michael Cofer	.35	.25	.14
12	Barry Sanders	3.00	2.25	1.25

1964 Lions White Border

Measuring 7-3/8" x 9-3/8", the 24-card set includes black-and-white photos that are bordered in white. The player's name and position, along with the Detroit Lions, are printed under the photo. The unnumbered cards could have been released in many series, as later cards have a date stamped on the otherwise blank backs.

		NM	E	VG
	Complete Set (24):	90.00	45.00	27.00
	Common Player:	4.00	2.00	1.25
1	Dick Compton	4.00	2.00	1.25
2	Larry Ferguson	4.00	2.00	1.25
3	Dennis Gaubatz	4.00	2.00	1.25
4	Jim Gibbons	5.00	2.50	1.50
5	John Gonzaga	4.00	2.00	1.25
6	John Gordy	5.00	2.50	1.50
7	Tom Hall	4.00	2.00	1.25
8	Roger LaLonde	4.00	2.00	1.25
9	Dan LaRose	4.00	2.00	1.25
10	Yale Lary	10.00	5.00	3.00
11	Dan Lewis	5.00	2.50	1.50
12	Gary Lowe	4.00	2.00	1.25
13	Bruce Maher	5.00	2.50	1.50
14	Hugh McInnis	4.00	2.00	1.25
15	Max Messner	4.00	2.00	1.25
16	Floyd Peters	6.00	3.00	1.75
17	Daryl Sanders	4.00	2.00	1.25
18	Joe Schmidt	12.00	6.00	3.50
19	Bob Scholtz	4.00	2.00	1.25
20	James Simon	4.00	2.00	1.25
21	J.D. Smith	5.00	2.50	1.50
22	Bill Quinlan	4.00	2.00	1.25
23	Bob Whitlow	4.00	2.00	1.25
24	Sam Williams	4.00	2.00	1.25

1990 Little Big Leaguers

Boyhood photos and the highlights of the player's early athletic career are included in this 45-card set. The book, published by Simon and Schuster, included five 8-1/2" x 11" sheets, which included nine perforated cards. The card fronts included a black-and-white photo of the athlete as a child. A white border surrounds the card, with the player's name printed in a blue band at the top and "Little Football Big Leaguers" printed in a blue band at the bottom. The backs include the player's name, position, team, bio and write-up. The cards are unnumbered.

		NM/M	NM	E
	Complete Set (45):	40.00	30.00	16.00
	Common Player:	.50	.40	.20
1	Troy Aikman	10.00	7.50	4.00
2	Morten Andersen	.50	.40	.20
3	Jerry Ball	.50	.40	.20
4	Carl Banks	.75	.60	.30
5	Bennie Blades	.50	.40	.20
6	Brian Blades	.75	.60	.30
7	Joey Browner	.50	.40	.20
8	Keith Byars	.75	.60	.30
9	Anthony Carter	.75	.60	.30
10	Deron Cherry	.50	.40	.20
11	Roger Craig	.75	.60	.30
12	John Elway	7.00	5.25	2.75
13	Doug Flutie	1.00	.70	.40
14	Tim Goad	.50	.40	.20
15	Bob Golic	.50	.40	.20
16	Dino Hackett	.50	.40	.20
17	Dan Hampton	.75	.60	.30
18	Bobby Hebert	.75	.60	.30
19	Darryl Henley	.50	.40	.20
20	Wes Hopkins	.50	.40	.20
21	Hank Ilesic	.50	.40	.20
22	Tunch Ilkin	.50	.40	.20
23	Perry Kemp	.50	.40	.20
24	Bernie Kosar	.75	.60	.30
25	Mike Lansford	.50	.40	.20
26	Shawn Lee	.50	.40	.20
27	Charles Mann	.75	.60	.30
28	Dan Marino	14.00	10.50	5.50
29	Bruce Matthews	.75	.60	.30
30	Clay Matthews	.75	.60	.30
31	Freeman McNeil	.75	.60	.30
32	Warren Moon	2.00	1.50	.80
33	Anthony Munoz	.75	.60	.30

34	Andre Reed	1.00	.70	.40
35	Andre Rison	.75	.60	.30
36	Phil Simms	.75	.60	.30
37	Mike Singletary	.75	.60	.30
38	Rohn Stark	.50	.40	.20
39	Kelly Stouffer	.50	.40	.20
40	Vinny Testaverde	.75	.60	.30
41	Doug Williams	.50	.40	.20
42	Marc Wilson	.50	.40	.20
43	Craig Wolfley	.50	.40	.20
44	Ron Wolfley	.50	.40	.20
45	Steve Young	7.00	5.25	2.75

1981 Louisville Police

		NM/M	NM	E
	Complete Set (64):	125.00	94.00	50.00
	Common Player:	1.00	.70	.40
1	**Title Card SP** (Catch That Cardinal Spirit)	50.00	37.00	20.00
2	Bob Weber (CO)	1.00	.70	.40
3	**Assistant Coaches**	1.00	.70	.40
4	Jay Trautwein	1.00	.70	.40
5	Darrell Wimberly	1.00	.70	.40
6	Jeff Van Camp	1.00	.70	.40
7	Joe Welch	1.00	.70	.40
8	Fred Blackmon	1.00	.70	.40
9	Lamar "Toot" Evans	1.00	.70	.40
10	Tom Blair	1.00	.70	.40
11	Joe Kader	1.00	.70	.40
12	Mike Trainor	1.00	.70	.40
13	Richard Tharpe	1.00	.70	.40
14	Gene Hagan	1.00	.70	.40
15	Greg Jones	1.00	.70	.40
16	Leon Williams	1.00	.70	.40
17	Ellsworth Larkins	1.00	.70	.40
18	Sebastian Curry	1.00	.70	.40
19	Frank Minnifield	6.00	4.50	2.50
20	Roger Clay	1.00	.70	.40
21	Mark Blasinsky	1.00	.70	.40
22	Mike Cruz	1.00	.70	.40
23	David Arthur	1.00	.70	.40
24	Johnny Unitas (In front background, list of Cardinals who played pro ball)	15.00	11.00	6.00
25	John DeMarco	1.00	.70	.40
26	Eric Rollins	1.00	.70	.40
27	Jack Pok	1.00	.70	.40
28	Pete McCartney	1.00	.70	.40
29	Mark Clayton	15.00	11.00	6.00
30	Jeff Hortert	1.00	.70	.40
31	Pete Bowen	1.00	.70	.40
32	Robert Niece	1.00	.70	.40
33	Todd McMahan	1.00	.70	.40
34	John Wall	1.00	.70	.40
35	Kelly Stickrod	1.00	.70	.40
36	Jim Miller	1.00	.70	.40
37	Tom Moore	1.00	.70	.40
38	Kurt Knop	1.00	.70	.40
39	Mark Musgrave	1.00	.70	.40
40	Tony Campbell	1.00	.70	.40
41	Mark Wilson	1.00	.70	.40
42	Robert Mitchell	1.00	.70	.40
43	Courtney Jeter	1.00	.70	.40
44	Wayne Taylor	1.00	.70	.40
45	Jeff Speedy	1.00	.70	.40
46	Donald Craft	1.00	.70	.40
47	Glenn Hunter	1.00	.70	.40
48	**1981 Louisville Schedule**	1.00	.70	.40
49	Greg Hickman	1.00	.70	.40
50	Nate Dozier	1.00	.70	.40
51	Pat Patterson	1.00	.70	.40
52	Scott Gannon	1.00	.70	.40
53	Dean May	1.00	.70	.40
54	David Hatfield	1.00	.70	.40
55	Mike Nuzzolese	1.00	.70	.40
56	John Ayers	1.00	.70	.40
57	Lamar Cummins	1.00	.70	.40
58	Bill Olsen (AD)	1.00	.70	.40
59	**Tailgating**	1.00	.70	.40
60	**Football Complex**	1.00	.70	.40
61	**Marching Band**	1.00	.70	.40
62	**Cheerleaders**	1.00	.70	.40
63	**Administration Bldg.**	1.00	.70	.40
64	**Cardinal Bird**	1.00	.70	.40

1990 Louisville Smokey

		NM/M	NM	E
	Complete Set (16):	25.00	18.50	10.00
	Common Player:	1.25	.90	.50
1	Greg Brohm	1.25	.90	.50
2	Jeff Brohm	1.50	1.25	.60
3	Pete Burkey	1.25	.90	.50
4	Mike Flores	1.25	.90	.50
5	Dan Gangwer	1.25	.90	.50
6	Reggie Johnson	1.50	1.25	.60

7	Scott McAllister	1.25	.90	.50
8	Ken McKay	1.25	.90	.50
9	Browning Naglo	4.00	3.00	1.50
10	Ed Reynolds	1.25	.90	.50
11	Mark Sander	1.25	.90	.50
12	Howard Schnellenberger (CO)	5.00	3.75	2.00
13	Ted Washington	2.50	2.00	1.00
14	Klaus Wilmsmeyer	2.00	1.50	.80
15	**Cardinal Bird** (Mascot)	1.25	.90	.50
16	**Cardinal Stadium**	1.25	.90	.50

1985 LSU Police

		NM/M	NM	E
	Complete Set (16):	8.00	6.00	3.25
	Common Player:	.50	.40	.20
1	Mitch Andrews	.50	.40	.20
2	Bill Arnsparger (CO)	.75	.60	.30
3	Roland Barbay	.50	.40	.20
4	Michael Brooks	1.00	.70	.40
5	Shawn Burks	.50	.40	.20
6	Tommy Clapp	.50	.40	.20
7	Matt DeFrank	.50	.40	.20
8	Kevin Guidry	.50	.40	.20
9	Dalton Hilliard	1.50	1.25	.60
10	Garry James	.75	.60	.30
11	Norman Jefferson	.50	.40	.20
12	Rogie Magee	.50	.40	.20
13	**Mike the Tiger** (Mascot)	.50	.40	.20
14	Craig Rathjen	.50	.40	.20
15	Jeff Wickersham	.75	.60	.30
16	Karl Wilson	.75	.60	.30

1986 LSU Police

		NM/M	NM	E
	Complete Set (16):	8.00	6.00	3.25
	Common Player:	.50	.40	.20
1	Nacho Albergamo	.50	.40	.20
2	Eric Andolsek	1.00	.70	.40
3	Bill Arnsparger (CO)	.75	.60	.30
4	Roland Barbay	.50	.40	.20
5	Michael Brooks	1.00	.70	.40
6	Chris Carrier	.50	.40	.20
7	Toby Caston	1.00	.70	.40
8	Wendell Davis	1.50	1.25	.60
9	Kevin Guidry	.50	.40	.20
10	John Hazard	.50	.40	.20
11	Oliver Lawrence	.50	.40	.20
12	Rogie Magee	.50	.40	.20
13	Sam Martin	.75	.60	.30
14	Darrell Phillips	.50	.40	.20
15	Steve Rehage	.50	.40	.20
16	Ron Sancho	.75	.60	.30

1987 LSU Police

		NM/M	NM	E
	Complete Set (16):	10.00	7.50	4.00
	Common Player:	.50	.40	.20
1	Nacho Albergamo	.50	.40	.20
2	Eric Andolsek	.75	.60	.30
3	Mike Archer (CO)	.75	.60	.30
4	David Browndyke	.50	.40	.20
5	Chris Carrier	.50	.40	.20
6	Wendell Davis	1.00	.70	.40
7	Matt DeFrank	.50	.40	.20
8	Nicky Hazard	.50	.40	.20
9	Eric Hill	1.00	.70	.40
10	Tommy Hodson	1.50	1.25	.60
11	Greg Jackson	1.00	.70	.40
12	Brian Kinchen	1.00	.70	.40
13	Darren Malbrough	.50	.40	.20
14	Sam Martin	.50	.40	.20
15	Ron Sancho	.50	.40	.20
16	Harvey Williams	3.50	2.75	1.50

1988 LSU Police

		NM/M	NM	E
	Complete Set (16):	8.00	6.00	3.25
	Common Player:	.50	.40	.20
1	Mike the Tiger (Mascot)	.50	.40	.20
2	Mike Archer (CO)	.75	.60	.30
3	Tommy Hodson	1.50	1.25	.60
4	Harvey Williams	2.50	2.00	1.00
5	David Browndyke	.50	.40	.20
6	Karl Dunbar	.50	.40	.20
7	Eddie Fuller	.50	.40	.20
8	Mickey Guidry	.50	.40	.20
9	Greg Jackson	.75	.60	.30
10	Clint James	.50	.40	.20
11	Victor Jones	.50	.40	.20
12	Tony Moss	.50	.40	.20
13	Ralph Norwood	.50	.40	.20
14	Darrell Phillips	.50	.40	.20
15	Ruffin Rodrigue	.50	.40	.20
16	Ron Sancho	.50	.40	.20

1989 LSU Police

		NM/M	NM	E
	Complete Set (16):	8.00	6.00	3.25
	Common Player:	.50	.40	.20
1	Mike the Tiger (Mascot)	.50	.40	.20
2	David Browndyke	.50	.40	.20
3	Mike Archer (CO)	.75	.60	.30
4	Ruffin Rodrigue (68)	.50	.40	.20
5	Marc Boutte (95)	1.00	.70	.40
6	Clint James (70)	.50	.40	.20
7	Jimmy Young (5)	.50	.40	.20
8	Alvin Lee (26)	.50	.40	.20
9	Eddie Fuller (33)	.50	.40	.20
10	Tiger Stadium	.50	.40	.20
11	Harvey Williams (22)	2.00	1.50	.80
12	Verge Ausberry (98)	.50	.40	.20
13	Karl Dunbar (63)	.50	.40	.20
14	Tommy Hodson (13)	1.25	.90	.50
15	Tony Moss (6)	.50	.40	.20
16	The Golden Girls (Cheerleaders)	.75	.60	.30

1983 LSU Sunbeam

		NM/M	NM	E
	Complete Set (100):	12.00	9.00	4.75
	Common Player:	.10	.08	.04
1	1958 LSU National Championship Team	.20	.15	.08
2	Abe Mickal	.10	.08	.04
3	Carlos Carson	.20	.15	.08
4	Charles Alexander	.20	.15	.08
5	Steve Ensminger	.10	.08	.04
6	Ken Kavanaugh Sr.	.20	.15	.08
7	Bert Jones	.50	.40	.20
8	David Woodley	.20	.15	.08
9	Jerry Marchand	.10	.08	.04
10	Clyde Lindsey	.10	.08	.04
11	James Britt	.10	.08	.04
12	Warren Rabb	.20	.15	.08
13	Mike Hillman	.10	.08	.04
14	Nelson Stokley	.10	.08	.04
15	Abner Wimberly	.10	.08	.04
16	Terry Robiskie	.20	.15	.08
17	Steve Van Buren	.30	.25	.12
18	Doug Moreau	.20	.15	.08
19	George Tarasovic	.10	.08	.04
20	Billy Cannon	.30	.25	.12
21	Jerry Stovall	.20	.15	.08
22	Joe Labruzzo	.10	.08	.04
23	Mickey Mangham	.10	.08	.04
24	Craig Burns	.10	.08	.04
25	Y.A. Tittle	.75	.60	.30
26	Wendell Harris	.20	.15	.08
27	Leroy Labat	.10	.08	.04
28	Hokie Gajan	.20	.15	.08
29	Mike Williams	.10	.08	.04
30	Sammy Grezaffi	.20	.15	.08
31	Clinton Burrell	.10	.08	.04
32	Orlando McDaniel	.10	.08	.04
33	George Bevan	.10	.08	.04
34	Johnny Robinson	.20	.15	.08
35	Billy Masters	.10	.08	.04
36	J.W. Brodnax	.10	.08	.04
37	Tommy Casanova	.20	.15	.08
38	Fred Miller	.10	.08	.04
39	George Rice	.10	.08	.04
40	Earl Gros	.20	.15	.08
41	Lynn LeBlanc	.10	.08	.04
42	Jim Taylor	.40	.30	.15
43	Joe Tumenello	.10	.08	.04
44	Tommy Davis	.20	.15	.08
45	Alvin Dark	.30	.25	.12
46	Richard Picou	.10	.08	.04
47	Chaille Percy	.10	.08	.04
48	John Garlington	.20	.15	.08
49	Mike Morgan	.10	.08	.04
50	Charles "Bo" Strange	.10	.08	.04
51	Max Fugler	.30	.25	.12
52	Don Schwab	.10	.08	.04
53	Dennis Gaubatz	.20	.15	.08
54	Jimmy Field	.10	.08	.04
55	Warren Capone	.10	.08	.04
56	Albert Richardson	.10	.08	.04
57	Charley Cusiman	.10	.08	.04
58	Brad Davis	.10	.08	.04
59	Gaynell "Gus" Kinchen	.10	.08	.04
60	Roy "Moonie" Winston	.20	.15	.08
61	Mike Anderson	.10	.08	.04
62	Jesse Fatherree	.10	.08	.04
63	Gene "Red" Knight	.10	.08	.04
64	Tyler LaFauci	.10	.08	.04
65	Emile Fournet	.10	.08	.04
66	Gaynell "Gus" Tinsley	.20	.15	.08
67	Remi Prudhomme	.20	.15	.08
68	Marvin "Moose" Stewart	.10	.08	.04
69	Jerry Guillot	.10	.08	.04
70	Steve Cassidy	.10	.08	.04
71	Bo Harris	.20	.15	.08
72	Robert Dugas	.10	.08	.04
73	Malcolm Scott	.10	.08	.04
74	Charles "Pinky" Rohm	.10	.08	.04
75	Gerald Keigley	.10	.08	.04
76	Don Alexander	.10	.08	.04
77	A.J. Duhe	.20	.15	.08
78	Ronnie Estay	.10	.08	.04
79	John Wood	.10	.08	.04
80	Andy Hamilton	.20	.15	.08
81	Jay Michaelson	.10	.08	.04
82	Kenny Konz	.20	.15	.08
83	Tracy Porter	.10	.08	.04
84	Billy Truax	.20	.15	.08
85	Alan Risher	.10	.08	.04
86	John Adams	.10	.08	.04
87	Tommy Neck	.10	.08	.04
88	Brad Boyd	.10	.08	.04
89	Greg LaFleur	.10	.08	.04
90	Bill Elko	.10	.08	.04
91	Binks Miciotto	.10	.08	.04
92	Lew Sibley	.10	.08	.04
93	Willie Teal	.10	.08	.04
94	Lyman White	.10	.08	.04
95	Chris Williams	.10	.08	.04
96	Sid Fournet	.10	.08	.04
97	Leonard Marshall	.20	.15	.08
98	Ramsey Dardar	.10	.08	.04
99	Kenny Bordelon	.10	.08	.04
100	Fred "Skinny" Hall	.10	.08	.04

M

1980 Marketcom

These white-bordered posters, measuring 5-1/2" x 8-1/2", feature 50 NFL stars. The player's name appears at the top of the card; Marketcom, the set's producer, is credited in the bottom lower right corner. A white facsimile autograph also appears on the card front. The back has the player's name at the top, and a card number on the bottom (Mini-Poster 1 of 50, etc.). Marketcom, of St. Louis, sold the posters in packs of five.

		NM	E	VG
	Complete Set (50):	25.00	12.50	7.50
	Common Player:	.50	.25	.15
1	Ottis Anderson	1.00	.50	.30
2	Brian Sipe	.60	.30	.20
3	Lawrence McCutcheon	.60	.30	.20
4	Ken Anderson	1.25	.60	.40
5	Roland Harper	.50	.25	.15
6	Chuck Foreman	.75	.40	.25
7	Gary Danielson	.50	.25	.15
8	Wallace Francis	.50	.25	.15
9	John Jefferson	.75	.40	.25
10	Charlie Waters	.75	.40	.25
11	Jack Ham	1.00	.50	.30
12	Jack Lambert	1.25	.60	.40
13	Walter Payton	5.00	2.50	1.50
14	Bert Jones	1.00	.50	.30
15	Harvey Martin	.75	.40	.25
16	Jim Hart	.60	.30	.20
17	Craig Morton	.75	.40	.25
18	Reggie McKenzie	.50	.25	.15
19	Keith Wortman	.50	.25	.15
20	Otis Armstrong	.75	.40	.25
21	Steve Grogan	.75	.40	.25
22	Jim Zorn	.75	.40	.25
23	Bob Griese	2.00	1.00	.60
24	Tony Dorsett	2.00	1.00	.60
25	Wesley Walker	.75	.40	.25
26	Dan Fouts	2.00	1.00	.60
27	Dan Dierdorf	1.00	.50	.30
28	Steve Bartkowski	.75	.40	.25
29	Archie Manning	1.00	.50	.30
30	Randy Gradishar	.75	.40	.25
31	Randy White	1.25	.60	.40
32	Joe Theismann	2.00	1.00	.60
33	Tony Galbreath	.50	.25	.15
34	Cliff Harris	.75	.40	.25
35	Ray Guy	1.00	.50	.30
36	Dave Casper	.75	.40	.25
37	Ron Jaworski	.75	.40	.25
38	Greg Pruitt	.75	.40	.25
39	Ken Burrough	.60	.30	.20
40	Robert Brazile	.60	.30	.20
41	Pat Haden	1.00	.50	.30
42	Dan Pastorini	.60	.30	.20
43	Lee Roy Selmon	.75	.40	.25
44	Franco Harris	2.00	1.00	.60
45	Jack Youngblood	1.25	.60	.40
46	Terry Bradshaw	5.00	2.50	1.50
47	Roger Staubach	6.00	3.00	1.75
48	Earl Campbell	5.00	2.50	1.50
49	Phil Simms	3.00	1.50	.90
50	Delvin Williams	.50	.25	.15

1981 Marketcom

The 1981 Marketcom posters are the first set to include detailed information on the back of the poster. Along with biographical and statistical information for 1980 and for the player's career, a comprehensive summary of the player's accomplishments is provided. A poster number is also given. Each poster, measuring 5-1/2" x 8-1/2", has a full-color action photo of the player on the front, along with his facsimile signature. His name is listed in the upper left corner.

		NM/M	NM	E
	Complete Set (50):	32.00	24.00	13.00
	Common Player:	.50	.40	.20
1	Ottis Anderson	.75	.60	.30
2	Brian Sipe	.60	.45	.25
3	Rocky Bleier	.75	.60	.30
4	Ken Anderson	1.00	.70	.40
5	Roland Harper	.50	.40	.20
6	Steve Furness	.50	.40	.20
7	Gary Danielson	.50	.40	.20

8	Wallace Francis	.60	.45	.25
9	John Jefferson	.60	.45	.25
10	Charlie Waters	75	.60	.30
11	Jack Ham	.75	.60	.30
12	Jack Lambert	1.25	.90	.50
13	Walter Payton	5.00	3.75	2.00
14	Bert Jones	1.00	.70	.40
15	Harvey Martin	.75	.60	.30
16	Jim Hart	.75	.60	.30
17	Craig Morton	.75	.60	.30
18	Reggie McKenzie	.50	.40	.20
19	Keith Wortman	.50	.40	.20
20	Joe Greene	1.50	1.25	.60
21	Steve Grogan	.75	.60	.30
22	Jim Zorn	.75	.60	.30
23	Bob Griese	2.00	1.50	.80
24	Tony Dorsett	2.50	2.00	1.00
25	Wesley Walker	.75	.60	.30
26	Dan Fouts	2.00	1.50	.80
27	Dan Dierdorf	1.00	.70	.40
28	Steve Bartkowski	.75	.60	.30
29	Archie Manning	1.00	.70	.40
30	Randy Gradishar	.75	.60	.30
31	Randy White	1.25	.90	.50
32	Joe Theismann	2.00	1.50	.80
33	Tony Galbreath	.50	.40	.20
34	Cliff Harris	.75	.60	.30
35	Ray Guy	1.00	.70	.40
36	Joe Ferguson	.75	.60	.30
37	Ron Jaworski	.75	.60	.30
38	Greg Pruitt	.75	.60	.30
39	Ken Burrough	.60	.45	.25
40	Robert Brazile	.50	.40	.20
41	Pat Haden	1.00	.70	.40
42	Ken Stabler	2.00	1.50	.80
43	Lee Roy Selmon	.75	.60	.30
44	Franco Harris	2.00	1.50	.80
45	Jack Youngblood	1.25	.90	.50
46	Terry Bradshaw	6.00	4.50	2.50
47	Roger Staubach	6.00	4.50	2.50
48	Earl Campbell	4.00	3.00	1.50
49	Phil Simms	1.50	1.25	.60
50	Delvin Williams	.50	.40	.20

1982 Marketcom

These 50 mini-posters from Marketcom are similar in design to the previous year's issue. Each poster is 5-1/2" x 8-1/2" and has a full-color action photo on the front, along with a facsimile signature in white letters. The backs are similar to the backs of the 1981 posters - they have a detailed career summary and biographical information, plus statistics for the player's career and 1981 season. In addition to a number, the back also says "St. Louis - Marketcom - Series C".

		NM/M	NM	E
Complete Set (48):		175.00	100.00	85.00
Common Player:		2.00	1.50	.80
1	Joe Ferguson	2.50	2.00	1.00
2	Kellen Winslow	3.00	2.25	1.25
3	Jim Hart	2.50	2.00	1.00
4	Archie Manning	4.00	3.00	1.50
5	Earl Campbell	15.00	11.00	6.00
6	Wallace Francis	2.00	1.50	.80
7	Randy Gradishar	2.50	2.00	1.00
8	Ken Stabler	5.00	3.75	2.00
9	Danny White	3.00	2.25	1.25
10	Jack Ham	4.00	3.00	1.50
11	Lawrence Taylor	20.00	15.00	8.00
12	Eric Hipple	2.00	1.50	.80
13	Ron Jaworski	2.50	2.00	1.00
14	George Rogers	2.00	1.50	.80
15	Jack Lambert	5.00	3.75	2.00
16	Randy White	5.00	3.75	2.00
17	Terry Bradshaw	20.00	15.00	8.00
18	Ray Guy	3.00	2.25	1.25
19	Rob Carpenter	2.00	1.50	.80
20	Reggie McKenzie	2.00	1.50	.80
21	Tony Dorsett	7.50	5.75	3.00
22	Wesley Walker	2.50	2.00	1.00
23	Tommy Kramer	2.50	2.00	1.00
24	Dwight Clark	3.00	2.25	1.25
25	Franco Harris	5.00	3.75	2.00
26	Craig Morton	2.50	2.00	1.00
27	Harvey Martin	2.50	2.00	1.00
28	Jim Zorn	2.50	2.00	1.00
29	Steve Bartkowski	2.50	2.00	1.00
30	Joe Theismann	5.00	3.75	2.00
31	Dan Dierdorf	3.00	2.25	1.25
32	Walter Payton	25.00	18.50	10.00
33	John Jefferson	2.50	2.00	1.00
34	Phil Simms	5.00	3.75	2.00
35	Lee Roy Selmon	2.50	2.00	1.00
36	Joe Montana	40.00	30.00	16.00
37	Robert Brazile	2.00	1.50	.80
38	Steve Grogan	2.50	2.00	1.00
39	Dave Logan	2.00	1.50	.80
40	Ken Anderson	4.00	3.00	1.50

41	Richard Todd	2.50	2.00	1.00
42	Jack Youngblood	3.00	2.25	1.25
43	Ottis Anderson	3.00	2.25	1.25
44	Brian Sipe	2.50	2.00	1.00
45	Mark Gastineau	2.50	2.00	1.00
46	Mike Pruitt	2.00	1.50	.80
47	Cris Collinsworth	2.50	2.00	1.00
48	Dan Fouts	5.00	3.75	2.00

1982 Marketcom Cowboys

Measuring 5-1/2" x 8-1/2", these nine NFL mini-posters feature the player's name at the top left, with a color photo dominating the white-bordered fronts. The player's facsimile autograph also appears on the photo. The unnumbered card backs showcase the player's name at the top, with his bio directly underneath. His career highlights are also included. "St. Louis Marketcom" is printed in the lower right of the back. Some experts say a 10th card may exist.

		NM/M	NM	E
Complete Set (9):		50.00	37.00	20.00
Common Player:		5.00	3.75	2.00
1	Bob Breunig	5.00	3.75	2.00
2	Pat Donovan	5.00	3.75	2.00
3	Michael Downs	5.00	3.75	2.00
4	Butch Johnson	6.00	4.50	2.50
5	Harvey Martin	6.00	4.50	2.50
6	Timmy Newsome	5.00	3.75	2.00
7	Drew Pearson	6.00	4.50	2.50
8	Danny White	8.00	6.00	3.25
9	Randy White	10.00	7.50	4.00

1977 Marketcom Test

With posters measuring approximately 5-1/2" x 8-1/2", the set boasts only two confirmed mini-posters. The unnumbered posters each have folds in them. They are blank-backed, except for a Marketcom 1977 copyright tag line at the bottom.

		NM	E	VG
Complete Set (2):		100.00	75.00	40.00
Common Player:		50.00	25.00	15.00
1	Greg Pruitt	50.00	25.00	15.00
2	Jack Youngblood	50.00	25.00	15.00

1978 Marketcom Test

These unnumbered posters, featuring 32 NFL stars, measure 5-1/2" x 8-1/2". The fronts feature full-color photos, along with the player's name in the upper left corner. Marketcom, which produced the set, is listed in the lower right corner. The backs are blank.

		NM	E	VG
Complete Set (32):		225.00	112.00	67.00
Common Player:		4.00	2.00	1.25
(1)	Otis Armstrong	6.00	3.00	1.75
(2)	Steve Bartkowski	9.00	4.50	2.75
(3)	Terry Bradshaw	25.00	12.50	7.50
(4)	Earl Campbell	25.00	12.50	7.50
(5)	Dave Casper	5.00	2.50	1.50
(6)	Dan Dierdorf	10.00	5.00	3.00
(7)	Dan Fouts	15.00	7.50	4.50
(8)	Tony Galbreath	4.00	2.00	1.25
(9)	Randy Gradishar	7.00	3.50	2.00
(10)	Bob Griese	12.00	6.00	3.50
(11)	Steve Grogan	5.00	2.50	1.50
(12)	Ray Guy	6.00	3.00	1.75
(13)	Pat Haden	8.00	4.00	2.50
(14)	Jack Ham	7.00	3.50	2.00
(15)	Cliff Harris	7.00	3.50	2.00
(16)	Franco Harris	8.00	4.00	2.50
(17)	Jim Hart	5.00	2.50	1.50
(18)	Ron Jaworski	5.00	2.50	1.50
(19)	Bert Jones	10.00	5.00	3.00
(20)	Jack Lambert	10.00	5.00	3.00
(21)	Reggie McKenzie	4.00	2.00	1.25
(22)	Karl Mecklenberg	7.00	3.50	2.00
(23)	Craig Morton	5.00	2.50	1.50
(24)	Dan Pastorini	4.00	2.00	1.25
(25)	Walter Payton	25.00	12.50	7.50
(26)	Lee Roy Selmon	5.00	2.50	1.50
(27)	Roger Staubach	25.00	12.50	7.50
(28)	Joe Theismann (misspelled Theisman)	9.00	4.50	2.75
(29)	Wesley Walker	7.00	3.50	2.00
(30)	Randy White	7.00	3.50	2.00
(31)	Jack Youngblood	12.00	6.00	3.50
(32)	Jim Zorn	5.00	2.50	1.50

1991 Maryland HS Big 33

		NM/M	NM	E
Complete Set (34):		18.00	13.50	7.25
Common Player:		.75	.60	.30
1	Asim Penny	1.00	.70	.40
2	Louis Jason	1.00	.70	.40

3	Mark McCain	1.00	.70	.40
4	Matthew Byrne	.75	.60	.30
5	Mike Gillesple	.75	.60	.30
6	Ricky Rowe	.75	.60	.30
7	David DeArmas	1.00	.70	.40
8	Duane Ashman	.75	.60	.30
9	James Cunningham	.75	.60	.30
10	Keith Kormanik	.75	.60	.30
11	Leonard Green	.75	.60	.30
12	Larry Washington	.75	.60	.30
13	Raphael Wall	.75	.60	.30
14	Kai Hebron	.75	.60	.30
15	Coy Gibbs	1.00	.70	.40
16	Lenard Marcus	.75	.60	.30
17	John Taliaferro	1.00	.70	.40
18	J.C. Price	.75	.60	.30
19	Jamal Cox	1.00	.70	.40
20	Rick Budd	.75	.60	.30
21	Shaun Marshall	.75	.60	.30
22	Allan Jenkins	.75	.60	.30
23	Bryon Turner	.75	.60	.30
24	Ryan Foran	.75	.60	.30
25	John Summerday	.75	.60	.30
26	Joshua Austin	.75	.60	.30
27	Emile Palmer	.75	.60	.30
28	John Teter	.75	.60	.30
29	John Kennedy	.75	.60	.30
30	Clarence Collins	.75	.60	.30
31	Daryl Smith	.75	.60	.30
32	David Wilkins	.75	.60	.30
33	David Thomas	.75	.60	.30
34	Russell Thomas	1.00	.70	.40

1969 Maryland Team Sheets

		NM	E	VG
Complete Set (6):		25.00	12.50	7.50
Common Panel:		6.00	3.00	1.75
1	Bill Backus, Lou Bracken, Sonny Demczuk, Roland Merritt, Rich Slaninka, Ralph Sonntag, Mike Stubljar, Jim Stull	6.00	3.00	1.75
2	Bill Bell CO, George Boutselis CO, Albert Ferguson CO, James Kehoe CO, Roy Lester CO, Dim Montero CO, Lee Royer CO	6.00	3.00	1.75
3	Pat Burke, John Dyer, Craig Gienger, Tony Greene, Bob MacBride, Bill Meister, Russ Nolan, Ray Soporowski	6.00	3.00	1.75
4	Steve Ciambor, Kenny Dutton, Dan Kecman, Bob Mahnic, Len Santacroce, David Seifert, Len Spicer, Rick Stoll	6.00	3.00	1.75
5	Bob Colbert, John Dill, Henry Gareis, Bill Grant, Glenn Kubany, Bill Reilly, Wally Stalnaker, Gary Vansickler	6.00	3.00	1.75
6	Paul Fitzpatrick, Larry Marshall, Tom Miller, Will Morris, Dennis O'Hara, Scott Shank, Jeff Shugars, Al Thomas	6.00	3.00	1.75

1971 Mattel Mini-Records

Measuring approximately 2-1/2" in diameter, each of the 17 discs in the set were to be played on a specially made Mattel mini-record player. Some discs were packaged four to a pack, like Olsen, Hayes, Sayers and Brodie or Mackey, Lamonica, Simpson and Butkus. Other packs showcased eight discs and a Joe Namath or Bart Starr booklet. The discs have color artwork on one side and the recording on the reverse. The recording side has the player's name and "Instant Replay."

		NM	E	VG
Complete Set (17):		200.00	100.00	60.00
Common Player:		4.00	2.00	1.25
1	Donny Anderson	4.00	2.00	1.25
2	Lem Barney	6.00	3.00	1.75
3	John Brodie (DP)	6.00	3.00	1.75
4	Dick Butkus (DP)	15.00	7.50	4.50
5	Bob Hayes (DP)	6.00	3.00	1.75
6	Sonny Jurgenson	10.00	5.00	3.00
7	Alex Karras	10.00	5.00	3.00
8	Leroy Kelly	9.00	4.50	2.75

		NM	E	VG
9	Daryle Lamonica (DP)	4.00	2.00	1.25
10	John Mackey (DP)	6.00	3.00	1.75
11	Earl Morrall	4.00	2.00	1.25
12	Joe Namath	50.00	25.00	15.00
13	Merlin Olsen (DP)	6.00	3.00	1.75
14	Alan Page	9.00	4.50	2.75
15	Gale Sayers (DP)	20.00	10.00	6.00
16	O.J. Simpson (DP)	25.00	12.50	7.50
17	Bart Starr	30.00	15.00	9.00
NNO	**Record Player**	100.00	50.00	30.00

1894 Mayo

Thirty-five Ivy League college football players are included in this 35-card set. The card fronts include a sepia-toned photo and a black border. The player's name, college and Mayo Cut Plug advertisement are listed at the bottom. The unnumbered cards measure 1-5/8" x 2-7/8".

		NM	E	VG
Complete Set (35):		87,500	40,000	20,000
Common Player:		3,250	1,625	975.00
1	R Acton (Harvard)	3,250	1,625	975.00
2	George Adee (Yale AA94)	4,000	2,000	1,200
3	R. Armstrong (Yale)	3,250	1,625	975.00
4	H.W. Barnett (Princeton)	3,250	1,625	975.00
5	A.M. Beale (Harvard)	3,250	1,625	975.00
6	Anson Beard (Yale)	3,250	1,625	975.00
7	Charles Brewer (Harvard AA92/93/95)	4,500	2,250	1,350.00
8	Brown (Princeton)	3,250	1,625	975.00
9	Burt (Princeton)	3,250	1,625	975.00
10	Frank Butterworth (Yale AA93/94)	4,000	2,000	1,200
11	Eddie Crowdis (Princeton)	3,250	1,625	975.00
12	Robert Emmons (Harvard)	3,250	1,625	975.00
13	M.G. Gonterman (UER Harvard) (Misspelled Gouterman)	3,225	1,625	975.00
14	G.A. Grey (Harvard)	3,250	1,625	975.00
15	John Greenway (Yale)	4,000	2,000	1,200
16	William Hickok (Yale AA93/94)	4,500	2,250	1,350
17	Frank Hinkey (Yale AA91/92/93/94)	4,500	2,250	1,350
18	Augustus Holly (Princeton)	3,250	1,625	975.00
19	Langdon Lea (Princeton AA93/94/95)	5,500	2,750	1,650
20	W.C. Mackie (Harvard)	3,250	1,625	975.00
21	T.J. Manahan (Harvard)	3,250	1,625	975.00
22	Jim McCrea (Yale)	3,250	1,625	975.00
23	Frank Morse (Princeton AA93)	4,500	2,250	1,350
24	Fred Murphy (Yale AA95/96)	4,500	2,250	1,350
25	Poe (Princeton thought to be Neilson or Arthur)	6,000	3,000	1,800
26	Dudley Riggs (Princeton AA95)	6,000	3,000	1,800
27	Phillip Stillman (Yale AA94)	4,500	2,225	1,350
28	Knox Taylor (Princeton)	3,250	1,675	975.00
29	Brinck Thorne (Yale AA95)	4,500	2,250	1,350
30	Thomas Trenchard (Princeton AA93)	4,500	2,250	1,350
31	William Ward (Princeton)	3,250	1,675	975.00
32	Bert Waters (Harvard AA92/94)	4,500	2,250	1,350
33	Arthur Wheeler (Princeton AA92/93/94)	4,500	2,250	1,350
34	Edgar Wrightington (Harvard AA96)	3,250	1,625	975.00
35	**Anonymous** (John Dunlop- Harvard)	60,000	30,000	18,000

1986 McDonald's All-Stars

Measuring 3-1/16" x 4-11/16" with the tab intact or 3-1/16" x 3-5/8" without, this 30-card set was for participating McDonald's outside of an NFL market. Released over four weeks, the set featured different colored tabs -- with blue (first week), black or gray (second week), gold or orange (third week) and green (fourth week). The backs feature McDonald's All-Star Team printed at the top. Also included on the backs are the player's name, jersey number, career and 1985 highlights and a 1986 copyright date.

		NM/M	NM	E
Complete Set (Blue):		6.00	4.50	2.50
Complete Set (Black):		6.00	4.50	2.50
Complete Set (Gold):		6.00	4.50	2.50
Complete Set (Green):		6.00	4.50	2.50
Common Player:		.15	.11	.06
9	Jim McMahon	.35	.25	.14
11	Phil Simms	.35	.25	.14
13	Dan Marino	2.50	2.00	1.00
14	Dan Fouts	.35	.25	.14
16	Joe Montana	2.00	1.50	.80
20A	Deron Cherry	.15	.11	.06
20B	Joe Morris	.15	.11	.06
32	Marcus Allen	.35	.25	.14
33	Roger Craig	.25	.20	.10
34A	Kevin Mack	.15	.11	.06
35B	Walter Payton	1.75	1.25	.70
42	Gerald Riggs	.15	.11	.06
45	Kenny Easley	.15	.11	.06
47A	Joey Browner	.15	.11	.06
47B	LeRoy Irvin	.15	.11	.06
52	Mike Webster	.25	.20	.10
54A	E.J. Junior	.15	.11	.06
54B	Randy White	.25	.20	.10
56	Lawrence Taylor	.35	.25	.14
63	Mike Munchak	.15	.11	.06
66	Joe Jacoby	.15	.11	.06
73	John Hannah	.25	.20	.10
75A	Chris Hinton	.15	.11	.06
75B	Rulon Jones	.15	.11	.06
75C	Howie Long	.25	.20	.10
78	Anthony Munoz	.25	.20	.10
81	Art Monk	.35	.25	.14
82A	Ozzie Newsome	.35	.25	.14
82B	Mike Quick	.15	.11	.06
99	Mark Gastineau	.15	.11	.06

1986 McDonald's Atlanta Falcons

Released over a four-week time span at Atlanta-area McDonald's, the 24-card set measures 3-1/16" x 4-11/16" with the tab and 3-1/16" x 3-5/8" without. The card fronts are anchored with a color photo, with the McDonald's logo in the upper left and Falcons' helmet in the upper right. The NFL shield and NFLPA logo are located at the bottom, left and right respectively. The player's name, number and position are printed below the photo. The card backs include the player's name, number, position, bio and highlights. Each week featured a different colored tab: blue (first), black or gray (second), gold or orange (third) and green (fourth). The values listed are for cards with the tabs intact.

		NM/M	NM	E
Complete Set (Blue):		60.00	45.00	24.00
Complete Set (Black):		200.00	150.00	80.00
Complete Set (Gold):		40.00	30.00	16.00
Complete Set (Green):		15.00	11.00	6.00
Common Player:		.60	.45	.25
3	Rick Donnelly	.60	.45	.25
16	Dave Archer (DP)	1.00	.70	.40
18	Mick Luckhurst	.60	.45	.25
23	Bobby Butler	.60	.45	.25
26	James Britt (DP)	.60	.45	.25
37	Kenny Johnson	.60	.45	.25
39	Cliff Austin	.60	.45	.25
42	Gerald Riggs	.75	.60	.30
50	Buddy Curry	.60	.45	.25
56	Al Richardson	.60	.45	.25
57	Jeff Van Note	.75	.60	.30
58	David Frye	.60	.45	.25
61	John Scully	.60	.45	.25
62	Brett Miller	.60	.45	.25
74	Mike Pitts	.60	.45	.25
76	Mike Gann	.60	.45	.25
77	Rick Bryan	.60	.45	.25
78	Mike Kenn	.75	.60	.30
79	Bill Fralic	1.00	.70	.40
81	Billy Johnson	.75	.60	.30
82	Stacey Bailey (DP)	.60	.45	.25
87	Cliff Benson (DP)	.60	.45	.25
88	Arthur Cox	.60	.45	.25
89	Charlie Brown (DP)	.75	.60	.30

1985 McDonald's Bears

This 32-card set picturing only Chicago Bears was issued by McDonald's in the Chicago area, apparently to test the concept of using football cards as a promotion. The full-color cards have three different tab colors (blue, orange, yellow), each referring to a specific week in the playoffs or Super Bowl. The cards measure approximately 4-1/2" x 5-7/8" with the tab intact. The prices below are for cards with the tab intact. Cards without the tabs have little collector value and are worth considerably less. Because of space limitations, only players with a significant value over common price are listed individually. Players not listed are worth approximately the common price (or perhaps slightly above for minor stars). The individual values listed are for the least expensive color tabs (yellow or orange). Cards with blue tabs are worth about twice as much as values listed. Card numbers refer to a player's uniform number.

		NM/M	NM	E
Complete Set (Blue):		45.00	34.00	18.00
Complete Set (Orange):		25.00	18.50	10.00
Complete Set (Yellow):		20.00	15.00	8.00
Common Player:		.50	.40	.20
4	Steve Fuller	.75	.60	.30
6	Kevin Butler	1.00	.70	.40
8	Maury Buford	.50	.40	.20
9	Jim McMahon	2.50	2.00	1.00
21	Leslie Frazier	.50	.40	.20
22	Dave Duerson	.50	.40	.20
26	Matt Suhey	.75	.60	.30
27	Mike Richardson	.50	.40	.20
29	Dennis Gentry	.50	.40	.20
33	Calvin Thomas	.50	.40	.20
34	Walter Payton	7.00	5.25	2.75
45	Gary Fencik	.75	.60	.30
50	Mike Singletary	2.50	2.00	1.00
55	Otis Wilson	.50	.40	.20
58	Wilber Marshall	1.00	.70	.40
62	Mark Bortz	.50	.40	.20
63	Jay Hilgenberg	.75	.60	.30
72	William Perry	1.25	.90	.50
73	Mike Hartenstine	.50	.40	.20
74	Jim Covert	.75	.60	.30
75	Stefan Humphries	.50	.40	.20
76	Steve McMichael	1.00	.70	.40
78	Keith Van Horne	.50	.40	.20
80	Tim Wrightman	.50	.40	.20
82	Ken Margerum	.50	.40	.20
83	Willie Gault	1.00	.70	.40
85	Dennis McKinnon	.75	.60	.30
87	Emery Moorehead	.50	.40	.20
95	Richard Dent	2.00	1.50	.80
99	Dan Hampton	2.00	1.50	.80
	Mike Ditka (CO)	2.50	2.00	1.00
	Buddy Ryan (ACO)	1.50	1.25	.60

1976 McDonald's Buffalo Bills

Given away one per week in November with a sandwich purchase, these 8" x 10" color photocards have a player portrait with facsimile autograph on front. Backs have personal data, stats and ads for McDonald's and WBEN-TV. A fourth card was apparently planned but not issued.

		NM	E	VG
Complete Set (3):		75.00	37.50	22.00
Common Player:		30.00	15.00	9.00
(1)	Bob Chandler	30.00	15.00	9.00
(2)	Joe Ferguson	35.00	17.50	10.50
(3)	Reggie McKenzie	35.00	17.50	10.50

1986 McDonald's Buffalo Bills

Measuring 3-1/16" x 4-11/16" with the tab and 3-1/16" x 3-5/8" without, the 24-card set was distributed over four weeks of the 1986 season in the Buffalo area. In the top corners of the color action photo on the card front were the McDonald's logo and Bills helmet. At the bottom corners of the photo were the NFL shield and NFLPA logo. The player's name, number and position appear under the photo. The card backs have the player's name, jersey number and highlights. Each week featured a different colored tab: blue (first), black or gray (second), gold or orange (third) and green (fourth).

	NM/M	NM	E
Complete Set (Blue):	150.00	112.00	60.00
Complete Set (Black):	30.00	22.00	12.00
Complete Set (Gold):	15.00	11.00	6.00
Complete Set (Green):	15.00	11.00	6.00
Common Player:	.75	.60	.30

		NM/M	NM	E
4	John Kidd	.75	.60	.30
7	Bruce Mathison	.75	.60	.30
11	Scott Norwood	1.00	.70	.40
22	Steve Freeman	.75	.60	.30
26	Charles Romes	.75	.60	.30
28	Greg Bell (DP)	1.00	.70	.40
29	Derrick Burroughs (DP)	.75	.60	.30
43	Martin Bayless (DP)	.75	.60	.30
51	Jim Ritcher	1.00	.70	.40
54	Eugene Marve	.75	.60	.30
55	Jim Haslett	.75	.60	.30
57	Lucius Sanford	.75	.60	.30
63	Justin Cross	.75	.60	.30
65	Tim Vogler	.75	.60	.30
70	Joe Devlin	.75	.60	.30
72	Ken Jones	.75	.60	.30
76	Fred Smerlas	1.00	.70	.40
77	Ben Williams	1.00	.70	.40
78	Bruce Smith	5.00	3.75	2.00
80	Jerry Butler (DP)	1.00	.70	.40
83	Andre Reed	5.00	3.75	2.00
85	Chris Burkett (DP)	1.00	.70	.40
87	Eason Ramson	.75	.60	.30
95	Sean McNanie	.75	.60	.30

1986 McDonald's Chicago Bears

Released in the Chicago area, the 24-card set was released over four weeks at participating McDonald's. The tab colors were as follows: blue (first week), black or gray (second), gold or orange (third) and green (fourth). With the tab intact, the cards measure 3-1/16" x 4-11/16" and 3-1/16" x 3-5/8" without. The card fronts have the McDonald's logo in the upper left, Bears helmet in the upper right, NFL shield in the lower left and the NFLPA logo in the lower right. The card backs have "Super Bowl Collectors Edition" at the top. The player's name, uniform number, bio and 1986 and career highlights are also listed on the backs.

		NM/M	NM	E
	Complete Set (Blue):	15.00	11.00	6.00
	Complete Set (Black):	7.50	5.75	3.00
	Complete Set (Gold):	7.50	5.75	3.00
	Complete Set (Green):	7.50	5.75	3.00
	Common Player:	.30	.25	.12
6	Kevin Butler (DP)	.40	.30	.15
8	Maury Buford	.30	.25	.12
9	Jim McMahon (DP)	1.25	.90	.50
22	Dave Duerson	.30	.25	.12
26	Matt Suhey	.40	.30	.15
27	Mike Richardson	.30	.25	.12
34	Walter Payton (DP)	1.75	1.25	.70
45	Gary Fencik	.40	.30	.15
50	Mike Singletary (DP)	1.25	.90	.50
55	Otis Wilson	.30	.25	.12
57	Tom Thayer	.30	.25	.12
58	Wilber Marshall	.50	.40	.20
62	Mark Bortz (DP)	.30	.25	.12
63	Jay Hilgenberg	.40	.30	.15
72	William Perry (DP)	.50	.40	.20
74	Jim Covert	.40	.30	.15
76	Steve McMichael	.50	.40	.20
78	Keith Van Horne	.30	.25	.12
80	Tim Wrightman	.30	.25	.12
82	Ken Margerum	.30	.25	.12
83	Willie Gault	.50	.40	.20
87	Emery Moorehead	.30	.25	.12
95	Richard Dent	1.00	.70	.40
99	Dan Hampton	1.00	.70	.40

1986 McDonald's Cincinnati Bengals

The Cincinnati area received the benefits of this 24-card set, which was part of the McDonald's promotion of 1986. The card fronts showcase the McDonald's logo in the upper left, with the Cincinnati helmet in the upper right. The NFL shield and NFLPA logos appear in the bottom left and right, respectively, of the color action photo. Card backs feature the player's number, name, bio, stats and highlights. The cards measure 3-1/16" x 4-11/16" with the tab and 3-1/16" x 3-5/8" without. Released over four weeks, the first week's cards had blue tabs, second had black or gray, third had gold or orange and the fourth week tabs were green.

		NM/M	NM	E
	Complete Set (Blue):	25.00	18.50	10.00
	Complete Set (Black):	12.50	9.50	5.00
	Complete Set (Gold):	12.50	9.50	5.00
	Complete Set (Green):	12.50	9.50	5.00
	Common Player:	.50	.40	.20
7	Boomer Esiason	2.50	2.00	1.00
14	Ken Anderson (DP)	1.00	.70	.40
20	Ray Horton	.60	.45	.25
21	James Brooks (DP)	1.00	.70	.40
22	James Griffin	.50	.40	.20
28	Larry Kinnebrew	.60	.45	.25
34	Louis Breeden (DP)	.50	.40	.20
37	Robert Jackson	.50	.40	.20
52	Charles Alexander (DP)	.50	.40	.20
52	Dave Rimington	.60	.45	.25
57	Reggie Williams	.75	.60	.30
65	Max Montoya	.60	.45	.25
69	Tim Krumrie	.75	.60	.30
73	Eddie Edwards	.60	.45	.25
74	Brian Blados (DP)	.50	.40	.20
77	Mike Wilson	.50	.40	.20
78	Anthony Munoz	1.25	.90	.50
79	Ross Browner	.60	.45	.25
80	Cris Collinsworth	1.00	.70	.40
81	Eddie Brown (DP)	.75	.60	.30
82	Rodney Holman	.60	.45	.25
83	M.L. Harris	.50	.40	.20
90	Emanuel King	.50	.40	.20
91	Carl Zander	.50	.40	.20

1986 McDonald's Cleveland Browns

Issued over four weeks of the 1986 season in the Cleveland area, the 24-card set measure 3-1/16" x 4-11/16" with the tab and 3-1/16" x 3-5/8" without. The card fronts feature a color photo, with the McDonald's logo in the upper left and Browns helmet in the upper right. The NFL shields and NFLPA logo are on the bottom corners, left and right respectively. The card backs have the player's name, jersey number, bio and highlights. Each week's cards featured different colored tabs: blue (first), black or gray (second), gold or orange (third) and green (fourth).

	NM/M	NM	E
Complete Set (Blue):	10.00	7.50	4.00
Complete Set (Black):	6.00	4.50	2.50
Complete Set (Gold):	6.00	4.50	2.50
Complete Set (Green):	6.00	4.50	2.50
Common Player:	.25	.20	.10

		NM/M	NM	E
9	Matt Bahr (DP)	.25	.20	.10
18	Gary Danielson	.25	.20	.10
19	Bernie Kosar (DP)	1.75	1.25	.70
27	Al Gross	.25	.20	.10
29	Hanford Dixon	.35	.25	.14
31	Frank Minnifield	.35	.25	.14
34	Kevin Mack	.50	.40	.20
37	Chris Rockins	.25	.20	.10
44	Earnest Byner	.75	.60	.30
51	Eddie Johnson	.25	.20	.10
55	Curtis Weathers	.25	.20	.10
56	Chip Banks (DP)	.25	.20	.10
57	Clay Matthews	.50	.40	.20
60	Tom Cousineau	.25	.20	.10
61	Mike Baab (DP)	.25	.20	.10
63	Cody Risien	.35	.25	.14
77	Rickey Bolden (DP)	.25	.20	.10
78	Carl Hairston	.25	.20	.10
79	Bob Golic	.35	.25	.14
82	Ozzie Newsome	1.00	.70	.40
84	Glen Young	.25	.20	.10
85	Clarence Weathers	.25	.20	.10
86	Brian Brennan (DP)	.35	.25	.14
96	Reggie Camp	.25	.20	.10

1986 McDonald's Dallas Cowboys

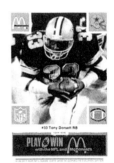

Issued over four weeks at Dallas-area McDonald's, the 25-card set measures 3-1/16" x 4-11/16" with the tab and 3-1/16" x 3-5/8" without. The card fronts boast a color photo, with the McDonald's logo in the upper left and Dallas helmet in the upper right. The NFL shield and NFLPA logo are located in the lower corners, left and right respectively. The player's name, number and position are printed under the photo. The card backs feature the player's name, number, bio and highlights. Each week's cards featured a different colored tab: blue (first), black or gray (second), gold or orange (third) and green (fourth).

		NM/M	NM	E
	Complete Set (Blue):	10.00	7.50	4.00
	Complete Set (Black):	10.00	7.50	4.00
	Complete Set (Gold):	10.00	7.50	4.00
	Complete Set (Green):	10.00	7.50	4.00
	Common Player:	.25	.20	.10
1	Rafael Septien	.25	.20	.10
11	Danny White	.50	.40	.20
24	Everson Walls	.35	.25	.14
26	Michael Downs (DP)	.25	.20	.10
27	Ron Fellows	.25	.20	.10
30	Timmy Newsome	.25	.20	.10
33	Tony Dorsett (DP)	1.50	1.25	.60
34	Herschel Walker	2.00	1.50	.80
40	Bill Bates (DP)	.50	.40	.20
47	Dexter Clinkscale (DP)	.25	.20	.10
50	Jeff Rohrer	.25	.20	.10
54	Randy White	.75	.60	.30
56	Eugene Lockhart	.35	.25	.14
58	Mike Hegman	.25	.20	.10
61	Jim Cooper (DP)	.25	.20	.10
63	Glen Titensor	.25	.20	.10
64	Tom Rafferty	.25	.20	.10
65	Kurt Peterson	.25	.20	.10
72	Ed "Too Tall" Jones	.75	.60	.30
75	Phil Pozderac	.25	.20	.10
77	Jim Jeffcoat	.50	.40	.20
78	John Dutton	.35	.25	.14
80	Tony Hill	.35	.25	.14
82	Mike Renfro	.25	.20	.10
84	Doug Cosbie (DP)	.25	.20	.10

1986 McDonald's Denver Broncos

Released over four weeks in the Denver area during the 1986 season, this 24-card set measured 3-1/16" x 4-11/16" with the tab and 3-1/16" x 3-5/8" without. The card fronts and backs followed the same format as the other McDonald's sets of that season. Each week's cards featured a different colored tab: blue (first), black or gray (second), gold or orange (third) and green (fourth).

		NM/M	NM	E
	Complete Set (Blue):	25.00	18.50	10.00
	Complete Set (Black):	8.00	6.00	3.25
	Complete Set (Gold):	8.00	6.00	3.25
	Complete Set (Green):	8.00	6.00	3.25
	Common Player:	.30	.25	.12
3	Rich Karlis	.30	.25	.12
7	John Elway	3.50	2.75	1.50
20	Louis Wright	.40	.30	.15
22	Tony Lily	.30	.25	.12
23	Sammy Winder	.40	.30	.15
30	Steve Sewell	.40	.30	.15
31	Mike Harden	.40	.30	.15
43	Steve Foley	.40	.30	.15
47	Gerald Wilhite	.40	.30	.15
49	Dennis Smith	.50	.40	.20
50	Jim Ryan	.30	.25	.12
54	Keith Bishop (DP)	.30	.25	.12
55	Rick Dennison (DP)	.30	.25	.12
57	Tom Jackson	1.25	.90	.50
60	Paul Howard	.30	.25	.12
64	Bill Bryan (DP)	.30	.25	.12
68	Rubin Carter (DP)	.30	.25	.12
70	Dave Studdard	.30	.25	.12
75	Rulon Jones	.40	.30	.15
77	Karl Mecklenburg	.60	.45	.25
79	Barney Chavous (DP)	.30	.25	.12
81	Steve Watson	.40	.30	.15
82	Vance Johnson	.60	.45	.25
84	Clint Sampson	.30	.25	.12

1986 McDonald's Detroit Lions

Released over a four-week time span at Detroit-area McDonald's, the 24-card set measures 3-1/16" x 4-11/16" with the tab and 3-1/16" x 3-5/8" without. The card fronts are anchored with a color photo, with the McDonald's logo in the upper left and Lions' helmet in the upper right. The NFL shield and NFLPA logo are located at the bottom, left and right respectively. The player's name, number and position are printed below the photo. The card backs include the player's name, number, position, bio and highlights. Each week featured a different colored tab: blue (first), black or gray (second), gold or orange (third) and green (fourth). The values listed are for cards which have the tabs intact.

		NM/M	NM	E
	Complete Set (Blue):	6.00	4.50	2.50
	Complete Set (Black):	6.00	4.50	2.50
	Complete Set (Gold):	6.00	4.50	2.50
	Complete Set (Green):	6.00	4.50	2.50
	Common Player:	.25	.20	.10
3	Eddie Murray	.35	.25	.14
11	Michael Black (DP)	.25	.20	.10
17	Eric Hipple	.35	.25	.14
20	Billy Sims	.50	.40	.20
21	Demetrious Johnson	.25	.20	.10
27	Bobby Watkins	.25	.20	.10
29	Bruce McNorton	.25	.20	.10
30	James Jones	.35	.25	.14
33	William Graham	.25	.20	.10
35	Alvin Hall	.25	.20	.10
39	Leonard Thompson	.35	.25	.14
50	August Curley (DP)	.25	.20	.10
52	Steve Mott	.25	.20	.10
55	Mike Cofer (DP)	.35	.25	.14
59	Jimmy Williams	.25	.20	.10
70	Keith Dorney (DP)	.25	.20	.10

71	Rich Strenger	.25	.20	.10
75	Lomas Brown (DP)	.35	.25	.14
76	Eric Williams	.25	.20	.10
79	William Gay	.25	.20	.10
82	Pete Mandley	.25	.20	.10
86	Mark Nichols	.25	.20	.10
87	David Lewis	.25	.20	.10
89	Jeff Chadwick (DP)	.25	.20	.10

1986 McDonald's Green Bay Packers

#12 Lynn Dickey QB

Released over a four-week time span at Green Bay-area McDonald's, the 24-card set measures 3-1/16" x 4-11/16" with the tab and 3-1/16" x 3-5/8" without. The card fronts are anchored with a color photo, with the McDonald's logo in the upper left and Packers' helmet in the upper right. The NFL shield and NFLPA logo are located at the bottom, left and right respectively. The player's name, number and position are printed below the photo. The card backs include the player's name, number, position, bio and highlights. Each week featured a different colored tab: blue (first), black or gray (second), gold or orange (third) and green (fourth). The values listed are for cards which have the tabs intact.

		NM/M	NM	E
	Complete Set (Blue):	6.00	4.50	2.50
	Complete Set (Black):	6.00	4.50	2.50
	Complete Set (Gold):	6.00	4.50	2.50
	Complete Set (Green):	6.00	4.50	2.50
	Common Player:	.25	.20	.10
10	Al Del Greco (DP)	.25	.20	.10
12	Lynn Dickey	.35	.25	.14
16	Randy Wright	.35	.25	.14
18	Jim Zorn	.35	.25	.14
22	Mark Lee	.25	.20	.10
26	Tim Lewis	.25	.20	.10
31	Gerry Ellis	.25	.20	.10
33	Jessie Clark (DP)	.25	.20	.10
37	Mark Murphy	.35	.25	.14
41	Tom Flynn	.25	.20	.10
42	Gary Ellerson	.25	.20	.10
55	Mike Douglass	.25	.20	.10
55	Randy Scott	.25	.20	.10
59	John Anderson (DP)	.25	.20	.10
67	Karl Swanke	.25	.20	.10
75	Ken Ruettgers	.25	.20	.10
76	Alphonso Carreker (DP)	.25	.20	.10
77	Mike Butler (DP)	.25	.20	.10
79	Donnie Humphrey	.25	.20	.10
82	Paul Coffman (DP)	.25	.20	.10
85	Phillip Epps	.35	.25	.14
90	Ezra Johnson	.25	.20	.10
91	Brian Noble	.35	.25	.14
94	Charles Martin	.25	.20	.10

1986 McDonald's Houston Oilers

Released over a four-week time span at Houston-area McDonald's, the 24-card set measures 3-1/16" x 4-11/16" with the tab and 3-1/16" x 3-5/8" without. The card fronts are anchored with a color photo, with the McDonald's logo in the upper left and Oilers' helmet in the upper right. The NFL shield and NFLPA logo are located at the bottom, left and right respectively. The player's name, number and position are printed below the photo. The card backs include the player's name, number, position, bio and highlights. Each week featured a different colored tab: blue (first), black or gray (second), gold or orange (third) and green (fourth). The values listed are for cards which have the tabs intact.

		NM/M	NM	E
	Complete Set (Blue):	12.00	9.00	4.75
	Complete Set (Black):	8.00	6.00	3.25
	Complete Set (Gold):	8.00	6.00	3.25
	Complete Set (Green):	8.00	6.00	3.25
	Common Player:	.30	.25	.12
1	Warren Moon	4.00	3.00	1.50
7	Tony Zendejas	.30	.25	.12

10	Oliver Luck	.40	.30	.15
21	Bo Eason	.30	.25	.12
23	Richard Johnson	.30	.25	.12
24	Steve Brown (DP)	.30	.25	.12
25	Keith Bostic (DP)	.30	.25	.12
29	Patrick Allen (DP)	.30	.25	.12
33	Mike Rozier	.50	.40	.20
40	Butch Woolfolk	.30	.25	.12
53	Avon Riley	.30	.25	.12
56	Robert Abraham (DP)	.30	.25	.12
63	Mike Munchak	.40	.30	.15
67	Mike Stensrud	.30	.25	.12
70	Doan Steinkuhler	.40	.30	.15
71	Richard Byrd (DP)	.30	.25	.12
73	Harvey Salem	.30	.25	.12
74	Bruce Matthews	.75	.60	.30
79	Ray Childress	.75	.60	.30
83	Tim Smith	.30	.25	.12
85	Drew Hill	.75	.60	.30
87	Jamie Williams	.30	.25	.12
91	Johnny Meads	.30	.25	.12
94	Frank Bush (DP)	.30	.25	.12

1986 McDonald's Indianapolis Colts

#25 Nesby Glasgow S

Released during a four-week time span at Indianapolis McDonald's, the 24-card set measures 3-1/16" x 4-11/16" with the tab and 3-1/16" x 3-5/8" without. Anchored with a color photo, the card fronts have a McDonald's logo in the upper left and a Colts' helmet in the upper right. The NFL shield and NFLPA logo are in the bottom corners, left and right respectively. The player's name, number and position are printed below the photo. The card backs showcase the player's name, number, bio and highlights. Each week's cards featured different colored tabs: blue (first), black or gray (second), gold or orange (third) and green (fourth).

		NM/M	NM	E
	Complete Set (Blue):	100.00	75.00	40.00
	Complete Set (Black):	20.00	15.00	8.00
	Complete Set (Gold):	15.00	11.00	6.00
	Complete Set (Green):	20.00	15.00	8.00
	Common Player:	.60	.45	.25
2	Raul Allegre (DP)	.60	.45	.25
3	Rohn Stark	.75	.60	.30
25	Nesby Glasgow	.60	.45	.25
27	Preston Davis	.60	.45	.25
32	Randy McMillian	.75	.60	.30
34	George Wonsley	.60	.45	.25
38	Eugene Daniel	.75	.60	.30
44	Owen Gill	.60	.45	.25
47	Leonard Coleman	.60	.45	.25
50	Duane Bickett (DP)	1.00	.70	.40
53	Ray Donaldson	.75	.60	.30
55	Barry Krauss	.60	.45	.25
64	Ben Utt	.60	.45	.25
66	Ron Solt	.60	.45	.25
72	Karl Baldischwiler (DP)	.60	.45	.25
75	Chris Hinton	.75	.60	.30
81	Pat Beach (DP)	.60	.45	.25
85	Matt Bouza (DP)	.60	.45	.25
87	Wayne Capers (DP)	.60	.45	.25
88	Robbie Martin	.60	.45	.25
92	Brad White	.60	.45	.25
93	Cliff Odom	.60	.45	.25
96	Blaise Winter	.60	.45	.25
98	Johnie Cooks	.60	.45	.25

1986 McDonald's Kansas City Chiefs

Released over a four-week time span at Kansas City area McDonald's, the 24-card set measures 3-1/16" x 4-11/16" with the tab and 3-1/16" x 3-5/8" without. Anchored with a color photo on the card front, the McDonald's logo is in the upper left and Chiefs' helmet in the upper right. The NFL shield and NFLPA logo are in the bottom corners, left and right respectively. The player's name, jersey number and position are located under the photo. The card backs have the player's name, jersey number, position, bio and career highlights. Each week's cards had different colored tabs: blue (first), black or gray (second), gold or orange (third) and green (fourth).

		NM/M	NM	E
Complete Set (Blue):		20.00	15.00	8.00
Complete Set (Black):		40.00	30.00	16.00
Complete Set (Gold):		20.00	15.00	8.00
Complete Set (Green):		20.00	15.00	8.00
Common Player:		.75	.60	.30
6	Jim Arnold (DP)	.75	.60	.30
8	Nick Lowery	1.00	.70	.40
9	Bill Kenney	.75	.60	.30
14	Todd Blackledge (DP)	1.00	.70	.40
20	Deron Cherry (DP)	1.25	.90	.50
29	Albert Lewis	1.50	1.25	.60
31	Kevin Ross	1.25	.90	.50
34	Lloyd Burruss (DP)	.75	.60	.30
41	Garcia Lane	.75	.60	.30
42	Jeff Smith	.75	.60	.30
43	Mike Pruitt	1.00	.70	.40
44	Herman Heard	.75	.60	.30
50	Calvin Daniels	.75	.60	.30
59	Gary Spani	.75	.60	.30
63	Bill Maas	.75	.60	.30
64	Bob Olderman	.75	.60	.30
66	Brad Budde (DP)	.75	.60	.30
67	Art Still	.75	.60	.30
72	David Lutz	.75	.60	.30
83	Stephone Paige	1.25	.90	.50
85	Jonathan Hayes	1.00	.70	.40
88	Carlos Carson (DP)	1.00	.70	.40
89	Henry Marshall	.75	.60	.30
97	Scott Radecic	.75	.60	.30

1986 McDonald's Los Angeles Raiders

Released over a four-week time span at Los Angeles-area McDonald's, the 24-card set measures 3-1/16" x 4-11/16" with the tab and 3-1/16" x 3-5/8" without. The card fronts are anchored with a color photo, with the McDonald's logo in the upper left and Raiders' helmet in the upper right. The NFL shield and NFLPA logo are located at the bottom, left and right respectively. The player's name, number and position are printed below the photo. The card backs include the player's name, number, position, bio and highlights. Each week featured a different colored tab: blue (first), black or gray (second), gold or orange (third) and green (fourth). The values listed are for cards which have the tabs intact.

		NM/M	NM	E
Complete Set (Blue):		20.00	15.00	8.00
Complete Set (Black):		10.00	7.50	4.00
Complete Set (Gold):		6.00	4.50	2.50
Complete Set (Green):		6.00	4.50	2.50
Common Player:		.25	.20	.10
1	Marc Wilson	.35	.25	.14
8	Ray Guy (DP)	.50	.40	.20
10	Chris Bahr (DP)	.25	.20	.10
16	Jim Plunkett	.50	.40	.20
22	Mike Haynes	.35	.25	.14
26	Vann McElroy	.25	.20	.10
27	Frank Hawkins	.25	.20	.10
32	Marcus Allen (DP)	1.50	1.25	.60
36	Mike Davis (DP)	.25	.20	.10
37	Lester Hayes	.35	.25	.14
46	Todd Christensen (DP)	.50	.40	.20

53	Rod Martin	.35	.25	.14
54	Reggie McKenzie	.25	.20	.10
55	Matt Millen	.35	.25	.14
70	Henry Lawrence	.25	.20	.10
71	Bill Pickel	.25	.20	.10
72	Don Mosebar	.35	.25	.14
73	Charley Hannah	.25	.20	.10
75	Howie Long	1.00	.70	.40
79	Bruce Davis (DP)	.25	.20	.10
84	Jessie Hester	.50	.40	.20
85	Dokie Williams	.25	.20	.10
91	Brad Van Pelt	.25	.20	.10
99	Sean Jones	.50	.40	.20

1986 McDonald's Los Angeles Rams

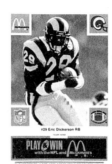

Released over a four-week time span at Los Angeles-area McDonald's, the 24-card set measures 3-1/16" x 4-11/16" with the tab and 3-1/16" x 3-5/8" without. The card fronts are anchored with a color photo, with the McDonald's logo in the upper left and Rams' helmet in the upper right. The NFL shield and NFLPA logo are located at the bottom, respectively. The player's name, number and position are printed below the photo. The card backs include the player's name, number, position, bio and highlights. Each week featured a different colored tab: first week (blue), second (black or gray), third (gold or orange) and fourth (green). The values listed are for cards which have the tabs intact.

		NM/M	NM	E
Complete Set (Blue):		9.00	6.75	3.50
Complete Set (Black):		6.00	4.50	2.50
Complete Set (Gold):		6.00	4.50	2.50
Complete Set (Green):		6.00	4.50	2.50
Common Player:		.25	.20	.10
1	Mike Lansford	.25	.20	.10
3	Dale Hatcher	.25	.20	.10
5	Dieter Brock (DP)	.25	.20	.10
20	Johnnie Johnson	.25	.20	.10
21	Nolan Cromwell (DP)	.35	.25	.14
22	Vince Newsome	.25	.20	.10
27	Gary Green	.25	.20	.10
29	Eric Dickerson (DP)	1.00	.70	.40
44	Mike Guman	.25	.20	.10
47	LeRoy Irvin	.35	.25	.14
50	Jim Collins (DP)	.25	.20	.10
54	Mike Wilcher	.25	.20	.10
55	Carl Ekern	.25	.20	.10
56	Doug Smith	.25	.20	.10
58	Mel Owens	.25	.20	.10
60	Dennis Harrah	.25	.20	.10
71	Reggie Doss (DP)	.25	.20	.10
72	Kent Hill	.25	.20	.10
75	Irv Pankey	.25	.20	.10
78	Jackie Slater	.50	.40	.20
80	Henry Ellard	.75	.60	.30
81	David Hill	.25	.20	.10
87	Tony Hunter	.25	.20	.10
89	Ron Brown (DP)	.35	.25	.14

1986 McDonald's Miami Dolphins

Issued over four weeks at Miami-area McDonald's, the 25-card set measure 3-1/16" x 4-11/16" with the tab and 3-1/16" x 3-5/8" without. Each card front is anchored with a color photo, with the McDonald's logo in the upper left and Miami helmet in the upper right. The NFL shield and NFLPA logo are in the bottom corners, left and right respectively. Below the photo are the player's name, number and position. The card backs showcase the player's name, number, position and highlights. Each week's cards featured a different colored tab: blue (first), black or gray (second), gold or orange (third) and green (fourth).

		NM/M	NM	E
Complete Set (Blue):		40.00	30.00	16.00
Complete Set (Black):		20.00	15.00	8.00
Complete Set (Gold):		20.00	15.00	8.00

Complete Set (Green):		20.00	15.00	8.00
Common Player:		.50	.40	.20
4	Reggie Roby	.75	.60	.30
7	Fuad Reveiz	.75	.60	.30
10	Don Strock	.75	.60	.30
13	Dan Marino	10.00	7.50	4.00
22	Tony Nathan	.75	.60	.30
23A	Joe Carter (ERR) (Photo actually Tony Nathan 22)	.75	.60	.30
23B	Joe Carter (COR)	.50	.40	.20
27	Lorenzo Hampton	.50	.40	.20
30	Ron Davenport	.50	.40	.20
43	Bud Brown (DP)	.50	.40	.20
47	Glenn Blackwood (DP)	.50	.40	.20
49	William Judson	.50	.40	.20
55	Hugh Green	.75	.60	.30
57	Dwight Stephenson	.75	.60	.30
58	Kim Bokamper (DP)	.50	.40	.20
59	Bob Brudzinski (DP)	.50	.40	.20
61	Roy Foster	.50	.40	.20
71	Mike Charles	.50	.40	.20
75	Doug Betters (DP)	.50	.40	.20
79	Jon Giesler	.50	.40	.20
83	Mark Clayton	2.00	1.50	.80
84	Bruce Hardy	.50	.40	.20
85	Mark Duper	1.00	.70	.40
89	Nat Moore	.75	.60	.30
91	Mack Moore	.50	.40	.20

1986 McDonald's Minnesota Vikings

Released over a four-week time span at Minneapolis-area McDonald's, the 24-card set measures 3-1/16" x 4-11/16" with the tab and 3-1/16" x 3-5/8" without. The card fronts are anchored with a color photo, with the McDonald's logo in the upper left and Vikings' helmet in the upper right. The NFL shield and NFLPA logo are located at the bottom, left and right respectively. The player's name, number and position are printed below the photo. The card backs include the player's name, number, position, bio and highlights. Each week featured a different colored tab: blue (first), black or gray (second), gold or orange (third) and green (fourth). The values listed are for cards which have the tabs intact.

		NM/M	NM	E
Complete Set (Blue):		45.00	34.00	18.00
Complete Set (Black):		30.00	22.00	12.00
Complete Set (Gold):		15.00	11.00	6.00
Complete Set (Green):		15.00	11.00	6.00
Common Player:		.60	.45	.25
8	Greg Coleman (DP)	.60	.45	.25
9	Tommy Kramer	.75	.60	.30
11	Wade Wilson	.75	.60	.30
20	Darrin Nelson	.75	.60	.30
23	Ted Brown (DP)	.60	.45	.25
37	Willie Teal	.60	.45	.25
39	Carl Lee	.75	.60	.30
46	Alfred Anderson (DP)	.60	.45	.25
47	Joey Browner (DP)	.75	.60	.30
55	Scott Studwell	.60	.45	.25
56	Chris Doleman	.75	.60	.30
59	Matt Blair (DP)	.75	.60	.30
67	Dennis Swilley	.60	.45	.25
68	Curtis Rouse	.60	.45	.25
75	Keith Millard	.75	.60	.30
76	Tim Irwin	.60	.45	.25
77	Mark Mullaney	.60	.45	.25
79	Doug Martin	.60	.45	.25
81	Anthony Carter (DP)	1.25	.90	.50
83	Steve Jordan	.75	.60	.30
87	Leo Lewis	.75	.60	.30
89	Mike Jones	.60	.45	.25
96	Tim Newton	.60	.45	.25
99	David Howard	.60	.45	.25

1986 McDonald's New England Patriots

Released over a four-week time span at New England-area McDonald's, the 24-card set measures 3-1/16" x 4-11/16" with the tab and 3-1/16" x 3-5/8" without. The card fronts are anchored with a color photo, with the McDonald's logo in the upper left and Patriots' helmet in the upper right. The NFL shield and NFLPA logo are located at the bottom, left and right respectively. The player's name, number and position are printed below the photo. The card backs include the player's name, number, position, bio and highlights. Each week featured a different colored tab: blue (first), black or gray (second), gold or orange (third) and green (fourth). The values listed are for cards which have the tabs intact.

		NM/M	NM	E
Complete Set (Blue):		6.00	4.50	2.50
Complete Set (Black):		6.00	4.50	2.50
Complete Set (Gold):		6.00	4.50	2.50
Complete Set (Green):		6.00	4.50	2.50
Common Player:		.25	.20	.10
3	Rich Camarillo (DP)	.25	.20	.10
11	Tony Eason (DP)	.35	.25	.14
14	Steve Grogan	.50	.40	.20
24	Robert Weathers	.25	.20	.10
26	Raymond Clayborn (DP)	.25	.20	.10
30	Mosi Tatupu	.25	.20	.10
31	Fred Marion	.25	.20	.10
32	Craig James	.50	.40	.20
33	Tony Collins (DP)	.35	.25	.14
38	Roland James	.25	.20	.10
42	Ronnie Lippett	.25	.20	.10
50	Larry McGrew	.25	.20	.10
55	Don Blackmon (DP)	.25	.20	.10
56	Andre Tippett	.50	.40	.20
57	Steve Nelson	.25	.20	.10
58	Pete Brock (DP)	.25	.20	.10
60	Garin Veris	.25	.20	.10
61	Ron Wooten	.25	.20	.10
73	John Hannah	.50	.40	.20
77	Kenneth Sims	.25	.20	.10
80	Irving Fryar	1.00	.70	.40
81	Stephen Starring	.25	.20	.10
83	Cedric Jones	.25	.20	.10
86	Stanley Morgan	.50	.40	.20

1986 McDonald's New Orleans Saints

Released over a four-week time span at New Orleans-area McDonald's, the 24-card set measures 3-1/16" x 4-11/16" with the tab and 3-1/16" x 3-5/8" without. The card fronts are anchored with a color photo, with the McDonald's logo in the upper left and Saints' helmet in the upper right. The NFL shield and NFLPA logo are located at the bottom, left and right respectively. The player's name, number and position are printed below the photo. The card backs include the player's name, number, position, bio and highlights. Each week featured a different colored tab: blue (first), black or gray (second), gold or orange (third) and green (fourth). The values listed are for cards which have the tabs intact.

		NM/M	NM	E
Complete Set (Blue):		150.00	110.00	60.00

		NM/M	NM	E
Complete Set (Black):		30.00	22.00	12.00
Complete Set (Gold):		20.00	15.00	8.00
Complete Set (Green):		25.00	18.50	10.00
Common Player:		.75	.60	.30
3	Bobby Hebert	2.00	1.50	.80
7	Morten Andersen (DP)	1.00	.70	.40
10	Brian Hansen	.75	.60	.30
18	Dave Wilson	.75	.60	.30
20	Russell Gary	.75	.60	.30
25	Johnnie Poe	.75	.60	.30
30	Wayne Wilson	.75	.60	.30
44	Dave Waymer	.75	.60	.30
46	Hokie Gajan	.75	.60	.30
49	Frank Wattelett	.75	.60	.30
50	Jack Del Rio (DP)	1.00	.70	.40
57	Rickey Jackson	1.00	.70	.40
60	Steve Korte	.75	.60	.30
61	Joel Hilgenberg	.75	.60	.30
63	Brad Edelman (DP)	.75	.60	.30
64	Dave Lafary	.75	.60	.30
67	Stan Brock (DP)	.75	.60	.30
73	Frank Warren	.75	.60	.30
75	Bruce Clark (DP)	.75	.60	.30
84	Eric Martin	1.50	1.25	.60
85	Hoby Brenner (DP)	.75	.60	.30
88	Eugene Goodlow	.75	.60	.30
89	Tyrone Young	.75	.60	.30
99	Tony Elliott	.75	.60	.30

1986 McDonald's New York Giants

Released over a four-week time span at New York-area McDonald's, the 24-card set measures 3-1/16" x 4-11/16" with the tab and 3-1/16" x 3-5/8" without. The card fronts are anchored with a color photo, with the McDonald's logo in the upper left and Giants' helmet in the upper right. The NFL shield and NFLPA logo are located at the bottom, left and right respectively. The player's name, number and position are printed below the photo. The card backs include the player's name, number, position, bio and highlights. Each week featured a different colored tab: blue (first), black or gray (second), gold or orange (third) and green (fourth). The values listed are for cards with the tabs intact.

		NM/M	NM	E
Complete Set (Blue):		12.00	9.00	4.75
Complete Set (Black):		10.00	7.50	4.00
Complete Set (Gold):		6.00	4.50	2.50
Complete Set (Green):		6.00	4.50	2.50
Common Player:		.25	.20	.10
5	Sean Landeta	.35	.25	.14
11	Phil Simms	1.00	.70	.40
20	Joe Morris	.50	.40	.20
23	Perry Williams	.25	.20	.10
26	Rob Carpenter (DP)	.25	.20	.10
33	George Adams (DP)	.25	.20	.10
34	Elvis Patterson	.35	.25	.14
43	Terry Kinard	.25	.20	.10
44	Maurice Carthon	.25	.20	.10
48	Kenny Hill	.25	.20	.10
53	Harry Carson	.35	.25	.14
54	Andy Headen	.25	.20	.10
56	Lawrence Taylor	1.50	1.25	.60
60	Brad Benson (DP)	.25	.20	.10
63	Karl Nelson	.25	.20	.10
64	Jim Burt (DP)	.35	.25	.14
67	Billy Ard (DP)	.25	.20	.10
70	Leonard Marshall	.35	.25	.14
75	George Martin	.35	.25	.14
80	Phil McConkey	.35	.25	.14
84	Zeke Mowatt	.25	.20	.10
85	Don Hasselbeck	.25	.20	.10
86	Lionel Manuel	.35	.25	.14
89	Mark Bavaro (DP)	.35	.25	.14

1986 McDonald's New York Jets

Released over a four-week time span at New York-area McDonald's, the 24-card set measures 3-1/16" x 4-11/16" with the tab and 3-1/16" x 3-5/8" without. The card fronts are anchored with a color photo, with the McDonald's logo in the upper left and Jets' helmet in the upper right. The NFL shield and NFLPA logo are located at the bottom, left and right respectively. The player's name, number and position are printed below the photo. The card backs include the player's name, number, position, bio and highlights. Each week featured a different colored tab: blue (first), black or gray (second), gold or orange (third) and green (fourth). The values listed are for cards with the tabs intact.

		NM/M	NM	E
Complete Set (Blue):		150.00	112.00	60.00
Complete Set (Black):		150.00	112.00	60.00
Complete Set (Gold):		25.00	18.50	10.00
Complete Set (Green):		25.00	18.50	10.00
Common Player:		1.00	.70	.40

5	Pat Leahy	1.00	.70	.40
7	Ken O'Brien	1.50	1.25	.60
21	Kirk Springs	1.00	.70	.40
24	Freeman McNeil	2.00	1.50	.80
27	Russell Carter (DP)	1.00	.70	.40
29	Johnny Lynn	1.00	.70	.40
34	Johnny Hector	1.00	.70	.40
39	Harry Hamilton	1.00	.70	.40
49	Tony Paige	1.00	.70	.40
53	Jim Sweeney	1.00	.70	.40
56	Lance Mehl	1.00	.70	.40
59	Kyle Clifton (DP)	1.00	.70	.40
60	Dan Alexander (DP)	1.00	.70	.40
65	Joe Fields (DP)	1.00	.70	.40
73	Joe Klecko	1.25	.90	.50
78	Barry Bennett (DP)	1.00	.70	.40
80	Johnny Lam Jones	1.00	.70	.40
82	Mickey Shuler	1.00	.70	.40
85	Wesley Walker	1.25	.90	.50
87	Kurt Sohn	1.00	.70	.40
88	Al Toon	2.00	1.50	.80
89	Rocky Klever	1.00	.70	.40
93	Marty Lyons	1.00	.70	.40
99	Mark Gastineau (DP)	1.50	1.25	.60

1984 McDonald's Ottawa

		NM/M	NM	E
Complete Set (4):		10.00	7.50	4.00
Common Player:		2.00	1.50	.80
1	Ken Miller, Rudy Phillips, Jim Reid	2.00	1.50	.80
2	Gary Dulin, Greg Marshall, Junior Robinson	2.00	1.50	.80
3	Kevin Powell, Tyron Gray, Skip Walker	2.00	1.50	.80
4	Rick Sowieta, Bruce Walker, J.C. Watts	5.00	3.75	2.00

1986 McDonald's Philadelphia Eagles

Issued over a four-week time span at Philadelphia-area McDonald's, the 24-card set measures 3-1/16" x 4-11/16" with the tab and 3-1/16" x 3-5/8" without. A color photo anchors the card front, with the McDonald's logo in the upper left and the Eagles' helmet in the upper right. The NFL shield and NFLPA logos are in the bottom corners, left and right respectively. The player's name, number and position are printed under the photo. The card backs have the player's name, number, bio and highlights. Each week's cards featured a different colored tab: blue (first), black or gray (second), gold or orange (third) and green (fourth).

		NM/M	NM	E
Complete Set (Blue):		60.00	45.00	24.00
Complete Set (Black):		20.00	15.00	8.00
Complete Set (Gold):		10.00	7.50	4.00
Complete Set (Green):		10.00	7.50	4.00
Common Player:		.25	.20	.10
7	Ron Jaworski	.50	.40	.20
8	Paul McFadden	.25	.20	.10
12	Randall Cunningham (DP)	2.00	1.50	.80
22	Brenard Wilson	.25	.20	.10
24	Ray Ellis	.25	.20	.10
29	Elbert Foules	.25	.20	.10
36	Herman Hunter	.35	.25	.14
41	Earnest Jackson	.35	.25	.14
43	Roynell Young	.35	.25	.14
48	Wes Hopkins	.25	.20	.10
50	Garry Cobb (DP)	.25	.20	.10
63	Ron Baker (DP)	.25	.20	.10
66	Ken Reeves	.25	.20	.10
71	Ken Clarke (DP)	.25	.20	.10
73	Steve Kenney	.25	.20	.10
74	Leonard Mitchell	.25	.20	.10

81	Kenny Jackson	.35	.25	.14
82	Mike Quick	.35	.25	.14
85	Ron Johnson	.25	.20	.10
88	John Spagnola	.25	.20	.10
91	Reggie White	4.00	3.00	1.50
93	Thomas Strauthers	.25	.20	.10
94	Byron Darby (DP)	.25	.20	.10
98	Greg Brown (DP)	.25	.20	.10

1986 McDonald's Pittsburgh Steelers

Released over a four-week time span at Pittsburgh-area McDonald's, the 24-card set measures 3-1/16" x 4-11/16" with the tab and 3-1/16" x 3-5/8" without. The card fronts are anchored with a color photo, with the McDonald's logo in the upper left and Steelers' helmet in the upper right. The NFL shield and NFLPA logo are located at the bottom, left and right respectively. The player's name, number and position are printed below the photo. The card backs include the player's name, number, position, bio and highlights. Each week featured a different colored tab: blue (first), black or gray (second), gold or orange (third) and green (fourth). The values listed are for cards which have the tabs intact.

		NM/M	NM	E
Complete Set (Blue):		50.00	37.00	20.00
Complete Set (Black):		25.00	18.50	10.00
Complete Set (Gold):		10.00	7.50	4.00
Complete Set (Green):		10.00	7.50	4.00
Common Player:		.40	.30	.15
1	Gary Anderson (K) (DP)	.50	.40	.20
16	Mark Malone	.50	.40	.20
21	Eric Williams	.40	.30	.15
24	Rich Erenberg (DP)	.40	.30	.15
30	Frank Pollard	.40	.30	.15
31	Donnie Shell	.50	.40	.20
34	Walter Abercrombie (DP)	.40	.30	.15
49	Dwayne Woodruff	.40	.30	.15
50	David Little	.40	.30	.15
52	Mike Webster	.50	.40	.20
53	Bryan Hinkle	.50	.40	.20
56	Robin Cole (DP)	.40	.30	.15
57	Mike Merriweather	.50	.40	.20
62	Tunch Ilkin	.40	.30	.15
65	Ray Pinney	.40	.30	.15
67	Gary Dunn (DP)	.40	.30	.15
73	Craig Wolfley	.40	.30	.15
74	Terry Long	.40	.30	.15
82	John Stallworth	.75	.60	.30
83	Louis Lipps	.75	.60	.30
87	Weegie Thompson	.40	.30	.15
92	Keith Gary (DP)	.40	.30	.15
93	Keith Willis	.40	.30	.15
99	Darryl Sims	.40	.30	.15

1975 McDonald's Quarterbacks

Measuring 2-1/2" x 3-7/16", this four-card set was a McDonald's promotion. The yellow-bordered card fronts showcase the player's name and team at the top, with a photo in the center. Printed below the photo is "Get a quarter back..." The McDonald's logo is in the lower right. The backs of each card have different colors. The unnumbered card backs have the player's name, position and team at the top, with his stats below. The perforated coupon below explains the promotion. Each card was good for one week. Prices are for cards which have the coupons intact.

		NM	E	VG
Complete Set (4):		10.00	5.00	3.00
Common Player:		.50	.25	.15
1	Terry Bradshaw	6.00	3.00	1.75
2	Joe Ferguson	1.00	.50	.30
3	Ken Stabler	4.00	2.00	1.25
4	Al Woodall	.50	.25	.15

1986 McDonald's San Diego Chargers

Released over four weeks in the San Diego area, the 24-card set measures 3-1/16" x 4-11/16" with the tab and 3-1/16" x 3-5/8" without. The card fronts showcase a color photo, with the McDonald's logo in the upper left, Chargers' helmet in the upper right, NFL shield in the bottom left and NFLPA logo in the lower right. The player's name, jersey number and position are printed under the photo. The card backs include the player's name, number, position, bio and highlights. Each week's cards had a different colored tab: blue (first), black or gray (second), gold or orange (third) and green (fourth).

		NM/M	NM	E
Complete Set (Blue):		20.00	15.00	8.00
Complete Set (Black):		15.00	11.00	6.00
Complete Set (Gold):		10.00	7.50	4.00
Complete Set (Green):		10.00	7.50	4.00
Common Player:		.40	.30	.15
9	Mark Herrmann	.40	.30	.15
14	Dan Fouts	1.50	1.25	.60
18	Charlie Joiner	1.25	.90	.50
21	Buford McGee	.40	.30	.15
22	Gill Byrd (DP)	.50	.40	.20
26	Lionel James	.50	.40	.20
29	John Hendy	.40	.30	.15
37	Jeff Dale (DP)	.40	.30	.15
40	Gary Anderson (RB) (DP)	.75	.60	.30
43	Tim Spencer	.40	.30	.15
51	Woodrow Lowe	.40	.30	.15
54	Bill Ray Smith	.50	.40	.20
60	Dennis McKnight	.40	.30	.15
62	Don Macek	.40	.30	.15
67	Ed White	.40	.30	.15
74	Jim Lachey	.50	.40	.20
78	Chuck Ehin (DP)	.40	.30	.15
80	Kellen Winslow	1.50	1.25	.60
83	Trumaine Johnson	.40	.30	.15
85	Eric Sievers	.40	.30	.15
88	Pete Holohan	.50	.40	.20
89	Wes Chandler (DP)	.50	.40	.20
93	Earl Wilson	.40	.30	.15
99	Lee Williams	.50	.40	.20

1986 McDonald's San Francisco 49ers

Released over a four-week time span at San Francisco-area McDonald's, the 24-card set measures 3-1/16" x 4-11/16" with the tab and 3-1/16" x 3-5/8" without. The card fronts are anchored with a color photo, with the McDonald's logo in the upper left and 49ers' helmet in the upper right. The NFL shield and NFLPA logo are located at the bottom, left and right respectively. The player's name, number and position are printed below the photo. The card backs include the player's name, number, position, bio and highlights. Each week featured a different colored tab: blue (first), black or gray (second), gold or orange (third) and green (fourth). The values listed are for cards with the tabs intact.

		NM/M	NM	E
Complete Set (Blue):		50.00	37.00	20.00
Complete Set (Black):		25.00	18.50	10.00
Complete Set (Gold):		25.00	18.50	10.00
Complete Set (Green):		25.00	18.50	10.00
Common Player:		.75	.60	.30
16	Joe Montana	12.00	9.00	4.75
21	Eric Wright	1.00	.70	.40
26	Wendell Tyler	1.00	.70	.40
27	Carlton Williamson	.75	.60	.30
33	Roger Craig (DP)	1.25	.90	.50
42	Ronnie Lott	2.00	1.50	.80
49	Jeff Fuller	.75	.60	.30
50	Riki Ellison	.75	.60	.30
51	Randy Cross (DP)	1.00	.70	.40
56	Fred Quillan	.75	.60	.30
58	Keena Turner	.75	.60	.30
62	Guy McIntyre	.75	.60	.30
68	John Ayers (DP)	.75	.60	.30
71	Keith Fahnhorst	.75	.60	.30
72	Jeff Stover	.75	.60	.30
76	Dwaine Board (DP)	.75	.60	.30

77	Bubba Paris	.75	.60	.30
78	Manu Tuiasosopo	.75	.60	.30
80	Jerry Rice	12.00	9.00	4.75
81	Russ Francis	1.00	.70	.40
86	John Frank	.75	.60	.30
87	Dwight Clark (DP)	1.00	.70	.40
90	Todd Shell	.75	.60	.30
95	Michael Carter (DP)	1.00	.70	.40

1986 McDonald's Seattle Seahawks

Released over a four-week time span at Seattle-area McDonald's, the 24-card set measures 3-1/16" x 4-11/16" with the tab and 3-1/16" x 3-5/8" without. The card fronts are anchored with a color photo, with the McDonald's logo in the upper left and Seahawks' helmet in the upper right. The NFL shield and NFLPA logo are located at the bottom, left and right respectively. The player's name, number and position are printed below the photo. The card backs include the player's name, number, position, bio and highlights. Each week featured a different colored tab: blue (first), black or gray (second), gold or orange (third) and green (fourth). The values listed are for cards which have the tabs intact.

		NM/M	NM	E
Complete Set (Blue):		10.00	7.50	4.00
Complete Set (Black):		7.00	5.25	2.75
Complete Set (Gold):		7.00	5.25	2.75
Complete Set (Green):		7.00	5.25	2.75
Common Player:		.25	.20	.10
9	Norm Johnson	.35	.25	.14
17	Dave Krieg	.50	.40	.20
20	Terry Taylor	.25	.20	.10
22	Dave Brown (DP)	.25	.20	.10
28	Curt Warner (DP)	.50	.40	.20
33	Dan Doornink	.25	.20	.10
44	John Harris	.25	.20	.10
45	Kenny Easley	.35	.25	.14
46	David Hughes	.25	.20	.10
50	Fredd Young	.25	.20	.10
53	Keith Butler (DP)	.25	.20	.10
55	Michael Jackson	.25	.20	.10
58	Bruce Scholtz	.25	.20	.10
59	Blair Bush (DP)	.25	.20	.10
61	Robert Pratt	.25	.20	.10
64	Ron Essink	.25	.20	.10
65	Edwin Bailey (DP)	.25	.20	.10
72	Joe Nash	.25	.20	.10
77	Jeff Bryant (DP)	.25	.20	.10
78	Bob Cryder (DP)	.25	.20	.10
79	Jacob Green	.35	.25	.14
80	Steve Largent	2.00	1.50	.80
81	Daryl Turner	.25	.20	.10
82	Paul Skansi	.25	.20	.10

1986 McDonald's St. Louis Cardinals

Released over four weeks in the St. Louis area during the 1986 season, the 24-card set measures 3-1/16" x 4-11/16" with the tabs and 3-1/16" x 3-5/8" without. The card fronts showcase a color photo, with the McDonald's logo in the upper left and the Cardinals' helmet in the upper right. The NFL shield and NFLPA logo appear at the bottom, left and right respectively. The player's name, jersey number and position are printed under the photo. The card backs showcase the player's name, jersey number, bio and highlights. Each week's card had a different colored tab: blue (first), black or gray (second), gold or orange (third) and green (fourth).

	NM/M	NM	E
Complete Set (Blue):	10.00	7.50	4.00
Complete Set (Black):	6.00	4.50	2.50
Complete Set (Gold):	6.00	4.50	2.50
Complete Set (Green):	6.00	4.50	2.50
Common Player:	.25	.20	.10
15 Neil Lomax	.50	.40	.20
18 Carl Birdsong (DP)	.25	.20	.10
30 Stump Mitchell	.35	.25	.14
32 Ottis Anderson (DP)	.75	.60	.30
43 Lonnie Young	.25	.20	.10
45 Leonard Smith	.25	.20	.10
47 Cedric Mack	.25	.20	.10
48 Lionel Washington	.25	.20	.10
53 Freddie Joe Nunn	.35	.25	.14
54 E.J. Junior	.35	.25	.14
57 Niko Noga	.25	.20	.10
60 Al "Bubba" Baker (DP)	.35	.25	.14
63 Tootie Robbins	.25	.20	.10
65 David Galloway	.25	.20	.10
66 Doug Dawson (DP)	.25	.20	.10
67 Luis Sharpe	.25	.20	.10
71 Joe Bostic (DP)	.25	.20	.10
73 Mark Duda (DP)	.25	.20	.10
75 Curtis Greer	.25	.20	.10
80 Doug Marsh	.25	.20	.10
81 Roy Green	.50	.40	.20
83 Pat Tilley	.25	.20	.10
84 J.T. Smith	.35	.25	.14
89 Greg Lafleur	.25	.20	.10

1986 McDonald's Tampa Bay Buccaneers

Issued over four weeks in the Tampa area during the 1986 season, the 24-card set measures 3-1/16" x 4-11/16" with the tab and 3-1/16" x 3-5/8" without. The card fronts have a color photo, with the McDonald's logo in the upper left and Tampa Bay helmet in the upper right. The NFL shield and NFLPA logo are in the bottom corners, left and right respectively. The card backs have the player's name, jersey number, bio and highlights. Each week's cards had different colored tabs: blue (first), black or gray (second), gold or orange (third) and green (fourth).

	NM/M	NM	E
Complete Set (Blue):	15.00	11.00	6.00
Complete Set (Black):	15.00	11.00	6.00
Complete Set (Gold):	15.00	11.00	6.00
Complete Set (Green):	15.00	11.00	6.00
Common Player:	.30	.25	.12
1 Donald Igwebuike	.30	.25	.12
8 Steve Young	8.00	6.00	3.25
17 Steve DeBerg	.75	.60	.30
21 John Holt	.30	.25	.12
23 Jeremiah Castille (DP)	.30	.25	.12
30 David Greenwood	.30	.25	.12
32 James Wilder	.50	.40	.20
44 Ivory Sully	.30	.25	.12
51 Chris Washington	.30	.25	.12
52 Scot Brantley (DP)	.30	.25	.12
54 Ervin Randle	.30	.25	.12
58 Jeff Davis (DP)	.30	.25	.12
60 Randy Grimes	.30	.25	.12
62 Sean Farrell	.40	.30	.15
66 George Yarno	.30	.25	.12
73 Ron Heller	.30	.25	.12
76 David Logan	.30	.25	.12
78 John Cannon (DP)	.30	.25	.12
82 Jerry Bell (DP)	.30	.25	.12
86 Calvin Magee	.30	.25	.12
87 Gerald Carter	.30	.25	.12
88 Jimmie Giles	.50	.40	.20
89 Kevin House	.50	.40	.20
90 Ron Holmes	.40	.30	.15

1986 McDonald's Washington Redskins

Released over a four-week time span at Washington, D.C.- area McDonald's, the 24-card set measures 3-1/16" x 4-11/16" with the tab and 3-1/16" x 3-5/8" without. The card fronts are anchored with a color photo, with the McDonald's logo in the upper left and Redskins' helmet in the upper right. The NFL shield and NFLPA logo are located at the bottom, left and right respectively. The player's name, number and position are printed below the photo. The card backs include the player's name, number, position, bio and highlights. Each week featured a different colored tab: blue (first), black or gray (second), gold or orange (third) and green (fourth). The values listed are for cards which have the tabs intact.

	NM/M	NM	E
Complete Set (Blue):	6.00	4.50	2.50
Complete Set (Black):	6.00	4.50	2.50
Complete Set (Gold):	6.00	4.50	2.50
Complete Set (Green):	6.00	4.50	2.50
Common Player:	.25	.20	.10
3 Mark Moseley	.25	.20	.10
10 Jay Schroeder	.50	.40	.20
22 Curtis Jordan	.25	.20	.10
28 Darrell Green	.50	.40	.20
32 Vernon Dean (DP)	.25	.20	.10
35 Keith Griffin	.25	.20	.10
37 Raphel Cherry (DP)	.25	.20	.10
38 George Rogers	.35	.25	.14
51 Monte Coleman (DP)	.35	.25	.14
52 Neal Olkewicz	.25	.20	.10
53 Jeff Bostic (DP)	.25	.20	.10
55 Mel Kaufman	.25	.20	.10
57 Rich Milot	.25	.20	.10
65 Dave Butz (DP)	.35	.25	.14
66 Joe Jacoby	.35	.25	.14
68 Russ Grimm	.35	.25	.14
71 Charles Mann	.50	.40	.20
72 Dexter Manley	.35	.25	.14
73 Mark May	.35	.25	.14
77 Darryl Grant	.25	.20	.10
81 Art Monk	1.00	.70	.40
84 Gary Clark (DP)	1.00	.70	.40
85 Don Warren	.35	.25	.14
86 Clint Didier	.25	.20	.10

1988 McNeese State McDag/Police

	NM/M	NM	E
Complete Set (16):	6.00	4.50	2.50
Common Player:	.50	.40	.20
1 Sonny Jackson (CO)	.50	.40	.20
2 Lance Wiley	.50	.40	.20
3 Brian McZeal	.50	.40	.20
4 Berwick Davenport	.50	.40	.20
5 Gary Irvin	.50	.40	.20
6 Glenn Koch	.50	.40	.20
7 Chad Habetz	.50	.40	.20
8 Pete Sinclair	.50	.40	.20
9 Tony Citizen	.50	.40	.20
10 Scott Dieterich	.50	.40	.20
11 Hud Jackson	.50	.40	.20
12 Darrin Andrus	.50	.40	.20
13 Jeff Mathews	.50	.40	.20

14 Devin Babineaux	.50	.40	.20
15 Jeff Delhomme	.50	.40	.20
16 Eric LeBlanc, Mike Pierce	.50	.40	.20

1989 McNeese State McDag/Police

	NM/M	NM	E
Complete Set (16):	6.00	4.50	2.50
Common Player:	.50	.40	.20
1 Marc Stampley	.50	.40	.20
2 Mark LeBlanc	.50	.40	.20
3 Kip Texada	.50	.40	.20
4 Brian Champagne	.50	.40	.20
5 Ronald Scott	.50	.40	.20
6 Jimmy Poirier	.50	.40	.20
7 Cliff Buckner	.50	.40	.20
8 Jericho Loupe	.50	.40	.20
9 Vaughn Calbert	.50	.40	.20
10 Rodney Burks	.50	.40	.20
11 Troy Jones	.50	.40	.20
12 Chris Andrus	.50	.40	.20
13 Robbie Vizier	.50	.40	.20
14 Kenneth Pierce	.50	.40	.20
15 Bobby Smith	.50	.40	.20
16 Trent Lee	.50	.40	.20

1990 McNeese State McDag/Police

	NM/M	NM	E
Complete Set (16):	6.00	4.50	2.50
Common Player:	.50	.40	.20
1 Hud Jackson	.50	.40	.20
2 Wes Watts	.50	.40	.20
3 Mark LeBlanc	.50	.40	.20
4 Jeff Delhomme	.50	.40	.20
5 Mike Reed	.50	.40	.20
6 Chuck Esponge	.50	.40	.20
7 Ronald Scott	.50	.40	.20
8 Ken Naquin	.50	.40	.20
9 Steve Aultman	.50	.40	.20
10 Sean Judge	.50	.40	.20
11 Greg Rayson	.50	.40	.20
12 Kip Texada	.50	.40	.20
13 Mike Pierce	.50	.40	.20
14 Jimmy Poirier	.50	.40	.20
15 Ronald Solomon	.50	.40	.20
16 Eric Foster	.50	.40	.20

1991 McNeese State McDag/Police

	NM/M	NM	E
Complete Set (16):	6.00	4.50	2.50
Common Player:	.50	.40	.20
1 Eric Roberts	.50	.40	.20
2 Irwin Brown	.50	.40	.20
3 Marcus Bowie	.50	.40	.20
4 Wes Watts	.50	.40	.20
5 Brian Brumfield	.50	.40	.20
6 Marc Stampley	.50	.40	.20
7 Sean Judge	.50	.40	.20
8 Joey Bernard	.50	.40	.20
9 Ken Naquin	.50	.40	.20
10 Bobby Smith	.50	.40	.20
11 Sam Breaux	.50	.40	.20
12 Ronald Scott	.50	.40	.20

13	Edward Dyer	.50	.40	.20
14	Blayne Rush	.50	.40	.20
15	Ronald Solomon	.50	.40	.20
16	Steve Aultman	.50	.40	.20

1991 Miami Police

		NM/M	NM	E
Complete Set (16):		15.00	11.00	6.00
Common Player:		1.00	.70	.40
1	Jessie Armstead	1.50	1.25	.60
2	Micheal Barrow	2.00	1.50	.80
3	Hurlie Brown	1.00	.70	.40
4	Dennis Erickson (CO)	2.00	1.50	.80
5	Anthony Hamlet	1.00	.70	.40
6	Carlos Huerta	1.50	1.25	.60
7	Herbert James	1.00	.70	.40
8	Claude Jones	1.00	.70	.40
9	Stephen McGuire	1.50	1.25	.60
10	Eric Miller	1.00	.70	.40
11	Joe Moore	1.00	.70	.40
12	Charles Pharms	1.00	.70	.40
13	Leon Searcy	2.00	1.50	.80
14	Darrin Smith	2.00	1.50	.80
15	Lamar Thomas	1.50	1.25	.60
16	Gino Torretta	2.00	1.50	.80

1990 Miami Smokey

		NM/M	NM	E
Complete Set (16):		18.00	13.50	7.25
Common Player:		.75	.60	.30
1	Randy Bethel (93)	.75	.60	.30
2	Wesley Carroll (81)	2.00	1.50	.80
3	Rob Chudzinski (84)	.75	.60	.30
4	Leonard Conley (28)	1.50	1.25	.60
5	Luis Cristobal (59)	.75	.60	.30
6	Maurice Crum (49)	.75	.60	.30
7	Shane Curry (44)	1.50	1.25	.60
8	Craig Erickson (7)	4.00	3.00	1.50
9	Dennis Erickson (CO)	2.00	1.50	.80
10	Darren Handy (66)	.75	.60	.30
11	Randal Hill (3)	4.00	3.00	1.50
12	Carlos Huerta (27)	1.50	1.25	.60
13	Russell Maryland (67)	3.00	2.25	1.25
14	Stephen McGuire (30)	1.50	1.25	.60
15	Roland Smith (16)	.75	.60	.30
16	Mike Sullivan (79)	.75	.60	.30

1977 Michigan

		NM	E	VG
Complete Set (21):		25.00	12.50	7.50
Common Player:		.75	.40	.25
1	John Anderson	1.25	.60	.40
2	Russell Davis	1.25	.60	.40
3	Mark Donahue	.75	.40	.25
4	Walt Downing	.75	.40	.25
5	Bill Dufek	1.25	.60	.40
6	Jon Giesler (SP)	2.00	1.00	.60
7	Steve Graves	.75	.40	.25
8	Curtis Greer	2.00	1.00	.60
9	Dwight Hicks	2.50	1.25	.70
10	Derek Howard	.75	.40	.25
11	Harlan Huckleby	2.50	1.25	.70
12	Gene Johnson	.75	.40	.25
13	Dale Keitz	.75	.40	.25
14	Mike Kenn	2.50	1.25	.70
15	Rick Leach	2.50	1.25	.70
16	Mark Schmerge	.75	.40	.25
17	Ron Simpkins	1.25	.60	.40
18	Curt Stephenson (SP)	2.00	1.00	.60
19	Gerry Szara (SP)	2.00	1.00	.60
20	Rick White	.75	.40	.25
21	Gregg Willner	.75	.40	.25

1989 Michigan

		NM/M	NM	E
Complete Set (22):		12.00	9.00	4.75
Common Player:		.50	.40	.20
1	H.O. "Fritz" Crisler (CO)	.60	.45	.25
2	Anthony Carter	1.50	1.25	.60
3	Willie Heston	.50	.40	.20
4	Reggie McKenzie	.50	.40	.20
5	Bo Schembechler (CO)	1.50	1.25	.60
6	Dan Dierdorf	1.50	1.25	.60
7	Jim Harbaugh	1.50	1.25	.60
8	Bennie Oosterbaan	.50	.40	.20
9	Jamie Morris	.60	.45	.25
10	Gerald R. Ford	1.50	1.25	.60
11	Curtis Greer	.60	.45	.25
12	Ron Kramer	.60	.45	.25
13	Calvin O'Neal	.50	.40	.20
14	Bob Chappuis	.50	.40	.20
15	Fielding Yost (CO)	.60	.45	.25
16	Dennis Franklin	.50	.40	.20
17	Benny Friedman	.60	.45	.25
18	Jim Mandich	.60	.45	.25
19	Rob Lytle	.60	.45	.25
20	Bump Elliott	.60	.45	.25
21	Harry Kipke	.50	.40	.20
22	Dave Brown	.60	.45	.25

1907 Michigan Dietsche Postcards

		NM	E	VG
Complete Set (15):		1,000	500.00	250.00
Common Player:		50.00	25.00	15.00
1	Dave Allerdice	50.00	25.00	12.00
2	William Casey	50.00	25.00	12.00
3	William Embs	50.00	25.00	12.00
4	Keene Fitzpatrick (TR)	30.00	15.00	9.00
5	Red Flanagan	50.00	25.00	12.00
6	Walter Graham	50.00	25.00	12.00
7	H.S. Hammond	50.00	25.00	12.00
8	John Loell	50.00	25.00	12.00
9	Paul Magoffin	50.00	25.00	12.00
10	James Miller	50.00	25.00	12.00
11	Walter Rheinschild	50.00	25.00	12.00
12	Mason Rumney	50.00	25.00	12.00
13	Adolph "Germany" Schultz	175.00	90.00	45.00
14	William Wasmund	50.00	25.00	12.00
15	Fielding Yost (CO)	180.00	90.00	45.00

1985 Miller Lite Beer

Measuring 4-3/4" x 7", the eight-card set is anchored on the front with a large player photo. The player's name, position, team helmet, player bio and NFL/Lite logo are beneath the photo. The card backs, which are unnumbered, have the Lite logo in the upper left, with the player's name and position on the upper right. The player's highlights on the field and off the field are printed at the bottom of the card.

		NM/M	NM	E
Complete Set (6):		150.00	112.00	60.00
Common Player:		15.00	11.00	6.00
1	Larry Csonka	35.00	26.00	14.00
2	John Hadl (CO)	15.00	11.00	6.00
3	Freeman McNeil (NFL Man of the Year)	15.00	11.00	6.00
4	Jack Reynolds (Lite Beer All-Stars)	15.00	11.00	6.00
5	Steve Young (USFL Man of the Year)	80.00	60.00	32.00
6	1985 LA Express (Cheerleaders)	15.00	11.00	6.00

1991 Mississippi Hoby

		NM/M	NM	E
Complete Set (42):		9.00	6.75	3.50
Common Player:		.25	.20	.10
439	Gary Abide	.25	.20	.10
440	Dwayne Amos	.25	.20	.10
441	Tyji Armstrong	1.00	.70	.40
442	Tyrone Ashley	.25	.20	.10
443	Darron Billings	.25	.20	.10
444	Danny Boyd	.25	.20	.10
445	Billy Brewer (CO)	.35	.25	.14
446	Chad Brown	.35	.25	.14
447	Tony Brown	.25	.20	.10
448	Vincent Brownlee	.25	.20	.10
449	Jeff Carter	.35	.25	.14
450	Richard Chisolm	.25	.20	.10
451	Clint Conlee	.25	.20	.10
452	Marvin Courtney	.25	.20	.10
453	Cliff Dew	.25	.20	.10
454	Johnny Dixon	.25	.20	.10
455	Artis Ford	.25	.20	.10
456	Chauncey Godwin	.25	.20	.10
457	Brian Harper	.25	.20	.10
458	David Harris	.25	.20	.10
459	Pete Harris	.25	.20	.10
460	David Herring	.25	.20	.10
461	James Holcombe	.25	.20	.10
462	Kevin Ingram	.25	.20	.10
463	Phillip Kent	.35	.25	.14
464	Derrick King	.25	.20	.10
465	Brian Lee	.25	.20	.10
466	Jim Lentz	.25	.20	.10
467	Everett Lindsay	.25	.20	.10
468	Tom Luke	.25	.20	.10
469	Thomas McLeish	.25	.20	.10
470	Wesley Melton	.25	.20	.10
471	Tyrone Montgomery	.75	.60	.30
472	Deano Orr	.25	.20	.10
473	Darrick Owens	.35	.25	.14
474	Lynn Ross	.25	.20	.10
475	Russ Shows	.25	.20	.10
476	Eddie Small	.35	.25	.14
477	Trea Southerland	.25	.20	.10
478	Gerald Vaughn	.25	.20	.10
479	Abner White	.25	.20	.10
480	Sebastian Williams	.25	.20	.10

1988 Mississippi McDag

		NM/M	NM	E
Complete Set (2):		4.00	3.00	1.50
Common Player:		2.00	1.50	.80
15	Mark Young	2.00	1.50	.80
16	Bryan Owen	2.00	1.50	.80

1991 Mississippi State Hoby

		NM/M	NM	E
Complete Set (42):		9.00	6.75	3.50
Common Player:		.25	.20	.10
481	Lance Aldridge	.25	.20	.10
482	Treddis Anderson	.25	.20	.10
483	Shea Bell	.25	.20	.10
484	Chris Bosarge	.25	.20	.10
485	Daniel Boyd	.25	.20	.10
486	Jerome Brown	.25	.20	.10
487	Torrance Brown	.25	.20	.10
488	Keith Carr	.25	.20	.10
489	Herman Carroll	.25	.20	.10
490	Keo Coleman	.35	.25	.14
491	Michael Davis	.25	.20	.10
492	Trenell Edwards	.25	.20	.10
493	Chris Firle	.25	.20	.10
494	Lee Ford	.25	.20	.10
495	Tay Galloway	.25	.20	.10
496	Chris Gardner	.25	.20	.10
497	Arleye Gibson	.25	.20	.10
498	Tony Harris	.25	.20	.10
499	Willie Harris	.25	.20	.10
500	Kevin Henry	.35	.25	.14
501	Jackie Sherrill (CO)	.50	.40	.20
502	John James	.25	.20	.10
503	Tony James	.25	.20	.10
504	Todd Jordan	.25	.20	.10
505	Keith Joseph	.25	.20	.10
506	Kelvin Knight	.25	.20	.10
507	Lee Lipscomb	.25	.20	.10
508	Juan Long	.25	.20	.10
509	Kyle McCoy	.25	.20	.10
510	Tommy Morrell	.25	.20	.10
511	Kelly Ray	.25	.20	.10
512	Mike Riley	.25	.20	.10
513	Kenny Roberts	.25	.20	.10
514	William Robinson	.25	.20	.10
515	Bill Sartin	.25	.20	.10
516	Kenny Stewart	.25	.20	.10
517	Rodney Stowers	.50	.40	.20
518	Anthony Thames	.25	.20	.10
519	Edward Williams	.25	.20	.10
520	Nate Williams	.25	.20	.10
521	Karl Williamson	.25	.20	.10
522	Marc Woodard	.25	.20	.10

1983 Mohawk B.C. Lions

		NM/M	NM	E
Complete Set (24):		18.00	13.50	7.25
Common Player:		.60	.45	.25
1	John Blain	.60	.45	.25
2	Tim Cowan	.60	.45	.25
3	Larry Crawford	1.00	.70	.40
4	Tyrone Crews	.60	.45	.25
5	James Curry	1.00	.70	.40
6	Roy Dewalt	1.50	1.25	.60
7	Mervyn Fernandez	3.00	2.25	1.25
8	Sammy Greene	.60	.45	.25
9	Jo Jo Heath	.60	.45	.25
10	Nick Hebeler	.60	.45	.25
11	Glen Jackson	.60	.45	.25
12	Tim Kearse	.60	.45	.25
13	Rick Klassen	1.00	.70	.40
14	Kevin Konar	1.00	.70	.40
15	Glenn Leonhard	.60	.45	.25
16	Nelson Martin	.60	.45	.25
17	Mack Moore	.60	.45	.25
18	John Pankratz	.60	.45	.25
19	Joe Paopao	1.25	.90	.50
20	Lui Passaglia	2.00	1.50	.80
21	Don Taylor	.60	.45	.25
22	Mike Washburn	.60	.45	.25
23	John Henry White	.60	.45	.25
24	Al Wilson	.60	.45	.25

1984 Mohawk B.C. Lions

		NM/M	NM	E
Complete Set (32):		18.00	13.50	7.25
Common Player:		.50	.40	.20
1	Ned Armour	.50	.40	.20
2	John Blain	.50	.40	.20
3	Melvin Byrd	.75	.60	.30
4	Darnell Clash	1.00	.70	.40
5	Tim Cowan	.50	.40	.20
6	Larry Crawford	.75	.60	.30
7	Tyrone Crews	.50	.40	.20

8	Roy DeWalt	1.50	1.25	.60
9	Mervyn Fernandez	3.00	2.25	1.25
10	Bernie Glier	.50	.40	.20
11	Dennis Guevin	.50	.40	.20
12	Nick Hebeler	.50	.40	.20
13	Bryan Illerbrun	.50	.40	.20
14	Glen Jackson	.50	.40	.20
15	Andre Jones	.50	.40	.20
16	Rick Klassen	.75	.60	.30
17	Kevin Konar	.75	.60	.30
18	Glenn Leonhard	.50	.40	.20
19	Nelson Martin	.50	.40	.20
20	Billy McBride	.50	.40	.20
21	Mack Moore	.50	.40	.20
22	John Pankratz	.50	.40	.20
23	James Parker	1.25	.90	.50
24	Lui Passaglia	1.50	1.25	.60
25	Ryan Potter	.50	.40	.20
26	Gerald Roper	.50	.40	.20
27	Jim Sandusky	2.00	1.50	.80
28	Don Taylor	.50	.40	.20
29	John Henry White	.50	.40	.20
30	Al Wilson	.50	.40	.20
31	**Team Card**	.75	.60	.30
32	**Checklist**	.75	.60	.30

1985 Mohawk B.C. Lions

	NM/M	NM	E
Complete Set (32):	18.00	13.50	7.25
Common Player:	.50	.40	.20

1	John Blain	.50	.40	.20
2	Jamie Buis	.50	.40	.20
3	Melvin Byrd	.75	.60	.30
4	Darnell Clash	1.00	.70	.40
5	Tim Cowan	.75	.60	.30
6	Tyrone Crews	.50	.40	.20
7	Mark DeBrueys	.50	.40	.20
8	Roy Dewalt	1.50	1.25	.60
9	Mervyn Fernandez	3.00	2.25	1.25
10	Bernie Glier	.50	.40	.20
11	Keith Gooch	.50	.40	.20
12	Dennis Guevin	.50	.40	.20
13	Nick Hebeler	.50	.40	.20
14	Bryan Illerbrun	.50	.40	.20
15	Glen Jackson	.50	.40	.20
16	Keyvan Jenkins	1.00	.70	.40
17	Andre Jones	.50	.40	.20
18	Rick Klassen	.75	.60	.30
19	Kevin Konar	.75	.60	.30
20	Glenn Leonhard	.50	.40	.20
21	Nelson Martin	.50	.40	.20
22	John Pankratz	.50	.40	.20
23	James Parker	1.25	.90	.50
24	Lui Passaglia	1.50	1.25	.60
25	Ryan Potter	.50	.40	.20
26	Ron Robinson	.75	.60	.30
27	Gerald Roper	.50	.40	.20
28	Jim Sandusky	2.00	1.50	.80
29	John Henry White	.50	.40	.20
30	Al Wilson	.50	.40	.20
31	**Team Photo**	.75	.60	.30
32	**Checklist**	.75	.60	.30

1988 Monte Gum

Monte Gum, in Europe, produced these 100 cards along with an album to hold them. The cards, 1-15/16" x 2-3/4", feature a generic team action photo and caption describing the play on the front. A card number is also included on the front, which has a yellow border around the photo. The backs are blank.

	NM/M	NM	E
Complete Set (100):	85.00	64.00	34.00
Common Player:	1.00	.70	.40

1	**Atlanta Falcons**	1.75	1.25	.70
2	**Atlanta Falcons**	1.00	.70	.40
3	**Atlanta Falcons**	1.00	.70	.40
4	**Buffalo Bills**	1.00	.70	.40
5	**Chicago Bears**	1.25	.90	.50
6	**Chicago Bears**	1.00	.70	.40
7	**Cincinnati Bengals**	1.00	.70	.40
8	**Cincinnati Bengals**	1.00	.70	.40
9	**Cincinnato Bengals**	5.00	3.75	2.00
10	**Cincinnati Bengals**	1.00	.70	.40
11	**Cincinnati Bengals**	1.50	1.25	.60
12	**Cleveland Browns**	1.00	.70	.40
13	**Cleveland Browns**	2.50	2.00	1.00
14	**Cleveland Browns**	1.00	.70	.40
15	**Cleveland Browns**	1.00	.70	.40
16	**Dallas Cowboys**	1.00	.70	.40
17	**Dallas Cowboys**	1.25	.90	.50
18	**Dallas Cowboys**	1.25	.90	.50
19	**Denver Broncos**	1.00	.70	.40
20	**Denver Broncos**	1.00	.70	.40
21	**Denver Broncos**	2.00	1.50	.80
22	**Detroit Lions**	1.00	.70	.40
23	**Green Bay Packers**	1.00	.70	.40
24	**Green Bay Packers**	1.00	.70	.40
25	**Houston Oilers**	1.00	.70	.40
26	**Houston Oliers**	1.00	.70	.40
27	**Indianapolis Colts**	1.00	.70	.40
28	**Kansas City Chiefs**	1.00	.70	.40
29	**Kansas City Chiefs**	1.00	.70	.40
30	**Kansas City Chiefs**	1.25	.90	.50
31	**Los Angeles Raiders**	1.00	.70	.40
32	**Los Angeles Raiders**	1.00	.70	.40
33	**Los Angeles Raiders**	1.00	.70	.40
34	**Los Angeles Raiders**	2.00	1.50	.80
35	**Los Angeles Rams**	1.00	.70	.40
36	**Los Angeles Rams**	2.00	1.50	.80
37	**Los Angeles Rams**	1.00	.70	.40
38	**Miami Dolphins**	1.25	.90	.50
39	**Miami Dolphins**	1.25	.90	.50
40	**Minnesota Vikings**	1.00	.70	.40
41	**Minnesota Vikings**	1.00	.70	.40
42	**New England Patriots**	1.00	.70	.40
43	**New England Patriots**	1.25	.90	.50
44	**New England Patriots**	3.00	2.25	1.25
45	**New Orleans Saints**	1.50	1.25	.60
46	**New Orleans Saints** (photo actually shows Washington and Michigan in '81 Rose Bowl game)	1.25	.90	.50
47	**New York Giants**	1.25	.90	.50
48	**New York Giants**	1.00	.70	.40
49	**New York Jets**	1.00	.70	.40
50	**New York Jets**	1.00	.70	.40
51	**Philadelphia Eagles**	1.00	.70	.40
52	**Philadelphia Eagles**	1.00	.70	.40
53	**Philadelphia Eagles**	1.00	.70	.40
54	**Philadelphia Eagles**	1.00	.70	.40
55	**Pittsburgh Steelers**	1.00	.70	.40
56	**Pittsburgh Steelers**	1.50	1.25	.60
57	**Pittsburgh Steelers**	1.00	.70	.40
58	**St. Louis Cardinals**	1.00	.70	.40
59	**St. Louis Cardinals**	1.00	.70	.40
60	**St. Louis Cardinals**	1.00	.70	.40
61	**St. Louis Cardinals**	1.00	.70	.40
62	**San Diego Chargers**	1.00	.70	.40
63	**San Diego Chargers**	1.00	.70	.40
64	**San Diego Chargers**	1.25	.90	.50
65	**San Diego Chargers**	1.00	.70	.40
66	**San Francisco 49ers**	1.00	.70	.40
67	**San Francisco 49ers**	1.25	.90	.50
68	**San Francisco 49ers**	10.00	7.50	4.00
69	**San Francisco 49ers**	1.25	.90	.50
70	**Seattle Seahawks**	1.00	.70	.40
71	**Seattle Seahawks**	1.00	.70	.40
72	**Tampa Bay Buccaneers**	1.00	.70	.40
73	**Tampa Bay Buccaneers**	1.00	.70	.40
74	**Tampa Bay Buccaneers**	1.00	.70	.40
75	**Tampa Bay Buccaneers**	1.00	.70	.40
76	**Washington Redskins**	1.00	.70	.40
77	**Washington Redskins**	1.00	.70	.40
78	**Washington Redskins**	1.00	.70	.40
79	**Washington Redskins**	1.00	.70	.40
80	**Official NFL Football**	1.00	.70	.40
81	**Helmets: Falcons/Bills**	1.00	.70	.40
82	**Helmets: Bears/Bengals**	1.00	.70	.40
83	**Helmets: Browns/ Cowboys**	1.00	.70	.40
84	**Helmets: Broncos/Lions**	1.00	.70	.40
85	**Helmets: Packers/Oilers**	1.00	.70	.40
86	**Helmets: Colts/Chiefs**	1.00	.70	.40
87	**Helmets: Raiders/Rams**	1.00	.70	.40
88	**Helmets: Dolphins/ Vikings**	1.00	.70	.40
89	**Helmets: Patriots/Saints**	1.00	.70	.40
90	**Helmets: Giants/Jets**	1.00	.70	.40
91	**Philadelphia Eagles Helmet**	1.00	.70	.40
92	**Pittsburgh Steelers Helmet**	1.00	.70	.40
93	**St. Louis Cardinals Helmet**	1.00	.70	.40
94	**San Diego Chargers Helmet**	1.00	.70	.40
95	**San Francisco 49ers Helmet**	1.00	.70	.40
96	**Seattle Seahawks Helmet**	1.00	.70	.40
97	**Tampa Bay Buccaneers Helmet**	1.00	.70	.40
98	**Washington Redskins Helmet**	1.00	.70	.40
99	**National Football League Logo**	1.00	.70	.40
100	**American Football Fans**	1.50	1.25	.60

N

1976 Nalley's Chips CFL

	NM	E	VG
Complete Set (30):	300.00	150.00	90.00
Common Player:	8.00	4.00	2.50

1	Bill Baker	20.00	10.00	6.00
2	Eric Guthrie	8.00	4.00	2.50
3	Lou Harris	10.00	5.00	3.00
4	Layne McDowell	8.00	4.00	2.50
5	Ray Nettles	8.00	4.00	2.50
6	Lui Passaglia	25.00	12.50	7.50
7	John Sciarra	15.00	7.50	4.50
8	Wayne Smith	8.00	4.00	2.50
9	Michael Strickland	8.00	4.00	2.50
10	Jim Young	20.00	10.00	6.00
11	Dave Cutler	15.00	7.50	4.50
12	Larry Highbaugh	12.00	6.00	3.50
13	John Koniszewski	8.00	4.00	2.50
14	Bruce Lemmerman	8.00	4.00	2.50
15	George McGowan	12.00	6.00	3.50
16	Dale Potter	8.00	4.00	2.50
17	Charlie Turner	8.00	4.00	2.50
18	Tyrone Walls	8.00	4.00	2.50
19	Don Warrington	8.00	4.00	2.50
20	Tom Wilkinson	25.00	12.50	7.50
21	Willie Burden	35.00	17.50	10.50
22	Larry Cates	8.00	4.00	2.50
23	Lloyd Fairbanks	12.00	6.00	3.50
24	Joe Forzani	8.00	4.00	2.50
25	Tom Forzani	8.00	4.00	2.50
26	Rick Galbos	8.00	4.00	2.50
27	John Helton	15.00	7.50	4.50
28	Harold Holton	8.00	4.00	2.50
29	Rudy Linterman	12.00	6.00	3.50
30	Joe Pisarcik	15.00	7.50	4.50

1963 Nalley's Coins

	NM	E	VG
Complete Set (160):	2,750	1,375	825.00
Common Player:	4.00	2.00	1.25

1	Jackie Parker	20.00	10.00	6.00
2	Dick Shatto	8.00	4.00	2.50
3	Dave Mann	5.00	2.50	1.50
4	Danny Nykoluk	4.00	2.00	1.25
5	Billy Shipp	4.00	2.00	1.25
6	Doug McNichol	4.00	2.00	1.25
7	Jim Rountree	4.00	2.00	1.25
8	Art Johnson	4.00	2.00	1.25
9	Walt Radzick	4.00	2.00	1.25
10	Jim Andreotti	4.00	2.00	1.25
11	Gerry Philip	20.00	10.00	6.00
12	Lynn Bottoms	20.00	10.00	6.00
13	Ron Morris (SP)	100.00	50.00	30.00
14	Nobby Wirkowski (CO)	20.00	10.00	6.00
15	John Wydareny	20.00	10.00	6.00
16	Gerry Wilson	20.00	10.00	6.00
17	Gerry Patrick (SP)	50.00	25.00	15.00
18	Aubrey Linne	20.00	10.00	6.00
19	Norm Stoneburgh	20.00	10.00	6.00
20	Ken Beck	20.00	10.00	6.00
21	Russ Jackson	15.00	7.50	4.50
22	Kaye Vaughan	8.00	4.00	2.50
23	Dave Thelen	8.00	4.00	2.50
24	Ron Stewart	8.00	4.00	2.50
25	Moe Racine	4.00	2.00	1.25
26	Jim Conroy	4.00	2.00	1.25
27	Joe Poirier	4.00	2.00	1.25
28	Mel Seminko	4.00	2.00	1.25
29	Whit Tucker	8.00	4.00	2.50
30	Ernie White	4.00	2.00	1.25
31	Frank Clair (CO)	20.00	10.00	6.00
32	Marv Bevan	20.00	10.00	6.00
33	Jerry Selinger	20.00	10.00	6.00
34	Jim Cain	20.00	10.00	6.00
35	Mike Snodgrass	20.00	10.00	6.00
36	Ted Smale	20.00	10.00	6.00
37	Billy Joe Booth	20.00	10.00	6.00
38	Len Chandler	20.00	10.00	6.00
39	Rick Black	20.00	10.00	6.00
40	Allen Schau	20.00	10.00	6.00
41	Bernie Faloney	15.00	7.50	4.50
42	Bobby Kuntz	4.00	2.00	1.25
43	Joe Zuger	4.00	2.00	1.25
44	Hal Patterson	12.00	6.00	3.50
45	Bronko Nagurski	10.00	5.00	3.00
46	Zeno Karcz	4.00	2.00	1.25
47	Hardiman Cureton	4.00	2.00	1.25
48	John Barrow	8.00	4.00	2.50
49	Tommy Grant	8.00	4.00	2.50

50	Garney Henley	8.00	4.00	2.50
51	Dick Easterly	20.00	10.00	6.00
52	Frank Cosentino	20.00	10.00	6.00
53	Geno DeNobile	20.00	10.00	6.00
54	Ralph Goldston	20.00	10.00	6.00
55	Chet Miksza	20.00	10.00	6.00
56	Bob Minihane	20.00	10.00	6.00
57	Don Sutherin	40.00	20.00	12.00
58	Ralph Sazio (CO)	20.00	10.00	6.00
59	Dave Viti (SP)	35.00	17.50	10.50
60	Angelo Mosca (SP)	100.00	50.00	30.00
61	Sandy Stephens	8.00	4.00	2.50
62	George Dixon	8.00	4.00	2.50
63	Don Clark	4.00	2.00	1.25
64	Don Paquette	4.00	2.00	1.25
65	Billy Wayte	4.00	2.00	1.25
66	Ed Nickla	4.00	2.00	1.25
67	Marv Luster	8.00	4.00	2.50
68	Joe Stracina	4.00	2.00	1.25
69	Bobby Jack Oliver	4.00	2.00	1.25
70	Ted Elsby	4.00	2.00	1.25
71	Jim Trimble (CO)	20.00	10.00	6.00
72	Bob Leblanc	20.00	10.00	6.00
73	Dick Schnell	20.00	10.00	6.00
74	Milt Crain	20.00	10.00	6.00
75	Dick Dalatri	20.00	10.00	6.00
76	Billy Roy	20.00	10.00	6.00
77	Dave Hoppmann	20.00	10.00	6.00
78	Billy Ray Locklin	20.00	10.00	6.00
79	Ed Learn (SP)	125.00	62.00	37.00
80	Meco Poliziani (SP)	40.00	20.00	12.00
81	Leo Lewis	8.00	4.00	2.50
82	Kenny Ploen	8.00	4.00	2.50
83	Steve Patrick	4.00	2.00	1.25
84	Farrell Funston	4.00	2.00	1.25
85	Charlie Shepard	4.00	2.00	1.25
86	Ronnie Latourelle	4.00	2.00	1.25
87	Gord Rowland	4.00	2.00	1.25
88	Frank Rigney	5.00	2.50	1.50
89	Cornel Piper	4.00	2.00	1.25
90	Ernie Pitts	4.00	2.00	1.25
91	Roger Hagberg	30.00	15.00	9.00
92	Herb Gray	50.00	25.00	15.00
93	Jack Delveaux	20.00	10.00	6.00
94	Roger Savoie	20.00	10.00	6.00
95	Nick Miller	20.00	10.00	6.00
96	Norm Rauhaus	20.00	10.00	6.00
97	Cec Luining	20.00	10.00	6.00
98	Hal Ledyard	20.00	10.00	6.00
99	Neil Thomas	20.00	10.00	6.00
100	Bud Grant (CO)	75.00	37.00	22.00
101	Eagle Keys (CO)	8.00	4.00	2.50
102	Mike Wicklum	4.00	2.00	1.25
103	Bill Mitchell	4.00	2.00	1.25
104	Mike Lashuk	4.00	2.00	1.25
105	Tommy Joe Coffey	8.00	4.00	2.50
106	Zeke Smith	4.00	2.00	1.25
107	Joe Hernandez	4.00	2.00	1.25
108	Johnny Bright	8.00	4.00	2.50
109	Don Getty	8.00	4.00	2.50
110	Nat Dye	4.00	2.00	1.25
111	James Earl Wright	20.00	10.00	6.00
112	Mike Volcan (SP)	35.00	17.50	10.50
113	Jon Rechner	20.00	10.00	6.00
114	Len Vella	20.00	10.00	6.00
115	Ted Frechette	20.00	10.00	6.00
116	Larry Fleisher	20.00	10.00	6.00
117	Oscar Kruger	20.00	10.00	6.00
118	Ken Peterson	20.00	10.00	6.00
119	Bobby Walden	30.00	15.00	9.00
120	Mickey Ording	20.00	10.00	6.00
121	Pete Manning	4.00	2.00	1.25
122	Harvey Wylie	4.00	2.00	1.25
123	Tony Pajaczkowski	8.00	4.00	2.50
124	Wayne Harris	10.00	5.00	3.00
125	Earl Lunsford	8.00	4.00	2.50
126	Don Luzzi	4.00	2.00	1.25
127	Ed Buckanan	4.00	2.00	1.25
128	Lovell Coleman	5.00	2.50	1.50
129	Hal Krebs	4.00	2.00	1.25
130	Eagle Day	8.00	4.00	2.50
131	Bobby Dobbs (CO)	20.00	10.00	6.00
132	George Hansen	20.00	10.00	6.00
133	Roy Jokanovich (SP)	75.00	37.00	22.00
134	Jerry Keeling	30.00	15.00	9.00
135	Larry Anderson	20.00	10.00	6.00
136	Bill Crawford	20.00	10.00	6.00
137	Ron Albright	20.00	10.00	6.00
138	Bill Britton	20.00	10.00	6.00
139	Jim Dillard	20.00	10.00	6.00
140	Jim Furlong	20.00	10.00	6.00
141	Dave Skrien (CO)	5.00	2.50	1.50
142	Willie Fleming	10.00	5.00	3.00
143	Nub Beamer	4.00	2.00	1.25
144	Norm Fieldgate	8.00	4.00	2.50
145	Joe Kapp	35.00	17.50	10.50
146	Tom Hinton	8.00	4.00	2.50
147	Pat Claridge	4.00	2.00	1.25
148	Bill Munsey	4.00	2.00	1.25
149	Mike Martin	4.00	2.00	1.25
150	Tom Brown	8.00	4.00	2.50
151	Ian Hagemoen	20.00	10.00	6.00
152	Jim Carphin	20.00	10.00	6.00
153	By Bailey	40.00	20.00	12.00
154	Steve Cotter	20.00	10.00	6.00
155	Mike Cacic	20.00	10.00	6.00
156	Neil Beaumont	20.00	10.00	6.00
157	Lonnie Dennis	20.00	10.00	6.00
158	Barney Therrien	20.00	10.00	6.00
159	Sonny Homer	20.00	10.00	6.00
160	Walt Bilicki	20.00	10.00	6.00
S1	**Toronto Shield**	50.00	2.00	15.00
S2	**Ottawa Shield**	50.00	25.00	15.00
S3	**Hamilton Shield**	50.00	25.00	15.00
S4	**Montreal Shield**	50.00	25.00	15.00
S5	**Winnipeg Shield**	50.00	25.00	15.00
S6	**Edmonton Shield**	50.00	25.00	15.00
S7	**Calgary Shield**	50.00	25.00	15.00
S8	**British Columbia Shield**	50.00	25.00	15.00

1964 Nalley's Coins

		NM	E	VG
Complete Set (100):		720.00	360.00	216.00
Common Player:		4.00	2.00	1.25
1	Joe Kapp	30.00	15.00	9.00
2	Willie Fleming	10.00	5.00	3.00
3	Norm Fieldgate	8.00	4.00	2.50
4	Bill Murray	4.00	2.00	1.25
5	Tom Brown	10.00	5.00	3.00
6	Neil Beaumont	4.00	2.00	1.25
7	Sonny Homer	4.00	2.00	1.25
8	Lonnie Dennis	4.00	2.00	1.25
9	Dave Skrien	4.00	2.00	1.25
10	Dick Fouts (CO)	4.00	2.00	1.25
11	Paul Seale	4.00	2.00	1.25
12	Peter Kempf	4.00	2.00	1.25
13	Steve Shafer	4.00	2.00	1.25
14	Tom Hinton	8.00	4.00	2.50
15	Pat Claridge	4.00	2.00	1.25
16	By Bailey	8.00	4.00	2.50
17	Nub Beamer	5.00	2.50	1.50
18	Steve Cotter	4.00	2.00	1.25
19	Mike Cacic	4.00	2.00	1.25
20	Mike Martin	4.00	2.00	1.25
21	Eagle Day	12.00	6.00	3.50
22	Jim Dillard	4.00	2.00	1.25
23	Pete Murray	4.00	2.00	1.25
24	Tony Pajaczkowski	8.00	4.00	2.50
25	Don Luzzi	4.00	2.00	1.25
26	Wayne Harris	10.00	5.00	3.00
27	Harvey Wylie	4.00	2.00	1.25
28	Bill Crawford	4.00	2.00	1.25
29	Jim Furlong	4.00	2.00	1.25
30	Lovell Coleman	5.00	2.50	1.50
31	Pat Haines	4.00	2.00	1.25
32	Bob Taylor	4.00	2.00	1.25
33	Ernie Danjean	4.00	2.00	1.25
34	Jerry Keeling	8.00	4.00	2.50
35	Larry Robinson	4.00	2.00	1.25
36	George Hansen	4.00	2.00	1.25
37	Ron Albright	4.00	2.00	1.25
38	Larry Anderson	4.00	2.00	1.25
39	Bill Miller	4.00	2.00	1.25
40	Bill Britton	4.00	2.00	1.25
41	Lynn Amadee	8.00	4.00	2.50
42	Mike Lashuk	4.00	2.00	1.25
43	Tommy Joe Coffey	8.00	4.00	2.50
44	Junior Hawthorne	4.00	2.00	1.25
45	Nat Dye	4.00	2.00	1.25
46	Al Ecuyer	4.00	2.00	1.25
47	Howie Schumm	4.00	2.00	1.25
48	Zeke Smith	4.00	2.00	1.25
49	Mike Wicklum	4.00	2.00	1.25
50	Mike Volcan	4.00	2.00	1.25
51	E.A. Sims	4.00	2.00	1.25
52	Bill Mitchell	4.00	2.00	1.25
53	Ken Reed	4.00	2.00	1.25
54	Len Vella	4.00	2.00	1.25
55	Johnny Bright	8.00	4.00	2.50
56	Don Getty	8.00	4.00	2.50
57	Oscar Kruger	4.00	2.00	1.25
58	Ted Frechette	4.00	2.00	1.25
59	James Earl Wright	4.00	2.00	1.25
60	Roger Nelson	4.00	2.00	1.25
61	Ron Lancaster	10.00	5.00	3.00
62	Bill Clarke	4.00	2.00	1.25
63	Bob Shaw	4.00	2.00	1.25
64	Ray Purdin	4.00	2.00	1.25
65	Ron Atchison	8.00	4.00	2.50
66	Ted Urness	8.00	4.00	2.50
67	Bob Ptacek	4.00	2.00	1.25
68	Neil Habig	4.00	2.00	1.25
69	Garner Ekstran	4.00	2.00	1.25
70	Gene Wlasiuk	4.00	2.00	1.25
71	Jack Gotta	4.00	2.00	1.25
72	Dick Cohee	4.00	2.00	1.25
73	Ron Meadmore	4.00	2.00	1.25
74	Martin Fabi	4.00	2.00	1.25
75	Bob Good	4.00	2.00	1.25
76	Len Legault	4.00	2.00	1.25
77	Al Benecick	4.00	2.00	1.25
78	Dale West	4.00	2.00	1.25
79	Reg Whitehouse	4.00	2.00	1.25
80	George Reed	10.00	5.00	3.00
81	Kenny Ploen	8.00	4.00	2.50
82	Leo Lewis	10.00	5.00	3.00
83	Dick Thornton	5.00	2.50	1.50
84	Steve Patrick	4.00	2.00	1.25
85	Frank Rigney	5.00	2.50	1.50
86	Cornel Piper	4.00	2.00	1.25
87	Sherwyn Thorson	4.00	2.00	1.25
88	Ernie Pitts	4.00	2.00	1.25
89	Roger Hagberg	5.00	2.50	1.50
90	Bud Grant (CO)	50.00	25.00	15.00
91	Jack Delveaux	4.00	2.00	1.25
92	Farrell Funston	4.00	2.00	1.25
93	Ronnie Latourelle	4.00	2.00	1.25
94	Roger Hamelin	4.00	2.00	1.25
95	Gord Rowland	4.00	2.00	1.25
96	Herb Gray	10.00	5.00	3.00
97	Nick Miller	4.00	2.00	1.25
98	Norm Rauhaus	4.00	2.00	1.25
99	Bill Whisler	4.00	2.00	1.25
100	Hal Ledyard	4.00	2.00	1.25
S1	**British Columbia Shield**	45.00	22.00	13.50
S2	**Calgary Shield**	45.00	22.00	13.50
S3	**Edmonton Shield**	45.00	22.00	13.50
S4	**Saskatchewan Shield**	45.00	22.00	13.50
S5	**Winnipeg Shield**	45.00	22.00	13.50

1935 National Chicle

The granddaddy of all football card sets, the 36-card National Chicle set was the first to be circulated nationally and the first set to feature only football players (all were pro football players except for Notre Dame coach Knute Rockne). Cards measure 2-3/8" x 2-7/8". The first 24 cards are easier to obtain than the final 12. Rookie cards in this set include Hall of Famers Earl "Dutch" Clark, Cliff Battles, Ken Strong, Turk Edwards, Clarke Hinkle and Bronko Nagurski. Nagurski's card is the most valuable football card in existence.

		NM	E	VG
Complete Set (36):		35,00.00	15,000	7,000
Common Player (1-24):		300.00	150.00	90.00
Common Player (25-36):		950.00	475.00	286.00
1	Earl "Dutch" Clark **RC**	800.00	400.00	225.00
2	Bo Molenda	500.00	250.00	125.00
3	George Kenneally	500.00	250.00	125.00
4	Ed Matesic	450.00	225.00	115.00
5	Glenn Presnell	450.00	225.00	115.00
6	Pug Rentner	300.00	150.00	90.00
7	Ken Strong **RC**	700.00	350.00	200.00
8	Jim Zyntell	300.00	150.00	90.00
9	Knute Rockne	2,200	1,100	600.00
10	Cliff Battles **RC**	400.00	200.00	120.00
11	Turk Edwards **RC**	400.00	200.00	120.00
12	Tom Hupke	300.00	150.00	90.00
13	Homer Griffiths	300.00	150.00	90.00
14	Phil Sorboe	300.00	150.00	90.00
15	Ben Ciccone	300.00	150.00	90.00
16	Ben Smith	300.00	150.00	90.00
17	Tom Jones	300.00	150.00	90.00
18	Mike Mikulak	300.00	150.00	90.00
19	Ralph Kercheval	300.00	150.00	90.00
20	Warren Heller	300.00	150.00	90.00
21	Cliff Montgomery	300.00	150.00	90.00
22	Shipwreck Kelley	300.00	150.00	90.00
23	Beattie Feathers **RC**	450.00	225.00	115.00
24	Clarke Hinkle	425.00	200.00	100.00
25	Dale Burnett	950.00	475.00	285.00
26	John Isola	950.00	475.00	285.00
27	Bill Tosi	950.00	475.00	285.00

28	Stan Kosta	950.00	475.00	285.00
29	Jim MacMurdo	950.00	475.00	285.00
30	Ernie Caddel	950.00	475.00	285.00
31	Nic Niccola	950.00	475.00	285.00
32	Swede Johnston	950.00	475.00	285.00
33	Ernie Smith	950.00	475.00	285.00
34	Bronko Nagurski **RC**	12,000	6,000	3,500
35	Luke Johnson	1,000	500.00	275.00
36	Bernie Masterson	1,800	900.00	500.00

1974 Nebraska

		NM	E	VG
	Complete Set (54):	65.00	32.00	19.50
	Common Player:	1.00	.50	.30
1	Tom Osborne (CO)	20.00	10.00	6.00
2	Terry Rogers	1.00	.50	.30
3	Tom Ruud	1.50	.70	.45
4	Jeff Schneider	1.00	.50	.30
5	Mark Heydorff	1.00	.50	.30
6	Dean Gissler	1.00	.50	.30
7	Jim Burrow	1.00	.50	.30
8	Al Eveland	1.00	.50	.30
9	Chuck Jones	1.00	.50	.30
10	Brad Jenkins	1.00	.50	.30
11	Dave Butterfield	1.00	.50	.30
12	Rich Duda	1.50	.70	.45
13	Steve Hoins	1.00	.50	.30
14	Ron Pruitt	1.00	.50	.30
15	Tony Davis	1.50	.70	.45
16	Mike Fultz	1.00	.50	.30
17	Chad Leonardi	1.00	.50	.30
18	John Starkebaum	1.00	.50	.30
19	Marvin Crenshaw	1.50	.70	.45
20	Larry Mushinskie	1.00	.50	.30
21	Tom Pate	1.00	.50	.30
22	David Humm	4.00	2.00	1.25
23	Willie Thornton	1.50	.70	.45
24	Dave Redding	1.00	.50	.30
25	Dave Shamblin	1.00	.50	.30
26	Earl Everett	1.00	.50	.30
27	Rik Bonness	1.50	.70	.45
28	Mark Doak	1.00	.50	.30
29	John Lee	1.00	.50	.30
30	Mike Coyle	1.00	.50	.30
31	George Kyros	1.00	.50	.30
32	Gary Higgs	1.00	.50	.30
33	Dennis Pavelka	1.00	.50	.30
34	Jeff Moran	1.00	.50	.30
35	John O'Leary	1.00	.50	.30
36	Percy Eichelberger	1.00	.50	.30
37	Greg Jorgensen	1.00	.50	.30
38	George Mills	1.00	.50	.30
39	Terry Luck	1.00	.50	.30
40	Don Westbrook	1.00	.50	.30
41	Mike Offner	1.00	.50	.30
42	Stan Waldemore	1.00	.50	.30
43	Stan Hegener	1.00	.50	.30
44	Bobby Thomas	1.00	.50	.30
45	Bob Martin	1.00	.50	.30
46	Ritch Bahe	1.00	.50	.30
47	Tom Heiser	1.00	.50	.30
48	Steve Wieser	1.00	.50	.30
49	Ardell Johnson	1.00	.50	.30
50	Chuck Malito	1.00	.50	.30
51	Bob Lingenfelter	1.00	.50	.30
52	Wonder Monds	1.50	.70	.45
53	Bob Nelson	1.50	.70	.45
54	**Memorial Stadium**	1.50	.70	.45

1977 Nebraska

		NM	E	VG
	Complete Set (54):	65.00	32.00	19.50
	Common Player:	1.00	.50	.30
1	Tom Osborne (CO)	15.00	7.50	4.50
2	Tom Alward	1.00	.50	.30
3	Dan Anderson	1.00	.50	.30
4	Frosty Anderson	1.00	.50	.30
5	Al Austin	1.00	.50	.30
6	Ritch Bahe	1.00	.50	.30
7	John Bell	1.00	.50	.30
8	Rik Bonness	1.50	.70	.45
9	Randy Borg	1.00	.50	.30
10	Rich Costanzo	1.00	.50	.30
11	Maury Damkroger	1.50	.70	.45
12	Tony Davis	1.50	.70	.45
13	Mark Doak	1.00	.50	.30
14	Richard Duda	1.50	.70	.45
15	John Dutton	3.00	1.50	.90
16	Pat Fischer	3.00	1.50	.90
17	Marvin Crenshaw	1.50	.70	.45
18	Dean Gissler	1.00	.50	.30

19	Dave Goeller	1.00	.50	.30
20	Percy Eichelberger	1.00	.50	.30
21	Stan Hegener	1.00	.50	.30
22	Dave Humm	2.50	1.25	.70
23	Ardell Johnson	1.00	.50	.30
24	Doug Johnson	1.00	.50	.30
25	Chuck Jones	1.00	.50	.30
26	Wonder Monds	1.50	.70	.45
27	Terry Rogers	1.00	.50	.30
28	Bob Revelle	1.00	.50	.30
29	Tom Pate	1.00	.50	.30
30	Mike O'Holleran	1.00	.50	.30
31	Ron Pruitt	1.50	.70	.45
32	Bob Nelson	1.50	.70	.45
33	Larry Mushinskie	1.00	.50	.30
34	Jeff Moran	1.00	.50	.30
35	Bob Martin	1.00	.50	.30
36	Ralph Powell	1.00	.50	.30
37	Steve Manstedt	1.00	.50	.30
38	Brent Longwell	1.00	.50	.30
39	George Kyros	1.00	.50	.30
40	Zaven Yaralian	1.00	.50	.30
41	Bob Wolfe	1.00	.50	.30
42	Steve Wieser	1.00	.50	.30
43	Daryl White	1.00	.50	.30
44	Bob Thornton	1.00	.50	.30
45	John Starkebaum	1.00	.50	.30
46	Dave Shamblin	1.00	.50	.30
47	Don Westbrook	1.50	.70	.45
48	Bob Schmit	1.50	.70	.45
49	Rich Sanger	1.00	.50	.30
50	Willie Thornton	1.50	.70	.45
51	Tom Ruud	1.50	.70	.45
52	Steve Runty	1.00	.50	.30
53	**Stadium** (Red)	1.50	.70	.45
54	**Stadium** (Black)	1.50	.70	.45

1989 Nebraska 100

		NM/M	NM	E
	Complete Set (100):	40.00	30.00	16.00
	Common Player:	.35	.25	.14
1	Tony Davis	.50	.40	.20
2	Keith Jones	.35	.25	.14
3	Turner Gill	1.25	.90	.50
4	Dave Butterfield	.35	.25	.14
5	Wonder Monds	.50	.40	.20
6	Dave Rimington	.75	.60	.30
7	John Dutton	.75	.60	.30
8	Irving Fryar	3.00	2.25	1.25
9	Dean Steinkuhler	.75	.60	.30
10	Mike Rozier	1.25	.90	.50
11	Jarvis Redwine	.75	.60	.30
12	Randy Schleusener	.35	.25	.14
13	Junior Miller	.50	.40	.20
14	Broderick Thomas	1.25	.90	.50
15	Steve Taylor	.50	.40	.20
16	Neil Smith	2.00	1.50	.80
17	John McCormick	.35	.25	.14
18	Danny Noonan	.50	.40	.20
19	Mike Fultz	.35	.25	.14
20	Vince Ferragamo	1.00	.70	.40
21	Jerry Tagge	.75	.60	.30
22	Jeff Kinney	.50	.40	.20
23	Rich Glover	.50	.40	.20
24	Johnny Rodgers	1.25	.90	.50
25	Rik Bonness	.50	.40	.20
26	Dave Humm	.50	.40	.20
27	Mark Traynowicz	.50	.40	.20
28	Harry Grimminger	.35	.25	.14
29	Bill Lewis	.50	.40	.20
30	Jim Skow	.50	.40	.20
31	Larry Kramer	.35	.25	.14
32	Tony Jeter	.50	.40	.20
33	Robert Brown	.35	.25	.14
34	Larry Wachholtz	.35	.25	.14
35	Wayne Meylan	.50	.40	.20
36	Bob Newton	.35	.25	.14
37	Willie Harper	.50	.40	.20
38	Bob Martin	.35	.25	.14
39	Jerry Murtaugh	.50	.40	.20
40	Daryl White	.35	.25	.14
41	Larry Jacobson	.35	.25	.14
42	Joe Armstrong	.35	.25	.14
43	Laverne Allers	.35	.25	.14
44	Freeman White	.50	.40	.20
45	Marvin Crenshaw	.50	.40	.20
46	Forrest Behm	.35	.25	.14
47	Jerry Minnick	.35	.25	.14
48	Tom Davis	.35	.25	.14
49	Kelvin Clark	.50	.40	.20
50	Tom Rathman	1.25	.90	.50
51	Sam Francis	.35	.25	.14
52	Joe Orduna	.50	.40	.20

53	Ed Weir	.35	.25	.14
54	Bill Thornton	.35	.25	.14
55	Bob Devaney (CO)	.75	.60	.30
56	Bret Clark	.35	.25	.14
57	Frank Solich	.35	.25	.14
58	Tim Smith	.35	.25	.14
59	George Andrews	.35	.25	.14
60	Rick Berns	.50	.40	.20
61	Monte Johnson	.50	.40	.20
62	Walt Barnes	.35	.25	.14
63	Jim McFarland	.35	.25	.14
64	Jimmy Williams	.35	.25	.14
65	Vic Halligan	.35	.25	.14
66	Guy Chamberlin	.35	.25	.14
67	Hugh Rhea	.35	.25	.14
68	George Sauer	.50	.40	.20
69	E.O. Stiehm (CO)	.35	.25	.14
70	Walter G. Booth (CO)	.35	.25	.14
71	**First Night Game** (Memorial Stadium)	.35	.25	.14
72	**Memorial Stadium**	.35	.25	.14
73	**M-Stadium Expansions**	.35	.25	.14
74	Andra Franklin	.75	.60	.30
75	Ron McDole	.50	.40	.20
76	Pat Fischer	.50	.40	.20
77	Dan McMullen	.35	.25	.14
78	Charles Brock	.35	.25	.14
79	Verne Lewellen	.35	.25	.14
80	Bob Nelson	.50	.40	.20
81	Roger Craig	3.00	2.25	1.25
82	Fred Shirey	.35	.25	.14
83	Tom Novak	.35	.25	.14
84	Ray Richards	.35	.25	.14
85	Warren Alfson	.35	.25	.14
86	Lawrence Ely	.35	.25	.14
87	Mike Rozier	1.25	.90	.50
88	Dean Steinkuhler	.75	.60	.30
89	John Dutton	.75	.60	.30
90	Dave Rimington	.75	.60	.30
91	Johnny Rodgers	1.25	.90	.50
92	**Herbie Husker** (Mascot)	.35	.25	.14
93	Tom Osborne (CO)	1.25	.90	.50
94	Broderick Thomas	1.25	.90	.50
95	Bob Reynolds	.35	.25	.14
96	Mike Tingelhoff (UER) (Name misspelled Tinglehoff)	.75	.60	.30
97	Lloyd Cardwell	.35	.25	.14
98	Johnny Rodgers	1.25	.90	.50
99	'70 National Champs (Team Photo)	.50	.40	.20
100	'71 National Champs (Team Photo)	.50	.40	.20
NNO	**Title Card** (Contest on back)	.50	.40	.20

1991 NFL Experience

These oversized cards feature artwork highlights from the first 25 Super Bowls. The black-bordered cards, which measure 2-1/2" x 4-3/4", were produced by the NFL, so each has an NFL Experience logo on the front. The back is in a horizontal format, with a pink bar at the top which says "The NFL Experience" written in it, plus the card number. A pink bar at the bottom carries a description of the action on the front. Sandwiched between the two bars is a brief comment about life in the NFL, plus a sponsor logo.

		NM/M	NM	E
	Complete Set (28):	4.00	3.00	1.50
	Common Player:	.20	.15	.08
1	**NFL Experience Theme Art**	.20	.15	.08
2	Super Bowl I (Max McGee)	.20	.15	.08
3	Super Bowl II (Vince Lombardi, Bart Starr)	.50	.40	.20
4	Super Bowl III (Don Shula, Joe Namath)	.75	.60	.30
5	**Super Bowl IV**	.20	.15	.08
6	**Super Bowl V - Colts vs. Cowboys**	.20	.15	.08
7	Super Bowl VI (Duane Thomas, Bob Lily, Roger Staubach, Tom Landry, Tex Schramm)	.60	.45	.25
8	**Super Bowl VII**	.20	.15	.08
9	Super Bowl VIII (Larry Csonka)	.30	.25	.12
10	**Super Bowl IX**	.20	.15	.08
11	Super Bowl X (Lynn Swann, Jack Lambert)	.30	.25	.12
12	Super Bowl XI - Raiders vs. Vikings (John Madden)	.30	.25	.12
13	Super Bowl XII (Randy White, Harvey Martin, Craig Morton)	.30	.25	.12

		NM	E	VG
14	**Super Bowl XIII - Steelers vs. Cowboys**	.20	.15	.08
15	Super Bowl XIV(Terry Bradshaw)	.60	.45	.25
16	**Super Bowl XV - Raiders vs. Eagles**	.20	.15	.08
17	**Super Bowl XVI - 49ers vs. Bengals**	.20	.15	.08
18	Super Bowl XVII(John Riggins)	.30	.25	.12
19	Super Bowl XVIII(Marcus Allen)	.30	.25	.12
20	**Super Bowl XIX - 49ers vs. Dolphins**	.20	.15	.08
21	Super Bowl XX(Richard Dent)	.30	.25	.12
22	**Super Bowl XXI**	.20	.15	.08
23	Super Bowl XXII(John Elway, Doug Williams)	.30	.25	.12
24	**Super Bowl XXIII - 49ers vs. Bengals**	.20	.15	.08
25	Super Bowl XXIV(Joe Montana)	1.00	.70	.40
26	**Super Bowl XXV**	.20	.15	.08
27	**Super Bowl XXVI - Lombardi Trophy**	.20	.15	.08
28	Joe Theismann	.30	.25	.12

1972 NFLPA Iron Ons

These 35 cards were created as cloth patches to be ironed onto clothes. Hence, the backs are blank. The front of the card has a full color head shot of the player, with his name and 1972 NFLPA copyright at the bottom. The player's name is above the photo, which is framed by a black border. The cards, which were sold through vending machines, measure 2-1/4" x 3-1/2" and are unnumbered.

		NM	E	VG
	Complete Set (35):	175.00	87.00	52.00
	Common Player:	2.00	1.00	.60
(1)	Donny Anderson	2.00	1.00	.60
(2)	George Blanda	7.50	3.75	2.25
(3)	Terry Bradshaw	20.00	10.00	6.00
(4)	John Brockington	2.00	1.00	.60
(5)	John Brodie	5.00	2.50	1.50
(6)	Dick Butkus	10.00	5.00	3.00
(7)	Larry Csonka	10.00	5.00	3.00
(8)	Mike Curtis	2.00	1.00	.60
(9)	Len Dawson	6.00	3.00	1.75
(10)	Carl Eller	3.00	1.50	.90
(11)	Mike Garrett	2.00	1.00	.60
(12)	Joe Greene	8.00	4.00	2.50
(13)	Bob Griese	9.00	4.50	2.75
(14)	Dick Gordon	2.00	1.00	.60
(15)	John Hadl	3.00	1.50	.90
(16)	Bob Hayes	3.00	1.50	.90
(17)	Ron Johnson	2.00	1.00	.60
(18)	Deacon Jones	3.00	1.50	.90
(19)	Sonny Jurgensen	6.00	3.00	1.75
(20)	Leroy Kelly	3.00	1.50	.90
(21)	Jim Kiick	2.50	1.25	.70
(22)	Greg Landry	2.00	1.00	.60
(23)	Floyd Little	3.00	1.50	.90
(24)	Mike Lucci	2.00	1.00	.60
(25)	Archie Manning	5.00	2.50	1.50
(26)	Joe Namath	35.00	17.50	10.50
(27)	Tommy Nobis	3.00	1.50	.90
(28)	Alan Page	3.00	1.50	.90
(29)	Jim Plunkett	4.00	2.00	1.25
(30)	Gale Sayers	10.00	5.00	3.00
(31)	O.J. Simpson	35.00	17.50	10.50
(32)	Roger Staubach	30.00	15.00	9.00
(33)	Duane Thomas	2.00	1.00	.60
(34)	Johnny Unitas	25.00	12.50	7.50
(35)	Paul Warfield	5.00	2.50	1.50

1979 NFLPA Pennant Stickers

Each of these 50 stickers, sponsored by the NFLPA, is shaped like a pennant and features a black-and-white head shot of a player inside a circle. The NFLPA football logo is also on the front of the sticker. Different colors are used for the backgrounds of the stickers; some stickers can be found with various colors for a background, too. The stickers measure 2-1/2" x 5" and have the player's name, position and team on the front.

		NM	E	VG
	Complete Set (50):	425.00	210.00	125.00
	Common Player:	2.50	1.25	.70
(1)	Lyle Alzado	5.00	2.50	1.50
(2)	Ken Anderson	7.50	3.75	2.25
(3)	Steve Bartkowski	10.00	5.00	3.00
(4)	Ricky Bell	4.00	2.00	1.25
(5)	Elvin Bethea	2.50	1.25	.70
(6)	Tom Blanchard	2.50	1.25	.70
(7)	Terry Bradshaw	25.00	12.50	7.50
(8)	Bob Breunig	4.00	2.00	1.25
(9)	Greg Brezina	5.00	2.50	1.50
(10)	Doug Buffone	9.00	4.50	2.75
(11)	Earl Campbell	50.00	25.00	15.00
(12)	John Cappelletti	3.00	1.50	.90
(13)	Harold Carmichael	4.00	2.00	1.25
(14)	Chuck Crist	15.00	7.50	4.50
(15)	Sam Cunningham	4.00	2.00	1.25
(16)	Joe DeLamielleure	2.50	1.25	.70
(17)	Tom Dempsey	4.00	2.00	1.25
(18)	Tony Dorsett	15.00	7.50	4.50
(19)	Dan Fouts	20.00	10.00	6.00
(20)	Roy Gerela	4.00	2.00	1.25
(21)	Bob Griese (misspelled Greise)	12.00	6.00	3.50
(22)	Franco Harris	15.00	7.50	4.50
(23)	Jim Hart	12.00	6.00	3.50
(24)	Charlie Joiner	6.00	3.00	1.75
(25)	Paul Krause	4.00	2.00	1.25
(26)	Bob Kuechenberg	4.00	2.00	1.25
(27)	Greg Landry	2.50	1.25	.70
(28)	Archie Manning	6.00	3.00	1.75
(29)	Chester Marcol	2.50	1.25	.70
(30)	Harvey Martin	4.00	2.00	1.25
(31)	Lawrence McCutcheon	12.00	6.00	3.50
(32)	Craig Morton	4.00	2.00	1.25
(33)	Haven Moses	2.50	1.25	.70
(34)	Steve Odom	3.00	1.50	.90
(35)	Morris Owens	2.50	1.25	.70
(36)	Dan Pastorini	9.00	4.50	2.75
(37)	Walter Payton	35.00	17.50	10.50
(38)	Greg Pruitt	14.00	7.00	4.25
(39)	John Riggins	9.00	4.50	2.75
(40)	Jake Scott	3.00	1.50	.90
(41)	Ken Stabler	20.00	10.00	6.00
(42)	Roger Staubach	30.00	15.00	9.00
(43)	Jan Stenerud	6.00	3.00	1.75
(44)	Art Still	9.00	4.50	2.75
(45)	Mick Tingelhoff	4.00	2.00	1.25
(46)	Richard Todd	2.50	1.25	.70
(47)	Phil Villapiano	9.00	4.50	2.75
(48)	Wesley Walker	5.00	2.50	1.50
(49)	Roger Werhli	9.00	4.50	2.75
(50)	Jim Zorn	12.00	6.00	3.50

1972 NFLPA Vinyl Stickers

These stickers feature 20 of the NFL's stars and were sold through vending machines. Each sticker is 2-3/4" x 4-3/4" and is copyrighted on the front by the NFLPA. Each player's head appears on a caricature drawing of him in a football uniform; the outline of his body is what can actually be used as a sticker. Consequently, the backs are blank. The stickers are unnumbered.

	NM	E	VG
Complete Set (20):	95.00	47.00	28.00
Common Player:	2.00	1.00	.60

		NM	E	VG
(1)	Donny Anderson	2.00	1.00	.60
(2)	George Blanda	5.00	2.50	1.50
(3)	Terry Bradshaw	17.00	8.50	5.00
(4)	John Brockington	2.00	1.00	.60
(5)	John Brodie	4.00	2.00	1.25
(6)	Dick Butkus	8.00	4.00	2.50
(7)	Dick Gordon	2.00	1.00	.60
(8)	Joe Greene	5.00	2.50	1.50
(9)	John Hadl	2.00	1.00	.60
(10)	Bob Hayes	3.00	1.50	.90
(11)	Ron Johnson	9.00	4.50	2.75
(12)	Floyd Little	3.00	1.50	.90
(13)	Joe Namath	25.00	12.50	7.50
(14)	Tommy Nobis	3.00	1.50	.90
(15)	Alan Page	15.00	7.50	4.50
(16)	Jim Plunkett	5.00	2.50	1.50
(17)	Gale Sayers	10.00	5.00	3.00
(18)	Roger Staubach	22.00	11.00	6.50
(19)	Johnny Unitas	18.00	9.00	5.50
(20)	Paul Warfield	4.00	2.00	1.25

1972 NFLPA Wonderful World Stamps

These numbered stamps, which each measure 1-15/16" x 2-7/8", feature stars from each team in the NFL. The front of each stamp has a color photo of the player; the back has player's name, a stamp number and a place for it to be glued so it can be put into an accompanying album. The 30-page 9-1/2" x 13-1/4" album traces the history of pro football in the United States and provides short biographies of the players who are featured on the stamps. The NFLPA sponsored the album, which is titled "The Wonderful World of Pro Football USA." Stamps which are listed in the checklist with an A were issued in 1971.

		NM	E	VG
	Complete Set (390):	275.00	137.00	82.00
	Common Player:	.35	.20	.11
1	Bob Berry	.50	.25	.15
2	Greg Brezina	.35	.20	.11
3	Ken Burrow	.35	.20	.11
4	Jim Butler	.40	.20	.12
5	Wes Chesson	.35	.20	.11
6	Claude Humphrey	.50	.25	.15
7	George Kunz	1.00	.50	.30
8	Tom McCauley	.35	.20	.11
9	Jim Mitchell	.50	.25	.15
10	Tommy Nobis	3.00	1.50	.90
11	Ken Reaves	.35	.20	.11
12	Bill Sandeman	.35	.20	.11
13	John Small	.35	.20	.11
14	Harmon Wages	.35	.20	.11
15	John Zook	.50	.25	.15
16	Norm Bulaich	.60	.30	.20
17	Bill Curry	.75	.40	.25
18	Mike Curtis	.75	.40	.25
19	Ted Hendricks	3.00	1.50	.90
20	Roy Hilton	.35	.20	.11
21	Eddie Hinton	.35	.20	.11
22	David Lee	.35	.20	.11
23	Jerry Logan	.35	.20	.11
24	John Mackey	2.00	1.00	.60
25	Tom Matte	.75	.40	.25
26	Jim O'Brien	.50	.25	.15
27	Glenn Ressler	.35	.20	.11
28	Johnny Unitas	15.00	7.50	4.50
29	Bob Vogel	.50	.25	.15
30	Rick Volk	.50	.25	.15
31	Paul Costa	.35	.20	.11
32	Jim Dunaway	.50	.25	.15
33	Paul Guidry	.35	.20	.11
34	Jim Harris	.35	.20	.11
35	Robert James	.35	.20	.11
36	Mike McBath	.35	.20	.11
37	Haven Moses	1.00	.50	.30
38	Wayne Patrick	.35	.20	.11
39	John Pitts	.35	.20	.11
40	Jim Reilly	.35	.20	.11
41	Pete Richardson	.35	.20	.11
42	Dennis Shaw	.50	.25	.15
43	O.J. Simpson	25.00	12.50	7.50
44	Mike Stratton	.50	.25	.15
45	Bob Tatarek	.35	.20	.11
46	Dick Butkus	8.00	4.00	2.50
47	Jim Cadile	.35	.20	.11
48	Jack Concannon	.50	.25	.15
49	Bobby Douglass	.75	.40	.25
50	George Farmer	.50	.25	.15
51	Dick Gordon	.50	.25	.15
52	Bobby Joe Green	.35	.20	.11
53	Ed O'Bradovich	.35	.20	.11
54A	Bob Hyland	.35	.20	.11
54B	Mac Percival	.35	.20	.11
55A	Ed O'Bradovich	.50	.25	.15
55B	Gale Sayers	9.00	4.50	2.75
56A	Mac Percival	.35	.20	.11
56B	George Seals	.35	.20	.11
57	Jim Seymour	.35	.20	.11

58A	George Seals	.35	.20	.11
58B	Ron Smith	.50	.25	.15
59	Bill Staley	.35	.20	.11
60	Cecil Turner	.40	.20	.12
61	Al Beauchamp	.45	.25	.14
62	Virgil Carter	.50	.25	.15
63	Vernon Holland	.35	.20	.11
64	Bob Johnson	.50	.25	.15
65	Ron Lamb	.35	.20	.11
66	Dave Lewis	.35	.20	.11
67	Rufus Mayes	.50	.25	.15
68	Horst Muhlmann	.35	.20	.11
69	Lemar Parrish	.75	.40	.25
70	Jess Phillips	.35	.20	.11
71	Mike Reid	2.00	1.00	.60
72	Ken Riley	1.00	.50	.30
73	Paul Robinson	.50	.25	.15
74	Bob Trumpy	2.25	1.25	.70
75	Fred Willis	.35	.20	.11
76	Don Cockroft	.50	.25	.15
77	Gary Collins	.50	.25	.15
78	Gene Hickerson	.50	.25	.15
79	Fair Hooker	.75	.40	.25
80	Jim Houston	.50	.25	.15
81	Walter Johnson	.50	.25	.15
82	Joe Jones	.35	.20	.11
83	Leroy Kelly	3.00	1.50	.90
84	Milt Morin	.50	.25	.15
85	Reece Morrison	.35	.20	.11
86	Bill Nelsen	.50	.25	.15
87	Mike Phipps	.75	.40	.25
88	Bo Scott	.50	.25	.15
89	Jerry Sherk	.50	.25	.15
90	Ron Snidow	.35	.20	.11
91	Herb Adderley	3.00	1.50	.90
92	George Andrie	.75	.40	.25
93	Mike Clark	.35	.20	.11
94	Dave Edwards	.50	.25	.15
95	Walt Garrison	1.50	.70	.45
96	Cornell Green	.75	.40	.25
97	Bob Hayes	2.00	1.00	.60
98	Calvin Hill	2.00	1.00	.60
99	Chuck Howley	.75	.40	.25
100	Lee Roy Jordan	2.50	1.25	.70
101	Dave Manders	.50	.25	.15
102	Craig Morton	1.25	.60	.40
103	Ralph Neely	.50	.25	.15
104	Mel Renfro	1.00	.50	.30
105	Roger Staubach	30.00	15.00	9.00
106	Bobby Anderson	.75	.40	.25
107	Sam Brunelli	.35	.20	.11
108	Dave Costa	.35	.20	.11
109	Mike Current	.35	.20	.11
110	Pete Duranko	.35	.20	.11
111	George Goeddeke	.35	.20	.11
112	Cornell Gordon	.35	.20	.11
113	Don Horn	.50	.25	.15
114	Rich Jackson	.35	.20	.11
115	Larry Kaminski	.35	.20	.11
116	Floyd Little	1.50	.70	.45
117	Marv Montgomery	.35	.20	.11
118	Steve Ramsey	.50	.25	.15
119	Paul Smith	.50	.25	.15
120	Billy Thompson	.75	.40	.25
121	Lem Barney	3.00	1.50	.90
122	Nick Eddy	.50	.25	.15
123	Mel Farr	.75	.40	.25
124	Ed Flanagan	.35	.20	.11
125	Larry Hand	.35	.20	.11
126	Greg Landry	.75	.40	.25
127	Dick LeBeau	.50	.25	.15
128	Mike Lucci	.50	.25	.15
129	Earl McCullouch	.50	.25	.15
130	Bill Munson	.75	.40	.25
131	Wayne Rasmussen	.35	.20	.11
132	Joe Robb	.35	.20	.11
133	Jerry Rush	.35	.20	.11
134	Altie Taylor	.50	.25	.15
135	Wayne Walker	.50	.25	.15
136	Ken Bowman	.35	.20	.11
137	John Brockington	.75	.40	.25
138	Fred Carr	.50	.25	.15
139	Carroll Dale	.50	.25	.15
140	Ken Ellis	.35	.20	.11
141	Gale Gillingham	.50	.25	.15
142	Dave Hampton	.50	.25	.15
143	Doug Hart	.35	.20	.11
144A	John Hilton	.35	.20	.11
144B	MacArthur Lane	.35	.20	.11
145	Mike McCoy	.50	.25	.15
146	Ray Nitschke	2.50	1.25	.70
147	Frank Patrick	.35	.20	.11
148	Francis Peay	.35	.20	.11
149	Dave Robinson	.75	.40	.25
150	Bart Starr	9.00	4.50	2.75
151	Bob Atkins	.35	.20	.11
152	Elvin Bethea	.75	.40	.25
153	Garland Boyette	.35	.20	.11

154	ken Burrough	.75	.40	.25
155	Woody Campbell	.35	.20	.11
156	John Charles	.35	.20	.11
157	Lynn Dickey	.75	.40	.25
158	Elbert Drungo	.35	.20	.11
159	Gene Ferguson	.35	.20	.11
160	Charlie Johnson	.75	.40	.25
161	Charlie Joyner	3.00	1.50	.90
162	Dan Patorini	.75	.40	.25
163	Ron Pritchard	.35	.20	.11
164	Walt Suggs	.35	.20	.11
165	Mike Tilleman	.35	.20	.11
166	Bobby Bell	3.00	1.50	.90
167	Aaron Brown	.50	.25	.15
168	Buck Buchanan	2.00	1.00	.60
169	Ed Buddle	.75	.40	.25
170	Curley Culp	1.00	.50	.30
171	Len Dawson	6.00	3.00	1.75
172	Willie Lanier	2.50	1.25	.70
173	Jim Lynch	.50	.25	.15
174	Jim Marsalis	.50	.25	.15
175	Mo Moorman	.35	.20	.11
176	Ed Podolak	.50	.25	.15
177	Johnny Robinson	.75	.40	.25
178	Jan Stenerud	2.00	1.00	.60
179	Otis Taylor	1.50	.70	.45
180	Jim Tyrer	.75	.40	.25
181	Kermit Alexander	.50	.25	.15
182	Coy Bacon	.35	.20	.11
183	Dick Buzin	.35	.20	.11
184	Roman Gabriel	1.00	.50	.30
185	Gene Howard	.35	.20	.11
186	Ken Iman	.35	.20	.11
187	Les Josephson	.50	.25	.15
188	Marlin McKeever	.50	.25	.15
189	Merlin Olsen	4.00	2.00	1.25
190A	Richie Petitbon	.75	.40	.25
190B	Phil Olsen	.35	.20	.11
191	David Ray	.35	.20	.11
192	Lance Rentzel	.75	.40	.25
193	Isiah Robertson	.50	.25	.15
194	Larry Smith	.35	.20	.11
195	Jack Snow	.75	.40	.25
196	Nick Buoniconti	2.00	1.00	.60
197	Doug Crusan	.35	.20	.11
198	Larry Csonka	8.00	4.00	2.50
199	Bob DeMarco	.50	.25	.15
200	Marv Fleming	.50	.25	.15
201	Bob Griese	10.00	5.00	3.00
202	Jim Klick	1.00	.50	.30
203	Bob Kuechenberg	1.00	.50	.30
204	Mercury Morris	1.25	.60	.40
205A	Jim Riley	.35	.20	.11
205B	John Richardson	.35	.20	.11
206	Jim Riley	.35	.20	.11
207	Jake Scott	.75	.40	.25
208	Howard Twilley	.75	.40	.25
209	Paul Warfield	5.00	2.50	1.50
210	Garo Yepremian	.75	.40	.25
211	Grady Alderman	.50	.25	.15
212	John Beasley	.35	.20	.11
213	John Henderson	.35	.20	.11
214	Wally Hilgenberg	.50	.25	.15
215	Clinton Jones	.50	.25	.15
216	Karl Kassulke	.35	.20	.11
217	Paul Krause	1.25	.60	.40
218	Dave Osborn	.50	.25	.15
219	Alan Page	2.00	1.00	.60
220	Ed Sharockman	.35	.20	.11
221	Fran Tarkenton	10.00	5.00	3.00
222	Mick Tingelhoff	.75	.40	.25
223	Charlie West	.35	.20	.11
224	Lonnie Warwick	.35	.20	.11
225	Gene Washington	.75	.40	.25
226	Hank Barton	.35	.20	.11
227A	Larry Carwell	.35	.20	.11
227B	Ron Berger	.35	.20	.11
228	Larry Carwell	.35	.20	.11
229A	Carl Garrett	.50	.25	.15
229B	Jim Cheyunski	.50	.25	.15
230A	Jim Hunt	.35	.20	.11
230B	Carl Garrett	.50	.25	.15
231	Rickie Harris	.35	.20	.11
232	Daryl Johnson	.35	.20	.11
233	Steve Kiner	.35	.20	.11
234	Jon Morris	.35	.20	.11
235	Jim Nance	.75	.40	.25
236	Tom Neville	.35	.20	.11
237	Jim Plunkett	4.00	2.00	1.25
238	Ron Sellers	.50	.25	.15
239	Len St. Jean	.35	.20	.11
240A	Gerald Warren	.35	.20	.11
240B	Don Webb	.35	.20	.11
241	Dan Abramowicz	.75	.40	.25
242A	Tony Baker	.35	.20	.11
242B	Dick Absher	.35	.20	.11
243	Leo Carroll	.35	.20	.11
244	Jim Duncan	.35	.20	.11

245	Al Dodd	.35	.20	.11
246	Jim Flanigan	.35	.20	.11
247	Hoyle Granger	.35	.20	.11
248	Edd Hargett	.75	.40	.25
249	Glen Ray Hines	.35	.20	.11
250	Hugo Hollas	.35	.20	.11
251	Jake Kupp	.35	.20	.11
252	Dave Long	.35	.20	.11
253	Mike Morgan	.35	.20	.11
254	Tom Roussel	.35	.20	.11
255	Del Williams	.35	.20	.11
256	Otto Brown	.35	.20	.11
257	Bobby Duhon	.50	.25	.15
258	Scott Eaton	.35	.20	.11
259	Jim Flies	.35	.20	.11
260	Tucker Fredrickson	.75	.40	.25
261A	Don Herrmann	.35	.20	.11
261B	Pete Gogolak	.50	.25	.15
262	Bob Grim	.50	.25	.15
263	Don Herrmann	.35	.20	.11
264A	Ernie Koy	.75	.40	.25
264B	Ron Johnson	1.00	.50	.30
265A	Spider Lockhart	.50	.25	.15
265B	Jim Kanicki	.35	.20	.11
266	Spider Lockhart	.50	.25	.15
267	Joe Morrison	.75	.40	.25
268	Bob Tucker	2.00	1.00	.60
269	Willie Williams	.35	.20	.11
270	Willie Young	.35	.20	.11
271	Al Atkinson	.35	.20	.11
272	Ralph Baker	.35	.20	.11
273	Emerson Boozer	.75	.40	.25
274	John Elliott	.35	.20	.11
275	Dave Herman	.35	.20	.11
276A	Dave Herman	.35	.20	.11
276B	Winston Hill	.50	.25	.15
277	Gus Hollomon	.35	.20	.11
278	Bob Howfield	.35	.20	.11
279	Pete Lammons	.50	.25	.15
280	Joe Namath (numbered 281)	22.00	11.00	6.50
281	Gerry Philbin	.50	.25	.15
282	Matt Snell	.75	.40	.25
283	Steve Tannen	.35	.20	.11
284	Earlie Thomas	.35	.20	.11
285	Al Woodall	.50	.25	.15
286	Fred Biletnikoff	4.00	2.00	1.25
287	George Blanda	6.00	3.00	1.75
288	Willie Brown	3.00	1.50	.90
289	Ray Chester	1.00	.50	.30
290	Tony Cline	.35	.20	.11
291	Dan Conners	.35	.20	.11
292	Ben Davidson	1.50	.70	.45
293	Hewritt Dixon	.50	.25	.15
294	Tom Keating	.50	.25	.15
295	Daryle Lamonica	1.50	.70	.45
296	Gus Otto	.35	.20	.11
297	Jim Otto	3.00	1.50	.90
298	Rod Sherman	.35	.20	.11
299	Bubba Smith	.35	.20	.11
300A	Warren Wells	.50	.25	.15
300B	Gene Upshaw	3.00	1.50	.90
301	Rick Arrington	.35	.20	.11
302	Gary Ballman	.50	.25	.15
303	Lee Bouggess	.35	.20	.11
304	Bill Bradley	.75	.40	.25
305A	Richard Harris	.35	.20	.11
305B	Happy Feller	.75	.40	.25
306A	Ben Hawkins	.35	.20	.11
306B	Richard Harris	.35	.20	.11
307	Ben Hawkins	.35	.20	.11
308	Harold Jackson	1.50	.70	.45
309	Pete Liske	.75	.40	.25
310	Al Nelson	.35	.20	.11
311	Gary Pettigrew	.35	.20	.11
312	Tim Rossovich	.75	.40	.25
313	Tom Woodeshick	.50	.25	.15
314	Adrian Young	.50	.25	.15
315	Steve Zabel	.50	.25	.15
316	Chuck Allen	.35	.20	.11
317	Warren Bankston	.50	.25	.15
318	Chuck Beatty	.35	.20	.11
319	Terry Bradshaw	20.00	10.00	6.00
320	John Fuqua	.50	.25	.15
321	Terry Hanratty	1.00	.50	.30
322	Ray Mansfield	.35	.20	.11
323	Ben McGee	.35	.20	.11
324	John Rowser	.35	.20	.11
325	Andy Russell	1.00	.50	.30
326	Ron Shanklin	.50	.25	.15
327	Dave Smith	.35	.20	.11
328	Bruce Van Dyke	.35	.20	.11
329	Lloyd Voss	.35	.20	.11
330	Bobby Walden	.35	.20	.11
331	Donny Anderson	.75	.40	.25
332	Jim Bakken	.75	.40	.25
333	Pete Beathard	.75	.40	.25
334A	Mel Gray	2.00	1.00	.60

334B	Miller Farr	.50	.25	.15
335A	Jim Hart	1.00	.50	.30
335B	Mel Gray	1.00	.50	.30
336	Jim Hart	1.00	.50	.30
337A	Chuck Latourette	.35	.20	.11
337B	Rol Krueger	.35	.20	.11
338	Chuck Latourette	.35	.20	.11
339A	Bob Reynolds	.35	.20	.11
339B	Ernie McMillan	.50	.25	.15
340	Bob Reynolds	.35	.20	.11
341	Jackie Smith	3.50	1.75	1.00
342	Larry Stallings	.50	.25	.15
343	Chuck Walker	.35	.20	.11
344	Roger Wehrli	.75	.40	.25
345	Larry Wilson	2.00	1.00	.60
346	Bob Babich	.35	.20	.11
347	Pete Barnes	.35	.20	.11
348A	Marty Domres	.50	.25	.15
348B	Steve DeLong	.50	.25	.15
349	Marty Domres	.50	.25	.15
350	Gary Garrison	.50	.25	.15
351A	Walker Gillette	.35	.20	.11
351B	John Hadl	1.25	.60	.40
352	Kevin Hardy	.35	.20	.11
353	Bob Howard	.35	.20	.11
354A	Jim Hill	.35	.20	.11
354B	Deacon Jones	1.75	.90	.50
355	Terry Owens	.75	.40	.25
356	Dennis Partee	.35	.20	.11
357A	Dennis Partee	.35	.20	.11
357B	Jeff Queen	.35	.20	.11
358	Jim Tolbert	.35	.20	.11
359	Russ Washington	.35	.20	.11
360	Doug Wilkerson	.35	.20	.11
361	John Brodie	3.50	1.75	1.00
362	Doug Cunningham	.35	.20	.11
363	Bruce Gossett	.35	.20	.11
364	Stan Hindman	.35	.20	.11
365	John Isenbarger	.50	.25	.15
366	Charlie Krueger	.50	.25	.15
367	Frank Nunley	.35	.20	.11
368	Woody Peoples	.35	.20	.11
369	Len Rohde	.35	.20	.11
370	Steve Spurrier	6.50	3.25	2.00
371	Gene Washington	1.00	.50	.30
372	Dave Wilcox	.75	.40	.25
373	Ken Willard	1.00	.50	.30
374	Bob Windsor	.50	.25	.15
375	Dick Witcher	.50	.25	.15
376	Verlon Biggs	.75	.40	.25
377	Larry Brown	3.00	1.50	.90
378	Speedy Duncan	.50	.25	.15
379	Chris Hanburger	1.00	.50	.30
380	Charlie Harraway	.50	.25	.15
381	Sonny Jurgensen	5.00	2.50	1.50
382	Bill Kilmer	1.50	.70	.45
383	Tommy Mason	.50	.25	.15
384	Ron McDole	.50	.25	.15
385	Brig Owens	.35	.20	.11
386	Jack Pardee	2.00	1.00	.60
387	Myron Pottios	1.00	.50	.30
388	Jerry Smith	.50	.25	.15
389	Diron Talbert	.50	.25	.15
390	Charley Taylor	4.00	2.00	1.25
---	**Album**	25.00	12.50	7.50

1988 North Carolina

		NM/M	NM	E
	Complete Set (16):	15.00	11.00	6.00
	Common Player:	1.00	.70	.40
1	Mack Brown (CO)	1.50	1.25	.60
2	Pat Crowley	1.00	.70	.40
3	Torin Dorn	2.00	1.50	.80
4	Jeff Garnica	1.00	.70	.40
5	Antonio Goss	1.25	.90	.50
6	Jonathan Hall	1.25	.90	.50
7	Darrell Hamilton	1.00	.70	.40
8	Creighton Incorminias	1.00	.70	.40
9	John Keller	1.00	.70	.40
10	Randy Marriott	1.00	.70	.40
11	Deems May	1.00	.70	.40
12	John Reed	1.00	.70	.40
13	James Thompson	1.25	.90	.50
14	Steve Steinbacher	1.00	.70	.40
15	Dan Vooletich	1.00	.70	.40
16	Mitch Wike	1.00	.70	.40

1979 North Schedules

		NM	E	VG
	Complete Set (4):	12.00	6.00	3.50
	Common Player:	3.00	1.50	.90
1	Ricky Barden	3.00	1.50	.90
2	Steve Junkman	3.00	1.50	.90
3	Matt Kupec	5.00	2.50	1.50
4	Doug Paschal	3.00	1.50	.90

1982 North Carolina Schedules

		NM/M	NM	E
	Complete Set (8):	25.00	18.50	10.00
	Common Player:	3.00	2.25	1.25
1	Kelvin Bryant	7.50	5.75	3.00
2	Alan Burrus	3.00	2.25	1.25
3	David Drechsler	3.00	2.25	1.25
4	Rod Elkins	4.00	3.00	1.50
5	Jack Parry	3.00	2.25	1.25
6	Greg Poole	3.00	2.25	1.25
7	Ron Spruill	3.00	2.25	1.25
8	Mike Wilcher	4.00	3.00	1.50

1986 North Carolina Schedules

		NM/M	NM	E
	Complete Set (4):	15.00	7.50	4.50
	Common Player:	3.00	2.25	1.25
1	Walter Bailey	3.00	2.25	1.25
2	Harris Barton	6.00	4.50	2.50
3	C.A. Brooks	3.00	2.25	1.25
4	Eric Streater	4.00	3.00	1.50

1991 North Carolina Schedules

		NM/M	NM	E
	Complete Set (3):	7.00	5.25	2.75
	Common Player:	2.00	1.50	.80
1	Eric Gash	2.00	1.50	.80
2	Dwight Hollier	4.00	3.00	1.50
3	Tommy Thigpen	2.00	1.50	.80

1989 North Texas McDag

		NM/M	NM	E
	Complete Set (16):	7.00	5.25	2.75
	Common Player:	.50	.40	.20
1	Clay Bode	.50	.40	.20
2	Scott Bowles	.50	.40	.20
3	Keith Chapman	.50	.40	.20
4	Darrin Collins	.50	.40	.20
5	Tony Cook	.50	.40	.20
6	Scott Davis	1.00	.70	.40
7	Byron Gross	.50	.40	.20
8	Larry Green	.50	.40	.20
9	Major Greene	1.00	.70	.40
10	Carl Brewer	.50	.40	.20
11	J.D. Martinez	.50	.40	.20
12	Charles Monroe	.50	.40	.20
13	Kregg Sanders	.50	.40	.20
14	Lou Smith	.50	.40	.20
15	Jeff Tutson	.50	.40	.20
16	Trent Touchstone	.50	.40	.20

1990 North Texas McDag

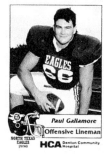

Paul Gallamore
Offensive Lineman

		NM/M	NM	E
	Complete Set (16):	9.00	6.75	3.50
	Common Player:	.50	.40	.20
1	Scott Davis	.75	.60	.30
2	Byron Gross	.50	.40	.20
3	Tony Cook	.50	.40	.20
4	Walter Casey	.50	.40	.20
5	Erric Pegram	4.00	3.00	1.50
6	Clay Bode	.50	.40	.20
7	Scott Bowles	.50	.40	.20
8	Shawn Wash	.50	.40	.20
9	Isaac Barnett	.50	.40	.20
10	Paul Gallamore	.50	.40	.20
11	J.D. Martinez	.50	.40	.20
12	Velton Morgan	.50	.40	.20
13	Major Greene	.75	.60	.30
14	Bart Helsley	.50	.40	.20
15	Jeff Tutson	.50	.40	.20
16	Tony Walker	.50	.40	.20

1988 Notre Dame

		NM/M	NM	E
	Complete Set (60).	20.00	15.00	8.00
	Common Player:	.25	.20	.10
1	**Golden Dome**	.50	.40	.20
2	Lou Holtz (CO)	2.00	1.50	.80
3	Mark Green	.50	.40	.20
4	Andy Heck	.75	.60	.30
5	Ned Bolcar	.50	.40	.20
6	Anthony Johnson	.50	.40	.20
7	Flash Gordon	.25	.20	.10
8	Pat Ellers	.25	.20	.10
9	Raghib Ismail	5.00	3.75	2.00
10	Ted FitzGerald	.25	.20	.10
11	Ted Healy	.25	.20	.10
12	Braxston Banks	.50	.40	.20
13	Steve Belles	.25	.20	.10
14	Steve Alaniz	.25	.20	.10
15	Chris Zorich	2.00	1.50	.80
16	Kent Graham	1.00	.70	.40
17	Mike Brennan	.25	.20	.10
18	Marty Lippincott	.25	.20	.10
19	Rod West	.25	.20	.10
20	Dean Brown	.25	.20	.10
21	Tom Gorman	.25	.20	.10
22	Tony Rice	1.50	1.25	.60
23	Steve Roddy	.25	.20	.10
24	Reggie Ho	.50	.40	.20
25	Pat Terrell	.75	.60	.30
26	Joe Jarosz	.25	.20	.10
27	Mike Stonebreaker	1.00	.70	.40
28	David Jandric	.25	.20	.10
29	Jeff Alm	.75	.60	.30
30	Pete Graham	.25	.20	.10
31	Corny Southall	.25	.20	.10
32	Joe Allen	.25	.20	.10
33	Jim Sexton	.25	.20	.10
34	Michael Crounse	.25	.20	.10
35	Kurt Zackrison	.25	.20	.10
36	Stan Smagala	.50	.40	.20
37	Mike Heidt	.25	.20	.10
38	Frank Stams	.75	.60	.30
39	D'Juan Francisco	.50	.40	.20
40	Tim Ryan	.50	.40	.20
41	Arnold Ale	.25	.20	.10
42	Andre Jones	.25	.20	.10
43	Wes Pritchett	.25	.20	.10
44	Tim Grunhard	.75	.60	.30
45	Chuck Killian	.25	.20	.10
46	Scott Kowalkowski	.50	.40	.20
47	George Streeter	.25	.20	.10
48	Donn Grimm	.25	.20	.10
49	Ricky Watters	6.00	4.50	2.50
50	Ryan Mihalko	.25	.20	.10
51	Tony Brooks	.75	.60	.30
52	Todd Lyght	1.00	.70	.40
53	Winston Sandri	.25	.20	.10
54	Aaron Robb	.25	.20	.10
55	Derek Brown (TE)	1.00	.70	.40
56	Bryan Flannery	.25	.20	.10
57	Kevin McShane	.25	.20	.10
58	Billy Hackett	.25	.20	.10
59	George Williams	.25	.20	.10
60	Frank Jacobs	.25	.20	.10

1989 Notre Dame 1903-32

		NM/M	NM	E
	Complete Set (22):	7.00	5.25	2.75
	Common Player:	.35	.25	.14
1	Hunk Anderson	.50	.40	.20
2	Bert Metzger	.35	.25	.14
3	Roger Kiley	.35	.25	.14
4	Nordy Hoffman	.35	.25	.14
5	Knute Rockne (CO)	2.00	1.50	.80
6	Elmer Layden	.75	.60	.30
7	Gus Dorais	.50	.40	.20
8	Ray Eichenlaub	.35	.25	.14
9	Don Miller	.50	.40	.20
10	Moose Krause	.75	.60	.30
11	Jesse Harper	.35	.25	.14
12	Jack Cannon	.35	.25	.14
13	Eddie Anderson	.35	.25	.14
14	Louis Salmon	.35	.25	.14
15	John Smith	.35	.25	.14
16	Harry Stuhldreher	.75	.60	.30
17	Joe Kurth	.35	.25	.14
18	Frank Carideo	.35	.25	.14
19	Marchy Schwartz	.35	.25	.14
20	Adam Walsh	.35	.25	.14
21	George Gipp	2.00	1.50	.80
22	Jim Crowley	.75	.60	.30

1989 Notre Dame 1935-59

		NM/M	NM	E
	Complete Set (22):	7.00	5.25	2.75
	Common Player:	.35	.25	.14
1	Frank Leahy (CO)	.75	.60	.30
2	John Lattner	.75	.60	.30
3	Jim Martin	.50	.40	.20
4	Joe Heap	.35	.25	.14
5	Paul Hornung	1.25	.90	.50
6	Bill Shakespeare	.75	.60	.30
7	Bob Dove	.35	.25	.14
8	Bob Williams	.35	.25	.14
9	Al Ecuyer	.35	.25	.14
10	George Connor	.75	.60	.30
11	Leon Hart	.75	.60	.30
12	Joe Beinor	.35	.25	.14
13	Bill Fischer	.35	.25	.14
14	Angelo Bertelli	.75	.60	.30
15	Ralph Guglielmi	.50	.40	.20
16	Pat Filley	.35	.25	.14
17	Emil (Red) Sitko	.50	.40	.20
18	Don Schaefer	.35	.25	.14
19	Monty Stickles	.50	.40	.20
20	Creighton Miller	.35	.25	.14
21	Chuck Sweeney	.35	.25	.14
22	John Lujack	1.00	.70	.40

1989 Notre Dame 1964-87

		NM/M	NM	E
	Complete Set (22):	7.00	5.25	2.75
	Common Player:	.35	.25	.14
1	Dan Devine (CO)	.50	.40	.20
2	Joe Theismann	1.00	.70	.40
3	Tom Gatewood	.50	.40	.20
4	Timmy Brown	1.25	.90	.50
5	Ara Parseghian (CO)	.75	.60	.30
6	Jim Lynch	.50	.40	.20
7	Luther Bradley	.35	.25	.14
8	Ross Browner	.50	.40	.20
9	John Huarte	1.00	.70	.40
10	Bob Crable	.50	.40	.20
11	Ken MacAfee	.50	.40	.20
12	Alan Page	.75	.60	.30
13	Vagas Ferguson	.50	.40	.20
14	Dick Arrington	.35	.25	.14
15	Bob Golic	.50	.40	.20
16	Mike Townsend	.35	.25	.14
17	Walt Patulski	.50	.40	.20
18	Allen Pinkett	.50	.40	.20
19	Terry Hanratty	.75	.60	.30
20	Dave Casper	.75	.60	.30
21	Jack Snow	.75	.60	.30
22	Nick Eddy	.50	.40	.20

1990 Notre Dame 200

		NM/M	NM	E
	Complete Set (200):	18.00	13.50	7.25
	Common Player:	.10	.08	.04
1	Joe Montana	1.25	.90	.50
2	Tim Brown	.50	.40	.20
3	Reggie Barnett	.20	.15	.08
4	Joe Theismann	.50	.40	.20
5	Bob Clasby	.10	.08	.04
6	Dave Casper	.20	.15	.08
7	George Kunz	.20	.15	.08
8	Vince Phelan	.10	.08	.04
9	Tom Gibbons	.10	.08	.04
10	Tom Thayer	.10	.08	.04
11	Notre Dame Helmet	.10	.08	.04
12	John Scully	.10	.08	.04
13	Lou Holtz (CO)	.30	.25	.12
14	Larry Dinardo	.20	.15	.08
15	Greg Marx	.10	.08	.04
16	Greg Dingens	.10	.08	.04
17	Jim Seymour	.20	.15	.08
18	1979 Cotton Bowl (Program)	.10	.08	.04
19	Mike Kadish	.20	.15	.08
20	Bob Crable	.20	.15	.08
21	Tony Rice	.20	.15	.08
22	Phil Carter	.10	.08	.04
23	Ken MacAfee	.20	.15	.08
24	Nick Eddy	.20	.15	.08
25	1988 National Champs (Trophies)	.20	.15	.08
26	Clarence Ellis	.20	.15	.08
27	Joe Restic	.10	.08	.04
28	Dan Devine (CO)	.20	.15	.08
29	John K. Carney	.10	.08	.04
30	Stacey Toran	.20	.15	.08
31	47th Sugar Bowl (Program)	.10	.08	.04
32	J. Heavens	.10	.08	.04
33	Mike Fanning	.10	.08	.04
34	Dave Vinson	.10	.08	.04
35	Ralph Gugliemi	.10	.08	.04
36	Reggie Ho	.10	.08	.04
37	Allen Pinkett	.20	.15	.08
38	Jim Browner	.20	.15	.08
39	Blair Kiel	.20	.15	.08
40	Joe Montana	1.25	.90	.50
41	Rocky Bleier	.30	.25	.12
42	Terry Hanratty	.20	.15	.08
43	Tom Regner	.20	.15	.08
44	Pete Holohan	.10	.08	.04
45	Greg Bell	.20	.15	.08
46	Dave Duerson	.20	.15	.08
47	Frank Varrichione	.20	.15	.08
48	1988 Championship (Team Photo)	.20	.15	.08
49	Ted Burgmeier	.10	.08	.04
50	Ara Parseghian (CO)	.30	.25	.12
51	Mike Townsend	.10	.08	.04
52	Liberty Bowl 1983 (Program)	.10	.08	.04
53	Tony Furjanic	.10	.08	.04
54	Luther Bradley	.20	.15	.08
55	Steve Niehaus	.20	.15	.08
56	56th Orange Bowl (Program)	.10	.08	.04
57	32nd Gator Bowl (Program)	.10	.08	.04
58	40th Sugar Bowl (Program)	.10	.08	.04
59	52nd Cotton Bowl (Program)	.10	.08	.04
60	1975 Orange Bowl (Program)	.10	.08	.04
61	Wayne Bullock	.10	.08	.04
62	Larry Moriarty	.10	.08	.04
63	Jim Lynch	.20	.15	.08
64	Mike McCoy	.20	.15	.08
65	Tony Hunter	.20	.15	.08
66	1984 Aloha Bowl (Program)	.10	.08	.04
67	Dave Huffman	.10	.08	.04
68	John Lattner	.20	.15	.08
69	Tom Gatewood	.20	.15	.08
70	Knute Rockne (CO)	.35	.25	.14
71	Phil Pozderac	.10	.08	.04
72	Ross Browner	.20	.15	.08
73	Pete Demmerle	.10	.08	.04
74	Sunkist Fiesta Bowl (Program)	.10	.08	.04
75	Walt Patulski	.20	.15	.08
76	George Gipp	.50	.40	.20
77	LeRoy Leopold	.10	.08	.04
78	John Huarte	.30	.25	.12
79	Tony Yelovich (CO)	.10	.08	.04
80	John Lujack	.30	.25	.12
81	Cotton Bowl Classic (Program)	.10	.08	.04
82	Tim Huffman	.10	.08	.04
83	Bob Golic	.20	.15	.08
84	Tom Clements	.20	.15	.08
85	39th Orange Bowl (Program)	.10	.08	.04
86	James J. White (ADMIN)	.10	.08	.04
87	Frank Carideo	.10	.08	.04
88	Vinny Cerrato	.10	.08	.04
89	Louis Salmon	.10	.08	.04
90	Bob Burger	.10	.08	.04
91	Gerry Dinardo	.20	.15	.08
92	Mike Creaney	.10	.08	.04
93	John Krimm	.10	.08	.04
94	Vagas Ferguson	.20	.15	.08
95	Kris Haines	.10	.08	.04
96	Gus Dorais	.20	.15	.08
97	Tom Schoen	.10	.08	.04
98	Jack Robinson	.10	.08	.04
99	Joe Heap	.10	.08	.04
100	Checklist 1-99	.10	.08	.04
101	Gary Darnell (CO)	.10	.08	.04
102	Peter Vaas (CO)	.10	.08	.04
103	1924 National Champs (Team Photo)	.20	.15	.08
104	Wayne Millner	.20	.15	.08
105	Moose Krause	.20	.15	.08
106	Jack Cannon	.10	.08	.04
107	Christy Flanagan	.10	.08	.04
108	Bob Lehmann	.10	.08	.04
109	1947 Champions (Team Photo)		.15	.08
110	Joe Kurth	.10	.08	.04
111	Tommy Yarr	.10	.08	.04
112	Nick Buoniconti	.30	.25	.12
113	Jim Smithberger	.10	.08	.04
114	Joe Beinor	.10	.08	.04
115	Pete Cordelli (CO)	.10	.08	.04
116	Daryle Lamonica	.30	.25	.12
117	Kevin Hardy	.10	.08	.04
118	Creighton Miller	.20	.15	.08
119	Bob Gladieux	.20	.15	.08
120	Fred Miller (Later Miller Brewing)	.20	.15	.08
121	Gary Potempa	.10	.08	.04
122	Bob Kuechenberg	.20	.15	.08
123	Jesse Harper	.10	.08	.04
124	1929 National Champs (Team Photo)	.20	.15	.08
125	Alan Page	.30	.25	.12
126	Don Miller	.20	.15	.08
127	1943 National Champs (Team Photo)	.20	.15	.08
128	Bob Wetoska	.10	.08	.04
129	Skip Holtz (CO)	.10	.08	.04
130	Hunk Anderson (CO)	.10	.08	.04
131	Bob Williams	.10	.08	.04
132	1966 National Champs (Team Photo)	.10	.08	.04
133	Jim Reilly	.10	.08	.04
134	Earl "Curly" Lambeau	.20	.15	.08
135	Ernie Hughes	.10	.08	.04
136	Dick Bumpas (CO)	.10	.08	.04
137	Jay Haynes (CO)	.10	.08	.04
138	Harry Stuhldreher	.20	.15	.08
139	1971 Cotton Bowl (Game Photo)	.20	.15	.08
140	1930 National Champs (Team Photo)	.20	.15	.08
141	Larry Conjar	.20	.15	.08
142	1977 National Champs (Team Photo)	.20	.15	.08
143	Pete Duranko	.20	.15	.08
144	Heisman Winners (Seven Trophy Winners)	.30	.25	.12
145	Bill Fisher	.10	.08	.04
146	Marchy Schwartz	.10	.08	.04
147	Chuck Heater (CO)	.10	.08	.04
148	Bert Metzger	.10	.08	.04
149	Bill Shakespeare	.20	.15	.08
150	Adam Walsh	.10	.08	.04
151	Nordy Hoffman	.10	.08	.04
152	Ted Gradel	.10	.08	.04
153	Monty Stickles	.20	.15	.08
154	Neil Worden	.10	.08	.04
155	Pat Filley	.10	.08	.04
156	Angelo Bertelli	.20	.15	.08
157	Nick Pietrosante	.20	.15	.08
158	Art Hunter	.10	.08	.04
159	Ziggy Czarobski	.10	.08	.04
160	1925 Rose Bowl (Program)	.10	.08	.04
161	Al Ecuyer	.10	.08	.04
162	1949 Notre Dame Champs (Team Photo)	.10	.08	.04
163	Elmer Layden	.20	.15	.08
164	Joe Moore (CO)	.10	.08	.04
165	1946 National Champs (Team Photo)	.10	.08	.04
166	Frank Rydzewski	.10	.08	.04
167	Bud Boeringer	.10	.08	.04
168	Jerry Groom	.10	.08	.04
169	Jack Snow	.20	.15	.08
170	Joe Montana	1.25	.90	.50
171	John Smith	.10	.08	.04
172	Frank Leahy (CO)	.30	.25	.12
173	Emil "Red" Sitko	.20	.15	.08
174	Dick Arrington	.10	.08	.04
175	Eddie Anderson	.10	.08	.04
176	1928 Army (Logo and score)	.10	.08	.04
177	1913 Army (Logo and score)	.10	.08	.04
178	1935 Ohio State (Logo and game score)	.10	.08	.04
179	1946 Army (Logo and game score)	.10	.08	.04
180	1953 Georgia Tech (Logo and game score)	.10	.08	.04
181	Don Schaefer	.10	.08	.04
182	1973 Football Team (Team Photo)	.20	.15	.08
183	Bob Dove	.10	.08	.04
184	Dick Szymanski	.10	.08	.04
185	Jim Martin	.20	.15	.08
186	1957 Oklahoma (Logo and game score)	.10	.08	.04
187	1966 Michigan State (Logo and game score)	.10	.08	.04
188	1973 USC (Logo and game score)	.10	.08	.04
189	1980 Michigan (Logo and game score)	.10	.08	.04
190	1982 Michigan (Logo and game score)	.10	.08	.04
191	Chuck Sweeney	.10	.08	.04
192	Notre Dame Stadium	.10	.08	.04
193	Roger Kiley	.10	.08	.04
194	Ray Eichenlaub	.10	.08	.04
195	George Connor	.20	.15	.08
196	1982 Pittsburgh (Logo and game score)	.10	.08	.04
197	1986 USC (Logo and game score)	.10	.08	.04
198	1988 Miami (Logo and game score)	.10	.08	.04
199	1988 USC (Logo and game score)	.10	.08	.04
200	Checklist 101-199	.10	.08	.04

1990 Notre Dame 60

		NM/M	NM	E
	Complete Set (60):	25.00	18.50	10.00
	Common Player:	.35	.25	.14
1	Joe Allen	.35	.25	.14
2	William Pollard	.35	.25	.14
3	Tony Smith	.35	.25	.14
4	Tony Brooks	.75	.60	.30
5	Kenny Spears	.35	.25	.14
6	Mike Heldt	.35	.25	.14
7	Derek Brown (TE)	.75	.60	.30
8	Rodney Culver	.75	.60	.30
9	Ricky Watters	3.00	2.25	1.25
10	Raghib Ismail	2.50	2.00	1.00
11	Lou Holtz (CO)	.75	.60	.30
12	Chris Zorich	1.00	.70	.40
13	Erik Simien	.35	.25	.14
14	Shawn Davis	.35	.25	.14
15	Greg Davis	.35	.25	.14
16	Walter Boyd	.35	.25	.14
17	Tim Ryan	.50	.40	.20
18	Lindsay Knapp	.35	.25	.14
19	Junior Bryant	.35	.25	.14
20	Mike Stonebreaker	.50	.40	.20
21	Randy Scianna	.35	.25	.14
22	Rick Mirer	6.00	4.50	2.50
23	Ryan Mihalko	.35	.25	.14
24	Todd Lyght	.75	.60	.30
25	Andre Jones	.35	.25	.14
26	Rod Smith (DB)	.50	.40	.20
27	Winston Sandri	.35	.25	.14
28	Bob Dahl	.50	.40	.20
29	Stuart Tyner	.35	.25	.14
30	Brian Shannon	.35	.25	.14
31	Shawn Smith	.35	.25	.14
32	Jim Sexton	.35	.25	.14
33	Dorsey Levens	1.00	.70	.40
34	Lance Johnson	.35	.25	.14
35	George Poorman	.35	.25	.14
36	Irv Smith	1.00	.70	.40
37	George Williams	.35	.25	.14
38	George Marshall	.50	.40	.20
39	Reggie Brooks	2.00	1.50	.80
40	Scott Kowalkowski	.50	.40	.20
41	Jerry Bodine	.35	.25	.14
42	Karmeeleyah McGill	.35	.25	.14
43	Donn Grimm	.35	.25	.14
44	Billy Hackett	.35	.25	.14
45	Jordan Halter	.35	.25	.14
46	Mirko Jurkovic	.75	.60	.30
47	Mike Callan	.35	.25	.14
48	Justin Hall	.35	.25	.14
49	Nick Smith	.35	.25	.14
50	Brian Ratigan	.35	.25	.14
51	Eric Jones	.35	.25	.14
52	Todd Norman	.35	.25	.14
53	Devon McDonald	.50	.40	.20
54	Marc deManigold	.35	.25	.14
55	Bret Hankins	.35	.25	.14
56	Adrian Jarrell	.35	.25	.14
57	Craig Hentrich	.50	.40	.20
58	Demetrius DuBose	.75	.60	.30
59	Gene McGuire	.75	.60	.30
60	Ray Griggs	.35	.25	.14

1990 Notre Dame Greats

		NM/M	NM	E
	Complete Set (22):	8.00	6.00	3.25
	Common Player:	.35	.25	.14
1	Clarence Ellis	.50	.40	.20
2	Rocky Bleier	.75	.60	.30
3	Tom Regner	.50	.40	.20
4	Jim Seymour	.35	.25	.14
5	Joe Montana	3.00	2.25	1.25
6	Art Hunter	.50	.40	.20
7	Mike McCoy	.50	.40	.20
8	Bud Boeringer	.35	.25	.14
9	Greg Marx	.35	.25	.14
10	Nick Buoniconti	.75	.60	.30
11	Pete Demmerle	.35	.25	.14
12	Fred Miller	.35	.25	.14
13	Tommy Yarr	.35	.25	.14
14	Frank Rydzewski	.35	.25	.14
15	Dave Duerson	.50	.40	.20
16	Ziggy Czarobski	.35	.25	.14
17	Jim White	.50	.40	.20
18	Larry DiNardo	.50	.40	.20
19	George Kunz	.50	.40	.20
20	Jack Robinson	.35	.25	.14
21	Steve Niehaus	.50	.40	.20
22	John Scully	.50	.40	.20

1930 Notre Dame Postcards

		NM	E	VG
	Complete Set (25):	1,500	750.00	375.00
	Common Player:	50.00	25.00	15.00
1	Marty Brill	50.00	25.00	12.00
2	Frank Carideo	75.00	40.00	20.00
3	Tom Conley	50.00	25.00	15.00
4	Al Culver (October 25)	50.00	25.00	12.00
5	Dick Donaghue (October 18)	50.00	25.00	15.00
6	Nordy Hoffmann	50.00	25.00	15.00
7	Al Howard (November 15)	50.00	25.00	15.00
8	Chuck Jaskwich (November 22)	50.00	25.00	15.00
9	Clarence Kaplan (October 18)	50.00	25.00	15.00
10	Tom Kassis	50.00	25.00	15.00
11	Ed Koska (November 22)	50.00	25.00	15.00
12	Joe Kurth	65.00	37.00	18.00
13	Bernie Leahy	75.00	40.00	20.00
14	Frank Leahy	180.00	90.00	45.00
15	Dick Mahoney (November 8)	50.00	25.00	15.00
16	Art McManmon (November 1)	50.00	25.00	15.00
17	Bert Metzger	50.00	25.00	15.00
18	Larry "Moon" Mullins	75.00	40.00	20.00
19	John O'Brien	50.00	25.00	15.00
20	Bucky O'Connor	50.00	25.00	15.00
21	Joe Savoldi	80.00	40.00	20.00
22	Marchmont Schwartz	50.00	25.00	15.00
23	Robert Terlaak (November 8)	50.00	25.00	15.00
24	George Vik (October 25)	50.00	25.00	15.00
25	Tom Yarr	50.00	25.00	15.00

1990 Notre Dame Promos

		NM/M	NM	E
	Complete Set (10):	7.00	5.25	2.75
	Common Player:	.50	.40	.20
1	Knute Rockne (CO)	1.00	.70	.40
2	Joe Theismann	1.00	.70	.40
3	Joe Montana	4.00	3.00	1.50
4	George Gipp	1.00	.70	.40
5	Notre Dame Stadium	.50	.40	.20
6	Ara Parseghian (CO)	.75	.60	.30
7	Frank Leahy (CO)	.50	.40	.20
8	Lou Holtz (CO)	.75	.60	.30
9	Tony Rice	.50	.40	.20
10	Rocky Bleier	.75	.60	.30

1988 Notre Dame Smokey

		NM/M	NM	E
	Complete Set (14):	30.00	22.00	12.00
	Common Player (1-10):	1.50	1.25	.60
	Common Sport (11-14):	1.50	1.25	.60
1	Braxston Banks (39)	2.00	1.50	.80
2	Ned Bolcar (47)	2.00	1.50	.80
3	Tom Gorman (87)	1.50	1.25	.60
4	Mark Green (24)	2.00	1.50	.80
5	Andy Heck (66)	2.00	1.50	.80
6	Lou Holtz (CO)	3.50	2.75	1.50
7	Anthony Johnson (22)	2.00	1.50	.80
8	Wes Pritchett (34)	1.50	1.25	.60
9	George Streeter (27)	1.50	1.25	.60
10	Ricky Watters (12)	9.00	6.75	3.50
11	Men's Soccer	1.50	1.25	.60
12	Volleyball	1.50	1.25	.60
13	Women's Basketball	1.50	1.25	.60
14	Women's Tennis	1.50	1.25	.60

1961 Nu-Card

		NM	E	VG
	Complete Set (80):	175.00	87.00	52.00
	Common Player:	2.00	1.00	.60
101	Bob Ferguson	5.00	2.50	1.50
102	Ron Snidow	3.00	1.50	.90
103	Steve Barnett	2.00	1.00	.60
104	Greg Mather	2.00	1.00	.60
105	Vern Von Sydow	2.00	1.00	.60
106	John Hewitt	2.00	1.00	.60
107	Eddie Johns	2.00	1.00	.60
108	Walt Rappold	2.00	1.00	.60
109	Roy Winston	4.00	2.00	1.25
110	Bob Boyda	2.00	1.00	.60
111	Bill Neighbors	5.00	2.50	1.50
112	Don Purcell	2.00	1.00	.60
113	Ken Byers	2.00	1.00	.60
114	Ed Pine	2.00	1.00	.60
115	Fred Oblak	2.00	1.00	.60
116	Bobby Iles	2.00	1.00	.60
117	John Hadl	18.00	9.00	5.50
118	Charlie Mitchell	2.00	1.00	.60
119	Bill Swinford	2.00	1.00	.60
120	Bill King	2.00	1.00	.60

121	Mike Lucci	5.00	2.50	1.50
122	Dave Sarette	2.00	1.00	.60
123	Alex Kroll	3.00	1.50	.90
124	Steve Bauwens	2.00	1.00	.60
125	Jimmy Saxton	3.00	1.50	.90
126	Steve Simms	2.00	1.00	.60
127	Andy Timura	2.00	1.00	.60
128	Gary Collins	6.00	3.00	1.75
129	Ron Taylor	2.00	1.00	.60
130	Bobby Dodd	8.00	4.00	2.50
131	Curtis McClinton	6.00	3.00	1.75
132	Ray Poage	3.00	1.50	.90
133	Gus Gonzales	2.00	1.00	.60
134	Dick Locke	2.00	1.00	.60
135	Larry Libertore	2.00	1.00	.60
136	Stan Sczurek	2.00	1.00	.60
137	Pete Case	3.00	1.50	.90
138	Jesse Bradford	2.00	1.00	.60
139	Coolidge Hunt	2.00	1.00	.60
140	Walter Doleschal	2.00	1.00	.60
141	Bill Williamson	2.00	1.00	.60
142	Pat Trammell	6.00	3.00	1.75
143	Ernie Davis	65.00	32.00	19.50
144	Chuck Lamson	2.00	1.00	.60
145	Bobby Plummer	3.00	1.50	.90
146	Sonny Gibbs	3.00	1.50	.90
147	Joe Ellers	2.00	1.00	.60
148	Roger Kochman	2.00	1.00	.60
149	Norman Beal	2.00	1.00	.60
150	Sherwyn Torson	2.00	1.00	.60
151	Russ Hepner	2.00	1.00	.60
152	Joe Romig	2.00	1.00	.60
153	Larry Thompson	2.00	1.00	.60
154	Tom Perdue	2.00	1.00	.60
155	Ken Bolin	2.00	1.00	.60
156	Art Perkins	2.00	1.00	.60
157	Jim Sanderson	2.00	1.00	.60
158	Bob Asack	2.00	1.00	.60
159	Dan Celoni	2.00	1.00	.60
160	Bill McGuirt	2.00	1.00	.60
161	Dave Hoppmann	2.00	1.00	.60
162	Gary Barnes	2.00	1.00	.60
163	Don Lisbon	3.00	1.50	.90
164	Jerry Cross	2.00	1.00	.60
165	George Pierovich	2.00	1.00	.60
166	Roman Gabriel	25.00	12.50	7.50
167	Billy White	2.00	1.00	.60
168	Gale Weidner	2.00	1.00	.60
169	Charles Rieves	2.00	1.00	.60
170	Jim Furlong	2.00	1.00	.60
171	Tom Hutchinson	3.00	1.50	.90
172	Galen Hall	8.00	4.00	2.50
173	Wilburn Hollis	2.00	1.00	.60
174	Don Kasso	2.00	1.00	.60
175	Bill Miller	3.00	1.50	.90
176	Ron Miller	2.00	1.00	.60
177	Joe Williams	2.00	1.00	.60
178	Mel Mellin	2.00	1.00	.60
179	Tom Vassell	2.00	1.00	.60
180	Mike Cotton	3.00	1.50	.90

1961 Nu-Card Pennant Inserts

		NM	E	VG
	Complete Set (264):	800.00	400.00	240.00
	Common Player:	3.00	1.50	.90
1	Air Force/Georgetown	3.00	1.50	.90
2	Air Force/Queens	3.00	1.50	.90
3	Air Force/Upsala	3.00	1.50	.90
4	Alabama/Boston U	4.00	2.00	1.25
5	Alabama/Cornell	4.00	2.00	1.25
6	Alabama/Detroit	4.00	2.00	1.25
7	Alabama/Harvard	4.00	2.00	1.25
8	Alabama/Wisconsin	4.00	2.00	1.25
9	Allegheny/Colorado St.	3.00	1.50	.90
10	Allegheny/Oregon	3.00	1.50	.90
11	Allegheny/Piedmont	3.00	1.50	.90
12	Allegheny/Wm. and Mary	3.00	1.50	.90
13	Arizona/Kansas	3.00	1.50	.90
14	Arizona/Mississippi	3.00	1.50	.90
15	Arizona/Pennsylvania	3.00	1.50	.90
16	Arizona/S.M.U.	3.00	1.50	.90
17	Army/Ga. Tech	3.00	1.50	.90
18	Army/Iowa	3.00	1.50	.90
19	Army/Johns Hopkins	3.00	1.50	.90
20	Army/Maryland	3.00	1.50	.90
21	Army/Missouri	3.00	1.50	.90
22	Army/Pratt	3.00	1.50	.90
23	Army/Purdue	3.00	1.50	.90
24	Auburn/Florida	4.00	2.00	1.25
25	Auburn/Gettysburg	3.00	1.50	.90
26	Auburn/Illinois	4.00	2.00	1.25
27	Auburn/Syracuse	4.00	2.00	1.25
28	Auburn/Virginia	4.00	2.00	1.25
29	Barnard/Colombia	3.00	1.50	.90
30	Barnard/Maine	3.00	1.50	.90
31	Barnard/N. Carolina	3.00	1.50	.90
32	Baylor/Colorado St.	3.00	1.50	.90

33	Baylor/Drew	3.00	1.50	.90
34	Baylor/Oregon	3.00	1.50	.90
35	Baylor/Piedmont	3.00	1.50	.90
36	Boston Coll./Minnesota	3.00	1.50	.90
37	Boston Coll./Norwich	3.00	1.50	.90
38	Boston Coll./Winthrop	3.00	1.50	.90
39	Boston U./Cornell	3.00	1.50	.90
40	Boston U./Rensselaer	3.00	1.50	.90
41	Boston U./Stanford	3.00	1.50	.90
42	Boston U./Temple	3.00	1.50	.90
43	Boston U./Utah State	3.00	1.50	.90
44	Bridgeport/Holy Cross	3.00	1.50	.90
45	Bridgeport/N.Y.U.	3.00	1.50	.90
46	Bridgeport/Northwestern	3.00	1.50	.90
47	Bucknell/Illinois	3.00	1.50	.90
48	Bucknell/Syracuse	3.00	1.50	.90
49	Bucknell/Virginia	3.00	1.50	.90
50	California/Delaware	3.00	1.50	.90
51	California/Hofstra	3.00	1.50	.90
52	California/Kentucky	3.00	1.50	.90
53	California/Marquette	3.00	1.50	.90
54	California/Michigan	4.00	2.00	1.25
55	California/Notre Dame	7.50	3.75	2.25
56	California/Wingate	3.00	1.50	.90
57	Charleston/Dickinson	3.00	1.50	.90
58	Charleston/Lafayette	3.00	1.50	.90
59	Charleston/U. of Mass.	3.00	1.50	.90
60	Cincinnati/Maine	3.00	1.50	.90
61	Cincinnati/Ohio West	3.00	1.50	.90
62	Citadel/Columbia	3.00	1.50	.90
63	Citadel/Maine	3.00	1.50	.90
64	Citadel/N. Carolina	3.00	1.50	.90
65	Coast Guard/Drake	3.00	1.50	.90
66	Coast Guard/Penn St.	3.00	1.50	.90
67	Coast Guard/Yale	3.00	1.50	.90
68	Coker/UCLA	3.00	1.50	.90
69	Coker/Wingate	3.00	1.50	.90
70	Colby/Kings Point	3.00	1.50	.90
71	Colby/Queens	3.00	1.50	.90
72	Colby/Rice	3.00	1.50	.90
73	Colby/Upsala	3.00	1.50	.90
74	Colgate/Dickinson	3.00	1.50	.90
75	Colgate/Lafayette	3.00	1.50	.90
76	Colgate/U. of Mass.	3.00	1.50	.90
77	Colgate/Springfield	3.00	1.50	.90
78	Colgate/Texas AM	3.00	1.50	.90
79	C.O.P./Princeton	3.00	1.50	.90
80	C.O.P./Oklahoma St.	3.00	1.50	.90
81	C.O.P./Oregon St.	3.00	1.50	.90
82	Colorado St./Drew	3.00	1.50	.90
83	Colorado St./Oregon	3.00	1.50	.90
84	Colorado St./Piedmont	3.00	1.50	.90
85	Colorado St./Wm. and Mary	3.00	1.50	.90
86	Columbia/Dominican	3.00	1.50	.90
87	Columbia/Maine	3.00	1.50	.90
88	Columbia/N. Carolina	3.00	1.50	.90
89	Cornell/Harvard	3.00	1.50	.90
90	Cornell/Rensselaer	3.00	1.50	.90
91	Cornell/Stanford	3.00	1.50	.90
92	Cornell/Wisconsin	3.00	1.50	.90
93	Dartmouth/Michigan St.	3.00	1.50	.90
94	Dartmouth/Ohio U.	3.00	1.50	.90
95	Dartmouth/Wagner	3.00	1.50	.90
96	Davidson/Ohio Wesl.	3.00	1.50	.90
97	Davidson/S. Carolina	3.00	1.50	.90
98	Davidson/Texas Tech	3.00	1.50	.90
99	Delaware/Marquette	3.00	1.50	.90
100	Delaware/Michigan	3.00	1.50	.90
101	Delaware/Notre Dame	5.00	2.50	1.50
102	Delaware/UCLA	3.00	1.50	.90
103	Denver/Florida State	4.00	2.00	1.25
104	Denver/Indiana	3.00	1.50	.90
105	Denver/Iowa State	3.00	1.50	.90
106	Denver/USC	3.00	1.50	.90
107	Denver/VMI	3.00	1.50	.90
108	Detroit/Harvard	3.00	1.50	.90
109	Detroit/Rensselaer	3.00	1.50	.90
110	Detroit/Stanford	3.00	1.50	.90
111	Detroit/Utah State	3.00	1.50	.90
112	Dickinson/U. of Mass.	3.00	1.50	.90
113	Dickinson/Regis	3.00	1.50	.90
114	Dickinson/Springfield	3.00	1.50	.90
115	Dickinson/Texas AM	3.00	1.50	.90
116	Dominican/North Carolina	3.00	1.50	.90
117	Drake/Duke	3.00	1.50	.90
118	Drake/Kentucky	3.00	1.50	.90
119	Drake/Middlebury	3.00	1.50	.90
120	Drake/Penn St.	3.00	1.50	.90
121	Drake/St. Peters	3.00	1.50	.90
122	Drake/Yale	3.00	1.50	.90
123	Drew/Middlebury	3.00	1.50	.90
124	Drew/Oregon	3.00	1.50	.90
125	Drew/Piedmont	3.00	1.50	.90
126	Drew/Wm. and Mary	3.00	1.50	.90
127	Duke/Middlebury	3.00	1.50	.90
128	Duke/Rhode Island	3.00	1.50	.90

129	Duke/Seton Hall	3.00	1.50	.90
130	Duke/Yale	3.00	1.50	.90
131	Finch/Long Island AT	3.00	1.50	.90
132	Finch/Michigan St.	3.00	1.50	.90
133	Finch/Ohio U.	3.00	1.50	.90
134	Finch/Wagner	3.00	1.50	.90
135	Florida/Gettysburg	3.00	1.50	.90
136	Florida/Illinois	4.00	2.00	1.25
137	Florida/Syracuse	4.00	2.00	1.25
138	Florida/Virginia	4.00	2.00	1.25
139	Florida St./Indiana	4.00	2.00	1.25
140	Florida St./Iowa St.	4.00	2.00	1.25
141	Florida St./So. Cal.	4.00	2.00	1.25
142	Florida St./VMI	4.00	2.00	1.25
143	Georgetown/Kings Point	3.00	1.50	.90
144	Georgetown/Rice	3.00	1.50	.90
145	Georgia/Missouri	4.00	2.00	1.25
146	Georgia/Ohio Wesleyan	3.00	1.50	.90
147	Georgia/Rutgers	3.00	1.50	.90
148	Georgia/So. Carolina	4.00	2.00	1.25
149	Ga. Tech/Johns Hopkins	3.00	1.50	.90
150	Ga. Tech/Maryland	3.00	1.50	.90
151	Ga. Tech/Missouri	3.00	1.50	.90
152	Gettysburg/Syracuse	3.00	1.50	.90
153	Harvard/Miami	4.00	2.00	1.25
154	Harvard/NC State	3.00	1.50	.90
155	Harvard/Stanford	3.00	1.50	.90
156	Harvard/Utah State	3.00	1.50	.90
157	Harvard/Wisconsin	3.00	1.50	.90
158	Hofstra/Marquette	3.00	1.50	.90
159	Hofstra/Michigan	4.00	2.00	1.25
160	Hofstra/Navy	3.00	1.50	.90
161	Hofstra/UCLA	3.00	1.50	.90
162	Holy Cross/Navy	3.00	1.50	.90
163	Holy Cross/New York	3.00	1.50	.90
164	Holy Cross/Northwestern	3.00	1.50	.90
165	Holy Cross/Nyack	3.00	1.50	.90
166	Howard/Kentucky	3.00	1.50	.90
167	Howard/Villanova	3.00	1.50	.90
168	Illinois/Syracuse	3.00	1.50	.90
169	Indiana/Iowa State	3.00	1.50	.90
170	Indiana/VMI	3.00	1.50	.90
171	Iowa/Maryland	3.00	1.50	.90
172	Iowa/Missouri	3.00	1.50	.90
173	Iowa/Pratt	3.00	1.50	.90
174	Iowa State/So. Cal.	4.00	2.00	1.25
175	Johns Hopkins/Pratt	3.00	1.50	.90
176	Johns Hopkins/Purdue	3.00	1.50	.90
177	Kansas/St. Francis	3.00	1.50	.90
178	Kansas/S.M.U.	3.00	1.50	.90
179	Kansas State/N.Y.U.	3.00	1.50	.90
180	Kansas State/T.C.U.	3.00	1.50	.90
181	Kentucky/Maryland	3.00	1.50	.90
182	Kentucky/Middlebury	3.00	1.50	.90
183	Kentucky/New Hampshire	3.00	1.50	.90
184	Kentucky/Penn State	5.00	2.50	1.50
185	Kentucky/St. Peter's	3.00	1.50	.90
186	Kentucky/Seton Hall	3.00	1.50	.90
187	Kentucky/Villanova	3.00	1.50	.90
188	Kings Point/Queens	3.00	1.50	.90
189	Kings Point/Rice	3.00	1.50	.90
190	Kings Point/Upsala	3.00	1.50	.90
191	Lafayette/U. of Mass.	3.00	1.50	.90
192	Lafayette/Regis	3.00	1.50	.90
193	Long Isl. AT/Michigan St.	3.00	1.50	.90
194	Long Isl. AT/Ohio U.	3.00	1.50	.90
195	Long Isl. At/Wagner	3.00	1.50	.90
196	Loyola/Minnesota	3.00	1.50	.90
197	Loyola/Norwich	3.00	1.50	.90
198	Loyola/Winthrop	3.00	1.50	.90
199	Marquette/Michigan	4.00	2.00	1.25
200	Marquette/Navy	3.00	1.50	.90
201	Marquette/New Paltz	3.00	1.50	.90
202	Marquette/Notre Dame	5.00	2.50	1.50
203	Marquette/UCLA	3.00	1.50	.90
204	Maryland/Missouri	3.00	1.50	.90
205	Mass./Regis	3.00	1.50	.90
206	Mass./Springfield	3.00	1.50	.90
207	Mass./Texas AM	3.00	1.50	.90
208	Michigan/Navy	4.00	2.00	1.25
209	Michigan/New Paltz	3.00	1.50	.90
210	Michigan/UCLA	4.00	2.00	1.25
211	Michigan St./Ohio U.	3.00	1.50	.90
212	Michigan St./Wagner	3.00	1.50	.90
213	Middlebury/Penn St.	3.00	1.50	.90
214	Middlebury/Yale	3.00	1.50	.90
215	Minnesota/Norwich	3.00	1.50	.90
216	Minnesota/Winthrop	3.00	1.50	.90
217	Mississippi/Penn	3.00	1.50	.90
218	Mississippi/St. Francis	3.00	1.50	.90
219	Missouri/Purdue	3.00	1.50	.90
220	Navy/Notre Dame	7.50	3.75	2.25
221	Navy/UCLA	4.00	2.00	1.25
222	Navy/Wingate	3.00	1.50	.90
223	New Hampshire/Villanova	3.00	1.50	.90
224	N.Y.U./Northwestern	3.00	1.50	.90

225	NCE/Temple	3.00	1.50	.90
226	NCE/Wisconsin	3.00	1.50	.90
227	NC State/Temple	3.00	1.50	.90
228	Northwestern/TCU	3.00	1.50	.90
229	Norwich/Winthrop	3.00	1.50	.90
230	Notre Dame/UCLA	7.50	3.75	2.25
231	Notre Dame/Wingate	5.00	2.50	1.50
232	Ohio U./Wagner	3.00	1.50	.90
233	Ohio Wesl./Roberts	3.00	1.50	.90
234	Ohio Wesl./S. Carolina	3.00	1.50	.90
235	Oklahoma St./Oregon St.	3.00	1.50	.90
236	Oklahoma St./Princeton	3.00	1.50	.90
237	Oregon/Piedmont	3.00	1.50	.90
238	Oregon/Wm. and Mary	3.00	1.50	.90
239	Oregon St./Princeton	3.00	1.50	.90
240	Penn State/St. Peter's	3.00	1.50	.90
241	Penn State/Seton Hall	3.00	1.50	.90
242	Penn State/Yale	3.00	1.50	.90
243	Penn/S.M.U.	3.00	1.50	.90
244	Penn/St. Francis	3.00	1.50	.90
245	Queens/Rice	3.00	1.50	.90
246	Queens/Upsala	3.00	1.50	.90
247	Rensselaer/Stanford	3.00	1.50	.90
248	Rensselaer/Temple	3.00	1.50	.90
249	Rensselaer/Utah State	3.00	1.50	.90
250	Rhode Island/Yale	3.00	1.50	.90
251	Rice/Upsala	3.00	1.50	.90
252	Roberts/So. Carolina	3.00	1.50	.90
253	Roberts/Texas Tech	3.00	1.50	.90
254	Rutgers/So. Carolina	3.00	1.50	.90
255	St. Francis/S.M.U.	3.00	1.50	.90
256	St. Peter's/Villanova	3.00	1.50	.90
257	St. Peter's/Yale	3.00	1.50	.90
258	So. California/VMI	4.00	2.00	1.25
259	So. Carolina/Texas Tech	3.00	1.50	.90
260	Syracuse/Virginia	3.00	1.50	.90
261	Temple/Wisconsin	3.00	1.50	.90
262	UCLA/Wingate	4.00	2.00	1.25
263	Utah State/Wisconsin	3.00	1.50	.90
264	Villanova/Yale	3.00	1.50	.90

O

1991 Oberlin College Heisman Club

		NM/M	NM	E
Complete Set (5):		5.00	3.75	2.00
Common Player:		1.00	.70	.40
1	50 Years, Two Careers (C.W. "Doc" Savage, J.H. Nichols) (Athletic Directors)	1.00	.70	.40
2	John W. Heisman (CO)	2.00	1.50	.80
3	Oberline's 1892 Team	1.00	.70	.40
4	Oberlin's Fauver Twins (Doc Edgar Fauver, Doc Edwin Fauver)	1.00	.70	.40
5	Oberlin's Four Horsemen (Carl Semple, C arl Williams, H.K. Regal, C.W. "Doc" Savage)	1.00	.70	.40

1979 Ohio State Greats

		NM	E	VG
Complete Set (53):		35.00	17.50	10.50
Common Player:		.75	.40	.25
1C	Chris Ward	.75	.40	.25
1D	Jan White	1.00	.50	.30
1H	Ernest R. Godfrey (ACO)	.75	.40	.25
1S	Ray Pryor	.75	.40	.25
2C	Ray Griffin	1.00	.50	.30
2D	Tom Deleone	1.00	.50	.30
2H	Francis A. Schmidt (CO)	.75	.40	.25
2S	Dave Foley	1.00	.50	.30
3C	Tom Cousineau	1.25	.60	.40
3D	Randy Gradishar	2.00	1.00	.60
3H	Jim Parker	2.00	1.00	.60
3S	Rufus Mayes	1.00	.50	.30
4C	Aaron Brown	1.00	.50	.30
4D	John Hicks	1.25	.60	.40
4H	Vic Janowicz	1.50	.70	.45
4S	Rex Kern	1.50	.70	.45
5C	Chris Ward	.75	.40	.25
5D	Van Decree	.75	.40	.25
5H	Les Horvath	1.50	.70	.45
5S	Jim Otis	1.50	.70	.45
6C	Tom Skladany	1.25	.60	.40
6D	Randy Gradishar	2.00	1.00	.60

6H	Bill Willis	1.25	.60	.40
6S	Ted Provost	.75	.40	.25
7C	Bob Brudzinski	1.00	.50	.30
7D	Archie Griffin	2.50	1.25	.70
7H	James Daniell	.75	.40	.25
7S	Jim Stillwagon	1.25	.60	.40
8C	Ted Smith	.75	.40	.25
8D	John Hicks	1.25	.60	.40
8H	Gust Zarnas	.75	.40	.25
8S	Jack Tatum	1.50	.70	.45
9C	Tom Skladany	1.25	.60	.40
9D	Neal Colzie	1.00	.50	.30
9H	Gomer Jones	.75	.40	.25
9S	Tim Anderson	.75	.40	.25
10C	Archie Griffin	2.50	1.25	.70
10D	Pete Cusick	.75	.40	.25
10H	Wes Fesler	1.00	.50	.30
10S	John Brockington	1.50	.70	.45
11C	Tim Fox	1.00	.50	.30
11D	Van Decree	.75	.40	.25
11H	Gaylord Stinchcomb	.75	.40	.25
11S	Mike Sensibaugh	1.00	.50	.30
12C	Tom Skladany	1.25	.60	.40
12D	Archie Griffin	2.50	1.25	.70
12H	Chic Harley	.75	.40	.25
12S	Jim Stillwagon	1.25	.60	.40
13C	Kurt Schumacher	1.00	.50	.30
13D	Steve Meyers	1.00	.50	.30
13H	Tom Cousineau	1.25	.60	.40
13S	Jack Tatum	1.50	.70	.45
JK	Howard Jones (CO)	1.00	.50	.30

1988 Ohio State

WOODY HAYES
HEAD COACH

		NM/M	NM	E
Complete Set (22):		40.00	20.00	12.00
Common Player:		.40	.30	.15
1	Bob Brudzinski	.50	.40	.20
2	Keith Byars	1.50	1.25	.60
3	Hopalong Cassady	1.00	.70	.40
4	Arnold Chonko	.50	.40	.20
5	Wes Fesler	.40	.30	.15
6	Randy Gradishar	1.00	.70	.40
7	Archie Griffin	1.50	1.25	.60
8	Chic Harley	.40	.30	.15
9	Woody Hayes (CO)	1.00	.70	.40
10	John Hicks	.50	.40	.20
11	Les Horvath	1.00	.70	.40
12	Jim Houston	.75	.60	.30
13	Vic Janowicz	1.00	.70	.40
14	Pepper Johnson	.75	.60	.30
15	Ike Kelley	.40	.30	.15
16	Rex Kern	.75	.60	.30
17	Jim Lachey	.75	.60	.30
18	Jim Parker	1.00	.70	.40
19	Tom Skladany	.40	.30	.15
20	Chris Spielman	1.00	.70	.40
21	Jim Stillwagon	.75	.60	.30
22	Jack Tatum	1.00	.70	.40

1989 Ohio State

		NM/M	NM	E
Complete Set (22):		8.00	6.00	3.25
Common Player:		.40	.30	.15
1	Mike Tomczak	1.00	.70	.40
2	Paul Warfield	1.50	1.25	.60
3	Kirk Lowdermilk	.50	.40	.20
4	Bob Ferguson	.50	.40	.20
5	Jack Graf	.40	.30	.15
6	Tim Fox	.50	.40	.20
7	Eric Kumerow	.50	.40	.20
8	Neal Colzie	.50	.40	.20
9	Jim Otis	.75	.60	.30
10	John Brockington	1.00	.70	.40
11	Cornelius Greene	.40	.30	.15
12	Jim Marshall	1.00	.70	.40
13	Tim Spencer	.50	.40	.20
14	Don Scott	.40	.30	.15
15	Chris Ward	.50	.40	.20
16	Marcus Marek	.50	.40	.20

17	Dave Foley	.50	.40	.20
18	Bill Willis	.75	.60	.30
19	John Frank	75	.60	.30
20	Rufus Mayes	.50	.40	.20
21	Tom Tupa	.75	.60	.30
22	Jan White	.50	.40	.20

1990 Ohio State

		NM/M	NM	E
Complete Set (22):		8.00	6.00	3.25
Common Player:		.35	.25	.14
1	Jeff Uhlenhake	.50	.40	.20
2	Ray Ellis	.35	.25	.14
3	Todd Bell	.50	.40	.20
4	Jeff Logan	.35	.25	.14
5	Pete Johnson	.75	.60	.30
6	Van DeCree	.35	.25	.14
7	Ted Provost	.35	.25	.14
8	Mike Lanese	.35	.25	.14
9	Aaron Brown	.50	.40	.20
10	Pete Cusick	.35	.25	.14
11	Vlade Janakievski	.35	.25	.14
12	Steve Myers	.35	.25	.14
13	Ted Smith	.35	.25	.14
14	Doug Donley	.50	.40	.20
15	Ron Springs	.50	.40	.20
16	Ken Fritz	.35	.25	.14
17	Jeff Davidson	.35	.25	.14
18	Art Schlichter	.75	.60	.30
19	Tom Cousineau	.75	.60	.30
20	Call Murray	.35	.25	.14
21	Brian Baschnagel	.50	.40	.20
22	Joe Staysniak	.35	.25	.14

1961 Oilers Jay Publishing

Measuring 5" x 7", the 24-card set is anchored by a black-and-white player photo on the front. The player's name and team appear in the white border beneath the photo. The player's facsimile signature is printed on the photo. The cards are unnumbered and have blank backs. Originally, the cards were sold in 12-card packs for 25 cents.

		NM	E	VG
Complete Set (24):		125.00	62.00	37.00
Common Player:		5.00	2.50	1.50
1	Dalva Allen	5.00	2.50	1.50
2	Tony Banfield	5.00	2.50	1.50
3	George Blanda	12.00	6.00	3.50
4	Billy Cannon	6.00	3.00	1.75
5	Doug Cline	5.00	2.50	1.50
6	Willard Dewveall	5.00	2.50	1.50
7	Mike Dukes	5.00	2.50	1.50
8	Don Floyd	6.00	3.00	1.75
9	Freddy Glick	6.00	3.00	1.75
10	Bill Groman	6.00	3.00	1.75
11	Charlie Hennigan	6.00	3.00	1.75
12	Ed Husmann	5.00	2.50	1.50
13	Al Jamison	5.00	2.50	1.50
14	Mark Johnston	5.00	2.50	1.50
15	Jacky Lee	6.00	3.00	1.75
16	Bob McLeod	5.00	2.50	1.50
17	Rich Michael	5.00	2.50	1.50
18	Dennit Morris	5.00	2.50	1.50
19	Jim Norton	6.00	3.00	1.75
20	Bob Schmidt	5.00	2.50	1.50
21	Dave Smith	5.00	2.50	1.50
22	Bob Talamini	6.00	3.00	1.75
23	Charles Tolar	6.00	3.00	1.75
24	Hogan Wharton	5.00	2.50	1.50

1964-65 Oilers Color Team Issue

Measuring 7-3/4" x 9-3/4", the 16-photo set is anchored by a color photo on the front, bordered in white. A facsimile signature is printed over the photo. The photos are unnumbered and have blank backs. The photos were sold in eight-photo packs for 50 cents.

		NM	E	VG
Complete Set (16):		80.00	40.00	24.00
Common Player:		5.00	2.50	1.50
1	Scott Appleton	6.00	3.00	1.75
2	Tony Banfield	6.00	3.00	1.75
3	Sonny Bishop	6.00	3.00	1.75
4	George Blanda	12.00	6.00	3.50
5	Sid Blanks	6.00	3.00	1.75
6	Danny Brabham	5.00	2.50	1.50
7	Ode Burrell	6.00	3.00	1.75
8	Doug Cline	5.00	2.50	1.50
9	Don Floyd	6.00	3.00	1.75
10	Freddy Glick	6.00	3.00	1.75
11	Charlie Hennigan	6.00	3.00	1.75
12	Ed Husmann	5.00	2.50	1.50
13	Walt Suggs	6.00	3.00	1.75
14	Bob Talamini	5.00	2.50	1.50
15	Charley Tolar	6.00	3.00	1.75
16	Don Trull	6.00	3.00	1.75

1967 Oilers Team Issue

Measuring 5-1/8" x 7", the 14-card set is anchored on the front with a black-and-white photo. The cards, which are un-numbered, have blank backs.

		NM	E	VG
Complete Set (14):		45.00	22.00	13.50
Common Player:		4.00	2.00	1.25
1	Pete Barnes	4.00	2.00	1.25
2	Sonny Bishop	5.00	2.50	1.50
3	Ode Burrell	5.00	2.50	1.50
4	Ronnie Caveness	4.00	2.00	1.25
5	Joe Childress (CO)	4.00	2.00	1.25
6	Glen Ray Hines	5.00	2.50	1.50
7	Pat Holmes	4.00	2.00	1.25
8	Bobby Jancik	5.00	2.50	1.50
9	Pete Johns	4.00	2.00	1.25
10	Jim Norton	5.00	2.50	1.50
11	Willie Parker	4.00	2.00	1.25
12	Bob Poole	4.00	2.00	1.25
13	Alvin Reed	4.00	2.00	1.25
14	Olen Underwood	4.00	2.00	1.25

1969 Oilers Team Issue

Measuring 8" x 10", the 39-photo set is anchored by a large black-and-white photo on the front, bordered in white. The player's name, team and position are located beneath the photo. The unnumbered photos have blank backs.

		NM	E	VG
Complete Set (39):		125.00	62.00	37.00
Common Player:		3.00	1.50	.90
1	Jim Beirne (Wide receiver)	4.00	2.00	1.25
2	Jim Beirne (Split end)	4.00	2.00	1.25
3	Elvin Bethea	5.00	2.50	1.50
4	Sonny Bishop	4.00	2.00	1.25
5	Garland Boyette	4.00	2.00	1.25
6	Ode Burrell	4.00	2.00	1.25
7	Ed Carrington	3.00	1.50	.90
8	Joe Childress (CO)	3.00	1.50	.90
9	Bob Davis	3.00	1.50	.90
10	Hugh Devore (CO)	3.00	1.50	.90
11	Tom Domres	3.00	1.50	.90
12	F.A. Dry	3.00	1.50	.90
13	Miller Farr	4.00	2.00	1.25
14	Mac Haik (Action shot)	3.00	1.50	.90
15	Mac Haik (Portrait)	3.00	1.50	.90
16	W.K. Hicks	3.00	1.50	.90
17	Glen Ray Hines	4.00	2.00	1.25
18	Pat Holmes	3.00	1.50	.90
19	Roy Hopkins	3.00	1.50	.90
20	Charlie Joiner	18.00	9.00	5.50
21	Jim LeMoine	3.00	1.50	.90
22	Bobby Maples	4.00	2.00	1.25
23	Richard Marshall	3.00	1.50	.90
24	Zeke Moore	4.00	2.00	1.25
25	Willie Parker	3.00	1.50	.90
26	Johnny Peacock	3.00	1.50	.90
27	Ron Pritchard (Back peddling)	3.00	1.50	.90
28	Ron Pritchard (Cutting left)	3.00	1.50	.90
29	Ron Pritchard (Preparing to fend off blocker)	3.00	1.50	.90
30	Tom Regner	3.00	1.50	.90
31	George Rice	3.00	1.50	.90
32	George Rice	3.00	1.50	.90
33	Bob Robertson	3.00	1.50	.90
34	Walt Suggs	3.00	1.50	.90
35	Don Trull	4.00	2.00	1.25
36	Olen Underwood	3.00	1.50	.90
37	Loyd Wainscott	3.00	1.50	.90
38	Wayne Walker	4.00	2.00	1.25
39	Glenn Woods	3.00	1.50	.90

1971 Oilers Team Issue

Measuring 4" x 5-1/2", the 23-card set showcases a black-and-white photo on the front, with an Oilers' helmet in the upper left, "Houston Oilers" at the top center and the NFL shield in the upper right. The player's name and position are printed beneath the photo. The blank-backed cards are un-numbered.

		NM	E	VG
Complete Set (23):		50.00	25.00	15.00
Common Player:		2.00	1.00	.60
1	Willie Alexander	2.50	1.25	.70
2	Jim Beirne	2.50	1.25	.70
3	Elvin Bethea	3.00	1.50	.90
4	Ron Billingsley	2.00	1.00	.60
5	Garland Boyette	2.50	1.25	.70
6	Leo Brooks	2.00	1.00	.60
7	Ken Burrough	4.00	2.00	1.25
8	Woody Campbell	2.00	1.00	.60
9	Lynn Dickey	4.00	2.00	1.25
10	Elbert Drungo	2.00	1.00	.60

11	Pat Holmes	2.00	1.00	.60
12	Robert Holmes	2.50	1.25	.70
13	Ken Houston	10.00	5.00	3.00
14	Charlie Johnson	4.00	2.00	1.25
15	Charlie Joiner	12.00	6.00	3.50
16	Zeke Moore	2.50	1.25	.70
17	Mark Moseley	4.00	2.00	1.25
18	Dan Pastorini	5.00	2.50	1.50
19	Alvin Reed	2.00	1.00	.60
20	Tom Regner	2.00	1.00	.60
21	Floyd Rice	2.00	1.00	.60
22	Mike Tilleman	2.00	1.00	.60
23	George Webster	3.00	1.50	.90

1972 Oilers Team Issue

Measuring 5" x 7", the 11-card set showcases full-bleed black-and-white photos on the front. The unnumbered backs are blank.

		NM	E	VG
Complete Set (11):		25.00	12.50	7.50
Common Player:		2.00	1.00	.60
1	Ron Billingsley	2.00	1.00	.60
2	Garland Boyette	2.00	1.00	.60
3	Levert Carr	2.00	1.00	.60
4	Walter Highsmith	2.00	1.00	.60
5	Albert Johnson	2.00	1.00	.60
6	Benny Johnson	2.00	1.00	.60
7	Guy Murdock	2.00	1.00	.60
8	Ron Saul	3.00	1.50	.90
9	Mike Tilleman	2.00	1.00	.60
10	Ward Walsh	2.00	1.00	.60
11	George Webster	4.00	2.00	1.25

1973 Oilers McDonald's

Measuring 8" x 10", the three-photo card set is anchored by a color photo on the front, with the player's name and team beneath it. The fronts are bordered in white. The backs, which are unnumbered, have the player's name, bio, highlights and stats, along with the 1973 Oilers' schedule. The McDonald's logo is printed in the lower right.

		NM	E	VG
Complete Set (3):		25.00	12.50	7.50
Common Player:		6.00	3.00	1.75
1	John Matuszak	12.00	6.00	3.50
2	Zeke Moore	6.00	3.00	1.75
3	Dan Pastorini	12.00	6.00	3.50

1973 Oilers Team Issue

Measuring 5" x 8", the 17-card set is anchored by a large black-and-white photo on the front of the white-bordered cards. The blank-backed cards are unnumbered.

		NM	E	VG
Complete Set (17):		35.00	17.50	10.50
Common Player:		2.00	1.00	.60
1	Mack Alston	2.00	1.00	.60
2	Bob Atkins	2.00	1.00	.60
3	Skip Butler	2.00	1.00	.60
4	Al Cowlings	3.00	1.50	.90
5	Lynn Dickey	3.00	1.50	.90
6	Mike Fanucci	2.00	1.00	.60
7	Edd Hargett	2.50	1.25	.70
8	Lewis Jolley	2.00	1.00	.60
9	Clifton McNeil	2.50	1.25	.70
10	Ralph Miller	2.00	1.00	.60
11	Zeke Moore	2.50	1.25	.70
12	Dave Parks	2.50	1.25	.70
13	Willie Rodgers	2.00	1.00	.60
14	Greg Sampson	2.00	1.00	.60
15	Finn Seemann	2.00	1.00	.60
16	Jeff Severson	2.00	1.00	.60
17	Fred Willis	2.50	1.25	.70

1980 Oilers Police

The 14-card, 2-5/8" x 4-1/8" set, sponsored by Kiwanis, local law enforcement and the Oilers, features front color action photos with "Oilers Tips" appearing on the backs.

		NM	E	VG
Complete Set (14):		12.00	6.00	3.50
Common Player:		.75	.40	.25
1	Gregg Bingham	1.00	.50	.30
2	Robert Brazile	.75	.40	.25
3	Ken Burrough	1.50	.70	.45
4	Rob Carpenter	1.00	.50	.30
5	Ronnie Coleman	1.00	.50	.30
6	Curley Culp	1.00	.50	.30
7	Carter Hartwig	.75	.40	.25
8	Billy Johnson	1.50	.70	.45
9	Carl Mauck	.75	.40	.25
10	Gifford Nielsen	1.00	.50	.30
11	Cliff Parsley	.75	.40	.25
12	Bum Phillips (CO)	1.00	.50	.30
13	Mike Renfro	1.00	.50	.30
14	Ken Stabler	4.00	2.00	1.25

1982 Oklahoma Playing Cards

		NM/M	NM	E
Complete Set (56):		40.00	30.00	16.00
Common Player:		.50	.40	.20
C1	Action Shot (Joe Washington)	1.00	.70	.40
C2	Coaches 1895-1934	.50	.40	.20
C3	All-Americans 1946-48 (Buddy Burris)	1.00	.70	.40
C4	All-Americans 1953-54 (Buck McPhail, J.D. Roberts, Max Boydston, Kurt Burris)	1.00	.70	.40
C5	All-Americans 1963-69 (Ralph Neely, Carl McAdams, Bob Kalsu, Steve Owens)	1.00	.70	.40
C6	All-Americans 1974-75 (Kyle Davis, Tinker Owens, Dewey Selmon, Lee Roy Selmon)	1.00	.70	.40
C7	1951(Jim Weatherall)	1.00	.70	.40
C8	1952(Billy Vessels)	1.00	.70	.40
C9	NCAA Champions 1955	1.00	.70	.40
C10	Action Shot (Uwe Von Schamann)	.50	.40	.20
C11	Action Shot (Tony DiRienzo)	.50	.40	.20
C12	Action Shot (Joe Washington)	1.00	.70	.40
C13	Action Shot (Tinker Owens)	.50	.40	.20
D1	Action Shot (Joe Washington)	1.00	.70	.40
D2	Coaches 1935-1982	.50	.40	.20
D3	All-Americans 1949 (Jimmy Owens, Darrell Royal)	1.00	.70	.40
D4	All-Americans 1955-56 (Bo Bolinger, Ed Gray, Jerry Tubbs, Terry McDonald)	1.00	.70	.40
D5	All-Americans 1966-71 (Granville Liggins, Steve Zabel, Ken Mendenhall, Jack Mildren)	1.00	.70	.40
D6	All-Americans 1975-76 (Terry Webb, Billy Brooks, Jimbo Elrod, Mike Vaughan)	1.00	.70	.40
D7	1953(J.D. Roberts)	1.00	.70	.40
D8	1969(Steve Owens)	1.50	1.25	.60
D9	NCAA Champions 1956	1.00	.70	.40
D10	Barry Switzer (CO)	.50	.40	.20
D11	Action Shot (Lucius Selmon)	.50	.40	.20
D12	Action Shot (Elvis Peacock)	.50	.40	.20
D13	Action Shot(Billy Sims)	1.00	.70	.40
H1	Action Shot(Jimbo Elrod)	.50	.40	.20
H2	All-Americans 1913-37	1.00	.70	.40
H3	All-Americans 1949-51(Jim Weatherall)	1.00	.70	.40
H4	All-Americans 1957-59 (Bill Krisher, Clendon Thomas, Bob Harrison, Jerry Thompson)	1.00	.70	.40
H5	All-Americans 1971-74 (Greg Pruitt, Tom Brahaney, Derland Moore, Rod Shoate)	1.00	.70	.40
H6	All-Americans 1976-78 (Zac Henderson, Greg Roberts, Daryl Hunt, George Cumby)	1.00	.70	.40
H7	1975(Lee Roy Selmon)	1.50	1.25	.60
H8	1978(Billy Sims)	1.50	1.25	.60
H9	NCAA Champions 1974	1.00	.70	.40
H10	Action Shot (Lee Roy Selmon)	1.00	.70	.40
H11	Action Shot(Tinker Owens)	.50	.40	.20
H12	Action Shot	.50	.40	.20
H13	Action Shot (Lee Roy Selmon)	1.00	.70	.40
S1	Action Shot (Horace Ivory)	.50	.40	.20
S2	All-Americans 1938-46	1.00	.70	.40
S3	All-Americans 1951-52 (Tom Catlin, Billy Vessels, Eddie Crowder)	1.00	.70	.40
S4	All-Americans 1962-63 (Leon Cross, Wayne Lee, Jim Grisham, Joe Don Looney)	1.00	.70	.40
S5	All-Americans 1973-75 (Lucius Selmon, Eddie Foster, John Roush, Joe Washington)	1.00	.70	.40
S6	All-Americans 1978-81 (Reggie Kinlaw, Billy Sims, Louis Oubre, Terry Crouch)	1.00	.70	.40
S7	1978(Greg Roberts)	1.00	.70	.40
S8	NCAA Champions 1950	1.00	.70	.40
S9	NCAA Champions 1975	1.00	.70	.40
S10	Action Shot(Bobby Proctor) (CO)	.50	.40	.20
S11	Action Shot(Steve Davis)	.50	.40	.20
S12	Action Shot(Greg Pruitt)	1.00	.70	.40
S13	Action Shot(Elvis Peacock)	.50	.40	.20
JK1	Sooner Schooner	.50	.40	.20
JK2	Sooner Schooner	.50	.40	.20
NNO	Mail Order Card	.50	.40	.20
NNO	Mail Order Card	.50	.40	.20

1986 Oklahoma

		NM/M	NM	E
Complete Set (16):		8.00	6.00	3.25
Common Player:		.35	.25	.14
1	Championship Ring - 1985 National Champs	.50	.40	.20
2	Orange Bowl (In Bowl Play)	.35	.25	.14
3	On The Road To Record	.35	.25	.14
4	Graduation Record	.35	.25	.14
5	President of Exxon (Lawrence G. Rawl)	.35	.25	.14
6	Barry Switzer (Winners)	1.50	1.25	.60
7	Win Streaks Hold Records	.35	.25	.14
8	Brian Bosworth	1.00	.70	.40
9	Heisman Trophy (Billy Vessels 1952, Steve Owens 1969, Billy Sims 1978)	.75	.60	.30
10	All-America Sooners (Tony Casillas)	.75	.60	.30
11	Jamelle Holieway	.50	.40	.20
12	Sooner Strength	.35	.25	.14
13	Sooner Support	.35	.25	.14
14	Go Sonners (Crimson and Cream)	.35	.25	.14
15	Border Battle (Oklahoma vs. Texas)	.50	.40	.20

1986 Oklahoma McDag

		NM/M	NM	E
Complete Set (16):		20.00	15.00	8.00
Common Player:		1.00	.70	.40
1	Brian Bosworth	3.00	2.25	1.25
2	Sonny Brown	1.00	.70	.40
3	Steve Bryan	1.00	.70	.40
4	Lydell Carr	1.50	1.25	.60
5	Patrick Collins	1.50	1.25	.60
6	Jamelle Holieway	2.00	1.50	.80
7	Mark Hutson	1.00	.70	.40
8	Keith Jackson	6.00	4.50	2.50
9	Troy Johnson	1.00	.70	.40
10	Dante Jones	3.00	2.25	1.25
11	Tim Lashar	1.00	.70	.40
12	Paul Migliazzo	1.00	.70	.40
13	Anthony Phillips	1.00	.70	.40
14	Darrell Reed	1.00	.70	.40
15	Derrick Shepard	1.50	1.25	.60
16	Spencer Tillman	1.50	1.25	.60

1987 Oklahoma Police

		NM/M	NM	E
Complete Set (16):		18.00	13.50	7.25
Common Player:		.75	.60	.30
1	Eric Mitchel	1.25	.90	.50
4	Jamelle Holieway	2.00	1.50	.80
10	David Vickers	.75	.60	.30
25	Anthony Stafford	1.25	.90	.50
29	Rickey Dixon	2.00	1.50	.80
33	Patrick Collins	1.25	.90	.50
40	Darrell Reed	.75	.60	.30
45	Lydell Carr	1.25	.90	.50
50	Dante Jones	2.00	1.50	.80
66	Jon Phillips	.75	.60	.30
68	Anthony Phillips	.75	.60	.30
75	Greg Johnson	.75	.60	.30
79	Mark Hutson	.75	.60	.30
80	Troy Johnson	.75	.60	.30
88	Keith Jackson	6.00	4.50	2.50
98	Dante Williams	.75	.60	.30
NNO	Barry Switzer (CO)	3.00	2.25	1.25

1988 Oklahoma Greats

		NM/M	NM	E
	Complete Set (30):	7.00	5.25	2.75
	Common Player:	.20	.15	.08
1	Jerry Anderson	.20	.15	.08
2	Dee Andros	.30	.25	.12
3	Dean Blevins	.20	.15	.08
4	Rick Bryan	.50	.40	.20
5	Paul (Buddy) Burris	.20	.15	.08
6	Eddie Crowder	.30	.25	.12
7	Jack Ging	.20	.15	.08
8	Jim Grisham	.30	.25	.12
9	Jimmy Harris	.30	.25	.12
10	Scott Hill	.20	.15	.08
11	Eddie Hinton	.30	.25	.12
12	Earl Johnson	.20	.15	.08
13	Don Key	.20	.15	.08
14	Tim Lashar	.20	.15	.08
15	Granville Liggins	.50	.40	.20
16	Thomas Lott	.30	.25	.12
17	Carl McAdams	.30	.25	.12
18	Jack Mitchell	.30	.25	.12
19	Billy Pricer	.20	.15	.08
20	John Roush	.20	.15	.08
21	Darrell Royal	.50	.40	.20
22	Lucius Selmon	.30	.25	.12
23	Ron Shotts	.20	.15	.08
24	Jerry Tubbs	.30	.25	.12
25	Bob Warmack	.30	.25	.12
26	Joe Washington	.50	.40	.20
27	Jim Weatherall	.30	.25	.12
28	'86 Sooner Great Game	.20	.15	.08
29	'75 Sooners	.20	.15	.08
30	Checklist Card	.30	.25	.12

1988 Oklahoma Police

		NM/M	NM	E
	Complete Set (16):	18.00	13.50	7.25
	Common Player:	1.00	.70	.40
1	Rotnei Anderson	2.00	1.50	.80
2	Eric Bross	1.00	.70	.40
3	Mike Gaddis	2.50	2.00	1.00
4	Scott Garl	1.00	.70	.40
5	James Goode	1.00	.70	.40
6	Jamelle Holieway	2.00	1.50	.80
7	Bob Latham	1.00	.70	.40
8	Ken McMichel	1.00	.70	.40
9	Eric Mitchel	1.50	1.25	.60
10	Leon Perry	1.50	1.25	.60
11	Anthony Phillips	1.00	.70	.40
12	Anthony Stafford	1.50	1.25	.60
13	Barry Switzer (CO)	4.00	3.00	1.50
14	Mark Vankeirsbilck	1.00	.70	.40
15	Curtice Williams	1.00	.70	.40
16	Dante Williams	1.00	.70	.40

1989 Oklahoma Police

		NM/M	NM	E
	Complete Set (16):	15.00	11.00	6.00
	Common Player:	1.00	.70	.40
1	Tom Backes	1.00	.70	.40
2	Frank Blevins	1.00	.70	.40
3	Eric Bross	1.00	.70	.40
4	Adrian Cooper	3.00	2.25	1.25
5	Scott Evans	1.00	.70	.40
6	Mike Gaddis	2.00	1.50	.80
7	Gary Gibbs (CO)	1.50	1.25	.60
8	James Goode	1.00	.70	.40
9	Ken McMichel	1.00	.70	.40
10	Leon Perry	1.50	1.25	.60
11	Mike Sawatzky	1.00	.70	.40
12	Don Smitherman	1.00	.70	.40
13	Kevin Thompson	1.00	.70	.40
14	Mark VanKeirsbilck	1.00	.70	.40
15	Mike Wise	1.00	.70	.40
16	Dante Williams	1.00	.70	.40

1991 Oklahoma Police

		NM/M	NM	E
	Complete Set (16):	15.00	11.00	6.00
	Common Player:	1.00	.70	.40
1	Gary Gibbs (CO)	1.50	1.25	.60
2	Cale Gundy	2.00	1.50	.80
3	Charles Franks	1.00	.70	.40
4	Mike Gaddis	1.50	1.25	.60
5	Brad Reddell	1.00	.70	.40
6	Brandon Houston	1.00	.70	.40
7	Chris Wilson	1.00	.70	.40
8	Darnell Walker	1.00	.70	.40
9	Mike McKinley	1.00	.70	.40
10	Kenyon Rasheed	2.00	1.50	.80
11	Joe Bowden	2.00	1.50	.80
12	Jason Belser	2.00	1.50	.80
13	Steve Collins	1.00	.70	.40

14	Reggie Barnes	1.00	.70	.40
15	Randy Wallace	1.00	.70	.40
16	Proctor Land	1.00	.70	.40

1968 O-Pee-Chee CFL

		NM	E	VG
	Complete Set (132):	1,100	550.00	325.00
	Common Player:	6.00	3.00	1.75
1	Roger Murphy	15.00	7.50	4.50
2	Charlie Parker	6.00	3.00	1.75
3	Mike Webster	6.00	3.00	1.75
4	Carroll Williams	6.00	3.00	1.75
5	Phil Brady	6.00	3.00	1.75
6	Dave Lewis	6.00	3.00	1.75
7	John Baker	6.00	3.00	1.75
8	Basil Bark	6.00	3.00	1.75
9	Donnie Davis	6.00	3.00	1.75
10	Pierre Desjardins	6.00	3.00	1.75
11	Larry Fairholm	6.00	3.00	1.75
12	Peter Paquette	6.00	3.00	1.75
13	Ray Lychak	6.00	3.00	1.75
14	Ted Collins	6.00	3.00	1.75
15	Margene Adkins	15.00	7.50	4.50
16	Ron Stewart	20.00	10.00	6.00
17	Russ Jackson	35.00	17.50	10.50
18	Bo Scott	15.00	7.50	4.50
19	Joe Poirier	6.00	3.00	1.75
20	Wayne Giardino	6.00	3.00	1.75
21	Gene Gaines	15.00	7.50	4.50
22	Billy Joe Booth	6.00	3.00	1.75
23	Whit Tucker	15.00	7.50	4.50
24	Rick Black	6.00	3.00	1.75
25	Ken Lehmann	12.00	6.00	3.50
26	Bob Brown	6.00	3.00	1.75
27	Moe Racine	6.00	3.00	1.75
28	Dick Thornton	8.00	4.00	2.50
29	Bob Taylor	6.00	3.00	1.75
30	Mel Profit	12.00	6.00	3.50
31	Dave Mann	8.00	4.00	2.50
32	Marv Luster	12.00	6.00	3.50
33	Ed Buchanan	6.00	3.00	1.75
34	Ed Harrington	8.00	4.00	2.50
35	Jim Dillard	6.00	3.00	1.75
36	Bob Taylor	6.00	3.00	1.75
37	Ron Arends	6.00	3.00	1.75
38	Mike Wadsworth	6.00	3.00	1.75
39	Wally Gabler	12.00	6.00	3.50
40	Pete Martin	6.00	3.00	1.75
41	Danny Nykoluk	6.00	3.00	1.75
42	Bill Frank	6.00	3.00	1.75
43	Gordon Christian	6.00	3.00	1.75
44	Tommy Joe Coffey	20.00	10.00	6.00
45	Ellison Kelly	20.00	10.00	6.00
46	Angelo Mosca	30.00	15.00	9.00
47	John Barrow	20.00	10.00	6.00
48	Bill Danychuk	12.00	6.00	3.50
49	Jon Hohman	6.00	3.00	1.75
50	Bill Redell	6.00	3.00	1.75
51	Joe Zuger	8.00	4.00	2.50
52	Willie Bethea	12.00	6.00	3.50
53	Dick Cohee	6.00	3.00	1.75
54	Tommy Grant	15.00	7.50	4.50
55	Garney Henley	20.00	10.00	6.00
56	Ted Page	6.00	3.00	1.75
57	Bob Krouse	6.00	3.00	1.75
58	Phil Minnick	6.00	3.00	1.75
59	Butch Pressley	6.00	3.00	1.75
60	Dave Raimey	8.00	4.00	2.50
61	Sherwyn Thorson	6.00	3.00	1.75
62	Bill Whisler	6.00	3.00	1.75
63	Roger Hamelin	6.00	3.00	1.75
64	Chuck Harrison	6.00	3.00	1.75
65	Ken Nielsen	12.00	6.00	3.50
66	Ernie Pitts	6.00	3.00	1.75
67	Mitch Zainasky	6.00	3.00	1.75
68	John Schneider	6.00	3.00	1.75
69	Ron Kirkland	6.00	3.00	1.75
70	Paul Desjardins	6.00	3.00	1.75
71	Luther Selbo	6.00	3.00	1.75
72	Don Gilbert	6.00	3.00	1.75
73	Bob Lueck	6.00	3.00	1.75
74	Gerry Shaw	6.00	3.00	1.75
75	Chuck Zickefoose	6.00	3.00	1.75
76	Frank Andruski	6.00	3.00	1.75
77	Lanny Boleski	6.00	3.00	1.75
78	Terry Evanshen	20.00	10.00	6.00
79	Jim Furlong	6.00	3.00	1.75
80	Wayne Harris	20.00	10.00	6.00
81	Jerry Keeling	15.00	7.50	4.50
82	Roger Kramer	8.00	4.00	2.50
83	Pete Liske	20.00	10.00	6.00
84	Dick Suderman	12.00	6.00	3.50
85	Granville Liggins	20.00	10.00	6.00
86	George Reed	30.00	15.00	9.00
87	Ron Lancaster	30.00	15.00	9.00
88	Alan Ford	6.00	3.00	1.75
89	Gordon Barwell	6.00	3.00	1.75

90	Wayne Shaw	6.00	3.00	1.75
91	Bruce Bennett	15.00	7.50	4.50
92	Henry Dorsch	6.00	3.00	1.75
93	Ken Reed	6.00	3.00	1.75
94	Ron Atchison	15.00	7.50	4.50
95	Clyde Brock	6.00	3.00	1.75
96	Alex Benecick	6.00	3.00	1.75
97	Ted Urness	12.00	6.00	3.50
98	Wally Dempsey	6.00	3.00	1.75
99	Don Gerhardt	6.00	3.00	1.75
100	Ted Dushinski	6.00	3.00	1.75
101	Ed McQuarters	12.00	6.00	3.50
102	Bob Kosid	6.00	3.00	1.75
103	Gary Brandt	6.00	3.00	1.75
104	John Wydareny	6.00	3.00	1.75
105	Jim Thomas	6.00	3.00	1.75
106	Art Perkins	6.00	3.00	1.75
107	Frank Cosentino	12.00	6.00	3.50
108	Earl Edwards	8.00	4.00	2.50
109	Garry Lefebvre	6.00	3.00	1.75
110	Greg Pipes	8.00	4.00	2.50
111	Ian MacLeod	6.00	3.00	1.75
112	Dick Dupuis	6.00	3.00	1.75
113	Ron Forwick	6.00	3.00	1.75
114	Jerry Griffin	6.00	3.00	1.75
115	John LaGrone	12.00	6.00	3.50
116	E.A. Sims	6.00	3.00	1.75
117	Greenard Poles	6.00	3.00	1.75
118	Leroy Sledge	6.00	3.00	1.75
119	Ken Sugarman	6.00	3.00	1.75
120	Jim Young	30.00	15.00	9.00
121	Garner Ekstran	12.00	6.00	3.50
122	Jim Evenson	12.00	6.00	3.50
123	Greg Findlay	6.00	3.00	1.75
124	Ted Gerela	8.00	4.00	2.50
125	Lach Heron	8.00	4.00	2.50
126	Mike Martin	6.00	3.00	1.75
127	Craig Murray	6.00	3.00	1.75
128	Pete Ohler	6.00	3.00	1.75
129	Sonny Homer	6.00	3.00	1.75
130	Bill Lasseter	6.00	3.00	1.75
131	John McDowell	6.00	3.00	1.75
132	Checklist Card	60.00	30.00	18.00

1968 O-Pee-Chee CFL Poster Inserts

		NM	E	VG
	Complete Set (16):	325.00	160.00	97.50
	Common Player:	15.00	7.50	4.50
1	Margene Adkins	20.00	10.00	6.00
2	Tommy Joe Coffey	25.00	12.50	7.50
3	Frank Cosentino	18.00	9.00	5.50
4	Terry Evanshen	25.00	12.50	7.50
5	Larry Fairholm	15.00	7.50	4.50
6	Wally Gabler	15.00	7.50	4.50
7	Russ Jackson	35.00	17.50	10.50
8	Ron Lancaster	30.00	15.00	9.00
9	Pete Liske	25.00	12.50	7.50
10	Dave Mann	18.00	9.00	5.50
11	Ken Nielsen	18.00	9.00	5.50
12	Dave Raimey	18.00	9.00	5.50
13	George Reed	30.00	15.00	9.00
14	Carroll Williams	15.00	7.50	4.50
15	Jim Young	30.00	15.00	9.00
16	Joe Zuger	15.00	7.50	4.50

1970 O-Pee-Chee CFL

		NM	E	VG
	Complete Set (115):	300.00	150.00	90.00
	Common Player:	2.00	1.00	.60
1	Ed Harrington	5.00	2.50	1.50
2	Danny Nykoluk	2.00	1.00	.60
3	Marv Luster	4.00	2.00	1.25
4	Dave Raimey	3.00	1.50	.90
5	Bill Symons	3.00	1.50	.90
6	Tom Wilkinson	20.00	10.00	6.00
7	Mike Wadsworth	2.00	1.00	.60
8	Dick Thornton	3.00	1.50	.90
9	Jim Tomlin	2.00	1.00	.60
10	Mel Profit	3.00	1.50	.90
11	Bob Taylor	4.00	2.00	1.25
12	Dave Mann	3.00	1.50	.90
13	Tommy Joe Coffey	5.00	2.50	1.50
14	Angelo Mosca	15.00	7.50	4.50
15	Joe Zuger	3.00	1.50	.90
16	Garney Henley	10.00	5.00	3.00
17	Mike Strofolino	2.00	1.00	.60
18	Billy Ray Locklin	2.00	1.00	.60
19	Ted Page	2.00	1.00	.60
20	Bill Danychuk	3.00	1.50	.90
21	Bob Krouse	2.00	1.00	.60
22	John Reid	2.00	1.00	.60
23	Dick Wesolowski	2.00	1.00	.60
24	Willie Bethea	3.00	1.50	.90
25	Ken Sugarman	2.00	1.00	.60
26	Rich Robinson	2.00	1.00	.60
27	Dave Tobey	2.00	1.00	.60

28	Paul Brothers	2.00	1.00	.60
29	Charlie Brown	2.00	1.00	.60
30	Jerry Bradley	2.00	1.00	.60
31	Ted Gerela	3.00	1.50	.90
32	Jim Young	8.00	4.00	2.50
33	Gary Robinson	2.00	1.00	.60
34	Bob Howes	2.00	1.00	.60
35	Greg Findlay	2.00	1.00	.60
36	Trevor Ekdahl	3.00	1.50	.90
37	Ron Stewart	6.00	3.00	1.75
38	Joe Poirier	3.00	1.50	.90
39	Wayne Giardino	2.00	1.00	.60
40	Tom Schuette	2.00	1.00	.60
41	Roger Perdrix	2.00	1.00	.60
42	Jim Mankins	2.00	1.00	.60
43	Jay Roberts	2.00	1.00	.60
44	Ken Lehmann	3.00	1.50	.90
45	Jerry Campbell	3.00	1.50	.90
46	Billy Joe Booth	3.00	1.50	.90
47	Whit Tucker	5.00	2.50	1.50
48	Moe Racine	2.00	1.00	.60
49	Corey Colehour	3.00	1.50	.90
50	Dave Gasser	2.00	1.00	.60
51	Jerry Griffin	2.00	1.00	.60
52	Greg Pipes	3.00	1.50	.90
53	Roy Shatzko	2.00	1.00	.60
54	Ron Forwick	2.00	1.00	.60
55	Ed Molstad	2.00	1.00	.60
56	Ken Ferguson	2.00	1.00	.60
57	Terry Swarn	5.00	2.50	1.50
58	Tom Nettles	2.00	1.00	.60
59	John Wydareny	2.00	1.00	.60
60	Bayne Norrie	2.00	1.00	.60
61	Wally Gabler	3.00	1.50	.90
62	Paul Desjardins	2.00	1.00	.60
63	Peter Francis	2.00	1.00	.60
64	Bill Frank	2.00	1.00	.60
65	Chuck Harrison	2.00	1.00	.60
66	Gene Lakusiak	2.00	1.00	.60
67	Phil Minnick	2.00	1.00	.60
68	Doug Strong	2.00	1.00	.60
69	Glen Schapansky	2.00	1.00	.60
70	Ed Ulmer	2.00	1.00	.60
71	Bill Whisler	2.00	1.00	.60
72	Ted Collins	2.00	1.00	.60
73	Larry DeGraw	2.00	1.00	.60
74	Henry Dorsch	2.00	1.00	.60
75	Alan Ford	2.00	1.00	.60
76	Ron Lancaster	20.00	10.00	6.00
77	Bob Kosid	2.00	1.00	.60
78	Bobby Thompson	2.00	1.00	.60
79	Ted Dushinski	2.00	1.00	.60
80	Bruce Bennett	4.00	2.00	1.25
81	George Reed	15.00	7.50	4.50
82	Wayne Shaw	2.00	1.00	.60
83	Cliff Shaw	2.00	1.00	.60
84	Jack Abendschan	2.00	1.00	.60
85	Ed McQuarters	5.00	2.50	1.50
86	Jerry Keeling	5.00	2.50	1.50
87	Gerry Shaw	2.00	1.00	.60
88	Basil Bark (UER) (Misspelled Back)	2.00	1.00	.60
89	Wayne Harris	6.00	3.00	1.75
90	Jim Furlong	2.00	1.00	.60
91	Larry Robinson	2.00	1.00	.60
92	John Helton	10.00	5.00	3.00
93	Dave Cranmer	2.00	1.00	.60
94	Lanny Boleski (UER) (Misspelled Larry)	2.00	1.00	.60
95	Herman Harrison	5.00	2.50	1.50
96	Granville Liggins	5.00	2.50	1.50
97	Joe Forzani	3.00	1.50	.90
98	Terry Evanshen	8.00	4.00	2.50
99	Sonny Wade	6.00	3.00	1.75
100	Dennis Duncan	2.00	1.00	.60
101	Al Phaneuf	2.00	1.00	.60
102	Larry Fairholm	2.00	1.00	.60
103	Moses Denson	4.00	2.00	1.25
104	Gino Baretta	2.00	1.00	.60
105	Gene Ceppetelli	2.00	1.00	.60
106	Dick Smith	2.00	1.00	.60
107	Gordon Judges	2.00	1.00	.60
108	Harry Olszewski	2.00	1.00	.60
109	Mike Webster	2.00	1.00	.60
110	**Checklist 1-115**	30.00	15.00	9.00
111	**Outstanding Player** (list from 1953-1969)	8.00	4.00	2.50
112	**Player of the Year** (list from 1954-1969)	8.00	4.00	2.50
113	**Lineman of the Year** (list from 1955-1969)	6.00	3.00	1.75
114	**CFL Coaches** (listed on card front)	6.00	3.00	1.75
115	**Identifying Player** (explanation of uniform numbering system)	15.00	7.50	4.50

1970 O-Pee-Chee CFL Push-Out Inserts

		NM	E	VG
Complete Set (16):		200.00	100.00	60.00
Common Player:		10.00	5.00	3.00
1	Ed Harrington	10.00	5.00	3.00
2	Danny Nykoluk	10.00	5.00	3.00
3	Tommy Joe Coffey	25.00	12.50	7.50
4	Angelo Mosca	30.00	15.00	9.00
5	Ken Sugarman	12.00	6.00	3.50
6	Jay Roberts	10.00	5.00	3.00
7	Joe Poirier	12.00	6.00	3.50
8	Corey Colehour	10.00	5.00	3.00
9	Dave Gasser	10.00	5.00	3.00
10	Wally Gabler	15.00	7.50	4.50
11	Paul Desjardins	10.00	5.00	3.00
12	Larry DeGraw	10.00	5.00	3.00
13	Jerry Keeling	20.00	10.00	6.00
14	Gerry Shaw	10.00	5.00	3.00
15	Terry Evanshen	25.00	12.50	7.50
16	Sonny Wade	12.00	6.00	3.50

1971 O-Pee-Chee CFL

		NM	E	VG
Complete Set (132):		250.00	125.00	75.00
Common Player:		1.00	.50	.30
1	Bill Symons	5.00	2.50	1.50
2	Mel Profit	1.50	.70	.45
3	Jim Tomlin	1.00	.50	.30
4	Ed Harrington	1.50	.70	.45
5	Jim Corrigall	4.00	2.00	1.25
6	Chip Barrett	1.00	.50	.30
7	Marv Luster	3.00	1.50	.90
8	Ellison Kelly	4.00	2.00	1.25
9	Charlie Bray	1.00	.50	.30
10	Pete Martin	1.00	.50	.30
11	Tony Moro	1.00	.50	.30
12	Dave Raimey	1.50	.70	.45
13	Joe Theismann	100.00	50.00	30.00
14	Greg Barton	6.00	3.00	1.75
15	Leon McQuay	6.00	3.00	1.75
16	Don Jonas	6.00	3.00	1.75
17	Doug Strong	1.00	.50	.30
18	Paul Brule	1.00	.50	.30
19	Bill Frank	1.00	.50	.30
20	Joe Critchlow	1.00	.50	.30
21	Chuck Liebrock	1.00	.50	.30
22	Rob McLaren	1.00	.50	.30
23	Bob Swift	1.00	.50	.30
24	Rick Shaw	1.00	.50	.30
25	Ross Richardson	1.00	.50	.30
26	Benji Dial	1.00	.50	.30
27	Jim Heighton	1.00	.50	.30
28	Ed Ulmer	1.00	.50	.30
29	Glen Schapansky	1.00	.50	.30
30	Larry Slagle	1.00	.50	.30
31	Tom Cassese	1.00	.50	.30
32	Ted Gerela	1.00	.50	.30
33	Bob Howes	1.00	.50	.30
34	Ken Sugarman	1.50	.70	.45
35	A.D. Whitfield	1.50	.70	.45
36	Jim Young	6.00	3.00	1.75
37	Tom Wilkinson	10.00	5.00	3.00
38	Lefty Hendrickson	1.00	.50	.30
39	Dave Golinsky	1.00	.50	.30
40	Gerry Herron	1.00	.50	.30
41	Jim Evenson	1.50	.70	.45
42	Greg Findlay	1.00	.50	.30
43	Garrett Hunsperger	1.00	.50	.30
44	Jerry Bradley	1.00	.50	.30
45	Trevor Ekdahl	1.50	.70	.45
46	Bayne Norrie	1.00	.50	.30
47	Henry King	1.00	.50	.30
48	Terry Swarn	1.50	.70	.45
49	Jim Thomas	1.50	.70	.45
50	Bob Houmard	1.00	.50	.30
51	Don Trull	3.00	1.50	.90
52	Dave Cutler	8.00	4.00	2.50
53	Mike Law	1.00	.50	.30
54	Dick Dupuis	1.50	.70	.45
55	Dave Gasser	1.00	.50	.30
56	Ron Forwick	1.00	.50	.30
57	John LaGrone	1.50	.70	.45
58	Greg Pipes	1.50	.70	.45
59	Ted Page	1.00	.50	.30
60	John Wydareny	1.50	.70	.45
61	Joe Zuger	1.50	.70	.45
62	Tommy Joe Coffey	6.00	3.00	1.75
63	Rensi Perdoni	1.00	.50	.30
64	Bob Taylor	2.50	1.25	.70
65	Garney Henley	6.00	3.00	1.75
66	Dick Wesolowski	1.00	.50	.30
67	Dave Fleming	1.00	.50	.30
68	Bill Danychuk	1.50	.70	.45
69	Angelo Mosca	15.00	7.50	4.50
70	Bob Krouse	1.00	.50	.30
71	Tony Gabriel	18.00	9.00	5.50
72	Wally Gabler	1.50	.70	.45
73	Bob Steiner	1.00	.50	.30
74	John Reid	1.00	.50	.30
75	Jon Hohman	1.00	.50	.30
76	Barry Ardern	1.00	.50	.30
77	Jerry Campbell	1.50	.70	.45
78	Billy Cooper	1.00	.50	.30
79	Dave Braggins	1.00	.50	.30
80	Tom Schuette	1.00	.50	.30
81	Dennis Duncan	1.00	.50	.30
82	Moe Racine	1.00	.50	.30
83	Rod Woodward	1.00	.50	.30
84	Al Marcelin	1.50	.70	.45
85	Garry Wood	5.00	2.50	1.50
86	Wayne Giardino	1.00	.50	.30
87	Roger Perdrix	1.00	.50	.30
88	Hugh Oldham	1.00	.50	.30
89	Rick Cassatta	2.50	1.25	.70
90	Jack Abendschan	1.50	.70	.45
91	Don Bahnuik	1.00	.50	.30
92	Bill Baker	10.00	5.00	3.00
93	Gordon Barwell	1.00	.50	.30
94	Gary Brandt	1.00	.50	.30
95	Henry Dorsch	1.00	.50	.30
96	Ted Dushinski	1.00	.50	.30
97	Alan Ford	1.00	.50	.30
98	Ken Frith	1.00	.50	.30
99	Ralph Galloway	1.00	.50	.30
100	Bob Kosid	1.00	.50	.30
101	Ron Lancaster	15.00	7.50	4.50
102	Silas McKinnie	1.00	.50	.30
103	George Reed	8.00	4.00	2.50
104	Gene Ceppetelli	1.00	.50	.30
105	Merl Code	1.00	.50	.30
106	Peter Dalla Riva	8.00	4.00	2.50
107	Moses Denson	2.50	1.25	.70
108	Pierre Desjardins	1.00	.50	.30
109	Terry Evanshen	6.00	3.00	1.75
110	Larry Fairholm	1.50	.70	.45
111	Gene Gaines	5.00	2.50	1.50
112	Ed George	1.50	.70	.45
113	Gordon Judges	1.00	.50	.30
114	Garry Lefebvre	1.00	.50	.30
115	Al Phaneuf	1.50	.70	.45
116	Steve Smear	5.00	2.50	1.50
117	Sonny Wade	3.00	1.50	.90
118	Frank Andruski	1.00	.50	.30
119	Basil Bark	1.00	.50	.30
120	Lanny Boleski	1.00	.50	.30
121	Joe Forzani	1.50	.70	.45
122	Jim Furlong	1.00	.50	.30
123	Wayne Harris	6.00	3.00	1.75
124	Herman Harrison	4.00	2.00	1.25
125	John Helton	4.00	2.00	1.25
126	Wayne Holm	1.00	.50	.30
127	Fred James	1.00	.50	.30
128	Jerry Keeling	4.00	2.00	1.25
129	Rudy Linterman	1.50	.70	.45
130	Larry Robinson	1.50	.70	.45
131	Gerry Shaw	1.00	.50	.30
132	**Checklist Card**	25.00	12.50	7.50
	1.00	.50	.30	

1971 O-Pee-Chee CFL Poster Inserts

		NM	E	VG
Complete Set (16):		150.00	75.00	45.00
Common Player:		6.00	3.00	1.75
1	Tommy Joe Coffey	15.00	7.50	4.50
2	Herman Harrison	15.00	7.50	4.50
3	Bill Frank	6.00	3.00	1.75
4	Ellison Kelly	10.00	5.00	3.00
5	Charlie Bray	6.00	3.00	1.75
6	Bill Danychuk	7.50	3.75	2.25
7	Saskatchewan Roughriders (Ron Lancaster)	20.00	10.00	6.00
8	Bill Symons	7.50	3.75	2.25
9	Steve Smear	10.00	5.00	3.00
10	Angelo Mosca	20.00	10.00	6.00
11	Wayne Harris	15.00	7.50	4.50
12	Greg Findlay	6.00	3.00	1.75
13	John Wydareny	7.50	3.75	2.25
14	Garney Henley	15.00	7.50	4.50
15	Al Phaneuf	7.50	3.75	2.25
16	Ed Harrington	6.00	3.00	1.75

1972 O-Pee-Chee CFL

		NM	E	VG
Complete Set (132):		175.00	87.00	52.00
Common Player:		1.00	.50	.30
1	Bob Krouse	2.50	1.25	.70
2	John Williams	1.00	.50	.30
3	Garney Henley	6.00	3.00	1.75
4	Dick Wesolowski	1.00	.50	.30
5	Paul McKay	1.00	.50	.30
6	Bill Danychuk	1.50	.70	.45
7	Angelo Mosca	10.00	5.00	3.00

8	Tommy Joe Coffey	5.00	2.50	1.50
9	Tony Gabriel	10.00	5.00	3.00
10	Mike Blum	1.00	.50	.30
11	Doug Mitchell	1.00	.50	.30
12	Emery Hicks	1.00	.50	.30
13	Max Anderson	1.00	.50	.30
14	Ed George	1.50	.70	.45
15	Mark Kosmos	1.50	.70	.45
16	Ted Collins	1.00	.50	.30
17	Peter Dalla Riva	5.00	2.50	1.50
18	Pierre Desjardins	1.00	.50	.30
19	Terry Evanshen	6.00	3.00	1.75
20	Larry Fairholm	1.50	.70	.45
21	Jim Foley	1.50	.70	.45
22	Gordon Judges	1.00	.50	.30
23	Barry Randall	1.00	.50	.30
24	Brad Upshaw	1.00	.50	.30
25	Jorma Kuisma	1.00	.50	.30
26	Mike Widger	1.00	.50	.30
27	Joe Theismann	50.00	25.00	15.00
28	Greg Barton	4.00	2.00	1.25
29	Bill Symons	3.00	1.50	.90
30	Leon McQuay	4.00	2.00	1.25
31	Jim Corrigall	4.00	2.00	1.25
32	Jim Stillwagon	4.00	2.00	1.25
33	Dick Thornton	1.50	.70	.45
34	Marv Luster	4.00	2.00	1.25
35	Paul Desjardins	1.00	.50	.30
36	Mike Eben	1.00	.50	.30
37	Eric Allen	5.00	2.50	1.50
38	Chip Barrett	1.00	.50	.30
39	Noah Jackson	3.00	1.50	.90
40	Jim Young	6.00	3.00	1.75
41	Trevor Ekdahl	1.50	.70	.45
42	Garrett Hunsperger	1.00	.50	.30
43	Willie Postler	1.00	.50	.30
44	George Anderson	1.00	.50	.30
45	Ron Estay	1.00	.50	.30
46	Johnny Musso	15.00	7.50	4.50
47	Eric Guthrie	1.00	.50	.30
48	Monroe Eley	1.00	.50	.30
49	Don Bunce	5.00	2.50	1.50
50	Jim Evenson	1.50	.70	.45
51	Ken Sugarman	1.50	.70	.45
52	Dave Golinsky	1.00	.50	.30
53	Wayne Harris	5.00	2.50	1.50
54	Jerry Keeling	4.00	2.00	1.25
55	Herman Harrison	4.00	2.00	1.25
56	Larry Robinson	1.50	.70	.45
57	John Helton	4.00	2.00	1.25
58	Gerry Shaw	1.00	.50	.30
59	Frank Andruski	1.00	.50	.30
60	Basil Bark	1.00	.50	.30
61	Joe Forzani	1.50	.70	.45
62	Jim Furlong	1.00	.50	.30
63	Rudy Linterman	1.50	.70	.45
64	Granville Liggins	4.00	2.00	1.25
65	Lanny Boleski	1.00	.50	.30
66	Hugh Oldham	1.00	.50	.30
67	Dave Braggins	1.00	.50	.30
68	Jerry Campbell	1.50	.70	.45
69	Al Marcelin	1.50	.70	.45
70	Tom Pullen	1.00	.50	.30
71	Rudy Sims	1.00	.50	.30
72	Marshall Shirk	1.00	.50	.30
73	Tom Laputka	1.00	.50	.30
74	Barry Ardern	1.00	.50	.30
75	Billy Cooper	1.00	.50	.30
76	Dan Deever	1.00	.50	.30
77	Wayne Giardino	1.00	.50	.30
78	Terry Wellesley	1.00	.50	.30
79	Ron Lancaster	12.00	6.00	3.50
80	George Reed	10.00	5.00	3.00
81	Bobby Thompson	1.00	.50	.30
82	Jack Abendschan	1.00	.50	.30
83	Ed McQuarters	3.00	1.50	.90
84	Bruce Bennett	3.00	1.50	.90
85	Bill Baker	5.00	2.50	1.50
86	Don Bahnuik	1.00	.50	.30
87	Gary Brandt	1.00	.50	.30
88	Henry Dorach	1.00	.50	.30
89	Ted Dushinski	1.00	.50	.30
90	Alan Ford	1.00	.50	.30
91	Bob Kosid	1.00	.50	.30
92	Greg Pipes	1.50	.70	.45
93	John LaGrone	1.50	.70	.45
94	Dave Gasser	1.00	.50	.30
95	Bob Taylor	1.50	.70	.45
96	Dave Cutler	5.00	2.50	1.50
97	Dick Dupuis	1.00	.50	.30
98	Ron Forwick	1.00	.50	.30
99	Bayne Norrie	1.00	.50	.30
100	Jim Henshall	1.00	.50	.30
101	Charlie Turner	1.00	.50	.30

102	Fred Dunn	1.00	.50	.30
103	Sam Scarber	1.00	.50	.30
104	Bruce Lemmerman	5.00	2.50	1.50
105	Don Jonas	6.00	3.00	1.75
106	Doug Strong	1.00	.50	.30
107	Ed Williams	1.00	.50	.30
108	Paul Markle	1.00	.50	.30
109	Gene Lakusiak	1.00	.50	.30
110	Bob LaRose	1.00	.50	.30
111	Rob McLaren	1.00	.50	.30
112	Pete Ribbins	1.00	.50	.30
113	Bill Frank	1.00	.50	.30
114	Bob Swift	1.00	.50	.30
115	Chuck Liebrock	1.00	.50	.30
116	Joe Critchlow	1.00	.50	.30
117	Paul Williams	1.00	.50	.30
118	**Pro Action**	1.00	.50	.30
119	**Pro Action**	1.00	.50	.30
120	**Pro Action**	1.00	.50	.30
121	**Pro Action**	1.00	.50	.30
122	**Pro Action**	1.00	.50	.30
123	**Pro Action**	1.00	.50	.30
124	**Pro Action**	1.00	.50	.30
125	**Pro Action**	1.00	.50	.30
126	**Pro Action**	1.00	.50	.30
127	**Pro Action**	1.00	.50	.30
128	**Pro Action**	1.00	.50	.30
129	**Pro Action**	1.00	.50	.30
130	**Pro Action**	1.00	.50	.30
131	**Pro Action**	1.00	.50	.30
132	**Checklist Card**	30.00	15.00	9.00

1953 Oregon

		NM	E	VG
Complete Set (20):		340.00	170.00	102.00
Common Player:		15.00	7.50	4.50
1	Farrell Albright	20.00	10.00	6.00
2	Ted Anderson	15.00	7.50	4.50
3	Len Berrie	15.00	7.50	4.50
4	Tom Elliott	15.00	7.50	4.50
5	Tim Flaherty	15.00	7.50	4.50
6	Cecil Hodges	15.00	7.50	4.50
7	Barney Holland	15.00	7.50	4.50
8	Dick James	25.00	12.50	7.50
9	Harry Johnson	15.00	7.50	4.50
10	Dave Lowe	15.00	7.50	4.50
11	Jack Patera	35.00	17.50	10.50
12	Ron Pheister	20.00	10.00	6.00
13	John Reed	15.00	7.50	4.50
14	Hal Reeve	20.00	10.00	6.00
15	Larry Rose	15.00	7.50	4.50
16	George Shaw	25.00	12.50	7.50
17	Lon Stiner Jr.	15.00	7.50	4.50
18	Ken Sweitzer	15.00	7.50	4.50
19	Keith Tucker	15.00	7.50	4.50
20	Dean Van Leuven	15.00	7.50	4.50

1956 Oregon

		NM	E	VG
Complete Set (19):		285.00	142.50	85.50
Common Player:		15.00	7.50	4.50
1	Bruce Brenn	15.00	7.50	4.50
2	Jack Brown	15.00	7.50	4.50
3	Reanous Cochran	15.00	7.50	4.50
4	Jack Crabtree	20.00	10.00	6.00
5	Tom Crabtree	15.00	7.50	4.50
6	Tom Hale	15.00	7.50	4.50
7	Spike Hillstrom	15.00	7.50	4.50
8	Jim Linden	15.00	7.50	4.50
9	Hank Loumena	15.00	7.50	4.50
10	Nick Markulis	15.00	7.50	4.50
11	Phil McHugh	15.00	7.50	4.50
13	Harry Mondale	15.00	7.50	4.50
14	Leroy Phelps	15.00	7.50	4.50
15	Jack Pocock	15.00	7.50	4.50
16	John Roventos	15.00	7.50	4.50
17	Jim Shanley	15.00	7.50	4.50
18	Ron Stover	20.00	10.00	6.00
19	J.C. Wheeler	15.00	7.50	4.50

1958 Oregon

		NM	E	VG
Complete Set (20):		260.00	130.00	78.00
Common Player:		15.00	7.50	4.50
1	Greg Altenhofen	15.00	7.50	4.50
2	Darrel Aschbacher	20.00	10.00	6.00
3	Dave Fish	15.00	7.50	4.50
4	Sandy Fraser	15.00	7.50	4.50
5	Dave Grosz	20.00	10.00	6.00
6	Bob Grottkau	20.00	10.00	6.00

7	Marlan Holland	15.00	7.50	4.50
8	Tom Keele	15.00	7.50	4.50
9	Alden Kimbrough	15.00	7.50	4.50
10	Don Laudenslager	15.00	7.50	4.50
11	Riley Mattson	25.00	12.50	7.50
12	Bob Peterson	15.00	7.50	4.50
13	Dave Powell	15.00	7.50	4.50
14	Len Read	15.00	7.50	4.50
15	Will Reeve	15.00	7.50	4.50
16	Joe Schafeld	15.00	7.50	4.50
17	Charlie Tourville	15.00	7.50	4.50
18	Dave Urell	15.00	7.50	4.50
19	Pete Welch	15.00	7.50	4.50
20	Willie West	25.00	12.50	7.50

1988 Oregon State Smokey

		NM/M	NM	E
Complete Set (12):		12.00	9.00	4.75
Common Player:		1.25	.90	.50
1	Troy Bussanich	1.25	.90	.50
2	Andre Harris	1.25	.90	.50
3	Teddy Johnson	1.25	.90	.50
4	Jason Kent	1.25	.90	.50
5	Dave Kragthorpe (CO)	1.25	.90	.50
6	Mike Matthews	1.25	.90	.50
7	Phil Ross	1.25	.90	.50
8	Brian Taylor	1.25	.90	.50
9	Robb Thomas	2.50	2.00	1.00
10	Esera Tuaolo	2.50	2.00	1.00
11	Erik Wilhelm	2.50	2.00	1.00
12	Dowell Williams	1.25	.90	.50

1990 Oregon State Smokey

		NM/M	NM	E
Complete Set (16):		10.00	7.50	4.00
Common Player:		1.00	.70	.40
1	Brian Beck	1.00	.70	.40
2	Martin Billings	1.00	.70	.40
3	Matt Booher	1.00	.70	.40
4	George Breland	1.00	.70	.40
5	Brad D'Ancona	1.00	.70	.40
6	Dennis Edwards	1.00	.70	.40
7	Brent Huff	1.00	.70	.40
8	James Jones	1.00	.70	.40
9	Dave Kragthorpe (CO)	1.00	.70	.40
10	Todd McKinney	1.00	.70	.40
11	Torey Overstreet	1.00	.70	.40
12	Reggie Pitchford	1.00	.70	.40
13	Todd Sahlfeld	1.00	.70	.40
14	Scott Thompson	1.00	.70	.40
15	Esera Tuaolo	2.00	1.50	.80
16	Maurice Wilson	1.00	.70	.40

1991 Oregon Smokey

		NM/M	NM	E
Complete Set (12):		12.00	9.00	4.75
Common Player:		1.00	.70	.40
1	Bud Bowie	1.00	.70	.40
2	Rich Brooks (CO)	3.00	2.25	1.25
3	Sean Burwell	1.00	.70	.40
4	Eric Castle	1.50	1.25	.60
5	Andy Conner	1.00	.70	.40
6	Joe Farwell	1.00	.70	.40
7	Matt LaBounty	1.50	1.25	.60
8	Gregg McCallum	1.00	.70	.40
9	Daryle Smith	1.00	.70	.40
10	Jeff Thomason	1.50	1.25	.60
11	Tommy Thompson	1.00	.70	.40
12	Marcus Woods	1.50	1.25	.60

1991 Oregon State Smokey

		NM/M	NM	E
Complete Set (12):		10.00	7.50	4.00
Common Player:		1.00	.70	.40
1	Adam Albaugh	1.00	.70	.40
2	Jamie Burke	1.00	.70	.40
3	Chad de Sully	1.00	.70	.40
4	Dennis Edwards	1.00	.70	.40
5	James Jones	1.00	.70	.40
6	Fletcher Keister	1.00	.70	.40
7	Tom Nordquist	1.00	.70	.40
8	Tony O'Billovich	1.00	.70	.40
9	Jerry Pettibone (CO)	1.25	.90	.50
10	Mark Price	1.00	.70	.40
11	Todd Sahlfeld	1.00	.70	.40
12	Earl Zackery	1.00	.70	.40

P

1984 Pacific Legends

The 30-card, regular-size set features well-known athletes from the Pac 10 football conference, including John Wayne, Pop Warner, Jackie Robinson, Frank Gifford and Lynn Swann.

		NM/M	NM	E
	Complete Set (30):	20.00	15.00	8.00
	Common Player:	.30	.25	.12
1	O.J. Simpson	5.00	3.75	2.00
2	Mike Garrett	.50	.40	.20
3	Pop Warner	.50	.40	.20
4	Bob Schloredt	.30	.25	.12
5	Pat Haden	.60	.45	.25
6	Ernie Nevers	.50	.40	.20
7	Jackie Robinson	2.50	2.00	1.00
8	Arnie Weinmeister	.50	.40	.20
9	Gary Beban	.50	.40	.20
10	Jim Plunkett	.60	.45	.25
11	Bobby Grayson	.30	.25	.12
12	Craig Morton	.50	.40	.20
13	Ben Davidson	.60	.45	.25
14	Jim Hardy	.30	.25	.12
15	Vern Burke	.30	.25	.12
16	Hugh McElhenny	.75	.60	.30
17	John Wayne	4.00	3.00	1.50
18	Ricky Bell (UER) (Name spelled Rickey on both sides)	.50	.40	.20
19	George Wildcat Wilson	.30	.25	.12
20	Bob Waterfield	.75	.60	.30
21	Charlie Mitchell	.30	.25	.12
22	Donn Moomaw	.30	.25	.12
23	Don Heinrich	.30	.25	.12
24	Terry Baker	.50	.40	.20
25	Jack Thompson	.50	.40	.20
26	Charles White	.50	.40	.20
27	Frank Gifford	1.50	1.25	.60
28	Lynn Swann	1.75	1.25	.70
29	Brick Muller	.30	.25	.12
30	Ron Yary	.50	.40	.20

1989 Pacific Steve Largent

This 110-card set is devoted to Hall of Fame wide receiver Steve Largent and commemorates his career with the Seattle Seahawks. Each card front, with a silver border, captures an event in Largent's career. The horizontally-designed backs describe the action on the front and have light blue borders. There were 85 cards in the set which were numbered; the remaining 25 cards form a 12-1/2" x 17-1/2" poster of Largent. The entire set was available as a factory set or wax packs of 10 cards each. Pacific Trading Cards produced them.

		NM/M	NM	E
	Complete Set (110):	25.00	18.50	10.00
	Common Player (1-85):	.25	.20	.10
1	Title Card (Steve Largent) (Checklist 1-42 On Back)	1.00	.70	.40
2	Santa, Can You Please (Steve Largent)	.25	.20	.10
3	Age 9(Steve Largent)	.25	.20	.10
4	Junior High 1968 (Steve Largent)	.25	.20	.10
5	High School 1971 (Steve Largent)	.25	.20	.10
6	Baseball or Football (Steve Largent)	.25	.20	.10
7	Tulsa, Senior Bowl (Steve Largent)	.25	.20	.10
8	Led Nation in TD's (Steve Largent)	.25	.20	.10

		NM/M	NM	E
9	Coach Patera, Coach Jerry Rhome	.40	.30	.15
10	Rookie 1976 (Steve Largent)	.50	.40	.20
11	First NFL TD (Steve Largent)	.25	.20	.10
12	Seahawk's First Win (Steve Largent)	.25	.20	.10
13	First Team All-Rookie (Steve Largent)	.40	.30	.15
14	Beats Buffalo 56-7 (Steve Largent)	.25	.20	.10
15	The Huddle (Steve Largent)	.25	.20	.10
16	Captains (Steve Largent, Norm Evans)	.40	.30	.15
17	First Win Against Raiders (Steve Largent)	.25	.20	.10
18	3000 Yards Receiving (Steve Largent)	.25	.20	.10
19	Jerry Rhome, Steve Largent	.50	.40	.20
20	Great Hands (Steve Largent)	.25	.20	.10
21	Climbs Mt. Rainier (Steve Largent)	.25	.20	.10
22	Zorn Connection (Steve Largent)	.40	.30	.15
23	Steve Largent, Jim Zorn	.40	.30	.15
24	First Team All-AFC (Steve Largent)	.25	.20	.10
25	Seahawks MVP 1981 (Steve Largent)	.40	.30	.15
26	Strike Season 1982 (Steve Largent)	.25	.20	.10
27	Training Camp 1983 (Steve Largent)	.25	.20	.10
28	Head Coach(Chuck Knox)	.40	.30	.15
29	50 Career TD's (Steve Largent)	.25	.20	.10
30	7000 Yards Receiving (Steve Largent)	.25	.20	.10
31	**Tilley and Largent**	.50	.40	.20
32	Cold Day in Cincy (Steve Largent)	.25	.20	.10
33	Catches 3 TD Passes (Steve Largent)	.25	.20	.10
34	Seahawks 12-4 in 1984 (Steve Largent)	.25	.20	.10
35	Defeated in AFC Championships (Steve Largent)	.25	.20	.10
36	Preparing for 1985 (Steve Largent)	.25	.20	.10
37	Career High 79 Catches (Steve Largent)	.25	.20	.10
38	Career High 1287 Yards (Steve Largent)	.25	.20	.10
39	10000 Yards Receiving (Steve Largent)	.25	.20	.10
40	Throws a Pass (Steve Largent)	.25	.20	.10
41	Game Day 1985 (Steve Largent)	.25	.20	.10
42	Seattle Sports Star of the Year(Steve Largent)	.40	.30	.15
43	A Very Sore Elbow (Steve Largent)	.25	.20	.10
44	The Concentration (Steve Largent)	.25	.20	.10
45	Steve Largent, Eugene Robinson	.40	.30	.15
46	Breaks Carmichael's Record (Steve Largent)	.35	.20	.10
47	Seahawks 37, Raiders 0 (Steve Largent)	.25	.20	.10
48	11000 Yards Receiving (Steve Largent)	.25	.20	.10
49	Rough Game (Steve Largent)	.25	.20	.10
50	Streak Continues (Steve Largent)	.25	.20	.10
51	**Captains Lane, Brown and Largent**	.40	.30	.15
52	Steve & Kyle Catch a Big One(Steve Largent)	.25	.20	.10
53	Krieg Connection (Steve Largent)	.40	.30	.15
54	Seahawk Camp (Steve Largent)	.25	.20	.10
55	NFL All-Time Leading Receiver(Steve Largent)	.40	.30	.15
56	Hall of Fame Bowl (Steve Largent)	.25	.20	.10
57	Steve Largent, Coach Knox	.40	.30	.15
58	1987 Seahawks MVP (Steve Largent)	.40	.30	.15

		NM/M	NM	E
59	Largent at Quarterback (Steve Largent)	.50	.40	.20
60	NFL All-Time Great (Steve Largent)	.40	.30	.15
61	Travelers' NFL Man of the Year 1988 (Steve Largent)	.40	.30	.15
62	Steve Largent, Terry Largent	.25	.20	.10
63	Holding for Norm Johnson (Steve Largent)	.40	.30	.15
64	Great Moves (Steve Largent)	.25	.20	.10
65	Great Hands (Steve Largent)	.25	.20	.10
66	Seven-Time Pro Bowl Selection (Steve Largent)	.25	.20	.10
67	Agee, Steve Largent, Paul Skansi	.40	.30	.15
68	Signing for Fans (Steve Largent)	.25	.20	.10
69	Miller, Joe Nash, Steve Largent, Bryan Millard	.25	.20	.10
70	Pro Bowl Greats (Steve Largent, John Elway)	1.50	1.25	.60
71	Hanging onto the Ball (Steve Largent)	.25	.20	.10
72	1618 Career Yards vs. Denve r(Steve Largent)	.25	.20	.10
73	17 Pro Bowl Receptions (Steve Largent)	.25	.20	.10
74	Jim Zorn, Steve Largent	.40	.30	.15
75	Mr. Seahawk (Steve Largent)	.40	.30	.15
76	Sets NFL Career Yardage Record(Steve Largent)	.40	.30	.15
77	Two of the Greatest (Steve Largent)	.50	.40	.20
78	Steve Largent, Jerry Rhome, Charlie Joiner	.50	.40	.20
79	NFL All-Time Leader in Receptions (Steve Largent)	.40	.30	.15
80	Leader in Consecutive Game Receptions (Steve Largent)	.40	.30	.15
81	All-Time Leader 12686 Receiving Yards (Steve Largent)	.25	.20	.10
82	NFL All-Time Leader 1000 Yard Seasons (Steve Largent)	.40	.30	.15
83	First Recipient of the Bart Starr Trophy (Steve Largent)	.50	.40	.20
84	Steve Largent	.40	.30	.15
85	Future Hall of Famer (Steve Largent)	.75	.60	.30

1991 Pacific

Pacific's inaugural issue features full-color fronts with ultra-violet coating and full-color backs. Cards began shipping in late June and were numbered alphabetically by city name and player name. Pacific's border colors echo the player's team colors.

		NM/M	NM	E
	Complete Set (660):	20.00		
		15.00	8.00	
	Complete Series 1 (550):	10.00	7.50	4.00
	Complete Series 2 (110):	10.00	7.50	4.00
	Common Player:	.04	.03	.02
	Series 1 Pack (14):	.50		
	Series 1 Wax Box (36):	10.00		
	Series 2 Pack (14):	.75		
	Series 2 Wax Box (36):	15.00		
1	Deion Sanders	.25	.20	.10
2	Steve Broussard	.04	.03	.02
3	Aundray Bruce	.04	.03	.02

4	Rick Bryant	.04	.03	.02
5	John Rade	.04	.03	.02
6	Scott Case	.04	.03	.02
7	Tony Casillas	.04	.03	.02
8	Shawn Collins	.04	.03	.02
9	Darion Conner	.04	.03	.02
10	Tory Epps	.04	.03	.02
11	Bill Fralic	.04	.03	.02
12	Mike Gann	.04	.03	.02
13	Tim Green	.04	.03	.02
14	Chris Hinton	.04	.03	.02
15	Houston Hoover	.04	.03	.02
16	Chris Miller	.04	.03	.02
17	Andre Rison	.25	.20	.10
18	Mike Rozier	.04	.03	.02
19	Jessie Tuggle	.04	.03	.02
20	Don Beebe	.04	.03	.02
21	Ray Bentley	.04	.03	.02
22	Shane Conlan	.04	.03	.02
23	Kent Hull	.04	.03	.02
24	Mark Kelso	.04	.03	.02
25	James Lofton	.04	.03	.02
26	Scott Norwood	.04	.03	.02
27	Andre Reed	.20	.15	.08
28	Leonard Smith	.04	.03	.02
29	Bruce Smith	.04	.03	.02
30	Leon Seals	.04	.03	.02
31	Darryl Talley	.04	.03	.02
32	Steve Tasker	.04	.03	.02
33	Thurman Thomas	.50	.40	.20
34	James Williams	.04	.03	.02
35	Will Wolford	.04	.03	.02
36	Frank Reich	.04	.03	.02
37	Jeff Wright RC	.12	.09	.05
38	Neal Anderson	.10	.08	.04
39	Trace Armstrong	.04	.03	.02
40	Johnny Bailey	.04	.03	.02
41	Mark Bortz	.04	.03	.02
42	Cap Boso	.04	.03	.02
43	Kevin Butler	.04	.03	.02
44	Mark Carrier	.04	.03	.02
45	Jim Covert	.04	.03	.02
46	Wendell Davis	.10	.08	.04
47	Richard Dent	.04	.03	.02
48	Shaun Gayle	.04	.03	.02
49	Jim Harbaugh	.10	.08	.04
50	Jay Hilgenberg	.04	.03	.02
51	Brad Muster	.04	.03	.02
52	William Perry	.04	.03	.02
53	Mike Singletary	.04	.03	.02
54	Peter Tom Willis	.04	.03	.02
55	Donnell Woolford	.04	.03	.02
56	Steve McMichael	.04	.03	.02
57	Eric Ball	.04	.03	.02
58	Lewis Billups	.04	.03	.02
59	Jim Breech	.04	.03	.02
60	James Brooks	.04	.03	.02
61	Eddie Brown	.04	.03	.02
62	Rickey Dixon	.04	.03	.02
63	Boomer Esiason	.15	.11	.06
64	James Francis	.04	.03	.02
65	David Fulcher	.04	.03	.02
66	David Grant	.04	.03	.02
67	Harold Green	.15	.11	.06
68	Rodney Holman	.04	.03	.02
69	Stanford Jennings	.04	.03	.02
70	Tim Krumrie	.04	.03	.02
71	Tim McGee	.04	.03	.02
72	Anthony Munoz	.04	.03	.02
73	Mitchell Price	.04	.03	.02
74	Eric Thomas	.04	.03	.02
75	Ickey Woods	.04	.03	.02
76	Mike Baab	.04	.03	.02
77	Thane Gash	.04	.03	.02
78	David Grayson	.04	.03	.02
79	Mike Johnson	.04	.03	.02
80	Reggie Langhorne	.04	.03	.02
81	Kevin Mack	.04	.03	.02
82	Clay Matthews	.04	.03	.02
83	Eric Metcalf	.04	.03	.02
84	Frank Minnifield	.04	.03	.02
85	Mike Oliphant	.04	.03	.02
86	Mike Pagel	.04	.03	.02
87	John Talley	.04	.03	.02
88	Lawyer Tillman	.04	.03	.02
89	Felix Wright	.04	.03	.02
90	Bryan Wagner	.04	.03	.02
91	Bob Burnett RC	.10	.08	.04
92	Tommie Agee	.04	.03	.02
93	Troy Aikman	1.00	.70	.40
94	Bill Bates	.04	.03	.02
95	Jack Del Rio	.04	.03	.02
96	Issiac Holt	.04	.03	.02
97	Michael Irvin	.50	.40	.20
98	Jim Jeffcoat	.04	.03	.02
99	Jimmy Jones	.04	.03	.02
100	Kelvin Martin	.04	.03	.02
101	Nate Newton	.04	.03	.02
102	Danny Noonan	.04	.03	.02
103	Ken Norton	.04	.03	.02
104	Jay Novacek	.15	.11	.06
105	Mike Saxon	.04	.03	.02
106	Derrick Sheppard	.04	.03	.02
107	Emmitt Smith	2.00	1.50	.80
108	Daniel Stubbs	.04	.03	.02
109	Tony Tolbert	.04	.03	.02
110	Alexander Wright	.09	.07	.04
111	Steve Atwater	.04	.03	.02
112	Melvin Bratton	.04	.03	.02
113	Tyrone Braxton	.04	.03	.02
114	Alphonso Carreker	.04	.03	.02
115	John Elway	.35	.25	.14
116	Simon Fletcher	.04	.03	.02
117	Bobby Humphrey	.04	.03	.02
118	Mark Jackson	.04	.03	.02
119	Vance Johnson	.04	.03	.02
120	Greg Kragen	.04	.03	.02
121	Karl Mecklenburg	.04	.03	.02
122	Orson Mobley	.04	.03	.02
123	Alton Montgomery	.04	.03	.02
124	Rickey Nattiel	.04	.03	.02
125	Steve Sewell	.04	.03	.02
126	Shannon Sharpe	.50	.40	.20
127	Dennis Smith	.04	.03	.02
128	Andre Townsend	.50	.40	.20
129	Mike Horan	.04	.03	.02
130	Jerry Ball	.04	.03	.02
131	Bennie Blades	.04	.03	.02
132	Lomas Brown	.04	.03	.02
133	Jeff Campbell	.04	.03	.02
134	Robert Clark	.04	.03	.02
135	Michael Cofer	.04	.03	.02
136	Dennis Gibson	.04	.03	.02
137	Mel Gray	.04	.03	.02
138	LeRoy Irvin	.04	.03	.02
139	George Jamison RC	.12	.09	.05
140	Eric Johnson	.04	.03	.02
141	Eddie Murray	.04	.03	.02
142	Dan Owens	.04	.03	.02
143	Rodney Peete	.04	.03	.02
144	Barry Sanders	1.25	.90	.50
145	Chris Spielman	.04	.03	.02
146	Mark Spindler	.04	.03	.02
147	Andre Ware	.12	.09	.05
148	William White	.04	.03	.02
149	Tony Bennett	.04	.03	.02
150	Robert Brown	.04	.03	.02
151	LeRoy Butler	.04	.03	.02
152	Anthony Dilweg	.04	.03	.02
153	Michael Haddix	.04	.03	.02
154	Ron Hallstrom	.04	.03	.02
155	Tim Harris	.04	.03	.02
156	Johnny Holland	.04	.03	.02
157	Chris Jacke	.04	.03	.02
158	Perry Kemp	.04	.03	.02
159	Mark Lee	.04	.03	.02
160	Don Majkowski	.04	.03	.02
161	Tony Mandarich	.04	.03	.02
162	Mark Murphy	.04	.03	.02
163	Brian Noble	.04	.03	.02
164	Shawn Patterson	.04	.03	.02
165	Jeff Query	.04	.03	.02
166	Sterling Sharpe	.60	.45	.25
167	Darrell Thompson	.12	.09	.05
168	Ed West	.04	.03	.02
169	Ray Childress	.04	.03	.02
170	Chris Dishman RC	.35	.25	.14
171	Curtis Duncan	.04	.03	.02
172	William Fuller	.04	.03	.02
173	Ernest Givins	.04	.03	.02
174	Drew Hill	.04	.03	.02
175	Haywood Jeffires	.20	.15	.08
176	Sean Jones	.04	.03	.02
177	Lamar Lathon	.04	.03	.02
178	Bruce Matthews	.04	.03	.02
179	Bubba McDowell	.04	.03	.02
180	Johnny Meads	.04	.03	.02
181	Warren Moon	.15	.11	.06
182	Mike Munchak	.04	.03	.02
183	Allen Pinkett	.04	.03	.02
184	Dean Steinkuhler	.04	.03	.02
185	Lorenzo White	.25	.20	.10
186	John Grimsby	.04	.03	.02
187	Pat Beach	.04	.03	.02
188	Albert Bentley	.04	.03	.02
189	Dean Biasucci	.04	.03	.02
190	Duane Bickett	.04	.03	.02
191	Bill Brooks	.04	.03	.02
192	Eugene Daniel	.04	.03	.02
193	Jeff George	.30	.25	.12
194	Jon Hand	.04	.03	.02
195	Jeff Herrod	.04	.03	.02
196	Jesse Hester	.04	.03	.02
197	Mike Prior	.04	.03	.02
198	Stacey Simmons	.04	.03	.02
199	Rohn Stark	.04	.03	.02
200	Pat Tomborlin	.04	.03	.02
201	Clarence Verdin	.04	.03	.02
202	Keith Taylor	.04	.03	.02
203	Jack Trudeau	.04	.03	.02
204	Chip Banks	.04	.03	.02
205	John Alt	.04	.03	.02
206	Deron Cherry	.04	.03	.02
207	Steve DeBerg	.04	.03	.02
208	Tim Grunhard	.04	.03	.02
209	Albert Lewis	.04	.03	.02
210	Nick Lowery	.04	.03	.02
211	Bill Maas	.04	.03	.02
212	Chris Martin	.04	.03	.02
213	Todd McNair	.04	.03	.02
214	Christian Okoye	.04	.03	.02
215	Stephone Paige	.04	.03	.02
216	Steve Pelluer	.04	.03	.02
217	Kevin Porter	.04	.03	.02
218	Kevin Ross	.04	.03	.02
219	Dan Sealeaumua	.04	.03	.02
220	Neil Smith	.04	.03	.02
221	David Szott	.04	.03	.02
222	Derrick Thomas	.25	.20	.10
223	Barry Word	.12	.09	.05
224	Percy Snow	.04	.03	.02
225	Marcus Allen	.04	.03	.02
226	Eddie Anderson	.04	.03	.02
227	Steve Beuerlein	.25	.20	.10
228	Tim Brown	.20	.15	.08
229	Scott Davis	.04	.03	.02
230	Mike Dyal	.04	.03	.02
231	Mervyn Fernandez	.04	.03	.02
232	Willie Gault	.04	.03	.02
233	Ethan Horton	.04	.03	.02
234	Bo Jackson	.50	.40	.20
235	Howie Long	.04	.03	.02
236	Terry McDaniel	.04	.03	.02
237	Max Montoya	.04	.03	.02
238	Don Mosebar	.04	.03	.02
239	Jay Schroeder	.04	.03	.02
240	Steve Smith	.04	.03	.02
241	Greg Townsend	.04	.03	.02
242	Aaron Wallace	.04	.03	.02
243	Lionel Washington	.04	.03	.02
244	Steve Wisniewski	1.00	.70	.40
245	Willie Anderson	.04	.03	.02
246	Latin Berry	.04	.03	.02
247	Robert Delpino	.04	.03	.02
248	Marcus Dupree	.04	.03	.02
249	Henry Ellard	.04	.03	.02
250	Jim Everett	.04	.03	.02
251	Cleveland Gary	.04	.03	.02
252	Jerry Gray	.04	.03	.02
253	Kevin Greene	.04	.03	.02
254	Pete Holohan	.04	.03	.02
255	Buford McGee	.04	.03	.02
256	Tom Newberry	.04	.03	.02
257	Irv Pankey	.04	.03	.02
258	Jackie Slater	.04	.03	.02
259	Doug Smith	.04	.03	.02
260	Frank Stams	.04	.03	.02
261	Michael Stewart	.04	.03	.02
262	Fred Strickland	.04	.03	.02
263	J.D. Brown	.04	.03	.02
264	Mark Clayton	.04	.03	.02
265	Jeff Cross	.04	.03	.02
266	Mark Dennis	.08	.06	.03
267	Mark Duper	.04	.03	.02
268	Ferrell Edmunds	.04	.03	.02
269	Dan Marino	2.00	1.50	.80
270	John Offerdahl	.04	.03	.02
271	Louis Oliver	.04	.03	.02
272	Tony Paige	.04	.03	.02
273	Reggie Roby	.04	.03	.02
274	Sammie Smith	.04	.03	.02
275	Keith Sims	.04	.03	.02
276	Brian Sochia	.04	.03	.02
277	Pete Stoyanovich	.04	.03	.02
278	Richmond Webb	.04	.03	.02
279	Jarvis Williams	.04	.03	.02
280	Tim McKyer	.04	.03	.02
281	Jim Jensen	.04	.03	.02
282	Scott Secules RC	.12	.09	.05
283	Ray Berry	.04	.03	.02
284	Joey Browner	.04	.03	.02
285	Anthony Carter	.04	.03	.02
286	Cris Carter	.25	.20	.10
287	Chris Doleman	.04	.03	.02
288	Mark Dusbabek	.04	.03	.02
289	Hassan Jones	.04	.03	.02
290	Steve Jordan	.04	.03	.02
291	Carl Lee	.04	.03	.02
292	Kirk Lowdermilk	.04	.03	.02
293	Randall McDaniel	.04	.03	.02
294	Mike Merriweather	.04	.03	.02

Num	Name				Num	Name				Num	Name			
295	Keith Millard	.04	.03	.02	392	Clyde Simmons	.04	.03	.02	489	Chris Warren	.50	.40	.20
296	Al Noga	.04	.03	.02	393	Ben Smith	.04	.03	.02	490	John L. Williams	.04	.03	.02
297	Scott Studwell	.04	.03	.02	394	Andre Waters	.04	.03	.02	491	Terry Wooden	.04	.03	.02
298	Henry Thomas	.04	.03	.02	395	Reggie White	.20	.15	.08	492	Tony Woods	.04	.03	.02
299	Herschel Walker	.04	.03	.02	396	Calvin Williams	.15	.11	.06	493	Brian Blades	.04	.03	.02
300	Gary Zimmerman	.04	.03	.02	397	Al Harris	.04	.03	.02	494	Paul Skansi	.04	.03	.02
301	Rich Gannon	.10	.08	.04	398	Anthony Toney	.04	.03	.02	495	Gary Anderson	.04	.03	.02
302	Wade Wilson	.04	.03	.02	399	Mike Quick	.04	.03	.02	496	Mark Carrier	.04	.03	.02
303	Vincent Brown	.04	.03	.02	400	Anthony Bell	.04	.03	.02	497	Chris Chandler	.04	.03	.02
304	Marv Cook	.04	.03	.02	401	Rich Camarillo	.04	.03	.02	498	Steve Christie	.04	.03	.02
305	Hart Lee Dykes	.04	.03	.02	402	Roy Green	.04	.03	.02	499	Reggie Cobb	.25	.20	.10
306	Irving Fryar	.04	.03	.02	403	Ken Harvey	.04	.03	.02	500	Reuben Davis	.04	.03	.02
307	Tom Hodson	.04	.03	.02	404	Eric Hill	.04	.03	.02	501	Willie Drewery	.04	.03	.02
308	Maurice Hurst	.04	.03	.02	405	Garth Jax RC	.07	.05	.03	502	Randy Grimes	.04	.03	.02
309	Ronnie Lippett	.04	.03	.02	406	Ernie Jones	.04	.03	.02	503	Paul Gruber	.04	.03	.02
310	Fred Marion	.04	.03	.02	407	Cedric Mack	.04	.03	.02	504	Wayne Haddix	.04	.03	.02
311	Greg McMurty	.04	.03	.02	408	Dexter Manley	.04	.03	.02	505	Ron Hall	.04	.03	.02
312	Johnny Rembert	.04	.03	.02	409	Tim McDonald	.04	.03	.02	506	Harry Hamilton	.04	.03	.02
313	Chris Singleton	.04	.03	.02	410	Freddie Joe Nunn	.04	.03	.02	507	Bruce Hill	.04	.03	.02
314	Ed Reynolds	.04	.03	.02	411	Ricky Proehl	.10	.08	.04	508	Eugene Marve	.04	.03	.02
315	Andre Tippett	.04	.03	.02	412	Moe Gardner RC	.12	.09	.05	509	Keith McCants	.04	.03	.02
316	Garin Veris	.04	.03	.02	413	Timm Rosenbach	.04	.03	.02	510	Winston Moss	.04	.03	.02
317	Brent Williams	.04	.03	.02	414	Luis Sharpe	.04	.03	.02	511	Kevin Murphy	.04	.03	.02
318	John Stephens	.75	.60	.30	415	Vai Sikahema	.04	.03	.02	512	Mark Robinson	.04	.03	.02
319	Sammy Martin	.04	.03	.02	416	Anthony Thompson	.04	.03	.02	513	Vinny Testaverde	.08	.06	.03
320	Bruce Armstrong	.04	.03	.02	417	Ron Wolfley	.04	.03	.02	514	Broderick Thomas	.04	.03	.02
321	Morten Andersen	.10	.08	.04	418	Lonnie Young	.04	.03	.02	515	Jeff Bostic	.04	.03	.02
322	Gene Atkins	.04	.03	.02	419	Gary Anderson	.04	.03	.02	516	Todd Bowles	.04	.03	.02
323	Vince Buck	.04	.03	.02	420	Bubby Brister	.04	.03	.02	517	Earnest Byner	.04	.03	.02
324	John Fourcade	.04	.03	.02	421	Thomas Everett	.04	.03	.02	518	Gary Clark	.20	.15	.08
325	Kevin Haverdink	.04	.03	.02	422	Eric Green	.10	.08	.04	519	Craig Erickson RC	.50	.40	.20
326	Bobby Hebert	.04	.03	.02	423	Delton Hall	.04	.03	.02	520	Darryl Grant	.04	.03	.02
327	Craig Heyward	.04	.03	.02	424	Bryan Hinkle	.04	.03	.02	521	Darrell Green	.04	.03	.02
328	Dalton Hilliard	.04	.03	.02	425	Merril Hoge	.04	.03	.02	522	Russ Grimm	.04	.03	.02
329	Rickey Jackson	.04	.03	.02	426	Carnell Lake	.04	.03	.02	523	Stan Humphries	.30	.25	.12
330	Vaughan Johnson	.04	.03	.02	427	Louis Lipps	.04	.03	.02	524	Joe Jacoby	.04	.03	.02
331	Eric Martin	.04	.03	.02	428	David Little	.04	.03	.02	525	Jim Lachey	.04	.03	.02
332	Wayne Martin	.04	.03	.02	429	Greg Lloyd	.04	.03	.02	526	Chip Lohmiller	.04	.03	.02
333	Rueben Mayes	.04	.03	.02	430	Mike Mularkey	.04	.03	.02	527	Charles Mann	.04	.03	.02
334	Sam Mills	.04	.03	.02	431	Keith Willis	.04	.03	.02	528	Wilber Marshall	.04	.03	.02
335	Brett Perriman	.04	.03	.02	432	Dwayne Woodruff	.04	.03	.02	529	Art Monk	.04	.03	.02
336	Pat Swilling	.04	.03	.02	433	Rod Woodson	.04	.03	.02	530	Tracy Rocker	.04	.03	.02
337	Renaldo Turnbull	.04	.03	.02	434	Tim Worley	.04	.03	.02	531	Mark Rypien	.12	.09	.05
338	Lonzell Hill	.04	.03	.02	435	Warren Williams	.04	.03	.02	532	Ricky Sanders	.04	.03	.02
339	Steve Walsh	.04	.03	.02	436	Terry Long	.04	.03	.02	533	Alvin Walton	.04	.03	.02
340	Carl Banks	.04	.03	.02	437	Martin Bayless	.04	.03	.02	534	Todd Marinovich RC	.15	.11	.06
341	Mark Bavaro	.04	.03	.02	438	Jarrod Bunch RC	.15	.11	.06	535	Mike Dumas	.04	.03	.02
342	Maurice Carthon	.04	.03	.02	439	Marion Butts	.04	.03	.02	536	Russell Maryland	.50	.40	.20
343	Pat Harlow RC	.08	.06	.03	440	Gill Byrd	.04	.03	.02	537	Eric Turner RC	.20	.15	.08
344	Eric Dorsey	.04	.03	.02	441	Arthur Cox	.04	.03	.02	538	Ernie Mills RC	.20	.15	.08
345	John Elliott	.04	.03	.02	442	John Friesz	.15	.11	.06	539	Ed King RC	.10	.08	.04
346	Rodney Hampton	.50	.40	.20	443	Leo Goeas	.04	.03	.02	540	Michael Stonebreaker	.04	.03	.02
347	Jeff Hostetler	.20	.15	.08	444	Burt Grossman	.04	.03	.02	541	Chris Zorich RC	.25	.20	.10
348	Erik Howard	.04	.03	.02	445	Courtney Hall	.04	.03	.02	542	Mike Croel	.35	.25	.14
349	Pepper Johnson	.04	.03	.02	446	Ronnie Harmon	.04	.03	.02	543	Eric Moten RC	.10	.08	.04
350	Sean Landeta	.50	.40	.20	447	Nate Lewis RC	.25	.20	.10	544	Dan McGwire RC	.15	.11	.06
351	Leonard Marshall	.04	.03	.02	448	Anthony Miller	.04	.03	.02	545	Keith Cash RC	.10	.08	.04
352	David Meggett	.04	.03	.02	449	Leslie O'Neal	.04	.03	.02	546	Kenny Walker RC	.12	.09	.05
353	Bart Oates	.04	.03	.02	450	Gary Plummer	.04	.03	.02	547	Leroy Hoard	.08	.06	.03
354	Gary Reasons	.04	.03	.02	451	Junior Seau	.30	.25	.12	548	Luis Chrisobol	.04	.03	.02
355	Phil Simms	.10	.08	.04	452	Billy Ray Smith	.04	.03	.02	549	Stacy Danley	.04	.03	.02
356	Lawrence Taylor	.10	.08	.04	453	Billy Joe Tolliver	.04	.03	.02	550	Todd Lyght RC	.10	.08	.04
357	Reyna Thompson	.04	.03	.02	454	Broderick Thompson	.04	.03	.02	551	Brett Favre RC	6.00	4.50	2.50
358	Brian Williams	.04	.03	.02	455	Lee Williams	.04	.03	.02	552	Mike Pritchard RC	.50	.40	.20
359	Matt Boyer	.04	.03	.02	456	Michael Carter	.04	.03	.02	553	Moe Gardner	.05	.04	.02
360	Mark Ingram	.04	.03	.02	457	Mike Cofer	.04	.03	.02	554	Tim McKyer	.05	.04	.02
361	Brad Baxter	.15	.11	.06	458	Kevin Fagan	.04	.03	.02	555	Erric Pegram RC	.50	.40	.20
362	Mark Boyer	.04	.03	.02	459	Charles Haley	.04	.03	.02	556	Norm Johnson	.05	.04	.02
363	Dennis Byrd	.04	.03	.02	460	Pierce Holt	.04	.03	.02	557	Bruce Pickens RC	.10	.08	.04
364	Dave Cadigan	.04	.03	.02	461	Johnny Jackson	.04	.03	.02	558	Henry Jones RC	.35	.25	.14
365	Kyle Clifton	.04	.03	.02	462	Brent Jones	.04	.03	.02	559	Phil Hansen RC	.20	.15	.08
366	James Hasty	.04	.03	.02	463	Guy McIntyre	.04	.03	.02	560	Cornelius Bennett	.05	.04	.02
367	Joe Kelly	.04	.03	.02	464	Joe Montana	1.00	.70	.40	561	Stan Thomas	.05	.04	.02
368	Jeff Lageman	.04	.03	.02	465	Bubba Paris	.04	.03	.02	562	Chris Zorich	.10	.08	.04
369	Pat Leahy	.04	.03	.02	466	Tom Rathman	.04	.03	.02	563	Anthony Morgan RC	.15	.11	.06
370	Terance Mathis	.10	.08	.04	467	Jerry Rice	1.00	.70	.40	564	Darren Lewis RC	.30	.25	.12
371	Erik McMillan	.04	.03	.02	468	Mike Sherrard	.04	.03	.02	565	Mike Stonebreaker	.05	.04	.02
372	Rob Moore	.25	.20	.10	469	John Taylor	.15	.11	.06	566	Alfred Williams RC	.15	.11	.06
373	Ken O'Brien	.04	.03	.02	470	Steve Young	.75	.60	.30	567	Lamar Rogers	.05	.04	.02
374	Tony Stargell	.04	.03	.02	471	Dennis Brown	.04	.03	.02	568	Erik Wilhelm RC	.30	.25	.12
375	Jim Sweeney	.04	.03	.02	472	Dexter Carter	.04	.03	.02	569	Ed King	.05	.04	.02
376	Al Toon	.04	.03	.02	473	Bill Romanowski	.04	.03	.02	570	Michael Jackson RC	.75	.60	.30
377	Johnny Hector	.04	.03	.02	474	Dave Waymer	.04	.03	.02	571	James Jones RC	.15	.11	.06
378	Jeff Criswell	.04	.03	.02	475	Robert Blackmon	.04	.03	.02	572	Russell Maryland	.15	.11	.06
379	Mike Haight	.04	.03	.02	476	Derrick Fenner	.10	.08	.04	573	Dixon Edwards RC	.10	.08	.04
380	Troy Benson	.04	.03	.02	477	Nesby Glasgow	.04	.03	.02	574	Derrick Brownlow	.05	.04	.02
381	Eric Allen	.04	.03	.02	478	Jacob Green	.04	.03	.02	575	Larry Brown RC	.50	.40	.20
382	Fred Barnett	.15	.11	.06	479	Andy Heck	.04	.03	.02	576	Mike Croel	.20	.15	.08
383	Jerome Brown	.04	.03	.02	480	Norm Johnson	.04	.03	.02	577	Keith Traylor RC	.08	.06	.03
384	Keith Byars	.04	.03	.02	481	Tommy Kane	.04	.03	.02	578	Kenny Walker	.05	.04	.02
385	Randall Cunningham	.20	.15	.08	482	Cortez Kennedy	.30	.25	.12	579	Reggie Johnson RC	.12	.09	.05
386	Byron Evans	.04	.03	.02	483	Dave Krieg	.04	.03	.02	580	Herman Moore RC	2.50	2.00	1.00
387	Wes Hopkins	.04	.03	.02	484	Bryan Millard	.04	.03	.02	581	Kelvin Pritchett RC	.10	.08	.04
388	Keith Jackson	.20	.15	.08	485	Joe Nash	.04	.03	.02	582	Kevin Scott RC	.10	.08	.04
389	Seth Joyner	.04	.03	.02	486	Rufus Porter	.04	.03	.02	583	Vinnie Clark RC	.10	.08	.04
390	Bobby Wilson RC	.10	.08	.04	487	Eugene Robinson	.04	.03	.02	584	Esera Tuaolo RC	.10	.08	.04
391	Heath Sherman	.10	.08	.04	488	Mike Tice RC	.10	.08	.04	585	Don Davey	.05	.04	.02

586	Blair Kiel **RC**	.12	.09	.05
587	Mike Dumas	.05	.04	.02
588	Darryll Lewis **RC**	.10	.08	.04
589	John Flannery **RC**	.10	.08	.04
590	Kevin Donnally	.05	.04	.02
591	Shane Curry	.05	.04	.02
592	Mark Vander Poel **RC**	.08	.06	.03
593	Dave McCloughan	.05	.04	.02
594	Mel Agee **RC**	.10	.08	.04
595	Kerry Cash **RC**	.12	.09	.05
596	Harvey Williams **RC**	.50	.40	.20
597	Joe Valerio	.05	.04	.02
598	Tim Barnett **RC**	.30	.25	.12
599	Todd Marinovich	.05	.04	.02
600	Nick Bell **RC**	.20	.15	.08
601	Roger Craig	.05	.04	.02
602	Ronnie Lott	.10	.08	.04
603	Mike Jones **RC**	.10	.08	.04
604	Todd Lyght	.10	.08	.04
605	Roman Phifer **RC**	.10	.08	.04
606	David Lang **RC**	.15	.11	.06
607	Aaron Craver **RC**	.10	.08	.04
608	Mark Higgs **RC**	.75	.60	.30
609	Chris Green	.05	.04	.02
610	Randy Baldwin **RC**	.10	.08	.04
611	Pat Harlow	.05	.04	.02
612	Leonard Russell **RC**	.20	.15	.08
613	Jerome Henderson **RC**	.10	.08	.04
614	Scott Zolak **RC**	.20	.15	.08
615	Jon Vaughn **RC**	.15	.11	.06
616	Harry Colon **RC**	.12	.09	.05
617	Wesley Carroll **RC**	.15	.11	.06
618	Quinn Early	.05	.04	.02
619	Reggie Jones **RC**	.15	.11	.06
620	Jarrod Bunch	.10	.08	.04
621	Kanavis McGhee **RC**	.15	.11	.06
622	Ed McCaffrey **RC**	3.00	2.25	1.25
623	Browning Nagle **RC**	.35	.25	.14
624	Mo Lewis **RC**	.10	.08	.04
625	Blair Thomas	.10	.08	.04
626	Antone Davis	.10	.08	.04
627	Jim McMahon	.05	.04	.02
628	Scott Kowalkowski **RC**	.10	.08	.04
629	Brad Goebel **RC**	.15	.11	.06
630	William Thomas **RC**	.10	.08	.04
631	Eric Swann **RC**	.20	.15	.08
632	Mike Jones **RC**	.10	.08	.04
633	Aeneas Williams **RC**	.12	.09	.05
634	Dexter Davis	.05	.04	.02
635	Tom Tupa	.05	.04	.02
636	Johnny Johnson	.20	.15	.08
637	Randal Hill	.30	.25	.12
638	Jeff Graham **RC**	.75	.60	.30
639	Ernie Mills	.10	.08	.04
640	Adrian Cooper **RC**	.15	.11	.06
641	Stanley Richard **RC**	.35	.25	.14
642	Eric Bieniemy **RC**	.15	.11	.06
643	Eric Moten	.05	.04	.02
644	Shawn Jefferson **RC**	.35	.25	.14
645	Ted Washington **RC**	.10	.08	.04
646	John Johnson **RC**	.10	.08	.04
647	Dan McGwire	.10	.08	.04
648	Doug Thomas **RC**	.05	.04	.02
649	David Daniels	.05	.04	.02
650	John Kasay **RC**	.12	.09	.05
651	Jeff Kemp	.05	.04	.02
652	Charles McRae **RC**	.08	.06	.03
653	Lawrence Dawsey **RC**	.20	.15	.08
654	Robert Wilson	.05	.04	.02
655	Dexter Manley	.05	.04	.02
656	Chuck Weatherspoon	.05	.04	.02
657	Tim Ryan	.05	.04	.02
658	Bobby Wilson	.05	.04	.02
659	Ricky Ervins **RC**	.35	.25	.14
660	Matt Millen	.05	.04	.02

1991 Pacific Checklists

These checklists were issued for Pacific's first series of 1991 football cards and were randomly included in late-issue foil and wax packs. Pacific stated it only produced 10,000 checklist sets. Cards were numbered on the back.

		NM/M	NM	E
Complete Set (5):		2.00	7.50	4.00
Common Player:		.50	2.00	1.00
1	**Checklist 1**	.50	2.00	1.00
2	**Checklist 2**	.50	2.00	1.00
3	**Checklist 3**	.50	2.00	1.00
4	**Checklist 4**	.50	2.00	1.00
5	**Checklist 5**	.50	2.00	1.00

1991 Pacific Flash Cards

These mathematical flash cards contain a problem on the front which, when worked out correctly, equals the uniform number of the player pictured on the card back. The back of the card has a glossy picture of the player and either a career summary or highlights from the previous season. A card number also appears on the back. The cards are standard size.

Complete Set (110):		6.00	3.25	2.00
Common Player:		.04	.02	
1	Steve Young	.30	.15	.06
2	Hart Lee Dykes	.04	.02	.04
3	Timm Rosenbach	.04	.02	.04
4	Andre Collins	.04	.02	.01
5	Johnny Johnson	.15	.08	.02
6	Nick Lowery	.04	.02	.01
7	John Stephens	.04	.02	.01
8	Jim Arnold	.04	.02	.01
9	Steve DeBerg	.11	.06	.01
10	Christian Okoye	.04	.02	.02
11	Eric Swann	.08	.04	.02
12	Jerry Robinson	.04	.02	.01
13	Steve Wisniewski	.04	.02	.01
14	Jim Harbaugh	.08	.04	.01
15	Steve Broussard	.04	.02	.02
16	Mike Singletary	.11	.06	.01
17	Tim Green	.04	.02	.01
18	Roger Craig	.11	.06	.02
19	Maury Buford	.04	.02	.01
20	Marcus Allen	.20	.10	.02
21	Deion Sanders	.30	.15	.03
22	Chris Miller	.15	.08	.02
23	Joey Browner	.08	.04	.01
24	Bubby Brister	.08	.04	.01
25	Buford McGee	.04	.02	.01
26	Ed West	.04	.02	.01
27	Mark Murphy	.04	.02	.01
28	Tim Worley	.08	.04	.01
29	Keith Willis	.04	.02	.01
30	Rich Gannon	.04	.02	.01
31	Jim Everett	.11	.06	.02
32	Duval Love	.04	.02	.01
33	Bob Nelson	.04	.02	.01
34	Anthony Munoz	.11	.06	.01
35	Boomer Esiason	.15	.08	.02
36	Kenny Walker	.04	.02	.03
37	Mike Horan	.04	.02	.01
38	Gary Kubiak	.04	.02	.01
39	David Treadwell	.04	.02	.01
40	Robert Wilson	.04	.02	.01
41	Lewis Billups	.04	.02	.01
42	Kevin Mack	.04	.02	.01
43	John Elway	.40	.20	.02
44	Lee Johnson	.04	.02	.01
45	Ken Willis	.04	.02	.01
46	Herman Moore	.30	.15	.03
47	Eddie Murray	.04	.02	.01
48	Mike Saxon	.04	.02	.01
49	John L. Williams	.08	.04	.01
50	Barry Sanders	.70	.40	.10
51	Andre Ware	.11	.06	.02
52	Dave Krieg	.08	.04	.01
53	Cortez Kennedy	.20	.10	.01
54	Bo Jackson	.40	.20	.10
55	Derrick Fenner	.04	.02	.02
56	Steve Walsh	.08	.04	.01
57	Brett Maxie	.04	.02	.01
58	Stan Brock	.04	.02	.01
59	DeMond Winston	.04	.02	.01
60	Sam Mills	.08	.04	.01
61	Eric Martin	.08	.04	.01
62	Michael Carter	.08	.04	.01
63	Steve Wallace	.04	.02	.01
64	Jesse Sapolu	.04	.02	.01
65	Bill Romanowski	.04	.02	.01
66	Joe Montana	1.50	.80	.10
67	Sean Landeta	.04	.02	.01
68	Doug Riesenberg	.04	.02	.01
69	Myron Guyton	.04	.02	.01
70	Andre Reed	.11	.06	.01
71	John Elliott	.04	.02	.01
72	Jeff Hostetler	.11	.06	.01
73	Rohn Stark	.04	.02	.01
74	Jeff George	.15	.08	.03
75	Duane Bickett	.04	.02	.01
76	Emmitt Smith	1.50	.80	.15
77	Michael Irvin	.40	.20	.02
78	Tony Stargell	.04	.02	.01
79	Kyle Clifton	.04	.02	.01
80	John Booty	.04	.02	.01
81	Fred Barnett	.15	.08	.02
82	Blair Thomas	.08	.04	.05
83	Erik McMillan	.04	.02	.01
84	Broderick Thomas	.08	.04	.01
85	Jim Skow	.04	.02	.01
86	Gary Anderson	.08	.04	.01
87	Mark Robinson	.04	.02	.01
88	Steve Christie	.04	.02	.01
89	Cody Carlson	.11	.06	.01
90	Warren Moon	.25	.14	.03
91	Lorenzo White	.08	.04	.01
92	Reggie Roby	.04	.02	.01
93	Jim C. Jensen	.04	.02	.01
94	Mark Clayton	.08	.04	.01
95	Willie Gault	.08	.04	.01
96	Don Mosebar	.04	.02	.01
97	Gary Plummer	.04	.02	.01
98	Leslie O'Neal	.08	.04	.01
99	Neal Anderson	.11	.06	.02
100	Derrick Thomas	.20	.10	.02
101	Luis Sharpe	.04	.02	.01
102	D.J. Dozier	.04	.02	.01
103	Jarrod Bunch	.04	.02	.01
104	Mark Ingram	.04	.02	.01
105	James Lofton	.11	.06	.01
106	Jay Schroeder	.08	.04	.01
107	Ronnie Lott	.11	.06	.01
108	Todd Marinovich	.08	.04	.07
109	Chris Zorich	.11	.06	.02
110	Charles McRae	.04	.02	.01

1991 Pacific Prototypes

These cards were produced by Pacific Trading Cards to promote its 1991 set, its debut set. The cards, which are numbered on the back, use different numbers than their counterparts in the regular set, and can also be identified from the regulars by the statistics line on the card back. The prototype cards use zeroes to fill in the stats on the back. Approximately 5,000 sets were made and distributed to dealers.

		NM/M	NM	E
Complete Set (5):		100.00	150.00	80.00
Common Player:		6.00	18.50	10.00
1	Joe Montana	25.00	18.50	10.00
2	Barry Sanders	25.00	18.50	10.00
3	Bo Jackson	10.00	7.50	4.00
4	Eric Metcalf	6.00	4.50	2.50
5	Troy Aikman	20.00	15.00	8.00

1961 Packers Lake to Lake

The 36-card, 2-1/2" x 3-1/4" set was issued by Lake to Lake out of Sheboygan, Wis. The card fronts feature a player shot with the card number and the player's number, height, weight and college attended. The card backs give offers for premium upgrades, such as a football or a ceramic figurine. Cards 1-8 and 17-24 are much more difficult to obtain.

		NM	E	VG
Complete Set (36):		625.00	312.00	187.00
Common Player (1-8/17-24):		25.00	12.50	7.50
Common Player (9-16/25-32):		2.50	1.25	.70
Common Player (33-36):		5.00	2.50	1.50
Common SP:		25.00	12.50	7.50
1	Jerry Kramer (SP)	45.00	22.00	13.50
2	Norm Masters (SP)	25.00	12.50	7.50
3	Willie Davis (SP)	50.00	25.00	15.00

		NM	E	VG
4	Bill Quinlan (SP)	25.00	12.50	7.50
5	Jim Temp (SP)	25.00	12.50	7.50
6	Emlen Tunnell (SP)	45.00	22.00	13.50
7	Gary Knafelc (SP)	25.00	12.50	7.50
8	Hank Jordan (SP)	45.00	22.00	13.50
9	Bill Forester	25.00	12.50	7.50
10	Paul Hornung	15.00	7.50	4.50
11	Jesse Whittenton	2.50	1.25	.70
12	Andy Cverko	2.50	1.25	.70
13	Jim Taylor	15.00	7.50	4.50
14	Hank Gremminger	2.50	1.25	.70
15	Tom Moore	3.00	1.50	.90
16	John Symank	2.50	1.25	.70
17	Max McGee (SP)	40.00	20.00	12.00
18	Bart Starr (SP)	85.00	42.00	25.00
19	Ray Nitschke (SP)	65.00	32.00	19.50
20	Dave Hanner (SP)	30.00	15.00	9.00
21	Tom Bettis (SP)	25.00	12.50	7.50
22	Fuzzy Thurston (SP)	30.00	15.00	9.00
23	Lew Carpenter (SP)	25.00	12.50	7.50
24	Boyd Dowler (SP)	30.00	15.00	9.00
25	Ken Iman	2.50	1.25	.70
26	Bob Skoronski	2.50	1.25	.70
27	Forrest Gregg	7.50	3.75	2.25
28	Jim Ringo	7.50	3.75	2.25
29	Ron Kramer	3.00	1.50	.90
30	Herb Adderley	12.00	6.00	3.50
31	Dan Currie	2.50	1.25	.70
32	John Roach	2.50	1.25	.70
33	Dale Hackbart	5.00	2.50	1.50
34	Larry Hickman	5.00	2.50	1.50
35	Nelson Toburen	5.00	2.50	1.50
36	Willie Wood	12.00	6.00	3.50

1966 Packers Mobil Posters

The eight-poster, 11" x 14" set features color action art with blank backs. The posters were available with envelopes which gave the art's title and number.

		NM	E	VG
	Complete Set (8):	80.00	40.00	24.00
	Common Player:	10.00	5.00	3.00
1	**The Pass** (Bart Star back to pass)	25.00	12.50	7.50
2	**The Block** (Jerry Kramer blocking for Elijah Pitts)	12.00	6.00	3.50
3	**The Punt** (Don Chandler punting)	10.00	5.00	3.00
4	**The Sweep** (Jim Taylor following blocking)	15.00	7.50	4.50
5	The Catch (Boyd Dowler)	12.00	6.00	3.50
6	**The Tackle**	10.00	5.00	3.00
7	**The Touchdown** (Tom Moore scoring)	12.00	6.00	3.50
8	**The Extra Point** (Don Chandler with Bart Starr holding)	12.00	6.00	3.50

1969 Packers Drenks Potato Chip Pins

The 20-pin, 1-1/8" in diameter set were issued by Drenks Potato Chips. The pins have a black and white headshot with green and white backgrounds. "Green Bay Packers" appears on the top edge while the bottom edge has the player's name and position.

		NM	E	VG
	Complete Set (20):	80.00	40.00	24.00
	Common Player:	2.00	1.00	.60
1	Herb Adderley	8.00	4.00	2.50
2	Lionel Aldridge	2.00	1.00	.60
3	Donny Anderson	3.00	1.50	.90
4	Ken Bowman	2.00	1.00	.60
5	Carroll Dale	2.00	1.00	.60
6	Willie Davis	8.00	4.00	2.50
7	Boyd Dowler	3.00	1.50	.90
8	Marv Fleming	3.00	1.50	.90
9	Gale Gillingham	2.00	1.00	.60
10	Jim Grabowski	3.00	1.50	.90
11	Forrest Gregg	8.00	4.00	2.50
12	Don Horn	2.00	1.00	.60
13	Bob Jeter	2.00	1.00	.60
14	Hank Jordan	8.00	4.00	2.50
15	Ray Nitschke	10.00	5.00	3.00
16	Elijah Pitts	3.00	1.50	.90
17	Dave Robinson	3.00	1.50	.90
18	Bart Starr	16.00	8.00	4.75
19	Travis Williams	3.00	1.50	.90
20	Willie Wood	8.00	4.00	2.50

1969 Packers Tasco Prints

The seven-piece, 11" x 16" print set features artwork of the player with his name and position, with the backs blank.

		NM	E	VG
	Complete Set (7):	50.00	30.00	18.00
	Common Player:	10.00	5.00	3.00
1	Donny Anderson	10.00	5.00	3.00
2	Boyd Dowler	10.00	5.00	3.00
3	Jim Grabowski	10.00	5.00	3.00
4	Hank Jordan	15.00	7.50	4.50
5	Ray Nitschke	25.00	12.50	7.50
6	Bart Starr	30.00	15.00	9.00
7	Willie Wood	15.00	7.50	4.50

1972 Packers Team Issue

The 45-card, 8" x 10" set was printed on glossy paper and featured posed player shots. The card front bottoms have the player's name and position while the backs are blank.

		NM	E	VG
	Complete Set (45):	50.00	30.00	18.00
	Common Player:	2.00	1.00	.60
1	Ken Bowman	2.00	1.00	.60
2	John Brockington	4.00	2.00	1.25
3	Bob Brown (DT)	2.00	1.00	.60
4	Willie Buchanon	3.00	1.50	.90
5	Fred Carr	3.00	1.50	.90
6	Jim Carter	2.00	1.00	.60
7	Carroll Dale	3.00	1.50	.90
8	Carroll Dale (Action pose)	3.00	1.50	.90
9	Dan Devine (CO/GM)	3.00	1.50	.90
10	Ken Ellis	2.00	1.00	.60
11	Len Garrett	2.00	1.00	.60
12	Gale Gillingham	2.00	1.00	.60
13	Leland Glass	2.00	1.00	.60
14	Charlie Hall	2.00	1.00	.60
15	Jim Hill	2.00	1.00	.60
16	Dick Himes	2.00	1.00	.60
17	Bob Hudson (Head shot)	2.00	1.00	.60
18	Bob Hudson (Kneeling pose)	2.00	1.00	.60
19	Kevin Hunt	2.00	1.00	.60
20	Scott Hunter	3.00	1.50	.90
21	Dave Kopay	2.00	1.00	.60
22	Bob Kroll	2.00	1.00	.60
23	Pete Lammons	2.00	1.00	.60
24	MacArthur Lane	4.00	2.00	1.25
25	Bill Lueck	2.00	1.00	.60
26	Al Matthews	2.00	1.00	.60
27	Mike McCoy	2.00	1.00	.60
28	Rich McGeorge	2.00	1.00	.60
29	Charlie Napper	2.00	1.00	.60
30	Ray Nitschke	10.00	5.00	3.00
31	Charles Pittman	3.00	1.50	.90
32	Malcolm Snider (action pose, Falcons Uniform)	2.00	1.00	.60
33	Malcolm Snider (Kneeling pose)	2.00	1.00	.60
34	Jon Staggers	3.00	1.50	.90
35	Bart Starr	12.00	6.00	3.50
36	Jerry Tagge	3.00	1.50	.90
37	Isaac Thomas (Action pose)	2.00	1.00	.60
38	Isaac Thomas (Kneeling pose)	2.00	1.00	.60
39	Vern Vanoy	2.00	1.00	.60
40	Ron Widby (Action pose, Cowboys uniform)	2.00	1.00	.60
41	Ron Widby (Kneeling pose)	2.00	1.00	.60
42	Clarence Williams	2.00	1.00	.60
43	Perry Williams	2.00	1.00	.60
44	Keith Wortman	2.00	1.00	.60
45	Coaching Staff (Bart Starr, Hank Kuhlmann, Dave Hanner, Burt Gustafson, John Polonchek, Don Doll, Red Cochran, Dan Devine, Rollie Dotsch)	12.00	6.00	3.50

1974 Packers Team Issue

The 14-card, 6" x 9" set featured the players in posed shots with facsimile autographs and blank backs.

		NM	E	VG
	Complete Set (14):	25.00	15.00	9.00
	Common Player:	3.00	1.50	.90
1	John Brockington	5.00	2.50	1.50
2	Willie Buchanon	4.00	2.00	1.25
3	Fred Carr	4.00	2.00	1.25
4	Jim Carter	4.00	2.00	1.25
5	Jack Concannon	4.00	2.00	1.25
6	Bill Curry	5.00	2.50	1.50

		NM	E	VG
7	John Hadl	5.00	2.50	1.50
8	Bill Lueck	3.00	1.50	.90
9	Chester Marcol	4.00	2.00	1.25
10	Rich McGeorge	4.00	2.00	1.25
11	Alden Roche	3.00	1.50	.90
12	Barry Smith	3.00	1.50	.90
13	Barty Smith	3.00	1.50	.90
14	Clarence Williams	3.00	1.50	.90

1983 Packers Police

The 19-card, 2-5/8" x 4-1/8" set featured action shots on white card stock with three different card backs: First Wisconsin Bank, Waukesha Police and without First Wisconsin Bank, with the latter one being the most rare set. "Packer Tips" are given on the back.

		NM/M	NM	E
	Complete Set (19):	20.00	15.00	8.00
	Common Player:	1.00	.70	.40
10	Jan Stenerud	2.00	1.50	.80
12	Lynn Dickey	1.50	1.25	.60
24	Johnnie Gray	1.00	.70	.40
29	Mike McCoy	1.25	.90	.50
31	Gerry Ellis	1.00	.70	.40
40	Eddie Lee Ivery	1.50	1.25	.60
52	George Cumby	1.00	.70	.40
53	Mike Douglass	1.25	.90	.50
54	Larry McCarren	1.00	.70	.40
59	John Anderson	1.25	.90	.50
63	Terry Jones	1.00	.70	.40
64	Sid Kitson	1.00	.70	.40
68	Greg Koch	1.00	.70	.40
80	James Lofton	4.00	3.00	1.50
82	Paul Coffman	1.50	1.25	.60
83	John Jefferson	2.00	1.50	.80
85	Phillip Epps	1.50	1.25	.60
90	Ezra Johnson	1.00	.70	.40
	Bart Starr (CO)	4.00	3.00	1.50

1984 Packers Police

83 • John Jefferson

The 25-card, 2-5/8" x 4" set was sponsored by First Wisconsin Bank, local law enforcement and the Packers. The card backs contain "Packer Tips."

		NM/M	NM	E
	Complete Set (25):	10.00	7.50	4.00
	Common Player:	.40	.30	.15
1	John Jefferson	.60	.45	.25
2	Forrest Gregg (CO)	2.00	1.50	.80
3	John Anderson	.50	.40	.20
4	Eddie Garcia	.40	.30	.15
5	Tim Lewis	.40	.30	.15
6	Jessie Clark	.40	.30	.15
7	Karl Swanke	.40	.30	.15
8	Lynn Dickey	1.00	.70	.40
9	Eddie Lee Ivery	.60	.45	.25
10	Dick Modzelewski (CO) (Defensive Coord.)	.40	.30	.15
11	Mark Murphy	.40	.30	.15
12	Dave Drechsler	.40	.30	.15
13	Mike Douglass	.40	.30	.15
14	James Lofton	2.50	2.00	1.00
15	Bucky Scribner	.40	.30	.15
16	Randy Scott	.40	.30	.15
17	Mark Lee	.50	.40	.20
18	Gerry Ellis	.40	.30	.15
19	Terry Jones	.40	.30	.15
20	Bob Schnelker (CO) (Offensive Coord.)	.40	.30	.15
21	George Cumby	.40	.30	.15
22	George Cumby	.40	.30	.15
23	Larry McCarren	.40	.30	.15
24	Sid Kitson	.40	.30	.15
25	Paul Coffman	.50	.40	.20

1985 Packers Police

80 • James Lofton

63" Wide Receiver
197 lbs Stanford

The 25-card, 2-3/4" x 4" set, as with the previous year's, was issued by First Wisconsin Bank, local law enforcement and Green Bay and contains "Packer Tips" on the card backs.

		NM/M	NM	E
Complete Set (25):		8.00	6.00	3.25
Common Player:		.40	.30	.15
1	Forrest Gregg (CO)	1.75	1.25	.70
2	Paul Coffman	.60	.45	.25
3	Terry Jones	.40	.30	.15
4	Ron Hallstrom	.40	.30	.15
5	Eddie Lee Ivery	.60	.45	.25
6	John Anderson	.40	.30	.15
7	Tim Lewis	.40	.30	.15
8	Bob Schnelker (CO)			
	(Offensive Coord.)	.40	.30	.15
9	Al Del Greco	.40	.30	.15
10	Mark Murphy	.40	.30	.15
11	Tim Huffman	.40	.30	.15
12	Del Rodgers	.40	.30	.15
13	Mark Lee	.40	.30	.15
14	Tom Flynn	.40	.30	.15
15	Dick Modzelewski (CO)			
	(Defensive Corrd.)	.40	.30	.15
16	Randy Scott	.40	.30	.15
17	Bucky Scribner	.40	.30	.15
18	George Cumby	.40	.30	.15
19	James Lofton	2.50	2.00	1.00
20	Mike Douglass	.50	.40	.20
21	Alphonso Carreker	.40	.30	.15
22	Greg Koch	.40	.30	.15
23	Gerry Ellis	.40	.30	.15
24	Ezra Johnson	.40	.30	.15
25	Lynn Dickey	.75	.60	.30

1986 Packers Police

The 25-card, 2-3/4" x 4" set was sponsored by local law enforcement, First Wisconsin Bank and the Packers. The card backs feature player bios and stats, as well as a safety tip.

		NM/M	NM	E
Complete Set (25):		8.00	6.00	3.25
Common Player:		.35	.25	.14
10	Al Del Greco	.35	.25	.14
12	Lynn Dickey	.60	.45	.25
16	Randy Wright	.60	.45	.25
26	Tim Lewis	.35	.25	.14
31	Gerry Ellis	.35	.25	.14
33	Jessie Clark	.35	.25	.14
37	Mark Murphy	.50	.40	.20
40	Eddie Lee Ivery	.50	.40	.20
41	Tom Flynn	.35	.25	.14
42	Gary Ellerson	.35	.25	.14
55	Randy Scott	.35	.25	.14
58	Mark Cannon	.35	.25	.14
59	John Anderson	.50	.40	.20
65	Ron Hallstrom	.35	.25	.14
67	Karl Swanke	.35	.25	.14
76	Alphonso Carreker	.35	.25	.14
80	James Lofton	1.50	1.25	.60
82	Paul Coffman	.50	.40	.20
85	Phillip Epps	.50	.40	.20
90	Ezra Johnson	.35	.25	.14
91	Brian Noble	.50	.40	.20
93	Robert Brown	.35	.25	.14
94	Charles Martin	.35	.25	.14
99	John Dorsey	.35	.25	.14
	Forrest Gregg (CO)	1.25	.90	.50

1987 Packers Police

Measuring 2-3/4" x 4", the 22-card set showcased "1987 Packers" at the top, with a photo in the center and the Packers' helmet, player's jersey number and name under the photo. The card backs, printed in green on white paper stock, has the player's name and jersey number at the top, his bio and highlights follow. A safety tip is also included on the back. The cards were sponsored by local law enforcement agencies, the Packers, Employers Health Insurance Co. and Arson Task Force. Approximately 35,000 sets were handed out. Card Nos. 5, 6 and 20 were never distributed as they featured players who were waived or traded before the set was released.

		NM/M	NM	E
Complete Set (22):		8.00	6.00	3.25
Common Player:		.35	.25	.14
1	Forrest Gregg (CO)	1.00	.70	.40
2	George Greene	.35	.25	.14
3	Ron Hallstrom	.35	.25	.14
4	Ezra Johnson	.35	.25	.14
7	Robert Brown	.35	.25	.14
8	Tom Neville	.35	.25	.14
9	Rich Moran	.35	.25	.14
10	Ken Ruettgers	.50	.40	.20
11	Alan Veingrad	.35	.25	.14
12	Mark Lee	.50	.40	.20
13	John Dorsey	.35	.25	.14
14	Paul Ott Carruth	.35	.25	.14
15	Randy Wright	.50	.40	.20
16	Phillip Epps	.50	.40	.20
17	Al Del Greco	.35	.25	.14
18	Tim Harris	1.00	.70	.40
19	Kenneth Davis	1.00	.70	.40
21	John Anderson	.50	.40	.20
22	Mark Murphy	.50	.40	.20
23	Ken Stills	.35	.25	.14
24	Brian Noble	.50	.40	.20
25	Mark Cannon	.35	.25	.14

1988 Packers Police

Measuring 2-3/4" x 4", the 25-card set was anchored by a large photo on the front, with the player's name, number, height, weight and position listed at the bottom. The Packers' helmet appears in the lower right. The card backs included a Packers' helmet at the top, with a "Packers Tips" boxed in section underneath. The set was sponsored by Copps, Brown County Arson Task Force, local law enforcement agencies and the Packers.

		NM/M	NM	E
Complete Set (25):		10.00	7.50	4.00
Common Player:		.40	.30	.15
1	John Anderson	.50	.40	.20
2	Jerry Boyarsky	.40	.30	.15
3	Don Bracken	.40	.30	.15
4	Dave Brown	.40	.30	.15
5	Mark Cannon	.40	.30	.15
6	Alphonso Carreker	.40	.30	.15
7	Paul Ott Carruth	.40	.30	.15
8	Kenneth Davis	.75	.60	.30
9	John Dorsey	.40	.30	.15
10	Brent Fullwood	.40	.30	.15
11	Tiger Greene	.40	.30	.15
12	Ron Hallstrom	.40	.30	.15
13	Tim Harris	.75	.60	.30
14	Johnny Holland	.50	.40	.20
15	Lindy Infante (CO)	.75	.60	.30
16	Mark Lee	.50	.40	.20
17	Don Majkowski	.75	.60	.30
18	Rich Moran	.40	.30	.15
19	Mark Murphy	.40	.30	.15
20	Ken Ruettgers	.50	.40	.20
21	Walter Stanley	.60	.45	.25
22	Keith Uecker	.40	.30	.15
23	Ed West	.50	.40	.20
24	Randy Wright	.40	.30	.15
25	Max Zendejas	.40	.30	.15

1989 Packers Police

Measuring 2-3/4" x 4", the 15-card set showcases a photo on the card front, with the player's name, jersey number, position and year in the league listed below. The Packers' helmet is at the bottom center. The backs have a Packers Tip boxed in the center, with the Packers' logo at the top. The card number is listed at the bottom center of the text box. The front photo is bordered in yellow, with the card printed on white stock.

		NM/M	NM	E
Complete Set (15):		5.00	3.75	2.00
Common Player:		.35	.25	.14
1	Lindy Infante (CO)	.50	.40	.20
2	Don Majkowski	.60	.45	.25
3	Brent Fullwood	.35	.25	.14
4	Mark Lee	.50	.40	.20
5	Dave Brown	.35	.25	.14
6	Mark Murphy	.50	.40	.20
7	Johnny Holland	.50	.40	.20
8	John Anderson	.50	.40	.20
9	Ken Ruettgers	.50	.40	.20
10	Sterling Sharpe	2.00	1.50	.80
11	Ed West	.35	.25	.14
12	Walter Stanley	.50	.40	.20
13	Brian Noble	.50	.40	.20
14	Shawn Patterson	.35	.25	.14
15	Tim Harris	.50	.40	.20

1990 Packers 25th Anniversary

Pacific Trading Cards produced this 45-card standard sized set, while Champion Cards released it. The card fronts feature a 25th Anniversary pennant in the upper left, either a color or sepia-toned photo and the player's name and position. The Packers' helmet is pictured in the lower right corner. The backs feature the player's name, position and number at the top. His bio and career highlights are also listed. The card's number is printed in the lower right.

		NM/M	NM	E
Complete Set (45):		10.00	7.50	4.00
Common Player:		.25	.20	.10
1	**Introduction Card**	.50	.40	.20
2	Bart Starr	2.00	1.50	.80
3	Herb Adderley	.75	.60	.30
4	Bob Skoronski	.25	.20	.10
5	Tom Brown	.35	.25	.14
6	Lee Roy Caffey	.35	.25	.14
7	Ray Nitschke	1.00	.70	.40
8	Carroll Dale	.35	.25	.14
9	Jim Taylor	1.25	.90	.50
10	Ken Bowman	.25	.20	.10
11	Gale Gillingham	.35	.25	.14
12	Jim Grabowski	.50	.40	.20
13	Dave Robinson	.50	.40	.20
14	Donny Anderson	.50	.40	.20
15	Willie Wood	.75	.60	.30
16	Zeke Bratkowski	.50	.40	.20
17	Doug Hart	.25	.20	.10
18	Jerry Kramer	.75	.60	.30
19	Marv Fleming	.35	.25	.14
20	Lionel Aldridge	.35	.25	.14
21	Red Mack (UER) (Text reads returned to football before the following season should be retired)	.25	.20	.10
22	Ron Kostelnik	.25	.20	.10
23	Boyd Dowler	.50	.40	.20
24	Vince Lombardi (CO)	1.25	.90	.50
25	Forrest Gregg	.75	.60	.30
26	Max McGee (Superstar)	.35	.25	.14
27	Fuzzy Thurston	.50	.40	.20
28	Bob Brown (DT)	.35	.25	.14
29	Willie Davis	.75	.60	.30
30	Elijah Pitts	.50	.40	.20
31	Hank Jordan	.75	.60	.30
32	Bart Starr	2.00	1.50	.80
33	Super Bowl I (Jim Taylor)	.75	.60	.30
34	**1996 Packers**	.50	.40	.20
35	Max McGee	.50	.40	.20
36	Jim Weatherwax	.25	.20	.10
37	Bob Long	.25	.20	.10
38	Don Chandler	.35	.25	.14
39	Bill Anderson	.25	.20	.10
40	Tommy Crutcher	.35	.25	.14
41	Dave Hathcock	.25	.20	.10
42	Steve Wright	.25	.20	.10
43	Phil Vandersea	.25	.20	.10
44	Bill Curry	.50	.40	.20
45	Bob Jeter	.35	.25	.14

1990 Packers Police

Measuring 2-3/4" x 4", the 20-card set is anchored by a large photo on the front. "Packers '90" is printed at the top, with the player's name, number, position and year in the league listed under the photo. The Packers' helmet is located in the lower left.

		NM/M	NM	E
Complete Set (20):		5.00	3.75	2.00
Common Player:		.25	.20	.10
1	Lindy Infante (CO)	.35	.25	.14
2	Keith Woodside	.25	.20	.10
3	Chris Jacke	.35	.25	.14
4	Chuck Cecil	.35	.25	.14
5	Tony Mandarich	.25	.20	.10
6	Brent Fullwood	.25	.20	.10
7	Robert Brown	.25	.20	.10
8	Scott Stephen	.25	.20	.10
9	Anthony Dilweg	.25	.20	.10
10	Mark Murphy	.25	.20	.10
11	Johnny Holland	.35	.25	.14
12	Sterling Sharpe	1.00	.70	.40

13	Tim Harris	.35	.25	.14
14	Ed West	.25	.20	.10
15	Jeff Query	.25	.20	.10
16	Mark Lee	.25	.20	.10
17	Rich Moran	.25	.20	.10
18	Perry Kemp	.35	.25	.14
19	Brian Noble	.35	.25	.14
20	Don Majkowski	.50	.40	.20

1991 Packers Police

The green-bordered, 20-card set features a yellow banner in the upper left corner of the card front which includes "1991 Packers." The photo is surrounded by a green and yellow border. The player's name and position are printed in the upper right, while his year in the league and his college are printed inside a yellow band at the bottom of the card. The Packers' logo is printed in the lower right of the photo. Numbered "of 20," the card backs feature "1991 Packer Tips." The sponsors' logos appear at the bottom of the standard-sized card backs. Each card back is vertical, except for the Lambeau Field card which is horizontal.

	NM/M	NM	E
Complete Set (20):	5.00	3.75	2.00
Common Player:	.30	.25	.12

1	**Lambeau Field**	.30	.25	.12
2	Sterling Sharpe	1.00	.70	.40
3	James Campen	.30	.25	.12
4	Chuck Cecil	.40	.30	.15
5	Lindy Infante (CO)	.40	.30	.15
6	Keith Woodside	.30	.25	.12
7	Perry Kemp	.30	.25	.12
8	Johnny Holland	.40	.30	.15
9	Don Majkowski	.40	.30	.15
10	Tony Bennett	.50	.40	.20
11	Leroy Butler	.40	.30	.15
12	Tony Mandarich	.30	.25	.12
13	Darrell Thompson	.40	.30	.15
14	Matt Brock	.30	.25	.12
15	Charles Wilson	.50	.40	.20
16	Brian Noble	.40	.30	.15
17	Ed West	.30	.25	.12
18	Chris Jacke	.30	.25	.12
19	Blair Kiel	.40	.30	.15
20	Mark Murphy	.30	.25	.12

1991 Packers Super Bowl II

The 25th anniversary of the Packers' Super Bowl II victory is honored on this standard-sized 50-card set. The card fronts include a photo which is surrounded by a dark green border. The player's name, Packers' logo and Super Bowl II are located inside a yellow band at the bottom of the card. The card backs feature the player's name, bio and highlights, along with his stats. A photo credit and "Copyright Champion Cards" appear at the bottom left. The card number is printed at the bottom center inside a football.

	NM/M	NM	E
Complete Set (50):	10.00	7.50	4.00
Common Player:	.25	.20	.10

1	**Intro Card Super Bowl Trophy**	.50	.40	.20
2	Steve Wright	.25	.20	.10
3	Jim Flanigan	.25	.20	.10
4	Tom Brown	.35	.25	.14
5	Tommy Joe Crutcher	.35	.25	.14
6	Doug Hart	.35	.25	.14
7	Bob Hyland	.25	.20	.10
8	John Rowser	.25	.20	.10
9	Bob Skoronski	.25	.20	.10
10	Jim Weatherwax	.25	.20	.10
11	Ben Wilson	.25	.20	.10
12	Don Horn	.35	.25	.14
13	Allen Brown	.25	.20	.10
14	Dick Capp	.25	.20	.10
15	Super Bowl II Action (Donny Anderson)	.50	.40	.20
16	Ice Bowl: The Play (Bart Starr)	1.00	.70	.40
17	Chuck Mercein	.35	.25	.14
18	Herb Adderley	.75	.60	.30
19	Ken Bowman	.25	.20	.10
20	Lee Roy Caffey	.35	.25	.14
21	Carroll Dale	.35	.25	.14
22	Marv Fleming	.35	.25	.14
23	Jim Grabowski	.50	.40	.20
24	Bob Jeter	.35	.25	.14
25	Jerry Kramer	.75	.60	.30
26	Max McGee	.50	.40	.20
27	Elijah Pitts	.50	.40	.20
28	Bart Starr	1.50	1.25	.60
29	Fuzzy Thurston	.50	.40	.20
30	Willie Wood	.75	.60	.30
31	Lionel Aldridge	.35	.25	.14
32	Donny Anderson	.50	.40	.20
33	Zeke Bratkowski	.50	.40	.20
34	Bob Brown (DT)	.35	.25	.14
35	Don Chandler	.35	.25	.14
36	Willie Davis	.75	.60	.30
37	Boyd Dowler	.50	.40	.20
38	Gale Gillingham	.35	.25	.14
39	Hank Jordan	.75	.60	.30
40	Ron Kostelnik	.25	.20	.10
41	Vince Lombardi (CO)	1.25	.90	.50
42	Bob Long	.25	.20	.10
43	Ray Nitschke	1.00	.70	.40
44	Dave Robinson	.50	.40	.20
45	Bart Starr (MVP)	1.25	.90	.50
46	Travis Williams	.35	.25	.14
47	**1967 Packers Team**	.50	.40	.20
48	**Ice Bowl Game Summary**	.25	.20	.10
49	**Ice Bowl**	.25	.20	.10
50	**NNO Packer Pro Shop**	.25	.20	.10

1988 Panini Stickers

These stickers, which each measure 2-1/8" x 2-3/4", were made to be stored in a special collector's album which was produced. John Elway is featured on the cover of the album, which has the stickers arranged on pages according to the way they are numbered. The sticker number appears on both sides of the sticker. The front of the sticker has a close-up shot of the player, between two team color-coded bars. His team's name is above the photo; his name is below the photo. The stickers were sold in packs which also included one of three types of foil stickers - team name stickers, team helmet stickers, and team uniform stickers. Each team name sticker was produced with a player sticker, listed in parenthesis. Backs for the team name stickers had a referee signal, while helmet foils had a stadium shot and uniform foils had a mascot cartoon on the back.

	NM/M	NM	E
Complete Set (447):	35.00	26.00	14.00
Common Player:	.05	.04	.02

1	**Super Bowl XXII Program Cover**	.15	.11	.06
2	**Bills Helmet**	.05	.04	.02
3	**Bills Action**	.05	.04	.02
4	Cornelius Bennett	.50	.40	.20
5	Chris Burkett	.05	.04	.02
6	Derrick Burroughs	.05	.04	.02
7	Shane Conlan	.25	.20	.10
8	Ronnie Harmon	.25	.20	.10
9	Jim Kelly	.80	.60	.30
10	**Buffalo Bills**	.05	.04	.02
11	Mark Kelso	.05	.04	.02
12	Nate Odomes	.05	.04	.02
13	Andre Reed	.25	.20	.10
14	Fred Smerlas	.05	.04	.02
15	Bruce Smith	.25	.20	.10
16	**Uniform**	.05	.04	.02
17	**Bengals Helmet**	.05	.04	.02
18	**Bengals Action**	.05	.04	.02
19	Jim Breech	.05	.04	.02
20	James Brooks	.10	.08	.04
21	Eddie Brown	.10	.08	.04
22	Cris Collinsworth	.10	.08	.04
23	Boomer Esiason	.20	.15	.08
24	Rodney Holman	.10	.08	.04
25	**Bengals**	.05	.04	.02
26	Larry Kinnebrew	.05	.04	.02
27	Tim Krumrie	.05	.04	.02
28	Anthony Munoz	.15	.11	.06
29	Reggie Williams	.10	.08	.04
30	Carl Zander	.05	.04	.02
31	**Uniform**	.05	.04	.02
32	**Browns Helmet**	.05	.04	.02
33	**Browns Action**	.15	.11	.06
34	Earnest Byner	.10	.08	.04
35	Hanford Dixon	.05	.04	.02
36	Bob Golic	.10	.08	.04
37	Mike Johnson	.05	.04	.02
38	Bernie Kosar	.30	.25	.12
39	Kevin Mack	.10	.08	.04
40	**Browns**	.05	.04	.02
41	Clay Matthews	.15	.11	.06
42	Gerald McNeil	.05	.04	.02
43	Frank Minnifield	.05	.04	.02
44	Ozzie Newsome	.15	.11	.06
45	Cody Risien	.05	.04	.02
46	**Uniform**	.05	.04	.02
47	**Broncos Helmet**	.05	.04	.02
48	**Broncos Action**	.05	.04	.02
49	Keith Bishop	.05	.04	.02
50	Tony Dorsett	.35	.25	.14
51	John Elway	1.25	.90	.50
52	Simon Fletcher	.25	.20	.10
53	Mark Jackson	.10	.08	.04
54	Vance Johnson	.10	.08	.04
55	**Broncos**	.05	.04	.02
56	Rulon Jones	.05	.04	.02
57	Rick Karlis	.05	.04	.02
58	Karl Mecklenburg	.10	.08	.04
59	Ricky Nattiel	.10	.08	.04
60	Sammy Winder	.05	.04	.02
61	**Uniform**	.05	.04	.02
62	**Oilers Helmet**	.05	.04	.02
63	**Oilers Action**	.25	.20	.10
64	Keith Bostic	.05	.04	.02
65	Steve Brown	.05	.04	.02
66	Ray Childress	.15	.11	.06
67	Jeff Donaldson	.05	.04	.02
68	John Grimsley	.05	.04	.02
69	Robert Lyles	.05	.04	.02
70	**Oilers**	.05	.04	.02
71	Drew Hill	.10	.08	.04
72	Warren Moon	.85	.60	.35
73	Mike Munchak	.15	.11	.06
74	Mike Rozier	.10	.08	.04
75	Johnny Meads	.05	.04	.02
76	**Uniform**	.05	.04	.02
77	**Colts Helmet**	.05	.04	.02
78	**Colts Action**	.15	.11	.06
79	Albert Bentley	.10	.08	.04
80	Dean Biasucci	.05	.04	.02
81	Duane Bickett	.15	.11	.06
82	Bill Brooks	.15	.11	.06
83	Johnny Cooks	.05	.04	.02
84	Eric Dickerson	.40	.30	.15
85	**Colts**	.05	.04	.02
86	Ray Donaldson	.05	.04	.02
87	Chris Hinton	.10	.08	.04
88	Cliff Odom	.05	.04	.02
89	Barry Krauss	.10	.08	.04
90	Jack Trudeau	.15	.11	.06
91	**Uniform**	.05	.04	.02
92	**Chiefs Helmet**	.05	.04	.02
93	**Chiefs Action**	.05	.04	.02
94	Carlos Carson	.05	.04	.02
95	Deron Cherry	.10	.08	.04
96	Dino Hackett	.05	.04	.02
97	Bill Kenney	.05	.04	.02
98	Albert Lewis	.10	.08	.04
99	Nick Lowery	.10	.08	.04
100	**Chiefs**	.05	.04	.02
101	Bill Maas	.05	.04	.02
102	Christian Okoye	.15	.11	.06
103	Stephone Paige	.10	.08	.04
104	Paul Palmer	.05	.04	.02
105	Kevin Ross	.05	.04	.02
106	**Uniform**	.05	.04	.02
107	**Raiders Helmet**	.05	.04	.02
108	**Raiders Action**	.25	.20	.10
109	Marcus Allen	.35	.25	.14
110	Todd Christensen	.15	.11	.06
111	Mike Haynes	.15	.11	.06
112	Bo Jackson	.60	.45	.25
113	James Lofton	.20	.15	.08
114	Howie Long	.15	.11	.06
115	**Raiders**	.05	.04	.02
116	Rod Martin	.05	.04	.02
117	Vann McElroy	.05	.04	.02
118	Bill Pickel	.05	.04	.02
119	Don Mosebar	.05	.04	.02
120	Stacey Toran	.05	.04	.02
121	**Uniform**	.05	.04	.02
122	**Dolphins Helmet**	.05	.04	.02
123	**Dolphins Action**	.05	.04	.02
124	John Bosa	.05	.04	.02
125	Mark Clayton	.15	.11	.06
126	Mark Duper	.10	.08	.04
127	Lorenzo Hampton	.05	.04	.02
128	William Judson	.05	.04	.02
129	Dan Marino	2.50	2.00	1.00
130	**Dolphins**	.05	.04	.02
131	John Offerdahl	.10	.08	.04
132	Reggie Roby	.05	.04	.02
133	Jackie Shipp	.05	.04	.02
134	Dwight Stephenson	.10	.08	.04
135	Troy Stradford	.10	.08	.04
136	**Uniform**	.05	.04	.02
137	**Patriots Helmet**	.05	.04	.02
138	**Patriots Action**	.05	.04	.02
139	Bruce Armstrong	.05	.04	.02
140	Raymond Clayborn	.05	.04	.02
141	Reggie Dupard	.05	.04	.02
142	Steve Grogan	.10	.08	.04
143	Craig James	.25	.20	.10
144	Ronnie Lippett	.05	.04	.02
145	**Patriots**	.05	.04	.02
146	Fred Marion	.05	.04	.02
147	Stanley Morgan	.15	.11	.06
148	Mosi Tatupu	.05	.04	.02
149	Andre Tippett	.10	.08	.04
150	Garin Veris	.05	.04	.02
151	**Uniform**	.05	.04	.02
152	**Jets Helmet**	.05	.04	.02
153	**Jets Action**	.05	.04	.02
154	Bob Crable	.05	.04	.02
155	Mark Gastineau	.10	.08	.04
156	Pat Leahy	.05	.04	.02

157	Johnny Hector	.10	.08	.04
158	Marty Lyons	.10	.08	.04
159	Freeman McNeil	.15	.11	.06
160	**Jets**	.05	.04	.02
161	Ken O'Brien	.10	.08	.04
162	Mickey Shuler	.05	.04	.02
163	Al Toon	.10	.08	.04
164	Roger Vick	.05	.04	.02
165	Wesley Walker	.10	.08	.04
166	**Uniform**	.05	.04	.02
167	**Steelers Helmet**	.05	.04	.02
168	**Steelers Action**	.05	.04	.02
169	Walter Abercrombie	.05	.04	.02
170	Gary Anderson	.05	.04	.02
171	Todd Blackledge	.05	.04	.02
172	Thomas Everett	.15	.11	.06
173	Delton Hall	.05	.04	.02
174	Bryan Hinkle	.05	.04	.02
175	**Steelers**	.05	.04	.02
176	Earnest Jackson	.10	.08	.04
177	Louis Lipps	.10	.08	.04
178	David Little	.05	.04	.02
179	Mike Merriweather	.10	.08	.04
180	Mike Webster	.15	.11	.06
181	**Uniform**	.05	.04	.02
182	**Chargers Helmet**	.05	.04	.02
183	**Chargers Action**	.05	.04	.02
184	Gary Anderson	.15	.11	.06
185	Chip Banks	.10	.08	.04
186	Martin Bayless	.05	.04	.02
187	Chuck Ehin	.05	.04	.02
188	Venice Glenn	.05	.04	.02
189	Lionel James	.05	.04	.02
190	**Chargers**	.05	.04	.02
191	Mark Malone	.05	.04	.02
192	Ralf Mojsiejenko	.05	.04	.02
193	Billy Ray Smith	.10	.08	.04
194	Lee Williams	.15	.11	.06
195	Kellen Winslow	.15	.11	.06
196	**Uniform**	.05	.04	.02
197	**Seahawks Helmet**	.05	.04	.02
198	**Seahawks Action**	.10	.08	.04
199	Eugene Robinson	.05	.04	.02
200	Jeff Bryant	.05	.04	.02
201	Ray Butler	.05	.04	.02
202	Jacob Green	.10	.08	.04
203	Norm Johnson	.10	.08	.04
204	Dave Krieg	.10	.08	.04
205	**Seahawks**	.05	.04	.02
206	Steve Largent	.75	.60	.30
207	Joe Nash	.05	.04	.02
208	Curt Warner	.10	.08	.04
209	Bobby Joe Edmonds	.10	.08	.04
210	Daryl Turner	.05	.04	.02
211	**Uniform**	.05	.04	.02
212	**AFC Logo**	.05	.04	.02
213	Bernie Kosar	.35	.25	.14
214	Curt Warner	.10	.08	.04
215	Jerry Rice, Steve Largent	1.25	.90	.50
216	Mark Bavaro, Anthony Munoz	.15	.11	.06
217	Gary Zimmerman, Bill Fralic	.10	.08	.04
218	Dwight Stephenson, Mike Munchak	.10	.08	.04
219	Joe Montana	3.00	2.25	1.25
220	Charles White, Eric Dickerson	.40	.30	.15
221	Morten Andersen, Vai Sikahema	.10	.08	.04
222	Bruce Smith, Reggie White	.30	.25	.12
223	Michael Carter, Steve McMichael	.10	.08	.04
224	Jim Arnold	.05	.04	.02
225	Carl Banks, Andre Tippett	.10	.08	.04
226	Barry Wilburn, Mike Singletary	.10	.08	.04
227	Hanford Dixon, Frank Minnifield	.05	.04	.02
228	Ronnie Lott, Joey Browner	.15	.11	.06
229	**NFC Logo**	.05	.04	.02
230	Gary Clark	.15	.11	.06
231	Richard Dent	.15	.11	.06
232	**Falcons Helmet**	.05	.04	.02
233	**Falcons Action**	.05	.04	.02
234	Rick Bryan	.10	.08	.04
235	Bobby Butler	.05	.04	.02
236	Tony Casillas	.15	.11	.06
237	Floyd Dixon	.05	.04	.02
238	Rick Donnelly	.05	.04	.02
239	Bill Fralic	.10	.08	.04
240	**Falcons**	.05	.04	.02
241	Mike Gann	.05	.04	.02
242	Chris Miller	.40	.30	.15
243	Robert Moore	.05	.04	.02
244	John Rade	.05	.04	.02
245	Gerald Riggs	.10	.08	.04
246	**Uniform**	.05	.04	.02
247	**Bears Helmet**	.05	.04	.02
248	**Bears Action**	.15	.11	.06
249	Neal Anderson	.30	.25	.12
250	Jim Covert	.10	.08	.04
251	Richard Dent	.15	.11	.06
252	Dave Duerson	.05	.04	.02
253	Dennis Gentry	.05	.04	.02
254	Jay Hilgenberg	.10	.08	.04
255	**Bears**	.05	.04	.02
256	Jim McMahon	.20	.15	.08
257	Steve McMichael	.10	.08	.04
258	Matt Suhey	.05	.04	.02
259	Mike Singletary	.20	.15	.08
260	Otis Wilson	.10	.08	.04
261	**Uniform**	.05	.04	.02
262	**Cowboys Helmet**	.05	.04	.02
263	**Cowboys Action**	.15	.11	.06
264	Bill Bates	.10	.08	.04
265	Doug Crosbie	.05	.04	.02
266	Ron Francis	.05	.04	.02
267	Jim Jeffcoat	.15	.11	.06
268	Ed "Too Tall" Jones	.20	.15	.08
269	Eugene Lockhart	.05	.04	.02
270	**Cowboys**	.05	.04	.02
271	Danny Noonan	.05	.04	.02
272	Steve Pelleur	.10	.08	.04
273	Herschel Walker	.10	.08	.04
274	Everson Walls	.20	.15	.08
275	Randy White	.05	.04	.02
276	**Uniform**	.05	.04	.02
277	**Lions Helmet**	.05	.04	.02
278	**Lions Action**	.05	.04	.02
279	Jim Arnold	.10	.08	.04
280	Jerry Ball	.05	.04	.02
281	Michael Cofer	.05	.04	.02
282	Keith Ferguson	.05	.04	.02
283	Dennis Gibson	.05	.04	.02
284	James Griffin	.05	.04	.02
285	**Lions**	.05	.04	.02
286	James Jones	.10	.08	.04
287	Chuck Long	.10	.08	.04
288	Pete Mandley	.05	.04	.02
289	Eddie Murray	.05	.04	.02
290	Garry James	.05	.04	.02
291	**Uniform**	.05	.04	.02
292	**Packers Helmet**	.05	.04	.02
293	**Packers Action**	.05	.04	.02
294	John Anderson	.05	.04	.02
295	Dave Brown	.10	.08	.04
296	Alphonso Carreker	.05	.04	.02
297	Kenneth Davis	.20	.15	.08
298	Phillip Epps	.05	.04	.02
299	Brent Fullwood	.05	.04	.02
300	**Packers**	.05	.04	.02
301	Tim Harris	.15	.11	.06
302	Johnny Holland	.10	.08	.04
303	Mark Murphy	.05	.04	.02
304	Brian Noble	.05	.04	.02
305	Walter Stanley	.10	.08	.04
306	**Uniform**	.05	.04	.02
307	**Rams Helmet**	.05	.04	.02
308	**Rams Action**	.05	.04	.02
309	Jim Collins	.05	.04	.02
310	Henry Ellard	.15	.11	.06
311	Jim Everett	.30	.25	.12
312	Jerry Gray	.05	.04	.02
313	LeRoy Irvin	.05	.04	.02
314	Mike Lansford	.05	.04	.02
315	**Los Angeles Rams**	.05	.04	.02
316	Mel Owens	.05	.04	.02
317	Jackie Slater	.10	.08	.04
318	Doug Smith	.05	.04	.02
319	Charles White	.10	.08	.04
320	Mike Wilcher	.05	.04	.02
321	**Uniform**	.05	.04	.02
322	**Vikings Helmet**	.05	.04	.02
323	**Vikings Action**	.05	.04	.02
324	Joey Browner	.10	.08	.04
325	Anthony Carter	.15	.11	.06
326	Chris Doleman	.15	.11	.06
327	D.J. Dozier	.10	.08	.04
328	Steve Jordan	.10	.08	.04
329	Tommy Kramer	.10	.08	.04
330	**Vikings**	.05	.04	.02
331	Darrin Nelson	.10	.08	.04
332	Jesse Solomon	.10	.08	.04
333	Scott Studwell	.10	.08	.04
334	Wade Wilson	.35	.25	.14
335	Gary Zimmerman	.05	.04	.02
336	**Uniform**	.05	.04	.02
337	**Saints Helmet**	.05	.04	.02
338	**Saints Action**	.15	.11	.06
339	Morten Andersen	.10	.08	.04
340	Bruce Clark	.05	.04	.02
341	Brad Edelman	.05	.04	.02
342	Bobby Hebert	.15	.11	.06
343	Dalton Hilliard	.10	.08	.04
344	Rickey Jackson	.15	.11	.06
345	**Saints**	.05	.04	.02
346	Vaughan Johnson	.10	.08	.04
347	Rueben Mayes	.10	.08	.04
348	Sam Mills	.10	.08	.04
349	Lionel Manuel	.35	.25	.14
350	Dave Waymer	.05	.04	.02
351	**Uniform**	.05	.04	.02
352	**Giants Helmet**	.05	.04	.02
353	**Giants Action**	.05	.04	.02
354	Carl Banks	.15	.11	.06
355	Mark Bavaro	.15	.11	.06
356	Jim Burt	.05	.04	.02
357	Harry Carson	.10	.08	.04
358	Terry Kinard	.05	.04	.02
359	Lionel Manuel	.05	.04	.02
360	**Giants**	.05	.04	.02
361	Leonard Marshall	.10	.08	.04
362	George Martin	.05	.04	.02
363	Joe Morris	.10	.08	.04
364	Phil Simms	.50	.40	.20
365	George Adams	.05	.04	.02
366	**Uniform**	.05	.04	.02
367	**Eagles Helmet**	.05	.04	.02
368	**Eagles Action**	.25	.20	.10
369	Jerome Brown	.30	.25	.12
370	Keith Byars	.15	.11	.06
371	Randall Cunningham	.40	.30	.15
372	Terry Hoage	.05	.04	.02
373	Seth Joyner	.20	.15	.08
374	Mike Quick	.15	.11	.06
375	**Eagles**	.05	.04	.02
376	Clyde Simmons	.20	.15	.08
377	Anthony Toney	.05	.04	.02
378	Andre Waters	.10	.08	.04
379	Reggie White	.35	.25	.14
380	Roynell Young	.05	.04	.02
381	**Uniform**	.05	.04	.02
382	**Cardinals Helmet**	.05	.04	.02
383	**Cardinals Action**	.05	.04	.02
384	Robert Awalt	.05	.04	.02
385	Roy Green	.15	.11	.06
386	Neil Lomax	.10	.08	.04
387	Stump Mitchell	.10	.08	.04
388	Niko Noga	.06	.05	.02
389	Freddie Joe Nunn	.05	.04	.02
390	**Cardinals**	.05	.04	.02
391	Luis Sharpe	.10	.08	.04
392	Vai Sikahema	.10	.08	.04
393	J.T. Smith	.10	.08	.04
394	Leonard Smith	.05	.04	.02
395	Lonnie Young	.05	.04	.02
396	**Uniform**	.05	.04	.02
397	**49ers Helmet**	.05	.04	.02
398	**49ers Action**	1.50	1.25	.60
399	Dwaine Board	.05	.04	.02
400	Michael Carter	.10	.08	.04
401	Roger Craig	.25	.20	.10
402	Jeff Fuller	.05	.04	.02
403	Don Griffin	.05	.04	.02
404	Ronnie Lott	.20	.15	.08
405	**49ers**	.05	.04	.02
406	Joe Montana	3.00	2.25	1.25
407	Tom Rathman	.25	.20	.10
408	Jerry Rice	1.50	1.25	.60
409	Keena Turner	.05	.04	.02
410	Michael Walter	.05	.04	.02
411	**Uniform**	.05	.04	.02
412	**Bucs Helmet**	.05	.04	.02
413	**Bucs Action**	.05	.04	.02
414	Mark Carrier	.25	.20	.10
415	Gerald Carter	.05	.04	.02
416	Ron Holmes	.10	.08	.04
417	Rod Jones	.05	.04	.02
418	Calvin Magee	.05	.04	.02
419	Ervin Randle	.05	.04	.02
420	**Buccaneers**	.05	.04	.02
421	Donald Igwebuike	.05	.04	.02
422	Vinny Testaverde	.25	.20	.10
423	Jackie Walker	.05	.04	.02
424	Chris Washington	.05	.04	.02
425	James Wilder	.10	.08	.04
426	**Uniform**	.05	.04	.02
427	**Redskins Helmet**	.05	.04	.02
428	**Redskins Action**	.10	.08	.04
429	Gary Clark	.15	.11	.06
430	Monte Coleman	.05	.04	.02
431	Darrell Green	.10	.08	.04
432	Charles Mann	.10	.08	.04
433	Kelvin Bryant	.10	.08	.04
434	Art Monk	.25	.20	.10
435	**Redskins**	.05	.04	.02
436	Ricky Sanders	.15	.11	.06
437	Jay Schroeder	.15	.11	.06
438	Alvin Walton	.05	.04	.02
439	Barry Wilburn	.10	.08	.04
440	Doug Williams	.10	.08	.04

		NM/M	NM	E
441	**Uniform**	.05	.04	.02
442	**Super Bowl Action**	.05	.04	.02
443	**Super Bowl Action**	.05	.04	.02
444	**Doug Williams**			
	(Super Bowl MVP)	.15	.11	.06
445	**Super Bowl Action**	.05	.04	.02
446	**Super Bowl Action**	.05	.04	.02
447	**Super Bowl Action**	.05	.04	.02
----	**Panini Album** (John Elway			
	on cover)	2.00	1.50	.80

1989 Panini Stickers

KANSAS CITY CHIEFS™

LLOYD BURRUSS

These 1989 stickers from Panini are slightly larger than those issued in 1988, measuring 1-15/16" x 3."

		NM/M	NM	E
	Complete Set (416):	30.00	22.00	12.00
	Common Player:	.05	.04	.02
1	**SB XXIII Program**	.10	.08	.04
2	**SB XXIII Program**	.05	.04	.02
3	Floyd Dixon	.05	.04	.02
4	Tony Casillas	.10	.08	.04
5	Bill Fralic	.10	.08	.04
6	Aundray Bruce	.05	.04	.02
7	Scott Case	.05	.04	.02
8	Rick Donnelly	.05	.04	.02
9	**Atlanta logo**	.05	.04	.02
10	**Helmet**	.05	.04	.02
11	Marcus Cotton	.05	.04	.02
12	Chris Miller	.25	.20	.10
13	Robert Moore	.05	.04	.02
14	Bobby Butler	.05	.04	.02
15	Rick Bryan	.05	.04	.02
16	John Settle	.10	.08	.04
17	Jim McMahon	.15	.11	.06
18	Neal Anderson	.15	.11	.06
19	Dave Duerson	.05	.04	.02
20	Steve McMichael	.05	.04	.02
21	Jay Hilgenberg	.05	.04	.02
22	Dennis McKinnon	.05	.04	.02
23	**Chicago logo**	.05	.04	.02
24	**Helmet**	.05	.04	.02
25	Richard Dent	.15	.11	.06
26	Dennis Gentry	.05	.04	.02
27	Mike Singletary	.15	.11	.06
28	Vestee Jackson	.05	.04	.02
29	Mike Tomczak	.15	.11	.06
30	Dan Hampton	.15	.11	.06
31	Michael Irvin	1.75	1.25	.70
32	Eugene Lockhart	.10	.08	.04
33	Herschel Walker	.30	.25	.12
34	Kelvin Martin	.15	.11	.06
35	Jim Jeffcoat	.10	.08	.04
36	Everson Walls	.10	.08	.04
37	**Dallas logo**	.05	.04	.02
38	**Helmet**	.05	.04	.02
39	Danny Noonan	.05	.04	.02
40	Ray Alexander	.05	.04	.02
41	Garry Cobb	.05	.04	.02
42	Ed "Too Tall" Jones	.15	.11	.06
43	Kevin Brooks	.05	.04	.02
44	Bill Bates	.10	.08	.04
45	**Detroit logo**	.05	.04	.02
46	Chuck Long	.10	.08	.04
47	Jim Arnold	.05	.04	.02
48	Michael Cofer	.05	.04	.02
49	Eddie Murray	.05	.04	.02
50	Keith Ferguson	.05	.04	.02
51	Pete Mandley	.05	.04	.02
52	**Helmet**	.05	.04	.02
53	Jerry Ball	.05	.04	.02
54	Bennie Blades	.15	.11	.06
55	Dennis Gibson	.05	.04	.02
56	Chris Spielman	.15	.11	.06
57	Eric Williams	.05	.04	.02
58	Lomas Brown	.05	.04	.02
59	Johnny Holland	.10	.08	.04
60	Tim Harris	.15	.11	.06
61	Mark Murphy	.05	.04	.02
62	Walter Stanley	.10	.08	.04
63	Brent Fullwood	.05	.04	.02
64	Ken Ruettgers	.10	.08	.04
65	**Green Bay logo**	.05	.04	.02
66	**Helmet**	.05	.04	.02
67	John Anderson	.05	.04	.02
68	Brian Noble	.05	.04	.02
69	Sterling Sharpe	1.50	1.25	.60
70	Keith Woodside	.10	.08	.04
71	Mark Lee	.05	.04	.02
72	Don Majkowski	.15	.11	.06
73	Aaron Cox	.10	.08	.04
74	LeRoy Irvin	.05	.04	.02
75	Jim Everett	.15	.11	.06
76	Mike Lansford	.05	.04	.02
77	Mike Wilcher	.05	.04	.02
78	Henry Ellard	.10	.08	.04
79	**Rams helmet**	.05	.04	.02
80	Jerry Gray	.05	.04	.02
81	Doug Smith	.05	.04	.02
82	Tom Newberry	.10	.08	.04
83	Jackie Slater	.10	.08	.04
84	Greg Bell	.10	.08	.04
85	Kevin Greene	.10	.08	.04
86	Chris Doleman	.10	.08	.04
87	Steve Jordan	.10	.08	.04
88	Jesse Solomon	.05	.04	.02
89	Randall McDaniel	.05	.04	.02
90	Hassan Jones	.10	.08	.04
91	Joey Browner	.10	.08	.04
92	**Vikings logo**	.05	.04	.02
93	**Helmet**	.05	.04	.02
94	Anthony Carter	.10	.08	.04
95	Gary Zimmerman	.05	.04	.02
96	Wade Wilson	.15	.11	.06
97	Scott Studwell	.10	.08	.04
98	Keith Millard	.10	.08	.04
99	Carl Lee	.10	.08	.04
100	Morten Andersen	.10	.08	.04
101	Bobby Hebert	.15	.11	.06
102	Rueben Mayes	.10	.08	.04
103	Sam Mills	.10	.08	.04
104	Vaughan Johnson	.10	.08	.04
105	Pat Swilling	.15	.11	.06
106	**Saints logo**	.05	.04	.02
107	**Helmet**	.05	.04	.02
108	Brad Edelman	.05	.04	.02
109	Craig Heyward	.15	.11	.06
110	Eric Martin	.10	.08	.04
111	Dalton Hilliard	.10	.08	.04
112	Lonzell Hill	.05	.04	.02
113	Rickey Jackson	.10	.08	.04
114	Erik Howard	.05	.04	.02
115	Phil Simms	.35	.25	.14
116	Leonard Marshall	.10	.08	.04
117	Joe Morris	.10	.08	.04
118	Bart Oates	.10	.08	.04
119	Mark Bavaro	.10	.08	.04
120	**Giants logo**	.05	.04	.02
121	**Helmet**	.05	.04	.02
122	Terry Kinard	.05	.04	.02
123	Carl Banks	.10	.08	.04
124	Lionel Manuel	.05	.04	.02
125	Stephen Baker	.15	.11	.06
126	Pepper Johnson	.10	.08	.04
127	Jim Burt	.05	.04	.02
128	Cris Carter	.35	.25	.14
129	Mike Quick	.10	.08	.04
130	Terry Hoage	.05	.04	.02
131	Keith Jackson	.80	.60	.30
132	Clyde Simmons	.15	.11	.06
133	Eric Allen	.05	.04	.02
134	**Eagles logo**	.05	.04	.02
135	**Helmet**	.05	.04	.02
136	Randall Cunningham	.40	.30	.15
137	Mike Pitts	.05	.04	.02
138	Keith Byars	.10	.08	.04
139	Seth Joyner	.15	.11	.06
140	Jerome Brown	.15	.11	.06
141	Reggie White	.30	.25	.12
142	Jay Novacek	.30	.25	.12
143	Neil Lomax	.10	.08	.04
144	Ken Harvey	.10	.08	.04
145	Freddie Joe Nunn	.05	.04	.02
146	Robert Awalt	.05	.04	.02
147	Niko Noga	.05	.04	.02
148	**Phoenix logo**	.05	.04	.02
149	**Helmet**	.05	.04	.02
150	Tim McDonald	.25	.20	.10
151	Roy Green	.10	.08	.04
152	Stump Mitchell	.10	.08	.04
153	J.T. Smith	.10	.08	.04
154	Luis Sharpe	.05	.04	.02
155	Vai Sikahema	.10	.08	.04
156	Jeff Fuller	.05	.04	.02
157	Joe Montana	3.00	2.25	1.25
158	Harris Barton	.05	.04	.02
159	Michael Carter	.10	.08	.04
160	Jeff Fuller	.05	.04	.02
161	Jerry Rice	2.00	1.50	.80
162	**49ers logo**	.05	.04	.02
163	**Helmet**	.05	.04	.02
164	Tom Rathman	.15	.11	.06
165	Roger Craig	.20	.15	.08
166	Ronnie Lott	.30	.25	.12
167	Charles Haley	.15	.11	.06
168	John Taylor	.50	.40	.20
169	Michael Walter	.05	.04	.02
170	Ron Hall	.05	.04	.02
171	Ervin Randle	.05	.04	.02
172	James Wilder	.10	.08	.04
173	Ron Holmes	.05	.04	.02
174	Mark Carrier	.15	.11	.06
175	William Howard	.05	.04	.02
176	**Tampa Bay logo**	.05	.04	.02
177	**Helmet**	.05	.04	.02
178	Lars Tate	.05	.04	.02
179	Vinny Testaverde	.20	.15	.08
180	Paul Gruber	.15	.11	.06
181	Bruce Hill	.10	.08	.04
182	Reuben Davis	.05	.04	.02
183	Ricky Reynolds	.05	.04	.02
184	Ricky Sanders	.15	.11	.06
185	Gary Clark	.15	.11	.06
186	Mark May	.05	.04	.02
187	Darrell Green	.10	.08	.04
188	Jim Lachey	.10	.08	.04
189	Doug Williams	.10	.08	.04
190	**Helmet**	.05	.04	.02
191	**Redskins logo**	.05	.04	.02
192	Kelvin Bryant	.05	.04	.02
193	Charles Mann	.05	.04	.02
194	Alvin Walton	.05	.04	.02
195	Art Monk	.20	.15	.08
196	Barry Wilburn	.05	.04	.02
197	Mark Rypien	.25	.20	.10
198	**NFC logo**	.05	.04	.02
199	Scott Case	.05	.04	.02
200	Herschel Walker	.30	.25	.12
201	Herschel Walker,			
	Roger Craig	.25	.20	.10
202	Henry Ellard, Jerry Rice	.65	.50	.25
203	Bruce Matthews,			
	Tom Newberry	.05	.04	.02
204	Gary Zimmerman,			
	Anthony Munoz	.10	.08	.04
205	Boomer Esiason	.15	.11	.06
206	Jay Hilgenberg	.10	.08	.04
207	Keith Jackson	.25	.20	.10
208	Reggie White,			
	Bruce Smith	.25	.20	.10
209	Keith Millard, Tim Krumrie	.10	.08	.04
210	Carl Lee, Frank Minnifield	.05	.04	.02
211	Joey Browner,			
	Deron Cherry	.10	.08	.04
212	Shane Conlan	.10	.08	.04
213	Mike Singletary	.15	.11	.06
214	Cornelius Bennett	.15	.11	.06
215	**AFC logo**	.05	.04	.02
216	Boomer Esiason	.25	.20	.10
217	Erik McMillan	.10	.08	.04
218	Jim Kelly	.60	.45	.25
219	Cornelius Bennett	.15	.11	.06
220	Fred Smerlas	.10	.08	.04
221	Shane Conlan	.10	.08	.04
222	Scott Norwood	.05	.04	.02
223	Mark Kelso	.05	.04	.02
224	**Bills logo**	.05	.04	.02
225	**Helmet**	.05	.04	.02
226	Thurman Thomas	1.50	1.25	.60
227	Pete Metzelaars	.05	.04	.02
228	Bruce Smith	.25	.20	.10
229	Art Still	.10	.08	.04
230	Kent Hull	.10	.08	.04
231	Andre Reed	.25	.20	.10
232	Tim Krumrie	.05	.04	.02
233	Boomer Esiason	.25	.20	.10
234	Ickey Woods	.10	.08	.04
235	Eric Thomas	.10	.08	.04
236	Rodney Holman	.10	.08	.04
237	Jim Skow	.05	.04	.02
238	**Bengals helmet**	.05	.04	.02
239	James Brooks	.10	.08	.04
240	David Fulcher	.10	.08	.04
241	Carl Zander	.05	.04	.02
242	Eddie Brown	.10	.08	.04
243	Max Montoya	.05	.04	.02
244	Anthony Munoz	.15	.11	.06
245	Felix Wright	.05	.04	.02
246	Clay Matthews	.15	.11	.06
247	Hanford Dixon	.05	.04	.02
248	Ozzie Newsome	.15	.11	.06
249	Bernie Kosar	.25	.20	.10
250	Kevin Mack	.10	.08	.04
251	**Bengals Helmet**	.05	.04	.02
252	Brian Brennan	.05	.04	.02

253	Reggie Langhorne	.05	.04	.02
254	Cody Risien	.05	.04	.02
255	Webster Slaughter	.15	.11	.06
256	Mike Johnson	.05	.04	.02
257	Frank Minnifield	.05	.04	.02
258	Mike Horan	.05	.04	.02
259	Dennis Smith	.10	.08	.04
260	Ricky Nattiel	.05	.04	.02
261	Karl Mecklenburg	.10	.08	.04
262	Keith Bishop	.05	.04	.02
263	John Elway	1.50	1.25	.60
264	**Broncos helmet**	.05	.04	.02
265	**Broncos logo**	.05	.04	.02
266	Simon Fletcher	.15	.11	.06
267	Vance Johnson	.10	.08	.04
268	Tony Dorsett	.35	.25	.14
269	Greg Kragen	.10	.08	.04
270	Mike Harden	.05	.04	.02
271	Mark Jackson	.05	.04	.02
272	Warren Moon	.75	.60	.30
273	Mike Rozier	.10	.08	.04
274	**Houston logo**	.05	.04	.02
275	Allen Pinkett	.10	.08	.04
276	Tony Zendejas	.05	.04	.02
277	Alonzo Highsmith	.10	.08	.04
278	Johnny Meads	.05	.04	.02
279	**Helmet**	.05	.04	.02
280	Mike Munchak	.10	.08	.04
281	John Grimsley	.05	.04	.02
282	Ernest Givins	.15	.11	.06
283	Drew Hill	.10	.08	.04
284	Bruce Matthews	.10	.08	.04
285	Ray Childress	.10	.08	.04
286	**Colts logo**	.05	.04	.02
287	Chris Hinton	.10	.08	.04
288	Clarence Verdin	.10	.08	.04
289	Jon Hand	.15	.11	.06
290	Chris Chandler	.15	.11	.06
291	Eugene Daniel	.05	.04	.02
292	Dean Biasucci	.05	.04	.02
293	**Helmet**	.05	.04	.02
294	Duane Bickett	.10	.08	.04
295	Rohn Stark	.05	.04	.02
296	Albert Bentley	.10	.08	.04
297	Bill Brooks	.10	.08	.04
298	O'Brien Alston	.05	.04	.02
299	Ray Donaldson	.05	.04	.02
300	Carlos Carson	.05	.04	.02
301	Lloyd Burruss	.05	.04	.02
302	Steve DeBerg	.15	.11	.06
303	Irv Eatman	.05	.04	.02
304	Dino Hackett	.05	.04	.02
305	Albert Lewis	.10	.08	.04
306	**Chiefs helmet**	.05	.04	.02
307	**Chiefs logo**	.05	.04	.02
308	Deron Cherry	.10	.08	.04
309	Paul Palmer	.05	.04	.02
310	Neil Smith	.40	.30	.15
311	Christian Okoye	.10	.08	.04
312	Stephone Paige	.10	.08	.04
313	Bill Maas	.05	.04	.02
314	Marcus Allen	.40	.30	.15
315	Vann McElroy	.05	.04	.02
316	Mervyn Fernandez	.10	.08	.04
317	Bill Pickel	.05	.04	.02
318	Greg Townsend	.10	.08	.04
319	Tim Brown	1.25	.90	.50
320	**Raiders logo**	.05	.04	.02
321	**Helmet**	.05	.04	.02
322	James Lofton	.15	.11	.06
323	Willie Gault	.10	.08	.04
324	Jay Schroeder	.10	.08	.04
325	Matt Millen	.05	.04	.02
326	Howie Long	.10	.08	.04
327	Bo Jackson	.50	.40	.20
328	Lorenzo Hampton	.05	.04	.02
329	Jarvis Williams	.05	.04	.02
330	Jim C. Jensen	.05	.04	.02
331	Dan Marino	2.50	2.00	1.00
332	John Offerdahl	.10	.08	.04
333	Brian Sochia	.05	.04	.02
334	**Miami logo**	.05	.04	.02
335	**Helmet**	.05	.04	.02
336	Ferrell Edmunds	.05	.04	.02
337	Mark Brown	.05	.04	.02
338	Mark Duper	.10	.08	.04
339	Troy Stradford	.05	.04	.02
340	T.J. Turner	.05	.04	.02
341	Mark Clayton	.15	.11	.06
342	**Patriots logo**	.05	.04	.02
343	Johnny Rembert	.05	.04	.02
344	Garin Veris	.05	.04	.02
345	Stanley Morgan	.10	.08	.04
346	John Stephens	.15	.11	.06
347	Fred Marion	.05	.04	.02
348	Irving Fryar	.15	.11	.06
349	**Helmet**	.05	.04	.02
350	Andre Tippett	.10	.08	.04

351	Roland James	.05	.04	.02
352	Brent Williams	.05	.04	.02
353	Raymond Clayborn	.05	.04	.02
354	Tony Eason	.10	.08	.04
355	Bruce Armstrong	.05	.04	.02
356	**Jets logo**	.05	.04	.02
357	Marty Lyons	.10	.08	.04
358	Bobby Humphrey	.05	.04	.02
359	Pat Leahy	.05	.04	.02
360	Mickey Shuler	.10	.08	.04
361	James Hasty	.05	.04	.02
362	Ken O'Brien	.10	.08	.04
363	**Helmet**	.05	.04	.02
364	Alex Gordon	.05	.04	.02
365	Al Toon	.10	.08	.04
366	Erik McMillan	.10	.08	.04
367	Johnny Hector	.10	.08	.04
368	Wesley Walker	.10	.08	.04
369	Freeman McNeil	.10	.08	.04
370	**Steelers logo**	.05	.04	.02
371	Gary Anderson	.05	.04	.02
372	Rodney Carter	.05	.04	.02
373	Merril Hoge	.10	.08	.04
374	David Little	.05	.04	.02
375	Bubby Brister	.15	.11	.06
376	Thomas Everett	.10	.08	.04
377	**Helmet**	.05	.04	.02
378	Rod Woodson	.40	.30	.15
379	Bryan Hinkle	.05	.04	.02
380	Tunch Ilkin	.05	.04	.02
381	Aaron Jones	.05	.04	.02
382	Louis Lipps	.10	.08	.04
383	Warren Williams	.05	.04	.02
384	Anthony Miller	.75	.60	.30
385	Gary Anderson	.15	.11	.06
386	Lee Williams	.10	.08	.04
387	Lionel James	.10	.08	.04
388	Gary Plummer	.05	.04	.02
389	Gill Byrd	.10	.08	.04
390	**Chargers helmet**	.05	.04	.02
391	Ralf Mojsiejenko	.05	.04	.02
392	Rod Bernstine	.25	.20	.10
393	Keith Browner	.05	.04	.02
394	Billy Ray Smith	.10	.08	.04
395	Leslie O'Neal	.15	.11	.06
396	Jamie Holland	.05	.04	.02
397	Tony Woods	.10	.08	.04
398	Bruce Scholtz	.05	.04	.02
399	Joe Nash	.05	.04	.02
400	Curt Warner	.10	.08	.04
401	John L. Williams	.10	.08	.04
402	Bryan Millard	.05	.04	.02
403	**Seahawks logo**	.05	.04	.02
404	**Helmet**	.05	.04	.02
405	Steve Largent	.30	.25	.12
406	Norm Johnson	.10	.08	.04
407	Jacob Green	.10	.08	.04
408	Dave Krieg	.10	.08	.04
409	Paul Moyer	.05	.04	.02
410	Brian Blades	.50	.40	.20
411	**SB XXIII**	.05	.04	.02
412	Jerry Rice	1.50	1.25	.60
413	**SB XXIII**	.10	.08	.04
414	**SB XXIII**	.10	.08	.04
415	**SB XXIII**	.10	.08	.04
416	**SB XXIII**	.10	.08	.04
----	**Panini Album** (Joe Montana on conver)	4.00	3.00	1.50

1990 Panini Stickers

DEION SANDERS

These stickers were intended to be stored in an album titled "The Hitters." Ronnie Lott, Mike Singletary and Lawrence Taylor are featured on the album cover. The stickers measure 1-7/8" x 2-15/16" and have a color action photo on the front, using a design distinctly different from those used the two years before.

	NM/M	NM	E
Complete Set (396):	20.00	15.00	8.00
Common Player:	.05	.04	.02

1	**Super Bowl XXIV Program Cover (top)**	.15	.11	.06
2	**Super Bowl XXIV Program Cover (bottom)**	.10	.08	.04
3	**Bills Crest**	.05	.04	.02
4	Thurman Thomas	.50	.40	.20
5	Nate Odomes	.05	.04	.02
6	Jim Kelly	.45	.35	.20
7	Cornelius Bennett	.20	.15	.08
8	Scott Norwood	.05	.04	.02
9	Mark Kelso	.05	.04	.02
10	Kent Hull	.05	.04	.02
11	Jim Ritcher	.05	.04	.02
12	Darryl Talley	.10	.08	.04
13	Bruce Smith	.15	.11	.06
14	Shane Conlan	.10	.08	.04
15	Andre Reed	.15	.11	.06
16	Jason Buck	.05	.04	.02
17	David Fulcher	.10	.08	.04
18	Jim Skow	.05	.04	.02
19	Anthony Munoz	.15	.11	.06
20	Eric Thomas	.05	.04	.02
21	Eric Ball	.05	.04	.02
22	Tim Krumrie	.05	.04	.02
23	James Brooks	.10	.08	.04
24	**Bengals Crest**	.05	.04	.02
25	Rodney Holman	.05	.04	.02
26	Boomer Esiason	.25	.20	.10
27	Eddie Brown	.10	.08	.04
28	Tim McGee	.10	.08	.04
29	**Browns Crest**	.05	.04	.02
30	Mike Johnson	.05	.04	.02
31	David Grayson	.05	.04	.02
32	Thane Gash	.05	.04	.02
33	Robert Banks	.05	.04	.02
34	Eric Metcalf	.20	.15	.08
35	Kevin Mack	.10	.08	.04
36	Reggie Langhorne	.05	.04	.02
37	Webster Slaughter	.10	.08	.04
38	Felix Wright	.05	.04	.02
39	Bernie Kosar	.25	.20	.10
40	Frank Minnifield	.05	.04	.02
41	Clay Matthews	.15	.11	.06
42	Vance Johnson	.10	.08	.04
43	Ron Holmes	.05	.04	.02
44	Melvin Bratton	.10	.08	.04
45	Greg Kragen	.05	.04	.02
46	Karl Mecklenburg	.10	.08	.04
47	Dennis Smith	.10	.08	.04
48	Bobby Humphrey	.10	.08	.04
49	Simon Fletcher	.10	.08	.04
50	**Broncos Crest**	.05	.04	.02
51	Michael Brooks	.05	.04	.02
52	Steve Atwater	.10	.08	.04
53	John Elway	.80	.60	.30
54	David Treadwell	.05	.04	.02
55	**Oilers Crest**	.05	.04	.02
56	Bubba McDowell	.05	.04	.02
57	Ray Childress	.10	.08	.04
58	Bruce Matthews	.05	.04	.02
59	Allen Pinkett	.10	.08	.04
60	Warren Moon	.55	.40	.20
61	John Grimsley	.05	.04	.02
62	Alonzo Highsmith	.10	.08	.04
63	Mike Munchak	.10	.08	.04
64	Ernest Givins	.10	.08	.04
65	Johnny Meads	.05	.04	.02
66	Drew Hill	.10	.08	.04
67	William Fuller	.05	.04	.02
68	Duane Bickett	.10	.08	.04
69	Jack Trudeau	.10	.08	.04
70	Jon Hand	.10	.08	.04
71	Chris Hinton	.10	.08	.04
72	Bill Brooks	.10	.08	.04
73	Donnell Thompson	.05	.04	.02
74	Jeff Herrod	.05	.04	.02
75	Andre Rison	.25	.20	.10
76	**Colts Crest**	.05	.04	.02
77	Chris Chandler	.10	.08	.04
78	Ray Donaldson	.05	.04	.02
79	Albert Bentley	.10	.08	.04
80	Keith Taylor	.05	.04	.02
81	**Chiefs Crest**	.05	.04	.02
82	Leonard Griffin	.05	.04	.02
83	Dino Hackett	.05	.04	.02
84	Christian Okoye	.10	.08	.04
85	Chris Martin	.10	.08	.04
86	John Alt	.05	.04	.02
87	Kevin Ross	.05	.04	.02
88	Steve DeBerg	.10	.08	.04
89	Albert Lewis	.10	.08	.04
90	Stephone Paige	.10	.08	.04
91	Derrick Thomas	.40	.30	.15
92	Neil Smith	.15	.11	.06
93	Pete Mandley	.05	.04	.02
94	Howie Long	.10	.08	.04

95	Greg Townsend	.05	.04	.02
96	Mervyn Fernandez	.10	.08	.04
97	Scott Davis	.05	.04	.02
98	Steve Beuerlein	.40	.30	.15
99	Mike Dyal	.05	.04	.02
100	Willie Gault	.10	.08	.04
101	Eddie Anderson	.05	.04	.02
102	**Raiders Crest**	.05	.04	.02
103	Trey McDaniel	.05	.04	.02
104	Bo Jackson	.30	.25	.12
105	Steve Wisniewski	.05	.04	.02
106	Steve Smith	.10	.08	.04
107	**Dolphins Crest**	.05	.04	.02
108	Mark Clayton	.15	.11	.06
109	Louis Oliver	.10	.08	.04
110	Jarvis Williams	.05	.04	.02
111	Ferrell Edmunds	.05	.04	.02
112	Jeff Cross	.05	.04	.02
113	John Offerdahl	.10	.08	.04
114	Brian Sochia	.05	.04	.02
115	Dan Marino	2.00	1.50	.80
116	Jim C. Jensen	.05	.04	.02
117	Sammie Smith	.05	.04	.02
118	Reggie Roby	.05	.04	.02
119	Roy Foster	.05	.04	.02
120	Bruce Armstrong	.05	.04	.02
121	Steve Grogan	.10	.08	.04
122	Hart Lee Dykes	.05	.04	.02
123	Andre Tippett	.10	.08	.04
124	Johnny Rembert	.05	.04	.02
125	Ed Reynolds	.05	.04	.02
126	Cedric Jones	.05	.04	.02
127	Vincent Brown	.05	.04	.02
128	**Patriots Crest**	.05	.04	.02
129	Brent Williams	.05	.04	.02
130	John Stephens	.10	.08	.04
131	Eric Sievers	.05	.04	.02
132	Maurice Hurst	.05	.04	.02
133	**Jets Crest**	.05	.04	.02
134	Johnny Hector	.10	.08	.04
135	Eric McMillan	.05	.04	.02
136	Jeff Lageman	.05	.04	.02
137	Al Toon	.10	.08	.04
138	James Hasty	.05	.04	.02
139	Kyle Clifton	.05	.04	.02
140	Ken O'Brien	.10	.08	.04
141	Jim Sweeney	.05	.04	.02
142	JoJo Townsell	.10	.08	.04
143	Dennis Byrd	.20	.15	.08
144	Mickey Shuler	.10	.08	.04
145	Alex Gordon	.05	.04	.02
146	Keith Willis	.05	.04	.02
147	Louis Lipps	.10	.08	.04
148	David Little	.05	.04	.02
149	Greg Lloyd	.10	.08	.04
150	Carnell Lake	.05	.04	.02
151	Tim Worley	.10	.08	.04
152	Dwayne Woodruff	.05	.04	.02
153	Gerald Williams	.05	.04	.02
154	**Steelers Crest**	.05	.04	.02
155	Merril Hoge	.10	.08	.04
156	Bubby Brister	.10	.08	.04
157	Tunch Ilkin	.05	.04	.02
158	Rod Woodson	.15	.11	.06
159	**Charger Crest**	.05	.04	.02
160	Leslie O'Neal	.10	.08	.04
161	Billy Ray Smith	.05	.04	.02
162	Marion Butts	.15	.11	.06
163	Lee Williams	.10	.08	.04
164	Gill Byrd	.10	.08	.04
165	Jim McMahon	.15	.11	.06
166	Courtney Hall	.05	.04	.02
167	Burt Grossman	.15	.11	.06
168	Gary Plummer	.05	.04	.02
169	Anthony Miller	.40	.30	.15
170	Billy Joe Tolliver	.15	.11	.06
171	Venice Glenn	.05	.04	.02
172	Andy Heck	.05	.04	.02
173	Brian Blades	.15	.11	.06
174	Bryan Millard	.05	.04	.02
175	Tony Woods	.05	.04	.02
176	Rufus Porter	.05	.04	.02
177	Dave Wyman	.05	.04	.02
178	John L. Williams	.10	.08	.04
179	Jacob Green	.05	.04	.02
180	**Seahawks Crest**	.05	.04	.02
181	Eugene Robinson	.05	.04	.02
182	Jeff Bryant	.05	.04	.02
183	Dave Krieg	.10	.08	.04
184	Joe Nash	.05	.04	.02
185	Christian Okoye	.05	.04	.02
186	Felix Wright	.05	.04	.02
187	Rod Woodson	.10	.08	.04
188	Barry Sanders, Christian Okoye	.75	.60	.30
189	Jerry Rice, Sterling Sharpe	1.00	.70	.40

190	Bruce Matthews	.05	.04	.02
191	Jay Hilgenberg	.05	.04	.02
192	Tom Newbury	.05	.04	.02
193	Anthony Munoz	.10	.08	.04
194	Jim Lachey	.05	.04	.02
195	Keith Jackson	.15	.11	.06
196	Joe Montana	1.50	1.25	.60
197	David Fulcher, Ronnie Lott	.10	.08	.04
198	Albert Lewis, Eric Allen	.05	.04	.02
199	Reggie White	.20	.15	.08
200	Keith Millard	.05	.04	.02
201	Chris Doleman	.05	.04	.02
202	Mike Singletary	.15	.11	.06
203	Tim Harris	.05	.04	.02
204	Lawrence Taylor	.20	.15	.08
205	Rich Camarrilo	.05	.04	.02
206	Sterling Sharpe	.25	.20	.10
207	Chris Doleman	.05	.04	.02
208	Barry Sanders	.55	.40	.20
209	**Falcons Crest**	.05	.04	.02
210	Michael Haynes	.30	.25	.12
211	Scott Case	.05	.04	.02
212	Marcus Cotton	.05	.04	.02
213	Chris Miller	.15	.11	.06
214	Keith Jones	.05	.04	.02
215	Tim Green	.05	.04	.02
216	Deion Sanders	.50	.40	.20
217	Shawn Collins	.10	.08	.04
218	John Settle	.05	.04	.02
219	Bill Fralic	.05	.04	.02
220	Aundray Bruce	.05	.04	.02
221	Jessie Tuggle	.05	.04	.02
222	James Thornton	.05	.04	.02
223	Dennis Gentry	.05	.04	.02
224	Richard Dent	.15	.11	.06
225	Jay Hilgenberg	.05	.04	.02
226	Steve McMichael	.05	.04	.02
227	Brad Muster	.10	.08	.04
228	Donnell Woodford	.05	.04	.02
229	Mike Singletary	.15	.11	.06
230	**Bears Crest**	.05	.04	.02
231	Mark Bortz	.05	.04	.02
232	Kevin Butler	.05	.04	.02
233	Neal Anderson	.10	.08	.04
234	Trace Armstrong	.05	.04	.02
235	**Cowboys Crest**	.05	.04	.02
236	Mark Tuinei	.10	.08	.04
237	Tony Tolbert	.05	.04	.02
238	Eugene Lockhart	.10	.08	.04
239	Daryl Johnston	.25	.20	.10
240	Troy Aikman	3.00	2.25	1.25
241	Jim Jeffcoat	.10	.08	.04
242	James Dixon	.05	.04	.02
243	Jesse Solomon	.05	.04	.02
244	Ken Norton	.25	.20	.10
245	Kelvin Martin	.05	.04	.02
246	Danny Noonan	.05	.04	.02
247	Michael Irvin	.50	.40	.20
248	Eric Williams	.05	.04	.02
249	Richard Johnson	.05	.04	.02
250	Michael Cofer	.05	.04	.02
251	Chris Spielman	.10	.08	.04
252	Rodney Peete	.20	.15	.08
253	Bennie Blades	.10	.08	.04
254	Jerry Ball	.05	.04	.02
255	Eddie Murray	.08	.06	.03
256	**Lions Crest**	.05	.04	.02
257	Barry Sanders	1.75	1.25	.70
258	Jerry Holmes	.05	.04	.02
259	Dennis Gibson	.05	.04	.02
260	Lomas Brown	.05	.04	.02
261	**Packers Crest**	.05	.04	.02
262	Dave Brown	.05	.04	.02
263	Mark Murphy	.05	.04	.02
264	Perry Kemp	.05	.04	.02
265	Don Majkowski	.10	.08	.04
266	Chris Jacke	.05	.04	.02
267	Keith Woodside	.10	.08	.04
268	Tony Mandarich	.05	.04	.02
269	Robert Brown	.05	.04	.02
270	Sterling Sharpe	.75	.60	.30
271	Tim Harris	.10	.08	.04
272	Brent Fullwood	.05	.04	.02
273	Brian Noble	.05	.04	.02
274	Alvin Wright	.05	.04	.02
275	Flipper Anderson	.10	.08	.04
276	Jackie Slater	.10	.08	.04
277	Kevin Greene	.10	.08	.04
278	Pete Holohan	.05	.04	.02
279	Tom Newberry	.05	.04	.02
280	Jerry Gray	.05	.04	.02
281	Henry Ellard	.10	.08	.04
282	**Rams Crest**	.05	.04	.02
283	LeRoy Irvin	.05	.04	.02
284	Jim Everett	.15	.11	.06
285	Greg Bell	.10	.08	.04
286	Doug Smith	.05	.04	.02

287	**Vikings Crest**	.05	.04	.02
288	Joey Browner	.10	.08	.04
289	Wade Wilson	.15	.11	.06
290	Chris Doleman	.10	.08	.04
291	Al Noga	.05	.04	.02
292	Herschel Walker	.20	.15	.08
293	Henry Thomas	.10	.08	.04
294	Steve Jordan	.10	.08	.04
295	Anthony Carter	.10	.08	.04
296	Keith Millard	.10	.08	.04
297	Carl Lee	.05	.04	.02
298	Randall McDaniel	.05	.04	.02
299	Gary Zimmerman	.05	.04	.02
300	Morten Andersen	.05	.04	.02
301	Rickey Jackson	.10	.08	.04
302	Sam Mills	.05	.04	.02
303	Hoby Brenner	.05	.04	.02
304	Dalton Hilliard	.05	.04	.02
305	Robert Massey	.05	.04	.02
306	John Fourcade	.10	.08	.04
307	Lonzell Hill	.05	.04	.02
308	**Saints Crest**	.05	.04	.02
309	Jim Dombrowski	.05	.04	.02
310	Pat Swilling	.15	.11	.06
311	Vaughan Johnson	.05	.04	.02
312	Eric Martin	.10	.08	.04
313	**Giants Crest**	.05	.04	.02
314	Ottis Anderson	.10	.08	.04
315	Myron Guyton	.05	.04	.02
316	Terry Kinard	.05	.04	.02
317	Mark Bavaro	.10	.08	.04
318	Phil Simms	.25	.20	.10
319	Lawrence Taylor	.30	.25	.12
320	Odessa Turner	.05	.04	.02
321	Erik Howard	.05	.04	.02
322	Mark Collins	.05	.04	.02
323	Dave Meggett	.15	.11	.06
324	Leonard Marshall	.05	.04	.02
325	Carl Banks	.10	.08	.04
326	Anthony Toney	.05	.04	.02
327	Seth Joyner	.15	.11	.06
328	Cris Carter	.20	.15	.08
329	Eric Allen	.05	.04	.02
330	Keith Jackson	.20	.15	.08
331	Clyde Simmons	.10	.08	.04
332	Byron Evans	.05	.04	.02
333	Keith Byars	.10	.08	.04
334	**Eagles Crest**	.05	.04	.02
335	Reggie White	.25	.20	.10
336	Izel Jenkins	.05	.04	.02
337	Jerome Brown	.15	.11	.06
338	David Alexander	.05	.04	.02
339	**Cardinals Crest**	.05	.04	.02
340	Rich Camarillo	.05	.04	.02
341	Ken Harvey	.05	.04	.02
342	Luis Sharpe	.05	.04	.02
343	Timm Rosenbach	.10	.08	.04
344	Tim McDonald	.15	.11	.06
345	Vai Sikahema	.05	.04	.02
346	Freddie Joe Nunn	.05	.04	.02
347	Ernie Jones	.05	.04	.02
348	J.T. Smith	.10	.08	.04
349	Eric Hill	.05	.04	.02
350	Roy Green	.10	.08	.04
351	Anthony Bell	.05	.04	.02
352	Kevin Fagan	.05	.04	.02
353	Roger Craig	.15	.11	.06
354	Ronnie Lott	.20	.15	.08
355	Mike Cofer	.05	.04	.02
356	John Taylor	.20	.15	.08
357	Joe Montana	3.00	2.25	1.25
358	Charles Haley	.10	.08	.04
359	Guy McIntyre	.05	.04	.02
360	**49ers Crest**	.05	.04	.02
361	Pierce Holt	.15	.11	.06
362	Tom Rathman	.15	.11	.06
363	Jerry Rice	1.50	1.25	.60
364	Michael Carter	.10	.08	.04
365	**Buccaneers Crest**	.05	.04	.02
366	Lars Tate	.05	.04	.02
367	Paul Gruber	.10	.08	.04
368	Winston Moss	.05	.04	.02
369	Reuben Davis	.05	.04	.02
370	Mark Robinson	.05	.04	.02
371	Bruce Hill	.05	.04	.02
372	Kevin Murphy	.05	.04	.02
373	Ricky Reynolds	.05	.04	.02
374	Harry Hamilton	.05	.04	.02
375	Vinny Testaverde	.15	.11	.06
376	Mark Carrier	.15	.11	.06
377	Ervin Randle	.05	.04	.02
378	Ricky Sanders	.10	.08	.04
379	Charles Mann	.10	.08	.04
380	Jim Lachey	.10	.08	.04
381	Wilber Marshall	.10	.08	.04
382	A.J. Johnson	.05	.04	.02
383	Darrell Green	.10	.08	.04

384	Mark Rypien	.15	.11	.06
385	Gerald Riggs	.10	.08	.04
386	**Redskins Crest**	.05	.04	.02
387	Alvin Walton	.05	.04	.02
388	Art Monk	.15	.11	.06
389	Gary Clark	.15	.11	.06
390	Earnest Byner	.10	.08	.04
391	**SB XXIV Action** (Jerry Rice)	.75	.60	.30
392	**SB XXIV Action** (49er Offensive Line)	.15	.11	.06
393	**SB XXIV Action** (Tom Rathman)	.25	.20	.10
394	**SB XXIV Action** (Chet Brooks)	.10	.08	.04
395	**SB XXIV Action** (John Elway)	1.00	.70	.40
396	**SB XXIV Action** (Joe Montana)	3.00	2.25	1.25
----	**Panini Album**	2.00	1.50	.80

1974 Parker Brothers Pro Draft

These 50 cards were included inside a Parker Brothers board game called Pro Draft. The cards, featuring only offensive players, were produced by Topps and use the identical design as the 1974 Topps set. However, some differences can be noted on certain cards. Some of the game cards have 1972 statistics on the card backs, and others have different player poses on the front (#s 23, 49, 116, 124, 126 and 127). Players with an * have 1972 statistics. Card numbers in this set are identical to the card numbers the players have in the regular 1974 Topps set.

		NM	E	VG
	Complete Set (50):	75.00	37.00	22.00
	Common Player:	1.25	.60	.40
4	Ken Bowman	1.25	.60	.40
6	Jerry Smith	3.00	1.50	.90
7	Ed Podolak	2.50	1.25	.70
9	Pat Matson	1.25	.60	.40
11	Frank Pitts	2.00	1.00	.60
15	Winston Hill	1.25	.60	.40
18	Rich Coady	2.00	1.00	.60
19	Ken Willard	3.75	2.00	1.25
21	Ben Hawkins	2.00	1.00	.60
23	Norm Snead (vertical pose)	10.00	5.00	3.00
24	Jim Yarborough	2.00	1.00	.60
28	Bob Hayes	5.00	2.50	1.50
32	Dan Dierdorf	8.00	4.00	2.50
35	Essex Johnson	2.00	1.00	.60
39	Mike Siani	1.25	.60	.40
42	Del Williams	1.25	.60	.40
43	Don McCauley	2.00	1.00	.60
44	Randy Jackson	2.00	1.00	.60
46	Gene Washington	3.50	1.75	1.00
49	Bob Windsor (vertical pose)	6.00	3.00	1.75
50	John Hadl	4.00	2.00	1.25
52	Steve Owens	4.00	2.00	1.25
54	Rayfield Wright	2.00	1.00	.60
57	Milt Sunde	2.00	1.00	.60
58	Bill Kilmer	5.50	2.75	1.75
61	Rufus Mayes	2.00	1.00	.60
63	Gene Washington	2.50	1.25	.70
65	Eugene Upshaw	4.50	2.25	1.25
75	Fred Willis	2.00	1.00	.60
77	Tom Neville	1.25	.60	.40
78	Ted Kwalick	3.00	1.50	.90
80	John Niland	2.00	1.00	.60
81	Ted Fritsch Jr.	1.25	.60	.40
83	Jack Snow	3.00	1.50	.90
87	Mike Phipps	3.00	1.50	.90
90	MacArthur Lane	3.00	1.50	.90
95	Calvin Hill	3.50	1.75	1.00
98	Len Rohde	1.25	.60	.40
101	Gary Garrison	2.50	1.25	.70
103	Len St. Jean	1.25	.60	.40
107	Jim Mitchell	2.00	1.00	.60
109	Harry Schuh	1.25	.60	.40
110	Greg Pruitt	5.00	2.50	1.50
111	Ed Flanagan	1.25	.60	.40
113	Chuck Foreman	6.00	3.00	1.75
116	Charlie Johnson (vertical pose)	8.00	4.00	2.50
119	Roy Jefferson	4.00	2.00	1.25
124	Forrest Blue (not All-Pro on card)	6.00	3.00	1.75
126	Tom Mack (not All-Pro on card)	8.00	4.00	2.50
127	Bob Tucker (not All-Pro on card)	6.00	3.00	1.75

1989 Parker Brothers Talking Football

Licensed by the NFL Players Association, the 34-card set features a "Superstar Lineup Talking Football" logo in the upper left. Up to three player photos can appear on the front of the card. The NFLPA logo also appears on the front of the card. The backs of the cards, which are unnumbered, include the name of player(s), bio and highlights. The bottom right of the card back carries a Parker Brothers copyright.

		NM/M	NM	E
	Complete Set (34):	90.00	67.00	36.00
	Common Player:	2.00	1.50	.80
1	**AFC Team Roster**	2.00	1.50	.80
2	Marcus Allen	5.00	3.75	2.00
3	Cornelius Bennett, John Offerdahl	3.00	2.25	1.25
4	Keith Bishop, Mike Munchak	2.00	1.50	.80
5	Keith Bostic, Deron Cherry, Hanford Dixon	2.00	1.50	.80
6	Carlos Carson, Stanley Morgan	2.00	1.50	.80
7	Todd Christensen, Mickey Shuler	2.50	2.00	1.00
8	Eric Dickerson	4.00	3.00	1.50
9	Ray Donaldson, Irving Fryar	2.00	1.50	.80
10	Jacob Green, Bruce Smith	2.00	1.50	.80
11	Mark Haynes, Frank Minnifield, Dennis Smith	2.00	1.50	.80
12	Chris Hinton, Anthony Munoz	2.50	2.00	1.00
13	Steve Largent, Al Toon	5.00	3.75	2.00
14	Howie Long, Bill Maas	3.00	2.25	1.25
15	Nick Lowery, Reggie Roby	2.00	1.50	.80
16	Dan Marino	25.00	18.50	10.00
17	Karl Mecklenburg, Andre Tippett	2.50	2.00	1.00
18	**NFC Team Roster**	2.00	1.50	.80
19	Morten Andersen, Jim Arnold	2.00	1.50	.80
20	Carl Banks, Mike Singletary	3.00	2.25	1.25
21	Mark Bavaro, Doug Cosbie	2.50	2.00	1.00
22	Joey Browner, Darrell Green, Leonard Smith	2.00	1.50	.80
23	Anthony Carter, Jerry Rice	12.00	9.00	4.75
24	Gary Clark, Mike Quick	4.00	3.00	1.50
25	Richard Dent, Chris Doleman	3.00	2.25	1.25
26	Brad Edelman, Bill Fralic	2.00	1.50	.80
27	Carl Ekern, Rickey Jackson	2.00	1.50	.80
28	Jerry Gray, LeRoy Irvin, Ronnie Lott	2.50	2.00	1.00
29	Mel Gray, Jay Hilgenberg	3.00	2.25	1.25
30	Dexter Manley, Reggie White	2.50	2.00	1.00
31	Rueben Mayes	2.00	1.50	.80
32	Joe Montana	20.00	15.00	8.00
33	Jackie Slater, Gary Zimmerman	2.00	1.50	.80
34	Herschel Walker	3.00	2.25	1.25

1952 Parkhurst CFL

		NM	E	VG
	Complete Set (100):	3,000	1,500	900.00
	Common Player (1-19):	20.00	10.00	6.00
	Common Player (20-100):	30.00	15.00	9.00
1	**Watch The Games**	50.00	25.00	15.00
2	**Teamwork**	20.00	10.00	6.00
3	**Football Equipment**	20.00	10.00	6.00
4	**Hang Onto The Ball**	20.00	10.00	6.00
5	**The Head On Tackle**	20.00	10.00	6.00
6	**The Football Field**	20.00	10.00	6.00
7	**The Lineman's Stance**	20.00	10.00	6.00
8	**Centre's Spiral Pass**	20.00	10.00	6.00
9	**The Lineman**	20.00	10.00	6.00
10	**The Place Kick**	20.00	10.00	6.00
11	**The Cross-Body Block**	20.00	10.00	6.00
12	**T Formation**	20.00	10.00	6.00
13	**Falling On The Ball**	20.00	10.00	6.00
14	**The Throw**	20.00	10.00	6.00
15	**Breaking From Tackle**	20.00	10.00	6.00
16	**How To Catch A Pass**	20.00	10.00	6.00
17	**The Punt**	20.00	10.00	6.00
18	**Shifting The Ball**	20.00	10.00	6.00
19	**Penalty Signals**	20.00	10.00	6.00
20	Leslie Ascott	30.00	15.00	9.00
21	Robert Marshall	30.00	15.00	9.00
22	Tom Harpley	30.00	15.00	9.00
23	Robert McClelland	30.00	15.00	9.00

24	Rod Smylie	30.00	15.00	9.00
25	Bill Bass	30.00	15.00	9.00
26	Fred Black	30.00	15.00	9.00
27	Jack Carpenter	30.00	15.00	9.00
28	Bob Hack	30.00	15.00	9.00
29	Ulysses Curtis	30.00	15.00	9.00
30	Nobby Wirkowski	50.00	25.00	15.00
31	George Arnett	30.00	15.00	9.00
32	Lorne Parkin	30.00	15.00	9.00
33	Alex Toogood	30.00	15.00	9.00
34	Marshall Haymes	30.00	15.00	9.00
35	Shanty McKenzie	30.00	15.00	9.00
36	Byron Karrys	30.00	15.00	9.00
37	George Rooks	30.00	15.00	9.00
38	Red Ettinger	30.00	15.00	9.00
39	Al Bruno	40.00	20.00	12.00
40	Stephen Karrys	30.00	15.00	9.00
41	Herb Trawick	50.00	25.00	15.00
42	Sam Etcheverry	350.00	175.00	105.00
43	Marv Melrowitz	30.00	15.00	9.00
44	John Red O'Quinn	50.00	25.00	15.00
45	Jim Ostendarp	30.00	15.00	9.00
46	Tom Tofaute	30.00	15.00	9.00
47	Joey Pal	30.00	15.00	9.00
48	Ray Cicia	30.00	15.00	9.00
49	Bruce Coulter	35.00	17.50	10.50
50	Jim Mitchener	30.00	15.00	9.00
51	Lally Lalonde	30.00	15.00	9.00
52	Jim Staton	30.00	15.00	9.00
53	Glenn Douglas	30.00	15.00	9.00
54	Dave Tomlinson	30.00	15.00	9.00
55	Ed Salem	30.00	15.00	9.00
56	Virgil Wagner	50.00	25.00	15.00
57	Dawson Tilley	30.00	15.00	9.00
58A	Cec Findlay	40.00	20.00	12.00
58B	Tommy Manastersky	40.00	20.00	12.00
59	Frank Nable	30.00	15.00	9.00
60	Chuck Anderson	30.00	15.00	9.00
61	Charlie Hubbard	30.00	15.00	9.00
63	Benny MacDonnell	30.00	15.00	9.00
64	Peter Karpuk	30.00	15.00	9.00
65	Tom O'Malley	30.00	15.00	9.00
66	Bill Stanton	30.00	15.00	9.00
67	Matt Anthony	30.00	15.00	9.00
68	John Morneau	30.00	15.00	9.00
69	Howie Turner	30.00	15.00	9.00
70	Alton Baldwin	30.00	15.00	9.00
71	John Bovey	30.00	15.00	9.00
72	Bruno Bitkowski	35.00	17.50	10.50
73	Gene Roberts	30.00	15.00	9.00
74	John Wagoner	30.00	15.00	9.00
75	Ted MacLarty	30.00	15.00	9.00
76	Jerry Lefebvre	30.00	15.00	9.00
77	Buck Rogers	30.00	15.00	9.00
78	Bruce Cummings	30.00	15.00	9.00
79	Hal Wagner	40.00	20.00	12.00
80	Joe Shinn	30.00	15.00	9.00
81	Eddie Bevan	30.00	15.00	9.00
82	Ralph Sazio	50.00	25.00	15.00
83	Bob McDonald	30.00	15.00	9.00
84	Vince Scott	40.00	20.00	12.00
85	Jack Stewart	30.00	15.00	9.00
86	Ralph Bartolini	30.00	15.00	9.00
87	Blake Taylor	30.00	15.00	9.00
88	Richard Brown	30.00	15.00	9.00
89	Douglas Gray	30.00	15.00	9.00
90	Alex Muzyka	30.00	15.00	9.00
91	Pete Neumann	50.00	25.00	15.00
92	Jack Rogers	30.00	15.00	9.00
93	Bernie Custis	40.00	20.00	12.00
94	Cam Fraser	30.00	15.00	9.00
95	Vince Mazza	40.00	20.00	12.00
96	Peter Wooley	30.00	15.00	9.00
97	Earl Valiquette	30.00	15.00	9.00
98	Floyd Cooper	30.00	15.00	9.00
99	Louis DiFrancisco	30.00	15.00	9.00
100	Robert Simpson	125.00	62.00	37.00

1956 Parkhurst CFL

		NM	E	VG
	Complete Set (50):	3,500	1,750	1,050
	Common Player:	40.00	20.00	12.00
1	Art Walker	80.00	40.00	24.00
2	Frank Anderson	40.00	20.00	12.00
3	Normie Kwong	150.00	75.00	45.00
4	Johnny Bright	150.00	75.00	45.00
5	Jackie Parker	500.00	250.00	150.00
6	Bob Dean	40.00	20.00	12.00
7	Don Getty	125.00	62.00	37.00
8	Rollie Miles	100.00	50.00	30.00
9	Ted Tully	40.00	20.00	12.00
10	Frank Morris	90.00	45.00	27.00
11	Martin Ruby	80.00	40.00	24.00
12	Mel Beckett	80.00	40.00	24.00
13	Bill Clarke	40.00	20.00	12.00
14	John Wozniak	40.00	20.00	12.00
15	Larry Isbell	40.00	20.00	12.00

16	Ken Carpenter	80.00	40.00	24.00
17	Sully Glasser	40.00	20.00	12.00
18	Bobby Marlow	90.00	45.00	27.00
19	Paul Anderson	40.00	20.00	12.00
20	Gord Sturtridge	80.00	40.00	24.00
21	Alex Macklin	40.00	20.00	12.00
22	Duke Cook	40.00	20.00	12.00
23	Bill Stevenson	40.00	20.00	12.00
24	Lynn Bottoms	80.00	40.00	24.00
25	Aramis Dandoy	40.00	20.00	12.00
26	Peter Muir	40.00	20.00	12.00
27	Harvey Wylie	80.00	40.00	24.00
28	Joe Yamauchi	40.00	20.00	12.00
29	John Alderton	40.00	20.00	12.00
30	Bill McKenna	40.00	20.00	12.00
31	Edward Kotowich	40.00	20.00	12.00
32	Herb Gray	100.00	50.00	30.00
33	Calvin Jones	100.00	50.00	30.00
34	Herman Day	40.00	20.00	12.00
35	Buddy Leake	40.00	20.00	12.00
36	Robert McNamara	40.00	20.00	12.00
37	Bud Grant	300.00	150.00	90.00
38	Gord Rowland	80.00	40.00	24.00
39	Glen McWhinney	40.00	20.00	12.00
40	Lorne Benson	40.00	20.00	12.00
41	Sam Etcheverry	300.00	150.00	90.00
42	Joey Pal	40.00	20.00	12.00
43	Tom Hugo	40.00	20.00	12.00
44	Tex Coulter	80.00	40.00	24.00
45	Doug McNichol	40.00	20.00	12.00
46	Tom Moran	40.00	20.00	12.00
47	Red O'Quinn	80.00	40.00	24.00
48	Hal Patterson	200.00	100.00	60.00
49	Jacques Belec	40.00	20.00	12.00
50	Pat Abruzzi	100.00	50.00	30.00

1988 Patriots Holsum

Available only in specially marked packages of Holsum Bread, the 12 standard-sized cards feature the Holsum logo in the upper left, with "1988 Annual Collectors' Edition" printed in the upper right. The player photo dominates the front, while the player's name and team are located inside a box beneath the photo. The card backs include the player's facsimile autograph, jersey number, bio and card number "of 12" printed at the top. The remainder of the card back is filled with stats and various logos.

		NM/M	NM	E
Complete Set (12):		40.00	30.00	16.00
Common Player:		4.00	3.00	1.50
1	Andre Tippett	4.00	3.00	1.50
2	Stanley Morgan	6.00	4.50	2.50
3	Steve Grogan	6.00	4.50	2.50
4	Ronnie Lippett	4.00	3.00	1.50
5	Kenneth Sims	4.00	3.00	1.50
6	Pete Brock	4.00	3.00	1.50
7	Sean Farrell	4.00	3.00	1.50
8	Garin Veris	4.00	3.00	1.50
9	Mosi Tatupu	4.00	3.00	1.50
10	Raymond Clayborn	5.00	3.75	2.00
11	Tony Franklin	4.00	3.00	1.50
12	Reggie Dupard	4.00	3.00	1.50

1988 Penn State Police

JOE PATERNO
Head Football Coach

		NM/M	NM	E
Complete Set (12):		25.00	18.50	10.00
Common Player:		1.25	.90	.50
5	Michael Timpson	4.00	3.00	1.50
20	John Greene	1.25	.90	.50
28	Brian Chizmar	1.25	.90	.50
31	Andre Collins	4.00	3.00	1.50
32	Blair Thomas	4.00	3.00	1.50
39	Eddie Johnson	1.25	.90	.50
66	Steve Wisniewski	4.00	3.00	1.50
75	Rich Schonewolf	1.25	.90	.50
78	Roger Duffy	1.25	.90	.50
84	Keith Karpinski	1.25	.90	.50
NNO	Joe Paterno (CO)	5.00	3.75	2.00
NNO	**Penn State Mascot - The Nittany Lion**	1.50	1.25	.60

1989 Penn State Police

		NM/M	NM	E
Complete Set (15):		20.00	15.00	8.00
Common Player:		1.00	.70	.40
1	Brian Chizmar	1.00	.70	.40
2	Andre Collins	2.50	2.00	1.00
3	David Daniels	2.50	2.00	1.00
4	Roger Duffy	1.00	.70	.40
5	Tim Freeman	1.00	.70	.40
6	Scott Gob	1.00	.70	.40
7	David Jakob	1.00	.70	.40
8	Geoff Japchen	1.00	.70	.40
9	Joe Paterno (CO)	4.00	3.00	1.50
10	Sherrod Rainge	1.00	.70	.40
11	Rich Schonewolf	1.00	.70	.40
12	Dave Szott	2.50	2.00	1.00
13	Blair Thomas	2.50	2.00	1.00
14	Leroy Thompson	4.00	3.00	1.50
15	**Nittany Lion** (Mascot)	1.00	.70	.40

1990 Penn State Police

		NM/M	NM	E
Complete Set (16):		15.00	11.00	6.00
Common Player:		.75	.60	.30
1	Gerry Collins	.75	.60	.30
2	David Daniels	1.25	.90	.50
3	Jim Deter	.75	.60	.30
4	Mark D'Onofrio	1.25	.90	.50
5	Sam Gash	2.00	1.50	.80
6	Frank Giannetti	.75	.60	.30
7	Keith Goganious	1.25	.90	.50
8	Doug Helkowski	.75	.60	.30
9	Hernon Henderson	.75	.60	.30
10	Matt McCartin	.75	.60	.30
11	Joe Paterno (CO)	3.00	2.25	1.25
12	Darren Perry	2.00	1.50	.80
13	Tony Sacca	2.00	1.50	.80
14	Terry Smith	.75	.60	.30
15	Willie Thomas	.75	.60	.30
16	Leroy Thompson	2.50	2.00	1.00

1991-92 Penn State Legends

		NM/M	NM	E
Complete Set (51):		15.00	11.00	6.00
Common Player:		.35	.25	.14
1	Joe Paterno (CO)	2.00	1.50	.80
2	Kurt Allerman	.35	.25	.14
3	Chris Bahr	.50	.40	.20
4	Matt Bahr	.35	.25	.14
5	Bruce Bannon	.35	.25	.14
6	Greg Buttle	.50	.40	.20
7	John Capelletti	.75	.60	.30
8	Bruce Clark	.35	.25	.14
9	Andre Collins	.75	.60	.30
10	Shane Conlan	.75	.60	.30
11	Chris Conlin	.35	.25	.14
12	Randy Crowder	.35	.25	.14
13	Keith Dorney	.50	.40	.20
14	D.J. Dozier	.75	.60	.30
15	Bill Dugan	.35	.25	.14
16	Chuck Fusina	.50	.40	.20
17	Leon Gajecki	.35	.25	.14
18	Jack Ham	1.25	.90	.50
19	Bob Higgins	.35	.25	.14
20	John Hufnagel	.75	.60	.30
21	Kenny Jackson	.50	.40	.20
22	Tim Johnson	.35	.25	.14
23	Dave Joyner	.35	.25	.14
24	Roger Kochman	.35	.25	.14
25	Ted Kwalick	.50	.40	.20
26	Richie Lucas	.75	.60	.30
27	Matt Millen	.75	.60	.30
28	Lydell Mitchell	.75	.60	.30
29	Bob Mitinger	.35	.25	.14
30	John Nessel	.35	.25	.14
31	Ed O'Neil	.50	.40	.20
32	Dennis Onkotz	.35	.25	.14
33	Darren Perry	.50	.40	.20
34	Charlie Pittman	.50	.40	.20
35A	Tom Rafferty (ERR) (Photo actually T. Quinn)	5.00	3.75	2.00
35B	Tom Rafferty (COR)	1.25	.90	.50
36	Mike Reid (UER) (Reversed negative)	1.25	.90	.50
37	Glenn Ressler	.50	.40	.20
38	Dave Robinson	.50	.40	.20
39	Mark Robinson	.35	.25	.14
40	Randy Sidler	.35	.25	.14
41	John Skorupan	.50	.40	.20
42	Neal Smith	.35	.25	.14
43	Steve Suhey	.50	.40	.20
44	Sam Tamburo	.35	.25	.14
45	Blair Thomas	1.25	.90	.50
46	Curt Warner	1.50	1.25	.60
47	Steve Wisniewski	.75	.60	.30
48	Charlie Zapiec	.35	.25	.14
49	Michael Zordich	.50	.40	.20
50	Harry Wilson, Joe Bedenk	.35	.25	.14
P1	Joe Paterno (CO) (Promo)	4.00	3.00	1.50
P10	Shane Conlan (Promo)	2.00	1.50	.80
P18	Jack Ham (Promo)	2.50	2.00	1.00
NNO	**Checklist Card**	.35	.25	.14

1991 Pennsylvania HS Big 33

		NM/M	NM	E
Complete Set (36):		35.00	26.00	14.00
Common Player:		.50	.40	.20
PA1	Dietrich Jells	2.00	1.50	.80
PA2	Mike Archie	3.00	2.25	1.25
PA3	Tony Miller	.50	.40	.20
PA4	Edmund Robinson	.50	.40	.20
PA5	Brian Miller	.75	.60	.30
PA6	Marvin Harrison	5.00	3.75	2.00
PA7	Mike Cawley	.50	.40	.20
PA8	Thomas Marchese	.50	.40	.20
PA9	Scott Milanovich	2.00	1.50	.80
PA10	Shawn Wooden	1.00	.70	.40
PA11	Curtis Martin	12.00	9.00	4.75
PA12	William Khayat	.50	.40	.20
PA13	Jermell Fleming	.50	.40	.20
PA14	Ray Zellars	4.00	3.00	1.50
PA15	Jon Witman	.75	.60	.30
PA16	Chris McCartney	.50	.40	.20
PA17	David Rebar	.50	.40	.20
PA18	Mark Zataveski	.75	.60	.30
PA19	Todd Atkins	.75	.60	.30
PA20	Shannon Stevens	.50	.40	.20
PA21	Keith Conlin	.75	.60	.30
PA22	John Bowman	.50	.40	.20
PA23	Maurice Lawrence	.50	.40	.20
PA24	Mike Halapin	.50	.40	.20
PA25	Steve Keim	.50	.40	.20
PA26	Dennis Martin	.50	.40	.20
PA27	Keith Morris	.50	.40	.20
PA28	Chris Villarrial	.50	.40	.20
PA29	Thomas Tumulty	.50	.40	.20
PA30	Jason Augustino	.50	.40	.20
PA31	Gregory Delong	.50	.40	.20
PA32	James Moore	.50	.40	.20
PA33	Eric Clair	.75	.60	.30
PA34	Tyler Young	.50	.40	.20
PA35	Jeffrey Sauve	.50	.40	.20
PA36	Terry Hammons	.50	.40	.20

1976 Pepsi Discs

This set was regionally produced in the Cincinnati area; hence the majority of the discs feature members of the Cincinnati Bengals (#s 21-40). The remaining discs feature top NFL stars. The cards are valued with the tab intact; this is how they are commonly found. The tab was used to hang the disc from a bottle included in six packs of Pepsi products. Each disc is 3-1/2" in diameter and features a player photo, biographical information and 1975 statistics on the front. Discs 1, 5, 7, 8 and 14 are reportedly scarcer than the others because they were short-printed. A free, personalized T-shirt was also offered to those who sent in 200 capliners which read "Pepsi Players." The shirt would picture either Ken Anderson or Archie Griffin, with the collector's first name. It would say "To my buddy xxxx, Best Wishes, Ken Anderson."

		NM	E	VG
Complete Set (40):		90.00	45.00	27.00
Common Player:		.50	.25	.15
1	Steve Bartkowski	22.00	11.00	6.50
2	Lydell Mitchell	1.50	.70	.45
3	Wally Chambers	.50	.25	.15
4	Doug Buffone	.50	.25	.15
5	Jerry Sherk	22.00	11.00	6.50
6	Drew Pearson	1.00	.50	.30
7	Otis Armstrong	22.00	11.00	6.50
8	Charlie Sanders	20.00	10.00	6.00
9	John Brockington	.75	.40	.25
10	Curley Culp	.75	.40	.25
11	Jan Stenerud	1.50	.70	.45
12	Lawrence McCutcheon	.75	.40	.25
13	Chuck Foreman	1.00	.50	.30
14	Bob Pollard	20.00	10.00	6.00
15	Ed Marinaro	12.00	6.00	3.50
16	Jack Lambert	5.00	2.50	1.50
17	Terry Metcalf	.75	.40	.25
18	Mel Gray	.75	.40	.25
19	Russ Washington	.50	.25	.15
20	Charley Taylor	2.50	1.25	.70
21	Ken Anderson	2.50	1.25	.70
22	Bob Brown	.50	.25	.15
23	Ron Carpenter	.50	.25	.15
24	Tom Casanova	1.25	.60	.40
25	Boobie Clark	1.00	.50	.30

		NM	E	VG
26	Isaac Curtis	1.00	.50	.30
27	Lenvil Elliott	.50	.25	.15
28	Stan Fritts	.50	.25	.15
29	Vernon Holland	.50	.25	.15
30	Bob Johnson	1.00	.50	.30
31	Ken Johnson	.50	.25	.15
32	Bill Kollar	.50	.25	.15
33	Jim LeClair	.75	.40	.25
34	Chip Myers	.50	.25	.15
35	Lemar Parrish	.75	.40	.25
36	Rob Pritchard	.50	.25	.15
37	Bob Trumpy	1.50	.70	.45
38	Sherman White	.50	.25	.15
39	Archie Griffin	1.50	.70	.45
40	John Shinners	.50	.25	.15

1964 Philadelphia

MERLIN OLSEN
LOS ANGELES RAMS   TACKLE

This was Philly's first of four straight 198-card sets, and Philly covered the NFL players while Topps, possibly unable to reach an agreement with the NFL, showcased only American Football League players. For the first time, a card with a team play and a black-and-white photo of the coach was included in a football card set. As would be the case throughout the Philly run, cards are numbered alphabetically by player's last name and by city name. Two checklists appear at the end of each of the four Philly sets. Rookies in this set include John Mackey, Tom Matte, Jack Pardee, Mick Tingelhoff, Irv Cross, and Hall of Famers Herb Adderly, Willie Davis and Merlin Olsen. Making their debut on cards on coaches' issues were Don Shula, Vince Lombardi and Allie Sherman. Second-year cards in the set include Bob Lilly and Jim Marshall. This set held the final regular-issue cards of Gino Marchetti, Night Train Lane, Joe Schmidt, Jerry Kramer, Frank Gifford, Y.A. Tittle, and Bob St. Clair. One error does exist in the set -- card #169 does not picture Garland Boyette as advertised, it's unclear who the player actually is.

	NM	E	VG
Complete Set (198):	1,400	700.00	425.00
Common Player:	7.00	3.50	2.10
Minor Stars:	2.50		
Unlisted Stars:	4.00		
Wax Pack (5):	190.00		

		NM	E	VG
1	Raymond Berry	25.00	13.00	8.00
2	Tom Gilburg	7.00	3.50	2.10
3	John Mackey RC	40.00	20.00	12.00
4	Gino Marchetti	10.00	5.00	3.00
5	Jim Martin	7.00	3.50	2.10
6	Tom Matte RC	10.00	5.00	3.00
7	Jimmy Orr	7.00	3.50	2.10
8	Jim Parker	10.00	5.00	3.00
9	Bill Pellington	7.00	3.50	2.10
10	Alex Sandusky	7.00	3.50	2.10
11	Dick Szymanski	7.00	3.50	2.10
12	Johnny Unitas	40.00	20.00	12.00
13	**Baltimore Colts Team**	7.00	3.50	2.10
14	Don Shula	20.00	10.00	6.00
15	Doug Atkins	10.00	5.00	3.00
16	Ron Bull	7.00	3.50	2.10
17	Mike Ditka	35.00	18.00	11.00
18	Joe Fortunato	7.00	3.50	2.10
19	Willie Galimore	7.00	3.50	2.10
20	Joe Marconi	7.00	3.50	2.10
21	Bennie McRae RC	7.00	3.50	2.10
22	Johnny Morris	7.00	3.50	2.10
23	Richie Petitbon RC	7.00	3.50	2.10
24	Mike Pyle	7.00	3.50	2.10
25	Roosevelt Taylor RC	10.00	5.00	3.00
26	Bill Wade	7.00	3.50	2.10
27	**Chicago Bears Team**	7.00	3.50	2.10
28	George Halas	15.00	7.50	4.50
29	Johnny Brewer	7.00	3.50	2.10
30	Jim Brown	90.00	45.00	27.00
31	Gary Collins RC	15.00	7.50	4.50
32	Vince Costello	7.00	3.50	2.10
33	Galen Fiss	7.00	3.50	2.10
34	Bill Glass	7.00	3.50	2.10

		NM	E	VG
35	Ernie Green RC	7.00	3.50	2.10
36	Rich Kreitling	7.00	3.50	2.10
37	John Morrow	7.00	3.50	2.10
38	Frank Ryan	7.00	3.50	2.10
39	Charlie Scales RC	7.00	3.50	2.10
40	Dick Schafrath RC	7.00	3.50	2.10
41	**Cleveland Browns Team**	7.00	3.50	2.10
42	Cleveland Browns Play of the Year(Blanton Collier)	7.00	3.50	2.10
43	Don Bishop	7.00	3.50	2.10
44	Frank Clarke RC	7.00	3.50	2.10
45	Mike Connelly	7.00	3.50	2.10
46	Lee Folkins	7.00	3.50	2.10
47	Cornell Green RC	15.00	7.50	4.50
48	Bob Lilly	40.00	20.00	12.00
49	Amos Marsh	7.00	3.50	2.10
50	Tommy McDonald	10.00	5.00	3.00
51	Don Meredith	35.00	17.50	10.50
52	Pettis Norman RC	700	3.50	2.10
53	Don Perkins	10.00	5.00	3.00
54	Guy Reese	7.00	3.50	2.10
55	**Dallas Cowboys Team**	7.00	3.50	2.10
56	Tom Landry	30.00	15.00	9.00
57	Terry Barr	7.00	3.50	2.10
58	Roger Brown	7.00	3.50	2.10
59	Gail Cogdill	7.00	3.50	2.10
60	John Gordy	7.00	3.50	2.10
61	Dick "Night Train" Lane	10.00	5.00	3.00
62	Yale Lary	10.00	5.00	3.00
63	Dan Lewis	7.00	3.50	2.10
64	Darris McCord	7.00	3.50	2.10
65	Earl Morrall	7.00	3.50	2.10
66	Joe Schmidt	10.00	5.00	3.00
67	Pat Studstill RC	7.00	3.50	2.10
68	Wayne Walker RC	7.00	3.50	2.10
69	**Detroit Lions Team**	7.00	3.50	2.10
70	Detroit Lions Player of the Year(George Wilson)	7.00	3.50	2.10
71	Herb Adderley RC	40.00	20.00	12.00
72	Willie Davis RC	40.00	20.00	12.00
73	Forrest Gregg	10.00	5.00	3.00
74	Paul Hornung	35.00	18.00	11.00
75	Henry Jordan	10.00	5.00	3.00
76	Jerry Kramer	10.00	5.00	3.00
77	Tom Moore	7.00	3.50	2.10
78	Jim Ringo	10.00	5.00	3.00
79	Bart Starr	45.00	23.00	14.00
80	Jim Taylor	30.00	15.00	9.00
81	Jess Whittenton RC	7.00	3.50	2.10
82	Willie Wood	15.00	7.50	4.50
83	**Green Bay Packers Team**	15.00	7.50	4.50
84	Vince Lombardi	35.00	18.00	11.00
85	Jon Arnett	7.00	3.50	2.10
86	Pervis Atkins RC	7.00	3.50	2.10
87	Dick Bass	7.00	3.50	2.10
88	Carroll Dale	10.00	5.00	3.00
89	Roman Gabriel	10.00	5.00	3.00
90	Ed Meador	7.00	3.50	2.10
91	Merlin Olsen RC	50.00	25.00	15.00
92	Jack Pardee RC	10.00	5.00	3.00
93	Jim Phillips	7.00	3.50	2.10
94	Carver Shannon	7.00	3.50	2.10
95	Frank Varrichione	7.00	3.50	2.10
96	Danny Villanueva	7.00	3.50	2.10
97	**Los Angeles Rams team**	7.00	3.50	2.10
98	Los Angeles Rams Play of the Year(Harland Svare)	7.00	3.50	2.10
99	Grady Alderman RC	7.00	3.50	2.10
100	Larry Bowie	7.00	3.50	2.10
101	Bill Brown RC	10.00	5.00	3.00
102	Paul Flatley RC	7.00	3.50	2.10
103	Rip Hawkins	7.00	3.50	2.10
104	Jim Marshall	15.00	7.50	4.50
105	Tommy Mason	7.00	3.50	2.10
106	Jim Prestel	7.00	3.50	2.10
107	Jerry Reichow	7.00	3.50	2.10
108	Ed Sharockman	7.00	3.50	2.10
109	Fran Tarkenton	50.00	30.00	18.00
110	Mick Tingelhoff RC	10.00	5.00	3.00
111	**Minnesota Vikings Team**	7.00	3.50	2.10
112	Norm Van Brocklin	10.00	5.00	3.00
113	Erich Barnes	7.00	3.50	2.10
114	Roosevelt Brown	10.00	5.00	3.00
115	Don Chandler	7.00	3.50	2.10
116	Darrell Dess	7.00	3.50	2.10
117	Frank Gifford	35.00	18.00	11.00
118	Dick James	7.00	3.50	2.10
119	Jim Katcavage	7.00	3.50	2.10
120	John Lovetere	7.00	3.50	2.10
121	Dick Lynch RC	7.00	3.50	2.10

		NM	E	VG
122	Jim Patton	7.00	3.50	2.10
123	Del Shofner	7.00	3.50	2.10
124	Y.A. Tittle	30.00	15.00	9.00
125	**New York Giants Team**	7.00	3.50	2.10
126	Player of the year(Allie Sherman)	7.00	3.50	2.10
127	Sam Baker	7.00	3.50	2.10
128	Maxie Baughan	7.00	3.50	2.10
129	Timmy Brown	7.00	3.50	2.10
130	Mike Clark	7.00	3.50	2.10
131	Irv Cross RC	7.00	3.50	2.10
132	Ted Dean	7.00	3.50	2.10
133	Ron Goodwin	7.00	3.50	2.10
134	King Hill	7.00	3.50	2.10
135	Clarence Peaks	7.00	3.50	2.10
136	Pete Retzlaff	7.00	3.50	2.10
137	Jim Schrader	7.00	3.50	2.10
138	Norm Snead	7.00	3.50	2.10
139	**Philadelphia Eagles Team**	7.00	3.50	2.10
140	Philadelphia Eagles Play of the Year (Joe Kuharich)	7.00	3.50	2.10
141	Gary Ballman RC	7.00	3.50	2.10
142	Charley Bradshaw	7.00	3.50	2.10
143	Ed Brown	7.00	3.50	2.10
144	John Henry Johnson	10.00	5.00	3.00
145	Joe Krupa	7.00	3.50	2.10
146	Bill Mack	7.00	3.50	2.10
147	Lou Michaels	7.00	3.50	2.10
148	Buzz Nutter	7.00	3.50	2.10
149	Myron Pottios	7.00	3.50	2.10
150	John Reger	7.00	3.50	2.10
151	Mike Sandusky	7.00	3.50	2.10
152	Clendon Thomas	7.00	3.50	2.10
153	**Pittsburgh Steelers Team**	7.00	3.50	2.10
154	Pittsburgh Steelers Play of the Year (Buddy Parker)	7.00	3.50	2.10
155	Kermit Alexander RC	7.00	3.50	2.10
156	Bernie Casey	7.00	3.50	2.10
157	Dan Colchico	7.00	3.50	2.10
158	Clyde Conner	7.00	3.50	2.10
159	Tommy Davis	7.00	3.50	2.10
160	Matt Hazeltine	7.00	3.50	2.10
161	Jim Johnson RC	30.00	15.00	9.00
162	Don Lisbon RC	7.00	3.50	2.10
163	Lamar McHan	7.00	3.50	2.10
164	Bob St. Clair	10.00	5.00	3.00
165	J.D. Smith	7.00	3.50	2.10
166	Abe Woodson	7.00	3.50	2.10
167	**San Francisco 49ers Team**	7.00	3.50	2.10
168	San Francisco 49ers Play of the Year(Red Hickey)	7.00	3.50	2.10
169	Garland Boyette	7.00	3.50	2.10
170	Bobby Joe Conrad	7.00	3.50	2.10
171	Bob DeMarco RC	7.00	3.50	2.10
172	Ken Gray RC	7.00	3.50	2.10
173	Jimmy Hill	7.00	3.50	2.10
174	Charlie Johnson	7.00	3.50	2.10
175	Ernie McMillan	7.00	3.50	2.10
176	Dale Meinert	7.00	3.50	2.10
177	Luke Owens	7.00	3.50	2.10
178	Sonny Randle	7.00	3.50	2.10
179	Joe Robb	7.00	3.50	2.10
180	Bill Stacy	7.00	3.50	2.10
181	**St. Louis Cardinals Team**	7.00	3.50	2.10
182	St. Louis Cardinals Play of the Year(Wally Lem)	7.00	3.50	2.10
183	Bill Barnes	7.00	3.50	2.10
184	Don Bosseler	7.00	3.50	2.10
185	Sam Huff	10.00	5.00	3.00
186	Sonny Jurgensen	30.00	15.00	9.00
187	Ed Khayat	7.00	3.50	2.10
188	Riley Mattson	7.00	3.50	2.10
189	Bobby Mitchell	10.00	5.00	3.00
190	John Nisby	7.00	3.50	2.10
191	Vince Promuto	7.00	3.50	2.10
192	Joe Rutgens	7.00	3.50	2.10
193	Lonnie Sanders	7.00	3.50	2.10
194	Jim Steffen	7.00	3.50	2.10
195	**Washington Redskins Team**	7.00	3.50	2.10
196	Washington Redskins Play of the Year(Bill McPeak)	7.00	3.50	2.10
197	**Checklist 1**	40.00	20.00	12.00
198	**Checklist 2**	30.00	15.00	9.00

1965 Philadelphia

This Philly set was the second one of NFLers issued in its four-year run during the mid-60s. The standard-size 198-card set lists players alphabetically by last name, and alphabetically by city name. Card fronts show the player name in a black box below the photo, with the NFL logo to the right. Card backs had a rub-off game below the statistics. Play of the year cards displayed a diagrammed play the team had used; accompanying it on the front of the card is a small black-and-white picture of the coach. Team cards were once again issued, as were set checklists. One error in the set has Merlin Olsen spelled "Olson" on the checklist card. Rookies in this set include Hall of Famers Paul Warfield and Charley Taylor; all-time interception leader Paul Krause; future NFL head coach Floyd Peters; Carl Eller; Fred Cox; Jack Concannon; Jim Bakken and Pat Fischer. Second-year cards in the set depict Hall of Famers Herb Adderly, Willie Davis, Ray Nitschke (his first Philly card), Vince Lombardi, Deacon Jones, and Merlin Olsen. Others include Mick Tinglehoff, Allie Sherman and Irv Cross. The final regular-issue cards of these players are also in the set: Hall of Famers Yale Lary, Norm Van Brocklin (on a play of the year card), John Henry Johnson, and Sam Huff. This set also had the last regular-issue card of Roosevelt Grier.

	NM	E	VG
Complete Set (198):	1,200	600.00	350.00
Common Player:	7.00	3.50	2.10
Minor Stars:	3.00		
Unlisted Stars:	4.00		
Wax Pack (5):	190.00		

1	**Baltimore Colts Team**	20.00	10.00	6.00
2	Raymond Berry	15.00	7.50	4.50
3	Bob Boyd	7.00	3.50	2.10
4	Wendell Harris	7.00	3.50	2.10
5	Jerry Logan	7.00	3.50	2.10
6	Tony Lorick	7.00	3.50	2.10
7	Lou Michaels	7.00	3.50	2.10
8	Lenny Moore	15.00	7.50	4.50
9	Jimmy Orr	7.00	3.50	2.10
10	Jim Parker	10.00	5.00	3.00
11	Dick Szymanski	7.00	3.50	2.10
12	Johnny Unitas	50.00	25.00	15.00
13	Bob Vogel **RC**	7.00	3.50	2.10
14	Don Shula	20.00	10.00	5.00
15	**Chicago Bears Team**	7.00	3.50	2.10
16	Jon Arnett	7.00	3.50	2.10
17	Doug Atkins	7.00	3.50	2.10
18	Rudy Bukich **RC**	3.00	1.50	.90
19	Mike Ditka	40.00	20.00	12.00
20	Dick Evey	7.00	3.50	2.10
21	Joe Fortunato	7.00	3.50	2.10
22	Bobby Joe Green **RC**	7.00	3.50	2.10
23	Johnny Morris	7.00	3.50	2.10
24	Mike Pyle	7.00	3.50	2.10
25	Roosevelt Taylor	7.00	3.50	2.10
26	Bill Wade	7.00	3.50	2.10
27	Bob Wetoska	7.00	3.50	2.10
28	George Halas	15.00	7.50	4.50
29	**Cleveland Browns Team**	7.00	3.50	2.10
30	Walter Beach	7.00	3.50	2.10
31	Jim Brown	80.00	40.00	24.00
32	Gary Collins	7.00	3.50	2.10
33	Bill Glass	7.00	3.50	2.10
34	Ernie Green	7.00	3.50	2.10
35	Jim Houston **RC**	7.00	3.50	2.10
36	Dick Modzelewski	7.00	3.50	2.10
37	Bernie Parrish	7.00	3.50	2.10
38	Walter Roberts	7.00	3.50	2.10
39	Frank Ryan	7.00	3.50	2.10
40	Dick Schafrath	7.00	3.50	2.10
41	Paul Warfield **RC**	75.00	37.00	22.00
42	Cleveland Browns Play of the Year(Blanton Collier)	7.00	3.50	2.10
43	**Dallas Cowboys Team**	7.00	3.50	2.10
44	Frank Clarke	7.00	3.50	2.10
45	Mike Connelly	7.00	3.50	2.10
46	Buddy Dial	7.00	3.50	2.10
47	Bob Lilly	40.00	20.00	12.00
48	Tony Liscio **RC**	7.00	3.50	2.10
49	Tommy McDonald	7.00	3.50	2.10
50	Don Meredith	30.00	15.00	9.00
51	Pettis Norman	7.00	3.50	2.10
52	Don Perkins	7.00	3.50	2.10
53	Mel Renfro **RC**	75.00	38.00	23.00
54	Jim Ridlon	7.00	3.50	2.10
55	Jerry Tubbs	7.00	3.50	2.10
56	Tom Landry	20.00	10.00	6.00
57	**Detroit Lions Team**	7.00	3.50	2.10
58	Terry Barr	7.00	3.50	2.10
59	Roger Brown	7.00	3.50	2.10
60	Gail Cogdill	7.00	3.50	2.10
61	Jim Gibbons	7.00	3.50	2.10
62	John Gordy	7.00	3.50	2.10
63	Yale Lary	7.00	3.50	2.40
64	Dick LeBeau **RC**	7.00	3.50	2.10
65	Earl Morrall	7.00	3.50	2.10
66	Nick Pietrosante	7.00	3.50	2.10
67	Pat Studstill	7.00	3.50	2.10
68	Wayne Walker	7.00	3.50	2.10
69	Tom Watkins	7.00	3.50	2.10
70	Detroit Lions Play of the Year(George Wilson)	7.00	3.50	2.10
71	**Green Bay Packers Team**	15.00	7.50	4.50
72	Herb Adderley	15.00	7.50	4.50
73	Willie Davis	15.00	7.50	4.50
74	Boyd Dowler	7.00	3.50	2.10
75	Forrest Gregg	10.00	5.00	3.00
76	Paul Hornung	40.00	20.00	12.00
77	Henry Jordan	7.00	3.50	2.10
78	Tom Moore	7.00	3.50	2.10
79	Ray Nitschke	30.00	15.00	9.00
80	Elijah Pitts **RC**	15.00	7.50	4.50
81	Bart Starr	40.00	20.00	12.00
82	Jim Taylor	25.00	13.00	8.00
83	Willie Wood	15.00	7.50	4.50
84	Vince Lombardi	30.00	15.00	9.00
85	**Los Angeles Rams Team**	7.00	3.50	2.10
86	Dick Bass	7.00	3.50	2.10
87	Roman Gabriel	15.00	7.50	4.50
88	Roosevelt Grier	7.00	3.50	2.10
89	Deacon Jones	15.00	7.50	4.50
90	Lamar Lundy **RC**	7.00	3.50	2.10
91	Marlin McKeever	7.00	3.50	2.10
92	Ed Meador	7.00	3.50	2.10
93	Bill Munson **RC**	7.00	3.50	2.10
94	Merlin Olsen	20.00	10.00	6.00
95	Bobby Smith	7.00	3.50	2.10
96	Frank Varrichione	7.00	3.50	2.10
97	Ben Wilson	7.00	3.50	2.10
98	Los Angeles Rams Play of the Year(Harland Svare)	7.00	3.50	2.10
99	**Minnesota Vikings Team**	7.00	3.50	2.10
100	Grady Alderman	7.00	3.50	2.10
101	Hal Bedsole **RC**	7.00	3.50	2.10
102	Bill Brown	7.00	3.50	2.10
103	Bill Butler	7.00	3.50	2.10
104	Fred Cox **RC**	7.00	3.50	2.10
105	Carl Eller **RC**	40.00	20.00	12.00
106	Paul Flatley	7.00	3.50	2.10
107	Jim Marshall	7.00	3.50	2.10
108	Tommy Mason	7.00	3.50	2.10
109	George Rose	7.00	3.50	2.10
110	Fran Tarkenton	40.00	20.00	12.00
111	Mick Tingelhoff	7.00	3.50	2.10
112	Norm Van Brocklin	7.00	3.50	2.10
113	**New York Giants Team**	7.00	3.50	2.10
114	Erich Barnes	7.00	3.50	2.10
115	Roosevelt Brown	7.00	3.50	2.10
116	Clarence Childs	7.00	3.50	2.10
117	Jerry Hillebrand	7.00	3.50	2.10
118	Greg Larson	7.00	3.50	2.10
119	Dick Lynch	7.00	3.50	2.10
120	Joe Morrison **RC**	7.00	3.50	2.10
121	Lou Slaby	7.00	3.50	2.10
122	Aaron Thomas **RC**	7.00	3.50	2.10
123	Steve Thurlow	7.00	3.50	2.10
124	Ernie Wheelwright	7.00	3.50	2.10
125	Gary Wood **RC**	7.00	3.50	2.10
126	New York Giants Play of the Year(Allie Sherman)	7.00	3.50	2.10
127	**Philadelphia Eagles Team**	7.00	3.50	2.10
128	Sam Baker	7.00	3.50	2.10
129	Maxie Baughan	7.00	3.50	2.10
130	Timmy Brown	7.00	3.50	2.10
131	Jack Concannon **RC**	7.00	3.50	2.10
132	Irv Cross	7.00	3.50	2.10
133	Earl Gros	7.00	3.50	2.10
134	Dave Lloyd	7.00	3.50	2.10
135	Floyd Peters	7.00	3.50	2.10
136	Nate Ramsey	7.00	3.50	2.10
137	Pete Retzlaff	7.00	3.50	2.10
138	Jim Ringo	7.00	3.50	2.10
139	Norm Snead	7.00	3.50	2.10
140	Philadelphia Eagles Play of the Year(Joe Kuharich)	7.00	3.50	2.10
141	**Pittsburgh Steelers Team**	7.00	3.50	2.10
142	John Baker	7.00	3.50	2.10
143	Gary Ballman	7.00	3.50	2.10
144	Charley Bradshaw	7.00	3.50	2.10
145	Ed Brown	7.00	3.50	2.10
146	Dick Haley	7.00	3.50	2.10
147	John Henry Johnson	10.00	5.00	3.00
148	Brady Keys	7.00	3.50	2.10
149	Ray Lemek	7.00	3.50	2.10
150	Ben McGee	7.00	3.50	2.10
151	Clarence Peaks	7.00	3.50	2.10
152	Myron Pottios	7.00	3.50	2.10
153	Clendon Thomas	7.00	3.50	2.10
154	Pittsburgh Steelers Play of the Year(Buddy Parker)	7.00	3.50	2.10
155	**St. Louis Cardinals Team**	7.00	3.50	2.10
156	Jim Bakken **RC**	7.00	3.50	2.10
157	Joe Childress	7.00	3.50	2.10
158	Bobby Joe Conrad	7.00	3.50	2.10
159	Bob DeMarco	7.00	3.50	2.10
160	Pat Fischer **RC**	10.00	5.00	3.00
161	Irv Goode	7.00	3.50	2.10
162	Ken Gray	7.00	3.50	2.10
163	Charlie Johnson	7.00	3.50	2.10
164	Bill Koman	7.00	3.50	2.10
165	Dale Meinert	7.00	3.50	2.10
166	Jerry Stovall **RC**	7.00	3.50	2.10
167	Abe Woodson	7.00	3.50	2.10
168	St. Louis Cardinals Play of the Year(Wally Lemon)	7.00	3.50	2.10
169	**San Francisco 49ers Team**	7.00	3.50	2.10
170	Kermit Alexander	7.00	3.50	2.10
171	John Brodie	15.00	7.50	4.50
172	Bernie Casey	7.00	3.50	2.10
173	John David Crow	7.00	3.50	2.10
174	Tommy Davis	7.00	3.50	2.10
175	Matt Hazeltine	7.00	3.50	2.10
176	Jim Johnson	10.00	5.00	3.00
177	Charlie Krueger	7.00	3.50	2.10
178	Roland Lakes	7.00	3.50	2.10
179	George Mira **RC**	7.00	3.50	2.10
180	Dave Parks **RC**	7.00	3.50	2.10
181	John Thomas	7.00	3.50	2.10
182	Jack Christiansen	7.00	3.50	2.10
183	**Washington Redskins Team**	7.00	3.50	2.10
184	Pervis Atkins	7.00	3.50	2.10
185	Preston Carpenter	7.00	3.50	2.10
186	Angelo Coia	7.00	3.50	2.10
187	Sam Huff	15.00	7.50	4.50
188	Sonny Jurgensen	20.00	10.00	6.00
189	Paul Krause **RC**	35.00	18.00	11.00
190	Jim Martin	7.00	3.50	2.10
191	Bobby Mitchell	10.00	5.00	3.00
192	John Nisby	7.00	3.50	2.10
193	John Paluck	7.00	3.50	2.10
194	Vince Promuto	7.00	3.50	2.10
195	Charley Taylor **RC**	60.00	30.00	18.00
196	Bill McPeak	7.00	3.50	2.10
197	**Checklist 1**	30.00	15.00	9.00
198	**Checklist 2**	60.00	30.00	18.00

1966 Philadelphia

This 198-card set of NFL players is best known for the inclusion of rookie cards of Gale Sayers and Dick Butkus (the other significant rookie card is that of Bob Hayes). This was the final year regular-issue cards were produced of players including Hall of Famers Lenny Moore, Jim Parker, Jim Brown, Roosevelt Brown, and Jim Ringo. The 198-card set lists players in alphabetical order according to city. The play card for each team features a color action photo on the front, with a description of the play on the back.

	NM	E	VG
Complete Set (198):	1,500	750.00	450.00
Common Player:	8.00	4.00	2.40
Minor Stars:	2.00		
Unlisted Stars:	4.00		
Wax Pack (5):	400.00		

1	**Falcons Logo**	20.00	10.00	6.00
2	Larry Benz	8.00	4.00	2.40
3	Dennis Claridge	8.00	4.00	2.40
4	Perry Lee Dunn	8.00	4.00	2.40

5	Dan Grimm	8.00	4.00	2.40
6	Alex Hawkins	8.00	4.00	2.40
7	Ralph Heck	8.00	4.00	2.40
8	Frank Lasky	8.00	4.00	2.40
9	Guy Reese	8.00	4.00	2.40
10	Bob Richards	8.00	4.00	2.40
11	Ron Smith	8.00	4.00	2.40
12	Ernie Wheelwright	8.00	4.00	2.40
13	**Atlanta Falcons Roster**	8.00	4.00	2.40
14	**Baltimore Colts Team Card**	8.00	4.00	2.40
15	Raymond Berry	15.00	7.50	4.50
16	Bob Boyd	8.00	4.00	2.40
17	Jerry Logan	8.00	4.00	2.40
18	John Mackey	8.00	4.00	2.40
19	Tom Matte	8.00	4.00	2.40
20	Lou Michaels	8.00	4.00	2.40
21	Lenny Moore	15.00	7.50	4.50
22	Jimmy Orr	8.00	4.00	2.40
23	Jim Parker	8.00	4.00	2.40
24	Johnny Unitas	60.00	30.00	18.00
25	Bob Vogel	8.00	4.00	2.40
26	**Baltimore Colts Play Card**	10.00	5.00	3.00
27	**Chicago Bears Team Card**	8.00	4.00	2.40
28	Doug Atkins	8.00	4.00	2.40
29	Rudy Bukich	8.00	4.00	2.40
30	Ron Bull	8.00	4.00	2.40
31	Dick Butkus **RC**	300.00	150.00	90.00
32	Mike Ditka	40.00	20.00	12.00
33	Joe Fortuanto	8.00	4.00	2.40
34	Bobby Joe Green	8.00	4.00	2.40
35	Roger LeClerc	8.00	4.00	2.40
36	Johnny Morris	8.00	4.00	2.40
37	Mike Pyle	8.00	4.00	2.40
38	Gale Sayers **RC**	225.00	115.00	70.00
39	Gale Sayers (Bears)	40.00	20.00	12.00
40	**Cleveland Browns Team Card**	8.00	4.00	2.40
41	Jim Brown	90.00	45.00	27.00
42	Gary Collins	8.00	4.00	2.40
43	Ross Fichtner	8.00	4.00	2.40
44	Ernie Green	8.00	4.00	2.40
45	Gene Hickerson **RC**	8.00	4.00	2.40
46	Jim Houston	8.00	4.00	2.40
47	John Morrow	8.00	4.00	2.40
48	Walter Roberts	8.00	4.00	2.40
49	Frank Ryan	8.00	4.00	2.40
50	Dick Schafrath	8.00	4.00	2.40
51	Paul Wiggin **RC**	8.00	4.00	2.40
52	**Cleveland Browns Play Card**	8.00	4.00	2.40
53	**Dallas Cowboys Team Card**	8.00	4.00	2.40
54	George Andrie **RC**	8.00	4.00	2.40
55	Frank Ryan	8.00	4.00	2.40
56	Mike Connelly	8.00	4.00	2.40
57	Cornell Green	8.00	4.00	2.40
58	Bob Hayes **RC**	55.00	28.00	17.00
59	Chuck Howley **RC**	20.00	10.00	6.00
60	Bob Lilly	25.00	13.00	8.00
61	Don Meredith	25.00	13.00	8.00
62	Don Perkins	30.00	15.00	9.00
63	Mel Renfro	15.00	7.50	4.50
64	Danny Villanueva	8.00	4.00	2.40
65	**Dallas Cowboys Play Card**	8.00	4.00	2.40
66	**Detroit Lions Team Card**	8.00	4.00	2.40
67	Roger Brown	8.00	4.00	2.40
68	John Gordy	8.00	4.00	2.40
69	Alex Karras	15.00	7.50	4.50
70	Dick LeBeau	8.00	4.00	2.40
71	Amos Marsh	8.00	4.00	2.40
72	Milt Plum	8.00	4.00	2.40
73	Bobby Smith	8.00	4.00	2.40
74	Wayne Rasmussen	8.00	4.00	2.40
75	Pat Studstill	8.00	4.00	2.40
76	Wayne Walker	8.00	4.00	2.40
77	Tom Watkins	8.00	4.00	2.40
78	**Detroit Lions Play Card**	8.00	4.00	2.40
79	**Green Bay Packers Team Card**	10.00	5.00	3.00
80	Herb Adderley	8.00	4.00	2.40
81	Lee Roy Caffey **RC**	8.00	4.00	2.40
82	Don Chandler	8.00	4.00	2.40
83	Willie Davis	8.00	4.00	2.40
84	Boyd Dowler	8.00	4.00	2.40
85	Forrest Gregg	8.00	4.00	2.40
86	Tom Moore	8.00	4.00	2.40
87	Ray Nitschke	25.00	13.00	8.00
88	Bart Starr	50.00	25.00	15.00
89	Jim Taylor	25.00	13.00	8.00
90	Willie Wood	8.00	4.00	2.40
91	**Green Bay Packers Play Card**	8.00	4.00	2.40
92	**Los Angeles Rams Team Card**	8.00	4.00	2.40
93	Willie Brown	8.00	4.00	2.40
94	Dick Bass, Roman Gabriel	8.00	4.00	2.40
95	Bruce Gossett	8.00	4.00	2.40
96	Deacon Jones	8.00	4.00	2.40
97	Tommy McDonald	8.00	4.00	2.40
98	Marlin McKeever	8.00	4.00	2.40
99	Aaron Martin	8.00	4.00	2.40
100	Ed Meador	8.00	4.00	2.40
101	Bill Munson	8.00	4.00	2.40
102	Merlin Olsen	20.00	10.00	6.00
103	Jim Stiger	8.00	4.00	2.40
104	**Los Angeles Rams Play Card**	8.00	4.00	2.40
105	**Minnesota Vikings Team Card**	8.00	4.00	2.40
106	Grady Alderman	8.00	4.00	2.40
107	Bill Brown	8.00	4.00	2.40
108	Fred Cox	8.00	4.00	2.40
109	Paul Flatley	8.00	4.00	2.40
110	Rip Hawkins	8.00	4.00	2.40
111	Tommy Mason	8.00	4.00	2.40
112	Ed Sharockman	8.00	4.00	2.40
113	Gordon Smith	8.00	4.00	2.40
114	Fran Tarkenton	50.00	25.00	15.00
115	Mick Tinglehoff	8.00	4.00	2.40
116	Bobby Walden **RC**	8.00	4.00	2.40
117	**Minnesota Vikings Play Card**	8.00	4.00	2.40
118	**New York Giants Team Card**	8.00	4.00	2.40
119	Roosevelt Brown	8.00	4.00	2.40
120	Henry Carr **RC**	8.00	4.00	2.40
121	Clarence Childs	8.00	4.00	2.40
122	Tucker Frederickson **RC**	8.00	4.00	2.40
123	Jerry Hillebrand	8.00	4.00	2.40
124	Greg Larson	8.00	4.00	2.40
125	Spider Lockhart **RC**	8.00	4.00	2.40
126	Dick Lynch	8.00	4.00	2.40
127	Earl Morrall, Bob Scholtz	8.00	4.00	2.10
128	Joe Morrison	8.00	4.00	2.40
129	Steve Thurlow	8.00	4.00	2.40
130	**New York Giants Play Card**	8.00	4.00	2.40
131	**Philadelphia Ealges Team Card**	8.00	4.00	2.40
132	Sam Baker	8.00	4.00	2.40
133	Maxie Baughan	8.00	4.00	2.40
134	Bob Brown **RC**	20.00	10.00	6.00
135	Timmy Brown	8.00	4.00	2.40
136	Irv Cross	8.00	4.00	2.40
137	Earl Gros	8.00	4.00	2.40
138	Ray Poage	8.00	4.00	2.40
139	Nate Ramsey	8.00	4.00	2.40
140	Pete Retzlaff	8.00	4.00	2.40
141	Jim Ringo	8.00	4.00	2.40
142	Norm Snead	10.00	5.00	3.00
143	**Philadelphia Eagles Play Card**	8.00	4.00	2.40
144	**Pittsburgh Steelers Team Card**	8.00	4.00	2.40
145	Gary Ballman	8.00	4.00	2.40
146	Charley Bradshaw	1.50	.70	.45
147	Jim Butler	8.00	4.00	2.40
148	Mike Clark	8.00	4.00	2.40
149	Dick Hoak **RC**	8.00	4.00	2.40
150	Roy Jefferson **RC**	8.00	4.00	2.40
151	Frank Lambert	8.00	4.00	2.40
152	Mike Lind	8.00	4.00	2.40
153	Bill Nelsen **RC**	8.00	4.00	2.40
154	Clarence Peaks	8.00	4.00	2.40
155	Clendon Thomas	8.00	4.00	2.40
156	**Pittsburgh Steelers Play Card**	8.00	4.00	2.40
157	**St. Louis Cardinals Team Card**	8.00	4.00	2.40
158	Jim Bakken	8.00	4.00	2.40
159	Bobby Joe Conrad	8.00	4.00	2.40
160	Willis Crenshaw **RC**	8.00	4.00	2.40
161	Bob DeMarco	8.00	4.00	2.40
162	Pat Fischer	8.00	4.00	2.40
163	Charlie Johnson	8.00	4.00	2.40
164	Dale Meinert	8.00	4.00	2.40
165	Sonny Randle	8.00	4.00	2.40
166	Sam Silas **RC**	8.00	4.00	2.40
167	Bill Triplett	8.00	4.00	2.40
168	Larry Wilson	10.00	5.00	3.00
169	**St. Louis Cardinals Play Card**	8.00	4.00	2.40
170	**San Francisco 49ers Team Card**	8.00	4.00	2.40
171	Kermit Alexander	8.00	4.00	2.40
172	Bruce Bosley	8.00	4.00	2.40
173	John Brodie	10.00	5.00	3.00
174	Bernie Casey	8.00	4.00	2.40
175	John David Crow	8.00	4.00	2.40
176	Tommy Davis	8.00	4.00	2.40
177	Jim Johnson	8.00	4.00	2.40
178	Gary Lewis	8.00	4.00	2.40
179	Dave Parks	8.00	4.00	2.40
180	Walter Rock	8.00	4.00	2.40
181	Ken Willard **RC**	8.00	4.00	2.40
182	**San Francisco 49ers Play Card**	8.00	4.00	2.40
183	**Washington Redskins Team Card**	8.00	4.00	2.40
184	Rickie Harris	8.00	4.00	2.40
185	Sonny Jurgensen	15.00	7.50	4.50
186	Paul Krause	8.00	4.00	2.40
187	Bobby Mitchell	10.00	5.00	3.00
188	Vince Promuto	8.00	4.00	2.40
189	Pat Richter **RC**	8.00	4.00	2.40
190	Joe Rutgens	8.00	4.00	2.40
191	John Sample	8.00	4.00	2.40
192	Lonnie Sanders	8.00	4.00	2.40
193	Jim Steffen	8.00	4.00	2.40
194	Charley Taylor	25.00	13.00	8.00
195	**Washington Redskins Play Card**	8.00	4.00	2.40
196	**Referee signals**	8.00	4.00	2.40
197	**Checklist 1**	25.00	13.00	8.00
198	**Checklist 2**	50.00	25.00	15.00

1967 Philadelphia

This was the last time until 1989 that Topps would face a direct challenge in the football card market, as the Philadelphia Chewing Gum Corp. ceased production of football cards after this issue. (The company returned with sets of NFL Hall of Famers in 1988 and 1989). The 198-card set has yellow borders on the front, and backs were printed on white or brown card stock. As usual, teams were grouped alphabetically by city name, players were grouped alphabetically by last name. Team logo cards rounded out the grouping of each team. There is an error in the set: on card #14, Raymond Berry, the picture actually shows Bob Boyd. Also, the roster for the New Orleans Saints team card (#121) was included on the back of the logo card (#132); the set includes team picture cards and team logo cards for all other teams except the expansion Saints (The front of the card reads, "On the back of this card are names of New Orleans players and the teams from which they were picked" while the back simply has a capsule on the Saints' New Orleans impact). Another error, on card #26 reads "Bukich" on the front and "Buckich" on the back. Rookies in this set include Tommy Nobis, Leroy Kelly, Lee Roy Jordan, and Chris Hanburger. Second-year cards include Dick Butkus, Gale Sayers, Bob Brown, Roy Jefferson, Jim Bakken and Ken Willard. This was the last year for regular-issue cards of Hall of Famers Forrest Gregg and Paul Hornung. The first members of the New Orleans Saints made their debut in the '67 Philly set.

	NM	E	VG
Complete Set (198):	1,400	700.00	425.00
Common Player:	7.00	3.50	2.10
Minor Stars:	2.00		
Unlisted Stars:	3.50		
Wax Pack (5):	180.00		

1	**Falcons Team**	20.00	10.00	6.00
2	Junior Coffey **RC**	7.00	3.50	2.10
3	Alex Hawkins	7.00	3.50	2.10
4	Randy Johnson **RC**	7.00	3.50	2.10
5	Lou Kirouac	7.00	3.50	2.10
6	Billy Martin	7.00	3.50	2.10
7	Tommy Nobis **RC**	20.00	10.00	6.00
8	Jerry Richardson **RC**	10.00	5.00	3.00
9	Marion Rushing	7.00	3.50	2.10
10	Ron Smith	7.00	3.50	2.10
11	Ernie Wheelwright	7.00	3.50	2.10
12	**Atlanta Falcons Insignia**	7.00	3.50	2.10
13	**Baltimore Colts Team**	7.00	3.50	2.10
14	Raymond Berry	15.00	7.50	4.50
15	Bob Boyd	7.00	3.50	2.10
16	Ordell Braase	7.00	3.50	2.10
17	Alvin Haymond	7.00	3.50	2.10
18	Tony Lorick	7.00	3.50	2.10
19	Lenny Lyles	7.00	3.50	2.10
20	John Mackey	10.00	5.00	3.00
21	Tom Matte	7.00	3.50	2.10

22	Lou Michaels	7.00	3.50	2.10
23	Johnny Unitas	45.00	23.00	14.00
24	**Baltimore Colts Insignia**	7.00	3.50	2.10
25	**Chicago Bears Team**	7.00	3.50	2.10
26	Rudy Bukich	7.00	3.50	2.10
27	Ron Bull	7.00	3.50	2.10
28	Dick Butkus	75.00	38.00	23.00
29	Mike Ditka	35.00	18.00	11.00
30	Dick Gordon **RC**	7.00	3.50	2.10
31	Roger LeClerc	7.00	3.50	2.10
32	Bennie McRae	7.00	3.50	2.10
33	Richie Petibon	7.00	3.50	2.10
34	Mike Pyle	7.00	3.50	2.10
35	Gale Sayers	75.00	37.00	22.00
36	**Chicago Bears Insignia**	7.00	3.50	2.10
37	**Cleveland Browns Team**	7.00	3.50	2.10
38	Johnny Brewer	7.00	3.50	2.10
39	Gary Collins	7.00	3.50	2.10
40	Ross Fichtner	7.00	3.50	2.10
41	Ernie Green	7.00	3.50	2.10
42	Gene Hickerson	7.00	3.50	2.10
43	Leroy Kelly **RC**	80.00	40.00	24.00
44	Frank Ryan	7.00	3.50	2.10
45	Dick Schafrath	7.00	3.50	2.10
46	Paul Warfield	20.00	10.00	6.00
47	John Wooten	7.00	3.50	2.10
48	**Cleveland Browns Insignia**	7.00	3.50	2.10
49	**Dallas Cowboys Team**	7.00	3.50	2.10
50	George Andrie	7.00	3.50	2.10
51	Cornell Green	7.00	3.50	2.10
52	Bob Hayes	7.00	3.50	2.10
53	Chuck Howley	7.00	3.50	2.10
54	Lee Roy Jordan **RC**	30.00	15.00	9.00
55	Bob Lilly	20.00	10.00	6.00
56	Dave Manders **RC**	7.00	3.50	2.10
57	Don Meredith	20.00	10.00	6.00
58	Dan Reeves **RC**	40.00	20.00	12.00
59	Mel Renfro	50.00	25.00	15.00
60	**Dallas Cowboys Insignia**	7.00	3.50	2.10
61	**Detroit Lions Team**	7.00	3.50	2.10
62	Roger Brown	7.00	3.50	2.10
63	Gail Cogdill	7.00	3.50	2.10
64	John Gordy	7.00	3.50	2.10
65	Ron Kramer	7.00	3.50	2.10
66	Dick LeBeau	7.00	3.50	2.10
67	Mike Lucci **RC**	10.00	5.00	3.00
68	Amos Marsh	7.00	3.50	2.10
69	Tom Nowatzke	7.00	3.50	2.10
70	Pat Studstill	7.00	3.50	2.10
71	Karl Sweetan	7.00	3.50	2.10
72	**Detroit Lions Insignia**	7.00	3.50	2.10
73	**Green Bay Packers Team**	20.00	10.00	6.00
74	Herb Adderley	10.00	5.00	3.00
75	Lee Roy Caffey	7.00	3.50	2.10
76	Willie Davis	10.00	5.00	3.00
77	Forrest Gregg	10.00	5.00	3.00
78	Henry Jordan	10.00	5.00	3.00
79	Ray Nitschke	20.00	10.00	6.00
80	Dave Robinson **RC**	10.00	5.00	3.00
81	Bob Skoronski	7.00	3.50	2.10
82	Bart Starr	40.00	20.00	12.00
83	Willie Wood	10.00	5.00	3.00
84	**Green Bay Packers Insignia**	7.00	3.50	2.10
85	**Los Angeles Rams Team**	7.00	3.50	2.10
86	Dick Bass	7.00	3.50	2.10
87	Maxie Baughan	7.00	3.50	2.10
88	Roman Gabriel	10.00	5.00	3.00
89	Bruce Gossett	7.00	3.50	2.10
90	Deacon Jones	10.00	5.00	3.00
91	Tommy McDonald	10.00	5.00	3.00
92	Marlin McKeever	7.00	3.50	2.10
93	Tom Moore	7.00	3.50	2.10
94	Merlin Olsen	10.00	5.00	3.00
95	Clancy Williams	7.00	3.50	2.10
96	**Los Angeles Rams Insignia**	7.00	3.50	2.10
97	**Minnesota Vikings Team**	7.00	3.50	2.10
98	Grady Alderman	7.00	3.50	2.10
99	Bill Brown	7.00	3.50	2.10
100	Fred Cox	7.00	3.50	2.10
101	Paul Flatley	7.00	3.50	2.10
102	Dale Hackbart	7.00	3.50	2.10
103	Jim Marshall	10.00	5.00	3.00
104	Tommy Mason	7.00	3.50	2.10
105	Milt Sunde	7.00	3.50	2.10
106	Fran Tarkenton	30.00	15.00	9.00
107	Mick Tingelhoff	7.00	3.50	2.10
108	**Minnesota Vikings Insignia**	7.00	3.50	2.10
109	**New York Giants Team**	7.00	3.50	2.10
110	Henry Carr	7.00	3.50	2.10
111	Clarence Childs	7.00	3.50	2.10
112	Allen Jacobs	7.00	3.50	2.10
113	Homer Jones **RC**	7.00	3.50	2.10
114	Tom Kennedy	7.00	3.50	2.10
115	Spider Lockhart	7.00	3.50	2.10
116	Joe Morrison	7.00	3.50	2.10
117	Francis Peay	7.00	3.50	2.10
118	Jeff Smith	7.00	3.50	2.10
119	Aaron Thomas	7.00	3.50	2.10
120	**New York Giants Team**	7.00	3.50	2.10
121	**New Orleans Saints Team**	7.00	3.50	2.10
122	Charley Bradshaw	7.00	3.50	2.10
123	Paul Hornung	30.00	15.00	9.00
124	Elbert Kimbrough	7.00	3.50	2.10
125	Earl Leggett	7.00	3.50	2.10
126	Obert Logan	7.00	3.50	2.10
127	Riley Mattson	7.00	3.50	2.10
128	John Morrow	7.00	3.50	2.10
129	Bob Scholtz	7.00	3.50	2.10
130	Dave Whitsell **RC**	7.00	3.50	2.10
131	Gary Wood	7.00	3.50	2.10
132	**New Orleans Saints Insignia**	7.00	3.50	2.10
133	**Philadelphia Eagles Team**	7.00	3.50	2.10
134	Sam Baker	7.00	3.50	2.10
135	Bob Brown	7.00	3.50	2.10
136	Tim Brown	7.00	3.50	2.10
137	Earl Gros	7.00	3.50	2.10
138	Dave Lloyd	7.00	3.50	2.10
139	Floyd Peters	7.00	3.50	2.10
140	Pete Retzlaff	7.00	3.50	2.10
141	Joe Scarpati	7.00	3.50	2.10
142	Norm Snead	7.00	3.50	2.10
143	Jim Skaggs	7.00	3.50	2.10
144	**Philadelphia Eagles Insignia**	7.00	3.50	2.10
145	**Pittsburgh Steelers Team**	7.00	3.50	2.10
146	Bill Asbury	7.00	3.50	2.10
147	John Baker	7.00	3.50	2.10
148	Gary Ballman	7.00	3.50	2.10
149	Mike Clark	7.00	3.50	2.10
150	Riley Gunnels	7.00	3.50	2.10
151	John Hilton	7.00	3.50	2.10
152	Roy Jefferson	7.00	3.50	2.10
153	Brady Keys	7.00	3.50	2.10
154	Ben McGee	7.00	3.50	2.10
155	Bill Nelsen	7.00	3.50	2.10
156	**Pittsburgh Steelers Insignia**	7.00	3.50	2.10
157	**St. Louis Cardinals Team**	7.00	3.50	2.10
158	Jim Bakken	7.00	3.50	2.10
159	Bobby Joe Conrad	7.00	3.50	2.10
160	Ken Gray	7.00	3.50	2.10
161	Charlie Johnson	7.00	3.50	2.10
162	Joe Robb	7.00	3.50	2.10
163	Johnny Roland **RC**	7.00	3.50	2.10
164	Roy Shivers	7.00	3.50	2.10
165	Jackie Smith **RC**	40.00	20.00	12.00
166	Jerry Stovall	7.00	3.50	2.10
167	Larry Wilson	10.00	5.00	3.00
168	**St. Louis Cardinals Insignia**	7.00	3.50	2.10
169	**San Francisco 49ers Team**	7.00	3.50	2.10
170	Kermit Alexander	7.00	3.50	2.10
171	Bruce Bosley	7.00	3.50	2.10
172	John Brodie	10.00	5.00	3.00
173	Bernie Casey	7.00	3.50	2.10
174	Tommy Davis	7.00	3.50	2.10
175	Howard Mudd	7.00	3.50	2.10
176	Dave Parks	7.00	3.50	2.10
177	John Thomas	7.00	3.50	2.10
178	Dave Wilcox **RC**	40.00	20.00	12.00
179	Ken Willard	7.00	3.50	2.10
180	**San Francisco 49ers Insignia**	7.00	3.50	2.10
181	**Washington Redskins Team**	7.00	3.50	2.10
182	Charlie Gogolak **RC**	7.00	3.50	2.10
183	Chris Hanburger **RC**	10.00	5.00	3.00
184	Len Hauss **RC**	7.00	3.50	2.10
185	Sonny Jurgensen	15.00	7.50	4.50
186	Bobby Mitchell	10.00	5.00	3.00
187	Bris Owens	7.00	3.50	2.10
188	Jim Shorter	7.00	3.50	2.10
189	Jerry Smith **RC**	7.00	3.50	2.10
190	Charley Taylor	15.00	7.50	4.50
191	A.D. Whitfield	7.00	3.50	2.10
192	**Washington Redskins Insignia**	7.00	3.50	2.10
193	**Cleveland Browns**	15.00	7.50	4.50
194	New York Giants Play Card (Joe Morrison)	7.00	3.50	2.10
195	Atlanta Falcons Play Card (Ernie Wheelwright)	7.00	3.50	2.10
196	**Referee Signals**	7.00	3.50	2.10
197	**Checklist 1**	10.00	5.00	3.00
198	**Checklist 2**	25.00	13.00	8.00

1991 Pinnacle

Score's first effort at a premium edition is its 415-card 1991 Pinnacle set. Each card front features an action shot and a mug shot against a black background with white borders. The back has an action photo superimposed against a black background, plus statistics, a profile and a biography. An anti-counterfeit band appears on the back of each card. Subsets include Head-to-Head, Technicians, Game Winners, Idols and Sidelines. There are also 58 rookies featured in the set; their cards have green backgrounds on the front, and a mug shot on the back. A standard-size Emmitt Smith promotional card was also created. It is identical in design to its regular set's counterpart, except the text on the back of the promo card mentions Smith's holdout before the season. Twelve four-card panels (5" x 7" each) were also made and use the same design as the regular 1991 cards. Each card in the panel has the same number as its counterpart in the regular set, but the panel is unnumbered.

	NM/M	NM	E
Complete Set (415):	35.00	26.00	14.00
Common Player:	.10	.08	.04
Minor Stars:	.20	.15	.08
Foil Pack (12):	1.00		
Foil Wax Box (36):	25.00		

1	Warren Moon	.30	.25	.12
2	Morten Andersen	.10	.08	.04
3	Rohn Stark	.10	.08	.04
4	Mark Bortz	.10	.08	.04
5	Mark Higgs **RC**	.10	.08	.04
6	Troy Aikman	4.00	3.00	1.50
7	John Elway	1.50	1.25	.60
8	Neal Anderson	.10	.08	.04
9	Chris Doleman	.10	.08	.04
10	Jay Schroeder	.10	.08	.04
11	Sterling Sharpe	.40	.30	.15
12	Steve DeBerg	.10	.08	.04
13	Ronnie Lott	.10	.08	.04
14	Sea Landeta	.10	.08	.04
15	Jim Everett	.10	.08	.04
16	Jim Breech	.10	.08	.04
17	Barry Foster	.10	.08	.04
18	Mike Merriweather	.10	.08	.04
19	Eric Metcalf	.40	.30	.15
20	Mark Carrier	.10	.08	.04
21	James Brooks	.10	.08	.04
22	Nate Odomes	.10	.08	.04
23	Rodney Hampton	.50	.40	.20
24	Chris Miller	.10	.08	.04
25	Roger Craig	.10	.08	.04
26	Louis Oliver	.10	.08	.04
27	Allen Pinkett	.10	.08	.04
28	Bubby Brister	.10	.08	.04
29	Reyna Thompson	.10	.08	.04
30	Issiac Holt	.10	.08	.04
31	Steve Broussard	.10	.08	.04
32	Christian Okoye	.10	.08	.04
33	Dave Meggett	.10	.08	.04
34	Andre Reed	.20	.15	.08
35	Shane Conlan	.10	.08	.04
36	Eric Ball	.10	.08	.04
37	Johnny Bailey	.10	.08	.04
38	Don Majkowski	.10	.08	.04
39	Gerald Williams	.10	.08	.04
40	Kevin Mack	.10	.08	.04
41	Jeff Herrod	.10	.08	.04
42	Emmitt Smith	6.00	4.50	2.50
43	Wendell Davis	.10	.08	.04
44	Lorenzo White	.10	.08	.04
45	Andre Rison	.20	.15	.08
46	Jerry Gray	.10	.08	.04
47	Dennis Smith	.10	.08	.04
48	Gaston Green	.10	.08	.04
49	Dermontti Dawson	.10	.08	.04
50	Jeff Hostetler	.30	.25	.12
51	Nick Lowery	.10	.08	.04
52	Merril Hoge	.10	.08	.04
53	Bobby Hebert	.10	.08	.04
54	Scott Case	.10	.08	.04
55	Jack Del Rio	.10	.08	.04
56	Cornelius Bennett	.10	.08	.04
57	Tony Mandarich	.10	.08	.04
58	Bill Brooks	.10	.08	.04
59	Jessie Tuggle	.10	.08	.04
60	Hugh Millen **RC**	.10	.08	.04
61	Tony Bennett	.10	.08	.04
62	Chris Dishman **RC**	.10	.08	.04
63	Darryl Henley **RC**	.10	.08	.04
64	Duane Bickett	.10	.08	.04
65	Jay Hilgenberg	.10	.08	.04
66	Joe Montana	3.50	2.75	1.50
67	Bill Fralic	.10	.08	.04
68	Sam Mills	.10	.08	.04
69	Bruce Armstrong	.10	.08	.04
70	Dan Marino	5.00	3.75	2.00
71	Jim Lachey	.10	.08	.04
72	Rod Woodson	.10	.08	.04
73	Simon Fletcher	.10	.08	.04

74	Bruce Matthews	.10	.08	.04
75	Howie Long	.10	.08	.04
76	John Friesz	.10	.08	.04
77	Karl Mecklenburg	.10	.08	.04
78	John L. Williams	.10	.08	.04
79	Rob Burnett **RC**	.10	.08	.04
80	Anthony Carter	.10	.08	.04
81	Henry Ellard	.10	.08	.04
82	Don Beebe	.10	.08	.04
83	Louis Lipps	.10	.08	.04
84	Greg McMurty	.10	.08	.04
85	Will Wolford	.10	.08	.04
86	Eric Green	.20	.15	.08
87	Irving Fryar	.10	.08	.04
88	John Offerdahl	.10	.08	.04
89	John Alt	.10	.08	.04
90	Tom Tupa	.10	.08	.04
91	Don Mosebar	.10	.08	.04
92	Jeff George	.50	.40	.20
93	Vinny Testaverde	.20	.15	.08
94	Greg Townsend	.10	.08	.04
95	Derrick Fenner	.10	.08	.04
96	Brian Mitchell	.20	.15	.08
97	Herschel Walker	.10	.08	.04
98	Ricky Proehl	.10	.08	.04
99	Mark Clayton	.10	.08	.04
100	Derrick Thomas	.20	.15	.08
101	Jim Harbaugh	.50	.40	.20
102	Barry Word	.10	.08	.04
103	Jerry Rice	4.00	3.00	1.50
104	Keith Byars	.10	.08	.04
105	Marion Butts	.10	.08	.04
106	Rich Moran	.10	.08	.04
107	Thurman Thomas	.75	.60	.30
108	Stephone Paige	.10	.08	.04
109	David Johnson	.10	.08	.04
110	William Perry	.10	.08	.04
111	Haywood Jeffires	.10	.08	.04
112	Rodney Peete	.10	.08	.04
113	Andy Heck	.10	.08	.04
114	Kevin Ross	.10	.08	.04
115	Michael Carter	.10	.08	.04
116	Tim McKyer	.10	.08	.04
117	Kenneth Davis	.10	.08	.04
118	Richmond Webb	.10	.08	.04
119	Rich Camarillo	.10	.08	.04
120	James Francis	.10	.08	.04
121	Craig Heyward	.10	.08	.04
122	Hardy Nickerson	.10	.08	.04
123	Michael Brooks	.10	.08	.04
124	Fred Barnett	.30	.25	.12
125	Cris Carter	.40	.30	.15
126	Brian Jordan	.10	.08	.04
127	Pat Leahy	.10	.08	.04
128	Kevin Greene	.10	.08	.04
129	Trace Armstrong	.10	.08	.04
130	Eugene Lockhart	.10	.08	.04
131	Albert Lewis	.10	.08	.04
132	Ernie Jones	.10	.08	.04
133	Eric Martin	.10	.08	.04
134	Anthony Thompson	.10	.08	.04
135	Tim Krumrie	.10	.08	.04
136	James Lofton	.10	.08	.04
137	John Taylor	.10	.08	.04
138	Jeff Cross	.10	.08	.04
139	Tommy Kane	.10	.08	.04
140	Robb Thomas	.10	.08	.04
141	Gary Anderson	.10	.08	.04
142	Mark Murphy	.10	.08	.04
143	Rickey Jackson	.10	.08	.04
144	Ken O'Brien	.10	.08	.04
145	Ernest Givins	.10	.08	.04
146	Jessie Hester	.10	.08	.04
147	Deion Sanders	1.75	1.25	.70
148	Keith Henderson **RC**	.10	.08	.04
149	Chris Singleton	.10	.08	.04
150	Rod Bernstine	.10	.08	.04
151	Quinn Early	.10	.08	.04
152	Boomer Esiason	.10	.08	.04
153	Mike Gann	.10	.08	.04
154	Dino Hackett	.10	.08	.04
155	Perry Kemp	.10	.08	.04
156	Mark Ingram	.10	.08	.04
157	Daryl Johnston	.75	.60	.30
158	Eugene Daniel	.10	.08	.04
159	Dalton Hilliard	.10	.08	.04
160	Rufus Porter	.10	.08	.04
161	Tunch Ilkin	.10	.08	.04
162	James Hasty	.10	.08	.04
163	Keith McKeller	.10	.08	.04
164	Heath Sherman	.10	.08	.04
165	Vai Sikahema	.10	.08	.04
166	Pat Terrell	.10	.08	.04
167	Anthony Munoz	.10	.08	.04
168	Brad Edwards **RC**	.10	.08	.04
169	Tom Rathman	.10	.08	.04
170	Steve McMichael	.10	.08	.04
171	Vaughan Johnson	.10	.08	.04
172	Nate Lewis **RC**	.10	.08	.04
173	Mark Rypien	.10	.08	.04
174	Rob Moore	.10	.08	.04
175	Tim Green	.10	.08	.04
176	Tony Casillas	.10	.08	.04
177	Jon Hand	.10	.08	.04
178	Todd McNair	.10	.08	.04
179	Toi Cook **RC**	.10	.08	.04
180	Eddie Brown	.10	.08	.04
181	Mark Jackson	.10	.08	.04
182	Pete Stoyanovich	.10	.08	.04
183	Bryce Paup **RC**	2.00	1.50	.80
184	Anthony Miller	.20	.15	.08
185	Dan Saleaumua	.10	.08	.04
186	Guy McIntyre	.10	.08	.04
187	Broderick Thomas	.10	.08	.04
188	Frank Warren	.10	.08	.04
189	Drew Hill	.10	.08	.04
190	Reggie White	.40	.30	.15
191	Chris Hinton	.10	.08	.04
192	David Little	.10	.08	.04
193	David Fulcher	.10	.08	.04
194	Clarence Verdin	.10	.08	.04
195	Junior Seau	1.00	.70	.40
196	Blair Thomas	.10	.08	.04
197	Stan Brock	.10	.08	.04
198	Gary Clark	.10	.08	.04
199	Michael Irvin	.75	.60	.30
200	Ronnie Harmon	.10	.08	.04
201	Steve Young	3.00	2.25	1.25
202	Brian Noble	.10	.08	.04
203	Dan Stryzinski	.10	.08	.04
204	Darryl Talley	.10	.08	.04
205	David Alexander	.10	.08	.04
206	Pat Swilling	.10	.08	.04
207	Gary Plummer	.10	.08	.04
208	Robert Delpino	.10	.08	.04
209	Norm Johnson	.10	.08	.04
210	Mike Singletary	.10	.08	.04
211	Anthony Johnson	.10	.08	.04
212	Eric Allen	.10	.08	.04
213	Gill Fenerty	.10	.08	.04
214	Neil Smith	.10	.08	.04
215	Joe Phillips	.10	.08	.04
216	Ottis Anderson	.10	.08	.04
217	LeRoy Butler	.10	.08	.04
218	Ray Childress	.10	.08	.04
219	Rodney Holman	.10	.08	.04
220	Kevin Fagan	.10	.08	.04
221	Bruce Smith	.10	.08	.04
222	Brad Muster	.10	.08	.04
223	Mike Horan	.10	.08	.04
224	Steve Atwater	.10	.08	.04
225	Rich Gannon	.10	.08	.04
226	Anthony Pleasant	.10	.08	.04
227	Steve Jordan	.10	.08	.04
228	Lomas Broan	.10	.08	.04
229	Jackie Slater	.10	.08	.04
230	Brad Baxter	.10	.08	.04
231	Joe Morris	.10	.08	.04
232	Marcus Allen	.20	.15	.08
233	Chris Warren	1.00	.70	.40
234	Johnny Johnson	.10	.08	.04
235	Phil Simms	.10	.08	.04
236	Dave Krieg	.10	.08	.04
237	Jim McMahon	.10	.08	.04
238	Richard Dent	.10	.08	.04
239	John Washington **RC**	.10	.08	.04
240	Sammie Smith	.10	.08	.04
241	Brian Brennan	.10	.08	.04
242	Cortez Kennedy	.20	.15	.08
243	Tim McDonald	.10	.08	.04
244	Charles Haley	.10	.08	.04
245	Joey Browner	.10	.08	.04
246	Eddie Murray	.10	.08	.04
247	Bob Golic	.10	.08	.04
248	Myron Guyton	.10	.08	.04
249	Dennis Byrd	.10	.08	.04
250	Barry Sanders	4.00	3.00	1.50
251	Clay Matthews	.10	.08	.04
252	Pepper Johnson	.10	.08	.04
253	Eric Swann **RC**	1.00	.70	.40
254	Lamar Lathon	.10	.08	.04
255	Andre Tippett	.10	.08	.04
256	Tom Newberry	.10	.08	.04
257	Kyle Clifton	.10	.08	.04
258	Leslie O'Neal	.10	.08	.04
259	Bubba McDowell	.10	.08	.04
260	Scott Davis	.10	.08	.04
261	Wilber Marshall	.10	.08	.04
262	Marv Cook	.10	.08	.04
263	Jeff Lageman	.10	.08	.04
264	Mike Young	.10	.08	.04
265	Gary Zimmerman	.10	.08	.04
266	Mike Munchak	.10	.08	.04
267	David Treadwell	.10	.08	.04
268	Steve Wisniewski	.10	.08	.04
269	Mark Duper	.10	.08	.04
270	Chris Spielman	.10	.08	.04
271	Brett Perriman	.50	.40	.20
272	Lionel Washington	.10	.08	.04
273	Lawrence Taylor	.20	.15	.08
274	Mark Collins	.10	.08	.04
275	Mark Carrier	.10	.08	.04
276	Paul Gruber	.10	.08	.04
277	Earnest Byner	.10	.08	.04
278	Andre Collins	.10	.08	.04
279	Reggie Cobb	.10	.08	.04
280	Art Monk	.20	.15	.08
281	Henry Jones **RC**	.20	.15	.08
282	Mike Pritchard **RC**	.75	.60	.30
283	Moe Gardner **RC**	.20	.15	.08
284	Chris Zorich **RC**	.50	.40	.20
285	Keith Traylor **RC**	.20	.15	.08
286	Mike Dumas **RC**	.20	.15	.08
287	Ed King **RC**	.20	.15	.08
288	Russell Maryland **RC**	.20	.15	.08
289	Alfred Williams **RC**	.20	.15	.08
290	Derek Russell **RC**	.20	.15	.08
291	Vinnie Clark **RC**	.20	.15	.08
292	Mike Croel **RC**	.20	.15	.08
293	Todd Marinovich **RC**	.20	.15	.08
294	Phil Hansen **RC**	.20	.15	.08
295	Aaron Craver **RC**	.20	.15	.08
296	Nick Bell **RC**	.20	.15	.08
297	Kenny Walker **RC**	.20	.15	.08
298	Roman Phifer **RC**	.20	.15	.08
299	Kanavis McGhee **RC**	.20	.15	.08
300	Ricky Ervins **RC**	.20	.15	.08
301	Jim Price **RC**	.20	.15	.08
302	John Johnson **RC**	.20	.15	.08
303	George Thornton	.10	.08	.04
304	Huey Richardson	.10	.08	.04
305	Harry Colon **RC**	.20	.15	.08
306	Antone Davis **RC**	.20	.15	.08
307	Todd Lyght **RC**	.30	.25	.12
308	Bryan Cox **RC**	1.00	.70	.40
309	Brad Goebel **RC**	.20	.15	.08
310	Eric Moten **RC**	.20	.15	.08
311	John Kasay **RC**	.30	.25	.12
312	Esera Tuaolo **RC**	.20	.15	.08
313	Bobby Wilson **RC**	.20	.15	.08
314	Mo Lewis **RC**	.20	.15	.08
315	Harvey Williams **RC**	1.00	.70	.40
316	Mike Stonebreaker	.10	.08	.04
317	Charles McRae **RC**	.20	.15	.08
318	John Flannery **RC**	.20	.15	.08
319	Ted Washington **RC**	.20	.15	.08
320	Stanley Richard **RC**	.20	.15	.08
321	Browning Nagle **RC**	.20	.15	.08
322	Ed McCaffery **RC**	3.50	2.75	1.50
323	Jeff Graham **RC**	.50	.40	.20
324	Stan Thomas	.10	.08	.04
325	Lawrence Dawsey **RC**	.20	.15	.08
326	Eric Bieniemy **RC**	.30	.25	.12
327	Tim Barnett **RC**	.20	.15	.08
328	Erric Pegram **RC**	1.50	1.25	.60
329	Lamar Rogers	.10	.08	.04
330	Ernie Mills **RC**	.20	.15	.08
331	Pat Harlow **RC**	.20	.15	.08
332	Greg Lewis **RC**	.20	.15	.08
333	Jarrod Bunch **RC**	.20	.15	.08
334	Dan McGwire **RC**	.20	.15	.08
335	Randal Hill **RC**	.50	.40	.20
336	Leonard Russell **RC**	.50	.40	.20
337	Carnell Lake	.10	.08	.04
338	Brian Blades	.10	.08	.04
339	Darrell Green	.10	.08	.04
340	Bobby Humphrey	.10	.08	.04
341	Mervyn Fernandez	.10	.08	.04
342	Ricky Sanders	.10	.08	.04
343	Keith Jackson	.20	.15	.08
344	Carl Banks	.10	.08	.04
345	Gill Byrd	.10	.08	.04
346	Al Toon	.10	.08	.04
347	Stephen Baker	.10	.08	.04
348	Randall Cunningham	.10	.08	.04
349	Flipper Anderson	.10	.08	.04
350	Jay Novacek	.10	.08	.04
351	**Young/Smith** (HH)	.40	.30	.15
352	**Sanders/Browner** (HH)	.75	.60	.30
353	**Montana/Carrier** (HH)	.50	.40	.20
354	**Thomas/Taylor** (HH)	.20	.15	.08
355	**Rice/Green** (HH)	.50	.40	.20
356	Warren Moon (TECH)	.20	.15	.08
357	Anthony Munoz (TECH)	.10	.08	.04
358	Barry Sanders (TECH)	1.50	1.25	.60
359	Jerry Rice (TECH)	1.00	.70	.40
360	Joey Browner (TECH)	.10	.08	.04
361	Morten Andersen (TECH)	.10	.08	.04
362	Sean Landeta (TECH)	.10	.08	.04
363	Thurman Thomas (GW)	.20	.15	.08
364	Emmitt Smith (GW)	3.00	2.25	1.25
365	Gaston Green (GW)	.10	.08	.04
366	Barry Sanders (GW)	2.00	1.50	.80
367	Christian Okoye (GW)	.10	.08	.04

368	Earnest Byner (GW)	.10	.08	.04
369	Neal Anderson (GW)	.10	.08	.04
370	Herschel Walker (GW)	.10	.08	.04
371	Rodney Hampton (GW)	.20	.15	.08
372	Darryl Talley (IDOL)	.10	.08	.04
373	Mark Carrier (IDOL)	.10	.08	.04
374	Jim Breech (IDOL)	.10	.08	.04
375	Rodney Hampton (IDOL)	.20	.15	.08
376	Kevin Mack (IDOL)	.10	.08	.04
377	Steve Jordan (IDOL)	.10	.08	.04
378	Boomer Esiason (IDOL)	.10	.08	.04
379	Steve DeBerg (IDOL)	.10	.08	.04
380	Al Toon (IDOL)	.10	.08	.04
381	Ronnie Lott (IDOL)	.10	.08	.04
382	Henry Ellard (IDOL)	.10	.08	.04
383	Troy Aikman (IDOL)	1.25	.90	.50
384	Thurman Thomas	.50	.40	.20
385	Dan Marino (IDOL)	1.75	1.25	.70
386	Howie Long (IDOL)	.10	.08	.04
387	Immaculate Reception			
	(Franco Harris)	.10	.08	.04
388	Esera Tuaolo	.10	.08	.04
389	**Super Bowl XXVI** (Super			
	Bowl Records)	.10	.08	.04
390	Charles Mann	.10	.08	.04
391	Kenny Walker	.10	.08	.04
392	Reggie Roby	.10	.08	.04
393	Bruce Pickens **RC**	.20	.15	.08
394	Ray Childress (SL)	.10	.08	.04
395	Karl Mecklenburg (SL)	.10	.08	.04
396	Dean Biasucci (SL)	.10	.08	.04
397	John Alt (SL)	.10	.08	.04
398	Marcus Allen (SL)	.10	.08	.04
399	John Offerdahl (SL)	.10	.08	.04
400	Richard Tardits (SL)	.10	.08	.04
401	Al Toon (SL)	.10	.08	.04
402	Joey Browner (SL)	.10	.08	.04
403	Spencer Tillman (SL)	.10	.08	.04
404	Jay Novacek (SL)	.10	.08	.04
405	Stephen Braggs (SL)	.10	.08	.04
406	Mike Tice (SL)	.10	.08	.04
407	Kevin Greene (SL)	.10	.08	.04
408	Reggie White (SL)	.20	.15	.08
409	Brian Noble (SL)	.10	.08	.04
410	Bart Oates (SL)	.10	.08	.04
411	Art Monk (SL)	.10	.08	.04
412	Ron Wolfley (SL)	.10	.08	.04
413	Louis Lipps (SL)	.10	.08	.04
414	Dante Jones **RC** (SL)	.20	.15	.08
415	Kenneth Davis (SL)	.10	.08	.04

1991 Pinnacle Promo Panels

The 18-card, 5" x 7" panel set each features four preview cards from Pinnacle's 1991 football debut and were issued at the Super Bowl XXVI Card Show. The four-card panels have the same design as the regular-issue set.

		NM/M	NM	E
Complete Set (18):		100.00	75.00	40.00
Common Player:		3.00	2.25	1.25

1	John Alt, Eric Green, Don Mosebar, Greg Townsend	3.00	2.25	1.25
2	Bruce Armstrong, Joe Montana, Jim Lachey, Bruce Matthews	8.00	6.00	3.25
3	Don Beebe, Irving Fryar, Ricky Proehl, Vinny Testaverde	4.00	3.00	1.50
4	Duane Bickett, Tony Bennett, John Friesz, Rob Burnett	3.00	2.25	1.25
5	Mark Bortz, Warren Moon, Jim Breech, Eric Metcalf	4.00	3.00	1.50
6	Roger Craig, Issiac Holt, Kevin Mack, Shane Conlan	4.00	3.00	1.50
7	Wendell Davis, Gaston Green, Tony Mandarich, Merril Hoge	3.00	2.25	1.25
8	Dermontti Dawson, Jerry Gray, Nick Lowery, Scott Case	3.00	2.25	1.25
9	Chris Doleman, Troy Aikman, Sterling Sharpe, Sean Landeta	8.00	6.00	3.25
10	Darryl Henley, Karl Mecklenburg, Sam Mills, Rod Woodson	4.00	3.00	1.50
11	Mark Higgs, Jay Schroeder, Mark Carrier, Jim Everett	4.00	3.00	1.50
12	Jay Hilgenberg, Dan Marino, Anthony Carter, Howie Long	15.00	11.00	6.00
13	Louis Lipps, John Offerdahl, Herschel Walker, Jeff George	4.00	3.00	1.50

14	Greg McMurtry, Henry Ellard, Brian Mitchell, Mark Clayton	4.00	3.00	1.50
15	Nate Odomes, Allen Pinkett, Don Majkowski, Dave Meggett	3.00	2.25	1.25
16	Andre Rison, Jeff Hostetler, Hugh Millen, Jack Del Rio	4.00	3.00	1.50
17	Emmitt Smith, Dennis Smith, Bill Brooks, Bobby Hebert	18.00	13.50	7.25
18	Reyna Thompson, Louis Oliver, Steve Broussard, Andre Reed	4.00	3.00	1.50

1989 Pittsburgh

		NM/M	NM	E
Complete Set (22):		10.00	7.50	4.00
Common Player:		.30	.25	.12

1	Tony Dorsett	2.00	1.50	.80
2	Pop Warner (CO)	.40	.30	.15
3	Hugh Green	.60	.45	.25
4	Matt Cavanaugh	.50	.40	.20
5	Mike Gottfried	.40	.30	.15
6	Jimbo Covert	.50	.40	.20
7	Bob Peck	.30	.25	.12
8	Gibby Welch	.30	.25	.12
9	Bill Daddio	.40	.30	.15
10	Jock Sutherland (CO)	.40	.30	.15
11	Joe Walton	.40	.30	.15
12	Dan Marino	4.00	3.00	1.50
13	Russ Grimm	.40	.30	.15
14	Mike Ditka	2.00	1.50	.80
15	Marshall Goldberg	.50	.40	.20
16	Bill Fralic	.40	.30	.15
17	Paul Martha	.40	.30	.15
18	Joe Schmidt	.75	.60	.30
19	Rickey Jackson	.60	.45	.25
20	Ave Daniell	.30	.25	.12
21	Bill Maas	.40	.30	.15
22	Mark May	.40	.30	.15

1990 Pitt Foodland

		NM/M	NM	E
Complete Set (12):		8.00	6.00	3.25
Common Player:		.50	.40	.20

1	Curtis Bray	.50	.40	.20
2	Craig Gob	.50	.40	.20
3	Paul Hackett (CO)	.50	.40	.20
4	Keith Hamilton	1.50	1.25	.60
5	Ricardo McDonald	1.50	1.25	.60
6	Ronald Redmon	.50	.40	.20
7	Curvin Richards	.50	.40	.20
8	Louis Riddick	1.50	1.25	.60
9	Chris Sestili	.50	.40	.20
10	Olanda Truitt	1.50	1.25	.60
11	Alex Van Pelt	1.50	1.25	.60
12	Nelson Walker	.50	.40	.20

1991 Pitt Foodland

		NM/M	NM	E
Complete Set (12):		7.00	5.25	2.75
Common Player:		.75	.60	.30

1	Richard Allen	.75	.60	.30
2	Curtis Bray	.75	.60	.30
3	Jeff Christy	.75	.60	.30
4	Steve Israel	1.00	.70	.40
5	Scott Kaplan	.75	.60	.30
6	Ricardo McDonald	1.00	.70	.40
7	Dave Moore	.75	.60	.30
8	Eric Seaman	.75	.60	.30
9	Chris Sestili	.75	.60	.30
10	Alex Van Pelt	1.50	1.25	.60
11	Nelson Walker	.75	.60	.30
12	Kevin Williams (HB)	.75	.60	.30

1991 Pitt State

		NM/M	NM	E
Complete Set (18):		12.00	9.00	4.75
Common Player:		.60	.45	.25

1	Chuck Broyles (CO)	.60	.45	.25
2	Darren Dawson	.60	.45	.25
3	Kendall Gammon	.60	.45	.25
4	Jamie Goodson	.60	.45	.25
5	Brian Hoover	.60	.45	.25
6	James Jenkins	.60	.45	.25
7	Ky Kiger	.60	.45	.25
8	Phil McCoy	.60	.45	.25
9	Kline Minniefield	.60	.45	.25
10	Ron Moore	4.00	3.00	1.50
11	Jeff Mundhenke	.60	.45	.25
12	Brian Pinamonti	.60	.45	.25
13	Michael Rose	.60	.45	.25

14	Shane Tafoya	.60	.45	.25
15	Ronnie West	1.25	.90	.50
16	Michael Wilber	.60	.45	.25
17	Troy Wilson	1.50	1.25	.60
18	**Team Photo**	1.25	.90	.50

1981 Police Saskatchewan

		NM/M	NM	E
Complete Set (10):		15.00	11.00	6.00
Common Player:		1.25	.90	.50

1	Roger Aldag (44)	2.00	1.50	.80
2	Joe Barnes (7)	1.25	.90	.50
3	Lester Brown (22)	1.25	.90	.50
4	Dwight Edwards (33)	1.25	.90	.50
5	Vince Goldsmith (78)	2.00	1.50	.80
6	John Hufnagel (12)	5.00	3.75	2.00
7	Ken McEachern (20)	1.25	.90	.50
8	Mike Samples (66)	1.25	.90	.50
9	Joey Walters (17)	1.25	.90	.50
10	Lyall Woznesensky (76)	1.25	.90	.50

1982 Police Hamilton

		NM/M	NM	E
Complete Set (35):		20.00	15.00	8.00
Common Player:		.50	.40	.20

1	Marv Allemang	.50	.40	.20
2	Jeff Arp	.50	.40	.20
3	Keith Baker	.50	.40	.20
4	Gerald Bess	.75	.60	.30
5	Mark Bragagnolo	.50	.40	.20
6	Carmelo Carteri	.50	.40	.20
7	Tom Clements	7.50	5.75	3.00
8	Grover Covington	3.00	2.25	1.25
9	Rocky DiPietro	4.00	3.00	1.50
10	Howard Fields	.50	.40	.20
11	Ross Francis	.50	.40	.20
12	Ed Fulton	.50	.40	.20
13	Peter Gales	.50	.40	.20
14	Ed Gataveckas	.50	.40	.20
15	Dave Graffi	.50	.40	.20
16	Obie Graves	.50	.40	.20
17	Hazen Henderson	.50	.40	.20
18	Ron Johnson	1.25	.90	.50
19	Dave Marler	.75	.60	.30
20	Jim Muller	.50	.40	.20
21	Leroy Paul	.50	.40	.20
22	John Priestner	.75	.60	.30
23	Dave Purves	.50	.40	.20
24	James Ramey	.50	.40	.20
25	Doug Redl	.50	.40	.20
26	Bernie Ruoff	.75	.60	.30
27	David Sauve	.50	.40	.20
28	David Shaw	.50	.40	.20
29	Kerry Smith	.50	.40	.20
30	Steve Stapler	.75	.60	.30
31	Kyle Stevens	.50	.40	.20
32	Mike Walker	2.00	1.50	.80
33	Henry Waszczuk	.50	.40	.20
34	Harold Woods	.50	.40	.20
35	Ben Zambiasi	2.50	2.00	1.00

1982 Police Saskatchewan

		NM/M	NM	E
Complete Set (16):		12.00	9.00	4.75
Common Player:		.75	.60	.30

2	Greg Fieger	.75	.60	.30
7	Joe Adams	.75	.60	.30
12	John Hufnagel	4.00	3.00	1.50
17	Joey Walters	.75	.60	.30
20	Ken McEachern	.75	.60	.30
21	Marcellus Greene	.75	.60	.30
25	Steve Dennis	.75	.60	.30
29	Fran McDermott	.75	.60	.30
37	Frank Robinson	1.00	.70	.40
44	Roger Aldag	1.25	.90	.50
57	Bob Poley	.75	.60	.30
66	Mike Samples	.75	.60	.30
69	Don Swafford	.75	.60	.30
74	Chris DeFrance	.75	.60	.30
76	Lyall Woznesensky	.75	.60	.30
78	Vince Goldsmith	1.50	1.25	.60

1982 Police Winnipeg

		NM/M	NM	E
Complete Set (24):		10.00	7.50	4.00
Common Player:		.40	.30	.15

1	Nick Bastaja	.40	.30	.15
2	Paul Bennett	.40	.30	.15
3	John Bonk	.40	.30	.15
4	Dieter Brock	2.50	2.00	1.00
5	Peter Catan	.40	.30	.15
6	Leo Ezerins	.40	.30	.15
7	Eugene Goodlow	.40	.30	.15
8	John Helton	1.50	1.25	.60

		NM/M	NM	E
9	Rick House	.60	.45	.25
10	Mark Jackson	.60	.45	.25
11	Ray Jauch (CO)	.40	.30	.15
12	Milson Jones	1.00	.70	.40
13	Trevor Kennerd	1.25	.90	.50
14	Stan Mikawos	.40	.30	.15
15	William Miller	.60	.45	.25
16	Tony Norman	.40	.30	.15
17	Vince Phason	.40	.30	.15
18	Reggie Pierson	.40	.30	.15
19	Joe Poplawski	.60	.45	.25
20	James Reed	.40	.30	.15
21	Franky Smith	.40	.30	.15
22	Bobby Thompson	.40	.30	.15
23	Chris Walby	1.00	.70	.40
24	Charles Williams	.40	.30	.15

1983 Police Hamilton

		NM/M	NM	E
	Complete Set (37):	20.00	15.00	8.00
	Common Player:	.50	.40	.20
1	Marv Allemang	.50	.40	.20
2	Jeff Arp	.50	.40	.20
3	Keith Baker	.50	.40	.20
4	Harold E. Ballard (PRES)	2.00	1.50	.80
5	Mike Barker	.50	.40	.20
6	Gerald Bess	.75	.60	.30
7	Pat Brady	.50	.40	.20
8	Mark Bragagnolo	.50	.40	.20
9	Tom Clements	7.50	5.75	3.00
10	Grover Covington	3.00	2.25	1.25
11	Rufus Crawford	2.00	.40	.80
12	Rocky DiPietro	4.00	3.00	1.50
13	Leo Ezerins	.50	.40	.20
14	Howard Fields	.50	.40	.20
15	Ross Francis	.50	.40	.20
16	Peter Gales	.50	.40	.20
17	Ed Gataveckas	.50	.40	.20
18	Paul Gohier	.50	.40	.20
19	Dave Graffi	.50	.40	.20
20	Ron Johnson	1.25	.90	.50
21	Steve Kearns	.50	.40	.20
22	Wayne Lee	.50	.40	.20
23	Mike McIntyre	.50	.40	.20
24	Paul Palma	.50	.40	.20
25	George Piva	.50	.40	.20
26	Mitchell Price	.75	.60	.30
27	John Priestner	.75	.60	.30
28	Bernie Ruoff	.75	.60	.30
29	David Sauve	.50	.40	.20
30	Johnny Shepherd	.50	.40	.20
31	Steve Stapler	1.00	.70	.40
32	Mark Streeter	.50	.40	.20
33	Jeff Tedford	.50	.40	.20
34	Mike Walker	2.00	1.50	.80
35	Henry Waszczuk	.50	.40	.20
36	Felix Wright	2.50	2.00	1.00
37	Ben Zambiasi	2.50	2.00	1.00

1983 Police Saskatchewan

		NM/M	NM	E
	Complete Set (16):	12.00	9.00	4.75
	Common Player:	.75	.60	.30
9	Ron Robinson	1.00	.70	.40
12	John Hufnagel	3.00	2.25	1.25
13	Ken Clark	1.00	.70	.40
18	Mike Washington	1.00	.70	.40
24	Marshall Hamilton	.75	.60	.30
25	Mike Emery	.75	.60	.30
30	Duane Galloway	.75	.60	.30
33	Dwight Edwards	1.00	.70	.40
36	Dave Ridgway	2.00	1.50	.80
42	Eddie Lowe	.75	.60	.30
58	J.C. Pelusi	.75	.60	.30
60	Karl Morgan	.75	.60	.30
61	Bryan Illerbrun	.75	.60	.30
65	Neil Quilter	.75	.60	.30
72	Ray Elgaard	3.00	2.25	1.25
74	Chris DeFrance	.75	.60	.30

1984 Police Ottawa

		NM/M	NM	E
	Complete Set (10):	30.00	22.00	12.00
	Common Player:	.75	.60	.30
1	Greg Marshall	1.25	.90	.50
2	Dave Newman	.75	.60	.30
3	Rudy Phillips	1.25	.90	.50
4	Jim Reid	1.25	.90	.50
5	Mark Seale (SP)	20.00	15.00	8.00
6	Rick Sowieta	1.25	.90	.50
7	Pat Stoqua	1.25	.90	.50
8	Skip Walker	2.50	2.00	1.00
9	Al Washington	.75	.60	.30
10	J.C. Watts	8.00	6.00	3.25

1985 Police Ottawa

		NM/M	NM	E
	Complete Set (10):	6.00	4.50	2.50
	Common Player:	.50	.40	.20
1	Ricky Barden	.50	.40	.20
2	Michel Bourgeau	.75	.60	.30
3	Roger Cattelan	.50	.40	.20
4	Ken Clark	.75	.60	.30
5	Dean Dorsey	.75	.60	.30
6	Greg Marshall	.75	.60	.30
7	Kevin Powell	.50	.40	.20
8	Jim Reid	.75	.60	.30
9	Rick Sowieta	.75	.60	.30
10	J.C. Watts	3.00	2.25	1.25

1985 Police Raiders/Rams

Broken down into two 15-card subsets for each team, the cards are not numbered, except with the player's uniform numerals. It was sponsored by KIIS Radio, the Rams and Raiders and the Los Angeles County Sheriff's Department. Card fronts include a photo of the player, with his name underneath, along with his team's helmet and sponsor logo. Card backs have the player's name, uniform number, position, bio and a safety message printed in black. The cards measure 2-13/16 x 4-1/8".

		NM/M	NM	E
	Complete Set (30):	20.00	15.00	8.00
	Common Raiders (1-15):	.75	.60	.30
	Common Rams (16-30):	.50	.40	.20
1	Marcus Allen	4.00	3.00	1.50
2	Lyle Alzado	1.50	1.25	.60
3	Todd Christensen	1.00	.70	.40
4	Dave Dalby	.75	.60	.30
5	Mike Davis	.75	.60	.30
6	Ray Guy	1.00	.70	.40
7	Frank Hawkins	.75	.60	.30
8	Lester Hayes	1.00	.70	.40
9	Mike Haynes	1.00	.70	.40
10	Howie Long	2.00	1.50	.80
11	Rod Martin	.75	.60	.30
12	Mickey Marvin	.75	.60	.30
13	Jim Plunkett	1.25	.90	.50
14	Brad Van Pelt	.75	.60	.30
15	Dokie Williams	.75	.60	.30
16	Bill Bain	.50	.40	.20
17	Mike Barber	.50	.40	.20
18	Dieter Brock	.75	.60	.30
19	Nolan Cromwell	.75	.60	.30
20	Eric Dickerson	3.00	2.25	1.25
21	Reggie Doss	.50	.40	.20
22	Carl Ekern	.50	.40	.20
23	Kent Hill	.50	.40	.20
24	LeRoy Irvin	.75	.60	.30
25	Johnnie Johnson	.50	.40	.20
26	Jeff Kemp	.50	.40	.20
27	Mike Lansford	.50	.40	.20
28	Mel Owens	.50	.40	.20
29	Barry Redden	.50	.40	.20
30	Mike Wilcher	.50	.40	.20

1986 Police Bears/Patriots

Featuring the two teams from Super Bowl XX, this 17-card set measures 2-5/8" x 4-1/4". The card fronts boast a photo of the player, with his name, uniform number and position at the bottom. The card backs have "Super Bowl Superstars 1986 presents" at the top, with a safety tip listed at the bottom of the card. The card number is located in the lower right. Chicago players are on card #s 2-9, while New England players are highlighted on #s 10-17.

		NM/M	NM	E
	Complete Set (17):	15.00	11.00	6.00
	Common Player:	.50	.40	.20
1	**Title Card** (Checklist on back of card)	.75	.60	.30
2	Richard Dent	2.00	1.50	.80
3	Walter Payton	6.00	4.50	2.50
4	William Perry	1.00	.70	.40
5	Jim McMahon	1.50	1.25	.60
6	Dave Duerson	.75	.60	.30
7	Gary Fencik	.75	.60	.30
8	Otis Wilson	.75	.60	.30
9	Willie Gault	1.00	.70	.40
10	Craig James	1.00	.70	.40
11	Fred Marion	.50	.40	.20
12	Ronnie Lippett	.50	.40	.20
13	Stanley Morgan	1.00	.70	.40
14	John Hannah	1.00	.70	.40
15	Andre Tippett	1.00	.70	.40
16	Tony Franklin	.50	.40	.20
17	Tony Eason	1.00	.70	.40

1976 Popsicle Teams

Each NFL team is represented in this 28-card set, which features a color action shot on the front of each card, plus the corresponding team's helmet. The back provides a historical overview of the team. The cards, which are unnumbered, are listed below alphabetically. Each one is 3-3/8" x 2-1/8" and resembles a thin plastic credit card with rounded corners. A title card, which says "Pro Quarterback, Pro Football's Leading Magazine," was also produced.

		NM	E	VG
	Complete Set (30):	40.00	20.00	12.00
	Common Player:	2.50	1.25	.70
(1)	**Atlanta Falcons**	2.50	1.25	.70
(2)	**Baltimore Colts**	2.50	1.25	.70
(3)	**Buffalo Bills**	2.50	1.25	.70
(4)	**Chicago Bears**	4.00	2.00	1.25
(5)	**Cincinnati Bengals**	2.50	1.25	.70
(6)	**Cleveland Browns**	2.50	1.25	.70
(7)	**Dallas Cowboys**	4.00	2.00	1.25
(8)	**Denver Broncos**	2.50	1.25	.70
(9)	**Detroit Lions**	2.50	1.25	.70
(10)	**Green Bay Packers**	2.50	1.25	.70
(11)	**Houston Oilers**	2.50	1.25	.70
(12)	**Kansas City Chiefs**	2.50	1.25	.70
(13)	**Los Angeles Rams**	2.50	1.25	.70
(14)	**Miami Dolphins**	4.00	2.00	1.25
(15)	**Minnesota Vikings**	2.50	1.25	.70
(16)	**New England Patriots**	2.50	1.25	.70
(17)	**New Orleans Saints**	2.50	1.25	.70
(18A)	**New York Giants** (Giants on helmet)	3.50	1.75	1.00
(18B)	**New York Giants** (New York on helmet)	4.50	2.25	1.25
(19)	**New York Jets**	2.50	1.25	.70
(20)	**Oakland Raiders**	4.00	2.00	1.25
(21)	**Philadelphia Eagles**	2.50	1.25	.70
(22)	**Pittsburgh Steelers**	4.00	2.00	1.25
(23)	**St. Louis Cardinals**	2.50	1.25	.70
(24)	**San Diego Chargers**	2.50	1.25	.70
(25)	**San Francisco 49ers**	3.00	1.50	.90
(26)	**Seattle Seahawks**	2.50	1.25	.70
(27)	**Tampa Bay Buccaneers**	2.50	1.25	.70
(28)	**Washington Redskins**	3.50	1.75	1.00
----	**Title Card, Pro Quarterback**	30.00	15.00	9.00

1962 Post Booklets

Measuring 5" x 3", each of the four booklets included 15 pages. The booklet covers include a drawing of the player, with his name, position and team, along with the title. The book covers are numbered in the upper right with a prefix of "book."

		NM	E	VG
	Complete Set (4):	65.00	49.00	26.00
	Common Player:	10.00	5.00	3.00
1	Football Formations To Watch (Jon Arnett) (Important Rules of the Game)	10.00	5.00	3.00
2	Fundamentals of Football(Paul Hornung)	25.00	12.50	7.50
3	How To Play On Offense (Sonny Jurgensen) (How To Call Signals And Key Plays)	20.00	10.00	6.00
4	How To Play Defense (Sam Huff)	15.00	7.50	4.50

1962 Post Cereal

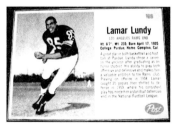

Post Cereal's only U.S. football issue, the 1962 set is complete at 200 cards. The blank-backed cards were printed on the back panels of various Post cereals and measure the standard 2-1/2" x 3-1/2" when properly cut. Like the Post Cereal baseball issues from the same period, the cards must be very carefully cut from the boxes to be considered in top condition. Players who were pictured on boxes of the less-popular cereals are scarcer and more valuable, explaining the higher prices on about two dozen of the cards listed below.

		NM	E	VG
	Complete Set (200):	2,500	1,250	750.00
	Common Player:	3.50	1.75	1.00

	Minor Stars:	5.00		
	Unlisted Stars:	7.00		
1	Dan Currie	3.50	1.75	1.00
2	Boyd Dowler	3.50	1.75	1.00
3	Bill Forester	3.50	1.75	1.00
4	Forrest Gregg	4.00	2.00	1.25
5	Dave Hanner	3.50	1.75	1.00
6	Paul Hornung	14.00	7.00	4.25
7	Henry Jordan	3.50	1.75	1.00
8	Jerry Kramer	12.00	6.00	3.50
9	Max McGee	3.50	1.75	1.00
10	Tom Moore	100.00	50.00	30.00
11	Jim Ringo	6.00	3.00	1.75
12	Bart Starr	20.00	10.00	6.00
13	Jim Taylor	12.00	6.00	3.50
14	Fred Thurston	3.50	1.75	1.00
15	Kess Whittenton	3.50	1.75	1.00
16	Erich Barnes	3.50	1.75	1.00
17	Roosevelt Grier	5.00	2.50	1.50
18	Bob Gaiters	3.50	1.75	1.00
19	Roosevelt Brown	5.00	2.50	1.50
20	Sam Huff	8.00	4.00	2.50
21	Jim Katcavage	3.50	1.75	1.00
22	Cliff Livingston	3.50	1.75	1.00
23	Dick Lynch	3.50	1.75	1.00
24	Joe Morrison	20.00	10.00	6.00
25	Dick Nolan	18.00	9.00	5.50
26	Andy Robustelli	5.00	2.50	1.50
27	Kyle Rote	7.00	3.50	2.00
28	Del Shofner	25.00	12.50	7.50
29	Y.A. Tittle	60.00	30.00	18.00
30	Alex Webster	3.50	1.75	1.00
31	Bill Barnes	3.50	1.75	1.00
32	Maxie Baughan	3.50	1.75	1.00
33	Chuck Bednarik	8.00	4.00	1.00
34	Tom Brookshier	6.00	3.00	1.75
35	Jimmy Carr	3.50	1.75	1.00
36	Ted Dean	3.50	1.75	1.00
37	Sonny Jurgensen	12.00	6.00	3.50
38	Tommy McDonald	3.50	1.75	1.00
39	Clarence Peaks	3.50	1.75	1.00
40	Pete Retzlaff	3.50	1.75	1.00
41	Jesse Richardson	30.00	15.00	9.00
42	Leo Sugar	3.50	1.75	1.00
43	Bobby Walston	40.00	20.00	12.00
44	Chuck Weber	3.50	1.75	1.00
45	Ed Khayat	3.50	1.75	1.00
46	Howard Cassady	3.50	1.75	1.00
47	Gail Cogdill	3.50	1.75	1.00
48	Jim Gibbons	3.50	1.75	1.00
49	Bill Glass	3.50	1.75	1.00
50	Alex Karras	3.50	1.75	1.00
51	Dick "Night Train" Lane	3.50	1.75	1.00
52	Yale Lary	3.50	1.75	1.00
53	Dan Lewis	3.50	1.75	1.00
54	Darris McCord	50.00	25.00	15.00
55	Jim Martin	3.50	1.75	1.00
56	Earl Morrall	3.50	1.75	1.00
57	Jim Ninowski	3.50	1.75	1.00
58	Nick Pietrosante	3.50	1.75	1.00
59	Joe Schmidt	50.00	25.00	15.00
60	Harley Sewell	3.50	1.75	1.00
61	Jim Brown	60.00	30.00	18.00
62	Galen Fiss	40.00	20.00	12.00
63	Bob Gain	3.50	1.75	1.00
64	Jim Houston	3.50	1.75	1.00
65	Mike McCormack	3.50	1.75	1.00
66	Gene Hickerson	3.50	1.75	1.00
67	Bob Mitchell	3.50	1.75	1.00
68	John Morrow	3.50	1.75	1.00
69	Bernie Parrish	3.50	1.75	1.00
70	Milt Plum	3.50	1.75	1.00
71	Ray Renfro	3.50	1.75	1.00
72	Dick Schafrath	3.50	1.75	1.00
73	Jim Ray Smith	3.50	1.75	1.00
74	Sam Baker	220.00	110.00	66.00
75	Paul Wiggin	3.50	1.75	1.00
76	Raymond Berry	3.50	1.75	1.00
77	Bob Boyd	3.50	1.75	1.00
78	Ordell Braase	3.50	1.75	1.00
79	Art Donovan	3.50	1.75	1.00
80	Dee Mackey	3.50	1.75	1.00
81	Gino Marchetti	3.50	1.75	1.00
82	Lenny Moore	3.50	1.75	1.00
83	Jim Mutscheller	3.50	1.75	1.00
84	Steve Myhra	3.50	1.75	1.00
85	Jimmy Orr	3.50	1.75	1.00
86	Jim Parker	3.50	1.75	1.00
87	Bill Pellington	3.50	1.75	1.00
88	Alex Sandusky	3.50	1.75	1.00
89	Dick Szymanski	3.50	1.75	1.00
90	Johnny Unitas	25.00	12.50	7.50
91	Bruce Bosley	3.50	1.75	1.00
92	John Brodie	12.00	6.00	3.75
93	Dave Baker	125.00	62.00	37.00
94	Tommy Davis	3.50	1.75	1.00
95	Bob Harrison	3.50	1.75	1.00
96	Matt Hazeltine	3.50	1.75	1.00
97	Jim Johnson	50.00	25.00	15.00
98	Bill Kilmer	8.00	4.00	2.50
99	Jerry Mertens	3.50	1.75	1.00
100	Frank Morze	3.50	1.75	1.00
101	R.C. Owens	3.50	1.75	1.00
102	J.D. Smith	3.50	1.75	1.00
103	Bob St. Clair	60.00	30.00	18.00
104	Monty Stickles	3.50	1.75	1.00
105	Abe Woodson	3.50	1.75	1.00
106	Doug Atkins	3.50	1.75	1.00
107	Ed Brown	3.50	1.75	1.00
108	J.C. Caroline	3.50	1.75	1.00
109	Rick Casares	3.50	1.75	1.00
110	Angelo Coia	175.00	90.00	50.00
111	Mike Ditka	20.00	10.00	6.00
112	Joe Fortunato	3.50	1.75	1.00
113	Willie Galimore	3.50	1.75	1.00
114	Bill George	5.50	2.75	1.60
115	Stan Jones	3.50	1.75	1.00
116	Johnny Morris	5.50	2.75	1.60
117	Larry Morris	40.00	20.00	12.00
118	Rich Pettibon	3.50	1.75	1.00
119	Bill Wade	4.00	2.00	1.00
120	Maury Youmans	3.50	1.75	1.00
121	Preston Carpenter	3.50	1.75	1.00
122	Buddy Dial	3.50	1.75	1.00
123	Bobby Joe Green	3.50	1.75	1.00
124	Mike Henry	3.50	1.75	1.00
125	John Henry Johnson	5.50	2.75	1.60
126	Bobby Layne	15.00	7.50	4.50
127	Gene Lipscomb	5.50	2.75	1.60
128	Lou Michaels	3.50	1.75	1.00
129	John Nisby	3.50	1.75	1.00
130	John Reger	3.50	1.75	1.00
131	Mike Sandusky	3.50	1.75	1.00
132	George Tarasovic	3.50	1.75	1.00
133	Tom Tracy	40.00	20.00	12.00
134	Glynn Gregory	3.50	1.75	1.00
135	Frank Clarke	40.00	20.00	12.00
136	Mike Connelly	40.00	20.00	12.00
137	L.G. Dupre	3.50	1.75	1.00
138	Bob Fry	3.50	1.75	1.00
139	Allen Green	60.00	30.00	18.00
140	Bill Howton	3.50	1.75	1.00
141	Bob Lilly	12.00	6.00	3.75
142	Don Meredith	16.00	8.00	5.00
143	Dick Moegle	3.50	1.75	1.00
144	Don Perkins	5.50	2.75	1.60
145	Jerry Tubbs	60.00	30.00	18.00
146	J.W. Lockett	3.50	1.75	1.00
147	Ed Cook	3.50	1.75	1.00
148	John David Crow	5.50	2.75	1.60
149	Sam Etcheverry	5.50	2.75	1.60
150	Frank Fuller	3.50	1.75	1.00
151	Prentice Gautt	3.50	1.75	1.00
152	Jimmy Hill	3.50	1.75	1.00
153	Bill Koman	40.00	20.00	12.00
154	Larry Wilson	5.50	2.75	1.60
155	Dale Meinert	3.50	1.75	1.00
156	Ed Henke	3.50	1.75	1.00
157	Sonny Randle	3.50	1.75	1.00
158	Ralph Guglielmi	40.00	20.00	12.00
159	Joe Childress	3.50	1.75	1.00
160	Jon Arnett	5.50	2.75	1.60
161	Dick Bass	3.50	1.75	1.00
162	Zeke Bratkowski	5.50	2.75	1.60
163	Carroll Dale	3.50	1.75	1.00
164	Art Hunter	3.50	1.75	1.00
165	John Lovetere	3.50	1.75	1.00
166	Lamar Lundy	3.50	1.75	1.00
167	Ollie Matson	8.00	4.00	2.50
168	Ed Meador	3.50	1.75	1.00
169	Jack Pardee	60.00	30.00	18.00
170	Jim Phillips	3.50	1.75	1.00
171	Les Richter	3.50	1.75	1.00
172	Frank Ryan	3.50	1.75	1.00
173	Frank Varrichione	3.50	1.75	1.00
174	Grady Alderman	3.50	1.75	1.00
175	Rip Hawkins	3.50	1.75	1.00
176	Don Joyce	60.00	30.00	18.00
177	Bill Lapham	3.50	1.75	1.00
178	Tommy Mason	3.50	1.75	1.00
179	Hugh McElhenny	3.50	1.75	1.00
180	Dave Middleton	3.50	1.75	1.00
181	Dick Pesonen	3.50	1.75	1.00
182	Karl Rubke	3.50	1.75	1.00
183	George Shaw	3.50	1.75	1.00
184	Fran Tarkenton	35.00	17.50	10.00
185	Mel Triplett	3.50	1.75	1.00
186	Frank Youso	40.00	20.00	12.00
187	Bill Bishop	3.50	1.75	1.00
188	Bill Anderson	40.00	20.00	12.00
189	Don Bosseler	3.50	1.75	1.00
190	Fred Hageman	3.50	1.75	1.00
191	Sam Horner	3.50	1.75	1.00
192	Jim Kerr	3.50	1.75	1.00
193	Joe Krakoski	150.00	75.00	45.00
194	Fred Dugan	3.50	1.75	1.00
195	John Paluck	3.50	1.75	1.00
196	Vince Promuto	3.50	1.75	1.00
197	Joe Rutgens	3.50	1.75	1.00
198	Norm Snead	5.50	2.75	1.60
199	Andy Stynchula	3.50	1.75	1.00
200	Bob Toneff	3.50	1.75	1.00

1962 Post Cereal CFL

		NM	E	VG
	Complete Set (137):	1,600	800.00	400.00
	Common Player:	7.50	3.75	2.25
1A	Don Clark (Brown Back)	20.00	10.00	6.00
1B	Don Clark (SP) (White Back)	60.00	30.00	18.00
2	Ed Meadows	7.50	3.75	2.25
3	Meco Poliziani	7.50	3.75	2.25
4	George Dixon	20.00	10.00	6.00
5	Bobby Jack Oliver	10.00	5.00	3.00
6	Ross Buckle	7.50	3.75	2.25
7	Jack Espenship	7.50	3.75	2.25
8	Howard Cissell	7.50	3.75	2.25
9	Ed Nickla	7.50	3.75	2.25
10	Ed Learn	7.50	3.75	2.25
11	Billy Ray Locklin	7.50	3.75	2.25
12	Don Paquette	7.50	3.75	2.25
13	Milt Crain	7.50	3.75	2.25
14	Dick Schnell	7.50	3.75	2.25
15	Dick Cohee	7.50	3.75	2.25
16	Joe Francis	7.50	3.75	2.25
17	Gilles Archambeault	7.50	3.75	2.25
18	Angelo Mosca	25.00	12.50	7.50
19	Ernie White	7.50	3.75	2.25
20	George Brancato	7.50	3.75	2.25
21	Ron Lancaster	35.00	17.50	10.50
22	Jim Cain	7.50	3.75	2.25
23	Gerry Nesbitt	7.50	3.75	2.25
24	Russ Jackson	30.00	15.00	9.00
25	Bob Simpson	18.00	9.00	5.50
26	Sam Scoccia	7.50	3.75	2.25
27	Tom Jones	7.50	3.75	2.25
28	Kaye Vaughan	15.00	7.50	4.50
29	Chuck Stanley	7.50	3.75	2.25
30	Dave Thelen	15.00	7.50	4.50
31	Gary Schreider	7.50	3.75	2.25
32	Jim Reynolds	7.50	3.75	2.25
33	Doug Daigneault	7.50	3.75	2.25
34	Joe Poirier	10.00	5.00	3.00
35	Clare Exelby	7.50	3.75	2.25
36	Art Johnson	7.50	3.75	2.25
37	Menan Schriewer	7.50	3.75	2.25
38	Art Darch	7.50	3.75	2.25
39	Cookie Gilchrist	25.00	12.50	7.50
40	Brian Aston	7.50	3.75	2.25
41	Bobby Kuntz (SP)	50.00	25.00	15.00
42	Gerry Patrick	7.50	3.75	2.25
43	Norm Stoneburgh	7.50	3.75	2.25
44	Billy Shipp	7.50	3.75	2.25
45	Jim Andreotti	15.00	7.50	4.50
46	Tobin Rote	20.00	10.00	6.00
47	Dick Shatto	15.00	7.50	4.50
48	Dave Mann	10.00	5.00	3.00
49	Ron Morris	7.50	3.75	2.25
50	Lynn Bottoms	10.00	5.00	3.00
51	Jim Rountree	7.50	3.75	2.25
52	Bill Mitchell	7.50	3.75	2.25
53	Wes Gideon (SP)	50.00	25.00	15.00
54	Boyd Carter	7.50	3.75	2.25
55	Ron Howell	10.00	5.00	3.00
56	John Barrow	15.00	7.50	4.50
57	Bernie Faloney	30.00	15.00	9.00
58	Ron Ray	7.50	3.75	2.25
59	Don Sutherin	15.00	7.50	4.50
60	Frank Cosentino	10.00	5.00	3.00
61	Hardiman Cureton	7.50	3.75	2.25
62	Hal Patterson	20.00	10.00	6.00
63	Ralph Goldston	7.50	3.75	2.25
64	Tommy Grant	15.00	7.50	4.50
65	Larry Hickman	7.50	3.75	2.25
66	Zeno Karcz	10.00	5.00	3.00
67	Garney Henley	20.00	10.00	6.00
68	Gerry McDougall	10.00	5.00	3.00
69	Vince Scott	12.00	6.00	3.50
70	Gerry James	15.00	7.50	4.50
71	Roger Hagberg	10.00	5.00	3.00
72	Gord Rowland	10.00	5.00	3.00
73	Ernie Pitts	7.50	3.75	2.25
74	Frank Rigney	12.00	6.00	3.50
75	Norm Rauhaus	12.00	6.00	3.50
76	Leo Lewis	20.00	10.00	6.00
77	Mike Wright	7.50	3.75	2.25
78	Jack Delveaux	7.50	3.75	2.25
79	Steve Patrick	7.50	3.75	2.25
80	Dave Burkholder	7.50	3.75	2.25
81	Charlie Shepard	7.50	3.75	2.25
82	Kenny Ploen	20.00	10.00	6.00

83	Ronnie Latourelle	7.50	3.75	2.25
84	Herb Gray	15.00	7.50	4.50
85	Hal Ledyard	7.50	3.75	2.25
86	Cornel Piper (SP)	50.00	25.00	15.00
87	Farrell Funston	7.50	3.75	2.25
88	Ray Smith	7.50	3.75	2.25
89	Clair Branch	7.50	3.75	2.25
90	Fred Burket	7.50	3.75	2.25
91	Dave Grosz	7.50	3.75	2.25
92	Bob Golic	10.00	5.00	3.00
93	Billy Gray	7.50	3.75	2.25
94	Neil Habig	7.50	3.75	2.25
95	Reg Whitehouse	7.50	3.75	2.25
96	Jack Gotta	10.00	5.00	3.00
97	Bob Ptacek	10.00	5.00	3.00
98	Jerry Keeling	15.00	7.50	4.50
99	Ernie Danjean	7.50	3.75	2.25
100	Don Luzzi	12.00	6.00	3.50
101	Wayne Harris	20.00	10.00	6.00
102	Tony Pajaczkowski	15.00	7.50	4.50
103	Earl Lunsford	15.00	7.50	4.50
104	Ernie Warlick	12.00	6.00	3.50
105	Gene Filipski	12.00	6.00	3.50
106	Eagle Day	15.00	7.50	4.50
107	Bill Crawford	7.50	3.75	2.25
108	Oscar Kruger	7.50	3.75	2.25
109	Gino Fracas	10.00	5.00	3.00
110	Don Stephenson	7.50	3.75	2.25
111	Jim Letcavits	7.50	3.75	2.25
112	Howie Schumm	7.50	3.75	2.25
113	Jackie Parker	45.00	22.00	13.50
114	Rollie Miles	15.00	7.50	4.50
115	Johnny Bright	20.00	10.00	6.00
116	Don Getty	15.00	7.50	4.50
117	Bobby Walden	10.00	5.00	3.00
118	Roger Nelson	15.00	7.50	4.50
119	Al Ecuyer	7.50	3.75	2.25
120	Ed Gray	7.50	3.75	2.25
121	Vic Chapman (SP)	50.00	25.00	15.00
122	Earl Keeley	7.50	3.75	2.25
123	Sonny Homer	7.50	3.75	2.25
124	Bob Jetter	20.00	10.00	6.00
125	Jim Carphin	7.50	3.75	2.25
126	By Bailey	15.00	7.50	4.50
127	Norm Fieldgate	15.00	7.50	4.50
128	Vic Kristopaitis	7.50	3.75	2.25
129	Willie Fleming	20.00	10.00	6.00
130	Don Vicic	7.50	3.75	2.25
131	Tom Brown (SP)	50.00	25.00	15.00
132	Tom Hinton (SP)	50.00	25.00	15.00
133	Pat Claridge	7.50	3.75	2.25
134	Bill Britton	7.50	3.75	2.25
135	Neal Beaumont	10.00	5.00	3.00
136	Nub Beamer (SP)	50.00	25.00	15.00
137	Joe Kapp	60.00	30.00	18.00
NNO	**Post Album**	75.00	37.00	22.00

1963 Post Cereal CFL

		NM	E	VG
	Complete Set (160):	900.00	450.00	270.00
	Common Player:	5.00	2.50	1.50
1	Larry Hickman	7.50	3.75	2.25
2	Dick Schnell	5.00	2.50	1.50
3	Don Clark	7.50	3.75	2.25
4	Ted Page	5.00	2.50	1.50
5	Milt Crain	7.50	3.75	2.25
6	George Dixon	10.00	5.00	3.00
7	Ed Nickla	5.00	2.50	1.50
8	Barrie Hansen	5.00	2.50	1.50
9	Ed Learn	5.00	2.50	1.50
10	Billy Ray Locklin	5.00	2.50	1.50
11	Bobby Jack Oliver	7.50	3.75	2.25
12	Don Paquette	5.00	2.50	1.50
13	Sandy Stephens	12.00	6.00	3.50
14	Billy Wayte	5.00	2.50	1.50
15	Jim Reynolds	5.00	2.50	1.50
16	Ross Buckle	5.00	2.50	1.50
17	Bob Geary	5.00	2.50	1.50
18	Bobby Lee Thompson	5.00	2.50	1.50
19	Mike Snodgrass	5.00	2.50	1.50
20	Billy Joe Booth	7.50	3.75	2.25
21	Jim Cain	5.00	2.50	1.50
22	Kaye Vaughan	10.00	5.00	3.00
23	Doug Daigneault	5.00	2.50	1.50
24	Millard Flemming	5.00	2.50	1.50
25	Russ Jackson	25.00	12.50	7.50
26	Joe Poirier	7.50	3.75	2.25
27	Moe Racine	5.00	2.50	1.50
28	Norb Roy	5.00	2.50	1.50
29	Ted Smale	5.00	2.50	1.50
30	Ernie White	5.00	2.50	1.50
31	Whit Tucker	10.00	5.00	3.00
32	Dave Thelen	10.00	5.00	3.00
33	Len Chandler	5.00	2.50	1.50
34	Jim Conroy	7.50	3.75	2.25
35	Jerry Selinger	5.00	2.50	1.50
36	Ron Stewart	12.00	6.00	3.50
37	Jim Andreotti	7.50	3.75	2.25
38	Jackie Parker	25.00	12.50	7.50
39	Lynn Bottoms	7.50	3.75	2.25
40	Gerry Patrick	5.00	2.50	1.50
41	Gerry Philip	5.00	2.50	1.50
42	Art Johnson	5.00	2.50	1.50
43	Aubrey Linne	5.00	2.50	1.50
44	Dave Mann	7.50	3.75	2.25
45	Marty Martinello	5.00	2.50	1.50
46	Doug McNichol	5.00	2.50	1.50
47	Ron Morris	5.00	2.50	1.50
48	Walt Radzick	5.00	2.50	1.50
49	Jim Rountree	5.00	2.50	1.50
50	Dick Shatto	10.00	5.00	3.00
51	Billy Shipp	5.00	2.50	1.50
52	Norm Stoneburgh	5.00	2.50	1.50
53	Gerry Wilson	5.00	2.50	1.50
54	Danny Nykoluk	5.00	2.50	1.50
55	John Barrow	10.00	5.00	3.00
56	Frank Cosentino	7.50	3.75	2.25
57	Hardiman Cureton	7.50	3.75	2.25
58	Bobby Kuntz	7.50	3.75	2.25
59	Bernie Faloney	20.00	10.00	6.00
60	Garney Henley	12.00	6.00	3.50
61	Zeno Karcz	7.50	3.75	2.25
62	Dick Easterly	5.00	2.50	1.50
63	Bronko Nagurski	12.00	6.00	3.50
64	Hal Patterson	15.00	7.50	4.50
65	Ron Ray	5.00	2.50	1.50
66	Don Sutherin	8.00	4.00	2.50
67	Dave Viti	5.00	2.50	1.50
68	Joe Zuger	7.50	3.75	2.25
69	Angelo Mosca	20.00	10.00	6.00
70	Ralph Goldston	5.00	2.50	1.50
71	Tommy Grant	10.00	5.00	3.00
72	Geno DeNobile	5.00	2.50	1.50
73	Dave Burkholder	5.00	2.50	1.50
74	Jack Delveaux	5.00	2.50	1.50
75	Farrell Funston	5.00	2.50	1.50
76	Herb Gray	10.00	5.00	3.00
77	Roger Hagberg	7.50	3.75	2.25
78	Henry Janzen	7.50	3.75	2.25
79	Ronnie Latourelle	5.00	2.50	1.50
80	Leo Lewis	10.00	5.00	3.00
81	Cornel Piper	5.00	2.50	1.50
82	Ernie Pitts	5.00	2.50	1.50
83	Kenny Ploen	10.00	5.00	3.00
84	Norm Rauhaus	7.50	3.75	2.25
85	Charlie Shepard	5.00	2.50	1.50
86	Gar Warren	5.00	2.50	1.50
87	Dick Thornton	7.50	3.75	2.25
88	Hal Ledyard	5.00	2.50	1.50
89	Frank Rigney	7.50	3.75	2.25
90	Gord Rowland	7.50	3.75	2.25
91	Don Walsh	5.00	2.50	1.50
92	Bill Burrell	5.00	2.50	1.50
93	Ron Atchison	9.00	4.50	2.75
94	Billy Gray	5.00	2.50	1.50
95	Neil Habig	5.00	2.50	1.50
96	Bob Ptacek	7.50	3.75	2.25
97	Ray Purdin	5.00	2.50	1.50
98	Ted Urness	8.00	4.00	2.50
99	Dale West	7.50	3.75	2.25
100	Reg Whitehouse	5.00	2.50	1.50
101	Clair Branch	5.00	2.50	1.50
102	Bill Clarke	5.00	2.50	1.50
103	Garner Ekstran	7.50	3.75	2.25
104	Jack Gotta	7.50	3.75	2.25
105	Len Legault	5.00	2.50	1.50
106	Larry Dumelie	5.00	2.50	1.50
107	Bill Britton	5.00	2.50	1.50
108	Ed Buchanan	5.00	2.50	1.50
109	Lovell Coleman	7.50	3.75	2.25
110	Bill Crawford	5.00	2.50	1.50
111	Ernie Danjean	5.00	2.50	1.50
112	Eagle Day	9.00	4.50	2.75
113	Jim Furlong	5.00	2.50	1.50
114	Wayne Harris	15.00	7.50	4.50
115	Roy Jakanovich	5.00	2.50	1.50
116	Phil Lohmann	5.00	2.50	1.50
117	Earl Lunsford	8.00	4.00	2.50
118	Don Luzzi	8.00	4.00	2.50
119	Tony Pajaczkowski	8.00	4.00	2.50
120	Pete Manning	7.50	3.75	2.25
121	Harvey Wylie	8.00	4.00	2.50
122	George Hansen	5.00	2.50	1.50
123	Pat Holmes	5.00	2.50	1.50
124	Larry Robinson	7.50	3.75	2.25
125	Johnny Bright	15.00	7.50	4.50
126	Jon Rechner	5.00	2.50	1.50
127	Al Ecuyer	5.00	2.50	1.50
128	Don Getty	12.00	6.00	3.50
129	Ed Gray	5.00	2.50	1.50
130	Oscar Kruger	5.00	2.50	1.50
131	Jim Letcavits	5.00	2.50	1.50
132	Mike Lashuk	7.50	3.75	2.25
133	Don Duncalfe	5.00	2.50	1.50
134	Bobby Walden	7.50	3.75	2.25
135	Tommy Joe Coffey	12.00	6.00	3.50
136	Nat Dye	5.00	2.50	1.50
137	Roy Stevenson	5.00	2.50	1.50
138	Howie Schumm	5.00	2.50	1.50
139	Roger Nelson	8.00	4.00	2.50
140	Larry Fleisher	7.50	3.75	2.25
141	Dunc Harvey	5.00	2.50	1.50
142	James Earl Wright	7.50	3.75	2.25
143	By Bailey	8.00	4.00	2.50
144	Nub Beamer	5.00	2.50	1.50
145	Neal Beaumont	7.50	3.75	2.25
146	Tom Brown	8.00	4.00	2.50
147	Pat Claridge	5.00	2.50	1.50
148	Lonnie Dennis	7.50	3.75	2.25
149	Norm Fieldgate	8.00	4.00	2.50
150	Willie Fleming	12.00	6.00	3.50
151	Dick Fouts	7.50	3.75	2.25
152	Tom Hinton	8.00	4.00	2.50
153	Sonny Homer	7.50	3.75	2.25
154	Joe Kapp	30.00	15.00	9.00
155	Tom Larscheid	5.00	2.50	1.50
156	Mike Martin	5.00	2.50	1.50
157	Mel Mein	5.00	2.50	1.50
158	Mike Cacic	5.00	2.50	1.50
159	Walt Bilicki	5.00	2.50	1.50
160	Earl Keeley	7.50	3.75	2.25
NNO	**Post Album**	75.00	37.00	22.00

1977 Pottsville Maroons

This 1977 17-card set commemorates the 1925 NFL champion team with photos of the players on the front. The player's name, number and team are printed at the bottom of the card front. The back include the player's name, number, bio, position and career highlights. At the bottom of the card back is the 1977 copyright line, which attributes the set to the estate of Joseph C. Zacko Sr. and executor Russel F. Zacko.

		NM	E	VG
	Complete Set (17):	25.00	12.50	7.50
	Common Player:	1.50	.70	.45
1	**Team History**	1.50	.70	.45
2	**The Symbolic Shoe**	1.50	.70	.45
3	Jack Ernst	1.50	.70	.45
4	Tony Latone	1.50	.70	.45
5	Duke Osborn	1.50	.70	.45
6	Frank Bucher	1.50	.70	.45
7	Frankie Racis	1.50	.70	.45
8	Russ Hathaway	1.50	.70	.45
9	W.H. Flanagan	1.50	.70	.45
10	Charlie Berry	3.00	1.50	.90
11	Russ Stein, Herb Stein	1.50	.70	.45
12	Howard Lebengood	1.50	.70	.45
13	Denny Hughes	1.50	.70	.45
14	Barney Wentz	1.50	.70	.45
15	Eddie Doyle (UER) (Bio says American troops landed in Africa 1943; should be 1942)	1.50	.70	.45
16	Walter French	1.50	.70	.45
17	Dick Rauch	3.00	1.50	.90

1990 Pro Line Samples

These Pro Line samples can be identified from the regular set's card by several factors, including having the word SAMPLE written on the card back next to a player head shot. The card fronts have photos which are entirely different, or cropped differently, than their regular counterparts. The front also has a silver border; the regular cards are full-bleed. Some backs also have different photos than those used in the regular set and quotes. Card numbers are from 1-37, using all the odd numbers except 15.

		NM/M	NM	E
	Complete Set (18):	45.00	90.00	47.50
	Common Player:	2.00	5.25	2.75
1	Charles Mann	2.00	5.25	2.75
3	Troy Aikman	10.00	7.50	4.00
5	Boomer Esiason	5.00	3.75	2.00
7	Warren Moon	5.00	3.75	2.00
9	Bill Fralic	2.00	5.25	2.75
11	Lawrence Taylor	5.00	3.75	2.00
13	George Seifert	2.00	5.25	2.75
17	Dan Marino	10.00	7.50	4.00
19	Jim Everett	3.00	2.25	1.25
21	John Elway	6.00	4.50	2.50
23	Jeff George	2.00	1.50	.80
25	Lindy Infante	2.00	5.25	2.75
27	Dan Reeves	2.00	5.25	2.75
29	Steve Largent	5.00	3.75	2.00
31	Roger Craig	4.00	3.00	1.50
33	Marty Schottenheimer	2.00	5.25	2.75
35	Mike Ditka	5.00	3.75	2.00
37	Sam Wyche	2.00	5.25	2.75

1991 Pro Line Portraits

This set of high-end cards issued by NFL Properties shows a number of past and present NFL players in posed shots, wearing team apparel without football equipment. These cards were issued in August 1991 in 12-card wax packs. Some 250,000 autographed, embossed and unnumbered were randomly packed. Cards are not licensed by the NFL Players Association, so non-association members such as Eric Dickerson, Michael Dean Perry, Jim Kelly, Bernie Kosar, Webster Slaughter and Cornelius Bennett appear here while they don't appear in any other 1991 sets. A subset, Spirit Collectibles, shows seven player wives. Two other cards, Pro Line Portraits Collectible #1 (Ahmad Rashad and family) and #2 (Payne Stewart), were limited to 10,000 randomly issued cards. Each card in the regular set was also autographed.

	NM/M	NM	E
Complete Set (300):	4.50	3.50	1.75
Common Player:	.03	.02	.01
Pack (12):	.40		
Wax Box (36):	12.00		

#		NM/M	NM	E
1	Jim Kelly	.20	.15	.08
2	Carl Banks	.03	.02	.01
3	Neal Anderson	.03	.02	.01
4	James Brooks	.03	.02	.01
5	Reggie Langhorne	.03	.02	.01
6	Robert Awalt	.03	.02	.01
7	Greg Kragen	.03	.02	.01
8	Steve Young	.50	.40	.20
9	Nick Bell RC	.10	.08	.04
10	Ray Childress	.03	.02	.01
11	Albert Bentley	.03	.02	.01
12	Albert Lewis	.03	.02	.01
13	Howie Long	.03	.02	.01
14	Willie Anderson	.03	.02	.01
15	Mark Clayton	.03	.02	.01
16	Jarrod Bunch RC	.10	.08	.04
17	Bruce Armstrong	.03	.02	.01
18	Vinnie Clark RC	.10	.08	.04
19	Rob Moore	.10	.08	.04
20	Eric Allen	.03	.02	.01
21	Timm Rosenbach	.03	.02	.01
22	Gary Anderson	.03	.02	.01
23	Martin Bayless	.03	.02	.01
24	Kevin Fagan	.03	.02	.01
25	Brian Blades	.03	.02	.01
26	Gary Anderson	.03	.02	.01
27	Earnest Bymer	.03	.02	.01
28	O.J. Simpson	1.00	.70	.40
29	Dan Henning	.03	.02	.01
30	Sean Landeta	.03	.02	.01
31	James Lofton	.03	.02	.01
32	Mike Singletary	.03	.02	.01
33	David Fulcher	.03	.02	.01
34	Mark Murphy	.03	.02	.01
35	Issiac Holt	.03	.02	.01
36	Dennis Smith	.03	.02	.01
37	Lomas Brown	.03	.02	.01
38	Ernest Givins	.03	.02	.01
39	Duane Bickett	.03	.02	.01
40	Barry Word	.03	.02	.01
41	Tony Mandarich	.03	.02	.01
42	Cleveland Gary	.03	.02	.01
43	Ferrell Edmunds	.03	.02	.01
44	Randal Hill RC	.25	.20	.10
45	Irving Fryar	.03	.02	.01
46	Henry Jones RC	.10	.08	.04
47	Blair Thomas	.03	.02	.01
48	Andre Waters	.03	.02	.01
49	J.T. Smith	.03	.02	.01
50	Thomas Everett	.03	.02	.01
51	Marion Butts	.03	.02	.01
52	Tom Rathman	.03	.02	.01
53	Vann McElroy	.03	.02	.01
54	Mark Carrier (T.B.)	.03	.02	.01
55	Jim Lachey	.03	.02	.01
56	Joe Theismann	.03	.02	.01
57	Jerry Glanville	.03	.02	.01
58	Doug Riesenberg	.03	.02	.01
59	Cornelius Bennett	.03	.02	.01
60	Mark Carrier (Chi.)	.03	.02	.01
61	Rodney Holman	.03	.02	.01
62	Leroy Hoard	.03	.02	.01
63	Michael Irvin	.65	.50	.25
64	Bobby Humphrey	.03	.02	.01
65	Mel Gray	.03	.02	.01
66	Brian Noble	.03	.02	.01
67	Al Smith	.03	.02	.01
68	Eric Dickerson	.10	.08	.04
69	Steve DeBerg	.03	.02	.01
70	Jay Schroeder	.03	.02	.01
71	Irv Pankey	.03	.02	.01
72	Reggie Roby	.03	.02	.01
73	Wade Wilson	.03	.02	.01
74	Reggie Rembert	.03	.02	.01
75	Russell Maryland RC	.40	.30	.15
76	Al Toon	.03	.02	.01
77	Randall Cunningham	.10	.08	.04
78	Lonnie Young	.03	.02	.01
79	Carnell Lake	.03	.02	.01
80	Brut Grossman	.03	.02	.01
81	Jim Mora	.03	.02	.01
82	Dave Krieg	.03	.02	.01
83	Bruce Hill	.03	.02	.01
84	Ricky Sanders	.03	.02	.01
85	Roger Staubach	.10	.08	.04
86	Richard Williamson	.03	.02	.01
87	Everson Walls	.03	.02	.01
88	Shane Conlan	.03	.02	.01
89	Mike Ditka	.10	.08	.04
90	Mark Bortz	.03	.02	.01
91	Tim McGee	.03	.02	.01
92	Michael Dean Perry	.10	.08	.04
93	Danny Noonan	.03	.02	.01
94	Mark Jackson	.03	.02	.01
95	Chris Miller	.03	.02	.01
96	Ed McCaffrey RC	.50	.40	.20
97	Lorenzo White	.10	.08	.04
98	Ray Donaldson	.03	.02	.01
99	Nick Lowery	.03	.02	.01
100	Steve Smith	.03	.02	.01
101	Jackie Slater	.03	.02	.01
102	Louis Oliver	.03	.02	.01
103	Kanavis McGhee RC	.10	.08	.04
104	Ray Agnew	.03	.02	.01
105	Sam Mills	.03	.02	.01
106	Bill Pickel	.03	.02	.01
107	Keith Byars	.03	.02	.01
108	Ricky Proehl	.10	.08	.04
109	Merril Hoge	.03	.02	.01
110	Rod Berstine	.03	.02	.01
111	Andy Heck	.03	.02	.01
112	Broderick Thomas	.03	.02	.01
113	Andre Reed	.03	.02	.01
114	Paul Warfield	.03	.02	.01
115	Bill Belichick	.03	.02	.01
116	Ottis Anderson	.03	.02	.01
117	Andre Reed	.10	.08	.04
118	Andre Rison	.20	.15	.08
119	Dexter Carter	.03	.02	.01
120	Anthony Munoz	.03	.02	.01
121	Bernie Kosar	.03	.02	.01
122	Alonzo Highsmith	.03	.02	.01
123	David Treadwell	.03	.02	.01
124	Rodney Peete	.03	.02	.01
125	Haywood Jeffires	.15	.11	.06
126	Clarence Verdin	.03	.02	.01
127	Christian Okoye	.03	.02	.01
128	Greg Townsend	.03	.02	.01
129	Tom Newberry	.03	.02	.01
130	Keith Sims	.03	.02	.01
131	Myron Guyton	.03	.02	.01
132	Andre Tippett	.03	.02	.01
133	Steve Walsh	.03	.02	.01
134	Erik McMillan	.03	.02	.01
135	Jim McMahon	.03	.02	.01
136	Derek Hill	.03	.02	.01
137	David Johnson	.03	.02	.01
138	Leslie O'Neal	.03	.02	.01
139	Pierce Holt	.03	.02	.01
140	Cortez Kennedy	.20	.15	.08
141	Danny Peebles	.03	.02	.01
142	Alvin Walton	.03	.02	.01
143	Drew Pearson	.03	.02	.01
144	Dick MacPherson	.03	.02	.01
145	Erik Howard	.03	.02	.01
146	Steve Tasker	.03	.02	.01
147	Bill Fralic	.03	.02	.01
148	Don Warren	.03	.02	.01
149	Eric Thomas	.03	.02	.01
150	Jack Pardee	.03	.02	.01
151	Gary Zimmerman	.03	.02	.01
152	Leonard Marshall	.03	.02	.01
153	Chris Spielman	.03	.02	.01
154	Sam Wyche	.03	.02	.01
155	Rohn Stark	.03	.02	.01
156	Stephone Paige	.03	.02	.01
157	Lionel Washington	.03	.02	.01
158	Henry Ellard	.03	.02	.01
159	Dan Marino	.75	.60	.30
160	Lindy Infante	.03	.02	.01
161	Dan McGwire RC	.10	.08	.04
162	Ken O'Brien	.03	.02	.01
163	Tim McDonald	.03	.02	.01
164	Louis Lipps	.03	.02	.01
165	Billy Joe Tolliver	.03	.02	.01
166	Harris Barton	.03	.02	.01
167	Tony Woods	.03	.02	.01
168	Matt Millen	.03	.02	.01
169	Gale Sayers	.03	.02	.01
170	Ron Meyer	.03	.02	.01
171	William Roberts	.03	.02	.01
172	Thurman Thomas	.25	.20	.10
173	Steve McMichael	.03	.02	.01
174	Ickey Woods	.03	.02	.01
175	Eugene Lockhart	.03	.02	.01
176	George Seifert	.03	.02	.01
177	Keith Jones	.03	.02	.01
178	Jack Trudeau	.03	.02	.01
179	Kevin Porter	.03	.02	.01
180	Ronnie Lott	.10	.08	.04
181	Marty Schottenheimer	.03	.02	.01
182	Morten Andersen	.03	.02	.01
183	Anthony Thompson	.03	.02	.01
184	Tim Worley	.03	.02	.01
185	Billy Ray Smith	.03	.02	.01
186	David Whitmore	.03	.02	.01
187	Jacob Green	.03	.02	.01
188	Browning Nagle RC	.15	.11	.06
189	Franco Harris	.10	.08	.04
190	Art Shell	.03	.02	.01
191	Bart Oates	.03	.02	.01
192	William Perry	.03	.02	.01
193	Chuck Noll	.03	.02	.01
194	Troy Aikman	1.00	.70	.40
195	Jeff George	.15	.11	.06
196	Derrick Thomas	.15	.11	.06
197	Roger Craig	.03	.02	.01
198	John Fourcade	.03	.02	.01
199	Rod Woodson	.03	.02	.01
200	Anthony Miller	.03	.02	.01
201	Jerry Rice	.75	.60	.30
202	Eugene Robinson	.03	.02	.01
203	Charles Mann	.03	.02	.01
204	Mel Blount	.03	.02	.01
205	Don Shula	.03	.02	.01
206	John Elliott	.03	.02	.01
207	Jay Hilgenberg	.03	.02	.01
208	Deron Cherry	.03	.02	.01
209	Dan Reeves	.03	.02	.01
210	Roman Phifer RC	.10	.08	.04
211	David Little	.03	.02	.01
212	Lee Williams	.03	.02	.01
213	John Taylor	.10	.08	.04
214	Monte Coleman	.03	.02	.01
215	Walter Payton	.10	.08	.04
216	John Robinson	.03	.02	.01
217	Pepper Johnson	.03	.02	.01
218	Tom Thayer	.03	.02	.01
219	Dan Saleaumua	.03	.02	.01
220	Ernest Spears	.03	.02	.01
221	Bubby Brister	.03	.02	.01
222	Junior Seau	.20	.15	.08
223	Brent Jones	.03	.02	.01
224	Rufus Porter	.03	.02	.01
225	Jack Kemp	.10	.08	.04
226	Wayne Fontes	.03	.02	.01
227	Phil Simms	.10	.08	.04
228	Shaun Gayle	.03	.02	.01
229	Bill Maas	.03	.02	.01
230	Renaldo Turnbull	.03	.02	.01
231	Bryan Hinkle	.03	.02	.01
232	Gary Plummer	.03	.02	.01
233	Jerry Burns	.03	.02	.01
234	Lawrence Taylor	.10	.08	.04
235	Joe Gibbs	.03	.02	.01
236	Neil Smith	.03	.02	.01
237	Rich Kotite	.03	.02	.01
238	Jim Covert	.03	.02	.01
239	Tim Grunhard	.03	.02	.01
240	Joe Bugel	.03	.02	.01
241	Dave Wyman	.03	.02	.01
242	Maruy Buford	.03	.02	.01
243	Kevin Ross	.03	.02	.01
244	Jimmy Johnson	.03	.02	.01
245	Jim Morrissey	.03	.02	.01
246	Jeff Hostetler	.20	.15	.08
247	Andre Ware	.10	.08	.04
248	Steve Largent	.10	.08	.04
249	Chuck Knox	.03	.02	.01
250	Boomer Esiason	.10	.08	.04
251	Kevin Butler	.03	.02	.01
252	Bruce Smith	.03	.02	.01
253	Webster Slaughter	.03	.02	.01
254	Mike Sherrard	.03	.02	.01
255	Steve Broussard	.03	.02	.01
256	Warren Moon	.15	.11	.06

257	John Elway	.25	.20	.10
258	Bob Golic	.03	.02	.01
259	Jim Everett	.03	.02	.01
260	Bruce Coslet	.03	.02	.01
261	James Francis	.03	.02	.01
262	Eric Dorsey	.03	.02	.01
263	Marcus Dupree	.03	.02	.01
264	Hart Lee Dykes	.03	.02	.01
265	Vinny Testaverde	.03	.02	.01
266	Chip Lohmiller	.03	.02	.01
267	John Riggins	.03	.02	.01
268	Mike Schad	.03	.02	.01
269	Kevin Greene	.03	.02	.01
270	Dean Biasucci	.03	.02	.01
271	Mike Pritchard **RC**	.40	.30	.15
272	Ted Washington **RC**	.10	.08	.04
273	Alfred Williams **RC**	.10	.08	.04
274	Chris Zorich **RC**	.15	.11	.06
275	Reggie Barrett	.03	.02	.01
276	Chris Hinton	.03	.02	.01
277	Tracy Johnson	.10	.08	.04
278	Jim Harbaugh	.03	.02	.01
279	John Roper	.03	.02	.01
280	Mike Dumas	.03	.02	.01
281	Herman Moore **RC**	3.50	2.75	1.50
282	Eric Turner **RC**	.15	.11	.06
283	Steve Atwater	.03	.02	.01
284	Michael Cofer (Det.)	.03	.02	.01
285	Darion Conner	.03	.02	.01
286	Darryl Talley	.03	.02	.01
287	Donnell Woolford	.03	.02	.01
288	Keith McCants	.03	.02	.01
289	Ray Handley	.03	.02	.01
290	Ahmad Rashad	.03	.02	.01
291	Eric Swann **RC**	.15	.11	.06
292	Dalton Hilltiard	.03	.02	.01
293	Rickey Jackson	.03	.02	.01
294	Vaughan Johnson	.03	.02	.01
295	Eric Martin	.03	.02	.01
296	Pat Swilling	.03	.02	.01
297	Anthony Carter	.03	.02	.01
298	Guy McIntyre	.03	.02	.01
299	Bennie Blades	.03	.02	.01
300	Paul Farren	.03	.02	.01

1991 Pro Line Portraits Autographs

Each card in the regular set was also autographed. The card is the same as the regular one, except it is not numbered. These cards command premium prices and were random inserts in packs, about one every three boxes.

	NM/M	NM	E
Complete Set (301):	5,250	3,850	2,100
Common Player:	6.00	4.50	2.50
Minor Stars:	12.00	9.00	4.75

1A	Jim Kelly (Autopenned)	20.00	15.00	8.00
1B	Jim Kelly (Real Signature)	250.00	185.00	100.00
2	Carl Banks	6.00	4.50	2.50
3	Neal Anderson	6.00	4.50	2.50
4	James Brooks	6.00	4.50	2.50
5	Reggie Langhorne	60.00	45.00	24.00
6	Robert Awalt	6.00	4.50	2.50
7	Greg Kragen	6.00	4.50	2.50
8	Steve Young	125.00	94.00	50.00
9	Nick Bell	6.00	4.50	2.50
10	Ray Childress	12.00	9.00	4.75
11	Albert Bentley	6.00	4.50	2.50
12	Albert Lewis (Most signatures are cut off)	60.00	45.00	24.00
13	Howie Long	35.00	26.00	14.00
14	Flipper Anderson	12.00	9.00	4.75
15	Mark Clayton	12.00	9.00	4.75
16	Jarrod Bunch	6.00	4.50	2.50
17	Bruce Armstrong	6.00	4.50	2.50
18	Vinnie Clark	6.00	4.50	2.50
19	Rob Moore	20.00	15.00	8.00
20	Eric Allen	6.00	4.50	2.50
21	Timm Rosenbach	6.00	4.50	2.50
22	Gary Anderson (K)	6.00	4.50	2.50
23	Martin Bayless	6.00	4.50	2.50
24	Kevin Fagan	6.00	4.50	2.50
25	Brian Blades	12.00	9.00	4.75
26	Gary Anderson (RB)	6.00	4.50	2.50
27	Earnest Byner	6.00	4.50	2.50
28	O.J. Simpson (RET)	300.00	225.00	120.00
29	Dan Henning (CO)	6.00	4.50	2.50
30	Sean Landeta	6.00	4.50	2.50
31	James Lofton	25.00	18.50	10.00
32	Mike Singletary	40.00	30.00	16.00
33	David Fulcher	6.00	4.50	2.50
34	Mark Murphy	6.00	4.50	2.50
35	Issiac Holt	6.00	4.50	2.50
36	Dennis Smith	6.00	4.50	2.50
37	Lomas Brown	6.00	4.50	2.50
38	Ernest Givins	12.00	9.00	4.75
39	Duane Bickett	6.00	4.50	2.50
40	Barry Word	6.00	4.50	2.50
41	Tony Mandarich	12.00	9.00	4.75
42	Cleveland Gary	12.00	9.00	4.75
43	Ferrell Edmunds	6.00	4.50	2.50
44	Randal Hill	12.00	9.00	4.75
45	Irving Fryar	12.00	9.00	4.75
46	Henry Jones	6.00	4.50	2.50
47	Blair Thomas	6.00	4.50	2.50
48	Andre Waters	6.00	4.50	2.50
49	J.T. Smith	6.00	4.50	2.50
50	Thomas Everett	6.00	4.50	2.50
51	Marion Butts	6.00	4.50	2.50
52	Tom Rathman	12.00	9.00	4.75
53	Vann McElroy	6.00	4.50	2.50
54	Mark Carrier (WR)	6.00	4.50	2.50
55	Jim Lachey	6.00	4.50	2.50
56	Joe Theismann (RET)	30.00	22.00	12.00
57	Jerry Glanville (CO)	12.00	9.00	4.75
58	Doug Riesenberg	6.00	4.50	2.50
59	Cornelius Bennett	12.00	9.00	4.75
60	Mark Carrier (DB)	100.00	75.00	40.00
61	Rodney Holman	225.00	170.00	90.00
62	Leroy Hoard	12.00	9.00	4.75
63	Michael Irvin	35.00	26.00	14.00
64	Bobby Humphrey	6.00	4.50	2.50
65	Mel Gray	12.00	9.00	4.75
66	Brian Noble	6.00	4.50	2.50
67	Al Smith	6.00	4.50	2.50
68	Eric Dickerson	30.00	22.00	12.00
69	Steve DeBerg	12.00	9.00	4.75
70	Jay Schroeder	12.00	9.00	4.75
71	Irv Pankey	6.00	4.50	2.50
72	Reggie Roby	12.00	9.00	4.75
73	Wade Wilson	12.00	9.00	4.75
74	Johnny Rembert	6.00	4.50	2.50
75	Russell Maryland	12.00	9.00	4.75
76	Al Toon	12.00	9.00	4.75
77	Randall Cunningham	30.00	22.00	12.00
78	Lonnie Young	6.00	4.50	2.50
79	Carnell Lake	12.00	9.00	4.75
80	Brut Grossman	6.00	4.50	2.50
81	Jim Mora (CO)	6.00	4.50	2.50
82	Dave Krieg	12.00	9.00	4.75
83	Bruce Hill	6.00	4.50	2.50
84	Ricky Sanders	12.00	9.00	4.75
85	Roger Staubach (RET)	150.00	112.00	60.00
86	Richard Williamson (CO)	6.00	4.50	2.50
87	Everson Walls	12.00	9.00	4.75
88	Shane Conlan	6.00	4.50	2.50
89	Mike Ditka (CO)	40.00	30.00	16.00
90	Mark Bortz	6.00	4.50	2.50
91	Tim McGee	6.00	4.50	2.50
92	Michael Dean Perry	12.00	9.00	4.75
93	Danny Noonan	6.00	4.50	2.50
94	Mark Jackson	12.00	9.00	4.75
95	Chris Miller	12.00	9.00	4.75
96	Ed McCaffrey	25.00	18.50	10.00
97	Lorenzo White	12.00	9.00	4.75
98	Ray Donaldson	6.00	4.50	2.50
99	Nick Lowery (May be autopenned)	6.00	4.50	2.50
100	Steve Smith	6.00	4.50	2.50
101	Jackie Slater	12.00	9.00	4.75
102	Louis Oliver	6.00	4.50	2.50
103	Kanavis McGhee	6.00	4.50	2.50
104	Ray Agnew	6.00	4.50	2.50
105	Sam Mills	12.00	9.00	4.75
106	Bill Pickel	12.00	9.00	4.75
107	Keith Byars	12.00	9.00	4.75
108	Ricky Proehl	12.00	9.00	4.75
109	Merril Hoge	6.00	4.50	2.50
110	Rod Berstine	6.00	4.50	2.50
111	Andy Heck	6.00	4.50	2.50
112	Broderick Thomas	6.00	4.50	2.50
113	Andre Collins	6.00	4.50	2.50
114	Paul Warfield (RET)	25.00	18.50	10.00
115	Bill Belichick (CO)	12.00	9.00	4.75
116	Ottis Anderson	12.00	9.00	4.75
117	Andre Reed	25.00	18.50	10.00
118A	Andre Rison (Ball-point pen)	15.00	11.00	6.00
118B	Andre Rison (Signed in Sharpie)	30.00	22.00	12.00
119	Dexter Carter	12.00	9.00	4.75
120	Anthony Munoz	12.00	9.00	4.75
121	Bernie Kosar	15.00	11.00	6.00
122	Alonzo Highsmith	60.00	45.00	24.00
123	David Treadwell	6.00	4.50	2.50
124	Rodney Peete	12.00	9.00	4.75
125	Haywood Jeffires	12.00	9.00	4.75
126	Clarence Verdin	6.00	4.50	2.50
127	Christian Okoye	12.00	9.00	4.75
128	Greg Townsend	125.00	94.00	50.00
129	Tom Newberry	6.00	4.50	2.50
130	Keith Sims	6.00	4.50	2.50
131	Myron Guyton	6.00	4.50	2.50
132	Andre Tippett	6.00	4.50	2.50
133	Steve Walsh	12.00	9.00	4.75
134	Erik McMillan	6.00	4.50	2.50
135	Jim McMahon	280.00	210.00	110.00
136	Derek Hill	6.00	4.50	2.50
137	D.J. Johnson	6.00	4.50	2.50
138	Leslie O'Neal	12.00	9.00	4.75
139	Pierce Holt	6.00	4.50	2.50
140	Cortez Kennedy	12.00	9.00	4.75
141	Danny Peebles	6.00	4.50	2.50
142	Alvin Walton	6.00	4.50	2.50
143	Drew Pearson (RET)	12.00	9.00	4.75
144	Dick MacPherson (CO)	6.00	4.50	2.50
145	Erik Howard	6.00	4.50	2.50
146	Steve Tasker	6.00	4.50	2.50
147	Bill Fralic	6.00	4.50	2.50
148	Don Warren	6.00	4.50	2.50
149	Eric Thomas	6.00	4.50	2.50
150	Jack Pardee (CO)	6.00	4.50	2.50
151	Gary Zimmerman	6.00	4.50	2.50
152	Leonard Marshall (Frequently miscut)	12.00	9.00	4.75
153	Chris Spielman	12.00	9.00	4.75
154	Sam Wyche (CO)	6.00	4.50	2.50
155	Rohn Stark	6.00	4.50	2.50
156	Stephone Paige	6.00	4.50	2.50
157	Lionel Washington (Most signatures are cut off)	120.00	90.00	48.00
158	Henry Ellard	12.00	9.00	4.75
159	Dan Marino	200.00	150.00	80.00
160	Lindy Infante (CO)	6.00	4.50	2.50
161	Dan McGwire	6.00	4.50	2.50
162	Ken O'Brien	12.00	9.00	4.75
163	Tim McDonald	6.00	4.50	2.50
164	Louis Lipps	6.00	4.50	2.50
165	Billy Joe Tolliver	12.00	9.00	4.75
166	Harris Barton	6.00	4.50	2.50
167	Tony Woods	6.00	4.50	2.50
168	Matt Millen	12.00	9.00	4.75
169	Gale Sayers (RET)	35.00	26.00	14.00
170	Ron Meyer (CO)	12.00	9.00	4.75
171	William Roberts	6.00	4.50	2.50
172	Thurman Thomas	30.00	22.00	12.00
173	Steve McMichael	6.00	4.50	2.50
174	Ickey Woods	6.00	4.50	2.50
175	Eugene Lockhart	6.00	4.50	2.50
176	George Seifert (CO)	12.00	9.00	4.75
177	Keith Jones	6.00	4.50	2.50
178	Jack Trudeau	6.00	4.50	2.50
179	Kevin Porter	6.00	4.50	2.50
180	Ronnie Lott	15.00	11.00	6.00
181	Marty Schottenhelmer (CO)	12.00	9.00	4.75
182	Morten Andersen	12.00	9.00	4.75
183	Anthony Thompson	6.00	4.50	2.50
184	Tim Worley	6.00	4.50	2.50
185	Billy Ray Smith	6.00	4.50	2.50
186	David Whitmore	6.00	4.50	2.50
187	Jacob Green	6.00	4.50	2.50
188	Browning Nagle	6.00	4.50	2.50
189	Franco Harris (RET) (Most signatures are cut off)	45.00	34.00	18.00
190	Art Shell (CO)	15.00	11.00	6.00
191	Bart Oates	6.00	4.50	2.50
192	William Perry	12.00	9.00	4.75
193	Chuck Noll (CO)	30.00	22.00	12.00
194	Troy Aikman	100.00	75.00	40.00
195	Jeff George	25.00	18.50	10.00
196	Derrick Thomas	40.00	30.00	16.00
197	Roger Craig	12.00	9.00	4.75
198	John Fourcade	6.00	4.50	2.50
199	Rod Woodson	12.00	9.00	4.75
200	Anthony Miller	12.00	9.00	4.75
201	Jerry Rice	150.00	110.00	60.00
202	Eugene Robinson	6.00	4.50	2.50
203	Charles Mann	6.00	4.50	2.50
204	Mel Blount (RET)	12.00	9.00	4.75
205	Don Shula (CO)	45.00	34.00	18.00
206	John Elliott	6.00	4.50	2.50
207	Jay Hilgenberg	6.00	4.50	2.50
208	Deron Cherry	6.00	4.50	2.50
209	Dan Reeves (CO)	12.00	9.00	4.75
210	Roman Phifer	6.00	4.50	2.50
211	David Little	6.00	4.50	2.50
212	Lee Williams	6.00	4.50	2.50
213	John Taylor	12.00	9.00	4.75
214	Monte Coleman	6.00	4.50	2.50
215	Walter Payton (RET)	150.00	110.00	60.00
216	John Robinson (CO)	6.00	4.50	2.50
217	Pepper Johnson	6.00	4.50	2.50
218	Tom Thayer	6.00	4.50	2.50
219	Dan Saleumua	6.00	4.50	2.50

220	Ernest Spears	6.00	4.50	2.50
221	Bubby Brister			
	(Signed Bubby 6)	12.00	9.00	4.75
222	Junior Seau	20.00	15.00	8.00
223	Brent Jones	12.00	9.00	4.75
224	Rufus Porter	6.00	4.50	2.50
225	Jack Kemp (RET)			
	(Autopenned)	30.00	22.00	12.00
226	Wayne Fontes (CO)	6.00	4.50	2.50
227	Phil Simms	30.00	22.00	12.00
228	Shaun Gayle	6.00	4.50	2.50
229	Bill Maas	6.00	4.50	2.50
230	Renaldo Turnbull	6.00	4.50	2.50
231	Bryan Hinkle	6.00	4.50	2.50
232	Gary Plummer	6.00	4.50	2.50
233	Jerry Burns (CO)	6.00	4.50	2.50
234	Lawrence Taylor	40.00	30.00	16.00
235	Joe Gibbs (CO)	20.00	15.00	8.00
236	Neil Smith (Most			
	signatures are cut off)	60.00	45.00	24.00
237	Rich Kotite (CO)	6.00	4.50	2.50
238	Jim Covert	6.00	4.50	2.50
239	Tim Grunhard			
	(Two different signatures			
	known for this card)	6.00	4.50	2.50
240	Joe Bugel (CO)	6.00	4.50	2.50
241	Dave Wyman	6.00	4.50	2.50
242	Maruy Buford	6.00	4.50	2.50
243	Kevin Ross	6.00	4.50	2.50
244	Jimmy Johnson (CO)	40.00	30.00	16.00
245	Jim Morrissey	6.00	4.50	2.50
246	Jeff Hostetler	12.00	9.00	4.75
247	Andre Ware	12.00	9.00	4.75
248	Steve Largent (RET)	40.00	30.00	16.00
249	Chuck Knox (CO)	12.00	9.00	4.75
250	Boomer Esiason	12.00	9.00	4.75
251	Kevin Butler	6.00	4.50	2.50
252	Bruce Smith	12.00	9.00	4.75
253	Webster Slaughter	6.00	4.50	2.50
254	Mike Sherrard	6.00	4.50	2.50
255	Steve Broussard	6.00	4.50	2.50
256	Warren Moon	35.00	26.00	14.00
257	John Elway	100.00	75.00	40.00
258	Bob Golic	6.00	4.50	2.50
259	Jim Everett	12.00	9.00	4.75
260	Bruce Coslet (CO)	6.00	4.50	2.50
261	James Francis	280.00	210.00	110.00
262	Eric Dorsey	6.00	4.50	2.50
263	Marcus Dupree	6.00	4.50	2.50
264	Hart Lee Dykes	6.00	4.50	2.50
265	Vinny Testaverde	15.00	11.00	6.00
266	Chip Lohmiller	6.00	4.50	2.50
267	John Riggins (RET)	50.00	37.00	20.00
268	Mike Schad	6.00	4.50	2.50
269	Kevin Greene	12.00	9.00	4.75
270	Dean Biasucci	6.00	4.50	2.50
271	Mike Pritchard	6.00	4.50	2.50
272	Ted Washington	6.00	4.50	2.50
273	Alfred Williams	6.00	4.50	2.50
274	Chris Zorich	6.00	4.50	2.50
275	Reggie Barrett	6.00	4.50	2.50
276	Chris Hinton	6.00	4.50	2.50
277	Tracy Johnson	6.00	4.50	2.50
278	Jim Harbaugh	12.00	9.00	4.75
279	John Roper	6.00	4.50	2.50
280	Mike Dumas	6.00	4.50	2.50
281	Herman Moore	60.00	45.00	24.00
282	Eric Turner	6.00	4.50	2.50
283	Steve Atwater	6.00	4.50	2.50
284	Michael Cofer	6.00	4.50	2.50
285	Darion Conner	6.00	4.50	2.50
286	Darryl Talley	6.00	4.50	2.50
287	Donnell Woolford	6.00	4.50	2.50
288	Keith McCants	6.00	4.50	2.50
289	Ray Handley (CO)	6.00	4.50	2.50
290	Ahmad Rashad (RET)	175.00	131.00	70.00
291	Eric Swann	12.00	9.00	4.75
292	Dalton Hilliard (Signatures			
	usually miscut)	25.00	18.50	10.00
293	Rickey Jackson	6.00	4.50	2.50
294	Vaughan Johnson	6.00	4.50	2.50
295	Eric Martin	6.00	4.50	2.50
296	Pat Swilling	12.00	9.00	4.75
297	Anthony Carter (Signatures			
	usually miscut)	25.00	18.50	10.00
298	Guy McIntyre	75.00	56.00	30.00
299	Bennie Blades	6.00	4.50	2.50
300	Paul Farren	6.00	4.50	2.50
PLC2	Payne Stewart (Golfer)	85.00	64.00	34.00
NNO	**Santa Claus Sendaway**			
	(Signed)	30.00	22.00	12.00
	Santa Claus Sendaway			
	(Signed and numbered)	60.00	45.00	24.00

1991 Pro Line Portraits Wives

Wives of some of the most popular NFL players are featured in this seven-card "Spirit" set. The cards are numbered on the back and were included in the 1991 Pro Line Portraits set.

		NM/M	NM	E
Common Wife:		.05	.04	.02
1	Jennifer Montana	.25	.20	.10
2	Babette Kosar	.05	.04	.02
3	Janet Elway	.05	.04	.02
4	Michelle Oates	.05	.04	.02
5	Toni Lipps	.05	.04	.02
6	Stacey O'Brien	.05	.04	.02
7	Phylicia Rashad	.20	.15	.08

1991 Pro Line Portraits Wives Autographs

The seven-card, standard-size set featured wives of top NFL players and was inserted in packs of 1991 NFL Pro Line. The Rashad signed card was limited to 15, thus giving it its high value. The cards are identical to the seven wives featured in the base set, except with signatures.

		NM/M	NM	E
Complete Set (7):		550.00	412.00	220.00
Common Player:		15.00	11.00	6.00
1	Jennifer Montana	75.00	56.00	30.00
2	Babette Kosar	15.00	11.00	6.00
3	Janet Elway	15.00	11.00	6.00
4	Michelle Oates	15.00	11.00	6.00
5	Toni Lipps	15.00	11.00	6.00
6	Stacey O'Brien	15.00	11.00	6.00
7	Phylicia Rashad	450.00	337.00	180.00

1991 Pro Line Profiles Anthony Munoz

Cincinnati Bengals lineman Anthony Munoz is profiled in this set of cards, which was included inside Super Bowl XXVI programs. The cards chronicle Munoz's career and are listed below according to the topic presented on the card back. Each back is also numbered. A full-color photo appears on the card front, along with the Pro Line Profiles logo. The back has a smaller photo and provides information and quotes from Munoz about his life, community service projects, his family and his NFL career.

		NM/M	NM	E
Complete Set (9):		4.00	3.00	1.50
Common Player:		.50	.40	.20
1	**1991 NFL Man of Year**	.50	.40	.20
2	**Little League player**	.50	.40	.20
3	**1980 Rose Bowl**	.50	.40	.20
4	**Community Service**	.50	.40	.20
5	**Portrait**	.50	.40	.20
6	**1981 AFC**			
	Championship Game	.50	.40	.20
7	**1992 Pro Bowl**	.50	.40	.20
8	**Super Bowl XVI and**			
	XXIII	.50	.40	.20
9	**Physical Fitness Video**	.50	.40	.20

1991 Pro Line Punt, Pass and Kick

Eleven NFL quarterbacks are featured in this 12-card set issued to promote nationwide Punt, Pass and Kick competitions. Each card front has a full bleed posed shot of the player, along with Pro Line Portraits and Punt, Pass and Kick logos. The card back is numbered and includes a player head shot and a quote from him about being a successful NFL quarterback. A checklist card was also produced.

		NM/M	NM	E
Complete Set (11):		50.00	56.00	30.00
Common Player:		3.00	3.75	2.00
1	Troy Aikman	10.00	7.50	4.00
2	Bubby Brister	3.00	3.75	2.00
3	Randall Cunningham	5.00	3.75	2.00
4	John Elway	8.00	6.00	3.25
5	Boomer Esiason	5.00	3.75	2.00
6	Jim Everett	3.00	3.75	2.00
7	Jim Kelly	5.00	3.75	2.00

8	Bernie Kosar	7.00	5.25	2.75
9	Dan Marino	12.00	9.00	4.75
10	Warren Moon	5.00	3.75	2.00
11	Phil Simms	4.00	3.00	1.50

1988 Pro Set Test

These promotional cards, used to preview Pro Set's debut set in 1989, can be distinguished from regular cards in several manners. First, each of the card backs is designed in a vertical fashion; the regular cards use a horizontal format. Also, the card number includes a # symbol before it. Plus, all the photos used for the fronts, except for the Jerry Rice photo, are different than those used on the regular cards.

		NM/M	NM	E
Complete Set (8):		200.00	150.00	80.00
Common Player:		10.00	7.50	4.00
1	Dan Marino	80.00	60.00	32.00
2	Jerry Rice	65.00	49.00	26.00
3	Eric Dickerson	25.00	18.50	10.00
4	Reggie White	25.00	18.50	10.00
5	Mike Singletary	15.00	11.00	6.00
6	Frank Minnifield	10.00	7.50	4.00
7	Phil Simms	25.00	18.50	10.00
8	Jim Kelly	45.00	34.00	18.00

1988 Pro Set Test Designs

Philadelphia Eagles quarterback Randall Cunningham is featured on these five prototype cards, used to preview Pro Set's 1989 debut set. The card numbers are the same on each card, but five different designs were used for the fronts. These are indicated with the corresponding card. Each card back is designed horizontally, with a mug shot, statistics, player profile and biographical information provided.

		NM/M	NM	E
Complete Set (5):		160.00	120.00	64.00
Common Player:		40.00	30.00	16.00
315A	Randall Cunningham (No team or name listed on card front; borderless; logo is vertical)	40.00	30.00	16.00
315B	Randall Cunningham (No team or name listed on card front; border is silver; logo is vertical)	40.00	30.00	16.00
315C	Randall Cunningham (Name and team listed on card front; borderless; logo is horizontal)	40.00	30.00	16.00
315D	Randall Cunningham (Team and name listed on card front; border is black; logo is horizontal)	40.00	30.00	16.00
315E	Randall Cunningham (Team and name listed on card front; border is gray; logo is horizontal)	40.00	30.00	16.00

1989 Pro Set

Pro Set's premier football issue was released in two series in the summer and fall of 1989. Printed on heavy white cardboard stock, the standard-size cards come in a variety of colors and feature full-color action shots on the front, full-color head shots on the back, and biographical notes and statistics on the back. The 615-card set (541 player/coach cards, 23 Super Bowl cards, 30 announcer cards, 20 Final Update cards, one commissioner card) was not released in factory-issued sets. Pro Set is the only one of the three 1989 football card sets featuring coaches cards. Pro Set released its first series in late July 1989, and its second series in September 1989. The third series, labeled "Final Update" on the boxes only, contained 20 additional cards of traded players, rookies and players not previously included in the set. Along with the re-released Art Shell card, these blue-bordered cards were included with Series I and II cards. Art Shell cards were printed on separate sheets and were inserted into late Series

II and all Final Update print runs; the card was usually found on top of the pack.

	NM/M	NM	E
Complete Set (561):	30.00	22.00	12.00
Complete Series 1 (440):	8.00	6.00	3.25
Complete Series 2 (100):	20.00	15.00	8.00
Complete Series 3 (21):	2.00	1.50	.80
Common Player:	.03	.02	.01
Minor Stars:	.10	.08	.04
Series 1 Pack (14):	.45		
Series 1 Box (36):	8.50		
Series 2 or 3 Pack (14):	1.00		
Series 2 or 3 Wax Box (36):	24.00		

1	Stacey Bailey	.03	.02	.01
2	Aundray Bruce **RC**	.03	.02	.01
3	Rick Bryan	.03	.02	.01
4	Bobby Butler	.03	.02	.01
5	Scott Case **RC**	.10	.08	.04
6	Tony Casillas	.03	.02	.01
7	Floyd Dixon	.03	.02	.01
8	Rick Donnelly	.03	.02	.01
9	Bill Fralic	.03	.02	.01
10	Mike Gann	.03	.02	.01
11	Mike Kenn	.03	.02	.01
12	Chris Miller **RC**	.25	.20	.10
13	John Rade	.03	.02	.01
14	Gerald Riggs	.03	.02	.01
15	John Settle **RC**	.10	.08	.04
16	Marion Campbell	.03	.02	.01
17	Cornelius Bennett	.10	.08	.04
18	Derrick Burroughs	.03	.02	.01
19	Shane Conlan	.03	.02	.01
20	Ronnie Harmon	.03	.02	.01
21	Kent Hull **RC**	.10	.08	.04
22	Jim Kelly	.50	.40	.20
23	Mark Kelso	.03	.02	.01
24	Pete Metzelaars	.03	.02	.01
25	Scott Norwood	.03	.02	.01
26	Andre Reed	.10	.08	.04
27	Fred Smerlas	.03	.02	.01
28	Bruce Smith	.10	.08	.04
29	Leonard Smith	.03	.02	.01
30	Art Still	.03	.02	.01
31	Darryl Talley	.03	.02	.01
32	Thurman Thomas **RC**	1.50	1.25	.60
33	Will Wolford	.03	.02	.01
34	Marv Levy (C)	.03	.02	.01
35	Neal Anderson	.03	.02	.01
36	Kevin Butler	.03	.02	.01
37	Jim Covert	.03	.02	.01
38	Richard Dent	.10	.08	.04
39	Dave Duerson	.03	.02	.01
40	Dennis Gentry	.03	.02	.01
41	Dan Hampton	.03	.02	.01
42	Jay Hilgenberg	.03	.02	.01
43	Dennis McKinnon	.03	.02	.01
44	Jim McMahon	.10	.08	.04
45	Steve McMichael	.03	.02	.01
46	Brad Muster **RC**	.10	.08	.04
47	William Perry ERR	3.00	2.25	1.25
48	Ron Rivera	.03	.02	.01
49	Vestee Jackson **RC**	.03	.02	.01
50	Mike Singletary	.10	.08	.04
51	Mike Tomczak	.03	.02	.01
52	Keith Van Horne **RC**	.03	.02	.01
53	Mike Ditka (C HOF stripe)	.10	.08	.04
54	Lewis Billups	.03	.02	.01
55	James Brooks	.03	.02	.01
56	Eddie Brown	.03	.02	.01
57	Jason Buck **RC**	.03	.02	.01
58	Boomer Esiason	.10	.08	.04
59	David Fulcher	.03	.02	.01
60	Rodney Holman **RC**	.10	.08	.04
61	Reggie Williams	.03	.02	.01
62	Joe Kelly **RC**	.03	.02	.01
63	Tim Krumrie	.03	.02	.01
64	Tim McGee	.03	.02	.01
65	Max Montoya	.03	.02	.01
66	Anthony Munoz	.10	.08	.04
67	Jim Skow	.03	.02	.01
68	Eric Thomas **RC**	.03	.02	.01
69	Leon White	.03	.02	.01
70	Ickey Woods	.03	.02	.01
71	Carl Zander	.03	.02	.01
72	Sam Wyche (C)	.03	.02	.01
73	Brian Brennan	.03	.02	.01
74	Earnest Byner	.03	.02	.01
75	Hanford Dixon	.03	.02	.01
76	Mike Pagel	.03	.02	.01
77	Bernie Kosar	.10	.08	.04
78	Reggie Langhorne **RC**	.10	.08	.04
79	Kevin Mack	.03	.02	.01
80	Clay Matthews	.03	.02	.01
81	Gerald McNeil	.03	.02	.01
82	Frank Minnifield	.03	.02	.01
83	Cody Risien	.03	.02	.01
84	Webster Slaughter	.10	.08	.04
85	Felix Wright	.03	.02	.01
86	Bud Carson (C)	.03	.02	.01
87	Bill Bates	.03	.02	.01
88	Kevin Brooks	.03	.02	.01
89	Michael Irvin **RC**	1.00	.70	.40
90	Jim Jeffcoat	.03	.02	.01
91	Too Tall Jones	.03	.02	.01
92	Eugene Lockhart	.03	.02	.01
93	Nate Newton **RC**	.20	.15	.08
94	Danny Noonan	.03	.02	.01
95	Steve Pelluer	.03	.02	.01
96	Herschel Walker	.10	.08	.04
97	Everson Walls	.03	.02	.01
98	Jimmy Johnson (C)	.10	.08	.04
99	Keith Bishop	.03	.02	.01
100	John Elway DRAFT	4.00	3.00	1.50
100a	John Elway TRADE	2.00	1.50	.80
101	Simon Fletcher **RC**	.10	.08	.04
102	Mike Harden	.03	.02	.01
103	Mike Horan	.03	.02	.01
104	Mark Jackson	.03	.02	.01
105	Vance Johnson	.03	.02	.01
106	Rulon Jones	.03	.02	.01
107	Clarence Kay	.03	.02	.01
108	Karl Mecklenburg	.03	.02	.01
109	Ricky Nattiel	.03	.02	.01
110	Steve Sewell **RC**	.10	.08	.04
111	Dennis Smith	.03	.02	.01
112	Gerald Willhite	.03	.02	.01
113	Sammy Winder	.03	.02	.01
114	Dan Reeves	.10	.08	.04
115	Jim Arnold	.03	.02	.01
116	Jerry Ball **RC**	.10	.08	.04
117	Bennie Blades **RC**	.10	.08	.04
118	Lomas Brown	.03	.02	.01
119	Michael Cofer	.03	.02	.01
120	Garry James	.03	.02	.01
121	James Jones	.03	.02	.01
122	Chuck Long	.03	.02	.01
123	Pete Mandley	.03	.02	.01
124	Eddie Murray	.03	.02	.01
125	Chris Speilman **RC**	.10	.08	.04
126	Dennis Gibson	.03	.02	.01
127	Wayne Fontes (C)	.03	.02	.01
128	John Anderson	.03	.02	.01
129	Brent Fullwood	.03	.02	.01
130	Mark Cannon	.03	.02	.01
131	Tim Harris	.03	.02	.01
132	Mark Lee	.03	.02	.01
133	Don Majkowski **RC**	.10	.08	.04
134	Mark Murphy	.03	.02	.01
135	Brian Noble	.03	.02	.01
136	Ken Ruettgers **RC**	.03	.02	.01
137	Johnny Holland	.03	.02	.01
138	Randy Wright	.03	.02	.01
139	Lindy Infante (C)	.03	.02	.01
140	Steve Brown	.03	.02	.01
141	Ray Childress	.03	.02	.01
142	Jeff Donaldson	.03	.02	.01
143	Ernest Givins	.10	.08	.04
144	John Grimsley	.03	.02	.01
145	Alonzo Highsmith	.03	.02	.01
146	Drew Hill	.03	.02	.01
147	Robert Lyles	.03	.02	.01
148	Bruce Matthews **RC**	.10	.08	.04
149	Warren Moon	.25	.20	.10
150	Mike Munchak	.03	.02	.01
151	Allen Pinkett **RC**	.10	.08	.04
152	Mike Rozier	.03	.02	.01
153	Tony Zendejas	.03	.02	.01
154	Jerry Glanville (C)	.10	.08	.04
155	Albert Bentley	.03	.02	.01
156	Dean Biasucci	.03	.02	.01
157	Duane Bickett	.03	.02	.01
158	Bill Brooks	.03	.02	.01
159	Chris Chandler **RC**	2.00	1.50	.80
160	Pat Beach	.03	.02	.01
161	Ray Donaldson	.03	.02	.01
162	Jon Hand	.03	.02	.01
163	Chris Hinton	.03	.02	.01
164	Rohn Stark	.03	.02	.01
165	Fredd Young	.03	.02	.01
166	Ron Meyer (C)	.03	.02	.01
167	Lloyd Burruss	.03	.02	.01
168	Carlos Carson	.03	.02	.01
169	Deron Cherry	.03	.02	.01
170	Irv Eatman	.03	.02	.01
171	Dino Hackett	.03	.02	.01
172	Steve DeBerg	.03	.02	.01
173	Albert Lewis	.03	.02	.01
174	Nick Lowery	.03	.02	.01
175	Bill Maas	.03	.02	.01
176	Christian Okoye	.10	.08	.04
177	Stephone Paige	.03	.02	.01
178	Mark Addickes	.03	.02	.01
179	Kevin Ross **RC**	.10	.08	.04
180	Neil Smith **RC**	.50	.40	.20
181	Marty Schottenheimer (C)	.03	.02	.01
182	Marcus Allen	.25	.20	.10
183	Tim Brown **RC**	1.50	1.25	.60
184	Willie Gault	.03	.02	.01
185	Bo Jackson	.25	.20	.10
186	Howie Long	.10	.08	.04
187	Vann McElroy	.03	.02	.01
188	Matt Millen	.10	.08	.04
189	Don Mosebar **RC**	.03	.02	.01
190	Bill Pickel	.03	.02	.01
191	Jerry Robinson	.03	.02	.01
192	Jay Schroeder	.03	.02	.01
193	Stacey Toran	.10	.08	.04
193a	Stacey Toran (1961-1989)	.50	.40	.20
194	Mike Shanahan (C)	.10	.08	.04
195	Greg Bell	.03	.02	.01
196	Ron Brown	.03	.02	.01
197	Aaron Cox **RC**	.03	.02	.01
198	Henry Ellard	.03	.02	.01
199	Jim Everett	.10	.08	.04
200	Jerry Gray	.03	.02	.01
201	Kevin Greene	.10	.08	.04
202	Pete Holohan	.03	.02	.01
203	LeRoy Irvin	.03	.02	.01
204	Mike Lansford	.03	.02	.01
205	Tom Newberry **RC**	.10	.08	.04
206	Mel Owens	.03	.02	.01
207	Jackie Slater	.03	.02	.01
208	Doug Smith	.03	.02	.01
209	Mike Wilcher	.03	.02	.01
210	John Robinson (C)	.03	.02	.01
211	John Bosa	.03	.02	.01
212	Mark Brown	.03	.02	.01
213	Mark Clayton	.03	.02	.01
214	Ferrell Edmunds **RC** (corrected)	.10	.08	.04
214a	Ferrell Edmunds **RC** (error)	.50	.40	.20
215	Roy Foster	.03	.02	.01
216	Lorenzo Hampton	.03	.02	.01
217	Jim Jensen	.03	.02	.01
218	William Judson	.03	.02	.01
219	Eric Kumerow **RC**	.03	.02	.01
220	Dan Marino	2.00	1.50	.80
221	John Offerdahl	.03	.02	.01
222	Fuad Reveiz	.03	.02	.01
223	Reggie Roby	.03	.02	.01
224	Brian Sochia	.03	.02	.01
225	Don Shula (C)	.20	.15	.08
226	Alfred Anderson	.03	.02	.01
227	Joey Browner	.03	.02	.01
228	Anthony Carter	.03	.02	.01
229	Chris Doleman	.03	.02	.01
230	Hassan Jones **RC**	.03	.02	.01
231	Steve Jordan	.03	.02	.01
232	Tommy Kramer	.03	.02	.01
233	Carl Lee **RC**	.03	.02	.01
234	Kirk Lowdermilk **RC**	.10	.08	.04
235	Randall McDaniel **RC**	.10	.08	.04
236	Doug Martin	.03	.02	.01
237	Keith Millard	.03	.02	.01
238	Darrin Nelson	.03	.02	.01
239	Jesse Solomon	.03	.02	.01
240	Scott Studwell	.03	.02	.01
241	Wade Wilson	.03	.02	.01
242	Gary Zimmerman	.03	.02	.01
243	Jerry Burns (C)	.03	.02	.01
244	Bruce Armstrong **RC**	.10	.08	.04
245	Raymond Clayburn	.03	.02	.01
246	Reggie Dupard	.03	.02	.01
247	Tony Eason	.03	.02	.01
248	Sean Farrell	.03	.02	.01
249	Doug Flutie	.75	.60	.30
250	Brent Williams **RC**	.03	.02	.01
251	Roland James	.03	.02	.01
252	Ronnie Lippett	.03	.02	.01
253	Fred Marion	.03	.02	.01
254	Lawrence McGrew	.03	.02	.01
255	Stanley Morgan	.03	.02	.01
256	Johnny Rembert **RC**	.03	.02	.01
257	John Stephens **RC**	.10	.08	.04
258	Andre Tippett	.03	.02	.01
259	Garin Veris	.03	.02	.01
260	Ray Berry (C HOF stripe)	.10	.08	.04
261	Morten Andersen	.10	.08	.04
262	Hoby Brenner	.03	.02	.01
263	Stan Brock	.03	.02	.01
264	Brad Edelmann	.03	.02	.01
265	James Geathers	.03	.02	.01
266	Bobby Hebert ("touchdown passers")	.50	.40	.20
266a	Bobby Hebert ("touchdown passes")	.10	.08	.04
267	Craig Heyward **RC**	.10	.08	.04
268	Lonzell Hill	.03	.02	.01
269	Dalton Hilliard	.03	.02	.01
270	Rickey Jackson	.03	.02	.01
271	Steve Korte	.03	.02	.01
272	Eric Martin	.03	.02	.01

273	Reuben Mayes	.03	.02	.01
274	Sam Mills	.03	.02	.01
275	Brett Perriman **RC**	.25	.20	.10
276	Pat Swilling	.10	.08	.04
277	John Tice	.03	.02	.01
278	Jim Mora (C)	.03	.02	.01
279	Eric Moore	.03	.02	.01
280	Carl Banks	.03	.02	.01
281	Mark Bavaro	.03	.02	.01
282	Maurice Carthon	.03	.02	.01
283	Mark Collins **RC**	.10	.08	.04
284	Erik Howard	.03	.02	.01
285	Terry Kinard	.03	.02	.01
286	Sean Landeta	.03	.02	.01
287	Lionel Manuel	.03	.02	.01
288	Leonard Marshall	.03	.02	.01
289	Joe Morris	.03	.02	.01
290	Bart Oates	.03	.02	.01
291	Phil Simms	.10	.08	.04
292	Lawrence Taylor	.20	.15	.08
293	Bill Parcells (C)	.10	.08	.04
294	Dave Cadigan	.03	.02	.01
295	Kyle Clifton **RC**	.10	.08	.04
296	Alex Gordon	.03	.02	.01
297	James Hasty **RC**	.10	.08	.04
298	Johnny Hector	.03	.02	.01
299	Bobby Humphery	.03	.02	.01
300	Pat Leahy	.03	.02	.01
301	Marty Lyons	.03	.02	.01
302	Reggie McElroy **RC**	.10	.08	.04
303	Erik McMillan **RC**	.10	.08	.04
304	Freeman McNeil	.03	.02	.01
305	Ken O'Brien	.03	.02	.01
306	Pat Ryan	.03	.02	.01
307	Mickey Shuler	.03	.02	.01
308	Al Toon	.03	.02	.01
309	JoJo Townsell	.03	.02	.01
310	Roger Vick	.03	.02	.01
311	Joe Walton (C)	.03	.02	.01
312	Jerome Brown	.03	.02	.01
313	Keith Byars	.03	.02	.01
314	Cris Carter **RC**	2.00	1.50	.80
315	Randall Cunningham	.40	.30	.15
316	Terry Hoage	.03	.02	.01
317	Wes Hopkins	.03	.02	.01
318	Keith Jackson **RC**	.20	.15	.08
319	Mike Quick	.03	.02	.01
320	Mike Reichenbach	.03	.02	.01
321	Dave Rimington	.03	.02	.01
322	John Teltschik	.03	.02	.01
323	Anthony Toney	.03	.02	.01
324	Andre Waters	.03	.02	.01
325	Reggie White	.25	.20	.10
326	Luis Zendejas	.03	.02	.01
327	Buddy Ryan (C)	.03	.02	.01
328	Robert Awalt	.03	.02	.01
329	Tim McDonald **RC**	.10	.08	.04
330	Roy Green	.03	.02	.01
331	Neil Lomax	.03	.02	.01
332	Cedric Mack	.03	.02	.01
333	Stump Mitchell	.03	.02	.01
334	Niko Noga	.03	.02	.01
335	Jay Novacek **RC**	.25	.20	.10
336	Freddie Joe Nunn	.03	.02	.01
337	Luis Sharpe	.03	.02	.01
338	Vai Sikahema	.03	.02	.01
339	J.T. Smith	.03	.02	.01
340	Ron Wolfley	.03	.02	.01
341	Gene Stallings (C)	.03	.02	.01
342	Gary Anderson (Pit.)	.03	.02	.01
343	Bubby Brister **RC**	.75	.60	.30
344	Dermontti Dawson **RC**	.10	.08	.04
345	Thomas Everett **RC**	.10	.08	.04
346	Delton Hall	.03	.02	.01
347	Bryan Hinkle **RC**	.10	.08	.04
348	Merril Hoge **RC**	.10	.08	.04
349	Tunch Ilken	.03	.02	.01
350	Aaron Jones **RC**	.10	.08	.04
351	Louis Lipps	.03	.02	.01
352	David Little	.03	.02	.01
353	Hardy Nickerson **RC**	.20	.15	.08
354	Rod Woodson **RC**	.75	.60	.30
355	Chuck Noll ("One of the only three") (C)	.15	.11	.06
355a	Chuck Noll ("One of only two") (C)	.15	.11	.06
356	Gary Anderson (S.D.)	.03	.02	.01
357	Rod Berstine **RC**	.10	.08	.04
358	Gill Byrd	.03	.02	.01
359	Vencie Glenn	.03	.02	.01
360	Dennis McKnight	.03	.02	.01
361	Lionel James	.03	.02	.01
362	Mark Malone	.03	.02	.01
363	Anthony Miller 14.8 **RC**	.40	.30	.15
363a	Anthony Miller 3 **RC**	.40	.30	.15
364	Ralf Mojsiejenko	.03	.02	.01
365	Leslie O'Neal	.03	.02	.01
366	Jamie Holland	.03	.02	.01
367	Lee Williams	.03	.02	.01
368	Dan Henning	.03	.02	.01
369	Harris Barton **RC**	.10	.08	.04
370	Michael Carter	.03	.02	.01
371	Mike Cofer **RC** (S.F.)	.10	.08	.04
372	Roger Craig	.10	.08	.04
373	Riki Ellison	.03	.02	.01
374	Jim Fahnhorst	.03	.02	.01
375	John Frank	.03	.02	.01
376	Jeff Fuller	.03	.02	.01
377	Don Griffin	.03	.02	.01
378	Charles Haley	.10	.08	.04
379	Ronnie Lott	.10	.08	.04
380	Tim McKyer	.03	.02	.01
381	Joe Montana	2.00	1.50	.80
382	Tom Rathman	.03	.02	.01
383	Jerry Rice	1.50	1.25	.60
384	John Taylor **RC**	.25	.20	.10
385	Keena Turner	.03	.02	.01
386	Michael Walter	.03	.02	.01
387	Bubba Paris	.03	.02	.01
388	Steve Young	1.00	.70	.40
389	George Siefert **RC** (C)	.10	.08	.04
390	Brian Blades **RC**	.20	.15	.08
391	Brian Bosworth (Seahawks)	.10	.08	.04
391a	Brian Bosworth (Seattle)	.10	.08	.04
392	Jeff Bryant	.03	.02	.01
393	Jacob Green	.03	.02	.01
394	Norm Johnson	.03	.02	.01
395	Dave Krieg	.03	.02	.01
396	Steve Largent	.15	.11	.06
397	Bryan Millard	.03	.02	.01
398	Paul Moyer	.03	.02	.01
399	Joe Nash	.03	.02	.01
400	Rufus Porter	.03	.02	.01
401	Eugene Robinson **RC**	.20	.15	.08
402	Bruce Scholtz	.03	.02	.01
403	Kelly Stouffer **RC**	.10	.08	.04
404	Curt Warner 1455 (yards 1,455)	1.00	.70	.40
404a	Curt Warner (yards 6,074)	.15	.11	.06
405	John L. Williams	.03	.02	.01
406	Tony Woods **RC**	.10	.08	.04
407	David Wyman	.03	.02	.01
408	Chuck Knox (C)	.03	.02	.01
409	Mark Carrier **RC**	.50	.40	.20
410	Randy Grimes	.03	.02	.01
411	Paul Gruber **RC**	.10	.08	.04
412	Harry Hamilton	.03	.02	.01
413	Ron Holmes	.03	.02	.01
414	Donald Igwebuike	.03	.02	.01
415	Dan Turk	.03	.02	.01
416	Ricky Reynolds	.03	.02	.01
417	Bruce Hill	.03	.02	.01
418	Lars Tate	.03	.02	.01
419	Vinny Testaverde	.30	.25	.12
420	James Wilder	.03	.02	.01
421	Ray Perkins (C)	.03	.02	.01
422	Jeff Bostic	.03	.02	.01
423	Kelvin Bryant	.03	.02	.01
424	Gary Clark	.10	.08	.04
425	Monte Coleman	.03	.02	.01
426	Darrell Green	.03	.02	.01
427	Joe Jacoby	.03	.02	.01
428	Jim Lachey	.03	.02	.01
429	Charles Mann	.03	.02	.01
430	Dexter Manley	.03	.02	.01
431	Darryl Grant	.03	.02	.01
432	Mark May **RC**	.10	.08	.04
433	Art Monk	.15	.11	.06
434	Mark Rypien **RC**	.20	.15	.08
435	Ricky Sanders	.03	.02	.01
436	Alvin Walton **RC**	.10	.08	.04
437	Don Warren	.03	.02	.01
438	Jamie Morris	.03	.02	.01
439	Doug Williams	.03	.02	.01
440	Joe Gibbs (C)	.10	.08	.04
441	Marcus Cotton	.03	.02	.01
442	Joel Williams	.03	.02	.01
443	Joe Devlin	.03	.02	.01
444	Robb Riddick	.03	.02	.01
445	William Perry	.03	.02	.01
446	Thomas Sanders **RC**	.03	.02	.01
447	Brian Blades	.03	.02	.01
448	Cris Collinsworth	.10	.08	.04
449	Stanford Jennings	.03	.02	.01
450	Barry Krauss	.03	.02	.01
451	Ozzie Newsome	.10	.08	.04
452	Mike Oliphant	.03	.02	.01
453	Tony Dorsett	.15	.11	.06
454	Bruce McNorton	.03	.02	.01
455	Eric Dickerson	.20	.15	.08
456	Keith Bostic	.03	.02	.01
457	Sam Clancy	.03	.02	.01
458	Jack Del Rio	.03	.02	.01
459	Mike Webster	.03	.02	.01
460	Bob Golic	.03	.02	.01
461	Otis Wilson	.03	.02	.01
462	Mike Haynes	.03	.02	.01
463	Greg Townsend	.03	.02	.01
464	Mark Duper	.03	.02	.01
465	E.J. Junior	.03	.02	.01
466	Troy Stradford	.03	.02	.01
467	Mike Merriweather	.03	.02	.01
468	Irving Fryar	.10	.08	.04
469	Vaughan Johnson **RC**	.10	.08	.04
470	Pepper Johnson	.03	.02	.01
471	Gary Reasons	.03	.02	.01
472	Perry Williams **RC**	.10	.08	.04
473	Wesley Walker	.03	.02	.01
474	Anthony Bell	.03	.02	.01
475	Earl Ferrell	.03	.02	.01
476	Craig Wolfley	.03	.02	.01
477	Billy Ray Smith	.03	.02	.01
478	Jim McMahon	.10	.08	.04
478a	Jim McMahon (traded)	.40	.30	.15
479	Eric Wright	.03	.02	.01
480	Earnest Byner	.10	.08	.04
480a	Earnest Byner (traded)	.30	.25	.12
481	Russ Grimm	.03	.02	.01
482	Wilber Marshall	.03	.02	.01
483	Gerald Riggs	.03	.02	.01
484	Brian Davis **RC**	.10	.08	.04
485	Shawn Collins **RC**	.10	.08	.04
486	Deion Sanders **RC**	2.00	1.50	.80
487	Trace Armstrong **RC**	.10	.08	.04
488	Donnell Woolford **RC**	.20	.15	.08
489	Eric Metcalf **RC**	.25	.20	.10
490	Troy Aikman **RC**	3.00	2.25	1.25
491	Steve Walsh **RC**	.20	.15	.08
492	Steve Atwater **RC**	.30	.25	.12
493	Bobby Humphrey **RC**	.10	.08	.04
494	Barry Sanders **RC**	15.00	11.00	6.00
495	Tony Mandarich **RC**	.20	.15	.08
496	David Williams **RC**	.10	.08	.04
497	Andre Rison **RC**	1.00	.70	.40
498	Derrick Thomas **RC**	1.00	.70	.40
499	Cleveland Gary **RC**	.20	.15	.08
500	Bill Hawkins **RC**	.10	.08	.04
501	Louis Oliver **RC**	.10	.08	.04
502	Sammie Smith **RC**	.10	.08	.04
503	Hart Lee Dykes **RC**	.10	.08	.04
504	Wayne Martin **RC**	.10	.08	.04
505	Brian Williams **RC**	.10	.08	.04
506	Jeff Lageman **RC**	.10	.08	.04
507	Eric Hill **RC**	.10	.08	.04
508	Joe Wolf **RC**	.10	.08	.04
509	Timm Rosenbach **RC**	.10	.08	.04
510	Tom Ricketts **RC**	.10	.08	.04
511	Tim Worley **RC**	.10	.08	.04
512	Burt Grossman **RC**	.10	.08	.04
513	Keith DeLong **RC**	.10	.08	.04
514	Andy Heck **RC**	.10	.08	.04
515	Broderick Thomas **RC**	.10	.08	.04
516	Don Beebe **RC**	.25	.20	.10
517	James Thornton **RC**	.10	.08	.04
518	Eric Kattus **RC**	.10	.08	.04
519	Bruce Kozerski **RC**	.10	.08	.04
520	Brian Washington **RC**	.10	.08	.04
521	Rodney Peete **RC**	.25	.20	.10
522	Erik Affholter **RC**	.10	.08	.04
523	Anthony Dilweg **RC**	.10	.08	.04
524	O'Brien Alston **RC**	.10	.08	.04
525	Mike Elkins **RC**	.10	.08	.04
526	Jonathan Hayes **RC**	.10	.08	.04
527	Terry McDaniel **RC**	.10	.08	.04
528	Frank Stams **RC**	.10	.08	.04
529	Darryl Ingram **RC**	.10	.08	.04
530	Henry Thomas **RC**	.10	.08	.04
531	Eric Coleman **RC**	.10	.08	.04
532	Sheldon White **RC**	.10	.08	.04
533	Eric Allen **RC**	.20	.15	.08
534	Robert Drummond	.03	.02	.01
535	Gizmo Williams ("Scouting Photo")	10.00	7.50	4.00
535a	Gizmo Williams (no "Scouting Photo")	.25	.20	.10
535b	Gizmo Williams (no "Scouting Photo," "Canadian Football" on back)	.15	.11	.06
536	Billy Joe Tolliver **RC**	.20	.15	.08
537	Danny Stubbs **RC**	.10	.08	.04
538	Wesley Walls **RC**	.40	.30	.15
539	James Jefferson (no stripe)	.30	.25	.12
539a	James Jefferson (Pro Set Prospect stripe)	.10	.08	.04
540	Tracy Rocker	.03	.02	.01
541	Art Shell (C)	.10	.08	.04
542	Lemuel Stinson **RC**	.15	.11	.06
543	Tyrone Braxton **RC**	.10	.08	.04
543a	Tyrone Braxton **RC** (back photo actually Ken Bell)	.10	.08	.04

544	David Treadwell RC	.10	.08	.04
545	Willie Anderson RC	.20	.15	.08
546	Dave Meggett RC	.25	.20	.10
547	Lewis Tillman RC	.20	.15	.08
548	Carnell Lake RC	.20	.15	.08
549	Marion Butts RC	.20	.15	.08
550	Sterling Sharpe RC	1.00	.70	.40
551	Ezra Johnson	.03	.02	.01
552	Clarence Verdin RC	.10	.08	.04
553	Mervyn Fernandez	.03	.02	.01
554	Ottis Anderson	.10	.08	.04
555	Gary Hogeboom	.03	.02	.01
556	Paul Palmer	.03	.02	.01
557	Jesse Solomon	.03	.02	.01
558	Chip Banks	.03	.02	.01
559	Steve Pelluer	.03	.02	.01
560	Darrin Nelson	.03	.02	.01
561	Herschel Walker	.10	.08	.04
CC1	Pete Rozelle	.50	.40	.20

1989 Pro Set Announcer Inserts

This set of 30 cards was issued in Pro Set's Series II wax packs, one per pack. Like the Super Bowl inserts, the glossy cards are standard size. They feature color photos (bordered in bright orange) of the announcer on the front and back - if the announcer is a former player, a shot of him in action is shown. If the announcer made it to the Hall of Fame as a player (Terry Bradshaw, O.J. Simpson), a yellow stripe bearing a "Hall of Fame" label is in the lower left corner of his action picture. Pro Set had announced the names of the players of its first 20 cards in its premier issue of Pro Set Gazette. Since the initial announcement, Pro Set acquired the rights to NBC announcers and added them shortly before the presses began to roll. Verne Lundquist was apparently substituted for Dan Jiggetts just before the print run began.

		NM/M	NM	E
Complete Set (30):		5.00	3.75	2.00
Common Player:		.08	.06	.03
1	Dan Dierdorf	.25	.20	.10
2	Frank Gifford	.75	.60	.30
3	Al Michaels	.15	.11	.06
4	Pete Axthelm	.08	.06	.03
5	Chris Berman	.25	.20	.10
6	Tom Jackson	.15	.11	.06
7	Mike Patrick	.08	.06	.03
8	John Saunders	.08	.06	.03
9	Joe Theismann	.30	.25	.12
10	Steve Sabol	.08	.06	.03
11	Jack Buck	.08	.06	.03
12	Terry Bradshaw	.50	.40	.20
13	James Brown	.08	.06	.03
14	Dan Fouts	.30	.25	.12
15	Dick Butkus	.50	.40	.20
16	Irv Cross	.08	.06	.03
17	Brent Musberger	.15	.11	.06
18	Ken Stabler	.25	.20	.10
19	Dick Stockton	.08	.06	.03
20	Hank Stram	.08	.06	.03
21	Verne Lundquist	.08	.06	.03
22	Will McDonough	.08	.06	.03
23	Bob Costas	.25	.20	.10
24	Dick Enberg	.15	.11	.06
25	Joe Namath	.65	.50	.25
26	Bob Trumpy	.08	.06	.03
27	Merlin Olsen	.25	.20	.10
28	Ahmad Rashad	.30	.25	.12
29	O.J. Simpson	2.00	1.50	.80
30	Bill Walsh	.30	.25	.12

1989 Pro Set GTE SB Album

This 40-card set was made available to those who attended the Super Bowl XXIV game in New Orleans in 1990. Players from the participants in the game, the San Francisco 49ers and Denver Broncos, are represented in the set. The card numbers are identical to those in the regular set, but these cards can be distinguished from the regulars by the NFC or AFC Champs designation on the card front, along with the Super Bowl logo. GTE issued the cards in conjunction with Pro Set, and created a card album to hold the set.

		NM/M	NM	E
Complete Set (40):		30.00	22.00	12.00
Common Player:		.40	.30	.15
99	Keith Bishop	.40	.30	.15
100	John Elway	6.00	4.50	2.50
101	Simon Fletcher	.60	.45	.25
103	Mike Horan	.40	.30	.15
104	Mark Jackson	.70	.50	.30
105	Vance Johnson	.60	.45	.25
107	Clarence Kay	.40	.30	.15
108	Karl Mecklenburg	.60	.45	.25
109	Ricky Nattiel	.60	.45	.25
110	Steve Sewell	.50	.40	.20
111	Dennis Smith	.50	.40	.20
113	Sammy Winder	.50	.40	.20
114	Dan Reeves CO	.60	.45	.25
369	Harris Barton	.40	.30	.15
370	Michael Carter	.60	.45	.25
371	Mike Cofer	.40	.30	.15
372	Roger Craig	1.75	1.25	.70
374	Jim Fahnhorst	.40	.30	.15
377	Don Griffin	.50	.40	.20
378	Charles Haley	.60	.45	.25
379	Ronnie Lott	2.50	2.00	1.00
380	Tim McKyer	.50	.40	.20
381	Joe Montana	11.00	8.25	4.50
382	Tom Rathman	.75	.60	.30
383	Jerry Rice	8.00	6.00	3.25
384	John Taylor	2.00	1.50	.80
385	Keena Turner	.50	.40	.20
386	Michael Walter	.40	.30	.15
387	Bubba Paris	.40	.30	.15
388	Steve Young	4.00	3.00	1.50
389	George Seifert CO	.50	.40	.20
479	Eric Wright	.60	.45	.25
492	Steve Atwater	1.00	.70	.40
493	Bobby Humphrey	.75	.60	.30
537	Danny Stubbs	.40	.30	.15
543	Tyrone Braxton	.50	.40	.20
544	David Treadwell	.40	.30	.15
----	AFC Logo XXIV Collectible	.60	.45	.25
----	NFC logo XXIV Collectible	.60	.45	.25
----	Superdome XXIV Collectible	.60	.45	.25

1989 Pro Set Promos

These five cards preview Pro Set's 1989 card design. The Santa Claus card was given to dealers, NFL representatives and members of the hobby press in December 1989. The Super Bowl card was given to those who attended the card show at Super Bowl XXIV in New Orleans in January 1990. The three player cards were samples which were mistakenly handed out at card shows in San Francisco and Chicago. The Bush and Lofton cards were intended to be included in Pro Set's Series II cards, but were bumped for Eric Dickerson and Greg Townsend. Sanders was given #446.

		NM/M	NM	E
Complete Set (5):		45.00	94.00	50.00
Common Player:		5.00	7.50	4.00
445	Thomas Sanders	10.00	7.50	4.00
455	Blair Bush	5.00	3.75	2.00
463	James Lofton	15.00	11.00	6.00
1989	Santa Claus	15.00	11.00	6.00

1989 Pro Set Super Bowl Inserts

Pro Set included a glossy Super Bowl card (1 through 23) in each wax pack of its 1989 Series I cards. The standard-size cards show the official logo of each Super Bowl surrounded by a bright orange border on the front of the card, with the stylized names of the two participating teams in the background. Card backs include a recap of the game and a line score.

		NM/M	NM	E
Complete Set (23):		5.00	3.75	2.00
Common Player:		.25	.20	.10

1	Super Bowl I	.25	.20	.10
2	Super Bowl II	.25	.20	.10
3	Super Bowl IV	.25	.20	.10
4	Super Bowl IV	.25	.20	.10
5	Super Bowl V	.25	.20	.10
6	Super Bowe VI	.25	.20	.10
7	Super Bowl VII	.25	.20	.10
8	Super Bowl VIII	.25	.20	.10
9	Super Bowl IX	.25	.20	.10
10	Super Bowl X	.25	.20	.10
11	Super Bowl XI	.25	.20	.10
12	Super Bowl XII	.25	.20	.10
13	Super Bowl XIII	.25	.20	.10
14	Super Bowl XIV	.25	.20	.10
15	Super Bowl XV	.25	.20	.10
16	Super Bowl XVI	.25	.20	.10
17	Super Bowl XVII	.25	.20	.10
18	Super Bowl XVIII	.25	.20	.10
19	Super Bowl XIX	.25	.20	.10
20	Super Bowl XX	.25	.20	.10
21	Super Bowl XXI	.25	.20	.10
22	Super Bowl XXII	.25	.20	.10
23	Super Bowl XXIII	.25	.20	.10

1990 Pro Set

Pro Set's Series I was issued in late May of 1990. The sophomore set for the Dallas-based company was its first using its own printing press, and that allowed Pro Set to create die-cut borderless cards. Again, several insert cards were included throughout Series I: Paul Tagliabue was randomly included in early Series I wax packs; golfer Payne Stewart was added to the rotation; and Jeff George completed the rotating triumverate in late Series I printings. Because of a squabble over what card companies he wanted to appear with, Eric Dickerson was not to appear in any 1990 card sets. Pro Set already had a card of him created, however, and was forced to pull them by hand from Series I. Some, however, did get through to the hobby. Issued in November 1990, the second series of Pro Set was, unlike the year before, not included in Series I wax boxes. In addition, space was saved in the middle of the set for the mail-in Final Update offer. Five cards were inserted on a rotating basis in every 50th pack: Paul Tagliabue (carried over from Series I), Payne Stewart (same), Santa Claus, Joe Robbie, and Marvel Comics Super Pro. The Final Update was available in late January through a mail-in offer. It included 28 cards, plus three other special cards: card 799, which featured Ronnie Lott in his role as a spokesman for the NFL's "Stay in School" program; the Series I Andre Rison card with a traded stripe; and cards 800, Emmitt Smith and Mark Carrier, the 1990 NFL Pro Set Rookies of the Year in the 1991 Pro Set design. One correction was made very early in the print run. The text on the back of card 772, Dexter Manley, originally read, "Reinstated by Paul Tagliabue 11 weeks into the 1990 season after suspension for violating the league's substance-abuse policy." According to reports, Manley's agent objected to the wording, and it was changed to "After missing the first 10 weeks of the 1990 season, Dexter returned to the NFL." Very few of the original cards were issued.

	NM/M	NM	E
Complete Set (801):	15.00	11.00	6.00
Complete Series 1 (377):	6.00	4.50	2.50
Complete Series 2 (392):	6.00	4.50	2.50
Complete Series 3 (32):	3.00	2.25	1.25
Common Player:	.03	.02	.01
Series 1 Pack (14+1):	.50		
Series 1 Wax Box (36):	10.00		
Series 2 Pack (14+1):	.50		
Series 2 Wax Box (36):	10.00		

1	Barry Sanders (ROY)	.75	.60	.30
2	Joe Montana (SPL)(back reads "Kelly-3,521 yards")	.50	.40	.20
2a	Joe Montana (SPL)(back corrected to "Kelly: 3,130 yards")	.75	.60	.30
3	Lindy Infante (SPL)	.03	.02	.01
4	Warren Moon (SPL)	.10	.08	.04
5	Keith Millard (SPL)	.03	.02	.01

6	Derrick Thomas (SPL)	.10	.08	.04
7	Ottis Anderson (SPL)	.03	.02	.01
8	Joe Montana (LL)	.50	.40	.20
9	Christian Okoye (SPL)	.03	.02	.01
10	Thurman Thomas	.25	.20	.10
11	Mike Cofer (SPL)	.03	.02	.01
12	Dalton Hilliard (SPL)	.03	.02	.01
13	Sterling Sharpe (LL)	.20	.15	.08
14	Rich Camarillo (LL)	.03	.02	.01
15	Walter Stanley (SPL)(#8 on back)	.10	.08	.04
15a	Walter Stanley (SPL)(#86 on back)	.10	.08	.04
16	Rod Woodson (LL)	.03	.02	.01
17	Felix Wright (LL)	.03	.02	.01
18	Chris Doleman (SPL) (error back)	.10	.08	.04
18a	Chris Doleman (SPL) (back corrected to 104.5 sacks for Taylor; "Townsent" corrected to "Townsend")	.10	.08	.04
19	Andre Ware (SPL)	.10	.08	.04
19a	Andre Ware (SPL)(drafted stripe added)	.10	.08	.04
20	Mohammed Elewonibi (SPL)	.05	.04	.02
20a	Mohammed Elewonibi (SPL)(drafted stripe added)	.05	.04	.02
21	Percy Snow (SPL)	.05	.04	.02
21a	Percy Snow (SPL)(drafted stripe added)	.05	.04	.02
22	Anthony Thompson (SPL)	.10	.08	.04
22a	Anthony Thompson (SPL) (drafted stripe added)	.10	.08	.04
23	Buck Buchanan (HOF)	.03	.02	.01
24	Bob Griese (HOF)	.03	.02	.01
25	Franco Harris (HOF)	.05	.04	.02
25a	Franco Harris (HOF) (corrected birthdate: 3/7/50)	.05	.04	.02
26	Ted Hendricks (HOF)	.03	.02	.01
27	Jack Lambert (HOF)	.08	.06	.03
27a	Jack Lambert (HOF) (corrected birthdate 7/8/52)	.08	.06	.03
28	Tom Landry (HOF)	.06	.05	.02
29	Bob St. Clair (HOF)	.03	.02	.01
30	Aundray Bruce	.06	.05	.02
31	Tony Casillas	.03	.02	.01
32	Shawn Collins	.03	.02	.01
33	Marcus Cotton	.03	.02	.01
34	Bill Fralic	.03	.02	.01
35	Chris Miller	.06	.05	.02
36	Deion Sanders	.30	.25	.12
37	John Settle	.03	.02	.01
38	Jerry Glanville	.03	.02	.01
39	Cornelius Bennett	.03	.02	.01
40	Jim Kelly	.35	.25	.14
41	Mark Kelso	.03	.02	.01
42	Scott Norwood	.03	.02	.01
43	Nate Odomes **RC**	.30	.25	.12
44	Scott Radecic	.03	.02	.01
45	Jim Ritcher	.03	.02	.01
46	Leonard Smith	.03	.02	.01
47	Darryl Talley	.03	.02	.01
48	Marv Levy (C)	.03	.02	.01
49	Neal Anderson	.03	.02	.01
50	Kevin Butler	.03	.02	.01
51	Jim Covert	.03	.02	.01
52	Richard Dent	.03	.02	.01
53	Jay Hilgenberg	.03	.02	.01
54	Steve McMichael	.03	.02	.01
55	Ron Morris	.03	.02	.01
56	John Roper	.03	.02	.01
57	Mike Singletary	.03	.02	.01
59	Mike Ditka (C)	.03	.02	.01
60	Lewis Billups	.03	.02	.01
61	Eddie Brown	.03	.02	.01
62	Jason Buck	.03	.02	.01
63	Rickey Dixon (no bio notes under photo)	.10	.08	.04
63a	Rickey Dixon (with bio notes)	.10	.08	.04
64	Tim McGee	.03	.02	.01
65	Eric Thomas	.03	.02	.01
66	Ickey Woods	.03	.02	.01
67	Carl Zander	.03	.02	.01
68	Sam Wyche (C)(no bio notes under photo)	.05	.04	.02
68a	Sam Wyche (C) (corrected)	.05	.04	.02
69	Paul Farren	.03	.02	.01
70	Thane Gash	.03	.02	.01
71	David Grayson	.03	.02	.01
72	Bernie Kosar	.03	.02	.01
73	Reggie Langhorne	.03	.02	.01
74	Eric Metcalf	.03	.02	.01
75	Ozzie Newsome	.10	.08	.04
75a	Ozzie Newsome (corrected hometown: Muscle Shoals, AL)	.10	.08	.04
75	Cody Risien (SP)	.10	.08	.04
76	Felix Wright	.03	.02	.01
77	Bud Carson (C)	.03	.02	.01
78	Troy Aikman	1.00	.70	.40
79	Michael Irvin	.30	.25	.12
80	Jim Jeffcoat	.03	.02	.01
81	Crawford Ker	.03	.02	.01
82	Eugene Lockhart	.03	.02	.01
83	Kelvin Martin **RC**	.25	.20	.10
84	Ken Norton Jr. **RC**	.50	.40	.20
85	Jimmy Johnson (C)	.03	.02	.01
86	Steve Atwater	.03	.02	.01
87	Tyrone Braxton	.03	.02	.01
88	John Elway	.40	.30	.15
89	Simon Fletcher	.03	.02	.01
90	Ron Holmes	.03	.02	.01
91	Bobby Humphrey	.03	.02	.01
92	Vance Johnson	.03	.02	.01
93	Ricky Nattiel	.03	.02	.01
94	Dan Reeves	.03	.02	.01
95	Jim Arnold	.03	.02	.01
96	Jerry Ball	.03	.02	.01
97	Bennie Blades	.03	.02	.01
98	Lomas Brown	.03	.02	.01
99	Michael Cofer	.03	.02	.01
100	Richard Johnson	.03	.02	.01
101	Eddie Murray	.03	.02	.01
102	Barry Sanders	1.25	.90	.50
103	Chris Spielman	.03	.02	.01
104	William White **RC**	.08	.06	.03
105	Eric Williams **RC**	.08	.06	.03
106	Wayne Fontes (C)	.03	.02	.01
107	Brent Fullwood	.03	.02	.01
108	Ron Hallstrom **RC**	.08	.06	.03
109	Tim Harris	.03	.02	.01
110	Johnny Holland (no name, number on back)	1.00	.70	.40
110a	Johnny Holland (corrected)	.15	.11	.06
111	Perry Kemp (Ken Stills photo on back)	.10	.08	.04
111a	Perry Kemp (corrected)	.10	.08	.04
112	Don Majkowski	.03	.02	.01
113	Mark Murphy	.03	.02	.01
114	Sterling Sharpe	.20	.15	.08
114a	Sterling Sharpe (corrected birthplace: Chicago, IL)	.20	.15	.08
115	Ed West	.03	.02	.01
116	Lindy Infante (C)	.03	.02	.01
117	Steve Brown	.03	.02	.01
118	Ray Childress	.03	.02	.01
119	Ernest Givins	.03	.02	.01
120	John Grimsley	.03	.02	.01
121	Alonzo Highsmith	.03	.02	.01
122	Drew Hill	.03	.02	.01
123	Bubba McDowell	.03	.02	.01
124	Dean Steinkuhler	.03	.02	.01
125	Lorenzo White	.10	.08	.04
126	Tony Zendejas	.03	.02	.01
127	Jack Pardee (C)	.03	.02	.01
128	Albert Bentley	.03	.02	.01
129	Dean Biasucci	.03	.02	.01
130	Duane Bickett	.03	.02	.01
131	Bill Brooks	.03	.02	.01
132	John Hand	.03	.02	.01
133	Mike Prior	.03	.02	.01
134	Andre Rison (no stripe)	.25	.20	.10
134a	Andre Rison (with stripe)	.50	.40	.20
135	Rohn Stark	.03	.02	.01
136	Donnell Thompson	.03	.02	.01
137	Clarence Verdin	.03	.02	.01
138	Fredd Young	.03	.02	.01
139	Ron Meyer (C)	.03	.02	.01
140	John Alt **RC**	.08	.06	.03
141	Steve DeBerg	.03	.02	.01
142	Irv Eatman	.03	.02	.01
143	Dino Hackett	.03	.02	.01
144	Nick Lowery	.03	.02	.01
145	Bill Maas	.03	.02	.01
146	Stephone Paige	.03	.02	.01
147	Neil Smith	.25	.20	.10
148	Marty Schottenheimer (C)	.03	.02	.01
149	Steve Beuerlein	.25	.20	.10
150	Tim Brown	.35	.25	.14
151	Mike Dyal	.03	.02	.01
152	Mervyn Fernandez	.10	.08	.04
152a	Mervyn Fernandez (status corrected to "Drafted 10th round '83")	.10	.08	.04
153	Willie Gault	.03	.02	.01
154	Bob Golic	.03	.02	.01
155	Bo Jackson	.40	.30	.15
156	Don Mosebar	.03	.02	.01
157	Steve Smith	.03	.02	.01
158	Greg Townsend	.03	.02	.01
159	Bruce Wilkerson **RC**	.08	.06	.03
160	Steve Wisniewski	.03	.02	.01
161	Art Shell (C)	.10	.08	.04
161a	Art Shell (C)(birthdate corrected to 11/26/46)	.10	.08	.04
162	Willie Anderson	.10	.08	.04
163	Greg Bell	.03	.02	.01
164	Henry Ellard	.03	.02	.01
165	Jim Everett	.03	.02	.01
166	Jerry Gray	.03	.02	.01
167	Kevin Greene	.03	.02	.01
168	Pete Holohan	.03	.02	.01
169	Larry Kelm **RC**	.08	.06	.03
170	Tom Newberry	.03	.02	.01
171	Vince Newsome	.03	.02	.01
172	Irv Pankey	.03	.02	.01
173	Jackie Slater	.03	.02	.01
174	Fred Strickland **RC**	.08	.06	.03
175	Mike Wilcher	.03	.02	.01
176	John Robinson (C)	.03	.02	.01
177	Mark Clayton	.03	.02	.01
178	Roy Foster	.03	.02	.01
179	Harry Galbreath **RC**	.08	.06	.03
180	Jim Jensen	.03	.02	.01
181	Dan Marino	.75	.60	.30
182	Louis Oliver	.03	.02	.01
183	Sammie Smith	.03	.02	.01
184	Brian Sochia	.03	.02	.01
185	Don Shula (C)	.03	.02	.01
186	Joey Browner	.03	.02	.01
187	Anthony Carter	.03	.02	.01
188	Chris Doleman	.03	.02	.01
189	Steve Jordan	.03	.02	.01
190	Carl Lee	.03	.02	.01
191	Randall McDaniel	.03	.02	.01
192	Mike Merriweather	.03	.02	.01
193	Keith Millard	.03	.02	.01
194	Al Noga	.03	.02	.01
195	Scott Studwell	.03	.02	.01
196	Henry Thomas	.03	.02	.01
197	Herschel Walker	.03	.02	.01
198	Wade Wilson	.03	.02	.01
199	Gary Zimmerman	.03	.02	.01
200	Jerry Burns (C)	.03	.02	.01
201	Vincent Brown **RC**	.15	.11	.06
202	Hart Lee Dykes	.03	.02	.01
203	Sean Farrell	.03	.02	.01
204	Fred Marion (49er with belt)	.05	.04	.02
204a	Fred Marion (corrected)	.05	.04	.02
205	Stanley Morgan	.03	.02	.01
206	Eric Sievers	.03	.02	.01
207	John Stephens	.03	.02	.01
208	Andre Tippett	.03	.02	.01
209	Rod Rust (C)	.03	.02	.01
210	Morten Andersen (name in white on back)	.10	.08	.04
210a	Morten Andersen (corrected)	.10	.08	.04
211	Brad Edelman	.03	.02	.01
212	John Fourcade	.03	.02	.01
213	Dalton Hilliard	.03	.02	.01
214	Rickey Jackson	.03	.02	.01
215	Vaughan Johnson	.03	.02	.01
216	Eric Martin (name in white on back)	.05	.04	.02
216a	Eric Martin (corrected)	.05	.04	.02
217	Sam Mills	.03	.02	.01
218	Pat Swilling	.03	.02	.01
219	Frank Warren **RC**	.08	.06	.03
220	Jim Wilks	.03	.02	.01
221	Jim Mora (C)(name in white on back)	.03	.02	.01
221a	Jim Mora (C)(corrected)	.03	.02	.01
222	Raul Allegre	.03	.02	.01
223	Carl Banks	.03	.02	.01
224	John Elliot	.03	.02	.01
225	Erik Howard	.03	.02	.01
226	Pepper Johnson	.03	.02	.01
227	Leonard Marshall	.03	.02	.01
228	David Meggett	.10	.08	.04
229	Bart Oates	.03	.02	.01
230	Phil Simms	.10	.08	.04
231	Lawrence Taylor	.10	.08	.04
232	Bill Parcells (C)	.03	.02	.01
233	Troy Benson	.03	.02	.01
234	Kyle Clifton	.03	.02	.01

235	Johnny Hector	.03	.02	.01
236	Jeff Lageman	.03	.02	.01
237	Pat Leahy	.03	.02	.01
238	Freeman McNeil	.03	.02	.01
239	Ken O'Brien	.03	.02	.01
240	Al Toon	.03	.02	.01
241	JoJo Townsell	.03	.02	.01
242	Bruce Coslet (C)	.03	.02	.01
243	Eric Allen	.03	.02	.01
244	Jerome Brown	.03	.02	.01
245	Keith Byars	.03	.02	.01
246	Cris Carter	.35	.25	.14
247	Randall Cunningham	.15	.11	.06
248	Keith Jackson	.25	.20	.10
249	Mike Quick	.03	.02	.01
250	Clyde Simmons	.03	.02	.01
251	Andre Waters	.03	.02	.01
252	Reggie White	.15	.11	.06
253	Buddy Ryan (C)	.03	.02	.01
254	Rich Camarillo	.03	.02	.01
255	Earl Ferrell	.03	.02	.01
256	Roy Green	.03	.02	.01
257	Ken Harvey **RC**	.08	.06	.03
258	Ernie Jones **RC**	.10	.08	.04
259	Tim McDonald	.03	.02	.01
260	Timm Rosenbach	.03	.02	.01
261	Luis Sharpe	.03	.02	.01
262	Vai Sikahema	.03	.02	.01
263	J.T. Smith	.03	.02	.01
264	Ron Wolfley	.03	.02	.01
265	Joe Bugel (C)	.03	.02	.01
266	Gary Anderson	.03	.02	.01
267	Bubby Brister	.10	.08	.04
268	Merril Hoge	.03	.02	.01
269	Carnell Lake	.03	.02	.01
270	Louis Lipps	.03	.02	.01
271	David Little	.03	.02	.01
272	Greg Lloyd	.03	.02	.01
273	Keith Willie	.03	.02	.01
274	Tim Worley	.03	.02	.01
275	Chuck Noll (C)	.03	.02	.01
276	Marion Butts	.06	.05	.02
277	Gill Byrd	.03	.02	.01
278	Vencie Glenn	.03	.02	.01
279	Burt Grossman	.03	.02	.01
280	Gary Plummer	.03	.02	.01
281	Billy Ray Smith	.03	.02	.01
282	Billy Joe Tolliver	.03	.02	.01
283	Dan Henning (C)	.03	.02	.01
284	Harris Barton	.03	.02	.01
285	Michael Carter	.03	.02	.01
286	Mike Cofer	.03	.02	.01
287	Roger Craig	.03	.02	.01
288	Don Griffin	.03	.02	.01
289	Charles Haley	.05	.04	.02
289a	Charles Haley (stats corrected to 5 total fumble recoveries)	.05	.04	.02
290	Pierce Holt **RC**	.10	.08	.04
291	Ronnie Lott	.10	.08	.04
292	Guy McIntyre	.03	.02	.01
293	Joe Montana	1.00	.70	.40
294	Tom Rathman	.03	.02	.01
295	Jerry Rice	.75	.60	.30
296	Jesse Sapolu **RC**	.05	.04	.02
297	John Taylor	.20	.15	.08
298	Michael Walter	.03	.02	.01
299	George Seifert (C)	.03	.02	.01
300	Jeff Bryant	.03	.02	.01
301	Jacob Green	.03	.02	.01
302	Norm Johnson	.03	.02	.01
303	Bryan Millard	.03	.02	.01
304	Joe Nash	.03	.02	.01
305	Eugene Robinson	.03	.02	.01
306	John L. Williams	.03	.02	.01
307	Dave Wyman	.03	.02	.01
308	Chuck Knox (C)	.03	.02	.01
309	Mark Carrier	.03	.02	.01
310	Paul Gruber	.03	.02	.01
311	Harry Hamilton	.03	.02	.01
312	Bruce Hill	.03	.02	.01
313	Donald Igwebuike	.03	.02	.01
314	Kevin Murphy	.03	.02	.01
315	Ervin Randle	.03	.02	.01
316	Mark Robinson	.03	.02	.01
317	Lars Tate	.03	.02	.01
318	Vinny Testaverde	.08	.06	.03
319	Ray Perkins (C)(no name, number on back)	.05	.04	.02
319a	Ray Perkins (C) (corrected)	.05	.04	.02
320	Earnest Byner	.03	.02	.01
321	Gary Clark	.15	.11	.06
322	Darryl Grant	.03	.02	.01
323	Darrell Green	.03	.02	.01
324	Jim Lachey	.03	.02	.01
325	Charles Mann	.03	.02	.01

326	Wilber Marshall	.03	.02	.01
327	Ralf Mojsienjenko	.03	.02	.01
328	Art Monk	.03	.02	.01
329	Gerald Riggs	.03	.02	.01
330	Mark Rypien	.10	.08	.04
331	Ricky Sanders	.03	.02	.01
332	Alvin Walton	.03	.02	.01
333	Joe Gibbs (C)	.03	.02	.01
334	**Aloha Stadium - PB**	.03	.02	.01
335	Brian Blades (PB)	.03	.02	.01
336	James Brooks (PB)	.03	.02	.01
337	Shane Conlan (PB)	.03	.02	.01
338	Eric Dickerson	4.00	3.00	1.50
339	Ray Donaldson (PB)	.03	.02	.01
340	Ferrell Edmunds	.03	.02	.01
341	Boomer Esiason (PB)	.06	.05	.02
342	David Fulcher (PB)	.03	.02	.01
343	Chris Hinton (PB)(no traded stripe)	.05	.04	.02
343a	Chris Hinton (PB)(traded)	.05	.04	.02
344	Rodney Holman (PB)	.06	.05	.02
345	Kent Hull (PB)	.03	.02	.01
346	Tunch Ilkin (PB)	.03	.02	.01
347	Mike Johnson (PB)	.03	.02	.01
348	Greg Kragen (PB)	.03	.02	.01
349	Dave Krieg (PB)	.03	.02	.01
350	Albert Lewis (PB)	.03	.02	.01
351	Howie Long (PB)	.03	.02	.01
352	Bruce Matthews	.03	.02	.01
353	Clay Matthews (PB)	.03	.02	.01
354	Erik McMillan (PB)	.03	.02	.01
355	Karl Mecklenberg (PB)	.03	.02	.01
356	Anthony Miller (PB)	.25	.20	.10
357	Frank Minnifield (PB)	.03	.02	.01
358	Max Montoya (PB)	.03	.02	.01
359	Warren Moon (PB)	.08	.06	.03
360	Mike Munchak (PB)	.03	.02	.01
361	Anthony Munoz (PB)	.03	.02	.01
362	John Offerdahl (PB)	.03	.02	.01
363	Christian Okoye (PB)	.03	.02	.01
364	Leslie O'Neal (PB)	.06	.05	.02
365	Rufus Porter (PB)	.03	.02	.01
366	Andre Reed (PB)	.06	.05	.02
367	Johnny Rembert (PB)	.03	.02	.01
368	Reggie Roby (PB)	.03	.02	.01
369	Kevin Ross (PB)	.03	.02	.01
370	Webster Slaughter (PB)	.03	.02	.01
371	Bruce Smith (PB)	.06	.05	.02
372	Dennis Smith	.03	.02	.01
373	Derrick Thomas (PB)	.06	.05	.02
374	Thurman Thomas	.25	.20	.10
375	David Treadwell (PB)	.03	.02	.01
376	Lee Williams (PB)	.03	.02	.01
377	Rod Woodson (PB)	.03	.02	.01
378	Bud Carson (PB)	.03	.02	.01
379	Eric Allen (PB)	.03	.02	.01
380	Neal Anderson (PB)	.03	.02	.01
381	Jerry Ball (PB)	.03	.02	.01
382	Joey Browner (PB)	.03	.02	.01
383	Rich Camarillo (PB)	.03	.02	.01
384	Mark Carrier (PB)	.03	.02	.01
385	Roger Craig (PB)	.03	.02	.01
386	Randall Cunningham (PB)	.10	.08	.04
387	Chris Doleman (PB)	.03	.02	.01
388	Henry Ellard (PB)	.03	.02	.01
389	Bill Fralic (PB)	.03	.02	.01
390	Brent Fullwood (PB)	.03	.02	.01
391	Jerry Gray (PB)	.03	.02	.01
392	Kevin Greene (PB)	.03	.02	.01
393	Tim Harris (PB)	.03	.02	.01
394	Jay Hilgenberg (PB)	.03	.02	.01
395	Dalton Hilliard (PB)	.03	.02	.01
396	Keith Jackson (PB)	.08	.06	.03
397	Vaughan Johnson (PB)	.03	.02	.01
398	Steve Jordan (PB)	.03	.02	.01
399	Carl Lee (PB)	.03	.02	.01
400	Ronnie Lott (PB)	.06	.05	.02
401	Don Majkowski (PB)	.03	.02	.01
402	Charles Mann (PB)	.03	.02	.01
403	Randall McDaniel (PB)	.03	.02	.01
404	Tim McDonald (PB)	.03	.02	.01
405	Guy McIntyre (PB)	.03	.02	.01
406	Dave Meggett (PB)	.03	.02	.01
407	Keith Millard (PB)	.03	.02	.01
408	Joe Montana (PB)	.50	.40	.20
409	Eddie Murray	.03	.02	.01
410	Tom Newberry (PB)	.03	.02	.01
411	Jerry Rice (PB)	.40	.30	.15
412	Mark Rypien (PB)	.03	.02	.01
413	Barry Sanders (PB)	.75	.60	.30
414	Luis Sharpe (PB)	.03	.02	.01
415	Sterling Sharpe (PB)	.20	.15	.08
416	Mike Singletary (PB)	.03	.02	.01
417	Jackie Slater (PB)	.03	.02	.01
418	Doug Smith (PB)	.03	.02	.01
419	Chris Spielman (PB)	.03	.02	.01

420	Pat Swilling (PB)	.03	.02	.01
421	John Taylor (PB)	.10	.08	.04
422	Lawrence Taylor (PB)	.10	.08	.04
423	Reggie White (PB)	.08	.06	.03
424	Ron Wolfley (PB)	.03	.02	.01
425	Gary Zimmerman (PB)	.03	.02	.01
426	John Robinson (PB)	.03	.02	.01
427	Scott Case	.03	.02	.01
428	Mike Kenn	.03	.02	.01
429	Mike Gann	.03	.02	.01
430	Tim Green **RC**	.08	.06	.03
431	Michael Haynes **RC**	.30	.25	.12
432	Jessie Tuggle **RC**	.20	.15	.08
433	John Rade	.03	.02	.01
434	Andre Rison	.25	.20	.10
435	Don Beebe	.03	.02	.01
436	Ray Bentley	.03	.02	.01
437	Shane Conlan	.03	.02	.01
438	Kent Hull	.03	.02	.01
439	Pete Metzelaars	.03	.02	.01
440	Andre Reed	.15	.11	.06
441	Frank Reich	.15	.11	.06
442	Leon Seals	.08	.06	.03
443	Bruce Smith	.03	.02	.01
444	Thurman Thomas	.40	.30	.15
445	Will Wolford	.03	.02	.01
446	Trace Armstrong	.03	.02	.01
447	Mark Bortz **RC**	.10	.08	.04
448	Tom Thayer **RC**	.10	.08	.04
449	Dan Hampton (DE back)	.05	.04	.02
449a	Dan Hampton (DT back)	.05	.04	.02
451	Dennis Gentry	.03	.02	.01
452	Jim Harbaugh	.10	.08	.04
453	Vestee Jackson	.03	.02	.01
454	Brad Muster	.03	.02	.01
455	William Perry	.03	.02	.01
456	Ron Rivera	.03	.02	.01
457	James Thornton	.03	.02	.01
458	Mike Tomczak	.03	.02	.01
459	Donnell Woolford	.03	.02	.01
460	Eric Ball	.03	.02	.01
461	James Brooks	.03	.02	.01
462	David Fulcher	.03	.02	.01
463	Boomer Esiason	.10	.08	.04
464	Rodney Holman	.03	.02	.01
465	Bruce Kozerski	.03	.02	.01
466	Tim Krumrie	.03	.02	.01
467	Anthony Munoz	.03	.02	.01
468	Brian Blados	.03	.02	.01
469	Mike Baab	.03	.02	.01
470	Brian Brennan	.03	.02	.01
471	Raymond Clayborn	.03	.02	.01
472	Mike Johnson	.03	.02	.01
473	Kevin Mack	.03	.02	.01
474	Clay Matthews	.03	.02	.01
475	Frank Minnifield	.03	.02	.01
476	Gregg Rakoczy	.03	.02	.01
477	Webster Slaughter	.03	.02	.01
478	James Dixon	.03	.02	.01
479	Robert Awalt	.03	.02	.01
480	Dennis McKinnon	.03	.02	.01
481	Danny Noonan	.03	.02	.01
482	Jesse Soloman	.03	.02	.01
483	Danny Stubbs	.03	.02	.01
484	Steve Walsh	.03	.02	.01
485	Michael Brooks **RC**	.25	.20	.10
486	Mark Jackson	.03	.02	.01
487	Greg Kragen	.03	.02	.01
488	Ken Lanier **RC**	.08	.06	.03
489	Karl Mecklenburg	.03	.02	.01
490	Steve Sewell	.03	.02	.01
491	Dennis Smith	.03	.02	.01
492	David Treadwell	.03	.02	.01
493	Michael Young **RC**	.08	.06	.03
494	Robert Clark **RC**	.10	.08	.04
495	Dennis Gibson	.03	.02	.01
496	Kevin Glover **RC** (C-G back)	.15	.11	.06
496a	Kevin Glover **RC** (G back)	.10	.08	.04
497	Mel Gray	.03	.02	.01
498	Rodney Peete	.10	.08	.04
499	Dave Brown	.03	.02	.01
500	Jerry Holmes	.03	.02	.01
501	Chris Jacke	.03	.02	.01
502	Alan Veingrad	.03	.02	.01
503	Mark Lee	.03	.02	.01
504	Tony Mandarich	.03	.02	.01
505	Brian Noble	.03	.02	.01
506	Jeff Query	.03	.02	.01
507	Ken Ruettgers	.03	.02	.01
508	Patrick Allen	.03	.02	.01
509	Curtis Duncan	.03	.02	.01
510	William Fuller	.03	.02	.01
511	Haywood Jeffires **RC**	.50	.40	.20
512	Sean Jones	.03	.02	.01
513	Terry Kinard	.03	.02	.01
514	Bruce Matthews	.03	.02	.01

#	Player	NM/M	NM	E
515	Gerald McNeil	.03	.02	.01
516	Greg Montgomery RC	.08	.06	.03
517	Warren Moon	.20	.15	.08
518	Mike Munchak	.03	.02	.01
519	Allen Pinkett	.03	.02	.01
520	Pat Beach	.03	.02	.01
521	Eugene Daniel	.03	.02	.01
522	Kevin Call	.03	.02	.01
523	Ray Donaldson	.03	.02	.01
524	Jeff Herrod RC	.08	.06	.03
525	Keith Taylor	.03	.02	.01
526	Jack Trudeau	.03	.02	.01
527	Deron Cherry	.03	.02	.01
528	Jeff Donaldson	.03	.02	.01
529	Albert Lewis	.03	.02	.01
530	Pete Mandley	.03	.02	.01
531	Chris Martin RC	.08	.06	.03
532	Christian Okoye	.03	.02	.01
533	Steve Pelluer	.03	.02	.01
534	Kevin Ross	.03	.02	.01
535	Dan Saleaumua	.03	.02	.01
536	Derrick Thomas	.25	.20	.10
537	Mike Webster	.03	.02	.01
538	Marcus Allen	.03	.02	.01
539	Greg Bell	.03	.02	.01
540	Thomas Benson	.03	.02	.01
541	Ron Brown	.03	.02	.01
542	Scott Davis	.03	.02	.01
543	Riki Ellison	.03	.02	.01
544	Jamie Holland	.03	.02	.01
545	Howie Long	.03	.02	.01
546	Terry McDaniel	.03	.02	.01
547	Max Montoya	.03	.02	.01
548	Jay Schroeder	.03	.02	.01
549	Lionel Washington	.03	.02	.01
550	Robert Delpino	.03	.02	.01
551	Bobby Humphery	.03	.02	.01
552	Mike Lansford	.03	.02	.01
553	Michael Stewart RC	.08	.06	.03
554	Doug Smith	.03	.02	.01
555	Curt Warner	.03	.02	.01
556	Alvin Wright	.03	.02	.01
557	Jeff Cross	.03	.02	.01
558	Jeff Dellenbach RC	.08	.06	.03
559	Mark Duper	.03	.02	.01
560	Ferrell Edmunds	.03	.02	.01
561	Tim McKyer	.03	.02	.01
562	John Offerdahl	.03	.02	.01
563	Reggie Roby	.03	.02	.01
564	Pete Stovanovich	.03	.02	.01
565	Alfred Anderson	.03	.02	.01
566	Ray Berry	.03	.02	.01
567	Rick Fenney	.03	.02	.01
568	Rich Gannon RC	2.00	1.50	.80
569	Tim Irwin	.03	.02	.01
570	Hassan Jones	.03	.02	.01
571	Cris Carter	.30	.25	.12
572	Kirk Lowdermilk	.03	.02	.01
573	Reggie Rutland RC	.08	.06	.03
574	Ken Stills	.03	.02	.01
575	Bruce Armstrong	.03	.02	.01
576	Irving Fryar	.03	.02	.01
577	Roland James	.03	.02	.01
578	Robert Perryman	.03	.02	.01
579	Cedric Jones	.03	.02	.01
580	Steve Grogan	.03	.02	.01
581	Johnny Rembert	.03	.02	.01
582	Ed Reynolds	.03	.02	.01
583	Brent Williams	.03	.02	.01
584	Marc Wilson	.03	.02	.01
585	Hoby Brenner	.03	.02	.01
586	Stan Brock	.03	.02	.01
587	Jim Dombrowski RC	.08	.06	.03
588	Joel Hilgenberg RC	.10	.08	.04
589	Robert Massey	.03	.02	.01
590	Floyd Turner	.10	.08	.04
591	Ottis Anderson	.03	.02	.01
592	Mark Bavaro	.03	.02	.01
593	Maurice Carthon	.03	.02	.01
594	Eric Dorsey RC	.10	.08	.04
595	Myron Guyton	.03	.02	.01
596	Jeff Hostetler RC	.75	.60	.30
597	Sean Landeta	.03	.02	.01
598	Lionel Manuel	.03	.02	.01
599	Odessa Turner RC	.10	.08	.04
600	Perry Williams	.03	.02	.01
601	James Hasty	.03	.02	.01
602	Erik McMillan	.03	.02	.01
603	Alex Gordon	.03	.02	.01
604	Ron Stallworth	.03	.02	.01
605	Byron Evans RC	.10	.08	.04
606	Ron Heller RC	.10	.08	.04
607	Wes Hopkins (black, red fumble/interceptions head)	.10	.08	.04
607a	Wes Hopkins (red fumble/interceptions head)	.10	.08	.04

#	Player	NM/M	NM	E
608	Mickey Shuler	.03	.02	.01
609	Seth Joyner	.03	.02	.01
610	Jim McMahon	.03	.02	.01
611	Mike Pitts	.03	.02	.01
612	Izel Jenkins	.03	.02	.01
613	Anthony Bell	.03	.02	.01
614	David Galloway	.03	.02	.01
615	Eric Hill	.03	.02	.01
616	Cedric Mack	.03	.02	.01
617	Freddie Joe Nunn	.03	.02	.01
618	Tootie Robbins	.03	.02	.01
619	Tom Tupa RC	.10	.08	.04
620	Joe Wolf	.03	.02	.01
621	Dermontti Dawson	.03	.02	.01
622	Thomas Everett	.03	.02	.01
623	Tunch Ilken	.03	.02	.01
624	Hardy Nickerson	.03	.02	.01
625	Gerald Williams RC	.08	.06	.03
626	Rod Woodson (black, red fumbles/interceptions head)	.25	.20	.10
626a	Rod Woodson (red fumbles/interceptions head)	.25	.20	.10
627	Rod Bernstine (error TE)	.25	.20	.10
627a	Rod Bernstine (corrected RB)	.15	.11	.06
628	Courtney Hall	.03	.02	.01
629	Ronnie Harmon	.03	.02	.01
630	Anthony Miller (WR back)	.25	.20	.10
630a	Anthony Miller (WR-KR back)	.20	.15	.08
630b	Anthony Miller (WR-KR back, front)	.20	.15	.08
631	Joe Philips	.03	.02	.01
632	Leslie O'Neal (LB-DE front)	.20	.15	.08
632a	Leslie O'Neal (LB front)	.15	.11	.06
633	David Richards (G-T back)	.05	.04	.02
633a	David Richards (G back)	.05	.04	.02
634	Mark Vlasic	.08	.06	.03
635	Lee Williams	.03	.02	.01
636	Chet Brooks	.03	.02	.01
637	Keena Turner	.03	.02	.01
638	Kevin Fagan	.03	.02	.01
639	Brent Jones RC	.70	.50	.30
640	Matt Millen	.03	.02	.01
641	Bubba Paris	.03	.02	.01
642	Bill Romanowski RC	.10	.08	.04
643	Fred Smerlas	.03	.02	.01
644	Dave Waymer	.03	.02	.01
645	Steve Young	.40	.30	.15
646	Brian Blades	.10	.08	.04
647	Andy Heck	.03	.02	.01
648	Dave Krieg	.03	.02	.01
649	Rufus Porter	.03	.02	.01
650	Kelly Stouffer	.03	.02	.01
651	Tony Woods	.03	.02	.01
652	Gary Anderson	.03	.02	.01
653	Reuben Davis	.03	.02	.01
654	Randy Grimes	.03	.02	.01
655	Ron Hall	.03	.02	.01
656	Eugene Marve	.03	.02	.01
657	Curt Jarvis (no "Official NFL card")	.05	.04	.02
657a	Curt Jarvis ("Official NFL card" added)	.05	.04	.02
658	Ricky Reynolds	.03	.02	.01
659	Broderick Thomas	.03	.02	.01
660	Jeff Bostic	.03	.02	.01
661	Todd Bowles RC	.10	.08	.04
662	Ravin Caldwell	.03	.02	.01
663	Russ Grimm	.03	.02	.01
664	Joe Jacoby	.03	.02	.01
665	Mark May	.03	.02	.01
666	Walter Stanley	.03	.02	.01
667	Don Warren	.03	.02	.01
668	Stan Humphries RC	.75	.60	.30
669	Jeff George (Illinois)	1.00	.70	.40
670	Blair Thomas RC (R1)	.10	.08	.04
671	Cortez Kennedy RC	.25	.20	.10
672	Keith McCants RC (R1)	.08	.06	.03
673	Junior Seau RC	1.00	.70	.40
674	Mark Carrier RC	.25	.20	.10
675	Andre Ware RC (R1)	.10	.08	.04
676	Chris Singleton RC (R1)	.10	.08	.04
677	Richmond Webb RC (R1)	.15	.11	.06
678	Ray Agnew RC (R1)	.08	.06	.03
679	Anthony Smith RC	.30	.25	.12
680	James Francis RC (R1)	.10	.08	.04
681	Percy Snow (R1)	.03	.02	.01
682	Renaldo Turnbull RC	.35	.25	.14
683	Lamar Lathon RC (R1)	.10	.08	.04
684	James Williams RC (R1)	.10	.08	.04
685	Emmitt Smith RC	6.00	4.50	2.50
686	Tony Bennett RC	.25	.20	.10

#	Player	NM/M	NM	E
687	Darrell Thompson RC	.20	.15	.08
688	Steve Broussard (R1)	.08	.06	.03
689	Eric Green RC	.25	.20	.10
690	Ben Smith RC (R1)	.08	.06	.03
691	Bern Brostek RC (R1)	.08	.06	.03
692	Rodney Hampton RC	1.25	.90	.50
693	Dexter Carter RC (R1)	.10	.08	.04
694	Rob Moore RC	1.50	1.25	.60
695	Alexander Wright RC (R2)	.20	.15	.08
696	Darion Conner RC (R2)	.10	.08	.04
697	Reggie Rembert (R2)	.03	.02	.01
698	Terry Wooden RC (R2) (back number 51)	.05	.04	.02
698a	Terry Wooden RC (R2) (back number 90)	.05	.04	.02
699	Reggie Cobb RC	.60	.45	.25
700	Anthony Thompson (R2)	.03	.02	.01
701	Fred Washington (R2)	.05	.04	.02
701a	Fred Washington (Final Update memorial)	.05	.04	.02
702	Ron Cox RC (R2)	.10	.08	.04
703	Robert Blackmon RC (R2)	.10	.08	.04
704	Dan Owens RC (R2)	.10	.08	.04
705	Anthony Johnson RC (R2)	.15	.11	.06
706	Aaron Wallace RC (R2)	.15	.11	.06
707	Harold Green RC	.35	.25	.14
708	Keith Sims RC (R2)	.10	.08	.04
709	Tim Grunhard RC (R2)	.10	.08	.04
710	Jeff Alm (R2)	.03	.02	.01
711	Carwell Gardner RC	.10	.08	.04

1990 Pro Set Collect-A-Books

These 2-1/2" x 3-1/2" 8-page booklets were issued in three series of 12. Each series came in its own box, and included one player who was a rookie. The front of the booklet has an action photo of the player, along with his name, and set logos. Page two has a color mug shot of the player; pages 3-4 provide a career summary in text form. Pages 6-7 are a double-page action photo of the player; page 8 has statistics and trademark information. Two players who have booklets - Eric Dickerson and Michael Dean Perry - were not included in Pro Set's regular 1990 card set.

	NM/M	NM	E
Complete Set (36):	7.50	5.75	3.00
Common Player:	.15	.11	.06

#	Player	NM/M	NM	E
1	Jim Kelly	.50	.40	.20
2	Andre Ware	.20	.15	.08
3	Phil Simms	.25	.20	.10
4	Bubby Brister	.20	.15	.08
5	Bernie Kosar	.25	.20	.10
6	Eric Dickerson	.25	.20	.10
7	Barry Sanders	.75	.60	.30
8	Jerry Rice	1.00	.70	.40
9	Keith Millard	.15	.11	.06
10	Erik McMillan	.15	.11	.06
11	Ickey Woods	.15	.11	.06
12	Mike Singletary	.25	.20	.10
13	Randall Cunningham	.30	.25	.12
14	Boomer Esiason	.25	.20	.10
15	John Elway	.25	.20	.10
16	Wade Wilson	.20	.15	.08
17	Troy Aikman	1.50	1.25	.60
18	Dan Marino	1.50	1.25	.60
19	Lawrence Taylor	.35	.25	.14
20	Roger Craig	.25	.20	.10
21	Merril Hoge	.15	.11	.06
22	Christian Okoye	.15	.11	.06
23	Blair Thomas	.15	.11	.06
24	William Perry	.20	.15	.08
25	Bill Fralic	.15	.11	.06
26	Warren Moon	.30	.25	.12
27	Jim Everett	.20	.15	.08
28	Jeff George	.50	.40	.20
29	Shane Conlan	.15	.11	.06
30	Carl Banks	.15	.11	.06
31	Charles Mann	.15	.11	.06
32	Anthony Munoz	.25	.20	.10
33	Dan Hampton	.25	.20	.10
34	Michael Dean Perry	.15	.11	.06
35	Joey Browner	.15	.11	.06
36	Ken O'Brien	.20	.15	.08

1990 Pro Set Draft Day

Each of these cards, numbered 669, was issued by Pro Set on the day of the 1990 NFL draft to present various scenarios for the draft. The card fronts preview Pro Set's 1990 main set design; each back uses a horizontal format and includes a mug shot, biographical information and a player profile.

	NM/M	NM	E
Complete Set (3):	5.00	18.50	10.00
Common Player:	1.00	2.25	1.25
669A Jeff George	2.00	1.50	.80
669B Jeff George	2.00	1.50	.80
669D Keith McCants	1.00	.70	.40

1990 Pro Set Pro Bowl 106

Participants in the annual Pro Bowl game are honored in this 106-card set produced by Pro Set. The set includes a white binder which features the Pro Bowl game logo on the front cover. The cards, except for four, are identical to their corresponding numbered counterparts in the regular set; there is no indication they were in the Pro Bowl set. However, four players who are featured in the Final Update set have "1990 Final Update" on the front (#s 754, 766, 771 and 778). This is not written on the fronts of the regular update cards.

Complete Set (106):	10.00	7.50	4.00
Common Player:	.03	.02	.01
39 Cornelius Bennett	.10	.08	.04
40 Jim Kelly	.25	.20	.10
49 Neal Anderson	.05	.04	.02
52 Richard Dent	.05	.04	.02
53 Jay Hilgenberg	.03	.02	.01
57 Mike Singletary	.08	.06	.03
86 Steve Atwater	.05	.04	.02
91 Bobby Humphrey	.03	.02	.01
96 Jerry Ball	.03	.02	.01
98 Lomas Brown	.03	.02	.01
102 Barry Sanders	1.00	.70	.40
114 Sterling Sharpe	.75	.60	.30
118 Ray Childress	.05	.04	.02
119 Ernest Givins	.05	.04	.02
122 Drew Hill	.05	.04	.02
135 Rohn Stark	.03	.02	.01
137 Clarence Verdin	.03	.02	.01
144 Nick Lowery	.03	.02	.01
155 Bo Jackson	.40	.30	.15
156 Don Mosebar	.03	.02	.01
158 Greg Townsend	.05	.04	.02
160 Steve Wisniewski	.03	.02	.01
173 Jackie Slater	.05	.04	.02
186 Joey Browner	.05	.04	.02
188 Chris Doleman	.05	.04	.02
189 Steve Jordan	.03	.02	.01
190 Carl Lee	.03	.02	.01
191 Randall McDaniel	.05	.04	.02
210 Morten Andersen	.05	.04	.02
215 Vaughan Johnson	.03	.02	.01
218 Pat Swilling	.05	.04	.02
226 Pepper Johnson	.03	.02	.01
229 Bart Oates	.03	.02	.01
231 Lawrence Taylor	.15	.11	.06
244 Jerome Brown	.03	.02	.01
247 Randall Cunningham	.15	.11	.06
248 Keith Jackson	.15	.11	.06
252 Reggie White	.25	.20	.10
271 David Little	.03	.02	.01
276 Marion Butts	.10	.08	.04
289 Charles Haley	.05	.04	.02
291 Ronnie Lott	.10	.08	.04
292 Guy McIntyre	.03	.02	.01
293 Joe Montana	1.00	.70	.40
295 Jerry Rice	.75	.60	.30
320 Earnest Byner	.03	.02	.01
321 Gary Clark	.05	.04	.02
323 Darrell Green	.05	.04	.02
324 Jim Lachey	.03	.02	.01
334 Pro Bowl Aloha Stadium	.03	.02	.01
434 Andre Rison	.25	.20	.10
438 Kent Hull	.03	.02	.01
440 Andre Reed	.15	.11	.06
443 Bruce Smith	.10	.08	.04
444 Thurman Thomas	.25	.20	.10
447 Mark Bortz	.03	.02	.01
462 David Fulcher	.03	.02	.01
464 Rodney Holman	.03	.02	.01
467 Anthony Munoz	.10	.08	.04
491 Dennis Smith	.03	.02	.01
497 Mel Gray	.03	.02	.01
514 Bruce Matthews	.03	.02	.01
517 Warren Moon	.25	.20	.10
529 Albert Lewis	.05	.04	.02
534 Kevin Ross	.03	.02	.01
536 Derrick Thomas	.20	.15	.08
557 Jeff Cross	.03	.02	.01
560 Ferrell Edmunds	.03	.02	.01
562 John Offerdahl	.05	.04	.02

575 Bruce Armstrong	.03	.02	.01
597 Sean Landeta	.03	.02	.01
626 Rod Woodson	.20	.15	.08
630 Anthony Miller	.10	.08	.04
632 Leslie O'Neal	.05	.04	.02
677 Richmond Webb	.05	.04	.02
754 Steve Tasker	8.00	6.00	3.25
766 Reyna Thompson	8.00	6.00	3.25
771 Johnny Johnson	12.00	9.00	4.75
778 Wayne Haddix	8.00	6.00	3.25
800 Mark Carrier	.10	.08	.04
SB1 Super Bowl I	.15	.11	.06
SB2 Super Bowl II	.15	.11	.06
SB3 Super Bowl III	.15	.11	.06
SB4 Super Bowl IV	.15	.11	.06
SB5 Super Bowl V	.15	.11	.06
SB6 Super Bowl VI	.15	.11	.06
SB7 Super Bowl VII	.15	.11	.06
SB8 Super Bowl VIII	.15	.11	.06
SB9 Super Bowl IX	.15	.11	.06
SB10 Super Bowl X	.15	.11	.06
SB11 Super Bowl XI	.15	.11	.06
SB12 Super Bowl XII	.15	.11	.06
SB13 Super Bowl XIII	.15	.11	.06
SB14 Super Bowl XIV	.15	.11	.06
SB15 Super Bowl XV	.15	.11	.06
SB16 Super Bowl XVI	.15	.11	.06
SB17 Super Bowl XVII	.15	.11	.06
SB18 Super Bowl XVIII	.15	.11	.06
SB19 Super Bowl XIX	.15	.11	.06
SB20 Super Bowl XX	.15	.11	.06
SB21 Super Bowl XXI	.15	.11	.06
SB22 Super Bowl XXII	.15	.11	.06
SB23 SUper Bowl XXIII	.15	.11	.06
SB24 Super Bowl XXIV	.15	.11	.06

1990 Pro Set Super Bowl 160

This set was issued in its own commemorative box and traces the history of the Super Bowl in four categories - Super Bowl Tickets, Super Bowl Supermen, Super Bowl Super Moments, and puzzle cards, which make up art for Super Bowl XXV. Cards were also sold in packs of eight and were originally given away at Texas Stadium during the Dallas Cowboys Pro Set Sports Collectors Show.

	NM/M	NM	E
Complete Set (160):	5.00	3.75	2.00
Common Player:	.05	.04	.02
Common Puzzle:	.03	.02	.01
1 SB 1 Ticket	.10	.08	.04
2 SB II Ticket	.05	.04	.02
3 SB III Ticket	.05	.04	.02
4 SB IV Ticket	.05	.04	.02
5 SB V Ticket	.05	.04	.02
6 SB VI Ticket	.05	.04	.02
7 SB VII Ticket	.05	.04	.02
8 SB VIII Ticket	.05	.04	.02
9 SB IV Ticket	.05	.04	.02
10 SB X Ticket	.05	.04	.02
11 SB XI Ticket	.05	.04	.02
12 SB XII Ticket	.05	.04	.02
13 SB XIII Ticket	.05	.04	.02
14 SB XIV Ticket	.05	.04	.02
15 SB XV Ticket	.05	.04	.02
16 SB XVI Ticket	.05	.04	.02
17 SB XVII Ticket	.05	.04	.02
18 SB XVIII Ticket	.05	.04	.02
19 SB XIX Ticket	.05	.04	.02
20 SB XX Ticket	.05	.04	.02
21 SB XXI Ticket	.05	.04	.02
22 SB XXII Ticket	.05	.04	.02
23 SB XXIII Ticket	.05	.04	.02
24 SB XXIV Ticket	.05	.04	.02
25 Tom Flores (CO)	.05	.04	.02
26 Joe Gibbs (CO)	.05	.04	.02
27 Tom Landry (CO)	.15	.11	.06
28 Vince Lombardi (CO)	.15	.11	.06
29 Chuck Noll (CO)	.10	.08	.04
30 Don Shula (CO)	.15	.11	.06
31 Bill Walsh (CO)	.15	.11	.06

32 Terry Bradshaw	.25	.20	.10
33 Joe Montana	.50	.40	.20
34 Joe Namath	.35	.25	.14
35 Jim Plunkett	.10	.08	.04
36 Bart Starr	.20	.15	.08
37 Roger Staubach	.35	.25	.14
38 Marcus Allen	.20	.15	.08
39 Roger Craig	.10	.08	.04
40 Larry Csonka	.10	.08	.04
41 Franco Harris	.10	.08	.04
42 John Riggins	.10	.08	.04
43 Timmy Smith	.05	.04	.02
44 Matt Snell	.05	.04	.02
45 Fred Biletnikoff	.10	.08	.04
46 Cliff Branch	.05	.04	.02
47 Max McGee	.10	.08	.04
48 Jerry Rice	.50	.40	.20
49 Ricky Sanders	.05	.04	.02
50 George Sauer	.05	.04	.02
51 John Stallworth	.10	.08	.04
52 Lynn Swann	.15	.11	.06
53 Dave Casper	.05	.04	.02
54 Marv Fleming	.05	.04	.02
55 Dan Ross	.05	.04	.02
56 Forrest Gregg	.10	.08	.04
57 Winston Hill	.05	.04	.02
58 Joe Jacoby	.05	.04	.02
59 Anthony Munoz	.10	.08	.04
60 Art Shell	.10	.08	.04
61 Rayfield Wright	.05	.04	.02
62 Ron Yary	.05	.04	.02
63 Randy Cross	.05	.04	.02
64 Jerry Kramer	.10	.08	.04
65 Bob Kuechenberg	.05	.04	.02
66 Larry Little	.05	.04	.02
67 Gerry Mullins	.05	.04	.02
68 John Niland	.05	.04	.02
69 Gene Upshaw	.10	.08	.04
70 Dave Dalby	.05	.04	.02
71 Jim Langer	.05	.04	.02
72 Dwight Stephenson	.05	.04	.02
73 Mike Webster	.10	.08	.04
74 Ross Browner	.05	.04	.02
75 Willie Davis	.10	.08	.04
76 Richard Dent	.10	.08	.04
77 L.C. Greenwood	.10	.08	.04
78 Ed "Too Tall" Jones	.10	.08	.04
79 Harvey Martin	.05	.04	.02
80 Dwight White	.05	.04	.02
81 Buck Buchanan	.10	.08	.04
82 Curley Culp	.05	.04	.02
83 Manny Fernandez	.05	.04	.02
84 Joe Greene	.15	.11	.06
85 Bob Lilly	.15	.11	.06
86 Alan Page	.15	.11	.06
87 Randy White	.10	.08	.04
88 Nick Buoniconti	.10	.08	.04
89 Lee Roy Jordan	.10	.08	.04
90 Jack Lambert	.15	.11	.06
91 Willie Lanier	.10	.08	.04
92 Ray Nitschke	.15	.11	.06
93 Mike Singletary	.15	.11	.06
94 Carl Banks	.05	.04	.02
95 Charles Haley	.05	.04	.02
96 Jack Ham	.10	.08	.04
97 Ted Hendricks	.10	.08	.04
98 Chuck Howley	.05	.04	.02
99 Rod Martin	.05	.04	.02
100 Herb Adderley	.10	.08	.04
101 Mel Blount	.10	.08	.04
102 Willie Brown	.10	.08	.04
103 Lester Hayes	.05	.04	.02
104 Mike Haynes	.05	.04	.02
105 Ronnie Lott	.15	.11	.06
106 Mel Renfro	.05	.04	.02
107 Eric Wright	.05	.04	.02
108 Dick Anderson	.05	.04	.02
109 David Fulcher	.05	.04	.02
110 Cliff Harris	.05	.04	.02
111 Johnny Robinson	.05	.04	.02
112 Jake Scott	.05	.04	.02
113 Donnie Shell	.05	.04	.02
114 Mike Wagner	.05	.04	.02
115 Willie Wood	.10	.08	.04
116 Ray Guy	.10	.08	.04
117 Lee Johnson	.05	.04	.02
118 Larry Seiple	.05	.04	.02
119 Jerrel Wilson	.05	.04	.02
120 Kevin Butler	.05	.04	.02
121 Don Chandler	.05	.04	.02
122 Jan Stenerud	.10	.08	.04
123 Jim Turner	.05	.04	.02
124 Ray Wersching	.05	.04	.02
125 Larry Anderson	.05	.04	.02
126 Stanford Jennings	.05	.04	.02
127 Mike Nelms	.05	.04	.02
128 John Taylor	.10	.08	.04
129 Fulton Walker	.05	.04	.02

130	E.J. Holub	.05	.04	.02
131	George Siefert CO	.05	.04	.02
132	Jim Taylor	.10	.08	.04
133	Joe Theismann	.15	.11	.06
134	Johnny Unitas	.25	.20	.10
135	Reggie Williams	.05	.04	.02
136	Two Networks (Paul Christman, Frank Gifford)	.05	.04	.02
137	**First Fly-Over** (Military jets)	.05	.04	.02
138	Weeb Ewbank (Super Bowl Super Moment)	.05	.04	.02
139	Otis Taylor (Super Bowl Super Moment)	.05	.04	.02
140	Jim O'Brien (Super Bowl Super Moment)	.05	.04	.02
141	Garo Yepremian (Super Bowl Super Moment)	.05	.04	.02
142	Pete Rozelle, Art Rooney	.05	.04	.02
143	Percy Howard (Super Bowl Super Moment)	.05	.04	.02
144	Jackie Smith (Super Bowl Super Moment)	.05	.04	.02
145	**Record Crowd** (Super Bowl Super Moment)	.05	.04	.02
146	**Yellow Ribbon UER** (Fourth line says more than year, should say more than a year)	.05	.04	.02
147	Dan Bunz, Charles Alexander (Super Bowl Super Moment)	.05	.04	.02
148	**Smurfs** (Redskins) (Super Bowl Super Moment)	.05	.04	.02
149	William "The Fridge" Perry (Scores)(Super Bowl Super Moment)	.05	.04	.02
150	Phil McConkey (Super Bowl Super Moment)	.05	.04	.02
151	Doug Williams (Super Bowl Super Moment)	.05	.04	.02
152	**Top row left**	.03	.02	.01
153	**Top row middle XXV Theme Art Puzzle**	.03	.02	.01
154	**Top row left XXV Theme Art Puzzle**	.03	.02	.01
155	**Center row left XXV Theme Art Puzzle**	.03	.02	.01
156	**Center row right XXV Theme Art Puzzle**	.03	.02	.01
157	**Center row right XXV Theme Art Puzzle**	.03	.02	.01
158	**Bottom row left VVX Theme Art Puzzle**	.03	.02	.01
159	**Bottom row right XXV Theme Art Puzzle**	.03	.02	.01
160	**Bottom row right XXV Theme Art Puzzle**	.03	.02	.01
	Special Offer Card	.10	.08	.04

1990 Pro Set Super Bowl Binder

This 56-card set, with Buick as its sponsor, was given to those who attended Super Bowl XXV between the New York Giants and Buffalo Bills. Included within the set are a cover card for Buick, a commemorative card for the 2-millionth Super Bowl fan, cards for the NFC and AFC Championship trophies, and a Ronnie Lott Stay in School card from Pro Set's Final Update set. Players from the two participating Super Bowl teams are featured in the set, along with 27 cards featuring fans' choices for the Silver Anniversary Super Bowl Team. Super Bowl participants' cards have the same photos as their counterparts in the regular set, but have NFC or AFC Champions designated on the front. A binder with pages that hold four cards per page was also issued to store the cards in.

Complete Set (56):		25.00	18.50	10.00
Common Player:		.25	.20	.10
1	Vince Lombardi	.35	.25	.14
2	Joe Montana	4.00	3.00	1.50
3	Larry Csonka	.50	.40	.20
4	Franco Harris	.50	.40	.20
5	Jerry Rice	3.00	2.25	1.25
6	Lynn Swann	.50	.40	.20
7	Forrest Gregg	.35	.25	.14
8	Art Shell	.35	.25	.14
9	Jerry Kramer	.25	.20	.10
10	Gene Upshaw	.35	.25	.14
11	Mike Webster	.35	.25	.14
12	Dave Casper	.25	.20	.10
13	Jan Stenerud	.35	.25	.14
14	John Taylor	.35	.25	.14
15	L.C. Greenwood	.25	.20	.10
16	Ed "Too Tall" Jones	.35	.25	.14
17	Joe Greene	.50	.40	.20
18	Randy White	.50	.40	.20

19	Jack Lambert	.50	.40	.20
20	Mike Singletary	.35	.25	.14
21	Jack Ham	.35	.25	.14
22	Ted Hendricks	.35	.25	.14
23	Mel Blount	.35	.25	.14
24	Ronnie Lott	.50	.40	.20
25	Donnie Shell	.25	.20	.10
26	Willie Wood	.35	.25	.14
27	Ray Guy	.35	.25	.14
SC1	**2,000,000th Fan**	.50	.40	.20
SC2	**Buick Checklist Card**	.50	.40	.20
SC3	**Lamar Hunt Trophy**	.50	.40	.20
SC4	**George Halas Trophy**	.50	.40	.20
799	**Ronnie Lott Education**	.35	.25	.14
39	Cornelius Bennett	.50	.40	.20
40	Jim Kelly	1.50	1.25	.60
47	Darryl Talley	.25	.20	.10
48	Marv Levy (CO)	.25	.20	.10
437	Shane Conlan	.25	.20	.10
438	Kent Hull	.25	.20	.10
440	Andre Reed	1.00	.70	.40
443	Bruce Smith	1.00	.70	.40
444	Thurman Thomas	2.50	2.00	1.00
725	Howard Ballard	.25	.20	.10
753	James Lofton	.50	.40	.20
754	Steve Tasker	.25	.20	.10
223	Carl Banks	.25	.20	.10
226	Pepper Johnson	.25	.20	.10
228	Dave Meggett	.25	.20	.10
230	Phil Simms	.50	.40	.20
231	Lawrence Taylor	.75	.60	.30
232	Bill Parcells (CO)	.35	.25	.14
591	Ottis Anderson	.50	.40	.20
592	Mark Bavaro	.25	.20	.10
596	Jeff Hostetler	.35	.25	.14
692	Rodney Hampton	1.00	.70	.40
765	Stephen Baker	.25	.20	.10
766	Reyna Thompson	.25	.20	.10

1990 Pro Set Super Bowl MVPs

These 1990 Pro Set Series II inserts feature the 24 players who were named MVP of a Super Bowl. Each card front has a portrait of the player done by artist Merv Corning. Two silver panels are also on the front, one on top, the other at the bottom. The player's name is in the bottom panel, which is bordered by two stripes featuring the player's team colors. The horizontal card back has a color action photo and summary of the player's Super Bowl achievement. The cards are numbered on the back in a chronological manner, beginning with Super Bowl I.

		NM/M	NM	E
Complete Set (24):		4.00	3.00	1.50
Common Player:		.10	.08	.04
1	Super Bowl I (Bart Starr)	.30	.25	.12
2	Super Bowl II (Bart Starr)	.30	.25	.12
3	Super Bowl III (Joe Namath)	.50	.40	.20
4	Super Bowl IV (Len Dawson)	.20	.15	.08
5	Super Bowl V (Chuck Howley)	.10	.08	.04
6	Super Bowl VI (Roger Staubach)	.50	.40	.20
7	Super Bowl VII (Jake Scott)	.10	.08	.04
8	Super Bowl VIII (Larry Csonka)	.30	.25	.12
9	Super Bowl IX (Franco Harris)	.30	.25	.12
10	Super Bowl X (Lynn Swann)	.20	.15	.08
11	Super Bowl XI (Fred Biletnikoff)	.20	.15	.08
12	Super Bowl XII (Harvey Martin)	.10	.08	.04
13	Super Bowl XIII (Terry Bradshaw)	.40	.30	.15
14	Super Bowl XIV (Terry Bradshaw)	.40	.30	.15
15	Super Bowl XV (Jim Plunkett)	.20	.15	.08
16	Super Bowl XVI (Joe Montana)	.50	.40	.20
17	Super Bowl XVII (John Riggins)	.20	.15	.08
18	Super Bowl XVIII (Marcus Allen)	.20	.15	.08
19	Super Bowl XIX (Joe Montana)	.50	.40	.20
20	Super Bowl XX (Richard Dent)	.10	.08	.04
21	Super Bowl XXI (Phil Simms)	.20	.15	.08
22	Super Bowl XXII (Doug Williams)	.10	.08	.04

23	Super Bowl XXIII (Jerry Rice)	.30	.25	.12
24	Super Bowl XXIV (Joe Montana)	.50	.40	.20

1990 Pro Set Theme Art

The 25-card set spotlights Super Bowl theme art on the front, which resembles the cover art of Super Bowl programs. The Pro Set logo is in the lower left, with the Super Bowl listed in the lower right, with the site and city name listed beneath. Card backs include a photo of the winning team's championship ring. The Super Bowl number and date, along with the score, are listed at the top, with background text also included. The cards were seeded one per 1990 Pro Set Series I pack.

		NM/M	NM	E
Complete Set (24):		3.00	2.25	1.25
Common Player:		.15	.11	.06
1	**Super Bowl I**	.15	.11	.06
2	**Super Bowl II**	.15	.11	.06
3	**Super Bowl III**	.15	.11	.06
4	**Super Bowl IV**	.15	.11	.06
5	**Super Bowl V**	.15	.11	.06
6	**Super Bowl VI**	.15	.11	.06
7	**Super Bowl VII**	.15	.11	.06
8	**Super Bowl VIII**	.15	.11	.06
9	**Super Bowl IX**	.15	.11	.06
10	**Super Bowl X**	.15	.11	.06
11	**Super Bowl XI**	.15	.11	.06
12	**Super Bowl XII**	.15	.11	.06
13	**Super Bowl XIII UER** (Colgate University 7, sould be Colgate 13)	.15	.11	.06
14	**Super Bowl XIV**	.15	.11	.06
15	**Super Bowl XV**	.15	.11	.06
16	**Super Bowl XVI**	.15	.11	.06
17	**Super Bowl XVII**	.15	.11	.06
18	**Super Bowl XVIII**	.15	.11	.06
19	**Super Bowl XIX**	.15	.11	.06
20	**Super Bowl XX**	.15	.11	.06
21	**Super Bowl XXI**	.15	.11	.06
22A	**Super Bowl XXII ERR** (Jan. 31, 1989 on back)	.50	.40	.20
22B	**Super Bowl XXII COR** (Jan. 31, 1988 on back)	.15	.11	.06
23	**Super Bowl XXIII**	.15	.11	.06
24	**Super Bowl XXIV Theme Art**	.15	.11	.06

1991 Pro Set

Released in late April, Pro Set's third annual football set was again divided into two series. Subsets added this year to Series I include Heisman Heroes, Super Bowl XXV Replay, NFL Officials, and Think About It cards. World League of American Football cards made their debut in Series I as well. Again, randomly-packed insert cards were included in Series I: Super Bowl XXV logo, Walter Payton and Team 34, a mini Pro Set Gazette, Red Grange, Russell Maryland 31 Draft Pick (only in Series I), and 1,000 autographed Lawrence Taylor cards. (Key: L - leader, M - milestone, HOF - Hall of Fame, AW - college award winner, HH - Heisman hero, SBR - Super Bowl XXV replay, R - 1990 replay, NR - newsreel, O - official, M - NFL message, NFC - all-NFC team, C - coach).

		NM/M	NM	E
Complete Set (850):		18.00	13.50	7.25
Complete Series 1 (405):		7.00	5.25	2.75
Complete Series 2 (407):		7.00	5.25	2.75
Complete Final (38):		4.00	3.00	1.50
Common Player:		.03	.02	.01
Series 1 Pack (14):		.20		
Series 1 Wax Box (36):		10.00		
Series 2 Pack (14):		.30		
Series 2 Wax Box (36):		15.00		
1	Emmitt Smith (LL)	1.00	.70	.40
2	Mark Carrier (LL)	.25	.20	.10
3	Joe Montana (LL)	.50	.40	.20
4	Art Shell (LL)	.03	.02	.01
5	Mike Singletary (LL)	.03	.02	.01

6	Bruce Smith (LL)	.04	.03	.02
7	Barry Word (LL)	.03	.02	.01
8	Jim Kelly (LL)(with NFLPA logo)	.25	.20	.10
8a	Jim Kelly (LL)(without NFLPA logo)	.20	.15	.08
8b	Jim Kelly (LL)(without NFLPA logo, with registered symbol)	6.00	4.50	2.50
9	Warren Moon (LL)	.08	.06	.03
10	Barry Sanders (LL)	.50	.40	.20
11	Jerry Rice (LL)	.40	.30	.15
12	Jay Novacek (LL)	.05	.04	.02
13	Thurman Thomas (LL)	.20	.15	.08
14	Nick Lowery (LL)	.03	.02	.01
15	Mike Horan (LL)	.03	.02	.01
16	Clarence Verdin (LL)	.03	.02	.01
17	Kevin Clark (LL)	.03	.02	.01
18	Mark Carrier (LL)	.03	.02	.01
19	Derrick Thomas (LL) (error: Bills helmet on front)	15.00	11.00	6.00
19a	Derrick Thomas (LL) (corrected: Chiefs helmet on front)	.25	.20	.10
20	Ottis Anderson (M)	.03	.02	.01
21	Roger Craig (M)	.03	.02	.01
22	Art Monk (M)	.05	.04	.02
23	Chuck Noll (M)	.03	.02	.01
24	Randall Cunningham (M)	.08	.06	.03
25	Dan Marino (M)	.40	.30	.15
26	Charles Haley (M)	.03	.02	.01
27	Earl Campbell (HOF)	.10	.08	.04
28	John Hannah (HOF)	.03	.02	.01
29	Stan Jones (HOF)	.03	.02	.01
30	Tex Schramm (HOF)	.03	.02	.01
31	Jan Stenerud (HOF)	.03	.02	.01
32	Russell Maryland **RC** (AW)	.40	.30	.15
33	Chris Zorich **RC** (AW)	.15	.11	.06
34	Darryl Lewis **RC** (AW)	.03	.02	.01
35	Alfred Williams **RC** (AW)	.08	.06	.03
36	Raghib Ismail **RC** (AW)	1.00	.70	.40
37	Ty Detmer **RC** (HH)	1.00	.70	.40
38	Andre Ware (HH)	.05	.04	.02
39	Barry Sanders (HH)	.50	.40	.20
40	Tim Brown (HH)	.05	.04	.02
41	Vinny Testaverde (HH)	.03	.02	.01
42	Bo Jackson (HH)	.15	.11	.06
43	Mike Rozier (HH)	.03	.02	.01
44	Herschel Walker (HH)	.03	.02	.01
45	Marcus Allen (HH)	.04	.03	.02
46	James Lofton (SBR)(with NFLPA logo)	.05	.04	.02
46a	James Lofton (SBR) (NFLPA logo removed)	.08	.06	.03
47	Bruce Smith (SBR) ("Official NFL Card" in white)	.15	.11	.06
47a	Bruce Smith (SBR) ("Official NFL Card" in black)	.10	.08	.04
48	**Myron Guyton** (SBR)	.03	.02	.01
49	Stephen Baker (SBR)	.03	.02	.01
50	Mark Ingram (SBR)	.03	.02	.01
51	O.J. Anderson (SBR)	.03	.02	.01
52	Thurman Thomas (SBR)	.20	.15	.08
53	Matt Bahr (SBR)	.03	.02	.01
54	Scott Norwood (SBR)	.03	.02	.01
55	Stephen Baker	.03	.02	.01
56	Carl Banks	.03	.02	.01
57	Mark Collins	.03	.02	.01
58	Steve DeOssie	.03	.02	.01
59	Eric Dorsey	.03	.02	.01
60	John Elliott	.03	.02	.01
61	Myron Guyton	.03	.02	.01
62	Rodney Hampton	.50	.40	.20
63	Jeff Hostetler	.15	.11	.06
64	Erik Howard	.03	.02	.01
65	Mark Ingram	.03	.02	.01
66	Greg Jackson **RC**	.08	.06	.03
67	Leonard Marshall	.03	.02	.01
68	David Meggett	.03	.02	.01
69	Eric Moore	.03	.02	.01
70	Bart Oates	.03	.02	.01
71	Gary Reasons	.03	.02	.01
72	Bill Parcells (C)	.03	.02	.01
73	Howard Ballard	.03	.02	.01
74	Cornelius Bennett (with NFLPA logo)	.25	.20	.10
74a	Cornelius Bennett (NFLPA logo removed)	.10	.08	.04
75	Shane Conlan	.03	.02	.01
76	Kent Hull	.03	.02	.01
77	Kirby Jackson	.03	.02	.01
78	Jim Kelly (w/o logo)	.35	.25	.14
79	Mark Kelso	.03	.02	.01
80	Nate Odomes	.03	.02	.01
81	Andre Reed	.08	.06	.03
82	Jim Ritcher	.03	.02	.01
83	Bruce Smith	.03	.02	.01
84	Darryl Talley	.03	.02	.01
85	Steve Tasker	.03	.02	.01
86	Thurman Thomas	.35	.25	.14
87	James Williams	.03	.02	.01
88	Will Wolford	.03	.02	.01
89	Jeff Wright	.03	.02	.01
90	Marv Levy (C)	.03	.02	.01
91	Steve Broussard	.03	.02	.01
92	Darion Conner (error: "Drafted 1st Round '99")	6.00	4.50	2.50
92a	Darion Conner (corrected: "Drafted 2nd Round '90")	.15	.11	.06
93	Bill Fralic	.03	.02	.01
94	Tim Green	.03	.02	.01
95	Michael Haynes	.03	.02	.01
96	Chris Hinton	.03	.02	.01
97	Chris Miller	.03	.02	.01
98	Deion Sanders	.20	.15	.08
99	Jerry Glanville (C)	.03	.02	.01
100	Kevin Butler	.03	.02	.01
101	Mark Carrier (Chi.)	.03	.02	.01
102	Jim Covert	.03	.02	.01
103	Richard Dent	.03	.02	.01
104	Jim Harbaugh	.08	.06	.03
105	Brad Muster	.03	.02	.01
106	Lemuel Stinson	.03	.02	.01
107	Keith Van Horne	.03	.02	.01
108	Mike Ditka (C)	.05	.04	.02
109	Lewis Billups	.03	.02	.01
110	James Brooks	.03	.02	.01
111	Boomer Esiason	.10	.08	.04
112	James Francis	.03	.02	.01
113	David Fulcher	.03	.02	.01
114	Rodney Holman	.03	.02	.01
115	Tim McGee	.03	.02	.01
116	Anthony Munoz	.03	.02	.01
117	Sam Wyche (C)	.03	.02	.01
118	Paul Farren	.03	.02	.01
119	Thane Gash	.03	.02	.01
120	Mike Johnson	.03	.02	.01
121	Bernie Kosar (with NFLPA logo)	.05	.04	.02
121a	Bernie Kosar (NFLPA logo removed)	.10	.08	.04
122	Clay Matthews	.03	.02	.01
123	Eric Metcalf	.03	.02	.01
124	Frank Minnifield	.03	.02	.01
125	Webster Slaughter (with NFLPA logo)	.05	.04	.02
125a	Webster Slaughter (NFLPA logo removed)	.05	.04	.02
126	Bill Belichick (C)	.03	.02	.01
127	Tommie Agee	.03	.02	.01
128	Troy Aikman	1.00	.70	.40
129	Jack Del Rio	.03	.02	.01
130	John Gesek **RC**	.06	.05	.02
131	Issiac Holt	.03	.02	.01
132	Michael Irvin	.55	.40	.20
133	Ken Norton	.03	.02	.01
134	Daniel Stubbs	.03	.02	.01
135	Jimmy Johnson (C)	.05	.04	.02
136	Steve Atwater (AW)	.03	.02	.01
137	Michael Brooks	.03	.02	.01
138	John Elway	.35	.25	.14
139	Wymon Henderson	.03	.02	.01
140	Bobby Humphery	.03	.02	.01
141	Mark Jackson	.03	.02	.01
142	Karl Mecklenburg	.03	.02	.01
143	Doug Widell	.03	.02	.01
144	Dan Reeves (C)	.03	.02	.01
145	Eric Andolsek	.03	.02	.01
146	Jerry Ball	.03	.02	.01
147	Bennie Blades	.03	.02	.01
148	Lomas Brown	.03	.02	.01
149	Robert Clark	.03	.02	.01
150	Michael Cofer	.03	.02	.01
151	Dan Owens	.03	.02	.01
152	Rodney Peete	.03	.02	.01
153	Wayne Fontes (C)	.03	.02	.01
154	Tim Harris	.03	.02	.01
155	Johnny Holland	.03	.02	.01
156	Don Majkowski	.03	.02	.01
157	Tony Mandarich	.03	.02	.01
158	Mark Murphy	.03	.02	.01
159	Brian Noble	.03	.02	.01
160	Jeff Query	.03	.02	.01
161	Sterling Sharpe	.20	.15	.08
162	Lindy Infante (C)	.03	.02	.01
163	Ray Childress	.03	.02	.01
164	Ernest Givins	.03	.02	.01
165	Richard Johnson	.03	.02	.01
166	Bruce Matthews	.03	.02	.01
167	Warren Moon	.15	.11	.06
168	Mike Munchak	.03	.02	.01
169	Al Smith	.03	.02	.01
170	Lorenzo White	.08	.06	.03
171	Jack Pardee (C)	.03	.02	.01
172	Albert Bentley	.03	.02	.01
173	Duane Bickett	.03	.02	.01
174	Bill Brooks	.03	.02	.01
175	Eric Dickerson (with NFLPA logo)(error text: 667)	.50	.40	.20
175a	Eric Dickerson (NFLPA logo removed)(error text: 667)	1.25	.90	.50
175b	Eric Dickerson (NFLPA logo removed) (corrected text: 677))	.25	.20	.10
176	Ray Donaldson	.03	.02	.01
177	Jeff George	.20	.15	.08
178	Jeff Herrod	.03	.02	.01
179	Clarence Verdin	.03	.02	.01
180	Ron Meyer (C)	.03	.02	.01
181	John Alt	.03	.02	.01
182	Steve DeBerg	.03	.02	.01
183	Albert Lewis	.03	.02	.01
184	Nick Lowery	.03	.02	.01
185	Christian Okoye	.03	.02	.01
186	Stephone Paige	.03	.02	.01
187	Kevin Porter	.03	.02	.01
188	Derrick Thomas	.15	.11	.06
189	Marty Schottenheimer (C)	.03	.02	.01
190	Willie Gault	.03	.02	.01
191	Howie Long	.03	.02	.01
192	Terry McDaniel	.03	.02	.01
193	Jay Schroeder	.03	.02	.01
194	Steve Smith	.03	.02	.01
195	Greg Townsend	.03	.02	.01
196	Lionel Washington	.03	.02	.01
197	Steve Wisniewski	.03	.02	.01
198	Art Shell (C)	.03	.02	.01
199	Henry Ellard	.03	.02	.01
200	Jim Everett	.03	.02	.01
201	Jerry Gray	.03	.02	.01
202	Kevin Greene	.03	.02	.01
203	Buford McGee	.03	.02	.01
204	Tom Newberry	.03	.02	.01
205	Frank Stams, David Wyman	.03	.02	.01
206	Alvin Wright	.03	.02	.01
207	John Robinson (C)	.03	.02	.01
208	Jeff Gross	.03	.02	.01
209	Mark Duper	.03	.02	.01
210	Dan Marino	.75	.60	.30
211	Tim McKyer	.05	.04	.02
211a	Tim McKyer (traded stripe added)	.05	.04	.02
212	John Offerdahl	.03	.02	.01
213	Sammie Smith	.03	.02	.01
214	Richmond Webb	.03	.02	.01
215	Jarvis Williams	.03	.02	.01
216	Don Shula (C)	.03	.02	.01
217	Darrell Fullington (missing registered symbol by NFLPA logo)	.05	.04	.02
217a	Darrell Fullington (corrected)	.05	.04	.02
218	Tim Irwin	.03	.02	.01
219	Mike Merriweather	.03	.02	.01
220	Keith Millard	.03	.02	.01
221	Al Noga	.03	.02	.01
222	Henry Thomas	.03	.02	.01
223	Wade Wilson	.03	.02	.01
224	Gary Zimmerman	.03	.02	.01
225	Jerry Burns (C)	.03	.02	.01
226	Bruce Armstrong	.03	.02	.01
227	Marv Cook	.03	.02	.01
228	Hart Lee Dykes	.03	.02	.01
229	Tom Hodson	.03	.02	.01
230	Ronnie Lippett	.03	.02	.01
231	Ed Reynolds	.03	.02	.01
232	Chris Singleton	.03	.02	.01
233	John Stephens	.03	.02	.01
234	Dick MacPherson (C)	.03	.02	.01
235	Stan Brock	.03	.02	.01
236	Craig Heyward	.03	.02	.01
237	Vaughan Johnson	.03	.02	.01
238	Robert Massey	.03	.02	.01
239	Brett Maxie	.03	.02	.01
240	Rueben Mayes	.03	.02	.01
241	Pat Swilling	.03	.02	.01
242	Renaldo Turnbull	.03	.02	.01
243	Jim Mora (C)	.03	.02	.01
244	Kyle Clifton	.03	.02	.01
245	Jeff Criswell	.03	.02	.01
246	James Hasty	.03	.02	.01
247	Erik McMillan	.03	.02	.01
248	Scott Mersereau **RC**	.05	.04	.02
249	Ken O'Brien	.03	.02	.01

250	Blair Thomas (with NFLPA logo)	.30	.25	.12
250a	Blair Thomas (NFLPA logo removed)	.10	.08	.04
251	Al Toon	.03	.02	.01
252	Bruce Coslet (C)	.03	.02	.01
253	Eric Allen (AW)(FC)	.03	.02	.01
254	Fred Barnett	.10	.08	.04
255	Keith Byars	.03	.02	.01
256	Randall Cunningham	.10	.08	.04
257	Seth Joyner	.03	.02	.01
258	Clyde Simmons	.03	.02	.01
259	Jessie Small	.03	.02	.01
260	Andre Waters	.03	.02	.01
261	Rich Kotite (C)	.03	.02	.01
262	Roy Green	.03	.02	.01
263	Ernie Jones	.03	.02	.01
264	Tim McDonald	.03	.02	.01
265	Timm Rosenbach	.03	.02	.01
266	Rod Saddler	.03	.02	.01
267	Luis Sharpe	.03	.02	.01
268	Anthony Thompson	.03	.02	.01
269	Marcus Turner RC	.08	.06	.03
270	Joe Bugel (C)	.03	.02	.01
271	Gary Anderson (Pit.)	.03	.02	.01
272	Dermontti Dawson	.03	.02	.01
273	Eric Green	.10	.08	.04
274	Merril Hoge	.03	.02	.01
275	Tunch Ilkin	.03	.02	.01
276	David Johnson	.03	.02	.01
277	Louis Lipps	.03	.02	.01
278	Rod Woodson	.05	.04	.02
279	Chuck Noll (C)	.03	.02	.01
280	Martin Bayless	.03	.02	.01
281	Marion Butts	.05	.04	.02
282	Gill Byrd	.03	.02	.01
283	Burt Grossman	.03	.02	.01
284	Courtney Hall	.03	.02	.01
285	Anthony Miller	.03	.02	.01
286	Leslie O'Neal	.03	.02	.01
287	Billy Joe Tolliver	.03	.02	.01
288	Dan Henning (C)	.03	.02	.01
289	Dexter Carter	.03	.02	.01
290	Michael Carter	.03	.02	.01
291	Kevin Fagan	.03	.02	.01
292	Pierce Holt	.03	.02	.01
293	Guy McIntyre	.03	.02	.01
294	Tom Rathman	.03	.02	.01
295	John Taylor	.08	.06	.03
296	Steve Young	.50	.40	.20
297	George Seifert (C)	.03	.02	.01
298	Brian Blades	.03	.02	.01
299	Jeff Bryant	.03	.02	.01
300	Norm Johnson	.03	.02	.01
301	Tommy Kane	.03	.02	.01
302	Cortez Kennedy	.20	.15	.08
303	Bryan Millard	.03	.02	.01
304	John L. Williams	.03	.02	.01
306	Chuck Knox (C)(with NFLPA logo)	.10	.08	.04
306a	Chuck Knox (NFLPA logo removed)	.40	.30	.15
307	Gary Anderson (T.B.)	.03	.02	.01
308	Reggie Cobb	.10	.08	.04
309	Randy Grimes	.03	.02	.01
310	Harry Hamilton	.03	.02	.01
311	Bruce Hill	.03	.02	.01
312	Eugene Marve	.03	.02	.01
313	Ervin Randle	.03	.02	.01
314	Vinny Testaverde	.08	.06	.03
315	Richard Williamson (C)	.03	.02	.01
316	Ernest Byner	.03	.02	.01
317	Gary Clark	.08	.06	.03
318	Andre Collins (with NFLPA logo)	.05	.04	.02
318a	Andre Collins (NFLPA logo removed)	.05	.04	.02
319	Darryl Grant	.03	.02	.01
320	Chip Lohmiller	.03	.02	.01
321	Martin Mayhew	.03	.02	.01
322	Mark Rypien	.08	.06	.03
323	Alvin Walton	.03	.02	.01
324	Joe Gibbs	.03	.02	.01
325	Jerry Glanville (R)	.03	.02	.01
326	Nate Odomes (with NFLPA logo)	.05	.04	.02
326a	Nate Odomes (NFLPA logo removed)	.05	.04	.02
327	Boomer Esiason	.03	.02	.01
328	Steve Tasker (with NFLPA logo)	.05	.04	.02
328a	Steve Tasker (NFLPA logo removed)	.05	.04	.02
329	Jerry Rice	.25	.20	.10
330	Jeff Rutledge	.03	.02	.01
331	KC defense (R)	.03	.02	.01
332	Rams (R)	.03	.02	.01
333	John Taylor (R)	.03	.02	.01

334	Randall Cunningham (with NFLPA logo)	.10	.08	.04
334a	Randall Cunningham (NFLPA logo removed)	.10	.08	.04
335	Bo Jackson	.10	.08	.04
336	Lawrence Taylor	.08	.06	.03
337	Warren Moon	.10	.08	.04
338	Alan Grant	.03	.02	.01
339	Steve DeBerg	.03	.02	.01
340	Playoff(Mark Clayton) (TM on Chief #27's shoulder)	.05	.04	.02
340a	Playoff(Mark Clayton) (TM away from Chief #27)	.05	.04	.02
341	Playoff(Jim Kelly) (with NFLPA logo)	.05	.04	.02
341a	Playoff(Jim Kelly) (NFLPA logo removed)	.05	.04	.02
342	NFC Championship(Matt Bahr) (R)	.03	.02	.01
343	Robert Tisch RC	.08	.06	.03
344	Sam Jankovich	.03	.02	.01
345	John Elway	.08	.06	.03
346	Bo Jackson	.08	.06	.03
347	Paul Tagliabue	.03	.02	.01
348	Ronnie Lott	.05	.04	.02
349	**Super Bowl XXV Teleclinic**	.03	.02	.01
350	Whitney Houston	.08	.06	.03
351	**U.S. Troops**	.03	.02	.01
352	Art McNally (O)	.03	.02	.01
353	Dick Jorgensen (O)	.03	.02	.01
354	Jerry Seeman (O)	.03	.02	.01
355	Jim Tunney (O)	.03	.02	.01
356	Gerry Austin (O)	.03	.02	.01
357	Gene Barth (O)	.03	.02	.01
358	Red Cashion (O)	.03	.02	.01
359	Tom Dooley (O)	.03	.02	.01
360	Johnny Grier (O)	.03	.02	.01
361	Pat Haggerty (O)	.03	.02	.01
362	Dale Hamer (O)	.03	.02	.01
363	Dick Hantak (O)	.03	.02	.01
364	Jerry Markbreit (O)	.03	.02	.01
365	Gordon McCarter (O)	.03	.02	.01
366	Bob McElwee (O)	.03	.02	.01
367	Howard Roe (O)	.03	.02	.01
368	Tom White (O)	.03	.02	.01
369	Norm Schachter (O)	.03	.02	.01
370	Warren Moon (small type)	.12	.09	.05
370a	Warren Moon (large type)	.10	.08	.04
371	Boomer Esiason (small type)	.05	.04	.02
371a	Boomer Esiason (large type)	.05	.04	.02
372	Troy Aikman (small type)	.50	.40	.20
372a	Troy Aikman (large type)	.50	.40	.20
373	Carl Banks (small type)	.05	.04	.02
373a	Carl Banks (large type)	.05	.04	.02
374	Jim Everett (small type)	.05	.04	.02
374a	Jim Everett (large type)	.05	.04	.02
375	Anthony Munoz (small type)(error back: "dificul," "latrapar") (error front: "Quadante," "Antony")	.05	.04	.02
375a	Anthony Munoz (small type)(corrected back: "dicifil", "atrapar")(error front: "Quadante," "Antony")	.05	.04	.02
375b	Anthony Munoz (large type)(error front: "Quadante," "Antony")	.05	.04	.02
375c	Anthony Munoz (large type)(corrected front: "Quedate," "Anthony")	.05	.04	.02
376	Ray Childress (small type)	.05	.04	.02
376a	Ray Childress (large type)	.05	.04	.02
377	Charles Mann (small type)	.05	.04	.02
377a	Charles Mann (large type)	.05	.04	.02
378	Jackie Slater (small type)	.05	.04	.02
378a	Jackie Slater (large type)	.05	.04	.02
379	Jerry Rice (NFC)	.25	.20	.10
380	Andre Rison (NFC)	.10	.08	.04
381	Jim Lachey (NFC)	.03	.02	.01
382	Jackie Slater (NFC)	.03	.02	.01
383	Randall McDaniel (NFC)	.03	.02	.01
384	Mark Bortz (NFC)	.03	.02	.01
385	Jay Hilgenberg (NFC)	.03	.02	.01
386	Keith Jackson (NFC)	.05	.04	.02
387	Joe Montana (NFC)	.50	.40	.20
388	Barry Sanders (NFC)	.50	.40	.20
389	Neal Anderson (NFC)	.03	.02	.01
390	Reggie White (NFC)	.05	.04	.02
391	Chris Doleman (NFC)	.03	.02	.01

392	Jerome Brown (NFC)	.03	.02	.01
393	Charles Haley (NFC)	.03	.02	.01
394	Lawrence Taylor (NFC)	.05	.04	.02
395	Pepper Johnson (NFC)	.03	.02	.01
396	Mike Singletary (NFC)	.03	.02	.01
397	Darrell Green (NFC)	.03	.02	.01
398	Carl Lee (NFC)	.03	.02	.01
399	Joey Browner (NFC)	.03	.02	.01
400	Ronnie Lott (NFC)	.05	.04	.02
401	Sean Landeta (NFC)	.03	.02	.01
402	Morten Andersen (NFC)	.03	.02	.01
403	Mel Gray (NFC)	.03	.02	.01
404	Reyna Thompson (NFC)	.03	.02	.01
405	Jimmy Johnson (NFC)	.03	.02	.01
406	Andre Reed	.05	.04	.02
407	Anthony Miller	.03	.02	.01
408	Anthony Munoz	.03	.02	.01
409	Bruce Armstrong	.03	.02	.01
410	Bruce Matthews	.03	.02	.01
411	Mike Munchak	.03	.02	.01
412	Kent Hull	.03	.02	.01
413	Rodney Holman	.03	.02	.01
414	Warren Moon	.10	.08	.04
415	Thurman Thomas	.15	.11	.06
416	Marion Butts	.05	.04	.02
417	Bruce Smith	.03	.02	.01
418	Greg Townsend	.03	.02	.01
419	Ray Childress	.03	.02	.01
420	Derrick Thomas	.08	.06	.03
421	Leslie O'Neal	.03	.02	.01
422	John Offerdahl	.03	.02	.01
423	Shane Conlan	.03	.02	.01
424	Rod Woodson	.04	.03	.02
425	Albert Lewis	.03	.02	.01
426	Steve Atwater	.03	.02	.01
427	David Fulcher	.03	.02	.01
428	Rohn Stark	.03	.02	.01
429	Nick Lowery	.03	.02	.01
430	Clarence Verdin	.03	.02	.01
431	Steve Tasker	.03	.02	.01
432	Art Shell	.03	.02	.01
433	Scott Case	.03	.02	.01
434	Tory Epps	.03	.02	.01
435	Mike Gann	.03	.02	.01
436	Brian Jordan	.03	.02	.01
437	Mike Kenn	.03	.02	.01
438	John Rade	.03	.02	.01
439	Andre Rison	.30	.25	.12
440	Mike Rozier	.03	.02	.01
441	Jessie Tuggle	.03	.02	.01
442	Don Beebe	.03	.02	.01
443	John Davis RC	.08	.06	.03
444	James Lofton	.03	.02	.01
445	Keith McKeller	.03	.02	.01
446	Frank Reich	.03	.02	.01
447	Scott Norwood	.03	.02	.01
448	Frank Reich	.03	.02	.01
449	Leon Seals	.03	.02	.01
450	Leonard Smith	.03	.02	.01
451	Neal Anderson	.03	.02	.01
452	Trace Armstrong	.03	.02	.01
453	Mark Bortz	.03	.02	.01
454	Wendell Davis	.05	.04	.02
455	Shaun Gayle	.03	.02	.01
456	Jay Hilgenberg	.03	.02	.01
457	Steve McMichael	.03	.02	.01
458	Mike Singletary	.05	.04	.02
459	Donnell Woolford	.03	.02	.01
460	Jim Breech	.03	.02	.01
461	Eddie Brown	.03	.02	.01
462	Barney Bussey	.03	.02	.01
463	Bruce Kozerski	.03	.02	.01
464	Tim Krumrie	.03	.02	.01
465	Bruce Reimers	.03	.02	.01
466	Kevin Walker RC	.08	.06	.03
467	Ickey Woods	.03	.02	.01
468	Carl Zander	.03	.02	.01
469	Mike Baab	.03	.02	.01
470	Brian Brennan	.03	.02	.01
471	Rob Burnett RC	.08	.06	.03
472	Raymond Clayborn	.03	.02	.01
473	Reggie Langhorne	.03	.02	.01
474	Kevin Mack	.03	.02	.01
475	Anthony Pleasant	.03	.02	.01
476	Joe Morris	.03	.02	.01
477	Dan Fike	.03	.02	.01
478	Ray Horton	.03	.02	.01
479	Jim Jeffcoat	.03	.02	.01
480	Jimmie Jones	.03	.02	.01
481	Kelvin Martin	.03	.02	.01
482	Nate Newton	.03	.02	.01
483	Danny Noonan	.03	.02	.01
484	Jay Novacek	.10	.08	.04
485	Emmitt Smith	2.00	1.50	.80
486	James Washington RC	.08	.06	.03
487	Simon Fletcher	.03	.02	.01
488	Ron Holmes	.03	.02	.01
489	Mike Horan	.03	.02	.01

490	Vance Johnson	.03	.02	.01
491	Keith Kartz	.03	.02	.01
492	Greg Kragen	.03	.02	.01
493	Ken Lanier	.03	.02	.01
494	Warren Powers	.03	.02	.01
495	Dennis Smith	.03	.02	.01
496	Jeff Campbell	.03	.02	.01
497	Ken Dallafior	.03	.02	.01
498	Dennis Gibson	.03	.02	.01
499	Kevin Glover	.03	.02	.01
500	Mel Gray	.03	.02	.01
501	Eddie Murray	.03	.02	.01
502	Barry Sanders	1.25	.90	.50
503	Chris Spielman	.03	.02	.01
504	William White	.03	.02	.01
505	Matt Brock RC	.08	.06	.03
506	Robert Brown	.03	.02	.01
507	LeRoy Butler	.03	.02	.01
508	James Campen	.03	.02	.01
509	Jerry Holmes	.03	.02	.01
510	Perry Kemp	.03	.02	.01
511	Ken Ruettgers	.03	.02	.01
512	Scott Stephen	.03	.02	.01
513	Ed West	.03	.02	.01
514	Cris Dishman RC	.08	.06	.03
515	Curtis Duncan	.03	.02	.01
516	Drew Hill	.03	.02	.01
517	Haywood Jeffires	.10	.08	.04
518	Sean Jones	.03	.02	.01
519	Lamar Lathon	.03	.02	.01
520	Don Maggs	.03	.02	.01
521	Bubba McDowell	.03	.02	.01
522	Johnny Meads	.03	.02	.01
523	Chip Banks (error no text)	.03	.02	.01
523a	Chip Banks (corrected)	.03	.02	.01
524	Pat Beach	.03	.02	.01
525	Sam Clancy	.03	.02	.01
526	Eugene Daniel	.03	.02	.01
527	Jon Hand	.03	.02	.01
528	Jessie Hester	.03	.02	.01
529	Mike Prior (error no textual information)	.08	.06	.03
529a	Mike Prior (corrected)	.03	.02	.01
530	Keith Taylor	.03	.02	.01
531	Donnell Thompson	.03	.02	.01
532	Dino Hackett	.05	.04	.02
533	David Lutz	.03	.02	.01
534	Chris Martin	.03	.02	.01
535	Kevin Ross	.03	.02	.01
536	Dan Saleaumua	.03	.02	.01
537	Neil Smith	.05	.04	.02
538	Percy Snow	.03	.02	.01
539	Robb Thomas	.03	.02	.01
540	Barry Word	.08	.06	.03
541	Marcus Allen	.03	.02	.01
542	Eddie Anderson	.03	.02	.01
543	Scott Davis	.03	.02	.01
544	Mervyn Fernandez	.03	.02	.01
545	Ethan Horton	.03	.02	.01
546	Ronnie Lott	.08	.06	.03
547	Don Mosebar	.03	.02	.01
548	Jerry Robinson	.03	.02	.01
549	Aaron Wallace	.03	.02	.01
550	Flipper Anderson	.05	.04	.02
551	Cleveland Gary	.03	.02	.01
552	Damone Johnson	.03	.02	.01
553	Duval Love	.03	.02	.01
554	Irv Pankey	.03	.02	.01
555	Mike Piel	.03	.02	.01
556	Jackie Slater	.03	.02	.01
557	Michael Stewart	.03	.02	.01
558	Pat Terrell	.03	.02	.01
559	J.B. Brown	.03	.02	.01
560	Mark Clayton	.03	.02	.01
561	Ferrell Edmunds	.03	.02	.01
562	Harry Galbreath	.03	.02	.01
563	David Griggs	.03	.02	.01
564	Jim C. Jensen	.03	.02	.01
565	Louis Oliver	.03	.02	.01
566	Tony paige	.05	.04	.02
567	Keith Sims	.03	.02	.01
568	Joey Browner	.03	.02	.01
569	Anthony Carter	.05	.04	.02
570	Chris Doleman	.05	.04	.02
571	Rich Gannon	.05	.04	.02
572	Hassan Jones	.03	.02	.01
573	Steve Jordan	.03	.02	.01
574	Carl Lee	.03	.02	.01
575	Randall McDaniel	.03	.02	.01
576	Herschel Walker	.05	.04	.02
577	Ray Agnew	.03	.02	.01
578	Vincent Brown	.03	.02	.01
579	Irving Fryar	.05	.04	.02
580	Tim Goad	.03	.02	.01
581	Maurice Hurst	.03	.02	.01
582	Fred Marion	.03	.02	.01
583	Johnny Rembert	.03	.02	.01
584	Andre Tippett	.03	.02	.01

585	Brent Williams	.03	.02	.01
586	Morten Andersen	.03	.02	.01
587	Toi Cook RC	.08	.06	.03
588	Jim Dombrowski	.03	.02	.01
589	Dalton Hilliard	.05	.04	.02
590	Rickey Jackson	.03	.02	.01
591	Eric Martin	.03	.02	.01
592	Sam Mills	.03	.02	.01
593	Bobby Hebert	.03	.02	.01
594	Steve Walsh	.03	.02	.01
595	Ottis Anderson	.03	.02	.01
596	Pepper Johnson	.03	.02	.01
597	Bob Kratch RC	.05	.04	.02
598	Sean Landeta	.03	.02	.01
599	Doug Riesenberg	.03	.02	.01
600	William Roberts	.03	.02	.01
601	Phil Simms	.05	.04	.02
602	Lawrence Taylor	.08	.06	.03
603	Everson Walls	.03	.02	.01
604	Brad Baxter	.05	.04	.02
605	Dennis Byrd	.03	.02	.01
606	Jeff Lageman	.03	.02	.01
607	Pat Leahy	.03	.02	.01
608	Rob Moore	.08	.06	.03
609	Joe Mott	.03	.02	.01
610	Tony Stargell	.03	.02	.01
611	Brian Washington	.03	.02	.01
612	Marvin Washington RC	.15	.11	.06
613	David Alexander	.03	.02	.01
614	Jerome Brown	.03	.02	.01
615	Byron Evans	.03	.02	.01
616	Ron Heller	.03	.02	.01
617	Wes Hopkins	.03	.02	.01
618	Keith Jackson	.10	.08	.04
619	Heath Sherman	.03	.02	.01
620	Reggie White	.10	.08	.04
621	Calvin Williams	.10	.08	.04
622	Ken Harvey	.03	.02	.01
623	Eric Hill	.03	.02	.01
624	Johnny Johnson	.20	.15	.08
625	Freddie Joe Nunn	.03	.02	.01
626	Ricky Proehl	.08	.06	.03
627	Tootie Robbins	.03	.02	.01
628	Jay Taylor	.03	.02	.01
629	Tom Tupa	.03	.02	.01
630	Jim Wahler RC	.08	.06	.03
631	Bubby Brister	.03	.02	.01
632	Thomas Everett	.03	.02	.01
633	Bryan Hinkle	.03	.02	.01
634	Carnell Lake	.03	.02	.01
635	David Little	.03	.02	.01
636	Hardy Nickerson	.03	.02	.01
637	Gerald Williams	.03	.02	.01
638	Keith Willis	.03	.02	.01
639	Tim Worley	.03	.02	.01
640	Rod Bernstine	.03	.02	.01
641	Frank Cornish	.03	.02	.01
642	Gary Plummer	.03	.02	.01
643	Henry Rolling RC	.08	.06	.03
644	Sam Seale	.03	.02	.01
645	Junior Seau	.20	.15	.08
646	Billy Ray Smith	.03	.02	.01
647	Broderick Thompson	.03	.02	.01
648	Derrick Walker RC	.08	.06	.03
649	Todd Bowles	.03	.02	.01
650	Don Griffin	.03	.02	.01
651	Charles Haley	.03	.02	.01
652	Brent Jones	.03	.02	.01
653	Joe Montana	1.00	.70	.40
654	Jerry Rice	.75	.60	.30
655	Bill Romanowski	.03	.02	.01
656	Michael Walter	.03	.02	.01
657	Dave Waymer	.03	.02	.01
658	Jeff Chadwick	.03	.02	.01
659	Derrick Fenner	.03	.02	.01
660	Nesby Glasgow	.03	.02	.01
661	Jacob Green	.03	.02	.01
662	Dwayne Harper RC	.08	.06	.03
663	Andy Heck	.03	.02	.01
664	Dave Krieg	.03	.02	.01
665	Rufus Porter	.03	.02	.01
666	Eugene Robinson	.03	.02	.01
667	Mark Carrier	.03	.02	.01
668	Steve Christie	.03	.02	.01
669	Reuben Davis	.03	.02	.01
670	Paul Gruber	.03	.02	.01
671	Wayne Haddix	.03	.02	.01
672	Ron Hall	.03	.02	.01
673	Keith McCants	.03	.02	.01
674	Ricky Reynolds	.03	.02	.01
675	Mark Robinson	.03	.02	.01
676	Jeff Bostic	.03	.02	.01
677	Darrell Green	.05	.04	.02
678	Markus Koch	.03	.02	.01
679	Jim Lachey	.03	.02	.01
680	Charles Mann	.03	.02	.01
681	Wilber Marshall	.03	.02	.01
682	Art Monk	.05	.04	.02

683	Gerald Riggs	.03	.02	.01
684	Ricky Sanders	.03	.02	.01
685	Ray Handley replaces Bill Parcels	.03	.02	.01
686	NFL Announces Expansion	.03	.02	.01
687	Miami Gets Super Bowl XXIX	.03	.02	.01
688	George Young named NFL Executive of yea	.03	.02	.01
689	Five-millionith fan visits Pro FB HOF	.03	.02	.01
690	Sports Illustrated poll pro football #1	.03	.02	.01
691	American Bowl London	.03	.02	.01
692	American Bowl Berlin	.03	.02	.01
693	American Bowl Tokyo	.03	.02	.01
694	Joe Ferguson (LEG)	.03	.02	.01
695	Carl Hairston (LEG)	.03	.02	.01
696	Dan Hampton (LEG)	.03	.02	.01
697	Mike Haynes (LEG)	.03	.02	.01
698	Marty Lyons (LEG)	.03	.02	.01
699	Ozzie Newsome (LEG)	.08	.06	.03
700	Scott Studwell (LEG)	.03	.02	.01
701	Mike Webster (LEG)	.04	.03	.02
702	Dwayne Woodruff (LEG)	.03	.02	.01
703	Larry Kennan (CO)	.03	.02	.01
704	Stan Gelbaugh RC	.08	.06	.03
705	John Brantley	.03	.02	.01
706	Danny Lockett	.03	.02	.01
707	Anthony Parker RC	.08	.06	.03
708	Dan Crossman	.03	.02	.01
709	Eric Wilkerson	.03	.02	.01
710	Judd Garrett RC	.08	.06	.03
711	Tony Baker	.03	.02	.01
712	1st Place BW(Randall Cunningham)	.06	.05	.02
713	2nd Place BW(Mark Ingram)	.03	.02	.01
714	3rd Place BW(Pete Holohan, Barney Bussey, Carl Carter)	.03	.02	.01
715	1st Place Color Action(Sterling Sharpe)	.08	.06	.03
716	2nd Place Color Action(Jim Harbaugh)	.04	.03	.02

1991 Pro Set Cinderella Story

This nine-card perforated sheet was available inside The Official NFL Pro Set Card Book. The card fronts are similar to the design Pro Set used for its 1991 set, except there are four cards which have black-and-white photos instead of color ones. Each card back is numbered indicating it is in the Cinderella Story set, which profiles players who have achieved success in the NFL despite formidable roadblocks in their paths. If a card is perforated from the sheet, it measures standard 2-1/2" x 3-1/2".

		NM/M	NM	E
Complete Set (9):		8.00	6.00	3.25
Common Player:		.60	.45	.25
1	Rocky Bleier	1.00	.70	.40
2	Tom Dempsey	.60	.45	.25
3	Dan Hampton	.75	.60	.30
4	Charlie Hennigan	.60	.45	.25
5	Dante Lavelli	.75	.60	.30
6	Jim Plunkett	.75	.60	.30
7	1968 New York Jets (Joe Namath Handing Off)	1.50	1.25	.60
8	1981 San Francisco 49ers (Joe Montana Passing)	3.00	2.25	1.25
9	1979 Tampa Bay Bucs (Ricky Bell Running)	.60	.45	.25

1991 Pro Set Draft Day

These cards, issued in conjunction with the 1991 NFL draft, create different scenarios regarding the first selection in the draft. Each card is numbered 694 and features the player in his collegiate uniform. The card back is in a horizontal format and has another player photo on it, plus biographical information and statistics.

Complete Set (8):		50.00	185.00	100.00
Common Player:		5.00	15.00	8.00
694A	Nick Bell	5.00	3.75	2.00
694B	Mike Croel	5.00	3.75	2.00
694C	Raghib (Rocket) Ismail (Cowboys)	15.00	11.00	6.00
694D	Raghib (Rocket) Ismail (Falcons)	15.00	11.00	6.00
694E	Raghib (Rocket) Ismail (Patriots)	15.00	11.00	6.00
694F	Todd Lyght	5.00	15.00	8.00
694G	Russell Maryland	5.00	3.75	2.00
694H	Dan McGwire	5.00	3.75	2.00

1991 Pro Set Inserts

These cards were random inserts in 1991 Pro Set Series I and Series II packs. The Super Bowl XXV logo card is a continuation of the set which was issued in 1989. The Pro Set Gazette card highlights Pro Set's 1991 cards. The Lawrence Taylor cards were autographed; 500 of each were made. The Walter Payton card details the Hall of Famer's post-NFL career in auto racing, while the card for Red Grange honors the Galloping Ghost, who passed away in 1991. Grange's card front features a sepia-toned photo. The previous six cards were Series I inserts; Series II inserts included full-bleed photos on the card front and have horizontal backs. They are also numbered, except for the Pro Set Gazette and Santa Claus cards.

	NM/M	NM	E
Complete Set (16):	400.00	300.00	150.00
Common Player:	.15	.11	.06

1991 Pro Set National Banquet

Each of these cards can be identified by the National Sports Collectors Convention logo on the front. The cards, which feature full-bleed color photos, were given away during the convention, held in Anaheim, Calif. Each card back is numbered and includes a player profile, biographical information and a mug shot.

		NM/M	NM	E
	Complete Set (5):	5.00	3.75	2.00
	Common Player:	.50	.40	.20
1	Ronnie Lott	1.50	1.25	.60
2	Roy Firestone (Television celebrity)	1.25	.90	.50
3	Roger Craig	1.25	.90	.50
4	ProFiles Television Show(Craig James, Tim Brant)	1.00	.70	.40
5	**Title Card**	.50	.40	.20

1991 Pro Set Platinum

Pro Set issued this 315-card set in two series - 150 and 165 cards each. The glossy cards have full-bleed color action photos on the front, along with the Pro Set Platinum logo. The card backs use a horizontal format and include another action photo, plus the player's name, team and position. A "Platinum Performer" feature is also included, highlighting an outstanding performance by the player. Each series is numbered alphabetically by team, beginning with Atlanta. Subsets include "Special Teams" (#s 128-135), "Platinum Performance" (#s 136-150) and "Platinum Prospects" (#s 286-315). Random insert cards include "Special Collectibles" (numbered PC1-PC10) and redemption cards for a limited-edition Platinum card of Paul Brown or Emmitt Smith.

		NM/M	NM	E
	Complete Set (315):	12.00	9.00	4.75
	Complete Series 1 (150):	5.00	3.75	2.00
	Complete Series 2 (165):	7.00	5.25	2.75
	Common Player:	.05	.04	.02
	Pack (16):	.20		
	Wax Box (36):	6.00		
1	Chris Miller	.05	.04	.02
2	Andre Rison	.25	.20	.10
3	Tim Green	.05	.04	.02
4	Jessie Tuggle	.05	.04	.02
5	Thurman Thomas	.40	.30	.15
6	Darryl Talley	.05	.04	.02
7	Kent Hull	.05	.04	.02
8	Bruce Smith	.05	.04	.02
9	Shane Conlan	.05	.04	.02
10	Jim Harbaugh	.08	.06	.03
11	Neal Anderson	.08	.06	.03
12	Mark Bortz	.05	.04	.02
13	Richard Dent	.05	.04	.02
14	Steve McMichael	.05	.04	.02
15	James Brooks	.05	.04	.02
16	Boomer Esiason	.08	.06	.03
17	Tim Krumrie	.05	.04	.02
18	James Francis	.05	.04	.02
19	Lewis Billups	.05	.04	.02
20	Eric Metcalf	.05	.04	.02
21	Kevin Mack	.05	.04	.02

22	Clay Matthews	.05	.04	.02
23	Mike Johnson	.05	.04	.02
24	Troy Aikman	1.00	.70	.40
25	Emmitt Smith	2.00	1.50	.80
26	Daniel Stubbs	.05	.04	.02
27	Ken Norton	.05	.04	.02
28	John Elway	.40	.30	.15
29	Bobby Humphrey	.05	.04	.02
30	Simon Fletcher	.05	.04	.02
31	Karl Mecklenburg	.05	.04	.02
32	Rodney Peete	.05	.04	.02
33	Barry Sanders	1.00	.70	.40
34	Michael Cofer	.05	.04	.02
35	Jerry Ball	.05	.04	.02
36	Sterling Sharpe	.20	.15	.08
37	Tony Mandarich	.05	.04	.02
38	Brian Noble	.05	.04	.02
39	Tim Harris	.05	.04	.02
40	Warren Moon	.15	.11	.06
41	Ernest Givins	.05	.04	.02
42	Mike Munchak	.05	.04	.02
43	Sean Jones	.05	.04	.02
44	Ray Childress	.05	.04	.02
45	Jeff George	.30	.25	.12
46	Albert Bentley	.05	.04	.02
47	Duane Bickett	.05	.04	.02
48	Steve DeBerg	.05	.04	.02
49	Christian Okoye	.05	.04	.02
50	Neil Smith	.05	.04	.02
51	Derrick Thomas	.25	.20	.10
52	Willie Gault	.05	.04	.02
53	Don Mosebar	.05	.04	.02
54	Howie Long	.05	.04	.02
55	Greg Townsend	.05	.04	.02
56	Terry McDaniel	.05	.04	.02
57	Jackie Slater	.05	.04	.02
58	Jim Everett	.05	.04	.02
59	Cleveland Gary	.05	.04	.02
60	Mike Piel	.05	.04	.02
61	Jerry Gray	.05	.04	.02
62	Dan Marino	.75	.60	.30
63	Sammie Smith	.05	.04	.02
64	Richmond Webb	.05	.04	.02
65	Louis Oliver	.05	.04	.02
66	Ferrell Edmunds	.05	.04	.02
67	Jeff Cross	.05	.04	.02
68	Wade Wilson	.05	.04	.02
69	Chris Doleman	.05	.04	.02
70	Joey Browner	.05	.04	.02
71	Keith Millard	.05	.04	.02
72	John Stephens	.05	.04	.02
73	Andre Tippett	.05	.04	.02
74	Brent Williams	.05	.04	.02
75	Craig Heyward	.05	.04	.02
76	Eric Martin	.05	.04	.02
77	Pat Swilling	.05	.04	.02
78	Sam Mills	.05	.04	.02
79	Jeff Hostetler	.25	.20	.10
80	Ottis Anderson	.05	.04	.02
81	Lawrence Taylor	.10	.08	.04
82	Pepper Johnson	.05	.04	.02
83	Blair Thomas	.05	.04	.02
84	Al Toon	.05	.04	.02
85	Ken O'Brien	.05	.04	.02
86	Erik McMillan	.05	.04	.02
87	Dennis Byrd	.05	.04	.02
88	Randall Cunningham	.10	.08	.04
89	Fred Barnett	.15	.11	.06
90	Seth Joyner	.05	.04	.02
91	Reggie White	.15	.11	.06
92	Timm Rosenbach	.05	.04	.02
93	Johnny Johnson	.25	.20	.10
94	Tim McDonald	.05	.04	.02
95	Freddie Joe Nunn	.05	.04	.02
96	Bubby Brister	.08	.06	.03
97	Gary Anderson	.05	.04	.02
98	Merril Hoge	.05	.04	.02
99	Keith Willis	.05	.04	.02
100	Rod Woodson	.08	.06	.03
101	Billy Joe Tolliver	.05	.04	.02
102	Marion Butts	.08	.06	.03
103	Rod Bernstine	.05	.04	.02
104	Lee Williams	.05	.04	.02
105	Burt Grossman	.05	.04	.02
106	Tom Rathman	.05	.04	.02
107	John Taylor	.10	.08	.04
108	Michael Carter	.05	.04	.02
109	Guy McIntyre	.05	.04	.02
110	Pierce Holt	.05	.04	.02
111	John L. Williams	.05	.04	.02
112	Dave Krieg	.05	.04	.02
113	Bryan Millard	.05	.04	.02
114	Cortez Kennedy	.30	.25	.12
115	Derrick Fenner	.05	.04	.02
116	Vinny Testaverde	.08	.06	.03
117	Reggie Cobb	.25	.20	.10
118	Gary Anderson	.05	.04	.02
119	Bruce Hill	.05	.04	.02

120	Wayne Haddix	.05	.04	.02
121	Broderick Thomas	.05	.04	.02
122	Keith McCants	.05	.04	.02
123	Andre Collins	.05	.04	.02
124	Earnest Byner	.05	.04	.02
125	Jim Lachey	.05	.04	.02
126	Mark Rypien	.10	.08	.04
127	Charles Mann	.05	.04	.02
128	Nick Lowery	.05	.04	.02
129	Chip Lohmiller	.05	.04	.02
130	Mike Horan	.05	.04	.02
131	Rohn Stark	.05	.04	.02
132	Sean Landeta	.05	.04	.02
133	Clarence Verdin	.05	.04	.02
134	Johnny Bailey	.05	.04	.02
135	Herschel Walker	.05	.04	.02
136	Bo Jackson	.40	.30	.15
137	Dexter Carter	.05	.04	.02
138	Warren Moon	.10	.08	.04
139	Joe Montana	1.00	.70	.40
140	Jerry Rice	.75	.60	.30
141	Deion Sanders	.30	.25	.12
142	Ronnie Lippett	.05	.04	.02
143	Terance Mathis	.05	.04	.02
144	Gaston Green	.05	.04	.02
145	Dean Biasucci	.05	.04	.02
146	Charles Haley	.05	.04	.02
147	Derrick Thomas	.25	.20	.10
148	Lawrence Taylor	.10	.08	.04
149	Art Shell	.05	.04	.02
150	Bill Parcells	.05	.04	.02
151	Steve Broussard	.05	.04	.02
152	Darion Conner	.05	.04	.02
153	Bill Fralic	.05	.04	.02
154	Mike Gann	.05	.04	.02
155	Tim McKyer	.05	.04	.02
156	Don Beebe	.05	.04	.02
157	Cornelius Bennett	.05	.04	.02
158	Andre Reed	.10	.08	.04
159	Leonard Smith	.05	.04	.02
160	Will Wolford	.05	.04	.02
161	Mark Carrier	.05	.04	.02
162	Wendell Davis	.10	.08	.04
163	Jay Hilgenberg	.05	.04	.02
164	Brad Muster	.05	.04	.02
165	Mike Singletary	.05	.04	.02
166	Eddie Brown	.05	.04	.02
167	David Fulcher	.05	.04	.02
168	Rodney Holman	.05	.04	.02
169	Anthony Munoz	.05	.04	.02
170	Craig Taylor	.05	.04	.02
171	Mike Baab	.05	.04	.02
172	David Grayson	.05	.04	.02
173	Reggie Langhorne	.05	.04	.02
174	Joe Morris	.05	.04	.02
175	Kevin Gogan	.10	.08	.04
176	Jack Del Rio	.05	.04	.02
177	Issiac Holt	.05	.04	.02
178	Michael Irvin	.60	.45	.25
179	Jay Novacek	.15	.11	.06
180	Steve Atwater	.05	.04	.02
181	Mark Jackson	.05	.04	.02
182	Ricky Nattiel	.05	.04	.02
183	Warren Powers	.05	.04	.02
184	Dennis Smith	.05	.04	.02
185	Bennie Blades	.05	.04	.02
186	Lomas Brown	.05	.04	.02
187	Robert Clark	.05	.04	.02
188	Mel Gray	.05	.04	.02
189	Chris Spielman	.05	.04	.02
190	Johnny Holland	.05	.04	.02
191	Don Majkowski	.05	.04	.02
192	Bryce Paup **RC**	.50	.40	.20
193	Darrell Thompson	.15	.11	.06
194	Ed West	.05	.04	.02
195	Cris Dishman	.15	.11	.06
196	Drew Hill	.05	.04	.02
197	Bruce Matthews	.05	.04	.02
198	Bubba McDowell	.05	.04	.02
199	Allen Pinkett	.05	.04	.02
200	Bill Brooks	.05	.04	.02
201	Jeff Herrod	.05	.04	.02
202	Anthony Johnson	.10	.08	.04
203	Mike Prior	.05	.04	.02
204	John Alt	.05	.04	.02
205	Stephone Paige	.05	.04	.02
206	Kevin Ross	.05	.04	.02
207	Dan Saleaumua	.05	.04	.02
208	Barry Word	.10	.08	.04
209	Marcus Allen	.05	.04	.02
210	Roger Craig	.05	.04	.02
211	Ronnie Lott	.10	.08	.04
212	Winston Moss	.05	.04	.02
213	Jay Schroeder	.05	.04	.02
214	Robert Delpino	.05	.04	.02
215	Henry Ellard	.05	.04	.02
216	Kevin Greene	.05	.04	.02
217	Tom Newberry	.05	.04	.02

218	Michael Stewart	.05	.04	.02
219	Mark Duper	.05	.04	.02
220	Mark Higgs RC	.30	.25	.12
221	John Offerdahl	.05	.04	.02
222	Keith Sims	.05	.04	.02
223	Anthony Carter	.05	.04	.02
224	Cris Carter	.05	.04	.02
225	Steve Jordan	.05	.04	.02
226	Randall McDaniel	.05	.04	.02
227	Al Noga	.05	.04	.02
228	Ray Agnew	.05	.04	.02
229	Bruce Armstrong	.05	.04	.02
230	Bruce Armstrong	.05	.04	.02
231	Greg McMurtry	.05	.04	.02
232	Chris Singleton	.05	.04	.02
233	Morten Andersen	.05	.04	.02
234	Vince Buck	.05	.04	.02
235	Gill Fenerty	.05	.04	.02
236	Rickey Jackson	.05	.04	.02
237	Vaughan Johnson	.05	.04	.02
238	Carl Banks	.05	.04	.02
239	Mark Collins	.05	.04	.02
240	Rodney Hampton	.50	.40	.20
241	David Meggett	.05	.04	.02
242	Bart Oates	.05	.04	.02
243	Kyle Clifton	.05	.04	.02
244	Jeff Lageman	.05	.04	.02
245	Freeman McNeil	.05	.04	.02
246	Rob Moore	.20	.15	.08
247	Eric Allen	.05	.04	.02
248	Keith Byars	.05	.04	.02
249	Keith Jackson	.10	.08	.04
250	Jim McMahon	.05	.04	.02
251	Andre Waters	.05	.04	.02
252	Ken Harvey	.05	.04	.02
253	Ernie Jones	.05	.04	.02
254	Luis Sharpe	.05	.04	.02
255	Anthony Thompson	.05	.04	.02
256	Tom Tupa	.05	.04	.02
257	Eric Green	.10	.08	.04
258	Barry Foster	.50	.40	.20
259	Bryan Hinkle	.05	.04	.02
260	Tunch Ilkin	.05	.04	.02
261	Louis Lipps	.05	.04	.02
262	Gill Byrd	.05	.04	.02
263	John Friesz	.10	.08	.04
264	Anthony Miller	.05	.04	.02
265	Junior Seau	.25	.20	.10
266	Ronnie Harmon	.05	.04	.02
267	Harris Barton	.05	.04	.02
268	Todd Bowles	.05	.04	.02
269	Don Griffin	.05	.04	.02
270	Bill Romanowski	.05	.04	.02
271	Steve Young	.50	.40	.20
272	Brian Blades	.05	.04	.02
273	Jacob Green	.05	.04	.02
274	Rufus Porter	.05	.04	.02
275	Eugene Robinson	.05	.04	.02
276	Mark Carrier	.05	.04	.02
277	Reuben Davis	.05	.04	.02
278	Paul Gruber	.05	.04	.02
279	Gary Clark	.10	.08	.04
280	Darrell Green	.05	.04	.02
281	Wilber Marshall	.05	.04	.02
282	Matt Millen	.05	.04	.02
283	Alvin Walton	.05	.04	.02
284	Joe Gibbs	.05	.04	.02
285	Don Shula	.05	.04	.02
286	Larry Brown RC	.15	.11	.06
287	Mike Croel RC	.30	.25	.12
288	Antone Davis RC	.10	.08	.04
289	Ricky Ervins RC	.25	.20	.10
290	Brett Favre RC	5.00	3.75	2.00
291	Pat Harlow RC	.10	.08	.04
292	Michael Jackson RC	.60	.45	.25
293	Henry Jones RC	.25	.20	.10
294	Aaron Craver RC	.10	.08	.04
295	Nick Bell RC	.25	.20	.10
296	Todd Lyght RC	.15	.11	.06
297	Todd Marinovich RC	.10	.08	.04
298	Russell Maryland RC	.35	.25	.14
299	Kanavis McGhee RC	.10	.08	.04
300	Dan McGwire RC	.15	.11	.06
301	Charles McRae	.10	.08	.04
302	Eric Moten	.10	.08	.04
303	Jerome Henderson	.10	.08	.04
304	Browning Nagle RC	.25	.20	.10
305	Mike Pritchard RC	.35	.25	.14
306	Stanley Richard RC	.30	.25	.12
307	Randal Hill RC	.25	.20	.10
308	Leonard Russell RC	1.00	.70	.40
309	Eric Swann RC	.15	.11	.06
310	Phil Hansen RC	.15	.11	.06
311	Moe Gardner RC	.15	.11	.06
312	Jon Vaughn RC	.15	.11	.06
313	Aeneas Williams RC	.10	.08	.04
314	Alfred Williams RC	.15	.11	.06
315	Harvey Williams RC	.35	.25	.14

1991 Pro Set Platinum PC

These 10 insert cards were randomly included in Series II Platinum packs. Each is numbered on the card back using a "PC" prefix. The card front has a full-bleed color action photo, plus the set logo. The back has another photo and player summary, all designed in a horizontal format. The cards were divided into three subsets - Platinum Profile, Platinum Photo and Platinum Game Breaker.

		NM/M	NM	E
Complete Set (10):		10.00	7.50	4.00
Common Player:		.50	.40	.20
1	Bobby Hebert	.50	.40	.20
2	Art Monk	.50	.40	.20
3	Kenny Walker	.50	.40	.20
4	**Low Fives**	.50	.40	.20
5	Kevin Mack	.50	.40	.20
6	Neal Anderson	.50	.40	.20
7	Gaston Green	.50	.40	.20
8	Barry Sanders	3.00	2.25	1.25
9	Emmitt Smith	5.00	3.75	2.00
10	Thurman Thomas	1.50	1.25	.60

1991 Pro Set Promos

These six promotional cards were distributed in various manners. Each is unnumbered. The Kids on the Block card was given away during the Super Bowl XXV Football Clinic, which featured NFL stars talking about drug education. The card was sponsored by Pro Set, Sports Illustrated for Kids and The Learning Channel, which broadcast the clinic. The Super Bowl XXV Card Show II card is similiar to the Card Show I issued in 1989, except the front gives the date of the second card show, which occurred Jan. 24-27, 1991. The cards for William Roberts and Michael Dean Perry (there were two versions for the Perry card) were intended to be in the previously issued Pro Bowl set, but were withdrawn. The Emmitt Smith card was a mail-in offer through the Pro Set Gazette, a quarterly publication designed to provide an overview of the hobby to young collectors.

		NM/M	NM	E
Complete Set (6):		25.00	110.00	60.00
Common Player:		.50	1.50	.80
NNO	**NLF Kids on the Block** (Tele-clinic)	.50	1.50	.80
NNO	**Super Bowl XXV** (Card Show II)	5.00	3.75	2.00
NNO	Michael Dean Perry Pro Bowl (unnumbered, with Pro Set logo)	6.00	4.50	2.50
NN0	Michael Dean Perry Pro Bowl (unnumbered, without Pro Set logo)	6.00	4.50	2.50
NNO	William Roberts Pro Bowl (unnumbered)	6.00	4.50	2.50
NNO	Emmitt Smith Gazette (Pro Set Gazette)	4.00	3.00	1.50

1991 Pro Set Spanish

These cards have the same photos on them as their regular 1991 Pro Set counterparts, but the card numbers have been changed. Also, the big difference is that all text and information on the card is in Spanish. Five insert cards (ES1-ES5) were also randomly included in packs.

Complete Set (300):		10.00	7.50	4.00
Common Player:		.03	.02	.01
1	Steve Broussard	.03	.02	.01
2	Darion Conner	.03	.02	.01
3	Tory Epps	.03	.02	.01
4	Bill Fralic	.03	.02	.01
5	Mike Gann	.03	.02	.01
6	Chris Miller	.15	.11	.06
7	Andre Rison	.20	.15	.08
8	Deion Sanders	.25	.20	.10
9	Jessie Tuggle	.03	.02	.01
10	Cornelius Bennett	.10	.08	.04
11	Shane Conlan	.05	.04	.02
12	Kent Hull	.03	.02	.01
13	Kirby Jackson	.03	.02	.01
14	James Lofton	.15	.11	.06
15	Andre Reed	.15	.11	.06
16	Bruce Smith	.15	.11	.06
17	Darryl Talley	.05	.04	.02
18	Thurman Thomas	.50	.40	.20
19	Neal Anderson	.15	.11	.06
20	Trace Armstrong	.03	.02	.01
21	Mark Carrier	.07	.05	.03
22	Wendell Davis	.03	.02	.01
23	Richard Dent	.15	.11	.06
24	Jim Harbaugh	.10	.08	.04
25	Ron Rivera	.03	.02	.01
26	Mike Singletary	.15	.11	.06
27	Lemuel Stinson	.03	.02	.01
28	James Brooks	.03	.02	.01
29	Eddie Brown	.03	.02	.01
30	Boomer Esiason	.15	.11	.06
31	James Francis	.03	.02	.01
32	David Fulcher	.03	.02	.01
33	Rodney Holman	.03	.02	.01
34	Anthony Munoz	.10	.08	.04
35	Bruce Reimers	.03	.02	.01
36	Ickey Woods	.05	.04	.02
37	Mike Baab	.03	.02	.01
38	Brian Brennan	.03	.02	.01
39	Raymond Clayborn	.03	.02	.01
40	Mike Johnson	.03	.02	.01
41	Clay Matthews	.03	.02	.01
42	Eric Metcalf	.07	.05	.03
43	Frank Minnifield	.03	.02	.01
44	Joe Morris	.05	.04	.02
45	Anthony Pleasant	.03	.02	.01
46	Troy Aikman	1.00	.70	.40
47	Jack Del Rio	.03	.02	.01
48	Issiac Holt	.03	.02	.01
49	Michael Irvin	.50	.40	.20
50	Jimmie Jones	.03	.02	.01
51	Nate Newton	.03	.02	.01
52	Danny Noonan	.03	.02	.01
53	Jay Novacek	.07	.05	.03
54	Emmitt Smith	2.00	1.50	.80
55	Steve Atwater	.05	.04	.02
56	Michael Brooks	.03	.02	.01
57	John Elway	.25	.20	.10
58	Mike Horan	.03	.02	.01
59	Mark Jackson	.03	.02	.01
60	Karl Mecklenburg	.03	.02	.01
61	Warren Powers	.03	.02	.01
62	Dennis Smith	.03	.02	.01
63	Doug Widell	.03	.02	.01
64	Jerry Ball	.05	.04	.02
65	Bennie Blades	.05	.04	.02
66	Robert Clark	.03	.02	.01
67	Ken Dallafior	.03	.02	.01
68	Mel Gray	.07	.05	.03
69	Eddie Murray	.05	.04	.02
70	Rodney Peete	.05	.04	.02
71	Barry Sanders	.75	.60	.30
72	Chris Spielman	.07	.05	.03
73	Robert Brown	.03	.02	.01
74	LeRoy Butler	.07	.05	.03
75	Perry Kemp	.03	.02	.01
76	Don Majkowski	.05	.04	.02
77	Tony Mandarich	.03	.02	.01
78	Mark Murphy	.03	.02	.01
79	Brian Noble	.03	.02	.01
80	Sterling Sharpe	.50	.40	.20
81	Ed West	.03	.02	.01
82	Ray Childress	.03	.02	.01
83	Cris Dishman	.03	.02	.01
84	Ernest Givins	.07	.05	.03
85	Drew Hill	.05	.04	.02
86	Haywood Jeffires	.07	.05	.03
87	Lamar Lathon	.03	.02	.01
88	Bruce Matthews	.07	.05	.03
89	Bubba McDowell	.03	.02	.01
90	Warren Moon	.25	.20	.10
91	Chip Banks	.03	.02	.01
92	Albert Bentley	.05	.04	.02
93	Duane Bickett	.03	.02	.01
94	Bill Brooks	.03	.02	.01
95	Sam Clancy	.03	.02	.01

96	Ray Donaldson	.03	.02	.01
97	Jeff George	.25	.20	.10
98	Mike Prior	.03	.02	.01
99	Clarence Verdin	.03	.02	.01
100	Steve DeBerg	.05	.04	.02
101	Albert Lewis	.03	.02	.01
102	Christian Okoye	.05	.04	.02
103	Kevin Ross	.03	.02	.01
104	Stephone Paige	.03	.02	.01
105	Kevin Porter	.03	.02	.01
106	Percy Snow	.03	.02	.01
107	Derrick Thomas	.20	.15	.08
108	Barry Word	.05	.04	.02
109	Marcus Allen	.20	.15	.08
110	Mervyn Fernandez	.03	.02	.01
111	Howie Long	.07	.05	.03
112	Ronnie Lott	.15	.11	.06
113	Terry McDaniel	.03	.02	.01
114	Max Montoya	.03	.02	.01
115	Don Mosebar	.03	.02	.01
116	Jay Schroeder	.10	.08	.04
117	Greg Townsend	.03	.02	.01
118	Flipper Anderson	.07	.05	.03
119	Henry Ellard	.07	.05	.03
120	Jim Everett	.10	.08	.04
121	Kevin Greene	.07	.05	.03
122	Damone Johnson	.03	.02	.01
123	Buford McGee	.03	.02	.01
124	Tom Newberry	.05	.04	.02
125	Michael Stewart	.03	.02	.01
126	Alvin Wright	.03	.02	.01
127	Mark Clayton	.05	.04	.02
128	Jeff Cross	.03	.02	.01
129	Mark Duper	.05	.04	.02
130	Ferrell Edmunds	.03	.02	.01
131	Dan Marino	.75	.60	.30
132	Tim McKyer	.03	.02	.01
133	John Offerdahl	.05	.04	.02
134	Louis Oliver	.03	.02	.01
135	Sammie Smith	.03	.02	.01
136	Joey Browner	.05	.04	.02
137	Anthony Carter	.10	.08	.04
138	Chris Doleman	.05	.04	.02
139	Hassan Jones	.03	.02	.01
140	Steve Jordan	.05	.04	.02
141	Carl Lee	.03	.02	.01
142	Al Noga	.03	.02	.01
143	Henry Thomas	.03	.02	.01
144	Herschel Walker	.15	.11	.06
145	Ray Agnew	.03	.02	.01
146	Bruce Armstrong	.03	.02	.01
147	Marv Cook	.05	.04	.02
148	Irving Fryar	.07	.05	.03
149	Tommy Hodson	.07	.05	.03
150	Fred Marion	.03	.02	.01
151	Johnny Rembert	.03	.02	.01
152	Chris Singleton	.03	.02	.01
153	Andre Tippett	.07	.05	.03
154	Morten Andersen	.10	.08	.04
155	Toi Cook	.03	.02	.01
156	Craig Heyward	.05	.04	.02
157	Dalton Hilliard	.03	.02	.01
158	Rickey Jackson	.07	.05	.03
159	Vaughan Johnson	.07	.05	.03
160	Rueben Mayes	.03	.02	.01
161	Pat Swilling	.07	.05	.03
162	Bobby Hebert	.07	.05	.03
163	Ottis Anderson	.10	.08	.04
164	Carl Banks	.05	.04	.02
165	Rodney Hampton	.25	.20	.10
166	Jeff Hostetler	.15	.11	.06
167	Mark Ingram	.05	.04	.02
168	Leonard Marshall	.03	.02	.01
169	David Meggett	.05	.04	.02
170	Lawrence Taylor	.25	.20	.10
171	Everson Walls	.03	.02	.01
172	Brad Baxter	.03	.02	.01
173	Jeff Lageman	.03	.02	.01
174	Pat Leahy	.03	.02	.01
175	Erik McMillan	.03	.02	.01
176	Scott Mersereau	.03	.02	.01
177	Rob Moore	.10	.08	.04
178	Ken O'Brien	.07	.05	.03
179	Blair Thomas	.10	.08	.04
180	Al Toon	.07	.05	.03
181	Eric Allen	.03	.02	.01
182	Jerome Brown	.03	.02	.01
183	Keith Byars	.05	.04	.02
184	Randall Cunningham	.15	.11	.06
185	Byron Evans	.03	.02	.01
186	Keith Jackson	.05	.04	.02
187	Heath Sherman	.03	.02	.01
188	Clyde Simmons	.05	.04	.02
189	Reggie White	.20	.15	.08
190	Rich Camarillo	.03	.02	.01
191	Johnny Johnson	.15	.11	.06
192	Ernie Jones	.03	.02	.01
193	Tim McDonald	.03	.02	.01
194	Freddie Joe Nunn	.03	.02	.01
195	Luis Sharpe	.03	.02	.01
196	Jay Taylor	.03	.02	.01
197	Anthony Thompson	.03	.02	.01
198	Tom Tupa	.03	.02	.01
199	Gary Anderson	.05	.04	.02
200	Bubby Brister	.10	.08	.04
201	Eric Green	.07	.05	.03
202	Bryan Hinkle	.03	.02	.01
203	Merril Hoge	.03	.02	.01
204	Carnell Lake	.03	.02	.01
205	Louis Lipps	.03	.02	.01
206	Keith Willis	.03	.02	.01
207	Rod Woodson	.10	.08	.04
208	Rod Bernstine	.05	.04	.02
209	Marion Butts	.07	.05	.03
210	Anthony Miller	.10	.08	.04
211	Leslie O'Neal	.03	.02	.01
212	Henry Rolling	.03	.02	.01
213	Junior Seau	.15	.11	.06
214	Billy Ray Smith	.03	.02	.01
215	Broderick Thompson	.03	.02	.01
216	Derrick Walker	.03	.02	.01
217	Dexter Carter	.03	.02	.01
218	Don Griffin	.03	.02	.01
219	Charles Haley	.05	.04	.02
220	Pierce Holt	.03	.02	.01
221	Joe Montana	1.00	.70	.40
222	Jerry Rice	.75	.60	.30
223	John Taylor	.10	.08	.04
224	Michael Walter	.03	.02	.01
225	Steve Young	.25	.20	.10
226	Brian Blades	.05	.04	.02
227	Jeff Bryant	.03	.02	.01
228	Jacob Green	.03	.02	.01
229	Tommy Kane	.03	.02	.01
230	Dave Krieg	.07	.05	.03
231	Bryan Millard	.03	.02	.01
232	Rufus Porter	.03	.02	.01
233	Eugene Robinson	.03	.02	.01
234	John L. Williams	.03	.02	.01
235	Gary Anderson	.05	.04	.02
236	Mark Carrier	.05	.04	.02
237	Reggie Cobb	.03	.02	.01
238	Rueben Davis	.03	.02	.01
239	Paul Gruber	.05	.04	.02
240	Harry Hamilton	.03	.02	.01
241	Keith McCants	.03	.02	.01
242	Ricky Reynolds	.03	.02	.01
243	Vinny Testaverde	.10	.08	.04
244	Earnest Byner	.05	.04	.02
245	Gary Clark	.10	.08	.04
246	Andre Collins	.03	.02	.01
247	Darrell Green	.07	.05	.03
248	Jim Lachey	.03	.02	.01
249	Charles Mann	.03	.02	.01
250	Wilber Marshall	.05	.04	.02
251	Art Monk	.10	.08	.04
252	Mark Rypien	.10	.08	.04
253	Russell Maryland	.15	.11	.06
254	Mike Croel	.03	.02	.01
255	Stanley Richard	.03	.02	.01
256	Leonard Russell	.03	.02	.01
257	Dan McGwire	.10	.08	.04
258	Todd Marinovich	.05	.04	.02
259	Eric Swann	.03	.02	.01
260	Mike Pritchard	.05	.04	.02
261	Alfred Williams	.03	.02	.01
262	Brett Favre	5.00	3.75	2.00
263	Browning Nagle	.07	.05	.03
264	Darryll Lewis	.03	.02	.01
265	Nick Bell	.03	.02	.01
266	Jeff Graham	.05	.04	.02
267	Eric Moten	.03	.02	.01
268	Roman Phifer	.03	.02	.01
269	Eric Bieniemy	.03	.02	.01
270	Phil Hansen	.03	.02	.01
271	Reggie Barrett	.03	.02	.01
272	Aeneas Williams	.07	.05	.03
273	Aaron Craver	.03	.02	.01
274	Lawrence Dawsey	.03	.02	.01
275	Ricky Ervins	.03	.02	.01
276	Jake Reed	.05	.04	.02
277	Eric Williams	.10	.08	.04
278	Tim Barnett	.10	.08	.04
279	Keith Traylor	.03	.02	.01
280	Jerry Rice	.25	.20	.10
281	Jim Lachey	.03	.02	.01
282	Barry Sanders	.50	.40	.20
283	Neal Anderson	.07	.05	.03
284	Reggie White	.15	.11	.06
285	Lawrence Taylor	.15	.11	.06
286	Mike Singletary	.10	.08	.04
287	Joey Browner	.05	.04	.02
288	Morten Andersen	.05	.04	.02
289	Andre Reed	.10	.08	.04
290	Anthony Munoz	.07	.05	.03
291	Warren Moon	.20	.15	.08
292	Thurman Thomas	.25	.20	.10
293	Ray Childress	.05	.04	.02
294	Derrick Thomas	.15	.11	.06
295	Rod Woodson	.10	.08	.04
296	Steve Atwater	.05	.04	.02
297	David Fulcher	.03	.02	.01
298	Anthony Munoz	.10	.08	.04
299	Ron Rivera	.03	.02	.01
300	Cornelius Bennett	.10	.08	.04
E1	Tom Flores	2.00	1.50	.80
E2	Anthony Munoz	2.00	1.50	.80
E3	Tony Casillas	2.00	1.50	.80
E4	Super Bowl XXVI	2.00	1.50	.80
E5	Felicidades	2.00	1.50	.80

1991 Pro Set Super Bowl XXVI AMEX Binder

American Express sponsored this 49-card set which was sold to commemorate Super Bowl XXVI in Minneapolis. The cards were included in an album, which holds four cards per page. Representatives from the Super Bowl teams - the Buffalo Bills and Washington Redskins - are included in the set. The cards have the same photos and numbers as their regular set counterparts, except these are marked with an AFC or NFC Champs logo on the front.

		NM/M	NM	E
	Complete Set (49):	25.00	18.50	10.00
	Common Player:	.40	.30	.15
1	**The NFL Experience**	1.00	.70	.40
2	**Super Bowl XXVI**	.50	.40	.20
3	**AFC Standings**	.50	.40	.20
4	**NFC Standings**	.50	.40	.20
5	**The Metrodome**	.50	.40	.20
73	Howard Ballard	.40	.30	.15
74	Cornelius Bennett	.75	.60	.30
75	Shane Conlan	.50	.40	.20
76	Kent Hull	.50	.40	.20
77	Kirby Jackson	.40	.30	.15
79	Mark Kelso	.40	.30	.15
80	Nate Odomes	.40	.30	.15
81	Andre Reed	.90	.70	.35
82	Jim Ritcher	.40	.30	.15
83	Bruce Smith	.75	.60	.30
84	Darryl Talley	.50	.40	.20
86	Thurman Thomas	3.00	2.25	1.25
88	Will Wolford	.40	.30	.15
89	Jeff Wright	.40	.30	.15
90	Marv Levy	.40	.30	.15
300	Cornelius Bennett	.50	.40	.20
316	Earnest Byner	.60	.45	.20
317	Gary Clark	.90	.70	.35
318	Andre Collins	.50	.40	.20
320	Chip Lohmiller	.40	.30	.15
321	Martin Mayhew	.40	.30	.15
322	Mark Rypien	.75	.60	.30
323	Alvin Walton	.40	.30	.15
324	Joe Gibbs	.50	.40	.20
370	Warren Moon	.75	.60	.30
444	James Lofton	.75	.60	.30
445	Keith McKeller	.50	.40	.20
449	Leon Seals	.40	.30	.15
450	Leonard Smith	.40	.30	.15
676	Jeff Bostic	.40	.30	.15
677	Darrell Green	.75	.60	.30
678	Markus Koch	.40	.30	.15
679	Jim Lachey	.50	.40	.20
680	Charles Mann	.50	.40	.20
681	Wilber Marshall	.50	.40	.20
682	Art Monk	.75	.60	.30
683	Gerald Riggs	.50	.40	.20
684	Ricky Sanders	.75	.60	.30
725	Howie Long	.75	.60	.30
726	Dan Marino	2.00	1.50	.80
746	Bobby Wilson	.50	.40	.20
805	Ricky Ervins	.75	.60	.30
848	Brian Mitchell	.75	.60	.30
(1)	Jim Kelly	20.00	15.00	8.00

1991 Pro Set UK Sheets

Measuring 5-1/8" x 11-3/4", the five six-card strips were used as a promotion in a Middlesex, England, newspaper called Today. Released one strip per week in Sunday papers during Fall 1991, the unperforated strips were numbered 1-5. Each player card is numbered identically to his 1991 regular-issue cards.

		NM/M	NM	E
	Complete Set (5):	25.00	18.50	10.00
	Common Player:	2.00	1.50	.80
1	Quarterbacks(200 Jim Everett, 167 Warren Moon, 111 Boomer Esiason, 128 Troy Aikman, 726 Dan Marino, 138 John Elway)	10.00	7.50	4.00

2	Running Backs(576 Herschel Walker, 213 Sammie Smith, 722 Earnest Byner, 123 Eric Metcalf, 485 Emmitt Smith)	10.00	7.50	4.00
3	Receivers(209 Mark Duper, 654 Jerry Rice, 251 Al Toon, 161 Sterling Sharpe, 618 Keith Jackson, 115 Tim McGee)	6.00	4.50	2.50
4	Kickers(460 Jim Breech, 447 Scott Norwood, 489 Mike Horan, 300 Norm Johnson, 184 Nick Lowery, 401 Sean Landeta)	2.00	1.50	.80
5	Defensive(728 Mike Singletary, 56 Carl Banks, 98 Deion Sanders, 191 Howie Long, 131 Issiac Holt, 241 Pat Swilling)	3.00	2.25	1.25

1991 Pro Set WLAF

These cards feature players from the World League of American Football. This logo and a notation that the card is an "Official World League Card" are on the front, which has a full-bleed color action photo. The back has a card number, player profile, biographical information and a mug shot. Each back is designed in a horizontal format.

	NM/M	NM	E
Complete Set (150):	5.00	3.75	2.00
Common Player:	.05	.04	.02

1	**World League Logo**	.15	.11	.06
2	Mike Lynn	.15	.11	.06
3	**First Weekend**	.15	.11	.06
4	**World Bowl Trophy**	.30	.25	.12
5	Jon Horton	.05	.04	.02
6	Stan Gelbaugh	.50	.40	.20
7	Dan Crossman	.05	.04	.02
8	Marlon Brown	.10	.08	.04
9	Judd Garrett	.25	.20	.10
10	**Barcelona Dragons**	.05	.04	.02
11	**Birmingham Fire**	.05	.04	.02
12	**Frankfurt Galaxy**	.05	.04	.02
13	**London Monarchs**	.05	.04	.02
14	**Montreal Machine**	.05	.04	.02
15	**NY-NJ Knights**	.05	.04	.02
16	**Orlando Thunder**	.05	.04	.02
17	**Raleigh-Durham Skyhawks**	.05	.04	.02
18	**Sacramento Surge**	.05	.04	.02
19	**San Antonio Riders**	.05	.04	.02
20	Eric Wilkerson	.05	.04	.02
21	Stan Gelbaugh	.35	.25	.14
22	Judd Garrett	.15	.11	.06
23	Tony Baker	.05	.04	.02
24	Byron Williams	.05	.04	.02
25	Chris Mohr	.10	.08	.04
26	Errol Tucker	.05	.04	.02
27	Carl Painter	.05	.04	.02
28	Anthony Parker	.10	.08	.04
29	Danny Lockett	.10	.08	.04
30	Scott Adams	.05	.04	.02
31	Jim Bell	.05	.04	.02
32	Lydell Carr	.15	.11	.06
33	Bruce Clark	.15	.11	.06
34	Demetrius Davis	.10	.08	.04
35	Scott Erney	.10	.08	.04
36	Ron Goetz	.05	.04	.02
37	Xisco Marcos	.05	.04	.02
38	Paul Palmer	.15	.11	.06
39	Tony Rice	.40	.30	.15
40	Bobby Sign	.05	.04	.02
41	Gene Taylor	.05	.04	.02
42	Barry Voorhees	.05	.04	.02
43	Jack Bicknell	.10	.08	.04

44	Kenny Bell	.05	.04	.02
45	Willie Bouyer	.05	.04	.02
46	John Brantley	.10	.08	.04
47	Elroy Harris	.05	.04	.02
48	James Henry	.05	.04	.02
49	John Holland	.10	.08	.04
50	Arhur Hunter	.05	.04	.02
51	Eric Jones	.05	.04	.02
52	Kirk Maggio	.05	.04	.02
53	Paul McGowan	.05	.04	.02
54	John Miller	.10	.08	.04
55	Maurice Oliver	.05	.04	.02
56	Darrel Phillips	.05	.04	.02
57	Chan Gailey	.05	.04	.02
58	Tony Baker	.10	.08	.04
59	Tim Broady	.05	.04	.02
60	Garry Frank	.05	.04	.02
61	Jason Johnson	.05	.04	.02
62	Stefan Maslo	.05	.04	.02
63	Mark Mraz	.05	.04	.02
64	Yepi Pau'u	.05	.04	.02
65	Mike Perez	.25	.20	.10
66	Mike Teeter	.05	.04	.02
67	Chris Williams	.05	.04	.02
68	Jack Elway	.20	.15	.08
69	Theo Adams	.05	.04	.02
70	Jeff Alexander	.05	.04	.02
71	Phillip Alexander	.05	.04	.02
72	Paul Berardelli	.10	.08	.04
73	Dana Brinson	.05	.04	.02
74	Marlon Brown	.05	.04	.02
75	Dedrick Dodge	.05	.04	.02
76	Victor Ebubedike	.05	.04	.02
77	Corris Ervin	.10	.08	.04
78	Steve Gabbard	.05	.04	.02
79	Judd Garrett	.15	.11	.06
80	Stan Gelbaugh	.75	.60	.30
81	Roy Hart	.05	.04	.02
82	Jon Horton	.05	.04	.02
83	Danny Lockett	.15	.11	.06
84	Doug Marrone	.05	.04	.02
85	Ken Sale	.05	.04	.02
86	Larry Kennan	.05	.04	.02
87	Mike Cadore	.05	.04	.02
88	K.D. Dunn	.05	.04	.02
89	Ricky Johnson	.05	.04	.02
90	Chris Mohr	.05	.04	.02
91	Bjorn Nittmo	.10	.08	.04
92	Michael Proctor	.05	.04	.02
93	Richard Shelton	.15	.11	.06
94	Tracy Simien	.30	.25	.12
95	Jacques Dussault	.05	.04	.02
96	Cornell Burbage	.10	.08	.04
97	Joe Campbell	.05	.04	.02
98	Monty Gilbreath	.05	.04	.02
99	Jeff Graham	.25	.20	.10
100	Kip Lewis	.05	.04	.02
101	Bob Lilljedahl	.05	.04	.02
102	Falanda Newton	.10	.08	.04
103	Anthony Parker	.10	.08	.04
104	Caesar Rentie	.05	.04	.02
105	Ron Sancho	.10	.08	.04
106	Craig Schlicting	.10	.08	.04
107	Lonnie Turner	.05	.04	.02
108	Eric Wilkerson	.05	.04	.02
109	Tony Woods	.10	.08	.04
110	Darrell "Mouse" Davis	.15	.11	.06
111	Kerwin Bell	.30	.25	.12
112	Wayne Davis	.05	.04	.02
113	John Guerrero	.05	.04	.02
114	Myron Jones	.05	.04	.02
115	Eric Mitchel	.20	.15	.08
116	Billy Owens	.05	.04	.02
117	Carl Painter	.10	.08	.04
118	Rob Sterling	.05	.04	.02
119	Errol Tucker	.05	.04	.02
120	Byron Williams	.05	.04	.02
121	Mike Withycombe	.05	.04	.02
122	Don Matthews	.05	.04	.02
123	Jon Carter	.05	.04	.02
124	Marvin Hargrove	.05	.04	.02
125	Clarkston Hines	.05	.04	.02
126	Ray Jackson	.05	.04	.02
127	Bobby McAllister	.25	.20	.10
128	Darryl McGill	.05	.04	.02
129	Pat McGuirk	.10	.08	.04
130	Shawn Woodson	.05	.04	.02
131	Roman Gabriel	.25	.20	.10
132	Greg Coauette	.05	.04	.02
133	Mike Eklins	.15	.11	.06
134	Victor Floyd	.05	.04	.02
135	Shawn Knight	.10	.08	.04
136	Pete Najarian	.05	.04	.02
137	Carl Parker	.10	.08	.04
138	Richard Stephens	.05	.04	.02
139	Curtis Wilson	.05	.04	.02
140	Kay Stephenson	.10	.08	.04
141	Ricky Blake	.25	.20	.10

142	Donnie Gardner	.05	.04	.02
143	Jason Garrett	.25	.20	.10
144	Mike Johnson	.05	.04	.02
145	Undra Johnson	.10	.08	.04
146	John Layfield	.05	.04	.02
147	Mark Ledbetter	.05	.04	.02
148	Gary Richard	.05	.04	.02
149	Tim Walton	.05	.04	.02
150	Mike Riley	.05	.04	.02

1991 Pro Set WLAF Helmets

Each of these 10 cards features a helmet for a team in the World League of American Football in its initial season. The cards, random inserts in 1991 Pro Set Series I packs, are numbered on the back and include information about the team depicted on the front, plus a schedule.

	NM/M	NM	E
Complete Set (10):	3.00	2.25	1.25
Common Helmet:	.30	.25	.12

1	**Barcelona Dragons**	.30	.25	.12
2	**Birmingham Fire**	.30	.25	.12
3	**Frankfurt Galaxy**	.30	.25	.12
4	**London Monarchs**	.30	.25	.12
5	**Montreal Machine**	.30	.25	.12
6	**NY-NJ Knights**	.30	.25	.12
7	**Orlando Thunder**	.30	.25	.12
8	**Raleigh-Durham Skyhawks**	.30	.25	.12
9	**Sacramento Surge**	.30	.25	.12
10	**San Antonio Riders**	.30	.25	.12

1991 Pro Set WLAF Inserts

These cards, featuring players from each of the 10 teams in the World League of American Football during its initial season in 1991, were random inserts in 1991 Pro Set Series I packs. Each team is represented by its quarterback and head coach, at least. The card front has the set's logo in an upper corner and indicates it is an official World League card. The back also has the set logo, plus a player profile and head shot. Card numbering includes "World League Collectible" above the number.

	NM/M	NM	E
Complete Set (32):	6.00	4.50	2.50
Common Player:	.10	.08	.04

1	Mike Lynn	.35	.25	.14
2	Larry Kennan	.10	.08	.04
3	Jack Bicknell	.10	.08	.04
4	Scott Erney	.20	.15	.08
5	A.J. Green	.25	.20	.10
6	Chan Gailey	.10	.08	.04
7	Paul McGowan	.15	.11	.06
8	Brent Pease	.20	.15	.08
9	Jack Elway	.30	.25	.12
10	Mike Perez	.30	.25	.12
11	Mike Tetter	.10	.08	.04
12	Larry Kennan	.10	.08	.04
13	Corris Ervin	.10	.08	.04
14	John Witkowski	.25	.20	.10
15	Jacques Dussault	.10	.08	.04
16	Ray Savage	.10	.08	.04
17	Kevin Sweeney	.50	.40	.20
18	Mouse Davis	.50	.40	.20
19	Todd Hammel	.20	.15	.08
20	Anthony Parker	.30	.25	.12
21	Don Matthews	.15	.11	.06
22	Kerwin Bell	.30	.25	.12
23	Wayne Davis	.10	.08	.04
24	Roman Gabriel	.60	.45	.25
25	John Carter	.20	.15	.08
26	Mark Maye	.20	.15	.08
27	Kay Stephenson	.20	.15	.08
28	Ben Bennett	.50	.40	.20
29	Shawn Knight	.20	.15	.08
30	Mike Riley	.10	.08	.04
31	Jason Garrett	.15	.11	.06
32	Greg Gilbert	.20	.15	.08

1991 Pro Set WLAF World Bowl Combo 43

This set combines Pro Set's helmet and 32-card insert sets into one issue. Fans who attended the World Bowl Game at Wembley Stadium in London, England, received the set. The cards have been renumbered from the original sets, and the helmet cards can be identified by the chronological text which is on the back instead of a team schedule.

	NM/M	NM	E
Complete Set (43):	15.00	11.00	6.00
Common Player:	.25	.20	.10

1	PRES(Mike Lynn)	.75	.60	.30
2	**League Opener London 24, Frankfurt 11**	.50	.40	.20
3	Jack Bicknell	.50	.40	.20
4	Scott Erney	.40	.30	.15
5	Anthony Greene	.50	.40	.20

6	Chan Gailey	.50	.40	.20
7	Paul McGowan	.25	.20	.10
8	Brent Pease	.50	.40	.20
9	Jack Elway	.80	.60	.30
10	Mike Perez	.75	.60	.30
11	Mike Teeter	.25	.20	.10
12	Larry Kennan	.25	.20	.10
13	Corris Ervin	.25	.20	.10
14	John Witkowski	.50	.40	.20
15	Jacques Dussault	.25	.20	.10
16	Ray Savage	.35	.25	.14
17	Kevin Sweeney	.65	.50	.25
18	Mouse Davis	.65	.50	.25
19	Todd Hammel	.50	.40	.20
20	Anthony Parker	.50	.40	.20
21	Don Matthews	.25	.20	.10
22	Kerwin Bell	.75	.60	.30
23	Wayne Davis	.25	.20	.10
24	Roman Gabriel	.75	.60	.30
25	Jon Carter	.50	.40	.20
26	Bobby McAllister	1.00	.70	.40
27	Kay Stephenson	.25	.20	.10
28	Mike Elkins	1.00	.70	.40
29	Shawn Knight	.50	.40	.20
30	Mike Riley	.25	.20	.10
31	Jason Garrett	.75	.60	.30
32	Greg Gilbert	.50	.40	.20
33	**World Bowl Trophy**	4.00	3.00	1.50
34	**Barcelona Dragons Helmet**	.60	.45	.25
35	**Birmingham Fire Helmet**	.60	.45	.25
36	**Frankfurt Galaxy Helmet**	.60	.45	.25
37	**London Monarchs Helmet**	.60	.45	.25
38	**Montreal Machine Helmet**	.60	.45	.25
39	**NY-NJ Knights Helmet**	.60	.45	.25
40	**Orlando Thunder Helmet**	.60	.45	.25
41	**Ral.-Durham Skyhawks Helmet**	.60	.45	.25
42	**Sacramento Surge Helmet**	.60	.45	.25
43	**San Antonio Riders Helmet**	.60	.45	.25

1989 Purdue Legends Smokey

		NM/M	NM	E
Complete Set (16):		25.00	18.50	10.00
Common Player:		1.25	.90	.50
1	Fred Akers (CO)	1.50	1.25	.60
2	Jim Everett (LEG)	4.00	3.00	1.50
3	Bob Griese (LEG)	6.00	4.50	2.50
4	Mark Herrmann (LEG)	2.00	1.50	.80
5	Bill Hitchcock	1.25	.90	.50
6	Steve Jackson	1.50	1.25	.60
7	Derrick Kelson	1.25	.90	.50
8	Leroy Keyes (LEG)	2.00	1.50	.80
9	Shawn McCarthy	1.50	1.25	.60
10	Dwayne O'Connor	1.25	.90	.50
11	Mike Phipps (LEG)	2.00	1.50	.80
12	Darren Trieb	1.25	.90	.50
13	Tony Vinson	1.25	.90	.50
14	Calvin Williams	3.00	2.25	1.25
15	Rod Woodson (LEG)	5.00	3.75	2.00
16	Dave Young (LEG)	1.25	.90	.50

Q

1991 Quarterback Legends

This 50-card set, produced by NFL Quarterback Legends, comes in a special commemorative box. Each card front has a full-bleed color action photo, with the set logo and name given at the bottom of the card in a checkerboard pattern. The card back has the sponsors' logos, a card number, a color photo, statistics and a career summary. The design is horizontal. Cards were released at the Quarterback Legends Show in Nashville, Tenn., in January 1992.

		NM/M	NM	E
Complete Set (50):		20.00	15.00	8.00
Common Player:		.25	.20	.10
1	Ken Anderson	.75	.60	.30
2	Steve Bartkowski	.35	.25	.14
3	George Blanda	1.50	1.25	.60
4	Terry Bradshaw	2.00	1.50	.80
5	Zeke Bratkowski	.25	.20	.10
6	John Brodie	.50	.40	.20

7	Charley Conerly	.50	.40	.20
8	Len Dawson	.50	.40	.20
9	Lynn Dickey	.25	.20	.10
10	Joe Ferguson	.25	.20	.10
11	Vince Ferragamo	.25	.20	.10
12	Tom Flores	.35	.25	.14
13	Dan Fouts	1.00	.70	.40
14	Roman Gabriel	.35	.25	.14
15	Otto Graham	.75	.60	.30
16	Bob Griese	1.25	.90	.50
17	Steve Grogan	.35	.25	.14
18	John Hadl	.35	.25	.14
19	James Harris	.25	.20	.10
20	Jim Hart	.25	.20	.10
21	Ron Jaworski	.25	.20	.10
22	Charlie Johnson	.25	.20	.10
23	Bert Jones	.35	.25	.14
24	Sonny Jurgensen	.75	.60	.30
25	Joe Kapp	.25	.20	.10
26	Billy Kilmer	.50	.40	.20
27	Daryle Lamonica	.35	.25	.14
28	Greg Landry	.25	.20	.10
29	Neil Lomax	.25	.20	.10
30	Archie Manning	.40	.30	.15
31	Earl Morrall	.35	.25	.14
32	Craig Morton	.35	.25	.14
33	Gifford Nielsen	.25	.20	.10
34	Dan Pastorini	.25	.20	.10
35	Jim Plunkett	.35	.25	.14
36	Norm Snead	.25	.20	.10
37	Ken Stabler	.75	.60	.30
38	Bart Starr	1.50	1.25	.60
39	Roger Staubach	3.00	2.25	1.25
40	Joe Theismann	.75	.60	.30
41	Y.A. Tittle	.75	.60	.30
42	Johnny Unitas	1.50	1.25	.60
43	Bill Wade	.25	.20	.10
44	Danny White	.35	.25	.14
45	Doug Williams	.25	.20	.10
46	Jim Zorn	.35	.25	.14
47	Legendary Feats(Otto Graham)	1.00	.70	.40
48	Legendary Feats(Johnny Unitas)	1.00	.70	.40
49	Legendary Feats(Bart Starr)	1.00	.70	.40
50	Legendary Feats(Terry Bradshaw)	1.75	1.25	.70

1991 Queen's University

		NM/M	NM	E
Complete Set (52):		12.00	9.00	4.75
Common Card (1-51):		.30	.25	.12
Common Card (P1-P5):		3.00	2.25	1.25
1	**First Rugby Team** (Team Photo)	.75	.60	.30
2	Grey Cup Years(Harry Batstone, Frank R. Leadlay)	.75	.60	.30
3	**1978 Vanier Cup Champs**	.30	.25	.12
4	**1978 Vanier Cup Champs**	.30	.25	.12
5	Tim Pendergast	.30	.25	.12
6	Brad Elberg	.30	.25	.12
7	Ken Kirkwood	.30	.25	.12
8	Kyle Wanzel	.30	.25	.12
9	Brian Alford	.30	.25	.12
10	Paul Kozan	.30	.25	.12
11	Paul Beresford	.30	.25	.12
12	Ron Herman	.30	.25	.12
13	Mike Ross	.30	.25	.12
14	Tom Black	.30	.25	.12
15	Steve Yovetich	.30	.25	.12
16	Mark Robinson	.30	.25	.12
17	Don Rorwick	.30	.25	.12
18	Ed Kidd	.30	.25	.12
19	Jamie Galloway	.30	.25	.12
20	Dan Wright	.30	.25	.12
21	Scott Gray	.30	.25	.12
22	Dan McCullough	.30	.25	.12
23	Steve Othen	.30	.25	.12
24	Doug Hargreaves (CO)	.30	.25	.12
25	Sue Bolton (CO)	.30	.25	.12
26	**Coaching Staff**	.50	.40	.20
27	Joel Dagnone	.30	.25	.12
28	Mark Morrison	.30	.25	.12
29	Rob Krog	.30	.25	.12
30	Dan Pawliw	.30	.25	.12
31	Greg Bryk	.30	.25	.12
32	Eric Dell	.30	.25	.12
33	Mike Boone	.30	.25	.12
34	James Paterson	.30	.25	.12
35	Jeff Yach	.30	.25	.12
36	Peter Pain	.30	.25	.12
37	Aron Campbell	.30	.25	.12
38	Chris McCormick	.30	.25	.12

39	Jason Moller	.30	.25	.12
40	Terry Huhtala	.30	.25	.12
41	Matt Zarowny	.30	.25	.12
42	David St. Amour	.30	.25	.12
43	Frank Tindall	.30	.25	.12
44	Ron Stewart	1.00	.70	.40
45	Jim Young	1.00	.70	.40
46	Bob Howes	.30	.25	.12
47	Stu Lang	.30	.25	.12
48	Mike Schad (In College Uniform)	.75	.60	.30
49	Mike Schad (In Philadelphia Eagles Uniform)	.75	.60	.30
50	Jock Climie	1.00	.70	.40
51	**Checklist**	.30	.25	.12
P1	Jock Climie	3.00	2.25	1.25
P1AU	Jock Climie (AU/100)	30.00	22.00	12.00
P2	Ron Stewart	4.00	3.00	1.50
P2AU	Ron Stewart (AU/300)	30.00	22.00	12.00
P3	Jim Young	4.00	3.00	1.50
P4	Stu Lang	3.00	2.25	1.25
P5	Mike Schad	3.00	2.25	1.25
P5AU	Mike Schad (AU/100)	30.00	22.00	12.00
NNO	**Title Card**	.75	.60	.30

R

1935 R311-2 Premium Photos

Measuring 6" x 8", these 17 photos feature both collegiate and professional players. The black-and-white photos have blank backs. The photos could be ordered from National Chicle in exchange for 20 wrappers given to the retailer. The photos are listed in alphabetical order by the player's name or team.

		NM	E	VG
Complete Set (17):		3,000	1,500	900.00
Common Player:		175.00	87.00	52.00
1	Joe Bach	175.00	87.00	52.00
2	Eddie Casey	175.00	87.00	52.00
3	George Christensen	175.00	87.00	52.00
4	Harold "Red" Grange	525.00	260.00	155.00
5	TD Next Stop(Stan Kostka)	175.00	87.00	52.00
6	Fordham Back(Joe Maniaci) (26 with ball, shown trying to gain around left end)	175.00	87.00	52.00
7	Harry Newman	175.00	87.00	52.00
8	Walter Switzer (Cornell quarterback)	175.00	87.00	52.00
9	**Chicago Bears, 1934 Western Champs**	300.00	150.00	90.00
10	**New York Giants, 1934 World's Champs**	350.00	175.00	105.00
11	**1934**	220.00	110.00	66.00
12	**Navy 1945**	175.00	87.00	52.00
13	**Pittsburgh Pirates, 1935 Football Club**	250.00	125.00	75.00
14	**Touchdown: Morton of Yale**	175.00	87.00	52.00
15	**A Tight Spot**	175.00	87.00	52.00
16	**Cotton Goes Places**	175.00	87.00	52.00
17	Picture Ever Photographed(Ace Gutowky, Steve Hokuf)	220.00	110.00	66.00

1985 Raiders Shell Oil Posters

Measuring 11-5/8" x 18", the five posters were available at participating Southern California Shell gas stations during the 1985 season. Color artwork of Raider players in action are included on the poster fronts. The backs are blank, except for the Pro Bowl poster which has the Raiders and Shell logos and the release schedule of the posters.

		NM/M	NM	E
Complete Set (5):		25.00	18.50	10.00
Common Player:		5.00	3.75	2.00
1	**Pro Bowl** (No release date)	6.00	4.50	2.50
2	**Defensive Front** (September)	6.00	4.50	2.50
3	**Deep Secondary** (October)	5.00	3.75	2.00
4	**Big Offensive Line** (November)	5.00	3.75	2.00
5	**Scores** (December)	5.00	3.75	2.00

1985 Raiders Smokey

Measuring 2-5/8" x 4-1/8", the four-card set is anchored by a photo on the front, with the player's name, position and team at the bottom. The Raiders' logo and Kodak logo are printed on the lower left and right, respectively. The card backs have the player's name and his highlights on the left. A fire safety tip and cartoon are included on the right. The cards are numbered on the backs. The sponsors and Kodak logos are printed at the bottom of the card backs.

		NM/M	NM	E
Complete Set (4):		3.00	2.25	1.25
Common Player:		.35	.25	.14
1	Marcus Allen	1.50	1.25	.60
2	Tom Flores (CO)	.50	.40	.20
3	Howie Long	1.25	.90	.50
4	Rod Martin	.35	.25	.14

1987 Raiders Smokey Color-Grams

This 14-page booklet includes 13 player drawings and one of Smokey and Huddles. Featured on a page are a 5-5/8" x 3-11/16" postcard and a perforated card which measures 2-1/2" x 3-11/16". Each booklet measures 8-1/8" x 3-11/16". The postcard fronts have "Arsonbusters" printed at the top, with a Smokey the Bear and two Raiders logos printed at the bottom. The cards, which are unnumbered, are listed by page number.

		NM/M	NM	E
Complete Set (14):		25.00	18.50	10.00
Common Player:		1.25	.90	.50
1	**Smokey and Huddles**	1.25	.90	.50
2	Matt Millen	1.50	1.25	.60
3	Rod Martin	1.50	1.25	.60
4	Sean Jones	2.50	2.00	1.00
5	Dokie Williams	1.25	.90	.50
6	Don Mosebar	1.50	1.25	.60
7	Todd Christensen	2.50	2.00	1.00
8	Bill Pickel	1.25	.90	.50
9	Marcus Allen	8.00	6.00	3.25
10	Charley Hannah	1.25	.90	.50
11	Howie Long	3.00	2.25	1.25
12	Vann McElroy	1.50	1.25	.60
13	Reggie McKenzie	1.25	.90	.50
14	Mike Haynes	2.00	1.50	.80

1988 Raiders Police

Measuring 2-3/4" x 4-1/8", the 12-card set is anchored by a large photo on the front, with "Los Angeles Raiders," Texaco logo and Raiders' logo printed at the top. The player's number, name and position are listed beneath the photo. The card backs, which are numbered, have the player's name, number, position, bio, safety tip and L.A.P.D. shield.

		NM/M	NM	E
Complete Set (12):		8.00	6.00	3.25
Common Player:		.40	.30	.15
1	Vann McElroy	.40	.30	.15
2	Bill Pickel	.40	.30	.15
3	Marcus Allen	2.00	1.50	.80
4	Rod Martin	.50	.40	.20
5	Lionel Washington	.50	.40	.20
6	Don Mosebar	.50	.40	.20
7	Reggie McKenzie	.40	.30	.15
8	Todd Christensen	.75	.60	.30
9	Bo Jackson	2.50	2.00	1.00
10	James Lofton	1.25	.90	.50
11	Howie Long	1.00	.70	.40
12	Mike Shanahan (CO)	.75	.60	.30

1988 Raiders Smokey

Measuring 3" x 5", the 14-card set showcases "Arsonbusters" at the top of the photo. The player's name and position are printed at the bottom of the photo. The Smokey the Bear and Raiders' logos are printed at the bottom of the black-bordered card fronts. The unnumbered card backs have the player's name, position, bio and safety tip cartoon.

		NM/M	NM	E
Complete Set (14):		10.00	7.50	4.00
Common Player:		.75	.60	.30
1	Marcus Allen	4.00	3.00	1.50
2	Todd Christensen	1.00	.70	.40
3	Bo Jackson	4.00	3.00	1.50
4	James Lofton	2.00	1.50	.80
5	Howie Long	1.50	1.25	.60
6	Rod Martin	1.00	.70	.40
7	Vann McElroy	.75	.60	.30
8	Don Mosebar	1.00	.70	.40
9	Bill Pickel	.75	.60	.30
10	Jerry Robinson	.75	.60	.30
11	Mike Shanahan (CO)	1.50	1.25	.60
12	**Smokey Bear**	.75	.60	.30
13	Stacey Toran	.75	.60	.30
14	Greg Townsend	1.00	.70	.40

1989 Raiders Swanson

The three cards were printed on a perforated strip, which also included two Swanson Hungry-Man dinner coupons. The cards measure 2-1/2" x 3-3/4". The card fronts have a black-and-white player photo inside an oval, with "Hungry Man" printed in a stripe in the upper left corner. The player's name is printed at the bottom. The card backs, which are unnumbered, showcase the player's name, bio and highlights. The Swanson Hungry-Man logo is printed at the top of the horizontal card backs.

		NM/M	NM	E
Complete Set (3):		8.00	6.00	3.25
Common Player:		2.50	2.00	1.00
1	Marcus Allen	5.00	3.75	2.00
2	Howie Long	3.00	2.25	1.25
3	Jim Plunkett	2.50	2.00	1.00

1990-91 Raiders Main Street Dairy

The six half-pint milk cartons have the Raiders logo, player head shot, his name, position, team and safety tip printed on a panel. The cartons measure 4-1/2" x 6" when they are collapsed. Released in the Los Angeles metro area, the cartons were produced in three colors -- brown (chocolate lowfat), red (vitamin D) and blue (two percent lowfat).

		NM/M	NM	E
Complete Set (6):		15.00	11.00	6.00
Common Player:		2.50	2.00	1.00
1	Bob Golic (Blue)	3.50	2.75	1.50
2	Terry McDaniel (Brown)	2.50	2.00	1.00
3	Don Mosebar (Red)	2.50	2.00	1.00
4	Jay Schroeder (Blue)	3.50	2.75	1.50
5	Art Shell (CO) (Red)	5.00	3.75	2.00
6	Steve Wisniewski (Brown)	2.50	2.00	1.00

1990 Raiders Smokey

The 16-card set is anchored on the front with a large photo. "Los Angeles Raiders" is printed above the photo, while the player's name and number are printed beneath the photo. The Smokey the Bear logo is in the lower left. The card fronts are bordered in black. The unnumbered card backs have the player's name, position, bio, Raiders' logos and safety tip cartoon.

		NM/M	NM	E
Complete Set (16):		10.00	7.50	4.00
Common Player:		.75	.60	.30
1	Eddie Anderson	1.00	.70	.40
2	Tom Benson	.75	.60	.30
3	Mervyn Fernandez	1.25	.90	.50
4	Bob Golic	1.00	.70	.40
5	Jeff Gossett	.75	.60	.30
6	Rory Graves	.75	.60	.30
7	Jeff Jaeger	.75	.60	.30
8	Howie Long	2.00	1.50	.80
9	Don Mosebar	1.00	.70	.40
10	Jay Schroeder	1.25	.90	.50
11	Art Shell (CO)	2.00	1.50	.80
12	Greg Townsend	1.25	.90	.50
13	Lionel Washington	1.00	.70	.40
14	Steve Wisniewski	1.25	.90	.50
15	**Commitment to Excellence** (Helmet and Super Bowl trophies)	.75	.60	.30
16	**Denise Franzen** (Cheerleader)	.75	.60	.30

1991 Raiders Adohr Farms Dairy

These 10 half-pint milk cartons have the Raiders' logo, player headshot, safety tip, player's name, position and team printed on one of the panels. The cartons measure 4-1/2" x 6" when collapsed. The cartons were printed in two colors -- blue (two percent lowfat) and red (vitamin D). The Greg Townsend carton was the only one to be released in both colors. The cartons are unnumbered.

		NM/M	NM	E
Complete Set (10):		25.00	18.50	10.00
Common Player:		2.50	2.00	1.00
1	Jeff Gossett (Red)	2.50	2.00	1.00
2	Ethan Horton (Blue)	2.50	2.00	1.00
3	Jeff Jaeger (Red)	2.50	2.00	1.00
4	Ronnie Lott (Blue)	5.00	3.75	2.00
5	Terry McDaniel (Red)	2.50	2.00	1.00
6	Don Mosebar (Red)	2.50	2.00	1.00
7	Jay Schroeder (Red)	3.50	2.75	1.50
8	Art Shell (CO) (Red)	5.00	3.75	2.00
9	Greg Townsend (Red or blue)	3.50	2.75	1.50
10	Steve Wisniewski (Red)	2.50	2.00	1.00

1991 Raiders Police

The 12-card set showcases a color action photo on the front, with the player's name printed in a gray stripe above the photo. The Raiders and sponsor logos are printed at the bottom of the card front. The card backs are numbered, have the player's name, position, bio and safety tip. The sponsors are listed at the bottom, while the card number is printed inside a football in the upper right.

		NM/M	NM	E
Complete Set (12):		15.00	11.00	6.00
Common Player:		1.00	.70	.40
1	Art Shell (CO)	3.00	2.25	1.25
2	Marcus Allen	3.00	2.25	1.25
3	Mervyn Fernandez	1.50	1.25	.60
4	Willie Gault	1.50	1.25	.60
5	Howie Long	2.00	1.50	.80
6	Don Mosebar	1.25	.90	.50
7	Winston Moss	1.00	.70	.40
8	Jay Schroeder	1.50	1.25	.60
9	Steve Wisniewski	1.25	.90	.50
10	Ethan Horton	1.00	.70	.40
11	Lionel Washington	1.25	.90	.50
12	Greg Townsend	1.50	1.25	.60

1950 Rams Admiral

Measuring 3-1/2" x 5-1/2", the 35-card set features a posed black-and-white photo on the front of the card, with "Your Admiral dealer presents..." and the player's name printed in a black area at the top. Beneath the photo are the card number and player bio. The backs have a Rams schedule on one half, while the other half is blank. Card Nos. 26-35 are blank-backed and are a bit smaller than the other cards in the set.

		NM	E	VG
Complete Set (35):		110.00	55.00	33.00
Common Player:		20.00	10.00	6.00
1	Joe Stydahar (CO)	30.00	15.00	9.00
2	Hampton Pool (CO)	20.00	10.00	6.00
3	Fred Naumetz	20.00	10.00	6.00
4	Jack Finlay	20.00	10.00	6.00
5	Gil Bouley	20.00	10.00	6.00
6	Bob Reinhard	20.00	10.00	6.00
7	Bob Boyd	25.00	12.50	7.50
8	Bob Waterfield	100.00	50.00	30.00
9	Mel Hein (CO)	40.00	20.00	12.00
10	Howard Hickey (CO)	25.00	12.50	7.50
11	Ralph Pasquariello	20.00	10.00	6.00
12	Jack Zilly	20.00	10.00	6.00
13	Tom Kalmanir	20.00	10.00	6.00
14	Norm Van Brocklin	125.00	62.00	37.00
15	Woodley Lewis	25.00	12.50	7.50
16	Glenn Davis	50.00	25.00	15.00
17	Dick Hoerner	20.00	10.00	6.00
18	Bob Kelley (ANN)	20.00	10.00	6.00
19	Paul (Tank) Younger	30.00	15.00	9.00
20	George Sims	20.00	10.00	6.00
21	Dick Huffman	20.00	10.00	6.00
22	Tom Fears	50.00	25.00	15.00
23	Vitamin Smith	25.00	12.50	7.50
24	Elroy Hirsch	75.00	37.00	22.00
25	Don Paul	25.00	12.50	7.50
26	Bill Lange	20.00	10.00	6.00
27	Paul Barry	20.00	10.00	6.00
28	Deacon Dan Towler	30.00	15.00	9.00
29	Vic Vasicek	20.00	10.00	6.00
30	Bill Smyth	20.00	10.00	6.00
31	Larry Brink	20.00	10.00	6.00
32	Jerry Williams	20.00	10.00	6.00
33	Stan West	20.00	10.00	6.00
34	Art Statuto	20.00	10.00	6.00
35	Ed Champagne	20.00	10.00	6.00

1953 Rams Black Border

Measuring 4-1/4" x 6-3/8", the 36-card set is anchored by a large photo and bordered in black. A facsimile autograph is printed near the bottom of the photo. The unnumbered card backs have the player's name, bio and highlights. The set was available from the Rams. Some cards from the 1953-55 and 1957 Rams Black Border sets are very similar, with the excepton of different information on the card backs.

		NM	E	VG
Complete Set (36):		175.00	87.00	52.00
Common Player:		3.00	1.50	.90
1	Ben Agajanian	3.00	1.50	.90
2	Bob Boyd (Born in Riverside)	3.00	1.50	.90
3	Larry Brink	3.00	1.50	.90
4	Rudy Bukich	5.00	2.50	1.50
5	Tom Dahms (4 text lines)	3.00	1.50	.90
6	Dick Daugherty (Regular Ram ...)	3.00	1.50	.90
7	Jack Dwyer (Played 1951 ...)	3.00	1.50	.90

		NM	E	VG
8	Tom Fears (1952 stats)	10.00	5.00	3.00
9	Bob Fry (Was sprinter)	3.00	1.50	.90
10	Frank Fuller (Attended ...)	3.00	1.50	.90
11	Norbert Hecker	3.00	1.50	.90
12	Elroy Hirsch (1952 stats)	12.00	6.00	3.50
13	John Hock (Just completed ...)	3.00	1.50	.90
14	Bob Kelley (ANN) (Signature in upper left of photo)	3.00	1.50	.90
15	Dick "Night Train" Lane	12.00	6.00	3.50
16	Woodley Lewis (Ram utility ...)	4.00	2.00	1.25
17	Tom McCormick (Set three ...)	3.00	1.50	.90
18	Lewis Bud McFadin (Came to Rams ...)	3.00	1.50	.90
19	Leon McLaughlin (Played every ...)	3.00	1.50	.90
20	Brad Myers	3.00	1.50	.90
21	Don Paul (A five year ...)	4.00	2.00	1.25
22	Hampton Pool (CO) (Hampton Pool ...)	3.00	1.50	.90
23	Duane Putnam (As rookie ...)	4.00	2.00	1.25
24	Volney Quinlan (Nickname ...)	4.00	2.00	1.25
25	Herb Rich	3.00	1.50	.90
26	Andy Robustelli (Rams' regular ...)	10.00	5.00	3.00
27	Vitamin Smith	4.00	2.00	1.25
28	Harland Svare (Attended ...)	3.00	1.50	.90
29	Len Teeuws	3.00	1.50	.90
30	Harry Thompson (Used at ...)	3.00	1.50	.90
31	Charley Toogood (Been defensive ...)	3.00	1.50	.90
32	Deacon Dan Towler (National football)	7.00	3.50	2.00
33	Norm Van Brocklin (1952 stats)	20.00	10.00	6.00
34	Stan West (Rams' regular)	3.00	1.50	.90
35	Paul (Tank) Younger (1952 stats)	6.00	3.00	1.75
36	Coaches(John Sauer, William Battles, Howard (Red) Hickey)	4.00	2.00	1.25

1954 Rams Black Border

Measuring 4-1/4" x 6-3/8", the front is anchored by a large black-and-white photo, bordered in black. A facsimile autograph also appears near the bottom of the photo. The unnumbered backs have the player's name, bio and career highlights. The 36-card set was available from the Rams.

		NM	E	VG
	Complete Set (36):	175.00	87.00	52.00
	Common Player:	3.00	1.50	.90
1	Bob Boyd (One of fastest ...)	3.00	1.50	.90
2	Bob Carey	3.00	1.50	.90
3	Bobby Cross	3.00	1.50	.90
4	Tom Dahms (5 text lines)	3.00	1.50	.90
5	Don Doll	3.00	1.50	.90
6	Jack Dwyer (Regular defensive ...)	3.00	1.50	.90
7	Tom Fears (1953 stats)	20.00	10.00	6.00
8	Bob Griffin (All American ...)	3.00	1.50	.90
9	Art Hauser (Was fastest ...)	3.00	1.50	.90
10	Hall Haynes	3.00	1.50	.90
11	Elroy Hirsch (1953 stats)	12.00	6.00	3.50
12	Ed Hughes	3.00	1.50	.90
13	Bob Kelley (ANN) (Signature across photo)	3.00	1.50	.90
14	Woodley Lewis (Established ...)	4.00	2.00	1.25
15	Gene Lipscomb	10.00	5.00	3.00
16	Tom McCormick (Rams' regular)	3.00	1.50	.90
17	Bud McFadin (Although ...)	3.00	1.50	.90
18	Leon McLaughlin (Started every ...)	3.00	1.50	.90
19	Paul Miller (Lettered at ...)	3.00	1.50	.90
20	Don Paul (One of two ...)	4.00	2.00	1.25
21	Hampton Pool (CO) (Since taking ...)	3.00	1.50	.90
22	Duane Putnam (Offensive guard)	4.00	2.00	1.25
23	Volney Quinlan (Had best ...)	4.00	2.00	1.25
24	Les Richter (Rated one ...)	7.00	3.50	2.00
25	Andy Robustelli (L.A.'s regular ...)	10.00	5.00	3.00
26	Willard Sherman (Played at ...)	4.00	2.00	1.25
27	Harland Svare (An outside ...)	3.00	1.50	.90
28	Harry Thompson (Played offensive ...)	3.00	1.50	.90
29	Charley Toogood	3.00	1.50	.90
30	Deacon Dan Towler (Since becoming ...)	7.00	3.50	2.00
31	Norm Van Brocklin (1953 stats)	20.00	10.00	6.00
32	Bill Wade (Selected as)	8.00	4.00	2.50
33	Duane Wardlow	3.00	1.50	.90
34	Stan West (Virtually ...)	3.00	1.50	.90
35	Paul (Tank) Younger (1953 stats)	7.00	3.50	2.00
36	Coaches(Bill Battles, Howard Hickey, John Sauer, Dick Voris, Buck Weaver, Hampton Pool)	4.00	2.00	1.25

1955 Rams Black Border

Measuring 4-1/4" x 6-3/8", the 37-card set is anchored by a large black-and-white photo on the front and bordered in black. A facsimile autograph appears near the bottom of the photo. The backs include the player's name, bio and career highlights. The cards are unnumbered and were available as a set from the Rams.

		NM	E	VG
	Complete Set (37):	175.00	87.00	52.00
	Common Player:	3.00	1.50	.90
1	Jack Bighead	3.00	1.50	.90
2	Bob Boyd	3.00	1.50	.90
3	Don Burroughs	3.00	1.50	.90
4	Jim Cason	3.00	1.50	.90
5	Bobby Cross	3.00	1.50	.90
6	Jack Ellena	3.00	1.50	.90
7	Tom Fears	10.00	5.00	3.00
8	Sid Fournet	3.00	1.50	.90
9	Frank Fuller	4.00	2.00	1.25
10	Sid Gillman (and staff)	7.00	3.50	2.00
11	Bob Griffin	3.00	1.50	.90
12	Art Hauser	3.00	1.50	.90
13	Hall Haynes	3.00	1.50	.90
14	Elroy Hirsch	12.00	6.00	3.50
15	John Hock	3.00	1.50	.90
16	Glenn Holtzman	3.00	1.50	.90
17	Ed Hughes	3.00	1.50	.90
18	Woodley Lewis	4.00	2.00	1.25
19	Gene Lipscomb	10.00	5.00	3.00
20	Tom McCormick	3.00	1.50	.90
21	Bud McFadin	3.00	1.50	.90
22	Leon McLaughlin	3.00	1.50	.90
23	Paul Miller	3.00	1.50	.90
24	Larry Morris	3.00	1.50	.90
25	Don Paul	4.00	2.00	1.25
26	Duane Putnam	4.00	2.00	1.25
27	Volney Quinlan	4.00	2.00	1.25
28	Les Richter	7.00	3.50	2.00
29	Andy Robustelli	10.00	5.00	3.00
30	Willard Sherman	4.00	2.00	1.25
31	Corky Taylor	3.00	1.50	.90
32	Charley Toogood	3.00	1.50	.90
33	Deacon Dan Towler	7.00	3.50	2.00
34	Norm Van Brocklin	20.00	10.00	6.00
35	Bill Wade	8.00	4.00	2.50
36	Ron Waller	3.00	1.50	.90
37	Paul (Tank) Younger	7.00	3.50	2.00

1956 Rams White Border

Measuring 4-1/4" x 6-3/8", the 37-card set is anchored by a black-and-white photo on the front and bordered in white. A facsimile autograph appears near the bottom of the photo. The unnumbered card backs have the player's name, bio and career highlights. The set was available from the Rams.

		NM	E	VG
	Complete Set (37):	175.00	87.00	52.00
	Common Player:	3.00	1.50	.90
1	Bob Boyd	3.00	1.50	.90
2	Rudy Bukich	5.00	2.50	1.50
3	Don Burroughs	3.00	1.50	.90
4	Jim Cason	3.00	1.50	.90
5	Leon Clarke	4.00	2.00	1.25
6	Dick Daugherty	3.00	1.50	.90
7	Jack Ellena	3.00	1.50	.90
8	Tom Fears	10.00	5.00	3.00
9	Sid Fournet	3.00	1.50	.90
10	Bob Fry	3.00	1.50	.90
11	Sid Gillman, Joseph Madro, Jack Faulkner, Joe Thomas, Lowell Storm (Coaches)	7.00	3.50	2.00
12	Bob Griffin	3.00	1.50	.90
13	Art Hauser	3.00	1.50	.90
14	Elroy Hirsch	12.00	6.00	3.50
15	John Hock	3.00	1.50	.90
16	Bobby Holladay	3.00	1.50	.90
17	Glenn Holtzman	3.00	1.50	.90
18	Bob Kelley (ANN)	3.00	1.50	.90
19	Joe Marconi	4.00	2.00	1.25
20	Bud McFadin	3.00	1.50	.90
21	Paul Miller	3.00	1.50	.90
22	Ron Miller	3.00	1.50	.90
23	Larry Morris	3.00	1.50	.90
24	John Morrow	3.00	1.50	.90
25	Brad Myers	3.00	1.50	.90
26	Hugh Pitts	3.00	1.50	.90
27	Duane Putnam	3.00	1.50	.90
28	Les Richter	7.00	3.50	2.00
29	Willard Sherman	4.00	2.00	1.25
30	Charley Toogood	3.00	1.50	.90
31	Norm Van Brocklin	20.00	10.00	6.00
32	Bill Wade	7.00	3.50	2.00
33	Ron Waller	4.00	2.00	1.25
34	Duane Wardlow	3.00	1.50	.90
35	Jesse Whittenton	4.00	2.00	1.25
36	Tom Wilson	4.00	2.00	1.25
37	Paul (Tank) Younger	7.00	3.50	2.00

1957 Rams Black Border

Measuring 4-1/4" x 6-3/8", the 38-card set is anchored by a large photo on the front bordered in black. A facsimile autograph appears near the bottom of the photo. The card backs include the player's name, bio and career highlights. The cards are unnumbered and were sold as a set by the Rams.

		NM	E	VG
	Complete Set (38):	175.00	87.00	52.00
	Common Player:	3.00	1.50	.90
1	Jon Arnett	8.00	4.00	2.50
2	Bob Boyd (Frequently called ...)	4.00	2.00	1.25
3	Alex Bravo	3.00	1.50	.90
4	Bill Brundige (ANN)	3.00	1.50	.90
5	Don Burroughs	3.00	1.50	.90
6	Jerry Castete	3.00	1.50	.90
7	Leon Clarke	4.00	2.00	1.25
8	Paige Cothren	3.00	1.50	.90
9	Dick Daugherty (Has the ...)	3.00	1.50	.90
10	Bob Dougherty	3.00	1.50	.90
11	Bob Fry (One of the ...)	3.00	1.50	.90
12	Frank Fuller (One of the ...)	3.00	1.50	.90
13	Coaches(Sid Gillman, Joseph Madro, George Allen, Jack Faulkner, Lowell Storm)	10.00	5.00	3.00
14	Bob Griffin (After four ...)	3.00	1.50	.90
15	Art Hauser (One of the ...)	3.00	1.50	.90
16	Elroy Hirsch (A legendary ...)	12.00	6.00	3.50
17	John Hock (Teamed with ...)	3.00	1.50	.90
18	Glenn Holtzman	3.00	1.50	.90
19	John Houser	3.00	1.50	.90
20	Bob Kelley (ANN) (Signature near right border of photo)	3.00	1.50	.90
21	Lamar Lundy	8.00	4.00	2.50
22	Joe Marconi	3.00	1.50	.90
23	Paul Miller (From a ...)	3.00	1.50	.90
24	Larry Morris	3.00	1.50	.90
25	Ken Panfil	3.00	1.50	.90
26	Jack Pardee	12.00	6.00	3.50
27	Duane Putnam (Named to a ...)	4.00	2.00	1.25
28	Les Richter (One of the ...)	7.00	3.50	2.00
29	Willard Sherman (One of the ...)	4.00	2.00	1.25
30	Del Shofner	8.00	4.00	2.50
31	Bill Ray Smith	6.00	3.00	1.75
32	George Strugar	3.00	1.50	.90
33	Norm Van Brocklin (When Van Brocklin ...)	25.00	12.50	7.50
34	Bill Wade (In the first ...)	7.00	3.50	2.00
35	Ron Waller	3.00	1.50	.90
36	Jesse Whittenton	4.00	2.00	1.25
37	Tom Wilson	4.00	2.00	1.25
38	Paul (Tank) Younger (One of a ...)	7.00	3.50	2.00

1959 Rams Bell Brand

The 40-card set is anchored by a color photo on the front, with the player's name, position and team at the bottom. The numbered card backs have the player's name, position, bio and career highlights, along with an advertisement for Bell Snacks on the left side. The right side has an ad for fans to buy L.A. Rams' Signature Merchandise. The card number is located in the upper left corner. The cards were included in specially marked bags of Bell's potato chips and corn chips.

		NM	E	VG
Complete Set (40):		1,500	750.00	450.00
Common Player:		30.00	15.00	9.00
1	Bill Wade	45.00	22.00	13.50
2	Buddy Humphrey	30.00	15.00	9.00
3	Frank Ryan	50.00	25.00	15.00
4	Ed Meador	40.00	20.00	12.00
5	Tom Wilson	30.00	15.00	9.00
6	Don Burroughs	30.00	15.00	9.00
7	Jon Arnett	45.00	22.00	13.50
8	Del Shofner	45.00	22.00	13.50
9	Jack Pardee	50.00	25.00	15.00
10	Ollie Matson	75.00	37.00	22.00
11	Joe Marconi	30.00	15.00	9.00
12	Jim Jones	30.00	15.00	9.00
13	Jack Morris	30.00	15.00	9.00
14	Willard Sherman	40.00	20.00	12.00
15	Clendon Thomas	40.00	20.00	12.00
16	Les Richter	40.00	20.00	12.00
17	John Morrow	30.00	15.00	9.00
18	Lou Michaels	40.00	20.00	12.00
19	Bob Reifsnyder	30.00	15.00	9.00
20	John Guzik	30.00	15.00	9.00
21	Duane Putnam	30.00	15.00	9.00
22	John Houser	30.00	15.00	9.00
23	Buck Lansford	30.00	15.00	9.00
24	Gene Selawski	30.00	15.00	9.00
25	John Baker	30.00	15.00	9.00
26	Bob Fry	30.00	15.00	9.00
27	John Lovetere	30.00	15.00	9.00
28	George Strugar	30.00	15.00	9.00
29	Roy Wilkins	30.00	15.00	9.00
30	Charley Bradshaw	30.00	15.00	9.00
31	Gene Brito	40.00	20.00	12.00
32	Jim Phillips	40.00	20.00	12.00
33	Leon Clarke	40.00	20.00	12.00
34	Lamar Lundy	45.00	22.00	13.50
35	Sam Williams	30.00	15.00	9.00
36	Sid Gillman (CO)	60.00	30.00	18.00
37	Jack Faulkner (CO)	30.00	15.00	9.00
38	Joseph Madro (CO)	30.00	15.00	9.00
39	Don Paul (CO)	30.00	15.00	9.00
40	Lou Rymkus (CO)	40.00	20.00	12.00

1960 Rams Bell Brand

The 39-card standard sized set features the identical design on the front and back as the 1959 set, except the fronts of the 1960 set has yellow borders (the 1959 set had white borders). Card Nos. 1-18, with the exception of No. 2, are duplicate photos from the 1959 set. These cards were also inserted into specially marked bags of Bell's Snacks. Card No. 2 of Gene Selawski was pulled from the set early in the season because he was waived from the team. However, the card was available from the company.

		NM	E	VG
Complete Set (39):		2,000	1,000	600.00
Common Player (1-18):		25.00	12.50	7.50
Common Player (19-39):		50.00	25.00	15.00
1	Joe Marconi	25.00	12.50	7.50
2	Gene Selawski (SP)	1,200	600.00	360.00
3	Frank Ryan	40.00	20.00	12.00
4	Ed Meador	30.00	15.00	9.00
5	Tom Wilson	25.00	12.50	7.50
6	Gene Brito	30.00	15.00	9.00
7	Jon Arnett	35.00	17.50	10.50
8	Buck Lansford	25.00	12.50	7.50
9	Jack Pardee	45.00	22.00	13.50
10	Ollie Matson	65.00	32.00	19.50
11	John Lovetere	25.00	12.50	7.50
12	Bill Jolko	25.00	12.50	7.50
13	Jim Phillips	30.00	15.00	9.00
14	Lamar Lundy	35.00	17.50	10.50
15	Del Shofner	40.00	20.00	12.00
16	Les Richter	30.00	15.00	9.00
17	Bill Wade	35.00	17.50	10.50
18	Lou Michaels	30.00	15.00	9.00
19	Dick Bass	60.00	30.00	18.00
20	Charley Britt	50.00	25.00	15.00
21	Willard Sherman	60.00	30.00	18.00
22	George Strugar	50.00	25.00	15.00
23	Bob Long	50.00	25.00	15.00
24	Danny Villanueva	60.00	30.00	18.00
25	Jim Boeke	50.00	25.00	15.00
26	Clendon Thomas	50.00	25.00	15.00
27	Art Hunter	50.00	25.00	15.00
28	Carl Karilivacz	50.00	25.00	15.00

29	John Baker	50.00	25.00	15.00
30	Charley Bradshaw	50.00	25.00	15.00
31	John Guzik	50.00	25.00	15.00
32	Buddy Humphrey	50.00	25.00	15.00
33	Carroll Dale	60.00	30.00	18.00
34	Don Ellensick	50.00	25.00	15.00
35	Ray Hord	50.00	25.00	15.00
36	Charles Janerette	50.00	25.00	15.00
37	John Kenerson	50.00	25.00	15.00
38	Jerry Stalcup	50.00	25.00	15.00
39	Bob Waterfield (CO)	125.00	62.00	37.00

1973 Rams Team Issue

Measuring 7" x 8-3/4", the six sheets are anchored on the front by color photos. Bordered in white, the fronts have the player's name and team listed beneath the photo. The blank-backed cards are unnumbered.

		NM	E	VG
Complete Set (6):		32.00	16.00	9.60
Common Player:		2.50	1.25	.70
1	Jim Bertelsen	2.50	1.25	.70
2	John Hadl	7.00	3.50	2.00
3	Harold Jackson	5.00	2.50	1.50
4	Merlin Olsen	10.00	5.00	3.00
5	Isiah Robertson	3.50	1.75	1.00
6	Jack Snow	3.50	1.75	1.00

1980 Rams Police

Measuring 2-5/8" x 4-1/8", the 14-card set is anchored by a large photo. The player's name, number, position and team are printed beneath the photo. The Rams' and Kiwanis' logos appear in the lower left and right, respectively, on the card fronts. The backs have Rams' tips inside a box, with the sponsors listed at the bottom. The cards are unnumbered. The cards were handed out by police officers for 14 weeks.

		NM	E	VG
Complete Set (14):		20.00	10.00	6.00
Common Player:		1.00	.50	.30
11	Pat Haden	3.50	1.75	1.00
15	Vince Ferragamo	2.50	1.25	.70
21	Nolan Cromwell	2.50	1.25	.70
26	Wendell Tyler	2.50	1.25	.70
32	Cullen Bryant	1.25	.60	.40
53	Jim Youngblood	1.25	.60	.40
59	Bob Brudzinski	1.00	.50	.30
61	Rich Saul	1.00	.50	.30
77	Doug France	1.00	.50	.30
82	Willie Miller	1.00	.50	.30
85	Jack Youngblood	4.00	2.00	1.25
88	Preston Dennard	1.00	.50	.30
90	Larry Brooks	1.00	.50	.30
xx0	Ray Malavasi (CO)	1.00	.50	.30

1985 Rams Smokey

Measuring 4" x 6", the 24-card set showcases the player's last name at the top of the card, with a photo of the player standing with Smokey the Bear printed in the center of the card front. The Rams' logo, helmet and Smokey the Bear logo are printed beneath the photo on the front. The backs include the card number, player name, position and bio, along with a safety tip cartoon.

		NM/M	NM	E
Complete Set (24):		15.00	11.00	6.00
Common Player:		.50	.40	.20
1	George Andrews	.50	.40	.20
2	Bill Bain	.50	.40	.20
3	Russ Bolinger	.50	.40	.20
4	Jim Collins	.50	.40	.20
5	Nolan Cromwell	1.00	.70	.40
6	Reggie Doss	.50	.40	.20
7	Carl Ekern	.50	.40	.20
8	Vince Ferragamo	1.00	.70	.40
9	Gary Green	.50	.40	.20
10	Mike Guman	.50	.40	.20
11	David Hill	.50	.40	.20
12	LeRoy Irvin (SP)	4.00	3.00	1.50
13	Mark Jerue	.50	.40	.20
14	Johnnie Johnson	.75	.60	.30
15	Jeff Kemp	1.00	.70	.40
16	Mel Owens	.50	.40	.20
17	Irv Pankey	.50	.40	.20
18	Doug Smith	.75	.60	.30
19	Ivory Sully	.50	.40	.20
20	Jack Youngblood	1.50	1.25	.60
21	Mike McDonald	.50	.40	.20
22	Norwood Vann	.50	.40	.20
23	**Smokey Bear** (Unnumbered)	.50	.40	.20
24	Smokey Bear(Reggie Doss, Gary Green, Johnnie Johnson, Carl Ekern) (Unnumbered)	.75	.60	.30

1987 Rams Jello/General Foods

Jello and Bird's Eye sponsored this 10-card set, which features a large photo, with the Rams' helmet in the upper left and the NFL shield in the upper right. The Jello and Bird's Eye logos are in the lower left and right, respectively, with the player's name and position printed in the bottom center of the card front. The card backs have the player's name and number at the top, with his bio inside an oval in the center. His career highlights are listed at the bottom of the card, along with the Jello and Bird's Eye logos. The cards are unnumbered.

		NM/M	NM	E
Complete Set (10):		5.00	3.75	2.00
Common Player:		.35	.25	.14
1	Ron Brown	.50	.40	.20
2	Nolan Cromwell	.60	.45	.25
3	Eric Dickerson	2.00	1.50	.80
4	Carl Ekern	.35	.25	.14
5	Jim Everett	2.00	1.50	.80
6	Dennis Harrah	.35	.25	.14
7	LeRoy Irvin	.50	.40	.20
8	Mike Lansford	.35	.25	.14
9	Jackie Slater	.60	.45	.25
10	Doug Smith	.50	.40	.20

1987 Rams Oscar Mayer

This 19-card set celebrated the Rams Special Teams Player of the Week. The player's photo appears inside a ripped-out hole in the center of the card. The Rams' helmet and Oscar Mayer logo are on the lower left and right, respectively. The player's name and position are listed beneath the photo. The fronts have a baby blue background. The unnumbered card backs have the player's name, bio Rams' helmet and Oscar Mayer logo.

		NM/M	NM	E
Complete Set (19):		14.00	10.50	5.50
Common Player:		.75	.60	.30
1	Sam Anno	.75	.60	.30
2	Ron Brown	1.00	.70	.40
3	Nolan Cromwell	1.25	.90	.50
4	Henry Ellard	1.50	1.25	.60
5	Jerry Gray	1.00	.70	.40
6	Kevin Greene	3.00	2.25	1.25
7	Mike Guman	.75	.60	.30
8	Dale Hatcher	.75	.60	.30
9	Clifford Hicks	.75	.60	.30
10	Mark Jerue	.75	.60	.30
11	Johnnie Johnson	1.00	.70	.40
12	Larry Kelm	.75	.60	.30
13	Mike Lansford	.75	.60	.30
14	Vince Newsome	.75	.60	.30
15	Michael Stewart	.75	.60	.30
16	Mickey Sutton	.75	.60	.30
17	Tim Tyrrell	.75	.60	.30
18	Norwood Vann	.75	.60	.30
19	Charles White	1.25	.90	.50

1989 Rams Police

Released as a 16-card perforated sheet, the cards have a photo of the player, with his name and position, along with the Rams' helmet and Frito-Lay logos beneath the helmet. The card backs, numbered "of 16," have the Rams' helmet and Frito-Lay logo in the upper corners, followed by the player's name, position and quote. McGruff the Crime Dog's safety tip is also included on the back. The 7-11 and police badge logos are in the lower corners, with the card number centered at the bottom.

		NM/M	NM	E
Complete Set (16):		10.00	7.50	4.00
Common Player:		1.00	.70	.40
1	John Robinson	2.00	1.50	.80
2	Jim Everett	2.50	2.00	1.00
3	Doug Smith	1.25	.90	.50
4	Duval Love	1.00	.70	.40
5	Henry Ellard	2.00	1.50	.80
6	Mel Owens	1.00	.70	.40
7	Jerry Gray	1.25	.90	.50
8	Kevin Greene	2.00	1.50	.80
9	Vince Newsome	1.00	.70	.40
10	Irv Pankey	1.00	.70	.40
11	Tom Newberry	1.25	.90	.50
12	Pete Holohan	1.00	.70	.40
13	Mike Lansford	1.00	.70	.40
14	Greg Bell	1.25	.90	.50
15	Jackie Slater	1.25	.90	.50
16	Dale Hatcher	1.00	.70	.40

1990 Rams Smokey

Full-bleed photos are on the fronts of this 12-card set, while the backs have a black-and-white photo of the player and his bio. The cards are unnumbered and sponsored by local fire departments. The cards measure 3-3/4" x 5-3/4".

		NM/M	NM	E
Complete Set (12):		8.00	6.00	3.25
Common Player:		.75	.60	.30
1	Aaron Cox	.75	.60	.30
2	Henry Ellard	1.25	.90	.50
3	Jim Everett	1.50	1.25	.60
4	Jerry Gray	1.00	.70	.40
5	Kevin Greene	1.50	1.25	.60
6	Pete Holohan	.75	.60	.30
7	Mike Lansford	.75	.60	.30
8	Vince Newsome	.75	.60	.30
9	Doug Reed	.75	.60	.30
10	Jackie Slater	1.00	.70	.40
11	Fred Strickland	.75	.60	.30
12	Mike Wilcher	.75	.60	.30

1981 Red Rooster Calgary Stampeders

		NM/M	NM	E
Complete Set (40):		25.00	18.50	10.00
Common Player:		.60	.45	.25
1	Willie Armstead	.60	.45	.25
2	Doug Battershill	.60	.45	.25
3	Willie Burden (From waist up)	3.00	2.25	1.25
4	Willie Burden (Head and shoulders)	3.00	2.25	1.25
5	Scott Burk (UER) (Misspelled Burke 4th line of bio)	.60	.45	.25
6	Al Burleson	.60	.45	.25
7	Ken Dombrowski	.60	.45	.25
8	Lloyd Fairbanks	1.25	.90	.50
9	Rob Forbes	.60	.45	.25
10	Tom Forzani	1.00	.70	.40
11	Miles Gorrell	.60	.45	.25
12	J.T. Hay	.60	.45	.25
13	John Holland	1.00	.70	.40
14	Norm Hopely	.60	.45	.25
15	Jeff Inglis	.60	.45	.25
16	Lepoleon Ingram	.60	.45	.25
17	Terry Irvin	.60	.45	.25
18	Ken Johnson	1.00	.70	.40
19	Franklin King	.60	.45	.25
20	Dave Kirzinger	.60	.45	.25
21	Frank Kosec	.60	.45	.25
22	Tom Krebs	.60	.45	.25
23	Reggie Lewis	.60	.45	.25
24	Robert Lubig	.60	.45	.25
25	Scott MacArthur	.60	.45	.25
26	Ed McAleney	.60	.45	.25
27	Mike McTague	1.00	.70	.40
28	Mark Moors	.60	.45	.25
29	Bernie Morrison	.60	.45	.25
30	Mark Nelson	.60	.45	.25
31	Ray Odums	.60	.45	.25
32	Ronnie Paggett	.60	.45	.25
33	John Palazeti	.60	.45	.25
34	John Prassas	.60	.45	.25
35	Tom Reimer	.60	.45	.25
36	James Sykes (Close-up)	3.00	2.25	1.25
37	James Sykes (From waist up)	3.00	2.25	1.25
38	Bruce Threadgill	.60	.45	.25
39	Bob Viccars	.60	.45	.25
40	Merv Walker	.60	.45	.25

1981 Red Rooster Edmonton Eskimos

		NM/M	NM	E
Complete Set (40):		50.00	37.00	20.00
Common Player:		.60	.45	.25
1	Leo Blanchard	.60	.45	.25
2	David Boone	.60	.45	.25
3	Brian Broomell	.60	.45	.25
4	Hugh Campbell (CO)	1.25	.90	.50
5	Dave Cutler	2.50	2.00	1.00
6	Marco Cyncar	1.00	.70	.40
7	Ron Estay	.60	.45	.25
8	Dave Fennell	1.00	.70	.40
9	Emilio Fraietta	.60	.45	.25
10	Brian Fryer	.60	.45	.25
11	Jim Germany	1.00	.70	.40
12	Gary Hayes	.60	.45	.25
13	Larry Highbaugh	1.25	.90	.50
14	Joe Hollimon	.60	.45	.25
15	Hank Ilesic	1.25	.90	.50
16	Ed Jones	.60	.45	.25
17	Dan Kearns	.60	.45	.25

18	Sean Kehoe	.60	.45	.25
19	Brian Kelly	2.50	2.00	1.00
20	Dan Kepley	1.25	.90	.50
21	Stu Lang	.60	.45	.25
22	Pete Lavorato	.60	.45	.25
23	Neil Lumsden	1.00	.70	.40
24	Bill Manchuk	.60	.45	.25
25	Mike McLeod	.60	.45	.25
26	Ted Milian	.60	.45	.25
27	Warren Moon	25.00	18.50	10.00
28	James Parker	2.00	1.50	.80
29	John Pointer	.60	.45	.25
30	Hector Pothier	.60	.45	.25
31	Dale Potter	.60	.45	.25
32	Angelo Santucci	.60	.45	.25
33	Tom Scott	1.00	.70	.40
34	Waddell Smith	1.00	.70	.40
35	Bill Stevenson	.60	.45	.25
36	Tom Towns	.60	.45	.25
37	Eric Upton	.60	.45	.25
38	Mark Wald	.60	.45	.25
39	Ken Walter	.60	.45	.25
40	Tom Wilkinson	3.00	2.25	1.25

1939 Redskins Matchbooks

Measuring 1-1/2" x 4-1/2" when folded out, the 20 matchbooks have a black-and-white headshot of the player at the top, with his facsimile autograph, position, college and bio listed underneath. The back side says, "This is one of 20 autographed pictures of the Washington Redskins. Compliments of The Ross Jewelry Co." The inside of the matchbook has the official 1939 Redskins schedule. The matchbooks are unnumbered.

		NM	E	VG
Complete Set (20):		525.00	262.50	157.50
Common Matchbook:		10.00	5.00	3.00
1	Jim Barber (SP)	125.00	62.00	37.00
2	Sammy Baugh	65.00	32.00	19.50
3	Hal Bradley	10.00	5.00	3.00
4	Vic Carroll	10.00	5.00	3.00
5	Bud Erickson	10.00	5.00	3.00
6	Andy Farkas	12.00	6.00	3.50
7	Frank Filchock	12.00	6.00	3.50
8	Ray Flaherty (CO)	18.00	9.00	5.50
9	Don Irwin	10.00	5.00	3.00
10	Ed Justice	10.00	5.00	3.00
11	Jim Karcher	10.00	5.00	3.00
12	Max Krause	10.00	5.00	3.00
13	Charley Malone	10.00	5.00	3.00
14	Bob Masterson	10.00	5.00	3.00
15	Wayne Millner	20.00	10.00	6.00
16	Mickey Parks	10.00	5.00	3.00
17	Ernie Pinckert	12.00	6.00	3.50
18	Steve Slivinski (SP)	125.00	62.00	37.00
19	Clem Stralka	10.00	5.00	3.00
20	Jay Turner	10.00	5.00	3.00

1940 Redskins Matchbooks

This 20-matchbook set is very similar in design to the 1939 set. The 1940 set has a headshot of the player, a facsimile autograph, his position, college and bio showcased on the front. The backside of the matchbook states, "This is one of 20 autographed pictures of the Washington Redskins. Compliments of Ross Jewelry Co." The inside of the matchbooks have the official 1940 Redskins' schedule. Prices listed here are for matchbooks missing the matches, but with the strikers intact.

		NM	E	VG
Complete Set (20):		225.00	112.50	67.50
Common Player:		10.00	5.00	3.00
1	Jim Barber	10.00	5.00	3.00
2	Sammy Baugh	45.00	22.00	13.50
3	Vic Carroll	10.00	5.00	3.00
4	Glen Edwards	25.00	12.50	7.50
5	Andy Farkas	12.00	6.00	3.50
6	Dick Farman	10.00	5.00	3.00
7	Bob Hoffman	10.00	5.00	3.00
8	Don Irwin	10.00	5.00	3.00
9	Charley Malone	10.00	5.00	3.00
10	Bob Masterson	10.00	5.00	3.00
11	Wayne Millner	20.00	10.00	6.00
12	Mickey Parks	10.00	5.00	3.00
13	Ernie Pinckert	12.00	6.00	3.50
14	Bo Russell	10.00	5.00	3.00
15	Clyde Shugart	10.00	5.00	3.00
16	Steve Slivinski	10.00	5.00	3.00
17	Clem Stralka	10.00	5.00	3.00
18	Dick Todd	12.00	6.00	3.50
19	Bill Young	10.00	5.00	3.00
20	Roy Zimmerman	10.00	5.00	3.00

1941 Redskins Matchbooks

Measuring 1-1/2" x 4-1/2" when folded out, the 20 matchbooks have a headshot of the player at the top of the front, with his facsimile autograph, position, college and bio listed beneath. The backside of the cover states, "This is one of 20 autographed pictures of the Washington Redskins. Compliments of Home Laundry is also included. The phone number Atlantic 2400 is also included. The inside features the 1941 official Redskins' schedule.

		NM	E	VG
Complete Set (20):		195.00	97.50	58.50
Common Player:		8.00	4.00	2.50
1	Ki Aldrich	10.00	5.00	3.00
2	Jim Barber	8.00	4.00	2.50
3	Sammy Baugh	40.00	20.00	12.00
4	Vic Carroll	8.00	4.00	2.50
5	Fred Davis	8.00	4.00	2.50
6	Andy Farkas	10.00	5.00	3.00
7	Dick Farman	8.00	4.00	2.50
8	Frank Filchock	10.00	5.00	3.00
9	Ray Flaherty (CO)	12.00	6.00	3.50
10	Bob Masterson	8.00	4.00	2.50
11	Bob McChesney	8.00	4.00	2.50
12	Wayne Millner	15.00	7.50	4.50
13	Wilbur Moore	10.00	5.00	3.00
14	Bob Seymour	8.00	4.00	2.50
15	Clyde Shugart	8.00	4.00	2.50
16	Clem Stralka	8.00	4.00	2.50
17	Robert Titchenal	8.00	4.00	2.50
18	Dick Todd	10.00	5.00	3.00
19	Bill Young	8.00	4.00	2.50
20	Roy Zimmerman	8.00	4.00	2.50

1942 Redskins Matchbooks

Measuring 1-1/2" x 4-1/2" when folded out, the 20 matchbooks follow the same design as the previous sets. A player headshot is showcased on the front, with his facsimile signature, position, college and bio printed beneath. The back of the cover states, "This is one of 20 autographed pictures of the Washington Redskins. Compliments of Home Laundry Atlantic 2400." The inside of the covers have the official 1942 Redskins' schedule, plus an ad for Home Laundry.

		NM	E	VG
Complete Set (20):		195.00	97.50	58.50
Common Player:		8.00	4.00	2.50
1	Ki Aldrich	10.00	5.00	3.00
2	Sammy Baugh	45.00	22.00	13.50
3	Joe Beinor	8.00	4.00	2.50
4	Vic Carroll	8.00	4.00	2.50
5	Ed Cifers	8.00	4.00	2.50
6	Fred Davis	8.00	4.00	2.50
7	Glen Edwards	16.00	8.00	4.75
8	Andy Farkas	10.00	5.00	3.00
9	Dick Farman	8.00	4.00	2.50
10	Ray Flaherty (CO)	12.00	6.00	3.50
11	Al Krueger	8.00	4.00	2.50
12	Bob Masterson	8.00	4.00	2.50
13	Bob McChesney	8.00	4.00	2.50
14	Wilbur Moore	10.00	5.00	3.00
15	Bob Seymour	8.00	4.00	2.50
16	Clyde Shugart	8.00	4.00	2.50
17	Clem Stralka	8.00	4.00	2.50
18	Dick Todd	10.00	5.00	3.00
19	Willie Wilkin	8.00	4.00	2.50
20	Bill Young	8.00	4.00	2.50

1951-52 Redskins Matchbooks

Measuring 1-1/2" x 4-1/2" when folded out, the 20 matchbooks have the player headshot on the front, followed by a facsimile signature, position, college and bio. The backs state, "This is one of 20 autographed pictures of the Washington Redskins. Compliments of Jack Blank, President, Arcade Pontiac Co. ADams 8500." The outside of the matchbooks have the Redskins' logo on black and gold. An advertisement for Arcade Pontiac is printed on the back, also in color. The matchbooks are unnumbered.

		NM	E	VG
Complete Set (25):		225.00	112.00	67.00
Common Player:		8.00	4.00	2.50
1	John Badaczewski	8.00	4.00	2.50
2A	Head Coach(Herman Ball) (CO)	8.00	4.00	2.50
2B	Assistant Coach(Herman Ball) (CO)	8.00	4.00	2.50
3	Sammy Baugh	40.00	20.00	12.00
4	Ed Berrang (1951)	10.00	5.00	3.00
5	Dan Brown (1951)	10.00	5.00	3.00
6	Al DeMao	8.00	4.00	2.50
7	Harry Dowda (1952)	10.00	5.00	3.00
8	Chuck Drazenovich	8.00	4.00	2.50
9	Bill Dudley (1951)	15.00	7.50	4.50
10	Harry Gilmer	12.00	6.00	3.50
11	Robert Goode (1951)	10.00	5.00	3.00
12	Leon Heath (1952)	10.00	5.00	3.00

13	Charlie Justice (1952)	15.00	7.50	4.50
14	Lou Karras	8.00	4.00	2.50
15	Eddie LeBaron (1952)	12.00	6.00	3.50
16	Paul Lipscomb	0.00	4.00	2.50
17	Laurie Niemi	8.00	4.00	2.50
18	John Papit (1952)	10.00	5.00	3.00
19	James Peebles (1951)	10.00	5.00	3.00
20	Ed Quirk	8.00	4.00	2.50
21	Jim Ricca (1952)	10.00	5.00	3.00
22	James Staton (1951)	10.00	5.00	3.00
23	Hugh Taylor	10.00	5.00	3.00
24	Joe Tereshinski	8.00	4.00	2.50
25	Dick Todd (CO) (1952)	10.00	5.00	3.00

1958-59 Redskins Matchbooks

Measuring 1-1/2" x 4-1/2" when folded out, the 20 matchbooks went with a totally different design than in years past. This set features a cutout of a player headshot printed below the Redskins' logo and "Famous Redskins." The years he played with the Redskins are listed to the left of the headshot. The back of the cover has an ad for First Federal Savings. The inside includes the player's name and bio, along with an ad for First Federal Savings. The matchbooks, which are unnumbered, are printed on gray cardboard.

		NM	E	VG
Complete Set (20):		195.00	92.50	58.50
Common Player:		8.00	4.00	2.50
1	Steve Bagarus (58)	8.00	4.00	2.50
2	Cliff Battles (58)	15.00	7.50	4.50
3	Sammy Baugh (58)	40.00	20.00	12.00
4	Gene Brito (58)	10.00	5.00	3.00
5	Jim Castiglia (58)	8.00	4.00	2.50
6	Al DeMao (58)	8.00	4.00	2.50
7	Chuck Drazenovich (59)	10.00	5.00	3.00
8	Bill Dudley (59)	18.00	9.00	5.50
9	Al Fiorentino (59)	8.00	4.00	2.50
10	Don Irwin (59)	8.00	4.00	2.50
11	Eddie LeBaron (58)	10.00	5.00	3.00
12	Wayne Millner (58)	12.00	6.00	3.50
13	Wilbur Moore (58)	10.00	5.00	3.00
14	Jim Schrader (59)	8.00	4.00	2.50
15	Riley Smith (59)	8.00	4.00	2.50
16	Mike Sommer (59)	8.00	4.00	2.50
17	Joe Tereshinski (58)	8.00	4.00	2.50
18	Dick Todd (59)	10.00	5.00	3.00
19	Willie Wilkin (59)	8.00	4.00	2.50
20	Casimir Witucki	8.00	4.00	2.50

1960 Redskins Jay Publishing

Measuring 5" x 7", the 12-card set is anchored by a black-and-white posed photo on the front. The cards are unnumbered and blank-backed. Originally, the cards were sold for 25 cents in 12-photo packs.

		NM	E	VG
Complete Set (12):		50.00	25.00	15.00
Common Player:		5.00	2.50	1.50
1	Sam Baker	6.00	3.00	1.75
2	Don Bosseler	6.00	3.00	1.75
3	Gene Brito	5.00	2.50	1.50
4	Johnny Carson	5.00	2.50	1.50
5	Chuck Drazenovich	5.00	2.50	1.50
6	Ralph Guglielmi	6.00	3.00	1.75
7	Dick James	6.00	3.00	1.75
8	Eddie LeBaron	7.50	3.75	2.25
9	Jim Podoley	5.00	2.50	1.50
10	Jim Schrader	5.00	2.50	1.50
11	Ed Sutton	5.00	2.50	1.50
12	Albert Zagers	5.00	2.50	1.50

1960-61 Redskins Matchbooks

Measuring 1-1/2" x 4-1/2" when folded out, the 20 matchbooks are very similar in design to the 1958-59 set except this 1960-61 set is printed on off-white cardboard. The front has a headshot of the player, along with the Redskins' logo and "Famous Redskins." The player's bio is printed on the back, along with "This is one of twenty famous Redskins presented for you by your 1st Federal Savings and Loan Association of Washington, Bethesda Branch." The matchbooks are not numbered.

		NM	E	VG
Complete Set (20):		175.00	87.00	52.00
Common Player:		8.00	4.00	2.50
1	Bill Anderson (61)	10.00	5.00	3.00
2	Don Bosseler (60)	10.00	5.00	3.00
3	Glen Edwards (60)	15.00	7.50	4.50
4	Ralph Guglielmi (61)	10.00	5.00	3.00
5	Bill Hartman (60)	8.00	4.00	2.50
6	Norbert Hecker (61)	8.00	4.00	2.50
7	Dick James (61)	10.00	5.00	3.00

8	Charlie Justice (60)	15.00	7.50	4.50
9	Ray Krause (61)	8.00	4.00	2.50
10	Ray Lemek (61)	8.00	4.00	2.50
11	Tommy Mont (60)	8.00	4.00	2.50
12	John Olszewski (61)	10.00	5.00	3.00
13	John Paluck (60)	8.00	4.00	2.50
14	Jim Peebles (60)	8.00	4.00	2.50
15	Bo Russell (60)	8.00	4.00	2.50
16	Jim Schrader (61)	8.00	4.00	2.50
17	Louis Stephens (61)	8.00	4.00	2.50
18	Ed Sutton (60)	8.00	4.00	2.50
19	Bob Toneff (60)	10.00	5.00	3.00
20	Lavern Torgeson (60)	10.00	5.00	3.00

1969 Redskins High's Dairy

Measuring 8" x 10", the eight-card set includes Alex Fournier artwork on the front. The player's facsimile signature is printed near the bottom of the artwork. On the left side of the unnumbered card backs is the player's name, bio and stats, while on the right side is data on Fournier. The portraits were available two ways - they could be purchased at High's Dairy Stores or consumers could purchase two half gallons of milk and recieve a free portrait.

		NM	E	VG
Complete Set (8):		100.00	50.00	30.00
Common Player:		6.00	3.00	1.75
1	Chris Hanburger	10.00	5.00	3.00
2	Len Hauss	8.00	4.00	2.50
3	Sam Huff	15.00	7.50	4.50
4	Sonny Jurgensen	25.00	12.50	7.50
5	Carl Kammerer	6.00	3.00	1.75
6	Brig Owens	6.00	3.00	1.75
7	Pat Richter	8.00	4.00	2.50
8	Charley Taylor	20.00	10.00	6.00

1972 Redskins Caricature

Dick Shuman and Compu-Set, Inc. produced this 15-card set. The 8" x 10" cards feature a caricature of a Washington Redskin player. The cards are unnumbered and blank-backed.

		NM	E	VG
Complete Set (16):		130.00	65.00	40.00
Common Player:		8.00	4.00	2.50
1	Mike Bass	10.00	5.00	3.00
2	Verlon Biggs	8.00	4.00	2.50
3	Mike Bragg	8.00	4.00	2.50
4	Speedy Duncan	10.00	5.00	3.00
5	Pat Fischer	10.00	5.00	3.00
6	Chris Hanburger	10.00	5.00	3.00
7	Curt Knight	8.00	4.00	2.50
8	Ron McDole	8.00	4.00	2.50
9	Brig Owens	8.00	4.00	2.50
10	Jack Pardee	10.00	5.00	3.00
11	Richie Petibon	10.00	5.00	3.00
12	Myron Pottios	8.00	4.00	2.50
13	Manny Sistrunk	8.00	4.00	2.50
14	Diron Talbert	8.00	4.00	2.50
15	Ted Vactor	8.00	4.00	2.50
16	Cover Card (Jack Pardee, Mike Bass, Manny Sistrunk, Chris Hanburger)	10.00	5.00	3.00

1981 Redskins Frito-Lay Schedules

Measuring 3-1/2" x 7-1/2", the 30 schedules are anchored by a color photo on the inside. Included on the collectibles are the 1981 Redskins' schedule, player photo and his name and bio, along with sponsor logos. The schedules are unnumbered.

		NM/M	NM	E
Complete Set (30):		30.00	22.00	12.00
Common Player:		.50	.40	.20
1	Coy Bacon	.75	.60	.30
2	Perry Brooks	.50	.40	.20
3	Dave Butz	.75	.60	.30
4	Rickey Claitt	.50	.40	.20
5	Monte Coleman	.75	.60	.30
6	Mike Connell	.50	.40	.20
7	Brad Dusek	.75	.60	.30
8	Ike Forte	.50	.40	.20
9	Clarence Harmon	.50	.40	.20
10	Terry Hermeling	.50	.40	.20
11	Wilbur Jackson	.50	.40	.20
12	Mike Kruczek	.50	.40	.20
13	Bob Kuziel	.50	.40	.20
14	Joe Lavender	.75	.60	.30
15	Karl Lorch	.50	.40	.20
16	LeCharls McDaniel	.50	.40	.20
17	Rich Milot	.50	.40	.20
18	Art Monk	3.00	2.25	1.25

19	Mark Moseley	1.00	.70	.40
20	Mark Murphy	.75	.60	.30
21	Mike Nelms	.50	.40	.20
22	Neal Olkewicz	.50	.40	.20
23	Lemar Parrish	.75	.60	.30
24	Tony Peters	.50	.40	.20
25	Ron Saul	.50	.40	.20
26	George Starke	.50	.40	.20
27	Joe Theismann	2.00	1.50	.80
28	Ricky Thompson	.50	.40	.20
29	Don Warren	.75	.60	.30
30	Jeris White	.50	.40	.20

1982 Redskins Frito-Lay Schedules

Measuring 3-1/2" x 7-1/2", the 15 schedule set boasts a color photo of the player on the inside, with "Redskins '82 Schedule" printed on another panel. The player's name and bio are also included on the schedules.

		NM/M	NM	E
Complete Set (15):		15.00	11.00	6.00
Common Player:		.50	.40	.20
1	Dave Butz	.75	.60	.30
2	Monte Coleman	.75	.60	.30
3	Brad Dusek	.50	.40	.20
4	Joe Lavender	.75	.60	.30
5	Art Monk	2.00	1.50	.80
6	Mark Moseley	1.00	.70	.40
7	Mark Murphy	.75	.60	.30
8	Mike Nelms	.50	.40	.20
9	Neal Olkewicz	.50	.40	.20
10	Tony Peters	.50	.40	.20
11	John Riggins	3.00	2.25	1.25
12	George Starke	.50	.40	.20
13	Joe Theismann	2.00	1.50	.80
14	Don Warren	.75	.60	.30
15	Joe Washington	1.00	.70	.40

1982 Redskins Police

Measuring 2-5/8" x 4-1/8", the 15-card set includes a photo of the player on the front, with the Redskins' helmet on the lower left. On the bottom right are the player's number, name, position and team. The backs have a boxed-in "Redskins/PACT Tips." The Frito-Lay and PACT logos appear at the bottom corners. The cards are numbered.

		NM/M	NM	E
Complete Set (15):		10.00	7.50	4.00
Common Player:		.50	.40	.20
1	Dave Butz	.75	.60	.30
2	Art Monk	2.50	2.00	1.00
3	Mark Murphy	.50	.40	.20
4	Monte Coleman	.75	.60	.30
5	Mark Moseley	.75	.60	.30
6	George Starke	.50	.40	.20
7	Perry Brooks	.50	.40	.20
8	Joe Washington	.75	.60	.30
9	Don Warren	.75	.60	.30
10	Joe Lavender	.50	.40	.20
11	Joe Theismann	2.00	1.50	.80
12	Tony Peters	.50	.40	.20
13	Neal Olkewicz	.50	.40	.20
14	Mike Nelms	.50	.40	.20
15	John Riggins	2.00	1.50	.80

1983 Redskins Frito-Lay Schedules

Measuring 2-1/2" x 3-1/2", the 15-schedule set showcases an action photo, along with the player's name and bio. The schedules are unnumbered.

		NM/M	NM	E
Complete Set (15):		15.00	11.00	6.00
Common Player:		.50	.40	.20
1	Charlie Brown	.75	.60	.30
2	Dave Butz	.75	.60	.30
3	The Hogs	.75	.60	.30
4	Dexter Manley	.75	.60	.30
5	Rich Milot	.50	.40	.20
6	Art Monk	1.50	1.25	.60
7	Mark Moseley	.75	.60	.30
8	Mark Murphy	.50	.40	.20
9	Mike Nelms	.50	.40	.20
10	Neal Olkewicz	.50	.40	.20
11	Tony Peters	.50	.40	.20
12	John Riggins	2.00	1.50	.80
13	Joe Theismann	2.00	1.50	.80
14	Joe Washington	.75	.60	.30
15	Jeris White	.50	.40	.20

1983 Redskins Police

#81 • Art Monk
Wide Receiver
Washington Redskins

Measuring 2-5/8" x 4-1/8", the 16-card set was handed out one per week by police officers. The card fronts are anchored by a large photo, with the player's number, position, name and bio beneath it. The Redskins' helmet is in the lower left corner, with "Washington Redskins, Super Bowl XVII Champions" printed at the bottom right. The backs, numbered "of 16," have a boxed-in "Redskins PACT Tips" and the player's bio and highlights. The Frito-Lay and PACT logos are printed in the lower left and right corners, respectively. Jeris White's card is tough to locate, as his card was never handed out because he held out during the season.

		NM/M	NM	E
Complete Set (16):		10.00	7.50	4.00
Common Player:		.50	.40	.20
1	Joe Washington	1.00	.70	.40
2	The Hogs (Offensive Line)	.75	.60	.30
3	Mark Moseley	1.00	.70	.40
4	Monte Coleman	.50	.40	.20
5	Mike Nelms	.50	.40	.20
6	Neal Olkewicz	.50	.40	.20
7	Joe Theismann	3.00	2.25	1.25
8	Charlie Brown	.75	.60	.30
9	Dave Butz	.75	.60	.30
10	Jeris White (SP)	1.50	1.25	.60
11	Mark Murphy	.50	.40	.20
12	Dexter Manley	.75	.60	.30
13	Art Monk	3.00	2.25	1.25
14	Rich Milot	.50	.40	.20
15	Vernon Dean	.50	.40	.20
16	John Riggins	2.00	1.50	.80

1984 Redskins Frito-Lay Schedules

Measuring 3-1/2" x 7-1/2", the 15 schedules boast a color photo of the player, along with his name and bio. The schedules are unnumbered.

		NM/M	NM	E
Complete Set (15):		15.00	11.00	6.00
Common Player:		.50	.40	.20
1	Charlie Brown	.75	.60	.30
2	Dave Butz	.75	.60	.30
3	Ken Coffey	.50	.40	.20
4	Clint Didier	.50	.40	.20
5	Darryl Grant	.50	.40	.20
6	Darrell Green	1.00	.70	.40
7	Jeff Hayes	.50	.40	.20
8	The Hogs	.75	.60	.30
9	Rich Milot	.50	.40	.20
10	Art Monk	1.50	1.25	.60
11	Mark Murphy	.50	.40	.20
12	John Riggins	1.50	1.25	.60
13	Joe Theismann	1.50	1.25	.60
14	Don Warren	.75	.60	.30
15	Joe Washington	.75	.60	.30

1984 Redskins Police

Measuring 2-5/8" x 4-1/8", the 16-card set showcases a color photo on the front, with the player's name, number and position printed beneath the photo. The player's facsimile signature and "NFC Champion Redskins" is printed in the lower right. The Redskins' helmet is located in the lower left. The card backs, numbered "of 16," have the "Redskins/PACT Tip" at the top, while the player's name, bio and highlights are printed below. The Frito-Lay and PACT logos are printed in the lower left and right, respectively.

		NM/M	NM	E
Complete Set (16):		8.00	6.00	3.25
Common Player:		.35	.25	.14
1	John Riggins	1.25	.90	.50
2	Darryl Grant	.35	.25	.14
3	Art Monk	1.50	1.25	.60
4	Neal Olkewicz	.35	.25	.14
5	The Hogs	.50	.40	.20
6	Jeff Hayes	.35	.25	.14

7	Joe Theismann	1.25	.90	.50
8	Clint Didier	.35	.25	.14
9	Mark Murphy	.35	.25	.14
10	Don Warren	.50	.40	.20
11	Darrell Green	1.00	.70	.40
12	Dave Butz	.50	.40	.20
13	Ken Coffey	.35	.25	.14
14	Rich Milot	.35	.25	.14
15	Charlie Brown	.50	.40	.20
16	Joe Washington	.50	.40	.20

1985 Redskins Frito-Lay Schedules

Measuring 3-1/2" x 7-1/2", the 16 schedules showcase a photo of a legendary Washington Redskins' player. The schedules are unnumbered.

		NM/M	NM	E
Complete Set (16):		15.00	11.00	6.00
Common Player:		.50	.40	.20
1	Cliff Battles	.75	.60	.30
2	Sammy Baugh	1.50	1.25	.60
3	Larry Brown	.75	.60	.30
4	Bill Dudley	.75	.60	.30
5	Turk Edwards	.75	.60	.30
6	Pat Fischer	.50	.40	.20
7	Chris Hanburger	.50	.40	.20
8	Len Hauss	.50	.40	.20
9	Ken Houston	.75	.60	.30
10	Sam Huff	1.00	.70	.40
11	Sonny Jurgenson	1.00	.70	.40
12	Billy Kilmer	.50	.40	.20
13	Wayne Millner	.50	.40	.20
14	Bobby Mitchell	.75	.60	.30
15	Brig Owens	.50	.40	.20
16	Charley Taylor	1.00	.70	.40

1985 Redskins Police

Measuring 2-5/8" x 4-1/8", the 16-card set has the Washington Redskins' logo at the top of the card front, with the player photo in the center. Beneath the player's number, position and name. The backs, numbered "of 16," have "Redskins/PACT Tips" at the top. Printed in the center of the back are the player's name, number, position, bio and career highlights. The Frito-Lay and PACT logos are located in the lower left and right, respectively.

		NM/M	NM	E
Complete Set (16):		5.00	3.75	2.00
Common Player:		.35	.25	.14
1	Darrell Green	.75	.60	.30
2	Clint Didier	.35	.25	.14
3	Neal Olkewicz	.35	.25	.14
4	Darryl Grant	.35	.25	.14
5	Joe Jacoby	.50	.40	.20
6	Vernon Dean	.35	.25	.14
7	Joe Theismann	1.00	.70	.40
8	Mel Kaufman	.35	.25	.14
9	Calvin Muhammad	.35	.25	.14
10	Dexter Manley	.50	.40	.20
11	John Riggins	1.00	.70	.40
12	Mark May	.50	.40	.20
13	Dave Butz	.35	.25	.14
14	Art Monk	1.25	.90	.50
15	Russ Grimm	.50	.40	.20
16	Charles Mann	.50	.40	.20

1986 Redskins Frito-Lay Schedules

These 16 schedules feature the Redskins' 50th Anniversary logo on the front and Frito-Lay's logos on the back. When opened, the left panel contains the preseason and postseason schedules, the center panel has a player photo and the right panel features the regular season schedule. The other panel has basic player information. The schedules are unnumbered.

		NM/M	NM	E
Complete Set (16):		20.00	15.00	8.00
Common Player:		1.00	.70	.40
1	Cliff Battles	1.50	1.25	.60
2	Sammy Baugh	2.00	1.50	.80
3	Larry Brown	1.00	.70	.40
4	Bill Dudley	1.50	1.25	.60
5	Turk Edwards	1.00	.70	.40
6	Pat Fischer	1.00	.70	.40
7	Chris Hanburger	1.00	.70	.40
8	Len Hauss	1.00	.70	.40
9	Sam Huff	2.00	1.50	.80
10	Ken Houston	1.50	1.25	.60
11	Sonny Jurgensen	2.00	1.50	.80
12	Billy Kilmer	1.50	1.25	.60
13	Wayne Millner	1.50	1.25	.60
14	Bobby Mitchell	2.00	1.50	.80
15	Brig Owens	1.00	.70	.40
16	Charley Taylor	2.00	1.50	.80

1986 Redskins Police

Measuring 2-5/8" x 4-1/8", the 16-card set has a Washington Redskins' pennant in the upper left corner of the front. Inside the pennant is a facsimile signature of the player. His number, name and position is printed to the right of the pennant. The photo fills up the bottom portion of the card front. The backs, numbered "of 16," have the player's name inside a pennant at the top, with his number, position, bio and career highlights printed beneath it. Quick quiz and crime prevention tips are also included on the back. The Frito-Lay, PACT and WMAL radio logos are printed at the bottom.

		NM/M	NM	E
Complete Set (16):		5.00	3.75	2.00
Common Player:		.35	.25	.14
1	Darrell Green	.75	.60	.30
2	Joe Jacoby	.50	.40	.20
3	Charles Mann	.50	.40	.20
4	Jay Schroeder	.50	.40	.20
5	Raphel Cherry	.35	.25	.14
6	Russ Grimm	.50	.40	.20
7	Mel Kaufman	.35	.25	.14
8	Gary Clark	1.25	.90	.50
9	Vernon Dean	.35	.25	.14
10	Mark May	.50	.40	.20
11	Dave Butz	.50	.40	.20
12	Jeff Bostic	.50	.40	.20
13	Dean Hamel	.35	.25	.14
14	Dexter Manley	.50	.40	.20
15	George Rogers	.50	.40	.20
16	Art Monk	1.00	.70	.40

1987 Redskins Frito-Lay Schedules

Measuring 3-1/2" x 7-1/2", the 16 schedule set includes an action photo of the player. The schedules are unnumbered.

		NM/M	NM	E
Complete Set (16):		15.00	11.00	6.00
Common Player:		.50	.40	.20
1	Jeff Bostic	.75	.60	.30
2	Kelvin Bryant	.75	.60	.30
3	Dave Butz	.75	.60	.30
4	Gary Clark	1.00	.70	.40
5	Steve Cox	.50	.40	.20
6	Clint Didier	.50	.40	.20
7	Darryl Grant	.50	.40	.20
8	Darrell Green	.75	.60	.30
9	Joe Jacoby	.75	.60	.30
10	Dexter Manley	.75	.60	.30
11	Charles Mann	.75	.60	.30
12	Mark May	.75	.60	.30
13	Art Monk	1.00	.70	.40
14	Jay Schroeder	.75	.60	.30
15	Alvin Walton	.50	.40	.20
16	Don Warren	.75	.60	.30

1987 Redskins Police

Measuring 2-5/8" x 4-1/8", the 16-card set has the Washington Redskins' logo at the top, with the player photo anchoring the middle. The player's name is printed at the bottom of the card front. The backs, numbered "Week X of 16," have the player's number inside a football in the upper left. The player's name, position, bio and career highlights are also listed on the back. "Did you know?" and a tip from McGruff the Crime Dog round out the back, along with Frito-Lay and PACT logos at the bottom right.

		NM/M	NM	E
Complete Set (16):		5.00	3.75	2.00
Common Player:		.30	.25	.12
1	Joe Jacoby	.40	.30	.15
2	Gary Clark	.75	.60	.30
3	Dexter Manley	.40	.30	.15
4	Darrell Green	.40	.30	.15
5	Alvin Walton	.30	.25	.12
6	Clint Didier	.30	.25	.12
7	Art Monk	1.00	.70	.40
8	Darryl Grant	.30	.25	.12
9	Kelvin Bryant	.40	.30	.15
10	Jay Schroeder	.40	.30	.15
11	Don Warren	.40	.30	.15
12	Steve Cox	.30	.25	.12
13	Mark May	.40	.30	.15
14	Jeff Bostic	.40	.30	.15
15	Charles Mann	.40	.30	.15
16	Dave Butz	.40	.30	.15

1988 Redskins Frito-Lay Schedules

Measuring 3-1/2" x 7-1/2", the 16 schedules boast an action photo of a player, with his name and bio. A photo of the Super Bowl trophy is showcased on these schedules, which are unnumbered.

		NM/M	NM	E
Complete Set (16):		15.00	11.00	6.00
Common Player:		.50	.40	.20

1	Jeff Bostic	.75	.60	.30
2	Dave Butz	.75	.60	.30
3	Gary Clark	1.00	.70	.40
4	Brian Davis	.50	.40	.20
5	Joe Jacoby	.75	.60	.30
6	Markus Koch	.50	.40	.20
7	Charles Mann	.75	.60	.30
8	Wilbur Marshall	.75	.60	.30
9	Mark May	.75	.60	.30
10	Raleigh McKenzie	.50	.40	.20
11	Art Monk	1.00	.70	.40
12	Ricky Sanders	.75	.60	.30
13	Alvin Walton	.50	.40	.20
14	Don Warren	.75	.60	.30
15	Barry Wilburn	.50	.40	.20
16	Doug Williams	1.00	.70	.40

1988 Redskins Police

Measuring 2-5/8" x 4-1/8", the 16-card set has the Washington Redskins' logo (with the Vince Lombardi Super Bowl Trophy printed where the "i" in Redskins would appear) located in the upper left. The player's number and name are printed in the upper right. A color photo covers the remaining portion of the card front. The backs, numbered with a "Week X," have the player's name and number at the top, followed by his bio, career highlights and a safety tip. The logos printed at the bottom from left to right are Mobil, PACT and Jello.

		NM/M	NM	E
Complete Set (16):		5.00	3.75	2.00
Common Player:		.30	.25	.12
1	Jeff Bostic	.40	.30	.15
2	Dave Butz	.40	.30	.15
3	Gary Clark	.75	.60	.30
4	Brian Davis	.30	.25	.12
5	Joe Jacoby	.40	.30	.15
6	Markus Koch	.30	.25	.12
7	Charles Mann	.40	.30	.15
8	Wilbur Marshall	.40	.30	.15
9	Mark May	.40	.30	.15
10	Raleigh McKenzie	.30	.25	.12
11	Art Monk	1.00	.70	.40
12	Ricky Sanders	.75	.60	.30
13	Alvin Walton	.30	.25	.12
14	Don Warren	.40	.30	.15
15	Barry Wilburn	.30	.25	.12
16	Doug Williams	.75	.60	.30

1989 Redskins Mobil Schedules

Measuring 3-1/2" x 7-1/2", the 16 schedules showcase a color player photo, along with the 1989 schedule. These schedules are unnumbered.

		NM/M	NM	E
Complete Set (16):		10.00	7.50	4.00
Common Player:		.40	.30	.15
1	Ravin Caldwell	.40	.30	.15
2	Gary Clark	1.00	.70	.40
3	Monte Coleman	.60	.45	.25
4	Brian Davis	.40	.30	.15
5	Joe Jacoby	.60	.45	.25
6	Jim Lachey	.60	.45	.25
7	Chip Lohmiller	.60	.45	.25
8	Charles Mann	.60	.45	.25
9	Wilbur Marshall	.60	.45	.25
10	Mark May	.60	.45	.25
11	Raleigh McKenzie	.40	.30	.15
12	Art Monk	1.00	.70	.40
13	Mark Rypien	.60	.45	.25
14	Ricky Sanders	.60	.45	.25
15	Don Warren	.60	.45	.25
16	Doug Williams	.75	.60	.30

1989 Redskins Police

Measuring 2-5/8" x 4-1/8", the 16-card set has "Washington" in a stripe at the top of the card front, with "Redskins" printed beneath it. The player photo has the player's name and number inside a stripe near the bottom. The unnum-

---

bered card backs have the player's number and name at the top, along with his bio, career highlights, safety tip and "Did you know?" The Mobil, PACT and Fox-TV 5 logos are printed at the bottom of the card backs.

		NM/M	NM	E
Complete Set (16):		5.00	3.75	2.00
Common Player:		.30	.25	.12
11	Mark Rypien	.60	.45	.25
17	Doug Williams	.60	.45	.25
21	Earnest Byner	.40	.30	.15
22	Jamie Morris	.30	.25	.12
28	Darrell Green	.40	.30	.15
34	Brian Davis	.30	.25	.12
37	Gerald Riggs	.40	.30	.15
50	Ravin Caldwell	.30	.25	.12
52	Neal Olkewicz	.30	.25	.12
58	Wilber Marshall	.40	.30	.15
73	Mark May	.40	.30	.15
74	Markus Koch	.30	.25	.12
81	Art Monk	1.00	.70	.40
83	Ricky Sanders	.60	.45	.25
84	Gary Clark	.75	.60	.30
85	Don Warren	.40	.30	.15

1990 Redskins Mobil Schedules

Measuring 3-1/2" x 7-1/2", the 16 pocket schedules boast a color action photo of the player. The schedules are unnumbered.

		NM/M	NM	E
Complete Set (16):		10.00	7.50	4.00
Common Player:		.40	.30	.15
1	Jeff Bostic	.60	.45	.25
2	Earnest Byner	.60	.45	.25
3	Gary Clark	.75	.60	.30
4	Darryl Grant	.40	.30	.15
5	Darrell Green	.60	.45	.25
6	Jim Lachey	.60	.45	.25
7	Chip Lohmiller	.60	.45	.25
8	Charles Mann	.60	.45	.25
9	Wilbur Marshall	.60	.45	.25
10	Ralf Mojsiejenko	.40	.30	.15
11	Art Monk	1.00	.70	.40
12	Gerald Riggs	.60	.45	.25
13	Mark Rypien	.60	.45	.25
14	Ricky Sanders	.60	.45	.25
15	Alvin Walton	.40	.30	.15
16	Don Warren	.60	.45	.25

1990 Redskins Police

Measuring 3-1/2" x 7-1/2", the 16-card set includes a Washington Redskins' logo at the top, with the player's name and number at the bottom of the card front. The unnumbered card backs have the player's name, number, bio, career highlights, safety tip and "Did you know?" Printed at the bottom of the card backs are the Mobil, PACT and Fox-TV 5 logos.

		NM/M	NM	E
Complete Set (16):		5.00	3.75	2.00
Common Player:		.25	.20	.10
1	Todd Bowles	.25	.20	.10
2	Earnest Byner	.35	.25	.14
3	Ravin Caldwell	.25	.20	.10
4	Gary Clark	.60	.45	.25
5	Darrell Green	.35	.25	.14
6	Jimmie Johnson	.25	.20	.10
7	Jim Lachey	.35	.25	.14
8	Chip Lohmiller	.35	.25	.14
9	Charles Mann	.35	.25	.14
10	Greg Manusky	.25	.20	.10
11	Wilber Marshall	.35	.25	.14
12	Art Monk	.75	.60	.30
13	Gerald Riggs	.35	.25	.14
14	Mark Rypien	.35	.25	.14
15	Alvin Walton	.25	.20	.10
16	Don Warren	.35	.25	.14

1991 Redskins Mobil Schedules

Measuring 2-1/2" x 3-1/2", the 16 pocket schedules boast a photo of the player on the front. The player's name and bio also are printed on the unnumbered schedule.

		NM/M	NM	E
Complete Set (16):		10.00	7.50	4.00
Common Player:		.40	.30	.15
1	Earnest Byner	.60	.45	.25
2	Gary Clark	.75	.60	.30
3	Andre Collins	.60	.45	.25
4	Kurt Gouveia	.40	.30	.15
5	Darrell Green	.60	.45	.25
6	Jimmie Johnson	.40	.30	.15
7	Markus Koch	.40	.30	.15
8	Jim Lachey	.60	.45	.25
9	Chip Lohmiller	.40	.30	.15
10	Charles Mann	.60	.45	.25
11	Martin Mayhew	.40	.30	.15
12	Art Monk	1.00	.70	.40

13	Mark Rypien	.60	.45	.25
14	Mark Schlereth	.40	.30	.15
15	Ed Simmons	.40	.30	.15
16	Eric Williams	.40	.30	.15

1991 Redskins Police

Measuring 2-5/8" x 4-1/8", the 16-card set has "Washington" printed inside a gold stripe at the top, while "Redskins" is printed vertically along the left side. The player photo is to the right of "Redskins." The player's number is printed inside a circle at the bottom, with his name inside a black stripe at the bottom. The backs have the player's name, number, bio, career highlights, safety tip and "Did you know?" The logos printed on the bottom, from left to right, are Mobil, PACT and Fox-TV 5. The cards are unnumbered.

		NM/M	NM	E
Complete Set (16):		5.00	3.75	2.00
Common Player:		.25	.20	.10
1	John Brandes	.25	.20	.10
2	Earnest Byner	.35	.25	.14
3	Gary Clark	.60	.45	.25
4	Andre Collins	.35	.25	.14
5	Darrell Green	.35	.25	.14
6	Joey Howard	.25	.20	.10
7	Tim Johnson	.25	.20	.10
8	Jim Lachey	.35	.25	.14
9	Chip Lohmiller	.25	.20	.10
10	Charles Mann	.35	.25	.14
11	Art Monk	.75	.60	.30
12	Mark Rypien	.35	.25	.14
13	Mark Schlereth	.25	.20	.10
14	Fred Stokes	.25	.20	.10
15	Don Warren	.35	.25	.14
16	Eric Williams	.25	.20	.10

1990 Rice Aetna

		NM/M	NM	E
Complete Set (12):		12.00	9.00	4.75
Common Player:		1.00	.70	.40
1	O.J. Brigance	1.50	1.25	.60
2	Trevor Cobb	2.50	2.00	1.00
3	Tim Fitzpatrick	1.00	.70	.40
4	Fred Goldsmith (CO)	2.00	1.50	.80
5	David Griffin	1.00	.70	.40
6	Eric Henley	1.50	1.25	.60
7	Donald Hollas	2.50	2.00	1.00
8	Richard Segina	1.00	.70	.40
9	Matt Sign	1.00	.70	.40
10	Bill Stone	1.00	.70	.40
11	Trey Teichelman (UER) (Misspelled Tichelman on front and back)	1.00	.70	.40
12	Alonzo Williams	1.00	.70	.40

1991 Rice Aetna

		NM/M	NM	E
Complete Set (12):		12.00	9.00	4.75
Common Player:		1.00	.70	.40
1	Mike Appelbaum	1.00	.70	.40
2	Louis Balady	1.00	.70	.40
3	Nathan Bennett	1.00	.70	.40
4	Trevor Cobb	2.00	1.50	.80
5	Herschel Crowe	1.00	.70	.40
6	David Griffin	1.00	.70	.40
7	Eric Henley	1.50	1.25	.60
8	Matt Sign	1.00	.70	.40
9	Larry Stuppy	1.00	.70	.40
10	Trey Teichelman	1.00	.70	.40
11	Alonzo Williams	1.00	.70	.40
12	Greg Willig	1.00	.70	.40

1971 Royal Bank B.C. Lions

		NM	E	VG
Complete Set (16):		50.00	25.00	15.00
Common Player:		2.50	1.25	.70
1	George Anderson	2.50	1.25	.70
2	Paul Brothers	2.50	1.25	.70
3	Brian Donnelly	2.50	1.25	.70
4	Dave Easley	2.50	1.25	.70
5	Trevor Ekdahl	3.50	1.75	1.00
6	Jim Evenson	3.50	1.75	1.00
7	Greg Findlay	2.50	1.25	.70
8	Lefty Hendrickson	2.50	1.25	.70
9	Bob Howes	2.50	1.25	.70
10	Garrett Hunsperger	2.50	1.25	.70
11	Wayne Matherne	2.50	1.25	.70
12	Don Moorhead	2.50	1.25	.70
13	Ken Phillips	2.50	1.25	.70
14	Ken Sugarman	3.50	1.75	1.00
15	Tom Wilkinson	10.00	5.00	3.00
16	Jim Young	10.00	5.00	3.00

1972 Royal Bank B.C. Lions

		NM	E	VG
	Complete Set (16):	50.00	25.00	15.00
	Common Player:	2.50	1.25	.70
1	George Anderson	2.50	1.25	.70
2	Brian Donnelly	2.50	1.25	.70
3	Dave Easley	2.50	1.25	.70
4	Trevor Ekdahl	3.50	1.75	1.00
5	Ron Estay	2.50	1.25	.70
6	Jim Evenson	3.50	1.75	1.00
7	Dave Golinsky	2.50	1.25	.70
8	Larry Highbaugh	3.50	1.75	1.00
9	Garrett Hunsperger	2.50	1.25	.70
10	Don Moorhead	2.50	1.25	.70
11	Johnny Musso	7.50	3.75	2.25
12	Ray Nettles	2.50	1.25	.70
13	Willie Postler	2.50	1.25	.70
14	Carl Weathers	15.00	7.50	4.50
15	Jim Young	7.50	3.75	2.25
16	Coaching Staff(Bud Tynes, Ken McCullough, Owen Dejanovich, Eagle Keys)	2.50	1.25	.70

1973 Royal Bank B.C. Lions

		NM	E	VG
	Complete Set (16):	50.00	25.00	15.00
	Common Player:	2.50	1.25	.70
1	Barry Ardern	2.50	1.25	.70
2	Monroe Eley	3.50	1.75	1.00
3	Bob Friend	2.50	1.25	.70
4	Eric Guthrie	2.50	1.25	.70
5	Garrett Hunsperger	2.50	1.25	.70
6	Wayne Matherne	2.50	1.25	.70
7A	Don Moorhead (Black border)	2.50	1.25	.70
7B	Don Moorhead (Silver border)	2.50	1.25	.70
8	Johnny Musso	7.50	3.75	2.25
9	Ray Nettles	2.50	1.25	.70
10	Pete Palmer	2.50	1.25	.70
11	Gary Robinson (SP)	20.00	10.00	6.00
12	Al Wilson	2.50	1.25	.70
13	Mike Wilson	2.50	1.25	.70
14	Jim Young	7.50	3.75	2.25
15	Coaches(Bud Tynes, Ken McCullough, Owen Dejanovich, Eagle Keys)	2.50	1.25	.70

1974 Royal Bank B.C. Lions

		NM	E	VG
	Complete Set (14):	40.00	20.00	12.00
	Common Player:	2.50	1.25	.70
1	Bill Baker	6.00	3.00	1.75
2	Karl Douglas	2.50	1.25	.70
3	Layne McDowell	2.50	1.25	.70
4	Ivan MacMillan	2.50	1.25	.70
5	Bud Magrum	2.50	1.25	.70
6	Don Moorhead	2.50	1.25	.70
7	Johnny Musso	7.50	3.75	2.25
8	Ray Nettles	2.50	1.25	.70
9	Brian Sopatyk	2.50	1.25	.70
10	Curtis Wester	3.50	1.75	1.00
11	Slade Willis	2.50	1.25	.70
12	Al Wilson	2.50	1.25	.70
13	Jim Young	7.50	3.75	2.25
14	**Coaching Staff**	3.50	1.75	1.00

1975 Royal Bank B.C. Lions

		NM	E	VG
	Complete Set (14):	40.00	20.00	12.00
	Common Player:	2.50	1.25	.70
1	Brock Ansley	2.50	1.25	.70
2	Terry Bailey	2.50	1.25	.70
3	Bill Baker	6.00	3.00	1.75
4	Elton Brown	2.50	1.25	.70
5	Grady Cavness	3.50	1.75	1.00
6	Ross Clarkson	2.50	1.25	.70
7	Joe Fourqurean	2.50	1.25	.70
8	Lou Harris	3.50	1.75	1.00
9	Layne McDowell	2.50	1.25	.70
10	Don Moorhead	2.50	1.25	.70
11	Tony Moro	2.50	1.25	.70
12	Ray Nettles	2.50	1.25	.70
13	Curtis Wester	3.50	1.75	1.00
14	Jim Young	7.50	3.75	2.25

1976 Royal Bank B.C. Lions

		NM	E	VG
	Complete Set (15):	40.00	20.00	12.00
	Common Player:	2.50	1.25	.70
1	Terry Bailey	2.50	1.25	.70
2	Bill Baker	6.00	3.00	1.75
3	Ted Dushinski	2.50	1.25	.70
4	Eric Guthrie	2.50	1.25	.70
5	Lou Harris	3.50	1.75	1.00
6	Glen Jackson	2.50	1.25	.70
7	Rocky Long	2.50	1.25	.70
8	Layne McDowell	2.50	1.25	.70
9	Ray Nettles	2.50	1.25	.70
10	Gary Robinson	2.50	1.25	.70
11	John Sciarra	6.00	3.00	1.75
12	Wayne Smith	2.50	1.25	.70
13	Michael Strickland	2.50	1.25	.70
14	Al Wilson	2.50	1.25	.70
15	Jim Young	7.50	3.75	2.25

1977 Royal Bank B.C. Lions

		NM	E	VG
	Complete Set (12):	40.00	20.00	12.00
	Common Player:	2.50	1.25	.70
1	Doug Carlson	2.50	1.25	.70
2	Sam Cvijanovich	2.50	1.25	.70
3	Ted Dushinski	2.50	1.25	.70
4	Paul Giroday	2.50	1.25	.70
5	Glen Jackson	2.50	1.25	.70
6	Frank Landy	2.50	1.25	.70
7	Lui Passaglia	7.50	3.75	2.25
8	John Sciarra	6.00	3.00	1.75
9	Michael Strickland	2.50	1.25	.70
10	Jerry Tagge	7.50	3.75	2.25
11	Al Wilson	2.50	1.25	.70
12	Jim Young	7.50	3.75	2.25

1978 Royal Bank B.C. Lions

		NM	E	VG
	Complete Set (12):	40.00	20.00	12.00
	Common Player:	2.50	1.25	.70
1	Terry Bailey	2.50	1.25	.70
2	Leon Bright	5.00	2.50	1.50
3	Doug Carlson	2.50	1.25	.70
4	Grady Cavness	3.50	1.75	1.00
5	Al Charuk	2.50	1.25	.70
6	Paul Giroday	2.50	1.25	.70
7	Larry Key	2.50	1.25	.70
8	Frank Landy	2.50	1.25	.70
9	Lui Passaglia	7.50	3.75	2.25
10	Jerry Tagge	7.50	3.75	2.25
11	Al Wilson	2.50	1.25	.70
12	Jim Young	7.50	3.75	2.25

1987 Royal Studios Saskatchewan Roughriders

		NM/M	NM	E
	Complete Set (40):	35.00	26.00	14.00
	Common Player:	.75	.60	.30
1	Dave Albright	.75	.60	.30
2	Roger Aldag	1.00	.70	.40
3	Mike Anderson	.75	.60	.30
4	Tron Armstrong	.75	.60	.30
5	Terry Baker	1.00	.70	.40
6	Walter Bender	1.25	.90	.50
7	Jeff Bentrim	1.25	.90	.50
8	Todd Brown	.75	.60	.30
9	Tom Burgess	3.00	2.25	1.25
10	Coaching Staff(John Hufnagel, Dick Adams, John Gregory, Ted Heath, Gary Hoffman, M. Samples)	1.00	.70	.40
11	Terry Cochrane	.75	.60	.30
12	David Conrad	.75	.60	.30
13	Steve Crane	.75	.60	.30
14	James Curry	2.00	1.50	.80
15	Tony Dennis	.75	.60	.30
16	Ray Elgaard	3.00	2.25	1.25
17	Denny Ferdinand	1.00	.70	.40
18	Roderick Fisher	.75	.60	.30
19	Joe Fuller	.75	.60	.30
20	**Gainer The Gopher** (Team Mascot)	.75	.60	.30
21	Norris Gibbs	.75	.60	.30
22	Nick Hebeler	.75	.60	.30
23	Bryan Illerbrun	1.00	.70	.40
24	Alan Johns	.75	.60	.30
25	Bobby Jurasin	3.00	2.25	1.25
26	Eddie Lowe	1.00	.70	.40
27	Tracey Mack	.75	.60	.30
28	Tim McCray	1.50	1.25	.60
29	Mike McGruder	1.00	.70	.40
30	Ken Moore	.75	.60	.30
31	Dan Rashovich	.75	.60	.30
32	Scott Redl	.75	.60	.30
33	Dave Ridgway	1.25	.90	.50
34	Dave Sidoo	.75	.60	.30
35	Harry Skipper	1.00	.70	.40
36	Lawrie Skolrood	.75	.60	.30
37	Vic Stevenson	.75	.60	.30
38	Glen Suitor	1.00	.70	.40
39	Brendan Taman Asst. EQ MG, Ivan Gutfriend Athletic Therapist, Norm Fong EQ MG	.75	.60	.30
40	Mark Urness	.75	.60	.30

1988 Royal Studios Saskatchewan Roughriders

		NM/M	NM	E
	Complete Set (54):	40.00	30.00	16.00
	Common Player:	.50	.40	.20
1	Dave Albright	.50	.40	.20
2	Roger Aldag (DP)	.75	.60	.30
3	Mike Anderson	.50	.40	.20
4	Kent Austin (DP)	4.00	3.00	1.50
5	Terry Baker	.75	.60	.30
6	Jeff Bentrim	.75	.60	.30
7	Rob Bresciani	.50	.40	.20
8	Albert Brown	.50	.40	.20
9	Tom Burgess (DP)	2.50	2.00	1.00
10	Coaching Staff(Gary Hoffman, Dick Adams, Dan Daniel, Ted Heath, John Gregory, Steve Goldman)	.75	.60	.30
11	**Dick Cohee and The Store** (and The Store)	.50	.40	.20
12	David Conrad	.50	.40	.20
13	Steve Crane	.50	.40	.20
14	James Curry (DP)	1.25	.90	.50
15	**Dream Team** (Cheerleaders)	1.25	.90	.50
16	Ray Elgaard	2.50	2.00	1.00
17	James Ellingson	.50	.40	.20
18	Jeff Fairholm	1.25	.90	.50
19	Denny Ferdinand	.75	.60	.30
20	**The Flame** (Team Mascot)	.50	.40	.20
21	Norm Fong, Ivan Gutfriend (Equipment/Trainer)	.50	.40	.20
22	Joe Fuller	.50	.40	.20
23	**Gainer The Gopher** (Team Mascot)	.50	.40	.20
24	Vince Goldsmith	1.00	.70	.40
25	John Gregory (CO)	.75	.60	.30
26	Richie Hall	.50	.40	.20
27	Bill Henry	.50	.40	.20
28	James Hood	.50	.40	.20
29	Bryan Illerbrun (UER) (Name misspelled Brian on front and back)	.75	.60	.30
30	Milson Jones	1.25	.90	.50
31	Bobby Jurasin (DP)	2.50	2.00	1.00
32	Tim Kearse	.50	.40	.20
33	Rick Klassen	.75	.60	.30
34	Gary Lewis	.75	.60	.30
35	Eddie Lowe	.75	.60	.30
36	Greg McCormack	.50	.40	.20
37	Tim McCray	1.00	.70	.40
38	Ray McDonald	.75	.60	.30
39	Mike McGruder	.75	.60	.30
40	Ken Moore	.50	.40	.20
41	Donald Narcisse	2.00	1.50	.80
42	Dan Rambo, Brendan Taman (Rider Scouting)	.50	.40	.20
43	Dan Rashovich	.75	.60	.30
44	Dameon Reilly	.75	.60	.30
45	Dave Ridgway (DP)	1.00	.70	.40
46	Rocco Romano	.50	.40	.20
47	Harry Skipper	.75	.60	.30
48	Vic Stevenson	.50	.40	.20
49	Glen Suitor	.75	.60	.30
50	Jeff Treftlin	.50	.40	.20
51	Mark Urness	.50	.40	.20
52	Eddie Ray Walker	.50	.40	.20
53	John Walker	.75	.60	.30
54	Jeff Watson	.50	.40	.20

1989 Royal Studios Saskatchewan Roughriders

		NM/M	NM	E
	Complete Set (54):	35.00	26.00	14.00
	Common Player:	.50	.40	.20
1	Dave Albright	.50	.40	.20
2	Roger Aldag (DP)	.75	.60	.30
3	Tuineau Alipate	.75	.60	.30
4	Mike Anderson	.50	.40	.20
5	Kent Austin	3.00	2.25	1.25
6	Terry Baker	.75	.60	.30
7	Jeff Bentrim	.75	.60	.30
8	Rob Bresciani	.50	.40	.20
9	Albert Brown	.50	.40	.20
10	Tom Burgess (DP)	2.50	2.00	1.00
11	**Coaching Staff**	.75	.60	.30

12	Steve Crane	.50	.40	.20
13	James Curry	1.25	.90	.50
14	Kevin Dixon	.50	.40	.20
15	**Dream Team**			
	(Cheerleaders			
	sponsored by CKRM)	1.00	.70	.40
16	Wayne Drinkwalter	.75	.60	.30
17	Ray Elgaard	2.00	1.50	.80
18	James Ellingson	.50	.40	.20
19	Jeff Fairholm	.75	.60	.30
20	**The Flame**	.50	.40	.20
21	Norm Fong, Ivan			
	Gutfriend (Equipment/			
	Trainer)	.50	.40	.20
22	**Gainer The Gopher** (DP)			
	(Team Mascot)	.50	.40	.20
23	John Gregory (CO)	.75	.60	.30
24	Vince Goldsmith	.75	.60	.30
25	Mark Guy	.50	.40	.20
26	Richie Hall (DP)	.50	.40	.20
27	John Hoffman	.50	.40	.20
28	Bryan Illerbrun (UER)			
	(Name misspelled			
	Brian on front and			
	back)	.75	.60	.30
29	Milson Jones	.75	.60	.30
30	Bobby Jurasin (DP)	2.00	1.50	.80
31	Chuck Klingbeil	.75	.60	.30
32	Gary Lewis	.75	.60	.30
33	Eddie Lowe	.75	.60	.30
34	Greg McCormack	.50	.40	.20
35	Tim McCray	1.00	.70	.40
36	Ray McDonald	.50	.40	.20
37	Ken Moore	.50	.40	.20
38	Cedric Moses	.50	.40	.20
39	Donald Narcisse	1.50	1.25	.60
40	Dan Payne	.50	.40	.20
41	Bob Poley	.50	.40	.20
42	Dan Rashovich	.50	.40	.20
43	Dave Ridgway (DP)	1.00	.70	.40
44	Junior Robinson	.75	.60	.30
45	Harry Skipper	.75	.60	.30
46	Vic Stevenson	.50	.40	.20
47	Glen Suitor	1.00	.70	.40
48	Jeff Treftlin	.50	.40	.20
49	Kelly Trithart	.50	.40	.20
50	Mark Urness	.50	.40	.20
51	Lionel Vital	.50	.40	.20
52	Eddie Ray Walker	.75	.60	.30
53	Steve Wiggins	.50	.40	.20
54	Donovan Wright	.50	.40	.20

1990 Royal Studios Saskatchewan Roughriders

		NM/M	NM	E
Complete Set (60):		35.00	26.00	14.00
Common Player:		.50	.40	.20
1	Dick Adams (CO)	.50	.40	.20
2	Dave Albright	.50	.40	.20
3	Roger Aldag	.75	.60	.30
4	Tuineau Alipate	.75	.60	.30
5	Mike Anderson	.50	.40	.20
6	Kent Austin	3.00	2.25	1.25
7	Tony Belser	.50	.40	.20
8	Jeff Bentrim	.75	.60	.30
9	Bruce Boyko	.75	.60	.30
10	Albert Brown	.75	.60	.30
11	Paul Bushey	.50	.40	.20
12	Larry Donovan (CO)	.50	.40	.20
13	**Dream Team**			
	(Cheerleaders			
	sponsored by CKRM)	.75	.60	.30
14	Wayne Drinkwalter	.75	.60	.30
15	Sean Dykes	.50	.40	.20
16	Ray Elgaard	2.00	1.50	.80
17	Jeff Fairholm	1.00	.70	.40
18	Norman Fong MG, Ivan			
	Gutfriend MG	.50	.40	.20
19	Alan Ford (GM)	.50	.40	.20
20	Lucius Floyd	.75	.60	.30
21	**Gainer The Gopher** (Team			
	Mascot)	.50	.40	.20
22	Chris Gioskos	.50	.40	.20
23	Vince Goldsmith	1.00	.70	.40
24	John Gregory (CO)	.75	.60	.30
25	Mark Guy	.75	.60	.30
26	Stacey Hairston	.75	.60	.30
27	Richie Hall	.75	.60	.30
28	Greg Harris	.50	.40	.20
29	Ted Heath (CO)	.50	.40	.20
30	Gary Hoffman (CO)	.50	.40	.20
31	John Hoffman	.50	.40	.20
32	Larry Hogue	.75	.60	.30
33	Bobby Jurasin	2.00	1.50	.80
34	Milson Jones	1.00	.70	.40
35	James King	.50	.40	.20
36	Chuck Klingbeil	1.00	.70	.40
37	Mike Lazecki	.50	.40	.20

38	Orville Lee	1.50	1.25	.60
39	Gary Lewis	.75	.60	.30
40	Eddie Lowe	.75	.60	.30
41	Greg McCormack	.50	.40	.20
42	Tim McCray	1.00	.70	.40
43	Ken Moore	.50	.40	.20
44	Donald Narcisse	1.50	1.25	.60
45	Dave Pitcher	.50	.40	.20
46	Bob Poley	.50	.40	.20
47	Brent Pollack	.50	.40	.20
48	Dan Rashovich	.50	.40	.20
49	Tony Rice	1.50	1.25	.60
50	Dave Ridgway	1.00	.70	.40
51	Pal Sartori	.50	.40	.20
52	**Saskatchewan**			
	Roughriders	1.00	.70	.40
53	Glen Scrivner	.50	.40	.20
54	Tony Simmons	.50	.40	.20
55	Vic Stevenson	.50	.40	.20
56	Glen Suitor	1.00	.70	.40
57	Jeff Treftlin	.75	.60	.30
58	Kelly Trithart (UER)			
	(Name misspelled			
	Trihart on front and			
	back)	.75	.60	.30
59	Lionel Vital	.50	.40	.20
60	Slater Zaleski	.50	.40	.20

1991 Royal Studios Saskatchewan Roughriders

		NM/M	NM	E
Complete Set (66):		35.00	26.00	14.00
Common Player:		.40	.30	.15
1	Dick Adams (CO)	.40	.30	.15
2	Dave Albright	.40	.30	.15
3	Roger Aldag	.60	.45	.25
4	Mike Anderson	.40	.30	.15
5	Kent Austin	3.00	2.25	1.25
6	John Bankhead	.60	.45	.25
7	1990 Miss Grey			
	Cup(Kerry Beutler)	.60	.45	.25
8	Allan Boyko	.60	.45	.25
9	Bruce Boyko	.60	.45	.25
10	Doug Brewster	.40	.30	.15
11	Albert Brown	.60	.45	.25
12	Paul Bushey	.40	.30	.15
13	**Coaching Staff**	.40	.30	.15
14	Larry Donovan (CO)	.40	.30	.15
15	Wayne Drinkwalter	.60	.45	.25
16	Sean Dykes	.40	.30	.15
17	Ray Elgaard	2.00	1.50	.80
18	Jeff Fairholm	1.00	.70	.40
19	Dan Farthing	.40	.30	.15
20	Lucius Ford	.60	.45	.25
21	**Gainer The Gopher** (Team			
	Mascot)	.40	.30	.15
22	Chris Gioskos (UER)			
	(Name misspelled			
	Gioskas on front)	.60	.45	.25
23	Sonny Gordon	.40	.30	.15
24	John Gregory (CO)	.60	.45	.25
25	Stacey Hairston	.60	.45	.25
26	Richie Hall	.60	.45	.25
27	Greg Harris	.40	.30	.15
28	Major Harris	1.50	1.25	.60
29	Ted Heath (CO)	.40	.30	.15
30	Gary Hoffman (CO)	.40	.30	.15
31	John Hoffman	.40	.30	.15
32	Larry Hogue	.60	.45	.25
33	Willis Jacox	1.50	1.25	.60
34	Ray Jauch (CO)	.60	.45	.25
35	Gene Jelks	1.50	1.25	.60
36	Milson Jones	1.00	.70	.40
37	Bobby Jurasin	2.00	1.50	.80
38	James King	.40	.30	.15
39	Mike Lazecki	.40	.30	.15
40	Orville Lee	1.50	1.25	.60
41	Gary Lewis	.60	.45	.25
42	Eddie Lowe	.60	.30	.25
43	Paul Maines	.40	.30	.15
44	Don Matthews (CO)	.40	.30	.15
45	Dane McArthur	.40	.30	.15
46	David McCrary	.40	.30	.15
47	Don Narcisse	1.50	1.25	.60
48	**Offensive Line**	.40	.30	.15
49	David Pitcher	.60	.45	.25
50	Bob Poley	.40	.30	.15
51	Brent Pollack	.40	.30	.15
52	Basil Proctor	.40	.30	.15
53	Dan Rashovich	.40	.30	.15
54	Dave Ridgway (UER)			
	(Name misspelled			
	Ridgeway on back)	1.00	.70	.40
55	**Roughriders vs The**			
	Rocket	1.00	.70	.40
56	**Roughriders Team**	.60	.45	.25
57	Glen Scrivner	.40	.30	.15
58	Keith Stephens	.40	.30	.15

59	Vic Stevenson	.40	.30	.15
60	Glen Suitor	1.00	.70	.40
61	Chris Thieneman	.40	.30	.15
62	Jeff Treftlin	.60	.45	.25
63	Kelly Trithart	.60	.45	.25
64	Paul Vaida	.40	.30	.15
65	Ted Wahl	.40	.30	.15
66	Rick Worman	1.00	.70	.40

S

1976 Saga Discs

Cards from this set parallel the 1976 Crane Disk singles. Instead of having the Crane logo on the back they have the Saga logo. Cards from this set are much tougher to find than the Crane singles.

		NM/M	NM	E
Complete Set (30):		1,000	750.00	400.00
Common Player:		12.00	9.00	4.75
1	Ken Anderson	30.00	9.00	4.75
2	Otis Armstrong	12.00	9.00	4.75
3	Steve Barkowski	15.00	9.00	4.75
4	Terry Bradshaw	250.00	9.00	4.75
5	John Brockington	12.00	9.00	4.75
6	Doug Buffone	12.00	9.00	4.75
7	Wally Chambers	12.00	9.00	4.75
8	Isaac Curtis	12.00	9.00	4.75
9	Chuck Foreman	15.00	9.00	4.75
10	Roman Gabriel	15.00	9.00	4.75
11	Mel Gray	12.00	9.00	4.75
12	Joe Greene	125.00	9.00	4.75
13	James Harris	12.00	9.00	4.75
14	Jim Hart	15.00	9.00	4.75
15	Billy Kilmer	15.00	9.00	4.75
16	Greg Landry	12.00	9.00	4.75
17	Ed Marinaro	12.00	9.00	4.75
18	Lawrence McCutcheon	12.00	9.00	4.75
19	Terry Metcalf	12.00	9.00	4.75
20	Lydell Mitchell	12.00	9.00	4.75
21	Jim Otis	12.00	9.00	4.75
22	Alan Page	30.00	9.00	4.75
23	Walter Payton	350.00	9.00	4.75
24	Greg Pruitt	15.00	9.00	4.75
25	Charlie Sanders	12.00	9.00	4.75
26	Ron Shanklin	12.00	9.00	4.75
27	Roger Staubach	275.00	9.00	4.75
28	Jan Stenerud	15.00	9.00	4.75
29	Charley Taylor	50.00	9.00	4.75
30	Roger Wehrli	12.00	9.00	4.75

1968-69 Saints 8x10

Measuring 8" x 10", the 35 black-and-white photo cards feature members of the 1968-69 Saints teams. The backs are unnumbered and blank.

		NM	E	VG
Complete Set (35):		120.00	60.00	36.00
Common Player:		3.00	1.50	.90
1	Dan Abramowicz	6.00	3.00	1.75
2	Doug Atkins	7.50	3.75	2.25
3	Tom Barrington	4.00	2.00	1.25
4	Jim Boeke	3.00	1.50	.90
5	Johnny Brewer	4.00	2.00	1.25
6	Bo Burris	3.00	1.50	.90
7	Bill Cody	3.00	1.50	.90
8	Ted Davis	3.00	1.50	.90
9	John Douglas	3.00	1.50	.90
10	Charles Durkee	3.00	1.50	.90
11	John Gilliam	4.00	2.00	1.25
12	Jim Hester	3.00	1.50	.90
13	Gene Howard	3.00	1.50	.90
14	Les Kelley	3.00	1.50	.90
15	Jake Kupp	4.00	2.00	1.25
16	Earl Leggett	3.00	1.50	.90
17	Archie Manning	20.00	10.00	6.00
18	Don McCall	3.00	1.50	.90
19	Tom McNeill	3.00	1.50	.90
20	Richard Neal	3.00	1.50	.90
21	Dave Parks	4.00	2.00	1.25
22	Dave Parks (with small			
	inset photo)	4.00	2.00	1.25
23	Ray Poage	3.00	1.50	.90
24	David Rowe	3.00	1.50	.90
25	Roy Schmidt	3.00	1.50	.90
26	Randy Schultz	3.00	1.50	.90
27	Brian Schweda	3.00	1.50	.90

28	Monty Stickles	3.00	1.50	.90
29	Steve Stonebreaker	4.00	2.00	1.25
30	Jerry Sturm	3.00	1.50	.90
31	Mike Tilleman	3.00	1.50	.90
32	Joe Wendryhoski	3.00	1.50	.90
33	Ernie Wheelwright	4.00	2.00	1.25
34	Fred Whittingham	3.00	1.50	.90
35	Del Williams	3.00	1.50	.90

1974 Saints Circle Inset

Measuring 8" x 10", the 22 photos showcase a black-and-white action photo on the front, with a player headshot pictured inside a circle inset. Printed at the bottom of the card are the player's name, position and team name. The backs are unnumbered and blank.

		NM	E	VG
	Complete Set (22):	120.00	60.00	36.00
	Common Player:	5.00	2.50	1.50
1	John Beasley	5.00	2.50	1.50
2	Tom Blanchard	6.00	3.00	1.75
3	Larry Cipa	5.00	2.50	1.50
4	Don Coleman	5.00	2.50	1.50
5	Wayne Colman	5.00	2.50	1.50
6	Jack DeGrenier	5.00	2.50	1.50
7	Rick Kingrea	5.00	2.50	1.50
8	Phil LaPorta	5.00	2.50	1.50
9	Odell Lawson	5.00	2.50	1.50
10	Archie Manning	20.00	10.00	6.00
11	Alvin Maxson	6.00	3.00	1.75
12	Bill McClard	5.00	2.50	1.50
13	Bill McNeill	5.00	2.50	1.50
14	Jim Merlo	6.00	3.00	1.75
15	Rick Middleton	5.00	2.50	1.50
16	Derland Moore	5.00	2.50	1.50
17	Jerry Moore	5.00	2.50	1.50
18	Joel Parker	5.00	2.50	1.50
19	Jess Phillips	5.00	2.50	1.50
20	Terry Schmidt	5.00	2.50	1.50
21	Paul Seal	5.00	2.50	1.50
22	Dave Thompson	5.00	2.50	1.50

1979 Saints Coke

The 45 cards are anchored by a black-and-white player headshot, with the Coca-Cola logo in an oval in the upper right. The Saints logo is in the lower left and the player's name is printed in the lower right. The fronts of the cards are bordered in red. The card backs have the card number inside a helmet in the upper left, while the player's name is to the right of the helmet. His position is printed inside a banner. Beneath the banner is the player's bio. The Coca-Cola logo is located at the bottom center.

		NM	E	VG
	Complete Set (45):	60.00	30.00	18.00
	Common Player:	1.00	.50	.30
1	Archie Manning	8.00	4.00	2.50
2	Ed Burns	1.00	.50	.30
3	Bobby Scott	1.50	.70	.45
4	Russell Erxleben	1.50	.70	.45
5	Eric Felton	1.00	.50	.30
6	David Gray	1.00	.50	.30
7	Ricky Ray	1.00	.50	.30
8	Clarence Chapman	1.00	.50	.30
9	Kim Jones	1.00	.50	.30
10	Mike Strachan	1.00	.50	.30
11	Tony Galbreath	2.00	1.00	.60
12	Tom Myers	1.50	.70	.45
13	Chuck Muncie	3.00	1.50	.90
14	Jack Holmes	1.00	.50	.30
15	Don Schwartz	1.00	.50	.30
16	Ralph McGill	1.00	.50	.30
17	Ken Bordelon	1.00	.50	.30
18	Jim Kovach	1.00	.50	.30
19	Pat Hughes	1.00	.50	.30
20	Reggie Mathis	1.00	.50	.30
21	Jim Merlo	1.00	.50	.30
22	Joe Federspiel	1.00	.50	.30
23	Don Reese	1.00	.50	.30
24	Roger Finnie	1.00	.50	.30
25	John Hill	1.00	.50	.30
26	Barry Bennett	1.00	.50	.30
27	Dave Lafary	1.00	.50	.30
28	Robert Woods	1.00	.50	.30
29	Conrad Dobler	1.50	.70	.45
30	John Watson	1.00	.50	.30
31	Fred Sturt	1.00	.50	.30
32	J.T. Taylor	1.00	.50	.30
33	Mike Fultz	1.00	.50	.30
34	Joe Campbell	1.00	.50	.30
35	Derland Moore	1.00	.50	.30
36	Elex Price	1.00	.50	.30
37	Elois Grooms	1.00	.50	.30
38	Emanuel Zanders	1.00	.50	.30
39	Ike Harris	1.00	.50	.30
40	Tinker Owens	1.50	.70	.45
41	Rich Mauti	1.00	.50	.30
42	Henry Childs	1.50	.70	.45
43	Larry Hardy	1.00	.50	.30
44	Brooks Williams	1.00	.50	.30
45	Wes Chandler	3.50	1.75	1.00
---	**Cover Card**	3.00	1.50	.90

1962 Salada Coins

These coins, featuring 154 pro football players, are color- color-coded according to the team the player plays for; each team has a specific rim color. The fronts feature a color head-and-shoulders shot of the player without his helmet on. The backs are numbered and contain advertising for Salada Tea and Junket brand desserts. Brief biographical information, including the collegiate school the player attended, is also given. Each coin measures 1-1/2" diameter. The set can sometimes be found as a complete set in its own custom box. Double- and triple-printed coins are indicated by (DP) and (TP) and are easier to find than the others.

		NM	E	VG
	Complete Set (154):	3,000	1,500	900.00
	Common Player DP:	7.50	5.50	3.00
	Common Player SP:	25.00	12.50	7.50
1	Johnny Unitas	175.00	87.00	52.00
2	Lenny Moore	85.00	42.00	25.00
3	Jim Parker	50.00	25.00	15.00
4	Gino Marchetti	60.00	30.00	18.00
5	Dick Szymanski	25.00	12.50	7.50
6	Alex Sandusky	25.00	12.50	7.50
7	Raymond Berry	90.00	45.00	27.00
8	Jimmy Orr	30.00	15.00	9.00
9	Ordell Braase	25.00	12.50	7.50
10	Bill Pellington	25.00	12.50	7.50
11	Bob Boyd	25.00	12.50	7.50
12	Paul Hornung (DP)	25.00	12.50	7.50
13	Jim Taylor (DP)	20.00	10.00	6.00
14	Henry Jordan (DP)	8.00	4.00	2.50
15	Dan Currie (DP)	8.00	4.00	2.50
16	Bill Forester (DP)	8.00	4.00	2.50
17	Dave Hanner (DP)	8.00	4.00	2.50
18	Bart Starr (DP)	30.00	15.00	9.00
19	Max McGee (DP)	7.50	3.75	2.25
20	Jerry Kramer (DP)	9.00	4.50	2.75
21	Forrest Gregg (DP)	15.00	7.50	4.50
22	Jim Ringo (DP)	15.00	7.50	4.50
23	Billy Kilmer	55.00	27.00	16.50
24	Charlie Krueger	25.00	12.50	7.50
25	Bob St. Clair	50.00	25.00	15.00
26	Abe Woodson	25.00	12.50	7.50
27	Jimmy Johnson	65.00	32.00	19.50
28	Matt Hazeltine	25.00	12.50	7.50
29	Bruce Bosley	25.00	12.50	7.50
30	Dan Conners	25.00	12.50	7.50
31	John Brodie	80.00	40.00	24.00
32	J.D. Smith	25.00	12.50	7.50
33	Monty Stickles	25.00	12.50	7.50
34	Johnny Morris (DP)	9.00	4.50	2.75
35	Stan Jones (DP)	15.00	7.50	4.50
36	J.C. Caroline (DP)	8.00	4.00	2.50
37	Richie Petitbon (DP)	9.00	4.50	2.75
38	Joe Fortunato (DP)	9.00	4.50	2.75
39	Larry Morris (DP)	6.00	3.00	1.75
40	Doug Atkins (DP)	12.00	6.00	3.50
41	Billy Wade (DP)	7.50	3.75	2.25
42	Rick Casares (DP)	9.00	4.50	2.75
43	Willie Galimore (DP)	9.00	4.50	2.75
44	Angelo Coia (DP)	8.00	4.00	2.50
45	Ollie Matson	65.00	32.00	19.50
46	Carroll Dale	30.00	15.00	9.00
47	Ed Meador	30.00	15.00	9.00
48	Jon Arnett	35.00	17.50	10.50
49	Joe Marconi	25.00	12.50	7.50
50	John LoVetere	25.00	12.50	7.50
51	Red Phillips	25.00	12.50	7.50
52	Zeke Bratkowski	35.00	17.50	10.50
53	Dick Bass	30.00	15.00	9.00
54	Les Richter	30.00	15.00	9.00
55	Art Hunter (DP)	8.00	4.00	2.50
56	Jim Brown (TP)	65.00	32.00	19.50
57	Mike McCormack (DP)	12.00	6.00	3.50
58	Bob Gain (DP)	8.00	4.00	2.50
59	Paul Wiggin (DP)	7.50	3.75	2.25
60	Jim Houston (DP)	7.50	3.75	2.25
61	Ray Renfro (DP)	7.50	3.75	2.25
62	Galen Fiss (DP)	8.00	4.00	2.50
63	J.R. Smith (DP)	8.00	4.00	2.50
64	John Morrow (DP)	8.00	4.00	2.50
65	Gene Hickerson (DP)	8.00	4.00	2.50
66	Jim Ninowski (DP)	7.50	3.75	2.25
67	Tom Tracy	30.00	15.00	9.00
68	Buddy Dial	30.00	15.00	9.00
69	Mike Sandusky	30.00	15.00	9.00
70	Lou Michaels	30.00	15.00	9.00
71	Preston Carpenter	25.00	12.50	7.50
72	John Reger	25.00	12.50	7.50
73	John Henry Johnson	65.00	32.00	19.50
74	Gene Lipscomb	40.00	20.00	12.00
75	Mike Henry	30.00	15.00	9.00
76	George Tarasovic	25.00	12.50	7.50
77	Bobby Layne	70.00	35.00	21.00
78	Harley Sewell (DP)	8.00	4.00	2.50
79	Darris McCord (DP)	8.00	4.00	2.50
80	Yale Lary (DP)	12.00	6.00	3.50
81	Jim Gibbons (DP)	8.00	4.00	2.50
82	Gail Codgill (DP)	8.00	4.00	2.50
83	Nick Pietrosante (DP)	9.00	4.50	2.75
84	Alex Karras (DP)	15.00	7.50	4.50
85	Dick "Night Train" Lane (DP)	12.00	6.00	3.50
86	Joe Schmidt (DP)	15.00	7.50	4.50
87	John Gordy (DP)	8.00	4.00	2.50
88	Milt Plum (DP)	7.50	3.75	2.25
89	Andy Stynchula	25.00	12.50	7.50
90	Bob Toneff	25.00	12.50	7.50
91	Bill Anderson	30.00	15.00	9.00
92	Sam Horner	25.00	12.50	7.50
93	Norm Snead	30.00	15.00	9.00
94	Bobby Mitchell	65.00	32.00	19.50
95	Billy Barnes	25.00	12.50	7.50
96	Rod Breedlove	25.00	12.50	7.50
97	Fred Hageman	25.00	12.50	7.50
98	Vince Promuto	25.00	12.50	7.50
99	Joe Rutgens	25.00	12.50	7.50
100	Maxie Baughan (DP)	9.00	4.50	2.75
101	Pete Retzlaff (DP)	7.50	3.75	2.25
102	Tom Brookshier (DP)	9.00	4.50	2.75
103	Sonny Jurgensen (DP)	25.00	12.50	7.50
104	Ed Khayat (DP)	6.00	3.00	1.75
105	Chuck Bednarik (DP)	15.00	7.50	4.50
106	Tommy McDonald (DP)	9.00	4.50	2.75
107	Bobby Walston (DP)	8.00	4.00	2.50
108	Ted Dean (DP)	8.00	4.00	2.50
109	Clarence Peaks (DP)	8.00	4.00	2.50
110	Jimmy Carr (DP)	8.00	4.00	2.50
111	Sam Huff (DP)	15.00	7.50	4.50
112	Erich Barnes (DP)	7.50	3.75	2.25
113	Del Shofner (DP)	9.00	4.50	2.75
114	Bob Gaiters (DP)	8.00	4.00	2.50
115	Alex Webster (DP)	9.00	4.50	2.75
116	Dick Modzelewski (DP)	7.50	3.75	2.25
117	Jim Katcavage (DP)	7.50	3.75	2.25
118	Roosevelt Brown (DP)	15.00	7.50	4.50
119	Y.A. Tittle (DP)	25.00	12.50	7.50
120	Andy Robustelli (DP)	12.00	6.00	3.50
121	Dick Lynch (DP)	7.50	3.75	2.25
122	Don Webb (DP)	8.00	4.00	2.50
123	Larry Eisenhauer (DP)	8.00	4.00	2.50
124	Babe Parilli (DP)	7.50	3.75	2.25
125	Charles Long (DP)	8.00	4.00	2.50
126	Billy Lott (DP)	8.00	4.00	2.50
127	Harry Jacobs (DP)	8.00	4.00	2.50
128	Bob Dee (DP)	8.00	4.00	2.50
129	Ron Burton (DP)	7.50	3.75	2.25
130	Jim Colclough (TP)	3.00	1.50	.90
131	Gino Cappelletti (DP)	9.00	4.50	2.75
132	Tommy Addison (DP)	8.00	4.00	2.50
133	Larry Grantham (DP)	7.50	3.75	2.25
134	Dick Christy (DP)	8.00	4.00	2.50
135	Bill Mathis (DP)	7.50	3.75	2.25
136	Butch Songin (DP)	8.00	4.00	2.50
137	Dainard Paulson (DP)	8.00	4.00	2.50
138	Roger Ellis (DP)	8.00	4.00	2.50
139	Mike Hudock (DP)	8.00	4.00	2.50
140	Don Maynard (DP)	20.00	10.00	6.00
141	Al Dorow (DP)	7.50	3.75	2.25
142	Jack Klotz (DP)	8.00	4.00	2.50
143	Lee Riley (DP)	8.00	4.00	2.50
144	Bill Atkins (DP)	8.00	4.00	2.50
145	Art Baker (DP)	8.00	4.00	2.50
146	Stew Barber (DP)	8.00	4.00	2.50
147	Glen Bass (DP)	8.00	4.00	2.50
148	Al Bemiller (DP)	8.00	4.00	2.50
149	Richie Lucas (DP)	7.50	3.75	2.25
150	Archie Matsos (DP)	8.00	4.00	2.50
151	Warren Rabb (DP)	8.00	4.00	2.50
152	Ken Rice (DP)	8.00	4.00	2.50
153	Billy Shaw (DP)	7.50	3.75	2.25
154	Laverne Torczon (DP)	8.00	4.00	2.50

1959 San Giorgio Flipbooks

Measuring 5-3/4" x 3-9/16", the 17 flipbooks showcase movement of a player on 14 different photos. When the photos are separated and sorted, the photos go into motion when they are flipped. Players from the Washington Redskins, Philadelphia Eagles and Pittsburgh Steelers are pictured in the set. Many collectors prefer the flipbooks to be intact and uncut.

		NM	E	VG
	Complete Set (17):	2,500	1,250	750.00
	Common Player:	150.00	75.00	45.00
1	Sam Baker	175.00	87.00	52.00

2	Bill Barnes	150.00	75.00	45.00
3	Chuck Bednarik	300.00	150.00	90.00
4	Don Bosseler	150.00	75.00	45.00
5	Darrell Drewster	150.00	75.00	45.00
6	Jack Butler	150.00	75.00	45.00
7	Proverb Jacobs	150.00	75.00	45.00
8	Eddie LeBaron	200.00	100.00	60.00
9	Tommy McDonald	175.00	87.00	52.00
10	Ed Meadows	150.00	75.00	45.00
11	Gern Nagler	150.00	75.00	45.00
12	Clarence Peaks	150.00	75.00	45.00
13	Pete Retzlaff	175.00	87.00	52.00
14	Mike Sommer	150.00	75.00	45.00
15	Tom Tracy	175.00	87.00	52.00
16	Bobby Walston	150.00	75.00	45.00
17	Chuck Weber	150.00	75.00	45.00

1990 San Jose State Smokey

		NM/M	NM	E
	Complete Set (15):	10.00	7.50	4.00
	Common Player:	.75	.60	.30
1	Bob Bleisch (90)	.75	.60	.30
2	Sheldon Canley (20)	.75	.60	.30
3	Paul Franklin (37)	.75	.60	.30
4	Anthony Gallegos (72)	.75	.60	.30
5	Steve Hieber (48)	.75	.60	.30
6	Everett Lampkins (43)	.75	.60	.30
7	Kelly Liebengood (21)	.75	.60	.30
8	Ralph Martini (9)	.75	.60	.30
9	Lyneil Mayo (62)	.75	.60	.30
10	Mike Powers (57)	.75	.60	.30
11	Mike Scialabba (46)	.75	.60	.30
12	Terry Shea (CO)	.75	.60	.30
13	Freddie Smith (4)	.75	.60	.30
14	Eddie Thomas (26)	.75	.60	.30
15	Brian Woods (64)	.75	.60	.30

1971 Sargent Promotions Stamps

		NM	E	VG
	Complete Set (225):	240.00	120.00	72.50
	Common Player:	.75	.40	.25
1	Jim Young	7.50	3.75	2.25
2	Trevor Ekdahl	1.25	.60	.40
3	Ted Gerela	1.25	.60	.40
4	Jim Evenson	1.25	.60	.40
5	Ray Lychak	.75	.40	.25
6	Dave Golinsky	.75	.40	.25
7	Ted Warkentin	.75	.40	.25
8	A.D. Whitfield	1.25	.60	.40
9	Lach Heron	1.25	.60	.40
10	Ken Phillips	.75	.40	.25
11	Lefty Hendrickson	.75	.40	.25
12	Paul Brothers	.75	.40	.25
13	Eagle Keys (CO)	1.50	.70	.45
14	Garrett Hunsperger	.75	.40	.25
15	Greg Findlay	.75	.40	.25
16	Dave Easley	.75	.40	.25
17	Barrie Hansen	.75	.40	.25
18	Wayne Dennis	.75	.40	.25
19	Jerry Bradley	.75	.40	.25
20	Gerry Herron	.75	.40	.25
21	Gary Robinson	.75	.40	.25
22	Bill Whisler	.75	.40	.25
23	Bob Howes	.75	.40	.25
24	Tom Wilkinson	6.00	3.00	1.75
25	Tom Cassese	.75	.40	.25
26	Dick Suderman	1.25	.60	.40
27	Jerry Keeling	4.00	2.00	1.25
28	John Helton	4.00	2.00	1.25
29	Jim Furlong	.75	.40	.25
30	Fred James	.75	.40	.25
31	Howard Starks	.75	.40	.25
32	Craig Koinzan	.75	.40	.25
33	Frank Andruski	.75	.40	.25
34	Joe Forzani	1.25	.60	.40
35	Herb Schumn	.75	.40	.25
36	Gerry Shaw	.75	.40	.25
37	Lanny Boleski	.75	.40	.25
38	Jim Duncan (CO)	.75	.40	.25
39	Hugh McKinnis	.75	.40	.25
40	Basil Bark	.75	.40	.25
41	Herman Harrison	4.00	2.00	1.25
42	Larry Robinson	1.25	.60	.40
43	Larry Lawrence	.75	.40	.25
44	Granville Liggins	2.00	1.00	.60
45	Wayne Harris	4.00	2.00	1.25
46	John Atamian	.75	.40	.25
47	Wayne Holm	.75	.40	.25
48	Rudy Linterman	1.25	.60	.40
49	Jim Sillye	.75	.40	.25
50	Terry Wilson	.75	.40	.25
51	Don Trull	2.00	1.00	.60
52	Rusty Clark	.75	.40	.25
53	Ted Page	.75	.40	.25
54	Ken Ferguson	.75	.40	.25
55	Alan Pitcaithley	.75	.40	.25

56	Bayne Norrie	.75	.40	.25
57	Dave Gasser	.75	.40	.25
58	Jim Thomas	.75	.40	.25
59	Terry Swarn	1.25	.60	.40
60	Ron Forwick	.75	.40	.25
61	Henry King	.75	.40	.25
62	John Wydareny	1.25	.60	.40
63	Ray Jauch (CO)	1.25	.60	.40
64	Jim Henshall	.75	.40	.25
65	Dave Cutler	4.00	2.00	1.25
66	Fred Dunn	.75	.40	.25
67	Dick Dupuis	1.25	.60	.40
68	Fritz Greenlee	.75	.40	.25
69	Jerry Griffin	1.25	.60	.40
70	Allen Ische	.75	.40	.25
71	John LaGrone	1.25	.60	.40
72	Mike Law	.75	.40	.25
73	Ed Molstad	.75	.40	.25
74	Greg Pipes	1.25	.60	.40
75	Roy Shatzko	.75	.40	.25
76	Joe Zuger	1.25	.60	.40
77	Wally Gabler	1.25	.60	.40
78	Tony Gabriel	6.00	3.00	1.75
79	John Reid	.75	.40	.25
80	Dave Fleming	.75	.40	.25
81	Jon Hohman	.75	.40	.25
82	Tommy Joe Coffey	5.00	2.50	1.50
83	Dick Wesolowski	.75	.40	.25
84	Gordon Christian	.75	.40	.25
85	Steve Worster	6.00	3.00	1.75
86	Bob Taylor	1.50	.70	.45
87	Doug Mitchell	.75	.40	.25
88	Al Dorow (CO)	1.25	.60	.40
89	Angelo Mosca	7.50	3.75	2.25
90	Bill Danychuk	1.25	.60	.40
91	Mike Blum	.75	.40	.25
92	Garney Henley	6.00	3.00	1.75
93	Bob Steiner	.75	.40	.25
94	John Manel	.75	.40	.25
95	Bob Krouse	.75	.40	.25
96	John Williams	.75	.40	.25
97	Scott Henderson	.75	.40	.25
98	Ed Chalupka	.75	.40	.25
99	Paul McKay	.75	.40	.25
100	Rensi Perdoni	.75	.40	.25
101	Ed George	1.25	.60	.40
102	Al Phaneuf	1.25	.60	.40
103	Sonny Wade	2.00	1.00	.60
104	Moses Denson	2.00	1.00	.60
105	Terry Evanshen	6.00	3.00	1.75
106	Pierre Desjardins	.75	.40	.25
107	Larry Fairholm	.75	.40	.25
108	Gene Gaines	4.00	2.00	1.25
109	Bobby Lee Thompson	.75	.40	.25
110	Mike Widger	.75	.40	.25
111	Gene Ceppetelli	.75	.40	.25
112	Barry Randall	.75	.40	.25
113	Sam Etcheverry (CO)	2.50	1.25	.70
114	Mark Kosmos	1.25	.60	.40
115	Peter Dalla Riva	4.00	2.00	1.25
116	Ted Collins	.75	.40	.25
117	John Couture	.75	.40	.25
118	Tony Passander	.75	.40	.25
119	Garry Lefebvre	.75	.40	.25
120	George Springate	.75	.40	.25
121	Gordon Judges	.75	.40	.25
122	Steve Smear	2.50	1.25	.70
123	Tom Pullen	.75	.40	.25
124	Merl Code	.75	.40	.25
125	Steve Booras	.75	.40	.25
126	Hugh Oldham	.75	.40	.25
127	Moe Racine	.75	.40	.25
128	John Kruspe	.75	.40	.25
129	Ken Lehmann	1.25	.60	.40
130	Billy Cooper	.75	.40	.25
131	Marshall Shirk	.75	.40	.25
132	Tom Schuette	.75	.40	.25
133	Doug Specht	.75	.40	.25
134	Dennis Duncan	.75	.40	.25
135	Jerry Campbell	1.25	.60	.40
136	Wayne Giardino	.75	.40	.25
137	Roger Perdrix	.75	.40	.25
138	Jack Gotta (CO)	.75	.40	.25
139	Terry Wellesley	.75	.40	.25
140	Dave Braggins	.75	.40	.25
141	Dave Pivec	.75	.40	.25
142	Rod Woodward	.75	.40	.25
143	Garry Wood	2.00	1.00	.60
144	Al Marcelin	1.25	.60	.40
145	Dan Dever	.75	.40	.25
146	Ivan MacMillan	.75	.40	.25
147	Wayne Smith	.75	.40	.25
148	Barry Ardern	.75	.40	.25
149	Rick Cassatta	1.25	.60	.40
150	Bill Van Burkleo	.75	.40	.25
151	Ron Lancaster	5.00	2.50	1.50
152	Wayne Shaw	.75	.40	.25
153	Bob Kosid	.75	.40	.25

154	George Reed	7.50	3.75	2.25
155	Don Bahnuik	.75	.40	.25
156	Gordon Barwell	.75	.40	.25
157	Clyde Brock	.75	.40	.25
158	Alan Ford	.75	.40	.25
159	Jack Abendschan	.75	.40	.25
160	Steve Molnar	.75	.40	.25
161	Al Rankin	.75	.40	.25
162	Bobby Thompson	.75	.40	.25
163	Dave Skrien (CO)	.75	.40	.25
164	Nolan Bailey	.75	.40	.25
165	Bill Baker	5.00	2.50	1.50
166	Bruce Bennett	1.50	.70	.45
167	Gary Brandt	.75	.40	.25
168	Charlie Collins	.75	.40	.25
169	Henry Dorsch	.75	.40	.25
170	Ted Dushinski	.75	.40	.25
171	Bruce Gainer	.75	.40	.25
172	Ralph Galloway	.75	.40	.25
173	Ken Frith	.75	.40	.25
174	Cliff Shaw	.75	.40	.25
175	Silas McKinnie	.75	.40	.25
176	Mike Eben	.75	.40	.25
177	Greg Barton	2.00	1.00	.60
178	Joe Theismann	20.00	10.00	6.00
179	Charlie Bray	.75	.40	.25
180	Roger Scales	.75	.40	.25
181	Bob Hudspeth	.75	.40	.25
182	Bill Symons	1.50	.70	.45
183	Dave Raimey	1.25	.60	.40
184	Dave Cranmer	1.25	.60	.40
185	Mel Profit	1.25	.60	.40
186	Paul Desjardins	.75	.40	.25
187	Tony Moro	.75	.40	.25
188	Leo Cahill (CO)	.75	.40	.25
189	Chip Barrett	.75	.40	.25
190	Pete Martin	.75	.40	.25
191	Walt Balasiuk	.75	.40	.25
192	Jim Corrigall	1.50	.70	.45
193	Ellison Kelly	5.00	2.50	1.50
194	Jim Tomlin	.75	.40	.25
195	Marv Luster	2.00	1.00	.60
196	Jim Thorpe	2.00	1.00	.60
197	Jim Stillwagon	4.00	2.00	1.25
198	Ed Harrington	.75	.40	.25
199	Jim Dye	.75	.40	.25
200	Leon McQuay	2.50	1.25	.70
201	Rob McLaren	.75	.40	.25
202	Benji Dial	.75	.40	.25
203	Chuck Liebrock	.75	.40	.25
204	Glen Schapansky	.75	.40	.25
205	Ed Ulmer	.75	.40	.25
206	Ross Richardson	.75	.40	.25
207	Lou Andrus	.75	.40	.25
208	Paul Robson	.75	.40	.25
209	Paul Brule	.75	.40	.25
210	Doug Strong	.75	.40	.25
211	Dick Smith	.75	.40	.25
212	Bill Frank	.75	.40	.25
213	Jim Spavital (CO)	.75	.40	.25
214	Rick Shaw	.75	.40	.25
215	Joe Critchlow	.75	.40	.25
216	Don Jonas	3.00	1.50	.90
217	Bob Swift	.75	.40	.25
218	Larry Kerychuk	.75	.40	.25
219	Bob McCarthy	.75	.40	.25
220	Gene Lakusiak	.75	.40	.25
221	Jim Heighton	.75	.40	.25
222	Chuck Harrison	.75	.40	.25
223	Lance Fletcher	.75	.40	.25
224	Larry Slagle	.75	.40	.25
225	Wayne Giesbrecht	.75	.40	.25

1981 Michael Schechter Associates Test Discs

These discs, produced by Michael Schecter Associates, were included in specially-marked packages of bread. The front shows a head shot of the player, but team logos have been airbrushed off the helmets. An NFLPA logo appears on the card front, along with the player's name, team, position and biographical information. Four stars appear at the top of the card. The unnumbered cards have blank backs. Holsum and Gardner's are among the brands of bread which included the cards inside packages. These two companies also made different posters which were intended to be used to display the discs.

	NM/M	NM	E
Complete Set (32):	175.00	131.00	70.00
Common Player:	2.50	2.00	1.00
(1) Ken Anderson	4.00	3.00	1.50
(2) Ottis Anderson	6.00	4.50	2.50
(3) Steve Bartkowski	3.00	2.25	1.25
(4) Ricky Bell	3.00	2.25	1.25
(5) Terry Bradshaw	17.50	13.00	7.00
(6) Harold Carmichael	3.00	2.25	1.25
(7) Joe Cribbs	2.50	2.00	1.00
(8) Gary Danielson	2.50	2.00	1.00
(9) Lynn Dickey	2.50	2.00	1.00
(10) Dan Doornink	2.50	2.00	1.00
(11) Vince Evans	3.00	2.25	1.25
(12) Joe Ferguson	3.00	2.25	1.25
(13) Vagas Ferguson	2.50	2.00	1.00
(14) Dan Fouts	8.00	6.00	3.25
(15) Steve Fuller	2.50	2.00	1.00
(16) Archie Griffin	3.00	2.25	1.25
(17) Steve Grogan	3.00	2.25	1.25
(18) Bruce Harper	2.50	2.00	1.00
(19) Jim Hart	3.00	2.25	1.25
(20) Jim Jensen	2.50	2.00	1.00
(21) Bert Jones	3.00	2.25	1.25
(22) Archie Manning	4.00	3.00	1.50
(23) Ted McKnight	2.50	2.00	1.00
(24) Joe Montana	85.00	64.00	34.00
(25) Craig Morton	3.00	2.25	1.25
(26) Robert Newhouse	3.00	2.25	1.25
(27) Phil Simms	9.00	6.75	3.50
(28) Billy Taylor	2.50	2.00	1.00
(29) Joe Theismann	5.00	3.75	2.00
(30) Mark Van Eeghen	2.50	2.00	1.00
(31) Delvin Williams	2.50	2.00	1.00
(32) Tim Wilson	2.50	2.00	1.00

1990 Michael Schechter Associates Superstars

These unnumbered cards, produced by Michael Schechter Associates, were included two per box of Ralston Purina's Staff and Food Club Frosted Flakes cereal. Each card front has a color closeup shot of the player, with "Superstars" written at the top, and the player's name and team at the bottom. Three footballs are in different corners; an NFLPA logo is in the fourth corner. The card back also has the NFLPA logo, plus biographical information and statistics.

	NM/M	NM	E
Complete Set (12):	15.00	11.00	6.00
Common Player:	.75	.60	.30
(1) Carl Banks	.75	.60	.30
(2) Cornelius Bennett	.75	.60	.30
(3) Roger Craig	1.50	1.25	.60
(4) Jim Everett	1.00	.70	.40
(5) Bo Jackson	2.00	1.50	.80
(6) Ronnie Lott	1.50	1.25	.60
(7) Don Majkowski	.75	.60	.30
(8) Dan Marino	8.00	6.00	3.25
(9) Karl Mecklenburg	.75	.60	.30
(10) Christian Okoye	.75	.60	.30
(11) Mike Singletary	1.00	.70	.40
(12) Herschel Walker	1.00	.70	.40

1989 Score Franco Harris

This card, which has two versions, was given to those who received Franco Harris' autograph at the Super Bowl show in New Orleans. The unnumbered standard-size cards have identical fronts and are similar in design to Score's 1989 regular set. The difference on the card backs is in the text which describes Harris' status as a potential Hall of Famer. Earlier versions say Harris was a "sure-shot" to be elected to the Hall of Fame. He was elected during the show, so the text was changed to say "Hall of Famer." The "sure-shot" cards are scarcer.

	NM/M	NM	E
Complete Set (2):	100.00	101.00	54.00
Common Player:	40.00	49.00	26.00
1A Franco Harris (Sure-shot)	60.00	45.00	24.00
1B Franco Harris (Hall of Famer)	40.00	49.00	26.00

1989 Score Promos

These cards were used to promote Score's debut football set. They are basically identical to the 1989 regular issue, but these six promo cards can be distinguished from the regular set by the use of a registered symbol on them instead of a trademark symbol. Also, the stats on these promo cards are carried out to only one decimal place on the card back; the regular cards carry out the stats to two places. These cards were sent to dealers along with order forms for the 1989 set.

	NM/M	NM	E
Complete Set (6):	75.00	56.00	30.00
Common Player:	5.00	3.75	2.00
1 Joe Montana	35.00	26.00	14.00
2 Bo Jackson	15.00	11.00	6.00
3 Boomer Esiason	12.00	9.00	4.75
4 Roger Craig	8.00	6.00	3.25
5 Too Tall Jones (Registered seven sacks, regular card issue has registered 7.0 sacks)	5.00	3.75	2.00
6 Phil Simms (Moorehead State, should say Morehead State; photo cropping has Score logo blocking part of the ball)	8.00	6.00	3.25

1989 Score Supplemental

These 110 cards continue with numbers where the 1989 Score regular set left off at - 330. The cards are numbered using an "S" prefix, however. The design is similar to the regular issue's, but the supplemental cards have purple borders. The cards were distributed as a complete, boxed set only.

	NM/M	NM	E
Complete Set (110):	15.00	11.00	6.00
Common Player:	.05	.04	.02
Minor Stars:	.10	.08	.04
331 Herschel Walker	.10	.08	.04
332 Allen Pinkett RC	.05	.04	.02
333 Sterling Sharpe RC	3.00	2.25	1.25
334 Alvin Walton RC	.05	.04	.02
335 Frank Reich RC	.50	.40	.20
336 Jim Thornton RC	.05	.04	.02
337 David Fulcher	.05	.04	.02
338 Raul Allegre	.05	.04	.02
339 John Elway	2.00	1.50	.80
340 Michael Cofer	.05	.04	.02
341 Jim Skow	.05	.04	.02
342 Steve DeBerg	.05	.04	.02
343 Mervyn Fernandez	.05	.04	.02
344 Mike Lansford	.05	.04	.02
345 Reggie Roby	.05	.04	.02
346 Raymond Clayborn	.05	.04	.02
347 Lonzell Hill	.05	.04	.02
348 Ottis Anderson	.05	.04	.02
349 Erik McMillan RC	.05	.04	.02
350 Al Harris RC	.05	.04	.02
351 Jack Del Rio RC	1.00	.70	.40
352 Gary Anderson	.10	.08	.04
353 Jim McMahon	.10	.08	.04
354 Keena Turner	.05	.04	.02
355 Tony Woods RC	.05	.04	.02
356 Donald Igwebuike	.05	.04	.02
357 Gerald Riggs	.05	.04	.02
358 Eddie Murray	.05	.04	.02
359 Dino Hackett	.05	.04	.02
360 Brad Muster RC	.05	.04	.02
361 Paul Palmer	.05	.04	.02
362 Jerry Robinson	.05	.04	.02
363 Simon Fletcher RC	.50	.40	.20
364 Tommy Kramer	.05	.04	.02
365 Jim C. Jensen	.05	.04	.02
366 Lorenzo White RC	.50	.40	.20
367 Fredd Young	.05	.04	.02
368 Ron Jaworski	.05	.04	.02
369 Mel Owens	.05	.04	.02
370 Dave Waymer	.05	.04	.02
371 Sean Landeta	.05	.04	.02
372 Sam Mills	.05	.04	.02
373 Todd Blackledge	.05	.04	.02
374 JoJo Townsell	.05	.04	.02
375 Ron Wolfley	.05	.04	.02
376 Ralf Mojsiejenko	.05	.04	.02
377 Eric Wright	.05	.04	.02
378 Newsby Glasgow	.05	.04	.02
379 Darryl Talley	.05	.04	.02
380 Eric Allen RC	.40	.30	.15
381 Dennis Smith	.05	.04	.02
382 John Tice	.05	.04	.02
383 Jesse Solomon	.05	.04	.02
384 Bo Jackson	1.50	1.25	.60
385 Mike Merriweather	.05	.04	.02
386 Maurice Carthon	.05	.04	.02
387 Dave Grayson	.05	.04	.02
388 Wilber Marshall	.05	.04	.02
389 David Wyman	.05	.04	.02
390 Thomas Everett RC	.05	.04	.02
391 Alex Gordon	.05	.04	.02
392 D.J. Dozier	.05	.04	.02
393 Scott Radecic RC	.05	.04	.02
394 Eric Thomas	.05	.04	.02
395 Mike Gann	.05	.04	.02
396 William Perry	.05	.04	.02
397 Carl Hariston	.05	.04	.02
398 Billy Ard	.05	.04	.02
399 Donnell Thompson	.05	.04	.02
400 Mike Webster	.05	.04	.02
401 Scott Davis	.05	.04	.02
402 Sean Farrell	.05	.04	.02
403 Mike Golic RC	.05	.04	.02
404 Mike Kenn	.05	.04	.02
405 Keith Van Horne RC	.05	.04	.02
406 Bob Golic	.05	.04	.02
407 Neil Smith RC	1.00	.70	.40
408 Dermontti Dawson RC	.05	.04	.02
409 Leslie O'Neal	.10	.08	.04
410 Matt Bahr	.05	.04	.02
411 Guy McIntyre RC	.10	.08	.04
412 Bryan Millard	.05	.04	.02
414 Rob Taylor RC	.05	.04	.02
415 Tony Zendejas	.05	.04	.02
416 Vai Sikahema	.05	.04	.02
417 Gary Reasons	.05	.04	.02
418 Shawn Collins RC	.05	.04	.02
419 Mark Green RC	.05	.04	.02
420 Courtney Hall RC	.05	.04	.02
421 Bobby Humphrey RC	.05	.04	.02
422 Myron Guyton RC	.05	.04	.02
423 Darryl Ingram	.05	.04	.02
424 Chris Jacke RC	.10	.08	.04
425 Keith Jones	.05	.04	.02
426 Robert Massey RC	.05	.04	.02
427 Bubba McDowell RC	.05	.04	.02
428 Dave Meggett RC	1.00	.70	.40
429 Louis Oliver RC	.05	.04	.02
430 Danny Peebles	.05	.04	.02
431 Rodney Peete RC	1.00	.70	.40
432 Jeff Query RC	.10	.08	.04
433 Timm Rosenbach RC	.05	.04	.02
434 Frank Stams RC	.05	.04	.02
435 Lawyer Tillman RC	.05	.04	.02
436 Billy Joe Tolliver RC	.10	.08	.04
437 Floyd Turner RC	.30	.25	.12
438 Steve Walsh RC	.75	.60	.30
439 Joe Wolf RC	.05	.04	.02
440 Trace Armstrong RC	.05	.04	.02

1989 Score

Score's premier set of football cards, a 330-card edition, was released in August 1989. An additional 110 cards were released as a boxed updated set to hobby shops in January 1990 and were numbered 331-440 with an "S" following the number. Score expanded its print run and corrected several errors in the regular set: #101, Keith Jackson (wrong uniform number on back); #122, Ricky Sanders (wrong uniform number on back); #126, Ron Hall (wrong photos on front and back); #188 Mark Carrier (wrong photo -- original back showed Bruce Hill); #218, Willie Gault (photo showed Greg Townsend); #293, Keith Jackson's All Pro card (wrong uniform number on back); #305, Tim Brown (photo showed James Lofton); and #316, Eric Thomas (wrong uniform number on back). The corrected cards were issued in both wax boxes and in factory sets, a Score spokesman said. The corrected cards are scarcer than the error cards. Score was the first set to include the same year's first-round draft picks. Rookies in this set include Barry Sanders, Deion Sanders, Troy Aikman, Louis Oliver, Dave Meggett, Erik McMillan and Don Majkowski.

	NM/M	NM	E
Complete Set (330):	100.00	97.50	52.50
Comp. Factory Set (330):	125.00	90.00	50.00
Common Player:	1.00	.50	.30
Minor Stars:	.20	.15	.08

Pack (15):		8.00		
Wax Box (36):		200.00		
1	Joe Montana	3.00	2.25	1.25
2	Bo Jackson	1.00	.70	.40
3	Boomer Esiason	1.00	.50	.15
4	Roger Craig	1.00	.50	.15
5	Ed Jones	1.00	.50	.15
6	Phil Simms	1.00	.50	.15
7	Dan Hampton	1.00	.50	.15
8	John Settle RC	1.00	.50	.15
9	Bernie Kosar	1.00	.50	.15
10	Al Toon	1.00	.50	.15
11	Bubby Brister RC	3.00	2.50	1.25
12	Mark Clayton	1.00	.50	.15
13	Dan Marino	4.00	3.00	1.50
14	Joe Morris	1.00	.50	.15
15	Warren Moon	1.00	.70	.40
16	Chuck Long	1.00	.50	.15
17	Mark Jackson	1.00	.50	.15
18	Michael Irvin RC	2.50	1.25	.75
19	Bruce Smith	1.00	.50	.15
20	Anthony Carter	1.00	.50	.15
21	Charles Haley	1.00	.50	.15
22	Dave Duerson	1.00	.50	.15
23	Troy Stradford	1.00	.50	.15
24	Freeman McNeil	1.00	.50	.15
25	Jerry Gray	1.00	.50	.15
26	Bill Maas	1.00	.50	.15
27	Chris Chandler RC	1.00	.50	.30
28	Tom Newberry RC	1.00	.50	.15
29	Albert Lewis	1.00	.50	.15
30	Jay Schroeder	1.00	.50	.15
31	Dalton Hilliard	1.00	.50	.15
32	Tony Eason	1.00	.50	.15
33	Rick Donnelly	1.00	.50	.15
34	Herschel Walker	1.00	.50	.15
35	Wesley Walker	1.00	.50	.15
36	Chris Doleman	1.00	.50	.15
37	Pat Swilling	1.00	.50	.15
38	Joey Browner	1.00	.50	.15
39	Shane Conlan	1.00	.50	.15
40	Mike Tomczak	1.00	.50	.15
41	Webster Slaughter	1.00	.50	.15
42	Ray Donaldson	1.00	.50	.15
43	Christian Okoye	1.00	.50	.15
44	Jon Bosa	1.00	.50	.15
45	Aaron Cox RC	1.00	.50	.15
46	Bobby Hebert	1.00	.50	.15
47	Carl Banks	1.00	.50	.15
48	Jeff Fuller	1.00	.50	.15
49	Gerald Willhite	1.00	.50	.15
50	Mike Singletary	1.00	.50	.15
51	Stanley Morgan	1.00	.50	.15
52	Mark Bavaro	1.00	.50	.15
53	Mickey Shuler	1.00	.50	.15
54	Keith Millard	1.00	.50	.15
55	Andre Tippett	1.00	.50	.15
56	Vance Johnson	1.00	.50	.15
57	Bennie Blades RC	1.00	.50	.15
58	Tim Harris	1.00	.50	.15
59	Hanford Dixon	1.00	.50	.15
60	Chris Miller RC	1.00	.50	.15
61	Cornelius Bennett	.75	.60	.30
62	Neal Anderson	1.00	.50	.15
63	Ickey Woods	1.00	.50	.15
64	Gary Anderson	1.00	.50	.15
65	Vaughan Johnson RC	1.00	.50	.15
66	Ronnie Lippett	1.00	.50	.15
67	Mike Quick	1.00	.50	.15
68	Roy Green	1.00	.50	.15
69	Tim Krumrie	1.00	.50	.15
70	Mark Malone	1.00	.50	.15
71	James Jones	1.00	.50	.15
72	Cris Carter RC	3.00	1.50	.90
73	Ricky Nattiel	1.00	.50	.15
74	Jim Arnold	1.00	.50	.15
75	Randall Cunningham	1.00	.70	.40
76	John L. Williams	1.00	.50	.15
77	Paul Gruber RC	1.00	.50	.15
78	Rod Woodson RC	4.00	3.00	1.50
79	Ray Childress	1.00	.50	.15
80	Doug Williams	1.00	.50	.15
81	Deron Cherry	1.00	.50	.15
82	John Offerdahl	1.00	.50	.15
83	Louis Lipps	1.00	.50	.15
84	Neil Lomax	1.00	.50	.15
85	Wade Wilson	1.00	.50	.15
86	Tim Brown RC	2.50	1.25	.75
87	Chris Hinton	1.00	.50	.15
88	Stump Mitchell	1.00	.50	.15
89	Tunch Ilkin	1.00	.50	.15
90	Steve Pelluer	1.00	.50	.15
91	Brian Noble	1.00	.50	.15
92	Reggie White	1.00	.70	.40
93	Aundray Bruce RC	1.00	.50	.15

94	Garry James	1.00	.50	.15
95	Drew Hill	1.00	.50	.15
96	Anthony Munoz	1.00	.50	.15
97	James Wilder	1.00	.50	.15
98	Dexter Manley	1.00	.50	.15
99	Lee Williams	1.00	.50	.15
100	Dave Krieg	1.00	.50	.15
101	Keith Jackson ERR RC (incorrect number 84)	1.00	.70	.40
101a	Keith Jackson COR RC (correct number 88)	1.00	.70	.40
102	Luis Sharpe	1.00	.50	.15
103	Kevin Greene	1.00	.50	.15
104	Duane Bickett	1.00	.50	.15
105	Mark Rypien RC	.75	.60	.30
106	Curt Warner	1.00	.50	.15
107	Jacob Green	1.00	.50	.15
108	Gary Clark	1.00	.50	.15
109	Bruce Matthews RC	1.00	.70	.40
110	Bill Fralic	1.00	.50	.15
111	Bill Bates	1.00	.50	.15
112	Jeff Bryant	1.00	.50	.15
113	Charles Mann	1.00	.50	.15
114	Richard Dent	1.00	.50	.15
115	Bruce Hill	1.00	.50	.15
116	Mark May RC	1.00	.50	.15
117	Mark Collins RC	1.00	.50	.15
118	Ron Holmes	1.00	.50	.15
119	Scott Case RC	1.00	.50	.15
120	Tom Rathman	1.00	.50	.15
121	Dennis McKinnon	1.00	.50	.15
122	Ricky Sanders ERR (incorrect number 46)	1.00	.50	.15
122a	Ricky Sanders COR (correct number 83)	1.00	.50	.20
123	Michael Carter	1.00	.50	.15
124	Ozzie Newsome	1.00	.50	.15
125	Irving Fryar	1.00	.50	.15
126	Ron Hall ERR RC (wrong photo)	1.00	.50	.15
126a	Ron Hall COR RC (corrected photo)	1.00	.50	.20
127	Clay Matthews	1.00	.50	.15
128	Leonard Marshall	1.00	.50	.15
129	Kevin Mack	1.00	.50	.15
130	Art Monk	1.00	.50	.15
131	Garin Veris	1.00	.50	.15
132	Steve Jordan	1.00	.50	.15
133	Frank Minnifield	1.00	.50	.15
134	Eddie Brown	1.00	.50	.15
135	Stacey Bailey	1.00	.50	.15
136	Rickey Jackson	1.00	.50	.15
137	Henry Ellard	1.00	.50	.15
138	Jim Burt	1.00	.50	.15
139	Jerome Brown	1.00	.50	.15
140	Rodney Holman RC	1.00	.50	.15
141	Sammy Winder	1.00	.50	.15
142	Marcus Cotton	1.00	.50	.15
143	Jim Jeffcoat	1.00	.50	.15
144	Reuben Mayes	1.00	.50	.15
145	Jim McMahon	1.00	.50	.15
146	Reggie Williams	1.00	.50	.15
147	John Anderson	1.00	.50	.15
148	Harris Barton RC	1.00	.50	.15
149	Philip Epps	1.00	.50	.15
150	Jay Hilgenberg	1.00	.50	.15
151	Earl Ferrell	1.00	.50	.15
152	Andre Reed	1.00	.50	.20
153	Dennis Gentry	1.00	.50	.15
154	Max Montoya	1.00	.50	.15
155	Darrin Nelson	1.00	.50	.15
156	Jeff Chadwick	1.00	.50	.15
157	James Brooks	1.00	.50	.15
158	Keith Bishop	1.00	.50	.15
159	Robert Awalt	1.00	.50	.15
160	Marty Lyons	1.00	.50	.15
161	Johnny Hector	1.00	.50	.15
162	Tony Casillas	1.00	.50	.15
163	Kyle Clifton RC	1.00	.50	.15
164	Cody Risien	1.00	.50	.15
165	Jamie Holland	1.00	.50	.15
166	Merril Hoge RC	1.00	.50	.15
167	Chris Spielman RC	1.00	.50	.30
168	Carlos Carson	1.00	.50	.15
169	Jerry Ball RC	1.00	.50	.15
170	Don Majkowski RC	1.00	.50	.15
171	Everson Walls	1.00	.50	.15
172	Mike Rozier	1.00	.50	.15
173	Matt Millen	1.00	.50	.15
174	Karl Mecklenberg	1.00	.50	.15
175	Paul Palmer	1.00	.50	.15
176	Brian Blades RC	1.00	.70	.40
177	Brent Fullwood	1.00	.50	.15
178	Anthony Miller RC	1.00	.70	.40
179	Brian Sochia	1.00	.50	.15

180	Stephen Baker RC	1.00	.50	.15
181	Jesse Solomon	1.00	.50	.15
182	John Grimsley	1.00	.50	.15
183	Timmy Newsome	1.00	.50	.15
184	Steve Sewell RC	1.00	.50	.15
185	Dean Biasucci	1.00	.50	.15
186	Alonzo Highsmith	1.00	.50	.15
187	Randy Grimes	1.00	.50	.15
188	Mark Carrier ERR RC (back shows Bruce Hill)	1.00	.50	.30
188a	Mark Carrier COR (corrected)	1.00	.50	.30
189	Vann McElroy	1.00	.50	.15
190	Greg Bell	1.00	.50	.15
191	Quinn Early RC	2.00	1.50	.80
192	Lawrence Taylor	1.00	.50	.20
193	Albert Bentley	1.00	.50	.15
194	Ernest Givins	1.00	.50	.15
195	Jackie Slater	1.00	.50	.15
196	Jim Sweeney	1.00	.50	.15
197	Freddie Joe Nunn	1.00	.50	.15
198	Keith Byars	1.00	.50	.15
199	Hardy Nickerson RC	1.00	.50	.30
200	Steve Beuerlein RC	1.00	.50	.30
201	Bruce Armstrong RC	1.00	.50	.15
202	Lionel Manuel	1.00	.50	.15
203	J.T. Smith	1.00	.50	.15
204	Mark Ingram RC	1.00	.70	.40
205	Fred Smerlas	1.00	.50	.15
206	Bryan Hinkle RC	1.00	.50	.15
207	Steve McMichael	1.00	.50	.15
208	Nick Lowery	1.00	.50	.15
209	Jack Trudeau	1.00	.50	.15
210	Lorenzo Hampton	1.00	.50	.15
211	Thurman Thomas RC	2.50	1.25	.75
212	Steve Young	2.00	1.50	.80
213	James Lofton	1.00	.50	.15
214	Jim Covert	1.00	.50	.15
215	Ronnie Lott	1.00	.50	.15
216	Stephone Paige	1.00	.50	.15
217	Mark Duper	1.00	.50	.15
218	Willie Gault ERR (shows Greg Townsend)	.25	.20	.15
218a	Willie Gault COR (corrected)	1.00	.50	.20
219	Ken Ruettgers RC	1.00	.50	.15
220	Kevin Ross RC	1.00	.50	.15
221	Jerry Rice	3.00	2.50	1.25
222	Billy Ray Smith	1.00	.50	.15
223	Jim Kelly	1.00	.70	.40
224	Vinny Testaverde	.40	.30	.15
225	Steve Largent	.75	.60	.30
226	Warren Williams RC	1.00	.50	.15
227	Morten Andersen	1.00	.50	.15
228	Bill Brooks	1.00	.50	.15
229	Reggie Langhorne RC	1.00	.50	.15
230	Pepper Johnson	1.00	.50	.15
231	Pat Leahy	1.00	.50	.15
232	Fred Marion	1.00	.50	.15
233	Gary Zimmerman	1.00	.50	.15
234	Marcus Allen	1.00	.50	.20
235	Gaston Green RC	1.00	.50	.15
236	John Stephens RC	1.00	.50	.15
237	Terry Kinard	1.00	.50	.15
238	John Taylor RC	1.00	.50	.30
239	Brian Bosworth	1.00	.50	.15
240	Anthony Toney	1.00	.50	.15
241	Ken O'Brien	1.00	.50	.15
242	Howie Long	1.00	.50	.15
243	Doug Flutie	2.00	1.50	.80
244	Jim Everett	.30	.50	.15
245	Broderick Thomas RC	1.00	.50	.15
246	Deion Sanders RC	2.00	1.00	.60
247	Donnell Woolford RC	1.00	.70	.40
248	Wayne Martin RC	.75	.60	.30
249	David Williams RC	1.00	.50	.15
250	Bill Hawkins	1.00	.50	.15
251	Eric Hill RC	1.00	.50	.15
252	Burt Grossman RC	1.00	.50	.15
253	Tracy Rocker	1.00	.50	.15
254	Steve Wisniewski RC	1.00	.50	.15
255	Jessie Small RC	1.00	.50	.15
256	David Braxton	1.00	.50	.15
257	Barry Sanders RC	8.00	4.00	2.50
258	Derrick Thomas RC	2.00	1.00	.60
259	Eric Metcalf RC	1.00	.50	.30
260	Keith DeLong RC	1.00	.50	.15
261	Hart Lee Dykes	1.00	.50	.15
262	Sammie Smith RC	1.00	.50	.15
263	Steve Atwater RC	1.00	.70	.40
264	Eric Ball RC	1.00	.50	.15
265	Don Beebe RC	1.00	.70	.40
266	Brian Williams	1.00	.50	.15
267	Jeff Lageman RC	1.00	.50	.15

		NM/M	NM	E
268	Tim Worley **RC**	1.00	.50	.15
269	Tony Mandarich	1.00	.50	.15
270	Troy Aikman **RC**	7.00	3.50	2.10
271	Andy Heck **RC**	1.00	.50	.15
272	Andre Rison **RC**	1.00	.50	030
273	AFC Championship Game	1.00	.50	.15
274	NFC Championship(Joe Montana)	1.00	.70	.40
275	Joe Montana, Jerry Rice	3.00	2.50	1.25
276	Rodney Carter	1.00	.50	.15
277	Mark Jackson, Vance Johnson, Ricky Nattiel	1.00	.50	.15
278	John Williams, Curt Warner	1.00	.50	.15
279	Joe Montana, Jerry Rice	3.00	2.50	1.25
280	Roy Green, Neil Lomax	1.00	.50	.15
281	Randall Cunningham, Keith Jackson	1.00	.50	.15
282	Chris Doleman, Keith Millard	1.00	.50	.15
283	Mark Duper, Mark Clayton	1.00	.50	.15
284	Allen, Jackson	1.00	.50	.20
285	Frank Minnifield (AP)	1.00	.50	.15
286	Bruce Matthews (AP)	1.00	.50	.15
287	Joey Browner (AP)	1.00	.50	.15
288	Jay Hilgenberg (AP)	1.00	.50	.15
289	Carl Lee **RC** (AP)	1.00	.50	.15
290	Scott Norwood (AP)	1.00	.50	.15
291	John Taylor (AP)	1.00	.50	.20
292	Jerry Rice (AP)	1.00	.70	.40
293	Keith Jackson ERR (AP) (incorrect number)	1.00	.50	.20
293a	Keith Jackson COR (AP) (corrected)	1.00	.50	.20
294	Gary Zimmerman (AP)	1.00	.50	.15
295	Lawrence Taylor (AP)	1.00	.50	.15
296	Reggie White (AP)	1.00	.50	.15
297	Roger Craig (AP)	1.00	.50	.15
298	Boomer Esiason (AP)	1.00	.50	.15
299	Cornelius Bennett (AP)	1.00	.50	.15
300	Mike Horan (AP)	1.00	.50	.15
301	Deron Cherry (AP)	1.00	.50	.15
302	Tom Newberry (AP)	1.00	.50	.15
303	Mike Singletary (AP)	1.00	.50	.15
304	Shane Conlan (AP)	1.00	.50	.15
305	Tim Brown ERR (AP) (shows James Lofton)	2.00	1.50	.80
305a	Tim Brown COR (AP) (corrected)	2.00	1.50	.80
306	Henry Ellard (AP)	1.00	.50	.15
307	Bruce Smith (AP)	1.00	.50	.15
308	Tim Krumrie (AP)	1.00	.50	.15
309	Anthony Munoz (AP)	1.00	.50	.15
310	Darrell Green (SB)	1.00	.50	.15
311	Anthony Miller (SB)	1.00	.50	.20
312	Wesley Walker (SB)	1.00	.50	.15
313	Ron Brown (SB)	1.00	.50	.15
314	Bo Jackson (SB)	.40	.30	.15
315	Philip Epps (SB)	1.00	.50	.15
316	Eric Thomas ERR **RC** (SB)(wrong number)	1.00	.50	.30
316a	Eric Thomas COR **RC** (SB)(corrected)	1.00	.50	.20
317	Herschel Walker (SB)	1.00	.50	.15
318	Jacob Green (PD)	1.00	.50	.15
319	Andre Tippett (PD)	1.00	.50	.15
320	Freddie Joe Nunn (PD)	1.00	.50	.15
321	Reggie White (PD)	1.00	.50	.15
322	Lawrence Taylor (PD)	1.00	.50	.15
323	Greg Townsend (PD)	1.00	.50	.15
324	Tim Harris (PD)	1.00	.50	.15
325	Bruce Smith (PD)	1.00	.50	.15
326	Tony Dorsett (RB)	1.00	.50	.15
327	Steve Largent (RB)	1.00	.50	.20
328	Tim Brown (RB)	2.00	1.50	.80
329	Joe Montana (RB)	1.00	.50	.30
330	Tom Landry (Tribute)	1.00	.70	.40

1990 Score Final Five

These five cards were inserted in 1990 Score Football factory sets and feature the last five picks in the 1990 NFL Draft. The "Final Five" logo is on each card front, along with a color photo of the player selected. The back has his name, position and summary of his collegiate accomplishments. Cards are numbered with a "B" prefix.

		NM/M	NM	E
Complete Set (5):		.50	.40	.20
Common Player:		.05	.04	.02
1	Judd Garrett	.05	.04	.02
2	Matt Stover	.15	.11	.06
3	Ken McMichael	.05	.04	.02
4	Demetrius Davis	.05	.04	.02
5	Elliott Searcy	.05	.04	.02

1990 Score Franco Harris

This card was given away to collectors who acquired Franco Harris' autograph at the Super Bowl Card Show in Tampa. The card is unnumbered and features a Leroy Nieman painting of Harris on the front with a picture of him celebrating a Super Bowl win on the back. Production of this card was estimated between 1,500 and 5,000.

		NM/M	NM	E
Complete Set (1):		50.00	75.00	40.00
Common Player:		50.00	75.00	40.00
1	Franco Harris	50.00	75.00	40.00

1990 Score Hot Card

Score test-marketed a 100-card football blister pack subset in August 1990, available only at select retail accounts. Blister packs featuring 100 assorted cards from Series I and Series II. As an incentive to buy the blister packs, one "Hot Card" was included in each blister pack.

		NM/M	NM	E
Complete Set (10):		12.00	22.00	12.00
Common Player:		.50	1.25	.70
1	Joe Montana	3.00	2.25	1.25
2	Bo Jackson	1.00	.70	.40
3	Barry Sanders	2.00	1.50	.80
4	Jerry Rice	2.00	1.50	.80
5	Eric Metcalf	.50	1.25	.70
6	Don Majkowski	.50	1.25	.70
7	Christian Okoye	.50	1.25	.70
8	Bobby Humphrey	.50	1.25	.70
9	Dan Marino	3.00	2.25	1.25
10	Sterling Sharpe	1.00	.70	.40

1990 Score Promos

These cards were sent to dealers along with order forms for Score's 1990 regular set. The design is similar to the regular issue, except the photos are cropped tighter. They also use a registered symbol on them, not the trademark symbol which is used on the regular cards.

		NM/M	NM	E
Complete Set (3):		8.00	13.50	7.25
Common Player:		1.00	2.00	1.00
20	Barry Sanders	7.00	5.25	2.75
184	Robert Delpino	1.00	2.00	1.00
256	Cornelius Bennett	2.00	1.50	.80

1990 Score Update

These cards were sold in sets only to hobby stores and included traded players as well as rookies in team uniforms.

		NM/M	NM	E
Complete Set (110):		120.00	90.00	50.00
Common Player:		.10	.08	.04
Minor Stars:		.20	.15	.08
1	Marcus Dupree	.10	.08	.04
2	Jerry Kauric	.10	.08	.04
3	Everson Walls	.10	.08	.04
4	Elliott Smith	.10	.08	.04
5	Donald Evans **RC**	.10	.08	.04
6	Jerry Holmes	.10	.08	.04
7	Dan Stryzinski **RC**	.10	.08	.04
8	Gerald McNeil	.10	.08	.04
9	Rick Tuten **RC**	.10	.08	.04
10	Mickey Shuler	.10	.08	.04
11	Jay Novacek	1.00	.70	.40
12	Eric Williams **RC**	.20	.15	.08
13	Stanley Morgan	.10	.08	.04
14	Wayne Haddix **RC**	.20	.15	.08
15	Gary Anderson	.20	.15	.08
16	Stan Humphries **RC**	1.00	.70	.40
17	Raymond Clayborn	.10	.08	.04
18	Mark Boyer **RC**	.10	.08	.04
19	Dave Waymer	.10	.08	.04
20	Andre Rison	.50	.40	.20
21	Daniel Stubbs	.10	.08	.04
22	Mike Rozier	.10	.08	.04
23	Damian Johnson	.10	.08	.04
24	Don Smith	.10	.08	.04
25	Max Montoya	.10	.08	.04
26	Terry Kinard	.10	.08	.04
27	Herb Welch	.10	.08	.04
28	Cliff Odom	.10	.08	.04
29	John Kidd	.10	.08	.04
30	Barry Word **RC**	.20	.15	.08
31	Rich Karlis	.10	.08	.04
32	Mike Baab	.10	.08	.04
33	Ronnie Harmon	.10	.08	.04
34	Jeff Donaldson	.10	.08	.04
35	Riki Ellison	.10	.08	.04
36	Steve Walsh	.20	.15	.08
37	Bill Lewis **RC**	.10	.08	.04
38	Tim McKyer	.10	.08	.04
39	James Wilder	.10	.08	.04
40	Tony Paige	.10	.08	.04
41	Derrick Fenner **RC**	.20	.15	.08
42	Thane Gash	.10	.08	.04
43	Dave Duerson	.10	.08	.04
44	Clarence Weathers	.10	.08	.04
45	Matt Bahr	.10	.08	.04
46	Alonzo Highsmith	.10	.08	.04
47	Joe Kelly	.10	.08	.04
48	Chris Hinton	.10	.08	.04
49	Bobby Humphery	.10	.08	.04
50	Greg Bell	.10	.08	.04
51	Fred Smerlas	.10	.08	.04
52	Dennis McKinnon	.10	.08	.04
53	Jim Skow	.10	.08	.04
54	Renaldo Turnbull	.20	.15	.08
55	Bern Brostek	.10	.08	.04
56	Charles Wilson **RC**	.10	.08	.04
57	Keith McCants	.10	.08	.04
58	Alexander Wright	.20	.15	.08
59	Ian Beckles **RC**	.10	.08	.04
60	Eric Davis **RC**	.20	.15	.08
61	Chris Singleton	.10	.08	.04
62	Rob Moore **RC**	10.00	7.50	4.00
63	Darion Conner	.10	.08	.04
64	Tim Gunhard	.10	.08	.04
65	Junior Seau	5.00	3.75	2.00
66	Tony Stargell	.10	.08	.04
67	Anthony Thompson	.20	.15	.08
68	Cortez Kennedy	.50	.40	.20
69	Darrell Thompson	.10	.08	.04
70	Calvin Williams **RC**	.20	.15	.08
71	Rodney Hampton	1.50	1.25	.60
72	Terry Wooden	.10	.08	.04
73	Leo Goeas	.10	.08	.04

74	Ken Willis	.10	.08	.04
75	Ricky Proehl	.75	.60	.30
76	Steve Christie RC	.50	.40	.20
77	Andre Ware	.20	.15	.08
78	Jeff George	3.00	2.25	1.25
79	Walter Wilson	.10	.08	.04
80	Johnny Bailey RC	.20	.15	.08
81	Harold Green RC	.20	.15	.08
82	Mark Carrier	.50	.40	.20
83	Frank Cornish	.10	.08	.04
84	James Williams	.10	.08	.04
85	James Francis RC	.20	.15	.08
86	Percy Snow	.10	.08	.04
87	Anthony Johnson	1.00	.70	.40
88	Tim Ryan	.10	.08	.04
89	Dan Owens RC	.20	.15	.08
90	Aaron Wallace	.10	.08	.04
91	Steve Broussard	.20	.15	.08
92	Eric Green	.50	.40	.20
93	Blair Thomas	.20	.15	.08
94	Robert Blackmon RC	.20	.15	.08
95	Alan Grant RC	.10	.08	.04
96	Andre Collins	.10	.08	.04
97	Dexter Carter	.20	.15	.08
98	Reggie Cobb RC	.20	.15	.08
99	Dennis Brown	.10	.08	.04
100	Kenny Davidson RC	.10	.08	.04
101	Emmitt Smith RC	110.00	82.00	44.00
102	Jeff Alm	.10	.08	.04
103	Alton Montgomery	.10	.08	.04
104	Tony Bennett	.20	.15	.08
105	Johnny Johnson RC	.50	.40	.20
106	Leroy Hoard RC	1.50	1.25	.60
107	Ray Agnew	.10	.08	.04
108	Richmond Webb	.20	.15	.08
109	Keith Sims	.10	.08	.04
110	Barry Foster	.20	.15	.08

1990 Score Young Superstars

This 40-card glossy set was a 1990 Score mail-in offer featuring some of the top young players in the NFL. Each card front has an action photo framed by black borders. Each back has a full color close-up photo, plus statistics, a card number, team logo and career summary.

		NM/M	NM	E
Complete Set (40):		8.00	6.00	3.25
Common Player:		.10	.08	.04
1	Barry Sanders	1.50	1.25	.60
2	Bobby Humphrey	.40	.30	.15
3	Ickey Woods	.20	.15	.08
4	Shawn Collins	.10	.08	.04
5	Dave Meggett	.25	.20	.10
6	Keith Jackson	.25	.20	.10
7	Sterling Sharpe	.25	.20	.10
8	Troy Aikman	.75	.60	.30
9	Tim McDonald	.10	.08	.04
10	Tim Brown	.25	.20	.10
11	Trace Armstrong	.10	.08	.04
12	Eric Metcalf (Led Bears in rushing, should be Browns)	.20	.15	.08
13	Derrick Thomas	.35	.25	.14
14	Eric Hill	.10	.08	.04
15	Deion Sanders	.50	.40	.20
16	Steve Atwater	.15	.11	.06
17	Carnell Lake	.10	.08	.04
18	Andre Reed	.30	.25	.12
19	Chris Spielman	.15	.11	.06
20	Eric Allen	.10	.08	.04
21	Erik McMillan	.15	.11	.06
22	Louis Oliver	.10	.08	.04
23	Robert Massey	.10	.08	.04
24	John Roper	.10	.08	.04
25	Burt Grossman	.15	.11	.06
26	Chris Jacke	.10	.08	.04
27	Steve Wisniewski	.10	.08	.04
28	Alonzo Highsmith	.15	.11	.06
29	Mark Carrier	.20	.15	.08
30	Bruce Armstrong	.10	.08	.04
31	Jerome Brown	.10	.08	.04

32	Cornelius Bennett	.20	.15	.08
33	Flipper Anderson	.15	.11	.06
34	Brian Blades	.25	.20	.10
35	Anthony Miller	.20	.15	.08
36	Thurman Thomas	.90	.70	.35
37	Chris Miller	.35	.25	.14
38	Aundray Bruce	.15	.11	.06
39	Robert Clark	.15	.11	.06
40	Robert Delpino	.15	.11	.06

1990 Score

Variations in the set include #134, Kevin Butler (uncorrected photo on back shows him wearing a helmet; corrected photo shows him without helmet), #136, Vai Sikahema (uncorrected photo on back shows him wearing a helmet; corrected photo shows him without a helmet), #147, Joey Browner (uncorrected back shows him looking into the sun; corrected back show more of a profile); #208, Ralf Mojsiejenko (uncorrected stats read "Chargers"; corrected stats read "Redskins."); and #600, Buck Buchanan (uncorrected back says he was the first player selected in the '83 AFL draft; it was corrected to read the '63 draft). Note: Rookie cards in the first series contained no information on which NFL team the player was drafted by; thus they are considered first cards, not rookie cards. (Key: HG - Hot Gun; GF - Ground Force; DP - draft pick)

		NM/M	NM	E
Complete Set (660):		8.00	6.00	3.25
Complete Series 1 (1-330):		4.00	3.00	1.50
Complete Series 2 (331-660):		4.00	3.00	1.50
Common Player:		.04	.03	.02
Series 1 Pack (16):		.50		
Series 1 Wax Box (36):		9.00		
Series 2 Pack (6):		.50		
Series 2 Wax Box (36):		9.00		
1	Joe Montana	1.00	.70	.40
2	Christian Okoye	.04	.03	.02
3	Mike Singletary	.04	.03	.02
4	Jim Everett	.04	.03	.02
5	Phil Simms	.10	.08	.04
6	Brent Fullwood	.04	.03	.02
7	Bill Fralic	.04	.03	.02
8	Leslie O'Neal	.04	.03	.02
9	John Taylor	.20	.15	.08
10	Bo Jackson	.40	.30	.15
11	John Stephens	.04	.03	.02
12	Art Monk	.04	.03	.02
13	Dan Marino	1.50	1.25	.60
14	John Settle	.04	.03	.02
15	Don Majkowski	.04	.03	.02
16	Bruce Smith	.04	.03	.02
17	Brad Muster	.04	.03	.02
18	Jason Buck	.04	.03	.02
19	James Brooks	.04	.03	.02
20	Barry Sanders	1.25	.90	.50
21	Troy Aikman	1.00	.70	.40
22	Allen Pinkett	.04	.03	.02
23	Duane Bickett	.04	.03	.02
24	Kevin Ross	.04	.03	.02
25	John Elway	.40	.30	.15
26	Jeff Query	.04	.03	.02
27	Eddie Murray	.04	.03	.02
28	Richard Dent	.04	.03	.02
29	Lorenzo White	.15	.11	.06
30	Eric Metcalf	.10	.08	.04
31	Jeff Dellenbach RC	.10	.08	.04
32	Leon White	.04	.03	.02
33	Jim Jeffcoat	.04	.03	.02
34	Herschel Walker	.04	.03	.02
35	Mike Johnson	.04	.03	.02
36	Joe Phillips	.04	.03	.02
37	Willie Gault	.04	.03	.02
38	Keith Millard	.04	.03	.02
39	Fred Marion	.04	.03	.02
40	Boomer Esiason	.20	.15	.08
41	Dermontti Dawson	.04	.03	.02
42	Dino Hackett	.04	.03	.02
43	Reggie Roby	.04	.03	.02
44	Roger Vick	.04	.03	.02
45	Bobby Hebert	.15	.11	.06

46	Don Beebe	.15	.11	.06
47	Neal Anderson	.10	.08	.04
48	Johnny Holland	.04	.03	.02
49	Bobby Humphery	.04	.03	.02
50	Lawrence Taylor	.10	.08	.04
51	Billy Ray Smith	.04	.03	.02
52	Robert Perryman	.04	.03	.02
53	Gary Anderson	.04	.03	.02
54	Raul Allegre	.04	.03	.02
55	Pat Swilling	.04	.03	.02
56	Chris Doleman	.04	.03	.02
57	Andre Reed	.20	.15	.08
58	Seth Joyner	.04	.03	.02
59	Bart Oates	.04	.03	.02
60	Bernie Kosar	.04	.03	.02
61	Dave Krieg	.04	.03	.02
62	Lars Tate	.04	.03	.02
63	Scott Norwood	.04	.03	.02
64	Kyle Clifton	.04	.03	.02
65	Alan Veingrad	.04	.03	.02
66	Gerald Riggs	.04	.03	.02
67	Tim Worley	.04	.03	.02
68	Rodney Holman	.04	.03	.02
69	Tony Zendejas	.04	.03	.02
70	Chris Miller	.10	.08	.04
71	Wilber Marshall	.04	.03	.02
72	Skip McClendon RC	.10	.08	.04
73	Jim Covert	.04	.03	.02
74	Sam Mills	.04	.03	.02
75	Chris Hinton	.04	.03	.02
76	Irv Eatman	.04	.03	.02
77	Bubba Paris	.04	.03	.02
78	John Elliott	.04	.03	.02
79	Thomas Everett	.04	.03	.02
80	Steve Smith	.04	.03	.02
81	Jackie Slater	.04	.03	.02
82	Kelvin Martin RC	.25	.20	.10
83	JoJo Townsell	.04	.03	.02
84	Jim Jensen	.04	.03	.02
85	Bobby Humphrey	.04	.03	.02
86	Mike Dyal	.04	.03	.02
87	Andre Rison	.25	.20	.10
88	Brian Sochia	.04	.03	.02
89	Greg Bell	.04	.03	.02
90	Dalton Hilliard	.04	.03	.02
91	Carl Banks	.04	.03	.02
92	Dennis Smith	.04	.03	.02
93	Bruce Matthews	.04	.03	.02
94	Charles Haley	.04	.03	.02
95	Deion Sanders	.35	.25	.14
96	Stephone Paige	.04	.03	.02
97	Marion Butts RC	.10	.08	.04
98	Howie Long	.04	.03	.02
99	Donald Igwebuike	.04	.03	.02
100	Roger Craig	.04	.03	.02
101	Charles Mann	.04	.03	.02
102	Fredd Young	.04	.03	.02
103	Chris Jacke	.04	.03	.02
104	Scott Case	.04	.03	.02
105	Warren Moon	.25	.20	.10
106	Clyde Simmons	.04	.03	.02
107	Steve Atwater	.04	.03	.02
108	Morten Andersen	.04	.03	.02
109	Eugene Marve	.04	.03	.02
110	Thurman Thomas	.40	.30	.15
111	Carnell Lake	.04	.03	.02
112	Jim Kelly	.30	.25	.12
113	Stanford Jennings	.04	.03	.02
114	Jacob Green	.04	.03	.02
115	Karl Mecklenberg	.04	.03	.02
116	Ray Childress	.04	.03	.02
117	Erik McMillan	.04	.03	.02
118	Harry Newsome	.04	.03	.02
119	James Dixon	.04	.03	.02
120	Hassan Jones	.04	.03	.02
121	Eric Allen	.04	.03	.02
122	Felix Wright	.04	.03	.02
123	Merril Hoge	.04	.03	.02
124	Eric Ball	.04	.03	.02
125	Willie Anderson	.10	.08	.04
126	James Jefferson	.04	.03	.02
127	Tim McDonald	.04	.03	.02
128	Larry Kinnebrew	.04	.03	.02
129	Mark Collins	.04	.03	.02
130	Ickey Woods	.04	.03	.02
131	Jeff Donaldson	.04	.03	.02
132	Rich Camarillo	.04	.03	.02
133	Melvin Bratton	.04	.03	.02
134	Kevin Butler (helmet)	.05	.04	.02
134a	Kevin Butler (without helmet)	.05	.04	.02
135	Albert Bentley	.04	.03	.02
136	Vai Sikahema (helmet on back)	.08	.06	.03
136a	Vai Sikahema (without helmet)	.08	.06	.03
137	Todd McNair RC	.10	.08	.04
138	Alonzo Highsmith	.04	.03	.02

139	Brian Blades	.10	.08	.04
140	Jeff Lageman	.04	.03	.02
141	Eric Thomas	.04	.03	.02
142	Derek Hill	.04	.03	.02
143	Rick Fenney	.04	.03	.02
144	Herman Heard	.04	.03	.02
145	Steve Young	1.00	.70	.40
146	Kent Hull	.04	.03	.02
147	Joey Browner	.04	.03	.02
148	Frank Minnifield	.04	.03	.02
149	Robert Massey	.04	.03	.02
150	Dave Meggett	.10	.08	.04
151	Bubba McDowell	.04	.03	.02
152	Rickey Dixon **RC**	.10	.08	.04
153	Ray Donaldson	.04	.03	.02
154	Alvin Walton	.04	.03	.02
155	Mike Cofer	.04	.03	.02
156	Darryl Talley	.04	.03	.02
157	A.J. Johnson	.04	.03	.02
158	Jerry Gray	.04	.03	.02
159	Keith Byars	.04	.03	.02
160	Andy Heck	.04	.03	.02
161	Mike Munchak	.04	.03	.02
162	Dennis Gentry	.04	.03	.02
163	Timm Rosenbach	.04	.03	.02
164	Randall McDaniel	.04	.03	.02
165	Pat Leahy	.04	.03	.02
166	Bubby Brister	.10	.08	.04
167	Aundray Bruce	.04	.03	.02
168	Bill Brooks	.04	.03	.02
169	Eddie Anderson **RC**	.10	.08	.04
170	Ronnie Lott	.10	.08	.04
171	Jay Hilgenberg	.04	.03	.02
172	Joe Nash	.04	.03	.02
173	Simon Fletcher	.04	.03	.02
174	Shane Conlan	.04	.03	.02
175	Sean Landeta	.04	.03	.02
176	John Alt **RC**	.10	.08	.04
177	Clay Matthews	.04	.03	.02
178	Anthony Munoz	.04	.03	.02
179	Pete Holohan	.04	.03	.02
180	Robert Awalt	.04	.03	.02
181	Rohn Stark	.04	.03	.02
182	Vance Johnson	.04	.03	.02
184	Robert Delpino	.04	.03	.02
185	Drew Hill	.04	.03	.02
186	Reggie Langhorne	.04	.03	.02
187	Lonzell Hill	.04	.03	.02
188	Tom Rathman	.04	.03	.02
189	Greg Montgomery **RC**	.10	.08	.04
190	Leonard Smith	.04	.03	.02
191	Chris Spielman	.04	.03	.02
192	Tom Newberry	.04	.03	.02
193	Cris Carter	.35	.25	.14
194	Kevin Porter	.04	.03	.02
195	Donnell Thompson	.04	.03	.02
196	Vaughan Johnson	.04	.03	.02
197	Steve McMichael	.04	.03	.02
198	Jim Sweeney	.04	.03	.02
199	Rich Karlis	.04	.03	.02
200	Jerry Rice	1.00	.70	.40
201	Dan Hampton	.04	.03	.02
202	Jim Lachey	.04	.03	.02
203	Reggie White	.15	.11	.06
204	Jerry Ball	.04	.03	.02
205	Russ Grimm	.04	.03	.02
206	Tim Green **RC**	.08	.06	.03
207	Shawn Collins	.04	.03	.02
208	Ralf Mojsiejenko (Chargers on back)	.05	.04	.02
208a	Ralf Mojsiejenko (Redskins on back)	.05	.04	.02
209	Trace Armstrong	.04	.03	.02
210	Keith Jackson	.25	.20	.10
211	Jamie Holland	.04	.03	.02
212	Mark Clayton	.04	.03	.02
213	Jeff Cross	.04	.03	.02
214	Bob Gagliano	.04	.03	.02
215	Louis Oliver	.04	.03	.02
216	Jim Arnold	.04	.03	.02
217	Robert Clark **RC**	.08	.06	.03
218	Gill Byrd	.04	.03	.02
219	Rodney Peete	.08	.06	.03
220	Anthony Miller	.30	.25	.12
221	Steve Grogan	.04	.03	.02
222	Vince Newsome	.04	.03	.02
223	Tom Benson	.04	.03	.02
224	Kevin Murphy	.04	.03	.02
225	Henry Ellard	.04	.03	.02
226	Richard Johnson	.04	.03	.02
227	Jim Skow	.04	.03	.02
228	Keith Jones	.04	.03	.02
229	Dave Brown	.04	.03	.02
230	Marcus Allen	.04	.03	.02
231	Steve Walsh	.04	.03	.02
232	Jim Harbaugh	.10	.08	.04
233	Mel Gray	.04	.03	.02
234	David Treadwell	.04	.03	.02
235	John Offerdahl	.04	.03	.02
236	Gary Reasons	.04	.03	.02
237	Tim Krumrie	.04	.03	.02
238	Dave Duerson	.04	.03	.02
239	Gary Clark	.10	.08	.04
240	Mark Jackson	.04	.03	.02
241	Mark Murphy	.04	.03	.02
242	Jerry Holmes	.04	.03	.02
243	Tim McGee	.04	.03	.02
244	Mike Tomczak	.04	.03	.02
245	Sterling Sharpe	.10	.08	.04
246	Bennie Blades	.04	.03	.02
247	Ken Harvey **RC**	.10	.08	.04
248	Ron Heller	.04	.03	.02
249	Louis Lipps	.04	.03	.02
250	Wade Wilson	.04	.03	.02
251	Freddie Joe Nunn	.04	.03	.02
252	Jerome Brown	.04	.03	.02
253	Myron Guyton	.04	.03	.02
254	Nate Odomes **RC**	.25	.20	.10
255	Rod Woodson	.25	.20	.10
256	Cornelius Bennett	.04	.03	.02
257	Keith Woodside	.04	.03	.02
258	Jeff Uhlenhake	.04	.03	.02
259	Harry Hamilton	.04	.03	.02
260	Mark Bavaro	.04	.03	.02
261	Vinny Testaverde	.10	.08	.04
262	Steve DeBerg	.04	.03	.02
263	Steve Wisniewski	.04	.03	.02
264	Pete Mandley	.04	.03	.02
265	Tim Harris	.04	.03	.02
266	Jack Trudeau	.04	.03	.02
267	Mark Kelso	.04	.03	.02
268	Brian Noble	.04	.03	.02
269	Jessie Tuggle **RC**	.20	.15	.08
270	Ken O'Brien	.04	.03	.02
271	David Little	.04	.03	.02
272	Pete Stoyanovich	.04	.03	.02
273	Odessa Turner **RC**	.10	.08	.04
274	Anthony Toney	.04	.03	.02
275	Tunch Ilkin	.04	.03	.02
276	Carl Lee	.04	.03	.02
277	Hart Lee Dykes	.04	.03	.02
278	Al Noga	.04	.03	.02
279	Greg Lloyd	.04	.03	.02
280	Billy Joe Tolliver	.04	.03	.02
281	Kirk Lowdermilk	.04	.03	.02
282	Earl Ferrell	.04	.03	.02
283	Eric Sievers	.04	.03	.02
284	Steve Jordan	.04	.03	.02
285	Burt Grossman	.04	.03	.02
286	Johnny Rembert	.04	.03	.02
287	Jeff Jaeger **RC**	.10	.08	.04
288	James Hasty	.04	.03	.02
289	Tony Mandarich	.04	.03	.02
290	Chris Singleton **RC** (DP)	.10	.08	.04
291	Lynn James (DP)(FC)	.04	.03	.02
292	Andre Ware **RC** (DP)	.20	.15	.08
293	Ray Agnew **RC** (DP)	.10	.08	.04
294	Joel Smeenge **RC** (DP)	.10	.08	.04
295	Marc Spindler **RC** (DP)	.10	.08	.04
296	Renaldo Turnbull **RC** (DP)	.40	.30	.15
297	Reggie Rembert (DP)	.04	.03	.02
298	Jeff Alm (DP)	.04	.03	.02
299	Cortez Kennedy **RC** (DP)	.30	.25	.12
300	Blair Thomas **RC** (DP)	.10	.08	.04
301	Pat Terrell **RC** (DP)	.10	.08	.04
302	Junior Seau **RC** (DP)	1.00	.70	.40
303	Mohammed Elewonibi (DP)	.04	.03	.02
304	Tony Bennett **RC** (DP)	.35	.25	.14
305	Percy Snow **RC** (DP)	.08	.06	.03
306	Richmond Webb **RC** (DP)	.15	.11	.06
307	Rodney Hampton **RC** (DP)	1.00	.70	.40
308	Barry Foster **RC** (DP)	.10	.08	.04
309	John Friesz **RC** (DP)	.25	.20	.10
310	Ben Smith **RC** (DP)	.08	.06	.03
311	Joe Montana (HG)	.50	.40	.20
312	Jim Everett (HG)	.04	.03	.02
313	Mark Rypien (HG)	.08	.06	.03
314	Phil Simms (HG)	.08	.06	.03
315	Don Majkowski (HG)	.04	.03	.02
316	Boomer Esiason (HG)	.10	.08	.04
317	Warren Moon (HG)	.10	.08	.04
318	Jim Kelly (HG)	.10	.08	.04
319	Bernie Kosar (HG)	.04	.03	.02
320	Dan Marino (HG)	.40	.30	.15
321	Christian Okoye (GF)	.04	.03	.02
322	Thurman Thomas (GF)	.20	.15	.08
323	James Brooks (GF)	.04	.03	.02
324	Bobby Humphrey (GF)	.04	.03	.02
325	Barry Sanders (GF)	.75	.60	.30
326	Neal Anderson (GF)	.04	.03	.02
327	Dalton Hilliard (GF)	.04	.03	.02
328	Greg Bell (GF)	.04	.03	.02
329	Roger Craig (GF)	.04	.03	.02
330	Bo Jackson (GF)	.20	.15	.08
331	Don Warren	.04	.03	.02
332	Rufus Porter	.04	.03	.02
333	Sammie Smith	.04	.03	.02
334	Lewis Tillman	.20	.15	.08
335	Michael Walter	.04	.03	.02
336	Marc Logan	.04	.03	.02
337	Ron Hallstrom **RC**	.08	.06	.03
338	Stanley Morgan	.04	.03	.02
339	Mark Robinson	.04	.03	.02
340	Frank Reich	.20	.15	.08
341	Chip Lohmiller **RC**	.10	.08	.04
342	Steve Beuerlein	.25	.20	.10
343	John L. Williams	.04	.03	.02
344	Irving Fryar	.04	.03	.02
345	Anthony Carter	.04	.03	.02
346	Al Toon	.04	.03	.02
347	J.T. Smith	.04	.03	.02
348	Pierce Holt **RC**	.10	.08	.04
349	Ferrell Edmunds	.04	.03	.02
350	Mark Rypien	.15	.11	.06
351	Paul Gruber	.04	.03	.02
352	Ernest Givins	.04	.03	.02
353	Ervin Randle	.04	.03	.02
354	Guy McIntyre	.04	.03	.02
355	Webster Slaughter	.04	.03	.02
356	Reuben Davis	.04	.03	.02
357	Rickey Jackson	.04	.03	.02
358	Earnest Byner	.04	.03	.02
359	Eddie Brown	.04	.03	.02
360	Troy Stradford	.04	.03	.02
361	Pepper Johnson	.04	.03	.02
362	Ravin Caldwell	.04	.03	.02
363	Chris Mohr **RC**	.08	.06	.03
364	Jeff Bryant	.04	.03	.02
365	Bruce Collie	.04	.03	.02
366	Courtney Hall	.04	.03	.02
367	Jerry Olsavsky	.04	.03	.02
368	David Galloway	.04	.03	.02
369	Wes Hopkins	.04	.03	.02
370	Johnny Hector	.04	.03	.02
371	Clarence Verdin	.04	.03	.02
372	Nick Lowery	.04	.03	.02
373	Tim Brown	.45	.35	.20
374	Kevin Greene	.04	.03	.02
375	Leonard Marshall	.04	.03	.02
376	Roland James	.04	.03	.02
377	Scott Studwell	.04	.03	.02
378	Jarvis Williams	.04	.03	.02
379	Mike Saxon	.04	.03	.02
380	Kevin Mack	.04	.03	.02
381	Joe Kelly	.04	.03	.02
382	Tom Thayer **RC**	.10	.08	.04
383	Roy Green	.04	.03	.02
384	Michael Brooks **RC**	.20	.15	.08
385	Michael Cofer	.04	.03	.02
386	Ken Ruettgers	.04	.03	.02
387	Dean Steinkuhler	.04	.03	.02
388	Maurice Carthon	.04	.03	.02
389	Ricky Sanders	.04	.03	.02
390	Winton Moss **RC**	.10	.08	.04
391	Tony Woods	.04	.03	.02
392	Keith DeLong	.04	.03	.02
393	David Wyman	.04	.03	.02
394	Vencie Glenn	.04	.03	.02
395	Harris Barton	.04	.03	.02
396	Bryan Hinkle	.04	.03	.02
397	Derek Kennard	.04	.03	.02
398	Heath Sherman **RC**	.20	.15	.08
399	Troy Benson	.04	.03	.02
400	Gary Zimmerman	.04	.03	.02
401	Mark Duper	.04	.03	.02
402	Eugene Lockhart	.04	.03	.02
403	Tim Manoa	.04	.03	.02
404	Reggie Williams	.04	.03	.02
405	Mark Bortz **RC**	.10	.08	.04
406	Mike Kenn	.04	.03	.02
407	John Grimsley	.04	.03	.02
408	Bill Romanowski **RC**	.10	.08	.04
409	Perry Kemp	.04	.03	.02
410	Norm Johnson	.04	.03	.02
411	Broderick Thomas	.04	.03	.02
412	Joe Wolf	.04	.03	.02
413	Andre Waters	.04	.03	.02
414	Jason Staurovsky	.04	.03	.02
415	Eric Martin	.04	.03	.02
416	Joe Prokop	.04	.03	.02
417	Steve Sewell	.04	.03	.02
418	Cedric Jones	.04	.03	.02
419	Alphonso Carreker	.04	.03	.02
420	Keith Willis	.04	.03	.02
421	Bobby Butler	.04	.03	.02
422	John Roper	.04	.03	.02
423	Tim Spencer	.04	.03	.02
424	Jesse Sapolu **RC**	.08	.06	.03
425	Ron Wolfley	.04	.03	.02
426	Doug Smith	.04	.03	.02
427	William Howard	.04	.03	.02
428	Keith Van Horne	.04	.03	.02
429	Tony Jordan	.04	.03	.02

430	Mervyn Fernandez	.04	.03	.02
431	Shaun Gayle **RC**	.10	.08	.04
432	Ricky Nattiel	.04	.03	.02
433	Albert Lewis	.04	.03	.02
434	Fred Banks **RC**	.10	.08	.04
435	Henry Thomas	.04	.03	.02
436	Chet Brooks	.04	.03	.02
437	Mark Ingram	.04	.03	.02
438	Jeff Gossett	.04	.03	.02
439	Mike Wilcher	.04	.03	.02
440	Deron Cherry	.04	.03	.02
441	Mike Rozier	.04	.03	.02
442	Jon Hand	.04	.03	.02
443	Ozzie Newsome	.10	.08	.04
444	Sammy Martin	.04	.03	.02
445	Luis Sharpe	.04	.03	.02
446	Lee Williams	.04	.03	.02
447	Chris Martin **RC**	.10	.08	.04
448	Kevin Fagan	.04	.03	.02
449	Gene Lang	.04	.03	.02
450	Greg Townsend	.04	.03	.02
451	Robert Lyles	.04	.03	.02
452	Eric Hill	.04	.03	.02
453	John Teltschik	.04	.03	.02
454	Vestee Jackson	.04	.03	.02
455	Bruce Reimers	.04	.03	.02
456	Butch Rolle **RC**	.10	.08	.04
457	Lawyer Tillman	.04	.03	.02
458	Andre Tippett	.04	.03	.02
459	James Thornton	.04	.03	.02
460	Randy Grimes	.04	.03	.02
461	Larry Roberts	.04	.03	.02
462	Ron Holmes	.04	.03	.02
463	Mike Wise	.04	.03	.02
464	Danny Copeland **RC**	.10	.08	.04
465	Bruce Wilkerson **RC**	.10	.08	.04
466	Mike Quick	.04	.03	.02
467	Mickey Shuler	.04	.03	.02
468	Mike Prior	.04	.03	.02
469	Ron Rivera	.04	.03	.02
470	Dean Biasucci	.04	.03	.02
471	Perry Williams	.04	.03	.02
472	Darren Comeaux	.04	.03	.02
473	Freeman McNeil	.04	.03	.02
474	Tyrone Braxton	.04	.03	.02
475	Jay Schroeder	.04	.03	.02
476	Naz Worthen	.04	.03	.02
477	Lionel Washington	.04	.03	.02
478	Carl Zander	.04	.03	.02
479	Al Baker	.04	.03	.02
480	Mike Merriweather	.04	.03	.02
481	Mike Gann	.04	.03	.02
482	Brent Williams	.04	.03	.02
483	Eugene Robinson	.04	.03	.02
484	Ray Horton	.04	.03	.02
485	Bruce Armstrong	.04	.03	.02
486	John Fourcade	.04	.03	.02
487	Lewis Billups	.04	.03	.02
489	Ken Sims	.04	.03	.02
490	Chris Chandler	.04	.03	.02
491	Mark Lee	.04	.03	.02
492	Johnny Meads	.04	.03	.02
493	Tim Irwin	.04	.03	.02
494	E.J. Junior	.04	.03	.02
495	Hardy Nickerson	.04	.03	.02
496	Rob McGovern	.04	.03	.02
497	Fred Strickland **RC**	.10	.08	.04
498	Reggie Rutland **RC**	.10	.08	.04
499	Mel Owens	.04	.03	.02
500	Derrick Thomas	.25	.20	.10
501	Jerrol Williams	.04	.03	.02
502	Maurice Hurst **RC**	.10	.08	.04
503	Larry Kelm **RC**	.10	.08	.04
504	Herman Fontenot	.04	.03	.02
505	Pat Beach	.04	.03	.02
506	Haywood Jeffires **RC**	.85	.60	.35
507	Neil Smith	.25	.20	.10
508	Cleveland Gary	.10	.08	.04
509	William Perry	.04	.03	.02
510	Michael Carter	.04	.03	.02
511	Walker Lee Ashley	.04	.03	.02
512	Bob Golic	.04	.03	.02
513	Danny Villa **RC**	.08	.06	.03
514	Matt Millen	.04	.03	.02
515	Don Griffin	.04	.03	.02
516	Jonathan Hayes	.04	.03	.02
517	Gerald Williams **RC**	.08	.06	.03
518	Scott Fulhage	.04	.03	.02
519	Irv Pankey	.04	.03	.02
520	Randy Dixon **RC**	.08	.06	.03
521	Terry McDaniel	.04	.03	.02
522	Dan Saleaumua	.04	.03	.02
523	Darrin Nelson	.04	.03	.02
524	Leonard Griffin	.04	.03	.02
525	Michael Ball	.04	.03	.02
526	Ernie Jones **RC**	.25	.20	.10
527	Tony Eason	.04	.03	.02
528	Ed Reynolds	.04	.03	.02
529	Gary Hogeboom	.04	.03	.02
530	Don Mosebar	.04	.03	.02
531	Ottis Anderson	.04	.03	.02
532	Bucky Scribner	.04	.03	.02
533	Aaron Cox	.04	.03	.02
534	Sean Jones	.04	.03	.02
535	Doug Flutie	.75	.60	.30
536	Leo Lewis	.04	.03	.02
537	Art Still	.04	.03	.02
538	Matt Bahr	.04	.03	.02
539	Keena Turner	.04	.03	.02
540	Sammy Winder	.04	.03	.02
541	Mike Webster	.04	.03	.02
542	Doug Riesenberg **RC**	.10	.08	.04
543	Dan Fike	.04	.03	.02
544	Clarence Kay	.04	.03	.02
545	Jim Burt	.04	.03	.02
546	Mike Horan	.04	.03	.02
547	Al Harris	.04	.03	.02
548	Maury Buford	.04	.03	.02
549	Jerry Robinson	.04	.03	.02
550	Tracy Rocker	.04	.03	.02
551	Karl Mecklenburg (CC)	.04	.03	.02
552	Lawrence Taylor (CC)	.08	.06	.03
553	Derrick Thomas (CC)	.20	.15	.08
554	Mike Singletary (CC)	.04	.03	.02
555	Tim Harris (CC)	.04	.03	.02
556	Jerry Rice (RM)	.40	.30	.15
557	Art Monk (RM)	.04	.03	.02
558	Mark Carrier (RM)	.04	.03	.02
559	Andre Reed (RM)	.08	.06	.03
560	Sterling Sharpe (RM)	.30	.25	.12
561	Herschel Walker (GF)	.04	.03	.02
562	Ottis Anderson (GF)	.04	.03	.02
563	Randall Cunningham (HG)	.08	.06	.03
564	John Elway (HG)	.20	.15	.08
565	David Fulcher (AP)	.04	.03	.02
566	Ronnie Lott (AP)	.04	.03	.02
567	Jerry Gray (AP)	.04	.03	.02
568	Albert Lewis (AP)	.04	.03	.02
569	Karl Mecklenburg (AP)	.04	.03	.02
570	Mike Singletary (AP)	.04	.03	.02
571	Lawrence Taylor (AP)	.08	.06	.03
572	Tim Harris (AP)	.04	.03	.02
573	Keith Millard (AP)	.04	.03	.02
574	Reggie White (AP)	.04	.03	.02
575	Chris Doleman (AP)	.04	.03	.02
576	Dave Meggett (AP)	.04	.03	.02
577	Rod Woodson (AP)	.04	.03	.02
578	Sean Landeta (AP)	.04	.03	.02
579	Eddie Murray (AP)	.04	.03	.02
580	Barry Sanders (AP)	.75	.60	.30
581	Christian Okoye (AP)	.04	.03	.02
582	Joe Montana (AP)	.50	.40	.20
583	Jay Hilgenberg (AP)	.04	.03	.02
584	Bruce Matthews (AP)	.04	.03	.02
585	Tom Newberry (AP)	.04	.03	.02
586	Gary Zimmerman (AP)	.04	.03	.02
587	Anthony Munoz (AP)	.04	.03	.02
588	Keith Jackson (AP)	.08	.06	.03
589	Sterling Sharpe (AP)	.30	.25	.12
590	Jerry Rice (AP)	.40	.30	.15
591	Bo Jackson (RB)	.15	.11	.06
592	Steve Largent (RB)	.10	.08	.04
593	Flipper Anderson (RB)	.04	.03	.02
594	Joe Montana (RB)	.50	.40	.20
595	Franco Harris (HOF)	.08	.06	.03
596	Bob St. Clair (HOF)	.04	.03	.02
597	Tom Landry (HOF)	.08	.06	.03
598	Jack Lambert (HOF)	.04	.03	.02
599	Ted Hendricks (HOF)	.04	.03	.02
600	Buck Buchanan (HOF) ("drafted '83")	.05	.04	.02
600a	Buck Buchanan (HOF) ("drafted '63")	.05	.04	.02
601	Bob Griese (HOF)	.04	.03	.02
602	**Super Bowl**	.04	.03	.02
603	Vince Lombardi	.04	.03	.02
604	Mark Carrier	.04	.03	.02
605	Randall Cunningham	.10	.08	.04
606	Percy Snow (C90)	.04	.03	.02
607	Andre Ware (C90)	.10	.08	.04
608	Blair Thomas (C90)	.04	.03	.02
609	Eric Green (C90)	.10	.08	.04
610	Reggie Rembert (C90)	.04	.03	.02
611	Richmond Webb (C90)	.10	.08	.04
612	Bern Brostek (C90)	.04	.03	.02
613	James Williams (C90)	.04	.03	.02
614	Mark Carrier (C90)	.04	.03	.02
615	Renaldo Turnbull (C90)	.20	.15	.08
616	Cortez Kennedy (C90)	.40	.30	.15
617	Keith McCants (C90)	.04	.03	.02
618	Anthony Thompson **RC** (DP)	.10	.08	.04
619	LeRoy Butler **RC** (DP)	.20	.15	.08
620	Aaron Wallace **RC** (DP)	.10	.08	.04
621	Alexander Wright **RC** (DP)	.15	.11	.06
622	Keith McCants **RC** (DP)	.10	.08	.04
623	Jimmie Jones **RC** (DP)	.10	.08	.04
624	Anthony Johnson **RC** (DP)	.20	.15	.08
625	Fred Washington (DP)	.04	.03	.02
626	Mike Bellamy (DP)	.04	.03	.02
627	Mark Carrier **RC** (DP)	.20	.15	.08
628	Harold Green **RC** (DP)	.25	.20	.10
629	Eric Green **RC** (DP)	.40	.30	.15
630	Andre Collins **RC** (DP)	.10	.08	.04
631	Lamar Lathon **RC** (DP)	.10	.08	.04
632	Terry Wooden **RC** (DP)	.10	.08	.04
633	Jesse Anderson (DP)	.04	.03	.02
634	Jeff George **RC** (DP)	1.25	.90	.50
635	Carwell Gardner **RC** (DP)	.10	.08	.04
636	Darrell Thompson **RC**	.25	.20	.10
637	Vince Buck (DP)	.10	.08	.04
638	Mike Jones (DP)	.04	.03	.02
639	Charles Arbuckle **RC** (DP)	.10	.08	.04
640	Dennis Brown **RC** (DP)	.10	.08	.04
641	James Williams **RC** (DP)	.10	.08	.04
642	Bern Brostek **RC** (DP)	.10	.08	.04
643	Darion Conner **RC** (DP)	.08	.06	.03
644	Mike Fox **RC** (DP)	.08	.06	.03
645	Cary Conklin **RC** (DP)	.40	.30	.15
646	Tim Grunhard **RC** (DP)	.08	.06	.03
647	Ron Cox **RC** (DP)	.08	.06	.03
648	Keith Sims **RC** (DP)	.08	.06	.03
649	Alton Montgomery **RC** (DP)	.10	.08	.04
650	Greg McMurtry **RC** (DP)	.10	.08	.04
651	Scott Mitchell **RC** (DP)	.75	.60	.30
652	Tim Ryan (DP)	.04	.03	.02
653	Jeff Mills (DP)	.04	.03	.02
654	Ricky Proehl **RC** (DP)	.50	.40	.20
655	Steve Broussard **RC** (DP)	.08	.06	.03
656	Peter Tom Willis **RC** (DP)	.15	.11	.06
657	Dexter Carter **RC** (DP)	.15	.11	.06
658	Tony Casillas	.04	.03	.02
659	Joe Morris	.04	.03	.02
660	Greg Kragen	.04	.03	.02

1990 Score 100 Hottest

These cards featuring 100 top NFL players, have the same photos on them as the regular issue 1990 Score cards, but they are numbered differently. Publications International published a magazine to accompany the set; the magazine offered additional information about the players.

		NM/M	NM	E
Complete Set (100):		15.00	11.00	6.00
Common Player:		.10	.08	.04
1	Bo Jackson	.25	.20	.10
2	Joe Montana	2.00	1.50	.80
3	Deion Sanders	.50	.40	.20
4	Dan Marino	1.25	.90	.50
5	Barry Sanders	1.00	.70	.40
6	Neal Anderson	.15	.11	.06
7	Phil Simms	.20	.15	.08
8	Bobby Humphrey	.10	.08	.04
9	Roger Craig	.20	.15	.08
10	John Elway	.60	.45	.25
11	James Brooks	.15	.11	.06
12	Ken O'Brien	.10	.08	.04
13	Thurman Thomas	.50	.40	.20
14	Troy Aikman	2.00	1.50	.80
15	Karl Mecklenburg	.10	.08	.04
16	Dave Krieg	.10	.08	.04
17	Chris Spielman	.10	.08	.04
18	Tim Harris	.15	.11	.06
19	Tim Worley	.10	.08	.04
20	Clay Matthews	.15	.11	.06
21	Lars Tate	.10	.08	.04
22	Hart Lee Dykes	.10	.08	.04
23	Cornelius Bennett	.15	.11	.06
24	Anthony Miller	.15	.11	.06
25	Lawrence Taylor	.30	.25	.12
26	Jay Hilgenberg	.10	.08	.04
27	Tom Rathman	.15	.11	.06
28	Brian Blades	.25	.20	.10
29	David Fulcher	.10	.08	.04
30	Cris Carter	.40	.30	.15
31	Marcus Allen	.30	.25	.12
32	Eric Metcalf	.15	.11	.06
33	Bruce Smith	.15	.11	.06
34	Jim Kelly	.60	.45	.25
35	Wade Wilson	.15	.11	.06
36	Rich Camarillo	.10	.08	.04
37	Boomer Esiason	.20	.15	.08
38	John Offerdahl	.10	.08	.04
39	Vance Johnson	.10	.08	.04
40	Ronnie Lott	.20	.15	.08
41	Kevin Ross	.15	.11	.06
42	Greg Bell	.10	.08	.04
43	Erik McMillan	.10	.08	.04
44	Mike Singletary	.20	.15	.08
45	Roger Vick	.10	.08	.04
46	Keith Jackson	.30	.25	.12

47	Henry Ellard	.15	.11	.06
48	Gary Anderson	.15	.11	.06
49	Art Monk	.30	.25	.12
50	Jim Everett	.15	.11	.06
51	Anthony Munoz	.15	.11	.06
52	Ray Childress	.15	.11	.06
53	Howie Long	.20	.15	.08
54	Chris Hinton	.10	.08	.04
55	John Stephens	.20	.15	.08
56	Reggie White	.25	.20	.10
57	Rodney Peete	.15	.11	.06
58	Don Majkowski	.10	.08	.04
59	Michael Cofer	.10	.08	.04
60	Bubby Brister	.10	.08	.04
61	Jerry Gray	.10	.08	.04
62	Rodney Holman	.10	.08	.04
63	Vinny Testaverde	.20	.15	.08
64	Sterling Sharpe	.65	.50	.25
65	Keith Millard	.10	.08	.04
66	Jim Lachey	.10	.08	.04
67	Dave Meggett	.15	.11	.06
68	Brent Fullwood	.10	.08	.04
69	Bobby Hebert	.15	.11	.06
70	Joey Browner	.10	.08	.04
71	Flipper Anderson	.15	.11	.06
72	Tim McGee	.10	.08	.04
73	Eric Allen	.10	.08	.04
74	Charles Haley	.25	.20	.10
75	Christian Okoye	.15	.11	.06
76	Herschel Walker	.20	.15	.08
77	Kelvin Martin	.15	.11	.06
78	Bill Fralic	.10	.08	.04
79	Leslie O'Neal	.15	.11	.06
80	Bernie Kosar	.20	.15	.08
81	Eric Sievers	.10	.08	.04
82	Timm Rosenbach	.10	.08	.04
83	Steve DeBerg	.15	.11	.06
84	Duane Bickett	.10	.08	.04
85	Chris Doleman	.15	.11	.06
86	Carl Banks	.15	.11	.06
87	Vaughan Johnson	.10	.08	.04
88	Dennis Smith	.10	.08	.04
89	Billy Joe Tolliver	.15	.11	.06
90	Dalton Hilliard	.10	.08	.04
91	John Taylor	.20	.15	.08
92	Mark Rypien	.20	.15	.08
93	Chris Miller	.30	.25	.12
94	Mark Clayton	.15	.11	.06
95	Andre Reed	.25	.20	.10
96	Warren Moon	.50	.40	.20
97	Bruce Matthews	.10	.08	.04
98	Rod Woodson	.25	.20	.10
99	Pat Swilling	.15	.11	.06
100	Jerry Rice	1.25	.90	.50

1991 Score Dream Team Autographs

The 11-card, standard-size set was inserted every 5,000 packs of Series II packs. Each player autographed approximately 500 cards.

		NM/M	NM	E
Complete Set (11):				
Common Player:		10.00	18.50	10.00
676	Warren Moon	75.00	56.00	30.00
677	Barry Sanders	250.00	187.00	100.00
678	Thurman Thomas	65.00	49.00	26.00
679	Andre Reed	55.00	41.00	22.00
680	Andre Rison	50.00	37.00	20.00
681	Keith Jackson	50.00	37.00	20.00
682	Bruce Armstrong	10.00	18.50	10.00
683	Jim Lachey	10.00	18.50	10.00
684	Bruce Matthews	10.00	18.50	10.00
685	Mike Munchak	10.00	18.50	10.00
686	Don Mosebar	10.00	18.50	10.00

1991 Score National 10

These 10 cards were distributed at the 12th National Sports Collectors Covention in a cello wrapper. A panel on the card back indicates the cards were created for the convention. A mug shot, card number, biographical information and career summary are also provided on the back. The front has a color action photo of the player, with a player/football pattern above and below the photo.

Complete Set (10):		10.00	7.50	4.002.00
Common Player:		.75	.60	.30.10
1	Emmitt Smith	8.00	6.00	3.25 .80
2	Mark Carrier	1.00	.70	.40 .15
3	Steve Broussard	1.00	.70	.40 .15
4	Johnny Johnson	2.00	1.50	.80 .30
5	Steve Christie	1.00	.70	.40 .10
6	Richmond Webb	.75	.60	.30 .12
7	James Francis	.75	.60	.30 .15
8	Jeff George	2.00	1.50	.80 .40
9	Rodney Hampton	3.00	2.25	1.25 .40
10	Calvin Williams	1.00	.70	.40 .12

1991 Score Promos

These six cards were designed to preview Score's 1991 regular set. The card numbers, which are on the card back, are identical to those in the regular set, except for Lawrence Taylor, who is #529 in the regular set. The prototype cards can be distinguished from the regular cards by several differences, including: the statistics on the back are in blue-green, not green; the promo cards omit the tiny trademark symbol next to the Team NFL logo; and cards 1, 5 and 7 are cropped slightly different.

		NM/M	NM	E
Complete Set (6):		10.00	7.50	4.00
Common Player:		1.00	.70	.40
1	Joe Montana	5.00	3.75	2.00
4	Lawrence Taylor	1.25	.90	.50
5	Derrick Thomas	1.50	1.25	.60
6	Mike Singletary	1.00	.70	.40
7	Boomer Esiason	1.25	.90	.50
12	Randall Cunningham	1.50	1.25	.60

1991 Score Supplemental

Rookies and players who were traded during the regular season are featured in this 110-card update set. The fronts have the same design as the regular cards do, except the borders shade from blue-green to white. The backs have a mug shot and player information in a horizontal format framed by a gold border. Card numbering is done on the back with a "T" suffix.

		NM/M	NM	E
Complete Set (110):		8.00	6.00	3.25
Common Player:		.04	.03	.02
1	Ronnie Lott	.10	.08	.04
2	Matt Millen	.04	.03	.02
3	Tim McKyer	.04	.03	.02
4	Vince Newsome	.04	.03	.02
5	Gaston Green	.04	.03	.02
6	Brett Perriman	.08	.06	.03
7	Roger Craig	.06	.05	.02
8	Pete Holohan	.04	.03	.02
9	Tony Zendejas	.04	.03	.02
10	Lee Williams	.04	.03	.02
11	Mike Stonebreaker	.04	.03	.02
12	Felix Wright	.04	.03	.02
13	Lonnie Young	.04	.03	.02
14	Hugh Millen **RC**	.10	.08	.04
15	Roy Green	.04	.03	.02
16	Greg Davis **RC**	.10	.08	.04
17	Dexter Manley	.04	.03	.02
18	Ted Washington **RC**	.10	.08	.04
19	Norm Johnson	.04	.03	.02
20	Joe Morris	.04	.03	.02
21	Robert Perryman	.04	.03	.02
22	Mike Iaquaniello	.04	.03	.02
23	Gerald Perry **RC**	.10	.08	.04
24	Zeke Mowatt	.04	.03	.02
25	Rich Miano **RC**	.10	.08	.04
26	Nick Bell	.10	.08	.04
27	Terry Orr **RC**	.15	.11	.06
28	Matt Stover **RC**	.15	.11	.06
29	Bubba Paris	.04	.03	.02
30	Ron Brown	.04	.03	.02
31	Don Davey	.04	.03	.02
32	Lee Rouson	.04	.03	.02
33	Terry Hoage	.04	.03	.02
34	Tony Covington	.04	.03	.02
35	John Rienstra	.04	.03	.02
36	Charles Dimry **RC**	.08	.06	.03
37	Todd Marinovich	.08	.06	.03
38	Winston Moss	.04	.03	.02
39	Vestee Jackson	.04	.03	.02
40	Brian Hansen	.04	.03	.02
41	Irv Eatman	.04	.03	.02
42	Jarrod Bunch	.08	.06	.03
43	Kanavis McGhee **RC**	.10	.08	.04
44	Vai Sikahema	.04	.03	.02
45	Charles McRae **RC**	.10	.08	.04
46	Quinn Early	.04	.03	.02
47	Jeff Faulkner **RC**	.10	.08	.04
48	William Frizzell **RC**	.10	.08	.04
49	John Booty	.04	.03	.02
50	Tim Harris	.04	.03	.02
51	Derek Russell	.10	.08	.04
52	John Flannery **RC**	.10	.08	.04
53	Tim Barnett **RC**	.15	.11	.06
54	Alfred Williams **RC**	.15	.11	.06
55	Dan McGwire	.04	.03	.02
56	Ernie Mills	.10	.08	.04
57	Stanley Richard	.04	.03	.02
58	Huey Richardson	.04	.03	.02
59	Jerome Henderson **RC**	.10	.08	.04
60	Bryan Cox **RC**	.40	.30	.15
61	Russell Maryland	.25	.20	.10
62	Reggie Jones **RC**	.15	.11	.06
63	Mo Lewis **RC**	.10	.08	.04
64	Moe Gardner	.04	.03	.02
65	Wesley Carroll	.10	.08	.04
66	Michael Jackson **RC**	.25	.20	.10
67	Shawn Jefferson **RC**	.10	.08	.04
68	Chris Zorich	.10	.08	.04
69	Kenny Walker	.04	.03	.02
70	Erric Pegram **RC**	.10	.08	.04
71	Alvin Harper	.10	.08	.04
72	Harry Colon **RC**	.10	.08	.04
73	Scott Miller	.04	.03	.02
74	Lawrence Dawsey	.10	.08	.04
75	Phil Hansen **RC**	.15	.11	.06
76	Roman Phifer **RC**	.15	.11	.06
77	Greg Lewis	.04	.03	.02
78	Merton Hanks **RC**	.15	.11	.06
79	James Jones **RC**	.10	.08	.04
80	Vinnie Clark	.04	.03	.02
81	R.J. Kors	.04	.03	.02
82	Mike Pritchard	.25	.20	.10
83	Stan Thomas	.04	.03	.02
84	Lamar Rogers	.04	.03	.02
85	Eric Williams **RC**	.25	.20	.10
86	Keith Traylor **RC**	.10	.08	.04
87	Mike Dumas	.04	.03	.02
88	Mel Agee	.04	.03	.02
89	Harvey Williams	.25	.20	.10
90	Todd Lyght	.04	.03	.02
91	Jake Reed	.50	.40	.20
92	Pat Harlow	.04	.03	.02
93	Antone Davis **RC**	.10	.08	.04
94	Aeneas Williams **RC**	.10	.08	.04
95	Eric Bieniemy	.04	.03	.02
96	John Kasay **RC**	.10	.08	.04
97	Robert Wilson	.04	.03	.02
98	Ricky Ervins	.15	.11	.06
99	Mike Croel	.10	.08	.04
100	David Lang **RC**	.15	.11	.06
101	Esera Tuaolo **RC**	.10	.08	.04
102	Randal Hill	.20	.15	.08
103	Jon Vaughn **RC**	.25	.20	.10
104	Dave McCloughan	.04	.03	.02
105	David Daniels	.04	.03	.02
106	Eric Moten	.04	.03	.02
107	Anthony Morgan **RC**	.15	.11	.06
108	Ed King	.04	.03	.02
109	Leonard Russell **RC**	.10	.08	.04
110	Aaron Craver	.08	.06	.03

1991 Score Young Superstars

These cards, available in October 1990 via a mail-in offer found on Score wax packs, featured up-and-coming stars of the game. Each front has game-day photography surrounded by black borders and team colors. The card back shows a head shot, a player profile and a scouting report quote.

Complete Set (40):		7.00	5.25	2.752.75
Common Player:		.10	.08	.04.04
1	Johnny Balley	.15	.11	.06.06
2	Johnny Johnson	.20	.15	.08.08
3	Fred Barnett	.15	.11	.06.06
4	Keith McCants	.10	.08	.04.02
5	Brad Baxter	.10	.08	.04.02
6	Dan Owens	.10	.08	.04.01
7	Steve Broussard	.15	.11	.06.03
8	Ricky Proehl	.15	.11	.06.02
9	Marion Butts	.20	.15	.08.02
10	Reggie Cobb	.10	.08	.04.03
11	Dennis Byrd	.10	.08	.04.01
12	Emmitt Smith	3.00	2.25	1.25.15
13	Mark Carrier	.15	.11	.06.02
14	Keith Sims	.10	.08	.04.01
15	Dexter Carter	.15	.11	.06.02
16	Chris Singleton	.10	.08	.04.02
17	Steve Christie	.10	.08	.04.01
18	Frank Cornish	.10	.08	.04.01
19	Timm Rosenbach	.10	.08	.04.02
20	Sammie Smith	.10	.08	.04.02
21	Calvin Williams	.15	.11	.06.02
22	Merril Hoge	.10	.08	.04.01
23	Hart Lee Dykes	.10	.08	.04.01
24	Darrell Thompson	.10	.08	.04.03
25	James Francis	.10	.08	.04.02
26	John Elliott	.10	.08	.04.01
27	Jeff George	.25	.20	.10.05
28	Broderick Thomas	.15	.11	.06.02
29	Eric Green	.15	.11	.06.03
30	Steve Walsh	.10	.08	.04.02
31	Harold Green	.15	.11	.06.03
32	Andre Ware	.10	.08	.04.02
33	Richmond Webb	.10	.08	.04.02
34	Junior Seau	.40	.30	.15.02
35	Tim Grunhard	.10	.08	.04.01
36	Tim Worley	.10	.08	.04.01
37	Haywood Jeffires	.20	.15	.08.03
38	Rod Woodson	.20	.15	.08.02
39	Rodney Hampton	.20	.15	.08.05
40	Dave Szott	.10	.08	.04.01

1991 Score

Score's 1991 first series was released in May 1991. The size increased by 15 cards over the previous year's Series I. Carried over from Score baseball was the "Dream Team" subset - this time featuring card-size profile shots with a smaller action insert. Artist Chris Greco worked on the MVP and Top Leader cards. Because Draft Pick cards carry no NFL team designation, they technically are not considered true rookie cards. (Key: DP - Draft Pick, 90 - 90-Plus Club, TL - Top Leader, DT - Dream Team)

	NM/M	NM	E
Complete Set (686):	9.00	6.75	3.50
Factory Set (690):	9.00	6.75	3.50
Complete Series 1 (345):	4.50	3.50	1.75
Complete Series 2 (341):	4.50	3.50	1.75
Common Player:	.04	.03	.02
Pack (16):	.40		
Wax Box (36):	9.00		

		NM/M	NM	E
1	Joe Montana	1.00	.70	.40
2	Eric Allen	.04	.03	.02
3	Rohn Stark	.04	.03	.02
4	Frank Reich	.04	.03	.02
5	Derrick Thomas	.25	.20	.10
6	Mike Singletary	.04	.03	.02
7	Boomer Esiason	.10	.08	.04
8	Matt Millen	.04	.03	.02
9	Chris Spielman	.04	.03	.02
10	Gerald McNeil	.04	.03	.02
11	Nick Lowery	.04	.03	.02
12	Randall Cunningham	.10	.08	.04
13	Marion Butts	.04	.03	.02
14	Tim Brown	.25	.20	.10
15	Emmitt Smith	1.50	1.25	.60
16	Rich Camarillo	.04	.03	.02
17	Mike Merriweather	.04	.03	.02
18	Derrick Fenner	.10	.08	.04
19	Clay Matthews	.04	.03	.02
20	Barry Sanders	1.50	1.25	.60
21	James Brooks	.04	.03	.02
22	Alton Montgomery	.04	.03	.02
23	Steve Atwater	.04	.03	.02
24	Ron Morris	.04	.03	.02
25	Brad Muster	.04	.03	.02
26	Andre Rison	.25	.20	.10
27	Brian Brennan	.04	.03	.02
28	Leonard Smith	.04	.03	.02
29	Kevin Butler	.04	.03	.02
30	Tim Harris	.04	.03	.02
31	Jay Novacek	.15	.11	.06
32	Eddie Murray	.04	.03	.02
33	Keith Woodside	.04	.03	.02
34	Ray Crockett RC	.10	.08	.04
35	Eugene Lockhart	.04	.03	.02
36	Bill Romanowski	.04	.03	.02
37	Eddie Brown	.04	.03	.02
38	Eugene Daniel	.04	.03	.02
39	Scott Fulhage	.04	.03	.02
40	Harold Green	.10	.08	.04
41	Mark Jackson	.04	.03	.02
42	Sterling Sharpe	.10	.08	.04
43	Mel Gray	.04	.03	.02
44	Jerry Holmes	.04	.03	.02
45	Allen Pinkett	.04	.03	.02
46	Warren Powers	.04	.03	.02
47	Rodney Peete	.04	.03	.02
48	Lorenzo White	.10	.08	.04
49	Dan Owens	.04	.03	.02
50	James Francis	.04	.03	.02
51	Ken Norton	.04	.03	.02
52	Ed West	.04	.03	.02
53	Andre Reed	.10	.08	.04
54	John Grimsley	.04	.03	.02
55	Michael Cofer	.04	.03	.02
56	Chris Doleman	.04	.03	.02
57	Pat Swilling	.04	.03	.02
58	Jessie Tuggle	.04	.03	.02
59	Mike Johnson	.04	.03	.02
60	Steve Walsh	.04	.03	.02
61	Sam Mills	.04	.03	.02
62	Don Mosebar	.04	.03	.02
63	Jay Hilgenberg	.04	.03	.02
64	Cleveland Gary	.04	.03	.02
65	Andre Tippett	.04	.03	.02
66	Tom Newberry	.04	.03	.02
67	Maurice Hurst	.04	.03	.02
68	Louis Oliver	.04	.03	.02
69	Fred Marion	.04	.03	.02
70	Christian Okoye	.04	.03	.02
71	Marv Cook	.04	.03	.02
72	Darryl Talley	.04	.03	.02
73	Rick Fenney	.04	.03	.02
74	Kelvin Martin	.04	.03	.02
75	Howie Long	.04	.03	.02
76	Steve Wisniewski	.04	.03	.02
77	Karl Mecklenburg	.04	.03	.02
78	Dan Saleaumua	.04	.03	.02
79	Ray Childress	.04	.03	.02
80	Henry Ellard	.04	.03	.02
81	Ernest Givins	.04	.03	.02
82	Ferrell Edmunds	.04	.03	.02
83	Steve Jordan	.04	.03	.02
84	Tony Mandarich	.04	.03	.02
85	Eric Martin	.04	.03	.02
86	Rich Gannon	.10	.08	.04
87	Irving Fryar	.04	.03	.02
88	Tom Rathman	.04	.03	.02
89	Dan Hampton	.04	.03	.02
90	Barry Word	.10	.08	.04
91	Kevin Greene	.04	.03	.02
92	Sean Landeta	.04	.03	.02
93	Trace Armstrong	.04	.03	.02
94	Dennis Byrd	.04	.03	.02
95	Timm Rosenbach	.04	.03	.02
96	Anthony Toney	.04	.03	.02
97	Tim Krumrie	.04	.03	.02
98	Jerry Ball	.04	.03	.02
99	Tim Green	.04	.03	.02
100	Bo Jackson	.35	.25	.14
101	Myron Guyton	.04	.03	.02
102	Mike Mularkey	.04	.03	.02
103	Jerry Gray	.04	.03	.02
104	Scott Stephen	.04	.03	.02
106	Lomas Brown	.04	.03	.02
107	David Little	.04	.03	.02
108	Brad Baxter	.10	.08	.04
109	Freddie Joe Nunn	.04	.03	.02
110	Dave Meggett	.04	.03	.02
111	Mark Rypien	.10	.08	.04
112	Warren Williams	.04	.03	.02
113	Ron Rivera	.04	.03	.02
114	Terance Mathis	.10	.08	.04
115	Anthony Munoz	.04	.03	.02
116	Jeff Bryant	.04	.03	.02
117	Issaic Holt	.04	.03	.02
118	Steve Sewell	.04	.03	.02
119	Tim Newton	.04	.03	.02
120	Emile Harry	.04	.03	.02
121	Gary Anderson (Pitt.)	.04	.03	.02
122	Mark Lee	.04	.03	.02
123	Alfred Anderson	.04	.03	.02
124	Tony Blaylock	.04	.03	.02
125	Ernest Byner	.04	.03	.02
126	Bill Maas	.04	.03	.02
127	Keith Taylor	.04	.03	.02
128	Cliff Odom	.04	.03	.02
129	Bob Golic	.04	.03	.02
130	Bart Oates	.04	.03	.02
131	Jim Arnold	.04	.03	.02
132	Jerr Herrod	.04	.03	.02
133	Bruce Armstrong	.04	.03	.02
134	Craig Heyward	.06	.05	.02
135	Joey Browner	.04	.03	.02
136	Darren Comeaux	.04	.03	.02
137	Pat Beach	.04	.03	.02
138	Dalton Hilliard	.06	.05	.02
139	David Treadwell	.04	.03	.02
140	Gary Anderson (T.B.)	.04	.03	.02
141	Eugene Robinson	.04	.03	.02
142	Scott Case	.04	.03	.02
143	Paul Farren	.04	.03	.02
144	Gill Fenerty	.04	.03	.02
145	Tim Irwin	.04	.03	.02
146	Norm Johnson	.04	.03	.02
147	Willie Gault	.06	.05	.02
148	Clarence Verdin	.04	.03	.02
149	Jeff Uhlenhake	.04	.03	.02
150	Erik McMillan	.04	.03	.02
151	Kevin Ross	.04	.03	.02
152	Pepper Johnson	.04	.03	.02
153	Bryan Hinkle	.04	.03	.02
154	Gary Clark	.08	.06	.03
155	Robert Delpino	.04	.03	.02
156	Doug Smith	.04	.03	.02
157	Chris Martin	.04	.03	.02
158	Ray Berry	.04	.03	.02
159	Steve Christie	.04	.03	.02
160	Don Smith	.04	.03	.02
161	Greg McMurtry	.04	.03	.02
162	Jack Del Rio	.04	.03	.02
163	Floyd Dixon	.04	.03	.02
164	Buford McGee	.04	.03	.02
165	Brett Maxie	.04	.03	.02
166	Morten Andersen	.06	.05	.02
167	Kent Hull	.04	.03	.02
168	Skip McClendon	.04	.03	.02
169	Keith Sims	.04	.03	.02
170	Leonard Marshall	.04	.03	.02
171	Tony Woods	.04	.03	.02
172	Byron Evans	.04	.03	.02
173	Rob Burnett RC	.15	.11	.06
174	Tory Epps	.04	.03	.02
175	Toi Cook RC	.10	.08	.04
176	John Elliott	.04	.03	.02
177	Tommie Agee	.04	.03	.02
178	Keith Van Horne	.04	.03	.02
179	Dennis Smith	.04	.03	.02
180	James Lofton	.04	.03	.02
181	Art Monk	.04	.03	.02
182	Anthony Carter	.04	.03	.02
183	Louis Lipps	.04	.03	.02
184	Bruce Hill	.04	.03	.02
185	Mike Young	.04	.03	.02
186	Eric Green	.10	.08	.04
187	Barney Bussey RC	.10	.08	.04
188	Curtis Duncan	.04	.03	.02
189	Robert Awalt	.04	.03	.02
190	Johnny Johnson	.20	.15	.08
191	Jeff Cross	.04	.03	.02
192	Keith McKeller	.04	.03	.02
193	Robert Brown	.04	.03	.02
194	Vincent Brown	.04	.03	.02
195	Calvin Williams	.20	.15	.08
196	Sean Jones	.04	.03	.02
197	Willie Drewrey	.04	.03	.02
198	Bubba McDowell	.04	.03	.02
199	Al Noga	.04	.03	.02
200	Ronnie Lott	.10	.08	.04
201	Warren Moon	.20	.15	.08
202	Chris Hinton	.04	.03	.02
203	Jim Sweeney	.04	.03	.02
204	Wayne Haddix	.04	.03	.02
205	Tim Jorden RC	.10	.08	.04
206	Marvin Allen	.04	.03	.02
207	Jim Morrissey RC	.10	.08	.04
208	Ben Smith	.04	.03	.02
209	William White	.04	.03	.02
210	Jim Jensen	.04	.03	.02
211	Doug Reed	.04	.03	.02
212	Ethan Horton	.04	.03	.02
213	Chris Jacke	.04	.03	.02
214	Johnny Hector	.04	.03	.02
215	Drew Hill	.04	.03	.02
216	Roy Green	.04	.03	.02
217	Dean Steinhuhler	.04	.03	.02
218	Cedric Mack	.04	.03	.02
219	Chris Miller	.04	.03	.02
220	Keith Byars	.04	.03	.02
221	Lewis Billups	.04	.03	.02
222	Roger Craig	.04	.03	.02
223	Shaun Gayle	.04	.03	.02
224	Mike Rozier	.04	.03	.02
225	Troy Aikman	1.00	.70	.40
226	Bobby Humphrey	.04	.03	.02
227	Eugene Marve	.04	.03	.02
228	Michael Carter	.04	.03	.02
229	Richard Johnson	.04	.03	.02
230	Billy Joe Tolliver	.08	.06	.03
231	Mark Murphy	.04	.03	.02
232	John L. Williams	.04	.03	.02
233	Ronnie Harmon	.08	.06	.03
234	Thurman Thomas	.40	.30	.15
235	Martin Mayhew	.04	.03	.02
236	Richmond Webb	.04	.03	.02
237	Gerald Riggs	.04	.03	.02
238	Mike Prior	.04	.03	.02
239	Mike Gann	.04	.03	.02
240	Alvin Walton	.04	.03	.02
241	Tim McGee	.04	.03	.02
242	Bruce Matthews	.04	.03	.02
243	Johnny Holland	.04	.03	.02
244	Martin Bayless	.04	.03	.02
245	Eric Metcalf	.04	.03	.02
246	John Alt	.04	.03	.02
247	Max Montoya	.04	.03	.02
248	Rod Bernstine	.04	.03	.02
249	Paul Gruber	.04	.03	.02
250	Charles Haley	.04	.03	.02
251	Scott Norwood	.04	.03	.02
252	Michael Haddix	.04	.03	.02
253	Ricky Sanders	.06	.05	.02
254	Ervin Randle	.04	.03	.02
255	Duane Bickett	.04	.03	.02
256	Mike Munchak	.04	.03	.02
257	Keith Jones	.04	.03	.02
258	Riki Ellison	.04	.03	.02
259	Vince Newsome	.04	.03	.02
260	Lee Williams	.04	.03	.02

261	Steve Smith	.04	.03	.02
262	Sam Clancy	.04	.03	.02
263	Pierce Holt	.04	.03	.02
264	Jim Harbaugh	.08	.06	.03
265	Dino Hackett	.04	.03	.02
266	Andy Heck	.04	.03	.02
267	Leo Goeas	.04	.03	.02
268	Russ Grimm	.04	.03	.02
269	Gill Byrd	.04	.03	.02
270	Neal Anderson	.08	.06	.03
271	Jackie Slater	.04	.03	.02
272	Joe Nash	.04	.03	.02
273	Todd Bowles	.04	.03	.02
274	D.J. Dozier	.04	.03	.02
275	Kevin Fagan	.04	.03	.02
276	Don Warren	.04	.03	.02
277	Jim Jeffcoat	.04	.03	.02
278	Bruce Smith	.08	.06	.03
279	Cortez Kennedy	.25	.20	.10
280	Thane Gash	.04	.03	.02
281	Perry Kemp	.04	.03	.02
282	John Taylor	.10	.08	.04
283	Stephone Paige	.04	.03	.02
284	Paul Skansi	.04	.03	.02
285	Shawn Collins	.04	.03	.02
286	Mervyn Fernandez	.04	.03	.02
287	Daniel Stubbs	.04	.03	.02
288	Chip Lohmiller	.04	.03	.02
289	Brian Blades	.04	.03	.02
290	Mark Carrier	.04	.03	.02
291	Carl Zander	.04	.03	.02
292	David Wyman	.04	.03	.02
293	Jeff Bostic	.04	.03	.02
294	Irv Pankey	.04	.03	.02
295	Keith Millard	.04	.03	.02
296	Jamie Mueller	.04	.03	.02
297	Bill Fralic	.04	.03	.02
298	Wendell Davis	.08	.06	.03
299	Ken Clarke	.04	.03	.02
300	Wymon Henderson	.04	.03	.02
301	Jeff Campbell	.04	.03	.02
302	Cody Carlson **RC**	.35	.25	.14
303	Matt Brock **RC**	.10	.08	.04
304	Maurice Carthon	.04	.03	.02
305	Scott Mersereau **RC**	.10	.08	.04
306	Steve Wright	.04	.03	.02
307	J.B. Brown	.04	.03	.02
308	Ricky Reynolds	.04	.03	.02
309	Darryl Pollard	.04	.03	.02
310	Donald Evans	.04	.03	.02
311	Nick Bell **RC** (DP)	.20	.15	.08
312	Pat Harlow **RC** (DP)	.10	.08	.04
313	Dan McGwire **RC** (DP)	.10	.08	.04
314	Mike Dumas (DP)	.04	.03	.02
315	Mike Croel **RC** (DP)	.20	.15	.08
316	Chris Smith (DP)	.04	.03	.02
317	Kenny Walker **RC** (DP)	.10	.08	.04
318	Todd Lyght **RC** (DP)	.10	.08	.04
319	Mike Stonebreaker (DP)	.04	.03	.02
320	Randall Cunningham (90)	.08	.06	.03
321	Terance Mathis (90)	.04	.03	.02
322	Gaston Green (90)	.04	.03	.02
323	Johnny Bailey (90)	.04	.03	.02
324	Donnie Elder (90)	.04	.03	.02
325	Dwight Stone (90)	.04	.03	.02
326	J.J. Birden **RC** (90)	.35	.25	.14
327	Alex Wright (90)	.04	.03	.02
328	Eric Metcalf (90)	.04	.03	.02
329	Andre Rison (TL)	.15	.11	.06
330	Warren Moon (TL)	.10	.08	.04
331	Steve Tasker, Reyna Thompson (DT)	.04	.03	.02
332	Mel Gray (DT)	.04	.03	.02
333	Nick Lowery (DT)	.04	.03	.02
334	Sean Landeta (DT)	.04	.03	.02
335	David Fulcher (DT)	.04	.03	.02
336	Joey Browner (DT)	.04	.03	.02
337	Albert Lewis (DT)	.04	.03	.02
338	Rod Woodson (DT)	.06	.05	.02
339	Shane Conlan (DT)	.04	.03	.02
340	Pepper Johnson (DT)	.04	.03	.02
341	Chris Spielman (DT)	.06	.05	.02
342	Derrick Thomas (DT)	.08	.06	.03
343	Ray Childress (DT)	.04	.03	.02
344	Reggie White (DT)	.08	.06	.03
345	Bruce Smith (DT)	.06	.05	.02
346	Darrell Green	.04	.03	.02
347	Ray Bentley	.04	.03	.02
348	Herschel Walker	.06	.05	.02
349	Rodney Holman	.04	.03	.02
350	Al Toon	.04	.03	.02
351	Harry Hamilton	.04	.03	.02
352	Albert Lewis	.04	.03	.02
353	Renaldo Turnbull	.04	.03	.02
354	Junior Seau	.25	.20	.10
355	Merril Hoge	.04	.03	.02
356	Shane Conlan	.04	.03	.02
357	Jay Schroeder	.04	.03	.02
358	Steve Broussard	.04	.03	.02
359	Mark Bavaro	.04	.03	.02
360	Jim Lachey	.04	.03	.02
361	Greg Townsend	.04	.03	.02
362	Dave Krieg	.04	.03	.02
363	Jessie Hester	.04	.03	.02
364	Steve Tasker	.04	.03	.02
365	Ron Hall	.04	.03	.02
366	Pat Leahy	.04	.03	.02
367	Jim Everett	.06	.05	.02
368	Felix Wright	.04	.03	.02
369	Ricky Proehl	.04	.03	.02
370	Anthony Miller	.05	.04	.02
371	Keith Jackson	.08	.06	.03
372	Pete Stoyanovich	.04	.03	.02
373	Tommy Kane	.04	.03	.02
374	Richard Johnson	.04	.03	.02
375	Randall McDaniel	.04	.03	.02
376	John Stephens	.04	.03	.02
377	Haywood Jeffires	.15	.11	.06
378	Rodney Hampton	.50	.40	.20
379	Tim Grunhard	.04	.03	.02
380	Jerry Rice	1.00	.70	.40
381	Ken Harvey	.04	.03	.02
382	Vaughan Johnson	.04	.03	.02
383	J.T. Smith	.04	.03	.02
384	Carnell Lake	.04	.03	.02
385	Dan Marino	1.50	1.25	.60
386	Kyle Clifton	.04	.03	.02
387	Wilber Marshall	.04	.03	.02
388	Pete Holohan	.04	.03	.02
389	Gary Plummer	.04	.03	.02
390	William Perry	.04	.03	.02
391	Mark Robinson	.04	.03	.02
392	Nate Odomes	.06	.05	.02
393	Ickey Woods	.04	.03	.02
394	Reyna Thompson	.04	.03	.02
395	Deion Sanders	.40	.30	.15
396	Harris Barton	.04	.03	.02
397	Sammie Smith	.04	.03	.02
398	Vinny Testaverde	.04	.03	.02
399	Ray Donaldson	.04	.03	.02
400	Tim McKyer	.04	.03	.02
401	Nesby Glasgow	.04	.03	.02
402	Brent Williams	.04	.03	.02
403	Rob Moore	.10	.08	.04
404	Bubby Brister	.05	.04	.02
405	David Fulcher	.04	.03	.02
406	Reggie Cobb	.20	.15	.08
407	Jerome Brown	.04	.03	.02
408	Erik Howard	.04	.03	.02
409	Tony Paige	.04	.03	.02
410	John Elway	.35	.25	.14
411	Charles Mann	.04	.03	.02
412	Luis Sharpe	.04	.03	.02
413	Hassan Jones	.04	.03	.02
414	Frank Minnifield	.04	.03	.02
415	Steve DeBerg	.04	.03	.02
416	Mark Carrier	.04	.03	.02
417	Brian Jordan	.04	.03	.02
418	Reggie Langhorne	.04	.03	.02
419	Don Majkowski	.04	.03	.02
420	Marcus Allen	.05	.04	.02
421	Michael Brooks	.04	.03	.02
422	Vai Sikahema	.04	.03	.02
423	Dermontti Dawson	.04	.03	.02
424	Jacob Green	.04	.03	.02
425	Flipper Anderson	.04	.03	.02
426	Bill Brooks	.04	.03	.02
427	Keith McCants	.04	.03	.02
428	Ken O'Brien	.04	.03	.02
429	Fred Barnett	.10	.08	.04
430	Mark Duper	.04	.03	.02
431	Mark Kelso	.04	.03	.02
432	Leslie O'Neal	.04	.03	.02
433	Ottis Anderson	.05	.04	.02
434	Jesse Sapolu	.04	.03	.02
435	Gary Zimmerman	.04	.03	.02
436	Kevin Porter	.04	.03	.02
437	Anthony Thompson	.04	.03	.02
438	Robert Clark	.04	.03	.02
439	Chris Warren	.20	.15	.08
440	Gerald Williams	.04	.03	.02
441	Jim Skow	.04	.03	.02
442	Rick Donnelly	.04	.03	.02
443	Guy McIntyre	.04	.03	.02
444	Jeff Lageman	.04	.03	.02
445	John Offerdahl	.04	.03	.02
446	Clyde Simmons	.04	.03	.02
447	John Kidd	.04	.03	.02
448	Chip Banks	.04	.03	.02
449	Johnny Meads	.04	.03	.02
450	Rickey Jackson	.04	.03	.02
451	Lee Johnson	.04	.03	.02
452	Michael Irvin	.25	.20	.10
453	Leon Seals	.04	.03	.02
454	Darrell Thompson	.20	.15	.08
455	Everson Walls	.04	.03	.02
456	LeRoy Butler	.06	.05	.02
457	Marcus Dupree	.04	.03	.02
458	Kirk Lowdermilk	.04	.03	.02
459	Chris Singleton	.04	.03	.02
460	Seth Joyner	.04	.03	.02
461	Rueben Mayes (Hayes in bio should be Heyward)	.04	.03	.02
462	Ernie Jones	.04	.03	.02
463	Greg Kragen	.04	.03	.02
464	Bennie Blades	.04	.03	.02
465	Mark Bortz	.04	.03	.02
466	Tony Stargell	.04	.03	.02
467	Mike Cofer	.05	.04	.02
468	Randy Grimes	.04	.03	.02
469	Tim Worley	.04	.03	.02
470	Kevin Mack	.04	.03	.02
471	Wes Hopkins	.04	.03	.02
472	Will Wolford	.04	.03	.02
473	Sam Seale	.04	.03	.02
474	Jim Ritcher	.04	.03	.02
475	Jeff Hostetler	.20	.15	.08
476	Mitchell Price	.04	.03	.02
477	Ken Lanier	.04	.03	.02
478	Naz Worthen	.04	.03	.02
479	Ed Reynolds	.04	.03	.02
480	Mark Clayton	.05	.04	.02
481	Matt Bahr	.04	.03	.02
482	Gary Reasons	.04	.03	.02
483	Dave Szott	.04	.03	.02
484	Barry Foster	.45	.35	.20
485	Bruce Reimers	.04	.03	.02
486	Dean Biasucci	.04	.03	.02
487	Cris Carter	.05	.04	.02
488	Albert Bentley	.04	.03	.02
489	Robert Massey	.04	.03	.02
490	Al Smith	.04	.03	.02
491	Greg Lloyd	.08	.06	.03
492	Steve McMichael (Photo on back actually Dan Hampton)	.05	.04	.02
493	Jeff Wright **RC**	.08	.06	.03
494	Scott Davis	.04	.03	.02
495	Freeman McNeil	.04	.03	.02
496	Simon Fletcher	.04	.03	.02
497	Terry McDaniel	.04	.03	.02
498	Heath Sherman	.04	.03	.02
499	Jeff Jaeger	.04	.03	.02
500	Mark Collins	.04	.03	.02
501	Tim Goad	.04	.03	.02
502	Jeff George	.25	.20	.10
503	Jimmie Jones	.05	.04	.02
504	Henry Thomas	.04	.03	.02
505	Steve Young	.60	.45	.25
506	William Roberts	.04	.03	.02
507	Neil Smith	.04	.03	.02
508	Mike Saxon	.04	.03	.02
509	Johnny Bailey	.04	.03	.02
510	Broderick Thomas	.04	.03	.02
511	Wade Wilson	.04	.03	.02
512	Hart Lee Dykes	.04	.03	.02
513	Hardy Nickerson	.04	.03	.02
514	Tim McDonald	.05	.04	.02
515	Frank Cornish	.04	.03	.02
516	Jarvis Williams	.04	.03	.02
517	Carl Lee	.04	.03	.02
518	Carl Banks	.04	.03	.02
519	Mike Golic	.04	.03	.02
520	Brian Noble	.04	.03	.02
521	James Hasty	.04	.03	.02
522	Bubba Paris	.04	.03	.02
523	Kevin Walker **RC**	.08	.06	.03
524	William Fuller	.04	.03	.02
525	Eddie Anderson	.04	.03	.02
526	Roger Ruzek	.04	.03	.02
527	Robert Blackmon	.04	.03	.02
528	Vince Buck	.04	.03	.02
529	Lawrence Taylor	.10	.08	.04
530	Reggie Roby	.04	.03	.02
531	Doug Riesenberg	.04	.03	.02
532	Joe Jacoby	.04	.03	.02
533	Kirby Jackson	.04	.03	.02
534	Robb Thomas	.04	.03	.02
535	Don Griffin	.04	.03	.02
536	Andre Waters	.05	.04	.02
537	Marc Logan	.04	.03	.02
538	James Thornton	.04	.03	.02
539	Ray Agnew	.04	.03	.02
540	Frank Stams	.04	.03	.02
541	Brett Perriman	.05	.04	.02
542	Andre Ware	.10	.08	.04
543	Kevin Haverdink	.04	.03	.02
544	Greg Jackson **RC**	.08	.06	.03
545	Tunch Ilkin	.04	.03	.02
546	Dexter Carter	.04	.03	.02
547	Rod Woodson	.06	.05	.02
548	Donnell Woolford	.04	.03	.02
549	Mark Boyer	.04	.03	.02

550	Jeff Query	.04	.03	.02
551	Burt Grossman	.04	.03	.02
552	Mike Kenn	.04	.03	.02
553	Richard Dent	.04	.03	.02
554	Gaston Green	.04	.03	.02
555	Phil Simms	.10	.08	.04
556	Brent Jones	.05	.04	.02
557	Ronnie Lippett	.04	.03	.02
558	Mike Horan	.04	.03	.02
559	Danny Noonan	.04	.03	.02
560	Reggie White	.15	.11	.06
561	Rufus Porter	.04	.03	.02
562	Aaron Wallace	.04	.03	.02
563	Vance Johnson	.04	.03	.02
564	Aaron Craver (No copyright line on back)	.04	.03	.02
565A	Russell Maryland RC (No copyright line on back)	.40	.30	.15
565B	Russell Maryland RC	.40	.30	.15
566	Paul Justin	.04	.03	.02
567	Walter Dean	.04	.03	.02
568	Herman Moore RC	1.50	1.25	.60
569	Bill Musgrave RC	.10	.08	.04
570	Rob Carpenter RC	.10	.08	.04
571	Greg Lewis RC	.10	.08	.04
572	Ed King RC	.10	.08	.04
573	Ernie Mills RC	.08	.06	.03
574	Jake Reed RC	1.00	.70	.40
575	Ricky Watters RC	1.50	1.25	.60
576	Derek Russell RC	.25	.20	.10
577	Shawn Moore RC	.15	.11	.06
578	Eric Bieniemy RC	.15	.11	.06
579	Chris Zorich RC	.30	.25	.12
580	Scott Miller	.05	.04	.02
581	Jarrod Bunch RC	.10	.08	.04
582	Ricky Ervins RC	.20	.15	.08
583	Browning Nagle RC	.20	.15	.08
584	Eric Turner RC	.20	.15	.08
585	William Thomas RC	.08	.06	.03
586	Stanley Richard RC	.30	.25	.12
587	Adrian Cooper RC	.15	.11	.06
588	Harvey Williams RC	.10	.08	.04
589	Alvin Harper RC	.10	.08	.04
590	John Carney	.04	.03	.02
591	Mark Vander Poel	.04	.03	.02
592	Mike Pritchard RC	.35	.25	.14
593	Eric Moten RC	.08	.06	.03
594	Moe Gardner RC	.10	.08	.04
595	Wesley Carroll RC	.10	.08	.04
596	Eric Swann RC	.10	.08	.04
597	Joe Kelly	.05	.04	.02
598	Steve Jackson RC	.10	.08	.04
599	Kelvin Pritchett RC	.15	.11	.06
600	Jesse Campbell RC	.08	.06	.03
601	Darryll Lewis RC (Misspelled Darryl on card)	.08	.06	.03
602	Howard Griffith	.04	.03	.02
603	Blaise Bryant	.04	.03	.02
604	Vinnie Clark RC	.08	.06	.03
605	Mel Agee RC	.08	.06	.03
606	Bobby Wilson RC	.08	.06	.03
607	Kevin Donnalley	.04	.03	.02
608	Randal Hill RC	.35	.25	.14
609	Stan Thomas	.04	.03	.02
610	Mike Heldt	.04	.03	.02
611	Brett Favre RC	2.00	1.00	.60
612	Lawrence Dawsey RC	.25	.20	.10
613	Dennis Gibson	.04	.03	.02
614	Dean Dingman	.04	.03	.02
615	Bruce Pickens RC	.08	.06	.03
616	Todd Marinovich RC	.08	.06	.03
617	Gene Atkins	.04	.03	.02
618	Marcus Dupree (Comeback Player)	.04	.03	.02
619	Warren Moon (Man of the Year)	.10	.08	.04
620	Joe Montana (MVP)	.50	.40	.20
621	Neal Anderson (Team MVP)	.05	.04	.02
622	James Brooks (Team MVP)	.05	.04	.02
623	Thurman Thomas (Team MVP)	.20	.15	.08
624	Bobby Humphrey (Team MVP)	.04	.03	.02
625	Kevin Mack (Team MVP)	.04	.03	.02
626	Mark Carrier (Team MVP)	.04	.03	.02
627	Johnny Johnson (Team MVP)	.08	.06	.03
628	Marion Butts (Team MVP)	.05	.04	.02
629	Steve DeBerg (Team MVP)	.05	.04	.02
630	Jeff George (Team MVP)	.10	.08	.04
631	Troy Aikman (MVP)	.50	.40	.20
632	Dan Marino (MVP)	.25	.20	.10
633	Randall Cunningham (Team MVP)	.08	.06	.03

634	Andre Rison (Team MVP)	.08	.06	.03
635	Pepper Johnson (Team MVP)	.04	.03	.02
636	Pat Leahy (Team MVP)	.04	.03	.02
637	Barry Sanders (MVP)	.50	.40	.20
638	Warren Moon (Team MVP)	.08	.06	.03
639	Sterling Sharpe (MVP)	.25	.20	.10
640	Bruce Armstrong (Team MVP)	.04	.03	.02
641	Bo Jackson (Team MVP)	.10	.08	.04
642	Henry Ellard (Team MVP)	.05	.04	.02
643	Earnest Byner (Team MVP)	.04	.03	.02
644	Pat Swilling (Team MVP)	.04	.03	.02
645	John L. Williams (Team MVP)	.04	.03	.02
646	Rod Woodson (Team MVP)	.06	.05	.02
647	Chris Doleman (Team MVP)	.04	.03	.02
648	Joey Browner (Crunch Crew)	.04	.03	.02
649	Erik McMillan (Crunch Crew)	.04	.03	.02
650	David Fulcher (Crunch Crew)	.04	.03	.02
651A	Ronnie Lott (Front 47, back 42)	.08	.06	.03
651B	Ronnie Lott (Front 47, back 42 is now blacked out)	.05	.04	.02
652	Louis Oliver (Crunch Crew)	.04	.03	.02
653	Mark Robinson (Crunch Crew)	.04	.03	.02
654	Dennis Smith (Crunch Crew)	.04	.03	.02
655	Reggie White (Sack Attack)	.08	.06	.03
656	Charles Haley (Sack Attack)	.04	.03	.02
657	Leslie O'Neal (Sack Attack)	.04	.03	.02
658	Kevin Greene (Sack Attack)	.04	.03	.02
659	Dennis Byrd (Sack Attack)	.04	.03	.02
660	Bruce Smith (Sack Attack)	.08	.06	.03
661	Derrick Thomas (Sack Attack)	.10	.08	.04
662	Steve DeBerg (Top Leader)	.04	.03	.02
663	Barry Sanders (TL)	.50	.40	.20
664	Thurman Thomas (TL)	.20	.15	.08
665	Jerry Rice (TL)	.40	.30	.15
666	Derrick Thomas (Top Leader)	.10	.08	.04
667	Bruce Smith (Top Leader)	.08	.06	.03
668	Mark Carrier (Top Leader)	.04	.03	.02
669	Richard Johnson (Top Leader)	.04	.03	.02
670	Jan Stenerud (Hall of Fame)	.05	.04	.02
671	Stan Jones (Hall of Fame)	.05	.04	.02
672	John Hannah (Hall of Fame)	.05	.04	.02
673	Tex Schramm (Hall of Fame)	.05	.04	.02
674	Earl Campbell (Hall of Fame)	.10	.08	.04
675	Mark Carrier, Emmitt Smith (ROY ROY)	.25	.20	.10
676	Warren Moon (DT)	.10	.08	.04
677	Barry Sanders (DT)	.50	.40	.20
678	Thurman Thomas (DT)	.20	.15	.08
679	Andre Reed (DT)	.06	.05	.02
680	Andre Rison (DT)	.15	.11	.06
681	Keith Jackson (DT)	.05	.04	.02
682	Bruce Armstrong (DT)	.05	.04	.02
683	Jim Lachey (DT)	.04	.03	.02
684	Bruce Matthews (DT)	.04	.03	.02
685	Mike Munchak (DT)	.04	.03	.02
686	Don Mosebar (DT)	.04	.03	.02

1991 Score Hot Rookie

1991 Score blister packs contained these random inserts which have card fronts showing action shots of the players in their collegiate uniforms against a hot pink/yellow background. The fronts are bordered in black. Each card back is numbered and includes a close-up shot of the player, plus a brief career summary.

	NM/M	NM	E
Complete Set (10):	3.00	6.00	3.25
Common Player:	.40	.60	.30

1	Dan McGwire	.50	.40	.20
2	Todd Lyght	.50	.40	.20
3	Mike Dumas	.40	.60	.30
4	Pat Harlow	.40	.60	.30
5	Nick Bell	1.00	.70	.40
6	Chris Smith	.40	.60	.30
7	Mike Stonebreaker	.40	.60	.30
8	Mike Croel	.50	.40	.20
9	Kenny Walker	.50	.40	.20
10	Rob Carpenter	.40	.60	.30

1977 Seahawks Fred Meyer

The 13-card, 7-1/4" x 6" set, distributed by Fred Meyer Department Stores, feature a color action shot with a headshot inset in a lower corner (cards 3, 5, 12, and 13a have no insets). Seahawks quarterback Jim Zorn is represented on two No. 13 cards, one having no inset. All card backs are blank.

	NM	E	VG
Complete Set (14):	75.00	37.00	22.00
Common Player:	5.00	2.50	1.50

1	Steve August	5.00	2.50	1.50
2	Autry Beamon	5.00	2.50	1.50
3	Terry Beeson	5.00	2.50	1.50
4	Dennis Boyd	5.00	2.50	1.50
5	Norm Evans	5.00	2.50	1.50
6	Sammy Green	5.00	2.50	1.50
7	Ron Howard	5.00	2.50	1.50
8	Steve Largent	20.00	10.00	6.00
9	Steve Myer	5.00	2.50	1.50
10	Steve Niehaus	5.00	2.50	1.50
11	Sherman Smith	5.00	2.50	1.50
12	Don Testerman	5.00	2.50	1.50
13A	Jim Zorn (No inset photo)	12.00	6.00	3.50
13B	Jim Zorn (With inset photo)	12.00	6.00	3.50

1977 Seahawks Team Issue

The 10-card, 5" x 7" set features black and white headshots of Seattle players with blank backs. A facsimile autograph also appears on each card front.

	NM	E	VG
Complete Set (10):	75.00	37.00	22.00
Common Player:	5.00	2.50	1.50

1	Ron Howard	5.00	2.50	1.50
2	Steve Largent	25.00	12.50	7.50
3	John Leypoldt	5.00	2.50	1.50
4	Bob Lurtsema	5.00	2.50	1.50
5	Steve Myer	5.00	2.50	1.50
6	Steve Niehaus	5.00	2.50	1.50
7	Jack Patera (CO)	6.00	3.00	1.75
8	Sherman Smith	5.00	2.50	1.50
9	Don Testerman	5.00	2.50	1.50
10	Jim Zorn	12.00	6.00	3.50

1978-80 Seahawks Nalley's

The 24-card, 10-3/4" x 9" set was available on the box backs of eight-ounce Nally's potato chip products. The color posed fronts feature a facsimile autograph with Seattle's schedule and player stats on the box sides. Prices are for complete boxes.

	NM	E	VG
Complete Set (24):	750.00	375.00	225.00
Common Player (1-8):	25.00	12.50	7.50
Common Player (9-16):	20.00	10.00	6.00
Common Player (17-24):	15.00	7.50	4.50

1	Steve Largent	300.00	150.00	90.00
2	Autry Beamon	25.00	12.50	7.50
3	Jim Zorn	65.00	32.00	19.50
4	Sherman Smith	40.00	20.00	12.00
5	Ron Coder	25.00	12.50	7.50
6	Terry Beeson	25.00	12.50	7.50
7	Steve Niehaus	30.00	15.00	9.00
8	Ron Howard	25.00	12.50	7.50
9	Steve Myer	20.00	10.00	6.00
10	Tom Lynch	20.00	10.00	6.00
11	David Sims	20.00	10.00	6.00
12	John Yarno	20.00	10.00	6.00
13	Bill Gregory	25.00	12.50	7.50
14	Steve Raible	25.00	12.50	7.50
15	Dennis Boyd	20.00	10.00	6.00
16	Steve August	20.00	10.00	6.00
17	Keith Simpson	15.00	7.50	4.50
18	Michael Jackson	15.00	7.50	4.50
19	Manu Tuiasosopo	20.00	10.00	6.00
20	Sam McCullum	20.00	10.00	6.00
21	Keith Butler	15.00	7.50	4.50
22	Sam Akins	15.00	7.50	4.50
23	Dan Doornink	20.00	10.00	6.00
24	Dave Brown	20.00	10.00	6.00

1979 Seahawks Police

The 16-card, 2-5/8" x 4-1/8" set, sponsored by Coca-Cola, Kiwanis, the Washington State Crime Prevention Association and local law enforcement, contain "Tips from the Seahawks" on the card backs.

		NM	E	VG
Complete Set (16):		12.00	6.00	3.50
Common Player:		.75	.40	.25
1	Steve August	.75	.40	.25
2	Autry Beamon	.75	.40	.25
3	Terry Beeson	.75	.40	.25
4	Dennis Boyd	.75	.40	.25
5	Dave Brown	.75	.40	.25
6	Efren Herrera	.75	.40	.25
7	Steve Largent	8.00	4.00	2.50
8	Tom Lynch	.75	.40	.25
9	Bob Newton	.75	.40	.25
10	Jack Patera (CO)	1.00	.50	.30
11	Sea Gal(Keri Truscan)	.75	.40	.25
12	Seahawk (Mascot)	.75	.40	.25
13	David Sims	.75	.40	.25
14	Sherman Smith	.75	.40	.25
15	John Yarno	.75	.40	.25
16	Jim Zorn	3.00	1.50	.90

1980 Seahawks 7-Up

The 10-card, 2-3/8" x 3-1/4" set features a player closeup on the card fronts with player bio information on the card backs. Quarterback Jim Zorn and receiver Steve Largent do not appear due to their sponsorships with Darigold Dairy.

		NM	E	VG
Complete Set (10):		125.00	62.00	37.00
Common Player:		12.00	6.00	3.50
1	Steve August	12.00	6.00	3.50
2	Terry Beeson	12.00	6.00	3.50
3	Dan Doornink	12.00	6.00	3.50
4	Michael Jackson	12.00	6.00	3.50
5	Tom Lynch	12.00	6.00	3.50
6	Steve Myer	12.00	6.00	3.50
7	Steve Raible	20.00	10.00	6.00
8	Sherman Smith	20.00	10.00	6.00
9	Manu Tuiasosopo	12.00	6.00	3.50
10	John Yarno	12.00	6.00	3.50

1980 Seahawks Police

The 16-card, 2-5/8" x 4-1/8" set, sponsored by local law enforcement, Coca-Cola, Kiwanis, the Washington State Crime Prevention Association and Ernst Home Centers, features "tips from the Seahawks" on the card backs.

		NM	E	VG
Complete Set (16):		10.00	7.50	4.00
Common Player:		.60	.30	.20
1	Sam McCullum	.60	.30	.20
2	Dan Doornink	.60	.30	.20
3	Sherman Smith	.60	.30	.20
4	Efren Herrera	.60	.30	.20
5	Bill Gregory	.60	.30	.20
6	Keith Simpson	.60	.30	.20
7	Manu Tuiasosopo	.60	.30	.20
8	Michael Jackson	.60	.30	.20
9	Steve Raible	.60	.30	.20
10	Steve Largent	6.00	3.00	1.75
11	Jim Zorn	2.00	1.00	.60
12	Nick Bebout	.60	.30	.20
13	The Seahawk (mascot)	.60	.30	.20
14	Jack Patera (CO)	.75	.40	.25
15	Robert Hardy	.60	.30	.20
16	Keith Butler	.60	.30	.20

1981 Seahawks 7-Up

The 30-card, 3-1/2" x 5-1/2" set features color action shots and facsimile autographs on the card fronts. The card backs contain a brief player bio. As with the 1980 set, Zorn and Largent do not appear because of conflicting sponsorships.

		NM/M	NM	E
Complete Set (30):		85.00	64.00	34.00
Common Player:		3.00	2.25	1.25
1	Sam Adkins	3.00	2.25	1.25
2	Steve August	3.00	2.25	1.25
3	Terry Beeson	3.00	2.25	1.25
4	Dennis Boyd	3.00	2.25	1.25
5	Dave Brown	4.00	3.00	1.50
6	Louis Bullard	3.00	2.25	1.25
7	Keith Butler	3.00	2.25	1.25
8	Peter Cronan	3.00	2.25	1.25
9	Dan Doornink	4.00	3.00	1.50
10	Jacob Green	6.00	4.50	2.50
11	Bill Gregory	3.00	2.25	1.25
12	Robert Hardy	3.00	2.25	1.25
13	Efren Herrera	3.00	2.25	1.25
14	Michael Jackson	3.00	2.25	1.25
15	Art Kuehn	3.00	2.25	1.25
16	Steve Largent	20.00	15.00	8.00
17	Tom Lynch	3.00	2.25	1.25
18	Sam McCullum	4.00	3.00	1.50
19	Steve Myer	3.00	2.25	1.25
20	Jack Patera (CO)	4.00	3.00	1.50
21	Steve Raible	3.00	2.25	1.25
22	The Sea Gals	3.00	2.25	1.25
23	The Seahawk Mascot	3.00	2.25	1.25
24	Keith Simpson	3.00	2.25	1.25
25	Sherman Smith	3.00	2.25	1.25
26	Manu Tuiasosopo	3.00	2.25	1.25
27	Herman Weaver	3.00	2.25	1.25
28	Cornell Webster	3.00	2.25	1.25
29	John Yarno	3.00	2.25	1.25
30	Jim Zorn	8.00	6.00	3.25

1982 Seahawks 7-Up

The 15-card, 3-1/2" x 5-1/2" set features color action shots on the card fronts with "Seahawks Fan Mail Courtesy" printed, as well as a facsimile autograph. The card backs include "Tips from the Seahawks" and the cards of Zorn and Largent are included with Darigold logo on the backs.

		NM/M	NM	E
Complete Set (15):		75.00	56.00	30.00
Common Player:		3.00	2.25	1.25
1	Edwin Bailey	3.00	2.25	1.25
2	Dave Brown	3.00	2.25	1.25
3	Kenny Easley	5.00	3.75	2.00
4	Ron Essink	3.00	2.25	1.25
5	Jacob Green (No facsimile autograph)	5.00	3.75	2.00
6	Robert Hardy	3.00	2.25	1.25
7	John Harris	3.00	2.25	1.25
8	David Hughes	3.00	2.25	1.25
9	Paul Johns (HOR)	3.00	2.25	1.25
10	Kerry Justin	3.00	2.25	1.25
11	Dave Krieg	12.00	9.00	4.75
12	Steve Largent (Darigold logo or Gold-n-Soft)	20.00	15.00	8.00
13	Keith Simpson	3.00	2.25	1.25
14	Manu Tuiasosopo	3.00	2.25	1.25
15	Jim Zorn (HOR) (Darigold logo or Gold-n-Soft)	8.00	6.00	3.25

1982 Seahawks Police

The 16-card, 2-5/8" x 4-1/8" set, issued by the Washington State Crime Prevention Association, Kiwanis, Coca-Cola, local law enforcement and Ernst Home Centers, includes "Tips from the Seahawks" on the card backs and the set contains the card of team mascot Sea Gal (No. 4). Also, the cards of Sam McCullum and Jack Patera were distributed in lesser quantities.

		NM/M	NM	E
Complete Set (16):		12.00	9.00	4.75
Common Player:		.40	.30	.15
1	Sam McCullum (SP)	2.00	1.50	.80
2	Manu Tuiasosopo	.50	.40	.20
3	Sherman Smith	.60	.45	.25
4	Karen Godwin (Sea Gal)	.40	.30	.15
5	Dave Brown	.60	.45	.25
6	Keith Simpson	.40	.30	.15
7	Steve Largent	5.00	3.75	2.00
8	Michael Jackson	.40	.30	.15
9	Kenny Easley	.75	.60	.30
10	Dan Doornink	.40	.30	.15
11	Jim Zorn	2.00	1.50	.80
12	Jack Patera (CO SP)	2.00	1.50	.80
13	Jacob Green	.60	.45	.25
14	Dave Krieg	3.00	2.25	1.25
15	Steve August	.40	.30	.15
16	Keith Butler	.40	.30	.15

1984 Seahawks GTE

The 12-card, 3-1/2" x 5-1/2" set features a color shot with a headshot inset in a corner, along with a facsimile autograph on the card front. The card backs have a brief player bio.

		NM/M	NM	E
Complete Set (12):		40.00	30.00	16.00
Common Player:		2.00	1.50	.80
1	Kenny Easley	3.00	2.25	1.25
2	Jacob Green	3.00	2.25	1.25
3	John Harris	2.00	1.50	.80
4	Norm Johnson	4.00	3.00	1.50
5	Chuck Knox (CO)	2.00	1.50	.80
6	Dave Krieg	7.00	5.25	2.75
7	Steve Largent	16.00	12.00	6.50
8	Joe Nash	2.00	1.50	.80
9	Keith Simpson	2.00	1.50	.80
10	Mike Tice	2.00	1.50	.80
11	Curt Warner	7.00	5.25	2.75
12	Charley Young	3.00	2.25	1.25

1984 Seahawks Nalley's

The four-card, 10-3/4" x 9" set was available on the box backs of Nalley's potato chips. The box sides contain Seattle's schedule and player bio information. Prices are for complete boxes.

		NM/M	NM	E
Complete Set (4):		50.00	37.00	20.00
Common Player:		10.00	7.50	4.00
1	Kenny Easley	10.00	7.50	4.00
2	Dave Krieg	15.00	11.00	6.00
3	Steve Largent	25.00	18.50	10.00
4	Curt Warner	15.00	11.00	6.00

1985 Seahawks Police

The 16-card, 2-5/8" x 4-1/8" set was sponsored by Kiwanis, Coca-Cola, KOMO-TV4, McDonald's, the Washington State Crime Prevention Association and local law enforcement. The card backs contain "Tips from the Seahawks."

		NM/M	NM	E
Complete Set (16):		8.00	6.00	3.25
Common Player:		.40	.30	.15
1	Dave Brown	.50	.40	.20
2	Jeff Bryant	.50	.40	.20
3	Blair Bush	.50	.40	.20
4	Keith Butler	.40	.30	.15
5	Dan Doornink	.40	.30	.15
6	Kenny Easley	1.00	.70	.40
7	Jacob Green	.60	.45	.25
8	John Harris	.40	.30	.15
9	Norm Johnson	1.00	.70	.40
10	Chuck Knox (CO)	1.00	.70	.40
11	Dave Krieg	1.50	1.25	.60
12	Steve Largent	3.00	2.25	1.25
13	Joe Nash	.50	.40	.20
14	Bruce Scholtz	.40	.30	.15
15	Curt Warner	1.25	.90	.50
16	Fredd Young	.60	.45	.25

1986 Seahawks Police

The 16-card, 2-5/8" x 4-1/8" set, sponsored by local law enforcement, contain "Tips from the Seahawks" on the card backs.

		NM/M	NM	E
Complete Set (16):		8.00	6.00	3.25
Common Player:		.40	.30	.15
1	Edwin Bailey	.40	.30	.15
2	Dave Brown	.50	.40	.20
3	Jeff Bryant	.50	.40	.20
4	Blair Bush	.50	.40	.20
5	Keith Butler	.40	.30	.15
6	Kenny Easley	.60	.45	.25
7	Jacob Green	.60	.45	.25
8	Michael Jackson	.40	.30	.15
9	Chuck Knox (CO)	.60	.45	.25
10	Dave Krieg	1.50	1.25	.60
11	Steve Largent	3.00	2.25	1.25
12	Joe Nash	.50	.40	.20
13	Bruce Scholtz	.40	.30	.15
14	Terry Taylor	.40	.30	.15
15	Curt Warner	.75	.60	.30
16	Fredd Young	.60	.45	.25

1987 Seahawks GTE

The 24-card, 3-5/8" x 5-1/2" set features color fronts with a facsimile player signature. The card backs have a career summary and a greeting from the player with another autograph.

		NM/M	NM	E
Complete Set (24):		60.00	45.00	24.00
Common Player:		1.50	1.25	.60
1	Edwin Bailey	1.50	1.25	.60
2	Brian Bosworth	2.50	2.00	1.00
3	Dave Brown	2.00	1.50	.80
4	Jeff Bryant	2.00	1.50	.80
5	Bobby Joe Edmonds	3.00	2.25	1.25
6	Jacob Green	3.00	2.25	1.25
7	Michael Jackson	1.50	1.25	.60
8	Norm Johnson	3.00	2.25	1.25
9	Jeff Kemp	2.50	2.00	1.00
10	Chuck Knox (CO)	3.00	2.25	1.25
11	Dave Krieg	5.00	3.75	2.00
12	Steve Largent	10.00	7.50	4.00
13	Ron Mattes	1.50	1.25	.60
14	Bryan Millard	1.50	1.25	.60
15	Paul Moyer	1.50	1.25	.60
16	Eugene Robinson	2.00	1.50	.80
17	Paul Skansi	1.50	1.25	.60
18	Kelly Stouffer	2.00	1.50	.80

		NM/M	NM	E
19	Terry Taylor	1.50	1.25	.60
20	Mike Tice	1.50	1.25	.60
21	Daryl Turner	2.00	1.50	.80
22	Curt Warner	4.00	3.00	1.50
23	John L. Williams	4.00	3.00	1.50
24	Fredd Young	2.00	1.50	.80

1987 Seahawks Police

The 16-card, 2-5/8" x 4-1/8" set features a silver border with a blue/green Seahawks logo. The card backs contain a safety tip.

		NM/M	NM	E
	Complete Set (16):	5.00	3.75	2.00
	Common Player:	.35	.25	.14
1	Jeff Bryant	.35	.25	.14
2	Kenny Easley	.60	.45	.25
3	Bobby Joe Edmonds	.35	.25	.14
4	Jacob Green	.60	.45	.25
5	Chuck Knox (CO)	.60	.45	.25
6	Dave Krieg	1.50	1.25	.60
7	Steve Largent	2.50	2.00	1.00
8	Ron Mattes	.35	.25	.14
9	Bryan Millard	.35	.25	.14
10	Eugene Robinson	.60	.45	.25
11	Bruce Scholtz	.35	.25	.14
12	Paul Skansi	.35	.25	.14
13	Curt Warner	.75	.60	.30
14	John L. Williams	1.00	.70	.40
15	Mike Wilson	.35	.25	.14
16	Fredd Young	.35	.25	.14

1987 Seahawks Snyder's/Franz

The 12-card, standard-size set was distributed in the Spokane area (Snyder bread) and Portland area (Franz bread). The card fronts contain a color photo with blue borders while the backs feature a player career summary.

		NM/M	NM	E
	Complete Set (12):	60.00	45.00	24.00
	Common Player:	5.00	3.75	2.00
1	Jeff Bryant	5.00	3.75	2.00
2	Keith Butler	5.00	3.75	2.00
3	Randy Edwards	5.00	3.75	2.00
4	Byron Franklin	5.00	3.75	2.00
5	Jacob Green	7.00	5.25	2.75
6	Dave Krieg	10.00	7.50	4.00
7	Bryan Millard	5.00	3.75	2.00
8	Paul Moyer	5.00	3.75	2.00
9	Eugene Robinson	7.00	5.25	2.75
10	Mike Tice	5.00	3.75	2.00
11	Daryl Turner	6.00	4.50	2.50
12	Curt Warner	8.00	6.00	3.25

1988 Seahawks Domino's

The 50-card, 2-1/2" x 8-1/2" set was distributed in panel strips with coupons for each Domino's pizza ordered. The first panel contained nine-cards and included a 12-1/2" x 8-1/2" team photo. Cards 10-13, 14-17, 18-21, 22-25, 26-29, 30-33, 34-38, 39-42, 43-46 and 47-50 were issued on a weekly basis.

		NM/M	NM	E
	Complete Set (51):	45.00	34.00	18.00
	Common Player:	.60	.45	.25
1	Steve Largent	10.00	7.50	4.00
2	Kelly Stouffer	.75	.60	.30
3	Bobby Joe Edmonds	1.00	.70	.40
4	Patrick Hunter	.75	.60	.30
5	**Ventrella/Valle/Gellos**	.60	.45	.25
6	Edwin Bailey	.60	.45	.25
7	Alonzo Mitz	.60	.45	.25
8	Tommy Kane	1.00	.70	.40
9	Chuck Knox (CO)	1.00	.70	.40
10	Curt Warner	2.00	1.50	.80
11	Alvin Powell	.60	.45	.25
12	Joe Nash	.60	.45	.25
13	Brian Blades	3.00	2.25	1.25
14	Blair Bush	.75	.60	.30
15	Melvin Jenkins	.60	.45	.25
16	Ruben Rodriguez	.60	.45	.25
17	Tommie Agee	.60	.45	.25
18	Eugene Robinson	.75	.60	.30
19	Dwayne Harper	.60	.45	.25
20	Raymond Butler	.60	.45	.25
21	Jeff Kemp	1.00	.70	.40
22	Norm Johnson	.75	.60	.30
23	Bryan Millard	.60	.45	.25
24	Tony Woods	1.00	.70	.40
25	Paul Skansi	.60	.45	.25
26	Jacob Green	1.00	.70	.40
27	Randall Morris	.60	.45	.25
28	Mike Tice	.60	.45	.25
29	Kevin Harmon	.60	.45	.25
30	Dave Krieg	2.50	2.00	1.00
31	Nesby Glasgow	.75	.60	.30
32	Bruce Scholtz	.60	.45	.25
33	John Spagnola	.60	.45	.25
34	Jeff Bryant	.75	.60	.30
35	Stan Eisenhooth	.60	.45	.25
36	Dave Wyman	.60	.45	.25
37	Greg Gaines	.60	.45	.25
38	Charlie Jones (NBC ANN)	.60	.45	.25
39	Terry Taylor	.60	.45	.25
40	Vernon Dean	.60	.45	.25
41	Mike Wilson	.60	.45	.25
42	Darrin Miller	.60	.45	.25
43	John L. Williams	2.50	2.00	1.00
44	Grant Feasel	.60	.45	.25
45	M.L. Johnson	.60	.45	.25
46	Ken Clarke	.75	.60	.30
47	Brian Bosworth	.75	.60	.30
48	Ron Mattes	.60	.45	.25
49	Paul Moyer	.60	.45	.25
50	Rufus Porter	1.00	.70	.40
NNO	**Team Photo** (Large size)	7.00	5.25	2.75

1988 Seahawks Police

Steve Largent
Wide Receiver   5'11"   184 lbs.   Tulsa

The 16-card, 2-5/8" x 4-1/8" set features color photos with gray borders and the backs include safety tips. Terry Taylor's card was pulled from distribution after he was suspended from the team.

		NM/M	NM	E
	Complete Set (16):	10.00	7.50	4.00
	Common Player:	.50	.40	.20
1	Brian Bosworth	1.00	.70	.40
2	Jeff Bryant	.60	.45	.25
3	Raymond Butler	.50	.40	.20
4	Jacob Green	1.00	.70	.40
5	Patrick Hunter	.60	.45	.25
6	Norm Johnson	.75	.60	.30
7	Chuck Knox (CO)	.75	.60	.30
8	Dave Krieg	1.50	1.25	.60
9	Steve Largent	2.50	2.00	1.00
10	Ron Mattes	.50	.40	.20
11	Bryan Millard	.50	.40	.20
12	Paul Moyer	.50	.40	.20
13	Terry Taylor (SP)	2.50	2.00	1.00
14	Curt Warner	1.00	.70	.40
15	John L. Williams	1.25	.90	.50
16	Fredd Young (SP)	4.50	3.50	1.75

1988 Seahawks Snyder's/Franz

The 12-card, standard-size set was issued in the Spokane area in Snyder's bread and in the Portland area in Franz bread. The card fronts have a color photo with blue borders.

		NM/M	NM	E
	Complete Set (10):	125.00	95.00	50.00
	Common Player:	12.00	9.00	4.75
1	Steve August	12.00	9.00	4.75
2	Terry Beeson	12.00	9.00	4.75
3	Dan Doornink	15.00	11.00	6.00
4	Michael Jackson	12.00	9.00	4.75
5	Tom Lynch	12.00	9.00	4.75
6	Steve Myer	12.00	9.00	4.75
7	Steve Raible	20.00	15.00	8.00
8	Sherman Smith	20.00	15.00	8.00
9	Manu Tuiasosopo	15.00	11.00	6.00
10	John Yarno	12.00	9.00	4.75

1989 Seahawks Oroweat

Curt Warner
RUNNING BACK

The 20-card, standard-size set was produced for Oroweat by Pacific and features silver borders. The horizontal backs contain player bio and stat information with career highlights. Each card was available in Oroweat's Oatnut Bread with a total distribution of 1.5 million.

		NM/M	NM	E
	Complete Set (20):	25.00	18.50	10.00
	Common Player:	.60	.45	.25
1	Paul Moyer	.60	.45	.25
2	Dave Wyman	.60	.45	.25
3	Tony Woods	1.00	.70	.40
4	Kelly Stouffer	1.00	.70	.40
5	Brian Blades	3.00	2.25	1.25
6	Norm Johnson	1.50	1.25	.60
7	Curt Warner	2.00	1.50	.80
8	John L. Williams	2.00	1.50	.80
9	Edwin Bailey	.60	.45	.25
10	Jacob Green	1.00	.70	.40
11	Paul Skansi	.60	.45	.25
12	Jeff Bryant	.75	.60	.30
13	Bruce Scholtz	.60	.45	.25
14	Dave Krieg	3.00	2.25	1.25
15	Steve Largent	8.00	6.00	3.25
16	Joe Nash	.75	.60	.30
17	Mike Wilson	.60	.45	.25
18	Ron Mattes	.60	.45	.25
19	Grant Feasel	.60	.45	.25
20	Bryan Millard	.60	.45	.25

1989 Seahawks Police

The 16-card, 2-5/8" x 4-1/8" set feature light blue borders with color action shots. The card backs contain safety tips, except for Largent's card, which lists his NFL records.

		NM/M	NM	E
	Complete Set (16):	5.00	3.75	2.00
	Common Player:	.40	.30	.15
1	Brian Blades	1.00	.70	.40
2	Brian Bosworth	.50	.40	.20
3	Jeff Bryant	.50	.40	.20
4	Jacob Green	.60	.45	.25
5	Chuck Knox (CO)	.60	.45	.25
6	Dave Krieg	1.25	.90	.50
7	Steve Largent	2.00	1.50	.80
8	Bryan Millard	.40	.30	.15
9	Rufus Porter	.50	.40	.20
10	Paul Moyer	.40	.30	.15
11	Eugene Robinson	.50	.40	.20
12	Ruben Rodriguez	.40	.30	.15
13	Kelly Stouffer	.50	.40	.20
14	Curt Warner	1.00	.70	.40
15	John L. Williams	1.00	.70	.40
16	Tony Woods	.60	.45	.25

1990 Seahawks Oroweat

The 50-card, regular-size set, produced by Pacific, was available in loaves of Oroweat's Oat Nut, Health Nut and Twelve Grain breads. The first 20 cards of the set were issued before the season with the remaining cards issued during the season. No card No. 25 was produced.

		NM/M	NM	E
	Complete Set (50):	30.00	22.00	12.00
	Common Player (1-20):	.35	.25	.14
	Common Player (21-50):	.50	.40	.20
1	Dave Krieg	1.50	1.25	.60
2	Rick Donnelly	.35	.25	.14
3	Brian Blades	1.50	1.25	.60
4	Cortez Kennedy	1.75	1.25	.70
5	John L. Williams	1.50	1.25	.60
6	Jeff Chadwick	.35	.25	.14
7	Thom Kaumeyer	.35	.25	.14
8	Bryan Millard	.35	.25	.14
9	Eugene Robinson	.50	.40	.20
10	Jacob Green	.50	.40	.20
11	Willie Bouyer	.35	.25	.14
12	Jeff Bryant	.50	.40	.20
13	Chris Warren	3.00	2.25	1.25

14	Derrick Fenner	.75	.60	.30
15	Paul Skansi	.35	.25	.14
16	Joe Cain	.35	.25	.14
17	Tommy Kane	.60	.45	.25
18	Tom Flores (GM)	.60	.45	.25
19	Terry Wooden	.50	.40	.20
20	Tony Woods	.60	.45	.25
21	Ricky Andrews	.50	.40	.20
22	Joe Tofflemire	.50	.40	.20
23	Ned Bolcar	.50	.40	.20
24A	Kelly Stouffer	1.00	.70	.40
24B	Melvin Jenkins	.50	.40	.20
26	Norm Johnson	.75	.60	.30
27	Eric Hayes	.50	.40	.20
28	Mike Morris	.50	.40	.20
29	Edwin Bailey	.50	.40	.20
30	Ron Heller	.50	.40	.20
31	Darren Comeaux	.60	.45	.25
32	Andy Heck	.60	.45	.25
33	Ronnie Lee	.50	.40	.20
34	Robert Blackmon	.60	.45	.25
35	Joe Nash	.60	.45	.25
36	Patrick Hunter	.60	.45	.25
37	Darrick Brilz	.50	.40	.20
38	Ron Mattes	.50	.40	.20
39	Nesby Glasgow	.60	.45	.25
40	Dwayne Harper	.50	.40	.20
41	Chuck Knox (CO)	.75	.60	.30
42	Travis McNeal	.60	.45	.25
43	Derek Loville	1.50	1.25	.60
44	Dave Wyman	.50	.40	.20
45	Louis Clark	.50	.40	.20
46	Grant Feasel	.50	.40	.20
47	James Jones	.60	.45	.25
48	Rufus Porter	1.00	.70	.40
49	Jeff Kemp	1.00	.70	.40
50	James Jefferson	.60	.45	.25
NNO	**Title Card**	3.00	2.25	1.25
		.50	.40	.20

1990 Seahawks Police

Travis
McNeal
Tight End 6'3" 248 lbs. Tennessee-Chat.

The 16-card, 2-5/8" x 4-1/8" set has green borders around a color action shot with safety tips appearing on the backs.

		NM/M	NM	E
Complete Set (16):		5.00	3.75	2.00
Common Player:		.35	.25	.14
1	Brian Blades	.75	.60	.30
2	Grant Feasel	.35	.25	.14
3	Jacob Green	.75	.60	.30
4	Andy Heck	.50	.40	.20
5	James Jefferson	.50	.40	.20
6	Norm Johnson	.75	.60	.30
7	Cortez Kennedy	1.00	.70	.40
8	Chuck Knox (CO)	.75	.60	.30
9	Dave Krieg	1.00	.70	.40
10	Travis McNeal	.35	.25	.14
11	Bryan Millard	.35	.25	.14
12	Rufus Porter	.50	.40	.20
13	Paul Skansi	.35	.25	.14
14	John L. Williams	.75	.60	.30
15	Tony Woods	.50	.40	.20
16	David Wyman	.35	.25	.14

1991 Seahawks Oroweat

The 50-card, standard-size set, produced by Pacific, was distributed in loaves of Oroweat bread and in five-card packs at a Seattle home game. The cards are very similar to Pacific's 1991 inaugural NFL set, except for the Oroweat logo in the upper right corner of the card front.

		NM/M	NM	E
Complete Set (50):		30.00	22.00	12.00
Common Player:		.50	.40	.20
1	Tommy Kane	.50	.40	.20
2	Norm Johnson	.75	.60	.30
3	Robert Blackmon	.50	.40	.20
4	Mike Tice	.50	.40	.20

5	Cortez Kennedy	1.50	1.25	.60
6	Bryan Millard	.50	.40	.20
7	Tony Woods	.50	.40	.20
8	Paul Skansi	.50	.40	.20
9	John L. Williams	1.50	1.25	.60
10	Terry Wooden	.75	.60	.30
11	Brian Blades	1.25	.90	.50
12	Jacob Green	.75	.60	.30
13	Joe Nash	.75	.60	.30
14	Eugene Robinson	.75	.60	.30
15	Rufus Porter	.75	.60	.30
16	Andy Heck	.50	.40	.20
17	Derrick Fenner	1.00	.70	.40
18	Nesby Glasgow	.50	.40	.20
19	Chris Warren	3.00	2.25	1.25
20	Dave Krieg	1.50	1.25	.60
21	Vann McElroy	.50	.40	.20
22	Jeff Bryant	.50	.40	.20
23	Warren Wheat	.50	.40	.20
24	Marcus Cotton	.50	.40	.20
25	David Wyman	.50	.40	.20
26	Joe Cain	.50	.40	.20
27	Darrick Brilz	.50	.40	.20
28	Eric Hayes	.50	.40	.20
29	Ronnie Lee	.50	.40	.20
30	Louis Clark	.50	.40	.20
31	James Jones	.50	.40	.20
32	Dwayne Harper	.50	.40	.20
33	Grant Feasel	.50	.40	.20
34	Trey Junkin	.50	.40	.20
35	James Jefferson	.50	.40	.20
36	Edwin Bailey	.50	.40	.20
37	Derrick Loville	1.50	1.25	.60
38	Travis McNeal	.50	.40	.20
39	Rick Donnelly	.50	.40	.20
40	Rod Stephens	.50	.40	.20
41	Darren Comeaux	.50	.40	.20
42	Brian Davis	.50	.40	.20
43	Bill Hitchcock	.50	.40	.20
44	Jeff Chadwick	.75	.60	.30
45	Patrick Hunter	.75	.60	.30
46	David Daniels	.50	.40	.20
47	Doug Thomas	.50	.40	.20
48	Dan McGwire	.75	.60	.30
49	John Kasay	.75	.60	.30
50	Jeff Kemp	.75	.60	.30
NNO	**Title Card**	2.50	2.00	1.00

1982 Sears-Roebuck

The 12-card, 5" x 7" set, issued by 37 different Sears district stores, closely resembles the Marketcom posters. The card backs contain bio and career highlight information with the Sears Roebuck logo on the card back bottom. Because of the football strike in 1982, many of the cards were not distributed and were either destroyed or thrown out.

		NM/M	NM	E
Complete Set (12):		265.00	132.00	79.00
Common Player:		8.00	6.00	3.25
1	Ken Anderson	15.00	11.00	6.00
2	Terry Bradshaw	25.00	18.50	10.00
3	Earl Campbell	25.00	18.50	10.00
4	Dwight Clark	8.00	6.00	3.25
5	Cris Collinsworth	8.00	6.00	3.25
6	Tony Dorsett	20.00	15.00	8.00
7	Dan Fouts	18.00	13.50	7.25
8	Franco Harris	20.00	15.00	8.00
9	Joe Montana	75.00	56.00	30.00
10	Walter Payton	40.00	30.00	16.00
11	Randy White	15.00	11.00	6.00
12	Kellen Winslow	15.00	11.00	6.00

1972 7-11 Slurpee Cups

Each of these 60 white plastic cups measures 5-1/4" tall, 3-1/4" in diameter at the mouth and 2" in diameter at the base. The fronts feature a color player portrait with his name and team name. Most of the cups feature a facsimile autograph between the portrait and the player's name. The backs include biographical information, the player's team helmet and the 7-Eleven logo. Another set of 80 cups was released in 1973. The cups are similar except the 1972 cups have a smaller typeface for the player's name (1/16") and do not have "Made in USA" printed on the sides.

		NM	E	VG
Complete Set (60):		250.00	125.00	75.00
Common Player:		4.00	2.00	1.25
1	Donny Anderson	4.00	2.00	1.25
2	Elvin Bethea	4.00	2.00	1.25
3	Fred Biletnikoff	8.00	4.00	2.50
4	Bill Bradley	4.00	2.00	1.25
5	Terry Bradshaw	25.00	12.50	7.50
6	Larry Brown	4.00	2.00	1.25
7	Willie Brown	5.00	2.50	1.50
8	Norm Bulaich	4.00	2.00	1.25
9	Dick Butkus	15.00	7.50	4.50
10	Ray Chester	4.00	2.00	1.25

11	Bill Curry	4.00	2.00	1.25
12	Len Dawson	8.00	4.00	2.50
13	Willie Ellison	4.00	2.00	1.25
14	Ed Flanagan	4.00	2.00	1.25
15	Gary Garrison	4.00	2.00	1.25
16	Gale Gillingham	4.00	2.00	1.25
17	Joe Greene	8.00	4.00	2.50
18	Cedrick Hardman	4.00	2.00	1.25
19	Jim Hart	5.00	2.50	1.50
20	Ted Hendricks	5.00	2.50	1.50
21	Winston Hill	4.00	2.00	1.25
22	Ken Houston	5.00	2.50	1.50
23	Chuck Howley	4.00	2.00	1.25
24	Claude Humphrey	4.00	2.00	1.25
25	Roy Jefferson	4.00	2.00	1.25
26	Sonny Jurgensen	6.00	3.00	1.75
27	Leroy Kelly	5.00	2.50	1.50
28	Paul Krause	4.00	2.00	1.25
29	George Kunz	4.00	2.00	1.25
30	Jake Kupp	4.00	2.00	1.25
31	Ted Kwalick	4.00	2.00	1.25
32	Willie Lanier	5.00	2.50	1.50
33	Bob Lilly	6.00	3.00	1.75
34	Floyd Little	4.00	2.00	1.25
35	Larry Little	5.00	2.50	1.50
36	Tom Mack	4.00	2.00	1.25
37	Milt Morin	4.00	2.00	1.25
38	Mercury Morris	5.00	2.50	1.50
39	John Niland	4.00	2.00	1.25
40	Jim Otto	5.00	2.50	1.50
41	Steve Owens	4.00	2.00	1.25
42	Alan Page	5.00	2.50	1.50
43	Jim Plunkett	5.00	2.50	1.50
44	Mike Reid	5.00	2.50	1.50
45	Mel Renfro	5.00	2.50	1.50
46	Isiah Robertson	4.00	2.00	1.25
47	Andy Russell	4.00	2.00	1.25
48	Charlie Sanders	4.00	2.00	1.25
49	O.J. Simpson	15.00	7.50	4.50
50	Bubba Smith	5.00	2.50	1.50
51	Bill Stanfill	4.00	2.00	1.25
52	Jan Stenerud	5.00	2.50	1.50
53	Walt Sweeney	4.00	2.00	1.25
54	Bob Tucker	4.00	2.00	1.25
55	Jim Tyrer	4.00	2.00	1.25
56	Rick Volk	4.00	2.00	1.25
57	Gene Washington	4.00	2.00	1.25
58	Dave Wilcox	4.00	2.00	1.25
59	Del Williams	4.00	2.00	1.25
60	Ron Yary	4.00	2.00	1.25

1973 7-11 Slurpee Cups

This 80-cup series is similar to the 1972 series except the player's name is printed in larger type (1/8") and the words "Made in USA" are printed down the sides.

		NM	E	VG
Complete Set (80):		450.00	225.00	135.00
Common Player:		5.00	2.50	1.50
1	Dan Abramowicz	6.00	3.00	1.75
2	Ken Anderson	10.00	5.00	3.00
3	Jim Beirne	5.00	2.50	1.50
4	Ed Bell	5.00	2.50	1.50
5	Bob Berry	5.00	2.50	1.50
6	Jim Bertelsen	5.00	2.50	1.50
7	Marlin Briscoe	5.00	2.50	1.50
8	John Brockington	5.00	2.50	1.50
9	Larry Brown	6.00	3.00	1.75
10	Buck Buchanan	7.50	3.75	2.25
11	Dick Butkus	25.00	12.50	7.50
12	Larry Carwell	5.00	2.50	1.50
13	Rich Caster	5.00	2.50	1.50
14	Bobby Douglass	5.00	2.50	1.50
15	Pete Duranko	5.00	2.50	1.50
16	Cid Edwards	5.00	2.50	1.50
17	Mel Farr	5.00	2.50	1.50
18	Pat Fischer	5.00	2.50	1.50
19	Mike Garrett	5.00	2.50	1.50
20	Walt Garrison	6.00	3.00	1.75
21	George Goeddeke	5.00	2.50	1.50
22	Bob Gresham	5.00	2.50	1.50
23	Jack Ham	10.00	5.00	3.00
24	Chris Hanburger	5.00	2.50	1.50
25	Franco Harris	20.00	10.00	6.00
26	Calvin Hill	6.00	3.00	1.75
27	J.D. Hill	5.00	2.50	1.50
28	Marv Hubbard	5.00	2.50	1.50
29	Scott Hunter	5.00	2.50	1.50
30	Harold Jackson	6.00	3.00	1.75
31	Randy Jackson	5.00	2.50	1.50
32	Bob Johnson	5.00	2.50	1.50
33	Jim Johnson	7.50	3.75	2.25
34	Ron Johnson	5.00	2.50	1.50
35	Leroy Keyes	5.00	2.50	1.50
36	Greg Landry	6.00	3.00	1.75
37	Gary Larsen	5.00	2.50	1.50
38	Frank Lewis	5.00	2.50	1.50

39	Bob Lilly	10.00	5.00	3.00
40	Dale Lindsey	5.00	2.50	1.50
41	Larry Little	7.50	3.75	2.25
42	Carl (Spider) Lockhart	5.00	2.50	1.50
43	Mike Lucci	5.00	2.50	1.50
44	Jim Lynch	5.00	2.50	1.50
45	Art Malone	5.00	2.50	1.50
46	Ed Marinaro	6.00	3.00	1.75
47	Jim Marshall	7.50	3.75	2.25
48	Ray May	5.00	2.50	1.50
49	Don Maynard	10.00	5.00	3.00
50	Don McCauley	5.00	2.50	1.50
51	Mike McCoy	5.00	2.50	1.50
52	Tom Mitchell	5.00	2.50	1.50
53	Tommy Nobis	7.50	3.75	2.25
54	Dan Pastorini	6.00	3.00	1.75
55	Mac Percival	5.00	2.50	1.50
56	Mike Phipps	6.00	3.00	1.75
57	Ed Podolak	5.00	2.50	1.50
58	John Reaves	5.00	2.50	1.50
59	Tim Rossovich	5.00	2.50	1.50
60	Bo Scott	5.00	2.50	1.50
61	Ron Sellers	5.00	2.50	1.50
62	Dennis Shaw	5.00	2.50	1.50
63	Mike Siani	5.00	2.50	1.50
64	O.J. Simpson	25.00	12.50	7.50
65	Bubba Smith	7.50	3.75	2.25
66	Larry Smith	5.00	2.50	1.50
67	Jackie Smith	7.50	3.75	2.25
68	Norm Snead	6.00	3.00	1.75
69	Jack Snow	5.00	2.50	1.50
70	Steve Spurrier	20.00	10.00	6.00
71	Doug Swift	5.00	2.50	1.50
72	Jack Tatum	7.50	3.75	2.25
73	Bruce Taylor	5.00	2.50	1.50
74	Otis Taylor	6.00	3.00	1.75
75	Bob Trumpy	6.00	3.00	1.75
76	Jim Turner	5.00	2.50	1.50
77	Phil Villapiano	5.00	2.50	1.50
78	Roger Wehrli	5.00	2.50	1.50
79	Ken Willard	5.00	2.50	1.50
80	Jack Youngblood	7.50	3.75	2.25

1983 7-11 Discs

These discs were available at participating 7-Eleven stores in 1983. Each disc, which is numbered on the back as "x of Fifteen," has a portrait and an action picture on the front. The player's team name is at the top of the disc, while his name is at the bottom. His jersey number is on each side. The disc back has the player's career totals, pro honors, a Slurpee logo and the year, 1983.

		NM/M	NM	E
Complete Set (15):		30.00	22.00	12.00
Common Player:		1.00	.70	.40
1	Franco Harris	5.00	3.75	2.00
2	Dan Fouts	3.00	2.25	1.25
3	Lee Roy Selmon	1.25	.90	.50
4	Nolan Cromwell	1.25	.90	.50
5	Marcus Allen	5.00	3.75	2.00
6	Joe Montana	10.00	7.50	4.00
7	Kellen Winslow	2.00	1.50	.80
8	Hugh Green	1.00	.70	.40
9	Ted Hendricks	2.00	1.50	.80
10	Danny White	1.50	1.25	.60
11	Wes Chandler	1.00	.70	.40
12	Jimmie Giles	1.00	.70	.40
13	Jack Youngblood	2.00	1.50	.80
14	Lester Hayes	1.00	.70	.40
15	Vince Ferragamo	1.00	.70	.40

1984 7-11 Discs

These discs, available at participating 7-Eleven stores, were available in two regions, East and West, as indicated by the card number prefix. The disc has a diameter of 1-3/4" and is designed like the previous year's issue, except the year on the back is 1984.

		NM/M	NM	E
Complete Set (40):		60.00	45.00	24.00
Common Player:		.75	.60	.30
1E	Franco Harris	3.00	2.25	1.25
2E	Lawrence Taylor	2.00	1.50	.80
3E	Mark Gastineau	.75	.60	.30
4E	Lee Roy Selmon	1.00	.70	.40
5E	Ken Anderson	1.50	1.25	.60
6E	Walter Payton	4.00	3.00	1.50
7E	Ken Stabler	1.50	1.25	.60
8E	Marcus Allen	2.00	1.50	.80
9E	Fred Smerlas	.75	.60	.30
10E	Ozzie Newsome	1.25	.90	.50
11E	Steve Bartkowski	1.00	.70	.40
12E	Tony Dorsett	2.00	1.50	.80
13E	John Riggins	1.50	1.25	.60
14E	Billy Sims	.75	.60	.30
15E	Dan Marino	9.00	6.75	3.50
16E	Tony Collins	.75	.60	.30
17E	Curtis Dickey	.75	.60	.30
18E	Ron Jaworski	.75	.60	.30
19E	William Andrews	.75	.60	.30
20E	Joe Theismann	1.50	1.25	.60
1W	Franco Harris	2.00	1.50	.80
2W	Joe Montana	10.00	7.50	4.00
3W	Matt Blair	.75	.60	.30
4W	Warren Moon	6.00	4.50	2.50
5W	Marcus Allen	2.00	1.50	.80
6W	John Riggins	1.50	1.25	.60
7W	Walter Payton	4.00	3.00	1.50
8W	Vince Ferragamo	.75	.60	.30
9W	Billy Sims	.75	.60	.30
10W	Ken Anderson	1.25	.90	.50
11W	Lynn Dickey	.75	.60	.30
12W	Tony Dorsett	2.00	1.50	.80
13W	Bill Kenney	.75	.60	.30
14W	Ottis Anderson	1.00	.70	.40
15W	Dan Fouts	1.50	1.25	.60
16W	Eric Dickerson	3.00	2.25	1.25
17W	John Elway	6.00	4.50	2.50
18W	Ozzie Newsome	1.25	.90	.50
19W	Curt Warner	1.00	.70	.40
20W	Joe Theismann	1.50	1.25	.60

1981 Shell Posters

The works of three different artists are featured on these 10-7/8" x 13-7/8" posters available at participating Shell Oil stations across the country in 1981. Each poster has a black-and-white drawing of the featured player, as rendered by either K. Atkins, Nick Galloway or Tanenbawm (these signatures are on the corresponding poster fronts). There are, however, some posters which were not signed by the artist (#s 7, 11, 12 and 93). The posters are listed alphabetically by teams, then alphabetically by players. Team sets consist of six posters. A national set of six posters was also made (Payton, Griffin, Logan, Pearson, Campbell and O. Anderson) and was available in markets where a pro team did not exist.

		NM/M	NM	E
Complete Set (96):		400.00	300.00	160.00
Common Player:		4.00	3.00	1.50
(1)	William Andrews	5.00	3.75	2.00
(2)	Steve Bartkowski	7.00	5.25	2.75
(3)	Buddy Curry	3.50	2.75	1.50
(4)	Wallace Francis	5.00	3.75	2.00
(5)	Mike Kenn	5.00	3.75	2.00
(6)	Jeff Van Note	5.00	3.75	2.00
(7)	Mike Barnes	4.00	3.00	1.50
(8)	Roger Carr	4.00	3.00	1.50
(9)	Curtis Dickey	5.00	3.75	2.00
(10)	Bert Jones	7.00	5.25	2.75
(11)	Bruce Laird	4.00	3.00	1.50
(12)	Randy McMillan	5.00	3.75	2.00
(13)	Brian Baschnagel	4.00	3.00	1.50
(14)	Vince Evans	5.00	3.75	2.00
(15)	Gary Fencik	5.00	3.75	2.00
(16)	Roland Harper	4.00	3.00	1.50
(17)	Alan Page	9.00	6.75	3.50
(18)	Walter Payton	10.00	7.50	4.00
(19)	Ken Anderson	8.00	6.00	3.25
(20)	Ross Browner	5.00	3.75	2.00
(21)	Archie Griffin	4.00	3.00	1.50
(22)	Pat McInally	5.00	3.75	2.00
(23)	Anthony Munoz	8.00	6.00	3.25
(24)	Reggie Williams	5.00	3.75	2.00
(25)	Lyle Alzado	6.00	4.50	2.50
(26)	Joe DeLamielleure	4.00	3.00	1.50
(27)	Doug Dieken	4.00	3.00	1.50
(28)	Dave Logan	4.00	3.00	1.50
(29)	Reggie Rucker	5.00	3.75	2.00
(30)	Brian Sipe	5.00	3.75	2.00
(31)	Benny Barnes	4.00	3.00	1.50
(32)	Bob Breunig	4.00	3.00	1.50
(33)	D.D. Lewis	4.00	3.00	1.50
(34)	Harvey Martin	6.00	4.50	2.50
(35)	Drew Pearson	4.00	3.00	1.50
(36)	Rafael Septien	4.00	3.00	1.50
(37)	Al (Bubba) Baker	5.00	3.75	2.00
(38)	Dexter Bussey	4.00	3.00	1.50
(39)	Gary Danielson	5.00	3.75	2.00
(40)	Freddie Scott	4.00	3.00	1.50
(41)	Billy Sims	6.00	4.50	2.50
(42)	Tom Skladany	4.00	3.00	1.50
(43)	Robert Brazile	6.00	4.50	2.50
(44)	Ken Burrough	6.00	4.50	2.50
(45)	Earl Campbell	9.00	6.75	3.50
(46)	Leon Gray	5.00	3.75	2.00
(47)	Carl Mauck	5.00	3.75	2.00
(48)	Ken Stabler	8.00	6.00	3.25
(49)	Bob Baumhower	5.00	3.75	2.00
(50)	Jimmy Cefalo	5.00	3.75	2.00
(51)	A.J. Duhe	5.00	3.75	2.00
(52)	Nat Moore	6.00	4.50	2.50
(53)	Ed Newman	4.00	3.00	1.50
(54)	Uwe Von Schamann	4.00	3.00	1.50
(55)	Steve Grogan	7.00	5.25	2.75
(56)	John Hannah	4.50	3.50	1.75
(57)	Don Hasselbeck	4.00	3.00	1.50
(58)	Mike Haynes	6.00	4.50	2.50
(59)	Harold Jackson	5.00	3.75	2.00
(60)	Steve Nelson	4.00	3.00	1.50
(61)	Elois Grooms	5.00	3.75	2.00
(62)	Rickey Jackson	7.50	5.75	3.00
(63)	Archie Manning	8.00	6.00	3.25
(64)	Tommy Myers	5.00	3.75	2.00
(65)	Benny Ricardo	5.00	3.75	2.00
(66)	George Rogers	6.00	4.50	2.50
(67)	Harry Carson	7.00	5.25	2.75
(68)	Dave Jennings	4.00	3.00	1.50
(69)	Gary Jeter	4.00	3.00	1.50
(70)	Phil Simms	8.00	6.00	3.25
(71)	Lawrence Taylor	12.00	9.00	4.75
(72)	Brad Van Pelt	5.00	3.75	2.00
(73)	Greg Buttle	5.00	3.75	2.00
(74)	Bruce Harper	4.00	3.00	1.50
(75)	Joe Klecko	5.00	3.75	2.00
(76)	Randy Rasmussen	4.00	3.00	1.50
(77)	Richard Todd	5.00	3.75	2.00
(78)	Wesley Walker	6.00	4.50	2.50
(79)	Ottis Anderson	4.00	3.00	1.50
(80)	Dan Dierdorf	9.00	6.75	3.50
(81)	Mel Gray	5.00	3.75	2.00
(82)	Jim Hart	6.00	4.50	2.50
(83)	E.J. Junior	5.00	3.75	2.00
(84)	Pat Tilley	5.00	3.75	2.00
(85)	Jimmie Giles	5.00	3.75	2.00
(86)	Charley Hannah	4.00	3.00	1.50
(87)	Bill Kollar	4.00	3.00	1.50
(88)	David Lewis	4.00	3.00	1.50
(89)	Lee Roy Selmon	6.00	4.50	2.50
(90)	Doug Williams	5.00	3.75	2.00
(91)	Joe Lavender	4.00	3.00	1.50
(92)	Mark Moseley	5.00	3.75	2.00
(93)	Mark Murphy	4.00	3.00	1.50
(94)	Lemar Parrish	5.00	3.75	2.00
(95)	John Riggins	9.00	6.75	3.50
(96)	Joe Washington	5.00	3.75	2.00

1956 Shredded Wheat CFL

		NM	E	VG
Complete Set (105):		9,000	4,500	2,700
Common Player:		80.00	40.00	24.00
A1	Peter Muir	80.00	40.00	24.00
A2	Harry Langford	80.00	40.00	24.00
A3	Tony Pajaczkowski	150.00	75.00	45.00
A4	Bob Morgan	80.00	40.00	24.00
A5	Baz Nagle	80.00	40.00	24.00
A6	Alex Macklin	80.00	40.00	24.00
A7	Bob Geary	80.00	40.00	24.00
A8	Don Klosterman	125.00	62.00	37.00
A9	Bill McKenna	80.00	40.00	24.00
A10	Bill Stevenson	80.00	40.00	24.00
A11	Charles Baillie	80.00	40.00	24.00
A12	Berdett Hess	80.00	40.00	24.00
A13	Lynn Bottoms	90.00	45.00	27.00
A14	Doug Brown	80.00	40.00	24.00
A15	Jack Hennemier	80.00	40.00	24.00
B1	Frank Anderson	80.00	40.00	24.00
B2	Don Barry	80.00	40.00	24.00
B3	Johnny Bright	200.00	100.00	60.00
B4	Kurt Burris	80.00	40.00	24.00
B5	Bob Dean	80.00	40.00	24.00
B6	Don Getty	150.00	75.00	45.00
B7	Normie Kwong	200.00	100.00	60.00
B8	Earl Lindley	80.00	40.00	24.00
B9	Art Walker	100.00	50.00	30.00
B10	Rollie Miles	125.00	62.00	37.00
B11	Frank Morris	125.00	62.00	37.00
B12	Jackie Parker	300.00	150.00	90.00
B13	Ted Tully	80.00	40.00	24.00
B14	Frank Ivy	90.00	45.00	27.00
B15	Bill Rowekamp	80.00	40.00	24.00
C1	Al Sherman	80.00	40.00	24.00
C2	Larry Cabrelli	80.00	40.00	24.00
C3	Ron Kelly	80.00	40.00	24.00
C4	Edward Kotowich	80.00	40.00	24.00
C5	Buddy Leake	100.00	50.00	30.00
C6	Thomas Lumsden	80.00	40.00	24.00
C7	Bill Smitiuk	80.00	40.00	24.00

		NM	E	VG
C8	Buddy Tinsley	125.00	62.00	37.00
C9	Ron Vaccher	80.00	40.00	24.00
C10	Eagle Day	125.00	62.00	37.00
C11	Buddy Allison	80.00	40.00	24.00
C12	Bob Haas	90.00	45.00	27.00
C13	Steve Patrick	80.00	40.00	24.00
C14	Keith Pearce (UER) (Misspelled Pierce on front)	80.00	40.00	24.00
C15	Lorne Benson	80.00	40.00	24.00
D1	George Arnett	80.00	40.00	24.00
D2	Eddie Bevan	80.00	40.00	24.00
D3	Art Darch	80.00	40.00	24.00
D4	John Fedosoff	80.00	40.00	24.00
D5	Cam Fraser	80.00	40.00	24.00
D6	Ron Howell	90.00	45.00	27.00
D7	Alex Muzyka	80.00	40.00	24.00
D8	Chet Miksza	80.00	40.00	24.00
D9	Walt Nikorak	80.00	40.00	24.00
D10	Pete Neumann	125.00	62.00	37.00
D11	Steve Oneschuk	80.00	40.00	24.00
D12	Vince Scott	125.00	62.00	37.00
D13	Ralph Toohy	80.00	40.00	24.00
D14	Ray Truant	80.00	40.00	24.00
D15	Nobby Wirkowski	100.00	50.00	30.00
E1	Pete Bennett	80.00	40.00	24.00
E2	Fred Black	80.00	40.00	24.00
E3	Jim Copeland	80.00	40.00	24.00
E4	Al Pfeifer	90.00	45.00	27.00
E5	Ron Albright	80.00	40.00	24.00
E6	Tom Dublinski	80.00	40.00	24.00
E7	Billy Shipp	80.00	40.00	24.00
E8	Baz Mackie	80.00	40.00	24.00
E9	Bill McFarlane	80.00	40.00	24.00
E10	John Sopinka	100.00	50.00	30.00
E11	Dick Brown	80.00	40.00	24.00
E12	Gerry Doucette	80.00	40.00	24.00
E13	Dan Shaw	80.00	40.00	24.00
E14	Dick Shatto	175.00	87.00	52.00
E15	Bill Swiacki	100.00	50.00	30.00
F1	Ray Syrnyk	80.00	40.00	24.00
F2	Martin Ruby	125.00	62.00	37.00
F3	Bobby Marlow	125.00	62.00	37.00
F4	Doug Kiloh	80.00	40.00	24.00
F5	Gord Sturtridge	90.00	45.00	27.00
F6	Stan Williams	80.00	40.00	24.00
F7	Larry Isbell	80.00	40.00	24.00
F8	Ken Casner	80.00	40.00	24.00
F9	Mel Becket	100.00	50.00	30.00
F10	Reg Whitehouse	80.00	40.00	24.00
F11	Harry Lampman	80.00	40.00	24.00
F12	Mario DeMarco	90.00	45.00	27.00
F13	Ken Carpenter	100.00	50.00	30.00
F14	Frank Filchock	100.00	50.00	30.00
F15	Frank Tripucka	125.00	62.00	37.00
G1	Tom Tracy	150.00	75.00	45.00
G2	Pete Ladygo	80.00	40.00	24.00
G3	Sam Scoccia	80.00	40.00	24.00
G4	Joe Upton	80.00	40.00	24.00
G5	Bob Simpson	150.00	75.00	45.00
G6	Bruno Bitkowski	90.00	45.00	27.00
G7	Joe Stracini (UER) (Misspelled Straccini on card front)	80.00	40.00	24.00
G8	Hal Ledyard	80.00	40.00	24.00
G9	Milt Graham	80.00	40.00	24.00
G10	Bill Sowalski	80.00	40.00	24.00
G11	Avatus Stone	80.00	40.00	24.00
G12	John Boich	100.00	50.00	30.00
G13	Don Pinhey (UER) (Misspelled Bob Pinkney on card front)	80.00	40.00	24.00
G14	Peter Karpuk	80.00	40.00	24.00
G15	Frank Clair	125.00	62.00	37.00

1978 Slim Jim

Specially-marked Slim Jim products in 1978 contained a 3" x 5-3/4" panel featuring two football player discs. The discs, featuring a player mug shot, biographical data, an NFLPA logo and "Slim Jim Collection" on the front, were issued by Michael Schechter Associates. MSA is also on the disc front. Each disc has a diameter of 2-3/8" and is perforated so it can be cut out from the panel. The same two players were always on the same panel. They are listed according to the pairs on the panel, starting with 1A and 1B and ending 69-70. Note: The prices for each disc are actually the value of the panel. So, 1A and 1B would be $20, not $40.

		NM	E	VG
Complete Set (70):		350.00	175.00	105.00
Common Player:		8.00	4.00	2.50
1A	Lyle Alzado	20.00	10.00	6.00
1B	Archie Manning	20.00	10.00	6.00
2A	Bill Bergey	20.00	10.00	6.00

2B	John Riggins	20.00	10.00	6.00
3A	Fred Biletnikoff	20.00	10.00	6.00
3B	Dan Dierdorf	20.00	10.00	6.00
4A	John Cappelletti	8.00	4.00	2.50
4B	Bob Chandler	8.00	4.00	2.50
5A	Tommy Casanova	8.00	4.00	2.50
5B	Darryl Stingley	8.00	4.00	2.50
6A	Billy Joe Dupree	8.00	4.00	2.50
6B	Nat Moore	8.00	4.00	2.50
7A	John Dutton	8.00	4.00	2.50
7B	Paul Krause	8.00	4.00	2.50
8A	Leon Gray	8.00	4.00	2.50
8B	Richard Caster	8.00	4.00	2.50
9A	Mel Gray	8.00	4.00	2.50
9B	Claude Humphrey	8.00	4.00	2.50
10A	Joe Greene	12.00	6.00	3.50
10B	Dexter Bussey	12.00	6.00	3.50
11A	Jack Gregory	8.00	4.00	2.50
11B	Billy Johnson	8.00	4.00	2.50
12A	Steve Grogan	8.00	4.00	2.50
12B	Jerome Barkum	8.00	4.00	2.50
13A	John Hannah	10.00	5.00	3.00
13B	Isaac Curtis	10.00	5.00	3.00
14A	Jim Hart	9.00	4.50	2.75
14B	Otis Sistrunk	9.00	4.50	2.75
15A	Tommy Hart	8.00	4.00	2.50
15B	Ron Howard	8.00	4.00	2.50
16A	Wilbur Jackson	8.50	4.25	2.50
16B	Riley Odoms	8.50	4.25	2.50
17A	Ron Jaworski	10.00	5.00	3.00
17B	Mike Thomas	10.00	5.00	3.00
18A	Larry Little	12.00	6.00	3.50
18B	Isiah Robertson	12.00	6.00	3.50
19A	Ron McDole	8.00	4.00	2.50
19B	Willie Buchanon	8.00	4.00	2.50
20A	Lydell Mitchell	8.50	4.25	2.50
20B	Glen Edwards	8.50	4.25	2.50
21A	Robert Newhouse	8.00	4.00	2.50
21B	Glenn Doughty	8.00	4.00	2.50
22A	Alan Page	10.00	5.00	3.00
22B	Fred Carr	10.00	5.00	3.00
23A	Walter Payton	55.00	27.00	16.50
23B	Larry Csonka	55.00	27.00	16.50
24A	Greg Pruitt	8.00	4.00	2.50
24B	Doug Buffone	8.00	4.00	2.50
25A	Ahmad Rashad	12.00	6.00	3.50
25B	Jeff Van Note	12.00	6.00	3.50
26A	Golden Richards	10.00	5.00	3.00
26B	Rocky Bleier	10.00	5.00	3.00
27A	Clarence Scott	8.00	4.00	2.50
27B	Joe DeLamielleure	8.00	4.00	2.50
28A	Lee Roy Selmon	10.00	5.00	3.00
28B	Charlie Sanders	10.00	5.00	3.00
29A	Bruce Taylor	8.50	4.25	2.50
29B	Otis Armstrong	8.50	4.25	2.50
30A	Emmitt Thomas	8.00	4.00	2.50
30B	Elvin Bethea	8.00	4.00	2.50
31A	Brad Van Pelt	8.00	4.00	2.50
31B	Ted Washington	8.00	4.00	2.50
32A	Gene Washington	15.00	7.50	4.50
32B	Charlie Joiner	15.00	7.50	4.50
33A	Clarence Williams	8.00	4.00	2.50
33B	Lemar Parrish	8.00	4.00	2.50
34A	Roger Wehrli	12.00	6.00	3.50
34B	Gene Upshaw	12.00	6.00	3.50
35A	Don Woods	8.00	4.00	2.50
35B	Ron Jessie	8.00	4.00	2.50

1969 South Carolina Team Sheets

		NM	E	VG
Complete Set (6):		45.00	22.00	13.50
Common Player:		6.00	3.00	1.75
1	Tim Bice, Candler Boyd, Don Buckner, Ronald Bunch, Bob Cole, Carl Cowart, Don Dunning, Mike Fair, Tony Fusaro, Benny Galloway	6.00	3.00	1.75
2	Allen Brown, Don Somma, Billy Tharp, Scott Townsend, Pat Watson, Bob Wehmeyer, Bob White, Curtis Williams, Tom Wingard, Fred Zeigler	6.00	3.00	1.75
3	Andy Chavous, Wally Orrel, Ronnie Palmer, Hyrum Pierce, Jimmy Poole, Roy Don Reeves, Larry Royal, Gene Schwarting, Fletcher Spigner, Frank Tetterton	6.00	3.00	1.75

4	Paul Dietzel CO, Larry Jones CO, Johnny Menger CO, Pride Ratterree CO, Bill Rowe CO, Bill Shalosky CO, Lou Holtz CO, Don Purvis CO, Jack Powers CO, Dick Weldon CO	15.00	7.50	4.50
5	Ben Garnto, Gordon Gibson, Johnny Glass, Jimmy Gobble, Dave Grant, Johnny Gregory, Bob Harris, Rudy Holloman, Earl Hunter, Jack James	6.00	3.00	1.75
6	Jimmy Killen, Joe Komoroski, Dave Lucas, Bob Mauro, George McCarthy, Toy McCord, Wally Medlin, Bob Morris, Warren Muir, Jim Mulvihill	6.00	3.00	1.75

1974 Southern Cal Discs

		NM	E	VG
Complete Set (30):		75.00	37.00	22.00
Common Player:		2.00	1.00	.60
1	Bill Bain	2.50	1.25	.70
2	Otha Bradley	2.50	1.25	.70
3	Kevin Bruce	2.00	1.00	.60
4	Mario Celotto	2.00	1.00	.60
5	Marvin Cobb	4.00	2.00	1.25
6	Anthony Davis	8.00	4.00	2.50
7	Joe Davis	2.00	1.00	.60
8	Shelton Diggs	2.50	1.25	.70
9	Dave Farmer	2.50	1.25	.70
10	Pat Haden	10.00	5.00	3.00
11	Donnie Hickman	2.00	1.00	.60
12	Doug Hogan	2.00	1.00	.60
13	Mike Howell	2.00	1.00	.60
14	Gary Jeter	4.00	2.00	1.25
15	Steve Knutson	2.00	1.00	.60
16	Chris Limahelu	2.50	1.25	.70
17	Bob McCaffrey	2.00	1.00	.60
18	J.K. McKay	4.00	2.00	1.25
19	John McKay (CO)	5.00	2.50	1.50
20	Jim O'Bradovich	4.00	2.00	1.25
21	Charles Phillips	2.50	1.25	.70
22	Ed Powell	2.00	1.00	.60
23	Marvin Powell	4.00	2.00	1.25
24	Danny Reece	2.50	1.25	.70
25	Art Riley	2.00	1.00	.60
26	Traveller II(Richard Sako)	2.50	1.25	.70
27	Trojan Statue(Tommy Trojan)	2.50	1.25	.70
28	**USC Song Girls**	2.50	1.25	.70
29	**USC Song Girls**	2.50	1.25	.70
30	Richard Wood	4.00	2.00	1.25
---	**Holder**	25.00	12.50	7.50

1988 Southern Cal Smokey

		NM/M	NM	E
Complete Set (17):		12.00	9.00	4.75
Common Player:		.75	.60	.30
1	Erik Affholter	1.25	.90	.50
2	Gene Arrington	.75	.60	.30
3	Scott Brennan	.75	.60	.30
4	Jeff Brown	.75	.60	.30
5	Tracy Butts	.75	.60	.30
6	Martin Chesley	.75	.60	.30
7	Paul Green	.75	.60	.30
8	John Guerrero	.75	.60	.30
9	Chris Hale	.75	.60	.30
10	Rodney Peete	4.00	3.00	1.50
11	Dave Powroznik	.75	.60	.30
12	Mark Sager	.75	.60	.30
13	Mike Serpa	.75	.60	.30
14	Larry Smith (CO)	1.25	.90	.50
15	Chris Sperle	.75	.60	.30
16	Joe Walshe	.75	.60	.30
17	Steven Webster	.75	.60	.30

1988 Southern Cal Winners

		NM/M	NM	E
Complete Set (73):		15.00	11.00	6.00
Common Player:		.15	.11	.06
1	**Title Card** (schedule on back)	.25	.20	.10
2	George Achica	.25	.20	.10
3	Marcus Allen	2.00	1.50	.80
4	Jon Arnett	.35	.25	.14
5	Johnny Baker	.15	.11	.06
6	Damon Bame	.15	.11	.06
7	Chip Banks	.35	.25	.14

		NM/M	NM	E
8	Mike Battle	.25	.20	.10
9	Hal Bedsole	.25	.20	.10
10	Ricky Bell	.35	.25	.14
11	Jeff Bregel	.15	.11	.06
12	Tay Brown	.15	.11	.06
13	Brad Budde	.25	.20	.10
14	Dave Cadigan	.25	.20	.10
15	Pat Cannamela	.15	.11	.06
16	Paul Cleary	.15	.11	.06
17	Sam Cunningham	.35	.25	.14
18	Anthony Davis	.50	.40	.20
19	Clarence Davis	.25	.20	.10
20	Morley Drury	.15	.11	.06
21	John Ferraro	.15	.11	.06
22	Bill Fisk	.15	.11	.06
23	Roy Foster	.25	.20	.10
24	Mike Garrett	.35	.25	.14
25	Frank Gifford	1.25	.90	.50
26	Ralph Heywood	.15	.11	.06
27	Pat Howell	.15	.11	.06
28	Gary Jeter	.25	.20	.10
29	Dennis Johnson	.15	.11	.06
30	Mort Kaer	.15	.11	.06
31	Grenny Lansdell	.15	.11	.06
32	Ronnie Lott	1.25	.90	.50
33	Paul McDonald	.25	.20	.10
34	Tim McDonald	.35	.25	.14
35	Ron Mix	.35	.25	.14
36	Don Mosebar	.35	.25	.14
37	Artimus Parker	.25	.20	.10
38	Charles Phillips	.15	.11	.06
39	Erny Pinckert	.15	.11	.06
40	Marvin Powell	.25	.20	.10
41	Aaron Rosenberg	.15	.11	.06
42	Tim Rossovich	.25	.20	.10
43	Jim Sears	.15	.11	.06
44	Gus Shaver	.15	.11	.06
45	Nate Shaw	.15	.11	.06
46	O.J. Simpson	5.00	3.75	2.00
47	Ernie Smith	.15	.11	.06
48	Harry Smith	.15	.11	.06
49	Larry Stevens	.15	.11	.06
50	Lynn Swann	1.00	.70	.40
51	Brice Taylor	.15	.11	.06
52	Dennis Thurman	.25	.20	.10
53	Keith Van Horne	.25	.20	.10
54	Cotton Warburton	.15	.11	.06
55	Charles White	.50	.40	.20
56	Elmer Willhoite	.15	.11	.06
57	Richard Wood	.25	.20	.10
58	Ron Yary	.35	.25	.14
59	Adrian Young	.15	.11	.06
60	Charles Young (UER) (listed as Adrian Young on card front)	.25	.20	.10
61	Pete Adams, John Grant	.15	.11	.06
62	Bill Bain, Jim O'Bradovich	.25	.20	.10
63	Nate Barrager, Francis Tappan	.15	.11	.06
64	Booker Brown, Steve Riley	.15	.11	.06
65	Al Cowlings, Jimmy Gunn, Charles Weaver	1.00	.70	.40
66	Jack Del Rio, Duane Bickett	.50	.40	.20
67	Clay Matthews, Bruce Matthews	.50	.40	.20
68	Marlin McKeever, Mike McKeever	.35	.25	.14
69	Orv Mohler, Garrett Arbelbide	.15	.11	.06
70	Sid Smith, Marv Montgomery	.15	.11	.06
71	John Vella, Willie Hall	.25	.20	.10
72	Don Williams, Jesse Hibbs	.15	.11	.06
73	Stan Williamson, Tony Slaton	.15	.11	.06

1989 Southern Cal Smokey

		NM/M	NM	E
	Complete Set (23):	10.00	7.50	4.00
	Common Player:	.60	.45	.25
1	Dan Barnes	.60	.45	.25
2	Dwight Garner	.60	.45	.25
3	Delmar Chesley	.60	.45	.25
4	Cleveland Colter	.60	.45	.25
5	Aaron Emanuel	1.25	.90	.50
6	Scott Galbraith	1.25	.90	.50
7	Leroy Holt	.75	.60	.30
8	Randy Hord	.60	.45	.25
9	John Jackson	1.50	1.25	.60
10	Brad Leggett	.60	.45	.25
11	**Marching Band**	.60	.45	.25
12	Dan Owens	1.50	1.25	.60
13	Brent Parkinson	.60	.45	.25
14	Tim Ryan	1.50	1.25	.60
15	Bill Schultz	.60	.45	.25
16	Larry Smith (CO)	.75	.60	.30
17	Ernest Spears	.60	.45	.25
18	J.P. Sullivan	.60	.45	.25
19	Cordell Sweeney	.60	.45	.25
20	**Traveler** (Horse Mascot)	.60	.45	.25
21	Marlon Washington	.60	.45	.25
22	Michael Williams	.60	.45	.25
23	**Yell Leaders and Song Girls**	.75	.60	.30

1991 Southern Cal College Classics

		NM/M	NM	E
	Complete Set (100):	30.00	22.00	12.00
	Common Player:	.25	.20	.10
1	Charles White	.75	.60	.30
2	Anthony Davis	.75	.60	.30
3	Clay Matthews	.75	.60	.30
4	Hoby Brenner	.35	.25	.14
5	Mike Garrett	.50	.40	.20
6	Bill Sharman (Basketball)	1.25	.90	.50
7	Bob Seagren (Track)	.35	.25	.14
8	Mike McKeever	.35	.25	.14
9	Celso Kalache (Volleyball)	.25	.20	.10
10	John Williams (CO) (Water Polo)	.25	.20	.10
11	John Naber (Swimming)	.50	.40	.20
12	Brad Budde	.35	.25	.14
13	Tim Ryan	.35	.25	.14
14	Mark Tucker	.25	.20	.10
15	Rodney Peete	1.00	.70	.40
16	Art Mazmanian (Baseball)	.25	.20	.10
17	Red Badgro (Baseball)	.35	.25	.14
18	Sue Habernigg (Women's Swimming)	.25	.20	.10
19	Craig Fertig	.25	.20	.10
20	John Block (Basketball)	.50	.40	.20
21	Jen-Kai Liu (Volleyball)	.25	.20	.10
22	Kim Ruddins (Women's Volleyball)	.25	.20	.10
23	Al Cowlings	1.00	.70	.40
24	Ronnie Lott	1.00	.70	.40
25	Adam Johnson (Volleyball)	1.50	1.25	.60
26	Fred Lynn (Baseball)	.50	.40	.20
27	Rick Leach (Tennis)	.35	.25	.14
28	Tim Rossovich	.50	.40	.20
29	Marvin Powell	.35	.25	.14
30	Ron Yary	.50	.40	.20
31	Ken Ruettgers	.50	.40	.20
32	Bob Yoder (CO) (Men's Volleyball)	.25	.20	.10
33	Megan McCallister (Women's Volleyball)	.25	.20	.10
34	Dave Cadigan	.35	.25	.14
35	Jeff Bregel	.25	.20	.10
36	Michael Wayman (Tennis)	.25	.20	.10
37	**Sippy Woodhead-Kantzer** (Women's Swimming)	.50	.40	.20
38	Tim Hovland (Volleyball)	1.00	.70	.40
39	Steve Busby (Baseball)	.50	.40	.20
40	Tom Seaver (Baseball)	2.00	1.50	.80
41	Anthony Colorito	.25	.20	.10
42	Wayne Carlander (Basketball)	.35	.25	.14
43	Erik Affholter	.35	.25	.14
44	Jim Obradovich	.35	.25	.14
45	Duane Bickett	.50	.40	.20
46	Leslie Daland (Women's Swimming)	.25	.20	.10
47	Ole Oleson (Track)	.25	.20	.10
48	Ed Putnam (Baseball)	.25	.20	.10
49	Stan Smith (Tennis)	.75	.60	.30
50	Jeff Hart (Golf)	.25	.20	.10
51	Jack Del Rio	.50	.40	.20
52	Bob Boyd (CO) (Basketball)	.35	.25	.14
53	Pat Haden	1.00	.70	.40
54	John Lambert (Basketball)	.35	.25	.14
55	Pete Beathard	.75	.60	.30
56	Anna-Maria Fernandez (Women's Tennis)	.50	.40	.20
57	Marta Figueras-Dotti (Women's Golf)	.35	.25	.14
58	Don Mosebar	.35	.25	.14
59	Don Doll	.35	.25	.14
60	Dave Stockton (Golf)	.75	.60	.30
61	Trisha Laux (Women's Tennis)	.25	.20	.10
62	Roy Foster	.35	.25	.14
63	Bruce Matthews	.35	.25	.14
64	Steve Sogge	.35	.25	.14
65	Tracy Nakamura (Women's Golf)	.35	.25	.14
66	Marv Montgomery	.25	.20	.10
67	Jack Tingley (Swimming)	.25	.20	.10
68	Larry Stevens	.25	.20	.10
69	Harry Smith	.25	.20	.10
70	Bill Bain	.25	.20	.10
71	Mark McGwire (Baseball)	3.00	2.25	1.25
72	Brad Brink (Baseball)	.25	.20	.10
73	Rod Dedeaux (CO) (Baseball)	.35	.25	.14
74	Rod Dedeaux (CO) (Baseball)	.50	.40	.20
75	Paul Westphal (Basketball)	1.25	.90	.50
76	Al Krueger	.25	.20	.10
77	James McConica (Swimming)	.25	.20	.10
78	Rod Martin	.35	.25	.14
79	Bill Yardley (Volleyball)	.25	.20	.10
80	Bill Stetson (Volleyball)	.25	.20	.10
81	Ray Looze (Swimming)	.25	.20	.10
82	Dan Jorgensen (Swimming)	.25	.20	.10
83	Anna-Lucia Fernandez (Women's Tennis)	.50	.40	.20
84	Terri O'Loughlin (Women's Swimming)	.25	.20	.10
85	John Grant	.25	.20	.10
86	Chris Lewis (Tennis)	.25	.20	.10
87	Steve Timmons (Volleyball)	2.00	1.50	.80
88	Dr. Dallas Long (Track)	.35	.25	.14
89	John McKay (CO)	.50	.40	.20
90	Joe Bottom (Swimming)	.25	.20	.10
91	John Jackson	.35	.25	.14
92	Paul McDonald	.35	.25	.14
93	Jimmy Gunn	.25	.20	.10
94	Rod Sherman	.35	.25	.14
95	Cecilia Fernandez (Women's Tennis)	.25	.20	.10
96	Doug Adler (Tennis)	.25	.20	.10
97	Ron Orr (Swimming)	.25	.20	.10
98	Debbie Landreth Brown (Women's Volleyball)	.25	.20	.10
99	Debbie Green (Women's Volleyball)	.25	.20	.10
100	Pat Harrison (Baseball)	.25	.20	.10

1991 Southern Cal Smokey

		NM/M	NM	E
	Complete Set (16):	8.00	6.00	3.25
	Common Player:	.60	.45	.25
1	Kurt Barber	1.25	.90	.50
2	Ron Dale	.60	.45	.25
3	Derrick Deese	1.00	.70	.40
4	Michael Gaytan	.60	.45	.25
5	Matt Gee	.60	.45	.25
6	Calvin Holmes	1.00	.70	.40
7	Scott Lockwood	1.00	.70	.40
8	Michael Moody	.60	.45	.25
9	Marvin Pollard	.60	.45	.25
10	Mark Raab	.60	.45	.25
11	Larry Smith (CO)	.75	.60	.30
12	Raoul Spears	.60	.45	.25
13	Matt Willig	.60	.45	.25
14	Alan Wilson	.60	.45	.25
15	James Wilson	.60	.45	.25
16	**Traveler** (The Trojan Horse)	.60	.45	.25

1990S Sports Impressions football statues/plates

	NM/M	NM	ENMEVG
Troy Aikman (mini bronze plate)			15.00
Randall Cunningham (home or away, mini)			40.00
Randall Cunningham (mini bronze plate)			15.00
John Elway (home or away, mini)			40.00
John Elway (mini bronze plate)			15.00
Boomer Esiason (unsigned)			65.00
Boomer Esiason (home or away, mini)			40.00
Boomer Esiason (mini bronze plate)			15.00
Jim Everett (mini)			40.00
Jim Everett (mini bronze plate)			15.00
Bob Griese (3,950, mini)			40.00
Jim Harbaugh (mini)			40.00
Jim Harbaugh (mini bronze plate)			15.00
Jim Kelly (mini)			40.00
Jim Kelly (mini bronze plate)			15.00
Bernie Kosar (mini)			40.00
Bernie Kosar (mini bronze plate)			15.00
Vince Lombardi (mini bronze plate)			20.00
Dan Marino (unsigned)			65.00
Dan Marino (home or away, mini)			40.00
Dan Marino (mini bronze plate)			15.00
Art Monk (mini)			40.00
Joe Montana (home or away, mini)			50.00

Joe Montana (1,500, signed)	250.00	
Joe Montana (mini bronze plate)	20.00	
Warren Moon (mini)	40.00	
Warren Moon (mini bronze plate)	15.00	
Christian Okoye (mini)	40.00	
Christian Okoye (mini bronze plate)	15.00	
Walter Payton (3,950, mini)	40.00	
Walter Payton (mini bronze plate)	15.00	
Jerry Rice (unsigned)	65.00	
Jerry Rice (mini)	40.00	
Jerry Rice (mini bronze plate)	15.00	
Mark Rypien (mini)	40.00	
Mark Rypien (mini bronze plate)	15.00	
Barry Sanders (mini)	40.00	
Barry Sanders (mini bronze plate)	15.00	
Deion Sanders (mini)	40.00	
Gale Sayers (3,950, mini)	40.00	
Emmitt Smith (mini)	40.00	
Ken Stabler (3,950, mini)	40.00	
Lawrence Taylor (unsigned)	65.00	
Lawrence Taylor (home or away, mini)	40.00	
Lawrence Taylor (mini bronze plate)	15.00	
Thurman Thomas (mini)	40.00	
Thurman Thomas (mini bronze plate)	15.00	
Johnny Unitas (mini)	40.00	
Johnny Unitas (mini bronze plate)	15.00	
Steve Young (mini)	40.00	

1976 Sportstix

The 10-sticker, 3-1/2" in diameter set was numbered as a continuation of non-sport issues. The helmet logos on the stickers have been erased and two major errors exist: Drew Pearson's card actually has Gloster Richardson on the card while Fred Biletnikoff's last name is spelled wrong on card No. 32.

		NM	E	VG
Complete Set (11):		200.00	100.00	60.00
Common Player:		10.00	5.00	3.00
31	Carl Eller	20.00	10.00	6.00
32	Fred Biletnikoff (UER) (Misspelled Belitnikoff)	30.00	15.00	9.00
33	Terry Metcalf	15.00	7.50	4.50
34	Gary Huff	10.00	5.00	3.00
35	Steve Bartkowski	20.00	10.00	6.00
36	Dan Pastorini	15.00	7.50	4.50
37	Drew Pearson (UER) (photo is of Gloster Richardson)	20.00	10.00	6.00
38	Bert Jones	15.00	7.50	4.50
39	Otis Armstrong	15.00	7.50	4.50
40	Don Woods	10.00	5.00	3.00
C	Dick Butkus	60.00	30.00	18.00

1963 Stancraft Playing Cards

This 54-card set, titled "Official NFL All-Time Greats," commemorates the opening of the Pro Football Hall of Fame in Canton, Ohio. Each of the cards, designed as playing cards, features an artistic drawing of the player, with his name, position, team name and years played below the picture, which is done in brown ink. The Aces and Jokers, however, have NFL logos on them instead of artwork. Two styles were used for the card backs - an NFL logo in the center surrounded by the 14 NFL team logos in a checkerboard pattern, all against a red background, or a green background with the 14 team helmets contained within it. Cards, 2-1/4" x 3-1/2" with rounded corners, came in a plastic box.

		NM	E	VG
Complete Set (54):		125.00	62.00	37.00
Common Player:		1.50	.70	.45
AC	NFL Logo	1.50	.70	.45
2C	Johnny "Blood" McNally	2.00	1.00	.60
3C	Bobby Mitchell	3.00	1.50	.90
4C	Bill Howton	1.50	.70	.45
5C	Wilbur "Fats" Henry	2.00	1.00	.60
6C	Tony Canedeo	2.00	1.00	.60
7C	Bulldog Turner	3.00	1.50	.90
8C	Charlie Trippi	2.00	1.00	.60
9C	Tommy Mason	1.50	.70	.45
10C	Earl "Dutch" Clark	2.00	1.00	.60
JC	Y.A. Tittle	5.00	2.50	1.50
QC	Lou Groza	5.00	2.50	1.50
KC	Bobby Layne	6.00	3.00	1.75
AD	NFL Logo	1.50	.70	.45
2D	Frankie Albert	1.50	.70	.45
3D	Del Shofner	1.50	.70	.45
4D	Ollie Matson	4.00	2.00	1.25
5D	Mike Ditka	8.00	4.00	2.50
6D	Otto Graham	6.00	3.00	1.75
7D	Chuck Bednarik	4.00	2.00	1.25
8D	Jim Taylor	3.00	1.50	.90
9D	Mel Hein	2.00	1.00	.60
10D	Eddie Price	1.50	.70	.45
JD	Sonny Randle	1.50	.70	.45
QD	Joe Perry	4.00	2.00	1.25

KD	Bob Waterfield	5.00	2.50	1.50
AH	NFL Logo	1.50	.70	.45
2H	Paul Hornung	5.00	2.50	1.50
3H	Johnny Unitas	10.00	5.00	3.00
4H	Doak Walker	5.00	2.50	1.50
5H	Tom Fears	3.00	1.50	.90
6H	Jim Thorpe	10.00	5.00	3.00
7H	Gino Marchetti	3.00	1.50	.90
8H	Claude Buddy Young	1.50	.70	.45
9H	Jim Benton	2.00	1.00	.60
10H	Jim Brown	12.00	6.00	3.50
JH	George Halas	1.50	.70	.45
QH	Sammy Baugh	4.00	2.00	1.25
KH	Bill Dudley	2.50	1.25	.70
1S	NFL Logo	1.50	.70	.45
2S	Eddie LeBaron	2.00	1.00	.60
3S	Don Hutson	3.50	1.75	1.00
4S	Clarke Hinkle	2.00	1.00	.60
5S	Charley Conerly	2.50	1.25	.70
6S	Earl (Curly) Lambeau	2.00	1.00	.60
7S	Sid Luckman	5.00	2.50	1.50
8S	Pete Pihos	2.00	1.00	.60
9S	Dante Lavelli	2.00	1.00	.60
10S	Norm Van Brocklin	4.00	2.00	1.25
JS	Cloyce Box	1.50	.70	.45
QS	Joe Schmidt	3.00	1.50	.90
KS	Elroy Hirsch	3.00	1.50	.90
xx	Joker (NFL Logo)	2.00	1.00	.60
xx	Joker (NFL Logo)	2.00	1.00	.60

1991 Stanford All-Century

JIM PLUNKETT QB

		NM/M	NM	E
Complete Set (100):		100.00	75.00	40.00
Common Player:		.75	.60	.30
1	Frankie Albert	1.25	.90	.50
2	Lester Archambeau	1.00	.70	.40
3	Bruno Banducci	.75	.60	.30
4	Benny Barnes	1.00	.70	.40
5	Guy Benjamin	2.00	1.50	.80
6	Mike Boryla	1.25	.90	.50
7	Marty Brill	.75	.60	.30
8	John Brodie	6.00	4.50	2.50
9	Jackie Brown	.75	.60	.30
10	George Buehler	1.00	.70	.40
11	Don Bunce	1.25	.90	.50
12	Chris Burford	1.25	.90	.50
13	Walter Camp (CO)	2.50	2.00	1.00
14	Gordy Ceresino	.75	.60	.30
15	Jack Chapple	.75	.60	.30
16	Toi Cook	2.00	1.50	.80
17	Bill Corbus	.75	.60	.30
18	Steve Dils	2.50	2.00	1.00
19	Pat Donovan	1.25	.90	.50
20	John Elway	20.00	15.00	8.00
21	Chuck Evans	.75	.60	.30
22	Skip Face	.75	.60	.30
23	Hugh Gallarneau	.75	.60	.30
24	Rod Garcia	.75	.60	.30
25	Bob Garrett	.75	.60	.30
26	Rick Gervais	.75	.60	.30
27	Jim Gillory	.75	.60	.30
28	Bobby Grayson	1.00	.70	.40
29	Bones Hamilton	1.00	.70	.40
30	Ray Handley	2.00	1.50	.80
31	Mark Harmon	.75	.60	.30
32	Marv Harris	.75	.60	.30
33	Emile Harry	1.25	.90	.50
34	Tony Hill	2.50	2.00	1.00
35	Brian Holloway	1.25	.90	.50
36	John Hopkins	.75	.60	.30
37	Dick Horn	.75	.60	.30
38	Jeff James	1.00	.70	.40
39	Gary Kerkorian	.75	.60	.30
40	Gordon King	1.00	.70	.40
41	Younger Klippert	.75	.60	.30
42	Pete Kmetovic	.75	.60	.30
43	Jim Lawson	.75	.60	.30
44	Pete Lazetich	.75	.60	.30
45	Dave Lewis	1.00	.70	.40
46	Vic Lindskog	.75	.60	.30

47	James Lofton	6.00	4.50	2.50
48	Ken Margerum	1.25	.90	.50
49	Ed McCaffrey	2.00	1.50	.80
50	Charles McCloud	.75	.60	.30
51	Bill McColl	1.00	.70	.40
52	Duncan McColl	.75	.60	.30
53	Milt McColl	.75	.60	.30
54	Jim Merlo	1.00	.70	.40
55	Phil Moffatt	.75	.60	.30
56	Bob Moore	1.00	.70	.40
57	Sam Morley	.75	.60	.30
58	Monk Moscrip	.75	.60	.30
59	Brad Muster	2.50	2.00	1.00
60	Ken Naber	.75	.60	.30
61	Darrin Nelson	2.00	1.50	.80
62	Ernie Nevers	3.00	2.25	1.25
63	Dick Norman	.75	.60	.30
64	Blaine Nye	1.25	.90	.50
65	Don Parish	.75	.60	.30
66	John Paye	2.00	1.50	.80
67	Gary Pettigrew	1.00	.70	.40
68	Jim Plunkett	6.00	4.50	2.50
69	Randy Poltl	.75	.60	.30
70	Seraphim Post	.75	.60	.30
71	John Ralston (CO)	1.25	.90	.50
72	Bob Reynolds	.75	.60	.30
73	Don Robesky	.75	.60	.30
74	Doug Robison	.75	.60	.30
75	Greg Sampson	.75	.60	.30
76	John Sande	.75	.60	.30
77	Turk Schonert	2.00	1.50	.80
78	Jack Schultz	.75	.60	.30
79	Clark Shaughnessy (CO)	1.25	.90	.50
80	Ted Shipkey	.75	.60	.30
81	Jeff Siemon	2.00	1.50	.80
82	Andy Sinclair	.75	.60	.30
83	Malcolm Snider	1.00	.70	.40
84	Norm Standlee	1.00	.70	.40
85	Roger Stillwell	.75	.60	.30
86	Chuck Taylor (CO)	.75	.60	.30
87	Dink Templeton	.75	.60	.30
88	Tiny Thornhill (CO)	.75	.60	.30
89	Dave Tipton	.75	.60	.30
90	Keith Topping	.75	.60	.30
91	Randy Vataha	.75	.60	.30
92	Garin Veris	1.25	.90	.50
93	Jon Volpe	2.50	2.00	1.00
94	Bill Walsh (CO)	5.00	3.75	2.00
95	Pop Warner (CO)	2.00	1.50	.80
96	Gene Washington	2.00	1.50	.80
97	Vincent White	.75	.60	.30
98	Paul Wiggin	1.25	.90	.50
99	John Wilbur	1.00	.70	.40
100	Dave Wyman	1.25	.90	.50

1989 Star-Cal Decals

The 54-card, 3" x 4-1/2" sticker set featured players from six NFL teams, and was licensed by the NFL and the NFL Players' Association. The cards have rounded edges with a silver logo (First Edition 1989) in the upper left corner. Each decal also came with a pennant-shaped mini team banner decal in the player's team colors.

		NM/M	NM	E
Complete Set (54):		80.00	60.00	32.00
Common Player:		1.00	.70	.40
1	Raul Allegre	1.00	.70	.40
2	Carl Banks	1.00	.70	.40
3	Cornelius Bennett	1.50	1.25	.60
4	Brian Blades	1.50	1.25	.60
5	Kevin Butler	1.00	.70	.40
6	Harry Carson	1.00	.70	.40
7	Anthony Carter	1.00	.70	.40
8	Michael Carter	1.00	.70	.40
9	Shane Conlan	1.00	.70	.40
10	Roger Craig	1.50	1.25	.60
11	Richard Dent	1.25	.90	.50
12	Chris Doleman	1.00	.70	.40
13	Tony Dorsett	4.00	3.00	1.50
14	Dave Duerson	1.00	.70	.40
15	Charles Haley	1.50	1.25	.60
16	Dan Hampton	1.00	.70	.40
17	Al Harris	1.00	.70	.40
18	Mark Jackson	1.00	.70	.40
19	Vance Johnson	1.00	.70	.40
20	Steve Jordan	1.00	.70	.40
21	Clarence Kay	1.00	.70	.40
22	Jim Kelly	4.00	3.00	1.50
23	Tommy Kramer	1.00	.70	.40
24	Ronnie Lott	2.00	1.50	.80
25	Lionel Manuel	1.00	.70	.40
26	Guy McIntyre	1.00	.70	.40
27	Steve McMichael	1.25	.90	.50
28	Karl Mecklenburg	1.25	.90	.50
29	Orson Mobley	1.00	.70	.40
30	Joe Montana	20.00	15.00	8.00
31	Joe Morris	1.00	.70	.40

32	Joe Nash	1.00	.70	.40
33	Ricky Nattiel	1.00	.70	.40
34	Chuck Nelson	1.00	.70	.40
35	Darrin Nelson	1.00	.70	.40
36	Karl Nelson	1.00	.70	.40
37	Scott Norwood	1.00	.70	.40
38	Bart Oates	1.00	.70	.40
39	Rufus Porter	1.00	.70	.40
40	Andre Reed	2.00	1.50	.80
41	Phil Simms	2.00	1.50	.80
42	Mike Singletary	1.50	1.25	.60
43	Fred Smerlas	1.00	.70	.40
44	Bruce Smith	2.00	1.50	.80
45	Kelly Stouffer	1.00	.70	.40
46	Scott Studwell	1.00	.70	.40
47	Matt Suhey	1.00	.70	.40
48	Steve Tasker	1.00	.70	.40
49	Keena Turner	1.00	.70	.40
50	John L. Williams	1.25	.90	.50
51	Wade Wilson	1.00	.70	.40
52	Sammy Winder	1.00	.70	.40
53	Tony Woods	1.00	.70	.40
54	Eric Wright	1.00	.70	.40

1990 Star-Cal Decals

The 94-card, 3" x 4-1/2" decal set was similar to the 1989 release, complete with facsimile autographs. Six players each from 12 of the league's top teams are featured. Each player decal was issued with a pennant-shaped mini team banner (3-1/2" x 2"). The set is also known as the Grid-Star decal set.

		NM/M	NM	E
Complete Set (94):		160.00	120.00	65.00
Common Player:		1.00	.50	.30
1	Eric Allen	1.00	.50	.30
2	Marcus Allen	2.00	1.50	.80
3	Flipper Anderson	1.00	.70	.40
4A	Neal Anderson (printed name in black letters)	1.00	.70	.40
4B	Neal Anderson (printed name in white letters)	1.00	.70	.40
5A	Carl Banks (printed name in black letters)	1.00	.50	.30
5B	Carl Banks (printed name in white letters)	1.00	.50	.30
6	Mark Bavaro	1.00	.50	.30
7	Cornelius Bennett	1.50	1.25	.60
8	Brian Blades	1.00	.70	.40
9	Joey Browner	1.00	.50	.30
10	Keith Byars	1.00	.50	.30
11A	Anthony Carter (printed name in black letters)	1.00	.70	.40
11B	Anthony Carter (printed name in white letters)	1.00	.70	.40
12	Cris Carter	2.00	1.50	.80
13	Michael Carter	1.00	.50	.30
14	Gary Clark	1.00	.70	.40
15	Mark Collins	1.00	.50	.30
16	Shane Conlan	1.00	.50	.30
17	Jim Covert	1.00	.50	.30
18A	Roger Craig (printed name black letters)	1.50	1.25	.60
18B	Roger Craig (printed name white letters)	1.50	1.25	.60
19	Richard Dent	1.25	.90	.50
20	Chris Doleman	1.00	.70	.40
21	Dave Duerson	1.00	.50	.30
22	Henry Ellard	1.50	1.25	.60
23A	John Elway (printed name in black letters)	6.00	4.50	2.50
23B	John Elway (printed name in white letters)	8.00	6.00	3.25
24	Jim Everett	1.25	.90	.50
25	Mervyn Fernandez	1.00	.50	.30
26	Willie Gault	1.25	.90	.50
27	Bob Golic	1.00	.50	.30
28	Darrell Green	1.25	.90	.50
29	Kevin Greene	1.25	.90	.50
30	Charles Haley	1.25	.90	.50
31	Jay Hilgenberg	1.00	.50	.30
32	Pete Holohan	1.00	.50	.30
33	Kent Hull	1.00	.50	.30
34	Bobby Humphrey	1.00	.70	.40
35A	Bo Jackson (printed name in black letters)	2.00	1.50	.80
35B	Bo Jackson (printed name in white letters)	2.00	1.50	.80
36	Keith Jackson	1.25	.90	.50
37	Mark Jackson	1.25	.90	.50
38	Joe Jacoby	1.00	.50	.30
39	Vance Johnson	1.00	.50	.30
40	Jim Kelly	3.00	2.25	1.25
41	Bernie Kosar	1.25	.90	.50
42	Greg Kragen	1.00	.50	.30
43	Jeff Lageman	1.00	.50	.30
44	Pat Leahy	1.00	.50	.30

45	Howie Long	1.25	.90	.50
46A	Ronnie Lott (serial numbered 11419)	1.50	1.25	.60
46B	Ronnie Lott (serial numbered 11414)	1.50	1.25	.60
47	Kevin Mack	1.00	.50	.30
48	Charles Mann	1.00	.50	.30
49	Leonard Marshall	1.00	.50	.30
50	Clay Matthews	1.25	.90	.50
51	Eric McMillan	1.00	.50	.30
52	Karl Mecklenburg	1.25	.90	.50
53	Dave Meggett (UER) (name misspelled Megget)	1.25	.90	.50
54A	Eric Metcalf (serial numbered 11414)	2.00	1.50	.80
54B	Eric Metcalf (serial numbered 11424)	1.50	1.25	.60
55	Keith Millard	1.00	.50	.30
56	Frank Minnifield	1.00	.50	.30
57A	Joe Montana (printed name in black letters autograph covers only left leg)	12.00	9.00	4.75
57B	Joe Montana (printed name in black letters autograph covers both legs)	15.00	11.00	6.00
57C	Joe Montana (printed name in white letters autograph covers only left leg)	20.00	15.00	8.00
58	Joe Nash	1.00	.50	.30
59	Ken O'Brien	1.25	.90	.50
60	Rufus Porter	1.00	.50	.30
61	Andre Reed	1.50	1.25	.60
62	Mark Rypien	1.25	.90	.50
63	Gerald Riggs	1.00	.50	.30
64	Mickey Shuler	1.00	.50	.30
65	Clyde Simmons	1.25	.90	.50
66A	Phil Simms (printed name in black letters)	1.50	1.25	.60
66B	Phil Simms (printed name in white letters)	1.50	1.25	.60
67A	Mike Singletary (printed name in black letters)	1.50	1.25	.60
67B	Mike Singletary (printed name in white letters)	1.50	1.25	.60
68	Jackie Slater	1.00	.50	.30
69	Bruce Smith	1.50	1.25	.60
70A	Kelly Stouffer (serial numbered 11414)	1.00	.50	.30
70B	Kelly Stouffer (serial numbered 11427)	1.00	.50	.30
71	John Taylor	1.25	.90	.50
72	Lawyer Tillman	1.00	.50	.30
73	Al Toon	1.25	.90	.50
74A	Herschel Walker (printed name in black letters)	1.50	1.25	.60
74B	Herschel Walker (printed name in white letters)	1.50	1.25	.60
75	Reggie White	2.00	1.50	.80
76A	John L. Williams (printed name in black letters autograph below knees)	1.00	.50	.30
76B	John L. Williams (printed name in black letters autograph above knees)	1.00	.50	.30
76C	John L. Williams (printed name in white letters autograph below knees)	1.00	.50	.30
77	Tony Woods	1.00	.50	.30
78	Gary Zimmerman	1.00	.50	.30

1990 Star-Cal Decals Prototypes

The four-card, 3" x 4-1/2" set was issued as a preview to the 1990 94-card decal set.

		NM/M	NM	E
Complete Set (4):		5.00	3.75	2.00
Common Player:		1.00	.70	.40
1	Jeff Hostetler	1.00	.70	.40
2	Mike Kenn	1.00	.70	.40
3	Freeman McNeil	1.00	.70	.40
4	Steve Young	3.00	2.25	1.25

1988 Starline Prototypes

The four-card, regular-size set was never issued to the public and just 75 sets were produced. Each card in the set features a color photo with a blue border.

		NM/M	NM	E
Complete Set (4):		500.00	375.00	200.00
Common Player:		75.00	56.00	30.00

1	John Elway	150.00	110.00	60.00
2	Bernie Kosar	75.00	56.00	30.00
3	Joe Montana	276.00	205.00	110.00
4	Phil Simms	75.00	56.00	30.00

1991 Star Pics

The company's first set of college prospects was released in June 1991. The set features 44 out of 55 first- and second-round picks from the 1991 draft. All 91 players in the set -- the roster of which was set before the draft -- were selected. Subsets include the nine-card flashback issue (NFL players in college uniforms) and Top Pick Agents, featuring player representatives. At least one in 50 sets contained a ran-domly- inserted autograph. (Key: FL - flashback, A - agent). Two promo panels, each featuring two standard-size cards, were also produced to preview the regular 1991 set's design. The players paired together were 1) Mark Carrier, $1, and 2) Aaron Craver, $1, and 3) Dan McGwire, $1, and 4) Eric Turner, $1.

		NM/M	NM	E
Complete Set (112):		6.00	4.50	2.50
Common Player:		.05	.04	.02
Common Autograph:		6.00	4.50	2.50
Autograph Cards: 20-40X				
NFL Autographs: 200-400X				
1	1991 NFL Draft Overview	.05	.04	.02
2	Barry Sanders (FL)	.10	.08	.04
3	Nick Bell	.10	.08	.04
4	Kevin Pritchett	.05	.04	.02
5	Huey Richardson	.05	.04	.02
6	Mike Croel	.10	.08	.04
7	Paul Justin	.05	.04	.02
8	Ivory Lee Brown	.05	.04	.02
9	Herman Moore	1.25	.90	.50
10	Derrick Thomas (FL)	.15	.11	.06
11	Keith Taylor	.05	.04	.02
12	Joe Johnson	.05	.04	.02
13	Dan McGwire	.10	.08	.04
14	Harvey Williams	.50	.40	.20
15	Eric Moten	.05	.04	.02
16	Steve Zucker	.05	.04	.02
17	Randal Hill	.20	.15	.08
18	Browning Nagle	.05	.04	.02
19	Stan Thomas	.05	.04	.02
20	Emmitt Smith (FL)	.50	.40	.20
21	Ted Washington	.05	.04	.02
22	Lamar Rogers	.05	.04	.02
23	Kenny Walker	.05	.04	.02
24	Howard Griffith	.05	.04	.02
25	Reggie Johnson	.05	.04	.02
26	Lawrence Dawsey	.05	.04	.02
27	Joe Garten	.05	.04	.02
28	Moe Gardner	.05	.04	.02
29	Michael Stonebreaker	.05	.04	.02
30	Jeff George (FL)	.15	.11	.06
31	Leigh Steinberg (A)	.05	.04	.02
32	John Flannery	.05	.04	.02
33	Pat Harlow	.05	.04	.02
34	Kanavis McGhee	.05	.04	.02
35	Michael Dumas	.05	.04	.02
36	Godfrey Myles	.05	.04	.02
37	Shawn Moore	.05	.04	.02
38	Jeff Graham	.50	.40	.20
39	Ricky Watters	1.00	.70	.40
40	Andre Ware (FL)	.05	.04	.02
41	Henry Jones	.10	.08	.04
42	Eric Turner	.30	.25	.12
43	Bob Wolf (A)	.05	.04	.02
44	Randy Baldwin	.05	.04	.02
45	Morris Lewis	.05	.04	.02
46	Jerry Evans	.05	.04	.02
47	Derek Russell	.05	.04	.02
48	Merton Hanks	.40	.30	.15
49	Kevin Donnalley	.05	.04	.02
50	Troy Aikman (FL)	.30	.25	.12
51	William Thomas	.05	.04	.02
52	Chris Thome	.05	.04	.02
53	Ricky Ervins	.10	.08	.04
54	Jake Reed	.25	.20	.10

55	Jerome Henderson	.05	.04	.02
56	Mark Vander Poel	.05	.04	.02
57	Bernard Ellison	.05	.04	.02
58	Jack Mills (A)	.05	.04	.02
59	Jarrod Bunch	.05	.04	.02
60	Mark Carrier (FL)	.05	.04	.02
61	Rocen Keeton	.05	.04	.02
62	Louis Riddick	.05	.04	.02
63	Bobby Wilson	.05	.04	.02
64	Steve Jackson	.05	.04	.02
65	Brett Favre	2.50	2.00	1.00
66	Ernie Mills	.20	.15	.08
67	Joe Valerio	.05	.04	.02
68	Chris Smith	.05	.04	.02
69	Ralph Cindrich	.05	.04	.02
70	Christian Okoye (FL)	.05	.04	.02
71	Charles McRae	.05	.04	.02
72	Jon Vaughn	.05	.04	.02
73	Eric Swann	.30	.25	.12
74	Bill Musgrave	.05	.04	.02
75	Eric Bieniemy	.20	.15	.08
76	Pat Tyrance	.05	.04	.02
77	Vince Clark	.05	.04	.02
78	Eugene Williams	.05	.04	.02
79	Rob Carpenter	.05	.04	.02
80	Deion Sanders (FL)	.25	.20	.10
81	Roman Phifer	.10	.08	.04
82	Greg Lewis	.05	.04	.02
83	John Johnson	.05	.04	.02
84	Richard Howell (A)	.05	.04	.02
85	Jesse Campbell	.05	.04	.02
86	Stanley Richard	.05	.04	.02
87	Alfred Williams	.05	.04	.02
88	Mike Pritchard	.25	.20	.10
89	Mel Agee	.05	.04	.02
90	Aaron Craver	.05	.04	.02
91	Tim Barnett	.05	.04	.02
92	Wesley Carroll	.05	.04	.02
93	Kevin Scott	.05	.04	.02
94	Darren Lewis	.05	.04	.02
95	Tim Bruton	.05	.04	.02
96	Tim James	.05	.04	.02
97	Darryl Lewis	.05	.04	.02
98	Shawn Jefferson	.20	.15	.08
99	Mitch Donahue	.05	.04	.02
100	Marvin Demoff (A)	.05	.04	.02
101	Adrian Cooper	.05	.04	.02
102	Bruce Pickens	.05	.04	.02
103	Scott Zolak	.05	.04	.02
104	Phil Hansen	.05	.04	.02
105	Ed King	.05	.04	.02
106	Mike Jones	.05	.04	.02
107	Alvin Harper	.50	.40	.20
108	Robert Young	.05	.04	.02
109	**Offensive Top Prospects**	.05	.04	.02
110	**Defensive Top Prospects**	.05	.04	.02

1991 Star Pics Promos

Star Pics issued these cards to promote their 1991 set. They were distributed in two-card panels and inserted in an issue of Pro Football Weekly. The card fronts feature a color photo with a football border. The backs are green and include basic player information and a close-up photo.

		NM/M	NM	E
	Complete Set (4):	4.00	3.00	1.50
	Common Player:	1.00	.70	.40
1	Mark Carrier DB	1.00	.70	.40
2	Aaron Craver	1.00	.70	.40
3	Dan McGwire	1.00	.70	.40
4	Eric Turner	1.00	.70	.40

1988 Starting Lineup Football

The 1988 set was Kenner's first issue in football, with 137 players released. The figures were sold in single blister packs which included a card of the player. Prices are for mint condition packages.

	NM/M	NM	E
Complete Set (137):	8,200	6,150	3,280
Common Piece:	35.00		
Collector Stand:	30.00		
Marcus Allen	75.00	56.00	30.00
Neal Anderson	35.00	26.00	14.00
Chip Banks	100.00	75.00	40.00
Mark Bavaro	50.00	37.00	20.00
Cornelius Bennett	175.00	130.00	70.00
Albert Bentley	80.00	60.00	32.00
Duane Bickett	100.00	75.00	40.00
Todd Blackledge	60.00	45.00	24.00
Brian Bosworth	42.00	31.00	17.00
Brian Brennan	60.00	45.00	24.00
Bill Brooks	100.00	75.00	40.00
James Brooks	60.00	45.00	24.00

Eddie Brown	60.00	45.00	24.00
Joey Browner	80.00	60.00	32.00
Aundray Bruce	60.00	45.00	24.00
Chris Burkett	125.00	94.00	50.00
Keith Byars	50.00	37.00	20.00
Scott Campbell	140.00	105.00	56.00
Carlos Carson	75.00	56.00	30.00
Harry Carson	50.00	37.00	20.00
Anthony Carter	75.00	56.00	30.00
Gerald Carter	40.00	30.00	16.00
Michael Carter	65.00	49.00	26.00
Tony Casillas	75.00	56.00	30.00
Jeff Chadwick	75.00	56.00	30.00
Deron Cherry	75.00	56.00	30.00
Ray Childress	100.00	75.00	40.00
Todd Christensen	100.00	75.00	40.00
Gary Clark	80.00	60.00	32.00
Mark Clayton	100.00	75.00	40.00
Cris Collinsworth	100.00	75.00	40.00
Doug Cosbie	130.00	97.00	52.00
Roger Craig	40.00	30.00	16.00
Randall Cunningham	100.00	75.00	40.00
Jeff Davis	40.00	30.00	16.00
Ken Davis	120.00	90.00	48.00
Richard Dent	50.00	37.00	20.00
Eric Dickerson	60.00	45.00	24.00
Floyd Dixon	55.00	41.00	22.00
Tony Dorsett	275.00	205.00	110.00
Mark Duper	90.00	67.00	36.00
Tony Eason	150.00	110.00	60.00
Carl Ekern	80.00	60.00	32.00
Henry Ellard	60.00	45.00	24.00
John Elway	250.00	185.00	100.00
Phillip Epps	100.00	75.00	40.00
Boomer Esiason	80.00	60.00	32.00
Jim Everett	50.00	37.00	20.00
Brent Fullwood	85.00	64.00	34.00
Mark Gastineau	40.00	30.00	16.00
Willie Gault	110.00	82.00	44.00
Bob Golic	100.00	75.00	40.00
Jerry Gray	75.00	56.00	30.00
Darrell Green	325.00	245.00	130.00
Jacob Green	125.00	94.00	50.00
Roy Green	80.00	60.00	32.00
Steve Grogan	100.00	75.00	40.00
Ronnie Harmon	150.00	110.00	60.00
Bobby Hebert	150.00	110.00	60.00
Alonzo Highsmith	40.00	30.00	16.00
Drew Hill	40.00	30.00	16.00
Earnest Jackson	75.00	56.00	30.00
Rickey Jackson	120.00	90.00	48.00
Vance Johnson	50.00	37.00	20.00
Ed Jones	110.00	82.00	44.00
James Jones	50.00	37.00	20.00
Rod Jones	40.00	30.00	16.00
Rulon Jones	45.00	34.00	18.00
Steve Jordan	100.00	75.00	40.00
E.J. Junior	100.00	75.00	40.00
Jim Kelly	200.00	150.00	80.00
Bill Kenney	80.00	60.00	32.00
Bernie Kosar	40.00	30.00	16.00
Tommy Kramer	110.00	82.00	44.00
Dave Krieg	200.00	150.00	80.00
Tim Krumrie	110.00	82.00	44.00
Mark Lee	110.00	82.00	44.00
Ronnie Lippett	50.00	37.00	20.00
Louis Lipps	125.00	94.00	50.00
Neil Lomax	125.00	94.00	50.00
Chuck Long	60.00	45.00	24.00
Howie Long	125.00	94.00	50.00
Ronnie Lott	140.00	105.00	56.00
Kevin Mack	40.00	30.00	16.00
Mark Malone	175.00	130.00	70.00
Dexter Manley	40.00	30.00	16.00
Dan Marino	250.00	185.00	100.00
Eric Martin	50.00	37.00	20.00
Rueben Mayes	50.00	37.00	20.00
Jim McMahon	50.00	37.00	20.00
Freeman McNeil	40.00	30.00	16.00
Karl Mecklenburg	50.00	37.00	20.00
Mike Merriweather	90.00	67.00	36.00
Stump Mitchell	60.00	45.00	24.00
Art Monk	275.00	205.00	110.00
Joe Montana	225.00	170.00	90.00
Warren Moon	80.00	60.00	32.00
Stanley Morgan	50.00	37.00	20.00
Joe Morris	40.00	30.00	16.00
Darrin Nelson	100.00	75.00	40.00
Ozzie Newsome	100.00	75.00	40.00
Ken O'Brien	40.00	30.00	16.00
John Offerdahl	125.00	94.00	50.00
Christian Okoye	50.00	37.00	20.00
Mike Quick	40.00	30.00	16.00
Jerry Rice	300.00	225.00	120.00

Gerald Riggs	40.00	30.00	16.00
Reggie Rogers	50.00	37.00	20.00
Mike Rozier	40.00	30.00	16.00
Jay Schroeder	85.00	64.00	34.00
Mickey Shuler	40.00	30.00	16.00
Phil Simms	50.00	37.00	20.00
Mike Singletary	50.00	37.00	20.00
Bill Ray Smith	175.00	130.00	70.00
Bruce Smith	175.00	130.00	70.00
J.T. Smith	60.00	45.00	24.00
Troy Stradford	110.00	82.00	44.00
Lawrence Taylor	65.00	49.00	26.00
Vinnie Testaverde	75.00	56.00	30.00
Andre Tippett	40.00	30.00	16.00
Anthony Toney	40.00	30.00	16.00
Al Toon	40.00	30.00	16.00
Jack Trudeau	125.00	94.00	50.00
Herschel Walker	50.00	37.00	20.00
Curt Warner	45.00	34.00	18.00
Dave Waymer	100.00	75.00	40.00
Charles White	45.00	34.00	18.00
Danny White	125.00	94.00	50.00
Randy White	220.00	165.00	88.00
Reggie White	100.00	75.00	40.00
James Wilder	50.00	37.00	20.00
Doug Williams	50.00	37.00	20.00
Marc Wilson	275.00	205.00	110.00
Sammy Winder	45.00	34.00	18.00
Kellen Winslow	400.00	300.00	160.00
Rod Woodson	400.00	300.00	160.00
Randy Wright	160.00	120.00	64.00

1989 Starting Lineup Football

The 1989 set includes 123 players and is identifiable by the black-bordered cards. Included in the set is former New York Jets quarterback Ken O'Brien with his name misspelled.

	NM/M	NM	E
Complete Set (122):	7,000	5,200	2,800
Common Piece:	30.00		
Set price does not include O'Brien Err.			
Comp. Helmet Set (4):	275.00	210.00	110.00
Marcus Allen	50.00	37.00	20.00
Neal Anderson	30.00	22.00	12.00
Carl Banks **RC**	125.00	94.00	50.00
Bill Bates **RC**	350.00	260.00	140.00
Mark Bavaro	40.00	30.00	16.00
Cornelius Bennett	75.00	56.00	30.00
Duane Bickett	150.00	110.00	60.00
Bennie Blades **RC**	125.00	94.00	50.00
Bubby Brister **RC**	50.00	37.00	20.00
Bill Brooks **RC**	80.00	60.00	32.00
James Brooks	40.00	30.00	16.00
Eddie Brown	50.00	37.00	20.00
Jerome Brown **RC**	280.00	210.00	110.00
Tim Brown **RC**	95.00	71.00	38.00
Joey Browner	100.00	75.00	40.00
Kelvin Bryant **RC**	50.00	37.00	20.00
Jim Burt **RC**	150.00	110.00	60.00
Keith Byars	180.00	135.00	72.00
Dave Cadigan **RC**	300.00	225.00	120.00
Anthony Carter	40.00	30.00	16.00
Michael Carter	50.00	37.00	20.00
Chris Chandler **RC**	75.00	56.00	30.00
Gary Clark	40.00	30.00	16.00
Shane Conlan **RC**	100.00	75.00	40.00
Jimbo Covert **RC**	300.00	225.00	120.00
Roger Craig	30.00	22.00	12.00
Randall Cunningham	50.00	37.00	20.00
Richard Dent	35.00	26.00	14.00
Hanford Dixon **RC**	100.00	75.00	40.00
Chris Doleman **RC**	125.00	94.00	50.00
Tony Dorsett	125.00	94.00	50.00
Dave Duerson **RC**	65.00	49.00	26.00
John Elway	200.00	150.00	80.00
Boomer Esiason	50.00	37.00	20.00
Jim Everett	30.00	22.00	12.00
Thomas Everett **RC**	175.00	130.00	70.00
Sean Farrell **RC**	225.00	170.00	90.00
Bill Fralic **RC**	250.00	185.00	100.00
Irving Fryar **RC**	185.00	140.00	74.00
David Fulcher **RC**	110.00	82.00	44.00
Ernest Givins **RC**	60.00	45.00	24.00
Alex Gordon **RC**	125.00	94.00	50.00
Charles Haley **RC**	200.00	150.00	80.00
Bobby Hebert	50.00	37.00	20.00
Johnny Hector **RC**	100.00	75.00	40.00
Drew Hill	30.00	22.00	12.00
Dalton Hilliard **RC**	40.00	30.00	16.00
Bryan Hinkle **RC**	325.00	245.00	130.00
Michael Irvin **RC**	125.00	94.00	50.00
Keith Jackson **RC**	50.00	37.00	20.00
Garry James **RC**	50.00	37.00	20.00

	NM/M	NM	E
Sean Jones RC	100.00	75.00	40.00
Jim Kelly	225.00	170.00	90.00
Joe Kelly RC	70.00	52.00	28.00
Bernie Kosar	30.00	22.00	12.00
Tim Krumrie	100.00	75.00	40.00
Louis Lipps	150.00	110.00	60.00
Eugene Lockhart RC	150.00	110.00	60.00
James Lofton RC	90.00	67.00	36.00
Neil Lomax	40.00	30.00	16.00
Chuck Long	30.00	22.00	12.00
Howie Long	110.00	82.00	44.00
Ronnie Lott	100.00	75.00	40.00
Kevin Mack	30.00	22.00	12.00
Pete Mandley RC	30.00	22.00	12.00
Dexter Manley	30.00	22.00	12.00
Charles Mann RC	50.00	37.00	20.00
Lionel Manuel RC	30.00	22.00	12.00
Dan Marino	275.00	205.00	110.00
Leonard Marshall RC	110.00	82.00	44.00
Eric Martin	50.00	37.00	20.00
Rueben Mayes	50.00	37.00	20.00
Vann McElroy RC	60.00	45.00	24.00
Dennis McKinnon RC	100.00	75.00	40.00
Jim McMahon	35.00	26.00	14.00
Steve McMichael RC	250.00	185.00	100.00
Erik McMillan RC	65.00	49.00	26.00
Freeman McNeil	30.00	22.00	12.00
Keith Millard RC	100.00	75.00	40.00
Chris Miller RC	60.00	45.00	24.00
Frank Minnifield RC	100.00	75.00	40.00
Art Monk	80.00	60.00	32.00
Joe Montana	125.00	94.00	50.00
Warren Moon	75.00	56.00	30.00
Joe Morris	30.00	22.00	12.00
Anthony Munoz RC	275.00	205.00	110.00
Ricky Nattiel RC	40.00	30.00	16.00
Darrin Nelson	70.00	52.00	28.00
Danny Noonan RC	130.00	97.00	52.00
Ken O'Brien	30.00	22.00	12.00
Ken O'Brien error (Misspelled)	100.00	75.00	40.00
Steve Pelluer RC	100.00	75.00	40.00
Mike Quick	30.00	22.00	12.00
Andre Reed RC	125.00	94.00	50.00
Jerry Rice	60.00	45.00	24.00
Mike Rozier	40.00	30.00	16.00
Jay Schroeder	40.00	30.00	16.00
John Settle RC	60.00	45.00	24.00
Mickey Shuler	90.00	67.00	36.00
Phil Simms	30.00	22.00	12.00
Mike Singletary	35.00	26.00	14.00
Webster Slaughter RC	45.00	34.00	18.00
Bruce Smith	150.00	112.00	60.00
Chris Spielman RC	250.00	185.00	100.00
John Stephens RC	35.00	26.00	14.00
Kelly Stouffer RC	40.00	30.00	16.00
Pat Swilling RC	60.00	45.00	24.00
Lawrence Taylor	60.00	45.00	24.00
Vinny Testaverde	55.00	41.00	22.00
Thurman Thomas RC	150.00	110.00	60.00
Andre Tippett	40.00	30.00	16.00
Anthony Toney	30.00	22.00	12.00
Al Toon	30.00	22.00	12.00
Garin Veris RC	275.00	205.00	110.00
Herschel Walker	30.00	22.00	12.00
Curt Warner	40.00	30.00	16.00
Reggie White	60.00	45.00	24.00
Doug Williams	50.00	37.00	20.00
John Williams RC	80.00	60.00	32.00
Wade Wilson RC	100.00	75.00	40.00
Ickey Woods RC	30.00	22.00	12.00
Rod Woodson	300.00	225.00	120.00
Steve Young RC	375.00	281.00	150.00

1989 Starting Lineup Football Helmets

Kenner issued four different packages of NFL helmets: AFC Offensive, AFC Defensive, NFC Offensive and NFC Defensive. Every NFL team was included in the product, which was designed to provide SLU collectors with extra helmets. The offensive and defensive face masks differ.

	NM/M	NM	E
Complete Set (4):	275.00	210.00	110.00

1990 Starting Lineup Football

The third release of Starting Lineup football includes 66 players and is highlighted by rookie pieces of Troy Aikman, Barry Sanders and Deion Sanders. The figures of Neal Anderson, Roger Craig, John Elway, Boomer Esiason, Bernie Kosar, Joe Montana, Mike Singletary and Reggie White each have different jersey versions (home and away).

	NM/M	NM	E
Complete Set (66):	2,000	1,500	800.00
Common Piece:	15.00		
Set price does not include home uniforms			
Troy Aikman RC	50.00	37.00	20.00
Neal Anderson blue (Blue Uni.)	20.00	15.00	8.00
Neal Anderson white (White Uni.)	20.00	15.00	8.00
Mark Bavaro	70.00	52.00	28.00
Steve Beuerlein RC	50.00	37.00	20.00
Bubby Brister	75.00	56.00	30.00
James Brooks	30.00	22.00	12.00
Tim Brown	80.00	60.00	32.00
Cris Carter RC	250.00	185.00	100.00
Roger Craig red (Red Uni.)	25.00	18.50	10.00
Roger Craig white (White Uni.)	40.00	30.00	16.00
Randall Cunningham (Green Uni.)	30.00	22.00	12.00
Randall Cunningham (White Uni.)	60.00	45.00	24.00
Hart Lee Dykes RC	80.00	60.00	32.00
John Elway orange (Orange Uni.)	85.00	64.00	34.00
John Elway white (White Uni.)	85.00	64.00	34.00
Boomer Esiason black (Black Uni.)	20.00	15.00	8.00
Boomer Esiason white (White Uni.)	20.00	15.00	8.00
Jim Everett	15.00	11.00	6.00
Simon Fletcher RC	150.00	110.00	60.00
Doug Flutie RC	185.00	140.00	74.00
Dennis Gentry RC	50.00	37.00	20.00
Dan Hampton RC	100.00	75.00	40.00
Jim Harbaugh RC	75.00	56.00	30.00
Rodney Holman RC	60.00	45.00	24.00
Bobby Humphrey RC	25.00	18.50	10.00
Michael Irvin	80.00	60.00	32.00
Bo Jackson RC	16.00	12.00	6.50
Keith Jackson	30.00	22.00	12.00
Vance Johnson	125.00	94.00	50.00
Jim Kelly	35.00	26.00	14.00
Bernie Kosar brown (Brown Uni.)	70.00	52.00	28.00
Bernie Kosar white (White Uni.)	20.00	15.00	8.00
Louis Lipps	85.00	64.00	34.00
Don Majkowski RC	20.00	15.00	8.00
Charles Mann	50.00	37.00	20.00
Lionel Manuel	20.00	15.00	8.00
Dan Marino	200.00	150.00	80.00
Tim McGee RC	20.00	15.00	8.00
David Meggett RC	20.00	15.00	8.00
Mike Merriweather	75.00	56.00	30.00
Eric Metcalf RC	25.00	18.50	10.00
Keith Millard	35.00	26.00	14.00
Joe Montana red (Red Uni.)	75.00	56.00	30.00
Joe Montana white (White Uni.)	80.00	60.00	32.00
Warren Moon	35.00	26.00	14.00
Christian Okoye	20.00	15.00	8.00
Tom Rathman RC	60.00	45.00	24.00
Andre Reed	30.00	22.00	12.00
Gerald Riggs	18.00	13.50	7.25
Mark Rypien RC	20.00	15.00	8.00
Barry Sanders RC	125.00	94.00	50.00
Deion Sanders RC	50.00	37.00	20.00
Ricky Sanders RC	15.00	11.00	6.00
Clyde Simmons RC	90.00	67.00	36.00
Phil Simms	15.00	11.00	6.00
Mike Singletary blue (Blue Uni.)	30.00	22.00	12.00
Mike Singletary white (White Uni.)	30.00	22.00	12.00
Webster Slaughter	40.00	30.00	16.00
Bruce Smith	90.00	67.00	36.00
John Stephens	30.00	22.00	12.00
John Taylor RC	20.00	15.00	8.00
Thurman Thomas	40.00	30.00	16.00
Mike Tomczak RC	20.00	15.00	8.00
Greg Townsend RC	75.00	56.00	30.00
Odessa Turner RC	25.00	18.50	10.00
Herschel Walker	20.00	15.00	8.00
Steve Walsh RC	60.00	45.00	24.00
Reggie White green (Green Uni.)	40.00	30.00	16.00
Reggie White white (White Uni.)	30.00	22.00	12.00
Wade Wilson	65.00	49.00	26.00
Ickey Woods	20.00	15.00	8.00
Donnell Woolford RC	60.00	45.00	24.00
Tim Worley RC	80.00	60.00	32.00
Felix Wright RC	90.00	67.00	36.00

1991 Starting Lineup FB Headline Collection

The 1991 Headline series was the first for Kenner's football series. The six-figure set includes Joe Montana and Dan Marino.

	NM/M	NM	E
Complete Set (6):	200.00	150.00	80.00
John Elway	120.00	90.00	48.00
Boomer Esiason	18.00	13.50	7.25
Dan Marino	120.00	90.00	48.00
Joe Montana	50.00	37.00	20.00
Jerry Rice	50.00	37.00	20.00
Barry Sanders	60.00	45.00	24.00

1991 Starting Lineup Football

The 1991 Starting Lineup set included just 26 figures and each blister card also contained a card and a coin of the featured player. The set is highlighted by Emmitt Smith's first appearance in Starting Lineup.

	NM/M	NM	E
Complete Set (26):	550.00	410.00	220.00
Troy Aikman	75.00	56.00	30.00
Flipper Anderson RC	15.00	11.00	6.00
Neal Anderson	15.00	11.00	6.00
James Brooks	15.00	11.00	6.00
Eddie Brown	15.00	11.00	6.00
Mark Carrier RC	18.00	13.50	7.25
Boomer Esiason	15.00	11.00	6.00
James Francis RC	20.00	15.00	8.00
Jeff George RC	22.00	16.50	8.75
Rodney Hampton RC	25.00	18.50	10.00
Jim Harbaugh	50.00	37.00	20.00
Jeff Hostetler RC	25.00	18.50	10.00
Bobby Humphrey	14.00	10.50	5.50
Don Majkowski	18.00	13.50	7.25
Dan Marino	120.00	90.00	48.00
David Meggett	14.00	10.50	5.50
Joe Montana	30.00	22.00	12.00
Warren Moon	24.00	18.00	9.50
Christian Okoye	10.00	7.50	4.00
Jerry Rice	40.00	30.00	16.00
Andre Rison RC	25.00	18.50	10.00
Barry Sanders	70.00	52.00	28.00
Phil Simms	15.00	11.00	6.00
Emmitt Smith RC	150.00	110.00	60.00
Thurman Thomas	24.00	18.00	9.50
Herschel Walker	15.00	11.00	6.00

1961 Steelers Jay Publishing

The 12-card, 5" x 7" set features black and white photos with blank backs and were issued in 12-card packs for 25 cents.

		NM/M	NM	E
Complete Set (12):		60.00	30.00	18.00
Common Player:		5.00	2.50	1.50
1	Preston Carpenter	5.00	2.50	1.50
2	Dean Derby	5.00	2.50	1.50
3	Buddy Dial	5.00	2.50	1.50
4	John Henry Johnson	9.00	2.50	1.50
5	Bobby Layne	15.00	2.50	1.50
6	Gene Lipscomb	7.50	2.50	1.50

		NM/M	NM	E
7	Bill Mack	5.00	2.50	1.50
8	Fred Mautino	5.00	2.50	1.50
9	Lou Michaels	5.00	2.50	1.50
10	Buddy Parker (CO)	5.00	2.50	1.50
11	Myron Pottios	6.00	2.50	1.50
12	Tom Tracy	6.00	2.50	1.50

1963 Steelers IDL

The 26-card, 4" x 5" set features black and white photos with white borders and an IDL logo in the bottom left corner. The backs are blank.

		NM/M	NM	E
Complete Set (26):		150.00	75.00	45.00
Common Player:		6.00	3.00	1.75
1	Frank Atkinson	6.00	3.00	1.75
2	Jim Bradshaw	6.00	3.00	1.75
3	Ed Brown	6.00	3.00	1.75
4	John Burrell	6.00	3.00	1.75
5	Preston Carpenter	7.50	3.00	1.75
6	Lou Cordileone	6.00	3.00	1.75
7	Buddy Dial	10.00	3.00	1.75
8	Bob Ferguson	7.50	3.00	1.75
9	Glenn Glass	6.00	3.00	1.75
10	Dick Haley	6.00	3.00	1.75
11	Dick Hoak	10.00	3.00	1.75
12	John Henry Johnson	15.00	3.00	1.75
13	Brady Keys	6.00	3.00	1.75
14	Joe Krupa	6.00	3.00	1.75
15	Ray Lemek	6.00	3.00	1.75
16	Bill Mack	6.00	3.00	1.75
17	Lou Michaels	7.50	3.00	1.75
18	Bill Nelsen	10.00	3.00	1.75
19	Buzz Nutter	6.00	3.00	1.75
20	Myron Pottios	7.50	3.00	1.75
21	John Reger	6.00	3.00	1.75
22	Mike Sandusky	6.00	3.00	1.75
23	Ernie Stautner	15.00	3.00	1.75
24	George Tarasovic	6.00	3.00	1.75
25	Clendon Thomas	7.50	3.00	1.75
26	Tom Tracy	10.00	3.00	1.75

1968 Steelers KDKA

The 15-card, 2-3/8" x 4-1/8" set featured multiple players on each horizontal card front by position.

		NM/M	NM	E
Complete Set (15):		60.00	30.00	18.00
Common Player:		5.00	2.50	1.50
1	Centers:(John Knight, Ray Mansfield)	5.00	2.50	1.50
2	Coaches:(Bill Austin (Head), Fletcher, Torgeson, McLaughlin, Taylor, Heinrich, DePasqua, Berlin (trainer))	5.00	2.50	1.50
3	Defensive Backs:(Bob Hohn, Paul Martha, Marv Woodson)	6.00	2.50	1.50
4	Defensive Backs:(John Foruria, Clendon Thomas, Bob Morgan)	5.00	2.50	1.50
5	Defensive Linemen:(Ben McGhee, Chuck Hinton, Dick Arndt, Ken Kortas, Lloyd Voss)	5.00	2.50	1.50
6	Flankers:(Roy Jefferson, Ken Hebert (End-Kicker))	6.00	2.50	1.50
7	Fullbacks:(Earl Gros, Bill Asbury)	5.00	2.50	1.50
8	Guards:(Larry Granger, Sam Davis, Bruce Van Dyke)	5.00	2.50	1.50
9	Linebackers:(Andy Russell, Bill Saul, John Campbell, Ray May)	6.00	2.50	1.50
10	Quarterbacks:(Dick Shiner, Kent Nix)	6.00	2.50	1.50
11	Rookies:(Ken Hebert, Ernie Ruple, Mike Taylor)	5.00	2.50	1.50
12	Running Backs:(Dick Hoak, Don Shy, Jim Butler)	6.00	2.50	1.50
13	Split Ends:(J.R. Wilburn, Dick Compton)	5.00	2.50	1.50
14	Tackles:(Fran O'Brien, Mike Haggerty, John Brown)	5.00	2.50	1.50
15	Tight Ends:(John Hilton, Chet Anderson)	5.00	2.50	1.50

1972 Steelers Photo Sheets

The eight-card, 2" x 3" set was issued in 10" x 8" sheets. The card fronts feature a black and white photo with the Steelers helmet appearing in the lower left corner. The backs are blank.

		NM/M	NM	E
Complete Set (8):		60.00	30.00	18.00
Common Player:		3.00	1.50	.90
1	Ralph Anderson, Jim Clack, Bobby Maples, Henry Davis, Jon Kolb, Ray Mansfield, Sam Davis, Chuck Allen	3.00	1.50	.90
2	Jim Brumfield, Chuck Beatty, Bobby Walden, Frank Lewis, Lee Calland, Warren Bankston, Mel Blount, John Rowser	7.50	1.50	.90
3	Bud Carson (CO), Bob Fry (CO), Dick Hoak (CO), Babe Parilli (CO), George Perles (CO), Lou Riecke (CO), Charley Sumner (CO), Lionel Taylor (CO)	4.00	1.50	.90
4	Jack Ham, Ben McGee, Brian Stenger, Lloyd Voss, Bruce Van Dyke, L.C. Greenwood, Gerry Mullins, John Brown	7.50	1.50	.90
5	Joe Greene, Bert Askson (UER), Mel Holmes, Dwight White, Bob Adams, Larry Brown, Dave Smith, John McMakin (Misspelled Burt)	7.50	1.50	.90
6	Chuck Noll (CO), Jon Staggers, Terry Hanratty, Roy Gerela, Terry Bradshaw, Bob Leahy, Joe Gilliam, Rocky Bleier	15.00	1.50	.90
7	Dick Post, Franco Harris, Dennis Meyer, Lorenzo Brinkley, Steve Furness, Gordon Gravelle, Rick Sharp, Dave Kalina	15.00	1.50	.90
8	Mike Wagner, Ron Shanklin, Preston Pearson, Glen Edwards, Al Young, John Fuqua, Andy Russell, Steve Davis	5.00	1.50	.90

1978 Steelers Team Issue

This set consists of eight 8" x 10" sheets which feature eight black-and-white photos each. Each player photo measures 2" x 3". The sheets are blank-backed and unnumbered.

		NM	E	VG
Complete Set (8):		80.00	40.00	24.00
Common Panel:		10.00	5.00	3.00
1	B. Carr, Reggie Harrison RB, Mel Blount, Doug Becker, Tom Brzoza, Loren Toews, Mike Webster, Dennis Winston	12.00	6.00	3.50
2	Jack Deloplaine, Wentford Gains, Sidney Thornton, Rick Moser, Randy Reutershan, Nat Terry, Frank Lewis, Brad Wagner	10.00	5.00	3.00
3	Willie Fry, Steve Furness, Tom Beasley, Ted Petersen, Gary Dunn, L.C. Greenwood, Fred Anderson, Lance Reynolds	12.00	6.00	3.50
4	Dave LaCrosse, Jon Kolb, Robin Cole, Sam Davis G, Jack Lambert, Jack Ham, Brad Cousina, John Hicks	12.00	6.00	3.50
5	Gerry Mullins, Dave Pureifory, Ray Pinney, Joe Greene, John Banaszak, Steve Courson, Dwight White, Larry Brown	12.00	6.00	3.50

6	Chuck Noll CO, Craig Colquitt, Roy Gerela, Terry Bradshaw, Mike Kruczek, Cliff Stoudt, Rocky Bleier, Tony Dungy	18.00	9.00	5.50
7	John Stallworth, Theo Bell, Randy Grossman, Andre Keys, Jim Smith, L. McCarthey, Lynn Swann, Bennie Cunningham	15.00	7.50	4.50
8	Mike Wagner, R. Scott, Glen Edwards, Alvin Maxson, Ron Johnson DB, Larry Anderson, Donnie Shell, Franco Harris	12.00	6.00	3.50

1981 Steelers Police

The 16-card, 2-5/8" x 4-1/8" set was sponsored by the Steelers, Kiwanis, Coca-Cola and local law enforcement. The card fronts feature an action shot with the player's name, position, uniform number, height and weight. The card backs have "Steeler's Tips."

		NM/M	NM	E
Complete Set (16):		25.00	18.50	10.00
Common Player:		.75	.60	.30
9	Matt Bahr	1.25	.90	.50
12	Terry Bradshaw (Passing)	10.00	7.50	4.00
31	Donnie Shell (Referee back)	1.50	1.25	.60
32	Franco Harris (Running with ball)	6.00	4.50	2.50
47	Mel Blount (Running without ball)	3.00	2.25	1.25
52	Mike Webster (Standing)	1.50	1.25	.60
57	Sam Davis	.75	.60	.30
58	Jack Lambert (Facing left)	5.00	3.75	2.00
9	Jack Ham (Sportsmanship back)	3.00	2.25	1.25
64	Steve Furness	.75	.60	.30
68	L.C. Greenwood	2.00	1.50	.80
75	Joe Greene	5.00	3.75	2.00
76	John Banaszak	.75	.60	.30
82	John Stallworth (Running with ball)	2.50	2.00	1.00
88	Lynn Swann (Double coverage back)	6.00	4.50	2.50

1982 Steelers Police

The 16-card, 2-5/8" x 4-1/8" set is virtually identical in design with the 1981 set. The cards are sponsored by Coca-Cola, local law enforcement, Kiwanis and the Steelers. The card backs contain "Steeler's Tips."

		NM/M	NM	E
Complete Set (16):		12.00	9.00	4.75
Common Player:		.40	.30	.15
12	Terry Bradshaw (Portrait)	5.00	3.75	2.00
31	Donnie Shell (Double Coverage back)	.60	.45	.25
32	Franco Harris (Portrait)	2.50	2.00	1.00
44	Frank Pollard	.40	.30	.15
47	Mel Blount (Running with ball)	1.50	1.25	.60
52	Mike Webster (Portrait)	.75	.60	.30
58	Jack Lambert (Facing forward)	2.50	2.00	1.00
59	Jack Ham (Teamwork back)	1.50	1.25	.60
65	Tom Beasley	.40	.30	.15
67	Gary Dunn	.40	.30	.15
74	Ray Pinney	.40	.30	.15
82	John Stallworth (Posed shot)	1.25	.90	.50
88	Lynn Swann (Sportsmanship back)	3.00	2.25	1.25
89	Bennie Cunningham	.50	.40	.20
90	Bob Kohrs	.40	.30	.15

1983 Steelers Police

The 17-card, 2-5/8" x 4-1/8" set is similar to the Police sets from 1981 and 1982. Card No. 2 has two variations of the spelling of coach Chuck Noll's last name.

		NM/M	NM	E
Complete Set (16):		8.00	6.00	3.25
Common Player:		.25	.20	.10
1	Walter Abercrombie	.35	.25	.14
2	Gary Anderson (K)	.50	.40	.20
3	Mel Blount	.75	.60	.30
4	Terry Bradshaw	3.00	2.25	1.25
5	Robin Cole	.25	.20	.10

6	Steve Courson	.25	.20	.10
7	Bennie Cunningham	.35	.25	.14
8	Franco Harris	2.00	1.50	.80
9	Greg Hawthorne	.25	.20	.10
10	Jack Lambert	1.00	.70	.40
11A	Chuck Noll (CO ERRM) (Misspelled Knoll)	5.00	3.75	2.00
11B	Chuck Noll (CO COR)	1.00	.70	.40
12	Donnie Shell	.35	.25	.14
13	John Stallworth	1.00	.70	.40
14	Mike Webster	.75	.60	.30
15	Dwayne Woodruff	.25	.20	.10
16	Rick Woods	.25	.20	.10

1984 Steelers Police

The 16-card, 2-5/8" x 4-1/8" set, sponsored by McDonald's, Kiwanis, the Steelers and local law enforcement, features action shots with "Steeler Tips" on the card backs. The cards are similar to the previous Police sets, except for the McDonald's and Kiwanis logos on the card fronts.

		NM/M	NM	E
Complete Set (16):		8.00	6.00	3.25
Common Player:		.40	.30	.15
1	Gary Anderson (K)	.60	.45	.25
16	Mark Malone	.60	.45	.25
19	David Woodley	.60	.45	.25
30	Frank Pollard	.40	.30	.15
32	Franco Harris	2.00	1.50	.80
34	Walter Abercrombie	.50	.40	.20
49	Dwayne Woodruff	.40	.30	.15
52	Mike Webster	.75	.60	.30
57	Mike Merriweather	.60	.45	.25
58	Jack Lambert	1.50	1.25	.60
67	Gary Dunn	.40	.30	.15
73	Craig Wolfley	.40	.30	.15
82	John Stallworth	1.50	1.25	.60
83	Louis Lipps	1.00	.70	.40
92	Keith Gary	.40	.30	.15
92	Keith Willis	.50	.40	.20

1985 Steelers Police

The 16-card, 2-5/8" x 4-1/8" set was sponsored by local law enforcement, Giant Eagle, the Steelers and Kiwanis. The card backs have "Steeler Tips."

		NM/M	NM	E
Complete Set (16):		5.00	3.75	2.00
Common Player:		.40	.30	.15
1	Gary Anderson K (Kickoff back)	.50	.40	.20
16	Mark Malone (Playbook back)	.50	.40	.20
21	Eric Williams	.40	.30	.15
30	Frank Pollard (Second Effort back)	.40	.30	.15
31	Donnie Shell (Zone back)	.50	.40	.20
34	Walter Abercrombie (Teamwork back)	.50	.40	.20
49	Dwayne Woodruff (Turnover back)	.40	.30	.15
50	David Little	.50	.40	.20
52	Mike Webster (Offside back)	.75	.60	.30
53	Bryan Hinkle (Blindside back)	.40	.30	.15
56	Robin Cole (Timeout back)	.40	.30	.15
57	Mike Merriweather (Blitz back)	.60	.45	.25
82	John Stallworth (Captains back)	1.50	1.25	.60
83	Louis Lipps (Pride back)	.60	.45	.25
93	Keith Willis (QB Sack card)	.40	.30	.15
NNO	Chuck Noll CO (Coach back)	1.25	.90	.50

1986 Steelers Police

The 15-card, 2-5/8" x 4-1/8" set was issued by Kiwanis, Giant Eagle, local law enforcement and the Steelers. The card fronts are virtually identical to the 1985 set, with the Giant Eagle and Kiwanis logos found in the top corners and brief bio information located along the bottom edge. The card backs contain "Steeler Tips."

		NM/M	NM	E
Complete Set (15):		5.00	3.75	2.00
Common Player:		.35	.25	.14
1	Gary Anderson (K) (Field Goal back)	.60	.45	.25
16	Mark Malone (Quarterback back)	.60	.45	.25
24	Rich Erenberg	.50	.40	.20
30	Frank Pollard (Running Back back)	.50	.40	.20

31	Donnie Shell (Interception back)	.60	.45	.25
34	Walter Abercrombie (Penalty back)	.50	.40	.20
49	Dwayne Woodruff	.35	.25	.14
52	Mike Webster (Possession back)	.75	.60	.30
53	Bryan Hinkle (Prevent back)	.35	.25	.14
56	Robin Cole (Equipmen back)	.35	.25	.14
57	Mike Merriweather (Linebacker back)	.50	.40	.20
62	Tunch Ilkin	.50	.40	.20
64	Edmund Nelson	.35	.25	.14
67	Gary Dunn (Defensive Holding back)	.35	.25	.14
82	John Stallworth (Victory back)	1.00	.70	.40
83	Louis Lipps (Receiver back)	.75	.60	.30

1987 Steelers Police

CHUCK NOLL
Head Coach

The 16-card, 2-5/8" x 4-1/8" set has basically the same design as the 1985 and 1986 sets, complete with Kiwanis and Giant Eagle logos and "Steeler Tips."

		NM/M	NM	E
Complete Set (16):		5.00	3.75	2.00
Common Player:		.35	.25	.14
1	Walter Abercrombie (Option Pass back)	.50	.40	.20
2	Gary Anderson (K) (Extra Point back)	.60	.45	.25
3	Bubby Brister	.90	.70	.35
4	Gary Dunn (Neutral Zone back)	.35	.25	.14
5	Preston Gothard	.35	.25	.14
6	Bryan Hinkle (Outside Linebackers back)	.50	.40	.20
7	Earnest Jackson	.50	.40	.20
8	Louis Lipps (Corner Pattern back)	.75	.60	.30
9	Mark Malone (Adverse Conditions back)	.60	.45	.25
10	Mike Merriweather (Instant Replay back)	.50	.40	.20
11	Chuck Noll (CO) (Referee back)	.75	.60	.30
12	John Rienstra	.35	.25	.14
13	Donnie Shell (Defense back)	.60	.45	.25
14	John Stallworth (Crackback Block back)	1.00	.70	.40
15	Mike Webster (Sportsmanship back)	.75	.60	.30
16	Keith Willis (Down back)	.35	.25	.14

1988 Steelers Police

The 16-card, 2-5/8" x 4-1/8" set is similar in design to the previous mid-1980s Steelers Police set as it is sponsored by Giant Eagle and Kiwanis and features "Steeler Tips" on the card backs. The Steelers helmet on the card backs have three white diamonds as opposed to the previous three years' helmets which had two black diamonds.

		NM/M	NM	E
Complete Set (16):		5.00	3.75	2.00
Common Player:		.35	.25	.14
1	Gary Anderson (K)	.60	.45	.25
2	Bubby Brister	.75	.60	.30
3	Thomas Everett	.60	.45	.25
4	Delton Hall	.35	.25	.14
5	Bryan Hinkle	.50	.40	.20
6	Tunch Ilkin	.35	.25	.14
7	Earnest Jackson	.50	.40	.20
8	Louis Lipps	.60	.45	.25

9	David Little	.35	.25	.14
10	Mike Merriweather	.50	.40	.20
11	Frank Pollard	.35	.25	.14
12	John Rienstra	.35	.25	.14
13	Mike Webster	.75	.60	.30
14	Keith Willis	.35	.25	.14
15	Craig Wolfley	.35	.25	.14
16	Rod Woodson	1.50	1.25	.60

1989 Steelers Police

The 16-card, 2-5/8" x 4-1/8" set is virtually identical to previous Police sets with sponsorships by Kiwanis and Giant Eagle. The card backs contain "Steeler Tips '89."

		NM/M	NM	E
Complete Set (16):		5.00	3.75	2.00
Common Player:		.40	.30	.15
1	Gary Anderson	.60	.45	.25
6	Bubby Brister	.60	.45	.25
18	Harry Newsome	.40	.30	.15
24	Rodney Carter	.40	.30	.15
26	Rod Woodson	1.00	.70	.40
27	Thomas Everett	.60	.45	.25
33	Merril Hoge	.40	.30	.15
53	Bryan Hinkle	.40	.30	.15
54	Hardy Nickerson	.75	.60	.30
62	Tunch Ilkin	.40	.30	.15
63	Dermontti Dawson	.60	.45	.25
74	Terry Long	.40	.30	.15
78	Tim Johnson	.40	.30	.15
83	Louis Lipps	.75	.60	.30
97	Aaron Jones	.40	.30	.15
98	Gerald Williams	.40	.30	.15

1990 Steelers Police

The 16-card, 2-5/8" x 4-1/8" set features identical front designs as previous Police sets, with the Kiwanis and Giant Eagle logos. The card backs have "Steelers '90 Tips."

		NM/M	NM	E
Complete Set (16):		5.00	3.75	2.00
Common Player:		.35	.25	.14
1	Gary Anderson (K)	.35	.25	.14
2	Bubby Brister	.60	.45	.25
3	Thomas Everett	.35	.25	.14
4	Merril Hoge	.35	.25	.14
5	Tunch Ilkin	.35	.25	.14
6	Carnell Lake	.50	.40	.20
7	Louis Lipps	.75	.60	.30
8	David Little	.35	.25	.14
9	Greg Lloyd	.75	.60	.30
10	Mike Mularkey	.35	.25	.14
11	Hardy Nickerson	.75	.60	.30
12	Chuck Noll (CO)	.75	.60	.30
13	John Rienstra	.35	.25	.14
14	Keith Willis	.35	.25	.14
15	Rod Woodson	.90	.70	.35
16	Tim Worley	.50	.40	.20

1991 Steelers Police

The 16-card, 2-5/8" x 4-1/8" set features front and back designs which are similar to previous Police sets. The card backs contain "Steelers Tips '91" while the Giant Eagle and Kiwanis logos appear on both sides.

		NM/M	NM	E
Complete Set (16):		5.00	3.75	2.00
Common Player:		.35	.25	.14
1	Gary Anderson (K)	.35	.25	.14
2	Bubby Brister	.60	.45	.25
3	Dermontti Dawson	.35	.25	.14
4	Eric Green	.75	.60	.30
5	Bryan Hinkle	.35	.25	.14
6	Merril Hoge	.50	.40	.20
7	John Jackson	.35	.25	.14
8	D.J. Johnson	.35	.25	.14
9	Carnell Lake	.50	.40	.20
10	Louis Lipps	.60	.45	.25
11	Greg Lloyd	1.00	.70	.40
12	Mike Mularkey	.35	.25	.14
13	Chuck Noll (CO)	.75	.60	.30
14	Dan Stryzinski	.35	.25	.14
15	Gerald Williams	.35	.25	.14
16	Rod Woodson	.90	.70	.35

1979 Stop 'N' Go

These 18 3D cards were available at Stop 'N' Go markets in 1979. Each front has a 3D effect player photo on the front, along with his team's helmet at the top. His name and team name are in a panel at the bottom of the card; "NFL 3-D Football Stars" is written at the top. The back of the card is numbered 1 of 18, etc., and includes yearly stats, plus summaries of the player's professional and collegiate accomplishments. The Stop 'N' Go logo is also on the card back. The cards measure 2-1/8" x 3-1/4".

		NM	E	VG
Complete Set (18):		45.00	22.00	13.50
Common Player:		1.25	.60	.40
1	Gregg Bingham	1.25	.60	.40
2	Ken Burrough	1.50	.70	.45
3	Preston Pearson	1.50	.70	.45
4	Sam Cunningham	2.00	1.00	.60
5	Robert Newhouse	2.00	1.00	.60
6	Walter Payton	13.00	6.50	4.00
7	Robert Brazile	1.50	.70	.45
8	Rocky Bleier	2.50	1.25	.70
9	Toni Fritsch	1.25	.60	.40
10	Jack Ham	3.00	1.50	.90
11	Jay Saldi	1.25	.60	.40
12	Roger Staubach	15.00	7.50	4.50
13	Franco Harris	8.00	4.00	2.50
14	Otis Armstrong	2.00	1.00	.60
15	Lyle Alzado	2.00	1.00	.60
16	Billy Johnson	1.50	.70	.45
17	Elvin Bethea	1.50	.70	.45
18	Joe Greene	5.00	2.50	1.50

1980 Stop 'N' Go

These 3D cards were available with beverage purchases at participating Stop 'N' Go markets in 1980. The card design is similar to the previous year's design, except the card front has a star on each side of the panel at the bottom where the player's name is. The card back is somewhat different, however, with the main difference being the 1979 statistics and a 1980 copyright logo.

		NM	E	VG
Complete Set (48):		50.00	25.00	15.00
Common Player:		.75	.40	.25
1	John Jefferson	1.00	.50	.30
2	Herbert Scott	.75	.40	.25
3	Pat Donovan	.75	.40	.25
4	William Andrews	1.25	.60	.40
5	Frank Corral	.75	.40	.25
6	Fred Dryer	1.50	.70	.45
7	Franco Harris	5.00	2.50	1.50
8	Leon Gray	.75	.40	.25
9	Gregg Bingham	.75	.40	.25
10	Louis Kelcher	.75	.40	.25
11	Robert Newhouse	1.25	.60	.40
12	Preston Pearson	1.00	.50	.30
13	Wallace Francis	1.00	.50	.30
14	Pat Haden	2.00	1.00	.60
15	Jim Youngblood	.75	.40	.25
16	Rocky Bleier	1.50	.70	.45
17	Gifford Nielsen	.75	.40	.25
18	Elvin Bethea	1.00	.50	.30
19	Charlie Joiner	3.00	1.50	.90
20	Tony Hill	1.00	.50	.30
21	Drew Pearson	1.25	.60	.40
22	Alfred Jenkins	1.00	.50	.30
23	Dave Elmendorf	.75	.40	.25
24	Jack Reynolds	1.25	.60	.40
25	Joe Greene	3.00	1.50	.90
26	Robert Brazile	1.00	.50	.30
27	Mike Reinfeldt	.75	.40	.25
28	Bob Griese	4.50	2.25	1.25
29	Harold Carmichael	1.50	.70	.45
30	Ottis Anderson	4.00	2.00	1.25
31	Ahmad Rashad	3.50	1.75	1.00
32	Archie Manning	1.50	.70	.45
33	Ricky Bell	1.00	.50	.30
34	Jay Saldi	.75	.40	.25
35	Ken Burrough	1.00	.50	.30
36	Don Woods	.75	.40	.25
37	Henry Childs	.75	.40	.25
38	Wilbur Jackson	.75	.40	.25
39	Steve DeBerg	1.50	.70	.45
40	Ron Jessie	.75	.40	.25
41	Mel Blount	2.50	1.25	.70
42	Cliff Branch	1.50	.70	.45
43	Chuck Muncie	1.25	.60	.40
44	Ken MacAfee	.75	.40	.25
45	Charley Young	1.00	.50	.30
46	Cody Jones	.75	.40	.25
47	Jack Ham	2.00	1.00	.60
48	Ray Guy	1.50	.70	.45

1976 Sunbeam NFL Die Cuts

The 28-card, standard-sized set is die-cut so that each card can stand up when perforated. The team's helmet, name and player drawing appear on the card fronts while the backs have a brief team history with the Sunbeam logo. The cards were printed on white or gray stock, with or without the Sunbeam logo.

		NM	E	VG
Complete Set (29):		200.00	150.00	80.00
Common Player:		8.00	6.00	3.25
1	**Atlanta Falcons**	8.00	6.00	3.25
2	**Baltimore Colts**	8.00	6.00	3.25
3	**Buffalo Bills**	8.00	6.00	3.25
4	**Chicago Bears**	8.00	6.00	3.25
5	**Cincinnati Bengals**	8.00	6.00	3.25
6	**Cleveland Browns**	8.00	6.00	3.25
7	**Dallas Cowboys**	10.00	5.00	3.00
8	**Denver Broncos**	8.00	6.00	3.25
9	**Detroit Lions**	8.00	6.00	3.25
10	**Green Bay Packers**	10.00	5.00	3.00
11	**Houston Oilers**	8.00	6.00	3.25
12	**Kansas City Chiefs**	8.00	6.00	3.25
13	**Los Angeles Rams**	8.00	6.00	3.25
14	**Miami Dolphins**	10.00	5.00	3.00
15	**Minnesota Vikings**	8.00	6.00	3.25
16	**New England Patriots**	8.00	6.00	3.25
17	**New Orleans Saints**	8.00	6.00	3.25
18	**New York Giants**	8.00	6.00	3.25
19	**New York Jets**	8.00	6.00	3.25
20	**Oakland Raiders**	10.00	5.00	3.00
21	**Philadelphia Eagles**	8.00	6.00	3.25
22	**Pittsburgh Steelers**	8.00	6.00	3.25
23	**St. Louis Cardinals**	8.00	6.00	3.25
24	**San Diego Chargers**	8.00	6.00	3.25
25	**San Francisco 49ers**	10.00	5.00	3.00
26	**Seattle Seahawks**	8.00	6.00	3.25
27	**Tampa Bay Buccaneers**	8.00	6.00	3.25
28	**Washington Redskins**	10.00	5.00	3.00
NNO	**NFL Logo** (Blankbacked)	8.00	6.00	3.25

1976 Sunbeam SEC Die Cuts

The 20-card, standard-size set was die-cut so when each card was perforated, it could stand up. The set is similar in design to the NFL set of the same year, except with SEC teams. The card fronts feature the school's logo with the backs containing the school's 1976 schedule. The cards were distributed in Sunbeam bread packages.

		NM	E	VG
Complete Set (20):		125.00	62.00	37.00
Common Player:		5.00	2.50	1.50
1	**Alabama Crimson Tide** (Team Profile)	10.00	5.00	3.00
2	**Alabama Crimson Tide** (Schedule)	10.00	5.00	3.00
3	**Auburn War Eagle** (Team Profile)	6.00	3.00	1.75
4	**Auburn War Eagle** (Schedule)	6.00	3.00	1.75
5	**Florida Gators** (Team Profile)	7.00	3.50	2.00
6	**Florida Gators** (Schedule)	7.00	3.50	2.00
7	**Georgia Bulldogs** (Team Profile)	6.00	3.00	1.75
8	**Georgia Bulldogs** (Schedule)	6.00	3.00	1.75
9	**Kentucky Wildcats** (Team Profile)	6.00	3.00	1.75
10	**Kentucky Wildcats** (Schedule)	6.00	3.00	1.75
11	**Louisiana St. Tigers** (Team Profile)	6.00	3.00	1.75
12	**Louisiana St. Tigers** (Schedule)	6.00	3.00	1.75
13	**Miss. St. Bulldogs** (Team Profile)	5.00	2.50	1.50
14	**Miss. St. Bulldogs** (Schedule)	5.00	2.50	1.50
15	**Ole Miss Rebels** (Team Profile)	5.00	2.50	1.50
16	**Ole Miss Rebels** (Schedule)	5.00	2.50	1.50
17	**Tennessee Volunteers** (Team Profile)	7.00	3.50	2.00
18	**Tennessee Volunteers** (Schedule)	7.00	3.50	2.00
19	**Vanderbilt Commodores** (Team Profile)	5.00	2.50	1.50
20	**Vanderbilt Commodores** (Schedule)	5.00	2.50	1.50

1972 Sunoco Stamps

Each NFL team is represented by 24 players in this 624-stamp set - 12 offensive and 12 defensive players have been chosen. The stamps measure 1-5/8" x 2-3/8" and were given away in perforated sheets of nine at participating Sun Oil Co. gas stations. Each stamp, featuring an oval with a player photo inside against a corresponding team color-coded background, is unnumbered. Two albums were issued to hold the stamps - a 56-page "NFL Action '72" album and a 128-page album. The albums had specific spots for each sticker, as indicated by a square providing the player's name, uniform number, age, height, weight and college he attended. There were 16 additional perforated sheets inside the album, too. The stamps could be placed inside the album by using the tabs which were provided with the album, instead of licking them.

		NM	E	VG
Complete Set (624):		125.00	62.00	37.00
Common Player:		.10	.05	.03
(1)	Ken Burrow	.15	.08	.05
(2)	Bill Sandeman	.10	.05	.03
(3)	Andy Maurer	.10	.05	.03
(4)	Jeff Van Note	.20	.10	.06
(5)	Malcolm Snider	.10	.05	.03
(6)	George Kunz	.25	.13	.08
(7)	Jim Mitchell	.10	.05	.03
(8)	Wes Chesson	.10	.05	.03
(9)	Bob Berry	.20	.10	.06
(10)	Dick Shiner	.10	.05	.03
(11)	Jim Butler	.10	.05	.03
(12)	Art Malone	.10	.05	.03
(13)	Claude Humphrey	.25	.13	.08
(14)	John Small	.10	.05	.03
(15)	Glen Condren	.10	.05	.03
(16)	John Zook	.20	.10	.06
(17)	Don Hansen	.10	.05	.03
(18)	Tommy Nobis	1.25	.60	.40
(19)	Greg Brezina	.20	.10	.06
(20)	Ken Reaves	.10	.05	.03
(21)	Tom Hayes	.10	.05	.03
(22)	Tom McCauley	.10	.05	.03
(23)	Bill Bell	.15	.08	.05
(24)	Bill Lothridge	.20	.10	.06
(25)	Ed Hinton	.10	.05	.03
(26)	Bob Vogel	.10	.05	.03
(27)	Glenn Ressler	.10	.05	.03
(28)	Bill Curry	.30	.15	.09
(29)	John Williams	.10	.05	.03
(30)	Dan Sullivan	.10	.05	.03
(31)	Tom Mitchell	.10	.05	.03
(32)	John Mackey	1.50	.70	.45
(33)	Ray Perkins	2.00	1.00	.60
(34)	John Unitas	6.00	3.00	1.75
(35)	Tom Matte	.30	.15	.09
(36)	Norm Bulaich	.25	.13	.08
(37)	Bubba Smith	1.00	.50	.30
(38)	Bill Newsome	.10	.05	.03
(39)	Fred Miller	.10	.05	.03
(40)	Roy Hinton	.10	.05	.03
(41)	Ray May	.10	.05	.03
(42)	Ted Hendricks	1.50	.70	.45
(43)	Charlie Stukes	.10	.05	.03
(44)	Rex Kern	.30	.15	.09
(45)	Jerry Logan	.10	.05	.03
(46)	Rick Volk	.20	.10	.06
(47)	David Lee	.15	.08	.05
(48)	Jim O'Brien	.25	.13	.08
(49)	J.D. Hill	.20	.10	.06
(50)	Willie Young	.10	.05	.03
(51)	Jim Reilly	.10	.05	.03
(52)	Bruce Jarvis	.15	.08	.05
(53)	Levert Carr	.10	.05	.03
(54)	Donnie Green	.10	.05	.03
(55)	Jan White	.20	.10	.06
(56)	Marlin Briscoe	.40	.20	.12
(57)	Dennis Shaw	.15	.08	.05
(58)	O.J. Simpson	12.00	6.00	3.50
(59)	Wayne Patrick	.10	.05	.03
(60)	John Leypoldt	.10	.05	.03
(61)	Al Cowlings	.75	.40	.25
(62)	Jim Dunaway	.20	.10	.06
(63)	Bob Tatarek	.10	.05	.03
(64)	Cal Snowden	.10	.05	.03
(65)	Paul Guidry	.10	.05	.03
(66)	Edgar Chandler	.20	.10	.06
(67)	Al Andrews	.10	.05	.03
(68)	Robert James	.10	.05	.03
(69)	Alvin Wyatt	.10	.05	.03
(70)	John Pitts	.10	.05	.03
(71)	Pete Richardson	.15	.08	.05
(72)	Spike Jones	.10	.05	.03
(73)	Dick Gordon	.20	.10	.06
(74)	Randy Jackson	.10	.05	.03
(75)	Glen Holloway	.10	.05	.03
(76)	Rick Coady	.10	.05	.03
(77)	Jim Cadile	.10	.05	.03
(78)	Steve Wright	.10	.05	.03
(79)	Bob Wallace	.10	.05	.03
(80)	George Farmer	.15	.08	.05
(81)	Bobby Douglass	.40	.20	.12
(82)	Don Shy	.10	.05	.03
(83)	Cyril Pinder	.10	.05	.03
(84)	Mac Percival	.10	.05	.03
(85)	Willie Holman	.10	.05	.03
(86)	George Seals	.15	.08	.05
(87)	Bill Staley	.10	.05	.03
(88)	Ed O'Bradovich	.20	.10	.06
(89)	Doug Buffone	.10	.05	.03
(90)	Dick Butkus	3.00	1.50	.90
(91)	Ross Brupbacher	.20	.10	.06
(92)	Charlie Ford	.10	.05	.03
(93)	Joe Taylor	.10	.05	.03

(94) Ron Smith	.20	.10	.06
(95) Jerry Moore	.10	.05	.03
(96) Bobby Joe Green	.15	.08	.05
(97) Chip Myers	.10	.05	.03
(98) Rufus Mayes	.10	.05	.03
(99) Howard Fest	.10	.05	.03
(100) Bob Johnson	.30	.15	.09
(101) Pat Matson	.10	.05	.03
(102) Vern Holland	.10	.05	.03
(103) Bruce Coslet	.75	.40	.25
(104) Bob Trumpy	1.00	.50	.30
(105) Virgil Carter	.20	.10	.06
(106) Fred Willis	.10	.05	.03
(107) Jess Phillips	.10	.05	.03
(108) Horst Muhlmann	.15	.08	.05
(109) Royce Berry	.10	.05	.03
(110) Mike Reid	.50	.25	.15
(111) Steve Chomyszak	.10	.05	.03
(112) Ron Carpenter	.10	.05	.03
(113) Al Beauchamp	.15	.08	.05
(114) Bill Bergey	.50	.25	.15
(115) Ken Avery	.10	.05	.03
(116) Lemar Parrish	.40	.20	.12
(117) Ken Riley	.40	.20	.12
(118) Sandy Durko	.10	.05	.03
(119) Dave Lewis	.10	.05	.03
(120) Paul Robinson	.20	.10	.06
(121) Fair Hooker	.20	.10	.06
(122) Doug Dieken	.10	.05	.03
(123) John Demarie	.10	.05	.03
(124) Jim Copeland	.10	.05	.03
(125) Gene Hickerson	.10	.05	.03
(126) Bob McKay	.10	.05	.03
(127) Milt Morin	.20	.10	.06
(128) Frank Pitts	.10	.05	.03
(129) Mike Phipps	.50	.25	.15
(130) Leroy Kelly	1.50	.70	.45
(131) Bo Scott	.20	.10	.06
(132) Don Cockroft	.10	.05	.03
(133) Ron Snidow	.10	.05	.03
(134) Walter Johnson	.10	.05	.03
(135) Jerry Sherk	.30	.15	.09
(136) Jack Gregory	.10	.05	.03
(137) Jim Houston	.10	.05	.03
(138) Dale Lindsey	.10	.05	.03
(139) Bill Andrews	.25	.13	.08
(140) Clarence Scott	.20	.10	.06
(141) Ernie Kellerman	.10	.05	.03
(142) Walt Sumner	.10	.05	.03
(143) Mike Howell	.10	.05	.03
(144) Reece Morrison	.10	.05	.03
(145) Bob Hayes	1.00	.50	.30
(146) Ralph Neely	.20	.10	.06
(147) John Niland	.10	.05	.03
(148) Dave Manders	.20	.10	.06
(149) Blaine Nye	.10	.05	.03
(150) Rayfield Wright	.20	.10	.06
(151) Billy Truax	.10	.05	.03
(152) Lance Alworth	3.00	1.50	.90
(153) Roger Staubach	10.00	5.00	3.00
(154) Duane Thomas	.50	.25	.15
(155) Walt Garrison	.30	.15	.09
(156) Mike Clark	.10	.05	.03
(157) Larry Cole	.10	.05	.03
(158) Jethro Pugh	.20	.10	.06
(159) Bob Lilly	2.00	1.00	.60
(160) George Andrie	.20	.10	.06
(161) Dave Edwards	.10	.05	.03
(162) Lee Roy Jordan	.90	.45	.25
(163) Chuck Howley	.30	.15	.09
(164) Herb Adderley	1.00	.50	.30
(165) Mel Renfro	.75	.40	.25
(166) Cornell Green	.30	.15	.09
(167) Cliff Harris	.20	.10	.06
(168) Ron Widby	.10	.05	.03
(169) Jerry Simmons	.10	.05	.03
(170) Roger Shoals	.10	.05	.03
(171) Larron Jackson	.10	.05	.03
(172) George Goeddeke	.10	.05	.03
(173) Mike Schnitker	.10	.05	.03
(174) Mike Current	.10	.05	.03
(175) Billy Masters	.15	.08	.05
(176) Jack Gehrke	.10	.05	.03
(177) Don Horn	.20	.10	.06
(178) Floyd Little	1.00	.50	.30
(179) Bobby Anderson	.30	.15	.09
(180) Jim Turner	.20	.10	.06
(181) Rich Jackson	.10	.05	.03
(182) Paul Smith	.10	.05	.03
(183) Dave Costa	.10	.05	.03
(184) Lyle Alzado	1.00	.50	.30
(185) Olen Underwood	.10	.05	.03
(186) Fred Forsberg	.10	.05	.03
(187) Chip Myrtle	.10	.05	.03

(188) Leroy Mitchell	.10	.05	.03
(189) Billy Thompson	.20	.10	.06
(190) Charlie Greer	.10	.05	.03
(191) George Saimes	.20	.10	.06
(192) Billy Van Heusen	.10	.05	.03
(193) Earl McCullouch	.20	.10	.06
(194) Jim Yarbrough	.10	.05	.03
(195) Chuck Walton	.15	.08	.05
(196) Ed Flanagan	.10	.05	.03
(197) Frank Gallagher	.10	.05	.03
(198) Rockne Freitas	.10	.05	.03
(199) Charlie Sanders	.25	.13	.08
(200) Larry Walton	.10	.05	.03
(201) Greg Landry	.40	.20	.12
(202) Altie Taylor	.20	.10	.06
(203) Steve Owens	.40	.20	.12
(204) Errol Mann	.10	.05	.03
(205) Joe Robb	.10	.05	.03
(206) Dick Evey	.10	.05	.03
(207) Jerry Rush	.10	.05	.03
(208) Larry Hand	.15	.08	.05
(209) Paul Naumoff	.20	.10	.06
(210) Mike Lucci	.20	.10	.06
(211) Wayne Walker	.10	.05	.03
(212) Lem Barney	1.00	.50	.30
(213) Dick LeBeau	.20	.10	.06
(214) Mike Weger	.10	.05	.03
(215) Wayne Rasmussen	.10	.05	.03
(216) Herman Weaver	.10	.05	.03
(217) John Spilis	.10	.05	.03
(218) Francis Peay	.10	.05	.03
(219) Bill Lueck	.10	.05	.03
(220) Ken Bowman	.10	.05	.03
(221) Gale Gillingham	.20	.10	.06
(222) Dick Himes	.10	.05	.03
(223) Rich McGeorge	.10	.05	.03
(224) Carroll Dale	.20	.10	.06
(225) Bart Starr	3.50	1.75	1.00
(226) Scott Hunter	.30	.15	.09
(227) John Brockington	.30	.15	.09
(228) Dave Hampton	.20	.10	.06
(229) Clarence Williams	.10	.05	.03
(230) Mike McCoy	.20	.10	.06
(231) Bob Brown	.20	.10	.06
(232) Alden Roche	.10	.05	.03
(233) Dave Robinson	.25	.13	.08
(234) Jim Carter	.20	.10	.06
(235) Fred Carr	.20	.10	.06
(236) Ken Ellis	.15	.08	.05
(237) Doug Hart	.10	.05	.03
(238) Al Randolph	.10	.05	.03
(239) Al Matthews	.10	.05	.03
(240) Tim Webster	.10	.05	.03
(241) Jim Beirne	.10	.05	.03
(242) Bob Young	.10	.05	.03
(243) Elbert Drungo	.10	.05	.03
(244) Sam Walton	.20	.10	.06
(245) Alvin Reed	.10	.05	.03
(246) Charlie Joiner	1.50	.70	.45
(247) Dan Pastorini	.30	.15	.09
(248) Charlie Johnson	.30	.15	.09
(249) Lynn Dickey	.40	.20	.12
(250) Woody Campbell	.10	.05	.03
(251) Robert Holmes	.20	.10	.06
(252) Mark Moseley	.30	.15	.09
(253) Pat Holmes	.10	.05	.03
(254) Mike Tilleman	.10	.05	.03
(255) Leo Brooks	.10	.05	.03
(256) Elvin Bethea	.30	.15	.09
(257) George Webster	.30	.15	.09
(258) Garland Boyette	.10	.05	.03
(259) Ron Pritchard	.15	.08	.05
(260) Zeke Moore	.10	.05	.03
(261) Willie Alexander	.10	.05	.03
(262) Ken Houston	1.00	.50	.30
(263) John Charles	.10	.05	.03
(264) Linzy Cole	.10	.05	.03
(265) Elmo Wright	.25	.13	.08
(266) Jim Tyrer	.20	.10	.06
(267) Ed Buddle	.20	.10	.06
(268) Jack Rudnay	.10	.05	.03
(269) Mo Moorman	.10	.05	.03
(270) Dave Hill	.10	.05	.03
(271) Morris Stroud	.10	.05	.03
(272) Otis Taylor	.40	.20	.12
(273) Len Dawson	3.00	1.50	.90
(274) Ed Podolak	.30	.15	.09
(275) Wendell Hayes	.10	.05	.03
(276) Jan Stenerud	1.25	.60	.40
(277) Marvin Upshaw	.10	.05	.03
(278) Curley Culp	.30	.15	.09
(279) Buck Buchanan	1.00	.50	.30
(280) Aaron Brown	.10	.05	.03
(281) Bobby Bell	1.25	.60	.40

(282) Willie Lanier	1.50	.70	.45
(283) Jim Lynch	.20	.10	.06
(284) Jim Marsalis	.20	.10	.06
(285) Emmitt Thomas	.20	.10	.06
(286) Jim Kearney	.10	.05	.03
(287) Johnny Robinson	.40	.20	.12
(288) Jerrel Wilson	.10	.05	.03
(289) Jack Snow	.35	.20	.11
(290) Charlie Cowan	.10	.05	.03
(291) Tom Mack	.50	.25	.15
(292) Ken Iman	.10	.05	.03
(293) Joe Scibelli	.10	.05	.03
(294) Harry Schuh	.10	.05	.03
(295) Rob Klein	.20	.10	.06
(296) Lance Rentzel	.35	.20	.11
(297) Roman Gabriel	.60	.30	.20
(298) Les Josephson	.20	.10	.06
(299) Willie Ellison	.20	.10	.06
(300) David Ray	.10	.05	.03
(301) Jack Youngblood	1.25	.60	.40
(302) Merlin Olsen	1.75	.90	.50
(303) Phil Olsen	.10	.05	.03
(304) Coy Bacon	.10	.05	.03
(305) Jim Purnell	.10	.05	.03
(306) Marlin McKeever	.20	.10	.06
(307) Isiah Robertson	.30	.15	.09
(308) Jim Nettles	.10	.05	.03
(309) Gene Howard	.10	.05	.03
(310) Kermit Alexander	.20	.10	.06
(311) Dave Elmendorf	.10	.05	.03
(312) Pat Studstill	.20	.10	.06
(313) Paul Warfield	1.50	.70	.45
(314) Doug Crusan	.10	.05	.03
(315) Bob Kuechenberg	.50	.25	.15
(316) Bob DeMarco	.20	.10	.06
(317) Larry Little	1.00	.50	.30
(318) Norm Evans	.20	.10	.06
(319) Marv Fleming	.20	.10	.06
(320) Howard Twilley	.30	.15	.09
(321) Bob Griese	2.50	1.25	.70
(322) Jim Klick	.60	.30	.20
(323) Larry Csonka	2.00	1.00	.60
(324) Garo Yepremian	.30	.15	.09
(325) Jim Riley	.10	.05	.03
(326) Manny Fernandez	.30	.15	.09
(327) Bob Heinz	.10	.05	.03
(328) Bill Stanfill	.30	.15	.09
(329) Doug Swift	.10	.05	.03
(330) Nick Buoniconti	1.00	.50	.30
(331) Mike Kolen	.10	.05	.03
(332) Tim Foley	.30	.15	.09
(333) Curtis Johnson	.10	.05	.03
(334) Dick Anderson	.40	.20	.12
(335) Jake Scott	.50	.25	.15
(336) Larry Seiple	.10	.05	.03
(337) Gene Washington	.20	.10	.06
(338) Grady Alderman	.10	.05	.03
(339) Ed White	.25	.13	.08
(340) Mick Tingelhoff	.20	.10	.06
(341) Milt Sunde	.10	.05	.03
(342) Ron Yary	.50	.25	.15
(343) John Beasley	.10	.05	.03
(344) John Henderson	.10	.05	.03
(345) Fran Tarkenton	4.00	2.00	1.25
(346) Clint Jones	.20	.10	.06
(347) Dave Osborn	.20	.10	.06
(348) Fred Cox	.20	.10	.06
(349) Carl Eller	.50	.25	.15
(350) Gary Larsen	.10	.05	.03
(351) Alan Page	1.00	.50	.30
(352) Jim Marshall	1.00	.50	.30
(353) Roy Winston	.20	.10	.06
(354) Lonnie Warwick	.10	.05	.03
(355) Wally Hilgenberg	.10	.05	.03
(356) Bobby Bryant	.15	.08	.05
(357) Ed Sharockman	.10	.05	.03
(358) Charlie West	.10	.05	.03
(359) Paul Krause	.60	.30	.20
(360) Bob Lee	.20	.10	.06
(361) Randy Vataha	.40	.20	.12
(362) Mike Montler	.10	.05	.03
(363) Halvor Hagen	.10	.05	.03
(364) Jon Morris	.10	.05	.03
(365) Len St. Jean	.10	.05	.03
(366) Tom Neville	.10	.05	.03
(367) Tom Beer	.15	.08	.05
(368) Ron Sellers	.20	.10	.06
(369) Jim Plunkett	1.00	.50	.30
(370) Carl Garrett	.20	.10	.06
(371) Jim Nance	.30	.15	.09
(372) Charlie Gogolak	.20	.10	.06
(373) Ike Lassiter	.10	.05	.03
(374) Dave Rowe	.10	.05	.03
(375) Julius Adams	.20	.10	.06

(376) Dennis Wirgowski	.10	.05	.03
(377) Ed Weisacosky	.10	.05	.03
(378) Jim Cheyunski	.10	.05	.03
(379) Steve Kiner	.10	.05	.03
(380) Larry Carwell	.10	.05	.03
(381) John Outlaw	.10	.05	.03
(382) Rickie Harris	.10	.05	.03
(383) Don Webb	.10	.05	.03
(384) Tom Janik	.10	.05	.03
(385) Al Dodd	.20	.10	.06
(386) Don Morrison	.10	.05	.03
(387) Jake Kupp	.10	.05	.03
(388) John Didion	.10	.05	.03
(389) Del Williams	.10	.05	.03
(390) Glen Ray Hines	.10	.05	.03
(391) Dave Parks	.20	.10	.06
(392) Dan Abramowicz	.40	.20	.12
(393) Archie Manning	2.00	1.00	.60
(394) Bob Gresham	.10	.05	.03
(395) Virgil Robinson	.10	.05	.03
(396) Charlie Durkee	.10	.05	.03
(397) Richard Neal	.10	.05	.03
(398) Bob Pollard	.10	.05	.03
(399) Dave Long	.10	.05	.03
(400) Joe Owens	.10	.05	.03
(401) Carl Cunningham	.10	.05	.03
(402) Jim Flanigan	.15	.08	.05
(403) Wayne Colman	.10	.05	.03
(404) D'Artagnan Martin	.10	.05	.03
(405) Delles Howell	.10	.05	.03
(406) Hugo Hollas	.10	.05	.03
(407) Doug Wyatt	.10	.05	.03
(408) Julian Fagan	.10	.05	.03
(409) Don Hermann	.10	.05	.03
(410) Willie Young	.10	.05	.03
(411) Bob Hyland	.10	.05	.03
(412) Greg Larson	.10	.05	.03
(413) Doug Van Horn	.10	.05	.03
(414) Charlie Harper	.10	.05	.03
(415) Bob Tucker	.25	.13	.08
(416) Joe Morrison	.20	.10	.06
(417) Randy Johnson	.20	.10	.06
(418) Tucker Frederickson	.30	.15	.09
(419) Ron Johnson	.30	.15	.09
(420) Pete Gogolak	.20	.10	.06
(421) Henry Reed	.10	.05	.03
(422) Jim Kanicki	.10	.05	.03
(423) Roland Lakes	.10	.05	.03
(424) John Douglas	.10	.05	.03
(425) Ron Hornsby	.10	.05	.03
(426) Jim Files	.10	.05	.03
(427) Willie Williams	.10	.05	.03
(428) Otto Brown	.10	.05	.03
(429) Scott Eaton	.10	.05	.03
(430) Carl Lockhart	.20	.10	.06
(431) Tom Blanchard	.20	.10	.06
(432) Rocky Thompson	.20	.10	.06
(433) Rich Caster	.30	.15	.09
(434) Randy Rasmussen	.10	.05	.03
(435) John Schmitt	.10	.05	.03
(436) Dave Herman	.20	.10	.06
(437) Winston Hill	.20	.10	.06
(438) Pete Lammons	.20	.10	.06
(439) Don Maynard	2.00	1.00	.60
(440) Joe Namath	10.00	5.00	3.00
(441) Emerson Boozer	.30	.15	.09
(442) John Riggins	4.00	2.00	1.25
(443) George Nock	.10	.05	.03
(444) Bobby Howfield	.10	.05	.03
(445) Gerry Philbin	.10	.05	.03
(446) John Little	.10	.05	.03
(447) Chuck Hinton	.10	.05	.03
(448) Mark Lomas	.10	.05	.03
(449) Ralph Baker	.10	.05	.03
(450) Al Atkinson	.10	.05	.03
(451) Larry Grantham	.20	.10	.06
(452) John Dockery	.10	.05	.03
(453) Earlie Thomas	.10	.05	.03
(454) Phil Wise	.10	.05	.03
(455) W.K. Hicks	.10	.05	.03
(456) Steve O'Neal	.15	.08	.05
(457) Drew Buie	.10	.05	.03
(458) Art Shell	2.00	1.00	.60
(459) Gene Upshaw	2.00	1.00	.60
(460) Jim Otto	.75	.40	.25
(461) Geprge Buehler	.10	.05	.03
(462) Bob Brown	.40	.20	.12
(463) Ray Chester	.40	.20	.12
(464) Fred Biletnikoff	2.00	1.00	.60
(465) Daryle Lamonica	.60	.30	.20
(466) Marv Hubbard	.20	.10	.06
(467) Clarence Davis	.20	.10	.06
(468) George Blanda	2.00	1.00	.60
(469) Tony Cline	.10	.05	.03

(470) Art Thoms	.10	.05	.03
(471) Tom Keating	.20	.10	.06
(472) Ben Davidson	1.00	.50	.30
(473) Phil Villapiano	.40	.20	.12
(474) Dan Conners	.10	.05	.03
(475) Duane Benson	.10	.05	.03
(476) Nemiah Wilson	.10	.05	.03
(477) Willie Brown	1.00	.50	.30
(478) George Atkinson	.20	.10	.06
(479) Jack Tatum	.40	.20	.12
(480) Jerry DePoyster	.10	.05	.03
(481) Harold Jackson	.50	.25	.15
(482) Wade Key	.10	.05	.03
(483) Henry Allison	.10	.05	.03
(484) Mike Evans	.10	.05	.03
(485) Steve Smith	.20	.10	.06
(486) Harold Carmichael	1.25	.60	.40
(487) Ben Hawkins	.20	.10	.06
(488) Pete Liske	.40	.20	.12
(489) Rick Arrington	.10	.05	.03
(490) Lee Bouggess	.10	.05	.03
(491) Tom Woodeshick	.20	.10	.06
(492) Tom Dempsey	.50	.25	.15
(493) Richard Harris	.20	.10	.06
(494) Don Hultz	.10	.05	.03
(495) Ernie Calloway	.15	.08	.05
(496) Mel Tom	.10	.05	.03
(497) Steve Zabel	.20	.10	.06
(498) Tim Rossovich	.20	.10	.06
(499) Ron Porter	.10	.05	.03
(500) Al Nelson	.10	.05	.03
(501) Nate Ramsey	.10	.05	.03
(502) Leroy Keyes	.40	.20	.12
(503) Bill Bradley	.50	.25	.15
(504) Tom McNeill	.10	.05	.03
(505) Dave Smith	.10	.05	.03
(506) Jon Kolb	.10	.05	.03
(507) Gerry Mullins	.10	.05	.03
(508) Ray Mansfield	.10	.05	.03
(509) Bruce Van Dyke	.10	.05	.03
(510) John Brown	.10	.05	.03
(511) Ron Shanklin	.30	.15	.09
(512) Terry Bradshaw	7.50	3.75	2.25
(513) Terry Hanratty	.40	.20	.12
(514) Preston Pearson	.40	.20	.12
(515) John Fuqua	.20	.10	.06
(516) Roy Gerela	.10	.05	.03
(517) L.C. Greenwood	.75	.40	.25
(518) Joe Greene	2.50	1.25	.70
(519) Lloyd Voss	.10	.05	.03
(520) Dwight White	.20	.10	.06
(521) Jack Ham	2.50	1.25	.70
(522) Chuck Allen	.10	.05	.03
(523) Brian Stenger	.10	.05	.03
(524) Andy Russell	.75	.40	.25
(525) John Rowser	.10	.05	.03
(526) Mel Blount	2.00	1.00	.60
(527) Mike Wagner	.20	.10	.06
(528) Bobby Walden	.10	.05	.03
(529) Mel Gray	.30	.15	.09
(530) Bob Reynolds	.10	.05	.03
(531) Dan Dierdorf	.60	.30	.20
(532) Wayne Mulligan	.10	.05	.03
(533) Clyde Williams	.10	.05	.03
(534) Ernie McMillan	.10	.05	.03
(535) Jackie Smith	1.00	.50	.30
(536) John Gilliam	.20	.10	.06
(537) Jim Hart	.50	.25	.15
(538) Pete Beathard	.40	.20	.12
(539) Johnny Roland	.30	.15	.09
(540) Jim Bakken	.30	.15	.09
(541) Ron Yankowski	.10	.05	.03
(542) Fred Heron	.15	.08	.05
(543) Bob Rowe	.10	.05	.03
(544) Chuck Walker	.10	.05	.03
(545) Larry Stallings	.20	.10	.06
(546) Jamie Rivers	.10	.05	.03
(547) Mike McGill	.10	.05	.03
(548) Miller Farr	.10	.05	.03
(549) Roger Wehrli	.30	.15	.09
(550) Larry Willingham	.10	.05	.03
(551) Larry Wilson	1.00	.50	.30
(552) Chuck Latourette	.10	.05	.03
(553) Billy Parks	.20	.10	.06
(554) Terry Owens	.25	.13	.08
(555) Doug Wilkerson	.10	.05	.03
(556) Carl Mauck	.10	.05	.03
(557) Walt Sweeney	.10	.05	.03
(558) Russ Washington	.10	.05	.03
(559) Pettis Norman	.20	.10	.06
(560) Gary Garrison	.20	.10	.06
(561) John Hadl	.60	.30	.20
(562) Mike Montgomery	.10	.05	.03
(563) Mike Garrett	.30	.15	.09

(564) Dennis Partee	.10	.05	.03
(565) Deacon Jones	1.00	.50	.30
(566) Ron East	.10	.05	.03
(567) Kevin Hardy	.10	.05	.03
(568) Steve DeLong	.20	.10	.06
(569) Rick Redman	.10	.05	.03
(570) Bob Babich	.15	.08	.05
(571) Pete Barnes	.10	.05	.03
(572) Bob Howard	.10	.05	.03
(573) Joe Beauchamp	.10	.05	.03
(574) Bryant Salter	.10	.05	.03
(575) Chris Fletcher	.10	.05	.03
(576) Jerry LeVias	.20	.10	.06
(577) Dick Witcher	.10	.05	.03
(578) Len Rohde	.12	.06	.04
(579) Randy Beisler	.10	.05	.03
(580) Forrest Blue	.20	.10	.06
(581) Woody Peoples	.10	.05	.03
(582) Cas Banaszek	.10	.05	.03
(583) Ted Kwalick	.40	.20	.12
(584) Gene Washington	.50	.25	.15
(585) John Brodie	1.25	.60	.40
(586) Ken Willard	.40	.20	.12
(587) Vic Washington	.20	.10	.06
(588) Bruce Gossett	.10	.05	.03
(589) Tommy Hart	.15	.08	.05
(590) Charlie Krueger	.20	.10	.06
(591) Earl Edwards	.10	.05	.03
(592) Cedric Hardman	.20	.10	.06
(593) Dave Wilcox	.25	.13	.08
(594) Frank Nunley	.10	.05	.03
(595) Skip Vanderbundt	.10	.05	.03
(596) Jimmy Johnson	.60	.30	.20
(597) Bruce Taylor	.30	.15	.09
(598) Mel Phillips	.10	.05	.03
(599) Rosey Taylor	.20	.10	.06
(600) Steve Spurrier	2.50	1.25	.70
(601) Charley Taylor	1.50	.70	.45
(602) Jim Snowden	.10	.05	.03
(603) Ray Schoenke	.10	.05	.03
(604) Len Hauss	.20	.10	.06
(605) John Wilbur	.10	.05	.03
(606) Walt Rock	.10	.05	.03
(607) Jerry Smith	.20	.10	.06
(608) Roy Jefferson	.20	.10	.06
(609) Bill Kilmer	1.00	.50	.30
(610) Larry Brown	1.00	.50	.30
(611) Charlie Harraway	.20	.10	.06
(612) Curt Knight	.10	.05	.03
(613) Ron McDole	.10	.05	.03
(614) Manuel Sistrunk	.10	.05	.03
(615) Diron Talbert	.20	.10	.06
(616) Verlon Biggs	.10	.05	.03
(617) Jack Pardee	.75	.40	.25
(618) Myron Pottios	.20	.10	.06
(619) Chris Hanburger	.50	.25	.15
(620) Pat Fischer	.20	.10	.06
(621) Mike Bass	.10	.05	.03
(622) Richie Petitbon	.20	.10	.06
(623) Brig Owens	.10	.05	.03
(624) Mike Bragg	.15	.08	.05

1972 Sunoco Stamps Update

These unnumbered 1-5/8" x 2-3/8" stamps are identical to the 1972 Sunoco stamps, but were not listed in the album which was produced to house the stamps. They were issued as team sheets later in the year.

	NM	E	VG
Complete Set (82):	75.00	37.00	22.00
Common Player:	1.00	.50	.30
(1) Clarence Ellis	1.00	.50	.30
(2) Dave Hampton	1.50	.70	.45
(3) Dennis Havig	1.00	.50	.30
(4) John James	1.00	.50	.30
(5) Joe Profit	1.00	.50	.30
(6) Lonnie Hepburn	1.00	.50	.30
(7) Dennis Nelson	1.00	.50	.30
(8) Mike McBath	1.00	.50	.30
(9) Walt Patulski	1.00	.50	.30
(10) Bob Asher	1.00	.50	.30
(11) Steve DeLong	1.00	.50	.30
(12) Tony McGee	1.00	.50	.30
(13) James Osborne	1.00	.50	.30
(14) Jim Seymour	1.00	.50	.30
(15) Tommy Casanova	1.50	.70	.45
(16) Neil Craig	1.00	.50	.30
(17) Essex Johnson	1.25	.60	.40
(18) Sherman White	1.00	.50	.30
(19) Bob Briggs	1.00	.50	.30
(20) Thom Darden	1.25	.60	.40
(21) Marv Bateman	1.00	.50	.30
(22) Toni Fritsch	1.00	.50	.30
(23) Calvin Hill	3.00	1.50	.90
(24) Pat Toomay	1.25	.60	.40

(25)	Pete Duranko	1.00	.50	.30
(26)	Marv Montgomery	1.00	.50	.30
(27)	Rod Sherman	1.00	.50	.30
(28)	Bob Kowalkowski	1.00	.50	.30
(29)	Jim Mitchell	1.00	.50	.30
(30)	Larry Woods	1.00	.50	.30
(31)	Willie Buchanon	1.50	.70	.45
(32)	Leland Glass	1.00	.50	.30
(33)	MacArthur Lane	1.50	.70	.45
(34)	Chester Marcol	1.00	.50	.30
(35)	Ron Widby	1.00	.50	.30
(36)	Ken Burrough	1.50	.70	.45
(37)	Calvin Hunt	1.00	.50	.30
(38)	Ron Saul	1.00	.50	.30
(39)	Greg Simpson	1.00	.50	.30
(40)	Mike Sensibaugh	1.00	.50	.30
(41)	Dave Chapple	1.00	.50	.30
(42)	Jim Langer	6.00	3.00	1.75
(43)	Mike Eischeid	1.00	.50	.30
(44)	John Gilliam	1.25	.60	.40
(45)	Ron Acks	1.00	.50	.30
(46)	Bob Gladieux	1.00	.50	.30
(47)	Honoe Jackson	1.00	.50	.30
(48)	Reggie Rucker	1.50	.70	.45
(49)	Pat Studstill	1.00	.50	.30
(50)	Bob Windsor	1.00	.50	.30
(51)	Joe Federspiel	1.00	.50	.30
(52)	Bob Newland	4.00	2.00	1.25
(53)	Pete Athas	1.00	.50	.30
(54)	Charlie Evans	1.00	.50	.30
(55)	Jack Gregory	1.00	.50	.30
(56)	John Mendenhall	1.00	.50	.30
(57)	Ed Bell	1.00	.50	.30
(58)	John Elliott	1.00	.50	.30
(59)	Chris Farasopoulos	1.00	.50	.30
(60)	Bob Svihus	1.00	.50	.30
(61)	Steve Tannen	1.00	.50	.30
(62)	Cliff Branch	3.00	1.50	.90
(63)	Gus Otto	1.00	.50	.30
(64)	Otis Sistrunk	1.25	.60	.40
(65)	Charlie Smith	1.00	.50	.30
(66)	John Reaves	1.00	.50	.30
(67)	Larry Watkins	1.00	.50	.30
(68)	Henry Davis	1.00	.50	.30
(69)	Ben McGee	1.00	.50	.30
(70)	Donny Anderson	1.25	.60	.40
(71)	Walker Gillette	1.00	.50	.30
(72)	Martin Imhoff	1.00	.50	.30
(73)	Bobby Moore (aka Ahmad Rashad)	8.00	4.00	2.50
(74)	Norm Thompson	1.00	.50	.30
(75)	Lionel Aldridge	1.00	.50	.30
(76)	Dave Costa	1.00	.50	.30
(77)	Cid Edwards	1.00	.50	.30
(78)	Tim Rossovich	1.00	.50	.30
(79)	Dave Williams	1.00	.50	.30
(80)	Johnny Fuller	1.00	.50	.30
(81)	Terry Hermeling	1.00	.50	.30
(82)	Paul Laaveg	1.00	.50	.30

1991 Surge WLAF Police

The 39-card, 2-3/8" x 3-1/2" set, sponsored by American Airlines, features players from the WLAF Sacramento Surge team. The card fronts feature a color photo with an American Airlines logo appearing along the top border. The lower right corner contains a triangle with the Surge helmet. The card backs give bio information and a safety tip.

		NM/M	NM	E
	Complete Set (39):	20.00	15.00	8.00
	Common Player:	.60	.45	.25
1	Mike Adams	.75	.60	.30
2	Sam Archer	.60	.45	.25
3	John Buddenberg	.60	.45	.25
4	Jon Burman	.60	.45	.25
5	Tony Burse	.75	.60	.30
6	Ricardo Cartwright	.60	.45	.25
7	Greg Coauette	.60	.45	.25
8	Paco Craig	.60	.45	.25
9	John Dominic	.60	.45	.25
10	Mike Elkins	1.00	.70	.40
11	Oliver Erhorn	.60	.45	.25
12	Mel Farr	1.00	.70	.40
13	Victor Floyd	.60	.45	.25
14	Byron Forsythe	.60	.45	.25
15	Paul Frazier	.60	.45	.25
16	Tom Gerhart	.60	.45	.25
17	Mike Hall	.60	.45	.25
18	Anthony Henton	.60	.45	.25
19	Nate Hill	.60	.45	.25
20	Kubanai Kalombo	.60	.45	.25
21	Shawn Knight	1.00	.70	.40
22	Sean Kugler	.60	.45	.25
23	Matti Lindholm	.60	.45	.25
24	Art Malone	.75	.60	.30
25	Robert McWright	.60	.45	.25
26	Tim Moore	.60	.45	.25

27	Pete Najarian	.60	.45	.25
28	Mark Nua	.60	.45	.25
29	Carl Parker	.60	.45	.25
30	Leon Perry	.60	.45	.25
31	Juha Salo	.60	.45	.25
32	Saute Sapolu	.60	.45	.25
33	Paul Soltis	.60	.45	.25
34	Richard Stephens	.60	.45	.25
35	Kay Stephenson (CO)	.75	.60	.30
36	Kendall Trainor	.75	.60	.30
37	Mike Wallace	.60	.45	.25
38	Curtis Wilson	.60	.45	.25
39	Rick Zumwalt	.60	.45	.25

1988 Swell Football Greats

Swell's first set picturing members of the Pro Football Hall of Fame featured 144 players, coaches and executives. The set was released in 10-card wax packs and in complete sets in August 1988. A separate checklist was included. The standard-size cards feature full-color photos or sepia-toned black-and-white photos (in the case of older players) enclosed in a blue border. A red Swell logo is seen in the upper left corner; the Hall of Fame's 25th Anniversary logo is in the lower left, and the player's name and position is in white type in a red box in the lower right corner. Card backs feature blue borders and the player's biographical notes and career statistics in a white rectangle. Cards are printed on white cardboard stock. There have been some reports of small nicks and notches along the tops of some of the cards in the factory-issued sets.

		NM/M	NM	E
	Complete Set (144):	15.00	11.00	6.00
	Common Player:	.10	.08	.04
1	Pete Rozell	.30	.25	.12
2	Joe Namath	1.50	1.25	.60
3	Herb Gatski	.10	.08	.04
4	O.J. Simpson	2.00	1.50	.80
5	Roger Staubach	1.50	1.25	.60
6	Herb Adderly	.10	.08	.04
7	Lance Alworth	.25	.20	.10
8	Doug Atkins	.10	.08	.04
9	Red Badgro	.10	.08	.04
10	Cliff Battles	.10	.08	.04
11	Sammy Baugh	.35	.25	.14
12	Raymond Berry	.15	.11	.06
13	Charles Bidwell Sr.	.10	.08	.04
14	Chuck Bednarik	.15	.11	.06
15	Bert Bell	.10	.08	.04
16	Bobby Bell	.10	.08	.04
17	George Blanda	.25	.20	.10
18	Jim Brown	1.00	.70	.40
19	Paul Brown	.15	.11	.06
20	Roosevelt Brown	.10	.08	.04
21	Ray Flaherty	.10	.08	.04
22	Len Ford	.15	.11	.06
23	Dan Fortmann	.10	.08	.04
24	Bill George	.10	.08	.04
25	Art Donovan	.10	.08	.04
26	John (Paddy) Driscoll	.10	.08	.04
27	Jimmy Conzelman	.10	.08	.04
28	Willie Davis	.10	.08	.04
29	Earl "Dutch" Clark	.10	.08	.04
30	George Connor	.10	.08	.04
31	Guy Chamberlain	.10	.08	.04
32	Jack Christiansen	.10	.08	.04
33	Tony Canadeo	.15	.11	.06
34	Joe Carr	.10	.08	.04
35	Willie Brown	.10	.08	.04
36	Dick Butkus	.35	.25	.14
37	Bill Dudley	.10	.08	.04
38	Turk Edwards	.10	.08	.04
39	Weeb Ewbank	.20	.15	.08
40	Tom Fears	.10	.08	.04
41	Otto Graham	.40	.30	.15
42	Harold "Red" Grange	.50	.40	.20
43	Frank Gifford	.60	.45	.25
44	Sid Gillman	.10	.08	.04
45	Forrest Gregg	.10	.08	.04
46	Lou Groza	.25	.20	.10
47	Joe Guyon	.10	.08	.04

48	George Halas	.20	.15	.08
49	Ed Healy	.10	.08	.04
50	Mel Hein	.10	.08	.04
51	Pete Henry	.15	.11	.06
52	Arnie Herber	.10	.08	.04
53	Bill Hewitt	.10	.08	.04
54	Clark Hinkle	.10	.08	.04
55	Elroy Hirsch	.25	.20	.10
56	Robert Hubbard	.10	.08	.04
57	Sam Huff	.10	.08	.04
58	Lamar Hunt	.15	.11	.06
59	Don Hutson	.20	.15	.08
60	Deacon Jones	.10	.08	.04
61	Sonny Jurgensen	.15	.11	.06
62	Walt Kiesling	.10	.08	.04
63	Frank Kinard	.10	.08	.04
64	Curley Lambeau	.10	.08	.04
65	Dick "Night Train" Lane	.10	.08	.04
66	Yale Lary	.10	.08	.04
67	Dante Lavelli	.10	.08	.04
68	Bobby Lane	.20	.15	.08
69	Alphonse Leemans	.10	.08	.04
70	Bob Lilly	.15	.11	.06
71	Vince Lombardi	.35	.25	.14
72	Sid Luckman	.20	.15	.08
73	William Roy Lyman	.10	.08	.04
74	Tim Mara	.10	.08	.04
75	Gino Marchetti	.15	.11	.06
76	George Preston Marshall	.10	.08	.04
77	Ollie Matson	.15	.11	.06
78	George McAfee	.10	.08	.04
79	Mike McCormack	.10	.08	.04
80	Hugh McElhenny	.15	.11	.06
81	John McNally	.15	.11	.06
82	Mike Michalske	.10	.08	.04
83	Wayne Millner	.10	.08	.04
84	Bobby Mitchell	.10	.08	.04
85	Ron Mix	.15	.11	.06
86	Lenny Moore	.15	.11	.06
87	Marion Motley	.15	.11	.06
88	George Musso	.10	.08	.04
89	Bronko Nagurski	.35	.25	.14
90	Earle Neale	.10	.08	.04
91	Ernie Nevers	.20	.15	.08
92	Ray Nitschke	.20	.15	.08
93	Leo Nomellini	.10	.08	.04
94	Merlin Olsen	.15	.11	.06
95	Jim Otto	.10	.08	.04
96	Steve Owen	.10	.08	.04
97	Clarence Parker	.10	.08	.04
98	Jim Parker	.10	.08	.04
99	Joe Perry	.15	.11	.06
100	Pete Pihos	.10	.08	.04
101	Hugh Ray	.10	.08	.04
102	Dan Reeves	.10	.08	.04
103	Jim Ringo	.10	.08	.04
104	Andy Robustelli	.10	.08	.04
105	Art Rooney	.10	.08	.04
106	Gale Sayers	.50	.40	.20
107	Joe Schmidt	.10	.08	.04
108	Bart Starr	.75	.60	.30
109	Ernie Stautner	.15	.11	.06
110	Ken Strong	.10	.08	.04
111	Joe Stydahar	.15	.11	.06
112	Charley Taylor	.15	.11	.06
113	Jim Taylor	.15	.11	.06
114	Jim Thorpe	.75	.60	.30
115	Y.A. Tittle	.35	.25	.14
116	George Trafton	.10	.08	.04
117	Charley Trippi	.10	.08	.04
118	Emlen Tunnell	.10	.08	.04
119	Clyde Turner	.10	.08	.04
120	Johnny Unitas	1.75	1.25	.70
121	Norm Van Brocklin	.20	.15	.08
122	Steve Van Buren	.10	.08	.04
123	Paul Warfield	.10	.08	.04
124	Bob Waterfield	.20	.15	.08
125	Arnie Weinmeister	.10	.08	.04
126	Bill Willis	.10	.08	.04
127	Larry Wilson	.10	.08	.04
128	Alex Wojciechowicz	.10	.08	.04
129	Doak Walker	.25	.20	.10
130	Willie Lanier	.10	.08	.04
131	Paul Hornung	.25	.20	.10
132	Ken Houston	.10	.08	.04
133	Fran Tarkenton	.50	.40	.20
134	Don Maynard	.15	.11	.06
135	Larry Csonka	.30	.25	.12
136	Joe Greene	.15	.11	.06
137	Len Dawson	.15	.11	.06
138	Gene Upshaw	.10	.08	.04
139	Jim Langer	.10	.08	.04
140	John Henry Johnson	.10	.08	.04
141	Fred Biletnikoff	.15	.11	.06
142	Mike Ditka	.50	.40	.20
143	Jack Ham	.15	.11	.06
144	Alan Page	.15	.11	.06

1989 Swell Football Greats

The 1989 edition of Swell Football Greats again included every member of the Pro Football Hall of Fame inducted through 1989. Swell had released its initial set of HOFers in 1988. The standard-size cards featured white borders with red striping. The Swell logo is in the upper left corner, and a blue flag carries the "Football Greats" slogan across the bottom of the card, just above the player's name and position. Most of the photos are in color. Those that feature early greats are sepia-toned. Backs are printed in two colors and contain biographical notes and career highlights as well as the year of Hall of Fame induction. Cards, which were released in late August 1989, were issued in wax packs of 10 cards each. Collector's Sets were also released by Swell, which is a division of the Philadelphia Chewing Gum Corp. One variation exists in the set: In the upper right corner of card #27, Sid Luckman shows "Sid" and the first part of "Chicago" printed in white. This was airbrushed out in later versions. The set has so little collector interest, however, that the error has no real additional value.

		NM/M	NM	E
Complete Set (150):		15.00	11.00	6.00
Common Player:		.10	.08	.04
1	Terry Bradshaw	1.00	.70	.40
2	Bert Bell	.10	.08	.04
3	Joe Carr	.10	.08	.04
4	Earl "Dutch" Clark	.10	.08	.04
5	Harold "Red" Grange	.60	.45	.25
6	Wilbur "Pete" Henry	.10	.08	.04
7	Mel Hein	.10	.08	.04
8	Cal Hubbard	.10	.08	.04
9	George Halas	.30	.25	.12
10	Don Hutson	.15	.11	.06
11	Curley Lambeau	.10	.08	.04
12	Tim Mara	.10	.08	.04
13	George Preston Marshall	.10	.08	.04
14	John McNally	.10	.08	.04
15	Bronko Nagurski	.40	.30	.15
16	Ernie Nevers	.15	.11	.06
17	Jim Thorpe	.50	.40	.20
18	Ed Healy	.10	.08	.04
19	Clarke Hinkle	.10	.08	.04
20	Link Lyman	.10	.08	.04
21	Mike Michalske	.10	.08	.04
22	George Trafton	.10	.08	.04
23	Guy Chamberlain	.15	.11	.06
24	John "Paddy" Driscoll	.10	.08	.04
25	Dan Fortmann	.10	.08	.04
26	Otto Graham	.40	.30	.15
27A	Sid Luckman	.35	.25	.14
27B	Sid Luckman (corrected)	1.25	.90	.50
28	Steve Van Buren	.15	.11	.06
29	Bob Waterfield	.20	.15	.08
30	Bill Dudley	.15	.11	.06
31	Joe Guyon	.10	.08	.04
32	Arnie Herber	.10	.08	.04
33	Walt Kiesling	.10	.08	.04
34	Jimmy Conzelman	.10	.08	.04
35	Art Rooney	.10	.08	.04
36	Willie Wood	.10	.08	.04
37	Art Shell	.25	.20	.10
38	Sammy Baugh	.45	.35	.20
39	Mel Blount	.10	.08	.04
40	Lamar Hunt	.15	.11	.06
41	Norm Van Brocklin	.30	.25	.12
42	Y.A. Tittle	.35	.25	.14
43	Andy Robustelli	.10	.08	.04
44	Vince Lombardi	.35	.25	.14
45	Frank Kinard	.10	.08	.04
46	Bill Hewitt	.10	.08	.04
47	Jim Brown	1.00	.70	.40
48	Pete Pihos	.10	.08	.04
49	Hugh McElhenny	.15	.11	.06
50	Tom Fears	.15	.11	.06
51	Jack Christiansen	.10	.08	.04
52	Ernie Stautner	.15	.11	.06
53	Joe Perry	.15	.11	.06
54	Leo Nomellini	.15	.11	.06
55	Earl "Greasy" Neale	.10	.08	.04
56	Turk Edwards	.10	.08	.04
57	Alex Wojciechowicz	.10	.08	.04
58	Charley Trippi	.10	.08	.04
59	Marion Motley	.20	.15	.08
60	Wayne Miller	.10	.08	.04
61	Elroy Hirsch	.15	.11	.06
62	Art Donovan	.10	.08	.04
63	Cliff Battles	.10	.08	.04
64	Emlen Tunnell	.15	.11	.06
65	Joe Stydahar	.10	.08	.04
66	Ken Strong	.10	.08	.04
67	Dan Reeves	.10	.08	.04
68	Bobby Layne	.30	.25	.12
69	Paul Brown	.20	.15	.08
70	Charles Bidwell Sr.	.10	.08	.04
71	Chuck Bednarik	.15	.11	.06
72	Bulldog Turner	.10	.08	.04
73	Hugh "Shorty" Ray	.10	.08	.04
74	Steve Owen	.10	.08	.04
75	George McAfee	.10	.08	.04
76	Forrest Gregg	.15	.11	.06
77	Frank Gifford	.50	.40	.20
78	Jim Taylor	.15	.11	.06
79	Len Ford	.10	.08	.04
80	Ray Flaherty	.10	.08	.04
81	Lenny Moore	.15	.11	.06
82	Dante Lavelli	.10	.08	.04
83	George Connor	.15	.11	.06
84	Roosevelt Grier	.10	.08	.04
85	Dick "Night Train" Lane	.10	.08	.04
86	Lou Groza	.30	.25	.12
87	Bill George	.10	.08	.04
88	Tony Canadeo	.10	.08	.04
89	Joe Schmidt	.10	.08	.04
90	Jim Parker	.10	.08	.04
91	Wayne Millner	.10	.08	.04
92	Raymond Berry	.20	.15	.08
93	Ollie Matson	.15	.11	.06
94	Gino Marchetti	.10	.08	.04
95	Larry Wilson	.10	.08	.04
96	Ray Nitschke	.25	.20	.10
97	Tuffy Leemans	.10	.08	.04
98	Weeb Ewbank	.10	.08	.04
99	Lance Alworth	.30	.25	.12
100	Bill Willis	.10	.08	.04
101	Bart Starr	.35	.25	.14
102	Gale Sayers	.35	.25	.14
103	Herb Adderly	.10	.08	.04
104	Johnny Unitas	1.00	.70	.40
105	Ron Mix	.10	.08	.04
106	Yale Lary	.10	.08	.04
107	Red Badgro	.10	.08	.04
108	Jim Otto	.10	.08	.04
109	Bob Lilly	.15	.11	.06
110	Deacon Jones	.15	.11	.06
111	Doug Atkins	.10	.08	.04
112	Jim Ringo	.10	.08	.04
113	Willie Davis	.10	.08	.04
114	George Blanda	.35	.25	.14
115	Bobby Bell	.10	.08	.04
116	Merlin Olsen	.15	.11	.06
117	George Musso	.10	.08	.04
118	Sam Huff	.15	.11	.06
119	Paul Warfield	.25	.20	.10
120	Bobby Mitchell	.10	.08	.04
121	Sonny Jurgensen	.25	.20	.10
122	Sid Gilman	.10	.08	.04
123	Arnie Weinmeister	.10	.08	.04
124	Charley Taylor	.10	.08	.04
125	Mike McCormack	.10	.08	.04
126	Willie Brown	.10	.08	.04
127	O.J. Simpson	1.50	1.25	.60
128	Pete Rozelle	.25	.20	.10
129	Joe Namath	1.25	.90	.50
130	Frank Gatski	.10	.08	.04
131	Willie Lanier	.10	.08	.04
132	Ken Houston	.10	.08	.04
133	Paul Hornung	.25	.20	.10
134	Roger Staubach	1.25	.90	.50
135	Len Dawson	.15	.11	.06
136	Larry Csonka	.30	.25	.12
137	Doak Walker	.15	.11	.06
138	Fran Tarkenton	.60	.45	.25
139	Don Maynard	.15	.11	.06
140	Jim Langer	.15	.11	.06
141	John Henry Johnson	.10	.08	.04
142	Joe Greene	.20	.15	.08
143	Jack Ham	.10	.08	.04
144	Mike Ditka	.75	.60	.30
145	Alan Page	.10	.08	.04
146	Fred Biletnikoff	.15	.11	.06
147	Gene Upshaw	.10	.08	.04
148	Dick Butkus	.50	.40	.20
149	**Checklist 1 & 2**	.10	.08	.04
150	**Checklist 3 & 4**	.10	.08	.04

1990 Swell Football Greats

Swell, which had released two straight sets of Pro Football Hall of Famers, returned with this 160-card set, also featuring HOFers. Produced by the Philadelphia Gum Co., the set includes 155 HOFers, two checklists, and three Hall of Fame cards. Cards are standard size, with a white border and blue and yellow lines. As in previous issues, some cards of the older players may have sepia-toned, rather than full-color, photos.

		NM/M	NM	E
Complete Set (160):		15.00	11.00	6.00
Common Player:		.10	.08	.04
1	Terry Bradshaw	1.00	.70	.40
2	Bert Bell	.10	.08	.04
3	Joe Carr	.10	.08	.04
4	Dutch Clark	.15	.11	.06
5	Harold "Red" Grange	.40	.30	.15
6	Pete Henry	.10	.08	.04
7	Mel Hein	.10	.08	.04
8	Cal Hubbard	.10	.08	.04
9	George Halas	.25	.20	.10
10	Don Hutson	.15	.11	.06
11	Curly Lambeau	.15	.11	.06
12	Tim Mara	.10	.08	.04
13	G. Preston Marshall	.10	.08	.04
14	John McNally	.10	.08	.04
15	Bronko Nagurski	.35	.25	.14
16	Ernie Nevers	.15	.11	.06
17	Jim Thorpe	.75	.60	.30
18	Ed Healy	.10	.08	.04
19	Clark Hinkle	.10	.08	.04
20	Link Lyman	.10	.08	.04
21	Mike Michalske	.10	.08	.04
22	George Trafton	.10	.08	.04
23	Guy Chamberlain	.10	.08	.04
24	Paddy Driscoll	.10	.08	.04
25	Dan Fortmann	.10	.08	.04
26	Otto Graham	.50	.40	.20
27	Sid Luckman	.40	.30	.15
28	Steve Van Buren	.15	.11	.06
29	Bob Waterfield	.25	.20	.10
30	Bill Dudley	.10	.08	.04
31	Joe Guyon	.10	.08	.04
32	Arnie Herber	.10	.08	.04
33	Walt Kiesling	.10	.08	.04
34	Jimmy Conzelman	.10	.08	.04
35	Art Rooney	.15	.11	.06
36	Willie Wood	.10	.08	.04
37	Art Shell	.15	.11	.06
38	Sammy Baugh	.40	.30	.15
39	Mel Blount	.10	.08	.04
40	Lamar Hunt	.15	.11	.06
41	Norm Van Brocklin	.25	.20	.10
42	Y.A. Tittle	.30	.25	.12
43	Andy Robustelli	.10	.08	.04
44	Vince Lombardi	.25	.20	.10
45	Bruiser Kinard	.10	.08	.04
46	Bill Hewitt	.10	.08	.04
47	Jim Brown	1.00	.70	.40
48	Pete Pihos	.10	.08	.04
49	Hugh McElhenny	.15	.11	.06
50	Tom Fears	.15	.11	.06
51	Jack Christiansen	.10	.08	.04
52	Ernie Stautner	.15	.11	.06
53	Joe Perry	.15	.11	.06
54	Leo Nomellini	.10	.08	.04
55	Greasy Neale	.10	.08	.04
56	Turk Edwards	.10	.08	.04
57	Alex Wojciechowicz	.20	.15	.08
58	Charlie Trippi	.10	.08	.04
59	Marion Motley	.15	.11	.06
60	Wayne Miller	.10	.08	.04
61	Elroy Hirsch	.20	.15	.08
62	Art Donovan	.10	.08	.04
63	Cliff Battles	.10	.08	.04
64	Emlen Tunnell	.10	.08	.04
65	Joe Stydahar	.10	.08	.04
66	Ken Strong	.10	.08	.04

67	Dan Reeves	.15	.11	.06
68	Bobby Layne	.25	.20	.10
69	Paul Brown	.20	.15	.08
70	Charles Bidwell Sr.	.10	.08	.04
71	Chuck Bednarik	.15	.11	.06
72	Bulldog Turner	.10	.08	.04
73	Shorty Ray	.10	.08	.04
74	Steve Owen	.10	.08	.04
75	George McAfee	.10	.08	.04
76	Forrest Gregg	.10	.08	.04
77	Frank Gifford	.40	.30	.15
78	Jim Taylor	.15	.11	.06
79	Len Ford	.10	.08	.04
80	Ray Flaherty	.10	.08	.04
81	Lenny Moore	.15	.11	.06
82	Dante Lavelli	.10	.08	.04
83	George Connor	.15	.11	.06
84	Roosevelt Brown	.10	.08	.04
85	Dick "Night Train" Lane	.10	.08	.04
86	Lou Groza	.20	.15	.08
87	Bill George	.10	.08	.04
88	Tony Canadeo	.10	.08	.04
89	Joe Schmidt	.15	.11	.06
90	Jim Parker	.10	.08	.04
91	Raymond Berry	.15	.11	.06
92	Ace Parker	.10	.08	.04
93	Ollie Matson	.15	.11	.06
94	Gino Marchetti	.10	.08	.04
95	Larry Wilson	.10	.08	.04
96	Ray Nitschke	.15	.11	.06
97	Tuffy Leemans	.10	.08	.04
98	Weeb Ewbank	.15	.11	.06
99	Lance Alworth	.20	.15	.08
100	Bill Willis	.10	.08	.04
101	Bart Starr	.30	.25	.12
102	Gale Sayers	.30	.25	.12
103	Herb Adderly	.10	.08	.04
104	Johnny Unitas	1.00	.70	.40
105	Ron Mix	.10	.08	.04
106	Yale Lary	.10	.08	.04
107	Red Badgro	.10	.08	.04
108	Jim Otto	.10	.08	.04
109	Bob Lilly	.15	.11	.06
110	Deacon Jones	.10	.08	.04
111	Doug Atkins	.10	.08	.04
112	Jim Ringo	.15	.11	.06
113	Willie Davis	.10	.08	.04
114	George Blanda	.35	.25	.14
115	Bobby Bell	.10	.08	.04
116	Merlin Olsen	.15	.11	.06
117	George Musso	.10	.08	.04
118	Sam Huff	.10	.08	.04
119	Paul Warfield	.15	.11	.06
120	Bobby Mitchell	.10	.08	.04
121	Sonny Jurgensen	.15	.11	.06
122	Sid Gilman	.10	.08	.04
123	Arnie Weinmeister	.10	.08	.04
124	Charley Taylor	.10	.08	.04
125	Mike McCormack	.10	.08	.04
126	Willie Brown	.10	.08	.04
127	O.J. Simpson	1.50	1.25	.60
128	Pete Rozelle	.25	.20	.10
129	Joe Namath	1.25	.90	.50
130	Frank Gatski	.10	.08	.04
131	Willie Lanier	.15	.11	.06
132	Ken Houston	.10	.08	.04
133	Paul Hornung	.25	.20	.10
134	Roger Staubach	1.00	.70	.40
135	Len Dawson	.15	.11	.06
136	Larry Csonka	.25	.20	.10
137	Doak Walker	.15	.11	.06
138	Fran Tarkenton	.40	.30	.15
139	Don Maynard	.15	.11	.06
140	Jim Langer	.10	.08	.04
141	John H. Johnson	.10	.08	.04
142	Joe Greene	.20	.15	.08
143	Jack Ham	.10	.08	.04
144	Mike Ditka	.50	.40	.20
145	Alan Page	.10	.08	.04
146	Fred Biletnikoff	.15	.11	.06
147	Gene Upshaw	.10	.08	.04
148	Dick Butkus	.30	.25	.12
149	Buck Buchanan	.10	.08	.04
150	Franco Harris	.30	.25	.12
151	Tom Landry	.35	.25	.14
152	Ted Hendricks	.10	.08	.04
153	Bob St. Clair	.10	.08	.04
154	Jack Lambert	.20	.15	.08
155	Bob Griese	.20	.15	.08
156	**Admission Coupon**	.10	.08	.04
157	**Enshrinement Day**	.10	.08	.04
158	**Hall of Fame**	.10	.08	.04
159	**Checklist 1 & 2**	.10	.08	.04
160	**Checklist 3 & 4**	.10	.08	.04

1989 Syracuse Burger King

		NM/M	NM	E
Complete Set (15):		15.00	11.00	6.00
Common Player:		1.00	.70	.40
1	David Bavaro	1.50	1.25	.60
2	Blake Bednars	1.00	.70	.40
3	Alban Brown	1.00	.70	.40
4	Dan Burey	1.00	.70	.40
5	Rob Burnett	2.50	2.00	1.00
6	Fred DeRiggi	1.00	.70	.40
7	John Flannery	2.00	1.50	.80
8	Duane Kinnon	1.00	.70	.40
9	Dick MacPherson (CO)	2.00	1.50	.80
10	Rob Moore	5.00	3.75	2.00
11	Michael Owens	1.50	1.25	.60
12	Bill Scharr	1.00	.70	.40
13	Turnell Sims	1.00	.70	.40
14	Sean Whiteman	1.00	.70	.40
15	Terry Wooden	2.50	2.00	1.00

1991 Syracuse Program Cards

		NM/M	NM	E
Complete Set (36):		30.00	22.00	12.00
Common Player:		.75	.60	.30
1	George Rooks	.75	.60	.30
2	Marvin Graves	4.00	3.00	1.50
3	Andrew Dees	.75	.60	.30
4	Glen Young	1.00	.70	.40
5	Chris Gedney	2.00	1.50	.80
6	Paul Pasqualoni	1.00	.70	.40
7	Terrence Wisdom	.75	.60	.30
8	John Biskup	.75	.60	.30
9	Mark McDonald	.75	.60	.30
10	Dan Conley	1.00	.70	.40
11	Kevin Mitchell	.75	.60	.30
12	Qadry Ismail	6.00	4.50	2.50
13	John Lusardi	.75	.60	.30
14	David Walker	.75	.60	.30
15	John Capachione	.75	.60	.30
16	Shelby Hill	1.25	.90	.50
17	Dwayne Joseph	.75	.60	.30
18	Greg Walker	.75	.60	.30
19	Jerry Sharp	.75	.60	.30
20	Tim Sandquist	.75	.60	.30
21	Chuck Bull	.75	.60	.30
22	Jo Jo Wooden	.75	.60	.30
23	Terry Richardson	.75	.60	.30
24	Doug Womack	.75	.60	.30
25	Reggie Terry	.75	.60	.30
26	Garland Hawkins	.75	.60	.30
27	Tony Montemorra	.75	.60	.30
28	Chip Todd	.75	.60	.30
29	Pat O'Neill	1.00	.70	.40
30	Kevin Barker	.75	.60	.30
31	John Reagan	.75	.60	.30
32	Pat O'Rourke	.75	.60	.30
33	Jim Wentworth	.75	.60	.30
34	Ernie Brown	.75	.60	.30
35	John Nilsen	.75	.60	.30
36	Al Wooten	.75	.60	.30

1981 TCMA Greats

These standard-size cards were issued by TCMA in 1981. Each card front has a color photo of a player from the 1950s or '60s, framed by a white border. The card back is white and uses black ink to provide a career summary, biographical information, a TCMA copyright and a card number. Some cards, however, went unnumbered and command values about 2 times more than their numbered counterparts.

		NM/M	NM	E
Complete Set (78):		25.00	18.50	10.00
Common Player:		.25	.20	.10
1	Alex Karras	1.00	.70	.40
2	Fran Tarkenton	3.00	2.25	1.25
3	John Unitas	4.50	3.50	1.75
4	Bobby Layne	2.00	1.50	.80
5	Roger Staubach	6.00	4.50	2.50
6	Joe Namath	6.00	4.50	2.50
7	**1954 New York Giants**	.50	.40	.20
8	Jimmy Brown	6.00	4.50	2.50
9	Ray Wietecha	.25	.20	.10
10	R.C. Owens	.25	.20	.10
11	Alex Webster	.35	.25	.14
12	Jim Otto	1.00	.70	.40
13	Jim Taylor	1.00	.70	.40
14	Kyle Rote	.75	.60	.30
15	Roger Ellis	.25	.20	.10
16	Nick Pietrosante	.35	.25	.14
17	Milt Plum	.30	.25	.12
18	Eddie LeBaron	.50	.40	.20
19	Jimmy Patton	.25	.20	.10
20	Yale Lary	1.00	.70	.40
21	Leo Nomellini	1.25	.90	.50
22	Johnny Olszewski	.25	.20	.10
23	Ernie Koy	.35	.25	.14

24	Bill Wade	.35	.25	.14
25	Billy Wells	.25	.20	.10
26	Ron Wallor	.25	.20	.10
27	Pat Summerall	.60	.45	.25
28	Joe Schmidt	1.25	.90	.50
29	Bob St. Clair	.75	.60	.30
30	Dick Lynch	.35	.25	.14
31	Tommy McDonald	.50	.40	.20
32	Earl Morrall	.50	.40	.20
33	Jim Martin	.25	.20	.10
34	Dick Modzelewski	.30	.25	.12
35	Dick LeBeau	.35	.25	.14
36	Dick Post	.25	.20	.10
37	Les Richter	.35	.25	.14
38	Andy Robustelli	.75	.60	.30
39	Pete Retzlaff	.35	.25	.14
40	Fred Biletnikoff	1.50	1.25	.60
41	Timmy Brown	.35	.25	.14
42	Babe Parilli	.35	.25	.14
43	Lance Alworth	1.75	1.25	.70
44	Sammy Baugh	1.75	1.25	.70
45	Paul (Tank) Younger	.35	.25	.14
46	Chuck Bednarik	1.50	1.25	.60
47	Art Donovan	1.25	.90	.50
48	Len Dawson	2.00	1.50	.80
49	Don Maynard	1.25	.90	.50
50	Joe Morrison	.35	.25	.14
51	John Eliott	.25	.20	.10
52	Jim Ringo	.85	.60	.35
53	Max McGee	.35	.25	.14
54	Art Powell	.35	.25	.14
55	Galen Fiss	.25	.20	.10
56	Jack Stroud	.25	.20	.10
57	Bake Turner	.35	.25	.14
58	Mike McCormack	.75	.60	.30
59	L.G. Dupre	.35	.25	.14
60	Bill McPeak	.25	.20	.10
61	Art Spinney	.25	.20	.10
62	Fran Rogel	.25	.20	.10
63	Ollie Matson	1.25	.90	.50
64	Doak Walker	1.25	.90	.50
65	Lenny Moore	1.25	.90	.50
66	George Shaw, Bert Rechichar	.25	.20	.10
67	Kyle Rote, Jim Lee Howell, Ray Krause	.35	.25	.14
68	Andy Robustelli, Roosevelt Grier, Dick Modzelewski, Jim Katcavage	.65	.50	.25
69	Tucker Frederickson, Ernie Koy	.35	.25	.14
70	Gino Marchetti	1.00	.70	.40
71	Earl Morrall, Allie Sherman	.50	.40	.20
72	Roosevelt Brown	.75	.60	.30
73	Howard Cassady (Hopalong)	.35	.25	.14
74	Don Chandler	.35	.25	.14
75	Joe Childress	.25	.20	.10
76	Rick Casares	.35	.25	.14
77	Charley Conerly	1.00	.70	.40
78	1958 Giants QB's (Don Heinrich, Tom Dublinski, Charlie Conerly)	.50	.40	.20

1987 TCMA Update

This set, produced by TCMA's successor (CMC), is a reissue of TCMA's 1981 set, but 12 additional cards were added. The extra cards were numbered from were the first issue ended, at 79. The copyright on the card back is CMC 1987.

		NM/M	NM	E
Complete Set (12):		20.00	15.00	8.00
Common Player:		.75	.60	.30
79	Fred Dryer	1.00	.70	.40
80	Ed Marinaro	1.00	.70	.40
81	O.J. Simpson	10.00	7.50	4.00
82	Joe Theismann	2.50	2.00	1.00
83	Roman Gabriel	1.00	.70	.40
84	Terry Metcalf	.75	.60	.30
85	Lyle Alzado	1.50	1.25	.60
86	Jake Scott	.75	.60	.30
87	Cliff Branch	1.50	1.25	.60
88	Rocky Bleier	1.00	.70	.40
89	Cliff Harris	.75	.60	.30
90	Archie Manning	2.00	1.50	.80

1980 Tennessee Police

		NM/M	NM	E
Complete Set (19):		50.00	37.00	20.00
Common Player:		2.00	1.50	.80
1	Bill Bates	12.00	1.50	.80
2	James Berry	2.00	1.50	.80
3	Chris Bolton	2.00	1.50	.80

#	Player	NM/M	NM	E
4	Mike L. Cofer	6.00	1.50	.80
5	Glenn Ford	2.00	1.50	.80
6	Anthony Hancock	6.00	1.50	.80
7	Brian Ingram	2.00	1.50	.80
8	Tim Irwin	4.00	1.50	.80
9	Kenny Jones	2.00	1.50	.80
10	Wilbert Jones	2.00	1.50	.80
11	Johnny Majors (CO)	6.00	1.50	.80
12	Bill Marren	2.00	1.50	.80
13	Danny Martin	2.00	1.50	.80
14	Jim Noonan	2.00	1.50	.80
15	Lee North	2.00	1.50	.80
16	Hubert Simpson	3.00	1.50	.80
17	Danny Spradlin	3.00	1.50	.80
18	John Warren	3.00	1.50	.80
19	Brad White	2.00	1.50	.80

1990 Tennessee Centennial

#	Player	NM/M	NM	E
	Complete Set (294):	30.00	22.00	12.00
	Common Player:	.10	.08	.04
1	Vince Moore	.20	.15	.08
2	Steve Matthews	.10	.08	.04
3	Joey Chapman	.10	.08	.04
4	Terence Cleveland	.10	.08	.04
5	Thomas Wood	.10	.08	.04
6	J.J. McCleskey	.10	.08	.04
7	Jason Julian	.10	.08	.04
8	Andy Kelly	.20	.15	.08
9	Derrick Folsom	.10	.08	.04
10	Chip McCallum	.10	.08	.04
11	Lloyd Kerr	.10	.08	.04
12	Cory Fleming	.30	.25	.12
13	Kevin Zurcher	.10	.08	.04
14	Lee England	.10	.08	.04
15	Carl Pickens	2.00	1.50	.80
16	Sterling Henton	.10	.08	.04
17	Lee Wood	.10	.08	.04
18	Kent Elmore	.10	.08	.04
19	Craig Faulkner	.10	.08	.04
20	Keith Denson	.10	.08	.04
21	Preston Warren	.10	.08	.04
22	Floyd Miley	.10	.08	.04
23	Earnest Fields	.10	.08	.04
24	Tony Thompson	.10	.08	.04
25	Jeremy Lincoln	.30	.25	.12
26	David Bennett	.10	.08	.04
27	Greg Burke	.10	.08	.04
28	Tavio Henson	.10	.08	.04
29	Kevin Wendelboe	.10	.08	.04
30	Cedric Kline	.10	.08	.04
31	Keith Jeter	.10	.08	.04
32	Chris Russ	.10	.08	.04
33	DeWayne Dotson	.10	.08	.04
34	Mike Rapien	.10	.08	.04
35	Clemons McCroskey	.10	.08	.04
36	Mark Fletcher	.10	.08	.04
37	Chuck Smith	.20	.15	.08
38	Jeff Tullis	.10	.08	.04
39	Kelly Days	.10	.08	.04
40	Shazzon Bradley	.10	.08	.04
41	Reggie Ingram	.10	.08	.04
42	Roland Poles	.10	.08	.04
43	Tracy Smith	.10	.08	.04
44	Chuck Webb	.30	.25	.12
45	Shon Walker	.20	.15	.08
46	Eric Riffer	.10	.08	.04
47	Greg Amsler	.10	.08	.04
48	J.J. Surlas	.10	.08	.04
49	Brian Bradley	.10	.08	.04
50	Tom Myslinski	.20	.15	.08
51	John Fisher	.10	.08	.04
52	Craig Martin	.10	.08	.04
53	Carey Bailey	.10	.08	.04
54	Houston Thomas	.10	.08	.04
55	Ryan Patterson	.10	.08	.04
56	Chad Goodin	.10	.08	.04
57	Brian Spivey	.10	.08	.04
58	Todd Kelly	.10	.08	.04
59	Mike Stowell	.10	.08	.04
60	Jim Fenwick	.10	.08	.04
61	Marc Jones	.10	.08	.04
62	Chris Ragan	.10	.08	.04
63	Rodney Gordon	.10	.08	.04
64	Mark Needham	.10	.08	.04
65	Patrick Lenoir	.10	.08	.04
66	Martin Williams	.10	.08	.04
67	Brad Seiber	.10	.08	.04
68	Larry Smith	.10	.08	.04
69	Jerry Teel	.10	.08	.04
70	Charles McRae	.30	.25	.12
71	Rex Hargrove	.10	.08	.04
72	James Wilson	.10	.08	.04
73	Doug Baird	.10	.08	.04
74	Mark Moore	.10	.08	.04
75	Lance Nelson	.10	.08	.04
76	Robert Todd	.10	.08	.04
77	Greg Gerardi	.10	.08	.04
78	Antone Davis	.30	.25	.12
79	Eric Still	.10	.08	.04
80	Anthony Morgan	.75	.60	.30
81	Alvin Harper	1.00	.70	.40
82	Charles Longmire	.10	.08	.04
83	Mark Adams	.10	.08	.04
84	Chris Benson	.10	.08	.04
85	Horace Morris	.10	.08	.04
86	Harlan Davis	.10	.08	.04
87	Darryl Hardy	.10	.08	.04
88	Tracy Hayworth	.20	.15	.08
89	Von Reeves	.10	.08	.04
90	Marion Hobby	.10	.08	.04
91	John Ward (ANN)	.10	.08	.04
92	Roderick Lewis	.10	.08	.04
93	Orion McCants	.10	.08	.04
94	James Warren	.10	.08	.04
95	Mario Brunson	.10	.08	.04
96	Joe Davis	.10	.08	.04
97	Shawn Truss	.10	.08	.04
98	Keith Steed	.10	.08	.04
99	Kacy Rodgers	.10	.08	.04
100	Johnny Majors (CO)	.30	.25	.12
101	Phillip Fulmer (CO)	.30	.25	.12
102	Larry Lacewell (CO)	.20	.15	.08
103	Charlie Coe (CO)	.10	.08	.04
104	Tommy West (CO)	.10	.08	.04
105	David Cutcliffe (CO)	.10	.08	.04
106	Jack Sells (CO)	.10	.08	.04
107	Rex Norris (CO)	.10	.08	.04
108	John Chavis (CO)	.10	.08	.04
109	Tim Keane (CO)	.10	.08	.04
110	Recruiter (Tim Mingey)	.10	.08	.04
111	Sr. Admin. Asst. (Bill Higdon)	.10	.08	.04
112	Tim Kerin (TR)	.10	.08	.04
113	Bruno Pauletto (CO)	.10	.08	.04
114	Vols 17, Co. State 14 (Chuck Webb)	.20	.15	.08
115	Vols 24, UCLA 6 (Chuck Webb)	.20	.15	.08
116	**Vols 28, Duke 6** (Game Action Photo)	.10	.08	.04
117	**Vols 21, Auburn 14** (Game Action Photo)	.10	.08	.04
118	Vols 17, Georgia 14 (Jason Julian)	.10	.08	.04
119	Vols 30, Alabama 47 (Roland Poles)	.10	.08	.04
120	Vols 45, LSU 39 (Charles McRae)	.20	.15	.08
121	Vols 52, Akron 9 (Brian Spivey)	.10	.08	.04
122	Vols 33, Ole Miss 21 (Alvin Harper)	.30	.25	.12
123	Vols 31, Kentucky 10 (Kelly Days)	.10	.08	.04
124	**Vols 17, Vanderbilt 10** (Game Action Photo)	.10	.08	.04
125	'90 Mobil Cotton Bowl 1 (Jason Julian)	.10	.08	.04
126	'90 Mobil Cotton Bowl 2 (Andy Kelly)	.10	.08	.04
127	'90 Mobil Cotton Bowl 3 (Chuck Webb)	.20	.15	.08
128	**'90 Mobil Cotton Bowl 4** (Scoreboard)	.10	.08	.04
129	Eric Still	.10	.08	.04
130	Chris Benson	.10	.08	.04
131	Preston Warren	.10	.08	.04
132	Lee England	.10	.08	.04
133	Kent Elmore	.10	.08	.04
134	Eric Still	.10	.08	.04
135	Chuck Webb	.30	.25	.12
136	Marion Hobby	.10	.08	.04
137	Kent Elmore	.10	.08	.04
138	Antone Davis	.30	.25	.12
139	Thomas Woods	.10	.08	.04
140	Charles McRae	.30	.25	.12
141	Preston Warren	.10	.08	.04
142	Darryl Hardy	.10	.08	.04
143	Offense or Defense (Carl Pickens)	1.00	.70	.40
144	Carl Pickens	2.00	1.50	.80
145	Chuck Webb	.30	.25	.12
146	Thomas Woods	.10	.08	.04
147	Total Offense Game (Andy Kelly)	.10		.04
148	**The TVA** (Offensive Line)	.10	.08	.04
149	**Smokey** (Mascot)	.10	.08	.04
150	Director of Athletics (Doug Dickey)	.10	.08	.04
151	**Neyland Stadium**	.10	.08	.04
152	**Neyland-Thompson Ctr**	.10	.08	.04
153	**Gibbs Hall** (Dormitory)	.10	.08	.04
154	Asst. AD (Carmen Tegano) (Academics and Athletics)	.10	.08	.04
155	Gene McEver (HOF)	.10	.08	.04
156	Beattie Feathers (HOF)	.30	.25	.12
157	Robert Neyland (HOF) (CO)	.50	.40	.20
158	Herman Hickman (HOF)	.20	.15	.08
159	Bowden Wyatt (HOF)	.20	.15	.08
160	Hank Lauricella (HOF)	.10	.08	.04
161	Doug Atkins (HOF)	.30	.25	.12
162	Johnny Majors (HOF)	.30	.25	.12
163	Bobby Dodd (HOF)	.30	.25	.12
164	Bob Suffridge (HOF)	.10	.08	.04
165	Nathan Dougherty (HOF)	.10	.08	.04
166	George Cafego (HOF)	.10	.08	.04
167	Bob Johnson (HOF)	.20	.15	.08
168	Ed Molinski (HOF)	.10	.08	.04
169	Reggie White	2.00	1.50	.80
170	Willie Gault	.60	.45	.25
171	Doug Atkins	.30	.25	.12
172	Keith DeLong	.30	.25	.12
173	Ron Widby	.20	.15	.08
174	Bill Johnson	.20	.15	.08
175	Jack Reynolds	.30	.25	.12
176	Tim McGee	.50	.40	.20
177	Harry Galbreath	.20	.15	.08
178	Roland James	.20	.15	.08
179	Abe Shires	.10	.08	.04
180	Ted Daffer	.10	.08	.04
181	Bob Foxx	.10	.08	.04
182	Richmond Flowers	.30	.25	.12
183	Beattie Feathers	.30	.25	.12
184	Condredge Holloway	.50	.40	.20
185	Larry Sievers	.20	.15	.08
186	Johnnie Jones	.10	.08	.04
187	Carl Zander	.20	.15	.08
188	Dale Jones	.10	.08	.04
189	Bruce Wilkerson	.20	.15	.08
190	Terry McDaniel	.30	.25	.12
191	Craig Colquitt	.20	.15	.08
192	Stanley Morgan	.75	.60	.30
193	Curt Watson	.10	.08	.04
194	Bobby Majors	.10	.08	.04
195	Steve Kiner	.20	.15	.08
196	Paul Naumoff	.20	.15	.08
197	Bud Sherrod	.10	.08	.04
198	Murray Warmath	.20	.15	.08
199	Steve DeLong	.20	.15	.08
200	Bill Pearman	.10	.08	.04
201	Bobby Gordon	.10	.08	.04
202	John Michels	.10	.08	.04
203	Bill Mayo	.10	.08	.04
204	Andy Kozar	.10	.08	.04
205	1892 Volunteers (Team Photo)	.10	.08	.04
206	1900 Volunteers (Team Photo)	.10	.08	.04
207	1905 Volunteers (Team Photo)	.10	.08	.04
208	1907 Volunteers (Individual player photos)	.10	.08	.04
209	1916 Volunteers (Team Photo)	.10	.08	.04
210	1914 Volunteers (Team Photo)	.10	.08	.04
211	1896 Volunteers (Team Photo)	.10	.08	.04
212	1908 Volunteers (Team Photo)	.10	.08	.04
213	1926 Volunteers (Team Photo)	.10	.08	.04
214	1930 Volunteers (Team Photo)	.10	.08	.04
215	1934 Volunteers (Team Photo)	.10	.08	.04
216	1938 Volunteers (Team Photo)	.10	.08	.04
217	1940 Volunteers (Team Photo)	.10	.08	.04
218	1944 Volunteers (Team Photo)	.10	.08	.04
219	1945 Volunteers (Team Photo)	.10	.08	.04
220	1954 Volunteers (Team Photo)	.10	.08	.04
221	1969 Volunteers (Team Photo)	.10	.08	.04
222	1962 Volunteers (Team Photo)	.10	.08	.04
223	1976 Volunteers (Team Photo)	.10	.08	.04
224	1985 Volunteers (Team Photo)	.10	.08	.04
225	1978 Volunteers (Team Photo)	.10	.08	.04

226	1980 Volunteers (Team Photo)	.10	.08	.04
227	1984 Volunteers (Team Photo)	.10	.08	.04
228	1988 Volunteers (Team Photo)	.10	.08	.04
229	James Baird	.10	.08	.04
230	Condredge Holloway	.50	.40	.20
231	J.G. Lowe	.10	.08	.04
232	E.A. McLean	.10	.08	.04
233	Lemont Holt Jeffers	.10	.08	.04
234	Howard Johnson	.10	.08	.04
235	Malcolm Aiken	.10	.08	.04
236	Toby Palmer	.10	.08	.04
237	Sam Bartholomew	.10	.08	.04
238	Ray Graves	.10	.08	.04
239	Billy Bevis	.10	.08	.04
240	Bert Rechichar	.20	.15	.08
241	Jim Beutel	.10	.08	.04
242	Mike Lucci	.30	.25	.12
243	Hal Wantland	.10	.08	.04
244	Jackie Walker	.10	.08	.04
245	Ron McCartney	.10	.08	.04
246	Robert Shaw	.30	.25	.12
247	Lee North	.10	.08	.04
248	James Berry	.10	.08	.04
249	Carl Zander	.20	.15	.08
250	Chris White	.10	.08	.04
251	Timmy Sims	.10	.08	.04
252	Tim McGee	.50	.40	.20
253	Keith DeLong	.30	.25	.12
254	1931 NY Charity Game (Program)	.10	.08	.04
255	1941 Super Bowl (Program)	.10	.08	.04
256	1945 Rose Bowl (Program)	.10	.08	.04
257	1957 Gator Bowl (Program)	.10	.08	.04
258	1968 Orange Bowl (Program)	.10	.08	.04
259	1972 Bluebonnet Bowl (Program)	.10	.08	.04
260	1981 Graden State Bowl (Program)	.10	.08	.04
261	1968 Sugar Bowl (Program)	.10	.08	.04
262	Checklist 1-76	.10	.08	.04
263	Checklist 77-152	.10	.08	.04
264	Checklist 153-228	.10	.08	.04
265	Checklist 229-294	.10	.08	.04
266	Chris White	.10	.08	.04
267	Kelsey Finch	.10	.08	.04
268	Johnnie Jones	.10	.08	.04
269	Johnnie Jones	.10	.08	.04
270	Curt Watson	.10	.08	.04
271	William Howard	.10	.08	.04
272	Bubba Wyche	.10	.08	.04
273	Tony Robinson	.30	.25	.12
274	Daryl Dickey	.30	.25	.12
275	Alan Cockrell, Willie Gault	.30	.25	.12
276	Alan Cockrell	.30	.25	.12
277	Bobby Scott	.30	.25	.12
278	Tony Robinson	.30	.25	.12
279	Jeff Francis	.20	.15	.08
280	Alvin Harper	1.00	.70	.40
281	Johnny Mills	.10	.08	.04
282	Thomas Woods	.10	.08	.04
283	Bob Lund	.10	.08	.04
284	Gene McEver	.10	.08	.04
285	Stanley Morgan	.75	.60	.30
286	Fuad Reveiz	.30	.25	.12
287	Kent Elmore	.10	.08	.04
288	Jimmy Colquitt	.10	.08	.04
289	Willie Gault	.60	.45	.25
290	100 Years Celebration (Reggie White)	.75	.60	.30
291	The 100 Years Kickoff (Group Photo)	.10	.08	.04
292	Like Father, Like Son (Keith DeLong, Steve DeLong)	.30	.25	.12
293	Offense and Defense (Raleigh McKenzie, Reggie McKenzie)	.20	.15	.08
294	It's Football Time (1990 schedule on back)	.20	.15	.08

1991 Tennessee Hoby

		NM/M	NM	E
Complete Set (42):		25.00	18.50	10.00
Common Player:		.25	.20	.10
397	Mark Adams	.25	.20	.10
398	Carey Bailey	.25	.20	.10
399	David Bennett	.25	.20	.10
400	Shazzon Bradley	.25	.20	.10
401	Kenneth Campbell	.25	.20	.10

402	Dale Carter	1.50	1.25	.60
403	Joey Chapman	.25	.20	.10
404	Jerry Colquitt	.50	.40	.20
405	Bernard Daftney	.50	.40	.20
406	Craig Faulkner	.25	.20	.10
407	Earnest Fields	.25	.20	.10
408	John Fisher	.25	.20	.10
409	Cory Fleming	.75	.60	.30
410	Mark Fletcher	.25	.20	.10
411	Tom Fuhler	.25	.20	.10
412	Johnny Majors (CO)	.50	.40	.20
413	Darryl Hardy	.25	.20	.10
414	Aaron Hayden	3.00	2.25	1.25
415	Tavio Henson	.25	.20	.10
416	Reggie Ingram	.25	.20	.10
417	Andy Kelly	.50	.40	.20
418	Todd Kelly	.75	.60	.30
419	Patrick Lenoir	.25	.20	.10
420	Roderick Lewis	.25	.20	.10
421	Jeremy Lincoln	1.50	1.25	.60
422	J.J. McCleskey	.35	.25	.14
423	Floyd Miley	.25	.20	.10
424	Chris Mims	1.50	1.25	.60
425	Tom Myslinski	.35	.25	.14
426	Carl Pickens	5.00	3.75	2.00
427	Roc Powe	.25	.20	.10
428	Von Reeves	.25	.20	.10
429	Eric Riffer	.25	.20	.10
430	Kacy Rodgers	.25	.20	.10
431	Steve Session	.25	.20	.10
432	Heath Shuler	6.00	4.50	2.50
433	Chuck Smith	.35	.25	.14
434	James O. Stewart	3.00	2.25	1.25
435	Mike Stowell	.25	.20	.10
436	J.J. Surlas	.25	.20	.10
437	Shon Walker	.35	.25	.14
438	James Wilson	.25	.20	.10

1960 Texans 7-Eleven

The standard-sized cards feature a black and white photo of the player with his name, position and team along the bottom edge. The horizontal card backs have player highlights in typewriter-style print. Even though there are 11 cards checklisted, there may have been more in the unnumbered set.

		NM	E	VG
Complete Set (11):		400.00	200.00	120.00
Common Player:		35.00	17.50	10.50
1	Max Boydston	35.00	17.50	10.50
2	Mel Branch	35.00	17.50	10.50
3	Chris Burford	35.00	17.50	10.50
4	Ray Collins (UER) (No team name on front)	35.00	17.50	10.50
5	Cotton Davidson	35.00	17.50	10.50
6	Abner Haynes	60.00	30.00	18.00
7	Sherrill Headrick	35.00	17.50	10.50
8	Bill Krisher	35.00	17.50	10.50
9	Paul Miller	35.00	17.50	10.50
10	Johnny Robinson	60.00	30.00	18.00
11	Jack Spikes	35.00	17.50	10.50

1991 Texas HS Legends

		NM/M	NM	E
Complete Set (25):		18.00	13.50	7.25
Common Player:		.60	.45	.25
1	Marty Akins	.60	.45	.25
2	Gil Bartosh	.60	.45	.25
3	Bill Bradley	1.00	.70	.40
4	Chris Gilbert	1.25	.90	.50
5	Glynn Gregory	.75	.60	.30
6	Charlie Haas	.60	.45	.25
7	Craig James	2.00	1.50	.80
8	Boody Johnson	.60	.45	.25
9	Ernie Koy Jr.	.75	.60	.30
10	Glenn Lippman	.60	.45	.25
11	Jack Pardee	1.00	.70	.40
12	Billy Patterson	.60	.45	.25
13	Billy Sims	3.00	2.25	1.25
14	Byron Townsend	.60	.45	.25
15	Doyle Traylor	.60	.45	.25
16	Joe Washington Jr.	1.00	.70	.40
17	Allie White	.60	.45	.25
18	Wilson Whitley	.75	.60	.30
19	Gordon Wood	.75	.60	.30
20	Willie Zapalac	.60	.45	.25
21	Cover Card 1	.60	.45	.25
22	Cover Card 2	.60	.45	.25
23	Cover Card 3	.60	.45	.25
24	Cover Card 4	.60	.45	.25
25	Cover Card 5	.60	.45	.25

1961 Titans Jay Publishing

The 12-card, 5" x 7" set features black and white photos of the New York Titans, an original AFL team that eventually became the New York Jets. The cards were originally packaged 12 to a pack and sold for 25 cents. The backs are blank.

		NM	E	VG
Complete Set (12):		75.00	37.00	22.00
Common Player:		5.00	2.50	1.50
1	Al Dorow	5.00	2.50	1.50
2	Larry Grantham	6.00	3.00	1.75
3	Mike Hagler	5.00	2.50	1.50
4	Mike Hudock	5.00	2.50	1.50
5	Bob Jewett	5.00	2.50	1.50
6	Jack Klotz	5.00	2.50	1.50
7	Don Maynard	20.00	10.00	6.00
8	John McMullan	5.00	2.50	1.50
9	Bob Mischak	5.00	2.50	1.50
10	Art Powell	10.00	5.00	3.00
11	Bob Reifsnyder	6.00	3.00	1.75
12	Sid Youngelman	6.00	3.00	1.75

1950 Topps Felt Backs

BILLY CONN
All-American Halfback
GEORGETOWN U.

These 7/8" x 1-7/16" cards feature several top collegiate players of the era on the front; a mug shot has the player's name, position and college under it. The card back is felt and includes his college's team pennant. Cards come with either brown or yellow backgrounds; yellow backgrounds are generally twice the listed values. The following cards come in both versions: 5, 6, 9, 13, 30, 35, 36, 39, 46, 51, 52, 54, 55, 57, 61, 66, 71, 75, 76, 78, 84, 86, 87, 92, and 100.

		NM	E	VG
Complete Set (100):		11,500	5,750	3,000
Common Player:		125.00	65.00	39.00
Minor Stars:		75.00		
Common Player (Yellow Variation):		100.00		
1	Lou Allen	125.00	65.00	39.00
2	Morris Bailey	125.00	65.00	39.00
3	George Bell	125.00	65.00	39.00
4	Lindy Berry	125.00	65.00	39.00
5A	Mike Boldin BR	125.00	65.00	39.00
5B	Mike Boldin YE	150.00	75.00	45.00
6A	Bernie Botula BR	125.00	65.00	39.00
6B	Bernie Botula YE	175.00	90.00	54.00
7	Bob Bowlby	125.00	65.00	39.00
8	Bob Bucher	125.00	65.00	39.00
9A	Al Burnett BR	125.00	65.00	39.00
9B	Al Burnett YE	150.00	75.00	45.00
10	Don Burson	125.00	65.00	39.00
11	Paul Campbell	125.00	65.00	39.00
12	Herb Carey	125.00	65.00	39.00
13A	Bimbo Cecconi BR	125.00	65.00	39.00
13B	Bimbo Cecconi YE	150.00	75.00	45.00
14	Bill Chauncey	125.00	65.00	39.00
15	Dick Clark	125.00	65.00	39.00
16	Tom Coleman	125.00	65.00	39.00
17	Billy Conn	125.00	65.00	39.00
18	John Cox	125.00	65.00	39.00
19	Lou Creekmur RC	300.00	150.00	90.00
20	Glen Davis	125.00	65.00	39.00
21	Warren Davis	125.00	65.00	39.00
22	Bob Deuber	125.00	65.00	39.00
23	Ray Dooney	125.00	65.00	39.00
24	Tom Dublinski	125.00	65.00	39.00
25	Jeff Fleischman	125.00	65.00	39.00
26	Jack Friedland	125.00	65.00	39.00
27	Bob Fuchs	125.00	65.00	39.00
28	Arnold Galiffa	125.00	65.00	39.00
29	Dick Gilman	125.00	65.00	39.00
30A	Frank Gitschier BR	125.00	65.00	39.00
30B	Frank Gitschier YE	150.00	75.00	45.00
31	Gene Glick	125.00	65.00	39.00
32	Bill Gregus	125.00	65.00	39.00
33	Harold Hagan	125.00	65.00	39.00

34	Charles Hall	125.00	65.00	39.00
35A	Leon Hart BR	175.00	90.00	45.00
35B	Leon Hart YE	200.00		
36A	Bob Hester BR	125.00	65.00	39.00
36B	Bob Hester YE	150.00	75.00	45.00
37	George Hughes	125.00	65.00	39.00
38	Levi Jackson	125.00	65.00	39.00
39A	Jackie Jensen BR	250.00	125.00	65.00
39B	Jackie Jensen YE	400.00		
40	Charlie Justice	150.00	75.00	45.00
41	Gary Kerkorian	125.00	65.00	39.00
42	Bernie Krueger	125.00	65.00	39.00
43	Bill Kuhn	125.00	65.00	39.00
44	Dean Laun	125.00	65.00	39.00
45	Chet Leach	125.00	65.00	39.00
46A	Bobby Lee BR	125.00	65.00	39.00
46B	Bobby Lee YE	200.00	100.00	50.00
47	Roger Lehew	125.00	65.00	39.00
48	Glenn Lippman	125.00	65.00	39.00
49	Melvin Lyle	125.00	65.00	39.00
50	Len Makowski	125.00	65.00	39.00
51A	Al Malekoff BR	200.00	100.00	50.00
51B	Al Malekoff YE	115.00	60.00	30.00
52A	Jim Martin BR	140.00	70.00	42.00
52B	Jim Martin YE	175.00		
53	Frank Mataya	125.00	65.00	39.00
54A	Ray Matthews BR **RC**	140.00	70.00	42.00
54B	Ray Mathews YE **RC**	175.00		
55A	Dick McKissack BR	150.00	75.00	38.00
55B	Dick McKissack YE	115.00	60.00	30.00
56	Frank Miller	125.00	65.00	39.00
57A	John Miller BR	140.00	70.00	42.00
57B	John Miller YE	175.00	90.00	54.00
58	Ed Modzelewski	125.00	65.00	39.00
59	Don Mouser	125.00	65.00	39.00
60	James Murphy	125.00	65.00	39.00
61A	Ray Nagle BR	140.00	70.00	42.00
61B	Ray Nagle YE	175.00	90.00	54.00
62	Leo Nomellini	450.00	225.00	135.00
63	James O'Day	125.00	65.00	39.00
64	Joe Paterno **RC**	2,500	1,250	750.00
65	Andy Pavich	125.00	65.00	39.00
66A	Pete Perini BR	140.00	70.00	42.00
66B	Pete Perini YE	175.00	90.00	54.00
67	Jim Powers	125.00	65.00	39.00
68	Dave Rakestraw	125.00	65.00	39.00
69	Herb Rich	125.00	65.00	39.00
70	Fran Rogel	125.00	65.00	39.00
71A	Darrell Royal BR **RC**	500.00	250.00	150.00
71B	Darrell Royal YE **RC**	750.00		
72	Steve Sawle	125.00	65.00	39.00
73	Nick Sebeck	125.00	65.00	39.00
74	Herb Seidell	125.00	65.00	39.00
75A	Charles Shaw BR	140.00	70.00	42.00
75B	Charles Shaw YE	175.00	90.00	54.00
76A	Emil Sitko BR **RC**	140.00	70.00	35.00
76B	Emil Sitko YE **RC**	160.00		
77	Ed (Butch) Songin	125.00	65.00	39.00
78A	Mariano Stalloni BR	125.00	60.00	30.00
78B	Mariano Stalloni YE	125.00	65.00	39.00
79	Ernie Stautner **RC**	450.00	225.00	135.00
80	Don Stehley	125.00	65.00	39.00
81	Gil Stevenson	125.00	65.00	39.00
82	Bishop Strickland	125.00	65.00	39.00
83	Harry Szulborski	125.00	65.00	39.00
84A	Wally Teninga BR	140.00	70.00	42.00
84B	Wally Teninga YE	375.00	188.00	115.00
85	Clayton Tonnemaker	125.00	65.00	39.00
86A	Dan Towler BR **RC**	150.00	75.00	45.00
86B	Dan Towler YE **RC**	375.00		
87A	Bert Turek BR	140.00	70.00	42.00
87B	Bert Turek YE	375.00	188.00	115.00
88	Harry Ulinski	125.00	65.00	39.00
89	Leon Van Billingham	125.00	65.00	39.00
90	Langdon Viracola	125.00	65.00	39.00
91	Leo Wagner	125.00	65.00	39.00
92A	Doak Walker BR	600.00	300.00	180.00
92B	Doak Walker YE **RC**	900.00		
93	Jim Ward	125.00	65.00	39.00
94	Art Weiner	125.00	65.00	39.00
95	Dick Weiss	125.00	65.00	39.00
96	Froggie Williams	125.00	65.00	39.00
97	Robert (Red) Wilson	125.00	65.00	39.00
98	Roger (Red) Wilson	125.00	65.00	39.00
99	Carl Wren	125.00	65.00	39.00
100A	Pete Zinaich BR	140.00	70.00	42.00
100B	Pete Zinaich YE	175.00	90.00	54.00

1951 Topps

THOMAS SCOTT
END (CAVALIERS)

Refered to as the 1951 Topps "Magic" set, this 1951 issue was Topps' first major football card set. The 75-card set featured the nation's top college players. The backs of the cards include a football trivia question with the answer concealed under a scratch-off area.

		NM	E	VG
Complete Set (75):		1,100	500.00	300.00
Common Player:		18.00	8.00	4.75
Minor Stars:		25.00		
Back Unscratched: 2X				
1	Jimmy Monahan **RC**	30.00	15.00	9.00
2	Bill Wade **RC**	50.00	25.00	15.00
3	Bill Reichardt	18.00	9.00	5.50
4	Babe Parilli **RC**	50.00	25.00	15.00
5	Billie Burkhalter	18.00	9.00	5.50
6	Ed Weber	18.00	9.00	5.50
7	Tom Scott	18.00	9.00	5.50
8	Frank Guthridge	18.00	9.00	5.50
9	John Karras	18.00	9.00	5.50
10	Vic Janowicz **RC**	150.00	75.00	45.00
11	Lloyd Hill	18.00	9.00	5.50
12	Jim Weatherall **RC**	25.00	12.50	7.50
13	Howard Hansen	18.00	9.00	5.50
14	Lou D'Achille	18.00	9.00	5.50
15	Johnny Turco	18.00	9.00	5.50
16	Jerrell Price	18.00	9.00	5.50
17	John Coatta	18.00	9.00	5.50
18	Bruce Patton	18.00	9.00	5.50
19	Marion Campbell **RC**	35.00	17.50	10.50
20	Blaine Earon	18.00	9.00	5.50
21	Dewey McConnell	18.00	9.00	5.50
22	Ray Beck	18.00	9.00	5.50
23	Jim Prewett	18.00	9.00	5.50
24	Bob Steele	18.00	9.00	5.50
25	Art Betts	18.00	9.00	5.50
26	Walt Trillhaase	18.00	9.00	5.50
27	Gil Bartosh	18.00	9.00	5.50
28	Bob Bestwick	18.00	9.00	5.50
29	Tom Rushing	18.00	9.00	5.50
30	Bert Rechichar **RC**	35.00	17.50	10.50
31	Bill Owens	18.00	9.00	5.50
32	Mike Goggins	18.00	9.00	5.50
33	John Petitbon	18.00	9.00	5.50
34	Byron Townsend	18.00	9.00	5.50
35	Ed Rotticci	18.00	9.00	5.50
36	Steve Wadiak	18.00	9.00	5.50
37	Bobby Marlow **RC**	18.00	9.00	5.50
38	Bill Fuchs	18.00	9.00	5.50
39	Ralph Staub	18.00	9.00	5.50
40	Bill Vesprini	18.00	9.00	5.50
41	Zack Jordan	18.00	9.00	5.50
42	Bob Smith	18.00	9.00	5.50
43	Charles Hanson	18.00	9.00	5.50
44	Glenn Smith	18.00	9.00	5.50
45	Armand Kitto	18.00	9.00	5.50
46	Vinnie Drake	18.00	9.00	5.50
47	Bill Putich	18.00	9.00	5.50
48	George Young **RC**	40.00	20.00	12.00
49	Don McRae	18.00	9.00	5.50
50	Frank Smith	18.00	9.00	5.50
51	Dick Hightower	18.00	9.00	5.50
52	Clyde Pickard	18.00	9.00	5.50
53	Bob Reynolds	18.00	9.00	5.50
54	Dick Gregory	18.00	9.00	5.50
55	Dale Samuels	18.00	9.00	5.50
56	Gale Galloway	18.00	9.00	5.50
57	Vic Pujo	18.00	9.00	5.50
58	Dave Waters	18.00	9.00	5.50
59	Joe Ernest	18.00	9.00	5.50
60	Elmer Costa	18.00	9.00	5.50
61	Nick Liotta	18.00	9.00	5.50
62	John Dottley	18.00	9.00	5.50
63	Hi Faubion	18.00	9.00	5.50
64	David Harr	18.00	9.00	5.50
65	Bill Matthews	18.00	9.00	5.50
66	Carroll McDonald	18.00	9.00	5.50
67	Dick Dewing	18.00	9.00	5.50
68	Joe Johnson	18.00	9.00	5.50
69	Arnold Burwitz	18.00	9.00	5.50
70	Ed Dobrowolski	18.00	9.00	5.50
71	Joe Dudeck	18.00	9.00	5.50
72	John Bright **RC**	25.00	12.50	7.50
73	Harold Loehlein	18.00	9.00	5.50
74	Lawrence Hairston	18.00	9.00	5.50
75	Bob Carey **RC**	25.00	12.50	7.50

1955 Topps All-American

VIRGINIA
ALL AMERICAN
BILL DUDLEY
Halfback

This was the last Topps set to have college stars. The 100-card All-American set includes past and contemporary college stars. Cards measure 2-5/8" x 3-5/8" and feature a horizontal format. A number of the cards were short-printed in this set. Because the set featured many stars of the past, this set includes the only "regular issue" cards of several Hall of Famers (though technically these cards shouldn't qualify as "regular issue" cards since they weren't released during the player's career). Some of these rookie cards include Red Grange, Mel Hein, Jim Thorpe, Ernie Nevers, Bruiser Kinard, Ace parker, Don Hutson and Pete Henry. The only card issued of the Four Horsemen also appears in this set. The second (and last) "regular issue" cards of these players appear in this set: Knute Rockne, Ken Strong, Turk Edwards, and Alex Wojciechowicz. This set also includes the last cards of Bill Dudley, Otto Graham, Whizzer White (his second-year card, which actually should be his rookie card, since the 1954 Bowman card showed not Byron "Whizzer" White but Wilford White) and Sid Luckman. Two variations exist in the set. The backs on #14 Gaynell Tinsley and #21 Whizzer White were switched. The corrected versions are more plentiful than the errors. (Key: SP - short-printed)

		NM	E	VG
Complete Set (100):		5,250	2,625	1,575
Common Player:		35.00	18.00	11.00
Minor Stars:		42.00		
SP Cards:		50.00	25.00	
Glassine Pack (9):		2,500		
Cello Pack (20):		4,000		
1	Herman Hickman **RC**	150.00	75.00	45.00
2	John Kimbrough	35.00	18.00	11.00
3	Ed Weir	35.00	18.00	11.00
4	Ernie Pinckert	35.00	18.00	11.00
5	Bobby Grayson	35.00	18.00	11.00
6	Niles Kinnick **RC**	135.00	67.00	40.00
7	Andy Bershak	35.00	18.00	11.00
8	George Cafego	35.00	18.00	11.00
9	Tom Hamilton (SP)	50.00	25.00	13.00
10	Bill Dudley	60.00	30.00	18.00
11	Bobby Dodd (SP)	50.00	25.00	13.00
12	Otto Graham	175.00	87.00	52.00
13	Aaron Rosenberg	35.00	18.00	11.00
14	Gaynell "Gus" Tinsley **RC** (Whizzer White back)	200.00	100.00	60.00
14A	Gaynell "Gus" Tinsley **RC**	35.00	18.00	11.00
15	Ed Kaw (SP)	50.00	25.00	13.00
16	Knute Rockne	275.00	135.00	82.00
17	Bob Reynolds	35.00	18.00	11.00
18	Pudge Heffelfinger (SP)	50.00	25.00	13.00
19	Bruce A. Smith **RC**	50.00	25.00	13.00
20	Sammy Baugh	200.00	100.00	60.00
21	Whizzer White **RC** (SP (Gaynell Tinsley back)	250.00	125.00	75.00
21a	Whizzer White (SP)	100.00	50.00	30.00
22	Brick Muller	35.00	18.00	11.00
23	Dick Kazmaier **RC**	37.00	19.00	12.00
24	Ken Strong	35.00	18.00	11.00
25	Casimir Myslinski (SP)	50.00	25.00	13.00
26	Larry Kelley **RC** (SP)	50.00	25.00	13.00
27	Harold "Red" Grange	275.00	138.00	83.00
28	Mel Hein **RC** (SP)	75.00	37.00	22.00
29	Leo Nomellini (SP)	90.00	45.00	27.00
30	Wes E. Fesler	35.00	18.00	11.00
31	George Sauer Sr. **RC**	35.00	18.00	11.00
32	Hank Foldberg	35.00	18.00	11.00
33	Bob Higgins	35.00	18.00	11.00
34	Davey O'Brien **RC**	50.00	25.00	15.00
35	Tom Harmon **RC** (SP)	80.00	40.00	24.00
36	Turk Edwards (SP)	50.00	25.00	13.00
37	Jim Thorpe	425.00	215.00	129.00
38	Amos Alonzo Stagg **RC**	90.00	45.00	27.00
39	Jerome Holland	35.00	18.00	11.00
40	Donn Moomaw	35.00	18.00	11.00
41	Joseph Alexander (SP)	50.00	25.00	13.00
42	J. Edward Tryon (SP)	50.00	25.00	13.00

43	George Savitsky	35.00	18.00	11.00
44	Ed Garbisch	35.00	18.00	11.00
45	Elmer Oliphant	35.00	18.00	11.00
46	Arnold Lassman	36.00	18.00	11.00
47	Bo McMillan	35.00	18.00	11.00
48	Ed Widseth	35.00	18.00	11.00
49	Don Zimmerman	35.00	18.00	11.00
50	Ken Kavanaugh	35.00	18.00	11.00
51	Duane Purvis (SP)	50.00	25.00	13.00
52	John Lujack	80.00	40.00	24.00
53	John F. Green	35.00	18.00	11.00
54	Edwin Dooley (SP)	50.00	25.00	13.00
55	Frank Merritt (SP)	50.00	25.00	13.00
56	Ernie Nevers **RC**	100.00	50.00	30.00
57	Vic Hanson (SP)	50.00	25.00	13.00
58	Ed Franco	35.00	18.00	11.00
59	Doc Blanchard **RC**	80.00	40.00	24.00
60	Dan Hill	35.00	18.00	11.00
61	Charles Brickley (SP)	50.00	25.00	13.00
62	Harry Newman	35.00	18.00	11.00
63	Charlie Justice	35.00	18.00	11.00
64	Benny Friedman	35.00	18.00	11.00
65	Joe Donchess (SP)	50.00	25.00	13.00
66	Bruiser Kinard **RC**	60.00	30.00	18.00
67	Frankie Albert	35.00	18.00	11.00
68	**Four Horsemen** (SP)	500.00	250.00	150.00
69	Frank Sinkwich **RC**	35.00	19.00	11.00
70	Bill Daddio	35.00	18.00	11.00
71	Bob Wilson	35.00	18.00	11.00
72	Chub Peabody	35.00	18.00	11.00
73	Hugh Governali	35.00	18.00	11.00
74	Gene McEver	35.00	18.00	11.00
75	Hugh Gallarneau	35.00	18.00	11.00
76	Angelo Bertelli **RC**	35.00	18.00	11.00
77	Bowden Wyatt (SP)	50.00	25.00	13.00
78	Jay Berwanger **RC**	35.00	17.50	10.50
79	Pug Lund	35.00	18.00	11.00
80	Bennie Oosterbaan	35.00	18.00	11.00
81	Cotton Warburton	35.00	18.00	11.00
82	Alex Wojciechowicz	60.00	30.00	18.00
83	Ted Coy (SP)	50.00	25.00	13.00
84	Ace Parker **RC** (SP)	75.00	38.00	23.00
85	Sid Luckman	150.00	75.00	45.00
86	Albie Booth (SP)	50.00	25.00	13.00
87	Adolph Schultz (SP)	50.00	25.00	13.00
88	Ralph G. Kercheval	35.00	18.00	11.00
89	Marshall Goldberg	35.00	18.00	11.00
90	Charlie O'Rourke	70.00	35.00	21.00
91	Bob Odell	35.00	18.00	11.00
92	Biggie Munn	35.00	18.00	11.00
93	Willie Heston (SP)	50.00	25.00	13.00
94	Joe Bernard (SP)	50.00	25.00	13.00
95	Red Cagle (SP)	50.00	25.00	13.00
96	Bill Hollenbeck (SP)	50.00	25.00	13.00
97	Don Hutson **RC** (SP)	320.00	160.00	96.00
98	Beattie Feathers (SP)	130.00	65.00	39.00
99	Don Witmire (SP)	50.00	25.00	13.00
100	Wilbur "Fats" Henry **RC**	200.00	100.00	60.00

1956 Topps

This set of 120 cards plus an unnumbered (and probably short-printed) checklist was oversized, measuring 2-5/8" x 3-5/8". This was Topps' first set to feature only professional football players. Most notable about this set was the inclusion of the first team cards by any company (cards of the Chicago Cardinals and Washington Redskins players, however, were short-printed). Rookies in this set include Hall of Famers Roosevelt Brown, Joe Schmidt, Bill George and Lenny Moore, plus Rosey Grier. Second-year cards in this set are those of Alan Ameche, Art Donovan and Mike McCormack.

	NM	E	VG
Complete Set (120):	3,000	1,500	900.00
Common Player:	12.00	6.00	3.50
Minor Stars:	15.00		
Unlisted Stars:	20.00		
SP Cards:	20.00	10.00	6.00
Team Cards:	20.00	10.00	6.00
Checklist:	350.00	175.00	105.00
Wax Pack Dark Gr. (6):	400.00		

1	Jack Carson SP	200.00	100.00	60.00
2	Gordon Soltau	12.00	6.00	3.50
3	Frank Varrichione	12.00	6.00	3.50
4	Eddie Bell	12.00	6.00	3.50
5	Alex Webster **RC**	15.00	7.50	4.50
6	Norm Van Brocklin	15.00	7.50	4.50
7	**Green Bay Packers**	20.00	10.00	6.00
8	Lou Creekmur	12.00	6.00	3.50
9	Lou Groza	35.00	18.00	11.00
10	Tom Bienemann	20.00	10.00	6.00
11	George Blanda	48.00	24.00	14.00
12	Alan Ameche	15.00	7.50	4.50
13	Vic Janowicz SP	60.00	30.00	18.00
14	Dick Moegle	12.00	6.00	3.50
15	Fran Rogel	12.00	6.00	3.50
16	Harold Giancanelli	12.00	6.00	3.50
17	Emlen Tunnell	12.00	6.00	3.50
18	Tank Younger	12.00	6.00	3.50
19	Bill Howton	12.00	6.00	3.50
20	Jack Christiansen	12.00	6.00	3.50
21	Darrell Brewster	12.00	6.00	3.50
22	**Chicago Cardinals SP**	70.00	35.00	21.00
23	Ed Brown	12.00	6.00	3.50
24	Joe Campanella	12.00	6.00	3.50
25	Leon Heath	35.00	18.00	11.00
26	**San Francisco 49ers**	20.00	10.00	6.00
27	Dick Flanagan	12.00	6.00	3.50
28	Chuck Bednarik	35.00	18.00	11.00
29	Kyle Rote	15.00	8.00	5.00
30	Les Richter	12.00	6.00	3.50
31	Howard Ferguson	12.00	6.00	3.50
32	Dorne Dibble	12.00	6.00	3.50
33	Kenny Konz	12.00	6.00	3.50
34	Dave Mann	30.00	15.00	9.00
35	Rick Casares	12.00	6.00	3.50
36	Art Donovan	35.00	18.00	11.00
37	Chuck Drazenovich	35.00	18.00	11.00
38	Joe Arenas	12.00	6.00	3.50
39	Lynn Chandnois	12.00	6.00	3.50
40	**Philadelphia Eagles**	20.00	10.00	6.00
41	Roosevelt Brown **RC**	50.00	25.00	15.00
42	Tom Fears	35.00	18.00	11.00
43	Gary Knafelc	12.00	6.00	3.50
44	Joe Schmidt **RC**	50.00	25.00	15.00
45	**Cleveland Browns**	20.00	10.00	6.00
46	Len Teeuws	30.00	15.00	9.00
47	Bill George **RC**	50.00	25.00	15.00
48	**Baltimore Colts**	20.00	10.00	6.00
49	Eddie LeBaron SP	65.00	38.00	23.00
50	Hugh McElhenry	35.00	18.00	11.00
51	Ted Marchibroda	12.00	6.00	3.50
52	Adrian Burk	12.00	6.00	3.50
53	Frank Gifford	60.00	30.00	18.00
54	Charley Toogood	12.00	6.00	3.50
55	Tobin Rote	12.00	6.00	3.50
56	Bill Stits	12.00	6.00	3.50
57	Don Colo	12.00	6.00	3.50
58	Ollie Matson SP	80.00	40.00	24.00
59	Harlon Hill	12.00	6.00	3.50
60	Lenny Moore **RC**	115.00	58.00	35.00
61	**Washington Redskins SP**	80.00	40.00	24.00
62	Billy Wilson	12.00	6.00	3.50
63	**Pittsburgh Steelers**	20.00	10.00	6.00
64	Bob Pellegrini	12.00	6.00	3.50
65	Ken MacAfee	12.00	6.00	3.50
66	Willard Sherman	12.00	6.00	3.50
67	Roger Zatkoff	12.00	6.00	3.50
68	Dave Middleton	12.00	6.00	3.50
69	Ray Renfro	12.00	6.00	3.50
70	Don Stonesifer	20.00	10.00	6.00
71	Stan Jones **RC**	50.00	25.00	15.00
72	Jim Mutscheller	12.00	6.00	3.50
73	Volney Peters	35.00	18.00	11.00
74	Leo Nomellini	20.00	10.00	6.00
75	Ray Mathews	12.00	6.00	3.50
76	Dick Bielski	12.00	6.00	3.50
77	Charley Conerly	35.00	18.00	11.00
78	Elroy Hirsch	35.00	18.00	11.00
79	Bill Forester **RC**	12.00	6.00	3.50
80	Jim Doran	12.00	6.00	3.50
81	Fred Morrison	12.00	6.00	3.50
82	Jack Simmons	20.00	10.00	6.00
83	Bill McColl	12.00	6.00	3.50
84	Bert Rechichar	12.00	6.00	3.50
85	Joe Scudero	35.00	18.00	11.00
86	Y.A. Tittle	45.00	23.00	14.00
87	Ernie Stautner	30.00	15.00	9.00
88	Norm Willey	12.00	6.00	3.50
89	Bob Schnelker	12.00	6.00	3.50
90	Dan Towler	12.00	6.00	3.50
91	John Martinkovic	12.00	6.00	3.50
92	**Detroit Lions**	20.00	10.00	6.00
93	George Ratterman	12.00	6.00	3.50
94	Chuck Ulrich	20.00	10.00	6.00
95	Bobby Watkins	12.00	6.00	3.50
96	Buddy Young	12.00	6.00	3.50
97	Billy Wells	30.00	15.00	9.00
98	Bob Toneff	12.00	6.00	3.50
99	Bill McPeak	12.00	6.00	3.50
100	Bobby Thompason	12.00	6.00	3.50
101	Roosevelt Grier **RC**	50.00	25.00	15.00
102	Ron Waller	12.00	6.00	3.50
103	Bobby Dillon	12.00	6.00	3.50
104	Leon Hart	12.00	6.00	3.50
105	Mike McCormack	30.00	15.00	9.00
106	John Olszewski	30.00	15.00	9.00
107	Bill Wightkin	12.00	6.00	3.50
108	George Shaw **RC**	12.00	6.00	3.50
109	Dale Atkeson	35.00	18.00	11.00
110	Joe Perry	35.00	18.00	11.00
111	Dale Dodrill	12.00	6.00	3.50
112	Tom Scott	12.00	6.00	3.50
113	**New York Giants**	20.00	10.00	6.00
114	**Los Angeles Rams**	20.00	10.00	6.00
115	Al Carmichael	6.00	2.50	1.50
116	Bobby Layne	45.00	23.00	14.00
117	Ed Modzelewski	6.00	2.50	1.50
118	Lamar McHan	20.00	10.00	6.00
119	**Chicago Bears**	20.00	10.00	6.00
120	Billy Vessels **RC**	50.00	25.00	15.00
---	**Contest Card 1**	110.00	55.00	33.00
---	**Contest Card 2**	110.00	55.00	33.00
---	**Contest Card 3**	115.00	55.00	33.00
---	**Contest Card A**	125.00	65.00	39.00
---	**Contest Card B**	150.00	75.00	45.00

1957 Topps

This 154-card set (not including the unnumbered checklist) has a horizontal format with two different pictures of the player on each side -- a head shot and a posed action shot. Issued in two series, the second series is more difficult to obtain than the first. Rookie cards in this set include Night Train Lane, Ray Berry, Earl Morrall, Bart Starr, John Unitas and Paul Hornung. Second-year cards include Roosevelt Brown, Pat Summerall, John Henry Johnson, Bob St. Clair, Lenny Moore and Len Ford (this is also his last regular-issued card). The final regular-issue card of Elroy Hirsch is also in this set. One variation does exist: The scarce card #58 of Willard Sherman has no team name on the front. The corrected version reads "Los Angeles Rams." It's believed that a number of the high series cards are short-printed, including Starr, Unitas and Hornung.

	NM	E	VG
Complete Set (155):	4,250	2,125	1,275
Common Player (1-88):	12.00	6.00	3.50
Minor Stars (1-88):	6.00		
Unlisted Stars (1-88):	8.00		
Common Player (89-154):	20.00	10.00	6.00
Minor Stars (89-154):	15.00		
Unlisted Stars (89-154):	15.00		
Checklist:	900.00	450.00	270.00
Series 1 Wax Pack (6):	400.00		
Series 2 Wax Pack (6):	800.00		

1	Eddie LeBaron	55.00	28.00	17.00
2	Pete Retzlaff **RC**	20.00	10.00	6.00
3	Mike McCormack	20.00	10.00	6.00
4	Lou Baldacci	12.00	6.00	3.50
5	Gino Marchetti	25.00	13.00	8.00
6	Leo Nomellini	30.00	15.00	9.00
7	Bobby Watkins	12.00	6.00	3.50
8	Dave Middleton	12.00	6.00	3.50
9	Bobby Dillon	12.00	6.00	3.50
10	Les Richter	12.00	6.00	3.50
11	Roosevelt Brown	30.00	15.00	9.00
12	Lavern Torgeson **RC**	12.00	6.00	3.50
13	Dick Bielski	12.00	6.00	3.50
14	Pat Summerall	28.00	14.00	8.50
15	Jack Butler **RC**	20.00	10.00	6.00
16	John Henry Johnson	22.00	11.00	6.50
17	Art Spinney	12.00	6.00	3.50
18	Bob St. Clair	20.00	10.00	6.00
19	Perry Jeter	12.00	6.00	3.50
20	Lou Creekmur	20.00	10.00	6.00
21	Dave Hanner	12.00	6.00	3.50
22	Norm Van Brocklin	45.00	28.00	17.00
23	Don Chandler **RC**	12.00	6.00	3.50
24	Al Dorow	12.00	6.00	3.50
25	Tom Scott	12.00	6.00	3.50
26	Ollie Matson	30.00	15.00	9.00
27	Fran Rogel	12.00	6.00	3.50
28	Lou Groza	30.00	15.00	9.00
29	Billy Vessels	12.00	6.00	3.50

30	Y.A. Tittle	50.00	25.00	15.00
31	George Blanda	50.00	25.00	15.00
32	Bobby Layne	50.00	25.00	15.00
33	Bill Howton	12.00	6.00	3.50
34	Bill Wade	12.00	6.00	3.50
35	Emlen Tunnell	20.00	10.00	6.00
36	Leo Elter	12.00	6.00	3.50
37	Clarence Peaks **RC**	12.00	6.00	3.50
38	Don Stonesifer	12.00	6.00	3.50
39	George Tarasovic	12.00	6.00	3.50
40	Darrell Brewster	12.00	6.00	3.50
41	Bert Rechichar	12.00	6.00	3.50
42	Billy Wilson	12.00	6.00	3.50
43	Ed Brown	12.00	6.00	3.50
44	Gene Gedman	12.00	6.00	3.50
45	Gary Knafelc	12.00	6.00	3.50
46	Elroy Hirsch	30.00	15.00	9.00
47	Don Heinrich	12.00	6.00	3.50
48	Gene Brito	12.00	6.00	3.50
49	Chuck Bednarik	30.00	15.00	9.00
50	Dave Mann	12.00	6.00	3.50
51	Bill McPeak	12.00	6.00	3.50
52	Kenny Konz	12.00	6.00	3.50
53	Alan Ameche	15.00	9.00	6.00
54	Gordon Soltau	12.00	6.00	3.50
55	Rick Casares	12.00	6.00	3.50
56	Charlie Ane	12.00	6.00	3.50
57	Al Carmichael	12.00	6.00	3.50
58A	Willard Sherman ERR (no team name on front)	300.00	150.00	90.00
58B	Willard Sherman COR (Rams)	12.00	6.00	3.50
59	Kyle Rote	12.00	6.00	3.50
60	Chuck Drazenovich	12.00	6.00	3.50
61	Bobby Walston	12.00	6.00	3.50
62	John Olszewski	12.00	6.00	3.50
63	Ray Mathews	12.00	6.00	3.50
64	Maurice Bassett	12.00	6.00	3.50
65	Art Donovan	30.00	15.00	9.00
66	Joe Arenas	12.00	6.00	3.50
67	Harlon Hill	12.00	6.00	3.50
68	Yale Lary	25.00	13.00	8.00
69	Bill Forester	12.00	6.00	3.50
70	Bob Boyd	12.00	6.00	3.50
71	Andy Robustelli	30.00	15.00	9.00
72	Sam Baker **RC**	12.00	6.00	3.50
73	Bob Pellegrini	12.00	6.00	3.50
74	Leo Sanford	12.00	6.00	3.50
75	Sid Watson	12.00	6.00	3.50
76	Ray Renfro	12.00	6.00	3.50
77	Carl Taseff	12.00	6.00	3.50
78	Clyde Conner	12.00	6.00	3.50
79	J.C. Caroline	12.00	6.00	3.50
80	Howard Cassady **RC**	20.00	10.00	6.00
81	Tobin Rote	12.00	6.00	3.50
82	Ron Waller	12.00	6.00	3.50
83	Jim Patton **RC**	12.00	6.00	3.50
84	Volney Peters	12.00	6.00	3.50
85	Dick "Night Train" Lane **RC**	95.00	50.00	30.00
86	Royce Womble	12.00	6.00	3.50
87	Duane Putnam **RC**	12.00	6.00	3.50
88	Frank Gifford	60.00	30.00	18.00
89	Steve Meilinger	20.00	10.00	6.00
90	Buck Lansford	20.00	10.00	6.00
91	Lindon Crow	20.00	10.00	6.00
92	Ernie Stautner	30.00	15.00	9.00
93	Preston Carpenter **RC**	20.00	10.00	6.00
94	Raymond Berry **RC**	185.00	93.00	56.00
95	Hugh McElhenny	45.00	28.00	17.00
96	Stan Jones	30.00	15.00	9.00
97	Dorne Dibble	20.00	10.00	6.00
98	Joe Scudero	20.00	10.00	6.00
99	Eddie Bell	20.00	10.00	6.00
100	Joe Childress	20.00	10.00	6.00
101	Elbert Nickel	20.00	10.00	6.00
102	Walt Michaels	20.00	10.00	6.00
103	Jim Mutscheller	20.00	10.00	6.00
104	Earl Morrall **RC**	70.00	35.00	21.00
105	Larry Strickland	20.00	10.00	6.00
106	Jack Christiansen	20.00	10.00	6.00
107	Fred Cone	20.00	10.00	6.00
108	Bud McFadin **RC**	20.00	10.00	6.00
109	Charley Conerly	45.00	28.00	17.00
110	Tom Runnels	20.00	10.00	6.00
111	Ken Keller	20.00	10.00	6.00
112	James Root	20.00	10.00	6.00
113	Ted Marchibroda	20.00	10.00	6.00
114	Don Paul	20.00	10.00	6.00
115	George Shaw	20.00	10.00	6.00
116	Dick Moegle	20.00	10.00	6.00
117	Don Bingham	20.00	10.00	6.00
118	Leon Hart	30.00	15.00	9.00
119	Bart Starr **RC**	560.00	280.00	168.00
120	Paul Miller	20.00	10.00	6.00
121	Alex Webster	25.00	13.00	8.00
122	Ray Wietecha	20.00	10.00	6.00
123	Johnny Carson	20.00	10.00	6.00
124	Tommy McDonald **RC**	100.00	50.00	30.00
125	Jerry Tubbs **RC**	20.00	10.00	6.00
126	Jack Scarbath	20.00	10.00	6.00
127	Ed Modzelewski	20.00	10.00	6.00
128	Lenny Moore	60.00	30.00	18.00
129	Joe Perry	45.00	28.00	17.00
130	Bill Wightkin	20.00	10.00	6.00
131	Jim Doran	20.00	10.00	6.00
132	Howard Ferguson	20.00	10.00	6.00
133	Tom Wilson	20.00	10.00	6.00
134	Dick James	20.00	10.00	6.00
135	Jimmy Harris	20.00	10.00	6.00
136	Chuck Ulrich	20.00	10.00	6.00
137	Lynn Chandnois	20.00	10.00	6.00
138	Johnny Unitas **RC**	500.00	250.00	150.00
139	Jim Ridlon	20.00	10.00	6.00
140	Zeke Bratkowski	20.00	10.00	6.00
141	Ray Krouse	20.00	10.00	6.00
142	John Martinkovic	20.00	10.00	6.00
143	Jim Cason	20.00	10.00	6.00
144	Ken MacAfee	20.00	10.00	6.00
145	Sid Youngelman **RC**	20.00	10.00	6.00
146	Paul Larson	20.00	10.00	6.00
147	Len Ford	40.00	20.00	12.00
148	Bob Toneff	20.00	10.00	6.00
149	Ronnie Knox	20.00	10.00	6.00
150	Jim David **RC**	20.00	10.00	6.00
151	Paul Hornung **RC**	450.00	225.00	135.00
152	Tank Younger	20.00	10.00	6.00
153	Bill Svoboda	20.00	10.00	6.00
154	Fred Morrison	90.00	45.00	27.00

1958 Topps

This 132-card set features an oval photo of the player on the front and a bright red background on the back. The card set also includes team cards, which had been missing from the previous year's set. Rookies here include Jim Brown and Sonny Jurgensen. Second-year cards are those of Bart Starr, Jim Ringo (his rookie was in '55), Bill George, and Ray Berry. This set also includes the last Topps card of Jack Christiansen.

	NM	E	VG
Complete Set (132):	4,500	2,250	1,350
Common Player:	10.00	5.00	3.00
Minor Stars:	10.00		
Unlisted Stars:	15.00		
Wax Pack (6):	475.00		

1	Gene Filipski **RC**	35.00	18.00	11.00
2	Bobby Layne	40.00	20.00	12.00
3	Joe Schmidt	20.00	10.00	6.00
4	Bill Barnes	10.00	5.00	3.00
5	Milt Plum **RC**	15.00	7.50	4.50
6	Billie Howton	10.00	5.00	3.00
7	Howard Cassady	10.00	5.00	3.00
8	James Dooley	10.00	5.00	3.00
9	**Cleveland Browns Team**	15.00	7.50	4.50
10	Lenny Moore	30.00	15.00	9.00
11	Pete Brewster	10.00	5.00	3.00
12	Alan Ameche	15.00	7.50	4.50
13	Jim David	10.00	5.00	3.00
14	Jim Mutscheller	10.00	5.00	3.00
15	Andy Robustelli	15.00	7.50	4.50
16	Gino Marchetti	20.00	10.00	6.00
17	Ray Renfro	10.00	5.00	3.00
18	Yale Lary	15.00	7.50	4.50
19	Gary Glick	10.00	5.00	3.00
20	Jon Arnett **RC**	15.00	7.50	4.50
21	Bob Boyd	10.00	5.00	3.00
22	Johnny Unitas	150.00	75.00	45.00
23	Zeke Bratkowski	10.00	5.00	3.00
24	Sid Youngelman	10.00	5.00	3.00
25	Leo Elter	10.00	5.00	3.00
26	Ken Konz	10.00	5.00	3.00
27	**Washington Redskins Team**	15.00	7.50	4.50
28	C. Brettschneider	10.00	5.00	3.00
29	**Chicago Bears Team**	15.00	7.50	4.50
30	Alex Webster	10.00	5.00	3.00
31	Al Carmichael	10.00	5.00	3.00
32	Bobby Dillon	10.00	5.00	3.00
33	Steve Meilinger	10.00	5.00	3.00
34	Sam Baker	10.00	5.00	3.00
35	Chuck Bednarik	20.00	10.00	6.00
36	Vic Zucco	10.00	5.00	3.00
37	George Tarasovic	10.00	5.00	3.00
38	Bill Wade	10.00	5.00	3.00
39	Dick Stanfell	10.00	5.00	3.00
40	Jerry Norton	10.00	5.00	3.00
41	**San Francisco 49ers Team**	15.00	7.50	4.50
42	Emlen Tunnell	20.00	10.00	6.00
43	Jim Doran	10.00	5.00	3.00
44	Ted Marchibroda	10.00	5.00	3.00
45	Chet Hanulak	10.00	5.00	3.00
46	Dale Dodrill	10.00	5.00	3.00
47	John Carson	10.00	5.00	3.00
48	Dick Deschaine	10.00	5.00	3.00
49	Billy Wells	10.00	5.00	3.00
50	Larry Morris	10.00	5.00	3.00
51	Jack McClairen	10.00	5.00	3.00
52	Lou Groza	20.00	10.00	6.00
53	Rick Casares	10.00	5.00	3.00
54	Don Chandler	10.00	5.00	3.00
55	Duane Putnam	10.00	5.00	3.00
56	Gary Knafelc	10.00	5.00	3.00
57	Earl Morrall	12.00	6.00	3.50
58	Ron Kramer **RC**	10.00	5.00	3.00
59	Mike McCormack	10.00	5.00	3.00
60	Gern Nagler	10.00	5.00	3.00
61	**New York Giants Team**	15.00	7.50	4.50
62	Jim Brown **RC**	600.00	300.00	180.00
63	Joe Marconi **RC**	10.00	5.00	3.00
64	R.C. Owens **RC**	10.00	5.00	3.00
65	Jimmy Carr **RC**	10.00	5.00	3.00
66	Bart Starr	100.00	50.00	30.00
67	Tom Wilson	10.00	5.00	3.00
68	Lamar McHan	10.00	5.00	3.00
69	**Chicago Cardinals Team**	15.00	7.50	4.50
70	Jack Christiansen	10.00	5.00	3.00
71	Don McElhenny **RC**	10.00	5.00	3.00
72	Ron Waller	10.00	5.00	3.00
73	Frank Gifford	50.00	25.00	15.00
74	Bert Rechichar	10.00	5.00	3.00
75	John H. Johnson	10.00	5.00	3.00
76	Jack Butler	10.00	5.00	3.00
77	Frank Varrichione	10.00	5.00	3.00
78	Ray Mathews	10.00	5.00	3.00
79	Mary Matsuzak	10.00	5.00	3.00
80	Harlon Hill	10.00	5.00	3.00
81	Lou Creekmur	15.00	7.50	4.50
82	Woody Lewis	10.00	5.00	3.00
83	Don Heinrich	10.00	5.00	3.00
84	Charley Conerly	15.00	7.50	4.50
85	**Los Angeles Rams Team**	15.00	7.50	4.50
86	Y.A. Tittle	35.00	18.00	11.00
87	Bob Walston	10.00	5.00	3.00
88	Earl Putnam	10.00	5.00	3.00
89	Leo Nomellini	20.00	10.00	6.00
90	Sonny Jurgensen **RC**	125.00	65.00	39.00
91	Don Paul	10.00	5.00	3.00
92	Paige Cothren	10.00	5.00	3.00
93	Joe Perry	25.00	13.00	8.00
94	Tobin Rote	10.00	5.00	3.00
95	Billy Wilson	10.00	5.00	3.00
96	**Green Bay Packers Team**	15.00	7.50	4.50
97	Torgy Torgeson	10.00	5.00	3.00
98	Milt Davis	10.00	5.00	3.00
99	Larry Strickland	10.00	5.00	3.00
100	Matt Hazeltine **RC**	10.00	5.00	3.00
101	Walt Yowarski	10.00	5.00	3.00
102	Roosevelt Brown	20.00	10.00	6.00
103	Jim Ringo	20.00	10.00	6.00
104	Joe Krupa	10.00	5.00	3.00
105	Les Richter	10.00	5.00	3.00
106	Art Donovan	30.00	15.00	9.00
107	John Olszewski	10.00	5.00	3.00
108	Ken Keller	10.00	5.00	3.00
109	**Philadelphia Eagles Team**	15.00	7.50	4.50
110	**Baltimore Colts Team**	15.00	7.50	4.50
111	Dick Bielski	10.00	5.00	3.00
112	Eddie LeBaron	10.00	5.00	3.00
113	Gene Brito	10.00	5.00	3.00
114	William Galimore **RC**	12.00	6.00	3.50
115	**Detroit Lions Team**	15.00	7.50	4.50
116	**Pittsburgh Steelers Team**	15.00	7.50	4.50
117	L.G. Dupre	10.00	5.00	3.00
118	Babe Parilli	10.00	5.00	3.00
119	Bill George	10.00	5.00	3.00
120	Raymond Berry	50.00	25.00	15.00
121	Jim Podoley	10.00	5.00	3.00
122	Hugh McElhenny	25.00	13.00	8.00
123	Ed Brown	10.00	5.00	3.00
124	Dicky Moegle	10.00	5.00	3.00

#	Player	NM	E	VG
125	Tom Scott	10.00	5.00	3.00
126	Tom McDonald	10.00	5.00	3.00
127	Ollie Matson	30.00	15.00	9.00
128	Preston Carpenter	10.00	5.00	3.00
129	George Blanda	35.00	18.00	11.00
130	Gordy Soltau	10.00	5.00	3.00
131	Dick Nolan **RC**	10.00	5.00	3.00
132	Don Bosseler **RC**	40.00	20.00	12.00

1958 Topps CFL

	NM	E	VG
Complete Set (88):	500.00	250.00	150.00
Common Player:	5.00	2.50	1.50

#	Player	NM	E	VG
1	Paul Anderson	12.00	6.00	3.50
2	Leigh McMillan	5.00	2.50	1.50
3	Vic Chapman	5.00	2.50	1.50
4	Bobby Marlow	12.00	6.00	3.50
5	Mike Cacic	5.00	2.50	1.50
6	Ron Pawlowski	5.00	2.50	1.50
7	Frank Morris	9.00	4.50	2.75
8	Earl Keeley	6.00	3.00	1.75
9	Don Walsh	5.00	2.50	1.50
10	Bryan Engram	5.00	2.50	1.50
11	Bobby Kuntz	6.00	3.00	1.75
12	Jerry Janes	5.00	2.50	1.50
13	Don Bingham	5.00	2.50	1.50
14	Paul Fedor	5.00	2.50	1.50
15	Tommy Grant	12.00	6.00	3.50
16	Don Getty	20.00	10.00	6.00
17	George Brancato	6.00	3.00	1.75
18	Jackie Parker	40.00	20.00	12.00
19	Alan Valdes	5.00	2.50	1.50
20	Paul Dekker	5.00	2.50	1.50
21	Frank Tripucka	12.00	6.00	3.50
22	Gerry McDougall	9.00	4.50	2.75
23	Duke Dewveall	6.00	3.00	1.75
24	Ted Smale	5.00	2.50	1.50
25	Tony Pajaczkowski	12.00	6.00	3.50
26	Don Pinhey	5.00	2.50	1.50
27	Buddy Tinsley	12.00	6.00	3.50
28	Cookie Gilchrist	35.00	17.50	10.50
29	Larry Isbell	5.00	2.50	1.50
30	Bob Kelley	5.00	2.50	1.50
31	Tom "Corky" Tharp	6.00	3.00	1.75
32	Steve Patrick	5.00	2.50	1.50
33	Hardiman Cureton	5.00	2.50	1.50
34	Joe Mobra	5.00	2.50	1.50
35	Harry Lunn	5.00	2.50	1.50
36	Gord Rowland	6.00	3.00	1.75
37	Herb Gray	15.00	7.50	4.50
38	Bob Simpson	15.00	7.50	4.50
39	Cam Fraser	5.00	2.50	1.50
40	Kenny Ploen	18.00	9.00	5.50
41	Lynn Bottoms	6.00	3.00	1.75
42	Bill Stevenson	5.00	2.50	1.50
43	Jerry Selinger	5.00	2.50	1.50
44	Oscar Kruger	9.00	4.50	2.75
45	Gerry James	15.00	7.50	4.50
46	Dave Mann	12.00	6.00	3.50
47	Tom Dimitroff	5.00	2.50	1.50
48	Vince Scott	12.00	6.00	3.50
49	Fran Rogel	6.00	3.00	1.75
50	Henry Hair	5.00	2.50	1.50
51	Bob Brady	5.00	2.50	1.50
52	Gerry Doucette	5.00	2.50	1.50
53	Ken Carpenter	6.00	3.00	1.75
54	Bernie Faloney	25.00	12.50	7.50
55	John Barrow	20.00	10.00	6.00
56	George Druxman	5.00	2.50	1.50
57	Rollie Miles	12.00	6.00	3.50
58	Jerry Cornelison	5.00	2.50	1.50
59	Harry Langford	5.00	2.50	1.50
60	Johnny Bright	20.00	10.00	6.00
61	Ron Clinkscale	5.00	2.50	1.50
62	Jack Hill	5.00	2.50	1.50
63	Ron Quillian	5.00	2.50	1.50
64	Ted Tully	5.00	2.50	1.50
65	Pete Neft	5.00	2.50	1.50
66	Arvyd Buntins	5.00	2.50	1.50
67	Normie Kwong	20.00	10.00	6.00
68	Matt Phillips	5.00	2.50	1.50
69	Pete Bennett	5.00	2.50	1.50
70	Vern Lofstrom	5.00	2.50	1.50
71	Norm Stoneburgh	5.00	2.50	1.50
72	Danny Nykoluk	5.00	2.50	1.50
73	Chuck Dubuque	5.00	2.50	1.50
74	John Varone	5.00	2.50	1.50
75	Bob Kimoff	5.00	2.50	1.50
76	John Pyeatt	5.00	2.50	1.50
77	Pete Neumann	12.00	6.00	3.50
78	Ernie Pitts	9.00	4.50	2.75
79	Steve Oneschuk	5.00	2.50	1.50
80	Kaye Vaughan	12.00	6.00	3.50
81	Joe Yamauchi	5.00	2.50	1.50
82	Harvey Wylie	9.00	4.50	2.75
83	Berdett Hess	5.00	2.50	1.50
84	Dick Shatto	20.00	10.00	6.00
85	Floyd Harrawood	5.00	2.50	1.50
86	Ron Atchison	12.00	6.00	3.50
87	Bobby Judd	5.00	2.50	1.50
88	Keith Pearce	9.00	4.50	2.75

1959 Topps

This 176-card set, featuring alternating blue and red letters for player names, was issued in two series, with the first being more valuable than the second. Team cards also included checklists on the back of each, and pennant cards were included and numbered as part of the set. This set showcases the rookie cards of Max McGee, Sam Huff, Alex Karras, John David Crow, Jerry Kramer, Jim Parker, Bobby Mitchell, and Jim Taylor (actually not the HOFer; see below). Second-year cards in the set are those of Paul Hornung and Jim Brown. Card #155, Jim Taylor, does not show the HOF running back for the Packers, as the card reads; instead, it shows Chicago Cardinal linebacker Jim Taylor. This mistake was repeated the following year, meaning a card actually depicting Taylor did not appear until 1961.

	NM	E	VG
Complete Set (176):	4,000	2,000	1,200
Common Player (1-88):	10.00	5.00	3.00
Minor Stars (1-88):	5.00		
Unlisted Stars (1-88):	8.00		
Common Player (89-176):	10.00	5.00	3.00
Minor Stars (89-176):	3.00		
Unlisted Stars (89-176):	5.00		
Team Cards:	11.00	5.50	3.25
Series 1 Wax Pack (6):	350.00		
Series 2 Wax Pack (6):	300.00		

#	Player	NM	E	VG
1	Johnny Unitas	140.00	70.00	42.00
2	Gene Brito	10.00	5.00	3.00
3	**Detroit Lions Team Card**	11.00	5.50	3.25
4	Max McGee **RC**	25.00	13.00	8.00
5	Hugh McElhenny	25.00	13.00	8.00
6	Joe Schmidt	15.00	7.50	4.50
7	Kyle Rote	15.00	7.50	4.50
8	Clarence Peaks	10.00	5.00	3.00
9	**Pittsburgh Steelers Pennant Card**	11.00	5.50	3.25
10	Jim Brown	140.00	70.00	42.00
11	Ray Mathews	10.00	5.00	3.00
12	Bobby Dillon	10.00	5.00	3.00
13	Joe Childress	10.00	5.00	3.00
14	Terry Barr	10.00	5.00	3.00
15	Del Shofner **RC**	13.00	6.50	4.00
16	Bob Pellegrini	10.00	5.00	3.00
17	**Baltimore Colts Team Card**	11.00	5.50	3.25
18	Preston Carpenter	10.00	5.00	3.00
19	Leo Nomellini	20.00	10.00	6.00
20	Frank Gifford	45.00	23.00	14.00
21	Charlie Ane	10.00	5.00	3.00
22	Jack Butler	10.00	5.00	3.00
23	Bart Starr	60.00	30.00	18.00
24	**Chicago Cardinals Pennant Card**	11.00	5.50	3.25
25	Bill Barnes	10.00	5.00	3.00
26	Walt Michaels	12.00	6.00	3.60
27	Clyde Conner	10.00	5.00	3.00
28	Paige Cothren	10.00	5.00	3.00
29	Roosevelt Grier	20.00	10.00	6.00
30	Alan Ameche	15.00	7.50	4.50
31	**Philadelphia Eagles Team Card**	11.00	5.50	3.25
32	Dick Nolan	15.00	7.50	4.50
33	R.C. Owens	15.00	7.50	4.50
34	Dale Dodrill	10.00	5.00	3.00
35	Gene Gedman	10.00	5.00	3.00
36	Gene Lipscomb **RC**	15.00	7.50	4.50
37	Ray Renfro	10.00	5.00	3.00
38	**Cleveland Brown Pennant Card**	11.00	5.50	3.25
39	Bill Forester	10.00	5.00	3.00
40	Bobby Layne	35.00	18.00	11.00
41	Pat Summerall	25.00	13.00	8.00
42	Jerry Mertens	10.00	5.00	3.00
43	Steve Myhra	10.00	5.00	3.00
44	John Henry Johnson	15.00	7.50	4.50
45	Woody Lewis	10.00	5.00	3.00
46	**Green Bay Packers Team Card**	11.00	5.50	3.25
47	Don Owens	10.00	5.00	3.00
48	Ed Beatty	10.00	5.00	3.00
49	Don Chandler	10.00	5.00	3.00
50	Ollie Matson	25.00	13.00	8.00
51	Sam Huff **RC**	55.00	28.00	17.00
52	Tom Miner	10.00	5.00	3.00
53	**New York Giants Pennant Card**	11.00	5.50	3.25
54	Kenny Konz	10.00	5.00	3.00
55	Raymond Berry	30.00	15.00	9.00
56	Howard Ferguson	10.00	5.00	3.00
57	Chuck Ulrich	10.00	5.00	3.00
58	Bob St. Clair	15.00	7.50	4.50
59	Don Burroughs **RC**	10.00	5.00	3.00
60	Lou Groza	25.00	13.00	8.00
61	**San Francisco 49ers Team Card**	11.00	5.50	3.25
62	Andy Nelson	10.00	5.00	3.00
63	Hal Bradley	10.00	5.00	3.00
64	Dave Hanner	13.00	6.50	4.00
65	Chuck Connerly	20.00	10.00	6.00
66	Gene Cronin	10.00	5.00	3.00
67	Duane Putnam	10.00	5.00	3.00
68	**Baltimore Colts Pennant Card**	11.00	5.50	3.25
69	Ernie Stautner	18.00	9.00	5.50
70	Jon Arnett	10.00	5.00	3.00
71	Ken Panfil	10.00	5.00	3.00
72	Matt Hazeltine	10.00	5.00	3.00
73	Harley Sewell	10.00	5.00	3.00
74	Mike McCormack	15.00	7.50	4.50
75	Jim Ringo	15.00	7.50	4.50
76	**Los Angeles Rams Team Card**	11.00	5.50	3.25
77	Bob Gain **RC**	10.00	5.00	3.00
78	Buzz Nutter	10.00	5.00	3.00
79	Jerry Norton	10.00	5.00	3.00
80	Joe Perry	25.00	13.00	8.00
81	Carl Brettschneider	10.00	5.00	3.00
82	Paul Hornung	60.00	30.00	18.00
83	**Philadelphia Eagles Pennant Card**	11.00	5.50	3.25
84	Les Richter	10.00	5.00	3.00
85	Howard Cassady	15.00	7.50	4.50
86	Art Donovan	25.00	13.00	8.00
87	Jim Patton	15.00	7.50	4.50
88	Pete Retzlaff	15.00	7.50	4.50
89	Jim Mutscheller	10.00	5.00	3.00
90	Zeke Bratkowski	10.00	5.00	3.00
91	**Washington Redskins Team Card**	11.00	5.50	3.25
92	Art Hunter	10.00	5.00	3.00
93	Gern Nagler	10.00	5.00	3.00
94	Chuck Weber	10.00	5.00	3.00
95	Lew Carpenter **RC**	10.00	5.00	3.00
96	Stan Jones	15.00	7.50	4.50
97	Ralph Guglielmi	10.00	5.00	3.00
98	**Green Bay Packer Pennant Card**	11.00	5.50	3.25
99	Ray Wietecha	10.00	5.00	3.00
100	Lenny Moore	25.00	13.00	8.00
101	Jim Ray Smith **RC**	10.00	5.00	3.00
102	Abe Woodson **RC**	10.00	5.00	3.00
103	Alex Karras **RC**	45.00	23.00	14.00
104	**Chicago Bears Team Card**	11.00	5.50	3.25
105	Johnny Crow **RC**	25.00	13.00	8.00
106	Joe Fortunato **RC**	10.00	5.00	3.00
107	Babe Parilli	10.00	5.00	3.00
108	Proverb Jacobs	10.00	5.00	3.00
109	Gino Marchetti	15.00	7.50	4.50
110	Bill Wade	10.00	5.00	3.00
111	**San Francisco 49ers Pennant Card**	11.00	5.50	3.25
112	Karl Rubke	10.00	5.00	3.00
113	Dave Middleton	10.00	5.00	3.00
114	Roosevelt Brown	20.00	10.00	6.00
115	John Olszewski	10.00	5.00	3.00
116	Jerry Kramer **RC**	35.00	18.00	11.00
117	King Hill **RC**	10.00	5.00	3.00
118	**Chicago Cardinals Team Card**	11.00	5.50	3.25
119	Frank Viarrichione	10.00	5.00	3.00
120	Rick Casares	10.00	5.00	3.00
121	George Strugar	10.00	5.00	3.00
122	Bill Glass **RC**	10.00	5.00	3.00
123	Don Bosseler	10.00	5.00	3.00
124	John Reger	10.00	5.00	3.00
125	Jim Ninowski **RC**	10.00	5.00	3.00
126	**Los Angeles Rams Pennant Card**	11.00	5.50	3.25
127	Willard Sherman	10.00	5.00	3.00
128	Bob Schnelker	10.00	5.00	3.00
129	Ollie Spencer	10.00	5.00	3.00
130	Y.A. Tittle	35.00	18.00	11.00

131	Yale Lary	15.00	7.50	4.50
132	Jim Parker **RC**	30.00	15.00	9.00
133	**New York Giants Team Card**	11.00	5.50	3.25
134	Jim Schrader	10.00	5.00	3.00
135	M.C. Reynolds	10.00	5.00	3.00
136	Mike Sandusky	10.00	5.00	3.00
137	Ed Brown	10.00	5.00	3.00
138	Al Barry	10.00	5.00	3.00
139	**Detroit Lions Pennant Card**	11.00	5.50	3.25
140	Bobby Mitchell **RC**	30.00	15.00	9.00
141	Larry Morris	10.00	5.00	3.00
142	Jim Phillips **RC**	10.00	5.00	3.00
143	Jim David	10.00	5.00	3.00
144	Joe Krupa	10.00	5.00	3.00
145	Willie Galimore	10.00	5.00	3.00
146	**Pittsburgh Steelers Team Card**	11.00	5.50	3.25
147	Andy Robustelli	12.00	6.00	3.50
148	Bill Wilson	10.00	5.00	3.00
149	Leo Sanford	10.00	5.00	3.00
150	Eddie LeBaron	10.00	5.00	3.00
151	Bill McColl	10.00	5.00	3.00
152	Buck Lansford	10.00	5.00	3.00
153	**Chicago Bears Pennant Card**	11.00	5.50	3.25
154	Leo Sugar	10.00	5.00	3.00
155	Jim Taylor **RC**	35.00	17.50	10.50
156	Lindon Crow	10.00	5.00	3.00
157	Jack McClairen	10.00	5.00	3.00
158	Vince Costello **RC**	10.00	5.00	3.00
159	Stan Wallace	10.00	5.00	3.00
160	Mel Triplett **RC**	10.00	5.00	3.00
161	**Cleveland Browns Team Card**	11.00	5.50	3.25
162	Dan Currie	10.00	5.00	3.00
163	L.G. Dupre	10.00	5.00	3.00
164	John Morrow	10.00	5.00	3.00
165	Jim Podoley	10.00	5.00	3.00
166	Bruce Bosley **RC**	10.00	5.00	3.00
167	Harlon Hill	10.00	5.00	3.00
168	**Washington Redskins Pennant Card**	11.00	5.50	3.25
169	Junior Wren	10.00	5.00	3.00
170	Tobin Rote	10.00	5.00	3.00
171	Art Spinney	10.00	5.00	3.00
172	Chuck Drazenovich	10.00	5.00	3.00
173	Bobby Joe Conrad **RC**	10.00	5.00	3.00
174	Jesse Richardson	10.00	5.00	3.00
175	Sam Baker	10.00	5.00	3.00
176	Tom Tracy **RC**	20.00	10.00	6.00

1959 Topps CFL

	NM	E	VG
Complete Set (88):	400.00	200.00	120.00
Common Player:	4.00	2.00	1.25

1	Norm Rauhaus	10.00	5.00	3.00
2	Cornel Piper (UER) (Misspelled Cornell on both sides)	4.00	2.00	1.25
3	Leo Lewis	20.00	10.00	6.00
4	Roger Savoie	4.00	2.00	1.25
5	Jim Van Pelt	10.00	5.00	3.00
6	Herb Gray	10.00	5.00	3.00
7	Gerry James	10.00	5.00	3.00
8	By Bailey	12.00	6.00	3.50
9	Tom Hinton	8.00	4.00	2.50
10	Chuck Quilter	4.00	2.00	1.25
11	Mel Gillett	4.00	2.00	1.25
12	Ted Hunt	4.00	2.00	1.25
13	Sonny Homer	5.00	2.50	1.50
14	Bill Jessup	4.00	2.00	1.25
15	Al Dorow (Checklist 1-44 back)	20.00	10.00	6.00
16	Norm Fieldgate	12.00	6.00	3.50
17	Urban Henry	5.00	2.50	1.50
18	Paul Cameron	4.00	2.00	1.25
19	Bruce Claridge	4.00	2.00	1.25
20	Jim Bakhtiar	4.00	2.00	1.25
21	Earl Lunsford	12.00	6.00	3.50
22	Walt Radzick	4.00	2.00	1.25
23	Ron Albright	4.00	2.00	1.25
24	Art Scullion	4.00	2.00	1.25
25	Ernie Warlick	6.00	3.00	1.75
26	Nobby Wirkowski	5.00	2.50	1.50
27	Harvey Wylie	9.00	4.50	2.75
28	Gordon Brown	4.00	2.00	1.25
29	Don Luzzi	10.00	5.00	3.00
30	Hal Patterson	20.00	10.00	6.00
31	Jackie Simpson	15.00	7.50	4.50
32	Doug McNichol	4.00	2.00	1.25
33	Bob MacLellan	4.00	2.00	1.25
34	Ted Elsby	4.00	2.00	1.25
35	Mike Kovac	4.00	2.00	1.25
36	Bob Leary	4.00	2.00	1.25
37	Hal Krebs	4.00	2.00	1.25
38	Steve Jennings	4.00	2.00	1.25
39	Don Getty	12.00	6.00	3.50
40	Normie Kwong	12.00	6.00	3.50
41	Johnny Bright	15.00	7.50	4.50
42	Art Walker	5.00	2.50	1.50
43	Jackie Parker (UER) (Incorrectly listed as Tackle on card front)	35.00	17.50	10.50
44	Don Barry (Checklist 45-88 back)	20.00	10.00	6.00
45	Tommy Joe Coffey	25.00	12.50	7.50
46	Mike Volcan	4.00	2.00	1.25
47	Stan Renning	4.00	2.00	1.25
48	Gino Fracas	9.00	4.50	2.75
49	Ted Smale	4.00	2.00	1.25
50	Mack Yoho	5.00	2.50	1.50
51	Bobby Gravens	4.00	2.00	1.25
52	Milt Graham	4.00	2.00	1.25
53	Lou Bruce	4.00	2.00	1.25
54	Bob Simpson	12.00	6.00	3.50
55	Bill Sowalski	4.00	2.00	1.25
56	Russ Jackson	40.00	20.00	12.00
57	Don Clark	4.00	2.00	1.25
58	Dave Thelen	10.00	5.00	3.00
59	Larry Cowart	4.00	2.00	1.25
60	Dave Mann	5.00	2.50	1.50
61	Norm Stoneburgh (UER) (Misspelled Stoneburg)	4.00	2.00	1.25
62	Ronnie Knox	9.00	4.50	2.75
63	Dick Shatto	12.00	6.00	3.50
64	Bobby Kuntz	5.00	2.50	1.50
65	Phil Muntz	4.00	2.00	1.25
66	Gerry Doucette	4.00	2.00	1.25
67	Sam DeLuca	5.00	2.50	1.50
68	Boyd Carter	4.00	2.00	1.25
69	Vic Kristopaitis	9.00	4.50	2.75
70	Gerry McDougall (UER) (Misspelled Jerry)	5.00	2.50	1.50
71	Vince Scott	10.00	5.00	3.00
72	Angelo Mosca	35.00	17.50	10.50
73	Chet Miksza	4.00	2.00	1.25
74	Eddie Macon	5.00	2.50	1.50
75	Harry Lampman	4.00	2.00	1.25
76	Bill Graham	4.00	2.00	1.25
77	Ralph Goldston	5.00	2.50	1.50
78	Cam Fraser	4.00	2.00	1.25
79	Ron Dundas	4.00	2.00	1.25
80	Bill Clarke	4.00	2.00	1.25
81	Len Legault	4.00	2.00	1.25
82	Reg Whitehouse	4.00	2.00	1.25
83	Dale Parsons	4.00	2.00	1.25
84	Doug Kiloh	4.00	2.00	1.25
85	Tom Whitehouse	4.00	2.00	1.25
86	Mike Hagler	4.00	2.00	1.25
87	Paul Anderson	4.00	2.00	1.25
88	Danny Banda	5.00	2.50	1.50

1960 Topps

This 132-card set by Topps, featuring NFL players only (Fleer picked up teams from the AFL in its 1960 set), showcased the inclusion of the expansion Dallas Cowboys. Cards are again numbered alphabetically according to city name. Card backs had a "Football Funnies" quiz which revealed the answer underneath a scratch-off area. This set marks the rookie cards of HOFer Forrest Gregg, future announcer Tom Brookshier, and former Jets coach Joe Walton. Second-year cards in the set include Jim Parker, Doug Atkins (his rookie card was six years prior to his second-year card), Bobby Mitchell, and Sam Huff. There are three errors in the set. Card #52, Jim Taylor, shows not the HOF running back of the Packers, as advertised; it again shows Cardinals linebacker Jim Taylor. This mistake was made in the 1959 set as well. The other errors are reversed negatives; on the card of #97, Frank Varrichione, and on card #20, Doug Atkins.

	NM	E	VG
Complete Set (132):	1,200	600.00	350.00
Common Player:	10.00	5.00	3.00
Minor Stars:	2.50		
Unlisted Stars:	5.00		
Team Cards:	12.00	6.00	3.50
Wax Pack (6):	400.00		

1	Johnny Unitas	100.00	50.00	30.00
2	Alan Ameche	15.00	7.50	4.50
3	Lenny Moore	15.00	7.50	4.50
4	Raymond Berry	15.00	7.50	4.50
5	Jim Parker	15.00	7.50	4.50
6	George Preas	10.00	5.00	3.00
7	Art Spinney	10.00	5.00	3.00
8	Bill Pellington **RC**	10.00	5.00	3.00
9	Johnny Sample **RC**	10.00	5.00	3.00
10	Gene Lipscomb	10.00	5.00	3.00
11	**Baltimore Colts Team Card** (Checklist 67-132)	12.00	6.00	3.50
12	Ed Brown	10.00	5.00	3.00
13	Rick Casares	10.00	5.00	3.00
14	Willie Galimore	10.00	5.00	3.00
15	Jim Dooley	10.00	5.00	3.00
16	Harlon Hill	10.00	5.00	3.00
17	Stan Jones	12.00	6.00	3.50
18	Bill George	12.00	6.00	3.50
19	Erich Barnes **RC**	10.00	5.00	3.00
20	Doug Atkins	10.00	5.00	3.00
21	**Chicago Bears Team Card** (Checklist 1-66)	12.00	6.00	3.50
22	Milt Plum	10.00	5.00	3.00
23	Jim Brown	80.00	40.00	24.00
24	Sam Baker	10.00	5.00	3.00
25	Bobby Mitchell	15.00	7.50	4.50
26	Ray Renfro	10.00	5.00	3.00
27	Billy Howton	10.00	5.00	3.00
28	Jim Ray Smith	10.00	5.00	3.00
29	Jim Shofner **RC**	10.00	5.00	3.00
30	Bob Gain	10.00	5.00	3.00
31	**Cleveland Browns Team Card** (Checklist 1-66)	12.00	6.00	3.50
32	Don Heinrich	10.00	5.00	3.00
33	Ed Modzelewski	10.00	5.00	3.00
34	Fred Cone	10.00	5.00	3.00
35	L.G. Dupre	10.00	5.00	3.00
36	Dick Bielski	10.00	5.00	3.00
37	Charlie Ane	10.00	5.00	3.00
38	Jerry Tubbs	10.00	5.00	3.00
39	Doyle Nix	10.00	5.00	3.00
40	Ray Krouse	10.00	5.00	3.00
41	Earl Morrall	12.00	6.00	3.50
42	Hopalong Cassady	10.00	5.00	3.00
43	Dave Middleton	10.00	5.00	3.00
44	Jim Gibbons **RC**	10.00	5.00	3.00
45	Darris McCord	10.00	5.00	3.00
46	Joe Schmidt	15.00	7.50	4.50
47	Terry Barr	10.00	5.00	3.00
48	Yale Lary	12.00	6.00	3.50
49	Gil Mains	10.00	5.00	3.00
50	**Detroit Lions Team Card** (Checklist 1-66)	12.00	6.00	3.50
51	Bart Starr	40.00	20.00	12.00
52	Jim Taylor	15.00	7.50	4.50
53	Lew Carpenter	10.00	5.00	3.00
54	Paul Hornung	45.00	28.00	17.00
55	Max McGee	15.00	7.50	4.50
56	Forrest Gregg **RC**	40.00	20.00	12.00
57	Jim Ringo	12.00	6.00	3.50
58	Bill Forester	10.00	5.00	3.00
59	Dave Hanner	10.00	5.00	3.00
60	**Green Bay Packers Team Card** (Checklist 67-132)	12.00	6.00	3.50
61	Bill Wade	10.00	5.00	3.00
62	Frank Ryan **RC**	12.00	6.00	3.50
63	Ollie Matson	15.00	7.50	4.50
64	Jon Arnett	10.00	5.00	3.00
65	Del Shofner	10.00	5.00	3.00
66	Jim Phillips	10.00	5.00	3.00
67	Art Hunter	10.00	5.00	3.00
68	Les Richter	10.00	5.00	3.00
69	Lou Michaels **RC**	10.00	5.00	3.00
70	John Baker	10.00	5.00	3.00
71	**Los Angeles Rams Team Card** (Checklist 1-66)	12.00	6.00	3.50
72	Charley Conerly	15.00	7.50	4.50
73	Mel Triplett	10.00	5.00	3.00
74	Frank Gifford	40.00	20.00	12.00
75	Alex Webster	10.00	5.00	3.00
76	Bob Schnelker	10.00	5.00	3.00
77	Pat Summerall	15.00	7.50	4.50
78	Roosevelt Brown	10.00	5.00	3.00
79	Jimmy Patton	10.00	5.00	3.00
80	Sam Huff	25.00	13.00	8.00
81	Andy Robustelli	15.00	7.50	4.50
82	**New York Giants Team Card** (Checklist 1-66)	12.00	6.00	3.50
83	Clarence Peaks	10.00	5.00	3.00
84	Bill Barnes	10.00	5.00	3.00
85	Pete Retzlaff	10.00	5.00	3.00
86	Bobby Walston	10.00	5.00	3.00
87	Chuck Bednarik	15.00	7.50	4.50
88	Bob Pellagrini	10.00	5.00	3.00
89	Tom Brookshier **RC**	10.00	5.00	3.00

90	Marion Campbell	10.00	5.00	3.00
91	Jesse Richardson	10.00	5.00	3.00
92	**Philadelphia Eagles Team Card** (Checklist 1-66)	12.00	6.00	3.50
93	Bobby Layne	40.00	20.00	12.00
94	John Henry Johnson	15.00	7.50	4.50
95	Tom Tracy	10.00	5.00	3.00
96	Preston Carpenter	10.00	5.00	3.00
97	Frank Varrichione	10.00	5.00	3.00
98	John Nisby	10.00	5.00	3.00
99	Dean Derby	10.00	5.00	3.00
100	George Tarasovic	10.00	5.00	3.00
101	Ernie Stautner	15.00	7.50	4.50
102	**Pittsburgh Steelers Team Card** (Checklist 67-132)	12.00	6.00	3.50
103	King Hill	10.00	5.00	3.00
104	Mal Hammack	10.00	5.00	3.00
105	John Crow	10.00	5.00	3.00
106	Bobby Joe Conrad	10.00	5.00	3.00
107	Woodley Lewis	10.00	5.00	3.00
108	Don Gillis	10.00	5.00	3.00
109	Carl Brettschneider	10.00	5.00	3.00
110	Leo Sugar	10.00	5.00	3.00
111	Frank Fuller	10.00	5.00	3.00
112	**St. Louis Cardinals Team Card** (Checklist 67-132)	12.00	6.00	3.50
113	Y.A. Tittle	40.00	20.00	12.00
114	Joe Perry	15.00	7.50	3.50
115	J.D. Smith **RC**	10.00	5.00	3.00
116	Hugh McElhenny	15.00	7.50	4.50
117	Billy Wilson	10.00	5.00	3.00
118	Bob St. Clair	12.00	6.00	3.50
119	Matt Hazeltine	10.00	5.00	3.00
120	Abe Woodson	10.00	5.00	3.00
121	Leo Nomellini	12.00	6.00	3.50
122	**San Francisco 49ers Team Card** (Checklist 67-132)	12.00	6.00	3.50
123	Ralph Gugliemi	10.00	5.00	3.00
124	Don Bosseler	10.00	5.00	3.00
125	Johnny Olszewski	10.00	5.00	3.00
126	Bill Anderson	10.00	5.00	3.00
127	Joe Walton **RC**	10.00	5.00	3.00
128	Jim Schrader	10.00	5.00	3.00
129	Ralph Felton	10.00	5.00	3.00
130	Gary Glick	10.00	5.00	3.00
131	Bob Toneff	10.00	5.00	3.00
132	**Washington Redskins**	25.00	13.00	8.00

1960 Topps CFL

	NM	E	VG
Complete Set (88):	500.00	250.00	150.00
Common Player:	4.00	2.00	1.25

1	By Bailey	12.00	6.00	3.50
2	Paul Cameron	4.00	2.00	1.25
3	Bruce Claridge	4.00	2.00	1.25
4	Chuck Dubuque	4.00	2.00	1.25
5	Randy Duncan	12.00	6.00	3.50
6	Norm Fieldgate	10.00	5.00	3.00
7	Urban Henry	5.00	2.50	1.50
8	Ted Hunt	4.00	2.00	1.25
9	Bill Jessup	4.00	2.00	1.25
10	Ted Tully	4.00	2.00	1.25
11	Vic Chapman	4.00	2.00	1.25
12	Gino Fracas	5.00	2.50	1.50
13	Don Getty	10.00	5.00	3.00
14	Ed Gray	4.00	2.00	1.25
15	Oscar Kruger (Checklist 1-44 back)	20.00	10.00	6.00
16	Rollie Miles	10.00	5.00	3.00
17	Jackie Parker	30.00	15.00	9.00
18	Joe-Bob Smith (UER) (Misspelled Bob-Joe on both sides)	4.00	2.00	1.25
19	Mike Volcan	4.00	2.00	1.25
20	Art Walker	5.00	2.50	1.50
21	Ron Albright	4.00	2.00	1.25
22	Jim Bakhtiar	4.00	2.00	1.25
23	Lynn Bottoms	5.00	2.50	1.50
24	Jack Gotta	8.00	4.00	2.50
25	Joe Kapp	50.00	25.00	15.00
26	Earl Lunsford	9.00	4.50	2.75
27	Don Luzzi	9.00	4.50	2.75
28	Art Scullion	4.00	2.00	1.25
29	Hugh Simpson	4.00	2.00	1.25
30	Ernie Warlick	8.00	4.00	2.50
31	John Barrow	12.00	6.00	3.50
32	Paul Dekker	4.00	2.00	1.25
33	Bernie Faloney	20.00	10.00	6.00
34	Cam Fraser	4.00	2.00	1.25
35	Ralph Goldston	5.00	2.50	1.50
36	Ron Howell	5.00	2.50	1.50
37	Gerry McDougall (UER) (Misspelled Jerry)	4.00	2.00	1.25
38	Angelo Mosca	20.00	10.00	6.00
39	Pete Neumann	8.00	4.00	2.50
40	Vince Scott	8.00	4.00	2.50
41	Ted Elsby	4.00	2.00	1.25
42	Sam Etcheverry	25.00	12.50	7.50
43	Mike Kovac	4.00	2.00	1.25
44	Ed Learn	4.00	2.00	1.25
45	Ivan Livingstone (Checklist 45-88 back)	20.00	10.00	6.00
46	Hal Patterson	18.00	9.00	5.50
47	Jackie Simpson	12.00	6.00	3.50
48	Veryl Switzer	4.00	2.00	1.25
49	Bill Bewley	9.00	4.50	2.75
50	Joel Wells	4.00	2.00	1.25
51	Ron Atchison	9.00	4.50	2.75
52	Ken Carpenter	5.00	2.50	1.50
53	Bill Clarke	4.00	2.00	1.25
54	Ron Dundas	4.00	2.00	1.25
55	Mike Hagler	4.00	2.00	1.25
56	Jack Hill	4.00	2.00	1.25
57	Doug Kiloh	4.00	2.00	1.25
58	Bobby Marlow	10.00	5.00	3.00
59	Bob Mulgado	4.00	2.00	1.25
60	George Brancato	5.00	2.50	1.50
61	Lou Bruce	4.00	2.00	1.25
62	Hardiman Cureton	4.00	2.00	1.25
63	Russ Jackson	25.00	12.50	7.50
64	Gerry Nesbitt	4.00	2.00	1.25
65	Bob Simpson	10.00	5.00	3.00
66	Ted Smale	4.00	2.00	1.25
67	Dave Thelen	9.00	4.50	2.75
68	Kaye Vaughan	8.00	4.00	2.50
69	Pete Bennett	4.00	2.00	1.25
70	Boyd Carter	4.00	2.00	1.25
71	Gerry Doucette	4.00	2.00	1.25
72	Bobby Kuntz	5.00	2.50	1.50
73	Alex Panton	4.00	2.00	1.25
74	Tobin Rote	18.00	9.00	5.50
75	Jim Rountree	5.00	2.50	1.50
76	Dick Shatto	10.00	5.00	3.00
77	Norm Stoneburgh	4.00	2.00	1.25
78	Tom "Corky" Tharp	5.00	2.50	1.50
79	George Druxman	4.00	2.00	1.25
80	Herb Gray	10.00	5.00	3.00
81	Gerry James	10.00	5.00	3.00
82	Leo Lewis	10.00	5.00	3.00
83	Ernie Pitts	4.00	2.00	1.25
84	Kenny Ploen	15.00	7.50	4.50
85	Norm Rauhaus	4.00	2.00	1.25
86	Gord Rowland	4.00	2.00	1.25
87	Charlie Shepard	5.00	2.50	1.50
88	Don Clark	10.00	5.00	3.00

1960 Topps Team Emblem Stickers

One of each of these 33 metallic inserts was included in a wax pack of 1960 Topps football cards. The team emblem stickers are unnumbered and included NFL teams (1-13) and college teams (14-33). This was Topps' first football insert set. Future Topps inserts in the early '60s would also include college teams. These sticker fronts are bordered in black and show either a blue, silver or gold background. The stickers measure about 2" x 3".

	NM	E	VG
Complete Set (33):	175.00	87.50	52.50
Common Pro Team:	6.00	3.00	1.75
Common College Team:	4.50	2.25	1.35

(1)	**Baltimore Colts**	6.00	3.00	1.75
(2)	**Chicago Bears**	6.00	3.00	1.75
(3)	**Cleveland Browns**	6.00	3.00	1.75
(4)	**Dallas Cowboys**	8.00	4.00	2.50
(5)	**Detroit Lions**	8.00	4.00	2.50
(6)	**Green Bay Packers**	6.00	3.00	1.75
(7)	**Los Angeles Rams**	6.00	3.00	1.75
(8)	**New York Giants**	6.00	3.00	1.75
(9)	**Philadelphia Eagles**	6.00	3.00	1.75
(10)	**Pittsburgh Steelers**	6.00	3.00	1.75
(11)	**St. Louis Cardinals**	6.00	3.00	1.75
(12)	**San Francisco 49ers**	6.00	3.00	1.75
(13)	**Washington Redskins**	8.00	4.00	2.50
(14)	**Air Force**	4.50	2.25	1.35
(15)	**Army**	4.50	2.25	1.35
(16)	**California**	4.50	2.25	1.35
(17)	**Dartmouth**	4.50	2.25	1.35
(18)	**Duke**	4.50	2.25	1.35
(19)	**LSU**	4.50	2.25	1.35
(20)	**Michigan**	4.50	2.25	1.35
(21)	**Mississippi**	4.50	2.25	1.35
(22)	**Navy**	4.50	2.25	1.35
(23)	**Notre Dame**	15.00	7.50	4.50
(24)	**SMU**	4.50	2.25	1.35
(25)	**USC**	4.50	2.25	1.35
(26)	**Syracuse**	4.50	2.25	1.35
(27)	**Tennessee**	4.50	2.25	1.35
(28)	**Texas**	4.50	2.25	1.35
(29)	**UCLA**	4.50	2.25	1.35
(30)	**Minnesota**	4.50	2.25	1.35
(31)	**Washington**	4.50	2.25	1.35
(32)	**Wisconsin**	4.50	2.25	1.35
(33)	**Yale**	4.50	2.25	1.35

1961 Topps

This set of 198 cards was the last full Topps set to include both AFL players and NFL players. The AFL segment of the set (133-197) does not include team checklists. Cards are similar to the 1961 Topps baseball issue and feature a ruboff game on the back. The set is once again numbered in order of teams - alphabetically by city. Rookies in this set include John Brodie, Don Maynard, Jim Otto and Tom Flores. Second-year cards include Alex Karras, Henry Jordan, Sonny Jurgensen (three years after his rookie card debuted), Abner Haynes, Jack Kemp and Ron Mix. This set included the last regular-issue cards of Alan Ameche, Charley Conerly, Kyle Rote, Chuck Bednarik and Tom Brookshier. Card #41 could actually be considered Packer running back Jim Taylor's rookie card. His rookie and second- year cards Topps printed in 1959 and 1960 actually depicted Cardinal linebacker Jim Taylor instead of HOFer Jim Taylor.

	NM	E	VG
Complete Set (198):	2,750	1,375	825.00
Common Player:	8.00	4.00	2.40
Minor Stars:	3.00		
Unlisted Stars:	4.00		
Series 1 Wax Pack (5):	410.00		
Series 2 Wax Pack (5):	425.00		

1	Johnny Unitas	125.00	65.00	39.00
2	Lenny Moore	15.00	7.50	4.50
3	Alan Ameche	12.00	6.00	3.50
4	Raymond Berry	15.00	7.50	4.50
5	Jim Mutscheller	8.00	4.00	2.40
6	Jim Parker	12.00	6.00	3.50
7	Gino Marchetti	15.00	7.50	4.50
8	Gene Lipscomb	12.00	6.00	3.50
9	**Baltimore Colts**	10.00	5.00	3.00
10	Bill Wade	8.00	4.00	2.40
11	Johnny Morris **RC**	12.00	6.00	3.50
12	Rick Casares	8.00	4.00	2.40
13	Harlon Hill	8.00	4.00	2.40
14	Stan Jones	12.00	6.00	3.50
15	Doug Atkins	12.00	6.00	3.50
16	Bill George	12.00	6.00	3.50
17	J.C. Caroline	8.00	4.00	2.40
18	**Chicago Bears**	10.00	5.00	3.00
19	Big Time Football comes to Texas (Eddie LeBaron)	10.00	5.00	3.00
20	Eddie LeBaron	8.00	4.00	2.40
21	Don McElhenny	8.00	4.00	2.40
22	L.G. Dupre	8.00	4.00	2.40
23	Jim Doran	8.00	4.00	2.40
24	Billy Howton	8.00	4.00	2.40
25	Buzz Guy	8.00	4.00	2.40
26	Jack Patera **RC**	8.00	4.00	2.40
27	Tom Frankauser	8.00	4.00	2.40
28	**Dallas Cowboys**	15.00	7.50	4.50
29	Jim Ninowski	8.00	4.00	2.40
30	Dan Lewis **RC**	8.00	4.00	2.40
31	Nick Pietrosante **RC**	8.00	4.00	2.40
32	Gail Cogdill **RC**	8.00	4.00	2.40
33	Jim Gibbons	8.00	4.00	2.40
34	Jim Martin	8.00	4.00	2.40
35	Alex Karras	25.00	13.00	8.00
36	Joe Schmidt	8.00	4.00	2.40
37	**Detroit Lions**	10.00	5.00	3.00
38	Set Scoring Record (Paul Hornung)	25.00	13.00	8.00
39	Bart Starr	45.00	23.00	14.00
40	Paul Hornung	45.00	23.00	14.00
41	Jim Taylor	35.00	18.00	11.00
42	Max McGee	12.00	6.00	3.50

43	Boyd Dowler **RC**	15.00	7.50	4.50
44	Jim Ringo	15.00	7.50	4.50
45	Henry Jordan **RC**	45.00	23.00	14.00
46	Bill Forester	8.00	4.00	2.40
47	**Green Bay Packers**	13.00	6.50	4.00
48	Frank Ryan	8.00	4.00	2.40
49	Jon Arnett	8.00	4.00	2.40
50	Ollie Matson	15.00	7.50	4.50
51	Jim Phillips	8.00	4.00	2.40
52	Del Shofner	8.00	4.00	2.40
53	Art Hunter	8.00	4.00	2.40
54	Gene Brito	8.00	4.00	2.40
55	Lindon Crow	8.00	4.00	2.40
56	**Los Angeles Rams**	10.00	5.00	3.00
57	25-TD Passes (Johnny Unitas)	35.00	18.00	11.00
58	Y.A. Tittle	35.00	18.00	11.00
59	John Brodie **RC**	45.00	23.00	14.00
60	J.D. Smith	8.00	4.00	2.40
61	R.C. Owens	8.00	4.00	2.40
62	Clyde Conner	8.00	4.00	2.40
63	Bob St. Clair	12.00	6.00	3.50
64	Leo Nomellini	15.00	7.50	4.50
65	Abe Woodson	8.00	4.00	2.40
66	**San Francisco 49ers**	10.00	5.00	3.00
67	**Checklist**	50.00	25.00	15.00
68	Milt Plum	8.00	4.00	2.40
69	Ray Renfro	8.00	4.00	2.40
70	Bobby Mitchell	15.00	7.50	4.50
71	Jim Brown	100.00	50.00	30.00
72	Mike McCormack	12.00	6.00	3.50
73	Jim Ray Smith	8.00	4.00	2.40
74	Sam Baker	8.00	4.00	2.40
75	Walt Michaels	8.00	4.00	2.40
76	**Cleveland Browns**	10.00	5.00	3.00
77	Jim Brown IA	45.00	23.00	14.00
78	George Shaw	8.00	4.00	2.40
79	Hugh McElhenny	15.00	7.50	4.50
80	Clancy Osborne	8.00	4.00	2.40
81	Dave Middleton	8.00	4.00	2.40
82	Frank Youso	8.00	4.00	2.40
83	Don Joyce	8.00	4.00	2.40
84	Ed Culpepper	8.00	4.00	2.40
85	Charley Conerly	12.00	6.00	3.50
86	Mel Triplett	8.00	4.00	2.40
87	Kyle Rote	8.00	4.00	2.40
88	Roosevelt Brown	12.00	6.00	3.50
89	Ray Wietecha	8.00	4.00	2.40
90	Andy Robustelli	12.00	6.00	3.50
91	Sam Huff	15.00	7.50	4.50
92	Jim Patton	8.00	4.00	2.40
93	**New York Giants**	10.00	5.00	3.00
94	Leads Giants for 13th Year (Chas Conerly)	12.00	6.00	3.50
95	Sonny Jurgensen	20.00	10.00	6.00
96	Tommy McDonald	12.00	6.00	3.50
97	Billy Barnes	8.00	4.00	2.40
98	Bobby Waltson	8.00	4.00	2.40
99	Pete Retzlaff	8.00	4.00	2.40
100	Jim McCusker	8.00	4.00	2.40
101	Chuck Bednarik	15.00	7.50	4.50
102	Tom Brookshier	8.00	4.00	2.40
103	**Philadephia Eagles**	10.00	5.00	3.00
104	Bobby Layne	25.00	13.00	8.00
105	John Henry Johnson	12.00	6.00	3.50
106	Tom Tracy	8.00	4.00	2.40
107	Buddy Dial **RC**	8.00	4.00	2.40
108	Jim Orr **RC**	12.00	6.00	3.50
109	Mike Sandusky	8.00	4.00	2.40
110	John Reger	8.00	4.00	2.40
111	Junior Wren	8.00	4.00	2.40
112	**Pittsburgh Steelers**	10.00	5.00	3.00
113	Sets New Passing Record (Bobby Layne)	10.00	5.00	3.00
114	John Roach	8.00	4.00	2.40
115	Sam Etcheverry **RC**	8.00	4.00	2.40
116	John David Crow	8.00	4.00	2.40
117	Mal Hammack	8.00	4.00	2.40
118	Sonny Randle **RC**	8.00	4.00	2.40
119	Leo Sugar	8.00	4.00	2.40
120	Jerry Norton	8.00	4.00	2.40
121	**St. Louis Cardinals**	10.00	5.00	3.00
122	**Checklist**	45.00	23.00	14.00
123	Ralph Guglielmi	8.00	4.00	2.40
124	Dick James	8.00	4.00	2.40
125	Don Bosseler	2.00	1.00	.60
126	Joe Walton	8.00	4.00	2.40
127	Bill Anderson	8.00	4.00	2.40
128	Vince Promuto **RC**	8.00	4.00	2.40
129	Bob Toneff	8.00	4.00	2.40
130	John Paluck	8.00	4.00	2.40
131	**Washington Redskins**	10.00	5.00	3.00
132	Wins NFL Passing Title (Milt Plum)	8.00	4.00	2.40
133	Abner Haynes	15.00	7.50	4.50
134	Mel Branch	10.00	5.00	3.00
135	Jerry Cornelison	10.00	5.00	3.00
136	Bill Krisher	10.00	5.00	3.00
137	Paul Miller	10.00	5.00	3.00
138	Jack Spikes	10.00	5.00	3.00
139	Johnny Robinson **RC**	15.00	7.50	4.50
140	Cotton Davidson **RC**	10.00	5.00	3.00
141	Dave Smith	10.00	5.00	3.00
142	Bill Groman	10.00	5.00	3.00
143	Rich Michael	10.00	5.00	3.00
144	Mike Dukes	10.00	5.00	3.00
145	George Blanda	12.00	6.00	3.50
146	Billy Cannon	10.00	5.00	3.00
147	Dennit Morris	10.00	5.00	3.00
148	Jacky Lee	10.00	5.00	3.00
149	Al Dorrow	10.00	5.00	3.00
150	Don Maynard **RC**	55.00	28.00	17.00
151	Art Powell **RC**	10.00	5.00	3.00
152	Sid Youngelman	10.00	5.00	3.00
153	Bob Mischak	10.00	5.00	3.00
154	Larry Grantham	10.00	5.00	3.00
155	Tom Saidock	10.00	5.00	3.00
156	Roger Donnahoo	10.00	5.00	3.00
157	Lavern Torczon	10.00	5.00	3.00
158	Archie Matsos **RC**	10.00	5.00	3.00
159	Elbert Dubenion	10.00	5.00	3.00
160	Wray Carlton **RC**	10.00	5.00	3.00
161	Rich McCabe	10.00	5.00	3.00
162	Ken Rice	10.00	5.00	3.00
163	Art Baker	10.00	5.00	3.00
164	Tom Rychiec	10.00	5.00	3.00
165	Mack Yoho	10.00	5.00	3.00
166	Jack Kemp	40.00	20.00	12.00
167	Paul Lowe	10.00	5.00	3.00
168	Ron Mix	10.00	5.00	3.00
169	Paul Maguire	10.00	5.00	3.00
170	Volney Peters	10.00	5.00	3.00
171	Ernie Wright	10.00	5.00	3.00
172	Ron Nery	10.00	5.00	3.00
173	Dave Kocourek **RC**	10.00	5.00	3.00
174	Jim Colclough	10.00	5.00	3.00
175	Babe Parilli	10.00	5.00	3.00
176	Billy Lott	10.00	5.00	3.00
177	Fred Bruney	10.00	5.00	3.00
178	Ross O'Hanley	2.00	1.00	.60
179	Walt Cudzik	10.00	5.00	3.00
180	Charles Leo	10.00	5.00	3.00
181	Bob Dee	10.00	5.00	3.00
182	Jim Otto **RC**	40.00	20.00	12.00
183	Eddie Macon	10.00	5.00	3.00
184	Dick Christy	10.00	5.00	3.00
185	Alan Miller	10.00	5.00	3.00
186	Tom Flores **RC**	20.00	10.00	6.00
187	Joe Cannavino	10.00	5.00	3.00
188	Don Manoukian	10.00	5.00	3.00
189	Bob Coolbaugh	10.00	5.00	3.00
190	Lionel Taylor **RC**	15.00	7.50	4.50
191	Bud McFadin	10.00	5.00	3.00
192	Goose Gonsoulin	10.00	5.00	3.00
193	Frank Tripucka	10.00	5.00	3.00
194	Gene Mingo **RC**	10.00	5.00	3.00
195	Eldon Danenhauer	10.00	5.00	3.00
196	Bob McNamara	10.00	5.00	3.00
197	Dave Rolle	10.00	5.00	3.00
198	**Checklist**	50.00	25.00	14.00

1961 Topps CFL

	NM	E	VG
Complete Set (132):	900.00	450.00	270.00
Common Player:	6.00	3.00	1.75

1	By Bailey	15.00	7.50	4.50
2	Bruce Claridge	6.00	3.00	1.75
3	Norm Fieldgate	12.00	6.00	3.50
4	Willie Fleming	20.00	10.00	6.00
5	Urban Henry	7.50	3.75	2.25
6	Bill Herron	6.00	3.00	1.75
7	Tom Hinton	10.00	5.00	3.00
8	Sonny Homer	7.50	3.75	2.25
9	Bob Jeter	15.00	7.50	4.50
10	Vic Kristopaitis	6.00	3.00	1.75
11	Baz Nagle	6.00	3.00	1.75
12	Ron Watton	6.00	3.00	1.75
13	Joe Yamauchi	6.00	3.00	1.75
14	Bob Schloredt	15.00	7.50	4.50
15	**B.C. Lions Team**	12.00	6.00	3.50
16	Ron Albright	6.00	3.00	1.75
17	Gordon Brown	6.00	3.00	1.75
18	Gerry Doucette	6.00	3.00	1.75
19	Gene Filipski	12.00	6.00	3.50
20	Joe Kapp	30.00	15.00	9.00
21	Earl Lunsford	12.00	6.00	3.50
22	Don Luzzi	12.00	6.00	3.50
23	Bill McKenna	6.00	3.00	1.75
24	Ron Morris	6.00	3.00	1.75
25	Tony Pajaczkowski	12.00	6.00	3.50
26	Lorne Reid	6.00	3.00	1.75
27	Art Scullion	6.00	3.00	1.75
28	Ernie Warlick	10.00	5.00	3.00
29	**Stampeders Team**	12.00	6.00	3.50
30	Johnny Bright	15.00	7.50	4.50
31	Vic Chapman	6.00	3.00	1.75
32	Gino Fracas	7.50	3.75	2.25
33	Tommy Joe Coffey	18.00	9.00	5.50
34	Don Getty	15.00	7.50	4.50
35	Ed Gray	6.00	3.00	1.75
36	Oscar Kruger	7.50	3.75	2.25
37	Rollie Miles	12.00	6.00	3.50
38	Roger Nelson	12.00	6.00	3.50
39	Jackie Parker	35.00	17.50	10.50
40	Howie Schumm	6.00	3.00	1.75
41	Joe-Bob Smith (UER) (Misspelled Bob-Joe on both sides)	6.00	3.00	1.75
42	Art Walker	7.50	3.75	2.25
43	**Eskimos Team**	12.00	6.00	3.50
44	John Barrow	15.00	7.50	4.50
45	Paul Dekker	6.00	3.00	1.75
46	Tom Dublinski	6.00	3.00	1.75
47	Bernie Faloney	25.00	12.50	7.50
48	Cam Fraser	6.00	3.00	1.75
49	Ralph Goldston	7.50	3.75	2.25
50	Ron Howell	7.50	3.75	2.25
51	Gerry McDougall	7.50	3.75	2.25
52	Pete Neumann	12.00	6.00	3.50
53	Bronko Nagurski	15.00	7.50	4.50
54	Vince Scott	10.00	5.00	3.00
55	Steve Oneschuk	7.50	3.75	2.25
56	Hal Patterson	20.00	10.00	6.00
57	Jim Taylor	7.50	3.75	2.25
58	**Tiger-Cats Team**	12.00	6.00	3.50
59	Ted Elsby	6.00	3.00	1.75
60	Don Clark	7.50	3.75	2.25
61	Dick Cohee	10.00	5.00	3.00
62	George Dixon	20.00	10.00	6.00
63	Wes Gideon	6.00	3.00	1.75
64	Harry Lampman	6.00	3.00	1.75
65	Meco Poliziani	6.00	3.00	1.75
66	Charles Baillie	6.00	3.00	1.75
67	Howard Cissell	6.00	3.00	1.75
68	Ed Learn	6.00	3.00	1.75
69	Tom Moran	6.00	3.00	1.75
70	Jack Simpson	12.00	6.00	3.50
71	Bill Bewley	7.50	3.75	2.25
72	Tom Hugo	6.00	3.00	1.75
73	**Alouettes Team**	15.00	7.50	4.50
74	Gilles Archambeault	6.00	3.00	1.75
75	Lou Bruce	6.00	3.00	1.75
76	Russ Jackson	30.00	15.00	9.00
77	Tom Jones	6.00	3.00	1.75
78	Gerry Nesbitt	6.00	3.00	1.75
79	Ron Lancaster	40.00	20.00	12.00
80	Joe Kelly	6.00	3.00	1.75
81	Joe Poirier	7.50	3.75	2.25
82	Doug Daigneault	6.00	3.00	1.75
83	Kaye Vaughan	10.00	5.00	3.00
84	Dave Thelen	15.00	7.50	4.50
85	Ron Stewart	25.00	12.50	7.50
86	Ted Smale	6.00	3.00	1.75
87	Bob Simpson	15.00	7.50	4.50
88	**Ottawa Rough Riders Team**	12.00	6.00	3.50
89	Don Allard	6.00	3.00	1.75
90	Ron Atchison	12.00	6.00	3.50
91	Bill Clarke	6.00	3.00	1.75
92	Ron Dundas	6.00	3.00	1.75
93	Jack Gotta	10.00	5.00	3.00
94	Bob Golic	7.50	3.75	2.25
95	Jack Hill	6.00	3.00	1.75
96	Doug Kiloh	7.50	3.75	2.25
97	Len Legault	6.00	3.00	1.75
98	Doug McKenzie	6.00	3.00	1.75
99	Bob Ptacek	6.00	3.00	1.75
100	Roy Smith	6.00	3.00	1.75
101	**Saskatchewan Roughriders Team**	12.00	6.00	3.50
102	**Checklist 1-132**	90.00	45.00	27.00
103	Jim Andreotti	7.50	3.75	2.25
104	Boyd Carter	6.00	3.00	1.75
105	Dick Fouts	7.50	3.75	2.25
106	Cookie Gilchrist	25.00	12.50	7.50
107	Bobby Kuntz	7.50	3.75	2.25
108	Jim Rountree	7.50	3.75	2.25
109	Dick Shatto	15.00	7.50	4.50
110	Norm Stoneburgh	6.00	3.00	1.75
111	Dave Mann	10.00	5.00	3.00
112	Ed Ochiena	6.00	3.00	1.75
113	Bill Stribling	6.00	3.00	1.75
114	Tobin Rote	20.00	10.00	6.00
115	Stan Wallace	6.00	3.00	1.75
116	Billy Shipp	7.50	3.75	2.25
117	**Argonauts Team**	15.00	7.50	4.50
118	Dave Burkholder	6.00	3.00	1.75
119	Jack Delveaux	6.00	3.00	1.75
120	George Druxman	6.00	3.00	1.75
121	Farrell Funston	7.50	3.75	2.25
122	Herb Gray	12.00	6.00	3.50
123	Gerry James	12.00	6.00	3.50
124	Ronnie Latourelle	6.00	3.00	1.75

125	Leo Lewis	15.00	7.50	4.50
126	Steve Patrick	6.00	3.00	1.75
127	Ernie Pitts	6.00	3.00	1.75
128	Kenny Ploen	15.00	7.50	4.50
129	Norm Rauhaus	7.50	3.75	2.25
130	Gord Rowland	7.50	3.75	2.25
131	Charlie Shepard	7.50	3.75	2.25
132	**Winnipeg Blue Bombers Team Card**	20.00	10.00	6.00

1961 Topps CFL Transfers

	NM	E	VG
Complete Set (24):	700.00	350.00	210.00
Common Player (1-15):	25.00	12.50	7.50
Common Team (19-27):	20.00	10.00	6.00

1	Don Clark	30.00	15.00	9.00
2	Gene Filipski	30.00	15.00	9.00
3	Willie Fleming	40.00	20.00	12.00
4	Cookie Gilchrist	45.00	22.00	13.50
5	Jack Hill	25.00	12.50	7.50
6	Bob Jeter	30.00	15.00	9.00
7	Joe Kapp	65.00	32.00	19.50
8	Leo Lewis	40.00	20.00	12.00
9	Gerry McDougall	25.00	12.50	7.50
10	Jackie Parker	50.00	25.00	15.00
11	Hal Patterson	40.00	20.00	12.00
12	Kenny Ploen	40.00	20.00	12.00
13	Bob Ptacek	25.00	12.50	7.50
14	Ron Stewart	40.00	20.00	12.00
15	Dave Thelen	40.00	20.00	12.00
16	**British Columbia Lions Logo/Pennant**	20.00	10.00	6.00
20	**Calgary Stampeders Logo/Pennant**	20.00	10.00	6.00
21	**Edmonton Eskimos Logo/Pennant**	20.00	10.00	6.00
22	**Hamilton Tiger-Cats Logo/Pennant**	20.00	10.00	6.00
23	**Montreal Alouettes Logo/Pennant**	20.00	10.00	6.00
24	**Ottawa Rough Riders Logo/Pennant**	20.00	10.00	6.00
25	**Saskatchewan Roughriders Logo/ Pennant**	20.00	10.00	6.00
26	**Toronto Argonauts Logo/Pennant**	20.00	10.00	6.00
27	**Winnipeg Blue Bombers Logo/Pennant**	20.00	10.00	6.00

1961 Topps Stickers

This set of 48 stickers was included one per pack in the 1961 Topps football set. Stickers are unnumbered and are grouped according to NFL (1-15), AFL (16-24), and colleges (25-48). The stickers were issued with tabs that could be peeled off. For the sticker to be considered Mint, tabs would have to be intact.

	NM	E	VG
Complete Set (48):	175.00	87.50	52.50
Common Pro Team:	6.00	3.00	1.75
Common College Team:	3.50	1.75	1.00

(1)	**NFL Emblem**	6.00	3.00	1.75
(2)	**Baltimore Colts**	6.00	6.00	3.00
(3)	**Chicago Bears**	6.00	6.00	3.00
(4)	**Cleveland Browns**	6.00	3.00	1.75
(5)	**Dallas Cowboys**	8.00	4.00	2.50
(6)	**Detroit Lions**	6.00	3.00	1.75
(7)	**Green Bay Packers**	8.00	4.00	2.50
(8)	**Los Angeles Rams**	6.00	3.00	1.75
(9)	**Minnesota Vikings**	6.00	3.00	1.75
(10)	**New York Giants**	6.00	3.00	1.75
(11)	**Philadelphia Eagles**	6.00	3.00	1.75
(12)	**Pittsburgh Steelers**	6.00	3.00	1.75
(13)	**San Francisco 49ers**	6.00	3.00	1.75
(14)	**St. Louis Cardinals**	6.00	3.00	1.75
(15)	**Washington Redskins**	8.00	4.00	2.50
(16)	**AFL Emblem**	8.00	4.00	2.50
(17)	**Boston Patriots**	6.00	3.00	1.75
(18)	**Buffalo Bills**	8.00	4.00	2.50
(19)	**Dallas Texans**	8.00	4.00	2.50
(20)	**Denver Broncos**	6.00	3.00	1.75
(21)	**Houston Oilers**	6.00	3.00	1.75
(22)	**Oakland Raiders**	8.00	4.00	2.50
(23)	**San Diego Chargers**	6.00	3.00	1.75
(24)	**Titans of New York**	6.00	3.00	1.75
(25)	**Air Force**	3.50	1.75	1.00
(26)	**Alabama**	6.00	3.00	1.75
(27)	**Arkansas**	3.50	1.75	1.00
(28)	**Army**	5.00	2.50	1.50
(29)	**Baylor**	3.50	1.75	1.00
(30)	**California**	3.50	1.75	1.00
(31)	**Georgia Tech**	3.50	1.75	1.00
(32)	**Illinois**	3.50	1.75	1.00
(33)	**Kansas**	3.50	1.75	1.00
(34)	**Kentucky**	3.50	1.75	1.00
(35)	**Miami**	3.50	1.75	1.00
(36)	**Michigan**	6.00	3.00	1.75
(37)	**Missouri**	3.50	1.75	1.00
(38)	**Navy**	5.00	2.50	1.50
(39)	**Oregon**	3.50	1.75	1.00
(40)	**Penn State**	6.00	3.00	1.75
(41)	**Pittsburgh**	3.50	1.75	1.00
(42)	**Purdue**	3.50	1.75	1.00
(43)	**USC**	6.00	3.00	1.75
(44)	**Stanford**	3.50	1.75	1.00
(45)	**TCU**	3.50	1.75	1.00
(46)	**Virginia**	3.50	1.75	1.00
(47)	**Washington**	3.50	1.75	1.00
(48)	**Washington State**	3.50	1.75	1.00

1962 Topps

This 176-card set is one of the decade's toughest to complete in mint condition because of the easily-scuffed black borders. Like many of the Topps sets of this era, a good number of the cards in the set are short-printed, probably because the number of cards in the set didn't exactly match the amount that would fit onto printing sheets. Cards are again grouped by teams, which are listed in alphabetical order by city. This was the first time in five years Topps tried a horizontal format; Topps would try it again in 1966. Rookies in this set include Mike Ditka, Ernie Davis (his only regular-issue card), Roman Gabriel, Fran Tarkenton, Bill Kilmer and Norm Snead. Second-year cards in the set include Don Meredith (his first Topps card) and John Brodie. Last-year cards in the set include Max McGee and Hall of Famers Joe Perry, Ollie Matson and Bobby Layne. The last Topps cards of Frank Gifford and Andy Robustelli are also included. (Key: SP - short printed)

	NM	E	VG
Complete Set (176):	3,400	1,700	1,025
Common Player:	20.00	10.00	6.00
Minor Stars:	5.00		
Unlisted Stars:	7.50		
SP Cards:	30.00	15.00	9.00
Wax Pack (FB Bucks):	360.00		
Wax Pack (Pro Stars):	385.00		

1	Johnny Unitas	250.00	125.00	75.00
2	Lenny Moore	35.00	18.00	11.00
3	Alex Hawkins **RC** (SP)	30.00	15.00	9.00
4	Joe Perry	30.00	15.00	9.00
5	Raymond Berry (SP)	40.00	20.00	12.00
6	Steve Myhra	20.00	10.00	6.000
7	Tom Gilburg (SP)	30.00	15.00	9.00
8	Gino Marchetti	20.00	10.00	6.00
9	Bill Pellington	20.00	10.00	6.00
10	Andy Nelson	20.00	10.00	6.00
11	Wendell Harris (SP)	30.00	15.00	9.00
12	**Baltimore Colts Team**	25.00	13.00	8.00
13	Billy Wade (SP)	30.00	15.00	9.00
14	Willie Galimore	20.00	10.00	6.00
15	Johnny Morris (SP)	30.00	15.00	9.00
16	Rick Casares	20.00	10.00	6.00
17	Mike Ditka **RC**	275.00	140.00	84.00
18	Stan Jones	20.00	10.00	6.00
19	Roger LeClerc	20.00	10.00	6.00
20	Angelo Coia	20.00	10.00	6.00
21	Doug Atkins	20.00	10.00	6.00
22	Bill George	20.00	10.00	6.00
23	Richie Petitbon **RC**	20.00	10.00	5.00
24	Ron Bull (SP)	30.00	15.00	9.00
25	**Chicago Bears Team**	20.00	10.00	6.00
26	Howard Cassady	20.00	10.00	6.00
27	Ray Renfro (SP)	30.00	15.00	9.00
28	Jim Brown	225.00	115.00	70.00
29	Rick Kreitling	20.00	10.00	6.00
30	Jim Ray Smith	20.00	10.00	6.00
31	John Morrow	20.00	10.00	6.00
32	Lou Groza	20.00	10.00	6.00
33	Bob Gain	20.00	10.00	6.00
34	Bernie Parrish	20.00	10.00	6.00
35	Jim Shofner	20.00	10.00	6.00
36	Ernie Davis **RC** (SP)	200.00	100.00	60.00
37	**Cleveland Browns Team**	25.00	13.00	8.00
38	Eddie LeBaron	20.00	10.00	6.00
39	Don Meredith (SP)	125.00	65.00	39.00
40	J.W. Lockett (SP)	30.00	15.00	9.00
41	Don Perkins **RC**	35.00	18.00	11.00
42	Billy Howton	20.00	10.00	6.00
43	Dick Bielski	20.00	10.00	6.00
44	Mike Connelly **RC**	20.00	10.00	6.00
45	Jerry Tubbs (SP)	30.00	15.00	9.00
46	Don Bishop (SP)	30.00	15.00	9.00
47	Dick Moegle	20.00	10.00	6.00
48	Bobby Plummer (SP)	30.00	15.00	9.00
49	**Dallas Cowboys Team**	20.00	10.00	6.00
50	Milt Plum	20.00	10.00	6.00
51	Dan Lewis	20.00	10.00	6.00
52	Nick Pietrosante (SP)	30.00	15.00	9.00
53	Gail Cogdill	20.00	10.00	6.00
54	Jim Gibbons	20.00	10.00	6.00
55	Jim Martin	20.00	10.00	6.00
56	Yale Lary	20.00	10.00	6.00
57	Darris McCord	20.00	10.00	6.00
58	Alex Karras	20.00	10.00	6.00
59	Joe Schmidt	20.00	10.00	6.00
60	Dick "Night Train" Lane	20.00	10.00	6.00
61	John Lomakoski (SP)	30.00	15.00	9.00
62	**Detroit Lions Team** (SP)	35.00	18.00	11.00
63	Bart Starr (SP)	125.00	65.00	39.00
64	Paul Hornung (SP)	100.00	50.00	30.00
65	Tom Moore (SP)	30.00	15.00	9.00
66	Jim Taylor (SP)	65.00	38.00	23.00
67	Max McGee (SP)	30.00	15.00	9.00
68	Jim Ringo (SP)	30.00	15.00	9.00
69	Fuzzy Thurston **RC** (SP)	40.00	20.00	12.00
70	Forrest Gregg	20.00	10.00	6.00
71	Boyd Dowler	20.00	10.00	6.00
72	Henry Jordan (SP)	30.00	15.00	9.00
73	Bill Forester (SP)	30.00	15.00	9.00
74	Earl Gros (SP)	30.00	15.00	9.00
75	**Green Bay Packers** (SP)	50.00	25.00	15.00
76	**Checklist** (SP)	80.00	40.00	24.00
77	Zeke Bratkowski (SP)	30.00	15.00	9.00
78	Jon Arnett (SP)	30.00	15.00	9.00
79	Ollie Matson (SP)	40.00	20.00	12.00
80	Dick Bass (SP)	30.00	15.00	9.00
81	Jim Phillips	20.00	10.00	6.00
82	Carroll Dale **RC**	20.00	10.00	6.00
83	Frank Varrichione	20.00	10.00	6.00
84	Art Hunter	20.00	10.00	6.00
85	Danny Villanueva **RC**	20.00	10.00	6.00
86	Les Richter (SP)	30.00	15.00	9.00
87	Lindon Crow	20.00	10.00	6.00
88	Roman Gabriel **RC** (SP)	90.00	45.00	27.00
89	**Los Angeles Rams** (SP)	30.00	15.00	9.00
90	Fran Tarkenton **RC** (SP)	275.00	140.00	85.00
91	Jerry Reichow (SP)	30.00	15.00	9.00
92	Hugh McElhenny (SP)	40.00	20.00	12.00
93	Mel Triplett (SP)	30.00	15.00	9.00
94	Tommy Mason **RC** (SP)	30.00	15.00	9.00
95	Dave Middleton (SP)	30.00	15.00	9.00
96	Frank Youso (SP)	30.00	15.00	9.00
97	Mike Mercer (SP)	30.00	15.00	9.00
98	Rip Hawkins (SP)	30.00	15.00	9.00
99	Cliff Livingston (SP)	30.00	15.00	9.00
100	Roy Winston **RC** (SP)	30.00	15.00	9.00
101	**Minnesota Vikings Team** (SP)	40.00	20.00	12.00
102	Y.A. Tittle	50.00	25.00	15.00
103	Joe Walton	20.00	10.00	6.00
104	Frank Gifford	65.00	38.00	23.00
105	Alex Webster	20.00	10.00	6.00
106	Del Shofner	20.00	10.00	6.00
107	Don Chandler	20.00	10.00	6.00
108	Andy Robustelli	20.00	10.00	6.00
109	Jim Katcavage	20.00	10.00	6.00
110	Sam Huff (SP)	30.00	15.00	9.00
111	Erich Barnes	20.00	10.00	6.00
112	Jimmy Patton	20.00	10.00	6.00
113	Jerry Hillebrand (SP)	30.00	15.00	9.00
114	**New York Giants Team**	20.00	10.00	6.00
115	Sonny Jurgensen	50.00	25.00	15.00
116	Tommy McDonald	20.00	10.00	6.00
117	Ted Dean (SP)	30.00	15.00	9.00
118	Clarence Peaks	20.00	10.00	6.00
119	Bobby Walston	20.00	10.00	6.00
120	Pete Retzlaff (SP)	30.00	15.00	9.00
121	Jim Schrader (SP)	30.00	15.00	9.00
122	J.D. Smith	20.00	10.00	6.00
123	King Hill	20.00	10.00	6.00
124	Maxie Baughan	20.00	10.00	6.00
125	Pete Case (SP)	30.00	15.00	9.00
126	**Philadelphia Eagles Team**	20.00	10.00	6.00
127	Bobby Layne	50.00	25.00	15.00
128	Tom Tracy	20.00	10.00	6.00
129	John Henry Johnson	20.00	10.00	6.00
130	Buddy Dial (SP)	30.00	15.00	9.00
131	Preston Carpenter	20.00	10.00	6.00
132	Lou Michaels (SP)	30.00	15.00	9.00
133	Gene Lipscomb (SP)	30.00	15.00	9.00
134	Ernie Stautner (SP)	40.00	20.00	12.00
135	John Reger (SP)	30.00	15.00	9.00
136	Myron Pottios	20.00	10.00	6.00
137	Bob Ferguson (SP)	30.00	15.00	9.00
138	**Pittsburgh Steelers Team**	20.00	10.00	6.00

139	Sam Etcheverry	20.00	10.00	6.00
140	John David Crow (SP)	30.00	15.00	9.00
141	Bobby Joe Conrad (SP)	30.00	15.00	9.00
142	Prentice Gautt **RC** (SP)	20.00	10.00	6.00
143	Frank Mestnik	20.00	10.00	6.00
144	Sonny Randle	20.00	10.00	6.00
145	Gerry Perry	20.00	10.00	6.00
146	Jerry Norton	20.00	10.00	6.00
147	Jimmy Hill	20.00	10.00	6.00
148	Bill Stacy	20.00	10.00	6.00
149	Fate Echols (SP)	7.50	3.75	2.25
150	**St. Louis Cardinals Team**	20.00	10.00	6.00
151	Bill Kilmer **RC**	40.00	20.00	12.00
152	John Brodie	35.00	18.00	11.00
153	J.D. Smith	20.00	10.00	6.00
154	C.R. Roberts (SP)	30.00	15.00	9.00
155	Monty Stickles	20.00	10.00	6.00
156	Clyde Conner	20.00	10.00	6.00
157	Bob St. Clair	20.00	10.00	6.00
158	Tommy Davis **RC**	20.00	10.00	6.00
159	Leo Nomellini	20.00	10.00	6.00
160	Matt Hazeltine	20.00	10.00	6.00
161	Abe Woodson	20.00	10.00	6.00
162	Dave Baker	20.00	10.00	6.00
163	**San Francisco 49ers Team**	20.00	10.00	6.00
164	Norm Snead **RC** (SP)	40.00	20.00	12.00
165	Dick James	20.00	10.00	6.00
166	Bobby Mitchell	20.00	10.00	6.00
167	Sam Horner	20.00	10.00	6.00
168	Bill Barnes	20.00	10.00	6.00
169	Bill Anderson	20.00	10.00	6.00
170	Fred Dugan	20.00	10.00	6.00
171	John Aveni (SP)	30.00	15.00	9.00
172	Bob Toneff	20.00	10.00	6.00
173	Jim Kerr	20.00	10.00	6.00
174	Leroy Jackson (SP)	30.00	15.00	9.00
175	**Washington Redskins Team**	20.00	10.00	6.00
176	**Checklist**	115.00	60.00	35.00

1962 Topps Bucks

This 48-card set was issued one per wax pack in the 1962 Topps football issue. The 1-1/4" x 4-1/4" "cards" have a dollar bill motif with the player's head in the middle and his name underneath. Backs show the same motif, with the NFL and team logo encircled. The Topps Bucks were printed on white paper.

		NM	E	VG
	Complete Set (48):	400.00	200.00	120.00
	Common Player:	4.50	2.25	1.35
1	J.D. Smith	4.50	2.25	1.35
2	Bart Starr	25.00	12.50	7.50
3	Dick James	4.50	2.25	1.35
4	Alex Webster	6.00	3.00	1.75
5	Paul Hornung	18.00	9.00	5.50
6	John David Crow	6.00	3.00	1.75
7	Jimmy Brown	60.00	30.00	18.00
8	Don Perkins	4.50	2.25	1.35
9	Bobby Walston	4.50	2.25	1.35
10	Jim Phillips	4.50	2.25	1.35
11	Y.A. Tittle	20.00	10.00	6.00
12	Sonny Randle	4.50	2.25	1.35
13	Jerry Reichow	4.50	2.25	1.35
14	Yale Lary	7.00	3.50	2.25
15	Buddy Dial	4.50	2.25	1.35
16	Ray Renfro	4.50	2.25	1.35
17	Norm Snead	4.50	2.25	1.35
18	Leo Nemellini	6.00	3.00	1.75
19	Hugh McElhenny	8.00	4.00	2.50
20	Eddie LeBaron	4.50	2.25	1.35
21	Bill Howton	4.50	2.25	1.35
22	Bobby Mitchell	9.00	4.50	2.75
23	Nick Pietrosante	4.50	2.25	1.35
24	John Unitas	30.00	15.00	9.00
25	Raymond Berry	9.00	4.50	2.75
26	Billy Kilmer	7.00	3.50	2.25
27	Lenny Moore	8.00	4.00	2.50
28	Tommy McDonald	4.50	2.25	1.35
29	Del Shofner	4.50	2.25	1.35
30	Jim Taylor	12.00	6.00	3.75
31	Joe Schmidt	7.00	3.50	2.25
32	Bill George	6.00	3.00	1.75
33	Fran Tarkenton	65.00	32.50	20.00
34	Willie Galimore	4.50	2.25	1.35
35	Bobby Layne	17.00	8.50	5.00
36	Max McGee	4.50	2.25	1.35
37	Jon Arnett	4.50	2.25	1.35
38	Lou Groza	10.00	5.00	3.00
39	Frank Varrichione	4.50	2.25	1.35
40	Milt Plum	4.50	2.25	1.35
41	Prentice Gault	4.50	2.25	1.35
42	Billy Wade	6.00	3.00	1.75
43	Gino Marchetti	7.00	3.50	2.25
44	John Brodie	10.00	5.00	3.00
45	Sonny Jurgensen	10.00	5.00	3.00
46	Clarence Peaks	4.50	2.25	1.35
47	Mike Ditka	20.00	10.00	6.00
48	John Henry Johnson	7.00	3.50	2.25

1962 Topps CFL

		NM	E	VG
	Complete Set (169):	500.00	250.00	150.00
	Common Player:	2.00	1.00	.60
1	By Bailey	6.00	3.00	1.75
2	Nub Beamer	2.00	1.00	.60
3	Tom Brown	8.00	4.00	2.50
4	Mack Burton	2.00	1.00	.60
5	Mike Cacic	2.00	1.00	.60
6	Pat Claridge	2.00	1.00	.60
7	Steve Cotter	2.00	1.00	.60
8	Lonnie Dennis	2.00	1.00	.60
9	Norm Fieldgate	5.00	2.50	1.50
10	Willie Fleming	10.00	5.00	3.00
11	Tom Hinton	4.00	2.00	1.25
12	Sonny Homer	3.00	1.50	.90
13	Joe Kapp	14.00	7.00	4.25
14	Tom Larscheid	2.00	1.00	.60
15	Gordie Mitchell	2.00	1.00	.60
16	Baz Nagle	2.00	1.00	.60
17	Norris Stevenson	2.00	1.00	.60
18	Barney Therrien (UER) (Misspelled Therien on card front)	2.00	1.00	.60
19	Don Vicic	2.00	1.00	.60
20	**B.C. Lions Team**	8.00	4.00	2.50
21	Ed Buchanan	2.00	1.00	.60
22	Joe Carruthers	2.00	1.00	.60
23	Lovell Coleman	4.00	2.00	1.25
24	Barrie Cyr	2.00	1.00	.60
25	Ernie Danjean	3.00	1.50	.90
26	Gene Filipski	4.00	2.00	1.25
27	George Hansen	2.00	1.00	.60
28	Earl Lunsford	5.00	2.50	1.50
29	Don Luzzi	4.00	2.00	1.25
30	Bill McKenna	2.00	1.00	.60
31	Tony Pajaczkowski	4.00	2.00	1.25
32	Chuck Quilter	2.00	1.00	.60
33	Lorne Reid	2.00	1.00	.60
34	Art Scullion	2.00	1.00	.60
35	Jim Walden	2.00	1.00	.60
36	Harvey Wylie	4.00	2.00	1.25
37	**Calgary Stampeders Team Card**	8.00	4.00	2.50
38	Johnny Bright	10.00	5.00	3.00
39	Vic Chapman	2.00	1.00	.60
40	Marion Drew Deese	2.00	1.00	.60
41	Al Ecuyer	2.00	1.00	.60
42	Gino Fracas	3.00	1.50	.90
43	Don Getty	6.00	3.00	1.75
44	Ed Gray	2.00	1.00	.60
45	Urban Henry	3.00	1.50	.90
46	Bill Hill	2.00	1.00	.60
47	Mike Kmeche	2.00	1.00	.60
48	Oscar Kruger	3.00	1.50	.90
49	Mike Lashuk	2.00	1.00	.60
50	Jim Letcavits	2.00	1.00	.60
51	Roger Nelson	4.00	2.00	1.25
52	Jackie Parker	15.00	7.50	4.50
53	Howie Schumm	2.00	1.00	.60
54	Jim Shipka	2.00	1.00	.60
55	Bill Smith	2.00	1.00	.60
56	Jo Bob Smith	2.00	1.00	.60
57	Art Walker	3.00	1.50	.90
58	**Edmonton Eskimos Team Card**	8.00	4.00	2.50
59	John Barrow	8.00	4.00	2.50
60	Hardiman Cureton	2.00	1.00	.60
61	Geno DeNobile	2.00	1.00	.60
62	Tom Dublinski	2.00	1.00	.60
63	Bernie Faloney	12.00	6.00	3.50
64	Cam Fraser	2.00	1.00	.60
65	Ralph Goldston	3.00	1.50	.90
66	Tommy Grant	7.00	3.50	2.00
67	Garney Henley	15.00	7.50	4.50
68	Ron Howell	3.00	1.50	.90
69	Zeno Karcz	3.00	1.50	.90
70	Gerry McDougall (UER) (Misspelled Jerry)	3.00	1.50	.90
71	Chet Miksza	2.00	1.00	.60
72	Bronko Nagurski	6.00	3.00	1.75
73	Hal Patterson	10.00	5.00	3.00
74	George Scott	2.00	1.00	.60
75	Vince Scott	4.00	2.00	1.25
76	**Hamilton Tiger-Cats Team Card**	8.00	4.00	2.50
77	Ron Brewer	3.00	1.50	.90
78	Ron Brooks	2.00	1.00	.60
79	Howard Cissell	2.00	1.00	.60
80	Don Clark	3.00	1.50	.90
81	Dick Cohee	3.00	1.50	.90
82	John Conroy	2.00	1.00	.60
83	Milt Crain	3.00	1.50	.90
84	Ted Elsby	2.00	1.00	.60
85	Joe Francis	3.00	1.50	.90
86	Gene Gaines	8.00	4.00	2.50
87	Barrie Hansen	2.00	1.00	.60
88	Mike Kovac	2.00	1.00	.60
89	Ed Learn	2.00	1.00	.60
90	Billy Ray Locklin	2.00	1.00	.60
91	Marv Luster	6.00	3.00	1.75
92	Bobby Jack Oliver	3.00	1.50	.90
93	Sandy Stephens	8.00	4.00	2.50
94	**Montreal Alouettes Team Card**	10.00	5.00	3.00
95	Gilles Archambeault	2.00	1.00	.60
96	Bruno Bitkowski	3.00	1.50	.90
97	Jim Conroy	3.00	1.50	.90
98	Doug Daigneault	2.00	1.00	.60
99	Dick Desmarais	2.00	1.00	.60
100	Russ Jackson	15.00	7.50	4.50
101	Tom Jones	2.00	1.00	.60
102	Ron Lancaster	20.00	10.00	6.00
103	Angelo Mosca	15.00	7.50	4.50
104	Gerry Nesbitt	2.00	1.00	.60
105	Joe Poirier	3.00	1.50	.90
106	Moe Racine	2.00	1.00	.60
107	Gary Schreider	2.00	1.00	.60
108	Bob Simpson	6.00	3.00	1.75
109	Ted Smale	2.00	1.00	.60
110	Ron Stewart	7.00	3.50	2.00
111	Dave Thelen	6.00	3.00	1.75
112	Kaye Vaughan	4.00	2.00	1.25
113	**Ottawa Rough Ridgers Team Card**	8.00	4.00	2.50
114	Ron Atchison (UER) (Misspelled Atcheson on card front)	4.00	2.00	1.25
115	Danny Banda	2.00	1.00	.60
116	Al Benecick	2.00	1.00	.60
117	Clair Branch	2.00	1.00	.60
118	Fred Burket	2.00	1.00	.60
119	Bill Clarke	2.00	1.00	.60
120	Jim Copeland	2.00	1.00	.60
121	Ron Dundas	2.00	1.00	.60
122	Bob Golic	3.00	1.50	.90
123	Jack Gotta	4.00	2.00	1.25
124	Dave Grosz	2.00	1.00	.60
125	Neil Habig	3.00	1.50	.90
126	Jack Hill	2.00	1.00	.60
127	Len Legault	2.00	1.00	.60
128	Bob Ptacek	2.00	1.00	.60
129	Roy Smith	2.00	1.00	.60
130	**Saskatchewan Roughriders Team Card**	8.00	4.00	2.50
131	Lynn Bottoms	3.00	1.50	.90
132	Dick Fouts	3.00	1.50	.90
133	Wes Gideon	2.00	1.00	.60
134	Cookie Gilchrist	15.00	7.50	4.50
135	Art Johnson	2.00	1.00	.60
136	Bobby Kuntz	3.00	1.50	.90
137	Dave Mann	4.00	2.00	1.25
138	Marty Martinello	2.00	1.00	.60
139	Doug McNichol	2.00	1.00	.60
140	Bill Mitchell	2.00	1.00	.60
141	Danny Nykoluk	2.00	1.00	.60
142	Walt Radzick	2.00	1.00	.60
143	Tobin Rote	10.00	5.00	3.00
144	Jim Rountree	3.00	1.50	.90
145	Dick Shatto	8.00	4.00	2.50
146	Billy Shipp	3.00	1.50	.90
147	Norm Stoneburgh	2.00	1.00	.60
148	**Toronto Argonauts Team Card**	10.00	5.00	3.00
149	Dave Burkholder	2.00	1.00	.60
150	Jack Delveaux	2.00	1.00	.60
151	George Druxman	2.00	1.00	.60
152	Farrell Funston	3.00	1.50	.90
153	Herb Gray	5.00	2.50	1.50
154	Roger Hagberg	3.00	1.50	.90
155	Gerry James	6.00	3.00	1.75
156	Henry Janzen	3.00	1.50	.90
157	Ronnie Latourelle	2.00	1.00	.60
158	Hal Ledyard	2.00	1.00	.60
159	Leo Lewis	6.00	3.00	1.75
160	Steve Patrick	2.00	1.00	.60
161	Cornel Piper	2.00	1.00	.60
162	Ernie Pitts	2.00	1.00	.60
163	Kenny Ploen	8.00	4.00	2.50
164	Norm Rauhaus	3.00	1.50	.90

		NM	E	VG
165	Frank Rigney	6.00	3.00	1.75
166	Gord Rowland	3.00	1.50	.90
167	Roger Savoie	2.00	1.00	.60
168	Charlie Shepard	3.00	1.50	.90
169	**Winnipeg Blue Bombers Team Card**	20.00	10.00	6.00

1963 Topps

Topps' 170-card set of NFL players features teams grouped in alphabetical order by city name. As with many Topps sets in this era, numerous cards were short-printed because the number of cards didn't match the size of Topps' printing sheets, meaning some were produced in more quantities than others. Rookies in this set include Hall of Famers Deacon Jones, Bob Lilly, Willie Wood, and Ray Nitschke. Other important rookie cards include Jim Marshall and Charlie Johnson. The set also features the second-year cards of Roman Gabriel, Mike Ditka, Fran Tarkenton and Bill Kilmer. Last-year cards here include Eddie LeBaron, Fuzzy Thurston, Hugh McElhenny, Ernie Stautner and Leo Nomellini. The final Topps cards of such players as Night Train Lane, Yale Lary, Joe Schmidt, Y.A. Tittle, Rosey Grier, Sam Huff, John Henry Johnson and Bob St. Clair are also in this set. (Key: SP - short printed)

	NM	E	VG
Complete Set (170):	2,500	1,250	750.00
Common Player:	10.00	5.00	3.00
Minor Stars:	4.50		
Unlisted Stars:	6.00		
SP Commons	5.00		
Wax Pack (5):	375.00		

		NM	E	VG
1	Johnny Unitas	150.00	75.00	45.00
2	Lenny Moore	20.00	10.00	5.00
3	Jimmy Orr	10.00	5.00	3.00
4	Raymond Berry	20.00	10.00	5.00
5	Jim Parker	10.00	5.00	3.00
6	Alex Sandusky	10.00	5.00	3.00
7	Dick Szymanski	10.00	5.00	3.00
8	Gino Marchetti	15.00	7.50	4.50
9	Billy Ray Smith **RC**	10.00	5.00	3.00
10	Bill Pellington	10.00	5.00	3.00
11	Bob Boyd **RC**	10.00	5.00	3.00
12	**Baltimore Colts Team** (SP)	15.00	7.50	4.50
13	Frank Ryan (SP)	15.00	7.50	4.50
14	Jim Brown (SP)	200.00	100.00	60.00
15	Ray Renfro (SP)	15.00	7.50	4.50
16	Rich Kreitling (SP)	15.00	7.50	4.50
17	Mike McCormack (SP)	15.00	7.50	4.50
18	Jim Ray Smith (SP)	15.00	7.50	4.50
19	Lou Groza (SP)	30.00	15.00	9.00
20	Bill Glass (SP)	15.00	7.50	4.50
21	Galen Fiss (SP)	15.00	7.50	4.50
22	Don Fleming **RC** (SP)	10.00	5.00	3.00
23	Bob Gain (SP)	15.00	7.50	4.50
24	**Cleveland Browns** (SP)	15.00	7.50	4.50
25	Milt Plum	10.00	5.00	3.00
26	Dan Lewis	10.00	5.00	3.00
27	Nick Pietrosante	10.00	5.00	3.00
28	Gail Cogdill	10.00	5.00	3.00
29	Harley Sewell	10.00	5.00	3.00
30	Jim Gibbons	10.00	5.00	3.00
31	Carl Brettschneider	10.00	5.00	3.00
32	Dick "Night Train" Lane	10.00	5.00	3.00
33	Yale Lary	10.00	5.00	3.00
34	Roger Brown **RC**	10.00	5.00	3.00
35	Joe Schmidt	10.00	5.00	3.00
36	**Detroit Lions Team** (SP)	15.00	7.50	4.50
37	Roman Gabriel	20.00	10.00	6.00
38	Zeke Bratkowski	10.00	5.00	3.00
39	Dick Bass	10.00	5.00	3.00
40	Jon Arnett	10.00	5.00	3.00
41	Jim Phillips	10.00	5.00	3.00
42	Frank Varrichione	10.00	5.00	3.00
43	Danny Villanueva	10.00	5.00	3.00
44	Deacon Jones **RC**	60.00	30.00	18.00
45	Lindon Crow	10.00	5.00	3.00
46	Marlin McKeever	10.00	5.00	3.00
47	Ed Meador **RC**	10.00	5.00	3.00
48	**Los Angeles Rams Team**	10.00	5.00	3.00
49	Y.A. Tittle (SP)	60.00	30.00	18.00
50	Del Shofner (SP)	15.00	7.50	4.50
51	Alex Webster (SP)	15.00	7.50	4.50
52	Phil King (SP)	15.00	7.50	4.50
53	Jack Stroud (SP)	15.00	7.50	4.50
54	Darrell Dess (SP)	15.00	7.50	4.50
55	Jim Katcavage (SP)	15.00	7.50	4.50
56	Roosevelt Grier (SP)	20.00	10.00	6.00
57	Erich Barnes (SP)	15.00	7.50	4.50
58	Jim Patton (SP)	15.00	7.50	4.50
59	Sam Huff (SP)	30.00	15.00	9.00
60	**New York Giants Team**	10.00	5.00	3.00
61	Bill Wade	10.00	5.00	3.00
62	Mike Ditka	75.00	38.00	23.00
63	Johnny Morris	10.00	5.00	3.00
64	Roger LeClerc	10.00	5.00	3.00
65	Roger Davis	10.00	5.00	3.00
66	Joe Marconi	10.00	5.00	3.00
67	Herman Lee	10.00	5.00	3.00
68	Doug Atkins	10.00	5.00	3.00
69	Joe Fortunato	10.00	5.00	3.00
70	Bill George	10.00	5.00	3.00
71	Richie Petitbon	10.00	5.00	3.00
72	**Chicago Bears Team** (SP)	15.00	7.50	4.50
73	Eddie LeBaron (SP)	15.00	7.50	4.50
74	Don Meredith (SP)	65.00	33.00	20.00
75	Don Perkins (SP)	15.00	7.50	4.50
76	Amos Marsh (SP)	15.00	7.50	4.50
77	Bill Howton (SP)	15.00	7.50	4.50
78	Andy Cverko (SP)	15.00	7.50	4.50
79	Sam Baker (SP)	15.00	7.50	4.50
80	Jerry Tubbs (SP)	15.00	7.50	4.50
81	Don Bishop (SP)	15.00	7.50	4.50
82	Bob Lilly **RC**	170.00	85.00	51.00
83	Jerry Norton (SP)	15.00	7.50	4.50
84	**Dallas Cowboys**	20.00	10.00	6.00
85	**Checklist**	30.00	15.00	9.00
86	Bart Starr	70.00	35.00	21.00
87	Jim Taylor	30.00	15.00	9.00
88	Boyd Dowler	10.00	5.00	3.00
89	Forrest Gregg	10.00	5.00	3.00
90	Fuzzy Thurston	10.00	5.00	3.00
91	Jim Ringo	10.00	5.00	3.00
92	Ron Kramer	10.00	5.00	3.00
93	Hank Jordan	10.00	5.00	3.00
94	Bill Forester	10.00	5.00	3.00
95	Willie Wood **RC**	45.00	23.00	14.00
96	Ray Nitschke **RC**	80.00	40.00	24.00
97	**Green Bay Packers Team**	10.00	5.00	3.00
98	Fran Tarkenton	75.00	38.00	21.00
99	Tommy Mason	10.00	5.00	3.00
100	Mel Triplett	10.00	5.00	3.00
101	Jerry Reichow	10.00	5.00	3.00
102	Frank Youso	10.00	5.00	3.00
103	Hugh McElhenny	10.00	5.00	3.00
104	Gerry Huth	10.00	5.00	3.00
105	Ed Sharockman	10.00	5.00	3.00
106	Rip Hawkins	10.00	5.00	3.00
107	Jim Marshall **RC**	40.00	20.00	12.00
108	Jim Prestel	10.00	5.00	3.00
109	**Minnesota Vikings Team**	10.00	5.00	3.00
110	Sonny Jurgensen (SP)	15.00	7.50	4.50
111	Timmy Brown **RC** (SP)	15.00	7.50	4.50
112	Tommy McDonald (SP)	15.00	7.50	4.50
113	Clarence Peaks (SP)	15.00	7.50	4.50
114	Pete Retzlaff (SP)	15.00	7.50	4.50
115	Jim Schrader (SP)	15.00	7.50	4.50
116	Jim McCusker (SP)	15.00	7.50	4.50
117	Don Burroughs (SP)	15.00	7.50	4.50
118	Maxie Buaghan (SP)	15.00	7.50	4.50
119	Riley Gunnels (SP)	15.00	7.50	4.50
120	Jimmy Carr (SP)	15.00	7.50	4.50
121	**Philadelphia Eagles** (SP)	15.00	7.50	4.50
122	Ed Brown (SP)	25.00	13.00	8.00
123	John Henry Johnson	45.00	23.00	14.00
124	Buddy Dial (SP)	15.00	7.50	4.50
125	Red Mack (SP)	15.00	7.50	4.50
126	Preston Carpenter (SP)	15.00	7.50	4.50
127	Ray Lemek (SP)	15.00	7.50	4.50
128	Buzz Nutter (SP)	15.00	7.50	4.50
129	Ernie Stautner (SP)	30.00	15.00	9.00
130	Lou Michaels (SP)	15.00	7.50	4.50
131	Clendon Thomas **RC** (SP)	15.00	7.50	4.50
132	Tom Bettis (SP)	15.00	7.50	4.50
133	**Pittsburgh Steelers** (SP)	15.00	7.50	4.50
134	John Brodie	20.00	10.00	6.00
135	J.D. Smith	10.00	5.00	3.00
136	Bill Kilmer	10.00	5.00	3.00
137	Bernie Casey **RC**	10.00	5.00	3.00
138	Tommy Davis	10.00	5.00	3.00
139	Ted Connolly	10.00	5.00	3.00
140	Bob St. Clair	10.00	5.00	3.00
141	Abe Woodson	10.00	5.00	3.00
142	Matt Hazeltine	10.00	5.00	3.00
143	Leo Nomellini	10.00	5.00	3.00
144	Dan Colchico	10.00	5.00	3.00
145	**San Francisco 49ers** (SP)	15.00	7.50	4.50
146	Charlie Johnson **RC**	10.00	5.00	3.00
147	John David Crow	10.00	5.00	3.00
148	Bobby Joe Conrad	10.00	5.00	3.00
149	Sonny Randle	10.00	5.00	3.00
150	Prentice Gautt	10.00	5.00	3.00
151	Taz Anderson	10.00	5.00	3.00
152	Ernie McMillan **RC**	10.00	5.00	3.00
153	Jimmy Hill	10.00	5.00	3.00
154	Bill Koman	10.00	5.00	3.00
155	Larry Wilson **RC**	30.00	15.00	9.00
156	Don Owens	10.00	5.00	3.00
157	**St. Louis Cardinals** (SP)	15.00	7.50	4.50
158	Norm Snead (SP)	20.00	10.00	6.00
159	Bobby Mitchell **RC** (SP)	30.00	15.00	9.00
160	Billy Barnes (SP)	15.00	7.50	4.50
161	Fred Dugan (SP)	15.00	7.50	4.50
162	Don Bosseler (SP)	15.00	7.50	4.50
163	John Nisby (SP)	15.00	7.50	4.50
164	Riley Mattson (SP)	15.00	7.50	4.50
165	Bob Toneff (SP)	15.00	7.50	4.50
166	Rod Breedlove (SP)	15.00	7.50	4.50
167	Dick James (SP)	15.00	7.50	4.50
168	Claud Crabb (SP)	15.00	7.50	4.50
169	**Washington Redskins Team** (SP)	15.00	7.50	4.50
170	**Checklist**	50.00	25.00	15.00

1963 Topps CFL

	NM	E	VG
Complete Set (88):	300.00	150.00	90.00
Common Player:	2.50	1.25	.70

		NM	E	VG
1	Willie Fleming	12.00	6.00	3.50
2	Dick Fouts	3.50	1.75	1.00
3	Joe Kapp	15.00	7.50	4.50
4	Nub Beamer	2.50	1.25	.70
5	By Bailey	6.00	3.00	1.75
6	Tom Walker	2.50	1.25	.70
7	Sonny Homer	3.50	1.75	1.00
8	Tom Hinton	5.00	2.50	1.50
9	Lonnie Dennis	2.50	1.25	.70
10	**British Columbia Lions Team Card**	7.50	3.75	2.25
11	Ed Buchanan	2.50	1.25	.70
12	Ernie Danjean	2.50	1.25	.70
13	Eagle Day	6.00	3.00	1.75
14	Earl Lunsford	5.00	2.50	1.50
15	Don Luzzi	5.00	2.50	1.50
16	Tony Pajaczkowski	5.00	2.50	1.50
17	Jerry Keeling	15.00	7.50	4.50
18	Pat Holmes	2.50	1.25	.70
19	Wayne Harris	15.00	7.50	4.50
20	**Calgary Stampeders Team Card**	7.50	3.75	2.25
21	Tommy Joe Coffey	7.50	3.75	2.25
22	Mike Lashuk	2.50	1.25	.70
23	Bobby Walden	5.00	2.50	1.50
24	Don Getty	8.00	4.00	2.50
25	Len Vella	2.50	1.25	.70
26	Ted Frechette	2.50	1.25	.70
27	E.A. Sims	2.50	1.25	.70
28	Nat Dye	2.50	1.25	.70
29	**Edmonton Eskimos Team Card**	7.50	3.75	2.25
30	Bernie Faloney	10.00	5.00	3.00
31	Hal Patterson	8.00	4.00	2.50
32	John Barrow	6.00	3.00	1.75
33	Sam Fernandez	2.50	1.25	.70
34	Garney Henley	12.00	6.00	3.50
35	Joe Zuger	5.00	2.50	1.50
36	Hardiman Cureton	2.50	1.25	.70
37	Zeno Karcz	3.50	1.75	1.00
38	Bobby Kuntz	3.50	1.75	1.00
39	**Hamilton Tiger-Cats Team Card**	7.50	3.75	2.25
40	George Dixon	6.00	3.00	1.75
41	Don Clark	3.50	1.75	1.00
42	Marv Luster	6.00	3.00	1.75
43	Bobby Jack Oliver	3.50	1.75	1.00
44	Billy Ray Locklin	2.50	1.25	.70
45	Sandy Stephens	6.00	3.00	1.75
46	Milt Crain	3.50	1.75	1.00
47	Meco Poliziani	2.50	1.25	.70
48	Ted Elsby	2.50	1.25	.70
49	**Montreal Alouettes Team Card**	9.00	4.50	2.75
50	Russ Jackson	15.00	7.50	4.50
51	Ron Stewart	8.00	4.00	2.50
52	Dave Thelen	6.00	3.00	1.75
53	Kaye Vaughan	5.00	2.50	1.50
54	Joe Poirier	3.50	1.75	1.00
55	Moe Racine	2.50	1.25	.70
56	Whit Tucker	10.00	5.00	3.00
57	Ernie White	2.50	1.25	.70
58	**Ottawa Rough Ridgers Team Card**	7.50	3.75	2.25
59	Bob Ptacek	2.50	1.25	.70

60	Ray Purdin	2.50	1.25	.70
61	Dale West	3.50	1.75	1.00
62	Neil Habig	2.50	1.25	.70
63	Jack Gotta	3.50	1.75	1.00
64	Billy Gray	2.50	1.25	.70
65	Don Walsh	2.50	1.25	.70
66	Bill Clarke	2.50	1.25	.70
67	**Saskatchewan Roughriders Team Card**	7.50	3.75	2.25
68	Jackie Parker	15.00	7.50	4.50
69	Dave Mann	5.00	2.50	1.50
70	Dick Shatto	6.00	3.00	1.75
71	Norm Stoneburgh (UER) (Misspelled Stoneburg front)	2.50	1.25	.70
72	Clare Exelby	2.50	1.25	.70
73	Art Johnson	2.50	1.25	.70
74	Doug McNichol	2.50	1.25	.70
75	Danny Nykoluk	2.50	1.25	.70
76	Walt Radzick	2.50	1.25	.70
77	**Toronto Argonauts Team Card**	9.00	4.50	2.75
78	Leo Lewis	6.00	3.00	1.75
79	Kenny Ploen	7.00	3.50	2.00
80	Henry Janzen	3.50	1.75	1.00
81	Charlie Shepard	3.50	1.75	1.00
82	Roger Hagberg	3.50	1.75	1.00
83	Herb Gray	6.00	3.00	1.75
84	Frank Rigney	5.00	2.50	1.50
85	Jack Delveaux	2.50	1.25	.70
86	Ronnie Latourelle	2.50	1.25	.70
87	**Winnipeg Blue Bombers Team Card**	7.50	3.75	2.25
88	**Checklist Card**	50.00	25.00	15.00

1964 Topps

Considered to be one of the toughest sets of the decade, this 176-card set was Topps' first to feature only American Football League players. Because of the awkward size of the set and the inability to print the cards on two sheets, some of the cards in the set are short-printed. Cards are numbered by city and by player. This set contains the rookie cards of Daryle Lamonica, Buck Buchanan, John Hadi, and Hall of Famers Bobby Bell and Matt Snell. Second-year cards in the set include Nick Buoniconti, Len Dawson and Lance Alworth. An interesting error exists in the set: Bo Roberson, #151, has a helmet with the Raiders logo at the bottom of the card. Helmets were not part of the card design, and logos were always airbrushed. (Key: SP - short printed)

	NM	E	VG
Complete Set (176):	2,000	1,00.00	600.00
Common Player:	8.00	4.00	2.50
Minor Stars:	4.00		
Unlisted Stars:	6.00		
SP Cards:	10.00	5.00	3.00
Wax Pack (5):	420.00		
Wax Pack (8):	550.00		

1	Tommy Addison (SP)	35.00	18.00	11.00
2	Houston Antwine **RC**	8.00	4.00	2.50
3	Nick Buoniconti	20.00	10.00	6.00
4	Ron Burton (SP)	15.00	7.50	4.50
5	Gino Cappelletti	8.00	4.00	2.50
6	Jim Colclough (SP)	10.00	5.00	3.00
7	Bob Dee (SP)	10.00	5.00	3.00
8	Larry Eisenhauer	8.00	4.00	2.50
9	Dick Felt (SP)	10.00	5.00	3.00
10	Larry Garron	8.00	4.00	2.50
11	Art Graham	8.00	4.00	2.50
12	Ron Hall	8.00	4.00	2.50
13	Charles Long	8.00	4.00	2.50
14	Don McKinnon	8.00	4.00	2.50
15	Don Oakes (SP)	10.00	5.00	3.00
16	Ross O'Hanley (SP)	10.00	5.00	3.00
17	Babe Parilli (SP)	15.00	7.50	4.50
18	Jesse Richardson (SP)	10.00	5.00	3.00
19	Jack Rudolph (SP)	10.00	5.00	3.00
20	Don Webb **RC**	8.00	4.00	2.50
21	**Boston Patriots Team**	8.00	4.00	2.50
22	Ray Abbruzzese	8.00	4.00	2.50
23	Stew Barber **RC**	8.00	4.00	2.50
24	Dave Behrman	8.00	4.00	2.50
25	Al Bemiller	8.00	4.00	2.50
26	Elbert Dubenion (SP)	15.00	7.50	4.50
27	Jim Dunaway **RC** (SP)	10.00	5.00	3.00
28	Booker Edgerson (SP)	10.00	5.00	3.00
29	Cookie Gilchrist (SP)	20.00	10.00	6.00
30	Jack Kemp (SP)	200.00	100.00	60.00
31	Daryle Lamonica **RC**	75.00	38.00	23.00
32	Bill Miller	8.00	4.00	2.50
33	Herb Paterra **RC**	8.00	4.00	2.50
34	Ken Rice (SP)	10.00	5.00	3.00
35	Ed Rutkowski	8.00	4.00	2.50
36	George Saimes **RC**	8.00	4.00	2.50
37	Tom Sestak	8.00	4.00	2.50
38	Billy Shaw (SP)	20.00	10.00	6.00
39	Mike Stratton	8.00	4.00	2.50
40	Gene Sykes	8.00	4.00	2.50
41	John Tracey (SP)	10.00	5.00	3.00
42	Sid Youngelman (SP)	10.00	5.00	3.00
43	**Buffalo Bills Team**	8.00	4.00	2.50
44	Eldon Danenhauer (SP)	10.00	5.00	3.00
45	Jim Fraser (SP)	10.00	5.00	3.00
46	Chuck Gavin (SP)	10.00	6.00	3.00
47	Goose Gonsoulin (SP)	15.00	7.50	4.50
48	Ernie Barnes **RC**	8.00	4.00	2.50
49	Tom Janik	8.00	4.00	2.50
50	Billy Joe **RC**	8.00	4.00	2.50
51	Ike Lassiter **RC**	8.00	4.00	2.50
52	John McCormick (SP)	10.00	5.00	3.00
53	Lewis Bud McFadin (SP)	10.00	5.00	3.00
54	Gene Mingo (SP)	10.00	5.00	3.00
55	Charlie Mitchell	8.00	4.00	2.50
56	John Nocera (SP)	10.00	5.00	3.00
57	Tom Nomina	8.00	4.00	2.50
58	Harold Olson (SP)	10.00	5.00	3.00
59	Bob Scarpitto	8.00	4.00	2.50
60	John Sklopan	8.00	4.00	2.50
61	Mickey Slaughter	8.00	4.00	2.50
62	Don Stone	8.00	4.00	2.50
63	Jerry Sturm	8.00	4.00	2.50
64	Lionel Taylor (SP)	15.00	7.50	4.50
65	**Denver Broncos Team** (SP)	20.00	10.00	6.00
66	Scott Appleton **RC**	8.00	4.00	2.50
67	Tony Banfield (SP)	10.00	5.00	3.00
68	George Blanda (SP)	60.00	30.00	18.00
69	Billy Cannon	8.00	4.00	2.50
70	Doug Cline (SP)	10.00	5.00	3.00
71	Gary Cutsinger (SP)	10.00	5.00	3.00
72	Willard Dewveall (SP)	10.00	5.00	3.00
73	Don Floyd (SP)	10.00	5.00	3.00
74	Freddy Gick (SP)	10.00	5.00	3.00
75	Charlie Hennigan (SP)	15.00	7.50	4.50
76	Ed Husmann (SP)	10.00	5.00	3.00
77	Bobby Jancik (SP)	10.00	5.00	3.00
78	Jacky Lee (SP)	10.00	5.00	3.00
79	Bob McLeod (SP)	10.00	5.00	3.00
80	Rich Michael (SP)	10.00	5.00	3.00
81	Larry Onesti **RC**	8.00	4.00	2.50
82	**Checklist**	50.00	25.00	15.00
83	Bob Schmidt (SP)	10.00	5.00	3.00
84	Walt Suggs (SP)	10.00	5.00	3.00
85	Bob Talamini (SP)	10.00	5.00	3.00
86	Charley Tolar (SP)	10.00	5.00	3.00
87	Don Trull **RC**	8.00	4.00	2.50
88	**Houston Oilers Team**	8.00	4.00	2.50
89	Fred Arbanas	8.00	4.00	2.50
90	Bobby Bell **RC**	35.00	17.50	10.50
91	Mel Branch (SP)	10.00	5.00	3.00
92	Buck Buchanan **RC**	35.00	17.50	10.50
93	Ed Budde **RC**	8.00	4.00	2.50
94	Chris Burford (SP)	10.00	5.00	3.00
95	Walt Corey **RC**	8.00	4.00	2.50
96	Len Dawson (SP)	75.00	37.00	22.00
97	Dave Grayson **RC**	8.00	4.00	2.50
98	Abner Haynes	8.00	4.00	2.50
99	Sherrill Headrick (SP)	15.00	7.50	4.50
100	E.J. Holub	8.00	4.00	2.50
101	Bobby Hunt	8.00	4.00	2.50
102	Frank Jackson (SP)	10.00	5.00	3.00
103	Curtis McClinton	8.00	4.00	2.50
104	Jerry Mays (SP)	8.00	4.00	2.50
105	Johnny Robinson (SP)	15.00	7.50	4.50
106	Jack Spikes (SP)	10.00	5.00	3.00
107	Smokey Stover (SP)	10.00	5.00	3.00
108	Jim Tyrer **RC**	8.00	4.00	2.50
109	Duane Wood (SP)	10.00	5.00	3.00
110	**Kansas City Chiefs Team**	8.00	4.00	2.50
111	Dick Christy (SP)	10.00	5.00	3.00
112	Dan Ficca (SP)	10.00	5.00	3.00
113	Larry Grantham	8.00	4.00	2.50
114	Curley Johnson (SP)	10.00	5.00	3.00
115	Gene Heeter	8.00	4.00	2.50
116	Jack Klotz	8.00	4.00	2.50
117	Pete Liske **RC**	8.00	4.00	2.50
118	Bob McAdam	8.00	4.00	2.50
119	Dee Mackey (SP)	10.00	5.00	3.00
120	Bill Mathis (SP)	15.00	7.50	4.50
121	Don Maynard	35.00	18.00	11.00
122	Dainard Paulson (SP)	10.00	5.00	3.00
123	Gerry Philbin **RC**	8.00	4.00	2.50
124	Mark Smolinski (SP)	10.00	5.00	3.00
125	Matt Snell **RC**	20.00	10.00	6.00
126	Mike Taliaferro	8.00	4.00	2.50
127	Bake Turner **RC** (SP)	15.00	7.50	4.50
128	Jeff Ware	8.00	4.00	2.50
129	Clyde Washington	8.00	4.00	2.50
130	Dick Wood **RC**	8.00	4.00	2.50
131	**New York Jets Team**	8.00	4.00	2.50
132	Dalva Allen (SP)	10.00	5.00	3.00
133	Dan Birdwell	8.00	4.00	2.50
134	Dave Costa **RC**	8.00	4.00	2.50
135	Dobiue Craig	8.00	4.00	2.50
136	Clem Daniels	8.00	4.00	2.50
137	Cotton Davidson (SP)	15.00	7.50	4.50
138	Claude Gibson	8.00	4.00	2.50
139	Tom Flores	20.00	10.00	6.00
140	Wayne Hawkins (SP)	10.00	5.00	3.00
141	Ken Herock	8.00	4.00	2.50
142	Jon Jelacic (SP)	10.00	5.00	3.00
143	Joe Krakoski	8.00	4.00	2.50
144	Archie Matsos (SP)	10.00	5.00	3.00
145	Mike Mercer	8.00	4.00	2.50
146	Alan Miller (SP)	10.00	5.00	3.00
147	Bob Mischak (SP)	10.00	5.00	3.00
148	Jim Otto (SP)	35.00	18.00	11.00
149	Clancy Osborne (SP)	10.00	5.00	3.00
150	Art Powell (SP)	15.00	7.50	4.50
151	Bo Roberson	8.00	4.00	2.50
152	Fred Williamson (SP)	30.00	15.00	9.00
153	**Oakland Raiders Team**	8.00	4.00	2.50
154	Chuck Allen **RC** (SP)	15.00	7.50	4.50
155	Lance Alworth	50.00	25.00	15.00
156	George Blair	8.00	4.00	2.50
157	Earl Faison	8.00	4.00	2.50
158	Sam Gruniesen	8.00	4.00	2.50
159	John Hadl **RC**	45.00	23.00	14.00
160	Dick Harris (SP)	10.00	5.00	3.00
161	Emil Karas (SP)	10.00	5.00	3.00
162	Dave Kocourek (SP)	10.00	5.00	3.00
163	Ernie Ladd	8.00	4.00	2.50
164	Keith Lincoln	8.00	4.00	2.50
165	Paul Lowe (SP)	20.00	10.00	6.00
166	Charles McNeil	8.00	4.00	2.50
167	Jacque MacKinnon (SP)	10.00	5.00	3.00
168	Ron Mix (SP)	10.00	5.00	3.00
169	Don Norton (SP)	10.00	5.00	3.00
170	Don Rogers (SP)	10.00	5.00	3.00
171	Tobin Rote (SP)	15.00	7.50	4.50
172	Henry Schmidt (SP)	10.00	5.00	3.00
173	Bud Whitehead	8.00	4.00	2.50
174	Ernie Wright (SP)	15.00	7.50	4.50
175	**San Diego Chargers Team**	8.00	4.00	2.50
176	**Checklist** (SP)	125.00	65.00	39.00

1964 Topps CFL

	NM	E	VG
Complete Set (88):	300.00	150.00	90.00
Common Player:	2.50	1.25	.70

1	Willie Fleming	12.00	6.00	3.50
2	Dick Fouts	3.50	1.75	1.00
3	Joe Kapp	15.00	7.50	4.50
4	Nub Beamer	2.50	1.25	.70
5	Tom Brown	5.00	2.50	1.50
6	Tom Walker	2.50	1.25	.70
7	Sonny Homer	3.50	1.75	1.00
8	Tom Hinton	5.00	2.50	1.50
9	Lonnie Dennis	2.50	1.25	.70
10	**B.C. Lions Team**	7.50	3.75	2.25
11	Lovell Coleman	4.00	2.00	1.25
12	Ernie Danjean	2.50	1.25	.70
13	Eagle Day	5.00	2.50	1.50
14	Jim Furlong	2.50	1.25	.70
15	Don Luzzi	5.00	2.50	1.50
16	Tony Pajaczkowski	5.00	2.50	1.50
17	Jerry Keeling	6.00	3.00	1.75
18	Pat Holmes	2.50	1.25	.70
19	Wayne Harris	7.50	3.75	2.25
20	**Calgary Stampeders Team Card**	7.50	3.75	2.25
21	Tommy Joe Coffey	7.50	3.75	2.25
22	Al Ecuyer	2.50	1.25	.70
23	**Checklist Card**	35.00	17.50	10.50
24	Don Getty	6.00	3.00	1.75
25	Len Vella	2.50	1.25	.70
26	Ted Frechette	2.50	1.25	.70
27	E.A. Sims	2.50	1.25	.70
28	Nat Dye	2.50	1.25	.70
29	**Edmonton Eskimos Team Card**	7.50	3.75	2.25
30	Bernie Faloney	15.00	7.50	4.50
31	Hal Patterson	8.00	4.00	2.50

32	John Barrow	6.00	3.00	1.75
33	Tommy Grant	6.00	3.00	1.75
34	Garney Henley	9.00	4.50	2.75
35	Joe Zuger	3.50	1.75	1.00
36	Hardiman Cureton	2.50	1.25	.70
37	Zeno Karcz	3.50	1.75	1.00
38	Bobby Kuntz	3.50	1.75	1.00
39	**Hamilton Tiger-Cats Team Card**	7.50	3.75	2.25
40	George Dixon	7.50	3.75	2.25
41	Dave Hoppmann	2.50	1.25	.70
42	Dick Walton	2.50	1.25	.70
43	Jim Andreotti	3.50	1.75	1.00
44	Billy Ray Locklin	2.50	1.25	.70
45	Fred Burket	2.50	1.25	.70
46	Milt Crane	3.50	1.75	1.00
47	Meco Poliziani	2.50	1.25	.70
48	Ted Elsby	2.50	1.25	.70
49	**Montreal Alouettes Team Card**	9.00	4.50	2.75
50	Russ Jackson	15.00	7.50	4.50
51	Ron Stewart	8.00	4.00	2.50
52	Dave Thelen	5.00	2.50	1.50
53	Kaye Vaughan	5.00	2.50	1.50
54	Joe Poirier	3.50	1.75	1.00
55	Moe Racine	2.50	1.25	.70
56	Whit Tucker	6.00	3.00	1.75
57	Ernie White	2.50	1.25	.70
58	**Ottawa Roughriders Team Card**	7.50	3.75	2.25
59	Bob Ptacek	2.50	1.25	.70
60	Ray Purdin	2.50	1.25	.70
61	Dale West	3.50	1.75	1.00
62	Neil Habig	2.50	1.25	.70
63	Jack Gotta	3.50	1.75	1.00
64	Billy Gray	2.50	1.25	.70
65	Don Walsh	2.50	1.25	.70
66	Bill Clarke	2.50	1.25	.70
67	**Saskatchewan Roughriders Team Card**	7.50	3.75	2.25
68	Jackie Parker	15.00	7.50	4.50
69	Dave Mann	4.00	2.00	1.25
70	Dick Shatto	6.00	3.00	1.75
71	Norm Stoneburgh	2.50	1.25	.70
72	Clare Exelby	2.50	1.25	.70
73	Jim Christopherson	2.50	1.25	.70
74	Sherman Lewis	6.00	3.00	1.75
75	Danny Nykoluk	2.50	1.25	.70
76	Walt Radzick	2.50	1.25	.70
77	**Toronto Argonauts Team Card**	9.00	4.50	2.75
78	Leo Lewis	6.00	3.00	1.75
79	Kenny Ploen	6.00	3.00	1.75
80	Henry Janzen	3.50	1.75	1.00
81	Charlie Shepard	3.50	1.75	1.00
82	Roger Hagberg	3.50	1.75	1.00
83	Herb Gray	6.00	3.00	1.75
84	Frank Rigney	5.00	2.50	1.50
85	Jack Delveaux	2.50	1.25	.70
86	Ronnie Latourelle	2.50	1.25	.70
87	**Winnipeg Blue Bombers Team Card**	7.50	3.75	2.25
88	**Checklist Card**	50.00	25.00	15.00

1964 Topps Pennant Stickers

These 24 peel-off stickers (they measure about 2" x 4-1/2") were inserted one per wax pack of the 1964 Topps football cards. The unnumbered pennants covered AFL teams and major college teams. Since stickers were folded to fit into the backs, all of them are found with a crease.

	NM	E	VG
Complete Set (24):	240.00	120.00	72.50
AFL Team:	12.00	6.00	3.75
College Team:	7.00	3.50	2.25

(1)	**Boston Patriots**	12.00	6.00	3.75
(2)	**Buffalo Bills**	12.00	6.00	3.75
(3)	**Denver Broncos**	12.00	6.00	3.75
(4)	**Houston Oilers**	12.00	6.00	3.75
(5)	**K.C. Chiefs**	12.00	6.00	3.75
(6)	**New York Jets**	12.00	6.00	3.75
(7)	**Oakland Raiders**	12.00	6.00	3.75
(8)	**San Diego Chargers**	12.00	6.00	3.75
(9)	**Air Force**	7.00	3.50	2.25
(10)	**Army**	7.00	3.50	2.25
(11)	**Dartmouth**	7.00	3.50	2.25
(12)	**Duke**	7.00	3.50	2.25
(13)	**Michigan**	7.00	3.50	2.25
(14)	**Minnesota**	7.00	3.50	2.25
(15)	**Mississippi**	7.00	3.50	2.25
(16)	**Navy**	7.00	3.50	2.25
(17)	**Notre Dame**	15.00	7.50	4.50
(18)	**SMU**	7.00	3.50	2.25
(19)	**USC**	7.00	3.50	2.25
(20)	**Syracuse**	7.00	3.50	2.25
(21)	**Texas**	7.00	3.50	2.25
(22)	**Washington**	7.00	3.50	2.25
(23)	**Wisconsin**	7.00	3.50	2.25
(24)	**Yale**	7.00	3.50	2.25

1965 Topps

Topps' second set featuring only AFL players is easily the most valued set of the decade for several reasons - the oversized (about 2-1/2" x 5") cards are attractive; it includes Joe Namath's rookie card; and Topps' unorthodox printing method created an abundance of certain cards, but a scarcity of others - all throughout the 176-card set, too, not just in one sequentially-numbered series. There may be a variation on Namath's rookie card as well. There's a report of a card showing Broadway Joe with a butterfly tattoo on his arm; on other cards, this tattoo is airbrushed off. It's uncertain how many, or even if, this variation exists. Besides Namath, other rookies in this set include Fred Biletnikoff, Willie Brown, and Ben Davidson. Second-year cards include those of Daryle Lamonica, Bobby Bell, Buck Buchanon, Matt Snell and John Hadl. (Key: SP - short printed)

	NM	E	VG
Complete Set (176):	4,250	2,125	1,275
Common Player:	20.00	10.00	6.00
Minor Stars:	11.50		
Unlisted Stars:	18.00		
SP Cards:	30.00	15.00	9.00
Wax Pack (5):	675.00		

1	Tommy Addison (SP)	40.00	20.00	12.00
2	Houston Antwine (SP)	25.00	13.00	8.00
3	Nick Buoniconti (SP)	40.00	20.00	12.00
4	Ron Burton (SP)	35.00	18.00	11.00
5	Gino Cappelletti (SP)	30.00	15.00	9.00
6	Jim Colclough	20.00	10.00	6.00
7	Bob Dee (SP)	25.00	13.00	8.00
8	Larry Eisenhauer	20.00	10.00	6.00
9	J.D. Garrett	20.00	10.00	6.00
10	Larry Garron	20.00	10.00	6.00
11	Art Graham (SP)	25.00	13.00	8.00
12	Ron Hall	20.00	10.00	6.00
13	Charles Long	20.00	10.00	6.00
14	Jon Morris **RC**	20.00	10.00	6.00
15	Bill Neighbors (SP)	25.00	13.00	8.00
16	Ross O'Hanley	20.00	10.00	6.00
17	Babe Parilli (SP)	30.00	15.00	9.00
18	Tony Romeo (SP)	25.00	13.00	8.00
19	Jack Rudolph (SP)	25.00	13.00	8.00
20	Bob Schmidt	20.00	10.00	6.00
21	Don Webb (SP)	25.00	13.00	8.00
22	Jim Whalen (SP)	25.00	13.00	8.00
23	Stew Barber	20.00	10.00	6.00
24	Glenn Bass (SP)	25.00	13.00	8.00
25	Al Bemiller (SP)	25.00	13.00	8.00
26	Wray Carlton (SP)	25.00	13.00	8.00
27	Tom Day	20.00	10.00	6.00
28	Elbert Dubenion (SP)	30.00	15.00	9.00
29	Jim Dunaway	20.00	10.00	6.00
30	Pete Gogolak **RC** (SP)	30.00	15.00	9.00
31	Dick Hudson (SP)	25.00	13.00	8.00
32	Harry Jacobs (SP)	25.00	13.00	8.00
33	Billy Joe (SP)	30.00	15.00	9.00
34	Tom Keating **RC** (SP)	25.00	13.00	8.00
35	Jack Kemp (SP)	125.00	65.00	39.00
36	Daryle Lamonica (SP)	30.00	15.00	9.00
37	Paul Maguire (SP)	25.00	13.00	8.00
38	Ron McDole **RC** (SP)	25.00	13.00	8.00
39	George Saimes (SP)	25.00	13.00	8.00
40	Tom Sestak (SP)	25.00	13.00	8.00
41	Billy Shaw (SP)	25.00	13.00	8.00
42	Mike Stratton (SP)	25.00	13.00	8.00
43	John Tracey (SP)	25.00	13.00	8.00
44	Ernie Warlick	20.00	10.00	6.00
45	Odell Barry	20.00	10.00	6.00
46	Willie Brown **RC** (SP)	100.00	50.00	30.00
47	Gerry Bussell (SP)	25.00	13.00	8.00
48	Eldon Danehauer (SP)	25.00	13.00	8.00
49	Al Denson (SP)	25.00	13.00	8.00
50	Hewritt Dixon **RC** (SP)	30.00	15.00	9.00
51	Cookie Gilchrist (SP)	35.00	18.00	11.00
52	Goose Gonsoulin (SP)	30.00	15.00	9.00
53	Abner Haynes (SP)	30.00	15.00	9.00
54	Jerry Hopkins (SP)	25.00	13.00	8.00
55	Ray Jacobs (SP)	25.00	13.00	8.00
56	Jacky Lee (SP)	30.00	15.00	9.00
57	John McCormick	20.00	10.00	6.00
58	Bob McCullough (SP)	20.00	10.00	6.00
59	John McGeever	20.00	10.00	6.00
60	Charlie Mitchell (SP)	25.00	13.00	8.00
61	Jim Perkins (SP)	25.00	13.00	8.00
62	Bob Scarpitto (SP)	25.00	13.00	8.00
63	Mickey Slaughter (SP)	25.00	13.00	8.00
64	Jerry Sturm (SP)	25.00	13.00	8.00
65	Lionel Taylor (SP)	30.00	15.00	9.00
66	Scott Appleton (SP)	25.00	13.00	8.00
67	Johnny Baker (SP)	25.00	13.00	8.00
68	Sonny Bishop (SP)	25.00	13.00	8.00
69	George Blanda (SP)	100.00	50.00	30.00
70	Sid Blanks (SP)	25.00	13.00	8.00
71	Ode Burrell (SP)	25.00	13.00	8.00
72	Doug Cline (SP)	25.00	13.00	8.00
73	Willard Dewveall	20.00	10.00	6.00
74	Larry Elkins **RC**	20.00	10.00	6.00
75	Don Floyd (SP)	25.00	13.00	8.00
76	Freddy Glick	20.00	10.00	6.00
77	Tom Goode (SP)	25.00	13.00	8.00
78	Charlie Hennigan (SP)	30.00	15.00	9.00
79	Ed Husmann	20.00	10.00	6.00
80	Bobby Jancik (SP)	25.00	13.00	8.00
81	Bud McFadin (SP)	25.00	13.00	8.00
82	Bob McLeod (SP)	25.00	13.00	8.00
83	Jim Norton (SP)	25.00	13.00	8.00
84	Walt Suggs	20.00	10.00	6.00
85	Bob Talamini	20.00	10.00	6.00
86	Charley Tolar (SP)	25.00	13.00	8.00
87	**Checklist 1-88** (SP)	175.00	90.00	54.00
88	Don Trull (SP)	25.00	13.00	8.00
89	Fred Arbanas (SP)	25.00	13.00	8.00
90	Pete Beathard **RC** (SP)	22.00	11.00	6.50
91	Bobby Bell (SP)	35.00	18.00	11.00
92	Mel Branch (SP)	25.00	13.00	8.00
93	Tommy Brooker (SP)	25.00	13.00	8.00
94	Buck Buchanan (SP)	35.00	18.00	11.00
95	Ed Budde (SP)	25.00	13.00	8.00
96	Chris Burford (SP)	25.00	13.00	8.00
97	Walt Corey	20.00	10.00	6.00
98	Jerry Cornelison	20.00	10.00	6.00
99	Len Dawson (SP)	85.00	43.00	26.00
100	Jon Gilliam (SP)	25.00	13.00	8.00
101	Sherrill Headrick (SP)	25.00	13.00	8.00
102	Dave Hill (SP)	25.00	13.00	8.00
103	E.J. Holub (SP)	25.00	13.00	8.00
104	Bobby Hunt (SP)	25.00	13.00	8.00
105	Frank Jackson (SP)	25.00	13.00	8.00
106	Jerry Mays	20.00	10.00	6.00
107	Curtis McClinton (SP)	30.00	15.00	9.00
108	Bobby Ply (SP)	25.00	13.00	8.00
109	Johnny Robinson (SP)	30.00	15.00	9.00
110	Jim Tyrer (SP)	25.00	13.00	8.00
111	Bill Baird (SP)	25.00	13.00	8.00
112	Ralph Baker **RC** (SP)	25.00	13.00	8.00
113	Sam DeLuca (SP)	25.00	13.00	8.00
114	Larry Grantham (SP)	30.00	15.00	9.00
115	Gene Heeter (SP)	25.00	13.00	8.00
116	Winston Hill **RC** (SP)	30.00	15.00	9.00
117	John Huarte **RC** (SP)	35.00	18.00	11.00
118	Cosmo Iacavazzi (SP)	25.00	13.00	8.00
119	Curley Johnson (SP)	25.00	13.00	8.00
120	Dee Mackey	20.00	10.00	6.00
121	Don Maynard	50.00	25.00	15.00
122	Joe Namath **RC** (SP)	1,800	900.00	540.00
123	Dainard Paulson	20.00	10.00	6.00
124	Gerry Philbin (SP)	25.00	13.00	8.00
125	Sherman Plunkett **RC**	30.00	15.00	9.00
126	Mark Smolinski	20.00	10.00	6.00
127	Matt Snell (SP)	35.00	18.00	11.00
128	Mike Taliaferro (SP)	25.00	13.00	8.00
129	Bake Turner (SP)	25.00	13.00	8.00
130	Clyde Washington (SP)	25.00	13.00	8.00
131	Verlon Biggs **RC** (SP)	25.00	13.00	8.00
132	Dalva Allen	20.00	10.00	6.00
133	Fred Biletnikoff **RC** (SP)	275.00	140.00	84.00
134	Billy Cannon (SP)	30.00	15.00	9.00

135	Dave Costa (SP)	25.00	13.00	8.00
136	Clem Daniels (SP)	30.00	15.00	9.00
137	Ben Davidson **RC** (SP)	65.00	33.00	20.00
138	Cotton Davidson (SP)	30.00	15.00	9.00
139	Tom Flores (SP)	30.00	15.00	9.00
140	Claude Gibson	20.00	10.00	6.00
141	Wayne Hawkins	20.00	10.00	6.00
142	Archie Matsos (SP)	25.00	13.00	8.00
143	Mike Mercer (SP)	25.00	13.00	8.00
144	Bob Mischak (SP)	25.00	13.00	8.00
145	Jim Otto	35.00	18.00	11.00
146	Art Powell (SP)	25.00	13.00	8.00
147	Warren Powers (SP)	25.00	13.00	8.00
148	Ken Rice (SP)	25.00	13.00	8.00
149	Bo Roberson (SP)	25.00	13.00	8.00
150	Harry Schuh **RC**	20.00	10.00	6.00
151	Larry Todd (SP)	25.00	13.00	8.00
152	Fred Williamson (SP)	30.00	15.00	9.00
153	J.R. Williamson	20.00	10.00	6.00
154	Chuck Allen	20.00	10.00	6.00
155	Lance Alworth	85.00	43.00	26.00
156	Frank Buncom	20.00	10.00	6.00
157	Steve DeLong **RC** (SP)	30.00	15.00	9.00
158	Earl Faison (SP)	30.00	15.00	9.00
159	Kenny Graham (SP)	25.00	13.00	8.00
160	George Gross (SP)	25.00	13.00	8.00
161	John Hadl (SP)	35.00	18.00	11.00
162	Emil Karas (SP)	25.00	13.00	8.00
163	Dave Kocourek (SP)	25.00	13.00	8.00
164	Ernie Ladd (SP)	30.00	15.00	9.00
165	Keith Lincoln (SP)	30.00	15.00	9.00
166	Paul Lowe (SP)	30.00	15.00	9.00
167	Jacque MacKinnon	20.00	10.00	6.00
168	Ron Mix	30.00	15.00	9.00
169	Don Norton (SP)	25.00	13.00	8.00
170	Bob Petrich	20.00	10.00	6.00
171	Rick Redman (SP)	25.00	13.00	8.00
172	Pat Shea	20.00	10.00	6.00
173	Walt Sweeney **RC** (SP)	35.00	18.00	11.00
174	Dick Westmoreland **RC**	20.00	10.00	6.00
175	Ernie Wright (SP)	30.00	15.00	9.00
176	**Checklist 89-176** (SP)	215.00	110.00	66.00

1965 Topps CFL

		NM	E	VG
Complete Set (132):		325.00	162.00	97.00
Common Player:		2.00	1.00	.60
1	Neal Beaumont	6.00	3.00	1.75
2	Tom Brown	6.00	3.00	1.75
3	Mike Cacic	2.00	1.00	.60
4	Pat Claridge	2.00	1.00	.60
5	Steve Cotter	2.00	1.00	.60
6	Lonnie Dennis	2.00	1.00	.60
7	Norm Fieldgate	4.00	2.00	1.25
8	Willie Fleming	10.00	5.00	3.00
9	Dick Fouts	3.00	1.50	.90
10	Tom Hinton	4.00	2.00	1.25
11	Sonny Homer	3.00	1.50	.90
12	Joe Kapp	12.00	6.00	3.50
13	Paul Seale	2.00	1.00	.60
14	Steve Shafer	2.00	1.00	.60
15	Bob Swift	2.00	1.00	.60
16	Larry Anderson	2.00	1.00	.60
17	Lu Bain	2.00	1.00	.60
18	Lovell Coleman	3.00	1.50	.90
19	Eagle Day	4.00	2.00	1.25
20	Jim Furlong	2.00	1.00	.60
21	Wayne Harris	6.00	3.00	1.75
22	Herman Harrison	12.00	6.00	3.50
23	Jerry Keeling	5.00	2.50	1.50
24	Hal Krebs	2.00	1.00	.60
25	Don Luzzi	4.00	2.00	1.25
26	Tony Pajaczkowski	4.00	2.00	1.25
27	Larry Robinson	4.00	2.00	1.25
28	Bob Taylor	3.00	1.50	.90
29	Ted Woods	2.00	1.00	.60
30	Jon Anabo	2.00	1.00	.60
31	Jim Battle	2.00	1.00	.60
32	Charlie Brown	2.00	1.00	.60
33	Tommy Joe Coffey	7.50	3.75	2.25
34	Marcel Deleeuw	2.00	1.00	.60
35	Al Ecuyer	2.00	1.00	.60
36	Jim Higgins	2.00	1.00	.60
37	Oscar Kruger	3.00	1.50	.90
38	Barry Mitchelson	2.00	1.00	.60
39	Roger Nelson	4.00	2.00	1.25
40	Bill Redell	2.00	1.00	.60
41	E.A. Sims	2.00	1.00	.60
42	Jim Stinnette	2.00	1.00	.60
43	Jim Thomas	2.00	1.00	.60
44	Terry Wilson	2.00	1.00	.60
45	Art Baker	2.00	1.00	.60
46	John Barrow	6.00	3.00	1.75
47	Dick Cohee	3.00	1.50	.90
48	Frank Cosentino	4.00	2.00	1.25
49	Johnny Counts	2.00	1.00	.60
50	Tommy Grant	5.00	2.50	1.50
51	Garney Henley (See also number 57)	9.00	4.50	2.75
52	Zeno Karcz	3.00	1.50	.90
53	Ellison Kelly	12.00	6.00	3.50
54	Bobby Kuntz	3.00	1.50	.90
55	Angelo Mosca	12.00	6.00	3.50
56	Bronko Nagurski	6.00	3.00	1.75
57	Don Sutherin (UER) (number 51 on back)	12.00	6.00	3.50
58	Dave Viti	2.00	1.00	.60
59	Joe Zuger	3.00	1.50	.90
60	**Checklist 1-60**	25.00	12.50	7.50
61	Jim Andreotti	3.00	1.50	.90
62	Harold Cooley	2.00	1.00	.60
63	Nat Craddock	2.00	1.00	.60
64	George Dixon	6.00	3.00	1.75
65	Ted Elsby	2.00	1.00	.60
66	Clare Exelby	2.00	1.00	.60
67	Bernie Faloney	12.00	6.00	3.50
68	Al Irwin	2.00	1.00	.60
69	Ed Learn	2.00	1.00	.60
70	Moe Levesque	2.00	1.00	.60
71	Bob Minihane	2.00	1.00	.60
72	Jim Reynolds	2.00	1.00	.60
73	Billy Roy	2.00	1.00	.60
74	Billy Joe Booth	3.00	1.50	.90
75	Jim Cain	2.00	1.00	.60
76	Larry DeGraw	2.00	1.00	.60
77	Don Estes	2.00	1.00	.60
78	Gene Gaines	5.00	2.50	1.50
79	John Kennerson	2.00	1.00	.60
80	Roger Kramer	3.00	1.50	.90
81	Ken Lehmann	3.00	1.50	.90
82	Bob O'Billovich	2.00	1.00	.60
83	Joe Poirier	3.00	1.50	.90
84	Bill Quinter	2.00	1.00	.60
85	Jerry Selinger	2.00	1.00	.60
86	Bill Siekierski	2.00	1.00	.60
87	Len Sparks	2.00	1.00	.60
88	Whit Tucker	4.00	2.00	1.25
89	Ron Atchison	4.00	2.00	1.25
90	Ed Buchanan	2.00	1.00	.60
91	Hugh Campbell	10.00	5.00	3.00
92	Henry Dorsch	2.00	1.00	.60
93	Garner Ekstran	3.00	1.50	.90
94	Martin Fabi	2.00	1.00	.60
95	Bob Good	2.00	1.00	.60
96	Ron Lancaster	12.00	6.00	3.50
97	Bob Ptacek	2.00	1.00	.60
98	George Reed	25.00	12.50	7.50
99	Wayne Shaw	2.00	1.00	.60
100	Dale West	3.00	1.50	.90
101	Reg Whitehouse	2.00	1.00	.60
102	Jim Worden	2.00	1.00	.60
103	Ron Brewer	3.00	1.50	.90
104	Don Fuell	2.00	1.00	.60
105	Ed Harrington	3.00	1.50	.90
106	George Hughley	2.00	1.00	.60
107	Dave Mann	4.00	2.00	1.25
108	Marty Martinello	2.00	1.00	.60
109	Danny Nykoluk	2.00	1.00	.60
110	Jackie Parker	15.00	7.50	4.50
111	Dave Pivec	2.00	1.00	.60
112	Walt Radzick	2.00	1.00	.60
113	Lee Sampson	2.00	1.00	.60
114	Dick Shatto	5.00	2.50	1.50
115	Norm Stoneburgh	2.00	1.00	.60
116	Jim Vollenweider	2.00	1.00	.60
117	John Wydareny	3.00	1.50	.90
118	Billy Cooper	2.00	1.00	.60
119	Farrell Funston	3.00	1.50	.90
120	Herb Gray	5.00	2.50	1.50
121	Henry Janzen	3.00	1.50	.90
122	Leo Lewis	6.00	3.00	1.75
123	Brian Palmer	2.00	1.00	.60
124	Cornel Piper	2.00	1.00	.60
125	Ernie Pitts	2.00	1.00	.60
126	Kenny Ploen	6.00	3.00	1.75
127	Norm Rauhaus	3.00	1.50	.90
128	Frank Rigney	4.00	2.00	1.25
129	Roger Savoie	2.00	1.00	.60
130	Dick Thornton	4.00	2.00	1.25
131	Bill Whisler	2.00	1.00	.60
132	**Checklist 61-132**	40.00	20.00	12.00

1965 Topps CFL Transfers

		NM	E	VG
Complete Set (27):		500.00	250.00	150.00
Common Player:		20.00	10.00	6.00
1	**British Columbia Lions Crest**	20.00	10.00	6.00
2	**British Columbia Lions Pennant**	20.00	10.00	6.00
3	**Calgary Stampeders Crest**	20.00	10.00	6.00
4	**Calgary Stampeders Pennant**	20.00	10.00	6.00
5	**Edmonton Eskimos Crest**	20.00	10.00	6.00
6	**Edmonton Eskimos Pennant**	20.00	10.00	6.00
7	**Hamilton Tiger-Cats Crest**	20.00	10.00	6.00
8	**Hamilton Tiger-Cats Pennant**	20.00	10.00	6.00
9	**Montreal Alouettes Crest**	20.00	10.00	6.00
10	**Montreal Alouettes Pennant**	20.00	10.00	6.00
11	**Ottawa Rough Riders Crest**	20.00	10.00	6.00
12	**Ottawa Rough Riders Pennant**	20.00	10.00	6.00
13	**Saskatchewan Roughriders Crest**	20.00	10.00	6.00
14	**Saskatchewan Roughriders Pennant**	20.00	10.00	6.00
15	**Toronto Argonauts Crest**	20.00	10.00	6.00
16	**Toronto Argonauts Pennant**	20.00	10.00	6.00
17	**Winnipeg Blue Bombers Crest**	20.00	10.00	6.00
18	**Winnipeg Blue Bombers Pennant**	20.00	10.00	6.00
19	**Quebec Provincial Crest**	20.00	10.00	6.00
20	**Ontario Provincial Crest**	20.00	10.00	6.00
21	**Manitoba Provincial Crest**	20.00	10.00	6.00
22	**Saskatchewan Provincial Crest**	20.00	10.00	6.00
23	**Alberta Provincial Crest**	20.00	10.00	6.00
24	**British Columbia Provincial Crest**	20.00	10.00	6.00
25	**Northwest Territories Territorial Crest**	20.00	10.00	6.00
26	**Yukon Territory Territorial Crest**	20.00	10.00	6.00
27	**Canada**	30.00	15.00	9.00

1965 Topps Rub-Offs

This 36-card, unnumbered set was included one per pack in wax packs of 1965 Topps football. The set, which measures two by three inches, includes the eight American Football League teams plus 28 college team emblems. Similar in design to the 1961 Topps baseball rub-offs, the fronts carried a team logo and team name in reverse type, while the backs carried instructions on how to use the rub-offs.

	NM	E	VG
Complete Set (36):	400.00	200.00	120.00
Common AFL Team:	15.00	7.50	4.50
Common College Team:	10.00	5.00	3.00
(1) **Boston Patriots**	15.00	7.50	4.50
(2) **Buffalo Bills**	20.00	10.00	6.00
(3) **Denver Broncos**	25.00	12.50	7.50
(4) **Houston Oilers**	20.00	10.00	6.00
(5) **Kansas City Chiefs**	15.00	7.50	4.50
(6) **New York Jets**	20.00	10.00	6.00
(7) **Oakland Raiders**	35.00	17.50	10.50
(8) **San Diego Chargers**	15.00	7.50	4.50
(9) **Alabama**	15.00	7.50	4.50
(10) **Air Force Academy**	10.00	5.00	3.00
(11) **Arkansas**	15.00	7.50	4.50
(12) **Army**	15.00	7.50	4.50
(13) **Boston College**	10.00	5.00	3.00
(14) **Duke**	15.00	7.50	4.50
(15) **Illinois**	10.00	5.00	3.00
(16) **Kansas**	15.00	7.50	4.50
(17) **Kentucky**	10.00	5.00	3.00
(18) **Maryland**	10.00	5.00	3.00
(19) **Miami**	15.00	7.50	4.50
(20) **Minnesota**	15.00	7.50	4.50
(21) **Mississippi**	10.00	5.00	3.00
(22) **Navy**	15.00	7.50	4.50
(23) **Nebraska**	15.00	7.50	4.50
(24) **Notre Dame**	35.00	17.50	10.50
(25) **Penn State**	15.00	7.50	4.50
(26) **Purdue**	10.00	5.00	3.00
(27) **Southern California**	10.00	5.00	3.00
(28) **Southern Methodist**	15.00	7.50	4.50
(29) **Stanford**	10.00	5.00	3.00
(30) **Syracuse**	10.00	5.00	3.00
(31) **Texas**	10.00	5.00	3.00
(32) **Texas Christian**	15.00	7.50	4.50
(33) **Virginia**	10.00	5.00	3.00
(34) **Washington**	15.00	7.50	4.50
(35) **Wisconsin**	10.00	5.00	3.00
(36) **Yale**	10.00	5.00	3.00

1966 Topps

This set, which shows AFL players only (Topps' third straight) is quite popular with collectors. It uses a TV motif. Cards were once again grouped in alphabetical order by city name, then by the player's last name. Joe Namath's second-year card is the set's biggest selling player card, but "card" #15, the Funny Ring checklist, is a very difficult find and is easily the most expensive card in the set. Other key cards include rookie cards of Otis Taylor, Jim Turner and George Sauer Jr., second-year cards of Fred Biletnikoff and Ben Davidson, and cards showing Hall of Famers George Blanda, Bobby Bell, Len Dawson, Don Maynard, Ron Mix, Jim Otto and Lance Alworth. A Jack Kemp card is the set's third most expensive card; other high-priced cards are checklists, which are hard to find in mint.

	NM	E	VG
Complete Set (132):	1,500	750.00	450.00
Common Player:	10.00	5.00	3.00
Minor Stars:	5.00		
Unlisted Stars:	6.00		
Wax Pack (5+1):	325.00		

		NM	E	VG
1	Tom Addison	25.00	13.00	8.00
2	Houston Antwine	10.00	5.00	3.00
3	Nick Buoniconti	15.00	7.50	4.50
4	Gino Cappelletti	10.00	5.00	3.00
5	Bob Dee	10.00	5.00	3.00
6	Larry Garron	10.00	5.00	3.00
7	Art Graham	10.00	5.00	3.00
8	Ron Hall	10.00	5.00	3.00
9	Charles Long	10.00	5.00	3.00
10	Jon Morris	10.00	5.00	3.00
11	Don Oakes	10.00	5.00	3.00
12	Babe Parilli	10.00	5.00	3.00
13	Don Webb	10.00	5.00	3.00
14	Jim Whalen	10.00	5.00	3.00
15	**Funny Ring CL**	300.00	150.00	90.00
16	Stew Barber	10.00	5.00	3.00
17	Glenn Bass	10.00	5.00	3.00
18	Dave Behrman	10.00	5.00	3.00
19	Al Bemiller	10.00	5.00	3.00
20	Butch Byrd **RC**	10.00	5.00	3.00
21	Wray Carlton	10.00	5.00	3.00
22	Tom Day	10.00	5.00	3.00
23	Elbert Dubenion	10.00	5.00	3.00
24	Jim Dunaway	10.00	5.00	3.00
25	Dick Hudson	10.00	5.00	3.00
26	Jack Kemp	100.00	50.00	30.00
27	Daryle Lamonica	20.00	10.00	6.00
28	Tom Sestak	10.00	5.00	3.00
29	Billy Shaw	15.00	7.50	4.50
30	Mike Stratton	10.00	5.00	3.00
31	Eldon Danenhauer	10.00	5.00	3.00
32	Cookie Gilchrist	15.00	7.50	4.50
33	Goose Gonsoulin	10.00	5.00	3.00
34	Wendell Hayes **RC**	15.00	7.50	4.50
35	Abner Haynes	15.00	7.50	4.50
36	Jerry Hopkins	10.00	5.00	3.00
37	Ray Jacobs	10.00	5.00	3.00
38	Charlie Janerette	10.00	5.00	3.00
39	Ray Kubala	10.00	5.00	3.00
40	John McCormick	10.00	5.00	3.00
41	Leroy Moore	10.00	5.00	3.00
42	Bob Scarpitto	10.00	5.00	3.00
43	Mickey Slaughter	10.00	5.00	3.00
44	Jerry Sturm	10.00	5.00	3.00
45	Lionel Taylor	15.00	7.50	4.50
46	Scott Appleton	10.00	5.00	3.00
47	Johnny Baker	10.00	5.00	3.00
48	George Blanda	40.00	20.00	12.00
49	Sid Blanks	10.00	5.00	3.00
50	Danny Brabham	10.00	5.00	3.00
51	Ode Burrell	10.00	5.00	3.00
52	Gary Cutsinger	10.00	5.00	3.00
53	Larry Elkins	10.00	5.00	3.00
54	Don Floyd	10.00	5.00	3.00
55	Willie Frazier **RC**	10.00	5.00	3.00
56	Freddy Glick	10.00	5.00	3.00
57	Charles Henningan	10.00	5.00	3.00
58	Bobby Jancik	10.00	5.00	3.00
59	Rich Michael	10.00	5.00	3.00
60	Don Trull	10.00	5.00	3.00
61	**Checklist**	60.00	30.00	18.00
62	Fred Arbanas	10.00	5.00	3.00
63	Pete Beathard	10.00	5.00	3.00
64	Bobby Bell	10.00	5.00	3.00
65	Ed Budde	10.00	5.00	3.00
66	Chris Burford	10.00	5.00	3.00
67	Len Dawson	50.00	25.00	15.00
68	Jon Gilliam	10.00	5.00	3.00
69	Sherrill Headrick	10.00	5.00	3.00
70	E.J. Holub	10.00	5.00	3.00
71	Bobby Hunt	10.00	5.00	3.00
72	Curtis McClinton	10.00	5.00	3.00
73	Jerry Mays	10.00	5.00	3.00
74	Johnny Robinson	10.00	5.00	3.00
75	Otis Taylor **RC**	25.00	13.00	8.00
76	Tom Erlandson	10.00	5.00	3.00
77	Norman Evans **RC**	15.00	7.50	4.50
78	Tom Goode	10.00	5.00	3.00
79	Mike Hudock	10.00	5.00	3.00
80	Frank Jackson	10.00	5.00	3.00
81	Billy Joe	10.00	5.00	3.00
82	Dave Kocourek	10.00	5.00	3.00
83	Bo Roberson	10.00	5.00	3.00
84	Jack Spikes	10.00	5.00	3.00
85	Jim Warren **RC**	10.00	5.00	3.00
86	Willie West **RC**	10.00	5.00	3.00
87	Dick Westmoreland	10.00	5.00	3.00
88	Eddie Wilson	10.00	5.00	3.00
89	Dick Wood	10.00	5.00	3.00
90	Verlon Biggs	10.00	5.00	3.00
91	Sam DeLuca	10.00	5.00	3.00
92	Winston Hill	10.00	5.00	3.00
93	Dee Mackey	10.00	5.00	3.00
94	Bill Mathis	10.00	5.00	3.00
95	Don Maynard	25.00	12.50	7.50
96	Joe Namath	200.00	100.00	60.00
97	Dainard Paulson	10.00	5.00	3.00
98	Gerry Philbin	10.00	5.00	3.00
99	Sherman Plunkett	10.00	5.00	3.00
100	Paul Rochester	10.00	5.00	3.00
101	George Sauer Jr. **RC**	10.00	5.00	3.00
102	Matt Snell	15.00	7.50	4.50
103	Jim Turner **RC**	10.00	5.00	3.00
104	Fred Biletnikoff	60.00	30.00	18.00
105	Bill Budness	10.00	5.00	3.00
106	Billy Cannon	15.00	7.50	4.50
107	Clem Daniels	10.00	5.00	3.00
108	Ben Davidson	15.00	7.50	4.50
109	Cotton Davidson	10.00	5.00	3.00
110	Claude Gibson	10.00	5.00	3.00
111	Wayne Hawkins	10.00	5.00	3.00
112	Ken Herock	10.00	5.00	3.00
113	Bob Mischak	10.00	5.00	3.00
114	Gus Otto	10.00	5.00	3.00
115	Jim Otto	20.00	10.00	6.00
116	Art Powell	15.00	7.50	4.50
117	Harry Schuh	10.00	5.00	3.00
118	Chuck Allen	10.00	5.00	3.00
119	Lance Alworth	45.00	23.00	14.00
120	Frank Buncom	10.00	5.00	3.00
121	Steve DeLong	10.00	5.00	3.00
122	John Farris	10.00	5.00	3.00
123	Ken Graham	10.00	5.00	3.00
124	Sam Gruneison	10.00	5.00	3.00
125	John Hadl	15.00	7.50	4.50
126	Walt Sweeney	10.00	5.00	3.00
127	Keith Lincoln	15.00	7.50	4.50
128	Ron Mix	15.00	7.50	4.50
129	Don Norton	10.00	5.00	3.00
130	Pat Shea	10.00	5.00	3.00
131	Ernie Wright	15.00	7.50	4.50
132	**Checklist**	175.00	90.00	54.00

1966 Topps Funny Rings

The 24-card, 1-1/4" x 3" set was issued in each pack of 1966 Topps Football. The card fronts feature a ring that can be punched out and folded to make a ring. The backs are blank.

		NM	E	VG
Complete Set (24):		500.00	250.00	150.00
Common Player:		25.00	12.50	7.50

		NM	E	VG
1	**Funny Ring - Kiss Me**	25.00	12.50	7.50
2	**Funny Ring - Bloodshot Eye**	25.00	12.50	7.50
3	**Funny Ring - Big Mouth**	25.00	12.50	7.50
4	**Funny Ring - Tooth-ache**	25.00	12.50	7.50
5	**Funny Ring - Fish eats Fish**	25.00	12.50	7.50
6	**Funny Ring - Mrs. Skull**	25.00	12.50	7.50
7	**Funny Ring - Hot Dog**	25.00	12.50	7.50
8	**Funny Ring - Head with Nail**	25.00	12.50	7.50
9	**Funny Ring - Ah**	25.00	12.50	7.50
10	**Funny Ring - Apple with Worm**	25.00	12.50	7.50
11	**Funny Ring - Snake**	25.00	12.50	7.50
12	**Funny Ring - Yicch**	25.00	12.50	7.50
13	**Funny Ring - If You Can Read This**	25.00	12.50	7.50
14	**Funny Ring - Nuts to You**	25.00	12.50	7.50
15	**Funny Ring - Get Lost**	25.00	12.50	7.50
16	**Funny Ring - You Fink**	25.00	12.50	7.50
17	**Funny Ring - Hole in Shoe**	25.00	12.50	7.50
18	**Funny Ring - Head with One Eye**	25.00	12.50	7.50
19	**Funny Ring - Mr. Ugly**	25.00	12.50	7.50
20	**Funny Ring - Mr. Fang**	25.00	12.50	7.50
21	**Funny Ring - Mr. Fright**	25.00	12.50	7.50
22	**Funny Ring - Mr. Boo**	25.00	12.50	7.50
23	**Funny Ring - Mr. Glug**	25.00	12.50	7.50
24	**Funny Ring - Mr. Blech**	25.00	12.50	7.50

1967 Topps

This 132-card set is the last AFL-only set issued by Topps. Best-known for the inclusion of Joe-Namath's second-year card, the set also features another Jack Kemp card. Wahoo McDaniels' only card is also in this set. Cards are grouped according to each of the nine AFL teams. It's very difficult to find an unmarked checklist; consequently, prices are pretty high on those two cards.

	NM	E	VG
Complete Set (132):	1,000	500.00	300.00
Common Player:	2.50	1.25	.70
Minor Stars:	3.00		
Unlisted Stars:	5.00		
Wax Pack (5):	400.00		

		NM	E	VG
1	John Huarte	20.00	10.00	6.00
2	Babe Parilli	8.00	4.00	2.50
3	Gino Cappelletti	8.00	4.00	2.50
4	Larry Garron	8.00	4.00	2.50
5	Tom Addison	8.00	4.00	2.50
6	Jon Morris	8.00	4.00	2.50
7	Houston Antwine	8.00	4.00	2.50
8	Don Oakes	8.00	4.00	2.50
9	Larry Eisenhauer	8.00	4.00	2.50
10	Jim Hunt	8.00	4.00	2.50
11	Jim Whalen	8.00	4.00	2.50
12	Art Graham	8.00	4.00	2.50
13	Nick Buoniconti	10.00	5.00	3.00
14	Bob Dee	8.00	4.00	2.50
15	Keith Lincoln	10.00	5.00	3.00
16	Tom Flores	8.00	4.00	2.50
17	Art Powell	8.00	4.00	2.50
18	Stew Barber	8.00	4.00	2.50
19	Wray Carlton	8.00	4.00	2.50
20	Elbert Dubenion	8.00	4.00	2.50
21	Jim Dunaway	8.00	4.00	2.50
22	Dick Hudson	8.00	4.00	2.50
23	Harry Jacobs	8.00	4.00	2.50
24	Jack Kemp	40.00	20.00	12.00
25	Ron McDole	8.00	4.00	2.50
26	George Saimes	8.00	4.00	2.50
27	Tom Sestak	8.00	4.00	2.50
28	Billy Shaw	10.00	5.00	3.00
29	Mike Stratton	8.00	4.00	2.50
30	Nemiah Wilson **RC**	8.00	4.00	2.50
31	John McCormick	8.00	4.00	2.50
32	Rex Mirich	8.00	4.00	2.50
33	Dave Costa	8.00	4.00	2.50
34	Goose Gonsoulin	8.00	4.00	2.50
35	Abner Haynes	10.00	5.00	3.00
36	Wendell Hayes	8.00	4.00	2.50
37	Archie Matsos	2.50	1.25	.70

		NM	E	VG
38	John Bramlett	8.00	4.00	2.50
39	Jerry Sturm	8.00	4.00	2.50
40	Max Leetzow	8.00	4.00	2.50
41	Bob Scarpitto	8.00	4.00	2.50
42	Lionel Taylor	10.00	5.00	3.00
43	Al Denson	8.00	4.00	2.50
44	Miller Farr **RC**	8.00	4.00	2.50
45	Don Trull	8.00	4.00	2.50
46	Jacky Lee	8.00	4.00	2.50
47	Bobby Jancik	8.00	4.00	2.50
48	Ode Burrell	8.00	4.00	2.50
49	Larry Elkins	8.00	4.00	2.50
50	W.K. Hicks	8.00	4.00	2.50
51	Sid Blanks	8.00	4.00	2.50
52	Jim Norton	8.00	4.00	2.50
53	Bobby Maples **RC**	8.00	4.00	2.50
54	Bob Talamini	8.00	4.00	2.50
55	Walter Suggs	8.00	4.00	2.50
56	Gary Cutsinger	8.00	4.00	2.50
57	Danny Brabham	8.00	4.00	2.50
58	Ernie Ladd	10.00	5.00	3.00
59	**Checklist**	40.00	20.00	12.00
60	Pete Beathard	8.00	4.00	2.50
61	Len Dawson	35.00	18.00	11.00
62	Bobby Hunt	8.00	4.00	2.50
63	Bert Coan	8.00	4.00	2.50
64	Curtis McClinton	8.00	4.00	2.50
65	Johnny Robinson	8.00	4.00	2.50
66	E.J. Holub	8.00	4.00	2.50
67	Jerry Mays	8.00	4.00	2.50
68	Jim Tyrer	8.00	4.00	2.50
69	Bobby Bell	10.00	5.00	3.00
70	Fred Arbanas	8.00	4.00	2.50
71	Buck Buchanan	10.00	5.00	3.00
72	Chris Burford	8.00	4.00	2.50
73	Otis Taylor	10.00	5.00	3.00
74	Cookie Gilchrist	10.00	5.00	3.00
75	Earl Faison	8.00	4.00	2.50
76	George Wilson Jr.	8.00	4.00	2.50
77	Rick Norton	8.00	4.00	2.50
78	Frank Jackson	8.00	4.00	2.50
79	Joe Auer	8.00	4.00	2.50
80	Willie West	8.00	4.00	2.50
81	Jim Warren	8.00	4.00	2.50
82	Wahoo McDaniel **RC**	45.00	23.00	14.00
83	Ernie Park	8.00	4.00	2.50
84	Bill Neighbors	8.00	4.00	2.50
85	Norm Evans	8.00	4.00	2.50
86	Tom Nomina	8.00	4.00	2.50
87	Rich Zecher	8.00	4.00	2.50
88	Dave Kocourek	8.00	4.00	2.50
89	Bill Baird	8.00	4.00	2.50
90	Ralph Baker	8.00	4.00	2.50
91	Verlon Biggs	8.00	4.00	2.50
92	Sam DeLuca	8.00	4.00	2.50
93	Larry Grantham	8.00	4.00	2.50
94	Jim Harris	8.00	4.00	2.50
95	Winston Hill	8.00	4.00	2.50
96	Bill Mathis	8.00	4.00	2.50
97	Don Maynard	10.00	5.00	3.00
98	Joe Namath	135.00	70.00	42.00
99	Gerry Philbin	8.00	4.00	2.50
100	Paul Rochester	8.00	4.00	2.50
101	George Sauer	8.00	4.00	2.50
102	Matt Snell	10.00	5.00	3.00
103	Daryle Lamonica	15.00	7.50	4.50
104	Glenn Bass	8.00	4.00	2.50
105	Jim Otto	10.00	5.00	3.00
106	Fred Biletnikoff	30.00	15.00	9.00
107	Cotton Davidson	8.00	4.00	2.50
108	Larry Todd	8.00	4.00	2.50
109	Billy Cannon	10.00	5.00	3.00
110	Clem Daniels	8.00	4.00	2.50
111	Dave Grayson	8.00	4.00	2.50
112	Kent McCloughan **RC**	8.00	4.00	2.50
113	Bob Svihus	8.00	4.00	2.50
114	Isaac Lassiter	8.00	4.00	2.50
115	Harry Schuh	8.00	4.00	2.50
116	Ben Davidson	10.00	5.00	3.00
117	Tom Day	8.00	4.00	2.50
118	Scott Appleton	8.00	4.00	2.50
119	Steve Tensi **RC**	8.00	4.00	2.50
120	John Hadl	10.00	5.00	3.00
121	Paul Lowe	8.00	4.00	2.50
122	Jim Allison	8.00	4.00	2.50
123	Lance Alworth	35.00	18.00	11.00
124	Jacque MacKinnon	8.00	4.00	2.50
125	Ron Mix	10.00	5.00	3.00
126	Bob Petrich	8.00	4.00	2.50
127	Howard Kindig	8.00	4.00	2.50
128	Steve DeLong	8.00	4.00	2.50
129	Chuck Allen	8.00	4.00	2.50
130	Frank Buncom	8.00	4.00	2.50
131	Speedy Duncan **RC**	15.00	7.50	4.50
132	**Checklist**	60.00	30.00	18.00

1967 Topps Comic Pennants

The 31-card, standard-size sticker set was issued in packs of 1967 Topps and is considered to be scarce - the set was probably discontinued before the end of the shipping. The cards contain juvenile humor (Denver girls look like Broncos). The cards are numbered in the upper right corner.

		NM	E	VG
	Complete Set (31):	600.00	300.00	180.00
	Common Player:	20.00	10.00	6.00
1	Navel Academy	20.00	10.00	6.00
2	City College of Useless Knowledge	20.00	10.00	6.00
3	Notre Dame (Hunchback of)	40.00	20.00	12.00
4	Psychedelic State	20.00	10.00	6.00
5	Minneapolis Mini-skirts	20.00	10.00	6.00
6	School of Art - Go, Van Gogh	20.00	10.00	6.00
7	Washington Is Dead	25.00	12.50	7.50
8	School of Hard Knocks	20.00	10.00	6.00
9	Alaska (If I See Her ...)	20.00	10.00	6.00
10	Confused State	20.00	10.00	6.00
11	Yale Locks Are Tough to Pick	20.00	10.00	6.00
12	University of Transylvania	20.00	10.00	6.00
13	Down With Teachers	20.00	10.00	6.00
14	Cornell Caught Me Cheating	20.00	10.00	6.00
15	Houston Oilers (You're a Fink)	25.00	12.50	7.50
16	Harvard (Flunked Out)	25.00	12.50	7.50
17	Diskotech	20.00	10.00	6.00
18	Dropout U	20.00	10.00	6.00
19	Air Force (Gas Masks)	20.00	10.00	6.00
20	Nutstu U	20.00	10.00	6.00
21	Michigan State Pen	20.00	10.00	6.00
22	Denver Broncos (Girls Look Like)	25.00	12.50	7.50
23	Buffalo Bills (Without Paying My)	25.00	12.50	7.50
24	Army of Dropouts	20.00	10.00	6.00
25	Miami Dolphins (Bitten by Two)	30.00	15.00	9.00
26	Too Many) Chiefs	20.00	10.00	6.00
27	Boston Patriots (Banned In)	20.00	10.00	6.00
28	Icebox) Raiders	30.00	15.00	9.00
29	The Right Direction)	20.00	10.00	6.00
30	New York Jets (Skies Are Crowded With)	25.00	12.50	7.50
31	San Diego Chargers (Police Will Press)	20.00	10.00	6.00

1968 Topps

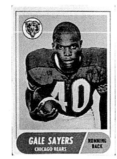

Topps' first set to clear 200 cards in number was also its first set in five years to feature NFL players as well as AFL players. Released in two series, the second series is a little tougher to find. First-series cards show blue printing on the backs, while second series issues green. The 219-card set features a special design for cards of players from the Super Bowl teams, the Oakland Raiders and Green Bay Packers. Cards of players from these teams show players in a horizontal format set against a stylized football backdrop. Remaining cards are in a vertical format. Each carries a player photo inside a white frame with the players team, position and team in an oval at the card bottom. A number of second-series card backs can be pieced together to show a picture of Bart Starr or Len Dawson (10 cards per player).

Puzzle-piece card backs are found on cards 141, 145, 146, 148, 151-53, 155, 163, 168, 170, 172, 186, 195 and 197. One error in the set is on #12, Kent McCloughan. The back spells his name "McCloughlan." Another mix-up occurs on card #70, Dick Van Raaphorst's card. The back lists his name as "Van Raap Horst." Also, there are two differnt checklist cards; the back of one is blue, the back of the other is green. Rookies in this set include Bob Griese, Jim Hart, Craig Morton, Joe Kapp, Jim Grabowski, Jack Snow, and Donny Anderson. Other valuable cards include Bart Starr, Don Meredith, Joe Namath, Gale Sayers, John Unitas, Dick Butkis, George Blanda, Jack Kemp, and Fran Tarkenton. This set featured the final regular-issue cards of Hall of Famers Mike Ditka and Jim Taylor.

	NM	E	VG
Complete Set (219):	1,250	625.00	375.00
Common Player (1-131):	7.00	3.50	2.10
Minor Stars (1-131):	1.25		
Unlisted Stars (1-131):	1.50		
Common Player (132-219):	7.00		
Minor Stars (132-219):	4.00		
Unlisted Stars (132-219):	5.00		
Series 1 Wax Pack (5+1):	220.00		
Series 1 Wax Box (24):	4,600		
Series 2 Wax Pack (5+1):	300.00		
Series 2 Wax Box (24):	6,375		

		NM	E	VG
1	Bart Starr	50.00	25.00	15.00
2	Dick Bass	7.00	3.50	2.10
3	Grady Alderman	7.00	3.50	2.10
4	Obert Logan	7.00	3.50	2.10
5	Ernie Koy **RC**	7.00	3.50	2.10
6	Don Hultz	7.00	3.50	2.10
7	Earl Gros	7.00	3.50	2.10
8	Jim Bakken	7.00	3.50	2.10
9	George Mira	7.00	3.50	2.10
10	Carl Kammerer	7.00	3.50	2.10
11	Willie Frazier	7.00	3.50	2.10
12	Kent McCloughan	7.00	3.50	2.10
13	George Sauer	7.00	3.50	2.10
14	Jack Clancy	7.00	3.50	2.10
15	Jim Tyrer	7.00	3.50	2.10
16	Bobby Maples	7.00	3.50	2.10
17	Bo Hickey	7.00	3.50	2.10
18	Frank Buncom	7.00	3.50	2.10
19	Keith Lincoln	7.00	3.50	2.10
20	Jim Whalen	7.00	3.50	2.10
21	Junior Coffey	7.00	3.50	2.10
22	Billy Ray Smith	7.00	3.50	2.10
23	Johnny Morris	7.00	3.50	2.10
24	Ernie Green	7.00	3.50	2.10
25	Don Meredith	25.00	13.00	8.00
26	Wayne Walker	7.00	3.50	2.10
27	Carroll Dale	20.00	10.00	6.00
28	Bernie Casey	7.00	3.50	2.10
29	Dave Osborn **RC**	7.00	3.50	2.10
30	Ray Poage	7.00	3.50	2.10
31	Homer Jones	7.00	3.50	2.10
32	Sam Baker	7.00	3.50	2.10
33	Bill Saul	7.00	3.50	2.10
34	Ken Willard	7.00	3.50	2.10
35	Bobby Mitchell	10.00	5.00	3.00
36	Gary Garrison	7.00	3.50	2.10
37	Billy Cannon	7.00	3.50	2.10
38	Ralph Baker	7.00	3.50	2.10
39	Howard Twilley **RC**	10.00	5.00	3.00
40	Wendell Hayes	7.00	3.50	2.10
41	Jim Norton	7.00	3.50	2.10
42	Tom Beer	7.00	3.50	2.10
43	Chris Burford	7.00	3.50	2.10
44	Stew Barber	7.00	3.50	2.10
45	Leroy Mitchell	7.00	3.50	2.10
46	Dan Grimm	7.00	3.50	2.10
47	Jerry Logan	7.00	3.50	2.10
48	Andy Livingston	7.00	3.50	2.10
49	Paul Warfield	20.00	10.00	6.00
50	Don Perkins	7.00	3.50	2.10
51	Ron Kramer	7.00	3.50	2.10
52	Bob Jeter	7.00	3.50	2.10
53	Les Josephson **RC**	7.00	3.50	2.10
54	Bobby Walden	7.00	3.50	2.10
55	**Checklist**	20.00	10.00	6.00
56	Walter Roberts	7.00	3.50	2.10
57	Henry Carr	7.00	3.50	2.10
58	Gary Ballman	7.00	3.50	2.10
59	J.R. Wilburn	7.00	3.50	2.10
60	Jim Hart **RC**	10.00	5.00	3.00
61	Jimmy Johnson	7.00	3.50	2.10
62	Chris Hanburger	7.00	3.50	2.10
63	John Hadl	7.00	3.50	2.10
64	Hewritt Dixon	7.00	3.50	2.10
65	Joe Namath	70.00	35.00	21.00
66	Jim Warren	7.00	3.50	2.10
67	Curtis McClinton	7.00	3.50	2.10
68	Bob Talamini	7.00	3.50	2.10
69	Steve Tensi	7.00	3.50	2.10
70	Dick Van Raaphorst	7.00	3.50	2.10
71	Art Powell	7.00	3.50	2.10
72	Jim Nance **RC**	10.00	5.00	3.00

73	Bob Riggle	7.00	3.50	2.10
74	John Mackey	15.00	7.50	4.50
75	Gale Sayers	50.00	25.00	15.00
76	Gene Hickerson	7.00	3.50	2.10
77	Dan Reeves	15.00	7.50	4.50
78	Tom Nowatzke	7.00	3.50	2.10
79	Elijah Pitts	7.00	3.50	2.10
80	Lamar Lundy	7.00	3.50	2.10
81	Paul Flatley	7.00	3.50	2.10
82	Dave Whitsell	7.00	3.50	2.10
83	Spider Lockhart	7.00	3.50	2.10
84	Dave Lloyd	7.00	3.50	2.10
85	Roy Jefferson	7.00	3.50	2.10
86	Jackie Smith	10.00	5.00	3.00
87	John David Crow	7.00	3.50	2.10
88	Sonny Jurgensen	10.00	5.00	3.00
89	Ron Mix	7.00	3.50	2.10
90	Clem Daniels	7.00	3.50	2.10
91	Cornell Gordon	7.00	3.50	2.10
92	Tom Goode	7.00	3.50	2.10
93	Bobby Bell	7.00	3.50	2.10
94	Walt Suggs	7.00	3.50	2.10
95	Eric Crabtree	7.00	3.50	2.10
96	Sherrill Headrick	7.00	3.50	2.10
97	Wray Carlton	7.00	3.50	2.10
98	Gino Cappelletti	7.00	3.50	2.10
99	Tommy McDonald	7.00	3.50	2.10
100	Johnny Unitas	30.00	15.00	9.00
101	Richie Petitbon	7.00	3.50	2.10
102	Erich Barnes	7.00	3.50	2.10
103	Bob Hayes	10.00	5.00	3.00
104	Milt Plum	7.00	3.50	2.10
105	Boyd Dowler	7.00	3.50	2.10
106	Ed Meador	7.00	3.50	2.10
107	Fred Cox	7.00	3.50	2.10
108	Steve Stonebreaker **RC**	7.00	3.50	2.10
109	Aaron Thomas	7.00	3.50	2.10
110	Norm Snead	7.00	3.50	2.10
111	Paul Martha **RC**	7.00	3.50	2.10
112	Jerry Stovall	7.00	3.50	2.10
113	Kay McFarland	7.00	3.50	2.10
114	Pat Richter	7.00	3.50	2.10
115	Rick Redman	7.00	3.50	2.10
116	Tom Keating	7.00	3.50	2.10
117	Matt Snell	7.00	3.50	2.10
118	Dick Westmoreland	7.00	3.50	2.10
119	Jerry Mays	7.00	3.50	2.10
120	Sid Blanks	7.00	3.50	2.10
121	Al Denson	7.00	3.50	2.10
122	Bobby Hunt	7.00	3.50	2.10
123	Mike Mercer	7.00	3.50	2.10
124	Nick Buoniconti	10.00	5.00	3.00
125	Ron Vanderkelen **RC**	7.00	3.50	2.10
126	Ordell Braase	7.00	3.50	2.10
127	Dick Butkus	50.00	25.00	15.00
128	Gary Collins	7.00	3.50	2.10
129	Mel Renfro	10.00	5.00	3.00
130	Alex Karras	10.00	5.00	3.00
131	Herb Adderley	10.00	5.00	3.00
132	Roman Gabriel	10.00	5.00	3.00
133	Bill Brown	7.00	3.50	2.10
134	Kent Kramer	7.00	3.50	2.10
135	Tucker Frederickson	10.00	5.00	3.00
136	Nate Ramsey	7.00	3.50	2.10
137	Marv Woodson	7.00	3.50	2.10
138	Ken Gray	7.00	3.50	2.10
139	John Brodie	10.00	5.00	3.00
140	Jerry Smith	7.00	3.50	2.10
141	Brad Hubbert	7.00	3.50	2.10
142	George Blanda	25.00	13.00	8.00
143	Pete Lammons **RC**	7.00	3.50	2.10
144	Doug Moreau	7.00	3.50	2.10
145	E.J. Holub	7.00	3.50	2.10
146	Ode Burrell	1.50	.70	.45
147	Bob Scarpitto	7.00	3.50	2.10
148	Andre White	7.00	3.50	2.10
149	Jack Kemp	30.00	15.00	9.00
150	Art Graham	7.00	3.50	2.10
151	Tommy Nobis	10.00	5.00	3.00
152	Willie Richardson **RC**	7.00	3.50	2.10
153	Jack Concannon	7.00	3.50	2.10
154	Bill Glass	7.00	3.50	2.10
155	Craig Morton **RC**	15.00	7.50	4.50
156	Pat Studstill	7.00	3.50	2.10
157	Ray Nitschke	20.00	10.00	6.00
158	Roger Brown	7.00	3.50	2.10
159	Joe Kapp	10.00	5.00	3.00
160	Jim Taylor	20.00	10.00	6.00
161	Fran Tarkenton	25.00	13.00	8.00
162	Mike Ditka	35.00	18.00	11.00
163	Andy Russell **RC**	15.00	7.50	4.50
164	Larry Wilson	10.00	5.00	3.00
165	Tommy Davis	7.00	3.50	2.10
166	Paul Krause	7.00	3.50	2.10
167	Leslie Duncan	7.00	3.50	2.10
168	Fred Biletnikoff	15.00	7.50	4.50
169	Don Maynard	15.00	7.50	4.50
170	Frank Emanuel	7.00	3.50	2.10
171	Len Dawson	20.00	10.00	6.00
172	Miller Farr	7.00	3.50	2.10
173	Floyd Little **RC**	35.00	18.00	11.00
174	Lonnie Wright	7.00	3.50	2.10
175	Paul Costa	7.00	3.50	2.10
176	Don Trull	7.00	3.50	2.10
177	Jerry Simmons	7.00	3.50	2.10
178	Tom Matte	7.00	3.50	2.10
179	Bennie McRae	7.00	3.50	2.10
180	Jim Kanicki	7.00	3.50	2.10
181	Bob Lilly	20.00	10.00	6.00
182	Tom Watkins	7.00	3.50	2.10
183	Jim Grabowski **RC**	10.00	5.00	3.00
184	Jack Snow **RC**	10.00	5.00	3.00
185	Gary Cuozzo **RC**	7.00	3.50	2.10
186	Billy Kilmer	10.00	5.00	3.00
187	Jim Katcavage	7.00	3.50	2.10
188	Floyd Peters	7.00	3.50	2.10
189	Bill Nelsen	7.00	3.50	2.10
190	Bobby J. Conrad	1.50	.70	.45
191	Kermit Alexander	7.00	3.50	2.10
192	Charley Taylor	10.00	5.00	3.00
193	Lance Alworth	25.00	13.00	8.00
194	Daryle Lamonica	10.00	5.00	3.00
195	Al Atkinson	7.00	3.50	2.10
196	Bob Griese **RC**	100.00	50.00	30.00
197	Buck Buchanan	10.00	5.00	3.00
198	Pete Beathard	7.00	3.50	2.10
199	Nemiah Wilson	7.00	3.50	2.10
200	Ernie Wright	7.00	3.50	2.10
201	George Saimes	7.00	3.50	2.10
202	John Charles	7.00	3.50	2.10
203	Randy Johnson	7.00	3.50	2.10
204	Tony Lorick	7.00	3.50	2.10
205	Dick Evey	7.00	3.50	2.10
206	Leroy Kelly	10.00	5.00	3.00
207	Lee Roy Jordan	10.00	5.00	3.00
208	Jim Gibbons	7.00	3.50	2.10
209	Donny Anderson **RC**	10.00	5.00	3.00
210	Maxie Baughan	7.00	3.50	2.10
211	Joe Morrison	7.00	3.50	2.10
212	Jim Snowden	7.00	3.50	2.10
213	Lenny Lyles	7.00	3.50	2.10
214	Bobby Joe Green	7.00	3.50	2.10
215	Frank Ryan	7.00	3.50	2.10
216	Cornell Green	7.00	3.50	2.10
217	Karl Sweetan	7.00	3.50	2.10
218	Dave Williams	7.00	3.50	2.10
219	**Checklist** (blue, green)	20.00	10.00	6.00

1968 Topps Posters

Sixteen players from both the AFL and NFL are included in this set. Posters, printed on paper, measure about 5" x 7" and were issued in gum packs, similar to the Topps baseball posters of the same year. A full-color posed action shot is on the front, with the players, name, team and position shown in an oval at the bottom of the front. Backs are blank.

		NM	E	VG
	Complete Set (16):	50.00	25.00	15.00
	Common Player:	1.50	.75	.45
1	Johnny Unitas	9.00	4.50	2.75
2	Leroy Kelly	1.50	.75	.45
3	Bob Hayes	1.50	.75	.45
4	Bart Starr	5.00	2.50	1.50
5	Charley Taylor	1.50	.75	.45
6	Fran Tarkenton	4.50	2.25	1.35
7	Jim Bakken	1.50	.75	.45
8	Gale Sayers	6.00	3.00	1.75
9	Gary Cuozzo	1.50	.75	.45
10	Les Josephson	1.50	.75	.45
11	Jim Nance	1.50	.75	.45
12	Brad Hubbert	1.50	.75	.45
13	Keith Lincoln	1.50	.75	.45
14	Don Maynard	2.00	1.00	.60
15	Len Dawson	3.00	1.50	1.75
16	Jack Clancy	1.50	.75	.45

1968 Topps Stand-Ups

These 22 unnumbered card-size (2-1/2" x 3-1/2") issues were meant to be punched and folded in order to make them stand. Cards lose much of their value if they're not complete; obviously, not too many complete sets have been found. Cards show a head shot of the player, with his name beneath the photo. Backs are blank. Cards are listed below in alphabetical order.

		NM	E	VG
	Complete Set (22):	350.00	175.00	105.00
	Common Player:	10.00	5.00	3.00
(1)	Sid Blanks	10.00	5.00	3.00
(2)	John Brodie	15.00	7.50	4.50
(3)	Jack Concannon	10.00	5.00	3.00
(4)	Roman Gabriel	10.00	5.00	3.00
(5)	Art Graham	10.00	5.00	3.00
(6)	Jim Grabowski	10.00	5.00	3.00
(7)	John Hadl	10.00	5.00	3.00
(8)	Jim Hart	10.00	5.00	3.00
(9)	Homer Jones	10.00	5.00	3.00
(10)	Sonny Jurgensen	15.00	7.50	4.50
(11)	Alex Karras	15.00	7.50	4.50
(12)	Billy Kilmer	10.00	5.00	3.00
(13)	Daryle Lamonica	10.00	5.00	3.00
(14)	Floyd Little	10.00	5.00	3.00
(15)	Curtis McClinton	10.00	5.00	3.00
(16)	Don Meredith	50.00	25.00	15.00
(17)	Joe Namath	100.00	50.00	30.00
(18)	Bill Nelsen	10.00	5.00	3.00
(19)	Dave Osborn	10.00	5.00	3.00
(20)	Willie Richardson	10.00	5.00	3.00
(21)	Frank Ryan	10.00	5.00	3.00
(22)	Norm Snead	10.00	5.00	3.00

1968 Topps Team Patch/Stickers

These patches, inserted into packs of Topps test team cards, feature team logos for each NFL team. One test team card and a sticker were in each pack; the stickers were supposed to be the main item inside, according to the wrapper. The stickers measure 2-1/2" x 3-1/2".

		NM	E	VG
	Complete Set (44):	1,600	800.00	480.00
	Common Sticker:	10.00	5.00	3.00
1	**1 and 2**	15.00	7.50	4.50
2	**3 and 4**	10.00	5.00	3.00
3	**5 and 6**	12.00	6.00	3.50
4	**7 and 8**	10.00	5.00	3.00
5	**9 and 0**	10.00	5.00	3.00
6	**A and B**	12.00	6.00	3.50
7	**C and D**	10.00	5.00	3.00
8	**E and F**	10.00	5.00	3.00
9	**G and H**	12.00	6.00	3.50
10	**I and W**	10.00	5.00	3.00
11	**J and X**	10.00	5.00	3.00
12	**Atlanta Falcons**	60.00	30.00	18.00
13	**Baltimore Colts**	65.00	32.00	19.50
14	**Chicago Bears**	80.00	40.00	24.00
15	**Cleveland Browns**	60.00	30.00	18.00
16	**Dallas Cowboys**	140.00	70.00	42.00
17	**Detroit Lions**	60.00	30.00	18.00
18	**Green Bay Packers**	80.00	40.00	24.00
19	**Los Angeles Rams**	60.00	30.00	18.00
20	**Minnesota Vikings**	65.00	32.00	19.50
21	**New Orleans Saints**	60.00	30.00	18.00
22	**New York Giants**	75.00	37.00	22.00
23	**K and L**	10.00	5.00	3.00
24	**M and O**	12.00	6.00	3.50
25	**N and P**	10.00	5.00	3.00
26	**Q and R**	10.00	5.00	3.00
27	**S and T**	12.00	6.00	3.50
28	**U and V**	10.00	5.00	3.00
29	**Y and Z**	10.00	5.00	3.00
30	**Philadelphia Eagles**	60.00	30.00	18.00
31	**Pittsburgh Steelers**	80.00	40.00	24.00
32	**St. Louis Cardinals**	60.00	30.00	18.00
33	**San Francisco 49ers**	75.00	37.00	22.00
34	**Washington Redskins**	120.00	60.00	36.00
35	**Boston Patriots**	60.00	30.00	18.00
36	**Buffalo Bills**	75.00	37.00	22.00
37	**Denver Broncos**	120.00	60.00	36.00
38	**Houston Oilers**	75.00	37.00	22.00
39	**Kansas City Chiefs**	60.00	30.00	18.00
40	**Miami Dolphins**	110.00	55.00	33.00
41	**New York Jets**	75.00	37.00	22.00
42	**Oakland Raiders**	140.00	70.00	42.00
43	**San Diego Chargers**	60.00	30.00	18.00
44	**Cincinnati Bengals**	70.00	35.00	21.00

1968 Topps Test Teams

These were printed in an extremely limited number by Topps. Cards are a bit oversize -- about 2-1/2" x 4-5/8" -- and show a posed shot of the entire team on the front. A nameplate is beneath the picture, and a "frame" features footballs in each of the corners. The back is a guide to the photo, complete with little footballs to indicate each row. Cards were issued in alphabetical order by city name, and are numbered on the back.

	NM	E	VG
Complete Set (25):	2,700	1,350	825.00
Common Team:	100.00	50.00	30.00

		NM	E	VG
1	**Atlanta Falcons**	100.00	50.00	30.00
2	**Baltimore Colts**	100.00	50.00	30.00
3	**Buffalo Bills**	100.00	50.00	30.00
4	**Chicago Bears**	135.00	70.00	40.00
5	**Cleveland Browns**	100.00	50.00	30.00
6	**Dallas Cowboys**	135.00	70.00	40.00
7	**Denver Broncos**	135.00	70.00	40.00
8	**Detroit Lions**	100.00	50.00	30.00
9	**Green Bay Packers**	135.00	70.00	40.00
10	**Houston Oilers**	100.00	50.00	30.00
11	**Kansas City Chiefs**	100.00	50.00	30.00
12	**Los Angeles Rams**	100.00	50.00	30.00
13	**Miami Dolphins**	135.00	70.00	40.00
14	**Minnesota Vikings**	100.00	50.00	30.00
15	**New England Patriots**	100.00	50.00	30.00
16	**New Orleans Saints**	100.00	50.00	30.00
17	**New York Giants**	135.00	70.00	40.00
18	**New York Jets**	135.00	70.00	40.00
19	**Oakland Raiders**	135.00	70.00	40.00
20	**Philadelphia Eagles**	100.00	50.00	30.00
21	**Pittsburgh Steelers**	135.00	70.00	40.00
22	**St. Louis Cardinals**	100.00	50.00	30.00
23	**San Diego Chargers**	100.00	50.00	30.00
24	**San Francisco 49ers**	135.00	70.00	40.00
25	**Washington Redskins**	100.00	50.00	30.00

1969 Topps

This 263-card set was printed in two series and in two different styles. The first series cards (1-132) have no borders, while the second series has white borders. In the borderless version, a player photo is set against a brightly colored background. A large team logo is in the lower right hand corner, and a player name and position and team name are in a white box at the card bottom. Second-series cards are of identical design, except for a white border around the player photo. This development is not pleasing for collectors searching for the first series in mint condition, since the lack of borders makes it tough to find any in superb condition. The variation in the set is the checklist card, #132, which is found with and without borders, depending on the series in which it was printed. Another variation in the set involved card #18, Tom Beer. In some versions of the card, the "B" in his last name is slightly raised above the rest of the name on the card front. Versions of each have been reported. The key card in this set is Brian Piccolo's rookie card; this and his Four In One issue are the only cards on which he appears. Other rookies in this set include Larry Csonka, Lance Rentzel, and Mike Curtis. Hall of Famers Doug Atkins and Bobby Mitchell were featured on their final regular-issue cards.

	NM	E	VG
Complete Set (263):	1,500	750.00	450.00
Common Player (1-132):	7.00	3.50	2.10
Minor Stars (1-132):	1.50		
Unlisted Stars (1-132):	3.00		
Common Player (133-263):	7.00	3.50	2.10
Minor Stars (133-263):	2.00		
Unlisted Stars (133-263):	3.00		
Series 1 Wax Pack (12+1):	340.00		
Series 1 Wax Box (24):	7,175		
Series 2 Wax Pack (12+2):	300.00		
Series 2 Wax Box (24):	6,300		

		NM	E	VG
1	LeRoy Kelly	20.00	10.00	5.00
2	Paul Flatley	7.00	3.50	2.10
3	Jim Cadile	7.00	3.50	2.10
4	Erich Barnes	7.00	3.50	2.10
5	Willie Richardson	7.00	3.50	2.10
6	Bob Hayes	10.00	5.00	2.50
7	Bob Jeter	7.00	3.50	2.10
8	Jim Colclough	7.00	3.50	2.10
9	Sherrill Headrick	7.00	3.50	2.10
10	Jim Dunaway	7.00	3.50	2.10
11	Bill Munson	7.00	3.50	2.10
12	Jack Pardee	7.00	3.50	2.10
13	Jim Lindsey	7.00	3.50	2.10
14	Dave Whitsell	7.00	3.50	2.10
15	Tucker Frederickson	7.00	3.50	2.10
16	Alvin Haymond	7.00	3.50	2.10
17	Andy Russell	7.00	3.50	2.10
18	Tom Beer	7.00	3.50	2.10
19	Bobby Maples	7.00	3.50	2.10
20	Len Dawson	15.00	7.50	4.50
21	Willis Crenshaw	7.00	3.50	2.10
22	Tommy Davis	7.00	3.50	2.10
23	Rickie Harris	7.00	3.50	2.10
24	Jerry Simmons	7.00	3.50	2.10
25	Johnny Unitas	45.00	23.00	14.00
26	Brian Piccolo **RC**	90.00	45.00	27.00
27	Bob Matheson	7.00	3.50	2.10
28	Howard Twilley	7.00	3.50	2.10
29	Jim Turner	7.00	3.50	2.10
30	Pete Banaszak **RC**	7.00	3.50	2.10
31	Lance Rentzel **RC**	7.00	3.50	2.10
32	Bill Triplett	7.00	3.50	2.10
33	Boyd Dowler	7.00	3.50	2.10
34	Merlin Olsen	10.00	5.00	3.00
35	Joe Kapp	7.00	3.50	2.10
36	Dan Abramowicz **RC**	10.00	5.00	3.00
37	Spider Lockhart	7.00	3.50	2.10
38	Tom Day	7.00	3.50	2.10
39	Art Graham	7.00	3.50	2.10
40	Bob Cappadona	7.00	3.50	2.10
41	Gary Ballman	7.00	3.50	2.10
42	Clendon Thomas	7.00	3.50	2.10
43	Jackie Smith	10.00	5.00	3.00
44	Dave Wilcox	7.00	3.50	2.10
45	Jery Smith	7.00	3.50	2.10
46	Dan Grimm	7.00	3.50	2.10
47	Tom Matte	7.00	3.50	2.10
48	John Stofa	7.00	3.50	2.10
49	Rex Mirich	7.00	3.50	2.10
50	Milloer Farr	7.00	3.50	2.10
51	Gale Sayers	50.00	25.00	15.00
52	Bill Nelsen	7.00	3.50	2.10
53	Bob Lilly	10.00	5.00	3.00
54	Wayne Walker	7.00	3.50	2.10
55	Ray Nitschke	15.00	7.50	4.50
56	Ed Meador	7.00	3.50	2.10
57	Lonnie Warwick	7.00	3.50	2.10
58	Wendell Hayes	7.00	3.50	2.10
59	Dick Anderson **RC**	10.00	5.00	3.00
60	Don Maynard	10.00	5.00	3.00
61	Tony Lorick	7.00	3.50	2.10
62	Pete Gogolak	7.00	3.50	2.10
63	Nate Ramsey	7.00	3.50	2.10
64	Dick Shiner	7.00	3.50	2.10
65	Larry Wilson	7.00	3.50	2.10
66	Ken Willard	7.00	3.50	2.10
67	Charley Taylor	10.00	5.00	3.00
68	Billy Cannon	7.00	3.50	2.10
69	Lance Alworth	15.00	7.50	4.50
70	Jim Nance	7.00	3.50	2.10
71	Nick Rassas	7.00	3.50	2.10
72	Lenny Lyles	7.00	3.50	2.10
73	Bennie McRae	7.00	3.50	2.10
74	Bill Glass	7.00	3.50	2.10
75	Don Meredith	20.00	10.00	6.00
76	Dick LeBeau	7.00	3.50	2.10
77	Carroll Dale	7.00	3.50	2.10
78	Ron McDole	7.00	3.50	2.10
79	Charley King	7.00	3.50	2.10
80	**Checklist 1-132**	15.00	7.50	4.50
81	Dick Bass	7.00	3.50	2.10
82	Roy Winston	7.00	3.50	2.10
83	Don McCall	7.00	3.50	2.10
84	Jim Katcavage	7.00	3.50	2.10
85	Norm Snead	7.00	3.50	2.10
86	Earl Gros	7.00	3.50	2.10
87	Don Brumm	7.00	3.50	2.10
88	Sonny Bishop	7.00	3.50	2.10
89	Fred Arbanas	7.00	3.50	2.10
90	Karl Noonan	7.00	3.50	2.10
91	Dick Witcher	7.00	3.50	2.10
92	Vince Promuto	7.00	3.50	2.10
93	Tommy Nobis	10.00	5.00	3.00
94	Jerry Hill	7.00	3.50	2.10
95	Ed O'Bradovich **RC**	7.00	3.50	2.10
96	Ernie Kellerman	7.00	3.50	2.10
97	Chuck Howley	7.00	3.50	2.10
98	Hewritt Dixon	7.00	3.50	2.10
99	Ron Mix	7.00	3.50	2.10
100	Joe Namath	65.00	33.00	20.00
101	Billy Gambrell	7.00	3.50	2.10
102	Elijah Pitts	7.00	3.50	2.10
103	Billy Truax	7.00	3.50	2.10
104	Ed Sharockman	7.00	3.50	2.10
105	Doug Atkins	7.00	3.50	2.10
106	Greg Larson	7.00	3.50	2.10
107	Israel Lang	7.00	3.50	2.10
108	Houston Antwine	7.00	3.50	2.10
109	Paul Guidry	7.00	3.50	2.10
110	Al Denson	7.00	3.50	2.10
111	Roy Jefferson	7.00	3.50	2.10
112	Chuck LaTourette	7.00	3.50	2.10
113	Jimmy Johnson	7.00	3.50	2.10
114	Bobby Mitchell	10.00	5.00	3.00
115	Randy Johnson	7.00	3.50	2.10
116	Lou Michaels	7.00	3.50	2.10
117	Rudy Kuechenberg	7.00	3.50	2.10
118	Walt Suggs	7.00	3.50	2.10
119	Goldie Sellers	7.00	3.50	2.10
120	Larry Csonka **RC**	70.00	35.00	21.00
121	Jim Houston	7.00	3.50	2.10
122	Craig Baynham	7.00	3.50	2.10
123	Alex Karras	10.00	5.00	3.00
124	Jim Grabowski	7.00	3.50	2.10
125	Roman Gabriel	7.00	3.50	2.10
126	Larry Bowie	7.00	3.50	2.10
127	Dave Parks	7.00	3.50	2.10
128	Ben Davidson	7.00	3.50	2.10
129	Steve DeLong	7.00	3.50	2.10
130	Fred Hill	7.00	3.50	2.10
131	Ernie Koy	7.00	3.50	2.10
132	**Checklist 133-263**	20.00	10.00	6.00
133	Dick Hoak	7.00	3.50	2.10
134	Larry Stallings **RC**	7.00	3.50	2.10
135	Clifton McNeil **RC**	7.00	3.50	2.10
136	Walter Rock	7.00	3.50	2.10
137	Billy Lothridge	7.00	3.50	2.10
138	Bob Vogel	7.00	3.50	2.10
139	Dick Butkus	45.00	23.00	14.00
140	Frank Ryan	7.00	3.50	2.10
141	Larry Garron	7.00	3.50	2.10
142	George Saimes	7.00	3.50	2.10
143	Frank Buncom	7.00	3.50	2.10
144	Don Perkins	7.00	3.50	2.10
145	Johnny Robinson	7.00	3.50	2.10
146	Lee Roy Caffey	7.00	3.50	2.10
147	Bernie Casey	7.00	3.50	2.10
148	Billy Martin	7.00	3.50	2.10
149	Gene Howard	7.00	3.50	2.10
150	Fran Tarkenton	30.00	15.00	9.00
151	Eric Crabtree	7.00	3.50	2.10
152	W.K. Hicks	7.00	3.50	2.10
153	Bobby Bell	7.00	3.50	2.10
154	Sam Baker	7.00	3.50	2.10
155	Marv Woodson	7.00	3.50	2.10
156	Dave Williams	7.00	3.50	2.10
157	Bruce Bosley	7.00	3.50	2.10
158	Carl Kammerer	7.00	3.50	2.10
159	Jim Burson	7.00	3.50	2.10
160	Roy Hilton	7.00	3.40	2.10
161	Bob Griese	30.00	15.00	9.00
162	Bob Talamini	7.00	3.50	2.10
163	Jim Otto	10.00	5.00	3.00
164	Ron Bull	7.00	3.50	2.10
165	Walter Johnson	7.00	3.50	2.10
166	Lee Roy Jordan	10.00	5.00	3.00
167	Mike Lucci	7.00	3.50	2.10
168	Willie Wood	10.00	5.00	3.00
169	Maxie Baughan	7.00	3.50	2.10
170	Bill Brown	7.00	3.50	2.10
171	John Hadl	10.00	5.00	3.00
172	Gino Cappelletti	7.00	3.50	2.10
173	George Byrd	7.00	3.50	2.10
174	Steve Stonebreaker	7.00	3.50	2.10
175	Joe Morrison	7.00	3.50	2.10
176	Joe Scarpati	7.00	3.50	2.10
177	Bobby Walden	7.00	3.50	2.10
178	Roy Shivers	7.00	3.50	2.10
179	Kermit Alexander	7.00	3.50	2.10
180	Pat Richter	7.00	3.50	2.10
181	Pete Perreault	7.00	3.50	2.10
182	Pete Duranko	7.00	3.50	2.10
183	Leroy Mitchell	7.00	3.50	2.10
184	Jim Simon	7.00	3.50	2.10
185	Billy Ray Smith	7.00	3.50	2.10
186	Jack Concannon	1.15	.60	.35
187	Ben Davis	7.00	3.50	2.10
188	Mike Clark	7.00	3.50	2.10
189	Jim Gobbons	7.00	3.50	2.10
190	Dave Robinson	7.00	3.50	2.10
191	Otis Taylor	7.00	3.50	2.10
192	Nick Buoniconti	10.00	5.00	3.00
193	Matt Snell	7.00	3.50	2.10
194	Bruce Gossett	7.00	3.50	2.10
195	Mick Tingelhoff	7.00	3.50	2.10
196	Earl Leggett	7.00	3.50	2.10
197	Pete Case	7.00	3.50	2.10
198	Tom Woodeshick **RC**	7.00	3.50	2.10
199	Ken Kortas	7.00	3.50	2.10
200	Jim Hart	10.00	5.00	3.00
201	Fred Biletnikoff	15.00	7.50	4.50

		NM	E	VG

202	Jacque MacKinnon	7.00	3.50	2.10
203	Jim Whalen	7.00	3.50	2.10
204	Matt Hazeltine	7.00	3.50	2.10
205	Charlie Gogolak	7.00	3.50	2.10
206	Ray Ogden	7.00	3.50	2.10
207	John Mackey	10.00	5.00	3.00
208	Rosey Taylor	7.00	3.50	2.10
209	Gene Hickerson	7.00	3.50	2.10
210	Dave Edwards RC	7.00	3.50	2.10
211	Tom Sestak	7.00	3.50	2.10
212	Ernie Wright	7.00	3.50	2.10
213	Dave Costa	7.00	3.50	2.10
214	Tom Vaughn	7.00	3.50	2.10
215	Bart Starr	40.00	20.00	12.00
216	Les Josephson	7.00	3.50	2.10
217	Fred Cox	7.00	3.50	2.10
218	Mike Tilleman	7.00	3.50	2.10
219	Darrell Dess	7.00	3.50	2.10
220	Dave Lloyd	7.00	3.50	2.10
221	Pete Beathard	7.00	3.50	2.10
222	Buck Buchanan	10.00	5.00	3.00
223	Frank Emanuel	7.00	3.50	2.10
224	Paul Martha	7.00	3.50	2.10
225	Johnny Roland	7.00	3.50	2.10
226	Gary Lewis	7.00	3.50	2.10
227	Sonny Jurgensen	10.00	5.00	3.00
228	Jim Butler	7.00	3.50	2.10
229	Mike Curtis RC	10.00	5.00	3.00
230	Richie Petitbon	7.00	3.50	2.10
231	George Sauer Jr.	7.00	3.50	2.10
232	George Blanda	20.00	10.00	6.00
233	Gary Garrison	7.00	3.50	2.10
234	Gary Collins	7.00	3.50	2.10
235	Craig Morton	10.00	5.00	3.00
236	Tom Nowatzke	7.00	3.50	2.10
237	Donny Anderson	7.00	3.50	2.10
238	Deacon Jones	10.00	5.00	3.00
239	Grady Alderman	7.00	3.50	2.10
240	Bill Kilmer	10.00	5.00	3.00
241	Mike Taliaferro	7.00	3.50	2.10
242	Stew Barber	7.00	3.50	2.10
243	Bobby Hunt	7.00	3.50	2.10
244	Homer Jones	7.00	3.50	2.10
245	Bob Brown	7.00	3.50	2.10
246	Bill Asbury	7.00	3.50	2.10
247	Charley Johnson	7.00	3.50	2.10
248	Chris Hanburger	7.00	3.50	2.10
249	John Brodie	10.00	5.00	3.00
250	Earl Morrall	7.00	3.50	2.10
251	Floyd Little	10.00	5.00	3.00
252	Jerrell Wilson RC	7.00	3.50	2.10
253	Jim Keyes	7.00	3.50	2.10
254	Mel Renfro	10.00	5.00	3.00
255	Herb Adderley	10.00	5.00	3.00
256	Jack Snow	7.00	3.50	2.10
257	Charlie Durkee	7.00	3.50	2.10
258	Charlie Harper	7.00	3.50	2.10
259	J.R. Wilburn	7.00	3.50	2.10
260	Charlie Krueger	7.00	3.50	2.10
261	Pete Jacquess	7.00	3.50	2.10
262	Gerry Philbin	7.00	3.50	2.10
263	Daryle Lamonica	15.00	7.50	4.50

1969 Topps Four In Ones

Issued one per pack in the 1969 Topps football wax packs, each "card" contained four perforated cards of NFL players which could be punched out and inserted into each team's mini-album. The cards are unnumbered, but appear here in alphabetical order according to the last name of the player who appears in the upper left corner of the card. One variation does exist: Cards #27 and 28 show the same four players, but Charlie Johnson on #27 has a red logo while #28 gives him a white one. Bill Triplett on #27 has a white logo, while #28 is red. Both seem to have been issued in equal quantities. Most of the cards in this set are of the key players, including Brian Piccolo and Larry Csonka rookies. A few of the lesser-known NFL players appeared in this set only and not the regular 1969 set (and vice versa). An important note: the entire card is priced here. The small, individual cards have very little value when separated from the rest of the card, as is the case with Topps' 1980-81 basketball issue.

		NM	E	VG
	Complete Set (66):	400.00	200.00	120.00
	Common Card:	8.00	4.00	2.40
(1)	Grady Alderman, Jerry Smith, Gale Sayers, Dick LeBeau	15.00	7.50	4.50
(2)	Jim Allison, Frank Buncom, Frank Emanuel, George Sauer Jr.	8.00	4.00	2.40
(3)	Lance Alworth, Don Maynard, Ron McDole, Billy Cannon	10.00	5.00	3.00
(4)	Dick Anderson, Mike Taliaferro, Fred Biletnikoff, Otis Taylor	10.00	5.00	3.00
(5)	Ralph Baker, Les Duncan, Eric Crabtree, Bobby Bell	10.00	5.00	3.00
(6)	Gary Ballman, Jerry Hill, Roy Jefferson, Boyd Dowler	8.00	4.00	2.40
(7)	Tom Beer, Miller Farr, Jim Colclough, Steve DeLong	8.00	4.00	2.40
(8)	Sonny Bishop, Pete Banaszak, Paul Guidry, Tom Day	8.00	4.00	2.40
(9)	Bruce Bosley, J.R. Wilburn, Tom Nowatzke, Jim Simon	8.00	4.00	2.40
(10)	Larry Bowie, Willis Crenshaw, Tommy Davis, Paul Flatley	8.00	4.00	2.40
(11)	Nick Buoniconti, George Saimes, Jacque MacKinnon, Pete Duranko	10.00	5.00	3.00
(12)	Jim Burson, Dan Abramowicz, Ed O'Bradovich, Dick Witcher	8.00	4.00	2.40
(13)	Reg Carolan, Larry Garron, W.K. Hicks, Pete Jacques	8.00	4.00	2.40
(14)	Bert Coan, John Hadl, Dan Birdwell, Sam Brunelli	8.00	4.00	2.40
(15)	Hewritt Dixon, Goldie Sellers, Joe Namath, Howard Twilley	35.00	18.00	11.00
(16)	Charlie Durkee, Clinton McNeil, Maxie Baughan, Fran Tarkenton	15.00	7.50	4.50
(17)	Pete Gogolak, Ron Bull, Chuck LaTourette, Willie Richardson	8.00	4.00	2.40
(18)	Bob Griese, Jim Lemoine, Dave Grayson, Walt Sweeney	15.00	7.50	4.50
(19)	Jim Hart, Darrell Dess, Kermit Alexander, Mick Tingelhoff	8.00	4.00	2.40
(20)	Alvin Haymond, Elijah Pitts, Billy Ray Smith, Ken Willard	8.00	4.00	2.40
(21)	Gene Hickerson, Donny Anderson, Dick Butkus, Mike Lucci	15.00	7.50	4.50
(22)	Fred Hill, Ernie Koy, Tommy Nobis, Bennie McRae	8.00	4.00	2.40
(23)	Dick Hoak, Roman Gabriel, Ed Sharockman, Dave Williams	8.00	4.00	2.40
(24)	Jim Houston, Roy Shivers, Carroll Dale, Bill Asbury	8.00	4.00	2.40
(25)	Gene Howard, Joe Morrison, Billy Martin, Ben Davis	8.00	4.00	2.40
(26)	Chuck Howley, Brian Piccolo, Chris Hanburger, Erich Barnes	20.00	10.00	6.00
(27)	Charlie Johnson, Jim Katcavage, Gary Lewis, Bill Triplett (red white)	10.00	5.00	3.00
(28)	Charlie Johnson, Jim Katcavage, Gary Lewis, Bill Triplett (white red)	8.00	4.00	2.40
(29)	Walter Johnson, Tucker Frederickson, Dave Lloyd, Bobby Walden	8.00	4.00	2.40
(30)	Sonny Jurgensen, Dick Bass, Paul Martha, Dave Parks	12.00	6.00	3.50
(31)	Leroy Kelly, Ed Meador, Bart Starr, Ray Ogden	20.00	10.00	6.00
(32)	Charlie King, Bob Cappadona, Fred Arbanas, Ben Davidson	8.00	4.00	2.40
(33)	Daryle Lamonica, Carl Cunningham, Bobby Hunt, Stew Barber	8.00	4.00	2.40
(34)	Israel Lang, Bob Lilly, Jim Butler, John Brodie	12.00	6.00	3.50
(35)	Jim Lindsey, Ray Nitschke, Rickie Harris, Bob Vogel	10.00	5.00	3.00
(36)	Billy Lothridge, Herb Adderly, Charlie Gogolak, John Mackey	10.00	5.00	3.00
(37)	Bobby Maples, Karl Noonan, Houston Antwine, Wendell Hayes	8.00	4.00	2.40
(38)	Don Meredith, Gary Collins, Homer Jones, Marv Woodson	15.00	7.50	4.50
(39)	Rex Mirich, Art Graham, Jim Turner, John Stofa	8.00	4.00	2.40
(40)	Leroy Mitchell, Sid Blanks, Paul Rochester, Pete Perreault	8.00	4.00	2.40
(41)	Jim Nance, Jim Dunaway, Larry Csonka, Ron Mix	15.00	7.50	4.50
(42)	Bill Nelsen, Bill Munson, Nate Ramsey, Mike Curtis	8.00	4.00	2.40
(43)	Jim Otto, Dave herman, Dave Costa, Dennis Randall	10.00	5.00	3.00
(44)	Jack Pardee, Norm Snead, Craig Baynham	8.00	4.00	2.40
(45)	Richie Petitbon, John Robinson, Mike Clark, Jack Snow	8.00	4.00	2.40
(46)	Nick Rassas, Tom Matte, Lance Rentzel, Bobby Mitchell	8.00	4.00	2.40
(47)	Pat Richter, Dave Whitsell, Joe Kapp, Bill Glass	8.00	4.00	2.40
(48)	Johnny Roland, Craig Morton, Bill Brown, Sam Baker	8.00	4.00	2.40
(49)	Andy Russell, Randy Johnson, Bob Matheson, Alex Karras	8.00	4.00	2.40
(50)	Joe Scarpati, Walter Rock, Jack Concannon, Bernie Casey	8.00	4.00	2.40
(51)	Tom Sestak, Ernie Wright, Doug Moreau, Matt Snell	8.00	4.00	2.40
(52)	Jerry Simmons, Bob Hayes, Doug Atkins, Spider Lockhart	10.00	5.00	3.00
(53)	Jackie Smith, Jim Grabowski, Jim Johnson, Charley Taylor	10.00	5.00	3.00
(54)	Larry Stallings, Roosevelt Taylor, Jim Gibbons, Bob Brown	8.00	4.00	2.40
(55)	Mike Stratton, Marion Rushing, Soloman Brannan, Jim Keyes	8.00	4.00	2.40
(56)	Walt Suggs, Len Dawson, Sherrill Headrick, Al Denson	10.00	5.00	3.00
(57)	Bob Talamini, George Blanda, Jim Whalen, Jack Kemp	10.00	5.00	3.00
(58)	Clendon Thomas, Don McCall, Earl Morrall, Lonnie Warwick	8.00	4.00	2.40
(59)	Don Trull, Gerry Philbin, Gary Garrison, Buck Buchanan	10.00	5.00	3.00
(60)	John Unitas, Les Josephson, Fred Cox, Mel Renfro	20.00	10.00	6.00
(61)	Wayne Walker, Tony Lorick, Dave Wilcox, Merlin Olsen	10.00	5.00	3.00
(62)	Willie West, Ken Herock, George Byrd, Gino Cappelletti	8.00	4.00	2.40
(63)	Jerrel Wilson, John Bramlett, Pete Beathard, Floyd Little	8.00	4.00	2.40
(64)	Larry Wilson, Lou Michaels, Billy Gambrell, Earl Gros	10.00	5.00	3.00
(65)	Willie Wood, Steve Stonebreaker, Vince Promuto, Jim Cadie	10.00	5.00	3.00
(66)	Tom Woodeshick, Greg Larson, Billy Kilmer, Don Perkins	8.00	4.00	2.40

1969 Topps mini-albums

The 26 team booklets were intended as stamp books for the 1969 Topps Four In Ones. You punched out the four players on the card and stuck them into this 2-1/2" x 3-1/2" book, right over the picture of the player. The booklets are numbered on the back and arranged in alphabetical order by city name. Aside from its condition, in order for a book to be considered mint, there must be no stamps in it.

Complete Set (26):		50.00	25.00	15.00
Common Booklet:		2.00	1.00	.60
1	**Atlanta Falcons**	2.00	1.00	.60
2	**Baltimore Colts**	2.00	1.00	.60
3	**Chicago Bears**	4.00	2.00	1.25
4	**Cleveland Browns**	2.00	1.00	.60
5	**Dallas Cowboys**	5.00	2.50	1.50
6	**Detroit Lions**	2.00	1.00	.60
7	**Green Bay Packers**	5.00	2.50	1.50
8	**Los Angeles Rams**	2.00	1.00	.60
9	**Minnesota Vikings**	2.00	1.00	.60
10	**New Orleans Saints**	2.00	1.00	.60
11	**New York Giants**	4.00	2.00	1.25
12	**Philadelphia Eagles**	2.00	1.00	.60
13	**Pittsburgh Steelers**	4.00	2.00	1.25
14	**St. Louis Cardinals**	2.00	1.00	.60
15	**San Francisco 49ers**	4.00	2.00	1.25
16	**Washington Redskins**	4.00	2.00	1.25
17	**Boston Patriots**	2.00	1.00	.60
18	**Buffalo Bills**	4.00	2.00	1.25
19	**Cincinnati Bengals**	2.00	1.00	.60
20	**Denver Broncos**	5.00	2.50	1.50
21	**Houston Oilers**	4.00	2.00	1.25
22	**Kansas City Chiefs**	2.00	1.00	.60
23	**Miami Dolphins**	4.00	2.00	1.25
24	**New York Jets**	4.00	2.00	1.25
25	**Oakland Raiders**	5.00	2.50	1.50
26	**San Diego Chargers**	2.00	1.00	.60

1970 Topps

The 1970 Topps set, which included 263 cards, was printed in two series. The second series is a little tougher to find than the first, since it was printed in lesser quantities. One variation that appears in the set is #113, Lance Rentzel. His name appears in red on the "common" card; on the hard-to-find variation, his name appears in black. Card #132, the second-series checklist card, was double- printed, a common practice for Topps during its multi-series production days. The set is best known for its inclusion of the O.J. Simpson rookie card, but other rookies in the set are Leroy Brown, Jan Stenerud, Alan Page, Bob Trumpy, Bubba Smith, Bill Bergey, Calvin Hill and Fred Dryer.

	NM	E	VG
Complete Set (263):	875.00	435.00	265.00
Common Player (1-132):	5.00	2.50	1.50
Minor Stars (1-132):	.75		
Unlisted Stars (1-132):	1.50		
Common Player (133-263):	5.00	2.50	1.50
Minor Stars (133-263):	1.00		
Unlisted Stars (133-263):	2.00		
Series 1 Wax Pack (10+1):	175.00		
Series 1 Wax Box (24):	3,650		
Series 2 Wax Pack (10+1):	182.50		
Series 2 Wax Box (24):	3,725		

1	Len Dawson	20.00	10.00	6.00
2	Doug Hart	5.00	2.50	1.50
3	Verlon Biggs	5.00	2.50	1.50
4	Ralph Neely **RC**	5.00	2.50	1.50
5	Harmon Wages	5.00	2.50	1.50
6	Dan Conners	5.00	2.50	1.50
7	Gino Cappelletti	5.00	2.50	1.50
8	Erich Barnes	5.00	2.50	1.50
9	**Checklist 1-132**	10.00	5.00	3.00
10	Bob Griese	15.00	7.50	4.50
11	Ed Flanagan	5.00	2.50	1.50
12	George Seals	5.00	2.50	1.50
13	Harry Jacobs	5.00	2.50	1.50
14	Mike Haffner	5.00	2.50	1.50
15	Bob Vogel	5.00	2.50	1.50
16	Bill Peterson	5.00	2.50	1.50
17	Spider Lockhart	5.00	2.50	1.50
18	Billy Truax	5.00	2.50	1.50
19	Jim Beirne	5.00	2.50	1.50
20	Leroy Kelly	7.00	3.50	2.10
21	Dave Lloyd	5.00	2.50	1.50
22	Mike Tilleman	5.00	2.50	1.50
23	Gary Garrison	5.00	2.50	1.50
24	Larry Brown **RC**	10.00	5.00	3.00
25	Jan Stenerud **RC**	15.00	7.50	4.50
26	Rolf Krueger	5.00	2.50	1.50
27	Roland Lakes	5.00	2.50	1.50
28	Dick Hoak	5.00	2.50	1.50
29	Gene Washington **RC** (Vikings)	5.00	2.50	1.50
30	Bart Starr	25.00	13.00	8.00
31	Dave Grayson	5.00	2.50	1.50
32	Jerry Rush	5.00	2.50	1.50
33	Len St. Jean	5.00	2.50	1.50
34	Randy Edmunds	5.00	2.50	1.50
35	Matt Snell	5.00	2.50	1.50
36	Paul Costa	5.00	2.50	1.50
37	Mike Pyle	5.00	2.50	1.50
38	Roy Hilton	5.00	2.50	1.50
39	Steve Tensi	5.00	2.50	1.50
40	Tommy Nobis	5.00	2.50	1.50
41	Pete Case	5.00	2.50	1.50
42	Andy Rice	5.00	2.50	1.50
43	Elvin Bethea **RC**	15.00	7.50	4.50
44	Jack Snow	5.00	2.50	1.50
45	Mel Renfro	5.00	2.50	1.50
46	Andy Livingston	5.00	2.50	1.50
47	Gary Ballman	5.00	2.50	1.50
48	Bob DeMarco	5.00	2.50	1.50
49	Steve DeLong	5.00	2.50	1.50
50	Daryle Lamonica	5.00	2.50	1.50
51	Jim Lynch **RC**	5.00	2.50	1.50
52	Mel Farr **RC**	5.00	2.50	1.50
53	Bob Long	5.00	2.50	1.50
54	John Elliott	5.00	2.50	1.50
55	Ray Nitschke	7.00	3.50	2.10
56	Jim Shorter	5.00	2.50	1.50
57	Dave Wilcox	5.00	2.50	1.50
58	Eric Crabtree	5.00	2.50	1.50
59	Alan Page **RC**	15.00	7.50	4.50
60	Jim Nance	5.00	2.50	1.50
61	Glen Ray Hines	5.00	2.50	1.50
62	John Mackey	5.00	2.50	1.50
63	Ron McDole	5.00	2.50	1.50
64	Tom Beier	5.00	2.50	1.50
65	Bill Nelsen	5.00	2.50	1.50
66	Paul Flatley	5.00	2.50	1.50
67	Sam Brunelli	5.00	2.50	1.50
68	Jack Pardee	5.00	2.50	1.50
69	Brig Owens	5.00	2.50	1.50
70	Gale Sayers	30.00	15.00	9.00
71	Lee Roy Jordan	5.00	2.50	1.50
72	Harold Jackson **RC**	7.00	3.50	2.10
73	John Hadl	5.00	2.50	1.50
74	Dave Parks	5.00	2.50	1.50
75	Lem Barney **RC**	15.00	7.50	4.50
76	Johnny Roland	5.00	2.50	1.50
77	Ed Budde	5.00	2.50	1.50
78	Ben McGee	5.00	2.50	1.50
79	Ken Bowman	5.00	2.50	1.50
80	Fran Tarkenton	20.00	10.00	6.00
81	Gene Washington **RC**	7.00	3.50	2.10
82	Larry Grantham	5.00	2.50	1.50
83	Bill Brown	5.00	2.50	1.50
84	John Charles	5.00	2.50	1.50
85	Fred Biletnikoff	10.00	5.00	3.00
86	Royce Berry	5.00	2.50	1.50
87	Bob Lilly	7.00	3.50	2.10
88	Earl Morrall	5.00	2.50	1.50
89	Jerry LeVias	5.00	2.50	1.50
90	O.J. Simpson **RC**	60.00	30.00	18.00
91	Mike Howell	5.00	2.50	1.50
92	Ken Gray	5.00	2.50	1.50
93	Chris Hanburger	5.00	2.50	1.50
94	Larry Seiple **RC**	5.00	2.50	1.50
95	Rich Jackson **RC**	5.00	2.50	1.50
96	Rockne Freitas	5.00	2.50	1.50
97	Dick Post **RC**	5.00	2.50	1.50
98	Ben Hawkins	5.00	2.50	1.50
99	Ken Reaves	5.00	2.50	1.50
100	Roman Gabriel	5.00	2.50	1.50
101	Dave Rowe	5.00	2.50	1.50
102	Dave Robinson	5.00	2.50	1.50
103	Otis Taylor	5.00	2.50	1.50
104	Jim Turner	5.00	2.50	1.50
105	Joe Morrison	5.00	2.50	1.50
106	Dick Evey	5.00	2.50	1.50
107	Ray Mansfield	5.00	2.50	1.50
108	Grady Alderman	5.00	2.50	1.50
109	Bruce Gossett	5.00	2.50	1.50
110	Bob Trumpy **RC**	5.00	2.50	1.50
111	Jim Hunt	5.00	2.50	1.50
112	Larry Stallings	5.00	2.50	1.50
113	Lance Rentzel (red)	5.00	2.50	1.50
113a	Lance Rentzel (black)	5.00	2.50	1.50
114	Bubba Smith **RC**	25.00	12.50	7.50
115	Norm Snead	5.00	2.50	1.50
116	Jim Otto	5.00	2.50	1.50
117	Bo Scott **RC**	5.00	2.50	1.50
118	Rick Redman	5.00	2.50	1.50
119	George Byrd	5.00	2.50	1.50
120	George Webster **RC**	5.00	2.50	1.50
121	Chuck Walton	5.00	2.50	1.50
122	Dave Costa	5.00	2.50	1.50
123	Al Dodd	5.00	2.50	1.50
124	Len Hauss	5.00	2.50	1.50
125	Deacon Jones	5.00	2.50	1.50
126	Randy Johnson	5.00	2.50	1.50
127	Ralph Heck	5.00	2.50	1.50
128	Emerson Boozer **RC**	5.00	2.50	1.50
129	Johnny Robinson	5.00	2.50	1.50
130	John Brodie	7.00	3.50	2.10
131	Gale Gillingham **RC**	1.00	.50	.30
132	**Checklist 133-263** (DP)	10.00	5.00	3.00
133	Chuck Walker	5.00	2.50	1.50
134	Bennie McRae	5.00	2.50	1.50
135	Paul Warfield	10.00	5.00	3.00
136	Dan Darragh	5.00	2.50	1.50
137	Paul Robinson **RC**	5.00	2.50	1.50
138	Ed Philpott	5.00	2.50	1.50
139	Craig Morton	5.00	2.50	1.50
140	Tom Dempsey **RC**	5.00	2.50	1.50
141	Al Nelson	5.00	2.50	1.50
142	Tom Matte	5.00	2.50	1.50
143	Dick Schafrath	5.00	2.50	1.50
144	Willie Brown	5.00	2.50	1.50
145	Charley Taylor	5.00	2.50	1.50
146	John Huard	5.00	2.50	1.50
147	Dave Osborn	5.00	2.50	1.50
148	Gene Mingo	5.00	2.50	1.50
149	Larry Hand	5.00	2.50	1.50
150	Joe Namath	45.00	23.00	14.00
151	Tom Mack **RC**	15.00	7.50	4.50
152	Kenny Graham	5.00	2.50	1.50
153	Don Herrmann	5.00	2.50	1.50
154	Bobby Bell	5.00	2.50	1.50
155	Hoyle Granger	5.00	2.50	1.50
156	Claude Humphrey **RC**	5.00	2.50	1.50
157	Clifton McNeil	5.00	2.50	1.50
158	Mick Tingelhoff	5.00	2.50	1.50
159	Don Horn **RC**	5.00	2.50	1.50
160	Larry Wilson	5.00	2.50	1.50
161	Tom Neville	5.00	2.50	1.50
162	Larry Csonka	25.00	12.50	7.50
163	Doug Buffone **RC**	5.00	2.50	1.50
164	Cornell Green	5.00	2.50	1.50
165	Haven Moses **RC**	5.00	2.50	1.50
166	Bill Kilmer	5.00	2.50	1.50
167	Tim Rossovich **RC**	5.00	2.50	1.50
168	Bill Bergey **RC**	5.00	2.50	1.50
169	Gary Collins	5.00	2.50	1.50
170	Floyd Little	5.00	2.50	1.50
171	Tom Keating	5.00	2.50	1.50
172	Pat Fischer	5.00	2.50	1.50
173	Walt Sweeney	5.00	2.50	1.50
174	Greg Larson	5.00	2.50	1.50
175	Carl Eller	5.00	2.50	1.50
176	George Sauer	5.00	2.50	1.50
177	Jim Hart	5.00	2.50	1.50
178	Bob Brown	5.00	2.50	1.50
179	Mike Garrett **RC**	5.00	2.50	1.50
180	Johnny Unitas	30.00	15.00	9.00
181	Tom Regner	5.00	2.50	1.50
182	Bob Jeter	5.00	2.50	1.50
183	Gail Cogdill	5.00	2.50	1.50
184	Earl Gros	5.00	2.50	1.50
185	Dennis Partee	5.00	2.50	1.50
186	Charlie Krueger	5.00	2.50	1.50
187	Martin Baccaglio	5.00	2.50	1.50
188	Charlie Long	5.00	2.50	1.50
189	Bob Hayes	5.00	2.50	1.50
190	Dick Butkus	20.00	10.00	6.00
191	Al Bemiller	5.00	2.50	1.50
192	Dick Westmoreland	5.00	2.50	1.50
193	Joe Scarpati	5.00	2.50	1.50
194	Ron Snidow	5.00	2.50	1.50
195	Earl McCullough **RC**	5.00	2.50	1.50
196	Jake Kupp	5.00	2.50	1.50
197	Bob Lurtsema	5.00	2.50	1.50
198	Mike Current	5.00	2.50	1.50
199	Charlie Smith	5.00	2.50	1.50
200	Sonny Jurgensen	10.00	5.00	3.00
201	Mike Curtis	5.00	2.50	1.50
202	Aaron Brown	5.00	2.50	1.50

203	Richie Petitbon	5.00	2.50	1.50
204	Walt Suggs	5.00	2.50	1.50
205	Roy Jefferson	5.00	2.50	1.50
206	Russ Washington **RC**	5.00	2.50	1.50
207	Woody Peoples **RC**	5.00	2.50	1.50
208	Dave Williams	5.00	2.50	1.50
209	John Zook **RC**	5.00	2.50	1.50
210	Tom Woodeshick	5.00	2.50	1.50
211	Howard Fest	5.00	2.50	1.50
212	Jack Concannon	5.00	2.50	1.50
213	Jim Marshall	5.00	2.50	1.50
214	Jon Morris	5.00	2.50	1.50
215	Dan Abramowicz	5.00	2.50	1.50
216	Paul Martha	5.00	2.50	1.50
217	Ken Willard	5.00	2.50	1.50
218	Walter Rock	5.00	2.50	1.50
219	Garland Boyette	5.00	2.50	1.50
220	Buck Buchanan	5.00	2.50	1.50
221	Bill Munson	5.00	2.50	1.50
222	David Lee **RC**	5.00	2.50	1.50
223	Karl Noonan	5.00	2.50	1.50
224	Harry Schuh	5.00	2.50	1.50
225	Jackie Smith	5.00	2.50	1.50
226	Gerry Philbin	5.00	2.50	1.50
227	Ernie Koy	5.00	2.50	1.50
228	Chuck Howley	5.00	2.50	1.50
229	Billy Shaw	5.00	2.50	1.50
230	Jerry Hillebrand	5.00	2.50	1.50
231	Bill Thompson **RC**	5.00	2.50	1.50
232	Carroll Dale	5.00	2.50	1.50
233	Gene Hickerson	5.00	2.50	1.50
234	Jim Butler	5.00	2.50	1.50
235	Greg Cook **RC**	5.00	2.50	1.50
236	Lee Roy Caffey	5.00	2.50	1.50
237	Merlin Olsen	5.00	2.50	1.50
238	Fred Cox	5.00	2.50	1.50
239	Nate Ramsey	5.00	2.50	1.50
240	Lance Alworth	10.00	5.00	3.00
241	Chuck Hinton	5.00	2.50	1.50
242	Jerry Smith	5.00	2.50	1.50
243	Tony Baker	5.00	2.50	1.50
244	Nick Buoniconti	5.00	2.50	1.50
245	Jim Johnson	5.00	2.50	1.50
246	Willie Richardson	5.00	2.50	1.50
247	Fred Dryer **RC**	15.00	7.50	4.50
248	Bobby Maples	5.00	2.50	1.50
249	Alex Karras	5.00	2.50	1.50
250	Joe Kapp	5.00	2.50	1.50
251	Ben Davidson	5.00	2.50	1.50
252	Mike Stratton	5.00	2.50	1.50
253	Les Josephson	5.00	2.50	1.50
254	Don Maynard	5.00	2.50	1.50
255	Houston Antwine	5.00	2.50	1.50
256	Mac Percival **RC**	5.00	2.50	1.50
257	George Goeddeke	5.00	2.50	1.50
258	Homer Jones	5.00	2.50	1.50
259	Bob Berry	5.00	2.50	1.50
260	Calvin Hill **RC**	15.00	7.50	4.50
261	Willie Wood	5.00	2.50	1.50
262	Ed Weisacosky	5.00	2.50	1.50
263	Jim Tyrer	5.00	2.50	1.50

1970 Topps posters

This 24-poster set was included one per pack in the first series of 1970 Topps football wax packs. The posters, which measure about 8" x 10", were folded several times; it's very difficult to find any in top condition.

		NM	E	VG
	Complete Set (24):	50.00	25.00	15.00
	Common Player:	1.00	.50	.30
1	Gale Sayers	9.00	4.50	2.75
2	Bobby Bell	3.00	1.50	.90
3	Roman Gabriel	3.25	1.65	1.00
4	Jim Tyrer	1.00	.50	.30
5	Willie Brown	3.00	1.50	.90
6	Carl Eller	3.00	1.50	.90
7	Tom Mack	1.50	.75	.45
8	Deacon Jones	3.00	1.50	.90
9	Johnny Robinson	1.00	.50	.30
10	Jan Stenerud	2.00	1.00	.60
11	Dick Butkus	5.00	2.50	1.50
12	Lem Barney	1.00	.50	.30
13	David Lee	1.00	.50	.30
14	Larry Wilson	2.00	1.00	.60
15	Gene Hickerson	1.00	.50	.30
16	Lance Alworth	3.00	1.50	.90
17	Merlin Olsen	3.00	1.50	.90
18	Bob Trumpy	2.00	1.00	.60
19	Bob Lilly	3.00	1.50	.90
20	Mick Tingelhoff	1.50	.75	.45
21	Calvin Hill	2.00	1.00	.60
22	Paul Warfield	3.00	1.50	.90
23	Chuck Howley	1.00	.50	.30
24	Bob Brown	1.00	.50	.30

1970 Topps Super Glossy

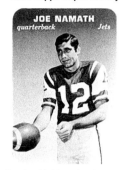

A collector favorite, this 33-card set is among the decade's most expensive subsets. These were found in the second series of 1970 Topps football wax packs and had full-color action-pose glossy fronts, heavy white cardboard stock, and rounded corners. The only information on the white backs is the player's name, team, position and card number.

		NM	E	VG
	Complete Set (33):	300.00	150.00	90.00
	Common Player:	1.00	.50	.30
1	Tommy Nobis	1.00	.50	.30
2	John Unitas	7.00	3.50	2.10
3	Tom Matte	1.00	.50	.30
4	Mac Percival	1.00	.50	.30
5	Leroy Kelly	1.00	.50	.30
6	Mel Renfro	1.00	.50	.30
7	Bob Hayes	1.00	.50	.30
8	Earl McCullouch	1.00	.50	.30
9	Bart Starr	6.00	3.00	1.80
10	Willie Wood	3.00	1.50	.90
11	Jack Snow	1.00	.50	.30
12	Joe Kapp	1.00	.50	.30
13	Dave Osborn	1.00	.50	.30
14	Dan Abramowicz	1.00	.50	.30
15	Fran Tarkenton	6.00	3.00	1.80
16	Tom Woodeshick	1.00	.50	.30
17	Roy Jefferson	1.00	.50	.30
18	Jackie Smith	1.00	.50	.30
19	Jim Johnson	1.00	.50	.30
20	Sonny Jurgensen	3.00	1.50	.90
21	Houston Antwine	1.00	.50	.30
22	O.J. Simpson	10.00	5.00	3.00
23	Greg Cook	1.00	.50	.30
24	Floyd Little	1.00	.50	.30
25	Rich Jackson	1.00	.50	.30
26	George Webster	1.00	.50	.30
27	Len Dawson	3.00	1.50	.90
28	Bob Griese	5.00	2.50	1.50
29	Joe Namath	15.00	7.50	4.50
30	Matt Snell	1.00	.50	.30
31	Daryle Lamonica	1.00	.50	.30
32	Fred Biletnikoff	3.00	1.50	.90
33	Dick Post	1.00	.50	.30

1970 Topps Supers

A 35-card set issued three per pack with a stick of gum, the cards featured an action pose of an NFL star with a fac-simile autograph. No other identification is on the front. Card backs show the reverse of the player's regular 1970 card. These were printed on heavy white cardboard stock and measure about 3-1/8" x 5-1/4". The final seven in the set were apparently short-printed (possibly added late) and are much harder to find than the first 28 cards.

		NM	E	VG
	Complete Set (35):	300.00	150.00	90.00
	Common Player:	2.75	1.40	.85
1	Fran Tarkenton	16.00	8.00	4.75
2	Floyd Little	3.00	1.50	.90
3	Bart Starr	16.00	8.00	4.75
4	Len Dawson	8.50	4.25	2.50

5	Dick Post	2.75	1.40	.85
6	Sonny Jurgensen	8.50	4.25	2.50
7	Deacon Jones	5.00	2.60	1.50
8	Leroy Kelly	2.75	1.40	.85
9	Larry Wilson	2.75	1.40	.85
10	Greg Cook	2.75	1.40	.85
11	Carl Eller	4.50	2.25	1.35
12	Lem Barney	2.75	1.40	.85
13	Lance Alworth	7.00	3.50	2.25
14	Dick Butkus	12.00	6.00	3.75
15	John Unitas	25.00	12.50	7.50
16	Roy Jefferson	2.75	1.40	.85
17	Bobby Bell	5.00	2.50	1.50
18	John Brodie	9.00	4.50	2.75
19	Dan Abramowicz	2.75	1.40	.85
20	Matt Snell	2.75	1.40	.85
21	Tom Matte	2.75	1.40	.85
22	Gale Sayers	20.00	10.00	6.00
23	Tom Woodeshick	2.75	1.40	.85
24	O.J. Simpson	50.00	25.00	15.00
25	Roman Gabriel	5.00	2.50	1.50
26	Jim Nance	2.75	1.40	.85
27	Joe Morrison	2.75	1.40	.85
28	Calvin Hill	2.75	1.40	.85
29	Tommy Nobis	6.50	3.25	2.00
30	Bob Hayes	6.50	3.25	2.00
31	Joe Kapp	6.50	3.25	2.00
32	Daryle Lamonica	6.50	3.25	2.00
33	Joe Namath	65.00	35.00	20.00
34	George Webster	6.50	3.25	2.00
35	Bob Griese	15.00	7.50	4.50

1971 Topps

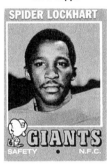

This 263-card set was released in two series, with the first containing cards #1-132 and the second with cards #133-263. The second-series checklist (card #106) is double-printed. There aren't any subsets in the 1971 issue, but the NFC players are designated by red borders and AFC players have blue borders. All-stars have blue borders. This, incidentally, is the last Topps set that would not contain some type of subset. Hall of Famers with rookie cards in this set include Terry Bradshaw, Joe Greene, Willie Lanier, and Ken Houston. Other rookies include Duane Thomas, Ron Johnson, Mercury Morris, Garo Yepremian, Mark Mosley, and Charlie Sanders.

		NM	E	VG
	Complete Set (263):	1,000	500.00	300.00
	Common Player (1-132):	5.00	2.50	1.50
	Minor Stars (1-132):	1.00		
	Unlised Stars (1-132):	2.00		
	Common Player (133-263):	5.00	2.50	1.50
	Minor Stars (133-263):	1.50		
	Unlisted Stars (133-263):	2.50		
	Series 1 Wax Pack (8+2):	250.00		
	Series 1 Wax Box (24):	5,300		
	Series 2 Wax Pack (8+2):	300.00		
	Series 2 Wax Box (24):	6,375		
1	Johnny Unitas	35.00	18.00	11.00
2	Jim Butler	5.00	2.50	1.50
3	Marty Schottenheimer **RC**	20.00	10.00	6.00
4	Joe O'Donnell	5.00	2.50	1.50
5	Tom Dempsey	5.00	2.50	1.50
6	Chuck Allen	5.00	2.50	1.50
7	Ernie Kellerman	5.00	2.50	1.50
8	Walt Garrison **RC**	5.00	2.50	1.50
9	Bill Van Heusen	5.00	2.50	1.50
10	Lance Alworth	10.00	5.00	3.00
11	Greg Landry **RC**	5.00	2.50	1.50
12	Larry Krause	5.00	2.50	1.50
13	Buck Buchanan	5.00	2.50	1.50
14	Roy Gerela **RC**	5.00	2.50	1.50
15	Clifton McNeil	5.00	2.50	1.50
16	Bob Brown	5.00	2.50	1.50
17	Lloyd Mumphord	5.00	2.50	1.50
18	Gary Cuozzo	5.00	2.50	1.50
19	Don Maynard	10.00	5.00	3.00
20	Larry Wilson	5.00	2.50	1.50
21	Charlie Smith	5.00	2.50	1.50
22	Ken Avery	5.00	2.50	1.50

23	Billy Walik	5.00	2.50	1.50
24	Jim Johnson	5.00	2.50	1.50
25	Dick Butkus	25.00	13.00	8.00
26	Charley Taylor	10.00	5.00	3.00
27	**Checklist 1-132**	15.00	7.50	4.50
28	Lionel Aldridge **RC**	5.00	2.50	1.50
29	Billy Lothridge	5.00	2.50	1.50
30	Terry Hanratty **RC**	5.00	2.50	1.50
31	Lee Roy Jordan	5.00	2.50	1.50
32	Rick Volk **RC**	5.00	2.50	1.50
33	Howard Kindig	5.00	2.50	1.50
34	Carl Garrett **RC**	5.00	2.50	1.50
35	Bobby Bell	5.00	2.50	1.50
36	Gene Hickerson	5.00	2.50	1.50
37	Dave Parks	5.00	2.50	1.50
38	Paul Martha	5.00	2.50	1.50
39	George Blanda	15.00	7.50	4.50
40	Tom Woodeshick	5.00	2.50	1.50
41	Alex Karras	5.00	2.50	1.50
42	Rick Redman	5.00	2.50	1.50
43	Zeke Moore	5.00	2.50	1.50
44	Jack Snow	5.00	2.50	1.50
45	Larry Csonka	20.00	10.00	6.00
46	Karl Kassulke	5.00	2.50	1.50
47	Jim Hart	5.00	2.50	1.50
48	Al Atkinson	5.00	2.50	1.50
49	Horst Muhlmann **RC**	5.00	2.50	1.50
50	Sonny Jurgensen	5.00	2.50	1.50
51	Ron Johnson **RC**	5.00	2.50	1.50
52	Cas Banaszek	5.00	2.50	1.50
53	Bubba Smith	10.00	5.00	3.00
54	Bobby Douglass **RC**	5.00	2.50	1.50
55	Willie Wood	5.00	2.50	1.50
56	Bake Turner	5.00	2.50	1.50
57	Mike Morgan	5.00	2.50	1.50
58	George Byrd	5.00	2.50	1.50
59	Don Horn	5.00	2.50	1.50
60	Tommy Nobis	5.00	2.50	1.50
61	Jan Stenerud	10.00	5.00	3.00
62	Altie Taylor **RC**	5.00	2.50	1.50
63	Gary Pettigrew	5.00	2.50	1.50
64	Spike Jones	5.00	2.50	1.50
65	Duane Thomas **RC**	5.00	2.50	1.50
66	Marty Domres **RC**	5.00	2.50	1.50
67	Dick Anderson	5.00	2.50	1.50
68	Ken Iman	5.00	2.50	1.50
69	Miller Farr	5.00	2.50	1.50
70	Daryle Lamonica	5.00	2.50	1.50
71	Alan Page	15.00	7.50	4.50
72	Pat Matson	5.00	2.50	1.50
73	Emerson Boozer	5.00	2.50	1.50
74	Pat Fischer	5.00	2.50	1.50
75	Gary Collins	5.00	2.50	1.50
76	John Fuqua **RC**	5.00	2.50	1.50
77	Bruce Gossett	5.00	2.50	1.50
78	Ed O'Bradovich	5.00	2.50	1.50
79	Bob Tucker **RC**	5.00	2.50	1.50
80	Mike Curtis	5.00	2.50	1.50
81	Rich Jackson	5.00	2.50	1.50
82	Tom Janik	5.00	2.50	1.50
83	Gale Gillingham	5.00	2.50	1.50
84	Jim Mitchell	5.00	2.50	1.50
85	Charlie Johnson	5.00	2.50	1.50
86	Edgar Chandler	5.00	2.50	1.50
87	Cyril Pinder	5.00	2.50	1.50
88	Johnny Robinson	5.00	2.50	1.50
89	Ralph Neely	5.00	2.50	1.50
90	Dan Abramowicz	5.00	2.50	1.50
91	Mercury Morris **RC**	10.00	5.00	3.00
92	Steve DeLong	5.00	2.50	1.50
93	Larry Stallings	5.00	2.50	1.50
94	Tom Mack	5.00	2.50	1.50
95	Hewritt Dixon	5.00	2.50	1.50
96	Fred Cox	5.00	2.50	1.50
97	Chris Hanburger	5.00	2.50	1.50
98	Gerry Philbin	5.00	2.50	1.50
99	Ernie Wright	5.00	2.50	1.50
100	John Brodie	10.00	5.00	3.00
101	Tucker Frederickson	5.00	2.50	1.50
102	Bobby Walden	5.00	2.50	1.50
103	Dick Gordon	5.00	2.50	1.50
104	Walter Johnson	5.00	2.50	1.50
105	Mike Lucci	5.00	2.50	1.50
106	**Checklist 133-263**	10.00	5.00	3.00
107	Ron Berger	5.00	2.50	1.50
108	Dan Sullivan	5.00	2.50	1.50
109	George Kunz **RC**	5.00	2.50	1.50
110	Floyd Little	5.00	2.50	1.50
111	Zeke Bratkowski	5.00	2.50	1.50
112	Haven Moses	5.00	2.50	1.50
113	Ken Houston **RC**	20.00	10.00	6.00
114	Willie Lanier **RC**	20.00	10.00	6.00
115	Larry Brown	5.00	2.50	1.50
116	Tim Rossovich	5.00	2.50	1.50
117	Errol Linden	5.00	2.50	1.50
118	Mel Renfro	5.00	2.50	1.50
119	Mike Garrett	5.00	2.50	1.50
120	Fran Tarkenton	20.00	10.00	6.00
121	Garo Yepremian **RC**	5.00	2.50	1.50
122	Glen Condren	5.00	2.50	1.50
123	Johnny Roland	5.00	2.50	1.50
124	Dave Herman	5.00	2.50	1.50
125	Merlin Olsen	10.00	5.00	3.00
126	Doug Buffone	5.00	2.50	1.50
127	Earl McCullouch	5.00	2.50	1.50
128	Spider Lockhart	5.00	2.50	1.50
129	Ken Willard	5.00	2.50	1.50
130	Gene Washington (MN)	5.00	2.50	1.50
131	Mike Phipps **RC**	5.00	2.50	1.50
132	Andy Russell	5.00	2.50	1.50
133	Ray Nitschke	10.00	5.00	3.00
134	Jerry Logan	5.00	2.50	1.50
135	MacArthur Lane **RC**	5.00	2.50	1.50
136	Jim Turner	5.00	2.50	1.50
137	Kent McCloughan	5.00	2.50	1.50
138	Paul Guidry	5.00	2.50	1.50
139	Otis Taylor	5.00	2.50	1.50
140	Virgil Carter **RC**	5.00	2.50	1.50
141	Joe Dawkins	5.00	2.50	1.50
142	Steve Preece	5.00	2.50	1.50
143	Mike Bragg **RC**	5.00	2.50	1.50
144	Bob Lilly	10.00	5.00	3.00
145	Joe Kapp	5.00	2.50	1.50
146	Al Dodd	5.00	2.50	1.50
147	Nick Buoniconti	5.00	2.50	1.50
148	Speedy Duncan	5.00	2.50	1.50
149	Cedrick Hardman **RC**	5.00	2.50	1.50
150	Gale Sayers	30.00	15.00	9.00
151	Jim Otto	5.00	2.50	1.50
152	Billy Truax	5.00	2.50	1.50
153	John Elliott	5.00	2.50	1.50
154	Dick LeBeau	5.00	2.50	1.50
155	Bill Bergey	5.00	2.50	1.50
156	Terry Bradshaw **RC**	200.00	100.00	60.00
157	Leroy Kelly	10.00	5.00	3.00
158	Paul Krause	5.00	2.50	1.50
159	Ted Vactor	5.00	2.50	1.50
160	Bob Griese	20.00	10.00	6.00
161	Ernie McMillan	5.00	2.50	1.50
162	Donny Anderson	5.00	2.50	1.50
163	John Pitts	5.00	2.50	1.50
164	Dave Costa	5.00	2.50	1.50
165	Gene Washington (SF)	5.00	2.50	1.50
166	John Zook	5.00	2.50	1.50
167	Pete Gogolak	5.00	2.50	1.50
168	Erich Barnes	5.00	2.50	1.50
169	Alvin Reed	5.00	2.50	1.50
170	Jim Nance	5.00	2.50	1.50
171	Craig Morton	5.00	2.50	1.50
172	Gary Garrison	5.00	2.50	1.50
173	Joe Scarpati	5.00	2.50	1.50
174	Adrian Young	5.00	2.50	1.50
175	John Mackey	5.00	2.50	1.50
176	Mac Percival	5.00	2.50	1.50
177	Preston Pearson **RC**	15.00	7.50	4.50
178	Fred Biletnikoff	10.00	5.00	3.00
179	Mike Battle **RC**	5.00	2.50	1.50
180	Len Dawson	10.00	5.00	3.00
181	Les Josephson	5.00	2.50	1.50
182	Royce Berry	5.00	2.50	1.50
183	Herman Weaver	5.00	2.50	1.50
184	Norm Snead	5.00	2.50	1.50
185	Sam Brunelli	5.00	2.50	1.50
186	Jim Kiick **RC**	5.00	2.50	1.50
187	Austin Denney	5.00	2.50	1.50
188	Roger Wehrli **RC**	20.00	10.00	6.00
189	Dave Wilcox	5.00	2.50	1.50
190	Bob Hayes	5.00	2.50	1.50
191	Joe Morrison	5.00	2.50	1.50
192	Manny Sistrunk	5.00	2.50	1.50
193	Don Cockroft **RC**	5.00	2.50	1.50
194	Lee Bouggess	5.00	2.50	1.50
195	Bob Berry	5.00	2.50	1.50
196	Ron Sellers	5.00	2.50	1.50
197	George Webster	5.00	2.50	1.50
198	Hoyle Granger	5.00	2.50	1.50
199	Bob Vogel	5.00	2.50	1.50
200	Bart Starr	20.00	10.00	6.00
201	Mike Mercer	5.00	2.50	1.50
202	Dave Smith	5.00	2.50	1.50
203	Lee Roy Caffey	5.00	2.50	1.50
204	Mick Tingelhoff	5.00	2.50	1.50
205	Matt Snell	5.00	2.50	1.50
206	Jim Tyrer	5.00	2.50	1.50
207	Willie Brown	5.00	2.50	1.50
208	Bob Johnson **RC**	5.00	2.50	1.50
209	Deacon Jones	5.00	2.50	1.50
210	Charlie Sanders **RC**	25.00	13.00	8.00
211	Jake Scott **RC**	10.00	5.00	3.00
212	Bob Anderson **RC**	5.00	2.50	1.50
213	Charlie Krueger	5.00	2.50	1.50
214	Jim Bakken	5.00	2.50	1.50
215	Harold Jackson	5.00	2.50	1.50
216	Bill Brundige	5.00	2.50	1.50
217	Calvin Hill	10.00	5.00	3.00
218	Claude Humphrey	5.00	2.50	1.50
219	Glen Ray Hines	5.00	2.50	1.50
220	Bill Nelsen	5.00	2.50	1.50
221	Roy Hilton	5.00	2.50	1.50
222	Don Herrmann	5.00	2.50	1.50
223	John Bramlett	5.00	2.50	1.50
224	Ken Ellis	5.00	2.50	1.50
225	Dave Osborn	5.00	2.50	1.50
226	Edd Hargett **RC**	5.00	2.50	1.50
227	Gene Mingo	5.00	2.50	1.50
228	Larry Grantham	5.00	2.50	1.50
229	Dick Post	5.00	2.50	1.50
230	Roman Gabriel	5.00	2.50	1.50
231	Mike Eischeid	5.00	2.50	1.50
232	Jim Lynch	5.00	2.50	1.50
233	Lemar Parrish **RC**	5.00	2.50	1.50
234	Cecil Turner	5.00	2.50	1.50
235	Dennis Shaw **RC**	5.00	2.50	1.50
236	Mel Farr	5.00	2.50	1.50
237	Curt Knight	5.00	2.50	1.50
238	Chuck Howley	5.00	2.50	1.50
239	Bruce Taylor **RC**	5.00	2.50	1.50
240	Jerry LeVias	5.00	2.50	1.50
241	Bob Lurtsema	5.00	2.50	1.50
242	Earl Morrall	5.00	2.50	1.50
243	Kermit Alexander	5.00	2.50	1.50
244	Jackie Smith	5.00	2.50	1.50
245	Joe Greene **RC**	60.00	30.00	18.00
246	Harmon Wages	5.00	2.50	1.50
247	Errol Mann	5.00	2.50	1.50
248	Mike McCoy	5.00	2.50	1.50
249	Milt Morin **RC**	5.00	2.50	1.50
250	Joe Namath	60.00	30.00	18.00
251	Jackie Burkett	5.00	2.50	1.50
252	Steve Chomyszak	5.00	2.50	1.50
253	Ed Sharockman	5.00	2.50	1.50
254	Robert Holmes **RC**	5.00	2.50	1.50
255	John Hadl	5.00	2.50	1.50
256	Cornell Gordon	5.00	2.50	1.50
257	Mark Moseley **RC**	5.00	2.50	1.50
258	Gus Otto	5.00	2.50	1.50
259	Mike Taliaferro	5.00	2.50	1.50
260	O.J. Simpson	20.00	10.00	6.00
261	Paul Warfield	10.00	5.00	3.00
262	Jack Concannon	5.00	2.50	1.50
263	Tom Matte	10.00	5.00	3.00

1971 Topps Game Cards

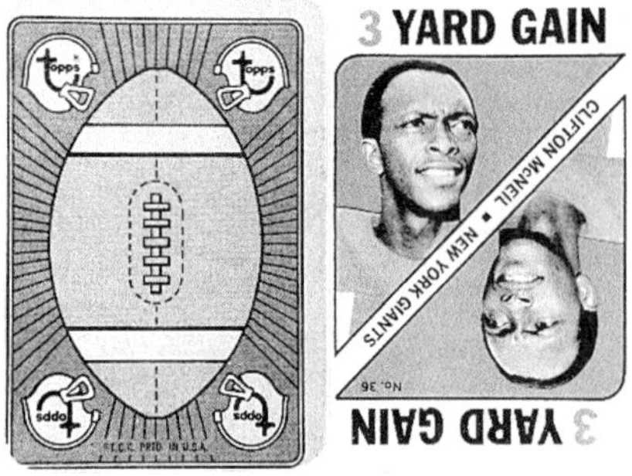

The 53 cards in this set came one per pack inside wax packs of 1971 Topps football cards. Intended for use in a card game, these cards are similar to playing cards and carry a head "Action" shot of the player, his name and team in a diagonal stripe across the front, and a play (such as "Interception," "Touchdown" and "Fumble") on the top and bottom. Card backs are light blue and show the Topps logo inside a football helmet surrounding a football. The set has 52 "playing cards" plus a "first down/field marker" for use with the game. Six of the cards in the series were double-printed: Dick Butkus, Bob Berry, Joe Namath, Andy Russell, Tom Woodeshick, and Bart Starr. (Key: DP -- double-printed)

		NM	E	VG
Complete Set (53):		125.00	65.00	40.00
Common Player:		.50	.25	.15
1	Dick Butkus (DP)	4.00	2.00	1.25
2	Bob Berry (DP)	.50	.25	.15
3	Joe Namath (DP)	17.00	8.50	4.75
4	Mike Curtis	.50	.25	.15
5	Jim Nance	.50	.25	.15
6	Ron Berger	.50	.25	.15
7	O.J. Simpson	20.00	10.00	6.00
8	Haven Moses	.50	.25	.15
9	Tommy Nobis	.50	.25	.15
10	Gale Sayers	9.00	4.50	2.75
11	Virgil Carter	.50	.25	.15
12	Andy Russell (DP)	.50	.25	.15
13	Bill Nelsen	.50	.25	.15
14	Gary Collins	.50	.25	.15
15	Duane Thomas	.50	.25	.15
16	Bob Hayes	.80	.40	.25
17	Floyd Little	.80	.40	.25

18	Sam Brunelli	.50	.25	.15
19	Charlie Sanders	.50	.25	.15
20	Mike Lucci	.50	.25	.15
21	Gene Washington (SF)	.80	.40	.25
22	Willie Wood	3.00	1.50	.90
23	Jerry LeVias	.50	.25	.15
24	Charlie Johnson	.80	.40	.25
25	Len Dawson	3.00	1.50	.90
26	Bobby Bell	2.00	1.00	.60
27	Merlin Olsen	3.00	1.50	.90
28	Roman Gabriel	2.00	1.00	.60
29	Bob Griese	4.00	2.00	1.25
30	Larry Csonka	4.00	2.00	1.25
31	Dave Osborn	.50	.25	.15
32	Gene Washington (MN)	.50	.25	.15
33	Dan Abramowicz	.50	.25	.15
34	Tom Dempsey	.50	.25	.15
35	Fran Tarkenton	9.00	4.50	2.75
36	Clifton McNeil	.50	.25	.15
37	Johnny Unitas	12.00	6.00	3.75
38	Matt Snell	.50	.25	.15
39	Daryle Lamonica	.80	.40	.25
40	Hewritt Dixon	.50	.25	.15
41	Tom Woodeshick (DP)	.50	.25	.15
42	Harold Jackson	.50	.25	.15
43	Terry Bradshaw	20.00	10.00	6.00
44	Ken Avery	.50	.25	.15
45	MacArthur Lane	.50	.25	.15
46	Larry Wilson	2.00	1.00	.60
47	John Hadl	1.00	.50	.30
48	Lance Alworth	2.00	1.00	.60
49	John Brodie	4.00	2.00	1.25
50	Bart Starr (DP)	6.00	3.00	1.75
51	Sonny Jurgensen	6.00	3.00	1.75
52	Larry Brown	.50	.25	.15
53	**Field Marker**	.50	.25	.15

1971 Topps Pin-Ups

These mini-posters (about 5" x 7") were folded twice and inserted into wax packs. The front features a head shot of the player, with his name in bold capitals above the photo and his team in smaller type at the bottom. Backs showed a football field with side markers, as well as the accompanying instructions. Because these posters were folded, it's very difficult, if not impossible, to find any in Mint condition.

		NM	E	VG
	Complete Set (32):	40.00	20.00	12.00
	Common Player:	.65	.32	.20
1	Gene Washington	.75	.37	.25
2	Andy Russell	.65	.32	.20
3	Harold Jackson	.65	.32	.20
4	Joe Namath	12.00	6.00	3.75
5	Fran Tarkenton	5.00	2.50	1.50
6	Dave Osborn	.65	.32	.20
7	Bob Griese	2.50	1.25	.75
8	Roman Gabriel	1.00	.50	.30
9	Jerry LeVias	.65	.32	.20
10	Bart Starr	5.00	2.50	1.50
11	Bob Hayes	1.00	.50	.30
12	Gale Sayers	5.50	2.25	1.10
13	O.J. Simpson	7.50	3.75	2.25
14	Sam Brunelli	.65	.32	.20
15	Jim Nance	.65	.32	.20
16	Bill Nelsen	.65	.32	.20
17	Sonny Jurgensen	2.50	1.25	.75
18	John Brodie	2.50	1.25	.75
19	Lance Alworth	1.50	.75	.45
20	Larry Wilson	1.00	.50	.30
21	Daryle Lamonica	.75	.37	.25
22	Dan Abramowicz	.65	.32	.20
23	Gene Washington (Minn)	.65	.32	.20
24	Bobby Bell	1.50	.75	.45
25	Merlin Olsen	2.00	1.00	.60
26	Charlie Sanders	.65	.32	.20
27	Virgil Carter	.65	.32	.20
28	Dick Butkus	2.50	1.25	.75
29	Johnny Unitas	7.00	3.50	2.25
30	Tommy Nobis	.75	.37	.25
31	Floyd Little	.65	.32	.20
32	Larry Brown	.65	.32	.20

1972 Topps

The 1972 set, a 351-card edition, was Topps' last to be issued in series form. The first series includes cards #1-132; the second - somewhat harder to find than the first - includes cards #133-263; and the final series - the difficult series - shows cards #264-351. Because of the difficulty in acquiring a complete set, this is easily the most expensive Topps set of the 1970s. Subsets in this issue include statistical leaders, playoffs, All-Pros and In Action cards. Rookies in the set include John Riggins, Archie Manning, Jim Plunkett, John Brockington, Ted Hendricks, L.C. Greenwood, Lyle Alzado, Dan Pastorini, Gene Upshaw, Charlie Joiner and Steve Spurrier. (Key: IA - in action, AP - All Pro)

		NM	E	VG
	Complete Set (351):	2,500	1,125	675.00
	Common Player (1-132):	4.00	2.00	1.25
	Minor Stars (1-132):	1.00		
	Unlisted Stars (1-132):	1.50		
	Common Player (133-263):	4.00	2.00	1.25
	Minor Stars (133-132):	1.50		
	Unlisted Stars (133-263):	2.50		
	Common Player (264-351):	10.00	5.00	3.00
	Minor Stars (264-351):	25.00		
	Unlisted Stars (264-351):	30.00		
	Series 1 Wax Pack (10):	75.00		
	Series 1 Wax Box (24):	1,525		
	Series 2 Wax Pack (10):	110.00		
	Series 2 Wax Box (24):	2,250		
	Series 3 Wax Pack (10):	310.00		
	Series 3 Wax Box (24):	6,325		
1	AFC rushing leaders (Floyd Little, Larry Csonka)	15.00	7.50	4.50
2	NFC rushing leaders (John Brockington, Steve Owens, Willie Ellison)	4.00	2.00	1.25
3	AFC passing leaders (Bob Griese, Len Dawson)	8.00	4.00	2.40
4	NFC passing leaders (Roger Staubach, Bill Kilmer)	8.00	4.00	2.40
5	AFC receiving leaders (Fred Biletnikoff, Otis Taylor, Randy Vataha)	4.00	2.00	1.25
6	NFC receiving leaders (Bob Tucker, Ted Kwalick, Harold Jackson, Roy Jefferson)	4.00	2.00	1.25
7	AFC scoring leaders (Garo Yepremian, Jan Stenerud)	4.00	2.00	1.25
8	NFC scoring leaders (Curt Knight, Errol Mann, Bruce Gossett)	4.00	2.00	1.25
9	Jim Kiick	4.00	2.00	1.25
10	Otis Taylor	4.00	2.00	1.25
11	Bobby Joe Green	4.00	2.00	1.25
12	Ken Ellis	4.00	2.00	1.25
13	John Riggins **RC**	15.00	7.50	4.50
14	Dave Parks	4.00	2.00	1.25
15	John Hadl	4.00	2.00	1.25
16	Ron Hornsby	4.00	2.00	1.25
17	Chip Myers	4.00	2.00	1.25
18	Bill Kilmer	4.00	2.00	1.25
19	Fred Hoaglin	4.00	2.00	1.25
20	Carl Eller	4.00	2.00	1.25
21	Steve Zabel	4.00	2.00	1.25
22	Vic Washington **RC**	4.00	2.00	1.25
23	Len St. Jean	4.00	2.00	1.25
24	Bill Thompson	4.00	2.00	1.25
25	Steve Owens **RC**	4.00	2.00	1.25
26	Ken Burrough **RC**	4.00	2.00	1.25
27	Mike Clark	4.00	2.00	1.25
28	Willie Brown	4.00	2.00	1.25
29	**Checklist 1-132**	10.00	5.00	3.00
30	Marlin Briscoe	4.00	2.00	1.25
31	Jerry Logan	4.00	2.00	1.25
32	Donny Anderson	4.00	2.00	1.25
33	Rich McGeorge	4.00	2.00	1.25
34	Charlie Durkee	4.00	2.00	1.25
35	Willie Lanier	5.00	2.50	1.50
36	Chris Farasopoulos	4.00	2.00	1.25
37	Ronnie Shanklin	4.00	2.00	1.25
38	Forrest Blue **RC**	4.00	2.00	1.25
39	Ken Reaves	4.00	2.00	1.25
40	Roman Gabriel	5.00	2.50	1.50
41	Mac Percival	4.00	2.00	1.25
42	Lem Barney	4.00	2.00	1.25
43	Nick Buoniconti	4.00	2.00	1.25
44	Charlie Gogolak	4.00	2.00	1.25
45	Bill Bradley **RC**	4.00	2.00	1.25
46	Joe Jones	4.00	2.00	1.25
47	Dave Williams	4.00	2.00	1.25
48	Pete Athas	4.00	2.00	1.25
49	Virgil Carter	4.00	2.00	1.25
50	Floyd Little	4.00	2.00	1.25
51	Curt Knight	4.00	2.00	1.25
52	Bobby Maples	4.00	2.00	1.25
53	Charlie West	4.00	2.00	1.25
54	Marv Hubbard **RC**	4.00	2.00	1.25
55	Archie Manning **RC**	15.00	7.50	4.50
56	Jim O'Brien **RC**	4.00	2.00	1.25
57	Wayne Patrick	4.00	2.00	1.25
58	Ken Bowman	4.00	2.00	1.25
59	Roger Wehrli	4.00	2.00	1.25
60	Charlie Sanders	4.00	2.00	1.25
61	Jan Stenerud	4.00	2.00	1.25
62	Willie Ellison	4.00	2.00	1.25
63	Walt Sweeney	4.00	2.00	1.25
64	Ron Smith	4.00	2.00	1.25
65	Jim Plunkett **RC**	15.00	7.50	4.50
66	Herb Adderly	4.00	2.00	1.25
67	Mike Reid **RC**	4.00	2.00	1.25
68	Richard Caster **RC**	4.00	2.00	1.25
69	Dave Wilcox	4.00	2.00	1.25
70	Leroy Kelly	4.00	2.00	1.25
71	Bob Lee **RC**	4.00	2.00	1.25
72	Verlon Biggs	4.00	2.00	1.25
73	Henry Allison	4.00	2.00	1.25
74	Steve Ramsey	4.00	2.00	1.25
75	Claude Humphrey	4.00	2.00	1.25
76	Bob Grim **RC**	4.00	2.00	1.25
77	John Fuqua	4.00	2.00	1.25
78	Ken Houston	8.00	4.00	2.40
79	**Checklist 133-263**	4.00	2.00	1.25
80	Bob Griese	10.00	5.00	3.00
81	Lance Rentzel	4.00	2.00	1.25
82	Ed Podolak **RC**	4.00	2.00	1.25
83	Ike Hill	4.00	2.00	1.25
84	George Farmer	4.00	2.00	1.25
85	John Brockington **RC**	4.00	2.00	1.25
86	Jim Otto	4.00	2.00	1.25
87	Richard Neal	4.00	2.00	1.25
88	Jim Hart	4.00	2.00	1.25
89	Bob Babich	4.00	2.00	1.25
90	Gene Washington (S.F.)	4.00	2.00	1.25
91	John Zook	4.00	2.00	1.25
92	Bobby Duhon	4.00	2.00	1.25
93	Ted Hendricks **RC**	20.00	10.00	6.00
94	Rockne Freitas	4.00	2.00	1.25
95	Larry Brown	4.00	2.00	1.25
96	Mike Phipps	4.00	2.00	1.25
97	Julius Adams	4.00	2.00	1.25
98	Dick Anderson	4.00	2.00	1.25
99	Fred Willis	4.00	2.00	1.25
100	Joe Namath	25.00	13.00	8.00
101	L.C. Greenwood **RC**	10.00	5.00	3.00
102	Mark Nordquist	4.00	2.00	1.25
103	Robert Holmes	4.00	2.00	1.25
104	Ron Yary **RC**	15.00	7.50	4.50
105	Bob Hayes	4.00	2.00	1.25
106	Lyle Alzado **RC**	10.00	5.00	3.00
107	Bob Berry	4.00	2.00	1.25
108	Phil Villapiano **RC**	4.00	2.00	1.25
109	Dave Elmendorf	4.00	2.00	1.25
110	Gale Sayers	20.00	10.00	6.00
111	Jim Tyrer	4.00	2.00	1.25
112	Mel Gray **RC**	4.00	2.00	1.25
113	Gerry Philbin	4.00	2.00	1.25
114	Bob James	4.00	2.00	1.25
115	Garo Yepremian	4.00	2.00	1.25
116	Dave Robinson	4.00	2.00	1.25
117	Jeff Queen	4.00	2.00	1.25
118	Norm Snead	4.00	2.00	1.25
119	Jim Nance (IA)	4.00	2.00	1.25
120	Terry Bradshaw (IA)	10.00	5.00	3.00
121	Jim Kiick (IA)	4.00	2.00	1.25
122	Roger Staubach (IA)	10.00	5.00	3.00
123	Bo Scott (IA)	4.00	2.00	1.25
124	John Brodie (IA)	4.00	2.00	1.25
125	Rick Volk (IA)	4.00	2.00	1.25
126	John Riggins (IA)	5.00	2.50	1.50
127	Bubba Smith (IA)	4.00	2.00	1.25
128	Roman Gabriel (IA)	4.00	2.00	1.25
129	Calvin Hill (IA)	4.00	2.00	1.25
130	Bill Nelsen (IA)	4.00	2.00	1.25
131	Tom Matte (IA)	4.00	2.00	1.25
132	Bob Griese (IA)	8.00	4.00	2.40

133	**AFC semi-final**	4.00	2.00	1.25
134	NFC semi-final (Duane Thomas)	4.00	2.00	1.25
135	AFC semi-final (Don Nottingham)	4.00	2.00	1.25
136	**NFC semi-final**	4.00	2.00	1.25
137	**AFC Championship**	4.00	2.00	1.25
138	**NFC Championship**	4.00	2.00	1.25
139	**Super Bowl**	8.00	4.00	2.40
140	Larry Csonka	10.00	5.00	3.00
141	Rick Volk	4.00	2.00	1.25
142	Roy Jefferson	4.00	2.00	1.25
143	Raymond Chester **RC**	4.00	2.00	1.25
144	Bobby Douglass	4.00	2.00	1.25
145	Bob Lilly	8.00	4.00	2.40
146	Harold Jackson	4.00	2.00	1.25
147	Pete Gogolak	4.00	2.00	1.25
148	Art Malone	4.00	2.00	1.25
149	Ed Flanagan	4.00	2.00	1.25
150	Terry Bradshaw	35.00	18.00	11.00
151	MacArthur Lane	4.00	2.00	1.25
152	Jack Snow	4.00	2.00	1.25
153	Al Beauchamp	4.00	2.00	1.25
154	Bob Anderson	4.00	2.00	1.25
155	Ted Kwalick **RC**	4.00	2.00	1.25
156	Dan Pastorini **RC**	4.00	2.00	1.25
157	Emmitt Thomas **RC**	15.00	7.50	4.50
158	Randy Vataha **RC**	4.00	2.00	1.25
159	Al Atkinson	4.00	2.00	1.25
160	O.J. Simpson	10.00	5.00	3.00
161	Jackie Smith	4.00	2.00	1.25
162	Ernie Kellerman	4.00	2.00	1.25
163	Dennis Partee	4.00	2.00	1.25
164	Jake Kupp	4.00	2.00	1.25
165	Johnny Unitas	15.00	7.50	4.50
166	Clint Jones	4.00	2.00	1.25
167	Paul Warfield	4.00	2.00	1.25
168	Roland McDole	4.00	2.00	1.25
169	Daryle Lamonica	4.00	2.00	1.25
170	Dick Butkus	20.00	10.00	6.00
171	Jim Butler	4.00	2.00	1.25
172	Mike McCoy	4.00	2.00	1.25
173	Dave Smith	4.00	2.00	1.25
174	Greg Landry	4.00	2.00	1.25
175	Tom Dempsey	4.00	2.00	1.25
176	John Charles	4.00	2.00	1.25
177	Bobby Bell	4.00	2.00	1.25
178	Don Horn	4.00	2.00	1.25
179	Bob Trumpy	4.00	2.00	1.25
180	Duane Thomas	4.00	2.00	1.25
181	Merlin Olsen	4.00	2.00	1.25
182	Dave Herman	4.00	2.00	1.25
183	Jim Nance	4.00	2.00	1.25
184	Pete Beathard	4.00	2.00	1.25
185	Bob Tucker	4.00	2.00	1.25
186	Gene Upshaw **RC**	14.00	7.00	4.25
187	Bo Scott	4.00	2.00	1.25
188	J.D. Hill **RC**	4.00	2.00	1.25
189	Bruce Gossett	4.00	2.00	1.25
190	Bubba Smith	4.00	2.00	1.25
191	Edd Hargett	4.00	2.00	1.25
192	Gary Garrison	4.00	2.00	1.25
193	Jake Scott	4.00	2.00	1.25
194	Fred Cox	4.00	2.00	1.25
195	Sonny Jurgensen	5.00	2.50	1.50
196	Greg Brezina **RC**	4.00	2.00	1.25
197	Ed O'Bradovich	4.00	2.00	1.25
198	John Rowser	4.00	2.00	1.25
199	Altie Taylor	4.00	2.00	1.25
200	Roger Staubach **RC**	150.00	75.00	45.00
201	Leroy Keyes **RC**	4.00	2.00	1.25
202	Garland Boyette	4.00	2.00	1.25
203	Tom Beer	4.00	2.00	1.25
204	Buck Buchanan	4.00	2.00	1.25
205	Larry Wilson	4.00	2.00	1.25
206	Scott Hunter **RC**	4.00	2.00	1.25
207	Ron Johnson	4.00	2.00	1.25
208	Sam Brunelli	4.00	2.00	1.25
209	Deacon Jones	4.00	2.00	1.25
210	Fred Biletnikoff	8.00	4.00	2.40
211	Bill Nelson	4.00	2.00	1.25
212	George Nock	4.00	2.00	1.25
213	Dan Abramowicz	4.00	2.00	1.25
214	Irv Goode	4.00	2.00	1.25
215	Isiah Robertson **RC**	4.00	2.00	1.25
216	Tom Matte	4.00	2.00	1.25
217	Pat Fischer	4.00	2.00	1.25
218	Gene Washington	4.00	2.00	1.25
219	Paul Robinson	4.00	2.00	1.25
220	John Brodie	8.00	4.00	2.40
221	Manny Fernandez **RC**	4.00	2.00	1.25
222	Errol Mann	4.00	2.00	1.25
223	Dick Gordon	4.00	2.00	1.25
224	Calvin Hill	4.00	2.00	1.25
225	Fran Tarkenton	10.00	5.00	3.00
226	Jim Turner	4.00	2.00	1.25
227	Jim Mitchell	4.00	2.00	1.25
228	Pete Liske	4.00	2.00	1.25
229	Carl Garrett	4.00	2.00	1.25
230	Joe Greene	20.00	10.00	6.00
231	Gale Gillingham	4.00	2.00	1.25
232	Norm Bulaich **RC**	4.00	2.00	1.25
233	Spider Lockhart	4.00	2.00	1.25
234	Ken Willard	4.00	2.00	1.25
235	George Blanda	10.00	5.00	3.00
236	Wayne Mulligan	4.00	2.00	1.25
237	Dave Lewis	4.00	2.00	1.25
238	Dennis Shaw	4.00	2.00	1.25
239	Fair Hooker	4.00	2.00	1.25
240	Larry Little **RC**	15.00	7.50	4.50
241	Mike Garrett	4.00	2.00	1.25
242	Glen Ray Hines	4.00	2.00	1.25
243	Myron Pottios	4.00	2.00	1.25
244	Charlie Joiner **RC**	15.00	7.50	4.50
245	Len Dawson	8.00	4.00	2.40
246	W.K. Hicks	4.00	2.00	1.25
247	Les Josephson	4.00	2.00	1.25
248	Lance Alworth	8.00	4.00	2.40
249	Frank Nunley	4.00	2.00	1.25
250	Mel Farr (IA)	4.00	2.00	1.25
251	Johnny Unitas (IA)	10.00	5.00	3.00
252	George Farmer (IA)	4.00	2.00	1.25
253	Duane Thomas (IA)	4.00	2.00	1.25
254	John Hadl (IA)	4.00	2.00	1.25
255	Vic Washington (IA)	4.00	2.00	1.25
256	Don Horn (IA)	4.00	2.00	1.25
257	L.C. Greenwood (IA)	4.00	2.00	1.25
258	Bob Lee (IA)	4.00	2.00	1.25
259	Larry Csonka (IA)	5.00	2.50	1.50
260	Mike McCoy (IA)	4.00	2.00	1.25
261	Greg Landry (IA)	4.00	2.00	1.25
262	Ray May (IA)	4.00	2.00	1.25
263	Bobby Douglass (IA)	4.00	2.00	1.25
264	Charlie Sanders (AP)	15.00	7.50	4.50
265	Ron Yary (AP)	15.00	7.50	4.50
266	Rayfield Wright (AP)	10.00	5.00	3.00
267	Larry Little (AP)	20.00	10.00	6.00
268	John Niland (AP)	10.00	5.00	3.00
269	Forrest Blue (AP)	10.00	5.00	3.00
270	Otis Taylor (AP)	15.00	7.50	4.50
271	Paul Warfield (AP)	20.00	10.00	6.00
272	Bob Griese (AP)	30.00	15.00	9.00
273	John Brockington (AP)	10.00	5.00	3.00
274	Floyd Little (AP)	20.00	10.00	6.00
275	Garo Yepremian (AP)	10.00	5.00	3.00
276	Jerrel Wilson (AP)	10.00	5.00	3.00
277	Carl Eller (AP)	15.00	7.50	4.50
278	Bubba Smith (AP)	15.00	7.50	4.50
279	Alan Page (AP)	20.00	10.00	6.00
280	Bob Lilly (AP)	25.00	13.00	8.00
281	Ted Hendricks (AP)	20.00	10.00	6.00
282	Dave Wilcox (AP)	10.00	5.00	3.00
283	Willie Lanier (AP)	20.00	10.00	6.00
284	Jim Johnson (AP)	10.00	5.00	3.00
285	Willie Brown (AP)	20.00	10.00	6.00
286	Bill Bradley (AP)	10.00	5.00	3.00
287	Ken Houston (AP)	20.00	10.00	6.00
288	Mel Farr	10.00	5.00	3.00
289	Kermit Alexander	10.00	5.00	3.00
290	John Gilliam **RC**	10.00	5.00	3.00
291	Steve Spurrier **RC**	60.00	30.00	18.00
292	Walter Johnson	10.00	5.00	3.00
293	Jack Pardee	15.00	7.50	4.50
294	**Checklist 264-351**	30.00	15.00	9.00
295	Winston Hill	10.00	5.00	3.00
296	Hugo Hollas	10.00	5.00	3.00
297	Ray May **RC**	10.00	5.00	3.00
298	Jim Bakken	10.00	5.00	3.00
299	Larry Carwell	10.00	5.00	3.00
300	Alan Page	30.00	15.00	9.00
301	Walt Garrison	10.00	7.50	4.50
302	Mike Lucci	10.00	5.00	3.00
303	Nemiah Wilson	10.00	5.00	3.00
304	Carroll Dale	10.00	5.00	3.00
305	Jim Kanicki	10.00	5.00	3.00
306	Preston Pearson	25.00	12.50	7.50
307	Lemar Parrish	15.00	7.50	4.50
308	Earl Morrall	10.00	5.00	3.00
309	Tommy Nobis	10.00	5.00	3.00
310	Rich Jackson	10.00	5.00	3.00
311	Doug Cunningham	10.00	5.00	3.00
312	Jim Marsalis	10.00	5.00	3.00
313	Jim Beirne	10.00	5.00	3.00
314	Tom McNeill	10.00	5.00	3.00
315	Milt Morin	10.00	5.00	3.00
316	Rayfield Wright **RC**	50.00	25.00	15.00
317	Jerry LeVias	15.00	7.50	4.50
318	Travis Williams **RC**	15.00	7.50	4.50
319	Edgar Chandler	10.00	5.00	3.00
320	Bob Wallace	10.00	5.00	3.00
321	Delles Howell	10.00	5.00	3.00
322	Emerson Boozer	10.00	5.00	3.00
323	George Atkinson **RC**	10.00	5.00	3.00
324	Mike Montler	10.00	5.00	3.00
325	Randy Johnson	10.00	5.00	3.00
326	Mike Curtis	15.00	7.50	4.50
327	Miller Farr	10.00	5.00	3.00
328	Horst Muhlmann	10.00	5.00	3.00
329	John Niland **RC**	10.00	5.00	3.00
330	Andy Russell	25.00	13.00	8.00
331	Mercury Morris	25.00	13.00	8.00
332	Jim Johnson	10.00	5.00	3.00
333	Jerrel Wilson	10.00	5.00	3.00
334	Charley Taylor	25.00	13.00	8.00
335	Dick LeBeau	10.00	5.00	3.00
336	Jim Marshall	10.00	5.00	3.00
337	Tom Mack	10.00	5.00	3.00
338	Steve Spurrier (IA)	25.00	13.00	8.00
339	Floyd Little (IA)	20.00	10.00	6.00
340	Len Dawson (IA)	20.00	10.00	6.00
341	Dick Butkus (IA)	35.00	18.00	11.00
342	Larry Brown (IA)	10.00	5.00	3.00
343	Joe Namath (IA)	75.00	38.00	23.00
344	Jim Turner (IA)	10.00	5.00	3.00
345	Doug Cunningham (IA)	10.00	5.00	3.00
346	Edd Hargett (IA)	10.00	5.00	3.00
347	Steve Owens (IA)	10.00	5.00	3.00
348	George Blanda (IA)	25.00	13.00	8.00
349	Ed Podolak (IA)	10.00	5.00	3.00
350	Rich Jackson (IA)	10.00	5.00	3.00
351	Ken Willard (IA)	30.00	15.00	9.00

1973 Topps

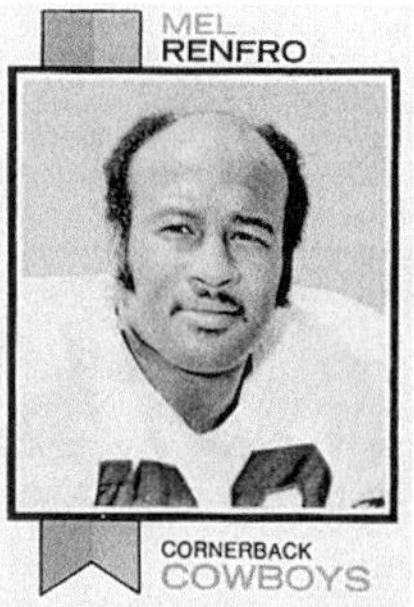
MEL
RENFRO
CORNERBACK
COWBOYS

This issue might have been Topps' most important of the decade for a number of reasons. The 1973 set was Topps' first of 10 consecutive football sets at 528 cards, and its first major set that was issued all at once instead of in a series. This coincides with its cutback in baseball cards (787 to 660) and emphasis on football and basketball; it also signaled the end of Topps' high-series release. Subsets in the 1973 release include the usual statistical leaders and playoffs, plus three cards depicting childhood photos of NFL stars. Rookies in this set include Ken Anderson, Lydell Mitchell, Franco Harris, Jack Ham, Art Shell, Ken Riley, Jack Tatum, Dan Dierdorf, Jim Langer, Jack Youngblood and Ken Stabler. Though he went on to play several more years with the Rams and Jets, Joe Namath's final regular-issue card appears in this set. Like Earl Campbell several years later, he apparently was unable to reach a contract agreement after this season. One other item of note: this set has a few of the most unique player names of any football issue: Chip Glass, Happy Feller, and the immortal Remi Prudhomme.

	NM	E	VG
Complete Set (528):	950.00	475.00	285.00
Common Player:	3.00	1.50	.90
Minor Stars:	.75		
Unlisted Stars:	1.00		
Wax Pack (10+1):	88.50		
Wax Box (24):	1,850		
Wax Pack (15):	115.00		
Wax Box (24):	2,450		

1	Rushing Leaders (Larry Brown, O.J. Simpson)	10.00	5.00	3.00
2	Passing Leaders (Norm Snead, Earl Morrall)	3.00	1.50	.90
3	Receiving Leaders (Harold Jackson, Fred Biletnikoff)	3.00	1.50	.90
4	Scoring Leaders (Chester Marcol, Bobby Howfield)	3.00	1.50	.90
5	Interception Leaders (Bill Bradley, Mike Sensibaugh)	3.00	1.50	.90
6	Punting Leaders (Dave Chapple, Jerrell Wilson)	3.00	1.50	.90
7	Bob Trumpy	3.00	1.50	.90
8	Mel Tom	3.00	1.50	.90
9	Clarence Ellis	3.00	1.50	.90
10	John Niland	3.00	1.50	.90
11	Randy Jackson	3.00	1.50	.90
12	Greg Landry	3.00	1.50	.90
13	Cid Edwards	3.00	1.50	.90
14	Phil Olsen	3.00	1.50	.90

15	Terry Bradshaw	15.00	7.50	4.50
16	Al Cowlings **RC**	4.00	2.00	.90
17	Walker Gillette	3.00	1.50	.90
18	Bob Atkins	3.00	1.50	.90
19	Diron Talbert **RC**	3.00	1.50	.90
20	Jim Johnson **RC**	3.00	1.50	.90
21	Howard Twilley	3.00	1.50	.90
22	Dick Enderle	3.00	1.50	.90
23	Wayne Colman	3.00	1.50	.90
24	John Schmitt	3.00	1.50	.90
25	George Blanda	5.00	2.50	1.50
26	Milt Morin	3.00	1.50	.90
27	Mike Current	3.00	1.50	.90
28	Rex Kern **RC**	3.00	1.50	.90
29	MacArthur Lane	3.00	1.50	.90
30	Alan Page	3.00	1.50	.90
31	Randy Vataha	3.00	1.50	.90
32	Jim Kearney	3.00	1.50	.90
33	Steve Smith	3.00	1.50	.90
34	Ken Anderson **RC**	15.00	7.50	4.50
35	Calvin Hill	3.00	1.50	.90
36	Andy Maurer	3.00	1.50	.90
37	Joe Taylor	3.00	1.50	.90
38	Deacon Jones	3.00	1.50	.90
39	Mike Weger	3.00	1.50	.90
40	Roy Gerela	3.00	1.50	.90
41	Les Josephson	3.00	1.50	.90
42	Dave Washington	3.00	1.50	.90
43	Bill Curry **RC**	3.00	1.50	.90
44	Fred Heron	3.00	1.50	.90
45	John Brodie	3.00	1.50	.90
46	Roy Winston	3.00	1.50	.90
47	Mike Bragg	3.00	1.50	.90
48	Mercury Morris	3.00	1.50	.90
49	Jim Files	3.00	1.50	.90
50	Gene Upshaw	3.00	1.50	.90
51	Hugo Hollas	3.00	1.50	.90
52	Rod Sherman	3.00	1.50	.90
53	Ron Snidow	3.00	1.50	.90
54	Steve Tannen	3.00	1.50	.90
55	Jim Carter	3.00	1.50	.90
56	Lydell Mitchell **RC**	3.00	1.50	.90
57	Jack Rudnay **RC**	3.00	1.50	.90
58	Halvor Hagen	3.00	1.50	.90
59	Tom Dempsey	3.00	1.50	.90
60	Fran Tarkenton	10.00	5.00	3.00
61	Lance Alworth	5.00	2.50	1.50
62	Vern Holland	3.00	1.50	.90
63	Steve DeLong	3.00	1.50	.90
64	Art Malone	3.00	1.50	.90
65	Isiah Robertson	3.00	1.50	.90
66	Jerry Rush	3.00	1.50	.90
67	Bryant Salter	3.00	1.50	.90
68	**Checklist 1-132**	3.00	1.50	.90
69	J.D. Hill	3.00	1.50	.90
70	Forrest Blue	3.00	1.50	.90
71	Myron Pottios	3.00	1.50	.90
72	Norm Thompson **RC**	3.00	1.50	.90
73	Paul Robinson	3.00	1.50	.90
74	Larry Grantham	3.00	1.50	.90
75	Manny Fernandez	3.00	1.50	.90
76	Kent Nix	3.00	1.50	.90
77	Art Shell **RC**	15.00	7.50	4.50
78	George Saimes	3.00	1.50	.90
79	Don Cockroft	3.00	1.50	.90
80	Bob Tucker	3.00	1.50	.90
81	Don McCauley **RC**	3.00	1.50	.90
82	Bob Brown	3.00	1.50	.90
83	Larry Carwell	3.00	1.50	.90
84	Mo Moorman	3.00	1.50	.90
85	John Gilliam	3.00	1.50	.90
86	Wade Key	3.00	1.50	.90
87	Ross Brupbacher	3.00	1.50	.90
88	Dave Lewis	3.00	1.50	.90
89	Franco Harris **RC**	40.00	20.00	12.00
90	Tom Mack	3.00	1.50	.90
91	Mike Tilleman	3.00	1.50	.90
92	Carl Mauck	3.00	1.50	.90
93	Larry Hand	3.00	1.50	.90
94	Dave Foley	3.00	1.50	.90
95	Frank Nunley	3.00	1.50	.90
96	John Charles	3.00	1.50	.90
97	Jim Bakken	3.00	1.50	.90
98	Pat Fischer	3.00	1.50	.90
99	Randy Rasmussen	3.00	1.50	.90
100	Larry Csonka	5.00	2.50	1.50
101	Mike Siani **RC**	3.00	1.50	.90
102	Tom Roussel	3.00	1.50	.90
103	Clarence Scott **RC**	3.00	1.50	.90
104	Charlie Johnson	3.00	1.50	.90
105	Rick Volk	3.00	1.50	.90
106	Willie Young	3.00	1.50	.90
107	Emmitt Thomas	3.00	1.50	.90
108	Jon Morris	3.00	1.50	.90
109	Clarence Williams	3.00	1.50	.90
110	Rayfield Wright	3.00	1.50	.90
111	Norm Bulaich	3.00	1.50	.90
112	Mike Eischeid	3.00	1.50	.90
113	Speedy Thomas	3.00	1.50	.90
114	Glen Holloway	3.00	1.50	.90
115	Jack Ham **RC**	20.00	10.00	6.00
116	Jim Nettles	3.00	1.50	.90
117	Errol Mann	3.00	1.50	.90
118	John Mackey	3.00	1.50	.90
119	George Kunz	3.00	1.50	.90
120	Bob James	3.00	1.50	.90
121	Garland Boyette	3.00	1.50	.90
122	Mel Phillips	3.00	1.50	.90
123	Johnny Roland	3.00	1.50	.90
124	Doug Swift	3.00	1.50	.90
125	Archie Manning	3.00	1.50	.90
126	Dave Herman	3.00	1.50	.90
127	Carleton Oats	3.00	1.50	.90
128	Bill Van Heusen	3.00	1.50	.90
129	Rich Jackson	3.00	1.50	.90
130	Len Hauss	3.00	1.50	.90
131	Billy Parks **RC**	3.00	1.50	.90
132	Ray May	3.00	1.50	.90
133	NFC Semi-Final (Roger Staubach)	8.00	4.00	2.40
134	**AFC Semi-Final**	3.00	1.50	.90
135	**NFC Semi-Final**	3.00	1.50	.90
136	AFC Semi-Final (Bob Griese, Larry Csonka)	3.00	1.50	.90
137	NFC Championship (Bill Kilmer, Larry Brown)	3.00	1.50	.90
138	**AFC Championship**	3.00	1.50	.90
139	**Super Bowl**	3.00	1.50	.90
140	Dwight White **RC**	3.00	1.50	.90
141	Jim Marsalis	3.00	1.50	.90
142	Doug Van Horn	3.00	1.50	.90
143	Al Matthews	3.00	1.50	.90
144	Bob Windsor	3.00	1.50	.90
145	Dave Hampton **RC**	3.00	1.50	.90
146	Horst Muhlmann	3.00	1.50	.90
147	Wally Hilgenberg **RC**	3.00	1.50	.90
148	Ron Smith	3.00	1.50	.90
149	Coy Bacon **RC**	3.00	1.50	.90
150	Winston Hill	3.00	1.50	.90
151	Ron Jessie **RC**	3.00	1.50	.90
152	Ken Iman	3.00	1.50	.90
153	Ron Saul	3.00	1.50	.90
154	Jim Braxton **RC**	3.00	1.50	.90
155	Bubba Smith	3.00	1.50	.90
156	Gary Cuozzo	3.00	1.50	.90
157	Charlie Krueger	3.00	1.50	.90
158	Tim Foley **RC**	3.00	1.50	.90
159	Lee Roy Jordan	3.00	1.50	.90
160	Bob Brown	3.00	1.50	.90
161	Margene Adkins	3.00	1.50	.90
162	Ron Widby	3.00	1.50	.90
163	Jim Houston	3.00	1.50	.90
164	Joe Dawkins	3.00	1.50	.90
165	L.C. Greenwood	5.00	2.50	1.50
166	Richmond Flowers	3.00	1.50	.90
167	Curley Culp **RC**	3.00	1.50	.90
168	Len St. Jean	3.00	1.50	.90
169	Walter Rock	3.00	1.50	.90
170	Bill Bradley	3.00	1.50	.90
171	Ken Riley **RC**	3.00	1.50	.90
172	Rich Coady	3.00	1.50	.90
173	Don Hansen	3.00	1.50	.90
174	Lionel Aldridge	3.00	1.50	.90
175	Don Maynard	5.00	2.50	1.50
176	Dave Osborn	3.00	1.50	.90
177	Jim Bailey	3.00	1.50	.90
178	John Pitts	3.00	1.50	.90
179	Dave Parks	3.00	1.50	.90
180	Chester Marcol **RC**	3.00	1.50	.90
181	Len Rohde	3.00	1.50	.90
182	Jeff Staggs	3.00	1.50	.90
183	Gene Hickerson	3.00	1.50	.90
184	Charlie Evans	3.00	1.50	.90
185	Mel Renfro	3.00	1.50	.90
186	Marvin Upshaw	3.00	1.50	.90
187	George Atkinson	3.00	1.50	.90
188	Norm Evans	3.00	1.50	.90
189	Steve Ramsey	3.00	1.50	.90
190	Dave Chapple	3.00	1.50	.90
191	Gerry Mullins	3.00	1.50	.90
192	John Didion	3.00	1.50	.90
193	Bob Gladieux	3.00	1.50	.90
194	Don Hultz	3.00	1.50	.90
195	Mike Lucci	3.00	1.50	.90
196	John Wilbur	3.00	1.50	.90
197	George Farmer	3.00	1.50	.90
198	Tommy Casanova **RC**	3.00	1.50	.90
199	Russ Washington	3.00	1.50	.90
200	Claude Humphrey	3.00	1.50	.90
201	Pat Hughes	3.00	1.50	.90
202	Zeke Moore	3.00	1.50	.90
203	Chip Glass	3.00	1.50	.90
204	Glenn Ressler	3.00	1.50	.90
205	Willie Ellison	3.00	1.50	.90
206	John Leypoldt	3.00	1.50	.90
207	Johnny Fuller	3.00	1.50	.90
208	Bill Hayhoe	3.00	1.50	.90
209	Ed Bell	3.00	1.50	.90
210	Willie Brown	3.00	1.50	.90
211	Carl Eller	3.00	1.50	.90
212	Mark Nordquist	3.00	1.50	.90
213	Larry Willingham	3.00	1.50	.90
214	Nick Buoniconti	3.00	1.50	.90
215	John Hadl	3.00	1.50	.90
216	Jethro Pugh **RC**	3.00	1.50	.90
217	Leroy Mitchell	3.00	1.50	.90
218	Billy Newsome	3.00	1.50	.90
219	John McMakin	3.00	1.50	.90
220	Larry Brown	3.00	1.50	.90
221	Clarence Scott	3.00	1.50	.90
222	Paul Naumoff	3.00	1.50	.90
223	Ted Fritsch	3.00	1.50	.90
224	**Checklist 133-264**	3.00	1.50	.90
225	Dan Pastorini	3.00	1.50	.90
226	Joe Beauchamp	3.00	1.50	.90
227	Pat Matson	3.00	1.50	.90
228	Tony McGee	3.00	1.50	.90
229	Mike Phipps	3.00	1.50	.90
230	Harold Jackson	3.00	1.50	.90
231	Willie Williams	3.00	1.50	.90
232	Spike Jones	3.00	1.50	.90
233	Jim Tyrer	3.00	1.50	.90
234	Roy Hilton	3.00	1.50	.90
235	Phil Villapiano	3.00	1.50	.90
236	Charley Taylor	3.00	1.50	.90
237	Malcolm Snider	3.00	1.50	.90
238	Vic Washington	3.00	1.50	.90
239	Grady Alderman	3.00	1.50	.90
240	Dick Anderson	3.00	1.50	.90
241	Ron Yankowski	3.00	1.50	.90
242	Billy Masters	3.00	1.50	.90
243	Herb Adderly	3.00	1.50	.90
244	David Ray	3.00	1.50	.90
245	John Riggins	9.00	4.50	2.75
246	Mike Wagner **RC**	3.00	1.50	.90
247	Don Morrison	3.00	1.50	.90
248	Earl McCullouch	3.00	1.50	.90
249	Dennis Wirgowksi	3.00	1.50	.90
250	Chris Hanburger	3.00	1.50	.90
251	Pat Sullivan **RC**	3.00	1.50	.90
252	Walt Sweeney	3.00	1.50	.90
253	Willie Alexander	3.00	1.50	.90
254	Doug Dressler	3.00	1.50	.90
255	Walter Johnson	3.00	1.50	.90
256	Ron Hornsby	3.00	1.50	.90
257	Ben Hawkins	3.00	1.50	.90
258	Donnie Green	3.00	1.50	.90
259	Fred Hoaglin	3.00	1.50	.90
260	Jerrill Wilson	3.00	1.50	.90
261	Horace Jones	3.00	1.50	.90
262	Woody Peoples	3.00	1.50	.90
263	Jim Hill	3.00	1.50	.90
264	John Fuqua	3.00	1.50	.90
265	Childhood Photo: (Donny Anderson)	3.00	1.50	.90
266	Childhood Photo: (Roman Gabriel)	3.00	1.50	.90
267	Childhood Photo: (Mike Garrett)	3.00	1.50	.90
268	Rufus Mayes	3.00	1.50	.90
269	Chip Myrtle	3.00	1.50	.90
270	Bill Stanfill **RC**	3.00	1.50	.90
271	Clint Jones	3.00	1.50	.90
272	Miller Farr	3.00	1.50	.90
273	Harry Schuh	3.00	1.50	.90
274	Bob Hayes	3.00	1.50	.90
275	Bobby Douglass	3.00	1.50	.90
276	Gus Hollomon	3.00	1.50	.90
277	Del Williams	3.00	1.50	.90
278	Julius Adams	3.00	1.50	.90
279	Herman Weaver	3.00	1.50	.90
280	Joe Greene	8.00	4.00	2.40
281	Wes Chesson	3.00	1.50	.90
282	Charlie Harraway	3.00	1.50	.90
283	Paul Guidry	3.00	1.50	.90
284	Terry Owens	3.00	1.50	.90
285	Jan Stenerud	3.00	1.50	.90
286	Pete Athas	3.00	1.50	.90
287	Dale Lindsey	3.00	1.50	.90
288	Jack Tatum **RC**	10.00	5.00	3.00
289	Floyd Little	3.00	1.50	.90
290	Bob Johnson	3.00	1.50	.90
291	Tommy Hart	3.00	1.50	.90
292	Tom Mitchell	3.00	1.50	.90
293	Walt Patulski **RC**	3.00	1.50	.90
294	Jim Skaggs	3.00	1.50	.90
295	Bob Griese	5.00	2.50	1.50
296	Mike McCoy	3.00	1.50	.90
297	Mel Gray	3.00	1.50	.90
298	Bobby Bryant	3.00	1.50	.90
299	Blaine Nye **RC**	3.00	1.50	.90
300	Dick Butkus	8.00	4.00	2.40
301	Charlie Cowan	3.00	1.50	.90
302	Mark Lomas	3.00	1.50	.90

303	Josh Ashton	3.00	1.50	.90
304	Happy Feller	3.00	1.50	.90
305	Ronnie Shanklin	3.00	1.50	.90
306	Wayne Rasmussen	3.00	1.50	.90
307	Jerry Smith	3.00	1.50	.90
308	Ken Reaves	3.00	1.50	.90
309	Ron East	3.00	1.50	.90
310	Otis Taylor	3.00	1.50	.90
311	John Garlington	3.00	1.50	.90
312	Lyle Alzado	3.00	1.50	.90
313	Remi Prudhomme	3.00	1.50	.90
314	Cornelius Johnson	3.00	1.50	.90
315	Lemar Parrish	3.00	1.50	.90
316	Jim Kiick	3.00	1.50	.90
317	Steve Zabel	3.00	1.50	.90
318	Alden Roche	3.00	1.50	.90
319	Tom Blanchard	3.00	1.50	.90
320	Fred Biletnikoff	4.00	2.00	1.25
321	Ralph Neely	3.00	1.50	.90
322	Dan Dierdorf **RC**	10.00	5.00	3.00
323	Richard Caster	3.00	1.50	.90
324	Gene Howard	3.00	1.50	.90
325	Elvin Bethea	3.00	1.50	.90
326	Carl Garrett	3.00	1.50	.90
327	Ron Billingsley	3.00	1.50	.90
328	Charlie West	3.00	1.50	.90
329	Tom Neville	3.00	1.50	.90
330	Ted Kwalick	3.00	1.50	.90
331	Rudy Redmond	3.00	1.50	.90
332	Henry Davis	3.00	1.50	.90
333	John Zook	3.00	1.50	.90
334	Jim Turner	3.00	1.50	.90
335	Len Dawson	5.00	2.50	1.50
336	Bob Chandler **RC**	3.00	1.50	.90
337	Al Beauchamp	3.00	1.50	.90
338	Tom Matte	3.00	1.50	.90
339	Paul Laaveg	3.00	1.50	.90
340	Ken Ellis	3.00	1.50	.90
341	Jim Langer **RC**	8.00	4.00	2.40
342	Ron Porter	3.00	1.50	.90
343	Jack Youngblood **RC**	15.00	7.50	4.50
344	Cornell Green	3.00	1.50	.90
345	Marv Hubbard	3.00	1.50	.90
346	Bruce Taylor	3.00	1.50	.90
347	Sam Havrilak	3.00	1.50	.90
348	Walt Sumner	3.00	1.50	.90
349	Steve O'Neal	3.00	1.50	.90
350	Ron Johnson	3.00	1.50	.90
351	Rockne Freitas	3.00	1.50	.90
352	Larry Stallings	3.00	1.50	.90
353	Jim Cadile	3.00	1.50	.90
354	Ken Burrough	3.00	1.50	.90
355	Jim Plunkett	4.00	2.00	1.25
356	Dave Long	3.00	1.50	.90
357	Ralph Anderson	3.00	1.50	.90
358	**Checklist 265-396**	3.00	1.50	.90
359	Gene Washington	3.00	1.50	.90
360	Dave Wilcox	3.00	1.50	.90
361	Paul Smith	3.00	1.50	.90
362	Alvin Wyatt	3.00	1.50	.90
363	Charlie Smith	3.00	1.50	.90
364	Royce Berry	3.00	1.50	.90
365	Dave Elmendorf	3.00	1.50	.90
366	Scott Hunter	3.00	1.50	.90
367	Bob Kuechenberg **RC**	3.00	1.50	.90
368	Pete Gogolak	3.00	1.50	.90
369	Dave Edwards	3.00	1.50	.90
370	Lem Barney	3.00	1.50	.90
371	Verlon Biggs	3.00	1.50	.90
372	John Reaves **RC**	3.00	1.50	.90
373	Ed Podolak	3.00	1.50	.90
374	Chris Faracopoulos	3.00	1.50	.90
375	Gary Garrison	3.00	1.50	.90
376	Tom Funchess	3.00	1.50	.90
377	Bobby Joe Green	3.00	1.50	.90
378	Don Brumm	3.00	1.50	.90
379	Jim O'Brien	3.00	1.50	.90
380	Paul Krause	3.00	1.50	.90
381	Leroy Kelly	3.00	1.50	.90
382	Ray Mansfield	3.00	1.50	.90
383	Dan Abramowicz	3.00	1.50	.90
384	John Outlaw **RC**	3.00	1.50	.90
385	Tommy Nobis	3.00	1.50	.90
386	Tom Domres	3.00	1.50	.90
387	Ken Willard	3.00	1.50	.90
388	Mike Stratton	3.00	1.50	.90
389	Fred Dryer	3.00	1.50	.90
390	Jake Scott	3.00	1.50	.90
391	Rich Houston	3.00	1.50	.90
392	Virgil Carter	3.00	1.50	.90
393	Tody Smith	3.00	1.50	.90
394	Ernie Calloway	3.00	1.50	.90
395	Charlie Sanders	3.00	1.50	.90
396	Fred Willis	3.00	1.50	.90
397	Curt Knight	3.00	1.50	.90
398	Nemiah Wilson	3.00	1.50	.90
399	Carroll Dale	3.00	1.50	.90
400	Joe Namath	18.00	9.00	5.50
401	Wayne Mulligan	3.00	1.50	.90
402	Jim Harrison	3.00	1.50	.90
403	Tim Rossovich	3.00	1.50	.90
404	David Lee	3.00	1.50	.90
405	Frank Pitts	3.00	1.50	.90
406	Jim Marshall	3.00	1.50	.90
407	Bob Brown	3.00	1.50	.90
408	John Rowser	3.00	1.50	.90
409	Mike Montler	3.00	1.50	.90
410	Willie Lanier	3.00	1.50	.90
411	Bill Bell	3.00	1.50	.90
412	Cedrick Hardman	3.00	1.50	.90
413	Bob Anderson	3.00	1.50	.90
414	Earl Morrall **RC**	3.00	1.50	.90
415	Ken Houston	3.00	1.50	.90
416	Jack Snow	3.00	1.50	.90
417	Dick Cunningham	3.00	1.50	.90
418	Greg Larson	3.00	1.50	.90
419	Mike Bass	3.00	1.50	.90
420	Mike Reid	3.00	1.50	.90
421	Walt Garrison	3.00	1.50	.90
422	Pete Liske	3.00	1.50	.90
423	Jim Yarbrough	3.00	1.50	.90
424	Rich McGeorge	3.00	1.50	.90
425	Bobby Howfield	3.00	1.50	.90
426	Pete Banaszak	3.00	1.50	.90
427	Willie Holman	3.00	1.50	.90
428	Dale Hackbart	3.00	1.50	.90
429	Fair Hooker	3.00	1.50	.90
430	Ted Hendricks	3.00	1.50	.90
431	Mike Garrett	3.00	1.50	.90
432	Glen Ray Hines	3.00	1.50	.90
433	Fred Cox	3.00	1.50	.90
434	Bobby Walden	3.00	1.50	.90
435	Bobby Bell	3.00	1.50	.90
436	David Rowe	3.00	1.50	.90
437	Bob Berry	3.00	1.50	.90
438	Bill Thompson	3.00	1.50	.90
439	Jim Beirne	3.00	1.50	.90
440	Larry Little	3.00	1.50	.90
441	Rocky Thompson	3.00	1.50	.90
442	Brig Owens	3.00	1.50	.90
443	Richard Neal	.40	.20	.12
444	Al Nelson	3.00	1.50	.90
445	Chip Myers	3.00	1.50	.90
446	Ken Bowman	3.00	1.50	.90
447	Jim Purnell	3.00	1.50	.90
448	Altie Taylor	3.00	1.50	.90
449	Linzy Cole	3.00	1.50	.90
450	Bob Lilly	5.00	2.50	1.50
451	Charlie Ford	3.00	1.50	.90
452	Milt Sunde	3.00	1.50	.90
453	Doug Wyatt	3.00	1.50	.90
454	Don Nottingham **RC**	3.00	1.50	.90
455	Johnny Unitas	10.00	5.00	3.00
456	Frank Lewis **RC**	3.00	1.50	.90
457	Roger Wehrli	3.00	1.50	.90
458	Jim Cheyunski	3.00	1.50	.90
459	Jerry Sherk **RC**	3.00	1.50	.90
460	Gene Washington	3.00	1.50	.90
461	Jim Otto	3.00	1.50	.90
462	Ed Budde	3.00	1.50	.90
463	Jim Mitchell	3.00	1.50	.90
464	Emerson Boozer	3.00	1.50	.90
465	Garo Yepremian	3.00	1.50	.90
466	Pete Duranko	3.00	1.50	.90
467	Charlie Joiner	3.00	1.50	.90
468	Spider Lockhart	3.00	1.50	.90
469	Marty Domres	3.00	1.50	.90
470	John Brockington	3.00	1.50	.90
471	Ed Flanagan	3.00	1.50	.90
472	Roy Jefferson	3.00	1.50	.90
473	Julian Fagan	3.00	1.50	.90
474	Bill Brown	3.00	1.50	.90
475	Roger Staubach	10.00	5.00	3.00
476	Jan White	3.00	1.50	.90
477	Pat Holmes	3.00	1.50	.90
478	Bob DeMarco	3.00	1.50	.90
479	Merlin Olsen	3.00	1.50	.90
480	Andy Russell	3.00	1.50	.90
481	Steve Spurrier	3.00	1.50	.90
482	Nate Ramsey	3.00	1.50	.90
483	Dennis Partee	3.00	1.50	.90
484	Jerry Simmons	3.00	1.50	.90
485	Donny Anderson	3.00	1.50	.90
486	Ralph Baker	3.00	1.50	.90
487	Ken Stabler **RC**	35.00	18.00	11.00
488	Ernie McMillan	3.00	1.50	.90
489	Ken Burrow	3.00	1.50	.90
490	Jack Gregory **RC**	3.00	1.50	.90
491	Larry Seiple	3.00	1.50	.90
492	Mick Tingelhoff	3.00	1.50	.90
493	Craig Morton	3.00	1.50	.90
494	Cecil Turner	3.00	1.50	.90
495	Steve Owens	3.00	1.50	.90
496	Richie Harris	3.00	1.50	.90
497	Buck Buchanan	3.00	1.50	.90
498	**Checklist 397-528**	4.00	2.00	1.25
499	Bill Kilmer	3.00	1.50	.90
500	O.J. Simpson	10.00	5.00	3.00
501	Bruce Gossett	3.00	1.50	.90
502	Art Thoms	3.00	1.50	.90
503	Larry Kaminski	3.00	1.50	.90
504	Larry Smith	3.00	1.50	.90
505	Bruce Van Dyke	3.00	1.50	.90
506	Alvin Reed	3.00	1.50	.90
507	Delles Howell	3.00	1.50	.90
508	Leroy Keyes	3.00	1.50	.90
509	Bo Scott	3.00	1.50	.90
510	Ron Yary	3.00	1.50	.90
511	Paul Warfield	5.00	2.50	1.50
512	Mac Percival	3.00	1.50	.90
513	Essex Johnson	3.00	1.50	.90
514	Jackie Smith	3.00	1.50	.90
515	Norm Snead	3.00	1.50	.90
516	Charlie Stukes	3.00	1.50	.90
517	Reggie Rucker **RC**	3.00	1.50	.90
518	Bill Sandeman	3.00	1.50	.90
519	Mel Farr	3.00	1.50	.90
520	Raymond Chester	3.00	1.50	.90
521	Fred Carr **RC**	3.00	1.50	.90
522	Jerry LeVias	3.00	1.50	.90
523	Jim Strong	3.00	1.50	.90
524	Roland McDole	3.00	1.50	.90
525	Dennis Shaw	3.00	1.50	.90
526	Dave Manders	3.00	1.50	.90
527	Skip Vanderbundt	3.00	1.50	.90
528	Mike Sensibaugh **RC**	3.00	1.50	.90

1973 Topps Team Checklists

This was the first time Topps issued separate team checklists in its 528-card sets, a practice that would end with the 1974 set. The cards showed an anonymous action shot at the top of the card, with a Topps logo in a football helmet facing the team name. The checklist was beneath all that, and showed the card number, name, uniform number and position (as it would in 1974). Card backs carried pieces to a puzzle of either Larry Brown or Joe Namath; or they carried a message that read, "Collect all 26 Team Checklists and complete your Joe Namath & Larry Brown Puzzles."

		NM	E	VG
Complete Set (26):		35.00	26.00	14.00
Common Team:		1.50	.75	.45
1	**Atlanta Falcons**	1.50	.75	.45
2	**Baltimore Colts**	1.50	.75	.45
3	**Buffalo Bills**	1.50	.75	.45
4	**Chicago Bears**	1.50	.75	.45
5	**Cincinnati Bengals**	1.50	.75	.45
6	**Cleveland Browns**	1.50	.75	.45
7	**Dallas Cowboys**	1.50	.75	.45
8	**Denver Broncos**	1.50	.75	.45
9	**Detroit Lions**	1.50	.75	.45
10	**Green Bay Packers**	1.50	.75	.45
11	**Houston Oilers**	1.50	.75	.45
12	**Kansas City Chiefs**	1.50	.75	.45
13	**Los Angeles Rams**	1.50	.75	.45
14	**Miami Dolphins**	1.50	.75	.45
15	**Minnesota Vikings**	1.50	.75	.45
16	**New England Patriots**	1.50	.75	.45
17	**New Orleans Saints**	1.50	.75	.45
18	**New York Giants**	1.50	.75	.45
19	**New York Jets**	1.50	.75	.45
20	**Oakland Raiders**	1.50	.75	.45
21	**Philadelphia Eagles**	1.50	.75	.45
22	**Pittsburgh Steelers**	1.50	.75	.45
23	**St. Louis Cardinals**	1.50	.75	.45
24	**San Diego Chargers**	1.50	.75	.45
25	**San Francisco 49ers**	1.50	.75	.45
26	**Washington Redskins**	1.50	.75	.45

1974 Topps

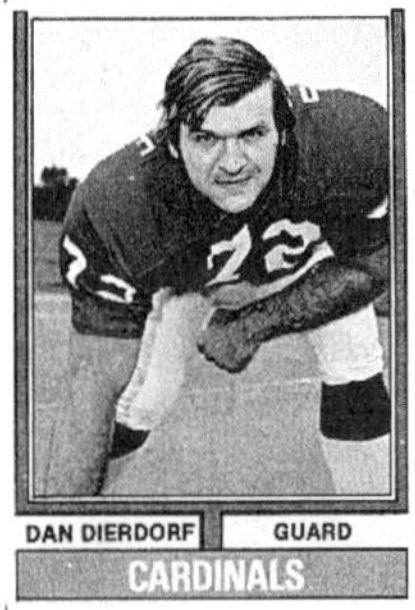

This was Topps' second 528-card set, and marked the second and last time team checklists would be issued unnumbered and separate from the set. Rookies in this set include Ahmad Rashad, Greg Pruitt, Chuck Foreman, Harold Carmichael, Ray Guy, John Matuszak, Conrad Dobler, Ed Marinaro, Darryl Stingley, Lynn Dickey, Billy Joe DuPree,

D.D. Lewis, John Hannah, Terry Metcalf, Joe Ferguson and Bert Jones. In addition, this set features the last regularly-issued card of Johnny Unitas. All Pro cards showing individual players are found on cards 121-144. Other subsets include statistical leader and playoff cards. There is one error in the set, on card #265, Bob Lee. The back of the card lists his team as the Atlanta Hawks instead of the Falcons.

	NM	E	VG
Complete Set (528):	400.00	200.00	120.00
Common Player:	3.00	1.50	.90
Minor Stars:	.75		
Unlisted Stars:	1.00		
Wax Pack (10-ALL 528):	41.00		
Wax Box (24):	865.00		
Wax Pack (10+1 - B.T.C.):	42.00		
Wax Box (36):	1,300		

		NM	E	VG
1	O.J. Simpson	10.00	5.00	3.00
2	Blaine Nye	3.00	1.50	.90
3	Don Hansen	3.00	1.50	.90
4	Ken Bowman	3.00	1.50	.90
5	Carl Eller	3.00	1.50	.90
6	Jerry Smith	3.00	1.50	.90
7	Ed Podolak	3.00	1.50	.90
8	Mel Gray	3.00	1.50	.90
9	Pat Matson	3.00	1.50	.90
10	Floyd Little	3.00	1.50	.90
11	Frank Pitts	3.00	1.50	.90
12	Vern Den Herder **RC**	3.00	1.50	.90
13	John Fuqua	3.00	1.50	.90
14	Jack Tatum	3.00	1.50	.90
15	Winston Hill	3.00	1.50	.90
16	John Beasley	3.00	1.50	.90
17	David Lee	3.00	1.50	.90
18	Rich Coady	3.00	1.50	.90
19	Ken Willard	3.00	1.50	.90
20	Coy Bacon	3.00	1.50	.90
21	Ben Hawkins	3.00	1.50	.90
22	Paul Guidry	3.00	1.50	.90
23	Norm Snead	3.00	1.50	.90
24	Jim Yarbrough	3.00	1.50	.90
25	Jack Reynolds **RC**	3.00	1.50	.90
26	Josh Ashton	3.00	1.50	.90
27	Donnie Green	3.00	1.50	.90
28	Bob Hayes	3.00	1.50	.90
29	John Zook	3.00	1.50	.90
30	Bobby Bryant	3.00	1.50	.90
31	Scott Hunter	3.00	1.50	.90
32	Dan Dierdorf	5.00	2.50	1.50
33	Curt Knight	3.00	1.50	.90
34	Elmo Wright **RC**	3.00	1.50	.90
35	Essex Johnson	3.00	1.50	.90
36	Walt Sumner	3.00	1.50	.90
37	Marv Montgomery	3.00	1.50	.90
38	Tim Foley	3.00	1.50	.90
39	Mike Siani	3.00	1.50	.90
40	Joe Greene	5.00	2.50	1.50
41	Bobby Howfield	3.00	1.50	.90
42	Del Williams	3.00	1.50	.90
43	Don McCauley	3.00	1.50	.90
44	Randy Jackson	3.00	1.50	.90
45	Ron Smith	3.00	1.50	.90
46	Gene Washington	3.00	1.50	.90
47	Po James	3.00	1.50	.90
48	Soloman Freelon	3.00	1.50	.90
49	Bob Windsor	3.00	1.50	.90
50	John Hadl	3.00	1.50	.90
51	Greg Larson	3.00	1.50	.90
52	Steve Owens	3.00	1.50	.90
53	Jim Cheyunski	3.00	1.50	.90
54	Rayfield Wright	3.00	1.50	.90
55	Dave Hampton	3.00	1.50	.90
56	Ron Widby	3.00	1.50	.90
57	Milt Sunde	3.00	1.50	.90
58	Bill Kilmer	3.00	1.50	.90
59	Bobby Bell	3.00	1.50	.90
60	Jim Bakken	3.00	1.50	.90
61	Rufus Mayes	3.00	1.50	.90
62	Vic Washington	3.00	1.50	.90
63	Gene Washington	3.00	1.50	.90
64	Clarence Scott	3.00	1.50	.90
65	Gene Upshaw	3.00	1.50	.90
66	Larry Seiple	3.00	1.50	.90
67	John McMakin	3.00	1.50	.90
68	Ralph Baker	3.00	1.50	.90
69	Lydell Mitchell	3.00	1.50	.90
70	Archie Manning	3.00	1.50	.90
71	George Farmer	3.00	1.50	.90
72	Ron East	3.00	1.50	.90
73	Al Nelson	3.00	1.50	.90
74	Pat Hughes	3.00	1.50	.90
75	Fred Willis	3.00	1.50	.90
76	Larry Walton	3.00	1.50	.90
77	Tom Neville	3.00	1.50	.90
78	Ted Kwalick	3.00	1.50	.90
79	Walt Patulski	3.00	1.50	.90
80	John Niland	3.00	1.50	.90
81	Ted Fritsch	3.00	1.50	.90
82	Paul Krause	3.00	1.50	.90
83	Jack Snow	3.00	1.50	.90
84	Mike Bass	3.00	1.50	.90
85	Jim Tyrer	3.00	1.50	.90
86	Ron Yankowski	3.00	1.50	.90
87	Mike Phipps	3.00	1.50	.90
88	Al Beauchamp	3.00	1.50	.90
89	Riley Odoms **RC**	3.00	1.50	.90
90	MacArthur Lane	3.00	1.50	.90
91	Art Thoms	3.00	1.50	.90
92	Marlin Briscoe	3.00	1.50	.90
93	Bruce Van Dyke	3.00	1.50	.90
94	Tom Myers	3.00	1.50	.90
95	Calvin Hill	3.00	1.50	.90
96	Bruce Laird	3.00	1.50	.90
97	Tony McGee	3.00	1.50	.90
98	Len Rohde	3.00	1.50	.90
99	Tom McNeill	3.00	1.50	.90
100	Delles Howell	3.00	1.50	.90
101	Gary Garrison	3.00	1.50	.90
102	Dan Goich	3.00	1.50	.90
103	Len St. Jean	3.00	1.50	.90
104	Zeke Moore	3.00	1.50	.90
105	Ahmad Rashad **RC**	10.00	5.00	3.00
106	Mel Renfro	3.00	1.50	.90
107	Jim Mitchell	3.00	1.50	.90
108	Ed Budde	3.00	1.50	.90
109	Harry Schuh	3.00	1.50	.90
110	Greg Pruitt **RC**	3.00	1.50	.90
111	Ed Flanagan	3.00	1.50	.90
112	Larry Stallings	3.00	1.50	.90
113	Chuck Foreman **RC**	3.00	1.50	.90
114	Royce Berry	3.00	1.50	.90
115	Gale Gillingham	3.00	1.50	.90
116	Charlie Johnson	3.00	1.50	.90
117	**Checklist 1-132**	3.00	1.50	.90
118	Bill Butler	3.00	1.50	.90
119	Roy Jefferson	3.00	1.50	.90
120	Bobby Douglass	3.00	1.50	.90
121	Harold Carmichael **RC**	8.00	4.00	2.40
122	George Kuntz (AP)	3.00	1.50	.90
123	Larry Little (AP)	3.00	1.50	.90
124	Forrest Blue (AP)	3.00	1.50	.90
125	Ron Yary (AP)	3.00	1.50	.90
126	Tom Mack (AP)	3.00	1.50	.90
127	Bob Tucker (AP)	3.00	1.50	.90
128	Paul Warfield (AP)	4.00	2.00	1.25
129	Fran Tarkenton (AP)	10.00	5.00	3.00
130	O.J. Simpson (AP)	10.00	5.00	3.00
131	Larry Csonka (AP)	7.00	3.50	2.10
132	Bruce Gossett (AP)	3.00	1.50	.90
133	Bill Stanfill (AP)	3.00	1.50	.90
134	Alan Page (AP)	3.00	1.50	.90
135	Paul Smith (AP)	3.00	1.50	.90
136	Claude Humphrey (AP)	3.00	1.50	.90
137	Jack Ham (AP)	7.00	3.50	2.00
138	Lee Roy Jordan (AP)	3.00	1.50	.90
139	Phil Villapiano (AP)	3.00	1.50	.90
140	Ken Ellis (AP)	3.00	1.50	.90
141	Willie Brown (AP)	3.00	1.50	.90
142	Dick Anderson (AP)	3.00	1.50	.90
143	Bill Bradley (AP)	3.00	1.50	.90
144	Jerrel Wilson (AP)	3.00	1.50	.90
145	Reggie Rucker	3.00	1.50	.90
146	Marty Domres	3.00	1.50	.90
147	Bob Kowalkowski	3.00	1.50	.90
148	John Matuszak **RC**	7.00	3.50	2.10
149	Mike Adamle **RC**	3.00	1.50	.90
150	Johnny Unitas	10.00	5.00	3.00
151	Charlie Ford	3.00	1.50	.90
152	Bob Klein **RC**	3.00	1.50	.90
153	Jim Merlo	3.00	1.50	.90
154	Willie Young	3.00	1.50	.90
155	Donny Anderson	3.00	1.50	.90
156	Brig Owens	3.00	1.50	.90
157	Bruce Jarvis	3.00	1.50	.90
158	Ron Carpenter	3.00	1.50	.90
159	Don Cockroft	3.00	1.50	.90
160	Tommy Nobis	3.00	1.50	.90
161	Craig Morton	3.00	1.50	.90
162	Jon Staggers	3.00	1.50	.90
163	Mike Eischeid	3.00	1.50	.90
164	Jerry Sisemore **RC**	3.00	1.50	.90
165	Cedric Hardman	3.00	1.50	.90
166	Bill Thompson	3.00	1.50	.90
167	Jim Lynch	3.00	1.50	.90
168	Bob Moore	3.00	1.50	.90
169	Glen Edwards	3.00	1.50	.90
170	Mercury Morris	3.00	1.50	.90
171	Julius Adams	3.00	1.50	.90
172	Cotton Speyrer	3.00	1.50	.90
173	Bill Munson	3.00	1.50	.90
174	Benny Johnson	3.00	1.50	.90
175	Burgess Owens **RC**	3.00	1.50	.90
176	Cid Edwards	3.00	1.50	.90
177	Doug Buffone	3.00	1.50	.90
178	Charlie Cowan	3.00	1.50	.90
179	Bob Newland	3.00	1.50	.90
180	Ron Johnson	3.00	1.50	.90
181	Bob Rowe	3.00	1.50	.90
182	Len Hauss	3.00	1.50	.90
183	Joe DeLamielleure **RC**	10.00	5.00	3.00
184	Sherman White **RC**	3.00	1.50	.90
185	Fair Hooker	3.00	1.50	.90
186	Nick Mike-Mayer	3.00	1.50	.90
187	Ralph Neely	3.00	1.50	.90
188	Rich McGeorge	3.00	1.50	.90
189	Ed Marinaro **RC**	3.00	1.50	.90
190	Dave Wilcox	3.00	1.50	.90
191	Joe Owens	3.00	1.50	.90
192	Bill Van Heusen	3.00	1.50	.90
193	Jim Kearney	3.00	1.50	.90
194	Otis Sistrunk **RC**	3.00	1.50	.90
195	Ronnie Shanklin	3.00	1.50	.90
196	Bill Lenkaitis	3.00	1.50	.90
197	Tom Drougas	3.00	1.50	.90
198	Larry Hand	3.00	1.50	.90
199	Mack Alston	3.00	1.50	.90
200	Bob Griese	7.00	3.50	2.10
201	Earlie Thomas	3.00	1.50	.90
202	Carl Gersbach	3.00	1.50	.90
203	Jim Harrison	3.00	1.50	.90
204	Jake Kupp	3.00	1.50	.90
205	Merlin Olsen	3.50	1.75	1.00
206	Spider Lockhart	3.00	1.50	.90
207	Walter Gillette	3.00	1.50	.90
208	Verlon Biggs	3.00	1.50	.90
209	Bob James	3.00	1.50	.90
210	Bob Trumpy	3.00	1.50	.90
211	Jerry Sherk	3.00	1.50	.90
212	Andy Maurer	3.00	1.50	.90
213	Fred Carr	3.00	1.50	.90
214	Mick Tingelhoff	3.00	1.50	.90
215	Steve Spurrier	5.00	2.50	1.50
216	Richard Harris	3.00	1.50	.90
217	Charlie Greer	3.00	1.50	.90
218	Buck Buchanan	3.00	1.50	.90
219	Ray Guy **RC**	15.00	7.50	4.50
220	Franco Harris	10.00	5.00	3.00
221	Darryl Stingley **RC**	3.00	1.50	.90
222	Rex Kern	3.00	1.50	.90
223	Toni Fritsch	3.00	1.50	.90
224	Levi Johnson	3.00	1.50	.90
225	Bob Kuechenberg	3.00	1.50	.90
226	Elvin Bethea	3.00	1.50	.90
227	Al Woodall **RC**	3.00	1.50	.90
228	Terry Owens	3.00	1.50	.90
229	Bivian Lee	3.00	1.50	.90
230	Dick Butkus	8.00	4.00	2.40
231	Jim Bertelsen **RC**	3.00	1.50	.90
232	John Mendenhall **RC**	3.00	1.50	.90
233	Conrad Dobler **RC**	3.00	1.50	.90
234	J.D. Hill	3.00	1.50	.90
235	Ken Houston	3.00	1.50	.90
236	Dave Lewis	3.00	1.50	.90
237	John Garlington	3.00	1.50	.90
238	Bill Sandeman	3.00	1.50	.90
239	Alden Roche	3.00	1.50	.90
240	John Gilliam	3.00	1.50	.90
241	Bruce Taylor	3.00	1.50	.90
242	Vern Winfield	3.00	1.50	.90
243	Bobby Maples	3.00	1.50	.90
244	Wendell Hayes	3.00	1.50	.90
245	George Blanda	7.00	3.50	2.00
246	Dwight White	3.00	1.50	.90
247	Sandy Durko	3.00	1.50	.90
248	Tom Mitchell	3.00	1.50	.90
249	Chuck Walton	3.00	1.50	.90
250	Bob Lilly	4.00	2.00	1.25
251	Doug Swift	3.00	1.50	.90
252	Lynn Dickey **RC**	3.00	1.50	.90
253	Jerome Barkum **RC**	3.00	1.50	.90
254	Clint Jones	3.00	1.50	.90
255	Billy Newsome	3.00	1.50	.90
256	Bob Asher	3.00	1.50	.90
257	Joe Scibelli	3.00	1.50	.90
258	Tom Blanchard	3.00	1.50	.90
259	Norm Thompson	3.00	1.50	.90
260	Larry Brown	3.00	1.50	.90
261	Paul Seymour	3.00	1.50	.90
262	**Checklist 133-264**	3.00	1.50	.90
263	Doug Dieken **RC**	3.00	1.50	.90
264	Lemar Parrish	3.00	1.50	.90
265	Bob Lee	3.00	1.50	.90
266	Bob Brown	3.00	1.50	.90
267	Roy Winston	3.00	1.50	.90
268	Randy Beisler	3.00	1.50	.90
269	Joe Dawkins	3.00	1.50	.90
270	Tom Dempsey	3.00	1.50	.90
271	Jack Rudnay	3.00	1.50	.90
272	Art Shell	3.00	1.50	.90
273	Mike Wagner	3.00	1.50	.90
274	Rick Cash	3.00	1.50	.90
275	Greg Landry	3.00	1.50	.90
276	Glenn Ressler	3.00	1.50	.90
277	Billy Joe DuPree **RC**	3.00	1.50	.90

No.	Player	NM	E	VG
278	Norm Evans	3.00	1.50	.90
279	Billy Parks	3.00	1.50	.90
280	John Riggins	5.00	2.50	1.50
281	Lionel Aldridge	3.00	1.50	.90
282	Steve O'Neal	3.00	1.50	.90
283	Craig Clemons	3.00	1.50	.90
284	Willie Williams	3.00	1.50	.90
285	Isiah Robertson	3.00	1.50	.90
286	Dennis Shaw	3.00	1.50	.90
287	Bill Brundige	3.00	1.50	.90
288	John Leypoldt	3.00	1.50	.90
289	John DeMarie	3.00	1.50	.90
290	Mike Reid	3.00	1.50	.90
291	Greg Brezina	3.00	1.50	.90
292	Willie Buchanon **RC**	3.00	1.50	.90
293	Dave Osborn	3.00	1.50	.90
294	Mel Phillips	3.00	1.50	.90
295	Haven Moses	3.00	1.50	.90
296	Wade Key	3.00	1.50	.90
297	Marvin Upshaw	3.00	1.50	.90
298	Ray Mansfield	3.00	1.50	.90
299	Edgar Chandler	3.00	1.50	.90
300	Marv Hubbard	3.00	1.50	.90
301	Herman Weaver	3.00	1.50	.90
302	Jim Bailey	3.00	1.50	.90
303	D.D. Lewis **RC**	3.00	1.50	.90
304	Ken Burrough	3.00	1.50	.90
305	Jake Scott	3.00	1.50	.90
306	Randy Rasmussen	3.00	1.50	.90
307	Pettis Norman	3.00	1.50	.90
308	Carl Johnson	3.00	1.50	.90
309	Joe Taylor	3.00	1.50	.90
310	Pete Gogolak	3.00	1.50	.90
311	Tony Baker	3.00	1.50	.90
312	John Richardson	3.00	1.50	.90
313	Dave Robinson	3.00	1.50	.90
314	Reggie McKenzie **RC**	3.00	1.50	.90
315	Isaac Curtis **RC**	3.00	1.50	.90
316	Tom Darden	3.00	1.50	.90
317	Ken Reaves	3.00	1.50	.90
318	Malcolm Snider	3.00	1.50	.90
319	Jeff Siemon **RC**	3.00	1.50	.90
320	Dan Abramowicz	3.00	1.50	.90
321	Lyle Alzado	3.00	1.50	.90
322	John Reaves	3.00	1.50	.90
323	Morris Stroud	3.00	1.50	.90
324	Bobby Walden	3.00	1.50	.90
325	Randy Vataha	3.00	1.50	.90
326	Nemiah Wilson	3.00	1.50	.90
327	Paul Naumoff	3.00	1.50	.90
328	Rushing Leaders (O.J. Simpson, John Brockington)	5.00	2.50	1.50
329	Passing Leaders (Ken Stabler, Roger Staubach)	7.00	3.50	2.10
330	Receiving Leaders (Fred Willis, Harold Carmichael)	3.00	1.50	.90
331	**Scoring Leaders** (Roy Gerela, David Ray)	3.00	1.50	.90
332	**Interception Leaders** (Dick Anderson, Mike Wagner, Bobby Bryan t)	3.00	1.50	.90
333	**Punting Leaders** (Jerrell Wilson, Tom Wittum)	3.00	1.50	.90
334	Dennis Nelson	3.00	1.50	.90
335	Walt Garrison	3.00	1.50	.90
336	Tody Smith	3.00	1.50	.90
337	Ed Bell	3.00	1.50	.90
338	Bryant Salter	3.00	1.50	.90
339	Wayne Colman	3.00	1.50	.90
340	Garo Yepremian	3.00	1.50	.90
341	Bob Newton	3.00	1.50	.90
342	Vince Clements **RC**	3.00	1.50	.90
343	Ken Iman	3.00	1.50	.90
344	Jim Tolbert	3.00	1.50	.90
345	Chris Hanburger	3.00	1.50	.90
346	Dave Foley	3.00	1.50	.90
347	Tommy Casanova	3.00	1.50	.90
348	John James	3.00	1.50	.90
349	Clarence Williams	3.00	1.50	.90
350	Leroy Kelly	3.00	1.50	.90
351	Stu Voigt **RC**	3.00	1.50	.90
352	Skip Vanderbundt	3.00	1.50	.90
353	Pete Duranko	3.00	1.50	.90
354	John Outlaw	3.00	1.50	.90
355	Jan Stenerud	3.00	1.50	.90
356	Barry Pearson	3.00	1.50	.90
357	Brian Dowling	3.00	1.50	.90
358	Dan Conners	3.00	1.50	.90
359	Bob Bell	3.00	1.50	.90
360	Rick Volk	3.00	1.50	.90
361	Pat Toomay	3.00	1.50	.90
362	Bob Gresham	3.00	1.50	.90
363	John Schmitt	3.00	1.50	.90
364	Mel Rogers	3.00	1.50	.90
365	Manny Fernandez	3.00	1.50	.90
366	Ernie Jackson	3.00	1.50	.90
367	Gary Huff **RC**	3.00	1.50	.90
368	Bob Grim	3.00	1.50	.90
369	Ernie McMillan	3.00	1.50	.90
370	Dave Elmendorf	3.00	1.50	.90
371	Mike Bragg	3.00	1.50	.90
372	John Skorupan	3.00	1.50	.90
373	Howard Fest	3.00	1.50	.90
374	Jerry Tagge **RC**	3.00	1.50	.90
375	Art Malone	3.00	1.50	.90
376	Bob Babich	3.00	1.50	.90
377	Jim Marshall	3.00	1.50	.90
378	Bob Hoskins	3.00	1.50	.90
379	Dan Zimmerman	3.00	1.50	.90
380	Ray May	3.00	1.50	.90
381	Emmitt Thomas	3.00	1.50	.90
382	Terry Hanratty	3.00	1.50	.90
383	John Hannah **RC**	15.00	7.50	4.50
384	George Atkinson	3.00	1.50	.90
385	Ted Hendricks	3.00	1.50	.90
386	Jim O'Brien	3.00	1.50	.90
387	Jethro Pugh	3.00	1.50	.90
388	Elbert Drungo	3.00	1.50	.90
389	Richard Caster	3.00	1.50	.90
390	Deacon Jones	3.00	1.50	.90
391	**Checklist 265-396**	3.00	1.50	.90
392	Jess Phillips	3.00	1.50	.90
393	Gary Lyle	3.00	1.50	.90
394	Jim Files	3.00	1.50	.90
395	Jim Hart	3.00	1.50	.90
396	Dave Chapple	3.00	1.50	.90
397	Jim Langer	3.00	1.50	.90
398	John Wilbur	3.00	1.50	.90
399	Dwight Harrison	3.00	1.50	.90
400	John Brockington	3.00	1.50	.90
401	Ken Anderson	5.00	2.50	1.50
402	Mike Tilleman	3.00	1.50	.90
403	Charlie Hall	3.00	1.50	.90
404	Tommy Hart	3.00	1.50	.90
405	Norm Bulaich	3.00	1.50	.90
406	Jim Turner	3.00	1.50	.90
407	Mo Moorman	3.00	1.50	.90
408	Ralph Anderson	3.00	1.50	.90
409	Jim Otto	3.00	1.50	.90
410	Andy Russell	3.00	1.50	.90
411	Glenn Doughty	3.00	1.50	.90
412	Altie Taylor	3.00	1.50	.90
413	Marv Bateman	3.00	1.50	.90
414	Willie Alexander	3.00	1.50	.90
415	Bill Zapalac	3.00	1.50	.90
416	Russ Washington	3.00	1.50	.90
417	Joe Federspiel	3.00	1.50	.90
418	Craig Cotton	3.00	1.50	.90
419	Randy Johnson	3.00	1.50	.90
420	Harold Jackson	3.00	1.50	.90
421	Roger Wehrli	3.00	1.50	.90
422	Charlie Harraway	3.00	1.50	.90
423	Spike Jones	3.00	1.50	.90
424	Bob Johnson	3.00	1.50	.90
425	Mike McCoy	3.00	1.50	.90
426	Dennis Havig	3.00	1.50	.90
427	Bob McKay	3.00	1.50	.190
428	Steve Zabel	3.00	1.50	.90
429	Horace Jones	3.00	1.50	.90
430	Jim Johnson	3.00	1.50	.90
431	Roy Gerela	3.00	1.50	.90
432	Tom Graham	3.00	1.50	.90
433	Curley Culp	3.00	1.50	.90
434	Ken Mendenhall	3.00	1.50	.90
435	Jim Plunkett	3.00	1.50	.90
436	Julian Fagan	3.00	1.50	.90
437	Mike Garrett	3.00	1.50	.90
438	Bobby Joe Green	3.00	1.50	.90
439	Jack Gregory	3.00	1.50	.90
440	Charlie Sanders	3.00	1.50	.90
441	Bill Curry	3.00	1.50	.90
442	Bob Pollard	3.00	1.50	.90
443	David Ray	3.00	1.50	.90
444	Terry Metcalf **RC**	3.00	1.50	.90
445	Pat Fischer	3.00	1.50	.90
446	Bob Chandler	3.00	1.50	.90
447	Bill Bergey	3.00	1.50	.90
448	Walter Johnson	3.00	1.50	.90
449	Charlie Young **RC**	3.00	1.50	.90
450	Chester Marcol	3.00	1.50	.90
451	Ken Stabler	10.00	5.00	3.00
452	Preston Pearson	3.00	1.50	.90
453	Mike Current	3.00	1.50	.90
454	Ron Bolton	3.00	1.50	.90
455	Mark Lomas	3.00	1.50	.90
456	Raymond Chester	3.00	1.50	.90
457	Jerry LeVias	3.00	1.50	.90
458	Skip Butler	3.00	1.50	.90
459	Mike Livingston **RC**	3.00	1.50	.90
460	AFC Semi-finals	3.00	1.50	.90
461	NFC Semi-finals (Roger Staubach)	3.00	1.50	.90
462	Playoff Championship (Ken Stabler, Fran Tarkenton)	3.00	1.50	.90
463	**Super Bowl**	3.00	1.50	.90
464	Wayne Mulligan	3.00	1.50	.90
465	Horst Muhlmann	3.00	1.50	.90
466	Milt Morin	3.00	1.50	.90
467	Don Parish	3.00	1.50	.90
468	Richard Neal	3.00	1.50	.90
469	Ron Jessie	3.00	1.50	.90
470	Terry Bradshaw	15.00	7.50	4.50
471	Fred Dryer	3.00	1.50	.90
472	Jim Carter	3.00	1.50	.90
473	Ken Burrow	3.00	1.50	.90
474	Wally Chambers **RC**	3.00	1.50	.90
475	Dan Pastorini	3.00	1.50	.90
476	Don Morrison	3.00	1.50	.90
477	Carl Mauck	3.00	1.50	.90
478	Larry Cole **RC**	3.00	1.50	.90
479	Jim Kiick	3.00	1.50	.90
480	Willie Lanier	3.00	1.50	.90
481	Don Herrmann	3.00	1.50	.90
482	George Hunt	3.00	1.50	.90
483	Bob Howard	3.00	1.50	.90
484	Myron Pottios	3.00	1.50	.90
485	Jackie Smith	3.00	1.50	.90
486	Vern Holland	3.00	1.50	.90
487	Jim Braxton	3.00	1.50	.90
488	Joe Reed	3.00	1.50	.90
489	Wally Hilgenberg	3.00	1.50	.90
490	Fred Biletnikoff	5.00	2.50	1.50
491	Bob DeMarco	3.00	1.50	.90
492	Mark Nordquist	3.00	1.50	.90
493	Larry Brooks	3.00	1.50	.90
494	Pete Athas	3.00	1.50	.90
495	Emerson Boozer	3.00	1.50	.90
496	L.C. Greenwood	3.00	1.50	.90
497	Rockne Freitas	3.00	1.50	.90
498	**Checklist 397-528**	3.00	1.50	.90
499	Joe Schmiesing	3.00	1.50	.90
500	Roger Staubach	15.00	7.50	4.50
501	Al Cowlings	3.00	1.50	.90
502	Sam Cunningham **RC**	3.00	1.50	.90
503	Dennis Partee	3.00	1.50	.90
504	John Didion	3.00	1.50	.90
505	Nick Buoniconti	3.00	1.50	.90
506	Carl Garrett	3.00	1.50	.90
507	Doug Van Horn	3.00	1.50	.90
508	Jamie Rivers	3.00	1.50	.90
509	Jack Youngblood	3.00	1.50	1.00
510	Charley Taylor	3.00	1.50	.90
511	Ken Riley	3.00	1.50	.90
512	Joe Ferguson **RC**	3.00	1.50	.90
513	Bill Lueck	3.00	1.50	.90
514	Ray Brown	3.00	1.50	.90
515	Fred Cox	3.00	1.50	.90
516	Joe Jones	3.00	1.50	.90
517	Larry Schreiber	3.00	1.50	.90
518	Dennis Wirgowski	3.00	1.50	.90
519	Leroy Mitchell	3.00	1.50	.90
520	Otis Taylor	3.00	1.50	.90
521	Henry Davis	3.00	1.50	.90
522	Bruce Barnes	3.00	1.50	.90
523	Charlie Smith	3.00	1.50	.90
524	Bert Jones **RC**	3.00	1.50	.90
525	Lem Barney	3.00	1.50	.90
526	John Fitzgerald **RC**	3.00	1.50	.90
527	Tom Funchess	3.00	1.50	.90
528	Steve Tannen	3.00	1.50	.90

1974 Topps Team Checklists

These unnumbered checklists were issued in wax packs of 1974 Topps cards. At the bottom of the card was an ad for a sendaway offer where collectors could buy the entire run of checklists through Topps. The back of the card carried instructions for a game that could be played with football cards. This was the last time Topps would issue team checklists separate from the rest of the set.

	NM	E	VG
Complete Set (26):	35.00	26.00	14.00
Common Team:	1.50	.75	.45

		NM	E	VG
(1)	Atlanta Falcons	1.50	.75	.45
(2)	Baltimore Colts	1.50	.75	.45
(3)	Buffalo Bills	1.50	.75	.45
(4)	Chicago Bears	1.50	.75	.45
(5)	Cincinnati Bengals	1.50	.75	.45
(6)	Cleveland Browns	1.50	.75	.45
(7)	Dallas Cowboys	1.50	.75	.45
(8)	Denver Broncos	1.50	.75	.45
(9)	Detroit Lions	1.50	.75	.45
(10)	Green Bay Packers	1.50	.75	.45
(11)	Houston Oilers	1.50	.75	.45
(12)	Kansas City Chiefs	1.50	.75	.45
(13)	Los Angeles Rams	1.50	.75	.45
(14)	Miami Dolphins	1.50	.75	.45
(15)	Minnesota Vikings	1.50	.75	.45
(16)	New England Patriots	1.50	.75	.45
(17)	New Orleans Saints	1.50	.75	.45
(18)	New York Giants	1.50	.75	.45
(19)	New York Jets	1.50	.75	.45
(20)	Oakland Raiders	1.50	.75	.45
(21)	Philadelphia Eagles	1.50	.75	.45
(22)	Pittsburgh Steelers	1.50	.75	.45
(23)	St. Louis Cardinals	1.50	.75	.45
(24)	San Diego Chargers	1.50	.75	.45
(25)	San Francisco 49ers	1.50	.75	.45
(26)	Washington Redskins	1.50	.75	.45

1975 Topps

FRED DRYER

The 528-card 1975 issue was arguably Topps' most attractive offering of the decade. Its clean design and white borders leaves room for the photo, player's name, a pennant with the team name, and the player's position in a green helmet. Most notable for the inclusion of the Dan Fouts rookie card, other rookies in this set are Mel Blount, Rocky Bleier, Drew Pearson, Lynn Swann, James Harris, Otis Armstrong, Lawrence McCutcheon and Joe Theismann. One feature of this set is the larger number of separate All-Pro cards, numbered 201-225. Each shows two star players. Other subsets include Statistical Leaders, Record Breakers, Highlights and Playoff Action. George Blanda has two "honorary" cards in this set, numbers 7 and 8. The first shows him in a black jersey and lists his career highlights on the back; the second shows him in a white Oakland jersey and documents his career statistics. No team checklists were issued for this set.

	NM	E	VG
Complete Set (528):	400.00	200.00	120.00
Common Player:	2.00	1.00	.60
Minor Stars:	.60		
Unlisted Stars:	1.25		
Wax Pack (10):	50.00		
Wax Box (36):	275.00		

		NM	E	VG
1	Rushing Leaders (Lawrence McCutcheon, Otis Armstrong)	2.00	1.00	.60
2	Passing Leaders (Sonny Jurgensen, Ken Anderson)	2.00	1.00	.60
3	Receiving Leaders (Charley Young, Lydell Mitchell)	2.00	1.00	.60
4	Scoring Leaders (Chester Marcol, Roy Gerela)	2.00	1.00	.60
5	Interception Leaders (Ray Brown, Emmitt Thomas)	2.00	1.00	.60
6	Punting Leaders (Tom Blanchard, Ray Guy)	2.00	1.00	.60
7	George Blanda (highlights, black jersey)	4.00	2.00	1.20
8	George Blanda (career, white jersey)	4.00	2.00	1.20
9	Ralph Baker	2.00	1.00	.60
10	Don Woods	2.00	1.00	.60
11	Bob Asher	2.00	1.00	.60
12	Mel Blount **RC**	10.00	5.00	3.00
13	Sam Cunningham	2.00	1.00	.60
14	Jackie Smith	2.00	1.00	.60
15	Greg Landry	2.00	1.00	.60
16	Buck Buchanan	2.00	1.00	.60

		NM	E	VG
17	Haven Moses	2.00	1.00	.60
18	Clarence Ellis	2.00	1.00	.60
19	Jim Carter	2.00	1.00	.60
20	Charley Taylor	2.25	1.25	.70
21	Jess Phillips	2.00	1.00	.60
22	Larry Seiple	2.00	1.00	.60
23	Doug Dieken	2.00	1.00	.60
24	Ron Saul	2.00	1.00	.60
25	Isaac Curtis	2.00	1.00	.25
26	Gary Larsen **RC**	2.00	1.00	.25
27	Bruce Jarvis	2.00	1.00	.60
28	Steve Zabel	2.00	1.00	.60
29	John Mendenhall	2.00	1.00	.60
30	Rick Volk	2.00	1.00	.60
31	**Checklist 1-132**	2.50	1.25	.70
32	Dan Abramowicz	2.00	1.00	.60
33	Bubba Smith	2.00	1.00	.60
34	David Ray	2.00	1.00	.60
35	Dan Dierdorf	2.00	1.00	.60
36	Randy Rasmussen	2.00	1.00	.60
37	Bob Howard	2.00	1.00	.60
38	Gary Huff	2.00	1.00	.60
39	Rocky Bleier **RC**	10.00	5.00	3.00
40	Mel Gray	2.00	1.00	.60
41	Tony McGee	2.00	1.00	.60
42	Larry Hand	2.00	1.00	.60
43	Wendell Hayes	2.00	1.00	.60
44	Doug Wilkerson **RC**	2.00	1.00	.60
45	Paul Smith	2.00	1.00	.60
46	Dave Robinson	2.00	1.00	.60
47	Bivian Lee	2.00	1.00	.60
48	Jim Mandich **RC**	2.00	1.00	.60
49	Greg Pruitt	2.00	1.00	.60
50	Dan Pastorini	2.00	1.00	.60
51	Ron Pritchard	2.00	1.00	.60
52	Dan Conners	2.00	1.00	.60
53	Fred Cox	2.00	1.00	.60
54	Tony Greene	2.00	1.00	.60
55	Craig Morton	2.00	1.00	.60
56	Jerry Sisemore	2.00	1.00	.60
57	Glenn Doughty	2.00	1.00	.60
58	Larry Schreiber	2.00	1.00	.60
59	Charlie Waters **RC**	2.00	1.00	.60
60	Jack Youngblood	2.00	1.00	.60
61	Bill Lenkaitis	2.00	1.00	.60
62	Greg Brezina	2.00	1.00	.60
63	Bob Pollard	2.00	1.00	.60
64	Mack Alston	2.00	1.00	.60
65	Drew Pearson **RC**	10.00	5.00	3.00
66	Charlie Stukes	2.00	1.00	.60
67	Emerson Boozer	2.00	1.00	.60
68	Dennis Partee	2.00	1.00	.60
69	Bob Newton	2.00	1.00	.60
70	Jack Tatum	2.00	1.00	.60
71	Frank Lewis	2.00	1.00	.60
72	Bob Young	2.00	1.00	.60
73	Julius Adams	2.00	1.00	.60
74	Paul Naumoff	2.00	1.00	.60
75	Otis Taylor	2.00	1.00	.60
76	Dave Hampton	2.00	1.00	.60
77	Mike Current	2.00	1.00	.60
78	Brig Owens	2.00	1.00	.60
79	Bobby Scott	2.00	1.00	.60
80	Harold Carmichael	2.00	1.00	.60
81	Bill Stanfill	2.00	1.00	.60
82	Bob Babich	2.00	1.00	.60
83	Vic Washington	2.00	1.00	.60
84	Mick Tingelhoff	2.00	1.00	.60
85	Bob Trumpy	2.00	1.00	.60
86	Earl Edwards	2.00	1.00	.60
87	Ron Hornsby	2.00	1.00	.60
88	Don McCauley	2.00	1.00	.60
89	Jimmy Johnson	2.00	1.00	.60
90	Andy Russell	2.00	1.00	.60
91	Cornell Green	2.00	1.00	.60
92	Charlie Cowan	2.00	1.00	.60
93	Jon Staggers	2.00	1.00	.60
94	Billy Newsome	2.00	1.00	.60
95	Willie Brown	2.00	1.00	.60
96	Carl Mauck	2.00	1.00	.60
97	Doug Buffone	2.00	1.00	.60
98	Preston Pearson	2.00	1.00	.60
99	Jim Bakken	2.00	1.00	.60
100	Bob Griese	3.00	1.50	.90
101	Bob Windsor	2.00	1.00	.60
102	Rockne Freitas	2.00	1.00	.60
103	Jim Marsalis	2.00	1.00	.60
104	Bill Thompson	2.00	1.00	.60
105	Ken Burrow	2.00	1.00	.60
106	Diron Talbert	2.00	1.00	.60
107	Joe Federspiel	2.00	1.00	.60
108	Norm Bulaich	2.00	1.00	.60
109	Bob DeMarco	2.00	1.00	.60
110	Tom Wittum	2.00	1.00	.60
111	Larry Hefner	2.00	1.00	.60
112	Tody Smith	2.00	1.00	.60
113	Stu Voigt	2.00	1.00	.60
114	Horst Muhlmann	2.00	1.00	.60

		NM	E	VG
115	Ahmad Rashad	2.00	1.00	.90
116	Joe Dawkins	2.00	1.00	.60
117	George Kunz	2.00	1.00	.60
118	D.D. Lewis	2.00	1.00	.60
119	Levi Johnson	2.00	1.00	.60
120	Len Dawson	5.00	2.50	1.50
121	Jim Bertelsen	2.00	1.00	.60
122	Ed Bell	2.00	1.00	.60
123	Art Thoms	2.00	1.00	.60
124	Joe Beauchamp	2.00	1.00	.60
125	Jack Ham	4.00	2.00	1.20
126	Carl Garrett	2.00	1.00	.60
127	Roger Finnie	2.00	1.00	.60
128	Howard Twilley	2.00	1.00	.60
129	Bruce Barnes	2.00	1.00	.60
130	Nate Wright	2.00	1.00	.60
131	Jerry Tagge	2.00	1.00	.60
132	Floyd Little	2.00	1.00	.60
133	John Zook	2.00	1.00	.60
134	Len Hauss	2.00	1.00	.60
135	Archie Manning	2.00	1.00	.60
136	Po James	2.00	1.00	.60
137	Walt Sumner	2.00	1.00	.60
138	Randy Beisler	2.00	1.00	.60
139	Willie Alexander	2.00	1.00	.60
140	Garo Yepremian	2.00	1.00	.60
141	Chip Myers	2.00	1.00	.60
142	Jim Braxton	2.00	1.00	.60
143	Doug Van Horn	2.00	1.00	.60
144	Stan White	2.00	1.00	.60
145	Roger Staubach	10.00	5.00	3.00
146	Herman Weaver	2.00	1.00	.60
147	Marvin Upshaw	2.00	1.00	.60
148	Bob Klein	2.00	1.00	.60
149	Earlie Thomas	2.00	1.00	.60
150	John Brockington	2.00	1.00	.60
151	Mike Siani	2.00	1.00	.60
152	Sam Davis	2.00	1.00	.60
153	Mike Wagner	2.00	1.00	.60
154	Larry Stallings	2.00	1.00	.60
155	Wally Chambers	2.00	1.00	.60
156	Randy Vataha	2.00	1.00	.60
157	Jim Marshall	2.00	1.00	.60
158	Jim Turner	2.00	1.00	.60
159	Walt Sweeney	2.00	1.00	.60
160	Ken Anderson	2.00	1.00	.60
161	Ray Brown	2.00	1.00	.60
162	John Didion	2.00	1.00	.60
163	Tom Dempsey	2.00	1.00	.60
164	Clarence Scott	2.00	1.00	.60
165	Gene Washington	2.00	1.00	.60
166	Willie Rodgers	2.00	1.00	.60
167	Doug Swift	2.00	1.00	.60
168	Rufus Mayes	2.00	1.00	.60
169	Marv Bateman	2.00	1.00	.60
170	Lydell Mitchell	2.00	1.00	.60
171	Ron Smith	2.00	1.00	.60
172	Bill Munson	2.00	1.00	.60
173	Bob Grim	2.00	1.00	.60
174	Ed Budde	2.00	1.00	.60
175	Bob Lilly	4.00	2.00	1.20
176	Jim Youngblood **RC**	2.00	1.00	.60
177	Steve Tannen	2.00	1.00	.60
178	Rich McGeorge	2.00	1.00	.60
179	Jim Tyrer	2.00	1.00	.60
180	Forrest Blue	2.00	1.00	.60
181	Jerry LeVias	2.00	1.00	.60
182	Joe Gilliam **RC**	2.00	1.00	.60
183	Jim Otis **RC**	2.00	1.00	.60
184	Mel Tom	2.00	1.00	.60
185	Paul Seymour	2.00	1.00	.60
186	George Webster	2.00	1.00	.60
187	Pete Duranko	2.00	1.00	.60
188	Essex Johnson	2.00	1.00	.60
189	Bob Lee	2.00	1.00	.60
190	Gene Upshaw	2.00	1.00	.60
191	Tom Myers	2.00	1.00	.60
192	Don Zimmerman	2.00	1.00	.60
193	John Garlington	2.00	1.00	.60
194	Skip Butler	2.00	1.00	.60
195	Tom Mitchell	2.00	1.00	.60
196	Jim Langer	2.00	1.00	.60
197	Ron Carpenter	2.00	1.00	.60
198	Dave Foley	2.00	1.00	.60
199	Bert Jones	2.00	1.00	.60
200	Larry Brown	2.00	1.00	.60
201	All Pro Receivers (Charley Taylor, Fred Biletnikoff)	2.00	1.00	.60
202	All Pro Tackles (Russ Washington, Rayfield Wright)	2.00	1.00	.60
203	All Pro Guards (Tom Mack, Larry Little)	2.00	1.00	.60
204	All Pro Center s (Jeff Van Note, Jack Rudnay)	2.00	1.00	.60
205	All Pro Guards (Gale Gillingham, John Hannah)	2.00	1.00	.60

206	All Pro Tackles (Winston Hill, Dan Dierdorf)	2.00	1.00	.60
207	All Pro Tight Ends (Riley Odoms, Charley Young)	2.00	1.00	.60
208	All Pro Quarterbacks (Fran Tarkenton, Ken Stabler)	3.00	1.50	.90
209	All Pro Backs (Lawrence McCutcheon, O.J. Simpson)	5.00	2.50	1.50
210	All Pro Backs (Otis Armstrong, Terry Metcalf)	2.00	1.00	.60
211	All Pro Receivers (Isaac Curtis, Mel Gray)	2.00	1.00	.60
212	All Pro Kickers (Roy Gerela, Chester Marcol)	2.00	1.00	.60
213	All Pro Ends (Elvin Bethea, Jack Youngblood)	2.00	1.00	.60
214	All Pro Tackles (Otis Sistrunk, Alan Page)	2.00	1.00	.60
215	All Pro Tackles (Merlin Olsen, Mike Reid)	2.00	1.00	.60
216	All Pro Ends (Carl Eller, Lyle Alzado)	2.00	1.00	.60
217	All Pro Linebackers (Ted Hendricks, Phil Villapiano)	2.00	1.00	.60
218	All Pro Linebackers (Willie Lanier, Lee Roy Jordan)	2.00	1.00	.60
219	All Pro Linebackers (Andy Russell, Isiah Robertson)	2.00	1.00	.60
220	All Pro Cornerbacks (Emmitt Thomas, Nate Wright)	2.00	1.00	.60
221	All Pro Cornerbacks (Lemar Parrish, Willie Buchanon)	2.00	1.00	.60
222	All Pro Safeties (Ken Houston, Dick Anderson)	2.00	1.00	.60
223	All Pro Safeties (Cliff Harris, Jack Tatum)	2.00	1.00	.60
224	All Pro Punters (Tom Wittum, Ray Guy)	2.00	1.00	.60
225	All Pro Returners (Greg Pruitt, Terry Metcalf)	2.00	1.00	.60
226	Ted Kwalick	2.00	1.00	.60
227	Spider Lockhart	2.00	1.00	.60
228	Mike Livingston	2.00	1.00	.60
229	Larry Cole	2.00	1.00	.60
230	Gary Garrison	2.00	1.00	.60
231	Larry Brooks	2.00	1.00	.60
232	Bobby Howfield	2.00	1.00	.60
233	Fred Carr	2.00	1.00	.60
234	Norm Evans	2.00	1.00	.60
235	Dwight White	2.00	1.00	.60
236	Conrad Dobler	2.00	1.00	.60
237	Garry Lyle	2.00	1.00	.60
238	Darryl Stingley	1.00	.50	.30
239	Tom Graham	2.00	1.00	.60
240	Chuck Foreman	2.00	1.00	.60
241	Ken Riley	2.00	1.00	.60
242	Don Morrison	2.00	1.00	.60
243	Lynn Dickey	2.00	1.00	.60
244	Don Cockroft	2.00	1.00	.60
245	Claude Humphrey	2.00	1.00	.60
246	John Skorupan	2.00	1.00	.60
247	Raymond Chester	2.00	1.00	.60
248	Cas Banaszek	2.00	1.00	.60
249	Art Malone	2.00	1.00	.60
250	Ed Flanagan	2.00	1.00	.60
251	Checklist 133-264	2.00	1.00	.60
252	Nemiah Wilson	2.00	1.00	.60
253	Ron Jessie	2.00	1.00	.60
254	Jim Lynch	2.00	1.00	.60
255	Bob Tucker	2.00	1.00	.60
256	Terry Owens	2.00	1.00	.60
257	John Fitzgerald	2.00	1.00	.60
258	Jack Snow	2.00	1.00	.60
259	Garry Puetz	2.00	1.00	.60
260	Mike Phipps	2.00	1.00	.60
261	Al Matthews	2.00	1.00	.60
262	Bob Kuechenberg	2.00	1.00	.60
263	Ron Yankowski	2.00	1.00	.60
264	Ron Shanklin	2.00	1.00	.60
265	Bobby Douglass	2.00	1.00	.60
266	Josh Ashton	2.00	1.00	.60
267	Bill Van Heusen	2.00	1.00	.60
268	Jeff Siemon	2.00	1.00	.60
269	Bob Newland	2.00	1.00	.60
270	Gale Gillingham	2.00	1.00	.60
271	Zeke Moore	2.00	1.00	.60
272	Mike Tilleman	2.00	1.00	.60
273	John Leypoldt	2.00	1.00	.60

274	Ken Mendenhall	2.00	1.00	.60
275	Norm Snead	2.00	1.00	.60
276	Bill Bradley	2.00	1.00	.60
277	Jerry Smith	2.00	1.00	.60
278	Clarence Davis	2.00	1.00	.60
279	Jim Yarbrough	2.00	1.00	.60
280	Lemar Parrish	2.00	1.00	.60
281	Bobby Bell	1.50	.70	.45
282	Lynn Swann **RC**	35.00	18.00	11.00
283	John Hicks	2.00	1.00	.60
284	Coy Bacon	2.00	1.00	.60
285	Lee Roy Jordan	2.00	1.00	.60
286	Willie Buchanon	2.00	1.00	.60
287	Al Woodall	2.00	1.00	.60
288	Reggie Rucker	2.00	1.00	.60
289	John Schmitt	2.00	1.00	.60
290	Carl Eller	2.00	1.00	.60
291	Jake Scott	2.00	1.00	.60
292	Donny Anderson	2.00	1.00	.60
293	Charley Wade	2.00	1.00	.60
294	John Tanner	2.00	1.00	.60
295	Charley Johnson	2.00	1.00	.60
296	Tom Blanchard	2.00	1.00	.60
297	Curley Culp	2.00	1.00	.60
298	Jeff Van Note **RC**	2.00	1.00	.60
299	Bob James	2.00	1.00	.60
300	Franco Harris	5.00	2.50	1.50
301	Tim Berra	2.00	1.00	.60
302	Bruce Gossett	2.00	1.00	.60
303	Berlon Biggs	2.00	1.00	.60
304	Bob Kowalkowski	2.00	1.00	.60
305	Marv Hubbard	2.00	1.00	.60
306	Ken Avery	2.00	1.00	.60
307	Mike Adamle	2.00	1.00	.60
308	Don Herrmann	2.00	1.00	.60
309	Chris Fletcher	2.00	1.00	.60
310	Roman Gabriel	2.00	1.00	.60
311	Billy Joe DuPree	2.00	1.00	.60
312	Fred Dryer	2.00	1.00	.60
313	John Riggins	4.00	2.00	1.20
314	Bob McKay	2.00	1.00	.60
315	Ted Hendricks	2.00	1.00	.60
316	Bobby Bryant	2.00	1.00	.60
317	Don Nottingham	2.00	1.00	.60
318	John Hannah	2.00	1.00	.60
319	Rich Coady	2.00	1.00	.60
320	Phil Villapiano	2.00	1.00	.60
321	Jim Plunkett	2.00	1.00	.60
322	Lyle Alzado	2.00	1.00	.60
323	Ernie Jackson	2.00	1.00	.60
324	Billy Parks	2.00	1.00	.60
325	Willie Lanier	2.00	1.00	.60
326	John James	2.00	1.00	.60
327	Joe Ferguson	2.00	1.00	.60
328	Ernie Holmes **RC**	2.00	1.00	.60
329	Bruce Laird	2.00	1.00	.60
330	Chester Marcol	2.00	1.00	.60
331	Dave Wilcox	2.00	1.00	.60
332	Pat Fischer	2.00	1.00	.60
333	Steve Owens	2.00	1.00	.60
334	Royce Berry	2.00	1.00	.60
335	Russ Washington	2.00	1.00	.60
336	Walker Gillette	2.00	1.00	.60
337	Mark Nordquist	2.00	1.00	.60
338	James Harris **RC**	2.00	1.00	.60
339	Warren Koegel	2.00	1.00	.60
340	Emmitt Thomas	2.00	1.00	.60
341	Walt Garrison	2.00	1.00	.60
342	Thom Darden	2.00	1.00	.60
343	Mike Eischeid	2.00	1.00	.60
344	Ernie McMillan	2.00	1.00	.60
345	Nick Buoniconti	2.00	1.00	.60
346	George Farmer	2.00	1.00	.60
347	Sam Adams	2.00	1.00	.60
348	Larry Cipa	2.00	1.00	.60
349	Bob Moore	2.00	1.00	.60
350	Otis Armstrong **RC**	4.00	2.00	1.25
351	George Blanda (RH)	4.00	2.00	1.25
352	Fred Cox (RH)	2.00	1.00	.60
353	Tom Dempsey (RH)	2.00	1.00	.60
354	Ken Houston (RH)	2.00	1.00	.60
355	O.J. Simpson (RH)	5.00	2.50	1.50
356	Ron Smith (RH)	2.00	1.00	.60
357	Bob Atkins	2.00	1.00	.60
358	Pat Sullivan	2.00	1.00	.60
359	Joe DeLamielleure	2.00	1.00	.60
360	L. McCutcheon **RC**	2.00	1.00	.60
361	David Lee	2.00	1.00	.60
362	Mike McCoy	2.00	1.00	.60
363	Skip Vanderbundt	2.00	1.00	.60
364	Mark Moseley	2.00	1.00	.60
365	Lem Barney	2.00	1.00	.60
366	Doug Dressler	2.00	1.00	.60
367	Dan Fouts **RC**	25.00	13.00	8.00
368	Bob Hyland	2.00	1.00	.60
369	John Outlaw	2.00	1.00	.60
370	Roy Gerela	2.00	1.00	.60
371	Isiah Robertson	2.00	1.00	.60

372	Jerome Barkum	2.00	1.00	.60
373	Ed Podolak	2.00	1.00	.60
374	Milt Morin	2.00	1.00	.60
375	John Niland	2.00	1.00	.60
376	Checklist 265-396	2.00	1.00	.60
377	Ken Iman	2.00	1.00	.60
378	Manny Fernandez	2.00	1.00	.60
379	Dave Gallagher	2.00	1.00	.60
380	Ken Stabler	5.00	2.50	1.50
381	Mack Herron	2.00	1.00	.60
382	Bill McClard	2.00	1.00	.60
383	Ray May	2.00	1.00	.60
384	Don Hansen	2.00	1.00	.60
385	Elvin Bethea	2.00	1.00	.60
386	Joe Scibelli	2.00	1.00	.60
387	Neal Craig	2.00	1.00	.60
388	Marty Domres	2.00	1.00	.60
389	Ken Ellis	2.00	1.00	.60
390	Charley Young	2.00	1.00	.60
391	Tommy Hart	2.00	1.00	.60
392	Moses Denson	2.00	1.00	.60
393	Larry Walton	2.00	1.00	.60
394	Dave Green	2.00	1.00	.60
395	Ron Johnson	2.00	1.00	.60
396	Ed Bradley	2.00	1.00	.60
397	J.T. Thomas	2.00	1.00	.60
398	Jim Bailey	2.00	1.00	.60
399	Barry Pearson	2.00	1.00	.60
400	Fran Tarkenton	4.00	2.00	1.25
401	Jack Rudnay	2.00	1.00	.60
402	Rayfield Wright	2.00	1.00	.60
403	Roger Wehrli	2.00	1.00	.60
404	Vern Den Herder	2.00	1.00	.60
405	Fred Biletnikoff	2.00	1.00	.60
406	Ken Grandberry	2.00	1.00	.60
407	Bob Adams	2.00	1.00	.60
408	Jim Merlo	2.00	1.00	.60
409	John Pitts	2.00	1.00	.60
410	Dave Osborn	2.00	1.00	.60
411	Dennis Havig	2.00	1.00	.60
412	Bob Johnson	2.00	1.00	.60
413	Ken Burrow	2.00	1.00	.60
414	Jim Cheyunski	2.00	1.00	.60
415	MacArthur Lane	2.00	1.00	.60
416	Joe Theismann **RC**	20.00	10.00	6.00
417	Mike Boryla **RC**	2.00	1.00	.60
418	Bruce Taylor	2.00	1.00	.60
419	Chris Hanburger	2.00	1.00	.60
420	Tom Mack	2.00	1.00	.60
421	Errol Mann	2.00	1.00	.60
422	Jack Gregory	2.00	1.00	.60
423	Harrison Davis	2.00	1.00	.60
424	Burgess Owens	2.00	1.00	.60
425	Joe Greene	5.00	2.50	1.50
426	Morris Stroud	2.00	1.00	.60
427	John DeMarie	2.00	1.00	.60
428	Mel Renfro	2.00	1.00	.60
429	Cid Edwards	2.00	1.00	.60
430	Mike Reid	2.00	1.00	.60
431	Jack Mildren	2.00	1.00	.60
432	Jerry Simmons	2.00	1.00	.60
433	Ron Yary	2.00	1.00	.60
434	Howard Stevens	2.00	1.00	.60
435	Ray Guy	2.00	1.00	.60
436	Tommy Nobis	2.00	1.00	.60
437	Solomon Freelon	2.00	1.00	.60
438	J.D. Hill	2.00	1.00	.60
439	Toni Linhart	2.00	1.00	.60
440	Dick Anderson	2.00	1.00	.60
441	Guy Morriss	2.00	1.00	.60
442	Bob Hoskins	2.00	1.00	.60
443	John Hadl	2.00	1.00	.60
444	Roy Jefferson	2.00	1.00	.60
445	Charlie Sanders	2.00	1.00	.60
446	Pat Curran	2.00	1.00	.60
447	David Knight	2.00	1.00	.60
448	Bob Brown	2.00	1.00	.60
449	Pete Gogolak	2.00	1.00	.60
450	Terry Metcalf	2.00	1.00	.60
451	Bill Bergey	2.00	1.00	.60
452	Dan Abramowicz (HL)	2.00	1.00	.60
453	Otis Armstrong (HL)	2.00	1.00	.60
454	Cliff Branch (HL)	2.00	1.00	.60
455	John James (HL)	2.00	1.00	.60
456	Lydell Mitchell (HL)	2.00	1.00	.60
457	Lemar Parrish (HL)	2.00	1.00	.60
458	Ken Stabler (HL)	3.00	1.50	.90
459	Lynn Swann (HL)	5.00	3.50	1.50
460	Emmitt Thomas (HL)	2.00	1.00	.60
461	Terry Bradshaw	10.00	5.00	3.00
462	Jerrel Wilson	2.00	1.00	.60
463	Walter Johnson	2.00	1.00	.60
464	Golden Richards	2.00	1.00	.60
465	Tommy Casanova	2.00	1.00	.60
466	Randy Jackson	2.00	1.00	.60
467	Ron Bolton	2.00	1.00	.60
468	Joe Owens	2.00	1.00	.60
469	Wally Hilgenberg	2.00	1.00	.60

		NM	E	VG
470	Riley Odoms	2.00	1.00	.60
471	Otis Sistrunk	2.00	1.00	.60
472	Eddie Ray	2.00	1.00	.60
473	Reggie McKenzie	2.00	1.00	.25
474	Elbert Drungo	2.00	1.00	.60
475	Mercury Morris	2.00	1.00	.60
476	Dan Dickel	2.00	1.00	.60
477	Merritt Kersey	2.00	1.00	.60
478	Mike Holmes	2.00	1.00	.60
479	Clarence Williams	2.00	1.00	.60
480	Bill Kilmer	2.00	1.00	.60
481	Altie Taylor	2.00	1.00	.60
482	Dave Elmendorf	2.00	1.00	.60
483	Bob Rowe	2.00	1.00	.60
484	Pete Athas	2.00	1.00	.60
485	Winston Hill	2.00	1.00	.60
486	Bo Mathews	2.00	1.00	.60
487	Earl Thomas	2.00	1.00	.60
488	Jan Stenerud	2.00	1.00	.60
489	Steve Holden	2.00	1.00	.60
490	Cliff Harris **RC**	4.00	2.00	1.25
491	Boobie Clark **RC**	2.00	1.00	.60
492	Joe Taylor	2.00	1.00	.60
493	Tom Neville	2.00	1.00	.60
494	Wayne Colman	2.00	1.00	.60
495	Jim Mitchell	2.00	1.00	.60
496	Paul Krause	2.00	1.00	.60
497	Jim Otto	2.00	1.00	.60
498	John Rowser	2.00	1.00	.60
499	Larry Little	2.00	1.00	.60
500	O.J. Simpson	8.00	4.00	2.40
501	John Dutton **RC**	2.00	1.00	.60
502	Pat Hughes	2.00	1.00	.60
503	Malcolm Snider	2.00	1.00	.60
504	Fred Willis	2.00	1.00	.60
505	Harold Jackson	2.00	1.00	.60
506	Mike Bragg	2.00	1.00	.60
507	Jerry Sherk	2.00	1.00	.60
508	Mirro Roder	2.00	1.00	.60
509	Tom Sullivan	2.00	1.00	.60
510	Jim Hart	2.00	1.00	.60
511	Cedrick Hardman	2.00	1.00	.60
512	Blaine Nye	2.00	1.00	.60
513	Elmo Wright	2.00	1.00	.60
514	Herb Orvis	2.00	1.00	.60
515	Richard Caster	2.00	1.00	.60
516	Doug Kotar **RC**	2.00	1.00	.60
517	**Checklist 397-528**	2.00	1.00	.60
518	Jesse Freitas	2.00	1.00	.60
519	Ken Houston	2.00	1.00	.60
520	Alan Page	2.00	1.00	.60
521	Tim Foley	2.00	1.00	.60
522	Bill Olds	2.00	1.00	.60
523	Bobby Maples	2.00	1.00	.60
524	Cliff Branch **RC**	8.00	4.00	2.40
525	Merlin Olsen	2.00	1.00	.60
526	AFC Champions (Terry Bradshaw, Franco Harris)	5.00	2.50	1.50
527	NFC Champions (Chuck Foreman)	5.00	2.50	1.50
528	Super Bowl (Terry Bradshaw)	5.00	2.50	1.50

1975 Topps Team Checklists

Each of the 26 NFL teams is represented in this set, which was available as a mail-in offer from Topps as an uncut sheet. Each card is standard size, and shows the team's 1975 schedule on the front. The card back is unnumbered and contains a checklist for the players in the team set.

		NM	E	VG
	Complete Set (26):	195.00	97.50	55.50
	Common Player:	8.00	4.00	2.50
(1)	Atlanta Falcons	8.50	4.25	2.50
(2)	Baltimore Colts	8.00	4.00	2.50
(3)	Buffalo Bills	8.00	4.00	2.50
(4)	Chicago Bears	9.00	4.50	2.75
(5)	Cincinnati Bengals	8.00	4.00	2.50
(6)	Cleveland Browns	9.00	4.50	2.75
(7)	Dallas Cowboys	10.00	5.00	3.00
(8)	Denver Broncos	10.00	5.00	3.00
(9)	Dotroit Lions	8.00	4.00	2.50
(10)	Green Bay Packers	8.00	4.00	2.50
(11)	Houston Oilers	8.00	4.00	2.50
(12)	Kansas City Chiefs	8.00	4.00	2.50
(13)	Los Angeles Rams	8.00	4.00	2.50
(14)	Miami Dolphins	10.00	5.00	3.00
(15)	Minnesota Vikings	9.00	4.50	2.75
(16)	New England Patriots	8.00	4.00	2.50
(17)	New York Giants	9.00	4.50	2.75
(18)	New York Jets	9.00	4.50	2.75
(19)	New Orleans Saints	8.00	4.00	2.50
(20)	Oakland Raiders	10.00	5.00	3.00
(21)	Philadelphia Eagles	8.00	4.00	2.50
(22)	Pittsburgh Steelers	9.00	4.50	2.75
(23)	St. Louis Cardinals	9.00	4.50	2.75
(24)	San Diego Chargers	8.00	4.00	2.50
(25)	San Francisco 49ers	9.00	4.50	2.75
(26)	Washington Redskins	10.00	5.00	3.00

1976 Topps

This is the most valuable of the 528-card sets issued by Topps, primarily because of the inclusion of Walter Payton's rookie card. Other rookies in this set include Steve Bartkowski, Harvey Martin, Russ Francis, Randy White, Jack Lambert, Randy Gradishar, Steve Grogan, and Ron Jaworski. The set also features the second-year card of Dan Fouts. Hall of Famers (and future Hall of Famers) showing up in the 1976 Topps issue include Payton, Fouts, Martin, White, Lambert, Willie Lanier, Fred Biletnikoff, Ray Guy, Alan Page, Bob Griese, Franco Harris, O.J. Simpson, John Riggins, Len Dawson, Paul Warfield, George Blanda, Roger Staubach, Ken Stabler, Larry Csonka, Charley Taylor and Fran Tarkenton. (Key: AP - All Pro)

	NM	E	VG
Complete Set (528):	450.00	225.00	135.00
Common Player:	2.00	1.00	.60
Minor Stars:	.50		
Unlisted Stars:	1.00		
Team Cards:	1.50	1.25	.60
Wax Pack (10):	70.00		
Wax Box (36):	1,800.		

1	George Blanda	4.00	2.00	1.20
2	Neil Colzie	2.00	1.00	.60
3	Chuck Foreman	2.00	1.00	.60
4	Jim Marshall	2.00	1.00	.60
5	Terry Metcalf	2.00	1.00	.60
6	O.J. Simpson	5.00	2.50	1.50
7	Fran Tarkenton	5.00	2.50	1.50
8	Charley Taylor	2.00	1.00	.60
9	Ernie Holmes	2.00	1.00	.60
10	Ken Anderson (AP)	2.00	1.00	.60
11	Bobby Bryant	2.00	1.00	.60
12	Jerry Smith	2.00	1.00	.60
13	David Lee	2.00	1.00	.60
14	Robert Newhouse **RC**	2.00	1.00	.60
15	Vern Den Herder	2.00	1.00	.60
16	John Hannah	2.00	1.00	.60
17	J.D. Hill	2.00	1.00	.60
18	James Harris	2.00	1.00	.60
19	Willie Buchanon	2.00	1.00	.60
20	Charley Young (AP)	2.00	1.00	.60
21	Jim Yarbrough	2.00	1.00	.60
22	Ronnie Coleman	2.00	1.00	.60
23	Don Cockroft	2.00	1.00	.60
24	Willie Lanier	2.00	1.00	.60
25	Fred Biletnikoff	2.00	1.00	.60
26	Ron Yankowski	2.00	1.00	.60
27	Spider Lockhart	2.00	1.00	.60
28	Bob Johnson	2.00	1.00	.60
29	J.T. Thomas	2.00	1.00	.60
30	Ron Yary (AP)	2.00	1.00	.60
31	Brad Dusek **RC**	2.00	1.00	.60
32	Raymond Chester	2.00	1.00	.60
33	Larry Little	2.00	1.00	.60
34	Pat Leahy **RC**	2.00	1.00	.60
35	Steve Bartkowski **RC**	2.00	1.00	.60
36	Tom Myers	2.00	1.00	.60
37	Bill Van Heusen	2.00	1.00	.60

38	Russ Washington	2.00	1.00	.60
39	Tom Sullivan	2.00	1.00	.60
40	Curley Culp (AP)	2.00	1.00	.60
41	Johnnie Gray	2.00	1.00	.60
42	Bob Klein	2.00	1.00	.60
43	Lem Barney	2.00	1.00	.60
44	Harvey Martin **RC**	10.00	5.00	3.00
45	Reggie Rucker	2.00	1.00	.60
46	Neil Clabo	2.00	1.00	.60
47	Ray Hamilton	2.00	1.00	.60
48	Joe Ferguson	2.00	1.00	.60
49	Ed Podolak	2.00	1.00	.60
50	Ray Guy (AP)	2.00	1.00	.60
51	Glen Edwards	2.00	1.00	.60
52	Jim LeClair	2.00	1.00	.60
53	Mike Barnes	2.00	1.00	.60
54	Nat Moore **RC**	2.00	1.00	.60
55	Bill Kilmer	2.00	1.00	.60
56	Larry Stallings	2.00	1.00	.60
57	Jack Gregory	2.00	1.00	.60
58	Steve Mike-Mayer	2.00	1.00	.60
59	Virgil Livers	2.00	1.00	.60
60	Jerry Sherk (AP)	2.00	1.00	.60
61	Guy Morriss	2.00	1.00	.60
62	Barty Smith	2.00	1.00	.60
63	Jerome Barkum	2.00	1.00	.60
64	Ira Gordon	2.00	1.00	.60
65	Paul Krause	2.00	1.00	.60
66	John McMakin	2.00	1.00	.60
67	Checklist 1-132	2.00	1.00	.60
68	Charley Johnson	2.00	1.00	.60
69	Tommy Nobis	2.00	1.00	.60
70	Lydell Mitchell	2.00	1.00	.60
71	Vern Holland	2.00	1.00	.60
72	Tim Foley	2.00	1.00	.60
73	Golden Richards	2.00	1.00	.60
74	Bryant Salter	2.00	1.00	.60
75	Terry Bradshaw	4.00	2.00	1.20
76	Ted Hendricks	2.00	1.00	.60
77	Rich Saul **RC**	2.00	1.00	.60
78	John Smith	2.00	1.00	.60
79	Altie Taylor	2.00	1.00	.60
80	Cedrick Hardman (AP)	2.00	1.00	.60
81	Ken Payne	2.00	1.00	.60
82	Zeke Moore	2.00	1.00	.60
83	Alvin Maxson	2.00	1.00	.60
84	Wally Hilgenberg	2.00	1.00	.60
85	John Niland	2.00	1.00	.60
86	Mike Sensibaugh	2.00	1.00	.60
87	Ron Johnson	2.00	1.00	.60
88	Winston Hill	2.00	1.00	.60
89	Charlie Joiner	2.00	1.00	.60
90	Roger Wehrli (AP)	2.00	1.00	.60
91	Mike Bragg	2.00	1.00	.60
92	Dan Dickel	2.00	1.00	.60
93	Earl Morrall	2.00	1.00	.60
94	Pat Toomay	2.00	1.00	.60
95	Gary Garrison	2.00	1.00	.60
96	Ken Geddes	2.00	1.00	.60
97	Mike Current	2.00	1.00	.60
98	Bob Avellini	2.00	1.00	.60
99	Dave Pureifory	2.00	1.00	.60
100	Franco Harris (AP)	5.00	2.50	1.50
101	Randy Logan	2.00	1.00	.60
102	John Fitzgerald	2.00	1.00	.60
103	Gregg Bingham **RC**	2.00	1.00	.60
104	Jim Plunkett	2.00	1.00	.60
105	Carl Eller	2.00	1.00	.60
106	Larry Walton	2.00	1.00	.60
107	Clarence Scott	2.00	1.00	.60
108	Skip Vanderbundt	2.00	1.00	.60
109	Boobie Clark	2.00	1.00	.60
110	Tom Mack (AP)	2.00	1.00	.60
111	Bruce Laird	2.00	1.00	.60
112	Dave Dalby **RC**	2.00	1.00	.60
113	John Leypoldt	2.00	1.00	.60
114	Barry Pearson	2.00	1.00	.60
115	Larry Brown	2.00	1.00	.60
116	Jackie Smith	2.00	1.00	.60
117	Pat Hughes	2.00	1.00	.60
118	Al Woodall	2.00	1.00	.60
119	John Zook	2.00	1.00	.60
120	Jake Scott (AP)	2.00	1.00	.60
121	Rich Glover	2.00	1.00	.60
122	Ernie Jackson	2.00	1.00	.60
123	Otis Armstrong	2.00	1.00	.60
124	Bob Grim	2.00	1.00	.60
125	Jeff Siemon	2.00	1.00	.60
126	Harold Hart	2.00	1.00	.60
127	John DeMarie	2.00	1.00	.60
128	Dan Fouts	3.00	1.50	.90
129	Jim Kearney	2.00	1.00	.60
130	John Dutton (AP)	2.00	1.00	.60
131	Calvin Hill	2.00	1.00	.60
132	Toni Fritsch	2.00	1.00	.60
133	Ron Jessie	2.00	1.00	.60
134	Don Nottingham	2.00	1.00	.60
135	Lemar Parrish	2.00	1.00	.60

136	Russ Francis **RC**	2.00	1.00	.60
137	Joe Reed	2.00	1.00	.60
138	C.L. Whittington	2.00	1.00	.60
139	Otis Sistrunk	2.00	1.00	.60
140	Lynn Swann (AP)	13.00	6.50	3.90
141	Jim Carter	2.00	1.00	.60
142	Mike Montler	2.00	1.00	.60
143	Walter Johnson	2.00	1.00	.60
144	Doug Kotar	2.00	1.00	.60
145	Roman Gabriel	2.00	1.00	.60
146	Billy Newsome	2.00	1.00	.60
147	Ed Bradley	2.00	1.00	.60
148	Walter Payton **RC**	150.00	75.00	45.00
149	Johnny Fuller	2.00	1.00	.60
150	Alan Page (AP)	2.00	1.00	.60
151	Frank Grant	2.00	1.00	.60
152	Dave Green	2.00	1.00	.60
153	Nelson Munsey	2.00	1.00	.60
154	Jim Mandich	2.00	1.00	.60
155	Lawrence McCutcheon	2.00	1.00	.60
156	Steve Ramsey	2.00	1.00	.60
157	Ed Flanagan	2.00	1.00	.60
158	Randy White **RC**	20.00	10.00	6.00
159	Gerry Mullins	2.00	1.00	.60
160	Jan Stenerud (AP)	2.00	1.00	.60
161	Steve Odom	2.00	1.00	.60
162	Roger Finnie	2.00	1.00	.60
163	Norm Snead	2.00	1.00	.60
164	Jeff Van Note	2.00	1.00	.60
165	Bill Bergey	2.00	1.00	.60
166	Allen Carter	2.00	1.00	.60
167	Steve Holden	2.00	1.00	.60
168	Sherman White	2.00	1.00	.60
169	Bob Berry	2.00	1.00	.60
170	Ken Houston (AP)	2.00	1.00	.60
171	Bill Olds	2.00	1.00	.60
172	Larry Seiple	2.00	1.00	.60
173	Cliff Branch	2.00	1.00	.00
174	Reggie McKenzie	2.00	1.00	.60
175	Dan Pastorini	2.00	1.00	.60
176	Paul Naumoff	2.00	1.00	.60
177	Checklist 133-265	2.00	1.00	.60
178	Durwood Keeton	2.00	1.00	.60
179	Earl Thomas	2.00	1.00	.60
180	L.C. Greenwood (AP)	2.00	1.00	.60
181	John Outlaw	2.00	1.00	.60
182	Frank Nunley	2.00	1.00	.60
183	Dave Jennings **RC**	2.00	1.00	.60
184	McArthur Lane	2.00	1.00	.60
185	Chester Marcol	2.00	1.00	.60
186	J.J. Jones	2.00	1.00	.60
187	Tom DeLeone	2.00	1.00	.60
188	Steve Zabel	2.00	1.00	.60
189	Ken Johnson	2.00	1.00	.60
190	Rayfield Wright (AP)	2.00	1.00	.60
191	Brent McClanahan	2.00	1.00	.60
192	Pat Fischer	2.00	1.00	.60
193	Roger Carr **RC**	2.00	1.00	.60
194	Manny Fernandez	2.00	1.00	.60
195	Roy Gerela	2.00	1.00	.60
196	Dave Elmendorf	2.00	1.00	.60
197	Bob Kowalkowski	2.00	1.00	.60
198	Phil Villapiano	2.00	1.00	.60
199	Will Wynn	2.00	1.00	.60
200	Terry Metcalf **RC**	2.00	1.00	.60
201	Passing Leaders: (Ken Anderson, Fran Tarkenton)	5.00	2.50	1.50
202	Receiving Leaders: (Reggie Rucker, Lydell Mitchell, Chuck Foreman)	2.00	1.00	.60
203	Rushing Leaders: (O.J. Simpson, Jim Otis)	3.00	1.50	.90
204	Scoring Leaders: (O.J. Simpson, Chuck Foreman)	4.00	2.00	1.20
205	Interception Leaders: (Mel Blount, Paul Krause)	2.00	1.00	.60
206	Punting Leaders: (Ray Guy, Herman Weaver)	2.00	1.00	.60
207	Ken Ellis	2.00	1.00	.60
208	Ron Saul	2.00	1.00	.60
209	Toni Linhart	2.00	1.00	.60
210	Jim Langer (AP)	2.00	1.00	.40
211	Jeff Wright	2.00	1.00	.60
212	Moses Denson	2.00	1.00	.60
213	Earl Edwards	2.00	1.00	.60
214	Walker Gillette	2.00	1.00	.60
215	Bob Trumpy	2.00	1.00	.60
216	Emmitt Thomas	2.00	1.00	.60
217	Lyle Alzado	2.00	1.00	.60
218	Carl Garrett	2.00	1.00	.60
219	Van Green	2.00	1.00	.60
220	Jack Lambert **RC** (AP)	25.00	13.00	8.00
221	Spike Jones	2.00	1.00	.60
222	John Hadl	2.00	1.00	.60
223	Billy Johnson **RC**	2.00	1.00	.60
224	Tony McGee	2.00	1.00	.60
225	Preston Pearson	2.00	1.00	.60
226	Isiah Robertson	2.00	1.00	.60
227	Errol Mann	2.00	1.00	.60
228	Paul Seal	2.00	1.00	.60
229	Roland Harper **RC**	2.00	1.00	.60
230	Ed White **RC**	2.00	1.00	.60
231	Joe Theismann	2.00	1.00	.60
232	Jim Cheyunski	2.00	1.00	.60
233	Bill Stanfill	2.00	1.00	.60
234	Marv Hubbard	2.00	1.00	.60
235	Tommy Casanova	2.00	1.00	.60
236	Bob Hyland	2.00	1.00	.60
237	Jesse Freitas	2.00	1.00	.60
238	Norm Thompson	2.00	1.00	.60
239	Charlie Smith	2.00	1.00	.60
240	John James (AP)	2.00	1.00	.60
241	Alden Roche	2.00	1.00	.60
242	Gordon Jolley	2.00	1.00	.60
243	Larry Ely	2.00	1.00	.60
244	Richard Caster	2.00	1.00	.60
245	Joe Greene	4.00	2.00	1.20
246	Larry Schreiber	2.00	1.00	.60
247	Terry Schmidt	2.00	1.00	.60
248	Jerrel Wilson	2.00	1.00	.60
249	Marty Domres	2.00	1.00	.60
250	Isaac Curtis (AP)	2.00	1.00	.60
251	Harold McLinton	2.00	1.00	.60
252	Fred Dryer	2.00	1.00	.60
253	Bill Lenkaitis	2.00	1.00	.60
254	Don Hardeman	2.00	1.00	.60
255	Bob Griese	4.00	2.00	1.25
256	Oscar Roan **RC**	2.00	1.00	.60
257	Randy Gradishar **RC**	2.00	1.00	.60
258	Bob Thomas **RC**	2.00	1.00	.60
259	Joe Owens	2.00	1.00	.60
260	Cliff Harris (AP)	2.00	1.00	.60
261	Frank Lewis	2.00	1.00	.60
262	Mike McCoy	2.00	1.00	.60
263	Rickey Young **RC**	2.00	1.00	.60
264	Brian Kelley **RC**	2.00	1.00	.60
265	Charlie Sanders	2.00	1.00	.60
266	Jim Hart	2.00	1.00	.60
267	Gregg Gantt	2.00	1.00	.60
268	John Ward	2.00	1.00	.60
269	Al Beauchamp	2.00	1.00	.60
270	Jack Tatum (AP)	2.00	1.00	.60
271	Jim Lash	2.00	1.00	.60
272	Diron Talbert	2.00	1.00	.60
273	Checklist 265-396	2.00	1.00	.60
274	Steve Spurrier	4.00	2.00	1.25
275	Greg Pruitt	2.00	1.00	.60
276	Jim Mitchell	2.00	1.00	.60
277	Jack Rudnay	2.00	1.00	.60
278	Freddie Solomon **RC**	2.00	1.00	.60
279	Frank LeMaster	2.00	1.00	.60
280	Wally Chambers (AP)	2.00	1.00	.60
281	Mike Collier	2.00	1.00	.60
282	Clarence Williams	2.00	1.00	.60
283	Mitch Hoopes	2.00	1.00	.60
284	Ron Bolton	2.00	1.00	.60
285	Harold Jackson	2.00	1.00	.60
286	Greg Landry	2.00	1.00	.60
287	Tony Greene	2.00	1.00	.60
288	Howard Stevens	2.00	1.00	.60
289	Roy Jefferson	2.00	1.00	.60
290	Jim Bakken (AP)	2.00	1.00	.60
291	Doug Sutherland	2.00	1.00	.60
292	Marvin Cobb	2.00	1.00	.60
293	Mack Alston	2.00	1.00	.60
294	Rod McNeil	2.00	1.00	.60
295	Gene Upshaw	2.00	1.00	.60
296	Dave Gallagher	2.00	1.00	.60
297	Larry Ball	2.00	1.00	.60
298	Ron Howard	2.00	1.00	.60
299	Don Strock **RC**	2.00	1.00	.60
300	O.J. Simpson (AP)	5.00	2.50	1.50
301	Ray Mansfield	2.00	1.00	.60
302	Larry Marshall	2.00	1.00	.60
303	Dick Himes	2.00	1.00	.60
304	Ray Wersching **RC**	2.00	1.00	.60
305	John Riggins	2.00	1.00	.60
306	Bob Parsons	2.00	1.00	.60
307	Ray Brown	2.00	1.00	.60
308	Len Dawson	4.00	2.00	1.20
309	Andy Maurer	2.00	1.00	.60
310	Jack Youngblood (AP)	2.00	1.00	.60
311	Essex Johnson	2.00	1.00	.60
312	Stan White	2.00	1.00	.60
313	Drew Pearson	2.00	1.00	.60
314	Rockne Freitas	2.00	1.00	.60
315	Mercury Morris	2.00	1.00	.60
316	Willie Alexander	2.00	1.00	.60
317	Paul Warfield	2.00	1.00	.60
318	Bob Chandler	2.00	1.00	.60
319	Bobby Walden	2.00	1.00	.60
320	Riley Odoms (AP)	2.00	1.00	.60
321	Mike Boryla	2.00	1.00	.60
322	Bruce Van Dyke	2.00	1.00	.60
323	Pete Banaszak	2.00	1.00	.60
324	Darryl Stingley	2.00	1.00	.60
325	John Mendenhall	2.00	1.00	.60
326	Dan Dierdorf	2.00	1.00	.60
327	Bruce Taylor	2.00	1.00	.60
328	Don McCauley	2.00	1.00	.60
329	John Reaves	2.00	1.00	.60
330	Chris Hanburger (AP)	2.00	1.00	.60
331	NFC Champions (Roger Staubach)	5.00	2.50	1.50
332	AFC Champions (Franco Harris)	2.00	1.00	.60
333	Super Bowl X (Terry Bradshaw)	5.00	2.50	1.50
334	Godwin Turk	2.00	1.00	.60
335	Dick Anderson	2.00	1.00	.60
336	Woody Green	2.00	1.00	.60
337	Pat Curran	2.00	1.00	.60
338	Council Rudolph	2.00	1.00	.60
339	Joe Lavender	2.00	1.00	.60
340	John Gilliam (AP)	2.00	1.00	.60
341	Steve Furness **RC**	2.00	1.00	.60
342	D.D. Lewis	2.00	1.00	.60
343	Duane Carrell	2.00	1.00	.60
344	Jon Morris	2.00	1.00	.60
345	John Brockington	2.00	1.00	.60
346	Mike Phipps	2.00	1.00	.60
347	Lyle Blackwood **RC**	2.00	1.00	.60
348	Julius Adams	2.00	1.00	.60
349	Terry Hermeling	2.00	1.00	.60
350	Rolland Lawrence **RC** (AP)	2.00	1.00	.60
351	Glenn Doughty	2.00	1.00	.60
352	Doug Swift	2.00	1.00	.60
353	Mike Strachan	2.00	1.00	.60
354	Craig Morton	2.00	1.00	.60
355	George Blanda	5.00	2.50	1.50
356	Garry Puetz	2.00	1.00	.60
357	Carl Mauck	2.00	1.00	.60
358	Walt Patulski	2.00	1.00	.60
359	Stu Voigt	2.00	1.00	.60
360	Fred Carr (AP)	2.00	1.00	.60
361	Po James	2.00	1.00	.60
362	Otis Taylor	2.00	1.00	.60
363	Jeff West	2.00	1.00	.60
364	Gary Huff	2.00	1.00	.60
365	Dwight White	2.00	1.00	.60
366	Dan Ryczek	2.00	1.00	.60
367	Jon Keyworth **RC**	2.00	1.00	.60
368	Mel Renfro	2.00	1.00	.60
369	Bruce Coslet **RC**	2.00	1.00	.60
370	Len Hauss (AP)	2.00	1.00	.60
371	Rick Volk	2.00	1.00	.60
372	Howard Twilley	2.00	1.00	.60
373	Cullen Bryant **RC**	2.00	1.00	.60
374	Bob Babich	2.00	1.00	.60
375	Herman Weaver	2.00	1.00	.60
376	Steve Grogan **RC**	2.00	1.00	.60
377	Bubba Smith	2.00	1.00	.60
378	Burgess Owens	2.00	1.00	.60
379	Alvin Matthews	2.00	1.00	.60
380	Art Shell	2.00	1.00	.60
381	Larry Brown	2.00	1.00	.60
382	Horst Muhlmann	2.00	1.00	.60
383	Ahmad Rashad	2.00	1.00	.60
384	Bobby Maples	2.00	1.00	.60
385	Jim Marshall	2.00	1.00	.60
386	Joe Dawkins	2.00	1.00	.60
387	Dennis Partee	2.00	1.00	.60
388	Eddie McMillan	2.00	1.00	.60
389	Randy Johnson	2.00	1.00	.60
390	Bob Kuechenberg (AP)	2.00	1.00	.60
391	Rufus Mayes	2.00	1.00	.60
392	Lloyd Mumphord	2.00	1.00	.60
393	Ike Harris	2.00	1.00	.60
394	Dave Hampton	2.00	1.00	.60
395	Roger Staubach	10.00	5.00	3.00
396	Doug Buffone	2.00	1.00	.60
397	Howard Fest	2.00	1.00	.60
398	Wayne Mulligan	2.00	1.00	.60
399	Bill Bradley	2.00	1.00	.60
400	Chuck Foreman (AP)	2.00	1.00	.60
401	Jack Snow	2.00	1.00	.60
402	Bob Howard	2.00	1.00	.60
403	John Matuszak	2.00	1.00	.60
404	Bill Munson	2.00	1.00	.60
405	Andy Russell	2.00	1.00	.60
406	Skip Butler	2.00	1.00	.60
407	Hugh McKinnis	2.00	1.00	.60
408	Bob Penchion	2.00	1.00	.60
409	Mike Bass	2.00	1.00	.60
410	George Kunz (AP)	2.00	1.00	.60
411	Ron Pritchard	2.00	1.00	.60
412	Barry Smith	2.00	1.00	.60
413	Norm Bulaich	2.00	1.00	.60
414	Marv Bateman	2.00	1.00	.60
415	Ken Stabler	5.00	2.50	1.50
416	Conrad Dobler	2.00	1.00	.60

417	Bob Tucker	2.00	1.00	.60
418	Gene Washington	2.00	1.00	.60
419	Ed Marinaro	2.00	1.00	.60
420	Jack Ham (AP)	5.00	2.50	1.50
421	Jim Turner	2.00	1.00	.60
422	Chris Fletcher	2.00	1.00	.60
423	Carl Barzilauskas	2.00	1.00	.60
424	Robert Brazile RC	2.00	1.00	.60
425	Harold Carmichael	2.00	1.00	.60
426	Ron Jaworski RC	10.00	5.00	3.00
427	Ed "Too Tall" Jones RC	15.00	7.50	4.50
428	Larry McCarren	2.00	1.00	.60
429	Mike Thomas RC	2.00	1.00	.60
430	Joe DeLamielleure (AP)	2.00	1.00	.60
431	Tom Blanchard	2.00	1.00	.60
432	Ron Carpenter	2.00	1.00	.60
433	Levi Johnson	2.00	1.00	.60
434	Sam Cunningham	2.00	1.00	.60
435	Garo Yapremian	2.00	1.00	.60
436	Mike Livingston	2.00	1.00	.60
437	Larry Csonka	2.00	1.00	.60
438	Doug Dieken	2.00	1.00	.60
439	Bill Lueck	2.00	1.00	.60
440	Tom MacLeod (AP)	2.00	1.00	.60
441	Mick Tingelhoff	2.00	1.00	.60
442	Terry Hanratty	2.00	1.00	.60
443	Mike Siani	2.00	1.00	.60
444	Dwight Harrison	2.00	1.00	.60
445	Jim Otis	2.00	1.00	.60
446	Jack Reynolds	2.00	1.00	.60
447	Jean Fugett RC	2.00	1.00	.60
448	Dave Beverly	2.00	1.00	.60
449	Bernard Jackson RC	1.00	.50	.30
450	Charley Taylor	2.00	1.00	.60
451	Atlanta Falcons Team	2.00	1.00	.60
452	Baltimore Colts Team	2.00	1.00	.60
453	Buffalo Bills Team	2.00	1.00	.60
454	Chicago Bears Team	2.00	1.00	.60
455	Cincinnati Bengals Team	2.00	1.00	.60
456	Cleveland Browns Team	2.00	1.00	.60
457	Dallas Cowboys Team	2.00	1.00	.60
458	Denver Broncos Team	2.00	1.00	.60
459	Detroit Lions Team	2.00	1.00	.60
460	Green Bay Packers Team	2.00	1.00	.60
461	Houston Oilers Team	2.00	1.00	.60
462	Kansas City Chiefs Team	2.00	1.00	.60
463	Los Angeles Rams Team	2.00	1.00	.60
464	Miami Dolphins Team	2.00	1.00	.60
465	Minnesota Vikings Team	2.00	1.00	.60
466	New England Patriots Team	2.00	1.00	.60
467	New Orleans Saints Team	2.00	1.00	.60
468	New York Giants Team	2.00	1.00	.60
469	New York Jets Team	2.00	1.00	.60
470	Oakland Raiders Team	2.00	1.00	.60
471	Philadelphia Eagles Team	2.00	1.00	.60
472	Pittsburgh Steelers Team	2.00	1.00	.60
473	St. Louis Cardinals Team	2.00	1.00	.60
474	San Diego Chargers Team	2.00	1.00	.60
475	San Francisco 49ers Team	2.00	1.00	.60
476	Seattle Seahawks Team	2.00	1.00	.60
477	Tampa Bay Bucaneers Team	2.00	1.00	.60
478	Washington Redskins Team	2.00	.70	.60
479	Fred Cox	2.00	1.00	.60
480	Mel Blount (AP)	5.00	2.50	1.50
481	John Bunting	2.00	1.00	.60
482	Ken Mendenhall	2.00	1.00	.60
483	Will Harrell	2.00	1.00	.60
484	Marlin Briscoe	2.00	1.00	.60
485	Archie Manning	2.00	1.00	.60
486	Tody Smith	2.00	1.00	.60
487	George Hunt	2.00	1.00	.60
488	Roscoe Word	2.00	1.00	.60
489	Paul Seymour	2.00	1.00	.60
490	Lee Roy Jordan (AP)	2.00	1.00	.60
491	Chip Myers	2.00	1.00	.60
492	Norm Evans	2.00	1.00	.60
493	Jim Bertelsen	2.00	1.00	.60
494	Mark Moseley	2.00	1.00	.60
495	George Buehler	2.00	1.00	.60
496	Charlie Hall	2.00	1.00	.60
497	Marvin Upshaw	2.00	1.00	.60
498	Tom Banks RC	2.00	1.00	.60
499	Randy Vataha	2.00	1.00	.60
500	Fran Tarkenton (AP)	5.00	2.50	1.50
501	Mike Wagner	2.00	1.00	.60
502	Art Malone	2.00	1.00	.60
503	Fred Cook	2.00	1.00	.60
504	Rich McGeorge	2.00	1.00	.60
505	Ken Burrough	2.00	1.00	.60
506	Nick Mike-Mayer	2.00	1.00	.60
507	Checklist 397-528	2.00	1.00	.60
508	Steve Owens	2.00	1.00	.60
509	Brad Van Pelt RC	2.00	1.00	.60
510	Ken Riley (AP)	2.00	1.00	.60
511	Art Thoms	2.00	1.00	.60

512	Ed Bell	2.00	1.00	.60
513	Tom Wittum	2.00	1.00	.60
514	Jim Braxton	2.00	1.00	.60
515	Nick Buoniconti	2.00	1.00	.60
516	Brian Sipe RC	5.00	2.50	1.50
517	Jim Lynch	2.00	1.00	.60
518	Prentice McCray	2.00	1.00	.60
519	Tom Dempsey	2.00	1.00	.60
520	Mel Gray (AP)	2.00	1.00	.60
521	Nate Wright	2.00	1.00	.60
522	Rocky Bleier	5.00	2.50	1.50
523	Dennis Johnson	2.00	1.00	.60
524	Jerry Sisemore	2.00	1.00	.60
525	Bert Jones	2.00	1.00	.60
526	Perry Smith	2.00	1.00	.60
527	Blaine Nye	2.00	1.00	.60
528	Bob Moore	2.00	1.00	.60

1976 Topps Team Checklists

The 30-card, standard-size set includes team checklist for each of the 28 NFL teams and two checklists. The set was available in uncut sheets from Topps and was unnumbered. The cards parallel the team checklists in the base sets (451-478), but come in thinner stock.

		NM	E	VG
	Complete Set (30):	130.00	65.00	40.00
	Common Player:	5.00	2.50	1.50
1	Atlanta Falcons	5.00	2.50	1.50
2	Baltimore Colts	5.00	2.50	1.50
3	Buffalo Bills	5.00	2.50	1.50
4	Chicago Bears	7.50	3.75	2.25
5	Cincinnati Bengals	5.00	2.50	1.50
6	Cleveland Browns	5.00	2.50	1.50
7	Dallas Cowboys	10.00	5.00	3.00
8	Denver Broncos	5.00	2.50	1.50
9	Detroit Lions	5.00	2.50	1.50
10	Green Bay Packers	5.00	2.50	1.50
11	Houston Oilers	5.00	2.50	1.50
12	Kansas City Chiefs	5.00	2.50	1.50
13	Los Angeles Rams	5.00	2.50	1.50
14	Miami Dolphins	7.50	3.75	2.25
15	Minnesota Vikings	5.00	2.50	1.50
16	New England Patriots	5.00	2.50	1.50
17	New York Giants	5.00	2.50	1.50
18	New York Jets	5.00	2.50	1.50
19	New Orleans Saints	5.00	2.50	1.50
20	Oakland Raiders	7.50	3.75	2.25
21	Philadelphia Eagles	5.00	2.50	1.50
22	Pittsburgh Steelers	7.50	3.75	2.25
23	St. Louis Cardinals	5.00	2.50	1.50
24	San Diego Chargers	5.00	2.50	1.50
25	San Francisco 49ers	7.50	3.75	2.25
26	Seattke Seahawks	5.00	2.50	1.50
27	Tampa Bay Buccaneers	5.00	2.50	1.50
28	Washington Redskins	7.50	3.75	2.25
29	Checklist 1-132	5.00	2.50	1.50
30	Checklist 133-264	5.00	2.50	1.50

1977 Topps

Known primarily for containing Steve Largent's rookie issue, this set of 528 cards also has the second-year card of Walter Payton. Other rookie cards included in the set are Pat Haden, Jim Zorn, John Cappeletti, Richard Todd, Harry Carson, Chuck Muncie, Archie Griffin and Dave Casper. All-Pro

designations were once again placed on the regular-issued card. Of the subsets, the "Record" run appears in the middle of the set; AFC/NFC championship and the Super Bowl card are the last three in the set; and the statistical leader cards are the first six. This was the last year in which team checklists were issued; future cards would show team leaders with the checklists.

		NM	E	VG
	Complete Set (528):	350.00	175.00	105.00
	Common Player:	2.00	1.00	.60
	Minor Stars:	.50		
	Unlisted Stars:	1.00		
	Wax Pack (10):	21.00		
	Wax Box (36):	640.00		
	Wax Pack (14):	25.00		
	Wax Box (36):	600.00		
1	Passing Leaders: (James Harris, Ken Stabler)	2.00	1.00	.60
2	Receiving Leaders: (Drew Pearson, MacArthur Lane)	2.00	1.00	.60
3	Rushing Leaders: (Walter Payton, O.J. Simpson)	8.00	4.00	2.40
4	Scoring Leaders: (Mark Moseley, Toni Linhart)	2.00	1.00	.60
5	Interception Leaders: (Monte Jackson, Ken Riley)	2.00	1.00	.60
6	Punting Leaders: (John James, Marv Bateman)	2.00	1.00	.60
7	Mike Phipps	2.00	1.00	.60
8	Rick Volk	2.00	1.00	.60
9	Steve Furness	2.00	1.00	.60
10	Isaac Curtis	2.00	1.00	.60
11	Nate Wright	2.00	1.00	.60
12	Jean Fugett	2.00	1.00	.60
13	Ken Mendenhall	2.00	1.00	.60
14	Sam Adams	2.00	1.00	.60
15	Charlie Waters	2.00	1.00	.60
16	Bill Stanfill	2.00	1.00	.60
17	John Holland	2.00	1.00	.60
18	Pat Haden RC	2.00	1.00	.60
19	Bob Young	2.00	1.00	.60
20	Wally Chambers (AP)	2.00	1.00	.60
21	Lawrence Gains	2.00	1.00	.60
22	Larry McCarren	2.00	1.00	.60
23	Horst Muhlmann	2.00	1.00	.60
24	Phil Villapiano	2.00	1.00	.60
25	Greg Pruitt	2.00	1.00	.60
26	Ron Howard	2.00	1.00	.60
27	Craig Morton	2.00	1.00	.60
28	Rufus Mayes	2.00	1.00	.60
29	Lee Roy Selmon RC	10.00	5.00	3.00
30	Ed White (AP)	2.00	1.00	.60
31	Harold McLinton	2.00	1.00	.60
32	Glenn Doughty	2.00	1.00	.60
33	Bob Kuechenberg	2.00	1.00	.60
34	Duane Carrell	2.00	1.00	.60
35	Riley Odoms	2.00	1.00	.60
36	Bobby Scott	2.00	1.00	.60
37	Nick Mike-Mayer	2.00	1.00	.60
38	Bill Lenkaitis	2.00	1.00	.60
39	Roland Harper	2.00	1.00	.60
40	Tommy Hart (AP)	2.00	1.00	.60
41	Mike Sensibaugh	2.00	1.00	.60
42	Rusty Jackson	2.00	1.00	.60
43	Levi Johnson	2.00	1.00	.60
44	Mike McCoy	2.00	1.00	.60
45	Roger Staubach	11.00	5.50	3.30
46	Fred Cox	2.00	1.00	.60
47	Bob Babich	2.00	1.00	.60
48	Reggie McKenzie	2.00	1.00	.60
49	Dave Jennings	2.00	1.00	.60
50	Mike Haynes RC (AP)	10.00	5.00	3.00
51	Larry Brown	2.00	1.00	.60
52	Marvin Cobb	2.00	1.00	.60
53	Fred Cook	2.00	1.00	.60
54	Freddie Solomon	2.00	1.00	.60
55	John Riggins	2.00	1.00	.60
56	John Bunting	2.00	1.00	.60
57	Ray Wersching	2.00	1.00	.60
58	Mike Livingston	2.00	1.00	.60
59	Billy Johnson	2.00	1.00	.60
60	Mike Wagner (AP)	2.00	1.00	.60
61	Waymond Bryant	2.00	1.00	.60
62	Jim Otis	2.00	1.00	.60
63	Ed Galigher	2.00	1.00	.60
64	Randy Vataha	2.00	1.00	.60
65	Jim Zorn RC	2.00	1.00	.60
66	John Keyworth	2.00	1.00	.60
67	Checklist 1-132	2.00	1.00	.60
68	Henry Childs	2.00	1.00	.60
69	Thom Darden	2.00	1.00	.60
70	George Kunz (AP)	2.00	1.00	.60
71	Lenvil Elliott	2.00	1.00	.60
72	Curtis Johnson	2.00	1.00	.60
73	Doug Van Horn	2.00	1.00	.60

74	Joe Theismann	2.00	1.00	.60
75	Dwight White	2.00	1.00	.60
76	Scott Laidlaw	2.00	1.00	.60
77	Monte Johnson	2.00	1.00	.60
78	Dave Beverly	2.00	1.00	.60
79	Jim Mitchell	2.00	1.00	.60
80	Jack Youngblood (AP)	2.00	1.00	.60
81	Mel Gray	2.00	1.00	.60
82	Dwight Harrison	2.00	1.00	.60
83	John Hadl	2.00	1.00	.60
84	Matt Blair **RC**	2.00	1.00	.60
85	Charlie Sanders	2.00	1.00	.60
86	Noah Jackson	2.00	1.00	.60
87	Ed Marinaro	2.00	1.00	.60
88	Bob Howard	2.00	1.00	.60
89	John McDaniel	2.00	1.00	.60
90	Dan Dierdorf (AP)	2.00	1.00	.60
91	Mark Moseley	2.00	1.00	.60
92	Cleo Miller	2.00	1.00	.60
93	Andre Tillman	2.00	1.00	.60
94	Bruce Taylor	2.00	1.00	.60
95	Bert Jones	2.00	1.00	.60
96	Anthony Davis **RC**	2.00	1.00	.60
97	Don Goode	2.00	1.00	.60
98	Ray Rhodes **RC**	2.00	1.00	.60
99	Mike Webster **RC**	10.00	5.00	3.00
100	O.J. Simpson (AP)	10.00	5.00	3.00
101	Doug Plank **RC**	2.00	1.00	.60
102	Efren Herrera	2.00	1.00	.60
103	Charlie Smith	2.00	1.00	.60
104	Carlos Brown	2.00	1.00	.60
105	Jim Marshall	2.00	1.00	.60
106	Paul Naumoff	2.00	1.00	.60
107	Walter White	2.00	1.00	.60
108	John Cappelletti **RC**	2.00	1.00	.60
109	Chip Myers	2.00	1.00	.60
110	Ken Stabler (AP)	5.00	2.50	1.50
111	Joe Ehrmann	2.00	1.00	.60
112	Rick Engles	2.00	1.00	.60
113	Jack Dolbin	2.00	1.00	.60
114	Ron Bolton	2.00	1.00	.60
115	Mike Thomas	2.00	1.00	.60
116	Mike Fuller	2.00	1.00	.60
117	John Hill	2.00	1.00	.60
118	Richard Todd **RC**	2.00	1.00	.60
119	Duriel Harris **RC**	2.00	1.00	.60
120	John James (AP)	2.00	1.00	.60
121	Lionel Antoine	2.00	1.00	.60
122	John Skorupan	2.00	1.00	.60
123	Skip Butler	2.00	1.00	.60
124	Bob Tucker	2.00	1.00	.60
125	Paul Krause	2.00	1.00	.60
126	Dave Hampton	2.00	1.00	.60
127	Tom Wittum	2.00	1.00	.60
128	Gary Huff	2.00	1.00	.60
129	Emmitt Thomas	2.00	1.00	.60
130	Drew Pearson (AP)	2.00	1.00	.60
131	Ron Saul	2.00	1.00	.60
132	Steve Niehaus	2.00	1.00	.60
133	Fred Carr	2.00	1.00	.60
134	Norm Bulaich	2.00	1.00	.60
135	Bob Trumpy	2.00	1.00	.60
136	Greg Landry	2.00	1.00	.60
137	George Buehler	2.00	1.00	.60
138	Reggie Rucker	2.00	1.00	.60
139	Julius Adams	2.00	1.00	.60
140	Jack Ham (AP)	2.00	1.00	.60
141	Wayne Morris	2.00	1.00	.60
142	Marv Bateman	2.00	1.00	.60
143	Bobby Maples	2.00	1.00	.60
144	Harold Carmichael	2.00	1.00	.60
145	Bob Avellini	2.00	1.00	.60
146	Harry Carson **RC**	12.00	6.00	3.60
147	Lawrence Pillers	2.00	1.00	.60
148	Ed Williams	2.00	1.00	.60
149	Dan Pastorini	2.00	1.00	.60
150	Ron Yary (AP)	2.00	1.00	.60
151	Joe Lavender	2.00	1.00	.60
152	Pat McInally	2.00	1.00	.60
153	Lloyd Mumphord	2.00	1.00	.60
154	Cullen Bryant	2.00	1.00	.60
155	Willie Lanier	2.00	1.00	.60
156	Gene Washington	2.00	1.00	.60
157	Scott Hunter	2.00	1.00	.60
158	Jim Merlo	2.00	1.00	.60
159	Randy Grossman	2.00	1.00	.60
160	Blaine Nye (AP)	2.00	1.00	.60
161	Ike Harris	2.00	1.00	.60
162	Doug Dieken	2.00	1.00	.60
163	Guy Morriss	2.00	1.00	.60
164	Bob Parsons	2.00	1.00	.60
165	Steve Grogan	2.00	1.00	.60
166	John Brockington	2.00	1.00	.60
167	Charlie Joiner	2.00	1.00	.60
168	Ron Carpenter	2.00	1.00	.60
169	Jeff Wright	2.00	1.00	.60
170	Chris Hanburger (AP)	2.00	1.00	.60
171	Roosevelt Leaks **RC**	2.00	1.00	.60
172	Larry Little	2.00	1.00	.60
173	John Matuszak	2.00	1.00	.60
174	Joe Ferguson	2.00	1.00	.60
175	Brad Van Pelt	2.00	1.00	.60
176	Dexter Bussey **RC**	2.00	1.00	.60
177	Steve Largent **RC**	20.00	10.00	6.00
178	Dewey Selmon	2.00	1.00	.60
179	Randy Gradishar	2.00	1.00	.60
180	Mel Blount (AP)	2.00	1.00	.60
181	Dan Neal	2.00	1.00	.60
182	Rich Szaro	2.00	1.00	.60
183	Mike Boryla	2.00	1.00	.60
184	Steve Jones	2.00	1.00	.60
185	Paul Warfield	2.00	1.00	.60
186	Greg Buttle **RC**	2.00	1.00	.60
187	Rich McGeorge	2.00	1.00	.60
188	Leon Gray **RC**	2.00	1.00	.60
189	John Shinners	2.00	1.00	.60
190	Toni Linhart (AP)	2.00	1.00	.60
191	Robert Miller	2.00	1.00	.60
192	Jake Scott	2.00	1.00	.60
193	Jon Morris	2.00	1.00	.60
194	Randy Crowder	2.00	1.00	.60
195	Lynn Swann	5.00	2.50	1.50
196	Marsh White	2.00	1.00	.60
197	Rod Perry **RC**	2.00	1.00	.60
198	Willie Hall	2.00	1.00	.60
199	Mike Hartenstine	2.00	1.00	.60
200	Jim Bakken (AP)	2.00	1.00	.60
201	Atlanta Falcons Team	2.00	1.00	.60
202	Baltimore Colts Team	2.00	1.00	.60
203	Buffalo Bills Team	2.00	1.00	.60
204	Chicago Bears Team	2.00	1.00	.60
205	Cincinnati Bengals Team	2.00	1.00	.60
206	Cleveland Browns Team	2.00	1.00	.60
207	Dallas Cowboys Team	2.00	1.00	.60
208	Denver Broncos Team	2.00	1.00	.60
209	Detroit Lions Team	2.00	1.00	.60
210	Green Bay Packers Team	2.00	1.00	.60
211	Houston Oilers Team	2.00	1.00	.60
212	Kansas City Chiefs Team	2.00	1.00	.60
213	Los Angeles Rams Team	2.00	1.00	.60
214	Miami Dolphins Team	2.00	1.00	.60
215	Minnesota Vikings Team	2.00	1.00	.60
216	New England Patriots Team	2.00	1.00	.60
217	New Orleans Saints Team	2.00	1.00	.60
218	New York Giants Team	2.00	1.00	.60
219	New York Jets Team	2.00	1.00	.60
220	Oakland Raiders Team	2.00	1.00	.60
221	Philadelphia Eagles Team	2.00	1.00	.60
222	Pittsburgh Steelers Team	2.00	1.00	.60
223	St. Louis Cardinals Team	2.00	1.00	.60
224	San Diego Chargers Team	2.00	1.00	.60
225	San Francisco 49ers Team	2.00	1.00	.60
226	Seattle Seahawks Team	2.00	1.00	.60
227	Tampa Bay Bucaneers Team	2.00	1.00	.60
228	Washington Redskins Team	2.00	1.00	.60
229	Sam Cunningham	2.00	1.00	.60
230	Alan Page (AP)	2.00	1.00	.60
231	Eddie Brown	2.00	1.00	.60
232	Stan White	2.00	1.00	.60
233	Vern Den Herder	2.00	1.00	.60
234	Clarence Davis	2.00	1.00	.60
235	Ken Anderson	2.00	1.00	.60
236	Karl Chandler	2.00	1.00	.60
237	Will Harrell	2.00	1.00	.60
238	Clarence Scott	2.00	1.00	.60
239	Bo Rather	2.00	1.00	.60
240	Robert Brazile (AP)	2.00	1.00	.60
241	Bob Bell	2.00	1.00	.60
242	Rolland Lawrence	2.00	1.00	.60
243	Tom Sullivan	2.00	1.00	.60
244	Larry Brunson	2.00	1.00	.60
245	Terry Bradshaw	8.00	4.00	2.40
246	Rich Saul	2.00	1.00	.60
247	Cleveland Elam	2.00	1.00	.60
248	Don Woods	2.00	1.00	.60
249	Bruce Laird	2.00	1.00	.60
250	Coy Bacon (AP)	2.00	1.00	.60
251	Russ Francis	2.00	1.00	.60
252	Jim Braxton	2.00	1.00	.60
253	Perry Smith	2.00	1.00	.60
254	Jerome Barkum	2.00	1.00	.60
255	Garo Yepremian	2.00	1.00	.60
256	Checklist 133-264	2.00	1.00	.60
257	Tony Galbreath **RC**	2.00	1.00	.60
258	Troy Archer	2.00	1.00	.60
259	Brian Sipe	2.00	1.00	.60
260	Billy Joe DuPree (AP)	2.00	1.00	.60
261	Bobby Walden	2.00	1.00	.60
262	Larry Marshall	2.00	1.00	.60
263	Ted Fritsch	2.00	1.00	.60
264	Larry Hand	2.00	1.00	.60
265	Tom Mack	2.00	1.00	.60
266	Ed Bradley	2.00	1.00	.60
267	Pat Leahy	2.00	1.00	.60
268	Louis Carter	2.00	1.00	.60
269	Archie Griffin **RC**	5.00	2.50	1.50
270	Art Shell (AP)	2.00	1.00	.60
271	Stu Voigt	2.00	1.00	.60
272	Prentice McCray	2.00	1.00	.60
273	MacArthur Lane	2.00	1.00	.60
274	Dan Fouts	3.00	1.50	.90
275	Charley Young	2.00	1.00	.60
276	Wilbur Jackson **RC**	2.00	1.00	.60
277	John Hicks	2.00	1.00	.60
278	Nat Moore	2.00	1.00	.60
279	Virgil Livers	2.00	1.00	.60
280	Curley Culp (AP)	2.00	1.00	.60
281	Rocky Bleier	2.00	1.00	.60
282	John Zook	2.00	1.00	.60
283	Tom DeLeone	2.00	1.00	.60
284	Danny White **RC**	6.00	3.00	1.80
285	Otis Armstrong	2.00	1.00	.60
286	Larry Walton	2.00	1.00	.60
287	Jim Carter	2.00	1.00	.60
288	Don McCauley	2.00	1.00	.60
289	Frank Grant	2.00	1.00	.60
290	Roger Wehrli (AP)	2.00	1.00	.60
291	Mick Tinglehoff	2.00	1.00	.60
292	Bernard Jackson	2.00	1.00	.60
293	Tom Owen **RC**	2.00	1.00	.60
294	Mike Esposito	2.00	1.00	.60
295	Fred Biletnikoff	2.00	1.00	.60
296	Revie Sorey **RC**	2.00	1.00	.60
297	John McMakin	2.00	1.00	.60
298	Dan Ryczek	2.00	1.00	.60
299	Wayne Moore	2.00	1.00	.60
300	Franco Harris (AP)	6.00	3.00	1.80
301	Rick Upchurch **RC**	2.00	1.00	.60
302	Jim Stienke	2.00	1.00	.60
303	Charlie Davis	2.00	1.00	.60
304	Don Cockroft	2.00	1.00	.60
305	Ken Burrough	2.00	1.00	.60
306	Clark Gaines	2.00	1.00	.60
307	Bobby Douglass	2.00	1.00	.60
308	Ralph Perretta	2.00	1.00	.60
309	Wally Hilgenberg	2.00	1.00	.60
310	Monte Jackson **RC** (AP)	2.00	1.00	.60
311	Chris Bahr **RC**	2.00	1.00	.60
312	Jim Cheyunski	2.00	1.00	.60
313	Mike Patrick	2.00	1.00	.60
314	Ed "Too Tall" Jones	5.00	2.50	1.50
315	Bill Bradley	2.00	1.00	.60
316	Benny Malone	2.00	1.00	.60
317	Paul Seymour	2.00	1.00	.60
318	Jim Laslavic	2.00	1.00	.60
319	Frank Lewis	2.00	1.00	.60
320	Ray Guy (AP)	2.00	1.00	.60
321	Allen Ellis	2.00	1.00	.60
322	Conrad Dobler	2.00	1.00	.60
323	Chester Marcol	2.00	1.00	.60
324	Doug Kotar	2.00	1.00	.60
325	Lemar Parrish	2.00	1.00	.60
326	Steve Holden	2.00	1.00	.60
327	Jeff Van Note	2.00	1.00	.60
328	Howard Stevens	2.00	1.00	.60
329	Brad Dusek	2.00	1.00	.60
330	Joe DeLamielleure (AP)	2.00	1.00	.60
331	Jim Plunkett	2.00	1.00	.60
332	Checklist 265-396	2.00	1.00	.60
333	Lou Piccone	2.00	1.00	.60
334	Ray Hamilton	2.00	1.00	.60
335	Jan Stenerud	2.00	1.00	.60
336	Jeris White	2.00	1.00	.60
337	Sherman Smith **RC**	2.00	1.00	.60
338	Dave Green	2.00	1.00	.60
339	Terry Schmidt	2.00	1.00	.60
340	Sammie White **RC** (AP)	2.00	.60	.40
341	Jon Kolb **RC**	2.00	1.00	.60
342	Randy White	4.00	2.00	1.20
343	Bob Klein	2.00	1.00	.60
344	Bob Kowalkowski	2.00	1.00	.60
345	Terry Metcalf	2.00	1.00	.60
346	Joe Danelo	2.00	1.00	.60
347	Ken Payne	2.00	1.00	.60
348	Neal Craig	2.00	1.00	.60
349	Dennis Johnson	2.00	1.00	.60
350	Bill Bergey (AP)	2.00	1.00	.60
351	Raymond Chester	2.00	1.00	.60
352	Bob Matheson	2.00	1.00	.60
353	Mike Kadish	2.00	1.00	.60
354	Mark Van Eeghen **RC**	2.00	1.00	.60
355	L.C. Greenwood	2.00	1.00	.60
356	Sam Hunt	2.00	1.00	.60
357	Darrell Austin	2.00	1.00	.60
358	Jim Turner	2.00	1.00	.60
359	Ahmad Rashad	2.00	1.00	.60
360	Walter Payton (AP)	25.00	13.00	8.00
361	Mark Arneson	2.00	1.00	.60
362	Jerrel Wilson	2.00	1.00	.60

363	Steve Bartkowski	2.00	1.00	.60
364	John Watson	2.00	1.00	.60
365	Ken Riley	2.00	1.00	.60
366	Gregg Bingham	2.00	1.00	.60
367	Golden Richards	2.00	1.00	.60
368	Clyde Powers	2.00	1.00	.60
369	Diron Talbert	2.00	1.00	.60
370	Lydell Mitchell	2.00	1.00	.60
371	Bob Jackson	2.00	1.00	.60
372	Jim Mandich	2.00	1.00	.60
373	Frank LeMaster	2.00	1.00	.60
374	Benny Ricardo	2.00	1.00	.60
375	Lawrence McCutcheon	2.00	1.00	.60
376	Lynn Dickey	2.00	1.00	.60
377	Phil Wise	2.00	1.00	.60
378	Tony McGee	2.00	1.00	.60
379	Norm Thompson	2.00	1.00	.60
380	Dave Casper RC (AP)	10.00	5.00	3.00
381	Glen Edwards	2.00	1.00	.60
382	Bob Thomas	2.00	1.00	.60
383	Bob Chandler	2.00	1.00	.60
384	Rickey Young	2.00	1.00	.60
385	Carl Eller	2.00	1.00	.60
386	Lyle Alzado	2.00	1.00	.60
387	John Leypoldt	2.00	1.00	.60
388	Gordon Bell	2.00	1.00	.60
389	Mike Bragg	2.00	1.00	.60
390	Jim Langer (AP)	2.00	1.00	.60
391	Vern Holland	2.00	1.00	.60
392	Nelson Munsey	2.00	1.00	.60
393	Mack Mitchell	2.00	1.00	.60
394	Tony Adams	2.00	1.00	.60
395	Preston Pearson	2.00	1.00	.60
396	Emanuel Zanders	2.00	1.00	.60
397	Vince Papale	4.00	2.00	1.20
398	Joe Fields RC	2.00	1.00	.60
399	Craig Clemons	2.00	1.00	.60
400	Fran Tarkenton (AP)	4.00	2.00	1.20
401	Andy Johnson	2.00	1.00	.60
402	Willie Buchanon	2.00	1.00	.60
403	Pat Curran	2.00	1.00	.60
404	Ray Jarvis	2.00	1.00	.60
405	Joe Greene	2.00	1.00	.60
406	Bill Simpson	2.00	1.00	.60
407	Ronnie Coleman	2.00	1.00	.60
408	J.K. McKay	2.00	1.00	.60
409	Pat Fischer	2.00	1.00	.60
410	John Dutton (AP)	2.00	1.00	.60
411	Boobie Clark	2.00	1.00	.60
412	Pat Tilley RC	2.00	1.00	.60
413	Don Strock	2.00	1.00	.60
414	Brian Kelley	2.00	1.00	.60
415	Gene Upshaw	1.00	.50	.30
416	Mike Montler	2.00	1.00	.60
417	**Checklist 397-528**	1.50	.70	.60
418	John Gilliam	2.00	1.00	.60
419	Brent McClanahan	2.00	1.00	.60
420	Jerry Sherk (AP)	2.00	1.00	.60
421	Roy Gerela	2.00	1.00	.60
422	Tim Fox	2.00	1.00	.60
423	John Ebersole	2.00	1.00	.60
424	James Scott	2.00	1.00	.60
425	Delvin Williams RC	2.00	1.00	.60
426	Spike Jones	2.00	1.00	.60
427	Harvey Martin	2.00	1.00	.60
428	Don Herrmann	2.00	1.00	.60
429	Calvin Hill	2.00	1.00	.60
430	Isiah Robertson (AP)	2.00	1.00	.60
431	Tony Greene	2.00	1.00	.60
432	Bob Johnson	2.00	1.00	.60
433	Lem Barney	2.00	1.00	.60
434	Eric Torkelson	2.00	1.00	.60
435	John Mendenhall	2.00	1.00	.60
436	Larry Seiple	2.00	1.00	.60
437	Art Kuehn	2.00	1.00	.60
438	John Vella	2.00	1.00	.60
439	Greg Latta	2.00	1.00	.60
440	Roger Carr (AP)	2.00	1.00	.60
441	Doug Sutherland	2.00	1.00	.60
442	Mike Kruczek	2.00	1.00	.60
443	Steve Zabel	2.00	1.00	.60
444	Mike Pruitt RC	2.00	1.00	.60
445	Harold Jackson	2.00	1.00	.60
446	George Jakowenko	2.00	1.00	.60
447	John Fitzgerald	2.00	1.00	.60
448	Terry Joyce	2.00	1.00	.60
449	Jim LeClair	2.00	1.00	.60
450	Ken Houston (AP)	2.00	1.00	.60
451	Record: (Steve Grogan)	2.00	1.00	.60
452	Record: (Jim Marshall)	2.00	1.00	.60
453	Record: (O.J. Simpson)	5.00	2.50	1.50
454	Record: (Tarkenton)	3.00	1.50	.90
455	Record: (Jim Zorn)	2.00	1.00	.60
456	Robert Pratt	2.00	1.00	.60
457	Walker Gillette	2.00	1.00	.60
458	Charlie Hall	2.00	1.00	.60
459	Robert Newhouse	2.00	1.00	.60
460	John Hannah (AP)	2.00	1.00	.60

461	Ken Reaves	2.00	1.00	.60
462	Herman Weaver	2.00	1.00	.60
463	James Harris	2.00	1.00	.60
464	Howard Twilley	2.00	1.00	.60
465	Jeff Siemon	2.00	1.00	.60
466	John Outlaw	2.00	1.00	.60
467	Chuck Muncie RC	2.00	1.00	.60
468	Bob Moore	2.00	1.00	.60
469	Robert Woods	2.00	1.00	.60
470	Cliff Branch (AP)	2.00	1.00	.60
471	Johnnie Gray	2.00	1.00	.60
472	Don Hardeman	2.00	1.00	.60
473	Steve Ramsey	2.00	1.00	.60
474	Steve Mike-Mayer	2.00	1.00	.60
475	Gary Garrison	2.00	1.00	.60
476	Walter Johnson	2.00	1.00	.60
477	Neil Clabo	2.00	1.00	.60
478	Len Hauss	2.00	1.00	.60
479	Darryl Stingley	2.00	1.00	.60
480	Jack Lambert (AP)	6.00	3.00	1.80
481	Mike Adamle	2.00	1.00	.60
482	David Lee	2.00	1.00	.60
483	Tom Mullen	2.00	1.00	.60
484	Claude Humphrey	2.00	1.00	.60
485	Jim Hart	2.00	1.00	.60
486	Bobby Thompson	2.00	1.00	.60
487	Jack Rudnay	2.00	1.00	.60
488	Rich Sowells	2.00	1.00	.60
489	Reuben Gant	2.00	1.00	.60
490	Cliff Harris (AP)	2.00	1.00	.60
491	Bob Brown	2.00	1.00	.60
492	Don Nottingham	2.00	1.00	.60
493	Ron Jessie	2.00	1.00	.60
494	Otis Sistrunk	2.00	1.00	.60
495	Bill Kilmer	2.00	1.00	.60
496	Oscar Roan	2.00	1.00	.60
497	Bill Van Heusen	2.00	1.00	.60
498	Randy Logan	2.00	1.00	.60
499	John Smith	2.00	1.00	.60
500	Chuck Foreman (AP)	2.00	1.00	.60
501	J.T. Thomas	2.00	1.00	.60
502	Steve Schubert	2.00	1.00	.60
503	Mike Barnes	2.00	1.00	.60
504	J.V. Cain	2.00	1.00	.60
505	Larry Csonka	3.00	1.50	.90
506	Elvin Bethea	2.00	1.00	.60
507	Ray Easterling	2.00	1.00	.60
508	Joe Reed	2.00	1.00	.60
509	Steve Odom	2.00	1.00	.60
510	Tommy Casanova (AP)	2.00	1.00	.60
511	Dave Dalby	2.00	1.00	.60
512	Richard Caster	2.00	1.00	.60
513	Fred Dryer	2.00	1.00	.60
514	Jeff Kinney	2.00	1.00	.60
515	Bob Griese	5.00	2.50	1.50
516	Butch Johnson RC	2.00	1.00	.60
517	Gerald Irons	2.00	1.00	.60
518	Don Calhoun	2.00	1.00	.60
519	Jack Gregory	2.00	1.00	.60
520	Tom Banks (AP)	2.00	1.00	.60
521	Bobby Bryant	2.00	1.00	.60
522	Reggie Harrison	2.00	1.00	.60
523	Terry Hermeling	2.00	1.00	.60
524	David Taylor	2.00	1.00	.60
525	Brian Baschnagel RC	2.00	1.00	.60
526	AFC Championship: (Ken Stabler)	2.00	1.00	.60
527	NFC Championship	2.00	1.00	.60
528	Super Bowl XI	2.00	1.00	.60

1977 Topps Holsum Packers/Vikings

The 22-card, standard-size set featuring 11 Green Bay players (1-11) and 11 Minnesota players (12-22) was issued in Holsum Bread packages. For an unapparent reason, Holsum did not print its name or logo anywhere on the cards.

		NM	E	VG
	Complete Set (22):	45.00	22.00	13.50
	Common Player:	1.00	.50	.30
1	Lynn Dickey	3.00	1.50	.90
2	John Brockington	2.00	1.00	.60
3	Will Harrell	1.00	.50	.30
4	Ken Payne	1.00	.50	.30
5	Rich McGeorge	1.00	.50	.30
6	Steve Odom	1.00	.50	.30
7	Jim Carter	1.00	.50	.30
8	Fred Carr	1.00	.50	.30
9	Willie Buchanon	2.00	1.00	.60
10	Mike McCoy	1.00	.50	.30
11	Chester Marcol	1.00	.50	.30
12	Chuck Foreman	4.00	2.00	1.25
13	Ahmad Rashad	7.00	3.50	2.00
14	Sammie White	3.00	1.50	.90
15	Stu Voigt	1.00	.50	.30
16	Fred Cox	1.00	.50	.30
17	Carl Eller	4.00	2.00	1.25
18	Alan Page	6.00	3.00	1.75
19	Jeff Siemon	1.00	.50	.30
20	Bobby Bryant	1.00	.50	.30
21	Paul Krause	3.00	1.50	.90
22	Ron Yary	2.00	1.00	.60

1977 Topps Mexican

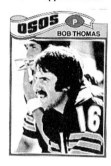

The 528-card, standard-size set is the Spanish parallel set to the standard 1977 Topps set. All text on the card fronts and backs is in Spanish. The wrappers are also deemed collectible as they depict various NFL stars.

		NM	E	VG
	Complete Set (528):	6,000	3,000	1,800
	Common Player:	10.00	5.00	3.00
	Common Checklist:	12.00	6.00	3.50
	Semistars:	10.00	5.00	3.00
	Pack (2):	6.00		
	Wax Box (36):	200.00		
1	Passing Leaders (James Harris, Ken Stabler)	125.00	65.00	38.00
2	Receiving Leaders (Drew Pearson, MacArthur Lane)	200.00	100.00	60.00
3	Rushing Leaders (Walter Payton, O.J. Simpson)	800.00	400.00	240.00
4	Scoring Leaders (Mark Moseley, Toni Linhart)	200.00	100.00	60.00
18	Pat Haden	10.00	5.00	3.00
29	Lee Roy Selmon (UER) (Misspelled Leroy)	125.00	65.00	38.00
45	Roger Staubach	125.00	65.00	38.00
50	Mike Haynes (AP)	80.00	40.00	24.00
55	John Riggins	10.00	5.00	3.00
65	Jim Zorn	20.00	10.00	6.00
74	Joe Theismann	25.00	13.00	8.00
80	Jack Youngblood (AP)	10.00	5.00	3.00
90	Dan Dierdorf (AP)	10.00	5.00	3.00
95	Bert Jones	10.00	5.00	3.00
96	Anthony Davis	10.00	5.00	3.00
98	Ray Rhodes	450.00	225.00	155.00
99	Mike Webster	50.00	25.00	15.00
100	O.J. Simpson (AP)	50.00	25.00	15.00
108	John Cappelletti	20.00	10.00	6.00
110	Ken Stabler (AP)	50.00	25.00	15.00
130	Drew Pearson (AP)	25.00	12.50	7.50
140	Jack Ham (AP)	30.00	15.00	9.00
144	Harold Carmichael	15.00	7.50	4.50
146	Harry Carson	75.00	38.00	23.00
165	Steve Grogan	20.00	10.00	6.00
167	Charlie Joiner	20.00	10.00	6.00
173	John Matuszak	20.00	10.00	6.00
177	Steve Largent	400.00	200.00	120.00
179	Randy Gradishar	15.00	7.50	4.50
180	Mel Blount (AP)	30.00	15.00	9.00
185	Paul Warfield	30.00	15.00	9.00
195	Lynn Swann	75.00	38.00	23.00
230	Alan Page (AP)	20.00	10.00	6.00
235	Ken Anderson	20.00	10.00	6.00
245	Terry Bradshaw	60.00	30.00	18.00
259	Brian Sipe	15.00	7.50	4.50
269	Archie Griffin	50.00	25.00	15.00
270	Art Shell (AP)	15.00	7.50	4.50
274	Dan Fouts	30.00	15.00	9.00

		NM	E	VG
281	Rocky Bleier	30.00	15.00	9.00
284	Danny White	65.00	33.00	20.00
295	Fred Biletnikoff	250.00	125.00	75.00
300	Franco Harris (AP)	100.00	50.00	30.00
314	Ed "Too Tall" Jones	100.00	50.00	30.00
320	Ray Guy (AP)	15.00	7.50	4.50
331	Jim Plunkett	30.00	15.00	9.00
342	Randy White	350.00	175.00	105.00
359	Ahmad Rashad	20.00	10.00	6.00
360	Walter Payton (AP)	400.00	200.00	120.00
380	Dave Casper (AP)	50.00	25.00	15.00
386	Lyle Alzado	15.00	7.50	4.50
400	Fran Tarkenton (AP)	50.00	25.00	15.00
405	Joe Greene	30.00	15.00	9.00
412	Pat Tilley	20.00	10.00	6.00
415	Gene Upshaw	20.00	10.00	6.00
427	Harvey Martin	30.00	15.00	9.00
433	Lem Barney	30.00	15.00	9.00
444	Mike Pruitt	550.00	225.00	135.00
450	Ken Houston (AP)	20.00	10.00	6.00
453	O.J. Simpson (RB)	250.00	125.00	75.00
454	Most Yardage, Passing, Lifetime (Fran Tarkenton) (RB)	20.00	10.00	6.00
455	Most Passing Yards Season, Rookie (Jim Zorn) (RB)	25.00	12.50	7.50
460	John Hannah (AP)	15.00	7.50	4.50
467	Chuck Muncie	15.00	7.50	4.50
470	Cliff Branch (AP)	180.00	90.00	54.00
480	Jack Lambert (AP)	120.00	60.00	36.00
505	Larry Csonka	30.00	15.00	9.00
515	Bob Griese	15.00	7.50	4.50
526	AFC Championship (Ken Stabler)	75.00	37.00	22.00
527	NFC Championship	75.00	37.00	22.00
528	Super Bowl XI	800.00	400.00	240.00

1977 Topps Team Checklists

The 30-card, standard-size set contains a 28 team checklist and two checklist cards and was available through Topps as an uncut sheet. The cards are identical to the checklists in the base set, except for the thinner stock.

		NM	E	VG
	Complete Set (30):	120.00	60.00	35.00
	Common Player:	5.00	2.50	1.50
1	Atlanta Falcons	5.00	2.50	1.50
2	Baltimore Colts	5.00	2.50	1.50
3	Buffalo Bills	5.00	2.50	1.50
4	Chicago Bears	8.00	4.00	2.50
5	Cincinnati Bengals	5.00	2.50	1.50
6	Cleveland Browns	5.00	2.50	1.50
7	Dallas Cowboys	10.00	5.00	3.00
8	Denver Broncos	5.00	2.50	1.50
9	Detroit Lions	5.00	2.50	1.50
10	Green Bay Packers	8.00	4.00	2.50
11	Houston Oilers	5.00	2.50	1.50
12	Kansas City Chiefs	5.00	2.50	1.50
13	Los Angeles Rams	5.00	2.50	1.50
14	Miami Dolphins	8.00	4.00	2.50
15	Minnesota Vikings	5.00	2.50	1.50
16	New England Patriots	5.00	2.50	1.50
17	New York Giants	5.00	2.50	1.50
18	New York Jets	5.00	2.50	1.50
19	New Orleans Saints	5.00	2.50	1.50
20	Oakland Raiders	8.00	4.00	2.50
21	Philadelphia Eagles	5.00	2.50	1.50
22	Pittsburgh Steelers	8.00	4.00	2.50
23	St. Louis Cardinals	5.00	2.50	1.50
24	San Diego Chargers	5.00	2.50	1.50
25	San Francisco 49ers	8.00	4.00	2.50
26	Seattle Seahawks	5.00	2.50	1.50
27	Tampa Bay Buccaneers	5.00	2.50	1.50
28	Washington Redskins	8.00	4.00	2.50
NN01	Checklist 1-132	5.00	2.50	1.50
NN02	Checklist 133-264	5.00	2.50	1.50

1978 Topps

BILLY JOE DuPREE
COWBOYS

Topps' fourth 528-card set featured a colorful design, with the team name in white inside a solid border of color down the left side of the card. The subsets in the 1978 set include highlights, conference leader cards, and team leader cards (the last cards in the set; the team leader cards are arranged alphabetically by city name). This is the first time Topps pictured the actual team leaders on its team cards. The set is most notable for the inclusion of the Dorsett rookie card, the Largent second-year card, and the Payton third-year card. Other rookies in the set include Johnny Rodgers, Joe Klecko, John Stallworth, Wesley Walker, Stanley Morgan and Pete Johnson. (Key: AP - All Pro)

		NM	E	VG
	Complete Set (528):	200.00	100.00	60.00
	Common Player:	1.50	.75	.45
	Minor Stars:	.40		
	Unlisted Stars:	.75		
	Wax Pack (14):	11.50		
	Wax Box (36):	345.00		
1	Gary Huff (HL)	.25	.13	.08
2	Craig Morton (HL)	.25	.13	.08
3	Walter Payton (HL)	3.00	1.50	.90
4	O.J. Simpson (HL)	3.00	1.50	.90
5	Fran Tarkenton (HL)	2.00	1.00	.60
6	Bob Thomas (HL)	1.50	.75	.45
7	Joe Pisarcik	1.50	.75	.45
8	Skip Thomas	1.50	.75	.45
9	Roosevelt Leaks	1.50	.75	.45
10	Ken Houston (AP)	1.50	.75	.45
11	Tom Blanchard	1.50	.75	.45
12	Jim Turner	1.50	.75	.45
13	Tom DeLeone	1.50	.75	.45
14	Jim LeClair	1.50	.75	.45
15	Bob Avellini	1.50	.75	.45
16	Tony McGee	1.50	.75	.45
17	James Harris	1.50	.75	.45
18	Terry Nelson	1.50	.75	.45
19	Rocky Bleier	1.50	.75	.45
20	Joe DeLamielleure (AP)	1.50	.75	.45
21	Richard Caster	1.50	.75	.45
22	A.J. Duhe **RC**	1.00	.50	.30
23	John Outlaw	1.50	.75	.45
24	Danny White	1.50	.70	.45
25	Larry Csonka	1.50	.70	.45
26	David Hill	1.50	.75	.45
27	Mark Arneson	1.50	.75	.45
28	Jack Tatum	1.50	.75	.45
29	Norm Thompson	1.50	.75	.45
30	Sammie White	1.50	.75	.45
31	Dennis Johnson	1.50	.75	.45
32	Robin Earl	1.50	.75	.45
33	Don Cockroft	1.50	.75	.45
34	Bob Johnson	1.50	.75	.45
35	John Hannah	1.50	.75	.45
36	Scott Hunter	1.50	.75	.45
37	Ken Burrough	1.50	.75	.45
38	Wilbur Jackson	1.50	.75	.45
39	Rich McGeorge	1.50	.75	.45
40	Lyle Alzado (AP)	1.50	.75	.45
41	John Ebersole	1.50	.75	.45
42	Gary Green **RC**	1.50	.75	.45
43	Art Kuehn	1.50	.75	.45
44	Glen Edwards	1.50	.75	.45
45	Lawrence McCutcheon	1.50	.75	.45
46	Duriel Harris	1.50	.75	.45
47	Rich Szaro	1.50	.75	.45
48	Mike Washington	1.50	.75	.45
49	Stan White	1.50	.75	.45
50	Dave Casper (AP)	1.50	.75	.45
51	Len Hauss	1.50	.75	.45
52	James Scott	1.50	.75	.45
53	Brian Sipe	1.50	.75	.45
54	Gary Shirk	1.50	.75	.45
55	Archie Griffin	1.50	.75	.45
56	Mike Patrick	1.50	.75	.45
57	Mario Clark	1.50	.75	.45
58	Jeff Siemon	1.50	.75	.45
59	Steve Mike-Mayer	1.50	.75	.45
60	Randy White (AP)	1.50	.75	.45
61	Darrell Austin	1.50	.75	.45
62	Tom Sullivan	1.50	.75	.45
63	Johnny Rodgers **RC**	1.50	.75	.45
64	Ken Reaves	1.50	.75	.45
65	Terry Bradshaw	5.00	2.50	1.50
66	Fred Steinfort	1.50	.75	.45
67	Curley Culp	1.50	.75	.45
68	Ted Hendricks	1.50	.75	.45
69	Raymond Chester	1.50	.75	.45
70	Jim Langer (AP)	1.50	.75	.45
71	Calvin Hill	1.50	.75	.45
72	Mike Hartenstine	1.50	.75	.45
73	Gerald Irons	1.50	.75	.45
74	Billy Brooks	1.50	.75	.45
75	John Mendenhall	1.50	.75	.45
76	Andy Johnson	1.50	.75	.45
77	Tom Wittum	1.50	.75	.45
78	Lynn Dickey	1.50	.75	.45
79	Carl Eller	1.50	.75	.45
80	Tom Mack	1.50	.75	.45
81	Clark Gaines	1.50	.75	.45
82	Lem Barney	1.50	.75	.45
83	Mike Montler	1.50	.75	.45
84	Jon Kolb	1.50	.75	.45
85	Bob Chandler	1.50	.75	.45
86	Robert Newhouse	1.50	.75	.45
87	Frank LeMaster	1.50	.75	.45
88	Jeff West	1.50	.75	.45
89	Lyle Blackwood	1.50	.75	.45
90	Gene Upshaw (AP)	1.50	.75	.45
91	Frank Grant	1.50	.75	.45
92	Tom Hicks	1.50	.75	.45
93	Mike Pruitt	1.50	.75	.45
94	Chris Bahr	1.50	.75	.45
95	Russ Francis	1.50	.75	.45
96	Norris Thomas	1.50	.75	.45
97	Gary Barbaro **RC**	1.50	.75	.45
98	Jim Merlo	1.50	.75	.45
99	Karl Chandler	1.50	.75	.45
100	Fran Tarkenton	2.50	1.25	.75
101	Abdul Salaam	1.50	.75	.45
102	Marv Kellum	1.50	.75	.45
103	Herman Weaver	1.50	.75	.45
104	Roy Gerela	1.50	.75	.45
105	Harold Jackson	1.50	.75	.45
106	Dewey Selmon	1.50	.75	.45
107	**Checklist 1-132**	1.50	.75	.45
108	Clarence Davis	1.50	.75	.45
109	Robert Pratt	1.50	.75	.45
110	Harvey Martin (AP)	1.50	.75	.45
111	Brad Dusek	1.50	.75	.45
112	Greg Latta	1.50	.75	.45
113	Tony Peters	1.50	.75	.45
114	Jim Braxton	1.50	.75	.45
115	Ken Riley	1.50	.75	.45
116	Steve Nelson	1.50	.75	.45
117	Rick Upchurch	1.50	.75	.45
118	Spike Jones	1.50	.75	.45
119	Doug Kotar	1.50	.75	.45
120	Bob Griese (AP)	1.50	.75	.45
121	Burgess Owens	1.50	.75	.45
122	Rolf Benirschke	1.50	.75	.45
123	Haskel Stanback	1.50	.75	.45
124	J.T. Thomas	1.50	.75	.45
125	Ahmad Rashad	1.50	.75	.45
126	Rick Kane	1.50	.75	.45
127	Elvin Bethea	1.50	.75	.45
128	Dave Dalby	1.50	.75	.45
129	Mike Barnes	1.50	.75	.45
130	Isiah Robertson	1.50	.75	.45
131	Jim Plunkett	1.50	.75	.45
132	Allan Ellis	1.50	.75	.45
133	Mike Bragg	1.50	.75	.45
134	Bob Jackson	1.50	.75	.45
135	Coy Bacon	1.50	.75	.45
136	John Smith	1.50	.75	.45
137	Chuck Muncie	1.50	.75	.45
138	Johnnie Gray	1.50	.75	.45
139	Jimmy Robinson	1.50	.75	.45
140	Tom Banks	1.50	.75	.45
141	Marvin Powell **RC**	1.50	.75	.45
142	Jerrell Wilson	1.50	.75	.45
143	Ron Howard	1.50	.75	.45
144	Rob Lytle **RC**	1.50	.75	.45
145	L.C. Greenwood	1.50	.75	.45
146	Morris Owens	1.50	.75	.45
147	Joe Reed	1.50	.75	.45
148	Mike Kadish	1.50	.75	.45
149	Phil Villapiano	1.50	.75	.45
150	Lydell Mitchell	1.50	.75	.45
151	Randy Logan	1.50	.75	.45
152	Mike Williams	1.50	.75	.45
153	Jeff Van Note	1.50	.75	.45
154	Steve Schubert	1.50	.75	.45
155	Bill Kilmer	1.50	.75	.45
156	Boobie Clark	1.50	.75	.45

157	Charlie Hall	1.50	.75	.45
158	Raymond Clayborn **RC**	1.50	.75	.45
159	Jack Gregory	1.50	.75	.45
160	Cliff Harris (AP)	1.50	.75	.45
161	Joe Fields	1.50	.75	.45
162	Don Nottingham	1.50	.75	.45
163	Ed White	1.50	.75	.45
164	Toni Fritsch	1.50	.75	.45
165	Jack Lambert	2.50	1.25	.75
166	NFC Champions (Roger Staubach)	1.50	.70	.45
167	AFC Champions: (Rob Lytle)	1.50	.75	.45
168	Super Bowl XII (Tony Dorsett)	1.50	.75	.45
169	Neal Colzie **RC**	1.50	.75	.45
170	Cleveland Elam (AP)	1.50	.75	.45
171	David Lee	1.50	.75	.45
172	Jim Otis	1.50	.75	.45
173	Archie Manning	1.50	.75	.45
174	Jim Carter	1.50	.75	.45
175	Jean Fugett	1.50	.75	.45
176	Willie Parker	1.50	.75	.45
177	Haven Moses	1.50	.75	.45
178	Horace King	1.50	.75	.45
179	Bob Thomas	1.50	.75	.45
180	Monte Jackson	1.50	.75	.45
181	Steve Zabel	1.50	.75	.45
182	John Fitzgerald	1.50	.75	.45
183	Mike Livingston	1.50	.75	.45
184	Larry Poole	1.50	.75	.45
185	Isaac Curtis	1.50	.75	.45
186	Chuck Ramsey	1.50	.75	.45
187	Bob Klein	1.50	.75	.45
188	Ray Rhodes	1.50	.75	.45
189	Otis Sistrunk	1.50	.75	.45
190	Bill Bergey	1.50	.75	.45
191	Sherman Smith	1.50	.75	.45
192	Dave Green	1.50	.75	.45
193	Carl Mauck	1.50	.75	.45
194	Reggie Harrison	1.50	.75	.45
195	Roger Carr	1.50	.75	.45
196	Steve Bartkowski	1.50	.75	.45
197	Ray Wershing	1.50	.75	.45
198	Willie Buchanon	1.50	.75	.45
199	Neil Clabo	1.50	.75	.45
200	Walter Payton (AP)	10.00	5.00	3.00
201	Sam Adams	1.50	.75	.45
202	Larry Gordon	1.50	.75	.45
203	Pat Tilley	1.50	.75	.45
204	Mack Mitchell	1.50	.75	.45
205	Ken Anderson	1.50	.75	.45
206	Scott Dierking	1.50	.75	.45
207	Jack Rudnay	1.50	.75	.45
208	Jim Stienke	1.50	.75	.45
209	Bill Simpson	1.50	.75	.45
210	Errol Mann	1.50	.75	.45
211	Bucky Dilts	1.50	.75	.45
212	Reuben Gant	1.50	.75	.45
213	Thomas Henderson **RC**	1.50	.75	.45
214	Steve Furness	1.50	.75	.45
215	John Riggins	1.50	.75	.45
216	Keith Krepfle **RC**	1.50	.75	.45
217	Fred Dean **RC**	1.50	.75	.45
218	Emanuel Zanders	1.50	.75	.45
219	Don Testerman	1.50	.75	.45
220	George Kunz	1.50	.75	.45
221	Darryl Stingley	1.50	.75	.45
222	Ken Sanders	1.50	.75	.45
223	Gary Huff	1.50	.75	.45
224	Gregg Bingham	1.50	.75	.45
225	Jerry Sherk	1.50	.75	.45
226	Doug Plank	1.50	.75	.45
227	Ed Taylor	1.50	.75	.45
228	Emery Moorehead	1.50	.75	.45
229	Reggie Williams **RC**	1.50	.75	.45
230	Claude Humphrey	1.50	.75	.45
231	Randy Cross **RC**	1.50	.75	.45
232	Jim Hart	1.50	.75	.45
233	Bobby Bryant	1.50	.75	.45
234	Larry Brown	1.50	.75	.45
235	Mark Van Eeghen	1.50	.75	.45
236	Terry Hermeling	1.50	.75	.45
237	Steve Odom	1.50	.75	.45
238	Jan Stenerud	1.50	.75	.45
239	Andre Tillman	1.50	.75	.45
240	Tom Jackson **RC** (AP)	1.50	.75	.45
241	Ken Mendenhall	1.50	.75	.45
242	Tim Fox	1.50	.75	.45
243	Don Herrmann	1.50	.75	.45
244	Eddie McMillan	1.50	.75	.45
245	Greg Pruitt	1.50	.75	.45
246	J.K. McKay	1.50	.75	.45
247	Larry Keller	1.50	.75	.45
248	Dave Jennings	1.50	.75	.45
249	Bo Harris	1.50	.75	.45
250	Revie Sorey	1.50	.75	.45
251	Tony Greene	1.50	.75	.45
252	Butch Johnson	1.50	.75	.45
253	Paul Naumoff	1.50	.75	.45
254	Rickey Young	1.50	.75	.45
255	Dwight White	1.50	.75	.45
256	Joe Lavender	1.50	.75	.45
257	**Checklist 133-264**	1.50	.75	.45
258	Ronnie Coleman	1.50	.75	.45
259	Charlie Smith	1.50	.75	.45
260	Ray Guy (AP)	1.50	.75	.45
261	David Taylor	1.50	.75	.45
262	Bill Lenkaitis	1.50	.75	.45
263	Jim Mitchell	1.50	.75	.45
264	Delvin Williams	1.50	.75	.45
265	Jack Youngblood	1.60	.30	.20
266	Chuck Crist	1.50	.75	.45
267	Richard Todd	1.50	.75	.45
268	Dave Logan **RC**	1.50	.75	.45
269	Rufus Mayes	1.50	.75	.45
270	Brad Van Pelt	1.50	.75	.45
271	Chester Marcol	1.50	.75	.45
272	J.V. Cain	1.50	.75	.45
273	Larry Seiple	1.50	.75	.45
274	Brent McClanahan	1.50	.75	.45
275	Mike Wagner	1.50	.75	.45
276	Diron Talbert	1.50	.75	.45
277	Brian Baschnagel	1.50	.75	.45
278	Ed Podolak	1.50	.75	.45
279	Don Goode	1.50	.75	.45
280	John Dutton	1.50	.75	.45
281	Don Calhoun	1.50	.75	.45
282	Monte Johnson	1.50	.75	.45
283	Ron Jessie	1.50	.75	.45
284	Jon Morris	1.50	.75	.45
285	Riley Odoms	1.50	.75	.45
286	Marv Bateman	1.50	.75	.45
287	Joe Klecko **RC**	1.50	.75	.45
288	Oliver Davis	1.50	.75	.45
289	John McDaniel	1.50	.75	.45
290	Roger Staubach	6.00	3.00	1.80
291	Brian Kelley	1.50	.75	.45
292	Mike Hogan	1.50	.75	.45
293	John Leypoldt	1.50	.75	.45
294	Jack Novak	1.50	.75	.45
295	Joe Greene	2.00	1.00	.60
296	John Hill	1.50	.75	.45
297	Danny Buggs	1.50	.75	.45
298	Ted Albrecht	1.50	.75	.45
299	Nelson Munsey	1.50	.75	.45
300	Chuck Foreman	1.50	.75	.45
301	Dan Pastorini	1.50	.75	.45
302	Tommy Hart	1.50	.75	.45
303	Dave Beverly	1.50	.75	.45
304	Tony Reed **RC**	1.50	.75	.45
305	Cliff Branch	1.50	.75	.45
306	Clarence Duren	1.50	.75	.45
307	Randy Rasmussen	1.50	.75	.45
308	Oscar Roan	1.50	.75	.45
309	Lenvil Elliott	1.50	.75	.45
310	Dan Dierdorf (AP)	1.50	.75	.45
311	Johnny Perkins	1.50	.75	.45
312	Rafael Septien **RC**	1.50	.75	.45
313	Terry Beeson	1.50	.75	.45
314	Lee Roy Selmon	1.50	.75	.45
315	Tony Dorsett **RC**	20.00	10.00	6.00
316	Greg Landry	1.50	.75	.45
317	Jake Scott	1.50	.75	.45
318	Dan Peiffer	1.50	.75	.45
319	John Bunting	1.50	.75	.45
320	John Stallworth **RC**	7.50	3.75	2.25
321	Bob Howard	1.50	.75	.45
322	Larry Little	1.50	.75	.45
323	Reggie McKenzie	1.50	.75	.45
324	Duane Carrell	1.50	.75	.45
325	Ed Simonini	1.50	.75	.45
326	John Vella	1.50	.75	.45
327	Wesley Walker **RC**	1.50	.75	.45
328	Jon Keyworth	1.50	.75	.45
329	Ron Bolton	1.50	.75	.45
330	Tommy Casanova	1.50	.75	.45
331	Passing Leaders: (Bob Griese, Roger Staubach)	2.50	1.25	.75
332	Receiving Leaders: (Lydell Mitchell, Ahmad Rashad)	1.50	.75	.45
333	Rushing Leaders: (Mark Van Eeghen, Walter Payton)	2.25	1.75	.70
334	Scoring Leaders: (Errol Mann, Walter Payton)	2.25	1.75	.70
335	Interception Leaders: s (Lyle Blackwood, Rolland Lawrence)	1.50	.75	.45
336	Punting Leaders: (Ray Guy, Tom Blanchard)	1.50	.75	.45
337	Robert Brazile	1.50	.75	.45
338	Charlie Joiner	1.50	.75	.45
339	Joe Ferguson	1.50	.75	.45
340	Bill Thompson	1.50	.75	.45
341	Sam Cunningham	1.50	.75	.45
342	Curtis Johnson	1.50	.75	.45
343	Jim Marshall	1.50	.75	.45
344	Charlie Sanders	1.50	.75	.45
345	Willie Hall	1.50	.75	.45
346	Pat Haden	1.50	.75	.45
347	Jim Bakken	1.50	.75	.45
348	Bruce Taylor	1.50	.75	.45
349	Barty Smith	1.50	.75	.45
350	Drew Pearson	1.00	.50	.45
351	Mike Webster	1.50	.75	.45
352	Bobby Hammond	1.50	.75	.45
353	Dave Mays	1.50	.75	.45
354	Pat McInally	1.50	.75	.45
355	Toni Linhart	1.50	.75	.45
356	Larry Hand	1.50	.75	.45
357	Ted Fritsch	1.50	.75	.45
358	Larry Marshall	1.50	.75	.45
359	Waymond Bryant	1.50	.75	.45
360	Louie Kelcher **RC**	1.50	.75	.45
361	Stanley Morgan **RC**	1.50	.75	.45
362	Bruce Harper **RC**	1.50	.75	.45
363	Bernard Jackson	1.50	.75	.45
364	Walter White	1.50	.75	.45
365	Ken Stabler	2.50	1.25	.75
366	Fred Dryer	1.50	.75	.45
367	Ike Harris	1.50	.75	.45
368	Norm Bulaich	1.50	.75	.45
369	Merv Krakau	1.50	.75	.45
370	John James	1.50	.75	.45
371	Bennie Cunningham **RC**	1.50	.75	.45
372	Doug Van Horn	1.50	.75	.45
373	Thom Darden	1.50	.75	.45
374	Eddie Edwards **RC**	1.50	.75	.45
375	Mike Thomas	1.50	.75	.45
376	Fred Cook	1.50	.75	.45
377	Mike Phipps	1.50	.75	.45
378	Paul Krause	1.50	.75	.45
379	Harold Carmichael	1.50	.75	.45
380	Mike Haynes (AP)	1.50	.75	.45
381	Wayne Morris	1.50	.75	.45
382	Greg Buttle	1.50	.75	.45
383	Jim Zorn	1.50	.75	.45
384	Jack Dolbin	1.50	.75	.45
385	Charlie Waters	1.50	.75	.45
386	Dan Ryczek	1.50	.75	.45
387	Joe Washington **RC**	1.50	.75	.30
388	Checklist 265-396	1.50	.75	.30
389	James Hunter	1.50	.75	.45
390	Billy Johnson	1.50	.75	.45
391	Jim Allen	1.50	.75	.45
392	George Buehler	1.50	.75	.45
393	Harry Carson	1.25	.60	.40
394	Cleo Miller	1.50	.75	.45
395	Gary Burley	1.50	.75	.45
396	Mark Moseley	1.50	.75	.45
397	Virgil Livers	1.50	.75	.45
398	Joe Ehrmann	1.50	.75	.45
399	Freddie Solomon	1.50	.75	.45
400	O.J. Simpson	2.50	1.25	.75
401	Julius Adams	1.50	.75	.45
402	Artimus Parker{	1.50	.75	.45
403	Gene Washington	1.50	.75	.45
404	Herman Edwards	1.50	.75	.45
405	Craig Morton	1.50	.75	.45
406	Alan Page	1.50	.75	.45
407	Larry McCarren	1.50	.75	.45
408	Tony Galbreath	1.50	.75	.45
409	Roman Gabriel	1.50	.75	.45
410	Efren Herrera (AP)	1.50	.75	.45
411	Jim Smith **RC**	1.50	.75	.45
412	Bill Bryant	1.50	.75	.45
413	Doug Dieken	1.50	.75	.45
414	Marvin Cobb	1.50	.75	.45
415	Fred Biletnikoff	1.50	.70	.45
416	Joe Theismann	1.50	.75	.45
417	Roland Harper	1.50	.75	.45
418	Derrel Luce	1.50	.75	.45
419	Ralph Perretta	1.50	.75	.45
420	Louis Wright **RC**	1.50	.75	.45
421	Prentice McCray	1.50	.75	.45
422	Garry Puetz	1.50	.75	.45
423	Alfred Jenkins **RC**	1.50	.75	.45
424	Paul Seymour	1.50	.75	.45
425	Garo Yepremian	1.50	.75	.45
426	Emmitt Thomas	1.50	.75	.45
427	Dexter Bussey	1.50	.75	.45
428	John Sanders	1.50	.75	.45
429	Ed "Too Tall" Jones	1.50	.75	.45
431	Frank Lewis	1.50	.75	.45
432	Jerry Golsteyn	1.50	.75	.45
433	Clarence Scott	1.50	.75	.45
434	Pete Johnson **RC**	1.50	.75	.45
435	Charley Young	1.50	.75	.45

436	Harold McLinton	1.50	.75	.45
437	Noah Jackson	1.50	.75	.45
438	Bruce Laird	1.50	.75	.45
439	John Matuszak	1.50	.75	.45
440	Nat Moore (AP)	1.50	.75	.45
441	Leon Gray	1.50	.75	.45
442	Jerome Barkum	1.50	.75	.45
443	Steve Largent	2.00	1.00	.60
444	John Zook	1.50	.75	.45
445	Preston Pearson	1.50	.75	.45
446	Conrad Dobler	1.50	.75	.45
447	Wilbur Summers	1.50	.75	.45
448	Lou Piccone	1.50	.75	.45
449	Ron Jaworski	1.60	.75	.45
450	Jack Ham (AP)	1.50	.70	.45
451	Mick Tingelhoff	1.50	.75	.45
452	Clyde Powers	1.50	.75	.45
453	John Cappelletti	1.50	.75	.45
454	Dick Ambrose	1.50	.75	.45
455	Lemar Parrish	1.50	.75	.45
456	Ron Saul	1.50	.75	.45
457	Bob Parsons	1.50	.75	.45
458	Glenn Doughty	1.50	.75	.45
459	Don Woods	1.50	.75	.45
460	Art Shell (AP)	1.50	.75	.45
461	Sam Hunt	1.50	.75	.45
462	Lawrence Pillers	1.50	.75	.45
463	Henry Childs	1.50	.75	.45
464	Roger Wehrli	1.50	.75	.45
465	Otis Armstrong	1.50	.75	.45
466	Bob Baumhower RC	1.50	.75	.45
467	Ray Jarvis	1.50	.75	.45
468	Guy Morriss	1.50	.75	.45
469	Matt Blair	1.50	.75	.45
470	Bill Joe DuPree	1.50	.75	.45
471	Roland Hooks	1.50	.75	.45
472	Joe Danelo	1.50	.75	.45
473	Reggie Rucker	1.50	.75	.45
474	Vern Holland	1.50	.75	.45
475	Mel Blount	1.50	.75	.45
476	Eddie Brown	1.50	.75	.45
477	Bo Rather	1.50	.75	.45
478	Don McCauley	1.50	.75	.45
479	Glen Walker	1.50	.75	.45
480	Randy Gradishar (AP)	1.50	.75	.45
481	Dave Rowe	1.50	.75	.45
482	Pat Leahy	1.40	.75	.45
483	Mike Fuller	1.50	.75	.45
484	David Lewis	1.50	.75	.45
485	Steve Grogan	1.50	.75	.45
486	Mel Gray	1.50	.75	.45
487	Eddie Payton RC	1.50	.75	.45
488	Checklist 397-528	1.50	.75	.45
489	Stu Voigt	1.50	.75	.45
490	Rolland Lawrence (AP)	1.50	.75	.45
491	Nick Mike-Mayer	1.50	.75	.45
492	Troy Archer	1.50	.75	.45
493	Benny Malone	1.50	.75	.45
494	Golden Richards	1.50	.75	.45
495	Chris Hanburger	1.50	.75	.45
496	Dwight Harrison	1.50	.75	.45
497	Gary Fencik RC	1.50	.75	.45
498	Rich Saul	1.50	.75	.45
499	Dan Fouts	2.50	1.25	.75
500	Franco Harris (AP)	3.00	1.50	.90
501	Atlanta Falcons Team: (Haskel Stanback, Alfred Jenkins, Claude Humphrey, Jeff Merrow, Rolland Lawrence)	1.50	.75	.45
502	Baltimore Colts Team: (Lydell Mitchell, Lyle Blackwood, Fred Cook)	1.50	.75	.45
503	Buffalo Bills Team: (Bob Chandler, O.J. Simpson, Tony Greene, Sherman White)	2.00	1.00	.60
504	Chicago Bears Team: (James Scott, Allan Ellis, Ron Rydalch, Walter Payton)	2.00	1.00	.60
505	Cincinnati Bengals Team: (Billy Brooks, Lemar Parrish, Reggie Williams, Gary Burley, Pete Johnson)	1.50	.75	.45
506	Cleveland Browns Team: (Reggie Rucker, Thom Darden, Mack Mitchell, Greg Pruitt)	1.50	.75	.45
507	Dallas Cowboys Team: (Drew Pearson, Cliff Harris, Harvey Martin, Tony Dorsett)	2.00	1.00	.60

508	Denver Broncos Team: (Otis Armstrong, Haven Moses, Bill Thompson, Rick Upchurch)	1.50	.75	.45
509	Detroit Lions Team: (Horace King, David Hill, James Hunter, Ken Sanders)	1.50	.75	.45
510	Green Bay Packers Team: (Barty Smith, Steve Odom, Steve Luke, M.C. McCoy, Dave Pureifory, Dave Roller)	1.50	.75	.45
511	Houston Oilers Team: (Ronnie Coleman, Ken Burrough, Mike Reinfeldt, James Young)	1.50	.75	.45
512	Kansas City Chiefs Team: (Ed Podolak, Walter White, Gary Barbaro, Wilbur Young)	1.50	.75	.45
513	Los Angeles Rams Team: (Lawrence McCutcheon, Harold Jackson, Bill Simpson, Jack Youngblood)	1.50	.75	.45
514	Miami Dolphins Team: (Benny Malone, Nat Moore, Curtis Johnson, A.J. Duhe)	1.50	.75	.45
515	Minnesota Vikings Team: (Chuck Foreman, Sammie White, Bobby Bryant, Carl Eller)	1.50	.75	.45
516	New England Patriots Team: (Sam Cunningham, Darryl Stingley, Mike Haynes, Tony McGee)	1.50	.75	.45
517	New Orleans Saints Team: (Chuck Muncie, Don Herrmann, Chuck Crist, Elois Grooms)	1.50	.75	.45
518	New York Giants Team: (Bobby Hammond, Jimmy Robinson, Bill Bryant, John Mendenhall)	1.50	.75	.45
519	New York Jets Team: (Clark Gaines, Wesley Walker, Burgess Owens, Joe Klecko)	1.50	.75	.45
520	Oakland Raiders Team: (Mark Van Eeghen, Dave Casper, Jack Tatum, Neal Colzie)	1.50	.75	.45
521	Philadelphia Eagles Team: (Mike Hogan, Harold Carmichael, Herman Edwards, John Sanders, Lem Burnham)	1.50	.75	.45
522	Pittsburgh Steelers Team: (Jim Smith, Mel Blount, Steve Furness, Franco Harris)	1.50	.75	.45
523	St. Louis Cardinals Team: (Terry Metcalf, Mel Gray, Roger Wehrli, Mike Dawson)	1.50	.75	.45
524	San Diego Chargers Team: (Rickey Young, Charlie Joiner, Mike Fuller, Gary Johnson)	1.50	.75	.45
525	San Francisco 49ers Team: (Delvin Williams, G. Washington, Mel Phillips, Dave Washington, Cleveland Elam)	1.50	.75	.45
526	Seattle Seahawks Team: (Steve Largent, Autry Beamon, Walter Packer, Sherman Smith)	1.50	.70	.45
527	Tampa Bay Buccaneers Team: (Morris Owens, Isaac Hagins, Mike Washington, Lee Roy Selmon)	1.50	.75	.45
528	Washington Redskins Team: (Jean Fugett, Ken Houston, Dennis Johnson, Mike Thomas)	1.50	.75	.45

1978 Topps Holsum

DAVE CASPER
RAIDERS
TE

The 33-card, standard-size set was produced by Topps and distributed with loaves of Holsum Bread. For whatever reason, the cards do not have the Holsum name or logo printed anywhere on the card. As with the 1977 Packers/Vikings Holsum set, an uncut sheet was offered by Topps at an archives auction in 1989.

		NM	E	VG
	Complete Set (33):	250.00	125.00	75.00
	Common Player:	3.00	1.50	.90
1	Rolland Lawrence	3.00	1.50	.90
2	Walter Payton	80.00	40.00	24.00
3	Lydell Mitchell	4.00	2.00	1.25
4	Joe DeLamielleure	3.00	1.50	.90
5	Ken Anderson	10.00	5.00	3.00
6	Greg Pruitt	4.00	2.00	1.25
7	Harvey Martin	5.00	2.50	1.50
8	Tom Jackson	5.00	2.50	1.50
9	Chester Marcol	3.00	1.50	.90
10	Jim Carter	3.00	1.50	.90
11	Will Harrell	3.00	1.50	.90
12	Greg Landry	4.00	2.00	1.25
13	Billy Johnson	4.00	2.00	1.25
14	Jan Stenerud	5.00	2.50	1.50
15	Lawrence McCutcheon	4.00	2.00	1.25
16	Bob Griese	20.00	10.00	6.00
17	Chuck Foreman	4.00	2.00	1.25
18	Sammie White	4.00	2.00	1.25
19	Jeff Siemon	3.00	1.50	.90
20	Mike Haynes	4.00	2.00	1.25
21	Archie Manning	6.00	3.00	1.75
22	Brad Van Pelt	3.00	1.50	.90
23	Richard Todd	4.00	2.00	1.25
24	Dave Casper	4.00	2.00	1.25
25	Bill Bergey	4.00	2.00	1.25
26	Franco Harris	20.00	10.00	6.00
27	Mel Gray	4.00	2.00	1.25
28	Louie Kelcher	3.00	1.50	.90
29	O.J. Simpson	30.00	15.00	9.00
30	Jim Zorn	4.00	2.00	1.25
31	Lee Roy Selmon	6.00	3.00	1.75
32	Ken Houston	6.00	3.00	1.75
33	Checklist Card	8.00	4.00	2.50

1979 Topps

MEL BLOUNT
STEELERS
CORNERBACK

Topps' fifth 528-card set was similar in design to its 1973 set, which also showed a small flag. This set, though, showed only the lower half of the flag in solid color, and showed the player's position in a football superimposed over the flag. The team name appeared in any one of a number of colors in capital letters above the photo. Subsets in this year's issue include conference leaders and playoff results. This set is notable for the inclusion of the only four cards Topps issued depicting running back Earl Campbell. Topps was apparently unable to reach a contract agreement with Campbell after this season - possibly similar to the Joe Namath situation after 1973. In addition to Campbell, other rookie cards in this set include Doug Williams, Steve DeBerg, Wilbert Montgomery, Tony Hill, James Jefferson, Ozzie Newsome, and James Lofton. This set also contains the second-year card of Tony Dorsett. (Key: AP - All Pro)

	NM	E	VG
Complete Set (528):	200.00	100.00	60.00
Common Player:	1.50	.75	.45
Minor Stars:	.50		
Unlisted Stars:	.75		
Wax Pack (12):	12.00		
Wax Box (36):	325.00		

#	Player	NM	E	VG
1	Passing Leaders (Roger Staubach, Terry Bradshaw)	4.00	2.00	1.20
2	Receiving Leaders (Rickey Young, Steve Largent)	1.50	.75	.45
3	Rushing Leaders (Walter Payton, Earl Campbell)	2.50	1.25	.75
4	Scoring Leaders (Frank Corral, Pat Leahy)	1.50	.75	.45
5	Interception Leaders (Willie Buchanon, Ken Stone, Thom Darden)	1.50	.75	.45
6	Punting Leaders (Tom Skladany, Pat McInally)	1.50	.75	.45
7	Johnny Perkins	1.50	.75	.45
8	Charles Phillips	1.50	.75	.45
9	Derrel Luce	1.50	.75	.45
10	John Riggins	1.50	.70	.45
11	Chester Marcol	1.50	.75	.45
12	Bernard Jackson	1.50	.75	.45
13	Dave Logan	1.50	.75	.45
14	Bo Harris	1.50	.75	.45
15	Alan Page	1.50	.75	.25
16	John Smith	1.50	.75	.45
17	Dwight McDonald	1.50	.75	.45
18	John Cappelletti	1.50	.75	.45
19	Pittsburgh Steelers Team (Franco Harris, Larry Anderson, Tim Dungy, L.C. Greenwood)	1.50	.75	.25
20	Bill Bergey (AP)	1.50	.75	.45
21	Jerome Barkum	1.50	.75	.45
22	Larry Csonka	1.50	.60	.40
23	Joe Ferguson	1.50	.75	.45
24	Ed "Too Tall" Jones	1.50	.50	.30
25	Dave Jennings	1.50	.75	.45
26	Horace King	1.50	.75	.45
27	Steve Little	1.50	.75	.45
28	Morris Bradshaw	1.50	.75	.45
29	Joe Ehrmann	1.50	.75	.45
30	Ahmad Rashad (AP)	1.50	.75	.25
31	Joe Lavender	1.50	.75	.45
32	Dan Neal	1.50	.75	.45
33	Johnny Evans	1.50	.75	.45
34	Pete Johnson	1.50	.75	.45
35	Mike Haynes (AP)	1.50	.75	.45
36	Tim Mazzetti	1.50	.75	.45
37	Mike Barber RC	1.50	.75	.45
38	San Francisco 49ers Team (O.J. Simpson, Freddie Solomon, Chuck Crist, Cedrick Hardman)	1.50	.75	.45
39	Bill Gregory	1.50	.75	.45
40	Randy Gradishar (AP)	1.50	.75	.45
41	Richard Todd	1.50	.75	.45
42	Henry Marshall	1.50	.75	.45
43	John Hill	1.50	.75	.45
44	Sidney Thornton	1.50	.75	.45
45	Ron Jessie	1.50	.75	.45
46	Bob Baumhower	1.50	.75	.45
47	Johnnie Gray	1.50	.75	.45
48	Doug Williams RC	4.00	2.00	1.20
49	Don McCauley	1.50	.75	.45
50	Ray Guy (AP)	1.50	.75	.45
51	Bob Klein	1.50	.75	.45
52	Golden Richards	1.50	.75	.45
53	Mark Miller	1.50	.75	.45
54	John Sanders	1.50	.75	.45
55	Gary Burley	1.50	.75	.45
56	Steve Nelson	1.50	.75	.45
57	Buffalo Bills Team (Miller, Frank Lewis, Mario Clark, Lucius Sanford)	1.50	.75	.45
58	Bobby Bryant	1.50	.75	.45
59	Rick Kane	1.50	.75	.45
60	Larry Little	1.50	.75	.45
61	Ted Fritsch	1.50	.75	.45
62	Larry Mallory	1.50	.75	.45
63	Marvin Powell	1.50	.75	.45
64	Jim Hart	1.50	.75	.45
65	Joe Greene (AP)	3.00	1.50	.90
66	Walter White	1.50	.75	.45
67	Gregg Bingham	1.50	.75	.45
68	Errol Mann	1.50	.75	.45
69	Bruce Laird	1.50	.75	.45
70	Drew Pearson	1.50	.75	.45
71	Steve Bartkowski	1.50	.75	.45
72	Ted Albrecht	1.50	.75	.45
73	Charlie Hall	1.50	.75	.45
74	Pat McInally	1.50	.75	.45
75	Al Baker RC (AP)	1.50	.75	.45
76	New England Patriots Team (Sam Cunningham, Stanley Morgan, Mike Haynes, Tony McGee)	1.50	.75	.45
77	Steve DeBerg RC	1.50	.75	.45
78	John Yarno	1.50	.75	.45
79	Stu Voight	1.50	.75	.45
80	Frank Corral (AP)	1.50	.75	.45
81	Troy Archer	1.50	.75	.45
82	Bruce Harper	1.50	.75	.45
83	Tom Jackson	1.50	.75	.25
84	Larry Brown	1.50	.75	.45
85	Wilbert Montgomery RC	1.50	.75	.45
86	Butch Johnson	1.50	.75	.45
87	Mike Kadish	1.50	.75	.45
88	Ralph Perretta	1.50	.75	.45
89	David Lee	1.50	.75	.45
90	Mark Van Eeghen	1.50	.75	.45
91	John McDaniel	1.50	.75	.45
92	Gary Fencik	1.50	.75	.45
93	Mack Mitchell	1.50	.75	.45
94	Cincinnati Bengals Team (Pete Johnson, Isaac Curtis, Dick Jauron, Ross Browner)	1.50	.75	.45
95	Steve Grogan	1.50	.75	.45
96	Garo Yepremian	1.50	.75	.45
97	Barty Smith	1.50	.75	.45
98	Frank Reed	1.50	.75	.45
99	Jim Clark	1.50	.75	.45
100	Chuck Foreman	1.50	.75	.45
101	Joe Klecko	1.50	.75	.45
102	Pat Tilley	1.50	.75	.45
103	Conrad Dobler	1.50	.75	.45
104	Craig Colquitt	1.50	.75	.45
105	Dan Pastorini	1.50	.75	.45
106	Rod Perry (AP)	1.50	.75	.45
107	Nick Mike-Mayer	1.50	.75	.45
108	John Matuszak	1.50	.75	.45
109	David Taylor	1.50	.75	.45
110	Billy Joe DuPree (AP)	1.50	.75	.45
111	Harold McLinton	1.50	.75	.45
112	Virgil Livers	1.50	.75	.45
113	Cleveland Browns Team (Greg Pruitt, Reggie Rucker, Thom Darden, Mack Mitchell)	1.50	.75	.45
114	Checklist 1-132	1.50	.75	.45
115	Ken Anderson	1.25	.60	.40
116	Bill Lenkaitis	1.50	.75	.45
117	Bucky Dilts	1.50	.75	.45
118	Tony Greene	1.50	.75	.45
119	Bobby Hammond	1.50	.75	.45
120	Nat Moore	1.50	.75	.45
121	Pat Leahy (AP)	1.50	.75	.45
122	James Harris	1.50	.75	.45
123	Lee Roy Selmon	1.50	.75	.45
124	Bennie Cunningham	1.50	.75	.45
125	Matt Blair (AP)	1.50	.75	.45
126	Jim Allen	1.50	.75	.45
127	Alfred Jenkins	1.50	.75	.45
128	Arthur Whittington	1.50	.75	.45
129	Norm Thompson	1.50	.75	.45
130	Pat Haden	1.50	.75	.45
131	Freddie Solomon	1.50	.75	.45
132	Chicago Bears Team (Walter Payton, James Scott, Gary Fencik, Alan Page)	2.00	1.00	.60
133	Mark Moseley	1.50	.75	.45
134	Cleo Miller	1.50	.75	.45
135	Ross Browner RC	1.30	.75	.45
136	Don Calhoun	1.50	.75	.45
137	David Whitehurst	1.50	.75	.45
138	Terry Beeson	1.50	.75	.45
139	Ken Stone	1.50	.75	.45
140	Brad Van Pelt AP	1.50	.75	.45
141	Wesley Walker (AP)	1.50	.75	.25
142	Jan Stenerud	1.50	.75	.45
143	Henry Childs	1.50	.75	.45
144	Otis Armstrong	1.25	.75	.45
145	Dwight White	1.50	.75	.45
146	Steve Wilson	1.50	.75	.45
147	Tom Skladany (AP)	1.50	.75	.45
148	Lou Piccone	1.50	.75	.45
149	Monte Johnson	1.50	.75	.45
150	Joe Washington	1.50	.75	.45
151	Philadelphia Eagles Team (Wilbert Montgomery, Harold Carmichael, Herman Edwards, Dennis Harrison)	1.50	.75	.45
152	Fred Dean	1.25	.75	.45
153	Rolland Lawrence	1.50	.75	.45
154	Brian Baschnagel	1.50	.75	.45
155	Joe Theismann	1.50	.70	.45
156	Marvin Cobb	1.50	75	45
157	Dick Ambrose	1.50	.75	.45
158	Mike Patrick	1.50	.75	.45
159	Gary Shirk	1.50	.75	.45
160	Tony Dorsett	5.00	2.50	1.50
161	Greg Buttle	1.50	.75	.45
162	A.J. Duhe	1.50	.75	.45
163	Mick Tingelhoff	1.50	.75	.45
164	Ken Burrough	1.50	.75	.45
165	Mike Wagner	1.50	.75	.45
166	AFC Championship (Franco Harris)	2.00	1.00	.60
167	NFC Championship	1.50	.75	.45
168	Super Bowl XII (Franco Harris)	1.25	.60	.40
169	Oakland Raiders Team (Mark Van Eeghen, Dave Casper, Charles Phillips, Ted Hendricks)	1.50	.75	.45
170	O.J. Simpson	3.00	1.50	.90
171	Doug Nettles	1.50	.75	.45
172	Dan Dierdorf (AP)	1.50	.75	.25
173	Dave Beverly	1.50	.75	.45
174	Jim Zorn	1.50	.75	.45
175	Mike Thomas	1.50	.75	.45
176	John Outlaw	1.50	.75	.45
177	Jim Turner	1.50	.75	.45
178	Freddie Scott	1.50	.75	.45
179	Mike Phipps	1.50	.75	.45
180	Jack Youngblood (AP)	1.50	.75	.15
181	Sam Hunt	1.50	.75	.45
182	Tony Hill RC	4.00	2.00	1.20
183	Gary Barbaro	1.50	.75	.45
184	Archie Griffin	1.40	.75	.45
185	Jerry Sherk	1.50	.75	.45
186	Bobby Jackson	1.50	.75	.45
187	Don Woods	1.50	.75	.45
188	New York Giants Team (Doug Kotar, Jimmy Robinson, Terry Jackson, George Martin)	1.50	.75	.45
189	Raymond Chester	1.50	.75	.45
190	Joe DeLamielleure (AP)	1.50	.75	.45
191	Tony Galbreath	1.50	.75	.45
192	Robert Brazile (AP)	1.50	.75	.45
193	Neil O'Donoghue	1.50	.75	.45
194	Mike Webster	1.50	.75	.25
195	Ed Simonini	1.50	.75	.45
196	Denny Malone	1.50	.75	.45
197	Tom Wittum	1.50	.75	.45
198	Steve Largent (AP)	2.50	1.25	.75
199	Tommy Hart	1.50	.75	.45
200	Fran Tarkenton	3.00	1.50	.90
201	Leon Gray (AP)	1.50	.75	.45
202	Leroy Harris	1.50	.75	.45
203	Eric Williams	1.50	.75	.45
204	Thom Darden (AP)	1.50	.75	.45
205	Ken Riley	1.50	.75	.45
206	Clark Gaines	1.50	.75	.45
207	Kansas City Chiefs Team (Tony Reed, Tim Gray, Art Still)	1.50	.75	.45
208	Joe Danelo	1.50	.75	.45
209	Glen Walker	1.50	.75	.45
210	Art Shell	1.50	.75	.45
211	Jon Keyworth	1.50	.75	.45
212	Herman Edwards	1.50	.75	.45
213	John Fitzgerald	1.50	.75	.45
214	Jim Smith	1.50	.75	.45
215	Coy Bacon	1.50	.75	.45
216	Dennis Johnson	1.50	.75	.45
217	John Jefferson RC	1.50	.75	.45
218	Gary Weaver	1.50	.75	.45
219	Tom Blanchard	1.50	.75	.45
220	Bert Jones	1.50	.75	.45
221	Stanley Morgan	1.50	.70	.45
222	James Hunter	1.50	.75	.45
223	Jim O'Bradovich	1.50	.75	.45
224	Carl Mauck	1.50	.75	.45
225	Chris Bahr	1.50	.75	.45
226	New York Jets Team (Kevin Long, Wesley Walker, Bobby Jackson, Burgess Owens, Joe Klecko)	1.60	.75	.45
227	Roland Harper	1.50	.75	.45
228	Randy Dean	1.50	.75	.45
229	Bob Jackson	1.50	.75	.45
230	Sammie White	1.25	.75	.45
231	Mike Dawson	1.50	.75	.45
232	Checklist 133-264	1.00	.50	.30
233	Ken MacAfee	1.50	.75	.45
234	Jon Kolb (AP)	1.50	.75	.45
235	Willie Hall	1.50	.75	.45

236	Ron Saul (AP)	1.50	.75	.45
237	Haskel Stanback	1.50	.75	.45
238	Zenon Andrusyshyn	1.50	.75	.45
239	Norris Thomas	1.50	.75	.45
240	Rick Upchurch	1.30	.75	.45
241	Robert Pratt	1.50	.75	.45
242	Julius Adams	1.50	.75	.45
243	Rich McGeorge	1.50	.75	.45
244	Seattle Seahawks Team (Sherman Smith, Steve Largent, Cornell Webster, Bill Gregory)	1.00	.50	.30
245	Blair Bush	1.50	.75	.45
246	Billy Johnson	1.50	.75	.45
247	Randy Rasmussen	1.50	.75	.45
248	Brian Kelley	1.50	.75	.45
249	Mike Pruitt	1.50	.75	.45
250	Harold Carmichael (AP)	1.50	.75	.45
251	Mike Hartenstine	1.50	.75	.45
252	Robert Newhouse	1.50	.75	.45
253	Gary Danielson	1.50	.75	.45
254	Mike Fuller	1.50	.75	.45
255	L.C. Greenwood (AP)	1.40	.75	.45
256	Lemar Parrish	1.50	.75	.45
257	Ike Harris	1.50	.75	.45
258	Ricky Bell RC	1.00	.50	.30
259	Willie Parker	1.50	.75	.45
260	Gene Upshaw	1.50	.75	.45
261	Glenn Doughty	1.50	.75	.45
262	Steve Zabel	1.50	.75	.45
263	Atlanta Falcons Team (Bubba Bean, Wallace Francis, Rolland Lawrence, Greg Brezina)	1.50	.75	.45
264	Ray Wersching	1.50	.75	.45
265	Lawrence McCutcheon	1.50	.75	.45
266	Willie Buchanon (AP)	1.50	.75	.45
267	Matt Robinson	1.50	.75	.45
268	Reggie Rucker	1.50	.75	.45
269	Doug Van Horn	1.50	.75	.45
270	Lydell Mitchell	1.50	.75	.45
271	Vern Holland	1.50	.75	.45
272	Eason Ramson	1.50	.75	.45
273	Steve Towle	1.50	.75	.45
274	Jim Marshall	1.40	.75	.45
275	Mel Blount	1.50	.75	.45
276	Bob Kuziel	1.50	.75	.45
277	James Scott	1.50	.75	.45
278	Tony Reed	1.50	.75	.45
279	Dave Green	1.50	.75	.45
280	Toni Linhart	1.50	.75	.45
281	Andy Johnson	1.50	.75	.45
282	Los Angeles Rams Team (Cullen Bryant, Willie Miller, Rod Perry, Pat Thomas, Larry Brooks)	1.50	.75	.45
283	Phil Villapiano	1.50	.75	.45
284	Dexter Bussey	1.50	.75	.45
285	Craig Morton	1.50	.75	.45
286	Guy Morriss	1.50	.75	.45
287	Lawrence Pillers	1.50	.75	.45
288	Gerald Irons	1.50	.75	.45
289	Scott Perry	1.50	.75	.45
290	Randy White	1.50	.75	.45
291	Jack Gregory	1.50	.75	.45
292	Bob Chandler	1.50	.75	.45
293	Rich Szaro	1.50	.75	.45
294	Sherman Smith	1.50	.75	.45
295	Tom Banks (AP)	1.50	.75	.45
296	Revie Sorey (AP)	1.50	.75	.45
297	Ricky Thompson	1.50	.75	.45
298	Ron Yary	1.50	.75	.45
299	Lyle Blackwood	1.50	.75	.45
300	Franco Harris	2.00	1.00	.60
301	Houston Oilers Team (Earl Campbell, Ken Burrough, Willie Alexander, Elvin Bethea)	2.50	1.25	.75
302	Scott Bull	1.50	.75	.45
303	Dewey Selmon	1.50	.75	.45
304	Jack Rudnay	1.50	.75	.45
305	Fred Biletnikoff	1.50	.75	.45
306	Jeff West	1.50	.75	.45
307	Shafer Suggs	1.50	.75	.45
308	Ozzie Newsome RC	10.00	5.00	3.00
309	Boobie Clark	1.50	.75	.45
310	James Lofton RC	10.00	5.00	3.00
311	Joe Pisarcik	1.50	.75	.45
312	Bill Simpson (AP)	1.50	.75	.45
313	Haven Moses	1.50	.75	.45
314	Jim Merlo	1.50	.75	.45
315	Preston Pearson	1.50	.75	.45
316	Larry Tearry	1.50	.75	.45
317	Tom Dempsey	1.50	.75	.45
318	Greg Latta	1.50	.75	.45

319	Washington Redskins Team (John Riggins, John McDaniel, Jake Scott, Coy Bacon)	1.50	.75	.45
320	Jack Ham (AP)	2.50	1.25	.75
321	Harold Jackson	1.50	.75	.45
322	George Roberts	1.50	.75	.45
323	Ron Jaworski	1.50	.75	.45
324	Jim Otis	1.50	.75	.45
325	Roger Carr	1.50	.75	.45
326	Jack Tatum	1.50	.75	.45
327	Derrick Gaffney	1.50	.75	.45
328	Reggie Williams	2.50	.75	.45
329	Doug Dieken	1.50	.75	.45
330	Efren Herrera	1.50	.75	.45
331	Record: (Campbell)	2.50	1.25	.75
332	Record: (Tony Galbreath)	1.50	.75	.45
333	Record: (Bruce Harper)	1.50	.75	.45
334	Record: (John James)	1.50	.75	.45
335	Record: (Walter Payton)	3.00	1.50	.90
336	Record: (Rickey Young)	1.50	.75	.45
337	Jeff Van Note	1.50	.75	.45
338	San Diego Chargers Team (Lydell Mitchell, John Jefferson, Mike Fuller, Fred Dean)	1.50	.75	.45
339	Stan Walters RC (AP)	1.50	.75	.45
340	Louis Wright (AP)	1.50	.75	.45
341	Horace Ivory	1.50	.75	.45
342	Andre Tillman	1.50	.75	.45
343	Greg Coleman	1.50	.75	.45
344	Doug English RC (AP)	1.50	.75	.45
345	Ted Hendricks	1.50	.75	.45
346	Rich Saul	1.50	.75	.45
347	Mel Gray	1.50	.75	.45
348	Toni Fritsch	1.50	.75	.45
349	Cornell Webster	1.50	.75	.45
350	Ken Houston	1.50	.75	.45
351	Ron Johnson	1.50	.75	.45
352	Doug Kotar	1.50	.75	.45
353	Brian Sipe	1.50	.75	.45
354	Billy Brooks	1.50	.75	.45
355	John Dutton	1.50	.75	.45
356	Don Goode	1.50	.75	.45
357	Detroit Lions Team (Dexter Bussey, David Hill, Jim Allen, Al Baker)	1.50	.75	.45
358	Reuben Gant	1.50	.75	.45
359	Bob Parsons	1.50	.75	.45
360	Cliff Harris (AP)	1.50	.75	.45
361	Raymond Clayborn	1.50	.75	.45
362	Scott Dierking	1.50	.75	.45
363	Bill Bryan	1.50	.75	.45
364	Mike Livingston	1.50	.75	.45
365	Otis Sistrunk	1.50	.75	.45
366	Charley Young	1.50	.75	.45
367	Keith Wortman	1.50	.75	.45
368	Checklist 265-396	1.50	.75	.45
369	Mike Michel	1.50	.75	.45
370	Delvin Williams	1.50	.75	.45
371	Steve Furness	1.50	.75	.45
372	Emery Moorehead	1.50	.75	.45
373	Clarence Scott	1.50	.75	.45
374	Rufus Mayes	1.50	.75	.45
375	Chris Hanberger	1.50	.75	.45
376	Baltimore Colts Team (Joe Washington, Roger Carr, Norm Thompson, John Dutton)	2.50	.75	.45
377	Bob Avellini	1.50	.75	.45
378	Jeff Siemon	1.50	.75	.45
379	Roland Hooks	1.50	.75	.45
380	Russ Francis	1.50	.75	.45
381	Roger Wehrli	1.50	.75	.45
382	Joe Fields	1.50	.75	.45
383	Archie Manning	1.50	.75	.45
384	Rob Lytle	1.50	.75	.45
385	Thomas Henderson	1.50	.75	.45
386	Morris Owens	1.50	.75	.45
387	Dan Fouts	2.50	1.50	.90
388	Chuck Crist	1.50	.75	.45
389	Ed O'Neil	1.50	.75	.45
390	Earl Campbell RC (AP)	20.00	10.00	6.00
391	Randy Grossman	1.50	.75	.45
392	Monte Jackson	1.50	.75	.45
393	John Mendenhall	1.50	.75	.45
394	Miami Dolphins Team (Delvin Williams, Duriel Harris, Tim Foley, Vern Den Herder)	1.50	.75	.45
395	Isaac Curtis	1.50	.75	.45
396	Mike Bragg	1.50	.75	.45
397	Doug Plank	1.50	.75	.45
398	Mike Barnes	1.50	.75	.45
399	Calvin Hill	1.50	.75	.45
400	Roger Staubach (AP)	4.00	2.00	1.20

401	Doug Beaudoin	1.50	.75	.45
402	Chuck Ramsey	1.50	.75	.45
403	Mike Hogan	1.50	.75	.45
404	Mario Clark	1.50	.75	.45
405	Riley Odoms	1.50	.75	.45
406	Carl Eller	1.50	.75	.45
407	Green Bay Packers Team (Terdell Middleton, James Lofton, Willie Buchanon, Ezra Johnson)	1.50	.75	.45
408	Mark Arenson	1.50	.75	.45
409	Vince Ferragamo RC	1.50	.75	.45
410	Cleveland Elam	1.50	.75	.45
411	Donnie Shell RC	6.00	3.00	1.80
412	Ray Rhodes	1.50	.75	.45
413	Don Cockroft	1.50	.75	.45
414	Don Bass	1.50	.75	.45
415	Cliff Branch	1.50	.75	.25
416	Diron Talbert	1.50	.75	.45
417	Tom Hicks	1.50	.75	.45
418	Roosevelt Leaks	1.50	.75	.45
419	Charlie Joiner	1.50	.75	.25
420	Lyle Alzado (AP)	1.50	.75	.25
421	Sam Cunningham	1.50	.75	.45
422	Larry Keller	1.50	.75	.45
423	Jim Mitchell	1.50	.75	.45
424	Randy Logan	1.50	.75	.45
425	Jim Langer	1.50	.75	.45
426	Gary Green	1.50	.75	.45
427	Luther Blue	1.50	.75	.45
428	Dennis Johnson	1.50	.75	.45
429	Danny White	1.50	.75	.25
430	Roy Gerela	1.50	.75	.45
431	Jimmy Robinson	1.50	.75	.45
432	Minnesota Vikings Team (Chuck Foreman, Ahmad Rashad, Bobby Bryant, Mark Mullaney)	1.50	.75	.45
433	Oliver Davis	1.50	.75	.45
434	Lenvill Elliott	1.50	.75	.45
435	Willie Miller	1.50	.75	.45
436	Brad Dusek	1.50	.75	.45
437	Bob Thomas	1.50	.75	.45
438	Ken Mendenhall	1.50	.75	.45
439	Clarence Davis	1.50	.75	.45
440	Bob Griese	1.50	.75	.45
441	Tony McGee	1.50	.75	.45
442	Ed Taylor	1.50	.75	.45
443	Ron Howard	1.50	.75	.45
444	Wayne Morris	1.50	.75	.45
445	Charlie Waters	1.50	.75	.45
446	Rick Danmeier	1.50	.75	.45
447	Paul Naumoff	1.50	.75	.45
448	Keith Krepfle	1.50	.75	.45
449	Rusty Jackson	1.50	.75	.45
450	John Stallworth	1.50	.75	.45
451	New Orleans Saints Team (Tony Galbreath, Henry Childs, Tom Myers, Elex Price)	1.50	.75	.45
452	Ron Mikolajczyk	1.50	.75	.45
453	Fred Dryer	1.50	.75	.25
454	Jim LeClair	1.50	.75	.45
455	Greg Pruitt	1.50	.75	.45
456	Jake Scott	1.50	.75	.45
457	Steve Schubert	1.50	.75	.45
458	George Kunz	1.50	.75	.45
459	Mike Williams	1.50	.75	.45
460	Dave Casper (AP)	1.50	.75	.45
461	Sam Adams	1.50	.75	.45
462	Abdul Salaam	1.50	.75	.45
463	Terdell Middleton	1.50	.75	.45
464	Mike Wood	1.50	.75	.45
465	Bill Thompson (AP)	1.50	.75	.45
466	Larry Gordon	1.50	.75	.45
467	Benny Ricardo	1.50	.75	.45
468	Reggie McKenzie	1.50	.75	.45
469	Dallas Cowboys Team (Tony Dorsett, Tony Hill, Benny Barnes, Harvey Martin, Randy White)	1.50	.75	.45
470	Rickey Young	1.50	.75	.45
471	Charlie Smith	1.50	.75	.45
472	Al Dixon	1.50	.75	.45
473	Tom DeLeone	1.50	.75	.45
474	Louis Breeden	1.50	.75	.45
475	Jack Lambert	2.50	1.25	.75
476	Terry Hermeling	1.50	.75	.45
477	J.K. McKay	1.50	.75	.45
478	Stan White	1.50	.75	.45
479	Terry Nelson	1.50	.75	.45
480	Walter Payton (AP)	10.00	5.00	3.00
481	Dave Dalby	1.50	.75	.45
482	Burgess Owens	1.50	.75	.45
483	Rolf Benirschke	1.50	.75	.45
484	Jack Dolbin	1.50	.75	.45

485	John Hannah (AP)	1.50	.75	.45
486	Checklist 397-528	1.50	.75	.45
487	Greg Landry	1.50	.75	.45
488	St. Louis Cardinals Team (Jim Otis, Pat Tilley, Ken Stone, Mike Dawson)	1.50	.75	.45
489	Paul Krause	1.50	.75	.45
490	John James	1.50	.75	.45
491	Merv Krakau	1.50	.75	.45
492	Dan Doornink	1.50	.75	.45
493	Curtis Johnson	1.50	.75	.45
494	Rafael Septien RC	1.50	.75	.45
495	Jean Fugett	1.50	.75	.45
496	Frank LeMaster	1.50	.75	.45
497	Allan Ellis	1.50	.75	.45
498	Billy Waddy RC	1.50	.75	.45
499	Hank Bauer	1.50	.75	.45
500	Terry Bradshaw (AP)	5.00	2.50	1.50
501	Larry McCarren	1.50	.75	.45
502	Fred Cook	1.50	.75	.45
503	Chuck Muncie	1.50	.75	.45
504	Herman Weaver	1.50	.75	.45
505	Eddie Edwards	1.50	.75	.45
506	Tony Peters	1.50	.75	.45
507	Denver Broncos Team (Lonnie Perrin, Riley Odoms, Steve Foley, Bernard Jackson, Lyle Alzado)	1.50	.75	.45
508	Jimbo Elrod	1.50	.75	.45
509	David Hill	1.50	.75	.45
510	Harvey Martin	1.50	.75	.45
511	Terry Miller	1.50	.75	.45
512	June Jones RC	1.50	.75	.45
513	Randy Cross	1.50	.75	.45
514	Duriel Harris	1.50	.75	.45
515	Harry Carson	1.50	.75	.45
516	Tim Fox	1.50	.75	.45
517	John Zook	1.50	.75	.45
518	Bob Tucker	1.50	.75	.45
519	Kevin Long	1.50	.75	.45
520	Ken Stabler	2.50	1.25	.75
521	John Bunting	1.50	.75	.45
522	Rocky Bleier	1.50	.75	.45
523	Noah Jackson	1.50	.75	.45
524	Cliff Parsley	1.50	.75	.45
525	Louie Kelcher (AP)	1.50	.75	.45
526	Tampa Bay Bucaneers (Ricky Bell, Morris Owens, Cedric Brown, Lee Roy Selmon)	1.50	.75	.45
527	Bob Brudzinski	1.50	.75	.45
528	Danny Buggs	1.50	.75	.45

1980 Topps

The cards in this set feature a football at the bottom of the card with the team name and position on either side of the player's name. The 528-card set has subsets featuring, as usual, record breakers and the previous year's playoff decisions. Rookies in this set include Ottis Anderson, Tommy Kramer, Phil Simms and Wes Chandler. (Key: AP - All Pro)

	NM	E	VG
Complete Set (528):	100.00	50.00	30.00
Common Player:	.50	.25	.15
Minor Stars:	.30		
Unlisted Stars:	.75		
Wax Pack (12):	4.00		
Wax Box (36):	100.00		

1	Record: (O. Anderson)	.50	.25	.15
2	Record: (Harold Carmichael)	.50	.25	.05
3	Record: (Dan Fouts)	.50	.25	.15
4	Record: (Paul Krause)	.50	.25	.15
5	Record: (Rick Upchurch)	.50	.25	.15
6	Record: (Garo Yepremian)	.50	.25	.15
7	Harold Jackson	.50	.25	.15
8	Mike Williams	.50	.25	.15
9	Calvin Hill	.50	.25	.15
10	Jack Ham	.50	.25	.15

11	Dan Melville	.50	.25	.15
12	Matt Robinson	.50	.25	.15
13	Billy Campfield	.50	.25	.15
14	Phil Tabor	.50	.25	.15
15	Randy Hughes	.50	.25	.15
16	Andre Tillman	.50	.25	.15
17	Isaac Curtis	.50	.25	.15
18	Charley Hannah	.50	.25	.15
19	Washington Redskins Team (John Riggins, Danny Buggs, Joe Lavender, Coy Bacon)	.50	.25	.15
20	Jim Zorn	.50	.25	.15
21	Brian Baschnagel	.50	.25	.15
22	Jon Keyworth	.50	.25	.15
23	Phil Villapiano	.50	.25	.15
24	Richard Osborne	.50	.25	.15
25	Rich Saul (AP)	.50	.25	.15
26	Doug Beaudoin	.50	.25	.15
27	Cleveland Elam	.50	.25	.15
28	Charlie Joiner	.50	.25	.15
29	Dick Ambrose	.50	.25	.15
30	Mike Reinfeldt RC (AP)	.50	.25	.15
31	Matt Bahr RC	.50	.25	.15
32	Keith Krepfle	.50	.25	.15
33	Herbert Scott	.50	.25	.15
34	Doug Kotar	.50	.25	.15
35	Bob Griese	3.00	1.50	.90
36	Jerry Butler RC	.40	.25	.12
37	Rolland Lawrence	.50	.25	.15
38	Gary Weaver	.50	.25	.15
39	Kansas City Chiefs Team (Ted McKnight, J.T. Smith, Gary Barbaro, Art Still)	.40	.25	.12
40	Chuck Muncie	.50	.25	.15
41	Mike Hartenstine	.50	.25	.15
42	Sammie White	.50	.25	.15
43	Ken Clark	.50	.25	.15
44	Clarence Harmon	.50	.25	.15
45	Bert Jones	.50	.15	.15
46	Mike Washington	.50	.25	.15
47	Joe Fields	.50	.25	.15
48	Mike Wood	.50	.25	.15
49	Oliver Davis	.50	.25	.15
50	Stan Walters (AP)	.50	.25	.15
51	Riley Odoms	.50	.25	.15
52	Steve Pisarkiewicz	.50	.25	.15
53	Tony Hill	.50	.25	.15
54	Scott Perry	.50	.25	.15
55	George Martin RC	.40	.25	.12
56	George Roberts	.50	.25	.15
57	Seattle Seahawks Team (Sherman Smith, Steve Largent, Dave Brown, Manu Tuiasosopo)	.50	.25	.15
58	Billy Johnson	.50	.25	.15
59	Reuben Johnson	.50	.25	.15
60	Dennis Harrah RC (AP)	.50	.25	.15
61	Rocky Bleier	.50	.25	.15
62	Sam Hunt	.50	.25	.15
63	Allan Ellis	.50	.25	.15
64	Ricky Thompson	.50	.25	.15
65	Ken Stabler	2.00	1.00	.60
66	Dexter Bussey	.50	.25	.15
67	Ken Mendenhall	.50	.25	.15
68	Woodrow Lowe	.50	.25	.15
69	Thom Darden	.50	.25	.15
70	Randy White (AP)	.50	.25	.15
71	Ken MacAfee	.50	.25	.15
72	Ron Jaworski	.50	.25	.15
73	William Andrews RC	.50	.25	.15
74	Jimmy Robinson	.50	.25	.15
75	Roger Wehrli (AP)	.50	.25	.15
76	Miami Dolphins Team (Larry Csonka, Nat Moore, Neal Colzie, Gerald Small, Vern Den Herder)	.50	.25	.15
77	Jack Rudnay	.50	.25	.15
78	James Lofton	.50	.25	.15
79	Robert Brazile	.50	.25	.15
80	Russ Francis	.50	.25	.15
81	Ricky Bell	.50	.25	.15
82	Bob Avellini	.50	.25	.15
83	Bobby Jackson	.50	.25	.15
84	Mike Bragg	.50	.25	.15
85	Cliff Branch	.50	.25	.15
86	Blair Bush	.50	.25	.15
87	Sherman Smith	.50	.25	.15
88	Glen Edwards	.50	.25	.15
89	Don Cockroft	.50	.25	.15
90	Louis Wright (AP)	.50	.25	.15
91	Randy Grossman	.50	.25	.15
92	Carl Hariston RC	.50	.25	.15
93	Archie Manning	.50	.25	.15
94	New York Giants Team (Billy Taylor, Earnest Gray, George Martin)	.50	.15	.15

95	Preston Pearson	.50	.25	.15
96	Rusty Chambers	.50	.25	.15
97	Greg Coleman	.50	.25	.15
98	Charley Young	.50	.25	.15
99	Matt Cavanaugh RC	.50	.25	.15
100	Jesse Baker	.50	.25	.15
101	Doug Plank	.50	.25	.15
102	Checklist 1-132	.50	.25	.15
103	Luther Bradley RC	.50	.25	.15
104	Bob Kuziel	.50	.25	.15
105	Craig Morton	.50	.25	.15
106	Sherman White	.50	.25	.15
107	Jim Breech RC	.50	.25	.15
108	Hank Bauer	.50	.25	.15
109	Tom Blanchard	.50	.25	.15
110	Ozzie Newsome (AP)	.65	.37	.25
111	Steve Furness	.50	.25	.15
112	Frank LeMaster	.50	.25	.15
113	Dallas Cowboys Team (Tony Dorsett, Tony Hill, Harvey Martin)	.50	.25	.15
114	Doug Van Horn	.50	.25	.15
115	Delvin Williams	.50	.25	.15
116	Lyle Blackwood	.50	.25	.15
117	Derrick Gaffney	.50	.25	.15
118	Cornell Webster	.50	.25	.15
119	Sam Cunningham	.50	.25	.15
120	Jim Youngblood (AP)	.50	.25	.15
121	Bob Thomas	.50	.25	.15
122	Jack Thompson RC	.50	.25	.15
123	Randy Cross	.50	.25	.15
124	Karl Lorch	.50	.25	.15
125	Mel Gray	.50	.25	.15
126	John James	.50	.25	.15
127	Terdell Middleton	.50	.25	.15
128	Leroy Jones	.50	.25	.15
129	Tom DeLeone	.50	.25	.15
130	John Stallworth (AP)	.50	.25	.15
131	Jimmie Giles RC	.50	.15	.15
132	Philadelphia Eagles Team (Wilbert Montgomery, Harold Carmichael, Brenard Wilson, Carl Hairston)	.50	.15	.15
133	Gary Green	.50	.25	.15
134	John Dutton	.50	.25	.15
135	Harry Carson (AP)	.50	.25	.15
136	Bob Kuechenberg	.50	.25	.15
137	Ike Harris	.50	.25	.15
138	Tommy Kramer RC	.50	.25	.15
139	Sam Adams	.50	.25	.15
140	Doug English (AP)	.50	.25	.15
141	Steve Schubert	.50	.25	.15
142	Rusty Jackson	.50	.25	.15
143	Reese McCall	.50	.25	.15
144	Scott Dierking	.50	.25	.15
145	Ken Houston (AP)	.50	.25	.15
146	Bob Martin	.50	.25	.15
147	Sam McCullum	.50	.25	.15
148	Tom Banks	.50	.25	.15
149	Willie Buchanon	.50	.25	.15
150	Greg Pruitt	.50	.25	.15
151	Denver Broncos Team (Otis Armstrong, Rick Upchurch, Steve Foley, Brison Manor)	.50	.25	.15
152	Don Smith	.50	.25	.15
153	Pete Johnson	.50	.25	.15
154	Charlie Smith	.50	.25	.15
155	Mel Blount	.50	.25	.15
156	John Mendenhall	.50	.25	.15
157	Danny White	.50	.25	.15
158	Jimmy Cefalo RC	.50	.15	.15
159	Richard Bishop (AP)	.50	.25	.15
160	Walter Payton (AP)	6.00	3.00	1.80
161	Dave Dalby	.50	.25	.15
162	Preston Dennard	.50	.25	.15
163	Johnnie Gray	.50	.25	.15
164	Russell Erxieben	.50	.25	.15
165	Toni Fritsch (AP)	.50	.25	.15
166	Terry Hermeling	.50	.25	.15
167	Roland Hooks	.50	.25	.15
168	Roger Carr	.50	.25	.15
169	San Diego Chargers Team (Clarence Williams, John Jefferson, Woodrow Lowe, Ray Preston, Wilbur Young)	.50	.15	.15
170	Ottis Anderson RC (AP)	3.00	1.50	.75
171	Brian Sipe	.50	.15	.15
172	Leonard Thompson	.50	.25	.15
173	Tony Reed	.50	.25	.15
174	Bob Tucker	.50	.25	.15
175	Joe Greene	.50	.25	.15
176	Jack Dolbin	.50	.25	.15
177	Chuck Ramsey	.50	.25	.15
178	Paul Hofer	.50	.25	.15
179	Randy Logan	.50	.25	.15

No.	Player			
180	David Lewis (AP)	.50	.25	.15
181	Duriel Harris	.50	.25	.15
182	June Jones	.50	.25	.15
183	Larry McCarren	.50	.25	.15
184	Ken Johnson	.50	.25	.15
185	Charlie Waters	.50	.25	.15
186	Noah Jackson	.50	.25	.15
187	Reggie Williams	.50	.25	.15
188	New England Patriots Team (Sam Cunningham, Harold Jackson, Raymond Clayborn, Tony McGee)	.50	.25	.15
189	Carl Eller	.35	.25	.15
190	Ed White (AP)	.50	.25	.15
191	Mario Clark	.50	.25	.15
192	Roosevelt Leaks	.50	.25	.15
193	Ted McKnight	.50	.25	.15
194	Danny Buggs	.50	.25	.15
195	Lester Hayes RC	.50	.25	.15
196	Clarence Scott	.50	.25	.15
197	New Orleans Saints Team (Chuck Muncie, Wes Chandler, Tom Myers, Elois Grooms, Don Reese)	.50	.25	.15
198	Richard Caster	.50	.25	.15
199	Louie Giammona	.50	.25	.15
200	Terry Bradshaw	3.50	1.75	1.00
201	Ed Newman	.50	.25	.15
202	Fred Dryer	.50	.25	.15
203	Dennis Franks	.50	.25	.15
204	Bob Breunig RC	.40	.25	.15
205	Alan Page	.50	.25	.15
206	Earnest Gray	.50	.25	.15
207	Minnesota Vikings Team (Rickey Young, Ahmad Rashad, Tommy Hannon, Nate Wright, Mark Mullaney)	.40	.25	.12
208	Horace Ivory	.50	.25	.15
209	Isaac Hagins	.50	.25	.15
210	Gary Johnson (Chargers) (AP)	.50	.25	.15
211	Kevin Long	.50	.25	.15
212	Bill Thompson	.50	.25	.15
213	Don Bass	.50	.25	.15
214	George Starke RC	.50	.25	.15
215	Efren Herrera	.50	.25	.15
216	Theo Bell	.50	.25	.15
217	Monte Jackson	.50	.25	.15
218	Reggie McKenzie	.50	.25	.15
219	Bucky Dilts	.50	.25	.15
220	Lyle Alzado	.50	.25	.15
221	Tim Foley	.50	.25	.15
222	Mark Arneson	.50	.25	.15
223	Fred Quillan	.50	.25	.15
224	Benny Ricardo	.50	.25	.15
225	Phil Simms RC	7.50	4.50	2.70
226	Chicago Bears Team (Walter Payton, Brian Baschnagel, Gary Fencik, Terry Schmidt, Jon Osborne)	2.50	1.25	.75
227	Max Runager	.50	.25	.15
228	Barty Smith	.50	.25	.15
229	Jay Saldi	.50	.25	.15
230	John Hannah (AP)	.50	.25	.15
231	Tim Wilson	.50	.25	.15
232	Jeff Van Note	.50	.25	.15
233	Henry Marshall	.50	.25	.15
234	Diron Talbert	.50	.25	.15
235	Garo Yepremian	.50	.25	.15
236	Larry Brown	.50	.25	.15
237	Clarence Williams	.50	.25	.15
238	Burgess Owens	.50	.25	.15
239	Vince Ferragamo	.50	.25	.15
240	Rickey Young	.50	.25	.15
241	Dave Logan	.50	.25	.15
242	Larry Gordon	.50	.25	.15
243	Terry Miller	.50	.25	.15
244	Baltimore Colts Team (Joe Washington, Fred Cook)	.50	.25	.15
245	Steve DeBerg	.50	.25	.15
246	Checklist 133-264	.50	.25	.15
247	Greg Latta	.50	.25	.15
248	Raymond Clayborn	.50	.25	.15
249	Jim Clack	.50	.25	.15
250	Drew Pearson	.50	.25	.15
251	John Bunting	.50	.25	.15
252	Rob Lytle	.50	.25	.15
253	Jim Hart	.50	.25	.15
254	John McDaniel	.50	.25	.15
255	Dave Pear (AP)	.50	.25	.15
256	Donnie Shell	.50	.25	.15
257	Dan Doornink	.50	.25	.15
258	Wallace Francis RC	.50	.25	.15
259	Dave Beverly	.50	.25	.15
260	Lee Roy Selmon (AP)	.50	.25	.15
261	Doug Dieken	.50	.25	.15
262	Gary David	.50	.25	.15
263	Bob Rush	.50	.25	.15
264	Buffalo Bills Team (Curtis Brown, Frank Lewis, Keith Moody, Sherman White)	.50	.25	.15
265	Greg Landry	.50	.25	.15
266	Jan Stenerud	.50	.25	.15
267	Tom Hicks	.50	.25	.15
268	Pat McInally	.50	.25	.15
269	Tim Fox	.50	.25	.15
270	Harvey Martin	.50	.25	.15
271	Dan Lloyd	.50	.25	.15
272	Mike Barber	.50	.25	.15
273	Wendell Tyler RC	.50	.25	.15
274	Jeff Komlo	.50	.25	.15
275	Wes Chandler RC	.50	.25	.15
276	Brad Dusek	.50	.25	.15
277	Charlie Johnson	.50	.25	.15
278	Dennis Swilley	.50	.25	.15
279	Johnny Evans	.50	.25	.15
280	Jack Lambert (AP)	.50	.25	.15
281	Vern Den Herder	.50	.25	.15
282	Tampa Bay Bucanees Team (Ricky Bell, Isaac Hagins, Lee Roy Selmon)	.50		
283	Bob Klein	.50	.25	.15
284	Jim Turner	.50	.25	.15
285	Marvin Powell (AP)	.50	.25	.15
286	Aaron Kyle	.50	.25	.15
287	Dan Neal	.50	.25	.15
288	Wayne Morris	.50	.25	.15
289	Steve Bartkowski	.50	.25	.15
290	Dave Jennings	.50	.25	.15
291	John Smith	.50	.25	.15
292	Bill Gregory	.50	.25	.15
293	Frank Lewis	.50	.25	.15
294	Fred Cook	.50	.25	.15
295	David Hill (AP)	.50	.25	.15
296	Wade Key	.50	.25	.15
297	Sidney Thornton	.50	.25	.15
298	Charlie Hall	.50	.25	.15
299	Joe Lavender	.50	.25	.15
300	Tom Rafferty RC	.50	.25	.15
301	Mike Renfro RC	.50	.25	.15
302	Wilbur Jackson	.50	.25	.15
303	Green Bay Packers Team (Terdell Middleton, James Lofton, Johnnie Gray, Robert Barber, Ezra Johnson)	.50	.25	.15
304	Henry Childs	.50	.25	.15
305	Russ Washington (AP)	.50	.25	.15
306	Jim LeClair	.50	.25	.15
307	Tommy Hart	.50	.25	.15
308	Gary Barbaro	.50	.25	.15
309	Billy Taylor	.50	.25	.15
310	Ray Guy	.50	.25	.15
311	Don Hasselbeck	.50	.25	.15
312	Doug Williams	.50	.25	.15
313	Nick Mike-Mayer	.50	.25	.15
314	Don McCauley	.50	.25	.15
315	Wesley Walker	.50	.25	.15
316	Dan Dierdorf	.50	.25	.15
317	Dave Brown RC	.50	.25	.15
318	Leroy Harris	.50	.25	.15
319	Pittsburgh Steelers Team (Franco Harris, John Stallworth, Jack Lambert, Steve Furness, L.C. Greenwood)	.50	.25	.15
320	Mark Moseley (AP)	.50	.25	.15
321	Mark Dennard	.50	.25	.15
322	Terry Nelson	.50	.25	.15
323	Tom Jackson	.50	.25	.15
324	Rick Kane	.50	.25	.15
325	Jerry Sherk	.50	.25	.15
326	Ray Preston	.50	.25	.15
327	Golden Richards	.50	.25	.15
328	Randy Dean	.50	.25	.15
329	Rick Danmeier	.50	.25	.15
330	Tony Dorsett	3.50	1.75	1.00
331	Passing Leaders (Dan Fouts, Roger Staubach)	2.50	1.25	.75
332	Receiving Leaders (Joe Washington, Ahmad Rashad)	.50	.25	.15
333	Sack Leaders (Jesse Baker, Al Baker, Jack Youngblood)	.50	.25	.15
334	Scoring Leaders (John Smith, Jack Moseley)	.50	.25	.15
335	Interception Leaders (Mike Reinfeldt, Lemar Parrish)	.50	.25	.15
336	Punting Leaders (Bob Grupp, Dave Jennings)	.50	.25	.15
337	Freddie Solomon	.50	.25	.15
338	Cincinnati Bengals Team (Pete Johnson, Don Bass, Dick Jauron, Gary Burley)	.50	.25	.15
339	Ken Stone	.50	.25	.15
340	Greg Buttle (AP)	.50	.25	.15
341	Bob Baumhower	.50	.25	.15
342	Billy Waddy	.50	.25	.15
343	Cliff Parsley	.50	.25	.15
344	Walter White	.50	.25	.15
345	Mike Thomas	.50	.25	.15
346	Neil O'Donoghue	.50	.25	.15
347	Freddie Scott	.50	.25	.15
348	Joe Ferguson	.50	.25	.15
349	Doug Nettles	.50	.25	.15
350	Mike Webster (AP)	.50	.25	.15
351	Ron Saul	.50	.25	.15
352	Julius Adams	.50	.25	.15
353	Rafael Septien	.50	.25	.15
354	Cleo Miller	.50	.25	.15
355	Keith Simpson (AP)	.50	.25	.15
356	Johnny Perkins	.50	.25	.15
357	Jerry Sisemore	.50	.25	.15
358	Arthur Wittington	.50	.25	.15
359	St. Louis Cardinals Team (Ottis Anderson, Pat Tilley, Ken Stone, Bob Pollard)	.50	.25	.15
360	Rick Upchurch	.50	.25	.15
361	Kim Bokamper	.50	.25	.15
362	Roland Harper	.50	.25	.15
363	Pat Leahy	.50	.25	.15
364	Louis Breeden	.50	.25	.15
365	John Jefferson	.50	.25	.15
366	Jerry Eckwood	.50	.25	.15
367	David Whitehurst	.50	.25	.15
368	Willie Parker	.50	.25	.15
369	Ed Simonini	.50	.25	.15
370	Jack Youngblood (AP)	.50	.25	.15
371	Don Warren RC	.50	.25	.15
372	Andy Johnson	.50	.25	.15
373	D.D. Lewis	.50	.25	.15
374	Beasley Reece RC	.50	.15	.15
375	L.C. Greenwood	.50	.15	.15
376	Cleveland Browns Team (Mike Pruitt, Dave Logan, Thom Darden, Jerry Sherk)	.50	.15	.15
377	Herman Edwards	.50	.25	.15
378	Rob Carpenter RC	.50	.25	.15
379	Herman Weaver	.50	.25	.15
380	Gary Fencik (AP)	.50	.25	.15
381	Don Strock	.50	.25	.15
382	Art Shell	.50	.25	.15
383	Tim Mazzetti	.50	.25	.15
384	Bruce Harper	.50	.25	.15
385	Al Baker	.50	.25	.15
386	Conrad Dobler	.50	.25	.15
387	Stu Voight	.50	.25	.15
388	Ken Anderson	.50	.25	.15
389	Pat Tilley	.50	.25	.15
390	John Riggins	50	.25	.15
391	Checklist 265-396	.65	.35	.20
392	Fred Dean (AP)	.50	.25	.15
393	Benny Barnes RC	.50	.25	.15
394	Los Angeles Rams Team (Wendell Tyler, Preston Dennard, Nolan Cromwell, Jim Youngblood)	.50	.25	.15
395	Brad Van Pelt	.50	.25	.15
396	Eddie Hare	.50	.25	.15
397	John Sciarra	.50	.25	.15
398	Bob Jackson	.50	.25	.15
399	John Yarno	.50	.25	.15
400	Franco Harris (AP)	.75	.38	.24
401	Ray Wersching	.50	.25	.15
402	Virgil Livers	.50	.25	.15
403	Raymond Chester	.50	.25	.15
404	Leon Gray	.50	.25	.15
405	Richard Todd	.50	.25	.15
406	Larry Little	.50	.25	.15
407	Ted Fritsch	.50	.25	.15
408	Larry Mucker	.50	.25	.15
409	Jim Allen	.50	.25	.15
410	Randy Grandishar	.40	.25	.12
411	Atlanta Falcons Team (William Andrews, Wallace Francis, Rolland Lawrence, Don Smith)	.50	.25	.15
412	Louie Kelcher	.50	.25	.15
413	Robert Newhouse	.50	.25	.15
414	Gary Shirk	.50	.25	.15
415	Mike Haynes (AP)	.50	.25	.15
416	Craig Colquitt	.50	.25	.15

417	Lou Piccone	.50	.25	.15
418	Clay Matthews **RC**	.50	.25	.15
419	Marvin Cobb	.50	.25	.15
420	Harold Carmichael (AP)	.50	.25	.15
421	Uwe Von Schamann	.50	.25	.15
422	Mike Phipps	.50	.25	.15
423	Nolan Cromwell **RC**	.50	.25	.15
424	Glenn Doughty	.50	.25	.15
425	Bob Young (AP)	.50	.25	.15
426	Tony Galbreath	.50	.25	.15
427	Luke Prestridge	.50	.25	.15
428	Terry Beeson	.50	.25	.15
429	Jack Tatum	.50	.25	.15
430	Lemar Parrish (AP)	.50	.25	.15
431	Chester Marcol	.50	.25	.15
432	Houston Oilers Team (Dan Pastorini, Ken Burrough, Mike Reinfeldt, Jesse Baker)	.50	.25	.15
433	John Fitzgerald	.50	.25	.15
434	Gary Jeter	.50	.25	.15
435	Steve Grogan	.40	.25	.12
436	Jon Kolb	.50	.25	.15
437	Jim O'Bradovich	.50	.25	.15
438	Gerald Irons	.50	.25	.15
439	Jeff West	.50	.25	.15
440	Wilbert Montgomery	.50	.25	.15
441	Norris Thomas	.50	.25	.15
442	James Scott	.50	.25	.15
443	Curtis Brown	.50	.25	.15
444	Ken Fantetti	.50	.25	.15
445	Pat Haden	.50	.25	.15
446	Carl Mauck	.50	.25	.15
447	Bruce Laird	.50	.25	.15
448	Otis Armstrong	.50	.25	.15
449	Gene Upshaw	.50	.15	.15
450	Steve Largent (AP)	3.00	1.50	.90
451	Benny Malone	.50	.25	.15
452	Steve Nelson	.50	.25	.15
453	Mark Cotney	.50	.25	.15
454	Joe Danelo	.50	.25	.15
455	Billy Joe DuPree	.50	.25	.15
456	Ron Johnson	.50	.25	.15
457	Archie Griffin	.50	.25	.15
458	Reggie Rucker	.50	.25	.15
459	Claude Humphrey	.50	.25	.15
460	Lydell Mitchell	.50	.25	.15
461	Steve Towle	.50	.25	.15
462	Revie Sorey	.50	.25	.15
463	Tom Skladany	.50	.25	.15
464	Clark Gaines	.50	.25	.15
465	Frank Corral	.50	.25	.15
466	Steve Fuller **RC**	.50	.25	.15
467	Ahmad Rashad (AP)	.50	.25	.15
468	Oakland Raiders Team (Mark Van Eeghen, Cliff Branch, Lester Hayes, Willie Jones)	.50	.25	.15
469	Brian Peets	.50	.25	.15
470	Pat Donovan **RC** (AP)	.50	.25	.15
471	Ken Burrough	.50	.25	.15
472	Don Calhoun	.50	.25	.15
473	Bill Bryan	.50	.25	.15
474	Terry Jackson	.50	.25	.15
475	Joe Theismann	.50	.25	.15
476	Jim Smith	.50	.25	.15
477	Joe DeLamielleure	.50	.25	.15
478	Mike Pruitt (AP)	.50	.25	.15
479	Steve Mike-Mayer	.50	.25	.15
480	Bill Bergey	.50	.25	.15
481	Mike Fuller	.50	.25	.15
482	Bob Parsons	.50	.25	.15
483	Billy Brooks	.50	.25	.15
484	Jerome Barkum	.50	.25	.15
485	Larry Csonka	.50	.25	.15
486	John Hill	.50	.25	.15
487	Mike Dawson	.50	.25	.15
488	Detroit Lions Team (Dexter Bussey, Freddie Scott, Jim Allen, Luther Bradley, Al Baker)	.50	.25	.15
489	Ted Hendricks	.50	.25	.15
490	Dan Pastorini	.50	.25	.15
491	Stanley Morgan	.50	.25	.15
492	AFC Championship (Rocky Bleier)	.50	.25	.15
493	NFC Championship (Vince Ferragamo)	.50	.25	.15
494	Super Bowl XIV	.50	.25	.15
495	Dwight White	.50	.25	.15
496	Haven Moses	.50	.25	.15
497	Guy Morriss	.50	.25	.15
498	Dewey Selmon	.50	.25	.15
499	Dave Butz **RC**	.50	.25	.15
500	Chuck Foreman	.50	.25	.15
501	Chris Bahr	.50	.25	.15
502	Mark Miller	.50	.25	.15
503	Tony Greene	.50	.25	.15

504	Brian Kelley	.50	.25	.15
505	Joe Washington	.50	.25	.15
506	Butch Johnson	.50	.25	.15
507	New York Jets Team (Clark Gaines, Wesley Walker, Burgess Owens, Joe Klecko)	.50	.25	.15
508	Steve Little	.50	.25	.15
509	Checklist 397-528	.50	.25	.15
510	Mark Van Eeghen	.50	.25	.15
511	Gary Danielson	.50	.25	.15
512	Manu Tuiasosopo	.50	.25	.15
513	Paul Coffman **RC**	.50	.25	.15
514	Cullen Bryant	.50	.25	.15
515	Nat Moore	.50	.25	.15
516	Bill Lenkaitis	.50	.25	.15
517	Lynn Cain **RC**	.50	.25	.15
518	Gregg Bingham	.50	.25	.15
519	Ted Albrecht	.50	.25	.15
520	Dan Fouts (AP)	2.50	1.50	.90
521	Bernard Jackson	.50	.25	.15
522	Bacon Bacon	.50	.25	.15
523	Tony Franklin **RC**	.50	.25	.15
524	Bo Harris	.50	.25	.15
525	Bob Grupp (AP)	.50	.25	.15
526	San Francisco 49ers Team (Paul Hofer, Freddie Solomon, James Owens, Dwaine Board)	.50	.25	.15
527	Steve Wilson	.50	.25	.15
528	Bennie Cunningham	.50	.25	.15

1980 Topps Super

Printed on heavy white cardboard stock, these oversize (around 5" x 7") cards featured 30 NFL stars. The front displays a color photo of the player and his name appears in a gold plaque atop the card; the back lists his name, position and team with the Topps logo in the center of the card. This is a set similar to the 1980 Topps Superstar Photo Baseball set.

		NM	E	VG
Complete Set (30):		15.00	7.50	4.50
Common Player:		.30	.15	.09
1	Franco Harris	1.00	.50	.30
2	Bob Griese	1.00	.50	.30
3	Archie Manning	.30	.15	.09
4	Harold Carmichael	.30	.15	.09
5	Wesley Walker	.30	.15	.09
6	Richard Todd	.30	.15	.09
7	Dan Fouts	.90	.45	.27
8	Ken Stabler	.60	.30	.18
9	Jack Youngblood	.30	.15	.09
10	Jim Zorn	.30	.15	.09
11	Tony Dorsett	1.50	.75	.45
12	Lee Roy Selmon	.30	.15	.09
13	Russ Francis	.30	.15	.09
14	John Stallworth	.30	.15	.09
15	Terry Bradshaw	1.50	.75	.45
16	Joe Theismann	1.00	.50	.30
17	Ottis Anderson	.30	.15	.09
18	John Jefferson	.30	.15	.09
19	Jack Ham	.30	.15	.09
20	Joe Greene	.30	.15	.09
21	Chuck Muncie	.30	.15	.09
22	Ron Jaworski	.30	.15	.09
23	John Hannah	.30	.15	.09
24	Randy Gradishar	.30	.15	.09
25	Jack Lambert	.30	.15	.09
26	Ricky Bell	.30	.15	.09
27	Drew Pearson	.30	.15	.09
28	Rick Upchurch	.30	.15	.09
29	Brad Van Pelt	.30	.15	.09
30	Walter Payton	3.50	1.75	1.00

1981 Topps

Just one phrase describes this set: Joe Montana rookie. Other rookie cards in this set include Mark Gastineau, Art Monk, Billy Sims, Kellen Winslow, Joe Cribbs, Dwight Clark, Curtis Dickey and Charles White. The 528-card set is bordered in white. Around the photos is black piping which leads

to a colored scroll at the bottom of the card showing the team and player. Super Action cards in this set - included along with the player's regular card - show the major stars in action. (Key: SA - Super Action, AP - All Pro)

		NM/M	NM	E
Complete Set (528):		250.00	185.00	100.00
Common Player:		.50	.25	.15
Minor Stars:		.25		
Unlisted Stars:		.75		
Wax Pack (12 - '79 WR):		12.25		
Wax Box (36):		350.00		
Wax Pack (15):		15.00		
Wax Box (36):		400.00		
1	Passing Leaders	.50	.25	.15
2	Receiving Leaders	.50	.25	.15
3	Sack Leaders	.50	.25	.15
4	Scoring Leaders	.50	.25	.15
5	Interception Leaders	.50	.25	.15
6	Punting Leaders	.50	.25	.15
7	Don Calhoun	.50	.25	.15
8	Jack Tatum	.50	.25	.15
9	Reggie Rucker	.50	.25	.15
10	Mike Webster (AP)	.50	.25	.15
11	Vince Evans **RC**	.50	.25	.15
12	Ottis Anderson	.50	.25	.15
13	Leroy Harris	.50	.25	.15
14	Gordon King	.50	.25	.15
15	Harvey Martin	.50	.25	.15
16	Johnny Lam Jones	.50	.25	.15
17	Ken Greene	.50	.25	.15
18	Frank Lewis	.50	.25	.15
19	Seattle Seahawks Team	.50	.25	.15
20	Lester Hayes (AP)	.50	.20	.15
21	Uwe Von Schamann	.50	.25	.15
22	Joe Washington	.50	.25	.15
23	Louie Kelcher	.50	.25	.15
24	Willie Miller	.50	.25	.15
25	Steve Grogan	.50	.25	.15
26	John Hill	.50	.25	.15
27	Stan White	.50	.25	.15
28	William Andrews (SA)	.50	.25	.15
29	Clarence Scott	.50	.25	.15
30	Leon Gray (AP)	.50	.25	.15
31	Craig Colquitt	.50	.25	.15
32	Doug Williams	.50	.25	.15
33	Bob Breunig	.50	.25	.15
34	Billy Taylor	.50	.25	.15
35	Harold Carmichael	.50	.25	.15
36	Ray Wersching	.50	.25	.15
37	Dennis Johnson	.50	.25	.15
38	Archie Griffin	.50	.25	.15
39	Los Angeles Rams Team (Cullen Bryant, Billy Waddy, Nolan Cromwell, Jack Youngblood)	.50	.25	.15
40	Gary Fencik (AP)	.50	.25	.15
41	Lynn Dickey	.15	.25	.15
42	Steve Bartkowski (SA)	.50	.25	.15
43	Art Shell	.50	.25	.15
44	Wilbur Jackson	.50	.25	.15
45	Frank Corral	.50	.25	.15
46	Ted McKnight	.50	.25	.15
47	Joe Klecko	.50	.25	.15
48	Don Doornink	.50	.25	.15
49	Doug Dieken	.50	.25	.15
50	Jerry Robinson **RC** (AP)	.50	.25	.15
51	Wallace Francis	.50	.25	.15
52	Dave Preston	.50	.25	.15
53	Jay Saldi	.50	.25	.15
54	Rush Brown	.50	.25	.15
55	Phil Simms	2.00	1.00	.60
56	Nick Mike-Mayer	.50	.25	.15
57	Washington Redskins Team	.50	.25	.15
58	Mike Renfro	.50	.25	.15
59	Ted Brown (SA)	.50	.25	.15
60	Steve Nelson (AP)	.50	.25	.15
61	Sidney Thornton	.50	.25	.15
62	Kent Hill	.50	.25	.15
63	Don Bessillieu	.50	.25	.15
64	Fred Cook	.50	.25	.15
65	Raymond Chester	.50	.25	.15
66	Rick Kane	.50	.25	.15
67	Mike Fuller	.50	.25	.15
68	Dewey Selmon	.50	.25	.15
69	Charles White **RC**	.50	.25	.15
70	Jeff Van Note (AP)	.50	.25	.15
71	Robert Newhouse	.50	.25	.15
72	Roynell Young **RC**	.50	.25	.15
73	Lynn Cain (SA)	.50	.25	.15
74	Mike Friede	.50	.25	.15
75	Earl Cooper	.50	.25	.15
76	New Orleans Saints Team	.50	.25	.15
77	Rick Danmeier	.50	.25	.15
78	Darrol Ray	.50	.25	.15
79	Gregg Bingham	.50	.25	.15
80	John Hannah (AP)	.50	.30	.15

81	Jack Thompson	.50	.25	.15
82	Rick Upchurch	.50	.25	.15
83	Mike Butler	.50	.25	.15
84	Don Warren	.50	.20	.15
85	Mark Van Eeghen	.50	.25	.15
86	J.T. Smith **RC**	.50	.25	.15
87	Herman Weaver	.50	.25	.15
88	Terry Bradshaw (SA)	2.00	1.00	.60
89	Charlie Hall	.50	.25	.15
90	Donnie Shell	.50	.25	.15
91	Ike Harris	.50	.25	.15
92	Charlie Johnson	.50	.25	.15
93	Rickey Watts	.50	.25	.15
94	New England Patriots Team	.50	.25	.15
95	Drew Pearson	.50	.25	.15
96	Neil O'Donoghue	.50	.25	.15
97	Conrad Dobler	.50	.25	.15
98	Jewerl Thomas	.50	.25	.15
99	Mike Barber	.50	.25	.15
100	Billy Sims **RC** (AP)	2.50	1.25	.75
101	Vern Den Herder	.50	.25	.15
102	Greg Landry	.50	.25	.15
103	Joe Cribbs (SA)	.50	.25	.15
104	Mark Murphy **RC**	.50	.25	.15
105	Chuck Muncie	.50	.25	.15
106	Alfred Jackson	.50	.25	.15
107	Chris Bahr	.50	.25	.15
108	Gordon Jones	.50	.25	.15
109	Willie Harper **RC**	.50	.25	.15
110	Dave Jennings (AP)	.50	.25	.15
111	Bennie Cunningham	.50	.25	.15
112	Jerry Sisemore	.50	.25	.15
113	**Cleveland Browns Team**	.50	.25	.15
114	Rickey Young	.50	.25	.15
115	Ken Anderson	.50	.25	.15
116	Randy Gradishar	.50	.25	.15
117	Eddie Lee Ivery **RC**	.50	.25	.15
118	Wesley Walker	.50	.25	.15
119	Chuck Foreman	.50	.25	.15
120	Nolan Cromwell (AP)	.50	.25	.15
121	Curtis Dickey (SA)	.50	.25	.15
122	Wayne Morris	.50	.25	.15
123	Greg Stemrick	.50	.25	.15
124	Coy Bacon	.50	.25	.15
125	Jim Zorn	.50	.25	.15
126	Henry Childs	.50	.25	.15
127	Checklist 1-132	.50	.20	.15
128	Len Waltersheid	.50	.25	.15
129	Johnny Evans	.50	.25	.15
130	Gary Barbaro (AP)	.50	.25	.15
131	Jim Smith	.50	.25	.15
132	New York Jets Team	.50	.25	.15
133	Curtis Brown	.50	.25	.15
134	D.D. Lewis	.50	.25	.15
135	Jim Plunkett	.50	.25	.15
136	Nat Moore	.50	.25	.15
137	Don McCauley	.50	.25	.15
138	Tony Dorsett (SA)	.50	.25	.15
139	Julius Adams	.50	.25	.15
140	Ahmad Rashad (AP)	.50	.25	.15
141	Rich Saul	.50	.25	.15
142	Ken Fantetti	.50	.25	.15
143	Kenny Johnson	.50	.25	.15
144	Clark Gaines	.50	.25	.15
145	Mark Moseley	.50	.25	.15
146	Vernon Perry **RC**	.15	.25	.15
147	Jerry Sherk	.50	.25	.15
148	Freddie Solomon	.50	.25	.15
149	Jerry Sherk	.50	.25	.15
150	Kellen Winslow **RC** (AP)	5.00	2.50	1.50
151	Green Bay Packers Team	.50	.25	.15
152	Ross Browner	.50	.25	.15
153	Dan Fouts (SA)	.50	.25	.15
154	Woody Peoples	.50	.25	.15
155	Jack Lambert	.50	.25	.15
156	Mike Dennis	.50	.25	.15
157	Rafael Septien	.50	.25	.15
158	Archie Manning	.50	.25	.15
159	Don Hasselbeck	.50	.25	.15
160	Alan Page (AP)	.50	.25	.15
161	Arthur Whittington	.50	.25	.15
162	Billy Waddy	.50	.25	.15
163	Horace Belton	.50	.25	.15
164	Luke Prestridge	.50	.25	.15
165	Joe Theismann	.50	.25	.15
166	Morris Towns	.50	.25	.15
167	Dave Brown	.50	.25	.15
168	Ezra Johnson	.50	.25	.15
169	Tampa Bay Bucaneers Team	.50	.25	.15
170	Joe DeLamielleure (AP)	.50	.25	.15
171	Earnest Gray (SA)	.50	.25	.15
172	Mike Thomas	.50	.25	.15
173	Jim Haslett	.50	.25	.15
174	David Woodley **RC**	.50	.25	.15
175	Al Bubba Baker	.50	.25	.15
176	Nesby Glasgow **RC**	.50	.25	.15
178	Ton Brahaney	.50	.25	.15
179	Herman Edwards	.50	.25	.15
180	Junior Miller **RC** (AP)	.50	.25	.15
181	Richard Wood	.50	.25	.15
182	Lenvil Elliott	.50	.25	.15
183	Sammie White	.50	.25	.15
184	Russell Erxieben	.50	.25	.15
185	Ed "Too Tall" Jones	.50	.25	.15
186	Ray Guy (SA)	.50	.25	.15
187	Haven Moses	.50	.25	.15
188	**New York Giants Team**	.50	.25	.15
189	David Whitehurst	.50	.25	.15
190	John Jefferson (AP)	.50	.25	.15
191	Terry Beeson	.50	.25	.15
192	Dan Ross **RC**	.50	.25	.15
193	Dave Williams	.50	.25	.15
194	Art Monk **RC**	5.00	2.50	1.50
195	Roger Wehrli	.50	.25	.15
196	Rickey Feacher	.50	.25	.15
197	Miami Dolphins Team (Tony Nathan, Gerald Small, Kim Bokamper, A.J. Duhe)	.50	.25	.15
198	Carl Roaches	.50	.25	.15
199	Cilly Campfield	.50	.25	.15
200	Ted Hendricks (AP)	.50	.25	.15
201	Fred Smerlas **RC**	.50	.25	.15
202	Walter Payton (SA)	6.00	3.00	1.80
203	Luther Bradley	.50	.25	.15
204	Herbert Scott	.50	.25	.15
205	Jack Youngblood	.50	.25	.15
206	Danny Pittman	.50	.25	.15
207	Houston Oilers Team (Carl Roaches, Mike Barber, Jack Tatum, Jesse Baker, Robert Brazile)	.50	.25	.15
208	Vagas Ferguson	.50	.25	.15
209	Mark Dennard	.50	.25	.15
210	Lemar Parrish (AP)	.50	.25	.15
211	Bruce Harper	.50	.25	.15
212	Ed Simonini	.50	.25	.15
213	Nick Lowery **RC**	.50	.25	.15
214	Kevin House **RC**	.50	.25	.15
215	Mike Kenn **RC**	.50	.25	.15
216	Joe Montana **RC**	50.00	25.00	15.00
217	Joe Senser	.50	.25	.15
218	Lester Hayes (SA)	.50	.25	.15
219	Gene Upshaw	.50	.25	.15
220	Franco Harris	2.50	1.25	.75
221	Ron Bolton	.50	.25	.15
222	Charles Alexander	.50	.25	.15
223	Matt Robinson	.50	.25	.15
224	Ray Oldham	.50	.25	.15
225	George Martin	.50	.25	.15
226	**Buffalo Bills Team**	.50	.25	.15
227	Tony Franklin	.50	.25	.15
228	George Cumby	.50	.25	.15
229	Butch Johnson	.50	.25	.15
230	Mike Haynes (AP)	.50	.25	.15
231	Rob Carpenter	.50	.25	.15
232	Steve Fuller	.50	.25	.15
233	John Sawyer	.50	.25	.15
234	Kenny King (SA)	.50	.25	.15
235	Jack Ham	.50	.25	.15
236	Jimmy Rogers	.50	.25	.15
237	Bob Parsons	.50	.25	.15
238	Marty Lyons **RC**	.50	.40	.20
239	Pat Tilley	.50	.25	.15
240	Dennis Harrah (AP)	.50	.25	.15
241	Thom Darden	.50	.25	.15
242	Rolf Benirschke	.50	.25	.15
243	Gerald Small	.50	.25	.15
244	Atlanta Falcons Team	.50	.25	.15
245	Roger Carr	.50	.25	.15
246	Sherman White	.50	.25	.15
247	Ted Brown	.50	.25	.15
248	Matt Cavanaugh	.50	.25	.15
249	John Dutton	.50	.25	.15
250	Bill Bergey (AP)	.50	.25	.15
251	Jim Allen	.50	.25	.15
252	Mike Nelms (SA)	.50	.25	.15
253	Tom Blanchard	.50	.25	.15
254	Ricky Thompson	.50	.25	.15
255	John Matuszak	.50	.25	.15
256	Randy Grossman	.50	.25	.15
257	Ray Griffin	.50	.25	.15
258	Lynn Cain	.50	.25	.15
259	Checklist 133-164	.50	.20	.15
260	Mike Pruitt (AP)	.50	.25	.15
261	Chris Ward	.50	.25	.15
262	Fred Steinfort	.50	.25	.15
263	James Owens	.50	.25	.15
264	Chicago Bears Team	2.50	1.25	.75
265	Dan Fouts	2.00	1.00	.60
266	Arnold Morgado	.50	.25	.15
267	John Jefferson (SA)	.50	.25	.15
268	Bill Lenkaitis	.50	.25	.15
269	James Jones	.50	.25	.15
270	Brad Van Pelt	.50	.25	.15
271	Steve Largent	1.50	.75	.45
272	Elvin Bethea	.50	.25	.15
273	Cullen Bryant	.50	.25	.15
274	Gary Danielson	.50	.25	.15
275	Tony Galbreath	.50	.25	.15
276	Dave Butz	.50	.25	.15
277	Steve Mike-Mayer	.50	.25	.15
278	Ron Johnson	.50	.25	.15
279	Tom DeLeone	.50	.25	.15
280	Ron Jaworski	.50	.25	.15
281	Mel Gray	.50	.25	.15
282	San Diego Chargers Team	.50	.25	.15
283	Mark Brammer	.50	.25	.15
284	Alfred Jenkins (SA)	.50	.25	.15
285	Greg Buttle	.50	.25	.15
286	Randy Hughes	.50	.25	.15
287	Delvin Williams	.50	.25	.15
288	Brian Baschnagel	.50	.25	.15
289	Gary Jeter	.50	.25	.15
290	Stanley Morgan (AP)	.50	.25	.15
291	Gerry Ellis	.50	.25	.15
292	Al Richardson	.50	.25	.15
293	Jimmie Giles	.50	.25	.15
294	Dave Jennings (SA)	.50	.25	.15
295	Wilbert Montgomery	.50	.25	.15
296	Dave Pureifory	.50	.25	.15
297	Greg Hawthorne	.50	.25	.15
298	Dick Ambrose	.50	.25	.15
299	Terry Hermeling	.50	.25	.15
300	Danny White	.50	.25	.15
301	Ken Burrough	.50	.25	.15
302	Paul Hofer	.50	.25	.15
303	Denver Broncos Team	.50	.25	.15
304	Eddie Payton	.50	.25	.15
305	Isaac Curtis	.50	.25	.15
306	Benny Ricardo	.50	.25	.15
307	Riley Odoms	.50	.25	.15
308	Bob Chandler	.50	.25	.15
309	Larry Heater	.50	.25	.15
310	Art Still **RC** (AP)	.50	.25	.15
311	Harold Jackson	.50	.25	.15
312	Charlie Joiner (SA)	.50	.25	.15
313	Jeff Nixon	.50	.25	.15
314	Aundra Thompson	.50	.25	.15
315	Richard Todd	.50	.25	.15
316	Dan Hampton **RC**	7.50	4.50	2.70
317	Doug Marsh	.50	.25	.15
318	Louie Giammona	.50	.25	.15
319	San Francisco 49ers Team	.50	.25	.15
320	Manu Tuiasosopo	.50	.25	.15
321	Rich Milot	.50	.25	.15
322	Mike Guman	.50	.25	.15
323	Bob Kuechenberg	.50	.25	.15
324	Tom Skladany	.50	.25	.15
325	Dave Logan	.50	.25	.15
326	Bruce Laird	.50	.25	.15
327	James Jones (SA)	.50	.25	.15
328	Joe Danelo	.50	.25	.15
329	Kenny King **RC**	.50	.25	.15
330	Pat Donovan (Ap)	.50	.25	.15
331	Record: (Earl Cooper)	.50	.25	.15
332	Record: (John Jefferson)	.50	.25	.15
333	Record: (Kenny King)	.50	.25	.15
334	Record: (Rod Martin)	.50	.25	.15
335	Record: (Jim Plunkett)	.50	.25	.15
336	Record: (Bill Thompson)	.50	.25	.15
337	John Cappelletti	.50	.25	.15
338	Detroit Lions Team	.50	.25	.15
339	Don Smith	.50	.25	.15
340	Rod Perry (AP)	.50	.25	.15
341	David Lewis	.50	.25	.15
342	Mark Gastineau **RC**	3.00	1.50	.90
343	Steve Largent (SA)	.50	.25	.15
344	Charley Young	.50	.25	.15
345	Toni Fritsch	.50	.25	.15
346	Matt Blair	.50	.25	.15
347	Don Bass	.50	.25	.15
348	Jim Jensen	.50	.25	.15
349	Karl Lorch	.50	.25	.15
350	Brian Sipe (AP)	.50	.25	.15
351	Theo Bell	.50	.25	.15
352	Sam Adams	.50	.25	.15
353	Paul Coffman	.50	.25	.15
354	Eric Harris	.50	.25	.15
355	Tony Hill	.50	.25	.15
356	J.T. Turner	.50	.25	.15
357	Frank LeMaster	.50	.25	.15
358	Jim Jodat	.50	.25	.15
359	Oakland Raiders Team	.50	.20	.15
360	Joe Cribbs **RC** (AP)	.50	.25	.15
361	James Lofton (SA)	.50	.25	.15
362	Dexter Bussey	.50	.25	.15
363	Bobby Jackson	.50	.25	.15
364	Steve DeBerg	.50	.25	.15
365	Ottis Anderson	.50	.25	.15
366	Tom Myers	.50	.25	.15
367	John James	.50	.25	.15

368	Reese McCall	.50	.25	.15
369	Jack Reynolds	.50	.25	.15
370	Gary Jonson (AP)	.50	.25	.15
371	Jimmy Cefalo	.50	.25	.15
372	Horace Ivory	.50	.25	.15
373	Garo Yepremian	.50	.25	.15
374	Brian Kelley	.50	.25	.15
375	Terry Bradshaw	5.00	2.50	1.50
376	Dallas Cowboys Team	.50	.25	.15
377	Randy Logan	.50	.25	.15
378	Tim Wilson	.50	.25	.15
379	Archie Manning (SA)	.50	.25	.15
380	Revie Sorey (AP)	.50	.25	.15
381	Randy Holloway	.50	.25	.15
382	Henry Lawrence	.50	.25	.15
383	Pat McInally	.50	.25	.15
384	Kevin Long	.50	.25	.15
385	Louis Wright	.50	.25	.15
386	Leonard Thompson	.50	.25	.15
387	Jan Stenerud	.50	.25	.15
388	Raymond Butler RC	.50	.25	.15
389	Checklist 265-396	.50	.25	.15
390	Steve Bartkowski (Ap)	.50	.25	.15
391	Clarence Harmon	.50	.25	.15
392	Wilbert Montgomery (SA)	.50	.25	.15
393	Billy Joe DuPree	.50	.25	.15
394	Kansas City Chiefs Team			
	(Ted McKnight, Henry Marshall, Gary Barbaro, Art Still)	.50	.25	.15
395	Earnest Gray	.50	.25	.15
396	Ray Hamilton	.50	.25	.15
397	Brenard Wilson	.50	.25	.15
398	Calvin Hill	.50	.25	.15
399	Robin Cole	.50	.25	.15
400	Walter Payton (AP)	4.50	2.25	1.35
401	Jim Hart	.50	.25	.15
402	Ron Yary	.50	.25	.15
403	Cliff Branch	.50	.30	.15
404	Roland Hooks	.50	.25	.15
405	Ken Stabler	2.00	1.00	.60
406	Chuck Ramsey	.50	.25	.15
407	Mike Nelms	.50	.25	.15
408	Ron Jaworski (SA)	.50	.25	.15
409	James Hunter	.50	.25	.15
410	Lee Roy Selmon	.50	.25	.15
411	Baltimore Colts Team			
	(Curtis Dickey, Roger Carr, Bruce Laird, Mike Barnes)	.50	.25	.15
412	Henry Marshall	.50	.25	.15
413	Preston Pearson	.50	.25	.15
414	Richard Bishop	.50	.25	.15
415	Greg Pruitt	.50	.25	.15
416	Matt Bahr	.50	.25	.15
417	Tony Mullady	.50	.25	.15
418	Glen Edwards	.50	.25	.15
419	Sam McCullum	.50	.25	.15
420	Stan Walters (AP)	.50	.25	.15
421	George Roberts	.50	.25	.15
422	Dwight Clark RC	3.50	1.75	1.00
423	Pat Thomas RC	.50	.25	.15
424	Bruce Harper (SA)	.50	.25	.15
425	Craig Morton	.50	.25	.15
426	Derrick Gaffney	.50	.25	.15
427	Pete Johnson	.50	.25	.15
428	Wes Chandler	.50	.40	.20
429	Burgess Owens	.50	.25	.15
430	James Lofton (AP)	.50	.25	.15
431	Tony Reed	.50	.25	.15
432	Minnesota Vikings Team	.50	.30	.15
433	Ron Springs RC	.50	.25	.15
434	Tim Fox	.50	.25	.15
435	Ozzie Newsome	.50	.25	.15
436	Steve Furness	.50	.25	.15
437	Will Lewis	.50	.25	.15
438	Mike Hartenstine	.50	.25	.15
439	John Bunting	.50	.25	.15
440	Eddie Murray RC	.50	.25	.15
441	Mike Pruitt (SA)	.50	.25	.15
442	Larry Swider	.50	.25	.15
443	Steve Freeman	.50	.25	.15
444	Bruce Hardy	.50	.25	.15
445	Pat Haden	.50	.25	.15
446	Curtis Dickey RC	.50	.25	.15
447	Doug Wilkerson	.50	.25	.15
448	Alfred Jenkins	.50	.25	.15
449	Dave Dalby	.50	.25	.15
450	Robert Brazile (AP)	.50	.25	.15
451	Bobby Hammond	.50	.25	.15
452	Raymond Clayborn	.50	.25	.15
453	Jim Miller	.50	.25	.15
454	Roy Simmons	.50	.25	.15
455	Charlie Waters	.50	.25	.15
456	Ricky Bell	.50	.25	.15
457	Ahmad Rashad (SA)	.50	.20	.15
458	Don Cockroft	.50	.25	.15
459	Keith Krepfle	.50	.25	.15

460	Marvin Powell (AP)	.50	.25	.15
461	Tommy Kramer	.50	.20	.15
462	Jim LeClair	.50	.25	.15
463	Freddie Scott	.50	.25	.15
464	Rob Lytle	.50	.25	.15
465	Johnnie Gray	.50	.25	.15
466	Doug France RC	.50	.25	.15
467	Carlos Carson RC	.50	.25	.15
468	St. Louis Cardinals Team	.50	.25	.15
469	Efren Herrera	.50	.25	.15
470	Randy White (AP)	.50	.25	.15
471	Richard Caster	.50	.25	.15
472	Andy Johnson	.50	.25	.15
473	Billy Sims (SA)	.50	.20	.15
474	Joe Lavender	.50	.25	.15
475	Harry Carson	.50	.25	.15
476	John Stallworth	.50	.25	.15
477	Bob Thomas	.50	.25	.15
478	Keith Wright	.50	.25	.15
479	Ken Stone	.50	.25	.15
480	Carl Hairston (AP)	.50	.25	.15
481	Reggie McKenzie	.50	.25	.15
482	Bob Griese	.50	.25	.15
483	Mike Bragg	.50	.25	.15
484	Scott Dierking	.50	.25	.15
485	David Hill	.50	.25	.15
486	Brian Sipe (SA)	.50	.25	.15
487	Rod Martin	.50	.25	.15
488	Cincinnati Bengals Team			
	(Pete Johnson, Dan Ross, Louis Breeden, Eddie Edwards)	.50	.25	.15
489	Preston Dennard	.50	.25	.15
490	John Smith (AP)	.50	.25	.15
491	Mike Reinfeldt	.50	.25	.15
492	NFC Championship (Ron Jaworski)	.50	.25	.15
493	AFC Championship (Jim Plunkett)	.50	.25	.15
494	Super Bowl XV (Jim Plunkett, King)	.50	.25	.15
495	Joe Greene	.50	.25	.15
496	Charlie Joiner	.50	.25	.15
497	Rolland Lawrence	.50	.25	.15
498	Bubba Baker (SA)	.50	.25	.15
499	Brad Dusek	.50	.25	.15
500	Tony Dorsett	2.50	1.25	.75
501	Robin Earl	.50	.25	.15
502	Theotis Brown	.50	.25	.15
503	Joe Ferguson	.15	.25	.15
504	Bealsey Reece	.50	.25	.15
505	Lyle Alzado	.50	.25	.15
506	Tony Nathan RC	.50	.25	.15
507	Philadelphia Eagles Team			
	(Wilbert Montgomery, Charlie Smith, Brenard Wilson, Claude Humphrey)	.50	.25	.15
508	Herb Orvis	.50	.25	.15
509	Clarence Williams	.50	.25	.15
510	Ray Guy (AP)	.50	.25	.15
511	Jeff Komlo	.50	.25	.15
512	Freddie Solomon (SA)	.50	.25	.15
513	Tim Mazzetti	.50	.25	.15
514	Elvis Peacock	.50	.25	.15
515	Russ Francis	.50	.25	.15
516	Roland Harper	.50	.25	.15
517	Checklist 397-528	.50	.20	.15
518	Billy Johnson	.50	.25	.15
519	Dan Dierdorf	.50	.30	.15
520	Fred Dean (AP)	.50	.25	.15
521	Jerry Butler	.50	.25	.15
522	Ron Saul	.50	.25	.15
523	Charlie Smith	.50	.25	.15
524	Kellen Winslow (SA)	.50	.25	.15
525	Bert Jones	.50	.25	.15
526	Pittsburgh Steelers Team	.50	.25	.15
527	Duriel Harris	.50	.25	.15
528	William Andrews	.50	.25	.15

1981 Topps Red Border Stickers

These stickers came in their own little containers and measure 1-15/16" x 2-9/16". Each of the 28 NFL teams is represented in the set, which features red borders on the front, framing a color photo. The player's name and position are also listed. The sticker back has the sticker number, player name, position and team, biographical information and instructions on how to apply the sticker.

		NM/M	NM	E
Complete Set (28):		20.00	15.00	8.00
Common Player:		.40	.30	.15
1	Steve Bartkowski	1.00	.70	.40
2	Bert Jones	1.00	.70	.40
3	Joe Cribbs	.60	.45	.25
4	Walter Payton	5.00	3.75	2.00
5	Ross Browner	.40	.30	.15

6	Brian Sipe	.75	.60	.30
7	Tony Dorsett	2.50	2.00	1.00
8	Randy Gradishar	.60	.45	.25
9	Billy Sims	1.00	.70	.40
10	James Lofton	1.75	1.25	.70
11	Mike Barber	.40	.30	.15
12	Art Still	.40	.30	.15
13	Jack Youngblood	.75	.60	.30
14	Dave Woodley	.50	.40	.20
15	Ahmad Rashad	1.25	.90	.50
16	Russ Francis	.50	.40	.20
17	Archie Manning	.75	.60	.30
18	Dave Jennings	.40	.30	.15
19	Richard Todd	.50	.40	.20
20	Lester Hayes	.60	.45	.25
21	Ron Jaworski	.50	.40	.20
22	Franco Harris	2.00	1.50	.80
23	Ottis Anderson	1.00	.70	.40
24	John Jefferson	.50	.40	.20
25	Freddie Solomon	.40	.30	.15
26	Steve Largent	3.50	2.75	1.50
27	Lee Roy Selmon	.75	.60	.30
28	Art Monk	8.00	6.00	3.25

1981 Topps Stickers

These stickers, which measure 1-15/16" x 2-9/16", are numbered alphabetically by teams within divisions. The front has a color photo with a white frame, plus the sticker number. That number is also on the back, along with the player's name, position, team and instructions on how to apply the sticker. A sticker album was also made available as a mail-in offer. The album cover features a Buffalo Bills player.

		NM/M	NM	E
Complete Set (262):		25.00	18.50	10.00
Common Player:		.05	.04	.02
1	AFC Passing Leader (Brian Sipe)	.10	.08	.04
2	AFC Passing Yardage Leader (Dan Fouts)	.50	.40	.20
3	AFC Receiving Yardage Leader (John Jefferson)	.08	.06	.03
4	AFC Kickoff Return Yardage Leader (Bruce Harper)	.05	.04	.02
5	AFC Punt Return Yardage Leader (J.T. Smith)	.05	.04	.02
6	AFC Punting Leader (Luke Prestidge)	.05	.04	.02
7	AFC Interceptions Leader (Lester Hayes)	.05	.04	.02
8	AFC Sacks Leader (Gary Johnson)	.05	.04	.02
9	Bert Jones	.15	.11	.06
10	Fred Cook	.05	.04	.02
11	Roger Carr	.10	.08	.04
12	Greg Landry	.08	.06	.03
13	Raymond Butler	.08	.06	.03
14	Bruce Laird	.05	.04	.02
15	Ed Simonini	.05	.04	.02
16	Curtis Dickey	.10	.08	.04
17	Joe Cribbs	.10	.08	.04
18	Joe Ferguson	.15	.11	.06
19	Ben Williams	.05	.04	.02
20	Jerry Butler	.08	.06	.03
21	Roland Hooks	.05	.04	.02
22	Fred Smerlas	.08	.06	.03
23	Frank Lewis	.05	.04	.02
24	Mark Brammer	.05	.04	.02
25	Dave Woodley	.08	.06	.03
26	Nat Moore	.10	.08	.04
27	Uwe Von Schamann	.05	.04	.02
28	Vern Den Herder	.05	.04	.02
29	Tony Nathan	.10	.08	.04
30	Duriel Harris	.08	.06	.03
31	Don McNeal	.05	.04	.02
32	Delvin Williams	.05	.04	.02
33	Stanley Morgan	.15	.11	.06
34	John Hannah	.15	.11	.06
35	Horace Ivory	.05	.04	.02
36	Steve Nelson	.05	.04	.02
37	Steve Grogan	.15	.11	.06
38	Vagas Ferguson	.10	.08	.04
39	John Smith	.05	.04	.02
40	Mike Haynes	.12	.09	.05
41	Mark Gastineau	.15	.11	.06
42	Wesley Walker	.15	.11	.06
43	Joe Klecko	.10	.08	.04
44	Chris Ward	.05	.04	.02
45	Johnny Lam Jones	.08	.06	.03
46	Marvin Powell	.08	.06	.03
47	Richard Todd	.15	.11	.06
48	Greg Buttle	.08	.06	.03
49	Eddie Edwards	.05	.04	.02
50	Dan Ross	.08	.06	.03
51	Ken Anderson	.50	.40	.20

52	Ross Browner	.08	.06	.03
53	Don Bass	.08	.06	.03
54	Jim LeClair	.05	.04	.02
55	Pete Johnson	.08	.06	.03
56	Anthony Munoz	1.25	.90	.50
57	Brian Sipe	.12	.09	.05
58	Mike Pruitt	.10	.08	.04
59	Greg Pruitt	.15	.11	.06
60	Thom Darden	.05	.04	.02
61	Ozzie Newsome	.40	.30	.15
62	Dave Logan	.05	.04	.02
63	Lyle Alzado	.15	.11	.06
64	Reggie Rucker	.08	.06	.03
65	Robert Brazile	.08	.06	.03
66	Mike Barber	.08	.06	.03
67	Carl Roaches	.10	.08	.04
68	Ken Stabler	.30	.25	.12
69	Gregg Bingham	.08	.06	.03
70	Mike Renfro	.08	.06	.03
71	Leon Gray	.05	.04	.02
72	Rob Carpenter	.10	.08	.04
73	Franco Harris	.50	.40	.20
74	Jack Lambert	.30	.25	.12
75	Jim Smith	.05	.04	.02
76	Mike Webster	.15	.11	.06
77	Sidney Thornton	.05	.04	.02
78	Joe Greene	.40	.30	.15
79	John Stallworth	.20	.15	.08
80	Tyrone McGriff	.05	.04	.02
81	Randy Gradishar	.12	.09	.05
82	Haven Moses	.08	.06	.03
83	Riley Odoms	.10	.08	.04
84	Matt Robinson	.05	.04	.02
85	Craig Morton	.12	.09	.05
86	Rulon Jones	.05	.04	.02
87	Rick Upchurch	.10	.08	.04
88	Jim Jensen	.05	.04	.02
89	Art Still	.12	.09	.05
90	J.T. Smith	.12	.09	.05
91	Steve Fuller	.05	.04	.02
92	Gary Barbaro	.05	.04	.02
93	Ted McKnight	.05	.04	.02
94	Bob Grupp	.05	.04	.02
95	Henry Marshall	.05	.04	.02
96	Mike Williams	.05	.04	.02
97	Jim Plunkett	.25	.20	.10
98	Lester Hayes	.12	.09	.05
99	Cliff Branch	.20	.15	.08
100	John Matuszak	.10	.08	.04
101	Matt Millen	.10	.08	.04
102	Kenny King	.05	.04	.02
103	Ray Guy	.15	.11	.06
104	Ted Hendricks	.20	.15	.08
105	John Jefferson	.12	.09	.05
106	Fred Dean	.12	.09	.05
107	Dan Fouts	.35	.25	.14
108	Charlie Joiner	.25	.20	.10
109	Kellen Winslow	1.25	.90	.50
110	Gary Johnson	.08	.06	.03
111	Mike Thomas	.05	.04	.02
112	Louie Kelcher	.12	.09	.05
113	Jim Zorn	.12	.09	.05
114	Terry Beeson	.05	.04	.02
115	Jacob Green	.35	.25	.14
116	Steve Largent	1.25	.90	.50
117	Dan Doornink	.05	.04	.02
118	Manu Tuiasosopo	.05	.04	.02
119	John Sawyer	.05	.04	.02
120	Jim Jodat	.05	.04	.02
121	Walter Payton (All-Pro)	2.00	1.50	.80
122	Brian Sipe (All-Pro)	.25	.20	.10
123	Joe Cribbs (All-Pro)	.25	.20	.10
124	James Lofton (All-Pro)	.60	.45	.25
125	John Jefferson (All-Pro)	.25	.20	.10
126	Leon Gray (All-Pro)	.15	.11	.06
127	Joe DeLamielleure (All-Pro)	.20	.15	.08
128	Mike Webster (All-Pro)	.30	.25	.12
129	John Hannah (All-Pro)	.30	.25	.12
130	Mike Kenn (All-Pro)	.20	.15	.08
131	Kellen Winslow (All-Pro)	1.50	1.25	.60
132	Lee Roy Selmon (All-Pro)	.30	.25	.12
133	Randy White (All-Pro)	.30	.25	.12
134	Gary Johnson (All-Pro)	.15	.11	.06
135	Art Still (All-Pro)	.20	.15	.08
136	Robert Brazile (All-Pro)	.20	.15	.08
137	Nolan Cromwell (All-Pro)	.20	.15	.08
138	Ted Hendricks (All-Pro)	.50	.40	.20
139	Lester Hayes (All-Pro)	.25	.20	.10
140	Randy Gradishar (All-Pro)	.35	.25	.14
141	Lemar Parrish (All-Pro)	.20	.15	.08
142	Donnie Shell (All-Pro)	.20	.15	.08
143	NFC Passing Leader (Ron Jaworski)	.12	.09	.05
144	NFC Passing Leader (Archie Manning)	.20	.15	.08
145	NFC Rushing Yardage Leader (Walter Payton)	.75	.60	.30

146	NFC Rushing Touchdowns Leader (Billy Sims)	.25	.20	.10
147	NFC Receiving Yardage Leader (James Lofton)	.25	.20	.10
148	NFC Punting Leader (Dave Jennings)	.05	.04	.02
149	NFC Interceptions Leader (Nolan Cromwell)	.08	.06	.03
150	NFC Sacks Leader (Al (Bubba) Baker)	.08	.06	.03
151	Tony Dorsett	.50	.40	.20
152	Harvey Martin	.15	.11	.06
153	Danny White	.25	.20	.10
154	Pat Donovan	.05	.04	.02
155	Drew Pearson	.15	.11	.06
156	Robert Newhouse	.10	.08	.04
157	Randy White	.40	.30	.15
158	Butch Johnson	.10	.08	.04
159	Dave Jennings	.05	.04	.02
160	Brad Van Pelt	.05	.04	.02
161	Phil Simms	.40	.30	.15
162	Mike Friede	.05	.04	.02
163	Billy Taylor	.08	.06	.03
164	Gary Jeter	.08	.06	.03
165	George Martin	.05	.04	.02
166	Earnest Gray	.05	.04	.02
167	Ron Jaworski	.15	.11	.06
168	Bill Bergey	.10	.08	.04
169	Wilbert Montgomery	.08	.06	.03
170	Charlie Smith	.05	.04	.02
171	Jerry Robinson	.08	.06	.03
172	Herman Edwards	.05	.04	.02
173	Harold Carmichael	.15	.11	.06
174	Claude Humphrey	.10	.08	.04
175	Ottis Anderson	.30	.25	.12
176	Jim Hart	.15	.11	.06
177	Pat Tilley	.08	.06	.03
178	Rush Brown	.05	.04	.02
179	Tom Brahaney	.05	.04	.02
180	Dan Dierdorf	.25	.20	.10
181	Wayne Morris	.05	.04	.02
182	Doug Marsh	.05	.04	.02
183	Art Monk	3.00	2.25	1.25
184	Clarence Harmon	.05	.04	.02
185	Lemar Parrish	.12	.09	.05
186	Joe Theismann	.35	.25	.14
187	Joe Lavender	.05	.04	.02
188	Wilbur Jackson	.05	.04	.02
189	Dave Butz	.05	.04	.02
190	Coy Bacon	.05	.04	.02
191	Walter Payton	1.50	1.25	.60
192	Alan Page	.15	.11	.06
193	Vince Evans	.20	.15	.08
194	Roland Harper	.08	.06	.03
195	Dan Hampton	.80	.60	.30
196	Gary Fencik	.08	.06	.03
197	Mike Hartenstine	.05	.04	.02
198	Robin Earl	.05	.04	.02
199	Billy Sims	.25	.20	.10
200	Leonard Thompson	.05	.04	.02
201	Jeff Komlo	.08	.06	.03
202	Al (Bubba) Baker	.10	.08	.04
203	Ed Murray	.15	.11	.06
204	Dexter Bussey	.05	.04	.02
205	Tom Ginn	.05	.04	.02
206	Freddie Scott	.08	.06	.03
207	James Lofton	.50	.40	.20
208	Mike Butler	.05	.04	.02
209	Lynn Dickey	.12	.09	.05
210	Gerry Ellis	.05	.04	.02
211	Edd Lee Ivery	.10	.08	.04
212	Ezra Johnson	.05	.04	.02
213	Paul Coffman	.08	.06	.03
214	Aundra Thompson	.05	.04	.02
215	Ahmad Rashad	.25	.20	.10
216	Tommy Kramer	.08	.06	.03
217	Matt Blair	.08	.06	.03
218	Sammie White	.08	.06	.03
219	Ted Brown	.08	.06	.03
220	Joe Senser	.08	.06	.03
221	Rickey Young	.08	.06	.03
222	Randy Holloway	.05	.04	.02
223	Lee Roy Selmon	.15	.11	.06
224	Doug Williams	.10	.08	.04
225	Ricky Bell	.10	.08	.04
226	David Lewis	.05	.04	.02
227	Gordon Jones	.08	.06	.03
228	Dewey Selmon	.08	.06	.03
229	Jimmie Giles	.10	.08	.04
230	Mike Washington	.05	.04	.02
231	William Andrews	.15	.11	.06
232	Jeff Van Note	.08	.06	.03
233	Steve Bartkowski	.15	.11	.06
234	Junior Miller	.08	.06	.03
235	Lynn Cain	.08	.06	.03
236	Joel Williams	.05	.04	.02
237	Alfred Jenkins	.08	.06	.03

238	Kenny Johnson	.05	.04	.02
239	Jack Youngblood	.20	.15	.08
240	Elvis Peacock	.08	.06	.03
241	Cullen Bryant	.10	.08	.04
242	Dennis Harrah	.05	.04	.02
243	Billy Waddy	.05	.04	.02
244	Nolan Cromwell	.10	.08	.04
245	Doug France	.05	.04	.02
246	Johnnie Johnson	.08	.06	.03
247	Archie Manning	.25	.20	.10
248	Tony Galbreath	.10	.08	.04
249	Wes Chandler	.15	.11	.06
250	Stan Brock	.05	.04	.02
251	Ike Harris	.05	.04	.02
252	Russell Erxleben	.05	.04	.02
253	Jimmy Rogers	.05	.04	.02
254	Tom Myers	.05	.04	.02
255	Dwight Clark	.75	.60	.30
256	Earl Cooper	.05	.04	.02
257	Steve DeBerg	.25	.20	.10
258	Randy Cross	.10	.08	.04
259	Freddie Solomon	.08	.06	.03
260	Jim Miller	.05	.04	.02
261	Charley Young	.08	.06	.03
262	Bobby Leopold	.05	.04	.02

1982 Topps

Topps' last 528-card set was issued in 1982, and the design was nearly a duplicate of the 1975 football set. Football helmets featuring the team's helmet design appeared on these cards for the first time. Also included in this set were in-action cards of top stars and a subset featuring NFL brother tandems. Cards are numbered alphabetically by team and by the last name of the player. Notable rookies in this set include Cris Collinsworth, Anthony Munoz, Freeman McNeil, George Rogers, Ronnie Lott, Lawrence Taylor and Neil Lomax. (Key: AP - All Pro, IA - In Action)

	NM/M	NM	E
Complete Set (528):	100.00	50.00	30.00
Common Player:	.50	.25	.15
Wax Pack (15):	4.00		
Wax Box (36):	120.00		

1	Ken Anderson (RB)	.50	.25	.15
2	Dan Fouts (RB)	.50	.25	.15
3	LeRoy Irvin (RB)	.50	.25	.15
4	Stump Mitchell (RB)	.50	.25	.15
5	George Rogers (RB)	.50	.25	.15
6	Dan Ross (RB)	.50	.25	.15
7	AFC Championship (Ken Anderson, Pete Johnson)	.50	.25	.15
8	NFC Championship (Earl Cooper)	.50	.25	.15
9	Super Bowl XVI (Anthony Munoz)	.50	.25	.15
10	Baltimore Colts Team	.50	.25	.15
11	Raymond Butler	.50	.25	.15
12	Roger Carr	.50	.25	.15
13	Curtis Dickey	.50	.25	.15
14	Zachary Dixon	.50	.25	.15
15	Nesby Glasgow	.50	.25	.15
16	Bert Jones	.50	.25	.15
17	Bruce Laird	.50	.25	.15
18	Reese McCall	.50	.25	.15
19	Randy McMillan	.50	.25	.15
20	Ed Simonini	.50	.25	.15
21	Buffalo Bills Team	.50	.25	.15
22	Mark Brammer	.50	.25	.15
23	Curtis Brown	.50	.25	.15
24	Jerry Butler	.50	.25	.15
25	Mario Clark	.50	.25	.15
26	Joe Cribbs	.50	.25	.15
27	Joe Cribbs (IA)	.50	.25	.15
28	Joe Ferguson	.50	.25	.15
29	Jim Haslett	.50	.25	.15
30	Frank Lewis (AP)	.50	.25	.15
31	Frank Lewis (IA)	.50	.25	.15
32	Shane Nelson	.50	.25	.15
33	Charles Romes	.50	.25	.15
34	Bill Simpson	.50	.25	.15

35	Fred Smerlas	.50	.25	.15
36	Cincinnati Bengals Team	.50	.25	.15
37	Charles Alexander	.50	.25	.15
38	Ken Anderson (AP)	.50	.25	.15
39	Ken Anderson (IA)	.50	.25	.15
40	Jim Breech	.50	.25	.15
41	Jim Breech (IA)	.50	.25	.15
42	Louis Breeden	.50	.25	.15
43	Ross Browner	.50	.25	.15
44	Cris Collinsworth **RC**	2.00	1.00	.60
45	Cris Collinsworth IA (IA)	.50	.25	.15
46	Isaac Curtis	.50	.25	.15
47	Pete Johnson	.50	.25	.15
48	Pete Johnson (IA)	.50	.25	.15
49	Steve Kreider	.50	.25	.15
50	Pat McInnaly (AP)	.50	.25	.15
51	Anthony Munoz **RC** (AP)	4.00	2.00	1.20
52	Dan Ross	.50	.25	.15
53	David Verser	.50	.25	.15
54	Reggie Williams	.50	.25	.15
55	Cleveland Browns Team	.50	.25	.15
56	Lyle Alzado	.50	.25	.15
57	Dick Ambrose	.50	.25	.15
58	Ron Bolton	.50	.25	.15
59	Steve Cox	.50	.25	.15
60	Joe DeLamielleure	.50	.25	.15
61	Tom DeLeone	.50	.25	.15
62	Doug Dieken	.50	.25	.15
63	Ricky Feacher	.50	.25	.15
64	Don Goode	.50	.25	.15
65	Robert L. Jackson	.50	.25	.15
66	Dave Logan	.50	.25	.15
67	Ozzie Newsome	.50	.25	.15
68	Ozzie Newsome (IA)	.50	.25	.15
69	Greg Pruitt	.50	.25	.15
70	Mike Pruitt	.50	.25	.15
71	Mike Pruitt (IA)	.50	.25	.15
72	Reggie Rucker	.50	.25	.15
73	Clarence Scott	.50	.25	.15
74	Brian Sipe	.50	.25	.15
75	Charles White	.50	.25	.15
76	Denver Broncos Team	.50	.25	.15
77	Rubin Carter	.50	.25	.15
78	Steve Foley	.50	.25	.15
79	Randy Gradishar	.50	.25	.15
80	Tom Jackson	.50	.25	.15
81	Craig Morton	.50	.25	.15
82	Craig Morton (IA)	.50	.25	.15
83	Riley Odoms	.50	.25	.15
84	Rick Parros	.50	.25	.15
85	Dave Preston	.50	.25	.15
86	Tony Reed	.50	.25	.15
87	Bob Swenson	.50	.25	.15
88	Bill Thompson	.50	.25	.15
89	Rick Upchurch	.50	.25	.15
90	Steve Watson **RC** (AP)	.50	.25	.15
91	Steve Watson (IA)	.50	.25	.15
92	Houston Oilers Team	.50	.25	.15
93	Mike Barber	.50	.25	.15
94	Elvin Bethea	.50	.25	.15
95	Gregg Bingham	.50	.25	.15
96	Robert Brazile (AP)	.50	.25	.15
97	Ken Burrough	.50	.25	.15
98	Toni Fritsch	.50	.25	.15
99	Leon Gray	.50	.25	.15
100	Gifford Nielsen **RC**	.50	.25	.15
101	Vernon Perry	.50	.25	.15
102	Mike Reinfeldt	.50	.25	.15
103	Mike Renfro	.50	.25	.15
104	Carl Roaches (AP)	.50	.25	.15
105	Ken Stabler	1.50	.75	.45
106	Greg Stemrick	.50	.25	.15
107	J.C. Wilson	.50	.25	.15
108	Tim Wilson	.50	.25	.15
109	Kansas City Chiefs Team	.50	.25	.15
110	Gary Barbaro (AP)	.50	.25	.15
111	Brad Budde (AP)	.50	.25	.15
112	Joe Delaney **RC** (AP)	.50	.25	.15
113	Joe Delaney (IA)	.50	.25	.15
114	Steve Fuller	.50	.25	.15
115	Gary Green	.50	.25	.15
116	James Hadnot	.50	.25	.15
117	Eric Harris	.50	.25	.15
118	Billy Jackson	.50	.25	.15
119	Bill Kenney	.50	.25	.15
120	Nick Lowery (AP)	.50	.25	.15
121	Nick Lowery (IA)	.50	.25	.15
122	Henry Marshall	.50	.25	.15
123	J.T. Smith	.50	.25	.15
124	Art Still	.50	.25	.15
125	Miami Dolphins Team	.50	.25	.15
126	Bob Baumhower (AP)	.50	.25	.15
127	Glenn Blackwood	.50	.25	.15
128	Jimmy Cefalo	.50	.25	.15
129	A.J. Duhe	.50	.25	.15
130	Andra Franklin	.50	.25	.15
131	Duriel Harris	.50	.25	.15
132	Nat Moore	.50	.25	.15

133	Tony Nathan	.50	.25	.15
134	Ed Newman	.50	.25	.15
135	Earnie Rhone	.50	.25	.15
136	Don Strock	.50	.25	.15
137	Tommy Vigorito	.50	.25	.15
138	Uwe Von Schamann	.50	.25	.15
139	Uwe Von Schamann (IA)	.50	.25	.15
140	David Woodley	.50	.25	.15
141	New England Patriots Team	.50	.25	.15
142	Julius Adams	.50	.25	.15
143	Richard Bishop	.50	.25	.15
144	Matt Cavanaugh	.50	.25	.15
145	Raymond Clayborn	.50	.25	.15
146	Tony Collins **RC**	.50	.25	.15
147	Vagas Ferguson	.50	.25	.15
148	Tim Fox	.50	.25	.15
149	Steve Grogan	.50	.25	.15
150	John Hannah (AP)	.50	.25	.15
151	John Hannah (IA)	.50	.25	.15
152	Don Hasselbeck	.50	.25	.15
153	Mike Haynes	.50	.25	.15
154	Harold Jackson	.50	.25	.15
155	Andy Johnson	.50	.25	.15
156	Stanley Morgan	.50	.25	.15
157	Stanley Morgan (IA)	.50	.25	.15
158	Steve Nelson	.50	.25	.15
159	Rod Shoate	.50	.25	.15
160	New York Jets Team	.50	.25	.15
161	Dan Alexander	.50	.25	.15
162	Mike Augustyniak	.50	.25	.15
163	Jerome Barkum	.50	.25	.15
164	Greg Buttle	.50	.25	.15
165	Scott Dierking	.50	.25	.15
166	Joe Fields	.50	.25	.15
167	Mark Gastineau (AP)	.50	.25	.15
168	Mark Gastineau (IA)	.50	.25	.15
169	Bruce Harper	.50	.25	.15
170	Johnny Lam Jones	.50	.25	.15
171	Joe Klecko (AP)	.50	.25	.15
172	Joe Klecko (IA)	.50	.25	.15
173	Pat Leahy	.50	.25	.15
174	Pat Leahy (IA)	.50	.25	.15
175	Marty Lyons	.50	.25	.15
176	Freeman McNeil **RC**	.50	.25	.15
177	Marvin Powell AP	.50	.25	.15
178	Chuck Ramsey	.50	.25	.15
179	Darrol Ray	.50	.25	.15
180	Abdul Salaam	.50	.25	.15
181	Richard Todd	.50	.25	.15
182	Richard Todd (IA)	.50	.25	.15
183	Wesley Walker	.50	.25	.15
184	Chris Ward	.50	.25	.15
185	Oakland Raiders Team	.50	.25	.15
186	Cliff Branch	.50	.25	.15
187	Bob Chandler	.50	.25	.15
188	Ray Guy	.50	.25	.15
189	Lester Hayes (AP)	.50	.25	.15
190	Ted Hendricks (AP)	.50	.25	.15
191	Monte Jackson	.50	.25	.15
192	Derrick Jensen	.50	.25	.15
193	Kenny King	.50	.25	.15
194	Rod Martin	.50	.25	.15
195	John Matuszak	.50	.25	.15
196	Matt Millen **RC**	.50	.25	.15
197	Derrick Ramsey	.50	.25	.15
198	Art Shell	.40	.30	.15
199	Mark Van Eeghen	.50	.25	.15
200	Arthur Whittington	.50	.25	.15
201	Marc Wilson **RC**	.20	.15	.08
202	Pittsburgh Steelers Team	.50	.40	.20
203	Mel Blount (AP)	.50	.25	.15
204	Terry Bradshaw	3.00	1.50	.90
205	Terry Bradshaw (IA)	.75	.60	.30
206	Craig Colquitt	.50	.25	.15
207	Bennie Cunningham	.50	.25	.15
208	Russell Davis	.50	.25	.15
209	Gary Dunn	.50	.25	.15
210	Jack Ham	.75	.60	.30
211	Franco Harris	.75	.60	.30
212	Franco Harris (IA)	.50	.40	.20
213	Jack Lambert (AP)	.75	.60	.30
214	Jack Lambert (IA)	.50	.40	.20
215	Mark Malone **RC**	.50	.25	.15
218	Jim Smith	.50	.25	.15
219	John Stallworth	.60	.45	.25
220	John Stallworth (IA)	.50	.25	.15
221	David Trout	.50	.25	.15
222	Mike Webster (AP)	.50	.25	.15
223	San Diego Chargers Team	.50	.25	.15
224	Rolf Bernirschke	.50	.25	.15
225	Rolf Benirschke (IA)	.50	.25	.15
226	James Brooks **RC**	.50	.25	.15
227	Willie Buchanon	.50	.25	.15
228	Wes Chandler	.50	.25	.15
229	Wes Chandler (IA)	.50	.25	.15
230	Dan Fouts	2.00	1.00	.50
231	Dan Fouts (IA)	.50	.25	.15
232	Gary Johnson (AP)	.50	.25	.15

233	Charlie Joiner	.50	.25	.15
234	Charlie Joiner (IA)	.50	.25	.15
235	Louie Kelchor	.50	.25	.15
236	Chuck Muncie (AP)	.50	.25	.15
237	Chuck Muncie (IA)	.50	.25	.15
238	George Roberts	.50	.25	.15
239	Ed White	.50	.25	.15
240	Doug Wilkerson (AP)	.50	.25	.15
241	Kellen Winslow (AP)	.50	.25	.15
242	Kellen Winslow IA (IA)	.50	.25	.15
243	Seattle Seahawks Team	.50	.25	.15
244	Theotis Brown	.50	.25	.15
245	Don Doornink	.50	.25	.15
246	John Harris	.50	.25	.15
247	Efren Herrera	.50	.25	.15
248	David Hughes	.50	.25	.15
249	Steve Largent	.50	.25	.15
250	Steve Largent (IA)	.90	.70	.35
251	Sam McCullum	.50	.25	.15
252	Sherman Smith	.50	.25	.15
253	Manu Tuiasosopo	.50	.25	.15
254	John Yarno	.50	.25	.15
255	Jim Zorn	.50	.25	.15
256	Jim Zorn (IA)	.50	.25	.15
257	Joe Montana, Ken Anderson	.50	.25	.15
258	Receiving Leaders (Kellen Winslow, Dwight Clark)	.50	.25	.15
259	Sack Leaders (Joe Klecko, Curtis Greer)	.50	.25	.15
260	Scoring Leaders (Jim Breech, Nick Lowery, Ed Murray, Rafael Septien)	.50	.25	.15
261	Interception Leaders (John Harris, Everson Walls)	.50	.25	.15
262	Punting Leaders (Pat McInally, Tom Skladany)	.50	.25	.15
263	Brothers: (Chris Bahr, Matt Bahr)	.50	.25	.15
264	Brothers: (Lyle Blackwood, Glenn Blackwood)	.50	.25	.15
265	Brothers: (Pete Brock, Stan Brock)	.50	.25	.15
266	Brothers: (Archie Griffin, Ray Griffin)	.50	.25	.15
267	Brothers: (John Hannah, Charley Hannah)	.50	.25	.15
268	Brothers: (Monte Jackson, Terry Jackson)	.50	.25	.15
269	Brothers: (Eddie Payton, Walter Payton)	2.00	1.00	.60
270	Brothers: (Dewey Selmon, Lee Roy Selmon)	.50	.25	.15
271	Atlanta Falcons Team	.50	.25	.15
272	Williams Andrews	.50	.25	.15
273	William Anderws (IA)	.50	.25	.15
274	Steve Bartkowski	.50	.25	.15
275	Steve Bartkowski	.50	.25	.15
276	Bobby Butler	.50	.25	.15
277	Lynn Cain	.50	.25	.15
278	Wallace Francis	.50	.25	.15
279	Alfred Jackson	.50	.25	.15
280	John James	.50	.25	.15
281	Alfred Jenkins (AP)	.50	.25	.15
282	Alfred Jenkins (IA)	.50	.25	.15
283	Kenny Johnson	.50	.25	.15
284	Mike Kenn (AP)	.50	.25	.15
285	Fulton Kuykendall	.50	.25	.15
286	Mike Luckhurst	.50	.25	.15
287	Mick Luckhurst (IA)	.50	.25	.15
288	Junior Miller	.50	.25	.15
289	Al Richardson	.50	.25	.15
290	R.C. Thielemann	.50	.25	.15
291	Jeff Van Note	.50	.25	.15
292	Chicago Bears Team	.50	.25	.15
293	Brian Baschnagel	.50	.25	.15
294	Robin Earl	.50	.25	.15
295	Vince Evans	.50	.25	.15
296	Gary Fencik (AP)	.50	.25	.15
297	Dan Hampton	.50	.25	.15
298	Noah Jackson	.50	.25	.15
299	Ken Margerum	.50	.25	.15
300	Jim Osborne	.50	.25	.15
301	Bob Parsons	.50	.25	.15
302	Walter Payton	4.00	2.00	1.20
303	Walter Payton IA (IA)	4.00	2.00	1.20
304	Revie Sorey	.50	.25	.15
305	Matt Suhey **RC**	.50	.25	.15
306	Rickey Watts	.50	.25	.15
307	Dallas Cowboys Team	.50	.25	.15
308	Bob Breunig	.50	.25	.15
309	Doug Cosbie **RC**	.50	.25	.15
310	Pat Donovan (AP)	.50	.25	.15
311	Tony Dorsett (AP)	1.50	.75	.45
312	Tony Dorsett (IA)	1.50	.75	.45
313	Michael Downs	.50	.25	.15
314	Billy Joe DuPree	.50	.25	.15
315	John Dutton	.50	.25	.15

316	Tony Hill	.50	.25	.15
317	Butch Johnson	.50	.25	.15
318	Ed "Too Tall" Jones (AP)	.60	.45	.25
319	James Jones	.50	.25	.15
320	Harvey Martin	.50	.25	.15
321	Drew Pearson	.50	.25	.15
322	Herbert Scott (AP)	.50	.25	.15
323	Rafael Septien (AP)	.50	.25	.15
324	Rafael Septien (IA)	.50	.25	.15
325	Ron Springs	.50	.25	.15
326	Dennis Thurman RC	.50	.25	.15
327	Everson Walls RC	.50	.25	.15
328	Everson Walls (IA)	.50	.25	.15
329	Danny White	.50	.25	.15
330	Danny White (IA)	.50	.25	.15
331	Randy White (AP)	.60	.25	.15
332	Randy White (IA)	.50	.25	.15
333	**Detroit Lions Team**	.50	.25	.15
334	Jim Allen	.50	.25	.15
335	Al Bubba Baker	.50	.25	.15
336	Dexter Bussey	.50	.25	.15
337	Doug English (AP)	.50	.25	.15
338	Ken Fantetti	.50	.25	.15
339	William Gay	.50	.25	.15
340	David Hill	.50	.25	.15
341	Eric Hipple RC	.50	.25	.15
342	Rick Kane	.50	.25	.15
343	Ed Murray	.50	.25	.15
344	Ed Murray (IA)	.50	.25	.15
345	Ray Oldham	.50	.25	.15
346	Dave Pureifory	.50	.25	.15
347	Freddie Scott	.50	.25	.15
348	Freddie Scott (IA)	.50	.25	.15
349	Billy Sims (AP)	.50	.25	.15
350	Billy Sims (IA)	.50	.25	.15
351	Tom Skladany (AP)	.50	.25	.15
352	Leonard Thompson	.50	.25	.15
353	Stan White	.50	.25	.15
354	Green Bay Packers Team	.50	.25	.15
355	Paul Coffman	.50	.25	.15
356	George Cumby	.50	.25	.15
357	Lynn Dickey	.50	.25	.15
358	Lynn Dickey (IA)	.50	.25	.15
359	Gerry Ellis	.50	.25	.15
360	Maurice Harvey	.50	.25	.15
361	Harlan Huckleby	.50	.25	.15
362	John Jefferson	.50	.25	.15
363	Mark Lee	.50	.25	.15
364	James Lofton (AP)	.50	.25	.15
365	James Lofton (IA)	.50	.25	.15
366	Jan Stenerud	.50	.25	.15
367	Jan Stenerud (IA)	.50	.25	.15
368	Rich Wingo	.50	.25	.15
369	Los Angeles Rams Team	.50	.25	.15
370	Frank Corral	.50	.25	.15
371	Nolan Cromwell (AP)	.50	.25	.15
372	Nolan Cromwell (IA)	.50	.25	.15
373	Preston Dennard	.50	.25	.15
374	Mike Fanning	.50	.25	.15
375	Doug France	.50	.25	.15
376	Mike Guman	.50	.25	.15
377	Pat Haden	.50	.25	.15
378	Dennis Harrah	.50	.25	.15
379	Drew Hill RC	.50	.25	.15
380	LeRoy Irvin RC	.40	.30	.15
381	Cody Jones	.50	.25	.15
382	Rod Perry	.50	.25	.15
383	Rich Saul (AP)	.50	.25	.15
384	Pat Thomas	.50	.25	.15
385	Wendell Tyler	.50	.25	.15
386	Wendell Tyler (IA)	.50	.25	.15
387	Billy Waddy	.50	.25	.15
388	Jack Youngblood	.50	.25	.15
389	Minnesota Vikings Team	.50	.25	.15
390	Matt Blair (AP)	.50	.25	.15
391	Ted Brown	.50	.25	.15
392	Ted Brown (IA)	.50	.25	.15
393	Rick Danmeier	.50	.25	.15
394	Tommy Kramer	.50	.25	.15
395	Mark Mullaney	.50	.25	.15
396	Eddie Payton	.50	.25	.15
397	Ahmad Rashad	.40	.20	.15
398	Joe Senser	.50	.25	.15
399	Joe Senser (IA)	.50	.25	.15
400	Sammy White	.50	.25	.15
401	Sammy White (IA)	.50	.25	.15
402	Ron Yary	.50	.25	.15
403	Rickey Young	.50	.25	.15
404	New Orleans Saints Team	.50	.40	.20
405	Russell Erxleben	.50	.25	.15
406	Elois Grooms	.50	.25	.15
407	Jack Holmes	.50	.25	.15
408	Archie Manning	.50	.25	.15
409	Derland Moore	.50	.25	.15
410	George Rogers RC	.50	.25	.15
411	George Rogers (IA)	.40	.20	.15
412	Toussaint Tyler	.50	.25	.15
413	Dave Waymer RC	.50	.25	.15

414	Wayne Wilson	.50	.25	.15
415	New York Giants Team	.50	.25	.15
416	Scott Brunner RC	.50	.25	.15
417	Rob Carpenter	.50	.25	.15
418	Harry Carson (AP)	.50	.25	.15
419	Bill Currier	.50	.25	.15
420	Joe Danelo	.50	.25	.15
421	Joe Danelo (IA)	.50	.25	.15
422	Mark Haynes RC	.50	.25	.15
423	Terry Jackson	.50	.25	.15
424	Dave Jennings	.50	.25	.15
425	Gary Jeter	.50	.25	.15
426	Brian Kelley	.50	.25	.15
427	George Martin	.50	.25	.15
428	Curtis McGriff	.50	.25	.15
429	Bill Neill	.50	.25	.15
430	Johnny Perkins	.50	.25	.15
431	Beasley Reece	.50	.25	.15
432	Gary Shirk	.50	.25	.15
433	Phil Simms	.50	.25	.15
434	Lawrence Taylor RC (AP)	10.00	5.00	3.00
435	Lawrence Taylor IA (IA)	10.00	5.00	3.00
436	Brad Van Pelt	.50	.25	.15
437	Philadelphia Eagles Team	.50	.25	.15
438	John Bunting	.50	.25	.15
439	Billy Campfield	.50	.25	.15
440	Harold Carmichael	.50	.25	.15
441	Harold Carmichael (IA)	.50	.25	.15
442	Herman Edwards	.50	.25	.15
443	Tony Franklin	.50	.25	.15
444	Tony Franklin (IA)	.50	.25	.15
445	Carl Hairston	.50	.25	.15
446	Dennis Harrison	.50	.25	.15
447	Ron Jaworski	.50	.25	.15
448	Charlie Johnson	.50	.25	.15
449	Keith Krepfle	.50	.25	.15
450	Frank LeMaster	.50	.25	.15
451	Randy Logan	.50	.25	.15
452	Wilbert Montgomery	.50	.25	.15
453	Wilbert Montgomery (IA)	.50	.25	.15
454	Hubert Oliver	.50	.25	.15
455	Jerry Robinson	.50	.25	.15
456	Jerry Robinson (IA)	.50	.25	.15
457	Jerry Sisemore	.50	.25	.15
458	Charlie Smith	.50	.25	.15
459	Stan Walters	.50	.25	.15
460	Brenard Wilson	.50	.25	.15
461	Roynell Young (AP)	.50	.25	.15
462	St. Louis Cardinals Team	.50	.25	.15
463	Ottis Anderson	.50	.25	.15
464	Ottis Anderson (IA)	.50	.25	.15
465	Carl Birdsong	.50	.25	.15
466	Rush Brown	.50	.25	.15
467	Mel Gray	.50	.25	.15
468	Ken Greene	.50	.25	.15
469	Jim Hart	.50	.25	.15
470	E.J. Junior RC	.50	.25	.15
471	Neil Lomax RC	.50	.25	.15
472	Stump Mitchell RC	.50	.25	.15
473	Wayne Morris	.50	.25	.15
474	Neil O'Donoghue	.50	.25	.15
475	Pat Tilley	.50	.25	.15
476	Pat Tilley (IA)	.50	.25	.15
477	San Francisco 49ers Team	.50	.25	.15
478	Dwight Clark	.50	.25	.15
479	Dwight Clark (IA)	.50	.25	.15
480	Earl Cooper	.50	.25	.15
481	Randy Cross (AP)	.50	.25	.15
482	Johnny Davis	.50	.25	.15
483	Fred Dean	.50	.25	.15
484	Fred Dean (IA)	.50	.25	.15
485	Dwight Hicks RC	.50	.25	.15
486	Ronnie Lott RC (AP)	8.00	4.00	2.40
487	Ronnie Lott IA (IA)	6.00	4.50	2.50
488	Joe Montana (AP)	6.00	3.00	1.80
489	Joe Montana IA (IA)	3.50	1.75	1.00
490	Ricky Patton	.50	.25	.15
491	Jack Reynolds	.50	.25	.15
492	Freddie Solomon	.50	.25	.15
493	Ray Wersching	.50	.25	.15
494	Charley Young	.50	.25	.15
495	Tampa Bay Bucaneers Team	.50	.25	.15
496	Cedric Brown	.50	.25	.15
497	Neal Colzie	.50	.25	.15
498	Jerry Eckwood	.50	.25	.15
499	Jimmy Giles (AP)	.50	.25	.15
500	Hugh Green RC	.50	.25	.15
501	Kevin House	.50	.25	.15
502	Kevin House (IA)	.50	.25	.15
503	Cecil Johnson	.50	.25	.15
504	James Owens	.50	.25	.15
505	Lee Roy Selmon (AP)	.50	.25	.15
506	Mike Washington	.50	.25	.15
507	James Wilder RC	.50	.25	.15
508	Doug Williams	.50	.25	.15
509	Washington Redskins Team	.50	.25	.15
510	Perry Brooks	.50	.25	.15

511	Dave Butz	.50	.25	.15
512	Wilbur Jackson	.50	.25	.15
513	Joe Lavender	.50	.25	.15
514	Terry Metcalf	.50	.25	.15
515	Art Monk	.50	.25	.15
516	Frank Pollard, Mark Moseley	.50	.25	.15
517	Donnie Shell, Mark Murphy (AP)	.50	.25	.15
518	Mike Neims (AP)	.50	.25	.15
519	Lemar Parrish	.50	.25	.15
520	John Riggins	.50	.25	.15
521	Joe Theismann	.50	.25	.15
522	Ricky Thompson	.50	.25	.15
523	Don Warren	.50	.25	.15
524	Joe Washington	.50	.25	.15
525	Checklist 1-132	.50	.25	.15
526	Checklist 133-264	.50	.25	.15
527	Checklist 265-396	.50	.25	.15
528	Checklist 397-528	.50	.25	.15

1982 Topps "Coming Soon" Stickers

These stickers were inserted in 1982 Topps football card packs. They are 1-15/16" x 2-9/16", making them the same size as Topps' regular 1982 stickers. They also share the same card numbers, which is why the set is skip-numbered. The card number is on the back, along with the words "Coming Soon!" The fronts of the stickers are gold-bordered foil stickers.

		NM/M	NM	E
	Complete Set (16):	5.00	3.75	2.00
	Common Player:	.10	.08	.04
5	MVP Super Bowl XVI (Joe Montana)	2.00	1.50	.80
6	**NFC Championship**	.10	.08	.04
9	Super Bowl XVI (Joe Montana)	1.50	1.25	.60
71	Tommy Kramer	.30	.25	.12
73	George Rogers	.30	.25	.12
75	Tom Skladany	.10	.08	.04
139	Nolan Cromwell	.30	.25	.12
143	Jack Lambert	.50	.40	.20
144	Lawrence Taylor	1.75	1.25	.70
150	Billy Sims	.40	.30	.15
154	Ken Anderson	.50	.40	.20
159	John Hannah	.40	.30	.15
160	Anthony Munoz	.75	.60	.30
220	Ken Anderson	.50	.40	.20
221	Dan Fouts	.50	.40	.20
222	Frank Lewis	.10	.08	.04

1982 Topps Stickers

These stickers follow the same format as the 1981 stickers, complete with an album featuring Joe Montana on the cover. However, these stickers have yellow borders and a 1982 copyright date on the back. Foil stickers were also produced again (#s 1-10, 70-77, 139-160, 220-227). Stickers 1 and 2 combine as a puzzle to form a picture of the San Francisco 49ers; 3 and 4 show Super Bowl theme art.

		NM/M	NM	E
	Complete Set (288):	30.00	22.00	12.00
	Common Player:	.05	.04	.02
1	**Super Bowl XVI (49er Team)**	.35	.25	.14
2	**Super Bowl XVI (49er Team)**	.15	.11	.06
3	**Super Bowl XVI (Theme Art Trophy)**	.15	.11	.06
4	**Super Bowl XVI (Theme Art Trophy)**	.15	.11	.06
5	MVP Super Bowl XVI (Joe Montana)	3.50	2.75	1.50
6	**1981 NFC Champions 49ers**	.15	.11	.06
7	1981 AFC Champions (Ken Anderson)	.25	.20	.10
8	Super Bowl XVI (Ken Anderson)	.25	.20	.10
9	Super Bowl XVI (Joe Montana)	3.00	2.25	1.25

10	**Super Bowl XVI** (line blocking)	.15	.11	.06
11	Steve Bartkowski	.15	.11	.06
12	William Andrews	.10	.08	.04
13	Lynn Cain	.08	.06	.03
14	Wallace Francis	.08	.06	.03
15	Alfred Jackson	.08	.06	.03
16	Alfred Jenkins	.10	.08	.04
17	Mike Kenn	.08	.06	.03
18	Junior Miller	.10	.08	.04
19	Vince Evans	.10	.08	.04
20	Walter Payton	1.25	.90	.50
21	Dave Williams	.05	.04	.02
22	Brian Baschnagel	.05	.04	.02
23	Rickey Watts	.05	.04	.02
24	Ken Margerum	.08	.06	.03
25	Revie Sorey	.05	.04	.02
26	Gary Fencik	.05	.04	.02
27	Matt Suhey	.05	.04	.02
28	Danny White	.20	.15	.08
29	Tony Dorsett	.50	.40	.20
30	Drew Pearson	.25	.20	.10
31	Rafael Septien	.08	.06	.03
32	Pat Donovan	.05	.04	.02
33	Herbert Scott	.05	.04	.02
34	Ed "Too Tall" Jones	.20	.15	.08
35	Randy White	.25	.20	.10
36	Tony Hill	.08	.06	.03
37	Eric Hipple	.08	.06	.03
38	Billy Sims	.25	.20	.10
39	Dexter Bussey	.05	.04	.02
40	Freddie Scott	.08	.06	.03
41	David Hill	.05	.04	.02
42	Ed Murray	.10	.08	.04
43	Tom Skladany	.05	.04	.02
44	Doug English	.08	.06	.03
45	Al (Bubba) Baker	.12	.09	.05
46	Lynn Dickey	.12	.09	.05
47	Gerry Ellis	.05	.04	.02
48	Harlan Huckleby	.05	.04	.02
49	James Lofton	.40	.30	.15
50	John Jefferson	.08	.06	.03
51	Paul Coffman	.05	.04	.02
52	Jan Stenerud	.20	.15	.08
53	Rich Wingo	.05	.04	.02
54	Wendell Tyler	.10	.08	.04
55	Preston Dennard	.05	.04	.02
56	Billy Waddy	.05	.04	.02
57	Frank Corral	.05	.04	.02
58	Jack Youngblood	.15	.11	.06
59	Pat Thomas	.05	.04	.02
60	Rod Perry	.08	.06	.03
61	Nolan Cromwell	.10	.08	.04
62	Tommy Kramer	.10	.08	.04
63	Rickey Young	.08	.06	.03
64	Ted Brown	.05	.04	.02
65	Ahmad Rashad	.25	.20	.10
66	Sammie White	.08	.06	.03
67	Joe Senser	.05	.04	.02
68	Ron Yary	.08	.06	.03
69	Matt Blair	.08	.06	.03
70	NFC Passing Leader (Joe Montana)	3.50	2.75	1.50
71	NFC Passing Yardage Leader (Tommy Kramer)	.20	.15	.08
72	NFC Receiving Yardage Leader (Alfred Jenkins)	.15	.11	.06
73	NFC Rushing Yardage Leader (George Rogers)	.25	.20	.10
74	NFC Rushing Touchdowns Leader (Wendell Tyler)	.30	.25	.12
75	NFC Punting Leader (Tom Skladany)	.15	.11	.06
76	NFC Interceptions Leader (Everson Walls)	.35	.25	.14
77	MFC Sacks Leader (Curtis Greer)	.15	.11	.06
78	Archie Manning	.25	.20	.10
79	Dave Waymer	.05	.04	.02
80	George Rogers	.20	.15	.08
81	Jack Holmes	.05	.04	.02
82	Toussaint Tyler	.05	.04	.02
83	Wayne Wilson	.05	.04	.02
84	Russell Erxleben	.05	.04	.02
85	Elois Grooms	.05	.04	.02
86	Phil Simms	.20	.15	.08
87	Scott Brunner	.10	.08	.04
88	Rob Carpenter	.08	.06	.03
89	Johnny Perkins	.05	.04	.02
90	Dave Jennings	.05	.04	.02
91	Harry Carson	.12	.09	.05
92	Lawrence Taylor	2.50	2.00	1.00
93	Beasley Reece	.05	.04	.02
94	Mark Haynes	.05	.04	.02
95	Ron Jaworski	.12	.09	.05
96	Wilbert Montgomery	.08	.06	.03
97	Hubert Oliver	.05	.04	.02
98	Harold Carmichael	.10	.08	.04
99	Jerry Robinson	.08	.06	.03
100	Stan Walters	.05	.04	.02
101	Charlie Johnson	.05	.04	.02
102	Roynell Young	.05	.04	.02
103	Tony Franklin	.05	.04	.02
104	Neil Lomax	.15	.11	.06
105	Jim Hart	.15	.11	.06
106	Ottis Anderson	.20	.15	.08
107	Stump Mitchell	.12	.09	.05
108	Pat Tilley	.08	.06	.03
109	Rush Brown	.05	.04	.02
110	E.J. Junior	.05	.04	.02
111	Ken Greene	.05	.04	.02
112	Mel Gray	.08	.06	.03
113	Joe Montana	2.50	2.00	1.00
114	Ricky Patton	.05	.04	.02
115	Earl Cooper	.05	.04	.02
116	Dwight Clark	.25	.20	.10
117	Freddie Solomon	.08	.06	.03
118	Randy Cross	.10	.08	.04
119	Fred Dean	.08	.06	.03
120	Ronnie Lott	1.75	1.25	.70
121	Dwight Hicks	.08	.06	.03
122	Doug Williams	.15	.11	.06
123	Jerry Eckwood	.08	.06	.03
124	James Owens	.08	.06	.03
125	Kevin House	.08	.06	.03
126	Jimmie Giles	.05	.04	.02
127	Charley Hannah	.05	.04	.02
128	Lee Roy Selmon	.15	.11	.06
129	Hugh Green	.12	.09	.05
130	Joe Theismann	.30	.25	.12
131	Joe Washington	.08	.06	.03
132	John Riggins	.25	.20	.10
133	Art Monk	.50	.40	.20
134	Ricky Thompson	.05	.04	.02
135	Don Warren	.08	.06	.03
136	Perry Brooks	.05	.04	.02
137	Mike Nelms	.05	.04	.02
138	Mark Moseley	.05	.04	.02
139	Nolan Cromwell (All-Pro)	.20	.15	.08
140	Dwight Hicks (All-Pro)	.15	.11	.06
141	Ronnie Lott (All-Pro)	2.00	1.50	.80
142	Harry Carson (All-Pro)	.20	.15	.08
143	Jack Lambert (All-Pro)	.40	.30	.15
144	Lawrence Taylor (All-Pro)	2.50	2.00	1.00
145	Mel Blount (All-Pro)	.30	.25	.12
146	Joe Klecko (All-Pro)	.15	.11	.06
147	Randy White (All-Pro)	.35	.25	.14
148	Doug English (All-Pro)	.10	.08	.04
149	Fred Dean (All-Pro)	.20	.15	.08
150	Billy Sims (All-Pro)	.25	.20	.10
151	Tony Dorsett (All-Pro)	.75	.60	.30
152	James Lofton (All-Pro)	.75	.60	.30
153	Alfred Jenkins (All-Pro)	.20	.15	.08
154	Ken Anderson (All-Pro)	.35	.25	.14
155	Kellen Winslow (All-Pro)	.50	.40	.20
156	Marvin Powell (All-Pro)	.10	.08	.04
157	Randy Cross (All-Pro)	.20	.15	.08
158	Mike Webster (All-Pro)	.30	.25	.12
159	John Hannah (All-Pro)	.30	.25	.12
160	Anthony Munoz (All-Pro)	1.25	.90	.50
161	Curtis Dickey	.08	.06	.03
162	Randy McMillan	.08	.06	.03
163	Roger Carr	.08	.06	.03
164	Raymond Butler	.05	.04	.02
165	Reese McCall	.05	.04	.02
166	Ed Simonini	.05	.04	.02
167	Herb Oliver	.05	.04	.02
168	Nesby Glasgow	.05	.04	.02
169	Joe Ferguson	.08	.06	.03
170	Joe Cribbs	.08	.06	.03
171	Jerry Butler	.08	.06	.03
172	Frank Lewis	.08	.06	.03
173	Mark Brammer	.05	.04	.02
174	Fred Smerlas	.10	.08	.04
175	Jim Haslett	.05	.04	.02
176	Charles Alexander	.05	.04	.02
177	Bill Simpson	.05	.04	.02
178	Ken Anderson	.20	.15	.08
179	Charles Alexander	.05	.04	.02
180	Pete Johnson	.05	.04	.02
181	Isaac Curtis	.05	.04	.02
182	Cris Collinsworth	.50	.40	.20
183	Pat McInally	.08	.06	.03
184	Anthony Munoz	.50	.40	.20
135	Louis Breeden	.05	.04	.02
186	Jim Breech	.10	.08	.04
187	Brian Sipe	.10	.08	.04
188	Charles White	.10	.08	.04
189	Mike Pruitt	.08	.06	.03
190	Reggie Rucker	.12	.09	.05
191	Dave Logan	.05	.04	.02
192	Ozzie Newsome	.30	.25	.12
193	Dick Ambrose	.05	.04	.02
194	Joe DeLamielleure	.05	.04	.02
195	Ricky Feacher	.05	.04	.02
196	Craig Morton	.12	.09	.05
197	Dave Preston	.05	.04	.02
198	Rick Parros	.05	.04	.02
199	Rick Upchurch	.08	.06	.03
200	Steve Watson	.10	.08	.04
201	Riley Odoms	.08	.06	.03
202	Randy Gradishar	.10	.08	.04
203	Steve Foley	.05	.04	.02
204	Ken Stabler	.30	.25	.12
205	Gifford Nielsen	.08	.06	.03
206	Tim Wilson	.05	.04	.02
207	Ken Burrough	.10	.08	.04
208	Mike Renfro	.10	.08	.04
209	Greg Stemrick	.05	.04	.02
210	Robert Brazile	.08	.06	.03
211	Gregg Bingham	.08	.06	.03
212	Steve Fuller	.08	.06	.03
213	Bill Kenney	.08	.06	.03
214	Joe Delaney	.20	.15	.08
215	Henry Marshall	.05	.04	.02
216	Nick Lowery	.10	.08	.04
217	Art Still	.08	.06	.03
218	Gary Green	.05	.04	.02
219	Gary Barbaro	.05	.04	.02
220	AFC PAssing Leader (Ken Anderson)	.35	.25	.14
221	AFC PAssing Yardage Leader (Dan Fouts)	.50	.40	.20
222	AFC Receiving Yardage Leader (Frank Lewis)	.20	.15	.08
223	AFC Kickoff Return Yardage Leader (James Brooks)	.75	.60	.30
224	AFC Rushing Touchdowns Leader (Chuck Muncie)	.20	.15	.08
225	AFC Punting Leader (Pat McInally)	.20	.15	.08
226	AFC Interceptions Leader (John Harris)	.20	.15	.08
227	AFC Sacks Leader (Joe Klecko)	.20	.15	.08
228	Dave Woodley	.08	.06	.03
229	Tony Nathan	.08	.06	.03
230	Andra Franklin	.05	.04	.02
231	Nat Moore	.08	.06	.03
232	Duriel Harris	.08	.06	.03
233	Uwe Von Schamann	.05	.04	.02
234	Bob Baumhower	.10	.08	.04
235	Glenn Blackwood	.10	.08	.04
236	Tommy Vigorito	.05	.04	.02
237	Steve Grogan	.12	.09	.05
238	Matt Cavanaugh	.08	.06	.03
239	Tony Collins	.08	.06	.03
240	Vagas Ferguson	.10	.08	.04
241	John Smith	.05	.04	.02
242	Stanley Morgan	.10	.08	.04
243	John Hannah	.15	.11	.06
244	Steve Nelson	.05	.04	.02
245	Don Hasselback	.05	.04	.02
246	Richard Todd	.12	.09	.05
247	Bruce Harper	.05	.04	.02
248	Wesley Walker	.12	.09	.05
249	Jerome Barkum	.08	.06	.03
250	Marvin Powell	.08	.06	.03
251	Mark Gastineau	.15	.11	.06
252	Joe Klecko	.08	.06	.03
253	Darrol Ray	.05	.04	.02
254	Marty Lyons	.08	.06	.03
255	Marc Wilson	.10	.08	.04
256	Kenny King	.08	.06	.03
257	Mark Van Eeghen	.08	.06	.03
258	Cliff Branch	.12	.09	.05
259	Bob Chandler	.08	.06	.03
260	Ray Guy	.15	.11	.06
261	Ted Hendricks	.20	.15	.08
262	Lester Hayes	.20	.15	.08
263	Terry Bradshaw	.60	.45	.25
264	Franco Harris	.35	.25	.14
265	John Stallworth	.15	.11	.06
266	Jim Smith	.05	.04	.02
267	Mike Webster	.12	.09	.05
268	Jack Lambert	.20	.15	.08
269	Mel Blount	.15	.11	.06
270	Donnie Shell	.12	.09	.05
271	Bennie Cunningham	.08	.06	.03
272	Dan Fouts	.40	.30	.15
273	Chuck Muncie	.10	.08	.04
274	James Brooks	.65	.50	.25
275	Charlie Joiner	.20	.15	.08
276	Wes Chandler	.12	.09	.05
277	Kellen Winslow	.25	.20	.10
278	Doug Wilkerson	.05	.04	.02
279	Gary Johnson	.08	.06	.03
280	Rolf Benirschke	.08	.06	.03
281	Jim Zorn	.12	.09	.05
282	Theotis Brown	.08	.06	.03
283	Dan Doornink	.05	.04	.02
284	Steve Largent	1.25	.90	.50
285	Sam McCullum	.08	.06	.03

286	Efren Herrera	.05	.04	.02
287	Manu Tuiasosopo	.05	.04	.02
288	John Harris	.05	.04	.02

1983 Topps

Presumably adjusting for an increase in the size of its baseball card set, Topps cut the number of cards in its annual football card set in 1983 from 528 to 396. Because Topps still printed the cards on four sheets, one-third of the cards were double-printed - accounting for some of the apparent price discrepancies in the list below. Cards in the set are bordered in white and feature the team name in white block letters at the top of the card. The player's name and position are found in a white rectangle near the bottom. All-Pro designations are found above this box. This set is notable for several rookies: Gerald Riggs, Jim McMahon, Mike Singletary, Roy Green and Marcus Allen. It also features Lawrence Taylor's second-year card. Cards are again listed alphabetically by city name and by player name. (Key: PB - Pro Bowl)

		NM/M	NM	E
Complete Set (396):		150.00	75.00	45.00
Common Player:		.50	.25	.15
Wax Pack (13+1):		2.50		
Wax Box (36):		65.00		

1	Ken Anderson (RB)	.50	.25	.15
2	Tony Dorsett (RB)	.50	.25	.15
3	Dan Fouts (RB)	.50	.25	.15
4	Joe Montana (RB)	2.00	1.00	.60
5	Mark Moseley (RB)	.50	.25	.15
6	Mike Nelms (RB)	.50	.25	.15
7	Darrol Ray (RB)	.50	.25	.15
8	John Riggins (RB)	.50	.25	.15
9	Fulton Walker (RB)	.50	.25	.15
10	NFC Championship (John Riggins)	.50	.25	.15
11	AFC Championship	.50	.25	.15
12	Super Bowl XVII (John Riggins)	.50	.25	.15
13	Atlanta Falcons Team (William Andrews)	.50	.25	.15
14	William Andrews (PB)	.50	.25	.15
15	Steve Bartkowski	.50	.25	.15
16	Bobby Butler	.50	.25	.15
17	Buddy Curry	.50	.25	.15
18	Alfred Jackson	.50	.25	.15
19	Alfred Jenkins	.50	.25	.15
20	Kenny Johnson	.50	.25	.15
21	Mike Kenn (PB)	.50	.25	.15
22	Mick Luckhurst	.50	.25	.15
23	Junior Miller	.50	.25	.15
24	Al Richardson	.50	.25	.15
25	Gerald Riggs RC	.50	.60	.30
26	R.C. Thielemann (PB)	.50	.25	.15
27	Jeff Van Note (PB)	.50	.25	.15
28	Walter Payton (TL)	1.50	.75	.45
29	Brian Baschnagel	.50	.25	.15
30	Dan Hampton (PB)	.50	.25	.15
31	Mike Hartenstine	.50	.25	.15
32	Noah Jackson	.50	.25	.15
33	Jim McMahon RC	3.00	1.50	.90
34	Emery Moorehead	.50	.25	.15
35	Bob Parsons	.50	.25	.15
36	Walter Payton	3.00	1.50	.90
37	Terry Schmidt	.50	.25	.15
38	Mike Singletary RC	4.50	2.25	1.35
39	Matt Suhey	.50	.25	.15
40	Rickey Watts	.50	.25	.15
41	Otis Wilson RC	.15	.11	.06
42	Tony Dorsett (TL)	.50	.25	.15
43	Bob Breunig (PB)	.50	.25	.15
44	Doug Cosbie	.50	.25	.15
45	Pat Donovan (PB)	.50	.25	.15
46	Tony Dorsett (PB)	1.50	.75	.45
47	Tony Hill	.50	.25	.15
48	Butch Johnson	.50	.25	.15
49	Ed "Too Tall" Jones (PB)	.50	.25	.15
50	Harvey Martin	.50	.25	.15
51	Drew Pearson	.50	.25	.15

52	Rafael Septien	.50	.25	.15
53	Ron Springs	.50	.25	.15
54	Dennis Thurman	.50	.25	.15
55	Everson Walls (PB)	.50	.25	.15
56	Danny White (PB)	.50	.25	.15
57	Randy White (PB)	.50	.25	.15
58	Detroit Lions Team (Billy Sims)	.50	.25	.15
59	Al "Bubba" Baker	.50	.25	.15
60	Dexter Bussey	.50	.25	.15
61	Gary Danielson	.50	.25	.15
62	Keith Dorney (PB)	.50	.25	.15
63	Doug English (PB)	.50	.25	.15
64	Ken Fantetti	.50	.25	.15
65	Alvin Hall	.50	.25	.15
66	David Hill	.50	.25	.15
67	Eric Hipple	.50	.25	.15
68	Ed Murray	.50	.25	.15
69	Freddie Scott	.50	.25	.15
70	Billy Sims (PB)	.50	.25	.15
71	Tom Skladany	.50	.25	.15
72	Leonard Thompson	.50	.25	.15
73	Bobby Watkins	.50	.25	.15
74	Green Bay Packers Team (Eddie Lee Ivery)	.50		
75	John Anderson	.50	.25	.15
76	Paul Coffman (PB)	.50	.25	.15
77	Lynn Dickey	.50	.25	.15
78	Mike Douglass	.50	.25	.15
79	Eddie Lee Ivery	.50	.25	.15
80	John Jefferson (PB)	.50	.25	.15
81	Ezra Johnson	.50	.25	.15
82	Mark Lee	.50	.25	.15
83	James Lofton (PB)	.50	.25	.15
84	Larry McCarren (PB)	.50	.25	.15
85	Jan Stenerud	.50	.25	.15
86	Los Angeles Rams Team (Wendell Tyler)	.50	.25	.15
87	Bill Bain	.50	.25	.15
88	Nolan Cromwell (PB)	.50	.25	.15
89	Preston Dennard	.50	.25	.15
90	Vince Ferragamo	.50	.25	.15
91	Mike Guman	.50	.25	.15
92	Kent Hill (PB)	.50	.25	.15
93	Mike Lansford	.50	.25	.15
94	Rod Perry	.50	.25	.15
95	Pat Thomas	.50	.25	.15
96	Jack Youngblood	.50	.25	.15
97	Minnesota Vikings Team (Ted Brown)	.50	.25	.15
98	Matt Blair (PB)	.50	.25	.15
99	Ted Brown	.50	.25	.15
100	Greg Coleman	.50	.25	.15
101	Randy Holloway	.50	.25	.15
102	Tommy Kramer	.50	.25	.15
103	Doug Martin	.50	.25	.15
104	Mark Mullaney	.50	.25	.15
105	Joe Senser	.50	.25	.15
106	Willie Teal	.50	.25	.15
107	Sammy White	.50	.25	.15
108	Rickey Young	.50	.25	.15
109	New Orleans Saints Team (George Rogers)	.50	.25	.15
110	Stan Brock RC	.50	.25	.15
111	Bruce Clark	.50	.25	.15
112	Russell Erxleben	.50	.25	.15
113	Russell Gary	.50	.25	.15
114	Jeff Groth	.50	.25	.15
115	John Hill	.50	.25	.15
116	Derland Moore	.50	.25	.15
117	George Rogers (PB)	.50	.25	.15
118	Ken Stabler	.50	.25	.15
119	Wayne Wilson	.50	.25	.15
120	New York Giants Team (Butch Woolfolk)	.50	.25	.15
121	Scott Brunner	.50	.25	.15
122	Rob Carpenter	.50	.25	.15
123	Harry Carson (PB)	.50	.25	.15
124	Joe Danelo	.50	.25	.15
125	Earnest Gray	.50	.25	.15
126	Mark Haynes (PB)	.50	.25	.15
127	Terry Jackson	.50	.25	.15
128	Dave Jennings (PB)	.50	.25	.15
129	Brian Kelley	.50	.25	.15
130	George Martin	.50	.25	.15
131	Tom Mullady	.50	.25	.15
132	Johnny Perkins	.50	.25	.15
133	Lawrence Taylor (PB)	.50	.25	.15
134	Brad Van Pelt	.50	.25	.15
135	Butch Woolfolk	.50	.25	.15
136	Philadelphia Eagles Team (Wilbert Montgomery)	.50	.25	.15
137	Harold Carmichael	.50	.25	.15
138	Herman Edwards	.50	.25	.15
139	Tony Franklin	.50	.25	.15

140	Carl Hairston	.50	.25	.15
141	Dennis Harrison (PB)	.50	.25	.15
142	Ron Jaworski	.50	.25	.15
143	Frank LeMaster	.50	.25	.15
144	Wilbert Montgomery	.50	.25	.15
145	Guy Morriss	.50	.25	.15
146	Jerry Robinson	.50	.25	.15
147	Max Runager	.50	.25	.15
148	Ron Smith	.50	.25	.15
149	John Spagnola	.50	.25	.15
150	Stan Walters	.50	.25	.15
151	Roynell Young	.50	.25	.15
152	St. Louis Cardinals Team (Ottis Anderson)	.50	.25	.15
153	Ottis Anderson	.50	.25	.15
154	Carl Birdsong	.50	.25	.15
155	Dan Dierdorf	.50	.25	.15
156	Roy Green RC	.50	.25	.15
157	Elois Grooms	.50	.25	.15
158	Neil Lomax	.50	.25	.15
159	Wayne Morris	.50	.25	.15
160	James Robbins	.50	.25	.15
161	Luis Sharpe RC	.50	.25	.15
162	Pat Tilley	.50	.25	.15
163	San Francisco 49ers Team (Jeff Moore)	.50	.25	.15
164	Dwight Clark (PB)	.50	.25	.15
165	Randy Cross (PB)	.50	.25	.15
166	Russ Francis	.50	.25	.15
167	Dwight Hicks (PB)	.50	.25	.15
168	Ronnie Lott (PB)	.50	.25	.15
169	Joe Montana	4.00	2.00	1.20
170	Jeff Moore	.50	.25	.15
171	Renaldo Nehemiah RC	.50	.25	.15
172	Freddie Solomon	.50	.25	.15
173	Ray Wersching	.50	.25	.15
174	Tampa Bay Buccaneers Team (James Wilder)	.50	.25	.15
175	Cedric Brown	.50	.25	.15
176	Bill Capece	.50	.25	.15
177	Neal Colzie	.50	.25	.15
178	Jimmie Giles (PB)	.50	.25	.15
179	Hugh Green (PB)	.50	.25	.15
180	Kevin House	.50	.25	.15
181	James Owens	.50	.25	.15
182	Lee Roy Selmon (PB)	.50	.25	.15
183	Mike Washington	.50	.25	.15
184	James Wilder	.50	.25	.15
185	Doug Williams	.50	.25	.15
186	Washington Redskins Team (John Riggins)	.50	.25	.15
187	Jeff Bostic	.50	.25	.15
188	Charlie Brown (PB)	.50	.25	.15
189	Vernon Dean	.50	.25	.15
190	Joe Jacoby RC	.50	.25	.15
191	Dexter Manley RC	.50	.25	.15
192	Rich Milot	.50	.25	.15
193	Art Monk	.50	.25	.15
194	Mark Mosely (PB)	.50	.25	.15
195	Mike Nelms (PB)	.50	.25	.15
196	Neal Olkewicz	.50	.25	.15
197	Tony Peters (PB)	.50	.25	.15
198	John Riggins	.50	.25	.15
199	Joe Theismann (PB)	.50	.25	.15
200	Don Warren	.50	.25	.15
201	Jeris White	.50	.25	.15
202	Passing Leaders (Joe Theismann, Ken Anderson)	.50	.25	.15
203	Receiving Leaders (Dwight Clark, Kellen Winslow)	.50	.25	.15
204	Rushing Leaders (Tony Dorsett, Freeman McNeil)	.50	.25	.15
205	Scoring Leaders (Marcus Allen, Wendell Tyler)	.50	.25	.15
206	Interception Leaders (Everson Walls)	.50	.25	.15
207	Punting Leaders (Carl Birdsong, Luke Prestridge)	.50	.25	.15
208	Baltimore Colts Team (Randy McMillan)	.50	.25	.15
209	Matt Bouza	.50	.25	.15
210	Johnnie Cooks	.50	.25	.15
211	Curtis Dickey	.50	.25	.15
212	Nesby Glasgow	.50	.25	.15
213	Derrick Hatchett	.50	.25	.15
214	Randy McMillan	.50	.25	.15
215	Mike Pagel RC	.50	.25	.15
216	Rohn Stark RC	.50	.25	.15
217	Donnell Thompson	.50	.25	.15
218	Leo Wisniewski	.50	.25	.15
219	Buffalo Bills Team (Joe Cribbs)	.50	.25	.15

220	Curtis Brown	.50	.25	.15
221	Jerry Butler	.50	.25	.15
222	Greg Cater	.50	.25	.15
223	Joe Cribbs	.50	.25	.15
224	Joe Ferguson	.50	.25	.15
225	Roosevelt Leaks	.50	.25	.15
226	Frank Lewis	.50	.25	.15
227	Eugene Marve	.50	.25	.15
228	Fred Smerlas (PB)	.50	.25	.15
229	Ben Williams (PB)	.50	.25	.15
230	Cincinnati Bengals Team			
	(Pete Johnson)	.50	.25	.15
231	Charles Alexander	.50	.25	.15
232	Ken Anderson (PB)	.50	.25	.15
233	Jim Breech	.50	.25	.15
234	Ross Browner	.50	.25	.15
235	Cris Collinsworth (PB)	.50	.25	.15
236	Isaac Curtis	.50	.25	.15
237	Pete Johnson	.50	.25	.15
238	Steve Kreider	.50	.25	.15
239	Max Montoya	.50	.25	.15
240	Anthony Munoz (PB)	.50	.25	.15
241	Ken Riley	.50	.25	.15
242	Dan Ross (PB)	.50	.25	.15
243	Reggie Williams	.50	.25	.15
244	Cleveland Browns Team			
	(Mike Pruitt)	.50	.25	.15
245	Chip Banks RC (PB)	.50	.25	.15
246	Tom Cousineau	.50	.25	.15
247	Joe DeLamielleure	.50	.25	.15
248	Doug Dieken	.50	.25	.15
249	Hanford Dixon RC	.50	.25	.15
250	Ricky Feacher	.50	.25	.15
251	Lawrence Johnson	.50	.25	.15
252	Dave Logan	.50	.25	.15
253	Paul McDonald	.50	.25	.15
254	Ozzie Newsome	.50	.25	.15
255	Mike Pruitt	.50	.25	.15
256	Clarence Scott	.50	.25	.15
257	Brian Sipe	.50	.25	.15
258	Dwight Walker	.50	.25	.15
259	Charles White	.50	.25	.15
260	Denver Broncos Team			
	(Gerald Wilhite)	.50	.25	.15
261	Steve DeBerg	.50	.25	.15
262	Randy Gradishar (PB)	.50	.25	.15
263	Rulon Jones	.50	.25	.15
264	Rick Karlis	.50	.25	.15
265	Don Latimer	.50	.25	.15
266	Rick Parros	.50	.25	.15
267	Luke Prestridge (PB)	.50	.25	.15
268	Rick Upchurch (PB)	.50	.25	.15
269	Steve Watson	.50	.25	.15
270	Gerald Wilhite	.50	.25	.15
271	Houston Oilers Team			
	(Gifford Nielson)	.50	.25	.15
272	Harold Bailey	.50	.25	.15
273	Jesse Baker	.50	.25	.15
274	Gregg Bingham	.50	.25	.15
275	Robert Brazile (PB)	.50	.25	.15
276	Donnie Craft	.50	.25	.15
277	Daryl Hunt	.50	.25	.15
278	Archie Manning	.50	.25	.15
279	Gifford Nielsen	.50	.25	.15
280	Mike Renfro	.50	.25	.15
281	Carl Roaches	.50	.25	.15
282	Kansas City Chiefs Team			
	(Joe Delaney)	.50	.25	.15
283	Gary Barbaro (PB)	.50	.25	.15
284	Joe Delaney	.50	.25	.15
285	Jeff Gossett RC	.50	.25	.15
286	Gary Green (PB)	.50	.25	.15
287	Eric Harris	.50	.25	.15
288	Billy Jackson	.50	.25	.15
289	Bill Kenney	.50	.25	.15
290	Nick Lowery	.50	.25	.15
291	Henry Marshall	.50	.25	.15
292	Art Still (PB)	.50	.25	.15
293	Marcus Allen (TL)	.50	.25	.15
294	Marcus Allen RC (PB)	5.00	2.50	1.50
295	Lyle Alzado	.50	.25	.15
296	Chris Bahr	.50	.25	.15
297	Cliff Branch	.50	.25	.15
298	Todd Christensen RC	.50	.25	.15
299	Ray Guy	.50	.25	.15
300	Frank Hawkins	.50	.25	.15
301	Lester Hayes (PB)	.50	.25	.15
302	Ted Hendricks (PB)	.50	.25	.15
303	Kenny King	.50	.25	.15
304	Rod Martin	.50	.25	.15
305	Matt Millen	.50	.25	.15
306	Burgess Owens	.50	.25	.15
307	Jim Plunkett	.50	.25	.15
308	Miami Dolphins Team			
	(Andra Franklin)	.50	.25	.15

309	Bob Baumhower (PB)	.50	.25	.15
310	Glenn Blackwood	.50	.25	.15
311	Lyle Blackwood	.50	.25	.15
312	A.J. Duhe	.50	.25	.15
313	Andra Franklin (PB)	.50	.25	.15
314	Duriel Harris	.50	.25	.15
315	Bob Kuechenberg (PB)	.50	.25	.15
316	Don McNeal	.50	.25	.15
317	Tony Nathan	.50	.25	.15
318	Ed Newman (PB)	.50	.25	.15
319	Earnie Rhone	.50	.25	.15
320	Joe Rose	.50	.25	.15
321	Don Strock	.50	.25	.15
322	Uwe Von Schamann	.50	.25	.15
323	David Woodley	.50	.25	.15
324	New England Patriots			
	Team (Tony Collins)	.50	.25	.15
325	Julius Adams	.50	.25	.15
326	Pete Brock	.50	.25	.15
327	Rich Camarillo RC	.50	.25	.15
328	Tony Collins	.50	.25	.15
329	Steve Grogan	.50	.25	.15
330	John Hannah (PB)	.50	.25	.15
331	Don Hasselbeck	.50	.25	.15
332	Mike Haynes (PB)	.50	.25	.15
333	Roland James	.50	.25	.15
334	Stanley Morgan	.50	.60	.30
335	Steve Nelson	.50	.25	.15
336	Kenneth Sims	.50	.25	.15
337	Mark Van Eeghen	.50	.25	.15
338	New York Jets Team			
	(Freeman McNeil)	.50	.25	.15
339	Greg Buttle	.50	.25	.15
340	Joe Fields (PB)	.50	.25	.15
341	Mark Gastineau (PB)	.50	.25	.15
342	Bruce Harper	.50	.25	.15
343	Bobby Jackson	.50	.25	.15
344	Bobby Jones	.50	.25	.15
345	Johnny "Lam" Jones	.50	.25	.15
346	Joe Klecko	.50	.25	.15
347	Marty Lyons	.50	.25	.15
348	Freeman McNeil (PB)	.50	.25	.15
349	Lance Mehl	.50	.25	.15
350	Marvin Powell (PB)	.50	.25	.15
351	Darrol Ray	.50	.25	.15
352	Abdul Salaam	.50	.25	.15
353	Richard Todd	.50	.25	.15
354	Wesley Walker (PB)	.50	.25	.15
355	Pittsburgh Steelers Team			
	(Franco Harris)	.50	.25	.15
356	Gary Anderson RC	1.50	.75	.45
357	Mel Blount	.50	.25	.15
358	Terry Bradshaw	1.50	.75	.45
359	Larry Brown (PB)	.50	.25	.15
360	Bennie Cunningham	.50	.25	.15
361	Gary Dunn	.50	.25	.15
362	Franco Harris	.50	.25	.15
363	Jack Lambert (PB)	.50	.25	.15
364	Frank Pollard	.50	.25	.15
365	Donnie Shell (PB)	.50	.25	.15
366	John Stallworth (PB)	.50	.25	.15
367	Loren Toews	.50	.25	.15
368	Mike Webster (PB)	.50	.25	.15
369	Dwayne Woodruff RC	.50	.25	.15
370	San Diego Chargers Team			
	(Chuck Muncie)	.50	.25	.15
371	Rolf Benirschke (PB)	.50	.25	.15
372	James Brooks	.50	.25	.15
373	Wes Chandler (PB)	.50	.25	.15
374	Dan Fouts (PB)	.50	.25	.15
375	Tim Fox	.50	.25	.15
376	Gary Johnson (PB)	.50	.25	.15
377	Charlie Joiner	.50	.25	.15
378	Louie Kelcher	.50	.25	.15
379	Chuck Muncie (PB)	.50	.25	.15
380	Cliff Thrift	.50	.25	.15
381	Doug Wilkerson (PB)	.50	.25	.15
382	Kellen Winslow (PB)	.50	.25	.15
383	Seattle Seahawks Team			
	(Sherman Smith)	.50	.25	.15
384	Kenny Easley RC (PB)	.50	.25	.15
385	Jacob Green RC	.50	.25	.15
386	John Harris	.50	.25	.15
387	Mike Jackson	.50	.25	.15
388	Norm Johnson RC	.50	.25	.15
389	Steve Largent	.50	.25	.15
390	Keith Simpson	.50	.25	.15
391	Sherman Smith	.50	.25	.15
392	Jeff West	.50	.25	.15
393	Jim Zorn	.50	.25	.15
394	Checklist 1-132	.50	.25	.15
395	Checklist 133-264	.50	.25	.15
396	Checklist 265-396	.50	.25	.15

1983 Topps Sticker Boxes

These boxes contained 35 stickers inside, but also had two 2-1/2" x 3-1/2" on them; an offensive player was on each box. The cards are not numbered, and there was no issue for #10, but the box is numbered with a tab. The prices below are for an uncut box.

		NM/M	NM	E
	Complete Set (12):	15.00	11.00	6.00
	Common Player:	.75	.60	.30
1	Pat Donovan,			
	Mark Gastineau	.75	.60	.30
2	Wes Chandler,			
	Nolan Cromwell	1.25	.90	.50
3	Marvin Powell,			
	Ed "Too Tall" Jones	1.25	.90	.50
4	Ken Anderson, Tony Peters	1.25	.90	.50
5	Freeman McNeil,			
	Lawrence Taylor	2.00	1.50	.80
6	Mark Moseley,			
	Dave Jennings	.75	.60	.30
7	Dwight Clark, Mark Haynes	1.50	1.25	.60
8	Jeff Van Note,			
	Harry Carson	.75	.60	.30
9	Tony Dorsett, Hugh Green	2.00	1.50	.80
11	Randy Cross,			
	Gary Johnson	1.00	.70	.40
12	Kellen Winslow,			
	Lester Hayes	1.25	.90	.50
13	John Hannah, Randy White	2.00	1.50	.80

1983 Topps Sticker Inserts

These 33 different inserts, which came in each wax pack of 1983 Topps football cards, pictured an NFL star on the front and a piece to one of three different puzzles on the backs. A gold plaque at the bottom of the card identifies the player.

	NM/M	NM	E
Complete Set (33):	20.00	15.00	8.00
Common Player:	.35	.25	.14

		NM/M	NM	E
1	Marcus Allen	5.00	3.75	2.00
2	Ken Anderson	.50	.40	.20
3	Ottis Anderson	.35	.25	.14
4	William Andrews	.35	.25	.14
5	Terry Bradshaw	1.25	.90	.50
6	Wes Chandler	.35	.25	.14
7	Dwight Clark	.50	.40	.20
8	Cris Collinsworth	.35	.25	.14
9	Joe Cribbs	.35	.25	.14
10	Nolan Cromwell	.35	.25	.14
11	Tony Dorsett	1.50	1.25	.60
12	Dan Fouls	1.00	.70	.40
13	Mark Gastineau	.35	.25	.14
14	Jimmie Giles	.35	.25	.14
15	Franco Harris	1.00	.70	.40
16	Ted Hendricks	.60	.45	.25
17	Tony Hill	.35	.25	.14
18	John Jefferson	.35	.25	.14
19	James Lofton	1.00	.70	.40
20	Freeman McNeil	.50	.40	.20
21	Joe Montana	6.00	4.50	2.50
22	Mark Moseley	.35	.25	.14
23	Ozzie Newsome	1.00	.70	.40
24	Walter Payton	3.00	2.25	1.25
25	John Riggins	1.00	.70	.40
26	Billy Sims	.35	.25	.14
27	John Stallworth	.50	.40	.20
28	Lawrence Taylor	3.00	2.25	1.25
29	Joe Theismann	1.25	.90	.50
30	Richard Todd	.35	.25	.14
31	Wesley Walker	.35	.25	.14
32	Danny White	.35	.25	.14
33	Kellen Winslow	.50	.40	.20

1983 Topps Stickers

These stickers are similar to those issued in previous years, but can be identified by the rounded frame around the picture on the front and the reference on the back to the 1983 sticker album which was produced. Once again, Topps included foil stickers in the set (#s 1-4, 73-80, 143-152 and 264-271. Foil stickers 1-2 are right and left sides of Franco Harris; 3 and 4 portray Walter Payton.

		NM/M	NM	E
Complete Set (330):		30.00	22.00	12.00
Common Player:		.05	.04	.02

		NM/M	NM	E
1	Franco Harris	.50	.40	.20
2	Franco Harris	.50	.40	.20
3	Walter Payton	1.25	.90	.50
4	Walter Payton	1.25	.90	.50
5	John Riggins	.35	.25	.14
6	Tony Dorsett	.40	.30	.15
7	Mark Van Eeghen	.05	.04	.02
8	Chuck Muncie	.08	.06	.03
9	Wilbert Montgomery	.08	.06	.03
10	Greg Pruitt	.08	.06	.03
11	Sam Cunningham	.10	.08	.04
12	Ottis Anderson	.20	.15	.08
13	Mike Pruitt	.08	.06	.03
14	Dexter Bussey	.05	.04	.02
15	Mike Pagel	.05	.04	.02
16	Curtis Dickey	.08	.06	.03
17	Randy McMillan	.08	.06	.03
18	Raymond Butler	.05	.04	.02
19	Nesby Glasgow	.05	.04	.02
20	Zachary Dixon	.05	.04	.02
21	Matt Bouza	.05	.04	.02
22	Johnie Cooks	.05	.04	.02
23	Curtis Brown	.05	.04	.02
24	Joe Cribbs	.10	.08	.04
25	Roosevelt Leaks	.08	.06	.03
26	Jerry Butler	.08	.06	.03
27	Frank Lewis	.08	.06	.03
28	Fred Smerlas	.05	.04	.02
29	Ben Williams	.05	.04	.02

30	Joe Ferguson	.15	.11	.06
31	Isaac Curtis	.08	.06	.03
32	Cris Collinsworth	.15	.11	.06
33	Anthony Munoz	.20	.15	.08
34	Max Montoya	.05	.04	.02
35	Ross Browner	.08	.06	.03
36	Reggie Williams	.10	.08	.04
37	Ken Riley	.10	.08	.04
38	Pete Johnson	.08	.06	.03
39	Ken Anderson	.20	.15	.08
40	Charles White	.10	.08	.04
41	Dave Logan	.05	.04	.02
42	Doug Dieken	.05	.04	.02
43	Ozzie Newsome	.20	.15	.08
44	Tom Cousineau	.05	.04	.02
45	Bob Golic	.08	.06	.03
46	Brian Sipe	.10	.08	.04
47	Paul McDonald	.05	.04	.02
48	Mike Pruitt	.10	.08	.04
49	Luke Prestridge	.05	.04	.02
50	Randy Gradishar	.10	.08	.04
51	Rulon Jones	.05	.04	.02
52	Rick Parros	.05	.04	.02
53	Steve DeBerg	.15	.11	.06
54	Tom Jackson	.10	.08	.04
55	Rick Upchurch	.08	.06	.03
56	Steve Watson	.08	.06	.03
57	Robert Brazile	.10	.08	.04
58	Willie Tullis	.05	.04	.02
59	Archie Manning	.15	.11	.06
60	Gifford Nielsen	.08	.06	.03
61	Harold Bailey	.05	.04	.02
62	Carl Roaches	.08	.06	.03
63	Gregg Bingham	.05	.04	.02
64	Daryl Hunt	.05	.04	.02
65	Gary Green	.05	.04	.02
66	Gary Barbaro	.08	.06	.03
67	Bill Kenney	.08	.06	.03
68	Joe Delaney	.10	.08	.04
69	Henry Marshall	.05	.04	.02
70	Nick Lowery	.10	.08	.04
71	Jeff Gossett	.05	.04	.02
72	Art Still	.10	.08	.04
73	AFC Passing Leader (Ken Anderson)	.40	.30	.15
74	AFC PAssing Yardage Leader (Dan Fouts)	.50	.40	.20
75	AFC Receiving Yardage Leader (Wes Chandler)	.25	.20	.10
76	AFC Kickoff Return Yardage Leader (James Brooks)	.40	.30	.15
77	AFC Punt Return Yardage Leader (Rick Upchurch)	.30	.25	.12
78	AFC Punting Leader (Luke Prestridge)	.15	.11	.06
79	AFC Sacks Leader (Jesse Baker)	.15	.11	.06
80	AFC Rushing Yardage Leader (Freeman McNeil)	.30	.25	.12
81	Ray Guy	.15	.11	.06
82	Jim Plunkett	.15	.11	.06
83	Lester Hayes	.08	.06	.03
84	Kenny King	.05	.04	.02
85	Cliff Branch	.12	.09	.05
86	Todd Christensen	.12	.09	.05
87	Lyle Alzado	.15	.11	.06
88	Ted Hendricks	.20	.15	.08
89	Rod Martin	.10	.08	.04
90	Dave Woodley	.10	.08	.04
91	Ed Newman	.05	.04	.02
92	Earnie Rhone	.05	.04	.02
93	Don McNeal	.05	.04	.02
94	Glenn Blackwood	.08	.06	.03
95	Andra Franklin	.08	.06	.03
96	Nat Moore	.12	.09	.05
97	Lyle Blackwood	.08	.06	.03
98	A.J. Duhe	.10	.08	.04
99	Tony Collins	.08	.06	.03
100	Stanley Morgan	.10	.08	.04
101	Pete Brock	.05	.04	.02
102	Steve Nelson	.05	.04	.02
103	Steve Grogan	.15	.11	.06
104	Mark Van Eeghen	.08	.06	.03
105	Don Hasselbeck	.05	.04	.02
106	John Hannah	.15	.11	.06
107	Mike Haynes	.15	.11	.06
108	Wesley Walker	.10	.08	.04
109	Marvin Powell	.05	.04	.02
110	Joe Klecko	.08	.06	.03
111	Bobby Jackson	.05	.04	.02
112	Richard Todd	.10	.08	.04
113	Lance Mehl	.08	.06	.03
114	Johnny Lam Jones	.10	.08	.04
115	Mark Gastineau	.10	.08	.04
116	Freeman McNeil	.15	.11	.06
117	Franco Harris	.30	.25	.12
118	Mike Webster	.15	.11	.06
119	Mel Blount	.15	.11	.06

120	Donnie Shell	.10	.08	.04
121	Terry Bradshaw	.75	.60	.30
122	John Stallworth	.12	.09	.05
123	Jack Lambert	.25	.20	.10
124	Dwayne Woodruff	.05	.04	.02
125	Bennie Cunningham	.05	.04	.02
126	Charlie Joiner	.20	.15	.08
127	Kellen Winslow	.20	.15	.08
128	Rolf Benirschke	.05	.04	.02
129	Louis Kelcher	.08	.06	.03
130	Chuck Muncie	.08	.06	.03
131	Wes Chandler	.10	.08	.04
132	Gary Johnson	.08	.06	.03
133	James Brooks	.15	.11	.06
134	Dan Fouts	.35	.25	.14
135	Jacob Green	.10	.08	.04
136	Michael Jackson	.05	.04	.02
137	Jim Zorn	.12	.09	.05
138	Sherman Smith	.08	.06	.03
139	Keith Simpson	.05	.04	.02
140	Steve Largent	1.25	.90	.50
141	John Harris	.08	.06	.03
142	Jeff West	.08	.06	.03
143	Ken Anderson (top)	.45	.35	.20
144	Ken Anderson (bottom)	.45	.35	.20
145	Tony Dorsett (top)	.40	.30	.15
146	Tony Dorsett (bottom)	.40	.30	.15
147	Dan Fouts (top)	.40	.30	.15
148	Dan Fouts (bottom)	.40	.30	.15
149	Joe Montana (top)	2.00	1.50	.80
150	Joe Montana (bottom)	2.00	1.50	.80
151	Mark Moseley (top)	.15	.11	.06
152	Mark Moseley (bottom)	.15	.11	.06
153	Richard Todd	.10	.08	.04
154	Butch Johnson	.10	.08	.04
155	Bill (Gary) Hogeboom	.08	.06	.03
156	A.J. Duhe	.08	.06	.03
157	Kurt Sohn	.05	.04	.02
158	Drew Pearson	.10	.08	.04
159	John Riggins	.35	.25	.14
160	Pat Donovan	.05	.04	.02
161	John Hannah	.15	.11	.06
162	Jeff Van Note	.10	.08	.04
163	Randy Cross	.10	.08	.04
164	Marvin Powell	.08	.06	.03
165	Kellen Winslow	.25	.20	.10
166	Dwight Clark	.20	.15	.08
167	Wes Chandler	.08	.06	.03
168	Tony Dorsett	.40	.30	.15
169	Freeman McNeil	.12	.09	.05
170	Ken Anderson	.25	.20	.10
171	Mark Moseley	.05	.04	.02
172	Mark Gastineau	.08	.06	.03
173	Gary Johnson	.05	.04	.02
174	Randy White	.30	.25	.12
175	Ed "Too Tall" Jones	.12	.09	.05
176	Hugh Green	.08	.06	.03
177	Harry Carson	.10	.08	.04
178	Lawrence Taylor	.30	.25	.12
179	Lester Hayes	.08	.06	.03
180	Mark Haynes	.05	.04	.02
181	Dave Jennings	.05	.04	.02
182	Nolan Cromwell	.08	.06	.03
183	Tony Peters	.05	.04	.02
184	Jimmy Cefalo	.05	.04	.02
185	A.J. Duhe	.08	.06	.03
186	John Riggins	.35	.25	.14
187	Charlie Brown	.05	.04	.02
188	Mike Nelms	.05	.04	.02
189	Mark Murphy	.05	.04	.02
190	Fulton Walker	.05	.04	.02
191	Marcus Allen	2.50	2.00	1.00
192	Chip Banks	.08	.06	.03
193	Charlie Brown	.05	.04	.02
194	Bob Crable	.05	.04	.02
195	Vernon Dean	.05	.04	.02
196	Jim McMahon	.75	.60	.30
197	James Robbins	.08	.06	.03
198	Luis Sharpe	.08	.06	.03
199	Rohn Stark	.05	.04	.02
200	Lester Williams	.05	.04	.02
201	Leo Wisniewski	.05	.04	.02
202	Butch Woolfolk	.10	.08	.04
203	Mike Kenn	.10	.08	.04
204	R.C. Thielemann	.05	.04	.02
205	Buddy Curry	.05	.04	.02
206	Steve Bartkowski	.12	.09	.05
207	Alfred Jenkins	.08	.06	.03
208	Don Smith	.05	.04	.02
209	Alfred Jenkins	.08	.06	.03
210	Fulton Kuykendall	.05	.04	.02
211	William Andrews	.10	.08	.04
212	Gary Fencik	.08	.06	.03
213	Walter Payton	1.50	1.25	.60
214	Mike Singletary	1.50	1.25	.60
215	Otis Wilson	.08	.06	.03
216	Matt Suhey	.05	.04	.02
217	Dan Hampton	.20	.15	.08

218	Emery Moorehead	.05	.04	.02
219	Mike Hartenstine	.05	.04	.02
220	Danny White	.20	.15	.08
221	Drew Pearson	.10	.08	.04
222	Rafael Septien	.05	.04	.02
223	Ed "Too Tall" Jones	.15	.11	.06
224	Everson Walls	.10	.08	.04
225	Randy White	.20	.15	.08
226	Harvey Martin	.10	.08	.04
227	Tony Hill	.08	.06	.03
228	John Jefferson	.30	.25	.12
229	Billy Sims	.20	.15	.08
230	Leonard Thompson	.05	.04	.02
231	Ed Murray	.05	.04	.02
232	Doug English	.05	.04	.02
233	Ken Fantetti	.05	.04	.02
234	Tom Skladany	.05	.04	.02
235	Freddie Scott	.05	.04	.02
236	Eric Hipple	.08	.06	.03
237	David Hill	.05	.04	.02
238	John Jefferson	.08	.06	.03
239	Paul Coffman	.05	.04	.02
240	Ezra Johnson	.05	.04	.02
241	Mike Douglass	.05	.04	.02
242	Mark Lee	.08	.06	.03
243	John Anderson	.10	.08	.04
244	Jan Stenerud	.15	.11	.06
245	Lynn Dickey	.10	.08	.04
246	James Lofton	.30	.25	.12
247	Vince Ferragamo	.12	.09	.05
248	Preston Dennard	.05	.04	.02
249	Jack Youngblood	.15	.11	.06
250	Mike Guman	.05	.04	.02
251	LeRoy Irvin	.08	.06	.03
252	Mike Lansford	.05	.04	.02
253	Kent Hill	.05	.04	.02
254	Nolan Cromwell	.05	.04	.02
255	Doug Martin	.05	.04	.02
256	Greg Coleman	.05	.04	.02
257	Ted Brown	.05	.04	.02
258	Mark Mullaney	.05	.04	.02
259	Joe Senser	.08	.06	.03
260	Randy Holloway	.05	.04	.02
261	Matt Blair	.08	.06	.03
262	Sammie White	.10	.08	.04
263	Tommy Kramer	.10	.08	.04
264	NFC Passing Leader (Joe Theismann)	.40	.30	.15
265	NFC Passing Yardage Leader (Joe Montana)	1.50	1.25	.60
266	NFC Receiving Yardage Leader (Dwight Clark)	.25	.20	.10
267	NFC Kickoff Return Yardage Leader (Mike Nelms)	.10	.08	.04
268	NFC Punting Leader (Carl Birdsong)	.10	.08	.04
269	NFC Interceptions Leader (Everson Walls)	.20	.15	.08
270	NFC Sacks Leader (Doug Martin)	.15	.11	.06
271	NFC Rushing Yardage Leader (Tony Dorsett)	.40	.30	.15
272	Russell Erxleben	.05	.04	.02
273	Stan Brock	.05	.04	.02
274	Jeff Groth	.05	.04	.02
275	Bruce Clark	.05	.04	.02
276	Ken Stabler	.30	.25	.12
277	George Rogers	.10	.08	.04
278	Derland Moore	.08	.06	.03
279	Wayne Wilson	.05	.04	.02
280	Lawrence Taylor	.35	.25	.14
281	Harry Carson	.10	.08	.04
282	Brian Kelley	.05	.04	.02
283	Brad Van Pit	.05	.04	.02
284	Earnest Gray	.05	.04	.02
285	Dave Jennings	.05	.04	.02
286	Rob Carpenter	.05	.04	.02
287	Scott Brunner	.05	.04	.02
288	Ron Jaworski	.15	.11	.06
289	Jerry Robinson	.08	.06	.03
290	Frank LeMaster	.05	.04	.02
291	Wilbert Montgomery	.08	.06	.03
292	Tony Franklin	.05	.04	.02
293	Harold Carmichael	.15	.11	.06
294	John Spagnola	.05	.04	.02
295	Herman Edwards	.05	.04	.02
296	Ottis Anderson	.15	.11	.06
297	Carl Birdsong	.05	.04	.02
298	Doug Marsh	.05	.04	.02
299	Neil Lomax	.12	.09	.05
300	Rush Brown	.05	.04	.02
301	Pat Tilley	.08	.06	.03
302	Wayne Morris	.08	.06	.03
303	Dan Dierdorf	.20	.15	.08
304	Roy Green	.30	.25	.12
305	Joe Montana	1.75	1.25	.70
306	Randy Cross	.10	.08	.04
307	Freddie Solomon	.08	.06	.03
308	Jack Reynolds	.10	.08	.04
309	Ronnie Lott	.50	.40	.20
310	Renaldo Nehemiah	.15	.11	.06
311	Russ Francis	.08	.06	.03
312	Dwight Clark	.20	.15	.08
313	Doug Williams	.12	.09	.05
314	Bill Capece	.05	.04	.02
315	Mike Washington	.05	.04	.02
316	Hugh Green	.10	.08	.04
317	Kevin House	.08	.06	.03
318	Lee Roy Selmon	.12	.09	.05
319	Neal Colzie	.10	.08	.04
320	Jimmie Giles	.08	.06	.03
321	Cedric Brown	.05	.04	.02
322	Tony Peters	.05	.04	.02
323	Neal Olkewicz	.05	.04	.02
324	Dexter Manley	.05	.04	.02
325	Joe Theismann	.30	.25	.12
326	Rich Milot	.05	.04	.02
327	Mark Moseley	.08	.06	.03
328	Art Monk	.40	.30	.15
329	Mike Nelms	.08	.06	.03
330	John Riggins	.35	.25	.14

1984 Topps USFL

This 132-card set was Topps' first issue of United States Football League cards, and it's proven to be the most valuable set Topps issued in the 1980s. Several key rookie cards can be found in this set, including Jim Kelly, Herschel Walker, Reggie White, Anthony Carter, Bobby Hebert, Kelvin Bryant and Mike Rozier. Issued as a factory set, cards were printed on white cardboard stock. Bordered in red and blue piping over white space with the USFL logo and "Premier Edition" at the top of the card, a team helmet appears at lower left with the team name in red and the player name in black over a yellow background below the photo. Cards were numbered alphabetically by city name and by the player's last name.

		NM/M	NM	E
Complete Set (132):		300.00	220.00	120.00
Common Player:		1.50	1.25	.60
1	Luther Bradley	1.50	1.25	.60
2	Frank Corral	1.50	1.25	.60
3	Trumaine Johnson	1.50	1.25	.60
4	Greg Landry	1.50	1.25	.60
5	Kit Lathrop	1.50	1.25	.60
6	Kevin Long	1.50	1.25	.60
7	Tim Spencer	1.50	1.25	.60
8	Stan White	1.50	1.25	.60
9	Buddy Aydelette	1.50	1.25	.60
10	Tom Banks	1.50	1.25	.60
11	Fred Bohannon	1.50	1.25	.60
12	Joe Cribbs	1.50	1.25	.60
13	Joey Jones	1.50	1.25	.60
14	Scott Norwood	1.50	1.25	.60
15	Jim Smith	1.50	1.25	.60
16	Cliff Stoudt	1.50	1.25	.60
17	Vince Evans	2.00	1.50	.80
18	Vagas Ferguson	1.50	1.25	.60
19	John Gillen	1.50	1.25	.60
20	Kris Haines	1.50	1.25	.60
21	Glenn Hyde	1.50	1.25	.60
22	Mark Keel	1.50	1.25	.60
23	Garry Lewis	1.50	1.25	.60
24	Doug Plank	1.50	1.25	.60
25	Neil Balholm	1.50	1.25	.60
26	David Dumars	1.50	1.25	.60
27	David Martin	1.50	1.25	.60
28	Craig Penrose	1.50	1.25	.60
29	Dave Stalls	1.50	1.25	.60
30	Harry Sydney RC	1.00	.70	.40
31	Vincent White	1.50	1.25	.60
32	George Yarno	1.50	1.25	.60
33	Kiki DeAyala	1.50	1.25	.60
34	Sam Harrell	1.50	1.25	.60
35	Mike Hawkins	1.50	1.25	.60
36	Jim Kelly RC	25.00	13.00	8.00
37	Mark Rush	1.50	1.25	.60
38	Ricky Sanders RC	3.00	1.50	.90

39	Paul Bergmann	1.50	1.25	.60
40	Tom Dinkel	1.50	1.25	.60
41	Wyatt Henderson	1.50	1.25	.60
42	Vaughan Johnson RC	1.50	1.25	.60
43	Willie McClendon	1.50	1.25	.60
44	Matt Robinson	1.50	1.25	.60
45	George Achica	1.50	1.25	.60
46	Mark Adickes	1.50	1.25	.60
47	Howard Carson	1.50	1.25	.60
48	Kevin Nelson	1.50	1.25	.60
49	Jeff Partridge	1.50	1.25	.60
50	JoJo Townsell	1.50	1.25	.60
51	Eddie Weaver	1.50	1.25	.60
52	Steve Young RC	60.00	30.00	18.00
53	Derrick Crawford	1.50	1.25	.60
54	Walter Lewis	1.50	1.25	.60
55	Phil McKinnely	1.50	1.25	.60
56	Vic Minore	1.50	1.25	.60
57	Gary Shirk	1.50	1.25	.60
58	Reggie White RC	25.00	13.00	8.00
59	Anthony Carter RC	5.00	2.50	1.50
60	John Corker	1.50	1.25	.60
61	David Greenwood	1.50	1.25	.60
62	Bobby Hebert RC	1.50	1.25	.60
63	Derek Holloway	1.50	1.25	.60
64	Ken Lacy	1.50	1.25	.60
65	Tyrone McGriff	1.50	1.25	.60
66	Ray Pinney	1.50	1.25	.60
67	Gary Barbaro	1.50	1.25	.60
68	Sam Bowers	1.50	1.25	.60
69	Clarence Collins	1.50	1.25	.60
70	Willie Harper	1.50	1.25	.60
71	Jim LeClair	1.50	1.25	.60
72	Bob Leopold	1.50	1.25	.60
73	Brian Sipe	2.00	1.50	.80
74	Herschel Walker RC	10.00	5.00	3.00
75	Junior Ah You	1.50	1.25	.60
76	Marcus Dupree RC	2.00	1.50	.80
77	Marcus Marek	1.50	1.25	.60
78	Tim Mazzetti	1.50	1.25	.60
79	Mike Robinson	1.50	1.25	.60
80	Dan Ross	1.50	1.25	.60
81	Mark Schellen	1.50	1.25	.60
82	Johnnie Walton	1.50	1.25	.60
83	Gordon Banks	1.50	1.25	.60
84	Fred Besana	1.50	1.25	.60
85	Dave Browning	1.50	1.25	.60
86	Eric Jordan	1.50	1.25	.60
87	Frank Manumaleuga	1.50	1.25	.60
88	Gary Plummer RC	1.50	1.25	.60
89	Stan Talley	1.50	1.25	.60
90	Arthur Whittington	1.50	1.25	.60
91	Terry Beeson	1.50	1.25	.60
92	Mel Gray RC	2.00	1.50	.80
93	Mike Katolin	1.50	1.25	.60
94	Dewey McClain	1.50	1.25	.60
95	Sidney Thorton	1.50	1.25	.60
96	Doug Williams	2.50	2.00	1.00
97	Kelvin Bryant RC	2.50	2.00	1.00
98	John Bunting	1.50	1.25	.60
99	Irv Eatman RC	2.00	1.50	.80
100	Scott Fitzkee	1.50	1.25	.60
101	Chuck Fusina	1.50	1.25	.60
102	Sean Landeta RC	1.50	1.25	.60
103	David Trout	1.50	1.25	.60
104	Scott Woerner	1.50	1.25	.60
105	Glenn Carano	1.50	1.25	.60
106	Ron Crosby	1.50	1.25	.60
107	Jerry Holmes	1.50	1.25	.60
108	Bruce Huther	1.50	1.25	.60
109	Mike Rozier RC	1.50	1.25	.60
110	Larry Swider	1.50	1.25	.60
111	Danny Buggs	1.50	1.25	.60
112	Putt Choate	1.50	1.25	.60
113	Rich Garza	1.50	1.25	.60
114	Joey Hackett	1.50	1.25	.60
115	Rick Neuheisel	1.50	1.25	.60
116	Mike St. Clair	1.50	1.25	.60
117	Gary Anderson RC	1.50	1.25	.60
118	Zenon Andrusyshyn	1.50	1.25	.60
119	Doug Beaudoin	1.50	1.25	.60
120	Mike Butler	1.50	1.25	.60
121	Willie Gillespie	1.50	1.25	.60
122	Fred Nordgren	1.50	1.25	.60
123	John Reaves	1.50	1.25	.60
124	Eric Truvillion	1.50	1.25	.60
125	Reggie Collier	1.50	1.25	.60
126	Mike Guess	1.50	1.25	.60
127	Mike Hohensee	1.50	1.25	.60
128	Craig James RC	1.50	1.25	.60
129	Eric Robinson	1.50	1.25	.60
130	Billy Taylor	1.50	1.25	.60
131	Joey Walters	1.50	1.25	.60
132	**Checklist 1-132**	3.00	1.50	.90

1984 Topps

Topps' most sought-after NFL set of the decade is notable for its excellent array of rookies: Dickerson, Elway, Marino, Curt Warner, Mark Duper, Willie Gault and Roger Craig are among them. This is one of the better-designed sets of the decade as well. The 396-card set is numbered alphabetically by city and by player name; AFC teams are listed first, while NFC teams are listed after the NFL leaders. Team leader cards, which had for years shown team leaders in several categories, this year showed just one leader. Card fronts show an angled photo in a yellow stripe. The team logo and name appear at the bottom also at an angle. The Pro Bowl designation appears above the team name. Instant Replay cards issued in this set in addition to the player's regular card featured NFL stars in action poses. The score on the Super Bowl card (#9) is incorrect: instead of 28-9, it should read 38-9. (Key: PB - Pro Bowl, IR - Instant Replay)

	NM/M	NM	E
Complete Set (396):	200.00	100.00	60.00
Common Player:	.50	.25	.15
Wax Pack (15):	16.00		
Wax Box (36):	425.00		

		NM/M	NM	E
1	Eric Dickerson (RB)	.50	.25	.15
2	Ali Haji-Sheikh (RB)	.50	.25	.15
3	Franco Harris (RB)	.50	.25	.15
4	Mark Moseley (RB)	.50	.25	.15
5	John Riggins (RB)	.50	.25	.15
6	Jan Stenerud (RB)	.50	.25	.15
7	AFC Championship	.50	.25	.15
8	NFC Championship	.50	.25	.15
9	Super Bowl XVIII	.50	.25	.15
10	Indianapolis Colts Team: (Curtis Dickey)	.50	.25	.15
11	Raul Allegre RC	.50	.25	.15
12	Curtis Dickey	.50	.25	.15
13	Ray Donaldson RC	.50	.25	.15
14	Nesby Glasgow	.50	.25	.15
15	Chris Hinton RC (PB)	.50	.25	.15
16	Vernon Maxwell RC	.50	.25	.15
17	Randy McMillan	.50	.25	.15
18	Mike Pagel	.50	.25	.15
19	Rohn Stark	.50	.25	.15
20	Leo Wisniewski	.50	.25	.15
21	Buffalo Bills Team: (Joe Cribbs)	.50	.25	.15
22	Jerry Butler	.50	.25	.15
23	Joe Danelo	.50	.25	.15
24	Joe Ferguson	.50	.25	.15
25	Steve Freeman	.50	.25	.15
26	Roosevelt Leaks	.50	.25	.15
27	Frank Lewis	.50	.25	.15
28	Eugene Marve	.50	.25	.15
29	Booker Moore	.50	.25	.15
30	Fred Smerlas (PB)	.50	.25	.03
31	Ben Williams	.50	.25	.15
32	Cincinnati Bengals Team: (Cris Collinsworth)	.50	.25	.15
33	Charles Alexander	.50	.25	.15
34	Ken Anderson	.50	.25	.15
35	Ken Anderson (IR)	.50	.25	.15
36	Jim Breech	.50	.25	.15
37	Cris Collinsworth (PB)	.50	.25	.15
38	Cris Collinsworth (IR)	.50	.25	.15
39	Isaac Curtis	.50	.25	.15
40	Eddie Edwards	.50	.25	.15
41	Ray Horton RC	.50	.25	.15
42	Pete Johnson	.50	.25	.15
43	Steve Kreider	.50	.25	.15
44	Max Montoya	.50	.25	.15
45	Anthony Munoz (PB)	.50	.25	.15
46	Reggie Williams	.50	.25	.15
47	Cleveland Browns Team: (Mike Pruitt)	.50	.25	.15
48	Matt Bahr	.50	.25	.15
49	Chip Banks (PB)	.50	.25	.15
50	Tom Cousineau	.50	.25	.15
51	Joe DeLamielleure	.50	.25	.15
52	Doug Dieken	.50	.25	.15
53	Bob Golic RC	.50	.25	.15
54	Bobby Jones	.50	.25	.15
55	Dave Logan	.50	.25	.15
56	Clay Matthews	.50	.25	.15
57	Paul McDonald	.50	.25	.15
58	Ozzie Newsome	.50	.25	.15
59	Ozzie Newsome (IR)	.50	.25	.15
60	Mike Pruitt	.50	.25	.15
61	Steve Watson	.50	.25	.15
62	Barney Chavous RC	.50	.25	.15
63	John Elway RC	20.00	10.00	6.00
64	Steve Foley	.50	.25	.15
65	Tom Jackson	.50	.25	.15
66	Rick Karlis	.50	.25	.15
67	Luke Prestridge	.50	.25	.15
68	Zack Thomas	.50	.25	.15
69	Rich Upchurch	.50	.25	.15
70	Steve Watson	.50	.25	.15
71	Sammy Winder RC	.50	.25	.15
72	Louis Wright (PB)	.50	.25	
73	Houston Oilers Team: (Tim Smith)	.50	.25	.15
74	Jesse Baker	.50	.25	.15
75	Gregg Bingham	.50	.25	.15
76	Robert Brazile	.50	.25	.15
77	Steve Brown	.50	.25	.15
78	Chris Dressel	.50	.25	.15
79	Doug France	.50	.25	.15
80	Florian Kempf	.50	.25	.15
81	Carl Roaches	.50	.25	.15
82	Tim Smith RC	.50	.25	.15
83	Willie Tullis	.50	.25	.15
84	Kansas City Chiefs Team: (Carlos Carson)			
85	Mike Bell	.50	.25	.15
86	Theotis Brown	.50	.25	.15
87	Carlos Carson (PB)	.50	.25	.15
88	Carlos Carson (IR)	.50	.25	.15
89	Deron Cherry RC (PB)	.50	.25	.15
90	Gary Green (PB)	.50	.25	.15
91	Billy Jackson	.50	.25	.15
92	Bill Kenney	.50	.25	.15
93	Bill Kenney (IR)	.50	.25	.15
94	Nick Lowery	.50	.25	.15
95	Henry Marshall	.50	.25	.15
96	Art Still	.50	.25	
97	Los Angeles Raiders Team: (Todd Christensen)	.50	.25	.15
98	Marcus Allen	.50	.25	.15
99	Marcus Allen IR (IR)	.50	.25	.15
100	Lyle Alzado	.50	.25	.15
101	Lyle Alzado (IR)	.50	.25	.15
102	Chris Bahr	.50	.25	.15
103	Malcolm Barnwell	.50	.25	.15
104	Cliff Branch	.50	.25	.15
105	Todd Christensen (PB)	.50	.25	.15
106	Todd Christensen (IR)	.50	.25	.15
107	Ray Guy	.50	.25	.15
108	Frank Hawkins	.50	.25	.15
109	Lester Hayes (PB)	.50	.25	.03
110	Ted Hendricks (PB)	.20	.15	.08
111	Howie Long RC (PB)	5.00	2.50	1.50
112	Rod Martin (PB)	.50	.25	.15
113	Vann McElroy RC (PB)	.50	.25	.15
114	Jim Plunkett	.50	.25	.15
115	Greg Pruitt (PB)	.50	.25	.15
116	Miami Dolphins Team: (Mark Duper)	.50	.25	.15
117	Bob Baumhower (PB)	.50	.25	.15
118	Doug Betters RC (PB)	.50	.25	.15
119	A.J. Duhe	.50	.25	.15
120	Mark Duper RC (PB)	.50	.25	.15
121	Andre Franklin (Andra)	.50	.25	.15
122	William Judson	.50	.25	.15
123	Dan Marino RC (PB)	20.00	10.00	6.00
124	Dan Marino IR (IR)	25.00	13.00	8.00
125	Nat Moore	.50	.25	.15
126	Ed Newman (PB)	.50	.25	.15
127	Reggie Roby RC	.50	.25	.15
128	Gerald Small	.50	.25	.15
129	Dwight Stephenson RC	3.00	1.50	.90
130	Uwe Von Schamann	.50	.25	.15
131	New England Patriots Team: (Tony Collins)	.50	.25	.15
132	Rich Camarillo (PB)	.50	.25	.15
133	Tony Collins (PB)	.50	.25	.15
134	Tony Collins (IR)	.50	.25	.15
135	Bob Cryder	.50	.25	.15
136	Steve Grogan	.50	.25	.15
137	John Hannah (PB)	.50	.25	.15
138	Brian Holloway RC (PB)	.50	.25	.15
139	Roland James	.50	.25	.15
140	Stanley Morgan	.50	.25	.15
141	Rick Sanford	.50	.25	.15
142	Mosi Tatupu	.50	.25	.15
143	Andre Tippett RC	2.00	1.00	.60
144	New York Jets Team: (Wesley Walker)	.50	.25	.15
145	Jerome Barkum	.50	.25	.15
146	Mark Gastineau (PB)	.50	.25	.03
147	Mark Gastineau (IR)	.50	.25	.15
148	Bruce Harper	.50	.25	.15
149	Johnny "Lam" Jones	.50	.25	.15
150	Joe Klecko (PB)	.50	.25	.15
151	Pat Leahy	.50	.25	.15
152	Freeman McNeil	.20	.15	.15
153	Lance Mehl	.50	.25	.15
154	Marvin Powell (PB)	.50	.25	.15
155	Darrol Ray	.50	.25	.15
156	Pat Ryan	.50	.25	.15
157	Kirk Springs	.50	.25	.15
158	Wesley Walker	.50	.25	.15
159	Pittsburgh Steelers Team: (Franco Harris)	.50	.25	.15
160	Walter Abercrombie RC	.50	.25	.15
161	Gary Anderson (PB)	.50	.25	.15
162	Terry Bradshaw	2.50	1.50	.90
163	Craig Colquitt	.50	.25	.15
164	Bennie Cunningham	.50	.25	.15
165	Franco Harris	.50	.25	.15
166	Franco Harris (IR)	.50	.25	.15
167	Jack Lambert (PB)	.50	.25	.15
168	Jack Lambert (IR)	.50	.25	.15
169	Frank Pollard	.50	.25	.15
170	Donnie Shell	.50	.25	.15
171	Mike Webster (PB)	.50	.25	.15
172	Keith Willis	.50	.25	.15
173	Rick Woods	.50	.25	.15
174	San Diego Chargers Team: (Kellen Winslow)	.50	.25	.15
175	Rolf Benirschke	.50	.25	.15
176	James Brooks	.50	.25	.15
177	Maury Buford	.50	.25	.15
178	Wes Chandler (PB)	.50	.25	.15
179	Dan Fouts (PB)	1.50	.75	.45
180	Dan Fouts (IR)	.50	.25	.15
181	Charlie Joiner	.50	.25	.15
182	Linden King	.50	.25	.15
183	Chuck Muncie	.50	.25	.15
184	Billy Ray Smith RC	.50	.25	.15
185	Danny Walters	.50	.25	.15
186	Kellen Winslow (PB)	.50	.25	.15
187	Kellen Winslow (IR)	.50	.25	.15
188	Seattle Seahawks Team: (Curt Warner)	.50	.25	.15
189	Steve August	.50	.25	.15
190	Dave Brown	.50	.25	.15
191	Zachary Dixon	.50	.25	.15
192	Kenny Easley	.50	.25	.15
193	Jacob Green	.50	.25	.15
194	Norm Johnson	.50	.25	.15
195	Dave Krieg RC	1.50	.75	.45
196	Steve Largent	.50	.25	.15
197	Steve Largent (IR)	.50	.25	.15
198	Curt Warner RC (PB)	.50	.25	.15
199	Curt Warner (IR)	.50	.25	.15
200	Jeff West	.50	.25	.15
201	Charley Young	.50	.25	.15
202	Passing Leaders: (Dan Marino, Steve Bartkowski) (LL)	2.00	1.00	.60
203	Receiving Leaders: (Todd Christensen, Charlie Brown, Earnest Gray, Roy Green)	.50	.25	.15
204	Rushing Leaders: (Curt Warner, Eric Dickerson)	.50	.25	.15
205	Scoring Leaders: (Gary Anderson, Mark Moseley)	.50	.25	.15
206	Interception Leaders: (Vann McElroy, Ken Riley, Mark Murphy)	.50	.25	.15
207	Punting Leaders: (Rich Camarillo, Greg Coleman)	.50	.25	.15
208	Atlanta Falcons Team: (William Andrews)	.50	.25	.15
209	William Andrews	.50	.25	.15
210	William Andrews (IR)	.50	.25	.15
211	Stacey Bailey RC	.50	.25	.15

212	Steve Bartkowski	.50	.25	.15
213	Steve Barkowski (IR)	.50	.25	.15
214	Ralph Giacomarro	.50	.25	.15
215	Billy Johnson (PB)	.50	.25	.15
216	Mike Kenn (PB)	.50	.25	.15
217	Mick Luckhurst	.50	.25	.15
218	Gerald Riggs	.50	.25	.15
219	R.C. Thielemann (PB)	.50	.25	.15
220	Jeff Van Note	.50	.25	.15
221	Walter Payton (TL)	1.50	.75	.45
222	Jim Covert RC	.50	.25	.15
223	Leslie Frazier	.50	.25	.15
224	Willie Gault RC	.50	.25	.15
225	Mike Hartenstine	.50	.25	.15
226	Noah Jackson	.50	.25	.15
227	Jim McMahon	.50	.25	.15
228	Walter Payton (PB)	5.00	2.50	1.50
229	Walter Payton IR (IR)	1.50	.75	.45
230	Mike Richardson RC	.50	.25	.15
231	Terry Schmidt	.50	.25	.15
232	Mike Singletary (PB)	.50	.25	.15
233	Matt Suhey	.50	.25	.15
234	Bob Thomas	.50	.25	.15
235	Dallas Cowboys Team:			
	(Tony Dorsett)	.50	.25	.15
236	Bob Breunig	.50	.25	.15
237	Doug Cosbie (PB)	.50	.25	.15
238	Tony Dorsett (PB)	1.50	.75	.45
239	Tony Dorsett (IR)	.50	.25	.15
240	John Dutton	.50	.25	.15
241	Tony Hill	.50	.25	.15
242	Ed "Too Tall" Jones (PB)	.50	.25	.15
243	Drew Pearson	.50	.25	.15
244	Rafael Septien	.50	.25	.15
245	Ron Springs	.50	.25	.15
246	Dennis Thurman	.50	.25	.15
247	Everson Walls (PB)	.50	.25	.15
248	Danny White	.50	.25	.15
249	Randy White (PB)	.50	.25	.15
250	Detroit Lions Team: (Billy			
	Sims)	.50	.25	.15
251	Jeff Chadwick RC	.50	.25	.15
252	Garry Cobb	.50	.25	.15
253	Doug English (PB)	.50	.25	.15
254	William Gay	.50	.25	.15
255	Eric Hipple	.50	.25	.15
256	James Jones RC	.50	.25	.15
257	Bruce McNorton	.50	.25	.15
258	Ed Murray	.50	.25	.15
259	Ulysses Norris	.50	.25	.15
260	Billy Sims	.50	.25	.15
261	Billy Sims (IR)	.50	.25	.15
262	Leonard Thompson	.50	.25	.15
263	Green Bay Packers			
	Team: (James Lofton)	.50	.25	.15
264	John Anderson	.50	.25	.15
265	Paul Coffman (PB)	.50	.25	.15
266	Lynn Dickey	.50	.25	.15
267	Gerry Ellis	.50	.25	.15
268	John Jefferson	.50	.25	.15
269	John Jefferson (IR)	.50	.25	.15
270	Ezra Johnson	.50	.25	.15
271	Tim Lewis	.50	.25	.15
272	James Lofton (PB)	.50	.25	.15
273	James Lofton (IR)	.50	.25	.15
274	Larry McCarren (PB)	.50	.25	.15
275	Jan Stenerud	.50	.25	.15
276	Eric Dickerson (TL)	.50	.25	.15
277	Mike Barber	.50	.25	.15
278	Jim Collins	.50	.25	.15
279	Nolan Cromwell (PB)	.50	.25	.15
280	Eric Dickerson RC (PB)	5.00	2.50	1.50
281	Eric Dickerson IR (IR)	2.00	1.50	.80
282	George Farmer	.50	.25	.15
283	Vince Ferragamo	.50	.25	.15
284	Kent Hill (PB)	.50	.25	.15
285	John Misko	.50	.25	.15
286	Jackie Slater RC (PB)	2.50	1.25	75
287	Jack Youngblood	.50	.25	.15
288	Minnesota Vikings Team:			
	(Darrin Nelson)	.50	.25	.15
289	Ted Brown	.50	.25	.15
290	Greg Coleman	.50	.25	.15
291	Steve Dils	.50	.25	.15
292	Tony Galbreath	.50	.25	.15
293	Tommy Kramer	.50	.25	.15
294	Doug Martin	.50	.25	.15
295	Darrin Nelson RC	.50	.25	.15
296	Benny Ricardo	.50	.25	.15
297	John Swain	.50	.25	.15
298	John Turner	.50	.25	.15

299	New Orleans Saints			
	Team: (George			
	Rogers)	.50	.25	.15
300	Morten Andersen RC	2.50	1.25	.75
301	Russell Erxleben	.50	.25	.15
302	Jeff Groth	.50	.25	.15
303	Rickey Jackson RC (PB)	5.00	2.50	1.50
304	Johnnie Poe	.50	.25	.15
305	George Rogers	.50	.25	.15
306	Richard Todd	.50	.25	.15
307	Jim Wilks	.50	.25	.15
308	Dave Wilson	.50	.25	.15
309	Wayne Wilson	.50	.25	.15
310	New York Giants Team:			
	(Earnest Gray)	.50	.25	.15
311	Leon Bright	.50	.25	.15
312	Scott Brunner	.50	.25	.15
313	Rob Carpenter	.50	.25	.15
314	Harry Carson (PB)	.50	.25	.15
315	Earnest Gray	.50	.25	.15
316	Ali Haji-Sheikh (PB)	.50	.25	.15
317	Mark Haynes (PB)	.50	.25	.15
318	Dave Jennings	.50	.25	.15
319	Brian Kelley	.50	.25	.15
320	Phil Simms	.50	.25	.15
321	Lawrence Taylor (PB)	1.00	.50	.25
322	Lawrence Taylor IR (IR)	.50	.25	.15
323	Brad Van Pelt	.50	.25	.15
324	Butch Woolfolk	.50	.25	.15
325	Philadelphia Eagles			
	Team: (Mike Quick)	.50	.25	.15
326	Harold Carmichael	.50	.25	.15
327	Herman Edwards	.50	.25	.15
328	Michael Haddix	.50	.25	.15
329	Dennis Harrison	.50	.25	.15
330	Ron Jaworski	.50	.25	.15
331	Wilbert Montgomery	.50	.25	.15
332	Hubert Oliver	.50	.25	.15
333	Mike Quick RC (PB)	.50	.25	.15
334	Jerry Robinson	.50	.25	.15
335	Max Runager	.50	.25	.15
336	Michael Williams	.50	.25	.15
337	St. Louis Cardinals Team:			
	(Ottis Anderson)	.50	.25	.15
338	Ottis Anderson	.50	.25	.15
339	Al "Bubba" Baker	.50	.25	.15
340	Carl Birdsong (PB)	.50	.25	.15
341	David Galloway	.50	.25	.15
342	Roy Green (PB)	.50	.25	.15
343	Roy Green (IR)	.50	.25	.15
344	Curtis Greer RC	.50	.25	.15
345	Neil Lomax	.50	.25	.15
346	Doug Marsh	.50	.25	.15
347	Stump Mitchell	.50	.25	.15
348	Lionel Washington RC	.50	.25	.15
349	San Francisco 49ers			
	Team: (Dwight Clark)	.50	.25	.15
350	Dwaine Board	.50	.25	.15
351	Dwight Clark	.50	.25	.15
352	Dwight Clark (IR)	.50	.25	.15
353	Roger Craig RC	3.00	1.50	.75
354	Fred Dean	.50	.25	.15
355	Fred Dean (IR)	.50	.25	.15
356	Dwight Hicks (PB)	.50	.25	.15
357	Ronnie Lott (PB)	.50	.25	.15
358	Joe Montana (PB)	3.00	1.50	.90
359	Joe Montana IR (IR)	1.50	.75	.45
360	Freddie Solomon	.50	.25	.15
361	Wendell Tyler	.50	.25	.15
362	Ray Wersching	.50	.25	.15
363	Eric Wright RC	.50	.25	.15
364	Tampa Bay Buccaneers			
	Team: (Kevin House)	.50	.25	.15
365	Gerald Carter	.50	.25	.15
366	Hugh Green (PB)	.50	.25	.15
367	Kevin House	.50	.25	.15
368	Michael Morton	.50	.25	.15
369	James Owens	.50	.25	.15
370	Booker Reese	.50	.25	.15
371	Lee Roy Selmon (PB)	.50	.25	.15
372	Jack Thompson	.50	.25	.15
373	James Wilder	.50	.25	.15
374	Steve Wilson	.50	.25	.15
375	Washington Redskins			
	Team: (John Riggins)	.50	.25	.15
376	Jeff Bostic (PB)	.50	.25	.15
377	Charlie Brown (PB)	.50	.25	.15
378	Charlie Brown (IR)	.50	.25	.15
379	Dave Butz (PB)	.50	.25	.15
380	Darrell Green RC	4.00	2.00	1.20
381	Russ Grimm RC (PB)	4.00	2.00	1.20
382	Joe Jacoby (PB)	.50	.25	.15
383	Dexter Manley	.50	.25	.15

384	Art Monk	.50	.25	.15
385	Mark Moseley	.50	.25	.15
386	Mark Murphy (PB)	.50	.25	.16
387	Mike Nelms	.50	.25	.15
388	John Riggins	.50	.25	.15
389	John Riggins (IR)	.50	.25	.15
390	Joe Theismann (PB)	.50	.25	.15
391	Joe Theismann (IR)	.50	.25	.15
392	Don Warren	.50	.25	.15
393	Joe Washington	.50	.25	.15
394	Checklist 1-132	.50	.25	.15
395	Checklist 133-264	.50	.25	.15
396	Checklist 265-396	.50	.25	.15

1984 Topps Glossy Send-In

This 30-card set was available only through a mail-in offer. Cards show an action pose of the player on the front with a blackboard diagram as a background. His name, team and position are at the bottom. Backs identify the player, set and card number.

		NM/M	NM	E
	Complete Set (30):	14.00	10.50	5.75
	Common Player:	.25	.20	.10
1	Marcus Allen	1.25	.90	.50
2	John Riggins	.40	.30	.20
3	Walter Payton	2.00	1.50	.80
4	Tony Dorsett	1.00	.75	.40
5	Franco Harris	.75	.57	.30
6	Curt Warner	.40	.30	.20
7	Eric Dickerson	2.50	1.85	1.00
8	Mike Pruitt	.25	.20	.10
9	Ken Anderson	.25	.20	.10
10	Dan Fouts	.50	.37	.20
11	Terry Bradshaw	.75	.57	.30
12	Joe Theismann	.40	.30	.20
13	Joe Montana	2.00	1.50	.80
14	Danny White	.25	.20	.10
15	Kellen Winslow	.25	.20	.10
16	Wesley Walker	.25	.20	.10
17	Drew Pearson	.25	.20	.10
18	James Lofton	.25	.20	.10
19	Cris Collinsworth	.25	.20	.10
20	Dwight Clark	.25	.20	.10
21	Mark Gastineau	.25	.20	.10
22	Lawrence Taylor	.40	.30	.20
23	Randy White	.25	.20	.10
24	Ed "Too Tall" Jones	.25	.20	.10
25	Jack Lambert	.25	.20	.10
26	Fred Dean	.25	.20	.10
27	Jan Stenerud	.40	.30	.20
28	Bruce Harper	.25	.20	.10
29	Todd Christensen	.25	.20	.10
30	Greg Pruitt	.25	.20	.10

1984 Topps NFL Stars

This 11-card set was included, one per pack, in the 1984 Topps football card wax packs. Styled almost exactly as the 1985 NFL Stars set a year later, the glossy cards included an action photo of the player bordered in blue, plus the NFL logo and the player name at the bottom of the card. Cards were printed on heavy white cardboard stock.

		NM/M	NM	E
	Complete Set (11):	6.00	4.50	2.50
	Common Player:	.25	.20	.10
1	Curt Warner	.40	.30	.20
2	Eric Dickerson	2.50	1.85	1.00
3	Dan Marino	2.00	1.50	.80
4	Steve Bartkowski	.25	.20	.10
5	Todd Christensen	.25	.20	.10
6	Roy Green	.25	.20	.10
7	Charlie Brown	.25	.20	.10
8	Earnest Gray	.25	.20	.10
9	Mark Gastineau	.25	.20	.10
10	Fred Dean	.25	.20	.10
11	Lawrence Taylor	.40	.30	.20

1984 Topps Play Cards

The 27-card, standard-size set was inserted in each pack of 1984 Topps Football. The card fronts describe prizes for the collectors and game rules, as well as the number of yards gained. Collectors had to collect at least 25 yards for five 1984 Glossy inserts. The card backs of the Play Cards contain game rules.

		NM/M	NM	E
Complete Set (27):		15.00	11.00	6.00
Common Player:		.60	.45	.25
1	**Houston Oilers** (2 yards gained)	.60	.45	.25
2	**Houston Oilers** (3 yards gained)	.60	.45	.25
3	**Cleveland Browns** (4 yards gained)	.60	.45	.25
4	**Cleveland Browns** (5 yards gained)	.60	.45	.25
5	**Cincinnati Bengals** (6 yards gained)	.60	.45	.25
6	**Pittsburgh Steelers** (7 yards gained)	.75	.60	.30
7	**New Orleans Saints** (8 yards gained)	.75	.60	.30
8	**New York Giants** (2 yards gained)	.60	.45	.25
9	**Washington Redskins** (3 yards gained)	.75	.60	.30
10	**Green Bay Packers** (4 yards gained)	.60	.45	.25
11	**Atlanta Falcons** (5 yards gained)	.60	.45	.25
12	**Detroit Lions** (6 yards gained)	.60	.45	.25
13	**New England Patriots** (7 yards gained)	.60	.45	.25
14	**New York Jets** (8 yards gained)	.75	.60	.30
15	**Buffalo Bills** (2 yards gained)	.60	.45	.25
16	**Kansas City Chiefs** (3 yards gained)	.60	.45	.25
17	**Miami Dolphins** (4 yards gained)	.75	.60	.30
18	**San Diego Chargers** (5 yards gained)	.60	.45	.25
19	**Seattle Seahawks** (6 yards gained)	.60	.45	.25
20	**Seattle Seahawks** (7 yards gained)	.60	.45	.25
21	**Dallas Cowboys** (8 yards gained)	1.00	.70	.40
22	**St. Louis Cardinals** (2 yards gained)	.60	.45	.25
23	**Chicago Bears** (3 yards gained)	.60	.45	.25
24	**San Francisco 49ers** (4 yards gained)	1.00	.70	.40
25	**Philadelphia Eagles** (5 yards gained)	.60	.45	.25
26	**Minnesota Vikings** (6 yards gained)	.60	.45	.25
27	**Los Angeles Rams** (7 yards gained)	.75	.60	.30

1984 Topps Stickers

Topps has followed its same format for these stickers, except some of the stickers come in pairs, which are listed in parentheses. Those without are full stickers, comprising the entire card. An album, featuring Charlie Joiner on the front and Dan Fouts on the back, was also issued, as were foil stickers.

		NM/M	NM	E
Complete Set (283):		35.00	26.00	14.00
Common Player:		.05	.04	.02
1	**Super Bowl XVIII** (Plunkett/ Allen)	.35	.25	.14
2	**Super Bowl XVIII** (Plunkett/ Allen)	.15	.11	.06
3	**Super Bowl XVIII** (Plunkett/ Allen)	.15	.11	.06
4	**Super Bowl XVIII** (Plunkett/ Allen)	.15	.11	.06
5	Marcus Allen (Super Bowl MVP)	.75	.60	.30
6	Walter Payton	1.00	.70	.40
7	Mike Richardson (157)	.03	.02	.01
8	Jim McMahon (158)	.10	.08	.04
9	Mike Hartenstine (159)	.05	.04	.02
10	Mike Singletary	.20	.15	.08
11	Willie Gault	.10	.08	.04
12	Terry Schmidt (162)	.05	.04	.02
13	Emery Moorehead (163)	.05	.04	.02
14	Leslie Frazier (164)	.06	.05	.02
15	Jack Thompson (165)	.05	.04	.02
16	Booker Reese (166)	.05	.04	.02
17	James Wilder (166)	.05	.04	.02
18	Lee Roy Selmon (167)	.08	.06	.03
19	Hugh Green	.06	.05	.02
20	Gerald Carter (170)	.05	.04	.02
21	Steve Wilson (171)	.05	.04	.02
22	Michael Morton (172)	.05	.04	.02
23	Kevin House	.05	.04	.02
24	Ottis Anderson	.12	.09	.05
25	Lionel Washington (175)	.08	.06	.03
26	Pat Tilley (176)	.05	.04	.02
27	Curtis Greer (177)	.05	.04	.02
28	Roy Green	.08	.06	.03
29	Carl Bridsong	.05	.04	.02
30	Neil Lomax (180)	.06	.05	.02
31	Lee Nelson (181)	.05	.04	.02
32	Stump Mitchell (182)	.04	.03	.02
33	Tony Hill (183)	.05	.04	.02
34	Everson Walls (184)	.05	.04	.02
35	Danny White (185)	.08	.06	.03
36	Tony Dorsett	.40	.30	.15
37	Ed "Too Tall" Jones	.12	.09	.05
38	Rafael Septien (188)	.05	.04	.02
39	Doug Crosbie (189)	.05	.04	.02
40	Drew Pearson (190)	.06	.05	.02
41	Randy White	.20	.15	.08
42	Ron Jaworski	.10	.08	.04
43	Anthony Griggs (193)	.05	.04	.02
44	Hubert Oliver (194)	.05	.04	.02
45	Wilbert Montgomery (195)	.05	.04	.02
46	Dennis Harrison	.05	.04	.02
47	Mike Quick	.08	.06	.03
48	Jerry Robinson (198)	.04	.03	.02
49	Michael Williams (199)	.05	.04	.02
50	Herman Edwards (200)	.05	.04	.02
51	Steve Bartkowski (201)	.06	.05	.02
52	Mick Luckhurst (202)	.05	.04	.02
53	Mike Pitts (203)	.05	.04	.02
54	William Andrews	.10	.08	.04
55	R.C. Thielemann	.05	.04	.02
56	Buddy Curry (206)	.05	.04	.02
57	Billy Johnson (207)	.04	.03	.02
58	Ralph Giacomaro (208)	.05	.04	.02
59	Mike Kenn	.08	.06	.03
60	Joe Montana	1.75	1.25	.70
61	Fred Dean (211)	.05	.04	.02
62	Dwight Clark (212)	.10	.08	.04
63	Wendell Tyler (213)	.05	.04	.02
64	Dwight Hicks	.05	.04	.02
65	Ronnie Lott	.25	.20	.10

		NM/M	NM	E
66	Roger Craig (216)	.40	.30	.15
67	Fred Solomon (217)	.05	.04	.02
68	Ray Wersching (218)	.05	.04	.02
69	Brad Van Pelt (219)	.05	.04	.02
70	Butch Woolfolk (220)	.05	.04	.02
71	Terry Kinard (221)	.05	.04	.02
72	Lawrence Taylor	.35	.25	.14
73	Aji Haji-Sheikh	.05	.04	.02
74	Mark Haynes (224)	.05	.04	.02
75	Rob Carpenter (225)	.05	.04	.02
76	Earnest Gray (226)	.05	.04	.02
77	Harry Carson	.10	.08	.04
78	Billy Sims	.15	.11	.06
79	Ed Murray (229)	.05	.04	.02
80	William Gay (230)	.05	.04	.02
81	Leonard Thompson (231)	.05	.04	.02
82	Doug English	.08	.06	.03
83	Eric Hipple	.08	.06	.03
84	Ken Fantetti (234)	.05	.04	.02
85	Bruce McNorton (235)	.05	.04	.02
86	James Jones (236)	.05	.04	.02
87	Lynn Dickey (237)	.06	.05	.02
88	Ezra Johnson (238)	.05	.04	.02
89	Jan Stenerud (239)	.08	.06	.03
90	James Lofton	.20	.15	.08
91	Larry McCarren	.05	.04	.02
92	John Jefferson (242)	.05	.04	.02
93	Mike Douglass (243)	.05	.04	.02
94	Gerry Ellis (244)	.05	.04	.02
95	Paul Coffman	.05	.04	.02
96	Eric Dickerson	1.00	.70	.40
97	Jackie Slater (247)	.20	.15	.08
98	Carl Ekern (248)	.05	.04	.02
99	Vince Ferragamo (249)	.06	.05	.02
100	Kent Hill	.05	.04	.02
101	Nolan Cromwell	.08	.06	.03
102	Jack Youngblood (252)	.10	.08	.04
103	John Misko (253)	.05	.04	.02
104	Mike Barber (254)	.07	.05	.03
105	Jeff Bostic (255)	.05	.04	.02
106	Mark Murphy (256)	.05	.04	.02
107	Joe Jacoby (257)	.05	.04	.02
108	John Riggins	.25	.20	.10
109	Joe Theismann	.30	.25	.12
110	Russ Grimm (260)	.05	.04	.02
111	Neal Olkewicz (261)	.07	.05	.03
112	Charlie Brown (262)	.05	.04	.02
113	Dave Butz	.08	.06	.03
114	George Rogers	.10	.08	.04
115	Jim Kovach (265)	.05	.04	.02
116	Dave Wilson (266)	.05	.04	.02
117	Johnnie Poe (267)	.05	.04	.02
118	Russell Erxleben	.05	.04	.02
119	Rickey Jackson	.50	.40	.20
120	Jeff Groth (270)	.05	.04	.02
121	Richard Todd (271)	.06	.05	.02
122	Wayne Wilson (272)	.05	.04	.02
123	Steve Dils (273)	.05	.04	.02
124	Benny Ricardo (274)	.05	.04	.02
125	John Turner (275)	.05	.04	.02
126	Ted Brown	.05	.04	.02
127	Greg Coleman	.05	.04	.02
128	Darrin Nelson (278)	.05	.04	.02
129	Scott Studwell (279)	.06	.05	.02
130	Tommy Kramer (280)	.06	.05	.02
131	Doug Martin	.05	.04	.02
132	Nolan Cromwell (144, All-Pro)	7.50	5.75	3.00
133	Carl Birdsong (145, All-Pro)	.10	.08	.04
134	Deron Cherry (146, All-Pro)	.20	.15	.08
135	Ronnie Lott (147, All-Pro)	.30	.25	.12
136	Lester Hayes (148, All-Pro)	.10	.08	.04
137	Lawrence Taylor (149, All-Pro)	.30	.25	.12
138	Jack Lambert (150, All-Pro)	.20	.15	.08
139	Chip Banks (151, All-Pro)	.10	.08	.04
140	Lee Roy Selmon (152, All-Pro)	.15	.11	.06
141	Fred Smerlas (153, All-Pro)	.10	.08	.04
142	Doug English (154, All-Pro)	.10	.08	.04
143	Doug Betters (155, All-Pro)	.10	.08	.04
144	Dan Marino (132, All-Pro)	3.00	2.25	1.25
145	Ali Haji-Sheikh (133, All-Pro)	.10	.08	.04
146	Eric Dickerson (134, All-Pro)	.65	.50	.25
147	Curt Warner (135, All-Pro)	.15	.11	.06
148	James Lofton (136, All-Pro)	.25	.20	.10
149	Todd Christensen (All-Pro)	.15	.11	.06

150	Cris Collinsworth (All-Pro)	.20	.15	.08
151	Mike Kenn (139, All-Pro)	.10	.08	.04
152	Russ Grimm (140, All-Pro)	.10	.08	.04
153	Jeff Bostic (141, All-Pro)	.10	.08	.04
154	John Hannah (142, All-Pro)	.15	.11	.06
155	Anthony Munoz (143, All-Pro)	.20	.15	.08
156	Ken Anderson	.35	.25	.14
157	Pete Johnson (7)	.05	.04	.02
158	Reggie Williams (8)	.06	.05	.02
159	Isaac Curtis (9)	.05	.04	.02
160	Anthony Munoz	.20	.15	.08
161	Cris Collinsworth	.15	.11	.06
162	Charles Alexander (12)	.05	.04	.02
163	Ray Horton (13)	.10	.08	.04
164	Steve Keider (14)	.05	.04	.02
165	Ben Williams (15)	.05	.04	.02
166	Frank Lewis (16)	.08	.06	.03
167	Roosevelt Leaks (17)	.05	.04	.02
168	Joe Ferguson	.08	.06	.03
169	Fred Smerlas	.08	.06	.03
170	Joe Danelo (20)	.05	.04	.02
171	Chris Keating (21)	.05	.04	.02
172	Jerry Butler (22)	.05	.04	.02
173	Eugene Marve	.05	.04	.02
174	Louis Wright	.08	.06	.03
175	Barney Chavous (25)	.10	.08	.04
176	Zack Thomas (26)	.05	.04	.02
177	Luke Prestridge (27)	.05	.04	.02
178	Steve Watson	.08	.06	.03
179	John Elway	5.00	3.75	2.00
180	Steve Foley (30)	.05	.04	.02
181	Sammy Winder (31)	.10	.08	.04
182	Rick Upchurch (32)	.05	.04	.02
183	Bobby Jones (33)	.08	.06	.03
184	Matt Bahr (34)	.05	.04	.02
185	Doug Dieken (35)	.05	.04	.02
186	Mike Pruitt	.08	.06	.03
187	Chip Banks	.10	.08	.04
188	Tom Cousineau (38)	.05	.04	.02
189	Paul McDonald (39)	.05	.04	.02
190	Clay Matthews (40)	.08	.06	.03
191	Ozzie Newsome	.20	.15	.08
192	Dan Fouts	.40	.30	.15
193	Chuck Muncie (43)	.05	.04	.02
194	Linden King (44)	.05	.04	.02
195	Charlie Joiner (45)	.08	.06	.03
196	Wes Chandler	.08	.06	.03
197	Kellen Winslow	.20	.15	.08
198	James Brooks (48)	.10	.08	.04
199	Mike Green (49)	.05	.04	.02
200	Rolf Benirschke (58)	.05	.04	.02
201	Henry Marshall (51)	.05	.04	.02
202	Nick Lowery (52)	.06	.05	.02
203	Jerry Blanton (53)	.05	.04	.02
204	Bill Kenney	.08	.06	.03
205	Carlos Carson	.08	.06	.03
206	Billy Jackson (56)	.05	.04	.02
207	Art Still (57)	.05	.04	.02
208	Theotis Brown (58)	.05	.04	.02
209	Deron Cherry	.25	.20	.10
210	Curtis Dickey	.08	.06	.03
211	Nesby Glasgow (61)	.05	.04	.02
212	Mike Pagel (62)	.05	.04	.02
213	Ray Donaldson (63)	.05	.04	.02
214	Raul Allegre	.05	.04	.02
215	Chris Hinton	.30	.25	.12
216	Rohn Stark (66)	.08	.06	.03
217	Randy McMillan (67)	.08	.06	.03
218	Vernon Maxwell (68)	.05	.04	.02
219	A.J. Duhe (69)	.10	.08	.04
220	Andra Franklin (70)	.05	.04	.02
221	Ed Newman (71)	.05	.04	.02
222	Dan Marino	7.50	5.75	3.00
223	Doug Betters	.08	.06	.03
224	Bob Baumhower (74)	.05	.04	.02
225	Reggie Roby (75)	.08	.06	.03
226	Dwight Stephenson (76)	.08	.06	.03
227	Mark Duper	.40	.30	.15
228	Mark Gastineau	.15	.11	.06
229	Freeman McNeil (79)	.08	.06	.03
230	Bruce Harper (80)	.05	.04	.02
231	Wesley Walker (81)	.06	.05	.02
232	Marvin Powell	.08	.06	.03
233	Joe Klecko	.08	.06	.03
234	Johnny Lam Jones (84)	.05	.04	.02
235	Lance Mehl (85)	.05	.04	.02
236	Pat Ryan (86)	.05	.04	.02
237	Florian Kempf (87)	.05	.04	.02
238	Carl Roaches (88)	.05	.04	.02
239	Gregg Bigham (89)	.05	.04	.02
240	Tim Smith	.05	.04	.02
241	Jesse Baker	.05	.04	.02
242	Doug France (92)	.08	.06	.03
243	Chris Dressel (93)	.05	.04	.02
244	Willie Tullis (94)	.05	.04	.02
245	Robert Brazile	.08	.06	.03
246	Tony Collins	.08	.06	.03
247	Brian Holloway (97)	.05	.04	.02
248	Stanley Morgan (98)	.06	.05	.02
249	Rick Sanford (99)	.05	.04	.02
250	John Hannah	.15	.11	.06
251	Rich Camarillo	.08	.06	.03
252	Andre Tippett (102)	.08	.06	.03
253	Steve Grogan (103)	.08	.06	.03
254	Clayton Weishuhn (104)	.05	.04	.02
255	Jim Plunkett (105)	.08	.06	.03
256	Rod Martin (106)	.08	.06	.03
257	Lester Hayes (107)	.05	.04	.02
258	Marcus Allen	.50	.40	.20
259	Todd Chistensen	.10	.08	.04
260	Ted Hendricks (110)	.08	.06	.03
261	Greg Pruitt (111)	.05	.04	.02
262	Howie Long (112)	.50	.40	.20
263	Vann McElroy	.05	.04	.02
264	Curt Warner	.25	.20	.10
265	Jacob Green (115)	.06	.05	.02
266	Bruce Scholtz (116)	.05	.04	.02
267	Steve Largent (117)	.50	.40	.20
268	Kenny Easley	.08	.06	.03
269	Dave Krieg	.35	.25	.14
270	Dave Brown (120)	.05	.04	.02
271	Zachary Dixon (121)	.05	.04	.02
272	Norm Johnson (122)	.05	.04	.02
273	Terry Bradshaw (123)	.30	.25	.12
274	Keith Willis (124)	.05	.04	.02
275	Gary Anderson (125)	.05	.04	.02
276	Franco Harris	.35	.25	.14
277	Mike Webster	.15	.11	.06
278	Calvin Sweeney (128)	.05	.04	.02
279	Rick Woods (129)	.05	.04	.02
280	Bennie Cunningham (130)	.08	.06	.03
281	Jack Lambert	.15	.11	.06
282	Curt Warner (283)	.35	.25	.14
283	Todd Christensen (282)	.15	.11	.06

1985 Topps USFL

This was the second and final year of Topps' production of United States Football League cards. The 132-card set was issued as a factory set. Cards were numbered alphabetically according to city and according to the player's last name. Printed on white cardboard stock, fronts show a bright red border with a white and blue stripe across the middle; the USFL logo appears in the upper right corner. The team name appears in heavy red type at the bottom of the card, and the player's name and position are in a yellow football above the team name. Card backs show a goalpost design in blue and red. The set includes rookies of Doug Flutie, Gary Clark and Gerald McNeil, plus Herschel Walker's second-year card.

		NM/M	NM	E
	Complete Set (132):	100.00	75.00	40.00
	Common Player:	.35	.25	.14
1	Case DeBruijn	.35	.25	.14
2	Mike Katolin	.35	.25	.14
3	Bruce Laird	.35	.25	.14
4	Kit Lathrop	.35	.25	.14
5	Kevin Long	.35	.25	.14
6	Karl Lorch	.35	.25	.14
7	Dave Tipton	.35	.25	.14
8	Doug Williams	.40	.30	.15
9	Luis Zendejas	.35	.25	.14
10	Kelvin Bryant	.75	.60	.30
11	Willie Collier	.35	.25	.14
12	Irv Eatman	.50	.40	.20
13	Scott Fitzkee	.35	.25	.14
14	William Fuller **RC**	1.00	.50	.25
15	Chuck Fusina	.35	.25	.14
16	Pete Kugler	.35	.25	.14
17	Garcia Lane	.35	.25	.14
18	Mike Lush	.35	.25	.14
19	Sam Mills **RC**	4.00	2.00	1.20
20	Buddy Aydelette	.35	.25	.14
21	Joe Cribbs	.50	.40	.20
22	David Dumars	.35	.25	.14
23	Robin Earl	.35	.25	.14
24	Joey Jones	.35	.25	.14
25	Leon Perry	.35	.25	.14
26	Dave Pureifory	.35	.25	.14
27	Bill Roe	.35	.25	.14
28	Doug Smith **RC**	2.00	1.50	.80
29	Cliff Stoudt	.35	.25	.14
30	Jeff Delaney	.35	.25	.14
31	Vince Evans	.50	.40	.20
32	Leonard Harris **RC**	2.00	1.50	.80
33	Bill Johnson	.35	.25	.14
34	Marc Lewis	.35	.25	.14
35	David Martin	.35	.25	.14
36	Bruce Thornton	.35	.25	.14
37	Craig Walls	.35	.25	.14
38	Vincent White	.35	.25	.14
39	Luther Bradley	.35	.25	.14
40	Pete Catan	.35	.25	.14
41	Kiki DeAyala	.35	.25	.14
42	Tony Fritsch	.35	.25	.14
43	Sam Harrell	.35	.25	.14
44	Richard Johnson **RC**	1.50	1.25	.60
45	Jim Kelly	5.00	2.50	1.50
46	Gerald McNeil **RC**	1.50	1.25	.60
47	Clarence Verdin **RC**	2.00	1.50	.80
48	Dale Walters	.35	.25	.14
49	Gary Clark **RC**	2.00	1.00	.60
50	Tom Dinkel	.35	.25	.14
51	Mike Edwards	.35	.25	.14
52	Brian Franco	.35	.25	.14
53	Bob Gruber	.35	.25	.14
54	Robbie Mahfouz	.35	.25	.14
55	Mike Rozier	1.75	1.25	.70
56	Brian Sipe	.50	.40	.20
57	J.T. Turner	.35	.25	.14
58	Howard Carson	.35	.25	.14
59	Wymon Henderson **RC**	.60	.45	.25
60	Kevin Nelson	.35	.25	.14
61	Jeff Partridge	.35	.25	.14
62	Ben Rudolph	.35	.25	.14
63	JoJo Townsell	.35	.25	.14
64	Eddie Weaver	.35	.25	.14
65	Steve Young	10.00	5.00	3.00
66	Tony Zendejas **RC**	.75	.60	.30
67	Mossy Cade	.35	.25	.14
68	Leonard Coleman **RC**	.50	.40	.20
69	John Corker	.35	.25	.14
70	Derrick Crawford	.35	.25	.14
71	Art Kuehn	.35	.25	.14
72	Walter Lewis	.35	.25	.14
73	Tyrone McGriff	.35	.25	.14
74	Tim Spencer	.35	.25	.14
75	Reggie White	6.00	3.00	1.80
76	Gizmo Williams **RC**	2.00	1.50	.80
77	Sam Bowers	.35	.25	.14
78	Maurice Carthon **RC**	1.25	.90	.50
79	Clarence Collins	.35	.25	.14
80	Doug Flutie **RC**	12.00	6.00	3.50
81	Freddie Gilbert	.35	.25	.14
82	Kerry Justin	.35	.25	.14
83	Dave Lapham	.35	.25	.14
84	Rick Partridge	.35	.25	.14
85	Roger Ruzek **RC**	1.00	.70	.40
86	Herschel Walker	4.00	2.00	1.20
87	Gordon Banks	.35	.25	.14
88	Monte Bennett	.35	.25	.14
89	Albert Bentley **RC**	1.00	.50	.25
90	Novo Bojovic	.35	.25	.14
91	Dave Browning	.35	.25	.14
92	Anthony Carter	1.00	.50	.25
93	Bobby Hebert	1.00	.50	.25
94	Ray Pinney	.35	.25	.14
95	Stan Talley	.35	.25	.14
96	Ruben Vaughan	.35	.25	.14
97	Curtis Bledsoe	.35	.25	.14
98	Reggie Collier	.35	.25	.14
99	Jerry Doerger	.35	.25	.14
100	Jerry Golsteyn	.35	.25	.14
101	Bob Niziolek	.35	.25	.14
102	Joel Patten	.35	.25	.14
103	Ricky Simmons	.35	.25	.14
104	Joey Walters	.35	.25	.14
105	Marcus Dupree	.35	.25	.14
106	Jeff Gossett	.50	.40	.20
107	Frank Lockett	.35	.25	.14
108	Marcus Marek	.35	.25	.14
109	Kenny Neil	.35	.25	.14
110	Robert Pennywell	.35	.25	.14
111	Matt Robinson	.35	.25	.14
112	Dan Ross	.35	.25	.14
113	Doug Woodward	.35	.25	.14
114	Danny Buggs	.35	.25	.14
115	Putt Choate	.35	.25	.14
116	Greg Fields	.35	.25	.14
117	Ken Hartley	.35	.25	.14
118	Nick Mike-Mayer	.35	.25	.14
119	Rick Neuheisel	.35	.25	.14
120	Peter Raeford	.35	.25	.14
121	Gary Worthy	.35	.25	.14

122	Gary Anderson	.50	.25	.15
123	Zenon Andrusyshyn	.35	.25	.14
124	Greg Boone	.35	.25	.14
125	Mike Butler	.35	.25	.14
126	Mike Clark	.35	.25	.14
127	Willie Gillespie	.35	.25	.14
128	James Harrell	.35	.25	.14
130	John Reaves	.35	.25	.14
131	Eric Truvillion	.35	.25	.14
132	Checklist 1-132	5.00	2.50	1.50

1985 Topps USFL New Jersey Generals

This nine-card sheet features members of the USFL's New Jersey Generals. The panel is 7-1/2" x 10-1/2"; individual cards would be the standard size if they were cut out of the panel. The card front has an action photo of the player, along with his name, team name and team logo. The back is numbered and includes biographical and statistical information, plus a brief player profile. The card stock is gray; the print is yellow and red on the back.

		NM/M	NM	E
	Complete Set (9):	35.00	26.00	14.00
	Common Player:	2.00	1.50	.80
1	Walt Michaels	2.00	1.50	.80
2	Sam Bowers	2.00	1.50	.80
3	Clarence Collins	2.00	1.50	.80
4	Doug Flutie	20.00	15.00	8.00
5	Gregory Johnson	2.00	1.50	.80
6	Jim LeClair	3.00	2.25	1.25
7	Bobby Leopold	2.00	1.50	.80
8	Herschel Walker	15.00	11.00	6.00
9	**Membership card** (schedule on back)	2.00	1.50	.80

1985 Topps

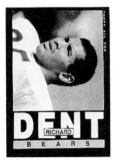

This was Topps' most radical card design in football cards in decades. Player photos were mounted horizontally in this 396-card set, with black borders surrounding the photo. The player's last name appeared in large white letters across the bottom of the card, with his first name in smaller letters in the middle of his last name. The team name appeared in smaller, darker type in the upper left corner. Cards in this issue were numbered alphabetically according to city name and conference, with NFC teams listed first and AFC teams listed after the league leader cards. This set includes rookie cards of Richard Dent, Henry Ellard, Joe Morris, Warren Moon, Mark Clayton, Tony Eason, Ken O'Brien and Louis Lipps. (Key: AP - All Pro)

		NM/M	NM	E
	Complete Set (396):	80.00	60.00	32.00
	Common Player:	1.00	.50	.30
	Wax Pack (15):	4.00		
	Wax Box (36):	100.00		
1	Record: (Mark Clayton)	1.00	.50	.25
2	Record: (Eric Dickerson)	1.00	.50	.25
3	Record: (Charlie Joiner)	1.00	.50	.25
4	Dan Marino RB	3.00	1.50	.75
5	Record: (Art Monk)	1.00	.50	.25
6	Walter Payton RB	4.00	2.00	1.20
7	NFC Championship: (Matt Suhey)	1.00	.50	.25
8	AFC Championship: (Bennett)	1.00	.50	.25
9	Super Bowl XIX: (Wendell Tyler)	1.00	.50	.25
10	Atlanta Falcons Team: (Gerald Riggs)	1.00	.50	.25
11	William Andrews	1.00	.50	.25
12	Stacey Bailey	1.00	.50	.25
13	Steve Bartkowski	1.00	.50	.25
14	Rick Bryan RC	1.00	.50	.25
15	Alfred Jackson	1.00	.50	.25
16	Kenny Johnson	1.00	.50	.25
17	Mike Ken (AP)	1.00	.50	.25
18	Mike Pitts RC	1.00	.50	.25
19	Gerald Riggs	1.00	.50	.25
20	Sylvester Stamps	1.00	.50	.25
21	R.C. Theileman	1.00	.50	.25

22	Chicago Bears Team:	2.50	1.25	.75
23	Todd Bell RC (AP)	.50	.25	.15
24	Richard Dent RC (AP)	8.00	4.00	2.50
25	Gary Fencik	1.00	.50	.25
26	Dave Finzer	1.00	.50	.25
27	Leslie Frazier	1.00	.50	.25
28	Steve Fuller	1.00	.50	.25
29	Willie Gault	1.00	.50	.25
30	Dan Hampton (AP)	1.00	.50	.25
31	Jim McMahon	1.00	.50	.25
32	Steve McMichael RC	1.00	.50	.25
33	Walter Payton (AP)	8.00	4.00	2.50
34	Mike Singletary	1.00	.60	.30
35	Matt Suhey	1.00	.50	.25
36	Bob Thomas	1.00	.50	.25
37	Dallas Cowboys Team: (Tony Dorsett)	1.00	.50	.25
38	Bill Bates RC	1.00	.50	.25
39	Doug Cosbie	1.00	.50	.25
40	Tony Dorsett	2.00	1.00	.60
41	Michael Downs	1.00	.50	.25
42	Mike Hegman	1.00	.50	.25
43	Tony Hill	1.00	.50	.25
44	Gary Hogeboom RC	1.00	.50	.25
45	Jim Jeffcoat RC	1.00	.50	.25
46	Ed "Too Tall" Jones	1.00	.50	.25
47	Mike Renfro	1.00	.50	.25
48	Rafael Septien	1.00	.50	.25
49	Dennis Thurman	1.00	.50	.25
50	Everson Walls	1.00	.50	.25
51	Danny White	1.00	.50	.25
52	Randy White	1.00	.50	.25
53	Detroit Lions Team	1.00	.50	.25
54	Jeff Chadwick	1.00	.50	.25
55	Mike Cofer RC	1.00	.50	.25
56	Gary Danielson	1.00	.50	.25
57	Keith Dorney	1.00	.50	.25
58	Doug English	1.00	.50	.25
59	William Gay	1.00	.50	.25
60	Ken Jenkins	1.00	.50	.25
61	James Jones	1.00	.50	.25
62	Ed Murray	1.00	.50	.25
63	Billy Sims	1.00	.50	.25
64	Leonard Thompson	1.00	.50	.25
65	Bobby Watkins	1.00	.50	.25
66	Green Bay Packers Team: (Lynn Dickey)	1.00	.50	.25
67	Paul Coffman	1.00	.50	.25
68	Lynn Dickey	1.00	.50	.25
69	Mike Douglass	1.00	.50	.25
70	Tom Flynn	1.00	.50	.25
71	Eddie Lee Ivery	1.00	.50	.25
72	Ezra Johnson	1.00	.50	.25
73	Mark Lee	1.00	.50	.25
74	Tim Lewis	1.00	.50	.25
75	James Lofton	1.00	.50	.25
76	Bucky Scribner	1.00	.50	.25
77	Los Angeles Rams Team: (Eric Dickerson)	1.00	.50	.25
78	Nolan Cromwell	1.00	.50	.25
79	Eric Dickerson (AP)	1.00	.70	.40
80	Henry Ellard RC	2.00	1.00	.60
81	Kent Hill	1.00	.50	.25
82	LeRoy Irvin	1.00	.50	.25
83	Jeff Kemp	1.00	.50	.25
84	Mike Lansford	1.00	.50	.25
85	Barry Redden	1.00	.50	.25
86	Jackie Slater	1.00	.50	.25
87	Doug Smith RC	1.00	.50	.25
88	Jack Youngblood	1.00	.50	.25
89	Minnesota Vikings Team	1.00	.50	.25
90	Alfred Anderson	1.00	.50	.25
91	Ted Brown	1.00	.50	.25
92	Greg Coleman	1.00	.50	.25
93	Tommy Hannon	1.00	.50	.25
94	Tommy Kramer	1.00	.50	.25
95	Leo Lewis RC	1.00	.50	.08
96	Doug Martin	1.00	.50	.25
97	Darrin Nelson	1.00	.50	.25
98	Jan Stenerud (AP)	1.00	.50	.25
99	Sammy White	1.00	.50	.25
100	New Orleans Saints Team	1.00	.50	.25
101	Morten Anderson	1.00	.60	.30
102	Hoby Brenner RC	1.00	.50	.25
103	Bruce Clark	1.00	.50	.25
104	Hokie Gajan	1.00	.50	.25
105	Brian Hansen RC	1.00	.50	.25
106	Rickey Jackson	1.00	.70	.40
107	George Rogers	1.00	.50	.25
108	Dave Wilson	1.00	.50	.25
109	Tyrone Young	1.00	.50	.25
110	New York Giants Team	1.00	.50	.25
111	Carl Banks RC	1.00	.70	.40
112	Jim Burt RC	1.00	.50	.25
113	Rob Carpenter	1.00	.50	.25
114	Harry Carson	1.00	.50	.25
115	Earnest Gray	1.00	.50	.25

116	Ali Haji-Sheikh	1.00	.50	.25
117	Mark Haynes (AP)	1.00	.50	.25
118	Bobby Johnson	1.00	.50	.25
119	Lionel Manuel RC	1.00	.50	.25
120	Joe Morris RC	1.00	.50	.25
121	Zeke Mowatt RC	1.00	.50	.25
122	Jeff Rutledge RC	1.00	.50	.25
123	Phil Simms	1.00	.45	.25
124	Lawrence Taylor (AP)	1.25	.90	.50
125	Philadelphia Eagles Team: (Wilbert Montgomery)	1.00	.50	.25
126	Greg Brown	1.00	.50	.25
127	Ray Ellis	1.00	.50	.25
128	Dennis Harrison	1.00	.50	.25
129	Wes Hopkins RC, Marvin Harvey	1.00	.50	.25
130	Mike Horan	1.00	.50	.25
131	Kenny Jackson RC	1.00	.50	.25
132	Ron Jaworski	1.00	.50	.25
133	Paul McFadden	1.00	.50	.25
134	Wilbert Montgomery	1.00	.50	.25
135	Mike Quick	1.00	.50	.25
136	John Spagnola	1.00	.50	.25
137	St. Louis Cardinals Team	1.00	.50	.25
138	Ottis Anderson	1.00	.50	.25
139	Al "Bubba" Baker	1.00	.50	.25
140	Roy Green	1.00	.50	.25
141	Curtis Greer	1.00	.50	.25
142	E.J. Junior (AP)	1.00	.50	.25
143	Neil Lomax	1.00	.50	.25
144	Stump Mitchell	1.00	.50	.25
145	Neil O'Donoghue	1.00	.50	.25
146	Pat Tilley	1.00	.50	.25
147	Lionel Washington	1.00	.50	.25
148	San Francisco 49ers	2.00	1.50	.75
149	Dwaine Board	1.00	.50	.25
150	Dwight Clark	1.00	.50	.25
151	Roger Craig	1.25	.90	.50
152	Randy Cross (AP)	1.00	.50	.25
153	Fred Dean	1.00	.50	.25
154	Keith Fahnhorst	1.00	.50	.25
155	Dwight Hicks	1.00	.50	.25
156	Ronnie Lott	1.00	.50	.25
157	Joe Montana	4.00	2.00	1.25
158	Renaldo Nehemiah	1.00	.50	.25
159	Fred Quillan	1.00	.50	.25
160	Jack Reynolds	1.00	.50	.25
161	Freddie Solomon	1.00	.50	.25
162	Keena Turner RC	1.00	.50	.25
163	Wendell Tyler	1.00	.50	.25
164	Ray Wersching	1.00	.50	.25
165	Carlton Williamson	1.00	.50	.25
166	Tampa Bay Buccaneers Team: (Steve DeBerg)	1.00	.50	.25
167	Gerald Carter	1.00	.50	.25
168	Mark Cotney	1.00	.50	.25
169	Steve DeBerg	1.00	.50	.25
170	Sean Farrell	1.00	.50	.25
171	Hugh Green	1.00	.50	.25
172	Kevin House	1.00	.50	.25
173	David Logan	1.00	.50	.25
174	Michael Morton	1.00	.50	.25
175	Lee Roy Selmon	1.00	.50	.25
176	James Wilder	1.00	.50	.25
177	Washington Redskins Team: (John Riggins)	1.00	.50	.25
178	Charlie Brown	1.00	.50	.25
179	Monte Coleman RC	1.00	.50	.25
180	Vernon Dean	1.00	.50	.25
181	Darrell Green	1.00	.50	.25
182	Russ Grimm	1.00	.50	.25
183	Joe Jacoby	1.00	.50	.25
184	Dexter Manley	1.00	.50	.25
185	Art Monk	1.00	.50	.25
186	Mark Moseley	1.00	.50	.25
187	Calvin Muhammad	1.00	.50	.25
188	Mike Nelms	1.00	.50	.25
189	John Riggins	1.00	.50	.25
190	Joe Theismann	1.00	.50	.25
191	Joe Washington	1.00	.50	.25
192	Passing Leaders: (Joe Montana, Dan Marino)	5.00	2.50	1.50
193	Receiving Leaders: (Ozzie Newsome, Art Monk)	1.00	.50	.25
194	Rushing Leaders: (Earnest Jackson, Eric Dickerson)	1.00	.50	.25
195	Scoring Leaders: (Gary Anderson, Ray Wersching)	1.00	.50	.25
196	Interception Leaders: (Kenny Easley, Tom Flynn)	1.00	.50	.25
197	Punting Leaders: (Jim Arnold, Brian Hansen)	1.00	.50	.25

198	Buffalo Bills Team: (Greg Bell)	1.00	.50	.25
199	Greg Bell RC	1.00	.50	.25
200	Preston Dennard	1.00	.50	.25
201	Joe Ferguson	1.00	.50	.25
202	Byron Franklin	1.00	.50	.25
203	Steve Freeman	1.00	.50	.25
204	Jim Haslett	1.00	.50	.25
205	Charles Romes	1.00	.50	.25
206	Fred Smerlas	1.00	.50	.25
207	Darryl Talley RC	2.00	1.50	.80
208	Van Williams	1.00	.50	.25
209	Cincinnati Bengals Team: (Ken Anderson, Larry Kinnebrew)	1.00	.50	.25
210	Ken Anderson	.20	.50	.25
211	Jim Breech	1.00	.50	.25
212	Louis Breeden	1.00	.50	.25
213	James Brooks	1.00	.50	.25
214	Ross Browner	1.00	.50	.25
215	Eddie Edwards	1.00	.50	.25
216	M.L. Harris	1.00	.50	.25
217	Bobby Kemp	1.00	.50	.25
218	Larry Kinnebrew RC	1.00	.50	.25
219	Anthony Munoz (AP)	1.00	.50	.25
220	Reggie Williams	1.00	.50	.25
221	Cleveland Browns Team: (Boyce Green)	1.00	.50	.25
222	Matt Bahr	1.00	.50	.25
223	Chip Banks	1.00	.50	.25
224	Reggie Camp	1.00	.50	.25
225	Tom Cousineau	1.00	.50	.25
226	Joe DeLamielleure	1.00	.50	.25
227	Ricky Feacher	1.00	.50	.25
228	Boyce Green	1.00	.50	.25
229	Al Gross	1.00	.50	.25
230	Clay Matthews	1.00	.50	.25
231	Paul McDonald	1.00	.50	.25
232	Ozzie Newsome (AP)	1.00	.50	.25
233	Mike Pruitt	1.00	.50	.25
234	Don Rogers	1.00	.50	.25
235	Denver Broncos (John Elway, Sammy Winder)	3.00	1.50	.90
236	Rubin Carter	1.00	.50	.25
237	Barney Chavous	1.00	.50	.25
238	John Elway	7.00	3.50	2.10
239	Steve Foley	1.00	.50	.25
240	Mike Harden	1.00	.50	.25
241	Tom Jackson	1.00	.50	.25
242	Butch Johnson	1.00	.50	.25
243	Rulon Jones	1.00	.50	.25
244	Rick Karlis	1.00	.50	.25
245	Steve Watson	1.00	.50	.25
246	Gerald Wilhite	1.00	.50	.25
247	Sammy Winder	1.00	.50	.25
248	Houston Oilers Team: (Larry Moriarty)	1.00	.50	.25
249	Jesse Baker	1.00	.50	.25
250	Carter Hartwig	1.00	.50	.25
251	Warren Moon RC	4.00	2.00	1.20
252	Larry Moriarty RC	1.00	.50	.25
253	Mike Munchak RC	3.00	1.50	.90
254	Carl Roaches	1.00	.50	.25
255	Tim Smith	1.00	.50	.25
256	Willie Tullis	1.00	.50	.25
257	Jamie Williams	1.00	.50	.25
258	Indianapolis Colts Team: (Art Schlichter)	1.00	.50	.25
259	Raymond Butler	1.00	.50	.25
260	Johnie Cooks	1.00	.50	.25
261	Eugene Daniel	1.00	.50	.25
262	Curtis Dickey	1.00	.50	.25
263	Chris Hinton	1.00	.50	.25
264	Vernon Maxwell	1.00	.50	.25
265	Randy McMillan	1.00	.50	.25
266	Art Schlichter	1.00	.50	.25
267	Rohn Stark	1.00	.50	.25
268	Leo Wisniewski	1.00	.50	.25
269	Kansas City Chiefs Team: (Bill Kenney)	1.00	.50	.25
270	Jim Arnold	1.00	.50	.25
271	Mike Bell	1.00	.50	.25
272	Todd Blackledge	1.00	.50	.25
273	Carlos Carson	1.00	.50	.25
274	Deron Cherry	1.00	.50	.25
275	Herman Heard RC	1.00	.50	.25
276	Bill Kenney	1.00	.50	.25
277	Nick Lowery	1.00	.50	.25
278	Bill Maas RC	1.00	.50	.25
279	Henry Marshall	1.00	.50	.25
280	Art Still	1.00	.50	.25
281	Los Angeles Raiders Team: (Marcus Allen)	1.00	.50	.25
282	Marcus Allen	1.00	.50	.25
283	Lyle Alzado	1.00	.50	.25
284	Chris Bahr	1.00	.50	.25
285	Malcolm Barnwell	1.00	.50	.25
286	Cliff Branch	1.00	.50	.25
287	Todd Christensen	1.00	.50	.25
288	Ray Guy	1.00	.50	.25
289	Lester Hayes	1.00	.50	.25
290	Mike Haynes (AP)	1.00	.50	.25
291	Henry Lawrence	1.00	.50	.25
292	Howie Long	2.50	1.25	.75
293	Rod Martin (AP)	1.00	.50	.25
294	Vann McElroy	1.00	.50	.25
295	Matt Millen	1.00	.50	.25
296	Bill Pickel RC	1.00	.50	.25
297	Jim Plunkett	1.00	.50	.25
298	Dokie Williams RC	1.00	.50	.25
299	Marc Wilson	1.00	.50	.25
300	Miami Dolphins Team: (Mark Duper)	1.00	.50	.25
301	Bob Baumhower	1.00	.50	.25
302	Doug Betters	1.00	.50	.25
303	Glenn Blackwood	1.00	.50	.25
304	Lyle Blackwood	1.00	.50	.25
305	Kim Bokamper	1.00	.50	.25
306	Charles Bowser	1.00	.50	.25
307	Jimmy Cefalo	1.00	.50	.25
308	Mark Clayton RC (AP)	1.00	.50	.25
309	A.J. Duhe	1.00	.50	.25
310	Mark Duper	1.00	.50	.25
311	Andra Franklin	1.00	.50	.25
312	Bruce Hardy	1.00	.50	.25
313	Pete Johnson	1.00	.50	.25
314	Dan Marino (AP)	5.00	2.50	1.50
315	Tony Nathan	1.00	.50	.25
316	Ed Newman	1.00	.50	.25
317	Reggie Roby (AP)	1.00	.50	.25
318	Dwight Stephenson (AP)	1.00	.50	.25
319	Uwe Von Schamann	1.00	.50	.25
320	New England Patriots Team: (Tony Collins)	1.00	.50	.25
321	Raymond Clayborn	1.00	.50	.25
322	Tony Collins	1.00	.50	.25
323	Tony Eason RC	1.00	.50	.25
324	Tony Franklin	1.00	.50	.25
325	Irving Fryar RC	3.00	1.50	.90
326	John Hannah (AP)	1.00	.50	.25
327	Brian Holloway	1.00	.50	.25
328	Craig James RC	1.00	.50	.25
329	Stanley Morgan	1.00	.50	.25
330	Steve Nelson (AP)	1.00	.50	.25
331	Derrick Ramsey	1.00	.50	.25
332	Stephen Starring	1.00	.50	.25
333	Mosi Tatupu	1.00	.50	.25
334	Andre Tippett	1.00	.50	.25
335	New York Jets Team: (Mark Gastineau, Ferguson)	1.00	.50	.25
336	Russell Carter	1.00	.50	.25
337	Mark Gastineau (AP)	1.00	.50	.25
338	Bruce Harper	1.00	.50	.25
339	Bobby Humphery	1.00	.50	.25
340	Johnny "Lam" Jones	1.00	.50	.25
341	Joe Klecko	1.00	.50	.25
342	Pat Leahy	1.00	.50	.25
343	Marty Lyons	1.00	.50	.25
344	Freeman McNeil	1.00	.50	.25
345	Lance Mehl	1.00	.50	.25
346	Ken O'Brien RC	1.00	.50	.25
347	Marvin Powell	1.00	.50	.25
348	Pat Ryan	1.00	.50	.25
349	Mickey Shuler RC	1.00	.50	.25
350	Wesley Walker	1.00	.50	.25
351	Pittsburgh Steelers Team (Mark Malone)	1.00	.50	.25
352	Walter Abercrombie	1.00	.50	.25
353	Gary Anderson	1.00	.50	.25
354	Robin Cole	1.00	.50	.25
355	Bennie Cunningham	1.00	.50	.25
356	Rich Erenberg	1.00	.50	.25
357	Jack Lambert	1.00	.50	.25
358	Louis Lipps RC	1.00	.50	.25
359	Mark Malone	1.00	.50	.25
360	Mike Merriweather RC	1.00	.50	.25
361	Frank Pollard	1.00	.50	.25
362	Donnie Shell	1.00	.50	.25
363	John Stallworth	1.00	.50	.25
364	Sam Washington	1.00	.50	.25
365	Mike Webster	1.00	.50	.25
366	Dwayne Woodruff	1.00	.50	.25
367	San Diego Chargers Team	1.00	.50	.25
368	Rolf Benirschke	1.00	.50	.25
369	Gill Byrd RC	1.00	.70	.40
370	Wes Chandler	1.00	.50	.25
371	Bobby Duckworth	1.00	.50	.25
372	Dan Fouts	1.00	.45	.25
373	Mike Green	1.00	.50	.25
374	Pete Holohan RC	1.00	.45	.25
375	Earnest Jackson	1.00	.50	.25
376	Lionel James	1.00	.50	.25
377	Charlie Joiner	1.00	.50	.25
378	Billy Ray Smith	1.00	.50	.25
379	Kellen Winslow	1.00	.50	.25
380	Seattle Seahawks Team (Dave Krieg)	1.00	.50	.25
381	Dave Brown	1.00	.50	.25
382	Jeff Bryant	1.00	.50	.25
383	Dan Doornink	1.00	.50	.25
384	Kenny Easley (AP)	1.00	.50	.25
385	Jacob Green	1.00	.50	.25
386	David Hughes	1.00	.50	.25
387	Norm Johnson	1.00	.50	.25
388	Dave Krieg	1.00	.50	.25
389	Steve Largent	1.00	.50	.25
390	Joe Nash RC	1.00	.50	.25
391	Daryl Turner	1.00	.50	.25
392	Curt Warner	1.00	.50	.25
393	Fredd Young RC	1.00	.50	.25
394	Checklist 1-132	1.00	.50	.25
395	Checklist 133-264	1.00	.50	.25
396	Checklist 265-396	1.00	.50	.25

1985 Topps "Coming Soon" Stickers

These stickers say "Coming Soon" on the backs and share identical card numbers with their counterparts in Topps' regular 1985 sticker set; thus, the checklist is skip-numbered. These stickers, which were random inserts in 1985 Topps football packs, measure 2-1/8" x 3" each but, unlike many of the regular stickers, feature only one player per sticker. The stickers have a colored photo on the front with a color frame and white border surrounding it.

		NM/M	NM	E
	Complete Set (30):	5.00	3.75	2.00
	Common Player:	.08	.06	.03
6	Ken Anderson	.30	.25	.12
15	Greg Bell	.15	.11	.06
24	John Elway	.75	.60	.30
33	Ozzie Newsome	.25	.20	.10
42	Charlie Joiner	.25	.20	.10
51	Bill Kenney	.15	.11	.06
60	Randy McMillan	.08	.06	.03
69	Dan Marino	2.00	1.50	.80
77	Mark Clayton	.50	.40	.20
78	Mark Gastineau	.08	.06	.03
87	Warren Moon	2.00	1.50	.80
96	Tony Eason	.15	.11	.06
105	Marcus Allen	.50	.40	.20
114	Steve Largent	.60	.45	.25
123	John Stallworth	.20	.15	.08
156	Walter Payton	1.00	.70	.40
165	James Wilder	.12	.09	.05
174	Neil Lomax	.15	.11	.06
183	Tony Dorsett	.35	.25	.14
192	Mike Quick	.15	.11	.06
201	William Andrews	.10	.08	.04
210	Joe Montana	2.50	2.00	1.00
214	Dwight Clark	.35	.25	.14
219	Lawrence Taylor	.35	.16	.04
228	Billy Sims	.15	.11	.06
237	James Lofton	.30	.25	.12
246	Eric Dickerson	.50	.40	.20
255	John Riggins	.25	.20	.10
268	George Rogers	.12	.09	.05
281	Tommy Kramer	.08	.06	.03

1985 Topps Box Bottoms

The bottoms of 1985 Topps wax pack boxes featured these cards, which are numbered using a letter instead of a number. The design is the same as a regular 1985 Topps card, except the front border is red and "Topps Superstars" is printed at the top. The backs are identical to the regular cards' backs except for the letters used as card numbers.

		NM/M	NM	E
	Complete Set (16):	15.00	11.00	6.00
	Common Player:	.30	.25	.12
A	Marcus Allen	1.50	1.25	.60
B	Ottis Anderson	.30	.25	.12
C	Mark Clayton	1.00	.70	.40
D	Eric Dickerson	1.00	.70	.40
E	Tony Dorsett	.75	.60	.30
F	Dan Fouts	.75	.60	.30
G	Mark Gastineau	.30	.25	.12
H	Charlie Joiner	.50	.40	.20
I	James Lofton	.75	.60	.30
J	Neil Lomax	.30	.25	.12
K	Dan Marino	6.00	4.50	2.50
L	Art Monk	.75	.60	.30
M	Joe Montana	6.00	4.50	2.50
N	Walter Payton	2.50	2.00	1.00
O	John Stallworth	.30	.25	.12
P	Lawrence Taylor	.75	.60	.30

1985 Topps Star Set

This 11-card glossy set was a follow-up to the 1984 insert set. Cards were printed on heavy white cardboard stock, with red borders surrounding an action picture of each player. Cards were issued one per wax pack with the 1985 cards. Card backs were printed in blue and red and show pretty much the same design, front and back, as the 1984 insert set, but with smaller type indicating the year of issue on the back. This was the second and final year of Topps' production of United States Football League cards. The 132-card set was issued as a factory set. Cards were numbered alphabetically according to city and according to the player's last name. Printed on white cardboard stock, fronts show a bright red border with a white and blue stripe across the middle; the USFL logo appears in the upper right corner. The team name appears in heavy red type at the bottom of the card, and the player's name and position is in a yellow football above the team name. Card backs show a goalpost design in blue and red. The set includes rookies Doug Flutie, Gary Clark and Gerald McNeill; plus Herschel Walker's second-year card.

		NM/M	NM	E
Complete Set (11):		6.50	4.75	2.75
Common Player:		.25	.20	.10
1	Mark Clayton	.25	.20	.10
2	Eric Dickerson	1.75	1.35	.70
3	John Elway	1.00	.75	.40
4	Mark Gastineau	.25	.20	.10
5	Ronnie Lott	.40	.30	.20
6	Dan Marino	1.25	.90	.50
7	Joe Montana	1.50	1.10	.60
8	Walter Payton	1.50	1.10	.60
9	John Riggins	.35	.27	.15
10	John Stallworth	.25	.20	.10
11	Lawrence Taylor	.35	.27	.15

1985 Topps Stickers

These stickers are different than those issued in previous years, because no foil stickers were produced. However, there were stickers issued in pairs on some cards; they are noted as being partners by the parenthesis which follows the player's name in the checklist. Charlie Joiner, Art Monk, Joe Montana, Dan Marino, Walter Payton and Eric Dickerson are all featured on the album cover; the 49ers team is on the back.

		NM/M	NM	E
Complete Set (285):		20.00	15.00	8.00
Common Player:		.05	.04	.02
1	Super Bowl XIX	1.50	1.25	.60
2	Super Bowl XIX	1.00	.70	.40
3	Super Bowl XIX	.10	.08	.04
4	Super Bowl XIX	.10	.08	.04
5	Super Bow XIX	.08	.06	.03
6	Ken Anderson	.30	.25	.12
7	M.L. Harris (157)	.05	.04	.02
8	Eddie Edwards (157)	.05	.04	.02
9	Louis Breeden (159)	.05	.04	.02
10	Larry Kinnebrew	.05	.04	.02
11	Isaac Curtis (161)	.06	.05	.02
12	James Brooks (162)	.12	.09	.05
13	Jim Breech (163)	.05	.04	.02
14	Boomer Esiason (164)	.75	.60	.30
15	Greg Bell	.10	.08	.04
16	Fred Smerlas (166)	.05	.04	.02
17	Joe Ferguson (167)	.06	.05	.02
18	Ken Johnson (168)	.05	.04	.02
19	Darryl Talley (169)	.25	.20	.10
20	Preston Dennard (170)	.05	.04	.02
21	Charles Romes (171)	.05	.04	.02
22	Jim Haslett (172)	.05	.04	.02
23	Byron Franklin	.05	.04	.02
24	John Elway	1.25	.90	.50
25	Rulon Jones (175)	.05	.04	.02
26	Butch Johnson (176)	.05	.04	.02
27	Rick Karlis (177)	.05	.04	.02
28	Sammy Winder	.05	.04	.02
29	Tom Jackson (179)	.10	.08	.04
30	Mike Harden (180)	.05	.04	.02
31	Steve Watson (181)	.05	.04	.02
32	Steve Foley (182)	.05	.04	.02
33	Ozzie Newsome	.25	.20	.10
34	Al Gross (184)	.05	.04	.02
35	Paul McDonald (185)	.05	.04	.02
36	Matt Bahr (186)	.07	.05	.03
37	Charles White (187)	.06	.05	.02
38	Don Rogers (188)	.05	.04	.02
39	Mike Pruitt (189)	.05	.04	.02
40	Reggie Camp (190)	.05	.04	.02
41	Boyce Green	.05	.04	.02
42	Charlie Joiner	.20	.15	.08
43	Dan Fouts (193)	.25	.20	.10
44	Keith Ferguson (194)	.05	.04	.02
45	Pete Holohan (195)	.05	.04	.02
46	Earnest Jackson	.08	.06	.03
47	Wes Chandler (197)	.06	.05	.02
48	Gill Byrd (198)	.15	.11	.06
49	Kellen Winslow (199)	.15	.11	.06
50	Billy Ray Smith (200)	.06	.05	.02
51	Bill Kenney	.08	.06	.03
52	Herman Heard (202)	.05	.04	.02
53	Art Still (203)	.05	.04	.02
54	Nick Lowery (204)	.05	.04	.02
55	Deron Cherry (205)	.08	.06	.03
56	Jenry Marshall (206)	.05	.04	.02
57	Mike Bell (207)	.05	.04	.02
58	Todd Blackledge (208)	.05	.04	.02
59	Carlos Carson	.08	.06	.03
60	Randy McMillan	.05	.04	.02
61	Donnell Thompson (211)	.05	.04	.02
62	Raymond Butler (212)	.05	.04	.02
63	Ray Donaldson (213)	.05	.04	.02
64	Art Schlichter	.15	.11	.06
65	Rohn Stark (215)	.05	.04	.02
66	Johnie Cooks (216)	.05	.04	.02
67	Mike Pagel (217)	.05	.04	.02
68	Eugene Daniel (218)	.05	.04	.02
69	Dan Marino	2.00	1.50	.80
70	Pete Johnson (220)	.05	.04	.02
71	Tony Nathan (221)	.05	.04	.02
72	Glenn Blackwood (222)	.05	.04	.02
73	Woody Bennett (223)	.05	.04	.02
74	Dwight Stephenson (224)	.05	.04	.02
75	Mark Duper (225)	.10	.08	.04
76	Doug Betters (226)	.05	.04	.02
77	Mark Clayton	.50	.40	.20
78	Mark Gastineau	.08	.06	.03
79	Johnny Lam Jones (229)	.05	.04	.02
80	Mickey Shuler (230)	.05	.04	.02
81	Tony Paige (231)	.15	.11	.06
82	Freeman McNeil	.15	.11	.06
83	Russell Carter (233)	.06	.05	.02
84	Wesley Walker (234)	.06	.05	.02
85	Bruce Harper (235)	.15	.11	.06
86	Ken O'Brien (236)	1.75	1.25	.70
87	Warren Moon	.05	.04	.02
88	Jesse Baker (238)	.05	.04	.02
89	Carl Roaches (239)	.05	.04	.02
90	Carter Hartwig (240)	.05	.04	.02
91	Larry Moriarty (241)	.05	.04	.02
92	Robert Brazile (242)	.05	.04	.02
93	Oliver Luck (243)	.05	.04	.02
94	Willie Tullis (244)	.05	.04	.02
95	Tim Smith	.05	.04	.02
96	Tony Eason	.12	.09	.05
97	Stanley Morgan (247)	.10	.08	.04
98	Mosi Tatupu (248)	.05	.04	.02
99	Raymond Clayborn (249)	.08	.06	.03
100	Andre Tippett	.10	.08	.04
101	Craig James (251)	.15	.11	.06
102	Derrick Ramsey (252)	.05	.04	.02
103	Tony Collins (253)	.05	.04	.02
104	Tony Franklin (254)	.05	.04	.02
105	Marcus Allen	.40	.30	.15
106	Chris Bahr (256)	.05	.04	.02
107	Marc Wilson (257)	.05	.04	.02
108	Howie Long (258)	.10	.08	.04
109	Bill Pickel (259)	.05	.04	.02
110	Mike Haynes (260)	.08	.06	.03
111	Malcolm Barnwell (261)	.05	.04	.02
112	Rod Martin (262)	.05	.04	.02
113	Todd Christensen	.10	.08	.04
114	Steve Largent	.75	.60	.30
115	Curt Warner (265)	.08	.06	.03
116	Kenny Easley (266)	.05	.04	.02
117	Jacob Green (267)	.05	.04	.02
118	Daryl Turner	.08	.06	.03
119	Norm Johnson (269)	.05	.04	.02
120	Dave Krieg (270)	.10	.08	.04
121	Eric Lane (271)	.05	.04	.02
122	Jeff Bryant (272)	.05	.04	.02
123	John Stallworth	.12	.09	.05
124	Donnie Shell (274)	.05	.04	.02
125	Gary Anderson (275)	.05	.04	.02
126	Mark Malone (276)	.05	.04	.02
127	Sam Washington (277)	.05	.04	.02
128	Frank Pollard (278)	.05	.04	.02
129	Mike Merriweather (279)	.10	.08	.04
130	Walter Abercrombie (280)	.05	.04	.02
131	Louis Lipps	.30	.25	.12
132	Mark Clayton (144)	.35	.25	.14
133	Randy Cross (145)	.06	.05	.02
134	Eric Dickerson (146)	.35	.25	.14
135	John Hannah (147)	.10	.08	.04
136	Mike Kenn (148)	.05	.04	.02
137	Dan Marino (149)	1.50	1.25	.60
138	Art Monk (151)	.15	.11	.06
139	Anthony Munoz (151)	.10	.08	.04
140	Ozzie Newsome (152)	.10	.08	.04
141	Walter Payton (153)	.40	.30	.15
142	Jan Stenerud (154)	.08	.06	.03
143	Dwight Stephenson (155)	.05	.04	.02
144	Todd Bell (132)	.05	.04	.02
145	Richard Dent (133)	.50	.40	.20
146	Kenny Easley (134)	.05	.04	.02
147	Mark Gastineau (135)	.06	.05	.02
148	Dan Hampton (136)	.10	.08	.04
149	Mark Haynes (137)	.05	.04	.02
150	Mike Haynes (138)	.06	.05	.02
151	E.J. Junior (139)	.05	.04	.02
152	Rod Martin (140)	.10	.08	.04
153	Steve Nelson (141)	.05	.04	.02
154	Reggie Roby (142)	.05	.04	.02
155	Lawrence Taylor (143)	.15	.11	.06
156	Walter Payton	.60	.45	.25
157	Dan Hampton (7)	.08	.06	.03
158	Willie Gault (8)	.06	.05	.02
159	Matt Suhey (9)	.05	.04	.02
160	Richard Dent	1.00	.70	.40
161	Mike Singletary (11)	.10	.08	.04
162	Gary Fencik (12)	.05	.04	.02
163	Jim McMahon (13)	.10	.08	.04
164	Bob Thomas (14)	.05	.04	.02
165	James Wilder	.08	.06	.03
166	Steve DeBerg (16)	.08	.06	.03
167	Mark Cotney (17)	.05	.04	.02
168	Adger Armstrong (18)	.05	.04	.02
169	Gerald Carter (19)	.05	.04	.02
170	David Logari (20)	.05	.04	.02
171	Hugh Green (21)	.05	.04	.02
172	Lee Roy Selmon (22)	.06	.05	.02
173	Kevin House	.10	.08	.04
174	Neil Lomax	.12	.09	.05
175	Ottis Anderson (25)	.10	.08	.04
176	Al (Bubba) Baker (26)	.05	.04	.02
177	E.J. Junior (27)	.08	.06	.03
178	Roy Green	.10	.08	.04
179	Pat Tilley (29)	.05	.04	.02
180	Stump Mitchell (30)	.05	.04	.02
181	Lionel Washington (31)	.05	.04	.02
182	Curtis Greer (32)	.05	.04	.02
183	Tony Dorsett	.25	.20	.10
184	Gary Hogeboom (34)	.06	.05	.02
185	Jim Jeffcoat (35)	.06	.05	.02
186	Danny White (36)	.08	.06	.03
187	Michael Downs (37)	.05	.04	.02
188	Doug Cosbie (38)	.08	.06	.03
189	Tony Hill (39)	.05	.04	.02
190	Rafael Septien (40)	.05	.04	.02
191	Randy White	.15	.11	.06
192	Mike Quick	.08	.06	.03
193	Ray Ellis (43)	.05	.04	.02
194	John Spagnola (44)	.05	.04	.02
195	Dennis Harrison (45)	.05	.04	.02
196	Wilbert Montgomery	.08	.06	.03
197	Greg Brown (47)	.05	.04	.02
198	Ron Jaworski (48)	.08	.06	.03
199	Paul McFadden (49)	.05	.04	.02
200	Wes Hopkins (50)	.05	.04	.02
201	William Andrews	.10	.08	.04
202	Mike Pitts (52)	.05	.04	.02
203	Steve Bartkowski (53)	.08	.06	.03
204	Gerald Riggs (54)	.08	.06	.03
205	Alfred Jackson (55)	.05	.04	.02
206	Don Smith (56)	.05	.04	.02
207	Mike Kenn (57)	.05	.04	.02
208	Kenny Johnson (58)	.05	.04	.02
209	Stacey Bailey	.05	.04	.02
210	Joe Montana	1.25	.90	.50
211	Wendell Tyler (61)	.05	.04	.02

212	Keena Turner (62)	.08	.06	.03
213	Ray Wersching (63)	.05	.04	.02
214	Dwight Clark	.15	.11	.06
215	Dwalne Board (65)	.05	.04	.02
216	Roger Craig (66)	.15	.11	.06
217	Ronnie Lott (67)	.15	.11	.06
218	Freddie Solomon (68)	.08	.06	.03
219	Lawrence Taylor	.25	.20	.10
220	Zeke Mowatt (70)	.05	.04	.02
221	Harry Carson (71)	.06	.05	.02
222	Rob Carpenter (72)	.05	.04	.02
223	Bobby Johnson (73)	.05	.04	.02
224	Joe Morris (74)	.07	.05	.03
225	Mark Haynes (75)	.05	.04	.02
226	Lionel Manuel (76)	.05	.04	.02
227	Phil Simms	.15	.11	.06
228	Billy Simms	.12	.09	.05
229	Leonard Thompson (79)	.03	.02	.01
230	James Jones (80)	.05	.04	.02
231	Ed Murray (81)	.05	.04	.02
232	William Gay	.05	.04	.02
233	Gary Danielson (83)	.05	.04	.02
234	Curtis Green (84)	.05	.04	.02
235	Bobby Watkins (85)	.05	.04	.02
236	Doug English (86)	.05	.04	.02
237	James Lofton	.20	.15	.08
238	Eddie Lee Ivery (88)	.06	.05	.02
239	Mike Douglas (89)	.05	.04	.02
240	Gerry Ellis (90)	.05	.04	.02
241	Tim Lewis (91)	.08	.06	.03
242	Paul Coffman (92)	.05	.04	.02
243	Tom Flynn (93)	.05	.04	.02
244	Ezra Johnson (94)	.05	.04	.02
245	Lynn Dickey	.08	.06	.03
246	Eric Dickerson	.60	.45	.25
247	Jack Youngblood (97)	.08	.06	.03
248	Doug Smith (98)	.05	.04	.02
249	Jeff Kemp (99)	.05	.04	.02
250	Kent Hill	.05	.04	.02
251	Mike Lansford (101)	.05	.04	.02
252	Henry Ellard (102)	.35	.25	.14
253	LeRoy Irvin (103)	.06	.05	.02
254	Ron Brown (104)	.20	.15	.08
255	John Riggins	.06	.05	.02
256	Dexter Manley (106)	.10	.08	.04
257	Darrell Green (107)	.15	.11	.06
258	Joe Theismann (108)	.05	.04	.02
259	Mark Moseley (109)	.05	.04	.02
260	Clint Didier (110)	.05	.04	.02
261	Vernon Dean (111)	.05	.04	.02
262	Calvin Muhammad (112)	.05	.04	.02
263	Art Monk	.20	.15	.08
264	Bruce Clark	.08	.06	.03
265	Hoby Brenner (115)	.05	.04	.02
266	Dave Wilson (116)	.06	.05	.02
267	Hokie Gajan (117)	.05	.04	.02
268	George Rogers	.10	.08	.04
269	Rickey Jackson (119)	.08	.06	.03
270	Brian Hansen (120)	.04	.03	.02
271	Dave Waymer (121)	.05	.04	.02
272	Richard Todd (122)	.05	.04	.02
273	Jan Stenerud	.15	.11	.06
274	Ted Brown (124)	.05	.04	.02
275	Leo Lewis (125)	.05	.04	.02
276	Scott Studwell (126)	.05	.04	.02
277	Alfred Anderson (127)	.05	.04	.02
278	Rufus Bess (128)	.05	.04	.02
279	Darrin Nelson (129)	.05	.04	.02
280	Greg Coleman (130)	.05	.04	.02
281	Tommy Kramer	.08	.06	.03
282	Joe Montana (283)	1.25	.90	.50
283	Dan Marino (282)	1.00	.70	.40
284	Brian Hansen (285)	.05	.04	.02
285	Jim Arnold (284)	.05	.04	.02

1986 Topps

Topps' 1986 offering was 396 cards for the fourth straight year. Cards showed a green background with diagonal white stripes; a photo of the player was enclosed in one of several colorful borders. The player's name is found at the bottom of the card; his team is at right. All-Pro cards show a small designation just above the player's name. Team cards show a yellow border. Cards were numbered according to the team's finish the previous season. Rookies in this set include William Perry, Al Toon, Jerry Rice, Keith Millard, Bernie Kosar, and Boomer Esiason. (Key: AP - All Pro)

		NM/M	NM	E
Complete Set (396):		180.00	135.00	72.50
Common Player:		.50	.25	.15
Wax Pack (17+1):		15.00		
Wax Box (36):		375.00		
1	Marcus Allen	.50	.25	.15
2	Eric Dickerson	.50	.25	.15
3	Lionel James	.50	.25	.15
4	Steve Largent	.50	.25	.15
5	George Martin	.50	.25	.15
6	Stephone Paige	.50	.25	.15
7	Walter Payton	2.50	1.25	.75
8	Super Bowl XX	.50	.25	.15
9	Chicago Bears Team (Walter Payton)	.50	.25	.15
10	Jim McMahon	.50	.25	.15
11	Walter Payton (AP)	3.00	1.50	.90
12	Matt Suhey	.50	.25	.15
13	Willie Gault	.50	.25	.15
14	Dennis McKinnon RC	.50	.25	.15
15	Emery Moorhead	.50	.25	.15
16	Jim Covert (AP)	.50	.25	.15
17	Jay Hilgenberg RC (AP)	.50	.25	.15
18	Kevin Butler RC	.50	.25	.15
19	Richard Dent (AP)	.50	.25	.15
20	William Perry RC	.80	.60	.30
21	Steve McMichael	.50	.25	.15
22	Dan Hampton	.50	.25	.10
23	Otis Wilson	.50	.25	.15
24	Mike Singletary	.60	.45	.25
25	Wilber Marshall RC	.50	.25	.15
26	Leslie Frazier	.50	.25	.15
27	Dave Duerson RC	.50	.25	.15
28	Gary Fencik	.50	.25	.15
29	New England Patriots Team (Craig James)	.50	.25	.15
30	Tony Eason	.50	.25	.15
31	Steve Grogan	.15	.11	.15
32	Craig James	.50	.25	.15
33	Tony Collins	.50	.25	.15
34	Irving Fryar	.50	.25	.15
35	Brian Holloway (AP)	.50	.25	.15
36	John Hannah (AP)	.50	.25	.15
37	Tony Franklin	.50	.25	.15
38	Garin Veris	.50	.25	.15
39	Andre Tippett (AP)	.50	.25	.15
40	Steve Nelson	.50	.25	.15
41	Raymond Clayborn	.50	.25	.15
42	Fred Marion RC	.50	.25	.15
43	Rich Camarillo	.50	.25	.15
44	Miami Dolphins Team (Dan Marino)	2.00	1.50	.80
45	Dan Marino (AP)	2.50	1.25	.75
46	Tony Nathan	.50	.25	.15
47	Ron Davenport	.50	.25	.15
48	Mark Duper	.50	.25	.15
49	Mark Clayton	.50	.25	.15
50	Nat Moore	.50	.25	.15
51	Bruce Hardy	.50	.25	.15
52	Roy Foster	.50	.25	.15
53	Dwight Stephenson	.50	.25	.15
54	Fuad Reveiz RC	.50	.25	.15
55	Bob Baumhower	.50	.25	.15
56	Mike Charles	.50	.25	.15
57	Hugh Green	.50	.25	.15
58	Glenn Blackwood	.50	.25	.15
59	Reggie Roby	.50	.25	.15
60	Los Angeles Raiders Team (Marcus Allen)	.50	.25	.15
61	Marc Wilson	.50	.25	.15
62	Marcus Allen (AP)	.50	.25	.15
63	Dokie Williams	.50	.25	.15
64	Todd Christensen	.50	.25	.15
65	Chris Bahr	.50	.25	.15
66	Fulton Walker	.50	.25	.15
67	Howie Long	.50	.25	.15
68	Bill Pickel	.50	.25	.15
69	Ray Guy	.50	.25	.15
70	Greg Townsend RC	.50	.25	.15
71	Rod Martin	.50	.25	.15
72	Matt Millen	.50	.25	.15
73	Mike Haynes (AP)	.50	.25	.15
74	Lester Hayes	.50	.25	.15
75	Vann McElroy	.50	.25	.15
76	Los Angeles Rams Team (Eric Dickerson)	.50	.25	.15
77	Dieter Brock	.50	.25	.15
78	Eric Dickerson	.50	.25	.15
79	Henry Ellard	.50	.25	.15
80	Ron Brown RC	.50	.25	.15
81	Tony Hunter	.50	.25	.15

82	Kent Hill (AP)	.50	.25	.15
83	Doug Smith	.50	.25	.15
84	Dennis Harrah	.50	.25	.15
85	Jackie Slater	.50	.25	.15
86	Mike Lansford	.50	.25	.15
87	Gary Jeter	.50	.25	.15
88	Mike Wilcher	.50	.25	.15
89	Jim Collins	.50	.25	.15
90	LeRoy Irvin	.50	.25	.15
91	Gary Green	.50	.25	.15
92	Nolan Cromwell	.50	.25	.15
93	Dale Hatcher	.50	.25	.15
94	New York Jets Team (Freeman McNeil)	.50	.25	.15
95	Ken O'Brien	.50	.25	.15
96	Freeman McNeil	.50	.25	.15
97	Tony Paige RC	.50	.25	.15
98	Johnny "Lam" Jones	.50	.25	.15
99	Wesley Walker	.50	.25	.15
100	Kurt Sohn	.50	.25	.15
101	Al Toon RC	.50	.25	.15
102	Mickey Shuler	.50	.25	.15
103	Marvin Powell	.50	.25	.15
104	Pat Leahy	.50	.25	.15
105	Mark Gastineau	.50	.25	.15
106	Joe Klecko (AP)	.50	.25	.15
107	Marty Lyons	.50	.25	.15
108	Lance Mehl	.50	.25	.15
109	Bobby Jackson	.50	.25	.15
110	Dave Jennings	.50	.25	.15
111	Denver Broncos Team (Sammy Winder)	.50	.25	.15
112	John Elway	2.50	1.50	.90
113	Sammy Winder	.50	.25	.15
114	Gerald Wilhite	.50	.25	.15
115	Steve Watson	.50	.25	.15
116	Vance Johnson RC	.50	.25	.15
117	Rick Karlis	.50	.25	.15
118	Rulon Jones	.50	.25	.15
119	Karl Mecklenburg RC (AP)	.50	.25	.15
120	Louis Wright	.50	.25	.15
121	Mike Harden	.50	.25	.15
122	Dennis Smith RC	.50	.25	.15
123	Steve Foley	.50	.25	.15
124	Dallas Cowboys Team (Tony Hill)	.50	.25	.15
125	Danny White	.50	.25	.15
126	Tony Dorsett	.50	.25	.15
127	Timmy Newsome	.50	.25	.15
128	Mike Renfro	.50	.25	.15
129	Tony Hill	.50	.25	.15
130	Doug Cosbie (AP)	.50	.25	.15
131	Rafael Septien	.50	.25	.15
132	Ed "Too Tall" Jones	.50	.25	.15
133	Randy White	.50	.25	.15
134	Jim Jeffcoat	.50	.25	.15
135	Everson Walls (AP)	.50	.25	.15
136	Dennis Thurman	.50	.25	.15
137	New York Giants Team (Joe Morris)	.50	.25	.15
138	Phil Simms	.50	.25	.15
139	Joe Morris	.50	.25	.15
140	George Adams RC	.50	.25	.15
141	Lionel Manuel	.50	.25	.15
142	Bobby Johnson	.50	.25	.15
143	Phil McConkey RC	.50	.25	.15
144	Mark Bavaro RC	.50	.25	.15
145	Zeke Mowatt	.50	.25	.15
146	Brad Benson	.50	.25	.15
147	Bart Oates RC	.50	.25	.15
148	Leonard Marshall RC (AP)	.50	.25	.15
149	Jim Burt	.50	.25	.15
150	George Martin	.50	.25	.15
151	Lawrence Taylor (AP)	.75	.60	.30
152	Harry Carson (AP)	.50	.25	.15
153	Elvis Patterson	.50	.25	.15
154	Sean Landeta	.50	.25	.15
155	San Francisco 49ers Team (Roger Craig)	.50	.25	.15
156	Joe Montana	4.00	2.00	1.20
157	Roger Craig	.50	.25	.15
158	Wendell Tyler	.50	.25	.15
159	Carl Monroe	.50	.25	.15
160	Dwight Clark	.50	.25	.15
161	Jerry Rice RC	30.00	15.00	9.00
162	Randy Cross	.50	.25	.15
163	Keith Fahnhorst	.50	.25	.15
164	Jeff Stover	.50	.25	.15
165	Michael Carter RC	.50	.25	.15
166	Dwaine Board	.50	.25	.15
167	Eric Wright	.50	.25	.15
168	Ronnie Lott	.50	.25	.15
169	Carlton Williamson	.50	.25	.15
170	Washington Redskins Team (Dave Butz)	.50	.25	.15
171	Joe Theismann	.50	.25	.15
172	Jay Schroeder RC	.50	.25	.15
173	George Rogers	.50	.25	.15

174	Ken Jenkins	.50	.25	.15
175	Art Monk (AP)	.50	.25	.15
176	Gary Clark **RC**	.50	.25	.15
177	Joe Jacoby	.50	.25	.15
178	Russ Grimm	.50	.25	.15
179	Mark Moseley	.50	.25	.15
180	Dexter Manely	.50	.25	.15
181	Charles Mann **RC**	.50	.25	.15
182	Vernon Dean	.50	.25	.15
183	Raphel Cherry **RC**	.50	.25	.15
184	Curtis Jordan	.50	.25	.15
185	Cleveland Browns Team			
	(Bernie Kosar)	.50	.25	.15
186	Gary Danielson	.50	.25	.15
187	Bernie Kosar **RC**	3.00	1.50	.90
188	Kevin Mack **RC**	.50	.25	.15
189	Earnest Byner **RC**	.50	.25	.15
190	Glen Young	.50	.25	.15
191	Ozzie Newsome	.50	.25	.15
192	Mike Baab	.50	.25	.15
193	Cody Risien	.50	.25	.15
194	Bob Golic	.50	.25	.15
195	Reggie Camp	.50	.25	.15
196	Chip Banks	.50	.25	.15
197	Tom Cousineau	.50	.25	.15
198	Frank Minnifield **RC**	.50	.25	.15
199	Al Gross	.50	.25	.15
200	Seattle Seahawks Team			
	(Curt Warner)	.50	.25	.15
201	Dave Krieg	.50	.25	.10
202	Curt Warner	.15	.11	.15
203	Steve Largent (AP)	.65	.50	.25
204	Norm Johnson	.50	.25	.15
205	Daryl Turner	.50	.25	.15
206	Jacob Green	.50	.25	.15
207	Joe Nash	.50	.25	.15
208	Jeff Bryant	.50	.25	.15
209	Randy Edwards	.50	.25	.15
210	Fredd Young	.50	.25	.15
211	Kenny Easley	.50	.25	.15
212	John Harris	.50	.25	.15
213	Green Bay Packers Team			
	(Paul Coffman)	.50	.25	.15
214	Lynn Dickey	.50	.25	.15
215	Gerry Ellis	.50	.25	.15
216	Eddie Lee Ivery	.50	.25	.15
217	Jessie Clark	.50	.25	.15
218	James Lofton	.50	.25	.15
219	Paul Coffman	.50	.25	.15
220	Alphonso Carreker	.50	.25	.15
221	Ezra Johnson	.50	.25	.15
222	Mike Douglass	.50	.25	.15
223	Tim Lewis	.50	.25	.15
224	Mark Murphy **RC**	.50	.25	.15
225	Passing Leaders (Joe			
	Montana, Ken O'Brien)	.50	.25	.15
226	Receiving Leaders			
	(Lionel James, Roger			
	Craig)	.50	.25	.15
227	Rushing Leaders (Marcus			
	Allen, Gerald Riggs)	.50	.25	.15
228	Scoring Leaders (Gary			
	Anderson, Kevin			
	Butler)	.50	.25	.15
229	Interception Leaders			
	(Eugene Daniel, Albert			
	Lewis, Everson Walls)	.50	.25	.15
230	San Diego Chargers			
	Team (Dan Fouts)	.50	.25	.15
231	Dan Fouts	.50	.25	.15
232	Lionel James	.50	.25	.15
233	Gary Anderson **RC**	.50	.25	.15
234	Tim Spencer **RC**	.50	.25	.15
235	Wes Chandler	.50	.25	.15
236	Charlie Joiner	.50	.25	.15
237	Kellen Winslow	.50	.25	.15
238	Jim Lachey **RC**	.50	.25	.15
239	Bob Thomas	.50	.25	.15
240	Jeffery Dale	.50	.25	.15
241	Ralf Mojsiejenko	.50	.25	.15
242	Detroit Lions Team (Eric			
	Hipple)	.50	.25	.15
243	Eric Hipple	.50	.25	.15
244	Billy Sims	.50	.25	.15
245	James Jones	.50	.25	.15
246	Pete Mandley **RC**	.50	.25	.15
247	Leonard Thompson	.50	.25	.15
248	Lomas Brown **RC**	.50	.25	.15
249	Ed Murray	.50	.25	.15
250	Curtis Green	.50	.25	.15
251	William Gay	.50	.25	.15
252	Jimmy Williams	.50	.25	.15
253	Bobby Watkins	.50	.25	.15
254	Cincinnati Bengals Team			
	(Boomer Esiason)	.50	.25	.15
255	Boomer Esiason **RC**	4.00	3.00	1.50
256	James Brooks	.50	.25	.15
257	Larry Kinnebrew	.50	.25	.15

258	Cris Collinsworth	.50	.25	.15
259	Mike Martin	.50	.25	.15
260	Eddie Brown **RC**	.50	.20	.15
261	Anthony Munoz	.50	.25	.15
262	Jim Breech	.50	.25	.15
263	Ross Browner	.50	.25	.15
264	Carl Zander	.50	.25	.15
265	James Griffin	.50	.25	.15
266	Robert Jackson	.50	.25	.15
267	Pat McInally	.50	.25	.15
268	Philadelphia Eagles Team			
	(Ron Jaworski)	.50	.25	.15
269	Ron Jaworski	.50	.25	.15
270	Earnest Jackson	.50	.25	.15
271	Mike Quick	.50	.25	.15
272	John Spagnola	.50	.25	.15
273	Mark Dennard	.50	.25	.15
274	Paul McFadden	.50	.25	.15
275	Reggie White **RC**	6.00	3.00	1.80
276	Greg Brown	.50	.25	.15
277	Herman Edwards	.50	.25	.15
278	Roynell Young	.50	.25	.15
279	Wes Hopkins (AP)	.50	.25	.15
280	Pittsburgh Steelers Team			
	(Walter Abercrombie)	.50	.25	.15
281	Mark Malone	.50	.25	.15
282	Frank Pollard	.50	.25	.15
283	Walter Abercrombie	.50	.25	.15
284	Louis Lipps	.50	.25	.15
285	John Stallworth	.50	.25	.15
286	Mike Webster	.50	.25	.15
287	Gary Anderson (AP)	.50	.25	.15
288	Keith Willis	.50	.25	.15
289	Mike Merriweather	.50	.25	.15
290	Dwayne Woodruff	.50	.25	.15
291	Donnie Shell	.50	.25	.15
292	Minnesota Vikings Team			
	(Tommy Kramer)	.50	.25	.15
293	Tommy Kramer	.50	.25	.15
294	Darrin Nelson	.50	.25	.15
295	Ted Brown	.50	.25	.15
296	Buster Rhymes	.15	.11	.15
297	Anthony Carter **RC**	2.00	1.50	.80
298	Steve Jordan **RC**	1.00	.70	.40
299	Keith Millard **RC**	.50	.40	.20
300	Joey Browner **RC**	.75	.60	.30
301	John Turner	.50	.25	.15
302	Greg Coleman	.50	.25	.15
303	Kansas City Chiefs Team			
	(Todd Blackledge)	.50	.25	.15
304	Bill Kenney	.50	.25	.15
305	Herman Heard	.50	.25	.15
306	Stephon Paige **RC**	.50	.25	.15
307	Carlos Carson	.50	.25	.15
308	Nick Lowery	.50	.25	.15
309	Mike Bell	.50	.25	.15
310	Bill Maas	.50	.25	.15
311	Art Still	.50	.25	.15
312	Albert Lewis **RC**	.50	.25	.15
313	Deron Cherry (AP)	.50	.25	.15
314	Indianapolis Colts Team			
	(Rohn Stark)	.50	.25	.15
315	Mike Pagel	.50	.25	.15
316	Randy McMillian	.50	.25	.15
317	Albert Bentley **RC**	.50	.25	.15
318	George Wonsley	.50	.25	.15
319	Robbie Martin	.50	.25	.15
320	Pat Beach	.50	.25	.15
321	Chris Hinton	.50	.25	.15
322	Duane Bickett **RC**	.50	.25	.15
323	Eugene Daniel	.50	.25	.15
324	Cliff Odom **RC**	.50	.25	.15
325	Rohn Stark (AP)	.50	.25	.15
326	St. Louis Cardinals Team			
	(Stump Mitchell)	.50	.25	.15
327	Neil Lomax	.50	.25	.15
328	Stump Mitchell	.50	.25	.15
329	Ottis Anderson	.50	.25	.15
330	J.T. Smith	.50	.25	.15
331	Pat Tilley	.50	.25	.15
332	Roy Green	.50	.25	.15
333	Lance Smith	.50	.25	.15
334	Curtis Greer	.50	.25	.15
335	Freddie Joe Nunn **RC**	.50	.25	.15
336	E.J. Junior			
337	Lonnie Young **RC**	.50	.25	.15
338	New Orleans Saints Team			
	(Wayne Wilson)	.50	.25	.15
339	Bobby Hebert **RC**	.50	.25	.15
340	Dave Wilson	.50	.25	.15
341	Wayne Wilson	.50	.25	.15
342	Hoby Brenner	.50	.25	.15
343	Stan Brock	.50	.25	.15
344	Morten Andersen	.50	.25	.15
345	Bruce Clark	.50	.25	.15
346	Rickey Jackson	.50	.25	.15
347	Dave Waymer	.50	.25	.15
348	Brian Hansen			

349	Houston Oilers Team			
	(Warren Moon)	.60	.45	.25
350	Warren Moon	4.00	3.00	1.50
351	Mike Rozier **RC**	.50	.25	.15
352	Butch Woolfolk	.50	.25	.15
353	Drew Hill	.50	.25	.15
354	Willie Drewrey **RC**	.50	.25	.15
355	Tim Smith	.50	.25	.15
356	Mike Munchak	.50	.25	.15
357	Ray Childress **RC**	1.50	1.25	.60
358	Frank Bush	.50	.25	.15
359	Steve Brown	.50	.25	.15
360	Atlanta Falcons Team			
	(Gerald Riggs)	.50	.25	.15
361	Dave Archer	.50	.25	.15
362	Gerald Riggs	.50	.25	.15
363	William Andrews	.50	.25	.15
364	Billy Johnson	.50	.25	.15
365	Arthur Cox	.50	.25	.15
366	Mike Kenn	.50	.25	.15
367	Bill Fralic **RC**	.50	.25	.15
368	Mick Luckhurst	.50	.25	.15
369	Rick Bryan	.50	.25	.15
370	Bobby Butler	.50	.25	.15
371	Rick Donnelly	.50	.25	.15
372	Tampa Bay Buccaneers			
	Team (James Wilder)	.50	.25	.15
373	Steve DeBerg	.50	.25	.10
374	Steve Young **RC**	15.00	7.50	4.50
375	James Wilder	.50	.25	.15
376	Kevin House	.50	.25	.15
377	Gerald Carter	.50	.25	.15
379	Sean Farrell	.50	.25	.15
380	Donald Igwebuike	.50	.25	.15
381	David Logan	.50	.25	.15
382	Jeremiah Castille **RC**	.50	.25	.15
383	Buffalo Bills Team (Greg			
	Bell)	.50	.25	.15
384	Bruce Mathison **RC**	.50	.25	.15
385	Joe Cribbs	.50	.25	.15
386	Greg Bell	.50	.25	.15
387	Jerry Butler	.50	.25	.15
388	Andre Reed **RC**	3.00	1.50	.90
389	Bruce Smith **RC**	5.00	2.50	1.50
390	Fred Smerlas	.50	.25	.15
391	Darryl Talley	.50	.50	.15
392	Jim Haslett	.50	.25	.15
393	Charles Romes	.50	.25	.15
394	Checklist 1-132	.50	.25	.15
395	Checklist 133-264	.50	.25	.15
396	Checklist 265-396	.50	.25	.15

1986 Topps 1000 Yard Club

Issued one card per wax pack with the 1986 regular-issue cards, this 26-card set shows each player who gained 1,000 yards rushing or receiving the previous year. The card order was determined by the number of yards gained, with Marcus Allen, 1985's leading ground-gainer, ending up first. (San Francisco's Roger Craig gained 1,000 yards rushing and receiving the previous year, but only his rushing yardage is listed). Printed on heavy white cardboard stock, card fronts show an ornate arch design in light green. Backs are printed in red and orange.

		NM/M	NM	E
	Complete Set (26):	6.00	4.50	2.50
	Common Player:	.10	.08	.04
1	Marcus Allen	.40	.30	.15
2	Gerald Riggs	.20	.15	.08
3	Walter Payton	1.00	.70	.40
4	Joe Morris	.30	.25	.12
5	Freeman McNeil	.20	.15	.08
6	Tony Dorsett	.50	.40	.20
7	James Wilder	.10	.08	.04
8	Steve Largent	1.00	.70	.40
9	Mike Quick	.10	.08	.04
10	Eric Dickerson	1.25	.90	.50
11	Craig James	.10	.08	.04
12	Art Monk	.20	.15	.08
13	Wes Chandler	.10	.08	.04

14	Drew Hill	.10	.08	.04
15	James Lofton	.20	.15	.08
16	Louis Lipps	.20	.15	.08
17	Cris Collinsworth	.10	.08	.04
18	Tony Hill	.10	.08	.04
19	Kevin Mack	.10	.08	.04
20	Curt Warner	.20	.15	.08
21	George Rogers	.10	.08	.04
22	Roger Craig	.40	.30	.15
23	Earnest Jackson	.10	.08	.04
24	Lionel James	.10	.08	.04
25	Stump Mitchell	.10	.08	.04
26	Earnest Byner	.10	.08	.04

1986 Topps Box Bottoms

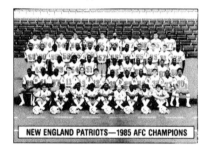

NEW ENGLAND PATRIOTS—1985 AFC CHAMPIONS

These four cards were featured on the sides of 1986 Topps wax pack boxes, one per box. The cards, which are standard size, feature the top four teams in the NFL in 1985 - the two Super Bowl participants and their opponents in the conference championship games. The team is pictured on the front; the back identifies those in the picture.

	NM/M	NM	E
Complete Set (4):	5.00	3.75	2.00
Common Player:	1.00	.70	.40
A **Chicago Bears**	2.50	2.00	1.00
B **New England Patriots**	1.00	.70	.40
C **Los Angeles Rams**	1.00	.70	.40
D **Miami Dolphins**	2.50	2.00	1.00

1986 Topps Stickers

Topps included foil stickers in its sticker set again in 1986, and followed the format it used for previous issues. The stickers use a shadow box for the frame on the front, around a color photo. A card number appears on both sides. The back has its information printed in brown ink against a white background. Some stickers were issued in pairs, as indicated by the parenthesis after the player's name in the checklist. The All-Pro players are foil stickers (#s 132-143) as are #s 282-285. The Chicago Bears are featured on the covers of the corresponding album which was issued to hold the stickers; Walter Payton is on the front.

		NM/M	NM	E
Complete Set (285):		20.00	15.00	8.00
Common Player:		.05	.04	.02
1	Walter Payton (left)	.60	.45	.25
2	Walter Payton (right)	.60	.45	.25
3	Richard Dent (left)	.10	.08	.04
4	Richard Dent (right)	.10	.08	.04
5	Richard Dent (Super Bowl MVP)	.40	.30	.15
6	Walter Payton	1.00	.70	.40
7	William Perry	.12	.09	.05
8	Jim McMahon (158)	.10	.08	.04
9	Richard Dent (159)	.10	.08	.04
10	Jim Covert (160)	.05	.04	.02
11	Dan Hampton (161)	.08	.06	.03
12	Mike Singletary (162)	.08	.06	.03
13	Jay Hilgenberg (163)	.06	.05	.02
14	Otis Wilson (164)	.04	.03	.02
15	Jimmie Giles	.05	.04	.02
16	Kevin House (166)	.03	.02	.01
17	Jeremiah Castille (167)	.03	.02	.01
18	James Wilder	.05	.04	.02
19	Donald Igwebuike (169)	.05	.04	.02
20	David Logan (170)	.05	.04	.02
21	Jeff Davis (171)	.05	.04	.02
22	Frank Garcia (172)	.05	.04	.02
23	Steve Young (173)	1.00	.70	.40
24	Stump Mitchell	.08	.06	.03
25	E.J. Junior	.08	.06	.03
26	J.T. Smith (176)	.05	.04	.02
27	Pat Tilley (177)	.05	.04	.02
28	Neil Lomax (178)	.06	.05	.02
29	Leonard Smith (179)	.05	.04	.02
30	Ottis Anderson (180)	.08	.06	.03
31	Curtis Greer (181)	.05	.04	.02
32	Roy Green (182)	.06	.05	.02
33	Tony Dorsett	.30	.25	.12
34	Tony Hill (184)	.05	.04	.02
35	Doug Cosbie (185)	.06	.05	.02
36	Everson Walls	.08	.06	.03
37	Randy White (187)	.10	.08	.04
38	Rafael Septien (188)	.05	.04	.02
39	Mike Renfro (189)	.05	.04	.02
40	Danny White (190)	.06	.05	.02
41	Ed "Too Tall" Jones (191)	.10	.08	.04
42	Earnest Jackson	.08	.06	.03
43	Mike Quick	.08	.06	.03
44	Wes Hopkins (194)	.05	.04	.02
45	Reggie White (195)	.75	.60	.30
46	Greg Brown (196)	.05	.04	.02
47	Paul McFadden (197)	.05	.04	.02
48	John Spagnola (198)	.05	.04	.02
49	Ron Jaworski (199)	.05	.04	.02
50	Herman Hunter (200)	.05	.04	.02
51	Gerald Riggs	.10	.08	.04
52	Mike Pitts (202)	.05	.04	.02
53	Buddy Curry (203)	.05	.04	.02
54	Billy Johnson	.12	.09	.05
55	Rick Donnelly (205)	.05	.04	.02
56	Rick Bryan (206)	.08	.06	.03
57	Bobby Butler (207)	.05	.04	.02
58	Mike Luckhurst (208)	.05	.04	.02
59	Mike Kenn (209)	.05	.04	.02
60	Roger Craig	.25	.20	.10
61	Joe Montana	1.75	1.25	.70
62	Michael Carter (212)	.10	.08	.04
63	Eric Wright (213)	.05	.04	.02
64	Dwight Clark (214)	.10	.08	.04
65	Ronnie Lott (215)	.12	.09	.05
66	Carlton Williamson (216)	.05	.04	.02
67	Wendell Tyler (217)	.08	.06	.03
68	Dwaine Board (218)	.05	.04	.02
69	Joe Morris	.12	.09	.05
70	Leonard Marshall (220)	.05	.04	.02
71	Lionel Manuel (221)	.05	.04	.02
72	Harry Carson	.10	.08	.04
73	Phil Simms (223)	.10	.08	.04
74	Sean Landeta (224)	.05	.04	.02
75	Lawrence Taylor (225)	.15	.11	.06
76	Elvis Patterson (226)	.05	.04	.02
77	George Adams (227)	.05	.04	.02
78	James Jones	.08	.06	.03
79	Leonard Thompson	.05	.04	.02
80	William Graham (230)	.05	.04	.02
81	Mark Nichols (231)	.05	.04	.02
82	William Gay (232)	.05	.04	.02
83	Jimmy Williams (233)	.05	.04	.02
84	Billy Sims (234)	.12	.09	.05
85	Bobby Watkins (235)	.05	.04	.02
86	Ed Murray (236)	.05	.04	.02
87	James Lofton	.25	.20	.10
88	Jessie Clark (238)	.05	.04	.02
89	Tim Lewis (239)	.05	.04	.02
90	Eddie Lee Ivery	.08	.06	.03
91	Phillip Epps (241)	.05	.04	.02
92	Ezra Johnson (242)	.05	.04	.02
93	Mike Douglass (243)	.05	.04	.02
94	Paul Coffman (244)	.05	.04	.02
95	Randy Scott (245)	.03	.02	.01
96	Eric Dickerson	.45	.35	.20
97	Dale Hatcher	.05	.04	.02
98	Ron Brown (248)	.06	.05	.02
99	LeRoy Irvin (249)	.05	.04	.02
100	Ken Hill (250)	.05	.04	.02
101	Dennis Harrah (251)	.05	.04	.02
102	Jackie Slater (252)	.08	.06	.03
103	Mike Wilcher (253)	.05	.04	.02
104	Doug Smith (254)	.05	.04	.02
105	Art Monk	.25	.20	.10
106	Joe Jacoby (256)	.05	.04	.02
107	Russ Grimm (257)	.05	.04	.02
108	George Rogers	.10	.08	.04
109	Dexter Manley (259)	.05	.04	.02
110	Jay Schroeder (260)	.12	.09	.05
111	Gary Calrk (261)	.50	.40	.20
112	Curtis Jordan (262)	.05	.04	.02
113	Charles Mann (263)	.08	.06	.03
114	Morten Andersen	.08	.06	.03
115	Rickey Jackson	.10	.00	.04
116	Glen Redd (266)	.05	.04	.02
117	Bobby Hebert (267)	.20	.15	.08
118	Hoby Brenner (268)	.05	.04	.02
119	Brian Hansen (269)	.05	.04	.02
120	Dave Waymer (270)	.05	.04	.02
121	Bruce Clark (271)	.05	.04	.02
122	Wayne Wilson (272)	.05	.04	.02
123	Joey Browner	.25	.20	.10
124	Darrin Nelson (274)	.08	.06	.03
125	Keith Millard (275)	.15	.11	.06
126	Anthony Carter	.35	.25	.14
127	Buster Rhymes (277)	.04	.03	.02
128	Steve Jordan (278)	.20	.15	.08
129	Greg Coleman (279)	.05	.04	.02
130	Ted Brown (280)	.05	.04	.02
131	John Turner (281)	.05	.04	.02
132	Harry Carson (144, All-Pro)	.20	.15	.08
133	Deron Cherry (145, All-Pro)	.10	.08	.04
134	Richard Dent (146, All-Pro)	.20	.15	.08
135	Mike Haynes (147, All-Pro)	.12	.09	.05
136	Wes Hopkins (148, All-Pro)	.10	.08	.04
137	Joe Klecko (149, All-Pro)	.10	.08	.04
138	Leonard Marshall (150, All-Pro)	.10	.08	.04
139	Karl Mecklenburg (151, All-Pro)	.12	.09	.05
140	Rohn Stark (152, All-Pro)	.10	.08	.04
141	Lawrence Taylor (153, All-Pro)	.25	.20	.10
142	Andre Tippett (154, All-Pro)	.12	.09	.05
143	Everson Walls (155, All-Pro)	.12	.09	.05
144	Marcus Allen (132, All-Pro)	.35	.25	.14
145	Gary Anderson (133, All-Pro)	.10	.08	.04
146	Doug Cosbie (134, All-Pro)	.15	.11	.06
147	Jim Covert (135, All-Pro)	.15	.11	.06
148	John Hannah (136, All-Pro)	.15	.11	.06
149	Jay Hilgenberg (137, All-Pro)	.12	.09	.05
150	Ken Hil (138, All-Pro)	.10	.08	.04
151	Brian Holloway (139, All-Pro)	.10	.08	.04
152	Steve Largent (140, All-Pro)	.75	.60	.30
153	Dan Marino (141, All-Pro)	1.50	1.25	.60
154	Art Monk (142, All-Pro)	.25	.20	.10
155	Walter Payton (143, All-Pro)	.75	.60	.30
156	Anthony Munoz	.15	.11	.06
157	Boomer Esiason	.40	.30	.15
158	Cris Collinsworth (8)	.06	.05	.02
159	Eddie Edwards (9)	.05	.04	.02
160	James Griffin (10)	.05	.04	.02
161	Jim Breech (11)	.05	.04	.02
162	Eddie Brown (12)	.05	.04	.02
163	Ross Browner (13)	.05	.04	.02
164	James Brooks (14)	.07	.05	.03
165	Greg Bell	.08	.06	.03
166	Jerry Butler (16)	.05	.04	.02
167	Don Wilson (17)	.05	.04	.02
168	Andre Reed	.75	.60	.30
169	Jim Haslett (19)	.05	.04	.02
170	Bruce Mathison (20)	.05	.04	.02
171	Bruce Smith (21)	.40	.30	.15
172	Joe Cribbs (22)	.05	.04	.02
173	Charles Romes (23)	.05	.04	.02
174	Karl Mecklenburg	.08	.06	.03
175	Rulon Jones	.05	.04	.02
176	John Elway (26)	.40	.30	.15
177	Sammy Winder (27)	.10	.08	.04
178	Louis Wright (28)	.05	.04	.02
179	Steve Watson (29)	.05	.04	.02
180	Dennis Smith (30)	.05	.04	.02
181	Mike Harden (31)	.05	.04	.02
182	Vance Johnson (32)	.10	.08	.04
183	Kevin Mack	.10	.08	.04
184	Chip Banks (34)	.05	.04	.02
185	Bob Golic (35)	.05	.04	.02
186	Earnest Byner	.35	.25	.14
187	Ozzie Newsome (37)	.12	.09	.05
188	Bernie Kosar (38)	.60	.45	.25
189	Don Rogers (39)	.05	.04	.02
190	Al Gross (40)	.05	.04	.02
191	Clarence Weathers (41)	.08	.06	.03

192	Lionel James	.08	.06	.03
193	Dan Fouts	.40	.30	.15
194	Wes Chandler (44)	.06	.05	.02
195	Kellen Winslow (45)	.10	.08	.04
196	Gary Anderson (46)	.07	.05	.03
197	Charlie Joiner (47)	.08	.06	.03
198	Ralf Mojsiejenko (48)	.05	.04	.02
199	Bob Thomas (49)	.05	.04	.02
200	Tim Spencer (50)	.05	.04	.02
201	Deron Cherry	.10	.08	.04
202	Bill Maas (52)	.05	.04	.02
203	Herman Heard (53)	.05	.04	.02
204	Carlos Carson	.08	.06	.03
205	Nick Lowery (55)	.08	.06	.03
206	Bill Kenney (56)	.05	.04	.02
207	Albert Lewis (57)	.25	.20	.10
208	Art Still (58)	.05	.04	.02
209	Stephone Paige (59)	.25	.20	.10
210	Rohn Stark	.05	.04	.02
211	Chris Hinton	.10	.08	.04
212	Albert Bentley (62)	.10	.08	.04
213	Eugene Daniel (63)	.05	.04	.02
214	Pat Beach (64)	.05	.04	.02
215	Cliff Odom (65)	.05	.04	.02
216	Duane Bickett (66)	.20	.15	.08
217	George Wonsley (67)	.05	.04	.02
218	Randy McMillan (68)	.05	.04	.02
219	Dan Marino	1.50	1.25	.60
220	Dwight Stephenson (70)	.08	.06	.03
221	Roy Foster (71)	.05	.04	.02
222	Mark Clayton	.20	.15	.08
223	Mark Duper (73)	.10	.08	.04
224	Fuad Reveiz (74)	.05	.04	.02
225	Reggie Roby (75)	.05	.04	.02
226	Tony Nathan (76)	.05	.04	.02
227	Ron Davenport (77)	.05	.04	.02
228	Freeman McNeil	.10	.08	.04
229	Joe Klecko	.08	.06	.03
230	Mark Gastineau (80)	.05	.04	.02
231	Ken O'Brien (81)	.06	.05	.02
232	Lance Mehl (82)	.05	.04	.02
233	Al Toon (83)	.20	.15	.08
234	Mickey Shuler (84)	.05	.04	.02
235	Pat Leahy (85)	.05	.04	.02
236	Wesley Walker (86)	.06	.05	.02
237	Drew Hill	.10	.08	.04
238	Warren Moon (88)	.40	.30	.15
239	Mike Rozier (89)	.10	.08	.04
240	Mike Munchak	.10	.08	.04
241	Tim Smith (91)	.05	.04	.02
242	Butch Woolfolk (92)	.05	.04	.02
243	Willie Drewrey (93)	.05	.04	.02
244	Keith Bostic (94)	.05	.04	.02
245	Jesse Baker (95)	.05	.04	.02
246	Craig James	.15	.11	.06
247	John Hannah	.12	.09	.05
248	Tony Eason (98)	.06	.05	.02
249	Andre Tippett (99)	.06	.05	.02
250	Tony Collins (100)	.05	.04	.02
251	Brian Holloway (101)	.05	.04	.02
252	Irving Fryar (102)	.10	.08	.04
253	Raymond Clayborn (103)	.05	.04	.02
254	Steve Nelson (104)	.05	.04	.02
255	Marcus Allen	.25	.20	.10
256	Mike Haynes (106)	.08	.06	.03
257	Todd Christensen (107)	.06	.05	.02
258	Howie Long	.12	.09	.05
259	Lester Hayes (109)	.05	.04	.02
260	Rod Martin (110)	.08	.06	.03
261	Dokie Williams (111)	.08	.06	.03
262	Chris Bahr (112)	.05	.04	.02
263	Bill Pickel (113)	.05	.04	.02
264	Curt Warner	.10	.08	.04
265	Steve Largent	.60	.45	.25
266	Fredd Young (116)	.06	.05	.02
267	Dave Krieg (117)	.08	.06	.03
268	Daryl Turner (118)	.05	.04	.02
269	John Harris (119)	.05	.04	.02
270	Randy Edwards (120)	.05	.04	.02
271	Kenny Easley (121)	.05	.04	.02
272	Jacob Green (122)	.05	.04	.02
273	Gary Anderson	.05	.04	.02
274	Mike Webster (124)	.07	.05	.03
275	Walter Abercombie (125)	.08	.06	.03
276	Louis Lipps	.10	.08	.04
277	Frank Pollard (127)	.05	.04	.02
278	Mike Merriweather (128)	.05	.04	.02
279	Mark Malone (129)	.05	.04	.02
280	Donnie Shell (130)	.08	.06	.03
281	John Stallworth (131)	.06	.05	.02
282	Marcus Allen (284)	.50	.40	.20
283	Ken O'Brien (285)	.15	.11	.06
284	Kevin Butler (282)	.15	.11	.06
285	Roger Craig (283)	.35	.25	.14

1987 Topps

Topps' fifth straight 396-card set was bordered in white and carried two flags at the top of the card - one indicating the team, the other indicating the player name. His position was listed in the border above the name. Cards were numbered in order of the team's finish the previous year. This set, which seems to be one of the hottest sets since the '84 issue, includes such rookies as Randall Cunningham, Jim Everett, Reuben Mayes, John Offerdahl, Ernest Givins and Tim Harris. This set also features the last regular-issue card of all-time rushing leader Walter Payton. Three errors have been found in the set: On the back of card #274, Rueben Mayes, the statistical heading reads "Comp" for completions, when it should read "yards." The statistical heading was apparently intended for a quarterback instead of a running back. Also, the back of card #288, John Stallworth, is missing statistics from the years 1982-86. Finally, the reverse of Ross Browner's card (#263) contains a reference to the Bengals' 1982 Super Bowl win. The Bengals, however, lost to the 49ers that year. Not only that, the card also lists the Super Bowl date as 1-10-82 when it was actually played 1-24-82. (Key: AP - All Pro)

	NM/M	NM	E
Complete Set (396):	90.00	45.00	27.00
Common Player:	.50	.25	.15
Wax Pack (15+1):	2.00		
Wax Box (36):	50.00		

1	Super Bowl XXI	.50	.25	.15
2	Todd Christensen	.50	.25	.15
3	Dave Jennings	.50	.25	.15
4	Charlie Joiner	.50	.25	.15
5	Steve Largent	.50	.25	.15
6	Dan Marino	.75	.38	.25
7	Donnie Shell	.50	.25	.15
8	Phil Simms	.50	.25	.15
9	Giants team (Mark Bavaro)	.50	.25	.15
10	Phil Simms	.50	.25	.15
11	Joe Morris (AP)	.50	.25	.15
12	Maurice Carthon **RC**	.50	.25	.15
13	Lee Rouson	.50	.25	.15
14	Bobby Johnson	.50	.25	.15
15	Lionel Manuel	.50	.25	.15
16	Phil McConkey	.50	.25	.15
17	Mark Bavaro (AP)	.50	.25	.15
18	Zeke Mowatt	.50	.25	.15
19	Raul Allegre	.50	.25	.15
20	Sean Landeta	.50	.25	.15
21	Brad Benson	.50	.25	.15
22	Jim Burt	.50	.25	.15
23	Leonard Marshall	.50	.25	.15
24	Carl Banks	.50	.25	.15
25	Harry Carson	.50	.25	.15
26	Lawrence Taylor (AP)	.50	.25	.15
27	Terry Kinard **RC**	.50	.25	.15
28	Pepper Johnson **RC**	.50	.25	.15
29	Erik Howard **RC**	.50	.25	.15
30	Broncos team (Gerald Wilhite)	.50	.05	.15
31	John Elway	1.50	.75	.45
32	Gerald Wilhite	.50	.25	.15
33	Sammy Winder	.50	.25	.15
34	Ken Bell	.50	.25	.15
35	Steve Watson	.50	.25	.15
36	Rick Karlis	.50	.25	.15
37	Keith Bishop	.50	.25	.15
38	Rulon Jones	.50	.25	.15
39	Karl Mecklenburg (AP)	.50	.25	.15
40	Louis Wright	.50	.25	.15
41	Mike Harden	.50	.25	.15
42	Dennis Smith	.50	.25	.15
43	Bears team (Walter Payton)	.50	.25	.15
44	Jim McMahon	.50	.25	.15
45	Doug Flutie **RC**	2.00	1.00	.60
46	Walter Payton	2.00	1.00	.60
47	Matt Suhey	.50	.25	.15
48	Willie Gault	.50	.25	.15
49	Dennis Gentry **RC**	.50	.25	.15
50	Kevin Butler	.50	.25	.15
51	Jim Covert (AP)	.50	.25	.15
52	Jay Hilgenberg	.50	.25	.15
53	Dan Hampton	.50	.25	.15
54	Steve McMichael	.50	.25	.15
55	William Perry	.50	.25	.15
56	Richard Dent	.50	.25	.15
57	Otis Wilson	.50	.25	.15
58	Mike Singletary (AP)	.50	.25	.15
59	Wilber Marshall	.50	.25	.15
60	Mike Richardson	.50	.25	.15
61	Dave Duerson	.50	.25	.15
62	Gary Fencik	.50	.25	.15
63	Redskins team (George Rogers)	.50	.25	.15
64	Jay Schroeder	.50	.25	.15
65	George Rogers	.50	.25	.15
66	Kelvin Bryant **RC**	.50	.25	.15
67	Ken Jenkins	.50	.25	.15
68	Gary Clark	.50	.25	.15
69	Art Monk	.50	.25	.15
70	Clint Didier **RC**	.50	.25	.15
71	Steve Cox	.50	.25	.15
72	Joe Jacoby	.50	.25	.15
73	Russ Grimm	.50	.25	.15
74	Charles Mann	.50	.25	.15
75	Dave Butz	.50	.25	.15
76	Dexter Manley (AP)	.50	.25	.15
77	Darrell Green (AP)	.50	.25	.15
78	Curtis Jordan	.50	.25	.15
79	**Browns team**	.50	.25	.15
80	Bernie Kosar	.50	.25	.15
81	Curtis Dickey	.50	.25	.15
82	Kevin Mack	.50	.25	.15
83	Herman Fontenot	.50	.25	.15
84	Brian Brennan **RC**	.50	.25	.15
85	Ozzie Newsome	.50	.25	.15
86	Jeff Gossett	.50	.25	.15
87	Cody Risien (AP)	.50	.25	.15
88	Reggie Camp	.50	.25	.15
89	Bob Golic	.50	.25	.15
90	Carl Hairston	.50	.25	.15
91	Chip Banks	.50	.25	.15
92	Frank Minnifield	.50	.25	.15
93	Hanford Dixon (AP)	.50	.25	.15
94	Gerald McNeil **RC**	.50	.25	.15
95	Dave Puzzuoli	.50	.25	.15
96	Patriots team (Andre Tippett)	.50	.25	.15
97	Tony Eason	.50	.25	.15
98	Craig James	.50	.25	.15
99	Tony Collins	.50	.25	.15
100	Mosi Tatupu	.50	.25	.15
101	Stanley Morgan	.50	.25	.15
102	Irving Fryar	.50	.25	.15
103	Stephen Starring	.50	.25	.15
104	Tony Franklin (AP)	.50	.25	.15
105	Rich Camarillo	.50	.25	.15
106	Garin Veris	.50	.25	.15
107	Andre Tippett (AP)	.50	.25	.15
108	Don Blackmon	.50	.25	.15
109	Ronnie Lippett **RC**	.50	.25	.15
110	Raymond Clayborn	.50	.25	.15
111	49ers team (Roger Craig)	.50	.25	.15
112	Joe Montana	2.00	1.00	.60
113	Roger Craig	.50	.25	.15
114	Joe Cribbs	.50	.25	.15
115	Jerry Rice (AP)	2.00	1.00	.60
116	Dwight Clark	.50	.25	.15
117	Ray Wersching	.50	.25	.15
118	Max Runager	.50	.25	.15
119	Jeff Stover	.50	.25	.15
120	Dwaine Board	.50	.25	.15
121	Tim McKyer **RC**	.50	.25	.15
122	Don Griffin **RC**	.50	.25	.15
123	Ronnie Lott (AP)	.50	.25	.12
124	Tom Holmoe	.50	.25	.15
125	Charles Haley **RC**	.50	.25	.15
126	Jets team (Mark Gastineau)	.50	.25	.15
127	Ken O'Brien	.50	.25	.15
128	Pat Ryan	.50	.25	.15
129	Freeman McNeil	.50	.25	.15
130	Johnny Hector **RC**	.50	.25	.15
131	Al Toon (AP)	.50	.25	.15
132	Wesley Walker	.50	.25	.15
133	Mickey Shuler	.50	.25	.15
134	Pat Leahy	.50	.25	.15
135	Mark Gastineau	.50	.25	.15
136	Joe Klecko	.50	.25	.15
137	Marty Lyons	.50	.25	.15
138	Bob Crable	.50	.25	.15
141	Harry Hamilton **RC**	.50	.25	.15
142	Lester Lyles	.50	.25	.15
143	Bobby Humphery	.50	.25	.15
144	Rams team (Eric Dickerson)	.50	.25	.15
145	Jim Everett **RC**	3.00	2.25	1.25
146	Eric Dickerson (AP)	.50	.40	.20
147	Barry Redden	.50	.25	.15
148	Ron Brown	.50	.25	.15

149	Kevin House	.50	.25	.15
150	Henry Ellard	.60	.45	.25
151	Doug Smith	.50	.25	.15
152	Dennis Harrah (AP)	.50	.25	.15
153	Jackie Slater	.50	.25	.15
154	Gary Jeter	.50	.25	.15
155	Carl Ekern	.50	.25	.15
156	Mike Wilcher	.50	.25	.15
157	Jerry Gray **RC**	.25	.25	.10
158	LeRoy Irvin	.50	.25	.15
159	Nolan Cromwell	.50	.25	.15
160	Chiefs team (Todd Blackledge)	.50	.05	.15
161	Bill Kenney	.50	.25	.15
162	Stephone Paige	.50	.25	.15
163	Henry Marshall	.50	.25	.15
164	Carlos Carson	.50	.25	.15
165	Nick Lowery	.50	.25	.15
166	Irv Eatman **RC**	.50	.25	.15
167	Brad Budde	.50	.25	.15
168	Art Still	.50	.25	.15
169	Bill Maas (AP)	.50	.25	.15
170	Lloyd Burruss **RC**	.50	.25	.15
171	Deron Cherry (AP)	.50	.25	.15
172	Seahawks team (Curt Warner)	.50	.25	.15
173	Dave Krieg	.50	.25	.15
174	Curt Warner	.50	.25	.15
175	John L. Williams **RC**	.50	.25	.15
176	Bobby Joe Edmonds **RC**	.50	.25	.15
177	Steve Largent	.50	.25	.15
178	Bruce Scholtz	.50	.25	.15
179	Norm Johnson	.50	.25	.15
180	Jacob Green	.50	.25	.15
181	Fredd Young	.50	.25	.15
182	Dave Brown	.50	.25	.15
183	Kenny Easley	.50	.25	.15
184	Bengals team (James Brooks)	.50	.25	.15
185	Boomer Esiason	.50	.25	.15
186	James Brooks	.50	.25	.15
187	Larry Kinnebrew	.50	.25	.15
188	Cris Collinsworth	.50	.25	.15
189	Eddie Brown	.50	.25	.15
190	Tim McGee **RC**	.50	.25	.15
191	Jim Breech	.50	.25	.15
192	Anthony Munoz	.50	.25	.15
193	Max Montoya	.50	.25	.15
194	Eddie Edwards	.50	.25	.15
195	Ross Browner	.50	.25	.15
196	Emanuel King	.50	.25	.15
197	Louis Breeden	.50	.25	.15
198	Vikings team (Darrin Nelson)	.50	.25	.15
199	Tommy Kramer	.50	.25	.15
200	Darrin Nelson	.50	.25	.15
201	Allen Rice	.50	.25	.15
202	Anthony Carter	.50	.25	.15
203	Leo Lewis	.50	.25	.15
204	Steve Jordan	.50	.25	.15
205	Chuck Nelson	.50	.25	.15
206	Greg Coleman	.50	.25	.15
207	Gary Zimmerman **RC**	.50	.25	.15
208	Doug Martin	.50	.25	.15
209	Keith Millard	.50	.25	.15
210	Issiac Holt **RC**	.50	.25	.15
211	Joey Browner	.50	.25	.15
212	Rufus Bess	.50	.25	.15
213	Raiders team (Marcus Allen)	.50	.25	.15
214	Jim Plunkett	.50	.25	.15
215	Marcus Allen	.50	.25	.15
216	Napoleon McCallum **RC**	.50	.25	.15
217	Dokie Williams	.50	.25	.15
218	Todd Christensen	.50	.25	.15
219	Chris Bahr	.50	.25	.15
220	Howie Long	.50	.25	.15
221	Bill Pickel	.50	.25	.15
222	Sean Jones **RC**	.50	.25	.15
223	Lester Hayes	.50	.25	.15
224	Mike Haynes	.50	.25	.15
225	Vann McElroy	.50	.25	.15
226	Fulton Walker	.50	.25	.15
227	Passing Leaders (Tommy Kramer, Dan Marino)	.50	.25	.15
228	Receiving Leaders (Jerry Rice, Todd Christensen)	.50	.25	.15
229	Rushing leaders (Eric Dickerson, Curt Warner)	.50	.25	.15
230	Scoring leaders (Kevin Butler, Tony Franklin)	.50	.25	.15
231	Interception leaders (Ronnie Lott, Deron Cherry)	.50	.25	.15
232	Dolphins team (Reggie Roby)	.50	.25	.15
233	Dan Marino (AP)	2.00	1.00	.60
234	Lorenzo Hampton **RC**	.50	.25	.15
235	Tony Nathan	.50	.25	.15
236	Mark Duper	.50	.25	.15
237	Mark Clayton	.50	.25	.15
238	Nat Moore	.50	.25	.15
239	Bruce Hardy	.50	.25	.15
240	Reggie Roby	.50	.25	.15
241	Roy Foster	.50	.25	.15
242	Dwight Stephenson (AP)	.50	.25	.15
243	Hugh Green	.50	.25	.15
244	John Offerdahl **RC**	.50	.25	.15
245	Mark Brown	.50	.25	.15
246	Doug Betters	.50	.25	.15
247	Bob Baumhower	.50	.25	.15
248	Falcons team (Gerald Riggs)	.50	.25	.15
249	Dave Archer	.50	.25	.15
250	Gerald Riggs	.50	.25	.15
251	William Andrews	.50	.25	.15
252	Charlie Brown	.50	.25	.15
253	Arthur Cox	.50	.25	.15
254	Rick Donnelly	.50	.25	.15
255	Bill Fralic (AP)	.30	.25	.15
256	Mike Gann **RC**	.50	.25	.15
257	Rick Bryan	.50	.25	.15
258	Bret Clark	.50	.25	.15
259	Mike Pitts	.50	.25	.15
260	Cowboys team (Tony Dorsett)	.50	.25	.15
261	Danny White	.50	.25	.15
262	Steve Pelluer **RC**	.50	.25	.15
263	Tony Dorsett	.50	.25	.15
264	Herschel Walker **RC**	1.50	.75	.45
265	Timmy Newsome	.50	.25	.15
266	Tony Hill	.50	.25	.15
267	Mike Sherrard **RC**	.50	.25	.15
268	Jim Jeffcoat	.50	.25	.15
269	Ron Fellows	.50	.25	.15
270	Bill Bates	.50	.25	.15
271	Michael Downs	.50	.25	.15
272	Saints team (Bobby Hebert)	.50	.25	.15
273	Dave Wilson	.50	.25	.15
274	Rueben Mayes **RC**	.50	.25	.15
275	Hoby Brenner	.50	.25	.15
276	Eric Martin **RC**	.50	.25	.15
277	Morten Andersen	.50	.25	.15
278	Brian Hansen	.50	.25	.15
279	Rickey Jackson	.50	.25	.15
280	Dave Waymer	.50	.25	.15
281	Bruce Clark	.50	.25	.15
282	James Geathers	.50	.25	.15
283	Steelers team (Walter Abercrombie)	.50	.25	.15
284	Mark Malone	.50	.25	.15
285	Earnest Jackson	.50	.25	.15
286	Walter Abercrombie	.50	.25	.15
287	Louis Lipps	.50	.25	.15
288	John Stallworth	.50	.25	.15
289	Gary Anderson	.50	.25	.15
290	Keith Willis	.50	.25	.15
291	Mike Merriweather	.50	.25	.15
292	Lupe Sanchez	.50	.25	.15
293	Donnie Shell	.50	.25	.15
294	Eagles team (Keith Byars)	.50	.25	.15
295	Mike Reichenbach	.50	.25	.15
296	Randall Cunningham **RC**	2.00	1.00	.60
297	Keith Byars **RC**	.50	.25	.15
298	Mike Quick	.50	.25	.15
299	Kenny Jackson	.50	.25	.15
300	John Teltschik **RC**	.50	.08	.15
301	Reggie White (AP)	.50	.25	.15
302	Ken Clarke	.50	.25	.15
303	Greg Brown	.50	.25	.15
304	Roynell Young	.50	.25	.15
305	Andre Waters **RC**	.50	.25	.15
306	Oilers team (Warren Moon)	.50	.25	.15
307	Warren Moon	.50	.25	.15
308	Mike Rozier	.50	.25	.15
309	Drew Hill	.50	.25	.15
310	Ernest Givins **RC**	.50	.25	.15
311	Lee Johnson	.50	.25	.15
312	Kent Hill	.50	.25	.15
313	Dean Steinkuhler **RC**	.50	.25	.15
314	Ray Childress	.50	.25	.15
315	John Grimsley **RC**	.50	.25	.15
316	Jesse Baker	.50	.25	.15
317	Lions team (Eric Hipple)	.50	.25	.15
318	Chuck Long **RC**	.50	.25	.15
319	James Jones	.50	.25	.15
320	Garry James	.50	.25	.15
321	Jeff Chadwick	.50	.25	.15
322	Leonard Thompson	.50	.25	.15
323	Pete Mandley	.50	.25	.15
324	Jimmie Giles	.50	.25	.15
325	Herman Hunter	.50	.25	.15
326	Keith Ferguson	.50	.25	.15
327	Devon Mitchell	.50	.25	.15
328	Cardinals team (Neil Lomax)	.50	.25	.15
329	Neil Lomax	.50	.25	.15
330	Stump Mitchell	.50	.25	.15
331	Earl Ferrell	.50	.25	.15
332	Vai Sikahema **RC**	.50	.25	.15
333	Ron Wolfley **RC**	.50	.25	.15
334	J.T. Smith	.50	.25	.15
335	Roy Green	.50	.25	.15
336	Al Baker	.50	.25	.15
337	Freddie Joe Nunn	.50	.25	.15
338	Cedrick Mack	.50	.25	.15
339	Chargers team (Gary Anderson)	.50	.25	.15
340	Dan Fouts	.50	.25	.15
341	Gary Anderson	.50	.25	.15
342	Wes Chandler	.50	.25	.15
343	Kellen Winslow	.50	.25	.15
344	Ralf Mojsiejenko	.50	.25	.15
345	Rolf Benirschke	.50	.25	.15
346	Lee Williams **RC**	.50	.25	.15
347	Leslie O'Neal **RC**	.50	.25	.15
348	Billy Ray Smith	.50	.25	.15
349	Gill Byrd	.50	.25	.15
350	Packers team (Paul Ott Caruth)	.50	.25	.15
351	Randy Wright	.50	.25	.15
352	Kenneth Davis **RC**	.50	.25	.15
353	Gerry Ellis	.50	.25	.15
354	James Lofton	.50	.25	.15
355	Phillip Epps	.50	.25	.15
356	Walter Stanley	.50	.25	.15
357	Eddie Lee Ivery	.50	.25	.15
358	Tim Harris **RC**	.50	.25	.15
359	Mark Lee	.50	.25	.15
360	Mossy Cade	.50	.25	.15
361	Bills team (Jim Kelly)	.50	.25	.15
362	Jim Kelly **RC**	2.00	1.00	.60
363	Robb Riddick	.50	.25	.15
364	Greg Bell	.50	.25	.15
365	Andre Reed	.50	.25	.15
366	Pete Metzelaars **RC**	.50	.25	.15
367	Sean McNanie	.50	.25	.15
368	Fred Smerlas	.50	.25	.15
369	Bruce Smith	.50	.25	.15
370	Darryl Talley	.50	.25	.15
371	Charles Romes	.50	.25	.15
372	Colts team (Rohn Stark)	.50	.25	.15
373	Jack Trudeau	.50	.25	.15
374	Gary Hogeboom	.50	.25	.15
375	Randy McMillan	.50	.25	.15
376	Albert Bentley	.50	.08	.15
377	Matt Bouza	.50	.25	.15
378	Bill Brooks **RC**	.50	.25	.15
379	Rohn Stark (AP)	.50	.25	.15
380	Chris Hinton	.50	.25	.15
381	Ray Donaldson	.50	.25	.15
382	Jon Hand **RC**	.50	.25	.15
383	Buccaneers team (James Wilder)	.50	.25	.15
384	Steve Young	2.00	1.00	.60
385	James Wilder	.50	.25	.15
386	Frank Garcia	.50	.25	.15
387	Gerald Carter	.50	.25	.15
388	Phil Freeman	.50	.25	.15
389	Calvin Magee	.50	.25	.15
390	Donald Igwebuike	.50	.25	.15
391	David Logan	.50	.25	.15
392	Jeff Davis	.50	.25	.15
393	Chris Washington	.50	.25	.15
394	Checklist 1-132	.50	.25	.15
395	Checklist 133-264	.50	.25	.15
396	Checklist 265-396	.50	.25	.15

1987 Topps 1000 Yard Club

Printed on heavy white cardboard stock, 1,000 Yard Club cards were found inside wax packs of 1987 Topps football cards. Each card pictures a player who gained 1,000 or more yards rushing or receiving. Cards feature a parthenon design on the front in blue; backs are light blue and carry a game-by-game yardage summary for each player.

		NM/M	NM	E
	Complete Set (24):	4.50	3.50	1.75
	Common Player:	.15	.11	.06
1	Eric Dickerson	.75	.60	.30
2	Jerry Rice	.75	.60	.30
3	Joe Morris	.30	.25	.12
4	Stanley Morgan	.15	.11	.06
5	Curt Warner	.20	.15	.08
6	Reuben Mayes	.25	.20	.10
7	Walter Payton	1.50	1.25	.60
8	Gerald Riggs	.20	.15	.08
9	Mark Duper	.15	.11	.06
10	Gary Clark	.15	.11	.06
11	George Rogers	.15	.11	.06
12	Al Toon	.25	.20	.10
13	Todd Christensen	.15	.11	.06
14	Mark Clayton	.15	.11	.06
15	Bill Brooks	.25	.20	.10
16	Drew Hill	.15	.11	.06
17	James Brooks	.15	.11	.06
18	Steve Largent	.60	.45	.25
19	Art Monk	.15	.11	.06
20	Ernest Givins	.20	.15	.08
21	Cris Collinsworth	.20	.15	.08
22	Wesley Walker	.15	.11	.06
23	J.T. Smith	.15	.11	.06
24	Mark Bavaro	.15	.11	.06

1987 Topps American/United Kingdom

These cards are smaller in size than their regular set counterparts, measuring 2-1/8" x 3". The cards, which were made available in the United Kingdom, also have different photos. However, the basic design remains similar to Topps' 1986 regular set. The back has a football term explained inside a football (Talking Football), plus a card number. A special collector's box was also produced to house the set. The box had a set checklist on its side. Cards 76-87 form a team action puzzle on one side and William Perry on the other.

		NM/M	NM	E
	Complete Set (88):	40.00	30.00	16.00
	Common Player:	.10	.08	.04
1	Phil Simms	.65	.50	.25
2	Joe Morris	.35	.25	.14
3	Mark Bavaro	.25	.20	.10
4	Sean Landeta	.10	.08	.04
5	Lawrence Taylor	2.00	1.50	.80
6	John Elway	4.00	3.00	1.50
7	Sammy Winder	.10	.08	.04
8	Rulon Jones	.10	.08	.04
9	Karl Mecklenburg	.15	.11	.06
10	Walter Payton	4.00	3.00	1.50
11	Dennis Gentry	.10	.08	.04
12	Kevin Butler	.10	.08	.04
13	Jim Covert	.10	.08	.04
14	Richard Dent	.35	.25	.14
15	Mike Singletary	.50	.40	.20
16	Jay Schroeder	.50	.40	.20
17	George Rogers	.25	.20	.10
18	Gary Clark	.50	.40	.20
19	Art Monk	.50	.40	.20
20	Dexter Manley	.10	.08	.04
21	Darrell Green	.35	.25	.14
22	Bernie Kosar	1.00	.70	.40
23	Cody Risien	.10	.08	.04
24	Hanford Dixon	.10	.08	.04
25	Tony Eason	.25	.20	.10
26	Stanley Morgan	.25	.20	.10
27	Tony Franklin	.10	.08	.04
28	Andre Tippett	.25	.20	.10
29	Joe Montana	8.00	6.00	3.25
30	Jerry Rice	8.00	6.00	3.25
31	Ronnie Lott	.75	.60	.30
32	Ken O'Brien	.25	.20	.10
33	Freeman McNeil	.15	.11	.06
34	Al Toon	.25	.20	.10
35	Wesley Walker	.25	.20	.10
36	Eric Dickerson	1.50	1.25	.60
37	Dennis Harrah	.10	.08	.04
38	Bill Maas	.10	.08	.04

39	Deron Cherry	.25	.20	.10
40	Curt Warner	.20	.15	.08
41	Bobby Joe Edmonds	.25	.20	.10
42	Steve Largent	2.00	1.50	.80
43	Boomer Esiason	2.00	1.50	.80
44	James Brooks	.25	.20	.10
45	Cris Collinsworth	.25	.20	.10
46	Tim McGee	.35	.25	.14
47	Tommy Kramer	.25	.20	.10
48	Marcus Allen	1.00	.70	.40
49	Todd Christensen	.35	.25	.14
50	Sean Jones	.35	.25	.14
51	Dan Marino	8.00	6.00	3.25
52	Mark Duper	.25	.20	.10
53	Mark Clayton	.30	.25	.12
54	Dwight Stephenson	.25	.20	.10
55	Gerald Riggs	.25	.20	.10
56	Bill Fralic	.25	.20	.10
57	Tony Dorsett	1.50	1.25	.60
58	Herschel Walker	1.50	1.25	.60
59	Rueben Mayes	.25	.20	.10
60	Lupe Sanchez	.10	.08	.04
61	Reggie White	2.50	2.00	1.00
62	Warren Moon	3.00	2.25	1.25
63	Ernest Givins	1.50	1.25	.60
64	Drew Hill	.25	.20	.10
65	Jeff Chadwick	.25	.20	.10
66	Herman Hunter	.10	.08	.04
67	Vai Sikhema	.25	.20	.10
68	J.T. Smith	.10	.08	.04
69	Dan Fouts	1.00	.70	.40
70	Lee Williams	.50	.40	.20
71	Randy Wright	.25	.20	.10
72	Jim Kelly	7.00	5.25	2.75
73	Bruce Smith	.75	.60	.30
74	Bill Brooks	.35	.25	.14
75	Rohn Stark	.10	.08	.04
76	**Team Action**	.10	.08	.04
77	**Team Action**	.10	.08	.04
78	**Team Action**	.10	.08	.04
79	**Team Action**	.10	.08	.04
80	**Team Action**	.10	.08	.04
81	**Team Action**	.10	.08	.04
82	**Team Action**	.10	.08	.04
83	**Team Action**	.10	.08	.04
84	**Team Action**	.10	.08	.04
85	**Team Action**	.10	.08	.04
86	**Team Action**	.10	.08	.04
87	**Team Action**	.10	.08	.04
88	**Checklist Card**	.10	.08	.04

1987 Topps Box Bottoms

These cards can be distinguished from Topps' regular cards by the yellow borders around the photo on the front. Plus, the cards were on the bottom of 1987 Topps wax pack boxes, and would have to be cut out to measure the standard-size Topps cards. It's better to leave them intact. The cards also use a letter for numbering, instead of a number.

		NM/M	NM	E
	Complete Set (16):	10.00	7.50	4.00
	Common Player:	.30	.25	.12
A	Mark Bavaro	.40	.30	.15
B	Todd Christensen	.50	.40	.20
C	Eric Dickerson	.65	.50	.25
D	John Elway	1.50	1.25	.60
E	Rulon Jones	.30	.25	.12
F	Dan Marino	3.00	2.25	1.25
G	Karl Mecklenburg	.30	.25	.12
H	Joe Montana	3.00	2.25	1.25
I	Joe Morris	.50	.40	.20
J	Walter Payton	1.25	.90	.50
K	Jerry Rice	3.50	2.75	1.50
L	Phil Simms	.50	.40	.20
M	Lawrence Taylor	.60	.45	.25
N	Al Toon	.35	.25	.14
O	Curt Warner	.40	.30	.15
P	Reggie White	1.25	.90	.50

1987 Topps Stickers

Each of these stickers is 2-1/8" x 3" and features a new design element from previous years' issues - four footballs are included in the frame around the picture on the front, one for each corner. A sticker number appears on both sides. All-Pro foils were again produced, as were stickers in pairs; they are matched up as indicated by the number in parenthesis. The backs have red ink on a white background. The album cover this time features artwork devoted to the New York Giants.

		NM/M	NM	E
	Complete Set (285):	15.00	11.00	6.00
	Common Player:	.05	.04	.02
1	Phil Simms (Super Bowl MVP)	.40	.30	.15
2	**Super Bowl XXI** (upper left)	.15	.11	.06
3	**Super Bowl XXI** (upper right)	.15	.11	.06
4	**Super Bowl XXI** (lower left)	.15	.11	.06
5	**Super Bowl XXI** (lower right)	.15	.11	.06
6	Mike Singletary	.12	.09	.05
7	Jim Covert (156)	.50	.40	.20
8	Willie Gault (157)	.06	.05	.02
9	Jim McMahon (158)	.08	.06	.03
10	Doug Flutie (159)	1.00	.70	.40
11	Richard Dent (160)	.08	.06	.03
12	Kevin Butler (161)	.05	.04	.02
13	Wilber Marshall (162)	.08	.06	.03
14	Walter Payton	.60	.45	.25
15	Calvin Magee	.05	.04	.02
16	David Logan (165)	.05	.04	.02
17	Jeff Davis (166)	.05	.04	.02
18	Gerald Carter (167)	.05	.04	.02
19	James Wilder	.05	.04	.02
20	Chris Washington (168)	.05	.04	.02
21	Phil Freeman (169)	.05	.04	.02
22	Frank Garcia (170)	.05	.04	.02
23	Donald Igwebuike (171)	.05	.04	.02
24	Al (Bubba) Baker (175)	.08	.06	.03
25	Vai Sikhema (176)	.05	.04	.02
26	Leonard Smith (177)	.05	.04	.02
27	Ron Wolgley (178)	.05	.04	.02
28	J.T. Smith	.08	.06	.03
29	Roy Green (179)	.06	.05	.02
30	Cedric Mack (180)	.05	.04	.02
31	Neil Lomax (181)	.06	.05	.02
32	Stump Mitchell	.08	.06	.03
33	Herschel Walker (184)	.50	.40	.20
34	Danny White (184)	.06	.05	.02
35	Michael Downs (185)	.05	.04	.02
36	Randy White (186)	.08	.06	.03
37	Eugene Lockhart (188)	.05	.04	.02
38	Mike Sherrard (189)	.20	.15	.08
39	Jim Jeffcoat (190)	.05	.04	.02
40	Tony Hill (191)	.06	.05	.02
41	Tony Dorsett	.35	.25	.14
42	Keith Byars (192)	.30	.25	.12
43	Andre Waters (193)	.06	.05	.02
44	Kenny Jackson (194)	.05	.04	.02
45	John Teltschik (195)	.05	.04	.02
46	Roynell Young (196)	.05	.04	.02
47	Randall Cunningham (197)	.60	.45	.25
48	Mike Reichenbach (198)	.05	.04	.02
49	Reggie White	.40	.30	.15
50	Mike Quick	.08	.06	.03
51	Bill Fralic (201)	.05	.04	.02
52	Sylvester Stamps (202)	.05	.04	.02
53	Bret Clark (203)	.05	.04	.02
54	William Andrews (204)	.05	.04	.02
55	Buddy Curry (205)	.05	.04	.02
56	Dave Archer (206)	.10	.08	.04
57	Rick Bryan (207)	.05	.04	.02
58	Gerald Riggs	.12	.09	.05
59	Charlie Brown	.05	.04	.02
60	Joe Montana	2.00	1.50	.80
61	Jerry Rice	1.50	1.25	.60
62	Carlton Williamson (212)	.05	.04	.02
63	Roger Craig (213)	.12	.09	.05
64	Ronnie Lott (214)	.15	.11	.06
65	Dwight Clark (215)	.15	.11	.06
66	Jeff Stover (216)	.05	.04	.02
67	Charles Haley (217)	.20	.15	.08
68	Ray Wersching (218)	.05	.04	.02
69	Lawrence Taylor	.30	.25	.12
70	Joe Morris	.12	.09	.05
71	Carl Banks (221)	.10	.08	.04
72	Mark Bavaro (222)	.06	.05	.02
73	Harry Carson (223)	.05	.04	.02
74	Phil Simms (224)	.10	.08	.04
75	Jim Burt (225)	.05	.04	.02
76	Brad Benson (226)	.05	.04	.02
77	Leonard Marshall (227)	.05	.04	.02
78	Jeff Chadwick	.05	.04	.02
79	Devon Mitchell (228)	.05	.04	.02
80	Chuck Long (229)	.06	.05	.02
81	Demetrious Johnson (230)	.05	.04	.02
82	Herman Hunter (231)	.05	.04	.02
83	Kieth Ferguson (232)	.05	.04	.02
84	Gary James (233)	.05	.04	.02
85	Leonard Thompson (234)	.05	.04	.02

86	James Jones	.08	.06	.03
87	Kenneth Davis	.35	.25	.14
88	Brian Noble (237)	.07	.05	.03
89	Al Del Greco (238)	.05	.04	.02
90	Mark Lee (239)	.05	.04	.02
91	Randy Wright	.05	.04	.02
92	Tim Harris (240)	.25	.20	.10
93	Phillip Epps (241)	.05	.04	.02
94	Walter Stanley (242)	.10	.08	.04
95	Eddie Lee Ivery (243)	.05	.04	.02
96	Doug Smith (247)	.05	.04	.02
97	Jerry Gray (248)	.05	.04	.02
98	Jim Everett (250)	.05	.04	.02
99	Jim Everett (250)	.60	.45	.25
100	Jackie Slater (251)	.06	.05	.02
101	Vince Newsome (252)	.10	.08	.04
102	LeRoy Irvin (253)	.10	.08	.04
103	Henry Ellard	.10	.08	.04
104	Eric Dickerson	.60	.45	.25
105	George Rogers (256)	.06	.05	.02
106	Darrell Green (257)	.07	.05	.03
107	Art Monk (258)	.10	.08	.04
108	Neal Olkewicz (260)	.05	.04	.02
109	Russ Grimm (261)	.05	.04	.02
110	Dexter Manley (262)	.05	.04	.02
111	Kelvin Bryant (263)	.05	.04	.02
112	Jay Schroeder	.15	.11	.06
113	Gary Clark	.15	.11	.06
114	Rickey Jackson	.08	.06	.03
115	Eric Martin (264)	.07	.05	.03
116	Dave Waymer (265)	.05	.04	.02
117	Morten Andersen (266)	.06	.05	.02
118	Bruce Clark (167)	.08	.06	.03
119	Hoby Brenner (269)	.07	.05	.03
120	Brian Hansen (270)	.05	.04	.02
121	Dave Wilson (271)	.05	.04	.02
122	Rueben Mayes	.10	.08	.04
123	Tommy Kramer	.08	.06	.03
124	Mark Malone (124)	.05	.04	.02
125	Anthony Carter (275)	.10	.08	.04
126	Keith Millard (276)	.08	.06	.03
127	Steve Jordan	.12	.09	.05
128	Chuck Nelson (277)	.06	.05	.02
129	Issiac Holt (278)	.05	.04	.02
130	Darrin Nelson (279)	.05	.04	.02
131	Gary Zimmerman (280)	.05	.04	.02
132	Mark Bavaro (146, All-Pro)	.10	.08	.04
133	Jim Covert (147, All-Pro)	.10	.08	.04
134	Eric Dickerson (148, All-Pro)	.35	.25	.14
135	Bill Fralic (149, All-Pro)	.10	.08	.04
136	Tony Franklin (150, All-Pro)	.10	.08	.04
137	Dennis Harrah (151, All-Pro)	.10	.08	.04
138	Dan Marino (152, All-Pro)	1.25	.90	.50
139	Joe Morris (153, All-Pro)	.25	.20	.10
140	Jerry Rice (154, All-Pro)	1.00	.70	.40
141	Cody Risien (155, All-Pro)	.10	.08	.04
142	Dwight Stephenson (282, All-Pro)	.12	.09	.05
143	Al Toon (283, All-Pro)	.20	.15	.08
144	Deron Cherry (284, All-Pro)	.12	.09	.05
145	Hanford Dixon (285, All-Pro)	.10	.08	.04
146	Darrell Green (132, All-Pro)	.15	.11	.06
147	Ronnie Lott (133, All-Pro)	.20	.15	.08
148	Bill Maas (134, All-Pro)	.10	.08	.04
149	Dexter Manley (135, All-Pro)	.10	.08	.04
150	Karl Mecklenburg (136, All-Pro)	.12	.09	.05
151	Mike Singletary (137, All-Pro)	.20	.15	.08
152	Rohn Stark (138, All-Pro)	.10	.08	.04
153	Lawrence Taylor 139, All-Pro)	.30	.25	.12
154	Andre Tippett (140, All-Pro)	.12	.09	.05
155	Reggie White (141, All-Pro)	.35	.25	.14
156	Boomer Esiason (7)	.15	.11	.06
157	Anthony Munoz (8)	.12	.09	.05
158	Tim McGee (9)	.20	.15	.08
159	Max Montoya (10)	.05	.04	.02
160	Jim Breech (11)	.05	.04	.02
161	Tim Krumrie (12)	.05	.04	.02
162	Eddie Brown (13)	.06	.05	.02
163	James Brooks	.10	.08	.04
164	Cris Collinsworth	.12	.09	.05
165	Charles Romes (16)	.05	.04	.02
166	Robb Riddick (17)	.05	.04	.02
167	Eugene Marve (18)	.05	.04	.02
168	Chris Burkett (20)	.10	.08	.04
169	Bruce Smith (21)	.12	.09	.05
170	Greg Bell (22)	.05	.04	.02
171	Pete Metzelaars (23)	.05	.04	.02
172	Jim Kelly	1.50	1.25	.60
173	Andre Reed	.30	.25	.12
174	John Elway	.60	.45	.25
175	Mike Harden (24)	.05	.04	.02
176	Gerald Willhite (25)	.05	.04	.02
177	Rulon Jones (26)	.05	.04	.02
178	Ricky Hunley (27)	.05	.04	.02
179	Mark Jackson (29)	.05	.04	.02
180	Rich Karlis (30)	.05	.04	.02
181	Sammy Winder (31)	.08	.06	.03
182	Karl Mecklenburg	.08	.06	.03
183	Bernie Kosar	.35	.25	.14
184	Kevin Mack (34)	.05	.04	.02
185	Bob Golic (35)	.08	.06	.03
186	Ozzie Newsome (36)	.08	.06	.03
187	Brian Brennan	.05	.04	.02
188	Gerald McNeil (37)	.05	.04	.02
189	Hanford Dixon (38)	.05	.04	.02
190	Cody Risien (39)	.05	.04	.02
191	Chris Rockins (40)	.05	.04	.02
192	Gill Byrd (42)	.05	.04	.02
193	Kellen Winslow (43)	.08	.06	.03
194	Billy Ray Smith (44)	.05	.04	.02
195	Wes Chandler (45)	.08	.06	.03
196	Leslie O'Neal (46)	.25	.20	.10
197	Ralf Mojsiejenko (47)	.05	.04	.02
198	Lee Williams (48)	.20	.15	.08
199	Gary Anderson	.08	.06	.03
200	Dan Fouts	.30	.25	.12
201	Stephone Paige (51)	.08	.06	.03
202	Irv Eatman (52)	.05	.04	.02
203	Bill Kenney (53)	.05	.04	.02
204	Dino Hackett (54)	.08	.06	.03
205	Carlos Carson (55)	.05	.04	.02
206	Art Still (56)	.06	.05	.02
207	Lloyd Burruss (57)	.05	.04	.02
208	Deron Cherry	.08	.06	.03
209	Bill Maas	.05	.04	.02
210	Gary Hogeboom	.08	.06	.03
211	Rohn Stark	.05	.04	.02
212	Cliff Odom (62)	.05	.04	.02
213	Randy McMillan (63)	.05	.04	.02
214	Chris Hinton (64)	.05	.04	.02
215	Matt Bouza (65)	.05	.04	.02
216	Ray Donaldson (66)	.05	.04	.02
217	Bill Brooks (67)	.08	.06	.03
218	Jack Trudeau (68)	.06	.05	.02
219	Mark Duper	.15	.11	.06
220	Dan Marino	1.50	1.25	.60
221	Dwight Stephenson (71)	.08	.06	.03
222	Mark Clayton (72)	.10	.08	.04
223	Roy Foster (73)	.05	.04	.02
224	John Offerdahl (74)	.20	.15	.08
225	Lorenzo Hampton (75)	.05	.04	.02
226	Reggie Roby (76)	.05	.04	.02
227	Tony Nathan (77)	.08	.06	.03
228	Johnny Hector (79)	.08	.06	.03
229	Wesley Walker (80)	.06	.05	.02
230	Mark Gastineau (81)	.10	.08	.04
231	Ken O'Brien (82)	.05	.04	.02
232	Dave Jennings (83)	.05	.04	.02
233	Mickey Shuler (84)	.05	.04	.02
234	Joe Klecko (85)	.05	.04	.02
235	Freeman McNeil	.10	.08	.04
236	Al Toon	.08	.06	.03
237	Warren Moon (88)	.35	.25	.14
238	Dean Steinkuhler (89)	.08	.06	.03
239	Mike Rozier (90)	.06	.05	.02
240	Ray Childress (92)	.08	.06	.03
241	Tony Zendejas (93)	.05	.04	.02
242	John Grimsley (94)	.05	.04	.02
243	Jesse Baker (95)	.05	.04	.02
244	Ernest Givins	.50	.40	.20
245	Drew Hill	.10	.08	.04
246	Tony Franklin	.05	.04	.02
247	Steve Grogan (96)	.06	.05	.02
248	Garin Veris (97)	.05	.04	.02
249	Stanley Morgan (98)	.06	.05	.02
250	Fred Morgan (98)	.05	.04	.02
251	Raymond Clayborn (100)	.07	.05	.03
252	Mosi Tatupu (101)	.05	.04	.02
253	Tony Eason (102)	.05	.04	.02
254	Andre Tippett	.08	.06	.03
255	Todd Christensen	.08	.06	.03
256	Howie Long (105)	.06	.05	.02
257	Marcus Allen (106)	.12	.09	.05
258	Vann McElroy (107)	.05	.04	.02
259	Dokie Williams	.05	.04	.02
260	Mike Haynes (108)	.08	.06	.03
261	Sean Jones	.10	.08	.04
262	Jim Plunkett (110)	.07	.05	.03
263	Chris Bahr (111)	.05	.04	.02
264	Dave Krieg (115)	.08	.06	.03
265	Jacob Green (116)	.05	.04	.02
266	Norm Johnson (117)	.05	.04	.02
267	Fredd Young (118)	.05	.04	.02
268	Steve Largent	.50	.40	.20
269	Dave Brown (119)	.05	.04	.02
270	Kenny Easley (120)	.05	.04	.02
271	Bobby Joe Edmonds (121)	.05	.04	.02
272	Curt Warner	.15	.11	.06
273	Mike Merriweather	.08	.06	.03
274	Mark Malone (124)	.05	.04	.02
275	Bryan Hinkle (125)	.05	.04	.02
276	Earnest Jackson (126)	.05	.04	.02
277	Keith Willis (128)	.05	.04	.02
278	Walter Abercrombie (129)	.06	.05	.02
279	Donnie Shell (130)	.08	.06	.03
280	John Stallworth (131)	.06	.05	.02
281	Louis Lipps	.10	.08	.04
282	Eric Dickerson (142)	.30	.25	.12
283	Dan Marino (143)	1.00	.70	.40
284	Tony Franklin (144)	.08	.06	.03
285	Todd Christensen	.12	.09	.05

1988 Topps

This set, issued in August 1988, was issued by teams in order of finish. These standard-size cards again showed the team helmets on front and All-Pro and Super Rookie designations (this was Topps' first year using Super Rookie labels). This set is noteworthy for the inclusion of Bo Jackson's rookie football card. (Key: AP - All Pro, SP - Super Rookie)

		NM/M	NM	E
Complete Set (396):		50.00	25.00	15.00
Common Player:		.50	.25	.15
Wax Pack (15+1):		.75		
Wax Box (36):		15.00		
1	Super Bowl XXII	.50	.25	.15
2	Vencie Glenn	.50	.25	.15
3	Steve Largent	.50	.25	.15
4	Joe Montana	.50	.25	.15
5	Walter Payton	4.00	2.00	1.20
6	Jerry Rice	4.00	2.00	1.20
7	Redskins team (Kelvin Bryant)	.50	.25	.15
8	Doug Williams	.50	.25	.15
9	George Rogers	.50	.25	.15
10	Kelvin Bryant	.50	.25	.15
11	Timmy Smith, Kent Hill (SR)	.50	.25	.15
12	Art Monk, Ray Childress	.50	.25	.15
13	Gary Clark	.50	.25	.15
14	Ricky Sanders **RC**	.50	.25	.15
15	Steve Cox	.50	.25	.15
16	Joe Jacoby	.50	.25	.15
17	Charles Mann	.50	.25	.15
18	Dave Butz	.50	.25	.15
19	Darrell Green (AP)	.50	.25	.15
20	Dexter Manley	.50	.25	.15
21	Barry Wilburn	.50	.25	.15
22	Broncos team (Sammy Winder)	.50	.25	.15
23	John Elway (AP)	2.00	1.00	.60
24	Sammy Winder	.50	.25	.15
25	Vance Johnson	.50	.25	.15
26	Mark Jackson **RC**	.50	.25	.15
27	Ricky Nattiel **RC** (SR)	.50	.25	.15
28	Clarence Kay	.50	.25	.15
29	Rich Karlis	.50	.25	.15
30	Keith Bishop	.50	.25	.15
31	Mike Horan	.50	.25	.15
32	Rulon Jones	.50	.25	.15
33	Karl Mecklenburg	.50	.25	.15
34	Jim Ryan	.50	.25	.15
35	Mark Haynes	.50	.25	.15
36	Mike Harden	.50	.25	.15
37	49ers team (Roger Craig)	.50	.25	.15
38	Joe Montana	2.00	1.00	.60
39	Steve Young	.50	.25	.15
40	Roger Craig	.50	.25	.15
41	Tom Rathman **RC**	.50	.40	.20
42	Joe Cribbs	.50	.25	.15
43	Jerry Rice (AP)	2.00	1.00	.60
44	Mike Wilson	.50	.25	.15
45	Ron Heller **RC**	.50	.25	.15
46	Ray Wersching	.50	.25	.15
47	Michael Carter	.50	.25	.15
48	Dwaine Board	.50	.25	.15
49	Michael Walter	.50	.25	.15
50	Don Griffin	.50	.25	.15
51	Ronnie Lott	.50	.25	.15
52	Charlie Haley	.50	.25	.15
53	Dana McLemore	.50	.25	.15
54	Saints Team (Bobby Hebert)	.50	.25	.15
55	Bobby Hebert	.50	.25	.15

56	Rueben Mayes	.50	.25	.15
57	Dalton Hilliard RC	.50	.25	.15
58	Eric Martin	.50	.25	.15
59	John Tice	.50	.25	.15
60	Brad Edelman	.50	.25	.15
61	Morten Andersen (AP)	.50	.25	.15
62	Brian Hansen	.50	.25	.15
63	Mel Gray RC	.50	.25	.15
64	Rickey Jackson	.50	.25	.15
65	Sam Mills RC	.50	.25	.15
66	Pat Swilling RC	.50	.25	.15
67	Dave Waymer	.50	.25	.15
68	Bears Team (Willie Gault)	.50	.25	.15
69	Jim McMahon	.50	.25	.15
70	Mike Tomczak RC	.50	.25	.15
71	Neal Anderson RC	.50	.25	.15
72	Willie Gault	.50	.25	.15
73	Dennis Gentry	.50	.25	.15
74	Dennis McKinnon	.50	.25	.15
75	Kevin Butler	.50	.25	.15
76	Jim Covert	.50	.25	.15
77	Jay Hilgenberg	.50	.25	.15
78	Steve McMichael	.50	.25	.15
79	William Perry	.50	.25	.15
80	Richard Dent	.20	.25	.15
81	Ron Rivera	.50	.25	.15
82	Mike Singletary (AP)	.50	.25	.15
83	Dan Hampton	.50	.08	.15
84	Dave Duerson	.50	.25	.15
85	Browns team (Bernie Kosar)	.50	.25	.15
86	Bernie Kosar	.50	.25	.15
87	Earnest Byner	.50	.25	.15
88	Kevin Mack	.50	.25	.15
89	Webster Slaughter RC	.50	.25	.15
90	Gerald McNeil	.50	.25	.15
91	Brian Brennan	.50	.25	.15
92	Ozzie Newsome	.50	.25	.15
93	Cody Risien	.50	.25	.15
94	Bob Golic	.50	.25	.15
95	Carl Hairston	.50	.25	.15
96	Mike Johnson RC	.50	.25	.15
97	Clay Matthews	.50	.25	.15
98	Frank Minnifield	.50	.25	.15
99	Hanford Dixon (AP)	.50	.25	.15
100	Dave Puzzuoli	.50	.25	.15
101	Felix Wright RC	.50	.25	.15
102	Oilers team (Warren Moon)	.50	.25	.15
103	Warren Moon	.50	.25	.15
104	Mike Rozier	.50	.25	.15
105	Alonzo Highsmith RC (SR)	.50	.25	.15
106	Drew Hill	.50	.25	.15
107	Ernest Givins	.50	.25	.15
108	Curtis Duncan RC	.50	.25	.15
109	Tony Zendejas RC	.50	.25	.15
110	Mike Munchak (AP)	.50	.25	.15
113	Al Smith RC	.50	.25	.15
114	Keith Bostic	.50	.25	.15
115	Jeff Donaldson	.50	.25	.15
116	Colts team (Eric Dickerson)	.50	.25	.15
117	Jack Trudeau	.50	.25	.15
118	Eric Dickerson (AP)	.50	.25	.15
119	Albert Bentley	.50	.25	.15
120	Matt Bouza	.50	.25	.15
121	Bill Brooks	.50	.25	.15
122	Dean Biasucci	.50	.25	.15
123	Chris Hinton	.50	.25	.15
124	Ray Donaldson	.50	.25	.15
125	Ron Solt RC	.50	.25	.15
126	Donnell Thompson	.50	.25	.15
127	Barry Krauss	.50	.25	.15
128	Duane Bickett	.50	.25	.15
129	Mike Prior RC	.50	.25	.15
130	Seahawks team (Curt Warner)	.50	.25	.15
131	Dave Krieg	.50	.25	.15
132	Curt Warner	.50	.25	.15
133	John L. Williams	.50	.25	.15
134	Bobby Joe Edmonds	.50	.25	.15
135	Steve Largent	.50	.25	.15
136	Raymond Butler	.50	.25	.15
137	Norm Johnson	.50	.25	.15
138	Ruben Rodriguez	.50	.25	.15
139	Blair Bush	.50	.25	.15
140	Jacob Green	.50	.25	.15
141	Joe Nash	.50	.25	.15
142	Jeff Bryant	.50	.25	.15
143	Fredd Young (AP)	.50	.25	.15
144	Brian Bosworth RC (SR)	2.00	1.00	.60
145	Kenny Easley (AP)	.50	.25	.15
146	Vikings team (Tommy Kramer)	.50	.25	.15
147	Wade Wilson RC	.50	.25	.15
148	Tommy Kramer	.50	.25	.15
149	Darrin Nelson	.50	.25	.15
150	D.J. Dozier RC (SR)	.50	.25	.15
151	Anthony Carter	.50	.25	.15
152	Leo Lewis	.50	.25	.15
153	Steve Jordan	.50	.25	.15
154	Gary Zimmerman	.50	.25	.15
155	Chuck Nelson	.50	.25	.15
156	Henry Thomas RC (SR)	.50	.25	.15
157	Chris Doleman RC	.50	.25	.15
158	Scott Studwell RC	.50	.25	.15
159	Jesse Solomon RC	.50	.25	.15
160	Joey Browner (AP)	.50	.25	.15
161	Neal Guggemos	.50	.25	.15
162	Steelers team (Louis Lipps)	.50	.25	.15
163	Mark Malone	.50	.25	.15
164	Walter Abercrombie	.50	.25	.15
165	Earnest Jackson	.50	.25	.15
166	Frank Pollard	.50	.25	.15
167	Dwight Stone RC	.50	.25	.15
168	Gary Anderson	.50	.25	.15
169	Harry Newsome RC	.50	.25	.15
170	Keith Willis	.50	.25	.15
171	Keith Gray	.50	.25	.15
172	David Little RC	.50	.25	.15
173	Mike Merriweather	.50	.25	.15
174	Dwayne Woodruff	.50	.25	.15
175	Patriots team (Irving Fryar)	.50	.25	.15
176	Steve Grogan	.50	.25	.15
177	Tony Eason	.50	.25	.15
178	Tony Collins	.50	.25	.15
179	Mosi Tatupu	.50	.25	.15
180	Stanley Morgan	.50	.25	.15
181	Irving Fryar	.50	.25	.15
182	Stephen Starring	.50	.25	.15
183	Tony Franklin	.50	.25	.15
184	Rich Camarillo	.50	.25	.15
185	Garin Veris	.50	.25	.15
186	Andre Tippett (AP)	.50	.25	.15
187	Ronnie Lippett	.50	.25	.15
188	Fred Marion	.50	.25	.15
189	Dolphins team (Dan Marino)	.50	.25	.15
190	Dan Marino	.50	.25	.15
191	Troy Stradford RC (SR)	.50	.25	.15
192	Lorenzo Hampton	.50	.25	.15
193	Mark Duper	.50	.25	.15
194	Mark Clayton	.50	.25	.15
195	Reggie Roby	.50	.25	.15
196	Dwight Stephenson (AP)	.50	.25	.15
197	T.J. Turner	.50	.25	.15
198	John Bosa (SR)	.50	.25	.15
199	Jackie Shipp	.50	.25	.15
200	John Offerdahl	.50	.25	.15
201	Mark Brown	.50	.25	.15
202	Paul Lankford	.50	.25	.15
203	Chargers Team (Kellen Winslow)	.50	.25	.15
204	Tim Spencer	.50	.25	.15
205	Gary Anderson	.50	.25	.15
206	Curtis Adams	.50	.25	.15
207	Lionel James	.50	.25	.15
208	Chip Banks	.50	.25	.15
209	Kellen Winslow	.50	.25	.15
210	Ralf Mojsiejenko	.50	.25	.15
211	Jim Lachey	.50	.25	.15
212	Lee Williams	.50	.25	.15
213	Billy Ray Smith	.50	.25	.15
214	Vencie Glenn RC	.50	.25	.15
215	NFL Passing Leaders (Bernie Kosar, Joe Montana)	.50	.25	.15
216	NFL Receiving Leaders (Al Toon, J.T. Smith)	.50	.25	.15
217	NFL Rushing Leaders (Charles White, Eric Dickerson)	.50	.25	.15
218	NFL Scoring Leaders (Jim Breech, Jerry Rice)	.50	.25	.15
219	NFL Interception Leaders (Keith Bostic, Mark Kelso, Mike Prior, Barry Wilburn)	.50	.25	.15
220	Bills team (Jim Kelly)	.50	.25	.15
221	Jim Kelly	.50	.25	.15
222	Ronnie Harmon RC	.50	.25	.15
223	Robb Riddick	.50	.25	.15
224	Andre Reed	.50	.25	.15
225	Chris Burkett RC	.50	.25	.15
226	Pete Metzelaars	.50	.25	.15
227	Bruce Smith (AP)	.50	.25	.15
228	Darryl Talley	.50	.25	.15
229	Eugene Marve	.50	.25	.15
230	Cornelius Bennett RC	.50	.25	.15
231	Mark Kelso RC	.20	.25	.15
232	Shane Conlan RC (SR)	.50	.25	.15
233	Eagles team (Randall Cunningham)	.50	.25	.15
234	Randall Cunningham	.50	.25	.15
235	Keith Byars	.50	.25	.15
236	Anthony Toney	.50	.25	.15
237	Mike Quick	.50	.25	.15
238	Kenny Jackson	.50	.25	.15
239	John Spagnola	.50	.25	.15
240	Paul McFadden	.50	.25	.15
241	Reggie White (AP)	.50	.25	.15
242	Ken Clarke	.50	.25	.15
243	Mike Pitts	.50	.25	.15
244	Clyde Simmons RC	.50	.25	.15
245	Seth Joyner RC	.50	.25	.15
246	Andre Waters	.50	.25	.15
247	Jerome Brown RC (SR)	.50	.25	.15
248	Cardinals team (Stump Mitchell)	.50	.25	.15
249	Neil Lomax	.50	.25	.15
250	Stump Mitchell	.50	.25	.15
251	Earl Ferrell	.50	.25	.15
252	Vai Sikahema	.50	.25	.15
253	J.T. Smith (AP)	.50	.25	.15
254	Roy Green	.50	.08	.04
255	Robert Awalt (SR)	.50	.25	.15
256	Freddie Joe Nunn	.50	.25	.15
257	Leonard Smith RC	.50	.08	.04
258	Travis Curtis	.50	.25	.15
259	Cowboys team (Herschel Walker)	.50	.25	.15
260	Danny White	.50	.25	.15
261	Herschel Walker	.50	.25	.15
262	Tony Dorsett	.50	.25	.15
263	Doug Cosbie	.50	.25	.15
264	Roger Ruzek RC	.50	.25	.15
265	Darryl Clack	.50	.25	.15
266	Ed "Too Tall" Jones	.50	.25	.15
267	Jim Jeffcoat	.50	.25	.15
268	Everson Walls	.50	.25	.15
269	Bill Bates	.50	.25	.15
270	Michael Downs	.50	.25	.15
271	Giants team (Mark Bavaro)	.50	.25	.15
272	Phil Simms	.50	.25	.15
273	Joe Morris	.50	.25	.15
274	Lee Rouson	.50	.25	.15
275	George Adams	.50	.25	.15
276	Lionel Manuel	.50	.25	.15
277	Mark Bavaro (AP)	.50	.25	.15
278	Raul Allegre	.50	.25	.15
279	Sean Landeta	.50	.25	.15
280	Erik Howard	.50	.25	.15
281	Leonard Marshall	.50	.25	.15
282	Carl Banks (AP)	.50	.25	.15
283	Pepper Johnson	.50	.25	.15
284	Harry Carson	.50	.25	.15
285	Lawrence Taylor	.50	.25	.15
286	Terry Kinard	.50	.25	.15
287	Rams team (Jim Everett)	.50	.25	.15
288	Jim Everett	.50	.25	.15
289	Charles White (AP)	.50	.25	.15
290	Ron Brown	.50	.25	.15
291	Henry Ellard	.50	.25	.15
292	Mike Lansford	.50	.25	.15
293	Dale Hatcher	.50	.25	.15
294	Doug Smith	.50	.25	.15
295	Jackie Slater (AP)	.50	.25	.15
296	Jim Collins	.50	.25	.15
297	Jerry Gray	.50	.25	.15
298	LeRoy Irvin	.50	.25	.15
299	Nolan Cromwell	.50	.25	.15
300	Kevin Greene RC	.50	.25	.15
301	Jets team (Ken O'Brien)	.50	.25	.15
302	Ken O'Brien	.50	.25	.15
303	Freeman McNeil	.50	.25	.15
304	Johnny Hector	.50	.25	.15
305	Al Toon	.50	.25	.15
306	JoJo Townsell	.50	.25	.15
307	Mickey Shuler	.50	.25	.15
308	Pat Leahy	.50	.25	.15
309	Roger Vick	.50	.25	.15
310	Alex Gordon	.50	.25	.15
311	Troy Benson	.50	.25	.15
312	Bob Crable	.50	.25	.15
313	Harry Hamilton	.50	.25	.15
314	Packers team (Phil Epps)	.50	.25	.15
315	Randy Wright	.50	.25	.15
316	Kenneth Davis	.50	.25	.15
317	Phillip Epps	.50	.25	.15
318	Walter Stanley	.50	.25	.15
319	Frankie Neal	.50	.25	.15
320	Don Bracken	.50	.25	.15
321	Brian Noble RC	.50	.25	.15
322	Johnny Holland RC (SR)	.50	.25	.15
323	Tim Harris	.50	.25	.15
324	Mark Murphy	.50	.25	.15
325	Raiders team (Bo Jackson)	.50	.25	.15
326	Marc Wilson	.50	.25	.15
327	Bo Jackson RC (SR)	4.00	2.00	1.20
328	Marcus Allen	.50	.25	.15

329	James Lofton	.50	.25	.15
330	Todd Christensen	.50	.25	.15
331	Chris Bahr	.50	.25	.15
332	Stan Talley	.50	.25	.15
333	Howie Long	.50	.25	.15
334	Sean Jones	.50	.25	.15
335	Matt Millen	.50	.25	.15
336	Stacey Toran	.50	.25	.15
337	Vann McElroy	.50	.25	.15
338	Greg Townsend	.50	.25	.15
339	Bengals team			
	(Boomer Esiason)	.50	.25	.15
340	Boomer Esiason	.50	.25	.15
341	Larry Kinnebrew	.50	.25	.15
342	Stanford Jennings	.50	.25	.15
343	Eddie Brown	.50	.25	.15
344	Jim Breech	.50	.25	.15
345	Anthony Munoz (AP)	.50	.25	.15
346	Scott Fulhage	.50	.25	.15
347	Tim Krumrie **RC**	.50	.25	.15
348	Reggie Williams	.50	.25	.15
349	David Fulcher **RC**	.50	.25	.15
350	Buccaneers team			
	(James Wilder)	.50	.25	.15
351	Frank Garcia	.50	.25	.15
352	Vinny Testaverde **RC** (SR)	3.00	1.50	.90
353	James Wilder	.50	.25	.15
354	Jeff Smith	.50	.25	.15
355	Gerald Carter	.50	.25	.15
356	Calvin Magee	.50	.25	.15
357	Donald Igwebuike	.50	.25	.15
358	Ron Holmes	.50	.25	.15
359	Chris Washington	.50	.25	.15
360	Ervin Randle	.50	.25	.15
361	Chiefs team (Bill Kenney)	.50	.25	.15
362	Bill Kenney	.50	.25	.15
363	Christian Okoye **RC** (SR)	.50	.25	.15
364	Paul Palmer	.50	.25	.15
365	Stephone Paige	.50	.25	.15
366	Carlos Carson	.50	.25	.15
367	Kelly Goodburn	.50	.25	.15
368	Bill Maas (AP)	.50	.25	.15
369	Mike Bell	.50	.25	.15
370	Dino Hackett **RC**	.50	.25	.15
371	Deron Cherry	.50	.25	.15
372	Lions team			
	(James Jones)	.50	.25	.15
373	Chuck Long	.50	.25	.15
374	Garry James	.50	.25	.15
375	James Jones	.50	.25	.15
376	Pete Mandley	.50	.25	.15
377	Gary Lee (SR)	.50	.25	.15
378	Ed Murray	.50	.25	.15
379	Jim Arnold	.50	.25	.15
380	Dennis Gibson (SR)	.50	.25	.15
381	Mike Cofer	.50	.25	.15
382	James Griffin	.50	.25	.15
383	Falcons team			
	(Gerald Riggs)	.50	.25	.15
384	Scott Campbell	.50	.25	.15
385	Gerald Riggs	.50	.25	.15
386	Floyd Dixon	.50	.25	.15
387	Rick Donnelly (AP)	.50	.25	.15
388	Bill Fralic (AP)	.50	.25	.15
389	Major Everett	.50	.25	.15
390	Mike Gann	.50	.25	.15
391	Tony Casillas **RC**	.50	.25	.15
392	Rick Bryan	.50	.25	.15
393	John Rade	.50	.25	.15
394	Checklist 1-132	.50	.25	.15
395	Checklist 133-264	.50	.25	.15
396	Checklist 265-396	.50	.25	.15

1988 Topps 1000 Yard Club

One card from this 28-card set was again issued in a wax pack of Topps football cards. The standard-size glossy cards on thick white cardboard stock feature "1000" in bold green border around a full-color action photo. Backs feature a game-by-game recap of the runner or receiver's yardage.

		NM/M	NM	E
Complete Set (28):		4.50	3.50	1.75
Common Player:		.10	.08	.04
1	Charles White	.10	.08	.04
2	Eric Dickerson	.75	.60	.30
3	J.T. Smith	.10	.08	.04
4	Jerry Rice	.75	.60	.30
5	Gary Clark	.10	.08	.04
6	Carlos Carson	.10	.08	.04
7	Drew Hill	.10	.08	.04
8	Curt Warner	.10	.08	.04
9	Al Toon	.10	.08	.04
10	Mike Rozier	.10	.08	.04
11	Ernest Givins	.10	.08	.04
12	Anthony Carter	.10	.08	.04
13	Reuben Mayes	.10	.08	.04
14	Steve Largent	.75	.60	.30
15	Herschel Walker	.75	.60	.30
16	James Lofton	.10	.08	.04
17	Gerald Riggs	.10	.08	.04
18	Mark Bavaro	.10	.08	.04
19	Roger Craig	.50	.40	.20
20	Webster Slaughter	.10	.08	.04
21	Henry Ellard	.10	.08	.04
22	Mike Quick	.10	.08	.04
23	Stump Mitchell	.10	.08	.04
24	Eric Martin	.10	.08	.04
25	Mark Clayton	.10	.08	.04
26	Chris Burkett	.10	.08	.04
27	Marcus Allen	.30	.25	.12
28	Andre Reed	.10	.08	.04

1988 Topps Box Bottoms

The bottoms of 1988 Topps wax pack boxes had these cards, which honor award-winning achievements by professional players while they were in college. Two players are featured on each card. The cards are numbered on the back using a letter and include a summary of the player's collegiate accomplishment. The cards are standard size.

		NM/M	NM	E
Complete Set (16):		5.00	3.75	2.00
Common Player:		.20	.15	.08
A	Vinny Testaverde	.50	.40	.20
B	Dean Steinkuhler	.20	.15	.08
C	George Rogers	.20	.15	.08
D	Kenneth Sims	.20	.15	.08
E	Cornelius Bennett	.50	.40	.20
F	Bo Jackson	1.00	.70	.40
G	Ross Browner	.35	.25	.14
H	Doug Flutie	1.00	.70	.40
I	Herschel Walker	.50	.40	.20
J	Jim Plunkett	.50	.40	.20
K	Charles White	.25	.20	.10
L	Brad Budde	.20	.15	.08
M	Marcus Allen	.50	.40	.20
N	Mike Rozier	.25	.20	.10
O	Tony Dorsett	.75	.60	.30
P	**Checklist**	.20	.15	.08

1988 Topps Sticker Backs

These cards were left after collectors would remove the 1988 Topps stickers from their card. Each card measures 2-1/8" x 3" and features a prominent offensive player. The sticker has "Superstar" written at the top, above the color player photo. His name and card number appear at the bottom in a stat box, using 1 of 67, etc.

		NM/M	NM	E
Complete Set (67):		5.00	3.75	2.00
Common Player:		.05	.04	.02
1	Doug Williams	.10	.08	.04
2	Gary Clark	.15	.11	.06
3	John Elway	.50	.40	.20
4	Sammy Winder	.05	.04	.02
5	Vance Johnson	.07	.05	.03
6	Joe Montana	1.50	1.25	.60
7	Roger Craig	.15	.11	.06
8	Jerry Rice	1.00	.70	.40
9	Rueben Mayes	.10	.08	.04
10	Eric Martin	.10	.08	.04
11	Neal Anderson	.30	.25	.12
12	Willie Gault	.10	.08	.04
13	Bernie Kosar	.25	.20	.10
14	Kevin Mack	.05	.04	.02
15	Webster Slaughter	.15	.11	.06
16	Warren Moon	.40	.30	.15
17	Mike Rozier	.10	.08	.04
18	Drew Hill	.10	.08	.04
19	Eric Dickerson	.30	.25	.12
20	Bill Brooks	.05	.04	.02
21	Curt Warner	.15	.11	.06
22	Steve Largent	.40	.30	.15
23	Darrin Nelson	.05	.04	.02
24	Anthony Carter	.15	.11	.06
25	Earnest Jackson	.05	.04	.02

26	Weegie Thompson	.05	.04	.02
27	Stephen Starring	.05	.04	.02
28	Stanley Morgan	.10	.08	.04
29	Dan Marino	1.50	1.25	.60
30	Troy Stadford	.10	.08	.04
31	Mark Clayton	.15	.11	.06
32	Curtis Adams	.05	.04	.02
33	Kellen Winslow	.15	.11	.06
34	Jim Kelly	.60	.45	.25
35	Ronnie Harmon	.25	.20	.10
36	Chris Burkett	.05	.04	.02
37	Randall Cunningham	.35	.25	.14
38	Anthony Toney	.05	.04	.02
39	Mike Quick	.10	.08	.04
40	Neil Lomax	.10	.08	.04
41	Stump Mitchell	.10	.08	.04
42	J.T. Smith	.05	.04	.02
43	Herschel Walker	.25	.20	.10
44	Herschel Walker	.25	.20	.10
45	Joe Morris	.12	.09	.05
46	Mark Bavaro	.10	.08	.04
47	Charles White	.15	.11	.06
48	Henry Ellard	.10	.08	.04
49	Ken O'Brien	.10	.08	.04
50	Freeman McNeil	.10	.08	.04
51	Al Toon	.12	.09	.05
52	Kenneth Davis	.10	.08	.04
53	Walter Stanley	.05	.04	.02
54	Marcus Allen	.30	.25	.12
55	James Lofton	.25	.20	.10
56	Boomer Esiason	.20	.15	.08
57	Larry Kinnebrew	.05	.04	.02
58	Eddie Brown	.10	.08	.04
59	James Wilder	.07	.05	.03
60	Gerald Carter	.05	.04	.02
61	Christian Okoye	.20	.15	.08
62	Carlos Carson	.05	.04	.02
63	James Jones	.05	.04	.02
64	Pete Mandley	.05	.04	.02
65	Gerald Riggs	.10	.08	.04
66	Floyd Dixon	.05	.04	.02
67	**Checklist Card**	.10	.08	.04

1988 Topps Stickers

These stickers can be distinguished from Topps' previous efforts by the two frames used on the front to border the color photograph. An inner frame of yellow footballs is adjacent to an outer red frame of the picture. Each sticker measures 2-1/8" x 3" and is numbered on both sides. All-Pro stickers were produced as foil stickers again, and pairs of stickers were also made, as indicated by parentheses. Stickers 2-5 form a puzzle of Doug Williams featured in action during Super Bowl XXII. Williams is also featured on the back of the album cover which was produced to hold the stickers; the Redskins in action are featured on the front.

		NM/M	NM	E
Complete Set (285):		15.00	11.00	6.00
Common Player:		.05	.04	.02
1	Doug Williams (Super Bowl XXII MVP)	.20	.15	.08
2	**Super Bowl XXII**	.08	.06	.03
3	**Super Bowl XXII**	.08	.06	.03
4	**Super Bowl XXII**	.08	.06	.03
5	**Super Bowl XXII**	.08	.06	.03
6	Neal Anderson (234)	.25	.20	.10
7	Willie Gault (224)	.08	.06	.03
8	Dennis Gentry (219)	.05	.04	.02
9	Dave Duerson (197)	.05	.04	.02
10	Steve McMichael (266)	.05	.04	.02
11	Dennis McKinnon (230)	.05	.04	.02
12	Mike Singletary (209)	.08	.06	.03
13	Jim McMahon	.12	.09	.05
14	Richard Dent	.10	.08	.04
15	Vinny Testaverde (167)	.20	.15	.08
16	Gerald Carter (187)	.05	.04	.02
17	Jeff Smith (185)	.05	.04	.02
18	Chris Washington (212)	.05	.04	.02
19	Bobby Futrell (231)	.05	.04	.02
20	Calvin Magee (182)	.05	.04	.02

21	Ron Holmes (169)	.05	.04	.02
22	Ervin Randle	.05	.04	.02
23	James Wilder	.08	.06	.03
24	Neil Lomax	.08	.06	.03
25	Robert Awalt (161)	.05	.04	.02
26	Leonard Smith (177)	.05	.04	.02
27	Stump Mitchell (178)	.05	.04	.02
28	Vai Sikahema (280)	.06	.05	.02
29	Freddie Joe Nunn (222)	.05	.04	.02
30	Earl Ferrell (223)	.05	.04	.02
31	Roy Green (157)	.10	.08	.04
32	J.T. Smith	.10	.08	.04
33	Michael Downs	.05	.04	.02
34	Herschel Walker	.30	.25	.12
35	Roger Ruzek (269)	.05	.04	.02
36	Ed "Too Tall" Jones (245)	.07	.05	.03
37	Everson Walls (252)	.05	.04	.02
38	Bill Bates (213)	.05	.04	.02
39	Doug Cosbie (179)	.05	.04	.02
40	Eugene Lockhart (186)	.05	.04	.02
41	Danny White (205)	.07	.05	.03
42	Randall Cunningham	.40	.30	.15
43	Reggie White	.30	.25	.12
44	Anthony Toney (256)	.05	.04	.02
45	Mike Quick (248)	.08	.06	.03
46	John Spagnola (235)	.05	.04	.02
47	Clyde Simmons (275)	.20	.15	.08
48	Andre Waters (261)	.05	.04	.02
49	Keith Byars (265)	.08	.06	.03
50	Jerome Brown (240)	.15	.11	.06
51	John Rade	.05	.04	.02
52	Rick Donnelly	.05	.04	.02
53	Scott Campbell (160)	.05	.04	.02
54	Floyd Dixon (246)	.05	.04	.02
55	Gerald Riggs (236)	.06	.05	.02
56	Bill Fralic (267)	.08	.06	.03
57	Mike Gann (165)	.05	.04	.02
58	Tony Casillas (168)	.15	.11	.06
59	Rick Bryan (257)	.05	.04	.02
60	Jerry Rice	1.00	.70	.40
61	Ronnie Lott	.25	.20	.10
62	Ray Wersching (220)	.05	.04	.02
63	Charles Haley (281)	.06	.05	.02
64	Joe Montana (190)	.75	.60	.30
65	Joe Cribbs (221)	.05	.04	.02
66	Mike Wilson (203)	.05	.04	.02
67	Roger Craig (251)	.12	.09	.05
68	Michael Walter (162)	.05	.04	.02
69	Mark Bavaro	.08	.06	.03
70	Carl Banks	.10	.08	.04
71	George Adams (274)	.03	.02	.01
72	Phil Simms (216)	.15	.11	.06
73	Lawrence Taylor (181)	.12	.09	.05
74	Joe Morris (198)	.06	.05	.02
75	Lionel Manuel (204)	.05	.04	.02
76	Sean Landeta (210)	.05	.04	.02
77	Harry Carson (159)	.05	.04	.02
78	Chuck Long (166)	.05	.04	.02
79	James Jones (159)	.08	.06	.03
80	Gary James (158)	.05	.04	.02
81	Gary Lee (176)	.05	.04	.02
82	Jim Arnold (260)	.05	.04	.02
83	Dennis Gibson (232)	.05	.04	.02
84	Mike Cofer (242)	.05	.04	.02
85	Pete Mandley	.05	.04	.02
86	James Griffin	.05	.04	.02
87	Randy Wright (206)	.05	.04	.02
88	Phillip Epps (191)	.05	.04	.02
89	Brian Noble (249)	.05	.04	.02
90	Johnny Holland (258)	.10	.08	.04
91	Dave Brown (156)	.05	.04	.02
92	Brent Fullwood (207)	.05	.04	.02
93	Kenneth Davis (194)	.08	.06	.03
94	Tim Harris	.15	.11	.06
95	Walter Stanley	.08	.06	.03
96	Charles White	.15	.11	.06
97	Jackie Slater	.08	.06	.03
98	Jim Everett (271)	.12	.09	.05
99	Mike Lansford (200)	.05	.04	.02
100	Henry Ellard (199)	.06	.05	.02
101	Dale Hatcher (170)	.05	.04	.02
102	Jim Collins (268)	.05	.04	.02
103	Jerry Gray (214)	.05	.04	.02
104	LeRoy Irvin (276)	.05	.04	.02
105	Darrell Green	.12	.09	.05
106	Doug Williams	.10	.08	.04
107	Gary Clark (247)	.10	.08	.04
108	Charles Mann (171)	.10	.08	.04
109	Art Monk (270)	.12	.09	.05
110	Barry Wilburn (196)	.05	.04	.02
111	Alvin Walton (188)	.05	.04	.02
112	Dexter Manley (233)	.05	.04	.02
113	Kelvin Bryant (180)	.04	.03	.02
114	Morten Andersen	.10	.08	.04
115	Rueben Mayes (244)	.06	.05	.02
116	Brian Hansen (279)	.05	.04	.02
117	Dalton Hilliard (241)	.10	.08	.04
118	Rickey Jackson (195)	.06	.05	.02
119	Eric Martin (189)	.06	.05	.02
120	Mel Gray (278)	.05	.04	.02
121	Bobby Hebert (215)	.08	.06	.03
122	Pat Swilling	.40	.30	.15
123	Anthony Carter	.12	.09	.05
124	Wade Wilson (225)	.20	.15	.08
125	Darrin Nelson (250)	.05	.04	.02
126	D.J. Dozier (239)	.06	.05	.02
127	Chris Doleman	.30	.25	.12
128	Henry Thomas (255)	.05	.04	.02
129	Jesse Solomon (211)	.05	.04	.02
130	Neal Guggemos (243)	.05	.04	.02
131	Joey Browner (208)	.06	.05	.02
132	Carl Banks (152, All-Pro)	.10	.08	.04
133	Joey Browner (145, All-Pro)	.10	.08	.04
134	Hanford Dixon (149, All-Pro)	.10	.08	.04
135	Rick Donnelly (147, All-Pro)	.10	.08	.04
136	Kenny Easley (155, All-Pro)	.15	.11	.06
137	Darrell Green (151, All-Pro)	.15	.11	.06
138	Bill Maas (148, All-Pro)	.10	.08	.04
139	Mike Singletary (153, All-Pro)	.15	.11	.06
140	Bruce Smith (154, All-Pro)	.20	.15	.08
141	Andre Tippett (146, All-Pro)	.10	.08	.04
142	Reggie White (150, All-Pro)	.20	.15	.08
143	Fredd Young (144, All-Pro)	.10	.08	.04
144	Morten Andersen (143, All-Pro)	.10	.08	.04
145	Mark Bavaro (133, All-Pro)	.10	.08	.04
146	Eric Dickerson (141, All-Pro)	.30	.25	.12
147	John Elway (134, All-Pro)	.75	.60	.30
148	Bill Fralic (138, All-Pro)	.10	.08	.04
149	Mike Munchak (135, All-Pro)	.10	.08	.04
150	Anthony Munoz (142, All-Pro)	.15	.11	.06
151	Jerry Rice (137, All-Pro)	1.00	.70	.40
152	Jackie Slater (132, All-Pro)	.12	.09	.05
153	J.T. Smith (139, All-Pro)	.10	.08	.04
154	Dwight Stephenson (140, All-Pro)	.12	.09	.05
155	Charles White (136, All-Pro)	.12	.09	.05
156	Larry Kinnebrew (91)	.05	.04	.02
157	Stanford Jennings (31)	.05	.04	.02
158	Eddie Brown (80)	.05	.04	.02
159	Scott Fulhage (77)	.05	.04	.02
160	Boomer Esiason (53)	.12	.09	.05
161	Tim Krumrie (25)	.05	.04	.02
162	Anthony Munoz (68)	.08	.06	.03
163	Jim Breech	.05	.04	.02
164	Reggie Williams	.08	.06	.03
165	Andre Reed (57)	.20	.15	.08
166	Cornelius Bennett (78)	.30	.25	.12
167	Ronnie Harmon (15)	.15	.11	.06
168	Shane Conlan (58)	.15	.11	.06
169	Chris Burkett (21)	.06	.05	.02
170	Mark Kelso (101)	.08	.06	.03
171	Robb Riddick (108)	.05	.04	.02
172	Bruce Smith	.15	.11	.06
173	Jim Kelly	.60	.45	.25
174	Jim Ryan	.05	.04	.02
175	John Elway	.60	.45	.25
176	Sammy Winder (81)	.05	.04	.02
177	Karl Mecklenburg (26)	.05	.04	.02
178	Mark Haynes (27)	.05	.04	.02
179	Rulon Jones (39)	.05	.04	.02
180	Ricky Nattiel (113)	.08	.06	.03
181	Vance Johnson (73)	.05	.04	.02
182	Mike Harden (20)	.05	.04	.02
183	Frank Minnifield	.05	.04	.02
184	Bernie Kosar	.25	.20	.10
185	Earnest Byner (17)	.12	.09	.05
186	Webster Slaughter (40)	.15	.11	.06
187	Brian Brennan (16)	.05	.04	.02
188	Carl Hairston (111)	.05	.04	.02
189	Mike Johnson (119)	.05	.04	.02
190	Clay Matthews (64)	.06	.05	.02
191	Kevin Mack (88)	.06	.05	.02
192	Kellen Winslow	.12	.09	.05
193	Billy Ray Smith	.08	.06	.03
194	Gary Anderson (93)	.06	.05	.02
195	Chip Banks (118)	.05	.04	.02
196	Elvis Patterson (110)	.05	.04	.02
197	Lee Williams (9)	.07	.05	.03
198	Curtis Adams (74)	.05	.04	.02
199	Vencie Glenn (100)	.05	.04	.02
200	Ralf Mojsiejenko (99)	.05	.04	.02
201	Carlos Carson	.05	.04	.02
202	Bill Maas	.05	.04	.02
203	Christian Okoye (66)	.15	.11	.06
204	Deron Cherry (75)	.08	.06	.03
205	Dino Hackett (41)	.05	.04	.02
206	Mike Bell (87)	.05	.04	.02
207	Stephone Paige (92)	.06	.05	.02
208	Bill Kenney (131)	.06	.05	.02
209	Paul Palmer (12)	.05	.04	.02
210	Jack Trudeau (76)	.06	.05	.02
211	Albert Bentley (129)	.06	.05	.02
212	Bill Brooks (18)	.06	.05	.02
213	Dean Biasucci (38)	.05	.04	.02
214	Cliff Odom (103)	.05	.04	.02
215	Barry Krauss (121)	.05	.04	.02
216	Mike Prior (72)	.06	.05	.02
217	Eric Dickerson	.35	.25	.14
218	Duane Bickett	.08	.06	.03
219	Dwight Stephenson (8)	.08	.06	.03
220	John Offerdahl (62)	.10	.08	.04
221	Troy Stradford (65)	.06	.05	.02
222	John Bosa (29)	.04	.03	.02
223	Jackie Shipp (30)	.05	.04	.02
224	Paul Lankford (7)	.05	.04	.02
225	Mark Duper (124)	.08	.06	.03
226	Dan Marino	1.50	1.25	.60
227	Mark Clayton	.15	.11	.06
228	Bob Crable	.05	.04	.02
229	Al Toon	.08	.06	.03
230	Freeman McNeil (11)	.06	.05	.02
231	Johnny Hector (19)	.05	.04	.02
232	Pat Leahy (83)	.05	.04	.02
233	Ken O'Brien (112)	.05	.04	.02
234	Alex Gordon (6)	.05	.04	.02
235	Harry Hamilton (46)	.05	.04	.02
236	Mickey Shuler (55)	.05	.04	.02
237	Mike Rozier	.08	.06	.03
238	Al Smith	.15	.11	.06
239	Ernest Givins (126)	.15	.11	.06
240	Warren Moon (50)	.25	.20	.10
241	Drew Hill (117)	.10	.08	.04
242	Alonzo Highsmith (84)	.15	.11	.06
243	Mike Munchak (130)	.06	.05	.02
244	Keith Bostic (115)	.05	.04	.02
245	Sean Jones (36)	.08	.06	.03
246	Stanley Morgan (54)	.06	.05	.02
247	Garin Veris (107)	.05	.04	.02
248	Stephen Starring (45)	.05	.04	.02
249	Steve Grogan (89)	.06	.05	.02
250	Irving Fryar (125)	.10	.08	.04
251	Rich Camarillo (67)	.05	.04	.02
252	Ronnie Lippett (37)	.05	.04	.02
253	Andre Tippett	.08	.06	.03
254	Fred Marion	.05	.04	.02
255	Howie Long (128)	.10	.08	.04
256	James Lofton (44)	.12	.09	.05
257	Vance Mueller (59)	.05	.04	.02
258	Jerry Robinson (90)	.05	.04	.02
259	Todd Christensen (79)	.06	.05	.02
260	Vann McElroy (82)	.05	.04	.02
261	Greg Townsend (48)	.10	.08	.04
262	Bo Jackson	.85	.60	.35
263	Marcus Allen	.30	.25	.12
264	Curt Warner	.08	.06	.03
265	Jacob Green (49)	.06	.05	.02
266	Norm Johnson (10)	.05	.04	.02
267	Brian Bosworth (56)	.05	.04	.02
268	Bobby Joe Edmonds (102)	.05	.04	.02
269	Dave Krieg (35)	.07	.05	.03
270	Kenny Easley (109)	.06	.05	.02
271	Steve Largent (98)	.30	.25	.12
272	Fredd Young	.05	.04	.02
273	David Little	.05	.04	.02
274	Frank Pollard (71)	.05	.04	.02
275	Dwight Stone (47)	.08	.06	.03
276	Mike Merriweather (104)	.06	.05	.02
277	Earnest Jackson	.05	.04	.02
278	Delton Hall (120)	.05	.04	.02
279	Gary Anderson (116)	.05	.04	.02
280	Harry Newsome (28)	.08	.06	.03
281	Dwayne Woodruff (63)	.05	.04	.02
282	J.T. Smith (283)	.05	.04	.02
283	Charles White (282)	.05	.04	.02
284	Reggie White (285)	.15	.11	.06
285	Morten Andersen (284)	.10	.08	.04

1989 Topps Traded

This 132-card set was released in March of 1990. It was a boxed set through only hobby dealers, similar to the baseball "Traded" sets that Topps had been issuing since 1981. The set includes 1989 rookies, players not included in the regular '89 set and players that had been traded (now shown with their new team).

	NM/M	NM	E
Complete Set (132):	12.00	9.00	4.75
Common Player:	.05	.04	.02

1	Eric Ball **RC**	.10	.08	.04
2	Tony Mandarich	.05	.04	.02
3	Shawn Collins **RC**	.10	.08	.04
4	Ray Bentley **RC**	.10	.08	.04
5	Tony Casillas	.10	.08	.04
6	Al Del Greco **RC**	.10	.08	.04
7	Dan Saleaumua **RC**	.10	.08	.04
8	Keith Bishop	.05	.04	.02
9	Rodney Peete **RC**	.40	.30	.15
10	Lorenzo White **RC**	.25	.20	.10

11	Steve Smith **RC**	.25	.20	.10
12	Pete Mandley	.05	.04	.02
13	Mervyn Fernandez	.05	.04	.02
14	Flipper Anderson **RC**	.30	.25	.12
15	Louis Oliver **RC**	.15	.11	.06
16	Rick Fenney	.05	.04	.02
17	Gary Jeter	.05	.04	.02
18	Greg Cox	.05	.04	.02
19	Bubba McDowell **RC**	.15	.11	.06
20	Ron Heller	.05	.04	.02
21	Tim McDonald **RC**	.25	.20	.10
22	Jerrol Williams **RC**	.10	.08	.04
23	Marion Butts **RC**	.40	.30	.15
24	Steve Young	1.00	.70	.40
25	Mike Merriweather	.05	.04	.02
26	Richard Johnson	.05	.04	.02
27	Gerald Riggs	.05	.04	.02
28	Dave Waymer	.05	.04	.02
29	Isaac Holt	.05	.04	.02
30	Deion Sanders **RC**	1.75	1.25	.70
31	Todd Blackledge	.05	.04	.02
32	Jeff Cross **RC**	.30	.25	.12
33	Steve Wisniewski **RC**	.20	.15	.08
34	Ron Brown	.05	.04	.02
35	Ron Bernstine **RC**	.35	.25	.14
36	Jeff Uhlenhake **RC**	.08	.06	.03
37	Donnell Woolford **RC**	.12	.09	.05
38	Bob Gagliano **RC**	.12	.09	.05
39	Ezra Johnson	.05	.04	.02
40	Ron Jaworski	.05	.04	.02
41	Lawyer Tillman **RC**	.10	.08	.04
42	Lorenzo Lynch **RC**	.10	.08	.04
43	Mike Alexander	.05	.04	.02
44	Tim Worley **RC**	.15	.11	.06
45	Guy Bingham	.05	.04	.02
46	Cleveland Gary **RC**	.25	.20	.10
47	Danny Peebles	.05	.04	.02
48	Clarence Weathers	.05	.04	.02
49	Jeff Lageman **RC**	.10	.08	.04
50	Eric Metcalf **RC**	.65	.50	.25
51	Myron Guyton **RC**	.10	.08	.04
52	Steve Atwater **RC**	.20	.15	.08
53	John Fourcade	.05	.04	.02
54	Randall McDaniel	.12	.09	.05
55	Al Noga **RC**	.15	.11	.06
56	Sammie Smith **RC**	.10	.08	.04
57	Jesse Solomon	.05	.04	.02
58	Greg Kragen **RC**	.10	.08	.04
59	Don Beebe **RC**	.50	.40	.20
60	Hart Lee Dykes	.05	.04	.02
61	Trace Armstrong **RC**	.15	.11	.06
62	Steve Pelluer	.05	.04	.02
63	Barry Krauss	.05	.04	.02
64	Kevin Murphy	.05	.04	.02
65	Steve Tasker **RC**	.30	.25	.12
66	Jessie Small **RC**	.10	.08	.04
67	Dave Meggett **RC**	.25	.20	.10
68	Dean Hamel	.05	.04	.02
69	Jim Covert	.05	.04	.02
70	Troy Aikman **RC**	3.00	2.25	1.25
71	Raul Allegre	.05	.04	.02
72	Chris Jacke **RC**	.15	.11	.06
73	Leslie O'Neal	.25	.20	.10
74	Keith Taylor **RC**	.10	.08	.04
75	Steve Walsh **RC**	.50	.40	.20
76	Tracy Rocker	.05	.04	.02
77	Robert Massey **RC**	.12	.09	.05
78	Bryan Wagner	.05	.04	.02
79	Steve DeOssie	.05	.04	.02
80	Carnell Lake **RC**	.12	.09	.05
81	Frank Reich **RC**	.50	.40	.20
82	Tyrone Braxton **RC**	.10	.08	.04
83	Barry Sanders **RC**	10.00	7.50	4.00
84	Pete Stoyanovich **RC**	.20	.15	.08
85	Paul Palmer	.05	.04	.02
86	Billy Joe Tolliver **RC**	.10	.08	.04
87	Eric Hill **RC**	.08	.06	.03
88	Gerald McNeil	.05	.04	.02
89	Bill Hawkins	.05	.04	.02
90	Derrick Thomas **RC**	.75	.60	.30
91	Jim Harbaugh **RC**	1.00	.70	.40
92	Brian Williams	.05	.04	.02
93	Jack Trudeau	.05	.04	.02
94	Leonard Smith	.05	.04	.02
95	Gary Hogeboom	.05	.04	.02
96	A.J. Johnson **RC**	.10	.08	.04
97	Jim McMahon	.05	.04	.02
98	David Williams **RC**	.12	.09	.05
99	Rohn Stark	.05	.04	.02
100	Sean Landeta	.05	.04	.02
101	Tim Johnson **RC**	.08	.06	.03
102	Andre Rison **RC**	.50	.40	.20
103	Earnest Byner	.05	.04	.02
104	Don McPherson **RC**	.08	.06	.03
105	Zefross Moss **RC**	.08	.06	.03
106	Frank Stams **RC**	.10	.08	.04
107	Courtney Hall **RC**	.10	.08	.04
108	Marc Logan **RC**	.15	.11	.06
109	James Lofton	.15	.11	.06
110	Lewis Tillman **RC**	.50	.40	.20
111	Irv Pankey	.05	.04	.02
112	Ralf Mojsiejenko	.05	.04	.02
113	Bobby Humphrey **RC**	.08	.06	.03
114	Chris Burkett	.05	.04	.02
115	Greg Lloyd **RC**	.40	.30	.15
116	Matt Millen	.05	.04	.02
117	Carl Zander	.05	.04	.02
118	Wayne Martin **RC**	.25	.20	.10
119	Mike Saxon	.05	.04	.02
120	Herschel Walker	.12	.09	.05
121	Andy Heck **RC**	.08	.06	.03
122	Mark Robinson	.05	.04	.02
123	Keith Van Horne **RC**	.08	.06	.03
124	Ricky Hunley	.05	.04	.02
125	Timm Rosenbach **RC**	.15	.11	.06
126	Steve Grogan	.05	.04	.02
127	Stephen Braggs **RC**	.08	.06	.03
128	Terry Long	.05	.04	.02
129	Evan Cooper	.05	.04	.02
130	Robert Lyles	.05	.04	.02
131	Mike Webster	.05	.04	.02
132	**Checklist**	.05	.04	.02

1989 Topps

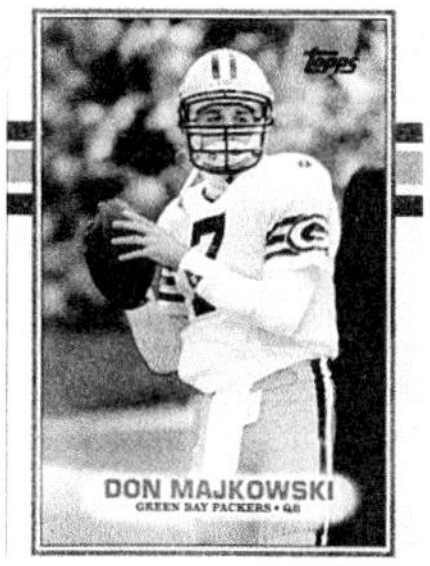

Topps released its seventh straight 396-card set in late August 1989. Cards are standard size, with white borders and a multicolored stripe about three-quarters from the bottom. Player names and teams are at the bottom of the card in an opaque circle. Card backs feature a dark green on yellow design. There are a few errors in the set: Card #24, Eddie Brown, lists his birthday as 12/18 and it's actually 12/17; card #27, Boomer Esiason, has him a native of East Islip, when it should be West Islip; the front of card #56, Mark Kelso, reads "BILL" instead of "BILLS"; on Jay Hilgenberg's card, a "g" is missing from "Chicago" on the card front. The back of Mark Rypien's card (#253) lists 14 as his 1988 completion total, while it should read 114. Card #125, Robert Delpino, correctly shows his team designation as "Rams" on the front, but lists "Los Angeles Raiders" on the back; card #247, Karl Mecklenberg, lists him as being drafted in the second round when it should be the 12th. Rodney Holman's card also features a problem with the card front: there are six different variations of "BENGALS". One has a small space between the "B" and "E"; the second has the "B" a little above the rest of the line of type; the third has it just a little below; the fourth shows just the "B" with no other letters behind it; another shows the "B" partially superimposed over the "E"; another shows "CINCINNATI B" without the rest of "Bengals"; and the last one is the correct version. Rookies in this set include Sterling Sharpe, Don Majkowski, Ickey Woods, John Stephens, John Taylor, Erik McMillan, Keith Jackson and Tom Newberry. (Key: AP - All Pro, SR - Super Rookie)

	NM/M	NM	E
Complete Set (396):	15.00	11.00	6.00
Common Player:	.25	.15	.09
Wax Pack (15+1):	.50		
Wax Box (36):	11.00		

1	**Super Bowl XXIII**	.25	.15	.09
2	Tim Brown	.25	.15	.09
3	Eric Dickerson	.25	.15	.09
4	Steve Largent	.25	.15	.09
5	Dan Marino	.60	.45	.25
6	49ers Team (Joe Montana)	.30	.25	.12
7	Jerry Rice (AP)	1.25	.75	.45
8	Roger Craig (AP)	.25	.15	.09
9	Ronnie Lott	.15	.11	.06
10	Michael Carter	.25	.15	.09
11	Charles Haley	.25	.15	.09
12	Joe Montana	2.00	1.00	.60
13	John Taylor **RC**	.25	.15	.09
14	Michael Walter	.25	.15	.09
15	Mike Cofer **RC**	.10	.08	.04
16	Tom Rathman	.25	.15	.09
17	Danny Stubbs **RC**	.12	.09	.05
18	Keena Turner	.25	.15	.09
19	Tim McKyer	.25	.15	.09
20	Larry Roberts	.25	.15	.09
21	Jeff Fuller	.25	.15	.09
22	Bubba Paris	.25	.15	.09
23	Bengals Team (Boomer Esiason)	.25	.15	.09
24	Eddie Brown (AP)	.25	.15	.09
25	Boomer Esiason (AP)	.30	.25	.12
26	Tim Krumrie (AP)	.25	.15	.09
27	Ickey Woods (SR)	.25	.15	.09
28	Anthony Munoz	.25	.15	.09
29	Tim McGee	.25	.15	.09
30	Max Montoya	.25	.15	.09
31	David Grant	.25	.15	.09
32	Rodney Holman **RC**	.25	.20	.10
33	David Fulcher	.25	.15	.09
34	Jim Skow	.25	.15	.09
35	James Brooks	.25	.15	.09
36	Reggie Williams	.25	.15	.09
37	Eric Thomas **RC**	.10	.08	.04
38	Stanford Jennings	.25	.15	.09
39	Jim Breech	.25	.15	.09
40	Bills Team (Jim Kelly)	.15	.11	.06
41	Shane Conlan (AP)	.15	.11	.06
42	Scott Norwood (AP)	.25	.15	.09
43	Cornelius Bennett	.30	.25	.12
44	Bruce Smith (AP)	.15	.11	.06
45	Thurman Thomas **RC** (SR)	.30	.15	.10
46	Jim Kelly	.50	.40	.20
47	John Kidd	.25	.15	.09
48	Kent Hull **RC**	.15	.11	.06
49	Art Still	.25	.15	.09
50	Fred Smerlas	.25	.15	.09
51	Derrick Burroughs	.25	.15	.09
52	Andre Reed	.30	.25	.12
53	Robb Riddick	.25	.15	.09
54	Chris Burkett	.25	.15	.09
55	Ronnie Harmon	.20	.15	.08
56	Mark Kelso	.25	.15	.09
57	Bears Team (Thomas Sanders)	.25	.15	.09
58	Mike Singletary (AP)	.10	.08	.04
59	Jay Hilgenberg (AP)	.25	.15	.09
60	Richard Dent	.25	.15	.09
61	Ron Rivera	.25	.15	.09
62	Jim McMahon	.25	.15	.09
63	Mike Tomczak	.12	.09	.05
64	Neal Anderson	.30	.25	.12
65	Dennis Gentry	.25	.15	.09
66	Dan Hampton	.25	.15	.09
67	David Tate	.25	.15	.09
68	Thomas Sanders **RC**	.10	.08	.04
69	Steve McMichael	.25	.15	.09
70	Dennis McKinnon	.25	.15	.09
71	Brad Muster **RC**	.20	.15	.08
72	Vestee Jackson **RC**	.10	.08	.04
73	Dave Duerson	.25	.15	.09
74	Vikings Team (Keith Millard)	.25	.15	.09
75	Joey Browner (AP)	.25	.15	.09
76	Carl Lee **RC** (AP)	.10	.08	.04
77	Gary Zimmerman (AP)	.25	.15	.09
78	Hassan Jones **RC**	.10	.08	.04
79	Anthony Carter	.25	.15	.09
80	Ray Berry	.25	.15	.09
81	Steve Jordan	.25	.15	.09
82	Issiac Holt	.25	.15	.09
83	Wade Wilson	.25	.15	.09
84	Chris Doleman	.20	.15	.08
85	Alfred Anderson	.25	.15	.09
86	Keith Millard	.25	.15	.09
87	Darrin Nelson	.25	.15	.09
88	D.J. Dozier	.25	.15	.09
89	Scott Studwell	.25	.15	.09
90	Oilers Team (Tony Zendejas)	.25	.15	.09
91	Bruce Matthews **RC** (AP)	.30	.25	.12
92	Curtis Duncan	.20	.15	.08
93	Warren Moon	.40	.30	.15
94	Johnny Meads **RC**	.10	.08	.04
95	Drew Hill	.25	.15	.09
96	Alonzo Highsmith	.25	.15	.09
97	Mike Munchak	.25	.15	.09
98	Mike Rozier	.25	.15	.09
99	Tony Zendejas	.25	.15	.09
100	Jeff Donaldson	.25	.15	.09
101	Ray Childress	.25	.15	.09
102	Sean Jones	.25	.15	.09
103	Ernest Givins	.20	.15	.08
104	William Fuller **RC**	.40	.30	.15
105	Allen Pinkett **RC**	.15	.11	.06
106	Eagles Team (Randall Cunningham)	.10	.08	.04
107	Keith Jackson **RC** (AP)	.50	.40	.20
108	Reggie White (AP)	.25	.20	.10
109	Clyde Simmons	.25	.20	.10
110	John Teltschik	.25	.15	.09
111	Wes Hopkins	.25	.15	.09
112	Keith Byars	.25	.15	.09

113	Jerome Brown	.25	.15	.09
114	Mike Quick	.25	.15	.09
115	Randall Cunningham	.40	.30	.15
116	Anthony Toney	.25	.15	.09
117	Ron Johnson	.25	.15	.09
118	Terry Hoage	.25	.15	.09
119	Seth Joyner	.25	.20	.10
120	Eric Allen RC	.40	.30	.15
121	Cris Carter RC	2.00	1.00	.60
122	Rams Team (Greg Bell)	.25	.15	.09
123	Tom Newberry RC (AP)	.15	.11	.06
124	Pete Holohan	.25	.15	.09
125	Robert Delpino RC	.35	.25	.14
126	Carl Ekern	.25	.15	.09
127	Greg Bell	.25	.15	.09
128	Mike Lansford	.25	.15	.09
129	Jim Everett	.15	.11	.06
130	Mike Wilcher	.25	.15	.09
131	Jerry Gray	.25	.15	.09
132	Dale Hatcher	.25	.15	.09
133	Doug Smith	.25	.15	.09
134	Kevin Greene	.15	.11	.06
135	Jackie Slater	.25	.15	.09
136	Aaron Cox RC	.12	.09	.05
137	Henry Ellard	.25	.15	.09
138	Browns Team (Bernie Kosar)	.25	.15	.09
139	Frank Minnifield (AP)	.25	.15	.09
140	Webster Slaughter	.25	.20	.10
141	Bernie Kosar	.20	.15	.08
142	Charles Buchanan	.25	.15	.09
143	Clay Matthews	.25	.15	.09
144	Reggie Langhorne RC	.30	.25	.12
145	Hanford Dixon	.25	.15	.09
146	Brian Brennan	.25	.15	.09
147	Earnest Byner	.25	.15	.09
148	Michael Dean Perry RC	.25	.15	.09
149	Kevin Mack	.25	.15	.09
150	Matt Bahr	.25	.15	.09
151	Ozzie Newsome	.20	.15	.08
152	Saints Team (Craig Heyward)	.25	.15	.09
153	Morten Andersen	.25	.15	.09
154	Pat Swilling	.25	.20	.10
155	Sam Mills	.25	.15	.09
156	Lonzell Hill	.25	.15	.09
157	Dalton Hilliard	.25	.15	.09
158	Craig Heyward RC	.50	.40	.20
159	Vaughan Johnson RC	.30	.25	.12
160	Reuben Mayes	.25	.15	.09
161	Gene Atkins RC	.10	.08	.04
162	Bobby Hebert	.20	.15	.08
163	Rickey Jackson	.25	.15	.09
164	Eric Martin	.25	.15	.09
165	Giants Team (Joe Morris)	.25	.15	.09
166	Lawrence Taylor (AP)	.15	.11	.06
167	Bart Oates	.25	.15	.09
168	Carl Banks	.25	.15	.09
169	Eric Moore	.25	.15	.09
170	Sheldon White RC	.12	.09	.05
171	Mark Collins RC	.12	.09	.05
172	Phil Simms	.15	.11	.06
173	Jim Burt	.25	.15	.09
174	Stephen Baker RC	.25	.20	.10
175	Mark Bavaro	.25	.15	.09
176	Pepper Johnson	.25	.15	.09
177	Lionel Manuel	.25	.15	.09
178	Joe Morris	.25	.15	.09
179	John Elliott RC	.15	.11	.06
180	Gary Reasons	.25	.15	.09
181	Seahawks Team (Dave Krieg)	.25	.15	.09
182	Brian Blades RC (SR)	.25	.15	.09
183	Steve Largent	.25	.20	.10
184	Rufus Porter RC	.15	.11	.06
185	Ruben Rodriguez	.25	.15	.09
186	Curt Warner	.25	.15	.09
187	Paul Moyer	.25	.15	.09
188	Dave Krieg	.25	.15	.09
189	Jacob Green	.25	.15	.09
190	John L. Williams	.25	.15	.09
191	Eugene Robinson RC	.15	.11	.06
192	Brian Bosworth	.25	.15	.09
193	Patriots Team (Tony Eason)	.25	.15	.09
194	John Stephens RC (SR)	.20	.15	.08
195	Robert Perryman RC	.10	.08	.04
196	Andre Tippett	.25	.15	.09
197	Fred Marion	.25	.15	.09
198	Doug Flutie	.75	.60	.30
199	Stanley Morgan	.25	.15	.09
200	Johnny Rembert RC	.10	.08	.04
201	Tony Eason	.25	.15	.09
202	Marvin Allen	.25	.15	.09
203	Raymond Clayborn	.25	.15	.09
204	Irving Fryar	.25	.15	.09
205	Colts Team (Chris Chandler)	.25	.15	.09
206	Eric Dickerson (AP)	.20	.15	.08
207	Chris Hinton (AP)	.25	.15	.09
208	Duane Bickett	.25	.15	.09
209	Chris Chandler RC	1.00	.50	.30
210	Jon Hand	.25	.15	.09
211	Ray Donaldson	.25	.15	.09
212	Dean Biasucci	.25	.15	.09
213	Bill Brooks	.25	.15	.09
214	Chris Goode RC	.10	.08	.04
215	Clarence Verdin RC	.20	.15	.08
216	Albert Bentley	.25	.15	.09
217	Passing Leaders (Wade Wilson, Boomer Esiason)	.25	.15	.09
218	Receiving Leaders (Henry Ellard, Al Toon)	.25	.15	.09
219	Rushing Leaders (Herschel Walker, Eric Dickerson)	.15	.11	.06
220	Scoring Leaders (Mike Cofer, Scott Norwood)	.25	.15	.09
221	Interception Leaders (Scott Case, Erik McMillan)	.25	.15	.09
222	Jets Team (Ken O'Brien)	.25	.15	.09
223	Erik McMillan (SR)	.10	.08	.04
224	James Hasty RC (SR)	.12	.09	.05
225	Al Toon	.25	.15	.09
226	John Booty RC	.12	.09	.05
227	Johnny Hector	.25	.15	.09
228	Ken O'Brien	.25	.15	.09
229	Marty Lyons	.25	.15	.09
230	Mickey Shuler	.25	.15	.09
231	Robin Cole	.25	.15	.09
232	Freeman McNeil	.25	.15	.09
233	Marion Barber	.25	.15	.09
234	JoJo Townsell	.25	.15	.09
235	Wesley Walker	.25	.15	.09
236	Roger Vick	.25	.15	.09
237	Pat Leahy	.25	.15	.09
238	Broncos Team (John Elway)	.10	.08	.04
239	Mike Horan (AP)	.25	.15	.09
240	Tony Dorsett	.25	.20	.10
241	John Elway	1.00	.50	.30
242	Mark Jackson	.25	.15	.09
243	Sammy Winder	.25	.15	.09
244	Rich Karlis	.25	.15	.09
245	Vance Johnson	.25	.15	.09
246	Steve Sewell RC	.10	.08	.04
247	Karl Mecklenburg	.25	.15	.09
248	Rulon Jones	.25	.15	.09
249	Simon Fletcher RC	.30	.25	.12
250	Redskins Team (Doug Williams)	.25	.15	.09
251	Chip Lohmiller RC (SR)	.30	.25	.12
252	Jamie Morris (SR)	.25	.15	.09
253	Mark Rypien RC (SR)	.40	.30	.15
254	Barry Wilburn	.25	.15	.09
255	Mark May	.10	.08	.04
256	Wilbur Marshall	.25	.15	.09
257	Charles Mann	.25	.15	.09
258	Gary Clark	.15	.11	.06
259	Doug Williams	.25	.15	.09
260	Art Monk	.15	.11	.06
261	Kelvin Bryant	.25	.15	.09
262	Dexter Manley	.25	.15	.09
263	Ricky Sanders	.25	.15	.09
264	Raiders Team (Marcus Allen)	.25	.15	.09
265	Tim Brown RC (AP)	1.00	.50	.25
266	Jay Schroeder	.25	.15	.09
267	Marcus Allen	.12	.09	.05
268	Mike Haynes	.25	.15	.09
269	Bo Jackson	.75	.60	.30
270	Steve Beuerlein RC	.25	.15	.09
271	Vann McElroy	.25	.15	.09
272	Willie Gault	.25	.15	.09
273	Howie Long	.25	.15	.09
274	Greg Townsend	.25	.15	.09
275	Mike Wise	.25	.15	.09
276	Cardinals Team (Neil Lomax)	.25	.15	.09
277	Luis Sharpe	.25	.15	.09
278	Scott Dill	.25	.15	.09
279	Vai Sikahema	.25	.15	.09
280	Ron Wolfley	.25	.15	.09
281	David Galloway	.25	.15	.09
282	Jay Novacek RC	.50	.25	.15
283	Neil Lomax	.25	.15	.09
284	Robert Awalt	.25	.15	.09
285	Cedric Mack	.25	.15	.09
286	Freddie Joe Nunn	.25	.15	.09
287	J.T. Smith	.25	.15	.09
288	Stump Mitchell	.25	.15	.09
289	Roy Green	.25	.15	.09
290	Dolphins Team (Dan Marino)	.25	.20	.10
291	Jarvis Williams RC (SR)	.10	.08	.04
292	Troy Stradford	.25	.15	.09
293	Dan Marino	1.50	.75	.45
294	T.J. Turner	.25	.15	.09
295	John Offerdahl	.25	.15	.09
296	Ferrell Edmunds RC	.15	.11	.06
297	Scott Schwedes	.25	.15	.09
298	Lorenzo Hampton	.25	.15	.09
299	Jim Jensen	.25	.15	.09
300	Brian Sochia	.25	.15	.09
301	Reggie Roby	.25	.15	.09
302	Mark Clayton	.25	.15	.09
303	Chargers Team (Tim Spencer)	.25	.15	.09
304	Lee Williams	.25	.15	.09
305	Gary Plummer RC	.15	.11	.06
306	Gary Anderson	.25	.15	.09
307	Gill Byrd	.25	.15	.09
308	Jamie Holland	.25	.15	.09
309	Billy Ray Smith	.25	.15	.09
310	Lionel James	.25	.15	.09
311	Mark Vlasic RC	.20	.15	.08
312	Curtis Adams	.25	.15	.09
313	Anthony Miller RC	.25	.15	.09
314	Steelers Team (Frank Pollard)	.25	.15	.09
315	Bubby Brister RC	.50	.40	.20
316	David Little	.25	.15	.09
317	Tunch Ilkin	.25	.15	.09
318	Louis Lipps	.25	.15	.09
319	Warren Williams RC	.10	.08	.04
320	Dwight Stone	.25	.15	.09
321	Merril Hoge RC	.20	.15	.08
322	Thomas Everett RC	.25	.20	.10
323	Rod Woodson RC	1.00	.50	.30
324	Gary Anderson	.25	.15	.09
325	Buccaneer Team (Ron Hall)	.25	.15	.09
326	Donnie Elder	.25	.15	.09
327	Vinny Testaverde	.15	.11	.06
328	Harry Hamilton	.25	.15	.09
329	James Wilder	.25	.15	.09
330	Lars Tate	.25	.15	.09
331	Mark Carrier RC	.65	.50	.25
332	Bruce Hill	.25	.15	.09
333	Paul Gruber RC	.12	.09	.05
334	Ricky Reynolds	.25	.15	.09
335	Eugene Marve	.25	.15	.09
336	Falcons Team (J. Williams)	.25	.15	.09
337	Aundray Bruce RC (SR)	.10	.08	.04
338	John Rade	.25	.15	.09
339	Scott Case RC	.10	.08	.04
340	Robert Moore	.25	.15	.09
341	Chris Miller RC	.60	.45	.25
342	Gerald Riggs	.25	.15	.09
343	Gene Lang	.25	.15	.09
344	Marcus Cotton	.25	.15	.09
345	Rick Donnelly	.25	.15	.09
346	John Settle RC	.10	.08	.04
347	Bill Fralic	.25	.15	.09
348	Chiefs Team (Dino Hackett)	.25	.15	.09
349	Steve DeBerg	.25	.15	.09
350	Mike Stensrud	.25	.15	.09
351	Dino Hackett	.25	.15	.09
352	Deron Cherry	.25	.15	.09
353	Christian Okoye	.12	.09	.05
354	Bill Maas	.25	.15	.09
355	Carlos Carson	.25	.15	.09
356	Albert Lewis	.25	.15	.09
357	Paul Palmer	.25	.15	.09
358	Nick Lowery	.25	.15	.09
359	Stephone Paige	.25	.15	.09
360	Lions Team (Chuck Long)	.25	.15	.09
361	Chris Spielman RC (SR)	.30	.25	.12
362	Jim Arnold	.25	.15	.09
363	Devon Mitchell	.25	.15	.09
364	Mike Cofer	.25	.15	.09
365	Bennie Blades RC	.15	.11	.06
366	James Jones	.25	.15	.09
367	Garry James	.25	.15	.09
368	Pete Mandley	.25	.15	.09
369	Keith Ferguson	.25	.15	.09
370	Dennis Gibson	.25	.15	.09
371	Packers Team (Johnny Holland)	.25	.15	.09
372	Brent Fullwood	.25	.15	.09
373	Don Majkowski	.20	.15	.08
374	Timothy Harris	.25	.15	.09
375	Keith Woodside RC	.10	.08	.04
376	Mark Murphy	.25	.15	.09
377	Dave Brown	.25	.15	.09
378	Perry Kemp RC	.10	.08	.04
379	Sterling Sharpe RC	1.50	.75	.45
380	Chuck Cecil RC	.25	.20	.10
381	Walter Stanley	.25	.15	.09

		NM/M	NM	E
382	Cowboys Team (Steve Pelleur)	.25	.15	.09
383	Michael Irvin **RC** (SR)	1.50	.75	.45
384	Bill Bates	.25	.15	.09
385	Herschel Walker	.15	.11	.06
386	Darryl Clack	.25	.15	.09
387	Danny Noonan	.25	.15	.09
388	Eugene Lockhart	.25	.15	.09
389	Ed "Too Tall" Jones	.25	.15	.09
390	Steve Pelleur	.25	.15	.09
391	Ray Alexander	.25	.15	.09
392	Nate Newton **RC**	.20	.15	.08
393	Garry Cobb	.25	.15	.09
394	**Checklist 1-132**	.25	.15	.09
395	**Checklist 133-264**	.25	.15	.09
396	**Checklist 265-396**	.25	.15	.09

1989 Topps 1000 Yard Club

These standard-size cards, printed on heavy white cardboard stock and featuring a full-color action shot of each NFL player who gained more tha 1,000 yards rushing or receiving during the 1988 season, were included in wax packs of 1989 Topps football cards. Fronts feature a yellow-and-blue ribbon from the upper right corner, across the top and leading to a "1000 Yard Club" medal at lower left. The photo and medal are bordered in red, with the player's name in white and his position in black also in the border. Card backs are in orange, with an ornate "1000 Yard Club" medal and ribbon reaching from the card number at upper left to the bottom center of the card. Statistics mark the game-by-game progress of the runner-receiver's season.

		NM/M	NM	E
	Complete Set (24):	4.00	3.00	1.50
	Common Player:	.10	.08	.04
1	Eric Dickerson	.60	.45	.25
2	Herschel Walker	.60	.45	.25
3	Roger Craig	.40	.30	.15
4	Henry Ellard	.10	.08	.04
5	Jerry Rice	.60	.45	.25
6	Eddie Brown	.10	.08	.04
7	Anthony Carter	.10	.08	.04
8	Greg Bell	.10	.08	.04
9	John Stephens	.10	.08	.04
10	Ricky Sanders	.10	.08	.04
11	Drew Hill	.10	.08	.04
12	Mark Clayton	.10	.08	.04
13	Gary Anderson	.10	.08	.04
14	Neal Anderson	.20	.15	.08
15	Roy Green	.10	.08	.04
16	Eric Martin	.10	.08	.04
17	Joe Morris	.10	.08	.04
18	Al Toon	.10	.08	.04
19	Ickey Woods	.20	.15	.08
20	Bruce Hill	.10	.08	.04
21	Lionel Manuel	.10	.08	.04
22	Curt Warner	.10	.08	.04
23	John Settle	.10	.08	.04
24	Mike Rozier	.10	.08	.04

1989 Topps American/United Kingdom

This boxed set of 33 cards was distributed in the United Kingdom using a design similar to Topps' regular 1989 set. However, the card stock for the back is not grey, like it is for the regular cards; these ones have white backs. The set's checklist is included on the box; card numbers do not match those in the regular set.

		NM/M	NM	E
	Complete Set (33):	35.00	26.00	14.00
	Common Player:	1.00	.70	.40
1	Anthony Carter	1.00	.70	.40
2	Jim Kelly	2.50	2.00	1.00
3	Bernie Kosar	1.50	1.25	.60
4	John Elway	4.00	3.00	1.50
5	Andre Tippett	1.00	.70	.40
6	Henry Ellard	1.50	1.25	.60
7	Eddie Brown	1.00	.70	.40
8	Gary Anderson	1.00	.70	.40
9	Eric Martin	1.00	.70	.40
10	Ickey Woods	1.00	.70	.40
11	Mike Singletary	1.00	.70	.40
12	Phil Simms	1.50	1.25	.60
13	Brian Bosworth	1.00	.70	.40
14	Mark Clayton	1.25	.90	.50
15	Eric Dickerson	1.50	1.25	.60
16	John Stephens	1.00	.70	.40
17	Neal Anderson	1.00	.70	.40
18	Al Toon	1.00	.70	.40
19	Lionel Manuel	.75	.60	.30
20	Joe Montana	7.00	5.25	2.75
21	Reggie White	2.00	1.50	.80
22	Randall Cunningham	1.75	1.25	.70
23	Lawrence Taylor	1.50	1.25	.60
24	Jim Everett	1.25	.90	.50
25	Neil Lomax	1.00	.70	.40

26	Herschel Walker	1.25	.90	.50
27	Roger Craig	1.25	.90	.50
28	Greg Bell	1.00	.70	.40
29	Ricky Sanders	1.00	.70	.40
30	Joe Morris	1.00	.70	.40
31	Curt Warner	1.00	.70	.40
32	Boomer Esiason	1.50	1.25	.60
33	Dan Marino	7.00	5.25	2.75

1989 Topps Box Bottoms

The 16-card, standard-size set featured the weekly offensive and defensive award winners for the 1988 season. The cards were included four to the bottom of each box of 1989 football. Two players (offensive and defensive) are on each card.

		NM/M	NM	E
	Complete Set (16):	5.00	3.75	2.00
	Common Player:	.25	.20	.10
A	Neal Anderson, Terry Hoage	.25	.20	.10
B	Boomer Esiason, Jacob Green	.50	.40	.20
C	Wesley Walker, Gary Jeter	.25	.20	.10
D	Jim Everett, Danny Noonan	.25	.20	.10
E	Neil Lomax, Dexter Manley	.25	.20	.10
F	Kelvin Bryant, Kevin Greene	.25	.20	.10
G	Roger Craig, Tim Harris	.50	.40	.20
H	Dan Marino, Carl Banks	2.00	1.50	.80
I	Drew Hill, Robin Cole	.25	.20	.10
J	Neil Lomax, Lawrence Taylor	.50	.40	.20
K	Roy Green, Tim Krumrie	.25	.20	.10
L	Bobby Hebert, Aundray Bruce	.25	.20	.10
M	Ickey Woods, Lawrence Taylor	.50	.40	.20
N	Louis Lipps, Greg Townsend	.25	.20	.10
O	Curt Warner, Tim Harris	.25	.20	.10
P	Dave Krieg, Kevin Greene	.35	.25	.14

1990 Topps Traded

Like its predecessor, the Topps football update again pictured rookies and traded players on white cardboard stock. The issue was sold as a boxed set and was available only through hobby shops.

		NM/M	NM	E
	Complete Set (132):	12.00	9.00	4.75
	Common Player:	.03	.02	.01
1	Gerald McNeil	.03	.02	.01
2	Andre Rison	.15	.11	.06
3	Steve Walsh	.10	.08	.04
4	Lorenzo White	.10	.08	.04
5	Max Montoya	.05	.04	.02
6	William Roberts	.03	.02	.01
7	Alonzo Highsmith	.10	.08	.04
8	Chris Hinton	.10	.08	.04
9	Stanley Morgan	.10	.08	.04
10	Mickey Shuler	.03	.02	.01
11	Bobby Humphrey	.03	.02	.01
12	Gary Anderson	.03	.02	.01
13	Mike Tomczak	.03	.02	.01
14	Anthony Pleasant	.03	.02	.01
15	Walter Stanley	.03	.02	.01
16	Greg Bell	.10	.08	.04
17	Tony Martin **RC**	2.00	1.50	.80
18	Terry Kinard	.03	.02	.01
19	Cris Carter	.50	.40	.20
20	James Wilder	.03	.02	.01
21	Jerry Kauric	.03	.02	.01
22	Irving Fryer	.03	.02	.01
23	Ken Harvey	.03	.02	.01
24	James Williams	.15	.11	.06
25	Ron Cox	.03	.02	.01
26	Andre Ware	.50	.40	.20
27	Emmitt Smith **RC**	10.00	7.50	4.00
28	Junior Seau	.50	.40	.20

29	Mark Carrier	.50	.40	.20
30	Rodney Hampton	.50	.40	.20
31	Rob Moore **RC**	1.25	.90	.50
32	Bern Brostek	.10	.08	.04
33	Dexter Carter	.40	.30	.15
34	Blair Thomas	.65	.50	.25
35	Harold Green	.30	.25	.12
36	Darrell Thompson	.20	.15	.08
37	Eric Green	.25	.20	.10
38	Renaldo Turnbull	.20	.15	.08
39	Leroy Hoard **RC**	.50	.40	.20
40	Anthony Thompson	.25	.20	.10
41	Jeff George	.50	.40	.20
42	Alexander Wright	.15	.11	.06
43	Richmond Webb	.25	.20	.10
44	Cortez Kennedy	.75	.60	.30
45	Ray Agnew	.10	.08	.04
46	Percy Snow	.15	.11	.06
47	Chris Singleton	.10	.08	.04
48	James Francis	.20	.15	.08
49	Tony Bennett	.10	.08	.04
50	Reggie Cobb **RC**	.20	.15	.08
51	Barry Foster	.10	.08	.04
52	Ben Smith	.10	.08	.04
53	Anthony Smith	.10	.08	.04
54	Steve Christie	.10	.08	.04
55	Johnny Bailey	.20	.15	.08
56	Alan Grant	.03	.02	.01
57	Eric Floyd	.03	.02	.01
58	Robert Blackmon	.03	.02	.01
59	Brent Williams	.03	.02	.01
60	Raymond Clayborn	.03	.02	.01
61	Dave Duerson	.07	.05	.03
62	Derrick Fenner	.50	.40	.20
63	Ken Willis	.03	.02	.01
64	Brad Baxter **RC**	.25	.20	.10
65	Tony Paige	.03	.02	.01
66	Jay Schroeder	.15	.11	.06
67	Jim Breech	.03	.02	.01
68	Barry Word	.50	.40	.20
69	Anthony Dilweg	.10	.08	.04
70	Rich Gannon **RC**	2.00	1.50	.80
71	Stan Humphries **RC**	.50	.40	.20
72	Jay Novacek	.50	.40	.20
73	Tommy Kane	.03	.02	.01
74	Everson Walls	.03	.02	.01
75	Mike Rozier	.10	.08	.04
76	Robb Thomas	.03	.02	.01
77	Terance Mathis **RC**	2.00	1.50	.80
78	Leroy Irvin	.03	.02	.01
79	Jeff Donaldson	.03	.02	.01
80	Ethan Horton	.03	.02	.01
81	J.B. Brown	.03	.02	.01
82	Joe Kelly	.03	.02	.01
83	John Carney	.03	.02	.01
84	Dan Stryzinski	.03	.02	.01
85	John Kidd	.03	.02	.01
86	Al Smith	.03	.02	.01
87	Travis McNeal	.03	.02	.01
88	Reyna Thompson	.10	.08	.04
89	Rick Donnelly	.03	.02	.01
90	Marv Cook	.03	.02	.01
91	Mike Farr	.03	.02	.01
92	Daniel Stubbs	.03	.02	.01
93	Jeff Campbell	.20	.15	.08
94	Tim McKyer	.10	.08	.04
95	Ian Beckles	.03	.02	.01
96	Lemuel Stinson	.03	.02	.01
97	Frank Cornish	.03	.02	.01
98	Riki Ellison	.03	.02	.01
99	Jamie Mueller	.03	.02	.01
100	Brian Hansen	.03	.02	.01
101	Warren Powers	.03	.02	.01
102	Howard Cross	.03	.02	.01
103	Tim Grunhard	.03	.02	.01
104	Johnny Johnson **RC**	.20	.15	.08
105	Calvin Williams **RC**	.65	.50	.25
106	Keith McCants	.15	.11	.06
107	Lamar Lathon	.10	.08	.04
108	Steve Broussard	.35	.25	.14
109	Glenn Parker	.03	.02	.01
110	Alton Montgomery	.07	.05	.03
111	Jim McMahon	.07	.05	.03
112	Aaron Wallace	.25	.20	.10
113	Keith Sims	.07	.05	.03
114	Ervin Randle	.03	.02	.01
115	Walter Wilson	.03	.02	.01
116	Terry Wooden	.07	.05	.03
117	Bernard Cook	.03	.02	.01
118	Tony Stargell	.03	.02	.01
119	Jimmie Jones	.07	.05	.03
120	Andre Collins	.03	.02	.01
121	Ricky Proehl **RC**	.40	.30	.15
122	Darion Conner	.07	.05	.03
123	Jeff Rutledge	.03	.02	.01
124	Heath Sherman	.25	.20	.10
125	Tommie Agee	.03	.02	.01
126	Tory Epps	.03	.02	.01

127	Tom Hodson	.25	.20	.10
128	Jessie Hester	.03	.02	.01
129	Alfred Oglesby	.03	.02	.01
130	Chris Chandler	.03	.02	.01
131	Fred Barnett **RC**	.50	.40	.20
132	**Checklist**	.03	.02	.01

1990 Topps

The 1990 Topps set, the largest since 1982, returned to 528 cards. A new addition to the Topps sets included 25 1990 draft pick cards; other subsets included four 1989 record breakers, four league leader cards and a Super Bowl card. Each wax pack included one of 31 glossy 1,000 Yard Club insert cards featuring players who gained 1,000 yards or more during the 1989 NFL season. Because NFL Properties denied Topps a license, cards have no free-standing team logos. A 196-card Bowman football set, also scheduled to be issued in 1990, was also scratched. Variations include cards #28, 193, 229 and 501-528 - all the Topps horizontal issues - which originally appeared without the small black vertical "hashmarks" running below the red border and underneath the Topps logo. These were corrected very early; no premium value has been put on them, but they should fetch 35-50 cents over the regular card price. Also, Topps issued "corrected" cards, presumably both in wax and in factory sets, that do not have the "unauthorized" tagline. These are thought to   be scarcer than the unauthorized cards. (Key: RB - Record Breaker).

		NM/M	NM	E
Complete Set (528):		10.00	7.50	4.00
Common Player:		.25	.15	.09
Wax Pack (15+1):		.50		
Wax Box (36):		8.50		

1	Joe Montana (RB)	.50	.40	.20
2	Flipper Anderson (RB)	.25	.15	.09
3	Troy Aikman (RB)	.50	.40	.20
4	Kevin Butler (RB)	.25	.15	.09
5	**Super Bowl XXIV**	.25	.15	.09
6	Dexter Carter **RC**	.20	.15	.08
7	Matt Millen	.25	.15	.09
8	Jerry Rice	.75	.60	.30
9	Ronnie Lott	.10	.08	.04
10	John Taylor	.20	.15	.08
11	Guy McIntryre	.25	.15	.09
12	Roger Craig	.25	.15	.09
13	Joe Montana	1.00	.50	.30
14	Brent Jones **RC**	.75	.60	.30
15	Tom Rathman	.25	.15	.09
16	Harris Barton	.25	.15	.09
17	Charles Haley	.25	.15	.09
18	Pierce Holt **RC**	.20	.1 5	.08
19	Michael Carter	.25	.15	.09
20	Chet Brooks	.25	.15	.09
21	Eric Wright	.25	.15	.09
22	Mike Cofer	.25	.15	.09
23	Jim Fahnhorst	.25	.15	.09
24	Keena Turner	.25	.15	.09
25	Don Griffin	.25	.15	.09
26	Kevin Fagan **RC**	.08	.06	.03
27	Bubba Paris	.25	.15	.09
28	**Rushing Leaders**	.15	.11	.06
29	Steve Atwater	.25	.15	.09
30	Tyrone Braxton	.25	.15	.09
31	Ron Holmes	.25	.15	.09
32	Bobby Humphrey	.25	.15	.09
33	Greg Kragen	.25	.15	.09
34	David Treadwell	.25	.15	.09
35	Karl Mecklenburg	.25	.15	.09
36	Dennis Smith	.25	.15	.09
37	John Elway	.40	.30	.15
38	Vance Johnson	.25	.15	.09
39	Simon Fletcher	.25	.15	.09
40	Jim Juriga	.25	.15	.09
41	Mark Jackson	.25	.15	.09
42	Melvin Bratton	.25	.15	.09
43	Wymon Henderson **RC**	.10	.08	.04
44	Ken Ball	.25	.15	.09
45	Sammy Winder	.25	.15	.09
46	Alphonso Carreker	.25	.15	.09

47	Orson Mobley	.25	.15	.09
48	Rodney Hampton **RC**	.25	.15	.09
49	Dave Meggett	.12	.09	.05
50	Myron Guyton	.25	.15	.09
51	Phil Simms	.10	.08	.04
52	Lawrence Taylor	.10	.08	.04
53	Carl Banks	.25	.15	.09
54	Pepper Johnson	.25	.15	.09
55	Leonard Marshall	.25	.15	.09
56	Mark Collins	.25	.15	.09
57	Erik Howard	.25	.15	.09
58	Eric Dorsey **RC**	.10	.08	.04
59	Ottis Anderson	.25	.15	.09
60	Mark Bavaro	.25	.15	.09
61	Odessa Turner **RC**	.12	.09	.05
62	Gary Reasons	.25	.15	.09
63	Maurice Carthon	.25	.15	.09
64	Lionel Manuel	.25	.15	.09
65	Sean Landeta	.25	.15	.09
66	Perry Williams	.25	.15	.09
67	Pat Terrell **RC**	.12	.09	.05
68	Flipper Anderson	.15	.11	.06
69	Jackie Slater	.25	.15	.09
70	Tom Newberry	.25	.15	.09
71	Jerry Gray	.25	.15	.09
72	Henry Ellard	.25	.15	.09
73	Doug Smith	.25	.15	.09
74	Kevin Greene	.25	.15	.09
75	Jim Everett	.25	.15	.09
76	Mike Lansford	.25	.15	.09
77	Greg Bell	.25	.15	.09
78	Pete Holohan	.25	.15	.09
79	Robert Delpino	.25	.15	.09
80	Mike Wilcher	.25	.15	.09
81	Mike Piel	.25	.15	.09
82	Mel Owens	.25	.15	.09
83	Michael Stewart **RC**	.10	.08	.04
84	Ben Smith **RC**	.10	.08	.04
85	Keith Jackson	.25	.20	.10
86	Reggie White	.15	.11	.06
87	Eric Allen	.25	.15	.09
88	Jerome Brown	.25	.15	.09
89	Robert Drummond	.25	.15	.09
90	Anthony Toney	.25	.15	.09
91	Keith Byars	.25	.15	.09
92	Cris Carter	.30	.25	.12
93	Randall Cunningham	.20	.15	.08
94	Ron Johnson	.25	.15	.09
95	Mike Quick	.25	.15	.09
96	Clyde Simmons	.25	.15	.09
97	Mike Pitts	.25	.15	.09
98	Izel Jenkins	.25	.15	.09
99	Seth Joyner	.25	.15	.09
100	Mike Schad	.25	.15	.09
101	Wes Hopkins	.25	.15	.09
102	Kirk Lowdermilk	.25	.15	.09
103	Rick Fenney	.25	.15	.09
104	Randall McDaniel	.25	.15	.09
105	Herschel Walker	.25	.15	.09
106	Al Noga	.25	.15	.09
107	Gary Zimmerman	.25	.15	.09
108	Chris Doleman	.25	.15	.09
109	Keith Millard	.25	.15	.09
110	Carl Lee	.25	.15	.09
111	Joey Browner	.25	.15	.09
112	Steve Jordan	.25	.15	.09
113	Reggie Rutland **RC**	.10	.08	.04
114	Wade Wilson	.25	.15	.09
115	Anthony Carter	.25	.15	.09
116	Rich Karlis	.25	.15	.09
117	Hassan Jones	.25	.15	.09
118	Henry Thomas	.25	.15	.09
119	Scott Studwell	.25	.15	.09
120	Ralf Mojsiejenko	.25	.15	.09
121	Earnest Byner	.25	.15	.09
122	Gerald Riggs	.25	.15	.09
123	Tracy Rocker	.25	.15	.09
124	A.J. Johnson	.25	.15	.09
125	Charles Mann	.25	.15	.09
126	Art Monk	.25	.15	.09
127	Rickey Sanders	.25	.15	.09
128	Gary Clark	.15	.11	.06
129	Jim Lachey	.25	.15	.09
130	Martin Mayhew **RC**	.15	.11	.06
131	Ravin Caldwell	.25	.15	.09
132	Don Warren	.25	.15	.09
133	Mark Rypien	.25	.20	.10
134	Ed Simmons **RC**	.10	.08	.04
135	Darryl Grant	.25	.15	.09
136	Darryl Green	.25	.15	.09
137	Chip Lommiller	.25	.15	.09
138	Tony Bennett **RC**	.35	.25	.14
139	Tony Mandarich	.25	.15	.09
140	Sterling Sharpe	.75	.60	.30
141	Tim Harris	.25	.15	.09
142	Don Majkowski	.25	.15	.09
143	Rich Moran	.25	.15	.09

144	Jeff Query	.25	.15	.09
145	Brent Fullwood	.25	.15	.09
146	Chris Jacke	.25	.15	.09
147	Keith Woodside	.25	.15	.09
148	Perry Kemp	.25	.15	.09
149	Herman Fontenot	.25	.15	.09
150	Dave Brown	.25	.15	.09
151	Brian Noble	.25	.15	.09
152	Johnny Holland	.25	.15	.09
153	Mark Murphy	.25	.15	.09
154	Bob Nelson	.25	.15	.09
155	Darrell Thompson **RC**	.25	.20	.10
156	Lawyer Tillman	.25	.15	.09
157	Eric Metcalf	.12	.09	.05
158	Webster Slaughter	.25	.15	.09
159	Frank Minnifield	.25	.15	.09
160	Brian Brennan	.25	.15	.09
161	Thane Gash	.25	.15	.09
162	Robert Banks	.25	.15	.09
163	Bernie Kosar	.25	.15	.09
164	David Grayson	.25	.15	.09
165	Kevin Mack	.25	.15	.09
166	Mike Johnson	.25	.15	.09
167	Tim Manoa	.25	.15	.09
168	Ozzie Newsome	.10	.08	.04
169	Felix Wright	.25	.15	.09
170	Al Baker	.25	.15	.09
171	Reggie Langhorne	.25	.15	.09
172	Clay Matthews	.25	.15	.09
173	Andrew Stewart	.25	.15	.09
174	Barry Foster **RC**	.10	.08	.04
175	Tim Worley	.25	.15	.09
176	Tim Johnson	.25	.15	.09
177	Carnell Lake	.25	.15	.09
178	Greg Lloyd	.25	.15	.09
179	Rod Woodson	.15	.11	.06
180	Tunch Ilkin	.25	.15	.09
181	Dermontti Dawson	.25	.15	.09
182	Gary Anderson	.25	.15	.09
183	Bubby Brister	.10	.08	.04
184	Louis Lipps	.25	.15	.09
185	Merril Hoge	.25	.15	.09
186	Mike Mularkey	.25	.15	.09
187	Derek Hill	.25	.15	.09
188	Rodney Carter	.25	.15	.09
189	Dwayne Carter	.25	.15	.09
190	Keith Willis	.25	.15	.09
191	Jerry Olsavsky	.25	.15	.09
192	Mark Stock	.25	.15	.09
193	**Sacks Leaders**	.25	.15	.09
194	Leonard Smith	.25	.15	.09
195	Darryl Talley	.25	.15	.09
196	Mark Kelso	.25	.15	.09
197	Kent Hull	.25	.15	.09
198	Nate Odomes **RC**	.30	.25	.12
199	Pete Metzelaars	.25	.15	.09
200	Don Beebe	.15	.11	.06
201	Ray Bentley	.25	.15	.09
202	Steve Tasker	.10	.08	.04
203	Scott Norwood	.25	.15	.09
204	Andre Reed	.20	.15	.08
205	Bruce Smith	.25	.15	.09
206	Thurman Thomas	.50	.40	.20
207	Jim Kelly	.35	.25	.14
208	Cornelius Bennett	.25	.15	.09
209	Shane Conlan	.25	.15	.09
210	Larry Kinnebrew	.25	.15	.09
211	Jeff Alm **RC**	.10	.08	.04
212	Robert Lyles	.25	.15	.09
213	Bubba McDowell	.25	.15	.09
214	Mike Munchak	.25	.15	.09
215	Bruce Matthews	.25	.15	.09
216	Warren Moon	.25	.20	.10
217	Drew Hill	.25	.15	.09
218	Ray Childress	.25	.15	.09
219	Steve Brown	.25	.15	.09
220	Alonzo Highsmith	.25	.15	.09
221	Allen Pinkett	.25	.15	.09
222	Sean Jones	.25	.15	.09
223	Johnny Meads	.25	.15	.09
224	John Grimsley	.25	.15	.09
225	Haywood Jeffires **RC**	.50	.40	.20
226	Curtis Duncan	.25	.15	.09
227	Greg Montgomery **RC**	.10	.08	.04
228	Ernest Givins	.25	.15	.09
229	**Passing Leaders**	.20	.15	.08
230	Robert Massey	.25	.15	.09
231	John Fourcade	.25	.15	.09
232	Dalton Hilliard	.25	.15	.09
233	Vaughan Johnson	.25	.15	.09
234	Hoby Brenner	.25	.15	.09
235	Pat Swilling	.25	.15	.09
236	Kevin Haverdink	.25	.15	.09
237	Bobby Hebert	.15	.11	.06
238	Sam Mills	.25	.15	.09
239	Eric Martin	.25	.15	.09
240	Lonzell Hill	.25	.15	.09

241	Steve Trapilo	.25	.15	.09
242	Rickey Jackson	.25	.15	.09
243	Craig Heyward	.25	.15	.09
244	Rueben Mayes	.25	.15	.09
245	Morten Anderson	.25	.15	.09
246	Percy Snow **RC**	.10	.08	.04
247	Pete Mandley	.25	.15	.09
248	Derrick Thomas	.30	.25	.12
249	Dan Saleaumua	.25	.15	.09
250	Todd McNair **RC**	.15	.11	.06
251	Leonard Griffin	.25	.15	.09
252	Jonathan Hayes	.25	.15	.09
253	Christian Okoye	.25	.15	.09
254	Albert Lewis	.25	.15	.09
255	Nick Lowery	.25	.15	.09
256	Kevin Ross	.25	.15	.09
257	Steve DeBerg	.25	.15	.09
258	Stephone Paige	.25	.15	.09
259	James Saxon **RC**	.10	.08	.04
260	Herman Heard	.25	.15	.09
261	Deron Cherry	.25	.15	.09
262	Dino Hackett	.25	.15	.09
263	Neil Smith	.20	.15	.08
264	Steve Pelluer	.25	.15	.09
265	Eric Thomas	.25	.15	.09
266	Eric Ball	.25	.15	.09
267	Leon White	.25	.15	.09
268	Tim Krumrie	.25	.15	.09
269	Jason Buck	.25	.15	.09
270	Boomer Esiason	.20	.15	.08
271	Carl Zander	.25	.15	.09
272	Eddie Brown	.25	.15	.09
273	David Fulcher	.25	.15	.09
274	Tim McGee	.25	.15	.09
275	James Brooks	.25	.15	.09
276	Rickey Dixon **RC**	.10	.08	.04
277	Ickey Woods	.25	.15	.09
278	Anthony Munoz	.25	.15	.09
279	Rodney Holman	.25	.15	.09
280	Mike Alexander	.25	.15	.09
281	Mervyn Fernandez	.25	.15	.09
282	Steve Wisniewski	.25	.15	.09
283	Steve Smith	.25	.15	.09
284	Howie Long	.25	.15	.09
285	Bo Jackson	.45	.35	.20
286	Mike Dyal	.25	.15	.09
287	Thomas Benson	.25	.15	.09
288	Willie Gault	.25	.15	.09
289	Marcus Allen	.25	.15	.09
290	Greg Townsend	.25	.15	.09
291	Steve Beurlein	.30	.25	.12
292	Scott Davis	.25	.15	.09
293	Eddie Anderson **RC**	.10	.08	.04
294	Terry McDaniel	.25	.15	.09
295	Tim Brown	.45	.35	.20
296	Bob Golic	.25	.15	.09
297	Jeff Jaeger **RC**	.12	.09	.05
298	Jeff George **RC**	.30	.15	.09
299	Chip Banks	.25	.15	.09
300	Andre Rison	.25	.20	.10
301	Rohn Stark	.25	.15	.09
302	Keith Taylor	.25	.15	.09
303	Jack Trudeau	.25	.15	.09
304	Chris Hinton	.25	.15	.09
305	Ray Donaldson	.25	.15	.09
306	Jeff Herrod **RC**	.10	.08	.04
307	Clarence Verdin	.25	.15	.09
308	Jon Hand	.25	.15	.09
309	Bill Brooks	.25	.15	.09
310	Albert Bentley	.25	.15	.09
311	Mike Prior	.25	.15	.09
312	Pat Beach	.25	.15	.09
313	Eugene Daniel	.25	.15	.09
314	Duane Bickett	.25	.15	.09
315	Dean Biasucci	.25	.15	.09
316	Richmond Webb **RC**	.25	.20	.10
317	Jeff Cross	.25	.15	.09
318	Louis Oliver	.25	.15	.09
319	Sammie Smith	.25	.15	.09
320	Pete Stovanovich	.25	.15	.09
321	John Offerdahl	.25	.15	.09
322	Ferrell Edmunds	.25	.15	.09
323	Dan Marino	.75	.60	.30
324	Andre Brown	.25	.15	.09
325	Reggie Roby	.25	.15	.09
326	Jarvis Williams	.25	.15	.09
327	Roy Foster	.25	.15	.09
328	Mark Clayton	.25	.15	.09
329	Brian Sochia	.25	.15	.09
330	Mark Duper	.25	.15	.09
331	T.J. Turner	.25	.15	.09
332	Jeff Uhlenhake	.25	.15	.09
333	Jim Jensen	.25	.15	.09
334	Cortez Kennedy **RC**	.25	.20	.10
335	Andy Heck	.25	.15	.09
336	Rufus Porter	.25	.15	.09
337	Brian Blades	.15	.11	.06
338	Dave Krieg	.25	.15	.09
339	John L. Williams	.25	.15	.09
340	David Wyman	.25	.15	.09
341	Paul Skansi **RC**	.10	.08	.04
342	Eugene Robinson	.25	.15	.09
343	Joe Nash	.25	.15	.09
344	Jacob Green	.25	.15	.09
345	Jeff Bryant	.25	.15	.09
346	Ruben Rodriguez	.25	.15	.09
347	Norm Johnson	.25	.15	.09
348	Darren Comeaux	.25	.15	.09
349	Andre Ware **RC**	.20	.15	.08
350	Richard Johnson	.25	.15	.09
351	Rodney Peete	.10	.08	.04
352	Barry Sanders	1.25	.75	.45
353	Chris Spielman	.25	.15	.09
354	Eddie Murray	.25	.15	.09
355	Jerry Ball	.25	.15	.09
356	Mel Gray	.25	.15	.09
357	Eric Williams **RC**	.10	.08	.04
358	Robert Clark **RC**	.10	.08	.04
359	Jason Phillips	.25	.15	.09
360	Terry Taylor **RC**	.08	.06	.03
361	Bennie Blades	.25	.15	.09
362	Michael Cofer	.25	.15	.09
363	Jim Arnold	.25	.15	.09
364	Marc Spindler **RC**	.10	.08	.04
365	Jim Covert	.25	.15	.09
366	Jim Harbaugh	.20	.15	.08
367	Neal Anderson	.15	.11	.06
368	Mike Singletary	.25	.15	.09
369	John Roper	.25	.15	.09
370	Steve McMichael	.25	.15	.09
371	Dennis Gentry	.25	.15	.09
372	Brad Muster	.25	.15	.09
373	Ron Morris	.25	.15	.09
374	James Thornton	.25	.15	.09
375	Kevin Butler	.25	.15	.09
376	Richard Dent	.25	.15	.09
377	Dan Hampton	.25	.15	.09
378	Jay Hilgenberg	.25	.15	.09
379	Donnell Woolford	.25	.15	.09
380	Trace Armstrong	.25	.15	.09
381	Junior Seau **RC**	1.00	.50	.30
382	Rod Bernstine	.15	.11	.06
383	Marion Butts	.15	.11	.06
384	Burt Grossman	.25	.15	.09
385	Darrin Nelson	.25	.15	.09
386	Leslie O'Neal	.25	.15	.09
387	Billy Joe Tolliver	.25	.15	.09
388	Courtney Hall	.25	.15	.09
389	Lee Williams	.25	.15	.09
390	Anthony Miller	.30	.25	.12
391	Gill Byrd	.25	.15	.09
392	Wayne Walker	.25	.15	.09
393	Billy Ray Smith	.25	.15	.09
394	Vencie Glenn	.25	.15	.09
395	Tim Spencer	.25	.15	.09
396	Gary Plummer	.25	.15	.09
397	Arthur Cox	.25	.15	.09
398	Jamie Holland	.25	.15	.09
399	Keith McCants **RC**	.10	.08	.04
400	Kevin Murphy	.25	.15	.09
401	Danny Peebles	.25	.15	.09
402	Mark Robinson	.25	.15	.09
403	Broderick Thomas	.25	.15	.09
404	Ron Hall	.25	.15	.09
405	Mark Carrier	.25	.15	.09
406	Paul Gruber	.25	.15	.09
407	Vinny Testaverde	.10	.08	.04
408	Bruce Hill	.25	.15	.09
409	Lars Tate	.25	.15	.09
410	Harry Hamilton	.25	.15	.09
411	Ricky Reynolds	.25	.15	.09
412	Donald Igwebuike	.25	.15	.09
413	Reuben Davis	.25	.15	.09
414	William Howard	.25	.15	.09
415	Winston Moss **RC**	.10	.08	.04
416	Chris Singleton **RC**	.10	.08	.04
417	Hart Lee Dykes	.25	.15	.09
418	Steve Grogan	.25	.15	.09
419	Bruce Armstrong	.25	.15	.09
420	Robert Perryman	.25	.15	.09
421	Andre Tippett	.25	.15	.09
422	Sammy Martin	.25	.15	.09
423	Stanley Morgan	.25	.15	.09
424	Cedric Jones	.25	.15	.09
425	Sean Farrell	.25	.15	.09
426	Marc Wilson	.25	.15	.09
427	John Stephens	.25	.15	.09
428	Eric Sievers	.25	.15	.09
429	Maurice Hurst **RC**	.10	.08	.04
430	Johnny Rembert	.25	.15	.09
431	**Receiving Leaders**	.25	.20	.10
432	Eric Hill	.25	.15	.09
433	Gary Hogeboom	.25	.15	.09
434	Timm Rosenbach	.25	.15	.09
435	Tim McDonald	.25	.15	.09
436	Rich Camarillo	.25	.15	.09
437	Luis Sharpe	.25	.15	.09
438	J.T. Smith	.25	.15	.09
439	Roy Green	.25	.15	.09
440	Ernie Jones **RC**	.15	.11	.06
441	Robert Awalt	.25	.15	.09
442	Vai Sikahema	.25	.15	.09
443	Joe Wolf	.25	.15	.09
444	Stump Mitchell	.25	.15	.09
445	David Galloway	.25	.15	.09
446	Ron Wolfley	.25	.15	.09
447	Freddie Joe Nunn	.25	.15	.09
448	Blair Thomas **RC**	.15	.11	.06
449	Jeff Lageman	.25	.15	.09
450	Tony Eason	.25	.15	.09
451	Eric McMillan	.25	.15	.09
452	Jim Sweeney	.25	.15	.09
453	Ken O'Brien	.25	.15	.09
454	Johnny Hector	.25	.15	.09
455	JoJo Townsell	.25	.15	.09
456	Roger Vick	.25	.15	.09
457	Dennis Hasty	.25	.15	.09
458	Dennis Byrd **RC**	.25	.20	.10
459	Ron Stallworth	.25	.15	.09
460	Mickey Shuler	.25	.15	.09
461	Bobby Humphery	.25	.15	.09
462	Kyle Clifton	.25	.15	.09
463	Al Toon	.25	.15	.09
464	Freeman McNeil	.25	.15	.09
465	Pat Leahy	.25	.15	.09
466	Scott Case	.25	.15	.09
467	Shawn Collins	.25	.15	.09
468	Floyd Dixon	.25	.15	.09
469	Deion Sanders	.35	.25	.14
470	Tony Casillas	.25	.15	.09
471	Michael Haynes **RC**	.50	.40	.20
472	Chris Miller	.25	.20	.10
473	John Settle	.25	.15	.09
474	Aundray Bruce	.25	.15	.09
475	Gene Lang	.25	.15	.09
476	Tim Gordon **RC**	.10	.08	.04
477	Scott Fulhage	.25	.15	.09
478	Bill Fralic	.25	.15	.09
479	Jessie Tuggle **RC**	.25	.20	.10
480	Marcus Cotton	.25	.15	.09
481	Steve Walsh	.25	.15	.09
482	Troy Aikman	.75	.45	.30
483	Ray Horton	.25	.15	.09
484	Tony Tolbert **RC**	.20	.15	.08
485	Steve Folsom	.25	.15	.09
486	Ken Norton Jr. **RC**	.50	.40	.20
487	Kelvin Martin **RC**	.25	.20	.10
488	Jack Del Rio	.25	.15	.09
489	Daryl Johnston **RC**	50	.25	.15
490	Bill Bates	.25	.15	.09
491	Jim Jeffcoat	.25	.15	.09
492	Vince Albritton	.25	.15	.09
493	Eugene Lockhart	.25	.15	.09
494	Mike Saxon	.25	.15	.09
495	James Dixon	.25	.15	.09
496	Willie Broughton	.25	.15	.09
497	**Checklist 1-132**	.25	.15	.09
498	**Checklist 133-264**	.25	.15	.09
499	**Checklist 265-396**	.25	.15	.09
500	**Checklist 397-528**	.25	.15	.09
501	**Bears Team**	.25	.15	.09
502	**Bengals Team**	.25	.15	.09
503	**Bills Team**	.25	.15	.09
504	**Broncos Team**	.25	.15	.09
505	**Browns Team**	.25	.15	.09
506	**Buccaneers Team**	.25	.15	.09
507	**Cardinals Team**	.25	.15	.09
508	**Chargers Team**	.25	.15	.09
509	**Chiefs Team**	.25	.15	.09
510	**Colts Team**	.25	.15	.09
511	**Cowboys Team**	.65	.50	.25
512	**Dolphins Team**	.25	.15	.09
513	**Eagles Team**	.25	.15	.09
514	**Falcons Team**	.25	.15	.09
515	**49ers Team**	.20	.15	.08
516	**Giants Team**	.25	.15	.09
517	**Jets Team**	.25	.15	.09
518	**Lions Team**	.25	.15	.09
519	**Oilers Team**	.10	.08	.04
520	**Packers Team**	.25	.15	.09
521	**Patriots Team**	.25	.15	.09
522	**Raiders Team**	.12	.09	.05
523	**Rams Team**	.25	.15	.09
524	**Redskins Team**	.25	.15	.09
525	**Saints Team**	.25	.15	.09
526	**Seahawks Team**	.25	.15	.09
527	**Steelers Team**	.25	.15	.09
528	**Vikings Team**	.25	.15	.09

1990 Topps 1000 Yard Club

ART MONK
WIDE RECEIVER

Players who gained more than 1,000 yards rushing or receiving during the 1989 NFL season are honored in this 30-card insert set. Cards were randomly included in 1990 Topps packs, one per pack. The front has a color picture, his and the set's name, plus the Topps' logo. Each back recaps each game from the 1989 season to show how the player reached the 1,000-yard milestone. The cards, numbered 1-30, are numbered according by yardage totals, with the leading yard gainer being #1, and so forth. The design for the card front is similar to the regular 1990 Topps football card design.

		NM/M	NM	E
Complete Set (30):		3.50	2.75	1.50
Common Player:		.05	.04	.02
1	Jerry Rice	.50	.40	.20
2	Christian Okoye	.15	.11	.06
3	Barry Sanders	1.00	.70	.40
4	Sterling Sharpe	.40	.30	.15
5	Mark Carrier	.15	.11	.06
6	Henry Ellard	.05	.04	.02
7	Andre Reed	.25	.20	.10
8	Neal Anderson	.25	.20	.10
9	Dalton Hilliard	.05	.04	.02
10	Anthony Miller	.20	.15	.08
11	Thurman Thomas	.25	.20	.10
12	James Brooks	.15	.11	.06
13	Webster Slaughter	.05	.04	.02
14	Gary Clark	.05	.04	.02
15	Tim McGee	.05	.04	.02
16	Art Monk	.15	.11	.06
17	Bobby Humphrey	.25	.20	.10
18	Flipper Anderson	.10	.08	.04
19	Ricky Sanders	.10	.08	.04
20	Greg Bell	.05	.04	.02
21	Vance Johnson	.05	.04	.02
22	Richard Johnson	.05	.04	.02
23	Eric Martin	.05	.04	.02
24	John Taylor	.25	.20	.10
25	Mervyn Fernandez	.10	.08	.04
26	Anthony Carter	.10	.08	.04
27	Brian Blades	.10	.08	.04
28	Roger Craig	.20	.15	.08
29	Ottis Anderson	.20	.15	.08
30	Mark Clayton	.07	.05	.03

1990 Topps Box Bottoms

These standard-size cards were included on the bottoms of 1990 Topps wax pack boxes. Each card has two photos on it; an offensive and defensive NFL Player of the Week from the 1989 season is featured. The back uses letters instead of card numbers and explains why the player was selected as the league's best performer for the week. The card design is similar to that which was used for Topps' regular 1990 set.

		NM/M	NM	E
Complete Set (16):		6.00	4.50	2.50
Common Player:		.30	.25	.12
A	Jim Kelly, Dave Grayson	.50	.40	.20
B	Henry Ellard, Derrick Thomas	.50	.40	.20
C	Joe Montana, Vince Newsome	1.50	1.25	.60
D	Bubby Brister, Tim Harris	.30	.25	.12
E	Christian Okoye, Keith Millard	.30	.25	.12
F	Warren Moon, Jerome Brown	.50	.40	.20
G	John Elway, Mike Merriweather	1.00	.70	.40
H	Webster Slaughter, Pat Swilling	.35	.25	.14
I	Rich Karlis, Lawrence Taylor	.35	.25	.14
J	Dan Marino, Greg Kragen	1.00	.70	.40
K	Boomer Esiason, Brent Williams	.35	.25	.14
L	Flipper Anderson, Pierce Holt	.30	.25	.12
M	Richard Johnson, David Fulcher	.30	.25	.12
N	John Taylor, Mike Prior	.50	.40	.20
O	Mark Rypien, Brett Faryniarz	.35	.25	.14
P	Greg Bell, Chris Doleman	.30	.25	.12

1991 Stadium Club

BRETT FARVE

Topps made its premiere edition debut with its 1991 Stadium Club set of 500 cards. The glossy cards feature full-bleed action photos on the front. The player's name is at the bottom in an aqua stripe that is bordered in gold. The back uses a horizontal format with a football field and stadium for a background. A biography, Sporting News Football Analysis Report and miniature replica of the player's Topps rookie card are also included on the back.

		NM/M	NM	E
Complete Set (500):		100.00	70.00	40.00
Common Player:		.20	.15	.08
Minor Stars:		.40	.30	.15
Pack (12):		3.00		
Wax Box (36):		100.00		
1	Pepper Johnson	.20	.15	.08
2	Emmitt Smith	10.00	7.50	4.00
3	Deion Sanders	3.00	2.25	1.25
4	Andre Collins	.20	.15	.08
5	Eric Metcalf	.30	.25	.12
6	Richard Dent	.30	.25	.12
7	Eric Martin	.20	.15	.08
8	Marcus Allen	.50	.40	.20
9	Gary Anderson	.20	.15	.08
10	Joey Browner	.20	.15	.08
11	Lorenzo White	.20	.15	.08
12	Bruce Smith	.20	.15	.08
13	Mark Boyer	.20	.15	.08
14	Mike Piel	.20	.15	.08
15	Albert Bentley	.20	.15	.08
16	Bennie Blades	.20	.15	.08
17	Jason Staurovsky	.20	.15	.08
18	Anthony Toney	.20	.15	.08
19	Dave Krieg	.20	.15	.08
20	Harvey Williams RC	2.00	1.50	.80
21	Bubba Paris	.20	.15	.08
22	Tim McGee	.20	.15	.08
23	Brian Noble	.20	.15	.08
24	Vinny Testaverde	.30	.25	.12
25	Doug Widell	.20	.15	.08
26	John Jackson	.20	.15	.08
27	Marion Butts	.20	.15	.08
28	Deron Cherry	.20	.15	.08
29	Don Warren	.20	.15	.08
30	Rod Woodson	.75	.60	.30
31	Mike Baab	.20	.15	.08
32	Greg Jackson	.20	.15	.08
33	Jerry Robinson	.20	.15	.08
34	Dalton Hilliard	.20	.15	.08
35	Brian Jordan	.20	.15	.08
36	James Thornton (Misspelled Thorton on cards back)	.20	.15	.08
37	Michael Irvin	1.00	.70	.40
38	Billy Joe Tolliver	.20	.15	.08
39	Jeff Herrod	.20	.15	.08
40	Scott Norwood	.20	.15	.08
41	Ferrell Edmunds	.20	.15	.08
42	Andre Waters	.20	.15	.08
43	Kevin Glover	.20	.15	.08
44	Ray Berry	.20	.15	.08
45	Timm Rosenbach	.20	.15	.08
46	Reuben Davis	.20	.15	.08
47	Charles Wilson	.20	.15	.08
48	Todd Marinovich RC	.20	.15	.08
49	Harris Barton	.20	.15	.08
50	Jim Breech	.20	.15	.08
51	Ron Holmes	.20	.15	.08
52	Chris Singleton	.20	.15	.08
53	Pat Leahy	.20	.15	.08
54	Tom Newberry	.20	.15	.08
55	Greg Montgomery	.20	.15	.08
56	Robert Blackmon	.20	.15	.08
57	Jay Hilgenberg	.20	.15	.08
58	Rodney Hampton	1.00	.70	.40
59	Brett Perriman	.75	.60	.30
60	Ricky Watters RC	7.00	5.25	2.75
61	Howie Long	.20	.15	.08
62	Frank Cornish	.20	.15	.08
63	Chris Miller	.20	.15	.08
64	Keith Taylor	.20	.15	.08
65	Tony Paige	.20	.15	.08
66	Gary Zimmerman	.20	.15	.08
67	Mark Royals	.20	.15	.08
68	Ernie Jones	.20	.15	.08
69	David Grant	.20	.15	.08
70	Shane Conlan	.20	.15	.08
71	Jerry Rice	5.00	3.75	2.00
72	Christian Okoye	.20	.15	.08
73	Eddie Murray	.20	.15	.08
74	Reggie White	.75	.60	.30
75	Jeff Graham RC	2.00	1.50	.80
76	Mark Jackson	.20	.15	.08
77	David Grayson	.20	.15	.08
78	Dan Stryzinski	.20	.15	.08
79	Sterling Sharpe	.75	.60	.30
80	Cleveland Gary	.20	.15	.08
81	Johnny Meads	.20	.15	.08
82	Howard Cross	.20	.15	.08
83	Ken O'Brien	.20	.15	.08
84	Brian Blades	.20	.15	.08
85	Ethan Horton	.20	.15	.08
86	Bruce Armstrong	.20	.15	.08
87	James Washington RC	.40	.30	.15
88	Eugene Daniel	.20	.15	.08
89	James Lofton	.20	.15	.08
90	Louis Oliver	.20	.15	.08
91	Boomer Esiason	.30	.25	.12
92	Seth Joyner	.20	.15	.08
93	Mark Carrier	.20	.15	.08
94	Brett Favre RC (Favre misspelled as Farve)	100.00	75.00	40.00
95	Lee Williams	.20	.15	.08
96	Neal Anderson	.20	.15	.08
97	Brent Jones	.20	.15	.08
98	John Alt	.20	.15	.08
99	Rodney Peete	.20	.15	.08
100	Steve Broussard	.20	.15	.08
101	Cedric Mack	.20	.15	.08
102	Pat Swilling	.20	.15	.08
103	Stan Humphries	2.00	1.50	.80
104	Darrell Thompson	.20	.15	.08
105	Reggie Langhorne	.20	.15	.08
106	Kenny Davidson	.20	.15	.08
107	Jim Everett	.30	.25	.12
108	Keith Millard	.20	.15	.08
109	Garry Lewis	.20	.15	.08
110	Jeff Hostetler	1.00	.70	.40
111	Lamar Lathon	.20	.15	.08
112	Johnny Bailey	.20	.15	.08
113	Cornelius Bennett	.20	.15	.08
114	Travis McNeal	.20	.15	.08
115	Jeff Lageman	.20	.15	.08
116	Nick Bell RC	.20	.15	.08
117	Calvin Williams	.50	.40	.20
118	Shawn Lee	.20	.15	.08
119	Anthony Munoz	.20	.15	.08
120	Jay Novacek	.40	.30	.15
121	Kevin Fagan	.20	.15	.08
122	Leo Goeas	.20	.15	.08
123	Vance Johnson	.20	.15	.08
124	Brent Williams	.20	.15	.08
125	Clarence Verdin	.20	.15	.08
126	Luis Sharpe	.20	.15	.08
127	Darrell Green	.20	.15	.08
128	Barry Word	.20	.15	.08
129	Steve Walsh	.40	.30	.15
130	Bryan Hinkle	.20	.15	.08
131	Ed West	.20	.15	.08
132	Jeff Campbell	.20	.15	.08
133	Dennis Byrd	.20	.15	.08
134	Nate Odomes	.20	.15	.08
135	Trace Armstrong	.20	.15	.08
136	Jarvis Williams	.20	.15	.08
137	Warren Moon	1.00	.70	.40
138	Eric Moten RC	.20	.15	.08
139	Tony Woods	.20	.15	.08
140	Phil Simms	.20	.15	.08
141	Ricky Reynolds	.20	.15	.08
142	Frank Stams	.20	.15	.08
143	Kevin Mack	.20	.15	.08
144	Wade Wilson	.20	.15	.08
145	Shawn Collins	.20	.15	.08
146	Roger Craig	.20	.15	.08
147	Jeff Feagles	.20	.15	.08
148	Norm Johnson	.20	.15	.08
149	Terrance Mathis	2.00	1.50	.80
150	Reggie Cobb	.20	.15	.08
151	Chip Banks	.20	.15	.08
152	Darryl Pollard	.20	.15	.08
153	Karl Mecklenburg	.20	.15	.08

#	Player			
154	Ricky Proehl	.20	.15	.08
155	Pete Stoyanovich	.20	.15	.08
156	John Stephens	.20	.15	.08
157	Ron Morris	.20	.15	.08
158	Steve DeBerg	.20	.15	.08
159	Mike Munchak	.20	.15	.08
160	Brett Maxie	.20	.15	.08
161	Don Beebe	.20	.15	.08
162	Martin Mayhew	.20	.15	.08
163	Merril Hoge	.20	.15	.08
164	Kelvin Pritchett	.20	.15	.08
165	Jim Jeffcoat	.20	.15	.08
166	Myron Guyton	.20	.15	.08
167	Ickey Woods	.20	.15	.08
168	Andre Ware	.20	.15	.08
169	Gary Plummer	.20	.15	.08
170	Henry Ellard	.20	.15	.08
171	Scott Davis	.20	.15	.08
172	Randall McDaniel	.20	.15	.08
173	Randal Hill RC	1.00	.70	.40
174	Anthony Bell	.20	.15	.08
175	Gary Anderson	.20	.15	.08
176	Byron Evans	.20	.15	.08
177	Tony Mandarich	.20	.15	.08
178	Jeff George	2.00	1.50	.80
179	Art Monk	.40	.30	.15
180	Mike Kenn	.20	.15	.08
181	Sean Landeta	.20	.15	.08
182	Shaun Gayle	.20	.15	.08
183	Michael Carter	.20	.15	.08
184	Robb Thomas	.20	.15	.08
185	Richmond Webb	.20	.15	.08
186	Carnell Lake	.20	.15	.08
187	Rueben Mayes	.20	.15	.08
188	Issiac Holt	.20	.15	.08
189	Leon Seals	.20	.15	.08
190	Al Smith	.20	.15	.08
191	Steve Atwater	.20	.15	.08
192	Greg McMurtry	.20	.15	.08
193	Al Toon	.20	.15	.08
194	Cortez Kennedy	.40	.30	.15
195	Gill Byrd	.20	.15	.08
196	Carl Zander	.20	.15	.08
197	Robert Brown	.20	.15	.08
198	Buford McGee	.20	.15	.08
199	Mervyn Fernandez	.20	.15	.08
200	Mike Dumas	.20	.15	.08
201	Rob Burnett RC	.40	.30	.15
202	Brian Mitchell	.20	.15	.08
203	Randall Cunningham	.50	.40	.20
204	Sammie Smith	.20	.15	.08
205	Ken Clarke	.20	.15	.08
206	Floyd Dixon	.20	.15	.08
207	Ken Norton	.20	.15	.08
208	Tony Siragusa	.20	.15	.08
209	Louis Lipps	.20	.15	.08
210	Chris Martin	.20	.15	.08
211	Jamie Mueller	.20	.15	.08
212	Dave Waymer	.20	.15	.08
213	Donnell Woolford	.20	.15	.08
214	Paul Gruber	.20	.15	.08
215	Ken Harvey	.20	.15	.08
216	Henry Jones RC	.40	.30	.15
217	Tommy Barnhardt	.20	.15	.08
218	Arthur Cox	.20	.15	.08
219	Pat Terrell	.20	.15	.08
220	Curtis Duncan	.20	.15	.08
221	Jeff Jaeger	.20	.15	.08
222	Scott Stephen	.20	.15	.08
223	Rob Moore	.20	.15	.08
224	Chris Hinton	.20	.15	.08
225	Marv Cook	.20	.15	.08
226	Patrick Hunter	.20	.15	.08
227	Earnest Byner	.20	.15	.08
228	Troy Aikman	4.00	3.00	1.50
229	Kevin Walker	.20	.15	.08
230	Keith Jackson	.20	.15	.08
231	Russell Maryland RC	.75	.60	.30
232	Charles Haley	.20	.15	.08
233	Nick Lowery	.20	.15	.08
234	Erik Howard	.20	.15	.08
235	Leonard Smith	.20	.15	.08
236	Tim Irwin	.20	.15	.08
237	Simon Fletcher	.20	.15	.08
238	Thomas Everett	.20	.15	.08
239	Leroy Hoard	.20	.15	.08
240	Wayne Haddix	.20	.15	.08
241	Gary Clark	.20	.15	.08
242	Eric Andolsek	.20	.15	.08
243	Jim Wahler	.20	.15	.08
244	Vaughan Johnson	.20	.15	.08
245	Kevin Butler	.20	.15	.08
246	Steve Tasker	.20	.15	.08
247	LeRoy Butler	.20	.15	.08
248	Eric Turner RC	1.00	.70	.40
250	Kevin Ross	.20	.15	.08
251	Stephen Baker	.20	.15	.08
252	Harold Green	.20	.15	.08
253	Rohn Stark	.20	.15	.08
254	Joe Nash	.20	.15	.08
255	Jesse Sapolu	.20	.15	.08
256	Willie Gault	.20	.15	.08
257	Jerome Brown	.20	.15	.08
258	Ken Willis	.20	.15	.08
259	Courtney Hall	.20	.15	.08
260	Hart Lee Dykes	.20	.15	.08
261	William Fuller	.20	.15	.08
262	Stan Thomas	.20	.15	.08
264	Dan Marino	6.00	4.50	2.50
265	Ron Cox	.20	.15	.08
266	Eric Green	.50	.40	.20
267	Anthony Carter	.20	.15	.08
268	Jerry Ball	.20	.15	.08
269	Ron Hall	.20	.15	.08
270	Dennis Smith	.20	.15	.08
271	Eric Hill	.20	.15	.08
272	Dan McGwire RC	.20	.15	.08
273	Lewis Billups	.20	.15	.08
274	Rickey Jackson	.20	.15	.08
275	Jim Sweeney	.20	.15	.08
276	Pat Beach	.20	.15	.08
277	Kevin Porter	.20	.15	.08
278	Mike Sherrard	.20	.15	.08
279	Andy Heck	.20	.15	.08
280	Ron Brown	.20	.15	.08
281	Lawrence Taylor	.50	.40	.20
282	Anthony Pleasant	.20	.15	.08
283	Wes Hopkins	.20	.15	.08
284	Jim Lachey	.20	.15	.08
285	Tim Harris	.20	.15	.08
286	Tony Epps	.20	.15	.08
287	Wendell Davis	.20	.15	.08
288	Bubba McDowell	.20	.15	.08
289	Reggie Roby, Bubby Brister	.20	.15	.08
290	Chris Zorich RC	1.00	.70	.40
291	Mike Merriweather	.20	.15	.08
292	Burt Grossman	.20	.15	.08
293	Eric McMillan	.20	.15	.08
294	John Elway	2.00	1.50	.80
295	Toi Cook	.20	.15	.08
297	Matt Bahr	.20	.15	.08
298	Chris Spielman	.20	.15	.08
299	Freddie Joe Nunn (Troy Aikman and Emmitt Smith shown in background)	.30	.25	.12
300	Jim C. Jenson	.20	.15	.08
301	David Fulcher (Rookie card should be '88, not '89)	.20	.15	.08
302	Tommy Hodson	.20	.15	.08
303	Stephone Page	.20	.15	.08
304	Greg Townsend	.20	.15	.08
305	Dean Biasucci	.20	.15	.08
306	Jimmie Jones	.20	.15	.08
307	Eugene Marve	.20	.15	.08
308	Flipper Anderson	.20	.15	.08
309	Darryl Talley	.20	.15	.08
310	Mike Croel RC	.40	.30	.15
311	Thane Gash	.20	.15	.08
312	Perry Kemp	.20	.15	.08
313	Heath Sherman	.20	.15	.08
314	Mike Singletary	.20	.15	.08
315	Chip Lohmiller	.20	.15	.08
316	Tunch Ilkin	.20	.15	.08
317	Junior Seau	2.00	1.50	.80
318	Mike Gann	.20	.15	.08
319	Tim McDonald	.20	.15	.08
320	Kyle Clifton	.20	.15	.08
321	Dan Owens	.20	.15	.08
322	Tim Grunhard	.20	.15	.08
323	Stan Brock	.20	.15	.08
324	Rodney Holman	.20	.15	.08
325	Mark Ingram	.20	.15	.08
326	Browning Nagle RC	.40	.30	.15
327	Joe Montana	5.00	3.75	2.00
328	Carl Lee	.20	.15	.08
329	John L. Williams	.20	.15	.08
330	David Griggs	.20	.15	.08
331	Clarence Kay	.20	.15	.08
332	Irving Fryar	.20	.15	.08
333	Doug Smith	.20	.15	.08
334	Kent Hull	.20	.15	.08
335	Mike Wilcher	.20	.15	.08
336	Ray Donaldson	.20	.15	.08
337	Mark Carrier (Rookie card should be '90, not '89)	.20	.15	.08
338	Kelvin Martin	.20	.15	.08
339	Keith Byars	.20	.15	.08
340	Wilber Marshall	.20	.15	.08
341	Ronnie Lott	.20	.15	.08
342	Blair Thomas	.20	.15	.08
343	Ronnie Harmon	.20	.15	.08
344	Brian Brennan	.20	.15	.08
345	Charles McRae RC	.20	.15	.08
346	Michael Cofer	.20	.15	.08
347	Keith Willis	.20	.15	.08
348	Bruce Kozerski	.20	.15	.08
349	Dave Meggett	.20	.15	.08
350	John Taylor	.20	.15	.08
351	Johnny Holland	.20	.15	.08
352	Steve Christie	.20	.15	.08
353	Ricky Ervins RC	1.00	.70	.40
354	Robert Massey	.20	.15	.08
355	Derrick Thomas	.50	.40	.20
356	Tommy Kane	.20	.15	.08
357	Melvin Bratton	.20	.15	.08
358	Bruce Matthews	.20	.15	.08
359	Mark Duper	.20	.15	.08
360	Jeff Wright	.20	.15	.08
361	Barry Sanders	6.00	4.50	2.50
362	Chuck Webb	.20	.15	.08
363	Darryl Grant	.20	.15	.08
364	William Roberts	.20	.15	.08
365	Reggie Rutland	.20	.15	.08
366	Clay Matthews	.20	.15	.08
367	Anthony Miller	.20	.15	.08
368	Mike Prior	.20	.15	.08
369	Jessie Tuggle	.20	.15	.08
370	Brad Muster	.20	.15	.08
371	Jay Schroeder	.20	.15	.08
372	Greg Lloyd	.20	.15	.08
373	Mike Cofer	.20	.15	.08
374	James Brooks	.20	.15	.08
375	Danny Noonan (Misspelled Noonen on card back)	.20	.15	.08
376	Latin Berry	.20	.15	.08
377	Brad Baxter	.20	.15	.08
378	Godfrey Myles	.20	.15	.08
379	Morten Andersen	.20	.15	.08
380	Keith Woodside	.20	.15	.08
381	Bobby Humphrey	.20	.15	.08
382	Mike Golic	.20	.15	.08
383	Keith McCants	.20	.15	.08
384	Anthony Thompson	.20	.15	.08
385	Mark Clayton	.20	.15	.08
386	Neil Smith	.20	.15	.08
387	Bryan Millard	.20	.15	.08
388	Mel Gray (Wrong Mel Gray pictured on card back)	.20	.15	.08
389	Ernest Givins	.20	.15	.08
390	Reyna Thompson	.20	.15	.08
391	Eric Bieniemy RC	.40	.30	.15
392	Jon Hand	.20	.15	.08
393	Mark Rypien	.20	.15	.08
394	Bill Romanowski	.20	.15	.08
395	Thurman Thomas	1.50	1.25	.60
396	Jim Harbaugh	.20	.15	.08
397	Don Mosebar	.20	.15	.08
398	Andre Rison	.50	.40	.20
399	Mike Johnson	.20	.15	.08
400	Dermontti Dawson	.20	.15	.08
401	Herschel Walker	.30	.25	.12
402	Joe Prokop	.20	.15	.08
403	Eddie Brown	.20	.15	.08
404	Nate Newton	.20	.15	.08
405	Damone Johnson	.20	.15	.08
406	Jessie Hester	.20	.15	.08
407	Jim Arnold	.20	.15	.08
408	Ray Agnew	.20	.15	.08
409	Michael Brooks	.20	.15	.08
410	Keith Sims	.20	.15	.08
411	Carl Banks	.20	.15	.08
412	Jonathan Hayes	.20	.15	.08
413	Richard Johnson	.20	.15	.08
414	Darryll Lewis RC	.20	.15	.08
415	Jeff Bryant	.20	.15	.08
416	Leslie O'Neal	.20	.15	.08
417	Andre Reed	.30	.25	.12
418	Charles Mann	.20	.15	.08
419	Ken DeLong	.20	.15	.08
420	Bruce Hill	.20	.15	.08
421	Matt Brock	.20	.15	.08
422	Johnny Johnson	.30	.25	.12
423	Mark Bortz	.20	.15	.08
424	Ben Smith	.20	.15	.08
425	Jeff Cross	.20	.15	.08
426	Irv Pankey	.20	.15	.08
427	Hassan Jones	.20	.15	.08
428	Andre Tippett	.20	.15	.08
429	Tim Worley	.20	.15	.08
430	Daniel Stubbs	.20	.15	.08
431	Max Montoya	.20	.15	.08
432	Jumbo Elliott	.20	.15	.08
433	Duane Bickett	.20	.15	.08
434	Nate Lewis RC	.50	.40	.20
435	Leonard Russell RC	1.00	.70	.40
436	Hoby Brenner	.20	.15	.08
437	Ricky Sanders	.20	.15	.08
438	Pierce Holt	.20	.15	.08
439	Derrick Fenner	.20	.15	.08

440	Drew Hill	.20	.15	.08
441	Will Wolford	.20	.15	.08
442	Albert Lewis	.20	.15	.08
443	James Francis	.20	.15	.08
444	Chris Jackie (Jacke)	.20	.15	.08
445	Mike Farr	.20	.15	.08
446	Stephen Braggs	.20	.15	.08
447	Michael Haynes	1.00	.70	.40
448	Freeman McNeil (2008 pounds, sic)	.20	.15	.08
449	Kevin Donnalley	.20	.15	.08
450	John Offerdahl	.20	.15	.08
451	Eric Allen	.20	.15	.08
452	Keith McKeller	.20	.15	.08
453	Kevin Greene	.20	.15	.08
454	Ronnie Lippett	.20	.15	.08
455	Ray Childress	.20	.15	.08
456	Mike Saxon	.20	.15	.08
457	Mark Robinson	.20	.15	.08
458	Greg Kragen	.20	.15	.08
459	Steve Jordan	.20	.15	.08
460	John Johnson	.20	.15	.08
461	Sam Mills	.20	.15	.08
462	Bo Jackson	.40	.30	.15
463	Mark Collins	.20	.15	.08
464	Percy Snow	.20	.15	.08
465	Jeff Bostic	.20	.15	.08
466	Jacob Green	.20	.15	.08
467	Dexter Carter	.20	.15	.08
468	Rich Camarillo	.20	.15	.08
469	Bill Brooks	.20	.15	.08
470	John Carney	.20	.15	.08
471	Don Majkowski	.20	.15	.08
472	Ralph Tamm	.20	.15	.08
473	Fred Barnett	1.00	.70	.40
474	Jim Covert	.20	.15	.08
475	Kenneth Davis	.20	.15	.08
476	Jerry Gray	.20	.15	.08
477	Broderick Thomas	.20	.15	.08
478	Chris Doleman	.20	.15	.08
479	Haywood Jeffires	.40	.30	.15
480	Craig Heyward	.20	.15	.08
481	Markus Koch	.20	.15	.08
482	Tim Krumrie	.20	.15	.08
483	Robert Clark	.20	.15	.08
484	Mike Rozier	.20	.15	.08
485	Danny Villa	.20	.15	.08
486	Gerald Williams	.20	.15	.08
487	Steve Wisniewski	.20	.15	.08
488	J.B. Brown	.20	.15	.08
489	Eugene Robinson	.20	.15	.08
490	Ottis Anderson	.20	.15	.08
491	Tony Stargell	.20	.15	.08
492	Jack Del Rio	.20	.15	.08
493	Lamar Rogers	.20	.15	.08
494	Ricky Nattiel	.20	.15	.08
495	Dan Saleaumua	.20	.15	.08
496	**Checklist Card**	.20	.15	.08
497	**Checklist Card**	.20	.15	.08
498	**Checklist Card**	.20	.15	.08
499	**Checklist Card**	.20	.15	.08
500	**Checklist Card**	.20	.15	.08

1991 Stadium Club Super Bowl XXVI

		NM/M	NM	E
Complete Set (300):		1,600	1,200	650.00
Common Player:		4.00	3.00	1.50
2	Emmitt Smith	60.00	45.00	24.00
3	Deion Sanders	20.00	15.00	8.00
7	Eric Martin	4.00	3.00	1.50
9	Gary Anderson	4.00	3.00	1.50
10	Joey Browner	4.00	3.00	1.50
11	Lorenzo White	4.00	3.00	1.50
14	Mike Piel	4.00	3.00	1.50
15	Albert Bentley	4.00	3.00	1.50
16	Bennie Blades	4.00	3.00	1.50
17	Jason Staurovsky	4.00	3.00	1.50
19	Dave Krieg	6.00	4.50	2.50
22	Tim McGee	4.00	3.00	1.50
23	Brian Noble	4.00	3.00	1.50
24	Vinny Testaverde	8.00	6.00	3.25
26	John Jackson	4.00	3.00	1.50
27	Marion Butts	6.00	4.50	2.50
28	Deron Cherry	4.00	3.00	1.50
30	Rod Woodson	8.00	6.00	3.25
32	Greg Jackson	4.00	3.00	1.50
34	Dalton Hilliard	4.00	3.00	1.50
35	Brian Jordan	8.00	6.00	3.25
37	Michael Irvin	12.00	9.00	4.75
38	Billy Joe Tolliver	4.00	3.00	1.50
42	Andre Waters	4.00	3.00	1.50
43	Kevin Glover	4.00	3.00	1.50
44	Ray Berry	4.00	3.00	1.50
45	Timm Rosenbach	4.00	3.00	1.50
48	Todd Marinovich	4.00	3.00	1.50
49	Harris Barton	4.00	3.00	1.50
52	Chris Singleton	4.00	3.00	1.50
53	Pat Leahy	4.00	3.00	1.50
60	Ricky Watters	25.00	18.50	10.00
61	Howie Long	8.00	6.00	3.25
62	Frank Cornish	4.00	3.00	1.50
64	Keith Taylor	4.00	3.00	1.50
66	Gary Zimmerman	4.00	3.00	1.50
67	Mark Royals	4.00	3.00	1.50
69	David Grant	4.00	3.00	1.50
70	Shane Conlan	4.00	3.00	1.50
71	Jerry Rice	40.00	30.00	16.00
72	Christian Okoye	6.00	4.50	2.50
73	Eddie Murray	4.00	3.00	1.50
74	Reggie White	12.00	9.00	4.75
76	Mark Jackson	4.00	3.00	1.50
77	David Grayson	4.00	3.00	1.50
82	Howard Cross	4.00	3.00	1.50
83	Ken O'Brien	4.00	3.00	1.50
84	Brian Blades	6.00	4.50	2.50
86	Bruce Armstrong	4.00	3.00	1.50
87	James Washington	4.00	3.00	1.50
88	Eugene Daniel	4.00	3.00	1.50
89	James Lofton	6.00	4.50	2.50
90	Louis Oliver	4.00	3.00	1.50
91	Boomer Esiason	8.00	6.00	3.25
94	Brett Favre UER (Favre misspelled as Farve)	300.00	225.00	120.00
95	Lee Williams	4.00	3.00	1.50
97	Brent Jones	6.00	4.50	2.50
99	Rodney Peete	6.00	4.50	2.50
101	Cedric Mack	4.00	3.00	1.50
103	Stan Humphries	8.00	6.00	3.25
105	Reggie Langhorne	4.00	3.00	1.50
108	Keith Millard	4.00	3.00	1.50
111	Lamar Lathon	4.00	3.00	1.50
112	Johnny Bailey	4.00	3.00	1.50
115	Jeff Lageman	4.00	3.00	1.50
116	Nick Bell	4.00	3.00	1.50
117	Calvin Williams	6.00	4.50	2.50
118	Shawn Lee	4.00	3.00	1.50
119	Anthony Munoz	8.00	6.00	3.25
120	Jay Novacek	6.00	4.50	2.50
121	Kevin Fagan	4.00	3.00	1.50
122	Leo Goeas	4.00	3.00	1.50
125	Clarence Verdin	4.00	3.00	1.50
127	Darrell Green	6.00	4.50	2.50
131	Ed West	4.00	3.00	1.50
132	Jeff Campbell	4.00	3.00	1.50
135	Trace Armstrong	4.00	3.00	1.50
136	Jarvis Williams	4.00	3.00	1.50
144	Wade Wilson	4.00	3.00	1.50
149	Terance Mathis	8.00	6.00	3.25
150	Reggie Cobb	4.00	3.00	1.50
151	Chip Banks	4.00	3.00	1.50
155	Pete Stoyanovich	4.00	3.00	1.50
156	John Stephens	4.00	3.00	1.50
163	Merril Hoge	4.00	3.00	1.50
165	Jim Jeffcoat	4.00	3.00	1.50
168	Andre Ware	6.00	4.50	2.50
169	Gary Plummer	4.00	3.00	1.50
170	Henry Ellard	6.00	4.50	2.50
172	Randall McDaniel	6.00	4.50	2.50
173	Randal Hill	6.00	4.50	2.50
174	Anthony Bell	4.00	3.00	1.50
176	Byron Evans	4.00	3.00	1.50
177	Tony Mandarich	4.00	3.00	1.50
183	Michael Carter	4.00	3.00	1.50
184	Robb Thomas	4.00	3.00	1.50
186	Carnell Lake	4.00	3.00	1.50
187	Rueben Mayes	4.00	3.00	1.50
188	Issiac Holt	4.00	3.00	1.50
189	Leon Seals	4.00	3.00	1.50
190	Al Smith	4.00	3.00	1.50
191	Steve Atwater	4.00	3.00	1.50
193	Al Toon	6.00	4.50	2.50
195	Gill Byrd	4.00	3.00	1.50
196	Carl Zander	4.00	3.00	1.50
197	Robert Brown	4.00	3.00	1.50
199	Mervyn Fernandez	4.00	3.00	1.50
200	Mike Dumas	4.00	3.00	1.50
201	Rob Burnett	4.00	3.00	1.50
205	Ken Clarke	4.00	3.00	1.50
206	Floyd Dixon	4.00	3.00	1.50
208	Tony Siragusa	4.00	3.00	1.50
209	Louis Lipps	4.00	3.00	1.50
211	Jamie Mueller	4.00	3.00	1.50
212	Dave Waymer	4.00	3.00	1.50
214	Paul Gruber	4.00	3.00	1.50
216	Henry Jones	6.00	4.50	2.50
217	Tommy Barnhardt	4.00	3.00	1.50
218	Arthur Cox	4.00	3.00	1.50
220	Curtis Duncan	4.00	3.00	1.50
221	Jeff Jaeger	4.00	3.00	1.50
222	Scott Stephen	4.00	3.00	1.50
223	Rob Moore	10.00	7.50	4.00
224	Chris Hinton	4.00	3.00	1.50
225	Marv Cook	4.00	3.00	1.50
226	Patrick Hunter	4.00	3.00	1.50
229	Kevin Walker	4.00	3.00	1.50
230	Keith Jackson	6.00	4.50	2.50
231	Russell Maryland UER (card back says Dallas Cowboy)	6.00	4.50	2.50
234	Erik Howard	4.00	3.00	1.50
235	Leonard Smith	4.00	3.00	1.50
236	Tim Irwin	4.00	3.00	1.50
237	Simon Fletcher	4.00	3.00	1.50
238	Thomas Everett	4.00	3.00	1.50
239	Reggie Roby	4.00	3.00	1.50
242	Gary Clark	6.00	4.50	2.50
243	Eric Andolsek	4.00	3.00	1.50
244	Jim Wahler	4.00	3.00	1.50
245	Vaughan Johnson	4.00	3.00	1.50
246	Kevin Butler	4.00	3.00	1.50
247	Steve Tasker	8.00	6.00	3.25
248	LeRoy Butler	6.00	4.50	2.50
249	Darion Conner	4.00	3.00	1.50
251	Kevin Ross	4.00	3.00	1.50
253	Harold Green	6.00	4.50	2.50
254	Rohn Stark	4.00	3.00	1.50
256	Jesse Sapolu	4.00	3.00	1.50
260	Courtney Hall	4.00	3.00	1.50
262	William Fuller	4.00	3.00	1.50
266	Eric Green	6.00	4.50	2.50
267	Anthony Carter	6.00	4.50	2.50
268	Jerry Ball	4.00	3.00	1.50
269	Ron Hall	4.00	3.00	1.50
270	Dennis Smith	4.00	3.00	1.50
271	Eric Hill	4.00	3.00	1.50
272	Dan McGwire	4.00	3.00	1.50
273	Lewis Billups UER (Louis on back)	4.00	3.00	1.50
274	Rickey Jackson	6.00	4.50	2.50
275	Jim Sweeney	4.00	3.00	1.50
276	Pat Beach	4.00	3.00	1.50
277	Kevin Porter	4.00	3.00	1.50
278	Mike Sherrard	6.00	4.50	2.50
279	Andy Heck	4.00	3.00	1.50
282	Anthony Pleasant	4.00	3.00	1.50
283	Wes Hopkins	4.00	3.00	1.50
284	Jim Lachey	4.00	3.00	1.50
285	Tim Harris	4.00	3.00	1.50
287	Wendell Davis	4.00	3.00	1.50
291	Mike Merriweather	4.00	3.00	1.50
292	Burt Grossman	4.00	3.00	1.50
293	Erik McMillan	4.00	3.00	1.50
296	Tom Rathman	4.00	3.00	1.50
297	Matt Bahr	4.00	3.00	1.50
299	Freddie Joe Nunn (Troy Aikman and Emmitt Smith shown in background)	8.00	6.00	3.25
301	David Fulcher UER (rookie card should be '88 not '89)	4.00	3.00	1.50
303	Stephon Paige	4.00	3.00	1.50
305	Dean Biasucci	4.00	3.00	1.50
306	Jimmie Jones	4.00	3.00	1.50
307	Eugene Marve	4.00	3.00	1.50
308	Flipper Anderson	4.00	3.00	1.50
309	Darryl Talley	4.00	3.00	1.50
310	Mike Croel	4.00	3.00	1.50
313	Heath Sherman	4.00	3.00	1.50
314	Mike Singletary	8.00	6.00	3.25
315	Chip Lohmiller	4.00	3.00	1.50
316	Tunch Ilkin	4.00	3.00	1.50
317	Junior Seau	10.00	7.50	4.00
318	Mike Gann	4.00	3.00	1.50
319	Tim McDonald	4.00	3.00	1.50
322	Tim Grunhard	4.00	3.00	1.50
323	Stan Brock	4.00	3.00	1.50
324	Rodney Holman	4.00	3.00	1.50
325	Mark Ingram	6.00	4.50	2.50
326	Browning Nagle	6.00	4.50	2.50
328	Carl Lee	4.00	3.00	1.50
329	John L. Williams	4.00	3.00	1.50
332	Irving Fryar	6.00	4.50	2.50
333	Doug Smith DT	4.00	3.00	1.50
335	Mike Wilcher	4.00	3.00	1.50
336	Ray Donaldson	4.00	3.00	1.50
337	Mark Carrier DB UER (rookie card should be '90 not '89)	4.00	3.00	1.50
338	Kelvin Martin	4.00	3.00	1.50
339	Keith Byars	6.00	4.50	2.50
340	Wilber Marshall	4.00	3.00	1.50
343	Ronnie Harmon	6.00	4.50	2.50
344	Brian Brennan	4.00	3.00	1.50
346	Michael Cofer	4.00	3.00	1.50
347	Keith Wills	4.00	3.00	1.50

348	Bruce Kozerski	4.00	3.00	1.50
349	Dave Meggett	6.00	4.50	2.50
350	John Taylor	6.00	4.50	2.50
351	Johnny Holland	4.00	3.00	1.50
352	Steve Christie	4.00	3.00	1.50
353	Ricky Ervins	6.00	4.50	2.50
354	Robert Massey	4.00	3.00	1.50
355	Derrick Thomas	8.00	6.00	3.25
356	Tommy Kane	4.00	3.00	1.50
357	Melvin Bratton	4.00	3.00	1.50
359	Mark Duper	6.00	4.50	2.50
360	Jeff Wright	4.00	3.00	1.50
361	Barry Sanders	80.00	60.00	32.00
362	Chuck Webb	4.00	3.00	1.50
363	Darryl Grant	4.00	3.00	1.50
368	Mike Prior	4.00	3.00	1.50
369	Jessie Tuggle	4.00	3.00	1.50
370	Brad Muster	4.00	3.00	1.50
371	Jay Schroeder	4.00	3.00	1.50
374	James Brooks	4.00	3.00	1.50
375	Danny Noonan UER (misspelled Noonen on card back)	4.00	3.00	1.50
378	Godfrey Myles	4.00	3.00	1.50
381	Bobby Humphrey	4.00	3.00	1.50
383	Keith McCants	4.00	3.00	1.50
386	Neil Smith	8.00	6.00	3.25
387	Bryan Millard	4.00	3.00	1.50
388	Mel Gray (wrong Mel Gray pictured on card back)	6.00	4.50	2.50
389	Ernest Givins	6.00	4.50	2.50
390	Reyna Thompson	4.00	3.00	1.50
393	Mark Rypien	6.00	4.50	2.50
394	Bill Romanowski	4.00	3.00	1.50
395	Thurman Thomas	12.00	9.00	4.75
397	Don Mosebar	4.00	3.00	1.50
399	Mike Johnson	4.00	3.00	1.50
401	Herschel Walker	6.00	4.50	2.50
402	Joe Prokop	4.00	3.00	1.50
403	Eddie Brown	4.00	3.00	1.50
404	Nate Newton	4.00	3.00	1.50
407	Joe Arnold	4.00	3.00	1.50
408	Ray Agnew	4.00	3.00	1.50
410	Keith Sims	4.00	3.00	1.50
41	Carl Banks	4.00	3.00	1.50
412	Jonathan Hayes	4.00	3.00	1.50
415	Jeff Bryant	4.00	3.00	1.50
416	Leslie O'Neal	6.00	4.50	2.50
419	Keith DeLong	4.00	3.00	1.50
420	Bruce Hill	4.00	3.00	1.50
421	Matt Brock	4.00	3.00	1.50
422	Johnny Johnson	6.00	4.50	2.50
423	Mark Bortz	4.00	3.00	1.50
425	Jeff Cross	4.00	3.00	1.50
426	Irv Pankey	4.00	3.00	1.50
428	Andre Tippett	4.00	3.00	1.50
429	Tim Worley	4.00	3.00	1.50
430	Daniel Stubbs	4.00	3.00	1.50
431	Max Montoya	4.00	3.00	1.50
432	Jumbo Elliott	4.00	3.00	1.50
434	Nate Lewis	4.00	3.00	1.50
436	Hoby Brenner	4.00	3.00	1.50
437	Ricky Sanders	6.00	4.50	2.50
438	Pierce Holt	4.00	3.00	1.50
439	Derrick Fenner	4.00	3.00	1.50
441	Will Wolford	4.00	3.00	1.50
447	Michael Haynes	8.00	6.00	3.25
448	Freeman McNeil UER (2,008 pounds for weight)	6.00	4.50	2.50
450	John Offerdahl	4.00	3.00	1.50
451	Eric Allen	6.00	4.50	2.50
454	Ronnie Lippett	4.00	3.00	1.50
455	Ray Childress	4.00	3.00	1.50
456	Mike Saxon	4.00	3.00	1.50
458	Greg Kragen	4.00	3.00	1.50
459	Steve Jordan	4.00	3.00	1.50
464	Percy Snow	4.00	3.00	1.50
465	Jeff Bostic	4.00	3.00	1.50
469	Bill Brooks	6.00	4.50	2.50
470	John Carney	4.00	3.00	1.50
474	Jim Covert	4.00	3.00	1.50
476	Jerry Gray	4.00	3.00	1.50
477	Broderick Thomas	4.00	3.00	1.50
479	Haywood Jeffires	6.00	4.50	2.50
480	Craig Heyward	6.00	4.50	2.50
482	Tim Krumrie	4.00	3.00	1.50
483	Robert Clark	4.00	3.00	1.50
484	Mike Rozier	4.00	3.00	1.50
486	Gerald Williams	4.00	3.00	1.50
490	Ottis Anderson	6.00	4.50	2.50
491	Tony Stargell	4.00	3.00	1.50
494	Ricky Nattiel	4.00	3.00	1.50

1991 Topps

Topps' largest-ever football set was issued in August 1991. The style of the cards is the same as in 1991 Topps baseball and hockey. Subsets include highlights, all-pros, draft picks and super rookies. (Key: HL - highlight, LL - league leader)

	NM/M	NM	E
Complete Set (660):	13.00	9.75	5.25
Complete Factory Set (660):	17.00	12.50	6.75
Common Player:	.25	.15	.09
Pack (16):	.40		
Wax Box (36):	10.00		

1	**Super Bowl XXV**	.08	.06	.03
2	Roger Craig (HL)	.25	.15	.09
3	Derrick Thomas (HL)	.12	.09	.05
4	Pete Stoyanovich (HL)	.25	.15	.09
5	Ottis Anderson (HL)	.25	.15	.09
6	Jerry Rice (HL)	.50	.25	.15
7	Warren Moon (HL)	.10	.08	.04
8	Warren Moon, Jim Everett (LL)	.10	.08	.04
9	Thurman Thomas, Barry Sanders (LL)	.50	.40	.20
10	Haywood Jeffries, Jerry Rice (LL)	.25	.20	.10
11	Richard Johnson, Mark Carrier (LL)	.25	.15	.09
12	Derrick Thomas, Charles Haley (LL)	.10	.08	.04
13	Jumbo Elliott	.25	.15	.09
14	Leonard Marshall	.25	.15	.09
15	William Roberts	.25	.15	.09
16	Lawrence Taylor	.10	.08	.04
17	Mark Ingram	.25	.15	.09
18	Rodney Hampton	.75	.60	.30
19	Carl Banks	.25	.15	.09
20	Ottis Anderson	.25	.15	.09
21	Mark Collins	.25	.15	.09
22	Pepper Johnson	.25	.15	.09
23	Dave Meggett	.25	.15	.09
24	Reyna Thompson	.25	.15	.09
26	Mike Fox	.25	.15	.09
27	Maurice Carthon	.25	.15	.09
28	Jeff Hostetler	.25	.20	.10
29	Greg Jackson **RC**	.10	.08	.04
30	Sean Landeta	.25	.15	.09
31	Bart Oates	.25	.15	.09
32	Phil Simms	.10	.08	.04
33	Erik Howard	.25	.15	.09
34	Myron Guyton	.25	.15	.09
35	Mark Bavaro	.25	.15	.09
36	Jarrod Bunch	.15	.11	.06
37	Will Wolford **RC**	.25	.15	.09
38	Ray Bentley	.25	.15	.09
39	Nate Odomes	.25	.15	.09
40	Scott Norwood	.25	.15	.09
41	Darryl Talley	.25	.15	.09
42	Carwell Gardner	.25	.15	.09
43	James Lofton	.25	.15	.09
44	Shane Conlan	.25	.15	.09
45	Steve Tasker	.25	.15	.09
46	James Williams	.25	.15	.09
47	Kent Hull	.25	.15	.09
48	Al Edwards	.25	.15	.09
49	Frank Reich	.25	.15	.09
50	Leon Seals	.25	.15	.09
51	Keith McKeller	.25	.15	.09
52	Thurman Thomas	.50	.40	.20
53	Leonard Smith	.25	.15	.09
54	Andre Reed	.15	.11	.06
55	Kenneth Davis	.25	.15	.09
56	Jeff Wright **RC**	.12	.09	.05
57	Jamie Mueller	.25	.15	.09
58	Jim Ritcher	.25	.15	.09
59	Bruce Smith	.25	.15	.09
60	Ted Washington **RC**	.10	.08	.04
61	Guy McIntyre	.25	.15	.09
62	Michael Carter	.25	.15	.09
63	Pierce Holt	.25	.15	.09
64	Darryl Pollard	.25	.15	.09
65	Mike Sherrard	.25	.15	.09

66	Dexter Carter	.25	.15	.09
67	Bubba Paris	.25	.15	.09
68	Harry Sydney	.25	.15	.09
69	Tom Rathman	.25	.15	.09
70	Jesse Sapolu	.25	.15	.09
71	Mike Cofer (S.F.)	.25	.15	.09
72	Keith DeLong	.25	.15	.09
73	Joe Montana	1.00	.50	.30
74	Bill Romanowski	.25	.15	.09
75	John Taylor	.15	.11	.06
76	Brent Jones	.25	.15	.09
77	Harris Barton	.25	.15	.09
78	Charles Haley	.25	.15	.09
79	Eric Davis	.25	.15	.09
80	Kevin Fagan	.25	.15	.09
81	Jerry Rice	.50	.25	.15
82	Dave Waymer	.25	.15	.09
83	Todd Marinovich **RC**	.25	.20	.10
84	Steve Smith	.25	.15	.09
85	Tim Brown	.12	.09	.05
86	Ethan Horton	.25	.15	.09
87	Marcus Allen	.25	.15	.09
88	Terry McDaniel	.25	.15	.09
89	Thomas Benson	.25	.15	.09
90	Roger Craig	.25	.15	.09
91	Don Mosebar	.25	.15	.09
92	Aaron Wallace	.25	.15	.09
93	Eddie Anderson	.25	.15	.09
94	Willie Gault	.25	.15	.09
95	Howie Long	.25	.15	.09
96	Jay Schroeder	.25	.15	.09
97	Ronnie Lott	.10	.08	.04
98	Bob Golic	.25	.15	.09
99	Bo Jackson	.35	.25	.14
100	Max Montoya	.25	.15	.09
101	Scott Davis	.25	.15	.09
102	Greg Townsend	.25	.15	.09
103	Garry Lewis	.25	.15	.09
104	Mervyn Fernandez	.25	.15	.09
105	Steve Wisniewski	.25	.15	.09
106	Jeff Jaeger	.25	.15	.09
107	Nick Bell **RC**	.20	.15	.08
108	Mark Dennis **RC**	.08	.06	.03
109	Jarvis Williams	.25	.15	.09
110	Mark Clayton	.25	.15	.09
111	Harry Galbreah	.25	.15	.09
112	Dan Marino	1.25	.75	.45
113	Louis Oliver	.25	.15	.09
114	Pete Styoyanovich	.25	.15	.09
115	Ferrell Edmunds	.25	.15	.09
116	Jeff Cross	.25	.15	.09
117	Richmond Webb	.25	.15	.09
118	Jim Jensen	.25	.15	.09
119	Keith Sims	.25	.15	.09
120	Mark Duper	.25	.15	.09
121	Shawn Lee **RC**	.12	.09	.05
122	Reggie Roby	.25	.15	.09
123	Jeff Uhlenhake	.25	.15	.09
124	Sammie Smith	.25	.15	.09
125	John Offerdahl	.25	.15	.09
126	Hugh Green	.25	.15	.09
127	Tony Paige	.25	.15	.09
128	David Griggs	.25	.15	.09
129	J.B. Brown	.25	.15	.09
130	Harvey Williams **RC**	.50	.40	.20
131	John Alt	.25	.15	.09
132	Albert Lewis	.25	.15	.09
133	Robb Thomas	.25	.15	.09
134	Neil Smith	.25	.15	.09
135	Stephone Paige	.25	.15	.09
136	Nick Lowery	.25	.15	.09
137	Steve DeBerg	.25	.15	.09
138	Rich Baldinger **RC**	.10	.08	.04
139	Percy Snow	.25	.15	.09
140	Kevin Porter	.25	.15	.09
141	Chris Martin	.25	.15	.09
142	Deron Cherry	.25	.15	.09
143	Derrick Thomas	.30	.25	.12
144	Tim Grunhard	.25	.15	.09
145	Todd McNair	.25	.15	.09
146	David Szott	.25	.15	.09
147	Dan Saleaumua	.25	.15	.09
148	Jonathan Hayes	.25	.15	.09
149	Christian Okoye	.25	.15	.09
150	Dino Hackett	.25	.15	.09
151	Bryan Barker **RC**	.10	.08	.04
152	Kevin Ross	.25	.15	.09
153	Barry Word	.15	.11	.06
154	Stan Thomas	.25	.15	.09
155	Brad Muster	.25	.15	.09
156	Donnell Woolford	.25	.15	.09
157	Neal Anderson	.10	.08	.04
158	Jim Covert	.25	.15	.09
159	Jim Harbaugh	.10	.08	.04
160	Shaun Gayle	.25	.15	.09
161	William Perry	.25	.15	.09
162	Ron Morris	.25	.15	.09
163	Mark Bortz	.25	.15	.09

164	James Thornton	.25	.15	.09
165	Ron Rivera	.25	.15	.09
166	Kevin Butler	.25	.15	.09
167	Jay Hilgenberg	.25	.15	.09
168	Peter Tom Willis	.25	.15	.09
169	Johnny Bailey	.25	.15	.09
170	Ron Cox	.25	.15	.09
171	Keith Van Horne	.25	.15	.09
172	Mark Carrier	.25	.15	.09
173	Richard Dent	.25	.15	.09
174	Wendell Davis	.10	.08	.04
175	Trace Armstrong	.25	.15	.09
176	Mike Singletary	.25	.15	.09
177	Chris Zorich **RC**	.35	.25	.14
178	Gerald Riggs	.25	.15	.09
179	Jeff Bostic	.25	.15	.09
180	Kurt Gouvela **RC**	.15	.11	.06
181	Stan Humphries	.15	.11	.06
182	Chip Lohmiller	.25	.15	.09
183	Raleigh McKenzie **RC**	.10	.08	.04
184	Alvin Walton	.25	.15	.09
185	Ernest Byner	.25	.15	.09
186	Markus Koch	.25	.15	.09
187	Art Monk	.25	.15	.09
188	Ed Simmons	.25	.15	.09
189	Bobby Wilson **RC**	.10	.08	.04
190	Charles Mann	.25	.15	.09
191	Darrell Green	.25	.15	.09
192	Mark Rypien	.15	.11	.06
193	Ricky Sanders	.25	.15	.09
194	Jim Lachey	.25	.15	.09
195	Martin Mayhew	.25	.15	.09
196	Gary Clark	.15	.11	.06
197	Wilber Marshall	.25	.15	.09
198	Darryl Grant	.25	.15	.09
199	Don Warren	.25	.15	.09
200	Ricky Ervins **RC**	.20	.15	.08
201	Eric Allen	.25	.15	.09
202	Anthony Toney	.25	.15	.09
203	Ben Smith	.25	.15	.09
204	David Alexander	.25	.15	.09
205	Jerome Brown	.25	.15	.09
206	Mike Golic	.25	.15	.09
207	Roger Ruzek	.25	.15	.09
208	Andre Waters	.25	.15	.09
209	Fred Barnett	.15	.11	.06
210	Randall Cunningham	.15	.11	.06
211	Mike Schad	.25	.15	.09
212	Reggie White	.15	.11	.06
213	Mike Bellamy	.25	.15	.09
214	Jeff Feagles **RC**	.08	.06	.03
215	Wes Hopkins	.25	.15	.09
216	Clyde Simmons	.25	.15	.09
217	Keith Byars	.25	.15	.09
218	Seth Joyner	.25	.15	.09
219	Byron Evans	.25	.15	.09
220	Keith Jackson	.15	.11	.06
221	Calvin Williams	.15	.11	.06
222	Mike Dumas	.25	.15	.09
223	Ray Childress	.25	.15	.09
224	Ernest Givins	.25	.15	.09
225	Lamar Lathon	.25	.15	.09
226	Greg Montgomery	.25	.15	.09
227	Mike Munchak	.25	.15	.09
228	Al Smith	.25	.15	.09
229	Bubba McDowell	.25	.15	.09
230	Haywood Jeffires	.15	.11	.06
231	Drew Hill	.25	.15	.09
233	Warren Moon	.25	.20	.10
234	Doug Smith **RC**	.10	.08	.04
235	Cris Dishman **RC**	.15	.11	.06
236	Teddy Garcia	.25	.15	.09
237	Richard Johnson	.25	.15	.09
238	Bruce Matthews	.25	.15	.09
239	Gerald McNeil	.25	.15	.09
240	Johnny Meads	.25	.15	.09
241	Curtis Duncan	.25	.15	.09
242	Sean Jones	.25	.15	.09
243	Lorenzo White	.10	.08	.04
244	Rob Carpenter **RC**	.12	.09	.05
245	Bruce Reimers	.25	.15	.09
246	Ickey Woods	.25	.15	.09
247	Lewis Billups	.25	.15	.09
248	Boomer Esiason	.15	.11	.06
249	Tim Krumrie	.25	.15	.09
250	David Fulcher	.25	.15	.09
251	Jim Breech	.25	.15	.09
252	Mitchell Price	.25	.15	.09
253	Carl Zander	.25	.15	.09
254	Barney Bussey **RC**	.10	.08	.04
255	Leon White	.25	.15	.09
256	Eddie Brown	.25	.15	.09
257	James Francis	.25	.15	.09
258	Harold Green	.15	.11	.06
259	Anthony Munoz	.25	.15	.09
260	James Brooks	.25	.15	.09
261	Kevin Walker **RC**	.12	.09	.05
262	Bruce Kozerski	.25	.15	.09
263	David Grant	.25	.15	.09
264	Tim McGee	.25	.15	.09
265	Rodney Holman	.25	.15	.09
266	Dan McGwire **RC**	.15	.11	.06
267	Andy Heck	.25	.15	.09
268	Dave Krieg	.25	.15	.09
269	David Wyman	.25	.15	.09
270	Robert Blackmon	.25	.15	.09
271	Grant Feasel	.25	.15	.09
272	Patrick Hunter **RC**	.12	.09	.05
273	Travis McNeal	.25	.15	.09
274	John L. Williams	.25	.15	.09
275	Tony Woods	.25	.15	.09
276	Derrick Fenner	.10	.08	.04
277	Jacob Green	.25	.15	.09
278	Brian Blades	.25	.15	.09
279	Eugene Robinson	.25	.15	.09
280	Terry Wooden	.25	.15	.09
281	Jeff Bryant	.25	.15	.09
282	Norm Johnson	.25	.15	.09
283	Joe Nash	.25	.15	.09
284	Rick Donnelly	.25	.15	.09
285	Chris Warren	.75	.60	.30
286	Tommy Kane	.25	.15	.09
287	Cortez Kennedy	.30	.25	.12
288	Ernie Mills **RC**	.15	.11	.06
289	Dermontti Dawson	.25	.15	.09
290	Tunch Ilkin	.25	.15	.09
291	Tim Worley	.25	.15	.09
293	Gary Anderson (Pit.)	.25	.15	.09
294	Chris Calloway	.25	.15	.09
295	Carnell Lake	.25	.15	.09
296	Dan Stryzinski	.25	.15	.09
297	Rod Woodson	.25	.15	.09
298	John Jackson **RC**	.10	.08	.04
299	Bubby Brister	.25	.15	.09
300	Thomas Everett	.25	.15	.09
301	Merril Hoge	.25	.15	.09
302	Eric Green	.10	.08	.04
303	Greg Lloyd	.25	.15	.09
304	Gerald Williams	.25	.15	.09
305	Bryan Hinkle	.25	.15	.09
306	Keith Willis	.25	.15	.09
307	Louis Lipps	.25	.15	.09
308	Donald Evans	.25	.15	.09
309	David Johnson	.25	.15	.09
310	Wesley Carroll **RC**	.10	.08	.04
311	Eric Martin	.25	.15	.09
312	Brett Maxie	.25	.15	.09
313	Rickey Jackson	.25	.15	.09
314	Robert Massey	.25	.15	.09
315	Pat Swilling	.25	.15	.09
316	Morten Andersen	.25	.15	.09
317	Toi Cook **RC**	.10	.08	.04
318	Sam Mills	.25	.15	.09
319	Steve Walsh	.25	.15	.09
320	Tommy Barnhardt **RC**	.10	.08	.04
321	Vince Buck	.25	.15	.09
322	Joel Hilgenberg	.25	.15	.09
323	Rueben Mayes	.25	.15	.09
325	Renaldo Turnbull	.25	.15	.09
326	Vaughan Johnson	.25	.15	.09
327	Gill Fenerty	.25	.15	.09
328	Stan Brock	.25	.15	.09
329	Dalton Hilliard	.25	.15	.09
330	Hoby Brenner	.25	.15	.09
331	Craig Heyward	.25	.15	.09
332	Jon Hand	.25	.15	.09
333	Duane Bickett	.25	.15	.09
334	Jessie Hester	.25	.15	.09
335	Rohn Stark	.25	.15	.09
336	Zefross Moss	.25	.15	.09
337	Bill Brooks	.25	.15	.09
338	Clarence Verdin	.25	.15	.09
339	Mike Prior	.25	.15	.09
340	Chip Banks	.25	.15	.09
341	Dean Biasucci	.25	.15	.09
342	Ray Donaldson	.25	.15	.09
343	Jeff Herrod	.25	.15	.09
344	Donnell Thompson	.25	.15	.09
345	Chris Goode	.25	.15	.09
346	Eugene Daniel	.25	.15	.09
347	Pat Beach	.25	.15	.09
348	Keith Taylor	.25	.15	.09
349	Jeff George	.30	.25	.12
350	Tony Siragusa **RC**	.10	.08	.04
351	Randy Dixon	.25	.15	.09
352	Albert Bentley	.25	.15	.09
353	Russell Maryland **RC**	.50	.40	.20
354	Mike Saxon	.25	.15	.09
355	Godfrey Myles	.08	.06	.03
356	Mark Stepnoski **RC**	.12	.09	.05
357	James Washington **RC**	.12	.09	.05
358	Jay Novacek	.25	.20	.10
359	Kelvin Martin	.25	.15	.09
360	Emmitt Smith	2.00	1.50	.80
361	Jim Jeffcoat	.25	.15	.09
362	Alexander Wright	.10	.08	.04
363	James Dixon	.25	.15	.09
364	Daniel Stubbs	.25	.15	.09
365	Jack Del Rio	.25	.15	.09
366	Jack Del Rio	.10	.08	.04
367	Mark Tuinei **RC**	.10	.08	.04
368	Michael Irvin	.25	.20	.10
369	John Gesek **RC**	.10	.08	.04
370	Ken Willis	.25	.15	.09
371	Troy Aikman	1.00	.70	.40
372	Jimmie Jones	.25	.15	.09
373	Nate Newton	.25	.15	.09
374	Issiac Holt	.25	.15	.09
375	Alvin Harper **RC**	.30	.25	.12
376	Todd Kalis	.25	.15	.09
377	Wade Wilson	.25	.15	.09
378	Joey Browner	.25	.15	.09
379	Chris Doleman	.25	.15	.09
380	Hassan Jones	.25	.15	.09
381	Henry Thomas	.25	.15	.09
382	Darrell Fullington	.25	.15	.09
383	Steve Jordan	.25	.15	.09
384	Gary Zimmerman	.25	.15	.09
385	Ray Berry	.25	.15	.09
386	Cris Carter	.25	.15	.09
387	Mike Merriweather	.25	.15	.09
388	Carl Lee	.25	.15	.09
389	Keith Millard	.25	.15	.09
390	Reggie Rutland	.25	.15	.09
391	Anthony Carter	.25	.15	.09
392	Mark Dusbabek	.25	.15	.09
393	Kirk Lowerdermilk	.25	.15	.09
394	Al Noga	.25	.15	.09
395	Herschel Walker	.25	.15	.09
396	Randall McDaniel	.25	.15	.09
397	Herman Moore **RC**	2.00	1.50	.80
398	John Jackson, Eddie Murray	.25	.15	.09
399	Lomas Brown	.25	.15	.09
400	Marc Spindler	.25	.15	.09
401	Bennie Blades	.25	.15	.09
402	Kevin Glover	.25	.15	.09
403	Aubrey Matthews **RC**	.10	.08	.04
404	Michael Cofer (Det.)	.25	.15	.09
405	Robert Clark	.25	.15	.09
406	Eric Clark	.25	.15	.09
407	William White	.25	.15	.09
408	Rodney Peete	.25	.15	.09
409	Mel Gray	.25	.15	.09
410	Jim Arnold	.25	.15	.09
411	Jeff Campbell	.25	.15	.09
412	Chris Spielman	.25	.15	.09
413	Jerry Ball	.25	.15	.09
414	Dan Owens	.25	.15	.09
415	Barry Sanders	1.25	.90	.50
416	Andre Ware	.12	.09	.05
417	Stanley Richard **RC**	.30	.25	.12
418	Gill Byrd	.25	.15	.09
419	John Kidd	.25	.15	.09
420	Sam Seale	.25	.15	.09
421	Gary Plummer	.25	.15	.09
422	Anthony Miller	.25	.15	.09
423	Ronnie Harmon	.25	.15	.09
424	Frank Cornish	.25	.15	.09
425	Marion Butts	.25	.15	.09
426	Leo Goeas	.25	.15	.09
427	Junior Seau	.30	.25	.12
428	Courtney Hall	.25	.15	.09
429	Leslie O'Neal	.25	.15	.09
430	Martin Bayless	.25	.15	.09
431	John Carney	.25	.15	.09
432	Lee Williams	.25	.15	.09
433	Arthur Cox	.25	.15	.09
434	Burt Grossman	.25	.15	.09
435	Nate Lewis **RC**	.25	.20	.10
436	Rod Bernstine	.25	.15	.09
437	Henry Rolling **RC**	.10	.08	.04
438	Billy Joe Tolliver	.25	.15	.09
439	Vince Clark **RC**	.10	.08	.04
440	Brian Noble	.25	.15	.09
441	Charles Wilson	.25	.15	.09
442	Don Majkowski	.25	.15	.09
443	Tim Harris	.25	.15	.09
444	Scott Stephen	.25	.15	.09
445	Perry Kemp	.25	.15	.09
446	Darrell Thompson	.15	.11	.06
447	Chris Jacke	.25	.15	.09
448	Mark Murphy	.25	.15	.09
449	Ed West	.25	.15	.09
450	LeRoy Butler	.25	.15	.09
451	Keith Woodside	.25	.15	.09
452	Tony Bennett	.25	.15	.09
453	Mark Lee	.25	.15	.09
454	James Campen **RC**	.08	.06	.03
455	Robert Brown	.25	.15	.09
456	Sterling Sharpe	.10	.08	.04
457	Tony Mandarich	.08	.06	.03
458	Johnny Holland	.25	.15	.09
459	Matt Brock **RC**	.12	.09	.05

460	Esera Tuaolo	.08	.06	.03
461	Freeman McNeil	.25	.15	.09
462	Terance Mathis	.10	.08	.04
463	Rob Moore	.20	.15	.08
464	Darrell Davis	.25	.15	.09
465	Chris Burkett	.25	.15	.09
466	Jeff Criswell	.25	.15	.09
467	Tony Stargell	.25	.15	.09
468	Ken O'Brien	.25	.15	.09
469	Erik McMillan	.25	.15	.09
470	Jeff Lageman	.25	.15	.09
471	Pat Leahy	.25	.15	.09
472	Dennis Byrd	.25	.15	.09
473	Jim Sweeney	.25	.15	.09
474	Brad Baxter	.15	.11	.06
475	Joe Kelly	.25	.15	.09
476	Al Toon	.25	.15	.09
477	Joe Prokop	.25	.15	.09
478	Mark Boyer	.25	.15	.09
479	Kyle Clifton	.25	.15	.09
480	James Hasty	.25	.15	.09
481	Browning Nagle **RC**	.25	.20	.10
482	Gary Anderson (T.B.)	.25	.15	.09
483	Mark Carrier (T.B.)	.25	.15	.09
484	Ricky Reynolds	.25	.15	.09
485	Bruce Hill	.25	.15	.09
486	Steve Christie	.25	.15	.09
487	Paul Gruber	.25	.15	.09
488	Jess Anderson	.25	.15	.09
489	Reggie Cobb	.30	.25	.12
490	Harry Hamilton	.25	.15	.09
491	Vinny Testaverde	.10	.08	.04
492	Mark Royals **RC**	.08	.06	.03
493	Keith McCants	.25	.15	.09
494	Ron Hall	.25	.15	.09
495	Ian Beckles	.25	.15	.09
496	Mark Robinson	.25	.15	.09
497	Reuben Davis	.25	.15	.09
498	Wayne Haddix	.25	.15	.09
499	Kevin Murphy	.25	.15	.09
500	Eugene Marve	.25	.15	.09
501	Broderick Thomas	.25	.15	.09
502	Eric Swann **RC**	.20	.15	.08
503	Ernie Jones	.25	.15	.09
504	Rich Camarillo	.25	.15	.09
505	Tim McDonald	.25	.15	.09
506	Freddie Joe Nunn	.25	.15	.09
507	Tim Jorden **RC**	.08	.06	.03
508	Johnny Johnson	.30	.25	.12
509	Eric Hill	.25	.15	.09
510	Derek Kennard	.25	.15	.09
511	Ricky Proehl	.12	.09	.05
512	Bill Lewis	.25	.15	.09
513	Roy Green	.25	.15	.09
514	Anthony Bell	.25	.15	.09
515	Timm Rosenbach	.25	.15	.09
516	Jim Wahler **RC**	.10	.08	.04
517	Anthony Thompson	.25	.15	.09
518	Ken Harvey	.25	.15	.09
519	Luis Sharpe	.25	.15	.09
520	Walter Reeves	.25	.15	.09
521	Lonnie Young	.25	.15	.09
522	Rod Saddler	.25	.15	.09
523	Todd Lyght **RC**	.15	.11	.06
524	Alvin Wright	.25	.15	.09
525	Flipper Anderson	.25	.15	.09
526	Jackie Slater	.25	.15	.09
527	Damone Johnson	.25	.15	.09
528	Cleveland Gary	.25	.15	.09
529	Mike Piel	.25	.15	.09
530	Buford McGee	.25	.15	.09
531	Michael Stewart	.25	.15	.09
532	Jim Everett	.25	.15	.09
533	Mike Wilcher	.25	.15	.09
534	Irv Pankey	.25	.15	.09
535	Bern Brostek	.25	.15	.09
536	Henry Ellard	.25	.15	.09
537	Doug Smith	.25	.15	.09
538	Larry Kelm	.25	.15	.09
539	Pat Terrell	.25	.15	.09
541	Jerry Gray	.25	.15	.09
542	Kevin Greene	.25	.15	.09
543	Duval Love **RC**	.10	.08	.04
544	Frank Stams	.25	.15	.09
545	Mike Croel **RC**	.20	.15	.08
546	Mark Jackson	.25	.15	.09
547	Greg Kragen	.25	.15	.09
548	Karl Mecklenburg	.25	.15	.09
549	Simon Fletcher	.25	.15	.09
550	Bobby Humphrey	.25	.15	.09
551	Ken Lanier	.25	.15	.09
552	Vance Johnson	.25	.15	.09
553	Ron Holmes	.25	.15	.09
554	John Elway	.40	.30	.15
555	Melvin Bratton	.25	.15	.09
556	Dennis Smith	.25	.15	.09
557	Ricky Nattiel	.25	.15	.09
558	Clarence Kay	.25	.15	.09

559	Michael Brooks	.25	.15	.09
560	Mike Horan	.25	.15	.09
561	Warren Powers	.25	.15	.09
562	Keith Karts	.25	.15	.09
563	Shannon Sharpe	.10	.08	.04
564	Wymon Henderson	.25	.15	.09
565	Steve Atwater	.25	.15	.09
566	David Treadwell	.25	.15	.09
567	Bruce Pickens **RC**	.10	.08	.04
568	Jessie Tuggle	.25	.15	.09
569	Chris Hinton	.25	.15	.09
570	Keith Jones	.25	.15	.09
571	Bill Fralic	.25	.15	.09
572	Mike Rozier	.25	.15	.09
573	Scott Fulhage	.25	.15	.09
574	Floyd Dixon	.25	.15	.09
575	Andre Rison	.25	.20	.10
576	Darion Conner	.25	.15	.09
577	Brian Jordan	.15	.11	.06
578	Michael Haynes	.35	.25	.14
579	Oliver Barnett	.25	.15	.09
580	Shawn Collins	.25	.15	.09
581	Tim Green	.25	.15	.09
582	Deion Sanders	.35	.25	.14
583	Mike Kenn	.25	.15	.09
584	Mike Gann	.25	.15	.09
585	Chris Miller	.25	.15	.09
586	Tory Epps	.25	.15	.09
587	Steve Broussard	.25	.15	.09
588	Gary Wilkins	.25	.15	.09
589	Eric Turner **RC**	.30	.25	.12
590	Thane Gash	.25	.15	.09
591	Clay Matthews	.25	.15	.09
592	Mike Johnson	.25	.15	.09
593	Raymond Clayborn	.25	.15	.09
594	Leroy Hoard	.10	.08	.04
595	Reggie Langhorne	.25	.15	.09
596	Mike Baab	.25	.15	.09
597	Anthony Pleasant	.25	.15	.09
598	David Grayson	.25	.15	.09
599	Rob Burnett **RC**	.12	.09	.05
600	Frank Minnifield	.25	.15	.09
601	Gregg Rakoczy	.25	.15	.09
602	Eric Metcalf	.25	.15	.09
603	Paul Farren	.25	.15	.09
604	Brian Brennan	.25	.15	.09
605	Tony Jones	.25	.15	.09
606	Stephen Braggs	.25	.15	.09
607	Kevin Mack	.25	.15	.09
608	Pat Harlow **RC**	.10	.08	.04
609	Marv Cook	.25	.15	.09
610	John Stephens	.25	.15	.09
611	Ed Reynolds	.25	.15	.09
612	Tim Goad	.25	.15	.09
613	Chris Singleton	.25	.15	.09
614	Bruce Armstrong	.25	.15	.09
615	Tom Hodson	.25	.15	.09
616	Sammy Martin	.25	.15	.09
617	Andre Tippett	.25	.15	.09
618	Johnny Rembert	.25	.15	.09
619	Maurice Hurst	.25	.15	.09
620	Vincent Brown	.25	.15	.09
621	Ray Agnew	.25	.15	.09
622	Ronnie Lippett	.25	.15	.09
623	Greg McMurtry	.25	.15	.09
624	Brent Williams	.25	.15	.09
625	Jason Staurovsky	.25	.15	.09
626	Marvin Allen	.25	.15	.09
627	Hart Lee Dykes	.25	.15	.09
628	**Falcons Team**	.25	.15	.09
629	**Bills Team**	.25	.15	.09
630	**Bears Team**	.25	.15	.09
631	**Bengals Team**	.25	.15	.09
632	**Browns Team**	.25	.15	.09
633	**Cowboys Team**	.25	.15	.09
634	**Broncos Team**	.25	.15	.09
635	**Lions Team**	.25	.15	.09
636	**Packers Team**	.25	.15	.09
637	**Oilers Team**	.10	.08	.04
638	**Colts Team**	.15	.11	.06
639	**Chiefs Team**	.25	.15	.09
640	Raiders Team (Tom Newberry)	.25	.15	.09
641	**Rams Team**	.25	.15	.09
642	**Dolphins Team**	.25	.15	.09
643	**Vikings Team**	.25	.15	.09
644	**Patriots Team**	.25	.15	.09
645	**Saints Team**	.25	.15	.09
646	**Giants Team**	.25	.15	.09
647	**Jets Team**	.25	.15	.09
648	**Eagles Team**	.08	.06	.03
649	**Cardinals Team**	.25	.15	.09
650	**Steelers Team**	.25	.15	.09
651	**Chargers Team**	.25	.15	.09
652	**49ers Team**	.25	.15	.09
653	**Seahawks Team**	.25	.15	.09
654	**Buccaneers Team**	.25	.15	.09
655	**Redskins Team**	.25	.15	.09

656	**Checklist**	.25	.15	.09
657	**Checklist**	.25	.15	.09
658	**Checklist**	.25	.15	.09
659	**Checklist**	.25	.15	.09
660	**Checklist**	.25	.15	.09

1991 Topps 1000 Yard Club

The 18 players featured in this insert set were receivers and running backs who gained more than 1,000 yards during the 1990 NFL season. Each card front has a color action photo, with the "1000 Yard Club" logo at the top. The photo has a red border at the top, while the player's name is at the bottom in an orange stripe. There is no border at the bottom or on the right, but the left side of the card has a red and purple border. The card back gives the player's game-by-game totals in blue and pink against a white background. A card number is in the upper right corner.

	NM/M	NM	E
Complete Set (18):	6.00	4.50	2.50
Common Player:	.25	.20	.10

1	Jerry Rice	1.50	1.25	.60
2	Barry Sanders	1.75	1.25	.70
3	Thurman Thomas	.75	.60	.30
4	Henry Ellard	.25	.20	.10
5	Marion Butts	.75	.60	.30
6	Earnest Byner	.25	.20	.10
7	Andre Rison	.50	.40	.20
8	Bobby Humphrey	.25	.20	.10
9	Gary Clark	.35	.25	.14
10	Sterling Sharpe	1.25	.90	.50
11	Flipper Anderson	.25	.20	.10
12	Neal Anderson	.35	.25	.14
13	Haywood Jeffires	.45	.35	.20
14	Stephone Paige	.35	.25	.14
15	Drew Hill	.25	.20	.10
16	Barry Word	.35	.25	.14
17	Anthony Carter	.30	.25	.12
18	James Brooks	.25	.20	.10

1977 Touchdown Club

These 50 black-and-white cards were issued as a set in 1977 to honor several Hall-of-Fame caliber retired players. Each front has photo of the player in uniform, with his name below the photo. A black frame borders the photo and his name. The card back has the player's name and number at the top, with his position listed just below them. A brief career summary, listing the player's main honors and accomplishments, is also given. "Touchdown, 1977" is written at the bottom. All of the information on the back is contained within a black box. The set was designed for collectors who wanted the players' autographs; a list of their home addresses was included with the set.

	NM	E	VG
Complete Set (50):	50.00	25.00	15.00
Common Player:	.75	.40	.25

1	Harold "Red" Grange	5.00	2.50	1.50
2	George Halas	2.00	1.00	.60
3	Benny Friedman	.75	.40	.25
4	Cliff Battles	1.00	.50	.30
5	Mike Michalske	.75	.40	.25
6	George McAfee	1.00	.50	.30
7	Beattle Feathers	1.25	.60	.40
8	Ernie Caddel	.75	.40	.25
9	George Musso	1.00	.50	.30
10	Sid Luckman	2.25	1.25	.70
11	Cecil Isbell	.75	.40	.25
12	Bronko Nagurski	3.00	1.50	.90
13	Hunk Anderson	.80	.40	.25
14	Dick Farman	.80	.40	.25
15	Aldo Forte	.90	.45	.25
16	Ki Aldrich	.80	.40	.25
17	Jim Lee Howell	.75	.40	.25
18	Ray Flaherty	.75	.40	.25
19	Hampton Pool	.80	.40	.25
20	Alex Wojciechowicz	1.00	.50	.30
21	Bill Osmanski	.75	.40	.25

22	Hank Soar	.75	.40	.25
23	Dutch Clark	1.00	.50	.30
24	Joe Muha	.75	.40	.25
25	Don Hutson	1.50	.70	.45
26	Jim Poole	.85	.45	.25
27	Charley Malone	.75	.40	.25
28	Charlie Trippi	1.25	.60	.40
29	Andy Farkas	.75	.40	.25
30	Clarke Hinkle	1.00	.50	.30
31	Gary Famiglietti	.75	.40	.25
32	Bulldog Turner	1.25	.60	.40
33	Sammy Baugh	3.00	1.50	.90
34	Pat Harder	.75	.40	.25
35	Tuffy Leemans	1.00	.50	.30
36	Ken Strong	1.00	.50	.30
37	Barney Poole	.75	.40	.25
38	Bruiser Kinard	1.00	.50	.30
39	Buford Ray	.75	.40	.25
40	Ace Parker	1.25	.60	.40
41	Buddy Parker	.75	.40	.25
42	Mel Hein	1.00	.50	.30
43	Ed Danowski	.75	.40	.25
44	Bill Dudley	1.25	.60	.40
45	Paul Stenn	.80	.40	.25
46	George Connor	1.00	.50	.30
47	George Connor	.75	.40	.25
48	Armand Niccolai	.75	.40	.25
49	Tony Canadeo	1.25	.60	.40
50	Bill Willis	1.50	.70	.45

1989 TV-4NFL Quarterbacks

The 20-card, 2-7/16" x 3-1/8" set features borderless portrait drawings by artist J.C. Ford. The card backs contain career highlights. The set was issued by a television station in Great Britain and were distributed to promote American football in the U.K.

		NM/M	NM	E
	Complete Set (20):	25.00	18.50	10.00
	Common Player:	.75	.60	.30
1	Dutch Clark	.75	.60	.30
2	Sammy Baugh	1.50	1.25	.60
3	Bob Waterfield	.75	.60	.30
4	Sid Luckman	.75	.60	.30
5	Otto Graham	1.00	.70	.40
6	Bobby Layne	.75	.60	.30
7	Norm Van Brocklin	.75	.60	.30
8	George Blanda	.75	.60	.30
9	Y.A. Tittle	1.00	.70	.40
10	Johnny Unitas	3.00	2.25	1.25
11	Bart Starr	1.25	.90	.50
12	Sonny Jurgensen	1.25	.90	.50
13	Joe Namath	2.50	2.00	1.00
14	Fran Tarkenton	1.50	1.25	.60
15	Roger Staubach	2.50	2.00	1.00
16	Terry Bradshaw	3.00	2.25	1.25
17	Dan Fouts	1.25	.90	.50
18	Joe Montana	5.00	3.75	2.00
19	John Elway	2.00	1.50	.80
20	Dan Marino	5.00	3.75	2.00

U

1991 UNLV

		NM/M	NM	E
	Complete Set (12):	8.00	6.00	3.25
	Common Player:	.75	.60	.30
1	**Cheerleaders and Songleaders**	.75	.60	.30
2	**Gang Tackle**	.75	.60	.30
3	Instant Offense (Hernandez Cooper)	.75	.60	.30
4	**No Escape**	.75	.60	.30
5	**On The Move**	.75	.60	.30
6	**Punching It In**	.75	.60	.30
7	Ready To Fire (Derek Stott)	.75	.60	.30
8	**Rebel Fever**	.75	.60	.30
9	**Rebel Sack**	.75	.60	.30
10	Silver Bowl (Sam Boyd)	.75	.60	.30
11	Jim Strong (CO)	.75	.60	.30
12	**Team Photo**	1.00	.70	.40

1991 Upper Deck

Issued in August, Upper Deck's premier football set was issued on foil packs. Upper Deck also randomly issued 2,500 autographed Joe Montana Heroes of Football cards. The set includes many of the elements from the baseball and hockey sets, including a "Star Rookies" subset. (Key: SR - star rookie, SL - season leader)

		NM/M	NM	E
	Complete Set (700):	15.00	11.00	6.00
	Complete Lo Series (500):	10.00	7.50	4.00
	Complete Hi Series (200):	5.00	3.75	2.00
	Complete Factory Set (700):	20.00	15.00	8.00
	Common Player:	.05	.04	.02
	Low or High Pack (12):	.50		
	Low or High Wax Box (36):	15.00		
1	**Star Rookie Checklist**	.10	.08	.04
2	Eric Bieniemy RC (SR)	.15	.11	.06
3	Mike Dumas (SR)	.05	.04	.02
4	Mike Croel RC (SR)	.15	.11	.06
5	Russell Maryland RC (SR)	.50	.40	.20
6	Charles McRae RC (SR)	.10	.08	.04
7	Dan McGwire RC (SR)	.10	.08	.04
8	Mike Pritchard RC (SR)	.35	.25	.14
9	Ricky Watters RC (SR)	1.75	1.25	.70
10	Chris Zorich RC (SR)	.30	.25	.12
11	Browning Nagle RC (SR)	.20	.15	.08
12	Wesley Carroll RC (SR)	.10	.08	.04
13	Brett Favre RC (SR)	15.00	11.00	6.00
14	Rob Carpenter RC (SR)	.15	.11	.06
15	Eric Swann RC (SR)	.25	.20	.10
16	Stanley Richard RC	.35	.25	.14
17	Herman Moore RC (SR)	2.00	1.50	.80
18	Todd Marinovich RC (SR)	.10	.08	.04
19	Aaron Craver (SR)	.10	.08	.04
20	Chuck Webb (SR)	.05	.04	.02
21	Todd Lyght RC (SR)	.10	.08	.04
22	Greg Lewis RC (SR)	.10	.08	.04
23	Eric Turner RC (SR)	.20	.15	.08
24	Alvin Harper RC (SR)	.30	.25	.12
25	Jarrod Bunch RC (SR)	.10	.08	.04
26	Bruce Pickens RC (SR)	.10	.08	.04
27	Harvey Williams RC (SR)	.50	.40	.20
28	Randal Hill RC (SR)	.40	.30	.15
29	Nick Bell RC (SR)	.15	.11	.06
30	Jim Everett, Henry Ellard	.05	.04	.02
31	Randall Cunningham, Keith Jackson	.10	.08	.04
32	Steve DeBerg, Stephone Paige	.05	.04	.02
33	Warren Moon, Drew Hill	.10	.08	.04
34	Dan Marino, Mark Clayton	.20	.15	.08
35	Montana, Rice	.40	.30	.15
36	Percy Snow	.05	.04	.02
37	Kelvin Martin	.05	.04	.02
38	Scott Case	.05	.04	.02
39	John Gesek RC	.10	.08	.04
40	Barry Word RC	.15	.11	.06
41	Cornelius Bennett	.05	.04	.02
42	Mike Kenn	.05	.04	.02
43	Andre Reed	.15	.11	.06
44	Bobby Hebert	.05	.04	.02
45	William Perry	.05	.04	.02
46	Dennis Byrd	.05	.04	.02
47	Martin Mayhew	.05	.04	.02
48	Issiac Holt	.05	.04	.02
49	William White	.05	.04	.02
50	JoJo Townsell	.05	.04	.02
51	Jarvis Williams	.05	.04	.02
52	Joey Browner	.05	.04	.02
53	Pat Terrell	.05	.04	.02
54	Joe Montana	1.00	.70	.40
55	Jeff Jerrod	.05	.04	.02
56	Cris Carter	.05	.04	.02
57	Jerry Rice	.75	.60	.30
58	Brett Perriman	.05	.04	.02
59	Kevin Fagen	.05	.04	.02
60	Wayne Haddix	.05	.04	.02

61	Tommy Kane	.05	.04	.02
62	Pat Beach	.05	.04	.02
63	Jeff Lageman	.05	.04	.02
64	Hassan Jones	.05	.04	.02
65	Bennie Blades	.05	.04	.02
66	Tim McGee	.05	.04	.02
67	Robert Blackmon	.05	.04	.02
68	Fred Stokes RC	.20	.15	.08
69	Barney Bussey RC	.10	.08	.04
70	Eric Metcalf	.05	.04	.02
71	Mark Kelso	.05	.04	.02
72	Bears Checklist (Neal Anderson)	.05	.04	.02
73	Bengals Checklist (Boomer Esiason)	.05	.04	.02
74	Bills Checklist (Thurman Thomas)	.25	.20	.10
75	Broncos Checklist (John Elway)	.15	.11	.06
76	Browns Checklist (Eric Metcalf)	.05	.04	.02
77	Buccaneers Checklist (Vinny Testaverde)	.05	.04	.02
78	Cardinals Checklist (Johnny Johnson)	.10	.08	.04
79	Chargers Checklist (Anthony Miller)	.05	.04	.02
80	Chiefs Checklist (Derrick Thomas)	.12	.09	.05
81	Colts Checklist (Jeff George)	.12	.09	.05
82	Cowboys Checklist (Troy Aikman)	.65	.50	.25
83	Dolphins Checklist (Dan Marino)	.30	.25	.12
84	Eagles Checklist (Randall Cunningham)	.10	.08	.04
85	Falcons Checklist (Deion Sanders)	.12	.09	.05
86	49ers Checklist (Jerry Rice)	.40	.30	.15
87	Giants Checklist (Lawrence Taylor)	.08	.06	.03
88	Jets Checklist (Al Toon)	.05	.04	.02
89	Lions Checklist (Barry Sanders)	.50	.40	.20
90	Oilers Checklist (Warren Moon)	.10	.08	.04
91	Packers Checklist (Sterling Sharpe)	.20	.15	.08
92	Patriots Checklist (Andre Tippett)	.05	.04	.02
93	Rams Checklist (Jim Everett)	.05	.04	.02
94	Raiders Checklist (Bo Jackson)	.25	.20	.10
95	Redskins Checklist (Art Monk)	.05	.04	.02
96	Saints Checklist (Morten Andersen)	.05	.04	.02
97	Seahawks Checklist (John L. Williams)	.05	.04	.02
98	Steelers Checklist (Rod Woodson)	.05	.04	.02
99	Vikings Checklist (Herschel Walker)	.05	.04	.02
100	**Checklist**	.05	.04	.02
101	Steve Young	.75	.60	.30
102	Jim Lachey	.05	.04	.02
103	Tom Rathman	.05	.04	.02
104	Earnest Byner	.05	.04	.02
105	Karl Mecklenburg	.05	.04	.02
106	Wes Hopkins	.05	.04	.02
107	Michael Irvin	.20	.15	.08
108	Burt Grossman	.05	.04	.02
109	Jay Novacek	.25	.20	.10
110	Ben Smith	.05	.04	.02
111	Rod Woodson	.05	.04	.02
112	Ernie Jones	.05	.04	.02
113	Bryan Hinkle	.05	.04	.02
114	Vai Sikahema	.05	.04	.02
115	Bubby Brister	.05	.04	.02
116	Brian Blades	.05	.04	.02
117	Don Majkowski	.05	.04	.02
118	Rod Bernstine	.05	.04	.02
119	Brian Noble	.05	.04	.02
120	Eugene Robinson	.05	.04	.02
121	John Taylor	.12	.09	.05
122	Vance Johnson	.05	.04	.02
123	Art Monk	.05	.04	.02
124	John Elway	.35	.25	.14
125	Dexter Carter	.05	.04	.02
126	Anthony Miller	.05	.04	.02
127	Keith Jackson	.15	.11	.06
128	Albert Lewis	.05	.04	.02
129	Bill Ray Smith	.05	.04	.02
130	Clyde Simmons	.05	.04	.02

#	Player				#	Player				#	Player			
131	Merril Hoge	.05	.04	.02	228	Vince Buck	.05	.04	.02	326	Carl Lee	.05	.04	.02
132	Ricky Proehl	.12	.09	.05	229	Mike Singletary	.05	.04	.02	327	Ken O'Brien	.05	.04	.02
133	Tim McDonald	.05	.04	.02	230	Rueben Mayes	.05	.04	.02	328	Dermontti Dawson	.05	.04	.02
134	Louis Lipps	.05	.04	.02	231	Mark Carrier (T.B.)	.05	.04	.02	329	Brad Baxter	.15	.11	.06
135	Ken Harvey	.05	.04	.02	232	Tony Mandarich	.05	.04	.02	330	Chris Doleman	.05	.04	.02
136	Sterling Sharpe	.20	.15	.08	233	Al Toon	.05	.04	.02	331	Louis Oliver	.05	.04	.02
137	Gill Byrd	.05	.04	.02	234	Renaldo Turnbull	.05	.04	.02	332	Frank Stams	.05	.04	.02
138	Tim Harris	.05	.04	.02	235	Broderick Thomas	.05	.04	.02	333	Mike Munchak	.05	.04	.02
139	Derrick Fenner	.10	.08	.04	236	Anthony Carter	.05	.04	.02	334	Fred Strickland	.05	.04	.02
140	Johnny Holland	.05	.04	.02	237	Flipper Anderson	.05	.04	.02	335	Mark Duper	.05	.04	.02
141	Ricky Sanders	.05	.04	.02	238	Jerry Robinson	.05	.04	.02	336	Jacob Green	.05	.04	.02
142	Bobby Humphrey	.05	.04	.02	239	Vince Newsome	.05	.04	.02	337	Tony Paige	.05	.04	.02
143	Roger Craig	.05	.04	.02	240	Keith Millard	.05	.04	.02	338	Jeff Bryant	.05	.04	.02
144	Steve Atwater	.05	.04	.02	241	Reggie Langhorne	.05	.04	.02	339	Lemuel Stinson	.05	.04	.02
145	Ickey Woods	.05	.04	.02	242	James Francis	.05	.04	.02	340	David Wyman	.05	.04	.02
146	Randall Cunningham	.15	.11	.06	243	Felix Wright	.05	.04	.02	341	Lee Williams	.05	.04	.02
147	Marion Butts	.05	.04	.02	244	Neal Anderson	.10	.08	.04	342	Trace Armstrong	.05	.04	.02
148	Reggie White	.15	.11	.06	245	Boomer Esiason	.15	.11	.06	343	Junior Seau	.30	.25	.12
149	Ronnie Harmon	.05	.04	.02	246	Pat Swilling	.05	.04	.02	344	John Roper	.05	.04	.02
150	Mike Saxon	.05	.04	.02	247	Richard Dent	.05	.04	.02	345	Jeff George	.30	.25	.12
151	Greg Townsend	.05	.04	.02	248	Craig Heyward	.05	.04	.02	346	Herschel Walker	.05	.04	.02
152	Troy Aikman	1.00	.70	.40	249	Ron Morris	.05	.04	.02	347	Sam Clancy	.05	.04	.02
153	Shane Conlan	.05	.04	.02	250	Eric Mann	.05	.04	.02	348	Steve Jordan	.05	.04	.02
154	Deion Sanders	.25	.20	.10	251	Jim Jensen	.05	.04	.02	349	Nate Odomes	.05	.04	.02
155	Bo Jackson	.35	.25	.14	252	Anthony Toney	.05	.04	.02	350	Martin Bayless	.05	.04	.02
156	Jeff Hostetler	.20	.15	.08	253	Sammie Smith	.05	.04	.02	351	Brent Jones	.05	.04	.02
157	Albert Bentley	.05	.04	.02	254	Calvin Williams	.20	.15	.08	352	Ray Agnew	.05	.04	.02
158	James Williams	.05	.04	.02	255	Dan Marino	.75	.60	.30	353	Charles Haley	.05	.04	.02
159	Bill Brooks	.05	.04	.02	256	Warren Moon	.20	.15	.08	354	Andre Tippett	.05	.04	.02
160	Nick Lowery	.05	.04	.02	257	Tommie Agee	.05	.04	.02	355	Ronnie Lott	.10	.08	.04
161	Ottis Anderson	.05	.04	.02	258	Haywood Jeffires	.25	.20	.10	356	Thurman Thomas	.50	.40	.20
162	Kevin Greene	.05	.04	.02	259	Eugene Lockhart	.05	.04	.02	357	Fred Barnett	.15	.11	.06
163	Neil Smith	.05	.04	.02	260	Drew Hill	.05	.04	.02	358	James Lofton	.05	.04	.02
164	Jim Everett	.05	.04	.02	261	Vinny Testaverde	.10	.08	.04	359	William Frizzell RC	.10	.08	.04
165	Derrick Thomas	.25	.20	.10	262	Jim Arnold	.05	.04	.02	360	Keith McKeller	.05	.04	.02
166	John L. Williams	.05	.04	.02	263	Steve Christie	.05	.04	.02	361	Rodney Holman	.05	.04	.02
167	Timm Rosenbach	.05	.04	.02	264	Chris Spielman	.05	.04	.02	362	Henry Ellard	.05	.04	.02
168	Leslie O'Neal	.05	.04	.02	265	Reggie Cobb	.25	.20	.10	363	David Fulcher	.05	.04	.02
169	Clarence Verdin	.05	.04	.02	266	John Stephens	.05	.04	.02	364	Jerry Gray	.05	.04	.02
170	Dave Krieg	.05	.04	.02	267	Jay Hilgenberg	.05	.04	.02	365	James Brooks	.05	.04	.02
171	Steve Broussard	.05	.04	.02	268	Brent Williams	.05	.04	.02	366	Tony Stargell	.05	.04	.02
172	Emmitt Smith	2.00	1.50	.80	269	Rodney Hampton	.75	.60	.30	367	Keith McCants	.05	.04	.02
173	Andre Rison	.25	.20	.10	270	Irving Fryar	.05	.04	.02	368	Lewis Billups	.05	.04	.02
174	Bruce Smith	.05	.04	.02	271	Terry McDaniel	.05	.04	.02	369	Ervin Randle	.05	.04	.02
175	Mark Clayton	.05	.04	.02	272	Reggie Roby	.05	.04	.02	370	Pat Leahy	.05	.04	.02
176	Christian Okoye	.05	.04	.02	273	Allen Pinkett	.05	.04	.02	371	Bruce Armstrong	.05	.04	.02
177	Duane Bickett	.05	.04	.02	274	Tim McKyer	.05	.04	.02	372	Steve DeBerg	.05	.04	.02
178	Stephone Paige	.05	.04	.02	275	Bob Golic	.05	.04	.02	373	Guy McIntyre	.05	.04	.02
179	Fredd Young	.05	.04	.02	276	Wilber Marshall	.05	.04	.02	374	Deron Cherry	.05	.04	.02
180	Mervyn Fernandez	.05	.04	.02	277	Ray Childress	.05	.04	.02	375	Fred Marion	.05	.04	.02
181	Phil Simms	.10	.08	.04	278	Charles Mann	.05	.04	.02	376	Michael Haddix	.05	.04	.02
182	Pete Holohan	.05	.04	.02	279	Cris Dishman RC	.15	.11	.06	377	Kent Hull	.05	.04	.02
183	Pepper Johnson	.05	.04	.02	280	Mark Rypien	.15	.11	.06	378	Jerry Holmes	.05	.04	.02
184	Jackie Slater	.05	.04	.02	281	Michael Cofer (Det.)	.05	.04	.02	379	Jim Richter	.05	.04	.02
185	Stephen Baker	.05	.04	.02	282	Keith Byars	.05	.04	.02	380	Ed West	.05	.04	.02
186	Frank Cornish	.05	.04	.02	283	Mike Rozier	.05	.04	.02	381	Richmond Webb	.05	.04	.02
187	Dave Waymer	.05	.04	.02	284	Seth Joyner	.05	.04	.02	382	Mark Jackson	.05	.04	.02
188	Terance Mathis	.10	.08	.04	285	Jessie Tuggle	.05	.04	.02	383	Tom Newberry	.05	.04	.02
189	Darryl Talley	.05	.04	.02	286	Mark Bavaro	.05	.04	.02	384	Ricky Nattiel	.05	.04	.02
190	James Hasty	.05	.04	.02	287	Eddie Anderson	.05	.04	.02	385	Keith Sims	.05	.04	.02
191	Jay Schroeder	.05	.04	.02	288	Sean Landeta	.05	.04	.02	386	Ron Hall	.05	.04	.02
192	Kenneth Davis	.05	.04	.02	289	Howie Long	.12	.09	.05	387	Ken Norton	.05	.04	.02
193	Chris Miller	.05	.04	.02	290	Reyna Thompson	.05	.04	.02	388	Paul Gruber	.05	.04	.02
194	Scott Davis	.05	.04	.02	291	Ferrell Edmunds	.05	.04	.02	389	Danny Stubbs	.05	.04	.02
195	Tim Green	.05	.04	.02	292	Willie Gault	.05	.04	.02	390	Ian Beckles	.05	.04	.02
196	Dan Saleaumua	.05	.04	.02	293	John Offerdahl	.05	.04	.02	391	Hoby Brenner	.05	.04	.02
197	Rohn Stark	.05	.04	.02	294	Tim Brown	.12	.09	.05	392	Tory Epps	.05	.04	.02
198	John Alt	.05	.04	.02	296	Kevin Ross	.05	.04	.02	393	Sam Mills	.05	.04	.02
199	Steve Tasker	.05	.04	.02	297	Lorenzo White	.10	.08	.04	394	Chris Hinton	.05	.04	.02
200	**Checklist**	.05	.04	.02	298	Dino Hackett	.05	.04	.02	395	Steve Walsh	.05	.04	.02
201	Freddie Joe Nunn	.05	.04	.02	299	Curtis Duncan	.05	.04	.02	396	Simon Fletcher	.05	.04	.02
202	Jim Breech	.05	.04	.02	300	**Checklist**	.05	.04	.02	397	Tony Bennett	.05	.04	.02
203	Roy Green	.05	.04	.02	301	Andre Ware	.12	.09	.05	398	Aundray Bruce	.05	.04	.02
204	Gary Anderson (T.B.)	.05	.04	.02	302	David Little	.05	.04	.02	399	Mark Murphy	.05	.04	.02
205	Rich Camarillo	.05	.04	.02	303	Jerry Ball	.05	.04	.02	400	**Checklist**	.05	.04	.02
206	Mark Bortz	.05	.04	.02	304	Dwight Stone	.05	.04	.02	401	Barry Sanders (SL)	.50	.40	.20
207	Eddie Brown	.05	.04	.02	305	Rodney Peete	.05	.04	.02	402	Jerry Rice (SL)	.35	.25	.14
208	Brad Muster	.05	.04	.02	306	Mike Baab	.05	.04	.02	403	Warren Moon (SL)	.10	.08	.04
209	Anthony Munoz	.05	.04	.02	307	Tim Worley	.05	.04	.02	404	Derrick Thomas (SL)	.12	.09	.05
210	Dalton Hilliard	.05	.04	.02	308	Paul Farren	.05	.04	.02	405	Nick Lowery (SL)	.05	.04	.02
211	Erik McMillan	.05	.04	.02	309	Carnell Lake	.05	.04	.02	406	Mark Carrier (Chi.) (SL)	.05	.04	.02
212	Perry Kemp	.05	.04	.02	310	Clay Matthews	.05	.04	.02	407	Michael Carter	.05	.04	.02
213	Jim Thornton	.05	.04	.02	311	Alton Montgomery	.05	.04	.02	408	Chris Singleton	.05	.04	.02
214	Anthony Dilweg	.05	.04	.02	312	Ernest Givins	.05	.04	.02	409	Matt Millen	.05	.04	.02
215	Cleveland Gary	.05	.04	.02	313	Mike Horan	.05	.04	.02	410	Ronnie Lippett	.05	.04	.02
216	Leo Goeas	.05	.04	.02	314	Sean Jones	.05	.04	.02	411	E.J. Junior	.05	.04	.02
217	Mike Merriweather	.05	.04	.02	315	Leonard Smith	.05	.04	.02	412	Ray Donaldson	.05	.04	.02
218	Courtney Hall	.05	.04	.02	316	Carl Banks	.05	.04	.02	413	Keith Willis	.05	.04	.02
219	Wade Wilson	.05	.04	.02	317	Jerome Brown	.05	.04	.02	414	Jessie Hester	.05	.04	.02
220	Billy Joe Tolliver	.05	.04	.02	318	Everson Walls	.05	.04	.02	415	Jeff Cross	.05	.04	.02
221	Harold Green	.10	.08	.04	319	Ron Heller	.05	.04	.02	416	Greg Jackson	.10	.08	.04
222	Al Baker	.05	.04	.02	320	Mark Collins	.05	.04	.02	417	Alvin Walton	.05	.04	.02
223	Carl Zander	.05	.04	.02	321	Eddie Murray	.05	.04	.02	418	Bart Oates	.05	.04	.02
224	Thane Gash	.05	.04	.02	322	Jim Harbaugh	.10	.08	.04	419	Chip Lohmiller	.05	.04	.02
225	Kevin Mack	.05	.04	.02	323	Mel Gray	.05	.04	.02	420	John Elliot	.05	.04	.02
226	Morten Andersen	.05	.04	.02	324	Keith Van Horne	.05	.04	.02	421	Randall McDaniel	.05	.04	.02
227	Dennis Gentry	.05	.04	.02	325	Lomas Brown	.05	.04	.02	422	Richard Johnson	.05	.04	.02

423	Al Noga	.05	.04	.02
424	Lamar Lathon	.05	.04	.02
425	Ricky Fenney	.05	.04	.02
426	Jack Del Rio	.05	.04	.02
427	Don Mosebar	.05	.04	.02
428	Luis Sharpe	.05	.04	.02
429	Steve Wisniewski	.05	.04	.02
430	Jimmie Jones	.05	.04	.02
431	Freeman McNeil	.05	.04	.02
432	Ron Rivera	.05	.04	.02
433	Hart Lee Dykes	.05	.04	.02
434	Mark Carrier (Chi.)	.05	.04	.02
435	Rob Moore	.15	.11	.06
436	Gary Clark	.12	.09	.05
437	Heath Sherman	.10	.08	.04
438	Darrell Greem	.05	.04	.02
439	Jessie Small	.05	.04	.02
440	Monte Coleman	.05	.04	.02
441	Leonard Marshall	.05	.04	.02
442	Richard Johnson	.05	.04	.02
443	Dave Meggett	.05	.04	.02
444	Barry Sanders	1.25	.90	.50
445	Lawrence Taylor	.10	.08	.04
446	Marcus Allen	.05	.04	.02
447	Johnny Johnson	.25	.20	.10
448	Aaron Wallace	.05	.04	.02
449	Anthony Thompson	.05	.04	.02
450	Garry Lewis	.05	.04	.02
451	Andre Rison (MVP)	.12	.09	.05
452	Thurman Thomas (MVP)	.25	.20	.10
453	Neal Anderson (MVP)	.05	.04	.02
454	Boomer Esiason (MVP)	.05	.04	.02
455	Eric Metcalf (MVP)	.05	.04	.02
456	Emmitt Smith (MVP)	1.00	.70	.40
457	Bobby Humphrey (MVP)	.05	.04	.02
458	Barry Sanders (MVP)	.50	.40	.20
459	Sterling Sharpe (MVP)	.20	.15	.08
460	Warren Moon (MVP)	.10	.08	.04
461	Albert Bentley (MVP)	.05	.04	.02
462	Steve DeBerg (MVP)	.05	.04	.02
463	Greg Townsend (MVP)	.05	.04	.02
464	Henry Ellard (MVP)	.05	.04	.02
465	Dan Marino (MVP)	.40	.30	.15
466	Anthony Carter (MVP)	.05	.04	.02
467	John Stephens (MVP)	.05	.04	.02
468	Pat Swilling (MVP)	.05	.04	.02
469	Ottis Anderson (MVP)	.05	.04	.02
470	Dennis Byrd (MVP)	.05	.04	.02
471	Randall Cunningham (MVP)	.10	.08	.04
472	Johnny Johnson (MVP)	.10	.08	.04
473	Rod Woodson (MVP)	.05	.04	.02
474	Anthony Miller (MVP)	.05	.04	.02
475	Jerry Rice (MVP)	.35	.25	.14
476	John L. Williams (MVP)	.05	.04	.02
477	Wayne Haddix (MVP)	.05	.04	.02
478	Earnest Byner (MVP)	.05	.04	.02
479	Doug Widell	.05	.04	.02
480	Tommy Hodson	.05	.04	.02
481	Shawn Collins	.05	.04	.02
482	Rickey Jackson	.05	.04	.02
483	Tony Casillas	.05	.04	.02
484	Vaughan Johnson	.05	.04	.02
485	Floyd Dixon	.05	.04	.02
486	Eric Green	.12	.09	.05
487	Harry Hamilton	.05	.04	.02
488	Gary Anderson (Pit.)	.05	.04	.02
489	Bruce Hill	.05	.04	.02
490	Gerald Williams	.05	.04	.02
491	Cortez Kennedy	.30	.25	.12
492	Chet Brooks	.05	.04	.02
493	Dwayne Harper	.15	.11	.06
494	Don Griffin	.05	.04	.02
495	Andy Heck	.05	.04	.02
496	David Treadwell	.05	.04	.02
497	Irv Pankey	.05	.04	.02
498	Dennis Smith	.05	.04	.02
499	Marcus Dupree	.05	.04	.02
500	**Checklist**	.05	.04	.02
501	Wendell Davis	.10	.08	.04
502	Matt Bahr	.05	.04	.02
503	Rob Burnett **RC**	.12	.09	.05
504	Maurice Carthon	.05	.04	.02
505	Donnell Woolford	.05	.04	.02
506	Howard Ballard	.05	.04	.02
507	Mark Boyer	.05	.04	.02
508	Eugene Marve	.05	.04	.02
509	Joe Kelly	.05	.04	.02
510	Will Wolford	.05	.04	.02
511	Robert Clark	.05	.04	.02
512	Matt Brock **RC**	.12	.09	.05
513	Chris Warren	.50	.40	.20
514	Ken Willis	.05	.04	.02
515	George Jamison **RC**	.12	.09	.05
516	Rufus Porter	.05	.04	.02
517	Mark Higgs **RC**	.25	.20	.10
518	Thomas Everett	.05	.04	.02
519	Robert Brown	.05	.04	.02
520	Gene Atkins	.05	.04	.02
521	Hardy Nickerson	.05	.04	.02
522	Johnny Bailey	.05	.04	.02
523	William Frizzell	.05	.04	.02
524	Steve McMichael	.05	.04	.02
525	Kevin Porter	.05	.04	.02
526	Carwell Gardner	.05	.04	.02
527	Eugene Daniel	.05	.04	.02
528	Vestee Jackson	.05	.04	.02
529	Chris Goode	.05	.04	.02
530	Leon Seals	.05	.04	.02
531	Darion Conner	.05	.04	.02
532	Stan Brock	.05	.04	.02
533	Kirby Jackson **RC**	.10	.08	.04
534	Marv Cook	.05	.04	.02
535	Bill Fralic	.05	.04	.02
536	Keith Woodside	.05	.04	.02
537	Hugh Green	.05	.04	.02
538	Grant Feasel	.05	.04	.02
539	Bubba McDowell	.05	.04	.02
540	Vai Sikahema	.05	.04	.02
541	Aaron Cox	.05	.04	.02
542	Roger Craig	.05	.04	.02
543	Robb Thomas	.05	.04	.02
544	Ronnie Lott	.10	.08	.04
545	Robert Delpino	.05	.04	.02
546	Greg McMurtry	.05	.04	.02
547	Jim Morrissey **RC**	.10	.08	.04
548	Johnny Rembert	.05	.04	.02
549	Markus Paul **RC**	.12	.09	.05
550	Karl Wilson **RC**	.12	.09	.05
551	Gaston Green	.05	.04	.02
552	Willie Drewrey	.05	.04	.02
553	Michael Young	.05	.04	.02
554	Tom Tupa	.05	.04	.02
555	John Friesz	.15	.11	.06
556	Cody Carlson **RC**	.35	.25	.14
557	Eric Allen	.05	.04	.02
558	Tom Bensen	.05	.04	.02
559	Scott Mersereau **RC**	.10	.08	.04
560	Lionel Washington	.05	.04	.02
561	Brian Brennan	.05	.04	.02
562	Jim Jeffcoat	.05	.04	.02
563	Jeff Jaeger	.05	.04	.02
564	David Johnson	.05	.04	.02
565	Danny Villa	.05	.04	.02
566	Don Beebe	.05	.04	.02
567	Michael Haynes	.30	.25	.12
568	Brett Faryniarz	.05	.04	.02
569	Mike Prior	.05	.04	.02
570	John Davis **RC**	.12	.09	.05
571	Vernon Turner **RC**	.12	.09	.05
572	Michael Brooks	.05	.04	.02
573	Mike Gann	.05	.04	.02
574	Ron Holmes	.05	.04	.02
575	Gary Plummer	.05	.04	.02
576	Bill Romanowski	.05	.04	.02
577	Chris Jacke	.05	.04	.02
578	Gary Reasons	.05	.04	.02
579	Tim Jorden **RC**	.08	.06	.03
580	Tim McKyer	.05	.04	.02
581	Johnny Jackson	.05	.04	.02
582	Ethan Horton	.05	.04	.02
583	Pete Stoyanovich	.05	.04	.02
584	Jeff Query	.05	.04	.02
585	Frank Reich	.05	.04	.02
586	Riki Ellison	.05	.04	.02
587	Eric Hill	.05	.04	.02
588	Anthony Shelton	.05	.04	.02
589	Steve Smith	.05	.04	.02
590	Garth Jax **RC**	.08	.06	.03
591	Greg Davis **RC**	.10	.08	.04
592	Bill Maas	.05	.04	.02
593	Henry Rolling **RC**	.10	.08	.04
594	Keith Jones	.05	.04	.02
595	Tootie Robbins	.05	.04	.02
596	Brian Jordan **RC**	.25	.20	.10
597	Derrick Walker **RC**	.12	.09	.05
598	Jonathan Hayes	.05	.04	.02
599	Nate Lewis **RC**	.25	.20	.10
600	**Checklist 501-600**	.05	.04	.02
601	AFC Checklist RF (Greg Lewis, Keith Traylor, Kenny Walker, Denver Broncos)	.15	.11	.06
602	James Jones **RC**	.15	.11	.06
603	Tim Barnett **RC**	.15	.11	.06
604	Ed King **RC**	.10	.08	.04
605	Shane Curry	.05	.04	.02
606	Mike Croel	.20	.15	.08
607	Bryan Cox **RC**	.50	.40	.20
608	Shawn Jefferson **RC**	.12	.09	.05
609	Kenny Walker **RC**	.25	.20	.10
610	Michael Jackson **RC**	.75	.60	.30
611	Jon Vaughn **RC**	.20	.15	.08
612	Greg Lewis	.05	.04	.02
613	Joe Valerio	.05	.04	.02
614	Pat Harlow **RC**	.10	.08	.04
615	Henry Jones **RC**	.20	.15	.08
616	Jeff Graham **RC**	.75	.60	.30
617	Darryll Lewis **RC**	.12	.09	.05
618	Keith Traylor **RC**	.10	.08	.04
619	Scott Miller	.05	.04	.02
620	Nick Bell	.10	.08	.04
621	John Flannery **RC**	.12	.09	.05
622	Leonard Russell **RC**	.50	.40	.20
623	Alfred Williams **RC**	.10	.08	.04
624	Browning Nagle	.15	.11	.06
625	Harvey Williams	.10	.08	.04
626	Dan McGwire	.10	.08	.04
627	Brett Favre, Moe Gardner, Erric Pegram, Bruce Pickens, Mike Pritchard (CL)	.50	.40	.20
628	William Thomas **RC**	.10	.08	.04
629	Lawrence Dawsey **RC**	.15	.11	.06
630	Aeneas Williams **RC**	.10	.08	.04
631	Stan Thomas	.05	.04	.02
632	Randal Hill	.15	.11	.06
633	Moe Gardner **RC**	.10	.08	.04
634	Alvin Harper	.25	.20	.10
635	Esera Tuaolo **RC**	.08	.06	.03
636	Russell Maryland	.20	.15	.08
637	Anthony Morgan	.15	.11	.06
638	Erric Pegram **RC**	.40	.30	.15
639	Herman Moore	.75	.60	.30
640	Ricky Ervins **RC**	.20	.15	.08
641	Kelvin Pritchett **RC**	.10	.08	.04
642	Roman Phifer **RC**	.10	.08	.04
643	Antone Davis **RC**	.10	.08	.04
644	Mike Pritchard	.40	.30	.15
645	Vinnie Clark **RC**	.10	.08	.04
646	Jake Reed **RC**	1.00	.70	.40
647	Brett Favre	3.00	2.25	1.25
648	Todd Lyght	.10	.08	.04
649	Bruce Pickens	.05	.04	.02
650	Darren Lewis **RC**	.25	.20	.10
651	Wesley Carroll	.10	.08	.04
652	James Joseph **RC**	.25	.20	.10
653	Robert Delpino	.05	.04	.02
654	Vencie Glenn	.05	.04	.02
655	Jerry Rice	.20	.15	.08
656	Barry Sanders	.50	.40	.20
657	Ken Tippins	.05	.04	.02
658	Christian Okoye	.05	.04	.02
659	Rich Gannon	.05	.04	.02
660	Johnny Meads	.05	.04	.02
661	J.J. Birden **RC**	.10	.08	.04
662	Bruce Kozerski	.05	.04	.02
663	Felix Wright	.05	.04	.02
664	Al Smith	.05	.04	.02
665	Stan Humphries	.30	.25	.12
666	Alfred Anderson	.05	.04	.02
667	Nate Newton	.05	.04	.02
668	Vince Workman **RC**	.10	.08	.04
669	Ricky Reynolds	.05	.04	.02
670	Bryce Paup **RC**	.75	.60	.30
671	Gill Generty	.05	.04	.02
672	Darrell Thompson	.20	.15	.08
673	Anthony Smith	.05	.04	.02
674	Darryl Henley **RC**	.08	.06	.03
675	Brett Maxie	.05	.04	.02
676	Craig Taylor	.05	.04	.02
677	Steve Wallace	.05	.04	.02
678	Jeff Feagles **RC**	.08	.06	.03
679	James Washington **RC**	.10	.08	.04
680	Tim Harris	.05	.04	.02
681	Dennis Gibson	.05	.04	.02
682	Toi Cook **RC**	.10	.08	.04
683	Lorenzo Lynch	.05	.04	.02
684	Brad Edwards **RC**	.10	.08	.04
685	Ray Crockett **RC**	.10	.08	.04
686	Harris Barton	.05	.04	.02
687	Byron Evans	.05	.04	.02
688	Eric Thomas	.05	.04	.02
689	Jeff Criswell	.05	.04	.02
690	Eric Ball	.05	.04	.02
691	Brian Mitchell	.20	.15	.08
692	Quinn Early	.05	.04	.02
693	Aaron Jones	.05	.04	.02
694	Jim Dombrowski	.05	.04	.02
695	Jeff Bostic	.05	.04	.02
696	Tony Casillas	.05	.04	.02
697	Ken Lanier	.05	.04	.02
698	Henry Thomas	.05	.04	.02
699	Steve Beuerlein	.20	.15	.08
700	**Checklist 601-700**	.05	.04	.02
SP1	Darrell Green	.50	.40	.20
SP2	Don Shula	1.00	.70	.40

1991 Upper Deck Game Breaker Holograms

Nine top running backs are featured on these insert cards, which were randomly included in 1991 Upper Deck packs. Series I packs contained cards 1-6; Series II packs had cards 7-9. Each card front has an action hologram against a background with a diagramed football play. "Gamebreakers" is in the bottom right corner, next to a stripe which has the player's name in it. The card backs are numbered with a "GB" prefix and contain the player's team logo and a career summary.

		NM/M	NM	E
Complete Set (9):		8.00	6.00	3.20
Common Player:		.60	.45	.25
1	Barry Sanders	4.00	3.00	1.60
2	Thurman Thomas	1.25	.90	.50
3	Bobby Humphrey	.60	.45	.25
4	Earnest Byner	.60	.45	.25
5	Emmitt Smith	4.50	3.50	1.75
6	Neal Anderson	.60	.45	.25
7	Marion Butts	.60	.45	.25
8	James Brooks	.60	.45	.25
9	Marcus Allen	.75	.60	.30

1991 Upper Deck Heroes Montana Box Bottoms

This eight-card set is identical to the Montana Heroes insert except they have blank backs and are oversized. Cards measure 5-1/4" x 7-1/4" and were found on the bottom of 1991 Upper Deck low series wax boxes.

		NM/M	NM	E
Complete Set (8):		5.00	3.75	2.00
Common Player:		1.00	.70	.40
1	1974-78 College Years	1.00	.70	.40
2	1981 A Star is Born	1.00	.70	.40
3	1984 Super Bowl MVP	1.00	.70	.40
4	1987 1st Passing Title	1.00	.70	.40
5	1988 Rematch	1.00	.70	.40
6	1989 NFL's MVP	1.00	.70	.40
7	1989 Back-to-Back	1.00	.70	.40
8	1990 Career Highs	1.00	.70	.40

1991 Upper Deck Heroes Namath Box Bottoms

This eight-card set has identical photos to the Namath Heroes insert, but has blank backs and printed on an oversized format. The cards measure 5-1/4" x 7-1/4" and are found on the bottom of 1991 Upper Deck high series football wax boxes.

		NM/M	NM	E
Complete Set (8):		5.00	3.75	2.00
Common Player:		1.00	.70	.40
10	1962-65 Crimson Tide	1.00	.70	.40
11	1965 Broadway Joe	1.00	.70	.40
12	1967 4,000 Yards Passing	1.00	.70	.40
13	1968 AFL MVP	1.00	.70	.40
14	1969 Super Bowl III	1.00	.70	.40
15	1969 All-Pro	1.00	.70	.40
16	1972 400 Yards	1.00	.70	.40
17	1985 Hall of Fame	1.00	.70	.40

1991 Upper Deck Joe Montana Heroes

This is the first set of Upper Deck's Football Heroes se-

ries. These 10 cards are devoted to 49er quarterback Joe Montana. Each card front has an oval framed with white and blue borders. A color photo is inside the oval. The card is two-toned - it shades from mustard to brown, and has the set logo in the bottom left corner. The card back is designed like a football field and includes a career summary and card number (1 of 9, etc.). Cards were random inserts in 1991 Upper Deck Series I packs. Montana autographed 2,500 of the cards. The tenth card is an unnumbered header card. A title appears on each card, too.

		NM/M	NM	E
Complete Set (10):		15.00	11.00	6.00
Common Player:		1.50	1.25	.60
Montana Header SP (NNO):		6.00	4.50	2.50
Montana Auto/2500:		200.00	150.00	80.00
1	1974-78 College Years(Joe Montana)	1.50	1.25	.60
2	1981 A Star is Born(Joe Montana)	1.50	1.25	.60
3	1984 Super Bowl MVP(Joe Montana)	1.50	1.25	.60
4	1987 1st Passing Title(Joe Montana)	1.50	1.25	.60
5	1988 Rematch(Joe Montana)	1.50	1.25	.60
6	1989 NFL's MVP(Joe Montana)	1.50	1.25	.60
7	1989 Back-to-Back(Joe Montana)	1.50	1.25	.60
8	1990 Career Highs(Joe Montana)	1.50	1.25	.60
9	Checklist Heroes 1-9(Joe Montana) (Vernon Wells potrait of Montana)	1.50	1.25	.60
----	Title/Header card SP(Joe Montana) (Unnumbered)	6.00	4.50	2.50

1991 Upper Deck Joe Namath Heroes

Hall of Fame quarterback Joe Namath is featured in this Football Heroes set which starts where the similar Joe Montana set ended. Cards are numbered 10-18 and were randomly inserted in 1991 Upper Deck Series II packs. The front has an oval with a picture in it, bordered with a white and blue frame. The player's name is in the bottom right corner, along with a title. A "Football Heroes" logo is in the lower left corner. The back has a football field design and includes a career summary and card number. Namath autographed 2,500 cards; he autographed every 100th card "Broadway Joe."

		NM/M	NM	E
Complete Set (10):		15.00	11.00	6.00
Common Player:		1.50	1.25	.60
Namath Header SP (NNO):		6.00	4.50	2.50
Namath Auto/2500:		200.00	150.00	80.00
10	1962-65 Crimson Tide(Joe Namath)	1.50	1.25	.60
11	1965 Broadway Joe(Joe Namath)	1.50	1.25	.60
12	1967 4,000 Yards Passing(Joe Namath)	1.50	1.25	.60
13	1968 AFL MVP(Joe Namath)	1.50	1.25	.60
14	1969 Super Bowl III(Joe Namath)	1.50	1.25	.60
15	1969 All-Pro(Joe Namath)	1.50	1.25	.60
16	1972 400 Yards(Joe Namath)	1.50	1.25	.60
17	1985 Hall of Fame(Joe Namath)	1.50	1.25	.60
18	Checklist Heroes 10-18(Joe Namath)	1.50	1.25	.60
----	Title/Header Card SP(Joe Namath) (Unnumbered)	6.00	4.50	2.50

1991 Upper Deck Promos

These two promo card preview Upper Deck's 1991 debut football set. The design is similar to that which was used for the regular set, but the photos and card numbers for the two players' corresponding cards are different. Cards were also available through 900-number promotion by Upper Deck. The Montana card is $4; the Sanders card is $2.50.

		NM/M	NM	E
Complete Set (2):		12.00	9.00	4.75
Common Player:		7.00	5.25	2.75
1	Joe Montana	7.00	5.25	2.75
500	Barry Sanders	8.00	6.00	3.25

1991 Upper Deck Sheets

Upper Deck offered two 8-1/2" x 11" sheets, with one commemorating the New York Giants Super Bowl XXV Champions and the second commemorating the 40th anniversary of the 1951 Rams championship team. The Giants sheet has the issue date, production run and issue number in the lower right hand corner. The Rams sheet was limited to 60,000.

		NM/M	NM	E
Complete Set (2):		10.00	7.50	4.00
Common Player:		5.00	3.75	2.00
1	October 1991 (60,000)	5.00	3.75	2.00
2	October 27, 1991 (Rodney Hampton, Lawrence Taylor, Dave Meggett, Jeff Hostetler, Mark Collins, Ottis Anderson) (SB XXV Champions) (72,000)	5.00	3.75	2.00

V

1988 Vachon CFL

		NM/M	NM	E
Complete Set (160):		135.00	101.00	54.00
Common Player:		.75	.60	.30
1	Dave Albright	1.00	.70	.40
2	Roger Aldag	1.00	.70	.40
3	Marv Allemang	.75	.60	.30
4	Damon Allen	2.50	2.00	1.00
5	Gary Allen	1.00	.70	.40
6	Randy Ambrosie	.75	.60	.30
7	Mike Anderson	.75	.60	.30
8	Kent Austin	4.00	3.00	1.50
9	Terry Baker	1.00	.70	.40
10	Danny Bass	3.00	2.25	1.25
11	Nick Bastaja	.75	.60	.30
12	Greg Battle	2.50	2.00	1.00
13	Lyle Bauer	.75	.60	.30
14	Jearld Baylis	2.00	1.50	.80
15	Ian Beckstead	.75	.60	.30
16	Walter Bender	1.50	1.25	.60
17	Nick Benjamin	1.00	.70	.40
18	David Black	.75	.60	.30
19	Leo Blanchard	.75	.60	.30
20	Trevor Bowles	.75	.60	.30
21	Ken Braden	.75	.60	.30
22	Rod Brown	.75	.60	.30
23	Less Browne	1.00	.70	.40
24	Jamie Buis	.75	.60	.30
25	Tom Burgess	3.50	2.75	1.50
26	Bob Cameron	1.00	.70	.40
27	Jan Carinci	.75	.60	.30
28	Tony Champion	2.50	2.00	1.00
29	Jacques Chapdelaine	.75	.60	.30
30	Tony Cherry	2.50	2.00	1.00
31	Lance Chomyc	1.00	.70	.40
32	John Congemi	2.00	1.50	.80
33	Rod Connop	.75	.60	.30
34	David Conrad	.75	.60	.30
35	Grover Covington	2.00	1.50	.80
36	Larry Crawford	1.25	.90	.50
37	James Curry	2.00	1.50	.80
38	Marco Cyncar	1.00	.70	.40
39	Gabriel DeLaGarza	.75	.60	.30
40	Mike Derks	.75	.60	.30
41	Blake Dermott	1.00	.70	.40
42	Roy DeWalt (SP)	4.00	3.00	1.50
43	Todd Dillon	1.25	.90	.50
44	Rocky DiPietro	2.00	1.50	.80
45	Kevin Dixon (SP)	2.00	1.50	.80
46	Tom Dixon	.75	.60	.30

47	Selwyn Drain	.75	.60	.30
48	Matt Dunigan	7.50	5.75	3.00
49	Ray Elgaard	3.00	2.25	1.25
50	Jerome Erdman	.75	.60	.30
51	Randy Fabi	.75	.60	.30
52	Gill Fenerty	2.00	1.50	.80
53	Denny Ferdinand	1.00	.70	.40
54	Dan Ferrone	1.00	.70	.40
55	Howard Fields	.75	.60	.30
56	Matt Finlay	.75	.60	.30
57	Rickey Foggie	2.00	1.50	.80
58	Delbert Fowler	1.00	.70	.40
59	Ed Gataveckas	.75	.60	.30
60	Keith Gooch	.75	.60	.30
61	Miles Gorrell	.75	.60	.30
62	Mike Gray	.75	.60	.30
63	Leo Groenewegen	.75	.60	.30
64	Ken Hailey	.75	.60	.30
65	Harold Hallman	1.00	.70	.40
66	Tracy Ham	5.00	3.75	2.00
67	Rodney Harding	2.00	1.50	.80
68	Glenn Harper	.75	.60	.30
69	J.T. Hay	.75	.60	.30
70	Larry Hogue	.75	.60	.30
71	Ron Hopkins (SP)	2.00	1.50	.80
72	Hank Llesic	2.00	1.50	.80
73	Bryan Illerbrun	.75	.60	.30
74	Lemont Jeffers	.75	.60	.30
75	James Jefferson	2.00	1.50	.80
76	Rick Johnson	2.00	1.50	.80
77	Chris Johnstone	.75	.60	.30
78	Johnnie Jones	.75	.60	.30
79	Milson Jones	1.50	1.25	.60
80	Stephen Jones	2.00	1.50	.80
81	Bobby Jurasin	2.50	2.00	1.00
82	Jerry Kauric	1.00	.70	.40
83	Dan Kearns	.75	.60	.30
84	Trevor Kennerd	2.00	1.50	.80
85	Mike Kerrigan	4.00	3.00	1.50
86	Rick Klassen	2.00	1.50	.80
87	Lee Knight	.75	.60	.30
88	Kevin Konar	1.00	.70	.40
89	Glenn Kulka	1.25	.90	.50
90	Doug (Tank) Landry	2.00	1.50	.80
91	Scott Lecky	.75	.60	.30
92	Orville Lee	1.50	1.25	.60
93	Marc Lewis	1.00	.70	.40
94	Eddie Lowe	.75	.60	.30
95	Lynn Madsen	.75	.60	.30
96	Chris Major	3.00	2.25	1.25
97	Doran Major	.75	.60	.30
98	Tony Martino	.75	.60	.30
99	Tim McCray	1.25	.90	.50
100	Michael McGruder	1.25	.90	.50
101	Sean McKeown (SP)	4.00	3.00	1.50
102	Andy McVey	.75	.60	.30
103	Stan Mikawos	.75	.60	.30
104	James Mills	2.00	1.50	.80
105	Larry Mohr	.75	.60	.30
106	Bernie Morrison	.75	.60	.30
107	James Murphy	2.00	1.50	.80
108	Paul Osbaldiston	1.00	.70	.40
109	Anthony Parker	1.50	1.25	.60
110	James Parker	2.00	1.50	.80
111	Greg Peterson	.75	.60	.30
112	Tim Petros	1.25	.90	.50
113	Reggie Pleasant	1.25	.90	.50
114	Willie Pless	2.00	1.50	.80
115	Bob Poley	.75	.60	.30
116	Tom Porras	1.50	1.25	.60
117	Hector Pothier	.75	.60	.30
118	Jim Reid	1.50	1.25	.60
119	Robert Reid	.75	.60	.30
120	Gilbert Renfroe	2.00	1.50	.80
121	Tom Richards	1.25	.90	.50
122	Dave Ridgway	2.00	1.50	.80
123	Rae Robirtis	.75	.60	.30
124	Gerald Roper	.75	.60	.30
125	Darryl Sampson	.75	.60	.30
126	Jim Sandusky	2.50	2.00	1.00
127	David Sauve	.75	.60	.30
128	Art Schlichter	2.00	1.50	.80
129	Ralph Scholz	.75	.60	.30
130	Mark Seale	1.00	.70	.40
131	Dan Sellers	.75	.60	.30
132	Lance Shields	1.00	.70	.40
133	Ian Sinclair	1.50	1.25	.60
134	Mike Siroishka	.75	.60	.30
135	Chris Skinner	.75	.60	.30
136	Harry Skipper	1.00	.70	.40
137	Darrell Smith	3.00	2.25	1.25
138	Tom Spoletini	.75	.60	.30
139	Steve Stapler	1.00	.70	.40
140	Bill Stevenson	.75	.60	.30
141	Gregg Stumon	1.25	.90	.50
142	Glen Suitor	.75	.60	.30
143	Emmanuel Tolbert	2.50	2.00	1.00
144	Perry Tuttle (SP)	4.00	3.00	1.50
145	Peter VandenBos	.75	.60	.30
146	Jake Vaughan	.75	.60	.30
147	Chris Walby	1.50	1.25	.60
148	Mike Walker	1.50	1.25	.60
149	Patrick Wayne	.75	.60	.30
150	James West	2.00	1.50	.80
151	Brett Williams	1.50	1.25	.60
152	David Williams	2.50	2.00	1.00
153	Henry Williams	8.00	6.00	3.25
154	Tommy Williams	.75	.60	.30
155	Larry Willis	1.00	.70	.40
156	Don Wilson	.75	.60	.30
157	Earl Winfield	2.50	2.00	1.00
158	Rick Worman	2.00	1.50	.80
159	Larry Wruck	.75	.60	.30
160	Kari Yli-Renko	.75	.60	.30

1989 Vachon CFL

	NM/M	NM	E
Complete Set (160):	125.00	94.00	50.00
Common Player:	.75	.60	.30

1	Tony Williams	1.00	.70	.40
2	Sean Foudy	.75	.60	.30
3	Tom Schimmer	.75	.60	.30
4	Ken Evraire	1.00	.70	.40
5	Gerald Wilcox	1.00	.70	.40
6	Damon Allen	2.00	1.50	.80
7	Tony Kimbrough	.75	.60	.30
8	Dean Dorsey	1.00	.70	.40
9	Rocco Romano	.75	.60	.30
10	Ken Braden	.75	.60	.30
11	Kari Yli-Renko	.75	.60	.30
12	Darrel Hopper	.75	.60	.30
13	Irv Daymond	.75	.60	.30
14	Orville Lee	1.00	.70	.40
15	Steve Howlett	.75	.60	.30
16	Kyle Hall	.75	.60	.30
17	Reggie Ward	.75	.60	.30
18	Gerald Alphin	2.00	1.50	.80
19	Troy Wilson	.75	.60	.30
20	Patrick Wayne	.75	.60	.30
21	Harold Hallman	1.25	.90	.50
22	John Congemi	1.50	1.25	.60
23	Doran Major	.75	.60	.30
24	Hank Llesic	1.50	1.25	.60
25	Gilbert Renfroe	2.00	1.50	.80
26	Rodney Harding	1.00	.70	.40
27	Todd Wiseman	.75	.60	.30
28	Chris Schultz	1.00	.70	.40
29	Carl Brazley	1.00	.70	.40
30	Darrell Smith	2.50	2.00	1.00
31	Glenn Kulka	1.00	.70	.40
32	Bob Skemp	.75	.60	.30
33	Don Moen	1.00	.70	.40
34	Jearld Baylis	2.00	1.50	.80
35	Lorenzo Graham	.75	.60	.30
36	Lance Chomyc	1.00	.70	.40
37	Warren Hudson	.75	.60	.30
38	Gill Fenerty	2.00	1.50	.80
39	Paul Masotti	1.00	.70	.40
40	Reggie Pleasant	1.25	.90	.50
41	Scott Flagel	.75	.60	.30
42	Mike Kerrigan	2.50	2.00	1.00
43	Frank Robinson	1.00	.70	.40
44	Jacques Chapdelaine	.75	.60	.30
45	Miles Gorrell	.75	.60	.30
46	Mike Walker	1.50	1.25	.60
47	Jason Riley	.75	.60	.30
48	Grover Covington	1.50	1.25	.60
49	Ralph Scholz	.75	.60	.30
50	Mike Derks	.75	.60	.30
51	Derrick McAdoo	1.50	1.25	.60
52	Rocky DiPietro	2.00	1.50	.80
53	Lance Shields	1.00	.70	.40
54	Dale Sanderson	.75	.60	.30
55	Tim Lorenz	.75	.60	.30
56	Rod Skillman	.75	.60	.30
57	Jed Tommy	.75	.60	.30
58	Paul Osbaldiston	1.00	.70	.40
59	Darrell Corbin	.75	.60	.30
60	Tony Champion	1.50	1.25	.60
61	Romel Andrews	.75	.60	.30
62	Bob Cameron	1.00	.70	.40
63	Greg Battle	2.00	1.50	.80
64	Rod Hill	1.00	.70	.40
65	Steve Rodehutskors	1.00	.70	.40
66	Trevor Kennerd	1.50	1.25	.60
67	Moustafa Ali	1.00	.70	.40
68	Mike Gray	.75	.60	.30
69	Bob Molle	.75	.60	.30
70	Tim Jessie	1.00	.70	.40
71	Matt Pearce	.75	.60	.30
72	Will Lewis	.75	.60	.30
73	Sean Salisbury	2.50	2.00	1.00
74	Chris Walby	1.00	.70	.40
75	Jeff Croonen	.75	.60	.30
76	David Black	.75	.60	.30
77	Buster Rhymes	2.00	1.50	.80
78	James Murphy	1.50	1.25	.60
79	Stan Mikawos	.75	.60	.30
80	Lee Saltz	2.00	1.50	.80
81	Bryan Illerbrun	.75	.60	.30
82	Donald Narcisse	3.00	2.25	1.25
83	Milson Jones	1.00	.70	.40
84	Dave Ridgway	1.50	1.25	.60
85	Glen Suitor	.75	.60	.30
86	Terry Baker	1.00	.70	.40
87	James Curry	1.50	1.25	.60
88	Harry Skipper	1.00	.70	.40
89	Bobby Jurasin	2.00	1.50	.80
90	Gary Lewis	.75	.60	.30
91	Roger Aldag	1.00	.70	.40
92	Jeff Fairholm	2.00	1.50	.80
93	Dave Albright	.75	.60	.30
94	Ray Elgaard	2.50	2.00	1.00
95	Kent Austin	3.50	2.75	1.50
96	Tom Burgess	3.00	2.25	1.25
97	Richie Hall	.75	.60	.30
98	Eddie Lowe	.75	.60	.30
99	Vince Goldsmith	1.00	.70	.40
100	Tim McCray	1.00	.70	.40
101	Leo Blanchard	.75	.60	.30
102	Tom Spoletini	.75	.60	.30
103	Dan Ferrone	1.00	.70	.40
104	Doug (Tank) Landry	1.50	1.25	.60
105	Chris Major	1.50	1.25	.60
106	Mike Palumbo	.75	.60	.30
107	Terrence Jones	2.00	1.50	.80
108	Larry Willis	1.25	.90	.50
109	Kent Warnock	.75	.60	.30
110	Tim Petros	1.00	.70	.40
111	Marshall Toner	.75	.60	.30
112	Ken Ford	.75	.60	.30
113	Ron Hopkins	.75	.60	.30
114	Eric Kramer	7.50	5.75	3.00
115	Stu Laird	.75	.60	.30
116	Vernell Quinn	.75	.60	.30
117	Lemont Jeffers	.75	.60	.30
118	Derrick Taylor	.75	.60	.30
119	Jay Christensen	1.00	.70	.40
120	Mitchell Price	.75	.60	.30
121	Rod Connop	.75	.60	.30
122	Mark Norman	.75	.60	.30
123	Andre Francis	1.00	.70	.40
124	Reggie Taylor	1.50	1.25	.60
125	Rick Worman	1.00	.70	.40
126	Marco Cyncar	1.00	.70	.40
127	Blake Dermott	.75	.60	.30
128	Jerry Kauric	1.00	.70	.40
129	Steve Taylor	2.00	1.50	.80
130	Dave Richardson	.75	.60	.30
131	John Mandarich	1.00	.70	.40
132	Gregg Stumon	1.00	.70	.40
133	Tracy Ham	4.00	3.00	1.50
134	Danny Bass	2.50	2.00	1.00
135	Blake Marshall	1.50	1.25	.60
136	Jeff Braswell	1.00	.70	.40
137	Larry Wruck	1.00	.70	.40
138	Warren Jones	.75	.60	.30
139	Stephen Jones	1.50	1.25	.60
140	Tom Richards	1.00	.70	.40
141	Tony Cherry	1.50	1.25	.60
142	Anthony Parker	1.50	1.25	.60
143	Gerald Roper	.75	.60	.30
144	Lui Passaglia	2.00	1.50	.80
145	Mack Moore	.75	.60	.30
146	Jamie Taras	.75	.60	.30
147	Rickey Foggie	1.50	1.25	.60
148	Matt Dunigan	6.00	4.50	2.50
149	Anthony Drawhorn	1.00	.70	.40
150	Eric Streater	1.25	.90	.50
151	Marcus Thomas	.75	.60	.30
152	Wes Cooper	.75	.60	.30
153	James Mills	1.00	.70	.40
154	Peter VandenBos	.75	.60	.30
155	Ian Sinclair	1.00	.70	.40
156	James Parker	1.50	1.25	.60
157	Andrew Murray	.75	.60	.30
158	Larry Crawford	1.25	.90	.50
159	Kevin Konar	1.00	.70	.40
160	David Williams	1.50	1.25	.60

1990 Versailles HS

	NM/M	NM	E
Complete Set (20):	8.00	6.00	3.25
Common Player:	.50	.40	.20

1	Kevin Bergman	.50	.40	.20
2	A.J. Bey	.50	.40	.20
3	Brad Bey	.50	.40	.20
4	Ed Dingman	.75	.60	.30
5	Brian Griesdorn	.50	.40	.20
6	Al Hetrick (CO)	.75	.60	.30
7	Garth Hoellrich	.50	.40	.20
8	Trent Huff	.50	.40	.20

		NM	E	VG
9	Brian Keiser	.50	.40	.20
10	Lane Knore	.50	.40	.20
11	Brian Kunk	.50	.40	.20
12	Keenan Leichty	.50	.40	.20
13	Marc Litten	.50	.40	.20
14	Craig Oliver	.50	.40	.20
15	Jon Pothast	.50	.40	.20
16	Joe Rush	.50	.40	.20
17	Shane Schultz	.50	.40	.20
18	Mark Siekman	.50	.40	.20
19	Matt Stall	.50	.40	.20
20	Nathan Subler	.50	.40	.20

1967-68 Vikings

The 29-card, 8" x 10" set features black-and-white photos with blank backs.

		NM	E	VG
	Complete Set (29):	120.00	60.00	35.00
	Common Player:	4.00	2.00	1.25
1	Grady Alderman (Tackle)	4.00	2.00	1.25
2	Grady Alderman (Offensive lineman)	4.00	2.00	1.25
3	John Beasley	4.00	2.00	1.25
4	Bob Berry	4.00	2.00	1.25
5	Larry Bowie	4.00	2.00	1.25
6	Gary Cuozzo	5.00	2.50	1.50
7	Doug Davis	4.00	2.00	1.25
8	Paul Dickinson	4.00	2.00	1.25
9	Paul Flatley	5.00	2.50	1.50
10	Bob Grim	5.00	2.50	1.50
11	Dale Hackbart	4.00	2.00	1.25
12	Don Hansen	4.00	2.00	1.25
13	Jim Hargrove	4.00	2.00	1.25
14	Clint Jones	5.00	2.50	1.50
15	Jeff Jordan	4.00	2.00	1.25
16	Joe Kapp	8.00	4.00	2.50
17	John Kirby	4.00	2.00	1.25
18	Gary Larsen	5.00	2.50	1.50
19	Earsell Mackbee	4.00	2.00	1.25
20	Marlin McKeever	5.00	2.50	1.50
21	Milt Sunde	5.00	2.50	1.50
22	David Tobey	4.00	2.00	1.25
23	Ron Vanderkelen	5.00	2.50	1.50
24	Jim Vellone	4.00	2.00	1.25
25	Bobby Walden	4.00	2.00	1.25
26	Lonnie Warwick	4.00	2.00	1.25
27	Gene Washington (Wide receiver)	5.00	2.50	1.50
28	Gene Washington (End)	5.00	2.50	1.50
29	Roy Winston	5.00	2.50	1.50

1969 Vikings Team Issue

The 27-card, 5" x 6-7/8" set features black-and-white borderless player portraits with blank backs.

		NM	E	VG
	Complete Set (27):	75.00	37.00	22.00
	Common Player:	3.00	1.50	.90
1	Bookie Bolin	3.00	1.50	.90
2	Bobby Bryant	4.00	2.00	1.25
3	John Beasley	3.00	1.50	.90
4	Gary Cuozzo	4.00	2.00	1.25
5	Doug Davis	3.00	1.50	.90
6	Paul Dickson	3.00	1.50	.90
7	Bob Grim	4.00	2.00	1.25
8	Dale Hackbart	3.00	1.50	.90
9	Jim Hargrove	3.00	1.50	.90
10	John Henderson	3.00	1.50	.90
11	Wally Hilgenberg	4.00	2.00	1.25
12	Clinton Jones	4.00	2.00	1.25
13	Karl Kassulke	4.00	2.00	1.25
14	Kent Kramer	3.00	1.50	.90
15	Gary Larsen	4.00	2.00	1.25
16	Bob Lee	3.00	1.50	.90
17	Jim Lindsey	3.00	1.50	.90
18	Earsell Mackbee	3.00	1.50	.90
19	Mike McGill	3.00	1.50	.90
20	Oscar Reed	3.00	1.50	.90
21	Ed Sharockman	3.00	1.50	.90
22	Steve Smith	3.00	1.50	.90
23	Milt Sunde	3.00	1.50	.90
24	Jim Vellone	3.00	1.50	.90
25	Lonnie Warwick	3.00	1.50	.90
26	Gene Washington	5.00	2.50	1.50
27	Charlie West	4.00	2.00	1.25

1971 Vikings Photos

The 52-card, 5" x 7-7/16" set consists of color close-up shots with blank backs. The player's name, position, and team name appear on the bottom border.

		NM	E	VG
	Complete Set (52):	125.00	94.00	50.00
	Common Player:	2.00	1.00	.60
1	Grady Alderman	2.00	1.00	.60

		NM	E	VG
2	Neil Armstrong (CO)	2.00	1.00	.60
3	John Beasley	2.00	1.00	.60
4	Bill Brown	4.00	2.00	1.25
5	Bob Brown	2.00	1.00	.60
6	Bobby Bryant	3.00	1.50	.90
7	Jerry Burns (CO)	3.00	1.50	.90
8	Fred Cox	3.00	1.50	.90
9	Gary Cuozzo	3.00	1.50	.90
10	Doug Davis	2.00	1.00	.60
11	Al Denson	2.00	1.00	.60
12	Paul Dickson	2.00	1.00	.60
13	Carl Eller	10.00	5.00	3.00
14	Bud Grant (CO)	12.00	6.00	3.50
15	Bob Grim	3.00	1.50	.90
16	Leo Hayden	2.00	1.00	.60
17	John Henderson	2.00	1.00	.60
18	Wally Hilgenberg	3.00	1.50	.90
19	Noel Jenke	2.00	1.00	.60
20	Clint Jones	3.00	1.50	.90
21	Karl Kassulke	3.00	1.50	.90
22	Paul Krause	5.00	2.50	1.50
23	Gary Larsen	2.00	1.00	.60
24	Bob Lee	2.00	1.00	.60
25	Jim Lindsey	2.00	1.00	.60
26	Jim Marshall	10.00	5.00	3.00
27	Bus Mertes (CO)	2.00	1.00	.60
28	John Michels (CO)	2.00	1.00	.60
29	Jocko Nelson (CO)	2.00	1.00	.60
30	Dave Osborn	4.00	2.00	1.25
31	Alan Page	12.00	6.00	3.50
32	Jack Patera (CO)	3.00	1.50	.90
33	Jerry Patton	2.00	1.00	.60
34	Pete Perreault	2.00	1.00	.60
35	Oscar Reed	2.00	1.00	.60
36	Ed Sharockman	2.00	1.00	.60
37	Norm Snead	6.00	3.00	1.75
38	Milt Sunde	3.00	1.50	.90
39	Doug Sutherland	2.00	1.00	.60
40	Mick Tingelhoff	4.00	2.00	1.25
41	Stu Voigt	4.00	2.00	1.25
42	John Ward	2.00	1.00	.60
43	Lonnie Warwick	2.00	1.00	.60
44	Gene Washington	6.00	3.00	1.75
45	Charlie West	2.00	1.00	.60
46	Ed White	4.00	2.00	1.25
47	Carl Winfrey	2.00	1.00	.60
48	Roy Winston	3.00	1.50	.90
49	Jeff Wright	2.00	1.00	.60
50	Nate Wright	2.00	1.00	.60
51	Ron Yary	4.00	2.00	1.25
52	Godfrey Zaunbrecher	2.00	1.00	.60

1971 Vikings Postcards

The 19-card, 5" x 7-7/16" set features color posed close-ups with the backs containing a typical postcard layout. Bio information appears in the upper left corner of the horizontal backs. The set was issued during the season.

		NM	E	VG
	Complete Set (19):	45.00	22.00	13.50
	Common Player:	2.00	1.00	.60
1	Grady Alderman	2.00	1.00	.60
2	Neil Armstrong (CO)	2.00	1.00	.60
3	John Beasley	2.00	1.00	.60
4	Paul Dickson	2.00	1.00	.60
5	Bud Grant (CO)	12.00	6.00	3.50
6	Wally Hilgenberg	2.00	1.00	.60
7	Noel Jenke	2.00	1.00	.60
8	Paul Krause	5.00	2.50	1.50
9	Gary Larsen	2.00	1.00	.60
10	Dave Osborn	4.00	2.00	1.25
11	Alan Page	12.00	6.00	3.50
12	Jerry Patton	2.00	1.00	.60
13	Doug Sutherland	2.50	1.25	.70
14	Mick Tingelhoff	4.00	2.00	1.25
15	Lonnie Warwick	2.00	1.00	.60
16	Charlie West	2.00	1.00	.60
17	Jeff Wright	2.00	1.00	.60
18	Nate Wright	2.00	1.00	.60
19	Godfrey Zaunbrecher	2.00	1.00	.60

1978 Vikings Country Kitchen

The seven-card, 5" x 7" set features a black-and-white player headshot with bio and stat information on the backs. The card fronts have a white border with the player's name and "Minnesota Vikings" printed.

		NM	E	VG
	Complete Set (7):	35.00	17.50	10.50
	Common Player:	4.00	2.00	1.25
1	Bobby Bryant	4.00	2.00	1.25
2	Tommy Kramer	6.00	3.00	1.75
3	Paul Krause	6.00	3.00	1.75
4	Ahmad Rashad	12.00	6.00	3.50

		NM	E	VG
5	Jeff Siemon	4.00	2.00	1.25
6	Mick Tingelhoff	5.00	2.50	1.50
7	Sammie White	6.00	3.00	1.75

1983 Vikings Police

#27 JOHN TURNER
CORNERBACK
MINNESOTA VIKINGS

The 17-card, 2-5/8" x 4-1/8" set was sponsored by Green Giant, Burger King, Pillsbury and Minnesota Crime Prevention Officers Association. The fronts contain an action photo with the back including bio and stat information.

		NM/M	NM	E
	Complete Set (17):	10.00	7.50	4.00
	Common Player:	.50	.40	.20
1	**Checklist Card**	.75	.60	.30
2	Tommy Kramer	1.00	.70	.40
3	Ted Brown	.50	.40	.20
4	Joe Senser	.50	.40	.20
5	Sammie White	1.00	.70	.40
6	Doug Martin	.50	.40	.20
7	Matt Blair	1.00	.70	.40
8	Bud Grant (CO)	2.00	1.50	.80
9	Scott Studwell	.75	.60	.30
10	Greg Coleman	.50	.40	.20
11	John Turner	.50	.40	.20
12	Jim Hough	.50	.40	.20
13	Joey Browner	1.00	.70	.40
14	Dennis Swilley	.50	.40	.20
15	Darrin Nelson	.75	.60	.30
16	Mark Mullaney	.50	.40	.20
17	Fran Tarkenton (All-Time Great)	3.00	2.25	1.25

1984 Vikings Police

The 18-card, 2-5/8" x 4-1/8" set, sponsored by Pillsbury, Burger King, the Minnesota Crime Prevention Officers Association and Green Giant, features an action shot on the card front with a crime prevention tip on the back.

		NM/M	NM	E
	Complete Set (18):	8.00	6.00	3.25
	Common Player:	.40	.30	.15
1	**Checklist Card**	.50	.40	.20
2	Keith Nord	.40	.30	.15
3	Joe Senser	.40	.30	.15
4	Tommy Kramer	1.25	.90	.50
5	Darrin Nelson	.50	.40	.20
6	Tim Irwin	.40	.30	.15
7	Mark Mullaney	.40	.30	.15
8	Les Steckel (CO)	.40	.30	.15
9	Greg Coleman	.40	.30	.15
10	Tommy Hannon	.40	.30	.15
11	Curtis Rouse	.40	.30	.15
12	Scott Studwell	.50	.40	.20
13	Steve Jordan	1.00	.70	.40
14	Willie Teal	.40	.30	.15
15	Ted Brown	.40	.30	.15
16	Sammie White	1.00	.70	.40
17	Matt Blair	.40	.30	.15
18	Jim Marshall (All-Time Great)	2.50	2.00	1.00

1985 Vikings Police

The 16-card, 2-5/8" x 4-1/8" set was sponsored by Frito-Lay, Pepsi-Cola, KS95-FM and local law enforcement. The cards are similar in design to previous Police sets, with crime prevention tips on the backs.

		NM/M	NM	E
	Complete Set (16):	8.00	6.00	3.25
	Common Player:	.40	.30	.15
1	**Checklist Card**	.50	.40	.20
2	Bud Grant (CO)	1.50	1.25	.60
3	Matt Blair	.50	.40	.20
4	Alfred Anderson	.50	.40	.20
5	Fred McNeill	.40	.30	.15

		NM/M	NM	E
6	Tommy Kramer	.75	.60	.30
7	Jan Stenerud	1.25	.90	.50
8	Sammie White	.75	.60	.30
9	Doug Martin	.40	.30	.15
10	Greg Coleman	.40	.30	.15
11	Steve Riley	.40	.30	.15
12	Walker Lee Ashley	.40	.30	.15
13	Tim Irwin	.40	.30	.15
14	Scott Studwell	.50	.40	.20
15	Darrin Nelson	.50	.40	.20
16	Mick Tingelhoff (All-Time Great)	.75	.60	.30

1986 Vikings Police

The 14-card, 2-5/8" x 4-1/8" set is similar to Police sets from previous years with a "Crime Prevention Tip" on the card back.

		NM/M	NM	E
Complete Set (14):		8.00	6.00	3.25
Common Player:		.40	.30	.15
1	Jerry Burns (CO) (Checklist back)	.50	.40	.20
2	Darrin Nelson	.50	.40	.20
3	Tommy Kramer	.75	.60	.30
4	Anthony Carter	1.50	1.25	.60
5	Scott Studwell	.50	.40	.20
6	Chris Doleman	1.50	1.25	.60
7	Joey Browner	.75	.60	.30
8	Steve Jordan	.50	.40	.20
9	David Howard	.40	.30	.15
10	Tim Newton	.40	.30	.15
11	Leo Lewis	.40	.30	.15
12	Keith Millard	1.00	.70	.40
13	Doug Martin	.40	.30	.15
14	Bill Brown (All-Time Great)	.75	.60	.30

1987 Vikings Police

The 14-card, 2-5/8" x 4-1/8" set features a color action shot on the front with a "Crime Prevention Tip" on the back. Card No. 1, Purple Power '87, is a Vikings montage by artist Cliff Spohn. Over 2 million sets were distributed over a 14-week period by the Vikings, Campbell's Soup, Frito-Lay, KSTP-FM and the Minnesota Crime Prevention Association.

		NM/M	NM	E
Complete Set (14):		8.00	6.00	3.25
Common Player:		.40	.30	.15
1	Purple Power '87 (checklist back)	.50	.40	.20
2	Jerry Burns (CO)	.50	.40	.20
3	Scott Studwell	.50	.40	.20
4	Tommy Kramer	.75	.60	.30
5	Gerald Robinson	.40	.30	.15
6	Wade Wilson	1.75	1.25	.70
7	Anthony Carter	1.00	.70	.40
8	Terry Tausch	.40	.30	.15
9	Leo Lewis	.40	.30	.15
10	Keith Millard	.75	.60	.30
11	Carl Lee	.50	.40	.20
12	Steve Jordan	.50	.40	.20
13	D.J. Dozier	.75	.60	.30
14	Alan Page (ATG)	1.75	1.25	.70

1988 Vikings Police

The 12-card, 2-5/8" x 4-1/8" set featured nine current players, one offense card, one defense card and one all-time great card (Paul Krause). The cards are similar in design to previous Police issues.

		NM/M	NM	E
Complete Set (12):		5.00	3.75	2.00
Common Player:		.40	.30	.15
1	Vikings Offense (Checklist on back)	.50	.40	.20
2	Jesse Solomon	.50	.40	.20
3	Kirk Lowdermilk	.40	.30	.15
4	Darrin Nelson	.50	.40	.20
5	Chris Doleman	1.00	.70	.40
6	D.J. Dozier	.50	.40	.20
7	Gary Zimmerman	.75	.60	.30
8	Allen Rice	.40	.30	.15
9	Joey Browner	.75	.60	.30
10	Anthony Carter	1.00	.70	.40
11	Vikings Defense	.50	.40	.20
12	Paul Krause (All-Time Great)	1.00	.70	.40

1989 Vikings Police

The 10-card, standard-size set features color photos on the gray-border fronts. The card backs are horizontal and contain safety tips, bio information and career highlights. Production was limited to 175,000 for each card.

		NM/M	NM	E
Complete Set (10):		5.00	3.75	2.00
Common Player:		.50	.40	.20
1	Team Card (schedule on back)	.75	.60	.30
2	Henry Thomas	1.00	.70	.40
3	Rick Fenney	.50	.40	.20
4	Chuck Nelson	.50	.40	.20
5	Jim Gustafson	.50	.40	.20
6	Wade Wilson	1.00	.70	.40
7	Randall McDaniel	.75	.60	.30
8	Jesse Solomon	.50	.40	.20
9	Anthony Carter	1.00	.70	.40
10	Joe Kapp (All-Time Great)	1.00	.70	.40

1989 Vikings Taystee Discs

The 12-disc, 2-3/4" in diameter set, features Minnesota players in closeups on the fronts with bio and stat information on the backs. Each disc was issued with a Taystee product in the Minnesota area.

		NM/M	NM	E
Complete Set (12):		5.00	3.75	2.00
Common Player:		.50	.40	.20
1	Anthony Carter	1.00	.70	.40
2	Chris Doleman	1.00	.70	.40
3	Joey Browner	.75	.60	.30
4	Steve Jordan	.75	.60	.30
5	Scott Studwell	.50	.40	.20
6	Wade Wilson	1.00	.70	.40
7	Kirk Lowdermilk	.50	.40	.20
8	Tommy Kramer	.75	.60	.30
9	Keith Millard	.75	.60	.30
10	Rick Fenney	.50	.40	.20
11	Gary Zimmerman	.50	.40	.20
12	Darrin Nelson	.75	.60	.30

1990 Vikings Police

The 10-card, standard-size set was sponsored by Gatorade, WCCO Radio and local law enforcement and contained a crime prevention tip on the card backs.

		NM/M	NM	E
Complete Set (10):		5.00	3.75	2.00
Common Player:		.50	.40	.20
1	Raymond Berry	.50	.40	.20
2	Anthony Carter	1.00	.70	.40
3	Chris Doleman	.75	.60	.30
4	Rick Fenney	.50	.40	.20
5	Hassan Jones	.75	.60	.30
6	Carl Lee	.50	.40	.20
7	Mike Merriweather	.50	.40	.20
8	Scott Studwell	.50	.40	.20
9	Herschel Walker	1.50	1.25	.60
10	Wade Wilson	1.00	.70	.40

1991 Vikings Police

The 10-card, standard-size set was sponsored by KFAN Radio, Gatorade, K102 Radio and Super Bowl XXVI. The cards were distributed on a weekly basis by area police departments in the order listed below.

		NM/M	NM	E
Complete Set (10):		5.00	3.75	2.00
Common Player:		.40	.30	.15
1	Rick Fenney	.40	.30	.15
2	Wade Wilson	.75	.60	.30
3	Mike Merriweather	.40	.30	.15
4	Hassan Jones	.40	.30	.15
5	Rich Gannon	1.00	.70	.40
6	Mark Dusbabek	.40	.30	.15
7	Sean Salisbury	.75	.60	.30
8	Reggie Rutland	.40	.30	.15

		NM/M	NM	E
9	Tim Irwin	.40	.30	.15
10	Chris Doleman	.75	.60	.30

1990 Virginia

		NM/M	NM	E
Complete Set (16):		25.00	18.50	10.00
Common Player:		1.25	.90	.50
1	Chris Borsari	1.25	.90	.50
2	Ron Carey	1.25	.90	.50
3	Paul Collins	1.25	.90	.50
4	Tony Covington	3.00	2.25	1.25
5	Derek Dooley	1.25	.90	.50
6	Joe Hall	1.25	.90	.50
7	Myron Martin	1.25	.90	.50
8	Bruce McGonnigal	1.50	1.25	.60
9	Jake McInerney	1.25	.90	.50
10	Keith McMeans	1.25	.90	.50
11	Herman Moore	12.00	9.00	4.75
12	Shawn Moore	4.00	3.00	1.50
13	Trevor Ryals	1.25	.90	.50
14	Chris Stearns	1.25	.90	.50
15	Jason Wallace	1.25	.90	.50
16	George Welsh (CO)	1.50	1.25	.60

W

1986 Waddingtons Game

Produced in England, this NFL card game consists of 40 cards measuring 3-1/2" x 5-11/16". The card fronts feature color illustrations of NFL teams. Five different teams are portrayed on seven cards each. The other five cards in the set are interception cards, which have the NFL logo on the front. The backs of all the cards feature the NFL logo.

		NM/M	NM	E
Complete Set (40):		60.00	45.00	24.00
Common Player:		.50	.40	.20
1	Bears 10(Walter Payton)	3.00	2.25	1.25
2	Bears 20(Walter Payton)	3.00	2.25	1.25
3	Bears 40(Walter Payton)	3.00	2.25	1.25
4	Bears 50(Walter Payton)	3.00	2.25	1.25
5	Bears First Down(Walter Payton)	3.00	2.25	1.25
6	Bears Punt(Walter Payton)	3.00	2.25	1.25
7	Bears Touchdown(Walter Payton)	3.00	2.25	1.25
8	Cowboys 10(Danny White, Tony Dorsett)	1.00	.70	.40
9	Cowboys 20(Danny White, Tony Dorsett)	1.00	.70	.40
10	Cowboys 40(Danny White, Tony Dorsett)	1.00	.70	.40
11	Cowboys 50(Danny White, Tony Dorsett)	1.00	.70	.40
12	Cowboys First Down(Danny White, Tony Dorsett)	1.00	.70	.40
13	Cowboys Punt(Danny White, Tony Dorsett)	1.00	.70	.40
14	Cowboys Touchdown(Danny White, Tony Dorsett)	1.00	.70	.40
15	Dolphins 10(Lorenzo Hampton, Eric Laakso)	.50	.40	.20
16	Dolphins 20(Lorenzo Hampton, Eric Laakso)	.50	.40	.20
17	Dolphins 40(Lorenzo Hampton, Eric Laakso)	.50	.40	.20
18	Dolphins 50(Lorenzo Hampton, Eric Laakso)	.50	.40	.20
19	Dolphins First Down(Lorenzo Hampton, Eric Laakso)	.50	.40	.20
20	Dolphins Punt(Lorenzo Hampton, Eric Laakso)	.50	.40	.20
21	Dolphins Touchdown(Lorenzo Hampton, Eric Laakso)	.50	.40	.20
22	Redskins 10(John Riggins, Joe Theismann)	1.00	.70	.40
23	Redskins 20(John Riggins, Joe Theismann)	1.00	.70	.40

		NM/M	NM	E
24	Redskins 40(John Riggins, Joe Theismann)	1.00	.70	.40
25	Redskins 50(John Riggins, Joe Theismann)	1.00	.70	.40
26	Redskins First Down(John Riggins, Joe Theismann)	1.00	.70	.40
27	Redskins Punt(John Riggins, Joe Theismann)	1.00	.70	.40
28	Redskins Touchdown(John Riggins, Joe Theismann)	1.00	.70	.40
29	Steelers 10(Terry Bradshaw, Lynn Swann)	2.00	1.50	.80
30	Steelers 20(Terry Bradshaw, Lynn Swann)	2.00	1.50	.80
31	Steelers 40(Terry Bradshaw, Lynn Swann)	2.00	1.50	.80
32	Steelers 50(Terry Bradshaw, Lynn Swann)	2.00	1.50	.80
33	Steelers First Down(Terry Bradshaw, Lynn Swann)	2.00	1.50	.80
34	Steelers Punt(Terry Bradshaw, Lynn Swann)	2.00	1.50	.80
35	Steelers Touchdown(Terry Bradshaw, Lynn Swann)	2.00	1.50	.80
36	Interception Card	.50	.40	.20
37	Interception Card	.50	.40	.20
38	Interception Card	.50	.40	.20
39	Interception Card	.50	.40	.20
40	Interception Card	.50	.40	.20

1988 Wagon Wheel

The eight-card, 6-5/16" x 4-5/16" set was issued in the United Kingdom by Burtons and each card was included in boxes of Chocolate Biscuits. Players are not specifically identified as the purpose of the set was to explain American football to the British by giving examples of positions.

		NM/M	NM	E
	Complete Set (8):	60.00	45.00	24.00
	Common Player:	6.00	4.50	2.50
1	Defensive Back (Todd Bowles covering Mark Bavaro)	6.00	4.50	2.50
2	Defensive Lineman (Ed "Too Tall" Jones, Neil Lomax)	8.00	6.00	3.25
3	Kicker (Kevin Butler)	6.00	4.50	2.50
4	Linebacker (Bob Brudzinski)	6.00	4.50	2.50
5	Offensive Lineman (Keith Van Horne leading Walter Payton)	15.00	11.00	6.00
6	Quarterback (John Elway)	20.00	15.00	8.00
7	Receiver (Steve Largent between Vann McElroy and Mike Haynes)	10.00	7.50	4.00
8	Running Back (Rodney Carter of the Steelers)	6.00	4.50	2.50

1988 Walter Payton Commemorative

Chicagoland Processing Corp. produced 16,726 of these sets to commemorate the total rushing yards Hall of Fame running back Walter Payton gained during his career with the Chicago Bears. The 132-card set chronicles his illustrious career; each card recaptures a significant moment. The standard-size cards were packaged in a blue plastic box and were issued in conjunction with a soft-cover book titled "Sweetness." Each card front has a dark blue border around an action photo. The Bears' logo and NFL logo are also on the front. The cards are numbered on the back and have a title and text which ties to the photo on the front. The cards are listed by the title used on the back.

		NM/M	NM	E
	Complete Set (132):	50.00	37.00	20.00
	Common Player:	.50	.40	.20
1	Leading Scorer in NCAA History	2.00	1.50	.80
2	1975 Game-by-Game	.50	.40	.20
3	Vs. New York Jets	.50	.40	.20
4	Vs. Miami Dolphins	.50	.40	.20
5	Vs. Baltimore/ Indianapolis Colts	.50	.40	.20
6	Vs. Buffalo Bills	.50	.40	.20
7	Vs. New England Patriots	.50	.40	.20
8	Vs. Houston Oilers	.50	.40	.20
9	Vs. Pittsburgh Steelers	.50	.40	.20
10	Vs. Cincinnati Bengals	.50	.40	.20
11	Vs. Cleveland Browns	.50	.40	.20
12	Vs. Kansas City Chiefs	.50	.40	.20
13	Vs. Oakland/Los Angeles Raiders	.50	.40	.20
14	Vs. San Diego Chargers	.50	.40	.20
15	Vs. Denver Broncos	.50	.40	.20
16	Vs. Seattle Seahawks	.50	.40	.20
17	Vs. Washington Redskins	.50	.40	.20
18	Vs. New York Giants	.50	.40	.20
19	Vs. Dallas Cowboys	.50	.40	.20
20	Vs. St. Louis Cardinals	.50	.40	.20
21	Vs. Philadelphia Eagles	.50	.40	.20
22	Vs. New Orleans Saints	.50	.40	.20
23	Vs. Atlanta Falcons	.50	.40	.20
24	Vs. Los Angeles Rams	.50	.40	.20
25	Vs. San Francisco 49ers	.50	.40	.20
26	Vs. Detroit Lions	.50	.40	.20
27	Vs. Minnesota Vikings	.50	.40	.20
28	Vs. Tampa Bay Buccaneers	.50	.40	.20
29	Vs. Green Bay Packers	.50	.40	.20
30	1976 Game-by-Game	.50	.40	.20
31	Appears in Nine Pro Bowls	.50	.40	.20
32	Post-Season Stats	.50	.40	.20
33	Owns 23 Bear Records	.50	.40	.20
34	Season-by-Season Statistics	.50	.40	.20
35	1977 Game-by-Game	.50	.40	.20
36	Most Yards Gained, Rushing	.50	.40	.20
37	Most Combined Yards, Career	.50	.40	.20
38	Most Rushing Touchdowns	.50	.40	.20
39	Most Games, 100 Yards Rushing, Career	.50	.40	.20
40	Consecutive Combined 2000-Yard Seasons	.50	.40	.20
41	Most Yards Gained, Rushing, Game	.50	.40	.20
42	Most Rushing Attempts, Career	.50	.40	.20
43	Most Combined Attempts, Career	.50	.40	.20
44	Most Seasons, 1000 Yards Rushing	.50	.40	.20
45	1978 Game-by-Game	.50	.40	.20
46	Top 10 Average Per Carry Days 1	.50	.40	.20
47	Top 10 Average Per Carry Days 2	.50	.40	.20
48	Top 10 Average Per Carry Days 3	.50	.40	.20
49	Top 10 Average Per Carry Days 4	.50	.40	.20
50	Top 10 Average Per Carry Days 5	.50	.40	.20
51	Top 10 Average Per Carry Days 6	.50	.40	.20
52	Top 10 Average Per Carry Days 7	.50	.40	.20
53	Top 10 Average Per Carry Days 8	.50	.40	.20
54	Top 10 Average Per Carry Days 9	.50	.40	.20
55	Top 10 Average Per Carry Days 10	.50	.40	.20
56	1979 Game-by-Game	.50	.40	.20
57	In Training Didn't Play Until 11th Grad	.50	.40	.20
58	In Training Running the Hill	.50	.40	.20
59	In Training Jumping Rope	.50	.40	.20
60	In Training	.50	.40	.20
61	Personal Life Interests Include...	.50	.40	.20
62	Personal Life Corporate Spokesman	.50	.40	.20
63	Personal Life Family Man	.50	.40	.20
64	Personal Life Realtives in NFL	.50	.40	.20
65	"Sweetness" autobiography written, 1978	.50	.40	.20
66	National Committee, Child Abuse Preven.	.50	.40	.20
67	Chicago 1986 Sports Father of the Year	.50	.40	.20
68	Active in Many Charities	.50	.40	.20
69	Personal Life Parade Grand Marshall	.50	.40	.20
70	1980 Game-by-Game	.50	.40	.20
71	1976 TSN MFC Player of the Year	.50	.40	.20
72	1976 Chicago Red Cloud Athlete of the Y	.50	.40	.20
73	1977 UPI Atlete of the Year	.50	.40	.20
74	1977 PFWA NFL MVP	.50	.40	.20
75	1977 UPI and TSN NFC Player of the Year	.50	.40	.20
76	1977 All Pro Pick AP, UPI, and NEA	.50	.40	.20
77	1977 PFWA,NEA,Mut. Radio,AP,FB Dig., POT	.50	.40	.20
78	TSN NFC All-Star 1976-79	.50	.40	.20
79	TSN NFL All-Star 1980,1984, and 1985	.50	.40	.20
80	1981 Game-by-Game	.50	.40	.20
81	As Quarterback	.50	.40	.20
82	Kickoff Return	.50	.40	.20
83	Complete Player	.50	.40	.20
84	Toouchdown	.50	.40	.20
85	1982 Game-by-Game	.50	.40	.20
86	Most Consecutive Games, Career	.50	.40	.20
87	Five Longest Runs	.50	.40	.20
88	Pass Receiving	.50	.40	.20
89	Ditka on Payton	.50	.40	.20
90	1983 Game-by-Game	.50	.40	.20
91	Breaks Career Rushing Record	.50	.40	.20
92	Breaks Career Rushing	.50	.40	.20
93	Breaks Career Rushing	.50	.40	.20
94	Breaks Career Rushing	.50	.40	.20
95	1984 Game-by-Game	.50	.40	.20
96	Bears Win 1985 NFC Champ. over Rams	.50	.40	.20
97	Super Bowl XX	.50	.40	.20
98	Super Bowl XX	.50	.40	.20
99	Super Bowl XX	.50	.40	.20
100	Super Bowl XX	.50	.40	.20
101	1985 Game-by-Game	.50	.40	.20
102	Sweetness	.50	.40	.20
103	Sweetness Choice to Pro Bowl Squad 1977	.50	.40	.20
104	Sweetness	.50	.40	.20
105	Sweetness 1979 Pro Bowl Starter,AP NFC	.50	.40	.20
106	Sweetness	.50	.40	.20
107	Sweetness	.50	.40	.20
108	Sweetness	.50	.40	.20
109	Sweetness	.50	.40	.20
110	1986 Game-by-Game	.50	.40	.20
111	Final Season Goodbye to Green Bay	.50	.40	.20
112	Final Season	.50	.40	.20
113	Last Regular Season Home Game	.50	.40	.20
114	Last Reg.Season Home Game,Number Retire	.50	.40	.20
115	Last Home Game,Presented with Portrait	.50	.40	.20
116	Last Regular Season Home Game	.50	.40	.20
117	Soldier Field,Known As Payton's Place	.50	.40	.20
118	Last Regular Season Home Game	.50	.40	.20
119	Last Regular Season Game vs. Raiders	.50	.40	.20
120	Last Regular Season Game	.50	.40	.20
121	Last Reg. Season Game, Catches 2 Passes	.50	.40	.20
122	Last Regular Season Game	.50	.40	.20

123	Last Regular Season Game	.50	.40	.20
124	Plays 190th Game, Bears All-Time Record	.50	.40	.20
125	Last Regular Season Game	.50	.40	.20
126	Ends Career with 21,803 Combined Yards	.50	.40	.20
127	Finishes w/4542 Career Receiving Yards	.50	.40	.20
128	16,726 Career Rushing Yards	.50	.40	.20
129	1987 Game-by-Game	.50	.40	.20
130	The End of an Era	.50	.40	.20
131	Thanks for the Memories	.50	.40	.20
132	Last Few Moments	2.00	1.50	.80

1973 Washington KFC

		NM	E	VG
	Complete Set (30):	350.00	175.00	105.00
	Common Player:	12.00	6.00	3.50
1	Jim Anderson	12.00	6.00	3.50
2	Jim Andrilenas	12.00	6.00	3.50
3	Glen Bonner	18.00	9.00	5.50
4	Bob Boustead	12.00	6.00	3.50
5	Skip Boyd	18.00	9.00	5.50
6	Gordie Bronson	12.00	6.00	3.50
7	Reggie Brown	12.00	6.00	3.50
8	Dan Celoni	12.00	6.00	3.50
9	Brian Daheny	12.00	6.00	3.50
10	Fred Dean	12.00	6.00	3.50
11	Pete Elswick	12.00	6.00	3.50
12	Dennis Fitzpatrick	12.00	6.00	3.50
13	Bob Graves	12.00	6.00	3.50
14	Pedro Hawkins	12.00	6.00	3.50
15	Rick Hayes	12.00	6.00	3.50
16	Barry Houlihan	12.00	6.00	3.50
17	Roberto Jourdan	12.00	6.00	3.50
18	Washington Keenan	12.00	6.00	3.50
19	Eddie King	12.00	6.00	3.50
20	Jim Kristoff	12.00	6.00	3.50
21	Murphy McFarland	12.00	6.00	3.50
22	Walter Oldes	12.00	6.00	3.50
23	Louis Quinn	12.00	6.00	3.50
24	Frank Reed	18.00	9.00	5.50
25	Dain Rodwell	12.00	6.00	3.50
26	Ron Stanley	12.00	6.00	3.50
27	Joe Tabor	12.00	6.00	3.50
28	Pete Taggares	12.00	6.00	3.50
29	John Whitacre	12.00	6.00	3.50
30	Hans Woldseth	12.00	6.00	3.50
NNO	Color Team Photo (Large 8x10)	18.00	9.00	5.50
NNO	Coaches Photo (Large 8x10)	25.00	12.50	7.50

1988 Washington Smokey

		NM/M	NM	E
	Complete Set (16):	15.00	11.00	6.00
	Common Player:	1.00	.70	.40
1	Ricky Andrews	1.00	.70	.40
2	Bern Brostek	2.00	1.50	.80
3	Dennis Brown	2.00	1.50	.80
4	Cary Conklin	2.00	1.50	.80
5	Tony Covington	1.00	.70	.40
6	Darryl Hall	1.00	.70	.40
7	Martin Harrison	2.00	1.50	.80
8	Don James (CO)	2.00	1.50	.80
9	Aaron Jenkins	1.00	.70	.40
10	Le-Lo Lang	2.00	1.50	.80
11	Art Malone	1.00	.70	.40
12	Andre Riley	1.00	.70	.40
13	Brian Slater	1.00	.70	.40
14	Vince Weathersby	1.00	.70	.40
15	Brett Wiese	1.00	.70	.40
16	Mike Zandofsky	1.50	1.25	.60

1988 Washington State Smokey

		NM/M	NM	E
	Complete Set (12):	12.00	9.00	4.75
	Common Player:	1.00	.70	.40
3	Timm Rosenbach	2.00	1.50	.80
18	Shawn Landrum	1.00	.70	.40
19	Artie Holmes	1.00	.70	.40
31	Steve Broussard	2.00	1.50	.80
42	Ron Lee	1.00	.70	.40
55	Tuineau Alipate	1.00	.70	.40
60	Mike Utley	4.00	3.00	1.50
68	Chris Dyko	1.00	.70	.40
74	Jim Michalczik	1.00	.70	.40
75	Tony Savage	1.00	.70	.40
76	Ivan Cook	1.00	.70	.40
82	Doug Wellsandt	1.00	.70	.40

1990 Washington Smokey

		NM/M	NM	E
	Complete Set (16):	15.00	11.00	6.00
	Common Player (1-12):	.75	.60	.30
	Common Player (13-16):	.75	.60	.30
1	Eric Briscoe (28)	.75	.60	.30
2	Mark Brunell (11)	6.00	4.50	2.50
3	James Clifford (53)	.75	.60	.30
4	John Cook (93)	.75	.60	.30
5	Ed Cunningham (79)	2.00	1.50	.80
6	Dana Hall (5)	2.50	2.00	1.00
7	Don James (CO)	1.50	1.25	.60
8	Donald Jones (48)	.75	.60	.30
9	Dean Kirkland (51)	.75	.60	.30
10	Greg Lewis (20)	2.00	1.50	.80
11	Orlando McKay (4)	.75	.60	.30
12	Travis Richardson (58)	.75	.60	.30
13	Kelley Larsen (Women's Volleyball)	.75	.60	.30
14	Michelle Reid (Women's Volleyball)	.75	.60	.30
15	Ashleigh Robertson (Women's Volleyball)	.75	.60	.30
16	Gail Thorpe (Women's Volleyball)	.75	.60	.30

1990 Washington State Smokey

		NM/M	NM	E
	Complete Set (16):	8.00	6.00	3.25
	Common Player:	.75	.60	.30
1	Lewis Bush (48)	.75	.60	.30
2	Carrie Couturier (Women's Volleyball)	.75	.60	.30
3	Steve Cromer (70)	.75	.60	.30
4	C.J. Davis (1)	.75	.60	.30
5	John Diggs (22)	.75	.60	.30
6	Alvin Dunn (27)	.75	.60	.30
7	Aaron Garcia (9)	.75	.60	.30
8	Bob Garman (74)	.75	.60	.30
9	Brad Gossen (12)	1.00	.70	.40
10	Calvin Griggs (5)	.75	.60	.30
11	Kelly Hankins (Women's Volleyball)	.75	.60	.30
12	Jason Hanson (4)	2.50	2.00	1.00
13	Kristen Hovde (Women's Volleyball)	.75	.60	.30
14	Keri Killebrew (Women's Volleyball)	.75	.60	.30
15	Chris Moton (6)	.75	.60	.30
16	Ron Ricard (26)	.75	.60	.30

1991 Washington Smokey

		NM/M	NM	E
	Complete Set (16):	15.00	11.00	6.00
	Common Player (1-12):	.75	.60	.30
	Common Player (13-16):	.75	.60	.30
1	Mario Bailey	1.50	1.25	.60
2	Beno Bryant	1.50	1.25	.60
3	Brett Collins	.75	.60	.30
4	Ed Cunningham	1.50	1.25	.60
5	Steve Emtman	2.00	1.50	.80
6	Dana Hall	2.00	1.50	.80
7	Billy Joe Hobert	4.00	3.00	1.50
8	Dave Hoffmann	.75	.60	.30
9	Don James (CO)	1.25	.90	.50
10	Donald Jones	.75	.60	.30
11	Siupeli Malamala	1.50	1.25	.60
12	Orlando McKay	.75	.60	.30
13	Diane Flick (Women's Volleyball)	.75	.60	.30
14	Kelley Larsen (Women's Volleyball)	.75	.60	.30
15	Ashleigh Robertson (Women's Volleyball)	.75	.60	.30
16	Dana Thompson (Women's Volleyball)	.75	.60	.30

1991 Washington State Smokey

		NM/M	NM	E
	Complete Set (16):	9.00	6.75	3.50
	Common Player (1-12):	.75	.60	.30
	Common Player (13-16):	.75	.60	.30
1	Lewis Bush	.75	.60	.30
2	Chad Cushing	.75	.60	.30
3	C.J. Davis	.75	.60	.30
4	Bob Garman	.75	.60	.30
5	Jason Hanson	2.00	1.50	.80
6	Gabriel Oladipo	.75	.60	.30
7	Anthony Prior	1.50	1.25	.60
8	Jay Reyna	.75	.60	.30
9	Lee Tilleman	.75	.60	.30
10	Kirk Westerfield	.75	.60	.30
11	Butch Williams	.75	.60	.30
12	Michael Wright	.75	.60	.30
13	Carrie Couturier (Women's Volleyball)	.75	.60	.30
14	Kelly Hankins (Women's Volleyball)	.75	.60	.30
15	Kristen Hovde (Women's Volleyball)	.75	.60	.30
16	Keri Killebrew (Women's Volleyball)	.75	.60	.30

1974 West Virginia

		NM	E	VG
	Complete Set (53):	80.00	40.00	24.00
	Common Player:	1.00	.50	.30
1C	Stu Wolpert	1.00	.50	.30
1D	Mountaineer Coaches	4.00	2.00	1.25
1H	Leland Byrd (AD)	1.00	.50	.30
1S	Bobby Bowden (CO)	25.00	12.50	7.50
2C	Jay Sheehan	1.00	.50	.30
2D	Tom Brandner	1.00	.50	.30
2H	Tom Bowden	1.00	.50	.30
2S	Chuck Smith	1.00	.50	.30
3C	Ray Marshall	1.00	.50	.30
3D	Randy Swinson	1.00	.50	.30
3H	Tom Loadman	1.00	.50	.30
3S	Bob Kaminski	1.00	.50	.30
4C	Ron Lee	3.00	1.50	.90
4D	Kirk Lewis	1.00	.50	.30
4H	Greg Dorn	1.00	.50	.30
4S	Emil Ros	1.00	.50	.30
5C	Mark Burke	1.00	.50	.30
5D	Rory Fields	1.00	.50	.30
5H	Gary Lombard	1.00	.50	.30
5S	Brian Gates	1.00	.50	.30
6C	John Schell	1.00	.50	.30
6D	Paul Jordan	1.00	.50	.30
6H	Mike Hubbard	1.00	.50	.30
6S	Chuck Kelly	1.00	.50	.30
7C	Rick Pennypacker	2.00	1.00	.60
7D	Heywood Smith	1.00	.50	.30
7H	Jack Eastwood	1.00	.50	.30
7S	Andy Peters	1.00	.50	.30
8C	Steve Dunlap	1.00	.50	.30
8D	Dave Wilcher	2.00	1.00	.60
8H	Greg Anderson	1.00	.50	.30
8S	Ken Culbertson	1.00	.50	.30
9C	David Van Halanger	1.00	.50	.30
9D	Rick Shaffer	1.00	.50	.30
9H	Rich Lukowski	1.00	.50	.30
9S	Al Gluchoski	1.00	.50	.30
10C	Dwayne Woods	1.00	.50	.30
10D	Ben Williams	2.00	1.00	.60
10H	John Adams	1.00	.50	.30
10S	Tom Florence	1.00	.50	.30
11C	Marcus Mauney	1.00	.50	.30
11D	John Spraggins	1.00	.50	.30
11H	Bruce Huffman	1.00	.50	.30
11S	Bernie Kirchner	1.00	.50	.30
12C	Artie Owens	2.00	1.00	.60
12D	Charlie Miller	1.00	.50	.30
12H	1974 Cheerleaders	1.00	.50	.30
12S	Eddie Russell	1.00	.50	.30
13C	Danny Buggs	4.00	2.00	1.25
13D	Marshall Mills	1.00	.50	.30
13H	John Everly	1.00	.50	.30
13S	Jeff Merrow	4.00	2.00	1.25
JK	Student Foundation	1.00	.50	.30

1988 West Virginia

		NM/M	NM	E
	Complete Set (16):	20.00	15.00	8.00
	Common Player:	1.00	.70	.40
1	Charlie Baumann	1.50	1.25	.60
2	Anthony Brown	1.00	.70	.40
3	Willie Edwards	1.00	.70	.40
4	Theron Ellis	1.50	1.25	.60
5	Chris Haering	1.00	.70	.40
6	Major Harris	4.00	3.00	1.50
7	Undra Johnson	1.50	1.25	.60

8	Kevin Koken	1.00	.70	.40
9	Pat Marlatt	1.00	.70	.40
10	Eugene Napoleon	1.00	.70	.40
11	Don Nehlen (CO)	2.00	1.50	.80
12	Bo Orlando	3.00	2.25	1.25
13	Chris Parker	1.00	.70	.40
14	Robert Pickett	1.00	.70	.40
15	Brian Smider	1.00	.70	.40
16	John Stroia	1.00	.70	.40

1990 West Virigina Program Cards

		NM/M	NM	E
Complete Set (49):		35.00	26.00	14.00
Common Player:		.75	.60	.30
1	Tarris Alexander	.75	.60	.30
2	Leroy Axem	.75	.60	.30
3	Michael Beasley	.75	.60	.30
4	Calvin Bell	.75	.60	.30
5	Matt Bland	.75	.60	.30
6	John Brown	1.25	.90	.50
7	Brad Carroll	.75	.60	.30
8	Mike Collins	.75	.60	.30
9	Mike Compton	1.25	.90	.50
10	Cecil Doggette	.75	.60	.30
11	Rick Dolly	.75	.60	.30
12	Theron Ellis	1.25	.90	.50
13	Charlie Fedorco	.75	.60	.30
14	Garrett Ford	.75	.60	.30
15	Scott Gaskins	.75	.60	.30
16	Boris Graham	.75	.60	.30
17	Keith Graley	.75	.60	.30
18	Chris Gray	.75	.60	.30
19	Greg Hertzog	.75	.60	.30
20	Ed Hill	.75	.60	.30
21	Verne Howard	.75	.60	.30
22	James Jett	4.00	3.00	1.50
23	Greg Jones	.75	.60	.30
24	Jon James	.75	.60	.30
25	Ted Kester	.75	.60	.30
26	Darroll Mitchell	.75	.60	.30
27	John Murphy	.75	.60	.30
28	Don Nehlen (CO)	2.50	2.00	1.00
29	Tim Newsom	.75	.60	.30
30	Joe Pabian	.75	.60	.30
31	John Ray	.75	.60	.30
32	Steve Redd	.75	.60	.30
33	Joe Ruth	.75	.60	.30
34	Alex Shook	.75	.60	.30
35	Jeff Sniffen	.75	.60	.30
36	Ray Staten	.75	.60	.30
37	Rick Stead	.75	.60	.30
38	Darren Studstill	2.00	1.50	.80
39	Lorenzo Styles	2.00	1.50	.80
40	Gary Tillis	.75	.60	.30
41	Rico Tyler	.75	.60	.30
42	Darrell Whitmore	2.00	1.50	.80
43	E.J. Wheeler	.75	.60	.30
44	Darrick Wiley	.75	.60	.30
45	Tim Williams	.75	.60	.30
46	Sam Wilson	.75	.60	.30
47	Dale Wolfley	.75	.60	.30
48	Rob Yachini	.75	.60	.30
49	**Mountaineer Field**	.75	.60	.30

1991 West Virginia ATG

		NM/M	NM	E
Complete Set (50):		15.00	11.00	6.00
Common Player:		.35	.25	.14
1	Jeff Hostetler	2.50	2.00	1.00
2	Tom Allman	.35	.25	.14
3	Russ Bailey	.35	.25	.14
4	Paul Bischoff	.35	.25	.14
5	Bruce Bosley	.50	.40	.20
6	Jim Braxton	.50	.40	.20
7	Danny Buggs	.50	.40	.20
8	Harry Clarke	.35	.25	.14
9	Ken Culbertson	.35	.25	.14
10	Willie Drewrey	.50	.40	.20
11	Steve Dunlap	.35	.25	.14
12	Garrett Ford	.35	.25	.14
13	Dennis Fowlkes	.35	.25	.14
14	Bob Gresham	.50	.40	.20
15	Chris Haering	.50	.40	.20
16	Major Harris	1.00	.70	.40
17	Steve Hathaway	.35	.25	.14
18	Rick Hollins	.35	.25	.14
19	Chuck Howley	1.00	.70	.40
20	Sam Huff	1.25	.90	.50
21	Brian Jozwiak	.50	.40	.20
22	Gene Lamone	.35	.25	.14
23	Oliver Luck	.75	.60	.30
24	Kerry Marbury	.35	.25	.14
25	Joe Marconi	.50	.40	.20
26	Jeff Merrow	.50	.40	.20
27	Steve Newberry	.35	.25	.14
28	Bob Orders	.35	.25	.14

29	Artie Owens	.50	.40	.20
30	Tom Pridemore	.50	.40	.20
31	Mark Raugh	.35	.25	.14
32	Heggie Hembert	.50	.40	.20
33	Ira Rodgers	.35	.25	.14
34	Mike Sherwood	.35	.25	.14
35	Joe Stydahar	.50	.40	.20
36	Renaldo Turnbull	1.25	.90	.50
37	Paul Woodside	.35	.25	.14
38	Fred Wyant	.35	.25	.14
39	Carl Leatherwood	.35	.25	.14
40	Darryl Talley	1.00	.70	.40
41	David Grant	.50	.40	.20
42	Bobby Bowden (CO)	1.00	.70	.40
43	Jim Carlen (CO)	.35	.25	.14
44	Frank Cignetti (CO)	.35	.25	.14
45	Gene Corum (CO)	.35	.25	.14
46	Art Lewis (CO)	.35	.25	.14
47	Don Nehlen (CO)	.50	.40	.20
48	**New Mountaineer Field**	.35	.25	.14
49	**Old Mountaineer Field**	.35	.25	.14
50	**Lambert Trophy**	.50	.40	.20

1991 West Virginia Program Cards

		NM/M	NM	E
Complete Set (42):		25.00	18.50	10.00
Common Player:		.75	.60	.30
1	Tarris Alexander	.75	.60	.30
2	Johnathan Allen	.75	.60	.30
3	Leroy Axem	.75	.60	.30
4	Joe Ayuso	.75	.60	.30
5	Michael Beasley	.75	.60	.30
6	Rich Braham	1.00	.70	.40
7	Tom Briggs	.75	.60	.30
8	John Cappa	.75	.60	.30
9	Mike Collins	1.00	.70	.40
10	Mike Compton	1.00	.70	.40
11	Doug Cooley	.75	.60	.30
12	Cecil Doggette	.75	.60	.30
13	Rick Dolly	.75	.60	.30
14	Garrett Ford	.75	.60	.30
15	Scott Gaskins	1.00	.70	.40
16	Boris Graham	.75	.60	.30
17	Keith Graley	.75	.60	.30
18	Chris Gray	.75	.60	.30
19	Barry Hawkins	.75	.60	.30
20	Ed Hill	1.00	.70	.40
21	James Jett	3.00	2.25	1.25
22	Jon Jones	.75	.60	.30
23	Jim LeBlanc	1.00	.70	.40
24	David Mayfield	1.00	.70	.40
25	Adrian Murrell	3.00	2.25	1.25
26	Sam Mustipher	.75	.60	.30
27	Tim Newsom	.75	.60	.30
28	Tommy Orr	.75	.60	.30
29	Joe Pabian	.75	.60	.30
30	John Ray	.75	.60	.30
31	Wes Richardson	1.00	.70	.40
32	Nate Rine	.75	.60	.30
33	Joe Ruth	.75	.60	.30
34	Alex Shook	.75	.60	.30
35	Kwame Smith	.75	.60	.30
36	Darren Studstill	2.00	1.50	.80
37	Lorenzo Styles	1.50	1.25	.60
38	Gary Tillis	.75	.60	.30
39	Ron Weaver	.75	.60	.30
40	Darrell Whitmore	2.50	2.00	1.00
41	Darrick Wiley	.75	.60	.30
42	Rodney Woodard	.75	.60	.30

1959 Wheaties CFL

		NM	E	VG
Complete Set (48):		4,000	2,000	1,200
Common Player:		60.00	30.00	18.00
1	Ron Adam	60.00	30.00	18.00
2	Bill Bewley	75.00	37.00	22.00
3	Lynn Bottoms	75.00	37.00	22.00
4	Johnny Bright	150.00	75.00	45.00
5	Ken Carpenter	75.00	37.00	22.00
6	Tony Curcillo	60.00	30.00	18.00
7	Sam Etcheverry	250.00	125.00	75.00
8	Bernie Faloney	200.00	100.00	60.00
9	Cam Fraser	75.00	37.00	22.00
10	Don Getty	125.00	62.00	37.00
11	Jack Gotta	75.00	37.00	22.00
12	Milt Graham	60.00	30.00	18.00
13	Jack Hill	60.00	30.00	18.00
14	Ron Howell	75.00	37.00	22.00
15	Russ Jackson	200.00	100.00	60.00
16	Gerry James	125.00	62.00	37.00
17	Doug Kiloh	60.00	30.00	18.00
18	Ronnie Knox	75.00	37.00	22.00
19	Vic Kristopaitis	60.00	30.00	18.00
20	Oscar Kruger	60.00	30.00	18.00
21	Bobby Kuntz	75.00	37.00	22.00
22	Normie Kwong	175.00	87.00	52.00

23	Leo Lewis	150.00	75.00	45.00
24	Harry Lunn	60.00	30.00	18.00
25	Don Luzzi	100.00	50.00	30.00
26	Dave Mann	75.00	37.00	22.00
27	Bobby Marlow	90.00	45.00	27.00
28	Gerry McDougall	75.00	37.00	22.00
29	Doug McNichol	60.00	30.00	18.00
30	Rollie Miles	100.00	50.00	30.00
31	Red O'Quinn	90.00	45.00	27.00
32	Jackie Parker	250.00	125.00	75.00
33	Hal Patterson	150.00	75.00	45.00
34	Don Pinhey	60.00	30.00	18.00
35	Kenny Ploen	125.00	62.00	37.00
36	Gord Rowland	75.00	37.00	22.00
37	Vince Scott	90.00	45.00	27.00
38	Art Scullion	60.00	30.00	18.00
39	Dick Shatto	125.00	62.00	37.00
40	Bob Simpson	125.00	62.00	37.00
41	Jackie Simpson (UER) (Misspelled Jacki)	100.00	50.00	30.00
42	Bill Sowalski	60.00	30.00	18.00
43	Norm Stoneburgh	60.00	30.00	18.00
44	Buddy Tinsley	90.00	45.00	27.00
45	Frank Tripucka	100.00	50.00	30.00
46	Jim Van Pelt	60.00	30.00	18.00
47	Ernie Warlick	75.00	37.00	22.00
48	Nobby Wirkowski	100.00	50.00	30.00

1964 Wheaties Stamps

These unnumbered stamps, which measure 2-1/2" x 2-3/4", were created to be stored in an accompanying stamp album titled "Pro Bowl Football Player Stamp Album." Each stamp has a color photo of the player, plus his facsimile signature, bordered by a white frame. The stamps were in panels of 12 inside the album and were perforated so they could be put on the corresponding spot within the album. Two stickers were attached to the inside front cover. Four team logo stamps and 70 players are represented on the stamps, but there were no spots in the album for the logo stamps or those for Y.A. Tittle or Joe Schmidt.

		NM	E	VG
Complete Set (74):		250.00	125.00	75.00
Common Player:		2.00	1.00	.60
(1)	Herb Adderley	6.00	3.00	1.75
(2)	Grady Alderman	2.00	1.00	.60
(3)	Doug Atkins	4.00	2.00	1.25
(4)	Sam Baker	2.00	1.00	.60
(5)	Erich Barnes	2.00	1.00	.60
(6)	Terry Barr	2.00	1.00	.60
(7)	Dick Bass	2.00	1.00	.60
(8)	Maxie Baughan	3.00	1.50	.90
(9)	Raymond Berry	6.00	3.00	1.75
(10)	Charley Bradshaw	2.50	1.25	.70
(11)	Jim Brown	35.00	17.50	10.50
(12)	Roger Brown	2.50	1.25	.70
(13)	Timmy Brown	3.00	1.50	.90
(14)	Gail Cogdill	2.00	1.00	.60
(15)	Tommy Davis	2.00	1.00	.60
(16)	Willie Davis	6.00	3.00	1.75
(17)	Bob DeMarco	2.00	1.00	.60
(18)	Darrell Dess	2.00	1.00	.60
(19)	Buddy Dial	3.00	1.50	.90
(20)	Mike Ditka	18.00	9.00	5.50
(21)	Galen Fiss	2.00	1.00	.60
(22)	Lee Folkins	2.00	1.00	.60
(23)	Joe Fortunato	2.00	1.00	.60
(24)	Bill Glass	3.00	1.50	.90
(25)	John Gordy	2.00	1.00	.60
(26)	Ken Gray	2.50	1.25	.70
(27)	Forrest Gregg	5.00	2.50	1.50
(28)	Rip Hawkins	2.00	1.00	.60
(29)	Charlie Johnson	3.00	1.50	.90
(30)	John Henry Johnson	5.00	2.50	1.50
(31)	Henry Jordan	3.00	1.50	.90
(32)	Jim Katcavage	2.00	1.00	.60
(33)	Jerry Kramer	5.00	2.50	1.50
(34)	Joe Krupa	2.00	1.00	.60
(35)	John LoVetere	2.00	1.00	.60
(36)	Dick Lynch	3.00	1.50	.90
(37)	Gino Marchetti	5.00	2.50	1.50
(38)	Joe Marconi	2.00	1.00	.60
(39)	Tommy Mason	3.00	1.50	.90
(40)	Dale Meinert	2.00	1.00	.60
(41)	Lou Michaels	2.00	1.00	.60
(42)	**Minnesota Vikings Emblem**	3.00	1.50	.90
(43)	Bobby Mitchell	6.00	3.00	1.75
(44)	John Morrow	2.00	1.00	.60
(45)	**New York Giants Emblem**	3.00	1.50	.90
(46)	Merlin Olsen	10.00	5.00	3.00
(47)	Jack Pardee	4.00	2.00	1.25
(48)	Jim Parker	4.00	2.00	1.25
(49)	Bernie Parrish	2.00	1.00	.60
(50)	Don Perkins	3.00	1.50	.90
(51)	Richie Petitbon	2.00	1.00	.60

(52)	Vince Promuto	2.00	1.00	.60
(53)	Myron Pottios	2.00	1.00	.60
(54)	Mike Pyle	2.00	1.00	.60
(55)	Pete Retzlaff	3.00	1.50	.90
(56)	Jim Ringo	5.00	2.50	1.50
(57)	Joe Rutgens	2.00	1.00	.60
(58)	**St. Louis Cardinals Emblem**	3.00	1.50	.90
(59)	**San Francisco 49ers Emblem**	3.00	1.50	.90
(60)	Dick Schafrath	2.00	1.00	.60
(61)	Joe Schmidt	6.00	3.00	1.75
(62)	Del Shofner	3.00	1.50	.90
(63)	Norm Snead	3.00	1.50	.90
(64)	Bart Starr	15.00	7.50	4.50
(65)	Jim Taylor	6.00	3.00	1.75
(66)	Roosevelt Taylor	2.00	1.00	.60
(67)	Clendon Thomas	2.00	1.00	.60
(68)	Y.A. Tittle	12.50	6.25	3.75
(69)	John Unitas	18.00	9.00	5.50
(70)	Bill Wade	3.00	1.50	.90
(71)	Wayne Walker	2.00	1.00	.60
(72)	Jesse Whittenton	2.00	1.00	.60
(73)	Larry Wilson	5.00	2.50	1.50
(74)	Abe Woodson	2.00	1.00	.60
---	**Album**	25.00	12.50	7.50

1987 Wheaties

Specially-marked boxes of Wheaties cereal each contained one of these 5" x 7" posters. The posters, which were wrapped in cellophane, were produced by Starline Inc. with the cooperation of the NFLPA and organizational efforts of Michael Schechter Associates. Each front has a color action photo, with the player's name, team, position and uniform number listed in a white box at the bottom. "Wheaties" is written in a banner in the upper left corner. The poster back is numbered and includes biographical information and career summary notes. Bernie Kosar's card was not listed in the set on the checklist Wheaties provided on the box. It is assumed Kosar was pulled from the set at some point - his card is listed as a short print.

		NM/M	NM	E
Complete Set (26):		130.00	97.00	52.00
Common Player:		2.50	2.00	1.00
1	Tony Dorsett	5.00	3.75	2.00
2	Herschel Walker	5.00	3.75	2.00
3	Marcus Allen	5.00	3.75	2.00
4	Eric Dickerson	6.00	4.50	2.50
5	Walter Payton	12.00	9.00	4.75
6	Phil Simms	4.00	3.00	1.50
7	Tommy Kramer	2.50	2.00	1.00
8	Joe Morris	2.50	2.00	1.00
9	Roger Craig	4.00	3.00	1.50
10	Curt Warner	3.50	2.75	1.50
11	Andre Tippett	2.50	2.00	1.00
12	Joe Montana	20.00	15.00	8.00
13	Jim McMahon	3.00	2.25	1.25
14	Bernie Kosar	25.00	18.50	10.00
15	Jay Schroeder	2.50	2.00	1.00
16	Al Toon	2.50	2.00	1.00
17	Mark Gastineau	2.50	2.00	1.00
18	Kenny Easley	2.50	2.00	1.00
19	Howie Long	2.50	2.00	1.00
20	Dan Marino	15.00	11.00	6.00
21	Karl Mecklenburg	3.25	2.50	1.25
22	John Elway	10.00	7.50	4.00
23	Boomer Esiason	5.00	3.75	2.00
24	Dan Fouts	4.00	3.00	1.50
25	Jim Kelly	10.00	7.50	4.00
26	Louis Lipps	3.00	2.25	1.25

1991 Wild Card College Draft Picks

Each of these cards features a glossy color action photo of a player in his college uniform. The card is black with an orange frame, which has different denominations running on top and down the right side. A circle with "1st Edition" appears in the lower left corner. The purple back has statistics, biographical information and a color photo. Striped, limited-edition Wild Card random inserts of each card were also

produced (1 out of every 100 is wild). These cards had denominations of 5, 10, 20, 50, 100 and 1,000; the higher numbers were made in scarcer numbers. The finder was able to redeem the card for a like amount of the player's regular card.

		NM	E	VG
Complete Set (160):		15.00	7.50	1.50
Common Player:		.05	.02	
1	Wild Card 1 (Todd Lyght)	.60	.30	.06
2	Kelvin Pritchett	.20	.10	.02
3	Robert Young	.05	.02	
4	Reggie Johnson	.05	.02	
5	Eric Turner	.50	.25	.05
6	Pat Tyrance	.10	.05	.01
7	Curvin Richards	.20	.10	.02
8	Calvin Stephens	.10	.05	.01
9	Corey Miller	.05	.02	
10	Michael Jackson	.30	.15	.03
11	Simmie Carter	.05	.02	
12	Roland Smith	.10	.05	.01
13	Pat O'Hara	.20	.10	.02
14	Scott Conover	.05	.02	
15	Wild Card 2 (Russell Maryland)	.75	.35	.07
16	Greg Amsler	.10	.05	.01
17	Moe Gardner	.30	.15	.03
18	Howard Griffith	.20	.10	.02
19	David Daniels	.10	.05	.01
20	Henry Jones	.10	.05	.01
21	Don Davey	.10	.05	.01
22	Wild Card 3 (Raghib (Rocket) Ismail)	1.00	.50	.10
23	Richie Andrews	.05	.02	
24	Shawn Moore	.25	.12	.02
25	Anthony Moss	.10	.05	.01
26	Vince Moore	.05	.02	
27	Leroy Thompson	.15	.07	.01
28	Darrick Brownlow	.20	.10	.02
29	Mel Agee	.10	.05	.01
30	Darryll Lewis	.25	.12	.02
31	Hyland Hickson	.05	.02	
32	Leonard Russell	1.00	.50	.10
33	Floyd Fields	.05	.02	
34	Esera Tuaolo	.15	.07	.01
35	Todd Marinovich	1.25	.60	.12
36	Gary Wellman	.10	.05	.01
37	Ricky Ervins	2.50	1.25	.25
38	Pat Harlow	.20	.10	.02
39	Mo Lewis	.25	.12	.02
40	John Kasay	.30	.15	.03
41	Phil Hansen	.10	.05	.01
42	Kevin Donnalley	.10	.05	.01
43	Dexter Davis	.10	.05	.01
44	Vance Hammond	.05	.02	
45	Chris Gardocki	.10	.05	.01
46	Bruce Pickens	.20	.10	.02
47	Godfrey Myles	.15	.07	.01
48	Ernie Mills	.25	.12	.02
49	Derek Russell	.35	.17	.03
50	Chris Zorich	.50	.25	.05
51	Alfred Williams	.25	.12	.02
52	Jon Vaughn	.45	.22	.04
53	Adrian Cooper	.25	.12	.02
54	Eric Bieniemy	.05	.02	
55	Robert Bailey	.05	.02	
56	Ricky Watters	.25	.12	.02
57	Mark Vander Poel	.10	.05	.01
58	James Joseph	.50	.25	.05
59	Darren Lewis	.45	.22	.04
60	Wesley Carroll	.40	.20	.04
61	Dave Key	.10	.05	.01
62	Mike Pritchard	.75	.35	.07
63	Craig Erickson	.40	.20	.04
64	Browning Nagle	.75	.35	.07
65	Mike Dumas	.20	.10	.02
66	Andre Jones	.05	.02	
67	Herman Moore	.75	.35	.07
68	Greg Lewis	.60	.30	.06
69	James Goode	.05	.02	
70	Stan Thomas	.10	.05	.01
71	Jerome Henderson	.10	.05	.01
72	Doug Thomas	.10	.05	.01
73	Tony Covington	.10	.05	.01
74	Charles Mincy	.10	.05	.01
75	Kanavis McGhee	.20	.10	.02
76	Tom Backes	.05	.02	
77	Fernandus Vinson	.05	.02	
78	Marcus Robertson	.05	.02	
79	Eric Harmon	.05	.02	
80	Rob Selby	.10	.05	.01
81	Ed King	.20	.10	.02
82	William Thomas	.10	.05	.01
83	Mike Jones	.10	.05	.01
84	Paul Justin	.20	.10	.02
85	Robert Wilson	.20	.10	.02
86	Jesse Campbell	.10	.05	.01
87	Hayward Haynes	.05	.02	
88	Mike Croel	.75	.35	.07

89	Jeff Graham	.20	.10	.02
90	Vinnie Clark	.25	.12	.02
91	Keith Cash	.20	.10	.02
92	Tim Ryan	.10	.05	.01
93	Jarrod Bunch	.20	.10	.02
94	Stanley Richard	.30	.15	.03
95	Alvin Harper	.60	.30	.06
96	Bob Dahl	.10	.05	.01
97	Mark Gunn	.05	.02	
98	Frank Blevins	.05	.02	
99	Harvey Williams	1.00	.50	.10
100	Dixon Edwards	.20	.10	.02
101	Blake Miller	.05	.02	
102	Bobby Wilson	.25	.12	.02
103	Chuck Webb	.25	.12	.02
104	Randal Hill	.75	.35	.07
105	Shane Curry	.05	.02	
106	Barry Sanders	.75	.35	.07
107	Richard Fain	.15	.07	.01
108	Joe Garten	.05	.02	
109	Dean Dingham	.05	.02	
110	Mark Tucker	.05	.02	
111	Dan McGwire	1.00	.50	.10
112	Paul Glonek	.05	.02	
113	Tom Dohring	.05	.02	
114	Joe Sims	.05	.02	
115	Bryan Cox	.30	.15	.03
116	Bobby Olive	.05	.02	
117	Blaise Bryant	.15	.07	.01
118	Charles Johnson	.15	.07	.01
119	Brett Favre	2.00	.80	.06
120	Luis Cristobal	.05	.02	
121	Don Gibson	.05	.02	
122	Scott Ross	.05	.02	
123	Huey Richardson	.15	.07	.01
124	Chris Smith	.10	.05	.01
125	Duane Young	.05	.02	
126	Eric Swann	.30	.15	.03
127	Jeff Fite	.05	.02	
128	Eugene Williams	.05	.02	
129	Harlan Davis	.05	.02	
130	James Bradley	.05	.02	
131	Rob Carpenter	.20	.10	.02
132	Dennis Ransom	.05	.02	
133	Mike Arthur	.05	.02	
134	Chuck Weatherspoon	.30	.15	.03
135	Darrell Malone	.05	.02	
136	George Thornton	.10	.05	.01
137	Lamar McGriggs	.05	.02	
138	Alex Johnson	.05	.02	
139	Eric Moten	.10	.05	.01
140	Joe Valerio	.10	.05	.01
141	Jake Reed	.20	.10	.02
142	Ernie Thompson	.10	.05	.01
143	Roland Poles	.05	.02	
144	Randy Bethel	.05	.02	
145	Terry Bagsby	.05	.02	
146	Tim James	.05	.02	
147	Kenny Walker	.60	.30	.06
148	Nolan Harrison	.05	.02	
149	Keith Traylor	.20	.10	.02
150	Nick Subis	.05	.02	
151	Scott Zolak	.25	.12	.02
152	Pio Sagapolutele	.15	.07	.01
153	James Jones	.10	.05	.01
154	Mike Sullivan	.05	.02	
155	Joe Johnson	.05	.02	
156	Todd Scott	.10	.05	.01
157	**Checklist 1**	.05	.02	
158	**Checklist 2**	.05	.02	
159	**Checklist 3**	.05	.02	
160	**Checklist 4**	.05	.02	

1991 Wild Card National Promos

This three-card set was given away as a promo at the 12th Annual National Convention in Anaheim. The cards are numbered on the back, starting with the Dan McGwire card as "Prototype-2." Striped versions of the cards with a hologram in the upper left corner were also issued.

		NM	E	VG
Complete Set (3):		12.00	6.00	1.20
Common Player:		2.50	1.25	.25
2	Dan McGwire	6.00	3.00	.60
3	Randal Hill	2.50	1.25	.25
4	Todd Marinovich	6.00	3.00	.60

1991 Wild Card NFL

These cards, similar in design to Wild Cards' collegiate draft picks set, have a full-color glossy action photo on the front, with a black and yellow border. Multi-color numbers appear in the upper right corner and along the right side of the card. The player's name and position are in the lower right corner, opposite a football with the words "NFL Premier Edition" inside. The card back has a mug shot, statistics, a card number and biographical information. Striped "Wild Cards," printed in limited editions, were also created for each card, in denominations of 10, 20, 50, 100 and 1,000. The card could be redeemed for a similar amount of the player's regular card, according to the denomination number in the stripe. A surprise Wild Card, #126, was also created; finders could redeem it for a 10-card NFL Experience subset which featured players from the Buffalo Bills and Washington Redskins. Also created were three bonus cards, which enabled finders to redeem them for the item pictured - either a case of cards, a box of cards, or a Wild Card cap.

		NM/M	NM	E
Complete Set (160):		10.00	7.50	4.00
Common Player:		.03	.02	.01
Wax Box:		6.00		
1	Jeff George	.35	.25	.14
2	Sean Jones	.03	.02	.01
3	Duane Bickett	.03	.02	.01
4	John Elway	.15	.11	.06
5	Christian Okoye	.08	.06	.03
6	Steve Atwater	.06	.05	.02
7	Anthony Munoz	.08	.06	.03
8	Dave Krieg	.08	.06	.03
9	Nick Lowery	.06	.05	.02
10	Albert Bentley	.06	.05	.02
11	Mark Jackson	.06	.05	.02
12	Jeff Bryant	.03	.02	.01
13	Johnny Hector	.03	.02	.01
14	John L. Williams	.08	.06	.03
15	Jim Everett	.15	.11	.06
16	Mark Duper	.06	.05	.02
17	Drew Hill	.08	.06	.03
18	Randal Hill	.60	.45	.25
19	Ernest Givins	.10	.08	.04
20	Ken O'Brien	.08	.06	.03
21	Blair Thomas	.40	.30	.15
22	Derrick Thomas	.15	.11	.06
23	Harvey Williams	.75	.60	.30
24	Simon Fletcher	.03	.02	.01
25	Stephone Paige	.06	.05	.02
26	Barry Wood	.25	.20	.10
27	Warren Moon	.20	.15	.08
28	Derrick Fenner	.12	.09	.05
29	Shane Conlan	.06	.05	.02
30	Karl Mecklenburg	.06	.05	.02
31	Gary Anderson	.06	.05	.02
32	Sammie Smith	.08	.06	.03
33	Steve DeBerg	.08	.06	.03
34	Dan McGwire	1.25	.90	.50
35	Roger Craig	.10	.08	.04
36	Tom Tupa	.10	.08	.04
37	Rod Woodson	.08	.06	.03
38	Junior Seau	.08	.06	.03
39	Bruce Pickens	.20	.15	.08
40	Greg Townsend	.03	.02	.01
41	Gary Clark	.12	.09	.05
42	Broderick Thomas	.06	.05	.02
43	Charles Mann	.06	.05	.02
44	Browning Nagle	.75	.60	.30
45	James Joseph	.45	.35	.20
46	Emmitt Smith	2.00	1.50	.80
47	Cornelius Bennett	.08	.06	.03
48	Maurice Hurst	.03	.02	.01
49	Art Monk	.10	.08	.04
50	Louis Lipps	.06	.05	.02
51	Mark Rypien	.20	.15	.08
52	Bubby Brister	.08	.06	.03
53	John Stephens	.06	.05	.02
54	Merril Hoge	.03	.02	.01
55	Kevin Mack	.06	.05	.02
56	Al Toon	.08	.06	.03
57	Ronnie Lott	.10	.08	.04
58	Eric Metcalf	.06	.05	.02
59	Vinny Testaverde	.08	.06	.03
60	Darrell Green	.10	.08	.04
61	Randall Cunningham	.15	.11	.06
62	Charles Haley	.06	.05	.02
63	Mark Carrier	.08	.06	.03
64	Jim Harbaugh	.10	.08	.04
65	Richard Dent	.08	.06	.03
66	Stan Thomas	.08	.06	.03
67	Neal Anderson	.15	.11	.06
68	Troy Aikman	1.25	.90	.50
69	Mike Pritchard **RC**	.40	.30	.15
70	Deion Sanders	.20	.15	.08
71	Andre Rison	.15	.11	.06
72	Keith Millard	.06	.05	.02
73	Jerry Rice	.85	.60	.35
74	Johnny Johnson	.25	.20	.10
75	Tim McDonald	.06	.05	.02
76	Leonard Russell **RC**	1.25	.90	.50
77	Keith Jackson	.08	.06	.03
78	Keith Byars	.06	.05	.02
79	Ricky Proehl	.10	.08	.04
80	Dexter Carter	.08	.06	.03
81	Alvin Harper **RC**	.75	.60	.30
82	Irving Fryar	.06	.05	.02
83	Marion Butts	.10	.08	.04
84	Alfred Williams	.15	.11	.06
85	Timm Rosenbach	.10	.08	.04
86	Steve Young	.60	.45	.25
87	Albert Lewis	.06	.05	.02
88	Rodney Peete	.08	.06	.03
89	Barry Sanders	.85	.60	.35
90	Bennie Blades	.06	.05	.02
91	Chris Spielman	.06	.05	.02
92	John Friesz	.35	.25	.14
93	Jerome Brown	.06	.05	.02
94	Reggie White	.08	.06	.03
95	Michael Irvin	.20	.15	.08
96	Keith McCants	.08	.06	.03
97	Vinnie Clark	.10	.08	.04
98	Louis Oliver	.03	.02	.01
99	Mark Clayton	.08	.06	.03
100	John Offerdahl	.03	.02	.01
101	Michael Carter	.06	.05	.02
102	John Taylor	.12	.09	.05
103	William Perry	.08	.06	.03
104	Gill Byrd	.06	.05	.02
105	Burt Grossman	.03	.02	.01
106	Herman Moore **RC**	1.50	1.25	.60
107	Howie Long	.06	.05	.02
108	Bo Jackson	.35	.25	.14
109	Kelvin Pritchett	.12	.09	.05
110	Jacob Green	.06	.05	.02
111	Chris Doleman	.06	.05	.02
112	Herschel Walker	.12	.09	.05
113	Russell Maryland	.45	.35	.20
114	Anthony Carter	.08	.06	.03
115	Joey Browner	.06	.05	.02
116	Tony Mandarich	.06	.05	.02
117	Don Majkowski	.08	.06	.03
118	Ricky Ervins	1.50	1.25	.60
119	Sterling Sharpe	.75	.60	.30
120	Tim Harris	.06	.05	.02
121	Hugh Millen	.75	.60	.30
122	Mike Rozier	.06	.05	.02
123	Chris Miller	.15	.11	.06
124	Morten Andersen	.06	.05	.02
125	Neil O'Donnell **RC**	1.50	1.25	.60
126	**Surprise Wild Card**	.25	.20	.10
127	Eddie Brown	.06	.05	.02
128	James Francis	.08	.06	.03
129	James Brookss	.08	.06	.03
130	David Fulcher	.03	.02	.01
131	Michael Jackson **RC**	.75	.60	.30
132	Clay Matthews	.03	.02	.01
133	Scott Norwood	.03	.02	.01
134	Wesley Carroll	.40	.30	.15
135	Thurman Thomas	.40	.30	.15
136	Mark Ingram	.03	.02	.01
137	Bobby Hebert	.08	.06	.03
138	Bobby Wilson	.08	.06	.03
139	Craig Heyward	.08	.06	.03
140	Dalton Hilliard	.06	.05	.02
141	Jeff Hostetler	.20	.15	.08
142	Dave Meggett	.10	.08	.04
143	Cris Dishman	.20	.15	.08
144	Lawrence Taylor	.10	.08	.04
145	Leonard Marshall	.06	.05	.02
146	Pepper Johnson	.06	.05	.02
147	Todd Marinovich	1.25	.90	.50
148	Mike Croel	.75	.60	.30
149	Erik McMillan	.06	.05	.02
150	Flipper Anderson	.06	.05	.02
151	Cleveland Gary	.06	.05	.02
152	Henry Ellard	.08	.06	.03
153	Kevin Greene	.06	.05	.02
154	Michael Cofer	.03	.02	.01
155	Todd Lyght	.40	.30	.15
156	Bruce Smith	.08	.06	.03
157	**Checklist 1**	.06	.05	.02
158	**Checklist 2**	.06	.05	.02
159	**Checklist 3**	.06	.05	.02
160	**Checklist 4**	.06	.05	.02

1991 Wild Card NFL Prototypes

The six-card set promoted Wild Card's upcoming 1991 NFL set. The card fronts showcase an action photo bordered in black with different colored numbers around the top and right border. The Wild Card logo is in the upper left, with "NFL Premier Edition" printed inside a football in the lower left. The player's name and position are in the lower right. The card backs, numbered by a prefix of "prototype," have a photo of the player, his name, position and bio at the top. The player's stats are included inside a box at the bottom.

		NM	E	VG
Complete Set (6):		40.00	20.00	4.00
Common Player:		5.00	2.50	.50
1	Troy Aikman	9.00	4.50	.90
2	Barry Sanders	10.00	5.00	1.00
3	Thurman Thomas	9.00	4.50	.90
4	Emmitt Smith	12.50	6.25	1.25
5	Jerry Rice	7.50	3.75	.75
6	Lawrence Taylor	5.00	2.50	.50

1991 Wild Card NFL Redemption Cards

This surprise Wild Card, #126, inserted randomly in 1991 Wild Card NFL packs, could be redeemed for the 10-card NFL Experience subset which is listed below. The cards feature members of the Buffalo Bills and Washington Redskins.

		NM	E	VG
Complete Set (10):		3.50	1.50	.30
Common Player:		.12	.06	.01
126A	Mark Rypien	.60	.25	.05
126B	Ricky Ervins	1.50	.60	.12
126C	Darrell Green	.25	.10	.02
126D	Charles Mann	.12	.06	.01
126E	Art Monk	.30	.12	.02
126F	Thurman Thomas	.90	.35	.07
126G	Bruce Smith	.30	.12	.02
126H	Cornelius Bennett	.25	.10	.02
126I	Scott Norwood	.12	.06	.01
126J	Shane Conlan	.18	.07	.01

1991 Wild Card NFL Super Bowl Promos

Super Bowl XXVI is honored on this 10-card set, which spotlights five players from each team. The cards were handed out to attendees at the Super Bowl Card Show. The card fronts have an action photo borded in black, with different colored numbers on the top and right borders. The NFL Experience logo is in the lower left. The player's name and position are located in the lower right. The card backs showcase a player photo, his name, position and bio at the top of the card. A text box at the bottom of the card explains that Wild Card was a corporate sponsor of the Super Bowl Card Show III.

		NM	E	VG
Complete Set (10):		30.00	15.00	3.00
Common Player:		1.00	.50	.10
1	Mark Rypien	5.00	2.50	.50
2	Ricky Ervins	10.00	5.00	1.00
3	Darrell Green	2.00	1.00	.20
4	Charles Mann	1.00	.50	.10
5	Art Monk	2.50	1.25	.25
6	Thurman Thomas	7.50	3.75	.75
7	Bruce Smith	2.50	1.25	.25
8	Cornelius Bennett	2.00	1.00	.20
9	Scott Norwood	1.00	.50	.10
10	Shane Conlan	1.50	.75	.15

1991-92 Wild Card Redemption Prototypes

The six-card, standard-size set was available to collectors via a redemption mail-in offer. In exchange for three Collegiate Football Surprise wild cards before April 30, 1992, collectors also received the set, which is similar to the 1992 Wild Card NFL set. The cards are numbered with the "P" prefix.

		NM/M	NM	E
Complete Set (6):		2.00	1.50	.80
Common Player:		.20	.15	.08
1	Edgar Bennett (Florida State)	1.00	.70	.40
2	Jimmy Smith (Jackson State)	.75	.60	.30
3	Will Furrer (Virginia Tech)	.20	.15	.08
4	Terrell Buckley (Florida State)	.30	.25	.12
5	Tommy Vardell (Stanford)	.30	.25	.12
6	Amp Lee (Florida State)	.30	.25	.12

1967 Williams Portraits

Measuring 8" x 10", these 512 charcoal portraits of NFL players were a Kraft Cheese promotion. Sold in eight-portrait sets for $1 and a proof of purchase from various Kraft Cheese products, the set was broken down into four eight-portrait groups for each of the 16 NFL teams. In addition, an album which held 32 portraits was available for $2. The unnumbered portraits featured the player's name and position under the player portrait. The backs of the portraits were blank. An 8" x 10" checklist sheet was also issued, but it is not considered a card.

		NM	E	VG
Complete Set (512):		5,000	2,500	1,500
Common Player:		6.00	3.00	1.75
1	Taz Anderson	10.00	7.50	4.00
2	Gary Barnes	10.00	7.50	4.00
3	Lee Calland	10.00	7.50	4.00
4	Junior Coffey	12.00	6.00	3.50
5	Ed Cook	10.00	7.50	4.00
6	Perry Lee Dunn	10.00	7.50	4.00
7	Dan Grimm	10.00	7.50	4.00
8	Alex Hawkins	15.00	7.50	4.50
9	Randy Johnson	12.00	6.00	3.50
10	Lou Kirouac	10.00	7.50	4.00
11	Errol Linden	10.00	7.50	4.00
12	Billy Lothridge	10.00	7.50	4.00
13	Frank Marchlewski	10.00	7.50	4.00
14	Richard Marshall	10.00	7.50	4.00

15	Billy Martin	10.00	7.50	4.00
16	Tom Moore	12.00	6.00	3.50
17	Tommy Nobis	20.00	10.00	6.00
18	Jim Norton	10.00	7.50	4.00
19	Nick Rassas	10.00	7.50	4.00
20	Ken Reaves	10.00	7.50	4.00
21	Bobby Richards	10.00	7.50	4.00
22	Jerry Richardson	15.00	7.50	4.50
23	Bob Riggle	10.00	7.50	4.00
24	Karl Rubke	10.00	7.50	4.00
25	Marion Rushing	10.00	7.50	4.00
26	Chuck Sieminski	10.00	7.50	4.00
27	Steve Sloan	12.00	6.00	3.50
28	Ron Smith	10.00	7.50	4.00
29	Don Talbert	10.00	7.50	4.00
30	Ernie Wheelwright	12.00	6.00	3.50
31	Sam Williams	10.00	7.50	4.00
32	Jim Wilson	10.00	7.50	4.00
33	Sam Ball	10.00	7.50	4.00
34	Raymond Berry	30.00	15.00	9.00
35	Bob Boyd	12.00	6.00	3.50
36	Ordell Braase	10.00	7.50	4.00
37	Barry Brown	10.00	7.50	4.00
38	Bill Curry	12.00	6.00	3.50
39	Mike Curtis	15.00	7.50	4.50
40	Alvin Haymond	10.00	7.50	4.00
41	Jerry Hill	10.00	7.50	4.00
42	David Lee	10.00	7.50	4.00
43	Jerry Logan	10.00	7.50	4.00
44	Tony Lorick	10.00	7.50	4.00
45	Lenny Lyles	10.00	7.50	4.00
46	John Mackey	18.00	9.00	5.50
47	Tom Matte	15.00	7.50	4.50
48	Lou Michaels	12.00	6.00	3.50
49	Fred Miller	10.00	7.50	4.00
50	Lenny Moore	30.00	15.00	9.00
51	Jimmy Orr	12.00	6.00	3.50
52	Jim Parker	18.00	9.00	5.50
53	Glenn Ressler	10.00	7.50	4.00
54	Willie Richardson	12.00	6.00	3.50
55	Don Shinnick	10.00	7.50	4.00
56	Billy Ray Smith	12.00	6.00	3.50
57	Bubba Smith	20.00	10.00	6.00
58	Dan Sullivan	10.00	7.50	4.00
59	Dick Szymanski	10.00	7.50	4.00
60	Johnny Unitas	50.00	25.00	15.00
61	Bob Vogel	10.00	7.50	4.00
62	Rick Volk	10.00	7.50	4.00
63	Jim Welch	10.00	7.50	4.00
64	Butch Wilson	10.00	7.50	4.00
65	Charlie Bivins	10.00	7.50	4.00
66	Charlie Brown	10.00	7.50	4.00
67	Doug Buffone	12.00	6.00	3.50
68	Rudy Bukich	12.00	6.00	3.50
69	Ron Bull	12.00	6.00	3.50
70	Dick Butkus	50.00	25.00	15.00
71	Jim Cadile	10.00	7.50	4.00
72	Jack Concannon	12.00	6.00	3.50
73	Frank Cornish	10.00	7.50	4.00
74	Don Croftcheck	10.00	7.50	4.00
75	Dick Evey	10.00	7.50	4.00
76	Joe Fortunato	12.00	6.00	3.50
77	Curtis Gentry	10.00	7.50	4.00
78	Bobby Joe Green	10.00	7.50	4.00
79	John Henry Johnson	15.00	7.50	4.50
80	Bob Jones	10.00	7.50	4.00
81	Jimmy Jones	10.00	7.50	4.00
82	Ralph Kurek	10.00	7.50	4.00
83	Roger LeClerc	10.00	7.50	4.00
84	Andy Livingston	10.00	7.50	4.00
85	Bennie McRae	10.00	7.50	4.00
86	Johnny Morris	12.00	6.00	3.50
87	Richie Petitbon	12.00	6.00	3.50
88	Loyd Phillips	10.00	7.50	4.00
89	Brian Piccolo	45.00	22.00	13.50
90	Jim Purnell	10.00	7.50	4.00
91	Mike Pyle	10.00	7.50	4.00
92	Mike Reilly	10.00	7.50	4.00
93	Gale Sayers	50.00	25.00	15.00
94	George Seals	10.00	7.50	4.00
95	Roosevelt Taylor	12.00	6.00	3.50
96	Bob Wetoska	10.00	7.50	4.00
97	Erich Barnes	12.00	6.00	3.50
98	Johnny Brewer	10.00	7.50	4.00
99	Monte Clark	10.00	7.50	4.00
100	Gary Collins	15.00	7.50	4.50
101	Larry Conjar	10.00	7.50	4.00
102	Vince Costello	10.00	7.50	4.00
103	Ross Fichtner	10.00	7.50	4.00
104	Bill Glass	12.00	6.00	3.50
105	Ernie Green	15.00	7.50	4.50
106	Jack Gregory	10.00	7.50	4.00
107	Charlie Harraway	12.00	6.00	3.50
108	Gene Hickerson	12.00	6.00	3.50
109	Fred Hoaglin	10.00	7.50	4.00
110	Jim Houston	12.00	6.00	3.50
111	Mike Howell	10.00	7.50	4.00
112	Joe Bob Isbell	10.00	7.50	4.00
113	Walter Johnson	12.00	6.00	3.50
114	Jim Kanicki	10.00	7.50	4.00
115	Ernie Kellerman	12.00	6.00	3.50
116	Leroy Kelly	20.00	10.00	6.00
117	Dale Lindsey	10.00	7.50	4.00
118	Clifton McNeil	12.00	6.00	3.50
119	Milt Morin	12.00	6.00	3.50
120	Nick Pietrosante	10.00	7.50	4.00
121	Frank Ryan	15.00	7.50	4.50
122	Dick Schafrath	12.00	6.00	3.50
123	Randy Schultz	10.00	7.50	4.00
124	Ralph Smith	10.00	7.50	4.00
125	Carl Ward	10.00	7.50	4.00
126	Paul Warfield	20.00	10.00	6.00
127	Paul Wiggin	12.00	6.00	3.50
128	John Wooten	12.00	6.00	3.50
129	George Andrie	10.00	7.50	4.00
130	Jim Boeke	10.00	7.50	4.00
131	Frank Clarke	12.00	6.00	3.50
132	Mike Connelly	10.00	7.50	4.00
133	Buddy Dial	12.00	6.00	3.50
134	Leon Donohue	10.00	7.50	4.00
135	Dave Edwards	12.00	6.00	3.50
136	Mike Gaechter	10.00	7.50	4.00
137	Walt Garrison	15.00	7.50	4.50
138	Pete Gent	12.00	6.00	3.50
139	Cornell Green	15.00	7.50	4.50
140	Bob Hayes	20.00	10.00	6.00
141	Chuck Howley	15.00	7.50	4.50
142	Lee Roy Jordan	18.00	9.00	5.50
143	Bob Lilly	30.00	15.00	9.00
144	Tony Liscio	10.00	7.50	4.00
145	Warren Livingston	10.00	7.50	4.00
146	Dave Manders	10.00	7.50	4.00
147	Don Meredith	30.00	15.00	9.00
148	Ralph Neely	12.00	6.00	3.50
149	John Niland	10.00	7.50	4.00
150	Pettis Norman	12.00	6.00	3.50
151	Don Perkins	15.00	7.50	4.50
152	Jethro Pugh	12.00	6.00	3.50
153	Dan Reeves	30.00	15.00	9.00
154	Mel Renfro	18.00	9.00	5.50
155	Jerry Rhome	15.00	7.50	4.50
156	Les Shy	10.00	7.50	4.00
157	J.D. Smith	10.00	7.50	4.00
158	Willie Townes	10.00	7.50	4.00
159	Danny Villanueva	10.00	7.50	4.00
160	John Wilbur	10.00	7.50	4.00
161	Mike Alford	10.00	7.50	4.00
162	Lem Barney	18.00	9.00	5.50
163	Charley Bradshaw	10.00	7.50	4.00
164	Roger Brown	12.00	6.00	3.50
165	Ernie Clark	10.00	7.50	4.00
166	Gail Cogdill	12.00	6.00	3.50
167	Nick Eddy	12.00	6.00	3.50
168	Mel Farr	12.00	6.00	3.50
169	Bobby Felts	10.00	7.50	4.00
170	Ed Flanagan	10.00	7.50	4.00
171	Jim Gibbons	12.00	6.00	3.50
172	John Gordy	12.00	6.00	3.50
173	Larry Hand	10.00	7.50	4.00
174	Wally Hilgenberg	10.00	7.50	4.00
175	Alex Karras	20.00	10.00	6.00
176	Bob Kowalkowski	10.00	7.50	4.00
177	Ron Kramer	12.00	6.00	3.50
178	Mike Lucci	15.00	7.50	4.50
179	Bruce Maher	10.00	7.50	4.00
180	Amos Marsh	10.00	7.50	4.00
181	Darris McCord	10.00	7.50	4.00
182	Tom Nowatzke	10.00	7.50	4.00
183	Milt Plum	15.00	7.50	4.50
184	Wayne Rasmussen	10.00	7.50	4.00
185	Roger Shoals	10.00	7.50	4.00
186	Pat Studstill	12.00	6.00	3.50
187	Karl Sweetan	10.00	7.50	4.00
188	Bobby Thompson	10.00	7.50	4.00
189	Doug Van Horn	12.00	6.00	3.50
190	Wayne Walker	12.00	6.00	3.50
191	Tommy Watkins	10.00	7.50	4.00
192	Garo Yepremian	15.00	7.50	4.50
193	Herb Adderley	12.00	6.00	3.50
194	Lionel Aldridge	6.00	3.00	1.75
195	Donny Anderson	8.00	4.00	2.50
196	Ken Bowman	6.00	3.00	1.75
197	Zeke Bratkowski	8.00	4.00	2.50
198	Bob Brown (DT)	6.00	3.00	1.75
199	Tom Brown	6.00	3.00	1.75
200	Lee Roy Caffey	6.00	3.00	1.75
201	Don Chandler	7.00	3.50	2.00
202	Tommy Crutcher	6.00	3.00	1.75
203	Carroll Dale	8.00	4.00	2.50
204	Willie Davis	15.00	7.50	4.50
205	Boyd Dowler	8.00	4.00	2.50
206	Marv Fleming	7.00	3.50	2.00
207	Gale Gillingham	6.00	3.00	1.75
208	Jim Grabowski	6.00	3.00	1.75
209	Forrest Gregg	15.00	7.50	4.50
210	Doug Hart	6.00	3.00	1.75
211	Bob Jeter	6.00	3.00	1.75
212	Hank Jordan	12.00	6.00	3.50
213	Ron Kostelnik	6.00	3.00	1.75
214	Jerry Kramer	15.00	7.50	4.50
215	Bob Long	6.00	3.00	1.75
216	Max McGee	8.00	4.00	2.50
217	Ray Nitschke	18.00	9.00	5.50
218	Elijah Pitts	7.00	3.50	2.00
219	Dave Robinson	7.00	3.50	2.00
220	Bob Skoronski	7.00	3.50	2.00
221	Bart Starr	25.00	12.50	7.50
222	Fred Thurston	7.00	3.50	2.00
223	Willie Wood	18.00	9.00	5.50
224	Steve Wright	6.00	3.00	1.75
225	Dick Bass	15.00	7.50	4.50
226	Maxie Baughan	12.00	6.00	3.50
227	Joe Carollo	10.00	7.50	4.00
228	Bernie Casey	15.00	7.50	4.50
229	Don Chuy	10.00	7.50	4.00
230	Charlie Cowan	10.00	7.50	4.00
231	Irv Cross	12.00	6.00	3.50
232	Willie Ellison	12.00	6.00	3.50
233	Roman Gabriel	18.00	9.00	5.50
234	Bruce Gossett	10.00	7.50	4.00
235	Roosevelt Grier	18.00	9.00	5.50
236	Anthony Guillory	10.00	7.50	4.00
237	Ken Iman	10.00	7.50	4.00
238	Deacon Jones	20.00	10.00	6.00
239	Les Josephson	12.00	6.00	3.50
240	Jon Kilgore	10.00	7.50	4.00
241	Chuck Lamson	10.00	7.50	4.00
242	Lamar Lundy	12.00	6.00	3.50
243	Tom Mack	15.00	7.50	4.50
244	Tommy Mason	12.00	6.00	3.50
245	Tommy McDonald	15.00	7.50	4.50
246	Ed Meador	12.00	6.00	3.50
247	Bill Munson	15.00	7.50	4.50
248	Bob Nichols	10.00	7.50	4.00
249	Merlin Olsen	25.00	12.50	7.50
250	Jack Pardee	15.00	7.50	4.50
251	Bucky Pope	10.00	7.50	4.00
252	Joe Scibelli	10.00	7.50	4.00
253	Jack Snow	15.00	7.50	4.50
254	Billy Truax	12.00	6.00	3.50
255	Clancy Williams	10.00	7.50	4.00
256	Doug Woodlief	10.00	7.50	4.00
257	Grady Alderman	12.00	6.00	3.50
258	John Beasley	10.00	7.50	4.00
259	Bob Berry	12.00	6.00	3.50
260	Larry Bowie	10.00	7.50	4.00
261	Bill Brown	15.00	7.50	4.50
262	Fred Cox	12.00	6.00	3.50
263	Doug Davis	10.00	7.50	4.00
264	Paul Dickson	10.00	7.50	4.00
265	Carl Eller	18.00	9.00	5.50
266	Paul Flatley	12.00	6.00	3.50
267	Dale Hackbart	10.00	7.50	4.00
268	Don Hansen	10.00	7.50	4.00
269	Clint Jones	10.00	7.50	4.00
270	Jeff Jordan	10.00	7.50	4.00
271	Karl Kassulke	12.00	6.00	3.50
272	John Kirby	10.00	7.50	4.00
273	Gary Larsen	12.00	6.00	3.50
274	Jim Lindsey	10.00	7.50	4.00
275	Earsell Mackbee	10.00	7.50	4.00
276	Jim Marshall	18.00	9.00	5.50
277	Marlin McKeever	10.00	7.50	4.00
278	Dave Osborn	15.00	7.50	4.50
279	Jim Phillips	10.00	7.50	4.00
280	Ed Sharockman	10.00	7.50	4.00
281	Jerry Shay	10.00	7.50	4.00
282	Milt Sunde	12.00	6.00	3.50
283	Archie Sutton	10.00	7.50	4.00
284	Mick Tingelhoff	15.00	7.50	4.50
285	Ron Vanderkelen	10.00	7.50	4.00
286	Jim Vellone	10.00	7.50	4.00
287	Lonnie Warwick	10.00	7.50	4.00
288	Roy Winston	12.00	6.00	3.50
289	Doug Atkins	20.00	10.00	6.00
290	Vern Burke	10.00	7.50	4.00
291	Bruce Cortez	10.00	7.50	4.00
292	Gary Cuozzo	12.00	6.00	3.50
293	Ted Davis	10.00	7.50	4.00
294	John Douglas	10.00	7.50	4.00
295	Jim Garcia	10.00	7.50	4.00
296	Tom Hall	10.00	7.50	4.00
297	Jim Heidel	10.00	7.50	4.00
298	Leslie Kelley	10.00	7.50	4.00
299	Billy Kilmer	18.00	9.00	5.50
300	Kent Kramer	10.00	7.50	4.00
301	Jake Kupp	10.00	7.50	4.00
302	Earl Leggett	10.00	7.50	4.00
303	Obert Logan	10.00	7.50	4.00
304	Tom McNeill	10.00	7.50	4.00
305	John Morrow	10.00	7.50	4.00

306	Ray Ogden	10.00	7.50	4.00
307	Ray Rissmiller	10.00	7.50	4.00
308	George Rose	10.00	7.50	4.00
309	David Rowe	10.00	7.50	4.00
310	Brian Schweda	10.00	7.50	4.00
311	Dave Simmons	10.00	7.50	4.00
312	Jerry Simmons	10.00	7.50	4.00
313	Steve Stonebreaker	12.00	6.00	3.50
314	Jim Taylor	20.00	10.00	6.00
315	Mike Tilleman	10.00	7.50	4.00
316	Phil Vandersea	10.00	7.50	4.00
317	Joe Wendryhoski	10.00	7.50	4.00
318	Dave Whitsell	12.00	6.00	3.50
319	Fred Whittingham	10.00	7.50	4.00
320	Gary Wood	10.00	7.50	4.00
321	Ken Avery	10.00	7.50	4.00
322	Bookie Bolin	10.00	7.50	4.00
323	Henry Carr	12.00	6.00	3.50
324	Pete Case	10.00	7.50	4.00
325	Clarence Childs	10.00	7.50	4.00
326	Mike Ciccolella	10.00	7.50	4.00
327	Glen Condren	10.00	7.50	4.00
328	Bob Crespino	10.00	7.50	4.00
329	Don Davis	10.00	7.50	4.00
330	Tucker Frederickson	15.00	7.50	4.50
331	Charlie Harper	10.00	7.50	4.00
332	Phil Harris	10.00	7.50	4.00
333	Allen Jacobs	10.00	7.50	4.00
334	Homer Jones	12.00	6.00	3.50
335	Jim Katcavage	12.00	6.00	3.50
336	Tom Kennedy	10.00	7.50	4.00
337	Ernie Koy	12.00	6.00	3.50
338	Greg Larson	12.00	6.00	3.50
339	Spider Lockhart	12.00	6.00	3.50
340	Chuck Mercein	12.00	6.00	3.50
341	Jim Moran	10.00	7.50	4.00
342	Earl Morrall	15.00	7.50	4.50
343	Joe Morrison	12.00	6.00	3.50
344	Francis Peay	10.00	7.50	4.00
345	Del Shofner	12.00	6.00	3.50
346	Jeff Smith	10.00	7.50	4.00
347	Fran Tarkenton	40.00	20.00	12.00
348	Aaron Thomas	12.00	6.00	3.50
349	Larry Vargo	10.00	7.50	4.00
350	Freeman White	10.00	7.50	4.00
351	Sidney Williams	10.00	7.50	4.00
352	Willie Young	10.00	7.50	4.00
353	Sam Baker	10.00	7.50	4.00
354	Gary Ballman	10.00	7.50	4.00
355	Randy Beisler	10.00	7.50	4.00
356	Bob Brown (OT)	12.00	6.00	3.50
357	Timmy Brown	15.00	7.50	4.50
358	Mike Ditka	45.00	22.00	13.50
359	Dave Graham	10.00	7.50	4.00
360	Ben Hawkins	10.00	7.50	4.00
361	Fred Hill	10.00	7.50	4.00
362	King Hill	12.00	6.00	3.50
363	Lynn Hoyem	10.00	7.50	4.00
364	Don Hultz	10.00	7.50	4.00
365	Dwight Kelley	10.00	7.50	4.00
366	Israel Lang	10.00	7.50	4.00
367	Dave Lloyd	10.00	7.50	4.00
368	Aaron Martin	10.00	7.50	4.00
369	Ron Medved	10.00	7.50	4.00
370	John Meyers	10.00	7.50	4.00
371	Mike Morgan	10.00	7.50	4.00
372	Al Nelson	10.00	7.50	4.00
373	Jim Nettles	10.00	7.50	4.00
374	Floyd Peters	12.00	6.00	3.50
375	Gary Pettigrew	10.00	7.50	4.00
376	Ray Poage	10.00	7.50	4.00
377	Nate Ramsey	10.00	7.50	4.00
378	Dave Recher	10.00	7.50	4.00
379	Jim Ringo	15.00	7.50	4.50
380	Joe Scarpati	10.00	7.50	4.00
381	Jim Skaggs	10.00	7.50	4.00
382	Norm Snead	18.00	9.00	5.50
383	Harold Wells	10.00	7.50	4.00
384	Tom Woodeshick	12.00	6.00	3.50
385	Bill Asbury	10.00	7.50	4.00
386	John Baker	10.00	7.50	4.00
387	Jim Bradshaw	10.00	7.50	4.00
388	Rod Breedlove	10.00	7.50	4.00
389	John Brown	10.00	7.50	4.00
390	Amos Bullocks	10.00	7.50	4.00
391	Jim Butler	10.00	7.50	4.00
392	John Campbell	10.00	7.50	4.00
393	Mike Clark	10.00	7.50	4.00
394	Larry Gagner	10.00	7.50	4.00
395	Earl Gros	12.00	6.00	3.50
396	John Hilton	10.00	7.50	4.00
397	Dick Hoak	12.00	6.00	3.50
398	Roy Jefferson	12.00	6.00	3.50
399	Tony Jeter	10.00	7.50	4.00
400	Brady Keys	10.00	7.50	4.00
401	Ken Kortas	10.00	7.50	4.00
402	Ray Mansfield	10.00	7.50	4.00
403	Paul Martha	10.00	7.50	4.00
404	Ben McGee	10.00	7.50	4.00
405	Bill Nelsen	15.00	7.50	4.50
406	Kent Nix	10.00	7.50	4.00
407	Fran O'Brien	10.00	7.50	4.00
408	Andy Russell	15.00	7.50	4.50
409	Bill Saul	10.00	7.50	4.00
410	Don Shy	10.00	7.50	4.00
411	Clendon Thomas	12.00	6.00	3.50
412	Bruce Van Dyke	10.00	7.50	4.00
413	Lloyd Voss	10.00	7.50	4.00
414	Ralph Wenzel	10.00	7.50	4.00
415	J.R. Wilburn	10.00	7.50	4.00
416	Marv Woodson	10.00	7.50	4.00
417	Jim Bakken	12.00	6.00	3.50
418	Don Brumm	10.00	7.50	4.00
419	Vidal Carlin	10.00	7.50	4.00
420	Bobby Joe Conrad	12.00	6.00	3.50
421	Willis Crenshaw	10.00	7.50	4.00
422	Bob DeMarco	10.00	7.50	4.00
423	Pat Fischer	12.00	6.00	3.50
424	Billy Gambrell	10.00	7.50	4.00
425	Prentice Gault	12.00	6.00	3.50
426	Ken Gray	10.00	7.50	4.00
427	Jerry Hillebrand	10.00	7.50	4.00
428	Charlie Johnson	15.00	7.50	4.50
429	Bill Koman	10.00	7.50	4.00
430	Dave Long	10.00	7.50	4.00
431	Ernie McMillan	10.00	7.50	4.00
432	Dave Meggysey	12.00	6.00	3.50
433	Dale Meinert	10.00	7.50	4.00
434	Mike Melinkovich	10.00	7.50	4.00
435	Dave O'Brien	10.00	7.50	4.00
436	Sonny Randle	12.00	6.00	3.50
437	Bob Reynolds	10.00	7.50	4.00
438	Joe Robb	10.00	7.50	4.00
439	Johnny Roland	12.00	6.00	3.50
440	Roy Shivers	10.00	7.50	4.00
441	Sam Silas	10.00	7.50	4.00
442	Jackie Smith	18.00	9.00	5.50
443	Rick Sortun	10.00	7.50	4.00
444	Jerry Stovall	10.00	7.50	4.00
445	Chuck Walker	10.00	7.50	4.00
446	Bobby Williams	10.00	7.50	4.00
447	Dave Williams	12.00	6.00	3.50
448	Larry Wilson	18.00	9.00	5.50
449	Kermit Alexander	10.00	7.50	4.00
450	Cas Banaszek	10.00	7.50	4.00
451	Bruce Bosley	10.00	7.50	4.00
452	John Brodie	20.00	10.00	6.00
453	Joe Cerne	10.00	7.50	4.00
454	John David Crow	12.00	6.00	3.50
455	Tommy Davis	12.00	6.00	3.50
456	Bob Harrison	10.00	7.50	4.00
457	Matt Hazeltine	10.00	7.50	4.00
458	Stan Hindman	10.00	7.50	4.00
459	Charlie Johnson	10.00	7.50	4.00
460	Jim Johnson	18.00	9.00	5.50
461	Dave Kopay	10.00	7.50	4.00
462	Charlie Krueger	12.00	6.00	3.50
463	Roland Lakes	10.00	7.50	4.00
464	Gary Lewis	10.00	7.50	4.00
465	Dave McCormick	10.00	7.50	4.00
466	Kay McFarland	10.00	7.50	4.00
467	Clark Miller	10.00	7.50	4.00
468	George Mira	12.00	6.00	3.50
469	Howard Mudd	10.00	7.50	4.00
470	Frank Nunley	10.00	7.50	4.00
471	Dave Parks	12.00	6.00	3.50
472	Walt Rock	10.00	7.50	4.00
473	Len Rohde	10.00	7.50	4.00
474	Steve Spurrier	35.00	17.50	10.50
475	Monty Stickles	10.00	7.50	4.00
476	John Thomas	10.00	7.50	4.00
477	Bill Tucker	10.00	7.50	4.00
478	Dave Wilcox	10.00	7.50	4.00
479	Ken Willard	12.00	6.00	3.50
480	Dick Witcher	10.00	7.50	4.00
481	Willie Adams	6.00	3.00	1.75
482	Walt Barnes	6.00	3.00	1.75
483	Jim Carroll	6.00	3.00	1.75
484	Dave Crossan	6.00	3.00	1.75
485	Charlie Gogolak	7.00	3.50	2.00
486	Tom Goosby	6.00	3.00	1.75
487	Chris Hanburger	8.00	4.00	2.50
488	Rickie Harris	6.00	3.00	1.75
489	Len Hauss	7.00	3.50	2.00
490	Sam Huff	18.00	9.00	5.50
491	Steve Jackson	6.00	3.00	1.75
492	Mitch Johnson	6.00	3.00	1.75
493	Sonny Jurgensen	18.00	9.00	5.50
494	Carl Kammerer	6.00	3.00	1.75
495	Paul Krause	12.00	6.00	3.50
496	Joe Don Looney	12.00	6.00	3.50
497	Ray McDonald	6.00	3.00	1.75
498	Bobby Mitchell	15.00	7.50	4.50
499	Jim Ninowski	7.00	3.50	2.00
500	Brig Owens	6.00	3.00	1.75
501	Vince Promuto	6.00	3.00	1.75
502	Pat Richter	7.00	3.50	2.00
503	Joe Rutgens	6.00	3.00	1.75
504	Lonnie Sanders	6.00	3.00	1.75
505	Ray Schoenke	6.00	3.00	1.75
506	Jim Shorter	6.00	3.00	1.75
507	Jerry Smith	8.00	4.00	2.50
508	Ron Snidow	6.00	3.00	1.75
509	Jim Snowden	6.00	3.00	1.75
510	Charley Taylor	18.00	9.00	5.50
511	Steve Thurlow	6.00	3.00	1.75
512	A.D. Whitfield	6.00	3.00	1.75

1974 Wonder Bread

Topps printed these 30 cards to be randomly included inside packages of Wonder Bread. Players from 18 NFL teams are represented on the cards, which have a closeup shot of the player and either a bright yellow or red border. The card back has biographical and statistical information about the player, plus a description and photograph illustrating a particular football play.

		NM	E	VG
Complete Set (30):		25.00	12.50	7.50
Common Player:		.40	.20	.12
1	Jim Bakken	.45	.25	.14
2	Forrest Blue	.40	.20	.12
3	Bill Bradley	.40	.20	.12
4	Willie Brown	1.50	.70	.45
5	Larry Csonka	4.00	2.00	1.25
6	Ken Ellis	.40	.20	.12
7	Bruce Gossett	.40	.20	.12
8	Bob Griese	4.00	2.00	1.25
9	Chris Hanburger	.75	.40	.25
10	Winston Hill	.40	.20	.12
11	Jim Johnson	1.25	.60	.40
12	Paul Krause	1.00	.50	.30
13	Ted Kwalick	.85	.45	.25
14	Willie Lanier	1.50	.70	.45
15	Tom Mack	1.00	.50	.30
16	Jim Otto	1.50	.70	.45
17	Alan Page	1.75	.90	.50
18	Frank Pitts	.40	.20	.12
19	Jim Plunkett	1.50	.70	.45
20	Mike Reid	1.00	.50	.30
21	Paul Smith	.40	.20	.12
22	Bob Tucker	.75	.40	.25
23	Jim Tryer	.75	.40	.25
24	Eugene Upshaw	1.50	.70	.45
25	Phil Villapiano	1.00	.50	.30
26	Paul Warfield	2.00	1.00	.60
27	Dwight White	.50	.25	.15
28	Steve Owens	.75	.40	.25
29	Jerrel Wilson	.40	.20	.12
30	Ron Yary	.75	.40	.25

1975 Wonder Bread

Once again, Topps produced this set for Wonder Bread to include the cards in specially-marked loaves of bread. The card front has a closeup shot of the player, with either a red or blue border surrounding it. The card back has statistics and biographical information about the player, plus questions and answers about the player and the game of football. The answers were written upside down.

		NM	E	VG
Complete Set (24):		25.00	12.50	7.50
Common Player:		.35	.20	.11
1	Alan Page	1.50	.70	.45
2	Emmitt Thomas	.40	.20	.12
3	John Mendenhall	.35	.20	.11
4	Ken Houston	1.25	.60	.40
5	Jack Ham	1.25	.60	.40
6	L.C. Greenwood	.75	.40	.25
7	Tom Mack	.75	.40	.25
8	Winston Hill	.35	.20	.11
9	Isaac Curtis	.50	.25	.15
10	Terry Owens	.50	.25	.15
11	Drew Pearson	.60	.30	.20
12	Don Cockroft	.35	.20	.11
13	Bob Griese	2.50	1.25	.70
14	Riley Odoms	.50	.25	.15
15	Chuck Foreman	.75	.40	.25
16	Forrest Blue	.35	.20	.11
17	Franco Harris	3.50	1.75	1.00
18	Larry Little	1.00	.50	.30
19	Bill Bergey	.60	.30	.20
20	Ray Guy	.90	.45	.25
21	Ted Hendricks	1.25	.60	.40
22	Levi Johnson	.35	.20	.11
23	Jack Mildren	.50	.25	.15
24	Mel Tom	.35	.20	.11

1976 Wonder Bread

These 24 cards use two different frames for the card front; red frames are used for defensive players, while blue frames are used for the offensive players in the set. A close-up shot of the player is featured prominently on the front. Each back has biographical information about the player, plus a diagram of a favorite play of coach Hank Stram. The corresponding text indicates the offensive players' assignments for that particular play. Topps produced the cards for Wonder Bread to insert into loaves of bread.

		NM	E	VG
Complete Set (24):		5.00	2.50	1.50
Common Player:		.20	.10	.06
1	Craig Morton	.35	.20	.11
2	Chuck Foreman	.35	.20	.11
3	Franco Harris	1.00	.50	.30
4	Mel Gray	.35	.20	.11
5	Charley Taylor	.60	.30	.20
6	Rich Caster	.20	.10	.06
7	George Kunz	.20	.10	.06
8	Rayfield Wright	.20	.10	.06
9	Gene Upshaw	.75	.40	.25
10	Tom Mack	.50	.25	.15
11	Len Hauss	.35	.20	.11
12	Garo Yepremian	.20	.10	.06
13	Cedrick Hardman	.20	.10	.06
14	Jack Youngblood	1.00	.50	.30
15	Wally Chambers	.20	.10	.06
16	Jerry Sherk	.20	.10	.06
17	Bill Bergey	.35	.20	.11
18	Jack Ham	.75	.40	.25
19	Fred Carr	.20	.10	.06
20	Jack Tatum	.35	.20	.11
21	Cliff Harris	.35	.20	.11
22	Emmitt Thomas	.20	.10	.06
23	Ken Riley	.20	.10	.06
24	Ray Guy	1.00	.50	.30

1984 Wranglers 8x10 Arizona

The eight-sheet, 8" x 10" set features two rows of four black and white cards, with the player's name printed below each card. The sheets are numbered.

		NM/M	NM	E
Complete Set (8):		40.00	30.00	16.00
Common Panel:		5.00	3.75	2.00
1	Edward Diethrich PRES, Bill Harris VP, George Allen CO, G. Bruce Allen GM, Robert Barnes, Dennis Bishop, Mack Boatner, Luther Bradley	8.00	6.00	3.25
2	Clay Brown, Eddie Brown, Wamon Buggs, Bob Clasby, Frank Corral, Doug Cozen, Doug Dennison, Robert Dillon	6.00	4.50	2.50
3	Larry Douglas, Joe Ehrmann, Nick Eyre, Jim Fahnhorst, Doak Field, Bruce Gheesling, Frank Giddens, Alfondia Hill	5.00	3.75	2.00
4	David Huffman, Hubert Hurst, Donnie Johnson, Randy Johnson, Trumaine Johnson, Jeff Kiewel, Bruce Laird, Greg Landry	7.00	5.25	2.75
5	Kit Lathrop, John Lee, Alva Liles, Dan Lloyd, Kevin Long, Karl Lorch, Andy Melontree, Frank Minnifield	5.00	3.75	2.00
6	Tom Piette, Tom Porras, Paul Ricker, Alan Risher, Don Schwartz, Bobby Scott, Lance Shields, Ed Smith	5.00	3.75	2.00
7	Robert Smith, Tim Spencer, John Stadnik, Mark Stevenson, Dave Steif, Gerry Sullivan, Ted Sutton, Motrandy Taylor	5.00	3.75	2.00
8	Rob Taylor, Tom Thayer, Todd Thomas, Ted Walton, Stan White, Lenny Willis, Tim Wrightman, Wilbur Young	5.00	3.75	2.00

1984 Wranglers Carl's Jr.

The 10-card, 2-1/2" x 3-5/8" set was sponsored by Carl's Jr. restaurants and the Tempe Police Department in Arizona and featured top players from the USFL Arizona Wranglers football team. Included in the set is coach George Allen and former longtime NFL quarterback Greg Landry. The card fronts have a black and white posed photo with bio information appearing on the back.

		NM/M	NM	E
Complete Set (10):		30.00	22.00	12.00
Common Player:		2.50	2.00	1.00
1	George Allen (CO)	8.00	6.00	3.25
2	Luther Bradley (27)	3.50	2.75	1.50
3	Trumaine Johnson (2)	3.50	2.75	1.50
4	Greg Landry (11)	6.00	4.50	2.50
5	Kit Lathrop (70)	2.50	2.00	1.00
6	John Lee (64)	2.50	2.00	1.00
7	Keith Long (33)	2.50	2.00	1.00
8	Alan Risher (7)	2.50	2.00	1.00
9	Tim Spencer (46)	3.50	2.75	1.50
10	Lenny Willis (89)	2.50	2.00	1.00

1990 Wyoming Smokey

		NM/M	NM	E
Complete Set (16):		20.00	15.00	8.00
Common Player:		1.50	1.25	.60
1	Tom Corontzos (18)	1.50	1.25	.60
2	Jay Daffer (34)	1.50	1.25	.60
3	Mitch Donahue (49)	2.00	1.50	.80
4	Sean Fleming (42)	1.50	1.25	.60
5	Pete Gosar (53)	1.50	1.25	.60
6	Robert Midgett (57)	1.50	1.25	.60
7	Bryan Mooney (9)	1.50	1.25	.60
8	Doug Rigby (77)	1.50	1.25	.60
9	Paul Roach (CO)	2.00	1.50	.80
10	Mark Timmer (48)	1.50	1.25	.60
11	Paul Wallace (29)	1.50	1.25	.60
12	Shawn Wiggins (15)	1.50	1.25	.60
13	Gordy Wood (95)	1.50	1.25	.60
14	Willie Wright (96)	1.50	1.25	.60
15	**Cowboy Joe Mascot**	1.50	1.25	.60
16	**Title Card Cowboy logo**	1.50	1.25	.60

Alphabetical Index

Chronological Index